# GENERAL MOTORS CORPORATION
## CHEVROLET VEHICLE INFORMATION

## GMC VEHICLE INFORMATION

## GMC VEHICLE INFORMATION— Continued

## GENERAL SERVICE

"The data reported herein has been compiled from authoritative sources While every effort is made by the editors to attain accuracy, manufacturing changes as well as typographical errors and omissions may occur. The publisher then cannot be responsible nor does it assume responsibility for such omissions, errors or changes."

# MOTOR
# LIGHT TRUCK & VAN
# REPAIR MANUAL

## 6th Edition
### First Printing

**Michael J. Kromida, SAE**
*Editor*

**John R. Lypen, SAE**
*Managing Editor*

**Warren Schildknecht, SAE**
*Senior Editor*

**Douglas Tasker**
*Assistant Editor*

**Richard F. Cahoon**
*Assistant Editor*

**James A. Jablonski**
*Assistant Editor*

**Gary L. Jones**
*Assistant Editor*

**Mark L. Kaufman**
*Assistant Editor*

**Salvatore Busuito**
*Assistant Editor*

**Mark C. Ferrand**
*Assistant Editor*

**Richard G. Glover**
*Assistant Editor*

**Michael A. Olech**
*Assistant Editor*

**Christopher P. Jakubowski**
*Assistant Editor*

**Timothy P. Kedzior**
*Assistant Editor*

**Donald R. Cobb**
*Assistant Editor*

**Published by**
# MOTOR

**Hearst Books/Business Publishing Group,
A Division of The Hearst Corp.**

**5600 Crooks Road, Troy, MI 48098**

Printed in the U.S.A.
© Copyright 1989 by The Hearst Corporation
ISBN 0-87851-721-9
1332

**Frank A. Bennack, Jr.**
*President*

**Gilbert C. Maurer**
*Executive Vice
President*

**Philip D. Shalala**
*Group Vice President
Business Publishing*

**Kevin F. Carr**
*Publisher
Motor Books*

**Randolph A. Hearst**
*Chairman*

**Gordon L. Jones**
*Vice President
Hearst Books/Business
Publishing Group*

**Nelson J. Maione**
*Vice President &
Resident Controller*

**Louis C. Forier, SAE**
*Vice President
Editorial Director
Motor Books*

# GASOLINE ENGINE TUNE UP SPECIFICATIONS & DIESEL ENGINE PERFORMANCE SPECIFICATIONS

**The following specifications are published from the latest information available. This data should be used only in the absence of a decal affixed in the engine compartment.**

## TABLE OF CONTENTS

Page No.

## JEEP EXC. COMANCHE & 1984–89 CHEROKEE & WAGONEER

| Year & Engine | Spark Plug Gap | Firing Order ① | Ignition Timing BTDC Man. Trans. | Ignition Timing BTDC Auto. Trans. | Mark Location | Curb Idle Speed ② Man. Trans. | Curb Idle Speed ② Auto. Trans. | Fast Idle Speed Man. Trans. | Fast Idle Speed Auto Trans. | Fuel Pump Pressure |
|---|---|---|---|---|---|---|---|---|---|---|
| **1987–89** | | | | | | | | | | |
| 4-151 | .035 | A | ⑥ | ⑥ | Damper | ⑥ | ⑥ | ⑥ | ⑥ | — |
| 6-258 | .035 | B | 9 ⑱ | 9 ⑱ | Damper | 680 | 600D | 1700 ⑰ | 1850 ⑰ | 4–5 |
| V8-360 | .033 | C | 12 ⑲ | 12 ⑲ | Damper | 600 | 600D | 1500 ⑰ | 1600 ⑰ | 5–6.5 |
| **1984–86** | | | | | | | | | | |
| 4-151 Exc. High Alt. | .035 | D | 12 ⑱ | 12 ⑱ | Damper | ③ | ④ | 2000 ⑰ | 2300 ⑰ | 4—5 |
| 4-151 High Alt. | .035 | D | 19 ⑱ | 19 ⑱ | Damper | ③ | ④ | 2000 ⑰ | 2300 ⑰ | 4–5 |
| 6-258 Exc. High Alt. | .035 | B | 9 ⑱ | 9 ⑱ | Damper | 680 ⑤ | 600D ⑦ | 1700 ⑰ | 1850 ⑰ | 4–5 |
| 6-258 High Alt. | .035 | B | 16 ⑱ | 16 ⑱ | Damper | 700 ⑤ | 650D ⑦ | 1700 ⑰ | 1850 ⑰ | 4–5 |
| V8-360 Exc. High Alt. | .035 | C | 10 ⑲ | 10 ⑲ | Damper | 600 | 600D | 1500 ⑰ | 1600 ⑰ | 5–6.5 |
| V8-360 High Alt. | .035 | C | 16 ⑲ | 16 ⑲ | Damper | 600 | 600D | 1550 ⑰ | 1550 ⑰ | 5–6.5 |
| **1983** | | | | | | | | | | |
| 4-151 Exc. High Alt. | .035 | D | 12° ⑱ | 12° ⑱ | Damper | 500 ③ | 500D ④ | 2000 ⑰ | 2000 ⑰ | 4–5 |
| 4-151 High Alt. | .035 | D | 19° ⑱ | 19° ⑱ | Damper | 500 ③ | 500D ④ | 2000 ⑰ | 2000 ⑰ | 4–5 |
| 4-151 | .060 | E | 12° ⑲ | — | Damper | 500/900 | — | 2500 ⑰ | — | 6½–8 |
| 6-258 Exc. Calif. & High Alt. | .035 | B | 6° ⑳ | 6° ⑳ | Damper | 600 ③ | 500D ⑧ | 1700 ⑰ | 18500 ⑰ | 4–5 |
| 6-258 Calif. | .035 | B | 6° ⑳ | 6° ⑳ | Damper | 650 ③ | 550° ⑧ | 1700 ⑰ | 1850 ⑰ | 4–5 |
| 6-258 High Alt. | .035 | B | 13° ⑳ | 13° ⑳ | Damper | 700 ⑨ | 650D ⑩ | 1700 ⑰ | 1850 ⑰ | 4–5 |
| V8-360 Exc. High Alt. | .035 | C | 10° ⑲ | 10° ⑲ | Damper | 500/600 | 500/600D | 1500 ⑰ | 1600 ⑰ | 5–6½ |
| V8-360 High Alt. | .035 | C | 16° ⑲ | 16° ⑲ | Damper | 500/600 | 500/600D | 1500 ⑰ | 1600 ⑰ | 5–6½ |
| **1982** | | | | | | | | | | |
| 4-151 Exc. Calif. & High Alt. | .060 | E | 12° ⑲ | — | Damper | 500/900 | — | 2400 ⑰ | — | 6½–8 |
| 4-151 Calif. | .060 | E | 8° ⑲ | — | Damper | 500/900 | — | 2400 ⑰ | — | 6½–8 |
| 4-151 High Alt. | .060 | E | 17° ⑲ | — | Damper | 500/900 | — | 2400 ⑰ | — | 6½–8 |
| 6-258 Exc. Calif. ⑪ | .035 | B | 8° ⑳ | 8° ⑳ | Damper | 650 ⑫ | 550D ⑬ | 1700 ⑰ | 1850 ⑰ | 4–5 |
| 6-258 Calif. ⑪ | .035 | B | 15° ⑳ | 15° ⑳ | Damper | 650 ⑫ | 550D ⑬ | 1700 ⑰ | 1850 ⑰ | 4–5 |
| 6-258 Exc. High Alt. ⑭ | .035 | B | 15° ⑳ | 15° ⑳ | Damper | 600 ⑫ | 500D ⑬ | 1700 ⑰ | 1850 ⑰ | 4–5 |
| 6-258 High Alt. | .035 | B | 19° ⑳ | 21° ⑳ | Damper | 600 ⑫ | 500D ⑬ | 1700 ⑰ | 1850 ⑰ | 4–5 |
| V8-360 Exc. High Alt. | .035 | C | 10° ⑲ | 10° ⑲ | Damper | 500/600 | 500/600D | 1500 ⑰ | 1600 ⑰ | 5–6½ |
| V8-360 High Alt. | .035 | C | 16° ⑲ | 16° ⑲ | Damper | 500/600 | 500/600D | 1500 ⑰ | 1600 ⑰ | 5–6½ |
| **1981** | | | | | | | | | | |
| 4-151 Exc. Calif. | .060 | E | 10° ⑲ | 12° ⑲ | Damper | 500/900 | 500/700D | 2400 ⑰ | 2600 ⑰ | 6½–8 |
| 4-151 Calif. | .060 | E | 10° ⑲ | 10° ⑲ | Damper | 500/900 | 500/700D | 2400 ⑰ | 2600 ⑰ | 6½–8 |
| 6-258 Exc. Calif. | .035 | B | 8° ⑲ | 8° ⑲ | Damper | 650 ⑫ | 550° ⑬ | 1700 ⑰ | 1850 ⑰ | 4–5 |
| 6-258 Calif. | .035 | B | 4° ⑲ | 6° ⑲ | Damper | 650 ⑫ | 550D ⑬ | 1700 ⑰ | 1850 ⑰ | 4–5 |
| V8-304 | .035 | C | 8° ⑮ ⑲ | 10° ⑲ | Damper | 600 ⑯ | 600D | 1500 ⑰ | 1600 ⑰ | 5–6½ |
| V8-360 | .035 | C | 10° ⑲ | 10° ⑲ | Damper | 600 | 600D | 1500 ⑰ | 1600 ⑰ | 5–6½ |
| **1980** | | | | | | | | | | |
| 4-151 | .060 | E | 12° ⑲ | — | Damper | 500/900 | — | 2400 ⑰ | — | 6½–8 |
| 6-258 Exc. Calif. ⑪ | .035 | B | 8° ⑲ | 10° ⑲ | Damper | 700 | 500/600D | 1700 ⑰ | 1850 ⑰ | 4–5 |
| 6-258 Calif. ⑪ | .035 | B | 6° ⑲ | 8° ⑲ | Damper | 700 | 500/600D | 1700 ⑰ | 1850 ⑰ | 4–5 |
| 6-258 Calif. ⑪ | .035 | B | 6° ⑲ | 8° ⑲ | Damper | 700 | 500/600D | 1700 ⑰ | 1850 ⑰ | 4–5 |
| 6-258 ⑭ | .035 | B | 8° ⑲ | 8° ⑲ | Damper | 700 | 700D | 1700 ⑰ | 1850 ⑰ | 4–5 |
| V8-304 Exc. Calif. | .035 | C | 8° ⑮ ⑲ | 10° ⑲ | Damper | 700 | 500/600D | 1500 ⑰ | 1600 ⑰ | 5–6½ |
| V8-304 Calif. | .035 | C | 5° ⑲ | 5° ⑲ | Damper | 700 | 500/600D | 1500 ⑰ | 1600 ⑰ | 5–6½ |
| V8-360 | .035 | C | 8° ⑲ | 8° ⑲ | Damper | 800 | 600D | 1500 ⑰ | 1600 ⑰ | 5–6½ |

## JEEP EXC. COMANCHE & 1984–89 CHEROKEE & WAGONEER—Continued

① —Before removing wires from distributor cap, determine location of No. 1 wire in cap, as distributor position may have been altered from that shown at the end of this chart.

② —Idle speed for man. trans. models is adjusted in Neutral. On auto. trans. models, idle speed is adjusted in Drive (D). When checking idle speed, set parking brake & block drive wheels.

③ —With holding solenoid energized, 750 RPM; with vacuum actuator energized, 950 RPM.

④ —With holding solenoid energized, 700D RPM; with vacuum actuator energized, 850D RPM.

⑤ —With holding solenoid energized, 900 RPM; with vacuum actuator energized, 1100 RPM.

⑥ —Non-adjustable.

⑦ —With holding solenoid energized, 800D RPM; with vacuum actuator energized, 900D RPM.

⑧ —With holding solenoid energized, 650D RPM; with vacuum actuator energized, 850D RPM.

⑨ —With holding solenoid energized, 950 RPM; with vacuum actuator energized, 1000 RPM.

⑩ —With holding solenoid energized, 750D RPM; with vacuum actuator energized, 850D RPM.

⑪ —CJ models.

⑫ —With holding solenoid energized, 750 RPM; with vacuum actuator energized, 900 RPM.

⑬ —With holding solenoid energized, 650D RPM; with vacuum actuator energized, 800D RPM.

⑭ —Cherokee, Wagoneer, J-10 & J-20.

⑮ —On hilly terrain, set at 12° BTDC.

⑯ —On hilly terrain, set at 700 RPM.

⑰ —With fast idle adjusting screw on second step of fast idle cam, engine at operating temperature & EGR vacuum hose disconnected & plugged.

⑱ —At 1600 RPM with vacuum switch electrical connector disconnected. Also disconnect & plug distributor vacuum advance hose.

⑲ —With distributor vacuum advance hose disconnected & plugged.

⑳ —On all models exc. Federal CJ models, at 1600 RPM with ignition module two wire (yellow & black) electrical connector disconnected & distributor vacuum advance hose disconnected. & plugged.

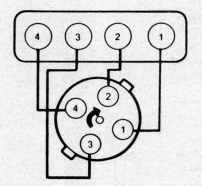

**Fig. A**

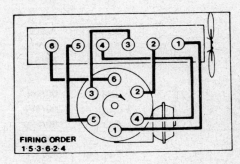

FIRING ORDER 1·5·3·6·2·4

**Fig. B**

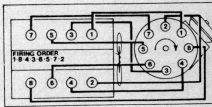

FIRING ORDER 1·8·4·3·6·5·7·2

**Fig. C**

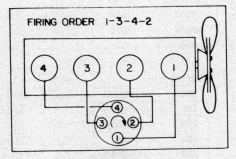

FIRING ORDER 1-3-4-2

**Fig. D**

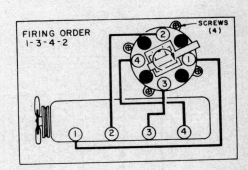

FIRING ORDER 1-3-4-2

SCREWS (4)

**Fig. E**

# TUNE UP SPECIFICATIONS

## JEEP COMANCHE & 1984–89 CHEROKEE & WAGONEER

| Year & Engine | Spark Plug Gap | Ignition Timing BTDC | | | | Curb Idle Speed② | | Fast Idle Speed | | Fuel Pump Pressure |
| | | Firing Order ① | Man. Trans. | Auto. Trans. | Mark Location | Man. Trans. | Auto. Trans. | Man. Trans. | Auto. Trans. | |
|---|---|---|---|---|---|---|---|---|---|---|
| **1987–89** | | | | | | | | | | |
| 4-151 | .035 | A | ⑤ | ⑤ | Damper | ⑤ | ⑤ | ⑤ | ⑤ | 31–39 |
| 6-243 | .035 | B | ⑤ | ⑤ | Damper | ⑤ | ⑤ | ⑤ | ⑤ | 31–39 |
| **1986** | | | | | | | | | | |
| 4-151 | .035 | A | ⑤ | ⑤ | Damper | ⑤ | ⑤ | ⑤ | ⑤ | — |
| V6-173 | .041 | C | ④ | 12 | Damper | 700 | 700D | 2000④ | 2300④ | 6-7.5 |
| **1984–85** | | | | | | | | | | |
| 4-151 | .035 | D | ③⑦ | ③⑦ | Damper | 750 | 700D | 2000⑥ | 2300⑥ | 4—5 |
| V6-173 | .041 | C | ④ | 12 | Damper | 700 | 700D | 2000⑥ | 2300⑥ | 6-7.5 |

①—Before removing wires from distributor cap, determine location of No. 1 wire in cap, as distributor position may have been altered from that shown at the end of this chart.

②—Idle speed on man. trans. models is adjusted in Neutral. On auto. trans. models, idle speed is adjusted in Drive (D). When checking idle speed, set parking brake & block drive wheels.

③—Exc. high alt., 12 BTDC; high alt., 19 BTDC.

④—Exc. Calif., 8 BTDC; California, 10 BTDC.

⑤—Non-adjustable.

⑥—On second step of fast idle cam with engine warm & EGR disconnected.

⑦—At 1600 RPM with vacuum switch electrical connector disconnected. Also disconnect and plug distributor vacuum advance hose.

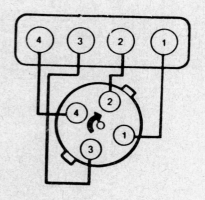

Fig. A

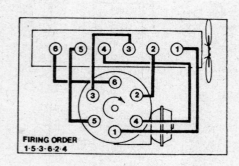

FIRING ORDER 1·5·3·6·2·4

Fig. B

FIRING ORDER 1-2-3-4-5-6

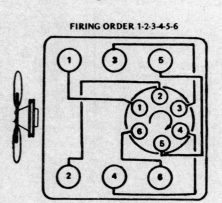

Fig. C

FIRING ORDER 1-3-4-2

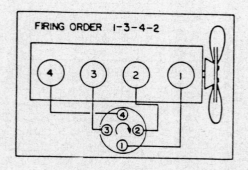

Fig. D

## DODGE & PLYMOUTH EXC. DAKOTA, MINI VANS, RAMPAGE & SCAMP

| Year & Engine | Spark Plug Gap | Firing Order ① | Ignition Timing BTDC Man. Trans. | Ignition Timing BTDC Auto. Trans. | Mark Location | Curb Idle Speed ② Man. Trans. | Curb Idle Speed ② Auto. Trans. | Fast Idle Speed Man. Trans. | Fast Idle Speed Auto. Trans. | Fuel Pump Pressure |
|---|---|---|---|---|---|---|---|---|---|---|
| **1988–89** | | | | | | | | | | |
| V6-239 | .035 | C | 10 | 10 | Damper | 750 | 750N | — | — | 5.75–7.25 |
| V8-318 | .035 | B | 10 | 10 | Damper | 700 | 700N | — | — | 5.75–7.25 |
| V8-360 Exc. High Alt. ④ | .035 | B | — | 12 | Damper | — | 800N | — | — | 5.75–7.25 |
| V8-360 High Alt. ④ | .035 | B | — | 12 | Damper | — | 750N | — | — | 5.75–7.25 |
| V8-360 Exc. Calif. & High Alt. ③⑨ | .035 | B | 10 | 10 | Damper | 710 | 710N | — | — | 5.75–7.25 |
| V8-360 Exc. Calif. & High Alt. ③⑩ | .035 | B | 13 | 13 | Damper | 800 | 800N | — | — | 5.75–7.25 |
| V8-360 Calif. ③ | .035 | B | 10 | 10 | Damper | 800 | 800N | — | — | 5.75–7.25 |
| V8-360 High Alt. ③ | .035 | B | — | 13 | Damper | — | 800N | — | — | 5.75–7.25 |
| **1987** | | | | | | | | | | |
| 6-225 Exc. Calif. | .035 | A | 12㉓ | 16㉓ | Damper | 725 | 750N | — | — | 4–5.5 |
| 6-225 Calif. | .035 | A | 12㉓ | 16㉓ | Damper | 775 | 775N | — | — | 4–5.5 |
| V8-318 | .035 | B | 8㉓ | 8㉓ | Damper | 650 | 650N | — | — | 5.75–7.25 |
| V8-360 Exc. High Alt. ④ | .035 | B | — | 12㉓ | Damper | — | 800N | — | — | 5.75–7.25 |
| V8-360 High Alt. ④ | .035 | B | — | 12㉓ | Damper | — | 750N | — | — | 5.75–7.25 |
| V8-360 Exc. Calif. ③⑨ | .035 | B | — | 10㉓ | Damper | — | 710N | — | — | 5.75–7.25 |
| V8-360 Calif. ③⑨ | .035 | B | — | 10㉓ | Damper | — | 800 | — | — | 5.75–7.25 |
| V8-360 ③⑩ | .035 | B | — | 13㉓ | Damper | — | 800 | — | — | 5.75–7.25 |
| **1986** | | | | | | | | | | |
| 6-225 Exc. Calif. | .035 | A | 12㉓ | 16㉓ | Damper | 725 | 750N | — | — | 4–5.5 |
| 6-225 Calif. | .035 | A | 12㉓ | 16㉓ | Damper | 775 | 775N | — | — | 4–5.5 |
| V8-318 Exc. Calif. & High Alt. | .035 | B | 12㉓ | 12㉓ | Damper | 700 | 700N | — | — | 5.75–7.25 |
| V8-318 Calif. & High Alt. | .035 | B | 8㉓ | 8㉓ | Damper | 650 | 650N | — | — | 5.75–7.25 |
| V8-360 Exc. High Alt. ④ | .035 | B | 12㉓ | 16㉓ | Damper | 800 | 800N | — | — | 5.75–7.25 |
| V8-360 High Alt. ④ | .035 | B | 12㉓ | 16㉓ | Damper | 750 | 710N | — | — | 5.75–7.25 |
| V8-360 Exc. Calif. ③ | .035 | B | 10㉓ | 10㉓ | Damper | 750 | 750N | — | — | 5.75–7.25 |
| V8-360 Calif. ③ | .035 | B | 10㉓ | 10㉓ | Damper | 800 | 800N | — | — | 5.75–7.25 |
| **1985** | | | | | | | | | | |
| 6-225 Exc. Calif. | .035 | A | 12㉓ | 16㉓ | Damper | 725 | 750 | 1600 | 1600 | 4–5.5 |
| 6-225 Calif. | .035 | A | 12㉓ | 16㉓ | Damper | 725 | 775N | 1600 | 1600 | 4–5.5 |
| V8-318 Exc. Calif. & High Alt. | .035 | B | 12㉓ | 12㉓ | Damper | 700 | 700N | 1600 | 1600 | 5.75–7.25 |
| V8-318 Calif. | .035 | B | 8㉓ | 8㉓ | Damper | 725 | 650N | 1400 | 1400 | 5.75–7.25 |
| V8-318 High Alt. | .035 | B | 8㉓ | 8㉓ | Damper | 650 | 650N | 1625 | 1450 | 5.75–7.25 |
| V8-360 Exc. High Alt. ④ | .035 | B | — | 16㉓ | Damper | 800 | 800N | 1350 | 1350 | 5.75–7.25 |
| V8-360 High Alt. ④ | .035 | B | — | 16㉓ | Damper | — | 750N | — | 1600 | 5.75–7.25 |
| V8-360 ③ | .035 | B | 6㉓ | 6㉓ | Damper | 800 | 800N | 1350 | 1350 | 5.75–7.25 |
| **1984** | | | | | | | | | | |
| 6-225 1 Bbl. ⑤ | .035 | A | 12㉓ | 16㉓ | Damper | 700 | 725N | 1600 | 1600 | 3–4.5 |
| V8-318 2Bbl. Exc. Calif. ⑤⑥ | .035 | B | 16㉓ | 16㉓ | Damper | 800 | 800N | 1400 | 1400 | 4.75–6.25 |
| V8-318 2Bbl. Exc. Calif. ⑤⑦ | .035 | B | 12㉓ | 12㉓ | Damper | 760 | 760N | 1400 | 1400 | 4.75–6.25 |
| V8-318 2 Bbl. Calif. ⑤⑥ | .035 | B | 16㉓ | 16㉓ | Damper | 740 | 700N | 1400 | 1400 | 4.75–6.25 |
| V8-318 4 Bbl. Exc. Calif. ④⑤ | .035 | B | — | 14㉓ | Damper | — | 760 | — | — | 4.75–6.25 |
| V8-318 4 Bbl. Exc. Calif. ④⑧ | .035 | B | — | 14㉓ | Damper | — | 700 | — | — | 4.75–6.25 |
| V8-318 4 Bbl. Exc. Calif. ③⑧ | .035 | B | — | 4㉓ | Damper | — | 700 | — | — | 4.75–6.25 |
| V8-360 4 Bbl. Calif. ③⑤ | .035 | B | — | 10㉓ | Damper | — | 750N | 1350 | 1350 | 4.75–6.25 |

## DODGE & PLYMOUTH EXC. DAKOTA, MINI VANS, RAMPAGE & SCAMP— Continued

| Year & Engine | Spark Plug Gap | Firing Order [1] | Ignition Timing BTDC Man. Trans. | Ignition Timing BTDC Auto. Trans. | Mark Location | Curb Idle Speed [2] Man. Trans. | Curb Idle Speed [2] Auto. Trans. | Fast Idle Speed Man. Trans. | Fast Idle Speed Auto. Trans. | Fuel Pump Pressure |
|---|---|---|---|---|---|---|---|---|---|---|
| **1983** | | | | | | | | | | |
| 6-225, 1 Bbl. Exc. Calif. | .035 | A | 12° [23] | 16° [23] | Damper | 600/800 | 650/800 | 1600 | 1600 | 3-4½ |
| 6-225, 1 Bbl. Calif. | .035 | A | 12° [23] | 16° [23] | Damper | 750/850 | 750/850 | 1600 | 1600 | 3-4½ |
| 6-225, 2 Bbl. Exc. Calif. | .035 | A | 12° [23] | — | Damper | 700/850 | — | 1600 | — | 3-4½ |
| V8-318, 2 Bbl. Exc. Calif. | .035 | B | 12° [23] | 12° [23] | Damper | 750/850 | 750/850 | 1500 | 1500 | 4¾-6¼ |
| V8-318, 2 Bbl. Calif. | .035 | B | 16° [23] | 16° [23] | Damper | 700/850 | 700/850 | 1400 | 1400 | 4¾-6¼ |
| V8-318, 2 Bbl. High Alt. | .035 | B | 16° [23] | 16° [23] | Damper | 700/850 | 700/850 | 1400 | 1400 | 4¾-6¼ |
| V8-318, 4 Bbl. Exc. Calif. [4] | .035 | B | 12° [23] | 16° [23] | Damper | 750 | 750 | 1600 | 1600 | 4¾-6¼ |
| V8-318, 4 Bbl. Calif. [4] | .035 | B | 12° [23] | — [23] | Damper | 750 | — | 1800 | — | 4¾-6¼ |
| V8-318, 4 Bbl. [3] | .035 | B | 8° [23] | 8° [23] | Damper | 750 | 750 | 1800 | 1800 | 4¾-6¼ |
| V8-360, 4 Bbl. Exc. Calif. | .035 | B | 4° [23] | 4° [23] | Damper | 700 | 700 | 1500 | 1500 | 4¾-6¼ |
| V8-360, 4 Bbl. Calif. [3] | .035 | B | 10° [23] | 10° [23] | Damper | 750 | 750 | 1700 | 1700 | 4¾-6¼ |
| **1982** | | | | | | | | | | |
| 6-225, Exc. Calif. | .035 | A | 12° [23] | 16° [23] | Damper | 600/800 | 600/800 | 1800 | 1600 | 3½-5 |
| 6-225, Calif. | .035 | A | 12° [23] | 16° [23] | Damper | 800 | 800 | 1800 | 1600 | 3½-5 |
| 6-225-2, 2 Bbl. | .035 | A | 12° [23] | — | Damper | 700 | — | 1600 | — | 3½-5 |
| V8-318, 2 Bbl. Exc. Calif. | .035 | B | 12° [23] | 12° [23] | Damper | 750 | 750 | 1500 | 1600 | 5-7 |
| V8-318, 4 Bbl. | .035 | B | 12° [23] | 16° [23] | Damper | 750 | 750 | [19] | [19] | 5-7 |
| V8-318, 4 Bbl. [3] | .035 | B | 8° [23] | 8° [23] | Damper | 750 | 750 | [19] | [19] | 5-7 |
| V8-360, 4 Bbl. Exc. Calif. [3] | .035 | B | 4° [23] | 4° [23] | Damper | 700 | 700 | — | — | 5-7 |
| V8-360, 4 Bbl. Calif. [3] | .035 | B | 10° [23] | 10° [23] | Damper | 750 | 750 | 1700 | 1700 | 5-7 |
| **1981** | | | | | | | | | | |
| 6-225, Exc. Calif. | .035 | A | 12° [24] | 16° [24] | Damper | 600/800 | 600/800 | 1600 | 1600 | 3½-5 |
| 6-225, Calif. | .035 | A | 12° [24] | 16° [24] | Damper | 800 | 800 | 1800 | 1600 | 3½-5 |
| V8-318, 2 Bbl. | .035 | B | 10° [24] | 16° [24] | Damper | 650/800 | 650/800 | 1500 | 1500 | 5-7 |
| V8-318, 4 Bbl. Exc. Calif. [4] | .035 | B | — | 16° [24] | Damper | — | 750/800 | 1800 | 1800 | 5-7 |
| V8-318, 4 Bbl. Calif. [4] [11] | .035 | B | 12° [24] | 16° [24] | Damper | 750/800 | 750/800 | 1500 | 1600 | 5-7 |
| V8-318, 4 Bbl. Calif. [4] [12] | .035 | B | 16° [24] | 16° [24] | Damper | 700/800 | 700/800 | 1500 | 1600 | 5-7 |
| V8-318, 4 Bbl. [3] | .035 | B | 12° [24] | 12° [24] | Damper | 750/800 | 750/800 | 1800 | 1800 | 5-7 |
| V8-360-1, Exc. Calif. | .035 | B | 12° [24] | 16° [24] | Damper | 600/800 | 625/800 | 1500 | 1500 | 5-7 |
| V8-360-1, Calif. [4] [13] | .035 | B | 12° [24] | 16° [24] | Damper | 750/800 | 750/800 | 1700 | 1700 | 5-7 |
| V8-360-1, Calif. [4] [14] | .035 | B | 16° [24] | 16° [24] | Damper | 700/800 | 700/800 | 1700 | 1700 | 5-7 |
| V8-360-1 [3] | .035 | b | — | 4° [24] | Damper | — | 700/800 | — | 1500 | 5-7 |
| V8-360-3 [15] | .035 | B | — | 4° [24] | Damper | — | 700/800 | — | 1500 | 5-7 |
| V8-360-3 [16] | .035 | B | — | 10° [24] | Damper | — | 750/800 | — | 1700 | 5-7 |
| **1980** | | | | | | | | | | |
| 6-225, Exc. Calif. | .035 | A | 12° [24] | 12° | Damper | 600 | 600 | 1600 | 1600 | 3½-5 |
| 6-225, Calif. | .035 | A | 12° [24] | 12° | Damper | 800 | 800 | 1600 | 1700 | 3½-5 |
| V8-318, 2 Bbl. | .035 | B | 12° [24] | 12° | Damper | 600 | 600 | 1600 | 1600 | 5-7 |
| V8-318, 4 Bbl. [17] | .035 | B | 6° [24] | 6° | Damper | 750 | 750 | 1500 | 1500 | 5-7 |
| V8-318, 4 Bbl. [3] | .035 | B | 8° [24] | 8° | Damper | 750 | 750 | 1800 | 1800 | 5-7 |
| V8-360-1, 4 Bbl. Exc. Calif. [4] | .035 | B | 12° [24] | 12° | Damper | 650 | 650 | 1600 | 1600 | 5-7 |
| V8-360-1, 4 Bbl. Exc. Calif. [3] | .035 | B | 4° [24] | 4° | Damper | 700 | 700 | 1600 | 1600 | 5-7 |
| V8-360-1, 4 Bbl. Calif. | .035 | B | 10° [24] | 10° | Damper | 750 | 750 | 1600 | 1600 | 5-7 |
| V8-360-3, 4 Bbl. Exc. Calif. | .035 | B | 4° [24] | 4° | Damper | 700 | 700 | — | 1600 | 5-7 |
| V8-360-3, 4 Bbl. Calif. [18] | .035 | B | 10° [24] | 10° | Damper | 750 | 750 | 1800 | 1800 | 5-7 |
| V8-360-3, 4 Bbl. Calif. [20] | .035 | B | 4° [24] | 4° | Damper | 700 | 700 | 1600 | 1600 | 5-7 |
| MV-446 | .035 | [21] | 5° [22] | 5° [22] | Damper | 525/575 | 625/675 | 2400 | 2400 | 4½-5¾ |

6

## DODGE & PLYMOUTH EXC. DAKOTA, MINI VANS, RAMPAGE & SCAMP— Continued

① —Before removing wires from distributor cap, determine location of No. 1 wire in cap, as distributor position may have been altered from that shown at the end of this chart.

② —Idle speed is adjusted with transmission in Neutral (N). When checking idle speed, set parking brake & block drive wheels.

③ —Heavy duty emissions, GVWR of 8501 lbs. & above.

④ —Light duty emissions, GVWR of 8500 lbs. & under.

⑤ —Models w/catalytic converter.

⑥ —Models w/electronic spark advance.

⑦ —Models less electronic spark advance.

⑧ —Models less catalytic converter.

⑨ —Models w/distributor part No. 4111950.

⑩ —Models w/distributor part No. 4145399.

⑪ —Models w/distributor No. 4111501 for man. trans., No. 4145602 for auto. trans.

⑫ —Models w/distributor No. 4145753.

⑬ —Models w/distributor No. 4145364 for man. trans., No. 4145604 for auto. trans.

⑭ —Models w/distributor No. 4145350.

⑮ —Models less catalytic converter.

⑯ —Models w/catalytic converter.

⑰ —Medium duty emission, GVWR 6001 to 8500 lbs.

⑱ —Exc. models w/carburetor No. TQ-9261S.

⑲ —W/carb. No. 4287013, 1600 RPM; w/carb. No. 4241752, 1800 RPM; w/carb. No. 4287016, 1500 RPM; w/carb. No. 4241753, 1700 RPM.

⑳ —Models w/carburetor No. TQ-9261S.

㉑ —Cylinder numbering (front to rear), right bank, 1-3-5-7; left bank, 2-4-6-8. Firing order, 1-2-7-3-4-5-6-8.

㉒ —There are two timing mark plates located on the engine front cover. If the upper timing plate is to be used to check timing, connect timing light to No. 1 cylinder. If the lower timing plate is used to check timing, connect timing light to No. 7 cylinder.

㉓ —On models less spark control computer, disconnect & plug distributor vacuum advance hose. On models with carburetor switch, connect jumper wire between carburetor switch & ground.

㉔ —With distributor vacuum advance hose disconnected & plugged.

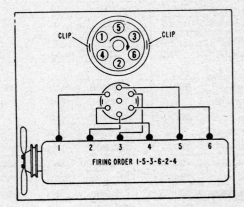

Fig. A

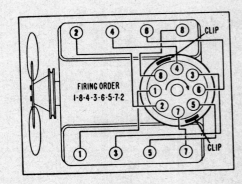

Fig. B

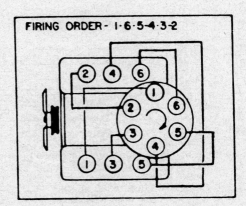

Fig. C

# TUNE UP SPECIFICATIONS

## DODGE RAMPAGE & PLYMOUTH SCAMP

| Year & Engine | Spark Plug Gap | Ignition Timing BTDC | | | | Curb Idle Speed ② | | Fast Idle Speed | | Fuel Pump Pressure |
| | | Firing Order ① | Man. Trans. | Auto. Trans. | Mark Location | Man. Trans. | Auto. Trans. | Man. Trans. | Auto. Trans. | |
|---|---|---|---|---|---|---|---|---|---|---|
| **1984** | | | | | | | | | | |
| 4-135 | .035 | A | 10③ | 10③ | Flywheel | 800 | 900N | 1500④ | ④⑤ | 4.5–6 |
| **1983** | | | | | | | | | | |
| 4-135 Exc. Calif. & High Alt. | .035 | A | 10°③ | 10°③ | Flywheel | 775 | 900N | 1300④ | 1500④ | 4.5–6 |
| 4-135 Calif. | .035 | A | 10°③ | 10°③ | Flywheel | 775 | 900N | 1400④ | 1500④ | 4.5–6 |
| 4-135 High Alt. | .035 | A | 6°③ | 6°③ | Flywheel | 900 | 900N | 1350④ | 1275④ | 4.5–6 |
| **1982** | | | | | | | | | | |
| 4-135 | .035 | A | 12°③ | 12°③ | Flywheel | 850 | 900N | ④⑥ | 1600④ | 4.5–6 |

①—Before removing wires from distributor cap, determine location of No. 1 wire in cap, as distributor position may have been altered from that shown at the end of this chart.

②—Idle speed is adjusted with transmission in Neutral (N). When checking idle speed, set parking brake & block drive wheels.

③—With spark control computer vacuum hose disconnected & plugged. On models equipped with carburetor switch, connect jumper wire between carburetor switch & ground.

④—On slowest speed step of fast idle cam.

⑤—On models w/Holley 5220 carburetor, 1700 RPM; on models w/Holley 6520 carburetor, 1600 RPM.

⑥—On models w/Holley 5220 carburetor, 1400 RPM; on models w/Holley 6520 carburetor, 1300 RPM.

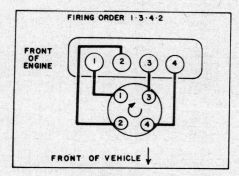

**Fig. A**

## DODGE DAKOTA

| Year & Engine | Spark Plug Gap | Ignition Timing BTDC | | | | Curb Idle Speed ② | | Fast Idle Speed | | Fuel Pump Pressure |
| | | Firing Order ① | Man. Trans. | Auto. Trans. | Mark Location | Man. Trans. | Auto. Trans. | Man. Trans. | Auto. Trans. | |
|---|---|---|---|---|---|---|---|---|---|---|
| **1988–89** | | | | | | | | | | |
| 4-135 | .035 | A | 12 | 12 | Flywheel | 850 | 850N | — | — | 4.5–6 |
| V6-239 | .035 | B | 10 | 10 | Damper | 750 | 750N | — | — | — |
| **1987** | | | | | | | | | | |
| 4-135 | .035 | A | 6③ | 6③ | Flywheel | 850 | 900N | — | — | 4.5–6 |
| V6-239 | .035 | B | 7④ | 7④ | Damper | 720 | 700N | — | — | 5.75–7.25 |

①—Before removing wires from distributor cap, determine location of No. 1 wire in cap, as distributor position may have been altered from that shown at the end of this chart.

②—Idle speed is adjusted with transmission in Neutral (N). When checking idle speed, set parking brake & block drive wheels.

③—With spark control computer vacuum hose disconnected & plugged.

④—With spark control computer & AIR switching valve vacuum hoses disconnected & plugged. Also connect jumper wire between carburetor switch & ground.

## DODGE DAKOTA — Continued

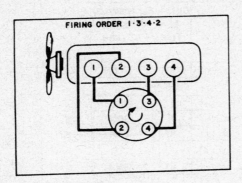

Fig. A

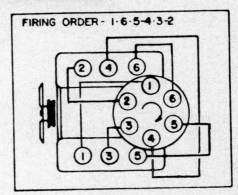

Fig. B

# DODGE CARAVAN, MINI RAM VAN & PLYMOUTH VOYAGER

| Year & Engine | Spark Plug Gap | Firing Order ① | Ignition Timing BTDC | | Mark Location | Curb Idle Speed ② | | Fast Idle Speed | | Fuel Pump Pressure |
|---|---|---|---|---|---|---|---|---|---|---|
| | | | Man. Trans. | Auto. Trans. | | Man. Trans. | Auto. Trans. | Man. Trans. | Auto. Trans. | |
| **1989** | | | | | | | | | | |
| 4-153 Exc. Turbo | .035 | A | 12⑥ | 12⑥ | Flywheel | 850 | 850N | — | — | — |
| 4-153 Turbo | .035 | A | 12⑥ | 12⑥ | Flywheel | 950 | 900N | — | — | — |
| V6-181 | .042 | C | 12⑥ | 12⑥ | Damper | 800 | 800N | — | — | — |
| **1987–88** | | | | | | | | | | |
| 4-153 | .035 | A | 12⑥ | 12⑥ | Flywheel | 850 | 850N | — | — | — |
| V6-181 | .042 | C | 12⑥ | 12⑥ | Damper | — | 700D | — | — | — |
| **1986–87** | | | | | | | | | | |
| 4-135 | .035 | A | 6⑦ | 6⑦ | Flywheel | 850 | 900N | — | — | 4.5–6 |
| 4-156 Exc. High Alt. | .035–.040 | B | | 7⑧ | Damper | — | 800N | — | — | 4.5–6 |
| 4-156 High Alt. | .035–.040 | B | | 12⑧ | Damper | — | 850N | — | — | 4.5–6 |
| **1985** | | | | | | | | | | |
| 4-135 | .035 | A | 10⑦ | 10⑦ | Flywheel | 800 | 900N | 1700④ | 1850④ | 4.5–6 |
| 4-156 Exc. High Alt. | .035–.040 | B | — | 7⑧ | Damper | — | 800 | — | ③⑤ | 4.5–6 |
| 4-156 High Alt. | .035–.040 | B | — | 7⑧ | Damper | — | 850 | — | 950⑤ | 4.5–6 |
| **1984** | | | | | | | | | | |
| 4-135 | .035 | A | 12⑦ | 12⑦ | Flywheel | 800 | 900N | 1500④ | 1700④ | 4.5–6 |
| 4-156 | .035–.040 | B | — | 7⑧ | Damper | — | 800N | — | ③⑤ | 4.5–6 |

①—Before removing wires from distributor cap, determine location of No. 1 wire in cap, as distributor position may have been altered from that shown at the end of this chart.

②—Idle speed is adjusted with transmission in Neutral (N). When checking idle speed, set parking brake & block drive wheels.

③—Exc. Calif., 1300 RPM; California, 950 RPM.

④—On slowest speed step of fast idle cam.

⑤—With tool No. C-4812-C installed on cam follower pin.

⑥—Disconnect coolant sensor wire connector when checking ignition timing.

⑦—With spark control computer vacuum hose disconnected & plugged. On models with carburetor switch, connect jumper wire between carburetor switch & ground.

⑧—With distributor vacuum advance hose disconnected & plugged.

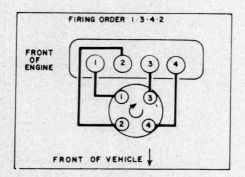

Fig. B

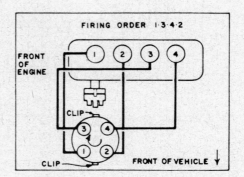

Fig. A

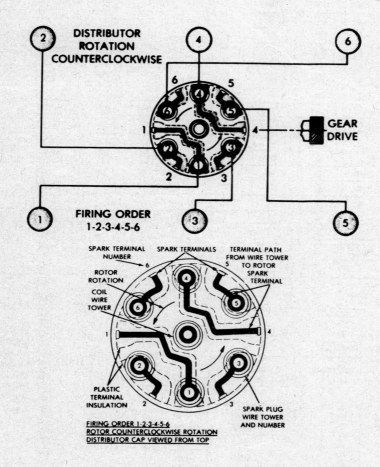

Fig. C

## FORD EXC. AEROSTAR, BRONCO II & 1983–89 RANGER

| Year & Engine | Spark Plug Gap | Firing Order [1] | Ignition Timing BTDC Man. Trans. | Auto. Trans. | Mark Location | Curb Idle Speed [2] Man. Trans. | Auto. Trans. | Fast Idle Speed Man. Trans. | Auto. Trans. | Fuel Pump Pressure |
|---|---|---|---|---|---|---|---|---|---|---|
| **1989** | | | | | | | | | | |
| 6-300 | .044 | [4] | 10[99] | 10[99] | Damper | [8] | [8] | — | — | 35-45[10] |
| V8-302 | .044 | A | 10[99] | 10[99] | Damper | [8] | [8] | — | — | 35-45[10] |
| V8-351 | .044 | B | 10[99] | 10[99] | Damper | [8] | [8] | — | — | 35-45[10] |
| V8-460 | .044 | [5] | 10[99] | 10[99] | Damper | [8] | [8] | — | — | 35-45[10] |
| **1988** | | | | | | | | | | |
| 6-300 | .044 | [4] | 10[99] | 10[99] | Damper | [8] | [8] | — | — | 35-45[10] |
| V8-302 | .044 | A | 10[99] | 10[99] | Damper | [8] | [8] | — | — | 35-45[10] |
| V8-351 | .044 | B | 10[99] | 10[99] | Damper | [8] | [8] | — | — | 35-45[10] |
| V8-460 | .044 | [5] | 10[99] | 10[99] | Damper | [8] | [8] | — | — | 35-45[10] |
| **1987** | | | | | | | | | | |
| 6-300 E150, 250 [86] | .044 | [4] | 10[99] | 10[99] | Damper | 625-725[8] | 525-625D[8] | [8] | [8] | 35-45[10] |
| 6-300 F150 [86][28] | .044 | [4] | 10[99] | 10[99] | Damper | [3][8][95] | [3][8][96] | [8] | [8] | 35-45[10] |
| 6-300 Bronco, F150 [86][28] | .044 | [4] | 10[99] | 10[99] | Damper | [3][8][97] | [3][8][98] | [8] | [8] | 35-45[10] |
| 6-300 F250 [86] | .044 | [4] | 10[99] | 10[99] | Damper | 625-725[8] | 525-625D[8] | [8] | [8] | 35-45[10] |
| 6-300 E & F250, 350 [87] | .044 | [4] | 10[99] | 10[99] | Damper | 650-750[8] | 590-690D[8] | [8] | [8] | 35-45[10] |
| V8-302 | .044 | A | 10[99] | 10[99] | Damper | [8] | 650-800D | — | 2200[79] | 6-8 |
| V8-351 Exc. High Alt. [86] | .044 | B | — | 10[100] | Damper | — | 650-800D | — | 2200[79] | 6-8 |
| V8-351 High Alt. [86] | .044 | B | — | 14[100] | Damper | — | 650-800D | — | 2200[79] | 6-8 |
| V8-351 [87] | .044 | B | 8[100] | 8[100] | Damper | 800 | 700D | 2200[79] | 2200[79] | 6-8 |
| V8-460 Exc. Calif. | .044 | [5] | 8[100] | 8[100] | Damper | 800 | 650D | 2200[79] | 2200[79] | 6-8 |
| V8-460 Calif. | .044 | [5] | 8[100] | 8[100] | Damper | 800 | 650D | 2200[79] | 1600[79] | 6-8 |
| **1986** | | | | | | | | | | |
| 6-300 [6] | .044 | [4] | 10[99] | 10[99] | Damper | [8] | [8] | 1600[78] | 1600[78] | 5-7 |
| 6-300 [7] | .044 | [4] | 6[99] | 8[99] | Damper | 750 | 600D | 1600[78] | 1600[78] | 5-7 |
| V8-302 2 Bbl. | .044 | A | — | 10[99] | Damper | — | 575D | — | 2000[79] | 6-8 |
| V8-302 EFI | .044 | A | 10[99] | 10[99] | Damper | [8] | [8] | [8] | [8] | 35-45[10] |
| V8-351 | .044 | B | 8[100] | 8[100] | Damper | 800 | 700D | 2000[79] | 2000[79] | 6-8 |
| V8-460 | .044 | [5] | 8[100] | 8[100] | Damper | 800 | 650D | 2000[79] | [9][79] | 6-8 |

| Year & Engine | Spark Plug Gap | Firing Order [1] | Ignition Timing BTDC Man. Trans. | Auto. Trans. | Mark Location | Curb Idle Speed [2] Man. Trans. | Auto. Trans. | Fast Idle Speed Man. Trans. | Auto. Trans. | Fuel Pump Pressure |
|---|---|---|---|---|---|---|---|---|---|---|
| **1985** | | | | | | | | | | |
| 6-300 | .044 | [4] | 10[101] | 10[101] | Damper | [8] | [8] | 1600[78] | 1600[78] | 5-7 |
| V8-302 2Bbl. | .044 | A | — | 10[101] | Damper | — | 575D | — | 2000[79] | 6-8 |
| V8-302 EFI [3][11] | .044 | A | 10[101] | 10[101] | Damper | [8] | [8] | [8] | [8] | 35-45[10] |
| V8-302 EFI [3][12] | .044 | A | 8[101] | — | Damper | [8] | — | [8] | [8] | 35-45[10] |
| V8-351 | .044 | B | 8[100] | 8[100] | Damper | 700 | 525/650D | 2000[79] | 2000[79] | 6-8 |
| V8-460 | .044 | [5] | 8[100] | 8[100] | Damper | 800 | 650D | 1600[78] | 1600[78] | 6-8 |
| **1984** | | | | | | | | | | |
| 6-300 [6] | .044 | [4] | 10[101] | 10[101] | Damper | 650 | 600D | 1600[78] | 1600[78] | 5-7 |
| 6-300 [7] | .044 | [4] | 12[101] | 12[101] | Damper | 500/700 | 550D | 1600[78] | 1600[78] | 5-7 |
| V8-302 [102] | .044 | A | 8[101] | 8[101] | Damper | 700/800 | 600/675D | 2100[79] | 2100[79] | 6-8 |
| V8-302 Calif. | .044 | A | — | 10[101] | Damper | — | 575D | — | 2000[79] | 6-8 |
| V8-302 High Alt. | .044 | A | 12[100] | 12[100] | Damper | 700/800 | 600/675D | 2100[79] | 2100[79] | 6-8 |
| V8-351 [3][6][13][102] | .044 | B | 10[100] | 10[100] | Damper | 750 | 600D | 2000[79] | 2000[79] | 6-8 |
| V8-351 [3][6][14][102] | .044 | B | — | 10[100] | Damper | — | 650/700D | — | 1900[79] | 6-8 |
| V8-351 Calif. [3][6] | .044 | B | — | 10[100] | Damper | — | 600D | — | 2000[79] | 6-8 |
| V8-351 High Alt. [3][6][15] | .044 | B | — | 10[100] | Damper | — | 600D | — | 2000[79] | 6-8 |

## FORD EXC. AEROSTAR, BRONCO II & 1983–89 RANGER—Continued

**1984—Con't**

| Year & Engine | Spark Plug Gap | Firing Order [1] | Ignition Timing BTDC Man. Trans. | Auto. Trans. | Mark Location | Curb Idle Speed [2] Man. Trans. | Auto. Trans. | Fast Idle Speed Man. Trans. | Auto. Trans. | Fuel Pump Pressure |
|---|---|---|---|---|---|---|---|---|---|---|
| V8-351 High Alt. [3][6][16] | .044 | B | — | 10[100] | Damper | — | 650/700D | — | 1900[79] | 6–8 |
| V8-351 [7] | .044 | B | 8[100] | 8[100] | Damper | 700 | 650D | — | 1900[79] | 6–8 |
| V8-460 | .044 | [5] | 8[100] | 8[100] | Damper | 800 | 650D [3][17] | 1500[78] | 1500[78] | 6–8 |
| **1983** | | | | | | | | | | |
| V6-232 | .044 | C | 2° | 10°[100] | Damper | 700/850 | 650/750D | 1300[78] | 2200[79] | 6–8 |
| [6][102] | .044 | [4] | 6°[3][70][100] | 10°[100] | Damper | 600/700[3][24] | 550/600D[3][72] | 1600[78] | 1600[78] | 5–7 |
| 6-300 Calif. [6] | .044 | [4] | 6°[100] | 10°[100] | Damper | 600/700 | 550/600D | 1600[78] | 1600[78] | 5–7 |
| 6-300 High Alt. [6] | .044 | [4] | 10°[100] | 10°[100] | Damper | 600/700 | 550/600D | 1600[78] | 1600[78] | 5–7 |
| 6-300 [7] | .044 | [4] | 12°[3][71][100] | 12°[100] | Damper | 500/700 | 550D | 1600[78] | 1600[78] | 5–7 |
| V8-302[102] | .044 | A | 8°[100] | 8°[100] | Damper | 700/800 | 600/675D | 2100[79] | 2100[79] | 6–8 |
| V8-302 Calif. | .044 | A | — | — | Damper | — | 575D | — | 2100[79] | 6–8 |
| V8-302 High Alt. | .044 | A | 12°[100] | 12°[100] | Damper | 700/800 | 600/675D | — | 2000[79] | 6–8 |
| V8-351 [6][102] | .044 | B | — | 10°[100] | Damper | 750/850[3][73] | 550/625D | 2100[79] | 2250[79] | 6–8 |
| V8-351 [6][104] | .044 | B | — | — | Damper | 600/900 | 550/625D | 1700[3][80][81] | 2000[79] | 6–8 |
| V8-351 High Alt. [6] | .044 | B | — | 14°[100] | Damper | 750/850[3][74] | — | 2000[80] | — | 6–8 |
| V8-351 [7] | .044 | B | 8°[100] | 8°[100] | Damper | 700 | 550/625D | 1700[3][80][82] | 2000[79] | 6–8 |
| V8-460 | .044 | [5] | [3][75][100] | [3][75][100] | Damper | 800 | [3][76] | 1500[78] | 1600[78] | 6–8 |

**1982**

| Year & Engine | Spark Plug Gap | Firing Order [1] | Ignition Timing BTDC Man. Trans. | Auto. Trans. | Mark Location | Curb Idle Speed [2] Man. Trans. | Auto. Trans. | Fast Idle Speed Man. Trans. | Auto. Trans. | Fuel Pump Pressure |
|---|---|---|---|---|---|---|---|---|---|---|
| V6-232 | .044 | C | 10°[100] | 12°[100] | Damper | 650/750 | [3][83] | 2100[79] | 2200[79] | 6–8 |
| V8-255 | .044 | A | 8°[100] | 8°[100] | Damper | 750 | 625/700D | 2250[78] | 2000[79] | 6–8 |
| 6-300 [6][102] | .044 | [4] | 6°[3][84][100] | 10°[100] | Damper | 600/700[3][85] | 550D | 1400[3][78][86] | 1400[78] | 5–7 |
| 6-300 Calif. [6] | .044 | [4] | 6°[100] | 10°[100] | Damper | 600/700 | [3][87] | 1600[78] | 1400[78] | 5–7 |
| 6-300 High Alt. [6] | .044 | [4] | 10°[100] | 14°[100] | Damper | 500/600 | 500N/550D | 1400[78] | 1400[78] | 5–7 |
| 6-300 [7] | .044 | [4] | [88][100] | 12°[100] | Damper | 500/700 | 500N/550D | 1600[78] | 1600[78] | 5–7 |
| V8-302[102] | .044 | A | 8°[100] | 8°[100] | Damper | 700 | 575/650D[3][89] | 2000[79] | 2000[79] | 6–8 |
| V8-302 Calif. | .044 | A | — | — | Damper | — | 575/650D | — | 1350[90] | 6–8 |
| V8-302 High Alt. | .044 | A | 12°[100] | 12°[100] | Damper | 730 | 575/650D | — | 2000[79] | 6–8 |
| V8-351 [3][6][27] | .044 | B | 10°[100] | 10°[100] | Damper | 550/625 | 550/625D | 2000[79] | 2100[79] | 6–8 |
| V8-351 [3][6][30] | .044 | B | 14°[100] | 14°[100] | Damper | 550/625 | 550/625D | 2000[79] | 2000[79] | 6–8 |
| V8-351 [3][6][31] | .044 | B | — | — | Damper | 750/850 | 550/625D | 2000[79] | 200[79] | 6–8 |
| V8-351 [3][7][52] | .044 | B | 5°[3][33][100] | [3][34][100] | Damper | 700[3][35] | 600D | [32] | 1650[80] | 6–8 |
| V8-351 [3][7][53] | .044 | B | 12°[100] | — | Damper | 700[3][35] | 525N/650D | 1500[78] | 1500[3][36][78] | 6–8 |
| V8-400 | .044 | B | 6°[100] | — | Damper | 500 | — | 1650[78] | — | 6–8 |
| V8-460 | .044 | A | 8°[100] | — | Damper | 600 | 500N/600D | 1750[79] | 2000[79] | 6–8 |
| **1981** | | | | | | | | | | |
| 6-300 Exc. E & F-350 | .044 | [4] | 6°[100] | 10°[100] | Damper | 600/700 | 550D | 1400[78] | 1400[78] | 5–7 |
| 6-300[103] | .044 | [4] | 12°[100] | 12°[100] | Damper | 500/700 | 500/550D | 1600[78] | 1400[78] | 5–7 |
| 6-300 F-350 Calif. | .044 | [4] | 10°[100] | — | Damper | 500/700 | — | 1600[78] | [37] | 5–7 |
| V8-255 | .044 | A | 4°[100] | 10°[100] | Damper | 750 | — | 1600[78] | — | 5–7 |
| V8-302 | .044 | A | 8°[100] | 8°[100] | Damper | 700 | 575/650D | 2200[79] | 2000[79] | 6–8 |
| V8-351W [49][66][102] | .044 | B | — | 10°[100] | Damper | — | 575/650D | 2200[79] | 2000[38][79] | 6–8 |
| V8-351W Exc. Calif. [49][87] | .044 | B | — | 6°[100] | Damper | — | 525/600D | — | 1700[79] | 6–8 |
| V8-351W Calif. | .044 | B | — | — | Damper | — | 600D | — | 1650[80] | 6–8 |
| V8-351W High Alt. | .044 | B | — | 8°[100] | Damper | — | 550/625D | — | 2000[79] | 6–8 |
| V8-351M [3][68][92] | .044 | B | 10°[100] | 6°[100] | Damper | 650 | 550/625D | — | 2000[79] | 6–8 |
| V8-351M [3][69][92] | .044 | B | 10°[100] | 10°[100] | Damper | 650 | 550/625D | 2000[79] | 2000[38][79] | 6–8 |
| V8-400 Exc. Calif. | .044 | B | 6°[100] | 3°[100] | Damper | 500/600 | 500/600D | 1750[79] | 1750[79] | 6–8 |
| V8-400 Calif. | .044 | B | 6°[100] | 6°[100] | Damper | 600 | 500/600D | 1750[79] | 2000[79] | 6–8 |
| V8-460 | .044 | A | — | 8°[100] | Damper | 650 | 650D | 1600[79] | 1600[79] | 6–8 |

## FORD EXC. AEROSTAR, BRONCO II & 1983–89 RANGER—Continued

| Year & Engine | Spark Plug Gap | Firing Order [1] | Ignition Timing BTDC Man. Trans. | Ignition Timing BTDC Auto. Trans. | Mark Location | Curb Idle Speed [2] Man. Trans. | Curb Idle Speed [2] Auto. Trans. | Fast Idle Speed Man. Trans. | Fast Idle Speed Auto. Trans. | Fuel Pump Pressure |
|---|---|---|---|---|---|---|---|---|---|---|
| **1980** | | | | | | | | | | |
| 6-300[103][106] | .044 | [4] | 6°[100] | 10°[100] | Damper | 600/700 | 550D | 1400[3][40][78] | 1400[3][40][78] | 5-7 |
| 6-300[105][106] | .044 | [4] | 6°[100] | [3][25] | Damper | 500/700 | 550D | 1400[3][40][41][78] | 1400[3][40][42][78] | 5-7 |
| 6-300 E & F-350[103] | .044 | [4] | 12°[100] | 12°[100] | Damper | 500/700 | 550D | 1400[78] | 1400[78] | 5-7 |
| 6-300 F-350 Calif.[103] | .044 | [4] | 10°[100] | 10°[100] | Damper | 500/700 | 550D | 1400[78] | 1400[78] | 5-7 |
| V8-302 E-100, 150[103] | .044 | A | 8°[100] | 10°[100] | Damper | 700 | 575D | 2000[79] | 2000[79] | 6-8 |
| V8-302 E-100 Calif. | .044 | A | — | 6°[100] | Damper | — | 650D | — | 2400 | 6-8 |
| V8-302 E-150 Calif. | .044 | A | — | [3][29][100] | Damper | — | 600D | — | 2000 | 6-8 |
| V8-302 E-250 Calif. | .044 | A | — | 10°[100] | Damper | — | 575D | — | 2100 | 6-8 |
| V8-302 F-100 | .044 | A | 6°[100] | 8°[100] | Damper | 700 | 575D | [43] | [44] | 6-8 |
| V8-302 F-150[28][103] | .044 | A | 2°[100] | 8°[100] | Damper | 550/800 | 575D | 2000[79] | 2000[79] | 6-8 |
| V8-302 F-150 Calif.[28] | .044 | A | [47] | 8°[100] | Damper | [48] | 650D | 2500[79] | 2400[79] | 6-8 |
| V8-302 F-150 & Bronco[28][103] | .044 | A | 8°[100] | [3][50][100] | Damper | 700 | 575D | 2000[79] | 2000[3][45][79] | 6-8 |
| V8-302 F-150 & Bronco[28][105] | .044 | A | 4°[100] | [3][51][100] | Damper | 750 | 575D | 2500[79] | 2100[79] | 6-8 |
| V8-302 F-250[28][103] | .044 | A | [77][100] | 8°[100] | Damper | 700 | 575D | 2000[79] | 2000[79] | 6-8 |
| V8-302 F-250 Calif.[28] | .044 | A | — | 10°[100] | Damper | — | 575D | — | 2000[79] | 6-8 |
| V8-302 F-250[28] | .044 | A | 8°[100] | 8°[100] | Damper | 700 | 575D | 2000[79] | 2000[3][46][79] | 6-8 |
| V8-351W E-100, 150[3][49][91][103] | .044 | B | — | 6°[100] | Damper | — | 525/650D | — | — | 6-8 |
| V8-351W E-100, 150[3][49][93][94][103] | .044 | B | — | 16°[100] | Damper | — | 500/600D | — | 1750[78] | 6-8 |
| V8-351W E-100, 150[3][18][49][93][103] | .044 | B | — | 14°[100] | Damper | — | 500/600D | — | 1750[78] | 6-8 |
| V8-351W E-100, 150[3][19][49][105] | .044 | B | — | 8°[100] | Damper | — | 500/600D | — | — | 6-8 |
| V8-351W E-100, 150[3][20][49][103] | .044 | B | — | 14°[100] | Damper | — | 500/600D | — | — | 6-8 |
| V8-351W E-100, 150[3][21][49] | .044 | B | — | 10°[100] | Damper | — | 500/600D | — | 1750[78] | 6-8 |
| V8-351W E-100, 150[3][22][49] | .044 | B | — | 8°[100] | Damper | — | 500/600D | — | 1750[78] | 6-8 |
| V8-351M E-250, 350[3][23][92] | .044 | B | — | 6°[100] | Damper | — | 550/625D | — | 2000[79] | 6-8 |
| V8-351M E-250, 350[3][54][92] | .044 | B | — | 4°[100] | Damper | — | 550/625D | — | 2000[79] | 6-8 |
| V8-351M[3][55][92][107] | .044 | B | 10°[56][100] | 10°[56][100] | Damper | 600 | 550/600D | 1750[79] | 2000[79] | 6-8 |
| V8-351M F-100-350[3][57][92] | .044 | B | 16°[56][100] | 14°[56][100] | Damper | 650 | 550/625D | 2000[79] | 2000[79] | 6-8 |
| V8-351M[3][58][92][107] | .044 | B | 10°[100] | 12°[56][100] | Damper | 650 | 550/625D | 2000[79] | 2000[79] | 6-8 |
| V8-351M[3][59][92][107] | .044 | B | 10°[100] | 8°[56][100] | Damper | 550/800 | 550/625D | 2000[79] | 1750[79] | 6-8 |
| V8-351M[3][60][92][107] | .044 | B | — | 6°[56][100] | Damper | — | 550/625D | — | 2000[79] | 6-8 |
| V8-351M[3][61][92][107] | .044 | B | — | 4°[56][100] | Damper | — | 550/625D | — | — | 6-8 |
| V8-400 E-250, 350 | .044 | B | — | 4°[100] | Damper | — | 550/625D | — | 2000[79] | 6-8 |
| V8-400[3][82] | .044 | B | 6°[56][100] | 3°[56][100] | Damper | 600 | 500/600D | 1750[79] | 2000[79] | 6-8 |
| V8-400 F-100-350[3][83] | .044 | B | 6°[56][100] | 6°[56][100] | Damper | 600 | 500/600D | 1750[79] | 2000[79] | 6-8 |
| V8-400 F-100-350[3][84] | .044 | B | — | 4°[56][100] | Damper | — | 550/625D | — | 2000[79] | 6-8 |
| V8-460 | .044 | A | — | 8°[100] | Damper | — | 650D | — | 1600[79] | 6-8 |

① —Before removing wires from distributor cap, determine location of No. 1 wire in cap, as distributor position may have been altered from that shown at the end of this chart.

② —Idle speed on man. trans. models is adjusted in Neutral. On auto. trans. models, idle speed is adjusted in Drive (D). When checking idle speed, set parking brake & block drive wheels. Where two idle speeds are listed, the higher speed is with the idle or A/C solenoid energized.

③ —Refer to engine calibration code on engine code information label, located at rear of left valve cover on V8 engines. The calibration code is located below or after the engine code number.

④ —Cylinder numbering front to rear 1, 2, 3, 4, 5, 6. Firing order 1-5-3-6-2-4.

⑤ —Cylinder numbering front to rear, right bank 1, 2, 3, 4; left bank 5, 6, 7, 8. Firing order 1-5-4-2-6-3-7-8.

## FORD EXC. AEROSTAR, BRONCO II & 1983–89 RANGER—Continued

(6)—Light duty models.
(7)—Heavy duty models.
(8)—Controlled by an idle speed control motor.
(9)—Exc. Calif., 2200 RPM; California, 1600 RPM.
(10)—Wrap shop towel around diagnostic valve to prevent fuel spillage. Connect a suitable fuel pressure gauge to fuel diagnostic valve. Energize fuel pump & note fuel pressure reading.
(11)—Exc. calibration code 5-53F-R01 & 5-53H-R01.
(12)—Calibration codes 5-53F-R01 & 5-53H-R01.
(13)—Calibration codes 4-63H-R0, 4-64H-R0 & 4-64H-R10.
(14)—Calibration codes 4-4-64G-R0 & 4-64G-R02.
(15)—Calibration code 4-64Y-R0.
(16)—Calibration code 4-64Z-R0.
(17)—Calibration code 3-98S-R10, 600D RPM.
(18)—Calibration codes 0-64B-R0 & R10.
(19)—Calibration codes 0-64T-R0, R10 & R11.
(20)—Calibration code 0-64B-R11.
(21)—Calibration codes 0-64G-R0, R10 & R11.
(22)—Calibration codes 0-64H-R0, R10 & R11.
(23)—Calibration codes 0-60D-R0 & R10.
(24)—Calibration code 3-51P-R00, 475/500 RPM; calibration code 3-51T-R10, 500/600 RPM.
(25)—Exc. calibration code 0-52S-R10, 10° BTDC; calibration code 0-52S-R10, 6° BTDC.
(26)—Exc. 4 wheel drive models.
(27)—Calibration code 1-64H-R2.
(28)—4 wheel drive models.
(29)—Calibration code 0-54T-R0, 12° BTDC; calibration code 0-54T-R10, 8° BTDC.
(30)—Calibration code 2-64X-R0.
(31)—Exc. calibration codes 1-64H-R2 & 2-64X-R0.
(32)—Exc. Calif., 1700 RPM; Calif., 1650 RPM.
(33)—Calibration code 7-75J-R14, 6°; calibration codes 2-75A-R10 & 2-75J-R20, 8°.
(34)—Calibration codes 2-76A-R10 & 2-76J-R20, 8°; calibration codes 2-76J-R17 & 2-76J-R18, 5°.
(35)—Calibration code 2-75A-R10, 800 RPM.
(36)—Calibration codes 7-76J-R11, 7-76J-R14 & 7-76J-R15, 1700 RPM.
(37)—Calibration code 9-78J-R0, 1500 RPM on kickdown step of cam; calibration code 9-78J-R11, 1600 RPM on high step of fast idle cam.
(38)—Calibration codes 1-54P-R0 & 1-54R-R0, 1350 on high step of fast idle cam.
(39)—Calibration codes 1-60A-R0 & 1-60B-R0, 2200 RPM.
(40)—Calibration code 0-51F-R0, 1600 RPM on kickdown step of cam.
(41)—Calibration codes 0-51S-R0 & 0-51T-R0, 1600 RPM on kickdown step of cam.
(42)—Calibration code 0-52S-R0, 1600 RPM on kickdown step of cam
(43)—Exc. Calif., 2000 RPM on high step of fast idle cam; Calif., 2500 RPM on high step of fast idle cam.
(44)—Exc. Calif., 2000 RPM on high step of fast idle cam; Calif., 2400 RPM on high step of fast idle cam.
(45)—Calibration code 0-54M-R0, 2100 RPM on high step of fast idle cam.
(46)—Calibration code 8-77M-R0, 2550 RPM on high step of fast idle cam.
(47)—Models w/3 spd. or 4 spd. overdrive man. trans., 2° BTDC; models w/4 spd. man. trans., 4° BTDC.
(48)—Models w/3 spd. or 4 spd. overdrive man. trans., 550/800 RPM; models w/4 spd. man. trans., 750 RPM.
(49)—Windsor engine.
(50)—Calibration code 0-54D-R0, 14° BTDC; 0-54D-R11, 12° BTDC; 0-54F-R0 & 0-54M-R0, 8° BTDC.
(51)—Calibration code 0-54M-R0, 8° BTDC; 0-54R-R0, 10° BTDC.
(52)—Exc. calibration code 7-76J-R13.
(53)—Calibration code 7-76J-R13.
(54)—Calibration code 0-62D-R10.
(55)—Calibration codes, man. trans. 9-71J-R10; auto. trans. 9-72J-R11.
(56)—On early 1980 Bronco & F Series, a sight hole located at the upper right hand corner of the fan shroud is used for viewing the pointer when adjusting ignition timing. It is recommended that the timing be set 2° less than the value observed on the engine damper through the sight hole, due to the angle employed when viewing the pointer.
(57)—Calibration codes, man. trans. 0-59C-R0; auto. trans. 0-60A-R0 & R10.
(58)—Calibration codes, man. trans. 0-59G-R0 & R10, 0-59H-R0 & R10 & 0-59J-R0 & R10; auto. trans. 0-60B-R0 & R10 & 0-60C-R0 & R10.
(59)—Calibration codes, man. trans. 0-59S-R0; auto. trans. 0-60G-R0, 0-60H-R11 & 0-60H-R13.
(60)—Calibration codes 0-60H-R0, 0-60H-R12, 0-60K-R0, R10, R11, R12 & 0-60J-R0.
(61)—Calibration code 0-60L-R10.
(62)—Calibration codes, man. trans. 9-73J-R11; auto. trans. 9-74J-R11.
(63)—Calibration codes, ma. trans. 9-73J-R12; auto. trans. 9-74J-R12.
(64)—Calibration code 0-62L-R0.
(65)—Calibration code 4-64Z-R00.
(66)—Models with G.V.W.R. less than 8500 lbs.
(67)—Models with G.V.W.R. 8500 lbs. & above.
(68)—Exc. calibration code 9-72J-R10.
(69)—Calibration code 9-71J-R10.
(70)—Exc. calibration code 3-51P-R00, 10°.
(71)—Exc. calibration code 9-77S-R10, 10°.
(72)—Calibration code 3-51Z-R00, 600/700D RPM.
(73)—Calibration code 1-64T-R15B, 600/900 RPM.
(74)—Calibration codes 2-63Y-R14B & 2-64Y-R14B, 600/900 RPM.
(75)—Calibration code 3-98S-R00, 6°; calibration code 9-97J-R13, 8°.
(76)—Calibration code 3-98S-R00, 600D RPM; calibration code 9-97J-R13, 650D RPM.
(77)—Models w/3 spd. or 4 spd. overdrive man. trans., 6° BTDC; models w/4 spd. man. trans., 8° BTDC.
(78)—On kickdown step of cam.
(79)—On high step of fast idle cam.
(80)—On second highest step of fast idle cam.
(81)—Calibration codes 1-64T-R12 & 1-64T-R13, 1650 RPM on second highest step of fast idle cam.
(82)—Calibration codes 2-64Y-R11 & 1-64Y-R12, 1650 RPM on second highest step of fast idle cam.
(83)—Calibration code 2-56D-R0, 550/600D RPM; calibration code 2-56D-R10, 600/700D RPM.
(84)—Calibration code, 2-51P-R0, 10°; calibration code 2-51P-R10, 12°.
(85)—Calibration codes 2-51P-R0 & 2-51P-R10, 500 RPM.
(86)—Calibration codes 2-51P-R0 & 2-51P-R10, 1600 RPM.
(87)—Calibration code 2-52S-R0, 550/600D RPM; calibration code 2-52T-R0, 550D RPM.
(88)—Calibration code 9-77J-R12, 12°; calibration code 9-77S-R10, 10°.
(89)—Calibration codes 2-54F-R0 & 2-54F-R10, 575D RPM.
(90)—On third highest step of fast idle cam.
(91)—Calibration code 7-76J-R11.
(92)—Modified engine.
(93)—Exc. high altitude.
(94)—Calibration codes 0-64A-R0, R10 & R11.
(95)—Exc. calibration code 7-51F-R0, 625-725 RPM; calibration code 7-51F-R0, 590-690 RPM.
(96)—Exc. calibration codes 7-52E-R11, 7-52G-R11 & 7-52Z-R11, 525-625D; calibration codes 7-52E-R11, 7-52G-R11 & 7-52Z-R11, 590-690D RPM.
(97)—Exc. calibration code 7-51H-R0, 625-725 RPM; calibration code 7-51H-R0, 590-690 RPM.
(98)—Exc. calibration codes 7-52E-R11 & 7-52Z-R11, 525-625D RPM; calibration codes 7-52E-R11 & 7-52Z-R11, 590-690D RPM.
(99)—With inline spout connector disconnected.
(100)— With distributor vacuum advance line disconnected & plugged.
(101)— With single wire connector near distributor disconnected.
(102)— Exc. Calif. & high altitude.
(103)— Exc. Calif.
(104)— Exc. high altitude.
(105)— Calif.
(106)— E & F-100-250 & Bronco.
(107)— E & F-100-350 & Bronco.

## FORD EXC. AEROSTAR, BRONCO II & 1983–89 RANGER—Continued

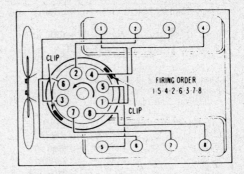

**Fig. A**

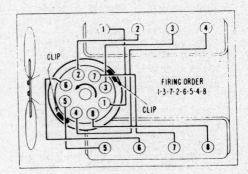

**Fig. B**

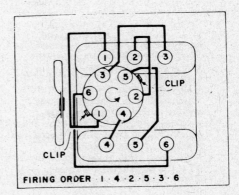

**Fig. C**

## FORD BRONCO II & 1983–89 RANGER

| Year & Engine | Spark Plug Gap | Firing Order [1] | Ignition Timing BTDC | | | Curb Idle Speed [2] | | Fast Idle Speed | | Fuel Pump Pressure |
|---|---|---|---|---|---|---|---|---|---|---|
| | | | Man. Trans. | Auto. Trans. | Mark Location | Man. Trans. | Auto. Trans. | Man. Trans. | Auto. Trans. | |
| **1989** | | | | | | | | | | |
| 4-140 | .044 | A | 10[20] | 10[20] | Damper | 725-875[9] | 725-875D[8] | [9] | [8] | 30-45[5] |
| V6-177 | .044 | B | 10[20] | 10[20] | Damper | 850[8] | 800N[8] | [8] | [8] | 30-45[5] |
| **1987–88** | | | | | | | | | | |
| 4-122 | .044 | A | 6[19] | — | Damper | 775-825[8] | — | 3200 | — | 5-7 |
| 4-140[15] | .044 | A | 10[20] | 10[20] | Damper | 645-795[8] | 645-795D[8] | [8] | [8] | 30-45[5] |
| 4-140[16] | .044 | A | 10[20] | 10[20] | Damper | [7][8][17] | 645-795D[8] | [8] | [8] | 30-45[5] |
| 4-140[18] | .044 | A | 10[20] | 10[20] | Damper | 725-875[8] | 725-875D[8] | [8] | [8] | 30-45[5] |
| V6-177 | .044 | B | 10[20] | 10[20] | Damper | 850[8] | 800N[8] | [8] | [8] | 30-45[5] |
| **1986** | | | | | | | | | | |
| 4-122 | .044 | A | 6[19] | — | Damper | 800 | — | 1700 | — | 4.5-6.5 |
| 4-140 | .044 | A | 10[20] | 10[20] | Damper | 800 | 800D | [8] | [8] | 35-45[5] |
| V6-177 Exc. Calif. | .044 | B | 10[20] | 10[20] | Damper | 850 | 800D | [8] | [8] | 35-45[5] |
| V6-177 Calif. | .044 | B | 10[20] | 10[20] | Damper | 900 | 800D | [8] | [8] | 35-45[5] |
| **1985** | | | | | | | | | | |
| 4-122 | .044 | A | 6[19] | — | Damper | 800 | — | 2000 | — | 4.5-6.5 |
| 4-140 | .044 | A | 10[21] | 10[21] | Damper | 650 | 700D | — | — | 4.5-6.5 |
| V6-171 Exc. Calif. | .044 | C | 10[21] | 10[21] | Damper | 850 | 750D | 3000 | 3000 | 4.5-6.5 |
| V6-171 Calif. | .044 | C | 14[21] | 10[21] | Damper | 850 | 750D | 3200 | 3000 | 4.5-6.5 |
| **1984** | | | | | | | | | | |
| 4-122 | .034 | A | 6[7][19] | — | Damper | 800 | — | 2000 | — | 5-7 |
| 4-140 Exc. High Alt. | .044 | A | 6[21] | 6[21] | Damper | [4] | 800D | 2000 | 2000 | 5-7 |
| 4-140 High Alt. | .044 | A | 10[21] | 10[21] | Damper | [4] | 800D | 2000 | 2000 | 5-7 |
| V6-171 | .044 | C | 10[21] | 10[21] | Damper | [3][7][8] | 750D | 3000 | 3000 | 4.5-6.5 |
| **1983** | | | | | | | | | | |
| 4-122 | .034 | A | 6°[19] | — | B | 800 | — | 2000 | — | 5-7 |
| 4-140 Exc. Calif. & High Alt. | .044 | A | 6°[19] | 6°[19] | B | [22] | 800 | 2000 | 2000 | 5-7 |
| 4-140 Calif.[7][9] | .044 | A | 6°[19] | 6°[19] | B | [22] | 800 | 2000 | 2000 | 5-7 |
| 4-140 Calif.[7][10] | .034 | A | 6°[19] | 8°[19] | B | [22] | [11] | 2000 | 2000 | 5-7 |
| 4-140 High Alt.[7][12] | .044 | A | 10°[19] | 10[19] | B | [22] | 800 | 2000 | 2000 | 5-7 |
| 4-140 High Alt.[7][13] | .034 | A | 10°[19] | [14] | B | 850 | 800 | 2000 | 2000 | 5-7 |

[1] —Before removing wires from distributor cap, determine location of No. 1 wire in cap, as distributor position may have been altered from that shown at the end of this chart.

[2] —Idle speed on man. trans. models is adjusted in Neutral. On auto. trans. models, idle speed is adjusted in Drive (D). When checking idle speed, set parking brake & block drive wheels.

[3] —Calibration codes 4-61G-R0 & 4-61G-R10, 750 RPM; calibration codes 4-61K-R01 & 4-61K-R10, 900 RPM; all other, 850 RPM.

[4] —Less power steer., 800 RPM; w/power steer., 850 RPM.

[5] —Wrap shop towel around fuel diagnostic valve to prevent fuel spillage. Connect a suitable fuel pressure gauge to fuel diagnostic valve. Energize fuel pump & note fuel pressure reading.

[6] —Calibration code 3-41P-R15, 8 BTDC; Calibration code 3-41S-R18, 9 BTDC.

[7] —Refer to engine calibration code on engine code information label, located at rear of left valve cover on V6 engine, on front of valve cover on 4 cylinder inline engine. The calibration code is located below or after the engine code number.

[8] —Controlled by automatic idle speed control.

[9] —Calibration codes 3-49S-R16, 3-49T-R20 & 3-50S-R18.

[10] —Exc. calibration codes 3-49S-R16 3-49T-R20 & 3-50S-R18.

[11] —Calibration code 3-50S-R11, 800 RPM; calibration code 3-50S-R01, 750 RPM.

[12] —Calibration codes 3-49Y-R19 & 3-50Y-R18.

[13] —Exc. calibration codes 3-49Y-R19 & 3-50Y-R18.

[14] —Calibration code 3-50X-R10, 8°; calibration code 3-50X-R11, 10°.

[15] —Ranger regular cab w/2 wheel drive.

[16] —Ranger regular cab w/4 wheel drive.

[17] —Calibration codes 7-49F-R0 & 7-49S-R0, 645-795 RPM; calibration codes 7-46H-R0 & 7-49T-R0, 725-875 RPM.

[18] —Ranger super cab.

[19] —With distributor vacuum advance hose disconnected & plugged.

[20] —With spout connector disconnected.

[21] —With single wire connector near distributor disconnected.

[22] —Less power steer., 800 RPM; w/power steer., 850 RPM.

## FORD BRONCO II & 1983-89 RANGER—Continued

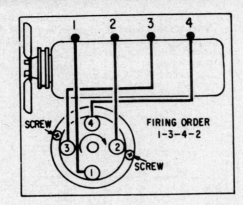

Fig. A

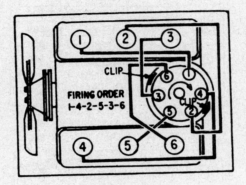

Fig. B

## FORD AEROSTAR

| Year & Engine | Spark Plug Gap | Ignition Timing BTDC | | | | Curb Idle Speed ② | | Fast Idle Speed | | Fuel Pump Pressure |
|---|---|---|---|---|---|---|---|---|---|---|
| | | Firing Order ① | Man. Trans. | Auto. Trans. | Mark Location | Man. Trans. | Auto. Trans. | Man. Trans. | Auto. Trans. | |
| **1989** | | | | | | | | | | |
| V6-182 | .044 | C | 10⑤ | 10⑤ | Damper | ③ | ③ | ③ | ③ | 30–45④ |
| **1987—88** | | | | | | | | | | |
| 4-140 Exc. Calif | .044 | A | 10⑤ | 10⑤ | Damper | 645-795③ | 645-795D③ | ③ | ③ | 30–45④ |
| 4-140 Calif. | .044 | A | 10⑤ | 10⑤ | Damper | 645-790③ | 645-790D③ | ③ | ③ | 35–45④ |
| V6-182 | .044 | C | 10⑤ | 10⑤ | Damper | ③ | ③ | ③ | ③ | |
| **1986** | | | | | | | | | | |
| 4-140 | .044 | A | 10⑤ | 10⑤ | Damper | 800 | 700D | ③ | ③ | 35–45④ |
| V6-171 | .044 | B | 10⑤ | 10⑤ | Damper | 850 | 750D | 3000⑥ | 3000⑥ | 4.5–6.5 |
| V6-182 | .044 | C | 10⑤ | 10⑤ | Damper | ③ | ③ | ③ | ③ | 35–45④ |

# TUNE UP SPECIFICATIONS

## FORD AEROSTAR—Continued

① —Before removing wires from cap, determine location of No. 1 wire in cap, as distributor position may have been altered from that shown at the end of this chart.

② —Idle speed on man. trans. models is adjusted in Neutral. On auto. trans.

models idle speed is adjusted in Drive (D). When checking idle speed, set parking brake & block drive wheels.

③ —Controlled by the idle control system.

④ —Wrap shop towel around fuel

diagnostic valve to prevent fuel spillage. Connect a suitable fuel pressure gauge to fuel diagnostic valve. Energize fuel pump & note pressure reading.

⑤ —With inline spout connector disconnected.

⑥ —On highest step of fast idle cam.

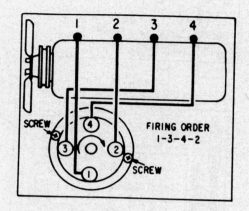

Fig. A

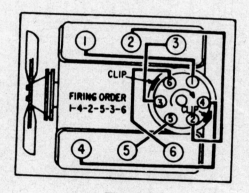

Fig. B

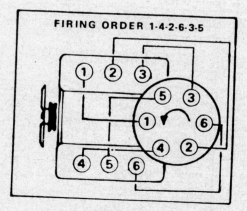

Fig. C

## CHEVROLET & GMC EXC. S/T-10 & 15 & ASTRO VAN & SAFARI VAN

The following specifications are published from the latest information available. This data should only be used in the absence of a decal affixed in the engine compartment.

| Year & Engine | Spark Plug Gap | Firing Order [1] | Ignition Timing BTDC [26] Man. Trans. | Ignition Timing BTDC [26] Auto. Trans. | Ignition Timing BTDC [26] Mark Location | Curb Idle Speed [2] Man. Trans. | Curb Idle Speed [2] Auto. Trans. | Fast Idle Speed Man. Trans. | Fast Idle Speed Auto. Trans. | Fuel Pump Pressure |
|---|---|---|---|---|---|---|---|---|---|---|
| **1988–89** | | | | | | | | | | |
| V6-262 | .035 | E | — | — | Damper | [7] | [7] | [7] | [7] | 9–13[6] |
| V8-305 | .035 | C | TDC[28] | TDC[28] | Damper | [7] | [7] | [7] | [7] | 9–13[6] |
| V8-350 | .035 | D | TDC[28] | TDC[28] | Damper | [7] | [7] | [7] | [7] | 9–13[6] |
| V8-454 | .035 | D | 4[28] | 4[28] | Damper | [7] | [7] | [7] | [7] | 9–13[6] |
| **1987** | | | | | | | | | | |
| V6-262 | .035 | E | — | — | Damper | [7] | [7] | [7] | [7] | 9–13[6] |
| 6-292 | .035 | C | — | — | Damper | — | — | — | — | 4.5–6 |
| V8-305 & 350 4 Bbl. | .035 | D | — | — | Damper | 700 | 500D | — | — | 4–6.5 |
| V8-305 & 350 TBI | .035 | D | — | — | Damper | [7] | [7] | [7] | [7] | 9–13[8] |
| V8-454 4 Bbl. | .045 | D | — | — | Damper | — | — | — | — | [4] |
| V8-454 TBI | .035 | D | — | — | Damper | [7] | [7] | [7] | [7] | 9–13[8] |
| **1986** | | | | | | | | | | |
| V6-262 TBI[3] | .035 | E | — | TDC | Damper | — | [7] | [7] | [7] | 9–13[6] |
| V6-262 4 Bbl. Exc. Calif. & High Alt. [9] | .035 | E | TDC | TDC | Damper | 600 | 500D | 1800[10] | 2200[10] | 4–6.5 |
| V6-262 4 Bbl. Calif. [9] | .035 | E | 4 | 4 | Damper | [7] | [7] | 1800[10] | 1800[10] | 4–6.5 |
| V6-262 4 Bbl. High Alt. [9] | .035 | E | 4 | 4 | Damper | 600 | 500D | 1800[10] | 1800[10] | 4–6.5 |
| 6-292 | .035 | C | 8 | 8 | Damper | 700 | 700N | 2400[10] | 2400[10] | 4.5–6 |
| V8-305 [3] | .035 | D | TDC | TDC | Damper | 700 | 500D | 1800[10] | 2200[10] | 5.5–6.5 |
| V8-305 Exc. Calif. & High Alt. [9] | .045 | D | 4 | 4 | Damper | 700 | 500D | 1700[10] | 1800[10] | [4] |
| V8-305 Calif. [9] | .045 | D | — | 6 | Damper | — | 550D | — | 1800[10] | [4] |
| V8-305 High Alt. [9] | .045 | D | 4 | 4 | Damper | 700 | 600D | 1500[10] | [10] [11] | [4] |
| V8-350 4 Bbl. Exc. High Alt. [8] | .045 | D | 8 | 8 | Damper | 700 | 550D | 1300[10] | 1600[10] | [4] |
| V8-350 4 Bbl. High Alt. [8] | .045 | D | 6 | 6 | Damper | 700 | 600D | 1400[10] | 1600[10] | [4] |
| V8-350 4 Bbl. Exc. Calif. [5] | .045 | D | 4 | 4 | Damper | 600/800 | 700N | 1900[10] | 1900[10] | [4] |
| V8-350 4 Bbl. Calif. [5] | .045 | D | 6 | 6 | Damper | 700 | 700N | 1900[10] | 1900[10] | [4] |
| V8-454 | .045 | D | 4 | 4 | Damper | 700 | 700N | 1900[10] | 1900[10] | [4] |
| **1985** | | | | | | | | | | |
| V6-262 [3] | .035 | E | — | TDC | Damper | — | [7] | — | [7] | 9–13[6] |
| V6-262 Exc. Calif. & High Alt. [9] | .035 | E | TDC | TDC | Damper | 600 | 500D | 1800[10] | 2200[10] | 4–6.5 |
| V6-262 Calif. [9] | .035 | E | 4 | 4 | Damper | [7] | [7] | 1800[10] | 1800[10] | 4–6.5 |
| V6-262 High Alt. [9] | .035 | E | 4 | 4 | Damper | 600 | 500D | 1800[10] | 2200[10] | 7.5–9 |
| V8-305 [3] | .045 | D | TDC | TDC | Damper | 700 | 500D | 1700[10] | 1800[10] | [4] |
| V8-305 Exc. Calif. & High Alt. [9] | .045 | D | 4 | 4 | Damper | — | 550D | — | 1800[10] | [4] |
| V8-305 Calif. [9] | .045 | D | — | 6 | Damper | — | 600D | 1500[10] | [10] [11] | [4] |
| V8-305 High Alt. | .045 | D | 4 | 4 | Damper | 700 | 550D | 1300[10] | 1600[10] | [4] |
| V8-350 4 Bbl. Exc. Calif. & High Alt. [8] | .045 | D | 8 | 8 | Damper | — | [7] | — | 1800[10] | [4] |
| V8-350 4 Bbl. Calif. [8] | .045 | D | — | 6 | Damper | 700 | 600D | 1400[10] | 1400[10] | [4] |
| V8-350 4 Bbl. High Alt. [8] | .045 | D | 8 | 8 | Damper | 700 | 600D | 1300[10] | 1600[10] | [4] |
| V8-350 4 Bbl. Exc. Calif. & High Alt. [5] | .045 | D | 4 | 4 | Damper | 700 | 700N | 1900[10] | 1900[10] | [4] |
| V8-350 4 Bbl. Calif. [5] | .045 | D | 6 | 6 | Damper | [7] | [7] | 1900[10] | 1900[10] | [4] |
| V8-350 4 Bbl. High Alt. [5] | .045 | D | 10 | 10 | Damper | 700 | 700N | 1900[10] | 1900[10] | [4] |
| V8-454 | .045 | D | 4 | 4 | Damper | 700 | 700N | 1900[10] | 1900[10] | [4] |

## CHEVROLET & GMC EXC. S/T-10 & 15 & ASTRO VAN & SAFARI VAN— Continued

| Year & Engine | Spark Plug Gap | Firing Order ① | Ignition Timing BTDC ㉖ Man. Trans. | Auto. Trans. | Mark Location | Curb Idle Speed ② Man. Trans. | Auto. Trans. | Fast Idle Speed Man. Trans. | Auto. Trans. | Fuel Pump Pressure |
|---|---|---|---|---|---|---|---|---|---|---|
| **1984** | | | | | | | | | | |
| V6-229 ③ | .045 | E | — | TDC | Damper | — | ⑦ | — | 2200 ⑩ | 4.5-6 |
| V6-231 ③ | .060 | B | — | 15 | Damper | — | 512D | — | 2200 ⑩ | 5.5-6.5 |
| 6-250 Exc. Calif & High Alt. | .035 | C | 10 | 10 | Damper | 550/700 | 525/650D | 2000 ⑩ | 2200 ⑩ | 4.5-6 |
| 6-250 Calif. | .035 | C | 6 | 6 | Damper | 700/850 | 650/700D | 2000 ⑩ | 2200 ⑩ | 4.5-6 |
| 6-250 High Alt | .035 | C | 10 | 10 | Damper | 600/700 | 600/650D | 2400 ⑩ | 2400 ⑩ | 4.5-6 |
| 6-292 | .035 | C | 8 | 8 | Damper | 700 | 700N | — | 2200 ⑩ | 4.5-6 |
| V8-305 ③ | .045 | D | — | 6 | Damper | — | 500/650D | 1500 ⑩ | 1600 ⑩ | 7.5-9 |
| V8-305 Exc. Calif & High Alt. ⑨ | .045 | D | 4 | 4 | Damper | 700/800 | 500/650D | — | 1800 ⑩ | ④ |
| V8-305 Calif. ⑨ | .045 | D | — | 6 | Damper | — | 550/650D | 1500 ⑩ | 1600 ⑩ | ④ |
| V8-305 High Alt. ⑨ | .045 | D | 4 | 4 | Damper | 700 | 600D | 1300 ⑩ | 1600 ⑩ | ④ |
| V8-350 4 Bbl.Exc. Calif. & High Alt. ⑧ | .045 | D | 8 | 8 | Damper | 700/800 | ㉗ | — | 1800 ⑩ | ④ |
| V8-350 4 Bbl. Calif. ⑧ | .045 | D | — | 6 | Damper | — | 550/650D | 1400 ⑩ | 1400 ⑩ | ④ |
| V8-350 High Alt. ⑧ | .045 | D | 8 | 8 | Damper | 700/800 | 600/650D | 1900 ⑩ | 1900 ⑩ | ④ |
| V8-350 4 Bbl. Exc. Calif. ⑤ | .045 | D | 4 | 4 | Damper | 700 | 700N | 1900 ⑩ | 1900 ⑩ | ④ |
| V8-350 4 Bbl. Calif. ⑤ | .045 | D | 6 | 6 | Damper | 700 | 700N | 1900 ⑩ | 1900 ⑩ | ④ |
| V8-454 | .045 | D | 4 | 4 | Damper | 700 | 700N | 1900 ⑩ | 1900 ⑩ | ④ |
| **1983** | | | | | | | | | | |
| V6-229 | .045 | E | — | TDC | Damper | — | ⑦ | — | 2200N | 4½-6 |
| V6-231 | .080 | B | — | 15° | Damper | — | 500D | — | 2200N | 5½-6½ |
| 6-250 Exc. Calif. & High Alt. | .035 | C | 10° | 10° | Damper | 550/750 | 525/650D | 2000 | 2200N | 4½-6 |
| 6-250 Calif. | .035 | C | 6° | 6° | Damper | 700/850 | ㉓ | 2000 | 2200N | 4½-6 |
| 6-250 High Alt. | .035 | C | 10° | 6° | Damper | 600/750 | 550/650D | 2000 | 2200N | 4½-6 |
| V6-292 | .035 | C | 8° | — | Damper | 700/1500 ⑭ | — | 2400 | — | 4-5 |
| V8-305 ③ | .045 | D | — | 6° | Damper | — | 500/650D | — | 2200N | 7½-9 |
| V8-305 Exc. Calif. & High Alt. | .045 | D | 4° | 4° | Damper | ⑮ | 500/600D | 1300 | 1600N | ④ |
| V8-305 Calif. | .045 | D | — | 8° | Damper | — | 550/600D | — | 1600N | ④ |
| V8-305 High Alt. | .045 | D | 4° | 4° | Damper | 700 | 600D | 1300 | 1600N | ④ |
| V8-350 Exc. Calif. & High Alt. ⑧ | .045 | D | 8° | 8° | Damper | 600/750 | 500/600D | 1300 | 1600N | ④ |
| V8-350 Calif. ⑧ | .045 | D | — | 8° | Damper | — | 500/600D | — | 1800N | ④ |
| V8-350 High Alt. | .045 | D | 8° | 8° | Damper | 700 | 600D | 1600 | 1600N | ④ |
| V8-350 Exc. Calif. ⑤ | .045 | D | 4° | 4° | Damper | 700/1600 ⑭ | 700/1600N ⑭ | 1900 | 1900N | ④ |
| V8-350 Calif. | .045 | D | 6° | 6° | Damper | 700/1500 ⑭ | ⑭ ㉕ | 1900 | 1900N | ④ |
| V8-454 | .045 | D | 4° | 4° | Damper | 700/1500 ⑭ | 700/1500N ⑭ | 1900 | 1900N | ④ |
| **1982** | | | | | | | | | | |
| V6-229 | .045 | E | — | TDC | Damper | — | ⑦ | — | 2200N | 4½-6 |
| V6-231 | .080 | A | — | 15° | Damper | — | 500D | — | 2200N | 3 Min. |
| 6-250 C10 Exc. Calif. & High Alt. | .035 | C | 10° | 10° | Damper | 450/625 | 550/600D | 2000 | 2200N | 4½-6 |
| 6-250 C10 Calif. | .035 | C | 10° | 10° | Damper | 450/700 | 450/650D | 2000 | 2000N | 4½-6 |
| 6-250 C10 High Alt. | .035 | C | — | 10° | Damper | — | 550/650D | — | 2200N | 4½-6 |
| 6-250 K10 Exc. High Alt. | .035 | C | 10° | 10° | Damper | 550/700 | 525/650D | 2000 | 2200N | 4½-6 |
| 6-250 K10 High Alt. | .035 | C | — | 10° | Damper | — | 550/650D | — | 2200N | 4½-6 |
| 6-250 C20 | .035 | C | 10° | 10° | Damper | 550/700 | 525/650D | 2000 | 2200N | 4½-6 |
| 6-250 G Series | .035 | C | 10° | 10° | Damper | 550/700 | 550/650D | 2000 | 2200N | 4½-6 |
| 6-292 | .035 | C | 8° | 8° | Damper | 450/700 | 450/700 | 2400 | 2400N | 4-5 |
| V8-267 | .045 | D | — | 2° | Damper | — | 500/600D | — | 2200N | 7½-9 |
| V8-305 ③ | .045 | D | — | 6° | Damper | — | 500/600D | — | 2200N | 7½-9 |
| V8-305 | .045 | D | 4° | 4° | Damper | 600/750 | 500/600D | 1300 | 1600N | ④ |

## CHEVROLET & GMC EXC. S/T-10 & 15 & ASTRO VAN & SAFARI VAN—Continued

| Year & Engine | Spark Plug Gap | Firing Order [1] | Ignition Timing BTDC [26] Man. Trans. | Auto. Trans. | Mark Location | Curb Idle Speed [2] Man. Trans. | Auto. Trans. | Fast Idle Speed Man. Trans. | Auto. Trans. | Fuel Pump Pressure |
|---|---|---|---|---|---|---|---|---|---|---|
| V8-305 CAlif. | .045 | D | — | 8° | Damper | — | 500/600D | — | 1800N | [4] |
| V8-305 High Alt. | .045 | D | 4° | 4° | Damper | 700 | 600D | 1300 | 1600N | 4° |
| V8-350 Exc. Calif. & High Alt. [8] | .045 | D | 8° | 8° | Damper | 600/750 | 500/600D | 1300 | 1600N | [4] |
| V8-350 Calif. [8] | .045 | D | — | 8° | Damper | — | 550/650D | — | 1800N | [4] |
| V8-350 High Alt. [8] | .045 | D | 8° | 8° | Damper | 700 | 600D | 1600 | 1600N | [4] |
| V8-350 Exc. Calif. [5] | .045 | D | 4° | 4° | Damper | 700 | 700N | 1900 | 1900N | [4] |
| V8-350 Calif. [5] | .045 | D | 6° | 6° | Damper | 700 | 700N | 1900 | 1900N | [4] |
| V8-454 | .045 | D | 4° | 4° | Damper | 700 | 700N | 1900 | 1900N | [4] |

**1982—Con't**

| Year & Engine | Spark Plug Gap | Firing Order [1] | Ignition Timing BTDC [26] Man. Trans. | Auto. Trans. | Mark Location | Curb Idle Speed [2] Man. Trans. | Auto. Trans. | Fast Idle Speed Man. Trans. | Auto. Trans. | Fuel Pump Pressure |
|---|---|---|---|---|---|---|---|---|---|---|
| **1981** | | | | | | | | | | |
| V6-229 | .045 | A | 6° | 6° | Damper | [7] | [7] | 2200 | 2200N | 4½-6 |
| V6-231 | .080 | B | — | 15° | Damper | — | [7] | — | 1800N | 3 Min. |
| 6-250 | .035 | C | 10° | 10° | Damper | 450/750 [18] | 450/650D [19] | 2000 | 2200N | 4½-6 |
| 6-292 | .035 | C | 8° | 8° | Damper | 450/700 | 450/700N | 2400 | 2400N | 4½-6 |
| V8-267 | .045 | D | — | 6° | Damper | — | 500/600D | — | 2200N | 7½-9 |
| V8-305 [3] | .045 | D | 6° | 6° | Damper | 700/800 | 500/600D | 2200 | 2200N | 7½-9 |
| V8-305 2 Barrel Carb. Series 10-30 | .045 | D | 8° | 8° | Damper | 600/700 | 500/600D | 1300 | 1600N | [4] |
| V8-305 4 Barrel Carb. C10-20, K10 Exc. Calif. | .045 | D | 4° | [20] | Damper | [21] | 500D | [24] | 1600N | [4] |
| V8-305 4 Barrel Carb. C10-20 Calif. | .045 | D | — | 8° | Damper | — | 550/650D | — | 1800N | [4] |
| V8-305 4 Barrel Carb. G10-20 | .045 | D | 6° | 4° | Damper | 700 | 500D | 1300 | 1600N | [4] |
| V8-350 Exc. Calif. [8] | .045 | D | 8° | 8° | Damper | — | 550/650D | — | 1800N | [4] |
| V8-350 C, K10 Calif. [8] | .045 | D | — | 6° | Damper | — | 550/650D | — | 1600N | [4] |
| V8-350 C, K20 Calif. [8] | .045 | D | — | [22] | Damper | — | 550/650D | — | 1800N | [4] |
| V8-350 G10-20 Calif. | .045 | D | — | 8° | Damper | — | 550/650D | — | 1800N | [4] |
| V8-350 C, K20-30 Exc. Calif. [5] | .045 | D | 4° | 6° | Damper | 700/1600 [14] | 700/1600N [14] | 1900 | 1900N | [4] |
| V8-350 G30, P20-30 Exc. Calif. [5] | .045 | D | 4° | 4° | Damper | 700/1600 [14] | 700/1600N [14] | 1900 | 1900N | [4] |
| V8-350 Calif. [5] | .045 | D | 6° | 6° | Damper | 700/1500 [14] | 700/1500N [14] | 1900 | 1900N | 7½-9 |
| V8-454 | .045 | D | 4° | 4° | Damper | 700/1500 [14] | 700/1500 [14] | 1900 | 1900N | |
| **1980** | | | | | | | | | | |
| V6-229 | .045 | A | 8° | 12° | Damper | 700/800 | 600/675D | 1300 | 1750N | 4½-6 |
| V6-231 Exc. Calif. | .060 | B | — | 15° | Damper | — | 560/670D | — | 2200N | 3 Min. |
| V6-231 Calif. | .060 | B | — | 15° | Damper | — | 600D | — | 2200N | 3 Min. |
| 6-250 Exc. Calif. | .035 | C | 10° | 10° | Damper | 450/750 | 450/650D | 2000 | 2200N | 4½-6 |
| 6-250 C, G-10 Calif. | .035 | C | 10° | 10° | Damper | 425/750 | 425/600D | 2000 | 2200N | 4½-6 |
| 6-250 | .035 | C | 10° | 8° | Damper | 425/750 | 425/600N | 2400 | 2400N | 4-5 |
| 6-292 | .035 | C | 8° | 8° | Damper | 700 | 700N | 2400 | 2400N | 7½-9 |
| V8-267 | .045 | D | — | 4° | Damper | — | 500/600D | — | 1850N | 7½-9 |
| V8-305 Exc. Calif. [3] | .045 | D | 4° | 4° | Damper | 700 | 500/600D | 1500 | 1850N | 7½-9 |
| V8-305 Calif. [3] | .045 | D | — | 4° | Damper | — | 550/650D | — | 2200N | 7½-9 |
| V8-305 Series 10-30 | .045 | D | [16] | 8° | Damper | 600/700 | 500/600D | 1300 | 1600N | [4] |
| V8-350 [12] | .045 | D | 8° [17] | 8° [17] | Damper | 700 | 500/600D | 1600 | 1600N | [4] |
| V8-350 Exc. Calif. [13] | .045 | D | 4° | 4° | Damper | 700 | 700N | 1900 | 1900N | [4] |
| V8-350 Calif. [13] | .045 | D | 6° | 6° | Damper | 700 | 700N | 1900 | 1900N | [4] |
| V8-400 G-20 | .045 | D | — | 4° | Damper | — | 500/600D | — | 1600N | [4] |
| V8-400 K-20, G & K-30 Exc. Calif. | .045 | D | — | 4° | Damper | — | 700N | — | 1900N | [4] |
| V8-400 K-20, G & K-30 Calif. | .045 | D | — | 6° | Damper | — | 700N | — | 1900N | [4] |
| V8-454 | .045 | D | 4° | 4° | Damper | 700/1500 [14] | 700/1500N [14] | 1900 | 1900N | 7½-9 |

## CHEVROLET & GMC EXC. S/T-10 & 15 & ASTRO VAN & SAFARI VAN— Continued

① —Before removing wires from distributor cap, determine location of No. 1 wire in cap, as distributor position may have been altered from that shown at the end of this chart.

② —Idle speed on man. trans. models is adjusted in Neutral. On auto. trans. models, idle speed is adjusted in Drive (D) or Neutral (N), as specified. When checking idle speed, set parking brake & block drive wheels. Where two idle speeds are listed, the higher speed is with the idle or A/C solenoid energized.

③ —Caballero & El Camino.

④ —With vapor return line, 5.5 to 7 psi.; less vapor return line, 7.5 to 9 psi.

⑤ —Chevrolet 10–30 & GMC 1500–3500 series w/heavy duty emissions, GVWR of 8501 lbs. & above.

⑥ —Wrap shop towel around fuel hose to steel line connection in engine compartment to prevent fuel spillage. Disconnect hose from steel line & install a suitable fuel pressure gauge between hose & line. Ensure pressure gauge connections are tight, then start engine & check fuel pressure readings.

⑦ —Equipped with Idle Speed Control (ISC) motor or Idle Air Control (IAC) valve.

⑧ —Chevrolet 10–30 & GMC 1500–3500 series w/light duty emissions, GVWR of 8500 lbs. or under.

⑨ —Chevrolet 10–30 or GMC 1500–3500 series.

⑩ —On high step of fast idle cam.

⑪ —C series, 1500 RPM; G & K series, 1600 RPM.

⑫ —Series 10–30 light duty emissions, GVWR 6000 lbs. & under.

⑬ —Series 10–30 heavy duty emissions, GVWR 6001 lbs. & above.

⑭ —Higher speed is throttle return control speed.

⑮ —Exc. C10/1500, 600/700 RPM; C10/1500, 600/750 RPM.

⑯ —Distributor model No. 1103381, set at 8° BTDC; distributor model No. 1103369, set at 6° BTDC.

⑰ —C-10 & 20 series with distributor model No. 1103339, set at 6° BTDC.

⑱ —G-10-20 w/emission control label code ADA, set at 450/800 RPM.

⑲ —G-10-20 w/emission control label code AAC, set at 450/700D RPM.

⑳ —Emission control label code AAH, 4°

BTDC; AAN, 6° BTDC; AAS, 2° BTDC.

㉑ —Exc. emission control label code AUS, 700 RPM; emission control label code AUS, 600 RPM.

㉒ —Exc. emission control label code AAZ, 6° BTDC; emission control label code AAZ, 8° BTDC.

㉓ —Less A/C, 500/650D RPM; w/A/C, 500/700D RPM.

㉔ —Exc. emission control label code AUS, 1300 RPM; emission control label code AUS, 1500 RPM.

㉕ —Exc. emission control label codes UDY, UFC, UFF, UKA & UKB, 4°; emission control label codes UDY, UFC, UFF, UKA & UKB, 0°.

㉖ —On models equipped w/EST, disconnect EST four wire connector at distributor. On models less EST, disconnect & plug distributor vacuum advance hose.

㉗ —C & K models, 500/650D RPM; G models, 550/650D RPM.

㉘ —Disconnect single wire EST connector (tan w/black stripe) at engine wiring harness, do not disconnect four wire connector at distributor.

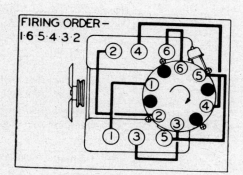

**Fig. A**

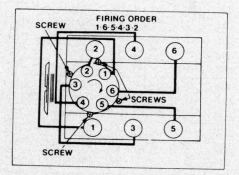

**Fig. B**

## CHEVROLET & GMC EXC. S/T-10 & 15 & ASTRO VAN & SAFARI VAN— Continued

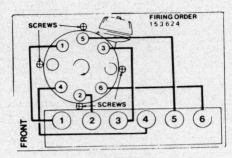

Fig. C

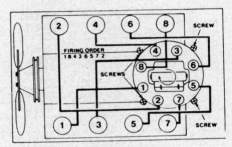

Fig. D

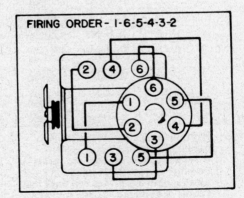

Fig. E

# TUNE UP SPECIFICATIONS

## CHEVROLET & GMC S/T-10 & 15

| Year & Engine | Spark Plug Gap | Firing Order ① | Ignition Timing BTDC ⑩ | | | Curb Idle Speed ② | | Fast Idle Speed | | Fuel Pump Pressure |
|---|---|---|---|---|---|---|---|---|---|---|
| | | | Man. Trans. | Auto. Trans. | Mark Location | Man. Trans. | Auto. Trans. | Man. Trans. | Auto. Trans. | |
| **1989** | | | | | | | | | | |
| 4-151 | .060 | D | — | — | Damper | ③ | ③ | ③ | ③ | 9–13 ④ |
| V6-173 | .045 | B | — | — | Damper | ③ | ③ | ③ | ③ | 9–13 ⑤ |
| V6-262 | .035 | E | — | — | Damper | ③ | ③ | ③ | ③ | 9–13 ⑥ |
| **1987–88** | | | | | | | | | | |
| 4-151 | .060 | D | — | — | Damper | ③ | ③ | ③ | ③ | 9–13 ④ |
| V6-173 | .045 | B | — | — | Damper | ③ | ③ | ③ | ③ | 9–13 ⑤ |
| **1986** | | | | | | | | | | |
| 4-151 | .060 | A | 8 | 8 | Damper | ③ | ③ | ③ | ③ | 9–13 ④ |
| V6-173 | .045 | B | 10 | 10 | Damper | ③ | ③ | ③ | ③ | 9–13 ⑤ |
| **1985** | | | | | | | | | | |
| 4-119 | .043 | A | 6 | — | Damper | 800/900 | — | 3200 ⑥ | 3200 ⑥ | 4.5 Min. |
| 4-151 | .060 | D | 8 | 8 | Damper | ③ | ③ | ③ | ③ | 9–13 ④ |
| V6-173 Exc. Calif. & High Alt. | .045 | B | 8 | 12 | Damper | 700/1100 | 700/850D | 2100 ⑥ | 2100 ⑥ | 6–7.5 |
| V6-173 Calif. | .045 | B | 10 | 10 | Damper | 750/950 | 650/850D | 2100 ⑥ | 2100 ⑥ | 6–7.5 |
| V6-173 High Alt. | .045 | B | 10 | 12 | Damper | 700/1100 | 700/850D | 2100 ⑥ | 2100 ⑥ | 6–7.5 |
| **1984** | | | | | | | | | | |
| 4-119 Exc. Calif. | A | .043 | 6 | — | Damper | 800/900 | — | 3200 ⑥ | 3200 ⑥ | 4.5 Min. |
| 4-119 Calif. | .043 | A | 6 | 6 | Damper | 900 | 900/1900P | 3200 ⑥ | 3200 ⑥ | 4.5 Min. |
| 4-121 | .035 | C | 2 | 2 | Damper | 800/1075 | 800/925D | 2400 ⑥ | 2300 ⑥ | 4.5 Min. |
| V6-173 Exc. Calif & High Alt. | .045 | B | 8 | 12 | Damper | 700/850 | 650/850D | 2100 ⑥ | 2100 ⑥ | 6–7.5 |
| V6-173 Calif. | .045 | B | 10 | 10 | Damper | 750/950 | 650/850D | 2100 ⑥ | 2100 ⑥ | 6–7.5 |
| V6-173 High Alt. | .045 | B | 10 | 14 | Damper | 700/850 | 700/850D | 2100 ⑥ | 2100 ⑥ | 6–7.5 |
| **1983** | | | | | | | | | | |
| 4-119 Exc. Calif. | .043 | A | 6° | 6° | Damper | 800/900 | 900/1900P | — | — | 3.6 |
| 4-119 Calif. | .043 | A | 6° | 6° | Damper | 800/900 | 900/1900P | — | — | 3.6 |
| 4-121 | .035 | C | — | 2° | Damper | — | 800/925D | — | 2600 | 4.5 |
| V6-173 Exc. Calif. & High Alt. | .045 | B | 8° | 12° | Damper | 650/850 | 650/850D | 1800 ⑥ | 2100 ⑥ | 6–7.5 |
| V6-173 Calif. | .045 | B | 10° | 10° | Damper | 750/950 | 650/850D | 2100 ⑥ | 2100 ⑥ | 6–7.5 |
| V6-173 High Alt. | .045 | B | 10° | 12° | Damper | 700/850 | 700/850D | 1800 | 2100 | 6–7.5 |
| **1982** | | | | | | | | | | |
| 4-119 | .043 | A | 6° | 6° | Damper | 800/900 | 900/1900P | — | — | 3.6 |
| V6-173 Exc. Calif. & High Alt. ⑦ | .045 | B | 6° | ⑧ | Damper | 650/850 | 650/850D | 1800 ⑥ | 2100 ⑥ | 6–7.5 |
| V6-173 Exc. Calif. & High Alt. ⑨ | .045 | B | 8° | 16° | Damper | 650/850 | 650/850D | 1800 ⑥ | 2100 ⑥ | 6–7.5 |
| V6-173 Calif. | .045 | B | 10° | 10° | Damper | 750/950 | 650/850D | 2100 ⑥ | 2100 ⑥ | 6–7.5 |
| V6-173 High Alt. | .045 | B | 10° | ⑧ | Damper | 750/850 | 650/850D | 1800 ⑥ | 2100 ⑥ | 6–7.5 |

① —Before removing wires from distributor cap, determine location of No. 1 wire in cap, as distributor position may have been altered from that shown at the end of this chart.

② —Idle speed on man. trans. models is adjusted in Neutral. On auto. trans. models, idle speed is adjusted in Drive (D) or Park (P) as specified. When checking idle speed, set parking brake & block drive wheels. Where two idle speeds are listed, the higher speed is with the Idle or A/C solenoid energized.

③ —Controlled by an idle speed control (ISC) motor or an Idle Air Control (IAC) valve.

④ —With transmission in Neutral, parking brake applied & drive wheels blocked, disconnect three terminal connector at fuel tank. Start engine & allow to run until fuel supply is depleted. Crank engine for approximately 3 seconds to relieve fuel pressure in lines. Remove air cleaner, gasket & adapter, then plug Thermac vacuum port on throttle body unit. Cover fitting to be disconnected with a shop towel, then connect a suitable pressure gauge at outlet side of inline fuel filter. Start engine & note fuel pressure reading. Before disconnecting fuel pressure gauge, relieve fuel system pressure.

⑤ —Wrap shop towel around fitting to be disconnected, then connect a suitable fuel pressure gauge at outlet side of inline fuel filter. Start engine & note fuel pressure reading.

⑥ —On high step of fast idle cam.

⑦ —Exc. cab-chassis & utility.

⑧ —Less A/C, 16° BTDC; w/A/C, 14° BTDC.

⑨ —Cab-chassis & utility.

⑩ —On models w/EST, disconnect EST four wire connector at distributor. On models less EST, disconnect & plug distributor vacuum advance hose.

## CHEVEROLET & GMC S/T
## 10 & 15—Continued

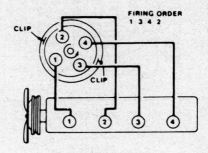

Fig. A

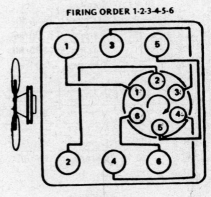

Fig. B

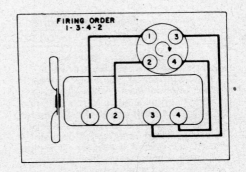

Fig. C

## CHEVEROLET & GMC S/T
## 10 & 15—Continued

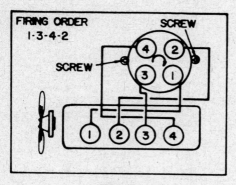

Fig. D

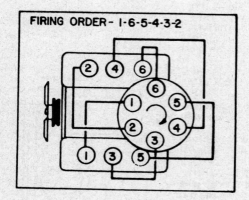

Fig. E

## CHEVROLET ASTRO VAN & GMC SAFARI VAN

| Year & Engine | Spark Plug Gap | Ignition Timing BTDC | | | | Curb Idle Speed ② | | Fast Idle Speed | | Fuel Pump Pressure |
| | | Firing Order ① | Man. Trans. | Auto. Trans. | Mark Location | Man. Trans. | Auto. Trans. | Man. Trans. | Auto. Trans. | |
|---|---|---|---|---|---|---|---|---|---|---|
| **1987–89** | | | | | | | | | | |
| 4-151 | .060 | A | — | — | Damper | ③ | ③ | ③ | ③ | 9–13 ⑥ |
| V6-262 | .035 | B | — | — | Damper | ③ | ③ | ③ | ③ | 9–13 ⑦ |
| **1986** | | | | | | | | | | |
| 4-151 | .060 | A | 8 ⑩ | 8 ⑩ | Damper | ③ | ③ | ③ | ③ | 9–13 ⑥ |
| V6-262 | .035 | B | TDC ⑩ | TDC ⑩ | Damper | ③ | ③ | ③ | ③ | 9–13 ⑦ |
| **1985** | | | | | | | | | | |
| 4-151 | .060 | A | 8 ⑩ | 8 ⑩ | Damper | ③ | ③ | ③ | ③ | 9–13 ⑥ |
| V6-262 | .035 | B | TDC ⑩ | TDC ⑩ | Damper | 600 ④ | 500D ⑤ | 1800 ⑧ | ⑧ ⑨ | 4–6.5 |

① —Before removing wires from distributor cap, determine location of No. 1 wire in cap, as distributor position may have been altered from that shown at the end of this chart.

② —Idle speed is adjusted in Neutral on man. trans. models. On auto. trans models, idle speed is adjusted in Drive (D). When checking idle speed, set parking brake & block drive wheels.

③ —Controlled by an Idle Speed Control (ISC) motor or an Idle Air Control (IAC) valve.

④ —Stepped speed control actuator RPM, less A/C, 800 RPM; w/A/C, 850 RPM.

⑤ —Stepped speed control actuator RPM, less A/C, 700 RPM; w/A/C 750 RPM.

⑥ —With transmission in Neutral, parking brake set & drive wheel blocked, disconnect three terminal connector at fuel tank. Start engine & allow to run until fuel supply is depleted. Crank engine for approximately 3 seconds to relieve fuel pressure in lines. Remove air cleaner, gasket & adapter, then plug Thermac vacuum port on throttle body unit. cover fitting to be disconnected with shop towel, then connect a suitable fuel pressure gauge at outlet side of inline fuel filter. Start engine & note fuel pressure reading. Before disconnecting fuel pressure gauge, relieve fuel system pressure.

⑦ —Wrap shop towel around fitting to be disconnected, then connect a suitable fuel pressure gauge at outlet side of inline fuel filter. Start engine & note fuel pressure reading.

⑧ —On high step of fast idle cam.

⑨ —Exc. Calif. & high alt., 2200 RPM; Calif. & high alt., 1800 RPM.

⑩ —With EST four wire connector at distributor disconnected.

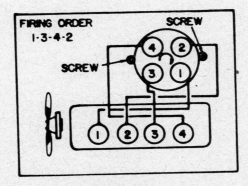

Fig. A

## CHEVROLET & GMC ASTRO VAN SAFARI —Continued

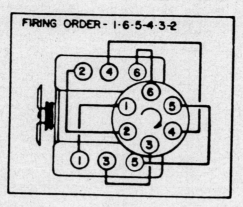

**Fig. B**

# DIESEL ENGINE PERFORMANCE

## CHEVROLET & GMC EXC. S/T-10 & 15

| Year | Engine | Injection Timing ① | Curb Idle Speed | Fast Idle Speed |
|---|---|---|---|---|
| 1980 | V8-350② | 4½° ④ ⑤ | 575D | 650D |
| 1980 | V8-350③ | 5½° ④ ⑤ | 575D | 650D |
| 1981 | V8-350② | 4° ④ ⑤ | ⑥ | ⑦ |
| 1981 | V8-350③ | 5° ④ ⑤ | ⑥ | ⑦ |
| 1982 | V8-379⑧ | — | 575N | 700N |
| 1982 | V8-379⑨ | — | 550D | 700N |
| 1982 | V8-379⑩ | — | 600D | 700N |
| 1982 | V8-379⑪ | — | 625N | 700N |
| 1983-84 | V8-350 | 4° ⑤ ⑫ | 600D | 750D |
| 1983-89 | V8-379 | | 650N | 800N |

① —ATDC: after top dead center.
② —Exc. high altitude.
③ —High altitude.
④ —At 1200 RPM.
⑤ —Using diesel timing meter J-33075 or equivalent.

⑥ —Exc. California, 575D; California, 600D.
⑦ —Exc. California, 650D; California, 750D.
⑧ —Engine codes CAF, CAH, CAK, CBK, CBN & CBS.

⑨ —Engine codes CBM, CBR & CBT.
⑩ —Engine codes CYF, CYJ & CYM.
⑪ —Engine codes CYC, CYD, CYH & CYK.
⑫ —At 1250 RPM.

## CHEVROLET & GMC S/T-10 & 15

| Year | Engine | Firing Order | Injection Timing B.T.D.C. ① | Cylinder Compression Pressure psi @ R.P.M. | Fuel Injection Starting Pressure Psi | Idle Speed |
|---|---|---|---|---|---|---|
| 1984-85 | 4-137 | 1-3-4-2 | 15° ② | 441 @ 220 | 1493 | 800 |

① —Plunger lift (inches) at degrees Before Top Dead Center (BTDC).
② —Exc. Calif., .020 inch @ 15°; Calif., .020 inch @ 13°.

## CHRYSLER/JEEP

| Year | Engine | Firing Order | Injection Timing B.T.D.C. (Static) |
|---|---|---|---|
| 1985-87 | 4-126 (2.1L) | 1-3-4-2 | TDC ① |

① —At .032 inch injection pump piston lift.

# DIESEL ENGINE PERFORMANCE SPECIFICATIONS

## FORD, EXC. 1983–88 RANGER

| Year | Engine | Compression Ratio | Firing Order | Injection Timing B.T.D.C. ① | Injection Nozzle Opening Pressure Psi | Idle Speed |
|------|--------|-------------------|--------------|------------------------------|---------------------------------------|------------|
| 1983-84 | V8-420 | 20.7 | 1-2-7-3-4-5-6-8 | ② | ③ | 600-700 |
| 1985-86 | V8-420 | 20.7 | 1-2-7-3-4-5-6-8 | ② | ④ | — |
| 1987 | V8-420 | 21.5 | 1-2-7-3-4-5-6-8 | ② | ⑤ | ⑥ |
| 1988 | V8-444 | 21.5 | 1-2-7-3-4-5-6-8 | ② | ⑤ | — |
| 1989 | V8-444 | 21.5 | 1-2-7-3-4-5-6-8 | ② | ⑤ | — |

①—B.T.D.C.: before top dead center.
②—Marks aligned.
③—Early 1984 & all 1983 calibration codes 3-68J-R10 & 3-68X-R10, 2000-2150 psi; 1984 calibration codes 4-68J-R00 & 4-68X-R00, 1800-1950 psi.
④—Calibration codes 4-68J-R00 & 4-68X-R0D, 1800-1950 psi.
⑤—New (+/- 75), 1875 psi; used (minimum), 1425 psi.
⑥—Early production, 750 RPM; late production, 675 RPM.

## FORD, 1983–88 RANGER

| Year | Engine | Firing Order | Injection Timing A.T.D.C. ① ② | Cylinder Compression Pressure Psi @ RPM | Injection Nozzle Opening Pressure Psi | Curb Idle Speed | Fast Idle Speed |
|------|--------|--------------|-------------------------------|------------------------------------------|---------------------------------------|-----------------|------------------|
| 1983-84 | 4-135 | 1-3-4-2 | 2° | 427 @ 200 | 1957 | 780-830 | 1150-1250 |
| 1985-88 | 4-143 | 1-3-4-2 | 5° | 341 @ 250 ③ | 1707-1849 | 750 | — |

①—A.T.D.C.: after top dead center.
②—Engine static.
③—Minimum.

# TROUBLESHOOTING
## TABLE OF CONTENTS

# Introduction

## STARTING A STALLED ENGINE

When an engine fails to start the chances are that 90 per cent of the cases will involve the ignition system and seldom the fuel system or other miscellaneous reasons. If a systematic procedure is followed the trouble can almost always be found without the use of special equipment.

To begin with, turn on the ignition switch and if the ammeter shows a slight discharge (or if the telltale lamp lights) it indicates that current is flowing. A glance at the gas gauge will indicate whether or not there is fuel in the tank.

Operate the starter and if the engine turns over freely, both the battery and starter are functioning properly. On the other hand, if the starter action is sluggish it may be due to a discharged or defective battery, loose, corroded or dirty battery terminals, mechanical failure in the starter, starter switch or starter drive. If the starter circuit is okay, skip this phase of the discussion and proceed to ignition.

## STARTER CIRCUIT CHECKOUT

To determine which part of the starter circuit is at fault, turn on the light switch and again operate the starter. Should the lights go out or become dim, the trouble is either in the battery, its connections or cables. A hydrometer test of the battery should indicate better than 1.250 specific gravity, while a voltmeter, placed across the positive and negative posts, should indicate about 12 volts. If either of these tests prove okay, clean and tighten the battery connections and cable terminals or replace any cable which seems doubtful.

If the lights remain bright when the starter is operated, the trouble is between the battery and the starter, or the starter switch is at fault, since it is evident that there is no electrical connection between these points. If these connections are clean and tight, it is safe to assume that the starter or starter switch is defective.

## NEUTRAL SAFETY SWITCH

If the ammeter shows a slight discharge (or if the telltale lamp lights) when the ignition is turned on, but the system goes dead when the starting circuit is closed, the neutral safety switch may be at fault. To check, bypass the switch with a suitable jumper. If the engine now starts, adjust or replace the switch.

**CAUTION:** With the safety switch bypassed, the truck can be started in any gear. Be sure the transmission is in neutral or park and the parking brake is applied.

## SEDONDARY IGNITION CHECKOUT

First of all, remove the wire from one of the spark plugs, turn on the ignition and operate the starter. While the engine is cranking, hold the terminal of the spark plug wire about ¼" away from the engine or spark plug base. If the spark is strong and jumps the gap, the trouble is confined to either the spark plugs or lack of fuel. Before going any further, wipe the outside of the plugs to remove any dirt or dampness which would create an easy path for the current to flow, then try to start the engine again. If it still fails to start, remove one of the spark plugs and if it is wet around the base, it indicates that the fuel system is okay, so it naturally follows that the spark plugs are at fault. Remove all the plugs, clean them and set the gaps. An emergency adjustment of spark plug gaps can be made by folding a piece of newspaper into 6 or 7 layers. When changing the gap, always bend the side (ground) electrode and never the center one as there is danger of breaking the insulation.

## FUEL SYSTEM CHECKOUT

If the spark plug that was removed showed no indication of dampness on its base, check the fuel system. A quick check can be made by simply removing the carburetor air cleaner and looking down into the carburetor. Open and close the throttle manually and if fuel is present in the carburetor, the throttle will operate the accelerating pump, causing it to push gasoline through the pump jet. If it does, check the choke valve. If the engine is cold, the choke valve should be closed. If the choke won't close, the engine can be started by covering the carburetor throat while the engine is cranking, provided, of course, that fuel is reaching the carburetor.

Check the operation of the fuel pump by disconnecting the fuel lines from the pump to the carburetor. Crank the engine and if the pump is working, fuel will pulsate out of the line. If not, either the pump isn't working or the line from the tank to the pump is clogged. Before blaming the pump, however, disconnect the line at the inlet side of the pump which leads to the tank and, while a companion listens at the tank blow through the line. If a gurgling sound is heard back in the tank, the line is open and the trouble is in the pump. Remove the sediment bowl, if so equipped and clean the screen, then replace the bowl and screen, being sure that you have an airtight fit. If the pump still refuses to function, it should be removed and repaired.

The foregoing discussion will, in most cases, uncover the cause of why an engine won't start. However, if further diagnosis is necessary, the following list will undoubtedly provide the answer.

## ENGINE NOISE TESTS

### LOOSE MAIN BEARING

A loose main bearing is indicated by a powerful but dull thud or knock when the engine is pulling. If all main bearings are loose a noticeable clatter will be audible.

The thud occurs regularly every other revolution. The knock can be confirmed by shorting spark plugs on cylinders adjacent to the bearing. Knock will disappear or be less when plugs are shorted. This test should be made at a fast idle equivalent to 15 mph in high gear. If bearing is not quite loose enough to produce a knock by itself, the bearing may knock if oil is too thin or if there is no oil at the bearing.

### LOOSE FLYWHEEL

A loose flywheel is indicated by a thud or click which is usually irregular. To test, idle the engine at about 20 mph and shut off the ignition. If thud is heard, the flywheel may be loose.

### LOOSE ROD BEARING

A loose rod bearing is indicated by a metallic knock which is usually loudest at about 30 mph with throttle closed. Knock can be reduced or even eliminated by shorting spark plug. If bearing is not loose enough to produce a knock by itself, the bearing may knock if oil is too thin or if there is no oil at the bearing.

### PISTON PIN

Piston pin, piston and connecting rod noises are difficult to tell apart.

A loose piston pin causes a sharp double knock which is usually heard when engine is idling. Severity of knock should increase when spark plug to this cylinder is short-circuited. However, on some engines the knock becomes more noticeable at 25 to 35 mph on the road.

Piston pin rubs against cylinder wall, caused by lock screw being loose or snap ring broken.

### HYDRAULIC LIFTERS

The malfunctioning of a hydraulic valve lifter is almost always accompanied by a clicking or tapping noise. More or less hydraulic lifter noise may be expected when the engine is cold but if lifters are functioning properly the noise should disappear when the engine warms up.

If all or nearly all lifters are noisy, they may be stuck because of dirty or gummy oil.

If all lifters are noisy, oil pressure to them may be inadequate. Foaming oil may also cause this trouble. If oil foams there will be bubbles on the oil level dipstick. Foaming may be caused by water in the oil or by too high an oil level or by a very low oil level.

If the hydraulic plungers require an initial adjustment, they will be noisy if this adjustment is incorrect.

If one lifter is noisy the cause may be:
1. Plunger too tight in lifter body.
2. Weak or broken plunger spring.
3. Ball valve leaks.
4. Plunger worn.
5. Lock ring (if any) improperly installed or missing.
6. Lack of oil pressure to this plunger.

If ball valve leaks, clean plunger in special solvent such as acetone and reinstall. Too often, plungers are condemned as faulty when all they need is a thorough cleaning.

Gum and dirty oil are the most common causes of hydraulic valve lifter trouble. Engine oil must be free of dirt. Select a standard brand of engine oil and use no other. Mixing up one standard brand with another may cause gummy oil and sticking plungers. Do not use any special oils unless recommended by the truck manufacturer and change oil filter or element at recommended intervals.

## LOOSE ENGINE MOUNTINGS

Occasional thud with truck in operation. Most likely to be noticed at the moment the throttle is opened or closed.

## EXCESSIVE CRANKSHAFT END PLAY

A rather sharp rap which occurs at idling speed but may be heard at higher speeds also. The noise should disappear when clutch is disengaged.

## FUEL PUMP NOISE

Diagnosis of fuel pumps suspected as noisy requires that some form of sounding device be used. Judgment by ear alone is not sufficient, otherwise a fuel pump may be needlessly replaced in attempting to correct noise contributed by some other component. Use of a stethoscope, a long screwdriver, or a sounding rod is recommended to locate the area or component causing the noise. The sounding rod can easily be made from a length of copper tubing ¼ to ⅜ inch in diameter.

If the noise has been isolated to the fuel pump, remove the pump and run the engine with the fuel remaining in the carburetor bowl. If the noise level does not change, the source of the noise is elsewhere and the original fuel pump should be reinstalled. On models using a fuel pump push rod, check for excessive wear and/or galling of the push rod.

## VAPOR LOCK

The term vapor lock means the flow of fuel to the mixing chamber in the carburetor has been stopped (locked) by the formation of vaporized fuel pockets or bubbles caused by overheating the fuel by hot fuel pump, hot fuel lines or hot carburetor.

The more volatile the fuel the greater the tendency for it to vapor lock. Vapor lock is encouraged by high atmospheric temperature, hard driving, defective engine cooling and high altitude.

A mild case of vapor lock will cause missing and hard starting when engine is warm. Somewhat more severe vapor lock will stop the engine which cannot be started again until it has cooled off enough so that any vaporized fuel has condensed to a liquid.

## PERCOLATION

Percolation means simply that gasoline in the carburetor bowl is boiling over into the intake manifold. This condition is most apt to occur immediately after a hot engine is shut off. Most carburetors have a provision for relieving the vapor pressure of overheated fuel in the carburetor bowl by means of ports. If, however, percolation should take place, the engine may be started by allowing it to cool slightly and then holding the throttle wide open while cranking to clear the intake manifold of excess fuel.

## SPARK KNOCK, PING, DETONATION

All three expressions mean the same thing. It is a sharp metallic knock caused by vibration of the cylinder head and block. The vibration is due to split-second high-pressure waves resulting from almost instantaneous abnormal combustion instead of the slower normal combustion.

The ping may be mild or loud. A mild ping does no harm but a severe ping will reduce power. A very severe ping may shatter spark plugs, break valves or crack pistons.

Pinging is most likely to occur on open throttle at low or moderate engine speed. Pinging is encouraged by:
1. Overheated engine.
2. Low octane fuel.
3. Too high compression.
4. Spark advanced too far.
5. Hot mixture due to hot engine or hot weather.
6. Heavy carbon deposit which increases the compression pressure.
7. Clogged or restricted EGR passages.

Tendency to ping increases with mixture temperature including high atmospheric temperature; intake manifold heater valve "on" when engine is warm; hot cooling water; hot interior engine surfaces due to sluggish water circulation or water jackets clogged with rust or dirt especially around exhaust valves. Some of these troubles may be confined to one or two cylinders.

If an engine pings objectionably even when using the highest octane fuel available, retard the spark setting, but first be sure the EGR system is functioning, the cooling system is in good condition, the mixture is not too lean, and the combustion chambers are free of carbon deposits.

## PRE-IGNITION

Pre-ignition means that the mixture is set on fire before the spark occurs, being ignited by a red hot spot in the combustion chamber such as an incandescent particle of carbon; a thin piece of protruding metal; an overheated spark plug, or a bright red hot exhaust valve. The result is reduction of power and overheating accompanied by pinging. The bright red hot exhaust valve may be due to a leak, to lack of tappet clearance, to valve sticking, or to a weak or broken spring.

Pre-ignition may not be noticed if not severe. Severe pre-ignition results in severe pinging. The most common cause of pre-ignition is a badly overheated engine.

When the engine won't stop when the ignition is shut off, the cause is often due to red hot carbon particles resting on heavy carbon deposit in a very hot engine.

## AFTER-BURNING

A subdued put-putting at the exhaust tail pipe may be due to leaky exhaust valves which permit the mixture to finish combustion in the muffler. If exhaust pipe or muffler is red hot, better let it cool, as there is some danger of setting the car on fire. Most likely to occur when mixture is lean.

## ENGINE CONTINUES TO RUN AFTER IGNITION IS TURNED OFF

This condition, known as "dieseling," "run on," or "after running," is caused by improper idle speed and/or high temperature. Idle speed and engine temperature are affected by:

**Carburetor Adjustment:** High idle speed will increase the tendency to diesel because of the inertia of the engine crankshaft and flywheel. Too low an idle speed, particularly with a lean mixture, will result in an increase in engine temperature, especially if the engine is allowed to idle for long periods of time.

**Ignition Timing:** Because advanced ignition timing causes a corresponding increase in idle speed and retarded timing reduces idle speed, ignition timing influences the tendency to diesel in the same manner as Carburetor Adjustment.

**Fuel Mixture:** Enriching the idle fuel mixture decreases the tendency to diesel by causing the engine to run cooler.

**Fuel Content:** High octane fuels tend to reduce dieseling. Increased fuel content of lead alkyl increases the tendency to diesel. Phosphates and nickel fuel additives help prevent dieseling.

**Spark Plugs:** Plugs of too high a heat range for the engine in question can cause dieseling.

**Throttle Plates:** If the throttle plates are not properly aligned in the carburetor bore,

a resulting leanness in fuel mixture occurs, contributing to dieseling.

**Electrical System:** Normally, during dieseling, ignition is self-supplied by a "hot spot," self-igniting fuel, etc. However, there is a possibility of the vehicle's electrical system supplying the necessary ignition. When the ignition switch is turned off, a small amount of current can flow from the generator into the primary of the ignition coil through the generator tell-tale light. This is particularly true when the warning light bulb has been changed for one of increased wattage.

**NOTE:** "Run on" is more prevalent in an engine when the ignition is turned off before the engine is allowed to return to idle. Therefore, it can be reduced by letting the engine return to idle before shutting off the ignition. "Run on" incidence can be reduced on automatic transmission units by turning off the engine when in gear.

A certain amount of "run on" can be expected from any gasoline engine regardless of make, size or configuration. (Diesel engines operate on this principle.) However, if the above suggestions are correctly employed, "Run on" will be reduced to an unnoticeable level.

# Gasoline Engine

NOTE: Refer to the appropriate truck chapters for diesel engine trouble shooting.

## ENGINE PERFORMANCE, LUBRICATION & NOISES

| Condition | Possible Cause | Correction |
|---|---|---|
| **ENGINE WILL NOT START** | 1. Weak battery. | 1. Test battery specific gravity. Recharge or replace as necessary. |
| | 2. Corroded or loose battery connections. | 2. Clean and tighten battery connections. Apply a coat of petroleum to terminals. |
| | 3. Faulty starter. | 3. Repair starter motor. |
| | 4. Moisture on ignition wires and distributor cap. | 4. Wipe wires and cap clean and dry. |
| | 5. Faulty ignition cables. | 5. Replace any cracked or shorted cables. |
| | 6. Open or shorted primary ignition circuit. | 6. Trace primary ignition circuit and repair as necessary. |
| | 7. Malfunctioning ignition points or condensor. | 7. Replace ignition points & condensor as necessary. |
| | 8. Faulty coil. | 8. Test and replace if necessary. |
| | 9. Incorrect spark plug gap. | 9. Set gap correctly. |
| | 10. Incorrect ignition timing. | 10. Reset timing. |
| | 11. Dirt or water in fuel line or carburetor. | 11. Clean lines and carburetor. Replace filter. |
| | 12. Carburetor flooded. | 12. Adjust float level—check seats. |
| | 13. Incorrect carburetor float setting. | 13. Adjust float level—check seats. |
| | 14. Faulty fuel pump. | 14. Install new fuel pump. |
| | 15. Carburetor percolating. No fuel in the carburetor. | 15. Measure float level. Adjust bowl vent. Inspect operation of manifold heat control valve. |
| **ENGINE STALLS** | 1. Idle speed set too low. | 1. Adjust carburetor. |
| | 2. Incorrect choke adjustment. | 2. Adjust choke. |
| | 3. Idle mixture too lean or too rich. | 3. Adjust carburetor. |
| | 4. Incorrect carburetor float setting. | 4. Adjust float setting. |
| | 5. Leak in intake manifold. | 5. Inspect intake manifold gasket and replace if necessary. |
| | 6. Worn or burned distributor rotor. | 6. Install new rotor. |
| | 7. Incorrect ignition wiring. | 7. Install correct wiring. |
| | 8. Faulty coil. | 8. Test and replace if necessary. |
| | 9. Incorrect tappet lash. | 9. Adjust to specifications. |
| **ENGINE LOSS OF POWER** | 1. Incorrect ignition timing. | 1. Reset timing. |
| | 2. Worn or burned distributor rotor. | 2. Install new rotor. |
| | 3. Worn distributor shaft. | 3. Remove and repair distributor. |
| | 4. Dirty or incorrectly gapped spark plugs. | 4. Clean plugs and set gap. |
| | 5. Dirt or water in fuel line, carburetor or filter. | 5. Clean lines, carburetor and replace filter. |
| | 6. Incorrect carburetor float setting. | 6. Adjust float level. |
| | 7. Faulty fuel pump. | 7. Install new pump. |

**34**

## ENGINE PERFORMANCE, LUBRICATION & NOISES—Continued

| Condition | Possible Cause | Correction |
|---|---|---|
| ENGINE LOSS OF POWER, Continued | 8. Incorrect valve timing. | 8. Check and correct valve timing. |
| | 9. Blown cylinder head gasket. | 9. Install new head gasket. |
| | 10. Low compression. | 10. Test compression of each cylinder. |
| | 11. Burned, warped or pitted valves. | 11. Install new valves. |
| | 12. Plugged or restricted exhaust system. | 12. Install new parts as necessary. |
| | 13. Faulty ignition cables. | 13. Replace any cracked or shorted cables. |
| | 14. Faulty coil. | 14. Test and replace as necessary. |
| ENGINE MISSES ON ACCELERATION | 1. Dirty, or gap too wide in spark plugs. | 1. Clean spark plugs and set gap. |
| | 2. Incorrect ignition timing. | 2. Reset timing. |
| | 3. Dirt in carburetor. | 3. Clean carburetor and replace filter. |
| | 4. Acceleration pump in carburetor. | 4. Install new pump. |
| | 5. Burned, warped or pitted valves. | 5. Install new valves. |
| | 6. Faulty coil. | 6. Test and replace if necessary. |
| ENGINE MISSES AT HIGH SPEED | 1. Dirty or gap set too wide in spark plug. | 1. Clean spark plugs and set gap. |
| | 2. Worn distributor shaft. | 2. Remove and repair distributor. |
| | 3. Worn or burned distributor rotor. | 3. Install new rotor. |
| | 4. Faulty coil. | 4. Test and replace if necessary. |
| | 5. Incorrect ignition timing. | 5. Reset timing. |
| | 6. Dirty jets in carburetor. | 6. Clean carburetor, replace filter. |
| | 7. Dirt or water in fuel line, carburetor or filter. | 7. Clean lines, carburetor and replace filter. |
| NOISY VALVES | 1. High or low oil level in crankcase. | 1. Check for correct oil level. |
| | 2. Thin or diluted oil. | 2. Change oil. |
| | 3. Low oil pressure. | 3. Check engine oil level. |
| | 4. Dirt in valve lifters. | 4. Clean lifters. |
| | 5. Bent push rod. | 5. Install new push rods. |
| | 6. Worn rocker arms. | 6. Inspect oil supply to rockers. |
| | 7. Worn tappets. | 7. Install new tappets. |
| | 8. Worn valve guides. | 8. Ream and install new valves with O/S Stems. |
| | 9. Excessive run-out of valve seats or valve faces. | 9. Grind valve seats and valves. |
| | 10. Incorrect tappet lash. | 10. Adjust to specifications. |
| CONNECTING ROD NOISE | 1. Insufficient oil supply. | 1. Check engine oil level. |
| | 2. Low oil pressure. | 2. Check engine oil level. Inspect oil pump relief valve and spring. |
| | 3. Thin or diluted oil. | 3. Change oil to correct viscosity. |
| | 4. Excessive bearing clearance. | 4. Measure bearings for correct clearance. |
| | 5. Connecting rod journals out-of-round. | 5. Replace crankshaft or regrind journals. |
| | 6. Misaligned (bent) connecting rods. | 6. Replace bent connecting rods. |
| MAIN BEARING NOISE | 1. Insufficient oil supply. | 1. Check engine oil level. |
| | 2. Low oil pressure. | 2. Check engine oil level. Inspect oil pump relief valve and spring. |
| | 3. Thin or diluted oil. | 3. Change oil to correct viscosity. |
| | 4. Excessive bearing clearance. | 4. Measure bearings for correct clearances. |
| | 5. Excessive end play. | 5. Check thrust bearing for wear on flanges. |
| | 6. Crankshaft journal worn out-of-round. | 6. Replace crankshaft or regrind journals. |
| | 7. Loose flywheel or torque converter. | 7. Tighten to correct torque. |
| OIL PUMPING AT RINGS | 1. Worn, scuffed, or broken rings. | 1. Hone cylinder bores and install new rings. |
| | 2. Carbon in oil ring slot. | 2. Install new rings. |
| | 3. Rings fitted too tight in grooves. | 3. Remove the rings. Check grooves. If groove is not proper width, replace piston. |

# TROUBLESHOOTING

## ENGINE PERFORMANCE, LUBRICATION & NOISES—Continued

| Condition | Possible Cause | Correction |
|---|---|---|
| OIL PRESSURE DROP | 1. Low oil level.<br>2. Faulty oil pressure sending unit.<br>3. Clogged oil filter.<br>4. Worn parts in oil pump.<br>5. Thin or diluted oil.<br>6. Excessive bearing clearance.<br><br>7. Oil pump relief valve stuck.<br><br>8. Oil pump suction tube loose, bent or cracked. | 1. Check engine oil level.<br>2. Install new sending unit.<br>3. Install new oil filter.<br>4. Replace worn parts or pump.<br>5. Change oil to correct viscosity.<br>6. Measure bearings for correct clearance.<br>7. Remove valve and inspect, clean, and reinstall.<br>8. Remove oil pan and install new tube if necessary. |
| NO OIL PRESSURE | 1. Low oil level.<br>2. Oil pressure gauge or sending unit inaccurate.<br>3. Oil pump malfunction.<br>4. Oil pressure relief valve sticking.<br><br>5. Oil passages on pressure side of pump obstructed.<br>6. Oil pickup screen or tube obstructed. | 1. Add oil to correct level.<br>2. Replace defective unit.<br><br>3. Repair oil pump.<br>4. Remove and inspect oil pressure relief valve assembly.<br>5. Inspect oil passages for obstructions.<br>6. Inspect oil pickup for obstructions. |
| LOW OIL PRESSURE | 1. Low oil level.<br>2. Oil excessively thin due to dilution, poor quality, or improper grade.<br>3. Oil pressure relief spring weak or sticking.<br>4. Oil pickup tube and screen assembly has restriction or air leak.<br><br>5. Excessive oil pump clearance.<br>6. Excessive main, rod, or camshaft bearing clearance. | 1. Add oil to correct level.<br>2. Drain and refill crankcase with recommended oil.<br>3. Remove and inspect oil pressure relief valve assembly.<br>4. Remove and inspect oil inlet tube and screen assembly. (Fill pickup with lacquer thinner to find leaks.)<br>5. Check clearances.<br>6. Measure bearing clearances, repair as necessary. |
| HIGH OIL PRESSURE | 1. Improper grade oil.<br><br>2. Oil pressure gauge or sending unit inaccurate.<br>3. Oil pressure relief valve sticking closed. | 1. Drain and refill crankcase with correct grade oil.<br>2. Replace defective unit.<br><br>3. Remove and inspect oil pressure relief valve assembly. |
| EXTERNAL OIL LEAK | 1. Fuel pump gasket broken or improperly seated.<br>2. Cylinder head cover gasket broken or improperly seated.<br><br>3. Oil filter gasket broken or improperly seated.<br>4. Oil pan side gasket broken or improperly seated.<br>5. Oil pan front oil seal broken or improperly seated.<br><br>6. Oil pan rear oil seal broken or improperly seated.<br><br><br>7. Timing chain cover oil seal broken or improperly seated.<br>8. Oil pan drain plug loose or has stripped threads.<br>9. Rear oil gallery plug loose.<br><br>10. Rear camshaft plug loose or improperly seated. | 1. Replace gasket.<br><br>2. Replace gasket; check cylinder head cover gasket flange and cylinder head gasket surface for distortion.<br>3. Replace oil filter.<br><br>4. Replace gasket; check oil pan gasket flange for distortion.<br>5. Replace seal; check timing chain cover and oil pan seal flange for distortion.<br>6. Replace seal; check oil pan rear oil seal flange; check rear main bearing cap for cracks, plugged oil return channels, or distortion in seal groove.<br>7. Replace seal.<br><br>8. Repair as necessary and tighten.<br><br>9. Use appropriate sealant on gallery plug and tighten.<br>10. Seat camshaft plug or replace and seal, as necessary. |

## ENGINE PERFORMANCE, LUBRICATION & NOISES—Continued

| Condition | Possible Cause | Correction |
|---|---|---|
| EXCESSIVE OIL CONSUMPTION | 1. Oil level too high. | 1. Lower oil level to specifications. |
| | 2. Oil too thin. | 2. Replace with specified oil. |
| | 3. Valve stem oil seals are damaged, missing, or incorrect type. | 3. Replace valve stem oil seals. |
| | 4. Valve stems or valve guides worn. | 4. Check stem-to-guide clearance and repair as necessary. |
| | 5. Piston rings broken, missing. | 5. Replace missing or broken rings. |
| | 6. Piston rings incorrect size. | 6. Check ring gap, repair as necessary. |
| | 7. Piston rings sticking or excessively loose in grooves. | 7. Check ring side clearance, repair as necessary. |
| | 8. Compression rings installed upside down. | 8. Repair as necessary. |
| | 9. Cylinder walls worn, scored, or glazed. | 9. Repair as necessary. |
| | 10. Piston ring gaps not properly staggered. | 10. Repair as necessary. |
| | 11. Excessive main or connecting rod bearing clearance. | 11. Check bearing clearance, repair as necessary. |

## OIL PRESSURE INDICATOR

| Condition | Possible Cause | Correction |
|---|---|---|
| LIGHT NOT LIT, IGNITION ON AND ENGINE NOT RUNNING. | 1. Bulb burned out. | 1. Replace bulb. |
| | 2. Open in light circuit. | 2. Locate and correct open. |
| | 3. Defective oil pressure switch. | 3. Replace oil pressure switch. |
| LIGHT ON, ENGINE RUNNING ABOVE IDLE SPEED. | 1. Grounded wiring between light and switch. | 1. Locate and repair ground. |
| | 2. Defective oil pressure switch. | 2. Replace oil pressure switch. |
| | 3. Low oil pressure. | 3. Locate cause of low oil pressure and correct. |

## IGNITION, STARTER & FUEL

| Condition | Possible Cause | Correction |
|---|---|---|
| NOTHING HAPPENS WHEN START ATTEMPT IS MADE | 1. Undercharged or defective battery. | 1. Check condition of battery and recharge or replace as required. |
| | 2. Loose battery cables. | 2. Clean and tighten cable connections. |
| | 3. Burned fusible link in starting circuit. | 3. Check for burned fusible link. Correct wiring problem. |
| | 4. Incorrectly positioned or defective neutral start switch. | 4. Check neutral start switch adjustment. If O.K., replace switch. |
| | 5. Loose or defective wiring between neutral start switch and ignition switch. | 5. Check for loose connections and opens between battery, horn relay, ignition switch, and solenoid "S" terminal. Check battery ground cable. Replace or repair defective item. |
| | 6. Defective starter motor. | 6. Repair or replace starter motor. |
| | 7. Defective starter interlock system. | 7. Use emergency button under hood. If car starts, repair circuit in interlock system. If car does not start, check and repair starter circuit. |
| SOLENOID SWITCH CLICKS BUT STARTER DOES NOT CRANK | 1. Undercharged or defective battery. | 1. Test battery. Recharge or replace battery. |
| | 2. Loose battery cables. | 2. Check and tighten battery connections. |
| | 3. Loose or defective wiring at starter. | 3. Tighten connections or repair wiring as required. |
| | 4. Defective solenoid. | 4. Replace solenoid. |
| | 5. "Hot stall" condition. | 5. Check engine cooling system. |
| | 6. Excessive engine rotational torque caused by mechanical problem within engine. | 6. Check engine torque for excessive friction. |
| | 7. Defective starter motor. | 7. Repair or replace starter motor. |

# TROUBLESHOOTING

## IGNITION, STARTER & FUEL—Continued

| Condition | Possible Cause | Correction |
|---|---|---|
| SLOW CRANKING | 1. Vehicle is overheating. | 1. Check engine cooling system and repair as required. |
| | 2. Undercharged or defective battery. | 2. Recharge or replace battery. |
| | 3. Loose or defective wiring between battery and engine block. | 3. Repair or replace wiring. |
| | 4. Loose or defective wiring between battery and solenoid "Bat" terminal. | 4. Repair or replace wiring. |
| | 5. Defective starter motor. | 5. Repair or replace starter. |
| STARTER SPINS AND/OR MAKES LOUD GRINDING NOISE BUT DOES NOT TURN ENGINE | 1. Defective starter motor. | 1. Repair or replace starter motor. |
| | 2. Defective ring gear. | 2. Replace ring gear. |
| STARTER KEEPS RUNNING AFTER IGNITION SWITCH IS RELEASED—FROM "START" TO "RUN" POSITION | 1. Defective ignition switch. | 1. Replace ignition switch. |
| | 2. Defective solenoid. | 2. Replace solenoid. |
| STARTER ENGAGES ("Clunks") BUT ENGINE DOES NOT CRANK | 1. Open circuit in solenoid armature or field coils. | 1. Repair or replace solenoid or starter motor. |
| | 2. Short or ground in field coil or armature. | 2. Repair or replace starter motor. |
| HARD STARTING (Engine Cranks Normally) | 1. Binding linkage, choke valve or choke piston. | 1. Repair as necessary. |
| | 2. Restricted choke vacuum and hot air passages. | 2. Clean passages. |
| | 3. Improper fuel level. | 3. Adjust float level. |
| | 4. Dirty, worn or faulty needle valve and seat. | 4. Repair as necessary. |
| | 5. Float sticking. | 5. Repair as necessary. |
| | 6. Exhaust manifold heat valve stuck. | 6. Repair as necessary. |
| | 7. Faulty fuel pump. | 7. Replace fuel pump. |
| | 8. Incorrect choke cover adjustment. | 8. Adjust choke cover. |
| | 9. Inadequate unloader adjustment. | 9. Adjust unloader. |
| | 10. Faulty ignition coil. | 10. Test and replace as necessary. |
| | 11. Improper spark plug gap. | 11. Adjust gap. |
| | 12. Incorrect initial timing. | 12. Adjust timing. |
| | 13. Incorrect valve timing. | 13. Check valve timing; repair as necessary. |
| ROUGH IDLE OR STALLING | 1. Incorrect curb or fast idle speed. | 1. Adjust curb or fast idle speed. |
| | 2. Incorrect initial timing. | 2. Adjust timing to specifications. |
| | 3. Improper idle mixture adjustment. | 3. Adjust idle mixture. |
| | 4. Damaged tip on idle mixture screw(s). | 4. Replace mixture screw(s). |
| | 5. Improper fast idle cam adjustment. | 5. Adjust fast idle. |
| | 6. Faulty PCV valve air flow. | 6. Test PCV valve and replace as necessary. |
| | 7. Exhaust manifold heat valve inoperative. | 7. Lubricate or replace heat valve as necessary. |
| | 8. Choke binding. | 8. Locate and eliminate binding condition. |
| | 9. Improper choke setting. | 9. Adjust choke. |
| | 10. Vacuum leak. | 10. Check manifold vacuum and repair as necessary. |
| | 11. Improper fuel level. | 11. Adjust fuel level. |
| | 12. Faulty distributor rotor or cap. | 12. Replace rotor or cap. |
| | 13. Leaking engine valves. | 13. Check cylinder leakdown rate or compression and repair as necessary. |
| | 14. Incorrect ignition wiring. | 14. Check wiring and correct as necessary. |
| | 15. Faulty coil. | 15. Test coil and replace as necessary. |
| | 16. Clogged air bleed or idle passages. | 16. Clean passages. |
| | 17. Restricted air cleaner. | 17. Clean or replace air cleaner. |
| | 18. Faulty EGR valve operation if equipped. | 18. Test EGR system and replace as necessary if equipped. |

## IGNITION, STARTER & FUEL—Continued

| Condition | Possible Cause | Correction |
|---|---|---|
| **FAULTY LOW-SPEED OPERATION** | 1. Clogged idle transfer slots. | 1. Clean transfer slots. |
| | 2. Restricted idle air bleeds and passages. | 2. Clean air bleeds and passages. |
| | 3. Restricted air cleaner. | 3. Clean or replace air cleaner. |
| | 4. Improper fuel level. | 4. Adjust fuel level. |
| | 5. Faulty spark plugs. | 5. Clean or replace spark plugs. |
| | 6. Dirty, corroded, or loose secondary circuit connections. | 6. Clean or tighten secondary circuit connections. |
| | 7. Faulty ignition cable. | 7. Replace ignition cable. |
| | 8. Faulty distributor cap. | 8. Replace cap. |
| **FAULTY ACCELERATION** | 1. Improper pump stroke. | 1. Adjust pump stroke. |
| | 2. Incorrect ignition timing. | 2. Adjust timing. |
| | 3. Inoperative pump discharge check ball or needle. | 3. Clean or replace as necessary. |
| | 4. Worn or damaged pump diaphragm or piston. | 4. Replace diaphragm or piston. |
| | 5. Leaking main body cover gasket. | 5. Replace gasket. |
| | 6. Engine cold and choke too lean. | 6. Adjust choke. |
| | 7. Faulty spark plug(s). | 7. Clean or replace spark plug(s). |
| | 8. Leaking engine valves. | 8. Check cylinder leakdown rate or compression, repair as necessary. |
| | 9. Faulty coil. | 9. Test coil and replace as necessary. |
| **FAULTY HIGH-SPEED OPERATION** | 1. Incorrect ignition timing. | 1. Adjust timing. |
| | 2. Faulty distributor centrifugal advance. | 2. Check centrifugal advance and repair as necessary. |
| | 3. Faulty distributor vacuum advance. | 3. Check vacuum advance and repair as necessary. |
| | 4. Low fuel pump volume. | 4. Replace fuel pump. |
| | 5. Improper spark plug gap. | 5. Adjust gap. |
| | 6. Faulty choke operation. | 6. Adjust choke. |
| | 7. Partially restricted exhaust manifold, exhaust pipe, muffler, or tailpipe. | 7. Eliminate restriction. |
| | 8. Clogged vacuum passages. | 8. Clean passages. |
| | 9. Improper size or obstructed main jets. | 9. Clean or replace as necessary. |
| | 10. Restricted air cleaner. | 10. Clean or replace as necessary. |
| | 11. Faulty distributor rotor or cap. | 11. Replace rotor or cap. |
| | 12. Worn distributor shaft. | 12. Replace shaft. |
| | 13. Faulty coil. | 13. Test coil and replace as necessary. |
| | 14. Leaking engine valve(s). | 14. Check cylinder leakdown or compression and repair as necessary. |
| | 15. Faulty valve spring(s). | 15. Inspect and test valve spring tension and replace as necessary. |
| | 16. Incorrect valve timing. | 16. Check valve timing and repair as necessary. |
| | 17. Intake manifold restricted. | 17. Pass chain through passages. |
| **MISFIRE AT ALL SPEEDS** | 1. Faulty spark plug(s). | 1. Clean or replace spark plug(s). |
| | 2. Faulty spark plug cable(s). | 2. Replace as necessary. |
| | 3. Faulty distributor cap or rotor. | 3. Replace cap or rotor. |
| | 4. Faulty coil. | 4. Test coil and replace as necessary. |
| | 5. Primary circuit shorted or open intermittently. | 5. Trace primary circuit and repair as necessary. |
| | 6. Leaking engine valve(s). | 6. Check cylinder leakdown rate or compression and repair as necessary. |
| | 7. Faulty hydraulic tappet(s). | 7. Clean or replace tappet(s). |
| | 8. Faulty valve spring(s). | 8. Inspect and test valve spring tension, repair as necessary. |
| | 9. Worn lobes on camshaft. | 9. Replace camshaft. |
| | 10. Vacuum leak. | 10. Check manifold vacuum and repair as necessary. |
| | 11. Improper carburetor settings. | 11. Adjust carburetor. |
| | 12. Fuel pump volume or pressure low. | 12. Replace fuel pump. |
| | 13. Blown cylinder head gasket. | 13. Replace gasket. |
| | 14. Intake or exhaust manifold passage(s) restricted. | 14. Pass chain through passages. |

# TROUBLESHOOTING

## IGNITION, STARTER & FUEL—Continued

| Condition | Possible Cause | Correction |
|---|---|---|
| POWER NOT UP TO NORMAL | 1. Incorrect ignition timing.<br>2. Faulty distributor rotor.<br>3. Worn distributor shaft.<br>4. Incorrect spark plug gap.<br>5. Faulty fuel pump.<br>6. Incorrect valve timing.<br><br>7. Faulty coil.<br>8. Faulty ignition cables.<br><br>9. Leaking engine valves.<br><br>10. Blown cylinder head gasket.<br>11. Leaking piston rings. | 1. Adjust timing.<br>2. Replace rotor.<br>3. Replace shaft.<br>4. Adjust gap.<br>5. Replace fuel pump.<br>6. Check valve timing and repair as necessary.<br>7. Test coil and replace as necessary.<br>8. Test cables and replace as necessary.<br>9. Check cylinder leakdown rate or compression and repair as necessary.<br>10. Replace gasket.<br>11. Check compression and repair as necessary. |
| INTAKE BACKFIRE | 1. Improper ignition timing.<br>2. Faulty accelerator pump discharge.<br>3. Improper choke operation.<br>4. Lean fuel mixture. | 1. Adjust timing.<br>2. Repair as necessary.<br>3. Repair as necessary.<br>4. Check float level or manifold vacuum for vacuum leak. |
| EXHAUST BACKFIRE | 1. Vacuum leak.<br><br>2. Faulty A.I.R. diverter valve.<br><br>3. Faulty choke operation.<br>4. Exhaust leak. | 1. Check manifold vacuum and repair as necessary.<br>2. Test diverter valve and replace as necessary.<br>3. Repair as necessary.<br>4. Locate and eliminate leak. |
| PING OR SPARK KNOCK | 1. Incorrect ignition timing.<br>2. Distributor centrifugal or vacuum advance malfunction.<br>3. Excessive combustion chamber deposits.<br>4. Carburetor set too lean.<br>5. Vacuum leak.<br><br>6. Excessively high compression.<br><br>7. Fuel octane rating excessively low.<br>8. Heat riser stuck in heat on position.<br>9. Insufficient EGR flow. | 1. Adjust timing.<br>2. Check advance and repair as necessary.<br>3. Use combustion chamber cleaner.<br>4. Adjust carburetor.<br>5. Check manifold vacuum and repair as necessary.<br>6. Check compression and repair as necessary.<br>7. Try alternate fuel source.<br>8. Free-up or replace heat riser.<br>9. Check EGR system operation. |
| SURGING (Cruising Speeds To Top Speeds) | 1. Low fuel level.<br>2. Low fuel pump pressure or volume.<br>3. Improper PCV valve air flow.<br><br>4. Vacuum leak.<br><br>5. Dirt in carburetor.<br>6. Undersize main jets.<br>7. Clogged fuel filter screen.<br>8. Restricted air cleaner.<br>9. Excessive EGR valve flow. | 1. Adjust fuel level.<br>2. Replace fuel pump.<br>3. Test PCV valve and replace as necessary.<br>4. Check manifold vacuum and repair as necessary.<br>5. Clean carburetor, replace filter.<br>6. Replace main jet(s).<br>7. Replace fuel filter.<br>8. Clean or replace air cleaner.<br>9. Check EGR system operation. |

## CHARGING SYSTEM

| Condition | Possible Cause | Correction |
|---|---|---|
| ALTERNATOR FAILS TO CHARGE (No Output or Low Output) | 1. Alternator drive belt loose.<br>2. Regulator base improperly grounded.<br>3. Worn brushes and/or slip rings.<br>4. Sticking brushes.<br><br>5. Open field circuit.<br><br>6. Open charging circuit. | 1. Adjust drive belt to specifications.<br>2. Connect regulator to a good ground.<br>3. Install new brushes and/or slip rings.<br>4. Clean slip rings and brush holders. Install new brushes if necessary.<br>5. Test all the field circuit connections, and correct as required.<br>6. Inspect all connections in charging circuit, and correct as required. |

## CHARGING SYSTEM—Continued

| Condition | Possible Cause | Correction |
|---|---|---|
| **ALTERNATOR FAILS TO CHARGE (No Output or Low Output), continued** | 7. Open circuit in stator windings. | 7. Remove alternator and disassemble. Test stator windings. Install new stator if necessary. |
| | 8. Open rectifiers. | 8. Remove alternator and disassemble. Test the rectifiers. Install new rectifier assemblies if necessary. |
| **LOW, UNSTEADY CHARGING RATE** | 1. High resistance in body to engine ground lead. | 1. Tighten ground lead connections. Install new ground lead if necessary. |
| | 2. Alternator drive belt loose. | 2. Adjust alternator drive belt. |
| | 3. High resistance at battery terminals. | 3. Clean and tighten battery terminals. |
| | 4. High resistance in charging circuit. | 4. Test charging circuit resistance. Correct as required. |
| | 5. Open stator winding. | 5. Remove and disassemble alternator. Test stator windings. Install new stator if necessary. |
| **LOW OUTPUT AND A LOW BATTERY** | 1. High resistance in charging circuit. | 1. Test charging circuit resistance and correct as required. |
| | 2. Shorted rectifier. Open rectifier. | 2. Perform current output test. Test the rectifiers and install new rectifier heat sink assembly as required. Remove and disassemble the alternator. |
| | 3. Grounded stator windings. | 3. Remove and disassemble alternator. Test stator windings. Install new stator if necessary. |
| | 4. Faulty voltage regulator. | 4. Test voltage regulator. Replace as necessary. |
| **EXCESSIVE CHARGING RATE TO A FULLY CHARGED BATTERY** | 1. Faulty ignition switch. | 1. Install new ignition switch. |
| | 2. Faulty voltage regulator. | 2. Test voltage regulator. Replace as necessary. |
| **NOISY ALTERNATOR** | 1. Alternator mounting loose. | 1. Properly install and tighten alternator mounting. |
| | 2. Worn or frayed drive belt. | 2. Install a new drive belt and adjust to specifications. |
| | 3. Worn bearings. | 3. Remove and disassemble alternator. Install new bearings as required. |
| | 4. Interference between rotor fan and stator leads. | 4. Remove and disassemble alternator. Correct interference as required. |
| | 5. Rotor or rotor fan damaged. | 5. Remove and disassemble alternator. Install new rotor. |
| | 6. Open or shorted rectifer. | 6. Remove and disassemble alternator. Test rectifers. Install new rectifier heat sink assemble as required. |
| | 7. Open or shorted winding in stator. | 7. Remove and disassemble alternator. Test stator windings. Install new stator if necessary. |
| **EXCESSIVE AMMETER FLUCTUATION** | 1. High resistance in the alternator and voltage regulator circuit. | 1. Clean and tighten all connections as necessary. |

## CHARGING SYSTEM INDICATOR

| | | |
|---|---|---|
| **LIGHT ON, IGNITION OFF** | 1. Shorted positive diode. | 1. Locate and replace shorted diode. |
| **LIGHT NOT ON, IGNITION ON AND ENGINE NOT RUNNING** | 1. Bulb burned out. | 1. Replace bulb. |
| | 2. Open in light circuit. | 2. Locate and correct open. |
| | 3. Open in field. | 3. Replace rotor. |
| **LIGHT ON, ENGINE RUNNING ABOVE IDLE SPEED** | 1. No generator output. | 1. Check and correct cause of no output. |
| | 2. Shorted negative diode. | 2. Locate and replace shorted diode. |
| | 3. Loose or broken generator belt. | 3. Tighten or replace and tighten generator belt. |

# TROUBLESHOOTING

## COOLING SYSTEM

| Condition | Possible Cause | Correction |
|---|---|---|
| **HIGH TEMPERATURE INDICATION— OVERHEATING** | 1. Coolant level low.<br>2. Fan belt loose.<br>3. Radiator hose(s) collapsed.<br>4. Radiator blocked to airflow.<br>5. Faulty radiator cap.<br>6. Car overloaded.<br>7. Ignition timing incorrect.<br>8. Idle speed low.<br>9. Air trapped in cooling system.<br>10. Car in heavy traffic.<br><br>11. Incorrect cooling system component(s) installed.<br>12. Faulty thermostat.<br>13. Water pump shaft broken or impeller loose.<br>14. Radiator tubes clogged.<br>15. Cooling system clogged.<br>16. Casting flash in cooling passages.<br><br><br><br>17. Brakes dragging.<br>18. Excessive engine friction.<br>19. Car working beyond cooling system capacity.<br>20. Antifreeze concentration over 68%.<br>21. Low anti-freeze concentration. | 1. Replenish coolant level.<br>2. Adjust fan belt.<br>3. Replace hose(s).<br>4. Remove restriction.<br>5. Replace cap.<br>6. Reduce load.<br>7. Adjust ignition timing.<br>8. Adjust idle speed.<br>9. Purge air.<br>10. Operate at fast idle intermittently to cool engine.<br>11. Install proper component(s).<br>12. Replace thermostat.<br>13. Replace water pump.<br><br>14. Flush radiator.<br>15. Flush system.<br>16. Repair or replace as necessary. Flash may be visible by removing cooling system components or removing core plugs.<br>17. Repair brakes.<br>18. Repair engine.<br>19. Install heavy-duty cooling fan and/or radiator.<br>20. Lower antifreeze content.<br>21. Add anti-freeze to provide a minimum 50% concentration. |
| **LOW TEMPERATURE INDICATION— OVERCOOLING** | 1. Improper fan being used.<br>2. Improper radiator.<br>3. Thermostat stuck open.<br>4. Improper fan pulley (too small). | 1. Install proper fan.<br>2. Install proper radiator.<br>3. Replace thermostat.<br>4. Install proper pulley. |
| **COOLANT LOSS—BOILOVER**<br><br>**NOTE:** Immediately after shutdown, the engine enters a period known as heat soak. This is caused because the cooling system is inoperative but engine temperature is still high. If coolant temperature rises above boiling point, it may push some coolant out of the radiator overflow tube. If this does not occur frequently, it is considered normal. | Refer to Overheating Causes in addition to the following:<br>1. Overfilled cooling system.<br><br>2. Quick shutdown after hard (hot) run.<br><br>3. Air in system resulting in occasional "burping" of coolant.<br>4. Insufficient antifreeze allowing coolant boiling point to be too low.<br>5. Antifreeze deteriorated because of age or contamination.<br>6. Leaks due to loose hose clamps, loose nuts, bolts, drain plugs, faulty hoses, or defective radiator.<br>7. Faulty head gasket.<br>8. Cracked head, manifold, or block. | <br><br>1. Reduce coolant level to proper specification.<br>2. Allow engine to run at fast idle prior to shutdown.<br>3. Purge system.<br><br>4. Add antifreeze to raise boiling point.<br><br>5. Replace coolant.<br><br>6. Pressure test system to locate leak then repair as necessary.<br><br>7. Replace head gasket.<br>8. Replace as necessary. |
| **COOLANT ENTRY INTO CRANKCASE OR CYLINDER** | 1. Faulty head gasket.<br>2. Crack in head, manifold or block. | 1. Replace head gasket.<br>2. Replace as necessary. |
| **COOLANT RECOVERY SYSTEM INOPERATIVE** | 1. Coolant level low.<br>2. Leak in system.<br><br>3. Pressure cap not tight or gasket missing or leaking.<br>4. Pressure cap defective.<br>5. Overflow tube clogged or leaking.<br>6. Recovery bottle vent plugged. | 1. Replenish coolant.<br>2. Pressure test to isolate leak and repair as necessary.<br>3. Repair as necessary.<br><br>4. Replace cap.<br>5. Repair as necessary.<br>6. Remove restriction. |
| **NOISE** | 1. Fan contacting shroud.<br><br>2. Loose water pump impeller.<br>3. Dry fan belt. | 1. Reposition shroud and check engine mounts.<br>2. Replace pump.<br>3. Apply belt dressing or replace belt. |

## COOLING SYSTEM—Continued

| Condition | Possible Cause | Correction |
|---|---|---|
| NOISE, continued | 4. Loose fan belt.<br>5. Rough surface on drive pulley.<br>6. Water pump bearing worn. | 4. Adjust fan belt.<br>5. Replace pulley.<br>6. Remove belt to isolate. Replace pump. |
| NO COOLANT FLOW THROUGH HEATER CORE | 1. Plugged return pipe in water pump.<br>2. Heater hose collapsed or plugged.<br>3. Plugged heater core.<br>4. Plugged outlet in thermostat housing.<br>5. Heater bypass hole in cylinder head plugged. | 1. Remove obstruction.<br>2. Remove obstruction or replace hose.<br>3. Remove obstruction or replace core.<br>4. Remove flash or obstruction.<br>5. Remove obstruction. |

## COOLANT TEMPERATURE INDICATOR

| Condition | Possible Cause | Correction |
|---|---|---|
| "HOT" INDICATOR; LIGHT NOT LIT WHEN CRANKING ENGINE | 1. Bulb burned out.<br>2. Open in light circuit.<br>3. Defective ignition switch. | 1. Replace bulb.<br>2. Locate and correct open.<br>3. Replace ignition switch. |
| LIGHT ON, ENGINE RUNNING | 1. Wiring grounded between light and switch.<br>2. Defective temperature switch.<br>3. Defective ignition switch.<br>4. High coolant temperature. | 1. Locate and correct grounded wiring.<br>2. Replace temperature switch.<br>3. Replace ignition switch.<br>4. Locate and correct cause of high coolant temperature. |

## EXHAUST SYSTEM

| Condition | Possible Cause | Correction |
|---|---|---|
| LEAKING EXHAUST GASES | 1. Leaks at pipe joints.<br>2. Damaged or improperly installed seals or packing.<br>3. Loose exhaust pipe heat tube extension connections.<br>4. Burned or rusted out exhaust pipe heat tube extensions. | 1. Tighten U-bolt nuts at leaking joints.<br>2. Replace seals or packing as necessary.<br>3. Replace seals or packing as required. Tighten stud nuts or bolts.<br>4. Replace heat tube extensions as required. |
| EXHAUST NOISES | 1. Leaks at manifold or pipe connections.<br><br>2. Burned or blown out muffler.<br>3. Burned or rusted out exhaust pipe.<br>4. Exhaust pipe leaking at manifold flange.<br>5. Exhaust manifold cracked or broken.<br>6. Leak between manifold and cylinder head. | 1. Tighten clamps at leaking connections to specified torque. Replace gasket or packing as required.<br>2. Replace muffler assembly.<br>3. Replace exhaust pipe.<br>4. Tighten attaching bolt nuts.<br>5. Replace manifold.<br>6. Tighten manifold to cylinder head stud nuts or bolts. |
| LOSS OF ENGINE POWER AND/OR INTERNAL RATTLES IN MUFFLER | 1. Dislodged turning tubes and or baffles in muffler. | 1. Replace muffler. |
| LOSS OF ENGINE POWER | 1. Imploding (inner wall collapse) of exhaust pipe. | 1. Replace exhaust pipe. |
| ENGINE HARD TO WARM UP OR WILL NOT RETURN TO NORMAL IDLE | 1. Heat control valve frozen in the open position. | 1. Free up manifold heat control using a suitable manifold heat control solvent. |
| MANIFOLD HEAT CONTROL VALVE NOISE | 1. Thermostat broken.<br>2. Broken, weak or missing anti-rattle spring. | 1. Replace thermostat.<br>2. Replace spring. |

# Clutch & Manual Transmission

| Condition | Possible Cause | Correction |
|---|---|---|
| CLUTCH CHATTER | 1. Worn or damaged disc assembly. | 1. Replace disc assembly. |
| | 2. Grease or oil on disc facings. | 2. Replace disc assembly and correct cause of contamination. |
| | 3. Improperly adjusted cover assembly. | 3. Replace cover assembly. |
| | 4. Broken or loose engine mounts. | 4. Replace or tighten mounts. |
| | 5. Misaligned clutch housing. | 5. Align clutch housing. |
| CLUTCH SLIPPING | 1. Insufficient pedal free play. | 1. Adjust release fork rod. |
| | 2. Burned, worn, or oil soaked facings. | 2. Replace disc assembly and correct cause of contamination. |
| | 3. Weak or broken pressure springs. | 3. Replace cover assembly. |
| DIFFICULT GEAR SHIFTING | 1. Excessive pedal free play. | 1. Adjust release fork rod. |
| | 2. Excessive deflection in linkage or firewall. | 2. Repair or replace linkage. |
| | 3. Worn or damaged disc assembly. | 3. Replace disc assembly. |
| | 4. Improperly adjusted cover assembly. | 4. Replace cover assembly. |
| | 5. Clutch disc splines sticking. | 5. Remove disc assembly and free up splines or replace disc. |
| | 6. Worn or dry pilot bushing. | 6. Lubricate or replace bushing. |
| | 7. Clutch housing misaligned. | 7. Align clutch housing. |
| CLUTCH NOISY | 1. Dry clutch linkage. | 1. Lubricate where necessary. |
| | 2. Worn release bearing. | 2. Replace release bearing. |
| | 3. Worn disc assembly. | 3. Replace disc assembly. |
| | 4. Worn release levers. | 4. Replace cover assembly. |
| | 5. Worn or dry pilot bushing. | 5. Lubricate or replace bushing. |
| | 6. Dry contact-pressure plate lugs in cover. | 6. Lubricate very lightly. |
| TRANSMISSION SHIFTS HARD | 1. Incorrect clutch adjustment. | 1. Adjust clutch pedal free-play. |
| | 2. Clutch linkage binding. | 2. Lubricate or repair linkage as required. |
| | 3. Gearshift linkage incorrectly adjusted, bent, or binding. | 3. Adjust linkage—correct any bind. Replace bent parts. |
| | 4. Bind in steering column, or column is misaligned. | 4. Disconnect shift rods at column. Check for bind/misalignment between tube and jacket by shifting lever into all positions. Correct as required. |
| | 5. Incorrect lubricant. | 5. Drain and refill transmission. |
| | 6. Internal bind in transmissions—e.g. shift rails, interlocks, shift forks, synchronizer teeth. | 6. Remove transmission and inspect shift mechanism. Repair as required. |
| | 7. Clutch housing misalignment. | 7. Check runout at rear face of clutch housing. |
| GEAR CLASH WHEN SHIFTING FROM ONE FORWARD GEAR TO ANOTHER | 1. Incorrect clutch adjustment. | 1. Adjust clutch. |
| | 2. Clutch linkage binding. | 2. Lubricate or repair linkage as required. |
| | 3. Gear shift linkage incorrectly adjusted, bent, or binding. | 3. Adjust linkage, correct binds, replace bent parts. |
| | 4. Clutch housing misalignment. | 4. Check runout at rear face of clutch housing. |
| | 5. Damaged or worn transmission components: shift forks, synchronizers, shift rails and interlocks. Excessive end play due to worn thrust washers. | 5. Inspect components. Repair or replace as required. |
| TRANSMISSION NOISY | 1. Insufficient lubricant. | 1. Check lubricant level and replenish as required. |
| | 2. Incorrect lubricant. | 2. Replace with proper lubricant. |
| | 3. Clutch housing to engine or transmission to clutch housing bolts loose. | 3. Check and correct bolt torque as required. |
| | 4. Dirt, chips in lubricant. | 4. Drain and flush transmission. |
| | 5. Gearshift linkage incorrectly adjusted, or bent or binding. | 5. Adjust linkage, correct binds, replace bent parts. |
| | 6. Clutch housing misalignment. | 6. Check runout at rear face of clutch housing. |

## CLUTCH & MANUAL TRANSMISSION—Continued

| Condition | Possible Cause | Correction |
|---|---|---|
| **TRANSMISSION NOISY, continued** | 7. Worn transmission components: front-rear bearings, worn gear teeth, damaged gear teeth or synchronizer components. | 7. Inspect components and repair as required. |
| **JUMPS OUT OF GEAR** | 1. Gearshift linkage incorrectly adjusted. | 1. Adjust linkage. |
| | 2. Gearshift linkage bent or binding. | 2. Correct bind, replace bent parts. |
| | 3. Clutch housing misaligned. | 3. Check runout at rear face of clutch housing. |
| | 4. Worn pilot bushing. | 4. Replace bushing. |
| | 5. Worn or damaged clutch shaft roller bearings. | 5. Replace bearings. |
| | 6. Worn, tapered gear teeth; synchronizer parts worn. | 6. Inspect and replace as required. |
| | 7. Shifter forks, shift rails, or detent-interlock parts worn, missing, etc. | 7. Inspect and replace as required. |
| | 8. Excessive end play of output shaft gear train, countershaft gear or reverse idler gear. | 8. Replace thrust washers, and snap rings (output shaft gear train). |
| **WILL NOT SHIFT INTO ONE GEAR—ALL OTHERS OK** | 1. Gearshift linkage not adjusted correctly. | 1. Adjust linkage. |
| | 2. Bent shift rod at transmission. | 2. Replace rod. |
| | 3. Transmission shifter levers reversed. | 3. Correctly position levers. |
| | 4. Worn or damaged shift rails, shift forks, detent-interlock plugs, loose setscrew in shifter fork, worn synchronizer parts. | 4. Inspect and repair or replace parts as required. |
| **LOCKED IN ONE GEAR—CANNOT BE SHIFTED OUT OF THAT GEAR** | 1. Gearshift linkage binding or bent. | 1. Correct bind, replace bent components. |
| | 2. Transmission shifter lever attaching nuts loose or levers are worn at shifter fork shaft hole. | 2. Tighten nuts, replace worn levers. |
| | 3. Shift rails worn or broken, shifter fork bent, setscrew loose, detent-interlock plug missing or worn. | 3. Inspect and replace worn or damaged parts. |
| | 4. Broken gear teeth on countershaft gear, clutch shaft, or reverse idler gear. | 4. Inspect and replace damaged part. |

# Transfer Case

| Condition | Possible Cause | Correction |
|---|---|---|
| **TRANSFER CASE NOISY**<br><br>**NOTE:** If the vehicle has not been driven for a week or more, noise may occur during initial operation. This is a normal condition and the noise will usually stop after continued operation. | 1. Incorrect tire inflation pressures and/or tire and wheel size. | 1. Check that all tire and wheel assemblies are the same size and inflation pressures are correct. |
| | 2. Incorrect lubricant level. | 2. Check and fill lubricant as required. |
| | 3. Worn or damaged bearings. | 3. Inspect and replace as required. |
| | 4. Worn or damaged drive chain. | 4. Inspect and replace as required. |
| | 5. Incorrectly aligned driveshafts or universal joints. | 5. Inspect and align as required. |
| | 6. Loose adapter bolts. | 6. Check and correct bolt torque as required. |
| **SHIFTER LEVER DIFFICULT TO MOVE** | 1. Dirty or contaminated linkage. | 1. Clean and lubricate as required. |
| | 2. Internal component damage. | 2. Inspect and replace as required. |
| **JUMPS OUT OF GEAR** | 1. Incorrectly adjusted or loose shift linkage. | 1. Adjust and/or tighten linkage bolts. |
| | 2. Loose mounting bolts. | 2. Check and correct bolt torque as required |
| | 3. Front and rear driveshaft slip yokes dry or loose. | 3. Lubricate and repair slip yokes as required. Correct bolt torque as required. |
| | 4. Internal case component damage. | 4. Inspect and replace worn and/or damaged case components as required. |

# TROUBLESHOOTING

## TRANSFER CASE—Continued

| Condition | Possible Cause | Correction |
|---|---|---|
| **FRONT AXLE SLIPS OUT OF ENGAGEMENT** | 1. Spring loose or broken.<br>2. Incorrect shift linkage or cable adjustment. | 1. Inspect and replace as required.<br>2. Adjust linkage or cable as required. |
| **TRANSFER CASE LEAKING** | 1. Excessive lubricant in case.<br>2. Worn and/or damaged seals or gaskets.<br>3. Loose mounting case bolts.<br>4. Scored yoke in seal contact area. | 1. Correct lubricant level as required.<br>2. Inspect and replace as required.<br>3. Check and correct bolt torque as required<br>4. Repair or replace as required. |

# Brakes

| | | |
|---|---|---|
| **LOW BRAKE PEDAL**<br>(Excessive pedal travel required to apply brake) | 1. Excessive clearance between linings and drums caused by inoperative automatic adjusters.<br><br>2. Worn brake lining.<br><br>3. Bent, distorted brakeshoes.<br>4. Caliper pistons corroded.<br>5. Power unit push rod height incorrect. | 1. Make 10 to 15 firm forward and reverse brake stops to adjust brakes. If brake pedal does not come up, repair or replace adjuster parts as necessary.<br>2. Inspect and replace lining if worn beyond minimum thickness specification.<br>3. Replace brakeshoes in axle sets.<br>4. Repair or replace calipers.<br>5. Check height with gauge (only). Replace power unit if push rod height is not within specifications. |
| **LOW BRAKE PEDAL**<br>(Pedal may go to floor under steady pressure) | 1. Leak in hydraulic system.<br><br><br>2. Air in hydraulic system.<br><br>3. Incorrect or non-recommended brake fluid (fluid boils away at below normal temp.). | 1. Fill master cylinder to within ¼-inch of rim; have helper apply brakes and check calipers, wheel cylinders combination valve, tubes, hoses and fittings for leaks. Repair or replace parts as necessary.<br>2. Bleed air from system. Refer to Brake Bleeding.<br>3. Flush hydraulic system with clean brake fluid. Refill with correct-type fluid. |
| **LOW BRAKE PEDAL**<br>(Pedal goes to floor on first application—OK on subsequent applications) | 1. Disc brakeshoe (pad) knock back; shoes push caliper piston back into bore. Caused by loose wheel bearings or excessive lateral runout of rotor (rotor wobble).<br>2. Calipers sticking on mounting surfaces of caliper and anchor. Caused by buildup of dirt, rust, or corrosion on abutment. | 1. Adjust wheel bearings and check lateral runout of rotor(s). Refinish rotors if runout is over limits. Replace rotor if refinishing would cause rotor to fall below minimum thickness limit.<br>2. Clean mounting surfaces and lubricate surfaces with molydisulphide grease or equivalent. |
| **FADING BRAKE PEDAL**<br>(Pedal falls away under steady pressure) | 1. Leak in hydraulic system.<br><br><br>2. Master cylinder piston cups worn, or master cylinder bore is scored, worn or corroded. | 1. Fill master cylinder reservoirs to within ¼-inch of rim; have helper apply brakes, check master cylinder, calipers, wheel cylinders combination valve, tubes, hoses, and fittings for leaks. Repair or replace parts as necessary.<br>2. Repair or replace master cylinder. |

## BRAKES—Continued

| Condition | Possible Cause | Correction |
|---|---|---|
| **DECREASING BRAKE PEDAL TRAVEL** (Pedal travel required to apply brakes decreases, may be accompanied by hard pedal) | 1. Caliper or wheel cylinder pistons sticking or seized.<br>2. Master cylinder compensator ports blocked (preventing fluid return to reservoirs) or pistons sticking or seized in master cylinder bore.<br>3. Power brake unit binding internally. | 1. Repair or replace calipers, or wheel cylinders.<br>2. Repair or replace master cylinder<br><br>3. Test unit as follows:<br>  a. Raise hood, shift transmission into neutral and start engine.<br>  b. Increase engine speed to 1500 RPM, close throttle and fully depress brake pedal.<br>  c. Slowly release brake pedal and stop engine.<br>  d. Remove vacuum check valve and hose from power unit. Observe for backward movement of brake pedal or power unit-to-brake pedal push rod.<br>  e. If pedal or push rod moves backward, power unit has internal bind—replace power brake unit. |
| | 4. Incorrect power unit push rod height. | 4. Adjust push rod height. |
| **SPONGY BRAKE PEDAL** (Pedal has abnormally soft, springy, spongy feel when depressed) | 1. Air in hydraulic system.<br>2. Brakeshoes bent or distorted.<br>3. Brake lining not yet seated to drums and rotors. | 1. Bleed brakes.<br>2. Replace brakeshoes.<br>3. Burnish brakes. |
| **HARD BRAKE PEDAL** (Excessive pedal pressure required to stop car. May be accompanied by brake fade) | 1. Loose or leaking power brake unit vacuum hose.<br>2. Brake lining contaminated by grease or brake fluid.<br>3. Incorrect or poor quality brake lining.<br>4. Bent, broken, distorted brakeshoes.<br>5. Calipers binding or dragging on anchor. Rear brakeshoes dragging on support plate. | 1. Tighten connections or replace leaking hose.<br>2. Determine cause of contaminations and correct. Replace contaminated brake lining in axle sets.<br>3. Replace lining in axle sets.<br>4. Replace brakeshoes and lining.<br>5. Sand or wire brush anchors and caliper mounting surfaces and lubricate surfaces lightly. Clean rust or burrs from rear brake support plate ledges and lubricate ledges.<br><br>**NOTE:** If ledges are deeply grooved or scored, do not attempt to sand or grind them smooth—replace support plate. |
| | 6. Rear brake drum(s) bell mouthed, flared or barrel shaped (distorted).<br>7. Caliper, wheel cylinder, or master cylinder pistons sticking or seized.<br>8. Power brake unit vacuum check valve malfunction. | 6. Replace rear drum(s).<br>7. Repair or replace parts as necessary.<br>8. Test valve as follows:<br>  a. Start engine, increase engine speed to 1500 RPM, close throttle and immediately stop engine.<br>  b. Wait at least 90 seconds then try brake action.<br>  c. If brakes are not vacuum assisted for 2 or more applications, check valve is faulty. |

# TROUBLESHOOTING

## BRAKES—Continued

| Condition | Possible Cause | Correction |
|---|---|---|
| **HARD BRAKE PEDAL, continued** | 9. Power brake unit has internal bind or incorrect push rod height (too long). | 9. Test unit as follows:<br>a. With engine stopped, apply brakes several times to exhaust all vacuum in system.<br>b. Shift transmission into neutral, depress brake pedal and start engine.<br>c. If pedal falls away under foot pressure and less pressure is required to hold pedal in applied position, power unit vacuum system is working. Test power unit as outlined in item (3) under "Decreasing Brake Pedal Travel." If power unit exhibits bind condition, replace power unit.<br>d. If power unit does not exhibit bind condition, disconnect master cylinder and check push rod height with appropriate gauge. If height is not within specifications, replace power unit. |
| | 10. Master cylinder compensator ports (at bottom of reservoirs) blocked by dirt, scale, rust, or have small burrs (blocked ports prevent fluid return to reservoirs). | 10. Repair or replace master cylinder.<br><br>**CAUTION:** Do not attempt to clean blocked ports with wire, pencils, or similar implements. |
| | 11. Brake hoses, tubes, fittings clogged or restricted. | 11. Use compressed air to check or unclog parts. Replace any damaged parts. |
| | 12. Brake fluid contaminated with improper fluids (motor oil, transmission fluid, or poor quality brake fluid) causing rubber components to swell and stick in bores. | 12. Replace all rubber components and hoses. Flush entire brake system. Refill with recommended brake fluid. |
| **GRABBING BRAKES**<br>**(Severe reaction to brake pedal pressure)** | 1. Brake lining(s) contaminated by grease or brake fluid. | 1. Determine and correct cause of contamination and replace brakeshoes and linings in axle sets. |
| | 2. Parking brake cables incorrectly adjusted or seized. | 2. Adjust cables. Free up or replace seized cables. |
| | 3. Power brake unit binding internally or push rod height incorrect. | 3. Test unit as outlined in item (3) under Decreasing Brake Pedal Travel. If O.K., check push rod height. If unit has internal bind or incorrect push rod height, replace unit. |
| | 4. Incorrect brake lining or lining loose on brakeshoes. | 4. Replace brakeshoes in axle sets. |
| | 5. Brakeshoes bent, cracked, distorted. | 5. Replace brakeshoes in axle sets. |
| | 6. Caliper anchor plate bolts loose. | 6. Tighten bolts. |
| | 7. Rear brakeshoes binding on support plate ledges. | 7. Clean and lubricate ledges. Replace support plate(s) if ledges are deeply grooved. Do not attempt to smooth ledges by grinding. |
| | 8. Rear brake support plates loose. | 8. Tighten mounting bolts. |
| | 9. Caliper or wheel cylinder piston sticking or seized. | 9. Repair or replace parts as necessary. |
| | 10. Master cylinder pistons sticking or seized in bore. | 10. Repair or replace master cylinder. |
| **BRAKES GRAB, PULL, OR WON'T HOLD IN WET WEATHER** | 1. Brake lining water soaked. | 1. Drive car with brakes lightly applied to dry out lining. If problem persists after lining has dried, replace brakeshoe lining in axle sets. |
| | 2. Rear brake support plate bent allowing excessive amount of water to enter drum. | 2. Replace support plate. |

## BRAKES—Continued

| Condition | Possible Cause | Correction |
|---|---|---|
| **DRAGGING BRAKES** (Slow or incomplete release of brakes) | 1. Brake pedal binding at pivot. | 1. Free up and lubricate. |
| | 2. Power brake unit push rod height incorrect (too high) or unit has internal bind. | 2. Replace unit if push rod height is incorrect. If height is O.K., check for internal bind as outlined in item (3) under "Decreasing Brake Pedal Travel." |
| | 3. Parking brake cables incorrectly adjusted or seized. | 3. Adjust cables. Free up or replace seized cables. |
| | 4. Brakeshoe return springs weak or broken. | 4. Replace return springs. Replace brakeshoe if necessary in axle sets. |
| | 5. Automatic adjusters malfunctioning. | 5. Repair or replace adjuster parts as required. |
| | 6. Caliper, wheel cylinder or master cylinder pistons sticking or seized. | 6. Repair or replace parts as necessary. |
| | 7. Master cylinder compensating ports blocked (fluid does not return to reservoirs). | 7. Use compressed air to clear ports. Do not use wire, pencils, or similar objects to open blocked ports. |
| **CAR PULLS TO ONE SIDE WHEN BRAKES ARE APPLIED** | 1. Incorrect front tire pressure. | 1. Inflate to recommended cold (reduced load) inflation pressures. |
| | 2. Incorrect front wheel bearing adjustment or worn—damaged wheel bearings. | 2. Adjust wheel bearings. Replace worn, damaged bearings. |
| | 3. Brakeshoe lining on one side contaminated. | 3. Determine and correct cause of contamination and replace brakeshoe lining in axle sets. |
| | 4. Brakeshoes on one side bent, distorted, or lining loose on shoe. | 4. Replace brakeshoes in axle sets. |
| | 5. Support plate bent or loose on one side. | 5. Tighten or replace support plate. |
| | 6. Brake lining not yet seated to drums and rotors. | 6. Burnish brakes. |
| | 7. Caliper anchor plate loose on one side. | 7. Tighten anchor plate bolts. |
| | 8. Caliper or wheel cylinder piston sticking or seized. | 8. Repair or replace caliper or wheel cylinder. |
| | 9. Brakeshoe linings watersoaked. | 9. Drive car with brakes lightly applied to dry linings. Replace brakeshoes in axle sets if problem persists. |
| | 10. Loose suspension component attaching or mounting bolts, incorrect front end alignment. Worn suspension parts. | 10. Tighten suspension bolts. Replace worn suspension components. Check and correct alignment as necessary. |
| **CHATTER OR SHUDDER WHEN BRAKES ARE APPLIED** (Pedal pulsation and roughness may also occur) | 1. Front wheel bearings loose. | 1. Adjust wheel bearings. |
| | 2. Brakeshoes distorted, bent, contaminated, or worn. | 2. Replace brakeshoes in axle sets. |
| | 3. Caliper anchor plate or support plate loose. | 3. Tighten mounting bolts. |
| | 4. Excessive thickness variation or lateral rim out of rotor. | 4. Refinish or replace rotor. |
| | 5. Rear drum(s) out of round, sharp spots. | 5. Refinish or replace drum. |
| | 6. Loose suspension component attaching or mounting bolts, incorrect front end alignment. Worn suspension parts. | 6. Tighten suspension bolts. Replace worn suspension components. Check and correct alignment as necessary. |
| **NOISY BRAKES** (Squealing, clicking, scraping sound when brakes are applied) | 1. Bent, broken, distorted brakeshoes. | 1. Replace brakeshoes in axle sets. |
| | 2. Brake lining worn out—shoes contacting drum or rotor. | 2. Replace brakeshoes and lining in axle sets. Refinish or replace drums or rotors. |
| | 3. Foreign material imbedded in brake lining. | 3. Replace brake lining. |
| | 4. Broken or loose hold-down or return springs. | 4. Replace parts as necessary. |
| | 5. Rough or dry drum brake support plate ledges. | 5. Lubricate support plate ledges. |
| | 6. Cracked, grooved, or scored rotor(s) or drum(s). | 6. Replace rotor(s) or drum(s). Replace brakeshoes and lining in axle sets if necessary. |

## BRAKES—Continued

| Condition | Possible Cause | Correction |
|---|---|---|
| PULSATING BRAKE PEDAL | 1. Out of round drums or excessive thickness variation or lateral runout in disc brake rotor(s). | 1. Refinish or replace drums or rotors. |
| | 2. Bent rear axle shaft. | 2. Replace axle shaft. |

# Steering

| Condition | Possible Cause | Correction |
|---|---|---|
| EXCESSIVE PLAY OR LOOSENESS IN STEERING | 1. Incorrectly adjusted front wheel bearings. | 1. Adjust bearings. |
| | 2. Worn steering shaft couplings. | 2. Inspect and replace as required. |
| | 3. Steering wheel loose on shaft, loose pitman arm, tie rods, steering arms or steering linkage ball studs. | 3. Check and correct steering attachment torques as required. |
| | 4. Worn ball joints. | 4. Inspect and replace as required. |
| | 5. Worn intermediate rod or tie rod sockets. | 5. Inspect and replace as required. |
| HARD OR ERRATIC STEERING | 1. Incorrect tire pressure. | 1. Inflate tires to recommended pressure. |
| | 2. Insufficient or incorrect lubrication. | 2. Lubricate as required. |
| | 3. Steering or linkage parts damaged or misaligned. | 3. Repair or replace parts as required. |
| | 4. Incorrect front wheel alignment. | 4. Adjust wheel alignment angles. |
| | 5. Incorrect steering gear adjustment. | 5. Adjust steering gear. |
| POOR STEERING RETURNABILITY | 1. Insufficient ball joint or linkage lubrication. | 1. Lubricate as required. |
| | 2. Steering gear adjusted too tightly. | 2. Adjust over center and thrust bearing preload. |
| | 3. Steering gear to column misaligned. | 3. Align steering column. |
| | 4. Incorrect front wheel alignment (caster). | 4. Check alignment and correct as required. |
| WHEEL SHIMMY OR TRAMP | 1. Improper tire pressure. | 1. Inflate tires to recommended pressures. |
| | 2. Wheels, tires, or brake drums out-of-balance or out-of-round. | 2. Inspect parts and replace unacceptable out-of-round parts. Rebalance parts. |
| | 3. Inoperative, worn, or loose shock absorbers or mounting parts. | 3. Repair or replace shocks or mountings. |
| | 4. Loose or worn steering or suspension parts. | 4. Tighten or replace as necessary. |
| | 5. Loose or worn wheel bearings. | 5. Adjust or replace bearings. |
| | 6. Incorrect steering gear adjustments. | 6. Adjust steering gear. |
| | 7. Incorrect front wheel alignment. | 7. Correct front wheel alignment. |
| TIRE WEAR | 1. Improper tire pressure. | 1. Inflate tires to recommended pressures. |
| | 2. Failure to rotate tires. | 2. Rotate tires. |
| | 3. Brakes grabbing. | 3. Adjust or repair brakes. |
| | 4. Incorrect front wheel alignment. | 4. Align incorrect angles. |
| | 5. Broken or damaged steering and suspension parts. | 5. Repair or replace defective parts. |
| | 6. Wheel runout. | 6. Replace faulty wheel. |
| | 7. Excessive speed on turns. | 7. Make driver aware of condition. |
| TRUCK LEADS TO ONE SIDE | 1. Improper tire pressures. | 1. Inflate tires to recommended pressures. |
| | 2. Front tires with uneven tread depth, wear pattern, or different cord design (i.e., one bias ply and one belted tire on front wheels). | 2. Install tires of same cord construction and reasonably even tread depth and wear pattern. |
| | 3. Incorrect front wheel alignment. | 3. Align incorrect angles. |
| | 4. Brakes dragging. | 4. Adjust or repair brakes. |
| | 5. Faulty power steering gear valve assembly. | 5. Replace valve assembly. |
| | 6. Pulling due to uneven tire construction. | 6. Replace faulty tire. |

# Suspension

| Condition | Possible Cause | Correction |
|---|---|---|
| **FRONT BOTTOMING OR RIDING LOW** | 1. Incorrect tire pressure. | 1. Inflate tires to recommended pressure. |
| | 2. Incorrect tire and wheel usage. | 2. Install correct tire and wheel assembly. |
| | 3. Truck overloaded or unevenly loaded. | 3. Correct as required. |
| | 4. Broken or incorrectly installed front springs. | 4. Repair or replace as required. |
| | 5. Loose or broken shock absorbers. | 5. Tighten or replace as required. |
| | 6. Loose or broken shackles. | 6. Tighten or replace as required. |
| | 7. Incorrect truck ride height. | 7. Measure vertical distance between axle(s) and spring tower flange/frame rail. If below ride, install shims. |
| | 8. Incorrect springs. | 8. Check springs and replace if necessary. |
| **DOG TRACKING OF REAR WHEELS** | 1. Loose or damaged front and/or rear suspension parts. | 1. Inspect, repair or replace as required. |
| | 2. Loose rear spring U-bolts. | 2. Check and correct bolt torque as required. |
| | 3. Rear springs incorrectly installed on axle. | 3. Repair as required. |
| | 4. Incorrectly installed front coil or leaf springs. | 4. Repair as required. |
| **SWAY OR ROLL** | 1. Unequal load distribution (side to side). | 1. Correct as required. |
| | 2. Excessive load or body height. | 2. Correct as required. |
| | 3. Incorrect tire pressure. | 3. Correct tire inflation pressure. |
| | 4. Loose wheel lug nuts. | 4. Torque lug nuts as required. |
| | 5. Worn or loose stabilizer bar assembly. | 5. Tighten or replace as required. |
| | 6. Loose or defective shock absorbers. | 6. Torque mounting bolts or replace as required. |
| | 7. Broken or sagging spring. | 7. Replace spring as required. |
| **FRONT END NOISE** | 1. Insufficient ball joint or linkage lubricant. | 1. Lubricate parts as required. |
| | 2. Worn bushings or loose shock absorber. | 2. Tighten bolts and/or replace bushings. |
| | 3. Worn control arm bushings. | 3. Replace bushings. |
| | 4. Worn tie rod ends. | 4. Replace tie rod ends. |
| | 5. Worn or loose wheel bearings. | 5. Adjust or replace wheel bearings. |
| | 6. Loose stabilizer bar. | 6. Torque all stabilizer bar attachments as required. |
| | 7. Loose wheel lug nuts. | 7. Torque lug nuts as required. |
| | 8. Incorrectly positioned spring. | 8. Correctly install spring. |
| | 9. Loose suspension bolts. | 9. Check and correct bolt torque as required. |
| **FRONT AXLE NOISE** | 1. Incorrect lubricant level. | 1. Check and fill lubricant as required. |
| | 2. Excessive pinion end-play. | 2. Check and adjust end play as required. |
| | 3. Incorrect pinion bearing preload. | 3. Check and adjust pinion bearing preload. |
| | 4. Worn and/or damaged pinion or differential bearings. | 4. Inspect and replace worn and/or damaged bearings. |
| | 5. Excessive differential bearing preload. | 5. Check and adjust differential bearing preload. |
| | 6. Damaged pinion gears. | 6. Replace gears. |

**NOTE:** A knocking noise heard at low speed or when coasting may be caused by loose differential side gears. If this is encountered, operate vehicle at speed where noise is loudest and apply brakes lightly. If loose gears are causing the problem, noise level should decrease as brakes are applied.

# TROUBLESHOOTING

# Exterior Lighting

## HEADLAMPS

| Condition | Possible Cause | Correction |
|---|---|---|
| ONE HEADLAMP INOPERATIVE OR INTERMITTENT | 1. Loose connection. | 1. Secure connections to sealed beam including ground. |
| | 2. Defective sealed beam. | 2. Replace sealed beam. |
| ONE OR MORE HEADLIGHTS ARE DIM | 1. Open ground connection at headlight. | 1. Repair ground wire connection between sealed beam and body ground. |
| | 2. Ground wire mislocated in headlight connector (type 2 sealed beam). | 2. Relocate ground wire in connector. |
| ONE OR MORE HEADLIGHTS SHORT LIFE | 1. Voltage regulator maladjusted. | 1. Readjust regulator to specifications. |
| ALL HEADLIGHTS INOPERATIVE OR INTERMITTENT | 1. Loose connection. | 1. Check and secure connections at dimmer switch and light switch. |
| | 2. Defective dimmer switch. | 2. Check voltage at dimmer switch with test lamp. If test lamp bulb lights only at switch "Hot" wire terminal, replace dimmer switch. |
| | 3. Open wiring—light switch to dimmer switch. | 3. Check wiring with test lamp. If bulb lights at light switch wire terminal, but not at dimmer switch, repair open wire. |
| | 4. Open wiring—light switch to battery. | 4. Check "Hot" wire terminal at light switch with test lamp. If lamp does not light, repair open wire circuit to battery (possible open fusible link). |
| | 5. Shorted ground circuit. | 5. If, after a few minutes operation, headlights flicker "ON" and "OFF" and/or a thumping noise can be heard from the light switch (circuit breaker opening and closing), repair short to ground in circuit between light switch and headlights. After repairing short, check for headlight flickering after one minute operation. If flickering occurs, the circuit breaker has been damaged and light switch must be replaced. |
| | 6. Defective light switch. | 6. Check light switch. Replace light switch, if defective. |
| UPPER OR LOWER BEAM WILL NOT LIGHT OR INTERMITTENT | 1. Open connection or defective dimmer switch. | 1. Check dimmer switch terminals with test lamp. If bulb lights at all wire terminals, repair open wiring between dimmer switch and headlights. If bulb will not light at one of these terminals, replace dimmer switch. |
| | 2. Short circuit to ground. | 2. Follow diagnosis above (all headlights inoperative or intermittent). |

## SIDE MARKER LAMPS

| Condition | Possible Cause | Correction |
|---|---|---|
| ONE LAMP INOPERATIVE | 1. Turn signal bulb burnt out (front lamp). | 1. Switch turn signals on. If signal bulb does not light, replace bulb. |
| | 2. Side marker bulb burnt out. | 2. Replace bulb. |
| | 3. Loose connection or open in wiring. | 3. Using test lamp, check "Hot" wire terminal at bulb socket. If test lamp lights, repair open ground circuit. If lamp does not light, repair open "Hot" wire circuit. |

## SIDE MARKER LAMPS—Continued

| Condition | Possible Cause | Correction |
|---|---|---|
| FRONT OR REAR LAMPS INOPERATIVE | 1. Loose connection or open ground connection. | 1. If associated tail or park lamps do not operate, secure all connectors in "Hot" wire circuit. If park and turn lamps operate, repair open ground connections. |
| | 2. Multiple bulbs burnt out. | 2. Replace burnt out bulbs. |
| ALL LAMPS INOPERATIVE | 1. Blown fuse. | 1. If park and tail lamps do not operate, replace blown fuse. If new fuse blows, check for short to ground between fuse panel and lamps. |
| | 2. Loose connection. | 2. Secure connector to light switch. |
| | 3. Open in wiring. | 3. Check tail light fuse with test lamp. If test lamp lights, repair open wiring between fuse and light switch. If not, repair open wiring between fuse and battery (possible open fusible link). |
| | 4. Defective light switch. | 4. Check light switch. Replace light switch, if defective. |

## TAIL, PARK AND LICENSE LAMPS

| Condition | Possible Cause | Correction |
|---|---|---|
| ONE SIDE INOPERATIVE | 1. Bulb burnt out. | 1. Replace bulb. |
| | 2. Open ground connection at bulb socket or ground wire terminal. | 2. Jump bulb base socket connection to ground. If lamp lights, repair open ground circuit. |
| BOTH SIDES INOPERATIVE | 1. Tail lamp fuse blown. | 1. Replace fuse. If new fuse blows, repair short to ground in "Hot" wire circuit between fuse panel through light switch to lamps. |
| | 2. Loose connection. | 2. Secure connector at light switch. |
| | 3. Open wiring. | 3. Using test light, check circuit on both sides of fuse. If lamp does not light on either side, repair open circuit between fuse panel and battery (possible open fusible link). If test lamp lights at light switch terminal, repair open wiring between light switch and lamps. |
| | 4. Multiple bulb burnout. | 4. If test lamp lights at lamp socket "Hot" wire terminal, replace bulbs. |
| | 5. Defective light switch. | 5. Check light switch. Replace light switch, if defective. |

## TURN SIGNAL AND HAZARD WARNING LAMP

| Condition | Possible Cause | Correction |
|---|---|---|
| TURN SIGNALS INOPERATIVE ONE SIDE | 1. Bulb(s) burnt out (flasher cannot be heard). | 1. Turn hazard warning system on. If one or more bulbs are inoperative replace necessary bulbs. |
| | 2. Open wiring or ground connection. | 2. Turn hazard warning system on. If one or more bulbs are inoperative, use test lamp and check circuit at lamp socket. If test lamp lights, repair open ground connection. If not, repair open wiring between bulb socket and turn signal switch. |
| | 3. Improper bulb or defective turn signal switch. | 3. Turn hazard warning system on. If all front and rear lamps operate, check for improper bulb. If bulbs are O.K., replace defective turn signal switch. |
| | 4. Short to ground (flasher can be heard, no bulbs operate). | 4. Locate and repair short to ground by disconnecting front and rear circuits separately. |

# TROUBLESHOOTING

## TURN SIGNAL AND HAZARD WARNING LAMP—Continued

| Condition | Possible Cause | Correction |
|---|---|---|
| **TURN SIGNALS INOPERATIVE** | 1. Blown turn signal fuse. | 1. Turn hazard warning system on. If all lamps operate, replace blown fuse. If new fuse blows, repair short to ground between fuse and lamps. |
| | 2. Defective flasher. | 2. If turn signal fuse is O.K. and hazard warning system will operate lamps, replace defective turn signal flasher. |
| | 3. Loose connection. | 3. Secure steering column connector. |
| **HAZARD WARNING LAMPS INOPERATIVE** | 1. Blown fuse. | 1. Switch turn signals on. If lamps operate, replace fuse if blown. If new fuse blows, repair short to ground. (could be in stop light circuit). |
| | 2. Defective hazard warning flasher. | 2. If fuse is O.K., switch turn signals on. If lamps operate, replace defective hazard flasher. |
| | 3. Open in wiring or defective turn signal switch. | 3. Using test lamp, check hazard switch feed wire in turn signal steering column connector. If lamp does not light on either side of connector, repair open circuit between flasher and connector. If lamp lights only on feed side of connector, clean connector contacts. If lamp lights on both sides of connector, replace defective turn signal switch assembly. |

## BACK-UP LAMP

| Condition | Possible Cause | Correction |
|---|---|---|
| **ONE LAMP INOPERATIVE OR INTERMITTENT** | 1. Loose or burnt out bulb. | 1. Secure or replace bulb. |
| | 2. Loose connection. | 2. Tighten connectors. |
| | 3. Open ground connections. | 3. Repair bulb ground circuit. |
| **BOTH LAMPS INOPERATIVE OR INTERMITTENT** | 1. Neutral start or back-up lamp switch maladjusted. | 1. Readjust or replace bulb. |
| | 2. Loose connection or open circuit. | 2. Secure all connectors. If O.K., check continuity of circuit from fuse to lamps with test lamp. If lamp does not light on either side of fuse, correct open circuit from battery to fuse. |
| | 3. Blown fuse. | 3. Replace fuse. If new fuse blows, repair short to ground in circuit from fuse through neutral start switch to back-up lamps. |
| | 4. Defective neutral start or back-up lamp switch. | 4. Check switch. Replace neutral start or back-up lamp switch, if defective. |
| | 5. Defective ignition switch. | 5. If test lamp lights at ignition switch battery terminal but not at output terminal, replace ignition switch. |
| **LAMP WILL NOT TURN OFF** | 1. Neutral start or back-up switch maladjusted. | 1. Readjust neutral start or back-up lamp switch. |
| | 2. Defective neutral start or back-up lamp switch. | 2. Check switch. Replace neutral start or back-up lamp switch, if defective. |

## STOP LIGHTS

| Condition | Possible Cause | Correction |
|---|---|---|
| **ONE BULB INOPERATIVE ONE SIDE INOPERATIVE** | 1. Bulb burnt out. | 1. Replace bulb. |
| | 1. Loose connection, open wiring or defective bulbs. | 1. Turn on directional signal. If lamp does not operate, check bulbs. If bulbs are O.K., secure all connections. If lamp still does not operate, use test lamp and check for open wiring. |

## STOP LIGHTS—Continued

| Condition | Possible Cause | Correction |
|---|---|---|
| ONE SIDE INOPERATIVE, continued | 2. Defective directional signal switch or cancelling cam. | 2. If lamp will operate by turning directional signal on, the switch is not centering properly during cancelling operation. Replace defective cancelling cam or directional signal switch. |
| ALL INOPERATIVE | 1. Blown fuse. | 1. Replace fuse. If new fuse blows, repair short to ground in circuit between fuse and lamps. |
| | 2. Stop-switch maladjusted or defective. | 2. Check stop switch. Adjust or replace stop switch, if required. |
| WILL NOT TURN OFF | 1. Stop switch maladjusted or defective. | 1. Readjust switch. If switch still malfunctions, replace. |

# Horns

| Condition | Possible Cause | Correction |
|---|---|---|
| HORNS WILL NOT OPERATE | 1. Loose connections in circuit. | 1. Check and tighten connections. Be sure to check ground straps. |
| | 2. Defective horn switch. | 2. Replace defective parts. |
| | 3. Defective horn relay. | 3. Replace relay. |
| | 4. Defects within horn. | 4. Replace horn. |
| HORNS HAVE POOR TONE | 1. Low available voltage at horn, or defects within horn. | 1. Check battery and charging circuit. Although horn should blow at any voltage above 7.0 volts, a weak or poor tone may occur at operating voltage below 11.0 volts. If horn has weak or poor tone at operating voltage of 11.0 volts or higher, remove horn and replace. |
| HORNS OPERATE INTERMITTENTLY | 1. Loose or intermittent connections in horn relay or horn switch. | 1. Check and tighten connections. |
| | 2. Defective horn switch. | 2. Replace switch. |
| | 3. Defective relay. | 3. Replace relay. |
| | 4. Defects within horn. | 4. Replace horn. |
| HORNS BLOW CONSTANTLY | 1. Sticking horn relay. | 1. Replace relay. |
| | 2. Horn relay energized by grounded or shorted wiring. | 2. Check and adjust wiring. |
| | 3. Horn button can be grounded by sticking closed. | 3. Adjust or replace damaged parts. |

# Speedometer

| Condition | Possible Cause | Correction |
|---|---|---|
| SPEEDOMETER NOT OPERATING PROPERLY | 1. Noisy speedometer cable. | 1. Loosen over-tightened casing nuts and snap-on at speedometer head. Replace housing and core. Replace broken cable. |
| | 2. Pointer and odometer inoperative. Inaccurate reading. | 2. Check tire size. Check for correct speedometer driven gear. |
| | 3. Kinked cable. | 3. Replace cable. Reroute casing so that bends have no less than 6″ radius. |
| | 4. Defective speedometer head. | 4. Replace speedometer. |
| | 5. Casing connector loose on speedometer case. | 5. Tighten connector. |

# Noise, Vibration & Harshness

## ROAD TEST

A road test and customer interview can provide much of the information needed to identify the specific condition which must be dealt with.

1. Make notes during diagnosis routine. This will ensure diagnosis is complete and systematic. Take care not to overlook details.
2. Road test vehicle and study condition by reproducing it several times during test.
3. When condition is reproduced, perform road test checks immediately. Refer to "Road Test Quick Checks" to identify proper section of diagnostic procedure. Perform checks several times to ensure valid conclusions. While the quick checks may not locate the problem, they will indicate the areas where there are no problems.
4. Do not make changes or adjustments before a road test and inspection of vehicle are performed. Any changes made can hide problems or add additional problems. Check and note tire pressures, any leaks, loose nuts or bolts, shiny spots where components may be rubbing, and if any unusually heavy items are loaded onto truck.

## ROAD TEST QUICK CHECKS

1. **25–50 mph**—Under light acceleration, a moaning noise can be heard possibly accompanied by a vibration in floor. Refer to "Tip-In Moan" diagnostic procedure.
2. **25–45 mph**—Under steady to heavy acceleration, a rumbling noise can be heard. Refer to "Incorrect Driveline Angle" diagnostic procedure.
3. **High Speed**—Under slow acceleration and deceleration, shaking is noticeable in steering column or wheel, seats, floor pan, trim panels, or front end sheet metal. Refer to "High Speed Shake" procedure.
4. **High Speed**—Vibration can be felt in floor pan or seats, with no visible shaking but with rumble, buzz, hum, or booming noise. Refer to "Driveline Vibration" procedure.
5. **High Speed**—Coast with clutch disengaged or with automatic transmission in neutral and engine idling. If vibration is present, refer to "Driveline Vibration" procedure. If vibration is no longer present, refer to "Engine and Accessory Vibration" or "High Speed Shake" procedures.
6. **0–High Speed**—Vibration can be felt when engine reaches particular RPM. Vibration can also be felt when vehicle

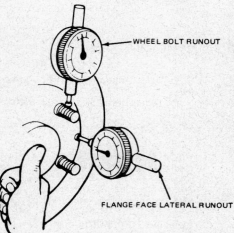

**Fig. 1   Checking axle flange & wheel bolt run-out**

is stationary. Refer to "Engine and Accessory Vibration."

## TYPES OF CONDITIONS

### HIGH SPEED SHAKE (35 MPH)

This condition involves a visible shake and pumping feeling in steering column, seats, or floor pan. The vibration is of low frequency (about 9–15 cycles per second) and may be seen as front end sheet metal shake. The condition may or may not be intensified by lightly applying brakes.

### TIP-IN MOAN (15–50 MPH)

Acceleration between 15–50 mph is accompanied by vibration which causes moan or high frequency resonance in floor pan. This condition is usually worse at a particular engine speed and at a particular throttle opening during acceleration at that speed. A moaning sound may also be caused depending on which component is producing the noise.

### DRIVELINE VIBRATION (50 MPH)

This condition does not involve a visible vibration, but is felt in floor pan as rumble, buzz, hum, drone, or boom. This condition is independent of engine speed and will occur at same speed in any gear, and is not sensitive to acceleration or deceleration and cannot be reduced by coasting in neutral. The condition can be duplicated by supporting vehicle on axle-type hoist and

operating driveline in gear at appropriate speed.

## ENGINE OR ACCESSORY VIBRATION (ALL SPEEDS)

This condition can occur at any vehicle speed but always at same engine RPM. Vibration will disappear during neutral coast and can be duplicated by operating engine at problem RPM with vehicle stationary. The condition can be caused by any component turning at engine speed when vehicle is stationary.

## HIGH SPEED SHAKE

1. Apply brakes gently. If shake increases, proceed to step 2; if shake does not increase, proceed to step 10.
2. Lightly apply parking brake. If shake increases, proceed to step 3; if shake does not increase, proceed to step 6.
3. Check clearance between rear drum and brake shoe. Loosen cable tension if necessary. If clearance is correct, proceed to step 4; if clearance is not correct, proceed to step 7.
4. Using dial indicator, check axle flange run-out, **Fig. 1**. If run-out is acceptable, proceed to step 5. If run-out is unacceptable, proceed to step 8.
5. Check run-out of rear brake drum or disc. If run-out is acceptable, proceed to step 10. If run-out is unacceptable, proceed to step 9.
6. Check run-out of front brake disc. If run-out is acceptable, proceed to step 10. If run-out is unacceptable, proceed to step 9.
7. Adjust parking brake cable tension and road test vehicle. If shake is not eliminated, proceed to step 4.
8. Replace axle shaft and road test vehicle. If shake is not eliminated, proceed to step 5.
9. Replace or machine brake drums or discs and road test vehicle. If shake is not eliminated, proceed to step 10.
10. Raise and support vehicle. Turn wheels by hand and check for abnormal wear, damage, wheel bearing play or roughness. If abnormal wear or damage is found, proceed to step 12. If wheel bearing displays excessive play or roughness, proceed to step 13. If brakes drag, proceed to steps 5 and 6.
11. Road test vehicle, noting carefully which area of vehicle is shaking. If front end sheet metal is shaking heavily, proceed to step 14. If shaking is felt more in floor pan, seat and steering column, proceed to step 15.
12. Replace worn or damaged tires and

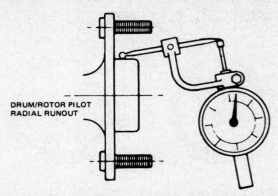

**Fig. 2  Checking drum/rotor pilot radial run-out**

check for any other damaged components such as shock absorbers. Road test vehicle. If vehicle still shakes, proceed to step 15.

13. Check and adjust wheel bearings. Replace damaged wheel bearings and road test vehicle. If shake is not eliminated, proceed to step 15.

14. Check and tighten all major front end sheet metal attaching bolts and adjust hood rests. Road test vehicle. If shake is not eliminated, proceed to step 15.

15. Balance wheels on vehicle and check tires and rims for run-out. If wheel balancing is not necessary, proceed to step 16. If wheel and tire run-out are found, proceed to step 19.

16. Road test vehicle at speed at which condition was most apparent. If shake is not eliminated, proceed to step 17.

17. Install a known good set of wheels and tires on vehicle and road test. If shake is eliminated, proceed to step 18. If shake is not eliminated, proceed to step 23.

18. If one or more of the tires has a construction irregularity which causes tire to contact the road in an irregular manner, substitute known good tires until irregular tires are located.

19. Attempt to reduce run-out by mounting wheel in different position in relation to axle. If run-out is now acceptable, proceed to step 16. If run-out is still excessive, proceed to step 17. If repositioning indicates axle shaft run-out, proceed to step 22. If repositioning indicates tire and wheel run-out, proceed to step 20.

20. Attempt to correct run-out by repositioning tire on rim. If run-out is acceptable, proceed to step 15. If run-out is still excessive, proceed to step 21.

21. Replace component shown to be unserviceable and recheck run-out. If run-out is acceptable, proceed to step 15. If run-out is excessive, proceed to step 22.

22. Measure axle shaft run-out, **Fig. 2.** Replace shaft if run-out is excessive and check run-out of new shaft. Install wheel and check run-out again. If run-out is acceptable, proceed to step 15. If run-out is excessive, proceed to step 20.

23. Raise and support vehicle. Remove rear wheels and tires. Check all axle and brake rotor run-out measurements if not already checked. If axle and brake run-out are acceptable, proceed to step 24. If axle run-out is excessive, proceed to step 8. If brake disc run-out is excessive, proceed to step 9.

24. Check driveshaft run-out. If run-out is acceptable, proceed to step 25. If run-out is excessive, proceed to step 27.

25. Remove driveshaft and inspect universal joints. If joints are O.K., proceed to step 26. If joints are defective, replace joints.

26. Install driveshaft and check for vibration. If vibration is unacceptable, proceed to step 27.

27. Measure ring gear run-out. If run-out is excessive, proceed to step 28.

28. Install new ring and pinion. Check run-out to ensure parts are within specifications. Recheck for vibration.

## MOANING NOISE DURING LIGHT ACCELERATION

1. Inspect air cleaner for correct positioning of gasket, lid and gasket, element and duct. Correct if necessary and check condition. If noise is unacceptable, proceed to step 2.

2. On vehicles where a transmission extension housing damper is specified, ensure damper is installed. Recheck condition, if noise is unacceptable, proceed to step 3.

3. Loosen engine mounts, start engine, and shift from Neutral to Drive and back to normalize engine mounts. Tighten engine mounts and check condition; if noise is unacceptable, proceed to step 4.

4. With exhaust system hot, loosen hangers, and operate engine while shifting from Neutral to Drive and back to normalize exhaust system. Tighten hangers and recheck condition; if noise is unacceptable, proceed to step 5.

5. Inspect accessory drive belts for prop-

er tension and accessory brackets for proper bolt torques. Adjust or tighten if necessary and check condition, if noise is unacceptable, proceed to step 6.

6. Loosen all bell housing bolts ¾ turn to test if noise is reduced. If noise is reduced, recheck step 2.

## DRIVELINE VIBRATION

**NOTE:** Driveline vibration is a higher frequency, lower amplitude vibration than high speed shake, directly related to road speeds of 45 mph and higher. This type of vibration will be felt in the floor pan or heard as a rumble, hum, buzz or boom and will be present in all driving modes. The vibration may vary during acceleration, deceleration or coasting conditions. A driveline vibration can usually be duplicated with the axle supported, through light braking applications while accelerating and decelerating to simulate road load resistance.

1. Raise and support vehicle with drive wheels free. Operate driveline at problem speed. If vibration is present, proceed to step 3; if vibration is not present, proceed to step 2.

2. Retest vehicle to observe reported condition.

3. Evaluate noise and vibration by operating driveline at problem speed. If audible boom or rumble occurs above 45 mph, proceed to step 5. If buzzy feel occurs in floor pan above 45 mph, proceed to step 5. If a gravelly feel or grinding sound occurs at low speeds, proceed to step 4.

4. Install rear spring dampers if available for vehicle. If condition is still unacceptable or dampers are not available, proceed to step 5.

5. Scribe a line to index rear axle companion flange to driveshaft flange. Inspect drive shaft for dents, undercoating, proper seating of U-joint bearing caps, and tight U-joints. If driveshaft is in acceptable condition, proceed to step 6. Replace driveshaft if damaged. Replace U-joints if worn or improperly positioned.

6. Inspect wheel bearings. If bearings are O.K., proceed to step 10; if wheel bearings are not in acceptable condition, proceed to step 7.

7. Replace wheel bearings and retest for vibration. If vibration is unacceptable proceed to step 10.

8. Repair or replace driveshaft. If vibration is unacceptable proceed to step 10.

9. Reposition U-joint bearing caps or replace U-joints. If vibration is unacceptable, proceed to step 10.

10. Disconnect driveshaft from rear axle companion flange and reconnect 180° from original position. Operate driveline at problem speed. If vibration is unacceptable, install rear axle pinion nose damper if available for vehicle. If

# TROUBLESHOOTING

pinion damper is not available or vibration is still unacceptable, proceed to step 11.

11. Disconnect driveshaft and return to original position. Refer to "Driveshaft Run-out," procedure and check run-out at front, center, and rear of driveshaft. If run-out is less than .035 inch at all positions, proceed to step 15 of "High Speed Shake" diagnosis. If run-out at front and/or center of driveshaft exceeds .035 inch while rear of shaft is acceptable, proceed to step 8. If run-out at rear of driveshaft exceeds .035 inch, proceed to "Driveshaft Run-out Check" procedure.

12. Balance driveshaft on vehicle and test vehicle at problem speed. If vibration is still unacceptable, proceed to step 17 of "High Speed Shake" diagnosis.

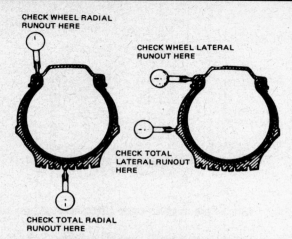

**Fig. 3  Checking tire/wheel radial run-out**

## INCORRECT PINION ANGLE

1. Ensure U-joints are tight and all bearing caps are in plate. If U-joints are in good condition, proceed to step 3; if not, proceed to step 2.
2. Make an index mark on driveshaft and rear axle companion flange. Remove driveshaft and replace U-joints. Retest vehicle; if vibration is unacceptable, proceed to step 3.
3. Refer to "Driveline Pinion Angle Check" procedure to check pinion angle.
4. If pinion angle is correct, proceed to step 1 of "Driveline Vibration."

## ENGINE OR ACCESSORY VIBRATION

1. With vehicle stationary, run engine at problem speed to check for condition. If vibration is present, proceed to step 2; if not, proceed to step 1 of "Driveline Vibration" diagnosis.
2. Inspect drive belts to check for wear or fraying. Ensure pulleys are not damaged or bent. Replace any damaged components and operate engine at problem speed. If vibration is present, proceed to step 3.
3. Check drive belt tension and adjust if necessary. Operate engine at problem speed. If vibration is still present, proceed to step 4.
4. Check torque of all accessory bracket bolts and retorque as necessary. Operate engine at problem speed; if vibration is still present, proceed to step 5.
5. Check pulley alignment and run-out visually at idle. Realign or replace pulleys if necessary. Operate engine at problem speed; if condition is still present, proceed to step 6.
6. Inspect belts for severe whipping at problem speed. If whip cannot be cor-

rected by adjusting tension, replace belts. Operate engine at problem speed; if condition is still present, proceed to step 7.
7. Check engine accessories for noise while operating engine at problem speed. If vibration is still present, proceed to step 9. If vibration is not present, proceed to step 8.
8. Repair or replace noisy accessory. Connect and tension drive belt. Operate engine at problem speed; if vibration is still present, proceed to step 9.
9. Remove accessory from bracket. Inspect all hardware and bracket. Repair or replace as necessary.

## CHECKS & ADJUSTMENTS
### TIRE/WHEEL RUN-OUT

1. After road test, promptly raise car on hoist to prevent flat spots in tires. Spin front wheels by hand to check for rough wheel bearings. Ensure bearings are not loose and adjust if necessary. If bearings are O.K., proceed to step 2. If bearings have rough feel, proceed to step 2.
2. Check total radial and lateral run-out of tire and wheel assembly, **Fig. 3**. If both run-out measurements are less than .070 inch, balance tires. If lateral run-out exceeds .070 inch, proceed to step 3. If radial run-out exceeds .070 inch, proceed to step 4.
3. Check wheel rim lateral run-out. If run-out is less than .045 inch, replace tire and proceed to step 2. If run-out exceeds .045 inch, replace wheel and proceed to step 2.
4. Mark point of maximum run-out on tire thread. Check radial run-out of wheel. If radial run-out of wheel exceeds .045 inch, replace wheel and proceed to step 2. If radial run-out of wheel is less than .045 inch, proceed to step 5.

5. Mark point of least run-out on wheel. Remove tire from wheel and match point of maximum tire run-out with point of least run-out on wheel. Mount tire in this position and check total radial run-out of wheel and tire assembly. If total radial run-out is less than .070 inch, balance tires. If run-out exceeds .070 inch, replace tire and proceed to step 2.

### DRIVESHAFT RUNOUT

1. Raise and support vehicle. Mark position of drive wheels or hub lugs for installation, then remove wheels.
2. On one piece driveshafts, proceed as follows:
   a. Using a suitable dial indicator, measure driveshaft run-out at front, center and rear of driveshaft. Rotate driveshaft by turning brake drum or brake rotor.
   b. If measured run-out exceeds .035 inch at front or center, replace driveshaft.
   c. If front and center run-out measurements are within specified amount and rear is not, mark rear run-out high point and proceed to step 4.
   d. If run-out exceeds specified amount at all test points, proceed to "Driveshaft Balance."
3. On two piece driveshafts, proceed as follows:
   a. Using a suitable dial indicator, measure run-out at areas A through F as shown in **Fig. 4**. Rotate coupling shaft or driveshaft by turning rear wheel or drum.
   b. Mark run-out high points on coupling shaft and driveshaft.
   c. If run-out exceeds .035 inch at areas A, B or C, replace coupling shaft.
   d. If run-out exceeds .035 inch at areas D or E, replace driveshaft.
   e. If run-out at front, center or rear is less than .035 inch, proceed to

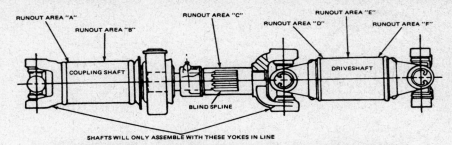

RUNOUT AREA "A"
RUNOUT AREA "B"
RUNOUT AREA "C"
RUNOUT AREA "D"
RUNOUT AREA "E"
RUNOUT AREA "F"
COUPLING SHAFT
DRIVESHAFT
BLIND SPLINE
SHAFTS WILL ONLY ASSEMBLE WITH THESE YOKES IN LINE

**Fig. 4   Two piece driveshaft run-out check areas**

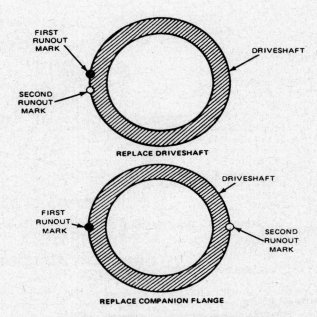

FIRST RUNOUT MARK
DRIVESHAFT
SECOND RUNOUT MARK
REPLACE DRIVESHAFT

DRIVESHAFT
FIRST RUNOUT MARK
SECOND RUNOUT MARK
REPLACE COMPANION FLANGE

**Fig. 5   Checking driveshaft run-out**

"Driveshaft Balance."

   f. If run-out at area F exceeds .035 inch, mark run-out high point on shaft.

4. Note or mark indexing of driveshaft to rear axle pinion flange. Disconnect driveshaft, turn 180° and reconnect. Check run-out at rear of shaft. If run-out exceeds .035 inch, mark run-out high point and proceed to step 5. If run-out is within specified amount, check for vibration at road test speed. If vibration is still present proceed to "Driveshaft Balance."

5. Excessive driveshaft run-out may originate in the driveshaft, pinion yoke or flange. To determine which, compare the two run-out high points marked in steps 2, 3 and 4, **Fig. 5.** If the marks are within 1 inch of each other, replace driveshaft and recheck for vibration. If the marks are on opposite sides of the driveshaft, approximately 180° apart, the yoke or flange is worn and/or damaged.

**NOTE:** During replacement of a yoke type flange, driveshaft run-out should not exceed .035 inch when reconnected. When run-out is within specified amount, check for vibration at road speed and road test if vibration is not present or substantially reduced. if vibration persists, proceed to "Driveshaft Balance."

## DRIVESHAFT BALANCE

Two methods are possible depending on the method of connecting the driveshaft to the differential. Some vehicles are equipped with a drilled companion flange at the differential which allows re-indexing of the driveshaft in 45° increments. Drive-shafts not equipped with this style flange can be balanced using worm-drive hose clamps, **Fig. 6.**

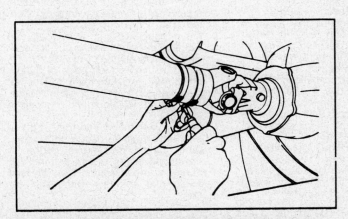

**Fig. 6   Balancing driveshaft using hose clamps**

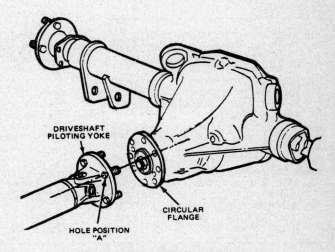

DRIVESHAFT PILOTING YOKE
CIRCULAR FLANGE
HOLE POSITION "A"

**Fig. 7   Driveshaft indexing**

# TROUBLESHOOTING

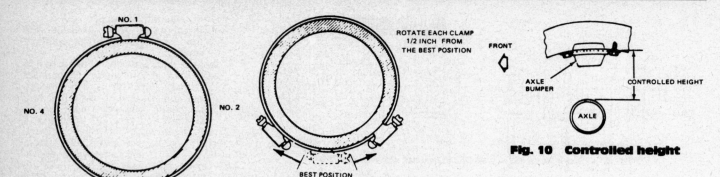

Fig. 8 Installing hose clamp

Fig. 9 Optimizing clamp location

Fig. 10 Controlled height

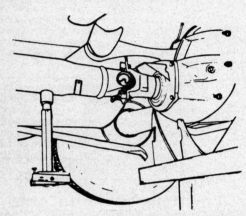

Fig. 11 Positioning driveline angle gauge on driveshaft

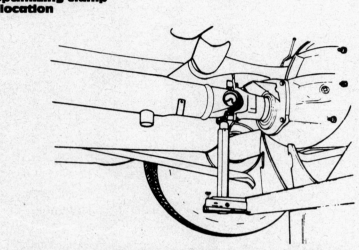

Fig. 12 Positioning driveline angle gauge on pinion U-joint cap

## Re-indexing Method

1. Mark one hole of rear U-joint yoke flange with letter A. Number rear axle pinion flange holes 1 through 8 starting with hole opposite yoke flange hole A, **Fig. 7.** Position A-1 will be considered original index position.

**NOTE:** Check U-joints for binding while re-indexing.

2. Index driveshaft 180° to position A-5. Road test vehicle. If condition is still unsatisfactory, check condition in position A-3 and position A-7.
3. If further improvement is necessary, evaluate remaining positions that are located between best of previous positions A-3 and A-7.
4. Coat flange bolts with suitable thread locking compound and torque to 70-95 ft. lbs.

## Hose Clamp Method

1. Make a mark to index rear axle companion flange to driveshaft. Disconnect driveshaft at flange, turn 180° and reconnect. If vibration increases, return driveshaft to original position. If vibration is reduced, proceed to step 2.
2. Mark rear of driveshaft with 4 equal sections numbered 1 through 4. Install a worm-drive hose clamp with screw at position 1 on driveshaft, **Fig. 8.** Operate driveline at problem speed. Check with clamp in each position. If vibration is worse in each position, proceed to step 5. If vibration is reduced in any one position, proceed to step 3. If vibration is reduced in any 2 positions, turn clamp between those positions and proceed to step 3.
3. Install additional clamp with screw in same position as first clamp in its best position. Operate driveline at problem speed. If vibration is same or increased, proceed to step 4.
4. Rotate each clamp screw ½ inch away in opposite directions, **Fig. 9.** If vibration is reduced, continue to move clamp screws apart until vibration is minimal. If vibration is still excessive, proceed to step 5.
5. Install wheels and road test vehicle to check if vibration might be acceptable on road. If vibration is unacceptable, proceed to step 17 of "High Speed Shake" diagnosis procedure.

## DRIVELINE PINION ANGLE CHECKING

1. Raise vehicle on drive-on hoist, ensuring vehicle is at proper controlled height, **Fig. 10.**
2. Turn driveshaft so pinion U-joint bearing cap is facing down.
3. Place Vee magnet from pinion angle measuring tool T68P-4602-A or equivalent on driveshaft. Working from left side of vehicle, position pinion angle gauge on Vee magnet with adjusting screw towards front of vehicle. Adjust screw so bubble just contacts zero line, **Fig. 11.**
4. Move gauge to U-joint bearing cap with tool in same relative position as it was on Vee magnet, **Fig. 12.**
5. Read position on left edge of bubble on scale to determine driveshaft pinion angle. If pinion angle is not correct, adjust. Recheck and proceed to step 6.
6. Position Vee magnet on front of driveshaft and position gauge on magnet. Zero bubble and move gauge to downward facing U-joint bearing cap at rear of transmission. Read driveline angle and compare with specification.

# Electrical

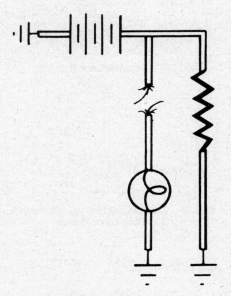

**Fig. 1   Open circuit**

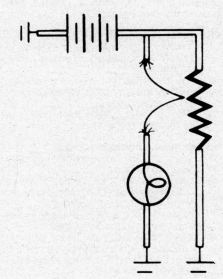

**Fig. 2   Short circuit**

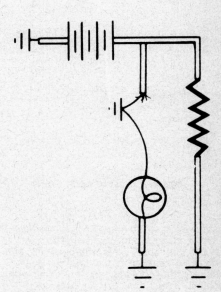

**Fig. 3   Grounded circuit**

## CIRCUIT MALFUNCTIONS

There are three types of electrical malfunctions that cause an inoperative circuit. They are the open circuit, short circuit and grounded circuit.

## OPEN CIRCUIT

When there is a complete break in the normal current patch such as a broken wire, **Fig. 1,** it prevents the flow of electricity from the source of power to the electrical unit or from the electrical unit to the ground. In the automotive electrical circuit, the current usually flows through wires or cables, through switches and an electrical component. The component may be grounded through its mounting attachments or another wire to ground and back to the source. A break anywhere along this route results in an open circuit and a complete loss of power. A break in the circuit is an infinite high resistance. However, symptoms will appear different than the typical high resistance circuit. For example, there will be no heat created by this type of malfunction since there is no current flow. An ammeter will not produce a reading since there is no current flow. A voltmeter, depending on where it is placed in the circuit in relation to the "Open", may or may not register a reading.

A high resistance in a circuit reduces current flow and causes the unit to operate intermittently or not at all. An open or high resistance circuit may be caused by a broken wire in the wiring harness, loose connections at terminals, broken leads or wiring within the units or poor ground connections between the unit and the ground.

## SHORT CIRCUIT

A short circuit, **Fig. 2,** is basically one that is completed the wrong way, such as two bare wires contacting each other so the current bypasses part of the circuit. When the current bypasses part of the circuit, it has found the path of least resistance and a higher current flow results. This causes blown fuses, wiring and component overheating, burned components and insulation, and inoperative components.

A short circuit causes more current flow through the conductor than the conductor can handle. This causes the conductor to overheat and, if the overload is severe or lasts long enough, will melt the wire and burn the insulation. If the wire melts through, there is no path for the current to flow and the circuit becomes an open circuit.

## GROUNDED CIRCUIT

A grounded circuit, **Fig. 3,** is similar to the short circuit since a grounded circuit also bypasses part of the normal circuit. However, the current flows directly to ground. A grounded circuit may be caused by a bare wire contacting the ground, or part of the circuit within a component contacting the frame or housing of the component. A grounded circuit may also be caused by deposits of dirt, oil or moisture around the connections or terminals since these deposits provide a path for the current to flow to ground. The current follows the path of least resistance to complete the circuit back to ground.

## CIRCUIT PROTECTION
### FUSES

The most common circuit protector in the automotive electrical system is the fuse. The fuse consists of a thin wire or strip of metal enclosed in a glass tube. Some vehicles use a new type fuse where the wire is enclosed in plastic. The wire or metal strip melts when there is an overload caused by a short or grounded circuit. The fuse is designed to melt before the wiring or electrical components are damaged. The cause of the overload must be located and repaired before the new fuse is installed since the new fuse will also blow.

Fuses are rated in amperes. Since different circuits carry various amounts of current, depending upon load components and wire gauge, the properly rated fuse must be installed in the circuit. Never install a fuse with a higher amperage rating than the original.

### CIRCUIT BREAKERS

Circuit breakers incorporate a bimetallic

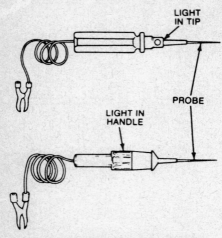

**Fig. 4   12 volt test light**

strip which, when heated by an overloaded circuit, moves and opens the contacts to break the circuit. When the bimetallic strip cools, it returns to the original position, closing the contacts and completing the circuit. The circuit breaker will open and close the circuit until the overload is located and repaired or the circuit is opened with a switch.

## FUSIBLE LINK

A fusible link is a short length of wire connected into a heavy feed circuit of the wiring system. The wire is generally four gauge sizes smaller than the circuit being protected and is used when the circuit is not protected by a fuse or circuit breaker. The fusible link is designed to melt in event of an overload before damage can occur to the circuit. Fusible links are marked on the insulation with the wire gauge size since the heavy insulation causes the link to appear heavier in wire size. Engine compartment wiring harnesses incorporate fusible links. When replacing a fusible link, the overload must be located and repaired and the same size fusible link installed in the circuit.

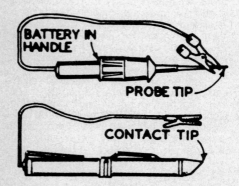

**Fig. 6   Self powered test light**

## TEST LAMP
### UNPOWERED TYPE

A test light consists of a 12 volt lamp bulb fitted with a pair of convenient test leads or one lead and a probe, **Fig. 4**. This test light is used with the power "On."

#### Check for Power
1. Connect one of the leads to a good ground or the battery negative terminal, **Fig. 5**.
2. Use the other test lead to check for power at the suspected wires, connectors or components.
3. If the light illuminates, power exists at the location being tested.

#### Blown Fuse Condition Check
1. Turn off all equipment powered through the fuse.
2. Disconnect all load items powered through the fuse. If a motor is present in the circuit, disconnect the motor connector. If a light is present in the circuit, remove the lamp bulb.
3. Turn ignition switch to "Run" position if necessary to supply power to the fuse, then turn "On" the equipment switches.
4. Connect one test lead to the "Hot" end of the blown fuse and the other lead to a good ground. The light should illuminate, indicating power to the fuse.
5. Disconnect the test lead connected to ground and connect lead to the other end of the blown fuse. If the light does not illuminate, it indicates that the short circuit has been removed by disconnecting the equipment. If the light illuminates, it indicates that a ground is present in the wiring. Isolate the ground by disconnecting the connectors in the circuit one at a time. Refer to the "Power Check".

### SELF-POWERED TYPE

The self-powered test light is a light and battery holder assembly fitted with test leads, or a test lead and a probe, **Fig. 6**. The light battery and test leads are connected in series so when the test leads are connected to two points of a continuous circuit, the light will illuminate, **Fig. 7**. This test light is used with the power "Off".

#### Continuity Check
Connect test leads to the ends of the suspected circuit. If the light illuminates, it indicates that the circuit is continuous and not broken. This test light may also be used to test a switch or other component. Connect the test leads to the switch terminals. If the light illuminates, the switch contacts are closed. At least one of the switch terminals should be disconnected from the normal switch circuit, so that only the switch is checked.

#### Ground Check
Connect one test lead to the suspected point and the other lead to the ground. If the light illuminates, it indicates that the

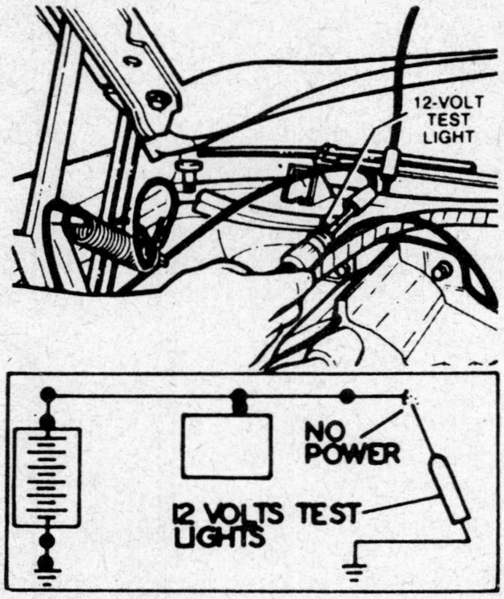

**Fig. 5   Checking for power with 12 volt test light**

point is grounded.

## JUMPER WIRE

A jumper wire is simply a length of wire with terminals at both ends, usually alligator clips, and is used to connect two points of a circuit or component, **Fig. 8**. The jumper wire is used for bypassing a portion of the circuit to temporarily prevent it from causing an open circuit. The jumper wire is used with the power "On."

In an open circuit consisting of a switch in series with a light or other load compo-

**Fig. 7   Checking for continuity with self powered test light**

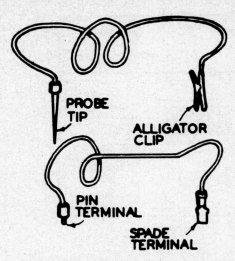

**Fig. 8 Typical jumper wires**

nent, connect the jumper wire to the switch terminals and apply power to the circuit, **Fig. 9**. If the connection of the jumper wire causes the circuit to operate, this indicates that the switch is open.

## TEST EQUIPMENT
### VOLTMETER

A DC voltmeter is used to measure DC voltage to ground. Connect the negative lead of the voltmeter to the ground and the positive lead to the point where voltage is to be measured, **Fig. 10**. This is called a parallel connection. The voltmeter is used with the power "On".

**CAUTION:** Do not use the jumper wire as a substitute for high resistance loads such as motors that are connected between the hot circuit and the ground.

### OHMMETER

The ohmmeter is used to measure resistance between two points in a circuit. Connect one lead of the ohmmeter to one point in the circuit and the other lead to the second point in the circuit being checked, **Fig. 11**. The ohmmeter is also used to check continuity of a circuit. For example, if you connect the ohmmeter leads to both ends of a length of wire, the reading will indicate some resistance or simply, a reading will be obtained. Now if the same length of wire is cut in half, the circuit is broken or open and no reading will be obtained, indicating an open circuit. The ohmmeter is used with the power "Off".

### AMMETER

A DC ammeter indicates current flow in amperes. The ammeter is connected into the circuit in series. Connect the positive lead of the ammeter to the power source and the negative lead into the remaining circuit so that all current must flow through the ammeter, **Fig. 12**. The ammeter is used with the power "On".

Some ammeters are equipped with a clamp-on probe. These ammeters are used to measure starter current.

### DIGITAL MULTIMETER

This test instrument, **Fig. 13**, combines the functions of all the above analog style instruments. The digital reading ensures more accurate voltage read out, which is especially important when testing low voltage circuits often used in microprocessor systems. When using such a device to test voltage or current of an unknown magnitude, be sure to set the range selector to the highest range first. Reduce setting as necessary to obtain satisfactory reading.

### SHORT CIRCUIT TESTER

A home-made short circuit tester can be made with a sealed beam, flasher or 7 amp. circuit breaker, wire and/or a buzzer as follows:
1. Connect test lead to two lengths of wire.
2. Connect one wire to the ground terminal of the sealed beam, **Fig. 14**.

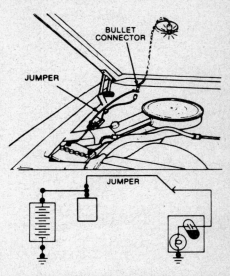

**Fig. 9 Bypassing part of circuit with jumper wire**

**NOTE:** It is desirable that a sealed beam connector be obtained since it will be easier to replace the sealed beam when it fails.

## VOLTMETER

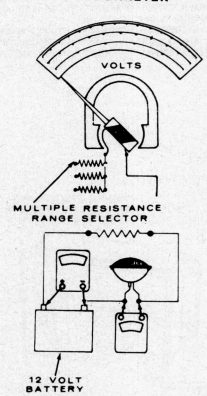

**Fig. 10 Voltmeter & connection into circuit**

## OHMMETER

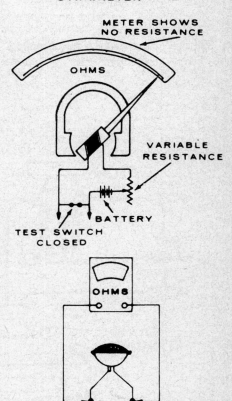

**Fig. 11 Ohmmeter & connection into circuit**

# TROUBLESHOOTING

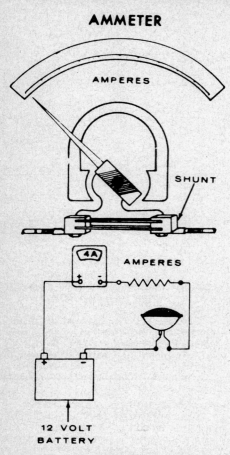

Fig. 12    Ammeter & connection into circuit

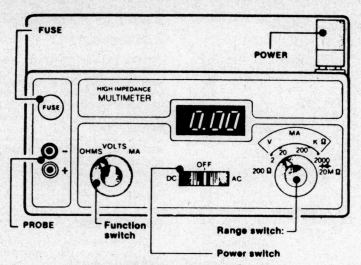

Fig. 13    Digital multimeter

3. Wire the high and low beam terminals and attach a length of wire to them.
4. Connect the flasher or circuit breaker in series with the sealed beam.
5. It is desirable but not necessary to connect a buzzer in parallel with the flasher. Also, an "On-Off" switch installed in one of the buzzer leads will make the signal optional during testing.
6. Various adapters can be made from old wiring harnesses so the tester leads can be connected at various points of the circuit such as fuse panel, connectors, etc.

**To Use the Tester**

Connect the tester in series with the cir-cuit being tested, using battery power as feed current, **Fig. 15.** When the circuit is closed and full power is supplied, the sealed beam will flash brightly and also, the buzzer will sound intermittently if connected in the circuit.

## COMPASS

An ordinary magnetic compass may be used for locating grounded circuits. The use of the compass utilizes the principle that a current carrying conductor creates a magnetic field.

In circuits protected by a circuit breaker, a short or ground can be located quickly. Activate the circuit and follow the conduc-

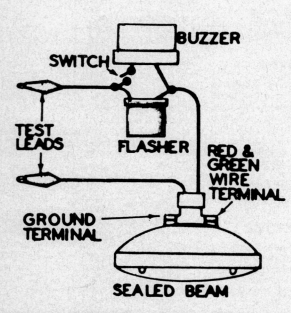

Fig. 14    Short circuit tester construction

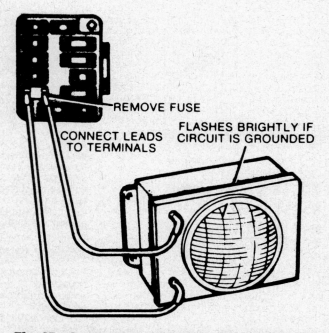

Fig. 15    Connecting a short circuit tester into circuit

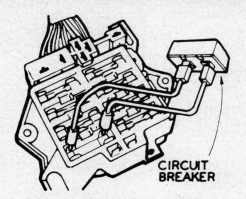

**Fig. 16 Connecting circuit breaker into circuit in place of fuse**

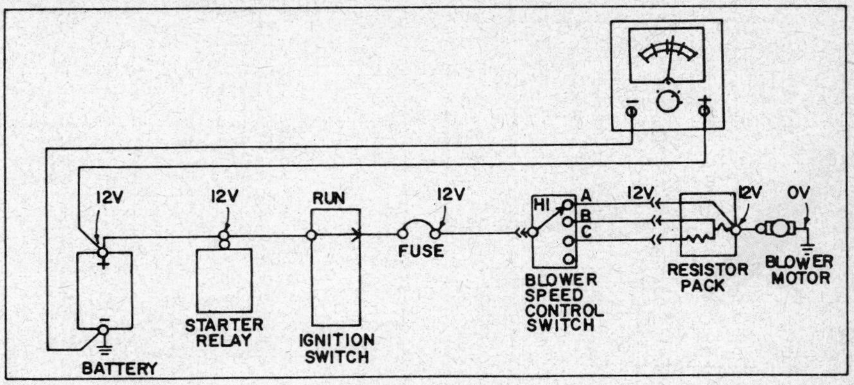

**Fig. 17 Three speed blower motor circuit. Typical**

tor with the compass. The compass will oscillate each time the circuit breaker closes. When the compass passes the point of the short or ground, the compass will stop oscillating, indicating the location of the malfunction.

The compass can be used without removing trim, cover plates or tape. If the circuit is protected by a fuse, the defect can be found with the compass by substituting a circuit breaker for the fuse.

## FUSE SUBSTITUTION

By using a circuit breaker in place of the fuse in the circuit being tested, **Fig. 16**, other tools can be effectively used. A turn signal flasher may be used as a circuit breaker. Solder a lead to each terminal of the flasher, solder the leads to each end cap of blown fuse. This unit may be installed in the fuse block in place of the fuse normally used. However, when attempting to locate a short or ground when using a magnetic compass, the flasher may operate too quickly to produce satisfactory needle deflection. To slow the flasher operation, insert a generator field control rheostat in series in one flasher lead. By adding additional resistance, the rate of flasher operation may be reduced to produce satisfactory compass needle deflection.

## CURRENT DRAW & VOLTAGE DROP

### AVAILABLE VOLTAGE & VOLTAGE DROP

Voltage drop is the amount of voltage lost as electricity passes through a resistance (lamp bulb, blower motor, resistor) and is measured using a voltmeter. The principle of voltage drop can best be demonstrated using a heater blower circuit where resistors are used to deliberately create voltage drops. In a typical three speed blower circuit the blower motor is

powered through a speed control switch. The switch has three wires leading to the resistor pack, **Fig. 17**. The amount of voltage available to the motor depends on which wire is fed from the switch. Resistors in the blower circuit allow for a change in blower speed by causing a voltage drop ahead of the motor. It must be remembered that available voltage and voltage drop must be measured under load; that is, with the circuit operating a load component such as a motor, or light bulb. In **Fig. 17** power to the blower is through wire A, by-passing the resistors. The blower is now operating at maximum speed. Available voltage may be measured by connecting the voltmeter negative lead to a ground and moving the positive lead various points along the blower circuit, **Fig. 17**. Battery voltage is available at the motor because there is little resistance in the circuit up to this point. Available voltage from the motor is zero volts because the circuit has used up the full 12 volts to operate the motor.

## VOLTAGE DROP IN A SERIES CIRCUIT

If the blower switch is positioned for medium speed, power to the motor must travel through wire B and through one of the resistors in the resistor pack, **Fig. 18**. A resistor has now been placed in series with the motor. The voltage drop is four volts through the resistor and eight volts through the motor for a total voltage drop of 12 volts. The motor now operates slower because there are only eight volts available to operate it.

**NOTE:** When resistances are connected in series, the voltage drops add up to the total available voltage at the source. Each voltage drop is proportional to the resistance of component the electricity flows through.

When the blower switch is positioned for low speed, the switch feeds wire C and there are now two resistors in series with the motor, **Fig. 19**. The available voltages are 12 volts into the resistor block, eight

volts into resistor B and 4 volts into the motor. The voltage drops are four volts at resistor A, four volts at resistor B and four volts at the motor for a total voltage drop of 12 volts. In each case zero volts are available out of the motor because the ground circuit has no resistance. If the ground circuit had resistance caused by a faulty ground connection, there would be a positive reading out of the motor. Also, each of the resistors would have proportionately lower voltage drops.

### Measuring Voltage Drop Directly

Voltage drop may be read directly from the meter by connecting the meter across the component or segment of the circuit, **Fig. 20**. Check that the voltmeter positive lead is connected to the battery side of the circuit and the negative lead is connected to the ground side. **Fig. 20** shows voltmeter connections for reading voltage drop across the resistor pack on the low blower circuit. The combined voltage drop through both resistors is eight volts.

### No Load Voltage

With the blower circuit operating on low blower and the motor disconnected from the circuit, connect two voltmeters as shown in **Fig. 21**. Meter A is connected as if to read resistor pack voltage drop. It will read zero because there is no voltage drop in a non-operating circuit. Meter B is connected as if to read available voltage. It is actually reading battery no load voltage. The circuit must be operating, that is, under load, to read voltage drop directly and to read available voltage in order to compute voltage drop. If the circuit is not under load, there will be no voltage drop.

### CURRENT DRAW

Current draw, or current, is the amount of electrical flow or volume and is measured using an ammeter. The ammeter is connected into the circuit, in series with the load, switch or resistor. It will measure current draw only when the circuit is closed and electricity is flowing. In **Fig. 22**, the ammeter is connected as if to read current draw from the battery. The positive battery cable is disconnected so that any current

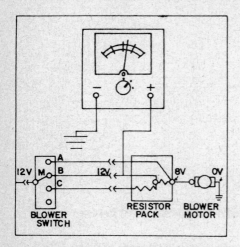

**Fig. 18 Measuring voltage drop through one resistor**

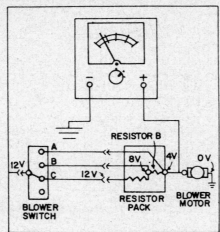

**Fig. 19 Measuring voltage drop through two resistors**

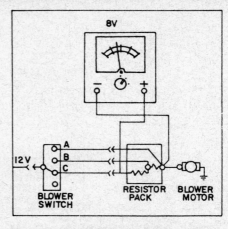

**Fig. 20 Measuring voltage drop directly**

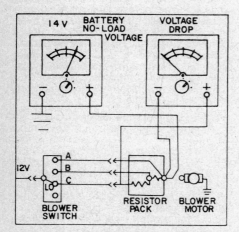

**Fig. 21 Measuring no-load voltage**

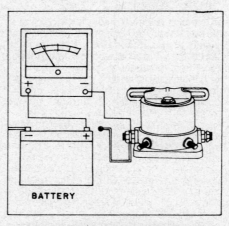

**Fig. 22 Measuring current draw from battery**

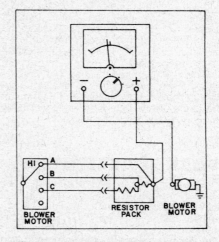

**Fig. 23 Measuring blower motor current draw**

flowing must go through the meter. If the vehicle's electrical systems were turned on one at a time, the meter would measure how much current each draws. The ammeter may be connected anywhere in a circuit, even between load and ground, as long as it is connected in series and correct polarity is observed.

### High Resistance Short To Ground

When a short circuit occurs and the current draw is not sufficient to cause the fuse to blow, but does cause a drain on the battery, an ammeter may be used to locate the short. If a current draw exists with everything off, then there is a short to ground.

**NOTE:** On some vehicles equipped with an electric clock, there will be a slight current draw at all times with all accessories off. This current draw should be taken into consideration when diagnosing a short circuit with an ammeter.

To locate the short, remove fuses one at a time until the meter reads zero. If this occurs, trouble shoot that circuit for a short to ground.

### Electric Motor Current Draw

Using the previous example of a blower circuit, an ammeter connected in series between the resistor pack and blower motor with the blower switch on high, **Fig. 23,** will show a reading of eight amps. This is a typical current draw for this type of motor. When the blower switch is moved to the medium position, the blower is being fed through a resistor and this reduces available voltage to the motor. The motor now draws about six amps and the motor operates slower. On low blower speed, the draw would decrease to 3 or 4 amps. If the switch were turned off, the ammeter would read zero.

**NOTE:** Current draw is highest with no

resistance and reduces as resistances are added in series.

If a second blower motor were connected in parallel and both were operated from the same switch, the electrical load would be doubled. The current draw, in the high speed position, would be 16 amps. Whenever electrical loads are added in parallel, the current draw increases. The effective resistance of the circuit decreases as parallel loads are added. If the two motors were connected in series, both would operate at reduced speed because one would act as a resistor for the other.

When an electric motor or solenoid has to work harder due to mechanical resistance, it draws more current. If the resistance is great, the motor will draw more current than that which can be safely handled by the circuit's fuse or circuit breaker. In this case the fuse blows or circuit breaker opens and interrupts the flow of current.

# METRICS & THREADED FASTENERS

## INDEX

## INTRODUCTION

Threaded fasteners are classified by specifications that define required mechanical properties, such as tensile strength, yield strength, proof load and hardness. These specifications are carefully considered during initial selection of fasteners for a given application.

Most fasteners are identified with markings or numbers that indicate the strength of the fastener. Also, some metric fasteners are colored blue. This metric blue idenfication is usually used as an aid during start of production and is discontinued afterwards.

## THREADED FASTENERS

Most vehicles covered in this service manual have some metric fasteners and some inch system fasteners. It is important that replacement fasteners be of the correct nominal diameter, thread pitch and strength. Original equipment fasteners (except for exposed bolts, such as bumper bolts and cross recess head screws) are identified by a number marking indicating the strength of the fastener. Metric cross recess screws are identified by a Posidriv or type 1-A cross recess.

## FASTENER STRENGTH IDENTIFICATION

Common metric fastener strength property classes are 9.8 and 10.9 with the class identification embossed on the head of each bolt. Inch strength classes range from grade 2 to 8 with line identification embossed on each bolt head. Markings correspond to two lines less than the actual grade of the bolt (i.e. grade 5 bolt will exhibit 3 embossed lines on the bolt head). Some metric nuts will be marked with single digit strength identification numbers on the nut face, while inch nuts will have a series of dots on the nut face.

Identification of metric u-nuts, studs, self-tapping, thread forming and certain other hardened screws will vary by the type of fastener, most often a variation of that used on bolts and nuts. U-nuts will usually have a number stamped on it. Large studs may carry the property class number, while smaller ones will be stamped on the end with a diamond or square (class 10.9), cross (class 9.8), or a circle (class 8.8).

Many types of metric and English fasteners may carry no special identification at all.

## BOLT STRENGTH IDENTIFICATION

### (ENGLISH) INCH SYSTEM

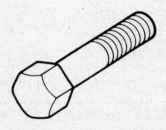          

Grade 1 or 2          Grade 5          Grade 8

English (Inch) bolts - Identification marks correspond to bolt strength - increasing number of slashes represent increasing strength.

### METRIC SYSTEM

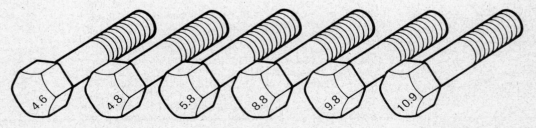

Metric bolts - Identification class numbers correspond to bolt strength - increasing numbers represent increasing strength. Common metric fastener bolt strength property are 9.8 and 10.9 with the class identification embossed on the bolt head.

# METRICS & THREADED FASTENERS

## HEX NUT STRENGTH IDENTIFICATION

| (ENGLISH) INCH SYSTEM | | METRIC SYSTEM | |
|---|---|---|---|
| Grade | Identification | Class | Identification |
| Hex Nut Grade 5 | 3 Dots | Hex Nut Property Class 9 | Arabic 9 |
| Hex Nut Grade 8 | 6 Dots | Hex Nut Property Class 10 | Arabic 10 |
| Increasing dots represent increasing strength. | | May also have blue finish or paint daub on hex flat. Increasing numbers represent increasing strength. | |

## FASTENER SELECTION

When replacing fasteners, make sure to select bolts and nuts of the same strength or greater (same strength marking or higher) than the original fastener. It is equally important to select the correct size and thread pitch fastener.

Correct replacement fasteners are available through the parts division of the vehicle manufacturer or after-market sources. However, many aftermarket fasteners are designed to standards of other countries other than the United States, and may be of lower strength, may not have the same strength identification markings and may be of a different thread pitch. The metric fasteners used on domestic vehicles are designed to standards that may not yet be manufactured by some suppliers.

## COMMON METRIC SIZES & PITCHES

Except for special applications, the most common sizes and pitches are:
M 6.0 × 1
M 8 × 1.25
M 10 × 1.5
M 12 × 1.75
M 14 × 2

## NOMENCLATURE FOR BOLTS

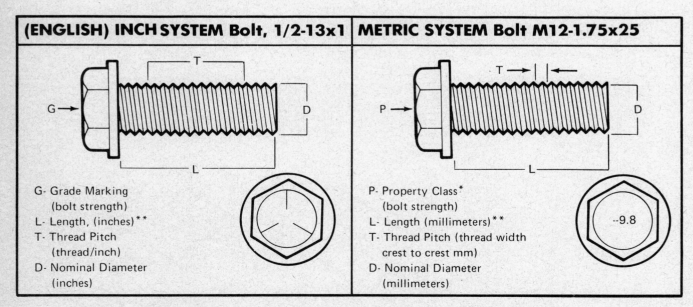

### (ENGLISH) INCH SYSTEM Bolt, 1/2-13x1

G- Grade Marking (bolt strength)
L- Length, (inches)**
T- Thread Pitch (thread/inch)
D- Nominal Diameter (inches)

### METRIC SYSTEM Bolt M12-1.75x25

P- Property Class* (bolt strength)
L- Length (millimeters)**
T- Thread Pitch (thread width crest to crest mm)
D- Nominal Diameter (millimeters)

*The property class is an Arabic numeral distinguishable from the slash SAE English grade system.
**The length of all bolts is measured from the underside of the head to the end.

## Other Types Of Parts

Metric identification schemes vary by type of part, most often a variation of that used on bolts and nuts. Note that many types of English and metric fasteners carry no special identification if they are otherwise unique.

**U-Nuts, Tapping Screws, Thread Forming Screws and Studs'**

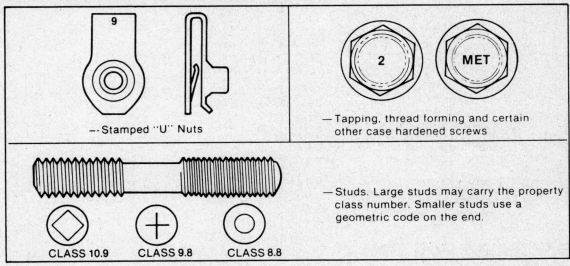

--Stamped "U" Nuts

— Tapping, thread forming and certain other case hardened screws

CLASS 10.9    CLASS 9.8    CLASS 8.8

— Studs. Large studs may carry the property class number. Smaller studs use a geometric code on the end.

## DECIMAL AND METRIC EQUIVALENTS

| Fractions | Decimal Inch | Metric mm | Fractions | Decimal Inch | Metric mm |
|-----------|--------------|-----------|-----------|--------------|-----------|
| 1/64 | .015625 | .397 | 33/64 | .515625 | 13.097 |
| 1/32 | .03125 | .794 | 17/32 | .53125 | 13.494 |
| 3/64 | .046875 | 1.191 | 35/64 | .546875 | 13.891 |
| 1/16 | .0625 | 1.588 | 9/16 | .5625 | 14.288 |
| 5/64 | .078125 | 1.984 | 36/64 | .578125 | 14.684 |
| 3/32 | .09375 | 2.381 | 19/32 | .59375 | 15.081 |
| 7/64 | .109375 | 2.778 | 39/64 | .609375 | 15.478 |
| 1/8 | .125 | 3.175 | 5/8 | .625 | 15.875 |
| 9/64 | .140625 | 3.572 | 41/64 | .640625 | 16.272 |
| 5/32 | .15625 | 3.969 | 21/32 | .65625 | 16.669 |
| 11/64 | .171875 | 4.366 | 43/64 | .671875 | 17.066 |
| 3/16 | .1875 | 4.763 | 11/16 | .6875 | 17.463 |
| 13/64 | .203125 | 5.159 | 45/64 | .703125 | 17.859 |
| 7/32 | .21875 | 5.556 | 23/32 | .71875 | 18.256 |
| 15/64 | .234375 | 5.953 | 47/64 | .734375 | 18.653 |
| 1/4 | .250 | 6.35 | 3/4 | .750 | 19.05 |
| 17/64 | .265625 | 6.747 | 49/64 | .765625 | 19.447 |
| 9/32 | .28125 | 7.144 | 25/32 | .78125 | 19.844 |
| 19/64 | .296875 | 7.54 | 51/64 | .796875 | 20.241 |
| 5/16 | .3125 | 7.938 | 13/16 | .8125 | 20.638 |
| 21/64 | .328125 | 8.334 | 53/64 | .828125 | 21.034 |
| 11/32 | .34375 | 8.731 | 27/32 | .84375 | 21.431 |
| 23/64 | .359375 | 9.128 | 55/64 | .859375 | 21.828 |
| 3/8 | .375 | 9.525 | 7/8 | .875 | 22.225 |
| 25/64 | .390625 | 9.922 | 57/64 | .890625 | 22.622 |
| 13/32 | .40625 | 10.319 | 29/32 | .90625 | 23.019 |
| 27/64 | .421875 | 10.716 | 59/64 | .921875 | 23.416 |
| 7/16 | .4375 | 11.113 | 15/16 | .9375 | 23.813 |
| 29/64 | .453125 | 11.509 | 61/64 | .953125 | 24.209 |
| 15/32 | .46875 | 11.906 | 31/32 | .96875 | 24.606 |
| 31/64 | .484375 | 12.303 | 63/64 | .984375 | 25.003 |
| 1/2 | .500 | 12.7 | 1 | 1.00 | 25.4 |

## ENGLISH METRIC CONVERSION

| | multiply | by | for equiv. no. of: |
|---|---|---|---|
| ACCELERATION | Foot/sec$^2$ | 0.304 8 | metre/sec$^2$ (m/s$^2$) |
| | Inch/sec$^2$ | 0.025 4 | metre/sec$^2$ |
| TORQUE | Pound-inch | 0.112 98 | newton-metres (N●m) |
| | Pound-foot | 1.355 8 | newton-metres |
| POWER | horsepower | 0.746 | kilowatts (kw) |
| PRESSURE or STRESS | inches of water | 0.2488 | kilopascals (kPa) |
| | pounds/sq. in. | 6.895 | kilopascals (kPa) |
| ENERGY or WORK | BTU | 1 055. | joules (J) |
| | foot-pound | 1.355 8 | joules (J) |
| | kilowatt-hour | 3 600 000.<br>or 3.6 x 10$^6$ | joules (J=one W's) |
| LIGHT | foot candle | 10.76 | lumens/metre$^2$ (lm/m$^2$) |
| FUEL PERFORMANCE | miles/gal | 0.425 1 | kilometres/litre (km/l) |
| | gal/mile | 2.352 7 | litres/kilometre (l/km) |
| VELOCITY | miles/hour | 1.609 3 | kilometres/hr. (km/h) |
| LENGTH | inch | 25.4 | millimetres (mm) |
| | foot | 0.304 8 | metres (m) |
| | yard | 0.914 4 | metres (m) |
| | mile | 1.609 | kilometres (km) |
| AREA | inch$^2$ | 645.2 | millimetres$^2$ (mm$^2$) |
| | | 6.45 | centimetres$^2$ (cm$^2$) |
| | foot$^2$ | 0.092 9 | metres$^2$ (m$^2$) |
| | yard$^2$ | 0.836 1 | metres$^2$ |
| VOLUME | inch$^3$ | 16 387. | mm$^3$ |
| | inch$^3$ | 16.387 | cm$^3$ |
| | quart | 0.016 4 | litres(1) |
| | quart | 0.946 4 | litres |
| | gallon | 3.785 4 | litres |
| | yard$^3$ | 0.764 6 | metres$^3$ (m$^3$) |
| MASS | pound | 0.453 6 | kilograms (kg) |
| | ton | 907.18 | kilograms (kg) |
| | ton | 0.90718 | tonne (t) |
| FORCE | kilogram | 9.807 | newtons (N) |
| | ounce | 0.278 0 | newtons |
| | pound | 4.448 | newtons |
| TEMPERATURE | degree farenheit | 0.556 ($^{\circ}$F −32) | degree Celsius ($^{\circ}$C) |

## TORQUE CONVERSION

| NEWTON METRES (N•m) | POUND-FEET (LB.-FT.) |
|---|---|
| 1 | 0.7376 |
| 2 | 1.5 |
| 3 | 2.2 |
| 4 | 3.0 |
| 5 | 3.7 |
| 6 | 4.4 |
| 7 | 5.2 |
| 8 | 5.9 |
| 9 | 6.6 |
| 10 | 7.4 |
| 15 | 11.1 |
| 20 | 14.8 |
| 25 | 18.4 |
| 30 | 22.1 |
| 35 | 25.8 |
| 40 | 29.5 |
| 50 | 36.9 |
| 60 | 44.3 |
| 70 | 51.6 |
| 80 | 59.0 |
| 90 | 66.4 |
| 100 | 73.8 |
| 110 | 81.1 |
| 120 | 88.5 |
| 130 | 95.9 |
| 140 | 103.3 |
| 150 | 110.6 |
| 160 | 118.0 |
| 170 | 125.4 |
| 180 | 132.8 |
| 190 | 140.1 |
| 200 | 147.5 |
| 225 | 166.0 |
| 250 | 184.4 |

| POUND-FEET (LB.-FT.) | NEWTON METRES (N•m) |
|---|---|
| 1 | 1.356 |
| 2 | 2.7 |
| 3 | 4.0 |
| 4 | 5.4 |
| 5 | 6.8 |
| 6 | 8.1 |
| 7 | 9.5 |
| 8 | 10.8 |
| 9 | 12.2 |
| 10 | 13.6 |
| 15 | 20.3 |
| 20 | 27.1 |
| 25 | 33.9 |
| 30 | 40.7 |
| 35 | 47.5 |
| 40 | 54.2 |
| 45 | 61.0 |
| 50 | 67.8 |
| 55 | 74.6 |
| 60 | 81.4 |
| 65 | 88.1 |
| 70 | 94.9 |
| 75 | 101.7 |
| 80 | 108.5 |
| 90 | 122.0 |
| 100 | 135.6 |
| 110 | 149.1 |
| 120 | 162.7 |
| 130 | 176.3 |
| 140 | 189.8 |
| 150 | 203.4 |
| 160 | 216.9 |
| 170 | 230.5 |
| 180 | 244.0 |

# GENERAL MAINTENANCE

## TABLE OF CONTENTS

## INDEX

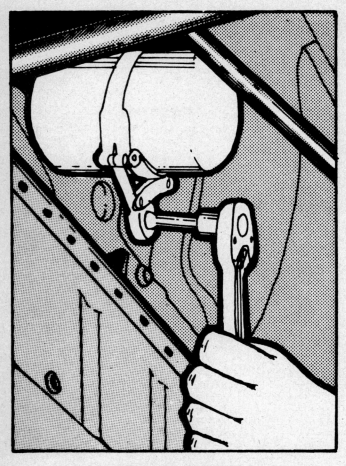

**Fig. 1   Oil filter removal (typical)**

Coat Gasket With Engine Oil

**Fig. 2   Oil filter installation (typical)**

# LUBRICATION & OIL CHANGE

## ENGINE OIL & FILTER CHANGE

**NOTE:** Engine oil and filter should be changed at intervals recommended by the vehicle manufacturer.

1. Operate engine and allow to reach operating temperature, then turn ignition off.
2. Place drain pan under engine oil pan, then using a suitable wrench remove drain plug.
3. Allow engine oil to thoroughly drain into pan, then replace drain plug.

**NOTE:** Do not overtighten drain plug, as this can strip the threads in oil pan.

4. If oil filter is to be replaced, position drain pan under filter, then install oil filter wrench and remove filter by turning counterclockwise, **Fig. 1.**

**NOTE:** Ensure old oil filter gasket is not on the filter adapter on the engine. Clean adapter before installing new filter.

5. Coat new oil filter gasket with engine oil, then position filter on adapter, **Fig. 2.** Hand tighten filter until gasket contacts adapter face, then tighten filter one additional turn. Wipe filter and adapter with a clean cloth.

**NOTE:** Ensure gasket is in position on filter before tightening. Do not use oil filter wrench to tighten filter. Hand tighten only.

6. Remove oil filler cap and add quantity of oil specified by manufacturer, then install filler cap.

**NOTE:** Only add oil which meets the vehicle manufacturer's specifications.

7. Start engine and check to ensure oil filter and drain plug are not leaking, then turn ignition off.
8. Check oil level to ensure crankcase is full but not overfilled. Add oil as necessary.

**NOTE:** Do not bring oil level above "Full" mark on dipstick. Overfilling could result in damage to engine gaskets or seals causing leaks.

# CHASSIS LUBRICATING

The first time you perform a grease job, you will spend much of the time looking for the fittings, **Figs. 3 and 4.**

As you find a fitting, wipe it off with a clean rag. This will help you spot it later and also prevent you from injecting dirt with the grease.

The injection tip of the grease gun should be a catch fit on the fitting nipple. That is, once in place it will not slip off. Slight, straight-on pressure is all that is necessary for the gun tip to engage the fitting. Once that is done, pump the handle. Follow the recommendations below to ensure proper lubrication and also prevent damage to the seals:

**Ford and Jeep**

Pump slowly until the rubber boot can be felt or seen to swell slightly.

**Chrysler Corp., General Motors**

Pump slowly until grease starts to flow from bleed holes at the base of the seals, or until the seals start to swell.

**NOTE:** If the fitting fails to take grease, the lubricant will ooze out between fitting and top of the gun. Do not just keep pumping, hoping some grease is getting in, or you will have a mess. It is normal for a bit of grease to seep out. However, if the fitting is obviously not taking grease, it should be replaced.

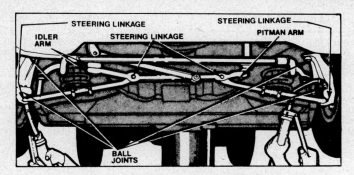

**Fig. 3   Fitting locations (typical)**

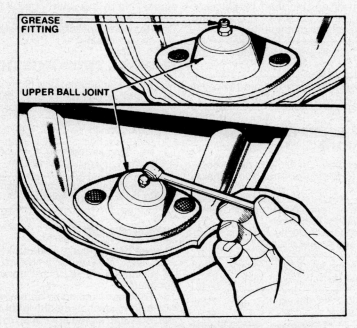

**Fig. 4   Identifying grease fittings (typical). If vehicle is equipped with plugs, the plugs must be removed and a grease fitting installed prior to lubricating**

## REPACKING FRONT WHEEL BEARINGS

1. Remove inner and outer bearings as outlined in truck chapters.
2. Clean old lubricant from hub and spindle.
3. Clean inner and outer bearings and bearing races with kerosene.

**NOTE:** Ensure all old lubricant is removed before repacking. Allow bearings and races to dry thoroughly. Do not use compressed air to clean bearings.

4. Inspect cones, rollers and races for cracks, nicks and wear, and replace as necessary.

**NOTE:** Bearings and race must be replaced as a unit.

5. Place a small amount of wheel bearing grease in palm of hand, then force grease into large end of roller cage until grease protrudes from small end.

**NOTE:** Use only wheel bearing grease which meets the vehicle manufacturer's specifications.

6. Lubricate remaining bearings in the same manner, then install and adjust bearings as outlined in truck chapter.

**NOTE:** Apply a light film of grease to lips of grease retainer before installing.

## CHECKING & MAINTAINING FLUID LEVELS

**NOTE:** When checking fluid levels, ensure vehicle is on a level surface. If vehicle is not level, an accurate fluid level reading cannot be obtained.

### ENGINE OIL LEVEL

1. Warm up engine, then turn ignition off and allow a few minutes for oil to return to crankcase.
2. Remove dipstick and wipe off.
3. Replace dipstick and ensure it is seated in tube.
4. Remove dipstick and inspect to see if oil level is between "Add" and "Full" marks.

**NOTE:** Add oil only if level is at or below "Add" mark.

5. If oil level is at "Add" mark, one quart of oil will bring level to "Full" mark. If oil level is below "Add" mark, add sufficient amount of oil to bring level between "Add" & "Full" marks.

**NOTE:** Do not bring oil level above "Full" mark, as overfilling of crankcase could result in damage to engine gaskets and seals and cause leaks. Only add oil meeting the vehicle manufacturer's specifications.

6. Replace dipstick.

### BATTERY

1. Remove filler cap and check fluid level in each cell.

**NOTE:** Keep flame and sparks away from top of battery as combustible gases present may explode. Do not allow battery electrolyte to contact skin, eyes, fabric or painted surfaces. Flush contacted area with water immediately and thoroughly and seek medical attention if necessary. Wear eye protection when working on or near battery. Do not wear rings or other metal jewelry when working on or near battery.

2. Add water as required to bring fluid level of each cell up to split ring located at bottom of filler well.

**NOTE:** In areas where water is known to be hard or have a high mineral or alkali content, distilled water must be used. If water is added during freezing temperatures, the vehicle should be driven several miles afterwards to mix the water and battery electrolyte.

3. Install filler caps.

## COOLING SYSTEM

**NOTE:** Add only permanent type antifreeze which meets the vehicle manufacturer's specifications.

**CAUTION:** Never add large quantities of water into radiator if truck has overheated before engine has cooled off. If necessary to service at this time, start engine and add water to coolant slowly. This will avoid damage to the engine.

### Less Coolant Recovery System

**NOTE:** Avoid checking coolant level if engine is hot. If coolant level must be checked when engine is hot, muffle radiator cap with a thick cloth, then turn cap counterclockwise until pressure starts to escape. After pressure has been completely relieved, finish removing cap.

1. With engine cold, remove radiator cap and inspect coolant level.
2. Coolant level should be approximately 1 inch below bottom of filler neck.
3. Add solution of 50% water–50% antifreeze as required.
4. Install radiator cap.

### With Coolant Recovery System

**NOTE:** On these type systems, do not remove radiator cap to check coolant level.

1. Start engine and allow to reach operating temperature.
2. Visually inspect coolant level in plastic reservoir.
3. On all models except Chrysler Corp. vehicles, coolant level should be between "Full" and "Add" marks or at "Full Hot" mark, depending on reservoir. On Chrysler Corp. vehicles, coolant level should be between the one and two quart marks with engine operating at idle speed.
4. Remove reservoir filler cap and add solution of 50% water-50% antifreeze as required.
5. Install reservoir filler cap.

## BRAKE MASTER CYLINDER RESERVOIR

1. Clean master cylinder reservoir cover, then using a screwdriver, unsnap

retainer(s) and remove cover.

**NOTE:** Do not hold cover over vehicle, as brake fluid may damage finish.

2. Brake fluid level should be ¼ inch from top of master cylinder reservoir.

**NOTE:** If brake fluid level is excessively low, the brake linings should be inspected for wear and brake system checked for leaks. Fluid level in reservoirs servicing disc brakes will decrease as disc brake pads wear.

3. Add brake fluid as required.

**NOTE:** Only add brake fluid which meets the vehicle manufacturer's specifications. Use only brake fluid which has been in a tightly closed container to prevent contamination from dirt and moisture. Do not allow petroleum base fluids to contaminate brake fluid, as seal damage may result.

4. Install cover and snap retainer into place.

**NOTE:** Ensure retainer is locked into cover grooves.

## POWER STEERING PUMP RESERVOIR

1. Start engine and allow to reach operating temperature, then turn ignition off.
2. Clean area around filler cap or dipstick, then remove filler cap or dipstick and inspect fluid level.
3. Fluid level should be between "Full" mark and end of dipstick.

**NOTE:** On models without dipstick, fluid level should be half way up filler neck.

4. Add fluid as necessary, then install filler cap or dipstick.

**NOTE:** Only add fluid recommended by the vehicle manufacturer.

## AUTOMATIC TRANSMISSION

1. Firmly apply parking brake, then start and run engine for approximately 10 minutes to bring transmission fluid to operating temperature.

**NOTE:** Do not run engine in unventilated area. Exhaust gases contain carbon monoxide which could be deadly in unventilated areas.

2. With engine running at idle speed, shift selector lever through all positions, then place lever in Neutral on Chrysler Corp. and Jeep vehicles, and in Park on Ford Motor Co. and General Motors Corp.
3. Clean dipstick cap, then remove dipstick and wipe off.

4. Replace dipstick and ensure it is seated in tube.
5. Remove dipstick and inspect to see if fluid level is between "Add" and "Full" marks.

**NOTE:** Add fluid only if level is at or below "Add" mark.

6. If fluid level is at "Add" mark, one pint of transmission fluid will bring level to "Full" mark. If fluid level is below "Add" mark, add sufficient amount of fluid to bring level between "Add" and "Full" marks. Transmission fluid is added through the dipstick tube.

**NOTE:** Do not bring level above "Full" mark, as overfilling could result in damage to transmission. Only add automatic transmission fluid of type and specification recommended by the vehicle manufacturer.

7. Replace dipstick and ensure it is seated in tube.

## MANUAL TRANSMISSION

1. Set parking brake and block wheels.
2. Clean area around filler plug, then using a suitable wrench or ratchet, remove filler plug.
3. Fluid should be level with bottom of filler plug hole.
4. Add fluid as required, then install filler plug.

**NOTE:** Only add lubricant recommended by the vehicle manufacturer.

## REAR AXLE

1. Set parking brake and block wheels.
2. Clean area around filler plug, then using a suitable ratchet, remove filler plug.
3. Fluid level should be approximately ½ inch below bottom of filler plug hole.
4. Add fluid as required, then install filler plug.

**NOTE:** Only add lubricant recommended by vehicle manufacturer.

## COOLING SYSTEM SERVICE

**CAUTION:** Do not attempt to perform any system servicing when the engine is hot or the cooling system is pressurized. Even a simple operation such as removing the radiator cap should be avoided since personal injury and loss of coolant may result.

### DRAINING THE SYSTEM

Most cooling systems incorporate a radiator petcock usually located on the engine side of the radiator at either of the lower corners. Some radiator petcocks are locat-

**Fig. 5   Replacing thermostat (typical)**

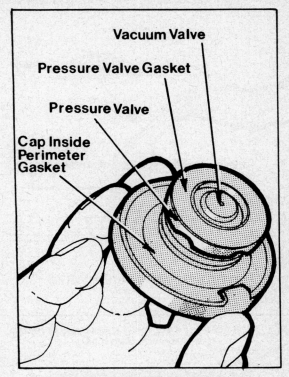

Vacuum Valve

Pressure Valve Gasket

Pressure Valve

Cap Inside
Perimeter
Gasket

**Fig. 6   Radiator cap (typical)**

ed on the side of the radiator. Not all cooling systems are equipped with a radiator petcock.

1. Place a suitable container under radiator to catch coolant.
2. On systems equipped with a radiator petcock, turn the tangs (ears) to open the petcock. However, do not apply excessive pressure in either direction as damage to the petcock may result because some petcocks turn clockwise and others counterclockwise to open.
3. On systems not equipped with a radiator petcock, it will be necessary to remove the lower hose from the radiator.
4. Dispose of coolant.

## FLUSHING THE SYSTEM

There are two flushing methods which can be performed without the use of special equipment. One method outlined below requires the use of a garden hose only. The second method requires the use of the garden hose and a "Tee" fitting spliced into one of the heater hoses. The "Tee" fitting and other items and instructions needed to perform this type of flushing are available through aftermarket manufacturers.

1. With coolant system drained, remove thermostat as outlined below:
    a. To locate the thermostat housing on most engines follow the upper radiator hose from the radiator to the engine block. On some engines, follow the lower radiator hose from the radiator to the engine block. The point at which these hoses connect is the thermostat housing.
    b. The thermostat housing is usually retained by two bolts or nuts. Remove these bolts or nuts and remove the housing.
    c. Lift the thermostat from the mounting flange, **Fig. 5,** noting the position in which it was installed. This is important to avoid reinstalling the thermostat upside down.
    d. Reinstall thermostat housing, however do not reinstall thermostat. Tighten retaining bolts.
2. Insert garden hose into radiator filler opening, open radiator petcock and turn on water.
3. Start engine and run engine for a few minutes. This should flush out any loose particles in the system.
4. Turn off engine and remove the garden hose.
5. Remove thermostat housing. Thoroughly clean the thermostat housing and engine surfaces of old gasket and sealer. This is necessary to prevent leakage between the housing and engine surfaces.
6. Install new thermostat housing gasket and the thermostat. Make certain the thermostat is installed exactly in the same position as it was removed.
7. Install thermostat housing and tighten retaining bolts and nuts.
8. Allow radiator to drain.
9. Close radiator petcock, if equipped.
10. Remove coolant overflow tank, if equipped. Thoroughly clean the inside of the tank and reinstall.

## REFILLING THE SYSTEM

1. Determine the amount of anti-freeze required to achieve a 50/50 solution in the cooling system. Refer to the "Cooling System & Capacity Data" tables in the individual truck chapters. Take the total number of quarts listed in the tables and divide by two. This number is the amount of anti-freeze, in quarts, required to achieve the 50/50 solution. This solution will generally provide protection to −35 degrees F.
2. Add the amount of anti-freeze to the radiator determined in the preceding step. If radiator fills before required amount of anti-freeze is installed, start engine and turn on heater. Add the anti-freeze as the coolant level sinks in the radiator.
3. Continue to run engine with the radiator cap removed until the upper radiator hose becomes hot to the touch.
4. Top up the coolant level in the radiator to the bottom of the filler neck with a 50/50 mixture of anti-freeze and water.
5. If equipped with an overflow tank, add a 50/50 mixture of anti-freeze and water to the cold level as marked on the side of the tank.

## RADIATOR CAP

The radiator filler cap contains a pressure relief valve and a vacuum relief valve, **Fig. 6.** The pressure relief valve is held

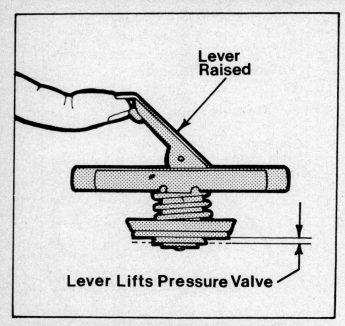

**Fig. 7 Radiator cap with pressure release mechanism (typical)**

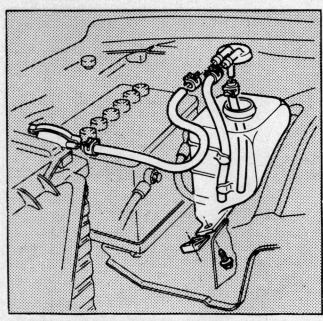

**Fig. 8 Factory installed coolant recovery system (typical)**

against its seat by a spring, which when compressed relieves excessive pressure out the radiator overflow. The vacuum valve is also held against its seat by a spring which when compressed opens the valve to relieve the vacuum created when the system cools.

**NOTE:** Some aftermarket radiator caps incorporate a pressure release mechanism to relieve cooling system pressure before rotating cap, **Fig. 7.**

The radiator cap should be washed with clean water and pressure checked at regular tune-up intervals. Inspect rubber seal on cap for tears or cracks. If the pressure cap will not hold pressure or does not release at the proper pressure, replace the cap.

## COOLANT RECOVERY SYSTEM

The coolant recovery system supplements the standard cooling system in that additional coolant is available from a plastic reservoir, **Fig. 8.**

As the coolant is heated it expands within the cooling system and overflows into the plastic reservoir. As the engine cools, the coolant contracts and is drawn back into the radiator by vacuum. In this way, the radiator is filled to capacity at all times, resulting in increased cooling efficiency.

Air or vapor entering the system will be forced to the reservoir under the coolant and will exit through the reservoir cap.

A special radiator cap is designed to discourage inadvertent removal. The finger grips have been eliminated, replaced by a round configuration.

**Fig. 9 Aftermarket coolant recovery system installation (typical)**

**Overflow Kit**

If your truck does not have an overflow reservoir, it is easy to fit it with one, **Fig. 9.** A kit should include the following:
1. A clear plastic reservoir with quart markings to indicate fluid level.
2. A replacement radiator cap, with an air sealing gasket in the cap's inside perimeter.
3. Necessary hoses and fittings.

## HOSE REPLACEMENT

The radiator, heater and the coolant

bypass hoses are held at each end by a clamp. All clamps but the spring design can be loosened with a screwdriver. To save yourself time after you have removed the hose from your radiator or heater, buy the replacement hose and any necessary clamps before starting the job.

**Removal**
1. Drain the radiator as outlined previously. Use a clean container, large enough to hold the coolant from your cooling system to save for refilling the system after replacing the hose. If you

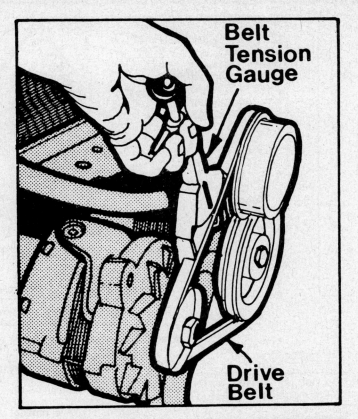

**Fig. 10  Checking belt tension with a tension gauge**

are removing the radiator upper hose or heater hoses, you need only drain the radiator. If you are removing the lower hose, also drain the block as follows: disconnect the lower hose at the radiator, bend it down and use it as a drain spout.

2. Loosen the clamps with a screwdriver at each end of the hose to be removed. If the clamps are old and corroded, they may be stuck to the hose. Loosening the screw may not be enough on some designs, in which case you'll have to pry the clamp.

**CAUTION:** Be very careful when prying under the clamp. The fittings are extremely fragile and might bend or break if too much force is exerted.

If the hose is held by spring clamps, you may be in for a struggle unless you have spring clamp pliers. There are many types of pliers designed for these clamps, including ordinary slip-joint pliers with recesses cut into the jaws to grip each end of the clamp. To release the clamp you must squeeze the ends together, and if you try to use ordinary pliers, the ends may slip off. The best procedure is to discard the spring type and install a wormdrive band clamp, but if you insist in reusing the one you have, at least invest in a pair of special pliers.

3. Twist the hose back and forth to loosen it from the connector. Slide the hose off the connections. If the hose is stuck, shove in a screwdriver and try to pry loose. If the working angle is poor for the screwdriver, or if the hose is really stuck, cut the hose off the neck with a single-edge razor blade. If the hose being removed is dried and cracked and remnants of it remain on either connection, clean the connection thoroughly with a scraper or putty knife.

**Installation**

1. With the old hose removed, wire brush the hose connections to remove foreign material.
2. To ease installation, coat hose neck with a soap solution.
3. Slide the hose in position so it is completely on the neck at each end, to avoid possibility of kinking and to provide room for proper positioning of the clamp. Except for the wormdrive clamp, which can be opened completely, the clamp must be loosely placed over the hose prior to fitting its end on the neck.
4. Make sure the clamps are beyond the head and placed in the center of the clamping surface of the connections.
5. Tighten the clamps.
6. Refill the cooling system as outlined previously.

## COOLING SYSTEM LEAKS

If the coolant level must be adjusted frequently, the cooling system may be leaking either internally or externally. To determine if the system is leaking internally, special equipment must be used such as a pressure tester. To determine if the system is leaking externally, check for leakage in the following locations: radiator and its seams, hoses and their connections, heater core, water pump, coolant temperature sending unit, thermostat housing, hot water choke housing, heater water valve, coolant recovery tank and core plugs.

## DRIVE BELTS

Proper belt tension is important not only to minimize noise and prolong belt life, but also to protect the accessories being driven.

Belts which are adjusted too tight may cause failure to the bearing of the accessory which it drives. Premature wear and breakage of the belt may also result. Belts which are too loose will slip on their pulleys and cause a screeching sound. Loose belts can also cause the battery to go dead, the engine to overheat, steering to become hard (if equipped with power steering) and air conditioner to malfunction.

### DRIVE BELT TENSION GAUGE

The use of a belt tension gauge will quickly indicate whether a belt is properly adjusted or not. Low cost tension gauges give spot readings while the more expensive ones give continuous readings as the belt tension is adjusted, **Fig. 10.**

### DRIVE BELT INSPECTION

All belts should be inspected at regular intervals for uneven wear, fraying and glazing.

**CAUTION:** Do not inspect belts while engine is running.

Small cracks on the underside of the belt can be enlarged for inspection by flexing the belt. Cracks expose the interior to damage, leading to breakage without warning.

Grease rots ordinary rubber belts. It also causes the belts to slip.

Glazed belts, indicated with a shiny friction surface cause the belts to slip. This can cause overheating, a low charging rate, and hard steering in the case of vehicles with power steering.

Always make sure to inspect the underside of belts. Belts that appear sound from the top, may be severely split on the sides and bottom, ready to fail.

### DRIVE BELT TENSION ADJUSTMENT

1. Run engine until it reaches normal operating temperature, then turn engine off.

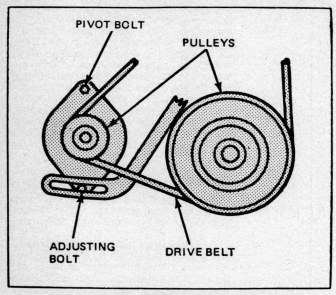

**Fig. 11  Pivot bolt and adjusting bolt arrangement**

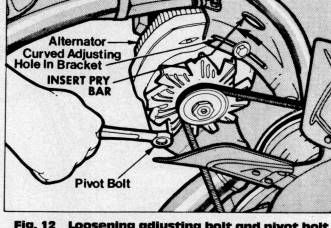

**Fig. 12  Loosening adjusting bolt and pivot bolt**

**CAUTION:** Do not attempt to check or adjust any drive belt while engine is running. Turn engine off.

2. Using belt tension gauge following manufacturer's instructions, check tension of each belt, individually. Refer to individual vehicle chapter for belt tension specifications.
3. If adjustment is necessary, proceed as follows:
   a. Pivot Bolt and Adjusting Bolt, **Figs. 11 and 12:** using a suitable wrench, loosen adjusting bolt and pivot bolt, then using a pry bar, move accessory toward or away from engine until tension gauge reaches specified reading. Make sure to tighten bolts before relieving force applied to pry bar.

**CAUTION:** Do not pry against power steering housing or air pump housing.

   b. Adjusting Bolt and Adjusting Bolt Slots, **Fig. 13,** loosen adjusting slot bolts, then loosen or tighten adjusting bolt until tension gauge reaches specified reading. Make sure to tighten adjusting slot bolts.
   c. Idler Pulley Pivot Bolt and Adjusting Bolt: loosen idler pulley pivot bolt and adjusting bolt, then insert a ½ inch flex handle into pulley arm slot and apply force on handle until tension gauge reaches specified reading. Make sure to tighten pivot and adjusting bolt before relieving force on handle.
4. To check tension on a belt without a belt tension gauge, proceed as follows:
   a. Place a straight edge along the belt from pulley to pulley, **Fig. 14.**
   b. Using a ruler, depress belt at midpoint between pulleys. Measure amount of deflection. For belt with a free span of less than 12 inches between pulleys, amount of deflection should be ¼ inch. For belts with a free span of more than 12 inches between pulleys, amount of deflection should be ½ inch.
   c. Adjust belt tension, if necessary, as described previously.
5. Recheck belt tension, and readjust if necessary.

## DRIVE BELT REPLACEMENT

To replace a belt, loosen the adjusting bolt and pivot bolt. Move accessory as required to obtain maximum slack on belt.

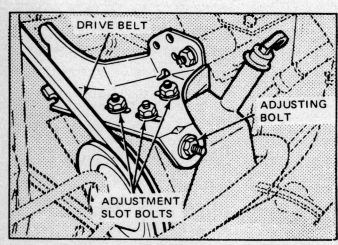

**Fig. 13  Adjustment bolt and adjustment slot arrangement**

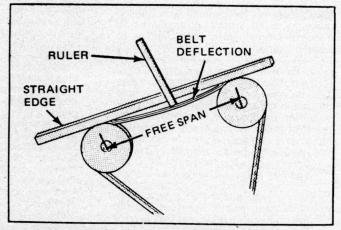

**Fig. 14  Checking belt tension without belt tension gauge**

**Fig. 15   Disconnecting lower shock absorber mount (typical)**

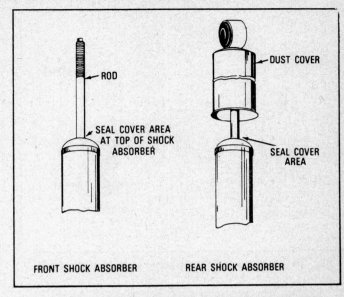

**Fig. 16   Possible source of shock absorber leakage**

Remove belt by lifting off the pulleys and working it around the fan or other accessories, as necessary. Occasionally on multiple belt arrangements, it will be necessary to remove one or more additional belts in order to remove the defective belt. To install belt, reverse the removal procedure and adjust belt tension as described previously.

**NOTE:** On accessories which are driven by dual belts, it is advisable to replace both belts even if only one needs replacement.

# SHOCK ABSORBERS
## ON VEHICLE CHECKS
### Bounce Test

Check each shock absorber by bouncing each corner of vehicle. This is best accomplished by alternately lifting up and pushing down at corner of vehicle until maximum up and down movement is reached. Let go of vehicle and ensure movement stops very quickly. Relative damping of shocks should be compared side to side but not front to rear.

### Shock Mounts

If noise appears to come from shock mounts, raise vehicle on hoist that supports wheels and check mountings for the following:
1. Worn or defective grommets.
2. Loose mounting nuts or bolts.
3. Possible interference condition.

4. Missing bump stops.
If no apparent faults can be found but noise condition exists when vehicle is bounced, proceed to next check.

### Leak Inspection & Manual Operation Check

1. Disconnect each shock lower mount, **Fig. 15,** and pull down on shock absorber until fully extended.
2. Check for leaks in seal cover area, **Fig. 16.** Shock absorber oil is a very thin hydraulic fluid that has a characteristic odor and dark brown color.

**NOTE:** Shock absorber seals are intended to allow slight seepage to lubricate rod. A trace of oil around seal cover area is not cause for shock absorber replacement since the unit has sufficient reserve fluid to compensate for this seepage.

Ensure oil spray is not from some other source. To check, wipe wet area clean and manually operate shock absorber as described in following step. Fluid will reappear if shock absorber is leaking.

**NOTE:** Air line must be disconnected from air adjustable shocks before they are manually operated.

3. If necessary, fabricate bracket or handle to enable a secure grip on shock absorber end, **Fig. 17.**
4. Check for internal binding, leakage, and improper or defective valving by

pulling down and pushing up shock absorber. Compare rebound resistance (downward) of both shock absorbers, then compression resistance. If any noticeable difference is detected during either stroke, the weaker unit is usually at fault.
5. If shock absorber operates noisily, it should be replaced. Noise conditions that require shock absorber replacement are as follows:
   a. Grunt or squeal after full stroke in both directions.
   b. Clicking noise during fast direction reversal.
   c. Skip or lag when reversing direction in mid-stroke.

## BENCH CHECKS

If a suitable hoist is not available to perform on-vehicle shock absorber checks, or there is still doubt as to whether the units are defective, the following bench test can be performed.

### Spiral Groove Reservoir Shock Absorbers

**NOTE:** If this style shock absorber is stored or left to lie in a horizontal position for any length of time, an air pocket will form in pressure chamber. If air pocket is not purged, shock absorber may be misdiagnosed as faulty. Purge air from pressure chamber as follows:
a. Extend shock absorber while holding it vertically and right side up, **Fig. 18.**
b. Invert shock absorber and fully compress unit.
c. Repeat steps a and b at least 5 times to ensure air is completely purged.

1. Obtain known good shock absorber with same part number.
2. Hold both shock absorbers in vertical

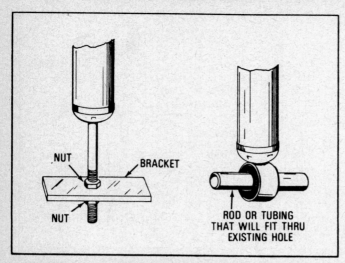

**Fig. 17    Methods of gripping shock absorbers**

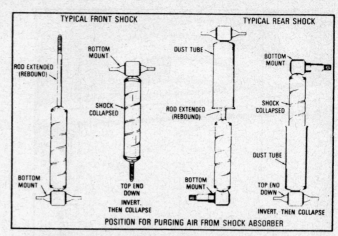

**Fig. 18    Purging air from shock absorbers**

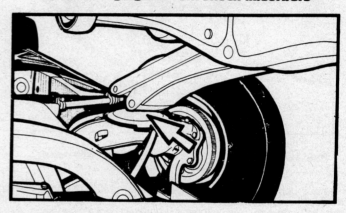

**Fig. 19    Supporting control arm on vehicles with spring on lower control arm**

position and clamp bottom mounts in vise. Do not clamp on mounting threads or on reservoir tube.

3. Operate shock absorbers by hand at different speeds and compare resistance of known good shock to the other. Rebound resistance (extension) is usually greater than compression resistance (about 2:1). Resistance should be smooth and consistent for each stroke rate.
4. Check for the following conditions which indicate a defective shock absorber:
   a. Skip or lag when reversing direction in mid-stroke.
   b. Seizing or binding except at extreme end of stroke.
   c. Noises such as grunt or squeal after completing full stroke in either direction.
   d. Clicking noise at fast reversal.
   e. Fluid leakage.
5. Check for loose piston by extending shock absorber to full rebound position, then give an extra hard pull. If any give is present, piston is loose and unit must be replaced.

### Gas Cell Shock Absorbers
These shock absorbers are equipped with a gas-filled cell which takes the place of air in the reservoir. Foaming of the fluid is eliminated since air and fluid cannot mix. Because of this feature, these style shock absorbers must be tested in an upside down position. If a lag is noticed when unit is stroked, gas cell has ruptured and unit must be replaced.

### Air Adjustable Shock Absorbers
These shock absorbers have an air chamber similar to the spiral groove reservoir type which must be purged. Refer to note under "Spiral Groove Reservoir Shock Absorbers" to purge air from shock absorbers.

1. Place shock absorber in vise in vertical position with larger diameter tube at top, and clamp at lower mounting

ring.
2. Operate unit manually at different speeds. A consistent degree of resistance should be felt through length of stroke. A gurgling noise is normal since unit is normally pressurized.
3. Refer to "Spiral Groove Reservoir Shock Absorbers" test procedure for remainder of bench checks.

# FRONT SUSPENSION & STEERING CHECKS

To perform the following wear checks, tension must be removed from the suspension parts. Raise the vehicle and support with jack stands. Relieve load from suspension as follows: on vehicles with the spring or torsion bar on the lower control arm, place a floor jack or single piston hydraulic jack under lower arm control as close to ball joint as possible, **Fig. 19,** and raise control arm until vehicle chassis is about to lift off jack stand, then stop; on vehicles with spring on upper control arm, jack up lower control arm as described previously, place block of wood between upper control arm and frame, **Fig. 20,** and slowly lower jack from lower control arm,

making sure that neither upper control nor wooden block move. Wooden block must be removed after inspection is completed.

## UPPER & LOWER CONTROL ARM BUSHINGS CHECK

1. Have assistant sit in vehicle and apply brake to lock front wheels.
2. Grasp front wheel with both hands and vigorously attempt to rotate it forward and backward. Observe control arms for excessive front-to-rear movement.
3. Repeat procedure on other front wheel.

## UPPER BALL JOINT CHECK

1. Grasp front wheel at top with one hand and at bottom with other.
2. Pull wheel out at bottom while simultaneously pushing in at top. Have assistant watch for play in upper ball joint.
3. Repeat on other front wheel.

## LOWER BALL JOINT CHECK

1. Place suitable bar or pipe directly under center of tire.
2. Wedge pipe against ground and lift. Several tries may be necessary to get

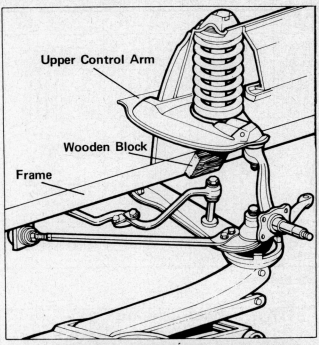

**Fig. 20 Blocking control arm of vehicles with spring on upper control arm**

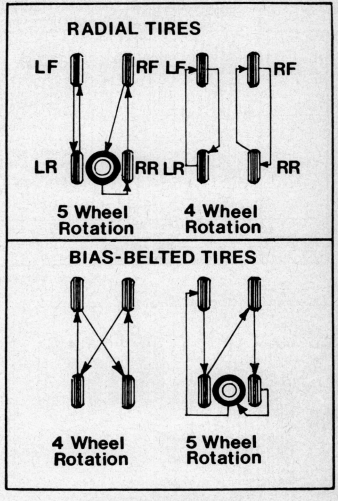

**Fig. 21 Tire rotation chart**

a good check.
3. Repeat procedure on other wheel.

## STEERING LINKAGE CHECK

1. Grasp wheel with both hands and vigorously shake tire from right to left. Have assistant check for wear in tie-rod ends, center link, and idler arm. Idler arm should not move up and down.
2. Repeat procedure on other wheel.

# TIRE CARE

## TIRE ROTATION

The purpose of tire rotation is to equalize normal wear. By equalizing this wear evenly over the entire tread surface, you extend tire life. Recommended rotation patterns are shown in **Fig. 21.**

It is wise to provide snow tires with rims of their own, so they do not have to be removed from rims in the late fall. They can be kept on rims of their own during both storage and use. In this way, you will protect tires from the bead damage which becomes a possibility when you break a tire away from a rim.

A studded snow tire should always be mounted on the same wheel of the car year after year. When storing studded snow tires, mark tire in chalk for either Right or Left, depending upon which side of the car the tire was mounted.

When storing tires, lay them flat, off the tread to prevent flat spots from developing. Keep tires away from electricity-producing machinery which creates ozone and can damage rubber.

## TIRE MAINTENANCE

Tires should be inspected regularly for excessive or abnormal tread wear, fabric breaks, cuts or other damage, **Fig. 22.** A bulge or bump in the sidewall or tread is reason for discarding a tire. A bulge indicates that the tread or sidewall has separated from the tire body. The tire is a candidate for a blowout. Look also for small stones or other foreign bodies wedged in the tread. These can be removed by prying them out carefully with a screwdriver.

# BATTERY SERVICE

## CONSTRUCTION & OPERATION

To understand why batteries malfunction, some knowledge of batteries is important. Simply stated, the battery is constructed of two unlike materials, a positive plate and a negative plate with a porous separator between the two plates, **Fig. 23.** This assembly placed in a suitable battery case and filled slightly above the top of the plates with electrolyte (sulphuric acid and distilled water) forms a cell. The 12 volt battery is composed of 6 cells interconnected by plate straps. Note that batteries have varying number of plates per cell, but each cell in any given battery has the same number of plates.

The battery performs the following four basic functions in a vehicle:
1. Supplies electrical energy to the starter motor to crank and start the engine and also to the ignition system while the engine is being started.
2. Supplies electrical energy for accessories such as radio, tape deck, heater, and lights when engine is not running and the ignition switch is in the "OFF" or the "Accessory" position.
3. Supplies additional electrical energy for accessories while the engine is running when the output alternator is exceeded by the various accessories.

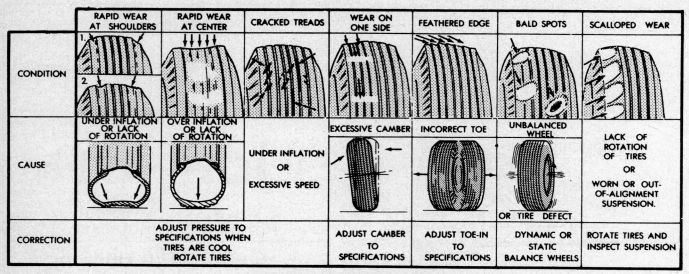

**Fig. 22    Tire tread wear patterns**

| | RAPID WEAR AT SHOULDERS | RAPID WEAR AT CENTER | CRACKED TREADS | WEAR ON ONE SIDE | FEATHERED EDGE | BALD SPOTS | SCALLOPED WEAR |
|---|---|---|---|---|---|---|---|
| CONDITION | | | | | | | |
| CAUSE | UNDER INFLATION OR LACK OF ROTATION | OVER INFLATION OR LACK OF ROTATION | UNDER INFLATION OR EXCESSIVE SPEED | EXCESSIVE CAMBER | INCORRECT TOE | UNBALANCED WHEEL OR TIRE DEFECT | LACK OF ROTATION OF TIRES OR WORN OR OUT-OF-ALIGNMENT SUSPENSION. |
| CORRECTION | ADJUST PRESSURE TO SPECIFICATIONS WHEN TIRES ARE COOL ROTATE TIRES | | | ADJUST CAMBER TO SPECIFICATIONS | ADJUST TOE-IN TO SPECIFICATIONS | DYNAMIC OR STATIC BALANCE WHEELS | ROTATE TIRES AND INSPECT SUSPENSION |

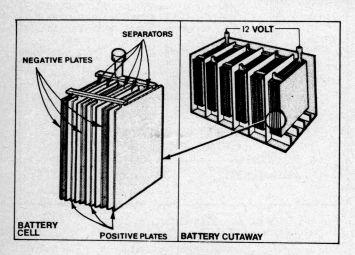

**Fig. 23    Battery construction**

4. Stabilizes voltage in the electrical system. Satisfactory operation of the ignition system and any other electrical device is impossible with a damaged, weak or even underpowered (low rating) battery.

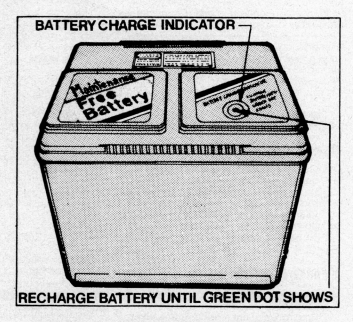

**Fig. 24    Typical maintenance free battery**

## SEALED BATTERIES

Sealed batteries, called "Maintenance Free" or "Freedom" batteries, **Fig. 24,** are available on some vehicles, and can also be purchased from other sources.

The sealed batteries have unique chemistry and construction methods which provide advantages.

Water never needs to be added to the battery.

The battery is completely sealed except for two small vent holes on the side. The vent holes allow what small amount of gases are produced in the battery to escape. The special chemical composition inside the battery reduces the production of gas to an extremely small amount at normal charging voltages.

The battery has a very strong ability to withstand damaging effects of overcharge, and the terminals are tightly sealed to minimize leakage. A charge indicator in the cover indicates state of charge.

Compared to a conventional battery in which performance decreases steadily with age, the sealed battery delivers more available power at any time during its life. The battery has a reduced tendency to self-discharge as compared to a conventional battery.

## SAFETY PRECAUTIONS

**CAUTION:** Electrolyte solution in the battery is a strong and dangerous acid. It is extremely harmful to eyes, skin and clothing. If acid contacts any part of the body, flush immediately with water for a period not less than 15 minutes. If acid is accidentally swallowed, drink large quantities of milk or water, followed by milk of magnesia, a beaten raw egg or vegetable oil. Call physician immediately.

When batteries are being charged, highly explosive hydrogen and oxygen gases form in each battery cell. Some of this gas escapes through the vent holes in the plugs on top of battery case and forms an explosive atmosphere surrounding the battery. This explosive gas will remain in and/or around the battery for several hours

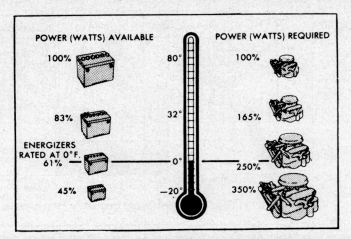

**Fig. 25  Battery energy versus falling temperature comparison chart**

after the battery has been charged. Sparks or flames can ignite this gas and cause a dangerous battery explosion.

The following precautions must be observed to avoid battery explosion, personal harm and damage to the vehicle's electrical system.

1. Do not smoke near batteries being charged or those which have been recently charged. It is a good practice never to smoke near a battery even though the battery is in the vehicle.
2. Always shield your eyes when working with batteries.
3. Do not disconnect live (working) circuits (lights or accessories operating) at the terminals of batteries since sparking usually occurs at a point where such a circuit is disconnected.
4. Use extreme caution when connecting or disconnecting booster leads or cable clamps from battery chargers. Make sure live (working) circuits are disconnected before connecting or disconnecting the booster leads or cable clamps. Poor booster lead connections are a common cause of electrical arcing causing battery explosions.

## CAUSES OF DISCHARGED BATTERIES

There are numerous reasons that could cause a battery to discharge and appear to be defective, therefore the battery should not be targeted as the primary source of electrical and/or starting problems before it has been tested.

The following are some common conditions that could discharge a good battery:
1. Lights left "ON" or doors not closed properly, leaving dome light "ON."
2. Excessive use of accessories with the engine not running.
3. Improper installation of aftermarket accessories.
4. Alternator belt loose or damaged.
5. Dirty battery case causing a self-discharge condition.
6. Loose battery cable terminals.
7. Low alternator output.
8. High resistance in charging circuits caused by other loose electrical connections.

## BATTERY RATING & CAPACITY

The two most commonly used ratings are the 20 hour rating of 80° F and the cold cranking load capacity of the battery at 0° F, specified in amps. Batteries are also rated by watts in the Peak Watt Rating (PWR) which is actually the cold cranking ability of the battery at 0° F.

Another battery rating method is the reserve capacity rating in minutes. The purpose of this rating is to determine the length of time a vehicle can be operated with a faulty charging system (malfunctioning alternator or regulator). Batteries are normally marketed by the Ampere-Hour rating which is based on the 20 hour rating. The Ampere-Hour rating is also normally stamped on the battery case or on a label attached to the battery. A battery capable of furnishing 4 amps for a period of 20 hours is classified as an 80 ampere hour battery (4 amps × 20 hours = 80).

The Ampere-Hour rating should not be confused with the cranking performance of a battery at 0° F. Batteries with the same Ampere-Hour ratings can have various 0° F cranking capacities. The higher quality battery will have a higher Ampere-Hour rating and a higher cranking capacity rating at 0° F. Note that battery capacity will increase with larger number of plates per cell, larger size of plates, and larger battery case size allowing for more electrolyte solution.

## SELECTING A REPLACEMENT BATTERY

Long and troublefree service can be better assured when the capacity or wattage rating of the replacement battery is at least equal to the wattage rating of the battery originally engineered for the application by the manufacturer.

The use of an undersized battery may result in poor performance and early failure. **Fig. 25** shows how battery power shrinks while the need for engine cranking power increases with falling temperatures. Sub-zero temperatures reduce capacity of a fully charged battery to 45% of its normal power and at the same time increase cranking load to 3½ times the normal warm weather load.

Hot weather can also place excessive electrical loads on the battery. Difficulty in starting may occur when cranking is attempted shortly after a hot engine has been turned off or stalls. High compression engines can be as difficult to start under such conditions as on the coldest day. Consequently, good performance can be obtained only if the battery has ample capacity to cope with these conditions.

A battery of greater capacity should be considered if the electrical load has been increased through the addition of accessories, or if driving conditions are such that the generator cannot keep the battery charged.

On applications where heavy electrical loads are encountered, a higher output generator that will supply a charge during low speed operation may be required to increase battery life and improve battery performance.

## TESTING BATTERY (SPECIFIC GRAVITY)

**NOTE:** The specific gravity of a sealed battery cannot be checked.

A hydrometer can be used to measure the specific gravity of the electrolyte in each cell. There are several types of hydrometers available, the least expensive consisting of a glass tube, a rubber bulb at the end of the tube and several balls within the tube. To use this type, the specific gravity of the battery must be interpreted by the number of balls which float to the surface of the electrolyte, according to the manufacturer's instructions.

The hydrometer indicates the concentration of the electrolyte.

## BOOST STARTING A VEHICLE WITH A DISCHARGED BATTERY

1. Be sure the ignition key is in the off position and all accessories and lights are off.
2. Shield eyes. Use goggles or similar eye protection.
3. Connect the booster cables from the positive (+) battery terminal of the discharged battery (vehicle to be started) to the positive (+) battery terminal of the vehicle used as the booster.
4. Connect one end of the other cable to negative (−) terminal of the good battery.
5. Connect one end of the other cable to

| Watt Rating | 5 Amperes | 10 Amperes | 20 Amperes | 30 Amperes | 40 Amperes | 50 Amperes |
|---|---|---|---|---|---|---|
| Below 2450 | 10 Hours | 5 Hours | 2½ Hours | 2 Hours | | |
| 2450–2950 | 12 Hours | 6 Hours | 3 Hours | 2 Hours | 1½ Hours | |
| Above 2950 | 15 Hours | 7½ Hours | 3¼ Hours | 2 Hours | 1¾ Hours | 1½ Hours |

**Fig. 26   Battery charging guide**

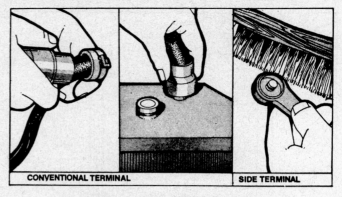

CONVENTIONAL TERMINAL                SIDE TERMINAL

**Fig. 27   Cleaning battery terminals**

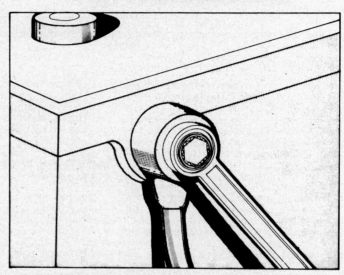

**Fig. 28   Removing side type battery terminal**

engine bolthead or similar good contact spot on the vehicle being started.

**CAUTION:** Never connect to negative terminal of dead battery.

**NOTE:** To prevent damage to other electrical components on the vehicle being started, make certain engine is at idle speed before disconnecting jumper cables.

## CHARGING THE BATTERY

There are two separate methods of recharging batteries which differ basically in the rate of charge.

### Slow Charging Method

Slow charging is the best and only method of completely recharging a battery. This method, when properly applied, may be used safely under all possible conditions providing the electrolyte is at proper level and the battery is capable of being fully charged. The normal charging rate is 5 amperes.

A fully charged battery is indicated when all cell specific gravities do not increase when checked at three one-hour intervals and all cells are gassing freely.

Charge periods of 24 hours or more may be required because of the low charging rate. See charging guide, **Fig. 26.**

### Quick Charging Method

In order to get a car back on the road in the least amount of time, it is sometimes necessary to quick charge a battery. The battery cannot be brought up to full charged condition by the quick charge method. It can, however, be substantially recharged or boosted but, in order to bring it to a fully charged condition, the charging cycle must be finished by charging at a low or normal rate. Some quick chargers have a provision for finishing the charging cycle at a low rate to bring the battery up to a fully charged condition.

**CAUTION:** Too high a current during quick charging will damage battery plates.

## BATTERY CABLE SERVICE

**NOTE:** At regular intervals, perform a visual inspection of the battery.

This inspection should be performed when any of the underhood maintenance items

such as engine oil, transmission fluid or radiator coolant level are checked.
1. Clean any heavy accumulation of dirt or corrosion on the battery terminals and battery tray with a wire brush, **Fig. 27.** Finish cleaning with a solution of baking soda and water. Diluted ammonia can also be used as a washing agent. Thoroughly flush battery with clean water.

**NOTE:** Baking soda and ammonia neutralize battery acid. Therefore make sure these agents are kept out of the battery by keeping the battery caps tightly in place.

2. Check for damaged cable insulation. Damaged insulation can cause the cable to short out against the body of the vehicle or other accessories. Cables in this condition should be replaced immediately.
3. Check level of electrolyte. If required, add water as described further on.
4. Make sure battery is securely held in place. A loose or broken bracket can result in battery damage (both internally and externally) from excessive vibration.

## BATTERY CABLE, REPLACE

**NOTE:** When disconnecting battery cables, first make sure all accessories are off, disconnect the negative battery cable and then the positive cable. Make sure to reconnect cables in the reverse order of removal.

1. On side terminal batteries, loosen the retaining bolts using a ⅚-inch wrench, and disconnect the cable from the battery, **Fig. 28.**
2. On all other type batteries, loosen the cable retaining bolt using a ½ inch or ⁹⁄₁₆ inch box wrench, **Fig. 29,** and lift the cable off the battery posts. Some cables can be removed by squeezing the tabs on the cable terminal using a pair of pliers, **Fig. 30,** and lifting the cable off the battery posts.
3. If the battery terminals are difficult to remove, use a terminal puller, **Fig. 31.** Place the legs of the puller underneath the terminal and tighten the puller screw until the terminal is removed.
4. Clean the cable terminals and battery

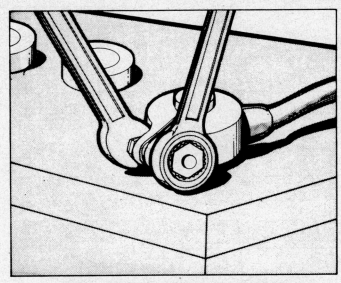

**Fig. 29    Removing bolt type terminal**

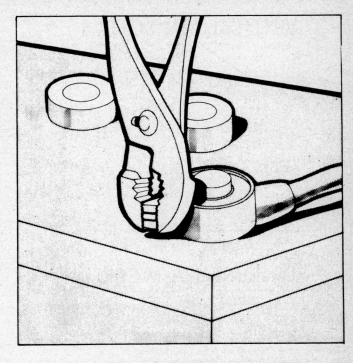

**Fig. 30    Removing spread type terminal**

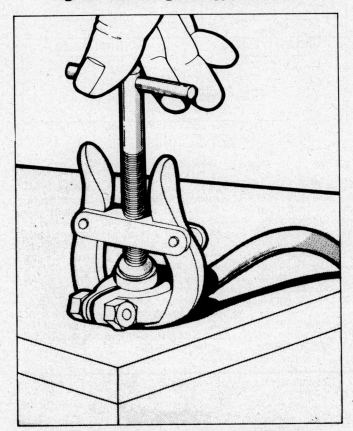

**Fig. 31    Removing battery cable terminal using cable terminal puller**

7. To install the cables on all other types of batteries, place the cables on the battery post and force them all the way down. If the cable is not completely bottomed, spread the cable terminal slightly with a screwdriver, until the terminal is properly positioned.
8. Tighten the terminal bolts using a ½ inch or $\frac{9}{16}$ inch box wrench.
9. Coat the outside of the terminals with petroleum jelly to prevent corrosion.

## BATTERY, REPLACE

Careless installation of a new battery can ruin the battery. In removing the old battery, note the location of the positive battery post so the new battery can be installed in the same position. Always remove the negative (ground) cable first.

Use an open-end wrench to loosen the clamp. If the nut is very tight, use one wrench on the head of the bolt and the other on the nut to avoid straining and possibly cracking the battery cover. A pair of battery pliers can be used to loosen the nut, but a wrench should always be used on the head of the bolt.

If a cable terminal is corroded to the post, do not try to loosen it by hammering, or by resting a tool on the battery and prying—either method can break the battery container. Use a screw type terminal puller, **Fig. 31,** or spread the cable terminals slightly with a screwdriver.

Clean any corrosion from the cables, battery case, or hold-downs, and inspect them. Paint any corroded steel parts with acid-proof paint. Make sure the cable is of the correct size and that its insulation and

posts using a terminal and post wire brush, **Fig. 27.**
5. Clean the battery top using a solution of soda and water. Ensure the battery is thoroughly cleaned and dried. Make sure you cover the battery caps to avoid entry of the soda and water solution into the battery.
6. To install the cables on a side terminal battery, place the cables onto the battery and tighten the retaining screws using a $\frac{5}{16}$ inch wrench.

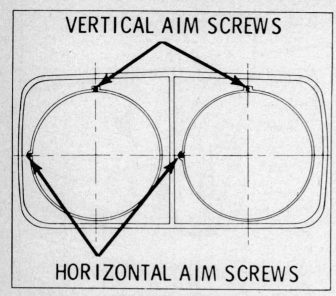

**Fig. 32  Headlamp adjusting screws (typical)**

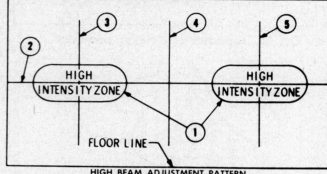

LOW BEAM ADJUSTMENT PATTERN
(VISUAL AIM AT 25 FEET)
5-3/4" TYPE 2 LAMPS (OUTBOARD ONLY) AND 7" TYPE 2 LAMPS

| | |
|---|---|
| LINE 1 | HIGH INTENSITY ZONES. |
| LINE 2 | HORIZONTAL AND VERTICAL AT CENTER OF HEADLAMPS. |
| LINES 3 & 5 | VERTICAL AT CENTER OF HEADLAMPS. |
| LINE 4 | VERTICAL AT CENTER OF CAR. |

HIGH BEAM ADJUSTMENT PATTERN
(VISUAL AIM AT 25 FEET)
5-3/4" TYPE 1 LAMPS (INBOARD ONLY)

**Fig. 33  Headlamp aiming**

clamp terminal are in good condition.

Put the new battery in position, making sure it sits level, and tighten the hold-downs a little at a time, alternately, to avoid distorting and breaking the battery case. The hold-downs should be snug enough to prevent bouncing, but should not be too tight.

**NOTE:** Before connecting the cables, check the battery terminals to be sure the battery is not reversed.

Clean the battery post bright with sandpaper or a wire brush.

Don't hammer the terminals down on the posts, as the battery case may crack. Spread the terminals slightly if necessary. Connect the starter cable first and the negative (ground) cable last, tightening the terminal bolts after making sure the cables don't interfere with the vent plugs or rub against the hold-downs.

## HEADLAMP AIMING

It is recommended that headlamps be checked for proper aim every 12 months or whenever front body work is repaired. On most vehicles, aiming can be performed without removing headlamp bezels. Vertical adjustment is usually accomplished with a screw at the top of the sealed beam retaining ring (12 o'clock position). Horizontal adjustment is provided by a screw at the right or left (3 or 9 o'clock position) of the sealed beam unit, **Fig. 32.** Headlamp aiming can be performed visually with a screen as follows:

1. Vehicle should be on level floor so headlamps are 25 ft. from screen or light colored wall. Fuel tank should be ½ full. Any heavy loads that are normally in vehicle should remain there. Driver and passengers should not be in vehicle during aiming. Tires should be inflated to specified pressures and headlamps lenses should be cleaned.
2. Mark screen or wall with four lines as shown in **Fig. 33.**
3. Adjust low beam pattern only as shown in top diagram in **Fig. 33.**
4. On vehicles with four headlamp systems, cover low beam (outboard or upper lamps) and adjust high beam lamp pattern as shown in bottom diagram of **Fig. 33.**

# TYPICAL LUBRICATION POINTS

**Jeep Combined (Heavy-Duty & Regular) Maintenance Schedule**

| | EACH FUEL FILL | 2,500 / 4 000 / 2.5 | 5,000 / 8 000 / 5 | 8,750 / 14 000 / 9 | 12,500 / 20 000 / 12½ | 16,250 / 26 000 / 16 | 20,000 / 32 000 / 20 | 23,750 / 38 000 / 24 | 27,500 / 44 000 / 27½ | 30,000 / 48 000 / 30 | 32,500 / 52 000 / 32 | 35,000 / 56 000 / 35 | 38,750 / 62 000 / 39 | 42,500 / 68 000 / 42½ | 46,250 / 74 000 / 46 | 50,000 / 80 000 / 50 |
|---|---|---|---|---|---|---|---|---|---|---|---|---|---|---|---|---|
| Miles / Kilometers / Months | | | | | | | | | | | | | | | | |
| 1) Check Axle Differentials (Front & Rear) | | HD | •HD | HD | •HD | HD | •HD | HD | •HD | | HD | •HD | HD | •HD | HD | •HD |
| 1) Replace Axle Differential Fluid (Front & Rear) | | | | | | | | | | • | | | | | | |
| 2) Lubricate Front Wheel Bearings (a) | | | | | HD | | | | •HD | | | | | HD | | |
| 2) Lubricate Manual Locking Hubs | | | | | HD | | | | •HD | | | | | HD | | |
| 3) Check Brakes & Chassis (b) | | | HD | | •HD | | HD | | •HD | | | HD | | •HD | | HD |
| 3) Lubricate Body Components (b) | | | HD | | •HD | | HD | | •HD | | | HD | | •HD | | HD |
| 4) Lubricate Clutch Lever & Linkage (CJ) | | HD | •HD | HD | •HD | HD | •HD | HD | •HD | HD | HD | •HD | HD | •HD | HD | •HD |
| 4) Lubricate Clutch Lever & Linkage (Cherokee, Wagoneer, Truck) | | | HD | | •HD | | HD | | •HD | | | HD | | •HD | | HD |
| 5) Inspect Exhaust System (c) | | HD | | | •HD | | •HD | | •HD | | | HD | | •HD | | •HD |
| 6) Check Manual Steering Gear | | HD | •HD | HD | •HD | HD | •HD | HD | •HD | HD | HD | •HD | HD | •HD | HD | •HD |
| 7) Lubricate Propeller Shafts (Front and Rear) (CJ) (d) | | HD | •HD | HD | •HD | HD | •HD | HD | •HD | HD | HD | •HD | HD | •HD | HD | •HD |
| 7) Lubricate Propeller Shafts (Front & Rear) (Cherokee, Wagoneer, Truck) (d) | | | HD | | •HD | | | | •HD | | | •HD | | •HD | | HD |
| 8) Check and Lubricate Steering Linkage (CJ) (e) | | HD | •HD | HD | •HD | HD | •HD | HD | •HD | HD | HD | •HD | HD | •HD | HD | •HD |
| 8) Check and Lubricate Steering Linkage (Cherokee, Wagoneer, Truck) (e) | | | HD | | •HD | | HD | | •HD | | | HD | | •HD | | HD |
| 9) Check Windshield Washer Level Fluid | • | | | | | | | | | | | | | | | |
| 10) Check Transfer Case Fluid | | HD | •HD | HD | •HD | HD | •HD | HD | •HD | | HD | •HD | HD | •HD | HD | •HD |
| 10) Replace Transfer Case Fluid | | | | | | | | | | • | | | | | | |
| 11) Check Manual Transmission Fluid | | HD | •HD | HD | •HD | HD | •HD | HD | •HD | | HD | •HD | HD | •HD | HD | •HD |
| 11) Replace Manual Transmission Fluid | | | | | | | | | | • | | | | | | |
| 11) Replace Automatic Transmission Fluid & Filter | | | | | HD | | HD | | | • | | HD | | HD | | |

(a) Replace spindle oil and bearing seals on front wheel bearings (rear wheel bearings do not require periodic or scheduled lubrication)

(b) Check the following items as indicated. Correct to specifications as necessary. BRAKES - Front and rear brake linings for wear; rear brake self-adjusting mechanism for proper operation, master cylinder, calipers, wheel cylinders and differential warning valves for leaks; brake lines, fittings and hoses for condition and leaks; parking brake for proper operation, overall brake condition and action. STEERING/SUSPENSION - Manual or power steering gear and linkage for leaks, looseness or wear; springs, shock absorbers, steering damper and bushings for leaks, looseness or wear; tire condition, overall steering/suspension condition and action. BODY LUBRICATION - Lubricate the following items with the recommended lubricants: ashtray slides; courtesy light buttons, door, hood, liftgate, tailgate latches and hinges; front seat tracks; glove box door latch and hinge; locks; windshield hinges and holddown knobs (CJ/Scrambler only.) ALSO - Adjust parking brake and manual transmission clutch free play, if necessary; adjust tire pressures to specifications; lubricate Model 300 transfer case linkage.

(c) Check exhaust system for leaks, damage, misalignment or grounding against body sheet metal or frame. Check catalytic converter for bulging or heat damage

(d) Lubricate sleeve yokes (splines) and single and double cardan U-joints.

(e) Inspect and replace torn or ruptured grease seals, replace damaged steering components, and lubricate ball joints.

**Jeep. Part 1 of 2 (Typical)**

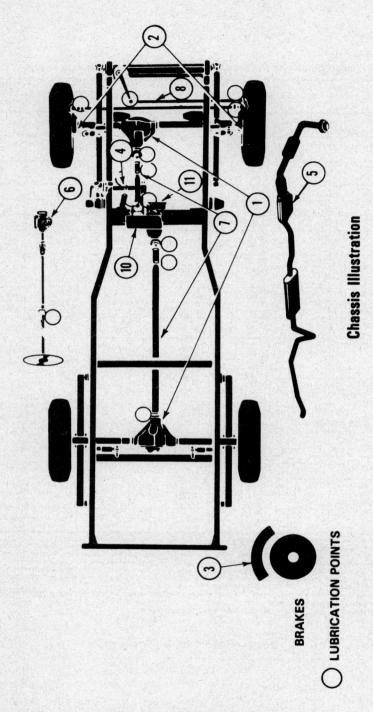

Chassis Illustration

BRAKES

LUBRICATION POINTS

**Jeep. Part 2 of 2 (Typical)**

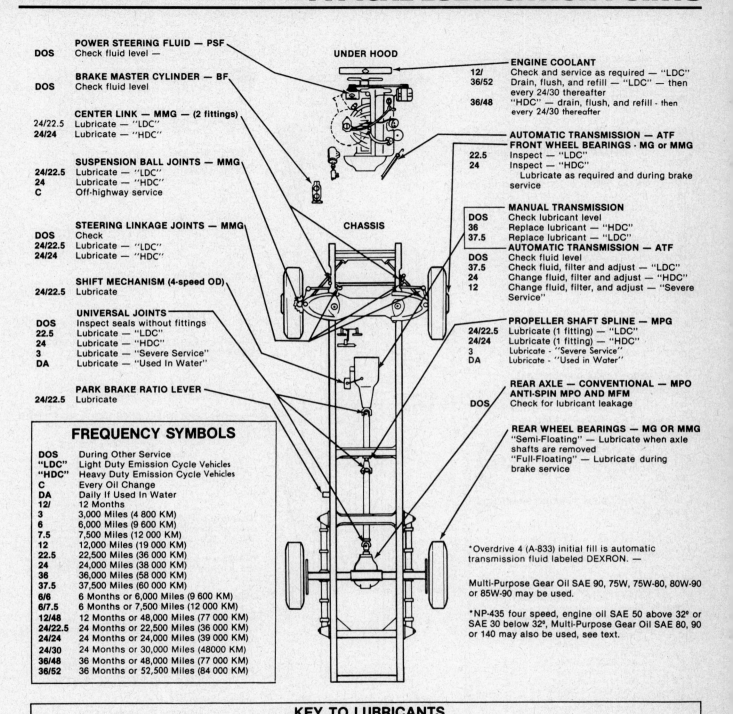

**POWER STEERING FLUID — PSF**

DOS — Check fluid level —

**BRAKE MASTER CYLINDER — BF**

DOS — Check fluid level

**CENTER LINK — MMG — (2 fittings)**

24/22.5 — Lubricate — "LDC"
24/24 — Lubricate — "HDC"

**SUSPENSION BALL JOINTS — MMG**

24/22.5 — Lubricate — "LDC"
24 — Lubricate — "HDC"
C — Off-highway service

**STEERING LINKAGE JOINTS — MMG**

DOS — Check
24/22.5 — Lubricate — "LDC"
24/24 — Lubricate — "HDC"

**SHIFT MECHANISM (4-speed OD)**

24/22.5 — Lubricate

**UNIVERSAL JOINTS**

DOS — Inspect seals without fittings
22.5 — Lubricate — "LDC"
24 — Lubricate — "HDC"
3 — Lubricate — "Severe Service"
DA — Lubricate — "Used In Water"

**PARK BRAKE RATIO LEVER**

24/22.5 — Lubricate

UNDER HOOD

CHASSIS

**ENGINE COOLANT**

12/ — Check and service as required — "LDC"
36/52 — Drain, flush, and refill — "LDC" — then every 24/30 thereafter
36/48 — "HDC" — drain, flush, and refill - then every 24/30 thereafter

**AUTOMATIC TRANSMISSION — ATF**
**FRONT WHEEL BEARINGS · MG or MMG**

22.5 — Inspect — "LDC"
24 — Inspect — "HDC"
   Lubricate as required and during brake service

**MANUAL TRANSMISSION**

DOS — Check lubricant level
36 — Replace lubricant — "HDC"
37.5 — Replace lubricant — "LDC"

**AUTOMATIC TRANSMISSION — ATF**

DOS — Check fluid level
37.5 — Check fluid, filter and adjust — "LDC"
24 — Change fluid, filter and adjust — "HDC"
12 — Change fluid, filter, and adjust — "Severe Service"

**PROPELLER SHAFT SPLINE — MPG**

24/22.5 — Lubricate (1 fitting) — "LDC"
24/24 — Lubricate (1 fitting) — "HDC"
3 — Lubricate - "Severe Service"
DA — Lubricate - "Used in Water"

**REAR AXLE — CONVENTIONAL — MPO**
**ANTI-SPIN MPO AND MFM**

DOS — Check for lubricant leakage

**REAR WHEEL BEARINGS — MG OR MMG**

"Semi-Floating" — Lubricate when axle shafts are removed
"Full-Floating" — Lubricate during brake service

## FREQUENCY SYMBOLS

| | |
|---|---|
| DOS | During Other Service |
| "LDC" | Light Duty Emission Cycle Vehicles |
| "HDC" | Heavy Duty Emission Cycle Vehicles |
| C | Every Oil Change |
| DA | Daily If Used In Water |
| 12/ | 12 Months |
| 3 | 3,000 Miles (4 800 KM) |
| 6 | 6,000 Miles (9 600 KM) |
| 7.5 | 7,500 Miles (12 000 KM) |
| 12 | 12,000 Miles (19 000 KM) |
| 22.5 | 22,500 Miles (36 000 KM) |
| 24 | 24,000 Miles (38 000 KM) |
| 36 | 36,000 Miles (58 000 KM) |
| 37.5 | 37,500 Miles (60 000 KM) |
| 6/6 | 6 Months or 6,000 Miles (9 600 KM) |
| 6/7.5 | 6 Months or 7,500 Miles (12 000 KM) |
| 12/48 | 12 Months or 48,000 Miles (77 000 KM) |
| 24/22.5 | 24 Months or 22,500 Miles (36 000 KM) |
| 24/24 | 24 Months or 24,000 Miles (39 000 KM) |
| 24/30 | 24 Months or 30,000 Miles (48000 KM) |
| 36/48 | 36 Months or 48,000 Miles (77 000 KM) |
| 36/52 | 36 Months or 52,500 Miles (84 000 KM) |

*Overdrive 4 (A-833) initial fill is automatic transmission fluid labeled DEXRON. —

Multi-Purpose Gear Oil SAE 90, 75W, 75W-80, 80W-90 or 85W-90 may be used.

*NP-435 four speed, engine oil SAE 50 above 32° or SAE 30 below 32°, Multi-Purpose Gear Oil SAE 80, 90 or 140 may also be used, see text.

## KEY TO LUBRICANTS

| | |
|---|---|
| **ATF** | DEXRON II — Automatic Transmission Fluid<br>1 qt (0.95 L), P/N 4271243<br>55 gal (208L), P/N 4271245 |
| **CC** | Carburetor Cleaner |
| **EO** | Engine Oil (SF/CC) |
| **BF** | Brake Fluid, Hi-Temp. — DOT 3 |
| **MG** | Multi-Purpose Grease, NLG1 grade 2 E.P. (P/N 4318063) |
| **MMG** | MOPAR Multi-Mileage Grease (P/N 4318062) |
| **MPO** | Multi-Purpose Gear Oil MOPAR Hypoid Lubricant<br>1 qt (0.95 L), P/N 4318058<br>16 gal (60.6 L), P/N 4318059 |
| **MFM** | MOPAR Friction Modifier |
| **PSF** | Power Steering Fluid (see text) |
| **S** | Manifold Heat Control Valve Solvent Or Equivalent |

**Dodge & Plymouth 2WD (Typical)**

# TYPICAL LUBRICATION POINTS

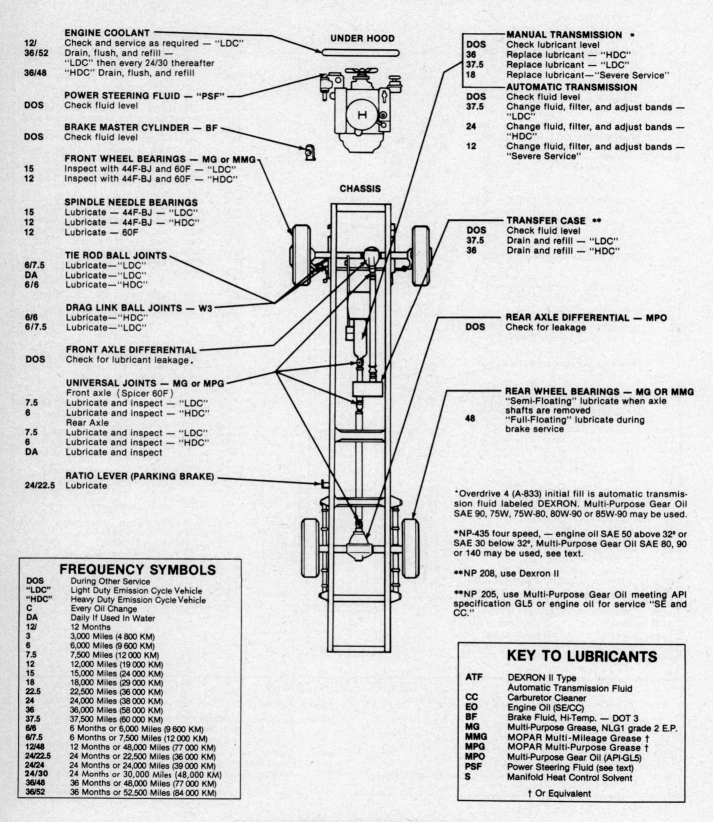

**ENGINE COOLANT**
12/ — Check and service as required — "LDC"
36/52 — Drain, flush, and refill — "LDC" then every 24/30 thereafter
36/48 — "HDC" Drain, flush, and refill

**POWER STEERING FLUID — "PSF"**
DOS — Check fluid level

**BRAKE MASTER CYLINDER — BF**
DOS — Check fluid level

**FRONT WHEEL BEARINGS — MG or MMG**
15 — Inspect with 44F-BJ and 60F — "LDC"
12 — Inspect with 44F-BJ and 60F — "HDC"

**SPINDLE NEEDLE BEARINGS**
15 — Lubricate — 44F-BJ — "LDC"
12 — Lubricate — 44F-BJ — "HDC"
12 — Lubricate — 60F

**TIE ROD BALL JOINTS**
6/7.5 — Lubricate — "LDC"
DA — Lubricate — "LDC"
6/6 — Lubricate — "HDC"

**DRAG LINK BALL JOINTS — W3**
6/6 — Lubricate — "HDC"
6/7.5 — Lubricate — "LDC"

**FRONT AXLE DIFFERENTIAL**
DOS — Check for lubricant leakage.

**UNIVERSAL JOINTS — MG or MPG**
Front axle (Spicer 60F)
7.5 — Lubricate and inspect — "LDC"
6 — Lubricate and inspect — "HDC"
Rear Axle
7.5 — Lubricate and inspect — "LDC"
6 — Lubricate and inspect — "HDC"
DA — Lubricate and inspect

**RATIO LEVER (PARKING BRAKE)**
24/22.5 — Lubricate

UNDER HOOD

CHASSIS

**MANUAL TRANSMISSION  ***
DOS — Check lubricant level
36 — Replace lubricant — "HDC"
37.5 — Replace lubricant — "LDC"
18 — Replace lubricant — "Severe Service"

**AUTOMATIC TRANSMISSION**
DOS — Check fluid level
37.5 — Change fluid, filter, and adjust bands — "LDC"
24 — Change fluid, filter, and adjust bands — "HDC"
12 — Change fluid, filter, and adjust bands — "Severe Service"

**TRANSFER CASE  ****
DOS — Check fluid level
37.5 — Drain and refill — "LDC"
36 — Drain and refill — "HDC"

**REAR AXLE DIFFERENTIAL — MPO**
DOS — Check for leakage

**REAR WHEEL BEARINGS — MG OR MMG**
"Semi-Floating" lubricate when axle shafts are removed
48 — "Full-Floating" lubricate during brake service

*Overdrive 4 (A-833) initial fill is automatic transmission fluid labeled DEXRON. Multi-Purpose Gear Oil SAE 90, 75W, 75W-80, 80W-90 or 85W-90 may be used.

*NP-435 four speed, — engine oil SAE 50 above 32º or SAE 30 below 32º, Multi-Purpose Gear Oil SAE 80, 90 or 140 may be used, see text.

**NP 208, use Dexron II

**NP 205, use Multi-Purpose Gear Oil meeting API specification GL5 or engine oil for service "SE and CC."

## FREQUENCY SYMBOLS

| | |
|---|---|
| DOS | During Other Service |
| "LDC" | Light Duty Emission Cycle Vehicle |
| "HDC" | Heavy Duty Emission Cycle Vehicle |
| C | Every Oil Change |
| DA | Daily If Used In Water |
| 12/ | 12 Months |
| 3 | 3,000 Miles (4 800 KM) |
| 6 | 6,000 Miles (9 600 KM) |
| 7.5 | 7,500 Miles (12 000 KM) |
| 12 | 12,000 Miles (19 000 KM) |
| 15 | 15,000 Miles (24 000 KM) |
| 18 | 18,000 Miles (29 000 KM) |
| 22.5 | 22,500 Miles (36 000 KM) |
| 24 | 24,000 Miles (38 000 KM) |
| 36 | 36,000 Miles (58 000 KM) |
| 37.5 | 37,500 Miles (60 000 KM) |
| 6/6 | 6 Months or 6,000 Miles (9 600 KM) |
| 6/7.5 | 6 Months or 7,500 Miles (12 000 KM) |
| 12/48 | 12 Months or 48,000 Miles (77 000 KM) |
| 24/22.5 | 24 Months or 22,500 Miles (36 000 KM) |
| 24/24 | 24 Months or 24,000 Miles (39 000 KM) |
| 24/30 | 24 Months or 30,000 Miles (48,000 KM) |
| 36/48 | 36 Months or 48,000 Miles (77 000 KM) |
| 36/52 | 36 Months or 52,500 Miles (84 000 KM) |

## KEY TO LUBRICANTS

| | |
|---|---|
| ATF | DEXRON II Type Automatic Transmission Fluid |
| CC | Carburetor Cleaner |
| EO | Engine Oil (SE/CC) |
| BF | Brake Fluid, Hi-Temp. — DOT 3 |
| MG | Multi-Purpose Grease, NLG1 grade 2 E.P. |
| MMG | MOPAR Multi-Mileage Grease † |
| MPG | MOPAR Multi-Purpose Grease † |
| MPO | Multi-Purpose Gear Oil (API-GL5) |
| PSF | Power Steering Fluid (see text) |
| S | Manifold Heat Control Solvent |

† Or Equivalent

**Dodge & Plymouth 4WD (Typical)**

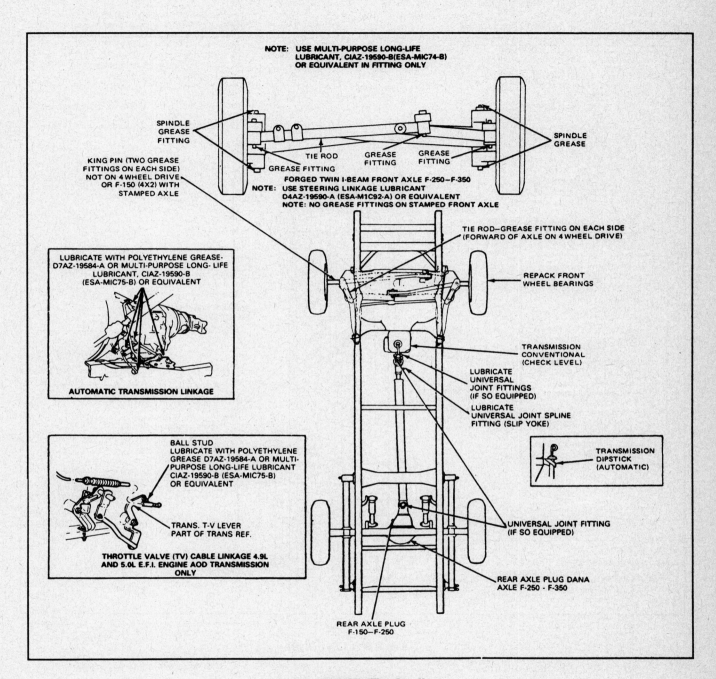

NOTE: USE MULTI-PURPOSE LONG-LIFE LUBRICANT, C1AZ-19590-B(ESA-MIC74-B) OR EQUIVALENT IN FITTING ONLY

SPINDLE GREASE FITTING

SPINDLE GREASE

KING PIN (TWO GREASE FITTINGS ON EACH SIDE) NOT ON 4 WHEEL DRIVE OR F-150 (4X2) WITH STAMPED AXLE

TIE ROD

GREASE FITTING

GREASE FITTING

GREASE FITTING

FORGED TWIN I-BEAM FRONT AXLE F-250—F-350
NOTE: USE STEERING LINKAGE LUBRICANT D4AZ-19590-A (ESA-M1C92-A) OR EQUIVALENT
NOTE: NO GREASE FITTINGS ON STAMPED FRONT AXLE

TIE ROD—GREASE FITTING ON EACH SIDE (FORWARD OF AXLE ON 4 WHEEL DRIVE)

REPACK FRONT WHEEL BEARINGS

LUBRICATE WITH POLYETHYLENE GREASE-D7AZ-19584-A OR MULTI-PURPOSE LONG- LIFE LUBRICANT, C1AZ-19590-B (ESA-MIC75-B) OR EQUIVALENT

AUTOMATIC TRANSMISSION LINKAGE

TRANSMISSION CONVENTIONAL (CHECK LEVEL)

LUBRICATE UNIVERSAL JOINT FITTINGS (IF SO EQUIPPED)

LUBRICATE UNIVERSAL JOINT SPLINE FITTING (SLIP YOKE)

TRANSMISSION DIPSTICK (AUTOMATIC)

BALL STUD LUBRICATE WITH POLYETHYLENE GREASE D7AZ-19584-A OR MULTI-PURPOSE LONG-LIFE LUBRICANT C1AZ-19590-B (ESA-MIC75-B) OR EQUIVALENT

TRANS. T-V LEVER PART OF TRANS REF.

THROTTLE VALVE (TV) CABLE LINKAGE 4.9L AND 5.0L E.F.I. ENGINE AOD TRANSMISSION ONLY

UNIVERSAL JOINT FITTING (IF SO EQUIPPED)

REAR AXLE PLUG DANA AXLE F-250 - F-350

REAR AXLE PLUG F-150—F-250

**Ford 2WD (Typical)**

# TYPICAL LUBRICATION POINTS

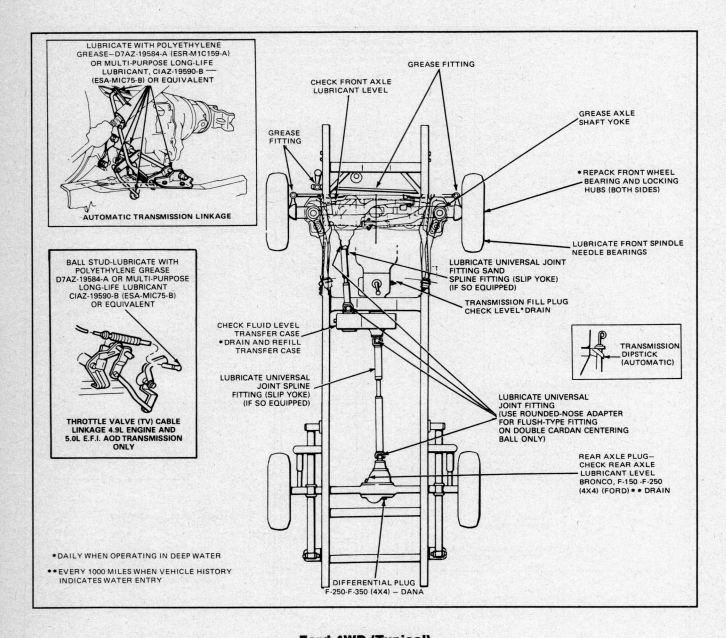

LUBRICATE WITH POLYETHYLENE GREASE—D7AZ-19584-A (ESR-M1C159-A) OR MULTI-PURPOSE LONG-LIFE LUBRICANT, CIAZ-19590-B (ESA-MIC75-B) OR EQUIVALENT

AUTOMATIC TRANSMISSION LINKAGE

BALL STUD-LUBRICATE WITH POLYETHYLENE GREASE D7AZ-19584-A OR MULTI-PURPOSE LONG-LIFE LUBRICANT CIAZ-19590-B (ESA-MIC75-B) OR EQUIVALENT

THROTTLE VALVE (TV) CABLE LINKAGE 4.9L ENGINE AND 5.0L E.F.I. AOD TRANSMISSION ONLY

GREASE FITTING

CHECK FRONT AXLE LUBRICANT LEVEL

GREASE FITTING

GREASE AXLE SHAFT YOKE

*REPACK FRONT WHEEL BEARING AND LOCKING HUBS (BOTH SIDES)

LUBRICATE FRONT SPINDLE NEEDLE BEARINGS

LUBRICATE UNIVERSAL JOINT FITTING SAND SPLINE FITTING (SLIP YOKE) (IF SO EQUIPPED)

TRANSMISSION FILL PLUG CHECK LEVEL*DRAIN

CHECK FLUID LEVEL TRANSFER CASE *DRAIN AND REFILL TRANSFER CASE

LUBRICATE UNIVERSAL JOINT SPLINE FITTING (SLIP YOKE) (IF SO EQUIPPED)

TRANSMISSION DIPSTICK (AUTOMATIC)

LUBRICATE UNIVERSAL JOINT FITTING (USE ROUNDED-NOSE ADAPTER FOR FLUSH-TYPE FITTING ON DOUBLE CARDAN CENTERING BALL ONLY)

REAR AXLE PLUG— CHECK REAR AXLE LUBRICANT LEVEL BRONCO, F-150 -F-250 (4X4) (FORD) ** DRAIN

*DAILY WHEN OPERATING IN DEEP WATER

**EVERY 1000 MILES WHEN VEHICLE HISTORY INDICATES WATER ENTRY

DIFFERENTIAL PLUG F-250-F-350 (4X4) — DANA

**Ford 4WD (Typical)**

## CONVENTIONAL AND FORWARD CONTROL MODELS

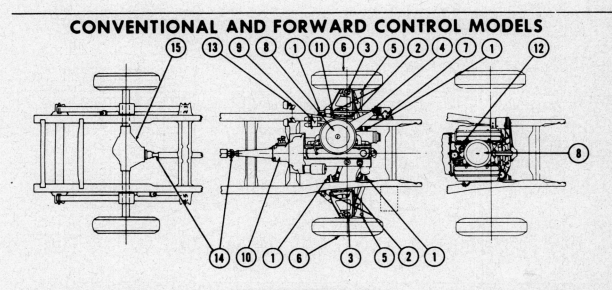

### LUBRICATION POINTS

| | | | | | |
|---|---|---|---|---|---|
| 1 | Lower Control Arms | 6 | Wheel Bearings | 11 | Throttle Bell Crank — L-6 |
| 2 | Upper Control Arms | 7 | Steering Gear | 12 | Carburetor Linkage — V-8 |
| 3 | Upper and Lower Control Arm Ball Joints | 8 | Air Cleaner — Element | 13 | Brake and Clutch Pedal Springs |
| 4 | Intermediate Steering Shaft (PA10) | 9 | Master Cylinder | 14 | Universal Joints |
| 5 | Tie Rod Ends | 10 | Transmission — Manual — Automatic | 15 | Rear Axle |

**Chevrolet & GMC 2WD (Typical)**

## FOUR WHEEL DRIVE MODELS

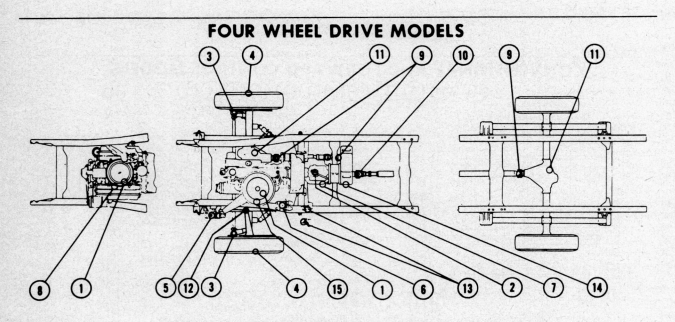

### LUBRICATION POINTS

| | | | | | | | |
|---|---|---|---|---|---|---|---|
| 1 | Air Cleaner | 6 | Master Cylinder | 11 | Front and Rear Axle |
| 2 | Control Linkage Points | 7 | Transmission — Manual | 12 | Drag Link |
| 3 | Tie Rod Ends | | — Automatic | 13 | Brake and Clutch |
| 4 | Wheel Bearings | 8 | Carburetor Linkage — V-8 | | Pedal Springs |
| 5 | Steering Gear | 9 | Universal Joints | 14 | Transfer Case |
| | | 10 | Propeller Shaft Slip Joints | 15 | Throttle Bell Crank — L-6 |

**Chevrolet & GMC 4WD (Typical)**

# CHRYSLER MOTORS/JEEP

# CHRYSLER MOTORS/JEEP

**NOTE:** Refer to the rear of this manual for vehicle manufacturers' special service tool suppliers.

# SPECIFICATIONS

## GENERAL ENGINE SPECIFICATIONS

| Year | Engine Code | Engine Model | Fuel System | Bore & Stroke | Comp. Ratio | Horsepower @ RPM | Torque Ft. Lbs. @ RPM | Normal Oil Pressure Lbs. |
|---|---|---|---|---|---|---|---|---|
| 1980 | 225 | 6-225/3.7L ① | 1 Bore | 3.40 x 4.125 | 8.4 | 95 @ 3600 | 170 @ 1600 | 30-80 |
| | 225 | 6-225/3.7L ③ ⑤ | 1 Bore | 3.40 x 4.125 | 8.4 | 90 @ 3600 | 150 @ 2000 | 30-80 |
| | 318 | V8-318/5.2L ① | 2 Bore | 3.91 x 3.31 | 8.7 | 135 @ 4000 | 240 @ 2000 | 30-80 |
| | 318 | V8-318/5.2L ① | 2 Bore | 3.91 x 3.31 | 8.7 | 140 @ 4000 | 240 @ 4000 | 30-80 |
| | 318 | V8-318/5.2L ③ | 4 Bore | 3.91 x 3.31 | 8.7 | 160 @ 4000 | 245 @ 2000 | 30-80 |
| | 318 | V8-318/5.2L ② ⑤ | 4 Bore | 3.91 x 3.31 | 8.0 | 155 @ 4000 | 240 @ 2000 | 30-80 |
| | 360-1 | V8-360/5.9L ① | 4 Bore | 4.00 x 3.58 | 8.6 | 170 @ 4000 | 270 @ 2000 | 30-80 |
| | 360-1 | V8-360/5.9L ③ | 4 Bore | 4.00 x 3.58 | 8.6 | 170 @ 4000 | 270 @ 2000 | 30-80 |
| | 360-1 | V8-360/5.9L ① | 4 Bore | 4.00 x 3.58 | 8.6 | 205 @ 4000 | 295 @ 3200 | 30-80 |
| | 360-1 | V8-360/5.9L ① ③ | 4 Bore | 4.00 x 3.58 | 8.6 | 175 @ 3600 | 260 @ 2800 | 30-80 |
| | 360-1 | V8-360/5.9L ② | 4 Bore | 4.00 x 3.58 | 8.2 | 180 @ 3600 | 270 @ 2000 | 30-80 |
| | 360-3 | V8-360/5.9L ② | 4 Bore | 4.00 x 3.58 | 8.0 | 180 @ 4000 | 260 @ 2400 | 30-80 |
| | 360-3 | V8-360/5.9L ② | 4 Bore | 4.00 x 3.58 | 8.0 | 210 @ 4000 | 285 @ 3200 | 30-80 |
| | 360-3 | V8-360/5.9L ② ⑤ | 4 Bore | 4.00 x 3.58 | 8.0 | 175 @ 3600 | 260 @ 2800 | 30-80 |
| | 360-3 | V8-360/5.9L ② ⑤ | 4 Bore | 4.00 x 3.58 | 8.0 | 200 @ 4000 | 280 @ 3200 | 30-80 |
| | 446 ⑥ | V8-446/7.3L ② | 4 Bore | 4.125 x 4.18 | 8.0 | 230 @ 3600 | 360 @ 2800 | 15-50 |
| 1981-82 | 225 | 6-225/3.7L ① ④ | 1 Bore | 3.40 x 4.125 | 8.4 | 95 @ 3600 | 170 @ 1600 | 30-70 |
| | 225 | 6-225/3.7L ③ ⑤ | 1 Bore | 3.40 x 4.125 | 8.4 | 90 @ 3600 | 165 @ 1200 | 30-70 |
| | 318 | V8-318/5.2L ① ④ | 2 Bore | 3.91 x 3.31 | 8.6 | 140 @ 3600 | 240 @ 2400 | 30-80 |
| | 318 | V8-318/5.2L ① ④ | 2 Bore | 3.91 x 3.31 | 8.6 | 135 @ 4000 | 240 @ 2000 | 30-80 |
| | 318 | V8-318/5.2L ① ④ | 4 Bore | 3.91 x 3.31 | 8.6 | 170 @ 4000 | 245 @ 2000 | 30-80 |
| | 318 | V8-318/5.2L ② | 4 Bore | 3.91 x 3.31 | 8.6 | 160 @ 4000 | 220 @ 3200 | 30-80 |
| | 318 | V8-318/5.2L ③ ⑤ | 4 Bore | 3.91 x 3.31 | 8.6 | 160 @ 4000 | 245 @ 2000 | 30-80 |
| | 360 | V8-360/5.9L ① ④ | 4 Bore | 4.00 x 3.58 | 8.5 | 175 @ 4000 | 260 @ 2000 | 30-80 |
| | 360 | V8-360/5.9L ① ⑤ | 4 Bore | 4.00 x 3.58 | 8.5 | 180 @ 4000 | 260 @ 2000 | 30-80 |
| | 360 | V8-360/5.9L ② ⑤ | 4 Bore | 4.00 x 3.58 | 8.5 | 170 @ 4000 | 265 @ 2400 | 30-80 |
| | 360 | V8-360/5.9L ② ④ | 4 Bore | 4.00 x 3.58 | 8.5 | 180 @ 3600 | 270 @ 2000 | 30-80 |
| 1983 | 225 | 6-225/3.7L ① | 1 Bore | 3.40 x 4.125 | 8.4 | 95 @ 3600 | 170 @ 1200 | 30-70 |
| | 225 | 6-225/3.7L ① | 2 Bore | 3.40 x 4.125 | 8.4 | 100 @ 3600 | 175 @ 1600 | 30-70 |
| | 225 | 6-225/3.7L ③ ⑤ | 1 Bore | 3.40 x 4.125 | 8.4 | 84 @ 3600 | 162 @ 1600 | 30-70 |
| | 318 | V8-318/5.2L ① | 2 Bore | 3.91 x 3.31 | 8.6 | 150 @ 4400 | 255 @ 2000 | 30-80 |
| | 318 | V8-318/5.2L ③ ⑤ ⑦ | 2 Bore | 3.91 x 3.31 | 8.6 | 143 @ 3600 | 253 @ 1600 | 30-80 |
| | 318 | V8-318/5.2L ① ⑤ ⑦ | 2 Bore | 3.91 x 3.31 | 8.6 | 143 @ 4000 | 250 @ 1600 | 30-80 |
| | 318 | V8-318/5.2L ① | 4 Bore | 3.91 x 3.31 | 8.6 | 167 @ 4000 | 245 @ 2000 | 30-80 |
| | 318 | V8-318/5.2L ② | 4 Bore | 3.91 x 3.31 | 8.6 | 158 @ 4000 | 240 @ 4000 | 30-80 |
| | 360 | V8-360/5.9L ② | 4 Bore | 4.00 x 3.58 | 8.5 | 190 @ 4000 | 265 @ 3200 | 30-80 |
| | 360 | V8-360/5.9L ② ⑤ | 4 Bore | 4.00 x 3.58 | 8.5 | 169 @ 4000 | 265 @ 3200 | 30-80 |
| 1984 | 225 | 6-225/3.7L ① ④ | 1 Bore | 3.40 x 4.125 | 8.4 | 95 @ 3600 | 170 @ 1600 | 30-70 |
| | 225 | 6-225/3.7L ③ ⑤ | 1 Bore | 3.40 x 4.125 | 8.4 | 85 @ 3600 | 170 @ 1600 | 30-70 |
| | 318 | V8-318/5.2L ③ ⑤ ⑦ | 2 Bore | 3.91 x 3.31 | 8.6 | 135 @ 4000 | 240 @ 2000 | 30-80 |
| | 318 | V8-318/5.2L ① ④ | 2 Bore | 3.91 x 3.31 | 8.6 | 150 @ 4000 | 250 @ 1600 | 30-80 |
| | 360 | V8-360/5.9L ① ④ | 4 Bore | 4.0 x 3.58 | 8.5 | 175 @ 4000 | 280 @ 2000 | 30-80 |
| | 360 | V8-360/5.9L ② ⑤ | 4 Bore | 4.0 x 3.58 | 8.5 | 175 @ 4000 | 225 @ 1600 | 30-80 |
| | 360 | V8-360/5.9L ② ④ | 4 Bore | 4.0 x 3.58 | 8.5 | 180 @ 3600 | 270 @ 2000 | 30-80 |

## GENERAL ENGINE SPECIFICATIONS-Continued

| Year | Engine Code | Engine Model | Fuel System | Bore & Stroke | Comp. Ratio | Horsepower @ RPM | Torque Ft. Lbs. @ RPM | Normal Oil Pressure Lbs. |
|---|---|---|---|---|---|---|---|---|
| 1985 | 225 | 6-225/3.7L ① ④ | 1 Bore | 3.40 x 4.125 | 8.4 | 90 @ 3600 | 165 @ 1600 | 30-70 |
| | 225 | 6-225/3.7L ③ ⑤ | 1 Bore | 3.40 x 4.125 | 8.4 | 90 @ 3600 | 160 @ 1600 | 30-70 |
| | 318 | V8-318/5.2L ① ④ | 2 Bore | 3.91 x 3.31 | 9.0 | 145 @ 4000 | 255 @ 2000 | 30-80 |
| | 318 | V8-318/5.2L ③ ⑤ | 2 Bore | 3.91 x 3.31 | 9.0 | 145 @ 3600 | 250 @ 1600 | 30-80 |
| | 360 | V8-360/5.9L ① ④ | 4 Bore | 4.0 x 3.58 | 8.5 | 175 @ 4000 | 280 @ 2000 | 30-80 |
| | 360 | V8-360/5.9L ② ④ | 4 Bore | 4.0 x 3.58 | 8.5 | 180 @ 3600 | 270 @ 2000 | 30-80 |
| | 360 | V8-360/5.9L ② ⑤ | 4 Bore | 4.0 x 3.58 | 8.5 | 175 @ 4000 | 255 @ 1600 | 30-80 |
| 1986 | 225 | 6-225/3.7L | 1 Bore | 3.40 x 4.125 | 8.4 | 95 @ 3600 | 170 @ 2000 | 25-70 |
| | 318 | V8-318/5.2L ④ | 2 Bore | 3.91 x 3.31 | 9.0 | 145 @ 3600 | 260 @ 2000 | 30-80 |
| | 318 | V8-318/5.2L ⑤ | 2 Bore | 3.91 x 3.31 | 9.0 | 145 @ 3600 | 250 @ 2000 | 30-80 |
| | 360 | V8-360/5.9L ① ④ | 4 Bore | 4.0 x 3.58 | 8.5 | 180 @ 4000 | 280 @ 1600 | 30-80 |
| | 360 | V8-360/5.9L ② ④ | 4 Bore | 4.0 x 3.58 | 8.5 | 170 @ 3600 | 260 @ 2000 | 30-80 |
| | 360 | V8-360/5.9L ② ⑤ | 4 Bore | 4.0 x 3.58 | 8.5 | 170 @ 4000 | 250 @ 1600 | 30-80 |
| 1987 | 225 | 6-225/3.7L | 1 Bore | 3.40 x 4.125 | 8.4 | 90 @ 3600 | — | 25-70 |
| | 318 | V8-318/5.2L | 2 Bore | 3.91 x 3.31 | 9.0 | 147 @ 3600 | — | 30-80 |
| | 360 | V8-360/5.9L | 4 Bore | 4.0 x 3.58 | 8.5 | 175 @ 4000 | — | 30-80 |
| 1988 | 238 | V6-238/3.9L | E.F.I. ⑧ | 3.91 x 3.31 | 9.0 | 125 @ 4000 | 195 @ 2000 | 30-80 |
| | 318 | V8-318/5.2L | E.F.I. ⑧ | 3.91 x 3.31 | 9.0 | 147 @ 3600 | — | 30-80 |
| | 360 | V8-360/5.9L | 4 Bore | 4.0 x 3.58 | 8.5 | 175 @ 4000 | — | 30-80 |
| 1989 | 239 | V6-239/3.9L | E.F.I. ⑧ | 3.91 x 3.31 | 9.0 | 125 @ 4000 | 195 @ 2000 | 30-80 |
| | 318 | V8-318/5.2L | E.F.I. ⑧ | 3.91 x 3.31 | 9.2 | 170 @ 4000 | 260 @ 2000 | 30-80 |
| | 360 | V8-360/5.9L ① | E.F.I. | 4.0 x 3.58 | 8.1 | 185 @ 4000 | 283 @ 1600 | 30-80 |
| | 360 | V8-360/5.9L ② | E.F.I. | 4.0 x 3.58 | 7.7 | 203 @ 4000 | 285 @ 1600 | 30-80 |
| | 360 | 6-360/5.9L | ⑨ | 4.0 x 4.7 | 17.5 | — | — | 30-70 |

①—Light duty vehicles.　④—Exc. Calif.　⑦—High alt.
②—Heavy duty vehicles.　⑤—Calif.　⑧—Electronic Fuel Injection.
③—Medium duty vehicles.　⑥—Motor home.　⑨—Turbo Diesel.

## ENGINE TIGHTENING SPECIFICATIONS*

*Torque specifications are for clean and lightly lubricated threads only. Dry or dirty threads produce increased friction which prevents accurate measurement of tightness.

| Year | Engine | Spark Plugs Ft. Lbs. | Cylinder Head Bolts Ft. Lbs. | Intake Manifold Ft. Lbs. | Exhaust Manifold Ft. Lbs. | Rocker Arm Shaft Bracket Ft. Lbs. | Rocker Arm Cover In. Lbs. | Connecting Rod Cap Bolts Ft. Lbs. | Main Bearing Cap Bolts Ft. Lbs. | Flywheel To Crankshaft Ft. Lbs. | Vibration Damper To Pulley Ft. Lbs. |
|---|---|---|---|---|---|---|---|---|---|---|---|
| 1980 | 6-225 | 10 | 70 | ⑤ | 120① | 25 | 40 | 45 | 85 | 55 | ② |
| | V8-318, V8-360 | 30 | ④ | 40 | ③ | 200① | 40 | 45 | 85 | 55 | 100 |
| | V8-446 | 15 | 105 | — | 18 | 20 | 72 | 41 | 95 | — | 90 |
| 1981-85 | 6-225 | 10 | 70 | ⑤ | 120① | 25 | 80 | 45 | 85 | 55 | ② |
| | V8-318, V8-360 | 30 | ④ | 40 | ③ | 200① | 80 | 45 | 85 | 55 | 100 |
| 1986-87 | 6-225 | 10 | 70 | ⑥ | 120① | 25 | 95 | 45 | 85 | 55 | ② |
| | V8-318, V8-360 | 30 | 105 | 45 | ③ | 200① | 80 | 45 | 85 | 55 | 100 |
| 1988 | V6-238 | 30 | 105 | 45 | ③ | 200① | ⑦ | 45 | 85 | 55 | 100 |
| | V8-318, V8-360 | 30 | 105 | 45 | ③ | 200① | 80 | 45 | 85 | 55 | 100 |
| 1989 | V6-238 | | 105 | 45 | ③ | 200① | ⑦ | 45 | 85 | 55 | 100 |
| | V8-318, V8-360 | 30 | 105 | 45 | ③ | 200① | 80 | 45 | 85 | 55 | 100 |
| | 6-360 | — | 93 | 45 | ③ | — | 18 | 73 | 129 | 101 | 92 |

①—Inch Lbs.
②—Press fit.
③—Screw, 20 ft. lbs.; Nut, 15 ft. lbs.
④—1981-84 V8-318, 95 ft. lbs.; 1981-84 V8-360, 105 ft. lbs.; All 1985-87, 105 ft. lbs.
⑤—Intake to exhaust manifold stud nut, 240 inch lbs. for Vans, Wagons & Front Sections or 360 inch lbs. on all others; Intake to exhaust manifold bolt, 200 inch lbs. for Vans, Wagons & Front Sections or 240 inch lbs. on
all others.
⑥—Intake to exhaust manifold stud nut, 300 inch lbs.; Intake to exhaust manifold bolt, 260 inch lbs.
⑦—Stud, 115 inch lbs.; Nut, 80 inch lbs.

# DODGE & PLYMOUTH FULL SIZE TRUCKS & VANS

## ALTERNATOR & REGULATOR SPECIFICATIONS

| Year | I.D. Tag Color | Ground Polarity | Field Coil Draw Amperes ① | Current Output | | | Operating Voltage | | |
|------|---------------|-----------------|---------------------------|----------------|--|--|-------------------|--|--|
| | | | | Engine RPM | Amperes ② | Volts | Engine RPM | Volts | Voltage @ 140°F ③ |
| 1980-83 | Violet 41 Amp | Neg. | 4.5-6.5 | 1250 | 40 | 15 | 1250 | 15 | 13.3-13.9 |
| | Yellow 60 Amp | Neg. | 4.5-6.5 | 1250 | 57 | 15 | 1250 | 15 | 13.3-13.9 |
| | Yellow 117 Amp | Neg. | 4.5-6.5 | 900 | 72 | 13 | 900 | 13 | 13.3-13.9 |
| 1984 | Violet 41 Amp | Neg. | 2.5-5.0 | 1250 | 32 | 15 | 1250 | 15 | 13.0-13.7 |
| | Yellow 60 Amp | Neg. | 2.5-5.0 | 1250 | 47 | 15 | 1250 | 15 | 13.0-13.7 |
| | Brown 78 Amp | Neg. | 2.5-5.0 | 1250 | 57 | 15 | 1250 | 15 | 13.0-13.7 |
| | Yellow 114 Amp | Neg. | 2.5-5.0 | 900 | 97 | 13 | 900 | 13 | 13.0-13.7 |
| 1985 | Violet 41 Amp | Neg. | 2.5-5.0 | 1250 | 32 | 15 | 1250 | 15 | 13.3-13.9 |
| | Yellow 60 Amp | Neg. | 2.5-5.0 | 1250 | 47 | 15 | 1250 | 15 | 13.3-13.9 |
| | Brown 78 Amp | Neg. | 2.5-5.0 | 1250 | 57 | 15 | 1250 | 15 | 13.3-13.9 |
| | Yellow 114 Amp | Neg. | 2.5-5.0 | 900 | 97 | 13 | 900 | 13 | 13.3-13.9 |
| 1986 | 60 Amp | Neg. | 2.5-5.0 | 1250 | 47 | 15 | 1250 | 15 | 13.3-13.9 |
| | 70 Amp | Neg. | 2.5-5.0 | 1250 | 57 | 15 | 1250 | 15 | 13.3-13.9 |
| | 114 Amp | Neg. | 2.5-5.0 | 900 | ④ | 13 | 900 | 13 | 13.3-13.9 |
| 1987 | 78 Amp | Neg. | 2.5-5.0 | 1250 | 56 | 15 | 1250 | 15 | 13.3-13.9 |
| | 50/120 Amp | Neg. | 2.5-5.0 | 1250 | 98 | 15 | 1250 | 15 | 13.3-13.9 |
| | 114 Amp | Neg. | 2.5-5.0 | 900 | 92 | 13 | 900 | 13 | 13.3-13.9 |
| 1988 | 75 Amp | Neg. | 2.5-5.0 | 1250 | 68 | 15 | — | — | — |
| | 90 Amp | Neg. | 2.5-5.0 | 1250 | 87 | 15 | 1250 | 15 | 13.0-13.9 |
| | 90 Amp | Neg. | 2.5-5.0 | 1250 | 87 | 15 | — | — | — |
| | 120 Amp | Neg. | 2.5-5.0 | 1250 | 98 | 15 | — | — | — |
| 1989 | 75 Amp | Neg. | 2.5-5.0 | 1250 | 68 | 15 | — | — | — |
| | 90 Amp | Neg. | 2.5-5.0 | 1250 | 87 | 15 | — | — | — |
| | 120 Amp | Neg. | 2.5-5.0 | 1250 | 98 | 15 | — | — | — |

①—Current draw at 12 volts while turning rotor shaft by hand.
②—If output is low, stator or rectifier is shorted.
③—Temperature is checked with a thermometer ¼ inch from voltage regulator.
④—Vans & Wagons, 92 amps; All others, 97 amps.

## STARTING MOTOR SPECIFICATIONS

| Model Number ① | Year | Brush Spring Tension, Oz. | No Load Test | | | Torque Test | |
|----------------|------|---------------------------|--------------|--|--|-------------|--|
| | | | Amperes | Volts | RPM | Amperes | Volts |
| 4111855 | 1980-85 | 32-36 | 90 | 11 | 3700 | 475-550 | 4 |
| 4111855 | 1986 | 32-36 | 100 | 11 | 5700 | 475-550 | 4 |
| 4111860 | 1984-85 | 32-36 | 90 | 11 | 5700 | 475-550 | 4 |
| 4111860 | 1986 | 32-36 | 100 | 11 | 5700 | 475-550 | 4 |
| 4111860 | 1987 | 32-36 | 90 | 11 | 5700 | 475-550 | 4 |
| 4379144 | 1988 | — | 82 | 11 | 3625 | — | — |
| 4379143 | 1989 | — | 82 | 11 | 3625 | — | — |
| 4379160 | 1988-89 | — | 82 | 11 | 3625 | — | — |

①—Stamped on plate riveted to housing.

## BRAKE SPECIFICATIONS

| Year | Model | Rear Drum I.D. | Wheel Cyl. Bore | | Disc Brake Rotor | | | | | Master Cyl. I.D. | |
|---|---|---|---|---|---|---|---|---|---|---|---|
| | | | Front Disc | Rear Drum | Nominal Thickness | Minimum Thickness | Thickness Variation (Parallelism) | Runout (TIR) | Finish (Microinch) | Manual Brakes | Power Brakes |
| **VANS, WAGONS & FRONT SECTIONS** | | | | | | | | | | | |
| 1980 | 100 | 10 | 3.10 | .938 | 1.250 | 1.180 | .0005 | .004 | 15-80 | 1.125 | 1.125 |
| | 200 | 10 | 3.10 | .938 | 1.250 | 1.180 | .0005 | .004 | 15-80 | 1.125 | 1.125 |
| | 300② | 12 | 3.10 | .875 | 1.250 | 1.180 | .0005 | .004 | 15-80 | 1.125 | 1.125 |
| | 300, 400③ | 12 | 3.10 | 1.00 | 1.190 | 1.125 | .0005 | .004 | 15-80 | 1.125 | 1.125 |
| | 400① | 13 | 3.10 | 1.125 | 1.190 | 1.125 | .0005 | .004 | 15-80 | 1.31 | 1.31 |
| 1981 | B-150 | 10 | 3.10 | .938 | 1.250 | 1.180 | .0005 | .004 | 15-80 | 1.125 | 1.125 |
| | B-250 | 10 | 3.10 | .938 | 1.250 | 1.180 | .0005 | .004 | 15-80 | 1.125 | 1.125 |
| | B-350② | 12 | 3.10 | 1.00 | 1.250 | 1.180 | .0005 | .004 | 15-80 | 1.125 | 1.125 |
| | B-350③ | 12 | 3.10 | 1.06 | 1.190 | 1.125 | .0005 | .004 | 15-80 | 1.125 | 1.125 |
| 1982 | B-150 | 10 | 3.10 | .938 | 1.250 | 1.180 | .0005 | .004 | 15-80 | 1.125 | 1.125 |
| | B-250 | 10 | 3.10 | .938 | 1.250 | 1.180 | .0005 | .004 | 15-80 | 1.125 | 1.125 |
| | B-350② | 12 | 3.10 | 1.00 | 1.250 | 1.180 | .0005 | .004 | 15-80 | 1.125 | 1.125 |
| | B-350③ | 12 | 3.10 | 1.06 | 1.190 | 1.125 | .0005 | .004 | 15-80 | 1.125 | 1.125 |
| 1983 | B-150 | 10 | 3.10 | .938 | 1.250 | 1.180 | .0005 | .004 | 15-80 | 1.125 | 1.125 |
| | B-250 | 10 | 3.10 | .938 | 1.250 | 1.180 | .0005 | .004 | 15-80 | 1.125 | 1.125 |
| | B-350② | 12 | 3.10 | 1.00 | 1.250 | 1.180 | .0005 | .004 | 15-80 | 1.125 | 1.125 |
| | B-350③ | 12 | 3.10 | 1.06 | 1.190 | 1.125 | .0005 | .004 | 15-80 | 1.125 | 1.125 |
| 1984 | B-150 | 11 | 3.10 | .938 | 1.250 | 1.180 | .0005 | .004 | 15-80 | 1.125 | 1.125 |
| | B-250 | 11 | 3.10 | .938 | 1.250 | 1.180 | .0005 | .004 | 15-80 | 1.125 | 1.125 |
| | B-350② | 12 | 3.10 | 1.00 | 1.250 | 1.180 | .0005 | .004 | 15-80 | 1.125 | 1.125 |
| | B-350③ | 12 | 3.10 | 1.06 | 1.190 | 1.125 | .0005 | .004 | 15-80 | 1.125 | 1.125 |
| 1985-89 | B-150 | 11 | 3.10 | .938 | 1.250 | 1.180 | .0005 | .004 | 15-80 | 1.125 | 1.125 |
| | B-250 | 11 | 3.10 | .938 | 1.250 | 1.180 | .0005 | .004 | 15-80 | 1.125 | 1.125 |
| | B-350② | 12 | 3.10 | .875 | 1.250 | 1.180 | .0005 | .004 | 15-80 | 1.125 | 1.125 |
| | B-350③ | 12 | 3.10 | 1.00 | 1.190 | 1.125 | .0005 | .004 | 15-80 | 1.125 | 1.125 |
| **RAMCHARGER & TRAIL DUSTER** | | | | | | | | | | | |
| 1980 | ALL④ | 10 | 3.10 | .938 | 1.250 | 1.180 | .0005 | .004 | 15-80 | 1.125 | 1.125 |
| | ALL⑤ | 10 | 3.10 | .938 | 1.250 | 1.180 | .001 | .005 | 15-80 | 1.125 | 1.125 |
| 1981 | ALL④ | 10 | 3.10 | .938 | 1.250 | 1.180 | .0005 | .004 | 15-80 | 1.125 | 1.125 |
| | ALL⑤ | 10 | 3.10 | .938 | 1.250 | 1.180 | .001 | .005 | 15-80 | 1.125 | 1.125 |
| 1982 | ALL④ | 10 | 3.10 | .938 | 1.250 | 1.180 | .0005 | .004 | 15-80 | 1.125 | 1.125 |
| | ALL⑤ | 10 | 3.10 | .938 | 1.250 | 1.180 | .001 | .005 | 15-80 | 1.125 | 1.125 |
| 1983 | ALL④ | 10 | 3.10 | .938 | 1.250 | 1.180 | .0005 | .004 | 15-80 | 1.125 | 1.125 |
| | ALL⑤ | 10 | 3.10 | .938 | 1.250 | 1.180 | .001 | .005 | 15-80 | 1.125 | 1.125 |
| 1984-87 | ALL④ | 11 | 3.10 | .938 | 1.250 | 1.180 | .0005 | .004 | 15-80 | — | 1.125 |
| | ALL⑤ | 11 | 3.10 | .938 | 1.250 | 1.180 | .001 | .005 | 15-80 | — | 1.125 |
| 1988-89 | ALL | 11 | 3.10 | .938 | 1.250 | 1.180 | .001 | .005 | 15-80 | — | 1.125 |
| **CONVENTIONAL CAB** | | | | | | | | | | | |
| 1980 | D-150 | 10 | 3.10 | .938 | 1.250 | 1.180 | .0005 | .004 | 15-80 | 1.125 | 1.125 |
| | W-150 | 10 | 3.10 | .938 | 1.250 | 1.180 | .001 | .005 | 15-80 | 1.125 | 1.125 |
| | D-200 | ⑧ | 3.10 | ⑨ | ⑩ | ⑪ | .001 | .005 | 15-80 | 1.125 | 1.125 |
| | W-200⑥ | 12 | 3.10 | 1.00 | 1.190 | 1.125 | .001 | .005 | 15-80 | 1.125 | 1.125 |
| | W-200⑦ | 12 | 3.38 | 1.00 | 1.190 | 1.125 | .001 | .005 | 15-80 | 1.125 | 1.125 |
| | D-300 | 12 | 3.10 | 1.00 | 1.190 | 1.125 | .001 | .005 | 15-80 | 1.125 | 1.125 |
| | W-300 | 12 | 3.38 | 1.06 | 1.190 | 1.125 | .001 | .005 | 15-80 | 1.125 | 1.125 |
| | D-400 | 12 | 3.10 | 1.06 | 1.190 | 1.125 | .001 | .005 | 15-80 | 1.125 | 1.125 |
| | W-400 | 12 | 3.38 | 1.06 | 1.190 | 1.125 | .001 | .005 | 15-80 | 1.125 | 1.125 |

## BRAKE SPECIFICATIONS —Continued

| Year | Model | Rear Drum I.D. | Wheel Cyl. Bore | | Disc Brake Rotor | | | | | Master Cyl. I.D. | |
|---|---|---|---|---|---|---|---|---|---|---|---|
| | | | Front Disc | Rear Drum | Nominal Thickness | Minimum Thickness | Thickness Variation (Parallelism) | Runout (TIR) | Finish (Microinch) | Manual Brakes | Power Brakes |
| 1981 | D-150 | 10 | 3.10 | .938 | 1.250 | 1.180 | .0005 | .004 | 15-80 | 1.125 | 1.125 |
| | W-150 | 10 | 3.10 | .938 | 1.250 | 1.180 | .001 | .005 | 15-80 | 1.125 | 1.125 |
| | D-250 | 12 | 3.10 | 1.00 | ⑩ | ⑪ | .001 | .005 | 15-80 | 1.125 | 1.125 |
| | W-250⑥ | 12 | 3.10 | 1.00 | 1.190 | 1.125 | .001 | .005 | 15-80 | 1.125 | 1.125 |
| | W-250⑦ | 12 | 3.38 | 1.00 | 1.190 | 1.125 | .001 | .005 | 15-80 | 1.125 | 1.125 |
| | D-350 | 12 | 3.10 | 1.00 | 1.190 | 1.125 | .001 | .005 | 15-80 | 1.125 | 1.125 |
| | W-350 | 12 | 3.38 | 1.06 | 1.190 | 1.125 | .001 | .005 | 15-80 | 1.125 | 1.125 |
| | D-450 | 12 | 3.10 | 1.00 | 1.190 | 1.125 | .001 | .005 | 15-80 | 1.125 | 1.125 |
| | W-450 | 12 | 3.38 | 1.06 | 1.190 | 1.125 | .001 | .005 | 15-80 | 1.125 | 1.125 |
| 1982 | D-150 | 10 | 3.10 | .938 | 1.250 | 1.180 | .0005 | .004 | 15-80 | 1.125 | 1.125 |
| | W-150 | 10 | 3.10 | .938 | 1.250 | 1.180 | .001 | .005 | 15-80 | 1.125 | 1.125 |
| | D-250 | 12 | 3.10 | 1.00 | ⑩ | ⑪ | .001 | .005 | 15-80 | 1.125 | 1.125 |
| | W-250⑥ | 12 | 3.10 | 1.00 | 1.190 | 1.125 | .001 | .005 | 15-80 | 1.125 | 1.125 |
| | W-250⑦ | 12 | 3.38 | 1.00 | 1.190 | 1.125 | .001 | .005 | 15-80 | 1.125 | 1.125 |
| | D-350 | 12 | 3.10 | 1.00 | 1.190 | 1.125 | .001 | .005 | 15-80 | 1.125 | 1.125 |
| | W-350 | 12 | 3.38 | 1.06 | 1.190 | 1.125 | .001 | .005 | 15-80 | 1.125 | 1.125 |
| 1983 | D-150 | 10 | 3.10 | .938 | 1.250 | 1.180 | .0005 | .004 | 15-80 | 1.125 | 1.125 |
| | W-150 | 10 | 3.10 | .938 | 1.250 | 1.180 | .001 | .005 | 15-80 | 1.125 | 1.125 |
| | D-250 | 12 | 3.10 | 1.00 | ⑩ | ⑪ | .001 | .005 | 15-80 | 1.125 | 1.125 |
| | W-250⑥ | 12 | 3.10 | 1.00 | 1.190 | 1.125 | .001 | .005 | 15-80 | 1.125 | 1.125 |
| | W-250⑦ | 12 | 3.38 | 1.00 | 1.190 | 1.125 | .001 | .005 | 15-80 | 1.125 | 1.125 |
| | D-350 | 12 | 3.10 | 1.00 | 1.190 | 1.125 | .001 | .005 | 15-80 | 1.125 | 1.125 |
| | W-350 | 12 | 3.38 | 1.06 | 1.190 | 1.125 | .001 | .005 | 15-80 | 1.125 | 1.125 |
| 1984 | D-100/150 | 11 | 3.10 | .938 | 1.250 | 1.180 | .0005 | .004 | 15-80 | — | 1.125 |
| | W-150 | 11 | 3.10 | .938 | 1.250 | 1.180 | .001 | .005 | 15-80 | — | 1.125 |
| | D-250 | 12 | 3.10 | ⑫ | ⑩ | ⑪ | .001 | .005 | 15-80 | — | 1.125 |
| | W-250⑥ | 12 | 3.10 | 1.00 | 1.190 | 1.125 | .001 | .005 | 15-80 | — | 1.125 |
| | W-250⑦ | 12 | 3.38 | 1.00 | 1.190 | 1.125 | .001 | .005 | 15-80 | — | 1.125 |
| | D-350 | 12 | 3.10 | 1.00 | 1.190 | 1.125 | .001 | .005 | 15-80 | — | 1.125 |
| | W-350 | 12 | 3.38 | 1.06 | 1.190 | 1.125 | .001 | .005 | 15-80 | — | 1.125 |
| 1985-87 | D-100/150 | 11 | 3.10 | .938 | 1.250 | 1.180 | .0005 | .004 | 15-80 | — | 1.125 |
| | W-150 | 11 | 3.10 | .938 | 1.250 | 1.180 | .001 | .005 | 15-80 | — | 1.125 |
| | D-250 | 12 | 3.10 | 1.00 | ⑩ | ⑪ | .001 | .005 | 15-80 | — | 1.125 |
| | W-250⑥ | 12 | 3.10 | 1.00 | 1.190 | 1.125 | .001 | .005 | 15-80 | — | 1.125 |
| | W-250⑦ | 12 | 3.38 | 1.00 | 1.190 | 1.125 | .001 | .005 | 15-80 | — | 1.125 |
| | D-350 | 12 | 3.10 | 1.125 | 1.190 | 1.125 | .001 | .005 | 15-80 | — | 1.125 |
| | W-350 | 12 | 3.38 | 1.125 | 1.190 | 1.125 | .001 | .005 | 15-80 | — | 1.125 |
| 1988-89 | D-100/150 | 11 | 3.10 | .938 | 1.250 | 1.180 | .001 | .005 | 15-80 | — | 1.125 |
| | W-150 | 11 | 3.10 | .938 | 1.250 | 1.180 | .001 | .005 | 15-80 | — | 1.125 |
| | D-250 | 12 | 3.10 | 1.00 | ⑩ | ⑪ | .001 | .005 | 15-80 | — | 1.125 |
| | W-250⑥ | 12 | 3.10 | 1.00 | 1.190 | 1.125 | .001 | .005 | 15-80 | — | 1.125 |
| | W-250⑦ | 12 | 3.38 | 1.00 | 1.190 | 1.125 | .001 | .005 | 15-80 | — | 1.125 |
| | D-350 | 12 | 3.10 | ⑬ | 1.190 | 1.125 | .001 | .005 | 15-80 | — | 1.125 |
| | W-350 | 12 | 3.38 | ⑬ | 1.190 | 1.125 | .001 | .005 | 15-80 | — | 1.125 |

**MOTOR HOME**

| Year | Model | Rear Drum I.D. | Front Disc | Rear Drum | Nominal Thickness | Minimum Thickness | Thickness Variation (Parallelism) | Runout (TIR) | Finish (Microinch) | Manual Brakes | Power Brakes |
|---|---|---|---|---|---|---|---|---|---|---|---|
| 1980 | M-300 | 12 | 2.38 | 1.06 | 1.550 | — | .0008 | .005 | 15-80 | — | 1.25 |
| | M-400 | 12 | 2.38 | 1.06 | 1.550 | — | .0008 | .005 | 15-80 | — | 1.31 |
| | M-500 | 15 | 2.38 | 1.375 | 1.550 | — | .0008 | .005 | 15-80 | — | 1.31 |
| | M-600 | 15 | 2.38 | 1.50 | 1.550 | — | .0008 | .005 | 15-80 | — | 1.31 |

①—Models with 163 inch wheel base.
②—Models with 3600 lb. front axle.
③—Models with 4000 lb. front axle.
④—Models less 4 wheel drive.
⑤—Models with 4 wheel drive.
⑥—Less Spicer 60 front axle.
⑦—With Spicer 60 front axle.
⑧—6200 G.V.W. exc. 165 inch wheel base crew cabs, 12.12 inches; others, 12 inches.
⑨—6200 G.V.W. exc. 165 inch wheel base crew cabs, .875 inch; others, 1.00 inch.
⑩—With 3300 lb. front axle, 1.25 inch; with 4000 lb. front axle, 1.19 inch.

## BRAKE SPECIFICATIONS—Continued

⑪—With 3300 lb. front axle, 1.180 inches; with 4000 lb. front axle, 1.125 inches.
⑫—With Spicer 60 rear axle, 1.00 inch;
with Spicer 60 HD rear axle, 1.125 inches.
⑬—Less Spicer 60 front axle, 1.00 inch;
with Spicer 60 front axle, 1.125 inches.

## WHEEL ALIGNMENT SPECIFICATIONS

| Model | Caster, Deg. | Camber, Deg. | Toe-In, Inch | Kingpin Inclination, Deg. |
|---|---|---|---|---|
| **1980** | | | | |
| AD-100, PD-100 | +½ ② | +¼ | +⅛ | — |
| AW-100, PW-100 ④ | — | — | — | — |
| B-100, B-200, B-300 | +2¼ ⑦ | +½ ⑧ | ⅛ ⑨ | — |
| PB-100, PB-200, PB-300 | +2¼ ⑦ | +½ ⑧ | +⅛ ⑨ | — |
| CB-300, CB-400 | +2¼ | +½ | ⅛ | — |
| MB-300, MB-400 | +2¼ | +½ | ⅛ | — |
| M-300 | — | — | — | — |
| M-400, M-500 | — | — | — | — |
| M-600 | — | — | — | — |
| D-100, D-150, D-200, D-300, D-400 | +½ ② | +¼ | ⅛ | — |
| W-150, W-200 | +3 ① | +1½ | 0 | 8½ |
| W-200, W-300, W-400 ① ④ ⑤ ⑩ | +3 ① | +½ | 0 | 8½ |
| **1981** | | | | |
| AD-150 | +½ | +¼ | ⅛ | — |
| B-150, B-250, B-350 | +2¼ | +½ | ⅛ | — |
| CB-350, CB-450 | +2¼ | +½ | ⅛ | — |
| D-150, D-250, D-350, D-450 | +½ | +¼ | ⅛ | — |
| MB-250, MB-350, MB-450 | +2¼ | +½ | ⅛ | — |
| PB-150, PB-250, PB-350 | +2¼ | +½ | ⅛ | — |
| PD-150 | +½ | +¼ | ⅛ | — |
| W-150, W-250 ⑩ | +3 | +1½ | 0 | 8½ |
| **1982** | | | | |
| AD-150, D-150, D-250, D-350 | +½ | +¼ | ⅛ | — |
| B-150, B-250, B-350 | +2¼ | +½ | ⅛ | — |
| PB-150, PB-250, PB-350 | +2¼ | +½ | ⅛ | — |
| W-150, W-250, W-350 ③ | +3 | +1½ | ⅛ | 8½ |
| W-250, W-350 ⑥ ⑩ | +3 | +½ | ⅛ | 8½ |
| **1983** | | | | |
| AD-150, D-150, D-250, D-350 | +½ | +½ | ⅛ | — |
| B-150, B-250, B-350 | +2¼ | +½ | ⅛ | — |
| PB-150, PB-250, PB-350 | +2¼ | +½ | ⅛ | — |
| W-150, W-250, W-350 | +2 ⑩ | +1 | ¼ | 8½ |
| **1984** | | | | |
| AD-150, D-100/150, D-250, D-350 | +½ ⑩ | +½ | ⅛ | — |
| B-150, B-250, B-350 | +2½ | +⅜ | ⅛ | — |
| W-150, W-250, W-350 | +2 ⑩ | +1 | ¼ | 8½ |
| **1985-86** | | | | |
| AD-150, D-100/150, D-250, D-350 | +½ ⑩ | +½ | ⅕ | — |
| B-150, B-250, B-350 | +2½ | +⅜ | ⅛ | — |
| W-150, W-250, W-350 | +2 ⑩ | +1 | ⅕ | 8½ |
| **1987** | | | | |
| AD-150, D100/150, D-250, D-350 | +½ ⑩ | +½ | ¼ | — |
| B-150, B-250, B-350 | +2½ | +⅜ | ⅛ | — |
| W-150, W-250, W-350 | +2 ⑩ | +1 | ⅕ | 8½ |
| **1988-89** | | | | |
| AD-150, D100/150, D-250, D-350 | +½ ⑩ | +½ | ¼ | — |
| B-150, B-250, B-350 | +2½ | 0 | 0 | — |
| W-150, W-250, W-350 | +2 ⑩ | +1 | ⅕ | 8½ |

## WHEEL ALIGNMENT SPECIFICATIONS-Continued

(1)—No load.
(2)—Loaded.
(3)—Models less 135" W.B. and 149" W.B.
(4)—Four wheel drive.
(5)—4500 lb. axle.
(6)—Models with 135" W.B. and 149" W.B.
(7)—Heavy front axle load applications, +1½.
(8)—Heavy front axle load applications, +⅝.
(9)—Heavy front axle load applications, 0.
(10)—Caster should be checked with vehicle loaded. If vehicle wanders, caster should be increased. If steering effort is very high, especially when cornering, caster should be decreased.

## DRIVE AXLE SPECIFICATIONS

| Year | Application | Ring Gear Size | Carrier Type | Ring Gear & Pinion Backlash | | Pinion Bearing Preload | | | Differential Bearing Preload | | |
|---|---|---|---|---|---|---|---|---|---|---|---|
| | | | | Method | Adjustment | Method | New Bearings Inch Lbs. | Used Bearings Inch Lbs. | Method | New Bearings Inch Lbs. | Used Bearings Inch Lbs. |
| **VANS, WAGONS & FRONT SECTIONS** | | | | | | | | | | | |
| 1980-83 | ALL | 8⅜ | (1) | .006-.008 | (2) | 20-35 | 10-25(3) | (1) | (5) | (5) | |
| | ALL | 9¼ | (1) | .006-.008 | (2) | 20-35 | 10-25(3) | (1) | (5) | (5) | |
| | ALL | 9¾(4) | Shims | .004-.009 | Shims | 10-20 | 10-20 | Shims | .015 | .015 | |
| | ALL | 10½(4) | Shims | .004-.009 | Shims | 10-20 | 10-20 | Shims | .015 | .015 | |
| 1984-85 | ALL | 8⅜ | (1) | .006-.008 | (2) | 20-35 | 10-25(3) | (1) | (5) | (5) | |
| | ALL | 9¼ | (1) | .006-.008 | (2) | 20-35 | 10-25(3) | (1) | (5) | (5) | |
| | ALL | 9¾ | Shims | .004-.009 | Shims | 10-20 | 10-20 | Shims | .015 | .015 | |
| 1986-89 | ALL | 8¾ | (1) | .005-.008 | (2) | 20-35 | 10-25(3) | (1) | (5) | (5) | |
| | ALL | 9¼ | (1) | .005-.008 | (2) | 20-35 | 10-25(3) | (1) | (5) | (5) | |
| | ALL | 9¾(4) | Shims | .004-.009 | Shims | 10-20 | 10-20 | Shims | .015 | .015 | |
| **RAMCHARGER & TRAIL DUSTER** | | | | | | | | | | | |
| 1980-87 | ALL(6) | 8⅜ | (1) | .006-.008 | (2) | 20-35 | 10-25(3) | (1) | (5) | (5) | |
| | ALL(6) | 9¼ | (1) | .006-.008 | (2) | 20-35 | 10-25(3) | (1) | (5) | (5) | |
| | ALL(7) | 8½(4) | Shims | .005-.009 | Shims | 20-40 | 10-20 | Shims | .015 | .015 | |
| 1988-89 | ALL(6) | 8⅜ | (1) | .006-.008 | (2) | 20-35 | (13) | (1) | (5) | (5) | |
| | ALL(6) | 9¼ | (1) | .006-.008 | (2) | 20-35 | (13) | (1) | (5) | (5) | |
| | ALL(7) | 8½(4) | Shims | .005-.009 | Shims | 20-40 | 10-20 | Shims | .015 | .015 | |
| **CONVENTIONAL CAB** | | | | | | | | | | | |
| 1980 | D-150, W-100(6) | 8⅜ | (1) | .006-.008 | (2) | 20-35 | 10-25(3) | (1) | (5) | (5) | |
| | D-150, W-100(6) | 9¼ | (1) | .006-.008 | (2) | 20-35 | 10-25(3) | (1) | (5) | (5) | |
| | D-200, W-200, D-300(6) | 9¾(4) | Shims | .004-.009 | Shims | 10-20 | 10-20 | Shims | .015 | .015 | |
| | D-300, W-300, D-400, W-400 (6) | 10½(4) | Shims | .004-.009 | Shims | 10-20 | 10-20 | Shims | .015 | .015 | |
| | W-150, W-200(7) | 8½(4) | Shims | .005-.009 | Shims | 20-40 | 10-20 | Shims | .015 | .015 | |
| | W-200, W-300, W-400(7) | 9¾(4) | Shims | .004-.009 | Shims | 10-20 | 10-20 | Shims | .015 | .015 | |
| 1981 | D-150, W-150(6) | 8⅜ | (1) | .006-.008 | (2) | 20-35 | 10-25(3) | (1) | (5) | (5) | |
| | D-150, W-150(6) | 9¼ | (1) | .006-.008 | (2) | 20-35 | 10-25(3) | (1) | (5) | (5) | |
| | D-250, W-250, D-350(6) | 9¾(4) | Shims | .004-.009 | Shims | 10-20 | 10-20 | Shims | .015 | .015 | |
| | D-350, W-350, D-450, W-450 (6) | 10½(4) | Shims | .004-.009 | Shims | 10-20 | 10-20 | Shims | .015 | .015 | |
| | W-150, W-250(7) | 8½(4) | Shims | .005-.009 | Shims | 20-40 | 10-20 | Shims | .015 | .015 | |
| | W-250, W-350, W-450(7) | 9¾(4) | Shims | .004-.009 | Shims | 10-20 | 10-20 | Shims | .015 | .015 | |
| 1982-83 | D-150, W-150(6) | 8⅜ | (1) | .006-.008 | (2) | 20-35 | 10-25(3) | (1) | (5) | (5) | |
| | D-150, W-150(6) | 9¼ | (1) | .006-.008 | (2) | 20-35 | 10-25(3) | (1) | (5) | (5) | |
| | D-250, W-250, D-350(6) | 9¾(4) | Shims | .004-.009 | Shims | 10-20 | 10-20 | Shims | .015 | .015 | |
| | D-350, W-350(6) | 10½(4) | Shims | .004-.009 | Shims | 10-20 | 10-20 | Shims | .015 | .015 | |
| | (7)(8) | 8½(4) | Shims | .005-.009 | Shims | 20-40 | 10-20 | Shims | .015 | .015 | |
| | (7)(9) | 9¾(4) | Shims | .004-.009 | Shims | 10-20 | 10-20 | Shims | .015 | .015 | |

## DRIVE AXLE SPECIFICATIONS-Continued

| Year | Application | Ring Gear Size | Carrier Type | Ring Gear & Pinion Backlash | | Pinion Bearing Preload | | | Differential Bearing Preload | | |
|---|---|---|---|---|---|---|---|---|---|---|---|
| | | | | Method | Adjustment | Method | New Bearings Inch Lbs. | Used Bearings Inch Lbs. | Method | New Bearings Inch Lbs. | Used Bearings Inch Lbs. |
| 1984 | D-100/150, W-150 ⑥ | 8⅜ | ① | .006-.008 | ② | 20-35 | 10-25 ③ | ① | ⑤ | ⑤ | |
| | D-100/150, W-150, D-250, W-250 ⑥ | 9¼ | ① | .006-.008 | ② | 20-35 | 10-25 ③ | ① | ⑤ | ⑤ | |
| | D-250, W-250, D-350 ⑥ | 9¾ ④ | Shims | .004-.009 | Shims | 10-20 | 10-20 | Shims | .015 | .015 | |
| | D-350, W-350 ⑥ | 10½ ④ | Shims | .004-.009 | Shims | 10-20 | 10-20 | Shims | .015 | .015 | |
| | ⑦ ⑧ | 8½ ④ | Shims | .005-.009 | Shims | 20-40 | 10-20 | Shims | .015 | .015 | |
| | ⑦ ⑨ | 9¾ ④ | Shims | .004-.009 | Shims | 10-20 | 10-20 | Shims | .015 | .015 | |
| 1985-87 | D-100/150 ⑥ | 8⅜ | ① | .006-.008 | ② | 20-35 | 10-25 ③ | ① | ⑤ | ⑤ | |
| | D-100/150, W-150, D-250, W-250 ⑥ | 9¼ | ① | .006-.008 | ② | 20-35 | 10-25 ③ | ① | ⑤ | ⑤ | |
| | D-250, W-250, W-350 ⑥ | 9¾ ④ | Shims | .004-.009 | Shims | 10-20 | 10-20 | Shims | .015 | .015 | |
| | D-350, W-350 ⑥ | 10½ ④ | Shims | .004-.009 | Shims | 10-20 | 10-20 | Shims | .015 | .015 | |
| | ⑦ ⑧ | 8½ | Shims | .005-.009 | Shims | 20-40 | 10-20 | Shims | .015 | .015 | |
| | ⑦ ⑨ | 9¾ ④ | Shims | .004-.009 | Shims | 10-20 | 10-20 | Shims | .015 | .015 | |
| 1988-89 | D-100/150 ⑥ | 8⅜ | ① | .006-.008 | ② | 20-35 | ⑬ | ① | ⑤ | ⑤ | |
| | D-100/150, W-150, D-250, W-250 ⑥ | 9¼ | ① | .006-.008 | ② | 20-35 | ⑬ | ① | ⑤ | ⑤ | |
| | D-250, W-250, W-350 ⑥ | 9¾ ④ | Shims | .004-.009 | Shims | 10-20 | 10-20 | Shims | .015 | .015 | |
| | D-350, W-350 ⑥ | 10½ ④ | Shims | .004-.009 | Shims | 10-20 | 10-20 | Shims | .015 | .015 | |
| | ⑦ ⑧ | 8½ | Shims | .005-.009 | Shims | 20-40 | 10-20 | Shims | .015 | .015 | |
| | ⑦ ⑨ | 9¾ ④ | Shims | .004-.009 | Shims | 10-20 | 10-20 | Shims | .015 | .015 | |

### MOTOR HOME

| Year | Application | Ring Gear Size | Carrier Type | Ring Gear & Pinion Backlash | | Pinion Bearing Preload | | | Differential Bearing Preload | | |
|---|---|---|---|---|---|---|---|---|---|---|---|
| 1980 | M-300, M-400, M-500 | 10½ ④ | Shims | .004-.009 | Shims | 10-20 | 10-20 | Shims | .015 | .015 | |
| | M-600 | 12½ ⑩ | ① ⑪ | .006-.012 | Shims | 5-15 | 5-15 | ① | ⑫ | ⑫ | |

①—Threaded adjuster.
②—Collapsible spacer.
③—With new front and used rear bearings.
④—Spicer axle.
⑤—Preload is correct when ring gear and pinion backlash is properly adjusted.
⑥—Rear axle.
⑦—Front axle.
⑧—W-150, W-250, W-350 with 131 inch wheel base and 149 inch wheel base.
⑨—W-250, W-350 with 135 inch wheel base and 149 inch wheel base.
⑩—Rockwell axle.
⑪—Low limit preferred for original bearings and high limit preferred for new bearings.
⑫—Tighten each adjusting nut one notch.
⑬—Set at 10 inch lbs. greater than reading taken at time of tear down with minimum of 210 ft. lbs. torque on pinion nut.

## COOLING SYSTEM & CAPACITY DATA

| Year | Model | Engine | Cooling Capacity, Qts. Less A/C | Cooling Capacity, Qts. With A/C | Radiator Cap Relief Pressure, Lbs. | Thermo. Opening Temp. | Fuel Tank Gals. | Engine Oil Refill Qts. ① | Transmission Oil 4 Speed Pints. | Transmission Oil 5 Speed Pints. | Transmission Oil Auto. Trans. Qts. ⑩ | Transfer Case Pints | Rear Axle Oil Pints |
|---|---|---|---|---|---|---|---|---|---|---|---|---|---|
| **VANS, WAGONS & FRONT SECTIONS** | | | | | | | | | | | | | |
| 1980 | ALL | 225 | 12 | 13 | 16 | 195 | 22 | 5 | 7½ | — | 8.3 | — | ② |
| | ALL | 318 | 16 | 17 | 16 | 195 | ③ | 5 | 7½ | — | 8.3 | — | ② |
| | ALL | 360 | 14½ | 15½ | 16 | 195 | ③ | 5 | 7½ | — | 8.3 | — | ② |
| 1981 | ALL | 225 | 12 | 13 | 16 | 195 | 22 | 5 | 7½ | — | 8.3 | — | ② |
| | ALL | 318 | 16 | 17 | 16 | 195 | ③ | 5 | 7½ | — | 8.3 | — | ② |
| | ALL | 360 | 14½ | 15½ | 16 | 195 | ③ | 5 | 7½ | — | 8.3 | — | ② |
| 1982 | ALL | 225 | 12 | 13 | 16 | 195 | 22 | 5 | 7½ | — | 8.3 | — | ② |
| | ALL | 318 | 16 | 17 | 16 | 195 | 22 | 5 | 7½ | — | 8.3 | — | ② |
| | ALL | 360 | 14½ | 15½ | 16 | 195 | 22 | 5 | 7½ | — | 8.3 | — | ② |
| 1983 | ALL | 225 | 12 | 13 | 16 | 195 | 22 | 5 | 7½ | — | 8.3 | — | ② |
| | ALL | 318 | 16 | 17 | 16 | 195 | 22 | 5 | 7½ | — | 8.3 | — | ② |
| | ALL | 360 | 14½ | 15½ | 16 | 195 | 22 | 5 | 7½ | — | 8.3 | — | ② |
| 1984 | ALL | 225 | 12 | 13 | 16 | 195 | 22 | 5 | 7½ | — | 8.5 | — | ② |
| | ALL | 318 | 16 | 17 | 16 | 195 | 22 | 5 | 7½ | — | 6.5 | — | ② |
| | ALL | 360 | 14½ | 15½ | 16 | 195 | 22 | 5 | 7½ | — | 6.5 | — | ② |
| 1985-86 | ALL | 225 | 12 | 14 | 16 | 195 | 22 | 5 | 7½ | — | 6.5 | — | ② |
| | ALL | 318 | 16 | 18 | 16 | 195 | 22 | 5 | 7½ | — | 6.5 | — | ② |
| | ALL | 360 | 14½ | 16½ | 16 | 195 | 22 | 5 | 7½ | — | 6.5 | — | ② |
| 1987 | ALL | 225 | 13.5 ⑱ | — | 16 | 195 | 22 | 5 | 7½ | — | 6.5 | — | ② |
| | ALL | 318 | 16½ ⑱ | 16½ ⑱ | 16 | 195 | 22 | 5 | 7½ | — | 6.5 | — | ② |
| | ALL | 360 | 15 | ⑲ | 16 | 195 | 22 | 5 | 7½ | — | 6.5 | — | ② |
| 1988 | ALL | 238 | 14½ | 14½ | 14-18 | 195 | 22 | 4 ㉑ | 7 | 8 | 8.5 ④ | — | ② |
| | ALL | 318 | 16½ | 16½ | 14-18 | 195 | 22 | 5 | 7 | 8 | 8.5 ④ | — | ② |
| | ALL | 360 | 15 | 15 | 14-18 | 195 | 22 | 5 | 7 | 8 | 8.5 ④ | — | ② |
| 1989 | ALL | 238 | 14½ | 14½ | 14-18 | 195 | ㉒ | 4 ㉑ | 7 | 4 | ㉓ | — | ② |
| | ALL | 318 | 16½ | 16½ | 14-18 | 195 | ㉒ | 5 | 7 | 4 | ㉓ | — | ② |
| | ALL | 360 | 15 ⑱ | 15 ⑱ | 14-18 | 195 | 35 | 5 | 7 | 4 | ㉓ | — | ② |
| **RAMCHARGER & TRAIL DUSTER** | | | | | | | | | | | | | |
| 1980 | ALL | 225 | 12 | 13 | 16 | 195 | 24 | 5 | ⑤ | — | 3.9 ④ | ⑥ | ② |
| | ALL | 318 | 16 | 17 | 16 | 195 | 24 | 5 | ⑤ | — | 8.5 ④ | ⑥ | ② ⑧ |
| | ALL | 360 | 14½ | 15½ | 16 | 195 | 24 | 5 | ⑤ | — | 8.5 ④ | ⑥ | ② ⑧ |
| 1981 | ALL | 318 | 16 | 17 | 16 | 195 | 35 | 5 | ⑤ | — | 8.5 ④ | ⑥ | ② ⑧ |
| | ALL | 360 | 14½ | 15½ | 16 | 195 | 35 | 5 | ⑤ | — | 8.5 ④ | ⑥ | ② ⑧ |
| 1982 | ALL | 318 | 16 | 17 | 16 | 195 | 35 | 5 | ⑤ | — | 8.5 ④ | ⑥ | ② ⑧ |
| | ALL | 360 | 14½ | 15½ | 16 | 195 | 35 | 5 | ⑤ | — | 8.5 ④ | ⑥ | ② ⑧ |
| 1983 | ALL | 318 | 16 | 17 | 16 | 195 | 35 | 5 | ⑤ | — | 8.5 ④ | ⑥ | ② ⑧ |
| 1984 | ALL | 318 | 16 | 17 | 16 | 195 | 35 | 5 | — | — | 8.5 ④ | ⑥ | ② ⑧ |
| | ALL | 360 | 14½ | 15½ | 16 | 195 | 35 | 5 | — | — | 8.5 ④ | ⑥ | ② ⑧ |
| 1985-87 | ALL | 318 | ⑪ | ⑪ | 16 | 195 | 35 | 5 | 7 | — | 8.5 ④ | ⑥ | ② ⑬ |
| | ALL | 360 | ⑫ | ⑫ | 16 | 195 | 35 | 5 | 7 | — | 8.5 ④ | ⑥ | ② ⑬ |
| 1988 | ALL | 318 | 16½ | 16½ | 14-18 | 195 | 34 | 5 | 7 | — | 8.5 ④ | ⑥ | ② ⑧ |
| | ALL | 360 | ⑳ | ⑳ | 14-18 | 195 | 34 | 5 | 7 | — | 8.5 ④ | ⑥ | ② ⑧ |
| 1989 | ALL | 318 | 17 | 17 | 14-18 | 195 | 34 | 5 | 7 | 4 | 8.5 | ⑥ | ② ⑧ |
| | ALL | 360 | ⑳ | ⑳ | 14-18 | 195 | 34 | 5 | 7 | 4 | 8.5 | ⑥ | ② ⑧ |

## COOLING SYSTEM & CAPACITY DATA-Continued

| Year | Model | Engine | Cooling Capacity, Qts. | | Radiator Cap Relief Pressure, Lbs. | Thermo. Opening Temp. | Fuel Tank Gals. | Engine Oil Refill Qts. ① | Transmission Oil | | | Transfer Case Pints | Rear Axle Oil Pints |
|---|---|---|---|---|---|---|---|---|---|---|---|---|---|
| | | | Less A/C | With A/C | | | | | 4 Speed Pints. | 5 Speed Pints. | Auto. Trans. Qts. ⑩ | | |
| **CONVENTIONAL CAB** | | | | | | | | | | | | | |
| 1980 | ALL | 225 | 12 | 13 | 16 | 195 | ⑨ | 5 | ⑤ | — | 3.9④ | ⑥ | ②⑧ |
| | ALL | 318 | 16 | 17 | 16 | 195 | ⑨ | 5 | ⑤ | — | 3.9④ | ⑥ | ②⑧ |
| | ALL | 360 | 14½ | 15½ | 16 | 195 | ⑨ | 5 | ⑤ | — | 3.9④ | ⑥ | ②⑧ |
| 1981 | ALL | 225 | 12 | 13 | 16 | 195 | 20 | 5 | ⑤ | — | ⑦ | ⑥ | ②⑧ |
| | ALL | 318 | 16 | 17 | 16 | 195 | 20 | 5 | ⑤ | — | ⑦ | ⑥ | ②⑧ |
| | ALL | 360 | 14½ | 15½ | 16 | 195 | 20 | 5 | ⑤ | — | ⑦ | ⑥ | ②⑧ |
| 1982 | ALL | 225 | 12 | 13 | 16 | 195 | 20 | 5 | ⑤ | — | ⑦ | ⑥ | ②⑧ |
| | ALL | 318 | 16 | 17 | 16 | 195 | 20 | 5 | ⑤ | — | ⑦ | ⑥ | ②⑧ |
| | ALL | 360 | 14½ | 15½ | 16 | 195 | 20 | 5 | ⑤ | — | ⑦ | ⑥ | ②⑧ |
| 1983 | ALL | 225 | 12 | 13 | 16 | 195 | 20 | 5 | ⑤ | — | ⑦ | ⑥ | ②⑧ |
| | ALL | 318 | 16 | 17 | 16 | 195 | 20 | 5 | ⑤ | — | ⑦ | ⑥ | ②⑧ |
| | ALL | 360 | 14½ | 15½ | 16 | 195 | 20 | 5 | ⑤ | — | ⑦ | ⑥ | ②⑧ |
| 1984 | ALL | 225 | 12 | 13 | 16 | 195 | 20 | 5 | ⑤ | — | ⑦ | ⑥ | ②⑧ |
| | ALL | 318 | 16 | 17 | 16 | 195 | 20 | 5 | ⑤ | — | ⑦ | ⑥ | ②⑧ |
| | ALL | 360 | 14½ | 15½ | 16 | 195 | 20 | 5 | ⑤ | — | ⑦ | ⑥ | ②⑧ |
| 1985-87 | ALL | 225 | ⑭ | ⑭ | 16 | 195 | 20 | 5 | ⑤ | — | ⑦ | ⑥ | ②⑬ |
| | ALL | 318 | ⑮ | ⑮ | 16 | 195 | 20 | 5 | ⑤ | — | ⑦ | ⑥ | ②⑬ |
| | ALL | 360 | ⑯ | ⑯ | 16 | 195 | 20 | 5 | ⑤ | — | ⑦ | ⑥ | ②⑬ |
| 1988 | ALL | 238 | 15 | 15 | 14-18 | 195 | 22 | 4㉑ | 7 | 8 | 8.5④ | ⑥ | ②⑧ |
| | ALL | 318 | 17 | 17 | 14-18 | 195 | 22 | 5 | 7 | 8 | 8.5④ | ⑥ | ②⑧ |
| | ALL | 360 | 15½ | 15½ | 14-18 | 195 | 22 | 5 | 7 | 8 | 8.5④ | ⑥ | ②⑧ |
| 1989 | ALL | 238 | 15 | 15 | 14-18 | 195 | ㉔ | 4㉑ | 7 | 4 | 8.5 | ⑥ | ②⑧ |
| | ALL | 318 | 17 | 17 | 14-18 | 195 | ㉔ | 5 | 7 | 4 | 8.5 | ⑥ | ②⑧ |
| | ALL | 360 | 15½ | 15½ | 14-18 | 195 | 30 | 5 | 7 | 4 | 8.5 | ⑥ | ②⑧ |
| | ALL | 360㉕ | ㉖ | ㉖ | 15 | 181-203 | 30 | 11 | — | — | 8.5 | ⑥ | ②⑧ |
| **MOTOR HOME** | | | | | | | | | | | | | |
| 1980 | ALL | 360-3 | 21 | — | 16 | 195 | 75 | 6 | — | — | 8.5 | — | ⑰ |
| | ALL | 446 | 24½ | — | 16 | 180 | 75 | 6 | — | — | 8.5 | — | ⑰ |

①—Including one qt. with filter change.
②—8⅜ inch ring gear, 4½ pts.; 9¼ inch ring gear, 4½ pts.; 9¾ inch ring gear, 6 pts.; 10½ inch ring gear, 6½ pts.
③—All 300 & 400 series front sections, 45 gals.; others, 22 gals.
④—Without torque converter drain.
⑤—A-833 trans., 7½ pts.; New Process 435 trans., 7 pts.; New Process 445 trans., 7½ pts.
⑥—New Process 208 transfer case, 6 pts.; New Process 205 transfer case, 4½ pts; New Process 241 transfer case, 4½ pts.
⑦—A-904T/A999 trans., 17.1 pts.; A-727 trans. (without torque converter drain), 7.7 pts.
⑧—Models equipped with 4 wheel drive, front axle 44 FBJ, 3½ pts.; front axle 60-F, 6½ pts.
⑨—Frame mount ahead of rear axle, 18 gals.; frame mount rear of rear axle, 21 gals.
⑩—Approximate. Make final check with dipstick.

⑪—With 22 x 18 inch radiator, 16 qts.; with 26 x 18 inch radiator, 17 qts. If equipped with A/C or increased cooling package, add one qt. to above capacities.
⑫—With 22 x 18 inch radiator, 14.5 qts.; with 26 x 18 inch radiator, 15.5 qts. If equipped with A/C or increased cooling package, add one qt. to above capacities.
⑬—Models equipped with 4 wheel drive, front axle 44-8FD, 5.6 pts.; front axle 60-F, 6.5 pts.
⑭—With 19 x 18 inch radiator, 12 qts.; with 22 x 18 inch radiator, 12 qts.; with 26 x 18 inch radiator, 13 qts. If equipped with A/C or increased cooling package, add one qt. to above cooling capacities.
⑮—With 22 x 18 inch radiator, 16 qts.; with 26 x 18 inch radiator, 17 qts.; with 26 x 20 inch radiator, 17.5 qts. If equipped with A/C or increased cooling package, add one qt. to above capacities.

⑯—With 22 x 18 inch radiator, 14.5 qts.; with 26 x 18 inch radiator, 15.5 qts.; with 26 x 20 inch radiator, 16 qts. If equipped with A/C or increased cooling package, add one qt. to above capacities.
⑰—9¾ inch ring gear, 6 pts.; 10½ inch ring gear, 6½ pts.; 12½ inch ring gear, 14 pts.
⑱—Add one quart if equipped with auxiliary heater.
⑲—With heavy duty cooling, 15.5 qts.; with A/C, 15 qts.
⑳—Two wheel drive, 15.5 qts.; four wheel drive, 15.0 qts.
㉑—With or without oil filter.
㉒—Standard tank; 22 gallon. Optional tank; 35 gallon.
㉓—With A-904, A-999 & A-727 trans; 8.5 quarts. With A-500 trans; 10.2
㉔—Standard tank; 22 gallon. Optional tank 30 gallon.
㉕—6-5.9L/360 diesel engine.
㉖—15½ with manual trans. 16½ with auto trans.

# ELECTRICAL

## INDEX

# FUSE PANEL & FLASHER LOCATION

## CONVENTIONAL CABS & RAMCHARGER

The fuse block is located directly below the steering column, on the lower steering column cover. The hazard flasher and turn signal flasher plug directly into the fuse block. To lower fuse panel, push fuse block locking tab on column cover downward.

## VANS, WAGONS & FRONT SECTIONS

The fuse block is located to the left side of the glove compartment, under the glove compartment door. The hazard flasher and turn signal flasher plug into designated slots next to the fuse panel. To access fuse panel, open glove box door and lift fuse block cover.

# STARTER
## REPLACE

1. Disconnect battery ground cable.
2. Disconnect starter cable at starter, then the solenoid lead wire from solenoid.
3. Remove heat shield attaching bolt, then the heat shield if equipped.
4. Remove starter motor attaching bolts, then the oil cooler tube bracket, if equipped with automatic transmission.
5. Remove starter from vehicle.
6. Reverse procedure to install.

# IGNITION SWITCH & LOCK

## REPLACE

### MODELS LESS TILT STEERING

1. Disconnect battery ground cable and remove turn signal switch as outlined in this chapter.
2. Remove ignition key lamp assembly attaching screws, then the assembly.
3. Remove snap ring from upper end of steering shaft.
4. Remove bearing housing to lock housing attaching screws, then the bearing housing from the shaft.
5. Remove buzzer switch attaching screws, then the buzzer switch, if equipped.
6. Remove lock lever guide plate attaching screws, then the lock plate.
7. Place lock cylinder in the "Lock" position and remove key. Using a suitable tool, depress spring loaded lock retainer and pull lock cylinder from housing bore, **Fig. 1.**
8. Remove ignition switch attaching screws, then the ignition switch.
9. Reverse procedure to install.

### MODELS WITH TILT STEERING

#### Ignition Lock, Replace

The ignition switch and lock assembly are separate units and must be replaced individually.
1. Disconnect battery ground cable and remove turn signal switch as outlined in this chapter.
2. Place lock cylinder in the "Lock" position and remove key. Insert suitable tool into slot next to switch mounting screw boss, **Fig. 2.**
3. Depress spring latch at bottom of slot, then remove lock.
4. To install ignition lock, place lock cylinder in the "Lock" position and remove key. Install lock cylinder assembly into housing, then press inward and move switch actuator rod up and down to align parts. **When parts align, the lock cylinder will move inward and a spring loaded retainer will snap into place, locking cylinder into housing.**

#### Ignition Switch, Replace

The ignition switch is located on the top of the steering column under the instrument panel. To replace it, the steering column should be lowered as follows:
1. Disconnect shift indicator link.
2. Remove nuts securing bracket to dash panel and carefully lower column.
3. Disconnect electrical connector from switch. Ensure switch is in "Accessory" position.
4. Remove switch attaching screws, then the switch.
5. To install ignition switch, place switch slider and lock in the "Accessory" position.
6. Fit actuator rod into switch and assemble to column.
7. Complete assembly in reverse of removal procedure.

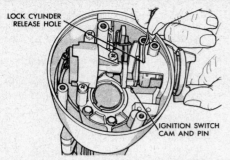

**Fig. 1  Lock cylinder removal. Less tilt steering wheel**

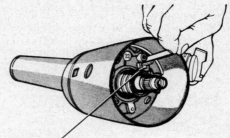

**Fig. 2  Lock cylinder removal. With tilt steering wheel**

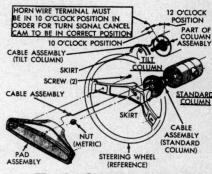

**Fig. 3  Steering wheel removal. Padded type, luxury & sport type similar**

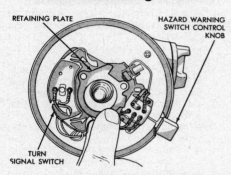

**Fig. 4  Turn signal switch retainer removal. Standard columns**

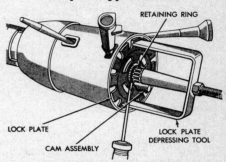

**Fig. 5  Lock plate retaining ring removal**

## LIGHT SWITCH
### REPLACE
#### VANS, WAGONS & FRONT SECTIONS

1. Disconnect battery ground cable.
2. Depress knob and stem release button located on bottom of switch housing, and pull knob and stem assembly from switch.
3. Remove instrument panel hood and bezel assembly.
4. Remove switch bezel attaching screws, then the switch bezel.
5. Remove switch attaching nut, then disconnect switch electrical connector and remove switch.
6. Reverse procedure to install.

#### RAMCHARGER, TRAIL DUSTER & CONVENTIONAL CABS
##### 1980

1. Disconnect battery ground cable.
2. Remove left air conditioner and air outlet assembly, if equipped.
3. Depress knob and stem release button located on bottom of switch housing, and pull knob and stem assembly from switch.
4. Remove switch attaching nut, then disconnect switch electrical connector and remove switch.
5. Reverse procedure to install.

##### 1981–89

1. Disconnect battery ground cable, then remove cluster face plate.

## STOP LIGHT SWITCH
### REPLACE
#### EXC. MOTOR HOME

1. Disconnect battery ground cable.
2. Disconnect wiring from switch and remove switch from brake pedal bracket.
3. Reverse procedure to install.
4. To adjust vehicles without speed control, proceed as follows:
   a. Loosen switch assembly to pedal bracket attaching screw and slide assembly away from pedal blade or striker plate.
   b. Push brake pedal down and allow to return to free position. **Do not pull brake pedal back at any time.**
   c. Place spacer gauge on pedal blade. **Models with speed control use a .070 inch spacer, 1980-83 models less speed control use a .130 inch spacer and 1984-89 models less speed control use a .140 inch spacer.**
   d. Slide switch assembly toward pedal blade until switch plunger is fully depressed against spacer gauge without moving the pedal.
   e. Tighten the switch bracket attaching screw and remove spacer. Ensure stop light switch does not prevent full pedal return.
5. To adjust vehicles with speed control, proceed as follows:
   a. Push switch through clip in mounting bracket until switch is seated against bracket, the brake pedal should move forward slightly.
   b. Gently pull back on brake pedal as far as it will go. The switch will ratchet backwards to the correct position.

#### MOTOR HOME

1. Disconnect battery ground cable.
2. Disconnect wiring from switch and remove switch from bracket.
3. Reverse procedure to install.
4. To adjust, proceed as follows:
   a. Loosen switch locknut, then the switch until plunger is no longer in contact with pedal blade.
   b. Disconnect pedal return spring and loosen pushrod locknut.
   c. Remove pushrod end bolt and pedal return spring bracket assembly.
   d. Position a .010-.015 inch spacer between pedal blade and pedal stop.
   e. Turn pushrod in or out until pushrod end bolt can be inserted through pedal blade. Ensure pushrod operates smoothly.
   f. Install pedal return spring bracket and torque attaching nut to 30 ft. lbs. Torque pushrod locknut to 120 inch lbs.
   g. Remove spacer and connect pedal return spring, then tighten stop light switch until it contacts pedal blade. Continue to tighten switch 2½ complete turns.
   h. Tighten switch locknut and ensure proper switch operation.

## NEUTRAL SAFETY & BACK-UP SWITCH
### REPLACE

1. Unscrew switch from transmission case, allowing fluid to drain into con-

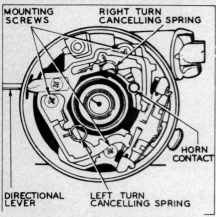

**Fig. 6 Turn signal switch removal. Tilt columns**

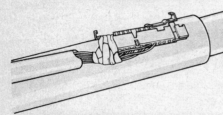

**Fig. 7 Taping turn signal connector and wires**

tainer.
2. Move shift lever to Park and then to Neutral positions and inspect to ensure switch operating lever is centered in switch opening in case.
3. Screw switch into transmission case, then add fluid to the proper level.
4. Check to ensure proper switch operation.

# HORN SOUNDER & STEERING WHEEL
## REPLACE
### LUXURY TYPE PADDED STEERING WHEEL

1. Disconnect battery ground cable.
2. Pry off pad, then disconnect electrical connector from horn ring terminal.
3. Remove each horn switch to steering wheel retaining screw and lift out horn button switches from wheel.
4. Remove steering wheel nut, then the wheel using a suitable puller. **Do not bump or hammer on steering shaft to remove wheel, as damage to shaft may result.**
5. Reverse procedure to install.

### PADDED TYPE EXC. LUXURY TYPE STEERING WHEEL

1. Disconnect battery ground cable.
2. Remove horn pad mounting screws located behind steering wheel spokes, then push pad out of wheel through access holes in back of the wheel. Do not pry pad off, **Fig. 3.**
3. Disconnect horn switch electrical connector.
4. Remove horn switch to retainer at-

taching screws, then the switch from retainer.
5. Remove steering wheel nut, then the steering wheel using a suitable puller. **Do not bump or hammer on steering shaft to remove wheel, as damage to shaft may result.**
6. Reverse procedure to install.

### SPORT STEERING WHEEL

1. Disconnect battery ground cable.
2. Lift horn button off wheel, then disconnect switch electrical connector.
3. Remove steering wheel nut.
4. Remove horn switch to steering wheel attaching screw, then the horn switch.
5. Remove steering wheel using suitable puller. **Do not bump or hammer on steering shaft to remove wheel, as damage to shaft may result.**
6. Reverse procedure to install.

# TURN SIGNAL/HAZARD WARNING SWITCH
## REPLACE
### 1980–88 MODELS

1. Disconnect battery ground cable.
2. On 1983-88 models, remove lower bezel from instrument panel.
3. On all models, remove horn sounder and steering wheel. Refer to "Horn Sounder & Steering Wheel, Replace" procedure.
4. On standard columns proceed as follows:
   a. Remove turn signal lever to switch attaching screw, then the lever. **If equipped with speed control, allow lever to hang free.**
   b. Remove switch retainer attaching screws, then the retainer, **Fig. 4.**
5. On tilt columns, proceed as follows:
   a. Remove plastic cover from lock plate, if equipped.
   b. Depress lock plate using tool C-4156 or equivalent, **Fig. 5,** then pry retaining ring out of groove using screwdriver. **The full load of the cancelling cam spring should not be relieved. If full load is relieved, retaining ring will turn too easily, making removal more difficult.**
   c. Remove lock plate, cancelling cam and spring, then place turn signal lever in right turn position.
   d. Remove turn signal lever to switch attaching screw, then the lever. **If equipped with speed control, allow lever to hang free.**
   e. Remove hazard warning switch knob attaching screw, then the turn signal switch attaching screws, **Fig. 6.**
6. On tilt columns, position steering wheel in midpoint position.
7. On models equipped with column shift, place selector lever in first or third gear position.
8. On all models, remove wire cover attaching clips, then the cover if equipped.
9. Disconnect turn signal electrical con-

nector. Wrap a piece of tape around the connector and wire to prevent snagging during switch removal, **Fig. 7.**
10. Remove turn signal/hazard warning switch assembly by pulling switch up from column while straightening and guiding wires up through column opening.
11. Reverse procedure to install.

### 1989 MODELS

1. Disconnect battery ground cable.
2. Remove lower bezel from instrument panel.
3. Remove horn sounder and steering wheel. Refer to "Horn Sounder & Steering Wheel, Replace" procedure.
4. Remove wiring trough from underside of steering column by prying out retainer buttons.
5. On standard columns, position gearshift to its full clock wise position. On tilt columns, position at mid-point.
6. On all models, disconnect turn signal switch electrical connectors.
7. On standard columns, proceed as follows:
   a. Remove upper bearing attaching screws, then the retainer.
   b. Remove screw holding wiper/washer switch to turn signal switch pivot. Leave turn signal lever in its installed position.
   c. Remove switch attaching screws from bearing housing, then the turn signal switch.
8. On tilt columns, proceed as follows:
   a. Depress lock plate using tool C-4156 or equivalent, **Fig. 5,** then pry retaining ring out of groove. **The full load of the upper bearing spring should not be relieved. If full load is relieved, retaining ring will turn too easily, making removal more difficult.**
   b. Remove lock plate, cancelling cam and upper bearing spring, then place turn signal lever in right turn position.
   c. Remove screw attaching link between turn signal switch and wiper/washer switch pivot. then the lever.
   d. Remove hazard warning switch knob attaching screw, then the turn signal switch attaching screws.
   e. Wrap a piece of tape around the connector and wire to prevent snagging during switch removal, remove turn signal/hazard warning switch assembly by pulling switch up from column while straightening and guiding wires up through column opening.
9. Reverse procedure to install.

# INSTRUMENT CLUSTER
## REPLACE
### 1980 MOTOR HOME

1. Disconnect battery ground cable.
2. Remove six instrument cluster to instrument panel attaching screws, then disconnect speedometer cable.

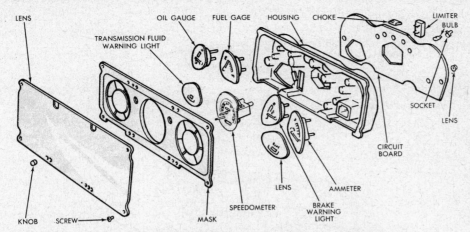

Fig. 8   Instrument cluster removal. 1980 Motor Home

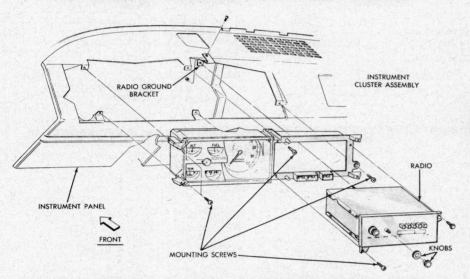

Fig. 10   Instrument cluster removal. 1980 Ramcharger, Trail Duster & Conventional Cabs

3. Disconnect instrument cluster electrical connectors, then remove cluster, **Fig. 8.**
4. Reverse procedure to install.

## VANS, WAGONS & FRONT SECTIONS

1. Disconnect battery ground cable.
2. Remove instrument panel hood and bezel assembly attaching screws, then pull bezel off upper retaining clips.
3. Disconnect selector lever actuator cable from steering column.
4. Remove cluster attaching screws, then pull cluster forward and disconnect speedometer cable.
5. Disconnect instrument cluster electrical connectors, then remove cluster, **Fig. 9.**
6. Reverse procedure to install.

## 1980 RAMCHARGER, TRAIL DUSTER & CONVENTIONAL CABS

1. Disconnect battery ground cable.
2. Cover steering column to prevent

damage to paint.
3. Remove bezel attaching screws, then the bezel.
4. Remove radio and left air conditioner duct if equipped.
5. Disconnect speedometer cable from cluster.
6. Remove cluster assembly attaching screws, then pull cluster forward and disconnect cluster electrical connectors.
7. Remove cluster assembly from panel, **Fig. 10.**
8. Reverse procedure to install.

## 1981 TRAIL DUSTER & 1981–89 RAMCHARGER & CONVENTIONAL CABS

1. Disconnect battery ground cable.
2. Cover steering column to prevent damage to paint.
3. Remove face plate, then four lower steering column cover attaching screws, **Figs. 11 and 12.**
4. Pry out upper steering column cover and slide downward.
5. Disconnect selector lever actuator ca-

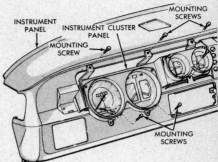

Fig. 9   Instrument cluster removal. Vans, Wagons & Front Sections

ble from steering column.
6. Loosen heater and A/C control. Pull rearward to clear forward mount on cluster housing.
7. Remove six cluster retaining screws, then pull cluster forward and disconnect speedometer cable.
8. Disconnect instrument cluster electrical connectors, then remove cluster.
9. Reverse procedure to install.

# WINDSHIELD WIPER MOTOR
## REPLACE

1. Disconnect battery ground cable.
2. Disconnect wiper motor electrical connectors, then remove motor attaching screws.
3. Lower motor down far enough to gain access to crank arm to drive link retainer bushing.
4. Remove crank arm from drive link by prying retainer bushing from crank arm pin using a suitable screwdriver.
5. Remove motor from vehicle.

# WINDSHIELD WIPER TRANSMISSION
## REPLACE
## VANS, WAGONS & FRONT SECTIONS

### Drive Link, Replace

1. Remove wiper arms and washer hoses, then the cowl cover grille.
2. Remove drive link from crank arm and connecting link pins by prying retainer bushing apart using a suitable screwdriver, **Fig. 13.**
3. Remove drive link through access hole.
4. Reverse procedure to install.

### Connecting Link, Replace

1. Remove cowl cover grille.
2. Remove connecting link from drivelink and pivot pins by prying retainer bushings apart using a suitable screwdriver, **Fig. 13.**
3. Remove connecting link through access hole.
4. Reverse procedure to install.

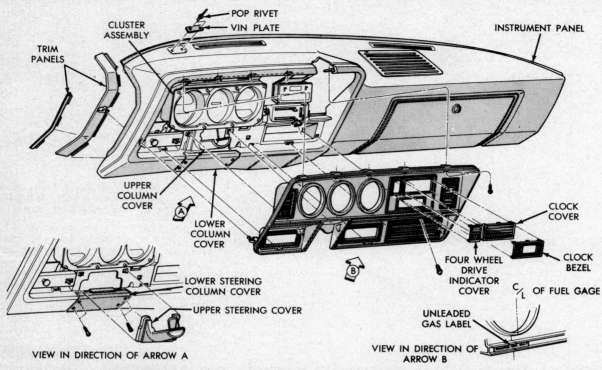

**Fig. 11  Instrument cluster removal. 1981 Trail Duster, 1981–85 Ramcharger & Conventional Cabs**

## Crank Arm, Replace

1. Remove wiper arms and washer hoses.
2. Remove cowl cover grille.
3. Remove drive link from crank arm pin by prying retainer bushing apart using a suitable screwdriver, **Fig. 13.**
4. Remove crank arm to motor attaching nut, then the crank arm through access hole.
5. Reverse procedure to install.

## Right Or Left Pivot, Replace

1. Remove wiper arms and washer hoses.
2. Remove cowl cover grille.
3. Remove connecting link from pivot pins by prying retainer bushing apart using a suitable screwdriver, **Fig. 13.**
4. Remove pivot attaching bolts, then lower pivot and remove through access hole.
5. Reverse procedure to install.

## 1980–89 RAMCHARGER & CONVENTIONAL CABS & 1980–81 TRAIL DUSTER

### Crank Arm, Replace

1. Remove wiper motor. Refer to "Windshield Wiper Motor, Replace" procedure.
2. Remove crank arm to motor drive shaft attaching nut, then the crank arm, **Fig. 14.**
3. Reverse procedure to install.

### Drive Link & Left Pivot Assembly, Replace

1. Remove wiper arms, then the cowl

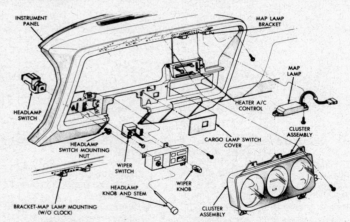

**Fig. 12  Instrument cluster removal. 1986–89 Ramcharger & Conventional Cabs**

cover attaching screws and cover.
2. Remove drive link from right pivot by prying retainer bushing apart using a suitable screwdriver, **Fig. 14.**
3. Remove crank arm from drive link by prying retainer bushing from crank arm pin using a suitable screwdriver.
4. Remove left pivot attaching screws and allow pivot to hang free.
5. Remove drive links and left pivot as an assembly.
6. Remove drive link from left pivot by prying retainer bushing from pivot pin using a suitable screwdriver.
7. Reverse procedure to install.

### Right Pivot Assembly, Replace

1. Remove wiper arms, then the cowl

cover attaching screws and cover.
2. Remove drive link from right pivot by prying retainer bushing from pivot pin using suitable screwdriver, **Fig. 14.**
3. Remove right pivot attaching screws, then the pivot through access hole.
4. Reverse procedure to install.

## WINDSHIELD WIPER SWITCH
### REPLACE
### VANS, WAGONS & FRONT SECTIONS

1. Disconnect battery ground cable.
2. Remove steering column cover, if equipped.

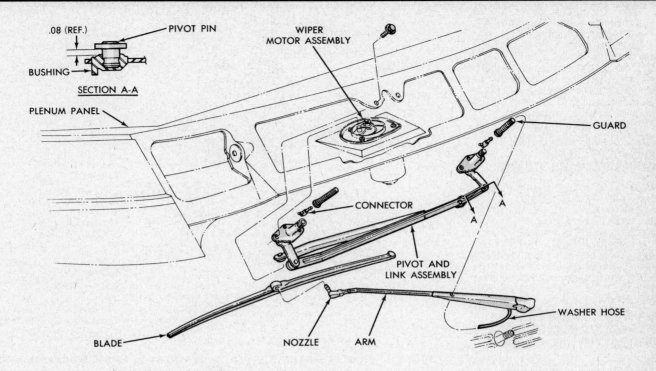

**Fig. 13   Windshield wiper transmission assembly. Vans, Wagons & Front Sections**

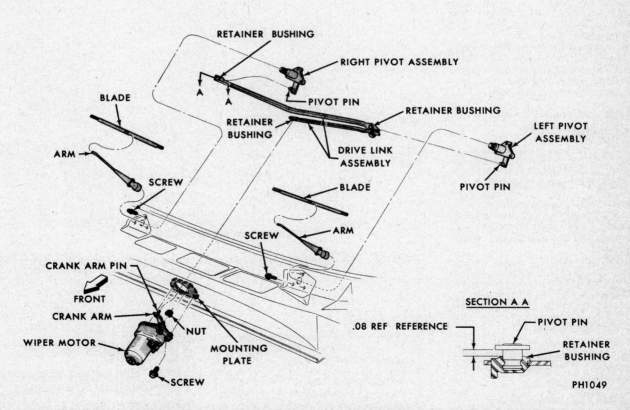

**Fig. 14   Windshield wiper transmission assembly. 1980–89 Ramcharger & Conventional Cabs & 1980–81 Trail Duster**

3. Remove two switch housing to instrument panel attaching screws.
4. Disconnect switch and bezel assembly electrical connectors.
5. Disconnect illumination lamp, then remove switch housing assembly from under instrument panel.
6. Remove switch to housing retaining screws, then the switch.
7. Reverse procedure to install.

### 1980 RAMCHARGER, TRAIL DUSTER & CONVENTIONAL CABS

1. Disconnect battery ground cable.
2. Remove ashtray housing.
3. Loosen knob attaching screw, then the knob from switch.
4. Remove switch to panel attaching nut, then working through ashtray opening, lower switch and disconnect switch electrical connector.
5. Remove lighting bracket, then the switch.
6. Reverse procedure to install.

### 1981 TRAIL DUSTER & 1981–89 RAMCHARGER & CONVENTIONAL CABS

1. Disconnect battery ground cable, then remove cluster face plate.
2. Depress head light knob and stem release button located on bottom of switch housing and pull knob and stem assembly from switch.
3. Pull wiper switch knob off wiper switch.
4. Remove bezel attaching screws, then the bezel.
5. Remove four wiper switch attaching screws.
6. Disconnect switch electrical connectors, then remove switch.
7. Reverse procedure to install.

## RADIO
### REPLACE
### 1980–81 TRAIL DUSTER & 1980–88 RAMCHARGER & CONVENTIONAL CABS

1. Disconnect battery ground cable.
2. Remove instrument cluster bezel attaching screws, then the bezel.
3. Remove left air conditioner duct if equipped.
4. Disconnect antenna lead, speaker leads and electrical connectors, then remove radio to mounting bracket attaching nut.
5. Remove radio to cluster attaching bolts, then remove radio through cluster housing opening.
6. Reverse procedure to install.

### VANS, WAGONS & FRONT SECTIONS & 1989 RAMCHARGER & CONVENTIONAL CABS

Do not operate radio with speaker leads detached, as damage to transistors may result.

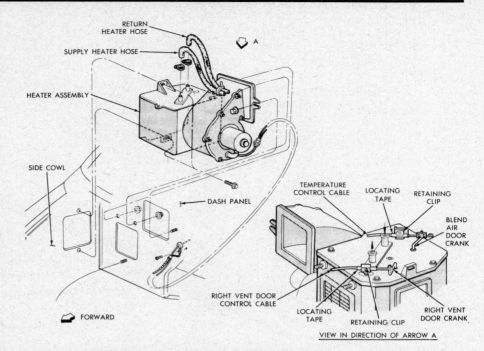

**Fig. 15   Heater assembly. Vans, Wagons & Front Sections less A/C**

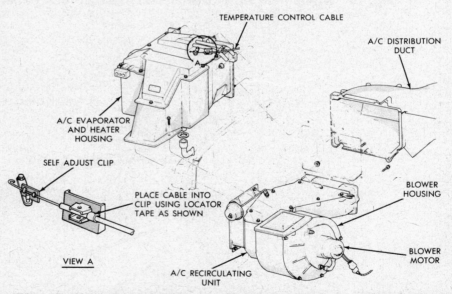

**Fig. 16   Heater assembly. Vans, Wagons & Front Sections with A/C**

1. Disconnect battery ground cable.
2. Remove cluster bezel attaching screws, then the bezel.
3. Remove radio attaching screws and ground strap screw.
4. Pull radio from panel, then disconnect antenna lead, speaker leads and electrical connectors.
5. Remove radio.
6. Reverse procedure to install.

## HEATER CORE
### REPLACE
### VANS, WAGONS & FRONT SECTIONS W/STANDARD HEATER

#### Less A/C

1. Disconnect battery ground cable and

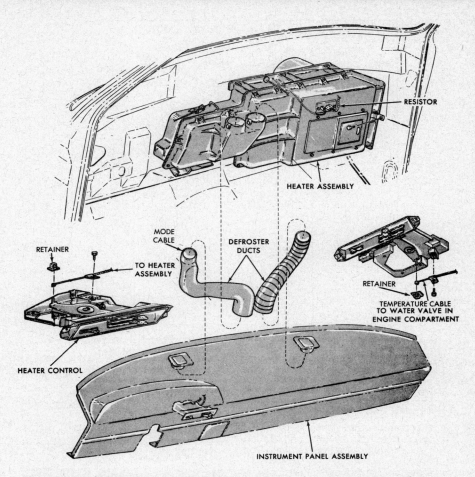

**Fig. 17   Heater assembly. 1980 Ramcharger, Trail Duster & Conventional Cabs less A/C**

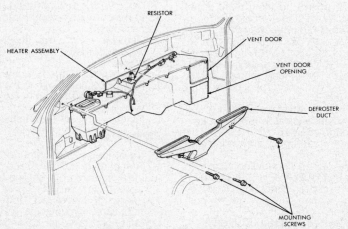

**Fig. 18   Heater assembly. Ramcharger, Trail Duster & Conventional Cabs less A/C. 1981–84 shown, 1985–89 similar**

drain cooling system.

2. Disconnect heater core hoses.
3. Disconnect temperature control cable from heater core cover and blend air door crank.
4. Disconnect blower motor feed wire from resistor block located on distribution duct in cab.
5. Set coolant overflow tank aside.
6. Remove nuts retaining heater assembly to side cowl and nuts retaining heater assembly to dash panel, then remove heater assembly from vehicle, **Fig. 15.**
7. Remove heater core cover, then remove the two heater core retaining screws and remove heater core.
8. Reverse procedure to install.

## With A/C

1. Discharge refrigerant from system.
2. Disconnect battery ground cable and drain cooling system.
3. Place a waterproof cover over alternator to prevent coolant from spilling over it, then disconnect and plug heater core hoses.
4. Disconnect refrigerant lines at H-valve, then remove two screws from filter drier bracket and position lines aside. Cap all refrigerant lines. Disconnect temperature control cable from cover.
5. From inside vehicle, remove glove box, spot cooler bezel and appearance shield.
6. Through glove box opening and under instrument panel, remove screws and nuts retaining evaporator housing to dash panel.
7. Remove the two screws from flange connection to blower housing. Separate evaporator housing from blower housing and carefully remove evaporator housing from vehicle, **Fig. 16.**
8. Remove cover from housing, then remove heater core strap retaining screw and remove heater core.
9. Reverse procedure to install.

## VANS, WAGONS & FRONT SECTIONS W/AUXILIARY HEATER

1. Disconnect battery ground cable, then drain cooling system.
2. Disconnect inlet and outlet hoses from heater.
3. On models with auxiliary air conditioning, proceed as follows:
   a. Remove auxiliary housing lower cover attaching screws, then the heater core tube seal and cover plate.
   b. Remove heater core support bracket attaching screws, then the support bracket.
   c. Remove heater core from housing.
4. On models less auxiliary air conditioning, proceed as follows:
   a. Remove heater to floor pan attaching nuts, then disconnect blower motor electrical connectors.
   b. Remove heater assembly from inside of vehicle.
   c. Remove heater cover to heater assembly attaching screws. The heater core is assembled to the

cover and will be removed as the cover is removed.

d. Remove heater core from heater cover.

5. On all models, reverse procedure to install.

## RAMCHARGER, TRAIL DUSTER & CONVENTIONAL CAB

### LESS A/C

### 1980 Models

1. Disconnect battery ground cable.
2. Drain cooling system and disconnect hoses from heater core.
3. Disconnect electrical connector from resistor.
4. Disconnect control cables and remove defroster ducts.
5. Disconnect ground wire and cooling tube from blower motor.
6. Remove bracket from right end of instrument panel and pull toward rear of cab.
7. Remove the seven retaining nuts from engine side of firewall and from inside of cab near right hand kick panel.
8. Remove heater from vehicle, **Fig. 17.**
9. Remove screws and separate heater housing.
10. Remove core retaining screws and carefully slide core out of heater housing.
11. Reverse procedure to install.

### 1981–89 Models

1. Disconnect battery ground cable.
2. Disconnect heater hoses on engine side and plug heater outlets.
3. Remove right side cowl trim if so equipped.
4. Remove glove box, then structural brace through glove box opening.
5. Remove right half of instrument panel lower reinforcement, making sure to disconnect ground strap.
6. Disconnect control cables, then blower motor wires on engine side.
7. Disconnect wires from resistor block, **Fig. 18.**
8. Remove screw holding heater to cowl side sheet metal.
9. Remove 6 heater retaining nuts on firewall, then remove heater.
10. Remove mode door crank and 15 screws to remove cover from housing, then slide heater core out.
11. Reverse procedure to install.

### WITH A/C

### 1980 Models

1. Disconnect battery ground cable.
2. Drain cooling system and disconnect hoses from heater core.
3. Remove glove box and ashtray.
4. Remove right and left A/C ducts, distribution duct and center air outlet and duct.
5. Disconnect wiring harness from resistor and vacuum lines from rear housing.
6. Remove the 24 retaining screws, then while holding defroster toward heat position, separate the units.
7. Remove one screw from engine side

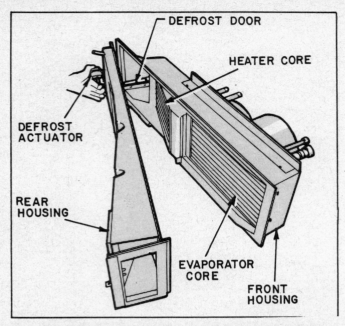

**Fig. 19   Heater assembly. 1980 Ramcharger, Trail Duster & Conventional Cabs with A/C**

and two screws from each end of core and slide core out, **Fig. 19.**
8. Reverse procedure to install.

### 1981–89 Models

1. Disconnect battery ground cable.
2. Discharge A/C system and disconnect refrigerant and heater lines from unit.
3. Move shift levers away from dash.
4. Remove right side cowl trim panel, if equipped.
5. Remove 4 screws at base and remove glove box, **Fig. 20.**
6. Remove brace through glove box opening and remove ashtray.
7. Remove right half of lower reinforcement (7 screws to instrument panel and 1 to cowl side of trim panel).
8. Disconnect radio ground strap.
9. Remove right upper air duct by removing mounting screw and pulling duct out through glove box opening.
10. Remove instrument panel center brace and right instrument panel cluster pivot bolt.
11. Remove instrument panel cluster, disconnect shift indicator cable and lower steering column.
12. Remove steering column studs and radio.
13. Remove scoop connecting heater to center distribution duct (2 screws).
14. Remove center distribution duct by pulling bottom of dash out to gain clearance.
15. Remove floor air distribution duct.
16. Disconnect temperature control cable through glove box.
17. Remove 7 retaining nuts from firewall and screw that retains assembly to cowl side sheet metal.
18. Flex dash out and remove heater assembly.
19. Remove nuts from door arms and remove door arms.
20. Remove 7 screws to remove cover from housing.
21. Remove evaporator core.
22. Reverse procedure to install.

## BLOWER MOTOR

### REPLACE

### VANS, WAGONS & FRONT SECTIONS W/STANDARD HEATER

### Less A/C

1. Disconnect battery ground cable and blower motor wires.
2. Remove 7 screws holding back plate to heater housing and remove blower assembly.
3. Remove spring clip holding blower wheel to motor and pull off blower wheel.
4. Remove vent tube from motor.
5. Remove 2 nuts holding blower motor to back plate and remove blower motor.
6. Reverse procedure to install.

### With A/C

1. Disconnect battery ground cable.
2. Remove top half of shroud by removing 2 screws from shroud to radiator support and two screws holding the halves of the shroud together. Top right screw on vehicles with six cylinder engine is hidden behind discharge line muffler. Move top half of shroud out of the way.
3. Disconnect blower motor electrical connector and remove blower motor cooling tube.
4. Remove the three retaining nuts from studs holding blower motor.
5. Pull A/C suction and discharge lines inboard and upward while pulling

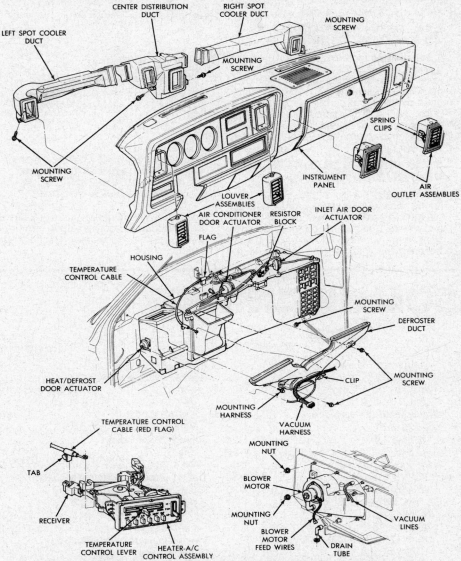

Fig. 20  Heater assembly. 1981 Trail Duster & 1981–89 Ramcharger & Conventional Cabs with A/C

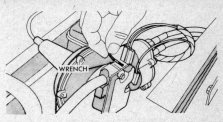

**Fig. 21  Speed control lock-in screw adjustment. 1980–82**

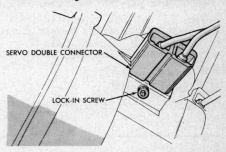

**Fig. 22  Speed control lock-in screw adjustment. 1983–88**

blower motor assembly from housing.
6. Remove blower motor.
7. Reverse procedure to install.

## VANS, WAGONS & FRONT SECTIONS W/AUXILIARY HEATER

### With Auxiliary Air Conditioning

1. Disconnect battery ground cable.
2. Disconnect blower motor electrical connectors.
3. Remove blower motor assembly to floor attaching screws, then the blower motor assembly.
4. Reverse procedure to install.

### Less Auxiliary Air Conditioning

1. Remove heater core, refer to "Heater Core, Replace" procedure.
2. Remove blower motor to heater assembly attaching screws, then the blower motor.

## RAMCHARGER, TRAIL DUSTER & CONVENTIONAL CABS

### LESS A/C

#### 1980 Models

1. Disconnect battery ground cable and blower motor wiring.
2. Disconnect blower motor vent tube.
3. Remove blower assembly mounting screws and blower assembly.
4. Separate wheel from motor, noting position of wheel on shaft.
5. Remove blower mounting plate from motor.
6. Reverse procedure to install.

#### 1981–89 Models

1. Disconnect battery ground cable and blower motor wiring.
2. Remove screws holding blower motor to heater housing on firewall.
3. Remove blower.

4. Reverse procedure to install.

### WITH A/C

#### 1980 Models

1. Disconnect battery ground cable and blower motor wiring.
2. Disconnect blower motor vent tube.
3. Remove blower assembly mounting screws and blower assembly.
4. Separate wheel from motor, noting position of wheel on shaft.
5. Remove blower mounting plate from motor.
6. Reverse procedure to install.

#### 1981–89 Models

1. Disconnect battery ground cable and blower motor wiring.
2. Remove screws holding blower motor to heater housing on firewall, **Fig. 20.**
3. Remove blower.
4. Reverse procedure to install.

## SPEED CONTROL

### ADJUST

#### LOCK-IN SCREW ADJUSTMENT

Lock-in accuracy will be affected by poor engine performance (need for tune up), loaded gross weight of car (trailering), or improper slack in control cable. After the foregoing items have been considered and the speed sags or drops more than 2 to 3 mph when the speed control is activated, the lock-in adjusting screw should be turned counterclockwise approximately 1/4 turn per one mph correction required.

If a speed increase of more than 2 to 3 mph occurs, the lock-in adjusting screw should be turned clockwise 1/4 turn per one mph correction required, **Figs. 21 and 22.** This adjustment must not exceed two turns in either direction or damage to the unit may occur.

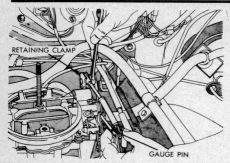

**Fig. 23 Speed control servo throttle cable adjustment. Exc. 1988–89 V6-238/3.9L & V8-318/5.2L engines**

## THROTTLE CABLE ADJUSTMENT

Optimum servo performance is obtained with a given amount of freeplay in the throttle control cable. To obtain proper freeplay, proceed as follows.

### Exc. 1988–89 V6-238/3.9L & V8-318/5.2L Engines

Insert a 1/16 inch diameter pin between forward end of slot in cable end of carburetor linkage pin (hair pin clip removed from linkage pin), **Fig. 23**. With choke in full open position and carburetor at curb idle, pull cable back toward dash until all freeplay is removed. Tighten cable clamp bolt to 45 inch lbs., remove 1/16 inch pin and install hair pin clip.

### 1988–89 V6-238/3.9L & V8-318/5.2L Engines

Grip speed control cable, **Fig. 24**, and lightly push toward servo. Lightly hold cable toward servo and mark next to protective sleeve. Pull speed control cable away from servo. There should be a .24 inch gap between the mark on the cable and the

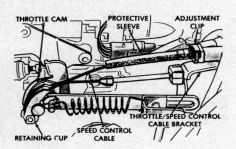

**Fig. 24 Speed control servo throttle cable adjustment. 1988–89 V6-238/3.9L & V8-318/5.2L engines**

sleeve. To correct gap, remove adjustment clip and push protective sleeve into or out of housing as necessary. Recheck gap and install clip.

# GASOLINE ENGINE

## INDEX

# ENGINE MOUNTS
## REPLACE
### FRONT

1. Raise hood, then position fan and related components to ensure necessary clearance.
2. Raise and support vehicle, then attach a suitable lifting device to engine.
3. Remove engine mount to frame attaching nuts.
4. Raise engine slightly, then remove mounts. **Some models incorporate a insulator between the engine mount and engine mount attaching bracket.**
5. Reverse procedure to install. Torque attaching nuts to 75 ft. lbs. and attaching bolts to 65 ft. lbs.

### REAR

1. Raise hood, then position fan and related components to ensure necessary clearance.
2. Raise and support vehicle, position a suitable jack under transmission assembly.
3. On four wheel drive vehicles equipped with skid plate, remove skid plate attaching bolts from the rear crossmember, then from the front crossmember and remove skid plate.
4. On all models, slightly raise transmission and engine assembly, then remove rear mount through bolts.

5. Remove U-shaped bracket from frame cross member.
6. Remove insulator from bottom face of transmission extension housing.
7. Reverse procedure to install. Torque attaching nuts to 75 ft. lbs. and attaching bolts to 65 ft. lbs.

# ENGINE
## REPLACE

If vehicle is equipped with manual transmission, transmission must be removed prior to engine removal. Refer to "Clutch & Manual Transmission" for transmission removal procedure.

## VANS, WAGONS & FRONT SECTIONS

### 6-225/3.7L Engine

1. Disconnect battery ground cable and remove oil dipstick.
2. Raise and support vehicle, then remove air pump tube from exhaust pipe.
3. Remove exhaust pipe, then the inspection cover from transmission.
4. Drain engine oil and remove engine to transmission strut.
5. Remove engine oil pan attaching screws, then the oil pan. It may be necessary to turn crankshaft to clear front of oil pan.
6. Turn pickup tube upward to protect from damage while removing engine, then remove flexplate to torque converter attaching bolts.
7. Remove lower transmission bellhousing attaching bolts, then the lower right engine mount insulator attaching nut.
8. Lower vehicle and drain cooling system.
9. Remove engine cover, then the carburetor air cleaner and carburetor.
10. On models equipped with A/C, discharge refrigerant from system and disconnect condenser lines.
11. On all models, remove fan shroud, windshield washer and over flow reservoirs, then the front bumper, grille and support brace.
12. Disconnect radiator hoses, then remove radiator and support as an assembly.
13. Remove power steering pump with hoses attached and position aside, then remove air pump.
14. Disconnect throttle linkage, vacuum hoses and all engine electrical connectors.
15. Remove alternator with brackets, fan blade, pulley and all drive belts, then disconnect fuel line from fuel pump.
16. Remove starter attaching bolts, then the starter.
17. Remove distributor cap with spark plug wires attached.
18. Remove upper left engine mount insulator attaching nut.
19. Attach suitable chain to cylinder heads to provide as an engine lifting fixture.
20. Install suitable engine hoist to lifting fixture, then place suitable floor jack under transmission.

21. Remove upper bellhousing attaching bolts.
22. Remove engine from front of vehicle.
23. Reverse procedure to install.

### V6-238/3.9L Engine

1. Disconnect battery ground cable, then remove oil dipstick.
2. Raise and support vehicle.
3. Remove exhaust crossover pipe, then the inspection cover from transmission.
4. Drain engine oil, then remove engine-to-transmission strut.
5. Remove engine oil pan attaching screws, then the oil pan. It may be necessary to turn crankshaft to clear front of oil pan.
6. Remove oil pump and pickup tube assembly, then the flexplate-to-torque converter attaching bolts.
7. Remove starter attaching bolts and the starter.
8. Remove lower transmission bellhousing attaching bolts, then the engine mount insulator lower attaching nuts.
9. Lower vehicle and drain cooling system.
10. Remove engine cover, then the throttle body air cleaner and throttle body.
11. On models equipped with A/C, discharge refrigerant from system and disconnect condenser lines.
12. On all models, remove front bumper, grille and support brace.
13. Disconnect radiator hoses, then remove radiator, condenser and support as an assembly.
14. Remove air conditioning compressor, if equipped, then plug all openings to keep out moisture and dirt.
15. Remove power steering pump with hoses attached and position aside, then remove air pump.
16. Disconnect throttle linkage, vacuum hoses and all engine electrical connectors.
17. Remove alternator, fan blade, pulley and all drive belts, then disconnect fuel line from fuel pump.
18. Remove left exhaust manifold and heat shield, then the distributor cap with spark plug wires attached.
19. Attach suitable chain to intake manifold to act as an engine lifting fixture.
20. Install suitable engine hoist to lifting fixture, then place suitable floor jack under transmission.
21. Remove upper bellhousing attaching bolts.
22. Remove engine from vehicle.
23. Reverse procedure to install.

### V8-318/5.2L & V8-360/5.9L Engines

1. Disconnect battery ground cable and remove oil dipstick.
2. Raise and support vehicle, then remove exhaust crossover pipe.
3. Remove inspection cover from transmission.
4. Drain engine oil and remove engine to transmission strut.
5. Remove engine oil pan attaching screws, then the oil pan. It may be necessary to turn crankshaft to clear front of oil pan.

6. Remove oil pump and pickup tube assembly, then the flexplate to torque converter attaching bolts.
7. Remove starter attaching bolts, then the starter.
8. Remove lower transmission bellhousing attaching bolts, then the engine mount insulator lower attaching nuts.
9. Lower vehicle and drain cooling system.
10. Remove engine cover, then the carburetor air cleaner and carburetor.
11. On models equipped with A/C, discharge refrigerant from system and disconnect condenser lines.
12. On all models, remove front bumper, grille and support brace.
13. Disconnect radiator hoses, then remove radiator, condenser and support as an assembly.
14. Remove air conditioning compressor, if equipped, then plug all openings to keep out moisture and dirt.
15. Remove power steering pump with hoses attached and position aside, then remove air pump.
16. Disconnect throttle linkage, vacuum hoses and all engine electrical connectors.
17. Remove alternator, fan blade, pulley and all drive belts, then disconnect fuel line from fuel pump.
18. Remove left exhaust manifold and heat shield, then the distributor cap with spark plug wires attached.
19. Attach suitable chain to intake manifold to provide as an engine lifting fixture.
20. Install suitable engine hoist to lifting fixture, then place suitable floor jack under transmission.
21. Remove upper bellhousing attaching bolts.
22. Remove engine from vehicle.
23. Reverse procedure to install.

## TRAIL DUSTER, RAMCHARGER & CONVENTIONAL CAB

1. Disconnect battery cables and remove battery, then drain cooling system.
2. Mark position of hinges for reassembly, then remove hood.
3. Remove radiator and heater hoses, then the radiator. Position fan shroud aside.
4. On models equipped with A/C, discharge refrigerant from system.
5. On all models, remove vacuum lines, then the distributor with spark plug wires attached.
6. On carbureted models, remove throttle linkage, then the carburetor.
7. On fuel injected models, remove throttle body linkage, then the throttle body.
8. On all models, remove all engine electrical connectors.
9. Remove air conditioning hoses and power steering hoses, if equipped.
10. Remove starter motor, alternator, charcoal canister and horns.
11. Disconnect exhaust pipe at manifold.
12. Remove bellhousing attaching bolts and inspection plate.
13. Attach C-clamp on bottom of trans-

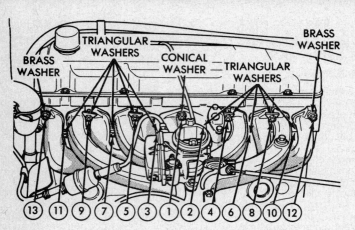

**Fig. 1   Intake manifold tightening sequence.
6-225/3.7L engine**

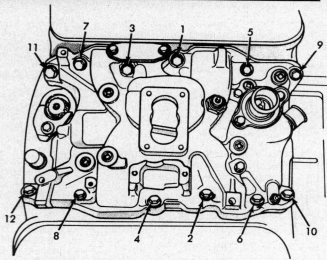

**Fig. 2   Intake manifold tightening sequence.
V6-238/3.9L engine**

mission torque converter housing to prevent torque converter from falling out.

14. Remove torque converter drive plate attaching bolts from torque converter drive plate. Mark converter and drive plate to aid in reassembly.
15. Support transmission using suitable floor jack, then disconnect engine from torque converter drive plate.
16. Install suitable lifting fixture to cylinder head.
17. Install suitable engine hoist to lifting fixture, then remove engine front mount bolts.
18. Remove engine from vehicle.
19. Reverse procedure to install.

## MOTOR HOME

1. Disconnect battery ground cable and drain cooling system.
2. Disconnect radiator hoses, then remove radiator.
3. Remove engine cover, passenger seat and other fixtures that may limit access to top of engine.
4. Disconnect heater hoses and all engine electrical connectors.
5. Remove air cleaner, fuel lines and carburetor.
6. Install engine lifting adapter to carburetor mounting pad on intake manifold.
7. Disconnect throttle linkage at transmission, then the exhaust pipes at both manifolds.
8. Remove line to fuel pump inlet.
9. Support engine using tool No. C-3487A or equivalent. With engine and transmission slightly raised, disconnect transmission rear mount, speedometer cable and hand brake.
10. Remove front bumper and frame front crossmember.
11. Install suitable engine hoist to lifting fixture, then disconnect front engine mounts from frame.
12. Remove engine from vehicle.
13. Reverse procedure to install.

## INTAKE MANIFOLD REPLACE

### 6-225/3.7L ENGINE
**Removal**

1. Disconnect battery ground cable.
2. Disconnect air cleaner vacuum line from carburetor, then the flexible connector between air cleaner and carburetor air heater.
3. Disconnect air cleaner line breather cap, then remove air cleaner.
4. Disconnect distributor vacuum control line, crankcase ventilator valve hose and carburetor bowl vent line, if equipped.
5. Remove carburetor air heater.
6. Disconnect fuel line, automatic choke rod and throttle linkage from carburetor, then remove carburetor.
7. Disconnect exhaust pipe from exhaust manifold.
8. Remove manifold assembly to cylinder head attaching nuts and washers, then the manifold assembly.
9. Remove three intake manifold to exhaust manifold attaching screws, then separate manifolds.

**Installation**

1. Install new gasket between the exhaust and intake manifolds, then the three long screws holding the manifolds together. **Do not tighten the three intake and exhaust manifold attaching screws at this point.**
2. Install new manifold to cylinder head gasket. Coat both sides of gasket with suitable sealing compound.
3. Install manifold assembly then the washers as specified in **Fig. 1.** Install steel conical washer with cup side facing nut and brass washer with flat side facing manifold. **Ensure all washers spanning intake and exhaust flanges are flat and free from distortion.**

4. Install nuts with cone side facing the washers, then torque all intake to exhaust manifold screws and manifold to cylinder head nuts to approximately 10 inch lbs.
5. Torque inboard intake to exhaust manifold screw to specifications, then the outboard intake to exhaust manifold screws to specifications.
6. Repeat step 5 until all three manifold screws are torqued to specifications.
7. Torque manifold to cylinder head nuts to 120 inch lbs. in sequence shown in **Fig. 1.**
8. Attach exhaust pipe to manifold flange, using a new gasket, then torque stud nuts to 35 ft. lbs.
9. Install carburetor air heater, then the air injection tube, if equipped. Torque tube to 200 inch lbs.
10. Install carburetor and connect fuel line, automatic choke rod and throttle linkage.
11. Install distributor vacuum control line and carburetor bowl vent line.
12. Install air cleaner, then connect breather cap to air cleaner line.
13. Install air cleaner vacuum line to carburetor, then the flexible connector between air cleaner and carburetor air heater.

### V6-238/3.9L ENGINE

1. Disconnect battery ground cable, then drain cooling system.
2. Remove alternator, throttle body air cleaner and fuel line, then disconnect accelerator linkage.
3. Remove distributor cap with wires attached, then disconnect coil wires, heat indicator sending unit wire, heater hoses and bypass hose.
4. Remove closed ventilation system, evaporation control system and cylinder head covers.
5. Remove intake manifold attaching bolts, then the intake manifold and throttle body as an assembly.
6. Reverse procedure to install, noting the following:

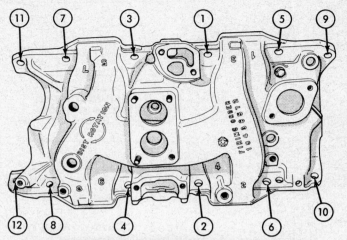

**Fig. 3  Intake manifold tightening sequence. V8-318/5.2L & V8-360/5.9L engines**

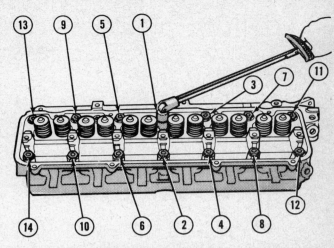

**Fig. 4  Cylinder head tightening sequence. 6-225/3.7L engine**

a. Coat intake manifold side gaskets with suitable sealer.
b. Apply a thin coating of suitable sealer to the intake manifold front and rear gaskets and cylinder block gasket surface.
c. When installing front and rear gaskets, ensure center holes in gasket engage dowels in block and end holes in seals are locked into tangs of head gasket.
d. Place a drop of suitable sealer onto each of the four manifold to cylinder head gasket corners.
e. Tighten intake manifold bolts in sequence shown in **Fig. 2.**

## V8-318/5.2L & V8-360/5.9L ENGINES

1. Disconnect battery ground cable, then drain cooling system.
2. Remove alternator, carburetor air cleaner and fuel line, then disconnect accelerator linkage.
3. Remove vacuum control hose between carburetor and distributor.
4. Remove distributor cap with wires attached, then disconnect coil wires, heat indicator sending unit wire, heater hoses and bypass hose.
5. Remove closed ventilation system, evaporation control system and cylinder head covers.
6. Remove intake manifold attaching bolts, then the intake manifold.
7. Reverse procedure to install, noting the following:
   a. On V8-318/5.2L engines, coat intake manifold side gaskets with suitable sealer.
   b. On V8-360/5.9L engines, do not use any sealer on side composition gaskets.
   c. Apply a thin coating of suitable sealer to the intake manifold front and rear gaskets and cylinder block gasket surface.
   d. When installing front and rear gaskets, ensure center holes in gasket engage dowels in block and end holes in seals are locked into tangs of head gasket.
   e. Place a drop of suitable sealer

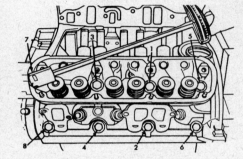

**Fig. 5  Cylinder head tightening sequence. V6-238/3.9L engine**

onto each of the four manifold to cylinder head gasket corners.
f. Tighten intake manifold bolts in sequence shown in **Fig. 3.**

## EXHAUST MANIFOLD REPLACE
### 6-225/3.7L ENGINE

Refer to "Intake Manifold, Replace" procedure.

## V6-238/3.9L, V8-318/5.2L & V8-360/5.9L ENGINES

1. Remove bolts and nuts attaching exhaust pipe to manifold.
2. Remove bolts, nuts and washers attaching manifold to cylinder head.
3. Remove manifold from cylinder head.
4. Reverse procedure to install, noting the following:
   a. If exhaust manifold studs came out with nuts, install new studs, applying suitable sealer on coarse thread ends. **If sealer is not applied to stud threads, water leaks may develop at the studs.**
   b. Install two bolts and conical washers at inner ends of outboard arms of manifold, then two bolts without washers on center arm of manifold.

## CYLINDER HEAD REPLACE
### 6-225/3.7L ENGINE

1. Disconnect battery ground cable and drain cooling system.
2. Remove carburetor air cleaner and fuel line.
3. Disconnect accelerator linkage, then remove vacuum control tube at carburetor and distributor.
4. Disconnect spark plug wires from the spark plugs.
5. Disconnect heater hose, then the clamp attaching bypass hose.
6. Disconnect heat indicator sending unit electrical connector.
7. Disconnect exhaust pipe at exhaust manifold flange.
8. Disconnect diverter valve vacuum line from intake manifold, then remove air tube assembly from cylinder head, if equipped.
9. Remove closed ventilation system, evaporation control system and cylinder head cover.
10. Remove rocker shaft assembly and pushrods. **During disassembly note location of pushrods so they can be installed in the same position.**
11. Remove 14 cylinder head attaching bolts, then the cylinder head, intake and exhaust manifold as an assembly.
12. Reverse procedure to install noting the following:
   a. Tighten head bolts in sequence shown in **Fig. 4.**
   b. Loosen bolts and nuts holding intake manifold to exhaust manifold. This is required to obtain proper alignment.
   c. Install intake and exhaust manifold and carburetor assembly to cylinder head with cup side of conical washers against manifold.

### V6-238/3.9L ENGINE

1. Disconnect battery ground cable and drain cooling system.
2. Remove alternator, then the throttle

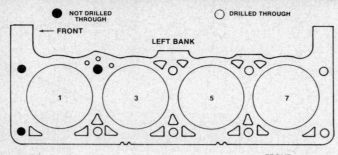

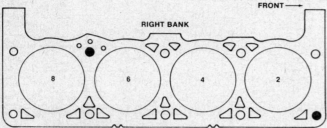

Fig. 6 Cylinder head bolt hole identification. Some V8-318/5.2L engines

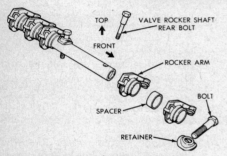

Fig. 9 Rocker arms & shaft. 6-225/3.7L engine

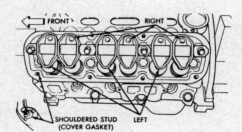

Fig. 10 Rocker arms & shaft. V6-238/3.9L engine

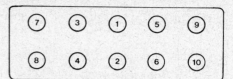

Fig. 8 Cylinder head tightening sequence. V8-446/7.3L engine

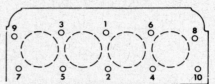

Fig. 7 Cylinder head tightening sequence. V8-318/5.2L & V8-360/5.9L engines

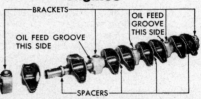

Fig. 11 Rocker arm & shaft assembly installed. V8-318/5.2L & V8-360/5.9L engines

body air cleaner and the fuel line.
3. Disconnect accelerator linkage.
4. Remove distributor cap with spark plug wires attached, then disconnect coil wires, heat indicator sending unit electrical connector, heater hose and bypass hose.
5. Remove closed ventilation system, evaporation control system and cylinder head covers.
6. Remove intake manifold and throttle body as an assembly.
7. Remove exhaust manifolds.
8. Remove rocker shaft assembly and pushrods. **During disassembly note location of pushrods so they can be installed in the same position.**
9. Remove cylinder head attaching bolts and the cylinder heads.
10. Reverse procedure to install, noting the following:
    a. Tighten head bolts in sequence shown in **Fig. 5**. Torque head bolts to 105 ft. lbs.
    b. Tighten intake manifold bolts in sequence shown in **Fig. 2**.

## V8-318/5.2L & V8-360/5.9L ENGINES

Some V8-318/5.2L engines have cylinder head bolt holes drilled through the block into the water jacket in cer-

tain locations, **Fig. 6**. Refer to **Fig. 6** and insert a screwdriver into the head bolt holes. If the screwdriver can be inserted at least two inches into a hole, that hole is open to the water jacket. Cylinder head bolts in these locations must have sealer 4057989 or equivalent applied to the threads to prevent engine coolant leakage. Be sure old sealer is cleaned from the threads before applying new sealer.

1. Disconnect battery ground cable and drain cooling system.
2. Remove alternator, then the carburetor air cleaner and fuel line.
3. Disconnect accelerator linkage.
4. Remove vacuum control hoses between carburetor and distributor.
5. Remove distributor cap with spark plug wires attached, then disconnect coil wires and heat indicator sending unit electrical connector.
6. Remove heater hoses and bypass hose.
7. Remove closed ventilation system, evaporation control system and cylinder head covers.
8. Remove intake manifold, ignition coil and carburetor as an assembly.
9. Remove exhaust manifolds.
10. Remove rocker shaft assembly and pushrods. **During disassembly note location of pushrods so they can**

be installed in the same position.
11. Remove cylinder head attaching bolts, then the cylinder heads.
12. Reverse procedure to install noting the following:
    a. Tighten head bolts in sequence shown in **Fig. 7**. Torque head bolts to 105 ft. lbs.
    b. Tighten intake manifold bolts in sequence shown in **Fig. 3**.

## V8-446/7.3L ENGINE

Cylinder heads should be tightened down by starting from the center, working outward from side to side and to the ends in the sequence shown in **Fig. 8**.

## ROCKER ARM SERVICE

When disassembling rocker arms, place all parts on the workbench in their proper sequence to ensure correct assembly.

Clean all sludge and gum formation from the inside and outside of the shafts. Clean oil holes and passages in the rocker arms and shafts. Inspect the shafts for wear.

### 6-225/3.7L ENGINE

Stamped steel rocker arms are arranged on a single rocker arm shaft, **Fig. 9**. Hardened steel spacers are used between the pairs of rocker arms. The rocker shaft is held in place by bolts and stamped steel retainers attached to the seven brackets on the cylinder head.

Install rocker assembly to cylinder head in the following order:

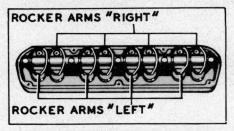

**Fig. 12  Rocker arm & shaft assembly. V8-446/7.3L engine**

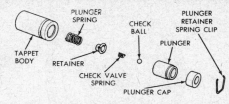

**Fig. 13  Hydraulic valve lifter. V6-238/3.9L, V8-318/5.2L & V8-360/5.9L Engines**

**Fig. 15  Removing stuck hydraulic lifter with special tool. Typical**

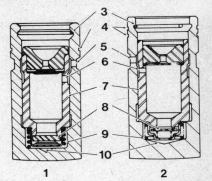

1. Type A
2. Type B
3. Snap ring
4. Identification rules
5. Tappet oil hole
6. Plunger oil hole
7. Plunger
8. Check valve
9. Spring
10. Oil Chamber

**Fig. 14  Hydraulic valve lifter. V8-446/7.3L engine**

1. Rocker arms and shaft assembly should be installed so the oil hole is positioned as shown in **Fig. 9.**
2. Install rocker shaft retainers between rocker arms. Ensure long retainer is installed in center position only.
3. Install rocker shaft bolts, then the special bolt at rear of engine. Torque to specifications.
4. Inspect cylinder head cover gasket flange for scratches or distortion, straighten if necessary.
5. Install new cylinder head cover gasket, then the cylinder head cover.
6. Install closed ventilation system and evaporation control system.

## V6-238/3.9L, V8-318/5.2L & V8-360/5.9L ENGINES

To provide proper lubrication of the rocker arms, the rocker shafts have a small notch machined at one end. Install rocker arm and shaft assemblies with notch on end of rocker shaft pointing to center line of engine and toward front of engine on the left bank and to the rear on the right bank. If rocker arms are removed from shaft, care must be taken to ensure proper reassembly. Some exhaust rocker arms have a relieved area on the underside for rotator clearance. Refer to **Figs. 10 and 11** for proper positioning of rocker arms. Note placement of long stamped steel retainers in the number two and four positions between the rocker arms.

## V8-446/7.3L ENGINE

The rocker arms on these engines are individually mounted and are retained by flange head bolts and pivot balls. Install the rocker arm components in original position, **Fig. 12.**

Inspect the pivot surfaces of the rocker arms and pivot balls for signs of scuffing, pitting or excessive wear. Inspect the valve stem contact surface of the rocker arms for pitting. Replace any component found unsatisfactory.

## VALVE CLEARANCE SPECIFICATIONS

Intake.............................10H
Exhaust...........................20H

## VALVE TIMING

### INTAKE OPENS BEFORE TDC

| | |
|---|---|
| 6-225 | 16 Degrees |
| 6-225 | 6 Degrees |
| V6-238 | 10 Degrees |
| V8-318 | 10 Degrees |
| V8-360 | 18 Degrees |
| V8-446 | 14 Degrees |

## VALVES

### ADJUST

#### 6-225/3.7L ENGINE, 1980

If the cylinder head has been removed it is a good practice to make an initial valve adjustment before starting the engine. Make two chalk marks spaced 120 degrees apart (1/3 of circumference) on the vibration damper so that with the timing mark, the damper is divided into thirds. With the crankshaft at TDC, temporarily set the intake valve lash for No. 1 cylinder at .012 inch and the exhaust at .028 inch. Repeat the procedure for the remaining valves, turning the crankshaft 1/3 turn in the

direction of normal rotation while adjusting the valves in the firing order sequence of 1-5-3-6-2-4. For final adjustment, start and run engine at 550 RPM idle until normal operating temperature is reached. Then adjust valve lash to clearance listed in "Valve Specifications."

## 1981—89 6-225/3.7L, V6 & V8 ENGINES

These engines are equipped with hydraulic lifters. No provision for adjustment is provided.

## VALVE GUIDES

### 6-225/3.7L, V6-238/3.9L, V8-318/5.2L & V8-360/5.9L ENGINES

These engines do not have removable valve guides. The valves operate in guide holes bored in the cylinder head. Valves with oversize valve stems are available for service replacement when necessary to ream the guide holes.

Standard production stem diameter should be .372-.373 inch for intake valves and .371-.372 inch for exhaust valves. If stem wear exceeds .002 inch, replace valve. When reaming guides for oversize valve stems do not attempt to ream from standard to .030 inch oversize. If necessary to ream to that size, use the step procedure of .005 inch, .015 inch and .030 inch. This must be done in order to maintain a true relationship of the guide to the valve seat. The following chart indicates reamer size and valve stem size.

| Reamer Oversize | Valve Stem Size |
|---|---|
| .005 inch | .379-.380 inch |
| .015 inch | .389-.390 inch |
| .030 inch | .404-.405 inch |

### V8-446/7.3L ENGINE

Clean valve guides with a suitable cleaning tool. Then check each valve guide with a GO and NO-GO gauge, if available; otherwise, use a new valve to check the fit. If the NO-GO portion of the

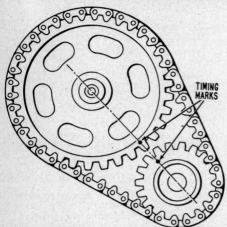

**Fig. 16   Valve timing. All inline six cylinder engines**

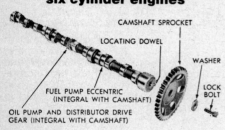

**Fig. 19   Camshaft assembly. 6-225/3.7L engine**

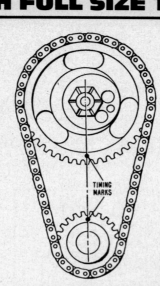

**Fig. 17   Valve Timing. V6 & V8 engines exc. V8-446/7.3L**

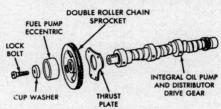

**Fig. 20   Camshaft assembly. V6-238/3.9L engine**

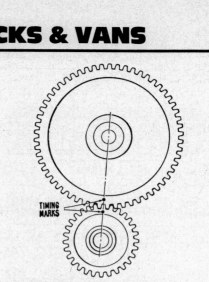

**Fig. 18   Valve Timing. V8-446/7.3L engine**

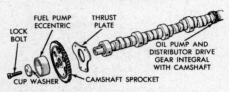

**Fig. 21   Camshaft assembly. V8-318/5.2L & V8-360/5.9L engines**

gauge enters, the guide must be replaced. Replacement is recommended for valve guides with diameters exceeding specifications, bell-mouthed more than .0005 inch or guides which are out of round.

New guides should be installed so that the distance from the cylinder head to the top of the guide is 27/32 inches for intake and 1 1/8 inch for exhaust.

When guides are properly installed, they should be reamed to .374–.375 inch.

## HYDRAULIC VALVE LIFTERS

**Figs. 13 and 14** illustrate the type of hydraulic valve lifters used. Before disassembling any part of the engine to check for noise, check the oil pressure at the gauge and the oil level in the oil pan. The oil level in the pan should never be above the "full" mark on the dipstick, nor below the "add oil" mark. Either of the two conditions could be responsible for noisy lifters.

### LIFTER, REPLACE

Worn valve guides or cocked springs are sometimes mistaken for noisy lifters. Determine which lifter is noisy. If the application of side thrust on the valve spring fails to noticeably reduce the noise, the lifter is probably faulty and should be removed for inspection. Removal of stuck lifters requires a special tool, **Fig. 15.** When installing hydraulic lifters in the engine, fill them with light engine oil to avoid excessive time required to quiet them during initial operation of engine.

## TIMING CHAIN COVER
### 6-225/3.7L ENGINE

1. To remove cover, drain cooling system and remove radiator and fan.
2. Remove vibration damper with a puller.
3. Loosen oil pan bolts to allow clearance and remove chain case cover.
4. Reverse above procedure to install cover.

### V6 & V8 ENGINES

To remove cover, first drain cooling system, remove radiator, fan belt, power steering pump and water pump assembly. Then, remove pulley from vibration damper and after removing bolt and washer, use puller to remove damper. Next, remove fuel lines and fuel pump. Loosen oil pan bolts and after removing front bolt at each side, timing cover may be removed. Reverse procedure to install cover, torque bolts to 30 ft. lbs. and install new oil seal.

## TIMING GEARS OR CHAIN
### REPLACE
### 6-225/3.7L ENGINE

1. After removing timing chain cover as outlined above, remove camshaft sprocket lock bolt, then remove timing chain and sprocket.
2. Clean all parts and inspect chain for broken or damaged links. Inspect

sprockets for cracks and chipped, worn or damaged teeth.
3. Turn crankshaft so sprocket timing mark is toward and directly in line with center line of camshaft.
4. Temporarily install camshaft sprocket. Rotate camshaft to position sprocket timing mark toward and directly in line with centerline of crankshaft: then remove camshaft sprocket.
5. Place chain on crankshaft sprocket and position camshaft sprocket in chain so sprocket can be installed with timing marks aligned and without moving camshaft, **Fig. 16.**
6. Install remaining components in reverse order of removal.

### V6-238/3.9L, V8-318/5.2L & V8-360/5.9L ENGINES

To install chain and sprockets, lay both camshaft and crankshaft sprockets on bench. Position sprockets so that the timing marks are next to each other. Place chain on both sprockets, then push sprockets apart as far as the chain will permit. Use a straightedge to form a line through the exact centers of both gears. The timing marks must be on this line.

Slide the chain with both sprockets on the camshaft and crankshaft at the same time, then recheck the alignment, **Fig. 17. Use Tool C-3509 to prevent camshaft from contacting welch plug in rear of engine block. Remove distributor and oil pump distributor drive gear. Position tool against rear side of camshaft gear and attach with distributor retainer plate bolt. Torque camshaft thrust plate bolts to 210 inch lbs. Torque camshaft bolt to 35 ft. lbs.**

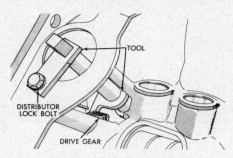

**Fig. 22 Install camshaft holding tool**

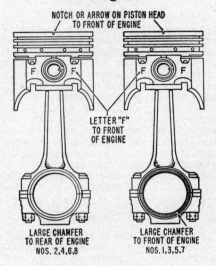

**Fig. 25 Piston & rod assembly. V8 engines exc. V8-446/7.3L**

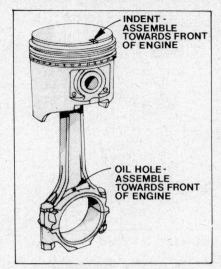

**Fig. 23 Piston & rod assembly. 6-225/3.7L engine**

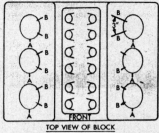

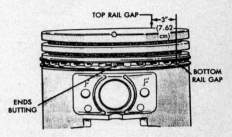

**Fig. 24 Oil ring installation. V6-238/3.9L engine**

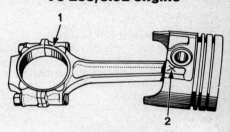

1 LARGE CHAMFER

2 PLACE MARK HERE

**Fig. 26 Piston & rod assembly. V8-446/7.3L engine**

## V8-446/7.3L ENGINE

When valves are correctly timed, the timing marks on the gears or sprockets should be adjacent to each other, **Fig. 18.**

## CAMSHAFT
## REPLACE

When removing camshaft or bearings, it is recommended that the engine be removed from chassis.

### 6-225/3.7L ENGINE

1. Remove lifters and pushrod using tool No. C-4129. Identify lifters to ensure correct position during installation.
2. Remove timing sprockets, distributor and oil pump.
3. Remove fuel pump.
4. Install long bolt into front of camshaft to facilitate removal, then remove camshaft from engine, **Fig. 19. Whenever new camshaft or lifters have been installed, add one pint of suitable crankcase conditioner to engine oil to aid lubrication during break-in.** Lifters should be inspected for crown using suitable straightedge. If negative crown (dishing) is observed, lifter should be replaced.

## V6-238/3.9L, V8-318/5.2L & V8-360/5.9L ENGINES

### Removal

1. Remove intake manifold, cylinder head covers, timing chain cover and timing chain.
2. Remove rocker arm and shaft assemblies.
3. Remove pushrods and lifters using suitable tool. Identify lifters to ensure correct position during installation.
4. Remove distributor, then lift out oil pump and distributor driveshaft.
5. Remove camshaft thrust plate noting location of oil tab.
6. Install long bolt into front of camshaft to facilitate removal, then remove camshaft from engine, **Figs. 20 and 21.**

### Installation

1. Lubricate camshaft lobes and bearing journals, then install camshaft within two inches of final position in cylinder block.
2. Install tool No. C-3509 as shown in **Fig. 22.**
3. Hold tool in position with distributor lock plate screw. **Tool should remain installed until camshaft, crankshaft sprockets and timing chain have been installed.**
4. Install camshaft thrust plate and chain oil tab attaching screws, ensuring tang enters lower right hole in thrust plate, then torque attaching screws to 210 inch lbs. **Top edge of tab should be flat against thrust plate in order to catch oil for chain lubrication.**
5. Install timing chain, refer to "Timing Gears Or Chain" procedure.
6. Install fuel pump eccentric, cup washer and camshaft bolt. Torque bolt to 35 ft. lbs.
7. Reverse remaining procedure to assemble.

### V8-446/7.3L ENGINE

1. Remove oil pump and distributor.
2. Remove valve lifters, water pump, crankshaft pulley and damper, then the timing case cover.
3. Remove camshaft thrust flange attaching bolts, then the camshaft. **Use caution when handling camshaft assembly to prevent chipping distributor gear teeth.**
4. Reverse procedure to install. To align timing marks refer to "Timing Gears Or Chain, Replace" procedure.

## PISTONS & RODS
## ASSEMBLE
### 6-225/3.7L ENGINE

Piston and rod assemblies should be installed as shown in **Fig. 23.**

### V6-238.3.9L ENGINE

When installing piston and rod assemblies in the cylinders, the compression ring gaps should be staggered and not in line with the oil ring gap. Ensure oil ring expander ends are butted and the rail gaps are located as shown in **Fig. 24.**

Immerse the piston head and rings in clean engine oil and, with a suitable piston ring compressor, insert the piston and rod assembly into the bore. Tap the piston down into the bore, using the handle of a hammer.

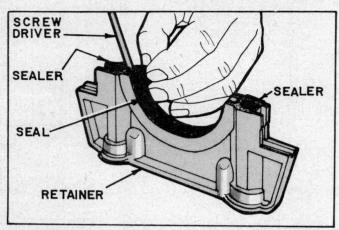

**Fig. 27 Lower oil seal & retainer. 6-225/3.7L engine**

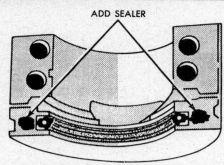

**Fig. 28 Rear main bearing cap. V8-360/5.9L engine**

Assemble and install the pistons and rods with the notch or groove on top of pistons pointing toward front of engine and the larger chamfer of the connecting rod bore installed toward crankshaft journal fillet.

## V8-318/5.2L & V8-360/5.9L ENGINES

When installing piston and rod assemblies in the cylinders, the compression ring gaps should be diametrically opposite one another and not in line with the oil ring gap. The oil ring expander gap should be toward the outside of the "V" of the engine. The oil ring gap should be turned toward the inside of the engine "V."

Immerse the piston head and rings in clean motor oil and, with a suitable piston ring compressor, insert the piston and rod assembly into the bore. Tap the piston down into the bore, using the handle of a hammer.

Assemble and install the pistons and rods as shown in **Fig. 25.**

## V8-446/7.3L ENGINE

Before disassembling, mark piston on same side as large chamfer on connecting rod, so they can be assembled in the same position. New pistons may be installed either way on connecting rod, **Fig. 26.**

When installing piston in engine the large chamfered side of each connecting rod must be located against the crankshaft face. The chamfer provides clearance at the crankshaft fillet.

## PISTONS, PINS & RINGS
### EXC. V8-446/7.3L ENGINE

Pistons are available in standard sizes and .020 inch oversize.

Pins are available in the following oversizes: V6-238/3.9L, V8-318/5.2L & V8-360/5.9L engines, .003, .008 inch. Oversize pins are not available on other engines.

Rings are available in the following oversizes: std. to .009, .020-.029, .040-.049 inch.

## V8-446/7.3L ENGINE

Pistons are available in standard sizes and the following oversizes: .010, .020, .030 inch.

Oversize pins are not available.

Rings are available in the following oversizes: .010, .020, .030 inch.

## MAIN & ROD BEARINGS
### EXC. V8-446/7.3L ENGINE

Main bearings are furnished in standard sizes and the following undersizes: .001, .002, .003, .010, .012 inch.

Rod bearings are furnished in standard sizes and the following undersizes: .001, .002, .003, .010, .012 inch.

## V8-446/7.3L ENGINE

Main and rod bearings are furnished in standard sizes and the following undersizes: .010, .020, .030 inch.

## CRANKSHAFT OIL SEAL REPLACE
### 6-225/3.7L ENGINE

When necessary to replace rear main bearing oil seal, removal of engine from vehicle or removal of crankshaft from engine block is not necessary. Remove engine oil pan as described under "Oil Pan, Replace," then the rear main bearing cap. Using oil seal replacement tool No. KD-492 or equivalent, remove defective upper seal, then, using same tool, install new seal. After installation, trim upper seal to eliminate frayed ends. Install rear main bearing cap, then the oil pan as described under "Oil Pan, Replace."

Replacement seals are of two piece rubber type composition which make possible the replacement of upper rear seal without removing crankshaft. Both halves must be used. After removing oil pan, rear main bearing cap and seal retainer, pry lower seal from retainer with small screwdriver. On models with rope type seal, screw a special tool into upper seal and carefully pull to remove seal while rotating crankshaft. On models with rubber type seal, remove upper seal by pressing with a suitable screwdriver on end of seal, being careful not to damage crankshaft. Wipe

crankshaft surface clean, then oil lightly before installing new upper seal. After oiling seal lip, hold seal with paint stripe to rear tightly against crankshaft with thumb. Carefully slide seal into groove in block making sure sharp edge does not shave or nick seal. Crankshaft may be rotated to ease seal into groove but sealing lip must not be damaged. Install other half of seal into lower seal retainer again with paint stripe to rear, then install rear main bearing cap and torque to specifications. Before installing seal retainer, apply a small amount of gasket sealer to mating surface of retainer but not on seal ends or seal lip, **Fig. 27.** Install retainer and torque to 30 ft. lbs.

## V6-238/3.9L, V8-318/5.2L & V8-360/5.9L ENGINES

When necessary to replace rear main bearing oil seal on V6-238 and V8-318 engines, removal of engine from vehicle or removal of crankshaft from engine block is not necessary. Remove engine oil pan as described under "Oil Pan, Replace," then the rear main bearing cap. Using oil seal replacement tool No. KD-492 or equivalent, remove defective upper seal, then, using same tool, install new seal. After installation, trim upper seal to eliminate frayed ends. Install rear main bearing cap, then the oil pan as described under "Oil Pan, Replace."

Replacement of rear main bearing oil seals is similar to procedure given above for inline 6 cylinder engines. A seal retainer is not found on these engines; lower half of seal is installed into groove in rear main bearing cap.

The 238 and 318 engines have cap seals in addition to lower seal secured by rear main bearing cap. Cap seal with yellow paint is installed, narrow sealing edge up, into right side with bearing cap in engine position. Cap seals must be flush with shoulder of bearing cap to prevent oil leakage.

The 360 engine requires sealer to be applied adjacent to rear main bearing oil seal, **Fig. 28,** as cap seals are not used. After applying sealer, quickly assemble rear main bearing cap to block and torque to specifications.

## V8-446/7.3L ENGINE

Crankshaft rear bearing oil seal consists of two pieces of special packing. One piece is installed in the groove in the rear bearing cap and the other piece is installed

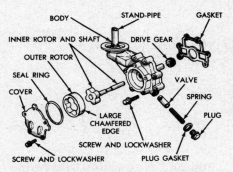

**Fig. 29 Oil pump exploded view. 6-225/3.7L engine**

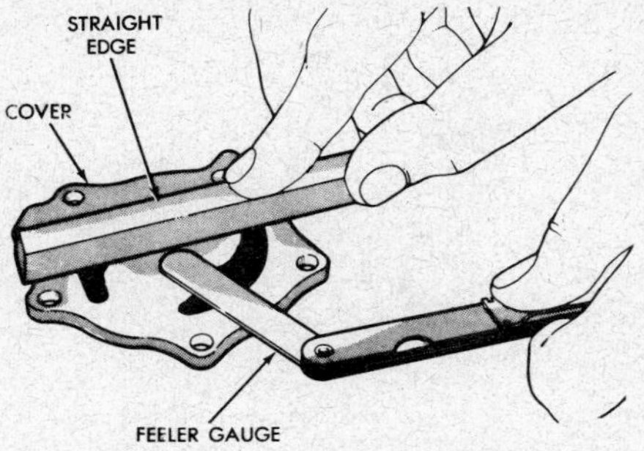

**Fig. 30 Checking oil pump cover flatness. Typical**

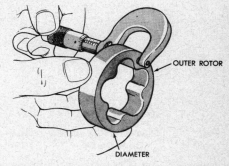

**Fig. 31 Measuring outer rotor thickness**

in a similar groove in the cylinder block.

Position the rear bearing seal in the groove in the cylinder block. Lay an improvised mandrel in the bearing bore and strike the mandrel with a hammer to drive the seal into the groove. Install the seal in the bearing cap in a similar manner. Using a sharp knife, cut off both ends of each seal which project out of the grooves. When cutting off the ends of the seals, do not leave frayed ends which would prevent proper seating of the bearing cap if the ends should extend between cap and cylinder block.

# OIL PAN
## REPLACE
### 6-225/3.7L ENGINE

1. Disconnect battery ground cable, then remove engine oil dipstick, dipstick tube, engine cover and air cleaner.
2. Raise and support front of vehicle, then drain crankcase and remove engine to transmission strut, if equipped.
3. On models equipped with automatic transmission, remove torque converter inspection cover.
4. Remove frame reinforcement if so equipped.
5. Remove oil pan attaching screws and position the crankshaft to permit clearance for oil pan removal. Remove oil pan.
6. Reverse procedure to install. On California models, left side gasket is of high temperature type. On all models, apply 1/8 inch drop of suitable sealer to all four corners of rubber seal and cork gasket.

### V6-238/3.9L ENGINES

1. Disconnect battery ground cable, then remove engine oil dipstick.
2. Raise and support vehicle.
3. Drain engine oil, then remove exhaust crossover pipe and left engine-to-transmission strut.
4. Remove oil pan attaching screws and the oil pan.
5. Reverse procedure to install. Clean the oil pan in solvent and inspect condition of oil screen. Using a new pan gasket, apply a drop of suitable sealant at corners of rubber and cork. Torque oil pan bolts to 200 inch lbs.

### V8-318/5.2L, V8-360/5.9L & 446/7.3L ENGINES

1. Drain engine oil and remove oil dipstick.
2. On 318 and 360 engines, disconnect crossover pipe from both manifolds. On Sport Utility vehicles, remove the left engine to transmission support only.
3. On all engines, remove the oil pan attaching screws and oil pan.
4. Reverse the procedure to install. Clean the oil pan in solvent and inspect the oil strainer alignment. On engines exc. V8-446/7.3L, use a new pan gasket set and add a drop of sealant 4026070 or equivalent at corners of rubber and cork. On V8-446/7.3L engines, a liquid gasket material is used. Apply 1/8 inch bead of sealer at corners and both ends and 1/16 inch bead of sealer on both sides. Torque oil pan bolts to 200 inch lbs.

# OIL PUMP SERVICE
### 6-225/3.7L ENGINE

Remove pump from side of engine by first unbolting oil pump cover, **Fig. 29**. Outer rotor will drop out when cover is removed. Do not allow rotor to be damaged by dropping it. Oil pump can now be unbolted and disassembled for inspection. Press off drive gear, supporting gear to keep load off aluminum body. Inner rotor and shaft can now be removed. Remove oil pressure relief valve plug and lift out spring and plunger. Clean all parts thoroughly. If mating surface of oil pump cover is scratched or grooved, replace pump assembly. Lay a straightedge across pump cover surface, **Fig. 30**. If a .0015 inch feeler gauge can be inserted between cover and straightedge, replace pump assembly. If outer rotor thickness measures .649 inch on 1980 or .825 inch or less on 1981-87 engines, and the diameter is 2.469 inches or less, replace shaft and both rotors, **Fig. 31**. Shaft and both rotors should also be replaced if inner rotor thickness measures .649 inch or less on 1980, or .825 or less on 1981-87 engines, **Fig. 32**. With outer rotor inserted into pump body, press rotor to one side with fingers. If clearance between rotor and pump body is .014 inch or more, replace oil pump assembly, **Fig. 33**. With inner rotor inserted into pump body,

place a straightedge across face between bolt holes. If a feeler gauge of .004 inch or more can be inserted between rotors and straightedge, replace oil pump assembly,

Using new parts as required, assemble pump except for outer rotor and cover. Install oil pump on engine then coat inside of pump with oil to assure priming. Install outer rotor and cover using new seal ring.

### V6-238.3.9L, V8-318/5.2L & V8-360/5.9L ENGINES

Removal of oil pump for servicing requires oil pan to be removed and oil pump unbolted from rear main bearing cap. With pump removed, disassemble pressure relief valve by pulling out cotter pins and drilling a 1/8 inch hole into center of relief valve retainer cap, **Fig. 36**. Insert a self-threading sheet metal screw into cap and secure head in vise. While supporting pump body, remove cap by tapping body with soft hammer. Discard retainer cap and remove spring and relief valve. On V8 engines, relief valve spring has a free length of $2^{1}/_{32}$ to $2^{3}/_{64}$ inch and should test between 16.2 and 17.2 lbs. when compressed to $1^{11}/_{32}$ inch. On V6 engines, relief valve spring has a free length of 1.95 inches and should test between 19.5 and 20.5 lbs. when compressed to $1^{11}/_{32}$ inch. Replace spring that fails to meet specifications. Unbolt oil pump cover and discard oil seal ring. Inner rotor and shaft can now be removed as well as outer rotor. Clean all parts thoroughly and inspect for damage or wear. If mating surface of oil pump cover is scratched or grooved, replace pump assembly. Lay a straightedge across pump cover surface. If a .0015 inch feeler gauge can be inserted between cover and straightedge, replace pump assembly, **Fig. 30**. If outer rotor thickness measures .825 inch or less on 238 and 318 engines, or less than .943 inch on 360 engine, or the diameter is 2.69 inches or less, replace the outer rotor, **Fig. 31**. If inner rotor measures .825 inch or less on 238 and 318 engines or less than .943 on 360 engine, replace inner rotor and shaft assembly, **Fig. 32**. With outer rotor inserted into pump body, press rotor to one side with fingers. If clearance between rotor and pump body is .014 inch or more, replace oil pump assembly, **Fig. 33**. With inner rotor inserted into pump body, place a straightedge across face between bolt holes. If a feeler gauge of .004 inch can be inserted between rotors and

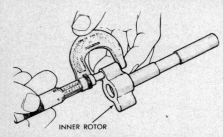

**Fig. 32   Measuring inner rotor thickness**

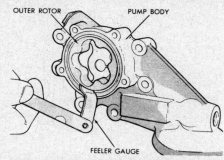

**Fig. 33   Measuring outer rotor clearance in pump body**

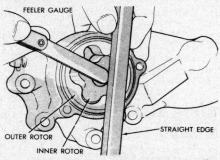

**Fig. 34   Measuring clearance over rotor**

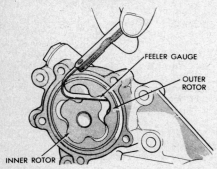

**Fig. 35   Measuring clearance between rotors**

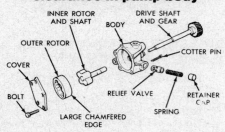

**Fig. 36   Oil pump. V6-238/3.9L, V8-318/5.2L & V8-360/5.9L engines**

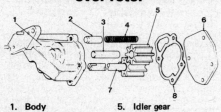

1. Body
2. Valve
3. Idler shaft
4. Spring
5. Idler gear
6. Cover
7. Drive shaft and gear
8. Gasket

**Fig. 37   Oil pump. V8-446/7.3L engine**

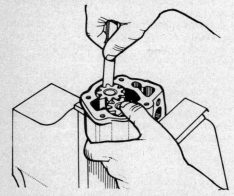

**Fig. 38   Measuring oil pump gear to body clearance. V8-446/7.3L engine**

ance between outside diameter of gear and bore of housing, **Fig. 38**. If clearance is not between .0014-.0054 inch, replace worn parts. Check pump shaft clearance in bore. If clearance is not between .001-.0025 inch, replace pump. Check backlash between pump body and gears. If clearance is more than .0107 inch, replace gear. Check body gear end clearance. Clearance should be .0015-.0065 inch. If endplay is not within specifications, add or remove oil pump cover gaskets to obtain specified clearance.

# WATER PUMP REPLACE

When it becomes necessary to remove a fan clutch of the silicone type, the assembly must be supported in the vertical position to prevent leaks of silicone fluid from the clutch mechanism. This loss of fluid will render the fan clutch inoperative.

## 6-225/3.7L ENGINE

1. Drain cooling system, then remove battery from vehicle.
2. Loosen alternator, air pump, power steering pump or idler pulley, if equipped, then remove all drive belts.
3. Remove fan, spacer or fluid unit, pulley and bolts as an assembly.
4. Remove fan shroud if equipped.
5. Remove A/C compressor and air pump bracket to water pump attaching bolts, if equipped, then position compressor and air pump aside. Keep compressor in upright position.
6. Disconnect heater hoses.
7. Remove water pump attaching bolts, then the water pump.
8. Reverse procedure to install.

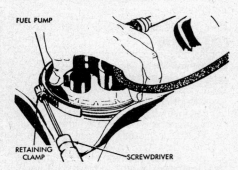

**Fig. 39   Removing fuel pump assembly from fuel tank. Fuel injected engines**

## V6-238/3.9L, V8-318/5.2L & V8-360/5.9L ENGINES

1. Drain cooling system, then remove battery from vehicle.
2. Remove radiator, if equipped with A/C.
3. Loosen alternator adjusting strap bolt and pivot bolt.
4. Loosen power steering and air pumps, if equipped, then remove all drive belts.
5. On engines less A/C, remove alternator bracket attaching bolts from water pump, then swing alternator out of way.
6. On engines with A/C, remove alternator, adjusting bracket and power steering pump attaching bolts and position aside.
7. On all models, remove fan blade, spacer or fluid unit, pulley and bolts as an assembly.
8. Disconnect heater and bypass hoses, then remove A/C compressor pulley

straightedge, replace oil pump assembly, **Fig. 34**. Shaft and both rotors should be replaced if tip clearance between inner and outer rotor exceeds .008 inch on V6 engines and .010 inch on V8 engines, **Fig. 35**. Using new parts as required, assemble pump. Prime pump before installation by filling rotor cavity with engine oil.

## V8-446/7.3L ENGINES

The oil pump, **Fig. 37**, consists of two gears and a pressure relief valve enclosed in the body. The pump is driven from the distributor drive gear. The body is equipped with a regulator valve that limits oil pressure to approximately 50 psi.

After removing the oil pan, the pump may be removed from its mounting and disassembled for repairs. With the pump cover removed, exert pressure against gear with the thumb so as to push gear from outlet side of pump. Measure clear-

and field coil assembly, if equipped.
9. Remove water pump to compressor front mount bracket attaching bolts and bracket.
10. Remove water pump attaching bolts, then the water pump.
11. Reverse procedure to install, Torque bolts to 30 ft. lbs.

## FUEL PUMP
## REPLACE
### CARBURETED ENGINES

Before installing the pump, it is good practice to crank the engine so that the nose of the camshaft eccentric is out of the way of the fuel pump rocker arm when the pump is installed. In this way there will be the least amount of tension on the rocker arm, thereby easing the installation of the pump.
1. Disconnect fuel lines from fuel pump.
2. Remove fuel pump attaching bolts and fuel pump.
3. Remove all gasket material from the pump and block gasket surfaces. Apply sealer to both sides of new gasket.
4. Position gasket on pump flange and hold pump in position against its mounting surface. Make sure rocker arm is riding on camshaft eccentric.
5. Press pump tight against its mounting. Install retaining screws and tighten them alternately.
6. Connect fuel lines. Then operate engine and check for leaks.

### FUEL INJECTED ENGINES
1. Depressurize fuel system as follows:
   a. Loosen gas cap to release fuel tank pressure.
   b. Disconnect electrical connector from injector harness.
   c. Ground one injector terminal using a jumper wire.
   d. Connect one end of jumper wire to second injector terminal and touch the other end to the battery positive terminal for no longer than 10 seconds.
   e. Remove jumper wires.
2. Disconnect battery ground cable.
3. Raise and support vehicle.
4. Drain fuel from fuel tank, then disconnect electrical connectors and lines from tank and remove ground strap.
5. Remove filler tube hose clamps, then disconnect hose from tank.
6. Position a suitable jack under fuel tank and raise slightly.
7. Remove tank retaining straps and lower tank from vehicle.
8. Hold fuel pump assembly down towards tank while loosening retaining clamp, **Fig. 39**, then release assembly and allow it to spring up from its position.
9. Remove fuel pump assembly from tank with O-ring and discard O-ring.
10. Reverse procedure to install, using a new O-ring.

# DIESEL ENGINE
## INDEX

## DESCRIPTION
### AIR INTAKE SYSTEM

The Cummins built engine is an inline six cylinder turbocharged diesel. On turbocharged engines, the flow is from the filter to the turbocharger and then through the air crossover to the manifold. From the intake manifold, air is forced into the cylinder. The exhaust gases flow through the turbocharger to rotate the turbine and impeller, using exhaust energy to force more air into the cylinders. The additional air provided by the turbocharger allows more fuel to be injected to increase power output from the engine, **Fig. 1**.

### FUEL SYSTEM

The function of the fuel system is to inject clean, atomized fuel into the engine cylinders at a precise time near the end of the compression stroke of each piston. The components of the system contribute to the delivery of fuel to the cylinders, **Fig. 2**.

The engine is equipped with a cam actuated lift pump. Fuel flow begins as the lift pump pulls fuel from the supply tank. This pump supplies low pressure fuel (3-5 psi) to the fuel filter head, through the filter and then to the distributor injection pump.

The Bosch distributor type fuel pump builds the high injection pressures required for combustion, and routes the fuel through individual high-pressure fuel lines to each injector. When the high pressure fuel reaches the injector, the pressure lifts the needle valve against the spring tension to let the fuel enter the combustion chamber. Any leakage past the needle valve enters the fuel drain manifold. The fuel drain manifold routes controlled venting from the distributor injection pump and leakage from the injectors back into the fuel tank.

### ELECTRICAL SYSTEM

The electrical system consists of the starting circuit, charging circuit, heaters and control devices. The injection pump uses an electrical fuel shut off valve. The engine has water temperature and oil pressure sensors connected to gauges on the instrument panel. In addition to the ammeter, water and oil gauges, a message center and run circuit is also used, **Fig. 3**. The heater circuits consist of an intake manifold heater system, fuel heater and coolant heater, **Figs. 4 through 6**.

### LUBRICATING SYSTEM

The lubricating gerotor type pump draws oil from the pan and forces it through the lubrication system. The pressure regulation valve controls the oil pressure in the system. This valve is designed to keep the oil pressure from exceeding 60 psi. When the oil pressure is greater than 60 psi, the valve opens uncovering the dump port so part of the oil is routed to the oil pan. The filter bypass valve ensures a supply of oil in the event the filter becomes plugged. The bypass valve, located on oil cooler cover, will let the oil flow bypass a plugged filter. The valve is designed to open when the pressure drop across the filter is more than 20 psi, as with a plugged filter. The piston pins are lubricated by the splash from the piston cooling nozzles. The oil pump idler gear bushing is pressure lubricated. The remainder of the front gear train is lubricated by oil carry over and splash, **Fig. 7**.

The oil coolers are full flow, plate type cooler. The oil flows through a cast passage in the cooler cover and through the element where it is cooled by engine coolant flowing past the plates of the element. After the oil is cooled, it flows through the filter. From the filter oil flows to the turbocharger and engine.

The turbocharger receives cooled and pressurized oil through a supply line from

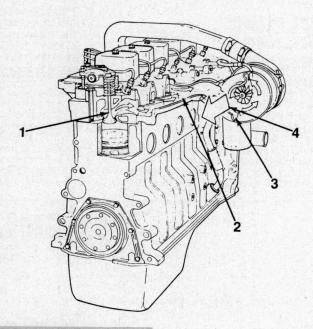

## Exhaust System

1. Exhaust Valve
2. Exhaust Manifold (Pulse-Type)
3. Dual Entry to Turbocharger
4. Turbocharger Exhaust Outlet

## Intake System

1. Intake Air Inlet to Turbocharger
2. Turbocharger Air to Intake Heater Unit
3. Intake Manifold Heater
4. Intake Manifold (Integral part of Cylinder Head)
5. Intake Valve

**Fig. 1   Air flow system**

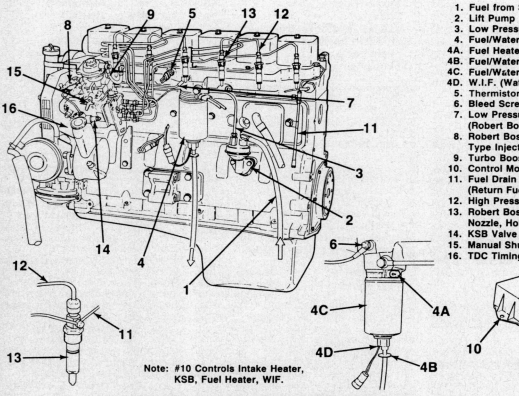

1. Fuel from Supply Tank
2. Lift Pump
3. Low Pressure Supply Line
4. Fuel/Water Separator Filter
4A. Fuel Heater
4B. Fuel/Water Drain Valve
4C. Fuel/Water Separator Filter
4D. W.I.F. (Water in Fuel)
5. Thermistor
6. Bleed Screw
7. Low Pressure Supply Line (Robert Bosch)
8. Robert Bosch VE Distributor Type Injection Pump
9. Turbo Boost Control Line
10. Control Module
11. Fuel Drain Manifold (Return Fuel to Tank)
12. High Pressure Lines
13. Robert Bosch, 17mm, Closed Nozzle, Hole Type Injectors
14. KSB Valve
15. Manual Shut Down
16. TDC Timing Pin

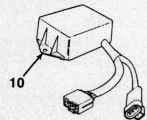

Note: #10 Controls Intake Heater, KSB, Fuel Heater, WIF.

**Fig. 2   Fuel system components & flow**

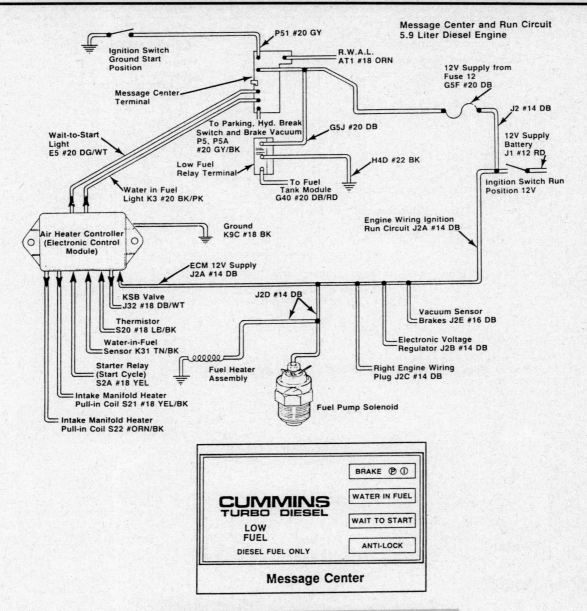

**Fig. 3  Message center & run circuit**

## SYSTEM TROUBLESHOOTING

the filter head. A drain line connected to the bottom of the turbocharger housing returns the oil to the oil pan.

The troubleshooting charts cover a partial list of symptoms of various engine systems. Refer to **Figs. 8 through 32** to diagnosis and correct a system malfunction.

## ENGINE
### REPLACE

If vehicle is equipped with manual transmission, transmission must be removed prior to engine removal. Refer to "Clutch & Manual Transmission" for transmission removal procedure.
1. Mark hood hinges locations and re-

move the hood.
2. Disconnect battery cables and drain cooling system.
3. Remove fan, fan clutch assembly and fan shroud. Disconnect radiator hoses and remove radiator.
4. Disconnect the air intake and exhaust pipes.
5. Discharge refrigerant from A/C system and disconnect air conditioner connections, then disconnect alternator loom.
6. Disconnect accelerator linkage, then disconnect throttle linkage from the control lever. **Do not remove control lever from the injection pump.**
7. Disconnect electrical connections from starter, then remove starter attaching bolts and the starter.
8. Disconnect all engine driven accessories.
9. Disconnect the torque converter, then

disconnect transmission cooler lines.
10. Drain engine oil.
11. Attach suitable chain to the engine by using the lifting eyes located on top of engine. Apply tension to the engine hoist to hold the engine for disconnecting engine mounts from the chassis.
12. Disconnect power steering lines and position aside.
13. Disconnect all lines including fuel lines to the lift pump and fuel return. Mark all lines accordingly, then cover all engine openings.
14. Remove the motor mounts.
15. Remove transmission bolts.
16. Remove engine from vehicle.
17. Reverse procedure to install, noting the following;
    a. Torque engine support bolts to 57 ft. lbs.
    b. Adjust the cable/rod to control le-

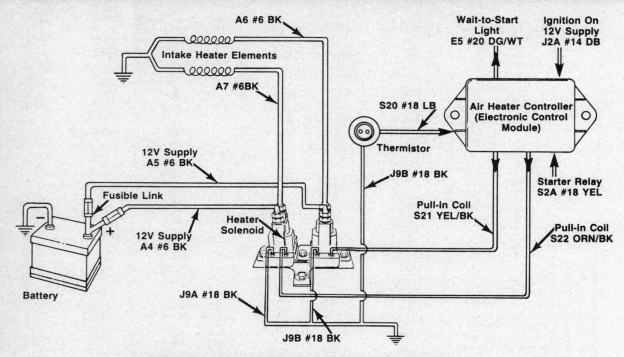

**Fig. 4   Intake manifold heater system**

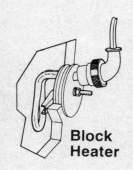

**Fig. 5   Fuel heater**

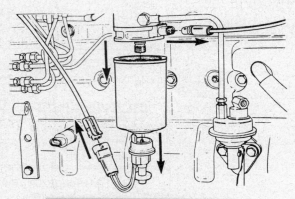

**Fig. 6   Coolant heater**

ver length so the lever has stop-to-stop movement.
c. Fuel filter filled with fuel and injection pump is primed. Bleeding of the fuel system may be required to start the engine.

## EXHAUST MANIFOLD
### REPLACE

1. Loosen air crossover hose clamps.
2. Disconnect air intake and exhaust piping from turbocharger.
3. Disconnect oil supply line and oil drain tube.
4. Remove turbocharger attaching nuts and the turbocharger and gasket.
5. Remove cab heater supply and return lines.
6. Remove manifold attaching bolts, then the manifold and gaskets.

7. Reverse procedure to install, noting the following:
   a. Torque manifold bolts to 32 ft. lbs. and in the sequence shown in **Fig. 33.**
   b. Torque turbocharger mounting nuts to 24 ft. lbs.
   c. Operate engine to check for leaks.

## INTAKE MANIFOLD COVER
### REPLACE

1. Remove throttle control bracket and linkage.
2. Disconnect high pressure lines from the injectors.
3. Remove the line clamp bolts from the intake cover.

4. Remove lines from the injection pump.
5. Disconnect intake manifold heater.
6. Disconnect fuel heater ground wire from intake manifold.
7. Loosen air crossover hose clamp and remove crossover mounting bolts, then remove air crossover tube.
8. Remove intake manifold heater.
9. Remove intake manifold cover attaching bolts, then the manifold cover and gasket.
10. Reverse procedure to install, noting the following:
    a. **Some of the manifold bolt holes are drilled through and must be sealed. Apply liquid teflon sealant to the bolts.** Install bolts and torque to 18 ft. lbs.
    b. Install and bleed high pressure fuel lines.

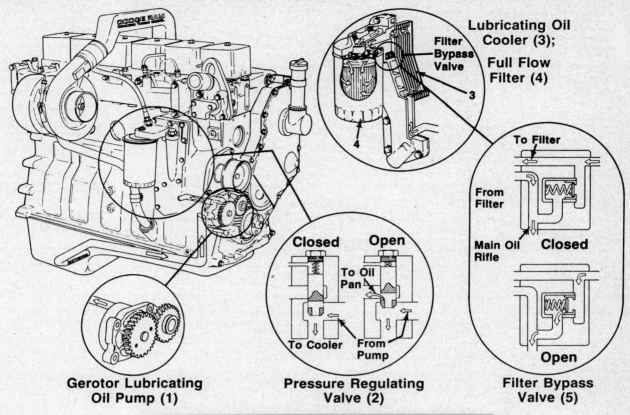

**Fig. 7 Lubrication system components & flow**

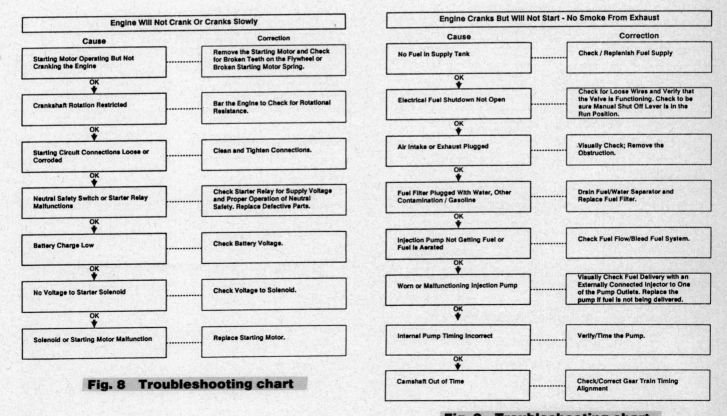

**Fig. 8 Troubleshooting chart**

**Fig. 9 Troubleshooting chart**

# DODGE & PLYMOUTH FULL SIZE TRUCKS & VANS

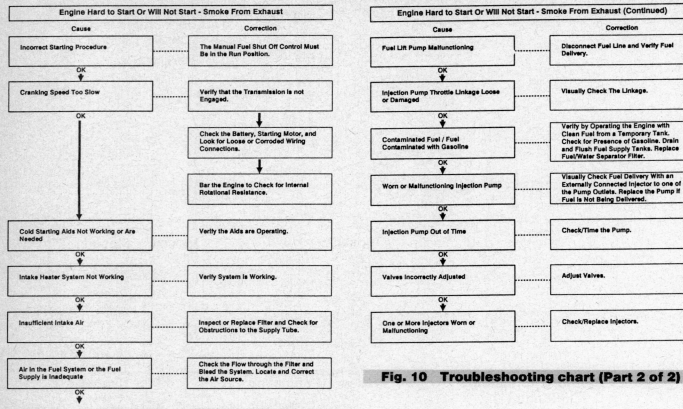

**Engine Hard to Start Or Will Not Start - Smoke From Exhaust**

| Cause | Correction |
|---|---|
| Incorrect Starting Procedure | The Manual Fuel Shut Off Control Must Be in the Run Position. |
| Cranking Speed Too Slow | Verify that the Transmission is not Engaged. |
| | Check the Battery, Starting Motor, and Look for Loose or Corroded Wiring Connections. |
| | Bar the Engine to Check for Internal Rotational Resistance. |
| Cold Starting Aids Not Working or Are Needed | Verify the Aids are Operating. |
| Intake Heater System Not Working | Verify System is Working. |
| Insufficient Intake Air | Inspect or Replace Filter and Check for Obstructions to the Supply Tube. |
| Air in the Fuel System or the Fuel Supply is Inadequate | Check the Flow through the Filter and Bleed the System. Locate and Correct the Air Source. |

**Fig. 10   Troubleshooting chart (Part 1 of 2)**

**Engine Hard to Start Or Will Not Start - Smoke From Exhaust (Continued)**

| Cause | Correction |
|---|---|
| Fuel Lift Pump Malfunctioning | Disconnect Fuel Line and Verify Fuel Delivery. |
| Injection Pump Throttle Linkage Loose or Damaged | Visually Check The Linkage. |
| Contaminated Fuel / Fuel Contaminated with Gasoline | Verify by Operating the Engine with Clean Fuel from a Temporary Tank. Check for Presence of Gasoline. Drain and Flush Fuel Supply Tanks. Replace Fuel/Water Separator Filter. |
| Worn or Malfunctioning Injection Pump | Visually Check Fuel Delivery With an Externally Connected Injector to one of the Pump Outlets. Replace the Pump if Fuel is Not Being Delivered. |
| Injection Pump Out of Time | Check/Time the Pump. |
| Valves Incorrectly Adjusted | Adjust Valves. |
| One or More Injectors Worn or Malfunctioning | Check/Replace Injectors. |

**Fig. 10   Troubleshooting chart (Part 2 of 2)**

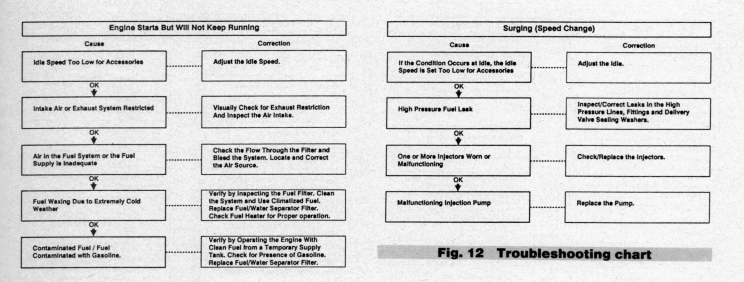

**Engine Starts But Will Not Keep Running**

| Cause | Correction |
|---|---|
| Idle Speed Too Low for Accessories | Adjust the Idle Speed. |
| Intake Air or Exhaust System Restricted | Visually Check for Exhaust Restriction And Inspect the Air Intake. |
| Air in the Fuel System or the Fuel Supply is Inadequate | Check the Flow Through the Filter and Bleed the System. Locate and Correct the Air Source. |
| Fuel Waxing Due to Extremely Cold Weather | Verify by Inspecting the Fuel Filter. Clean the System and Use Climatized Fuel. Replace Fuel/Water Separator Filter. Check Fuel Heater for Proper operation. |
| Contaminated Fuel / Fuel Contaminated with Gasoline. | Verify by Operating the Engine With Clean Fuel from a Temporary Supply Tank. Check for Presence of Gasoline. Replace Fuel/Water Separator Filter. |

**Fig. 11   Troubleshooting chart**

**Surging (Speed Change)**

| Cause | Correction |
|---|---|
| If the Condition Occurs at Idle, the Idle Speed is Set Too Low for Accessories | Adjust the Idle. |
| High Pressure Fuel Leak | Inspect/Correct Leaks in the High Pressure Lines, Fittings and Delivery Valve Sealing Washers. |
| One or More Injectors Worn or Malfunctioning | Check/Replace the Injectors. |
| Malfunctioning Injection Pump | Replace the Pump. |

**Fig. 12   Troubleshooting chart**

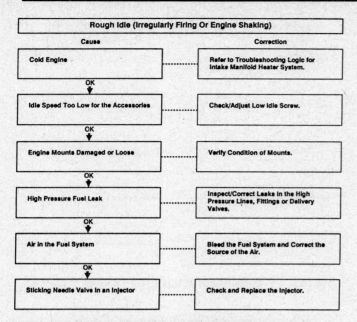

**Fig. 13 Troubleshooting chart**

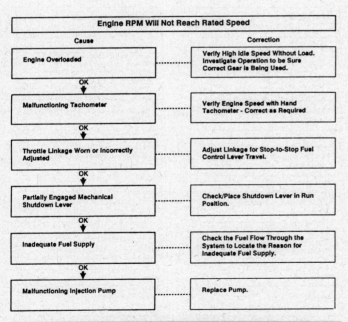

**Fig. 15 Troubleshooting chart**

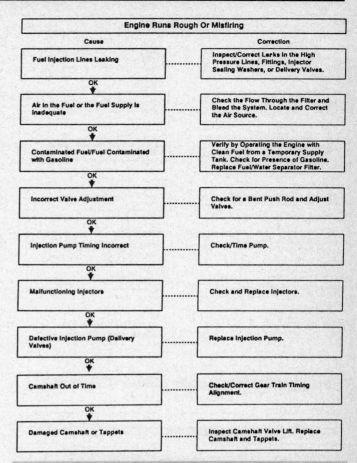

**Fig. 14 Troubleshooting chart**

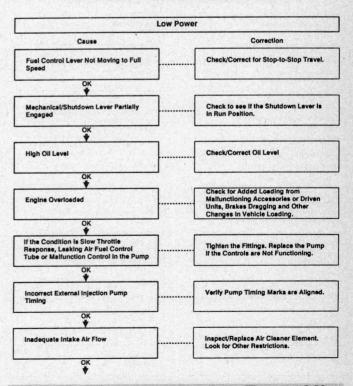

**Fig. 16 Troubleshooting chart (Part 1 of 3)**

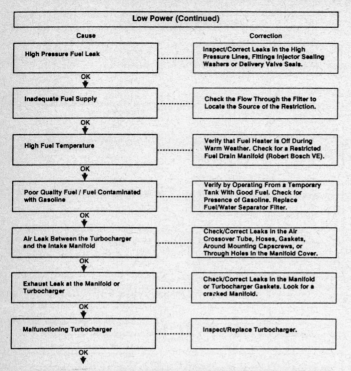

**Low Power (Continued)**

| Cause | Correction |
|---|---|
| High Pressure Fuel Leak | Inspect/Correct Leaks in the High Pressure Lines, Fittings Injector Sealing Washers or Delivery Valve Seals. |
| OK | |
| Inadequate Fuel Supply | Check the Flow Through the Filter to Locate the Source of the Restriction. |
| OK | |
| High Fuel Temperature | Verify that Fuel Heater is Off During Warm Weather. Check for a Restricted Fuel Drain Manifold (Robert Bosch VE). |
| OK | |
| Poor Quality Fuel / Fuel Contaminated with Gasoline | Verify by Operating From a Temporary Tank With Good Fuel. Check for Presence of Gasoline. Replace Fuel/Water Separator Filter. |
| OK | |
| Air Leak Between the Turbocharger and the Intake Manifold | Check/Correct Leaks in the Air Crossover Tube, Hoses, Gaskets, Around Mounting Capscrews, or Through Holes in the Manifold Cover. |
| OK | |
| Exhaust Leak at the Manifold or Turbocharger | Check/Correct Leaks in the Manifold or Turbocharger Gaskets. Look for a cracked Manifold. |
| OK | |
| Malfunctioning Turbocharger | Inspect/Replace Turbocharger. |
| OK | |

**Fig. 16   Troubleshooting chart (Part 2 of 3)**

**Low Power (Continued)**

| Cause | Correction |
|---|---|
| Valve Clearances Incorrect | Check/Adjust Valves. |
| OK | |
| Injection Pump Internal Malfunctioning | Check/Time Pump. |
| OK | |
| Worn or Malfunctioning Injectors | Check/Replace Injectors. |
| OK | |
| Malfunctioning Injection Pump | Replace Injection Pump. |
| OK | |
| Excessive Exhaust Restriction | Check/Correct Exhaust System. |

**Fig. 16   Troubleshooting chart (Part 3 of 3)**

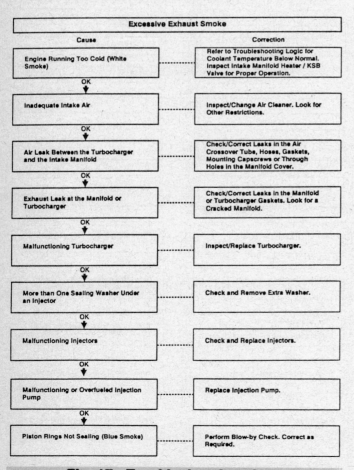

**Excessive Exhaust Smoke**

| Cause | Correction |
|---|---|
| Engine Running Too Cold (White Smoke) | Refer to Troubleshooting Logic for Coolant Temperature Below Normal. Inspect Intake Manifold Heater / KSB Valve for Proper Operation. |
| OK | |
| Inadequate Intake Air | Inspect/Change Air Cleaner. Look for Other Restrictions. |
| OK | |
| Air Leak Between the Turbocharger and the Intake Manifold | Check/Correct Leaks in the Air Crossover Tube, Hoses, Gaskets, Mounting Capscrews or Through Holes in the Manifold Cover. |
| OK | |
| Exhaust Leak at the Manifold or Turbocharger | Check/Correct Leaks in the Manifold or Turbocharger Gaskets. Look for a Cracked Manifold. |
| OK | |
| Malfunctioning Turbocharger | Inspect/Replace Turbocharger. |
| OK | |
| More than One Sealing Washer Under an Injector | Check and Remove Extra Washer. |
| OK | |
| Malfunctioning Injectors | Check and Replace Injectors. |
| OK | |
| Malfunctioning or Overfueled Injection Pump | Replace Injection Pump. |
| OK | |
| Piston Rings Not Sealing (Blue Smoke) | Perform Blow-by Check. Correct as Required. |

**Fig. 17   Troubleshooting chart**

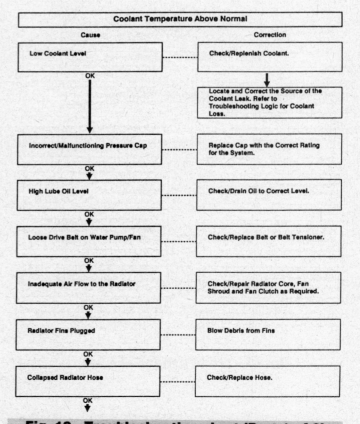

**Coolant Temperature Above Normal**

| Cause | Correction |
|---|---|
| Low Coolant Level | Check/Replenish Coolant. |
| OK | Locate and Correct the Source of the Coolant Leak. Refer to Troubleshooting Logic for Coolant Loss. |
| Incorrect/Malfunctioning Pressure Cap | Replace Cap with the Correct Rating for the System. |
| OK | |
| High Lube Oil Level | Check/Drain Oil to Correct Level. |
| OK | |
| Loose Drive Belt on Water Pump/Fan | Check/Replace Belt or Belt Tensioner. |
| OK | |
| Inadequate Air Flow to the Radiator | Check/Repair Radiator Core, Fan Shroud and Fan Clutch as Required. |
| OK | |
| Radiator Fins Plugged | Blow Debris from Fins |
| OK | |
| Collapsed Radiator Hose | Check/Replace Hose. |
| OK | |

**Fig. 18   Troubleshooting chart (Part 1 of 3)**

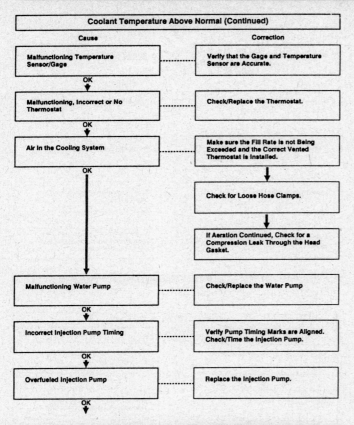

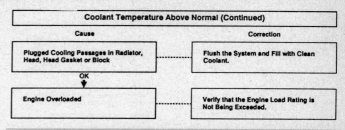

**Fig. 18  Troubleshooting chart (Part 3 of 3)**

**Fig. 18  Troubleshooting chart (Part 2 of 3)**

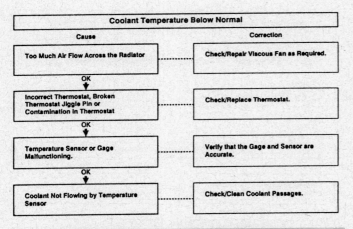

**Fig. 19  Troubleshooting chart**

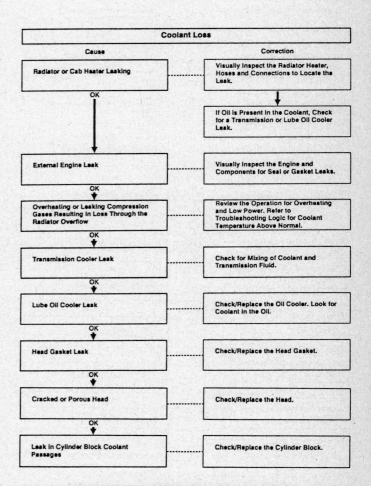

**Fig. 20  Troubleshooting chart**

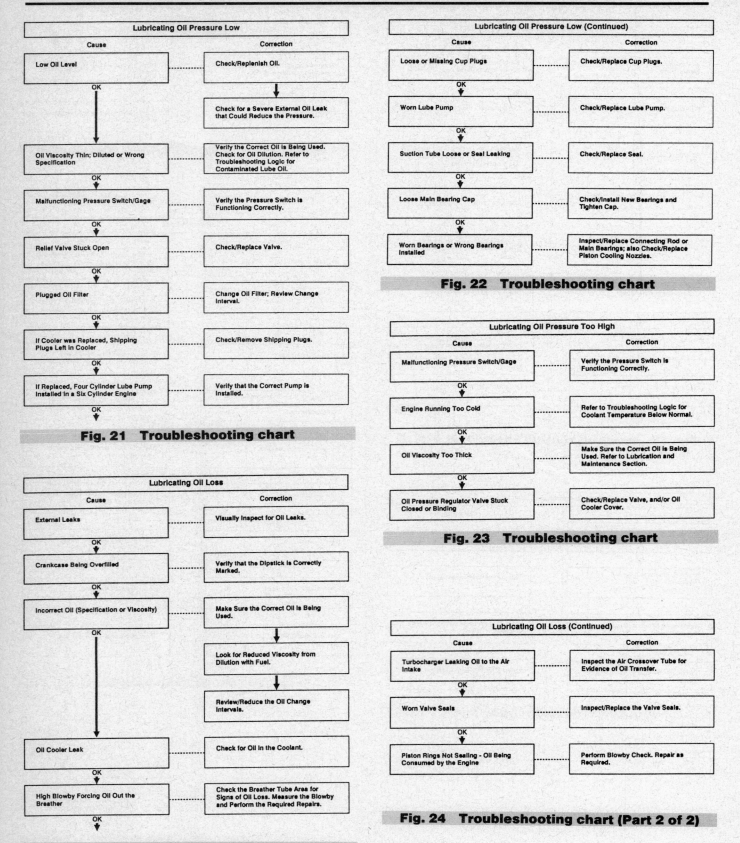

**Lubricating Oil Pressure Low**

| Cause | Correction |
|---|---|
| Low Oil Level | Check/Replenish Oil. |
| | Check for a Severe External Oil Leak that Could Reduce the Pressure. |
| Oil Viscosity Thin; Diluted or Wrong Specification | Verify the Correct Oil is Being Used. Check for Oil Dilution. Refer to Troubleshooting Logic for Contaminated Lube Oil. |
| Malfunctioning Pressure Switch/Gage | Verify the Pressure Switch is Functioning Correctly. |
| Relief Valve Stuck Open | Check/Replace Valve. |
| Plugged Oil Filter | Change Oil Filter; Review Change Interval. |
| If Cooler was Replaced, Shipping Plugs Left in Cooler | Check/Remove Shipping Plugs. |
| If Replaced, Four Cylinder Lube Pump Installed in a Six Cylinder Engine | Verify that the Correct Pump is Installed. |

**Fig. 21   Troubleshooting chart**

**Lubricating Oil Loss**

| Cause | Correction |
|---|---|
| External Leaks | Visually Inspect for Oil Leaks. |
| Crankcase Being Overfilled | Verify that the Dipstick is Correctly Marked. |
| Incorrect Oil (Specification or Viscosity) | Make Sure the Correct Oil is Being Used. |
| | Look for Reduced Viscosity from Dilution with Fuel. |
| | Review/Reduce the Oil Change Intervals. |
| Oil Cooler Leak | Check for Oil in the Coolant. |
| High Blowby Forcing Oil Out the Breather | Check the Breather Tube Area for Signs of Oil Loss. Measure the Blowby and Perform the Required Repairs. |

**Fig. 24   Troubleshooting chart (Part 1 of 2)**

**Lubricating Oil Pressure Low (Continued)**

| Cause | Correction |
|---|---|
| Loose or Missing Cup Plugs | Check/Replace Cup Plugs. |
| Worn Lube Pump | Check/Replace Lube Pump. |
| Suction Tube Loose or Seal Leaking | Check/Replace Seal. |
| Loose Main Bearing Cap | Check/Install New Bearings and Tighten Cap. |
| Worn Bearings or Wrong Bearings Installed | Inspect/Replace Connecting Rod or Main Bearings; also Check/Replace Piston Cooling Nozzles. |

**Fig. 22   Troubleshooting chart**

**Lubricating Oil Pressure Too High**

| Cause | Correction |
|---|---|
| Malfunctioning Pressure Switch/Gage | Verify the Pressure Switch is Functioning Correctly. |
| Engine Running Too Cold | Refer to Troubleshooting Logic for Coolant Temperature Below Normal. |
| Oil Viscosity Too Thick | Make Sure the Correct Oil is Being Used. Refer to Lubrication and Maintenance Section. |
| Oil Pressure Regulator Valve Stuck Closed or Binding | Check/Replace Valve, and/or Oil Cooler Cover. |

**Fig. 23   Troubleshooting chart**

**Lubricating Oil Loss (Continued)**

| Cause | Correction |
|---|---|
| Turbocharger Leaking Oil to the Air Intake | Inspect the Air Crossover Tube for Evidence of Oil Transfer. |
| Worn Valve Seals | Inspect/Replace the Valve Seals. |
| Piston Rings Not Sealing - Oil Being Consumed by the Engine | Perform Blowby Check. Repair as Required. |

**Fig. 24   Troubleshooting chart (Part 2 of 2)**

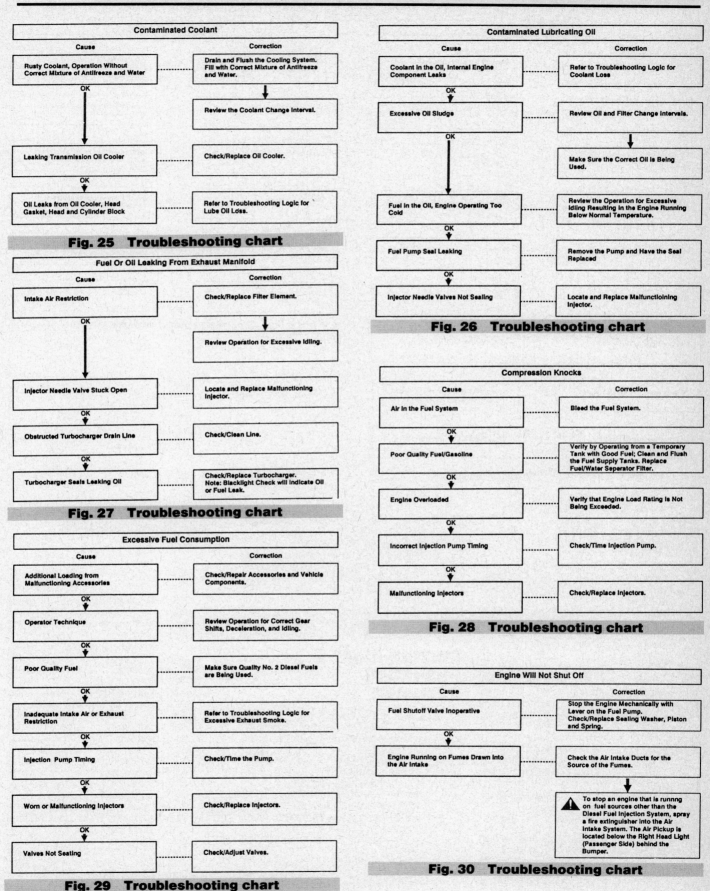

**Contaminated Coolant**

| Cause | Correction |
|---|---|
| Rusty Coolant, Operation Without Correct Mixture of Antifreeze and Water | Drain and Flush the Cooling System. Fill with Correct Mixture of Antifreeze and Water. |
| | Review the Coolant Change Interval. |
| Leaking Transmission Oil Cooler | Check/Replace Oil Cooler. |
| Oil Leaks from Oil Cooler, Head Gasket, Head and Cylinder Block | Refer to Troubleshooting Logic for Lube Oil Loss. |

**Fig. 25   Troubleshooting chart**

**Fuel Or Oil Leaking From Exhaust Manifold**

| Cause | Correction |
|---|---|
| Intake Air Restriction | Check/Replace Filter Element. |
| | Review Operation for Excessive Idling. |
| Injector Needle Valve Stuck Open | Locate and Replace Malfunctioning Injector. |
| Obstructed Turbocharger Drain Line | Check/Clean Line. |
| Turbocharger Seals Leaking Oil | Check/Replace Turbocharger. Note: Blacklight Check will Indicate Oil or Fuel Leak. |

**Fig. 27   Troubleshooting chart**

**Excessive Fuel Consumption**

| Cause | Correction |
|---|---|
| Additional Loading from Malfunctioning Accessories | Check/Repair Accessories and Vehicle Components. |
| Operator Technique | Review Operation for Correct Gear Shifts, Deceleration, and Idling. |
| Poor Quality Fuel | Make Sure Quality No. 2 Diesel Fuels are Being Used. |
| Inadequate Intake Air or Exhaust Restriction | Refer to Troubleshooting Logic for Excessive Exhaust Smoke. |
| Injection  Pump Timing | Check/Time the Pump. |
| Worn or Malfunctioning Injectors | Check/Replace Injectors. |
| Valves Not Seating | Check/Adjust Valves. |

**Fig. 29   Troubleshooting chart**

**Contaminated Lubricating Oil**

| Cause | Correction |
|---|---|
| Coolant in the Oil, Internal Engine Component Leaks | Refer to Troubleshooting Logic for Coolant Loss |
| Excessive Oil Sludge | Review Oil and Filter Change Intervals. |
| | Make Sure the Correct Oil is Being Used. |
| Fuel in the Oil, Engine Operating Too Cold | Review the Operation for Excessive Idling Resulting in the Engine Running Below Normal Temperature. |
| Fuel Pump Seal Leaking | Remove the Pump and Have the Seal Replaced |
| Injector Needle Valves Not Sealing | Locate and Replace Malfunctioning Injector. |

**Fig. 26   Troubleshooting chart**

**Compression Knocks**

| Cause | Correction |
|---|---|
| Air in the Fuel System | Bleed the Fuel System. |
| Poor Quality Fuel/Gasoline | Verify by Operating from a Temporary Tank with Good Fuel; Clean and Flush the Fuel Supply Tanks. Replace Fuel/Water Seperator Filter. |
| Engine Overloaded | Verify that Engine Load Rating is Not Being Exceeded. |
| Incorrect Injection Pump Timing | Check/Time Injection Pump. |
| Malfunctioning Injectors | Check/Replace Injectors. |

**Fig. 28   Troubleshooting chart**

**Engine Will Not Shut Off**

| Cause | Correction |
|---|---|
| Fuel Shutoff Valve Inoperative | Stop the Engine Mechanically with Lever on the Fuel Pump. Check/Replace Sealing Washer, Piston and Spring. |
| Engine Running on Fumes Drawn into the Air Intake | Check the Air Intake Ducts for the Source of the Fumes. |

⚠ To stop an engine that is runnng on fuel sources other than the Diesel Fuel Injection System, spray a fire extinguisher into the Air Intake System. The Air Pickup is located below the Right Head Light (Passenger Side) behind the Bumper.

**Fig. 30   Troubleshooting chart**

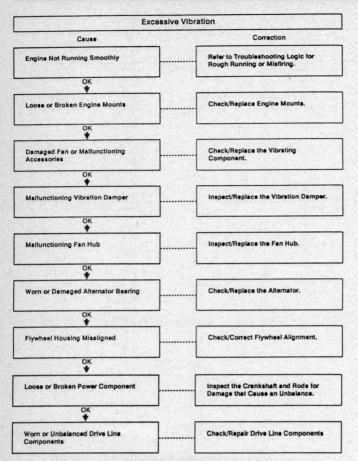

Fig. 31   Troubleshooting chart

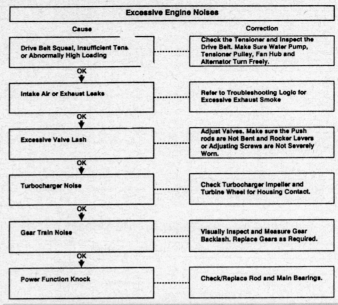

Fig. 32   Troubleshooting chart

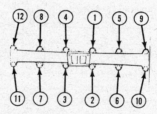

**Fig. 33   Exhaust manifold tightening sequence**

## CYLINDER HEAD
### REPLACE

1. Drain coolant, then engine oil.
2. Disconnect radiator and heater hoses.
3. Remove exhaust manifold as outlined previously.
4. Remove fuel lines and injector nozzles.
5. Remove the valve covers.
6. Remove rocker levers and push rods as follows:
   a. Loosen adjusting screw locknuts, then loosen the adjusting screws until they stop.
   b. Remove bolts from the rocker pedestals, then remove pedestals and rocker lever assemblies.
   c. Remove push rods.
7. Disconnect fuel heater electrical connector, then remove the fuel filter.
8. Remove cylinder head bolts in the sequence shown in **Fig. 34** if engine is hot, removal sequence is not important if engine is cold.
9. Remove cylinder head and gasket from cylinder block.
10. Reverse procedure to install, noting the following:
    a. Inspect coolant passages for rust and lime build up.
    b. Check top surface for flatness be-

tween each cylinder, maximum variation within any two inch diameter area is .003-.0004.
   c. Install head bolts in sequence shown in **Fig. 34**, torque bolts in three stages, step one: 29 ft. lbs., step two: 62 ft. lbs., step three: 93 ft. lbs.
   d. Torque rocker lever pedestal bolts to 18 ft. lbs., then adjust valve clearance.

## ROCKER ARMS & PUSHRODS
### REPLACE

1. Remove valve covers.
2. Loosen adjusting screw locknuts, then loosen the adjusting screws until they stop.
3. Remove bolts from the rocker pedestals, then remove pedestals and rocker lever assemblies, **Fig. 35**.
4. Remove push rods, place push rods and rocker assemblies in order so they may be installed in their original positions.
5. Disassemble rocker arm assembly as follows:
   a. Remove retaining rings and thrust washers.
   b. Remove rocker arm from shaft. **Do**

not disassemble rocker arm shaft and pedestal. Pedestal and shaft must be replaced as an assembly.
   c. Remove lock nut and adjusting screw.
6. Reverse procedure to install, noting the following:
   a. Inspect rocker for excessive wear in the bore (Maximum diameter; .75 inch) and contact surface for the valve stem. Measure rocker shaft diameter. Minimum diameter is .746 inch.
   b. Lubricate rocker shaft with engine oil. **Be sure to assemble intake and exhaust rocker levers in the correct location, Fig. 36.**
   c. Inspect push rod ball and socket for signs of scoring or cracks. Also check push rods for straightness and roundness.
   d. Torque 12mm bolt 93 ft. lbs. and in sequence shown in **Fig. 34.** Torque 8mm bolt to 18 ft. lbs.
   e. Adjust valve clearance.

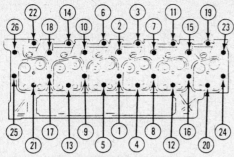

**Fig. 34 Cylinder head tightening sequence**

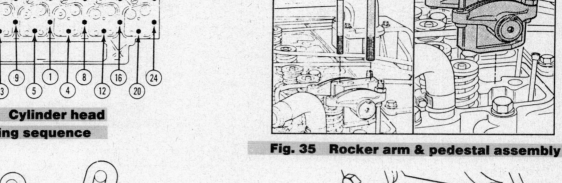

**Fig. 35 Rocker arm & pedestal assembly**

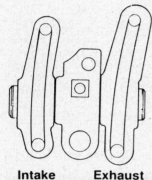

Intake      Exhaust

**Fig. 36 Rocker arm correct location on pedestal**

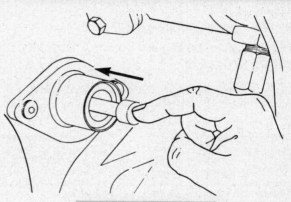

**Fig. 37 Timing pin**

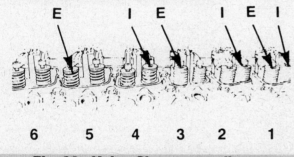

**Fig. 38 Valve Clearance adjustment**

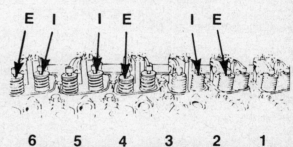

**Fig. 39 Valve Clearance adjustment**

## VALVE CLEARANCE ADJUST

Adjust valve clearance when engine is cold (Below 140°F). With lock nut loose, turn adjusting screw downward until desired clearance is reached using the following procedures.

1. Use the timing pin to locate top dead center for cylinder number one, **Fig. 37**. Be sure to disengage the timing pin after locating top dead center.
2. Adjust the clearance for valves shown in **Fig. 38**. Clearance specifications for intake valves: 0.10 inch, exhaust valves: 0.20 inch.
3. Mark the pulley and rotate crankshaft 360°. Be sure timing pin is disengage before rotating crankshaft.
4. Adjust the clearance for valves shown in **Fig. 39**. Clearance specifications

for intake valves: 0.10 inch, exhaust valves: 0.20 inch.

5. Torque adjusting screw lock nut to 18 ft. lbs.

## VALVE ARRANGEMENT

Front to rear . . . . . . . . I-E-I-E-I-E-I-E-I-E

## VALVE GUIDES REPLACE

To determine guide replacement, measure valve guide bore diameter, measurement should be .31257~.3185 inch. If valve guide bore is over maximum limit, install service guides using the following procedures. New valve guides must be reamed to size after they are installed.

1. Install thin wall guides as follows:
   a. Machine cylinder head valve guide bores to .4380-.0005 inch, **Fig. 40**.

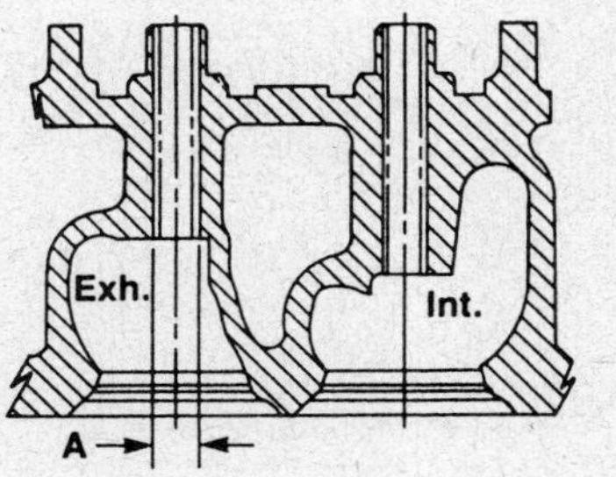

**Fig. 40 Valve guide removal (thin wall guide)**

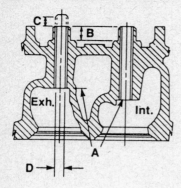

A = Lubricate with oil and press the guides flush to the bottom of the bosses.
B = [.4724 ± .0295 inch] reference
C = Trim off flush to top of guide bosses if necessary.
D = [.3161 ± .0004 inch]

**Fig. 41   Valve guide installation (thin wall guide)**

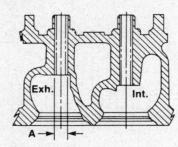

**Fig. 42   Valve guide removal (thick wall guide)**

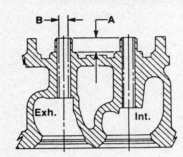

A = [0.4823 ± 0.020 inch]

B = [0.3161 ± 0.0004 inch]

**Fig. 43   Valve guide installation (thick wall guide)**

Service valve guides must be centered with valve seats within .01378 inch diameter and are to be square with the combustion face within .0004 inch at 1.9685 radius.

b. Using a suitable press, install valve guides, **Fig. 41.** Valve guide bore must be centered with valve seats within .0138 inch diameter and must be square with the combustion face within .0004 inch at 2.0 radius.

2. Install thick wall guides as follows:

a. Machine cylinder head valve guide bores to .5512-.0005 inch, **Fig. 42.** Valve guides must be centered with valve seats within .01378 inch diameter and are to be square with the combustion face within .0004 inch at 1.9685 radius.

b. Lubricate with oil and using a suitable press install valve guides to .4823-.020 inch, **Fig. 43.** Ream the bores to .3161-.0004 inch.

## FRONT OIL SEAL REPLACE
### REPLACE

1. Remove fan blade assembly.
2. Lift belt tensioner and remove fan belt.
3. Remove damper bolts and the vibration damper.
4. Drill two 1/8 holes into the seal face, 180° apart.
5. Using a slide hammer with a number ten screw, pull alternating from side to side until seal is free.
6. Before installing seal, apply a bead of Locktite 277 to outside diameter of the seal.
7. Install the pilot from the seal kit onto crankshaft, then place seal onto the pilot and start it into front cover seal bore. Remove the pilot.
8. Use the alignment/installation tool from seal kit and a plastic hammer to install seal to the correct depth.
9. Install vibration damper, but do not tighten bolts.
10. Install belt and torque damper bolts to 92 ft.lbs.

## ENGINE FRONT COVER
### REPLACE

1. Remove fan blade and drive assembly.
2. Lift belt tensioner and remove fan belt.
3. Remove tensioner bolts and belt tensioner.
4. Remove upper oil filler tube bolt, oil filler tube and adaptor.
5. Remove vibration damper and front oil seal as previously described.
6. Remove bolts holding gear cover to gear housing, then gently pry the cover away from the housing.
7. Remove cover from the engine.
8. Reverse procedure to install, noting the following:
   a. Install front cover and start cover bolts, then using alignment/installation tool from seal kit align cover to crankshaft. Torque bolts to 18 ft. lbs.
   b. Install front seal as previously described.

## CAMSHAFT, GEAR, & TAPPET
### REPLACE
#### REMOVAL

1. Remove valve covers.
2. Remove rocker lever assemblies, then the push rods.
3. Remove fan assembly, fan hub assembly and fan belt.
4. Remove vibration damper.
5. Remove oil filler tube, then the gear cover.
6. Remove lift pump.
7. Remove camshaft and gear as follows:
   a. Using camshaft removal service dowels, insert dowels through push rod tube holes and into the top of each tappet securely. Pull tappets up and wrap a rubber band around the top of the dowel rods, **Fig. 44.**
   b. Rotate camshaft to align crankshaft to camshaft timing marks, **Fig. 45.**
   c. Remove two bolts from camshaft thrust plate.
   d. Remove camshaft, gear and thrust plate.
   e. Using a suitable press, press camshaft out of the gear.
8. Remove tappets as follows:
   a. Using tappet removal service tool, **Fig. 46,** insert trough to the full length of the cam bore.
   b. Position trough so it will catch the tappet when dowel is removed. **Remove only one tappet at a time.** Remove rubber band from the two companion tappets, securing the tappet not to be removed with rubber band. Pull up dowel from the tappet bore allowing tappet to fall into the trough, **Fig. 47.**
   c. Carefully pull trough and tappet from the cam bore and remove tappet.
   d. Identify location of each tappet as it removed in order for tappets to

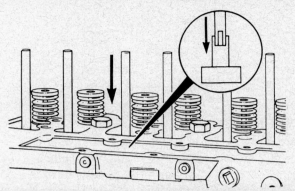

**Fig. 44   Dowels to hold tappets for camshaft removal**

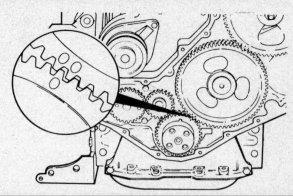

**Fig. 45   Crankshaft to camshaft timing mark alignment**

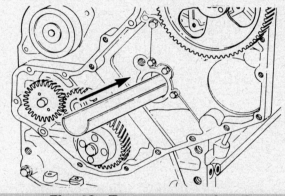

**Fig. 46   Tappet removal tool**

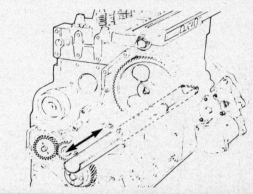

**Fig. 47   Trough position to remove tappets**

be installed in their original positions.

## INSTALLATION

1. Install tappets as follows:
    a. Insert trough full length of cam bore.
    b. Feed installation tool, **Fig. 48,** down tappet bore and into the trough. Carefully pull trough and installation tool out of the front.
    c. Lubricate tappet on stem and face with Lubriplate 105.
    d. Insert installation tool into tappet, then place tappet and tool in trough and slide trough back into cam bore.
    e. Pull tool and tappet through cam bore and up into tappet bore. After tappet has been pulled up into position, slide trough back into cam bore and rotate it ½ turn. This will position the round side of trough up, which will hold tappet in place.
    f. Remove installation tool, then install dowel into tappet and secure with rubber band.
2. Install gear on camshaft as follows:
    a. Install gear key in camshaft, then lubricate end of camshaft with Lubriplate 105.
    b. Heat gear in an oven at 250°F for 45 minutes.
    c. Install gear with timing marks away from the camshaft, be sure gear is seated against camshaft shoulder.
3. Lubricate camshaft lobes, journals and thrust plate and install camshaft and thrust washer. Align timing marks

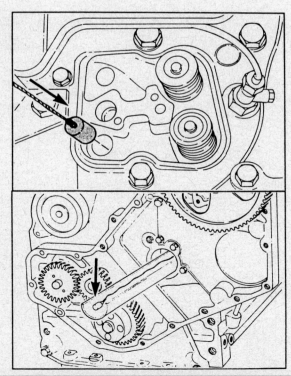

**Fig. 48   Tappet installation tool**

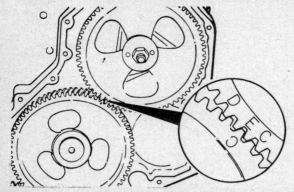

**Fig. 49   Camshaft to pump drive gear timing mark alignment**

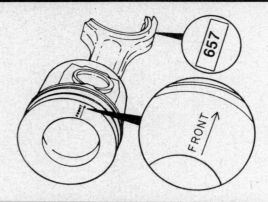

**Fig. 50   Piston & rod assembly**

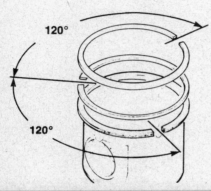

**Fig. 51   Ring position on piston**

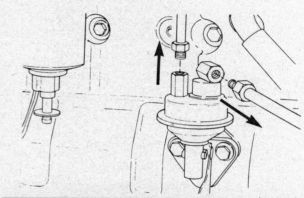

**Fig. 52   Lift pump replacement**

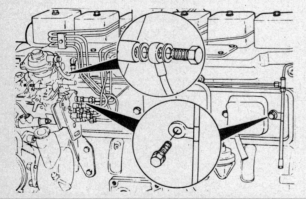

**Fig. 53   Fuel drain manifold removal**

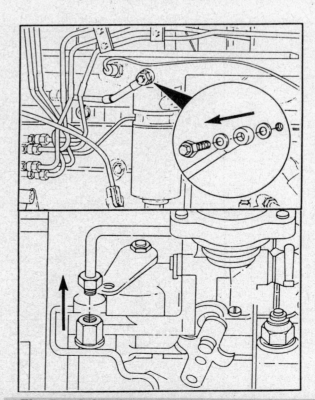

**Fig. 54   Injection pump supply line removal**

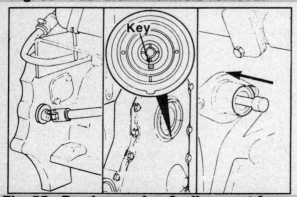

**Fig. 55   Barring engine & alignment for injection pump removal**

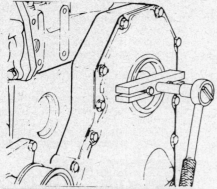

**Fig. 56  Injection pump drive gear removal**

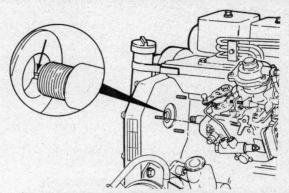

**Fig. 57  Injection pump alignment for installation**

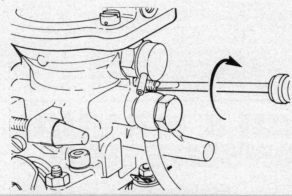

**Fig. 58  Idle speed adjustment**

as shown in **Fig. 49.**
4. Torque thrust washer bolts to 18 ft. lbs.

## PISTON & ROD ASSEMBLY

Assemble piston to rod, be sure the "Front" marking on piston and the numbers on rod and cap are oriented as shown in **Fig. 50.** Pistons do not require heating to install pin. Position piston and rod into cylinder bore with the word "Front" on piston towards front of cylinder block.

## PISTONS & RINGS

Pistons and rings are available in standard sizes and in two oversizes; .020 & .040 inch. There is also a cylinder bore sleeve available for salvage.

The top surface of all rings are identified with the word "Top" or suppliers "Mark." Position rings on piston as shown in **Fig. 51.**

## MAIN & ROD BEARINGS

Crankshaft main bearings are available in standard and undersize. Main bearing sizes are .0197 & .0394. Rod bearings are available in standard and oversizes. Rod bearing sizes are .0098, .0197, .0295 & .0394.

## CRANKSHAFT REAR OIL SEAL
### REPLACE

1. Raise and support vehicle, then remove transmission.
2. For manual transmissions, remove clutch cover & clutch plate.
3. On all models, remove flywheel.
4. Drill holes 180° apart into seal, then using a slide hammer and number ten screw, pull alternting from side to side until seal is free.
5. Install seal using seal pilot provided in seal kit. Push seal on pilot and onto crankshaft.
6. Remove pilot and drive seal on using alignment tool and hammer.
7. Reverse procedure to install.

## OIL PAN
### REPLACE

1. Remove engine. Refer to "Engine, Replace" section for procedures.
2. Remove oil pan bolts and oil pan.
3. Reverse procedure to install, use new gasket and with sealant, fill joint between the pan rail, gear housing and rear cover. Torque bolts to 60 ft. lbs.

## OIL PUMP
### SERVICE
### REMOVAL & INSTALLATION

1. Remove fan assembly, then the drive belt.
2. Remove radiator.
3. Remove fan clutch assembly, then the fan hub.
4. Remove oil filler tube.
5. Remove crankshaft vibration damper.
6. Remove front cover.
7. Remove pump attaching bolts, then the pump from the bore in cylinder block.
8. Reverse procedure to install, torque mounting bolts to 18 ft. lbs.

### DISASSEMBLY & ASSEMBLY

1. Remove back plate.
2. Remove gerotor planetary.
3. Clean all parts in solvent and dry with compressed air.
4. Check pump gears for chips, cracks or excessive wear. Inspect planetary for excessive wear.
5. Reverse procedure to assemble, install in original position of disassembly.

## WATER PUMP
### REPLACE

1. Drain coolant from system.
2. Remove fan belt.
3. Remove water pump bolts and the pump from the cylinder block.
4. Reverse procedure to install, torque pump bolts to 18 ft. lbs.

## FUEL PUMP
### REPLACE
### LIFT PUMP

1. Remove low pressure fuel lines.
2. Remove lift pump mounting bolts and lift pump from cylinder block, **Fig. 52.**
3. Install lift pump with a new gasket and torque bolts to 18 ft. lbs.
4. Install lines, then bleed system.

## INJECTION PUMP
### Removal

1. Remove throttle linkage and bracket.
2. Disconnect fuel drain manifold, **Fig. 53.**
3. Remove injection pump supply line, **Fig. 54,** then the high pressure lines.
4. Disconnect electrical connector from fuel shut off valve.
5. Remove fuel air control tube.
6. Remove pump support bracket.
7. Remove oil fill tube, bracket and adaptor from front gear cover, then the pump gear retainer nut and washer.
8. Insert a barring tool into flywheel housing opening on exhaust side of engine, **Fig. 55.** Place a 1/2 universal joint in barring tool and put enough drive extensions together to equal at least 36 inches. Place extension under turbocharger to the barring tool, then using a rachet turn barring tool. Bar the engine until key way on fuel pump shaft is in approximate position shown in **Fig. 55.** Locate TDC for cylinder number one by barring engine

6. If installing new or rebuilt pump without timing marks, take up gear lash by slowly while pushing in on TDC pin, stop when timing pin engages with gear timing hole, **Fig. 55.**
9. Loosen lockscrew and remove special washer from injection pump, then tighen lockscrew against the driveshaft.
10. Using a suitable puller, remove pump drive gear from the drive shaft, **Fig. 56.**
11. Remove pump mounting nuts and the injection pump.

### Installation

1. Verify cylinder number one is at TDC on the compression stroke.
2. Install new pump mounting gasket.
3. Align key with key slot and install pump, **Fig. 57.**
4. Install and finger tighten the pump mounting nuts, then install pump drive shaft nut and washer.
5. If installing original pump, rotate pump to align timing marks on pump flange and engine front cover. Torque to 18 ft. lbs.

rotating pump counter clockwise. Torque to 18 ft. lbs.
7. On all pumps, install pump support bracket and throttle support bracket.
8. Torque pump gear retaining nut to 48 ft.lbs.
9. Install and torque high pressure lines to 18 ft. lbs.
10. Connect cable to control lever and adjust length so lever has stop-to-stop movement.
11. Bleed air from fuel system, then if necessary, adjust idle speed, **Fig. 58**

## TURBOCHARGER
## REPLACE

1. Loosen air crossover hose.
2. Disconnect intake and exhaust piping.
3. Remove oil drain tube bolts, then the oil supply line.
4. Remove turbocharger mounting nuts and the turbocharger.
5. Reverse procedure to install, apply anti-seize compound to mounting studs and torque mounting nuts to 24 ft. lbs. Operate engine and check for leaks

# CLUTCH & MANUAL TRANSMISSION

### INDEX

## CLUTCH PEDAL
## ADJUST
### EXC. 1987 6-225/3.7L & ALL 1988-89

Adjust fork rod by turning self-locking adjusting nut to provide free movement at end of fork. Adjustment should be 3/32 inch. This movement will provide approximately 1-1 1/2 inches of freeplay at pedal.

### 1987 6-225/3.7L & ALL 1988-89

The pressure plate release levers on these models are preset during manufacture and no provision for adjustment is provided.

## CLUTCH
## REPLACE
### REMOVAL
#### 1980-1987

1. Remove transfer case, if equipped.
2. Remove transmission assembly.
3. Remove clutch housing pan, if equipped.

4. Disconnect return spring from clutch release fork and clutch housing.
5. Remove fork rod assembly spring washer from pin, then the rod with adjusting nut, washer and insulator.
6. Remove clutch release bearing and carrier assembly from clutch release fork, then the release fork and boot from clutch housing.
7. Mark clutch cover and flywheel to ensure correct position during installation.
8. Insert a special clutch aligning tool or a spare clutch shaft through the hub of the disc to prevent the disc from falling.
9. Loosen clutch cover attaching bolts one or two turns at a time to avoid bending cover flange.
10. Remove clutch assembly and disc from clutch housing.

#### 1988-89

1. Remove transmission assembly.
2. Remove clutch housing, release fork and bearing assembly.
3. Mark clutch cover and flywheel to ensure correct position during installation.
4. Insert a special clutch aligning tool or a spare clutch shaft through the hub

of the disc to prevent the disc from falling.
5. Loosen clutch cover attaching bolts one or two turns at a time to avoid bending cover flange.
6. Remove clutch assembly and disc from clutch housing.

### INSTALLATION

The pilot bushing requires a grease which will stay in place during high temperature operation. A small amount of grease should be placed in front of bushing and inner surface should be lightly coated.

Clean the surfaces of the flywheel and pressure plate, making certain no oil or grease remains on these parts. Hold the cover plate and disc in place and insert clutch aligning tool through the hub of the disc and into the pilot bearing in the crankshaft. Bolt the clutch cover loosely to the flywheel, being sure that punch marks previously made are lined up.

To avoid distortion of the clutch cover, tighten the cover bolts a few turns each in progression until all are tight.

Guide the transmission into place, using care to ensure the driven disc is not bent. Use a floor jack to support the transmission so that the clutch shaft may be guided through the driven disc safely. Finally, adjust the clutch pedal free travel where applicable.

## TRANSMISSION
### REPLACE
#### FOUR SPEED OVERDRIVE

1. Remove gear shift components, then drain fluid from transmission.
2. Disconnect propeller shaft at rear universal joint. Mark parts for reinstallation in same position, then carefully pull shaft yoke out of transmission housing.
3. Disconnect speedometer cable and back-up light switch.
4. Install engine lifting fixture and raise engine slightly.
5. Using a suitable jack, support transmission, then remove center crossmember.
6. Remove transmission to clutch housing bolts, then slide transmission rearward until drive pinion shaft clears clutch disc.
7. Lower transmission and remove from vehicle.

#### NEW PROCESS 4 SPEED

1. Remove transfer case, if equipped, as described under "Transfer Case, Replace."
2. Disconnect back-up light switch.
3. Install engine support fixture, then, using a suitable jack, support transmission and remove transmission crossmember.

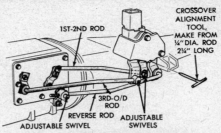

**Fig. 1   Gearshift linkage adjustment. Four-speed overdrive**

4. Remove transmission to clutch housing attaching bolts.
5. Slide transmission rearward until drive pinion shaft clears clutch disc, then lower transmission and remove from vehicle.

#### FIVE SPEED OVERDRIVE

1. Disconnect speedometer cable and back-up light switch.
2. Remove gear shift lever from shifter assembly, then drain fluid from transmission.
3. Disconnect propeller shaft at rear universal joint. Mark parts for reinstallation in same position, then carefully pull shaft yoke out of transmission housing.
4. Using a suitable jack, support transmission, then remove transmission to clutch housing bolts. Slide transmission rearward until input shaft clears clutch disc.
5. Lower transmission and remove from vehicle.

#### GETRAG FIVE SPEED

1. Disconnect back-up light switch, then remove case vent.
2. Remove gear shift lever from shifter assembly, then drain fluid from transmission.
3. Disconnect propeller shaft and remove.
4. Using a suitable jack, support transmission, then remove transmission to clutch housing bolts. Slide transmission rearward until input shaft clears clutch disc.
5. Lower transmission and remove from vehicle.

### GEARSHIFT
#### ADJUST
#### FOUR SPEED OVERDRIVE

1. Install gear shift lever aligning tool, **Fig. 1**, to hold levers in neutral crossover position.
2. With all rods removed from transmission shift levers, place levers in neutral detent position.
3. Adjust threaded shift rod levers so they enter transmission levers freely without any rearward or forward movement. **Start with 1-2 shift rod. It may be necessary to pull clip at shifter end to rotate this rod.**
4. Install washers and clips, then remove aligning tool and check linkage operation.

# TRANSFER CASE

## INDEX

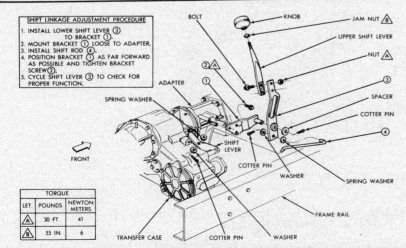

**Fig. 1   Transfer case shifter assembly and linkage adjustment. 1984–89 NP-205**

## TRANSFER CASE
### REPLACE

1. Remove skid plate, if equipped, and drain transfer case.
2. Disconnect speedometer cable and indicator switch electrical connector, then the parking brake cable guide from pivot, if necessary.
3. Disconnect vacuum switch hoses, if equipped.
4. Disconnect input and output shafts then support and position shafts aside. **Some 1980-81 models equipped with a single piece propeller shaft were assembled with the propeller shaft slip yoke positioned toward the rear axle assembly. When servicing these vehicles, the slip yoke should be positioned as assembled in production whether at the rear axle or at the transfer case.**
5. Disconnect shift rods and de-clutch rod, if equipped, from transfer case.

6. Support transfer case with a suitable jack.
7. If transfer case is supported by crossmember, or a support bracket, remove crossmember or the support bracket bolts, then lower transfer case from vehicle.
8. If transfer case is secured to an adapter, remove transfer case to adapter mounting bolts. Slide transfer case rearward to disengage front input spline and lower transfer case from vehicle.
9. Reverse procedure to install.

## TRANSFER CASE LINKAGE
### ADJUST
#### NEW PROCESS 205

On 1980-83 models, there is no provision for transfer case linkage adjustment. For transfer case linkage adjustment on 1984-89 models, refer to **Fig. 1**.

#### NEW PROCESS 208

On 1980-83 models, there is no provision for transfer case linkage adjustment. For transfer case linkage adjustment on 1984-87 models, refer to **Figs. 2 and 3**.

#### NEW PROCESS 241

For transfer case linkage adjustment on 1988-89 models, refer to **Fig. 3**.

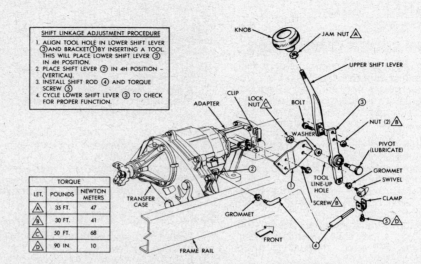

**Fig. 2   Transfer case shifter assembly and linkage adjustment. 1984 NP-208**

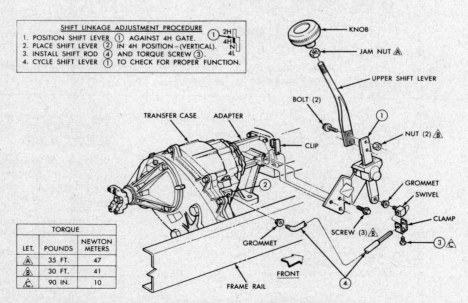

**Fig. 3   Transfer case shifter assembly & linkage adjustment. 1985–87 NP-208 & 1988–89 NP-214**

# REAR AXLES, SUSPENSION & BRAKES

## INDEX

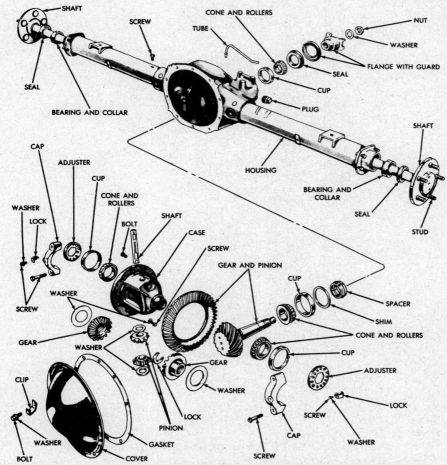

**Fig. 1   Typical 8³/₈ inch & 9¹/₄ inch integral carrier rear axle assembly.**

## DESCRIPTION

These axle assemblies, **Figs. 1 through 3**, are of the integral carrier housing hypoid gear type with the center line of the drive pinion mounted below the centerline of the ring gear. The drive pinion is supported by two preloaded taper roller bearings and the front and rear pinion bearing cones are pressed on the pinion stem. The front and rear pinion bearing cups are pressed against a shoulder that is recessed within the carrier casting. Drive pinion depth of mesh adjustment is controlled by installing metal shims between the rear pinion bearing cup and carrier casting.

## REAR AXLE
## REPLACE

1. Raise and support vehicle, then block brake pedal in the up position using a suitable block of wood.
2. Remove rear wheels, then the axle shafts, hub and drum assembly if equipped with Spicer axle.
3. Disconnect hydraulic brake lines at wheel cylinder. Cap fittings to prevent loss of brake fluid.
4. Disconnect parking brake cables, if necessary.
5. Scribe alignment marks on the propeller shaft universal joint and pinion flange to ensure correct position during installation. Disconnect propeller shaft at differential pinion flange and secure to one side.
6. Remove shock absorbers from spring plate studs, then the rear spring U-bolts.
7. Remove axle assembly from vehicle.
8. Reverse procedure to install.

## AXLE SHAFTS & BEARINGS
## REPLACE
## 8³/₈ & 9¹/₄ INCH

1. Raise and support vehicle and remove brake drum.
2. Clean area around housing cover, then loosen housing cover and allow lubricant to drain. Remove cover.
3. Turn differential case until pinion shaft lock screw is accessible and remove lock screw and pinion shaft, **Fig. 4**.
4. Push axle shaft inward and remove C-washer locks from axle shaft, **Fig. 5**, then pull axle shaft from housing being careful not to damage axle shaft bearing. **Inspect axle shaft bearing surfaces for signs of spalling or pitting. If any of these conditions exist, both shaft and bearing should be replaced. Normal bearing contact on shaft should be a dull gray and may appear lightly dented.**

5. Remove axle shaft bearing and seal from axle housing using tools C-4167 and C-637 on all models except 1984-88 9¼ inch HD axle, **Fig. 6**, or tool C-4828 on 1984-89 9¼ inch HD axle, **Fig. 7**. If bearing shows no sign of excessive wear or damage, it can be reused along with a new seal. Never reuse an axle shaft seal. **Remove any burrs that may be present in housing bearing shoulder, as bearing could become cocked during installation.**

6. Using suitable tools, install bearing, making sure it does not become cocked. Drive bearing until it bottoms against shoulder. **Do not use seal to position or bottom bearing as this will damage seal.**

7. Using seal installer, **Fig. 8**, install axle shaft bearing seal until outer flange of tool bottoms against housing flange face. This will position seal to the proper depth.

8. Reverse disassembly procedure to reassemble axle.

## AXLE SHAFT
### REPLACE
#### SPICER TYPE

1. Remove axle shaft flange nuts and lock washers.
2. Remove tapered dowels and axle shaft assembly by tapping axle shaft sharply in center of flange with a suitable hammer.
3. Reverse procedure to install.

## SERVICE BRAKE
### ADJUST
#### SELF ADJUSTING BRAKES

These brakes have self-adjusting shoe mechanisms that assure correct lining-to-drum clearances at all times. The automatic adjusters operate only when the brakes are applied as the car is moving rearward.

Although the brakes are self-adjusting, an initial adjustment is necessary when the brake shoes have been relined or replaced, or when the length of the star wheel adjuster has been changed during some other service operation.

Frequent usage of an automatic transmission forward range to halt reverse vehicle motion may prevent the automatic adjusters from functioning, thereby inducing low pedal heights. Should low pedal heights be encountered, it is recommended that numerous forward and reverse stops be made until satisfactory pedal height is obtained. **If a low pedal height condition cannot be corrected by making numerous reverse stops (provided the hydraulic system is free of air) it indicates that the self adjusting mechanism is not functioning. Therefore, it will be necessary to remove the drum, clean, free up and lubricate the adjusting mechanism. Then adjust the brakes, being sure the parking brake is fully released.**

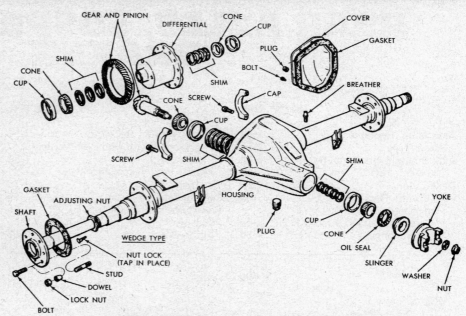

**Fig. 2   Spicer 60 (9¾ inch) rear axle assembly**

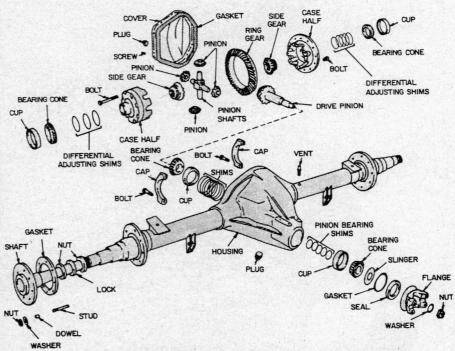

**Fig. 3   Spicer 70 (10½ inch) rear axle assembly**

### Adjustment

1. Raise vehicle so wheels are free to turn, then remove rear adjusting hole cover.
2. Back off parking brake cable adjustment so there is slack in the cable. Ensure parking brake lever is fully released.
3. On models equipped with release type adjuster, **Fig. 9**, insert adjusting tool into star wheel of adjusting screw. Move tool handle downward until slight drag is felt when wheel is rotated.
4. On models equipped with application type adjuster, **Fig. 10**, insert adjusting tool into star wheel of adjusting screw. Move tool handle upward until slight drag is felt when wheel is rotated.
5. On all models, insert a suitable screwdriver into brake adjusting hole and push adjusting lever out of engagement with star wheel. **Care should be taken not to bend adjusting lever.**

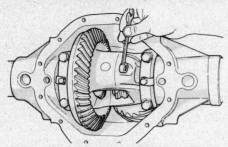

**Fig. 4   Removing differential pinion shaft lock pin**

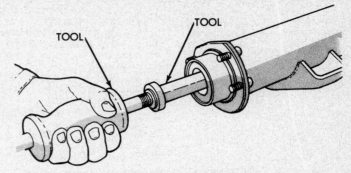

**Fig. 6   Removing axle shaft bearing and seal. Exc. 9¼ inch HD axle**

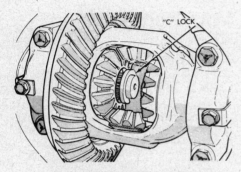

**Fig. 5   Removing C-lock washers**

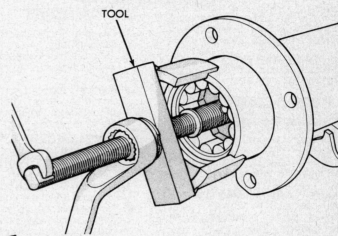

**Fig. 7   Removing axle shaft & bearing seal. 1984–89 9¼ inch HD axle**

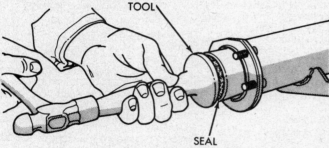

**Fig. 8   Installing axle shaft oil seal**

6. Back off star wheel 10 to 12 notches until wheel rotates freely with no drag.
7. Install adjusting hole cover. Adjust brakes on remaining wheels in the same manner.

## PARKING BRAKE
## ADJUST

1. Release parking brake lever and loosen cable adjusting nut to be sure cable is slack.
2. With rear wheel brakes properly adjusted tighten cable adjusting nut until a slight drag is felt when the rear wheels are rotated. Then loosen the cable adjusting nut until both rear wheels can be rotated freely.
3. To complete the operation, back off an additional two turns of the cable adjusting nut.
4. Apply and release parking brake several times to be sure rear wheels are not dragging when cable is in released position.

## MASTER CYLINDER
## REPLACE
## EXC. MODELS WITH ALUMINUM MASTER CYLINDER

1. Disconnect brake lines from master cylinder. Install plugs in outlets to prevent fluid leakage.
2. Remove nuts that attach master cylinder to cowl panel or power brake unit, if equipped.
3. Disconnect pedal pushrod (manual brakes) from brake pedal.
4. Slide master cylinder straight out from cowl panel and/or power brake unit.
5. Reverse procedure to install.

## MODELS WITH ALUMINUM MASTER CYLINDER
### Manual Brakes

1. Disconnect brake lines from master cylinder. Install plugs in outlets to prevent fluid leakage.
2. From under instrument panel, disconnect stop lamp switch mounting bracket and position aside.
3. Grasp brake pedal and pull backward to disengage pushrod from master cylinder piston. **This will require a pull of about 50 lbs. Also, the retention grommet will be destroyed.**
4. Remove master cylinder to cowl retaining nuts and remove master cylinder by pulling straight out. **Make sure to remove all traces of old grommet from pushrod groove and master cylinder piston.**
5. Reverse procedure to install. Install new grommet on pushrod, then lubricate grommet with water and align pushrod with master cylinder piston. Using brake pedal, apply pressure to fully seat pushrod into piston.

### Power Brakes

1. Disconnect primary and secondary brake tubes from master cylinder, then cap lines and master cylinder fitting.

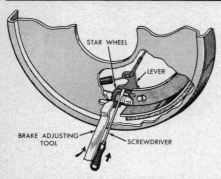

**Fig. 9 Release type brake adjuster**

2. Remove nuts attaching master cylinder to power brake unit, then slide master cylinder from power brake unit.
3. Reverse procedure to install.

## POWER BOOSTER
### REPLACE
### EXC. HYDRO-BOOST
**Transverse Mount**

1. Disconnect vacuum hose from power booster.
2. Remove master cylinder to booster attaching nuts, then the master cylinder.
3. Remove booster pushrod to pivot attaching bolts.
4. Remove power booster attaching nuts, then the power booster assembly.
5. Reverse procedure to install.

**Inline Mount**

1. Disconnect vacuum hose from check valve.
2. Remove master cylinder to booster attaching nuts.
3. Working from under instrument panel, position a suitable screwdriver between center tang on retainer clip and pin in brake pedal. Rotate screwdriver enough to allow retainer clip center tang to pass over end of brake pedal pin, then pull retainer clip from pin.
4. Remove power booster attaching nuts, then slide booster away from dash panel.
5. Reverse procedure to install.

## HYDRO-BOOST

1. Pump brake pedal several times to

ensure that all pressure is discharged from the accumulator prior to disconnecting hoses from booster.
2. Remove master cylinder attaching nuts and position master cylinder aside.
3. Disconnect and plug all fluid lines from booster ports, then disconnect brake pedal spring.
4. Remove pushrod to pedal attaching bolt.
5. Remove booster attaching nuts, then the booster.
6. Reverse procedure to install.

## SHOCK ABSORBER
### REPLACE
### MOTOR HOME

1. Remove shock absorber to frame attaching bolts.
2. Remove shock absorber lower bracket attaching nut, rubber bushing and washers.
3. Remove shock absorber and bracket assembly from vehicle, then the bracket from the shock.
4. Reverse procedure to install.

## RAMCHARGER, TRAIL DUSTER & CONVENTIONAL CAB

1. Remove two shock absorber bracket to frame attaching bolts.
2. On models equipped with 4 wheel drive, remove lower bracket attaching bolt, loosen upper attaching bolt, then rotate bracket until shock absorber clears upper bolt and remove.
3. On all models, remove shock absorber lower bracket attaching nut, rubber bushings and washers.
4. Remove shock absorber and bracket assembly from vehicle, then the bracket from the shock.
5. Reverse procedure to install.

## VANS, WAGONS & FRONT SECTIONS

1. Remove upper shock absorber attaching nut, bolt and washers.
2. Remove lower attaching nut at bushing end.
3. Swing shock absorber down, pivoting around lower bolt.
4. Remove shock absorber lower attaching bolt and washers, then the shock absorber from vehicle.
5. Reverse procedure to install.

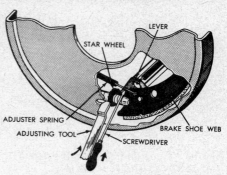

**Fig. 10 Application type brake adjuster**

## LEAF SPRING
### REPLACE
### RAMCHARGER, TRAIL DUSTER, CONVENTIONAL CAB & MOTOR HOME

1. Raise vehicle until weight is removed from springs and wheels are just touching ground, then support vehicle using suitable safety stands.
2. Remove nuts, lock washers and U-bolts attaching spring to axle.
3. Remove spring shackle attaching bolts, shackle and spring front bolt, then remove spring.
4. Reverse procedure to install.

## VANS, WAGONS & FRONT SECTIONS

1. Raise and support vehicle.
2. Remove U-bolt attaching nuts, U-bolts and plate.
3. Remove front pivot attaching bolt, then the rear shackle attaching nuts.
4. Remove outer shackle and bolt from hanger, then the spring. Some vehicles are equipped with one piece shackles.
5. Reverse procedure to install.

## SWAY BAR
### REPLACE

1. Remove link rod attaching nut from each end of sway bar.
2. Remove retainers and rubber bushings from sway bar link rods.
3. Remove sway bar support bracket attaching bolts, then the sway bar.
4. Reverse procedure to install.

# FRONT SUSPENSION & STEERING

## INDEX

Refer to "Front Wheel Drive" for 4 x 4 front axle service procedures not covered in this section.

## DESCRIPTION

### INDEPENDENT FRONT SUSPENSION

These vehicles are equipped with a coil spring front suspension system, **Figs. 1 through 4.** The upper control arms are mounted on longitudinal rails and the lower control arms are mounted on a removable crossmember. Both control arms have replaceable bushings on the inner ends and ball joints on the outer ends. The upper control arms also control caster and camber adjustments through eccentric pivot bolts at the inner ends or through slots in the upper control arm mounting bracket.

### EXC. INDEPENDENT FRONT SUSPENSION

The front axle assembly, **Figs. 5 and 6,** may be divided into three assemblies; axle I-beam, steering knuckles and steering linkage assemblies. It is unnecessary to remove the complete front axle assembly unless the I-beam is to be replaced.

## WHEEL ALIGNMENT

### CASTER & CAMBER, ADJUST

**Independent Front Suspension**

Front suspension height must be checked and corrected as necessary prior to checking wheel alignment.
1. Remove all foreign material from exposed threads of cam adjusting bolt nuts or pivot bar adjusting bolt nuts.
2. Record initial camber and caster readings before loosening cam bolt nuts or pivot bar bolt nuts, **Figs. 7 and 8.**
3. On vehicles using cam bolts, the camber and caster is adjusted by loosening the cam bolt nuts and turning the cam bolts as necessary until the desired setting is obtained. On vehicles using pivot bars, tool C-4581 or equiv-

alent is required to adjust caster and camber. When performing adjustments, the camber settings should be held as close as possible to the "desired" setting, and the caster setting should be held as nearly equal as possible on both wheels.

### Exc. Independent Front Suspension

No adjustment is provided for camber. If camber is not within specifications, axle or steering knuckle is bent and should be replaced.

Caster may be adjusted by inserting a wedge between the spring and axle, **Fig. 9.** To increase caster insert wedge so that the thick part faces rear of vehicle. To decrease caster insert wedge so that the thick end is toward front of vehicle.

### TOE-IN, ADJUST

With the front wheels in straight ahead position, loosen the clamps at each end of both adjusting tubes. Adjust toe-in by turning the tie rod sleeve which will "center" the steering wheel spokes. If the steering wheel was centered, make the toe-in adjustment by turning both sleeves an equal amount. Position sleeve clamps so ends do not align in the sleeve slot.

## WHEEL BEARINGS

## ADJUST

### EXC. MOTOR HOME & 4 WHEEL DRIVE

1. Torque adjusting nut to 360-480 inch lbs. for Vans, Wagons and Front Sections or 90 inch lbs. for Ramcharger, Trail Duster and Conventional Cabs while rotating wheel.
2. Stop wheel from rotating, then back off adjusting nut to completely release bearing preload.
3. Tighten adjusting nut finger tight, then install locknut and cotter key. Endplay should be .0001-.003 inch.
4. Clean grease cap, coat inside with suitable wheel bearing grease and install cap. Do not fill cap with grease.

### MOTOR HOME

1. Rotate wheel and tighten adjusting

nut until a slight binding is felt.
2. Back off adjusting nut so that the nearest slot indexes with the cotter pin hole in the spindle. **Never back off adjusting nut less than half the distance from one slot to the next slot.**
3. Install cotter pin to locknut and ensure that wheel rotates freely.

### 4 WHEEL DRIVE

#### Spicer 44FBJ & 44-8FD Axle

1. Raise and support vehicle.
2. Remove locking hub assembly, then the wheel bearing locknut and washer.
3. Torque adjusting nut to 50 ft. lbs., using tool No. C-4170 or equivalent, to seat the bearing.
4. Loosen adjusting nut and retorque to 30-40 ft. lbs. while rotating hub, then back off adjusting nut 135°-150°.
5. Install retaining washer and bearing locknut. Torque locknut to 50 ft. lbs. Endplay should be .001-.010 inch.

#### Spicer 60 Axle

1. Raise and support vehicle.
2. Remove hub cap, then the snap ring using suitable pliers.
3. Remove flange nuts and lock washers, then the drive flange or locking hub if equipped.
4. Straighten tang on lock ring, then using tool No. DD-1241-JD or equivalent, remove outer locknut and lock ring.
5. Torque locknut to 50 ft. lbs. to seat the bearing, loosen locknut and retorque to 30-40 ft. lbs. Back off locknut 135°-150°.
6. Install lock ring and outer locknut. Torque locknut to 65 ft. lbs.
7. Bend tangs of long ring over both locknuts. Endplay should be .001-.010 inch.

## BALL JOINTS

## REPLACE

### EXC. 4 WHEEL DRIVE

**Upper Ball Joint**

1. Place ignition switch in the "Off" posi-

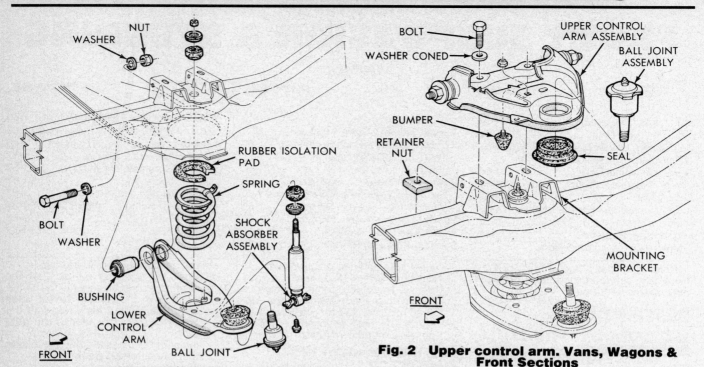

Fig. 1 **Lower control arm and coil spring. Vans, Wagons & Front Sections**

Fig. 2 **Upper control arm. Vans, Wagons & Front Sections**

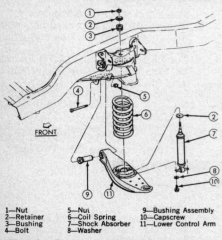

1—Nut  5—Nut  9—Bushing Assembly
2—Retainer  6—Coil Spring  10—Capscrew
3—Bushing  7—Shock Absorber  11—Lower Control Arm
4—Bolt  8—Washer

Fig. 3 **Lower control arm and coil spring. Ramcharger, Trail Duster & Conventional Cab except four wheel drive**

tion.
2. Using a suitable jack raise front of vehicle and position a jackstand under lower control arm as close to wheel and tire assembly as possible.
3. Remove wheel and tire assembly.
4. Remove cotter pin and nut from upper ball joint stud. Position tool No. C3564-A or equivalent over lower ball joint stud, allowing tool to rest on knuckle arm, then set tool securely against upper ball joint stud.
5. Tighten tool to apply pressure against upper ball joint stud, then strike knuckle with hammer to loosen stud.
6. Remove tool, then detach upper ball joint from knuckle. **Support knuckle and brake assembly to prevent**

damage to lower ball joint and **brake hoses.**
7. Remove upper ball joint from upper control arm, using tool No. C3561.
8. Reverse procedure to install. Thread upper ball joint into control arm as far as possible by hand. Torque upper ball joint into control arm to 125 ft. lbs. Install ball joint into steering knuckle, then torque attaching bolts to 135 ft. lbs. **Ball joint seals should be replaced whenever they have been removed.**

### Lower Ball Joint

1. Remove coil spring, refer to "Coil Spring, Replace" procedure.
2. Remove ball joint seal, then press ball joint out of lower control arm using tool No. C-4212 or equivalent.
3. Reverse procedure to install.

# SHOCK ABSORBER
## REPLACE

1. Raise and support vehicle.
2. Turn wheel as needed to gain access to upper shock absorber mount, then remove upper nut and retainer.
3. Remove two lower attaching bolts, then the shock.
4. Reverse procedure to install.

# COIL SPRING
## REPLACE
### VANS, WAGONS & FRONT SECTIONS

1. Block brake pedal in up position.
2. Raise and support vehicle.
3. Remove front wheels, then the caliper

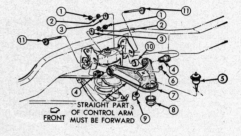

1—Nut  7—Upper Control Arm
2—Lockwasher  8—Upper Ball Joint
3—Cam  9—Bumper Assembly
4—Bushing Assembly  10—Sleeve
5—Ball Joint  11—Cam and Bolt Assembly
6—Lock Nut

Fig. 4 **Upper control arm. Ramcharger, Trail Duster & Conventional Cab except four wheel drive**

retainer and anti-rattle spring assemblies.
4. Remove caliper from disc and position caliper aside, then remove inboard shoe. **Do not allow caliper to hang or be supported by hydraulic brake hose.**
5. Remove shock absorber, upper bushing and sleeve, then the strut.
6. Install spring compressor tool No. DD-1278 finger tight, then back off one half turn.
7. Remove cotter keys and ball joint nuts.
8. Install ball joint breaker tool No. C-3564-A or equivalent over lower ball joint stud, then set tool securely against upper ball joint stud.
9. Tighten tool to apply pressure against upper ball joint stud, then strike knuckle with hammer to loosen stud.
10. Remove tool, then slowly loosen coil

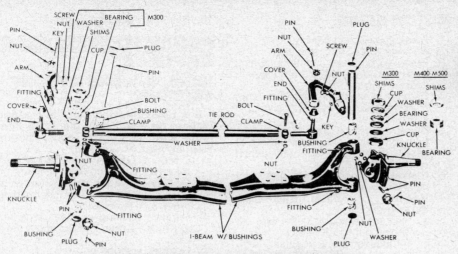

Fig. 5 Elliot type front axle assembly

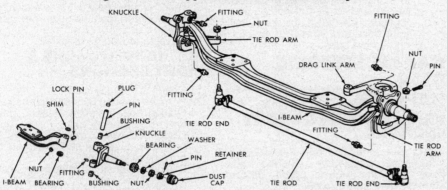

Fig. 6 Reverse Elliot type front axle assembly

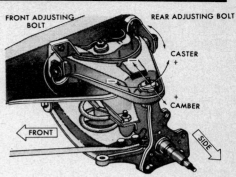

**Fig. 7 Alignment adjustment locations & directions. Cam bolt type**

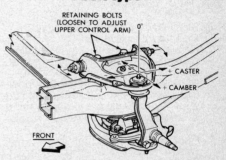

**Fig. 8 Alignment adjustment locations & directions. Pivot bolt type**

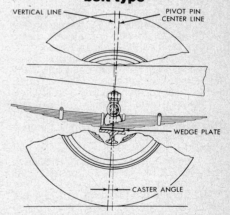

**Fig. 9 Caster angle adjustment. Exc. independent front suspension**

spring compressor until all tension is relieved from spring.

11. Remove spring compressor and spring.
12. Reverse procedure to install, noting the following:
    a. Torque ball joint nuts to 135 ft. lbs. for upper and lower $11/16$-16 inch nuts or 175 ft. lbs. for $3/4$-16 inch nuts.
    b. Inboard shoe anti-rattle spring should be installed on top of retainer spring plate. Torque retaining clips to 180 inch lbs.

## RAMCHARGER, TRAIL DUSTER & CONVENTIONAL CABS

1. Raise and support vehicle.
2. Remove front wheels, then the caliper retainer.
3. Remove caliper from disc and position caliper aside, then remove inboard shoe. **Do not allow caliper to hang or be supported by hydraulic brake hose.**
4. On 1980-84 models, proceed as follows:
    a. Remove grease cap, cotter key, locknut, adjusting nut, washer and outer bearing.
    b. Slide rotor from steering knuckle.

Use caution not to damage steering knuckle thread, bearing or oil seal when removing rotor.
    c. Remove splash shield attaching screws, then the splash shield, if equipped.
5. On all models, remove shock absorber, then disconnect sway bar at link, if equipped.
6. Remove spring pin from strut, then loosen strut attaching nut.
7. Install spring compressor tool No. DD-1278 finger tight, then back off half turn.
8. Remove cotter keys and ball joint nuts.
9. Install ball joint breaker tool No. C-3564-A or equivalent over lower ball joint stud, then set tool securely against upper ball joint stud.
10. Tighten tool to apply pressure against upper ball joint stud, then strike knuckle with hammer to loosen stud.
11. Remove tool, then slowly loosen coil spring compressor until all tension is relieved from spring.
12. Remove spring compressor and spring.
13. Reverse procedure to install noting the following:
    a. Torque ball joint nuts to 135 ft. lbs.
    b. Torque sway bar attaching bolt to 100 inch lbs.

## LEAF SPRING REPLACE

### MOTOR HOME & 4 WHEEL DRIVE MODELS

1. Raise vehicle until weight is removed from springs, then support spring using suitable jack.
2. Remove nuts, lock washers, U-bolts and U-bolt seat securing spring to axle.
3. Remove spring shackle attaching bolts, shackles and spring front eye bolt.
4. Remove spring from vehicle.
5. Reverse procedure to install.

## SWAY BAR
### REPLACE

1. Disconnect bar from right and left end links.
2. Disconnect attaching bolts from frame mounting brackets.
3. Remove bar assembly from vehicle.
4. Reverse procedure to install.

## STEERING KNUCKLE
### REPLACE
### EXC. MOTOR HOME & 4 WHEEL DRIVE

1. Block brake pedal in up position.
2. Raise and support vehicle.
3. Remove front wheels, then the caliper retainer and anti-rattle spring assembly.
4. Remove caliper from disc and position disc aside, then remove inboard shoe. **Do not allow caliper to hang or be supported by hydraulic brake hose.**
5. Remove hub cap, cotter key, nut, washer and outer bearing.
6. Slide disc from steering knuckle. Use caution not to damage steering knuckle thread, bearing or oil seal when removing disc.
7. Position suitable jack under outer end of lower control arm, then disconnect tie rod at steering knuckle arm using tool No. C-3894-A or equivalent.
8. Separate steering knuckle and steering knuckle arm from ball joints.
9. Remove splash shield attaching bolts, if equipped, then the brake adapter attaching bolts, steering knuckle arm and steering knuckle together.
10. Reverse procedure to install noting the following:
    a. Torque steering knuckle arm to steering knuckle attaching bolts to 215 ft. lbs. for 5/8-19 bolts or 225 ft. lbs. for 3/4-16 inch bolts.
    b. Torque ball joint nuts to 135 ft. lbs. for upper and lower 11/16-16 inch nuts or 175 ft. lbs. for 3/4-16 inch nuts.
    c. Torque tie rod end attaching nut to 45 ft. lbs. for 1/2-20 nuts, 55 ft. lbs. for 9/16-18 nuts or 75 ft. lbs. for 5/8-18 nuts.
    d. Torque anti-rattle spring fasteners to 180 inch lbs.

## MOTOR HOME

1. Raise and support vehicle.
2. Remove wheel, rotor and hub.
3. Remove disc brake adapter attaching bolts, then the adapter from steering knuckle.
4. Remove steering knuckle arm from steering knuckle, then the pivot pin lock.
5. Remove upper pivot pin oil seal plug, then drive pivot pin down and out of assembly using suitable drift punch and hammer.
6. Remove steering knuckle and pivot pin thrust washer.
7. Reverse procedure to install noting the following:
    a. Torque steering knuckle arm attaching nut to 200 ft. lbs.
    b. Torque disc brake adapter attaching bolts to: 175-245 ft. lbs. on all M-600 models; 85-135 ft. lbs. on M-300 and all M-400 and M-500 models; 140-180 ft. lbs. for lower front bolts and 90-140 ft. lbs. for upper front bolts.

## MANUAL STEERING GEAR
### REPLACE
### VANS, WAGONS & FRONT SECTIONS

It is recommended that the steering column be completely detached from floor and instrument panel before steering gear is removed.
1. Disconnect battery ground cable, then remove steering column.
2. Remove steering arm attaching nut and lock washer, located under vehicle.
3. Remove steering arm using tool No. C-4150.
4. Remove gear to frame attaching bolts or nuts, then the gear from vehicle.
5. Reverse procedure to install.

## TRAIL DUSTER, RAMCHARGER & CONVENTIONAL CAB

1. Disconnect battery ground cable.
2. Remove two wormshaft coupling attaching bolts.
3. Remove steering arm from steering gear using tool No. C-4150.
4. Remove steering gear to frame attaching bolts, then the gear from vehicle.

5. Reverse procedure to install.

## POWER STEERING GEAR
### REPLACE
### VANS, WAGONS & FRONT SECTIONS

It is recommended that the steering column be completely detached from floor and instrument panel before steering gear is removed.
1. Disconnect battery ground cable, then remove steering column.
2. Disconnect power steering hoses at gear. Cap all hoses and fluid ports to prevent oil leakage.
3. Remove steering arm attaching nut and lock washer, located under vehicle.
4. Remove steering arm using tool No. C-4150.
5. Remove three gear to frame attaching bolts or nuts, then the gear from vehicle.
6. Reverse procedure to install.

### EXC. VANS, WAGONS & FRONT SECTIONS

1. Center steering gear.
2. Remove steering gear arm to shaft attaching bolt, then the steering gear arm using suitable tool.
3. Disconnect power steering hoses at gear. Cap all hoses and fluid ports to prevent oil leakage.
4. Disconnect shaft coupling from steering gear.
5. Remove steering gear to frame attaching bolts, then the gear from vehicle. **On some Motor Homes, body location may require steering gear and bracket be removed as an assembly. If gear and bracket is removed as an assembly, support assembly with suitable transmission jack and remove frame to bracket attaching bolts.**

## POWER STEERING PUMP
### REPLACE

1. Loosen pump locking and attaching bolts, then remove drive belt.
2. Disconnect both fluid hoses from pump.
3. Remove pump locking and attaching bolts, then remove pump and bracket assembly.
4. Reverse procedure to install.

# FRONT WHEEL DRIVE

## INDEX

## SPICER 44FBJ & 44-8FD, FRONT AXLE

### AXLE ASSEMBLY, REPLACE

1. Disconnect battery ground cable, then secure brake pedal in the up position.
2. Raise and support vehicle , then disconnect front driveshaft at drive pinion yoke.
3. Disconnect drag link at steering knuckle arm (left side only).
4. Disconnect and plug brake line at frame crossmember.
5. Disconnect shock absorbers at lower mounts then disconnect sway bar link assembly, if equipped, from spring plates.
6. Disconnect vacuum lines and electrical connector from disconnect housing assembly if equipped.
7. Remove nuts and washers from U-bolt spring clips, then remove axle from vehicle.
8. Reverse procedure to install axle assembly. Lubricate all fittings, free brake pedal and bleed brakes.
9. Lower vehicle and check front wheel alignment.

### SERVICING ROTOR, HUB OR BEARINGS

#### MODELS W/FULL TIME 4WD
#### Removal & Inspection

1. Remove axle shaft cotter pin and loosen outer axle shaft nut.
2. Raise vehicle then remove wheel assembly.
3. After removing caliper retainer and anti-rattle spring assembly, slide caliper out and away from rotor. Hang caliper out of the way. Do not allow caliper to hang by hydraulic brake hose. Remove inboard brake pad.
4. Remove outer axle shaft nut and washer. Secure a suitable puller to wheel studs and tighten main screw of tool to remove hub and rotor assembly, **Fig. 1**.
5. Remove puller from hub and rotor assembly.
6. Assemble Modified Bearing Press, Tool C-293-PA, Extension, Tool C-293-3, and Adapters, Tool No. C-293-49, to hub and rotor assembly and position in a vise. Pull outer bearing cone from hub and rotor and discard outer seal, **Fig. 2**.

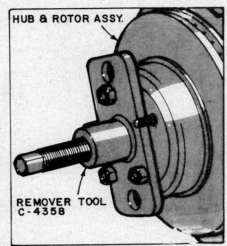

Fig. 1   Using puller to remove hub & rotor. 44 FBJ Units w/disc brakes. Models w/full time 4WD

7. Remove the six retainer bolts and retainer, **Fig. 3**, then remove brake caliper adapter from knuckle, if required.
8. Place a pry bar behind inner axle shaft yoke and push bearings out of knuckle, **Fig. 4**.
9. Remove and discard O-ring from knuckle, if equipped, then carefully remove axle shaft assembly. Examine inner seal surface and knuckle bore for wear or damage and replace knuckle if required. If outer axle shaft seal surface is grooved, repair as follows:
   a. Measure in from yoke shoulder of axle approximately 3/8 inch. Use a center punch and stake at 1/4 inch intervals around circumference of shaft. This will size shaft and ensure a tight fit of inner seal slinger, **Fig. 5**.
   b. Proper bearing clamp should be checked by installing bearing cups and spacer into knuckle bore and bolting bearing retainer to knuckle, **Figs. 6 and 7**. If a .004 inch feeler gauge can not be inserted between knuckle and retainer at the six places midway between retainer mounting ears, the knuckle must be replaced, **Fig. 8**. The brake dust shield may have to be removed to complete this check. If knuckle is serviceable, remove retainer, bearing cups and spacer and install

dust shield if removed.

### Assembly & Installation

1. Apply RTV sealer or equivalent to seal surface of axle shaft.
2. Using driver, Tool No. C-4398-1, install seal slinger with lip toward splines onto outer axle shaft, **Figs. 9 and 10**.
3. Carefully insert axle shaft into housing so as not to damage differential seal at side gears. After sliding axle shaft completely in, wedge a pry bar through universal joint to retain shaft, **Fig. 11**.
4. Install seal cup using adapter, Tool C-4398-2, and driver, Tool No. C-4398-1. Use a small amount of wheel bearing grease on adapter face to hold cup in position, then drive up until bottomed in knuckle, **Figs. 12 and 13**. Do not remove tool at this time.
5. Using a suitable tool, install new outer seal in retainer plate, then locate retainer plate over hub of rotor.
6. Thoroughly pack wheel bearings with Multi-Purpose grease and press outer bearing onto hub using Tool No. C-4246-A and adapters, **Fig. 14**. Remove tool and place grease coated outer bearing cup over bearing cone followed by spacer, grease coated inner bearing cup and inner bearing cone. Again use Tool No. C-4246-A and adapters to press components into position, **Fig. 14**. Remove tool.
7. Apply a 1/4 inch bead of RTV sealer to retainer face on the chamfer, **Fig. 15**. This replaces O-ring discarded during disassembly.
8. Carefully remove seal installing tool from knuckle bore so that outer axle shaft remains centered. If shaft is moved, be sure that lip seal is still riding inside cup. Correct if necessary.
9. Before assembling hub and rotor to knuckle, position bearing retainer in hub so that grease fitting is facing forward, if equipped. Using a crossing method, torque retainer plate bolts to 30 ft. lbs. **Bearing retainers that have a grease fitting must be positioned on knuckle so that fitting is facing directly forward, Fig. 16**.
10. Install brake adapter and remove pry bar from universal joint.
11. Install axle shaft washer and nut. Torque nut to 100 ft. lbs. and continue to tighten nut until next slot in nut aligns with hole in axle shaft. Install

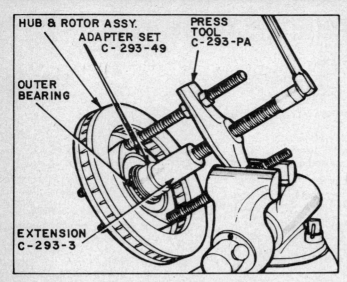

**Fig. 2 Removing outer bearing cone. 44 FBJ Units w/disc brakes. Models w/full time 4WD**

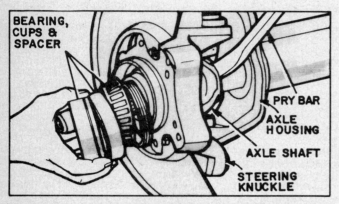

**Fig. 4 Using pry bar to remove bearing from knuckle. 44 FBJ Units w/disc brakes. Models w/full time 4WD**

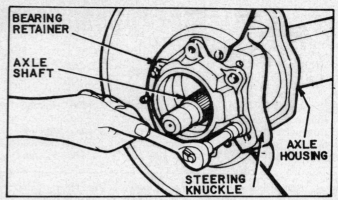

**Fig. 3 Removing bearing retainer. 44 FBJ Units w/disc brakes. Models w/full time 4WD**

**Fig. 5 Sizing axle shaft seal surface. 44 FBJ Units w/disc brakes. Models w/full time 4WD**

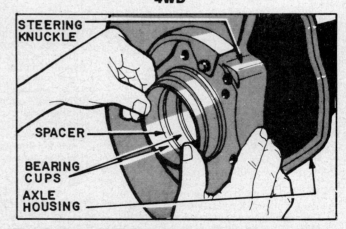

**Fig. 6 Installing bearing cups before checking bearing clamp. 44 FBJ Units w/disc brakes. Models w/full time 4WD**

cotter pin.

12. Through the access hole in hub, lubricate fitting in bearing retainer with multipurpose grease until grease flows through new inner seal. Seal may be viewed at the universal joint area. Spin hub several times and lubricate fitting again. Grease must flow from 1/2 of seal diameter.

13. Replace brake caliper assembly and wheel, then lower truck and test operation.

## MODELS LESS FULL TIME 4WD

### Removal & Inspection

1. Remove locking hub assembly, if equipped.
2. Raise and support vehicle, then remove wheel assembly.
3. Remove caliper retainer and anti-rattle assemblies.
4. Remove caliper from disc and support caliper to prevent damage to brake line.
5. Remove inboard brake shoe.
6. On 1985-89 models, remove grease cap and driving hub snap ring, then the driving hub and retaining spring.
7. On all models, remove wheel bearing adjusting locknut using tool C-4170 or equivalent, then the washer and adjusting nut.
8. Remove rotor assembly. The outer wheel bearing and retainer spring plate will slide out as rotor is removed.
9. Pry inner wheel bearing grease seal from hub, then remove bearing cone and the inner and outer bearing cups.

### Assembly & Installation

1. Install inner and outer bearing cups in rotor.
2. Lubricate and install inner bearings, then install the grease seal using suitable tools.
3. Install rotor, then the outer wheel bearing.
4. Install inner locknut and torque to 50

**Fig. 7  Installing bearing retainer to check bearing clamp. 44 FBJ Units w/disc brakes. Models w/full time 4WD**

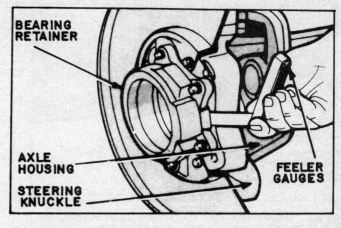

**Fig. 8  Checking bearing clamp. 44 FBJ Units w/disc brakes. Models w/full time 4WD**

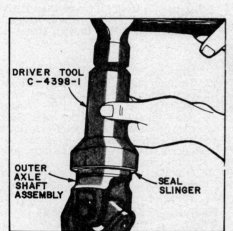

**Fig. 9  Installing seal slinger on outer axle shaft. 44 FBJ Units w/disc brakes. Models w/full time 4WD**

ft. lbs., using tool C-4170, to seat bearings.

5. Loosen inner locknut, then retorque to 30-40 ft. lbs. while rotating hub. Back off locknut 135° to 150°. Set retaining washer in position by turning nut so that the pin pressed into locknut will engage nearest hole in washer.
6. Install outer locknut and torque to 50 ft. lbs. Endplay after final bearing adjustment should be .001-.010 inch.
7. On 1985-88 models, install retaining spring plate, retaining spring with large end first, driving hub, snap ring and grease cap.
8. On all models, install inboard brake shoe on adapter with shoe flanges in adapter slots, then install caliper assembly. **Use care not to pull dust boot out of its grooves while sliding piston and boot over the inboard shoe.**
9. Install anti-rattle springs and retaining clips and torque to 180 inch lbs. **The inboard shoe anti-rattle spring must be installed on top of the retainer spring plate.**
10. Install wheel assembly, then lower truck and test operation.

## STEERING KNUCKLE & BALL JOINT

### MODELS W/FULL TIME 4WD

#### Removal & Disassembly

1. Remove axle shaft cotter pin and loosen outer axle shaft nut.
2. Raise vehicle, then remove wheel assembly.
3. After removing caliper retainer and anti-rattle spring assembly, slide caliper out and away from rotor. Hang caliper out of the way. Do not allow caliper to hang by hydraulic brake hose. Remove inboard brake pad.
4. Remove outer axle shaft nut and washer and through access hole in rotor assembly; remove the six bearing retainer bolts.
5. Secure a suitable puller to wheel studs and tighten main screw of tool to remove hub, rotor, bearings, retainer and outer seal as an assembly. Remove puller from rotor.
6. Remove brake caliper adapter from knuckle, then remove and discard O-ring from knuckle, if equipped.
7. Carefully pull axle shaft assembly out and remove seal and slinger from shaft.
8. Disconnect tie rod from steering knuckle using a suitable tool, **Fig. 17,** so as not to damage seal.
9. On left side only, disconnect drag link from steering knuckle arm again using a suitable tool to avoid seal damage, **Fig. 18.**
10. Remove nuts from steering knuckle arm on left side only. Tap arm to loosen tapered dowels. Remove dowels and arm.
11. Remove cotter pin from upper ball joint nut then remove upper and lower ball joint nuts. Discard lower nut.
12. Separate steering knuckle from axle housing yoke using a brass drift and a hammer, then, using a suitable tool, remove and discard sleeve from upper ball joint yoke on axle housing.
13. Secure steering knuckle upside down

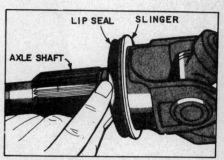

**Fig. 10  Installing lip seal on outer axle shaft. 44 FBJ Units w/disc brakes. Models w/full time 4WD**

in a vise and remove snap ring from lower ball joint.
14. Use proper tools to press upper and lower ball joints from steering knuckle. Replace ball joints if any looseness or endplay exists.

#### Assembly & Installation

1. Secure steering knuckle right side up in a vise and press upper and lower ball joints into position using proper tools. Install snap ring on lower joint and new boots on both joints.
2. Thread new sleeve into ball joint yoke on axle housing ensuring that two threads are exposed at the top.
3. Position steering knuckle on axle housing yoke, then install a new lower ball joint nut and torque to 80 ft. lbs.
4. Use Tool No. C-4169 and a torque wrench to torque sleeve in upper ball joint yoke to 40 ft. lbs., then install upper ball joint nut and torque to 100 ft. lbs. Install cotter pin if slot in nuts and hole in stud align. If not, tighten, do not loosen nut to align.
5. On left side only, position steering knuckle arm over studs on steering knuckle. Install tapered dowels and nuts, then torque nuts to 90 ft. lbs. Secure drag link to steering knuckle arm and torque nut to 60 ft. lbs.

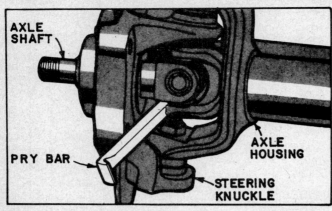

**Fig. 11   Using pry bar to retain axle shaft. 44 FBJ Units w/disc brakes. Models w/full time 4WD**

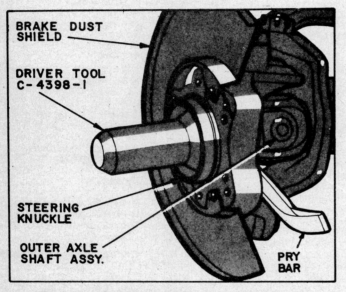

**Fig. 13   Tools in place after seal cup is installed. 44 FBJ Units w/disc brakes. Models w/full time 4WD**

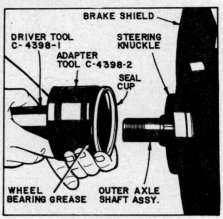

**Fig. 12   Using driving & adapter to install seal cup into knuckle. 44 FBJ Units w/disc brakes. Models w/full time 4WD**

6. Secure tie rod end to steering knuckle. Torque nut to 45 ft. lbs.
7. Install brake dust shield, if removed.
8. Inspect outer axle shaft seal surface for grooving. If surface is grooved, repair as described in "Servicing Rotor Hub or Bearings."
9. Apply RTV sealer to seal surface of axle shaft then using driver, C-4398-1, install seal slinger with lip toward splines onto outer axle shaft, **Figs. 9 and 10.**
10. Carefully insert axle shaft into housing so as not to damage differential seal at side gears. After sliding axle shaft completely in, wedge a pry bar through universal joint to retain shaft, **Fig. 11.**
11. Install seal cup using adapter C-4398-2, and driver C-4398-1. Use a small amount of wheel bearing grease on adapter face to hold cup in position, then drive cup until bottomed in knuckle, **Figs. 12 and 13.** Do not remove tool at this time.

12. Apply a ¼ inch bead of RTV sealer to retainer face on the chamfer, **Fig. 15.** This replaces the O-ring discarded during disassembly.
13. Carefully remove seal installing tool from knuckle bore so that outer axle shaft remains centered. If shaft is moved, ensure that lip seal is still riding inside cup. Correct if necessary.
14. Before installing hub, rotor, retainer and bearing assembly on knuckle, position bearing retainer in hub so that grease fitting is facing forward, if equipped. Use a crossing method and torque retainer plate bolts to 30 ft. lbs. **Bearing retainers that have a grease fitting must be positioned on knuckle so that fitting is facing directly forward, Fig. 16.**
15. Install brake adapter and remove any pry bar from universal joint.
16. Install axle shaft washer and nut. Torque nut to 100 ft. lbs. and continue to tighten nut until next slot in nut aligns with hole in axle shaft. Install

cotter pin.
17. Through the access hole in hub, lubricate fitting in bearing retainer with multipurpose grease until grease flows through new inner seal. Seal may be viewed through universal joint area. Spin hub several times and lubricate fitting again. Grease must flow from ½ of seal diameter.
18. Replace brake caliper assembly and wheel, then lower vehicle and test operation.

## MODELS LESS FULL TIME 4WD
### Removal & Disassembly

1. Remove locking hub assembly, if equipped.
2. Raise vehicle and remove wheel assembly.
3. Remove caliper retainer and anti-rattle spring assemblies.
4. Remove caliper from disc and support caliper to prevent damage to brake line.
5. Remove the inboard brake pad and disc.
6. Remove the caliper adapter from knuckle.
7. Remove the six nuts and washers from spindle to steering knuckle attaching bolts.
8. Remove brake splash shield.
9. Tap spindle lightly with soft faced hammer to free from steering knuckle.
10. Upon removal, examine bronze spacer between needle bearing and shaft joint assembly. If wear is evident, replace.
11. Clamp spindle in vise avoiding bearing carrying surfaces. Remove needle bearing grease seal.
12. Using a suitable puller remover inner axle needle bearings. **On 1985-87 models, left spindle does not have needle bearings.**
13. Carefully remove axle shaft, axle seal and stone shield, if equipped.
14. Remove the tie rod from the steering knuckle.

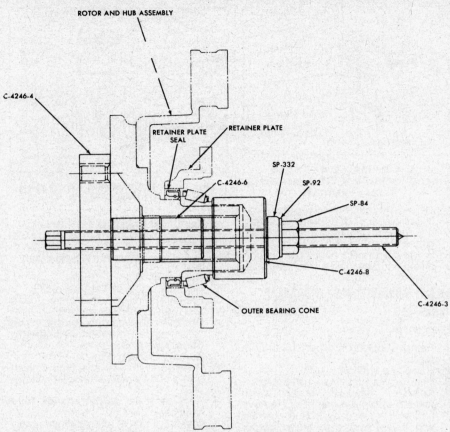

**Fig. 14 Tools positioned to press outer bearing onto hub. 44 FBJ Units w/disc brakes. Models w/full time 4WD**

## Cleaning & Inspection

1. Clean all parts using a suitable solvent.
2. Blow dry parts using compressed air.
3. Inspect all parts for cracks, wear, chips, burrs and distortion.
4. Replace any parts not suitable for further service.

## Assembly & Installation

1. Position steering knuckle right side up in a vise. Using tool C-4212-1 and adapter set C-4288, press the lower ball joint into position.
2. Using the same tool and adapter set as above, install the upper ball joint.
3. Install new boots on the ball joints and remove the steering knuckle from the vise.
4. Screw a new sleeve into the upper ball joint yoke leaving two threads showing at the top.
5. Position steering knuckle on axle housing yoke and torque new lower ball joint nut to 80 ft. lbs.
6. Using tool C-4169 and a torque wrench, torque sleeve in upper ball joint to 40 ft. lbs. Install upper ball joint and torque to 100 ft. lbs. Align slot in nut with hole in stud and install cotter pin. **Do not loosen to align.**
7. On left side only, position steering knuckle arm over studs on steering knuckle. Install cone washers and nuts and torque to 90 ft. lbs.
8. Install drag link on steering knuckle arm and torque to 60 ft. lbs. Install cotter pin.
9. Install the rod end to steering knuckle. Torque nut to 45 ft. lbs. and install cotter pin.
10. Install lip seal on stone shield with lip toward axle shaft spline.
11. On all except 1986–89 left side, carefully insert axle shaft into housing. Avoid damaging differential seal at right side gear or axle shaft seal on left side gear.
12. On 1986–89 left side, proceed as follows:
    a. Remove disconnect housing cover, then position shift collar onto

15. On the left side only, remove drag link from steering knuckle.
16. On the left side only, remove the nuts and cone washers from steering knuckle arm. Tap the steering knuckle arm to free knuckle. Remove arm.
17. Remove cotter pin from upper ball joint nut. Remove upper and lower ball joint nut. Discard lower nut.
18. Using a brass drift and hammer separate steering knuckle from axle housing yoke. Remove sleeve from upper ball joint using tool C-4169. Discard sleeve.

19. Install steering knuckle in vise and remove snap ring from lower ball joint with suitable snap ring pliers.
20. Using tool C-4212-1 and adapter set C-4288, press lower ball joint from steering knuckle.
21. Reposition tool, and press upper ball joint from steering knuckle. **Replace ball joints if any looseness or endplay exists.**

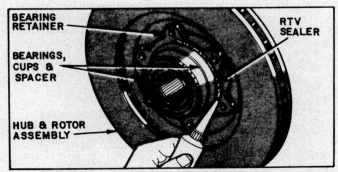

**Fig. 15 Forming a seal on bearing retainer face. 44 FBJ Units w/disc brakes. Models w/full time 4WD**

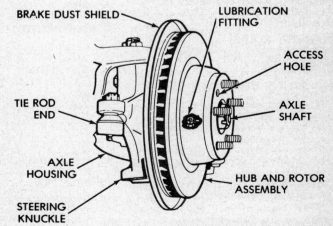

**Fig. 16 Bearing retainer positioned with grease fitting facing forward. 44 FBJ Units w/disc brakes. Models w/full time 4WD**

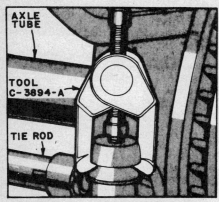

**Fig. 17 Using puller to remove tie rod (Typical)**

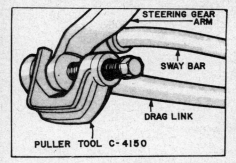

**Fig. 18 Using puller to remove drag link from steering arm. (Typical)**

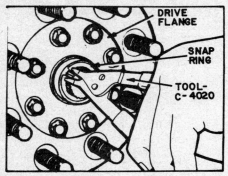

**Fig. 19 Removing snap ring. 60 Front Axle**

splined end of inner axle shaft.
b. Install intermediate axle shaft through axle shaft seal. Use caution not to damage seal.
c. Install disconnect housing cover assembly and gasket. Ensure shift fork is guided into groove of shift collar.
d. Install disconnect cover shield and shield attaching bolts. Torque bolts to 10 ft. lbs.
e. Connect vacuum lines and switch electrical connector.
13. Using tools D-122 and C-4171, install new needle bearings into spindle.
14. Fill seal area with NLG1 grease or equivalent, and install seal with tools D-155 and C-4171.
15. Install new bronze spacer on axle shaft, install spindle and brake splash shield.
16. Install new nuts and torque to 25-35 ft. lbs.
17. Mount braking disc assembly and outer wheel bearing cone onto spindle.
18. Install wheel bearing nuts and locking washer.
19. Install locking hub assembly.
20. Install brake adapter and torque attaching bolts to 85 ft. lbs.
21. Install the assembled brake caliper assembly.
22. Install the wheel and torque the nuts to 110 ft. lbs. Lower vehicle and test operation.

## 1985-89 AXLE DISCONNECT HOUSING ASSEMBLY

### Removal & Disassembly

1. Disconnect battery ground cable, then raise and support vehicle.
2. Disconnect vacuum lines and switch electrical connector.
3. Remove disconnect housing assembly, gasket and shield from axle housing.
4. Remove shift motor shaft E-clips, then the shift motor and shift fork.
5. Remove O-ring from shift motor shaft.

### Assembly & Installation

1. Install new O-ring on shift motor.
2. Install shift motor into disconnect housing and through shift fork.

3. Install shift motor shaft E-clips.
4. Install disconnect housing assembly and gasket, ensuring shift fork engages groove of shift collar.
5. Install disconnect housing assembly shield and attaching bolts. Torque attaching bolts to 10 ft. lbs.

## AXLE SHAFT ASSEMBLY

### 1980-84
### Removal

1. Remove locking hub assembly from vehicle.
2. Raise and support vehicle.
3. Remove tire and wheel assembly.
4. Remove caliper retainer and anti-rattle spring assemblies. Remove caliper from disc by sliding outward and away from disc. Hang caliper away from assembly. **Do not allow caliper to hang or be supported by the brake lines.**
5. Remove inboard shoe.
6. Remove outer axle shaft locknut washer and nut assembly.
7. Remove rotor and bearing assembly.
8. Remove six nuts attaching splash shield and spindle to knuckle assembly, if equipped.
9. Remove splash shield and spindle.
10. Remove brake caliper adapter from knuckle.
11. Carefully remove axle shaft assembly. Remove seal and stone shield from shaft.

### Installation

1. Install lip seal on axle shaft stone shield with lip of seal toward axle shaft spline.
2. Carefully insert axle shaft into housing.
3. Install spindle and brake splash shield. Install the six nuts and torque to 25-30 ft. lbs.
4. Install rotor, outer bearing nut, washer and locknut on spindle.
5. Install brake adapter and torque to 85 ft. lbs.
6. Install inboard brake shoe on adapter with shoe flanges located in adapter keyways. Slowly slide caliper assembly into position in adapter.
7. Install anti-rattle springs and retaining clips. Torque to 180 inch lbs.
8. Install locking hub assembly.
9. Install tire and wheel assembly.

Torque attaching nuts to 110 ft. lbs.

### 1985-89
### Right Axle Shaft, Removal

1. Raise and support vehicle.
2. Remove wheel and tire assembly.
3. Remove caliper retainer and anti-rattle spring assemblies.
4. Remove caliper from brake disc. Hang caliper aside. **Do not allow caliper to hang from brake lines.**
5. Remove braking disc.
6. Remove six nuts attaching splash shield and spindle to knuckle assembly.
7. Remove brake caliper adapter from knuckle.
8. Carefully remove axle shaft assembly from vehicle. Remove seal and stone shield.

### Right Axle Shaft, Installation

1. Install lip seal on axle shaft stone shield with lip toward axle shaft spline.
2. Carefully insert axle shaft into the housing.
3. Install spindle and splash shield. Install, then torque nuts to 25-30 ft. lbs.
4. Install braking disc, outer bearing, nut, washer and locknut onto spindle.
5. Install spring retainer, spring, drive gear and drive gear snap ring.
6. Apply RTV sealant or equivalent to seating edge of grease cap, then install the cap.
7. Install brake adapter and torque mounting bolts to 85 ft. lbs.
8. Position inboard brake shoe on adapter with shoe flanges in adapter keyways. Slowly slide caliper assembly into position in adapter and over braking disc. Align caliper on machined ways of adapter.
9. Install anti-rattle springs and retaining clips. Torque to 180 inch lbs.
10. Install tire and wheel assembly.

### Left Axle Shaft, Removal

1. Raise and support vehicle.
2. Remove wheel and tire assembly.
3. Remove caliper retainer and anti-rattle spring assemblies.
4. Remove caliper from brake disc.
5. Hang caliper aside. **Do not allow brake caliper to hang from brake lines.**

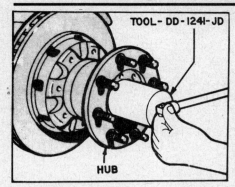

**Fig. 20  Removing hub lock nut. 60 Front Axle**

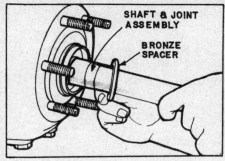

**Fig. 21  Removing or replacing axle shaft. 60 Front Axle**

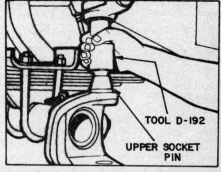

**Fig. 22  Removing or replacing upper socket pin. 60 Front Axle**

6. Remove inboard brake shoe.
7. Remove brake disc, splash shield and spindle.
8. Disconnect vacuum lines and electrical connector from disconnect housing assembly switch.
9. Remove disconnect housing assembly from vehicle as previously described.
10. Remove intermediate axle shaft assembly. **Carefully slide shaft through axle shaft seal to avoid damaging the seal assembly.**
11. Using tool D-330 or equivalent, remove needle bearing from intermediate axle shaft.
12. Remove shift collar from axle housing.
13. Loosen, then remove differential cover attaching screws. Remove cover and drain lubricant.
14. Push inner axle shaft toward center of vehicle and remove C-lock from shaft groove recess.
15. Using tools D-354-4 and D-354-1 or equivalents, remove inner axle shaft bearing.
16. Remove outer axle shaft bearing and seal from housing bore.

### Left Axle Shaft, Installation

1. Using tools D-354-4, D-354-2 and C-367 or equivalents, install inner axle shaft bearing.
2. Using a suitable tool, install inner axle shaft. Install C-lock into axle shaft groove recess.
3. Install shift collar on splined end of inner axle shaft.
4. Install axle shaft bearing and seal.
5. Install needle bearing into intermediate axle shaft.
6. Install intermediate axle shaft through seal.
7. Install disconnect housing assembly and gasket as previously described.
8. Install disconnect housing assembly shield and bolts. Torque bolts to 10 ft. lbs.
9. Connect vacuum lines and electrical connectors to switch assembly.
10. Install splash shield and spindle. Torque nuts to 25–30 ft. lbs.
11. Install brake disc, outer bearing, nut, washer and locknut on spindle assembly.

12. Install spring retainer, spring, drive gear and drive gear snap ring.
13. Apply RTV sealant to seating edge of grease cap, then install the cap.
14. Position inboard brake shoe on adapter with shoe flanges in adapter keyways. Slowly slide caliper assembly into position in adapter and over brake disc.
15. Install anti-rattle springs and retaining clips. Torque to 180 inch lbs.
16. Apply a 1/16 inch bead of suitable sealant along bolt circle of cover.
17. Allow sealant to cure and install on axle. Torque attaching bolts to 420 inch lbs.
18. Remove fill plug and fill axle with suitable lubricant.
19. Install tire and wheel assembly.

## SPICER 60 FRONT AXLE
### AXLE ASSEMBLY
#### Remove & Replace

1. Secure brake pedal in the up position, then raise vehicle.
2. Disconnect front drive shaft at drive pinion yoke.
3. Disconnect drag link at steering knuckle arm (left side only).
4. Disconnect and plug brake line at frame crossmember.
5. Disconnect shock absorbers at lower mounts then disconnect sway bar link assembly, if equipped, from spring plates.
6. Remove nuts and washers from universal bolt spring clips, then remove axle from vehicle.
7. Reverse procedure to install axle assembly. Lubricate all fittings, free brake pedal and bleed brakes.
8. Lower vehicle and check front wheel alignment.

### AXLE SHAFT, BALL JOINT & STEERING KNUCKLE REPAIRS
#### Removal & Disassembly

1. Block brake pedal in "Up" position.
2. Raise and support vehicle.
3. Remove wheel.
4. Remove brake caliper from adapter

and, using a piece of wire, suspend caliper. Do not hang caliper by brake hose. The inner brake pad will remain on adapter.
5. Remove hub cap and snap ring, **Fig. 19.**
6. Remove flange nuts and lock washers.
7. Remove drive flange and discard gasket, or remove locking hub, if equipped.
8. Straighten tang on lock ring, then remove outer locknut, lock ring, inner locknut and outer-bearing, **Fig. 20.** Slide hub and rotor assembly from spindle.
9. Remove inner brake pad from adapter.
10. Remove nuts and washers securing brake splash shield, brake adapter and spindle to steering knuckle.
11. Remove spindle from knuckle. Slide inner and outer axle shaft with bronze spacer, seal and slinger from axle, **Fig. 21.**
12. Remove cotter key and nut from tie rod. Disconnect tie rod from steering knuckle.
13. On left side only, remove cotter key and nut from drag link. Disconnect drag link from steering knuckle arm. Also, remove nuts and upper knuckle cap. Discard gasket. Remove spring and upper socket sleeve.
14. Remove capscrews from lower knuckle cap and free cap from knuckle and housing.
15. To remove knuckle from housing, swing outward at bottom, then lift up and off upper socket pin.
16. Using a suitable tool, loosen and remove upper socket pin, then the seal, **Fig. 22.**
17. Press lower ball socket from axle housing with suitable tools.
18. Referring to **Fig. 23,** disassemble shaft.

#### Assembly & Installation

1. Lubricate lower ball socket assembly with suitable grease.
2. With suitable tools, press seal and lower bearing cup into axle housing. Then, press lower bearing and seal into axle housing.
3. Using a suitable tool and torque

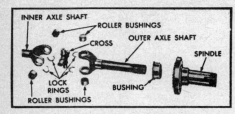

**Fig. 23 Universal joint, spindle and bushing assembly. (Typical)**

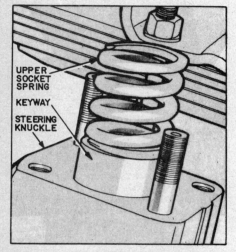

**Fig. 24 Correct alignment of upper socket pin to steering knuckle. 60 Front axle**

wrench, install and torque upper socket pin to 500-600 ft. lbs., **Fig. 22.** Install seal over socket pin.

4. Place steering knuckle over socket pin. Fill lower socket cavity with suitable grease. Work lower knuckle cap into place on knuckle and housing. Install capscrews and torque to 70-90 ft. lbs.

5. Lubricate upper socket pin with suitable grease. Align upper socket sleeve in keyway of steering knuckle and slide into position, **Fig. 24.**

6. Install new gasket over upper steering knuckle studs. Place spring over sleeve. Install cap on left side steering knuckle arm. Install nuts and torque to 70-90 ft. lbs.

7. On left side only, attach drag link to steering knuckle arm and install and torque nut to 60 ft. lbs.

8. Connect tie rod to steering knuckle and install and torque nut to 45 ft. lbs. Install cotter key.

9. Referring to **Fig. 23,** assemble shaft.

10. Slide axle shaft into position. Place bronze spacer on axle shaft with chamfer facing toward universal joint, **Fig. 21.**

11. Install spindle, brake adapter and splash shield. Install and torque nuts to 50-70 ft. lbs.

12. Place inner brake pad on adapter.

13. Install hub and rotor assembly onto spindle. Install outer bearing and inner locknut. Using tool DD-1241-JD and tool C-3952, torque locknut to 50 ft.

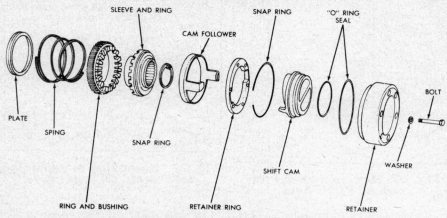

**Fig. 25 Manual locking hub assembly exploded view. Exc. Dualmatic**

lbs. to seat bearings. Then, back off locknut and retorque to 30-40 ft. lbs. while rotating hub and rotor. Back off nut 135 to 150 degrees. Assemble lock ring and outer locknut. Torque locknut to 65 ft. lbs. minimum. Bend one tang of lock ring over inner locknut and another tang over outer locknut. Bearing endplay should be .001-.010 inch.

14. Install new gasket on hub, then the drive flange, lock washers and nuts. Torque nuts to 30-40 ft. lbs. Install snap ring and hub cap, or locking hub, if equipped, **Fig. 19.**

15. Position caliper on adapter and torque Allen screw to 12-18 ft. lbs.

16. Install wheel and lower vehicle.

17. Remove block from brake pedal.

# FRONT WHEEL LOCKING HUB SERVICE
## MANUAL LOCKING HUB, EXC. DUALMATIC
### DESCRIPTION

As shown in **Fig. 25,** the splines on the inside diameter of the axle shaft sleeve and ring assembly mesh with the axle shaft splines. The assembly is retained on the axle shaft with a snap ring. The splines on the outside diameter of the inner clutch ring assembly mesh with the wheel hub splines. Therefore, when the actuator knob is turned towards the "L" position, the actuating cam body is forced outward towards the hub end, allowing the inner clutch to be forced under spring tension towards the axle shaft sleeve and ring assembly until the inner clutch assembly teeth are engaged in the axle shaft sleeve and ring assembly teeth, locking the axle and hub.

### OPERATION
#### "L" Position

When the transfer case is shifted into the position for driving the front axle, turn the actuating knob so that it is aligned with the letter L. If the clutch teeth do not engage with the knob turned to this position, the clutch teeth are butted and a slight

movement of the wheel in either direction complete the lock. The front axle will now drive the wheel.

#### "F" Position

When the transfer case is to be shifted into the position for driving the rear axle only, turn the actuating knob so that it is aligned with the letter F. This will disengage the clutch teeth and thus unlock the wheel hub from the axle shaft. The wheel will now turn free on the axle. **Be certain that the transfer case is shifted into two-wheel drive position before disengaging the Hub-Lok.**

### REMOVAL

1. Place hub in lock position, then remove six attaching bolts and washers from retainer using a suitable Allen wrench, **Fig. 25.**

2. Remove retainer and shift cam, then separate shift cam from retainer and discard O-rings.

3. Pry snap ring from hub internal groove, then slide retainer ring and cam follower from hub, **Fig. 26.**

4. Remove snap ring from axle shaft using suitable pliers.

5. Remove sleeve and ring, ring and bushing, spring and spring plate.

6. Inspect all parts for nicks, burrs or wear. Replace parts as necessary.

### ASSEMBLY

1. Install spring plate and spring, large coils first, into wheel hub housing.

2. Assemble ring and bushing, and sleeve and ring into one assembly, then slide into housing.

3. Install snap ring in axle shaft groove.

4. Position cam follower and retainer ring into housing, then lock into place with large internal snap ring.

5. Install small O-ring seal in shift cam groove, lubricate using suitable lubricant, then install retainer at lock position.

6. Install large O-ring seal in retainer groove, lubricate using suitable lubricant, then position assembly in hub.

7. Install washers and six attaching screws, then check for proper operation.

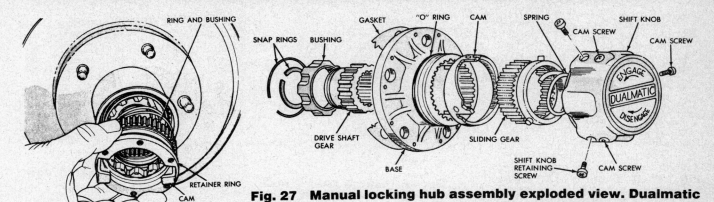

Fig. 26 **Retaining ring and cam follower removal**

**Fig. 27** **Manual locking hub assembly exploded view. Dualmatic**

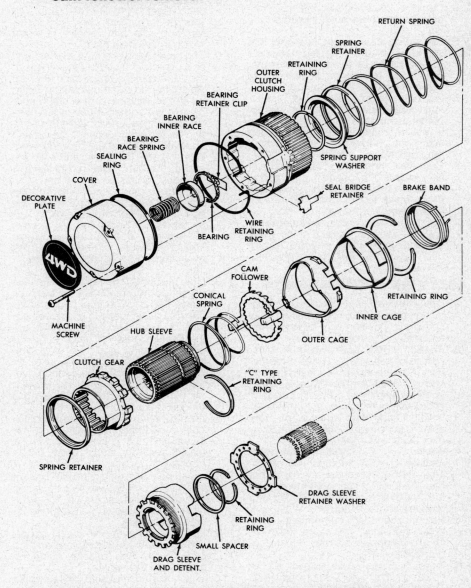

**Fig. 28** **Automatic locking hub assembly exploded view**

## DUALMATIC MANUAL LOCKING HUB

### REMOVAL & DISASSEMBLY

Do not remove cam (outer) screws from cover. If cam screws are removed, misalignment could occur causing damage to cam.

1. Turn to engage position.
2. Apply pressure to the face of the shift knob, remove three shift knob retaining screws, **Fig. 27**.
3. Pull shift knob from mounting base and remove snap ring from axle shaft.
4. Remove capscrews and lock washers from mounting flange.
5. Remove locking hub assembly from rotor hub and discard gasket.
6. Wash parts in mineral spirits and blow dry with compressed air. Inspect components for damage.

### ASSEMBLY & INSTALLATION

1. Lubricate parts with multipurpose lubricant part no. 2932524 or equivalent.
2. Install new gasket and locking hub onto rotor hub.
3. Install capscrews and lock washers and torque to 30-40 ft. lbs.
4. Install axle shaft snap ring and shift knob on mounting base.
5. Align the splines by pushing inward on shift knob and turning it clockwise to lock it in position.
6. Install and tighten three shift knob retaining screws.

## AUTOMATIC LOCKING HUB

Complaints of automatic locking hubs not engaging or disengaging on 1981 vehicles can be caused by the installation of the incorrect drag sleeve retainer washer, **Fig. 28**. To determine if the incorrect washer was installed, remove the automatic locking hub, then inspect the drag sleeve retainer washer located behind the wheel bearing locknut. There are four tabs on the drag sleeve retainer washer that should be visible, **Fig. 28**. If the four tabs are not visible, the incorrect drag sleeve retainer washer is installed and should be replaced with the correct part.

### DESCRIPTION

The Automatic Locking Hub, shown in **Fig. 28**, engages or disengages to lock the

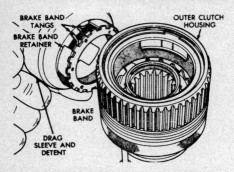

**Fig. 29 Removing drag sleeve and detent & brake band assembly**

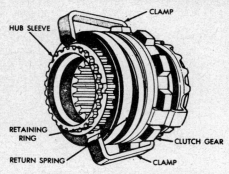

**Fig. 30 Clutch gear & hub sleeve assembly**

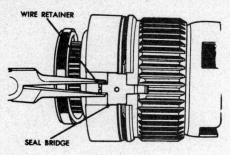

**Fig. 31 Install seal bridge**

front axle shaft to the hub of the front wheel. Engagement occurs whenever the vehicle is operated in 4WD. Disengagement occurs whenever 2WD has been selected and the vehicle is moving rearward. Disengagement will not occur when the vehicle is moved rearward if 4WD is selected and the hub has already been engaged.

Before disassembling a unit for a complaint of abnormal noise, note the following:

a. To obtain all-wheel drive, the transfer case lever must be placed in 4L or 4H, at which time the hub locks will automatically engage.
b. To unlock the hubs, shift the transfer case lever to 2H, then slowly reverse the vehicle direction approximately 10 feet.
c. An incomplete shift from 2WD to 4WD, or disengagement of only one hub lock may cause an abnormal sound from the front axle. Shift to 4WD to stop the noise, then unlock the hubs as previously stated.

## REMOVAL

1. Remove 5 screws retaining the cover to outer clutch housing.
2. Remove cover, seal, seal bridge and bearing components.
3. Compress the wire retaining ring and remove the remaining components from the hub.

## DISASSEMBLY

**Before disassembly, the hub must be unlocked. If hub is locked when removed from wheel, hold hub outer housing and rotate drag sleeve in either direction to unlock.**

1. Remove snap ring from groove in hub sleeve, then turn clutch gear until it falls into disengagement with the outer clutch housing. Lift and tilt the drag sleeve to unlock the tangs of the brake band from window of inner cage, **Fig. 29,** then remove the drag sleeve and brake assembly. **The brake band must never be removed from the drag sleeve. The spring tension of the brake band can be changed if the coils are over-expanded and could affect hub operation.**
2. Remove snap ring from groove in outer clutch housing, then pry plastic outer cage free from inner cage while in-

ner cage is being removed.
3. Pry plastic outer cage tabs free from groove in outer clutch housing, then remove outer cage.
4. Remove clutch sleeve and attached components from outer clutch housing.
5. Compress return spring and hold the spring with clamps, **Fig. 30,** then position the assembly in a vise so that the vise holds both ends of the clutch sleeve. Remove retaining ring.
6. Remove clamps holding the return spring, then slowly open the vise to permit the release of the return spring in a safe manner. Remove retainer seat, spring and spring support washers from the hub sleeve.
7. Remove C-ring from clutch sleeve. It is necessary to position sleeve assembly so that the C-ring ends are aligned with legs of cam follower, allowing removal between the legs.
8. Remove conical spring from between cam follower and clutch gear, then separate cam follower from clutch gear. Do not pry the legs of the cam follower apart.

## ASSEMBLY & INSTALLATION

1. Install tangs of cam follower over flats of clutch gear, then compress conical spring and position with large diameter located against clutch gear.
2. Position clutch gear assembly over splines of hub sleeve. The teeth of the cam follower should be located at the end of the hub sleeve with no splines, and the clutch gear and spring should slide freely over splines of hub sleeve.
3. Install C-ring into groove of hub sleeve, then install a spring retainer over each end of return spring.
4. Position one end of return spring with retainer against shoulder of clutch gear, then place support washer on end of the return spring. Compress return spring and install retainer ring into groove of hub sleeve.
5. Place assembled components into outer housing. The cam follower should be positioned with legs facing outward.
6. Install 3 of the cover screws into 3 holes of the outer clutch housing. These screws will support the component to permit the clutch hub to drop down so that the tangs of the brake band can be assembled.
7. Carefully install the plastic outer cage

into outer clutch housing with ramps facing toward cam follower. The small external tabs of the plastic cage should be located in wide groove of outer clutch housing.
8. Install steel inner cage into the outer cage aligning tab of outer cage with window of the inner cage, then install retaining ring into groove of outer clutch housing above outer cage.
9. The brake band and drag are serviced as a complete assembly. Install one of the 2 tangs of the brake band on each side of the lug of the outer cage, located in the window of the steel inner cage. It will be necessary to tilt these parts to engage the tangs in this position as the drag sleeve is positioned against the face of the cam follower.
10. Remove the 3 screws and rest the end of the hub sleeve on a suitable support, then install washer and snap ring above drag sleeve. **The following steps may be completed as the hub is installed into vehicle.**
11. Install wire retaining ring into groove of unsplined end of clutch housing. The tangs of retainer ring should point away from splined end of clutch housing.
12. Hold the tangs together and install the 2 bent down tabs of seal bridge over tangs, **Fig. 31.** The seal bridge holds the wire retainer ring in a clamped position in groove of outer clutch housing. Install O-ring into groove of outer clutch housing and over the seal bridge.
13. Lubricate and install the bearing over the inner race. The steel ball bearing should be visible when the bearing is properly installed.
14. Install bearing retainer clip into hole in outer race, then install bearing and retainer assembly in end of hub sleeve. Install seal ring over outer clutch housing.
15. Install bearing race spring into bore of cover, then install cover and spring assembly. Align holes in cover to holes in outer clutch housing and install 5 screws.
16. Install O-ring over seal bridge to prevent it from dislodging during handling prior to the hub bearing being installed into the vehicle.
17. The hub and attached parts should turn freely after installation. The 5 cover screws must be loosened to install the hub into the vehicle. After installation, torque the cover screws to 40-50 inch lbs.

# DODGE CARAVAN, MINI RAM VAN & PLYMOUTH VOYAGER

## INDEX OF SERVICE OPERATIONS

**NOTE:** Refer to the rear of this manual for vehicle manufacturer's special service tool suppliers.

# SPECIFICATIONS

## GENERAL ENGINE SPECIFICATIONS

| Year | Engine | Carb. | Bore & Stroke Inch (Millimeters) | Comp. Ratio | Horsepower @ RPM | Torque Ft. Lbs. @ RPM | Normal Oil Pressure Pounds |
|---|---|---|---|---|---|---|---|
| 1984 | 4-135/2.2L | 2 Bbl. | 3.44 x 3.62 (87.5 x 92) | 9.6 | 101 @ 5600 | 121 @ 3600 | 40 ① |
| | 4-156/2.6L | 2 Bbl. | 3.59 x 3.86 (91.1 x 98) | 8.7 | 99 @ 4800 | 143 @ 2000 | 85 ② |
| 1985 | 4-135/2.2L | 2 Bbl. | 3.44 x 3.62 (87.5 x 92) | 9.5 | 101 @ 5600 | 121 @ 3600 | 25-90 ③ |
| | 4-156/2.6L | 2 Bbl. | 3.59 x 3.86 (91.1 x 98) | 8.7 | 104 @ 4800 | 142 @ 2800 | 45-90 ③ |
| 1986 | 4-135/2.2L | 2 Bbl. | 3.44 x 3.62 (87.5 x 92) | 9.5 | ⑤ | ⑥ | 25-80 ③ |
| | 4-156/2.6L | 2 Bbl. | 3.59 x 3.86 (91.1 x 98) | 8.7 | 107 @ 5000 | 142 @ 2500 | 45-90 ③ |
| 1987 | 4-135/2.2L | 2 Bbl. | 3.44 x 3.62 (87.5 x 92) | 9.5 | 95 @ 5200 | 121 @ 3200 | 25-80 ③ |
| | 4-153/2.5L | Fuel Inj. | 3.44 x 4.09 (87.5 x 104) | 9.0 | 102 @ 4800 | 138 @ 2800 | 25-80 ③ |
| | 4-156/2.6L | 2 Bbl. | 3.59 x 3.856 (91.1 x 98) | 8.7 | 102 @ 4800 | 142 @ 2800 | 25-80 ③ |
| | V6-181/3.0L | Fuel Inj. | 3.59 x 2.99 (91.1 x 76) | 8.85 | 144 @ 4800 | 175 @ 2800 | 71-85 ④ |
| 1988 | 4-153/2.5L | Fuel Inj. | 3.44 x 4.09 (87.5 x 104) | 8.9 | 102 @ 4800 | 133 @ 3000 | 25-80 ③ |
| | V6-181/3.0L | Fuel Inj. | 3.59 x 2.99 (91.1 x 76) | 8.85 | 144 @ 4800 | 170 @ 2800 | 71-85 ④ |
| 1989 | 4-153/2.5L ⑦ | Fuel Inj. | 3.44 x 4.09 (87.5 x 104) | 8.9 | 100 @ 4800 | 135 @ 2800 | 25-80 ③ |
| | 4-153/2.5L ⑧ | Fuel Inj. | 3.44 x 4.09 (87.5 x 104) | 7.8 | 150 @ 4800 | 180 @ 2000 | 25-80 ③ |
| | V6-181/3.0L | Fuel Inj. | 3.59 x 2.99 (91.1 x 76) | 8.85 | 150 @ 5000 | 171 @ 3600 | 71-85 ④ |

①—At 2000 RPM.
②—At 2500 RPM.
③—At 3000 RPM.
④—Relief valve opening pressure.
⑤—Exc. Calif., 96 @ 5600; Calif., 94 @ 5200.
⑥—Exc. Calif., 121 @ 3600; Calif., 122 @ 3200.
⑦—Exc. turbocharged.
⑧—Turbocharged.

## ENGINE TIGHTENING SPECIFICATIONS*

*Torque specifications are for clean and lightly lubricated threads only. Dry or dirty threads produce increased friction which prevents accurate measurement of tightness.

| Year | Engine Model | Spark Plug Ft. Lbs. | Cylinder Head Bolts Ft. Lbs. | Intake Manifold Inch Lbs. | Exhaust Manifold Inch Lbs. | Camshaft Cover Inch Lbs. | Connecting Rod Cap Bolts Ft. Lbs. | Main Bearing Cap Bolts Ft. Lbs. | Flywheel To Crankshaft Ft. Lbs. | Crankshaft Pulley Ft. Lbs. |
|---|---|---|---|---|---|---|---|---|---|---|
| 1984-85 | 4-135 | 26 | 45 ① | 200 | 200 | 105 | 40 ① | 30 ① | 65 | 21 |
| | 4-156 | 18 | ② | 150 | 150 | 53 | 34 | 58 | 100 | 87 |
| 1986 | 4-135 | 26 | 65 ① | 200 | 200 | 105 | 40 ① | 30 ① | 70 | 21 |
| | 4-156 | 18 | ② | 150 | 150 | 53 | 34 | 58 | 70 | 87 |
| 1987 | 4-135 | 26 | 65 ① | 200 | 200 | 105 | 40 ① | 30 ① | 70 | 20.8 |
| | 4-153 | 26 | 65 ① | 200 | 200 | 105 | 40 ① | 30 ① | 70 | 20.8 |
| | 4-156 | 18 | ② | 150 | 150 | 53 | 34 | 58 | 70 | 87 |
| | V6-181 | 20 | 80 | 174 | ③ | 68 | 38 | 61 | 70 | 109 |
| 1988-89 | 4-153 | 26 | 65 ① | 200 | 200 | 105 | 40 ① | 30 ① | 70 | 24 |
| | V6-181 | 20 | 70 | 174 | ③ | 68 | 38 | 60 | 70 | 110 |

①—Turn torque wrench an additional ¼ turn after specified torque has been achieved.
②—Cold engine, 69 ft. lbs.; warm engine, 76 ft. lbs.
③—Rear exhaust manifold, 191 inch lbs.; front exhaust manifold, 174 inch lbs.

## ALTERNATOR & REGULATOR SPECIFICATIONS

| Year | | Alternator | | | Regulator | |
|---|---|---|---|---|---|---|
| | Identification | Rated Hot Output Amps. | Field Current 12 Volts @ 80°F. | Output @ 15 Volts 1250 RPM. | Part Number | Voltage @ 80°F. |
| 1984-85 | Yellow① | 60 | 2.5-5 | 47 | — | 13.9-14.4 |
| | Brown① | 78 | 2.5-5 | 56 | — | 13.9-14.4 |
| | A4T25191② | 75 | — | 63-70④ | Integral | 14.1-14.7③ |
| 1986 | 5213762⑤ | 60 | 2.5-5 | 47 | — | 13.9-14.4 |
| | 5213763⑤ | 78 | 2.5-5 | 56 | — | 13.9-14.4 |
| | 5226200⑤ | 40/90 | 2.5-5 | 82 | — | 13.9-14.4 |
| | A4T25191② | 75 | — | 64-72⑥ | Integral | 14.1-14.7③ |
| | ② | 90 | — | 80-91⑥ | Integral | 14.1-14.7③ |
| 1987 | ⑤ | 78 | 2.5-5 | 56 | — | 13.9-14.4 |
| | ⑤ | 40/90 | 2.5-5 | 82 | — | 13.9-14.4 |
| | A4T25191② | 75 | — | 64-72⑥ | Integral | 14.1-14.7③ |
| | ② | 90 | — | 80-91⑥ | Integral | 14.1-14.7③ |
| | 5227749⑦ | 40/90 | 2.5-5 | 87 | ⑧ | ⑨ |
| | 5227349⑩ | 40/90 | 2.5-5 | 87 | ⑧ | ⑨ |
| 1988 | 5227474 | 40/90 | 2.5-5 | 75 | ⑧ | ⑨ |
| | 5227749⑦ | 40/90 | 2.5-5 | 85 | ⑧ | ⑨ |
| | 5233474⑤ | 40/90 | 2.5-5 | 87 | ⑧ | ⑨ |
| | 5233508⑤ | 40/90 | 2.5-5 | 98 | ⑧ | ⑨ |
| | 5227349⑩ | 40/90 | 2.5-5 | 87 | ⑧ | ⑨ |
| 1989 | 5233618⑦ | 90HS | 2.5-5 | 87 | ⑧ | ⑨ |
| | 5233718⑦ | 90RS | 2.5-5 | 75 | ⑧ | ⑨ |
| | 5233449⑩ | 90HS | 2.5-5 | 87 | ⑧ | ⑨ |
| | 5233418⑩ | 90HS | 2.5-5 | 87 | ⑧ | ⑨ |
| | 5233660⑩ | 120HS | 2.5-5 | 98 | ⑧ | ⑨ |
| | 5233608⑩ | 120HS | 2.5-5 | 98 | ⑧ | ⑨ |

①—Chrysler alternators are identified by tag color.
②—Mitsubishi alternator.
③—68°F (20°C).
④—Output @ 13.5 volts, 1000 RPM
⑤—Chrysler Alternator
⑥—Output @ 13 volts, 1000 RPM
⑦—Bosch alternator.
⑧—In engine electronics.
⑨—Limited by voltage regulator in engine electronics.
⑩—Nippondenso alternator.

## STARTING MOTOR SPECIFICATIONS

| Year | Engine | Model | Ident. No. | Cranking Amperage Draw Test① | Free Speed Test | | |
|---|---|---|---|---|---|---|---|
| | | | | | Amps.② | Volts | RPM③ |
| 1984-85 | 4-135 | Bosch | 5213045 | 120-160 | 47 | 11 | 6600 |
| | | Nippondenso | 5213645 | 120-160 | 47 | 11 | 6600 |
| | 4-156 | Nippondenso | 5213235 | 150-210 | 85 | 11 | 3700 |
| 1986 | 4-135 | Bosch | 5226444 | 150-210 | 85 | 11 | 3700 |
| | 4-156 | Mitsubishi | 5213235 | 150-210 | 85 | 11 | 3700 |
| 1987 | 4-135 | Bosch | 5227282 | 150-210 | 85 | 11 | 3700 |
| | 4-153 | Bosch | 5227282 | 150-210 | 85 | 11 | 3700 |
| | 4-156 | Mitsubishi | 5213235 | 150-210 | 85 | 11 | 3700 |
| | V6-181 | Bosch | 5226948 | 150-220 | 90 | 11 | 3565 |
| | V6-181 | Nippondenso | 5227248 | 150-220 | 82 | 11 | 3625 |
| 1988 | 4-153 | Bosch | 5227282 | 150-220 | 85 | 11 | 3700 |
| | V6-181 | Bosch | 5226948 | 150-220 | 90 | 11 | 3565 |
| | V6-181 | Nippondenso | 5227248 | 150-220 | 82 | 11 | 3625 |
| 1989 | 4-153 | Bosch | 5233006 | 150-220 | 69 | 11 | 3447 |
| | V6-181 | Bosch | 5227548 | 150-220 | 69 | 11 | 3447 |
| | V6-181 | Nippondenso | 5227248 | 150-220 | 74 | 11 | 3980 |

**Continued**

## STARTING MOTOR SPECIFICATIONS-Continued

① —Engine should be at normal operating temperature.　　② —Maximum current drawn.　　③ —Minimum speed.

# WHEEL ALIGNMENT SPECIFICATIONS

| Year | Model | Caster Angle, Degrees | | Camber Angle, Degrees | | | | Toe In. Inch |
| | | Limits | Desired | Limits | | Desired | | |
| | | | | Left | Right | Left | Right | |
| 1984-85 | ALL① | — | — | −¼ to +¾ | −¼ to +¾ | +5/16 | +5/16 | ③ |
| | ALL② | — | — | −1⅛ to −⅛ | −1⅛ to −⅛ | −½ | −½ | ④ |
| 1986 | ALL① | — | — | −¼ to +¾ | −¼ to +¾ | +5/16 | +5/16 | ⑤ |
| | ALL② | — | — | — | — | — | — | 0 |
| 1987 | All① | — | ⑥ | −¼ to +¾ | −¼ to +¾ | +5/16 | +5/16 | ⑤ |
| | All② | — | — | −1⅜ to −¼ | −1⅜ to −¼ | −½ | −½ | 0 |
| 1988-89 | All | ⑥ | −¼ to +¾ | −¼ to +¾ | +5/16 | +5/16 | ⑤ | |
| | All② | — | — | −1⅜ to −¼ | −1⅜ to −¼ | −½ | −½ | 0 |

① —Front wheel alignment.
② —Rear wheel alignment.
③ —0 to ⅛" out.
④ —1984, 3/32"; 1985, zero.
⑤ —1/16".
⑥ —On Van, .4°; on Wagon, .7°.

# BRAKE SPECIFICATIONS

| Year | Model | Rear Drum I.D. | Wheel Cyl. Bore | | Disc Brake Rotor | | | | | Master Cyl. I.D. |
| | | | Front Disc | Rear Drum | Nominal Thickness | Minimum Thickness | Thickness Variation (Parallelism) | Runout (TIR)① | Finish (Microinch) | |
| 1984-88 | ALL | 9 | 2.362 | .748 | .861-.870 | .803 | .0005 | .004 | 15-80 | .944 |
| 1989 | ALL | 9 | 2.362 | .748 | .861-.870 | .803 | .0005 | .005 | 15-80 | .944 |

① —T.I.R.-Total indicator reading.

# COOLING SYSTEM & CAPACITY DATA

| Year | Engine | Cooling Capacity | | Radiator Cap Relief Pressure, Lbs. | Thermo. Opening Temp. Degrees F. (Centigrade) | Fuel Tank Gals. (Liters) | Engine Oil Refill Qts. (Liters) | Transaxle Oil | | Auto. Trans. Qts. (Liters) |
| | | Less A/C Qts. (Liters) | With A/C Qts. (Liters) | | | | | 4 Speed Pints (Liters) | 5 Speed Pints (Liters) | |
| 1984-86 | 4-135 | 8.5 (8.1) | 8.5 (8.1) | 14-18 | 195 (91) | 15 (56.8) | 4① (3.8) | 2 (1.8) | 4.6 (2.1) | 8.9③ (8.4) |
| | 4-156 | 9.5 (9) | 9.5 (9) | 14-18 | ④ | 15 (56.8) | 5② (4.8) | — | — | 8.9③ (8.4) |
| 1987 | 4-135 | 8.5 (8.1) | 8.5 (8.1) | 14-18 | 192-199 (88-93) | 15 (56.8) | 4① (3.8) | — | 4.8 (2.3) | 8.9③ (8.4) |
| | 4-153 | 8.5⑤ (8.1) | 8.5⑤ (8.1) | 14-18 | 192-199 (88-93) | 15 (56.8) | 4① (3.8) | — | — | 8.5 (8.0) |
| | 4-156 | 9.5 (9) | 9.5 (9) | 14-18 | 187-194 (86-90) | 15 (56.8) | 5② (4.8) | — | 4.8 (2.3) | 8.9③ (8.4) |
| | V6-181 | 10 (9.5) | 10 (9.5) | 14-18 | — | 15 (56.8) | 4① (3.8) | — | — | 8.5 (8.0) |
| 1988-89 | 4-153 | 8.5( 8.1)⑤ (8.1) | 8.5⑤ (8.1) | 14-18 | 192-199 (88-93) | 15 (56.8) | 4① (3.8) | —⑥ | —⑥ | 8.5 (8.0) |
| | V6-181 | 10 (9.5) | 10 (9.5) | 14-18 | — | 15 (56.8) | 4① (3.8) | —⑥ | —⑥ | 8.5 (8.0) |

① —With or without filter change.
② —Includes 1 pint (.47 liter) for filter.
③ —Replacement volume is approximately 4 qts. (3.8 liters).
　Make final check with dipstick.
④ —Except California, 190°F. (87°C); California, 180°F (84°C).
⑤ —Add .94 liters (1 qt.) when equipped
　with rear heater.
⑥ —Use SAE 5W30 engine oil as lubricant. Fill to bottom of fill hole in end cover.

# ELECTRICAL
## INDEX

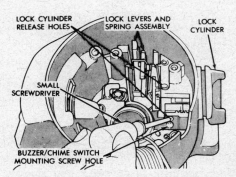

**Fig. 1   Ignition lock removal. Models w/standard column**

## FUSE PANEL & FLASHER LOCATION

The fuse panel is located under the left side of the instrument panel.

The turn signal flasher is located on the fuse panel and the hazard flasher is located below the fuse panel.

## STARTER REPLACE

### 4-135

1. Disconnect battery ground cable.
2. Remove heatshield clamp, then the heatshield if equipped.
3. Loosen air pump tube at exhaust manifold, then position tube bracket away from starter motor.
4. Disconnect battery cable at starter motor and solenoid leads at solenoid.
5. Remove starter to flywheel housing and rear bracket to engine or transaxle attaching bolts.
6. Remove starter.
7. Reverse procedure to install.

### 4-156

1. Disconnect battery ground cable.
2. Disconnect battery cable at starter motor and solenoid leads at solenoid.

3. Remove starter to flywheel housing attaching bolts, then the starter.
4. Reverse procedure to install.

### 4-153 & V6-181

1. Disconnect battery ground cable.
2. Remove starter motor attaching bolts from transaxle bellhousing.
3. Disconnect all electrical connectors from starter motor.
4. Remove starter.
5. Reverse procedure to install.

## IGNITION LOCK REPLACE
### MODELS LESS TILT COLUMN

1. Disconnect battery ground cable.
2. Remove turn signal switch as described under "Turn Signal/Hazard Warning Switch, Replace."
3. Disconnect horn and ignition key lamp ground wires, then remove ignition key lamp attaching screw and lamp.
4. Remove four screws attaching upper bearing housing to lock housing, then remove snap ring from upper end of steering shaft and remove upper bearing housing.
5. Remove lock plate spring and lock plate from steering shaft.
6. Position lock cylinder in Lock position and remove ignition key.
7. Remove key warning buzzer attaching screws, then remove buzzer.
8. Remove two screws attaching ignition switch to steering column, then remove switch by rotating it 90° and sliding from rod.
9. Remove two screws attaching dimmer switch, then disengage dimmer switch from actuator rod.
10. Remove two bell crank attaching screws, then slide bell crank up into lock housing until it can be disconnected from ignition switch actuator rod.
11. With lock cylinder in Lock position, insert a small diameter screwdriver into

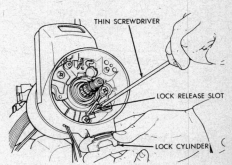

**Fig. 2   Ignition lock removal. Models w/tilt column**

lock cylinder release holes and push inward until spring loaded lock cylinder retainers release, **Fig. 1.**
12. Grasp lock cylinder and pull from lock housing bore.
13. Reverse procedure to install. The lock cylinder and ignition switch must be in the "Lock" position.

### MODELS W/TILT COLUMN

1. Disconnect battery ground cable.
2. Remove turn signal switch as described under "Turn Signal Switch, Replace."
3. Remove ignition key lamp.
4. Position ignition lock cylinder in the Lock position, then remove ignition key.
5. Insert a thin screwdriver into lock cylinder release slot and depress spring latch which releases lock cylinder, then grasp lock cylinder and remove from column, **Fig. 2.**
6. Reverse procedure to install.

## IGNITION SWITCH REPLACE

1. Disconnect battery ground cable.
2. Remove left lower instrument panel cover.
3. Position gear selector to "D" and disconnect indicator cable, if equipped with automatic transaxle.

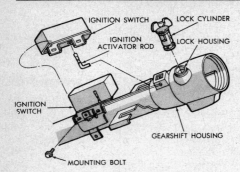

**Fig. 3   Ignition switch replacement**

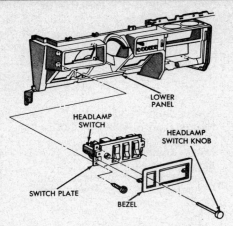

**Fig. 4   Light switch removal**

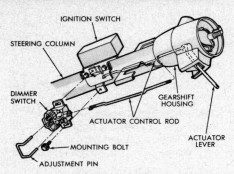

**Fig. 5   Dimmer switch replacement**

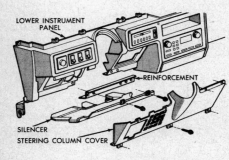

**Fig. 6   Steering column cover, silencer & reinforcement removal**

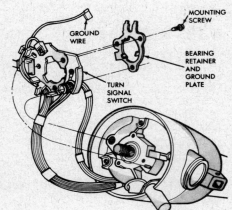

**Fig. 7   Turn signal switch replacement**

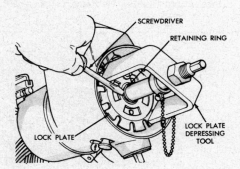

**Fig. 8   Lock plate removal. Models w/tilt column**

4. Remove lower panel reinforcement, then five steering column to support bracket attaching nuts.
5. Lower column and disconnect ignition switch electrical connector.
6. Position ignition lock cylinder in the Lock position.
7. Tape ignition switch rod to steering column to prevent rod from falling out of lock cylinder assembly.
8. Remove two ignition switch attaching screws, then the switch, **Fig. 3.**
9. Reverse procedure to install.

## STEERING WHEEL
### REPLACE

1. Disconnect battery ground cable.
2. On standard steering wheels, remove two horn pad assembly attaching screws.
3. On premium steering wheels, pry off horn pad using suitable screwdriver.
4. On all models, remove steering wheel nut.
5. Remove steering wheel using puller No. C-3428B or equivalent.
6. Reverse procedure to install. Torque steering wheel attaching nut to 45 ft. lbs.

## LIGHT SWITCH
### REPLACE

1. Disconnect battery ground cable.

2. Remove headlight and accessory switch trim bezel, **Fig. 4.**
3. Remove four switch plate to lower panel attaching screws.
4. Pull switch assembly rearward, then disconnect switch electrical connectors.
5. Remove switch knob and stem by depressing button on switch.
6. Remove two headlight switch plate to switch plate assembly attaching screws, then the headlight switch retainer and switch.
7. Reverse procedure to install.

## DIMMER SWITCH
### REPLACE

1. Disconnect battery ground cable.
2. Remove left lower instrument panel cover, then tape dimmer switch rod to steering column to prevent rod from falling out of notch in actuator lever.
3. Remove switch to column attaching screws.
4. Disconnect switch electrical connec-

tor, then remove switch from steering column, **Fig. 5.**
5. Reverse procedure to install. During installation, gently push up on switch to take up slack on rod.

## TURN SIGNAL/HAZARD WARNING SWITCH
### REPLACE

1. Remove steering wheel. Refer to "Steering Wheel, Replace" procedure.
2. Remove steering column cover, silencer and lower reinforcement, **Fig. 6.**
3. Pry off wiring trough from steering column, then disconnect turn signal/hazard warning switch electrical connector.
4. On models equipped with standard column, proceed as follows:
   a. Remove wiper/washer switch-to-turn signal switch pivot attaching screw. Leave turn signal lever in its installed position.
   b. Remove 3 bearing retainer and turn signal switch-to-upper bearing housing attaching screws, **Fig. 7.**
5. On models equipped with tilt column, proceed as follows:
   a. Remove plastic cover, if equipped, from lock plate.
   b. Depress lock plate using tool No. C-4156 or equivalent and pry retaining ring out of groove with a suitable screwdriver, **Fig. 8. The full load of the upper bearing**

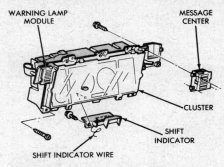

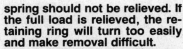

**Fig. 9 Instrument cluster removal**

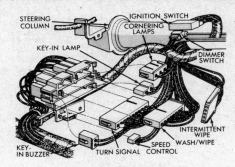

**Fig. 10 Steering column electrical connectors**

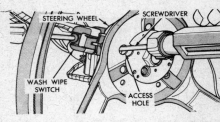

**Fig. 11 Access hole for turn signal lever**

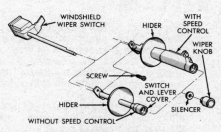

**Fig. 12 Control lever assembly**

spring should not be relieved. If the full load is relieved, the retaining ring will turn too easily and make removal more difficult.

c. Remove lock plate, cancelling cam and upper bearing spring, then place turn signal switch in right turn position.

d. Remove screw attaching link between turn signal switch and wiper/washer switch pivot.

e. Remove hazard warning switch knob attaching screw, then the 3 turn signal switch-to-steering column attaching screws.

6. On all models, remove turn signal/hazard warning switch assembly by gently pulling switch up from column while straightening and guiding wires up through column opening, **Fig. 7.**

7. Reverse procedure to install.

## INSTRUMENT CLUSTER
### REPLACE

1. Disconnect battery ground cable.
2. Remove instrument cluster bezel, then disconnect speedometer cable in engine compartment.
3. On models with automatic transaxle, remove instrument panel lower left cover, then disconnect shift indicator wire.
4. On all models, remove five instrument cluster to instrument panel attaching screws, **Fig. 9**, then disconnect speedometer cable from speedometer.
5. Disconnect cluster electrical connectors, then remove cluster from right side of steering column.
6. Reverse procedure to install.

## WASHER/WIPER SWITCH
### REPLACE
#### FRONT
##### Standard Column

1. Disconnect battery ground cable.
2. On standard steering wheels, remove two horn pad assembly attaching screws.
3. On premium steering wheels, pry off

horn pad using suitable screwdriver.
4. On all models, remove steering column cover, silencer and lower reinforcement, **Fig. 6.**
5. Pry off wiring trough from steering column, then remove washer/wiper switch cover attaching bolts and rotate cover upward.
6. Disconnect washer/wiper switch electrical connector, then the intermittent wipe switch and speed control electrical connectors if equipped, **Fig. 10.**
7. Place ignition in "Off" position and turn steering wheel so access hole in hub area is at 9 o'clock position. Using screwdriver, loosen turn signal lever screw through this access hole, **Fig. 11. Use tape to secure dimmer switch rod in place.**
8. Remove washer/wiper assembly.
9. Pull hider up control lever, then remove two control lever sleeve to washer/wiper switch attaching screws, **Fig. 12.**
10. Remove washer/wiper switch control knob from end of control lever.
11. Rotate control lever shaft clockwise and pull shaft straight out of switch.
12. Reverse procedure to install.

#### Tilt Column

1. Remove steering wheel. Refer to "Steering Wheel, Replace" procedure.
2. Remove steering column cover, silencer and lower reinforcement, **Fig. 6.**
3. Pry off wiring trough from steering column, then remove plastic cover from lock plate, if equipped.
4. Depress lock plate using depressing

tool No. C-4156 or equivalent and pry retaining ring out of groove with screwdriver, **Fig. 8.** Full load of upper bearing spring should not be relieved. If full load is relieved, retaining ring will turn too easily, making removal more difficult.

5. Remove lock plate, cancelling cam and upper bearing spring, then remove switch lever actuator attaching screw and lever.
6. Push in hazard warning knob, then remove by turning knob counterclockwise.
7. Disconnect washer/wiper switch electrical connector, then the intermittent wipe switch and speed control electrical connectors if equipped, **Fig. 10.**
8. Remove three turn signal switch attaching screws, then place selector lever in "1" position. Wrap a piece of tape around electrical connector and wires to prevent snagging during switch removal.
9. Remove turn signal switch and wiring, then the ignition key lamp.
10. Position ignition lock cylinder in the Lock position, then insert a small diameter screwdriver into lock cylinder release holes and push inward until spring loaded lock cylinder retainers release, **Fig. 2.**
11. Remove buzzer/chime switch by inserting a bent piece of stiff wire into the exposed loop of the switch and pull straight out. **Use caution not to drop switch into steering column.**
12. Remove three switch housing cover attaching screws, then the housing cover.
13. Remove washer/wiper switch pivot pin using a suitable punch, then remove washer/wiper switch assembly.
14. Pull hider up control lever, then remove control lever sleeve to washer/wiper switch attaching screws, **Fig. 12. Use tape to secure dimmer switch rod in place.**
15. Remove washer/wiper switch control knob from end of control lever.
16. Rotate control lever shaft clockwise and pull shaft straight out of switch.
17. Reverse procedure to install.

#### REAR

1. Disconnect battery ground cable.
2. Remove headlight and accessory switch trim bezel.
3. Remove four switch plate to lower panel attaching screws.

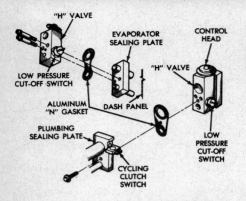

Fig. 13  H-valve assembly

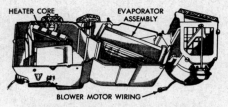

**Fig. 14  Evaporator heater assembly**

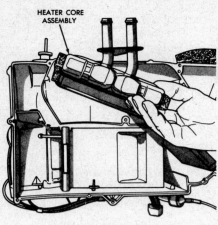

**Fig. 15  Heater core replacement**

4. Pull switch assembly rearward, then disconnect switch electrical connectors.
5. Remove switch lamp assembly attaching screw.
6. Remove two switch to switch plate assembly attaching screws, then the switch.
7. Reverse procedure to install.

## WIPER MOTOR
### REPLACE
### FRONT

1. Disconnect battery ground cable.
2. Remove wiper arms and blades, then disconnect fluid hoses from wiper arms.
3. Open hood assembly, then remove cowl top plenum grille and disconnect fluid hose from connector.
4. Remove cowl plenum chamber plastic screen, then the wiper pivot screws.
5. Disconnect pivots from cowl top mounting positions, then push pivots down into plenum chamber.
6. Disconnect wiper motor electrical connector, then remove three wiper motor attaching nuts.
7. Remove wiper motor assembly and linkage.
8. Remove cranks and linkage by clamping crank in vise and removing nut from end of motor shaft, then remove cranks and linkage from motor.
9. Reverse procedure to install.

### REAR

1. Disconnect battery ground cable.
2. Remove wiper arm assembly from output shaft using puller tool No. C-3982 or equivalent.
3. Open liftgate and remove liftgate trim panel.
4. Remove 4 wiper motor attaching screws, then disconnect wiper motor electrical connector.
5. Remove motor assembly from lift gate.
6. Reverse procedure to install.

## RADIO
### REPLACE

1. Disconnect battery ground cable.
2. Remove three attaching screws from top of bezel, then remove ashtray.
3. Remove two attaching screws at lower edge of bezel, then pull bezel rearward to release clip at left side of bezel.
4. Remove two radio to instrument panel attaching screws, then pull radio through front face of panel.
5. Disconnect radio electrical connector, antenna lead and ground strap.
6. Reverse procedure to install.

## HEATER CORE & BLOWER MOTOR
### REPLACE
### 1984–85

1. Disconnect battery ground cable, drain cooling system and discharge refrigerant from A/C system if equipped.
2. Disconnect heater hoses at heater core. Plug heater core tube openings to prevent coolant leakage.
3. Disconnect vacuum lines at brake booster and water valve, if equipped.
4. On models with A/C, remove expansion valve (H-valve) as follows:
   a. Disconnect low pressure cut-off switch electrical connector located on side of H-valve.
   b. Remove hex head bolt from center of plumbing sealing plate.
   c. Pull refrigerant line assembly towards front of vehicle.
   d. Remove two Allen head cap screws, then carefully remove the disassembled valve, **Fig. 13.**
5. Remove condensate drain tube, then the evaporator heater assembly to dash attaching nuts.
6. Remove resistor block electrical connector, push out grommet, then feed wire through grommet hole into passenger compartment.
7. Remove steering wheel. Refer to "Steering Wheel, Replace" procedure.
8. Remove lower instrument panel as follows:
   a. Remove left lower instrument panel cover, then the side cowl and sill molding.
   b. Loosen side cowl attaching bolts, then place selector lever in Neutral position and disconnect shift indicator cable if equipped with automatic transaxle.
   c. Remove instrument panel lower reinforcement, then the five steering column to support bracket attaching nuts. Lower steering column onto seat.
   d. Remove right instrument panel trim molding, then nine lower panel to upper panel and mid-reinforcement attaching screws.
   e. Drop lower panel down approximately six inches, then disconnect park brake release cable.
   f. Disconnect heater control cable, then the A/C control cable if equipped.
   g. Disconnect antenna and electrical connector from radio, then the electrical connections at cluster, bulkhead disconnect, side cowl, heater or A/C unit, blower motor and steering column.
   h. Disconnect fresh air duct, then remove garnish molding and weatherstrip.
   i. Remove lower instrument panel from vehicle.
9. Remove evaporator heater unit hanger strap, then pull assembly rearward and out of vehicle, **Fig. 14.**
10. Place evaporator heater assembly on workbench, then remove vacuum harness attaching screw. Feed harness through hole in cover.
11. Remove thirteen cover attaching screws, then the cover. Temperature control door will come out with cover.
12. Remove heater core tube retaining bracket attaching screw, then the heater core, **Fig. 15.**
13. Remove 5 sound helmet attaching screws, then the blower wheel by removing retainer clamp from blower wheel hub and sliding blower wheel from blower motor shaft.

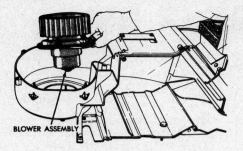

**Fig. 16 Blower motor replacement. (Typical)**

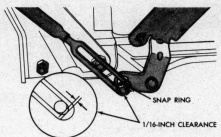

**Fig. 17 Throttle control cable adjustment. Exc. V6-181 engine**

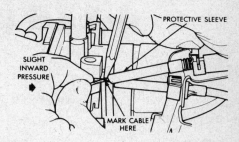

**Fig. 18 Throttle control cable adjustment. V6-181 engine.**

14. Remove blower motor attaching screws, then the blower motor, **Fig. 16.**
15. Reverse procedure to install.

## 1986–89

1. Disconnect battery ground cable and discharge A/C system, if equipped.
2. Remove 7 steering column cover to lower instrument panel attaching screws and the steering column cover.
3. Remove 3 steering column lower reinforcement attaching screws and the reinforcement.
4. Remove right side cowl and sill trim.
5. Remove bolt attaching right side instrument panel to right cowl.
6. Loosen 2 brackets supporting lower edge of instrument panel to A/C and heater or heater housing.
7. Remove instrument panel trim molding covering mid-reinforcement.
8. Disconnect vacuum lines at brake booster and, on A/C equipped vehicles, the water valve.
9. Drain cooling system, then disconnect heater hoses at heater core. Plug heater core tubes to prevent spilling coolant.
10. On models with A/C, remove expansion valve (H-valve) as follows:
    a. Disconnect low pressure cut-off switch electrical connector located on side of H-valve.
    b. Remove hex head bolt from center of plumbing sealing plate.
    c. Pull refrigerant line assembly toward front of vehicle.
    d. Remove 2 torx head cap screws, then carefully remove the disassembled valve, **Fig. 13.**
11. Remove 4 nuts from evaporator heater assembly mounting studs.
12. Pull right side of lower instrument panel rearward until it reaches passenger seat, disconnecting blower motor and resistor electrical connectors and the temperature control cable.
13. Disconnect hanger strap from evaporator heater assembly and bend rearward.
14. Pull evaporator heater assembly rearward from dash panel and remove from vehicle.

15. Perform steps 10 through 15 for 1984–85 vehicles.

## STOP LIGHT SWITCH
### REPLACE

1. Disconnect battery ground cable.
2. Disconnect stop light switch electrical connector, then remove switch assembly.
3. Install new switch and connect switch electrical connector. If adjustment of switch is required, proceed as follows:
   a. Push switch forward until fully seated. This will move brake pedal slightly forward.
   b. Pull back on brake pedal until it will go back no further. This will cause the switch to ratchet backward into correct position.

## NEUTRAL START & BACK-UP LIGHT SWITCH
### REPLACE

The following procedure applies to automatic transaxle equipped models only. On manual transaxle equipped models, a back-up switch is mounted on the transaxle case.
1. Disconnect battery ground cable.
2. Disconnect switch electrical connector.
3. Remove switch from transaxle case and allow fluid to drain into suitable container.
4. Install switch with new seal into trans case and connect switch electrical connector. Torque switch to 24 ft. lbs.

## SPEED CONTROL
### ADJUST
#### LOCK-IN SCREW ADJUSTMENT
##### 1984–85

Lock-in accuracy can be affected by poor engine performance, overloaded vehicle, or improper slack in throttle control cable.
1. If the above note has been taken into consideration and vehicle speed still varies or drops more than 2-3 mph

when speed control is activated, proceed as follows:
   a. Turn lock-in adjusting screw counterclockwise approximately 1/4 turn for every 1 mph out of adjustment.
2. If vehicle speed increases more than 2-3 mph when speed control is activated, proceed as follows:
   a. Turn lock-in adjusting screw clockwise approximately 1/4 turn for every 1 mph out of adjustment. **The above adjustments should not exceed two turns in either direction, or damage to unit may occur.**

## THROTTLE CONTROL CABLE ADJUSTMENT
### Exc. V6-181 Engine

1. Start engine and allow to reach normal operating temperature.
2. Remove snap ring, then check clearance between throttle stud and cable clevis, **Fig. 17.**
3. If adjustment is required, proceed as follows:
   a. Loosen cable clamp attaching nut.
   b. Pull all slack out of cable, using head of throttle stud as a gauge. **Do not pull cable so tight that it moves the throttle away from curb idle position.**
   c. Torque cable clamp attaching nut to 45 inch lbs. and move cable clevis back on round portion of stud.
4. Install snap ring and check for proper operation

### V6-181 Engine

1. Secure cable core wire, then lightly push toward servo.
2. While pushing toward servo, mark core wire next to protective sleeve as shown in **Fig. 18.**
3. Pull core wire away from servo. There should be a .24 inch (6 mm) gap between mark on core wire and the protective sleeve.
4. If gap is not as specified, remove adjustment clip and push protective sleeve into housing to decrease gap or pull sleeve out of housing to increase gap.
5. Install adjustment clip and check gap clearance.

# 4-135 (2.2L) & 4-153 (2.5L) ENGINES

## INDEX

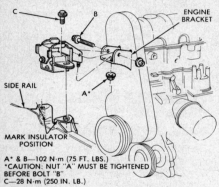

**Fig. 1  Right side engine mount**

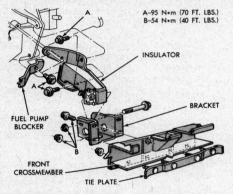

**Fig. 2  Front engine mount**

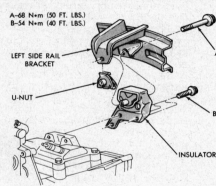

**Fig. 3  Left side engine mount**

## ENGINE MOUNTS
### REPLACE

When positioning the engine, check driveshaft length as outlined in "Front Suspension & Steering" under "Driveshaft Length, Adjust." The engine mounts incorporate slotted bolt holes and permit side-to-side positioning of the engine, thereby affecting the length of the driveshaft. Failure to properly position the engine may result in extensive damage to the engine.

Refer to **Figs. 1 through 3** when replacing engine mounts.

## ENGINE
### REPLACE

1. Disconnect battery ground cable.
2. Scribe hood hinge locations and remove hood.
3. Drain cooling system, then disconnect coolant hoses from radiator and engine.

4. Remove radiator and fan assembly, then the air cleaner and hoses.
5. On models equipped with A/C, unfasten A/C compressor and position aside, leaving refrigerant hoses attached.
6. On models equipped with power steering, unfasten power steering pump and position aside.
7. On all models, drain oil pan and remove oil filter.
8. Disconnect electrical connectors from alternator, carburetor and engine, **Fig. 4.**
9. Disconnect fuel line, heater hose and accelerator cable, **Fig. 5.**
10. On models equipped with manual transaxle, proceed as follows:
  a. Disconnect clutch cable.
  b. Remove transaxle case lower cover.
  c. Disconnect exhaust pipe from exhaust manifold.
  d. Unfasten starter motor and position aside.
11. On models equipped with automatic transaxle, proceed as follows:

  a. Disconnect exhaust pipe from exhaust manifold.
  b. Unfasten starter motor and position aside.
  c. Remove transaxle case lower cover, then mark flex plate to torque converter for assembly reference.
  d. Remove torque converter-to-flex plate attaching bolts.
  e. Position a C-clamp on front bottom of torque converter housing to prevent torque converter from falling out.
12. On all models, install a suitable transaxle holding fixture and attach a suitable lifting device.
13. Remove right side inner splash shield, then disconnect ground strap.
14. Remove long bolt through yoke bracket and insulator. **If yoke screws are to be removed, mark position on side rail for assembly reference.**
15. Remove transaxle case-to-cylinder block attaching bolts.
16. Remove front engine mount screw and nut.
17. On models equipped with manual

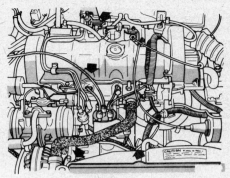

**Fig. 4  Electrical connector locations**

**Fig. 5  Fuel line, heater hose & accelerator cable connector locations**

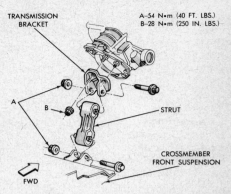

A–54 N•m (40 FT. LBS.)
B–28 N•m (250 IN. LBS.)

TRANSMISSION BRACKET
STRUT
CROSSMEMBER FRONT SUSPENSION
FWD

**Fig. 6  Engine anti-roll strut**

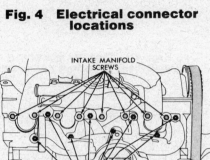

INTAKE MANIFOLD SCREWS

EXHAUST MANIFOLD NUTS

**Fig. 7  Intake & exhaust manifold replacement**

transaxle, proceed as follows:
a. Remove anti-roll strut, **Fig. 6.**
b. Remove insulator through bolt from inside wheel housing or the insulator bracket-to-transaxle attaching bolts.
18. Reverse procedure to install.

## INTAKE & EXHAUST MANIFOLD REPLACE

1. Disconnect battery ground cable.
2. Drain cooling system, then disconnect all vacuum lines, electrical connectors and fuel lines from carburetor.
3. Remove throttle linkage, then the power steering pump drive belt, if equipped.
4. Disconnect power brake vacuum hose, if equipped, from intake manifold.
5. Remove coolant hoses from water crossover.
6. Raise and support vehicle.
7. Remove exhaust pipe from exhaust manifold.
8. On models equipped with power steering, unfasten power steering pump and position aside.

9. On all models, remove intake manifold support bracket, then the EGR tube.
10. Remove intake manifold attaching bolts, then lower vehicle.
11. Remove intake and exhaust manifold assembly from engine, **Fig. 7.**
12. Remove exhaust manifold retaining nuts and separate exhaust manifold from intake manifold.
13. Reverse procedure to install, noting the following:
   a. Discard gaskets and clean gasket surfaces on both manifolds and cylinder head.
   b. Use a straightedge to ensure gasket surfaces on manifolds are flat within .006 inch per foot of manifold length.
   c. Install new gaskets with suitable sealant on manifold side.
   d. Torque exhaust manifold retaining nuts and intake manifold attaching bolts to 200 inch lbs., starting at center and working outward in both directions.

## TIMING SPROCKETS & OIL SEALS

### ALTERNATOR BELT REMOVAL

1. Disconnect battery ground cable.
2. Loosen alternator locking screw, then loosen adjusting screw and remove the alternator belt.
3. Reverse procedure to install.

### ALTERNATOR & COMPRESSOR MOUNTING BRACKET REMOVAL

For replacement of alternator and compressor mounting bracket, refer to **Figs. 8** and **9.**

### POWER STEERING PUMP MOUNTING BRACKET REMOVAL

1. Remove pump locking screw, **Fig. 10.**
2. Remove pivot bolt and pivot nut, then the drive belt.

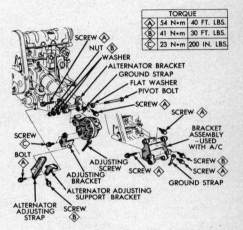

| TORQUE | | |
|---|---|---|
| Ⓐ | 54 N•m | 40 FT. LBS. |
| Ⓑ | 41 N•m | 30 FT. LBS. |
| Ⓒ | 23 N•m | 200 IN. LBS. |

SCREW Ⓐ
NUT Ⓑ
WASHER
ALTERNATOR BRACKET
GROUND STRAP
FLAT WASHER
PIVOT BOLT
SCREW Ⓐ
SCREW Ⓐ
BRACKET ASSEMBLY —USED WITH A/C
SCREW Ⓐ
BOLT Ⓐ
ADJUSTING SCREW
ADJUSTING BRACKET
ALTERNATOR ADJUSTING SUPPORT BRACKET
SCREW Ⓐ
SCREW Ⓑ
SCREW Ⓑ
GROUND STRAP
ALTERNATOR ADJUSTING STRAP
SCREW Ⓑ

**Fig. 8  Alternator & A/C compressor mounting bracket removal. 1984**

3. Remove power steering pump and lay aside.
4. Remove mounting bracket bolts, then the bracket.
5. Reverse procedure to install.

## CRANKSHAFT PULLEY & WATER PUMP PULLEY REMOVAL

1. Remove screws retaining water pump pulley to pump shaft, **Fig. 11.**
2. Remove bolts retaining crankshaft pulley.
3. Raise and support front of vehicle, then remove right inner splash shield and remove crankshaft pulley.
4. Reverse procedure to install.

## TIMING BELT COVER REMOVAL

1. Remove nuts securing timing belt cover to the cylinder head, **Fig. 12.**
2. Remove screws securing the cover to the cylinder head, then remove both halves of the timing belt cover.

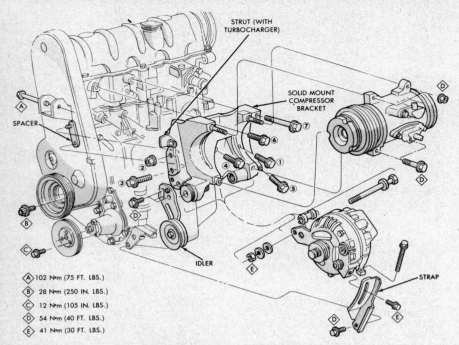

| TORQUES | | |
|---|---|---|
| Ⓐ | 54 N·m | 40 FT. LBS. |
| Ⓑ | 41 N·m | 30 FT. LBS. |

Ⓐ 102 N·m (75 FT. LBS.)
Ⓑ 28 N·m (250 IN. LBS.)
Ⓒ 12 N·m (105 IN. LBS.)
Ⓓ 54 N·m (40 FT. LBS.)
Ⓔ 41 N·m (30 FT. LBS.)

**Fig. 9  Alternator & A/C compressor mounting bracket removal. 1985—89**

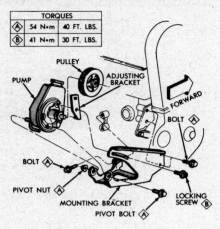

**Fig. 10  Power steering mounting bracket removal**

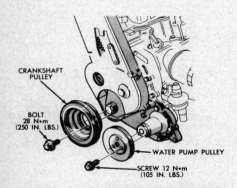

**Fig. 11  Crankshaft & water pump pulley removal**

3. Position a suitable jack under engine, then remove right hand engine mount bolt and raise engine slightly.
4. Loosen timing belt tensioner, then remove timing belt.
5. Reverse procedure to install.

## CRANKSHAFT SPROCKET REMOVAL

1. With the timing belt removed from engine, remove the crankshaft sprocket bolt.
2. Remove crankshaft sprocket using a suitable puller.

## CRANKSHAFT, INTERMEDIATE SHAFT & CAMSHAFT OIL SEAL SERVICE

Refer to **Figs. 13** and **14**, for removal and installation of crankshaft, intermediate shaft or camshaft seals.

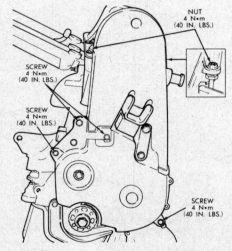

**Fig. 12  Timing belt cover removal**

## CRANKSHAFT & INTERMEDIATE SHAFT TIMING

1. Rotate crankshaft and intermediate shaft until markings on sprockets are aligned, **Fig. 15.**

## CAMSHAFT TIMING

1. Rotate camshaft until arrows on hub are aligned with No. 1 camshaft cap to cylinder head line. Small hole must be located along vertical center line.
2. Install timing belt. Refer to "Adjusting Drive Belt Tension" described else-

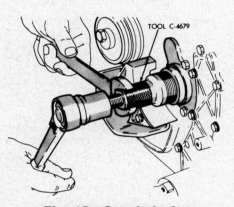

**Fig. 13  Crankshaft, intermediate shaft & camshaft oil seal removal**

where, for proper drive belt adjustment.
3. Rotate crankshaft two full revolutions and recheck timing. **Do not allow oil or solvents to contact the timing belt, since they will deteriorate the rubber and cause tooth slippage.**

## CAMSHAFT & INTERMEDIATE SHAFT SPROCKET REMOVAL & INSTALLATION

Refer to **Fig. 16**, for removal and installation of camshaft and intermediate shaft sprocket. Torque camshaft sprocket to 65 ft. lbs.

## ADJUSTING DRIVE BELT TENSION

1. Remove spark plugs, then rotate crankshaft to TDC position.
2. Using a suitable tool, loosen tensioner locknut, **Fig. 17.**
3. Reset tension so that belt tensioning tool's axis is within 15° of horizontal.
4. Rotate crankshaft two revolutions in a clockwise direction and position at TDC, then tighten tensioner locknut.

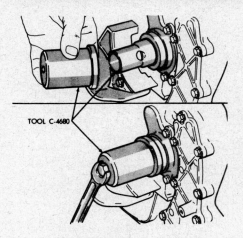

**Fig. 14  Crankshaft, intermediate shaft & camshaft oil seal installation**

**Fig. 15  Aligning crankshaft & intermediate shaft timing marks**

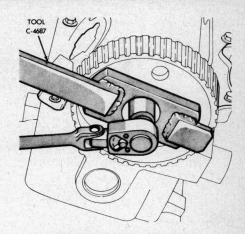

**Fig. 16  Camshaft & intermediate shaft sprocket replacement**

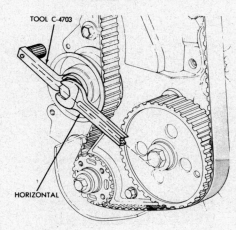

**Fig. 17  Adjusting drive belt tension**

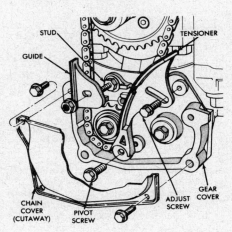

**Fig. 18  Removing chain cover, guide & tensioner**

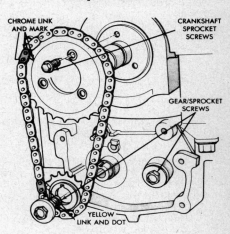

**Fig. 19  Removing drive chain & sprockets**

# BALANCE SHAFTS

The 4-153 engine is equipped with two balance shafts installed in a carrier attached to the lower crankcase.

The shafts are interconnected through gears to rotate in opposite directions. These gears are driven by a short chain from the crankshaft, to rotate at two times crankshaft speed. This counterbalances certain engine reciprocating masses.

## SHAFT, REPLACE

1. Remove oil pan, oil pickup, timing belt cover, belt, crankshaft belt sprocket and front crankshaft oil seal retainer.
2. Remove chain cover, guide and tensioner, **Fig. 18**.
3. Remove balance shaft gear and chain sprocket retaining screws and the crankshaft chain sprocket torx screws, then the chain and sprocket assembly, **Fig. 19**.
4. Remove double ended gear cover retaining stud, then the cover and balance shaft gears.

5. Remove carrier rear cover and the balance shafts.
6. Remove six carrier to crankshaft attaching bolts to separate carrier.
7. Reverse procedure to install, then adjust crankshaft to balance shaft timing.

## CARRIER ASSEMBLY, REPLACE

The gear cover, gears, balance shafts and rear cover will remain intact during carrier removal.

1. Remove chain cover and driven balance shaft chain sprocket screw.
2. Loosen tensioner pivot and adjusting screws, then move driven balance shaft inboard (through) driven chain sprocket. Sprocket will hang in lower chain loop.
3. Remove carrier to crankshaft attaching bolts and the carrier.
4. Reverse procedure to install, then adjust crankshaft to balance shaft timing.

# TIMING, ADJUST

1. With balance shafts installed in carrier, position carrier on crankshaft and install six attaching bolts, torquing to 40 ft. lbs.
2. Rotate balance shafts until both shaft keyways are parallel to vertical center line of engine, then install short hub drive gear on sprocket driven shaft. After installation, gear and balance shaft keyways must face up with gear timing marks meshed as shown, **Fig. 20**.
3. Install gear cover and torque double ended stud/washer fastener to 105 inch lbs.
4. Install crankshaft sprocket and torque socket head torx screws to 130 inch lbs.
5. Rotate crankshaft until number one cylinder is at top dead center (TDC). The timing marks on the chain sprocket should line up with the parting line on the left side of number one main bearing cap, **Fig. 21**.
6. Place chain over crankshaft sprocket

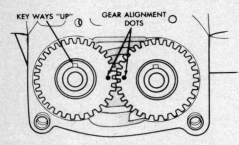

**Fig. 20   Setting gear timing**

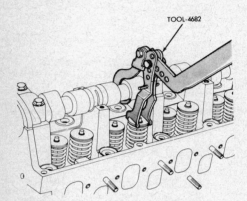

**Fig. 23   Valve spring removal & installation**

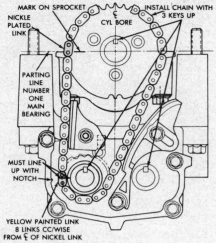

**Fig. 21   Setting balance shaft timing**

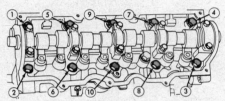

**Fig. 24   Cylinder head bolt removal sequence**

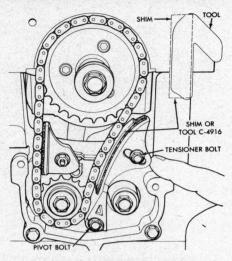

**Fig. 22   Adjusting chain tensioner**

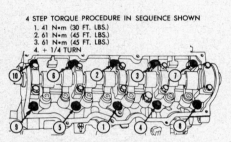

**Fig. 25   Cylinder head bolt tightening sequence**

so that nickel plated link of chain is over the timing mark on the crankshaft sprocket, **Fig. 21.**

7. Place balance shaft sprocket into timing chain so that timing mark on the sprocket (yellow dot) mates with yellow painted link on chain.

8. With balance shaft keyways at 12 o'clock, slide balance shaft sprocket onto nose of balance shaft. Balance shaft may have to be pushed in slightly to allow for clearance. **Balance shaft timing is correct if the timing mark on sprocket, the painted link and the arrow on the side of the gear cover are aligned.**

9. If sprockets are timed correctly, install balance shaft bolts, torquing to 250 inch lbs. A wood block placed between crankcase and crankshaft counterbalance will prevent gear rotation.

## TENSIONING CHAIN

1. Install chain tensioner loosely assembled.

2. Place a .039 inch thick by 2.75 inch long shim between tensioner and chain, push tensioner and shim up against chain and apply firm pressure directly behind the adjustment slot to take up all slack. Chain must have shoe radius contact as shown, **Fig. 22.**

3. With load applied, tighten top tensioner bolt first, then bottom pivot bolt, torquing both to 105 inch lbs., then remove shim.

4. Position guide on double ended stud, ensuring tab on guide fits into slot on gear cover, then install nut/washer assembly, torquing to 105 inch lbs.

5. Install carrier covers, torquing screws to 105 inch lbs.

## CYLINDER HEAD & VALVE ASSEMBLY

Some engines may be equipped with cylinder heads which have oversize journals. When servicing the cylinder head on these engines, proper replacement components must be installed. To identify oversize cylinder head journals, the top of the bearing caps are painted green and "O/S J" is stamped on air pump end of head.

## REMOVING & INSTALLING VALVE SPRINGS

### Cylinder Head On Engine

1. Rotate crankshaft until piston is at -DC on compression stroke.

2. Apply 90-120 psi of compressed air into spark plug hole of valve spring being removed.

3. Using valve compressor tool No. 4682 or equivalent, compress valve spring enough to remove valve stem locks, **Fig. 23.**

4. Remove valve spring and spring seat.

5. Remove valve seal.

## CYLINDER HEAD BOLT REMOVAL SEQUENCE

When removing cylinder head, remove cylinder head bolts in proper sequence, **Fig. 24.**

## CYLINDER HEAD BOLT TIGHTENING SEQUENCE

Refer to **Fig. 25** for cylinder head bolt tightening sequence. Torquing sequence for 1986 models is as shown, **Fig. 25**, but bolts should be torqued to 45 ft. lbs., then 65 ft. lbs., then 65 ft. lbs. again, then an additional 1/4 turn. Head bolt diameter on 1986-89 models has been increased to 11 mm. These bolts are identified by "11" stamped on the head of the bolt. Bolts used in previous years will thread into the holes but will strip the cylinder block bolt holes.

## CAMSHAFT BEARING CAPS

Some engines may be equipped with camshafts which have oversize journals. When servicing the camshaft on these engines, proper replacement components must be installed. To identify oversize camshaft journals, the barrel of the cam is painted green and "O/S J" is stamped on the air pump end of the camshaft. Never install an oversize journal camshaft in a

**Fig. 26  Camshaft bearing cap installation**

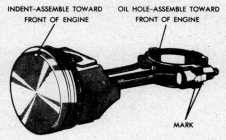

INDENT-ASSEMBLE TOWARD FRONT OF ENGINE

OIL HOLE-ASSEMBLE TOWARD FRONT OF ENGINE

MARK

**Fig. 27   Piston & connecting rod assembly**

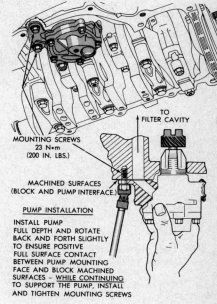

TO FILTER CAVITY

MOUNTING SCREWS 23 N•m (200 IN. LBS.)

MACHINED SURFACES (BLOCK AND PUMP INTERFACE.)

PUMP INSTALLATION

INSTALL PUMP FULL DEPTH AND ROTATE BACK AND FORTH SLIGHTLY TO ENSURE POSITIVE FULL SURFACE CONTACT BETWEEN PUMP MOUNTING FACE AND BLOCK MACHINED SURFACES – WHILE CONTINUING TO SUPPORT THE PUMP, INSTALL AND TIGHTEN MOUNTING SCREWS

**Fig. 28   Oil pump assembly**

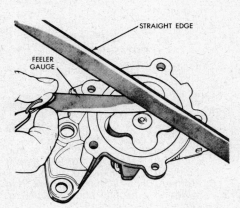

STRAIGHT EDGE

FEELER GAUGE

**Fig. 29   Checking oil pump endplay**

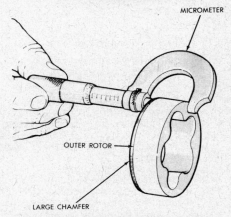

MICROMETER

OUTER ROTOR

LARGE CHAMFER

**Fig. 30   Measuring oil pump outer rotor thickness**

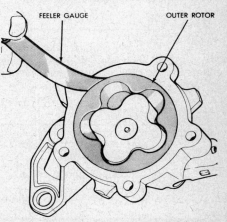

FEELER GAUGE

OUTER ROTOR

**Fig. 31   Measuring clearance between oil pump rotors**

cylinder head with standard size bores, or cam cap breakage could result.

1. With caps removed from engine, check oil holes for obstructions.
2. With caps aligned in proper sequence, make sure arrow on caps 1, 2, 3 and 4 point toward timing belt, **Fig. 26.**
3. Apply suitable sealant to No. 1 and 5 bearing caps.
4. Install caps before installing camshaft seals, then torque cap bolts to 165 inch lbs.

## PISTON & ROD ASSEMBLY

When installing the piston and rod assembly, the indentation on the top of piston must face the timing belt side of the engine, **Fig. 27.** The oil hole on connecting rod must also face the timing belt side of the engine and be on the same side as the indented mark on the piston.

## ENGINE LUBRICATION SYSTEM

### OIL PUMP ASSEMBLY

1. With oil pan removed, remove the screw securing oil pump to the cylinder block, **Fig. 28.**
2. Reverse procedure to install. Torque oil pump attaching screw to 200 inch lbs. Torque oil pan attaching screws to 200 inch lbs.

## OIL PUMP SERVICE

1. Measure the following oil pump clearances:
   a. Endplay, **Fig. 29.** Endplay should be .001-.004 inch on 1984-85 models, or .001-.003 inch on 1986-89 models.
   b. Outer rotor thickness, **Fig. 30.** Thickness should be .825 inch, minimum, on 1984-85 models, or .944 inch, minimum, on 1986-89 models. Install outer rotor with chamfered edge in pump body.
   c. Clearance between rotors, **Fig. 31,** should be .010 inch, maximum, on 1984-85 models, or .008 inch, maximum, on 1986-89 models.
   d. Outer rotor clearance, **Fig. 32.** Clearance should be .014 inch, maximum.
   e. Oil pump cover clearance, **Fig. 33,** should be no greater than .003 inch on 1984-86 models and .0015 inch on 1987-89 models.
   f. Oil pressure relief valve spring length should be 1.95 inches.

## WATER PUMP REPLACE

1. Disconnect battery ground cable.
2. Drain cooling system, then remove upper radiator hose.

3. Remove A/C compressor from mounting brackets and position aside with refrigerant lines attached, if equipped.
4. Remove alternator.
5. Disconnect lower radiator hose, bypass hose and four water pump to engine attaching screws, **Fig. 34,** then remove water pump from engine.
6. Reverse procedure to install.

## BELT TENSION DATA

On 1984 models, new drive belt tension should measure 95 lbs. for the A/C compressor and power steering pump and 115 lbs. for the alternator. Tension for all used belts should measure 80 lbs.

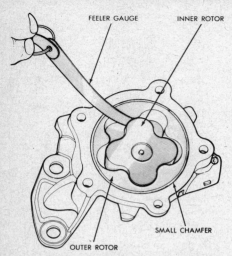

**Fig. 32  Measuring oil pump outer rotor clearance**

On 1985-89 models, new drive belt tension should measure 105 lbs. for the A/C compressor and 115 lbs. for the alternator and power steering pump. Tension for all used belts should measure 80 lbs.

## VALVES
### ADJUST

These engines use auto lash adjusters, therefore, no provisions for adjustment is provided.

## FUEL PUMP
### REPLACE
#### EXC. 4-153 ENGINE

1. Disconnect battery ground cable.
2. Remove oil filter.
3. Disconnect fuel lines from fuel pump.

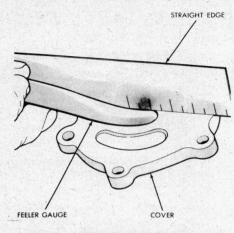

**Fig. 33  Measuring oil pump cover clearance**

4. Remove fuel pump blocker strut from front engine mount to blocker assembly.
5. Remove fuel pump attaching bolts, then fuel pump.
6. Remove and discard gasket.
7. Reverse procedure to install. Torque fuel pump attaching bolts to 250 inch lbs. and fuel lines to 175 inch lbs.

## 4-153 Engine

1. Release fuel system pressure as follows:
   a. Loosen gas cap to release any fuel tank pressure.
   b. Disconnect electrical connector from any injector.
   c. Ground one injector terminal using a jumper wire.
   d. Connect one end of jumper wire to one injector terminal and touch the other end to the battery positive

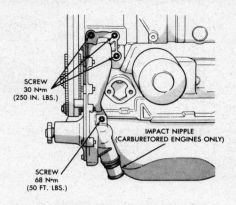

**Fig. 34  Water pump replacement**

terminal for no longer than 10 seconds.
   e. Remove jumper wires.
2. Raise and support vehicle, then drain fuel from fuel tank.
3. Remove bolts securing filler tube to inner and outer quarter panel.
4. Disconnect electrical connectors and lines from tank, then position a suitable jack under fuel tank.
5. Remove bolts securing fuel tank, then lower tank slightly and carefully remove filler tube from tank.
6. Lower tank, then disconnect vapor separator rollover valve hose and remove fuel tank and insulator pad from vehicle.
7. Using a hammer and a suitable non-metallic punch, tap lock ring counterclockwise to release pump.
8. Pull fuel pump assembly partially out of tank until return line hose connection is visible, then disconnect return line.
9. Remove fuel pump assembly from tank with 0-ring. Discard o-ring.
10. Reverse procedure to install.

# 4-156 (2.6L) ENGINE

## INDEX



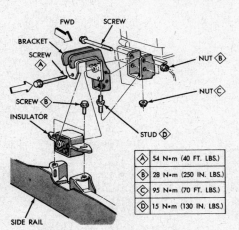

FWD
SCREW
BRACKET
SCREW Ⓐ
NUT Ⓑ
NUT Ⓒ
SCREW Ⓑ
INSULATOR
STUD Ⓓ
SIDE RAIL
Ⓐ 54 N•m (40 FT. LBS.)
Ⓑ 28 N•m (250 IN. LBS.)
Ⓒ 95 N•m (70 FT. LBS.)
Ⓓ 15 N•m (130 IN. LBS.)


**Fig. 1 Right side engine mount. 1984**

A
RIGHT YOKE BRACKET & INSULATOR
B
★C
SIDE RAIL
A-28 N·m (250 IN. LBS.)
B-C★ 102 N·m (75 IN. LBS.)
★CAUTION: NUT "C" MUST BE TIGHTENED BEFORE BOLT "B"


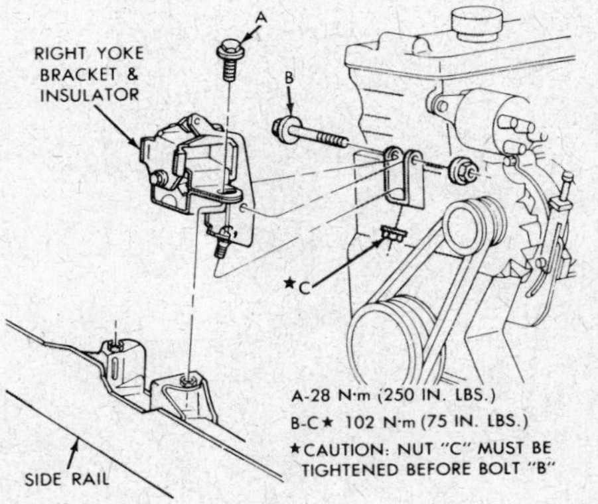

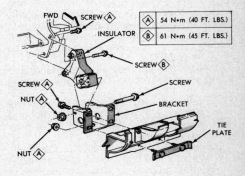

**Fig. 2 Right side engine mount. 1985–87**

FWD
SCREW Ⓐ
INSULATOR
Ⓐ 54 N•m (40 FT. LBS.)
Ⓑ 61 N•m (45 FT. LBS.)
SCREW Ⓑ
SCREW Ⓐ
SCREW
NUT Ⓐ
BRACKET
TIE PLATE
NUT Ⓐ


**Fig. 3 Front engine mount**

## ENGINE MOUNTS REPLACE

When positioning the engine, check driveshaft length as outlined in "Front Suspension & Steering" under "Driveshaft Length, Adjust." The engine mounts incorporate slotted bolt holes and permit side-to-side positioning of the engine, thereby affecting the length of the driveshaft. Failure to properly position the engine may result in extensive damage to the engine.

Refer to **Figs. 1 through 4** when replacing engine mounts.

## ENGINE REPLACE

1. Disconnect battery ground cable.
2. Scribe alignment marks on hood and hood hinge, then remove hood.
3. Drain cooling system, then disconnect radiator hoses at radiator and engine.
4. Remove radiator and fan shroud, then remove air cleaner.
5. On models equipped with A/C, remove A/C compressor from mounting bracket and position aside with hoses attached.
6. On models equipped with power steering, remove power steering pump from mounting bracket and position aside with hoses attached.
7. On all models, drain crankcase and remove oil filter.
8. Disconnect electrical connectors at alternator, carburetor and engine.
9. Disconnect fuel line, heater hose and accelerator cable.
10. Remove alternator from mounting bracket and position aside.
11. Disconnect exhaust pipe from exhaust manifold, then remove starter motor.
12. Remove transaxle case lower cover and place alignment marks on flex plate and torque converter, then remove converter to flex plate attaching screws. Attach a C-clamp to front lower portion of converter housing to retain torque converter in housing when engine is being removed.
13. Install a suitable transmission holding fixture and attach a suitable engine lifting device.
14. Remove right hand inner splash shield, then disconnect ground strap.
15. Remove right hand engine mount to insulator through bolt. Mark insulator position on side rail to assure correct positioning during installation.
16. Remove transmission case to engine block attaching bolts.
17. Remove front engine mount to bracket attaching bolt, then carefully lift engine from vehicle.
18. Reverse procedure to install.

## TIMING GEARS & OIL SEALS

A rattle from the camshaft and silent shaft chain area at the front of the engine accompanied by a broken camshaft timing chain guide may be caused by a blocked oil feed hole to the timing chain tensioner in the oil pump housing. This blockage occurs when a portion of the oil pump mount-

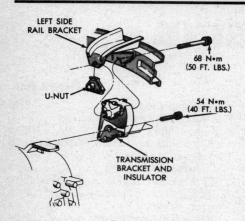

**Fig. 4   Left side engine mount**

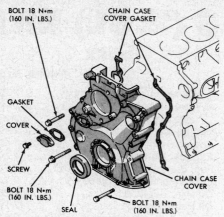

**Fig. 5   Chain case cover removal**

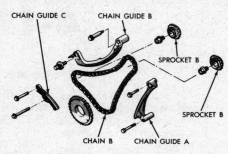

**Fig. 6   Silent shaft drive chain, replace**

ing gasket collapses into the channel in the pump cover which directs oil from the main gallery in the block to the chain tensioner feed hole. The lock washer between silent shaft chain guide B pivot bolt and timing chain guide may also be missing. This problem may be corrected as follows:

1. Remove chain case cover, silent shaft chain, camshaft chain and broken chain guide.
2. Remove engine oil pump, then clean all gasket material from pump and engine block.
3. Install new gasket (part No. MD060521), then the oil pump and new timing chain guide. Ensure gasket has hole cut in it.
4. Install timing chain, silent shaft chain, guides and chain case cover. Ensure chain guide B pivot bolt lock washer is in place before installing cover.

## TIMING CHAIN CASE COVER, REMOVAL

1. Disconnect battery ground cable.
2. Remove alternator locking screw, then loosen jam nut and adjusting screw. Remove drive belt.
3. Remove distributor attaching nut, then the distributor from cylinder head and position aside.
4. On models equipped with A/C, remove front and rear A/C compressor to bracket attaching screws, then the A/C compressor and position aside.
5. On models equipped with power steering, remove power steering pump pivot and lock screws, then the drive belt.
6. Remove power steering pump attaching screw and nut, then position power steering pump aside.
7. Remove power steering pump bracket to engine attaching screws, then the bracket.
8. On all models, raise and support vehicle, then remove right inner splash shield.
9. Drain crankcase, then remove crankshaft drive pulley.

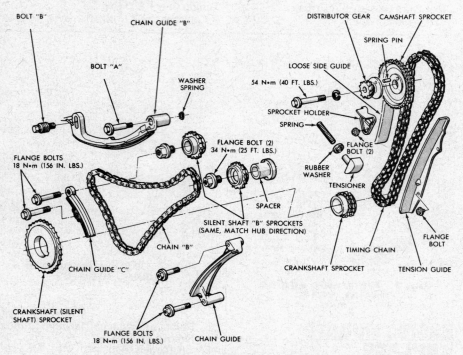

**Timing gears & chain assembly**

10. Lower vehicle and position a suitable jack under engine.
11. Remove engine mount to frame side rail through bolt, then remove engine oil dipstick.
12. Remove air cleaner assembly, then the spark plug wires.
13. Disconnect vacuum hoses from cylinder head cover.
14. Remove cylinder head cover attaching screws, then the cylinder head cover.
15. Remove two front cylinder head attaching bolts. Do not disturb any other cylinder head bolts.
16. Remove oil pan attaching bolts, then the oil pan.
17. Remove timing indicator plate from timing chain case cover.

18. Remove engine mounting plate from timing chain case cover.
19. Refer to **Fig. 5**, and remove remaining screws securing chain case cover to engine.

## SILENT SHAFT DRIVE CHAIN, REMOVAL

1. Remove timing chain case cover as previously described.
2. Remove sprocket screws, then the drive chain, crankshaft sprocket and silent shaft sprocket, **Fig. 6**.

## CAMSHAFT DRIVE CHAIN, REMOVAL

1. Remove timing chain case cover as previously described.

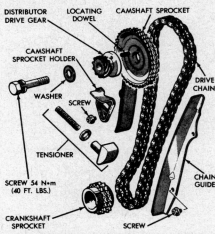

**Fig. 7   Camshaft drive chain, replace**

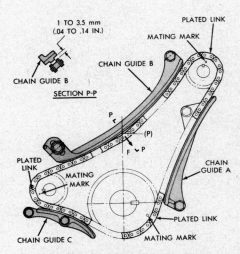

**Fig. 10   Silent shaft chain adjustment & installation w/engine removed**

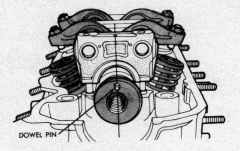

**Fig. 8   Camshaft timing mark alignment**

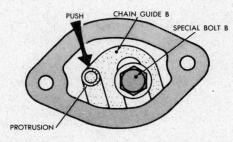

**Fig. 11   Silent shaft chain adjustment w/engine installed**

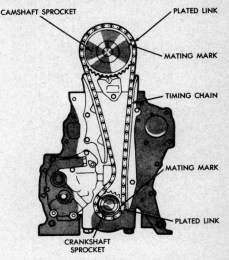

**Fig. 9   Timing chain installation**

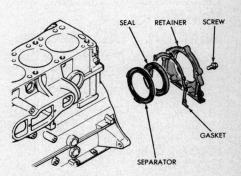

**Fig. 12   Rear oil seal, replace**

2. Remove camshaft sprocket holder, then the left and right timing chain guides, **Fig. 7.**
3. Depress tensioner to remove drive chain.
4. Remove crankshaft and camshaft sprockets.

## CAMSHAFT INSTALLATION

1. With camshaft bearing caps installed, rotate camshaft until timing marks are aligned as shown in **Fig. 8.**

## TIMING CHAIN INSTALLATION

1. Install sprocket holder, and the left and right chain guides, **Fig. 6.**
2. Rotate crankshaft until No. 1 piston is at TDC on compression stroke.
3. Install tensioner spring assembly onto oil pump body, **Fig. 7.**

4. Install timing chain on camshaft sprocket and crankshaft sprocket. Ensure timing marks are aligned, **Fig. 9.** Timing marks on sprockets are punch marks on the teeth, while timing marks on chain are plated links.
5. Align crankshaft sprocket to crankshaft keyway and slide into place. Align camshaft sprocket dowel hole to camshaft dowel hole.
6. Install dowel pin, then the distributor drive gear. Install sprocket attaching screw onto camshaft and torque to 40 ft. lbs.

## SILENT SHAFT CHAIN INSTALLATION & ADJUSTMENT

1. Install silent shaft chain drive pulley onto crankshaft.
2. Install silent shaft chain onto oil pump sprocket and silent shaft sprocket, **Fig. 10.**
3. Ensure timing marks are aligned. Timing marks on the sprockets are punch marks on the teeth, while marks on the chain are plated links.
4. Align crankshaft sprocket plated link with punch mark on sprocket.
5. Position chain on crankshaft sprocket, then install oil pump sprocket and silent shaft sprockets on their respective shafts.
6. Install oil pump and silent shaft sprocket attaching bolts. Torque attaching bolts to 25 ft. lbs.
7. Install three chain guides. Tighten

snug retaining bolts.
8. Refer to **Fig. 10** and adjust silent shaft chain tension as follows:
   a. Tighten chain guide "A" mounting screws.
   b. Tighten chain guide "C" mounting screws.
   c. Shake oil pump and silent shaft sprockets to collect slack at point "P."
   d. Adjust position of chain guide "B" so when the chain is pulled in direction of arrow "F," clearance between chain guide "B" and chain links will be .04-.14 inch. Tighten chain guide "B" mounting screws.
9. Install new gasket on chain case, coat gasket with suitable sealant, then install chain case to block and torque attaching screws to 156 inch lbs

## TENSION ADJUSTMENT W/ENGINE INSTALLED

1. Remove cover over access hole in chain case cover, **Fig. 11.**
2. Loosen bolt "B," **Fig. 11.**
3. Apply pressure by hand on boss indicated in **Fig. 11,** then torque bolt "B" to 160 inch lbs.

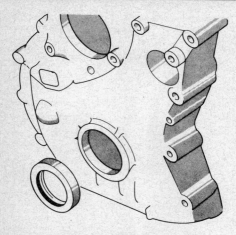

**Fig. 13   Front oil seal, replace**

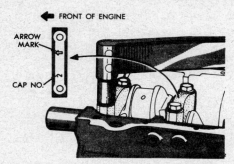

**Fig. 14   Main bearing cap installation**

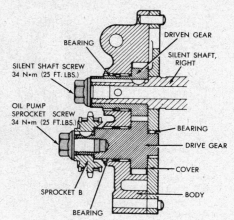

**Fig. 15   Oil pump & silent shaft, removal**

# CRANKSHAFT, BEARINGS & SILENT SHAFT

## REAR OIL SEAL, REPLACE

1. Remove screws attaching crankshaft rear oil seal retainer, then the retainer, **Fig. 12.**
2. Remove separator from retainer, then the oil seal.
3. Install new oil seal into retainer, then the separator. Ensure oil hole is positioned at separator bottom.

## FRONT OIL SEAL, REPLACE

1. Remove crankshaft pulley, then pry out oil seal, **Fig. 13.** Use caution not to nick or damage sealing surface.
2. Lightly apply suitable locking compound to outside portion of new oil seal, then install oil seal.
3. Install crankshaft drive pulley. Torque attaching bolt to 87 ft. lbs.

## MAIN BEARING CAPS

1. Install main bearing caps in sequence starting with cap nearest timing chain. Ensure arrows on caps are pointed in direction of timing chain, **Fig. 14.**

## OIL PUMP & SILENT SHAFT

1. Refer to **Fig. 15** and remove silent shaft screw, then the silent shaft.
2. Remove oil pump to cylinder block attaching screw, then the oil pump.

## LEFT SILENT SHAFT THRUST PLATE, REPLACE

1. Install two .31 inch screws into tapped holes in thrust plate, **Fig. 16.**
2. Turn both screws evenly until thrust plate loosens, then pull thrust plate from silent shaft.

## SILENT SHAFT CLEARANCES

Before installing silent shaft, measure outer diameter to outer bearing clearance.

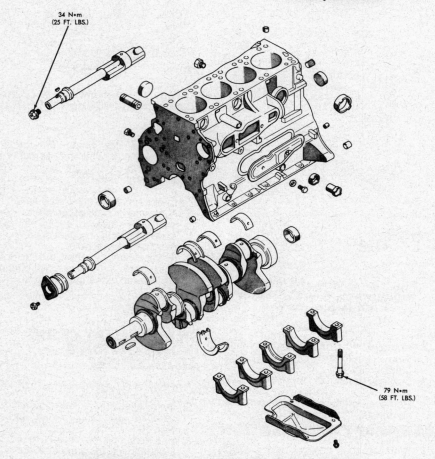

**Crankshaft, bearings & silent shaft assembly**

Clearance should be .0008-.0024 inch (.02-.06 mm). Measure inner diameter to inner bearing clearance. Clearance should be .0020 to .0035 inch (.05-.09 mm).

## PISTON & ROD ASSEMBLY

During installation of piston and rod assembly, arrow at top of piston must face toward front of engine (timing chain), **Fig. 17.** Refer to **Fig. 18** for correct piston ring installation.

1. Note the following ring groove clearances:
   a. No. 1 upper: .0024-.0039 inch (.06-.10 mm); wear limit, .004 inch (.1 mm).
   b. No. 2 intermediate: .0008-.0024 inch (.02-.06 mm); wear limit, .004 inch (.1 mm).

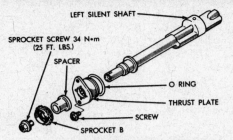

**Fig. 16  Left silent shaft thrust plate, removal**

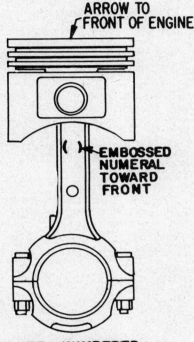

ARROW TO FRONT OF ENGINE

EMBOSSED NUMERAL TOWARD FRONT

NOTE: NUMBERED SIDE OF CAP SHOULD FACE NUMBERED SIDE OF ROD

**Fig. 17  Piston & rod assembly**

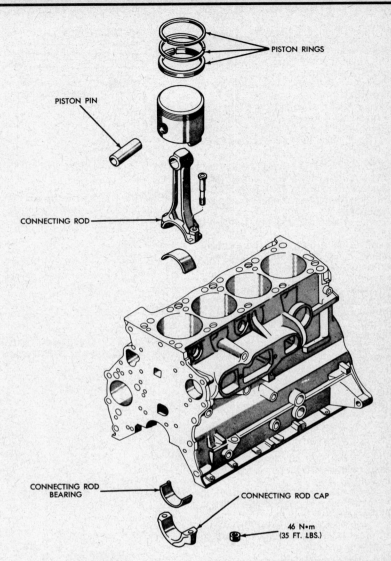

**Cylinder block, piston & connecting rod assembly**

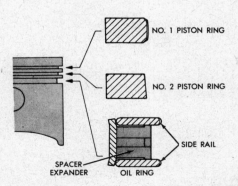

**Fig. 18  Piston ring installation**

c. Oil ring: oil ring side rails must be free to rotate after assembly.
2. Note the following end gap clearances:
 a. No. 1 upper: .010-.018 inch (.25-.45 mm); wear limit, .039 inch (.1 mm).
 b. No. 2 intermediate: .010-.018 inch (.25-.45 mm); wear limit, .039 inch (.1 mm).
 c. Oil ring side rail: .008-.035 inch (.2-.4 mm); wear limit .059 inch (1.5 mm).
3. Connecting rod side clearance should be .004-.010 inch (.1-.25 mm).

## INSTALLING PISTON RING SIDE RAIL

1. Place one end of side rail between piston ring groove and spacer ex-

pander, **Fig. 19.**
2. Hold end of ring firmly and press downward on portion to be installed until side rail is in position. Do not use piston ring extender.
3. Install upper side rail first, then the lower side rail.

## PISTON RING END GAP LOCATION

1. Position piston ring end gaps as shown in **Fig. 20.**
2. Position oil ring expander gap at least 45° from side rail gaps, but not on the piston pin center line or in thrust direction.

## CYLINDER HEAD & VALVE ASSEMBLY

### CYLINDER HEAD, REPLACE

1. Disconnect battery ground cable and

drain cooling system.

2. Remove upper radiator hose, then disconnect heater hoses.
3. Disconnect spark plug wires at spark plugs, then remove distributor.
4. Remove carburetor to valve cover bracket.
5. Disconnect fuel lines from fuel pump, then remove fuel pump.
6. Remove cylinder head cover attaching bolts, then the cylinder head cover.
7. Disconnect all electrical connectors and vacuum lines from cylinder head.
8. Disconnect throttle linkage from carburetor, then remove water pump belt and pulley.
9. Rotate crankshaft until No. 1 piston is at TDC.
10. Paint a white reference mark on the timing chain in line with timing mark on camshaft sprocket.
11. Remove camshaft sprocket bolt, sprocket and distributor drive gear.
12. Raise and support vehicle, then disconnect air feed lines.
13. Remove power steering pump and position aside.
14. Disconnect ground strap and remove dipstick tube.
15. Remove exhaust manifold heat shield, then disconnect exhaust pipe from catalytic converter and lower vehicle.
16. Remove cylinder head bolts in sequence shown in **Fig. 21**.
17. Reverse procedure to install. Refer to cylinder head bolt tightening sequence, **Fig. 22**, and torque cylinder head bolts in two steps as follows:
   a. Torque all bolts to 35 ft. lbs.
   b. Torque all bolts except No. 11 to 69 ft. lbs. on a cold engine or 75 ft. lbs. on a hot engine.
   c. Torque cylinder head to chain case cover bolts, No. 11, to 156 inch lbs.

## CAMSHAFT BEARING CAP

Align camshaft bearing caps with arrows pointing toward timing chain, **Fig. 23**. Install bearing caps in numerical order.

## ROCKER ARM SHAFT ASSEMBLY

1. Refer to **Fig. 24** and install bolts in front bearing caps.
2. Install wave washers, rocker arms, bearing caps and spring in order shown, **Fig. 24**.
3. Place rocker shaft assembly into position, then rotate camshaft until dowel pin hole is in vertical center line, **Fig. 8**.
4. Torque camshaft bearing cap bolts to 85 inch lbs., following the sequence listed below:
   a. No. 3 cap bolts.
   b. No. 2 cap bolts.
   c. No. 4 cap bolts.
   d. Front cap bolts.
   e. Rear cap bolts.
5. Repeat step 4, increasing torque to 175 inch lbs.

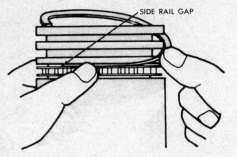

**Fig. 19  Installing oil ring side rail**

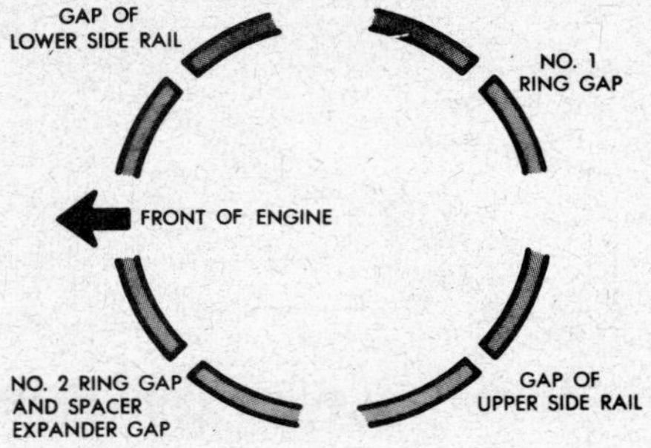

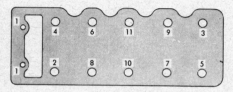

**Fig. 21  Cylinder head bolt removal sequence**

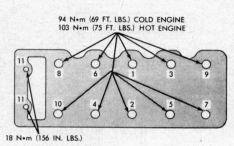

**Fig. 20  Piston ring end gap location**

**Fig. 22  Cylinder head bolt tightening sequence**

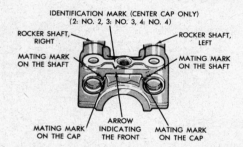

**Fig. 23  Camshaft bearing cap installation**

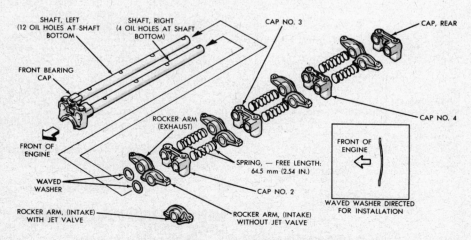

**Fig. 24  Rocker arm shaft assembly**

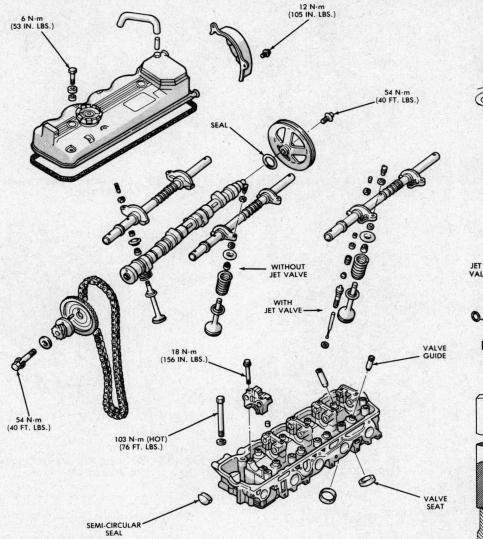

Cylinder head & valve assembly

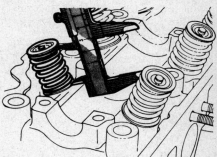

**Fig. 25  Measuring installed valve spring height**

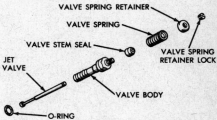

**Fig. 26  Exploded view of jet valve assembly**

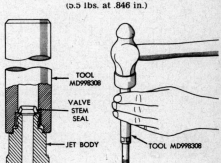

**Fig. 27  Installing jet valve stem seal**

## INSTALLED VALVE SPRING HEIGHT

1. Measure installed height of valve spring between spring seat and spring retainer, **Fig. 25.** Installed height should be 1.590 inches (40.4 mm). If height is greater than 1.629 inches (41.4 mm), replace spring.
2. Adjust valves as outlined under "Valves, Adjust."

## JET VALVE SERVICE

1. Using valve spring compressor tool MD 998309 or equivalent, compress spring, then remove retainer lock and retainer, **Fig. 26. Do not mix parts of jet valve assemblies.**
2. Pull off valve stem and seal with pliers.

3. Ensure valve stem diameter is .1693 inch (4.3 mm), face and seat angles are 45° and valve spring free length is 1.165 inch (29.6 mm).
4. Using valve stem seal installer tool MD 998308 or equivalent, install valve stem seal, **Fig. 27.**
5. Lubricate all jet valve components with engine oil.
6. Using valve spring depressing tool MD 998309 or equivalent, compress spring, then install retainer and retainer lock.
7. Install new O-ring, lubricated with engine oil, on jet valve body.
8. Install jet valve assembly finger tight.
9. Torque jet valve to 168 inch lbs. Ensure that jet valve socket wrench is not tilted with respect to center line of jet valve.

## JET VALVE CLEARANCE ADJUSTMENT

Refer to "Valves, Adjust," for jet valve clearance adjustment.

## VALVE CLEARANCE SPECIFICATIONS

INTAKE, .006 inch
EXHAUST, .010 inch
JET VALVE (if equipped), .006 inch

## VALVES
## ADJUST

Check hot engine torque on cylinder head bolts before performing valve adjustments.

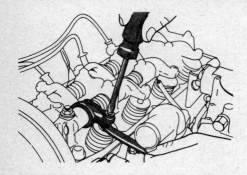

**Fig. 28 Adjusting valve clearance. Less jet valve**

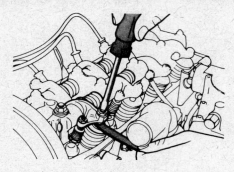

**Fig. 29 Adjusting valve clearance. With jet valve**

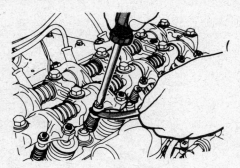

**Fig. 30 Adjusting jet valve clearance**

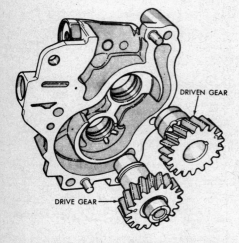

**Fig. 31 Oil pump bearing clearance**

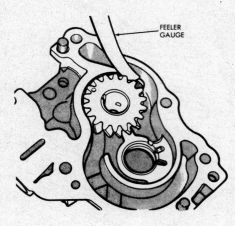

**Fig. 32 Driven gear to housing clearance**

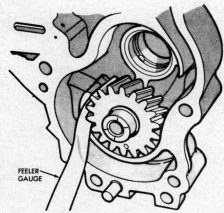

**Fig. 33 Drive gear to housing clearance**

## INTAKE & EXHAUST VALVES

On models equipped with jet valves, adjust jet valve clearance prior to adjusting intake valve clearance.

1. Allow engine to reach normal operating temperature, then position piston at TDC on compression stroke.
2. Loosen valve adjuster locknut, then adjust valve clearance by rotating adjusting screw while measuring with a feeler gauge, **Figs. 28 and 29.**
3. Check valve clearance. Valve clearance should be as specified.
4. Tighten locknut securely while holding adjusting screw with screwdriver.

## JET VALVE (IF EQUIPPED)

Adjust jet valve clearance before adjusting intake valve clearance.

1. Allow engine to reach normal operating temperature, then position piston at TDC on compression stroke.
2. Loosen valve adjuster locknut, then adjust valve clearance by rotating adjusting screw while measuring with a feeler gauge, **Fig. 30.**
3. Check valve clearance. Valve clearance should be as specified.
4. Tighten locknut securely while holding adjusting screw with screwdriver.

## INTAKE MANIFOLD
### REPLACE

1. Disconnect battery ground cable and drain cooling system.
2. Disconnect hose between water pump and intake manifold.
3. Disconnect carburetor air horn and position aside.
4. Disconnect carburetor and intake manifold vacuum hoses, throttle linkage and fuel line.
5. Remove fuel filter and fuel pump and position aside.
6. Remove mounting nuts and washers securing intake manifold, then the intake manifold.
7. Reverse procedure to install.

## EXHAUST MANIFOLD
### REPLACE

1. Disconnect battery ground cable and drain cooling system.
2. Remove air cleaner, then the power steering pump drive belt, if equipped.
3. Raise and support vehicle.
4. Disconnect exhaust pipe from exhaust manifold.
5. Disconnect air injection tube assembly from exhaust manifold, then lower vehicle.
6. Disconnect air injection tube assembly from air pump and position tube assembly aside.
7. Unfasten power steering pump, if equipped, and position aside.
8. Remove heat cowl from exhaust manifold.
9. Remove exhaust manifold retaining nuts and the exhaust manifold.
10. Reverse procedure to install.

## VALVE TIMING

The intake valves open at 25° before TDC on all applications.

## OIL PAN
### REPLACE

1. Drain crankcase oil from engine.
2. Remove oil pan attaching screws, then the oil pan.
3. Clean oil pan rail and oil pan.
4. Install oil pan using new gasket. Torque oil pan attaching screws to 60 inch lbs.

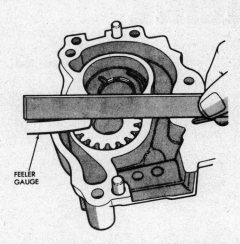

**Fig. 34  Driven gear endplay**

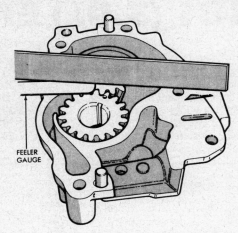

**Fig. 35  Drive gear endplay**

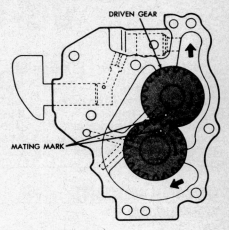

**Fig. 36  Oil pump gear alignment**

# OIL PUMP SERVICE

1. Measure drive gear to bearing clearance, **Fig. 31.** Clearance should be .0008–.0020 inch (.02–.05 mm).
2. Measure driven gear to bearing clearance, **Fig. 31.** Clearance should be .0008–.0020 inch (.02–.05 mm).
3. Measure driven gear to housing clearance, **Fig. 32.** Clearance should be .0043–.0059 inch (.11–.15 mm).
4. Measure drive gear to housing clearance, **Fig. 33.** Clearance should be .0043–.0059 inch (.11–.15 mm).
5. Measure driven gear endplay, **Fig. 34.** Endplay should be .0016–.0039 inch (.04–.10 mm).
6. Measure drive gear endplay, **Fig. 35.** Endplay should be .0020–.0043 inch (.05–.11 mm).
7. Measure relief valve spring free length. Free length should be 1.850

inch (47 mm).
8. Measure relief valve spring load. Spring load should be 9.5 lbs. @ 1.575 inch (42.2N @ 40 mm).
9. Refer to **Fig. 36** and align mating marks of drive and driven gears, then prime pump with clean oil and install on engine. Torque to 71 inch lbs.

# WATER PUMP
## REPLACE

1. Disconnect battery ground cable.
2. Drain cooling system.
3. Disconnect radiator hose, bypass hose, and heater hose from water pump.
4. Remove drive pulley shield.
5. Remove locking screw and pivot screws.
6. Remove drive belt, then the water

pump from engine.
7. Reverse procedure to install. Torque mounting bolts to 204 inch lbs.

# FUEL PUMP
## REPLACE

1. Disconnect battery ground cable.
2. Disconnect and plug fuel lines at fuel pump.
3. Remove fuel pump to cylinder block attaching bolts, then the fuel pump.
4. Reverse procedure to install.

# BELT TENSION DATA

New belt tension should measure 95 lbs. for the power steering pump and 115 lbs. for the A/C compressor and alternator. Used belt tension should measure 80 lbs. for all belts.

# V6-181 (3.0L) ENGINE

## INDEX

## ENGINE MOUNTS
## REPLACE

When positioning the engine, check driveshaft length as outlined in "Front Suspension & Steering" under "Driveshaft Length, Adjust." The engine mounts incorporates slotted bolt holes and permit side-to-side positioning of the engine, thereby affecting the length of the driveshaft. Failure to properly position the engine may result in extensive damage to the engine.

Refer to **Fig. 1** when replacing engine mounts.

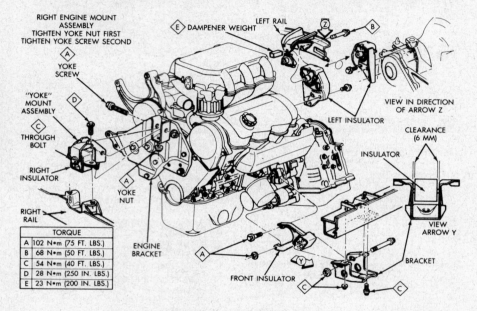

| TORQUE | |
|---|---|
| A | 102 N•m (75 FT. LBS.) |
| B | 68 N•m (50 FT. LBS.) |
| C | 54 N•m (40 FT. LBS.) |
| D | 28 N•m (250 IN. LBS.) |
| E | 23 N•m (200 IN. LBS.) |

**Fig. 1  Engine mounting**

## ENGINE
## REPLACE

1. Disconnect battery ground cable.
2. Scribe hood hinge locations and remove hood.
3. Drain cooling system, then disconnect hoses from radiator and engine.
4. Disconnect all electrical connections, then remove radiator and fan assembly.
5. Release fuel system pressure as follows:
   a. Loosen gas cap to release tank pressure.
   b. Disconnect electrical connector from injector.
   c. Ground one injector terminal using a jumper wire.
   d. Connect jumper wire to second terminal and touch battery positive terminal for no longer than 10 seconds, then remove jumper wire.
6. Disconnect fuel lines and accelerator cable.
7. Remove air cleaner assembly and drain engine oil, then raise and support vehicle.
8. On models equipped with A/C, unfasten A/C compressor and position aside, leaving refrigerant hoses attached.
9. On all models, disconnect exhaust pipe from manifold.
10. Remove transaxle inspection cover, then mark flex plate to torque converter for assembly reference.
11. Remove torque converter to flex plate attaching bolts, then position C-clamp on bottom of converter housing to prevent torque converter from falling out.
12. On models equipped with power steering, unfasten power steering pump and position aside.
13. On all models, remove two lower transaxle to block attaching bolts.
14. Remove starter.
15. Lower vehicle and disconnect all vacuum lines, then the ground strap.
16. Install a suitable transaxle holding fixture and attach a suitable lifting device.
17. Remove upper transaxle case to block attaching bolts.
18. Refer to **Fig. 1,** and remove engine mounts and insulators as follows:
   a. Mark right insulators on right rails support for assembly reference, then remove insulator to rails attaching bolts.
   b. Remove front engine mount through bolt and nut.
   c. Remove left insulator through bolt or insulator bracket to transaxle attaching bolts.
19. Remove engine.
20. Reverse procedure to install.

## INTAKE MANIFOLD
## REPLACE

1. Depressurize fuel system as follows:
   a. Loosen gas cap to release fuel tank pressure.
   b. Disconnect electrical connector from any injector.
   c. Ground injector terminal using a jumper wire.
   d. Connect one end of jumper wire to injector terminal, then touch the other end to the battery positive terminal for no longer than 10 seconds.
   e. Remove jumper wires.
2. Disconnect battery ground cable, then drain cooling system.
3. Remove air cleaner to throttle body hose, then disconnect throttle cable and transaxle kickdown linkage, **Fig. 2.**
4. Disconnect automatic idle speed (AIS) motor and throttle position sensor (TPS) electrical connectors from throttle body.
5. Disconnect vacuum hoses from throttle body.

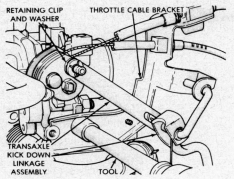

**Fig. 2  Throttle cable removal**

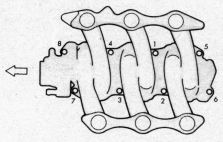

**Fig. 3  Intake manifold tightening sequence**

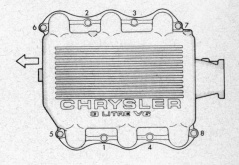

**Fig. 4  Intake plenum tightening sequence**

6. Remove EGR tube flange from intake plenum.
7. Disconnect coolant temperature sensor and charge temperature sensor electrical connectors.
8. Disconnect air intake plenum vacuum connector, then disconnect fuel hoses from fuel rail.
9. Remove air intake plenum to intake manifold attaching bolts, then the air intake plenum.
10. Disconnect vacuum hoses from fuel rail and fuel pressure regulator, then disconnect fuel injector electrical connector from engine wiring harness.
11. Remove fuel pressure regulator attaching bolts, then loosen hose clamps and remove regulator from rail.
12. Remove fuel rail attaching bolts, then lift fuel rail assembly from intake manifold.
13. Disconnect radiator hose from thermostat housing and heater hose from heater pipe.
14. Remove intake manifold attaching bolts, then the intake manifold.
15. Reverse procedure to install, noting the following:
    a. Discard gaskets and clean gasket surfaces on both manifolds and cylinder head.
    b. Use a straightedge to ensure gasket surfaces on manifolds are flat and within .004-.008 inch per foot of manifold length.
    c. Torque intake manifold bolts to 174 inch lbs. in sequence shown in **Fig. 3.**
    d. Torque fuel rail attaching bolts to 115 inch lbs.
    e. Torque air intake plenum attaching bolts to 115 inch lbs. in sequence shown in **Fig. 4.**
    f. Torque EGR tube flange nut to 200 inch lbs.

## EXHAUST MANIFOLD
### REPLACE

1. Disconnect battery ground cable, then raise and support vehicle.
2. Disconnect exhaust pipe from rear rear exhaust manifold.

3. Remove EGR tube from rear manifold, then disconnect oxygen sensor lead.
4. Remove cross over pipe attaching bolts, then the cross over pipe.
5. Remove rear manifold attaching bolts, then the rear manifold.
6. Lower vehicle, then remove heat shield attaching bolts from front exhaust manifold, then the heat shield.
7. Remove cross over pipe to front exhaust manifold attaching bolts.
8. Remove front exhaust manifold attaching bolts, then the front exhaust manifold.
9. Reverse procedure to install, noting the following:
   a. Discard gaskets and clean gasket surfaces on both manifolds and cylinder head.
   b. Use a straightedge to ensure gasket surfaces on manifolds are flat and within .004-.008 inch per foot of manifold length.
   c. Torque rear exhaust manifold attaching bolts to 191 inch lbs.
   d. Torque exhaust pipe to exhaust manifold attaching bolts to 250 inch lbs.
   e. Torque crossover pipe to manifold attaching bolts to 51 ft. lbs.
   f. Torque front exhaust manifold attaching bolts to 191 inch lbs, then install heat shield and torque bolts to 130 inch lbs.

## TIMING BELT
### REPLACE

1. Disconnect battery ground cable.
2. Remove accessory drive belts.
3. Remove A/C compressor, alternator, power steering pump, tensioners and mounting brackets as shown in **Fig. 5,** and set aside.
4. Raise and support vehicle, then remove right inner splash shield.
5. Remove crankshaft drive pulleys and torsional damper, **Fig. 6,** then lower vehicle and position a suitable jack under engine.
6. Remove engine mount insulator from engine mount bracket, raise engine slightly, then remove engine mount bracket as shown in **Fig. 7.**

7. Remove timing belt covers as shown in **Fig. 8.**
8. If belt is to be reused, mark belt running direction for reassembly reference.
9. Loosen timing belt tensioner, **Fig. 9,** then remove timing belt.
10. Remove crankshaft sprocket flange, if necessary.
11. Remove camshaft sprocket attaching bolts, then the sprockets, if necessary.
12. Install camshaft sprockets, then using camshaft sprocket holder tool MB990775, torque bolts to 73 ft. lbs.
13. Install timing belt tensioner and spring. Rotate tensioner counterclockwise, **Fig. 10,** then temporarily tighten bolt.
14. Install timing belt on crankshaft sprocket first, while keeping belt tight on tension side, then position belt over front camshaft sprocket, **Fig. 9.**
15. Then, install belt on water pump pulley and rear camshaft sprocket and finally on the timing belt tensioner, **Fig. 9.**
16. Rotate front camshaft sprocket in opposite direction and check that all timing marks align, **Fig. 9.**
17. Install crankshaft sprocket flange, then loosen tensioner bolt to allow spring to tension belt. Rotate crankshaft two complete revolutions, and check timing marks.
18. Tighten tensioner bolt to 23 ft. lbs.
19. Install timing belt covers as shown in **Fig. 8.**
20. Install engine brackets, pulleys, and accessories as shown in **Fig. 5,** then the drive belts.

## CAMSHAFT & ROCKER ARM SERVICE

Oil leak or seepage at rear cam plugs may be caused by defective or missing cam plug. This condition may be found on engines built prior to date codes of 7-593. Inspect at rear righthand side of engine on each cylinder head for evidence of oil leaks or seepage. If found, replace plugs, using a light coat of RTV sealer or equivalant.

| TORQUE | | |
|---|---|---|
| A | 30 FT. LBS. (41 N•m) |
| B | 250 IN. LBS. (28 N•m) |
| C | 40 FT. LBS. (54 N•m) |
| D | 70 FT. LBS. (95 N•m) |

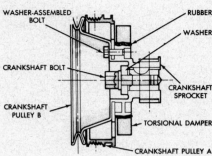

**Fig. 6  Crankshaft pulley removal**

**Fig. 5  Accessories & mounting brackets removal & installation**

Before removing rocker arms and camshafts, check auto adjusters for freeplay, **Fig. 11.** Insert a piece of wire through bleed hole in rocker arm and carefully push adjuster check ball down, **Fig. 3.** While pushing down on check ball, move rocker arm up and down to check for freeplay. If there is no play replace adjuster.

1. Install auto lash adjuster retainers M0998443 as shown in **Fig. 12.**
2. Remove distributor housing attaching bolts, then distributor housing and 0-ring.
3. **When removing camshaft bearing caps do not remove bolts from bearing caps.** Remove rocker arm, rocker shafts and bearing cap as an assembly.
4. Remove camshafts, oil seals and end seals.
5. Lubricate camshaft journals and cams with engine oil, then install camshafts on cylinder head.
6. Align camshaft bearing caps with arrows (depending on cylinder bank) as shown in **Fig. 13.**
7. Identify number 1 bearing cap as shown in **Fig. 14,** then install rocker shafts into bearing cap 1 with end notches positioned as shown in **Fig. 14,** and that machined portion of rocker shaft is facing down.
8. Install rocker arms, bearing caps and springs onto rocker arm shafts.
9. Temporarily install number 4 bearing cap bolts to retain assembly.
10. Apply a suitable sealant at bearing cap ends as shown in **Fig 13.**
11. Install rocker arm shaft assembly, ensuring that arrow on bearing cap and arrow mark on cylinder head are pointing in the same direction, **Fig. 13.**
12. Torque bearing caps as follows:
    a. Numbers 3, 2, 1, then 4 to 85 inch lbs.
    b. In the same sequence mentioned

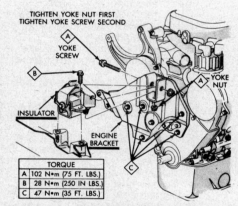

| TORQUE | |
|---|---|
| A | 102 N•m (75 FT. LBS.) |
| B | 28 N•m (250 IN. LBS.) |
| C | 47 N•m (35 FT. LBS.) |

**Fig. 7  Engine mount removal**

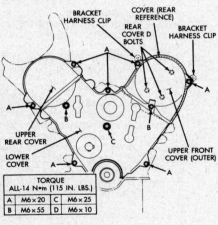

| TORQUE ALL-14 N•m (115 IN. LBS.) | | | |
|---|---|---|---|
| A | M6 × 20 | C | M6 × 25 |
| B | M6 × 55 | D | M6 × 10 |

**Fig. 8  Timing belt cover removal**

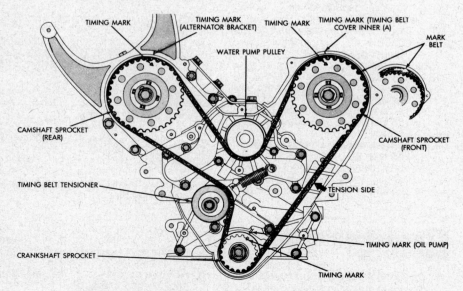

**Fig. 9  Timing belt installation**

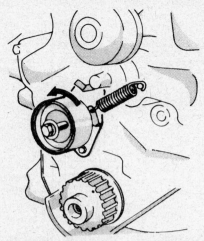

**Fig. 10 Positioning timing belt tensioner**

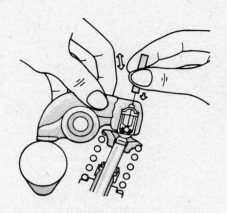

**Fig. 11 Checking auto lash adjuster**

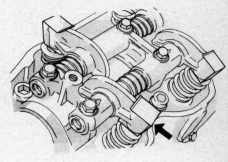

**Fig. 12 Installing auto lash adjuster retainers**

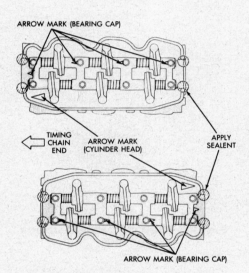

**Fig. 13 Camshaft bearing caps installation**

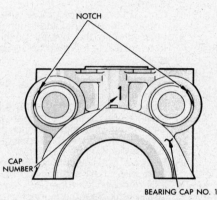

**Fig. 14 Identifying bearing caps**

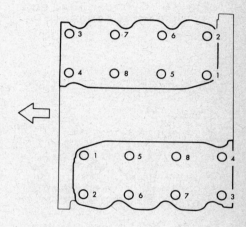

**Fig. 15 Cylinder head bolt removal sequence**

above, torque bearing cap bolts to 180 inch lbs.
13. Install distributor housing and torque bolts to 130 inch lbs.
14. Lubricate camshaft oil seals lip with engine oil, then using camshaft oil seal installer tool MD998713 or equivalent, install camshaft oil seals.
15. Using oil seal installer tool MB998306 or equivalent, install end seals.

## CYLINDER HEAD
### REPLACE

1. Refer to "Timing Belt, Replace," and remove timing belt as outlined.
2. Refer to "Camshaft & Rocker Arm Service," and remove camshaft and rocker arms as outlined.
3. Refer to "Intake Manifold & Exhaust

Manifold, Replace" procedures and remove intake and exhaust manifolds as outlined.
4. Remove distributor.
5. Remove cylinder head attaching bolts in sequence shown in **Fig. 15**, then the cylinder head.
6. Reverse procedure to install, torquing cylinder head bolts to 34 ft. lbs. in sequence shown in **Fig. 16**.

## PISTON & ROD ASSEMBLY

The piston and rod is assembled with front mark facing toward front of engine (toward timing belt), **Fig. 17**. Connecting rod front mark (72), must always face forward (toward timing belt), **Fig. 17**.

## OIL PUMP SERVICE
### REMOVAL

1. Refer to "Timing Belt, Replace," and remove timing belt as outlined.

2. Remove timing belt tensioner and crankshaft sprocket.
3. Remove oil pump assembly attaching bolts, then the oil pump.
4. Remove oil seal from oil pump housing.

### INSPECTION

1. Check oil pump case for cracks and damage.
2. Using a suitable feeler gauge, measure the following clearances referring to **Fig. 18**, as follows:
   a. Body clearance should be .004-.007 inch (0.10-0.18 mm).
   b. Side clearance should be .0015-.0035 inch (0.04-0.09 mm).
   c. Inner rotor to case clearance should be .001-.002 inch (0.03-0.07 mm).

### INSTALLATION

1. Install oil pump assembly and torque attaching bolts to 104 inch lbs.
2. Using oil seal installer tool MB998306, install new front oil seal into oil pump housing.

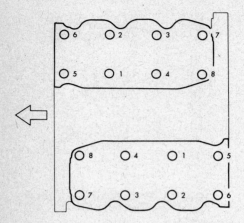

**Fig. 16   Cylinder head bolt tightening sequence**

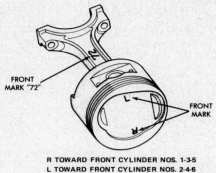

**Fig. 17   Piston & rod installation**

R TOWARD FRONT CYLINDER NOS. 1-3-5
L TOWARD FRONT CYLINDER NOS. 2-4-6

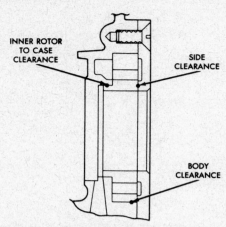

**Fig. 18   Oil pump clearance check locations**

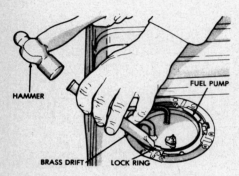

**Fig. 19   Fuel pump removal**

3. Reverse steps 1 and 2 in removal procedure, to install.

## VALVES
### ADJUST

This engine uses hydraulic lash adjusters. No provision for adjustment is provided.

## FUEL PUMP
### REPLACE

1. Depressurize fuel system as follows:
   a. Loosen gas cap to release any fuel tank pressure.
   b. Disconnect electrical connector from any injector.
   c. Ground one injector terminal using a jumper wire.
   d. Connect one end of jumper wire to one injector terminal and touch the other end to the battery positive terminal for no longer than 10 seconds.
   e. Remove jumper wires.
2. Raise and support vehicle, then drain fuel from fuel tank.
3. Remove bolts securing filler tube to inner and outer quarter panel.
4. Disconnect electrical connectors and lines from tank, then position a suitable jack under fuel tank.
5. Remove bolts securing fuel tank, then lower tank slightly and carefully remove filler tube from tank.
6. Lower tank, then disconnect vapor separator rollover valve hose and remove fuel tank and insulator pad from vehicle.
7. Using a hammer and a suitable nonmetallic punch, tap lock ring counterclockwise to release pump, **Fig. 19.**
8. Pull fuel pump assembly partially out of tank until return line hose connection is visible, then disconnect return line.
9. Remove fuel pump assembly from tank with O-ring. Discard O-ring.
10. Reverse procedure to install.

## WATER PUMP
### REPLACE

1. Refer to "Timing Belt, Replace," and remove timing belt as outlined.
2. Drain cooling system.
3. Disconnect water inlet pipe from water pump.
4. Remove water pump attaching bolts, then the water pump.
5. Reverse procedure to install, torquing water pump attaching bolts to 20 ft. lbs.

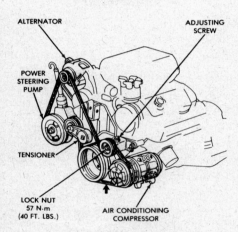

**Fig. 20   Belt deflection check points**

## BELT TENSION DATA

Belt deflection under a ten pound push or pull should be between 1/4 (6 mm) to 5/16 at locations shown in **Fig. 20.** Measure deflection while applying tension to the accessory, then torque mounting mounts to specification. Deflection on a new belt should be between 1/4 (6 mm) to 1/2 (12 mm); a belt is considered used after 15 minutes of engine operation, tension on a used belt should be 1/4 (6 mm) and 5/16 (8 mm) under a tension pound load.

# CLUTCH & MANUAL TRANSAXLE

## INDEX

### Page No.

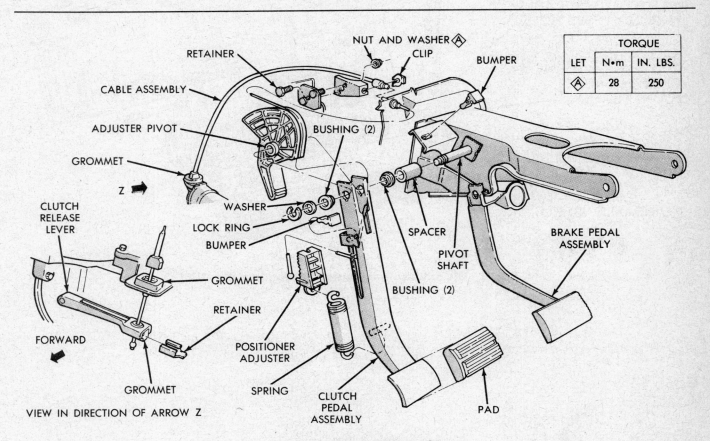

| TORQUE | | |
|---|---|---|
| LET | N•m | IN. LBS. |
| Ⓐ | 28 | 250 |

Fig. 1  Clutch cable routing

## CLUTCH
### ADJUST

The clutch release cable, **Fig. 1**, cannot be adjusted on these models. When the cable is properly routed, the spring between the clutch pedal and positioner adjuster will hold the clutch cable in proper position. An adjuster pivot is used to hold release cable in place to ensure complete clutch release when clutch pedal is depressed.

A broken clutch cable, slow clutch action or high clutch pedal effort on 1984 models may be the result of an improperly routed clutch cable. The transaxle cable mounting shelf contains two holes, **Fig. 2**.

One hole is for clutch cable retention and the other is for manufacturing purposes. If the cable is not routed as shown in **Fig. 2**, reroute as necessary, replacing cable if damaged.

## CLUTCH
### REPLACE

1. Remove transaxle as outlined under "Manual Transaxle, Replace" procedure.
2. Mark relationship between clutch cover and flywheel for reference during assembly, then install a suitable clutch disc aligning tool through clutch disc hub to prevent clutch disc from falling and damaging faces.
3. Gradually loosen clutch cover attaching bolts, then remove pressure plate, cover assembly and disc from flywheel.
4. Remove clutch release shaft and slide release bearing assembly off input shaft seal retainer. Remove fork from release bearing thrust plate.
5. Reverse procedure to install. Align reference marks made during disassembly, then using a clutch disc alignment tool, install disc, plate and cover to flywheel. Refer to **Fig. 3** for torque specifications.

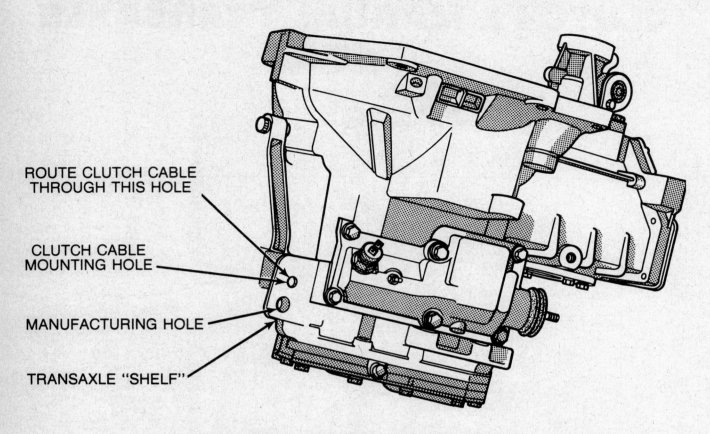

ROUTE CLUTCH CABLE THROUGH THIS HOLE

CLUTCH CABLE MOUNTING HOLE

MANUFACTURING HOLE

TRANSAXLE "SHELF"

Fig. 2   Clutch cable mounting hole identification

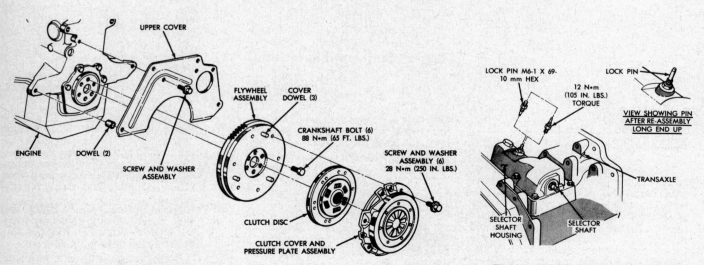

UPPER COVER

FLYWHEEL ASSEMBLY

COVER DOWEL (3)

CRANKSHAFT BOLT (6) 88 N•m (65 FT. LBS.)

SCREW AND WASHER ASSEMBLY (6) 28 N•m (250 IN. LBS.)

ENGINE

DOWEL (2)

SCREW AND WASHER ASSEMBLY

CLUTCH DISC

CLUTCH COVER AND PRESSURE PLATE ASSEMBLY

Fig. 3   Clutch assembly

LOCK PIN M6-1 X 69- 10 mm HEX

LOCK PIN

12 N•m (105 IN. LBS.) TORQUE

VIEW SHOWING PIN AFTER RE-ASSEMBLY LONG END UP

TRANSAXLE

SELECTOR SHAFT HOUSING

SELECTOR SHAFT

Fig. 4   Lock pin removal & installation

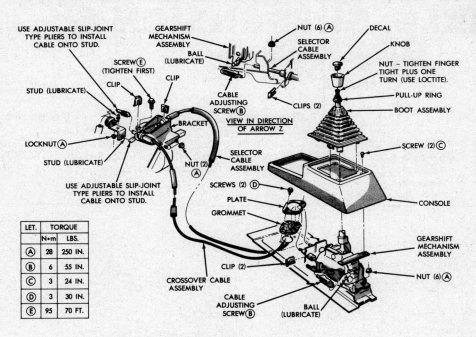

| LET. | TORQUE | |
|------|--------|------|
| | N·m | LBS. |
| Ⓐ | 28 | 250 IN. |
| Ⓑ | 6 | 55 IN. |
| Ⓒ | 3 | 24 IN. |
| Ⓓ | 3 | 30 IN. |
| Ⓔ | 95 | 70 FT. |

**Fig. 5   Gear shift linkage**

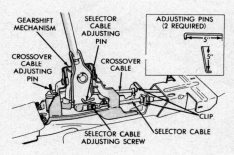

**Fig. 6   Cable adjusting pins**

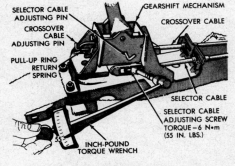

**Fig. 7   Adjusting selector cable**

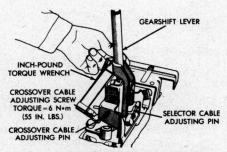

**Fig. 8   Adjusting crossover cable**

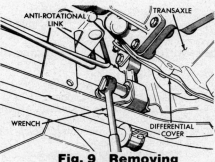

**Fig. 9   Removing anti-rotational link**

## GEARSHIFT LINKAGE
## ADJUST

1. Remove lock pin from transaxle selector shaft housing, **Fig. 4**.
2. Reverse lock pin so long end is facing downward, then insert lock pin into same threaded hole while pushing selector shaft into selector housing. This locks selector in 1-2 neutral position, **Fig. 4**.
3. Remove gearshift knob, retaining nut and pull-up ring, **Fig. 5**.
4. Remove boot assembly from console, then the console.
5. Fabricate two cable adjusting pins as shown in **Fig. 6**. Pin diameter should be 3/16 inch on 1984-85 models and 5/32 inch on 1986-89 models.
6. Adjust selector cable and torque adjusting screw to 55 inch lbs., **Fig. 7**. **The selector cable adjusting screw must be properly torqued.**
7. Adjust crossover cable and torque adjusting screw to 55 inch lbs., **Fig. 8**. **The crossover cable adjusting screw must be properly torqued.**
8. Install console and boot assembly, then the pull-up ring, retaining nut and gearshift knob. Apply suitable locking compound to retaining nut and tighten finger tight plus one turn.
9. Remove lock pin from selector shaft housing, then reinstall lock pin so long end is up in selector shaft housing, **Fig. 4**. Torque lock pin to 105 inch lbs.
10. Check for proper operation.

## MANUAL TRANSAXLE
## REPLACE

1. Disconnect battery ground cable.
2. Raise and support vehicle, then install suitable engine support fixture.
3. Disconnect gearshift linkage and clutch cable from transaxle.
4. Remove front wheel and tire assemblies.
5. Remove left front splash shield, then the left engine mount from transaxle.
6. Disconnect driveshafts. Refer to "Driveshaft, Replace" procedure under "Front Suspension & Steering."
7. Support transaxle and remove upper clutch housing attaching bolts.
8. Remove anti-rotational link, **Fig. 9**.
9. Pry transaxle rearward until mainshaft clears clutch, then lower transaxle from vehicle.
10. Reverse procedure to install. When installing left engine mount, refer to "Engine Mounts" procedure.

# REAR AXLE, SUSPENSION & BRAKES

## INDEX

| LET | TORQUE | |
|---|---|---|
| A | 35 FT. LBS. | 47 N·m |
| B | 70 IN. LBS. | 7 N·m |
| C | 95 FT. LBS. | 129 N·m |
| D | 80 FT. LBS. | 108 N·m |
| E | 60 FT. LBS. | 81 N·m |
| F | 45 FT. LBS. | 61 N·m |
| G | 85 FT. LBS. | 115 N·m |

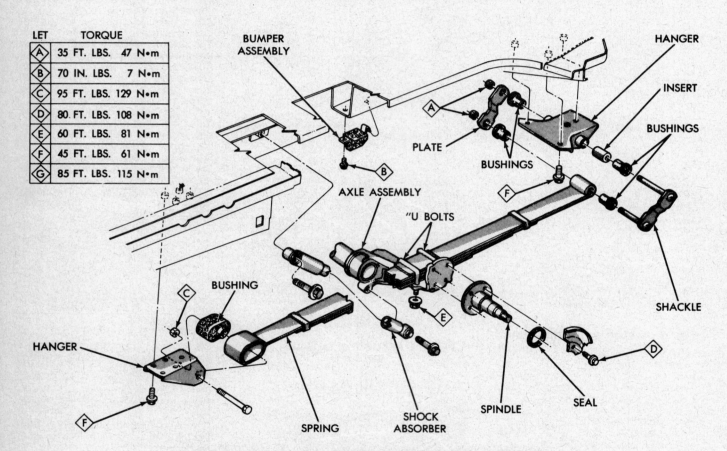

**Fig. 1 Rear axle & suspension assembly. 1984–85**

## REAR AXLE & SPRING REPLACE

### REMOVAL

1. Raise and support vehicle, then position suitable floor jack under axle assembly and raise axle assembly to relieve weight on rear springs.
2. On 1984-86 models, disconnect rear brake proportioning valve spring and on 1987-89 models, disconnect actuator assembly. Then on all models, lower ends of the rear shock absorbers at axle brackets, **Figs. 1 and 2.**
3. Remove U-bolt attaching nuts and washers, then the U-bolt.
4. Lower rear axle assembly, allowing rear spring to hang free.
5. Remove four attaching bolts from front spring hanger.
6. Remove rear spring shackle attaching nuts and plate, then the shackle from the spring.
7. Remove front pivot bolt from front spring hanger.
8. Remove springs from vehicle.

### INSTALLATION

1. Assemble shackle, bushings and plate on rear of spring and rear spring hanger, then install shackle bolt, **Figs. 1 and 2.** Do not tighten nut at this point.
2. Assemble front spring hanger to front of spring eye, then install pivot bolt. Do not tighten nut at this point. **Pivot bolt must face inboard to prevent structural damage during installation of spring.**
3. Raise front spring, then install four hanger attaching bolts. Torque bolts to 45 ft. lbs. and connect actuator assembly.
4. Raise axle assembly with axle centered under spring center bolt, then in-

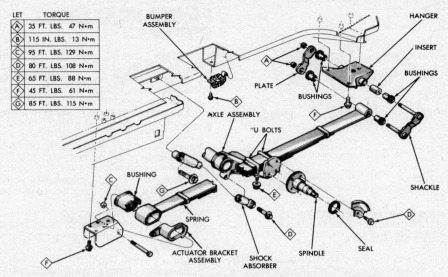

| LET | TORQUE | |
|-----|--------|--------|
| A | 35 FT. LBS. | 47 N•m |
| B | 115 IN. LBS. | 13 N•m |
| C | 95 FT. LBS. | 129 N•m |
| D | 80 FT. LBS. | 108 N•m |
| E | 65 FT. LBS. | 88 N•m |
| F | 45 FT. LBS. | 61 N•m |
| G | 85 FT. LBS. | 115 N•m |

**Fig. 2   Rear axle & suspension assembly. 1986–89**

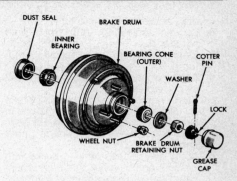

**Fig. 3   Wheel bearing assembly**

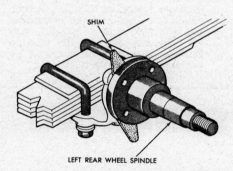

**Fig. 4   Shim installation for toe-out**

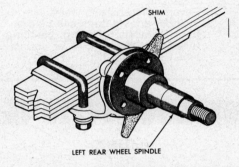

**Fig. 5   Shim installation for toe-in**

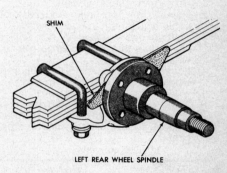

**Fig. 6   Shim installation for positive camber**

stall U-bolt and washer. Torque U-bolt attaching nut to 60 ft. lbs.
5. Install shock absorbers and attaching nuts. Do not tighten nuts at this point.
6. Lower vehicle to floor, allowing full weight of vehicle on wheels, then torque the following fasteners: front pivot bolt, 95 ft. lbs.; shackle nuts, 35 ft. lbs.; 1984 shock absorber bolts, 50 ft. lbs.; 1985–89 shock absorber upper bolts, 85 ft. lbs.; 1985–89 shock absorber lower bolts, 80 ft. lbs.
7. Connect rear brake proportioning valve spring.

## REAR WHEEL ALIGNMENT

Due to the design of the rear suspension and the incorporation of stub axles or wheel spindles, it is possible to adjust camber and toe of the rear wheels on these vehicles. Adjustment is controlled by adding shims approximately .010 inch thick between spindle mounting surface and spindle mounting plate. The amount of adjustment is approximately 3° per shim.

Refer to **Figs. 4 through 7** for proper replacement of shims.

## REAR WHEEL BEARING
### ADJUST

1. Raise and support rear of vehicle.
2. Torque adjusting nut to 270 inch lbs. while rotating wheel.
3. Stop wheel and loosen adjusting nut, **Fig. 3**.
4. Tighten adjusting nut finger tight. End play should be .0001-.0020 inch.
5. Install castle lock with slots aligned with cotter pin hole.
6. Install cotter pin and grease cap.

## SERVICE BRAKES
### ADJUST

The rear brakes are self-adjusting. An initial adjustment is necessary after the brake shoes have been relined or replaced, or when the length of the star wheel adjuster has been changed during other service operations. To adjust the rear brakes, proceed as follows:

1. Raise and support vehicle.
2. Remove adjusting hole covers from brake supports.
3. Release parking brake and back off adjustment to slacken cable.
4. Insert adjusting tool C-3784 or equivalent into star wheel of adjusting screw. Move handle of tool upward until a slight drag is felt.
5. Insert a suitable tool into brake adjusting hole and push adjusting lever out of engagement with star wheel, then back off star wheel to ensure there is no brake shoe drag. **Use caution not to bend adjusting lever or distort lever spring.**
6. Adjust parking brake, referring to "Parking Brake, Adjust" procedure.

## PARKING BRAKE
### ADJUST

Vehicles built prior to July 11, 1984 may experience high pedal effort when applying the parking brake. On these models, follow procedure "A," and all other models, follow procedure "B."

### PROCEDURE A

1. Raise and support vehicle.
2. Release parking brake, then tighten adjusting nut until both rear wheels

drag and are difficult to turn.

3. Loosen adjusting nut until both wheels turn freely. From this point, loosen adjusting nut an additional 25 turns.
4. Apply parking brake two times to seat all components.
5. Start engine and apply parking brake 15 clicks. With automatic transaxle in Drive or manual transaxle in 1st gear, both rear wheels should slide under engine torque.
6. Apply and release parking brake with ignition on to verify that instrument panel warning light shuts off. If light remains lit, tighten adjusting nut one turn at a time until system operates properly.

## PROCEDURE B

1. Raise and support vehicle.
2. Release parking brake and back off cable adjustment to slacken cable.
3. Tighten cable adjusting nut until a slight drag is obtained while rotating wheels.
4. Loosen cable adjusting nut until rear wheels rotate freely, then an additional two turns.
5. Apply and release parking brake to check for proper operation. The rear wheels should rotate without dragging.

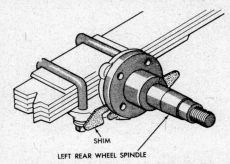

**Fig. 7  Shim installation for negative camber**

## MASTER CYLINDER REPLACE

1. Disconnect and plug brake tubes from master cylinder. Cap master cylinder ports.
2. Remove master cylinder attaching nuts.
3. Remove master cylinder from power brake unit.
4. Reverse procedure to install. **Master cylinder should be bench bled before installation, using bleeding tubes tool No. C-4546 or equivalent.**

## POWER BRAKE UNIT REPLACE

1. Remove master cylinder attaching nuts, slide master cylinder from mounting studs and support on fender shield. Do not disconnect brake tubes from master cylinder.
2. Disconnect vacuum hose from power brake unit. Do not remove check valve from booster.
3. Install suitable screwdriver between center tang on retainer clip and the brake pedal pin located under instrument panel. Rotate screwdriver so retainer clip center tang will pass over brake pedal pin.
4. Pull retainer clip from pin.
5. Remove brackets from steel heater water line at dash panel and left frame rail, if equipped.
6. On vehicles equipped with manual transaxle, remove clutch cable bracket at shock tower and position aside.
7. On all models, remove power brake unit attaching nuts, then the power brake unit from vehicle.
8. Reverse procedure to install. Torque power brake unit and master cylinder unit attaching nuts to 200-300 inch lbs. **Do not attempt to service booster, can only be serviced by replacing assembly.**

# FRONT SUSPENSION & STEERING

## INDEX

## DESCRIPTION

These vehicles use a MacPherson type front suspension with vertical shock absorber struts attached to upper fender reinforcement and steering knuckle, **Fig. 1.** The lower control arms are attached inboard to a crossmember and outboard to steering knuckle through a ball joint to provide lower steering knuckle position. During steering maneuvers, strut and steering knuckle rotate as an assembly.

The driveshafts are attached inboard to transaxle output drive flanges, and outboard to driven wheel hub.

## WHEEL ALIGNMENT

Prior to wheel alignment, ensure tires are at recommended pressure, are of equal size and have approximately the same wear pattern. Check front wheel and tire assembly for radial runout and inspect lower ball joints and steering linkage for looseness. Check front and rear springs for sagging or damage. Front suspension inspections should be performed on a level floor or alignment rack with fuel tank at capacity and vehicle free of luggage and

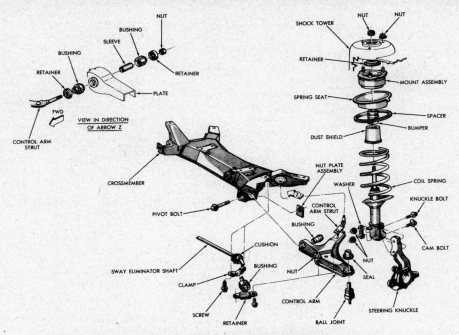

Fig. 1   Front suspension exploded view

Fig. 2   Camber adjustment

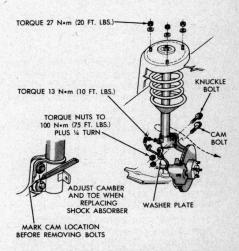

Fig. 4   Removing strut damper assembly

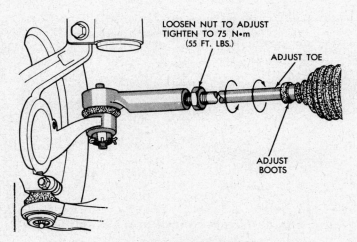

Fig. 3   Toe-in adjustment

passenger compartment load.

Prior to each alignment reading, the vehicle should be bounced an equal number of times from the center of the bumper alternating first from the rear, then the front, and releasing at bottom of down cycle.

## CASTER

The caster angle on these vehicles cannot be adjusted.

## CAMBER

To adjust camber, loosen cam and through bolts, **Fig. 2**. Rotate upper cam bolt to move top of wheel in or out to achieve specified camber angle. Torque attaching nuts to 75 ft. lbs. plus an additional 1/4 turn.

## TOE-IN

To adjust toe-in, center steering wheel and hold in position with a suitable tool. Loosen tie rod locknuts and rotate rod, **Fig. 3**, to adjust toe-in to specifications. Use care not to twist steering gear rubber boots. Torque tie rod locknuts to 55 ft. lbs. (75 Nm). Adjust position of steering gear rubber boots. Remove steering wheel holding tool.

# STRUT DAMPER ASSEMBLY
# REPLACE
## REMOVAL

1. Raise and support vehicle, then remove front wheels.
2. Mark position of camber adjusting cam, then remove camber adjusting bolt, through bolt and brake hose to damper bracket retaining screw, **Fig. 4.**
3. Remove strut damper to fender shield mounting nut and washer assemblies.
4. Remove strut damper from vehicle.

## INSTALLATION

1. Position strut assembly into fender reinforcement, then install retaining nut and washer assemblies. Torque retaining nut to 20 ft. lbs.
2. Position steering knuckle into strut, then install washer plate, cam bolts and knuckle bolts.
3. Attach brake hose retainers to damper. Torque to 10 ft. lbs.
4. Index cam bolt to alignment mark made during removal.
5. Position a 4 inch or larger C-clamp on

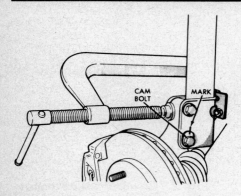

**Fig. 5 Installing strut damper assembly**

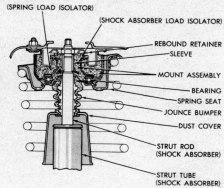

**Fig. 6 Strut damper mount assembly**

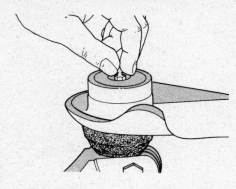

**Fig. 7 Checking ball joint for wear**

steering knuckle and strut, **Fig. 5,** then tighten clamp just enough to eliminate any looseness between strut and knuckle. Torque cam bolts to 75 ft. lbs. plus an additional 1/4 turn.
6. Remove C-clamp, then install wheel and tire assembly.

## COIL SPRING
## REPLACE

1. Remove strut damper assembly as previously outlined.
2. Compress coil spring using suitable tool.
3. Remove strut rod nut while holding strut rod to prevent rotation.
4. Remove the mount assembly, **Fig. 6.**
5. Remove coil spring from strut damper.
6. Inspect mount assembly for deterioration of rubber isolator, retainers for cracks and distortion, and bearings for blinding.
7. Install dust shield, jounce bumper, spacer and seat to top of spring. Mount assembly to rod, then install retainer and rod nut.
8. Position spring retainer alignment notch parallel to damper lower attaching bracket.
9. Torque strut rod nut to 60 ft. lbs., using suitable tool, then release spring compressor.
10. With weight of vehicle off front wheels, turn both strut rod and strut rod nut in same direction until upper spring seat is properly positioned, then recheck torque of strut rod nut.

## BALL JOINTS
## CHECKING BALL JOINTS

With weight of vehicle resting on wheel and tire assembly, attempt to move grease fitting with fingers, **Fig. 7.** Do not use tool or added force to attempt to move grease fitting. If grease fitting moves freely, ball joint is worn and should be replaced.

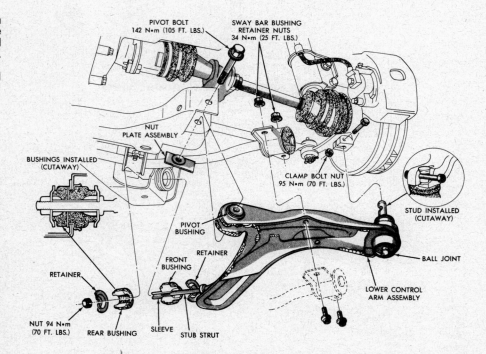

**Fig. 8 Lower control arm assembly**

## REPLACE

The ball joint is pressed into the lower control arm. On these models, the ball joint can be pressed from the lower control arm using a 1 1/16 inch deep socket and ball joint installer tool No. C-4699-2. When pressing ball joint into lower control arm, use ball joint installer tool Nos. C-4699-1 and C-4699-2. Install ball joint seal using a 1 1/2 inch socket and ball joint installer tool No. C-4699-2.

## LOWER CONTROL ARM
## REPLACE
### REMOVAL

1. Raise and support vehicle.

2. Remove front inner pivot through bolt, rear stub strut nut, retainer and bushing, then the ball joint to steering knuckle clamp bolt, **Fig. 8.**
3. Separate ball joint from steering knuckle by prying between ball stud retainer and lower control arm. **Pulling steering knuckle out from vehicle after releasing from ball joint can separate inner C/V joint.**
4. Remove sway bar to control arm nut, then rotate control arm over sway bar.
5. Remove rear stub strut bushing, sleeve and retainer.

### INSTALLATION

1. Install retainer, bushing and sleeve on stub strut.
2. Position control arm over sway bar

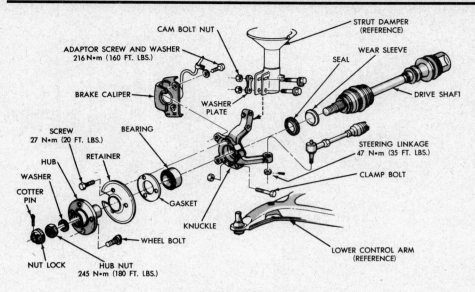

Fig. 9  Steering knuckle assembly

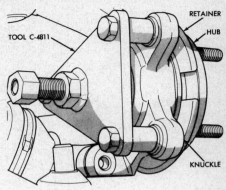

Fig. 10  Hub removal

and install rear stub strut and front pivot into crossmember.

3. Install front pivot bolt and loosely assemble nut, **Fig. 8.**
4. Install stub strut bushing and retainer and loosely assemble nut.
5. Install ball joint stud into steering knuckle, then the clamp bolt. Torque clamp bolt to 70 ft. lbs. (95 Nm).
6. Place sway bar end bushing retainer to control arm, then install retainer bolts. Torque retainer bolts to 25 ft. lbs. (34 Nm).
7. Lower vehicle so suspension fully supports vehicle, then torque front pivot bolt to 105 ft. lbs. (142 Nm) and stub strut nut to 70 ft. lbs. (95 Nm).

## STEERING KNUCKLE
## REPLACE
### REMOVAL

1. Remove cotter pin, locknut and spring washer.
2. Loosen hub nut with brakes applied, **Fig. 9. The hub and driveshaft are splined together through the knuckle (bearing) and retained by the hub nut.**
3. Raise and support vehicle, then remove front wheel and tire assembly.
4. Remove hub nut. Ensure splined driveshaft is free to separate from spline in hub during knuckle removal. A pulling force on shaft can separate inner C/V joint. Tap lightly with brass drift, if required.
5. Disconnect tie rod end from steering arm with a suitable puller.
6. Disconnect brake hose retainer from strut damper.
7. Remove clamp bolt securing ball joint stud into steering knuckle, then the brake caliper adapter screw and washer assemblies.

8. Support caliper with a piece of wire. Do not hang by brake hose.
9. Remove rotor, then separate ball joint stud from knuckle assembly.
10. Remove knuckle assembly from vehicle. **Support driveshaft during knuckle removal. Do not permit driveshaft to hang after separating steering knuckle from vehicle.**

## INSTALLATION

1. Place steering knuckle on lower ball joint stud and the driveshaft through hub.
2. Install and torque ball joint to steering knuckle clamp bolt to 70 ft. lbs. (95 Nm).
3. Install tie rod end into steering arm and torque nut to 35 ft. lbs. (47 Nm). Install cotter pin, **Fig. 9.**
4. Install rotor.
5. Install caliper over rotor and position adapter to steering knuckle. Install adapter to knuckle attaching bolts and torque to 160 ft. lbs. (216 Nm).
6. Attach brake hose retainer to strut damper and torque attaching screw to 10 ft. lbs. (13 Nm).
7. Install hub nut assembly as follows:
   a. With brakes applied, install hub nut and torque to 180 ft. lbs. (245 Nm).
   b. Install spring washer, locknut and new cotter pin.

## HUB & BEARING
## REPLACE
### EXC. 1987–89 EIGHT PASSENGER CARAVAN & VOYAGER & EXTENDED WHEELBASE MINI RAM VAN

#### Removal

1. Remove steering knuckle as previ-

ously outlined.
2. Remove hub using tool No. C-4811-14, **Fig. 10.**
3. Remove four bearing retainer to knuckle attaching screws, then the bearing retainer.
4. Pry bearing seal from machined recess in knuckle assembly.
5. Remove bearing from knuckle using tool No. C-4811-2, **Fig. 11.**

### Installation

1. Press new bearing into knuckle using tool No. C-4811-4, **Fig. 12.**
2. Install bearing retainer. Torque retainer attaching screws to 20 ft. lbs.
3. Press hub into bearing using tool No. C-4811-11, **Fig. 13.**
4. Position new seal in recess, then install using oil seal installer tool No. C-4698 or equivalent.
5. Install steering knuckle as described under "Steering Knuckle, Replace."

### 1987–89 EIGHT PASSENGER CARAVAN & VOYAGER & EXTENDED WHEELBASE MINI RAM VAN

#### Removal

1. Remove cotter pin, locknut and spring washer.
2. Loosen hub nut with brakes applied. **The hub and drive shaft are splined together through the knuckle (bearing) and retained by the hub nut.**
3. Raise and support vehicle, then remove front wheel and tire assembly.
4. Remove hub nut and washer.
5. Using puller tool C-3894-A or equivalent, disconnect tie rod end steering arm.
6. Remove bolt attaching ball joint stud to steering knuckle.
7. Remove caliper guide pins, then the caliper. Support caliper with wire and position aside. Do not hang by brake hose.
8. Remove rotor, then separate ball joint stud from knuckle assembly. **Care must be taken not to separate the inner CV joint during this procedure. Do not allow driveshaft to**

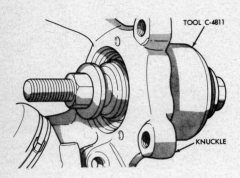

**Fig. 11  Removing bearing from knuckle**

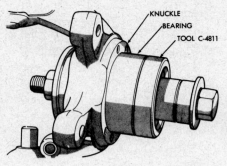

**Fig. 12  Installing bearing into knuckle**

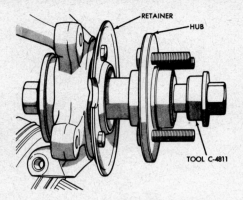

**Fig. 13  Installing hub into knuckle**

hang by inner CV joint, driveshafts must be supported.

9. Remove four hub and bearing assembly attaching screws from front of steering knuckle as shown in **Fig. 14.**
10. Remove hub and bearing assembly.

### Installation

1. Install hub and bearing assembly. Torque bolts in a crossing pattern to 45 ft. lbs. (65 Nm).
2. Using oil seal installer tool C-4698 or equivalent, install seal into knuckle, **Fig. 15.** Lubricate circumference of seal using a suitable lubricant.
3. Using oil seal installer tool C-4698 or equivalent, reverse driving head of tool and install wear sleeve. Lubricate circumference of wear sleeve using a suitable lubricant.
4. Install driveshaft through hub, then steering knuckle assembly on lower control arm ball joint stud.
5. Install ball joint to steering knuckle clamp bolt, and torque bolt to 70 ft. lbs. (95 Nm).
6. Install tie rod end into steering arm, then torque bolt to 35 ft. lbs. (47 Nm) and install cotter pin.
7. Install rotor, then position caliper over rotor and guide hold-down spring under machined guides on knuckle assembly.
8. Install guide pins and torque to 18-26 ft. lbs. (25-35 Nm).
9. Install washer and hub nut, then with brakes applied, torque nut to 180 ft. lbs. (244 Nm).
10. Install spring washer, locknut and cotter pin.

## SWAY BAR
### REPLACE

Some 1984 models may experience a low pitched squeak at the sway bar bushings and mounting cushions in ambient temperatures below 32°F. This noise will occur when the vehicle is bounced up and down, such as when hitting dips, bumps, etc. This problem can be corrected as follows:

1. Remove sway bar as described below.

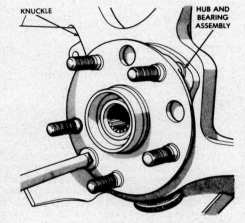

**Fig. 14  Removing hub & bearing assembly**

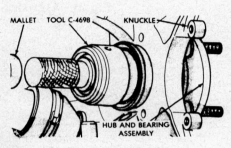

**Fig. 15  Installing seal.**

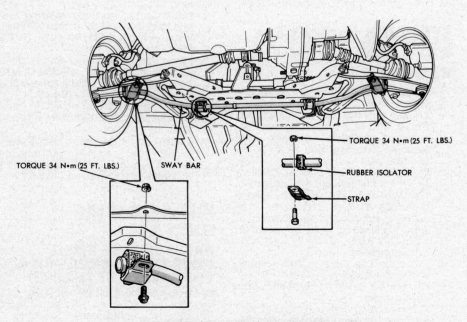

**Fig. 16  Sway bar assembly**

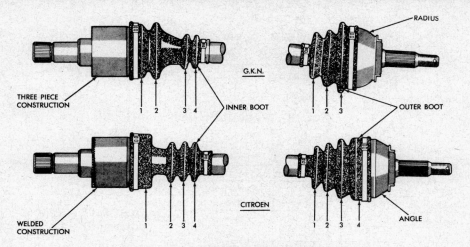

**Fig. 17  Driveshaft identification**

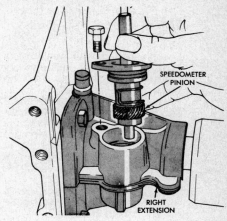

**Fig. 18  Speedometer pinion removal**

2. Remove and discard sway bar cushions.
3. Install new cushions (part No. 4322677, color coded beige), without using any type of lubricant.
4. Remove outer bushings using a hammer or other suitable tool. Do not cut bushings.
5. Clean inner diameter of bushing and bushing mating surface on sway bar.
6. Apply suitable sealant to inner surface of bushing and bushing mating surface on sway bar.
7. Install bushings onto sway bar until approximately ½ inch of bar protrudes at each end.
8. Install sway bar as described below.

## REMOVAL

1. Raise and support vehicle.
2. Remove nuts, bolts and retainers at the control arms, **Fig. 16**.
3. Remove crossmember clamp attaching bolts, then the crossmember clamps.
4. Remove sway bar from vehicle.

## INSTALLATION

1. Position crossmember bushings on sway bar with curved surface up and split to front of vehicle.
2. Position bar assembly onto crossmember, then install clamps and attaching bolts, **Fig. 16**.
3. Position retainers at control arms, then install bolts and attaching nuts.
4. Raise lower control arm to correct position, then torque attaching bolts to 25 ft. lbs.

# DRIVESHAFT IDENTIFICATION

Driveshafts are identified as "Citroen" or "G.K.N." assemblies, **Fig. 17**. Vehicles can be equipped with either of these assemblies, however they should not be intermixed. Procedures for installation and removal of driveshafts are essentially the same for either type assembly used.

# DRIVESHAFTS
## REPLACE
### REMOVAL

1. Remove cotter pin, locknut and spring washer from wheel hub.
2. Loosen hub nut with brakes applied.
3. Raise and support vehicle, then remove wheel and tire assembly.
4. If removing the right driveshaft, the speedometer pinion must be removed prior to driveshaft removal, **Fig. 18**.
5. Remove ball joint stud to steering knuckle clamp bolt, then separate ball joint stud from steering knuckle using a suitable pry bar. **Use caution not to damage ball joint or C/V joint boots.**
6. Separate outer C/V joint splined shaft from hub by holding C/V housing while moving knuckle/hub assembly away. **Do not use pry bar to separate hub from shaft or damage to outer wear sleeve on C/V joint may occur.**
7. Support driveshaft assembly at C/V joint housing and remove by pulling outward on the inner C/V joint housing. Do not pull on the shaft.
8. Remove driveshaft assembly from vehicle.

### INSTALLATION

During any service procedures where knuckle and driveshaft are separated, clean seal and wear sleeve with suitable solvent and apply a suitable lubricant to both components. **Solvent must not touch boot.**
1. Hold inner joint assembly at housing while aligning and guiding the inner joint spline into transaxle.
2. Push knuckle/hub assembly out and install outer C/V joint shaft into hub.
3. Install knuckle assembly on ball joint stud, then the clamp bolt. Torque bolt to 70 ft. lbs. **Steering knuckle clamp**

bolt is "prevailing torque type." Original or equivalent bolt must be installed during assembly.
4. Install speedometer pinion, right driveshaft only, **Fig. 18**.
5. Fill transaxle with suitable transaxle fluid.
6. Install washer and hub nut, then torque hub nut to 180 ft. lbs. Install nut lock and cotter pin.
7. If after installing driveshaft assembly in vehicle the inboard boot appears collapsed or deformed, vent the inner boot by inserting a round tipped, small diameter rod between boot and shaft. As venting occurs, the boot will return to its normal shape.
8. Install wheel and tire assembly. **After installation of driveshaft, check the driveshaft length as outlined in "Driveshaft Length, Adjust" procedure.**

# DRIVESHAFT LENGTH
## ADJUST

1. Position vehicle with wheels straight ahead and body weight distributed on all four tires.
2. Measure direct distance between inner edge of outboard boot to inner edge of inboard boot on both driveshafts. This measurement (dimension "A") should be taken at the bottom (six o'clock position) of driveshafts, **Fig. 19. Damper weights are used on left driveshaft assembly. Before measuring driveshaft length, damper should be removed from shaft. After specified measurement is completed, install damper weight and torque damper weight attaching bolts to 21 ft. lbs. (28 Nm).**
3. Driveshaft length (dimension "A") must be within specifications in chart, **Figs. 20, 21 and 22.** If measurement is not within specifications, engine position must be corrected as follows:

a. Remove load from engine mounts by carefully supporting engine and transaxle assembly using a suitable jack.
b. Loosen right engine mount vertical bolts, then the front engine mount bracket-to-crossmember attaching bolts.
c. Pry engine to right or left as necessary to bring driveshaft length within specifications. **The left engine mount is sleeved over long support bolt and shaft, Fig. 23, to provide lateral adjustment whether or not engine weight is removed.**
d. Torque engine mount vertical bolts to 250 inch lbs. and front engine mount bolts to 40 ft. lbs.
e. Center left engine mount, then recheck driveshaft length.

## INNER CONSTANT VELOCITY JOINT SERVICE

### DISASSEMBLE

Driveshaft assembly should be identified before starting service procedure. Refer to "Driveshaft Identification" procedure.

1. Remove boot clamps, then pull back boot to gain access to the tripod, **Fig. 24.**
2. On G.K.N. units, place driveshaft assembly in vise and hold housing as shown in **Fig. 25.** Lightly compress C/V joint retention spring while bending tabs back with suitable pliers, then remove tripod from housing.
3. On Citroen units, separate tripod from housing by slightly deforming retaining ring at three locations, **Fig. 26.** If necessary, cut retaining ring from housing and install replacement retaining ring by rolling the edge into machined groove in housing with suitable punch. **When removing tripod from housing, secure rollers. After tripod has been removed, secure assembly with tape.**
4. On all models, remove snap ring from end of shaft, then remove tripod using brass punch.

### INSPECTION

Remove grease from assembly and inspect bearing race, tripod components, spring, spring cup and spherical end of connecting shaft for excessive wear or damage and replace if necessary.

### ASSEMBLE

1. Slide small end of boot over shaft, then place clamp over groove on boot, **Fig. 24.**
2. Install tripod on shaft, then lock tripod assembly on shaft by installing retaining ring in shaft groove. **On G.K.N. units, slide tripod on shaft with non-chamfered end facing tripod retainer ring groove.**
3. Distribute packets of special grease provided in boot clamp kit as follows:

a. On G.K.N. units, distribute one packet of grease in the housing and remaining packets into the boot.
b. On Citroen units, distribute 2/3 of a packet of grease into the boot and remaining amount in the housing.
4. Position spring, with spring cup attached to exposed end, into spring pocket. Place a small amount of grease on spring cup.

5. Install tripod into housing as follows:
a. On G.K.N. units, slip tripod into housing and bend retaining tabs down to their original position. Ensure retaining tabs hold tripod in housing.
b. On Citroen units, remove tape holding rollers and needle bearings in place, then install tripod assembly into housing. Reform or install new retainer ring. Ensure

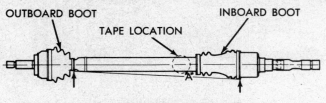

**Fig. 19   Measuring driveshaft**

| Driveshaft Identification | | | "A" Dimension | |
|---|---|---|---|---|
| Type | Side | Tape Color | M.M. | Inch |
| G.K.N. | Right | Green | 542–549 | 21.3–21.6 |
| G.K.N. | Left | Green | 270–285 | 10.6–11.2 |
| A.C.I. | Right | Blue | 520–532 | 20.5–20.9 |
| A.C.I. | Left | Blue | 255–270 | 10.0–10.6 |

**Fig. 20   Driveshaft length specifications. 1984–86**

| Driveshaft Identification | | "A" Dimension | |
|---|---|---|---|
| Type | Side | mm | Inch |
| G.K.N. | Right | 530–538 | 20.9–21.2 |
| | Left | 243–251 | 9.6– 9.9 |

**Fig. 21   Driveshaft length specifications. 1987**

| Driveshaft Identification | | "A" Dimension | |
|---|---|---|---|
| Type | Side | mm | Inch |
| G.K.N. | Right | 542–549 | 21.3–21.6 |
| | Left | 238–253 | 9.4–10.0 |
| Citroen | Right | 520–532 | 20.5–20.9 |
| | Left | 223–238 | 8.8– 9.4 |

**Fig. 22   Driveshaft length specifications. 1988–89**

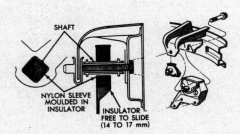

**Fig. 23   Left engine mount adjust**

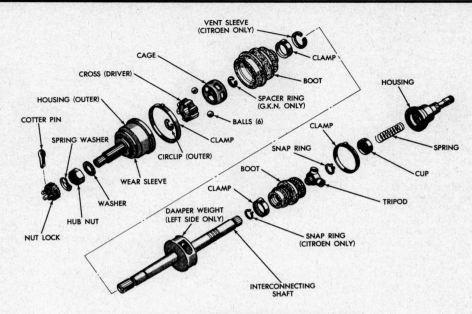

**Fig. 24   Driveshaft components**

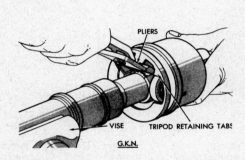

**Fig. 25   Removing inner C/V joint tripod. G.K.N. units**

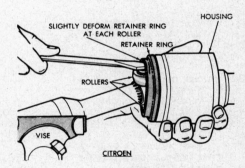

**Fig. 26   Removing inner C/V joint tripod. Citroen units**

retaining collar holds tripod in housing. **If new retainer ring is installed, hold ring in position with two C-clamps and roll the edge into machined groove in housing using a suitable punch.**

6. On all models, ensure proper spring positioning. The spring must remain centered in the housing spring pocket when tripod is installed and seated in the spring cup.

7. Position boot over boot groove in housing, then install clamp.

## OUTER CONSTANT VELOCITY JOINT SERVICE

### DISASSEMBLY

Driveshaft assembly should be identified before starting service procedure. Refer to "Driveshaft Identification" procedure.

1. Remove boot clamps, then pull back boot to gain access to joint, **Fig. 24.**
2. Clean grease from joint.
3. Place driveshaft assembly in suitable vise and support outer joint. Remove outer joint from shaft by tapping top of joint body with a soft hammer, **Fig. 27.**
4. Remove circlip from shaft groove and discard.
5. On G.K.N. units, remove heavy lock ring from shaft only if shaft needs replacement.
6. On all units, if constant velocity joint is operating satisfactorily and grease does not appear contaminated, proceed to "Assembly" procedure.
7. If constant velocity joint is noisy or badly worn, replace entire unit. The repair kit will include boot, clamps, circlip and lubricant. Clean and inspect joint outlined in the following steps.
8. Clean surplus grease and mark relative position of inner cross, cage and

housing with a dab of paint, **Fig. 28.**
9. Hold joint vertically in a soft jawed vise.
10. Press downward on one side of the inner race to tilt cage and remove ball from opposite side, **Fig. 28.** If joint is tight, use a hammer and brass drift to tap inner race. Do not strike the cage. Repeat this step until all balls have been removed. A screwdriver may be used to pry balls loose.
11. Tilt cage assembly vertically and position the two opposing, elongated cage windows in area between ball grooves. Remove cage and inner race assembly by pulling upward from the housing, **Fig. 29.**
12. Rotate inner cross 90° to cage and align one of the race spherical lands with an elongated cage window. Raise land into cage window and remove inner race by swinging outward, **Fig. 30.**

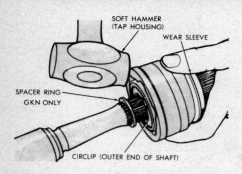

**Fig. 27   Removing outer C/V joint from shaft**

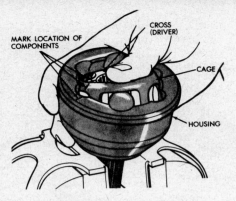

**Fig. 28   Ball removal. Outer C/V joint**

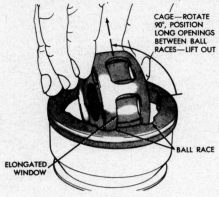

**Fig. 29   Cage & cross assembly removal. Outer C/V joint**

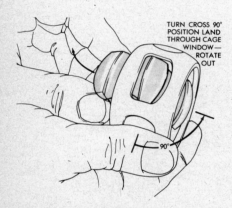

**Fig. 30   Removing cross from cage. Outer C/V joint**

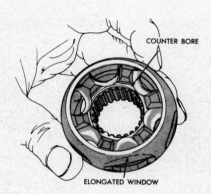

**Fig. 31   Cage & cross assembled. G.K.N. units**

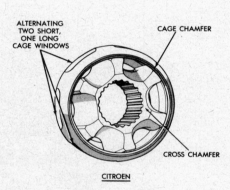

**Fig. 32   Cage & cross assembled. Citroen units**

## INSPECTION

1. Check housing ball races for excessive wear.
2. Check splined shaft and nut threads for damage.
3. Inspect the balls for pitting, cracks, scouring and wearing. Dulling of the surface is normal.
4. Inspect cage for excessive wear on inner and outer spherical surfaces, heavy brinelling of the cage, window cracks and chipping.
5. Inspect inner race (cross) for excessive wear or scoring of ball races.
6. If any of the defects listed in steps 1 through 5 are found, replace the C/V joint assembly as a unit. **Polished areas in races (cross and housing) and cage spheres are normal and do not indicate a need for joint replacement unless they are suspected of causing noise and vibration.**

## ASSEMBLY

1. If removed, position wear sleeve on joint housing, then tap sleeve onto housing using oil seal installer tool No. C-4698.
2. Lightly oil components, then align marks made during disassembly.
3. Align one of the inner race (cross) lands into cage window, then insert race into cage and pivot 90°, **Figs. 31 and 32.**
4. Align opposite elongated cage windows with housing land and insert cage assembly into housing. Pivot cage 90° to complete installation, **Fig. 33. When properly assembled, the cross counter bore should be facing outward from the joint on G.K.N. units, Figs. 31 and 34. On Citroen units, the cross and cage chamfers will be facing outward from the joint, Figs. 32 and 35.**
5. Apply lubricant to ball races between all sides of ball grooves.
6. Insert balls into raceway by tilting cage and inner race assembly.
7. Slide small end of boot over shaft, then place clamp over groove on boot, **Fig. 24.**
8. Insert new circlip in shaft groove. Do not over expand or twist circlip during assembly, **Fig. 36.**
9. Position joint housing on shaft, then engage by tapping sharply with a soft faced mallet.
10. Check to ensure snap ring is properly seated by attempting to pull joint from shaft.
11. Position boot over boot groove in housing, then install clamp.

## STEERING GEAR REPLACE

1. Raise and support vehicle, then remove front wheels.

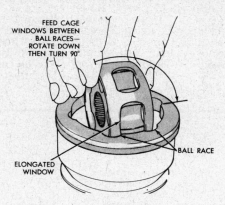

**Fig. 33 Installing cage & cross assembly into housing. Outer C/V joint**

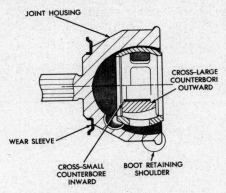

**Fig. 34 Cage & cross installed in housing. G.K.N. units**

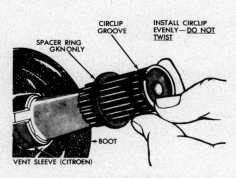

**Fig. 35 Cage & cross installed in housing. Citroen units**

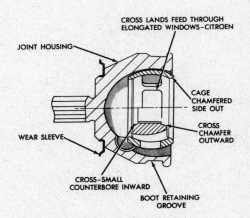

**Fig. 36 Installing circlip. Outer C/V joint**

2. Remove tie rod ends using a suitable puller.
3. On 1984-85, remove steering column as follows:
   a. Disconnect battery ground cable.
   b. On column shift vehicles, disconnect cable rod by prying rod out of grommet in shift lever, then remove cable clip from lower bracket.
   c. Disconnect all wiring connectors at steering column jacket and remove steering wheel center pad.
   d. Disconnect horn electrical connector and horn switch, then remove steering wheel using suitable puller.
   e. Expose steering column bracket, then remove instrument panel steering column cover and lower reinforcement. Remove bezel.
   f. Remove indicator set screw and shift indicator pointer from shift housing.
   g. Remove nuts attaching steering column bracket to instrument panel support, then lower bracket support to floor.

h. Remove four front suspension crossmember attaching bolts, then lower crossmember using suitable jack.
i. Remove coupling assembly to steering gear retaining pin.
j. Remove anti-rotational link from crossmember and air diverter valve bracket from left side of crossmember, if equipped.
k. Pull steering column and steering coupling rearward.
4. On all models, remove splash shields and boot seal shields, then the fluid lines to the pump on power steering gear only.
5. Disconnect tie rod ends from steering knuckles.
6. Remove crossmember to steering gear attaching bolts, then the steering gear from left side of vehicle.
7. Reverse procedure to install noting the following:
   a. For manual gear, make sure master serrations are in line.
   b. The right rear crossmember bolt is a pilot bolt that correctly locates the crossmember. Tighten this bolt

first. Torque all four crossmember bolts to 90 ft. lbs. **Proper torque is very important.**
   c. Torque four bolts attaching steering gear to crossmember to 250 inch lbs.

# POWER STEERING PUMP REPLACE
## 4-135 & 4-153 ENGINES

1. Disconnect battery ground cable.
2. Disconnect vapor separator hose from carburetor, then electrical connector from A/C cycling switch, if equipped.
3. Remove drive belt adjustment locking screw from front of pump, then the pump end hose bracket attaching nut, if equipped.
4. Raise and support vehicle, then disconnect return hose from gear tube and drain oil from pump through open end of hose. **Do not allow hoses to touch hot exhaust manifold or catalyst.**

5. Remove right side splash shield, then disconnect remaining fluid hoses from pump. Plug pump ports and hose ends to prevent contamination.
6. Remove pump lower stud nut and pivot screw.
7. Lower vehicle and remove belt from pulley, then move pump rearward to clear mounting bracket.
8. Remove pump adjustment bracket.
9. Rotate pump clockwise so pump faces rear of vehicle, then remove pump.
10. Reverse procedure to install.

## 4-156 ENGINES

1. Disconnect fluid hoses from pump. Plug pump ports and hose ends to prevent contamination.
2. Remove belt adjustment and pivot bolts, then the belt from pulley groove.
3. Remove pump and mounting bracket from vehicle as an assembly.
4. Reverse procedure to install.

**NOTE:** Refer to the rear of this manual for vehicle manufacturer's special service tool suppliers.

# Specifications

## GENERAL ENGINE SPECIFICATIONS

| Year | Engine CID/Liter | Fuel System | Bore and Stroke Inch (Millimeters) | Comp. Ratio | Horsepower @ RPM | Torque Ft. @ RPM | Normal Oil Pressure Pounds |
|---|---|---|---|---|---|---|---|
| 1987 | 4-135/2.2L | 2 Bbl.① | 3.44 x 3.62 (87.5 x 92) | 9.5 | 91 @ 5200 | 117 @ 2800 | 25-80② |
|  | V6-238/3.9L | 2 Bbl.③ | 3.91 x 3.31 (99.3 x 84) | 9.0 | 125 @ 4000 | 195 @ 2000 | 30-80② |
| 1988 | 4-135/2.2L | 2 Bbl.① | 3.44 x 3.62 (87.5 x 92) | 9.5 | 91 @ 5200 | 117 @ 2800 | 25-80② |
|  | V6-238/3.9L | Fuel Inj. | 3.91 x 3.31 (99.3 x 84) | 9.0 | 125 @ 4000 | 195 @ 2000 | 30-80② |
| 1989 | 4-153/2.5L | Fuel Inj. | 3.44 x 4.09 (87.5 x 104) | 8.9 | 100 @ 4800 | 135 @ 2500 | 25-90② |
|  | V6-238/3.9L | Fuel Inj. | 3.91 x 3.31 (99.3 x 84) | 9.2 | 125 @ 4000 | 195 @ 2000 | 30-80② |

①—Holley 6520 model carburetor.　　②—At 3000 RPM　　③—Holley 6280 model carburetor.

## ALTERNATOR & REGULATOR SPECIFICATIONS

| Year | Identification | Alternator Rated Hot Output Amps | Alternator Field Current 12 Volts @ 80°F. | Alternator Output @ 15 Volts 1250 RPM | Regulator Part Number | Regulator Voltage @ 80°F |
|---|---|---|---|---|---|---|
| 1987 | 5213763 | 78 | 2.5-5 | 56 | — | 13.9-14.4 |
|  | 5226457 | 50/120① | 2.5-5 | 98 | — | 13.9-14.4 |
| 1988 | 5227474 | 75 | 2.5-5 | 30 | — | 13.9-14.4 |
|  | 5227672 | 90 | 2.5-5 | 87 | — | — |
|  | 5227673 | 75 | 2.5-5 | 68 | — | — |
|  | 5227675 | 120 | 2.5-5 | 98 | — | — |
|  | 5233472 | 90 | 2.5-5 | 87 | — | — |
|  | 5233474 | 90 | 2.5-5 | 97 | — | 13.9-14.4 |
|  | 5233508 | 120 | 2.5-5 | 98 | — | 13.9-14.4 |
| 1989 | 5227672 | 90 | 2.5-5 | 87 | — | — |
|  | 5227673 | 75 | 2.5-5 | 68 | — | — |
|  | 5233199 | 120 | 2.5-5 | 98 | — | — |
|  | 5233416 | 75 | 2.5-5 | 68 | — | — |
|  | 5233418 | 90 | 2.5-5 | 87 | — | — |
|  | 5233472 | 90 | 2.5-5 | 87 | — | — |
|  | 5233599 | 98 | 2.5-5 | 120 | — | — |
|  | 5233608 | 120 | 2.5-5 | 98 | — | — |
|  | 5233616 | 75 | 2.5-5 | 30 | — | — |
|  | 5233618 | 90 | 2.5-5 | 75 | — | — |
|  | 5233718 | 90 | 2.5-5 | 75 | — | — |

①—50 amps at idle, 120 amps at rated speed.

## STARTING MOTOR SPECIFICATIONS

| Year | Engine | Model | Identification Number | Cranking Amps Draw Test① | Free Speed Test Amps.② | Free Speed Test Volts | Free Speed Test RPM③ |
|---|---|---|---|---|---|---|---|
| 1987 | 4-135 | Bosch | — | 120-160 | 47 | 11 | 6600 |
|  | 4-135 | Nippondenso | — | 120-160 | 47 | 11 | 6600 |
|  | V6-238 | Chrysler | 4111860 | 180-200 | 90④ | 11 | 5700 |
| 1988 | 4-135 | Bosch | 5227282 | 150-220 | 82 | 11 | 3700 |
|  | V6-238 | Nippondenso | 4379160 | 150-220 | 85 | 11 | 3625 |
| 1989 | 4-153 | Bosch | 5227282 | 150-220 | 85 | 11 | 3700 |
|  | V6-238 | Nippondenso | 4379160 | 150-220 | 82 | 11 | 3625 |

①—Engine should be at normal operating temperature.　　②—Maximum current drawn.　　③—Minimum speed.　　④—Minimum current drawn.

## ENGINE TIGHTENING SPECIFICATIONS*

*Torque specifications are for clean and lightly lubricated threads only. Dry or dirty threads produce increased friction which prevents accurate measurement of tightness.

| Year | Engine | Spark Plugs Ft. Lbs. | Cylinder Head Bolts Ft. Lbs. | Intake Manifold Inch Lbs. | Exhaust Manifold Inch Lbs. | Camshaft Cover Inch Lbs. | Connecting Rod Cap Bolts Ft. Lbs. | Main Bearing Cap Bolts Ft. Lbs. | Flywheel To Crankshaft Ft. Lbs. | Crankshaft Pulley Ft. Lbs. |
|---|---|---|---|---|---|---|---|---|---|---|
| 1987–88 | 4-135 | 26 | ① | 200 | 200 | 105 | ② | ③ | 55 | 50 ⑦ |
| | V6-238 | 30 | 105 | 45 ④ | ⑥ | ⑤ | 45 | 85 | 55 | 135 |
| 1989 | 4-153 | 26 | ① | 200 | 200 | 105 | ② | ③ | 55 | 50 ⑦ |
| | V6-238 | 30 | 105 | 45 ④ | ⑥ | ⑤ | 45 | 85 | 55 | 135 |

① —Torque bolts in four steps: first, to 45 ft. lbs.; second, to 65 ft. lbs.; third, to 65 ft. lbs.; fourth, torque bolts an additional ¼ turn.
② —Torque bolts, first to 40 ft. lbs., then turn bolts an additional ¼ turn each.
③ —Torque bolts, first to 30 ft. lbs., then turn bolts an additional ¼ turn each.
④ —Ft. lbs.
⑤ —Cylinder head cover nut, 80 in. lbs.; cylinder head cover stud, 115 in. lbs.
⑥ —Nut, 15 ft. lbs.; screw, 20 ft. lbs.
⑦ —Crankshaft sprocket bolt.

## WHEEL ALIGNMENT SPECIFICATIONS

| Year | Model | Caster Angle, Degrees Limits | Caster Angle, Degrees Desired | Camber Angle, Degrees Limits | Camber Angle, Degrees Desired | Toe-In Inch |
|---|---|---|---|---|---|---|
| 1987–89 | All | +½ to +2½ ① | +1½ | 0 to +1 | +½ | +⅛ |

① —Maximum left to right differential should not exceed +1¼.

## DRIVE AXLE SPECIFICATIONS

| Year | Model | Ring Gear Size | Carrier Type | Ring Gear & Pinion Backlash Method | Ring Gear & Pinion Backlash Adjustment | Pinion Bearing Preload Method | Pinion Bearing Preload New Bearings Inch Lbs. | Pinion Bearing Preload Used Bearings Inch Lbs. | Differential Bearing Preload Method | Differential Bearing Preload New Bearings Inch Lbs. | Differential Bearing Preload Used Bearings Inch Lbs. |
|---|---|---|---|---|---|---|---|---|---|---|---|
| 1987–89 | All | 7¼ | Integral | Shims | .003-.006 | ① | 10-20 | — | ② | ③ | ③ |
| | All | 8¼ | Integral | Shims | .005-.008 | ① | 10-20 | — | ② | ③ | ③ |

① —Collapsible spacer.
② —Threaded adjuster.
③ —Preload is correct when ring gear and pinion backlash is properly adjusted.

## BRAKE SPECIFICATIONS

| Year | Model | Rear Drum I.D. | Wheel Cyl. Bore Front Disc | Wheel Cyl. Bore Rear Drum | Disc Brake Rotor Nominal Thickness | Disc Brake Rotor Minimum Thickness | Disc Brake Rotor Thickness Variation (Parallelism) | Run Out (TIR) | Finish (Microinch) | Master Cyl. I.D. |
|---|---|---|---|---|---|---|---|---|---|---|
| 1987–89 | All | ① | 2.36 | ② | .861-.871 | .811 | .0005 | .004 | 15-80 | — |

① —Except heavy duty, 9"; heavy duty, 10".
② —Except heavy duty, ¾"; heavy duty, 13/16".

## COOLING SYSTEM & CAPACITY DATA

| Year | Engine | Cooling Capacity Less A/C Qts. | Cooling Capacity With A/C Qts. | Radiator Cap Relief Pressure, Lbs. | Thermo. Opening Temp. Degrees F. (Centigrade) | Fuel Tank Gals. | Engine Oil Refill Qts. | Transmission Oil 4 Speed Pints | Transmission Oil 5 Speed Pints | Transmission Oil Auto. Trans. Qts. |
|---|---|---|---|---|---|---|---|---|---|---|
| 1987 | 4-135 | 9.8 | 9.8 | 14-18 | 195 | ① | 4 | — | 4 ② | 7.8 ② |
| | V6-238 | 14 | 14 | 14-18 | 195 | ① | 5 | — | 4 ② | 8.6 ② |
| 1988 | 4-135 | 9.8 | 9.8 | 14-18 | 195 | ① | 4 | — | 4 ② | 7.8 ② |
| | V6-238 | 14 | 14 | 14-18 | 195 | ① | 4 | — | 4 ② | 8.6 ② |
| 1989 | 4-153 | 9.8 | 9.8 | 14-18 | 195 | ① | 4 | — | 4 ② | 7.8 ② |
| | V6-238 | 14 ③ | 14 ③ | 14-18 | 195 | ① | 3.8 | — | 4 ② | 10.2 ② |

① —Standard fuel tank, 15; optional fuel tank, 22.
② —Transfer case, 4.5 pints.
③ —With 26 inch radiator, 14.3 quarts.

# ELECTRICAL

## INDEX

## FUSE PANEL & FLASHER LOCATION

The fuse panel is located under the left side of the instrument panel.

The hazard and turn signal flashers are located in the fuse panel.

## STARTER
## REPLACE

### 4-135 & 4-153 ENGINES

1. Disconnect battery ground cable.
2. Remove heat shield clamp, then the heat shield if equipped.
3. On 4-135 engines, loosen air pump tube at exhaust manifold, then position tube bracket away from starter motor.
4. On all engines, disconnect battery cable at starter motor and solenoid leads at solenoid.
5. Remove starter to flywheel housing attaching bolts, then the starter.
6. On 4-153 engines, remove starter to engine mounting bracket.
7. Reverse procedure to install.

### V6-238 ENGINE

#### 1987

1. Disconnect battery ground cable.
2. Remove heat shield attaching nut and bolt.
3. Disconnect battery cable at starter motor and solenoid leads at solenoid.
4. Remove starter to flywheel housing attaching bolt and nut.
5. Slide automatic transmission oil cooler tube bracket off stud, if equipped and, on all models, remove starter motor from vehicle.
6. Reverse procedure to install.

#### 1988–89
#### 2 Wheel Drive

1. Disconnect battery ground cable.
2. Remove wire terminal connector from starter.
3. Remove starter-to-bellhousing attaching bolt and nut.
4. Move starter forward to clear lower mounting stud and starter housing nose, then allow starter to come down past the exhaust pipe and remove the starter.

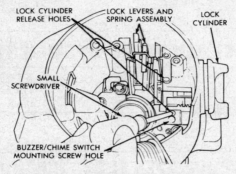

**Fig. 1   Ignition lock removal. Models w/standard column**

5. Reverse procedure to install.

#### 4 Wheel Drive

1. Disconnect battery ground cable.
2. Remove wire terminal connector from starter.
3. Disconnect steering column shaft coupling from steering gear and position aside.
4. Remove starter-to-bellhousing attaching bolt and nut.
5. Move starter forward to clear bellhousing, then lift starter upward and remove from vehicle.
6. Reverse procedure to install.

## IGNITION LOCK
## REPLACE

### MODELS W/STANDARD COLUMN

1. Disconnect battery ground cable.
2. Remove turn signal switch as described under "Turn Signal/Hazard Warning Switch, Replace."
3. Disconnect horn and ignition key lamp wires, then remove ignition key lamp attaching screw and lamp.
4. Remove four screws attaching upper bearing housing to lock housing, then remove snap ring from upper end of steering shaft and remove upper bearing housing.
5. Remove lock plate spring and lock plate from steering shaft.
6. Position lock cylinder in Lock position,

then remove ignition key.
7. Remove screw, then lift out buzzer/chime switch.
8. Remove screws attaching ignition switch.
9. Remove ignition switch by rotating the switch 90 degrees on the rod and sliding off rod.
10. Remove dimmer switch.
11. Remove screws attaching bell crank, then slide bell crank up into the lock housing until it can be disconnected from the ignition switch actuator rod.
12. Place lock cylinder into LOCK position, then insert two small screwdrivers into both lock cylinder release holes and push into release spring loaded lock retainers, **Fig. 1.**
13. Grasp lock lever and spring assembly and pull straight out of housing.
14. Remove four lock housing to column jacket attaching screws, then the lock housing plate and housing from jacket.
15. Turn lock housing 90 degrees to disengage from ignition switch actuator rod, then remove lock housing.
16. Reverse procedure to install.

### MODELS W/TILT COLUMN

1. Disconnect battery ground cable.
2. Remove turn signal switch as described under "Turn Signal Switch, Replace."
3. Remove ignition key lamp.
4. Position ignition lock cylinder in the Lock position, then remove ignition key.
5. Insert a thin screwdriver into lock cylinder release slot and depress spring latch which releases lock cylinder, then grasp lock cylinder and remove from column, **Fig. 2.**
6. Reverse procedure to install.

## IGNITION SWITCH
## REPLACE

1. Disconnect battery ground cable.
2. Remove left lower instrument panel cover.
3. If equipped with automatic transmission, disconnect gear position indicator cable.
4. Remove lower panel reinforcement, then steering column to support bracket attaching nuts.

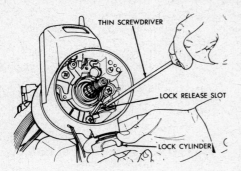

Fig. 2  Ignition lock removal. Models w/tilt column

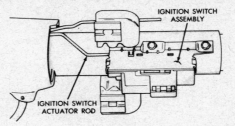

Fig. 3  Ignition switch replacement

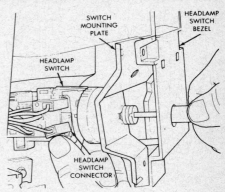

Fig. 4  Light switch removal

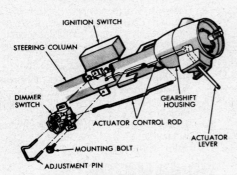

Fig. 5  Dimmer switch replacement

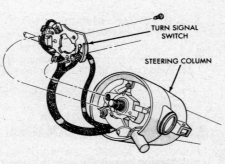

Fig. 6  Turn signal/hazard switch replacement

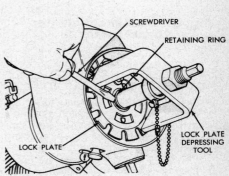

Fig. 7  Lock plate removal. Models w/tilt column

5. Lower column and disconnect ignition switch electrical connector.
6. Position ignition lock cylinder in the Lock position.
7. Tape ignition switch rod to steering column to prevent rod from falling out of lock cylinder assembly.
8. Remove two ignition switch attaching screws, then the switch, **Fig. 3**.
9. Reverse procedure to install.

## STEERING WHEEL REPLACE

1. Disconnect battery ground cable.
2. On standard steering wheels, remove two horn pad assembly attaching screws.
3. On premium steering wheels, pry off horn pad using suitable screwdriver.
4. Remove steering wheel nut.
5. Remove steering wheel using puller No. C-3428B or equivalent.
6. Reverse procedure to install. Torque steering wheel attaching nut to 45 ft. lbs.

## LIGHT SWITCH REPLACE

1. Disconnect battery ground cable.
2. Remove steering column cover and silencer pad (if equipped).
3. Remove instrument cluster bezel.
4. Remove light switch bezel assembly attaching screws.

5. Remove headlight and accessory switch trim bezel, **Fig. 4**.
6. Remove four switch plate to lower panel attaching screws.
7. Pull switch assembly rearward, then disconnect switch electrical connectors.
8. Remove switch knob and stem by depressing button on switch.
9. Remove two headlight switch plate to switch plate assembly attaching screws, then the headlight switch retainer and switch.
10. Reverse procedure to install.

## DIMMER SWITCH REPLACE

1. Disconnect battery ground cable.
2. Remove left lower instrument panel cover, then tape dimmer switch rod to steering column to prevent rod from falling out of notch in actuator lever.
3. Remove switch to column attaching screws.
4. Disconnect switch electrical connector, then remove switch from steering column, **Fig. 5**.
5. Reverse procedure to install. During installation, gently push up on switch to take up slack on rod.

## TURN SIGNAL/HAZARD WARNING SWITCH REPLACE

1. Remove steering wheel. Refer to "Steering Wheel, Replace" procedure.
2. Pry off wiring trough from steering col-

umn, then disconnect turn signal/hazard warning switch electrical connector.
3. On models equipped with standard column, proceed as follows:
   a. Remove wiper/washer switch-to-turn signal switch pivot attaching screw. Leave turn signal lever in its installed position.
   b. Remove 3 bearing retainer and turn signal switch-to-upper bearing housing attaching screws, **Fig. 6**.
4. On models equipped with tilt column, proceed as follows:
   a. Remove plastic cover, if equipped, from lock plate.
   b. Depress lock plate using tool No. C-4156 and pry retaining ring out of groove with a suitable screwdriver, **Fig. 7**. **The full load of the upper bearing spring should not be relieved. If the full load is relieved, the retaining ring will turn too easily and make removal difficult.**
   c. Remove lock plate, cancelling cam and upper bearing spring, then place turn signal switch in right turn position.
   d. Remove screw attaching link between turn signal switch and wiper/washer switch pivot.
   e. Remove hazard warning switch knob attaching screw, then the 3

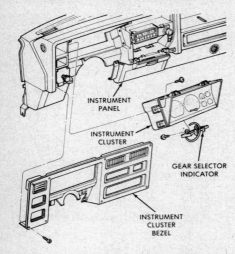

**Fig. 8  Instrument cluster & bezel removal**

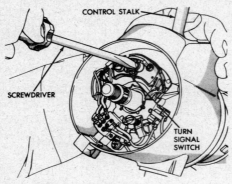

**Fig. 9  Washer/wiper switch removal**

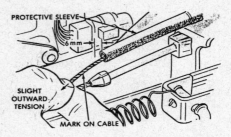

**Fig. 10  Speed control cable adjustment**

turn signal switch-to-steering column attaching screws.

5. On all models, remove turn signal/hazard warning switch assembly by gently pulling switch up from column while straightening and guiding wires up through column opening, **Fig. 6.**

6. Reverse procedure to install.

## INSTRUMENT CLUSTER
### REPLACE

1. Disconnect battery ground cable.
2. Remove steering column cover.
3. Remove instrument cluster bezel, **Fig. 8.**
4. On models equipped with automatic transmission, disconnect gearshift indicator cable from steering column.
5. Remove cluster to instrument panel attaching screws.
6. Pull cluster rearward and disconnect electrical connectors and speedometer cable.
7. Move cluster past steering wheel and remove cluster.
8. Reverse procedure to install.

## WASHER/WIPER SWITCH
### REPLACE

#### MODELS W/STANDARD COLUMN

1. Disconnect battery ground cable.
2. On models equipped with column shift, disconnect link rod.
3. Remove steering shaft coupling to wormshaft roll pin.
4. Disconnect electrical connectors from steering column jacket.
5. Disconnect horn wires and remove horn switch.
6. Remove steering wheel.
7. Pry out wiring trough retainers and lift off wiring trough.
8. Remove shift lever.

9. Remove two screws attaching lock housing cover to the lock housing.
10. Remove lock housing cover.
11. Remove washer/wiper switch assembly, **Fig. 9.**
12. Reverse procedure to install.

### MODELS W/TILT COLUMN

1. Remove steering wheel. Refer to "Steering Wheel, Replace" procedure.
2. Remove steering column cover, silencer and lower reinforcement.
3. Pry off wiring trough from steering column, then remove plastic cover from lock plate, if equipped.
4. Depress lock plate using tool No. C-4156 and pry retaining ring out of groove with screwdriver, **Fig. 7. Full load of upper bearing spring should not be relieved. If full load is relieved, retaining ring will turn too easily, making removal more difficult.**
5. Remove lock plate, cancelling cam and upper bearing spring, then remove switch lever actuator attaching screw and lever.
6. Push in hazard warning knob, then remove by turning knob counterclockwise.
7. Disconnect washer/wiper switch electrical connector, then the intermittent wipe switch and speed control electrical connectors if equipped.
8. Remove three turn signal switch attaching screws, then place selector lever in "1" position. Wrap a piece of tape around electrical connector and wires to prevent snagging during switch removal.
9. Remove turn signal switch and wiring, then the ignition key lamp.
10. Position ignition lock cylinder in the Lock position, then insert a small diameter screwdriver into lock cylinder release holes and push inward until spring loaded lock cylinder retainers release, **Fig. 2.**
11. Remove buzzer/chime switch by inserting a bent piece of stiff wire into the exposed loop of the switch and pull straight out. **Use caution not to drop switch into steering column.**
12. Remove three switch housing cover attaching screws, then the housing cover.

13. Remove washer/wiper switch pivot pin using a suitable punch, then remove washer/wiper switch assembly.
14. Pull hider up control lever, then remove control lever sleeve to washer/wiper switch attaching screws, **Fig. 9. Use tape to secure dimmer switch rod in place.**
15. Remove washer/wiper switch control knob from end of control lever.
16. Rotate control lever shaft clockwise and pull shaft straight out of switch.
17. Reverse procedure to install.

## WIPER MOTOR
### REPLACE

1. Disconnect battery ground cable.
2. Disconnect electrical connectors from wiper motor.
3. Remove three motor attaching nuts.
4. Remove cowl screen.
5. Hold drive crank, then remove crank nut.
6. Remove wiper motor from vehicle.
7. Reverse procedure to install.

## RADIO
### REPLACE

1. Disconnect battery ground cable.
2. Remove steering column cover, then the instrument cluster bezel, **Fig. 8.**
3. Remove two radio to instrument panel attaching screws, then pull radio through front face of panel.
4. Disconnect radio electrical connector, antenna lead and ground strap.
5. Reverse procedure to install.

## BLOWER MOTOR
### REPLACE

1. Disconnect battery ground cable.
2. Remove lower instrument panel module as follows:
   a. Remove steering column cover and silencer pad (if equipped).
   b. Remove ashtray and intermittent wipe control (if equipped) from bracket.
   c. Remove lower instrument panel module attaching screw, located to right of steering column at cluster bezel.
   d. Remove center air distribution duct

attaching screws from bottom of lower instrument panel module.
  e. Remove panel support screw from bottom of lower instrument panel module.
  f. Remove lower instrument panel module attaching screw located near ashtray location.
  g. Open glove box door, then remove screws attaching top edge of lower instrument panel module.
  h. Move module rearward and down until sufficient room is obtained to remove wiring harness and antenna cable from clips.
  i. Disconnect speaker wires and glove box light switch wire, then remove module.
3. On models equipped with A/C disconnect two vacuum lines from recirculating air door actuator.
4. On all models, disconnect blower motor wire, then remove blower housing to unit cover attaching screws and the cover.
5. Remove blower motor attaching screws, then the blower motor.
6. Reverse procedure to install.

# HEATER CORE
## REPLACE

1. Disconnect battery ground cable.
2. Discharge A/C system (if equipped).
3. Remove lower instrument panel module. Refer to step 2 under "Blower Motor, Replace" for procedure.
4. Remove heater A/C unit as follows:
   a. Remove center air distribution duct.
   b. Temporarily tape wiring harness aside.
   c. Remove antenna cable from retaining clip at right end of heater A/C unit.
   d. Disconnect blower motor lead wire, then remove terminal insulator retainer from heater A/C unit support brace.

  e. Disconnect demister hoses from tee at top of heater A/C unit.
  f. Disconnect vacuum hose harness connector, then the vacuum feed line.
  g. Disconnect temperature control cable flag retainer, then remove self-adjusting clip from blend air door crank.
  h. Drain engine cooling system, then disconnect refrigerant lines and remove expansion valve. **Plug all openings to prevent contamination of A/C system.**
  i. Disconnect heater hoses, then plug heater core inlet and outlet openings.
  j. Remove A/C condenser drainage tube.
  k. Remove four heater A/C unit attaching nuts from rear engine compartment dash panel.
  l. Remove heater A/C unit support brace attaching screw, then swing brace to the left.
  m. Pull heater A/C unit rearward until attaching studs clear the dashboard, then allow unit to drop down. Rotate unit in such a way so the attaching studs are facing downwards, and remove unit.
5. Remove heater A/C unit top cover.
6. Remove heater core bracket attaching screw, then the heater core.
7. Reverse procedure to install.

# SPEED CONTROL
## ADJUST
### LOCK-IN SCREW ADJUSTMENT

**Lock-in accuracy can be affected by poor engine performance, overloaded vehicle, or improper slack in throttle control cable.**
1. If the above note has been taken into consideration and vehicle speed still varies or drops more than 2-3 mph

when speed control is activated, proceed as follows:
   a. Turn lock-in adjusting screw counterclockwise approximately $1/4$ turn for every 1 mph out of adjustment.
2. If vehicle speed increases more than 2-3 mph when speed control is activated, proceed as follows:
   a. Turn lock-in adjusting screw clockwise approximately $1/4$ turn for every 1 mph out of adjustment. **The above adjustments should not exceed two turns in either direction, or damage to unit may occur.**

### SPEED CONTROL CABLE ADJUSTMENT
#### 4-135 & 1987 V6-238

1. Start and operate engine until normal operating temperature is reached.
2. Remove clevis retaining clip.
3. Clearance between the throttle stud and cable clevis should be $3/32$ inch.
4. To adjust, remove cable retaining clip at throttle bracket.
5. Pull all slack out of cable using a $3/32$ inch drill to adjust clearance.
6. Do not pull cable excessively, that it moves throttle away from curb idle position.
7. Install cable retaining clip onto throttle bracket.
8. Tighten clip at cable support bracket to 45 inch lbs.

#### 1988 V6-238

1. Grip cable core wire and lightly push toward servo.
2. Mark cable next to protective sleeve while lightly holding cable toward servo.
3. Pull core wire away from servo. Gap between protective sleeve and mark should be .24 inches, **Fig. 10.**
4. If cable requires adjustment, remove adjustment clip and push protective sleeve into housing to decrease gap or pull out of housing to increase gap.
5. Install adjustment clip.

# DODGE DAKOTA
# 4-135 (2.2L) ENGINE

**NOTE:** Refer to "4-135 (2.2L) Engine" in the Dodge Caravan, Mini Ram Van & Ply. Voyager chapter for service procedures not covered in this section.

## INDEX

| TORQUE | | |
|---|---|---|
| LET | FT.LBS. | N·m |
| A | 30 | 41 |
| B | 40 | 54 |
| C | 50 | 68 |
| D | 70 | 95 |
| E | 75 | 102 |

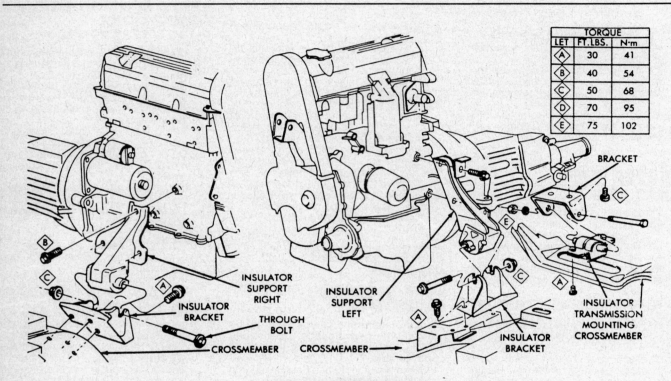

INSULATOR SUPPORT RIGHT — INSULATOR BRACKET — THROUGH BOLT — CROSSMEMBER — INSULATOR SUPPORT LEFT — CROSSMEMBER — INSULATOR BRACKET — BRACKET — INSULATOR TRANSMISSION MOUNTING CROSSMEMBER

**Fig. 1   Engine mount**

## ENGINE MOUNTS
## REPLACE
### FRONT MOUNTS

1. Disconnect battery ground cable.
2. Raise and support vehicle.
3. Remove insulator to crossmember bracket through bolts, **Fig. 1.**
4. Using suitable lifting device, raise engine slightly, then remove insulator.
5. Reverse procedure to install. Refer to **Fig. 1,** for torque specifications.

### REAR MOUNT

1. Raise and support vehicle.
2. Using suitable transmission jack, raise rear of transmission and engine slightly.
3. Remove rear mount through bolt, then screws and insulator from crossmem-

ber.
4. Remove insulator from top face of transmission mounting crossmember.
5. Reverse procedure to install. Refer to **Fig. 1,** for torque specifications.

## ENGINE
## REPLACE

1. Scribe hood hinge outlines on hood, then remove hood.
2. Drain cooling system, remove battery and air cleaner.
3. Disconnect all coolant hoses, then remove radiator.
4. Carefully discharge refrigerant from A/C system, if equipped.
5. Disconnect vacuum lines, remove distributor cap and wiring.
6. Remove carburetor, linkage, starter

wires and oil pressure wire.
7. Disconnect and cap A/C and power steering lines, if equipped.
8. Remove starter motor, alternator, charcoal canister and horns.
9. Disconnect exhaust pipe from exhaust manifold.
10. Remove front engine mount bolts.
11. Install suitable engine lifting equipment onto engine lifting eyes.
12. Lift engine until front engine mount insulators clear crossmember retaining brackets.
13. Place a suitable jack under transmission assembly.
14. Disconnect clutch release mechanism and remove transmission to clutch housing attaching bolts. Move engine forward until drive pinion shaft clears clutch disc.
15. Remove engine from vehicle.
16. Reverse procedure to install.

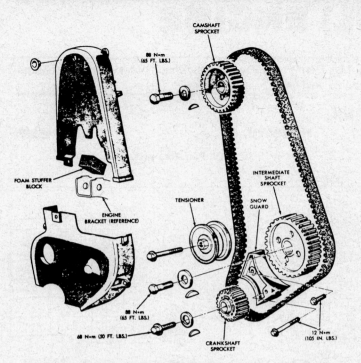

**Fig. A   Timing belt cover, belt & sprockets**

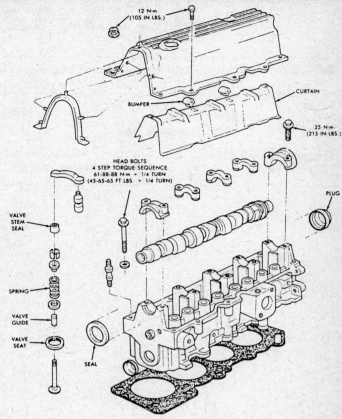

**Fig. B   Cylinder head & valve assembly**

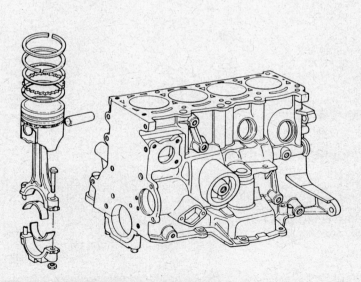

**Fig. C   Cylinder block & connecting rod assembly**

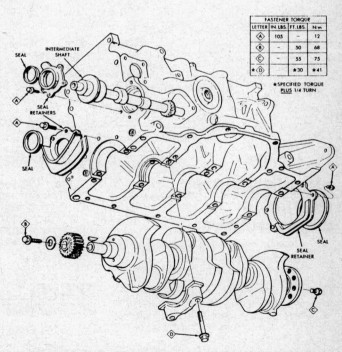

**Fig. D   Crankshaft, intermediate shaft & oil seals**

# 4-153 (2.5L) ENGINE

**NOTE:** Refer to "4-153 (2.5L) Engine" in the Dodge Caravan, Mini Ram Van & Ply. Voyager chapter for service procedures not covered in this section.

## INDEX

| TORQUE | | |
|---|---|---|
| LET | FT.LBS. | N·m |
| Ⓐ | 30 | 41 |
| Ⓑ | 40 | 54 |
| Ⓒ | 50 | 68 |
| Ⓓ | 70 | 95 |
| Ⓔ | 75 | 102 |

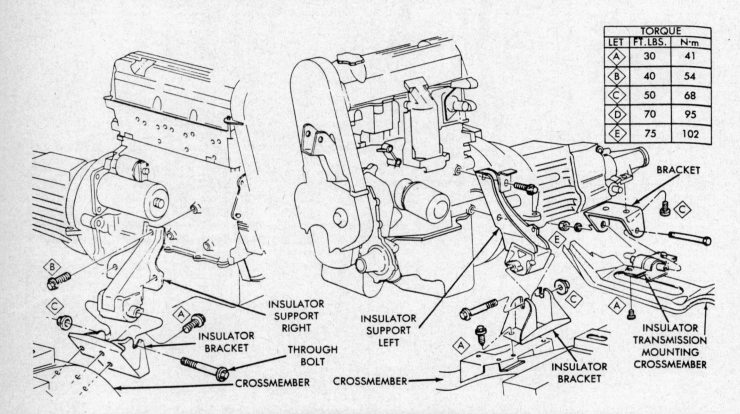

**Fig. 1  Engine mount replacement**

# ENGINE MOUNTS
## REPLACE
### FRONT MOUNTS

1. Disconnect battery ground cable.
2. Raise and support vehicle.
3. Remove insulator-to-crossmember bracket through bolts, **Fig. 1.**
4. Using suitable lifting device, raise engine slightly, then remove insulator.
5. Reverse procedure to install. Refer to **Fig. 1,** for torque specifications.

### REAR MOUNTS

1. Raise and support vehicle.
2. Using suitable transmission jack, raise rear of transmission and engine slightly.
3. Remove rear mount through bolt, then the screws and insulator from crossmember.
4. Remove insulator from top face of transmission mounting crossmember.
5. Reverse procedure to install. Refer to **Fig. 1,** for torque specifications.

# ENGINE
## REPLACE

1. Scribe hood hinge locations and remove hood.
2. Drain cooling system, then remove battery and air cleaner assembly.
3. Disconnect all coolant hoses, then remove radiator.
4. Discharge refrigerant from A/C system, if equipped.
5. Disconnect vacuum lines, remove distributor cap and wiring.
6. Remove throttle body, linkage, starter wires and oil pressure wire.
7. Disconnect and plug A/C and power steering lines, if equipped.
8. Remove starter motor, alternator, charcoal canister and horns.
9. Disconnect exhaust pipe from exhaust manifold.
10. Remove front engine mount bolts.
11. Install suitable engine lifting equipment onto engine lifting eyes.
12. Lift engine until front engine mount insulators clear crossmember retaining brackets.
13. Place a suitable jack under transmission assembly.
14. Disconnect clutch release mechanism and remove transmission to clutch housing attaching bolts. Move engine forward until drive pinion shaft clears clutch disc.

15. Remove engine from vehicle.
16. Reverse procedure to install.

## OIL PAN
### REPLACE

Raising the left side of engine is necessary for oil pan removal.
1. Disconnect air pump relief valve hose.
2. Raise and support vehicle, then drain engine oil.
3. Remove clutch housing block strut, **Fig. 2**, then the lower cover.
4. Remove lower radiator hose support

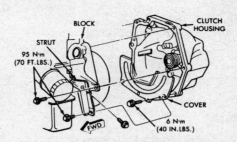

**Fig. 2   Clutch housing block strut removal**

bracket.
5. Loosen the following:
   a. Right insulator-to-bracket through bolt to relieve tension only.
   b. Left insulator-to-bracket through bolt enough to clear bracket.
   c. Transmission to crossmember mounting bracket.
6. Rotate left side of engine up slightly and remove oil pan.
7. Reverse procedure to install. Apply RTV to oil pan end seals, at junction of end seal, seal retainer and engine block. Torque oil pan bolts to 200 inch lbs. and clutch housing strut bolt to 70 ft. lbs.

# V6-238 (3.9L) ENGINE

## INDEX

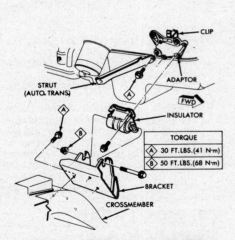

**Fig. 1   Right front engine mount. 2 wheel drive models**

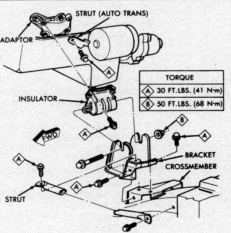

**Fig. 2   Left front engine mount. 2 wheel drive models**

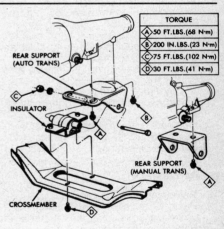

**Fig. 3   Rear engine mount. 2 wheel drive models**

## ENGINE MOUNTS
### REPLACE
#### 2 WHEEL DRIVE MODELS
##### Front Mounts

1. Raise hood and position fan to assure clearance for radiator top tank and hose.
2. Raise and support vehicle.
3. Install suitable engine lifting equipment onto engine.

4. Remove attaching bolts and washers from adapter and insulator through bolts, **Figs. 1 and 2**.
5. Raise engine enough to remove mount.
6. Reverse procedure to install. Refer to **Figs. 1 and 2**, for torque specifications.

##### Rear Mount

1. With vehicle raised and supported, position a transmission jack and raise rear of transmission and engine as-

semblies slightly.
2. Remove rear mount through bolt and attaching screws to frame crossmember, **Fig. 3**.
3. Raise rear of transmission enough to provide mount to crossmember clearance, then remove mount.
4. Reverse procedure to install. Refer to **Fig. 3**, for torque specifications.

#### 4 WHEEL DRIVE MODELS
##### Front Mounts

1. Raise hood and position fan to assure

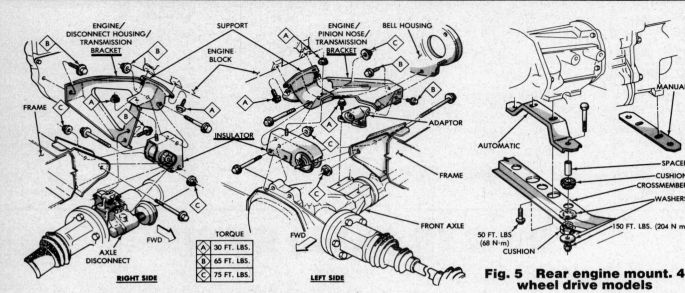

Fig. 4   Front engine mounts. 4 wheel drive models

TORQUE

| A | 30 FT. LBS. |
| B | 65 FT. LBS. |
| C | 75 FT. LBS. |

Fig. 5   Rear engine mount. 4 wheel drive models

clearance for radiator top tank and hose.
2. Install suitable lifting device to engine and raise engine slightly.
3. Install front axle lifting device and raise front axle slightly.
4. Remove mount through bolt, nut and washer assembly attaching engine mount bracket to insulator bracket, then raise engine slightly to clear insulator bracket stud.
5. On left side, remove insulator to axle carrier through bolt, **Fig. 4.**
6. On right side, remove insulator to axle disconnect housing through bolt, **Fig. 4.**
7. On both side, remove insulator to frame through bolt, then the insulator.
8. Reverse procedure to install. Refer to **Fig. 4,** for torque specifications.

### Rear Mount
1. Raise and support vehicle.
2. Position suitable transmission jack under transmission, then raise rear of transmission slightly.
3. Remove rear mount support bracket to transmission attaching bolts, **Fig. 5.**
4. Remove mount through bolt, spacers, cushions, washers and support bracket from crossmember.
5. Reverse procedure to install. Refer to **Fig. 5,** for torque specifications.

## ENGINE
## REPLACE

1. Scribe hood hinge outlines on hood, then remove hood.
2. Drain cooling system and remove battery and air cleaner.
3. Remove heater and radiator hoses, then the radiator.
4. Carefully discharge refrigerant from A/C system (if equipped).
5. Remove vacuum lines, distributor cap

and all electrical connectors.
6. Remove carburetor linkage, starter wires and oil pressure switch wires.
7. Disconnect A/C lines and hoses. Disconnect and cap power steering hoses.
8. Remove starter motor, alternator, charcoal canister and horns.
9. Disconnect exhaust pipe from exhaust manifold.
10. Remove bellhousing attaching bolts and inspection plate.
11. Attach a suitable C-clamp onto front bottom of torque converter housing to prevent converter from coming out.
12. Remove torque converter drive plate attaching bolts. Mark drive plate and torque converter for installation.
13. Place a suitable jack under transmission assembly.
14. Disconnect engine from torque converter drive plate.
15. Install suitable engine lifting equipment onto engine lifting eyes.
16. On 2 wheel drive models, remove engine front mount bolts.
17. On 4 wheel drive models, proceed as follows:
    a. Working on left side of vehicle, remove starter, then the two screws attaching bracket to transmission bellhousing and two bracket to pinion nose adapter screws. Separate engine from insulator by removing upper nut, washer and through bolt from engine support bracket.
    b. Working on right side of vehicle, remove two bracket to axle disconnect housing attaching bolts and one bracket to bellhousing attaching bolt. Separate engine from insulator by removing upper nut, washer and through bolt from engine support bracket.
18. Remove engine from vehicle.
19. Reverse procedure to install.

## ROCKER ARM & SHAFT
## REPLACE

1. Disconnect spark plug wires from spark plugs.
2. Disconnect PCV hose and fuel evaporation control system hoses from cylinder head cover.
3. Remove cylinder head cover and gasket.
4. Remove four rocker shaft bolts and retainers.
5. Remove rocker arm and shaft assembly.
6. If rocker arm assemblies are disassembled for cleaning or replacement, refer to **Fig. 6,** for rocker arm identification and **Fig. 7,** for positioning on the shaft. **On engines with exhaust valve rotators, exhaust rocker arm must have relief for clearance.**
7. Reverse procedure to install. Torque bolts to 200 inch lbs.

## CYLINDER HEAD
## REPLACE

1. Drain cooling system and disconnect battery ground cable.
2. Remove alternator and carburetor air cleaner, then disconnect fuel line.
3. Disconnect accelerator linkage.
4. Remove distributor cap and wires.
5. Disconnect coil wires, heat indicator sending unit wire, heater hoses and bypass hose.
6. Remove cylinder head cover and gasket.
7. Remove intake manifold and carburetor as an assembly.
8. Remove exhaust manifolds.
9. Remove rocker arm and shaft assemblies.
10. Remove pushrods. **Identify pushrods to ensure installation in origi-**

ROCKER ARM – "LEFT"    ROCKER ARM – "RIGHT"

RELIEVED FOR ROTATOR
CLEARANCE

INTAKE ROCKER ARM    EXHAUST ROCKER ARM

**Fig. 6   Intake & exhaust rocker arm identification**

nal locations.
11. Remove eight cylinder head bolts from each cylinder head, then the cylinder heads.
12. Reverse procedure to install. Torque cylinder head bolts to 50 ft. lbs., in sequence shown in **Fig 8**. Repeat procedure and torque all cylinder head bolts in sequence to 105 ft. lbs. When installing pushrods, rocker arm and shaft assemblies, ensure the word NOTCH on the end of the rocker shaft is pointing to the centerline of the engine and toward the front of the engine on the left bank and to the rear on the right bank. Ensure to install the long stamped steel retainers in the number two and four positions, torque to 200 inch lbs. When installing intake manifold, coat intake manifold side gaskets lightly with sealer part No. 4318035 or equivalent, **Fig. 9**. Install side gaskets onto cylinder head. Clean cylinder block front and rear gasket surfaces using a suitable solvent. Apply a thin, uniform coating of a quick drying cement to the intake manifold front and rear gaskets and cylinder block gasket surface. When installing gaskets, the center hole in the gasket must engage dowels in cylinder block. End holes in the seals must be locked into tangs of head gasket. Carefully install the front and rear intake manifold gaskets. Place a drop, approximately 1/4 inch in diameter, of rubber sealer part No. 4318025 or equivalent, onto each of the four manifold to cylinder head gasket corners, **Fig. 9**. Carefully lower intake manifold into position on the block and cylinder heads. After the intake manifold is in place, check to see if seals are correct in place. Install the twelve attaching bolts finger tight first. Torque bolts one through four to 25 ft. lbs. and remaining bolts to 25 ft. lbs. in sequence shown in, **Fig. 10.**. Retorque bolts one through four to 40 ft. lbs. and remaining bolts to 40 ft. lbs., in sequence shown in, **Fig. 10.**

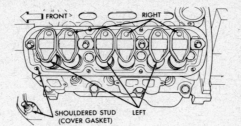

FRONT    RIGHT

SHOULDERED STUD    LEFT
(COVER GASKET)

**Fig. 7   Rocker arm location, left bank**

# VALVES & VALVE SPRINGS
## REPLACE

1. With cylinder head removed, compress valve springs using tool C-3422-A or equivalent.
2. Remove valve retaining locks, valve spring retainers, valve stem cup seals and valve springs.
3. Before removing valves, remove any burrs from the valve stem lock grooves to prevent damage to the valve guides. Identify valves to ensure installation in original locations.
4. Reverse procedure to install.

# VALVE TIMING CHECK

1. Turn crankshaft until No. 6 exhaust valve is closing and No. 6 intake valve is opening.
2. Insert a 1/4 inch spacer between rocker arm pad and stem tip of No. 1 intake valve. Allow spring load to bleed valve tappet down, giving in effect a solid tappet.
3. Install a suitable dial indicator so plunger contacts valve spring retainer as nearly perpendicular as possible. Zero dial indicator.
4. Rotate crankshaft clockwise until the valve has lifted .010 inch as indicated by the dial indicator. Do not turn crankshaft any further clockwise as valve spring might bottom and result in serious damage.
5. The timing of the crankshaft pulley should now read from 10 degrees before top dead center to 2 degrees after top dead center. Remove spacer.
6. If reading is not as specified, check sprocket index marks, timing chain for wear and accuracy of DC mark on timing indicator.

# TIMING CHAIN
## REPLACE

1. Drain cooling system.
2. Remove water pump.
3. Remove power steering pump.
4. Remove pulley from vibration damper and bolt and washer securing vibration damper on crankshaft.
5. Remove vibration damper.
6. Remove fuel lines and fuel pump.
7. Loosen oil pan bolts and remove the front bolts at each side.

**Fig. 8   Cylinder head bolt tightening sequence**

8. Remove timing chain case cover and gasket.
9. Place a scale next to the timing chain so that any movement of the chain can be measured.
10. Place a torque wrench and socket over camshaft sprocket attaching bolts and apply torque in direction of crankshaft rotation to take up slack; 30 ft. lbs. with cylinder head installed or 15 ft. lbs. with cylinder head removed. With a torque applied to the camshaft sprocket bolt, crankshaft should not be permitted to move.
11. Holding a scale with dimensional reading even with edge of a chain link, apply torque in reverse direction. Apply torque amount as stated in step 10 and note amount of chain movement.
12. If chain movement is less than 1/8 inch, timing chain is satisfactory.
13. If chain is not satisfactory, align timing marks as shown in **Fig. 11**, then remove camshaft sprocket attaching cup washer, fuel pump eccentric, timing chain and camshaft and crankshaft sprockets attached.
14. Ensure timing marks are still properly aligned, then install new timing chain and sprockets.
15. Install fuel pump eccentric, cup washer and camshaft bolt. Torque bolt to 35 ft.
16. Reverse procedure to install.

# CAMSHAFT
## REPLACE

1. With engine removed from vehicle, remove rocker arm and shaft assemblies.
2. Remove intake manifold, then the pushrods and lifters. Identify each pushrod and lifter for assembly reference.
3. Remove distributor and lift out oil pump and distributor driveshaft.
4. Remove timing chain, then the camshaft thrust plate. Note location of chain oil tab.
5. Remove camshaft.
6. Reverse procedure to install. Torque thrust plate bolt to 210 inch lbs. and camshaft bolt to 35 ft. lbs.

# PISTONS & CONNECTING RODS

Before installing pistons and connecting

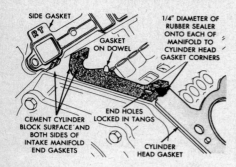

**Fig. 9   Intake manifold sealing**

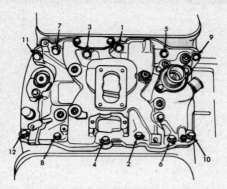

**Fig. 10   Intake manifold bolt tightening sequence**

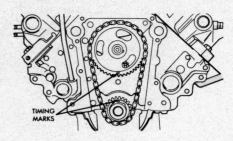

**Fig. 11   Aligning valve timing marks**

rods, ensure that the compression ring gaps are staggered so that neither is in line with the oil rail gap. Install piston and connecting rod assembly into engine with notch or groove on top of piston facing front of engine and the larger chamfer on connecting rod bore facing crankshaft journal fillet.

# CONNECTING ROD BEARINGS

Connecting rod bearings are available in .001, .002, .003, .010 and .012 inch undersize. Install bearings in pairs. Do not use a new bearing half with an old bearing half. Do not file the rods or bearing caps.

# MAIN BEARINGS

Crankshaft main bearings are not interchangeable and should be marked at removal to ensure correct assembly. Upper and lower bearing halves are not interchangeable. Lower main bearing halves of Nos. 1 and 3 are interchangeable. Bearings are available in standard size and undersizes of .001, .002, .003, .010 and .012 inch.

# VALVES
## ADJUST

These engines use hydraulic lifters. No provision for adjustment is provided.

# CRANKSHAFT REAR MAIN OIL SEAL
## REPLACE

The following procedure is used to repair a leaking (rotated) rear main oil seal. Do not remove upper half of rope oil seal during this procedure.
1. Remove oil pan, pump and rear main bearing cap.
2. Remove lower rope seal half from bearing cap.

3. Install a new lower seal half into bearing cap. Tap seal down into position using tool C-3511 or equivalent and cut the right bank seal end flush with the bearing cap. Remove the rope seal, rotate (end-for-end), and reinstall seal into cap with cut end protruding above the surface so as to tightly fill the block half seal end compressed above the block/cap parting line.
4. Press in rope seal into cap using tool C-3511 or equivalent, and cut left bank side flush with cap surface.
5. Lightly oil the lower seal half with clean engine oil and install side seals. **Ensure side seal identified with yellow paint is used on the right side.**
6. Install rear bearing cap.
7. Install main bearing cap, oil pump and oil pan.

# OIL PAN
## REPLACE
### 2 WHEEL DRIVE MODELS
1. Disconnect battery ground cable.
2. Remove oil dipstick, then disconnect distributor cap and position aside.
3. Raise and support vehicle.
4. Drain oil from engine, then remove exhaust crossover.
5. Loosen side engine mount bolts, **Figs. 1 and 2.**
6. Using suitable jack and block of wood positioned at oil pan, carefully and slightly raise engine assembly. Remove side engine mount bolts.
7. When the engine is high enough, place bolts (similar to engine mount bolts removed) in the engine mount attaching points on the frame brackets. Lower engine so bottom of engine mounts rest on the installed bolts.
8. Remove oil pan.

9. Reverse procedure to install. Place drop of RTV sealer at timing chain cover to cylinder block parting line, and where rubber and cork gaskets meet on oil pan gasket. Torque attaching bolts to 200 inch lbs.

### 4 WHEEL DRIVE MODELS
1. Disconnect battery ground cable, then remove oil dipstick.
2. Raise and support vehicle.
3. Remove front drive axle, exhaust crossover and transmission lower cover.
4. Remove oil pan.
5. Reverse procedure to install. Place drop of RTV sealer at timing chain cover to cylinder block parting line, and where rubber and cork gaskets meet on oil pan gasket. Torque attaching bolts to 200 inch lbs.

# FUEL PUMP
## REPLACE
### 1987
1. Disconnect battery ground cable.
2. Disconnect and plug fuel lines at fuel pump.
3. Remove fuel pump to cylinder block attaching bolts, then the fuel pump.
4. Reverse procedure to install.

### 1988–89
1. Disconnect battery ground cable.
2. Drain fuel tank, then remove the tank.
3. Apply downward pressure to fuel pump module, then release the holding clamp.
4. Remove module from tank.
5. Reverse procedure to install, noting the following:
   a. Clean sealing area on tank and replace O-ring seal.
   b. Ensure proper alignment of module with retaining bracket on bottom of tank.
   c. Torque module holding clamp to 40 inch lbs.

# CLUTCH & MANUAL TRANSMISSION

## INDEX

## CLUTCH
### ADJUST

This vehicle is equipped with a hydraulic clutch with no provision for adjustment.

## CLUTCH
### REPLACE

1. Remove transmission assembly.
2. Remove bellhousing assembly.
3. Mark relative position between flywheel and pressure plate to facilitate installation.
4. Insert a spare transmission drive pinion through clutch disc hub, then alternately and evenly loosen pressure plate attaching bolts.
5. Remove pressure plate and disc assembly.
6. Reverse procedure to install. Tighten pressure plate attaching bolts alternately and evenly to a final torque of 250 inch lbs.

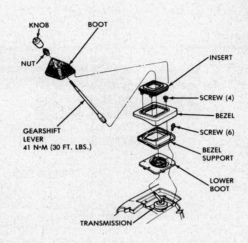

**Fig. 1  Gearshift lever removal**

## TRANSMISSION
### REPLACE
#### NEW PROCESS 2500 FIVE SPEED OVERDRIVE

1. Disconnect battery ground cable.
2. Remove gear shift lever, **Fig. 1.**
3. Raise and support vehicle.
4. Remove transfer case (if equipped). Refer to "Transfer Case" for procedure.
5. Disconnect all electrical connectors from transmission.
6. Remove front exhaust pipe from exhaust manifold.
7. Remove exhaust pipe brackets from transmission assembly.
8. Support engine and transmission assemblies, using suitable jacks.
9. Disconnect speedometer cable from transmission.
10. Remove crossmember.
11. If not removed previously, remove driveshaft.
12. Remove transmission to engine attaching bolts.
13. Lower transmission from vehicle.
14. Reverse procedure to install.

# TRANSFER CASE

## INDEX

## TRANSFER CASE, REPLACE
### REMOVAL

1. Raise and support vehicle.
2. Drain transfer case lubricant into suitable container.
3. Scribe reference marks between front and rear transfer case output shaft yokes and driveshafts.
4. Disconnect speedometer cable and vacuum switch hoses.
5. Disconnect transfer case shift lever linkage from gearshift assembly.
6. Support transmission with suitable jack, then remove rear crossmember.
7. Remove driveshafts from front and rear transfer case output shaft yokes, then wire driveshafts to frame. **Do not allow driveshafts to hang from axle flanges.**
8. If necessary, remove exhaust pipe support bracket attaching bolts from transfer case.
9. Remove transfer case to transmission attaching nuts, then pull transfer case rearward until clear of transmission output shaft.
10. Remove transfer case from vehicle. Remove all gasket material from transmission adapter housing.

### INSTALLATION

1. Apply Permatex No. 3 sealer, or equivalent, to both sides of transfer case to transmission gasket, then position gasket on transmission.
2. Install transfer case assembly on transmission. Ensure transfer case input shaft splines are aligned with transmission output shaft splines. If necessary, rotate transfer case rear output shaft flange to align splines. **Do not install any attaching nuts until transfer case mounting surface is completely seated against transmission mounting surface.**
3. Install transfer case attaching nuts. Torque attaching nuts to 35 ft. lbs.
4. Install transmission rear crossmember, then remove jack from transmission.
5. If removed, install exhaust pipe support bracket attaching bolts.
6. Install driveshafts. Align reference marks prior to installation.

7. Connect speedometer cable and vacuum switch hoses.
8. Connect shift linkage to gearshift assembly. Torque attaching locknut to 18 ft. lbs. on 1986-87 models, or 90 inch lbs. on 1989 models.
9. Fill transfer case with suitable fluid.
10. Lower vehicle.

## TRANSFER CASE LINKAGE
### ADJUST

1. Place transfer case shift lever in 4H position.

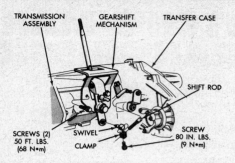

**Fig. 1  Transfer case linkage**

2. Remove shift boot attaching screws, then slide boot up to gain access to shift gate.
3. Insert a 1/8 inch (3 mm) spacer between shift lever and the forward edge of the shift linkage gate. Secure lever and spacer in this position.
4. Loosen adjusting linkage set screw enough to allow for free movement of linkage, **Fig. 1**.
5. Move transfer case lever to the 4H position.
6. Position linkage rod so it is a free fit in range lever, then tighten adjusting linkage set screw to 7 ft. lbs.
7. Remove spacer from shift gate, then install shift lever boot.
8. Check operation.

# REAR AXLES, SUSPENSION & BRAKES

## INDEX

## DESCRIPTION

These axle assemblies, **Figs. 1 and 2**, are of the integral carrier housing hypoid gear type with the centerline of the drive pinion mounted below the center line of the ring gear. The drive pinion is supported by two preloaded taper roller bearings and the front and rear pinion bearing cones are pressed on the pinion stem. The front and rear pinion bearing cups are pressed against a shoulder that is recessed within the carrier casting. Drive pinion depth of mesh adjustment is controlled by installing metal shims between the rear pinion bearing cup and carrier casting.

## REAR AXLE
### REPLACE

1. Raise and support vehicle, then block brake pedal in the up position using a suitable block of wood.
2. Remove rear wheels.
3. Disconnect hydraulic brake lines at wheel cylinders. Cap fittings to prevent loss of brake fluid.
4. Remove vent hose from brake tee nipple.
5. Remove brake tee nipple attaching bolt, then carefully detach hydraulic brake lines from clips.
6. Disconnect parking brake cables.
7. Scribe alignment marks on the propeller shaft universal joint and pinion flange to ensure correct position during installation. Disconnect propeller shaft at differential pinion flange and secure to one side.
8. Remove shock absorbers from spring plate studs, then the rear spring U-bolts.
9. Remove axle assembly from vehicle.
10. Reverse procedure to install.

## AXLE SHAFTS & BEARINGS
### REPLACE

1. Raise and support vehicle, then remove wheel assembly and brake drum.
2. Clean area around housing cover, then loosen housing cover and allow lubricant to drain. Remove cover.
3. Turn differential case until pinion shaft lock screw is accessible, then remove lock screw and pinion shaft, **Fig. 3**.
4. Push axle shaft inward and remove C-washer locks from axle shaft, **Fig. 4**, then pull axle shaft from housing being careful not to damage axle shaft bearing. **Inspect axle shaft bearing surfaces for signs of spalling or pitting. If any of these conditions exist, both shaft and bearing should be replaced. Normal bearing contact on shaft should be a dull gray and may appear lightly dented.**

5. Remove axle shaft bearing and seal from axle housing using tools C-4167 and C-637. **Remove any burrs that may be present in housing bearing shoulder, as bearing could become cocked during installation.**
6. Using suitable tools, install bearing, making sure it does not become cocked. Drive bearing until it bottoms against shoulder. **Do not use seal to position or bottom bearing as this will damage seal.**
7. Using tool Nos. C-4203 and C-4171 or equivalent, **Fig. 5**, install axle shaft bearing seal until outer flange of tool bottoms against housing flange face. This will position seal to the proper depth.
8. Reverse disassembly procedure to reassemble axle.

## SERVICE BRAKES
### ADJUST

These brakes have self-adjusting shoe mechanisms that assure correct lining-to-drum clearances at all times. The automatic adjusters operate only when the brakes are applied as the car is moving rearward.

Although the brakes are self-adjusting, an initial adjustment is necessary when the brake shoes have been relined or replaced, or when the length of the star

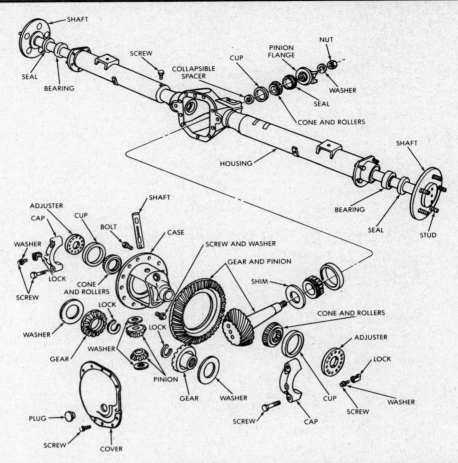

**Fig. 1  Exploded view of 7¼ inch inch integral carrier rear axle assembly.**

wheel adjuster has been changed during some other service operation.

Frequent usage of an automatic transmission forward range to halt reverse vehicle motion may prevent the automatic adjusters from functioning, thereby inducing low pedal heights. Should low pedal heights be encountered, it is recommended that numerous forward and reverse stops be made until satisfactory pedal height is obtained. **If a low pedal height condition cannot be corrected by making numerous reverse stops (provided the hydraulic system is free of air) it indicates that the self-adjusting mechanism is not functioning. Therefore, it will be necessary to remove the drum, clean, free up and lubricate the adjusting mechanism. Then adjust the brakes, being sure the parking brake is fully released.**

1. Raise vehicle so wheels are free to turn, then remove rear adjusting hole cover.
2. Back off parking brake cable adjustment so there is slack in the cable. Ensure parking brake lever is fully released.
3. Insert adjusting tool into star wheel of adjusting screw, **Fig. 6.** Move tool handle upward until slight drag is felt when wheel is rotated.
4. Insert a suitable screwdriver into

brake adjusting hole and push adjusting lever out of engagement with star wheel. **Care should be taken not to bend adjusting lever.**
5. Back off star wheel until wheel rotates freely with no drag.
6. Install adjusting hole cover. Adjust brakes on remaining wheels in the same manner.
7. Adjust parking brake.

# PARKING BRAKE
## ADJUST

Prior to adjusting the parking brake, ensure service brakes are adjusted properly.

1. Release parking brake lever and loosen cable adjusting nut to be sure cable is slack.
2. Tighten parking brake cable adjusting nut until a slight drag is felt when the rear wheels are rotated. Then loosen the cable adjusting nut until both rear wheels can be rotated freely.
3. To complete the operation, back off an additional two turns of the cable adjusting nut.
4. Apply and release parking brake several times to be sure rear wheels are not dragging when cable is in released position.

# MASTER CYLINDER
## REPLACE
### EXC. POWER BRAKES

1. Disconnect brake lines from master cylinder. Install plugs in outlets to prevent fluid leakage.
2. From under instrument panel, disconnect stop lamp switch mounting bracket, then position aside.
3. Pull pedal back and disengage pushrod from master cylinder piston. **This will require a pull of about 50 lbs. Also, the retention grommet will be destroyed.**
4. Remove master cylinder to cowl panel attaching bolts, then separate master cylinder from cowl panel.
5. Reverse procedure to install. Install new grommet on pushrod, then align pushrod with master cylinder piston. Using brake pedal, apply pressure to fully seat pushrod into piston.
6. Bleed brake system.

### POWER BRAKES

1. Disconnect primary and secondary brake tubes from master cylinder, then cap lines and master cylinder fitting.
2. Remove nuts attaching master cylinder to power brake unit, then slide

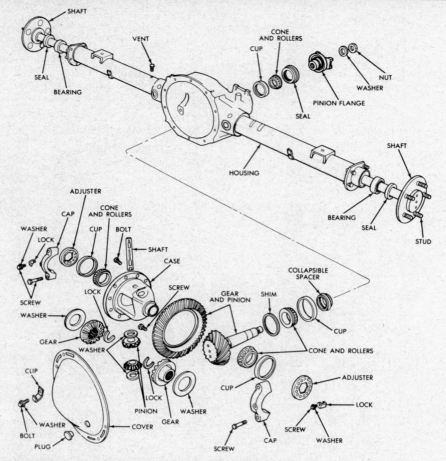

**Fig. 2   Exploded view of 8¼ inch inch integral carrier rear axle assembly.**

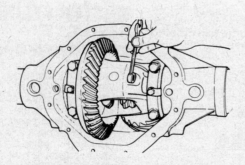

**Fig. 3   Removing differential pinion shaft lock pin**

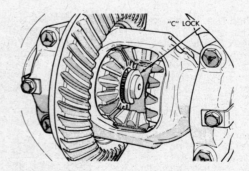

**Fig. 4   Removing C-lock washers**

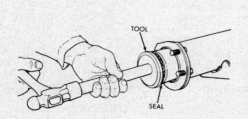

**Fig. 5   Installing axle shaft oil seal**

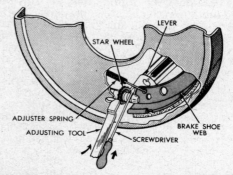

**Fig. 6   Release type brake adjuster**

master cylinder from power brake unit.
3. Reverse procedure to install.
4. Bleed brake system.

## REAR LEAF SPRING
### REPLACE

1. Raise and support rear of vehicle with suitable hoist lifting from frame side rail at crossmember behind the axle. Raise vehicle enough so rear wheels are just off the ground.

2. Remove nuts, lockwashers and U-bolts securing axle to leaf springs.
3. Remove spring shackle bolts and spring shackle, then the front spring nut, bolt and spring assembly.
4. Reverse procedure to install, noting the following:
   a. When installing spring, position spring center bolt so it enters hole in axle housing pad.
   b. Prior to fully tightening attaching nuts, lower vehicle to ground, then torque U-bolt nuts to 65 ft. lbs. Fully tighten all other attaching nuts.

## SHOCK ABSORBER
### REPLACE

1. Remove upper shock absorber attaching nut, bolt and washers.
2. Remove lower attaching nut at bushing end.
3. Swing shock absorber down, pivoting around lower bolt.
4. Remove shock absorber lower attaching bolt and washers, then the shock absorber from vehicle.
5. Reverse procedure to install.

# FRONT SUSPENSION & STEERING

**NOTE:** Refer to "Front Wheel Drive" for 4 x 4 front axle service procedures not covered in this section.

## INDEX

## DESCRIPTION

Two wheel drive models are equipped with a coil spring independent front suspension system, while four wheel drive models are equipped with a torsion bar sprung independent front suspension system, **Figs. 1, 2 and 3.** The upper and lower control arms are mounted on longitudinal rails. Both control arms have replaceable bushings on the inner ends and ball joints on the outer ends. The upper control arms control caster and camber adjustments through slots in the upper control arm mounting bracket.

## WHEEL ALIGNMENT
### CASTER & CAMBER, ADJUST

On four wheel drive models, front suspension height must be checked and corrected as necessary prior to checking wheel alignment. Refer to "Front Suspension Height, Adjust" for procedure.
1. Remove all foreign material from exposed threads of pivot bar adjusting nuts.
2. Record initial camber and caster readings before loosening pivot bar adjusting nuts, **Fig. 4.**
3. Moving only the rear pivot of the up-

per control arm in or out will greatly affect caster while changing camber only slightly. Moving the front pivot of the upper control arm in or out will greatly affect camber while changing caster only slightly.
4. Caster should be held as nearly equal as possible on both wheels.
5. Camber settings should be held as close as possible to desired specifications.
6. Torque pivot bar attaching nuts to 155 ft. lbs.

## TOE-IN, ADJUST
### 2 Wheel Drive Models

With the front wheels in a straight ahead position, retain steering wheel using a suitable tool. Loosen tie rod locknuts. Adjust toe-in by turning the both rods an equal amount. Do not twist tie rod to steering gear rubber boots during adjustment. Torque tie rod locknuts to 55 ft. lbs., then adjust steering gear to tie rod boots at tie rod. Remove steering wheel retaining tool.

### 4 Wheel Drive Models
1. With the front wheels in a straight ahead position, retain steering wheel with suitable tool. **On vehicles equipped with power steering, start engine before straightening wheels and leave running while adjusting toe-in.**

2. Loosen tie rod clamp bolts.
3. Adjust toe-in by turning tie rod sleeves evenly. **Each wheel should be set to be 1/2 the total specification to ensure steering wheel will remain centered.**
4. Shut off engine (if running), then tighten clamp nuts. **Ensure clamp nut does not project above top of tie rod sleeve.**

## FRONT SUSPENSION HEIGHT
### ADJUST
### 4 WHEEL DRIVE MODELS

**Check front suspension height before aligning front end.**
1. Ensure tire pressure is correct, gas tank is full and there is no load in vehicle.
2. Clean dirt off bottom side of lower control arm.
3. Jounce vehicle several times to settle suspension. Ensure bumper moves up and down at least 4 inches during operation.
4. Check front suspension height by measuring two points at lower control arm, **Fig. 5.** Front suspension height measurement is the difference between the two measurements. Correct measurement is 1.25 inches.

# DODGE DAKOTA

5. If measurement is not as specified, adjust by rotating the rear torsion bar anchor adjusting bolt as necessary, **Fig. 2.** After each adjustment, repeat step 3 and repeat measurement. **Both sides must be measured even though one side has been adjustment.**

6. Front suspension height should not vary more than ¼ inch from specifications and be within 1.4 inches side to side.

## WHEEL BEARINGS
### ADJUST
### 2 WHEEL DRIVE MODELS

1. Torque adjusting nut to 360-480 inch lbs. while rotating wheel.
2. Stop wheel from rotating, then back off adjusting nut to completely release bearing preload.
3. Tighten adjusting nut finger tight, then install locknut and cotter key. Endplay should be .0001-.003 inch.
4. Clean grease cap, coat inside with suitable wheel bearing grease and install cap. Do not fill cap with grease.

## BALL JOINT INSPECTION

Ball Joints should be inspected for excessive movement. If excessive movement is detected, replace faulty ball joints prior to performing front end alignment

## BALL JOINTS
### REPLACE
### 2 WHEEL DRIVE MODELS
#### Upper Ball Joint

1. Place ignition switch in the "Off" position.
2. Using a suitable jack raise front of vehicle and position a jackstand under lower control arm as close to wheel and tire assembly as possible.
3. Remove wheel and tire assembly.
4. Remove cotter pin and nut from upper ball joint nuts.
5. Using tool No. C-3564-A or equivalent, free upper ball joint from knuckle.
6. Using tool No. C-3561 or equivalent, unscrew ball joint from control arm. **Support knuckle and brake assembly to prevent damage to lower ball joint and brake hoses.**
7. Reverse procedure to install. Thread upper ball joint into control arm as far as possible by hand. Torque upper ball joint into control arm to 125 ft. lbs. Install ball joint seal using suitable 2 inch socket. Install ball joint into steering knuckle, then torque attaching bolts to 135 ft. lbs.

#### Lower Ball Joint

1. Raise and support vehicle, then remove wheel and tire assembly.
2. Remove brake caliper assembly and support aside with suitable rope or wire. **Do not allow brake caliper to hang by hydraulic hose.**

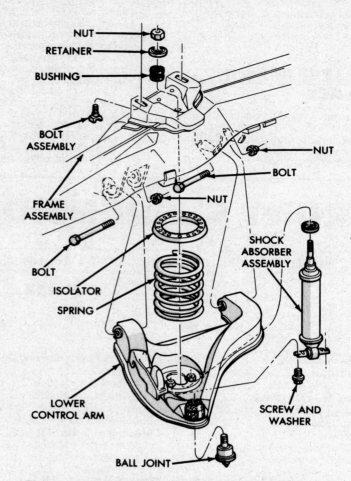

**Fig. 1   Lower control arm and coil spring. 2 wheel drive models**

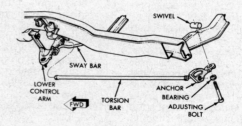

**Fig. 2   Lower control arm and torsion spring. 4 wheel drive models**

3. Remove shock absorber. Insert spring compressor tool DD-1278 and a piece of pipe to take up excessive space between tool and control arm. Tighten finger tight, then back off ½ turn.
4. Remove cotter pin and nut from lower ball joint.
5. Using tool No. C-3564-A or equivalent, free lower ball joint from knuckle.
6. Remove ball joint seal.
7. Press ball joint from lower control arm with tool C-4212.

8. Reverse procedure to install. Torque lower ball joint attaching nut to 135 ft. lbs.

### 4 WHEEL DRIVE MODELS
#### Upper Ball Joint

1. Remove cotter pin, locknut and spring washer from wheel hub.
2. While applying brakes, loosen hub nut.
3. Raise and support vehicle with front suspension in full rebound.

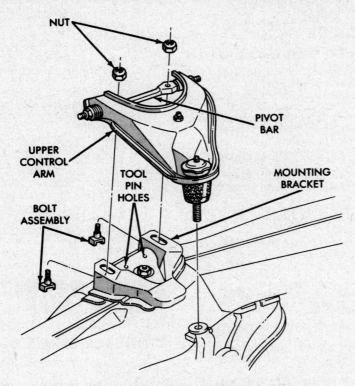

**Fig. 3   Upper control arm. 2 wheel drive models (similar to 4 wheel drive models)**

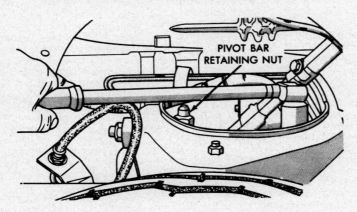

**Fig. 4   Loosening pivot bar adjusting nuts**

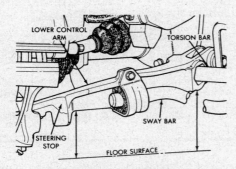

**Fig. 5   Front suspension height measuring points. 4 wheel drive models**

4. Remove hub nut and washer, then wheel and tire assembly.
5. Remove driveshaft to axle flange attaching bolts, then remove driveshafts.
6. Loosen rear torsion bar anchor adjusting bolt to unload suspension, **Fig. 2**.
7. Remove cotter pin and nut from upper ball joint.
8. Position ball joint removal tool C-3564-A on upper ball joint, then tighten tool and strike upper control arm with suitable hammer to remove ball joint.
9. Reverse procedure to install, noting the following:
   a. Press new ball joint into control arm with tool No. C-4212, then install new seal.
   b. Torque ball joint to steering knuckle attaching nut to 135 ft. lbs.
   c. Torque driveshaft to axle flange attaching bolts to 65 ft. lbs.
   d. Torque hub nut to 190 ft. lbs.
   e. Adjust torsion bars to set ride height. Refer to "Front Suspension Height, Adjust" for procedure.

## Lower Ball Joint

1. Remove cotter pin, locknut and spring washer from wheel hub.
2. While applying brakes, loosen hub nut.
3. Raise and support vehicle with front suspension in full rebound.
4. Remove hub nut and washer, then wheel and tire assembly.
5. Remove driveshaft to axle flange attaching bolts, then remove driveshafts.
6. Loosen rear torsion bar anchor adjusting bolt to unload suspension, **Fig. 2**.
7. Remove lower shock absorber mounting bolt.
8. Disconnect sway bar from lower control arm.
9. Remove cotter pin and nut from lower ball joint.
10. Separate lower ball joint from steering knuckle.
11. Remove lower ball joint.
12. Reverse procedure to install, noting the following:
    a. Torque ball joint to steering knuckle attaching nut to 120 ft. lbs.
    b. Torque sway bar attaching bolts to 20 ft. lbs.
    c. Torque lower shock absorber mounting bolt to 200 inch lbs.
    d. Torque driveshaft to axle flange attaching bolts to 65 ft. lbs.
    e. Torque hub nut to 190 ft. lbs.
    f. Adjust torsion bars to set ride height. Refer to "Front Suspension Height, Adjust" for procedure.

## SHOCK ABSORBER
## REPLACE

1. Raise and support vehicle.
2. Turn wheel as needed to gain access

# DODGE DAKOTA

to upper shock absorber mount, then remove upper nut and retainer.
3. Remove lower attaching bolt(s), then the shock.
4. Reverse procedure to install. Torque upper mount nut to 25 ft. lbs. and lower mount attaching bolt(s) to 200 inch lbs.

## COIL SPRING
### REPLACE
## 2 WHEEL DRIVE MODELS

1. Raise and support vehicle, then remove wheel and tire assembly.
2. Remove shock absorber, then loosely install spring compressor tool No. DD-1278 or equivalent.
3. Disconnect sway bar end link assembly from control arm.
4. Place suitable jackstands under control arm lower frames, ensuring they straddle control arm bushings.
5. Remove control arm mounting bolts from frame assembly.
6. Slowly lower jackstands until tension on coil spring is relieved, then remove spring compressor tool, coil spring and isolator pad.
7. Reverse procedure to install. Torque control arm front retaining nut to 130 ft. lbs. and rear nut to 80 ft. lbs. Torque top shock absorber retaining nut to 25 ft. lbs. and lower retaining bolts to 200 inch lbs.

## TORSION BAR
### REPLACE
## 4 WHEEL DRIVE MODELS

1. Remove upper control arm rebound bumper.
2. Raise and support front of vehicle with front suspension in full rebound.
3. Loosen rear torsion bar anchor adjusting bolt to unload suspension, **Fig. 2.**
4. Remove anchor adjusting bolt from swivel, then the torsion bar and anchor as an assembly.
5. Separate torsion bar from anchor and bearing.
6. Clean all parts as necessary, then inspect torsion bar adjusting bolt and swivel for signs of corrosion or other damage. Replace as necessary.
7. Reverse procedure to install, noting the following:
   a. Torque upper control arm rebound bumper attaching screws to 200 inch lbs.
   b. Lower vehicle to ground, then adjust torsion bars to set ride height. Refer to "Front Suspension Height, Adjust" for procedure.

## SWAY BAR
### REPLACE
## 2 WHEEL DRIVE MODELS

1. Remove link rod attaching nut from each end of sway bar.
2. Remove retainers and rubber bushings from sway bar link rods.
3. Remove sway bar support bracket attaching bolts, then the sway bar.
4. Reverse procedure to install.

## 4 WHEEL DRIVE MODELS

1. Remove sway bar to lower control arm bracket attaching bolts, then the brackets.
2. Remove sway bar to frame mounting bracket attaching brackets, then the brackets.
3. Remove sway bar from vehicle.
4. Reverse procedure to install. Torque bracket attaching bolts to 20 ft. lbs.

## STEERING KNUCKLE
### REPLACE
## 2 WHEEL DRIVE MODELS

1. Place a suitable jack under outer end of lower control arm, then raise and support vehicle.
2. Remove wheel and tire assembly.
3. Remove caliper from disc and position disc aside, then remove inboard shoe. **Do not allow caliper to hang or be supported by hydraulic brake hose.**
4. Disconnect tie rod end at steering knuckle arm.
5. Disconnect upper and lower ball joints from steering knuckle assembly, using tool No. C-3564-A.
6. Remove tool, then the steering knuckle assembly.
7. Remove splash shield and steering knuckle arm from steering knuckle.
8. Reverse procedure to install noting the following:
   a. Torque splash shield to steering knuckle attaching bolts to 220 inch lbs. and steering knuckle arm attaching bolts to 217 ft. lbs.
   b. Torque ball joint nuts to 135 ft. lbs.
   c. Torque tie rod end attaching nut to 40 ft. lbs.

## 4 WHEEL DRIVE MODELS

1. Remove cotter pin, locknut and spring washer from wheel hub.
2. While applying brakes, loosen hub nut.
3. Raise and support vehicle with front suspension in full rebound.
4. Remove hub nut and washer, then wheel and tire assembly.
5. Remove brake caliper and suspend aside with suitable wire or string. **Do not allow caliper to hang from hydraulic hose.**
6. Remove rotor, then the hub and bearing assembly attaching bolts and hub and bearing assembly.
7. Disconnect tie rod end from steering knuckle.
8. Separate steering knuckle from ball joints, then remove steering knuckle.
9. Reverse procedure to install, noting the following:
   a. Torque upper ball joint nut to 135 ft. lbs. and lower ball joint nut to 120 ft. lbs.
   b. Torque hub and bearing assembly attaching bolts to 110 ft. lbs.
   c. Torque tie rod end attaching nut to 40 ft. lbs.
   d. Torque hub nut to 190 ft. lbs.
   e. Lower vehicle to ground, then adjust torsion bars to set ride height. Refer to "Front Suspension Height, Adjust" for procedure.

## MANUAL & POWER STEERING GEAR
### REPLACE
## 2 WHEEL DRIVE MODELS

1. Disconnect tie rod ends from steering knuckle.
2. On models with power steering, remove power steering tubes.
3. On all models, remove steering shaft lower coupling to worm shaft roll pin.
4. Remove steering gear to front suspension crossmember attaching bolts, then the steering gear.
5. Reverse procedure to install. On models with manual steering gear, ensure master serrations are aligned. Torque attaching bolts to 150 ft. lbs.

## 4 WHEEL DRIVE MODELS

1. Center steering gear.
2. Remove steering gear arm using suitable puller.
3. Disconnect steering gear pressure and return lines.
4. Disconnect steering gear to steering shaft coupling.
5. Remove steering gear mounting bolts, then the steering gear.
6. Reverse procedure to install.

## POWER STEERING PUMP
### REPLACE

1. Loosen pump locking and attaching bolts, then remove drive belt.
2. Disconnect both fluid hoses from pump.
3. Remove pump locking and attaching bolts, then remove pump and bracket assembly.
4. Reverse procedure to install.

# FRONT WHEEL DRIVE

## INDEX

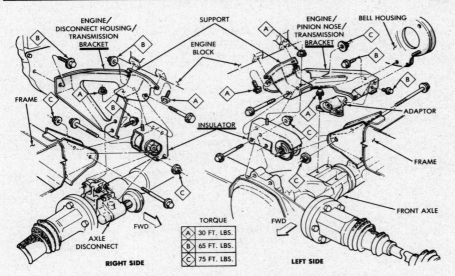

Fig. 1  Front drive axle removal & installation

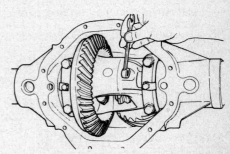

Fig. 2  Differential pinion shaft lock pin

## AXLE HOUSING ASSEMBLY REPLACE

1. Remove cotter pin, locknut and spring washer, then while applying brakes, loosen hub nut.
2. Disconnect battery ground cable, then raise and support vehicle and drain axle lubricant into suitable container. Remove skid plate.
3. Remove axle shafts using following procedure:
   a. Remove hub nut, washer, wheel and tire assembly.
   b. Remove six axle flange to axle shaft inner CV (constant velocity) joint attaching bolts.
   c. Support CV joint housing, then remove axle shaft from hub by pulling on outer CV joint.
4. Remove front driveshaft.
5. Disconnect vacuum lines and wire from switch on disconnect housing assembly.
6. Support axle housing assembly with suitable jack, then remove attaching bolts and lower axle housing assembly from vehicle, **Fig. 1.**
7. Reverse procedure to install, noting the following:

  a. Torque axle housing assembly attaching bolts to values shown in **Fig. 1.**
  b. Torque driveshaft universal joint brackets to axle flange bolts to 170 inch lbs. Torque driveshaft universal joint brackets to transfer case flange to 300 inch lbs.
  c. Torque inner axle shaft CV joint to axle flange attaching bolts to 65 ft. lbs.
  d. Torque skid plate attaching bolts to 200 inch lbs.

## LEFT SIDE AXLE SHAFT, BEARING & SEAL REPLACE
### REMOVAL

1. Disconnect battery ground cable, then raise and support vehicle and remove axle shaft.
2. Loosen axle housing cover and allow lubricant to drain into suitable container.
3. Remove axle housing cover.
4. Rotate differential case until pinion shaft lock screw is accessible, then remove lock screw and pinion shaft, **Fig. 2.**
5. Push axle shaft towards center of vehicle, then remove axle shaft C-lock, **Fig. 3.**
6. Carefully pull axle shaft from housing, using caution not to damage axle bearing remaining in axle housing, **Fig. 4.**
7. Inspect axle shaft for signs of damage. If damage is evident, replace shaft and bearing. **Axle shaft may have a dull gray color and may appear dented. This condition is considered normal.**
8. Remove axle seal from housing bore.
9. Remove axle shaft bearing with tool C-4167 and suitable slide hammer and inspect for signs of damage. If bearing appears satisfactory, it can be reused.
10. Inspect axle housing bearing bore for nicks and burrs. If present, they must be removed to prevent improper bearing installation.

### INSTALLATION

1. Install bearing into axle housing using tool No. C-4198 and handle C-4171. Drive bearing until fully seated in housing bore. Ensure bearing is driven straight in and is not cocked.
2. Install bearing seal using tool C-4203 and handle C-4171. Drive seal in until tool bottoms against axle housing flange face.
3. Lubricate bearing and seal lip, then slide axle shaft into housing, using care not to damage seal lips with axle splines.
4. Install axle shaft C-lock, then pull back on axle to lock in place.
5. Install differential shaft through case

and pinions. Align hole in shaft with lock screw hole, then install lock screw and torque to 100 inch lbs.
6. Install rear differential cover, then fill unit with gear oil.

## DISCONNECT HOUSING COVER ASSEMBLY
### REPLACE

1. Remove disconnect housing cover assembly attaching bolts, then the cover and gasket, **Fig. 5.**
2. Remove E-clip from shift motor housing and shaft, then remove shift motor and fork.
3. Remove O-ring and shift fork pads.
4. Clean and inspect parts. If any parts are worn or damaged, replace as necessary.
5. Reverse procedure to install, noting the following:
   a. When installing disconnect housing cover assembly, carefully guide the shift fork into shift collar groove.
   b. Torque cover attaching bolts to 10 ft. lbs.

## RIGHT SIDE OUTER & INNER AXLE SHAFT
### REPLACE

1. Disconnect battery ground cable, then raise and support vehicle and remove axle shaft.
2. Remove disconnect housing cover assembly.
3. Working through axle shaft hub, remove bearing seal retainer attaching screws, then the axle shaft, **Fig. 6.**
4. Remove snap ring and splined gear from axle shaft, then using suitable puller, remove bearing and seal from shaft.
5. Working through axle disconnect housing, remove shift collar.
6. Remove inner axle shaft. Refer to "Left Side Axle Shaft, Bearing And Seal, Replace" for procedure.
7. Remove needle bearing from inner axle shaft using tool D-330, **Fig. 7.**
8. Remove inner axle shaft bearing using tools D-354-1, D-354-4 and puller C-637.
9. Reverse procedure to install, noting the following:
   a. Install inner axle shaft bearing using tool D-354-2 and handle C-4171.
   b. Install needle bearing into inner axle shaft using tool D-328 and handle C-4171.
   c. Torque outer axle seal retainer attaching screws to 200 inch lbs.
   d. Torque disconnect housing cover assembly to 10 ft. lbs.

## AXLE SHAFTS
### REPLACE

1. Remove front hub cotter pin, locknut and spring washer, then with service

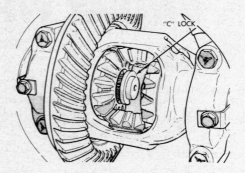

**Fig. 3   Axle shaft C-lock removal**

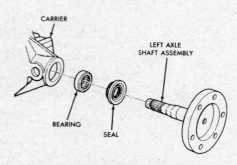

**Fig. 4   Left side axle shaft removal**

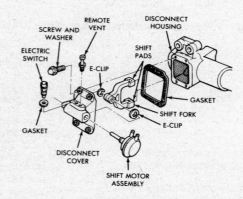

**Fig. 5   Disconnect housing cover assembly**

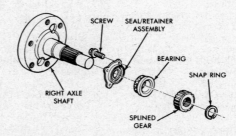

**Fig. 6   Right side outer axle shaft removal**

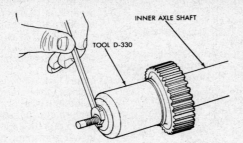

**Fig. 7 Inner axle shaft needle bearing removal**

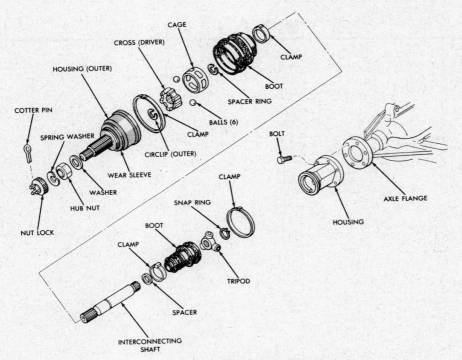

**Fig. 8 Axle shaft components**

## Inspection

1. Remove grease from housing and tripod.
2. Inspect housing roller raceways and tripod for damage and/or excessive wear.
3. Replace parts as necessary.

## Assembly

1. Install new boot over axle shaft, then insert axle shaft through housing.
2. Slide tripod onto axle shaft with non-chamfered end facing snap ring slot, then install snap ring.
3. Push tripod into housing, then install housing cover by lightly tapping into place.
4. Distribute grease included in service package into CV joint housing.
5. Install boot and clamps.

## OUTER CV JOINT
### Disassembly

1. Remove boot clamps, then pull back boot.
2. Wipe grease away to expose CV joint.
3. Support axle shaft in suitable soft jawed vise, then while supporting CV joint with one hand, tap top of joint body with a soft hammer to dislodge joint from internal circlip installed in groove at end of shaft.
4. Inspect wear sleeve on housing, **Fig. 8.** If wear sleeve is bent or damaged, pry from housing.
5. Remove circlip from end of shaft. **Do not remove spacer from shaft unless axle shaft requires replacement.**
6. Inspect CV joint. If joint was operating satisfactorily and grease does not appear to be contaminated, replace boot only. If joint is noisy and/or badly worn, replace entire joint assembly and boot. If joint is not noisy or excessively worn and grease appears slightly contaminated, proceed to step 7.
7. Remove excess grease from joint assembly, then using paint, mark relative positions of inner cross, cage and housing to be used during assembly.
8. Clamp axle shaft splines in suitable soft jawed vise to position axle shaft vertically. Press down on one side of inner race to tilt cage, then remove ball from opposite side. Repeat procedure until all balls are removed. **If joint is tight, use a hammer and brass drift to tilt race. Do not hit cage. If balls are tight, they can be pried loose with screwdriver.**
9. Tilt inner race and cage vertically and position two opposite cage windows in area between ball grooves. Pull inner race and cage assembly upwards to remove from housing.
10. Rotate inner race 90° to cage, then align one of the race spherical lands with cage window. Raise land into cage, then remove race by swinging away from cage.

### Inspection

1. Wash all parts in suitable solvent,

---

brake applied, loosen hub nut.
2. Raise and support front of vehicle.
3. Remove hub nut, washer, wheel and tire assembly.
4. Remove six axle flange to axle shaft inner CV (constant velocity) joint attaching bolts, **Fig. 8.**
5. Support CV joint housing, then remove axle shaft from hub by pulling on outer CV joint.
6. Reverse procedure to install, noting the following:
   a. Torque inner axle shaft CV joint to axle flange attaching bolts to 65 ft. lbs.
   b. Torque hub nut to 190 ft. lbs.
   c. Torque lug nuts to 85 ft. lbs. on 1986-87 models, or 95 ft. lbs. on 1989 models.

# CONSTANT VELOCITY (CV) JOINT SERVICE

## INNER CV JOINT
### Disassembly

1. Place inner CV joint housing in suitable vise, then remove boot clamps and pull boot back.
2. Move axle shaft rearward against housing cover, then using a soft faced hammer, tap lightly on end of axle shaft to force cover from housing.
3. Remove snap ring from end of shaft, then remove tripod.
4. Remove axle shaft from joint housing, then remove boot.

then dry with compressed air.

2. Check housing ball races for signs of excessive wear and scouring.
3. Check splined shaft and nut threads for damage.
4. Check balls for pitting, cracking, scouring and wear. **A slight dulling of ball surface is considered normal.**
5. Check cage for excessive wear on spherical surfaces, surface ripples on cage windows, cracks and chipping.
6. Check inner race for excessive wear or scouring of ball races.
7. If any of the above conditions exist, the CV joint assembly should be replaced.

## Assembly

1. Lightly lubricate all components with oil prior to assembly.
2. Align paint marks, then insert inner race lands into cage window, then feed race into cage. Pivot race 90° to complete installation.
3. Align opposing cage windows with housing land, then feed cage assembly into housing. Pivot cage 90° to complete installation. **Cage is installed correctly if inner race counterbore is facing outwards from joint housing.**
4. Distribute grease included in service package equally between all sides of ball grooves.
5. Tilt cage and inner race assembly and insert ball, then repeat procedure until all balls are installed.
6. Fasten boot to axle shaft.
7. Install new circlip on axle shaft. Do not bend or over extend circlip during installation.
8. Install joint on axle shaft, engage splines, then tap joint sharply with suitable mallet.
9. Ensure circlip is engaged by attempting to pull off joint.
10. Install boot over housing, then install clamp.
11. If removed, install wear sleeve on housing. Lubricate wear sleeve and seal with MOPAR multipurpose lubricant.

# DODGE RAMPAGE & PLYMOUTH SCAMP

## INDEX OF SERVICE OPERATIONS

---

**NOTE:** Refer to the rear of this manual for vehicle manufacturer's special service tool suppliers.

---

# SPECIFICATIONS

## GENERAL ENGINE SPECIFICATIONS

| Year | Engine | Carb. | Bore & Stroke | Comp. Ratio | Horsepower @ RPM | Torque Ft. @ RPM | Normal Oil Pressure psi. |
|---|---|---|---|---|---|---|---|
| 1982 | 4-135 | 2 Bbl. | 3.44 x 3.62 | 8.5:1 | 84 @ 4800 | 111 @ 2400 | 45–50 |
| 1983–84 | 4-135 | 2 Bbl. | 3.44 x 3.62 | 9:1 | 94 @ 5200 | 117 @ 3200 | 50 |

## ALTERNATOR & REGULATOR SPECIFICATIONS

| I.D. Tag Color | Ground Polarity | Field Coil Draw Amperes @ 12 Volts | Current Output | | | Operating Voltage | | |
|---|---|---|---|---|---|---|---|---|
| | | | Engine RPM | Amperes | Volts | Engine RPM | Volts | Voltage @ 140°F |
| Yellow Tag | Neg. | 4.5 to 6.5 | 1250 | 45 | 15 | 1250 | 15 | 13.3 to 13.9 |
| Brown Tag | Neg. | 4.5 to 6.5 | 1250 | 56 | 15 | 1250 | 15 | 13.3 to 13.9 |

## STARTING MOTOR SPECIFICATIONS

| Engine | Model | Ident. No.② | Brush Spring Tension Oz. | Free Speed Test | | |
|---|---|---|---|---|---|---|
| | | | | Amps.③ | Volts | RPM④ |
| 4-135 | Bosch | 5213045 | — | 47 | 11 | 6600 |
| 4-135① | Bosch | 5213395 | — | 47 | 11 | 6600 |
| 4-135 | Nippondenso | 5213645 | — | 47 | 11 | 6600 |

①—Manual transmission.
②—Number located on plate riveted to starter housing.
③—Maximum current drawn.
④—Minimum speed.

## ENGINE TIGHTENING SPECIFICATIONS*

*Torque specifications are for clean and lightly lubricated threads only. Dry or dirty threads produce increased friction which prevents accurate measurement of tightness.

| Year | Engine Model | Spark Plug Ft. Lbs. | Cylinder Head Bolts Ft. Lbs. | Intake Manifold Inch Lbs. | Exhaust Manifold Inch Lbs. | Camshaft Cover Inch Lbs. | Connecting Rod Cap Bolts Ft. Lbs. | Main Bearing Cap Bolts Ft. Lbs. | Flywheel To Crankshaft Ft. Lbs. | Crankshaft Pulley Ft. Lbs. |
|---|---|---|---|---|---|---|---|---|---|---|
| 1982–84 | 4-135 | 26 | 45① | 200 | 200 | 105 | 40① | 30① | 65② | 20.8 |

①—Turn torque wrench an additional ¼ turn after the specified torque has been achieved.
②—Manual trans.

## WHEEL ALIGNMENT SPECIFICATIONS

| Year | Model | Caster Angle, Degrees | | Camber Angle, Degrees | | | | Toe In. Inch |
|------|-------|-------|---------|------|-------|------|-------|------|
| | | | | Limits | | Desired | | |
| | | Limits | Desired | Left | Right | Left | Right | |
| 1982–84 | Rampage & Scamp ① | — | — | −¼ to +¾ | −¼ to +¾ | +5/16 | +5/16 | ③ |
| 1982–84 | Rampage & Scamp ② | — | — | −1¼ to −¼ | −1¼ to −¼ | −3-4 | −¾ | 3/32 |

① —Front wheel alignment.
② —Rear wheel alignment.
③ —Toe-out, 1/16 inch.

## BRAKE SPECIFICATIONS

| Year | Model | Rear Drum I.D. | Wheel Cyl. Bore | | Disc Brake Rotor | | | | | Master Cyl. I.D. |
|------|-------|------|-------------|-----------|-------------------|-------------------|-------------------------------------|------------------|----------------------|------|
| | | | Front Disc | Rear Drum | Nominal Thickness | Minimum Thickness | Thickness Variation (Parallelism) | Run Out (TIR) | Finish (Microinch) | |
| 1982 | Rampage | 7.87 | 1.893–1.895 | .625 | .490–.505 | .431 | .0005 | .004 | 15–80 | .875 |
| 1983–84 | Rampage & Scamp | 7.87 | 2.130 | .625 | .490–.505 | .431 | .0005 | .004 | 15–80 | .827 |

## COOLING SYSTEM & CAPACITY DATA

| Year | Engine & Model | Cooling Capacity | | Radiator Cap Relief Pressure, Lbs. | Thermo-Opening Temp. Degrees F. | Fuel Tank Gals. | Engine Oil Refill Qts. | Transaxle Oil | | Auto. Trans. Qts. |
|------|----------------|--------------|--------------|-------|-------|-------|-------|--------------|--------------|------|
| | | Less A/C Qts. | With A/C Qts. | | | | | 4 Speed Pts. | 5 Speed Pts. | |
| 1982 | Rampage 4-135 | 7 | 7 | 14–17 | 195 | 13① | 4② | 4 | — | 7.5③ |
| 1983 | Rampage & Scamp 4-135 | 9 | 9 | 14–18 | 195 | 13① | 4② | 4 | 4.6 | 8.9 |
| 1984 | Rampage 4-135 | 9 | 9 | 14–18 | 195 | 13① | 4② | 4 | 4.6 | 8.9 |

① —Approximate.
② —With or without filter.
③ —Some 1982 transaxles were manufactured with 1983 oil pans, therefore some 1982 capacities are increased to 8.9 qts. Use dipstick for final check.

# DODGE RAMPAGE & PLYMOUTH SCAMP

# ELECTRICAL

## INDEX

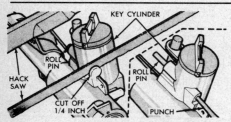

**Fig. 1 Ignition lock replacement**

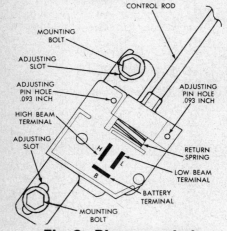

**Fig. 3 Dimmer switch replacement**

# STARTER
## REPLACE

1. Disconnect battery ground cable.
2. Remove starter to flywheel housing and rear bracket to engine or transaxle attaching bolts.
3. Loosen air pump tube at exhaust manifold, then position tube bracket away from starter motor.
4. If equipped, remove heat shield clamp and heat shield.
5. Disconnect battery cable at starter motor and solenoid leads at solenoid, then remove starter motor.
6. Reverse procedure to install.

# IGNITION LOCK
## REPLACE

Removal and installation of ignition lock must be done with key removed.
1. Disconnect battery ground cable.
2. Remove steering wheel, column covers and turn signal switch, refer to "Steering Wheel, Replace" and "Turn Signal Switch, Replace" procedures.
3. Cut upper 1/4 inch from key cylinder retainer pin boss using a hacksaw blade, **Fig. 1**.
4. Remove roll pin from housing using a suitable punch, then remove key cylinder.
5. Install new cylinder, ensuring it engages the lug or ignition switch driver.
6. Install roll pin and check for proper operation of lock.

# STEERING WHEEL & HORN SOUNDER
## REPLACE

1. Disconnect battery ground cable.
2. Remove horn button by carefully lifting with fingers, then remove steering wheel nut and horn switch.
3. Remove steering wheel using puller No. C-3428B.
4. To install, align master spline in wheel hub with missing tooth of shaft.
5. Install horn switch, then the steering wheel nut. Torque to 45 ft. lbs. **Do not torque steering wheel nut against column lock mechanism, as damage may occur.**
6. Install horn button and check for proper operation.

# IGNITION SWITCH
## REPLACE

1. Disconnect battery ground cable.
2. Remove electrical connector from ignition switch.
3. Place ignition lock in Lock position and remove key.
4. Remove two ignition switch attaching screws and permit switch and pushrod to drop below column jacket, **Fig. 2**.
5. Rotate the switch 90° for removal of switch from pushrod.
6. To install, position ignition switch in Lock position, second detent from top of switch.
7. Place switch at right angle to column and insert pushrod.

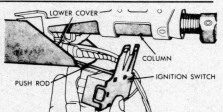

**Fig. 2 Ignition switch replacement**

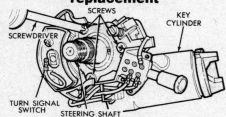

**Fig. 4 Turn signal switch replacement**

8. Align switch on bracket and loosely install screws.
9. Apply light rearward force to switch, then tighten attaching screws.
10. Connect ignition switch electrical connector and battery ground cable.
11. Check for proper operation of switch.

# LIGHT SWITCH
## REPLACE

1. Disconnect battery ground cable.
2. Reach under instrument panel and depress light switch knob release button, then pull light switch knob and shaft from switch.
3. Remove four bezel attaching screws, then the bezel.
4. Remove switch attaching screws and disconnect electrical connectors from switch.
5. Remove switch from panel.
6. Reverse procedure to install.

# DIMMER SWITCH
## REPLACE

1. Disconnect battery ground cable, then the electrical connector from switch.
2. Remove two switch mounting screws, then disengage switch from pushrod, **Fig. 3**.

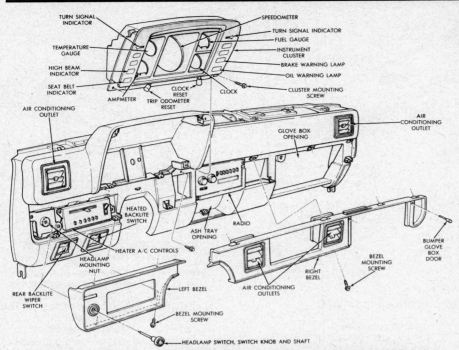

**Fig. 5   Instrument panel exploded view (Typical). 1982–83 models**

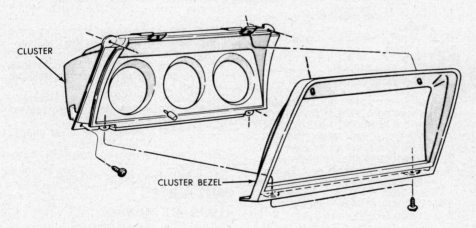

**Fig. 6   Instrument cluster & bezel. 1984 models**

3. To install switch, firmly seat pushrod into switch, then compress switch until two .093 inch drill shanks can be inserted into alignment holes. Position upper end of pushrod in pocket of wash/wipe switch. If necessary, remove lower column cover.
4. Apply light rearward force to switch, then install screws and remove drills. **Switch should click when lever is lifted, and again as lever returns, just before it reaches its stop in down position.**
5. Connect dimmer switch electrical connector, then the battery ground cable.

## TURN SIGNAL SWITCH
### REPLACE

1. Disconnect battery ground cable.

2. Remove horn button, three screws and the horn switch.
3. Remove steering wheel nut, then the steering wheel using a suitable puller.
4. Remove lower steering column cover attaching screws, then the column cover.
5. Remove wipe/wash switch attaching screw and position switch aside.
6. Disconnect turn signal and hazard warning switch electrical connector, then disengage wiring harness from support bracket.
7. Remove three turn signal switch attaching screws, **Fig. 4.**
8. Remove turn signal and hazard warning switch while guiding wire harness out from column.
9. Reverse procedure to install.

## INSTRUMENT CLUSTER
### REPLACE
#### 1982–83 MODELS

1. Disconnect battery ground cable.
2. Remove two mask-lens assembly lower attaching spring pins by pulling rearward with suitable pliers.
3. Pull mask-lens rearward, lower slightly and remove from cluster.
4. Remove two speedometer attaching screws, then the speedometer.
5. Disconnect wire harness electrical connectors.
6. Remove cluster attaching screws, **Fig. 5,** and pull cluster from dash.
7. Reach behind cluster and disconnect clock and tachometer wiring, if equipped.
8. Remove cluster from vehicle.
9. Reverse procedure to install.

#### 1984 MODELS

1. Disconnect battery ground cable.
2. Remove two lower cluster bezel attaching screws, **Fig. 6.**
3. Allow bezel to drop slightly, then remove bezel.
4. Remove four screws securing instrument cluster and pull cluster away from dash.
5. Disconnect electrical connectors and speedometer cable, then remove cluster.
6. Reverse procedure to install.

## WIPER SWITCH
### REPLACE

1. Disconnect battery ground cable.
2. Disconnect wiper switch and turn signal switch wiring harness connectors.
3. Remove lower column cover, then the horn button.
4. Place ignition switch in Off position and turn steering wheel so access hole in hub area is at 9 o'clock position on 1983–84 models, and in 3 o'clock position on 1982 models.
5. Loosen turn signal lever screw through access hole using a suitable screwdriver.
6. Disengage dimmer pushrod from wiper switch.
7. Unsnap wiring clip and remove wiper switch.
8. Reverse procedure to install.

## STOP LIGHT SWITCH
### REPLACE

1. Disconnect battery ground cable.
2. Disconnect stop light switch electrical connector, then remove switch assembly attaching screw and switch from brake pedal bracket.
3. Install new switch and connect switch electrical connector. Torque attaching bolt to 75 inch lbs.
4. If adjustment is required, proceed as follows:
   a. Loosen switch assembly to brake pedal bracket attaching screw and slide switch assembly away from

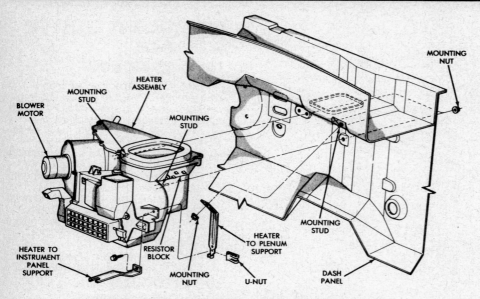

**Fig. 7 Heater assembly. Models less A/C**

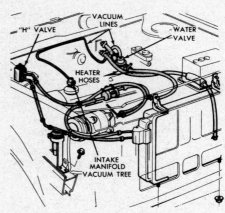

**Fig. 8 Air conditioning & heater hose routing**

brake pedal blade.

b. Depress brake pedal and allow it to return freely. **Do not pull brake pedal back at any time.**

c. Place a .130 inch spacer gauge on brake pedal blade.

d. Slide switch assembly toward pedal blade until switch plunger is fully depressed against spacer gauge without moving the pedal.

e. Torque stop light switch attaching screw to 75 inch lbs.

f. Remove spacer and ensure stop light switch does not prevent full brake pedal return.

## NEUTRAL START & BACK-UP LIGHT SWITCH
### REPLACE

The following procedure applies to automatic transaxle equipped models only. On manual transaxle equipped models, a back-up light switch is mounted on transaxle case.

1. Disconnect battery ground cable.
2. Disconnect switch wiring connector.
3. Remove switch from transaxle case, allow fluid to drain into a suitable container.
4. Install switch with new seal into transaxle case and connect switch wiring connector. Torque switch to 24 ft. lbs.

## WINDSHIELD WIPER MOTOR
### REPLACE

1. Disconnect battery ground cable.
2. Remove wiper arm assemblies.
3. Remove nuts from right and left pivots.
4. Open hood, then remove wiper motor plastic cover and washer hose attaching clip.
5. Disconnect wiper motor electrical connector.
6. Remove three bolts from wiper motor

mounting bracket.

7. Disengage pivots from cowl top mounting positions.
8. Remove wiper motor, cranks, pivots and drive link assembly from cowl plenum chamber.
9. Remove wiper motor from drive crank linkage.
10. Reverse procedure to install.

## RADIO
### REPLACE

1. Disconnect battery ground cable.
2. Remove right bezel attaching screws, then the bezel. On 1982-83 models, open glove box and guide bezel around glove box as needed.
3. Remove radio attaching screws.
4. Pull radio from panel and disconnect wiring ground strap and antenna lead from radio.
5. Remove radio from vehicle.
6. Reverse procedure to install.

## HEATER CORE
### REPLACE
#### LESS A/C

1. Disconnect battery ground cable, then drain cooling system.
2. Disconnect blower motor electrical connector, then remove ashtray.
3. Depress red color coded tab on end of temperature control cable, and pull control cable out of receiver on heater assembly.
4. Remove glove box and door assembly.
5. Disconnect heater hoses and plug heater core tube openings.
6. Remove two heater assembly to dash panel attaching nuts, **Fig. 7.**
7. Disconnect blower resistor electrical connector, then remove heater support brace to instrument panel attaching screws.
8. Remove heater support bracket nut,

then disconnect strap from plenum stud and lower heater assembly from under instrument panel.

9. Depress yellow color coded tab on end of mode door control cable out of receiver on heater assembly.
10. Move heater unit towards right side of vehicle, then out from under instrument panel.
11. Remove left heater outlet duct attaching screws, then the heater outlet duct.
12. Remove four blower motor mounting plate attaching screws, then the blower motor assembly.
13. Remove four outside air and defroster door cover attaching screws, then the door cover.
14. Remove defroster door assembly, then lift defroster door control rod out of heater assembly.
15. Remove 8 heater core cover attaching screws, then the core cover.
16. Slide heater core up and out of heater assembly.
17. Reverse procedure to install.

### WITH A/C
#### 1982–83 Models

1. Disconnect battery ground cable, then drain cooling system and discharge A/C system.
2. Disconnect heater hose at heater core. Plug heater core tube opening.
3. Disconnect vacuum lines at engine intake manifold and water valve, **Fig. 8.**
4. Remove expansion valve ("H" valve), **Fig. 8,** as follows:
   a. Disconnect low pressure cut-off switch electrical connector, located on side of "H" valve.
   b. Remove hex head bolt from center of plumbing sealing plate.
   c. Pull refrigerant line assembly towards front of vehicle.
   d. Remove two Allen head cap screws, then carefully remove the disassembled valve.
5. Remove hose clamp, then the condensate drain tube from evaporator heater assembly.
6. Remove evaporator heater assembly to dash panel attaching nuts, then depress red color coded tab on end of

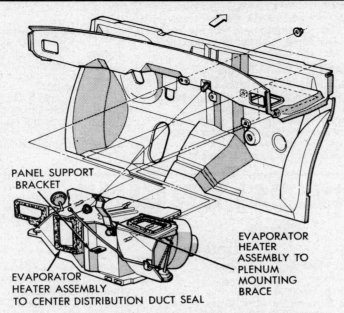

PANEL SUPPORT BRACKET

EVAPORATOR HEATER ASSEMBLY TO CENTER DISTRIBUTION DUCT SEAL

EVAPORATOR HEATER ASSEMBLY TO PLENUM MOUNTING BRACE

**Fig. 9  Heater assembly. Models with A/C**

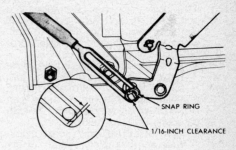

SNAP RING

1/16-INCH CLEARANCE

**Fig. 10  Throttle control cable**

temperature control cable and pull control cable out of receiver on heater assembly.

7. Remove glove box and door assembly, then disconnect vacuum harness from heater A/C control, located under instrument panel.
8. Disconnect blower motor electrical connector.
9. Remove right trim bezel to instrument panel attaching screws, then the right trim bezel.
10. Remove center distribution duct to instrument panel attaching screws, then the distribution duct.
11. Remove defroster duct adapter, then the panel support bracket.
12. Remove right side cowl lower panel, then the right side instrument panel pivot bracket screw.
13. Remove screws attaching lower instrument panel to steering column, then pull carpet from under evaporator heater assembly as far rearward as possible.
14. Remove nut attaching evaporator heater assembly to plenum mounting brace and blower motor ground cable, then support heater assembly with hands and remove mounting brace from its stud, **Fig. 9**.
15. Lift and pull evaporator heater assembly rearward to clear dash panel and liner. The panel will also have to be pulled rearward to allow assembly clearance.
16. Remove evaporator heater assembly from dash panel, taking care to prevent dash panel attaching studs from hanging up in dash liner.
17. Place evaporator assembly on workbench, then remove nut from mode door actuator arm on top cover.
18. Remove two retaining clips from front edge of cover, then the mode door actuator to cover attaching screws and mode door actuator.
19. Remove 15 heater assembly cover

attaching screws, then lift cover door out of heater assembly.
20. Remove heater core tube retaining bracket attaching screw, then lift core from heater assembly.
21. Reverse procedure to install.

## 1984 Models

1. Disconnect battery ground cable, then drain cooling system and discharge A/C system.
2. Disconnect blend air door cable and disengage from clip on heater air duct.
3. Remove glove box and door assembly.
4. Remove center bezel attaching screws, then the center bezel.
5. Remove center distribution duct and defroster duct adapter.
6. Disconnect heater hoses and A/C lines. Plug heater core tube openings.
7. Disconnect vacuum lines at engine and water valve, **Fig. 8**.
8. Remove four dash retaining nuts, then the right side cowl trim panel.
9. Remove right instrument panel pivot bracket attaching screw, then the two screws attaching lower instrument panel at steering column.
10. Remove panel top cover.
11. Remove all but left panel to fenceline attaching screw, then pull carpet from under A/C unit as far rearward as possible.
12. Remove support strap attaching nut and blower motor ground cable, then support heater unit with hands and remove strap from its plenum stud, **Fig. 9**.
13. Lift and pull evaporator heater assembly rearward to clear dash panel and liner. The panel will also have to be pulled rearward to allow assembly clearance.
14. Remove evaporator heater assembly from dash panel, taking care to prevent dash panel attaching studs from hanging up in dash liner.

15. Place evaporator heater assembly on workbench, then remove nut from mode door actuator arm on top cover.
16. Remove two retaining clips from front edge of cover, then the mode door actuator to cover attaching screws and mode door actuator.
17. Remove 15 heater unit cover attaching screws, then the cover. Lift mode door out of heater assembly.
18. Remove heater core tube retaining bracket attaching screw, then lift core from heater assembly.
19. Reverse procedure to install.

## BLOWER MOTOR
## REPLACE
### LESS A/C

1. Disconnect battery ground cable.
2. Disconnect blower motor wiring connector.
3. Remove left heater outlet duct.
4. Remove five blower mounting plate to heater assembly attaching screws.
5. Remove blower motor assembly.
6. Reverse procedure to install.

### WITH A/C

1. Disconnect battery ground cable.
2. Remove three glove box to instrument panel attaching screws, then the glove box.
3. Disconnect blower motor wiring connector. Remove wires from retaining clip on recirculating housing.
4. Disconnect blower motor vent tube from A/C unit.
5. Loosen recirculation door actuator from bracket and remove actuator from housing. Do not disconnect vacuum lines.
6. Remove seven recirculating housing to A/C unit attaching screws, then the recirculating housing.
7. Remove three blower motor mounting flange nuts, then the blower motor.
8. Reverse procedure to install.

## SPEED CONTROL
## ADJUST
### LOCK-IN SCREW ADJUSTMENT

Lock-in accuracy can be affected by poor engine performance, overloading of vehicle, or improper slack in throttle control cable.

1. If the above note has been taken into consideration and vehicle speed still varies or drops more than 2-3 mph when speed control is activated, proceed as follows:
   a. Turn lock-in adjusting screw counterclockwise approximately ¼ turn for every 1 mph out of adjustment.
2. If vehicle speed increases more than 2-3 mph when speed control is activated, proceed as follows:
   a. Turn lock-in adjusting screw clockwise approximately ¼ turn for every 1 mph out of adjustment.

**The above adjustments should not exceed two turns in either direction, as damage to unit may occur.**

## THROTTLE CONTROL CABLE ADJUSTMENT

1. Start engine and allow to reach normal operating temperature.
2. Remove snap ring, then check clearance between throttle stud and cable clevis, **Fig. 10.**
3. If adjustment is required, proceed as follows:
   a. Loosen cable clamp attaching nut.
   b. Pull all slack out of cable, using head of throttle stud as a gauge. **Do not pull cable so tight that it moves throttle away from curb idle position.**
   c. Torque cable clamp attaching nut to 45 inch lbs. and move cable clevis back on round portion of stud.
4. Install snap ring and check for proper operation.

# 4-135 (2.2L) ENGINE

## INDEX

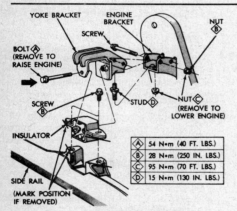

**Fig. 1 Engine mount. 1982-83, right side**

| | |
|---|---|
| Ⓐ | 54 N·m (40 FT. LBS.) |
| Ⓑ | 28 N·m (250 IN. LBS.) |
| Ⓒ | 95 N·m (70 FT. LBS.) |
| Ⓓ | 15 N·m (130 IN. LBS.) |

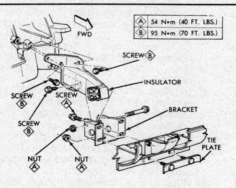

**Fig. 2 Front engine mount. 1982-83**

| | |
|---|---|
| Ⓐ | 54 N·m (40 FT. LBS.) |
| Ⓑ | 95 N·m (70 FT. LBS.) |

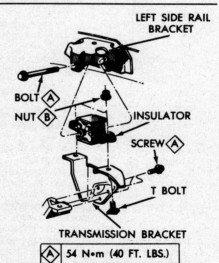

**Fig. 3 Engine mount. 1982-83, left side w/automatic transaxle**

| | |
|---|---|
| Ⓐ | 54 N·m (40 FT. LBS.) |
| Ⓑ | 75 N·m (55 FT. LBS.) |

## ENGINE MOUNTS
### REPLACE

Before removing engine mounts on 1982-83 models, driveshaft length should be measured to ensure correct engine and driveshaft positioning during installation. When positioning the engine on 1984 models, check driveshaft length as outlined in "Front Suspension & Steering" under "Driveshaft Length, Adjust." On all models, the engine mounts incorporate slotted bolt holes and permit side-to-side positioning of the engine, thereby affecting the length of the driveshaft. Failure to properly position the engine may result in extensive damage to the engine.

Refer to **Figs. 1 through 7** when replacing engine mounts.

On 1982-83 vehicles, the left engine mount is attached with two types of mounting screws. Two of the three are of the pilot type with extended tips. Extended tip screws must be installed in proper position, **Fig. 8.** Damage to shift cover or difficult shifting may occur if screws are incorrectly installed.

## ENGINE
### REPLACE
#### 1982-83 MODELS

1. Disconnect battery ground cable.
2. Scribe alignment marks on hood and hood hinge, then remove hood.
3. Drain cooling system, then disconnect radiator hoses at radiator and engine.
4. Remove radiator and fan shroud, then remove air cleaner.
5. If equipped with A/C, remove compressor from the mounting bracket and position aside with the hoses attached.
6. Remove power steering pump from mounting bracket and position aside with the hoses attached, if equipped.

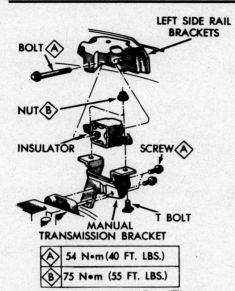

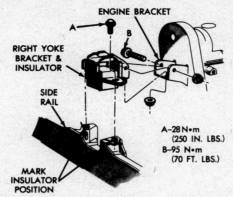

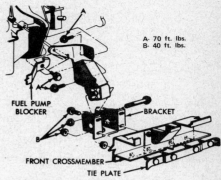

Fig. 6 Front engine mount. 1984

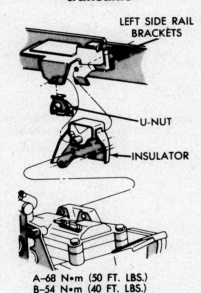

Fig. 8 Positioning of extended tip screws

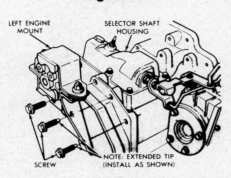

A–68 N•m (50 FT. LBS.)
B–54 N•m (40 FT. LBS.)

**Fig. 7 Engine mount. 1984, left side**

| | |
|---|---|
| A | 54 N•m (40 FT. LBS.) |
| B | 75 N•m (55 FT. LBS.) |

**Fig. 4 Engine mount. 1982–83, left side w/manual transaxle**

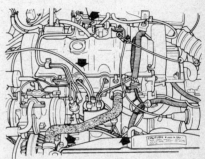

Fig. 9 Electrical connector location

7. Drain crankcase and remove the oil filter.
8. Disconnect the wire connectors at the alternator, carburetor and engine, **Fig. 9.**
9. Disconnect fuel line, heater hose and the accelerator cable, **Fig. 10.**
10. Remove alternator from mounting bracket and position aside.
11. On models equipped with manual transmission, disconnect clutch cable, then remove transmission lower cover.
12. Disconnect exhaust pipe at the manifold, then remove the starter motor, **Fig. 11.**
13. On models equipped with automatic transmission, remove transmission case lower cover and place alignment marks on the flexplate and torque

converter. Remove converter to flexplate attaching screws. Attach a C-clamp to the front lower position of the housing so as to retain the torque converter in the housing when removing the engine.
14. On all models, install a suitable transmission holding fixture and attach a suitable lifting device, **Fig. 12.**
15. Remove right inner splash shield, then disconnect ground strap, **Fig. 13.**
16. Remove right engine mount through bolts.
17. Remove transmission case-to-engine block attaching bolts.
18. Remove front engine mount bolt.
19. On 1983 vehicles with manual transmission, remove anti-roll strut, **Fig. 14.**
20. On all models, carefully lift engine from vehicle.
21. Reverse procedure to install. Torque transmission case-to-engine block attaching bolts to 70 ft. lbs.

## 1984 MODELS

1. Perform steps 1 through 15 for 1982–83 models.
2. Remove long bolt through yoke bracket and insulator. **If insulator screws are to be removed, mark position on side rail for exact reinstallation.**
3. Remove transmission case to cylinder block mounting screws.
4. Remove front engine mount screw and nut.
5. On vehicles with manual transmission, remove anti-roll strut, **Fig. 14.**

6. On vehicles with manual transmission, remove insulator through bolt from inside wheel house, or the insulator bracket to transmission screws.
7. On all vehicles, carefully remove engine from vehicle.
8. Reverse procedure to install. Torque transmission case-to-engine block attaching bolts to 70 ft. lbs.

## TIMING SPROCKETS & OIL SEAL
### REPLACE
### ALTERNATOR BELT REMOVAL

1. Disconnect battery ground cable.
2. Loosen alternator locking screw, then loosen adjusting screw and remove the alternator belt.
3. Reverse procedure to install.

### ALTERNATOR & COMPRESSOR MOUNTING BRACKET REMOVAL

For replacement of alternator and compressor mounting bracket, refer to **Fig. 15.**

### POWER STEERING PUMP MOUNTING BRACKET REMOVAL

1. Remove pump locking screw, **Fig. 16.**
2. Remove pivot bolt and pivot nut, then the drive belt.
3. Remove power steering pump and position aside.
4. Remove mounting bracket bolts, then the bracket.
5. Reverse procedure to install.

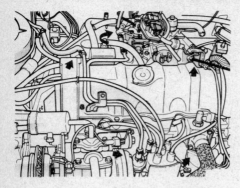

**Fig. 10   Fuel line, heater hose and accelerator connections**

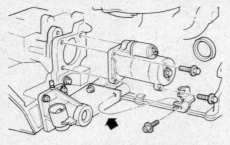

**Fig. 11   Removing starter motor**

A–22 N•m (16 FT. LBS.)
B–28 N•m (250 IN. LBS.)
C–54 N•m (40 FT. LBS.)

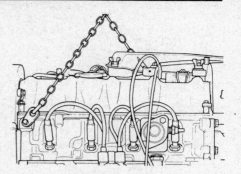

**Fig. 12   Engine lifting device**

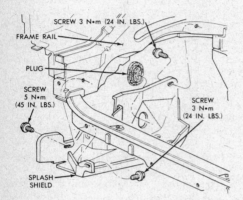

**Fig. 13   Right inner splash shield**

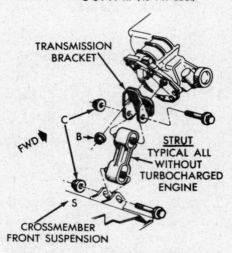

**Fig. 14   Anti-roll strut (Typical)**

| TORQUE | | |
|---|---|---|
| Ⓐ | 54 N•m | 40 FT. LBS. |
| Ⓑ | 41 N•m | 30 FT. LBS. |
| Ⓒ | 23 N•m | 200 IN. LBS. |

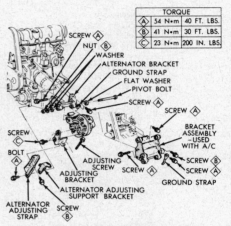

**Fig. 15   Removing alternator & compressor mounting bracket**

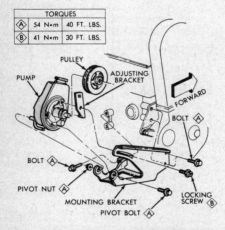

**Fig. 16   Power steering pump mounting bracket**

## TIMING BELT COVER REMOVAL

1. Remove nuts securing timing belt cover to the cylinder head, **Fig. 18.**
2. Remove screws securing the cover to the cylinder head, then remove both halves of the timing belt cover.
3. Position a suitable jack under engine, then remove right hand engine mount bolt and raise engine slightly.
4. Loosen timing belt tensioner, then remove timing belt.
5. Reverse procedure to install. **On 1983-84 models, torque all attaching hardware to 40 inch lbs.**

## CRANKSHAFT SPROCKET REMOVAL

1. With the timing belt removed from engine, remove the crankshaft sprocket bolt.
2. Remove crankshaft sprocket using a suitable puller.

## CRANKSHAFT, INTERMEDIATE SHAFT & CAMSHAFT OIL SEAL SERVICE

Refer to **Figs. 19** and **20,** for removal and installation of crankshaft, intermediate shaft or camshaft seals.

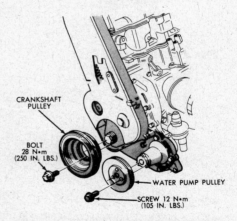

**Fig. 17   Removing crankshaft and water pump pulley**

## CRANKSHAFT & INTERMEDIATE SHAFT TIMING

1. Rotate crankshaft and intermediate shaft until markings on sprockets are aligned, **Fig. 21.**

## CAMSHAFT TIMING

1. Rotate camshaft until arrows on hub are aligned with No. 1 camshaft cap to cylinder head line. Small hole must be located along vertical center line.

## CRANKSHAFT PULLEY & WATER PUMP PULLEY REMOVAL

1. Remove screws retaining water pump pulley to pump shaft, **Fig. 17.**
2. Remove bolts retaining crankshaft pulley.
3. Raise and support front of vehicle, then remove right inner splash shield and remove crankshaft pulley.
4. Reverse procedure to install.

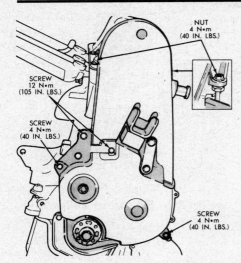

**Fig. 18  Removing timing belt cover**

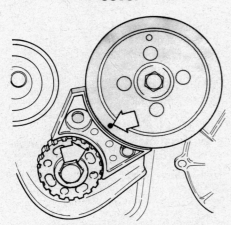

**Fig. 21  Aligning crankshaft & intermediate shaft timing marks**

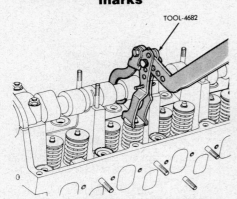

**Fig. 24  Valve spring removal and installation**

2. Install timing belt. Refer to "Adjusting Drive Belt Tension" described elsewhere, for proper drive belt adjustment.
3. Rotate crankshaft two full revolutions and recheck timing. **Do not allow oil or solvents to contact the timing belt, since they will deteriorate the belt and cause tooth slippage.**

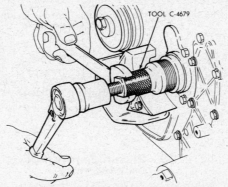

**Fig. 19  Removing crankshaft, intermediate shaft & camshaft oil seal**

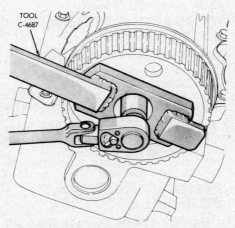

**Fig. 22  Replacing camshaft & intermediate shaft**

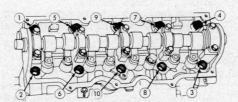

**Fig. 25  Cylinder head bolt removal sequence**

## CAMSHAFT & INTERMEDIATE SHAFT REMOVAL & INSTALLATION

Refer to **Fig. 22**, for removal and installation of camshaft and intermediate shaft sprocket.

## ADJUSTING DRIVE BELT TENSION

1. Remove spark plugs, then rotate crankshaft to TDC position.
2. Using a suitable tool, loosen tensioner locknut, **Fig. 23**.
3. Reset tension so that belt tensioning tool's axis is within 15° of horizontal.
4. Rotate crankshaft two revolutions in a clockwise direction and position at TDC, then tighten tensioner locknut.

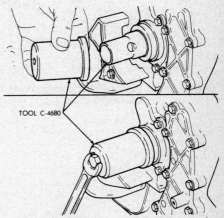

**Fig. 20  Installing crankshaft, intermediate shaft & camshaft oil seal**

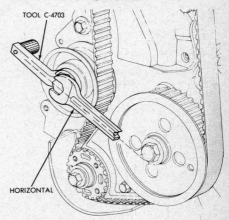

**Fig. 23  Adjusting drive belt tension**

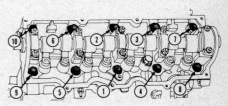

**Fig. 26  Cylinder head bolt tightening sequence**

## INTAKE & EXHAUST MANIFOLD REPLACE

1. Disconnect battery ground cable and drain cooling system.
2. Remove air cleaner and disconnect all vacuum and fuel lines, and electrical connectors from carburetor.
3. Disconnect throttle linkage, and remove power steering pump drive belt.
4. Disconnect power brake vacuum hose from carburetor, if equipped.
5. Disconnect hose from water crossover, then raise and support vehicle and disconnect exhaust pipe from exhaust manifold.

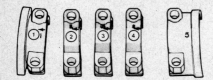

**Fig. 27   Installing camshaft bearing cap**

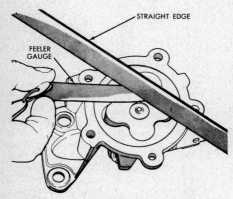

**Fig. 30   Checking oil pump endplay**

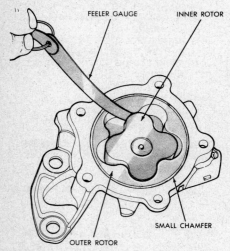

**Fig. 32   Measuring clearance between oil pump rotors**

6. Remove power steering pump and position aside, then remove intake manifold support bracket.
7. Remove EGR tube, then remove intake manifold retaining screws.
8. Lower vehicle and remove intake manifold.
9. Remove exhaust manifold retaining nuts, then the exhaust manifold.
10. Reverse procedure to install. Refer to "Engine Tightening Specifications" at the beginning of this chapter.

## CYLINDER HEAD & VALVE ASSEMBLY

Some engines may be equipped with cylinder heads which have oversize journals. When servicing the cylinder head on these engines, proper replace-

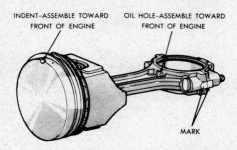

**Fig. 28   Piston & connecting rod assembly**

ment components must be installed. To identify over size cylinder head journals, the top of the bearing caps are painted green and "O/S J" is stamped on air pump end of head.

## REMOVING & INSTALLING VALVE SPRINGS
### Cylinder Head On Engine

1. Rotate crankshaft until piston is at TDC on compression stroke.
2. Apply 90-120 psi of compressed air into spark plug hole of valve spring being removed.
3. Using tool 4682, compress valve spring enough to remove valve stem locks, **Fig. 24.**
4. Remove valve spring and spring seat.
5. Remove valve seal.

## CYLINDER HEAD BOLT REMOVAL SEQUENCE

On 1982 models, oil leaks in the left front head gasket area may be found. If oil leakage is found, loosen cylinder head bolts 1/4 turn and retorque according to specifications.

When removing cylinder head, remove cylinder head bolts in proper sequence, **Fig. 25.**

## CYLINDER HEAD BOLT TIGHTENING SEQUENCE

Refer to **Fig. 26** for cylinder head bolt tightening sequence and to "Engine Tightening Specifications" at the beginning of this chapter.

## CAMSHAFT BEARING CAPS

Some engines may be equipped with camshafts which have oversize journals. When servicing the camshaft on these engines, proper replacement components must be installed. To identify oversize camshaft journals, the barrel of the cam is painted green and "O/S J" is stamped on the air pump end of the camshaft. Never install an oversize journal camshaft in a cylinder head with standard size bores, or cam cap breakage could result.

1. With caps removed from engine, check oil holes for obstructions.
2. With caps aligned in proper sequence, make sure arrow on caps 1, 2, 3 and 4 point toward timing belt, **Fig. 27.**
3. Apply suitable sealant to No. 1 and 5 bearing caps.

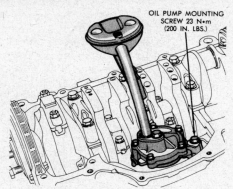

**Fig. 29   Oil pump assembly**

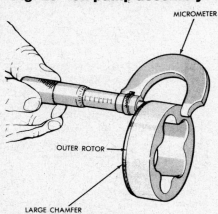

**Fig. 31   Measuring oil pump outer rotor thickness**

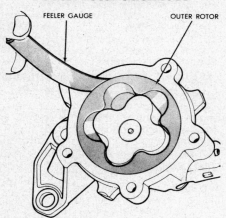

**Fig. 33   Measuring oil pump outer rotor clearance**

4. Install caps before installing camshaft seals, then torque cap bolts to 165 inch lbs.

## VALVES
### ADJUST

These engine are equipped with hydraulic lash adjuster. No provision for adjustment is provided.

## PISTON & ROD ASSEMBLY

When installing the piston and rod assembly, the indentation on the top of piston

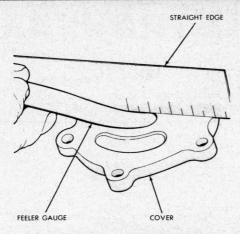

Fig. 34   Measuring oil pump cover clearance

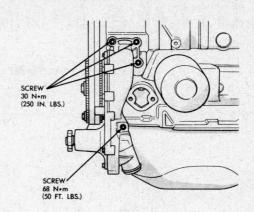

Fig. 35   Water pump to cylinder block attaching bolts

must face the timing belt side of the engine, **Fig. 28.** The oil hole on connecting rod must also face the timing belt side of the engine and be on the same side as the indented mark on the piston.

# ENGINE LUBRICATION SYSTEM

Some 1982 engines may exhibit a knock sound similar to a diesel engine. This noise occurs after a previously warmed up engine has sat for 4 hours or longer and been restarted. To alleviate this condition, a new oil filter adapter has been released which has an integral check valve. The new part No. is 4273323, and is used on all later models. When installing this adapter, inspect the check valve for proper operation by inserting a screwdriver in the oil filter end of the adapter and lightly pushing on the check valve. Under very light pressure, the valve should freely move 1/4 inch. If the valve sticks or binds, replace the oil filter adapter. A sticking valve may restrict oil pressure, possibly resulting in engine damage.

## OIL PUMP ASSEMBLY

1. With oil pan removed, remove the screw securing oil pump to the cylinder block, **Fig. 29.**

2. Reverse procedure to install. Torque oil pump attaching screw to 200 inch lbs.

## OIL PUMP SERVICE

1. Measure the following oil pump clearances:
   a. Endplay, **Fig. 30.** Endplay should be .001–.006 inch on 1982 vehicles, or .001–.004 inch on 1983–84 vehicles.
   b. Outer rotor thickness, **Fig. 31.** Thickness should be .825 inch, minimum. Install outer rotor with chamfered edge in pump body.
   c. Clearance between rotors, **Fig. 32,** should be .010 inch, maximum.
   d. Outer rotor clearance, **Fig. 33.** Clearance should be .014 inch, maximum.
   e. Oil pump cover clearance, **Fig. 34,** should be no greater than .015 inch on 1982 vehicles, or .003 inch on 1983–84 vehicles.
   f. Oil pressure relief valve spring length should be 1.95 inches.

## WATER PUMP
### REPLACE

1. Disconnect battery ground cable.
2. Drain cooling system, then remove upper radiator hose.

3. Remove A/C compressor from mounting brackets and position aside with refrigerant lines attached, if equipped.
4. Remove alternator.
5. Disconnect lower radiator hose, bypass hose and four water pump-to-engine attaching screws, **Fig. 35,** then remove water pump from engine.
6. Reverse procedure to install. Torque top three water pump-to-engine attaching screws to 250 inch lbs. and lower screw to 50 ft. lbs.

## FUEL PUMP
### REPLACE

1. Disconnect battery ground cable.
2. Disconnect and plug fuel line connections at fuel pump.
3. Remove fuel pump-to-cylinder block attaching bolts, then the fuel pump.
4. Reverse procedure to install.

## BELT TENSION DATA

| | | NEW | USED |
|---|---|---|---|
| 1982–84 | Air Cond. | 95 | 80 |
| | Alternator | 115 | 80 |
| | Power Steer. | 95 | 80 |

# CLUTCH & MANUAL TRANSAXLE

## INDEX

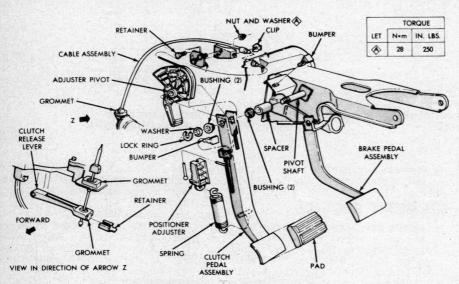

| TORQUE | | |
|---|---|---|
| LET | N•m | IN. LBS. |
| ◇ | 28 | 250 |

Fig. 1 Clutch cable routing

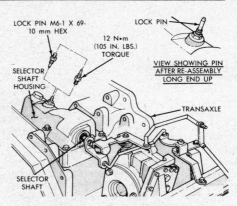

Fig. 2 Lock pin removal & installation

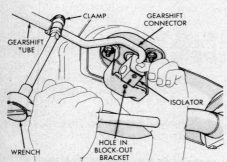

Fig. 3 Adjusting gear shift linkage

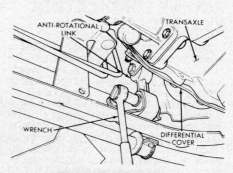

Fig. 4 Removing anti-rotational link

## CLUTCH
### ADJUST

The clutch release cable, **Fig. 1**, on these models cannot be adjusted. When the cable is properly routed, the spring between the clutch pedal and positioner adjuster will hold the clutch cable in the proper position. An adjuster pivot is used to hold release cable in place to ensure complete clutch release when the clutch pedal is depressed.

## CLUTCH
### REPLACE

1. Remove transmission as outlined under "Manual Transaxle, Replace" procedure.
2. Mark relationship between clutch cover and flywheel for reference during reassembly, then insert suitable clutch disc aligning tool through clutch disc hub.
3. Gradually loosen clutch cover attaching bolts, then remove pressure plate and cover assembly and disc from flywheel.
4. Remove clutch release shaft and slide release bearing assembly off input shaft seal retainer. Remove fork from release bearing thrust plate.
5. Reverse procedure to install. Align reference marks made during reassembly. Using clutch disc alignment tool, install disc, plate and cover to flywheel and torque bolts to 21 ft. lbs.

## GEARSHIFT LINKAGE
### ADJUST

1. Remove lock pin from transaxle selector shaft housing, **Fig. 2.**
2. Reverse lock pin, so long end is facing downward, and insert pin into same threaded hole while pushing selector shaft into selector housing.
3. Raise and support vehicle, then loosen clamp bolt that secures gearshift tube to gearshift rod.
4. Check that gearshift connector slides and rotates freely in gearshift tube.
5. Position shifter mechanism connector assembly so that isolater is spaced .050 inch away from upstanding flange. Align holes in block-out bracket, then hold connector isolater in this position while torquing nut on gearshift tube to 170 inch lbs, **Fig. 3.** Excessive force should not be used on linkage during this procedure.
6. Lower vehicle, remove lock pin from selector shaft housing and reinstall lock pin in reversed position. Torque pin to 105 inch lbs.
7. Check for proper operation.

## MANUAL TRANSAXLE
### REPLACE

1. Disconnect battery ground cable.
2. Raise and support vehicle and install suitable engine support fixture.
3. Disconnect gearshift linkage and clutch cable from transaxle.
4. Remove front wheel and tire assemblies.
5. Remove left front splash shield, then the impact bracket from transaxle if so equipped.
6. Refer to "Driveshafts, Replace" to disconnect driveshafts.
7. Support transaxle and remove upper clutch housing bolts.
8. Remove left engine mount from transaxle, noting location of bolts.

9. Remove anti-rotational link, if equipped, **Fig. 4.**
10. Move transaxle toward left side of ve-

hicle until mainshaft clears clutch, then lower and remove transaxle.
11. Reverse procedure to install. When in-

stalling left engine mount, refer to "Engine Mounts, Replace" in "Engine" section.

# REAR AXLE REAR SUSPENSION & BRAKES

## INDEX

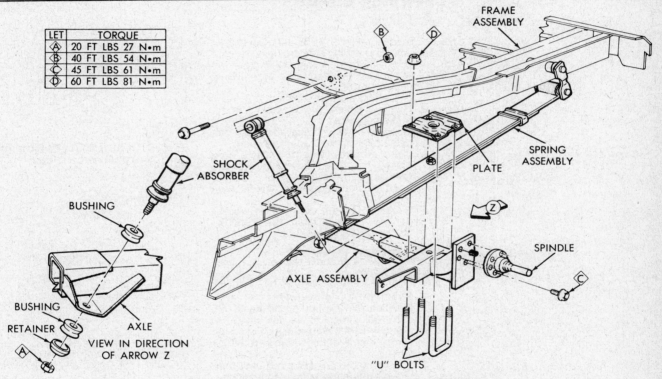

| LET | TORQUE |
|-----|--------|
| A | 20 FT LBS 27 N•m |
| B | 40 FT LBS 54 N•m |
| C | 45 FT LBS 61 N•m |
| D | 60 FT LBS 81 N•m |

**Fig. 1   Rear axle & suspension assembly**

## REAR AXLE & SPRING REPLACE
### REMOVAL

1. Raise and support vehicle, then position suitable floor jack under axle assembly and raise axle assembly to relieve weight on rear springs.
2. Disconnect rear brake proportioning valve spring, then the lower ends of rear shock absorbers at axle brackets, **Fig. 1.**
3. Remove U-bolt attaching nuts, then the U-bolt and spring plate.
4. Lower rear axle assembly, allowing rear spring to hang free.
5. Remove front pivot bolt from front spring hanger.
6. Remove rear spring shackle attaching

nuts, then the shackles from the spring.
7. Remove springs from vehicle.

### INSTALLATION

1. Assemble shackle and bushings in rear of spring and rear spring hanger, then install shackle bolt, **Figs. 1 and 2.** Do not tighten nut at this point.
2. Raise front of spring, then install pivot bolt and attaching nut. Do not tighten nut at this point.
3. Raise axle assembly into correct position with axle centered under spring center bolt.
4. Install spring plate, U-bolts and attaching nuts. Torque attaching nuts to 60 ft. lbs.
5. Install shock absorbers and attaching nuts. Do not tighten nuts at this point.

6. Lower vehicle to floor, allowing full weight of vehicle on wheels, then torque the following fasteners: front pivot bolt, 95 ft. lbs.; shackle nuts, 35 ft. lbs.; upper shock absorber attaching nut, 40 ft. lbs.
7. Connect rear brake proportioning valve spring.

## REAR WHEEL ALIGNMENT

Due to the design of the rear suspension and the incorporation of stub axles or wheel spindles, it is possible to adjust camber and toe of the rear wheels on these vehicles. Adjustment is controlled by adding shims approximately .010 inch thick between the spindle mounting surface and spindle mounting plate. The

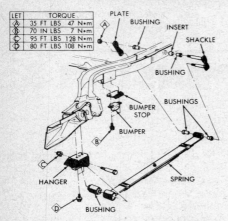

| LET | TORQUE | |
|---|---|---|
| A | 35 FT LBS | 47 N·m |
| B | 70 IN LBS | 7 N·m |
| C | 95 FT LBS | 128 N·m |
| D | 80 FT LBS | 108 N·m |

**Fig. 2   Rear spring installation**

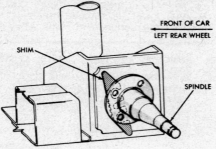

**Fig. 3   Shim installation for toe-out**

**Fig. 4   Shim installation for toe-in**

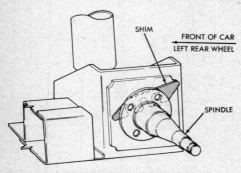

**Fig. 5   Shim installation for positive camber**

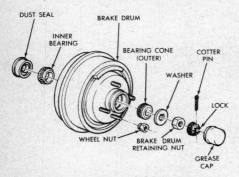

**Fig. 7   Wheel bearing assembly**

amount of adjustment is approximately 0°18' per shim for 1982 vehicles, and 3° per shim for 1983-84 vehicles. Refer to **Figs. 3 through 6** for proper replacement of shims.

## REAR WHEEL BEARING
### ADJUST

1. Raise and support rear of vehicle.
2. Torque adjusting nut to 270 inch lbs. while rotating wheel.
3. Stop wheel and loosen adjusting nut, **Fig. 7.**
4. Tighten adjusting nut finger tight. End play should be .001-.003 inch.
5. Install castle lock with slots aligned with cotter pin hole.
6. Install cotter pin and grease cap.

## SERVICE BRAKES
### ADJUST

The rear brakes on 1983-84 models are self-adjusting and no adjustment is necessary. On 1982 models, the rear brakes are not self-adjusting and periodic adjustment is required as follows:
1. Raise and support vehicle.
2. Remove adjusting hole covers from brake supports.
3. Release parking brake and back off cable adjustment to slacken cable.
4. Insert a narrow screwdriver into adjusting nut hole. Move screwdriver handle downward on left side or upward on right side until wheels are locked, **Fig. 8.**
5. Back off nut ten clicks, then adjust parking brake. Refer to "Parking Brake, Adjust" procedure.

## PARKING BRAKE
### ADJUST

1. Raise and support vehicle.
2. Release parking brake and back off cable adjustment to slacken cable.
3. Tighten cable adjusting nut until a slight drag is obtained while rotating wheels.
4. Loosen cable adjusting nut until the wheels rotate freely, then an additional two turns.
5. Apply and release parking brake to check for proper operation. The rear wheels should rotate without dragging.

## MASTER CYLINDER
### REPLACE
#### MANUAL BRAKES

1. Disconnect and plug brake tubes from master cylinder. Cap master cylinder ports to prevent fluid leakage.
2. Disconnect stop lamp switch mounting bracket from beneath instrument panel.
3. Pull brake pedal rearward to disengage pushrod from master cylinder. **Pulling the brake pedal rearward will destroy the grommet. Install a new grommet when installing the pushrod.**

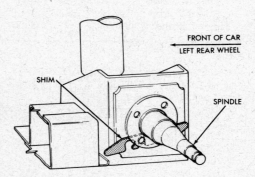

**Fig. 6   Shim installation for negative camber**

**Fig. 8   Adjusting service brake**

4. Remove master cylinder attaching nuts, then the master cylinder from vehicle.
5. Reverse procedure to install. **Master cylinder should be bench bled before installation using bleeder kit No. C-4546 or equivalent.**

### POWER BRAKES

1. Disconnect and plug brake tubes from master cylinder. Cap master cylinder ports to prevent fluid leakage.
2. Remove master cylinder attaching nuts, then master cylinder from power brake unit.
3. Reverse procedure to install. **Master cylinder should be bench bled before installation using bleeder kit No. C-4546 or equivalent.**

*REAR AXLE, SUSPENSION & BRAKES*

## POWER BRAKE UNIT
## REPLACE

1. Remove master cylinder attaching nuts, then slide master cylinder from mounting studs and support on fender shield. Do not disconnect brake tubes from master cylinder.
2. Disconnect vacuum hose from power brake unit.
3. Install a suitable screwdriver between center tang on retainer clip and the brake pedal pin, located under instrument panel. Rotate screwdriver so retainer clip center tang will pass over brake pedal pin.
4. Pull retainer clip from pin.
5. Remove power brake unit attaching nuts, then the power brake unit from vehicle.
6. Reverse procedure to install. Torque power brake unit and master cylinder unit attaching nuts to 200-300 inch lbs. for 1983-84 models, and 200-250 inch lbs. for 1982 models.

# FRONT SUSPENSION & STEERING

## INDEX

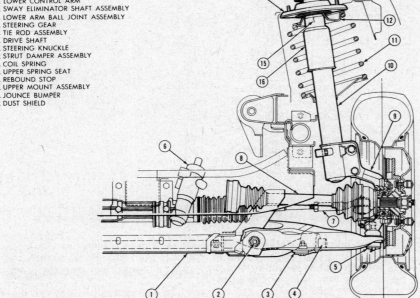

1. FRONT SUSPENSION CROSSMEMBER
2. FRONT PIVOT BOLT
3. LOWER CONTROL ARM
4. SWAY ELIMINATOR SHAFT ASSEMBLY
5. LOWER ARM BALL JOINT ASSEMBLY
6. STEERING GEAR
7. TIE ROD ASSEMBLY
8. DRIVE SHAFT
9. STEERING KNUCKLE
10. STRUT DAMPER ASSEMBLY
11. COIL SPRING
12. UPPER SPRING SEAT
13. REBOUND STOP
14. UPPER MOUNT ASSEMBLY
15. JOUNCE BUMPER
16. DUST SHIELD

**Fig. 1   Front suspension (typical)**

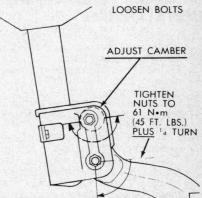

**Fig. 2   Camber adjustment**

## DESCRIPTION

These vehicles use a MacPherson-type front suspension with the vertical shock absorber struts attached to the upper fender reinforcement and the steering knuckle, **Fig. 1**. The lower control arms are attached inboard to a crossmember and outboard to the steering knuckle through a ball joint to provide lower steering knuckle position. During steering maneuvers, the strut and steering knuckle rotate as an assembly.

The driveshafts are attached inboard to the transaxle output drive flanges and outboard to the driven wheel hub.

## WHEEL ALIGNMENT

Prior to wheel alignment, ensure tires are at recommended pressure, are of equal size and have approximately the same wear pattern. Check front wheel and tire assembly for radial runout and inspect lower ball joints and steering linkage for looseness. Check front and rear springs for sagging or damage. Front suspension inspections should be performed on a level floor or alignment rack with fuel tank at capacity and vehicle free of luggage and passenger compartment load.

Prior to each alignment reading, the vehicle should be bounced an equal number of times from the center of the bumper alternately, first from the rear, then the front, releasing at bottom of down cycle.

## CASTER

The caster angle on these vehicles cannot be adjusted.

## CAMBER

To adjust camber, loosen the cam and through bolts, **Fig. 2**. Rotate the upper cam bolt to move the top of the wheel in or out to achieve the specified camber angle. Torque cam bolts to 45 ft. lbs., then advance bolts an additional 1/4 turn (90 degrees).

## TOE-IN

To adjust toe-in, center the steering wheel and hold in position using a steering wheel holding tool. Loosen the tie rod locknuts and rotate the rod, **Fig. 3**, to adjust toe-in to specifications. Use care not to twist the steering gear rubber boots. Torque the tie rod lock nuts to 55 ft. lbs. (75 Nm). Adjust position of steering gear rubber boots. Remove steering wheel holding tool.

## STRUT DAMPER ASSEMBLY
## REPLACE
### REMOVAL

1. Raise and support vehicle, then remove front wheels.
2. Mark position of camber adjusting cam, then remove the camber adjusting bolt, the through bolt and the brake hose to damper bracket retaining screw, **Figs. 4 and 5.**
3. Remove strut damper to fender shield mounting nut and washer assemblies.
4. Remove strut damper from vehicle.

### INSTALLATION

1. Position strut assembly into fender reinforcement, then install retaining nuts and washers and torque to 20 ft. lbs.
2. Position steering knuckle and washer plate to strut, then install upper cam and lower through bolts.
3. Install brake hose retainer on damper, then index cam bolt to alignment mark made during removal.
4. Position a 4-inch or larger, C-clamp on steering knuckle and strut, **Fig. 6.** Tighten clamp just enough to eliminate any looseness between strut and knuckle. Check alignment of marks made during removal, then tighten bolts to 45 ft. lbs. plus an additional 1/4 turn beyond the specified torque.
5. Remove C-clamp, then install wheel and tire assembly.

## COIL SPRING
## REPLACE

1. Remove strut damper assembly as outlined previously.
2. Using a suitable spring compressor, compress coil spring.
3. Remove strut rod nut while holding strut rod to prevent rotation.
4. Remove the mount assembly, **Fig. 7.**
5. Remove coil spring from strut damper.
6. Inspect mount assembly for deterioration of rubber isolator, retainers for cracks and distortion and bearings for binding.
7. Install the bumper dust shield assembly.
8. Install spring and seat, upper spring retainer, bearing and spacer, mount

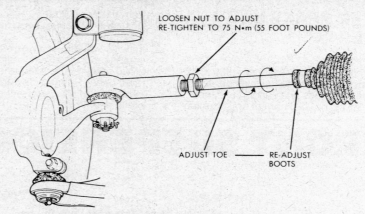

**Fig. 3   Toe-in adjustment**

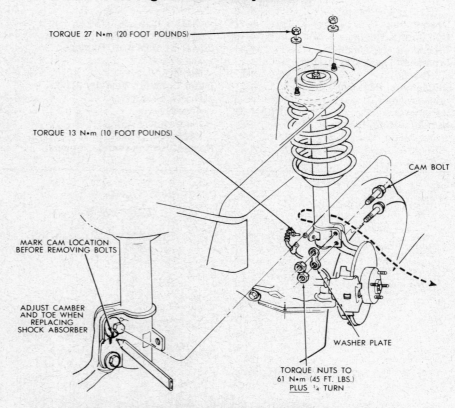

**Fig. 4   Replacing strut damper. 1982–83 models**

assembly and the rebound bumper, retainer and rod nut upper. **Position the spring retainer alignment notch parallel to the damper lower attaching brackets.**
9. Torque strut rod nut to 60 ft. lbs. (81 Nm). Do not release spring compressor before torquing nut.
10. Remove spring compressor.

## BALL JOINT SERVICE
## CHECKING

With weight of vehicle resting on wheel and tire assembly, attempt to move grease fitting with fingers, **Fig. 8.** Do not use a tool or added force to attempt to move grease fitting. If grease fitting moves freely, ball joint is worn and should be replaced.

## BALL JOINTS, REPLACE

The ball joint is pressed into the lower control arm. On these models, the ball joint can be pressed from the lower control arm using a 1 1/16 inch deep socket and receiver cup No. C-4699-2. When pressing ball joint into lower control arm, use ball joint installer No. C-4699-1 and receiver cup No. C-4699-2. Install ball joint seal using a 1 1/2 inch deep socket and receiver cup No. C-4699-2.

**On some models the ball joint is welded to the lower control arm. On these models, the ball joint and lower control arm must be replaced as an assembly.**

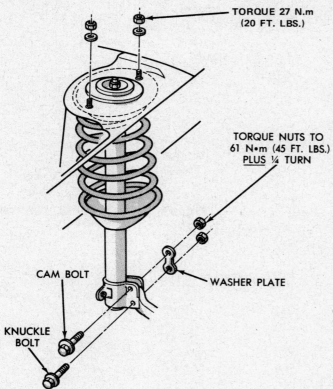

Fig. 5   Replacing strut damper. 1984 models

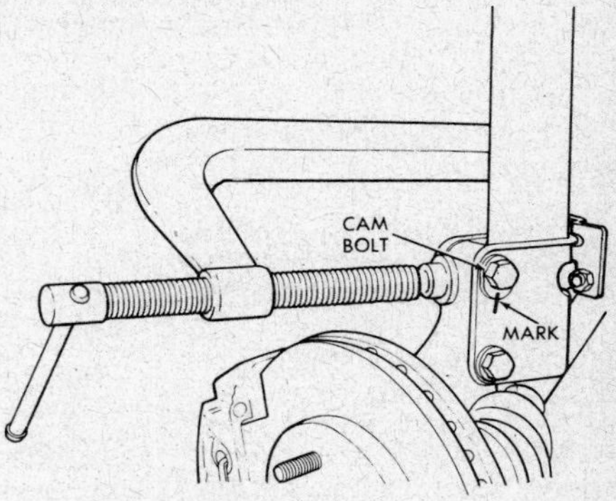

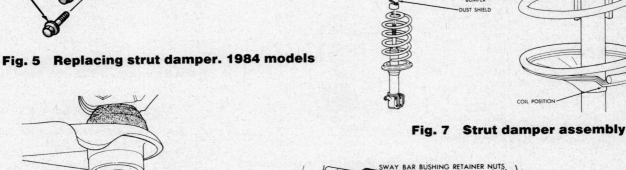

Fig. 6   Installing Strut damper

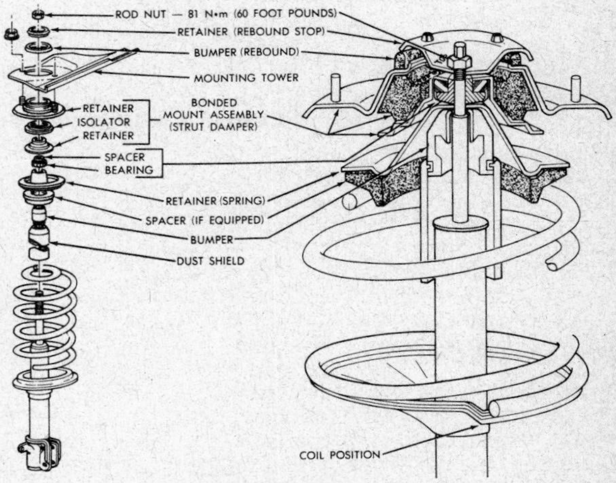

Fig. 7   Strut damper assembly

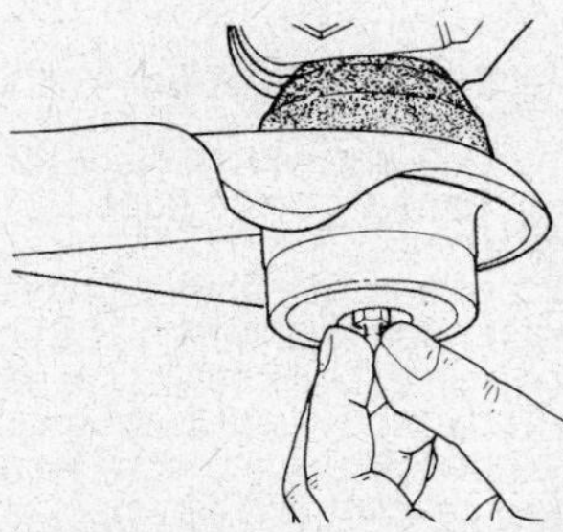

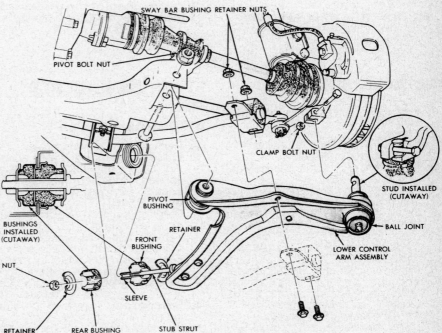

Fig. 8   Checking ball joint for wear

## LOWER CONTROL ARM
### REPLACE
#### REMOVAL

1. Raise and support vehicle.
2. Remove the front inner pivot through bolt, the rear stub strut nut, retainer and bushing and the ball joint to steering knuckle clamp bolt, **Fig. 9.**
3. Separate the ball joint from the steering knuckle by prying between the ball stud retainer and the lower control arm. **Pulling the steering knuckle "Out" from vehicle after releasing from ball joint can separate inner C/V joint.**
4. Remove sway bar to control arm nut and reinforcement and rotate control arm over sway bar. Remove rear stub strut bushing, sleeve and retainer.

Fig. 9   Lower control arm assembly

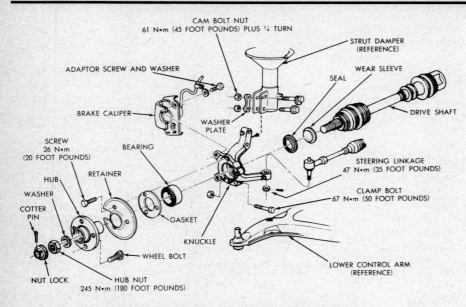

Fig. 10    Steering knuckle assembly

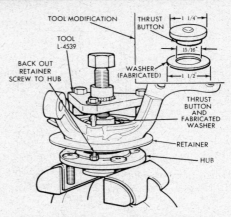

**Fig. 11    Hub removal. 1982–83 models**

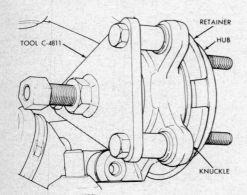

**Fig. 12    Hub removal. 1984 models**

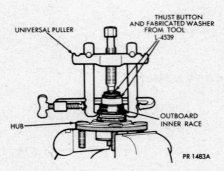

**Fig. 13    Removing outboard inner race. 1982–83 models**

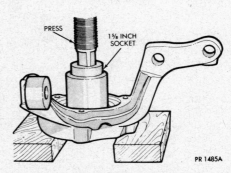

**Fig. 14    Removing bearing from knuckle. 1982–83 models**

## INSTALLATION

1. Install retainer, bushing and sleeve on stub strut.
2. Position control arm over sway bar and install rear stub strut and front pivot into crossmember.
3. Install front pivot bolt and loosely assemble nut, **Fig. 9.**
4. Install stub strut bushing and retainer and loosely assemble nut.
5. Install ball joint stud into steering knuckle, then the clamp bolt. Torque clamp bolt to 50 ft. lbs. (67 Nm) for 1982-83 models, 70 ft. lbs. (95 Nm) for 1984 models.
6. Place sway bar end bushing retainer to control arm, then install retainer bolts. Torque retainer bolts to 22 ft.lbs. (30 Nm) for 1982-83 models, 25 ft. lbs. (34 Nm) for 1984 models.
7. Lower vehicle so suspension fully supports vehicle, then torque front pivot bolt to 105 ft. lbs. (142 Nm) and stub strut nut to 70 ft. lbs. (95 Nm).

## STEERING KNUCKLE REPLACE
### REMOVAL

1. Remove cotter pin and locknut.
2. Loosen hub nut with brakes applied, **Fig. 10. The hub and driveshaft are splined together through the knuckle (bearing) and retained by the hub nut.**
3. Raise and support vehicle, then remove front wheel.
4. Remove hub nut. Ensure that the splined driveshaft is free to separate from spline in hub during knuckle removal. A pulling force on the shaft can separate the inner C/V joint. Tap lightly with a brass drift, if required.
5. Disconnect the tie rod end from steering arm with a suitable puller.
6. Disconnect brake hose retainer from strut damper.
7. Remove clamp bolt securing ball joint stud into steering knuckle and brake

caliper adapter screw and washer assemblies.
8. Support caliper with a piece of wire. Do not hang by brake hose.
9. Remove rotor.
10. Mark position of camber cam upper adjusting bolt and loosen both bolts.
11. Support steering knuckle and remove cam adjusting and through bolts. Move upper knuckle "neck" from strut damper bracket and lift knuckle from ball joint stud. **Support driveshaft during knuckle removal. Do not permit driveshaft to hang after separating steering knuckle from vehicle.**

## INSTALLATION

1. Place steering knuckle on lower ball joint stud and the driveshaft through hub.
2. Position upper "neck" of knuckle into strut damper bracket and install cam and through bolts. Place cam in original position. Place a 4-inch or larger, C-clamp on strut and steering knuckle, then tighten clamp just enough to eliminate looseness between knuckle and strut. Check to ensure that cam alignment marks made during removal are aligned, then tighten bolts to 45 ft. lbs. plus an additional 1/4 turn beyond specified torque. Remove C-clamp.
3. Install and torque ball joint to steering knuckle clamp bolt to 50 ft. lbs. (68 Nm).

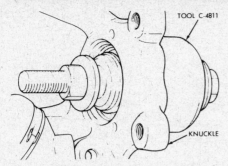

**Fig. 15 Removing bearing from knuckle. 1984 models**

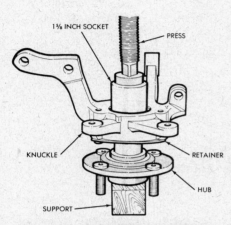

**Fig. 18 Installing hub into knuckle. 1982–83 models**

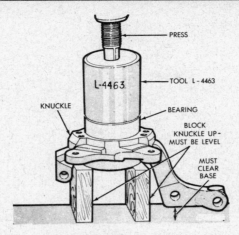

**Fig. 16 Installing bearing into knuckle. 1982–83 models**

4. On all models, remove bearing retainer attaching screws, then the retainer.
5. Remove bearing from knuckle using press and suitable socket for 1982-83 models, or tool No. C-4811 for 1984 models, **Figs. 14 and 15.**

## INSTALLATION

1. Press new bearing into knuckle using tool No. L-4463 and a suitable press for 1982-83 models, or tool No. C-4811 for 1984 models, **Figs. 16 and 17.**
2. Install bearing retainer. Torque retainer screws to 20 ft. lbs. (27 Nm).
3. Press hub into bearing using suitable press and socket for 1982-83 models, or tool No. C-4811 for 1984 models, **Figs. 18 and 19.**
4. Install steering knuckle as described under "Steering Knuckle, Replace."

## SWAY BAR
## REPLACE
### REMOVAL

1. Raise and support vehicle.
2. Remove nuts, bolts and retainers at the control arms, **Fig. 20.**
3. Remove crossmember clamp attaching bolts, then the crossmember clamps.
4. Remove sway bar from vehicle.

## INSTALLATION

A linkless sway bar is used in the front suspension. The sway bar is nearly symmetric looking, and it is possible to install the sway bar improperly in the vehicle when it is removed for service. Always mark the sway bar prior to removal to ensure proper installation. Sway bars used for production and service replacement are marked on the left (driver side) by a dab or stripe of paint.

1. Position crossmember bushings on the bar with the curved surface up and split to front of vehicle.
2. Position bar assembly onto crossmember, then install clamps and attaching bolts.
3. Position retainers at control arms,

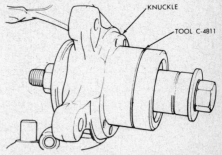

**Fig. 17 Installing bearing into knuckle. 1984 models**

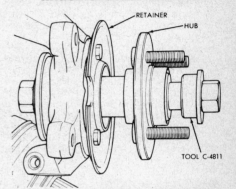

**Fig. 19 Installing hub into knuckle. 1984 models**

then install bolts and attaching nuts.
4. Raise lower control arm to correct position, then torque attaching bolts to 25 ft. lbs. for 1984 models, or 22 ft. lbs. for 1982-83 models. **A bushing retainer is not used on 1984 models.**

## DRIVESHAFT IDENTIFICATION

Driveshafts are identified as "A.C.I." or "G.K.N." assemblies, **Fig. 21.** Vehicles can be equipped with either of these assemblies, however they should not be intermixed. Procedures for installation and removal of driveshafts are essentially the same for either type assembly used.

## DRIVESHAFTS
## REPLACE
### REMOVAL

On early 1982 models, the inboard C/V joints have stub shafts splined into the differential side gears and are retained with circlips, **Fig. 22.** The circlip "Tangs" are located on a machined surface on the inner end of the stub shafts and are removed and installed with the shaft. On late 1982-84 models, the driveshafts are spring loaded and are retained to the side gears by constant spring pressure provided by the spring contained in the C/V joints, **Fig. 23.**

1. On early 1982 models, drain transaxle differential unit and remove cover.
2. If removing the right hand driveshaft, the speedometer pinion must be removed prior to driveshaft removal, **Fig. 24.**

4. Install tie rod end into steering arm and torque nut to 35 ft. lbs. (47 Nm). Install cotter pin.
5. Install rotor.
6. Install caliper over rotor and position adapter to steering knuckle. Install adapter to knuckle bolts and torque to 85 ft. lbs. (115 Nm). For 1982 vehicles, or 160 ft. lbs. (216 Nm) for 1983-84 vehicles.
7. Attach brake hose retainer to strut damper and torque screw to 10 ft. lbs. (13 Nm).
   a. Install washer and hub nut.
   b. With brakes applied, torque hub nut to 180 ft. lbs. (245 Nm).
   c. Install locknut and new cotter pin, **Fig. 10.**

## HUB & BEARING
## REPLACE
### REMOVAL

1. Remove steering knuckle as outlined previously.
2. Remove hub using tool No. L-4539 on 1982-83 vehicles, or tool No. C-4811 on 1984 vehicles, **Figs. 11 and 12. On 1982-83 models, the bearing inner races will separate and the outer race will remain in the hub.**
3. On 1982-83 models, remove bearing outer race from hub using suitable puller, **Fig. 13,** then remove brake dust shield, if equipped.

3. On early 1982 models, rotate driveshaft to expose circlip tangs, **Fig. 25.** Using needle nose pliers, compress circlip tangs while prying shaft into side gear splined cavity, **Fig. 26.** The circlip will be compressed in the cavity with the shaft.

4. Remove clamp bolt securing ball joint stud to steering knuckle, then, separate ball joint stud from steering knuckle. Do not damage ball joint or C/V joint boots.

5. Separate outer C/V joint splined shaft from hub by holding C/V housing while moving knuckle hub assembly away from C/V joint. **Do not damage slinger on outer C/V joint. Do not attempt to remove, repair or replace.**

6. Support assembly at C/V joint housings and remove by pulling outward on the inner C/V joint housing. Do not pull on the shaft. **If removing left hand driveshaft assembly, the removal may be aided by inserting a screwdriver blade between the differential pinion shaft and carefully prying against the end face of stub.**

7. Remove driveshaft assembly from vehicle.

## INSTALLATION

On early 1982 models, install new circlips on inner joint shaft before installation, **Fig. 27.**

1. On early 1982 units, be sure tangs on circlips are aligned with flattened end of shaft before inserting shaft into transaxle. If not, jamming or component damage may result.

2. Hold inner joint assembly at housing while aligning and guiding the inner joint spline into transaxle.

3. While holding the inner joint housing, quickly thrust the shaft into the differential. This will complete the lock-up of the driveshaft to the axle side gear. **On early 1982 models, inspect circlip positioning in side gears to verify lock-up.**

4. Push knuckle/hub assembly out and install splined outer C/V joint shaft into hub.

5. Install knuckle assembly on ball joint stud.

6. Install and torque clamp bolt to 50 ft. lbs. (68 Nm).

7. Install speedometer pinion, **Fig. 24.**

8. On early 1982 models, apply a $1/16$ inch bead of silicone sealant, part number 4026070, to differential cover sealing surface and mating surface of transaxle case after both have been properly cleaned and inspected.

9. On early 1982 models, install differential cover and torque retaining screws to 165 inch lbs. (19 Nm), then fill differential to bottom of filler plug hole with Dexron automatic transmission fluid.

10. Install washer and hub nut. Torque hub nut to 180 ft. lbs. (245 Nm). Install locknut and cotter pin.

11. If, after attaching driveshaft assembly in vehicle the inboard boot appears collapsed or deformed, vent the inner

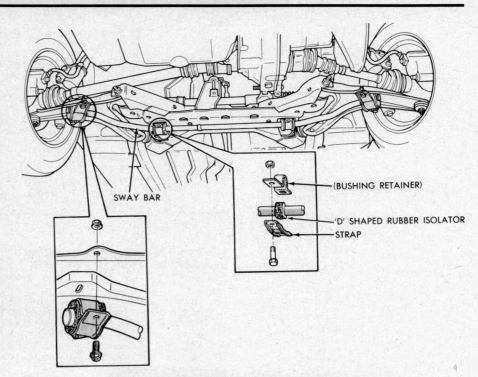

**Fig. 20  Sway bar assembly (Typical)**

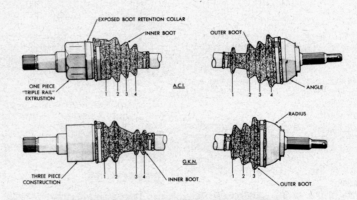

**Fig. 21  Driveshaft identification**

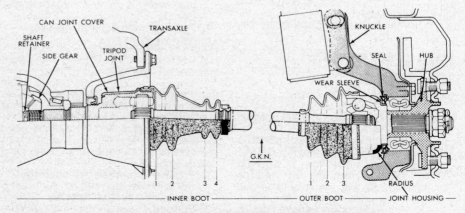

**Fig. 22  Driveshaft assembly. Early 1982**

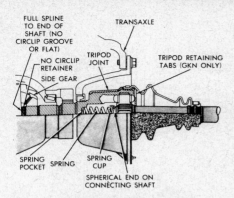

**Fig. 23 Driveshaft assembly. Late 1982–84 G.K.N. axles. (similar to 1984 A.I.S. axles)**

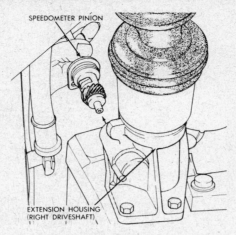

**Fig. 24 Replacing speedometer pinion**

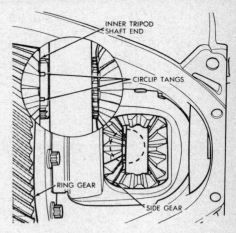

**Fig. 25 Exposing circlips. Early 1982 models**

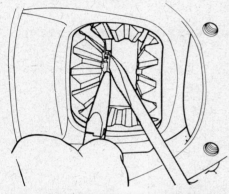

**Fig. 26 Compressing circlips. Early 1982 models**

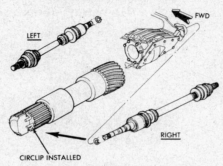

**Fig. 27 Installing circlips. Early 1982 models**

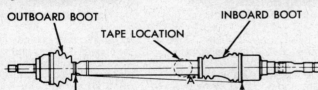

**Fig. 28 Measuring driveshaft**

| Driveshaft Identification | | | "A" Dimension | |
|---|---|---|---|---|
| Type | Side | Tape Color | M.M | Inch |
| G.K.N. | Right | Yellow | 498–509 | 19.6–20 |
| G.K.N. | Left | Yellow | 240–253 | 9.5–10 |
| A.C.I. | Right | Red | 469–478 | 18.5–19 |
| A.C.I. | Left | Red | 208–218 | 8.2–8.6 |

**Fig.29 Driveshaft length specification**

boot by inserting a round tipped, small diameter rod between the boot and shaft. As venting occurs, the boot will return to the normal shape.

## DRIVESHAFT LENGTH ADJUST
### 1983–84

1. Position vehicle with wheels straight ahead and body weight distributed on all four tires.
2. Measure direct distance between inner edge of outboard boot to inner edge of inboard boot on both driveshafts. This measurement (dimension "A") should be taken at the bottom (6 o'clock position) of driveshafts, **Fig. 28.** Damper weights are used on left driveshaft assembly. Before measuring driveshaft length, damper should be removed from shaft. After specified measurement is completed, install damper weight and torque damper weight attaching bolts to 8 ft. lbs. (11 Nm).

3. Driveshaft length (dimension "A") must be within specifications in chart, **Fig. 29.** If measurement is not within specifications, engine position must be corrected as follows:
   a. Remove load from engine mounts by carefully supporting engine and transaxle assembly using a suitable jack.
   b. Loosen right engine mount vertical bolts, then the front engine mount bracket-to-crossmember attaching bolts.
   c. Pry engine to the right or left as necessary to bring driveshaft length within specifications. **The left engine mount is sleeved over long support bolt and shaft, Fig. 30, to provide lateral adjustment whether or not engine weight is removed.**
   d. Torque engine mount vertical bolts to 250 inch lbs. and front engine mount bolts to 40 ft. lbs.
   e. Center left engine mount, then re-check driveshaft length.

## INNER CONSTANT VELOCITY JOINT SERVICE
### DISASSEMBLY

Driveshaft assembly should be identified before starting service procedure. Refer to "Driveshaft Identification."

1. Remove clamp and boot from joint and discard, **Fig. 31.**
2. On A.C.I. units, position tripod housing so all three rollers are flush with retaining tabs. Pull housing out by hand at a slight angle to pop one roller at a time out of the retaining tabs, **Fig. 32.** Do not hold joint at too severe an angle, as rollers may be damaged. **The retaining tabs must not be bent during removal or installation of tripod housing.**

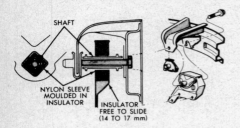

**Fig. 30  Left engine mount adjustment**

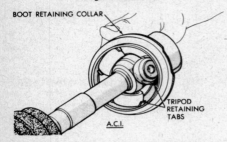

**Fig. 32  Removing inner C/V joint tripod housing. A.C.I. units**

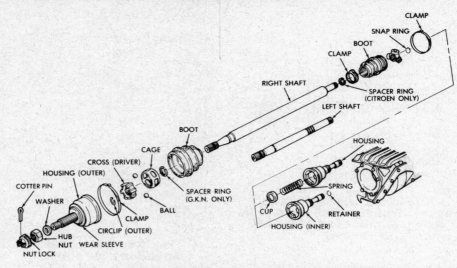

**Fig. 31  Driveshaft components. 1982–83 (Similar to 1984)**

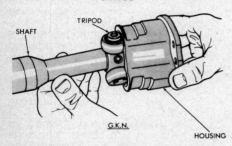

**Fig. 33  Removing inner C/V joint tripod housing. Early model G.K.N. units**

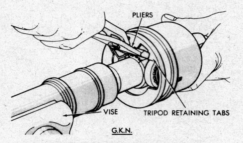

**Fig. 34  Removing inner C/V joint tripod housing. Late model G.K.N. units**

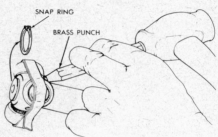

**Fig. 35  Removing snap ring & tripod inner C/V joints**

3. On early 1982 G.K.N. non-spring load-ed units, slide tripod from housing, **Fig. 33**. On late 1982-84 G.K.N. spring loaded units, bend tabs on joint cover using needle nose pliers, then remove tripod from housing, **Fig. 34**.
4. Remove snap ring from end of shaft, then remove tripod using brass punch, **Fig. 35**.

## INSPECTION

Remove grease from assembly and in-spect bearing race and tripod components for wear and damage and replace as nec-essary. On late 1982-84 spring loaded joints inspect spring, spring cup and spher-ical end of connecting shaft for wear and damage and replace as necessary.

**Components of spring loaded and non-spring loaded inner C/V joints cannot be interchanged.**

## ASSEMBLY

1. Slide small end of boot over shaft. On tubular type shafts, align boot lip with mark on shaft outer diameter. On solid type shafts, position small end of boot in groove on shaft.
2. Place rubber clamp over groove on boot.

3. Install tripod on shaft with non-chamfered face of tripod body facing shaft retainer groove.
4. Lock tripod assembly on shaft by in-stalling retaining ring in shaft groove.
5. Distribute packets of special grease provided in boot and clamp kit as fol-lows:
   a. On early 1982 G.K.N. units, distrib-ute one packet of grease in hous-ing before positioning housing over tripod.
   b. On late 1982-84 G.K.N. units, dis-tribute one packet of grease in housing, then position spring with spring cup attached to exposed end into spring pocket. Place a small amount of grease on spring cup.
   c. On A.C.I. units, distribute one pack-et of grease in boot and remaining packet in housing.
6. On early 1982 G.K.N. units, slip tripod into housing, then install boot over housing groove.
7. On late 1982-84 G.K.N. units, slip tri-pod into housing and bend retaining tabs down to their original position. In-stall boot over housing and ensure re-taining tabs hold tripod in housing.
8. On A.C.I. units, align tripod roller with retaining tabs and housing tracks. In-stall one roller at a time through re-taining tabs, and bend retaining tabs

down into their original position. Install boot over housing and ensure retain-ing tabs hold tripod in housing. **On all spring loaded joints, check to en-sure spring remains in pocket and centered in housing. Also ensure spring cup contacts spherical end of connecting shaft.**
9. On all models, install boot clamp.

## OUTER CONSTANT VELOCITY JOINT SERVICE

### DISASSEMBLY

Driveshaft assembly should be identi-fied before starting service procedure. Re-fer to "Driveshaft Identification."
1. Cut boot clamps from boot and dis-card, **Fig. 36**.
2. Clean grease from joint.
3. Support shaft in a soft jawed vise. Support the outer joint, and tap with a mallet to dislodge joint from internal circlip installed in a groove at the out-er end of the shaft, **Fig. 37**. Do not re-move slinger from housing.
4. Remove circlip from shaft groove and discard, **Fig. 38**.
5. Unless the shaft requires replace-ment, do not remove the heavy lock ring from shaft, **Fig. 38**.

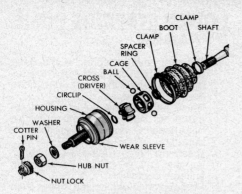

**Fig. 36   Outer C/V joint, disassembled view**

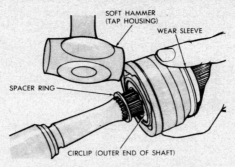

**Fig. 37   Removing joint from shaft. Outer C/V joints**

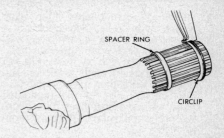

**Fig. 38   Circlip removal. Outer C/V joints**

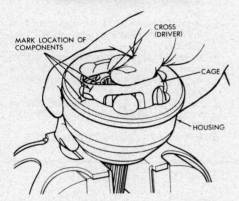

**Fig. 39   Ball removal. Outer C/V joints**

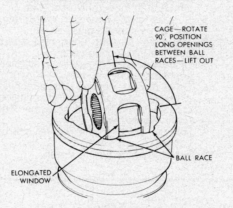

**Fig. 40   Cage & cross assemblyremoval. Outer C/V joints**

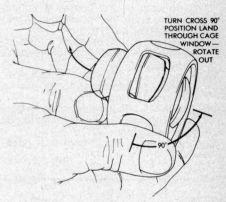

**Fig. 41   Removing cross from cage.Outer C/V joints**

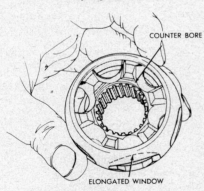

**Fig. 42   Cage & cross assembly.Outer C/V joints**

6. If constant velocity joint was operating satisfactorily and grease does not appear contaminated, proceed to "Assembly" procedure, step 7.
7. If the constant velocity joint is noisy orbadly worn, replace entire unit. The repair kit will include boot, clamps, circlip and lubricant. Clean and inspect the joint outlined in the following steps.
8. Clean surplus grease and mark relative position of inner cross, cage and housing with a dab of paint.
9. Hold joint vertically in a soft jawed vise.
10. Press downward on one side of the inner race to tilt cage and remove ball from opposite side, **Fig. 39**. If joint is

tight, use a hammer and a brass drift to tap inner race. Do not strike the cage. Repeat this step until all six balls are removed. A screwdriver may be used to pry the balls loose.
11. Tilt the cage assembly vertically and position the two opposing, elongated cage windows in area between ball grooves. Remove cage and inner race assembly by pulling upward from the housing, **Fig. 40**.
12. Rotate inner cross 90 degrees to cage and align one of the race spherical lands with an elongated cage window. Raise land into cage window and remove inner race by swinging outward, **Fig. 41**.

## INSPECTION

1. Check housing ball races for excessive wear.
2. Check splined shaft and nut threads for damage.
3. Inspect the balls for pitting, cracks, scoring and wearing. Dulling of the surface is normal.
4. Inspect cage for excessive wear on inner and outer spherical surfaces, heavy brinelling of cage, window cracks and chipping.
5. Inspect inner race (Cross) for excessive wear or scoring of ball races.
6. If any of the defects listed in steps 1 through 5, are found, replace the C/V assembly as a unit. **Polished areas in races (Cross and housing) and on**

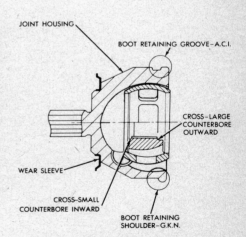

**Fig. 43   Cage & cross assembly installed in housing. Outer C/V joints**

cage spheres are normal and do not indicate a need for joint replacement unless they are suspected of causing noise and vibration.

## ASSEMBLY

1. If removed, position wear sleeve on joint housing, then tap sleeve onto housing, using sleeve installer tool No. C-4698.

# DODGE RAMPAGE & PLYMOUTH SCAMP

2. Lightly oil components, then align marks made during disassembly.
3. Align one of the inner race lands with elongated window of cage, then insert race into cage and pivot 90°, **Fig. 42.**
4. Align elongated cage windows with housing land, then pivot cage 90°. The curved side of the elongated cage windows and inner race counterbore should face outward from joint, **Fig. 43.**
5. Lubricate ball races with one packet of grease from kit.
6. Tilt cage and inner race assembly and insert balls.
7. With shaft supported in a soft jawed vise, install boot.
8. Slide small end of boot over spacer ring and shaft, then position boot end in machined groove.
9. Install snap ring on shaft. When installing use care not to overexpand snap ring.
10. Position joint housing on shaft, then engage by tapping sharply with a soft-faced mallet.
11. Check to ensure that snap ring is properly seated, by attempting to pull joint from shaft.
12. Locate large end of boot over housing.

13. On G.K.N. units, secure boot clamps using boot clamp installer No. C-4124.

## RACK & PINION STEERING GEAR
### REPLACE

1. Raise and support vehicle, then remove front wheels.
2. Remove tie rod ends with a suitable puller.
3. Remove splash shields and boot seal shields.
4. Drive out lower roll pin attaching pinion shaft to lower universal joint.
5. Support front suspension crossmember with a suitable jack.
6. On power steering units, disconnect hoses from steering gear.
7. Disconnect tie rod ends from steering knuckles.
8. On all models, remove bolts attaching steering gear to front suspension crossmember. Loosen crossmember from vehicle frame.
9. Remove steering gear from left side of vehicle.
10. Reverse procedure to install.

## POWER STEERING PUMP
### REPLACE

1. Remove power steering pump drive belt adjusting bolt and nut, then remove nut attaching pump end hose bracket, if equipped.
2. Raise and support vehicle, then remove nut attaching pump pressure hose locating bracket to crossmember.
3. Disconnect pressure hose from steering gear and allow fluid to drain into a suitable container.
4. Remove drive belt splash shield, then disconnect both pressure and return hoses at power steering pump. Cap hoses and fitting to prevent entry of dirt.
5. Remove lower stud nut and pivot bolt from power steering pump, then lower vehicle.
6. Remove drive belt pulley from pump, then move pump rearward to clear mounting bracket, and remove adjusting bracket.
7. Rotate pump so pulley faces rear of vehicle, then lift pump assembly from vehicle.
8. Reverse procedure to install.

# JEEP EXC. 1984–89 CHEROKEE & WAGONEER & 1986–89 COMANCHE

## INDEX OF SERVICE OPERATIONS

**NOTE:** Refer to back of this manual for vehicle manufacturer's special service tool suppliers.

# SPECIFICATIONS
## GENERAL ENGINE SPECIFICATIONS

| Year | Engine Model | Engine V.I.N. Code ① | Carb. Type | Bore x Stroke | Comp. Ratio | Horsepower @ R.P.M. | Torque Ft. Lbs. @ R.P.M. | Normal Oil Pressure Lbs. |
|---|---|---|---|---|---|---|---|---|
| 1980-81 | 4-151/2.5L | B | 2 Bore | 4.00 x 3.00 | 8.24 | — | — | 36-41 |
| | 6-258/4.2L | C | 2 Bore | 3.75 x 3.895 | 8.0 | — | — | 37-75 |
| | V8-304/5.0L | H | 2 Bore | 3.75 x 3.44 | 8.4 | 150 @ 4200 | 245 @ 2500 | 37-75 |
| | V8-360/5.9L | N | 2 Bore | 4.08 x 3.44 | 8.25 | 175 | 285 | 37-75 |
| 1982 | 4-151/2.5L | B | 2 Bore | 4.00 x 3.00 | 8.24 | — | — | 36-41 |
| | 6-258/4.2L | C | 2 Bore | 3.75 x 3.895 | 8.6 | — | — | 37-75 |
| | V8-360/5.9L | N | 2 Bore | 4.08 x 3.44 | 8.25 | 175 | — | 37-75 |
| 1983 | 4-150/2.46L | U | 1 Bore | 3.88 x 3.19 | 9.2 | — | 132 @ 3200 | 37-75 |
| | 4-151/2.5L | B | 2 Bore | 4.00 x 3.00 | 8.24 | — | — | 36-41 |
| | 6-258/4.2L | C | 2 Bore | 3.75 x 3.895 | 9.2 | 110 | — | 37-75 |
| | V8-360/5.9L | N | 2 Bore | 4.08 x 3.44 | 8.25 | 175 | — | 37-75 |
| 1984-85 | 4-150/2.46L | U | 1 Bore | 3.88 x 3.19 | 9.2 | — | 132 @ 3200 | 37-75 |
| | 6-258/4.2L | C | 2 Bore | 3.75 x 3.895 | 9.2 | 110 | — | 37-75 |
| | V8-360/5.9L | N | 2 Bore | 4.08 x 3.44 | 8.25 | 175 | — | 37-75 |
| 1986 | 4-150/2.46L | — | 1 Bore | 3.88 x 3.19 | 9.2 | 105 @ 5000 | 132 @ 3000 | 37-75 |
| 1986-88 | 6-258/4.2L | C | 2 Bore | 3.75 x 3.895 | 9.2 | 112 @ 3000 | 210 @ 2000 | 37-75 |
| | V8-360/5.9L | N | 2 Bore | 4.08 x 3.44 | 8.25 | 144 @ 3200 | 280 @ 1500 | 37-75 |
| 1987-88 | 4-150/2.46L | H | TBI② | 3.88 x 3.19 | 9.2 | 121 @ 5000 | 141 @ 3500 | 37-75 |
| 1989 | 4-150/2.46L | E | TBI② | 3.88 x 3.19 | 9.2 | 121 @ 5250 | 141 @ 3250 | 37-75 |
| | 6-258/4.2L | M | 2 Bore | 3.75 x 3.895 | 9.2 | 112 @ 3000 | 210 @ 2000 | 37-75 |
| | V8-360/5.9L | 7 | 2 Bore | 4.08 x 3.44 | 8.25 | 144 @ 3200 | 280 @ 1500 | 37-75 |

① —On vehicle identification plate located on left hand side of dash panel under the hood. On 1980 models, the 6th digit of the Vehicle Identification Number (V.I.N.) denotes engine code. On 1981-88 models, the fourth digit of the Vehicle Identification Number (V.I.N.) denotes engine code. On 1989 models, the eighth digit of the Vehicle Identification Number (V.I.N.) denotes engine code.
② —Throttle body injection.

---

## ENGINE TIGHTENING SPECIFICATIONS*

*Torque specifications are for clean and lightly lubricated threads only. Dry or dirty threads produce increased friction which prevents accurate measurement of tightness.

| Year | Engine | Spark Plug Ft. Lbs. | Cylinder Head Bolts Ft. Lbs. | Intake Manifold Ft. Lbs. | Exhaust Manifold Ft. Lbs. | Rocker Arm Cap Screw Ft. Lbs. | Rocker Arm Cover Inch Lbs. | Connecting Rod Cap Bolts Ft. Lbs. | Main Bearing Cap Bolts Ft. Lbs. | Flywheel To Crankshaft Ft. Lbs. | Vibration Damper Or Pulley Ft. Lbs. |
|---|---|---|---|---|---|---|---|---|---|---|---|
| 1980 | 6-258 | 28 | 105 | 23 | 23 | 19 | 50 | 33 | 80 | 105 | 80① |
| | V8-304, 360 | 28 | 110 | 43 | ② | 19 | 50 | 33 | 100 | 105 | 90① |
| | 4-151 | 7-15 | 92 | 37 | 39 | ③ | 84 | 30 | 65 | 68 | 160 |
| 1981 | 4-151 | 7-15 | 92 | 37 | 39 | 20 | 84 | 30 | 65 | 68 | 160 |
| | 6-258 | 11 | 85 | 23 | 23 | 19 | 28 | 33 | 65 | 105 | 80① |
| | V8-304, 360 | 28 | 110 | 43 | ② | 19 | 50 | 33 | 100 | 105 | 90① |
| 1982 | 4-151 | 7-15 | 92 | 37 | 37 | 20 | 84 | 30 | 65 | 68 | 160 |
| | 6-258 | 11 | 85 | 23 | 23 | 19 | 28 | 33 | 80 | 105 | 80① |
| | V8-360 | 28 | 110 | 43 | ② | 19 | 50 | 33 | 100 | 105 | 90① |
| 1983 | 4-150 | 27 | 85 | 23 | 23 | 19 | 55 | 33 | 80 | ④ | 80① |
| | 4-151 | 7-15 | 92 | 26 | 37 | 20 | 84 | 30 | 65 | 68 | 162 |
| | 6-258 | 11 | 85 | 23 | 23 | 19 | 28 | 33 | 80 | 105 | 80① |
| | V8-360 | 28 | 110 | 43 | ② | 19 | 50 | 33 | 100 | 105 | 90① |
| 1984-88 | 4-150 | 27 | 85 | 23 | 23 | 19 | 55 | 33 | 80 | ④ | 80 |
| | 6-258 | ⑥ | 85⑤ | 23 | 23 | 19 | 28⑦ | 33 | 80 | 105 | 80① |
| | V8-360 | 28 | 110 | 43 | ② | 19 | 50 | 33 | 100 | 105 | 90① |

## ENGINE TIGHTENING SPECIFICATIONS—Continued

| Year | Engine | Spark Plug Ft. Lbs. | Cylinder Head Bolts Ft. Lbs. | Intake Manifold Ft. Lbs. | Exhaust Manifold Ft. Lbs. | Rocker Arm Cap Screw Ft. Lbs. | Rocker Arm Cover Inch Lbs. | Connecting Rod Cap Bolts Ft. Lbs. | Main Bearing Cap Bolts Ft. Lbs. | Flywheel To Crankshaft Ft. Lbs. | Vibration Damper Or Pulley Ft. Lbs. |
|------|--------|------|------|------|------|------|------|------|------|------|------|
| 1989 | 4-150 | 27 | 85 | 23 | 30 | 19 | 44 | 33 | 80 | — | 80① |
| | 6-258 | 28 | 85⑤ | 23 | ⑨ | 19 | ⑦ | 33 | 80 | — | 80① |
| | V8-360 | 28 | 110 | 43 | ② | 19 | 55 | 33 | 100 | — | 90① |

①—Lubricate bolts with engine oil.
②—Center two bolts, 25 ft. lbs.; outer 4 bolts, 15 ft. lbs.
③—Rocker arm stud to cylinder head, 60 ft. lbs., rocker arm stud nut, 20 ft. lbs.
④—Torque bolts to 50 ft. lbs., then tighten bolts an additional 60 degrees.

⑤—Apply suitable sealer to threads of bolt 11 (left front) and reduce torque to 75 ft. lbs. Refer to text for torque sequence.
⑥—Exc. Wrangler, 11 ft. lbs.; Wrangler, 27 ft. lbs.

⑦—On Wrangler models, torque nuts to 28 inch lbs. and screws to 55 inch lbs.
⑧—Exc. bolt 8, 110 ft. lbs.; bolt 8, 100 ft. lbs.
⑨—Middle Nuts, 30 ft. lbs.; outside nuts, 23 ft. lbs.

## STARTING MOTOR SPECIFICATIONS

| Year | Engine Model | Brush Spring Tension Oz. | Free Speed Test | | |
|------|------|------|------|------|------|
| | | | Amps. | Volts | RPM |
| 1980-81 | 6-258, V8-304, V8-360 | — | 77 | 12 | 8900-9600 |
| 1980-83 | 4-151 | — | 45-70 | 9 | 7000-11900 |
| 1982-87 | V8-360 | — | 67 | 12 | 7380-9356 |
| 1982-88 | 6-258 | — | 67 | 12 | 7380-9356 |
| 1983-86 | 4-150 | — | 67 | 12 | 7380-9356 |
| 1987-89 | 4-150 | — | 75 | 11.5 | 2900 |
| 1988-89 | V8-360 | — | 80 | 11.5 | 2500 |
| 1989 | 6-258 | — | 80 | 11.5 | 2500 |

## ALTERNATOR SPECIFICATIONS

| Year | Make | Alternator | | Regulator | |
|------|------|------|------|------|------|
| | | Field Current @ 80°F | Rated Output Amps. ① | Model | Voltage @ 80°F |
| 1980 | Delco | 4.0-4.5 | 37 | Integral | 14.1-14.6 |
| | Delco | 4.0-4.5 | 63 | Integral | 14.1-14.6 |
| 1981-82 | Delco | 4.0-5.0 | 42 | Integral | 13.9-14.9 |
| | Delco | 4.0-5.0 | 63 | Integral | 13.9-14.9 |
| | Delco | 4.0-5.0 | 70 | Integral | 13.9-14.9 |
| | Delco | 4.0-5.0 | 85 | Integral | 13.9-14.9 |
| 1983-88 | Delco | 4.0-5.0 | 42 | Integral | 13.9-14.9 |
| | Delco | 4.0-5.0 | 56 | Integral | 13.9-14.9 |
| | Delco | 4.0-5.0 | 66 | Integral | 13.9-14.9 |
| | Delco | 4.0-5.0 | 78 | Integral | 13.9-14.9 |
| | Delco | 4.0-5.0 | 85 | Integral | 13.9-14.9 |
| 1989 | Delco | 4.0-5.0 | 56 | Integral | 13.9-14.9 |
| | Delco | 4.0-5.0 | 66 | Integral | 13.9-14.9 |
| | Delco | 4.0-5.0 | 78 | Integral | 13.9-14.9 |
| | Delco | 4.0-5.0 | 94 | Integral | 13.9-14.9 |

①—Stamped on alternator frame.

## BRAKE SPECIFICATIONS

| Year | Model | Rear Drum I.D. ① | Wheel Cyl. Bore Front Disc | Wheel Cyl. Bore Rear Drum | Disc Brake Rotor Minimum Thickness | Disc Brake Rotor Thickness Variation (Parallelism) | Disc Brake Rotor Run Out (TIR) | Disc Brake Rotor Finish (Microinch) | Master Cyl. Bore Dia. |
|---|---|---|---|---|---|---|---|---|---|
| 1980-83 | Cherokee, Wagoneer | 11.06 | 2.937 | .937 | 1.215 | .0010 | .005 | 20-60 | 1.125 |
| 1980-86 | CJ Models | 10.06 | 2.6 | .875 | .815 | .0010 | .005 | 15-80 | 1.0 |
| 1980-88 | J-10 | 11.06 | 2.937 | .937 | 1.215 | .0010 | .005 | 20-60 | 1.125 |
| | J-20 | 12.06 | 2.937 | 1.125 | 1.215 | .0010 | .005 | 20-60 | 1.125 |
| 1982-85 | Scrambler | 10.06 | 2.6 | .875 | .815 | .0010 | .005 | 15-80 | 1.0 |
| 1984-88 | Grand Wagoneer | 11.06 | 2.937 | .937 | 1.215 | .0010 | .005 | 20-60 | 1.125 |
| 1987-88 | Wrangler | 10.06 | 2.6 | .875 | .815 | — | .004 | — | .937 |
| 1989 | Grand Wagoneer | 11.06 | 2.9 | — | 1.215 | .0010 | .005 | — | — |
| | Wrangler | 10.06 | 2.6 | — | .815 | .0010 | .004 | — | — |

① —Maximum.

## WHEEL ALIGNMENT SPECIFICATIONS

| Year | Model | Caster Deg. | Camber Deg. | Toe-In Inch | Kingpin Inclination Deg. |
|---|---|---|---|---|---|
| 1980 | CJ | +3 | +1½ | 3/64 to 3/32 | 8½ |
| | Exc. CJ | +4 | +1½ | 3/64 to 3/32 | 8½ |
| 1981 | CJ | +6 | +1½ | 3/64 to 3/32 | 8½ |
| 1981-83 | Exc. CJ & Scrambler | +4 | Zero | 3/64 to 3/32 | 8½ |
| 1982-83 | CJ & Scrambler | +6 | Zero | 3/64 to 3/32 | 8½ |
| 1984-86 | CJ & Scrambler | +6 | Zero | 3/32 | 10 |
| 1984-88 | Grand Wagoneer & J-10, 20 | +4 | Zero | 3/64 to 3/32 | 8½ |
| 1987-88 | Wrangler | +8 | Zero | Zero | — |
| 1989 | Grand Wagoneer | +4 | Zero | 5/32 | — |
| | Wrangler | ① | Zero | Zero | — |

① —Auto. Trans., +6½°; Man. Trans., +8°

## DRIVE AXLE SPECIFICATIONS

| Year | Model | Carrier Type | Ring Gear & Pinion Backlash Method | Ring Gear & Pinion Backlash Adjustment | Pinion Bearing Preload Method | Pinion Bearing Preload New Bearings Inch Lbs. | Pinion Bearing Preload Used Bearings Inch Lbs. | Differential Bearing Preload Method | Differential Bearing Preload New Bearings Inch Lbs. | Differential Bearing Preload Used Bearings Inch Lbs. |
|---|---|---|---|---|---|---|---|---|---|---|
| 1980-88 | All ① ⑤ | Integral | Shims | .005-.010 | Shims | 20-40 | 10-20 | Shims | ③ | ③ |
| 1980-81 | CJ Models ② | Integral | Shims | .005-.009 | Sleeve | 17-25 | 17-25 | Shims | ④ | ④ |
| 1980-83 | Cherokee, Wagoneer ② | Integral | Shims | .005-.009 | Sleeve | 17-25 | 17-25 | Shims | ④ | ④ |
| 1980-88 | J-10 ② | Integral | Shims | .005-.009 | Sleeve | 17-25 | 17-25 | Shims | ④ | ④ |
| 1980-88 | J-20 ② | Integral | Shims | .005-.010 | Shims | 20-40 | 10-20 | Shims | ③ | ③ |
| 1982-86 | CJ, Scrambler ② | Integral | Shims | .005-.009 | Sleeve | 17-25 | 17-25 | Shims | ④ | ④ |
| 1984-88 | Grand Wagoneer ② | Integral | Shims | .005-.009 | Sleeve | 17-25 | 17-25 | Shims | ④ | ④ |
| 1986 | CJ-7 ② | Integral | Shims | .005-.009 | Sleeve | 17-25 | 17-25 | Shims | ④ | ④ |
| 1987-88 | Wrangler ① | Integral | Shims | .005-.010 | Shims | 20-40 | 15-25 | Shims | ③ | ③ |
| | Wrangler ② | Integral | Shims | .005-.009 | Spacer | 15-25 | 15-25 | Shims | ④ | ④ |
| 1989 | Grand Wagoneer ① | Integral | Shims | .005-.010 | Shims | 20-40 | 10-20 | Shims | .015 | .015 |
| | Grand Wagoneer ② | Integral | Shims | .005-.009 | Shims | 20-40 | 20-40 | Shims | ③ | ③ |
| | Wrangler ① | Integral | Shims | .005-.010 | Shims | 20-40 | 15-25 | Shims | .015 | .015 |
| | Wrangler ② | Integral | Shims | .005-.009 | Shims | 15-25 | 15-25 | Shims | ④ | ④ |

① —Front drive axle.
② —Rear drive axle.
③ —Slip fit in case (zero preload) plus .015 inch additional preload added to gear tooth side shim pack.
④ —Slip fit in case (zero preload) plus .004 inch additional preload added to each side.
⑤ —Exc. Wrangler.

## COOLING SYSTEM & CAPACITY DATA

| Year | Engine & Model | Cooling System Qts. | Radiator Cap Relief Pressure Lbs. | Thermo. Opening Temp. Deg. F. | Fuel Tank Gals. | Engine Oil Refill Qts. ① | Transmission Oil 4 Speed Pts. | 5 Speed Pts. | Auto. Trans. Qts. ② | Transfer Case Pts. | Drive Axle Front Pts. | Rear Pts. |
|---|---|---|---|---|---|---|---|---|---|---|---|---|
| 1980-81 | 4-151 CJ Models | 7.8 | 15 | 195 | 14.8 | 3③ | 3 | — | — | 4 | 2.5 | 4.8 |
| | 6-258, CJ Models | 10.5 | 15 | 195 | 14.8 | 5 | ④ | — | ⑤ | 4 | 2.5 | 4.8 |
| | 6-258, Cherokee & Wagoneer | 10.5 | 15 | 195 | 20.3 | 5 | 3.5 | — | ⑤ | ⑥ | 3 | 4.8 |
| | 6-258, J-10 Truck | 10.5 | 15 | 195 | 19 | 5 | 3.5 | — | ⑤ | ⑥ | 3 | 4.8 |
| | V8-304, CJ Models | 13 | 15 | 195 | 14.8 | 4 | 3.5 | — | ⑤ | 4 | 2.5 | 4.8 |
| | V8-360, Cherokee & Wagoneer | 14 | 15 | 195 | 20.3 | 4 | 3.5 | — | ⑤ | ⑥ | 3 | 4.8 |
| | V8-360, J-10 Truck | 14 | 15 | 195 | 19 | 4 | 3.5 | — | ⑤ | ⑥ | 3 | 4.8 |
| | V8-360, J-20 Truck | 14 | 15 | 195 | 19 | 4 | 6.5 | — | ⑤ | ⑥ | 3 | 6 |
| 1982-83 | 4-150, CJ & Scrambler | — | 15 | 195 | 14.8⑦ | 4③ | 3.9 | 4.5 | — | 4 | 2.5 | 4.8 |
| | 4-151, CJ & Scrambler | 7.8 | 15 | 195 | 14.8⑦ | 3③ | 3.9 | 4.5 | — | 4 | 2.5 | 4.8 |
| | 6-258, CJ & Scrambler | 10.5 | 15 | 195 | 14.8⑦ | 5 | 3.5 | 4.5 | ⑤ | 4 | 2.5 | 4.8 |
| | 6-258, Cherokee & Wagoneer | 10.5 | 15 | 195 | 20.3 | 5 | 3.5 | 4.5 | ⑤ | 7 | ⑧ | 4.8 |
| | 6-258, J-10 Truck | 10.5 | 15 | 195 | 18.2 | 5 | 3.5 | 4.5 | ⑤ | 7 | ⑧ | 4.8 |
| | V8-360, Cherokee & Wagoneer | 14 | 15 | 195 | 20.3 | 4 | 3.5 | — | ⑤ | 7 | ⑧ | 4.8 |
| | V8-360, J-10 Truck | 14 | 15 | 195 | 18.2 | 4 | 3.5 | — | ⑤ | 7 | ⑧ | 4.8 |
| | V8-360, J-20 Truck | 14 | 15 | 195 | 18.2 | 4 | 6 | — | ⑤ | 7 | 3 | 6 |
| 1984-85 | 4-150, CJ & Scrambler | 9 | 14 | 195 | 14.8⑦ | 4③ | 3.9 | 4.5 | — | 4 | 2.5 | 4.8 |
| | 6-258, CJ & Scrambler | 10.5 | 14 | 195 | 14.8⑦ | 5 | 3.9 | 4.5 | ⑤ | 4 | 2.5 | 4.8 |
| | 6-258, Grand Wagoneer | 10.5 | 15 | 195 | 20.3 | 5 | 3.5 | — | ⑤ | 7 | ⑧ | 4.8 |
| | 6-258, J-10 Truck | 10.5 | 15 | 195 | 18.2 | 5 | 3.5 | — | ⑤ | 7 | ⑧ | 4.8 |
| | V8-360, Grand Wagoneer | 14.8 | 15 | 195 | 20.3 | 4 | — | — | ⑤ | 7 | ⑧ | 4.8 |
| | V8-360, J-10 Truck | 14.8 | 15 | 195 | 18.2 | 4 | 3.5 | — | ⑤ | 7 | ⑧ | 4.8 |
| | V8-360, J-20 Truck | 14.8 | 15 | 195 | 18.2 | 4 | — | — | ⑤ | 7 | 3 | 6 |
| 1986 | 4-150, CJ-7 | 9 | 14 | 195 | 15⑦ | 4③ | 3.9 | 4.5 | — | 4 | 2.5 | 4.8 |
| | 6-258, CJ-7 | 10.5 | 14 | 195 | 15⑦ | 5 | 3.5 | 4.5 | ⑤ | 4 | 2.5 | 4.8 |
| | 6-258, Grand Wagoneer | 12.5 | 15 | 195 | 20.3 | 5 | — | — | ⑤ | 7 | 2.5 | 4.8 |
| | 6-258, J-10 Truck | 15.5 | 15 | 195 | 18.2 | 5 | 3.5 | — | ⑤ | 7 | ⑧ | 4.8 |
| | V8-360, Grand Wagoneer | 15.5 | 15 | 195 | 20.3 | 4 | — | — | ⑤ | 7 | ⑧ | 4.8 |
| | V8-360, J-10 Truck | 15.5 | 15 | 195 | 18.2 | 4 | — | — | ⑤ | 7 | ⑧ | 4.8 |
| | V8-360, J-20 Truck | 15.5 | 15 | 195 | 18.2 | 4 | — | — | ⑤ | 7 | 3 | 6 |
| 1987 | 4-150, Wrangler | 9 | 14 | 195 | 15⑦ | 4③ | — | ⑨ | ⑤ | 4.5 | 2.5 | 2.5 |
| | 6-258, Wrangler | 10.5 | 14 | 195 | 15⑦ | 5 | — | ⑨ | ⑤ | 4.5 | 2.5 | 2.5 |
| | 6-258, Grand Wagoneer | 12.5 | 15 | 195 | 20.3 | 5 | — | — | ⑤ | 6 | 3.75 | 3.75 |
| | 6-258, J-10 | 12.5 | 15 | 195 | 18.2 | 5 | 3.5 | — | ⑤ | 6 | 3.75 | 3.75 |
| | V8-360, Grand Wagoneer | 15.5 | 15 | 195 | 20.3 | 4 | — | — | ⑤ | 6 | 3.75 | 3.75 |
| | V8-360, J-10 | 15.5 | 15 | 195 | 18.2 | 4 | 3.5 | — | ⑤ | 6 | 3.75 | 3.75 |
| | V8-360, J-20 | 15.5 | 15 | 195 | 18.2 | 4 | 3.5 | — | ⑤ | 6 | 3.75 | 6 |
| 1988 | 4-150, Wrangler | 9 | 14 | 195 | 15⑦ | 4③ | — | ⑨ | ⑤ | 4.5 | 2.5 | 2.5 |
| | 6-258, Wrangler | 10.5 | 14 | 195 | 15⑦ | 6③ | — | ⑨ | ⑤ | 4.5 | 2.5 | 2.5 |
| | V8-360, Grand Wagoneer | 14.0 | 15 | 195 | 20.3 | 5③ | — | — | ⑤ | 6 | ⑧ | 4.8 |
| | V8-360, J-10 | 14.0 | 15 | 195 | 18.2 | 5③ | 3.5 | — | ⑤ | 6 | ⑧ | 4.8 |
| | V8-360, J-20 | 14.0 | 15 | 195 | 18.2 | 5③ | 3.5 | — | ⑤ | 6 | ⑧ | 6 |
| 1989 | 4-150, Wrangler | 9 | 14 | 195 | 15⑦ | 4③ | — | ⑨ | ⑤ | 3.3 | ⑩ | ⑩ |
| | 6-258, Wrangler | 10.5 | 14 | 195 | 15⑦ | 6③ | — | ⑨ | ⑤ | 3.3 | ⑩ | ⑩ |
| | V8-360, Grand Wagoneer | 15.5 | 15 | 195 | 20.3 | 5③ | — | — | ⑤ | 6 | ⑧ | 3.8 |

①—Add 1 qt. w/filter change unless otherwise noted.
②—Approximate. Make final check w/dipstick.
③—With or without filter change.
④—SR-4 trans., 3 pts.; T-176 trans., 3.5 pts.
⑤—Oil pan only, 4¼ qts.; total capacity, 8½ qts.
⑥—Model 208, 6 pts.; Model 219, 4 pts.
⑦—Optional fuel tank, 20 gals.
⑧—Less Selec-Trac, 3 pts.; w/Selec-Trac, 4.5 pts.
⑨—With BA10/5 trans. exc. 1989 models, 3.5 pts.; 1989 models with BA10/5 trans., 4.9 pts.; All models with AX5 trans., 7 pts.
⑩—With standard axle, 2.5 pts.; heavy duty axle 3.0 pts.

# ELECTRICAL

## INDEX

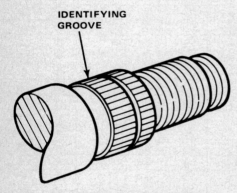

**Fig. 1 Metric steering shaft identification**

## FUSEPANEL & FLASHER LOCATION
### REPLACE

The fuse panel is located under the left side of the instrument panel.

Both the turn signal flasher and hazard flasher are located on the fuse panel.

## STARTER
### REPLACE

#### EXC. 1988-89 GRAND WAGONEER, 1988 J10 & 20 TRUCK

1. Disconnect battery ground cable.
2. Disconnect cable from starter motor terminal.
3. Remove bracket and mounting bolts, starter motor and shims, as equipped.
4. Reverse procedure to install.

## 1988-89 GRAND WAGONEER, 1988 J10 & 20 TRUCKS

1. Disconnect battery ground cable.
2. Raise and support vehicle.
3. Disconnect starter solenoid wires, then remove starter front and rear mounting bolts, and the starter.
4. Reverse procedure to install.

## IGNITION LOCK
### REPLACE

1. Disconnect battery ground cable.
2. Apply tape to painted areas of steering column.
3. Remove steering wheel nut and washer.
4. Paint or scribe an alignment mark on steering wheel and steering column shaft.
5. Using a suitable puller, remove steering wheel.
6. Using a suitable tool, remove lock plate cover from steering column.
7. Compress lock plate and remove steering shaft snap ring as follows:
  a. Check and identify steering shaft nut thread type. Metric type steering shafts have an identifying groove in the steering wheel locating splines, **Fig. 1**.
  b. If steering shaft is not a metric type, use lock plate compressor tool No. J-23653 to compress lock plate and remove snap ring, **Fig. 2**.
  c. If the steering shaft is of the metric type, replace compressor tool bolt with metric forcing bolt J-23653-A before installing compressor tool

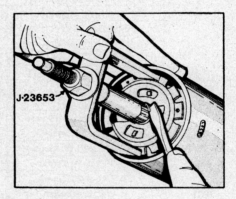

**Fig. 2 Compressing lock plate & removing snap ring**

onto steering shaft. The lock plate is under strong spring tension. Do not attempt to remove the steering shaft snap ring without using the specified lock plate compressor tool.

8. Remove compressor tool and snap ring.
9. Remove lock plate, canceling cam, and upper bearing preload spring.
10. Remove turn signal lever.
11. Remove hazard warning knob from steering column.
12. Remove turn signal switch attaching screws and position switch aside.
13. Position lock cylinder in On position.
14. Remove key warning switch switch and retaining clip with needle nose pliers or other suitable tool. Do not attempt to remove switch and clip separately, as clip could may drop into steering column jacket.

**Fig. 3  Lock cylinder removal. Models less ignition switch retaining screw**

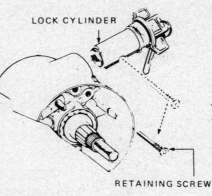

LOCK CYLINDER

RETAINING SCREW

**Fig. 4  Lock cylinder removal. Models w/ignition lock retaining screw**

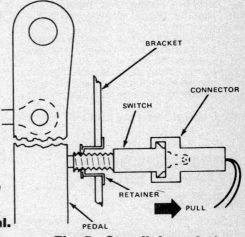

BRACKET

CONNECTOR

SWITCH

RETAINER

PULL

PEDAL

**Fig. 5  Stop light switch. Exc. Wrangler**

15. On models less lock cylinder retaining screw, rotate lock cylinder two detents clockwise beyond the Off-Unlock position. Insert a thin blade screwdriver through slot in steering column, then depress lock cylinder retaining tab and remove lock cylinder, **Fig. 3.**
16. On models with lock cylinder retaining screw, remove screw and pull lock cylinder from housing, **Fig. 4.**
17. Reverse procedure to install. On models with lock cylinder retaining screw, torque screw to 40 inch lbs.

## IGNITION SWITCH
### REPLACE

The ignition switch is mounted on the lower portion of the steering column and is connected to the steering lock by a remote actuator rod.

### REMOVAL

1. Disconnect battery ground cable.
2. Remove lower instrument panel trim panel, if equipped.
3. Place ignition in Off-Unlock position and remove switch attaching screws.
4. Disconnect switch from control rod and electrical connector from switch, then remove switch from steering column.

### INSTALLATION

1. Move switch slider to Accessory position.
2. Engage remote actuator rod into switch slider and position ignition switch onto steering column. Do not move switch slider when positioning ignition switch onto steering column jacket.
3. Install and torque switch retaining screws to 35 inch lbs.
4. Connect electrical connector onto switch.
5. Connect battery ground cable and check ignition switch for proper operation.
6. Install lower instrument panel trim panel, if equipped.

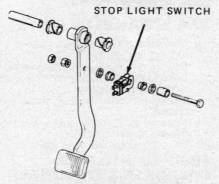

STOP LIGHT SWITCH

**Fig. 6  Stop light switch. Wrangler**

## STOP LIGHT SWITCH
### REPLACE
#### EXC. WRANGLER

The stop light switch is retained in its mounting bracket by a spring clip which engages the threaded portion of the switch housing, **Fig. 5.** To remove the stop light switch, pull switch straight out of the mounting bracket and retainer.

#### WRANGLER

1. Disconnect battery ground cable.
2. Disconnect electrical connector for stop light switch.
3. Remove bolt and locknuts attaching brake pedal to stop light switch and pushrod, **Fig. 6.**
4. Remove stop light switch and bushings from brake pedal.
5. Reverse procedure to install.

## NEUTRAL SAFETY & BACK-UP LAMP SWITCH
### REPLACE
#### 1980 MODELS

1. Disconnect battery ground cable.
2. Disconnect electrical switch harness from switch.
3. Remove neutral safety switch attaching screws, then the switch from steering column.

4. Reverse procedure to install.

### 1981-89 MODELS

1. Disconnect battery ground cable.
2. Raise and support vehicle.
3. Disconnect electrical connector from switch and remove switch from transmission. Allow transmission fluid to drain into a suitable container.
4. Move selector lever to Park and Neutral positions. Check switch operating fingers for proper operation.
5. Reverse procedure to install. Correct transmission fluid level as required.

## TURN SIGNAL SWITCH
### REPLACE

1. Disconnect battery ground cable.
2. Remove horn center button.
3. Remove horn button retainer attaching screws, bushing, retainer and spring.
4. Place alignment marks on steering wheel and steering column shaft for reference during installation.
5. Remove steering wheel retaining nut.
6. Using a suitable puller, remove steering wheel from column.
7. Using suitable tool, remove cover from lock plate, then remove lock plate as follows:
   a. Identify steering shaft thread type. Metric shafts have an identifying groove on steering wheel locating splines as shown in **Fig. 1.**
   b. Mount lock plate compressor J-23653 or equivalent on steering shaft, using forcing bolt J-23653-A on models with metric steering shafts.
   c. Tighten nut on tool to compress upper bearing preload spring, then remove and discard lock plate retaining ring, **Fig. 2.**
   d. Loosen nut on tool, then remove tool and lock plate.
8. Remove turn signal canceling cam, upper bearing preload spring and thrust washer from steering shaft.
9. Move turn signal actuating lever in

right turn position and remove lever.
10. Remove hazard warning switch button from steering column.
11. Remove turn signal electrical connector harness from column mounting bracket and disconnect connector.
12. Remove turn signal switch attaching screws, then pull switch and electrical connector harness from steering column.
13. Reverse procedure to install.

## HORN SOUNDER & STEERING WHEEL REPLACE

Some steering shafts have metric steering wheel nut threads. Check and identify shaft thread type before installing a replacement steering wheel nut. Metric steering shafts have an identifying groove in the steering wheel splines.

### CJ & SCRAMBLER

1. Disconnect battery ground cable.
2. Ensure front wheels are in straight ahead position.
3. Remove rubber boot, if equipped, and horn from steering wheel. Rotate button until lock tabs on button align with notches in contact cup, then pull upward and remove from steering wheel.
4. Remove steering wheel nut and washer.
5. Remove horn button receiver bushing attaching screws, then the bushing.
6. Remove horn button receiver and contact plate.
7. Paint or scribe an alignment mark on steering wheel and steering shaft for installation.
8. Using a suitable puller, remove steering wheel from steering shaft.
9. Reverse procedure to install.

### GRAND WAGONEER, J-10 & 20, WRANGLER & 1980-83 CHEROKEE & WAGONEER

1. Disconnect battery ground cable.
2. Ensure front wheels are in straight ahead position.
3. On models with standard steering wheel, remove horn cover attaching screws from underside of steering wheel, then disconnect the horn contact wire from cover and remove cover.
4. On models with sport type steering wheel, remove button, then the receiver bushing attaching screws, bushing, receiver and contact plate.
5. Paint or scribe an alignment mark on steering wheel and steering shaft for installation.
6. Remove steering wheel nut and washer.
7. Using a suitable puller, remove steering wheel from steering shaft.
8. Reverse procedure to install.

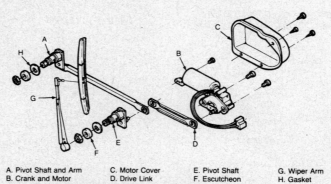

A. Pivot Shaft and Arm    C. Motor Cover    E. Pivot Shaft    G. Wiper Arm
B. Crank and Motor    D. Drive Link    F. Escutcheon    H. Gasket

**Fig. 7    Windshield wiper system. CJ, Scrambler & Wrangler**

## INSTRUMENT CLUSTER REPLACE

### CJ & SCRAMBLER

1. Disconnect battery ground cable.
2. On models equipped with air conditioning, remove evaporator assembly bolts, then lower evaporator assembly from instrument panel.
3. Disconnect speedometer cable from cluster.
4. Remove instrument cluster retaining screws, then the cluster.
5. Reverse procedure to install.

### 1980-83 J-10 & 20, CHEROKEE & WAGONEER

1. Disconnect battery ground cable.
2. Disconnect speedometer cable from cluster.
3. Remove cluster retaining screws, tilt top of cluster outward, then disconnect electrical connectors from cluster and ammeter. Mark installation position of ammeter wires, if equipped, to ensure proper assembly.
4. Disconnect electrical connectors and vacuum hoses from heater assembly.
5. Disconnect blend air door control cable.
6. Remove cluster from instrument panel.
7. Reverse procedure to install.

### 1984-85 GRAND WAGONEER, J-10 & 20

1. Disconnect battery ground cable.
2. Disconnect speedometer cable from cluster.
3. Remove cluster retaining screws, tilt top of cluster outward, then disconnect electrical connectors from cluster and ammeter. Mark installation position of ammeter wires, if equipped, to ensure proper assembly.
4. Disconnect electrical connectors and vacuum hoses from heater assembly.
5. Remove heater control panel lamps from control panel.
6. Disconnect blend air door control cable from control panel.
7. Remove cluster from instrument panel.
8. Reverse procedure to install.

### 1986-89 GRAND WAGONEER & 1986-88 J-10 & 20

1. Disconnect battery ground cable.
2. Release instrument panel bezel retaining tabs, then remove bezel.
3. Remove cluster retaining screws, tilt top of cluster outward, then disconnect speedometer cable & electrical connectors from cluster.
4. Remove cluster from instrument panel.
5. Reverse procedure to install.

### WRANGLER

#### Speedometer & Tachometer Cluster

1. Disconnect battery ground cable.
2. Remove five instrument panel shroud attaching screws.
3. Slide shroud outward toward steering wheel, then apply upward pressure to bottom shroud and downward pressure to upper shroud to release retaining tabs.
4. If speedometer is to be removed, remove two speedometer to instrument panel attaching screws. Pull speedometer slightly outward, then disconnect speedometer cable and remove speedometer.
5. If tachometer is to be removed, remove two tachometer to instrument panel attaching screws. Pull tachometer slightly outward, then disconnect electrical connector and remove tachometer.
6. Reverse procedure to install.

#### Gauge Cluster

1. Disconnect battery ground cable.
2. Remove six instrument cluster bezel attaching screw, then remove bezel.
3. Remove six instrument cluster to instrument panel attaching screws, then pull cluster outward to gain access to electrical connector.
4. Disconnect electrical connector and remove gauge cluster.
5. Reverse procedure to install.

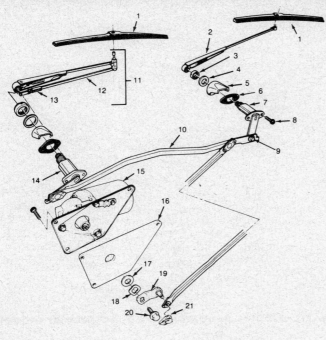

1. Blade
2. Arm
3. Nut
4. Washer
5. Escutcheon
6. Gasket
7. Right Pivot Shaft Body
8. Screw
9. Clip
10. Connecting Link
11. Articulating Arm
12. Aux. Arm
13. Clip
14. Left Pivot Shaft Body
15. Motor
16. Seal
17. Washer
18. Wave Washer
19. Crank Arm
20. Bolt
21. Clip

**Fig. 8   Windshield wiper system. Grand Wagoneer, J-10 & 20 Truck & 1980–83 Cherokee & Wagoneer**

## WINDSHIELD WIPER MOTOR
### REPLACE
#### CJ, SCRAMBLER & WRANGLER

1. Disconnect battery ground cable.
2. Remove necessary top components from windshield frame.
3. Remove right and left windshield hold-down knobs or bolts, as equipped, then fold windshield down.
4. On models without crash pad assembly, remove wiper motor cover.
5. Remove left access hole cover.
6. Disconnect drive link from left wiper pivot, **Fig. 7.**
7. Disconnect wiper motor electrical connector.
8. Remove wiper motor retaining bolts, then the wiper motor.
9. Reverse procedure to install.

#### GRAND WAGONEER, J-10 & 20 TRUCK & 1980–83 CHEROKEE & WAGONEER

1. Disconnect battery ground cable.
2. Remove bolts retaining wiper motor adapter plate to dash panel, **Fig. 8.**
3. Disconnect wiper motor electrical connector from motor.
4. Pull wiper motor and linkage outward to expose drive link to crank pin retaining clip.
5. Using a suitable screwdriver, raise locking tab up and slide retaining clip off of crank pin.
6. Remove wiper motor assembly from vehicle.
7. Reverse procedure to install.

## WINDSHIELD WIPER TRANSMISSION
### REPLACE
#### CJ, SCRAMBLER & WRANGLER

1. Remove both wiper arms, then remove nuts attaching pivots to windshield frame, **Fig. 7.**
2. Remove windshield hold-down knobs or bolts, as equipped, then tilt windshield forward.
3. Remove lefthand and righthand access hole covers, then disconnect wiper motor drive link from left wiper pivot.
4. Remove windshield wiper transmission through access hole.
5. Reverse procedure to install.

## GRAND WAGONEER, J-10 & 20 TRUCK & 1980–83 CHEROKEE & WAGONEER
### Models Less A/C

1. Remove both windshield wiper arms, then remove pivot shaft nuts, washers and gaskets, **Fig. 8.**
2. Disconnect drive arm from wiper motor crank.
3. Disconnect components as necessary to allow for removal of windshield wiper transmission with minimum interference.
4. Remove windshield wiper transmission from vehicle.
5. Reverse procedure to install.

### Models With A/C

1. Disconnect battery ground cable.
2. Remove wiper arms, then remove pivot shaft nuts, washers and gaskets, **Fig 8.**
3. Remove instrument cluster as describe under "Instrument Cluster, Replace."
4. Disconnect left defroster duct.
5. Disconnect drive arm from wiper motor crank.
6. Lower glove box assembly to gain access to righthand linkage clip, then remove clip.
7. Remove lefthand pivot shaft body attaching screw, then remove windshield transmission through instrument cluster opening.
8. Reverse procedure to install.

## WINDSHIELD WIPER SWITCH
### REPLACE
#### CJ & SCRAMBLER

1. Disconnect battery ground cable/
2. On models equipped with air conditioning, remove screws retaining evaporator assembly to instrument panel and lower assembly.
3. Remove switch control knob, nut and switch from instrument panel.
4. Mark wire color locations on switch, then disconnect electrical connector from wiper switch.
5. Reverse procedure to install.

#### 1980–83 CHEROKEE & WAGONEER, 1984–85 GRAND WAGONEER & J-10 & 20 TRUCK

1. Disconnect battery ground cable.
2. Locate small notch at base of switch knob, then insert a small screwdriver into notch to release knob from switch shaft.
3. Remove nut attaching front of switch to instrument panel.
4. Lower switch from rear of instrument panel, then disconnect electrical connector and remove switch.
5. Reverse procedure to install.

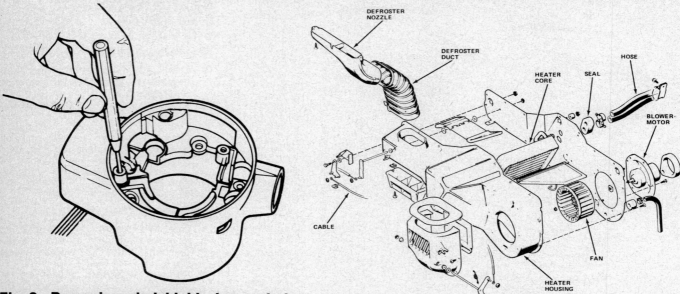

**Fig. 9   Removing windshield wiper switch retaining pin. Models w/tilt steering column**

**Fig. 10   Heater assembly. CJ & Scrambler models**

## WRANGLER & 1986–89 GRAND WAGONEER

1. Disconnect battery ground cable.
2. Remove turn signal switch as described under "Turn Signal Switch, Replace."
3. Remove ignition lock as described under "Ignition Lock, Replace."
4. Remove column-to-instrument panel mounting nuts, then disconnect wiper switch electrical connector.
5. Remove column mounting bracket-to-column attaching bolts, then the bracket and allow column to drop down.
6. Remove ignition and dimmer switches as described under "Ignition and Dimmer Switches, Replace."
7. On models less tilt steering column, proceed as follows:
   a. Remove housing attaching screws, then the housing and shroud assembly from steering column jacket.
   b. Turn assembly over and remove housing to shroud attaching screws and separate housing from shroud.
   c. Remove wiper pivot screw from housing, then remove wiper switch.
8. On models with tilt steering column, proceed as follows:
   a. Remove upper housing attaching screws, then the upper housing.
   b. Remove wiper switch side cover and dimmer switch operating cam.
   c. Using a 1/8 inch diameter punch, press out wiper switch retaining pin and remove wiper switch, **Fig. 9.**
9. Reverse procedure to install.

## RADIO
## REPLACE
### CJ & SCRAMBLER

1. Disconnect battery ground cable.

2. On models equipped with air conditioning, remove screws retaining evaporator assembly to instrument panel and lower assembly.
3. Remove radio control knobs, nuts and bezel.
4. Remove radio support bracket from instrument panel.
5. Pull and tilt radio downward toward steering wheel.
6. Disconnect antenna lead, speaker and power electrical connectors.
7. Remove radio from instrument panel.
8. Reverse procedure to install.

### J-10 & 20 TRUCK, 1980–83 CHEROKEE & WAGONEER, 1984–85 GRAND WAGONEER

1. Disconnect battery ground cable.
2. Remove glove compartment liner and lock striker.
3. Disconnect microphone lead connector from radio, if equipped.
4. Disconnect antenna lead(s).
5. Disconnect power wire connector from fuse panel.
6. Disconnect speaker electrical connectors from radio.
7. Remove rear support bracket from radio.
8. Remove radio control knobs, nuts and face plate.
9. Push radio back to clear instrument panel and remove radio through glove compartment.
10. Reverse procedure to install.

### 1986–89 GRAND WAGONEER

1. Disconnect battery ground cable.
2. Release instrument panel bezel retaining tabs, then remove bezel.
3. Remove radio attaching screws.
4. Disconnect electrical connector and antenna lead.
5. Remove radio.

6. Reverse procedure to install.

## WRANGLER

1. Disconnect battery ground cable.
2. Remove gauge cluster bezel attaching screws, then the bezel.
3. Remove radio attaching screws, then disconnect antenna lead and electrical connector.
4. Remove radio.
5. Reverse procedure to install.

## HEATER CORE
## REPLACE
### CJ, SCRAMBLER & WRANGLER

1. Disconnect battery ground cable, then drain cooling system.
2. Disconnect heater hoses from heater core.
3. Disconnect vent door control cables.
4. Disconnect blower motor electrical connector.
5. Disconnect water drain hose and defroster duct.
6. Remove nuts retaining heater housing assembly to instrument panel. Remove heater housing assembly by tilting heater downward to disengage it from air inlet duct and pulling toward rear of vehicle.
7. Remove heater core from heater housing, **Fig. 10.**
8. Reverse procedure to install.

### GRAND WAGONEER, J-10 & 20 TRUCK & 1980–83 CHEROKEE & WAGONEER

1. Disconnect battery ground cable.
2. Drain cooling system, then disconnect heater hoses from core.
3. Disconnect temperature control cable from blend air door.
4. Disconnect resistor harness electrical connector.

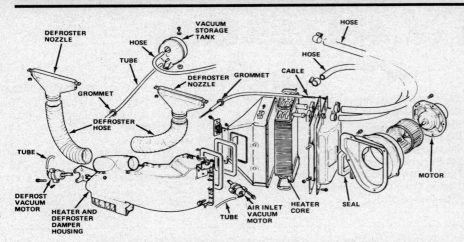

**Fig. 11 Heater assembly. Grand Wagoneer, Truck & 1980–83 Cherokee & Wagoneer**

5. Remove heater core housing to cowl panel retaining nuts, then the housing assembly.
6. Separate heater halves, **Fig. 11.**
7. Remove heater core retaining screws, then the heater core.
8. Reverse procedure to install.

# BLOWER MOTOR
## REPLACE
### LESS AIR CONDITIONING
#### CJ, Scrambler & Wrangler

1. Disconnect battery ground cable.
2. Remove heater housing as described under "Heater Core, Replace."
3. Remove blower motor assembly retaining screws, then the blower motor.
4. Reverse procedure to install.

#### Grand Wagoneer, J-10 & 20 Truck & 1980–83 Cherokee & Wagoneer

1. Disconnect battery ground cable.
2. Remove blower motor-to-housing attaching screws, then disconnect blower motor electrical connector.
3. Remove blower motor.
4. Reverse procedure to install.

### WITH AIR CONDITIONING

1. Disconnect battery ground cable.
2. Remove screws retaining evaporator assembly to instrument panel, then lower evaporator housing to gain access to blower motor attaching screws.
3. Disconnect blower motor electrical connector.
4. Remove blower motor attaching screws, then the blower motor.
5. Reverse procedure to install.

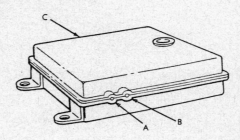

| CENTERING ADJUSTMENT | LOW SPEED SWITCH ADJUSTMENT | SENSITIVITY ADJUSTMENT |
| --- | --- | --- |
| A | B | C |

**Fig. 13 Centering adjusting screw location. 1981 4-151 & 6-258 engine & 1982–88 all**

# SPEED CONTROL
## ADJUST
### 1980 ALL & 1981 MODELS WITH V8-360 ENGINE

Before adjusting bellows chain, the carburetor throttle must be at idle position, ignition off and choke valve fully open. Ensure bellows bracket screws are tight. Adjust chain at bellows hook, one bead at a time until a free pin fit is obtained at throttle lever. After adjustment, there should be a slight deflection in the chain without moving either the throttle lever or bellows. Bend the bellows hook tabs together. The chain must be free in the hook after bending the bellows hook tabs.

### Centering Spring Adjustment

The centering spring adjustment is extremely sensitive and eccentric must never be turned more than 1/8 turn in either direction.

If speed control system engages at 2 or

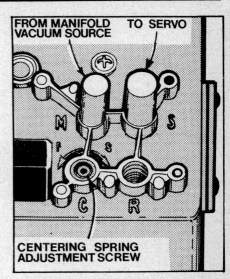

**Fig. 12 Centering spring adjustment. 1980 all & 1981 V8-360 engine**

more mph higher than selected speed, turn centering spring adjustment screw (C) toward (S) 1/32 inch or less, **Fig. 12.** If engagement speed is below selected speed, turn centering spring adjustment screw (C) toward (F) 1/32 inch or less.

# 1981 4-151 & 6-258 & ALL 1982–89 ENGINES
## Centering Adjustment

This adjustment is made by turning the centering adjusting screw on the regulator, **Fig. 13.** If speed control engages at 2 or more mph higher than selected speed, turn centering adjusting screw counterclockwise a small amount. If engagement speed is 2 or more mph below selected speed, turn centering adjusting screw clockwise a small amount. Check for proper centering adjustment on a level road after each adjustment.

## Sensitivity Adjustment

The sensitivity can be adjusted by turning the adjustment screw **Fig. 13,** clockwise to increase or counterclockwise to decrease sensitivity. Adjustment of sensitivity may affect centering setting, if necessary adjust centering.

## Low Speed Switch Adjustment

The cruise control should engage between 27 and 33 mph. If adjustment of the low speed setting is necessary, turn adjustment screw **Fig. 13,** clockwise to increase the speed or counterclockwise to decrease the speed.

## Vacuum Vent Valve

While holding brake pedal in the depressed position, move vacuum vent valve toward pedal bracket as far as possible, then release brake pedal

# 4-150 (2.46L) ENGINE

## INDEX

## ENGINE MOUNTS
### REPLACE

Removal or replacement of any cushion can be accomplished by supporting the weight of the engine or transmission at the area of the cushion to be replaced. If it is necessary to remove front mounts and/or crossmember an engine support fixture can be fabricated as shown in **Fig. 1**, and installed prior to raising vehicle.

## ENGINE
### REPLACE

1. Disconnect cables from battery, remove battery and drain cooling system.
2. Mark position of hood hinges for assembly, disconnect electrical connector to hood lamp if equipped, then remove hood.
3. Disconnect electrical connectors from alternator, ignition coil and distributor, oil pressure switch and starter motor, then separate CEC system engine harness connector.
4. On models equipped with carburetor, disconnect supply pipe to fuel pump and plug pipe and pump fitting.
5. On models equipped with TBI, disconnect fuel tubes at quick disconnect couplings, located at left inner fender apron.
6. On all models, remove air cleaner and disconnect engine ground strap.
7. Disconnect vacuum purge and bowl vent hoses from canister, throttle linkage, idle speed control and MC solenoid electrical connectors, fuel return hose (at filter), and remove vacuum check valve from brake booster.
8. Disconnect coolant temperature and oxygen sensor electrical connectors.
9. Disconnect coolant hoses from radiator, rear of intake manifold and thermostat housing.
10. Remove fan shroud and radiator mounting bolts, then the fan shroud and radiator assembly.
11. Remove fan and spacer or thermostatic clutch, as equipped.
12. Install 5/16 x 1/2 inch SAE bolt through fan pulley and thread into water pump in order to maintain pulley alignment as crankshaft is rotated.
13. On models with power steering, dis-

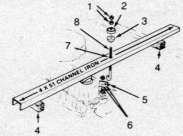

1 - 9/16-Inch – 12 Nuts
2 - Upper Trunnion Bearing
3 - Pivot or Sleeve
4 - 2 × 2 × 6-Inch Hardwood Block
5 - 1¼-Inch Angle Iron
6 - 1/2-Inch Holes
7 - 1-Inch Hole
8 - 9/16-Inch – 12 Trunnion

**Fig. 1 Engine support tool fabrication dimensions**

connect hoses from steering gear, drain fluid into suitable container, then plug hoses and open fittings.
14. On models with A/C (aftermarket system), disconnect hoses or remove compressor, following manufacturer's instructions.
15. Raise and support vehicle.
16. Remove starter motor, flywheel housing cover and front motor mount through bolts.
17. Disconnect exhaust pipe from manifold, remove upper flywheel housing bolts and loosen lower bolts.
18. Lower vehicle and attach suitable lifting equipment to engine.
19. Raise engine off mounts, place suitable support under flywheel housing and remove lower flywheel housing to engine bolts.
20. Separate engine from flywheel housing and remove from vehicle.
21. Reverse procedure to install.

## CYLINDER HEAD
### REPLACE

1. Disconnect battery ground cable, drain coolant and disconnect hoses from thermostat housing.
2. Remove air cleaner, then the rocker cover as follows:
  a. Remove PCV hose, shut-off valve and PCV valve.

b. On 1983-86 models, disconnect fuel pipe from fuel pump, loosen carburetor fitting and position pipe aside.
c. On all models, disconnect necessary vacuum and AIR hoses, noting position for assembly.
d. Remove rocker cover nuts and the cover, breaking RTV seal with suitable putty knife or cutter. Do not pry on cover until seal has been completely broken, and only pry cover at locations marked, or cover will be damaged.
3. Remove rocker arm, bridge and pivot assemblies, then the pushrods, keeping all components in order for assembly. Loosen retaining bolts alternately, 1 turn at a time, to avoid damaging bridges.
4. On 1983-88 models, remove power steering pump and bracket, then position aside.
5. On all models, remove intake manifolds as described under "Intake Manifold, Replace."
6. Remove exhaust manifold as described under "Exhaust Manifold, Replace."
7. Disconnect spark plug wires, temperature sensor lead and battery ground strap.
8. Remove cylinder head bolts, cylinder head and gasket, **Fig. 2**.
9. Reverse procedure to install, noting the following:
  a. On 1983-88 models, apply suitable sealing compound to head gasket and install gasket over dowel pins with "Top" mark facing up.
  b. On 1989 models, install head gasket.
  c. Install head and retaining bolts and torque bolts to specifications in sequence shown in **Fig. 3**. Coat threads of stud bolt in No. 8 position with suitable sealer.
  d. On 1983-88 models, apply a continuous bead of RTV sealer, 3/16 inch wide, to rocker cover, install cover and torque nuts to specifications.
  e. On 1983-88 models, remove temperature sensor and leave removed until cooling system is filled, allowing air to escape from block and head.

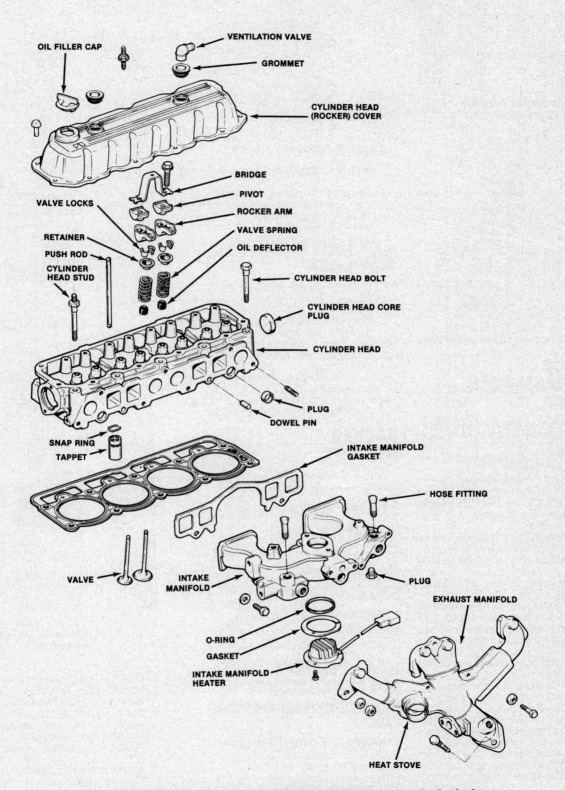

**Fig. 2  Cylinder head and manifold assemblies exploded view**

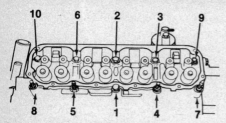

**Fig. 3   Cylinder head tightening sequence**

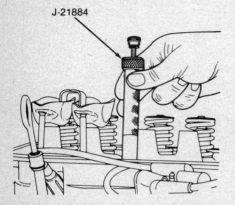

**Fig. 6   Hydraulic lifter removal**

## INTAKE MANIFOLD REPLACE

Mark installation position of all components, hoses and wiring prior to removal to aid reassembly.

1. Disconnect battery ground cable, then drain cooling system.
2. On 1983-86 models, disconnect fuel lines, air horn vent hose, idle speed control hose and electrical connector, choke heater connector and throttle linkages.
3. On 1987-89 models, disconnect fuel inlet and return hoses, idle speed actuator electrical connector and throttle cable.
4. On all models, disconnect coolant hoses from intake manifold.
5. Disconnect vacuum hoses from vacuum advance control valve and EGR valve, then electrical connectors from coolant sensor and intake manifold heater.
6. Disconnect PCV valve hose from intake manifold
7. On 1983-86 models, remove carburetor retaining nuts, then remove carburetor from manifold.
8. On 1987-89 models, remove throttle body retaining nuts, then remove throttle body from intake manifold.
9. On models with power steering, remove mounting bracket and position pump aside without disconnecting hoses.
10. On all models, disconnect EGR tube from intake manifold, then remove EGR tube-to-exhaust manifold attaching bolts.
11. Remove manifold-to-cylinder head at-

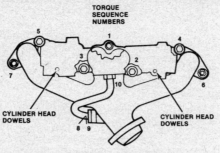

**Fig. 4   Intake manifold tightening sequence**

taching bolts, then the manifold, **Fig. 2.**
12. Reverse procedure to install, using new gaskets and torquing manifold bolts to specifications in sequence shown in **Fig. 4.**

## EXHAUST MANIFOLD REPLACE

1. Remove intake manifold as as described under "Intake Manifold, Replace."
2. Disconnect EGR tube and exhaust pipe from exhaust manifold.
3. Disconnect oxygen sensor electrical connector and remove sensor from exhaust pipe.
4. Remove manifold attaching nuts, then the manifold, **Fig. 2.**
5. Reverse procedure to install, torquing attaching bolts to specifications.

## VALVES ADJUST

These engines use hydraulic lifters. No provision for adjustment is provided.

## VALVE ARRANGEMENT FRONT TO REAR

4-150 . . . . . . . . . . . . . . . . . . . . E-I-I-E-E-I-I-E

## VALVE LIFT SPECIFICATIONS

| Engine | Year | Intake Exhaust | |
|---|---|---|---|
| 4-150 | 1983-89 | .424 | .424 |

## VALVE TIMING SPECIFICATIONS

### INTAKE OPENS BEFORE TDC

| Engine | Year | Degrees |
|---|---|---|
| 4-150 | 1983-89 | 12 |

## ROCKER ARMS REPLACE

1. Remove rocker arm cover attaching screws, then remove rocker arm cover as described under "Cylinder Head,

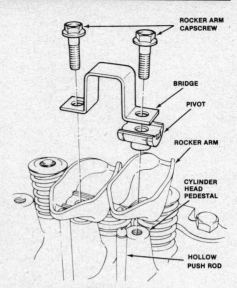

**Fig. 5   Rocker arm, bridge & pivot assembly**

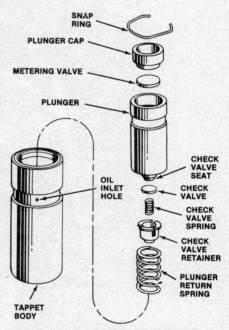

**Fig. 7   Hydraulic valve lifter assembly**

Replace." RTV sealant is used between rocker arm cover and cylinder head mating surfaces. To avoid damaging rocker arm cover, do not pry cover upward until seal has been completely broken. When prying cover upward, pry only in areas marked "Pry Here," which are located near rocker arm cover bolt holes.
2. Remove rocker arm cap screws by alternately loosening one turn at a time to prevent damage to bridge, **Fig. 5.**
3. Remove rocker arm bridge, pivots and rocker arms. Tag all components so they can be reinstalled in the same position as removed.

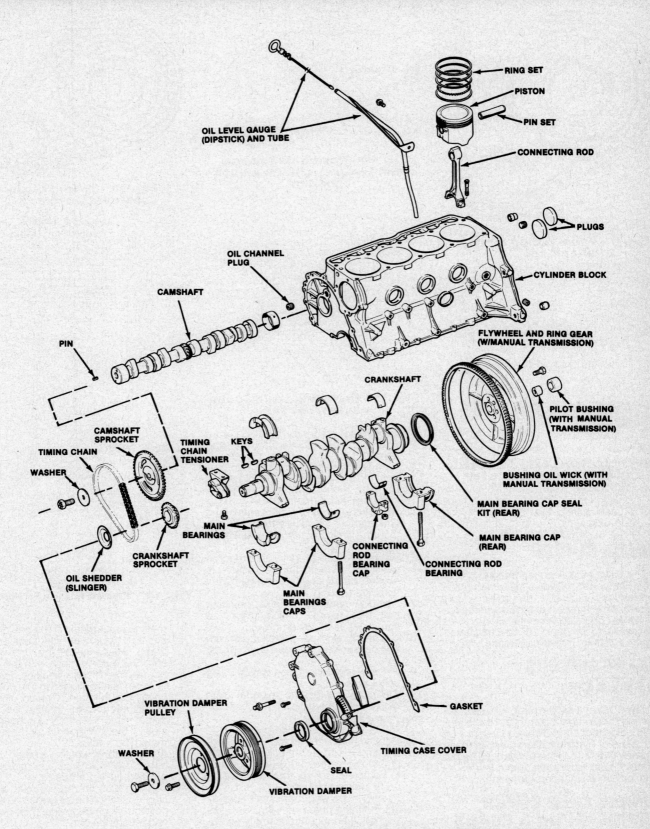

RING SET

PISTON

PIN SET

OIL LEVEL GAUGE
(DIPSTICK) AND TUBE

CONNECTING ROD

PLUGS

OIL CHANNEL
PLUG

CYLINDER BLOCK

CAMSHAFT

FLYWHEEL AND RING GEAR
(W/MANUAL TRANSMISSION)

PIN

CRANKSHAFT

PILOT BUSHING
(WITH MANUAL
TRANSMISSION)

CAMSHAFT
SPROCKET

TIMING
CHAIN
TENSIONER

KEYS

TIMING CHAIN

BUSHING OIL WICK (WITH
MANUAL TRANSMISSION)

WASHER

MAIN BEARING CAP SEAL
KIT (REAR)

MAIN
BEARINGS

MAIN BEARING CAP
(REAR)

CRANKSHAFT
SPROCKET

CONNECTING
ROD
BEARING
CAP

CONNECTING ROD
BEARING

OIL SHEDDER
(SLINGER)

MAIN
BEARINGS
CAPS

VIBRATION DAMPER
PULLEY

GASKET

WASHER

TIMING CASE COVER

SEAL

VIBRATION DAMPER

**Fig. 8   Cylinder block components exploded view**

**Fig. 9   Valve timing mark alignment**

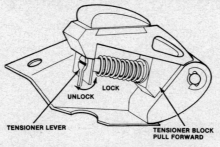

**Fig. 10   Positioning timing chain tensioner in the unlock position**

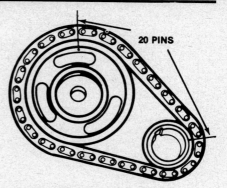

**Fig. 11   Timing chain installation check**

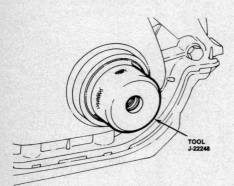

**Fig. 12   Using tool J-22248 to align timing case cover**

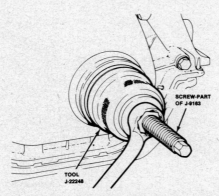

**Fig. 13   Installing timing case cover front seal**

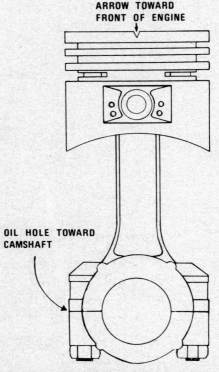

**Fig. 14   Piston & rod assembly**

4. Reverse procedure to install. When installing rocker arm cap screws, tighten each screw alternately and evenly approximately one turn at a time to prevent damage to bridge.

## VALVE GUIDES

The valve guides are an integral part of the cylinder head. If valve system to guide clearance is excessive, the guide should be reamed to the next oversize and the approximate oversize valve installed. Valves are available in standard size and oversizes of .003 inch and .015 inch.

## VALVE LIFTERS
### REPLACE

Valve lifters can be removed after removing rocker arm assemblies and pushrods, using tool J-21884 or equivalent, **Fig. 6.** Failure of hydraulic lifters used in these engines, **Fig. 7,** is generally caused by dirt or insufficient lubrication due to low oil levels, oil contamination or foaming.

## TIMING CASE COVER, TIMING CHAIN & GEARS
### REPLACE
#### REMOVAL

1. Disconnect battery ground cable, then remove accessory drive belts.
2. Remove engine cooling fan, hub and shroud.
3. Remove crankshaft damper hub bolt, then the damper, using suitable puller.
4. Remove alternator bracket assembly and position alternator aside.
5. Remove oil pan-to-timing cover and timing cover-to-block attaching bolts, then the timing cover and crankshaft oil slinger, **Fig. 8.**
6. Rotate crankshaft until zero degree mark on crankshaft sprocket is aligned with timing mark on camshaft sprocket (A), **Fig. 9.**
7. Remove camshaft sprocket retaining bolt, then remove timing chain and sprockets as an assembly.
8. Cut off oil pan side gaskets flush with engine block and remove ends of gaskets.
9. Pry oil seal from timing cover using suitable lever.
10. Clean all old gasket material from block, timing cover and front of oil pan.

#### INSTALLATION

1. Rotate lever on timing chain tensioner, **Fig. 10,** to unlocked position, pull tensioner block toward tensioner to compress spring, then rotate lever up to locked position.
2. Position cam and crankshaft sprockets in timing chain with timing marks aligned, then mount assembly on engine. Install camshaft sprocket retaining bolt and torque bolt to 80 ft. lbs. To verify proper installation of timing chain and gears, rotate crankshaft to position camshaft sprocket timing mark approximately at the one o'clock position, which should position the tooth adjacent to the crankshaft sprocket mark in mesh with the chain at the three o'clock position, **Fig. 11.** With sprockets aligned in this position, count the number of chain pins between the timing marks on both sprockets. If assembly is properly installed, there will be 20 pins between the timing marks.
3. Apply suitable sealing compound to both sides of timing cover gasket and position gasket on block.
4. Cut end tabs off replacement oil pan side gaskets to correspond to those cut from original gasket, then cement end tabs to oil pan.
5. Coat front pan seal end tabs with RTV sealer and apply sealer to pan side rail gasket joints, then install end seal on timing case cover.
6. Apply engine oil to the end seal/oil

| Crankshaft No. 1 Main Bearing Journal Color Codes and Diameter in Inches (mm) | Cylinder Block No. 1 Main Bearing Bore Color Code and Size in Inches (mm) | | Bearing Insert Color Code | |
|---|---|---|---|---|
| | | | Upper Insert Size | Lower Insert Size |
| Yellow — 2.5001 to 2.4996 (Standard) (63.5025 to 63.4898 mm) | Yellow — | 2.6910 to 2.6915 (68.3514 to 68.3641 mm) | Yellow — Standard | Yellow — Standard |
| | Black — | 2.6915 to 2.6920 (68.3641 to 68.3768 mm) | Yellow — Standard | Black — 0.001-inch Undersize (0.025 mm) |
| Orange — 2.4996 to 2.4991 (0.0005 Undersize) (63.4898 to 63.4771 mm) | Yellow — | 2.6910 to 2.6915 (68.3514 to 68.3641 mm) | Yellow — Standard | Black — 0.001-inch Undersize — (0.001 mm) |
| | Black — | 2.6915 to 2.6920 (68.3461 to 68.3768 mm) | Black — 0.001-inch Undersize (0.025 mm) | Black — 0.001-inch Undersize (0.025 mm) |
| Black — 2.4991 to 2.4986 (0.001 Undersize) (63.4771 to 63.4644 mm) | Yellow — | 2.6910 to 2.6915 (68.3514 to 68.3641 mm) | Black — 0.001-inch Undersize — (0.025 mm) | Black — 0.001-inch Undersize — (0.025 mm) |
| | Black — | 2.6915 to 2.6920 (68.3461 to 68.3768 mm) | Black — 0.001-inch Undersize (0.025 mm) | Green — 0.002-inch Undersize (0.051 mm) |
| Green — 2.4986 to 2.4981 (0.0015 Undersize) (63.4644 to63.4517 mm) | Yellow — | 2.6910 to 2.6915 (68.3514 to 68.3641 mm) | Black — 0.001-inch Undersize — (0.025 mm) | Green — 0.002-inch Undersize (0.051 mm) |
| Red — 2.4901 to 2.4896 (0.010 Undersize) (63.2485 to 63.2358 mm) | Yellow — | 2.6910 to 2.6915 (68.3514 to 68.3641 mm) | Red — 0.010-inch Undersize (0.254 mm) | Red — 0.010-inch Undersize — (0.254 mm) |

**Fig. 15  Main bearing selection chart. 4-150 No. 1 main bearing**

pan contact surface, install oil slinger, then position timing cover on block and install retaining bolts hand tight.

7. Install alignment tool J-22248 or equivalent in the timing cover seal opening, **Fig. 12**, then torque cover to block bolts to 5 ft. lbs. and oil pan bolts to 7 ft. lbs.
8. Remove alignment tool from cover, mount new oil seal on tool with seal lip facing out and coat outer surface of seal with suitable sealer.
9. Lightly coat crankshaft with engine oil, position tool over end of crankshaft and install screw J-9163-2 into tool and thread screw into crankshaft, **Fig. 13.**
10. Hold screw and tighten nut until body of installer contacts timing cover, then remove tool assembly.
11. Install crankshaft damper and bolt, torquing to 80 ft. lbs.
12. Install alternator bracket assembly and alternator.
13. Install engine cooling fan, hub and shroud.
14. Install accessory drive belts, then connect battery ground cable.

## CAMSHAFT
### REPLACE

1. Disconnect battery ground cable, then drain cooling system.
2. Remove radiator and condenser, if equipped with A/C.
3. On carbureted models, remove fuel pump.
4. Note position of distributor housing and rotor for reference during assembly.
5. Remove cylinder head cover and rocker arms as outlined under ""Rocker Arms, Replace."
6. Remove pushrods.
7. Remove valve lifters as outlined under "Valve Lifters, Replace."

8. Remove timing case cover, timing chain and gears as outlined under "Timing Case Cover, Timing Chain and Gears, Replace."
9. Remove camshaft.
10. Reverse procedure to install, noting the following:
    a. Torque timing case cover-to-block bolts to 5 ft. lbs.
    b. Torque oil pan-to-timing case cover bolts to 11 ft. lbs.
    c. Torque camshaft sprocket bolts to 80 ft. lbs.

## PISTON & ROD ASSEMBLE

Pistons are marked with an arrow on the top perimeter, **Fig. 14**. When installing piston in engine, the arrow must face toward front of engine. Always assemble rods and caps with oil spurt holes facing camshaft. Check side clearance between connecting rod and crankshaft journal. Clearance should be .010 to .019 inch.

## MAIN BEARINGS

The main bearing journal size (diameter) is identified by a color coded paint mark on adjacent cheek toward flanged (rear) end of crankshaft, except for rear main journal which is on crankshaft rear flange. Color codes used to indicate journal and corresponding bearing sizes are listed in **Figs. 15 and 16.**

## CONNECTING ROD BEARINGS

The connecting rod journal is identified by a color coded paint mark on adjacent cheek or counterweight toward flanged (rear) end of crankshaft. Color codes used to indicate journal sizes and corresponding bearing sizes are listed in **Fig. 17.**

## OIL PAN
### REPLACE

1. Disconnect battery ground cable.
2. Raise vehicle and support vehicle.
3. Drain engine oil, then remove starter motor.
4. Remove flywheel housing cover.
5. Disconnect exhaust pipe from exhaust manifold.
6. Disconnect exhaust hanger from catalytic convertor.
7. Remove oil pan retaining screws, then the oil pan.
8. Clean all old gasket material and sealer from oil pan, engine block and timing cover.
9. Install new oil pan front seal into timing case cover and liberally apply RTV sealer to recesses in ends of seal.
10. Install rear pan seal into recess in rear main bearing cap, ensuring that seal is fully seated.
11. If gasket is being used on pan side rails, coat both sides of gaskets with suitable "Hi-Tack" sealer and cement gaskets to block side rails, ensuring that gasket tabs are properly engaged in seal recesses. If RTV sealer is used in place of pan rail gaskets, apply a continuous bead of sealer to pan side rails, 3/16 inch wide, circling all bolt holes.
12. Install oil pan and attaching bolts.
13. Torque 1/4 inch bolts to 80 inch lbs. and 5/16 inch bolts to 11 ft. lbs.
14. Reverse remaining procedure to complete installation.

## OIL PUMP
### REPLACE

1. Drain crankcase, then remove oil pan.
2. Remove bolts attaching oil pump to cylinder block, then remove oil pump

| Crankshaft Main Bearing Journal 2-3-4-5 Color Code and Diameter in Inches (Journal Size) | Bearing Insert Color Code | |
| --- | --- | --- |
| | Upper Insert Size | Lower Insert Size |
| Yellow — 2.5001 to 2.4996 (Standard) (63.5025 to 63.4898 mm) | Yellow — Standard | Yellow — Standard |
| Orange — 2.4996 to 2.4991 (0.0005 Undersize) (63.4898 to 63.4771 mm) | Yellow — Standard | Black — 0.001-inch Undersize (0.025mm) |
| Black — 2.4991 to 2.4986 (0.001 Undersize) (63.4771 to 63.4644 mm) | Black — 0.001-inch Undersize (0.025 mm) | Black — 0.001-inch Undersize (0.025 mm) |
| Green — 2.4986 to 2.4981 (0.0015 Undersize) (63.4644 to 63.4517 mm) | Black — 0.001-inch Undersize (0.025 mm) | Green — 0.002-inch Undersize (0.051 mm) |
| Red — 2.4901 to 2.4896 (0.010 Undersize) (63.2485 to 63.2358 mm) | Red — 0.010-inch Undersize (0.054 mm) | Red — 0.010-inch Undersize (0.254 mm) |

**Fig. 16   Main bearing selection chart. 4-150 Nos. 2, 3, 4, 5 main bearings**

| Connecting Rod Bearing Journal 2-3-4-5 Color Code and Diameter in Inches (Journal Size) | Bearing Insert Color Code | |
| --- | --- | --- |
| | Upper Insert Size | Lower Insert Size |
| Yellow — 2.0955 to 2.0948 (53.2257 - 53.2079 mm) (Standard) | Yellow — Standard | Yellow — Standard |
| Orange — 2.0948 to 2.0941 (53.2079 - 53.1901 mm) (0.0007 Undersize) | Yellow — Standard | Black — 0.001-inch (0.025 mm) Undersize |
| Black — 2.0941 to 2.0943 (53.1901 to 53.1723 mm) (0.0014 Undersize) | Black — 0.001-inch (0.025 mm) Undersize | Black — 0.001-inch (0.025 mm) Undersize |
| Red — 2.0855 to 2.0848 (53.9717 to 53.9539 mm) (0.010 Undersize) | Red — 0.010-inch (0.254 mm) Undersize | Red — 0.010-inch (0.245 mm) Undersize |

**Fig. 17   Connecting rod bearing chart. 4-150**

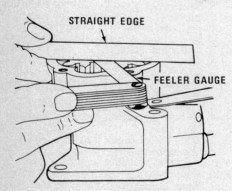

**Fig. 18   Checking oil pump gear end clearance**

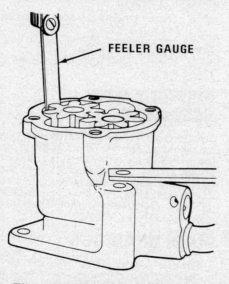

**Fig. 19   Checking oil pump gear to body clearance**

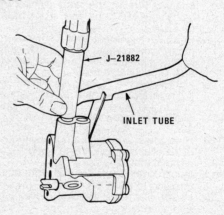

**Fig. 20   Installing oil pump pickup screen & tube assembly**

and gasket. Do not disturb positioning of oil pump strainer and tube. If tube is moved, a replacement tube and screen assembly must be installed.

3. Reverse procedure to install. Torque short attaching bolts to 10 ft. lbs. and long attaching bolts to 17 ft. lbs.

## OIL PUMP SERVICE

1. Remove oil pump cover retaining screws, then remove cover from pump body.
2. Check gear end clearance as follows:
   a. Place straightedge across ends of gears and pump body, **Fig. 18.**
   b. Check clearance using a suitable feeler gauge.
   c. Clearance should be .002 to .006 inch. If clearance is not within limits, replace oil pump assembly.

3. Check gear to pump body clearance as follows:
   a. Insert a suitable feeler gauge between gear tooth and pump body, **Fig. 19.**
   b. Clearance should be .002 to .004 inch. If clearance is not within limits, replace idler gear, idler shaft and drive gear assembly.
4. If pressure relief valve is to be checked, move pickup tube and screen assembly out of way. Remove spring retainer, spring and oil pressure

relief valve plunger. Check pressure relief valve components for binding and clean or replace as necessary. After reinstalling relief valve components, install a replacement pickup tube and screen assembly. When replacing relief valve plunger, ensure correct size is installed. Plungers are available in standard size and .010 inch oversize.

5. If a replacement pickup tube is to be installed, apply a light coating of Permatex No. 2 sealant or equivalent to end of tube. Install pickup tube and screen using tool No. J-21882, **Fig. 20.**
6. Before installing pump cover, fill pump with petroleum jelly.

7. When installing pump cover, torque attaching screws to 70 inch lbs.

## BELT TENSION DATA

|  | New Lbs. | Used Lbs. |
|---|---|---|
| V-Type Belts | 120-160 | 90-115 |
| Serpentine Type Belt | 180-200 | 140-160 |

## WATER PUMP
## REPLACE

1. Disconnect battery ground cable, then drain cooling system.
2. Disconnect radiator and heater hoses from water pump.
3. Remove drive belts.
4. If equipped, remove fan shroud attaching screws, then remove fan and fan shroud.
5. If equipped, remove power steering bracket.
6. Remove water pump attaching bolts, then remove water pump and gasket.
7. Reverse procedure to install. Torque water pump attaching bolts to 13 ft. lbs. **Engines with a serpentine drive belt use a reverse rotating water pump identified by "REV" cast on the pump body. Engines with V-type belts use a clockwise pump, installation of the wrong pump will cause overheating.**

## FUEL PUMP
## REPLACE
### ELECTRIC FUEL PUMP
#### 1987—89 Models

1. Disconnect battery ground cable.
2. Drain fuel from fuel tank into a suitable container.
3. Position a suitable jack under shield and fuel tank, then remove attaching bolts.
4. Disconnect fuel outlet hose, return hoses, fuel filler hose and vent hose.
5. Lower shield and fuel tank slightly, then disconnect fuel tank vapor hoses and fuel sender and fuel pump electrical connectors.
6. Lower fuel tank and remove from vehicle.
7. Using a suitable screwdriver remove fuel gauge sending unit retainer ring.
8. Remove fuel gauge sending unit and fuel pump from tank, then separate sending unit from fuel pump.
9. Reverse procedure to install. When installing fuel gauge sending unit and fuel pump, ensure retainer ring seal is properly seated. After completing installation, start engine and check for leaks.

## MECHANICAL FUEL PUMP
#### 1983—86 Models

1. Disconnect fuel lines from pump.
2. Remove retaining screws and fuel pump.
3. Remove all gasket material from the pump and block gasket surfaces. Apply sealer to both sides of new gasket.
4. Position gasket on pump flange and hold pump in position against its mounting surface. Make sure rocker arm is riding on camshaft eccentric.
5. Press pump tight against its mounting. Install retaining screws and tighten them alternately.
6. Connect fuel lines. Then operate engine and check for leaks. When installing pump, crank engine to place camshaft eccentric in a position as to place the least amount of tension on fuel pump rocker arm. This will ease pump installation.

# 4-151 (2.5L) ENGINE

## INDEX

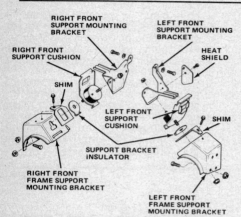

Fig. 1 Engine mounts. 4-151

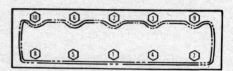

Fig. 2 Cylinder head bolt tightening sequence. 4-151

## ENGINE MOUNTS
### REPLACE

Remove fan shroud to radiator attaching screws to prevent damage to shroud. Removal or replacement of any cushion, **Fig. 1** can be accomplished by supporting the weight of the engine at the area of the cushion to be replaced.

## ENGINE
### REPLACE

1. Disconnect battery ground cable and body ground strap from firewall.
2. Remove air cleaner assembly.
3. Raise and support vehicle.
4. Disconnect electrical connector from oxygen sensor and exhaust pipe from exhaust manifold.
5. Disconnect battery cable and solenoid electrical connector from starter motor.
6. Remove starter motor attaching bolts, rear bracket nut, then the starter motor.
7. Disconnect electrical connectors from distributor and oil pressure sending unit.
8. Remove engine mount attaching nuts.
9. Remove hydraulic clutch slave cylinder and flywheel inspection plate.
10. Remove transmission clutch housing to engine attaching bolts.
11. Lower vehicle.
12. Support transmission using a suitable floor jack.
13. Mark and disconnect all vacuum hoses and electrical connector from engine.
14. Remove inlet and outlet heater hoses from heater core.
15. Drain radiator and remove lower radiator hose.
16. Remove upper radiator hose, fan shroud and radiator from vehicle.
17. Disconnect and cap power steering lines at power steering pump.
18. Install suitable engine lifting equipment to engine lifting eyes.
19. Remove engine from vehicle. If necessary, raise transmission slightly to provide a smooth engine from transmission separation.
20. Reverse procedure to install.

## CYLINDER HEAD
### REPLACE

1. Disconnect battery ground cable, then the cylinder head cover.
2. Drain coolant from radiator and engine block.
3. Disconnect electrical connector from oxygen sensor and exhaust pipe from exhaust manifold.
4. Mark and disconnect all vacuum hoses from cylinder head.
5. Remove alternator and position aside, then disconnect fuel line from carburetor.
6. Disconnect rear heater and upper radiator hoses from cylinder head.
7. Remove power steering pump and bracket and position aside. Do not disconnect power steering hoses.
8. Remove dipstick, rocker arm and pushrod assemblies. Tag rocker arms and pushrods so they can be installed in their original positions.
9. Remove cylinder head attaching bolts.
10. Remove cylinder head by inserting a suitable tool into alternator bracket and prying upward.
11. Reverse procedure to install. Torque cylinder head bolts to 92 ft. lbs. in sequence shown in **Fig. 2**.

## INTAKE MANIFOLD
### REPLACE

1. Disconnect battery ground cable.

2. Remove air cleaner assembly and disconnect PCV valve hose.
3. Drain cooling system.
4. Mark and disconnect all vacuum lines and electrical connectors from intake manifold and carburetor.
5. Disconnect fuel line from carburetor.
6. Disconnect throttle linkage from carburetor.
7. Remove carburetor and spacer plate from intake manifold.
8. Remove bell crank and throttle linkage brackets and position aside.
9. Disconnect heater hose from intake manifold.
10. Remove alternator and position aside.
11. Remove intake manifold to cylinder head bolts, then the intake manifold.
12. Reverse procedure to install. Torque cylinder head bolts in sequence shown in **Fig. 3**. Torque all bolts except bolt No. 7 to 25 ft. lbs. Torque bolt No. 7 to 37 ft. lbs.

## EXHAUST MANIFOLD
### REPLACE

1. Remove air cleaner assembly and heated air tube.
2. Remove oil dipstick tube bracket bolt.
3. On models equipped, remove oxygen sensor.
4. Disconnect exhaust pipe from exhaust manifold.
5. Remove exhaust manifold to cylinder head attaching bolts, then remove exhaust manifold.
6. Reverse procedure to install. Torque exhaust manifold attaching bolts to torque listed in "Engine Tightening Specifications" in sequence shown in **Fig. 4**.

## VALVES, ADJUST

These engines use hydraulic valve lift-

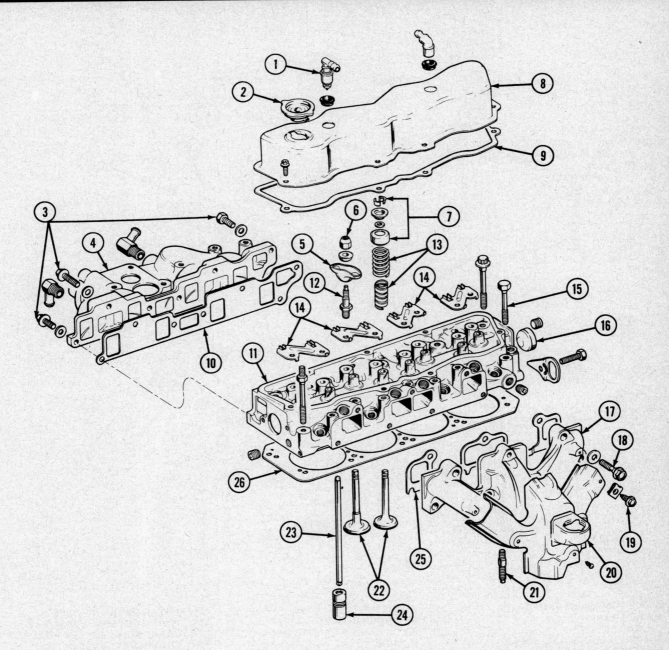

1. PCV VALVE
2. OIL FILLER CAP
3. INTAKE MANIFOLD ATTACHING BOLTS
4. INTAKE MANIFOLD
5. ROCKER ARM
6. ROCKER ARM PIVOT BALL AND NUT
7. VALVE SPRING RETAINER ASSEMBLY
8. CYLINDER HEAD COVER (ROCKER COVER)
9. CYLINDER HEAD COVER GASKET
10. INTAKE MANIFOLD GASKET
11. CYLINDER HEAD
12. ROCKER ARM STUD
13. VALVE SPRING
14. PUSH ROD GUIDE
15. CYLINDER HEAD BOLTS
16. CYLINDER HEAD CORE PLUG
17. EXHAUST MANIFOLD
18. EXHAUST MANIFOLD BOLT
19. OIL LEVEL INDICATOR TUBE ATTACHING SCREW
20. EXHAUST MANIFOLD HEAT SHROUD (HEAT SHIELD)
21. EXHAUST MANIFOLD TO EXHAUST PIPE STUD
22. VALVES
23. PUSH ROD
24. LIFTER
25. EXHAUST MANIFOLD GASKET
26. CYLINDER HEAD GASKET

**Exploded view of cylinder head, intake & exhaust manifolds. 4-151**

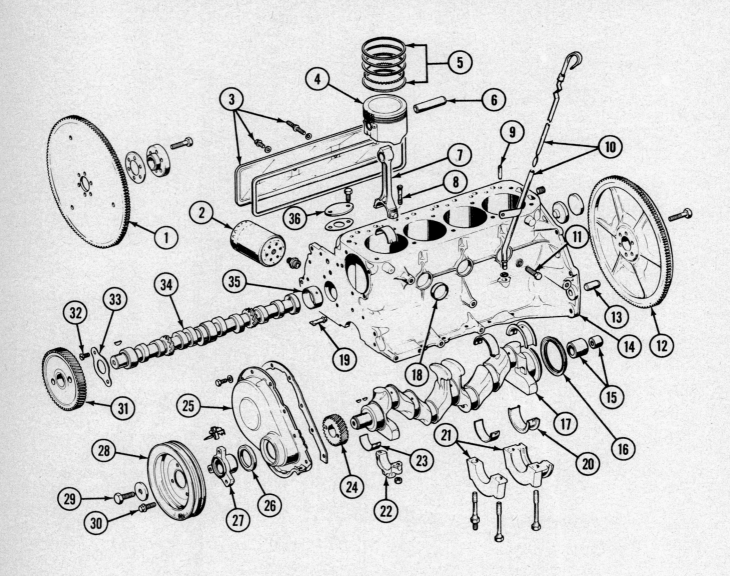

1. DRIVE PLATE AND RING (AUTO-MATIC TRANS)
2. OIL FILTER
3. PUSH ROD COVER AND BOLTS
4. PISTON
5. PISTON RING
6. PISTON PIN
7. CONNECTING ROD
8. CONNECTING ROD BOLT
9. DOWEL
10. OIL LEVEL INDICATOR AND TUBE
11. BLOCK DRAIN
12. FLYWHEEL AND RING GEAR (MAN-UAL TRANS)
13. DOWEL
14. CYLINDER BLOCK
15. PILOT AND/OR CONVERTER BUSHING
16. REAR OIL SEAL
17. CRANKSHAFT
18. BLOCK CORE PLUG
19. TIMING CHAIN OILER
20. MAIN BEARINGS
21. MAIN BEARING CAPS
22. CONNECTING ROD BEARING CAP
23. CONNECTING ROD BEARING
24. CRANKSHAFT GEAR
25. TIMING COVER (FRONT)
26. TIMING COVER OIL SEAL
27. CRANKSHAFT PULLEY HUB
28. CRANKSHAFT PULLEY
29. CRANKSHAFT PULLEY HUB BOLT
30. CRANKSHAFT PULLEY BOLT
31. CRANKSHAFT TIMING GEAR
32. CAMSHAFT THRUST PLATE SCREW
33. CAMSHAFT THRUST PLATE
34. CAMSHAFT
35. CAMSHAFT BEARING
36. OIL PUMP DRIVESHAFT RETAINER PLATE, GASKET AND BOLT

**Exploded view of cylinder block & components. 4-151**

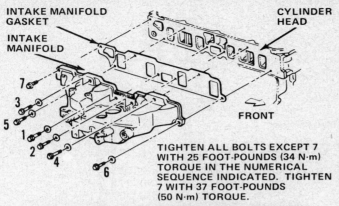

TIGHTEN ALL BOLTS EXCEPT 7 WITH 25 FOOT-POUNDS (34 N·m) TORQUE IN THE NUMERICAL SEQUENCE INDICATED. TIGHTEN 7 WITH 37 FOOT-POUNDS (50 N·m) TORQUE.

**Fig. 3   Intake manifold bolt tightening sequence. 4-151**

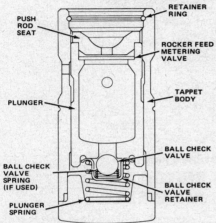

**Fig. 5   Sectional view of hydraulic valve lifter. 4-151**

ers. No provision for adjustment is provided.

## VALVE ARRANGEMENT
### FRONT TO REAR
4-151 . . . . . . . . . . . . . . . . . . . I-E-I-E-E-I-E-I

## CAM LOBE LIFT SPECIFICATIONS
4-151 . . . . . . . . . . . . . . . . . . . . . . . . . .230

## VALVE TIMING SPECIFICATIONS
### INTAKE OPENS BEFORE TDC

| Engine | Year | Degrees |
|--------|------|---------|
| 4-151 | 1980 | 33 |
| 4-151 | 1981-83 | 25 |

## ROCKER ARM SERVICE

To remove rocker arm assembly, proceed as follows:
1. Remove cylinder head cover.
2. Remove rocker arm nut and ball.
3. Remove rocker arm.
4. Reverse procedure to install. Clean all parts using a suitable cleaning solvent. Blow dry parts using compressed air. Inspect the pivot contact surface of each rocker arm, pivot ball and pushrod assembly. Replace any part that has been found unserviceable.

## VALVE GUIDES

Valves with oversize stems are available for both intake and exhaust valves. Valve guides should be reamed and replacement oversize valves installed whenever clearances exceed specification.

## HYDRAULIC LIFTERS

Failure of a hydraulic valve lifter, **Fig. 5**, is generally caused by an inadequate oil supply or dirt. An air leak at the intake side of the oil pump or excessive oil in the engine will cause air bubbles in the oil supply to the lifters causing them to collapse. This is a probable cause of trouble if several lifters fail to function, but air in oil is an unlikely cause of failure of a single unit.

Valve lifters can be removed after removing rocker arm cover, intake manifold and pushrod cover. Loosen rocker arm stud nut and rotate rocker arm so that pushrod can be removed, then remove valve lifter. If necessary, use valve lifter removal tool No. J-3049 to facilitate valve

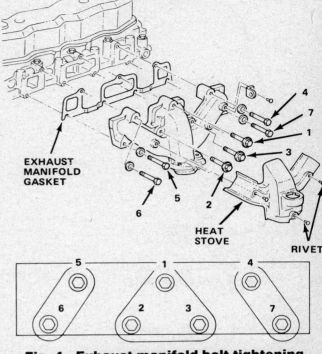

**Fig. 4   Exhaust manifold bolt tightening sequence. 4-151**

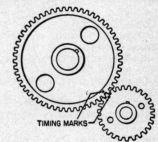

**Fig. 6   Aligning valve timing marks. 4-151**

lifter removal.

## PUSHROD COVER
### REPLACE

1. Remove intake manifold as described under "Intake Manifold, Replace."
2. Remove pushrod cover attaching bolts and pushrod cover.
3. Reverse procedure to install. Ensure pushrod cover and cylinder block sealing surfaces are thoroughly cleaned. Apply a 3/16 inch bead of RTV sealer to pushrod cover at cover to cylinder block sealing surface. Torque pushrod cover attaching bolts to 75 inch lbs.

## TIMING CASE COVER

1. Disconnect battery ground cable.
2. Remove crankshaft pulley hub, then remove alternator bracket.
3. Remove fan and shroud attaching nuts, then loosen drive belts and re-

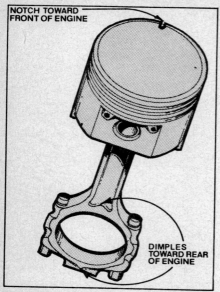

NOTCH TOWARD
FRONT OF ENGINE

DIMPLES
TOWARD REAR
OF ENGINE

**Fig. 7    Piston & rod assembly.
4-151**

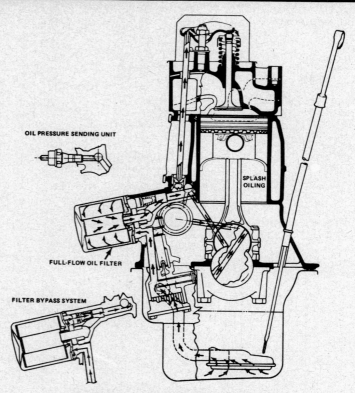

OIL PRESSURE SENDING UNIT

SPLASH
OILING

FULL-FLOW OIL FILTER

FILTER BYPASS SYSTEM

**Engine lubrication system. 4-151**

move fan and shroud.

4. Remove oil pan to timing case cover attaching screws, then pull cover slightly forward to permit cutting of oil pan front seal.
5. Using a suitable cutting tool, cut oil pan front seal flush with engine block at both sides of cover.
6. Remove front cover with attached portion of oil pan front seal.
7. Clean timing case cover and cylinder block gasket surfaces.
8. Cut tabs from a replacement oil pan front seal.
9. Install seal on timing case cover, inserting tips into holes provided in cover.
10. Coat gasket with gasket sealer, then position gasket on cover.
11. Apply a ⅛ inch bead of RTV sealer to joint surface formed at oil pan and cylinder block.
12. Position centering tool J-23042 into timing case cover oil seal, then position cover on block and install and partially tighten two oil pan to timing case cover attaching screws.
13. Install timing case cover to cylinder block attaching screws.
14. Torque all timing case cover attaching screws to 90 inch lbs., then remove centering tool.
15. Install alternator bracket, crankshaft pulley hub, fan and shroud.
16. Tighten all drive belts, then connect battery ground cable.

## TIMING GEARS
### REPLACE

The camshaft is driven by an iron crankshaft gear meshed with a fiber gear attached to the camshaft, **Fig. 6.** To remove the fiber timing gear requires the removal of the camshaft. Position camshaft and timing gear assembly in suitable press

plate and press camshaft out of gear using appropriate size socket and arbor press. Thrust plate must be properly aligned with camshaft woodruff key when pressing shaft out of gear or damage to thrust plate may result.

Reverse procedure to install timing gear. End clearance of thrust plate should be .0015-.0050 inch. If clearance is less than .0015 inch, replace spacer ring. If clearance is more than .0050 inch, replace thrust plate.

## CAMSHAFT
### REPLACE

To remove camshaft, remove timing case cover as outlined previously and proceed as follows:

1. Remove air cleaner. Do not remove block drain plugs or loosen radiator draincock with system under pressure. Scalding can occur from the hot coolant.
2. Drain radiator.
3. Disconnect radiator hoses at radiator, then remove radiator.
4. Remove camshaft thrust plate screws in camshaft gear.
5. Remove distributor, oil and fuel pumps.
6. Remove camshaft and gear assembly, withdraw assemblies through front of block. Secure shaft carefully when removing to prevent camshaft bearing damage.
7. Reverse procedure to install, aligning timing marks, **Fig. 6.** Thoroughly clean and inspect all parts. Any component found to be unserviceable should be replaced.

## PISTON & ROD
### ASSEMBLE

Assemble piston to rod with notch on piston facing toward front of engine and the raised notch side of rod at bearing end facing toward rear of engine, **Fig. 7.**

## PISTONS, PINS & RINGS

Pistons are available in standard size and oversizes of .005, .010, .020 and .030 inch. Piston pins are available in oversizes of .001 and .003 inch.

## MAIN & ROD BEARINGS

Main and rod bearings are available in standard size and undersizes of .001, .002 and .010 inch.

## CRANKSHAFT REAR OIL SEAL
### REPLACE

The rear main bearing oil seal is a one piece unit and can be removed or installed without removing the oil pan or the crankshaft.

1. Disconnect battery ground cable and raise and support vehicle.
2. Remove transmission and transfer case as a unit.
3. Remove starter motor.
4. On manual transmissions only, remove inspection plate from flywheel housing.

5. On manual transmissions only, remove hydraulic clutch slave cylinder from flywheel housing.
6. On all models, remove flywheel/drive plate housing from engine.
7. On manual transmissions, remove clutch pressure plate and disc assembly by loosening bolts 1/4 turn in equal amounts until pressure is relieved.
8. On all models, mark flywheel/drive plate location to ensure correct assembly.
9. Remove flywheel/drive plate.
10. Using a small screwdriver, pry out rear main oil seal, using care not to damage seating groove or crankshaft.
11. Center replacement seal over crankshaft with lip facing toward front of engine. Using a soft hammer, tap around perimeter of seal until it seats in groove taking care to prevent seal from binding on crankshaft and not seating properly.
12. Install flywheel/drive plate on crankshaft and torque to 68 ft. lbs.
13. On manual transmissions only, install clutch pressure plate and disc assembly. Alternately tighten bolts 1/4 turn at a time until assembly is flush against flywheel. Torque bolts to 18 ft. lbs. Using alignment tool J-5824-01 or equivalent align clutch disc prior to tightening bolts.
14. Install flywheel/drive plate housing and torque bolts to 35 ft. lbs.
15. On manual transmissions only, install inspection plate on flywheel housing, and install hydraulic clutch slave cylinder on flywheel housing. Torque bolts to 18 ft. lbs.
16. Install transmission/transfer case assembly. Torque transmission-to-engine bolt to 28 ft. lbs.
17. Install starter motor, lower vehicle, and connect battery ground cable.

## OIL PAN
### REPLACE

1. Disconnect battery ground cable.
2. Raise and support vehicle.
3. Drain engine oil from oil pan.
4. Disconnect battery cable and solenoid electrical connector from starter, then remove starter motor from vehicle.
5. Remove oil pan attaching bolts, then the oil pan.
6. Thoroughly clean oil pan and cylinder block gasket surfaces.
7. Install rear oil pan gasket into rear main bearing cap. Apply a suitable sealant to depression where pan gasket contacts cylinder block.

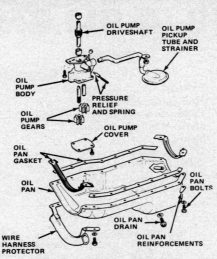

**Fig. 8  Oil pan & pump assembly. 4-151**

8. Position gasket onto oil pan. Apply a 1/8 x 1/4 inch bead of suitable sealer to split lines of front and side gasket.
9. Position oil pan onto cylinder block. Insert and torque pan side bolts to 75 inch lbs. Insert and torque oil pan to timing case cover bolts to 90 inch lbs.
10. Install starter motor. Torque 3/8 inch bolts to 27 ft. lbs. Torque No. 10 nut to 40 inch lbs.
11. Connect battery cable and solenoid electrical connector onto starter motor.
12. Lower vehicle.
13. Connect battery ground cable and add oil to engine.

## OIL PUMP
### REPLACE

1. Drain oil and remove oil pan.
2. Remove flange mounting bolts and nut from main bearing cap bolt and remove pump and pickup assembly as a unit.
3. Position oil pump gear shaft tang so it aligns with oil pump drive shaft slot. Install oil pump to block positioning flange over oil pump drive shaft lower bushing. Do not use gasket. Torque bolts to 18 ft. lbs. If oil pump does not slide easily into place, remove shaft and relocate slot.
4. Install oil pan with new gaskets and seals.

## OIL PUMP SERVICE
### DISASSEMBLY

1. Remove oil pump cover, idler gear

and drive gear and shaft, **Fig. 8.**
2. Remove pressure regulator valve and parts. The oil pickup pipe is attached during factory assembly and should not be disturbed.
3. The complete pump assembly should be replaced if any of the following conditions are observed during inspection:
   a. Pump body is cracked or shows excessive wear.
   b. Pump gears have cracks, excessive wear, and damage.
   c. Shaft is loose in housing.
   d. Inside of cover is worn enough to allow oil to leak past end of gears.
   e. Oil pickup assembly has damaged strainer screen or relief grommet. Remove any debris found on strainer screen surface.
   f. Pressure relief valve plunger does not fit properly in body.

### ASSEMBLY

1. Place drive gear and shaft in oil pump body.
2. Install idler gear so smooth side of gear will face cover.
3. Install cover and torque attaching screws to 9 ft. lbs. Make sure that shaft turns freely.
4. Install regulator valve plunger, spring, retainer, and pin.

## WATER PUMP
### REPLACE

1. Disconnect battery ground cable.
2. Drain cooling system.
3. Remove drive belt and fan.
4. Disconnect lower radiator and heater hoses from water pump.
5. Remove water pump attaching bolts, then the water pump.
6. Reverse procedure to install. Torque water pump attaching bolts to 25 ft. lbs.

## BELT TENSION DATA

|  | New Lbs | Used Lbs. |
|---|---|---|
| All | 125-155 | 90-115 |

## FUEL PUMP
### REPLACE

1. Disconnect battery ground cable.
2. Disconnect and cap fuel lines from fuel pump.
3. Remove fuel pump attaching bolts, then the fuel pump and gasket.
4. Reverse procedure to install.

# 6-258 (4.2L) ENGINE

## INDEX

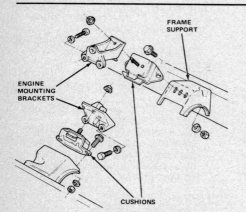

**Fig. 1  Engine mounts**

## ENGINE MOUNTS
### REPLACE

Removal or replacement of any cushion or bracket, **Fig. 1**, can be accomplished by fabricating an engine holding fixture to support the engine, **Fig. 2**. The engine may also be supported by a suitable jack positioned under the oil pan skid plate. Use a board between the jack and oil pan skid plate to distribute engine weight evenly.

## ENGINE
### REPLACE

1. Disconnect battery ground cable and drain cooling system.
2. Mark position of hood hinges, disconnect hood lamp if equipped, then remove hood.
3. Disconnect remaining cable and remove battery.
4. Remove air cleaner.
5. Disconnect fuel inlet pipe at pump and plug pipe and pump fitting.
6. Disconnect fuel return hose from pipe on frame or fuel filter, as equipped.
7. Disconnect heater hoses from engine and core fittings, remove fan shroud retaining screws, then disconnect hoses from radiator.
8. Disconnect electrical connectors and ground straps from engine, and remove vacuum switch and bracket from valve cover, if equipped.
9. Mark and disconnect all vacuum hos-

es from engine.
10. Disconnect throttle linkages and cables from throttle lever and engine mounted brackets.
11. Disconnect transmission cooler lines from radiator, if equipped, and plug lines and open fittings.
12. Remove radiator mounting bolts, radiator and fan shroud.
13. Remove fan and spacer or fan clutch, then install bolt through pulley and thread bolt into water pump hub to maintain pulley alignment.
14. On models with A/C proceed as follows:
    a. Remove service valve caps and rotate service valves fully clockwise to the front seated position.
    b. Slowly discharge refrigerant from compressor through service valve cores.
    c. Disconnect service valve assemblies from compressor and secure hoses aside. Plug open ports in compressor and service valves.
15. On models with power steering, disconnect hoses from steering gear and plug hose and gear fittings.
16. On all models, remove nut securing right front mount cushion to bracket and the bolt securing transmission filler tube, if equipped.
17. Raise and support vehicle.
18. Remove remaining mount cushion to bracket nuts.
19. Disconnect electrical connector to oxygen sensor, if equipped, then disconnect exhaust pipe from manifold.
20. Remove starter motor.
21. On models with manual transmission, remove flywheel shield and disconnect clutch linkage.
22. On models with automatic transmission, proceed as follows:
    a. Remove converter access cover and converter bolts, rotating crankshaft as needed to gain access to bolts.
    b. Remove oil pan bolts securing cooler line brackets to engine.
    c. Remove brace between converter housing and exhaust pipe, if equipped.
23. On all models, remove upper bellhousing to engine bolts and loosen lower bolts, then lower vehicle.
24. Remove A/C idler pulley and bracket, if equipped, then attach suitable lifting

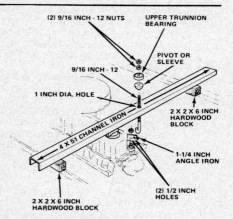

**Fig. 2  Engine holding fixture**

equipment to engine.
25. Raise engine off mounts, place suitable support under bellhousing, then remove lower bellhousing bolts.
26. Separate engine from bellhousing and remove from vehicle.
27. Reverse procedure to install. Prior to refilling cooling system, remove coolant temperature sending unit to allow air to escape from engine block. When system is filled, reinstall sending unit.

## ROCKER COVER

**REPLACE**

If excessive oil consumption is encountered on 1987 models with engine built prior to build date code 702C23, the rocker cover should be replaced, as the baffle seal maybe leaking.

1. Remove PCV valve and molded hose, and disconnect hose from PCV shut-off valve, if equipped.
2. Remove vacuum switch and bracket, and diverter valve and bracket assemblies from cover, if equipped.
3. Mark and disconnect necessary air and vacuum hoses to provide clearance for cover removal.
4. Remove cover bolts and break gasket/sealer seal using putty knife or suitable cutter. Do not pry on cover to break seal, as sealing surface may be damaged.
5. Rotate cover toward passenger side of vehicle and remove cover.

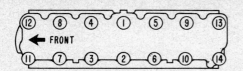

**Fig. 3  Cylinder head bolt tightening sequence**

6. Reverse procedure to install. Torque cover bolts to 55 inch lbs.

## CYLINDER HEAD
## REPLACE

1. Disconnect battery ground cable and drain cooling system.
2. Remove air cleaner, fuel pipe between carburetor and pump, and vacuum advance hose.
3. Remove rocker cover as described under "Rocker Cover, Replace."
4. Remove rocker arms, bridges and pivots, and the pushrods, keeping components in order for assembly. Alternately loosen rocker arm bolts, one turn at a time, to prevent damaging bridges.
5. Remove power steering and air pump mounting bolts, as equipped, and secure pumps aside.
6. Remove intake manifold as described under "Intake Manifold, Replace."
7. Remove exhaust manifold as described under "Exhaust Manifold, Replace."
8. On models with A/C, proceed as follows:
   a. Remove compressor belt idler pulley and bracket.
   b. Loosen alternator belt and disconnect alternator bracket from cylinder head.
   c. Remove compressor mounting bolts and position compressor aside.
9. On all models, disconnect spark plug wires and temperature sending unit electrical connector.
10. Remove spark plugs, ignition coil and coil bracket.
11. Remove cylinder head bolts, cylinder head and gasket. On some engines, cylinder head bolts installed on the spark plug (left) side of the engine were improperly hardened and may break under the bolt head or in the thread area. Whenever a broken bolt is found, all bolts on the spark plug side of the engine should be replaced. Engines included are code Nos. 310C06 through 310C14. The engine code is stamped on a machined surface on the distributor side of the engine.
12. Ensure that head and block gasket surfaces are clean and free from old gasket material, coat both sides of replacement gasket with suitable sealer and position gasket on block with "Top" mark facing up.
13. Ensure that gasket is properly seated on block, install cylinder head and head bolts, and torque bolts to specifi-

cations in sequence shown in **Fig. 3**. On 1980-86 models, apply suitable sealer to threads of left front head bolt (11), prior to installation.
14. Remove temperature sending unit and leave removed until cooling system is filled to allow air to escape from engine block.
15. Reverse remaining procedure to complete installation.

## INTAKE MANIFOLD
## REPLACE

1. Disconnect battery ground cable, drain coolant and remove air cleaner.
2. Disconnect fuel line, bowl vent and idle speed control hoses, and idle speed control and choke heater electrical connectors, as equipped.
3. Disconnect coolant and PCV hoses from manifold, and vacuum hoses from spark advance CTO valve.
4. Disconnect electrical connectors to manifold heater, temperature sensing unit and carburetor, as equipped.
5. Disconnect throttle cable and throttle valve rod, if equipped.
6. Disconnect EGR tube from manifolds and vacuum hose from EGR valve.
7. On models with AIR, disconnect hoses from pump and check valves, then remove diverter valve and hoses as an assembly.
8. On all models, remove carburetor along with vacuum hoses and base gasket.
9. Remove AIR/power steering pump lower bracket, if equipped, then the AIR pump.
10. Remove power steering pump and secure aside, leaving hoses connected.
11. Remove A/C compressor belt idler pulley and bracket, if equipped.
12. Remove intake manifold attaching bolts, then remove intake manifold and gasket, **Fig. 4**.
13. Position new gasket on cylinder head, install intake manifold and attaching bolts.
14. On 1980-88 models, torque bolts to specifications in sequence shown in **Fig. 5**. On 1989 models torque bolts 1 and 2 to 14 ft. lbs. and bolts 3 through 10 to 23 ft. lbs. in sequence as shown in **Fig. 6**.
15. Reverse procedure to complete installation, using new base gasket when installing carburetor. Remove coolant temperature sensor and leave removed until cooling system is filled to allow air to escape from block. When cooling system is filled, reinstall temperature sensor.

## EXHAUST MANIFOLD
## REPLACE

1. Remove intake manifold as outlined.
2. Disconnect exhaust pipe from manifold.
3. Disconnect electrical connector from oxygen sensor and remove sensor, if equipped.

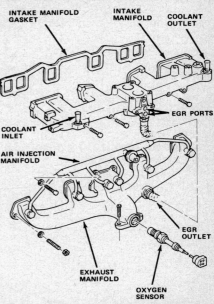

**Fig. 4  Manifold installation**

4. Remove nuts from end studs, then the exhaust manifold. **Fig. 4**.
5. Mount manifold on end studs and tighten retaining nuts hand tight.
6. Clean threads in oxygen sensor bore, coat sensor threads with suitable anti-seize compound, install sensor and torque to 35 ft. lbs.
7. Connect exhaust pipe to manifold.
8. Reinstall intake manifold and torque retaining bolts and nuts to specifications as outlined.

## ROCKER ARM SERVICE

1. Disconnect battery ground cable.
2. Remove cylinder head cover and gasket as described under "Rocker Cover, Replace."
3. Remove the two capscrews at each bridge and pivot assembly, **Fig. 7**. Alternately loosen capscrews one turn at a time to avoid damaging bridge.
4. Remove bridge and pivot assemblies with their rocker arms and pushrods and position aside. Bridge, pivot, rocker arms and pushrods must be installed in their original locations.
5. Clean all parts with a suitable solvent.
6. Using compressed air blow out rocker arm and pushrod oil passages.
7. Check rocker arms and pushrods for wear or damage. Replace as required.
8. Install pushrods into their original locations. Ensure bottom end of each pushrod is centered into hydraulic valve lifter plunger cap.
9. Install rocker arms, bridge and pivot assemblies into their original locations.
10. Loosely install bridge capscrews on each bridge and pivot assembly.
11. Torque capscrews alternately one turn at a time at each bridge and pivot assembly to 19 ft. lbs.
12. Install cylinder head cover and gasket.
13. Connect battery ground cable.

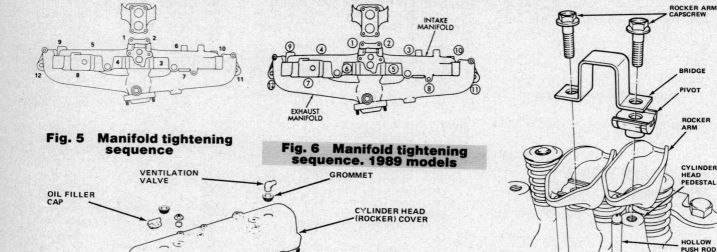

**Fig. 5   Manifold tightening sequence**

**Fig. 6   Manifold tightening sequence. 1989 models**

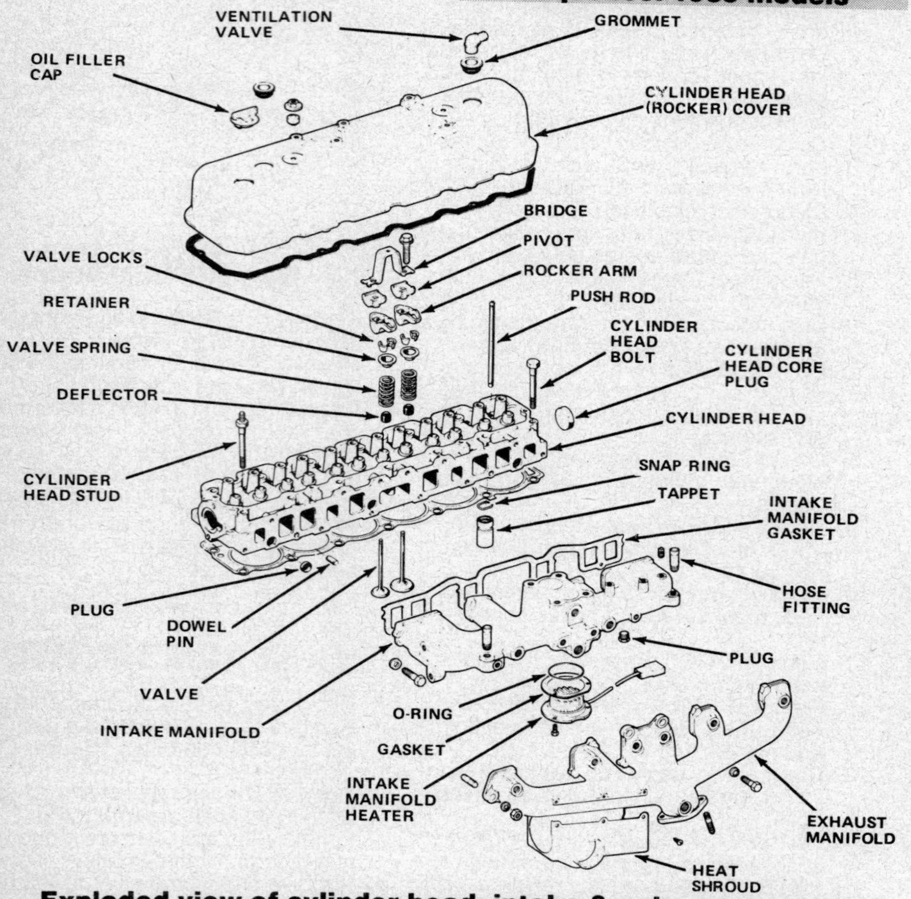

Exploded view of cylinder head, intake & exhaust manifold (Typical)

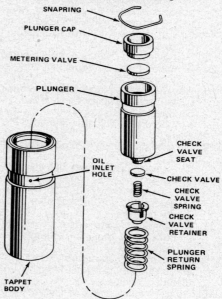

**Fig. 7   Rocker arm, bridge & pivot assembly**

**Fig. 8   Hydraulic valve lifter assembly**

# VALVES, ADJUST

These models use hydraulic valve lifters. No provision for adjustment is provided.

# VALVE ARRANGEMENT
## FRONT TO REAR

6-258 . . . . . . . . . . . . . E-I-I-E-I-E-E-I-E-I-I-E

# VALVE GUIDES

Valve guides are an integral part of the cylinder head and are not replaceable. When valve stem to guide clearance exceeds specification, ream the valve guide bores to accommodate the next larger oversize valve stem. Oversize valves are available with .003, .015 and .030 inch stem diameter sizes. Ream valve guides in steps, starting with the .003 inch oversize reamer and progressing to size required.

# HYDRAULIC VALVE LIFTERS

Valve lifters, **Fig. 8** may be removed from their bores after the cylinder head assembly is removed by using valve lifter removal tool No. J-21884.

# TIMING CASE COVER
## REPLACE

1. Disconnect battery ground cable.

2. Remove drive belt(s), engine fan, hub assembly, damper pulley and vibration damper.
3. Remove A/C compressor and alternator bracket assembly.
4. Remove oil pan to timing case cover and timing case cover to cylinder block bolts.
5. Remove timing case cover and gasket from engine, **Fig. 9.**
6. Using a suitable tool, cut oil pan gasket end tabs flush with front face of engine cylinder block and remove gasket tabs.
7. Clean timing case cover, oil pan and cylinder block gasket surfaces.
8. Remove crankshaft oil seal from timing case cover.

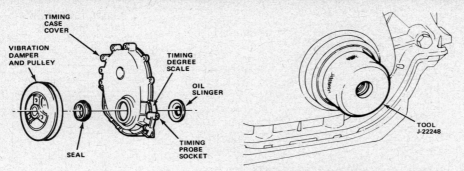

**Fig. 9   Timing case cover**

**Fig. 10   Using tool No. J-22248 to align timing case cover**

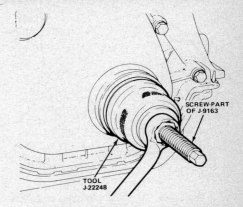

**Fig. 11   Installing timing case cover front seal**

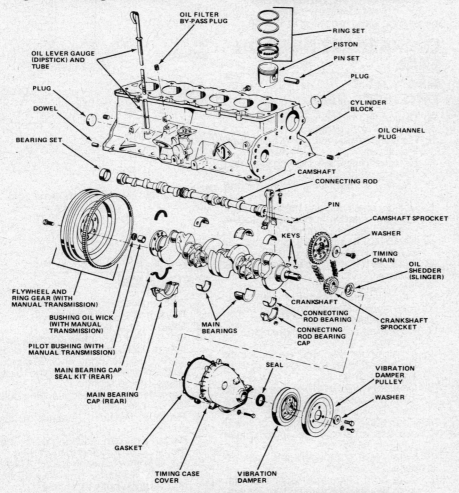

**Exploded view of cylinder block & components**

9. Apply a suitable sealer to timing case cover gasket and install onto cylinder block.
10. Cut end tabs off of replacement oil pan gasket corresponding to pieces cut from original gasket. Using a suitable sealer install cut pieces onto oil pan.
11. Coat oil pan seal end tabs with a suitable sealer and install seal onto timing case cover.
12. Install timing case cover onto engine. Position timing case cover alignment tool and seal installer J-22248 into crankshaft opening of case cover as shown in **Fig. 10**.
13. Install case cover to cylinder block bolts and oil pan to case cover bolts. Torque bolts to 5 ft. lbs. Torque oil pan to case cover bolts to 11 ft. lbs.
14. Remove case cover aligning tool and position oil seal onto tool with seal lip facing outward. Apply a suitable sealer to outer diameter to seal.
15. Insert screw No. J-9163 into seal tool. Tighten tool nut until tool contacts

timing case cover, **Fig. 11**.
16. Remove tool and apply clean engine oil to seal lip.

## TIMING CHAIN
### REPLACE

1. Disconnect battery ground cable.
2. Remove engine fan and hub assembly.
3. Remove vibration damper pulley and vibration damper.
4. Remove timing case cover.
5. Remove oil seal from timing case cover.
6. Remove camshaft sprocket retaining bolt and washer.
7. Rotate crankshaft until crankshaft sprocket timing marks is closest to and aligned with timing mark on camshaft sprocket, **Fig. 12**.
8. Remove timing chain and sprockets as an assembly.
9. Assemble timing chain, crankshaft and camshaft sprockets with timing marks aligned as shown in **Fig. 12**.
10. Install timing chain assembly onto engine.
11. Install camshaft sprocket retaining bolt and washer. On 1980-88 models, torque retaining bolt to 50 ft. lbs. On 1989 models torque retaining bolt to 80 ft. lbs. To verify correct installation of timing chain, position timing mark of the camshaft sprocket at approximately the one o'clock position. This positions crankshaft sprocket timing mark at a location where the adjacent tooth meshes with the timing chain, **Fig. 13**. Count the number of timing chain pins between timing marks of both crankshaft and camshaft sprockets. There must be 15 pins.
12. Install timing case cover and oil seal.
13. Install vibration damper. Torque damper bolt to 80 ft. lbs.
14. Install vibration damper pulley. Torque bolts to 20 ft. lbs.
15. Install engine fan and hub assembly.
16. Connect battery ground cable.

## CAMSHAFT
### REPLACE

1. Disconnect battery ground cable.

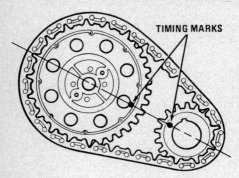

**Fig. 12    Valve timing marks**

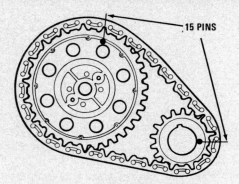

**Fig. 13    Timing chain installation check**

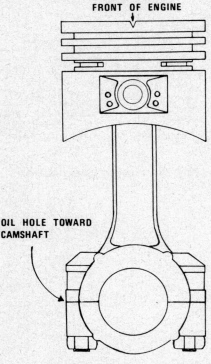

**Fig. 14    Piston and rod assembly**

2. Drain cooling system.
3. Remove air conditioner condenser and receiver assembly as a unit if equipped.
4. Remove radiator and fan assembly.
5. Remove fuel pump, distributor and spark plug wires.
6. Remove cylinder head cover.
7. Remove rocker arm, bridge and pivot assembly.
8. Remove pushrods. Ensure to install rocker arms, bridge, pivot and push-rod assemblies in their original locations.
9. Remove cylinder head and gasket.
10. Remove valve lifters.
11. Remove timing case cover, timing chain and sprockets.
12. Remove front bumper or grille.
13. Remove camshaft front engine.
14. Reverse procedure to install. During installation of distributor, rotate crankshaft until No. 1 piston is at TDC of compression stroke. Install distributor with rotor aligned with No. 1 terminal on distributor cap when distributor is completely seated on block.

## PISTON & ROD ASSEMBLE

Pistons are marked with a depression notch on the top perimeter, **Fig. 14**. When installed in the engine this notch must face toward the front of engine. Always assemble rods and caps with the cylinder numbers or oil squirt holes facing the camshaft side of engine.

## MAIN BEARINGS

The main bearing journal size (diameter) is identified by a color coded paint mark on adjacent cheek toward flanged (rear) end of crankshaft, except for rear main journal which is on crankshaft rear flange. Color codes used to indicate journal and corresponding bearing sizes are listed in **Figs. 15 through 17**.

## CONNECTING ROD BEARINGS

The connecting rod journal is identified by a color coded paint mark on adjacent cheek or counterweight toward flanged (rear) end of crankshaft. Color codes used to indicate journal sizes and correspond-ing bearing sizes are listed in **Fig. 18**.

## CRANKSHAFT REAR OIL SEAL
## REPLACE
## TWO PIECE SEAL

1. Disconnect battery ground cable.
2. Drain oil from engine.
3. Remove oil pan attaching bolts, then the oil pan.
4. Remove rear main bearing cap and lower oil seal.
5. Loosen all remaining main bearing caps.
6. Using a brass drift and hammer, tap oil seal until seal protrudes from groove. Pull oil seal from groove.
7. Remove oil pan front and rear oil seals and oil pan side gaskets.
8. Clean oil pan and engine block gasket surfaces.
9. Clean main bearing cap.
10. Clean sealing surface of crankshaft, then apply clean engine oil to crank-shaft sealing surface.
11. Coat lip of upper seal with engine oil, **Fig. 19**.
12. Install upper seal into engine block. Lip of seal must face toward front of engine.
13. Coat both sides of lower seal end tabs with RTV sealer or equivalent. Do not apply RTV to lip of seal.
14. Coat outer curved surface of lower seal with soap and seal lip with clean engine oil, **Fig. 19**.
15. Install seal completely into cap recess.
16. Coat both chamfered edges of rear main bearing cap with RTV or equivalent.
17. Install rear main bearing cap. Torque all main bearing cap bolts a little at a time to specification.
18. Install oil pan, if necessary, add engine oil and connect battery ground cable.

### ONE PIECE SEAL

1. Remove transmission assembly.
2. Remove flywheel or converter drive plate.
3. Using a suitable tool, remove seal from around crankshaft flange.
4. Reverse procedure to install, noting the following:
   a. Clean seal mounting surface.
   b. Lubricate seal with engine oil.

## OIL PAN
## REPLACE

1. Disconnect battery ground cable.
2. Raise and support vehicle.
3. Drain oil from engine.
4. On CJ and Scrambler models, position a suitable jack under transmission. Remove right engine support cushion bracket from engine block. Raise engine slightly.
5. Remove starter motor attaching bolts, then the starter motor.
6. Remove flywheel housing access cover.
7. Remove oil pan attaching bolts, then the oil pan by sliding toward rear.
8. Reverse procedure to install. Torque 1/4 inch oil pan bolts to 80 inch lbs., and 5/16 inch bolts to 11 ft. lbs.

## OIL PUMP
## REPLACE

1. Disconnect battery ground cable.
2. Raise and support vehicle.
3. Drain oil from engine.
4. Remove oil pan as described under "Oil Pan, Replace."
5. Remove oil pump attaching bolts, then the oil pump, **Fig. 20**.
6. Reverse procedure to install. Torque oil pump short bolts to 10 ft. lbs. Torque oil pump long bolts to 17 ft. lbs.

| Crankshaft No. 1 Main Bearing Journal Color Code and Diameter | Cylinder Block No. 1 Main Bearing Bore Color Code and Size | Bearing Insert Color Code | |
|---|---|---|---|
| | | Upper Insert Size | Lower Insert Size |
| Yellow – 63.5025-63.4898 mm (2.5001-2.4996 in.) (Standard) | Yellow – 68.3514-68.3641 mm (2.6910-2.6915 in.) | Yellow – Standard | Yellow – Standard |
| | Black – 68.3641-68.3768 mm (2.6915-2.6920 in.) | Yellow – Standard | Black – 0.025 mm Undersize (0.001 in.) |
| Orange – 63.4898-63.4771 mm (2.4996-2.4991 in.) (0.0005 Undersize) | Yellow – 68.3514-68.3641 mm (2.6910-2.6915 in.) | Yellow – Standard | Black – 0.025 mm Undersize (0.001 in.) |
| | Black – 68.3641-68.3768 mm (2.6915-2.6920 in.) | Black – 0.025 mm Undersize (0.001 in.) | Black – 0.025 mm Undersize (0.001 in.) |
| Black – 63.4771-63.4644 mm (2.4991-2.4986 in.) (0.001 Undersize) | Yellow – 68.3514-68.3641 mm (2.6910-2.6915 in.) | Black – 0.025 mm Undersize (0.001 in.) | Black – 0.025 mm Undersize (0.001 in.) |
| | Black – 68.3641-68.3768 mm (2.6915-2.6920 in.) | Black – 0.025 mm Undersize (0.001 in.) | Green – 0.051 mm Undersize (0.002 in.) |
| Green – 63.4644-63.4517 mm (2.4986-2.4981 in.) (0.0015 Undersize) | Yellow – 68.3514-68.3641 mm (2.6910-2.6915 in.) | Black – 0.025 mm Undersize (0.001 in.) | Green – 0.051 mm Undersize (0.002 in.) |
| Red – 63.2485-63.2358 mm (2.4901-2.4986 in.) (0.010 Undersize) | Yellow – 68.3514-68.3641 mm (2.6910-2.6915 in.) | Red – 0.254 mm Undersize (0.010 in.) | Red – 0.254 mm Undersize (0.010 in.) |

**Fig. 15 Main bearing selection chart. Main bearing No. 1**

| Crankshaft Main Bearing Journals 2-6 Color Code and Diameter (Journal Size) | Bearing Insert Color Code | |
|---|---|---|
| | Upper Insert Size | Lower Insert Size |
| Yellow – 63.5025-63.4898 mm (2.5001-2.4996 in.) (Standard) | Yellow – Standard | Yellow – Standard |
| Orange – 63.4898-63.4771 mm (2.4996-2.4991 in.) (0.0005 Undersize) | Yellow – Standard | Black – 0.025 mm Undersize (0.001 in.) |
| Black – 63.4771-63.4644 mm (2.4991-2.4986 in.) (0.001 Undersize) | Black – 0.025 mm Undersize (0.001 in.) | Black – 0.025 mm Undersize (0.001 in.) |
| Green – 63.4644-63.4517 mm (2.4986-2.4981 in.) (0.0015 Undersize) | Black – 0.025 mm Undersize (0.001 in.) | Green – 0.051 mm Undersize (0.002 in.) |
| Red – 63.2485-63.2358 mm (2.4901-2.4966 in.) (0.010 Undersize) | Red – 0.054 mm Undersize (0.010 in.) | Red – 0.254 mm Undersize (0.010 in.) |

**Fig. 16 Main bearing selection chart. Main bearing Nos. 2 through 6**

| Crankshaft Main Bearing Journal 7 Color Code and Diameter (Journal Size) | Bearing Insert Color Code | |
|---|---|---|
| | Upper Insert Size | Lower Insert Size |
| Yellow – 63.4873-63.4746 mm (2.4995-2.4990 in.) (Standard) | Yellow – Standard | Yellow – Standard |
| Orange – 63.4746-63.4619 mm (2.4990-2.4985 in.) (0.0005 Undersize) | Yellow – Standard | Black – 0.025 mm Undersize (0.001 in.) |
| Black – 63.4619-63.4492 mm (2.4985-2.4980 in.) (0.001 Undersize) | Black – 0.025 mm Undersize (0.001 in.) | Black – 0.025 mm Undersize (0.001 in.) |
| Green – 63.4492-63.4365 mm (2.4980-2.4975 in.) (0.0015 Undersize) | Black – 0.025 mm Undersize (0.001 in.) | Green – 0.051 mm Undersize (0.002 in.) |
| Red – 63.2333-63.2206 mm (2.4895-2.4890 in.) (0.010 Undersize) | Red – 0.254 mm Undersize (0.010 in.) | Red – 0.254 mm Undersize (0.010 in.) |

**Fig. 17 Main bearing selection chart. Main bearing No. 7**

| Crankshaft Connecting Rod Journal Color and Diameter in Inches (Journal Size) | Bearing Color Code | |
|---|---|---|
| | Upper Insert Size | Lower Insert Size |
| Yellow —2.0955 to 2.0948 (Standard)<br>Orange —2.0948 to 2.0941 (0.0007 Undersize)<br>Black —2.0941 to 2.0934 (0.0014 Undersize)<br>Red —2.0855 to 2.0848 (0.010 Undersize) | Yellow — Standard<br>Yellow — Standard<br>Black — .001-Inch Undersize<br>Red — .010-Inch Undersize | Yellow — Standard<br>Black — .001-inch Undersize<br>Black — .001-inch Undersize<br>Red — .010-inch Undersize |

**Fig. 18   Connecting rod bearing selection chart**

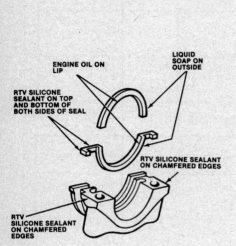

**Fig. 19   Crankshaft rear main oil seal & cap installation**

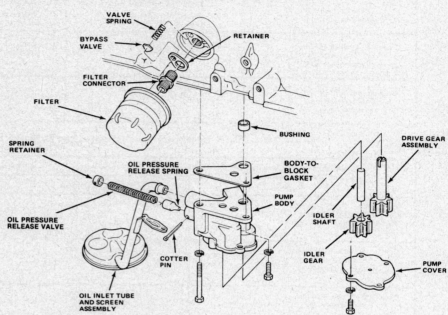

**Fig. 20   Oil pump assembly**

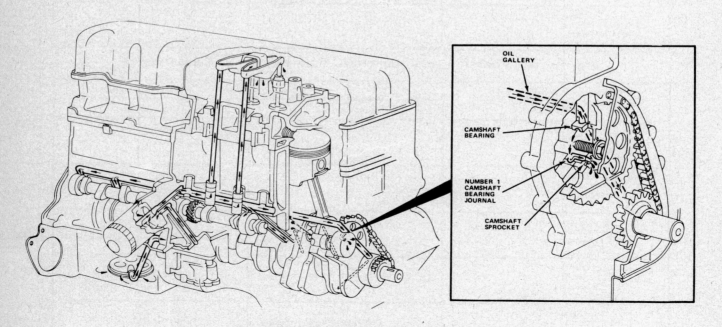

**6-258 engine lubrication system**

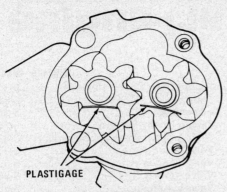

**Fig. 21  Installing Plastigage across oil pump gears**

# OIL PUMP SERVICE

1. Remove cover retaining bolts, cover and gasket.
2. Using the preferred method, check gear end clearance as follows:
   a. Place a strip of Plastigage across full width of each gear end, **Fig. 21.**
   b. Apply a bead of Loctite 515 or equivalent, around perimeter of oil pump cover and install onto oil pump.
   c. Torque cover bolts to 70 inch lbs.
   d. Remove oil pump cover and determine amount of end clearance by measuring width of compressed Plastigage.
   e. Clearance should be .002-.006 inch.
3. Using the alternate method, check gear end clearance as follows:
   a. Place a straightedge across ends of gears and pump body.
   b. Using a feeler gauge, measure gear end clearance. Clearance should be .004-.008 inch on 1980-88 models and .002-.006 inch on 1989 models.
   c. If clearance obtained exceeds specified amount, replace oil pump assembly.
4. Using a feeler gauge, measure clearance between gear tooth and oil pump body inner wall directly opposite point of gear mesh. Rotate pump gears and measure each gear tooth clearance. Clearance should be .0005-.0025 inch.
5. If clearance obtained exceeds specified amount, replace idler gear, idler shaft and drive gear assembly.
6. Remove cotter pin and slide spring retainer, spring and oil pressure release valve plunger out of oil pump body.

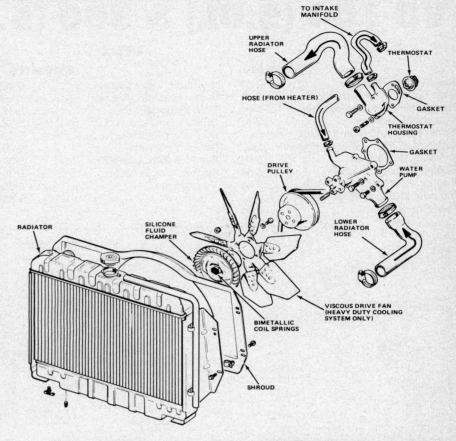

**Fig. 22  Water pump & cooling system components**

Check parts for wear or damage.
7. Install oil pressure release valve plunger, spring retainer and cotter pin.
8. Install idler shaft, idler gear and drive gear assembly.
9. Apply a suitable sealer to oil pump cover and install onto pump. Torque cover bolts to 70 inch lbs.

# BELT TENSION DATA

|  | New Lbs. | Used Lbs. |
|---|---|---|
| V-Type Belts | 120-160 | 90-115 |
| Serpentine Type Belt | 180-200 | 140-160 |

# WATER PUMP
## REPLACE

1. Disconnect battery ground cable.
2. Drain cooling system.
3. Disconnect radiator and heater hoses from water pump, **Fig. 22.**
4. Remove drive belts.
5. Remove fan shroud and fan.
6. Remove water pump attaching bolts, then the water pump and gasket.
7. Reverse procedure to install. Torque bolts to 13 ft. lbs.

# FUEL PUMP
## REPLACE

1. Disconnect battery ground cable.
2. Disconnect and cap fuel lines from fuel pump.
3. Remove fuel pump attaching bolts, then the fuel pump and gasket.
4. Reverse procedure to install. Torque bolts to 18 ft. lbs.

# V8-304 (5.0L) & 360 (5.9L) Engine

## INDEX

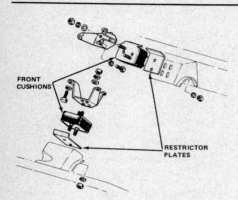

**Fig. 1  Engine mounts. V8 engine**

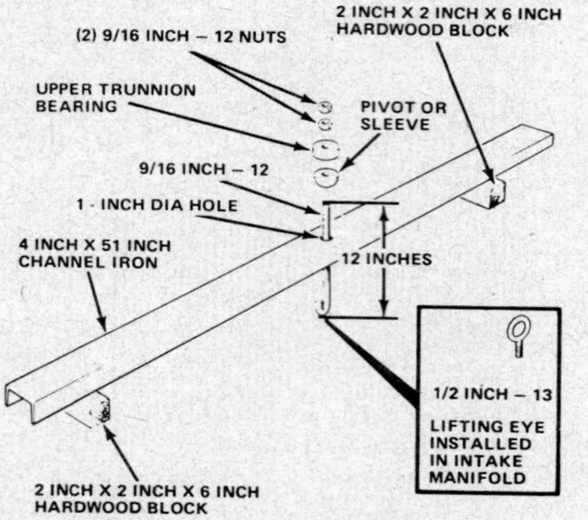

**Fig. 2  Engine holding fixture. V8 engine**

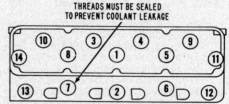

**Fig. 3  Cylinder head tightening sequence. V8 engine**

## ENGINE MOUNTS
### REPLACE

Removal or replacement of any cushion or bracket, **Fig. 1**, can be accomplished by fabricating an engine holding fixture to support the engine, **Fig. 2**.

## ENGINE
### REPLACE

1. Disconnect cables from battery and remove battery.
2. On all except CJ and Scrambler models, mark hood hinge location, disconnect hood lamp wiring if equipped and remove hood.
3. Remove air cleaner assembly from carburetor.
4. Drain cooling system, then disconnect upper, lower and heater hoses.
5. On models equipped with automatic transmission, disconnect fluid cooler lines from radiator and engine retaining brackets.
6. Remove fan shroud, if equipped.
7. Remove radiator and fan assembly from vehicle.
8. Disconnect and cap power steering lines from power steering pump, if equipped.
9. On models equipped with air conditioning, proceed as follows:
   a. Turn compressor service fitting valve stem to the front seated position.
   b. Loosen service fitting.
   c. Carefully and gradually discharge refrigerant from compressor. Do not allow refrigerant to contact eyes or skin.
   d. Remove service valve fitting from compressor.
10. Remove speed control vacuum servo bellows and mounting bracket as an assembly, if equipped.
11. Mark and disconnect all vacuum lines and electrical connectors from engine.
12. Disconnect fuel lines from frame hoses.
13. On models equipped with automatic transmission, disconnect filler tube bracket from engine.
14. Raise and support vehicle.
15. Remove both engine front support cushion to frame retaining nuts.
16. Disconnect exhaust pipe from manifolds and front bracket.
17. Remove starter motor.
18. On models equipped with automatic transmission, proceed as follows:
   a. Remove flywheel inspection cover and scribe matching mark between drive plate and torque converter.
   b. Remove torque converter bolts, ro-

tating crankshaft as needed to gain access to bolts.
   c. Remove support for lower throttle valve and inner manual linkage, then disconnect throttle valve rod from lower bell crank.
19. On all models, remove upper bellhousing to engine bolts and loosen lower bolts.
20. Lower vehicle and attach suitable lifting equipment to engine.
21. Raise engine to remove weight from mounts, place suitable support under transmission, and remove lower bellhousing bolts.
22. Separate engine from transmission and remove engine, taking care not to damage brake booster.
23. Reverse procedure to install.

## CYLINDER HEAD
### REPLACE

1. Remove air cleaner and drain cooling system, then if equipped with Air Guard emission system, disconnect air hose from injection manifold.
2. Disconnect all hoses and electrical leads from intake manifold, noting position for installation.
3. Remove valve covers, bridged pivot assemblies, rocker arms and pushrods. Loosen each bridged pivot bolt one turn at a time to avoid breaking the bridged pivot. Also, keep rocker arms, bridged pivot and pushrods in same order as removed so that they can be reinstalled in their original locations.

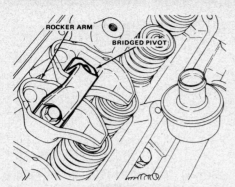

**Fig. 4   Rocker arm, bridge and pivot assembly. V8 engine**

4. Disconnect spark plug wires and remove spark plugs.
5. Remove intake manifold and disconnect exhaust manifolds from cylinder head.
6. Loosen all drive belts, then if equipped with air conditioning, remove compressor bracket attaching bolts and set compressor aside.
7. Disconnect alternator support brace, power steering mounting bracket and Air Guard pump (if used) mounting bracket from cylinder head.
8. Remove cylinder head bolts and cylinder head.
9. Reverse procedure to install. Torque head bolts in two steps using sequence shown in **Fig. 3**. First torque bolts to 80 ft. lbs., then torque bolts to value given in "Engine Tightening Specifications" chart. The cylinder block has two locating dowels on each bank to assist in lining up and holding the cylinder head and gasket in position during installation. The No. 7 bolt shown in **Fig. 3**, second from front on the left bank, must have the threads sealed to prevent coolant leakage. Permatex No. 2 or equivalent is recommended.

## INTAKE MANIFOLD
### REPLACE

1. Disconnect battery ground cable.
2. Drain cooling system.
3. Remove air cleaner assembly from carburetor.
4. Mark and disconnect ignition wires from spark plugs.
5. Disconnect upper radiator hose and bypass hose from intake manifold.
6. Disconnect electrical connectors from coolant temperature gauge valve.
7. Remove ignition coil bracket and position aside.
8. Disconnect heater hoses from intake manifold.
9. Mark and disconnect all vacuum hoses and electrical connectors from carburetor.
10. Disconnect throttle and throttle valve linkage from carburetor and intake manifold.
11. Disconnect air lines from air injection manifold.
12. Disconnect diverter valve from air

pump output line and position aside.
13. Remove carburetor from engine.
14. Remove intake manifold attaching bolts, then the intake manifold.
15. Reverse procedure to install. Torque intake manifold bolts to 43 ft. lbs.

## EXHAUST MANIFOLD
### REPLACE

1. Disconnect battery ground cable.
2. Disconnect ignition wires from spark plugs.
3. Disconnect air lines from air manifold.
4. Raise and support vehicle.
5. Disconnect front exhaust pipe from exhaust manifold.
6. Lower vehicle.
7. Remove exhaust manifold attaching bolts, then separate manifold from cylinder head.
8. Remove air injection manifold, service fittings and washers.
9. Reverse procedure to install. During installation of exhaust manifold, torque manifold center attaching bolts to 25 ft. lbs. Torque manifold outer bolts to 15 ft. lbs.

## ROCKER ARM SERVICE

The intake and exhaust rocker arms of each cylinder pivot on a bridge and pivot assembly which is secured with two capscrews as shown in **Fig. 4**. Each rocker arm is actuated by a hollow pushrod with a hardened ball at each end. The hollow pushrods route engine oil to the rocker arm assembly.

### REMOVAL

1. Disconnect battery ground cable.
2. Remove cylinder head cover and gasket.
3. Remove the two capscrews at each bridge and pivot assembly. Alternately loosen capscrews one turn at a time to avoid damaging bridge.
4. Remove bridge and pivot assemblies with their rocker arms and pushrods and position aside. Bridge, pivot, rocker arms and pushrods must be installed in their original locations.

### INSTALLATION

1. Clean all parts with a suitable solvent.
2. Using compressed air, blow out rocker arm and pushrod oil passages.
3. Check rocker arms and pushrods for wear or damage. Replace as required.
4. Install pushrods into their original locations. Ensure bottom end of each pushrod is centered into the hydraulic valve lifter plunger cap.
5. Install rocker arms, bridge and pivot assemblies into their original locations.
6. Loosely install bridge capscrews on each bridge and pivot assembly.
7. Torque capscrews alternately one turn at a time at each bridge and pivot assembly to 19 ft. lbs.
8. Install cylinder head cover and gasket.
9. Connect battery ground cable.

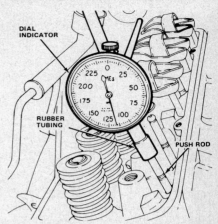

**Fig. 5   Measuring cam lobe lift. V8 engine**

## VALVE ARRANGEMENT
### FRONT TO REAR

All V8s . . . . . . . . . . . . . . . . . . . E-I-I-E-E-I-I-E

## VALVES
### ADJUST

These engine are equipped with hydraulic valve lifters which do not require adjustment. There should be zero valve clearance. If not, check pushrods, valve lifters, rocker arms and pivot assemblies for wear and damage and replace as necessary.

## VALVE GUIDES

Valve guides are an integral part of the cylinder head. When valve stem to guide clearance is excessive, ream valve guide bores to the next larger valve stem size. Valves are available with .003, .015 and .030 inch oversize stems. Ream valve guide bores in steps, starting with the .003 inch reamer and progressing to the size required.

## CAM LOBE LIFT MEASUREMENT

1. Disconnect battery ground cable.
2. Remove cylinder head cover, bridge and pivot assembly and rocker arms.
3. Remove spark plugs.
4. Position a suitable piece of rubber tubing over pushrod end, then install a dial indicator into other end of hose as shown in **Fig. 5**.
5. Rotate crankshaft until cam lobe base circle (pushrod down) is under valve tappet.
6. Set dial indicator to zero, then rotate crankshaft until point of maximum pushrod upward movement is obtained. Note dial indicator reading.
7. Refer to "Cam Lobe Lift Specifications" for specifications.

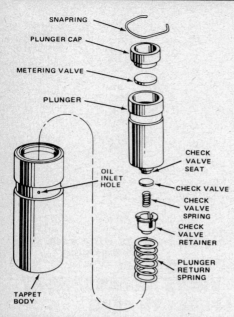

**Fig. 6 Hydraulic valve lifter assembly. V8 engine**

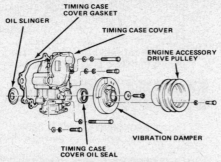

**Fig. 7 Timing case cover assembly. V8 engine**

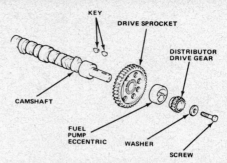

**Fig. 8 Camshaft assembly. V8 engine**

## CAM LOBE LIFT SPECIFICATIONS

V8-304, 360 ..........................266 inch

## VALVE TIMING

### INTAKE OPENS BEFORE TDC

V8-304, 360 .....................14.75°

## HYDRAULIC VALVE LIFTERS

The hydraulic valve lifters may be removed from their bores after removing cylinder head cover, bridge and pivot assembly, rocker arms, pushrods and intake manifold. Tool No. J-21884 may be used to remove valve lifters from their bores, **Fig. 6.**

## TIMING CASE COVER
### REPLACE

The timing chain cover is a die casting incorporating an oil seal at the vibration damper hub, **Fig. 7.** The front oil seal can be installed from either side of the cover, and the seal can be replaced after removing the damper. The timing cover does not have to be removed to replace the oil seal.

### REMOVAL

1. Disconnect battery ground cable and drain cooling system.
2. Disconnect lower radiator and bypass hoses from engine, then remove drive belts, cooling fan, and clutch or hub.
3. On models with A/C, remove compressor from bracket and secure aside, leaving hoses connected.
4. On all models, remove alternator, mounting bracket and rear idler pulley.
5. Remove power steering and AIR pumps, and the mounting brackets, as equipped. Leave power steering hoses connected and secure pumps aside.
6. Remove vibration damper assembly using suitable puller.
7. Remove distributor cap and disconnect electrical connectors from distributor.
8. Mark position fo distributor rotor and body, then remove distributor and fuel pump from front cover.
9. Remove 2 front oil pan bolt and bolts securing front cover to block, noting installation position for assembly.
10. Remove front cover, gasket and crankshaft oil slinger, then drive seal from cover using suitable drift and discard seal.

### INSTALLATION

1. Remove lower dowel pin from front of block and trim both protruding oil pan side gaskets flush with face of block. Retain gasket ends.
2. Apply suitable sealer to replacement front cover gasket, cement gasket to engine block, then install crankshaft oil slinger.
3. Apply suitable sealer to outer diameter of oil seal and install front seal in cover using J-26562 or equivalent to ensure that seal is properly seated.
4. On models with oil pan gasket, proceed as follows:
   a. Using original pieces as guide, trim ends of replacement gasket which correspond to gaskets removed previously.
   b. Install oil pan front seal onto timing case cover, align tabs of replacement pan gasket ends with oil pan seal and cement gaskets onto front cover.
   c. Apply suitable sealer to oil pan/engine block joint where pan gaskets were cut, mount cover in position on engine, then install front oil pan bolts.
   d. Tighten oil pan bolts slowly and evenly until front cover aligns with upper locating dowel, insert lower dowel through cover and drive dowel into place in engine block.
   e. Install remaining front cover bolts and torque all bolts to 25 ft. lbs.
5. On models where RTV sealer is used to seal oil pan, proceed as follows:
   a. Ensure that cover and oil pan sealing flanges are clean and free from oil, then apply a 1/8 inch wide bead of RTV sealer to cover flanges.
   b. Mount front cover on engine, aligning it with top locating dowel, then loosely install cover to block retaining bolts.
   c. Insert lower locating dowel through cover and drive into place in block, then torque cover bolts to 25 ft. lbs.
   d. Apply a small bead of RTV sealer to joint between pan and front cover and press sealer into place with finger.
   e. Apply suitable thread locking compound to front oil pan bolts, then install bolts and tighten until snug. Do not over tighten front oil pan bolts as pan will be distorted.
6. Reverse remaining procedure to complete installation.

## TIMING CHAIN
### REPLACE

1. Disconnect battery ground cable.
2. Remove vibration damper pulley, damper, timing case cover and gasket.
3. Remove crankshaft oil slinger.
4. Remove camshaft sprocket retaining bolt and washer.
5. Remove distributor drive gear and fuel pump eccentric, **Fig. 8.**
6. Rotate crankshaft until timing mark on crankshaft sprocket aligns with timing mark on camshaft sprocket, **Figs. 9 and 10.**
7. Remove crankshaft sprocket, camshaft sprocket and timing chain as an assembly.
8. Assemble timing chain, crankshaft sprocket and camshaft sprocket with timing marks positioned as shown in **Figs. 9 and 10.**
9. Install timing chain and sprocket assembly onto engine.
10. Install fuel pump eccentric and distributor drive gear. Install fuel pump eccentric with word "Rear" on eccentric facing toward camshaft.
11. Install camshaft washer and retaining bolt. Torque bolt to 30 ft. lbs.
12. To verify correct installation of timing chain, proceed as follows:

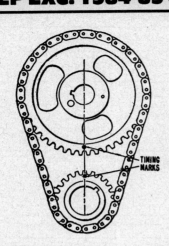

**Fig. 9   Valve timing. V8-304**

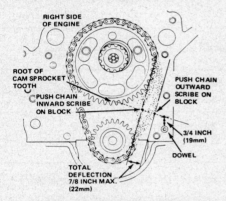

**Fig. 11   Measuring timing chain wear. V8 engine**

a. Rotate crankshaft until timing mark on camshaft is at the three o'clock position.
b. Starting with the pin directly adjacent to camshaft sprocket timing mark, count the number of pins downward to timing mark on crankshaft sprocket.
c. There must be 20 pins between these two points.
14. Install crankshaft oil slinger.
15. Remove original oil seal from timing case cover.
16. Install new seal into timing case cover, then position cover onto engine. Torque case cover bolts to 25 ft. lbs.
17. Install vibration damper and pulley.
18. Install battery ground cable.

## TIMING CHAIN WEAR MEASUREMENT

1. Disconnect battery ground cable.
2. Remove timing case cover.
3. Rotate camshaft or crankshaft sprocket until right side of timing chain is taut.
4. Determine a reference point for timing chain deflection measurement as follows:
   a. Measure 3/4 of an inch up from dowel pin located on right side of engine and mark location, **Fig. 11.**
   b. Position a suitable straightedge across timing chain from point at

lowest tooth of camshaft sprocket to point obtained (marked) in step 4a, **Fig. 11.**
   c. Grasp timing chain at point where straightedge dissects (cuts across) timing chain and use this point as a reference.
   d. Move timing chain inward toward center line of engine and mark engine block at point of maximum inward chain deflection, **Fig. 11.**
   e. Move timing chain outward from center line of engine and mark engine block at point of maximum outward chain deflection.
   f. Measure distance between inward and outward chain deflection marks placed on engine block.
   g. Replace timing chain assembly if deflection (wear) exceeds 7/8 inch.
5. Install timing case cover and connect battery ground cable.

## CAMSHAFT
### REPLACE

1. Disconnect battery ground cable.
2. Drain cooling system.
3. Remove radiator and fan assembly.
4. On models equipped with air conditioning, remove condenser and receiver assembly and position aside.
5. Remove cylinder head covers and gaskets.
6. Remove bridge and pivot assembly, rocker arms and pushrods. During removal of bridge and pivot assembly, alternately loosen capscrews one turn at a time to avoid damaging bridge.
7. Remove intake manifold assembly from engine.
8. Remove valve lifters.
9. Remove distributor.
10. Remove damper pulley and vibration damper.
11. Remove timing case cover.
12. Rotate crankshaft until timing mark on crankshaft sprocket aligns with timing mark on camshaft sprocket.
13. Remove camshaft and crankshaft sprocket retaining bolts.
14. Remove distributor drive gear and fuel pump eccentric from camshaft, **Fig. 8.**
15. Remove timing chain, camshaft and crankshaft sprockets as an assembly.
16. Remove hood latch support bracket, front bumper or grille, as required.
17. Remove camshaft from engine.
18. Reverse procedure to install. During installation of distributor, rotate crankshaft until No. 1 piston is at TDC of compression stroke. Install distributor with rotor aligned with No. 1 terminal on distributor cap when distributor is completely seated on engine block. During installation of timing chain, assemble crankshaft sprocket, camshaft sprocket with timing marks positioned as shown in **Figs. 9 and 10.**

## PISTON & ROD
### ASSEMBLE

Pistons and rods should be assembled

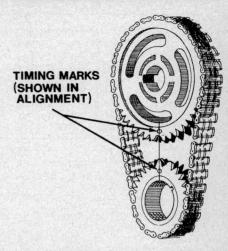

**Fig. 10   Valve timing. V8-360**

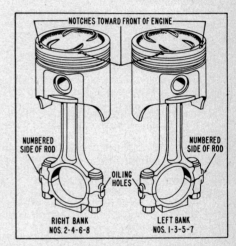

**Fig. 12   Piston & rod assembly. V8-304 & 360**

and installed as shown in **Fig. 12.**

## MAIN BEARINGS

The main bearing journal size (diameter) is identified by a color coded paint mark on adjacent cheek toward flanged (rear) end of crankshaft, except for rear main journal which is on crankshaft rear flange. Color codes used to indicate journal and corresponding bearing sizes are listed in **Fig. 13.**

## CONNECTING ROD BEARINGS

The connecting rod journal is identified by a color coded paint mark on adjacent cheek or counterweight toward flanged (rear) end of crankshaft. Color codes used to indicate journal sizes and corresponding bearing sizes are listed in **Fig. 14.**

## CRANKSHAFT REAR OIL SEAL
### REPLACE

1. Remove starter motor if necessary.

| Crankshaft Main Bearing Journal Color Code and Diameter in Inches (Journal Size) | Bearing Color Code | | |
|---|---|---|---|
| | | Upper Insert Size | Lower Insert Size |
| Yellow — 2.7489 to 2.7484 (Standard) | | Yellow — Standard | Yellow — Standard |
| Orange — 2.7484 to 2.7479 (0.0005 Undersize) | | Yellow — Standard | Black — .001-inch Undersize |
| Black — 2.7479 to 2.7474 (0.001 Undersize) | | Black — .001-inch Undersize | Black — .001-inch Undersize |
| Green — 2.7474 to 2.7469 (0.0015 Undersize) | | Black — .001-inch Undersize | Green — .002-inch Undersize |
| Red — 2.7389 to 2.7384 (0.010 Undersize) | | Red — .010-inch Undersize | Red — .010-inch Undersize |

**Fig. 13   Main bearing selection chart. V8 engine**

2. Remove oil pan as described under "Oil Pan, Replace."
3. Remove rear main bearing cap & oil seals, then clean cap thoroughly.
4. Loosen all remaining main bearing cap screws.
5. With a brass drift and hammer, tap upper seal until sufficient seal is protruding to permit pulling seal out completely with pliers.
6. Wipe seal surface of crankshaft clean, then oil lightly.
7. Coat back surface of upper seal with soap, and lip of seal with No. 40 engine oil.
8. Install upper seal into cylinder block, **Fig. 15.** Lip of seal must face to front of engine.
9. Coat cap and cylinder block mating surface portion of seal with Permatex No. 2 or equivalent, being careful not to apply sealer on lip of seal.
10. Coat back surface of lower seal with soap, and lip of seal with No. 40 engine oil. Place into cap, seating seal firmly into seal recess in cap.
11. Place Permatex No. 2 or equivalent on both chamfered edges of rear main bearing cap.
12. Install main bearing and cap. Torque cap to 100 ft. lbs.
13. Cement oil pan gasket to cylinder block with tongue of gasket at each end coated with Permatex or equivalent before installing into rear main bearing cap at joint of tongue and oil pan front neoprene seal.
14. Coat oil pan rear seal with soap. Place into recess of rear main bearing cap, making certain seal is firmly and evenly seated.
15. Install oil pan and tighten drain plug securely.
16. Install starter motor if removed.

## OIL PAN
### REPLACE

1. Disconnect battery ground cable.
2. Raise and support vehicle.
3. Drain oil from engine.
4. On vehicles equipped with manual transmission, bend dust shield tabs downward.
5. Remove oil pan attaching bolts, then the oil pan.
6. Reverse procedure to install. Torque 1/4 inch oil pan attaching bolts to 7 ft. lbs. and 5/16 inch bolts to 11 ft. lbs.

| Crankshaft Main Bearing Journal Color Code and Diameter | Corresponding Connecting Rod Bearing Insert Color Code | |
|---|---|---|
| | Upper Insert Size | Lower Insert Size |
| Yellow — 53.2257-53.2079 mm 2.0955-2.0948 in. Standard | Yellow — Standard | Yellow — Standard |
| Orange — 53.2079-53.1901 mm 2.0948-2.0941 in. Undersize (0.0178 mm or 0.0007 in.) | Yellow — Standard | Black — Undersize 0.025 mm 0.001 in. |
| Black — 53.1901-53.1723 mm 2.0941-2.0933 in. Undersize (0.0356 mm or 0.0014 in.) | Black — Undersize 0.025 mm 0.001 in. | Black — Undersize 0.025 mm 0.001 in. |
| Red — 52.9717-52.9539 mm 2.0855-2.0848 in. Undersize (0.254 mm or 0.010 in.) | Red — Undersize 0.254 mm 0.001 in. | Red — Undersize 0.254 mm 0.001 in. |

**Fig. 14   Connecting rod bearing selection chart. V8 engines**

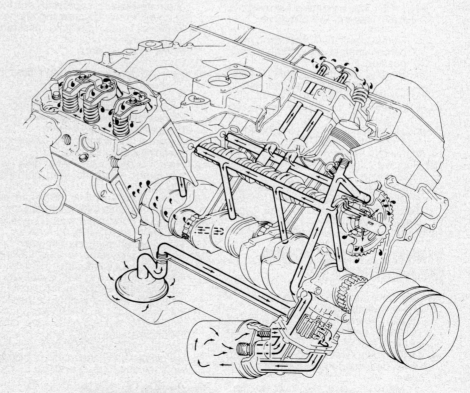

**Engine lubrication system. V8 engine**

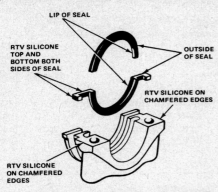

**Fig. 15 Installing crankshaft rear oil seal. V8 engine**

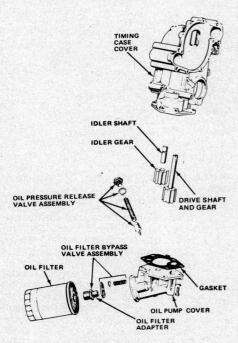

**Fig. 17 Oil pump & filter assembly. V8 engine**

## OIL PUMP
## REPLACE

1. Disconnect battery ground cable.
2. Refer to "Oil Pan, Replace" and remove oil pan.
3. Remove attaching bolts, then remove oil pump cover gasket and oil filter assembly, **Fig. 16.**
4. Install oil pressure relief valve into pump cover.
5. Install spring and retaining cap into pump cover.
6. Install idler shaft, idler gear and drive gear assembly into pump body.
7. Install pump cover and oil filter assembly. Torque pump cover screws to 55 inch lbs.

## OIL PUMP SERVICE

1. Remove drive gear and idler gear as-

sembly from pump body, **Fig. 17.**
2. Remove oil pressure relief, retaining cap and spring assembly.
3. Using the preferred method, measure gear end clearance as follows:
   a. Place a strip of Plastigage across full width of each oil pump gear.
   b. Install oil pump cover and gasket. Torque cover bolts to 55 inch lbs.
   c. Remove pump cover and measure width of compressed plastigage.
   d. Gear end clearance should be .002-.008 inch.
4. Using the alternate method, measure gear end clearance as follows:
   a. Place a suitable straightedge across gears and oil pump body.
   b. Place a feeler gauge between gears and straightedge.
   c. Gear end clearance should be .004-.008 inch.
   d. If gear end clearance is excessive measure gear length. If gear length is correct install a thinner oil pump cover gasket. If gear length is incorrect, replace gears and idler shaft.
5. Measure gear tooth to pump body clearance as follows:
   a. Place a suitable feeler gauge between gear tooth and pump body inner wall directly opposite point of gear mesh.
   b. Rotate gears and measure each gear tooth clearance.
   c. Clearance should be .0005-.0025 inch.
   d. If gear tooth to body clearance exceeds specified limit, use a micrometer and measure gear diameter. If gear diameter is correct and gear clearance is correct, replace cover. If gear diameter is incorrect, replace gears and idler shaft.

## BELT TENSION DATA

|  | New | Used |
|---|---|---|
|  | Lbs. | Lbs. |
| 1980-86 | 125-155 | 90-115 |
| 1987-89 | 120-160① | 90-115① |
| 1987-89 | 180-200② | 140-160② |

① —V-type belts.
② —Serpentine belts.

## WATER PUMP
## REPLACE

1. Disconnect battery ground cable.
2. Drain cooling system, then disconnect upper hose from radiator.
3. Loosen drive belts and remove fan shroud, if equipped.
4. Remove fan and hub assembly from water pump, **Fig. 18.**
5. On models equipped air conditioning, remove compressor bracket to water pump stud.
6. Remove alternator and mounting bracket assembly and position aside.
7. Remove power steering pump to rear mounting bracket nuts.
8. Remove front and rear power steering bracket to water pump mounting stud.

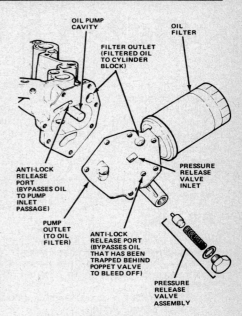

**Fig. 16 Oil pump cover assembly. V8 engine**

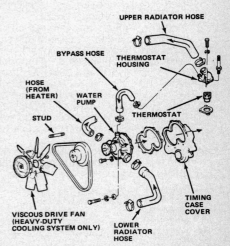

**Fig. 18 Engine cooling system components. V8 engine**

9. Disconnect heater hose, bypass hose and lower radiator hose from water pump.
10. Remove water pump and gasket from timing case cover.
11. Reverse procedure to install. Torque water pump-to-cylinder block attaching bolts to 28 ft. lbs. and pump-to-timing cover bolts to 48 inch lbs.

## FUEL PUMP
## REPLACE

1. Disconnect battery ground cable.
2. Disconnect and cap fuel lines from fuel pump.
3. Remove fuel pump attaching bolts, then the fuel pump.
4. Reverse procedure to install.

# Clutch & Manual Transmission

## INDEX

## CLUTCH PEDAL
### ADJUST

Some models use a hydraulic clutch mechanism, **Fig. 1**, which is self adjusting. Freeplay adjustments are not necessary and there is no provision for such an adjustment.

1. Position clutch pedal against pedal support bracket stop.
2. On Cherokee, Wagoneer, Grand Wagoneer and all truck models, adjust pedal to bell crank pushrod until bell crank inner lever is parallel to front face of clutch housing and slightly forward from the vertical position.
3. On all models, loosen jam nut on release rod adjuster and rotate adjuster as needed to obtain the following pedal freeplay: $3/8$–$5/8$ inch on all models with V-8 engines and 1980-81 Cherokee, Wagoneer and Truck models with 6 cylinder engines; $1 1/4$ inches on CJ, Scrambler, Grand Wagoneer, 1982-83 Cherokee and Wagoneer, and 1982-87 Truck models with 6 cylinder engines.
4. Tighten release rod adjuster jam nut and ensure that pedal freeplay is still within specification.

## CLUTCH HYDRAULIC SYSTEM
### BLEEDING
#### Exc. Wrangler

1. Ensure that clutch master cylinder is adequately filled.
2. Raise and support vehicle.
3. Remove slave cylinder from clutch housing and disconnect pushrod from cylinder.
4. Compress slave cylinder plunger using clamp J-24420-A or equivalent.
5. Attach suitable flexible tubing to slave cylinder bleed screw and immerse other end of tube in container filled halfway with clean brake fluid, ensuring that hose end remains submerged in fluid.
6. Loose bleed screw, have assistant fully depress and hold clutch pedal, tighten bleed screw, then release clutch pedal. Do not allow clutch pedal to be released while bleed screw is open, and do not allow master cylinder to run out of fluid during bleeding.

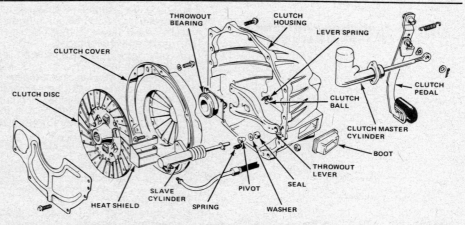

**Fig. 1   Hydraulic clutch release mechanism (Typical). 4 cylinder models**

7. Repeat step 5 until all air is purged from system, then reinstall slave cylinder, ensure that clutch master cylinder is adequately filled and check clutch release mechanism operation.

### Wrangler

1. Ensure clutch master cylinder is filled with DOT 3 brake fluid.
2. Raise and support vehicle.
3. Attach a suitable bleed hose to bleeder screw on slave cylinder, then insert other end of hose into a glass cylinder partially filled with brake fluid. Ensure end of hose is completely submerged in brake fluid.
4. Loosen bleed screw, have assistant fully depress and hold clutch pedal, tighten bleed screw, then release clutch pedal. Do not release clutch pedal while bleed screw is open. Also do not allow clutch master cylinder to run out of fluid during bleeding.
5. Repeat procedure until system is purged of air.

## CLUTCH MASTER CYLINDER, REPLACE

1. Disconnect hydraulic line at clutch cylinder.
2. Cap hydraulic line and master cylinder opening to prevent entry of dirt.
3. Remove cotter pin and washer retaining cylinder pushrod on clutch pedal and slide rod off pedal pivot.
4. Remove nuts attaching clutch cylinder to firewall and remove cylinder.

When servicing the clutch master cylinder, inspect the cylinder bore for nicks, scratches and scoring, corrosion, pitting or roughness, cracks, porosity and excessive wear. Do not attempt to repair a damaged master cylinder by honing, and replace the master cylinder if the bore is damaged in any way. While slight discoloration of the cylinder bore is acceptable, the master cylinder can only be overhauled (resealed) if the bore is clean and smooth.

5. Reverse procedure to install. Torque cylinder attaching nuts to 11 ft. lbs.

## CLUTCH SLAVE CYLINDER, REPLACE
### Exc. Wrangler

1. Raise and support vehicle.
2. Disconnect hydraulic line at cylinder, then remove throwout lever to cylinder pushrod retaining spring.
3. Remove slave cylinder, heat shield, throwout lever pivot, washer and seal from clutch housing. On some 1983-86 models, fluid leakage from one or both of the clutch cylinders may be caused by formation of an abrasive substance in the system fluid due to a chemical reaction between the master cylinder to slave cylinder hose and the fluid. If cylinder leaks are observed on these models, proceed as follows:

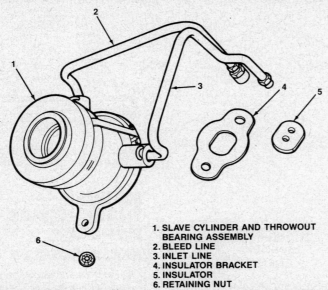

1. SLAVE CYLINDER AND THROWOUT BEARING ASSEMBLY
2. BLEED LINE
3. INLET LINE
4. INSULATOR BRACKET
5. INSULATOR
6. RETAINING NUT

**Fig. 2  Slave cylinder & throw-out bearing assembly. Wrangler**

a. Inspect system to determine which cylinder is leaking.
b. If slave cylinder is leaking, remove, clean and overhaul the cylinder. If master cylinder is leaking, remove and discard cylinder.
c. Remove and discard hose that connects master cylinder to slave cylinder.
d. Drain fluid from any cylinder not removed.
e. Install replacement master cylinder or repaired slave cylinder.
f. Install replacement hose 8953 004 162 for models with 4 cylinder engine, 8953 004 164 for models with 6 cylinder engines, or suitable equivalents.
g. Refill and bleed system as outlined, using DOT 3 brake fluid.
h. Verify proper clutch operation and ensure that all hose connections are tight and free from leaks.

## Wrangler

1. Disconnect clutch master cylinder fluid line at slave cylinder inlet line.
2. Remove transmission and transfer case.
3. Remove bolts attaching slave cylinder fluid line bracket to clutch housing, then remove insulator and bracket.
4. Remove cylinder and bearing retaining nut from mounting pin on transmission front case.
5. Slide cylinder and bearing, **Fig. 2**, from transmission input shaft. If cylinder and bearing are to be reinstalled, use care not to damage cylinder lines. If cylinder lines are damaged, the cylinder and bearing assembly must be replaced.
6. Reverse procedure to install. On replacement cylinder and bearing assemblies, nylon retaining straps are used to hold cylinder piston in place. Do not remove these straps, as they are designed to breakaway during piston movement after installation. After completing installation, bleed clutch

hydraulic system.

# CLUTCH
# REPLACE
## REMOVAL

1. Raise and support vehicle.
2. Remove transmission as described under "Transmission, Replace," then the starter motor.
3. On models except Wrangler with hydraulic release mechanism, remove slave cylinder bolts, disconnect pushrod from release fork and secure cylinder aside leaving hoses connected.
4. On all models, remove throwout bearing and clutch housing assembly, noting position of clutch housing shims, if equipped.
5. Mark position of pressure plate on flywheel for assembly reference.
6. Alternately loosen the pressure plate attaching bolts to relieve spring tension. The pressure plate bolts must be loosened evenly to prevent distortion of cover.
7. Remove pressure plate bolts, then the pressure plate and driven plate from flywheel. Place a mark on the side of the driven plate facing the flywheel for assembly reference.
8. Remove pilot bushing lubricating wick and soak wick in engine oil, if equipped.

## ADJUSTMENTS
### CLUTCH HOUSING ALIGNMENT CHECK
#### Exc. Wrangler

Clutch housing misalignment is caused by excessive face or bore runout of the clutch housing or transmission adapter. Misalignment causes improper clutch release, clutch noise and vibration, clutch plate and front transmission bearing failure, premature pilot bearing wear, and in severe cases, gear jumpout on decelera-

tion. If these malfunctions are evident, clutch housing alignment should be checked and corrected, as needed, using the following procedure.

1. With clutch housing assembly, pressure plate and clutch disc removed, remove one flywheel bolt.
2. Obtain a 1/2-20 bolt and nut to use as dial indicator support. Bolt should be 9 inches long for models less transmission adapter or 15 inches long for models with transmission adapter.
3. Install nut on bolt, thread bolt into crankshaft by hand, then tighten nut against flywheel to secure bolt.
4. Install clutch housing assembly, positioning shims as noted during removal, and torque bolts to 54 ft. lbs. for 4 cylinder engines, 30 ft. lbs. for V8 engines, or 35 ft. lbs. top and 45 ft. lbs. bottom for 6 cylinder engines.
5. Mount suitable dial indicator on support bolt with pointer bearing against transmission mounting face of clutch housing or adapter, approximately 1/8 inch from edge of bore, **Fig. 3**. Zero indicator.
6. Rotate crankshaft a full 360° while observing dial indicator and note readings. Face runout must not exceed .010 inch (total indicator reading) at any point in rotation. Crankshaft endplay must be held at zero to obtain accurate readings. Move and hold crankshaft with suitable lever to eliminate endplay.
7. Reposition dial indicator so that pointer bears against center of transmission front bearing adapter bore in clutch housing or adapter, then zero indicator.
8. Holding endplay at zero, rotate crankshaft a full 360° while observing indicator and note readings. Bore runout must not exceed .010 inch (total indicator reading).
9. If either face or bore runout exceed .010 inch on models without transmission adapter, proceed as follows:
   a. Move dial indicator aside and loosen clutch housing retaining bolts.
   b. Insert shims between clutch housing and engine or engine adapter to correct misalignment. When inserting shims, note that a change in face alignment will also change bore alignment.
   c. Shims inserted at point 1, **Fig. 4**, affect top to bottom alignment.
   d. Shims inserted at points 2 and 3, **Fig. 4**, affect side to side alignment.
   e. Shims inserted at points 4 and 5, **Fig. 4**, affect both top to bottom and side to side alignment.
   f. After inserting shims, torque housing bolts to specifications given in step 4, then recheck face and bore runout.
   g. If both bore and face alignment cannot be brought within specifications, housing should be replaced.
10. If face runout exceeds .010 inch on models with transmission adapter, adjust as outlined in step 9.
11. If both face and bore runout exceed specifications, correct face alignment,

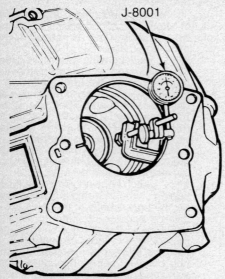

**Fig. 3   Clutch housing alignment check**

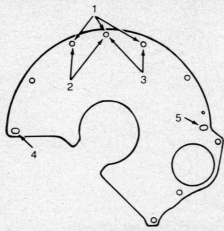

**Fig. 4   Clutch housing shim locations**

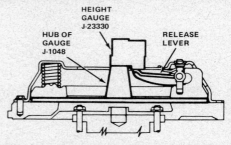

**Fig. 5   Pressure plate release lever height measurement**

then recheck and correct bore alignment as outlined in step 12. On models with transmission adapter, adjust adapter bore alignment as follows:

a. Move dial indicator aside, then loosen bolts securing adapter to clutch housing.

b. Reposition adapter on housing, moving adapter up or down, left or right, as needed.

c. Torque adapter bolts to 35 ft. lbs., then recheck bore runout.

13. On all models, replace clutch housing and transmission adapter, if equipped, if face and bore runout cannot be brought within specifications. Ensure that face and bore runout of replacement components is within specifications during installation.

14. When housing alignment has been set, remove dial indicator, then the housing assembly, noting installation position of shims.

15. Remove support bolt from crankshaft, install flywheel bolt and torque to specifications.

16. Install clutch disc and pressure plate assembly, then the clutch housing, insert housing shims in proper positions, then torque clutch housing bolts to specifications listed in step 4.

## PRESSURE PLATE (CLUTCH COVER) RELEASE LEVER ADJUSTMENT
### 1980–83

This procedure applies to all models not equipped with diaphragm spring type pressure plate (clutch cover).

1. Remove flywheel and position on flat surface with drive face up, then install gauge plate J-1048 on flywheel in hole normally occupied by clutch disc.

2. Position pressure plate assembly over gauge plate, rotate plate to align machined lands with pressure plate release levers and ensure that gauge

plate hub is centered.

3. Install pressure plate bolts and torque bolts alternately and evenly to 40 ft. lbs.

4. Compress each release lever several times to seat levers in operating position.

5. Measure height of each lever above gauge plate hub using height gauge J-23330, **Fig. 5.**

6. If release levers are not at specified height above gauge plate hub, adjust by turning lever height adjusting nuts until specified dimension is obtained, **Fig. 6.**

7. After each lever is adjusted, compress lever several times, recheck adjustment and correct as needed.

8. When all levers are at specified height, stake position of adjusting nuts to secure adjustment.

## INSTALLATION

1. Lightly lubricate release lever pivots.

2. Install pilot bushing lubricating wick into crankshaft bore, if equipped.

3. Install a suitable clutch alignment tool into clutch disc hub.

4. Install assembled disc and tool on flywheel. Ensure that alignment tool is seated fully in the pilot bushing. Ensure that the proper side of the disc faces the flywheel.

5. Place pressure plate on flywheel and over disc and alignment tool. Align pressure plate and flywheel using the marks made during removal. Install pressure plate attaching bolts finger tight.

6. Torque pressure plate evenly and alternately to 40 ft. lbs. except on CJ, Scrambler and Wrangler models with four cylinder engine. Torque these pressure plate bolts to 23 ft. lbs.

7. On all models except Wrangler, install clutch housing and starter motor.

8. On all models except Wrangler, install throwout bearing and waved washer, if used.

9. On all models, Install transmission.

10. On models with hydraulic clutch, bleed system as necessary.

## MANUAL TRANSMISSION REPLACE
### EXC. WRANGLER

1. Remove transmission shift lever boot attaching screws and slide boot upward.

2. On models with SR-4, T4 or T5 transmissions, remove bolts attaching transmission shift lever housing to transmission. Lift shift lever and housing upward and out of transmission.

3. On models with T-18A transmission, remove shift lever cap, gasket, spring seat, spring and shift lever as an assembly, then remove shift lever locating pins from housing.

4. On models with T-176 transmission, press and rotate transmission shift lever retainer, then remove lever, boot, spring and seat as an assembly.

5. Raise vehicle, then place alignment marks on propeller shaft and transfer case yoke. Disconnect propeller shaft at transfer case yoke and secure to underbody with wire.

6. On Cherokee and truck models, disconnect front parking brake cable at equalizer, then remove clip that retains rear cable to rear crossmember and position cable out of way.

7. Support engine by positioning a jack stand under clutch housing.

8. Remove bolts and nuts attaching rear crossmember to frame side rails and support cushion, then remove crossmember.

9. Disconnect speedometer cable, back-up lamp switch wire and four wheel drive indicator switch wire.

10. Disconnect transfer case vent hose at transfer case.

11. Place alignment marks on front propeller shaft and transfer case yoke, then disconnect propeller shaft and secure to underbody with wire.

12. On CJ models, remove transfer case shifter shaft retaining nut and control link pins, then remove shifter shaft and disengage shift lever from shift control links. Slide shift lever upward into boot to position lever out of way. On some units, it may be necessary to unthread shifter shaft to remove.

13. On Cherokee and truck models, remove cotter pin and washer that connect link to shift lever, then disconnect link.

| Year | Model | Lever Height |
|------|-------|--------------|
| 1980–82 | CJ, Scrambler① | .093–.1093 |
| | Cherokee, Wagoneer Truck | .1875 |
| 1980–83 | All② | 1.595–1.720 |
| 1982–83 | 6 cyl.③ | 2.04–2.16 |
| | V8 | .1875 |

①—Exc. 4 cyl. engines.    ②—4 Cyl. engines.
③—Using .305 gauge.

**Fig. 6   Pressure plate release lever height specifications**

14. Using a suitable jack, support transmission and transfer case assembly.
15. Remove transmission to clutch housing attaching bolts, then remove transmission and transfer case assembly.
16. Reverse procedure to install. Soak pilot bushing lubricating wick in engine oil before installing.

## WRANGLER
### Removal

1. Remove shift lever knobs from transmission and transfer case shifter levers.
2. Remove transmission and transfer case shift lever boots.
3. On models with AX-5 transmission, press stub shaft retainer downward and rotate counterclockwise to release from lugs, then lift shift lever, stub shaft and retainer from transmission. Do not remove shift lever from stub shaft.
4. On models with BA 10/5 transmission, remove shift tower dust boot, then remove stub shaft retainer plate and lift stub shaft and shifter lever from transmission. On some unit, a snap ring may be used in place of the retainer plate. Do not separate shift lever from stub shaft.
5. On all models, raise and support vehicle.
6. Drain lubricant from transmission and transfer case.
7. Place alignment marks on rear propeller shaft for reference during installation, then remove propeller shaft from vehicle.
8. Position a safety stand under transfer case for support, then remove rear crossmember.
9. Disconnect speedometer cable and back-up lamp switch from transmission.
10. Disconnect and tag vent and vacuum hoses from transmission and transfer case.
11. Disconnect range linkage from transfer case.
12. Place alignment marks on front propeller shaft for reference during installation, then remove propeller shaft.
13. Disconnect clutch master cylinder line from slave cylinder.
14. Position a suitable transmission jack under transmission and transfer case and secure with safety chains.
15. Remove clutch housing brace rod and clutch housing-to-engine attaching bolts, then lower transmission and transfer case from vehicle.
16. If necessary, remove bolts attaching transfer case to transmission and separate.
17. Remove clutch slave cylinder and throw-out bearing from transmission, then remove clutch housing.

### Installation

1. Install clutch housing on transmission, torque attaching bolts to 27 ft. lbs.
2. Install clutch slave cylinder and throw-out bearing.
3. Position transmission on suitable transmission jack, then align transmission input shaft splines with spline on clutch plate. Install transmission and torque clutch housing to engine attaching bolts to 28 ft. lbs.
4. Connect clutch master cylinder line to slave cylinder.
5. Position transfer case on suitable transmission jack, then align transfer case and transmission shaft splines.
6. Install transfer case on transmission and torque attaching bolts to 26 ft. lbs.
7. Remove transmission jack from transfer case and position a safety stand under transfer case for support.
8. Connect vacuum hose, vent hoses, back-up light switch, speedometer cable and transfer case range linkage.
9. Install rear crossmember. Torque crossmember to frame attaching bolts to 30 ft. lbs. Torque rear support to transmission attaching bolts and nuts to 33 ft. lbs.
10. On models equipped with AX-5 transmission, install shift lever, stub shaft and retainer on transmission tower. Lock retainer by rotating clockwise until lug are fully engaged. When installing, ensure nylon insulator at end of stab shaft is properly seated in shifter block located inside transmission tower.
11. On models equipped with BA 10/5 transmission, position shift lever and stub shaft on transmission tower, then install retaining plate or snap ring, depending on unit.
12. On all models, install shift tower dust boot and shift lever boots and knobs.
13. Install front and rear propeller shafts, aligning marks made during removal. Torque U-clamp bolts to 170 inch lbs.
13. Fill transmission and transfer case with lubricant and lower vehicle.

## MANUAL TRANSMISSION SHIFT MECHANISM
### EXC. WRANGLER

The shift mechanism on all manual transmission models is located within the shift control housing which also serves as the transmission top cover. The shift mechanism does not require adjustment and can be serviced separately from the transmission.

## WRANGLER

The shift mechanism on manual transmission models is located within the transmission assembly. The shift mechanism does not require adjustment and is serviced during transmission overhaul.

# Transfer Case

## INDEX

# TRANSFER CASE
## REPLACE
### ALL EXC. 1983–89 W/SELEC-TRAC
#### CJ & Scrambler Models

1. Remove shift lever knob, trim ring and boot from transmission and transfer case shift levers.
2. On all models, remove floor covering, if equipped, then the transmission access cover from floor pan.
3. Raise and support vehicle.
4. Drain lubricant from transfer case.
5. Place a jack stand under clutch housing to support engine and transmission, then remove rear crossmember.
6. Disconnect front and rear propeller shafts from output shaft yokes.
7. Disconnect speedometer cable from transfer case.
8. Disconnect parking brake cable at equalizer, if necessary.
9. Disconnect exhaust pipe support bracket from transfer case, if equipped.
10. Remove transfer case to transmission attaching bolts.
11. Remove transfer case from vehicle.
12. Remove and discard transfer case to transmission gasket.
13. Install new transfer case to transmission gasket.
14. Reverse steps 1 through 11 to install.

#### Grand Wagoneer, J-10 & 20 Truck & 1980–83 Cherokee & Wagoneer

1. Raise and support vehicle.
2. Drain transfer case lubricant.
3. Mark alignment of transfer case front and rear output shaft yokes and propeller shafts, then disconnect front and rear propeller shafts from output shaft yokes.
4. Disconnect speedometer cable and indicator switch wires from transfer case.
5. Support transmission with a suitable jack and remove rear crossmember.
6. Disconnect parking brake cable guide from pivot, located at right frame rail, if necessary.
7. Remove bolts attaching exhaust pipe support bracket to transfer case, if necessary.
8. Remove transfer case to transmission attaching bolts.
9. Remove transfer case from vehicle.
10. Remove transfer case to transmission gasket and discard.
11. Install new transfer case to transmission gasket.
12. Reverse steps 1 through 9 to install.

#### Wrangler

1. On model 207 transfer case, position transfer case shift lever into four-high range.
2. On model 231 transfer case, position transfer case shift lever into neutral.
3. Raise and support vehicle.
4. Drain lubricant from transfer case.
5. Place alignment marks on front and rear propeller shafts for use during installation, then remove front and rear propeller shafts.
6. Disconnect vent and vacuum hoses and range linkage from transfer case, then disconnect speedometer cable.
7. Using a safety stand to support transmission, remove rear crossmember.
8. Support transfer case using a suitable transmission jack, then remove transfer case to transmission attaching bolts and lower transfer case from vehicle.
9. Reverse procedure to install.

### 1983 SELEC-TRAC

1. Raise and support vehicle.
2. Drain lubricant from transfer case.
3. Disconnect speedometer cable and indicator switch wires, then the transfer case shift lever link at operating lever.
4. Disconnect parking brake cable guide from pivot on right frame rail, if necessary.
5. Place suitable support under transmission and remove rear crossmember.
6. Scribe alignment marks on transfer case front and rear output shafts at transfer case yokes and propeller shafts for proper assembly.
7. Disconnect front and rear propeller shafts at transfer case yokes and secure out of way.
8. Disconnect shift motor vacuum lines and the transfer case shift linkage.
9. Remove exhaust pipe support bracket to transfer case attaching bolts, if necessary.
10. Remove transfer case to transmission attaching bolts, then move transfer case assembly rearward until free of transmission output shaft and remove assembly.
11. Remove all gasket material from rear of transmission adapter housing.
12. Reverse procedure to install.

### 1984–89 SELEC-TRAC

1. Raise and support vehicle.
2. Drain lubricant from transfer case.
3. Disconnect speedometer cable and vent hose.
4. Disconnect shift motor vacuum hoses and the transfer case shift linkage.
5. Place suitable support under transmission and remove rear crossmember.
6. Scribe alignment marks on transfer case front and rear output shafts at transfer case yokes and propeller shafts for proper assembly.
7. Disconnect front and rear propeller shafts at transfer case yokes and secure shafts out of way.
8. Disconnect parking brake cable guide from pivot on right frame rail.
9. Remove transfer case to transmission attaching bolts.
10. Move transfer case rearward until clear of transmission output shaft and remove assembly.
11. Remove all gasket material from rear of transmission adapter housing.
12. Reverse procedure to install.

# FRONT/REAR YOKE OIL SEAL
## REPLACE
### MODEL 300 TRANSFER CASE

1. Raise and support vehicle.
2. Place suitable jack under transmission and remove rear crossmember.
3. Scribe alignment marks on pertinent propeller shaft and transfer case yoke for proper assembly, then disconnect

shaft from yoke.

4. Using suitable tools, remove transfer case yoke nut and washer, then the yoke.
5. Using suitable tools, remove oil seal and install new oil seal.
6. Install yoke, washer and nut, torquing nut to 120 ft. lbs.

## SHIFT ROD OIL SEAL
### REPLACE
### MODEL 300 TRANSFER CASE

1. When replacing left side shift rod seal, shift transfer case into 4L position.
2. Raise and support vehicle.
3. Remove pins connecting control links to transfer case shift rods.
4. Using suitable tools, remove shift rod oil seal and install new seal.
5. Install pins connecting control links to transfer case shift rods, securing with new cotter pins.

## REAR BEARING CAP/SPEEDOMETER DRIVE GEAR
### REPLACE
### MODEL 300 TRANSFER CASE

1. Disconnect rear propeller shaft at transfer case yoke and support out of way.
2. Disconnect speedometer cable, then remove speedometer driven gear sleeve and driven gear.
3. Remove transfer case vent hose.
4. Using suitable tools, remove output shaft yoke.
5. Remove bearing cap to transfer case bolts and remove bearing cap.
6. Remove shims and speedometer driven gear from output shaft, then the speedometer driven gear bushing from the bearing cap.
7. Using suitable tool, install speedometer driven gear bushing.
8. Install speedometer driven gear and shims on shaft.
9. Apply bead of suitable sealant to mating surface of cap and install cap, using two screws to align bolt holes, and tap cap into position with plastic mallet.
10. Torque bearing cap bolts to 35 ft. lbs.
11. Using suitable tools, install output shaft yoke, torquing locknut to 12 ft. lbs.
12. Check rear output shaft endplay as follows:
    a. Attach suitable dial indicator to bearing cap and position indicator stylus against output shaft.
    b. Pry output shaft back and forth to check endplay.
    c. If end play is not .001-.005 inches, remove or add shims between

speedometer drive gear and output shaft rear bearing.

13. Install transfer case vent hose and the speedometer driven gear sleeve and driven gear.
14. Install speedometer cable.
15. Install rear propeller shaft, torquing clamp strap bolts to 15 ft. lbs.

## SPEEDOMETER GEAR, SHAFT SEAL, REAR BEARING & RETAINER, OIL PUMP & PUMP SEAL
### REPLACE
### MODEL 208 TRANSFER CASE

1. Raise and support vehicle.
2. Remove fill and drain plugs and drain oil from transfer case.
3. Scribe alignment marks on propeller shaft and transfer case yoke for proper assembly, then disconnect propeller shaft.
4. Using suitable tools, remove and discard transfer case yoke retaining nut and yoke seal washer.
5. Remove yoke, using suitable tools as necessary.
6. Remove speedometer driven gear sleeve and driven gear from rear retainer.
7. Scribe alignment marks on rear retainer for proper assembly, then remove retainer attaching bolts and the retainer. Do not attempt to pry retainer off rear case. Tap retainer loose using only a rawhide or plastic mallet.
8. Remove speedometer drive gear, then the pump housing from retainer and seal from housing.
9. When replacing bearing or retainer, remove bearing retaining snap ring from rear retainer, and tap bearing out of retainer.
10. Remove oil pump from mainshaft, then remove output shaft seal.
11. Install oil pump on mainshaft, the seal into pump housing and the speedometer driven gear.
12. Install rear output bearing in rear retainer and install snap ring, ensuring that shielded side of bearing faces interior of transfer case.
13. Install pump housing in rear retainer, then apply suitable sealant to rear retainer mating surface and install retainer on case.
14. Install retainer attaching bolts, torquing to 23 ft. lbs., and install output shaft seal, then install yoke, yoke seal washer and yoke nut, torquing nut to 120 ft. lbs.
15. Install speedometer driven gear and sleeve, then the drain plug.
16. Fill transfer case to edge of fill plug with suitable lubricant, then install fill plug.
17. Contact propeller shaft, torquing clamp strap bolts to 14 ft. lbs.

## SPEEDOMETER GEAR, REAR BEARING, REAR SEAL & SHAFT YOKE
### REPLACE
### MODEL 219 TRANSFER CASE

1. Raise and support vehicle.
2. Remove fill and drain plugs and drain oil from transfer case.
3. Scribe alignment marks on propeller shaft and transfer case yoke for proper assembly, then disconnect shaft from yoke.
4. Using suitable tools, remove and discard transfer case yoke nut and seal washer, then remove yoke.
5. Remove speedometer cable from retainer, then scribe alignment marks on rear retainer for proper assembly and remove retainer.
6. Remove differential shims and speedometer driven gear.
7. Remove rear output bearing snap ring and remove bearing from retainer.
8. Using suitable tool, remove rear seal from retainer.
9. Install bearing in retainer, ensuring that shielded side of bearing faces case interior, then install bearing snap ring.
10. Using suitable tool, install rear yoke seal.
11. Install speedometer gear and differential shim.
12. Apply suitable sealant to mating surface of rear retainer and install retainer, torquing attaching bolts to 23 ft. lbs.
13. Install yoke seal, washer and yoke nut, torquing nut to 120 ft. lbs.
14. Install speedometer cable and connect propeller shaft.
15. Install drain plug and fill transfer case to bottom edge of fill plug hole with suitable lubricant.
16. Install fill plug.

## TORQUE BIAS TEST
### MODELS 219 & 229 TRANSFER CASES
### Exc. 1989 Models

1. Place vehicle on level surface, then shut off engine.
2. Place transmission shift lever in Neutral and transfer case shift lever in 4-HIGH position.
3. Raise and support vehicle so that one front wheel is off ground.
4. Remove hub cap from raised wheel.
5. Install torque wrench on a lug nut of raised wheel and rotate wheel with torque wrench to measure torque required to rotate wheel.
6. If required torque is at least 45 ft. lbs., viscous coupling is satisfactory.

## TESTING TRANSFER CASE SHIFT MOTOR

### MODEL 229 TRANSFER CASE

1. Disconnect vacuum harness from transfer case shift motor and connect suitable vacuum pump to shift motor front port.
2. Apply 15 inches vacuum to shift motor and rotate rear propeller shaft to fully engage transfer case in 4 wheel drive mode.
3. If shift motor does not retain vacuum for at least 30 seconds, replace motor.
4. Disconnect vacuum pump from front port of shift motor and connect to rear port, plug front axle connecting port and apply 15 inches vacuum to motor.
5. Place automatic transmission in Park or manual transmission in 1st gear.
6. If shift motor does not maintain vacuum for at least 30 seconds, replace motor.
7. Remove cap from shift motor axle connecting port and check for vacuum at port. If there is no vacuum, rotate rear propeller shaft as necessary to ensure total transfer case engagement. The transfer case must be fully engaged before shift motor stem will extend fully and open axle interconnecting port.
8. If vacuum is now present at shift motor axle connecting port, refer to **Fig. 1** on all except 1989 models, on 1989 models refer to **Fig. 2.**
9. If vacuum is still not present, slide boot away from shift motor stem and measure distance stem has extended. Stem should extend $5/8$ inch as measured from edge of shift motor housing to E-ring on stem.
10. If shift motor stem does not extend specified distance, refer to **Fig. 1.**
11. If shift motor stem extends specified distance but there is still no vacuum at axle connecting port, replace motor.

## TESTING FRONT AXLE SHIFT MOTOR

### MODEL 229 TRANSFER CASE

#### Exc. 1989 Models

1. Disconnect vacuum harness from front axle shift motor and connect suitable vacuum pump to shift motor front port.
2. Apply 15 inches vacuum to shift motor and rotate right front wheel to fully disengage axle.
3. If shift motor does not maintain vacuum for at least 30 seconds, replace motor.
4. Disconnect vacuum pump from shift motor front port and connect pump to shift motor rear port, cap transfer case connecting port and apply 15 inches vacuum to motor.
5. If shift motor does not maintain vacuum for at least 30 seconds, replace motor.

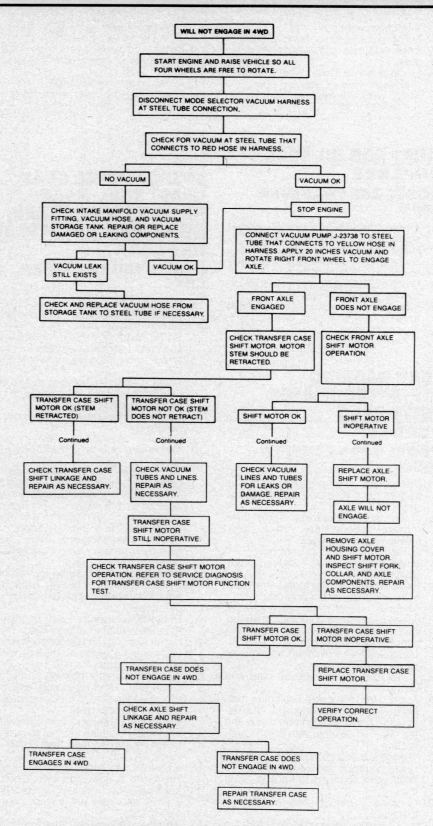

**Fig. 1   Selec-Trac diagnosis. Model 229 transfer case (Part 1 of 2)**

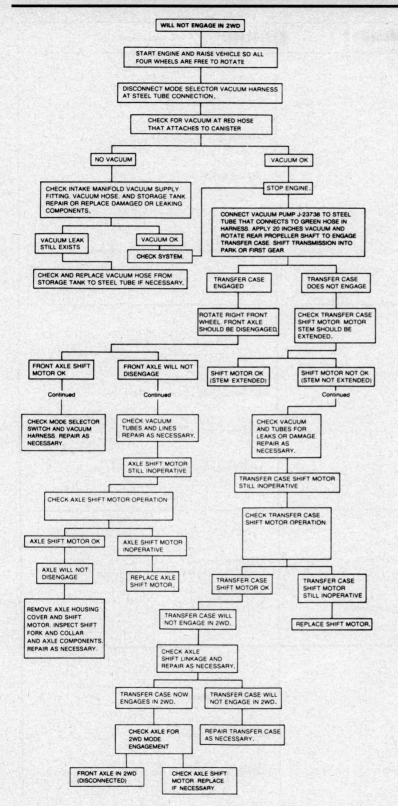

**Fig. 1   Selec-Trac diagnosis. Model 229 transfer case (Part 2 of 2)**

6. Remove cap from shift motor transfer case connecting port and check for vacuum at port.
7. If vacuum is not present, rotate right front wheel as necessary to ensure that axle has disengaged completely.
8. Check vacuum at shift motor transfer case connecting port again. If vacuum is now present, refer to **Fig. 1**.

## MODEL 231 TRANSFER CASE

1. Disconnect vacuum harness from front axle shift motor and connect suitable vacuum pump to shift motor front port.
2. Apply 15 inches vacuum to shift motor and rotate right front wheel to fully disengage axle.
3. If shift motor does not maintain vacuum for at least 30 seconds, replace motor.
4. Disconnect vacuum pump from shift motor front port and connect pump to shift motor rear port. Cap transfer case connecting port and apply 15 inches vacuum to motor.
5. If shift motor does not maintain vacuum for at least 30 seconds, replace motor.
6. Remove cap from shift motor transfer case connecting port and check for vacuum at port.
7. If vacuum is not present, rotate right front wheel as necessary to ensure that axle has disengaged completely.
8. Check vacuum at shift motor transfer case connecting port again. If vacuum is now present, refer to **Fig. 3**.

## MODE ROD
## ADJUST
## MODEL 229 TRANSFER CASE

### Exc. 1989 Models

With transfer case in 2WD/HI, both mode lever and range lever must be aligned on the same center line, **Fig. 4**, prior to mode rod adjustment. If levers are not properly aligned, the transfer case may not fully engage 2WD/HI, resulting in damage to the transfer case viscous coupling.

1. Ensure that all vacuum hoses are correctly routed and not loose or disconnected.
2. Adjust mode rod to approximately 5.9 inches, dimension A, **Fig. 4**.
3. Drive vehicle a short distance, shifting into 4WD and back to 2WD/HI.
4. Check mode lever position after test drive. If mode lever is not aligned with range lever, increase mode rod length one turn and repeat steps 1 and 2.
5. With transfer case vacuum motor shaft fully extended and transfer case in 2WD/HI, adjust mode rod so that pin "A" moves freely in hole through vacuum motor shaft and mode rod.

| Condition | Possible Cause | Correction |
|---|---|---|
| TRANSFER CASE WILL NOT SHIFT INTO 2WD OR 4WD MODE | (1) Vacuum leak in harness, connecting lines or tank.<br><br>(2) Shift motor malfunction.<br><br>(3) Check valve stuck/leaking.<br><br>(4) Mode switch malfunction.<br><br>(5) Transfer case shift mechanism worn/damaged. | (1) Locate/repair leak.<br><br>(2) Test and replace motor, if necessary.<br><br>(3) Replace valve.<br><br>(4) Check switch operation. Replace if necessary.<br><br>(5) Disassemble and repair as needed. |
| TRANSFER CASE WILL NOT SHIFT INTO HI OR LO RANGE | (1) Range lever misadjusted.<br><br>(2) Insufficient lubricant.<br><br>(3) Incorrect lubricant.<br><br>(4) Internal damage. | (1) Adjust lever shift rod.<br><br>(2) Check and correct lubricant level.<br><br>(3) Drain and refill.<br><br>(4) Disassemble and repair as needed. |
| NOISY IN ALL RANGES | (1) Insufficient or incorrect lubricant.<br><br>(2) Worn/damaged internal components. | (1) Drain and refill with DEXRON II® or MOPAR-MERCON® automatic transmission fluid.<br><br>(2) Disassemble and repair. |
| LUBRICANT LEAKS FROM OUTPUT SHAFT SEALS OR FROM VENT | (1) Transfer case overfilled.<br><br>(2) Vent restricted.<br><br>(3) Output shaft seals damaged or incorrectly installed. | (1) Drain to correct level.<br><br>(2) Replace/clear vent.<br><br>(3) Replace seals. Also replace yokes if seal surfaces are damaged. |

**Fig. 2  Selec-Trac diagnosis. Model 229 transfer case, 1989 models**

| Condition | Possible Cause | Correction |
|---|---|---|
| TRANSFER CASE DIFFICULT TO SHIFT OR WILL NOT SHIFT INTO DESIRED RANGE | (1) Vehicle speed too great to permit shifting.<br><br>(2) If vehicle was operated for extended period in 4H mode on dry paved surface, driveline torque load may cause difficulty.<br><br>(3) Transfer case external shift linkage binding.<br><br>(4) Insufficient or incorrect lubricant.<br><br>(5) Internal components binding, worn or damaged. | (1) Stop vehicle and shift into desired range. Or reduce speed to 3-4 km/h (2-3 mph) before attempting to shift.<br><br>(2) Stop vehicle, shift transmission to Neutral, shift transfer case to 2H mode and operate vehicle in 2H on dry paved surfaces.<br><br>(3) Lubricate, repair or replace linkage, or tighten loose components as necessary.<br><br>(4) Drain and refill to edge of fill hole with DEXRON II* or MOPAR-MERCON* Automatic Transmission Fluid.<br><br>(5) Disassemble unit and replace worn or damaged components as necessary. |
| TRANSFER CASE NOISY IN ALL DRIVE MODES | (1) Insufficient or incorrect lubricant. | (1) Drain and refill to edge of fill hole with DEXRON II* or MOPAR-MERCON* Automatic Transmission Fluid. Check for leaks and repair if necessary. **Note: If unit is still noisy after drain and refill, disassembly and inspection may be required to locate source of noise.** |
| NOISY IN – OR JUMPS OUT OF – FOUR WHEEL DRIVE LOW RANGE | (1) Transfer case not completely engaged in 4L position.<br><br>(2) Shift linkage loose or binding.<br><br>(3) Range fork damaged, inserts worn, or fork is binding on shift rail.<br><br>(4) Low range gear worn or damaged. | (1) Stop vehicle, shift transfer case to Neutral, then shift back into 4L position.<br><br>(2) Tighten, lubricate or repair linkage as necessary.<br><br>(3) Disassemble unit and repair as necessary.<br><br>(4) Disassemble and repair as necessary. |
| LUBRICANT LEAKING FROM OUTPUT SHAFT SEALS OR FROM VENT | (1) Transfer case overfilled.<br><br>(2) Vent closed or restricted.<br><br>(3) Output shaft seals damaged or installed incorrectly. | (1) Drain to correct level.<br><br>(2) Clear or replace vent if necessary.<br><br>(3) Replace seals. Be sure seal lip faces interior of case when installed. Also be sure yoke seal surfaces are not scored or nicked. Remove scores and nicks with fine sandpaper or replace yoke(s) if necessary. |
| ABNORMAL TIRE WEAR | (1) Extended operation on dry hard surface (paved) roads in 4H range. | (1) Operate in 2H on hard surface (paved) roads. |

**Fig. 3   Transfer case diagnosis. Model 231 transfer case**

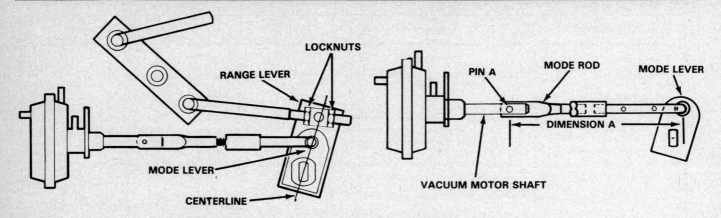

**Fig. 4   Adjusting mode & range rods. Model 229 transfer case**

# RANGE ROD
## ADJUST

### MODELS 207 & 231 TRANSFER CASES

1. Remove transfer case shift lever boot, then position shift lever (1), **Fig. 5,** in the two-high position.
2. Position a 1/8 inch spacer between forward edge of shift lever and shift lever gate.
3. Raise and support vehicle.
4. Loosen lock bolt (2), **Fig. 5,** on adjusting trunnion (3), then move range lever (5) fully rearward to the two-high position.
5. Position linkage rod (4), **Fig. 5,** so that it fits freely in range lever (5), then tighten adjusting trunnion bolt (2).
6. Lower vehicle and remove spacer from shift lever.

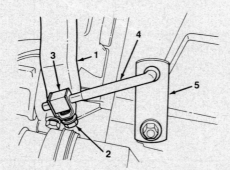

**Fig. 5   Range rod adjustment. Model 207 transfer case (model 229 similar)**

### MODEL 229 TRANSFER CASE
#### Exc. 1989 Models

After adjusting mode rod, check position of range lever inside vehicle. Range lever should be positioned 1/2 to 1 inch above floor when it is in 2WD/HI range. This en- sures sufficient travel for complete range engagement. Adjustment should be made at transfer case end of linkage.

1. Loosen locknuts and shorten or lengthen rod to correctly position floor lever.
2. Tighten locknuts to maintain rod adjustment.

#### 1989 Models

1. Remove transfer case shift lever boot, then position shift lever (1), **Fig. 5,** in the two-high position.
2. Position a 1/8 inch spacer between forward edge of shift lever and shift lever gate.
3. Raise and support vehicle.
4. Loosen lock bolt (2), **Fig. 5,** on adjusting trunnion (3), then move range lever (5) fully rearward to the two-high position.
5. Position linkage rod (4), **Fig. 5,** so that it fits freely in range lever (5), then tighten adjusting trunnion bolt (2).
6. Lower vehicle and remove spacer from shift lever.

# Rear Axle, Suspension & Brake

## INDEX

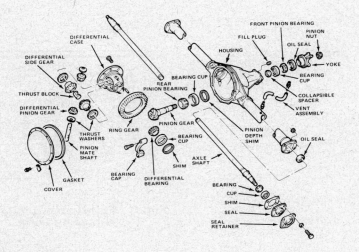

**Fig. 1  Semi-floating axle with tapered shaft**

## AXLE SHAFT, BEARING & OIL SEAL
### REPLACE
### SEMI-FLOATING TAPERED SHAFT

The hub and drum are separate units, and the hub and axle shaft are serrated to mate and fit together on the taper. Both are marked to insure correct assembly. The axle shaft and bearing assembly may be removed as follows:

1. Remove rear wheel, drum and hub, then disconnect parking brake cable at equalizer. Do not use a slide hammer or knockout type puller to remove hub from axle shaft. Damage to the axle bearings or other components will result.
2. Disconnect brake tube from wheel cylinder and remove brake support plate assembly, oil seal and axle shims from axle shaft. Axle shaft endplay shims are located on the left side only.
3. Using suitable puller, pull axle shaft and bearing from axle tube, **Fig. 1.** On models equipped with Trak-Lok differential, do not rotate differential unless

both axle shafts are in place.
4. Remove and install axle shaft bearing using a suitable arbor press. Remove old oil seal from axle housing bore, clean bore and install new seal.
5. If axle shaft bearing is replaced, pack bearing with generous amount of wheel bearing lubricant and press bearing onto shaft, ensuring that small diameter of bearing faces toward outer tapered end of shaft.
6. Coat inner seal with light lubricating oil, coat outer surface of seal metal retainer with non-hardening sealer, and install seal using suitable tool.
7. Install axle shafts, aligning shaft splines with differential side gear splines, and insert shaft into gear.
8. Install outer bearing cup, then inspect brake support plate for elongated bolt holes or other damage, replacing as necessary. During assembly, apply suitable sealant to axle tube flange and brake support plate mounting area to prevent entry of water and dust.
9. Install original axle endplay shims, oil seal assembly and brake support plate, torquing attaching bolts to 35 ft. lbs. The oil seal and retainer are located on the outside of the brake support

plate.
10. Connect brake line to wheel cylinder, then bleed and adjust brakes.
11. Check and adjust axle shaft endplay as follows:
  a. Axle shaft endplay is adjusted at the left side axle shaft only.
  b. Strike end of each axle shaft with lead hammer to seat bearing cups against support plate.
  c. Attach axle shaft endplay tool J-2092 or equivalent to end of left side axle shaft and mount dial indicator on support plate or tool, **Fig. 2,** then check endplay while pushing or pulling on axle shaft. Endplay should be .004-.008 inch.
  d. Adjust shim pack as necessary, adding shims to increase endplay or removing shims to decrease endplay.
12. When installing original hub, proceed as follows:
  a. Align keyway in hub with axle shaft key and slide hub onto axle shaft as far as possible.
  b. Install axle shaft nut and washer, then the brake drum, drum retaining screws and wheel assembly.
  c. Lower vehicle to ground, then torque axle shaft nut to 250 ft. lbs. and install cotter pin. If cotter pin hole is not aligned, tighten nut to next castellation, do not loosen nut to align cotter pin hole. When a replacement axle shaft is installed, a replacement hub must also be installed. A replacement hub may be installed on an original axle shaft if the serrations on the shaft are not worn or damaged.
13. When installing replacement hub, proceed as follows:
  a. Align keyway in hub with axle shaft key and slide hub onto shaft as far as possible.
  b. Lubricate two thrust washers with liberal amount of chassis grease and install washers on axle shaft.
  c. Install axle shaft nut, then the brake drum, drum retaining screws and wheel assembly.
  d. Lower vehicle to ground, then tighten axle shaft nut until distance from hub outer face to axle shaft outer end is 1 5/16 inches, **Fig. 3.**
  e. Remove axle shaft nut and one

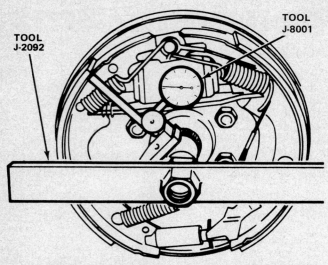

Fig. 2   Measuring axle shaft endplay

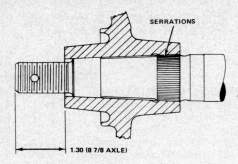

**Fig. 3   Replacement hub installation measurement. Semi-floating axle w/tapered shaft**

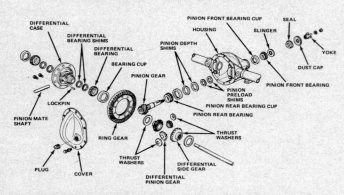

Fig. 4   Semi-floating flanged axle shaft

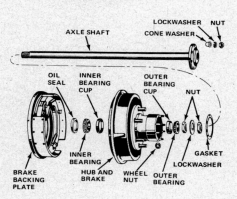

**Fig. 5   Full-floating axle with wheel bearing**

thrust washer.

f. Install axle shaft nut and torque to 250 ft. lbs.

g. Install new cotter pin. If cotter pin hole is not aligned, tighten nut to next castellation, do not loosen nut to align cotter pin hole.

## SEMI-FLOATING FLANGED SHAFT

1. Raise and support vehicle.
2. Remove remove rear wheels.
3. Remove brake drum, **Fig. 4.**
4. Remove axle retainer nuts using access hole in axle shaft flange.
5. Remove axle shaft from housing using suitable slide hammer. Remove bearing cup from housing.
6. Remove oil seal from housing bore, clean bore and install new seal.
7. To remove bearing, drill 1/4 inch hole in retainer ring. Hole depth should be 3/4 of the ring thickness. Do not allow drill to contact axle shaft.
8. Use a large chisel to split the retaining ring, then remove retaining ring. Ensure care is taken not to damage axle shaft.
9. Using suitable press, remove bearing

from axle shaft.

10. Remove retainer plate and seal.
11. When installing new bearing, pack bearing with wheel bearing grease and install with cup rib ring facing axle flange.
12. Lubricate outer diameter of bearing cup and install axle shaft and bearing assembly into axle housing using care not to damage oil seal.
13. Install axle shaft retainer and backing plate to housing. Torque retainer nuts to 30 ft. lbs.
14. Install cup plug into axle flange hole if required.
15. Install brake drum and wheel. Lower vehicle.

## FULL-FLOATING

It is not necessary to remove rear wheels to facilitate axle shaft replacement.

1. Remove axle flange nuts, lockwashers, and split washers retaining axle shaft flange.
2. Remove axle shaft from housing, **Fig. 5.**
3. If wheel bearings are to be replaced, proceed as follows:
   a. Bend lip of lockwasher and remove

locknut and lockwasher.

b. Raise and support vehicle.
c. Remove adjusting nut, outer wheel bearing and pull the wheel straight off the axle.
d. Service wheel bearings as required.
e. Reverse procedure to install, then adjust wheel bearings as described in "Wheel Bearings, Adjust."
4. Install new gasket on hub.
5. Install axle shaft and tighten nuts securely. It may be necessary to rotate wheel hub to align axle shaft splines with differential splines.

## WHEEL BEARING
## ADJUST
### FULL-FLOATING AXLE

1. Remove axle shaft as described in "Axle Shaft, Remove."
2. Straighten lip of lockwasher and remove locknut and lockwasher.
3. Raise and support vehicle.
4. Rotate wheel and torque adjusting nut to 50 ft. lbs. to seat bearings. Back off nut 1/6 turn or until wheel rotates freely without lateral movement.
5. Install locknut, torquing to 50 ft. lbs., and bend over lockwasher lip.

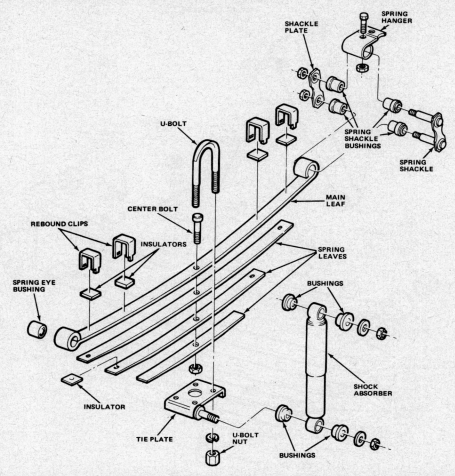

**Fig. 6  Rear spring & shock absorber assembly (Typical). Models w/ spring mounted below axle**

## REAR AXLE
### REPLACE

#### J-10 & 20 TRUCK, 1980–83 CHEROKEE, CJ, SCRAMBLER & WAGONEER, 1980–86 GRAND WAGONEER

1. Raise and support vehicle.
2. Remove rear wheels.
3. Scribe alignment marks on propeller shaft and axle for proper assembly, then disconnect propeller shaft from axle.
4. Disconnect shock absorbers at axle tubes.
5. Disconnect hydraulic brake hose at rear axle T-fitting, taping ends of hose and fitting.
6. Disconnect parking brake cable at equalizer.
7. Support axle with suitable jack.
8. Remove U-bolts and, on vehicles with spring mounted above axle, disconnect spring at rear shackle, then slide axle from under vehicle.
9. Reverse procedure to install.

#### 1984–86 CJ & 1984–85 SCRAMBLER

1. Apply parking brake and place manual transmission in 1st gear, or automatic transmission in Park.
2. Remove and discard cotter pins, then remove axle shaft nuts.
3. Raise and support rear of vehicle and remove rear wheels.
4. Remove brake drum retaining screws, then release parking brake and remove brake drums.
5. Using suitable puller, remove axle hub.
6. Disconnect brake lines at wheel cylinders, then remove support plates, oil seals and retainers and the endplay shims.
7. Using suitable tool, remove axle shafts.
8. Remove axle housing cover and drain lubricant, then reinstall cover.
9. Disconnect parking brake cables at equalizer.
10. Scribe alignment marks on propeller shaft and axle yokes for proper assembly, then disconnect propeller shaft at axle yoke.
11. Disconnect flexible brake hose at

body floor pan bracket, then the vent hose at the axle tube.
12. Support rear axle with suitable jack.
13. Disconnect shock absorbers at spring tie plates.
14. Remove spring U-bolts, spring plates and spring clip plate, if equipped.
15. Lower jack and remove axle.
16. Reverse procedure to install.

#### 1987–89 GRAND WAGONEER & WRANGLER

1. Raise and support vehicle.
2. Remove rear wheels.
3. Scribe alignment marks on propeller shaft and axle for proper assembly, then disconnect propeller shaft from axle.
4. Disconnect the track bar from axle mounting bracket.
5. Disconnect parking brake cable at equalizer.
6. Disconnect shock absorbers at axle tubes.
7. Disconnect hydraulic brake hose at rear axle Tee-fitting, then tape ends of hose and fitting to prevent contamination.
8. Disconnect axle vent tube from axle.

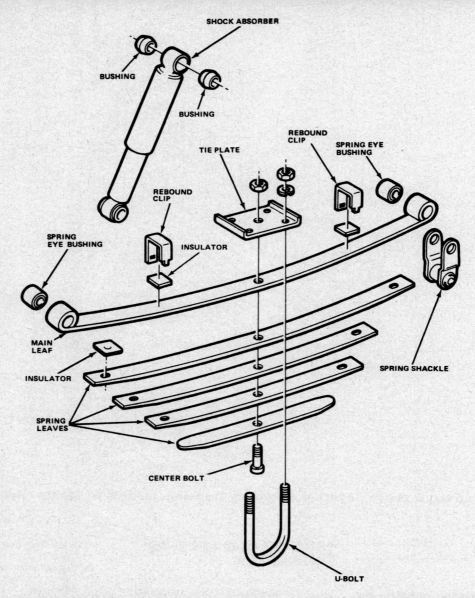

**Fig. 7   Rear spring & shock absorber assembly (Typical). Models w/spring mounted above axle**

9. Remove U-bolts and tie plates.
10. Loosen spring mounting bolts.
11. Support axle with suitable jack.
12. Remove spring-to-shackle attaching bolts and lower spring to the floor.
13. Remove axle assembly.
14. Reverse procedure to install.

## SHOCK ABSORBER REPLACE

1. Raise and support vehicle.
2. Position a suitable jack under axle assembly, then raise axle slightly.
3. Remove washers and locknuts attaching shock absorber to upper and lower mounting pins.
4. Remove shock absorber and bush-

ings from shock mounting eyes, **Figs. 6 and 7.**
5. Reverse procedure to install.

## LEAF SPRING REPLACE

### LEAF SPRING MOUNTED BELOW AXLE

1. Disconnect battery ground cable.
2. Raise and support vehicle.
3. Position a suitable jack under axle, then raise axle slightly.
4. Remove tie plate U-bolts, **Fig. 6.**
5. Remove bolt attaching spring rear eye to shackle.
6. Remove bolt attaching spring front

eye to frame mounting bracket.
7. Remove spring from vehicle.
8. Reverse procedure to install.

### LEAF SPRING MOUNTED ABOVE AXLE

1. Raise and support vehicle.
2. If left side leaf spring requires service, remove fuel tank skid plate, if necessary.
3. Position a suitable jack under axle, then raise axle slightly.
4. Disconnect shock absorber from mounting bracket.
5. Remove wheel assembly.
6. Remove tie plate U-bolts and tie plate.
7. Remove bolt attaching spring rear eye to shackle.

8. Remove bolt attaching spring front eye to frame rail bracket.
9. Remove spring from vehicle.
10. Reverse procedure to install.

## TRACK BAR
### REPLACE
#### GRAND WAGONEER & WRANGLER

1. Raise and support rear of vehicle.
2. Remove nut and bolt attaching track bar to frame rail bracket.
3. Remove bolt and nut attaching track bar to axle bracket, then remove track bar.
4. Reverse procedure to install. Torque track bar attaching bolts to 74 ft. lbs. on 1987-88 Wrangler models and 105 ft. lbs. on 1989 Grand Wagoneer and Wrangler models.

## DRUM BRAKE
### ADJUST

Two different rear drum brake designs are used. They are similar in construction and operation but differ in method of automatic adjustment. Rear drum brakes on CJ, Scrambler and Wrangler models have cable operated automatic adjusters while rear drum brakes on Grand Wagoneer J-10 and 20 Truck and 1980-83 Cherokee and Wagoneer models have linkage operated automatic adjusters. If the rear brakes are serviced, an initial adjustment must be performed before installing brake drums.
1. Remove access slot covers from brake support plates.
2. Using brake adjusting tool, rotate adjusting screw clockwise direction until brakes are locked.

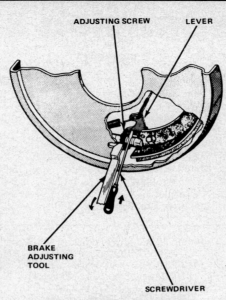

Fig. 8  Brake adjustment

3. Rotate brake adjuster screw counter-clockwise until wheel turns freely, **Fig. 8.** The automatic adjuster lever must be disengaged from the adjuster screw before screw can be turned.
4. Road test vehicle and apply 10-15 firm stops in reverse, applying one forward stop between each reverse stop to equalize adjustment.

## PARKING BRAKE
### ADJUST

Adjust service brakes before adjusting parking brake.
1. Release parking brakes.

2. Loosen equalizer locknuts, then adjustment nuts to release tension on cables.
3. Check cables for wear or damage. Replace damaged cables.
4. Tighten equalizer adjustment nuts until a slight drag is obtained at wheels.
5. Loosen equalizer adjustment nuts until wheel turns freely and brake drag is eliminated.
6. Tighten equalizer locknuts.

## BRAKE MASTER CYLINDER
### REPLACE

1. Disconnect brake lines from master cylinder. Cap lines and master cylinder ports.
2. On models with manual brakes, disconnect master cylinder pushrod at brake pedal.
3. On all models, remove nuts or bolts attaching master cylinder to dash panel or brake booster and remove master cylinder.
4. Reverse procedure to install.
5. Bleed the brake system.

## POWER BRAKE UNIT
### REPLACE

1. Disconnect booster pushrod from brake pedal.
2. Remove vacuum hose from check valve.
3. Remove nuts and washers securing master cylinder to booster unit, then separate master cylinder from booster unit. Do not disconnect brake lines from master cylinder.
4. Remove booster unit to firewall attaching nuts and remove booster unit.
5. Reverse procedure to install.

# Front Suspension & Steering

## INDEX

## CAMBER & CASTER

Camber is set into the axle assembly at time of manufacture and cannot be adjusted.

Caster may be adjusted by installing new front end components or caster shims between the axle pad and the springs.

## TOE-IN
### ADJUST

Position the wheels to a true straight ahead position with the steering gear also in a straight ahead driving position. Then turn both tie rod adjusting sleeves an equal amount until the desired toe-in setting is obtained.

## WHEEL BEARINGS
### REPLACE & ADJUST

Refer to "Front Wheel Drive" section under "Axle Shaft, Replace" for wheel bearing replacement and adjustment procedure.

## STEERING KNUCKLE
### REPLACE
#### EXC. WRANGLER
**Removal**

1. Remove axle shaft as described in "Front Wheel Drive" section under "Axle Shaft, Replace."
2. Disconnect tie rod from knuckle arm.
3. Remove lower ball stud jam nut and discard, Fig. 1. Loosen upper ball stud nut until top of nut is flush with top of stud.
4. Unseat ball studs using suitable hammer. Remove upper ball stud nut and steering knuckle.
5. Remove upper ball stud split ring seat using suitable nut wrench.

**Installation**

1. Install upper ball split ring seat until top of seat is flush with top of yoke.
2. Install steering knuckle on yoke, then a new lower ball stud jam nut finger tight.

3. On 1980 models position Nut Wrench J-25158, Button J-25211-3, Plate J-25211-3 and Puller J-25215. On 1981-88 models, position Nut Wrench J-23447, Button J-25211-3, Plate J-25211-1 and Puller J-25212 as shown, Fig. 2.
4. Tighten puller screw until lower ball stud is held firmly seated. Torque jam nut to 85 ft. lbs. on CJ and Scrambler models, and 75 ft. lbs. on all other models. Remove puller and plate.
5. Torque upper ball stud split ring seat to 50 ft. lbs.
6. Install upper ball stud nut and torque to 100 ft. lbs. Install cotter pin.
7. Install tie rod to steering knuckle. Torque tie rod end nuts to 50 ft. lbs.
8. Install axle shaft as described in "Front Wheel Drive" section under "Axle Shaft, Replace."

### WRANGLER
#### Removal

1. Remove axle shaft as described in "Front Wheel Drive" section under "Axle Shaft, Replace."
2. Remove caliper anchor plate from steering knuckle.
3. Remove upper and lower ball joint nuts.
4. Unseat ball studs using suitable hammer, then remove steering knuckle.
5. Remove ball stud split ring seat using seat removal tool J23447.

#### Installation

1. Install split ring seat to a depth of .206 inch in bottom ball joint bore of steering knuckle. Measure depth from notched end of seat to machined lower surface of steering knuckle joint bore, Fig. 3.
2. Install steering knuckle on ball studs, then torque retaining nuts to 75 ft. lbs.
3. Install caliper anchor plate and torque retaining bolt to 77 ft. lbs.
4. Install axle shaft as described in "Front Wheel Drive" section under "Axle Shaft, Replace."

## BALL STUDS
### REPLACE

1. Remove steering knuckle as de-

scribed in "Steering Knuckle, Replace."
2. Remove lower ball stud snap ring, if equipped.
3. Using suitable tools, press lower and upper ball studs from steering knuckle.
4. Reverse procedure to install. Install a new replacement snap ring on the lower ball stud, if equipped.

## BALL STUD PRELOAD MEASUREMENT
### EXC. WRANGLER

Ball stud preload is measured when vehicle exhibits high steering effort or slow return of the steering mechanism after turns. If this condition occurs and all other items affecting steering effort are normal, ball stud preload should be checked.

1. Raise and support vehicle.
2. Remove front wheels, then disconnect steering damper at tie rod if equipped.
3. Unlock steering column. Disconnect steering connecting rod at right side of steering knuckle on CJ and Scrambler models; and on all other models, at right side of tie rod.
4. Remove cotter pin and nut attaching tie rod to right side steering knuckle.
5. Rotate both steering knuckles completely several times, working from right side of vehicle.
6. Assemble a socket and 0-50 ft. lb. torque wrench onto right tie rod attaching nut. Torque wrench must be positioned parallel with the steering knuckle arm on 1980 vehicles, or perpendicular to arm on 1981-88 vehicles.
7. Rotate steering knuckles slowly and steadily through a complete arc and measure torque required to rotate knuckles.
   a. If reading is less than 25 ft. lbs., turning effort at knuckles is normal. Check other steering components for defects or binding.
   b. If reading is greater than 25 ft. lbs., proceed to step 8.
8. Disconnect tie rod from both steering knuckles. Install a 1/2 x 1 inch bolt, flat washer and nut in tie rod mounting

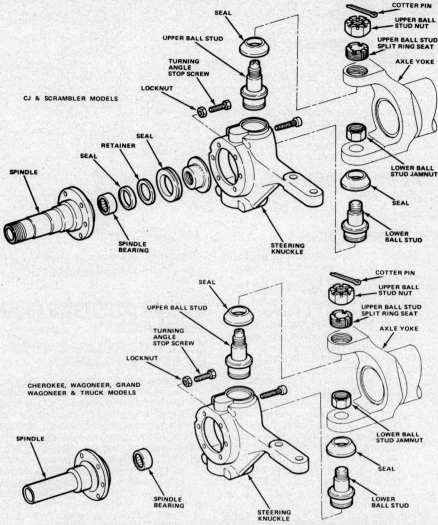

**Fig. 1 Exploded view of steering knuckle & components**

11. Install front axle shafts and steering spindles loosely and measure turning effort of each steering knuckle as described in "Ball Stud Preload, Measurement."
    a. If turning effort is less than 10 ft. lbs., proceed to next step.
    b. If turning effort is more than 10 ft. lbs., replace upper and lower ball studs as described in "Ball Studs, Replace."
12. Install front axle shafts and connect tie rod to steering knuckle arms. Torque tie rod end retaining nuts to 45 ft. lbs.
13. Attach connecting rod to tie rod. Torque connecting rod nut to 60 ft. lbs. on CJ and Scrambler models; and 75 ft. lbs. on all other models. Install steering damper if equipped.
14. Install front wheels and lower vehicle.

## SHOCK ABSORBER
### REPLACE
### EXC. WRANGLER

1. Raise and support vehicle.
2. Position a suitable jack under axle assembly, then raise axle slightly.
3. Remove washers and locknuts attaching shock absorber to upper and lower mounting pins.
4. Remove shock absorber and bushings from shock mounting eyes
5. Reverse procedure to install.

### WRANGLER

1. Remove nut and washer from upper shock absorber mounting.
2. Raise and support vehicle.
3. Remove lower shock absorber mounting bolt and shock absorber.
4. Reverse procedure to install. Torque shock absorber mounting nut to 8 ft. lbs. and lower mounting bolt to 45 ft. lbs.

## LEAF SPRING
### REPLACE
### GRAND WAGONEER

1. Raise and support vehicle.
2. Using suitable jack, raise front axle just enough to relieve weight from springs.
3. Disconnect stabilizer bar link from spring bracket, then remove spring U-bolts and brackets.
4. Remove bolt attaching front of spring to front shackle.
5. Remove bolt attaching rear of spring to frame, then remove spring.
6. Reverse procedure to install, noting the following:
    a. When installing spring, do not tighten front and rear spring eye mounting bolts until after vehicle has been lowered.
    b. Torque U-bolt nuts to 100 ft. lbs.
    c. Torque front spring shackle bolt to 100 ft. lbs.
    d. Torque spring to frame bracket bolt to 100 ft. lbs.
    e. Torque stabilizer bar connecting link to 55 ft. lbs.

hole in each of the steering knuckles.
9. Measure torque required to rotate each steering knuckle as described previously.
    a. If torque is less than 10 ft. lbs., steering effort is within specifications.
    b. If torque is more than 10 ft. lbs., perform "Ball Stud Preload, Adjust" procedure.
10. If both steering knuckles are within specification, check for damaged or tight tie rod ends.

## BALL STUD PRELOAD
### ADJUST
### EXC. WRANGLER

1. Remove front axle shafts as described in "Front Wheel Drive" section under "Axle Shaft, Replace."
2. Loosen lower ball stud jam nut, then remove upper ball stud nut.
3. Unseat ball studs from yoke using suitable hammer.

4. Remove upper ball stud split ring seat and discard.
5. Remove lower ball stud jam nut and steering knuckle. Discard jam nut.
6. Clean upper ball stud split ring seat threads, lower ball stud taper in steering knuckle, threads and tapered surfaces of ball studs, and upper ball stud retaining nut threads.
7. Position steering knuckle on axle and install a new lower ball stud jam nut finger tight.
8. Install upper ball stud nut and torque 10-20 ft. lbs. to draw upper ball stud into yoke. Do not install upper ball stud split ring seat at this time.
9. Torque lower ball stud jam nut to 80 ft. lbs.
10. Remove upper ball stud nut and install a new split ring seat. Torque split ring seat to 50 ft. lbs. Install upper ball stud nut and torque to 100 ft. lbs. Align and install cotter pin. Do not loosen nut to align cotter pin holes. Tighten only enough to align the holes and install cotter pin.

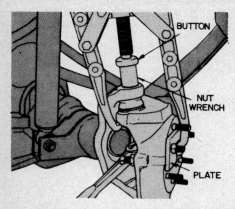

**Fig. 2  Steering knuckle installation tools**

## WRANGLER

1. Raise and support vehicle.
2. Remove wheel and tire assembly, then raise front axle just enough to relieve weight from springs.
3. Loosen stabilizer bar link nut, then remove spring U-bolts.
4. Position spring tie plates aside, then remove bolt attaching front of spring to front shackle.
5. Remove bolt attaching rear of spring to frame, then remove spring.
6. Reverse procedure to install. When installing spring, do not tighten front and rear spring eye mounting bolts until after vehicle has been lowered. Torque U-bolt nuts to 90 ft. lbs. Torque front spring shackle bolt to 95 ft. lbs. Torque spring to frame bracket bolt to 105 ft. lbs.

## STABILIZER BAR
### REPLACE
### WRANGLER

1. Raise and support vehicle.
2. Remove bolts attaching stabilizer bar to links.
3. Remove stabilizer bar mounting bracket to frame rail and steering gear bracket attaching bolts, then remove stabilizer bar.
4. Reverse procedure to install. Torque stabilizer bar mounting bracket bolts to 30 ft. lbs. Torque stabilizer bar link bolts to 45 ft. lbs.

### GRAND WAGONEER

1. Raise and support vehicle.
2. Remove stabilizer bar-to-link attaching bolts.
3. Remove stabilizer bar mounting bracket-to-frame rail attaching bolts, then remove stabilizer bar.
4. Reverse procedure to install. Torque stabilizer bar mounting bracket bolts to 35 ft. lbs. Torque stabilizer bar link bolts to 55 ft. lbs.

## TRACK BAR
### REPLACE
### GRAND WAGONEER & WRANGLER

1. Raise and support front of vehicle.
2. Remove nut and bolt attaching track bar to frame side rail.
3. Remove bolt and nut attaching track bar to axle bracket, then remove track bar.
4. Reverse procedure to install. Torque track bar attaching bolts to 74 ft. lbs.

## MANUAL STEERING GEAR
### REPLACE
### EXC. WRANGLER

1. Remove intermediate shaft to worm shaft coupling clamp bolt and disconnect intermediate shaft.
2. Remove pitman arm nut and lock washer, then separate pitman arm from steering gear shaft using a puller.
3. On all except CJ models, remove steering gear to frame bolts and remove steering gear.
4. On CJ and Scrambler models:
   a. Slightly raise left side of vehicle to relieve tension on left front spring, then place support stand under frame.
   b. Remove steering gear lower bracket to frame bolts.
   c. Remove steering gear upper bracket to crossmember bolts and remove gear.
   d. Remove bolts attaching upper bracket to tie plate and lower bracket to steering gear and remove brackets.
5. Reverse procedure to install. Apply Loctite 271 or equivalent to the steering gear to frame bolts, the bracket to gear bolts and the bracket to tie plate bolt. Torque steering gear to frame bolts and bracket to gear bolts to 70 ft. lbs., the bracket to tie plate bolt to 55 ft. lbs., the coupling pinch bolt and nut to 45 ft. lbs., and pitman arm nut to 185 ft. lbs. If there is a slightly rough feel after the steering gear is installed, turn the steering wheel completely to the left and then to the right for 10 to 15 complete cycles.

### WRANGLER

1. Disconnect intermediate shaft from steering gear.
2. Raise and support vehicle.
3. Disconnect center link from pitman arm, then remove front stabilizer bar.
4. Place align marks on pitman arm and shaft, then remove pitman arm using tool No. J-6632-01.
5. Remove steering gear attaching bolts and steering gear.
6. Reverse procedure to install. Torque steering gear to frame bolts to 75 ft. lbs. Torque pitman arm to steering gear nut to 185 ft. lbs. and stake in two places.

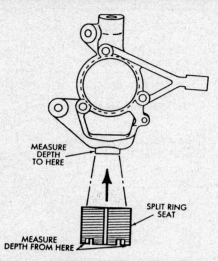

**Fig. 3  Ball stud split ring installation**

## POWER STEERING GEAR
### REPLACE
### EXC. WRANGLER & 1989 GRAND WAGONEER

1. Disconnect lines from gear. Plug lines to prevent entry of dirt and keep lines raised to avoid excessive fluid loss.
2. On all except CJ and Scrambler models, remove clamp bolt and nut attaching flex coupling to steering gear shaft and disconnect intermediate shaft.
3. On CJ and Scrambler models, remove clamp bolt and nut attaching intermediate shaft coupling to steering gear shaft and disconnect intermediate shaft.
4. Paint alignment marks on pitman shaft and pitman arm for assembly reference, then remove and discard the pitman arm nut and lockwasher. Use new nut and lockwasher.
5. Remove pitman using a puller.
6. On all except CJ and Scrambler models, remove steering gear to frame mounting bolts and remove steering gear.
7. On CJ and Scrambler models:
   a. Raise left side of vehicle to relieve tension on left front spring and place support stand under the frame.
   b. Remove the three lower steering gear mounting brackets to frame bolts.
   c. Remove the two upper steering gear mounting brackets to crossmember bolts and remove steering gear and mounting brackets.
   d. Remove mounting bracket to gear attaching bolts and remove upper and lower mounting brackets from steering gear.
8. Reverse procedure to install. Apply Loctite 271 or equivalent to mounting bracket to steering gear bolts and to steering gear to frame bolts. Torque steering gear to frame bolts to 75 ft.

lbs. on all except CJ and Scrambler models, and 55 ft. lbs. on CJ and Scrambler models, the mounting bracket to steering gear bolts to 70 ft. lbs., the flex coupling clamp bolt to 30 ft. lbs., the intermediate shaft coupling to steering gear bolt to 45 lbs. and the pitman arm nut to 185 ft. lbs.

## GRAND WAGONEER & WRANGLER

1. Position front wheels straight ahead.

2. Disconnect lines from gear. Plug lines to prevent entry of dirt and keep lines raised to avoid excessive fluid loss.
3. Remove clamp bolt and nut attaching flex coupling to steering gear shaft and disconnect intermediate shaft.
4. Raise and support vehicle.
5. Disconnect drag link from pitman arm.
6. Remove front stabilizer bar, if necessary.
7. Paint alignment marks on pitman shaft and pitman arm for assembly reference, then remove the pitman arm nut and lockwasher.

8. Remove pitman arm using a suitable puller.
9. Remove steering gear to frame mounting bolts, then the steering gear.
10. Reverse procedure to install, noting the following:
   a. Torque steering gear to frame bolts to 65 ft. lbs.
   b. Torque intermediate shaft coupling to steering gear bolt to 33 ft. lbs.
   c. Torque pitman arm nut to 185 ft. lbs.
   d. Torque drag link retaining nut to 60 ft. lbs.

# Front Wheel Drive

## INDEX

## AXLE SHAFT REPLACE

### MODELS LESS SELEC-TRAC EXC. CJ, SCRAMBLER & WRANGLER

1. Raise and support vehicle.
2. Remove disc brake caliper(s).
3. On models less front hubs, remove rotor hub cap, then the axle shaft snap ring, drive gear, pressure spring and spring retainer, **Fig. 1.**
4. On models with front hubs, proceed as follows:
   a. Remove socket head screws from hub body, then remove the body and large retaining ring.
   b. Remove small retaining ring from axle shaft.
   c. Remove hub clutch assembly from axle.
5. On all models, remove outer locknut, washer and inner locknut.
6. Remove rotor. The spring retainer and outer bearing are removed with the rotor.
7. Remove nuts and bolts attaching spindle and support shield and remove spindle and shield, tapping spindle with suitable mallet as necessary to remove it from knuckle.
8. Remove axle shaft.
9. Reverse procedure to install. Torque inner wheel bearing adjusting nut to 50 ft. lbs. while rotating wheel to seat bearings, then back off nut 1/6 turn. Turn inner adjusting locknut until peg engages nearest hole in lockwasher. Install outer locknut and torque to 50 ft. lbs. Torque socket head screws to 30 inch lbs. Install spring retainer with cupped side facing toward center of vehicle.

## MODELS w/SELEC-TRAC

### Exc. 1989 Models

To remove right side axle shaft refer to "Models Less Selec-Trac, Except CJ & Scrambler" for procedure. To remove left side axle shaft refer to "Models Less Selec-Trac, Except CJ & Scrambler" steps 1-8, then use following procedure.

1. Disconnect vacuum hoses from axle shift motor, then loosen axle housing cover bolts, allowing lubricant to drain from housing.
2. Remove axle housing cover and shift motor as an assembly, **Fig. 2.**
3. Remove retaining clip from inner axle shaft, then, using a suitable magnet remove inner axle shaft from axle tube. Remove shift collar from housing, **Fig. 3.**
4. Remove outer axle shaft bearing and seal using Tool J-26941 and J2619-01, **Fig. 4.**
5. Reverse procedure to install. Torque inner wheel bearing adjusting nut to 50 ft. lbs. while rotating wheel to seat bearings, then back nut off 1/6 turn. Install lockwasher with inner tab aligned with keyway in spindle. Turn inner adjusting nut until the peg engages nearest hole in lockwasher. Install outer locknut and torque to 50 ft. lbs. Install spring retainer with cupped side facing toward center of vehicle.

### 1989 Models

1. Raise and support vehicle.
2. Remove disc brake caliper(s).
3. Remove rotor hub cap, then the axle shaft snap ring, drive gear, pressure spring and spring retainer, **Fig. 1.**
4. Remove outer locknut, washer and inner locknut.
5. Remove rotor. The spring retainer and

outer bearing are removed with the rotor.
6. Remove nuts and bolts attaching spindle and support shield, then remove spindle and shield, tapping spindle with suitable mallet as necessary.
7. Remove axle shaft.
8. Reverse procedure to install. Torque inner wheel bearing adjusting nut to 50 ft. lbs. while rotating wheel to seat bearings, then back off nut 1/6 turn. Turn inner adjusting locknut until peg engages nearest hole in lockwasher. Install outer locknut and torque to 50 ft. lbs.

## CJ & SCRAMBLER MODELS

1. Raise and support vehicle.
2. Remove wheel, then the brake caliper.
3. Remove hub cap and drive flange snap ring, **Fig. 1.**
4. Remove rotor hub bolts, hub cover and gasket.
5. Remove axle flange.
6. Straighten lip of lockwasher and remove outer nut, lockwasher, inner adjusting nut and bearing lockwasher.
7. Remove outer bearing and drum/rotor assembly. Do not damage oil seal.
8. Remove brake support plate or caliper adapter and splash shield as equipped.
9. Remove spindle and spindle bearing, then slide out axle shaft assembly.
10. Reverse procedure to install. Torque inner adjusting nut to 50 ft. lbs. while rotating hub to seat bearings, then back off adjusting nut 1/6 turn. Install outer lockwasher and locknut. Torque locknut to 50 ft. lbs. and bend lip of washer over nut. Torque hub body bolts to 30 ft. lbs.

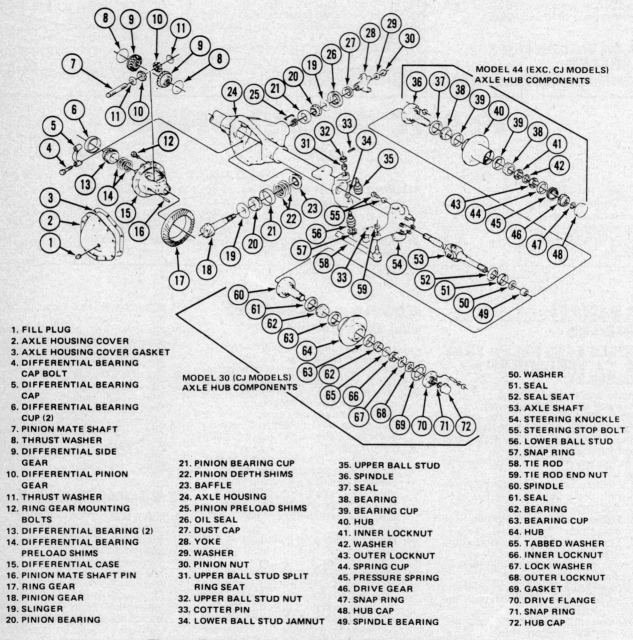

**Fig. 1   Front axle assembly. Open knuckle type**

MODEL 44 (EXC. CJ MODELS) AXLE HUB COMPONENTS

MODEL 30 (CJ MODELS) AXLE HUB COMPONENTS

1. FILL PLUG
2. AXLE HOUSING COVER
3. AXLE HOUSING COVER GASKET
4. DIFFERENTIAL BEARING CAP BOLT
5. DIFFERENTIAL BEARING CAP
6. DIFFERENTIAL BEARING CUP (2)
7. PINION MATE SHAFT
8. THRUST WASHER
9. DIFFERENTIAL SIDE GEAR
10. DIFFERENTIAL PINION GEAR
11. THRUST WASHER
12. RING GEAR MOUNTING BOLTS
13. DIFFERENTIAL BEARING (2)
14. DIFFERENTIAL BEARING PRELOAD SHIMS
15. DIFFERENTIAL CASE
16. PINION MATE SHAFT PIN
17. RING GEAR
18. PINION GEAR
19. SLINGER
20. PINION BEARING

21. PINION BEARING CUP
22. PINION DEPTH SHIMS
23. BAFFLE
24. AXLE HOUSING
25. PINION PRELOAD SHIMS
26. OIL SEAL
27. DUST CAP
28. YOKE
29. WASHER
30. PINION NUT
31. UPPER BALL STUD SPLIT RING SEAT
32. UPPER BALL STUD NUT
33. COTTER PIN
34. LOWER BALL STUD JAMNUT

35. UPPER BALL STUD
36. SPINDLE
37. SEAL
38. BEARING
39. BEARING CUP
40. HUB
41. INNER LOCKNUT
42. WASHER
43. OUTER LOCKNUT
44. SPRING CUP
45. PRESSURE SPRING
46. DRIVE GEAR
47. SNAP RING
48. HUB CAP
49. SPINDLE BEARING

50. WASHER
51. SEAL
52. SEAL SEAT
53. AXLE SHAFT
54. STEERING KNUCKLE
55. STEERING STOP BOLT
56. LOWER BALL STUD
57. SNAP RING
58. TIE ROD
59. TIE ROD END NUT
60. SPINDLE
61. SEAL
62. BEARING
63. BEARING CUP
64. HUB
65. TABBED WASHER
66. INNER LOCKNUT
67. LOCK WASHER
68. OUTER LOCKNUT
69. GASKET
70. DRIVE FLANGE
71. SNAP RING
72. HUB CAP

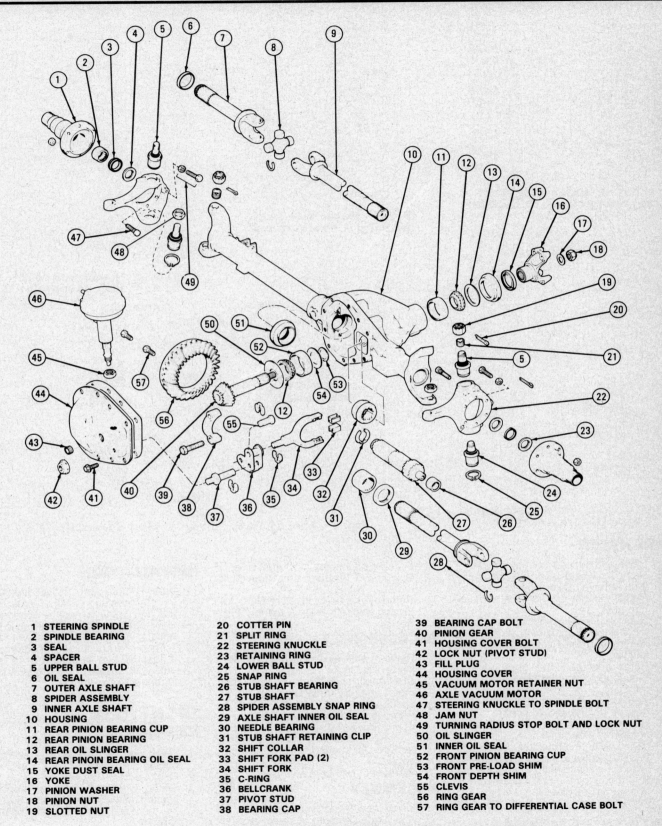

| | | |
|---|---|---|
| 1 STEERING SPINDLE | 20 COTTER PIN | 39 BEARING CAP BOLT |
| 2 SPINDLE BEARING | 21 SPLIT RING | 40 PINION GEAR |
| 3 SEAL | 22 STEERING KNUCKLE | 41 HOUSING COVER BOLT |
| 4 SPACER | 23 RETAINING RING | 42 LOCK NUT (PIVOT STUD) |
| 5 UPPER BALL STUD | 24 LOWER BALL STUD | 43 FILL PLUG |
| 6 OIL SEAL | 25 SNAP RING | 44 HOUSING COVER |
| 7 OUTER AXLE SHAFT | 26 STUB SHAFT BEARING | 45 VACUUM MOTOR RETAINER NUT |
| 8 SPIDER ASSEMBLY | 27 STUB SHAFT | 46 AXLE VACUUM MOTOR |
| 9 INNER AXLE SHAFT | 28 SPIDER ASSEMBLY SNAP RING | 47 STEERING KNUCKLE TO SPINDLE BOLT |
| 10 HOUSING | 29 AXLE SHAFT INNER OIL SEAL | 48 JAM NUT |
| 11 REAR PINION BEARING CUP | 30 NEEDLE BEARING | 49 TURNING RADIUS STOP BOLT AND LOCK NUT |
| 12 REAR PINION BEARING | 31 STUB SHAFT RETAINING CLIP | 50 OIL SLINGER |
| 13 REAR OIL SLINGER | 32 SHIFT COLLAR | 51 INNER OIL SEAL |
| 14 REAR PINION BEARING OIL SEAL | 33 SHIFT FORK PAD (2) | 52 FRONT PINION BEARING CUP |
| 15 YOKE DUST SEAL | 34 SHIFT FORK | 53 FRONT PRE-LOAD SHIM |
| 16 YOKE | 35 C-RING | 54 FRONT DEPTH SHIM |
| 17 PINION WASHER | 36 BELLCRANK | 55 CLEVIS |
| 18 PINION NUT | 37 PIVOT STUD | 56 RING GEAR |
| 19 SLOTTED NUT | 38 BEARING CAP | 57 RING GEAR TO DIFFERENTIAL CASE BOLT |

**Fig. 2   Selec-Trac front axle assembly. Open knuckle type**

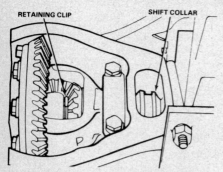

**Fig. 3   Inner axle shaft retaining clip & shift collar**

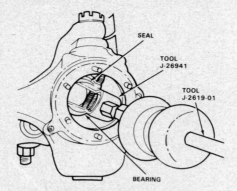

**Fig. 4   Outer axle shaft bearing & seal removal**

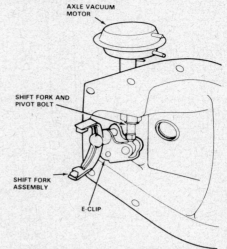

**Fig. 5   Axle vacuum motor & shift fork assembly**

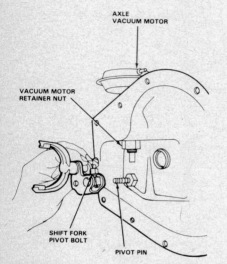

**Fig. 6   Removal & installation of shift fork assembly**

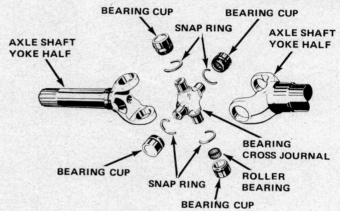

**Fig. 7   Axle shaft & universal joint assembly**

## WRANGLER

1. Raise and support front of vehicle.
2. Remove wheel and tire assembly, then remove brake caliper and rotor.
3. Remove cotter pin, nut lock and axle hub nut.
4. Remove steering knuckle-to-hub attaching bolts, then remove hub assembly and rotor splash shield from knuckle.
5. Remove left hand axle shaft.
6. Disconnect vacuum hoses from shift motor.
7. Remove shift motor from axle, then remove righthand axle shaft.
8. Reverse procedure to install. Ensure righthand axle shaft is properly engaged with intermediate shaft and that shift collar is properly positioned. When installing shift motor, ensure shift fork engages shift collar, Torque hub to knuckle attaching bolts to 75 ft. lbs.

## AXLE SHIFT MOTOR SERVICE
### REMOVAL

1. Raise and support front of vehicle,

then drain lubricant from front axle.
2. Disconnect vacuum lines from shift motor.
3. Remove axle housing cover, shift motor and shift fork as an assembly, **Fig. 5.**

### DISASSEMBLY

1. Remove shift fork to pivot pin retaining E-clip, **Fig. 5.**
2. Disconnect shift fork pivot from shift motor shaft by threading pivot out of shaft.
3. Remove shift fork assembly from pivot pin, **Fig. 6.**
4. Remove shift motor retaining nut and remove shift motor from axle housing cover.
5. Remove O-ring from shift motor.

### ASSEMBLY

1. Install new O-ring on motor.
2. Apply small amount of sealer around shift motor mounting hole and install shift motor and retaining nut, **Fig. 5.**
3. Install shift fork assembly on pivot pin and thread shift fork pivot into shift motor shaft. Install E-clip on shift fork pivot pin, **Fig. 5.**

## INSTALLATION

1. Apply RTV sealant to axle cover sealing surfaces and install on axle. Shift fork and fork tabs must be engaged in shift collar before installing cover bolts.
2. Torque axle housing cover bolts to 20 ft. lbs. Fill axle to bottom of fill plug hole with suitable gear lubricant and reconnect vacuum lines.

## FRONT AXLE
### REPLACE

1. Raise and support vehicle at frame behind front springs.
2. Remove front wheels.
3. Scribe alignment marks on propeller shaft and axle yoke for proper assembly, then disconnect propeller shaft at axle yoke.
4. Disconnect connecting rod at steering knuckles.
5. Disconnect shock absorbers at axle housing.
6. Remove stabilizer bar connecting links to spring tie plates attaching

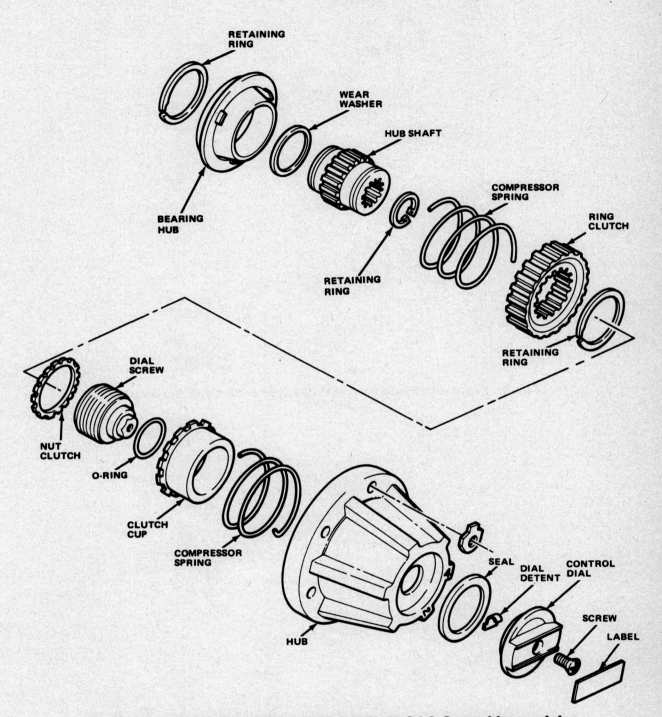

**Fig. 8   Front drive hub model M243. 1980–81 CJ & Scrambler models**

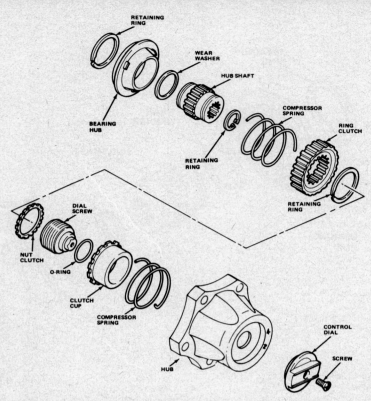

**Fig. 9   Front drive hub model M253. 1982–86 CJ & Scrambler models**

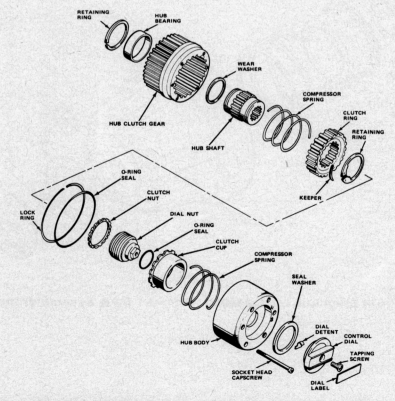

**Fig. 10   Front drive hub model M247. Cherokee, Wagoneer, Grand Wagoneer & all truck models**

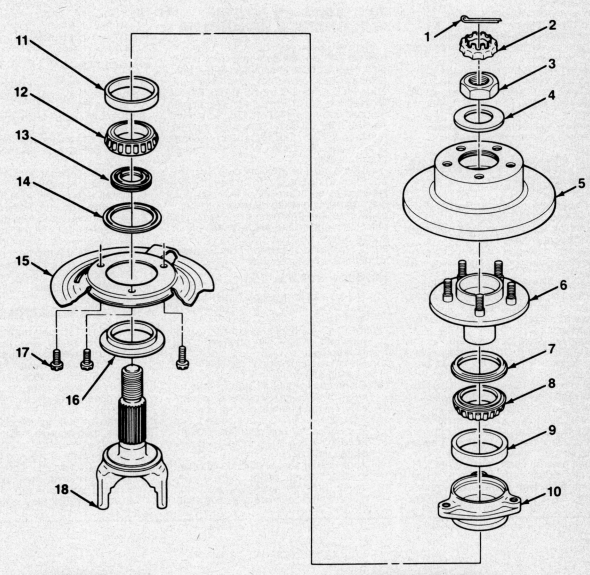

1. COTTER PIN
2. NUT RETAINER
3. NUT
4. WASHER
5. BRAKE ROTOR
6. HUB
7. OUTER BEARING SEAL
8. OUTER BEARING
9. OUTER BEARING RACE

10. BEARING CARRIER
11. INNER BEARING RACE
12. INNER BEARING
13. INNER BEARING SEAL
14. CARRIER SEAL
15. ROTOR SHIELD
16. AXLE SHAFT DUST SLINGER
17. BEARING CARRIER BOLTS
18. AXLE SHAFT

**Fig. 11   Front drive hub. Wrangler**

bolts, if equipped.

7. Disconnect breather tube at axle housing.
8. Disconnect stabilizer bar link bolts at spring clips.
9. Remove disc brake calipers, rotors and brake shields.
10. Remove U-bolts and tie plates.
11. Support axle assembly with suitable jack to relieve spring tension.
12. Loosen rear spring shackle to spring attaching bolts.
13. Remove front spring shackle to spring attaching bolts and lower spring to floor.
14. Remove axle from under vehicle.
15. Reverse procedure to install.

## AXLE SHAFT UNIVERSAL JOINT SERVICE

1. Remove axle shaft as described under "Axle Shaft, Replace."
2. Remove snap rings from universal joint bearing cups, **Fig. 7.**
3. Press on one end of bearing cup to remove opposite bearing cup from yoke half.
4. Press on exposed end of bearing cross journal and remove remaining bearing cup from yoke.
5. Repeat steps 3 and 4 for remaining bearing cups.
6. Clean universal joint components in a suitable solvent. Check parts for wear or damage. Replace damaged parts as required.
7. Pack bearing cups 1/3 full of suitable lubricant and install bearing rollers.
8. Install bearing cross journal.
9. Install bearing cups into axle shaft yoke halves. Ensure bearing cups are completely seated against bearing shoulders.
10. Install bearing cups onto journal.
11. Install bearing cup snap rings. If universal joint binds when assembled, gently tap on yoke to relieve tension

on bearing cups at each end of journal.

## FRONT DRIVE HUBS
### EXC. 1987–89 GRAND WAGONEER & WRANGLER

Manual front drive hubs are used on models 208 or 300 part-time front wheel drive transfer case assemblies only. Three different front drive hub assemblies are used. Hub assembly model M243, **Fig. 8,** is used on 1980-81 CJ and Scrambler models, hub model M253, **Fig. 9,** is used on 1982-86 CJ and Scrambler models, hub model M247, **Fig. 10,** is used on Cherokee, Wagoneer, Grand Wagoneer and all truck models.

All three hub assembly models are manually locked or unlocked. These hubs are serviced as an assembly or subassembly only. Do not attempt to disassemble these units. If an entire hub or subassembly is defective, replace the entire assembly or subassembly. The hubs may be removed for cleaning and inspection purposes and for periodic lubrication only.

### Models M243 & 253

1. Remove bolts and lock washers securing hub body to axle hub, **Figs. 8 and 9.**
2. Remove gasket and hub body. Do not turn hub control dial after removing hub body.
3. Remove retaining ring, hub clutch and bearing assembly.
4. Clean and inspect all components for wear or damage. Replace as necessary. Do not turn hub control dial until after hub control dial is installed. The hub clutch nut and cup can be damaged if dial is rotated while the hub is off the vehicle.
5. Apply a light coat of suitable lubricant to all hub components.
6. Install bearing assembly and hub clutch with retaining ring on axle shaft.

7. Install hub body and gasket. Install tabbed lockwashers and bolts into hub body and axle. Torque bolts to 30 ft. lbs.
8. Raise and support front of vehicle.
9. With dial in free position, rotate wheels. If wheels drag, check hub for correct installation.
10. Lower vehicle.

### Model M247

1. Remove socket head screws, axle hub retaining ring and axle shaft retaining ring.
2. Remove hub clutch assembly, **Fig. 10.**
3. Clean and inspect all components for wear or damage. Replace as necessary.
4. Apply a light coat of suitable lubricant to all hub components.
5. Install hub clutch, axle hub retaining ring and axle shaft retaining ring.
6. Install new O-ring into hub body and position into clutch. Install socket head screw and torque to 30 inch lbs.
7. Raise and support front of vehicle.
8. Turn dial to free position and rotate wheels. If wheels drag, check hub for correct installation.
9. Lower vehicle.

### 1987–89 WRANGLER

1. Raise and support front of vehicle.
2. Remove wheel and tire assembly, then remove brake caliper and suspend from frame with brake line attached using a piece of wire.
3. Remove brake rotor.
4. Remove cotter pin, lock and axle hub nut.
5. Remove hub to knuckle attaching bolts, then remove hub, **Fig. 11.**
6. Reverse procedure to install. Partially fill hub cavity of steering knuckle with chassis lubricant. Torque hub to steering knuckle attaching bolts to 75 ft. lbs. Torque hub nut to 175 ft. lbs., then install lock and cotter pin.

**NOTE:** Refer to rear of this manual for vehicle manufacturer's special service tool suppliers.

## GENERAL ENGINE SPECIFICATIONS

| Year | Engine CID ②/Liters | Carburetor | Bore & Stroke | Compression Ratio | Net H.P. @ R.P.M. | Maximum Torque Lbs. Ft. @ R.P.M. | Normal Oil Pressure Pounds |
|---|---|---|---|---|---|---|---|
| 1984-85 | 4-150/2.5L | YFA, 1 Bbl. ② | 3.88 x 3.19 | 9.2 | 105 @ 5000 | 132 @ 2800 | 37-75 |
| | V6-173/2.8L | 2 Bbl. ③ ④ | 3.50 x 2.99 | 8.5 | 110 @ 4800 | 145 @ 2100 | 50-65 |
| 1985-86 | 4-126/2.1L ⑤ | Fuel Inj. | 3.38 x 3.50 | 21.5 | 85 @ 3750 | 132 @ 2750 | 43.5 |
| 1986 | 4-150/2.5L | T.B.I. | 3.88 x 3.19 | 9.2 | 117 @ 5000 | 135 @ 3500 | 37-75 |
| | V6-173/2.8L | 2 Bbl. ③ | 3.50 x 2.99 | 8.5 | 115 @ 4800 | 150 @ 2100 | 50-65 |
| 1987 | 4-126/2.1L ⑤ | Fuel Inj. | 3.39 x 3.50 | 21.5 | 85 @ 3750 | 132 @ 2750 | 43.5 |
| | 4-150/2.5L | T.B.I. | 3.88 x 3.19 | 9.2 | 121 @ 5000 | 141 @ 3500 | 37-75 |
| | 6-243/4.0L | M.P.I. | 3.88 x 3.44 | 9.2 | 173 @ 4500 | 220 @ 2500 | 37-75 |
| 1988-89 | 4-150/2.5L | T.B.I. | 3.88 x 3.19 | 9.2 | 121 @ 5000 | 141 @ 3500 | 37-75 |
| | 6-243/4.0L | M.P.I. | 3.88 x 3.44 | 9.2⑥ | 177 @ 4500 | 224 @ 2500 | 37-75 |

①—Cubic Inch Displacement.
②—Carter feedback carburetor.
③—Rochester.
④—Exc. Calif., 2SE; Calif. models, E2SE fuel feedback carburetor.
⑤—Diesel engine.
⑥—1989, 8.8.

## ENGINE TIGHTENING SPECIFICATIONS*

*Torque specifications are for clean and lightly lubricated threads only. Dry or dirty threads produce increased friction which prevents accurate measurement of tightness.

| Year | Engine | Spark Plugs Ft. Lbs. | Cylinder Head Bolts Ft. Lbs. | Intake Manifold Ft. Lbs. | Exhaust Manifold Ft. Lbs. | Rocker Arm Shaft Bracket Ft. Lbs. | Rocker Arm Cover Ft. Lbs. | Connecting Rod Cap Bolts Ft. Lbs. | Main Bearing Cap Bolts Ft. Lbs. | Flywheel To Crankshaft Ft. Lbs. | Vibration Damper Or Pulley Ft. Lbs. |
|---|---|---|---|---|---|---|---|---|---|---|---|
| 1984-86 | 4-126/2.1L ⑤ | — | ⑦ | — | — | 18-22 | 35-53 ② | 46-50 | 67-72 | ⑧ | 96 |
| | 4-150/2.5L | 22-33 | 80 | 18-28 | 18-28 | 16-26 ① | 28 ② | 30-35 | 70-85 | ③ | 70-100 |
| | V6-173/2.8L | 7-15 | 65-75 | 20-25 | 22-28 | 43-49 ④ | 6-9 | 34-40 | 63-74 | 45-55 | 66-84 |
| 1987 | 4-126/2.1L ⑤ | — | ⑦ | — | — | 18-22 | 35-53 ② | 46-50 | 67-72 | 41-44 | 96 |
| | 4-150/2.5L | 7-15 | 85⑨ | 18-28 | 18-28 | 16-26 ① | 28 ② | 30-35 | 70-85 | ③ | 70-100 |
| | 6-243/4.0L | 28 | 85⑨ | 23 | 23 | 19 ① | ⑧ | 33 | 80 | 105 | 80 |
| 1988 | 4-150/2.5L | 22-33 | 85⑨ | 18-28 | 18-28 | 16-26 ① | 28 ② | 30-35 | 70-85 | ③ | 70-100 |
| | 6-243/4.0L | 28 | 85⑨ | 23 | 23 | 19 ① | ⑧ | 33 | 80 | 105 | 80 |
| 1989 | 4-150/2.5L | 22-33 | 85⑨ | ⑨ | ⑨ | 16-26 ① | 28 ② | 30-35 | 70-85 | ③ | 70-100 |
| | 6-243/4.0L | 28 | 85⑨ | ⑨ | ⑨ | 19 ① | ⑧ | 33 | 80 | 105 | 80 |

①—Rocker arm cap screw.
②—Inch pounds.
③—Torque bolts to 50 ft. lbs., then tighten bolts an additional 60°.
④—Rocker arm stud.
⑤—Diesel engine.
⑥—With manual trans., 41 ft. lbs.; with auto. trans., 52 ft. lbs.
⑦—Torque bolts in four steps, first to 22 ft. lbs., next to 37 ft. lbs., then to 70-77 ft. lbs. Finally recheck bolt torque and ensure bolt torque is 70-77 ft. lbs.
⑧—Some engines use a valve cover with precured sealer. On models with precured sealer on cover, torque attaching bolts to 50-70 inch lbs. On all other types, torque attaching bolts to 28 inch lbs.
⑨—Refer to text.

## STARTING MOTOR SPECIFICATIONS

| Year | Make | Starter Number | Free Speed Test | | |
|---|---|---|---|---|---|
| | | | Amps. | Volts | R.P.M. |
| 1984-89 | Bosch | — | 75 | 11.5 | 2900 |
| | Delco | 1109526 | 45-70 | 9 | 7000-11000 |
| | Mitsubishi | — | 80 | 11.2 | 2500 |
| | Motorcraft | — | 67 | 12 | 7380-9356 |
| 1985-87 | Paris Rhone | — | — | — | — |

# 1984-89 JEEP CHEROKEE & WAGONEER; 1986-89 COMANCHE

## ALTERNATOR SPECIFICATIONS

| Year | Make | Alternator Rated Output Amperes | Rated Output Volts | Field Current Amperes @ 80°F | Field Current Volts | Regulator Model ① | Regulator Volts @ 120°F |
|------|------|------|------|------|------|------|------|
| 1984-89 | Delco | 56 | — | 4-5 | 12 | 1116387 | 13.4-14.4 |
| | Delco | 66 | — | 4-5 | 12 | 1116387 | 13.4-14.4 |
| | Delco | 68 | — | 4-5 | 12 | 1116387 | 13.4-14.4 |
| | Delco | 78 | — | 4-5 | 12 | 1116387 | 13.4-14.4 |
| | Delco | 56 | — | 4-5 | 12 | 1116387 | 13.4-14.4 |
| | Delco | 68 | — | 4-5 | 12 | 1116387 | 13.4-14.4 |
| | Delco | 78 | — | 4-5 | 12 | 1116387 | 13.4-14.4 |
| 1985-86 | Paris Rhone | 60 | — | — | — | YL154 | — |
| | Paris Rhone | 70 | — | — | — | YH2654 | — |

①—Solid state integral assembly, no adjustment required.

## BRAKE SPECIFICATIONS

| Year | Model | Rear Drum I.D. | Wheel Cyl. Bore Front Disc | Wheel Cyl. Bore Rear Drum | Disc Brake Rotor Nominal Thickness | Minimum Thickness | Thickness Variation (Parallelism) | Run Out (TIR) | Finish (Microinch) | Master Cyl. I.D. |
|------|-------|------|------|------|------|------|------|------|------|------|
| 1984-89 | All | 10 | 2.60 | .875 | .880 | .815 | — | .004 | — | .937 |

## DRIVE AXLE SPECIFICATIONS

| Year | Axle | Carrier Type | Ring Gear & Pinion Backlash Method | Adjustment | Pinion Bearing Preload Method | New Bearings Inch Lbs. | Used Bearings Inch Lbs. | Differential Bearing Preload |
|------|------|------|------|------|------|------|------|------|
| 1984-89 | Front | Integral | Shims | .005-.010 | Shims | 20-40 | 15-25 | ① |
| | Rear | Integral | Shims | .005-.009 | Spacer | 15-25 | 15-25 | .008 |

## WHEEL ALIGNMENT SPECIFICATIONS

| Year | Model | Caster Deg. | Camber Deg. | Toe-In (Inches) |
|------|-------|------|------|------|
| 1984-89 | Cherokee, Wagoneer | 7 to 8 | −3/4 to +1/2 | −1/32 to +1/32 |
| 1986-88 | Comanche | 7 to 8 | −1/2 to +1/2 | −1/32 to +1/32 |
| 1989 | Comanche | 7 to 8 | −3/4 to +1/2 | −1/32 to +1/32 |

## COOLING SYSTEM & CAPACITY DATA

| Year | Model Or Engine | Cooling Capacity Qts. | | Radiator Cap Relief Pressure, Lbs. | Thermo. Opening Temp. | Fuel Tank Gals. | Engine Oil Refill Qts. | Transmission Oil | | | | Axle Oil Pts. |
|------|-----------------|------|------|------|------|------|------|------|------|------|------|------|
| | | Less A/C | With A/C | | | | | 4 Speed Pts. | 5 Speed Pts. | Auto. Trans. Qts. ② | Trans. Case Pts. | |
| 1984-86 | 4-150, 2.5L | 10③ | 10③ | 15 | 195 | ⑩ | 4 | ④ | ⑤ | 6.5 | ⑥ | ⑦ |
| | V6-173, 2.8L | 12③ | 12③ | 15 | 195 | ⑩ | 4 | ④ | ⑤ | 6.5 | ⑥ | ⑦ |
| 1985-86 | 4-126, 2.1⑧ | 9 | 9 | — | — | ⑩ | 6.3⑨ | ④ | ⑤ | 6.5 | ⑥ | ⑦ |
| 1987 | 4-126, 2.1L⑧ | 9 | 9 | — | — | ⑩ | 5.5⑨ | — | ⑫ | 7.9 | ⑬ | ⑦ |
| | 4-150, 2.5L | 10③ | 10③ | 15 | 195 | ⑩ | 4 | ⑪ | ⑫ | 7.9 | ⑬ | ⑦ |
| | 6-243, 4.0L | 12③ | 12③ | 15 | 195 | ⑩ | 5.5⑨ | ⑪ | ⑫ | 7.9 | ⑬ | ⑦ |
| 1988 | 4-150, 2.5L | 10③ | 10③ | 15 | 195 | ⑩ | 4 | ⑪ | ⑫ | 7.9 | ⑬ | ⑦ |
| | 6-243, 4.0L | 12③ | 12③ | 15 | 195 | ⑩ | 5.5⑨ | ⑪ | ⑫ | 7.9 | ⑬ | ⑦ |
| 1989 | 4-150, 2.5L | 10③ | 10③ | 15 | 195 | ⑮ | 4 | ⑪ | ⑭ | 7.9 | ⑯ | ⑦ |
| | 6-243, 4.0L | 12③ | 12③ | 15 | 195 | ⑮ | 5.5⑨ | ⑪ | ⑭ | 7.9 | ⑯ | ⑦ |

① —With or without filter change.
② —Approximate, make final check with dipstick.
③ —Includes coolant recovery bottle.
④ —Borg Warner, 3.9 pts.; Aisin, 7.4 pts.
⑤ —Borg Warner, 4.5 pts.; Aisin, 7.0 pts.
⑥ —New Process 207, 4.5 pts.; New Process 229, 6.0 pts.
⑦ —Front or rear, 2.5 pts.; models with Selec-Trac add 5 oz. for front axle disconnect housing.
⑧ —Diesel engine.
⑨ —With filter.
⑩ —13.5 gals. for Cherokee & Wagoneer; 16 gals. for Comanche.
⑪ —2WD models, 7.8 pints; 4WD models, 7.4 pints.
⑫ —2WD models, 7.4 pints; 4WD models, 7 pints.
⑬ —Command Trac 231, 2.2 pts.; Selec-Trac 242, 2.5 pts.
⑭ —BA 10/5 transmission; 2WD models, 4.9 pints; 4WD models, 5.2 pints.
⑮ —18.5/23.5, short/long-bed Comanche; 20.2, Cherokee & Wagoneer.
⑯ —Model 231, 3.25 pints; Model 242, 70 series only, 2.5 pints.

# ELECTRICAL

## INDEX

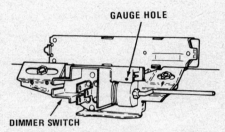

**Fig. 1  Adjusting dimmer switch**

GAUGE HOLE

DIMMER SWITCH

## FUSE PANEL & FLASHER LOCATION

The fuse panel is located on the lefthand side of the dash panel. The turn signal flasher is located at the upper left corner of the fuse block. The hazard warning flasher is located at the lower right corner of the fuse block.

## STARTER
### REPLACE
### 4-126 DIESEL

1. Disconnect battery ground cable.
2. Disconnect starter motor wiring.
3. Remove starter motor mounting bolts and nuts.
4. Remove starter assembly.
5. Reverse procedure to install.

### 6-242 & 1984-88 4-150

1. Disconnect battery ground cable.
2. Raise and support vehicle, then remove support bracket to starter retaining bolt and washer.
3. Remove starter motor attaching bolts and the starter motor. Remove shims, if used.
4. Reverse procedure to install. Reinstall any shims that were removed.

### 1989 4-150

1. Disconnect battery ground cable.
2. Remove exhaust clamp from bracket.
3. On automatic transmission models, remove bolt and nut from forward end

of brace rod, then remove brace rod and bracket.
4. On manual transmission models, remove bolt, nut and bracket from bellhousing.
5. On all models, disconnect solenoid feed wire from solenoid, then remove the starter.
6. Reverse procedure to install.

### V6-173

1. Disconnect battery ground cable.
2. Raise and support vehicle, then disconnect wiring from starter solenoid.
3. Remove starter motor attaching bolts and the starter motor. Remove shims, if used.
4. Reverse procedure to install. Reinstall any shims that were removed.

## HORN SOUNDER & STEERING WHEEL
### REPLACE

1. Disconnect battery ground cable.
2. Remove horn button and ring. On 1989 models with standard wheel, remove cover attaching screws from underside of wheel then remove the cover. Disconnect horn wire connectors from contact switch. On models with sport wheel, remove horn contact assembly and flex plate.
3. Remove steering wheel retaining nut, then scribe alignment marks on steering shaft and wheel to aid installation.
4. Using suitable puller, remove steering wheel from shaft.
5. Reverse procedure to install. Torque steering wheel retaining nut to 25 ft. lbs.

## DIMMER SWITCH
### REPLACE

1. Disconnect battery ground cable.
2. Remove instrument panel lower shroud.
3. Remove steering column to instrument panel retaining bolts, then lower steering column as necessary.
4. Tape actuator rod to column, then remove dimmer switch retaining screws

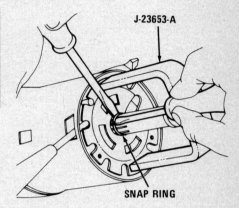

J-23653-A

SNAP RING

**Fig. 2  Removing steering shaft snap ring**

and pull switch from actuator rod.
5. Reverse procedure to install, then adjust dimmer switch as follows:
  a. Depress switch slightly, then insert a 3/32 inch drill bit into switch gauge hole, **Fig. 1**.
  b. Move switch toward steering wheel to remove excess lash from actuator rod, then torque switch retaining screws to 35 inch lbs.
  c. Remove drill bit, then test dimmer switch function by operating actuator lever.

## TURN SIGNAL SWITCH
### REPLACE
### 1984-88

1. Disconnect battery ground cable, then remove steering wheel as outlined previously.
2. Remove lockplate cover.
3. On models with tilt column, remove tilt lever. On all models, depress hazard warning knob, turn counterclockwise, then remove from steering column.
4. Compress lockplate using tool J-23653-A or equivalent, then remove steering shaft snap ring, **Fig. 2**.
5. Remove lockplate, canceling cam, upper bearing preload spring, spring seat and bearing race.
6. Disengage turn signal/wiper lever by

pulling it straight out, then disconnect turn signal switch harness connector from steering column lower bracket. **Wrap tape around switch harness connector to prevent snagging during removal.**

7. Remove turn signal switch retaining screws and actuator, then remove switch and harness by pulling switch straight up and out of column.
8. Reverse procedure to install.

## 1989

1. Disconnect battery ground cable.
2. On models with standard steering wheel, remove front cover retaining screws then the cover.
3. Turn key to Lock position. Using suitable puller, remove steering wheel and vibration damper, if equipped.
4. Using lockplate compressor tool No. C-4156, remove steering shaft snap ring.
5. Remove the following:
   a. Lockplate, cancelling cam and upper bearing pre-load spring.
   b. Hazard warning switch screw, actuator arm and turn signal switch attaching screws.
   c. Lower instrument trim cover panel and if equipped with column shift, remove PRNDL cable.
6. Remove steering column bracket-to-brake sled retaining nuts and steering column bracket-to-column bolts.
7. Loosen column brace mounting nut from driver's side kick panel to lower column.
8. Disconnect upper connector from turn signal connector, then remove from column bracket.
9. Tape connector flat-back against wire harness.
10. Pull plastic wire harness cover up and over weld nuts.
11. Pull turn signal switch straight up and out of housing.
12. Reverse procedure to install, noting the following:
    a. When installing switch, ensure wires are laying flat on bottom inside of column.
    b. Use new snap-ring on steering shaft.
    c. If PRNDL cable was removed, install clip with shift indicator on N.

## IGNITION LOCK
## REPLACE

1. Remove turn signal switch as outlined previously.
2. Turn ignition to "ON" position, then remove key warning buzzer and contacts using a needlenose pliers. **Do not attempt to remove switch and contacts separately, as contacts may fall into steering column.**
3. On models equipped with Type 1 lock cylinder, turn ignition to OFF-LOCK (tilt column) or two detents clockwise from OFF-LOCK (standard column) position, then depress retaining tab and pull lock cylinder from steering column. **The retaining tab is accessible through the slot adjacent to**

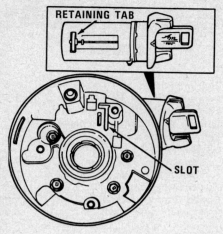

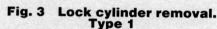

**Fig. 3  Lock cylinder removal. Type 1**

**Fig. 4  Lock cylinder removal. Type 2**

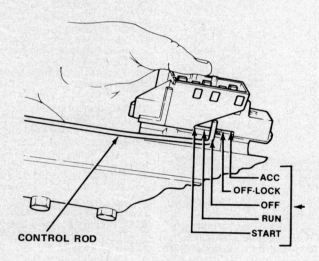

**Fig. 5  Ignition switch installation (Typical)**

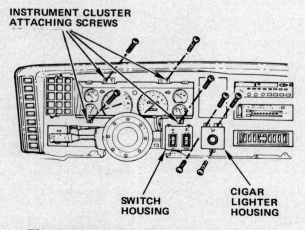

**Fig. 6  Removing instrument cluster**

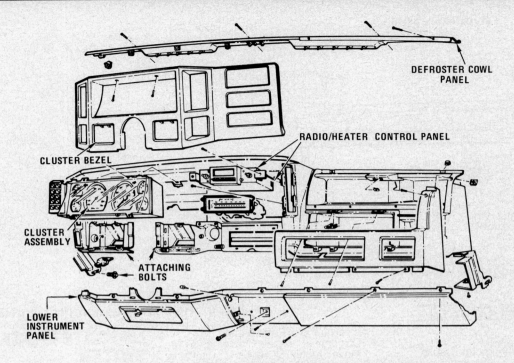

**Fig. 7  Instrument panel exploded view**

the turn signal switch mounting boss, **Fig. 3.**
4. On models equipped with Type 2 lock cylinder, turn ignition to On position, then remove lock cylinder retaining screw and pull lock from column, **Fig. 4.**
5. On all models, to install lock cylinder, insert key into lock, then hold cylinder sleeve and rotate key clockwise until key stops. Insert lock cylinder into housing bore, ensuring cylinder tab is aligned with keyway in housing. Push cylinder inward until it bottoms in housing, then rotate key counterclockwise until drive section of cylinder mates with sector.
6. On models equipped with Type 1 lock cylinder, push cylinder in fully until retaining tab engages housing groove.
7. On models equipped with Type 2 lock cylinder, push cylinder inward until it bottoms, then install lock retaining screw. Torque retaining screw to 40 inch lbs.

## IGNITION SWITCH
### REPLACE

1. Disconnect battery ground cable, then place ignition lock in OFF-LOCK position.
2. Remove instrument panel lower shroud.
3. Remove steering column to instrument panel retaining bolts, then lower steering column as necessary.
4. Disconnect control rod and electrical connector from switch, then remove switch attaching screws and the switch.
5. Position switch slider to the ACCESSORY position as shown, **Fig. 5.**

Place ignition key in ACCESSORY position, then insert control rod into switch and install attaching screws. On standard column vehicles, the accessory position is to the extreme left, with the left side of the ignition switch facing toward the steering wheel. On tilt column vehicles, the accessory position is to the extreme right, with the right side of the switch facing downward from the steering wheel.
6. Move switch downward to remove excess control rod lash, then torque attaching screws to 35 inch lbs.
7. Reconnect switch electrical connector.

## LIGHT SWITCH
### REPLACE

1. Disconnect battery ground cable, then pull control knob fully outward.
2. Working from underneath instrument panel, depress light switch shaft retainer button, then pull shaft from switch.
3. Remove light switch ferrule nut from front of instrument panel.
4. Disconnect switch electrical connector, then remove switch from vehicle.
5. Reverse procedure to install.

## STOP LIGHT SWITCH
### REPLACE

1. Disconnect battery ground cable.
2. Disconnect electrical connector from switch.
3. Remove brake pedal pivot bolt, nylon retaining rings, sleeve and switch.
4. Reverse procedure to install.

## NEUTRAL START/BACK-UP LIGHT SWITCH
### REPLACE
### AUTOMATIC TRANSMISSION VEHICLES

The neutral start and back-up light switches are an integral assembly and cannot be replaced separately.
1. Raise and support vehicle.
2. Disconnect electrical connector from switch.
3. Unscrew switch from transmission and allow fluid to drain into a suitable container.
4. Move shift linkage to PARK and NEUTRAL positions and observe switch operating fingers for proper positioning.
5. Reverse procedure to install. Correct transmission fluid as required, then check back up lights for proper operation.

## BACK-UP LIGHT SWITCH
### REPLACE
### MANUAL TRANSMISSION VEHICLES

1. Raise and support vehicle.
2. Disconnect electrical connector from switch.
3. Unscrew switch from transmission housing and remove from vehicle.
4. Reverse procedure to install. Correct transmission fluid level as required, then check back-up lights for proper operation.

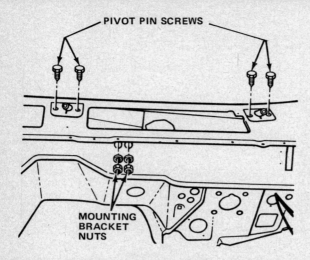

Fig. 8  Windshield wiper motor replacement

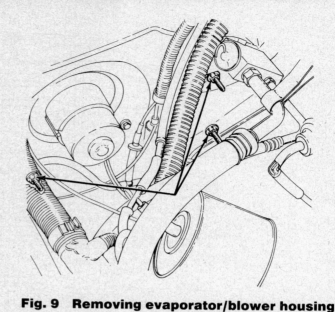

Fig. 9  Removing evaporator/blower housing

## INSTRUMENT CLUSTER
### REPLACE

1. Disconnect battery ground cable.
2. Remove the four instrument cluster bezel attaching screws, then carefully snap bezel from instrument panel.
3. Remove cigar lighter housing, switch housing and instrument cluster attaching screws, **Fig. 6.**
4. Disconnect speedometer cable.
5. Pull cluster out slightly, then disconnect electrical connectors and remove cluster from vehicle.
6. Reverse procedure to install.

## INSTRUMENT PANEL
### REPLACE

1. Disconnect battery ground cable.
2. Remove lower instrument panel attaching screws, then the lower instrument panel, **Fig. 7.**
3. Remove instrument cluster as outlined previously.
4. Remove radio and heater control panel attaching screws, then the control panel.
5. Remove instrument panel switches.
6. Remove defroster cowl panel to instrument panel attaching screws, then the defroster cowl panel.
7. Remove instrument panel attaching bolts, then the instrument panel assembly.
8. Reverse procedure to install. **The instrument panel wiring harness is attached to the rear of the instrument panel and must be installed in similar fashion to facilitate installation.**

## WINDSHIELD WIPER MOTOR
### REPLACE

1. Disconnect battery ground cable, then remove wiper arm assemblies.
2. Remove cowl trim panel attaching

screws and the trim panel.
3. Disconnect washer hose, then remove mounting bracket attaching nuts and pivot pin attaching screws, **Fig. 8.**
4. Disconnect wiper motor electrical connector, then remove wiper motor and linkage assembly. **The wiper motor is shrouded in a rubber protective boot. Exercise caution when removing or replacing wiper motor to avoid damaging boot.**
5. Reverse procedure to install.

## LIFTGATE WIPER MOTOR
### REPLACE

1. Disconnect battery ground cable, then remove wiper arm assembly.
2. Disconnect washer hose, then remove pin retaining nut.
3. Remove liftgate interior trim panel attaching screws and the trim panel.
4. Disconnect electrical connector from wiper motor.
5. Remove wiper motor attaching bolts and the wiper motor.
6. Reverse procedure to install.

## WINDSHIELD WIPER SWITCH
### REPLACE

1. Remove horn sounder and steering wheel as outlined previously.
2. Remove turn signal switch as outlined in "Turn Signal Switch, Replace" procedure.
3. Disconnect electrical connector, then remove pivot pin.
4. Remove wiper switch assembly.
5. Reverse procedure to install.

## LIFTGATE WIPER SWITCH
### REPLACE

1. Disconnect battery ground cable.
2. Remove instrument cluster bezel, then the switch housing panel.
3. Disconnect switch electrical connector.
4. Depress switch mounting tabs and remove switch from instrument panel.
5. Reverse procedure to install.

## RADIO
### REPLACE

When installing radio, adjust antenna trimmer for peak performance.
1. Disconnect battery ground cable.
2. Remove instrument cluster bezel attaching screws, then gently snap bezel from instrument panel.
3. Remove the two radio retaining screws, then pull radio out gently and disconnect electrical connector and antenna lead.
4. Remove radio from vehicle.
5. Reverse procedure to install.

## HEATER CORE
### REPLACE

1. Disconnect battery ground cable, then drain cooling system.
2. Disconnect hoses from heater core.
3. If equipped with A/C, remove evaporator/blower housing as follows:
   a. Discharge A/C system, then disconnect hoses from expansion valve.
   b. Disconnect electrical connector and vent tube from blower motor.
   c. Remove console, if equipped.
   d. Remove lower instrument panel attaching screws, then the lower panel.
   e. Disconnect electrical connections

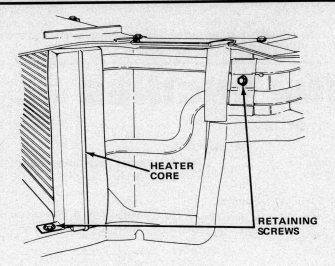

**Fig. 10  Removing heater core**

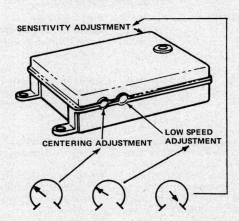

**Fig. 12  Speed control regulator adjustments**

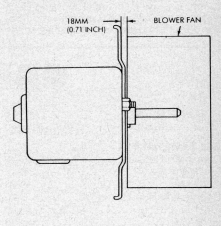

**Fig. 11  Blower fan installation**

blower motor, then remove blower motor/fan assembly.
5. Remove blower motor fan from motor shaft to gain access to attaching screws. **Ears A and B of retainer clip 3 must be over flat surface C on motor shaft 1 Fig. 11.**
6. Reverse procedure to install.

from A/C relay, blower motor resistors and A/C thermostat.
f. Disconnect vacuum hose from vacuum motor.
g. Cut evaporator/blower housing to heater core housing retaining strap, then disconnect heater control cable.
h. Pry retaining clip from rear of blower housing flange, then remove the three retaining screws.
i. Working from engine compartment, remove evaporator/blower housing attaching nuts, then the evaporator drain tube, **Fig. 9.**
j. Remove right kick panel, then the instrument panel support bolt.
k. Pull right side of dash outward, then rotate housing downward and towards rear of vehicle until studs clear dash panel. Remove housing from vehicle.
4. Remove heater core to housing retaining screws, then the heater core, **Fig. 10.**
5. Reverse procedure to install.

# BLOWER MOTOR
## REPLACE
### EXC. 1989 6-243

1. Disconnect battery ground cable.
2. Disconnect electrical connectors from blower motor.
3. Remove blower motor and fan assembly attaching nuts, then blower motor and fan.
4. Remove fan retaining clip from fan hub.
5. Remove fan from the motor shaft.
6. Reverse procedure to install.

### 1989 6-243

1. Remove retaining strap and mounting bracket from coolant bottle.
2. If equipped with anti-lock brakes, remove brake pump and bracket as an assembly, then position aside.
3. Remove hose bracket retaining screw located near hood prop rod.
4. Disconnect electrical connectors from

# SPEED CONTROL
## ADJUST
### REGULATOR ADJUSTMENTS

The regulator adjustments are pre-set by the manufacturer. However, if all of the other components of the system appear to be functioning normally and the speed control system remains inoperative, perform the adjustments below to determine if the regulator is working properly.

#### Pre-Adjustment

Turn the sensitivity adjustment screw fully clockwise, and the low speed and centering adjusting screws to the 10 o'clock position as shown in **Fig. 12.** The adjustment screws are extremely delicate. Insert the screwdriver into the slots carefully to avoid damaging regulator.

#### Centering Adjustment

Road test vehicle and observe engagement speed. If speed control engages at 2 mph or greater than the selected road speed, turn centering adjusting screw counterclockwise in small increments. If engagement speed is 2 or more mph below selected speed, turn adjusting screw clockwise in small increments. Check for proper centering adjustment by engaging speed control system on a level road after each adjustment is completed. If adjustments have no effect on system operation, replace the regulator.

# GASOLINE ENGINES

## INDEX

# ENGINE MOUNTS
## REPLACE
### FRONT MOUNT

1. Disconnect battery ground cable.
2. Remove through bolt retaining nut (1), **Fig. 1.** Do not remove through bolt at this time.
3. Remove engine mount upper retaining bolt (3), then raise and support vehicle.
4. Support engine with a suitable jack, then remove engine mount lower retaining nut (4) and through bolt (2). **On six cylinder engines, it may be necessary to remove the air pump and hose assembly to allow removal of through bolt.**
5. Raise engine slightly and remove engine mount (5).
6. Reverse procedure to install. Torque all nuts and bolts to 32 ft. lbs. On 1989 models, torque engine mount retaining bolts to 30 ft. lbs. and the through bolt to 48 ft. lbs.

### REAR MOUNT

1. Raise and support vehicle and transmission.
2. Remove rear mount to crossmember retaining nuts (1), **Fig. 2,** then the crossmember to frame retaining nuts and bolts (2). Remove crossmember from vehicle.
3. Remove rear mount to support bracket retaining nuts (4), then the rear mount.
4. Reverse procedure to install. Torque

crossmember to frame retaining nuts and bolts to 35 ft. lbs., mount to support bracket retaining nuts to 30 ft. lbs., and mount to crossmember retaining nuts to 18 ft. lbs. On 1989 models, torque crossmember nuts to 14 ft. lbs. and all bolts to 32 ft. lbs.

# ENGINE
## REPLACE
### 4-150 & 6-243

1. Disconnect battery ground cable, then remove air cleaner and hood.
2. Drain cooling system and remove upper and lower radiator hoses.
3. Remove fan shroud.
4. On vehicles equipped with automatic transmission, disconnect transmission cooling lines from radiator.
5. Remove radiator. On vehicles equipped with A/C, remove A/C condenser.
6. Remove fan assembly, then install a 5/16 x 1/2 inch bolt to retain fan pulley to water pump flange.
7. Disconnect heater hoses, throttle linkages, throttle valve rod and cruise control cable, if equipped.
8. Disconnect wires from starter motor.
9. Disconnect CEC wiring harness connector.
10. Disconnect fuel line from fuel pump and fuel return line from fuel filter.
11. On vehicles equipped with A/C, remove service valves and cap compressor ports.
12. If equipped with power brakes, re-

move vacuum check valve from brake booster.
13. If equipped with power steering, disconnect and plug hoses from steering gear, then drain power steering pump reservoir.
14. Disconnect all wires and vacuum hoses which will interfere with engine removal. Label wires and hoses to aid installation.
15. Raise and support vehicle, then remove starter motor.
16. Disconnect exhaust pipe from manifold.
17. Remove transmission housing inspection cover.
18. On automatic transmission equipped vehicles, mark torque converter to drive plate location, then remove converter to drive plate attaching bolts.
19. On all vehicles, remove upper transmission housing to engine attaching bolts and loosen bottom bolts.
20. Remove engine mount to support bracket attaching bolts, then install a suitable engine hoist.
21. Raise engine and support transmission with a suitable jack.
22. Remove the remaining transmission to engine attaching bolts.
23. Raise engine and remove from vehicle.
24. Reverse procedure to install.

### V6-173

1. Disconnect battery ground cable, then remove air cleaner and hood.
2. Drain cooling system and remove upper and lower radiator hoses.

3. Remove fan shroud, then disconnect automatic transmission cooling lines from radiator, if equipped.
4. Remove radiator and, if equipped with A/C, the A/C condenser.
5. Remove fan assembly.
6. Disconnect heater hoses, throttle linkage, throttle valve cable and cruise control cable, if equipped.
7. Disconnect hose from power brake booster.
8. Disconnect and label all wires and vacuum hoses which will interfere with engine removal.
9. Remove power steering pump and position aside.
10. Disconnect fuel line from fuel pump.
11. Disconnect hoses from A/C compressor, if equipped.
12. Raise and support vehicle, then disconnect exhaust pipes from exhaust manifolds.
13. Disconnect exhaust pipe from catalytic converter flange and allow pipe to drop to floor.
14. Remove transmission housing inspection cover.
15. If equipped with automatic transmission, mark torque converter to drive plate location, then remove converter to drive plate attaching bolts.
16. Disconnect wires from starter motor, then remove transmission housing to engine retaining bolts.
17. Lower vehicle and support transmission with suitable jack.
18. Remove air pump to support bracket retaining bolts, then position air pump aside.
19. Install a suitable engine hoist, then remove engine mount through bolts.
20. Disconnect ground strap at left side cylinder head.
21. Raise engine and remove from vehicle.
22. Reverse procedure to install.

## INTAKE MANIFOLD REPLACE

### 4-150

#### 1984–88

1. Disconnect battery ground cable and drain cooling system.
2. Remove air cleaner.
3. Disconnect fuel line, air horn vent hose and idle speed control hose and wire connector from carburetor or throttle body.
4. Disconnect coolant hoses from manifold and throttle cable from bell crank.
5. Disconnect PCV hose from manifold, then remove vacuum advance CTO valve vacuum hose.
6. Disconnect fuel feedback coolant temperature sender wire connector from manifold, then the air temperature sensor electrical connector, if equipped.
7. Disconnect vacuum hose from EGR valve.
8. If equipped with automatic transmission, disconnect throttle valve linkage, as required.
9. If equipped with power steering, remove power steering pump mounting

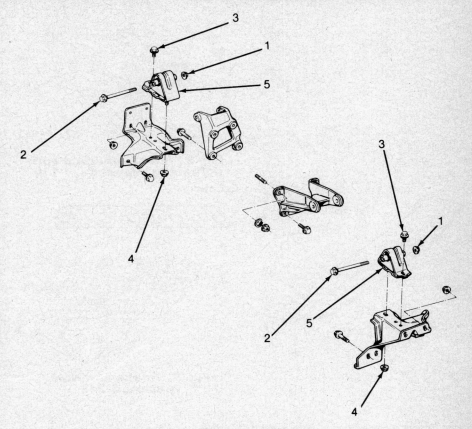

**Fig. 1  Front engine mount replacement**

bracket, then position pump and bracket aside. Do not disconnect hoses from pump.
10. Remove carburetor, if equipped.
11. Disconnect intake manifold heater wire connector, then remove EGR valve tube.
12. Remove intake manifold attaching nuts, bolts and clamps, then the intake manifold.
13. Reverse procedure to install. Torque manifold nuts and bolts to specification in sequence shown in **Fig. 3**.

#### 1989

1. Disconnect battery ground cable, drain cooling system and remove fuel tank filler cap to relieve pressure. Replace filler cap.
2. Remove air inlet hose from air cleaner.
3. Remove power steering pump, belt and brackets from water pump and intake manifold. Position power steering pump aside.
4. Disconnect fuel supply and return hoses from throttle body.
5. Disconnect throttle cable from throttle body. **When disconnecting cruise control, do not pry on connector. Use finger pressure only.**
6. Disconnect the following:
   a. Electrical connectors from throttle position sensor and idle speed control motor.
   b. Coolant temperature sensor, fuel injector, air temperature and oxygen sensors.
   c. Vacuum hoses from vacuum port on intake manifold, EGR transducer and brake booster.
   d. CCV hose from cylinder head.
7. Remove molded vacuum harness.
8. Loosen EGR tube nuts from intake manifold, then remove EGR-to-exhaust-manifold retaining bolts.
9. Remove bolts 2, 3, 4 and 5 retaining intake manifold to cylinder head **Fig. 6**. Loosen slightly bolt 1 and nuts 6 and 7, then remove intake manifold.
10. Reverse procedure to install. Torque bolts in sequence **Fig. 3** to the following specifications: bolts 1, 6 and 8 to 30 ft. lbs., bolts 2-5 to 23 ft. lbs. and bolts 9-10 to 14 ft. lbs.

### V6-173

1. Disconnect battery ground cable and remove air cleaner.
2. Drain cooling system.
3. Disconnect wire connectors, vacuum hoses, fuel line and control linkage from carburetor, then remove carburetor attaching nuts and the carburetor.
4. Remove A/C compressor, if equipped, and position aside. Do not disconnect hoses from compressor.
5. Disconnect wires from spark plugs and ignition coil, then remove distributor cap.
6. Mark distributor position in relation to cylinder block, then remove distributor hold-down bolt and the distributor.

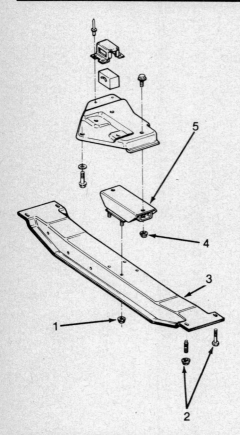

**Fig. 2   Rear engine mount replacement**

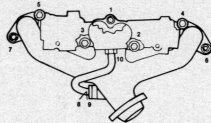

**Fig. 3   Intake manifold bolt tightening sequence. 4-150**

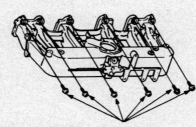

**Fig. 5   Intake manifold replace. 6-243**

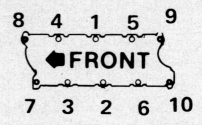

**Fig. 4   Intake manifold bolt tightening sequence. V6-173**

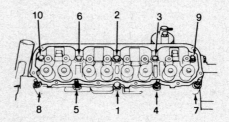

**Fig. 6   Cylinder head bolt tightening sequence. 4-150**

7. Remove EGR valve retaining bolts and the EGR valve.
8. Disconnect air injection and charcoal canister hoses.
9. Remove air injection pipe bracket from left valve cover.
10. Remove left valve cover and the diverter valve.
11. Remove diverter valve and coil retaining bracket, then the right valve cover.
12. Remove upper radiator hose, then disconnect heater hose.
13. Disconnect coolant temperature switch wire connectors.
14. Remove intake manifold retaining bolts, then the intake manifold.
15. Reverse procedure to install. Torque manifold bolts to specification in sequence shown in **Fig. 4**. When installing new intake manifold gaskets, note gaskets are marked right side and left side. Install them as indicated to maintain proper engine operation.

## 6-243

The intake and exhaust manifolds on the 4.0L engines must be removed together because the two manifolds share a common gasket at the cylinder head.

1. Disconnect battery ground cable, then drain cooling system.
2. Loosen EGR tube nuts from intake and exhaust manifolds, then the drive belt.

3. Remove air cleaner inlet hose then the air cleaner assembly.
4. Remove throttle, cruise control and transmission line pressure cables.
5. Disconnect vacuum connector from intake manifold by lifting the connector from thr bracket and depressing the lock tabs.
6. Disconnect electrical connectors from intake manifold.
7. Disconnect and remove fuel supply and return lines from fuel rail.
8. Remove the following:
   a. Power steering pump and bracket from intake manifold. Position aside.
   b. Fuel rail injectors and intake manifold heat shield.
9. Raise and support vehicle, then disconnect exhaust pipe downtube and oxygen sensor wire.
10. Lower vehicle then remove the intake/exhaust manifold/EGR tube assembly.
11. Remove EGR tube and seperate intake and exhaust manifolds.
12. Reverse procedure to install. Torque bolts in sequence to specifications. **Fig. 7.**

## CYLINDER HEAD
### REPLACE
### 4-150

1. Disconnect battery ground cable.
2. Drain cooling system and disconnect hoses from thermostat housing.
3. Remove air cleaner, then the valve cover.

4. Remove rocker arm cap screws, bridges and pivots, then the rocker arms and pushrods. **Retain pushrods, bridge, pivot and rocker arms in the same order as removed to facilitate installation in the original positions.**
5. If equipped with power steering, remove power steering pump retaining bracket, then position bracket and pump assembly aside. Do not disconnect hoses from pump.
6. Remove intake and exhaust manifolds from cylinder head.
7. If equipped with A/C, remove compressor drive belt and loosen alternator belt.
8. Remove A/C compressor/alternator bracket to cylinder head mounting screw, if equipped.
9. Remove remaining bolts and position alternator and A/C compressor aside.
10. Disconnect ignition wires and remove spark plugs.
11. Disconnect temperature sender wire connector, then remove cylinder head retaining bolts.
12. Remove cylinder head and gasket.
13. Reverse procedure to install. Torque cylinder head bolts to specification in sequence shown in **Fig. 6. Torque bolt No. 8 in sequence to 75 ft. lbs.** On 1989 models, torque bolts in sequence **Fig. 6,** using the following procedure: bolts 1-10 to 22 ft. lbs., bolts 1-10 to 45 ft. lbs.. Retorque all bolts to 45 ft. lbs. Torque bolts 1-7 to 110 ft. lbs., bolt 8 to 100 ft. lbs. and bolts 9 and 10 to 110 ft. lbs.

### V6-173

1. Remove intake manifold as outlined previously.
2. Drain coolant from cylinder block.

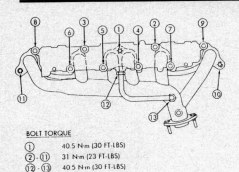

BOLT TORQUE
1   40.5 N·m (30 FT-LBS)
2 - 11   31 N·m (23 FT-LBS)
12 - 13   40.5 N·m (30 FT-LBS)

**Fig. 7   Intake/Exhaust manifold tightening sequence. 1989 6-243**

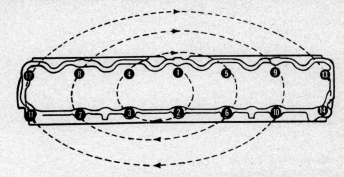

**Fig. 9   Cylinder head bolt tightening sequence. 6-243**

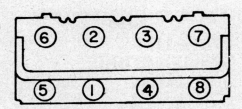

**Fig. 8   Cylinder head bolt tightening sequence. V6-173**

3. If removing left cylinder head, remove oil dipstick tube retaining nut and power steering pump and bracket assembly, if equipped.
4. Disconnect exhaust pipe from exhaust manifold, then remove exhaust manifold.
5. Loosen rocker arm retaining nuts, position rocker arms aside, then remove pushrods.
6. If removing right cylinder head, remove alternator/air pump retaining bracket assembly.
7. Remove cylinder head retaining bolts, then the cylinder head.
8. Reverse procedure to install. Torque cylinder head bolts to specification in sequence shown in **Fig. 8.**

## 1987—88

1. Disconnect battery ground cable.
2. Remove valve cover.
3. Remove rocker arm cap screws, bridges and pivots, then the rocker arms and pushrods. **Retain pushrods, bridge, pivot and rocker arms in the same order as removed to facilitate installation in the original positions.**
4. Remove spark plugs from cylinder head.
5. Remove cylinder head attaching bolts, then the cylinder head and gasket.
6. Reverse procedure to install, noting the following:
   a. Apply suitable sealing compound to both sides of new head gasket.
   b. Ensure head gasket identification mark faces up.
   c. Torque cylinder head attaching bolts to specification in sequence shown in **Fig. 9.** Apply suitable locking compound to threads of bolt No. 11 and torque in se-

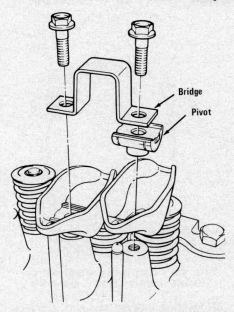

**Fig. 10   Rocker arm assembly. 4-150 (6-243 similar)**

quence to 75 ft. lbs.

## 1989

1. Disconnect battery ground cable, then drain cooling system.
2. Remove air cleaner assembly, fuel pipe and vacuum advance hose.
3. Remove cylinder head cover.
4. Remove in order, capscrews, bridge/pivot assemblies, rocker arms and push rods.
5. Disconnect power steering pump bracket and position aside.
6. Remove intake/exhaust manifolds as described under "Intake Manifold, Replace."
7. If equipped with A/C, remove drive belt. Loosen compressor mounting bolts and position aside. Remove alternator bracket-to-cylinder head.
8. Disconnect ignition wires and remove spark plugs.
9. Disconnect temperature sending unit.
10. Remove ignition coil and bracket assemblies, then remove cylinder head.
11. Reverse procedure to install. Torque bolts in sequence, **Fig. 9.** Coat threads of bolt No. 11 with Loctite 592

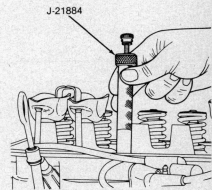

**Fig. 11   Valve lifter replacement. 4-150 (6-243 similar)**

or equivalent before installation. Torque all bolts to 22 ft. lbs. Torque all bolts to 45 ft. lbs., then recheck all bolts to 45 ft. lbs. Torque all bolts except No. 11 to 110 ft. lbs. Torque No. 11 to 100 ft. lbs.

# ROCKER ARM SERVICE
## 4-150 & 6-243

Remove rocker arm cap screws, bridge, pivot and rocker arms as shown in **Fig. 10.** Inspect pivot and rocker arm for excessive wear or scoring. Replace if necessary. To install, lubricate rocker arm and pivot, then position rocker arm, pivot and bridge onto cylinder head. Install cap screws, then tighten alternately one turn at a time until proper torque specification is reached.

## V6-173

Remove stud nut, pivot and rocker arm. Inspect pivot and rocker arm for excessive wear or scoring. Replace if necessary. Coat rocker arm and pivot friction surfaces with Molykote or equivalent, then install rocker arm, pivot and stud nut. Tighten stud nut until all lash is eliminated, ensuring pushrod is correctly seated in lifter and rocker arm socket. Adjust valves as outlined in "Valve Adjustment" procedure.

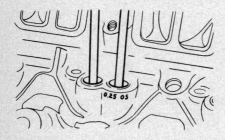

**Fig. 12   Oversize valve lifter stamping. V6-173**

## VALVE ARRANGEMENT
### FRONT TO REAR

```
4-150...................E-I-I-E-E-I-I-E
V6-173....................E-I-I-E-I-E
6-243.............E-I-I-E-I-E-I-E-I-I-E
```

## VALVES
### ADJUST
#### 4-150 & 6-243

These engines are equipped with hydraulic valve lifters. No provision for adjustment is provided.

### V6-173

1. Crank engine until mark on torsional damper is aligned with TDC mark on timing tab. Ensure engine is in No. 1 cylinder firing position by placing fingers on No. 1 cylinder rocker arms as mark on damper comes near TDC mark on timing tab. If valves are not moving, engine is in No. 1 firing position. If valves move as damper mark nears TDC mark on timing tab, engine is in No. 4 cylinder firing position and should be rotated one revolution to reach No. 1 cylinder firing position.
2. With engine in No. 1 cylinder firing position, adjust the following valves: exhaust: 1, 2, 3; intake: 1, 5, 6. To adjust valves, back off adjusting nut until lash is felt at pushrod, then tighten adjusting nut until all lash is removed. This can be determined by rotating pushrod while tightening adjusting nut. When all lash has been eliminated, turn adjusting nut an additional 1½ turns.
3. Crank engine one revolution until mark on torsional damper and TDC mark are again aligned. This is No. 4 cylinder firing position. With engine in this position, the following valves can be adjusted: exhaust: 4, 5, 6; intake: 2, 3, 4.
4. Install rocker arm covers, then start engine and check timing and idle speed.

## VALVE LIFTERS
### REPLACE
#### 4-150 & 6-243

1. Remove rocker arms as previously outlined.
2. Remove pushrods.

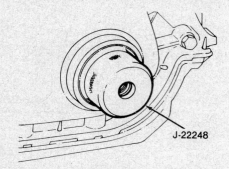

**Fig. 13   Timing case cover alignment tool. 4-150 & 6-243**

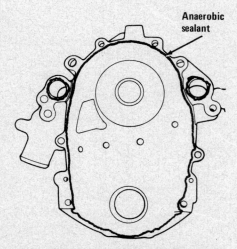

**Fig. 15   Applying sealant to timing case cover. V6-173**

Anaerobic sealant

3. Working through pushrod openings, remove valve lifters using tool J-21884 or equivalent, **Fig. 11**.
4. Reverse procedure to install, using service tool outlined above.

### V6-173

This engine may be equipped with both standard and .25mm. oversize valve lifters. Where oversized valve lifters are installed, the valve lifter boss will be marked by a dab of white paint and a ".25 OS" stamping as shown, **Fig. 12**.

1. Remove intake manifold and rocker arms as previously outlined.
2. Remove pushrods.
3. Using a suitable tool, remove valve lifters from cylinder block.
4. Reverse procedure to install. Coat base of lifter with Molykote or equivalent to prevent damage to lifter and/or camshaft.

## VALVE TIMING SPECIFICATIONS
### INTAKE OPENS BEFORE TDC

```
4-150.............................12°
V6-173 ............................7°
6-243.............................15°
```

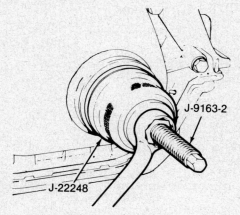

**Fig. 14   Installing front seal. 4-150**

## VALVE LIFT SPECIFICATIONS

| | | |
|---|---|---|
| 4-150 | .424 Intake | .424 Exhaust |
| V6-173 | .347 Intake | .394 Exhaust |
| 6-243 | .424 Intake | .424 Exhaust |

## VALVE GUIDES
### ALL ENGINES

The valve guides are an integral part of the cylinder head. If valve stem to guide clearance is excessive, the guide should be reamed to the next oversize and the appropriate oversized valve installed. Valves are available in .003 and .015 inch oversizes for 4-150 engines, .0035, .0155, and .0305 inch oversizes for V6-173 engines and .003 inch oversize for 6-243 engines. For 1989 models with 6-243, .015 and .030 oversizes are also available.

## TIMING CASE COVER & SEAL
### REPLACE
#### 4-150

1. Disconnect battery ground cable.
2. Remove drive belts, then the vibration damper and pulley.
3. Remove cooling fan and hub assembly, then the fan shroud.
4. Remove A/C compressor (if equipped) and alternator bracket assembly from cylinder head, and position aside.
5. Remove oil pan to cover retaining screws and cover to cylinder block retaining bolts.
6. Remove timing case cover, front seal and gasket.
7. Cut off oil pan side gasket end tabs and front seal tabs until they are flush with front face of cylinder block.
8. Clean timing case cover, oil pan and cylinder block sealing surfaces, then remove front crankshaft seal from timing cover.
9. Apply sealing compound to both sides of timing case cover gasket, then position gasket onto cylinder block.
10. Cut off end tabs from replacement oil

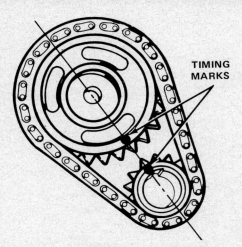

**Fig. 16 Aligning valve timing marks. 4-150 (6-243 similar)**

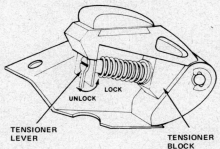

**Fig. 17 Timing chain tensioner. 4-150**

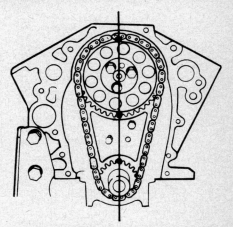

**Fig. 18 Aligning valve timing marks. V6-173**

pan side gaskets, then cement tabs to corresponding points on oil pan.

11. Coat front cover seal end tab recesses with RTV sealant, then position seal on timing case cover.
12. Apply engine oil to seal/oil pan contact surface, then position timing case cover onto cylinder block.
13. Install timing case cover alignment tool J-22248 or equivalent into opening in timing case cover as shown, **Fig. 13.**
14. Install cover to cylinder block retaining bolts and oil pan to cover retaining screws. Torque retaining bolts to 5 ft. lbs. and retaining screws to 11 ft. lbs.
15. Remove alignment tool, then position a new crankshaft seal onto tool, ensuring lip on seal faces outward. Apply a light coat of sealing compound to outside diameter of crankshaft seal, then coat crankshaft snout with engine oil.
16. Position alignment tool and seal over crankshaft snout, then insert installation tool J-9163-2 or equivalent into alignment tool as shown, **Fig. 14.** Tighten nut on installation tool until alignment tool contacts timing cover. Remove tool.
17. Install vibration damper and pulley. Torque vibration damper retaining nut to specification. **If engine is equipped with a serpentine drive belt, the pulley is integral with the vibration damper.**
18. Install A/C compressor (if equipped) and alternator bracket assembly, then the cooling fan, hub, and fan shroud.
19. Install drive belts, then reconnect battery ground cable.

## V6-173

1. Disconnect battery ground cable and drain cooling system.
2. Remove drive belts, then the radiator fan shroud.
3. Remove cooling fan and pulley.
4. If equipped with A/C, disconnect compressor from mounting bracket, position compressor aside and remove mounting bracket. Do not disconnect hoses from compressor.

5. Remove water pump retaining bolts and the water pump.
6. Remove vibration damper, then disconnect lower radiator hose from timing cover.
7. Remove timing cover attaching bolts, then the timing cover.
8. Pry crankshaft seal from timing cover, then position new seal so open end of seal faces towards inside of cover. Drive seal into position using tool J-23042 or equivalent.
9. Clean old sealant from timing cover and cylinder block.
10. Apply a continuous 3/32 inch bead of anaerobic sealant to timing cover sealing surface as shown, **Fig. 15,** then position cover onto cylinder block. Install bolts, then torque M8 x 1.25 bolts to 15 ft. lbs. and M10 x 1.50 bolts to 25 ft. lbs.
11. Install water pump.
12. Connect lower radiator hose, then install vibration damper.
13. Install A/C compressor mounting bracket, if equipped, then the cooling fan, pulley and fan shroud.
14. Install drive belts and fill cooling system.
15. Reconnect battery ground cable.

## 6-243

1. Disconnect battery ground cable.
2. Remove water pump from cylinder block.
3. Remove vibration damper using a suitable puller.
4. Remove timing case cover attaching bolts, then the timing case cover.
5. Remove timing case cover seal using a suitable tool.
6. Reverse procedure to install, noting the following:
   a. Install timing case cover and gasket, then align timing case cover using tool J-22248 or equivalent as shown, **Fig. 13.**
   b. Torque cover attaching bolts to 5 ft. lbs. and oil pan to cover attaching bolts to 11 ft. lbs.
   c. Apply suitable sealer to outside diameter of timing cover seal.
   d. Install seal into position. Seal can be installed by tapping on case cover seal installer tool J-22248 or equivalent with a suitable mallet until tool comes in contact with cover.
   e. Apply suitable oil to seal lip on inside diameter of timing cover seal.

## TIMING CHAIN & SPROCKETS
### REPLACE
#### 4-150 & 6-243

1. Remove timing case cover as previously outlined.
2. Rotate crankshaft until timing marks on camshaft and crankshaft sprockets align as shown in **Fig. 16**
3. Remove oil slinger from crankshaft snout.
4. Remove camshaft sprocket retaining bolt, then lift off sprockets and timing chain as an assembly.
5. On 4-150 engines, turn timing chain tensioner lever, **Fig. 17,** to its unlocked position, then pull tensioner block towards lever, to compress spring. While holding tensioner block in this position, lock tensioner lever as shown.
6. On all engines, install timing chain and sprockets, ensuring timing marks are properly aligned.
7. Install camshaft sprocket retaining bolt and torque to 80 ft. lbs. **To verify correct installation of timing chain, rotate crankshaft until camshaft sprocket timing mark is in one o'clock position. This should place crankshaft sprocket timing mark in three o'clock position. Count number of chain pins between timing marks. If valve timing is correct, there should be 20 chain pins between timing marks of both sprockets on 4-150 engines or 15 chain pins between timing marks of both sprockets on 6-243 engines.**
8. Install oil slinger, then the timing case cover.

#### V6-173

1. Remove timing case cover as outlined previously, then position No. 1 piston at TDC until marks on camshaft and crankshaft sprockets align as shown in **Fig. 18.**
2. Remove camshaft sprocket retaining

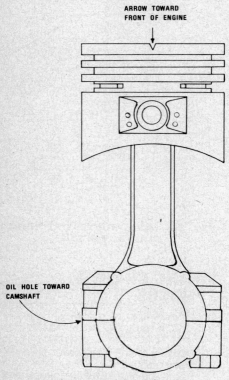

**Fig. 19 Piston & rod assembly. 4-150 (6-243 similar)**

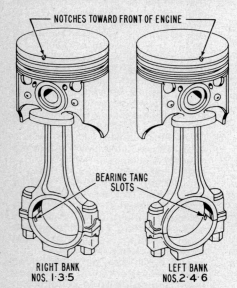

**Fig. 20 Piston & rod assembly. V6-173**

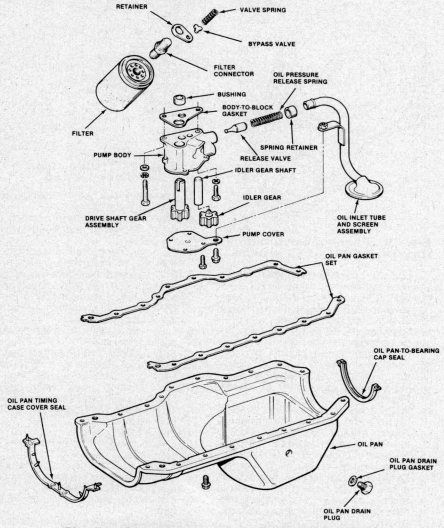

**Fig. 21 Oil pan & pump. 4-150 (6-243 similar)**

bolts, then the sprockets and timing chain.
3. Install timing chain on sprockets, then hold camshaft sprocket vertically to allow timing chain to hang downward. Align timing marks on sprockets as shown in **Fig. 18.**
4. Align dowel pin on camshaft with dowel pinhole on camshaft sprocket, then install sprockets onto camshaft and crankshaft.
5. Install camshaft sprocket retaining bolts and torque to 17 ft. lbs.

6. Lubricate timing chain, then install timing case cover as previously outlined.

## CAMSHAFT
### REPLACE
#### 4-150 & 6-243

1. Disconnect battery ground cable and drain cooling system.
2. Remove radiator and if equipped with A/C, the condenser.
3. Remove fuel pump, distributor and ignition wires.
4. Remove rocker arms, pushrods and valve lifters as previously outlined.
5. Remove timing case cover, then the timing chain and sprocket.
6. Carefully slide camshaft out of cylinder block.
7. Reverse procedure to install. Torque camshaft sprocket bolt to 80 ft. lbs.

#### V6-173

1. Disconnect battery ground cable and drain cooling system.

2. Remove radiator and if equipped with A/C, the condenser.
3. Remove intake manifold as previously outlined.
4. Remove fuel pump, push rods and valve lifters.
5. Remove timing case cover as previously outlined.
6. Remove timing chain and sprockets as outlined in "Timing Chain & Sprockets, Replace" procedure.
7. Carefully slide camshaft out of cylinder block.
8. Reverse procedure to install.

## PISTONS & RODS
### ASSEMBLE
#### 4-150 & 6-243

Pistons are marked with an arrow on the top perimeter. When assembling piston to rod, ensure arrow faces front of engine and oil spurt hole on connecting rod faces toward camshaft, as shown in **Fig. 19.** Check side clearance between connecting rod and crankshaft journal. Clearance

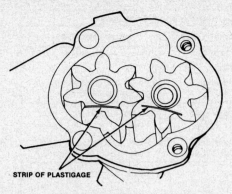

**Fig. 22 Checking oil pump gear end clearance. 4-150 & 6-243**

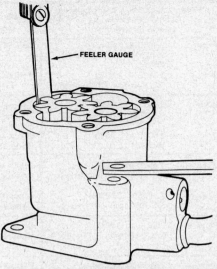

**Fig. 23 Checking oil pump gear to body clearance. 4-150 & 6-243**

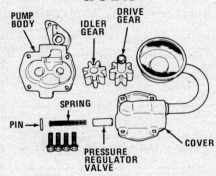

**Fig. 25 Oil pump disassembled view. V6-173**

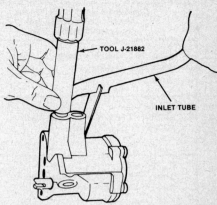

**Fig. 24 Installing oil pump pickup tube and screen assembly. 4-150 & 6-243**

should be .010 to .019 inch.

## V6-173

Assemble piston to connecting rod with notch on top of piston facing toward front of engine and connecting rod bearing tang opposite camshaft, as shown in **Fig. 20.** Check side clearance between connecting rod and crankshaft journal. Side clearance should be .006 to .017 inch.

## OIL PAN
## REPLACE
### 4-150 & 6-243

1. Disconnect battery ground cable.
2. Raise and support vehicle, then drain oil pan.
3. Disconnect exhaust pipe at manifold, then remove hanger at catalytic converter and allow pipe to drop to floor, if necessary.
4. Remove starter motor, then the transmission housing inspection cover.
5. Remove oil pan retaining bolts, then the oil pan and gaskets, **Fig. 21.**
6. Reverse procedure to install. Torque 1/4 bolts to 80 inch lbs. and 5/16 bolts to 11 ft. lbs.

### V6-173

1. Disconnect battery ground cable.
2. Disconnect right side exhaust pipe from manifold, then raise and support vehicle.
3. Drain oil pan.
4. Disconnect left side exhaust pipe from manifold, then remove starter motor.
5. Remove transmission housing inspection cover.
6. Disconnect exhaust pipe at catalytic converter flange, then lower "Y" pipe onto upper control arms.
7. Remove oil pan retaining bolts, then the oil pan and gasket.
8. Reverse procedure to install. **Before installing oil pan thoroughly clean all sealing surfaces, then apply a 1/8 inch bead of RTV sealant or equivalent to entire oil pan sealing flange.**

## OIL PUMP
## REPLACEMENT &
## SERVICING
### 4-150 & 6-243
**Removal**

1. Remove oil pan as previously outlined.
2. Remove oil pump to cylinder block retaining bolts, then the oil pump and gasket. **Do not disturb positioning of oil pump strainer and tube. If tube is moved, a replacement tube and screen assembly must be installed to prevent pump cavitation.**

**Inspection**

1. Remove pump cover to body retaining screws, then the pump cover.
2. Measure gear end clearance by positioning Plastigage across the full width of each gear as shown in **Fig. 22.** Reinstall pump cover and torque cover retaining bolts to 70 inch lbs. Remove cover and determine clear-

ance by comparing compressed Plastigage with scale on Plastigage envelope. Clearance should be .002-.006 inch. If clearance is excessive, replace oil pump.
3. Measure gear to pump body clearance by inserting a feeler gauge between each gear tooth and the pump body inner wall as shown in **Fig. 23.** Clearance should be .002-.004 inch. If clearance is excessive, replace idler gear, shaft and drive gear assembly.
4. If checking pressure relief valve, remove pickup tube and screen assembly and position aside. Remove cotter pin, then slide spring retainer, spring and pressure relief valve plunger out of pump body. If plunger binds during removal, clean or replace plunger as necessary. **Relief valve plungers are available in standard or .010 inch oversizes. When replacing plunger, ensure correct size is installed.**

**Assembly**

1. Install relief valve plunger, spring, retainer and cotter pin.
2. If pickup tube and screen assembly was removed, install replacement assembly as follows:
   a. Apply a light coat of Permatex No. 2 sealant or equivalent, to end of pickup tube.
   b. Using tool J-21882 or equivalent, drive tube into pump body as shown in **Fig. 24.** Ensure support bracket is aligned properly.
3. Before installing pump cover, fill pump with petroleum jelly.
4. Install pump cover and torque retaining screws to 70 inch lbs.

**Installation**

Install oil pump and new gasket onto cylinder block. Torque short retaining bolt to 10 ft. lbs and long retaining bolt to 17 ft. lbs., then install oil pan.

## V6-173
**Removal**

1. Remove oil pan as described under "Oil Pan, Replace."

| Crankshaft No. 1 Main Bearing Journal Color Codes and Diameter in inches (mm) | Cylinder Block No. 1 Main Bearing Bore Color Code and Size in inches (mm) | | Bearing Insert Color Code | |
|---|---|---|---|---|
| | | | Upper Insert Size | Lower Insert Size |
| Yellow — 2.5001 to 2.4996 (Standard) (63.5025 to 63.4898 mm) | Yellow — | 2.6910 to 2.6915 (68.3514 to 68.3641 mm) | Yellow — Standard | Yellow — Standard |
| | Black — | 2.6915 to 2.6920 (68.3641 to 68.3768 mm) | Yellow — Standard | Black — 0.001-inch Undersize (0.025 mm) |
| Orange — 2.4996 to 2.4991 (0.0005 Undersize) (63.4898 to 63.4771 mm) | Yellow — | 2.6910 to 2.6915 (68.3514 to 68.3641 mm) | Yellow — Standard | Black — 0.001-inch Undersize — (0.001 mm) |
| | Black — | 2.6915 to 2.6920 (68.3461 to 68.3768 mm) | Black — 0.001-inch Undersize (0.025 mm) | Black — 0.001-inch Undersize (0.025 mm) |
| Black — 2.4991 to 2.4986 (0.001 Undersize) (63.4771 to 63.4644 mm) | Yellow — | 2.6910 to 2.6915 (68.3514 to 68.3641 mm) | Black — 0.001-inch Undersize — (0.025 mm) | Black — 0.001-inch Undersize — (0.025 mm) |
| | Black — | 2.6915 to 2.6920 (68.3461 to 68.3768 mm) | Black — 0.001-inch Undersize (0.025 mm) | Green — 0.002-inch Undersize (0.051 mm) |
| Green — 2.4986 to 2.4981 (0.0015 Undersize) (63.4644 to 63.4517 mm) | Yellow — | 2.6910 to 2.6915 (68.3514 to 68.3641 mm) | Black — 0.001-inch Undersize — (0.025 mm) | Green — 0.002-inch Undersize — (0.051 mm) |
| Red — 2.4901 to 2.4896 (0.010 Undersize) (63.2485 to 63.2358 mm) | Yellow — | 2.6910 to 2.6915 (68.3514 to 68.3641 mm) | Red — 0.010-inch Undersize (0.254 mm) | Red — 0.010-inch Undersize — (0.254 mm) |

**Fig. 26   Main bearing selection chart. 4-150 & 6-243, No. 1 main bearing**

| Crankshaft Main Bearing Journal 2-3-4-5 Color Code and Diameter in inches (Journal Size) | Bearing Insert Color Code | |
|---|---|---|
| | Upper Insert Size | Lower Insert Size |
| Yellow — 2.5001 to 2.4996 (Standard) (63.5025 to 63.4898 mm) | Yellow — Standard | Yellow — Standard |
| Orange — 2.4996 to 2.4991 (0.0005 Undersize) (63.4898 to 63.4771 mm) | Yellow — Standard | Black — 0.001-inch Undersize (0.025mm) |
| Black — 2.4991 to 2.4986 (0.001 Undersize) (63.4771 to 63.4644 mm) | Black — 0.001-inch Undersize (0.025 mm) | Black — 0.001-inch Undersize (0.025 mm) |
| Green — 2.4986 to 2.4981 (0.0015 Undersize) (63.4644 to 63.4517 mm) | Black — 0.001-inch Undersize (0.025 mm) | Green — 0.002-inch Undersize (0.051 mm) |
| Red — 2.4901 to 2.4896 (0.010 Undersize) (63.2485 to 63.2358 mm) | Red — 0.010-inch Undersize (0.054 mm) | Red — 0.010-inch Undersize (0.254 mm) |

**Fig. 27   Main bearing selection chart. 4-150, Nos. 2, 3, 4, & 5 main bearings**

| Crankshaft Main Bearing Journals 2-6 Color Code and Diameter (Journal Size) | Bearing Insert Color Code | |
|---|---|---|
| | Upper Insert Size | Lower Insert Size |
| Yellow — 63.5025-63.4898 mm (2.5001-2.4996 in.) (Standard) | Yellow – Standard | Yellow – Standard |
| Orange – 63.4898-63.4771 mm (2.4996-2.4991 in.) (0.0005 Undersize) | Yellow – Standard | Black – 0.025 mm Undersize (0.001 in.) |
| Black – 63.4771-63.4644 mm (2.4991-2.4986 in.) (0.001 Undersize) | Black – 0.025 mm Undersize (0.001 in.) | Black – 0.025 mm Undersize (0.001 in.) |
| Green – 63.4644-63.4517 mm (2.4986-2.4981 in.) (0.0015 Undersize) | Black – 0.025 mm Undersize (0.001 in.) | Green – 0.051 mm Undersize (0.002 in.) |
| Red – 63.2485-63.2358 mm (2.4901-2.4986 in.) (0.010 Undersize) | Red – 0.054 mm Undersize (0.010 in.) | Red – 0.254 mm Undersize (0.010 in.) |

**Fig. 28   Main bearing selection chart. 6-243, Nos. 2, 3, 4, 5 & 6 main bearings**

| Crankshaft Main Bearing Journal 7 Color Code and Diameter (Journal Size) | Bearing Insert Color Code | |
|---|---|---|
| | Upper Insert Size | Lower Insert Size |
| Yellow – 63.4873-63.4746 mm (2.4995-2.4990 in.) (Standard) | Yellow – Standard | Yellow – Standard |
| Orange – 63.4746-63.4619 mm (2.4990-2.4985 in.) (0.0005 Undersize) | Yellow – Standard | Black – 0.025 mm Undersize (0.001 in.) |
| Black – 63.4619-63.4492 mm (2.4985-2.4980 in.) (0.001 Undersize) | Black – 0.025 mm Undersize (0.001 in.) | Black – 0.025 mm Undersize (0.001 in.) |
| Green – 63.4492-63.4365 mm (2.4980-2.4975 in.) (0.0015 Undersize) | Black – 0.025 mm Undersize (0.001 in.) | Green – 0.051 mm Undersize (0.002 in.) |
| Red – 63.2333-63.2206 mm (2.4895-2.4890 in.) (0.010 Undersize) | Red – 0.254 mm Undersize (0.010 in.) | Red – 0.254 mm Undersize (0.010 in.) |

**Fig. 29 Main bearing selection chart. 6-243, No. 7 main bearing**

| Crankshaft Connecting Rod Journal Color Code and Diameter in Inches ( Journal Size ) | Bearing Insert Color Code | |
|---|---|---|
| | Upper Insert Size | Lower Insert Size |
| Yellow — 2.0955 to 2.0948 (53.2257 - 53.2079 mm) (Standard) | Yellow — Standard | Yellow — Standard |
| Orange —2.0948 to 2.0941 (53.2079 - 53.1901 mm) (0.0007 Undersize) | Yellow — Standard | Black — 0.001-inch (0.025 mm) Undersize |
| Black — 2.0941 to 2.0943 (53.1901 to 53.1723 mm) (0.0014 Undersize) | Black — 0.001-inch (0.025 mm) Undersize | Black — 0.001-inch (0.025 mm) Undersize |
| Red — 2.0855 to 2.0848 (53.9717 to 53.9539 mm) (0.010 Undersize) | Red — 0.010-inch (0.254 mm) Undersize | Red — 0.010-inch (0.245 mm) Undersize |

**Fig. 30 Connecting rod bearing selection chart. 4-150 & 6-243**

2. Remove pump to rear main bearing cap bolt, and pump and extension shaft.

## Disassembly

1. Remove pump cover attaching bolts and pump cover, **Fig. 25.**
2. Mark drive and idler gear teeth so they can be installed in the same position, then remove idler and drive gear and shaft from pump body.
3. Remove pin, spring and pressure regulator valve from pump cover.
4. If pickup tube and screen assembly are to be replaced, mount pump cover in a soft jawed vise and remove pickup tube from cover. Do not remove screen from pickup tube, as these components are serviced as an assembly.

## Inspection

1. Inspect pump body and cover for excessive wear and cracks.
2. Inspect pump gear for damage or excessive wear. If pump gears are damaged or worn, the entire pump assembly must be replaced.
3. Check drive gear shaft for looseness in pump body.
4. Inspect pump cover for wear that

would allow oil to leak past gear teeth.
5. Inspect pickup tube and screen assembly for damage.
6. Check pressure regulator valve for fit in pump cover.

## Assembly

1. If pickup tube and screen were removed, apply sealer to end of pickup tube, mount pump cover in a soft jawed vise and using tool No. J-21882, tap pickup tube into position using a plastic mallet. **Whenever the pick-up tube and screen assembly has been removed, a new assembly should be installed. Use care when installing assembly so tube does not twist, shear or collapse. Loss of a press fit condition could result in an air leak and a loss of oil pressure.**
2. Install pressure regulator valve, spring and pin, **Fig. 25.**
3. Install drive gear and shaft in pump body.
4. Align marks made during disassembly, then install idler gear.
5. Install pump cover gasket, cover and attaching bolts. Torque bolts to 6 to 9 ft. lbs.
6. Rotate pump drive shaft by hand and check pump for smooth operation.

## Installation

1. Assemble pump and extension shaft with retainer to rear main bearing cap, aligning top end of hexagon extension shaft with hexagon socket on lower end of distributor shaft.
2. Install pump to rear main bearing cap bolt.
3. Install oil pan as described under "Oil Pan, Replace."

# MAIN BEARINGS
## 4-150 & 6-243

The main bearing journal diameter is identified by a color-coded paint mark located on the adjacent cheek toward the rear (flanged) end of the crankshaft, except for the rear main journal mark which is located on the crankshaft rear flange. Color codes used to indicate journal and corresponding bearing sizes are listed in **Figs. 26 through 29.**

## V6-173

Main bearings are available in standard size and undersizes of .013 and .026mm.

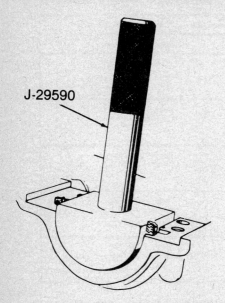

Fig. 31 Rear main oil seal repair. V6-173

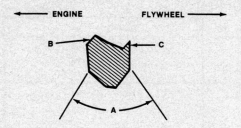

Fig. 32 Cross sectional view of two-piece type rear seal

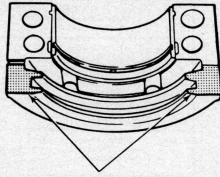

Fig. 33 Applying sealant to rear main cap

## CONNECTING ROD BEARINGS

### 4-150 & 6-243

The connecting rod journal is identified by a color coded paint mark on the adjacent cheek or counterweight near the rear of the crankshaft. Color codes used to indicate journal sizes and corresponding bearing sizes are listed in **Fig. 30**.

### V6-173

Connecting rod bearings are available in standard size and undersizes of .013 and .026mm.

## REAR MAIN OIL SEAL

### 4-150

1. Remove transmission as outlined in the "Clutch & Manual Transmission" section of this chapter.
2. Remove flywheel or converter drive plate.
3. Carefully pry seal out from around crankshaft flange.
4. Coat inner lip of replacement seal with engine oil, then carefully position seal around flange.
5. Using tool J-36306 or equivalent, tap seal until flush with cylinder block.
6. Install flywheel or converter drive plate, then the transmission.

### V6-173

Three different type rear main seals are used to replace the original rope-type seal. A two-piece seal is used on engines equipped with a knurled crankshaft built prior to May 17, 1984. A narrow one-piece seal is used on engines without a knurled crankshaft built after May 17, 1984, and a wide one-piece seal is used on all 1985-86 vehicles. The original rope-type seal can be repaired by fol-

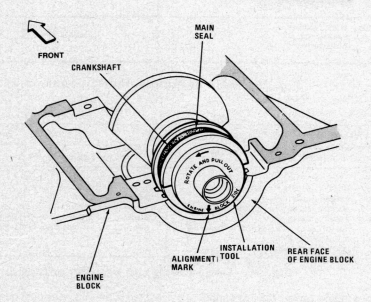

Fig. 34 Installing narrow one-piece type rear seal

lowing the procedure outlined below. Also found below will be the replacement procedures for the two-piece seal, and both narrow and wide one-piece seals.

#### Rope-Type Seal Repair

1. Remove oil pan and oil pump as previously described.
2. Remove rear main bearing cap.
3. Using tool No. J-29114-2, gently drive upper seal into groove approximately 1/4 in.
4. Repeat step 3 for other end of seal.
5. Measure the amount that was driven in on one side and add 1/16 in. Using a suitable cutting tool, cut this length from the oil rear main bearing cap lower seal using the main bearing cap as a guide. Repeat this step for the other end of seal.
6. Place piece of cut seal into groove of seal installer tool guide No. J-29114-1 and install tool guide onto engine block.
7. Using seal packing tool No. J-29114-2, drive piece of seal into block. Drive seal in until packing tool

contacts machined stop.
8. Remove tool guide and repeat steps 6 and 7 for other end of seal.
9. Install new seal in bearing cap.
10. Cut ends of seal flush with cap using tool J-29590, **Fig. 31**.
11. Place a piece of plastic gauging material on rear main journal, then install rear main bearing cap and torque to 70 ft. lbs.
12. Remove rear cap and check plastic gauge for bearing clearance. If clearance is not within specifications, recheck seal ends for fraying which may prevent cap from fully seating, and repair as necessary.
13. Clean plastic gauge from journal and bearing.
14. Apply a thin film of sealant No. 1052357 or equivalent to rear cap, then install cap. Use care not to allow sealant to contact the seal and bearing.

#### Two-Piece Seal Replacement

1. Remove oil pan and pump as outlined previously.

2. Remove rear main cap and both halves of original seal.
3. Loosen the number 2 and 3 main bearing cap bolts, then clean seal channels of both cylinder block and rear main cap with suitable solvent.
4. Apply a thin coating of sealant 8993539 or equivalent, to outer perimeter (A) of new seal halves, **Fig. 32.** Do not allow sealant to contact seal lips.
5. Install one seal half into cylinder block, ensuring that seal lips (B and C) are positioned as shown, **Fig. 32.** Slowly rotate crankshaft to help facilitate seal installation.
6. Install other seal half into rear main cap. Ensure seal lips (B and C) are positioned as outlined in previous step.
7. Coat shaded areas of rear main cap, **Fig. 33,** with Loctite 515 sealant or equivalent, then apply engine oil to seal contact surface of crankshaft.
8. Install rear main cap, torque all main bearing cap bolts to specification, then install oil pump and oil pan.

### Narrow One-Piece Seal Replacement

1. Remove engine as outlined previously.
2. Remove oil pan, oil pump and crankshaft.
3. Remove rear main seal, then clean main bearing cap, cylinder block and crankshaft with suitable solvent.
4. Apply a .040 inch bead of Loctite 515 sealant or equivalent, to outside diameter of replacement seal. **The replacement seal is pre-mounted on an installation tool. Do not remove seal from tool when applying sealant.**
5. Carefully install replacement seal/installation tool assembly onto crankshaft, ensuring that alignment mark of tool will be centered on rear main bearing when crankshaft is installed, **Fig. 34.**
6. Align replacement seal with seal groove in cylinder block, then carefully install crankshaft. Rotate installation tool counterclockwise and pull tool off crankshaft.
7. Coat crankshaft journals with engine oil, then apply Loctite sealant 515 or equivalent to shaded areas of rear main cap, **Fig. 33.**
8. Install main bearing and connecting rod caps and torque all cap bolts to specification.
9. Install oil pump and oil pan, then reinstall engine assembly into vehicle.

### Wide One-Piece Seal Replacement

1. Remove transmission.
2. Remove converter drive plate or flywheel.
3. Insert a screwdriver under main seal dust lip, then pry upward and remove seal from bore.
4. Inspect seal bore for nicks or scratches. Clean up nicks or scratches with crocus cloth to prevent damage to new seal, then clean bore with suit-

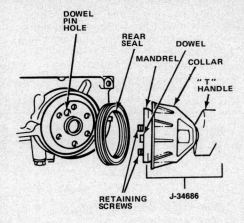

**Fig. 35   Installing wide one-piece type rear seal**

able solvent.
5. Thoroughly lubricate inner and outer surfaces of new seal with engine oil, fully retract mandrel of installation tool J-34686, then position replacement seal onto tool, **Fig. 35.** Ensure dust lip of seal faces toward collar of tool as shown.
6. Align dowel pin of installation tool with dowel pin hole in crankshaft flange, then install tool retaining screws and torque to 3 ft. lbs.
7. Tighten installation tool "T" handle until collar is firmly seated against cylinder block and bearing cap.
8. Loosen "T" handle of tool, then remove retaining screws and installation tool.
9. Install converter drive plate or flywheel, then the transmission.

### 6-243

This engine uses a two piece type rear main bearing oil seal. Replace both upper and lower seal halves as a unit.
1. Remove transmission and flywheel or drive plate.
2. Remove rear main bearing cap.
3. Remove upper and lower seal halves, then wipe seal surface area of crankshaft until it is clean.
4. Apply suitable oil to seal lips, then install upper seal in cylinder block. **Ensure lip of seal faces toward front of engine.**
5. Apply suitable sealing compound to both sides of lower seal end tabs. **Use caution not to apply sealant to lip of seal.**
6. Coat outer curved surface of lower seal with suitable soap and lip of seal with oil.
7. Install lower seal into bearing cap recess and seat it firmly. Apply sealing compound to both chamfered edges of rear main bearing cap, then install rear main bearing cap and cap attaching bolts. Torque cap attaching bolts to 80 ft. lbs. **Use caution not to apply sealant to cylinder block mating surfaces of rear main bearing cap because bearing to journal clearance could change.**

## MECHANICAL FUEL PUMP

### 4-150

1. Disconnect fuel lines from pump.
2. Remove retaining screws and fuel pump.
3. Remove all gasket material from the pump and block gasket surfaces. Apply sealer to both sides of new gasket.
4. Position gasket on pump flange and hold pump in position against its mounting surface. Ensure rocker arm is riding on camshaft eccentric.
5. Press pump tight against its mounting. Install retaining screws and tighten them alternately.
6. Connect fuel lines. Then operate engine and check for leaks. **When installing pump, crank engine to place camshaft eccentric in a position which will place the least amount of tension on fuel pump rocker arm. This will ease pump installation.**

### V6-173

1. Disconnect battery ground cable.
2. Disconnect inlet and outlet hoses from fuel pump.
3. Remove fuel pump attaching bolts, then the fuel pump and gasket.
4. Reverse procedure to install. **Before installing pump, rotate camshaft to "down stroke" position. When installation is completed, start engine and check for fuel leaks.** Torque bolts to 15 ft. lbs.

## ELECTRIC FUEL PUMP REPLACE

1. Disconnect battery ground cable.
2. Drain fuel from tank, then raise and support vehicle.
3. Remove fuel outlet and return hoses, then the fuel sending unit electrical connector.
4. Remove fuel sending unit retaining lock ring, then the sending unit and O-ring seal from fuel tank.
5. Disconnect fuel hose from pump, then the pump electrical connector.
6. Remove fuel pump to sending unit attaching nut, then separate fuel pump from sending unit.
7. Reverse procedure to install.

## WATER PUMP REPLACE

### 4-150 & 6-243

1. Drain cooling system, then disconnect hoses from pump.
2. Remove drive belts.
3. If equipped with power steering, remove power steering pump bracket from water pump boss.
4. Remove fan assembly and, if equipped, the radiator fan shroud.
5. Remove water pump retaining bolts, then the water pump and gasket.

6. Reverse procedure to install. Torque bolts to 13 ft. inch lbs.

## V6-173

1. Drain cooling system, then remove drive belts.
2. Remove fan assembly and, if equipped, the radiator shroud attaching screws and shroud.
3. Disconnect heater hose from pump, then remove water pump attaching bolts and nut and the water pump.
4. Reverse procedure to install.

## BELT TENSION DATA

Tension on new power steering pump drive belt should measure 120–140 lbs. All other V-belts should measure 120–160 lbs. when new and 90–115 lbs. when used. Serpentine drive belt tension should measure 180–200 lbs. when new and 140–160 lbs. when used.

# 4-126 (2.1L) DIESEL ENGINE

## INDEX

## ENGINE
### REPLACE

1. Scribe hood hinge locations and remove hood.
2. Disconnect battery cables and remove battery.
3. Remove skid plate, if equipped.
4. Drain cooling system and remove air cleaner assembly.
5. On models with A/C, seat service valve and remove them from the compressor.
6. On all models, disconnect radiator hoses and remove E-clip from bottom of radiator.
7. Raise and support vehicle.
8. On models equipped with automatic transmission, disconnect cooler lines.
9. Remove splash shield from the oil pan, then lower vehicle.
10. Loosen radiator shroud, then remove the radiator fan.
11. Remove shroud and splash shield.
12. Remove radiator.
13. On models equipped with A/C, remove condenser.
14. Remove intercooler.
15. On all models, remove the exhaust shield from manifold.
16. Disconnect oil hoses from filter, then remove oil filter.
17. Tag and disconnect all vacuum hoses and electrical connections.
18. Disconnect and plug the fuel inlet and return lines.
19. Remove left motor mount cushion through bolt attaching nut (automatic transmission), then the motor mount cushion attaching bolts.
20. Disconnect throttle cable, then raise vehicle.
21. On models equipped with power steering, disconnect power steering hoses, then drain power steering pump.
22. On all models, disconnect exhaust pipe at exhaust manifold.
23. Remove motor mount attaching nuts.
24. Support engine, then remove left motor mount bolts (automatic transmission).

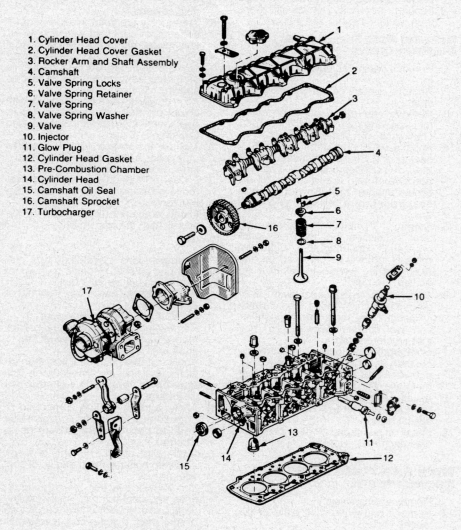

1. Cylinder Head Cover
2. Cylinder Head Cover Gasket
3. Rocker Arm and Shaft Assembly
4. Camshaft
5. Valve Spring Locks
6. Valve Spring Retainer
7. Valve Spring
8. Valve Spring Washer
9. Valve
10. Injector
11. Glow Plug
12. Cylinder Head Gasket
13. Pre-Combustion Chamber
14. Cylinder Head
15. Camshaft Oil Seal
16. Camshaft Sprocket
17. Turbocharger

**Fig. 1   Cylinder head exploded view**

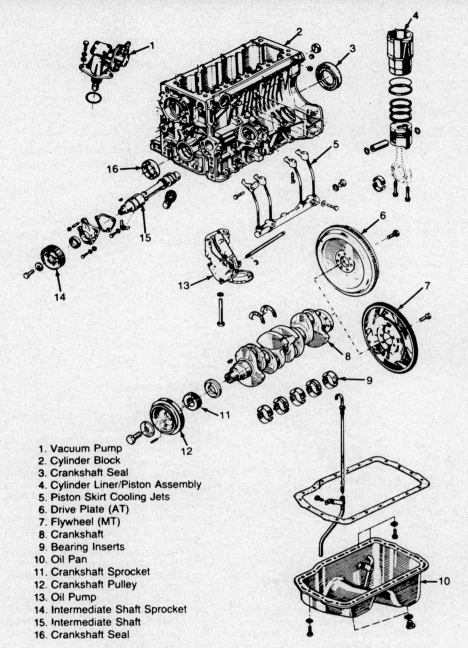

1. Vacuum Pump
2. Cylinder Block
3. Crankshaft Seal
4. Cylinder Liner/Piston Assembly
5. Piston Skirt Cooling Jets
6. Drive Plate (AT)
7. Flywheel (MT)
8. Crankshaft
9. Bearing Inserts
10. Oil Pan
11. Crankshaft Sprocket
12. Crankshaft Pulley
13. Oil Pump
14. Intermediate Shaft Sprocket
15. Intermediate Shaft
16. Crankshaft Seal

**Fig. 2  Cylinder block exploded view**

Mot. 861

**Fig. 3  TDC inspection plug location**

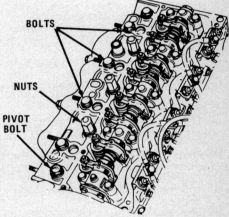

BOLTS

NUTS

PIVOT BOLT

**Fig. 4  Cylinder head removal**

25. Remove left motor mount.
26. Disconnect starter motor electrical connectors and attaching bolts, then remove starter motor.
27. Mark and remove the converter to drive plate bolts.
28. Remove the transmission to engine retaining bolts, then lower vehicle.
29. Remove remaining motor mount retaining bolts.
30. On models equipped with power steering, remove power steering reservoir.
31. On all models, remove the oil separator.
32. Disconnect heater hoses.
33. Remove the reference pressure regulator from dash panel. Attach suitable engine lifting equipment to engine. Support transmission with a suitable jack.
34. Remove engine from vehicle.
35. Reverse procedure to install.

# ENGINE DISASSEMBLY

Refer to Figs. 1 and 2 for disassembled view of engine.
1. Remove drive belts, alternator, starter and A/C compressor, if equipped.
2. Remove oil supply line and oil return hose from turbocharger.
3. Remove turbocharger attaching bolts, then the turbocharger.

4. Remove valve cover attaching bolts, then the cover and gasket.
5. Remove TDC inspection plug, **Fig. 3**. Rotate the crankshaft into position and insert TDC rod Mot. 861 into TDC slot in crankshaft countershaft. **Ensure rod is not inserted into crankshaft counterweight balance hole.**
6. Remove fan and water pump pulley assembly.
7. Drain cooling system and engine oil.
8. Remove timing belt cover attaching screws, then the cover.
9. Install sprocket holding tool Mot. 854 or equivalent, then remove the camshaft sprocket retaining bolt.
10. Loosen belt tensioner bolts and posi-

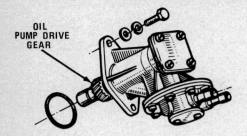

**Fig. 5  Vacuum pump with oil pump drive gear**

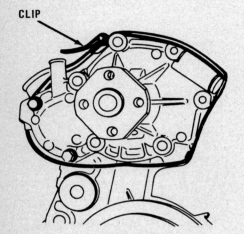

**Fig. 7  Water pump removal**

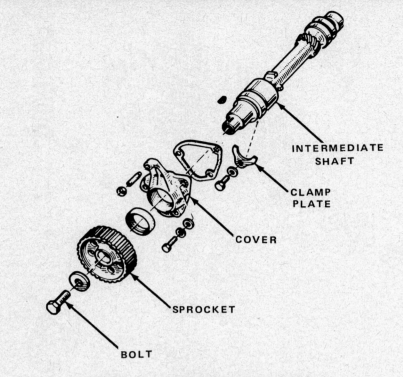

**Fig. 6  Intermediate shaft assembly**

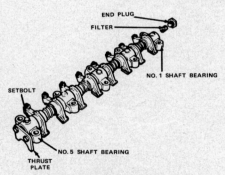

**Fig. 8  Rocker arm shaft assembly**

tion tensioner away from belt. Tighten tensioner bolts, then remove belt.

11. Disconnect fuel pipe fittings from injectors and injection pump. Cap all openings.
12. Disconnect and cap all hoses from fuel injection pump.
13. Remove mounting brackets and attaching bolts, then the injection pump assembly.
14. Remove cylinder head attaching nuts and bolts, then loosen pivot bolt, **Fig. 4.**
15. Remove the remaining cylinder head attaching bolts. Place a block of wood against the cylinder head and tap it lightly with a hammer to loosen cylinder head gasket.
16. Remove the pivot bolt and rocker arm shaft attaching bolts, then the rocker arm shaft assembly. **Do not lift cylinder head from the cylinder block until gasket is completely loosened from the cylinder liners, since liner seals could be damaged.**
17. Remove the cylinder head and gasket, then install cylinder liner clamps, Mot. 521-01 or equivalent, onto cylinder block.
18. Remove camshaft sprocket attaching bolt.
19. Install tool B.Vi 28-01 or equivalent, onto camshaft sprocket, then remove sprocket.
20. Disconnect fuel return hose fittings from injectors, then remove holders and injectors. Cap all openings. **Mark each injector with the corresponding cylinder number to facilitate installation.**

21. Remove copper washers and heat shields. **Copper washers and heat shields must be replaced when injectors are installed.**
22. Remove wire harness and glow plugs.
23. Remove intake and exhaust manifolds, then gaskets from the cylinder head.
24. Remove camshaft oil seal using a suitable puller, then remove camshaft from cylinder head.
25. Remove thermostat housing and gasket.
26. Remove vacuum pump along with pump drive gear, **Fig. 5.**
27. Loosen intermediate shaft drive sprocket bolt using sprocket holding tool Mot. 855 or equivalent, and suitable wrench.
28. Remove intermediate shaft bolt, sprocket, cover attaching screws, cover, clamp plate and intermediate shaft, **Fig. 6.**
29. Remove oil pan attaching screws, then the oil pan.

30. Remove oil pump assembly attaching screws, then the oil pump.
31. Using a long strap and clip, **Fig. 7,** retain timing belt tensioner plunger, then remove water pump attaching screws, water pump, inlet housing and gasket.
32. Remove crankshaft pulley attaching bolt, washer and pulley. **Remove pins from the crankshaft pulley.**
33. Using a suitable puller, remove the crankshaft sprocket and washer as follows:
    a. Position sprocket removal tool B.Vi 28-01 (with shaft end protector tool 15-01), with jaws inserted behind sprocket washer.
    b. Force sprocket washer and sprocket away from crankshaft until washer stops against Woodruff key. Do not force washer beyond this position.
    c. Remove tools installed in step (a), then install tools with jaws inserted between the sprocket washer and sprocket assembly.
    d. Force sprocket from crankshaft assembly.
    e. If there is not enough clearance between the washer and sprocket to insert sprocket removal tool jaws, insert two .078 inch metal strips between the washer and sprocket.
    f. Insert the removal tool jaws behind the washer and force the washer and sprocket assembly from crankshaft until the washer stops at the Woodruff key. Then repeat step (c).
34. Remove connecting rod bearing cap bolts, connecting rod bearing caps and bearing inserts.

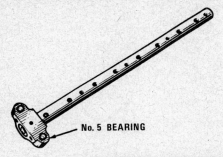

Fig. 9    Installing shaft bearing

Fig. 10    Foil installation

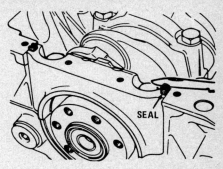

Fig. 11    Seal installation

35. Remove cylinder liner clamps.
36. Remove connecting rods, cylinder liners and pistons as an assembly. **Each piston and cylinder liner are a matched set. Mark each piston and liner to ensure installation in their original positions.**
37. Install holding plate Mot. 582 or equivalent to prevent the crankshaft from turning, then remove flywheel or drive plate from crankshaft.
38. Remove the crankshaft main bearing caps. **Mark the crankshaft main bearing caps according to their position, to facilitate installation in their original positions.**
39. Remove bearing inserts from the caps, then crankshaft and bearing upper inserts.
40. Using a suitable puller, remove clutch pilot bearing from the crankshaft, if equipped.

## ROCKER ARM SHAFT DISASSEMBLY

1. Remove camshaft thrust plate, Fig. 8.
2. Remove end plug and filter.
3. Remove No. 1 shaft bearing.
4. Remove set bolt and No. 5 shaft bearing.
5. Remove springs, rocker arms and remaining shaft bearings.
6. Retain all components in order removed to facilitate installation.

## CYLINDER HEAD DISASSEMBLY

1. Compress valve spring, then remove valve collets.
2. Release valve spring compressor, then remove spring retainer, spring, oil seal, spring seat and valve.
3. Place valve train components in their original order to facilitate installation.

## PISTON & ROD DISASSEMBLY

1. Remove piston rings.
2. Remove piston pin retaining clips, then the piston pin.
3. Keep disassembled parts in their original order to facilitate installation.

# ASSEMBLY

## CYLINDER HEAD ASSEMBLY

1. Insert valve into valve guide.
2. Install valve spring seat and stem oil seal.

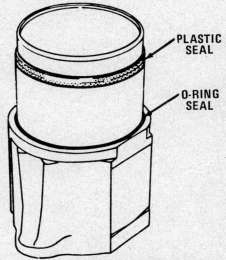

Fig. 12    Installing seals on liners

3. Install spring and valve spring retainer.
4. Compress valve spring and install valve collets.

## PISTON & ROD ASSEMBLY

1. Insert piston pin through piston and connecting rod, then install retaining clips.
2. Install piston rings.
3. Ensure that pistons, rods and cylinder liners for each cylinder assembly are installed in their original positions. **When installing rods, ensure that each connecting rod lubrication hole is adjacent to the oil pump side of the cylinder block.**

## ROCKER ARM SHAFT ASSEMBLY

1. Install No. 5 shaft bearing, then the set bolt in the bearing so that shaft oil holes face downward, Fig. 9. **The intake and exhaust valve rocker arms are identical.**
2. Install valve rocker arm, spring and another rocker arm.
3. Install intermediary shaft bearing with the offset facing toward the flywheel, or drive plate end of the cylinder head. Continue with the installation of the remaining components.
4. Install the No. 1 shaft bearing, filter and end plug.
5. Install thrust plate. Torque set bolts to 20 ft. lbs. and end plug to 15 ft. lbs.

# ENGINE ASSEMBLY

If main bearing inserts are being fitted to an out-of-round journal, ensure that the inserts are large enough for the maximum diameter of the journal. If inserts are fitted to the minimum diameter and the journal is out-of-round 0.001 inch or more, interference between bearing inserts and journal will result in rapid bearing failure.

1. Position crankshaft in cylinder block, then install main bearing cap Nos. 2, 3 and 4 with the replacement lower inserts in position.
2. Install the No. 1 main bearing cap, with a replacement lower insert, without the side seals. Tighten bolts and check endplay. **If endplay is not within specification, install thrust washers as necessary to obtain the correct endplay.**
3. Install No. 5 main bearing cap, with a replacement lower insert. Rotate crankshaft and ensure that it rotates smoothly.
4. Measure distance between the No. 1 main bearing cap and cylinder block, and No. 5 main bearing cap and cylinder block. If distance is .197 inch or less, use a .201 inch thick side seal. If distance is more than .197 inch, use a .212 inch thick seal.
5. Remove the No. 1 and No. 5 main bearing caps, then insert side seals in the main bearing cap slots, with grooves facing outward. **Each side seal should protrude approximately 0.008 inch outward from cap. Lubricate contact surfaces of side seals lightly with clean engine oil.**
6. Position a strip of suitable foil, Fig. 10, on each side of the main bearing caps. Torque caps to specifications.
7. Cut side seal ends so they protrude .020-.028 inch above the cylinder block surface, Fig. 11.
8. Using oil seal installation tool Mot. 788 or equivalent, for the seal at the flywheel/drive plate end and Mot. 789 or equivalent, for seal at the crankshaft sprocket end of cylinder block, install main bearing oil seals. **If oil seal lip has excessively worn the contact surface at either end of the crankshaft, a .06 inch washer must**

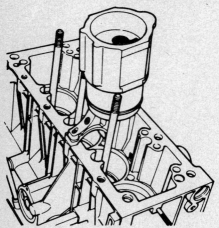

**Fig. 13  Piston, connecting rod and liner installation**

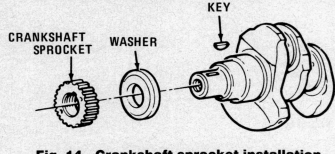

**Fig. 14  Crankshaft sprocket installation**

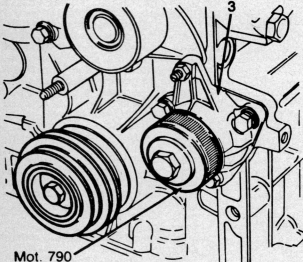

Mot. 790

**Fig. 15  Aligning intermediate shaft cover**

**Fig. 16  Oil pump assembly installation**

be placed between installation tool and replacement oil seal to position seal further inward on crankshaft.

9. Install a replacement O-ring seal and plastic ring on each cylinder liner and ensure that O-ring is not damaged, **Fig. 12.** If a connecting rod bearing upper insert is being fitted to an out-of-round journal, ensure that insert is large enough for the maximum diameter of the journal. If bearing insert is fitted to the minimum diameter and journal is out-of-round 0.001 inch or more, interference between the bearing insert and journal will result in rapid bearing failure. The bearing upper inserts have lubrication holes and the lower inserts do not. Ensure that the holes in upper insert are aligned with lubrication holes in the connecting rod.

10. Install piston, connecting rod and cylinder liner assemblies into cylinder

block with bearing upper inserts and rods positioned on crankshaft journals, **Fig. 13.** Ensure that cylinder liners are installed correctly. No. 1 cylinder liner assembly is adjacent to flywheel/drive plate end of block and liner flat surfaces are parallel. Ensure cylinder number stamped on each connecting rod and bearing cap is adjacent to the intermediate shaft side of block, and the combustion chamber in each piston crown faces toward the intermediate shaft side of block.

11. Install liner clamp tool Mot. 521-01 or equivalent, to cylinder head and torque bolts to 37 ft. lbs. to compress the liner seals to prevent liner seals from shifting.

12. Install each connecting rod bearing cap on its original connecting rod. Torque bearing cap bolts to 44-48 ft. lbs. **Tap each connecting rod lightly (parallel to the crankshaft) and ensure that there is adequate clearance. Rotate crankshaft and en-**

sure that the pistons, connecting rods and crankshaft function normally.

13. Install oil pump assembly and gasket. Ensure that locating dowels are in place. Torque oil pump retaining bolts to 30-33 ft. lbs.

14. Install oil pan and gasket. Torque bolts to 70-88 inch lbs.

15. Install water pump assembly. Continue to retain the timing belt tensioner plunger along with long strap and clip. Connect coolant hose and release strap, clip and timing belt tensioner.

16. Install clutch pilot bearing into end of crankshaft, if equipped. Seat bearing by gently tapping with a rubber mallet.

17. Apply Loctite 549, or equivalent, onto crankshaft to flywheel/drive plate mating surface.

18. Position flywheel/drive plate on to crankshaft and install holding tool Mot. 582 or equivalent. **The original flywheel/drive plate self-locking bolts are not reusable. Use replacement bolts for each installation.**

19. Lubricate threads of the replacement flywheel/drive plate bolts with Loctite 242, or equivalent, and torque flywheel bolts to 41 ft. lbs., and drive plate bolts to 52 ft. lbs. Bend locking plate tabs over flywheel/drive plate bolts. Remove holding tool.

20. Install washer, key and crankshaft sprocket, **Fig. 14.** The chamfered side of washer must face cylinder block and chamfered edge of sprocket bore faces washer.

**Fig. 17 Adjusting intermediate shaft cover clearance**

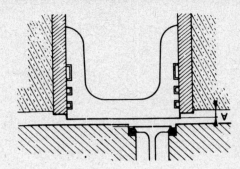

**Fig. 18 Piston protrusion measurement**

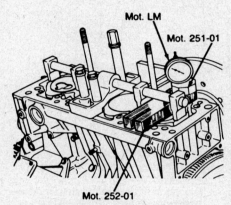

**Fig. 19 Dial indicator installation**

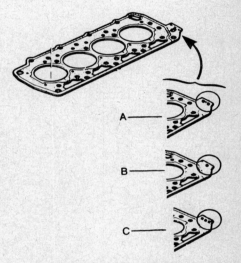

**Fig. 20 Head gasket identification**

21. Install the intermediate shaft, clamp plate, gasket and cover. Loosely install retaining bolt and nut.
22. Install intermediate shaft oil seal and align cover with installation tool Mot. 790, **Fig. 15. If oil seal lip contact surface on the intermediate shaft has been excessively worn by the original seal, insert a .04 inch washer between the seal and installation tool to position seal further inward on shaft. The intermediate shaft cover retaining bolt extends through cylinder block and oil could seep out around bolt unless properly sealed.**
23. Apply Loctite 242, or equivalent, to bolt threads, then install and tighten intermediate shaft cover retaining bolt and nut.
24. Install intermediate shaft sprocket, washer and bolt. Install sprocket with wider offset facing cylinder block.
25. Using holding tool Mot. 855 or equivalent, torque sprocket bolt to 37 ft. lbs.
26. Install oil pump drive shaft, gear, washer, and vacuum pump, **Fig. 16.** Clearance between the intermediate shaft cover and the timing belt tensioner must be adjusted to prevent lateral movement of the timing belt

when belt is tightened. The correct clearance is .004 inch. Adjust clearance by turning adjustment screw, **Fig. 17.**
27. Before the cylinder head can be installed, piston protrusion measurement must be done to determine correct size replacement gasket to be used. To determine piston protrusion, proceed as follows: **The piston protrusion measurement, (A), Fig. 18, procedure is necessary whenever major engine components have been replaced.**
   a. Rotate crankshaft one complete revolution and position No. 1 piston near (before) TDC of compression stroke.
   b. Place thrust plate tool Mot. 252-01 or equivalent, on top of piston, then insert dial indicator Mot. LM in block gauge Mot. 251-01 or equivalent. Tighten screw clamp and place assembly on one side of thrust plate. Zero dial indicator pointer with stem located on cylinder block face, **Fig. 19.** Place dial indicator stem on piston crown and rotate crankshaft clockwise until piston is at TDC. **Do not press on tools or piston since incorrect readings will result.**
   c. Record stem travel distance indicated by the dial indicator pointer. Repeat measurement procedure with dial indicator placed on the opposite side of thrust plate. Record stem travel distance indicated by dial indicator pointer.
   d. Calculate the average amount of piston protrusion from the two measurements. Note the following example: If protrusion at one side of piston is .033 inch and protrusion at the other side of piston is .043 inch, add .033 and .043 and divide by 2. Average piston protrusion is .038 inch.
   e. Use the same procedure described to determine average amount of protrusion for the remaining pistons. Use piston that has the largest amount of average

protrusion to determine required thickness of replacement cylinder head gasket.
   f. If the largest amount of piston average protrusion is less than .038 inch, use gasket (A) that is .063 inch thick or has 2 holes, **Fig. 20.** If between .038 and .041 inch, use gasket (B) that is .067 inch thick or has one hole. If more than .041 inch, use gasket (C) that is .071 inch thick or has three holes.
28. Remove cylinder liner clamps Mot. 588 and install cylinder head locating tool Mot. 720 or equivalent, at (A), **Fig. 21,** for alignment.
29. Position replacement gasket onto cylinder block and ensure that gasket has the correct thickness for piston protrusion.
30. Position camshaft in cylinder head, then install cylinder head and gasket onto block. Torque cylinder head bolts in 4 steps in sequence shown in **Fig. 22,** as follows:
   a. First, torque bolts to 22 ft. lbs.
   b. Second, torque bolts to 37 ft. lbs.
   c. Third, torque bolts to 70-77 ft. lbs.
   d. Finally, torque bolts again to 70-77 ft. lbs. Remove tool Mot. 720 or equivalent. **The cylinder head bolts must be retightened after**

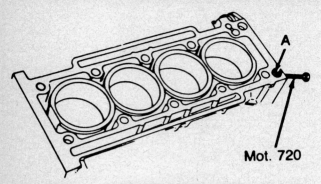

**Fig. 21 Cylinder head locating tool installation**

Mot. 720

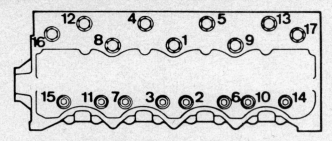

**Fig. 22 Cylinder head tightening sequence**

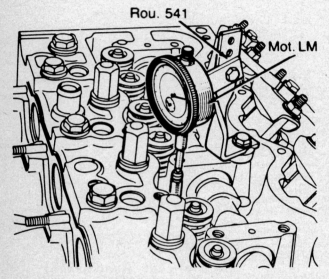

Rou. 541

Mot. LM

**Fig. 23 Piston to cylinder head clearance**

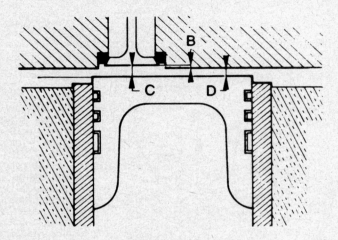

**Fig. 24 Valve travel distance**

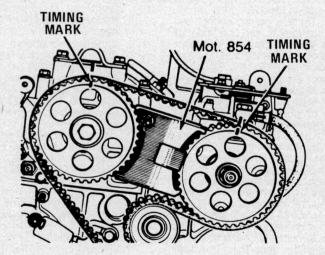

TIMING MARK

Mot. 854

TIMING MARK

**Fig. 25 Retaining timing mark position**

engine is installed in vehicle. Operate engine for a minimum of 20 minutes. Allow engine to cool for a minimum of 2.5 hours, then loosen each cylinder head bolt (in sequence) 1/2 turn and then torque in sequence to 70-77 ft. lbs. For final torquing, torque bolts again in sequence to 70-77 ft. lbs.

31. Check piston-to-cylinder head clearance. Clearance must be greater than .023 inch for proper operation.

32. Select a valve and use the following procedure to measure clearance between valve face (when seated) and the corresponding piston crown:

a. Rotate crankshaft clockwise and move selected piston to BTDC position. Compress valve spring using valve spring compressor Mot. 382 or equivalent, and remove locks and spring.

b. Push down on valve stem and ensure that piston is near TDC position. Attach bracket tool Rou. 541 or equivalent, to an adjacent rocker arm shaft bearing pedestal with a bearing hold down bolt, **Fig. 23**.

c. Attach dial indicator Mot. LM or equivalent to bracket tool and align it so that the stem rests on valve stem selected for measurement. With valve resting on piston crown, use dial indicator as a reference and rotate crankshaft to move piston up exactly to TDC position, then set dial indicator pointer to zero.

d. Lift valve up into its seat in the cylinder head and observe dial indicator valve travel distance between piston crown and valve seat. Record valve travel distance (C), **Fig. 24**.

e. Calculate piston-to-cylinder head clearance according to the following procedure: Subtract valve recess (B) dimension, **Fig. 24**, from valve travel distance (C) measured above. The result should be greater than .023 inch.

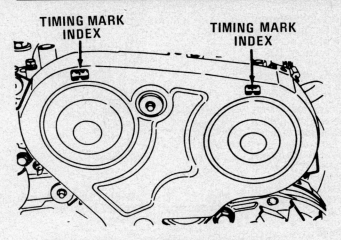

Fig. 26 Timing mark index location

Fig. 27 Injector clamp installation

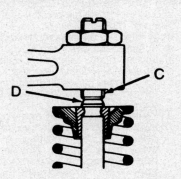

Fig. 28 Aligning adjustment screw with valve stem

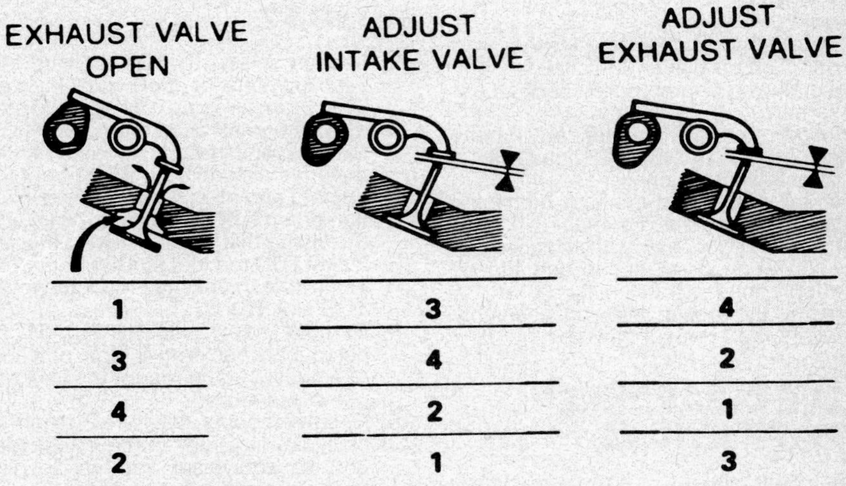

| EXHAUST VALVE OPEN | ADJUST INTAKE VALVE | ADJUST EXHAUST VALVE |
|---|---|---|
| 1 | 3 | 4 |
| 3 | 4 | 2 |
| 4 | 2 | 1 |
| 2 | 1 | 3 |

Fig. 29 Adjusting rocker arm clearance

f. Note the following example: If intake valve recess is .036 inch, and exhaust valve recess is .034 inch, both valve recess dimensions are within the valve recess tolerance of .031-.045 inch. The smallest valve recess dimension should always be used for the piston to cylinder head clearance calculation. Valve travel distance (C) is .061 inch, the clearance (D) equals (C) minus (B). (D) equals .061 inch minus .034 inch. (D) equals .027 inch and is an acceptable clearance.

g. Position valve spring over valve stem, compress spring with a compressor tool and install valve collets.

33. Install rocker arm shaft assembly into cylinder head. Torque shaft bearing hold-down bolts to specifications.

34. Install replacement camshaft oil seal, then measure camshaft endplay.

35. Install camshaft sprocket and retaining bolt. Using sprocket holding tool Mot. 855 or equivalent, torque camshaft sprocket bolt to 37 ft. lbs. Rotate camshaft until sprocket timing marks are at the 12 o'clock position.

36. Attach fuel injection pump mounting brackets and pump to cylinder head with the retaining bolts.

37. Remove inspection plug from cylinder block and install TDC rod Mot. 861 or equivalent into hole against crankshaft counterweight. Rotate crankshaft clockwise until TDC rod enters TDC slot in the crankshaft countershaft.

38. Install sprocket holding tool Mot. 854 or equivalent, to retain camshaft and fuel injection pump sprocket timing marks in place, **Fig. 25**.

39. Install timing belt on the sprockets. **There should be a total of 19 timing belt cogs (teeth) between camshaft sprocket timing mark and the fuel injection pump sprocket timing mark. Temporarily position timing belt cover over the sprockets and check camshaft and fuel injection pump sprocket timing marks with indexes on cover, Fig. 26.**

40. Remove timing belt cover and sprocket holding tool Mot. 854 or equivalent.

41. Adjust timing belt tension as follows:
a. Ensure that timing belt is correctly positioned around all the sprockets and loosen belt tensioner bolts 1/2 of a turn (maximum). The spring loaded belt tensioner, in contact with belt, will automatically adjust to the correct position.
b. Tighten tensioner bolts and re-

move TDC rod Mot. 861 or equivalent, and install inspection plug into cylinder block.
c. Rotate crankshaft clockwise, two complete revolutions and loosen timing belt tensioner bolts 1/2 of a turn, then tighten.
d. Measure timing belt tension. Belt deflection should be .118 to .197 inch. Install timing belt cover.

42. Install replacement copper washers and heat shields into cylinder head injector bores.

43. Install injectors in their original bores in the cylinder head. Place injector clamps over injectors and install retaining washers and nuts, **Fig. 27.** Torque clamp nuts to 12.5 ft. lbs.

44. Install glow plugs and connect injector fuel return hoses with replacement washers at each fitting.

45. Install glow plug wire harness. **Do not install injector high pressure fuel pipes at this time.**

46. Apply Loctite 549 or equivalent to crankshaft sprocket mating surface on the crankshaft pulley. Position crankshaft pulley on end of crankshaft.

47. Insert pins through the pulley and into the crankshaft sprocket.

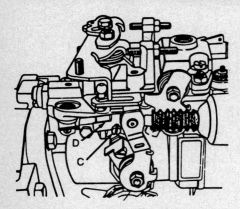

**Fig. 30    Adjusting control cable**

48. Apply a small amount of Loctite 242 or equivalent to the threads of crankshaft pulley bolt.
49. Install crankshaft pulley washer and bolt. Torque bolt to 96 ft. lbs.
50. Install water pump pulley and fan assembly.
51. Install starter, alternator, drive belts and, if equipped, A/C compressor. Check belt tension.
52. Install intake and exhaust manifolds with replacement gaskets.
53. Install turbocharger with replacement nuts. Connect all hoses and the oil supply line.
54. Install thermostat housing assembly with a replacement gasket.

## VALVE CLEARANCE SPECIFICATIONS

4-126 . . .008 Intake          . . .010Exhaust

## VALVES
### ADJUST

1. With engine cold, rotate crankshaft clockwise (as viewed from the front of the engine) until No. 1 cylinder exhaust valve is completely open.The No. 1 cylinder is located at the flywheel or drive plate assembly end

of the engine. As each adjustment screw (C), Fig. 28 is tightened, ensure that the bottom of the screw is aligned with the valve stem (D). If the adjustment screw is not aligned with the stem when tightened, stem damage can result.
2. Using adjustment tool Mot. 647 or equivalent, adjust rocker arm clearance for the No. 3 cylinder intake valve and No. 4 cylinder exhaust valve.
3. Rocker arm intake valve clearance should be as specified, refer to "Valve Clearance Specifications."
4. Refer to Fig. 29 and adjust rocker arm valve clearance to specification and in cylinder sequence shown.

## INJECTION PUMP TIMING
### ADJUST

1. Loosen screw (C), Fig. 30, and turn injection pump control cable clevis pin (D) ¼ turn, then disconnect cold start system control assembly.
2. Rotate crankshaft clockwise 2 revolutions (as viewed from the front of the engine) and align camshaft and injection pump sprocket timing marks with the timing belt cover indexes, Fig. 26.
3. Install TDC rod tool Mot. 861 or equivalent, into crankshaft counterweight TDC slot, Fig. 3.
4. Remove screw plug (1), Fig. 31, located between the 4 high pressure fuel outlets at the rear of the injection pump assembly.
5. Remove copper washer (2), then install dial indicator support tool Mot. 856 or equivalent into screw plug bore on injection pump assembly.
6. Insert stem of dial indicator tool Mot. LM, or equivalent, into support tool previously installed on injection pump.
7. Remove TDC rod tool Mot. 861 from crankshaft counterweight TDC slot.
8. Slowly turn crankshaft counterclockwise until dial indicator pointer stops moving.
9. Zero dial indicator pointer.
10. Slowly turn crankshaft clockwise until TDC rod Mot. 861 can be inserted into

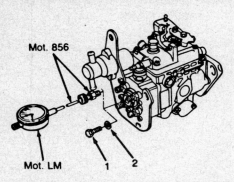

**Fig. 31    Install dial indicator & indicator support into screw plug**

TDC slot in crankshaft counterweight.
11. At TDC, the dial indicator pointer should indicate a piston lift travel distance of .032 inch.
12. If dial indicator reading obtained is not as specified, proceed as follows:
    a. Loosen pump adjustment bolts.
    b. Check dial indicator reading.
    c. To increase piston lift, rotate pump toward engine and then away from engine.
    d. To decrease piston lift, rotate pump away from engine. **Always adjust piston lift by rotating pump away from engine. This is the normal direction of pump rotation. When increasing the piston lift, rotate pump toward the engine until piston lift is greater than the specified tolerance and then rotate pump away from engine until the correct piston lift is indicated on the dial indicator.**
13. After adjustment is completed, tighten adjustment bolts and remove TDC rod from the crankshaft counterweight.

## BELT TENSION DATA

All V-belt tension should measure 155 lbs. when new and 115 lbs. when used. Serpentine drive belts should measure 180-200 lbs. when new and 140-160 lbs. when used.

# CLUTCH & MANUAL TRANSMISSION

## INDEX

## CLUTCH
### ADJUST

These vehicles are equipped with an hydraulic actuated clutch which requires no adjustment.

## CLUTCH ASSEMBLY
### REPLACE
#### REMOVAL

1. Raise and support vehicle.
2. Remove transmission as outlined in "Transmission, Replace" procedure.
3. Scribe marks on pressure plate and flywheel to aid installation, then loosen pressure plate attaching bolts one turn at a time to relieve spring tension. **The pressure plate bolts must be loosened evenly and in rotation to prevent distortion.**
4. Remove pressure plate attaching bolts, then the pressure plate and clutch disc.
5. Remove throwout bearing and clutch release lever from clutch housing.
6. Remove pilot bushing lubricating wick from crankshaft.

#### INSTALLATION

1. Lubricate and install pilot bushing lubricating wick.
2. Install clutch disc and pressure plate onto flywheel, then align disc and plate using alignment tool J-33169 or equivalent. **Ensure side of clutch disc marked "flywheel" is positioned against flywheel.**
3. Install attaching bolts, then torque bolts evenly to 23 ft. lbs. on gasoline engines or 16 ft. lbs. on diesel engines. On 1989 models with 4-150 engine, torque bolts to 23 ft. lbs. or with 6-243 engine to 40 ft. lbs.
4. Install throwout bearing and clutch release lever into clutch housing.
5. Install transmission, then lower vehicle.

## CLUTCH MASTER CYLINDER
### REPLACE

1. Disconnect hydraulic line from master cylinder, then plug opening to prevent dirt from entering line.
2. Remove cylinder pushrod to clutch pedal cotter pin and washer, then slide rod off pedal pivot. On 1989 models, it is necessary to remove the lower instrument panel cover to gain access to pushrod.
3. Remove master cylinder to dash panel attaching nuts, then the master cylinder.
4. Reverse procedure to install. Torque cylinder attaching nuts to 19 ft. lbs., then bleed hydraulic system.

## CLUTCH SLAVE CYLINDER
### REPLACE

1. Raise and support vehicle.
2. Disconnect hydraulic line from slave cylinder.
3. Remove slave cylinder to clutch housing attaching bolts, then the slave cylinder.
4. Reverse procedure to install, then bleed hydraulic system.

## CLUTCH SYSTEM
### BLEED

1. Ensure fluid reservoir is full. If reservoir is not full, replenish with brake fluid.
2. Raise and support vehicle.
3. Remove slave cylinder to clutch housing attaching bolts, then the slave cylinder.
4. Compress slave cylinder plunger using tool J-24420-A or equivalent.
5. Attach one end of suitable hose to slave cylinder bleed screw nipple. On 1989 models, attach suitable hose to throwout bearing bleed screw. Place the other end in a jar filled halfway with clean brake fluid. Ensure end of hose is submerged in brake fluid.
6. Loosen bleeder screw, then have an assistant depress and hold clutch pedal at end of travel.
7. Tighten bleeder screw, then have assistant release clutch pedal.
8. Repeat steps 6 and 7 until fluid entering jar is free of bubbles. **While bleeding clutch system, constantly check master cylinder fluid level and replenish as necessary to prevent master cylinder from running out of fluid.**
9. Remove tool from slave cylinder, then install slave cylinder.
10. Lower vehicle and check master cylinder level.

## TRANSMISSION
### REPLACE
#### REMOVAL

1. Remove outer gear shift lever boot, then remove upper console attaching screws and the upper console.
2. Remove lower console attaching screws and the lower console.
3. Remove shift lever inner boot.
4. Using tool J-34635 or equivalent, remove gearshift lever.
5. Raise and support vehicle, then drain transmission and transfer case lubricant, as required.
6. Scribe alignment marks on rear propeller shaft and axle yoke, then remove propeller shaft.
7. On 2WD models, position suitable safety stands under transmission. On 4WD models, position a suitable jack under transfer case to support transmission and transfer case.
8. On all models, remove rear crossmember to frame rail attaching bolts and nuts, then the rear crossmember.
9. Disconnect speedometer cable, back-up light switch electrical connector and transfer case vent hose, as required.
10. On 4WD models, disconnect transfer case vacuum hoses and linkage.
11. On all models, remove slave cylinder to clutch housing attaching nuts and position slave cylinder aside.
12. On 4WD models, scribe alignment marks on front propeller shaft and transfer case yoke, then disconnect propeller shaft and secure to underbody with suitable wire.
13. On 2WD models, install suitable transmission jack under transmission. On 4WD models, install a suitable transmission jack to transmission and transfer case.
14. On 2WD models, remove transmission clutch housing to engine attaching bolts, then lower transmission from vehicle.
15. On 4WD models, remove transmission clutch housing to engine attaching bolts, then lower transmission and transfer case assembly from vehicle.
16. On 4WD models, remove transmission to transfer case attaching bolts, then separate transfer case from transmission.

## INSTALLATION

1. Shift transmission into gear using shift lever or suitable screwdriver.
2. Install transmission onto transmission jack, then raise jack and align transmission input shaft with clutch disc splines.
3. Install transmission clutch housing to engine, then torque attaching bolts to 28 ft. lbs.
4. Install slave cylinder.
5. On 4WD models, position transfer case onto transmission jack, then raise jack and connect transfer case to transmission. Torque attaching nuts to 26 ft. lbs.
6. On all models, reconnect back-up light switch electrical connector and speedometer cable.
7. On 4WD models, install transfer case vent hose, linkage and vacuum hoses, then connect front propeller shaft to transfer case yoke, aligning scribe marks made during removal.
8. On all models, install rear crossmember, then torque attaching nuts and bolts to 30 ft. lbs.
9. Remove transmission jack, then connect rear propeller shaft to axle yoke, aligning scribe marks made during removal.
10. Fill transfer case and transmission with proper lubricant, as required, then lower vehicle.
11. Install gearshift lever, inner boot, lower and upper consoles, then the outer boot.

# TRANSFER CASE

## INDEX

## TRANSFER CASE REPLACE

### NEW PROCESS 207 & 231

1. Shift transfer case into 4-High position. On 1989 models with New Process 231, shift lever to Neutral.
2. Raise and support vehicle, then drain lubricant from case.
3. Scribe alignment marks on rear axle yoke and propeller shaft, then remove rear propeller shaft.
4. Disconnect speedometer cable, vacuum hoses and vent hose.
5. Raise transmission and transfer case, then remove crossmember attaching bolts and the crossmember.
6. Scribe alignment marks on front output shaft flange and propeller shaft, then disconnect front propeller shaft from transfer case.
7. Disconnect shift lever linkage rod, then remove shift lever bracket bolts.
8. Support transfer case, then remove attaching bolts.
9. Remove transfer case from vehicle.
10. Reverse procedure to install. Torque transfer case attaching bolts to 26 ft. lbs. and crossmember to frame attaching nuts and bolts to 30 ft. lbs.

### NEW PROCESS 228, 229 & 242

1. On 1989 models with New Process 242, shift lever to Neutral.
2. On all models, raise and support vehicle, then drain lubricant from case.

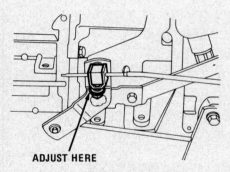

**ADJUST HERE**

**Fig. 1  Transfer case range control linkage adjustment (Typical)**

3. Disconnect speedometer cable and vent hose.
4. Disconnect transfer case shift lever link from operating lever.
5. Support transmission, then remove rear crossmember attaching bolts and the rear crossmember.
6. Scribe alignment marks on transfer case yokes and propeller shafts, then disconnect propeller shafts from transfer case.
7. Disconnect shift motor vacuum hoses.
8. Disconnect transfer case shift linkage, then remove transfer case to transmission attaching bolts.
9. Move transfer case rearward until clear of transmission output shaft and remove from vehicle.
10. Reverse procedure to install. Torque transfer case attaching bolts to 40 ft. lbs. or 26 ft. lbs. on 1989 models, and crossmember to frame attaching nuts and bolts to 30 ft. lbs.

## TRANSFER CASE RANGE CONTROL LINKAGE ADJUSTMENT

### 1984-88

1. Position range control lever in 2WD (Model 207 & 242), 2H (Model 231) or High (Model 228 and 229).
2. Install a 1/8 inch spacer between gate and lever while holding lever in position.
3. Position range control lever as noted in step 1, then adjust link as shown, **Fig. 1**, until a free pin fit is achieved at transfer case outer layer.

### 1989

1. On vehicles with models 231 and 242 transfer cases, move range lever to 4L position. On vehicles with model 229 transfer case, move range lever to Hi position.
2. Install .157 inch spacer between gate and lever while holding lever in position. On model 229 transfer cases, install 1/8 spacer.
3. Position range control lever as noted in step 1, then adjust link as shown, **Fig. 1**, until a free pin fit is achieved at transfer case outer layer.

# REAR AXLE, SUSPENSION & BRAKES

## INDEX

## AXLE HOUSING ASSEMBLY

### REPLACE

1. Raise and support vehicle, then remove wheels and brake drums.
2. Support axle, then disconnect shock absorbers at lower mount.
3. Disconnect brake hoses at frame rails and parking brake cables at equalizer.
4. Scribe alignment marks, then disconnect propeller shaft from axle.
5. Remove axle to spring U-bolts, then lower axle and remove from vehicle.
6. Reverse procedure to install. Torque U-bolt nuts to 52 ft. lbs. on 1984-88 models, or 90 ft. lbs. on 1989 models, then bleed brake system.

## AXLE SHAFT, BEARING & SEAL

### REMOVAL

1. Raise and support vehicle, then remove wheel and brake drum.
2. Working through holes in axle shaft flange, remove brake support plate attaching nuts.
3. Using a suitable slide hammer type puller, remove axle shaft from housing.

### DISASSEMBLY

1. Position axle shaft in a vise.
2. Drill a 1/4 inch hole approximately 3/4 of the way through bearing retaining ring, then chisel a deep groove in ring and remove from axle shaft, **Fig. 1.**
3. Using tool J-23674 or equivalent, press bearing from shaft, **Fig. 2.**
4. Remove seal, gasket and retainer plate from axle shaft.

### ASSEMBLY

1. Lubricate seal, then install retainer plate, gasket and seal onto axle shaft.
2. Lubricate bearing, then using tool J-23674 and a suitable press, install bearing and retaining ring onto axle shaft. Ensure bearing and ring are properly seated against axle shaft shoulder.

### INSTALLATION

1. Clean axle housing bearing bore, then apply a thin coat of grease to outer di-

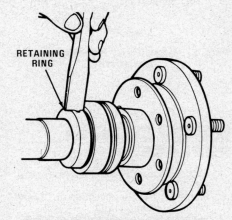

RETAINING RING

**Fig. 1　Removing retaining ring from axle shaft**

ameter of bearing cup.
2. Install axle shaft, then alternately torque brake support plate attaching nuts to 32 ft. lbs.
3. Install brake drum and wheel, then lower vehicle.

## SHOCK ABSORBER

### REPLACE

1. Raise vehicle and support rear axle with a suitable jack.
2. Raise jack slightly, then remove upper shock mount to body retaining bolts.
3. Remove lower retaining nut and washer, then the shock absorber.
4. Reverse procedure to install. Torque upper retaining bolts to 15 ft. lbs. and lower retaining nut to 44 ft. lbs. **If vehicle is equipped with Automatic Load Leveling System, disconnect lines from shock absorber before removing.**

## STABILIZER BAR

### REPLACE

#### CHEROKEE & WAGONEER

1. Raise and support vehicle.
2. Disconnect stabilizer bar at spring plates and frame rails, **Fig. 3.**
3. Remove stabilizer bar from vehicle.
4. Reverse procedure to install. Torque retaining bolts and nuts to 55 ft. lbs.

## LEAF SPRING & BUSHING

### REPLACE

1. Raise vehicle and support at side sills.
2. Position with a suitable jack under axle assembly, then raise jack slightly to relieve tension.
3. Disconnect shock absorber at lower mount, then remove wheel.
4. On Cherokee and Wagoneer, proceed as follows:
   a. Disconnect stabilizer bar from spring plate.
   b. Remove U-bolt attaching nuts, then the U-bolts and spring plate.
   c. Remove front and rear spring eye to bracket retaining nuts and bolts, then lower axle and remove spring from vehicle.
5. On Comanche, proceed as follows:
   a. Remove two spring plate U-bolts, then the spring plate.
   b. Remove rear eye-to-spring shackle bolt and front eye-to-bracket bolt.
   c. Remove spring from vehicle.
6. On all models, to replace bushing, position spring on an arbor press and press bushing from spring using a suitable rod or pipe.
7. Reverse procedure to install. Torque U-bolt attaching nuts to 52 ft. lbs. and front and rear spring eye retaining nuts to 110 ft. lbs.

## SERVICE BRAKES

### ADJUST

1. Raise and support vehicle.
2. Remove access slot cover at rear of brake support plate.
3. Rotate adjuster screw until wheel locks, then back off screw approximately one turn.
4. Install access slot cover, then lower vehicle and check for proper brake operation.
5. Drive vehicle in Reverse, making 10 to 15 firm brake applications with one forward stop between each reverse application to equalize adjustment.

## PARKING BRAKE

### ADJUST

Service brakes must be properly adjust-

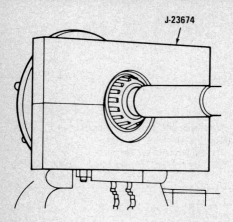

**Fig. 2 Replacing axle shaft bearing**

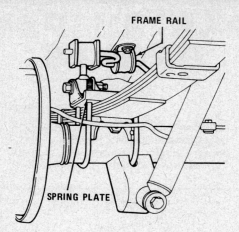

**Fig. 3 Stabilizer bar mounting locations**

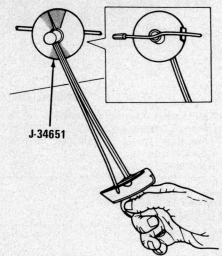

**Fig. 4 Adjusting parking brake using tool J-34651**

ed before adjusting parking brake mechanism.
1. Fully apply and release parking brake lever approximately five times.
2. Pull parking brake lever up to 5th click, then raise and support vehicle.
3. Install adjustment gauge tool J-34651 onto an inch lb. torque wrench, **Fig. 4,** then apply a 45-55 inch lb. load to cable.
4. Adjust equalizer nut until gauge pointer is in Green range, then repeat Step 1.
5. Recheck adjustment. If adjustment is correct, stake nut to maintain setting, then lower vehicle.

## MASTER CYLINDER REPLACE

1. Disconnect and plug lines from master cylinder.
2. Remove master cylinder to brake booster retaining nuts.
3. Remove master cylinder from vehicle.
4. Reverse procedure to install, then bleed brake hydraulic system.

## POWER BRAKE UNIT REPLACE

1. On 1989 models, remove lower instrument panel cover trim and disconnect stoplight switch.
2. On all models, disconnect power brake unit pushrod from brake pedal assembly.
3. Disconnect vacuum hose from booster check valve.
4. Remove master cylinder retaining nuts and position master cylinder aside. Do not disconnect brake lines from cylinder.
5. Remove power brake unit to dash panel retaining nuts.
6. Remove power brake unit from vehicle.
7. Reverse procedure to install. Torque retaining nuts to 30 ft. lbs.

# FRONT SUSPENSION & STEERING

**NOTE:** Refer to "Front Wheel Drive Section" for 4 x 4 front axle service procedures not covered in this section.

## INDEX

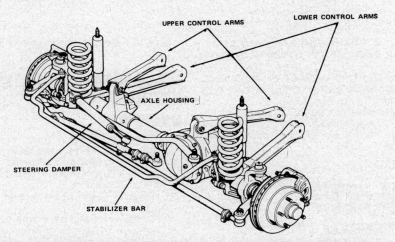

**Fig. 1  Typical front suspension. 4WD models (2WD models similar)**

## DESCRIPTION

The front suspension, **Fig. 1**, consists of a solid axle, four control arms, two coil springs, a stabilizer bar, dual action shock absorbers and a track bar.

## SHOCK ABSORBER
### REPLACE

1. Remove shock absorber upper attaching nut and washer.
2. Raise and support vehicle.
3. Remove lower attaching nuts and bolts, then the shock absorber.
4. Reverse procedure to install. Torque upper attaching nut to 8 ft. lbs. and lower attaching nuts and bolts to 14 ft. lbs.

## TRACK BAR
### REPLACE

1. Raise and support vehicle.
2. Remove track bar to frame rail bracket cotter pin and retaining nut.
3. Remove track bar to axle bracket retaining nut and bolt, then the track bar.
4. Reverse procedure to install. Torque track bar to frame rail bracket retaining nut to 35 ft. lbs. on 1984-88 models or 62 ft. lbs. on 1989 models and track bar to axle bracket retaining nut and bolt to 74 ft. lbs.

## CONTROL ARM
### REPLACE
#### UPPER ARM

1. On V6 equipped vehicles, disconnect right side engine mount, then raise engine until rear bolt is clear of exhaust pipe.
2. On all vehicles, raise and support vehicle, then remove control arm to axle attaching nuts and bolts.
3. Remove control arm to frame rail attaching bolt.
4. Remove control arm from vehicle.
5. Reverse procedure to install. Torque attaching nuts and bolts onto axle to 55 ft. lbs. and frame rail attaching nuts and bolts to 66 ft. lbs.

#### LOWER ARM

1. Raise and support vehicle.
2. Remove control arm to axle and control arm to rear bracket attaching nuts and bolts.
3. Remove control arm from vehicle.
4. Reverse procedure to install. Torque attaching nuts and bolts to 133 ft. lbs.

## STABILIZER BAR
### REPLACE

1. Raise and support vehicle.
2. Remove stabilizer bar to link attaching nuts, then the rubber bushings.
3. Remove stabilizer bar bracket to side sill retaining bolts.
4. Remove stabilizer bar.
5. Reverse procedure to install. Torque stabilizer bar to link attaching nuts to 27 ft. lbs. and stabilizer bar bracket to side sill retaining bolts to 55 ft. lbs.

## STEERING DAMPER
### REPLACE

1. Place front wheels in straight ahead position.
2. Remove cotter pin and retaining nut at center link.
3. Remove steering damper to axle bracket retaining nut and bolt, then the steering damper.
4. Reverse procedure to install. Torque steering damper to axle bracket retaining nut and bolt to 55 ft. lbs. and damper to center link retaining nut to 35 ft. lbs.

## COIL SPRING
### REPLACE

1. Raise and support vehicle.
2. Remove wheel, then position a suitable jack under axle.
3. Scribe alignment marks, then disconnect front propeller shaft from axle.
4. Disconnect lower control arm, stabilizer bar link and shock absorber from axle, then the track bar from side sill.
5. Disconnect center steering link from pitman arm.
6. Carefully lower axle assembly, then loosen spring retainer attaching nut

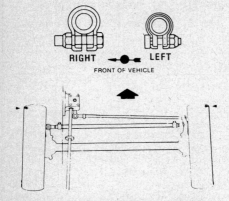

**Fig. 2  Positioning adjusting tube clamps**

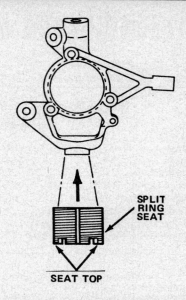

**Fig. 3  Steering knuckle split ring seat depth measurement**

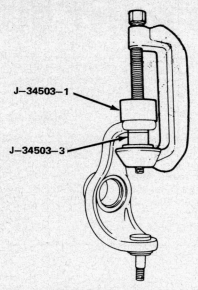

**Fig. 4  Removing upper ball joint**

and remove coil spring from vehicle.
7. Reverse procedure to install. Torque lower control arm retaining bolts and nuts to 133 ft. lbs., stabilizer bar link attaching nut to 70 ft. lbs., track bar to side sill retaining bolt to 35 ft. lbs. and center steering link to pitman arm retaining nut to 35 ft. lbs.

## WHEEL ALIGNMENT

Refer to "Wheel Alignment Specification Chart" at the beginning of this chapter for correct wheel alignment settings.

### CAMBER

Camber is preset at the factory and is not adjustable. If the camber angle is not within specifications, replace the suspension components responsible for the incorrect angles.

### CASTER

Caster is adjusted by adding or subtracting shims at the rear of the lower control arms.

### TOE ADJUSTMENT

To adjust toe setting, center steering gear, then lock steering wheel to hold in position. Adjust right wheel toe setting by loosening clamp bolt and rotating center link connecting pitman arm to right wheel. Adjust left wheel toe setting by loosening clamp bolt and rotating the tie rod connecting the center link to the left wheel.

After adjustments are completed, position clamps as shown, **Fig. 2.** Torque clamp bolts to 14 ft. lbs.

## STEERING KNUCKLE
### REPLACE

1. Remove axle shaft as outlined in "Front Wheel Drive Section."
2. Remove caliper anchor plate from knuckle, then the knuckle to ball joint cotter pins and retaining nuts.
3. Strike steering knuckle with a suitable mallet and remove from vehicle. **A split ring seat is located in the bottom end of steering knuckle. Before installing knuckle, set split ring seat to a depth of .206 inch,**

using tool J-23447 or equivalent. Measure depth to top of ring seat as shown, **Fig. 3.**
4. Reverse procedure to install. Torque steering knuckle retaining nuts to 75 ft. lbs. and anchor plate retaining bolts to 77 ft. lbs.

## BALL JOINTS
### REPLACE
#### UPPER BALL JOINT

1. Remove steering knuckle as previously outlined.
2. Position receiver tool J-34503-1 over top part of ball joint and adapter tool J-34503-3 onto C-clamp as shown, **Fig. 4.**
3. Tighten clamp and press ball joint from steering knuckle.
4. To install, place tool J-34503-5 over replacement ball joint and receiver tool J-34503-12 onto C-clamp. Position tool against yoke shoulder, then tighten clamp and press ball joint into knuckle.
5. Install steering knuckle.

#### LOWER BALL JOINT

1. Remove steering knuckle as previously outlined.
2. Position receiver tool J-34503-1 over ball joint stud and adapter tool J-34503-3 onto C-clamp as shown, **Fig. 5.**
3. Tighten clamp and press ball joint from steering knuckle.
4. To install, place tool J-34503-4 over replacement ball joint and receiver tool J-34503-2 onto C-clamp. Position tool against yoke shoulder, then tighten clamp and press ball joint into knuckle.
5. Install steering knuckle.

## AXLE HUB & BEARING SERVICE
### REMOVAL

1. Raise and support front of vehicle, then remove wheel and brake caliper.
2. Remove grease cap, cotter pin, nut retainer, adjusting nut and thrust washer from spindle, **Fig. 6.**
3. Remove outer wheel bearing from hub.
4. Remove hub and rotor from spindle.
5. Remove grease seal from hub and rotor, then the inner wheel bearing.

### INSTALLATION

1. Apply suitable grease in rotor hub cavity, then pack wheel bearings with grease.
2. Install inner wheel bearing and new grease seal in rotor.
3. Install hub and rotor on spindle.
4. Install outer bearing, thrust washer and spindle nut. Torque spindle nut to 17-25 ft. lbs. while rotating rotor to seat bearing.
5. Loosen spindle nut 1/2 turn while rotating wheel, then tighten spindle nut to 19 inch lbs.
6. Install nut retainer and cotter pin.
7. Install grease cap, caliper and wheel.

## STEERING GEAR
### REPLACE
#### MANUAL STEERING GEAR

1. Disconnect steering shaft from gear, then raise and support vehicle.
2. Disconnect center link from pitman arm.
3. Remove stabilizer bar as previously outlined.
4. Remove pitman arm retaining nut, then scribe alignment marks on sector shaft and arm.
5. Using puller tool J-6632-01 or equiva-

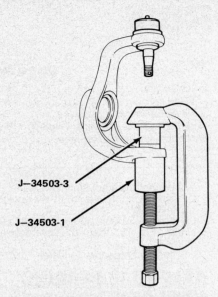

**Fig. 5 Removing lower ball joint**

J—34503-3

J—34503-1

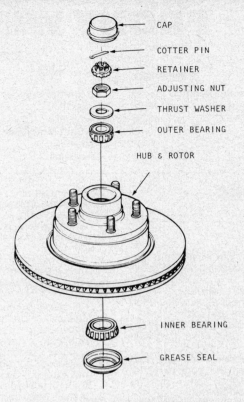

CAP

COTTER PIN

RETAINER

ADJUSTING NUT

THRUST WASHER

OUTER BEARING

HUB & ROTOR

INNER BEARING

GREASE SEAL

**Fig. 6 Axle hub & bearing assembly**

lent, remove pitman arm from shaft.

6. Remove steering gear retaining bolts, then the steering gear.
7. Reverse procedure to install. Torque steering gear retaining bolts to 65 ft. lbs., pitman arm retaining nut to 185 ft. lbs. and center link retaining nut to 35 ft. lbs. Stake pitman arm retaining nut to sector shaft for proper retention. On 1989 models, torque center link retaining nut to 60 ft. lbs.

## POWER STEERING GEAR

1. Place front wheels in straight ahead position.
2. Disconnect hoses from steering gear, then plug hoses to prevent dirt from entering.
3. Disconnect intermediate shaft from stub shaft.
4. Raise and support vehicle, then disconnect center link from pitman arm.
5. Remove stabilizer bar as outlined previously.
6. Remove pitman arm retaining nut, then scribe alignment marks on arm and sector shaft.
7. Using tool J-6632-01 or equivalent, remove pitman arm from shaft.
8. Remove steering gear retaining bolts, then the steering gear.
9. Reverse procedure to install. Torque steering gear retaining bolts to 65 ft.

lbs., pitman arm retaining nut to 185 ft. lbs. and center link retaining nut to 35 ft. lbs. On 1989 models, torque center link retaining nut to 60 ft. lbs. Stake pitman arm retaining nut to sector shaft for proper retention, then bleed hydraulic system as outlined in "Power Steering Pump, Replace" procedure.

## POWER STEERING PUMP REPLACE

1. Loosen pump adjusting bolt, then remove drive belt.
2. Remove air cleaner, if necessary.
3. Disconnect hoses from pump, then plug hoses to prevent dirt from entering.
4. Remove front bracket to engine retaining bolts and pump to rear bracket

retaining nuts.
5. Remove power steering pump together with front bracket.
6. Reverse procedure to install, then bleed hydraulic system as follows:
   a. Fill pump reservoir, then start engine and allow to reach normal operating temperature.
   b. Turn wheels to full left lock, stop engine, then add fluid to COLD mark on dipstick.
   c. Restart engine, then bleed system by turning wheels side to side until all air bubbles are eliminated. Do not allow wheels to hit stops.
   d. Return wheels to straight ahead position, allow engine to idle for approximately three minutes, then stop engine.
   e. Check fluid level. Fluid level should be at HOT mark on dipstick. If level is not at HOT, fill reservoir as necessary.

# FRONT WHEEL DRIVE

## INDEX

## AXLE HOUSING ASSEMBLY
### REPLACE

The axle code number is attached to a tag located on the differential housing cover.

1. Raise and support vehicle.
2. Remove tire/wheel assemblies, then the brake calipers and rotors.
3. Disconnect vacuum harness from shift motor and vent hose from axle housing.
4. Disconnect stabilizer bar, rod and center links, then the front propeller shaft, shock absorbers, steering damper and track bar from axle.
5. Position a suitable jack under axle, then disconnect upper and lower control arms at axle.
6. Carefully lower axle housing and remove from vehicle.
7. Reverse procedure to install. Torque upper control arm attaching bolts to 55 ft. lbs., lower control arm attaching bolts to 133 ft. lbs., stabilizer bar link to 70 ft. lbs., and steering damper and track bar attaching nuts to 74 ft. lbs. **When installing vent hose, secure hose away from the steering shaft U-joint.**

## AXLE HUB & BEARING SERVICE
### REMOVAL

1. Raise and support front of vehicle, then remove wheel, brake caliper and rotor.
2. Remove cotter pin, locknut, axle hub retaining nut and washer.
3. Remove hub/carrier assembly to steering knuckle attaching bolts, then the hub/carrier assembly.

### DISASSEMBLY

1. Press hub from carrier, then remove bearings and seals, **Fig. 1.**
2. Inspect bearing cups for wear or scoring. If replacement is necessary, drive bearing cups from carrier with a suitable drift. **If replacement is required, replace bearings and cups in matched sets only.**

### ASSEMBLY

1. Press new bearing cups into carrier, if applicable.
2. Fill steering knuckle and carrier cavities and coat seals with lithium base wheel bearing grease.
3. Repack, then install bearings into carrier.
4. Install new seal on hub side of carrier, then press hub through carrier.

### INSTALLATION

1. Fill steering knuckle hub cavity with chassis grease, then install hub/carrier assembly. Torque hub/carrier assembly to steering knuckle attaching bolts to 75 ft. lbs.
2. Install washer and axle hub retaining nut, torque retaining nut to 175 ft. lbs., then install locknut and cotter pin.
3. Install rotor, caliper and wheel, then lower vehicle.

## AXLE SHAFT
### REPLACE
#### REMOVAL

1. Remove axle hub as outlined previously.
2. Remove splash shield from steering knuckle.
3. If replacing left axle shaft, pull shaft from housing using a suitable puller.
4. If replacing right axle shaft, disconnect vacuum harness from shift motor, then disengage and remove motor from housing shift collar, **Fig. 2.** Pull axle shaft from housing.

#### INSTALLATION

1. If replacing left axle shaft, install axle shaft into housing, then install splash shield and axle hub.
2. If replacing right axle shaft, install shaft into housing, ensuring shaft is fully engaged over intermediate shaft end and shift collar is properly positioned in housing. Install shift motor so fork engages collar, then torque retaining bolts to 8 ft. lbs. Reconnect vacuum harness to shift motor, then install splash shield and axle hub.

## INTERMEDIATE SHAFT
### REPLACE

1. Raise and support vehicle.
2. Remove axle housing cover and drain lubricant from housing.
3. Remove right axle shaft as outlined previously.
4. Remove intermediate shaft retaining clip, **Fig. 3,** then the intermediate shaft.
5. Reverse procedure to install.

## AXLE TUBE BEARING
### REPLACE

1. Remove intermediate shaft as previously outlined.
2. Insert tools J-34659-3 and 4 or equivalents through outer end of axle tube, then working from access hole in shift motor housing, connect tool J-34659-1 to tools previously mentioned.
3. Position remover tool behind bearing, then tighten nut and remove bearing through access hole in shift motor housing.
4. Position new bearing into housing, then drive bearing into position using tool J-34659-2.
5. Install intermediate shaft.

## AXLE TUBE SEAL & GUARD
### REPLACE

1. Remove intermediate shaft as previously outlined.
2. Using tool J-34659-5 or equivalent, insert tool through outer end of axle tube, then drive seal and guard into shift motor housing and remove through access hole.
3. Position new seal and guard into shift motor housing, then using tool J-34659-2 or equivalent, tighten nut and pull seal and guard into position.
4. Install intermediate shaft.

## AXLE SHIFT MOTOR SERVICE
### REMOVAL

1. Raise and support vehicle.
2. Drain lubricant from pan, then disconnect vacuum harness from shift motor.
3. Remove shift motor housing retaining bolts, then the housing, shift motor and fork assembly.

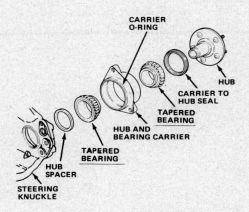

**Fig. 1   Axle hub & bearing assembly (Typical)**

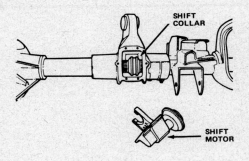

**Fig. 2   Axle shift motor & housing collar**

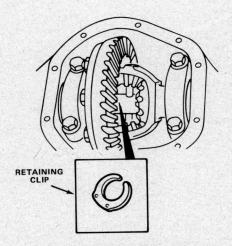

**Fig. 3   Intermediate shaft retaining clip**

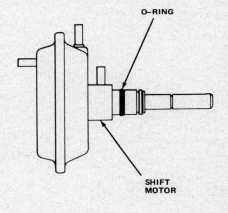

**Fig. 4   Front axle shift motor & O-ring**

## DISASSEMBLY

1. Scribe alignment marks on shift fork and housing to aid in assembly.
2. Rotate shift motor, then remove shift fork and motor retaining rings.
3. Remove shift motor from housing.
4. Remove O-ring from shift motor, **Fig. 4.**

## ASSEMBLY

1. Install replacement O-ring onto shift motor.
2. Install shift motor into housing, then slide shift fork onto shaft, aligning scribe marks made previously.
3. Install shift fork and motor retaining rings.

## INSTALLATION

1. Engage shift fork into collar, then install shift motor housing retaining bolts. Torque bolts to 8 ft. lbs.
2. Reconnect vacuum harness to shift motor, then add lubricant to proper level.
3. Lower vehicle.

# AIR CONDITIONING

## TABLE OF CONTENTS

# A/C System Testing

## INDEX

## GENERAL PRECAUTIONS

The Freon refrigerant used is also known as R-12 or F-12. It is colorless and odorless both as a gas and a liquid. Since it boils (vaporizes) at $-21.7°$ F, it will usually be in a vapor state when being handled in a repair shop. But if a portion of the liquid coolant should come in contact with the hands or face, note that its temperature momentarily will be at least $22°$ below zero.

Protective goggles should be worn when opening any refrigerant lines. If liquid coolant does touch the eyes, bathe the eyes quickly in cold water, then apply a bland disinfectant oil to the eyes. See an eye doctor.

When checking a system for leaks with a torch type leak detector, do not breathe the vapors coming from the flame. Do not discharge refrigerant in the area of a live flame. A poisonous phosgene gas is produced when R-12 or F-12 is burned. While the small amount of this gas produced by a leak detector is not harmful unless inhaled directly at the flame, the quantity of refrigerant released into the air when a system is purged can be extremely dangerous if allowed to come in contact with an open flame. Thus, when purging a system, be sure that the discharge hose is routed to a well ventilated place where no flame is present. Under these conditions the refrigerant will be quickly dissipated into the surrounding air.

Never allow the temperature of refrigerant drums to exceed $125°$ F. The resultant increase in temperature will cause a corresponding increase in pressure which may cause the safety plug to release or the drum to burst.

If it is necessary to heat a drum of refrigerant when charging a system, the drum should be placed in water that is no hotter than $125°$ F. Never use a blowtorch, or other open flame. If possible, a pressure release mechanism should be attached before the drum is heated.

When connecting and disconnecting service gauges on A/C system, ensure that gauge hand valves are fully closed and that compressor service valves, if equipped, are in the back-seated (fully counterclockwise) position. Do not disconnect gauge hoses from service port adapters, if used, while gauges are connected to A/C system. To disconnect hoses, always remove adapter from service port. Do not disconnect hoses from gauge manifold while connected to A/C system, as refrigerant will be rapidly discharged.

After disconnecting gauge lines, check the valve areas to be sure service valves are correctly seated and Schraeder valves, if used, are not leaking.

## EXERCISE SYSTEM

An important fact most owners ignore is that A/C units must be used periodically. Manufacturers caution that when the air conditioner is not used regularly, particularly during cold months, it should be turned on for a few minutes once every two or three weeks while the engine is running. This keeps the system in good operating condition.

Checking out the system for the effects of disuse before the onset of summer is one of the most important aspects of A/C servicing.

First clean out the condenser core, mounted in all cases at the front of the radiator. All obstructions, such as leaves, bugs, and dirt, must be removed, as they will reduce heat transfer and impair the efficiency of the system. Make sure the space between the condenser and the radiator also is free of foreign matter.

Make certain the evaporator water drain is open. Certain systems have two evaporators, one in the engine compartment and one toward the rear of the vehicle. The evaporator cools and dehumidifies the air before it enters the passenger compartment; there, the refrigerant is changed from a liquid to a vapor. As the core cools the air, moisture condenses on it but is prevented from collecting in the evaporator by the water drain.

## PERFORMANCE TEST

The system should be operated for at least 15 minutes to allow sufficient time for all parts to become completely stabilized. Determine if the system is fully charged by the use of test gauges and sight glass if one is installed on system. Head pressure will read from 180 psi to 220 psi or higher, depending upon ambient temperature and the type unit being tested. The sight glass should be free of bubbles if a glass is used in the system. Low side pressures should read approximately 15 psi to 30 psi, again depending on the ambient temperature and the unit being tested. It is not feasible to give a definite reading for all types of systems used, as the type control and component installation used on a particular system will directly influence the pres-

| Evaporator Pressure Gauge Reading | Evaporator Temperature F° | High Pressure Gauge Reading | Ambient Temperature |
|---|---|---|---|
| 0 | -21° | 45 | 20° |
| 0.6 | -20° | 55 | 30° |
| 2.4 | -15° | 72 | 40° |
| 4.5 | -10° | 86 | 50° |
| 6.8 | - 5° | 105 | 60° |
| 9.2 | 0° | 126 | 70° |
| 11.8 | 5° | 140 | 75° |
| 14.7 | 10° | 160 | 80° |
| 17.1 | 15° | 185 | 90° |
| 21.1 | 20° | 195 | 95° |
| 22.5 | 22° | 220 | 100° |
| 23.9 | 24° | 240 | 105° |
| 25.4 | 26° | 260 | 110° |
| 26.9 | 28° | 275 | 115° |
| 28.5 | 30° | 290 | 120° |
| 37.0 | 40° | 305 | 125° |
| 46.7 | 50° | 325 | 130° |
| 57.7 | 60° | | |
| 70.1 | 70° | | |
| 84.1 | 80° | | |
| 99.6 | 90° | | |
| 116.9 | 100° | | |
| 136.0 | 110° | | |
| 157.1 | 120° | | |
| 179.0 | 130° | | |

**Fig. 1   A/C system pressure/temperature relationship (Typical). Equivalent to 1750 RPM (30 mph)**

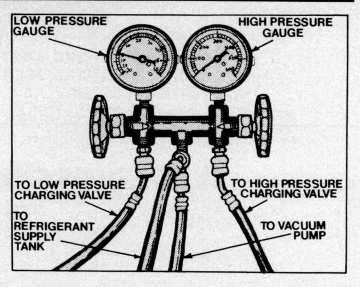

**Fig. 2   Gauge manifold hose connections. Exc. RV-2 compressor**

sure readings on the high and low sides, **Fig. 1.**

The high side pressure will definitely be affected by the ambient or outside air temperature. A system that is operating normally will indicate a high side gauge reading between 150-170 psi with an 80° F ambient temperature. The same system will register 210-230 psi with an ambient temperature of 100° F. No two systems will register exactly the same, which requires that allowance for variations in head pressures must be considered. Following are the most important normal readings likely to be encountered during the season.

| Ambient Temp. Side Pressure | High |
|---|---|
| 80 | 150-170 |
| 90 | 175-195 |
| 95 | 185-205 |
| 100 | 210-230 |
| 105 | 230-250 |
| 110 | 250-270 |

## RELATIVE TEMPERATURE OF HIGH AND LOW SIDES

The high side of the system should be uniformly hot to the touch throughout. A difference in temperature will indicate a partial blockage of liquid or gas at this point.

The low side of the system should be uniformly cool to the touch with no excessive sweating of the suction line or low side service valve. Excessive sweating or frosting of the low side service valve usually indicates an expansion valve is allowing an excessive amount of refrigerant into the evaporator.

## EVAPORATOR OUTPUT

At this point, provided all other inspection tests have been performed, and components have been found to operate as they should, a rapid cooling down of the interior of the vehicle should result. The use of a thermometer is not necessary to determine evaporator output. Bringing all units to the correct operating specifications will insure that the evaporator performs as intended.

## LEAK TEST

Testing the refrigerant system for leaks is one of the most important phases of troubleshooting. Several types of leak detectors are available that are suitable for detecting A/C system leaks. One or more of the following procedures will prove useful for detecting leaks and checking connections after service work has been performed. Prior to performing any leak test, prepare the vehicle as follows:

1. Attach a suitable gauge manifold to system and observe pressure readings.
2. If little or no pressure is indicated, the system must be partially charged.
3. If gauges indicate pressure, set engine to run at fast idle and operate system at maximum cooling for 10-15 minutes, then stop engine and perform leak tests.

## FLAME TYPE (HALIDE) LEAK DETECTORS

**Avoid inhaling fumes produced by burning refrigerant when using flame-type detectors. Use caution when using detector near flammable materials such as interior trim components. Do not use flame-type detector where concentrations of combustible or explosive gasses, dusts or vapors may exist.**

1. Light leak detector and adjust flame as low as possible to obtain maximum sensitivity.
2. Allow detector to warm until copper element is cherry-red. Flame should be almost colorless.
3. Test reaction plate sensitivity by passing end of sensor hose near an opened can of refrigerant. Flame should react violently, turning bright blue.
4. If flame does not change color, replace reaction plate following manufacturer's instructions.
5. Allow flame to clear, then slowly move sensor hose along areas suspected of leakage while observing flame. **Position sensor hose under areas of suspected leakage, as R-12 refrigerant is heavier than air.**

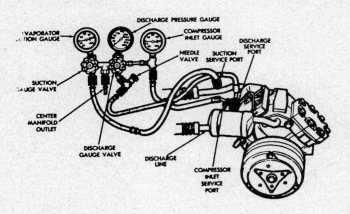

**Fig. 3   Gauge manifold hose connections. RV-2 compressor**

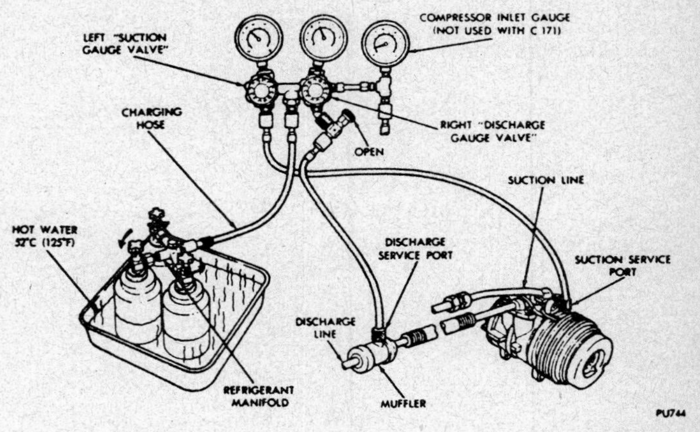

**Fig. 4   A/C system charging (Typical)**

6. Move sensor hose under all lines, fittings and components. Insert hose into evaporator case, if possible, and check compressor shaft seal.
7. The presence of refrigerant will cause flame to change color as follows: Pale blue, no refrigerant; yellow-yellow/green, slight leak; bright blue-purple/blue, major leak or concentration of refrigerant.
8. If detector indicates a large leak or heavy concentration of refrigerant, ventilate area using a small fan in order to pinpoint leak.
9. Repair leaks as needed, evacuate and recharge system, then recheck system for leaks.

## ELECTRONIC LEAK DETECTORS

The procedure for using an electronic leak detector is similar to the procedure for flame-type leak detectors, except that the presence of refrigerant is indicated by an audible tone or flashing light. Refer to operating instructions for unit being used, and observe the following procedures:
1. Move detector probe 1 inch per second along areas of suspected leakage.
2. Position probe under area to be tested as refrigerant is heavier than air.
3. Check gauge manifold, hoses and service ports for leakage.

## FLUID LEAK DETECTORS

Apply leak detector solution around joints to be tested. A cluster of bubbles will form immediately if there is a leak. A white foam that forms after a short while will indicate an extremely small leak. In some confined areas such as sections of the evaporator and condenser, electronic leak detectors will be more useful.

## DISCHARGING & EVACUATING SYSTEM
## DISCHARGING

1. Ensure that all gauge manifold or charging station hand valves are closed.
2. Connect compound (low) side gauge hose to the low (suction) side service port, and the high pressure gauge hose to the high (discharge) side port, **Figs. 2 and 3. Refer to "Charging Valve Location" chart in the "A/C System Servicing" section for service port locations.**
3. If charging station is being used, disconnect hose from vacuum pump inlet and ensure that vacuum valve is open.
4. Insert charging station vacuum hose or gauge manifold center hose into a suitable container that is vented to shop exhaust system.
5. If system is operational, set engine to run at fast idle and operate A/C system in maximum cooling position, with blower on high, for 10-15 minutes to return oil to compressor, then reduce idle and stop engine.
6. Slightly open low side control valve on manifold or charging station, and allow refrigerant to discharge slowly into container. **Do not allow refrigerant to discharge rapidly. Too rapid purging will draw the system oil charge out with the refrigerant.**
7. When system is nearly discharged, slightly open high side control valve on manifold to discharge remaining refrigerant from compressor and lines.
8. When system is completely discharged (gauges read zero), close high and low side control valves and measure amount of oil in discharge container
9. If more than 1/2 ounce of refrigeration oil is trapped in container, perform "Oil Level Check" as outlined in the "A/C System Servicing" section. **If addition of refrigeration oil is necessary, oil should be added prior to evacuating system.**

## EVACUATING SYSTEM WITH VACUUM PUMP

Vacuum pumps suitable for removing air and moisture from A/C systems are commercially available. The pump should be capable of drawing the system down to 26-28 1/2 inches Hg at sea level. For each 1000 foot increase in altitude, this specification should be decreased by 1 inch Hg. As an example, at 5000 feet elevation, only 23-24 1/2 inches Hg can be obtained.
1. Connect suitable gauge manifold and discharge system as outlined previously. **System must be completely discharged prior to evacuation. If pressurized refrigerant is allowed to enter vacuum pump, pump will be damaged.**
2. Connect hose from gauge manifold center port to vacuum pump inlet.
3. Fully open both gauge manifold hand valves.
4. Operate vacuum pump while observing low side compound gauge. If system does not "pump-down" to 28-29 1/2 inches Hg (at sea level) within approximately 5 minutes, recheck connections and leak test system.
5. Continue to operate vacuum pump for 15-30 minutes, longer if system was open for an extended period of time, then close both manifold valves and stop pump.
6. Check ability of system to hold vacuum. Watch low side compound gauge and ensure that reading does not rise at a rate faster than 1 inch Hg every 4-5 minutes.
7. f system fails to hold vacuum, recheck fittings and connections, and leak test system.
8. If system holds vacuum, charge system with refrigerant.

## EVACUATING SYSTEM WITH CHARGING STATION
### Jeep Models

A vacuum pump is built into the charging station that is constructed to withstand repeated and prolonged use without damage. Complete moisture removal from the A/C system is possible only with a pump of this type.

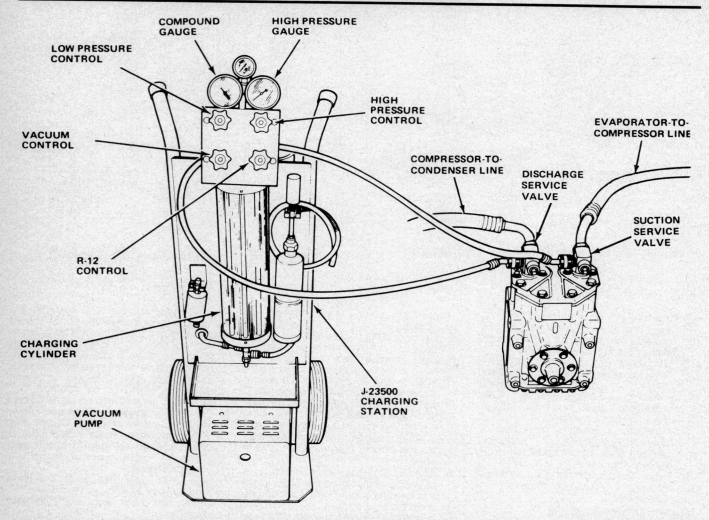

**Fig. 5   Charging station J-23500-01 hose connections. Shown with York type compressor**

1. Connect charging station and discharge system as outlined previously. **System must be completely discharged prior to evacuation. If pressurized refrigerant is allowed to enter vacuum pump, pump will be damaged.**
2. Reconnect vacuum hose to vacuum pump and ensure that vacuum control valve is closed.
3. Fully open low and high pressure control valves.
4. Connect station to a suitable voltage source and operate vacuum pump.
5. Slowly open vacuum control valve and observe low side compound gauge. If system does not "pump down" to 28-29½ inches Hg (at sea level) within approximately 5 minutes, recheck connections and leak test system.
6. Continue to operate vacuum pump for 15-30 minutes, longer if system was open for an extended period of time, then close all control valves and stop pump.
7. Check ability of system to hold vacu-

um. Watch low side compound gauge and ensure that reading does not rise at a rate faster than 1 inch Hg every 4-5 minutes.
8. If system fails to hold vacuum, recheck fittings and connections, and leak test system.
9. If system holds vacuum, charge system with refrigerant.

## CHARGING THE SYSTEM

Refer to "A/C Data Table" in the "A/C System Servicing" section for refrigerant capacities.

## CHARGING WITH 14 OUNCE CANS

Never use cans to charge into high pressure side of system (compressor discharge port) or into system at high temperature, as high system pressure transferred into charging can may cause it to explode.

1. Attach center hose from manifold gauge set to refrigerant dispensing manifold. Turn refrigerant manifold valves completely counter clockwise to open fully, and remove protective caps from refrigerant manifold.
2. Screw refrigerant cans into manifold, ensuring gasket is in place and in good condition. Torque can and manifold nuts to 6-8 ft. lbs.
3. Turn refrigerant manifold valves clockwise to puncture cans, and close manifold valves, **Fig. 4.**
4. Loosen charging hose at gauge set manifold and turn a refrigerant valve counterclockwise to release refrigerant and purge air from charging hose. When refrigerant gas escapes from loose connection, retighten hose.
5. Fully open all refrigerant manifold valves being used and place refrigerant cans into pan of hot water at 125° F to aid transfer of refrigerant gas. Place water pan and refrigerant cans on scale and note weight. **Do not heat refrigerant cans over 125° F. as they may explode.**

6. Connect jumper wire across terminals of cycling clutch switch connector located near "H" valve, if equipped, so that compressor clutch will remain engaged.
7. Start engine and set controls to A/C low blower position. Low pressure cut-out switch will prevent clutch from engaging until refrigerant is added to system. If clutch does engage, replace switch before continuing.
8. Charge through suction side of system by slowly opening suction manifold valve. Adjust valve so charging pressure does not exceed 50 psig.
9. Adjust engine speed to fast idle of 1400 RPM.
10. After specified refrigerant charge has entered system, close gauge set manifold valves, refrigerant manifold valves, and reconnect wiring.

## CHARGING WITH BULK REFRIGERANT SUPPLY

Only a charging bottle may be used to charge liquid refrigerant through the compressor discharge muffler. Never charge with liquid through compressor inlet or suction line ports, as damage to compressor is likely to occur. Do not run compressor while adding liquid refrigerant.
1. Warm charging bottle in pan of 125°

F. water. Do not heat R-12 with a torch, as it may explode.
2. Loosen charging hose at gauge set manifold and slowly open refrigerant supply valve until refrigerant has purged air from hose. Retighten the hose.
3. Place refrigerant container upside down on scale and note weight.
4. Open refrigerant supply valve and compressor discharge gauge valve to charge system. When scale indicates proper amount of charge has entered system, close valves.

If required amount of refrigerant does not enter system, close compressor discharge valve on manifold gauge set. Turn charging bottle right side up so gas, not liquid, will enter system. Start engine and set A/C control in A/C position. Slowly open suction line valve on manifold gauge set. The compressor will draw refrigerant into system. Charging line valve should be set so suction pressure does not exceed 50 psig.

## CHARGING STATION J-23500-01 METHOD
### Jeep Models

1. After discharging and evacuating system, close low pressure valve on charging station. Fully open left hand

refrigerant control valve at base of cylinder and high pressure valve on charging station and allow required charge of refrigerant to enter high side of system. When full charge has entered system, close refrigerant control valve and high pressure valve on charging station, **Fig. 5. Do not permit level of liquid to drop below zero mark on cylinder sight glass.**
2. After charging is completed, close manifold gauges and check high and low pressures and system operation. **Read gauges with high and low pressure valves closed on charging station. Low pressure gauge can be damaged if both high and low pressure valves are opened.**
3. Close all valves on charging station and close refrigerant drum valve when all operations are finished.
4. After completing operational check, back-seat suction and discharge service valves to their normal operating position by turning them fully counterclockwise.
5. Disconnect high and low pressure charging hoses from compressor.
6. Open valve on top of cylinder to remove remaining refrigerant as charging cylinder is not designed to store refrigerant.
7. Replace quick seal caps on compressor service valves.

# A/C System Servicing, Chrysler

## INDEX

## OIL LEVEL CHECK

Refer to "A/C Data Table" for oil level specifications and to Fig. 1, for oil dipstick dimensions.

### RV-2 COMPRESSOR

1. Connect gauge manifold and discharge system as outlined.
2. When system is nearly discharged, flush compressor dipstick with remaining refrigerant to ensure that dipstick is clean and at approximately the same temperature as oil in compressor sump.
3. Slowly loosen, then remove oil filler plug, Fig. 1. A suitable face shield should be worn when removing oil filler plug, as refrigerant dissolved in compressor oil may force oil out through plug opening.
4. Allow refrigerant vapors to clear and oil surface to stabilize, then measure oil level with dipstick.
5. Add oil to compressor, as needed, to bring level to within specifications list-

ed in "A/C Data Table." If other system components are replaced, refer to "Oil Charge."
6. Install filler plug, then evacuate and recharge system.

### A-590 & C-171 COMPRESSOR

These compressors must be removed from vehicle and drained to check the oil level. Refer to "Oil Charge" for service procedures.

## OIL CHARGE

### OIL CHARGE— COMPONENT REPLACEMENT

If there are no signs of external oil leakage, proceed as follows to add oil to system during component replacement.
1. Discharge system, as outlined, and measure amount of oil collected in

discharge container. **The amount of oil collected when discharging system must be replaced with new refrigeration oil to maintain proper oil charge.**
2. Remove defective components. Measure amount of oil remaining in compressor, if removed.
3. Add proper amount of new refrigeration oil to each replacement component as follows:
   a. If compressor is replaced, drain replacement compressor and add the same amount of oil as was drained from defective compressor.
   b. If condenser is replaced, add 1 ounce of oil to replacement condenser.
   c. If evaporator is replaced, add 2 ounces of oil to replacement evaporator.
   d. If filter/drier is replaced, add 1 ounce of oil to replacement filter/drier.
4. Install replacement components, then evacuate and recharge system.

## OIL LEVEL CHECK—LEAK CONDITION

### RV-2 Compressor

Refer to "Oil Level Check" for service procedures.

### A-590 & C-171 Compressor

Compressor oil level need only be checked when there is evidence of oil loss from the system as in the case of a broken line, leaking fitting or component, defective compressor seal or collision damage to system. A wet, shiny surface around a leak point is evidence of oil loss.

1. Discharge system as outlined, and re-

**Fig. 1 Dipstick fabrication & oil filler plug location. RV-2 compressor**

pair leak as needed.

2. Disconnect suction and discharge lines from compressor, then remove compressor and clutch assembly from vehicle.
3. Invert compressor and drain oil through suction and discharge ports.
4. On Dakota and front wheel drive vans and wagons, add 3 ounces of new refrigeration oil. On rear wheel drive vans and forward control models, add 7 ounces of new refrigeration oil. On all except above, add 5 ounces of new refrigeration oil. On all models, add oil to compressor through suction port.
5. Reinstall compressor using new gaskets on refrigerant line fittings, then evacuate and recharge system.

# A/C Data Table

| Year | Model | Refrigerant Capacity Lbs. | Viscosity | Refrigeration Oil | | | Compressor Clutch Air Gap Inches |
|---|---|---|---|---|---|---|---|
| | | | | Total System Capacity Ounces | Compressor Oil Level Check Inches | | |
| 1980 | Van & Forward Control ④ | 3 3/8 | 500 | ① | ② | | ③ |
| | Van & Forward Control ⑤ | 4 | 500 | ① | ② | | ③ |
| 1980-81 | Exc. Van & Forward Control | 2 5/8 | 500 | ① | ② | | ③ |
| 1981 | Van & Forward Control ④ | 3 | 500 | ① | ② | | ③ |
| | Van & Forward Control ⑤ | 4 | 500 | ① | ② | | ③ |
| 1982-83 | Van & Forward Control ④ | 3 | 500 | 9-10 | ⑥ | | .020-.035 |
| | Van & Forward Control ⑤ | 4 | 500 | 9-10 | ⑥ | | .020-.035 |
| 1982-84 | Exc. Van & Forward Control | 2 5/8 | 500 | 9-10 | ⑥ | | .020-.035 |
| | Rampage & Scamp | 2 1/8 | 500 | 9-10 | ⑥ | | .020-.035 |
| 1984 | Van & Forward Control ④ ⑦ | 3 | 500 | 9-10 | ⑥ | | .020-.035 |
| | Van & Forward Control ⑤ ⑦ | 4 | 500 | 9-10 | ⑥ | | .020-.035 |
| | Van & Wagon ⑧ | 2 1/3 | 500 | 9-10 | ⑥ | | .020-.035 |
| 1985-89 | Pickup & Ramcharger | 2 5/8 | 500 | 7-7.25 | ⑥ | | .020-.035 |
| | Van & Forward Control ④ ⑦ | 3 | 500 | 7-7 1/4 | ⑥ | | .020-.035 |
| | Van & Forward Control ⑤ ⑦ | 4 | 500 | 7-7 1/4 | ⑥ | | .020-.035 |
| | Van & Wagon ⑧ | 2 3/8 | 500 | 7-7 1/4 | ⑥ | | .020-.035 |
| 1987-89 | Dakota | 2 3/4 | 500 | 7-7.25 | ⑥ | | .020-.035 |

① —RV-2 comp., 10–12 oz.; C-171 comp., 9–10 oz.

② —RV-2 comp., 3–3.4 inch; C-171 comp., note that "Oil Level Inches" cannot be checked. Refer to total capacity and see text for checking procedure.

③ —C-171 comp., .020–.035 inch

④ —Models less auxiliary (rear, overhead etc.) system.

⑤ —Models with auxiliary (rear, overhead etc.) system.

⑥ —Note that "Oil Level Inches" cannot be checked. Refer to total capacity and see text for checking procedure.

⑦ —Rear wheel drive.

⑧ —Front wheel drive.

# Charging Valve Location

| Year | Model | High Pressure Fitting | Low Pressure Fitting |
|---|---|---|---|
| 1980-81 | Exc. Van & Front Section ① | Discharge Line Muffler | Suction Line at Compressor |
| | Van & Front Section ① | Discharge Line Muffler | Suction Hose |
| | All ② | Discharge Line Muffler | Compressor |
| 1982-89 | All | Discharge Line Muffler | Compressor |

① —RV-2 Compressor.

② —C-171 Compressor.

# A/C System Servicing, Jeep

## INDEX

## COMPRESSOR SERVICE VALVES

Most models are equipped with manual valves to isolate the compressor from the refrigerant system. These valves allow the compressor to be removed, or opened for oil level checks, without discharging the A/C system. Refrigerant system service access fittings are also included on most models.

During normal system operation, the manual valves are in the back-seated (fully counterclockwise) position, **Fig. 1.** To isolate the compressor, the valves are rotated to the front-seated (fully clockwise) position, closing off the refrigerant line passage to the compressor. To allow refrigerant system service access, the valves are rotated to the mid-position, **Fig. 1,** which opens the service port while still allowing refrigerant to flow through the system. **Manual compressor service valves should be in the back-seated (fully counterclockwise) position whenever service gauges are being connected or disconnected on the A/C system. Always install protective caps over manual valve stems and service ports, if equipped, after completing A/C service.**

## ISOLATING COMPRESSOR

1. Connect suitable gauge manifold to system and remove protective caps from manual valve stems.
2. Slightly open both service valves toward mid-position, then start engine and operate air conditioning.
3. Slowly rotate suction (low) side service valve clockwise toward front-seated position.
4. When suction (low) side gauge reads zero, stop engine, then rotate both low and high side valves to the fully clockwise (front-seated) position, **Fig. 1.**
5. Relieve internal compressor pressure on Sankyo 5 cylinder and York 2 cylinder compressors, by slightly loosening the oil sump filler plug. **A suitable face shield should be worn when relieving compressor pressure.**

## PURGING COMPRESSOR

The compressor must be purged of air whenever it has been isolated from the system for service.
1. Install oil plugs or reconnect refrigerant lines and manual valves to compressor as needed.
2. Cap service access ports on both manual valves, then rotate low

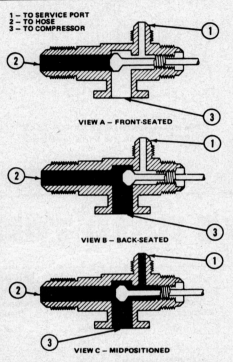

1 – TO SERVICE PORT
2 – TO HOSE
3 – TO COMPRESSOR

**VIEW A – FRONT-SEATED**

**VIEW B – BACK-SEATED**

**VIEW C – MIDPOSITIONED**

**Fig. 1  Compressor service valves, cross sectional view**

(suction) side service valve counterclockwise to the back-seated position.
3. Rotate high (discharge) side manual valve to mid-position, then slightly loosen cap on high side gauge port to allow refrigerant to force air out of compressor.
4. Back seat high side manual valve, then tighten gauge port cap.

## OIL LEVEL CHECK

Refer to "A/C Data Table" for oil level specifications.

### SANKYO COMPRESSOR

1. Isolate compressor as outlined in "Compressor Service Valves."
2. Remove compressor drive belt and rotate compressor so that filler plug faces straight up.
3. Slowly loosen, then remove oil filler plug. **A suitable face shield should be worn when removing filler plug.**
4. Rotate front clutch plate to position piston connecting rod in center of oil filler opening, **Fig. 3.**
5. Flush dipstick J-29642-12 or equivalent with refrigerant, then insert dipstick through opening to right of pis-

ton, **Fig. 3,** until stop bottoms against compressor housing.
6. Remove dipstick and note number of increments covered by oil. When properly filled, oil level should be between 4 and 6 increments.
7. Add suitable refrigeration oil, as needed, to obtain specified level.
8. Install oil filler plug and compressor drive belt, if removed, then purge air from compressor.

### YORK COMPRESSOR

**Compressor oil level should be checked whenever system is discharged for service part replacement or after rapid loss of refrigerant.**
1. Isolate compressor as outlined previously.
2. Slowly loosen crankcase oil check plug to relieve internal pressures, then after pressure is released, remove plug.
3. Hold dipstick, tool No. J-29642-12 in a vertical position, **Fig. 4,** then insert into check plug opening until dipstick bottoms in compressor. **If necessary, slightly rotate crankshaft to clear dipstick path.**
4. Remove dipstick and count number of dipstick increments covered with oil.
5. When properly filled, compressor should contain 7-10 increments of oil.
6. Add or remove oil as necessary.

## OIL CHARGE

Compressor oil level should be checked whenever the A/C system is discharged for repair or due to a malfunction. To ensure proper oil level after system service, proceed as follows:
1. Discharge system and repair as needed. **If compressor is replaced, ensure that oil level in replacement compressor is the same as the oil level in the defective compressor. If the evaporator or condenser is replaced, add 1 ounce of oil to each component prior to installation.**
2. Evacuate and recharge system, then operate A/C until pressure gauge readings stabilize (approximately 10 minutes).
3. Stop engine and perform "Oil Level Check."

## CHARGING VALVE LOCATION

Both high pressure and low pressure fittings are located on the compressor service valves.

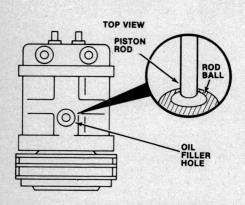

**Fig. 2 Positioning compressor piston rod for oil level check. Sankyo compressor**

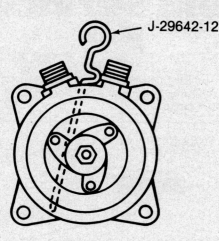

**Fig. 3 Compressor oil level check. Sankyo compressor**

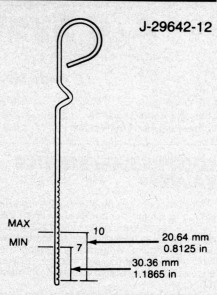

**Fig. 4 Compressor oil level check. York compressor**

# A/C Data Table

| Year | Model | Refrigerant Capacity Lbs. | Refrigerant Oil | | | Compressor Clutch Air Gap Inches |
|---|---|---|---|---|---|---|
| | | | Viscosity | Total System Capacity Ounces | Compressor Oil Level Check Inches | |
| 1980 | Exc. CJ Series | 2¼ | 500 | 7 | ① | — |
| | CJ Series | 2½ | 500 | 7 | ① | — |
| 1981-83 | Exc. CJ Series | 2¼ | 500 | ② | ③ | ④ |
| | CJ Series | 2½ | 500 | ② | ③ | ④ |
| 1984-86 | CJ Series | 2 | 500 | 6½ | ⑤ | ④ |
| | Grand Wagoneer & Truck | ⑥ | 500 | 6½ | ⑦ | ④ |
| | Cherokee & Wagoneer | 2 | 500 | 6½ | ⑤ | ④ |
| 1987-89 | Cherokee & Wagoneer | 2 | 500 | 6½ | ⑤ | ④ |
| | Commanche | 2 | 500 | 6½ | ⑤ | ④ |
| | Grand Wagoneer & Truck | ⑥ | 500 | 6½ | ⑦ | ④ |
| | Wrangler | 2 | 500 | 6 | ⑤ | ④ |

① —Horizontal mount, 13/16 inch; Vertical mount, 7/8–1⅛ inch.

② —Sankyo 5 cyl. comp., 7–8 oz.; York 2 cyl. comp., 7 oz.

③ —York 2 cyl. comp.: Horizontal mount, 13/16–1⅜ inch; Vertical mount, 7/8–1⅛ inch. Sankyo 5 cyl. comp., note that "Oil Level Inches" cannot be checked. Refer to total capacity and see text for checking procedure.

④ —Sankyo 5 cyl. comp., .016–.031 inch.

⑤ —Note that "Oil Level Inches" cannot be checked. Refer to total capacity and see text for checking procedure.

⑥ —In-line 6 cyl. engines, 2 lbs.; V8 engines, 2¼ lbs.

⑦ —York compressor, .8125–1.1865 inch.; Sankyo 5 cyl. compressor, note that "Oil Level Inches" cannot be checked. Refer to total capacity and see text for checking procedure.

# ENGINE COOLING FANS

## TABLE OF CONTENTS

# Electric Engine Cooling Fans, Chrysler

## INDEX

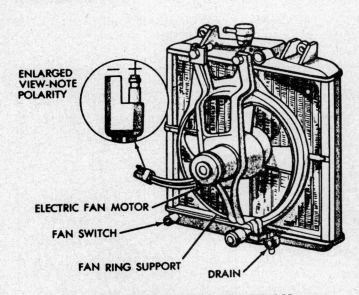

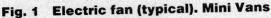

**Fig. 1  Electric fan (typical). Mini Vans**

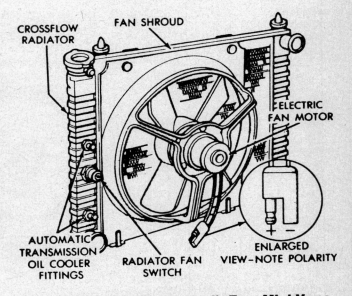

**Fig. 2  Electric fan (typical). Exc. Mini Vans**

## DESCRIPTION

On all except 1986-89 models with 4-135 (2.2L) engine and 1987-89 models with 4-153 (2.5L) and V6-181 (3.0L), the fan is controlled by a fan switch which is located on the radiator, **Figs. 1 and 2.** The switch will automatically turn on when coolant temperature reaches 200° F.

On 1986-89 models with 4-135 (2.2L) engine and 1987-89 models with 4-153 (2.5L) and V6-181 (3.0L), the fan is controlled by an on board computer. Coolant temperature is sensed by the computers temperature sensor which has two thermister sensors, one of which is for the cool-

ing system fan.

On models with A/C, when the A/C system is in operation, the fan motor will operate continually regardless of engine coolant temperature. When the ignition switch is turned off, the fan motor will stop operating, except on some 1984-87 Chrysler models equipped with 4-156 (2.6L) engines w/air conditioning. On some 1984-87 Chrysler models equipped with 4-156 (2.6L) engines and air conditioning, the fan will remain operating with ignition off for approximately 5-10 minutes if ambient temperature at radiator is above a predetermined level.

On all except 1986-89 models with 4-135 (2.2L) engine and 1989 models with

4-153 (2.5L) and V6-181 (3.0L), the radiator fan switch is located on the left side of the radiator tank. The switch is normally open and incorporates a bimetallic disc which pushes a plunger when coolant temperature reaches 200° F. Normal operation is indicated when fan motor turns on and off at appropriate temperatures.

The ambient temperature switch, used on some 4-156 (2.6L) engines w/air conditioning, is located on the radiator cooling fan mounting bracket and is used in conjunction with a time delay to activate the radiator cooling fan for approximately 5-10 minutes with engine off during periods of radiator ambient temperature of approximately 100° F or above.

## TROUBLESHOOTING

### AMBIENT TEMPERATURE SWITCH

#### Exc. 1986–89 Models W/4-135 (2.2L) & 1987-89 Models w/4-153 (2.5L) & V6-181 (3.0L)

Test switch using a suitable ohmmeter. When switch is cold, continuity should not exist. When switch is warmed to approximately 105° F or above, continuity should be present. Replace if defective.

### ELECTRIC FAN MOTOR

#### All Models

Disconnect wire connector from fan motor terminal, then connect a 14 gauge jumper wire from battery to fan motor terminal. If fan motor does not operate properly, replace fan motor.

### RADIATOR FAN SWITCH

#### Exc. 1986–89 Models W/4-135 (2.2L) & 1987-89 Models w/4-153 (2.5L) & V6-181 (3.0L)

To check switch continuity, drain coolant until level is below switch. The switch can be viewed by looking downward through the radiator filler neck. Disconnect electrical connector from switch and remove switch from radiator. Bring switch to a temperature of 208° F or higher using a suitable oil bath, then check for switch continuity using an ohmmeter or suitable test lamp. If continuity is not indicated, replace switch.

### ELECTRIC FAN MOTOR RELAY

#### Exc. 1986–89 Models w/4-135 (2.2L) & 1987–89 Models w/4-153 (2.5L) & V6-181 (3.0L)

The fan motor relay is used on Chrysler F.W.D. models equipped with A/C. The relay is located on the front lefthand shock absorber housing. If radiator fan switch and fan motor test results are satisfactory, but fan motor will not operate, the fan motor relay is suspected. Replace relay, then disconnect wire connector from radiator fan switch and connect a 14 gauge jumper wire between wire connector terminals. Place ignition switch in Accessory position. Fan motor should operate.

# VARIABLE SPEED FANS

## INDEX

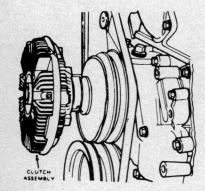

**Fig. 1 Fan drive clutch assembly. 1984–89 models (1980–83 models similar)**

**Fig. 2 Variable speed fan with coiled bimetallic thermostatic spring**

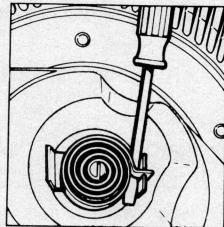

**Fig. 3 Bimetallic coiled spring removal**

## DESCRIPTION

Do not operate engine until fan has first been inspected for cracks and/or separations. If a fan blade is found to be bent or damaged in any way, do not attempt to repair or reuse damaged part. Proper balance is essential in fan assembly operation. Balance cannot be assured once a fan assembly has been found to be bent or damaged and failure may occur during operation, creating an extremely dangerous condition. Always replace damaged fan assembly.

The fan drive clutch, **Fig. 1**, is a fluid coupling containing silicone oil. Fan speed is regulated by the torque-carrying capacity of the silicone oil. The more silicone oil in the coupling, the greater the fan speed, and the less silicone oil, the slower the fan speed.

The fan drive clutch uses a heat-sensitive, coiled bimetallic spring connected to an opening plate, **Fig. 2**. This unit causes the fan speed to increase with a rise in temperature and to decrease as temperature decreases.

## TROUBLESHOOTING

### FAN DRIVE CLUTCH TEST

Do not operate the engine until the fan has been first checked for possible cracks and separations.

To check the clutch fan, disconnect the bimetal spring, **Fig. 3**, and rotate 90° counterclockwise. This disables the temperature-controlled, free-wheeling feature and the clutch performs like a conventional fan. If this cures the overheating condition, replace the clutch fan.

### FAN CLUTCH NOISE

Fan clutch noise can sometimes be noticed when clutch is engaged for maximum cooling. Clutch noise is also noticeable within the first few minutes after starting engine while clutch is redistributing the silicone fluid back to its normal, disengaged operating condition after settling for long periods of time (overnight). However, continuous fan noise or an excessive roar indicates the clutch assembly is locked-up due to internal failure. This condition can be checked by attempting to manually rotate fan. If fan cannot be rotated manually or there is a rough, abrasive feel as fan is rotated, the clutch should be replaced.

## FAN LOOSENESS

Lateral movement can be observed at the fan blade tip under various temperature conditions because of the type bearing used. This movement should not exceed 1/4 inch (6.5 mm) as measured at the fan tip. If this lateral movement does not exceed specifications, there is no cause for replacement.

## CLUTCH FLUID LEAK

Small fluid leaks do not generally affect the operation of the unit. These leaks generally occur around the area of the bearing assembly, but, if the leaks appear to be excessive, engine overheating may occur.

Check for clutch and fan free-wheeling by attempting to rotate fan and clutch assembly by hand five times. If no drag is felt, replace clutch.

## FAN BLADE INSPECTION

Place fan on flat surface with leading edge facing down. If there is a clearance between fan blade touching surface and opposite blade of more than .090 inch (2 mm), replace fan. (See caution at beginning of chapter.)

# ALTERNATORS
## TABLE OF CONTENTS

# Delco-Remy Alternators, Jeep

**NOTE:** For service procedures on these alternators, refer to "Alternator Systems" section of the Chevrolet/GMC chapter.

# Chrysler Alternators
## INDEX

## DESCRIPTION

The main components of the alternator are the rotor, stator, diodes, end shields and drive pulley. Direct current is available at the output "BAT" terminal. The function of the voltage regulator is to limit output voltage. This is accomplished by controlling the current flow in the rotor field coil, in turn controlling the strength of the rotor magnetic field. The electronic voltage regulator is a sealed, non-adjustable unit.

## TESTING SYSTEM ON VEHICLE
### ALTERNATOR OUTPUT WIRE RESISTANCE TEST
#### Testing

1. Disconnect battery ground cable.

2. Disconnect "Bat" lead at alternator output terminal.
3. Connect a 0-150 amp D.C. ammeter in series between alternator "Bat" terminal and disconnected "Bat" lead wire, **Fig. 1.**
4. Connect positive lead wire of a suitable voltmeter to disconnected "Bat" lead wire, then connect negative lead to battery positive post.
5. Disconnect voltage regulator wiring connector, then using suitable jumper wire, connect wiring connector green regulator field wire to a suitable ground. **Do not connect blue J2 lead or wiring connector to ground. Do not spread connector terminals with jumper wire.**
6. Connect a suitable engine tachometer, then reconnect battery ground cable.
7. Connect a variable carbon pile rheostat to battery terminals, ensuring car-

bon piles are in "open" or "off" position.
8. Start engine and operate at idle speed, then adjust carbon pile and engine speed to maintain a 20 amp circuit flow. Note voltmeter reading. Voltmeter reading should not exceed .7 volt on 1980-83 models, or .5 volt on 1984-89 models.

### Test Results

1. If a higher than specified voltage drop is indicated, clean and tighten all connectors in charging circuit. **A voltage drop test may be performed at each connector to locate point of excessive resistance.**
2. If charging circuit resistance test was satisfactory, disconnect battery ground cable, then the ammeter, voltmeter and carbon pile.

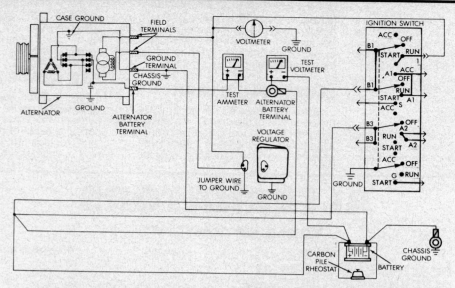

**Fig. 1   Alternator output wire resistance test (Typical)**

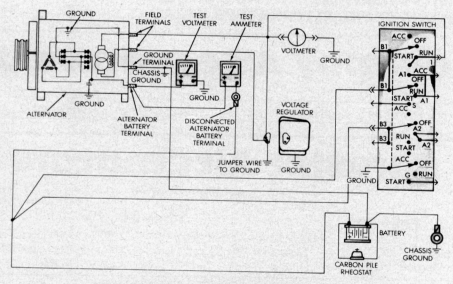

**Fig. 2   Current output test (Typical)**

3. Remove jumper wire, then connect regulator wire connector.
4. Connect battery ground cable.

## CURRENT OUTPUT TEST
### Testing

1. Disconnect battery ground cable.
2. Disconnect "Bat" lead at alternator output terminal.
3. Connect a 0-150 amp D.C. ammeter in series between alternator "Bat" terminal and disconnected "Bat" lead wire, **Fig. 2**.
4. Connect positive lead of a suitable voltmeter to "Bat" terminal of alternator, then connect negative lead to a suitable ground.

5. Disconnect voltage regulator wiring connector, then using suitable jumper wire, connect wiring connector green regulator field wire to a suitable ground. **Do not connect blue J2 lead or wiring connector to ground. Do not spread connector terminals with jumper wire.**
6. Connect a suitable engine tachometer, then reconnect battery ground cable.
7. Connect a variable carbon pile rheostat between battery terminals, ensuring carbon piles are in "open" or "off" position.
8. Start engine and operate at idle speed, then adjust carbon pile and engine speed in increments until a

speed of 1250 RPM at 15 volts is obtained on all units except 1980-84 100, 114 and 117 amp units. On 1980-84 100, 114 and 117 amp units, adjust carbon pile and engine speed to 900 RPM at 13 volts. **Do not allow voltmeter range to exceed 16 volts during testing.**

### Test Results

1. Note ammeter reading. Ammeter reading should be within specified limits noted in specification charts in individual truck chapters.
2. If reading is less than specified, alternator is defective.
3. After completion of current output test, turn off carbon pile and ignition

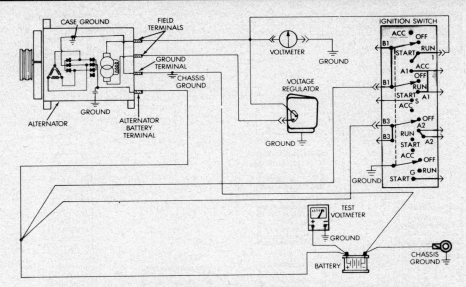

Fig. 3    Electronic voltage regulator test (Typical)

| Ambient Temperature Near Regulator | −20°F | 80°F | 140°F | Above 140°F |
|---|---|---|---|---|
| 1980-83 | 14.9-15.9 | 13.9-14.6 | 13.3-13.9 | Less than 13.6 |
| 1984 ① | 14.6-15.8 | 13.9-14.4 | 13.0-13.7 | Less than 13.6 |
| 1984 ② | 14.9-15.9 | 13,9-14.6 | 13.3-13.9 | Less than 13.6 |
| 1985-89 ③ | 14.9-15.8 | 13.9-14.4 | 13.0-13.7 | Less than 13.6 |
| 1985-89 ④ | 14.9-15.9 | 13.9-14.4 | 13.0-13.7 | Less than 13.6 |

①—Exc. R.W.D. Vans & Wagons.        ③—F.W.D. Mini-Vans.
②—R.W.D. Vans & Wagons.             ④—Exc. F.W.D. Mini-Vans.

Fig. 4    Regulator test specification chart

switch, then disconnect battery ground cable.
4. Remove ammeter, voltmeter, tachometer and carbon pile, then reconnect "Bat" lead to alternator output terminal.
5. Disconnect jumper wire from ground, then reconnect voltage regulator wiring connector.
6. Connect battery ground cable.

## VOLTAGE REGULATOR TEST

### Testing

**Battery must be fully charged for test to be accurate.**
1. Clean battery terminals, then connect positive lead of a suitable voltmeter to battery positive post and the negative lead to a suitable ground, **Fig. 3.**
2. Connect an engine tachometer, then start and operate engine at 1250 RPM with all lights and accessories in the "off" position.
3. Note voltmeter readings, then refer to voltage chart, **Fig. 4. An ammeter**

reading registering an immediate charge, then gradually returning to normal, is normal. The duration the ammeter remains positioned to the right depends on cranking time.

### Test Results
1. If voltage is fluctuating or below limits, proceed as follows:
   a. Ensure voltage regulator has a proper ground through regulator case, mounting screws and chassis.
   b. Place ignition switch in "off" position, then disconnect voltage regulator connector and inspect for a possible open circuit.
   c. Place ignition switch in "on" position. **Do not start engine or distort terminals with voltmeter probe.**
   d. Ensure battery voltage exists at blue and green leads at voltage regulator wiring harness terminals, then place ignition switch in "off"

position. **If steps a through d are satisfactory, replace voltage regulator.**
2. If voltage is above limits, **Fig. 4,** proceed as follows:
   a. Place ignition switch in "off" position, then disconnect voltage regulator connector.
   b. Place ignition switch in "on" position. **Do not start engine or distort terminals with voltmeter probe.**
   c. Ensure battery voltage exists at blue and green leads at voltage regulator wiring harness terminals, then place ignition switch in "off" position. **If results of steps a, b and c are not satisfactory, replace voltage regulator.**
3. Remove voltmeter and tachometer.

## ALTERNATOR & REGULATOR DIAGNOSIS

Ref+er to **Fig. 5** for alternator and regulator diagnosis.

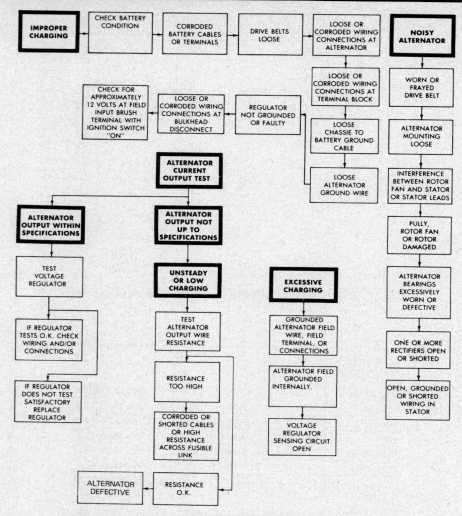

**Fig. 5   Charging system diagnosis chart**

# Mitsubishi Alternators, Chrysler

## INDEX

## DESCRIPTION

On these units, the regulator is incorporated into the alternator rear housing, **Fig. 1**. The electronic voltage regulator has the ability to vary regulated system voltage upward or downward as temperature changes. No voltage regulated adjustments are required on these units.

## IN-VEHICLE TESTS
### VOLTAGE REGULATOR TEST

1. With ignition switch in Off position, disconnect alternator battery lead at output terminal and connect ammeter in series between alternator and disconnected lead, **Fig. 2.**

2. Connect a voltmeter between alternator L terminal and ground, **Fig. 2.** Voltmeter should indicate zero voltage. If voltage is present, the alternator or charging system wiring is defective.

3. Place ignition switch in the On position and note voltmeter reading. Voltmeter reading should be 1 volt or less. If a higher reading is indicated, the alternator is defective.

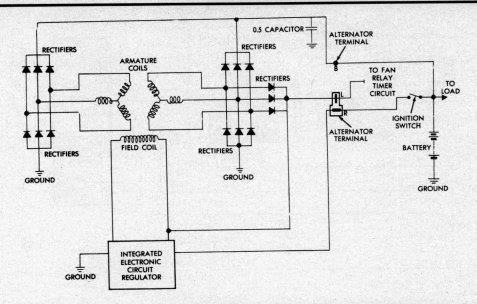

**Fig. 1  Wiring diagram of Mitsubishi alternator charging system**

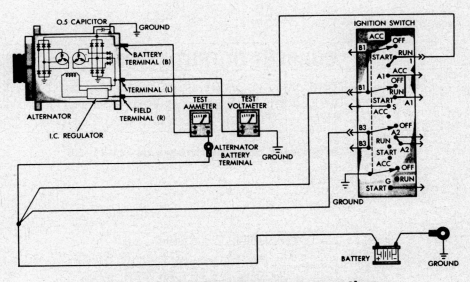

**Fig. 2  Voltage regulator test connections**

4. Connect a tachometer to engine, then start and operate engine at approximately 2000 to 3000 RPM and note ammeter reading. **When starting engine, ensure no starting current is applied to ammeter.**
5. If ammeter reading is 5 amps or less on 1981-83 units, or 10 amps or less on 1984-89 models, check voltmeter reading with engine operating at 2000 to 3000 RPM. The charging voltage should be 14.4 volts at 68° F.
6. If ammeter reading is above 5 amps on 1981-83 models or above 10 amps on 1984-89 models, continue to charge battery until reading drops to less than 5 amps on 1981-83 models, or to less than 10 amps on 1984-89 models. If voltage is not

within limits, alternator is defective. **An alternative method to limiting charging current is to connect a 1/4 ohm (25 watt) resistor in series with battery.**

## CURRENT OUTPUT TEST

1. With ignition switch in the Off position, disconnect battery ground cable, then disconnect battery lead from alternator output terminal.
2. Connect an ammeter set at the 0 to 100 amp scale between alternator output terminal and the disconnected battery lead, **Fig. 3.**
3. Connect positive lead of voltmeter to alternator output terminal and nega-

tive lead to ground, **Fig. 3.**
4. Connect suitable tachometer to engine and reconnect battery ground cable.
5. Connect a variable carbon pile regulator between battery terminals. When installing carbon pile regulator, ensure regulator is in Open or Off position.
6. Adjust carbon pile regulator and accelerate engine to the specified RPM, noting ammeter and voltmeter readings, **Figs. 4 and 5.**
7. If ammeter reading is less than specified, the alternator is defective.

## CHARGING CIRCUIT RESISTANCE TEST

1. Disconnect battery ground cable.
2. Disconnect "bat" lead at alternator

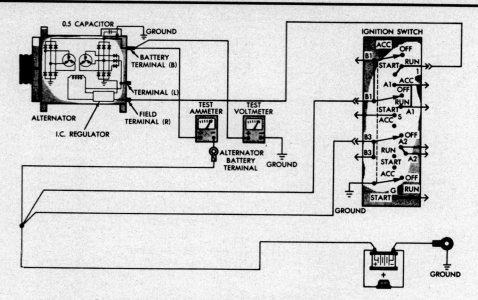

**Fig. 3  Current output test connections**

| CURRENT OUTPUT CHART | |
|---|---|
| Output current (Hot or Cold) at Engine RPM | 17-25A at 13.5 Volts and 500 RPM |
| | 63-70A at 13.5 Volts and 1000 RPM |
| | 74A at 13.5 Volts and 2000 RPM |

**Fig. 4  Alternator test specifications. 1981–85**

| 75 AMP CURRENT OUTPUT CHART | |
|---|---|
| Output current (Hot or Cold) at Engine RPM | 44-51A at 13.0 Volts and 750 RPM |
| | 64-72A at 13.0 Volts and 1000 RPM |
| | 74-78A at 13.0 Volts and 2000 RPM |
| **90 AMP CURRENT OUTPUT CHART** | |
| Output current (Hot or Cold) at Engine RPM | 58-71A at 13.0 Volts and 750 RPM |
| | 80-91A at 13.0 Volts and 1000 RPM |
| | 95-102A at 13.0 Volts and 2000 RPM |

**Fig. 5  Alternator test specifications. 1986–89**

output terminal.

3. Connect an ammeter set at 0 to 100 amp scale in series between alternator output terminal and disconnected lead wire, **Fig. 6.** Connect positive lead to "bat" terminal and negative lead to disconnected "bat" lead.
4. Connect positive lead of a suitable voltmeter to disconnected "bat" lead wire, then connect negative lead to battery positive post.
5. Connect a suitable tachometer to engine, then reconnect battery ground

cable.

6. Connect a variable carbon pile regulator between battery terminals. When installing regulator, ensure it is in "open" or "off" position.
7. Start engine, then adjust engine speed and carbon pile regulator to maintain 20 amp circuit flow. Ensure voltmeter reading does not exceed .5 volts. If a higher voltage drop is indicated, proceed as follows:
   a. Tighten all connections to locate possible source of resistance.

   b. Inspect and clean each connection.
8. If test proves satisfactory, disconnect battery ground cable, then remove ammeter, voltmeter and carbon pile.
9. Connect battery ground cable.

## ALTERNATOR & ELECTRONIC VOLTAGE REGULATOR DIAGNOSIS

For "Alternator and Electronic Voltage Regulator Diagnosis," refer to **Fig. 7.**

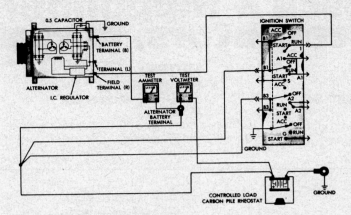

**Fig. 6  Charging circuit resistance test connections**

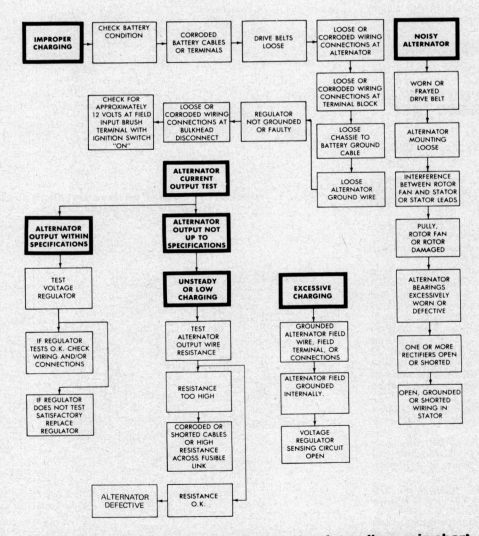

**Fig. 7  Alternator & electronic voltage regulator diagnosis chart**

# Bosch & Nippondenso Alternators, Chrysler

## INDEX

## DESCRIPTION

The main components of the alternator are the rotor, stator, rectifier, end shields and drive pulley. Direct current is available at the output "B+" terminal.

Alternator output is controlled by voltage regulator circuitry contained within the power and logic modules of the Single Module Engine Controller (SMEC).

## IN-VEHICLE TESTING

Prior to testing system, ensure battery is fully charged.

### ALTERNATOR OUTPUT WIRE RESISTANCE TEST

#### Testing

1. Disconnect battery ground cable.
2. Disconnect "B+" lead at alternator output terminal.
3. Connect a 0-150 amp D.C. ammeter in series between alternator "B+" terminal and disconnected "B+" lead wire, **Fig. 1.**
4. Connect positive lead wire of a suitable voltmeter to disconnected "B+" lead wire, then connect negative lead to battery positive post.
5. Remove air hose between Single Module Engine Controller (SMEC) and air cleaner, then ground one end of a suitable jumper wire and probe green R3 wire on dash side of black 8-way connector, **Fig. 1. Use caution not to ground J2 wire of 8-way dash connector. Both R3 and J2 wires are green on alternator side of wire connector. On dash side of connector, R3 wire is green, while J2 wire is blue.**
6. Connect a suitable engine tachometer, then reconnect battery ground cable.
7. Connect a variable carbon pile rheostat to battery terminals, ensuring carbon piles are in "open" or "off" position.
8. Start engine and operate at idle speed, then adjust carbon pile and engine speed to maintain a 20 amp circuit flow. Note voltmeter reading. Voltmeter reading should not exceed .5 volt.

#### Test Results

1. If a higher than specified voltage drop

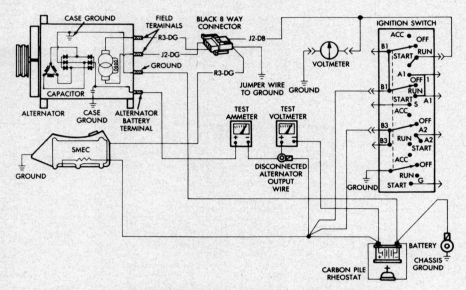

**Fig. 1   Alternator output wire resistance test. Bosch & Nippondenso alternators**

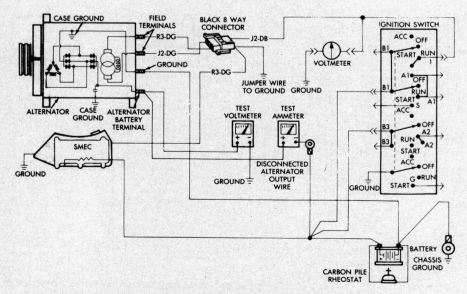

**Fig. 2   Alternator current output test. Bosch & Nippondenso alternators**

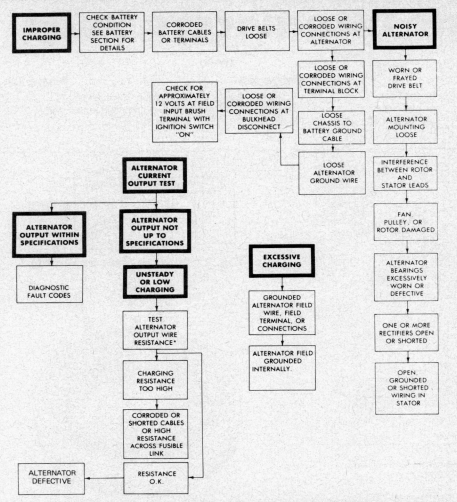

**Fig. 3   Charging System Diagnosis chart. Bosch & Nippondenso alternators**

is indicated, clean and tighten all connectors in charging circuit. **A voltage drop test may be performed at each connector to locate point of excessive resistance.**
2. If charging circuit resistance test was satisfactory, disconnect battery ground cable, then the ammeter, voltmeter and carbon pile.
3. Remove jumper wire.
4. Connect battery ground cable, then the hose between SMEC and air cleaner.

## CURRENT OUTPUT TEST
### Testing

1. Disconnect battery ground cable.
2. Disconnect "B+" lead at alternator output terminal.
3. Connect a 0-150 amp D.C. ammeter in series between alternator "B+" terminal and disconnected "B+" lead wire, **Fig. 2.**
4. Connect positive lead of a suitable

voltmeter to "B+" terminal of alternator, then connect negative lead to suitable ground.
5. Connect a suitable engine tachometer, then reconnect battery ground cable.
6. Connect a variable carbon pile rheostat between battery terminals, ensuring carbon piles are in "open" or "off" position.
7. Remove air hose between Single Module Engine Controller (SMEC) and air cleaner, then ground one end of a suitable jumper wire and probe green R3 wire on dash side of black 8-way connector, **Fig. 2.** Use caution not to ground J2 wire of 8-way dash connector. Both R3 and J2 wires are green on alternator side of wire connector. On dash side of connector, R3 wire is green, while J2 wire is blue.
8. Start engine and operate at idle speed, then adjust carbon pile and engine speed in increments until a speed of 1250 RPM at 15 volts is obtained. **Do not allow voltmeter range to exceed 16 volts during testing.**

### Test Results

1. Note ammeter reading. Ammeter reading should be within specified limits noted in specification charts in individual truck chapters.
2. If reading is less than specified, alternator is defective.
3. After completion of current output test, turn off carbon pile and ignition switch, then disconnect battery ground cable.
4. Remove ammeter, voltmeter, tachometer and carbon pile, then reconnect "B+" lead to alternator output terminal.
5. Disconnect jumper wire, then connect air hose from SMEC to air cleaner.
6. Connect battery ground cable.

## VOLTAGE REGULATOR TEST

Voltage regulation is controlled by the SMEC unit.

## CHARGING SYSTEM DIAGNOSIS

Refer to **Fig. 3** for charging system diagnosis.

# Paris-Rhone Alternators, Jeep

## INDEX

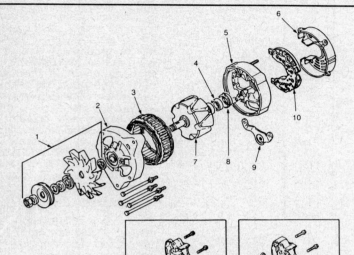

1. Pulley and Fan Assembly
2. Front Housing
3. Stator
4. Bearing
5. Rear Housing
6. Slip Ring End Frame Cover
7. Rotor
8. Race
9. Rear Lug
10. Rectifier Bridge

**Fig. 1  Exploded view of alternator assembly**

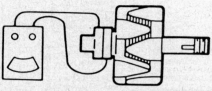

**Fig. 2  Testing rotor assembly**

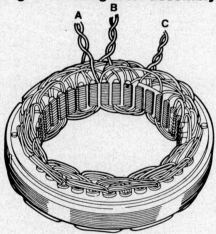

**Fig. 3  Testing stator assembly**

## DESCRIPTION

The Paris-Rhone alternator, **Fig. 1,** features a solid state built-in regulator that is available in two output capacities. These alternators are available in 60 amp and 70 amp ratings. All regulator components are enclosed in a solid mold with no need or provision for adjustment of the regulator. A rectifier bridge changes A.C. voltage to D.C. voltage which is available at the output terminal.

The alternator warning lamp is mounted on the instrument panel and illuminates when the ignition switch is turned on and goes out after the engine starts. If the lamp remains on or illuminates while the engine is running, a charging system malfunction is indicated.

## TROUBLESHOOTING

### ALTERNATOR LAMP DOES NOT ILLUMINATE WITH IGNITION SWITCH ON

1. Check if alternator connector is loose or disconnected.
2. Check ring terminal on alternator case for proper ground.

3. Ground wide terminal on connector, then check bulb by ensuring lamp lights.

### ALTERNATOR LAMP ILLUMINATES WITH IGNITION SWITCH ON

1. If warning lamp illuminates when engine is operating, a charging system defect is indicated. Check for loose or broken alternator drive belt, defective alternator or defective regulator.
2. If regulator voltage is less than 12.5 volts, check for defective diodes, an open stator winding, excessive carbon on slip rings and/or worn brushes.

## TESTING

### ALTERNATOR VOLTAGE TEST

1. Connect a suitable voltmeter across battery terminals.
2. Start engine, then increase RPM until voltmeter pointer remains steady. Voltage should be 12.5-15 volts.
3. Turn on as many accessories as pos-

sible with, then recheck voltage reading. Reading should be 12.5-15 volts.

### ROTOR TEST

1. Using a suitable ohmmeter, **Fig. 2,** check resistance between the two sections of the rotor slip rings. Take resistance readings at a minimum of four points around slip rings.
2. Resistance should be 2.9-3.5 ohms on 60 amp rotor or 3.0-3.6 ohms on 75 amp rotor. If resistance is not as specified, replace rotor.

### STATOR TEST

1. Using a suitable ohmmeter, check resistance across each stator wire connections.
2. Connect test leads to wires A and B, **Fig. 3,** then note resistance.
3. Connect test leads to wires B and C, then note resistance.
4. Connect test leads to wires A and C, then note resistance.
5. Resistance across each stator wire should not exceed .1 ± .01 ohms. on 60 amp stators or .08 ohms ±.008 ohms on 75 amp stators. Replace stator if resistance is not as specified.

# STARTER MOTORS & SWITCHES

## TABLE OF CONTENTS

# Delco-Remy Starters, Jeep

**NOTE:** For description, diagnosis & testing on this starter, refer to "Delco-Remy Starters" section in "Chevrolet & GMC" chapter.

# Bosch, Mitsubishi & Nippondenso Starters, Chrysler

## INDEX

## DESCRIPTION

Two types of starters are used. The first type is a direct drive starter motor with an overrunning clutch type starter drive. A solenoid switch is mounted on the starter motor. The second type is a permanent magnet reduction gear starter. A planetary gear train transmits power between starter motor and pinion shaft. The structure is different on both type starters, but electrical wiring is the same.

## DIAGNOSIS

Refer to **Fig. 1** when diagnosing starters.

## IN-VEHICLE TESTING

Before starting any tests, ensure that battery is fully charged and that all connections are good.

## AMPERAGE DRAW TEST

1. Run engine until it reaches operating temperature, then turn engine off.
2. Connect a suitable battery-starter tester according to manufacturer's instructions.
3. Turn battery-starter tester control knob to "off" position.
4. Turn voltmeter selector knob to "16 volt" position.
5. Turn battery-starter function selector to "starter system test" (0-500 amp scale).
6. Connect red positive ammeter lead to positive battery terminal and the black negative ammeter lead to negative battery terminal.
7. Connect red positive voltmeter lead to positive battery terminal and the black negative voltmeter lead to the negative battery terminal.
8. Connect a remote starter jumper according to manufacturer's instructions. **Do not crank engine excessively during testing.**
9. Disconnect coil wire from distributor cap center tower and secure to good ground.
10. Crank engine with remote starter switch and observe exact voltmeter reading, then stop cranking engine.
11. Turn tester control knob clockwise until voltmeter reads exactly the same as when engine was being cranked. Ammeter should read 120-160 amps on direct drive units or 150-210 amps on gear reduction units.

## CIRCUIT RESISTANCE TEST

On 1986-89 reduction gear starters, perform circuit resistance test, refer to "Chrysler Reduction Gear Starter" section.

## STARTER RESISTANCE TEST

1. Disconnect positive battery cable and connect a 0-300 scale ammeter between disconnected lead and battery terminal post.
2. Connect a voltmeter, graduated in tenths, between positive post on battery and starter relay terminal on starter solenoid.
3. Crank engine while observing reading on voltmeter and ammeter. A voltage reading exceeding .3 volt indicates high resistance caused by loose circuit connections, a faulty cable, burned starter relay or solenoid switch contacts. A high current combined with slow cranking speed indicates need for starter repair.
4. Reconnect positive battery lead to battery.

## INSULATED CIRCUIT TEST

1. Turn voltmeter selector knob to 4 volt position.
2. Disconnect ignition coil secondary cable.
3. Connect voltmeter positive lead to battery positive post and voltmeter negative lead to solenoid connector that connects to starter field coils. **It may be necessary to peel back**

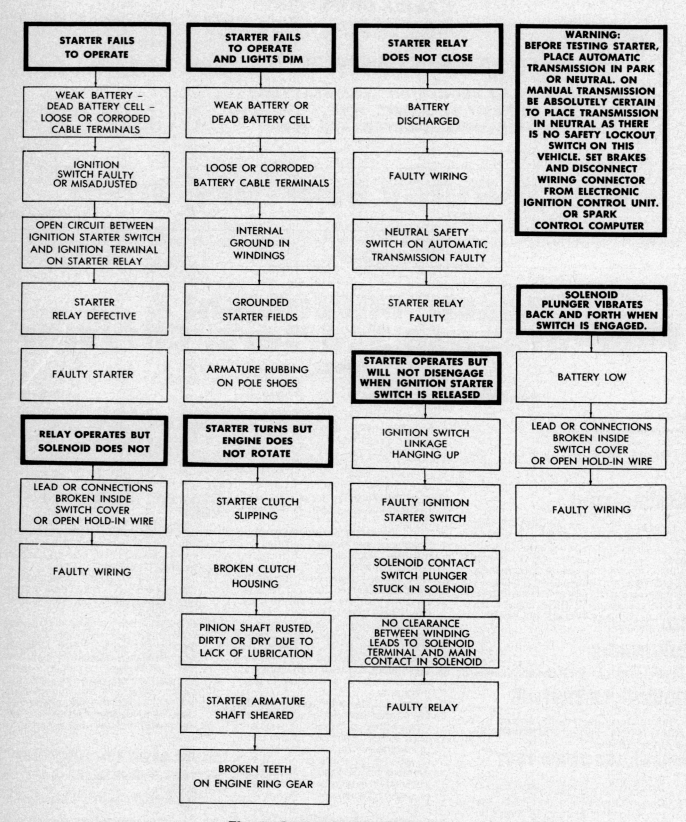

**Fig. 1  Starter motor diagnosis**

rubber boot on solenoid to reach solenoid connection. **Voltmeter will read off scale to right until starter is actuated.**
4. Connect remote control starter switch to battery solenoid terminal of starter relay.
5. Crank engine with remote control starter switch while observing voltmeter reading. If voltmeter reading exceeds .3 volt, there is high resistance in starter insulated circuit, proceed as follows:
  a. Remove voltmeter lead from solenoid connector and connect to following points, repeating test at each connection. Starter terminal of solenoid, battery terminal of solenoid, battery cable terminal at solenoid, starter relay and cable clamp at battery.
  b. A small change will occur each time a normal portion of circuit is removed from test. A definite change in voltmeter reading indicates that last part eliminated in test is at fault.

## STARTER GROUND TEST

1. Connect voltmeter positive lead to starter through bolt and negative voltmeter lead to battery negative post.
2. Crank engine with remote control starter switch and observe voltmeter reading.
3. If voltmeter reading exceeds .2 volt, make following tests to isolate point of excessive voltage loss, repeating test at each connection; starter drive housing, cable terminal at engine, cable clamp at battery.
4. A small change will occur each time a normal portion of circuit is removed from test. A definite change in voltmeter reading indicates last part eliminated in test is at fault.

## STARTER SOLENOID TEST

1. Connect heavy jumper wire on starter relay between battery and solenoid terminals. If engine cranks, perform starter relay test.
2. If engine does not crank or solenoid chatters, check wiring and connectors from relay to starter for loose or corroded connections.
3. Repeat test and, if engine still does not crank properly, repair or replace starter as necessary.

## STARTER RELAY TEST

1. Place transmission in Neutral and apply parking brake.
2. Check for battery voltage between starter relay battery terminal and ground.
3. Connect jumper wire on starter relay between battery and ignition terminals.
4. If engine does not crank, connect a second jumper wire to starter relay between ground terminal and good ground and repeat test.
5. If engine cranks in step 4, transmission linkage is misadjusted or neutral safety switch is defective.
6. If engine does not crank in step 4, starter relay is defective.

# Chrysler Reduction Gear Starter

## INDEX

## DESCRIPTION

This reduction gear starting motor, **Fig. 1,** has an armature-to-engine crankshaft ratio of 45 to 1; a 2 to 1 or 3½ to 1 reduction gear set is built into the motor assembly. The starter utilizes a solenoid shift. The housing of the solenoid is integral with the starter drive end housing.

## DIAGNOSIS

Refer to **Fig. 2** when diagnosing starter.

## IN-VEHICLE TESTING
## 1980-82 MODELS
### Starter Current Draw Test

1. Run engine until it reaches operating temperature, then shut engine off.
2. Connect suitable battery-starter tester according to manufacturer's instructions.
3. Turn variable resistor control knob to off or zero position.
4. Connect remote starter jumper according to manufacturer's instructions.
5. Crank engine just long enough to read cranking voltage on voltmeter.
6. Stop cranking engine, then turn variable resistor control knob until voltmeter reads cranking voltage previously noted. Ammeter should read 180-200 amps on V8-360 engine or 165-180 amps on other engines.

### Circuit Resistance Test

1. Connect voltmeter leads across each connection shown in circuit resistance chart, **Fig. 3.**
2. If readings are higher than specified, clean or repair connection, then repeat test.

### Starter Solenoid Test

1. Connect heavy jumper wire on starter relay between battery and solenoid terminals.
2. If starter does not crank, or solenoid chatters, check wiring and connectors from relay to starter for loose or corroded connections, then repeat test.
3. If engine still will not crank, repair or replace starter as necessary.

### Starter Relay Test

1. Place transmission in Neutral, then connect jumper wire on starter relay between battery and ignition terminals.
2. If engine does not crank, connect a second jumper wire on starter relay between ground terminal and good ground.

3. Repeat test. If engine cranks, transmission linkage is misadjusted or neutral safety switch is defective. If engine does not crank, starter relay is defective.

## 1983-89 MODELS
### Amperage Draw Test

Perform amperage draw test, refer to "Bosch, Mitsubishi & Nippondenso Starters" section. Amperage should be 165-180 amps for 1983-85 models with 6-225 and V8-318 engines, 180-200 amps for 1983-85 models with V8-360 engines or 165-180 amps for all 1986-89 models.

### Circuit Resistance Test

1. Connect voltmeter leads across each connection shown in circuit resistance chart, **Figs. 3 and 4.**
2. If readings are higher than specified, clean or repair connection, then repeat test.

### Starter Solenoid Test

Perform starter solenoid test, refer to "1980-82 models."

### Starter Solenoid Bench Test

Perform starter solenoid bench test, refer to "1980-82 models."

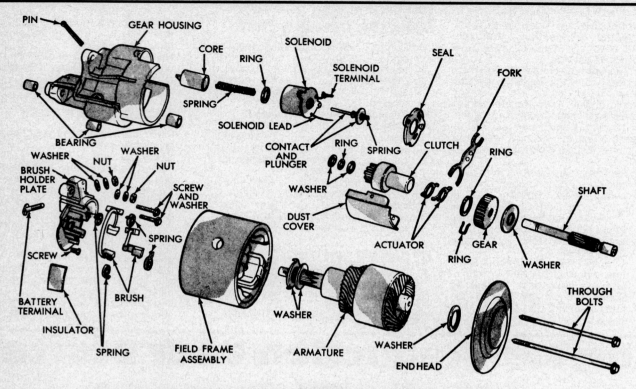

**Fig. 1 Chrysler built reduction gear starter. Gasoline engines**

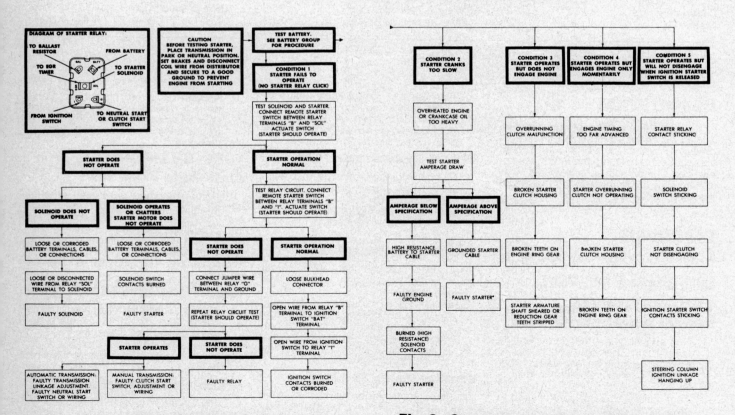

**Fig. 2 Starter motor diagnosis (Part 1 of 2)**   **Fig. 2 Starter motor diagnosis (Part 2 of 2)**

| CIRCUIT RESISTANCE CHART | | | |
|---|---|---|---|
| Connection | Voltmeter Lead Connection | | Voltmeter Reading |
| | Positive | Negative | |
| Positive post on battery to cable clamp | To post | To clamp | 0 |
| Negative post on battery to cable clamp | To post | To clamp | 0 |
| Battery ground cable to engine block. | To bolt | To cable connector | Not to exceed 0.2 volts |
| Battery cable to starter | To battery positive post | To battery terminal on starter | Not to exceed 0.2 volts |
| Starter housing to ground | To starter housing | To negative post on battery | Not to exceed 0.2 volts |

**Fig. 3   Circuit resistance chart. 1980–85**

| CIRCUIT RESISTANCE CHART | | | |
|---|---|---|---|
| Connection | Voltmeter Lead Connection | | Voltmeter Reading |
| | Positive | Negative | |
| Positive post on battery to battery cable clamp | Positive battery post | Battery cable clamp | 0 volts |
| Positive post on battery to starter battery terminal | Positive battery post | Battery terminal on starter | 0.2 volts |
| Positive post on battery to solenoid lead to field coils. | Positive battery post | Solenoid lead to field coils | 0.3 volts |
| Negative post on battery to cable clamp | Negative battery post | Battery cable clamp | 0 volts |
| Negative post on battery to engine block | Negative battery post | Battery cable connector on engine block | 0.2 volts |
| Starter housing to ground | Starter housing | Negative battery post | 0.2 volts |

**Fig. 4   Circuit resistance chart. 1986–89**

## Starter Relay Test (Automatic Transmissions)

Perform starter relay test, refer to "1980-82 models."

## Starter Relay Test (Manual Transmissions)

1. Depress clutch pedal, then connect suitable jumper wire on starter relay between battery and ignition terminals.

2. If engine cranks, starter relay is satisfactory. If engine does not crank, connect a second jumper on starter relay between ground terminal and good ground, then repeat test.
3. If engine does not crank, starter relay is defective and should be replaced.

# Ford Motorcraft Starters, Jeep

**NOTE:** For description & diagnosis procedures on these starters, refer to "Ford Motorcraft Starters" section in "Ford" chapter. For testing, refer to this section.

## INDEX

## ON-VEHICLE TESTING
### SOLENOID GROUND TEST

1. Connect one ohmmeter test probe to battery negative post and other probe to sheet metal adjacent to solenoid on manual transmission, or ground terminal on automatic transmission, and note resistance.
2. Move test probe to solenoid S termi-

nal. If resistance increases by more than 5 ohms, check solenoid ground.

### SOLENOID PULL-IN COIL WINDING TEST

1. Disconnect S terminal wire from solenoid.
2. Connect ohmmeter leads to S terminal and the mounting bracket on manual transmission, or ground terminal on automatic transmission.

3. If there is no continuity, replace solenoid.

### STARTER MOTOR FULL-LOAD CURRENT TEST

1. Ensure that battery is fully charged, then disconnect and ground ignition coil secondary wire.
2. Connect remote control starter switch between positive battery terminal and S terminal on solenoid.

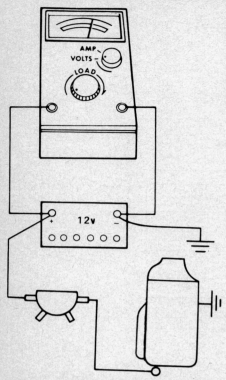

**Fig. 1  Full-load current test connections**

probe across adjacent commutator bars, then adjust voltage control until pointer indicates highest voltage on scale.
3. Test each commutator bar with adjacent bar. If any reading of zero volts is obtained, replace armature.

## ARMATURE GROUND TEST

1. Place armature in growler and turn power switch to "Test" position.
2. Place one lead of test lamp on armature core and other lead to each commutator bar.
3. If test lamp lights at any time, replace armature.

## ARMATURE SHORT TEST

1. Place armature in growler and turn power switch to "Growler" position.
2. Hold steel blade parallel to and touching armature core, then slowly rotate armature at least one full turn.
3. If steel blade vibrates, replace armature.

## FIELD WINDING TERMINAL-TO-BRUSH CONTINUITY TEST

1. Insert a piece of paper between contact points.
2. Touch ohmmeter leads to field winding terminal and insulated brush.
3. If resistance is greater than zero ohms, determine which solder joints have excessive resistance and repair with 600 watt soldering iron.

## HOLD-IN COIL WINDING RESISTANCE TEST

1. Insert piece of paper between contact points.
2. Using ohmmeter, measure resistance between S terminal and starter motor frame.
3. If resistance is not 2.0-3.5 ohms, replace field winding assembly.

## INSULATED BRUSH CONNECTION TEST

1. Using ohmmeter, test resistance through solder joint by touching leads to brush and the copper bus bar.
2. If resistance is more than zero ohms, resolder joint with 600 watt soldering iron.

## NO-LOAD CURRENT TEST

1. Connect test equipment as shown, **Fig. 2**, and turn tester load control knob fully counterclockwise, then operate starter and note voltage.
2. Using mechanical tachometer, determine exact motor RPM. Connect tachometer by removing seal from end of drive end housing and clean grease from end of armature shaft.

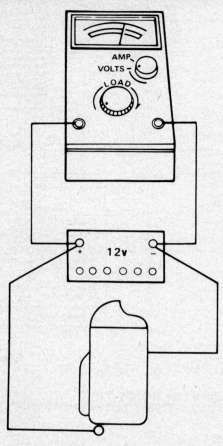

**Fig. 2  No-load current test connections**

3. Disconnect battery cable from starter.
4. Turn load control knob clockwise until voltage reading is exactly that obtained in step 1.
5. If ammeter does not read 77 amps with a starter motor RPM of 8900-9600 on 1980-81 models, or 67 amps with a starter motor RPM of 7380-9356 on 1982-89 models, repair or replace starter as necessary.

## SOLENOID CONTACT POINT TEST

1. Using ohmmeter, test resistance through solder joint.
2. If resistance is more than zero ohms, resolder joint using 600 watt soldering iron.

## TERMINAL BRACKET INSULATION TEST

1. Using ohmmeter, test resistance between terminal bracket and end cap.
2. If resistance is less than infinite, replace end cap.

3. Connect circuit tester, **Fig. 1**, then actuate remote starter switch and note voltmeter reading. **Note voltage after starter has reached maximum RPM.**
4. Turn off remote starter switch, then turn load control knob clockwise until indicated voltage is exactly the same as when starter was running.
5. If ammeter does not read as follows, bench test starter:
   a. All 1981-83 & 1984-89 Grand Wagoneer and Truck models w/6 cylinder engine, 150-180 amps.
   b. All 1981-83 & 1984-89 Grand Wagoneer and Truck models w/8 cylinder engine, 160-210 amps.
   c. All 1980 & 1984-89 exc. Grand Wagoneer and Truck models, 180-220 amps.

# OFF-VEHICLE TESTING

## ARMATURE BALANCE TEST

1. Place armature in growler and turn power switch to "Growler" position.
2. Place contact fingers of meter test

# DASH GAUGES & GRAPHIC DISPLAYS

## INDEX

## DASH GAUGES

Gauge failures are often caused by defective wiring or grounds. The first step in locating trouble should be a thorough inspection of all wiring, terminals and printed circuits. If wiring is secured by clamps, check to see whether the insulation has been severed, thereby grounding the wire. In the case of a fuel gauge installation, rust may cause failure by corrosion at the ground connection of the tank unit.

### CONSTANT VOLTAGE REGULATOR TYPE (CVR)

The Constant Voltage Regulator (CVR) type indicator is a bi-metal-resistance type system consisting of an Instrument Voltage Regulator (IVR), an indicator gauge, and a variable resistance sending unit. Current to the system is applied to the gauge terminals by the IVR, which maintains an average pulsating value of 5 volts.

The indicator gauge consists of a pointer which is attached to a wire-wound bi-metal strip. Current passing through the coil heats the bimetal strip, causing the pointer to move. As more current passes through the coil, heat increases, moving the pointer farther.

The circuit is completed through a sending unit which contains a variable resistor. When resistance is high, less current is allowed to pass through the gauge, and the pointer moves very little. As resistance decreases due to changing conditions in system being monitored, more current passes through gauge coil, causing pointer to move farther.

### Voltage Limiter Test

1. Connect one lead of a voltmeter to temperature sending unit and other lead to a good ground. Do not disconnect sending unit lead from sending

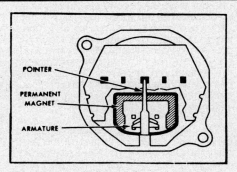

**Fig. 1   Typical conventional type ammeter**

unit.
2. Turn ignition switch to On position and observe voltmeter.
3. A fluctuating voltmeter indicates that voltage limiter is operating.

### VARIABLE VOLTAGE TYPE

The variable voltage type dash gauge consists of two magnetic coils to which battery voltage is applied. The coils act on the gauge pointer and pull in opposite directions. One coil is grounded directly to the chassis, while the other coil is grounded through a variable resistor within the sending unit. Resistance through the sending unit determines current flow through its coil, and therefore pointer position.

When resistance is high in the sending unit, less current is allowed to flow through its coil, causing the gauge pointer to move toward the directly grounded coil. When resistance in the sending unit decreases, more current is allowed to pass through its coil, increasing the magnetic field. The gauge pointer is then attracted toward the coil which is grounded through the sending unit.

### Dash Gauge Test

1. Disconnect electrical connector from sending unit.
2. Turn ignition to On position.
3. Ground sending unit lead and observe gauge. If gauge does not move to high side of scale, the gauge or wiring is defective. If gauge responds when grounded, replace sending unit.

## AMMETERS

The ammeter is an instrument used to indicate current flow into and out of the battery. When electrical accessories in the vehicle draw more current than the alternator can supply, current flows from the battery, and the ammeter indicates a discharge (−) condition. When electrical loads of the vehicle are less than alternator output, current is available to charge the battery, and the ammeter indicates a charge (+) condition. If battery is fully charged, the voltage regulator reduces alternator output to meet only immediate vehicle electrical loads. When this happens, ammeter reads zero.

### CONVENTIONAL AMMETER

A conventional ammeter must be connected between the battery and alternator in order to indicate current flow. This type ammeter, **Fig. 1**, consists of a frame to which a permanent magnet is attached. The frame also supports an armature and pointer assembly. Current in this system flows from the alternator through the ammeter, then to the battery or from the battery through the ammeter into the vehicle electrical system, depending on vehicle operating conditions.

When no current flows through the ammeter, the magnet holds the pointer armature so that the pointer stands at the center of the dial. When current passes in either direction through the ammeter, the resulting magnetic field attracts the armature away from the effect of the permanent magnet, thus giving a reading proportional to the strength of the current flowing.

## Troubleshooting

When the ammeter apparently fails to register correctly, there may be trouble in the wiring which connects the ammeter to the alternator and battery or in the alternator or battery itself.

To check the connections, first tighten the two terminal posts on the back of the ammeter. Then, following each wire from the ammeter, tighten all connections on the ignition switch, battery and alternator. Chafed, burned or broken insulation can be found by following each ammeter wire from end to end.

All wires with chafed, burned or broken insulation should be repaired or replaced. After this is done, and all connections are tightened, connect the battery cable and turn on the ignition switch. The needle should point slightly to the discharge (−) side.

Start the engine and run slightly above idling speed. The needle should move slowly to the charge side (+).

If the pointer does not move as indicated, the ammeter is out of order and should be replaced.

## SHUNT TYPE AMMETER

The shunt type ammeter is actually a specifically calibrated voltmeter. If it connected to read voltage drop across a resistance wire (shunt) between the battery and alternator. The shunt is located either in the vehicle wiring or within the ammeter itself.

When voltage is higher at the alternator end of the shunt, the meter indicates a charge (+) condition. When voltage is higher at the battery end of the shunt, the meter indicates a discharge (−) condition. When voltage is equal at both ends of the shunt, the meter reads zero.

## Troubleshooting

Ammeter accuracy can be determined by comparing reading with an ammeter of known accuracy.

1. With engine stopped and ignition switch in RUN position, switch on headlamps and heater fan. Meter should indicate a discharge (−) condition.
2. If ammeter pointer does not move, check ammeter terminals for proper connection and check for open circuit in wiring harness. If connections and wiring harness are satisfactory, ammeter is defective.
3. If ammeter indicates a charge (+) condition, wiring harness connections are reversed at ammeter.

## VOLTMETER

The voltmeter is a gauge which measures the electrical flow from the battery to indicate whether the battery output is within tolerances. The voltmeter reading can range from 13.5-14.0 volts under normal operating conditions. If an undercharge or overcharge condition is indicated for an extended period, the battery and charging system should be checked.

## TROUBLESHOOTING

To check voltmeter, turn key and headlights on with engine off. Pointer should move to 12.5 volts. If no needle movement is observed, check connections from battery to circuit breaker. If connections are tight and meter shows no movement, check wire continuity. If wire continuity is satisfactory, the meter is inoperative and must be replaced.

## OIL PRESSURE INDICATOR LIGHT

Many trucks utilize a warning light on the instrument panel in place of the conventional dash indicating gauge to warn the driver when the oil pressure is dangerously low. The warning light is wired in series with the ignition switch and the engine unit, which is an oil pressure switch.

The oil pressure switch contains a diaphragm and a set of contacts. When the ignition switch is turned on, the warning light circuit is energized and the circuit is completed through the closed contacts in the pressure switch. When the engine is started, build-up of oil pressure compresses the diaphragm, opening the contacts, thereby breaking the circuit and putting out the light.

## TROUBLESHOOTING

The oil pressure warning light should go on when the ignition is turned on. If it does not light, disconnect the wire from the engine unit and ground the wire to the frame or cylinder block. Then if the warning light still does not go on with the ignition switch on, replace the bulb.

If the warning light goes on when the wire is grounded to the frame or cylinder block, the engine unit should be checked for being loose or poorly grounded. If the unit is found to be tight and properly grounded, it should be removed and a new one installed. (The presence of sealing compound on the threads of the engine unit will cause a poor ground).

If the warning light remains lit when it normally should be out, replace the engine unit before proceeding further to determine the cause for a low pressure indication.

The warning light will sometimes light up or flicker when the engine is idling, even though the oil pressure is adequate. However, the light should go out when the engine speed is increased.

## TEMPERATURE INDICATOR LIGHT

A bimetal temperature switch located in the cylinder head controls the operation of a temperature indicator light with a red lens. If the engine cooling system is not functioning properly and coolant temperature exceeds a predetermined value, the warning light will illuminate.

## TROUBLESHOOTING

If the red light is not lit when the engine is being cranked, check for a burned out bulb, an open in the light circuit, or a defective ignition switch.

If the red light is lit when the engine is running, check the wiring between light and switch for a ground, defective temperature switch, or overheated cooling system.

As a test circuit to check whether the red bulb is functioning properly, a wire which is connected to the ground terminal of the ignition switch is tapped into its circuit. When the ignition is in the "Start" (engine cranking) position, the ground terminal is grounded inside the switch and the red bulb will be lit. When the engine is started and the ignition switch is in the "On" position, the test circuit is opened and the bulb is then controlled by the temperature switch.

## ELECTRICAL TEMPERATURE GAUGES

### CONSTANT VOLTAGE REGULATOR (CVR) TYPE

This temperature indicating system consists of a sending unit, located on the cylinder head, electrical temperature gauge and an instrument voltage regulator. As engine temperature increases or decreases, the resistance of the sending unit changes, in turn controlling current flow to the gauge. When engine temperature is low, the resistance of the sending unit is high, restricting current flow to the gauge, in turn indicating low engine temperature. As engine temperature increases, the resistance of the ending unit decreases, permitting an increased current flow to the gauge, resulting in an increased temperature reading.

## TROUBLESHOOTING

A special tester is required to diagnose this type gauge. Follow instructions included with the tester.

## ELECTRICAL OIL PRESSURE GAUGES

### CONSTANT VOLTAGE REGULATOR (CVR) TYPE

This oil pressure indicating system incorporates an instrument voltage regulator, electrical oil pressure gauge and a sending unit which are connected in series. The sending unit consists of a diaphragm, contact and a variable resistor. As oil pressure increases or decreases, the diaphragm actuated the contact on the variable resistor, in turn controlling current flow to the gauge. When oil pressure is low, the resistance of the variable resistor is high, restricting current flow to the gauge, in turn indicating low oil pressure.

As oil pressure increases, the resistance of the variable resistor is lowered, permitting an increased current flow to the gauge, resulting in an increased gauge reading.

## TROUBLESHOOTING

A special tester is required to diagnose this type gauge. Follow instructions included with the tester.

## FUEL LEVEL INDICATING SYSTEM

A hinged float arm in the fuel tank contacts a variable resistor in the gauge sending unit. The varying resistance in the fuel gauge circuit registers on the instrument panel gauge. Resistance in the circuit is lowest when the fuel tank is full and float arm is raised. The resulting high current flow causes the instrument panel gauge to indicate Full.

## TROUBLESHOOTING

1. Disconnect electrical connector from fuel tank sending unit and attach connector to a known good sending unit.
2. Connect a jumper wire between sending unit fuel pickup tube and a good ground.
3. Secure sending unit float arm in the empty stop position and turn ignition On. Within two minutes, the gauge should read Empty, plus one pointer width or minus two pointer widths.
4. Move float arm and secure in the full stop position. Within two minutes, the gauge should read Full, plus two pointer widths, or minus one pointer width.
5. If fuel gauge does not operate as specified, check the following:
   a. Wiring and electrical connections between sending unit and connector.
   b. Wiring and electrical connections between connector and printed circuit board terminals.
   c. Circuit continuity between printed circuit board terminals and gauge terminals.
   d. Voltage limiter performance.
6. If fuel gauge operates as specified with known good sending unit, check fuel tank and original sending unit as follows:
   a. Remove sending unit from fuel tank.
   b. Connect sending unit wire and jumper wire as previously described.
   c. If fuel gauge now operates as specified, check sending unit for damage, obstructions or improper installation and correct as necessary.

## SPEEDOMETERS

The following material covers only that service on speedometers which is feasible to perform. Repairs on the units themselves are not included as they require special tools and extreme care when mak-

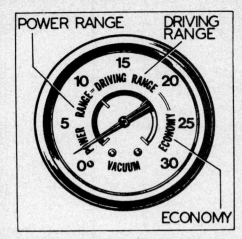

**Fig. 2   Typical vacuum gauge**

ing repairs and adjustments that only an experienced speedometer mechanic should attempt.

The speedometer has two main parts, the speedometer head and the speedometer drive cable. When the speedometer fails to indicate speed or mileage, the cable or cable housing is probably broken.

## SPEEDOMETER CABLE

Most cables are broken due to lack of lubrication, or a sharp bend or kink in the housing.

A cable might break because of the speedometer head mechanism binds. In such cases, the speedometer head should be repaired or replaced before a new cable or housing is installed.

A "jumpy" pointer condition, together with a scraping noise, is due, in most instances, to a dry or kinked speedometer cable. The kinked cable rubs on the housing and winds up, slowing down the pointer. The cable then unwinds and the pointer "jumps."

To check for kinks, remove the cable, lay it on a flat surface and twist one end with the fingers. If it turns over smoothly the cable is not kinked. But if part of the cable flops over as it is twisted, the cable is kinked and should be replaced.

## LUBRICATION

The speedometer cable should be lubricated with special cable lubricant. Fill the ferrule on the upper end of the housing with the cable lubricant. Insert the cable in the housing, starting at the upper end. Turn the cable around carefully while feeding it into the housing. Repeat filling the ferrule except for the last six inches of cable. Too much lubricant at this point may cause the lubricant to work into the speedometer head.

## INSTALLING CABLE

During installation, if the cable sticks when inserted in the housing and will not go through, the housing is damaged inside or kinked. Be sure to check the housing from one end to the other. Straighten any

sharp bends by relocating clamps or elbows. Replace housing if it is badly kinked or broken. Position the cable and housing so that they lead into the head as straight as possible.

Check the new cable for kinks before installing it. Use wide, sweeping, gradual curves where the cable comes out of the transmission and connects to the head so the cable will not be damaged during installation.

Arrange the housing so it does not lean against the engine because heat from the engine may dry out the lubricant.

If inspection indicates that the cable and housing are in good condition, yet pointer action is erratic, check the speedometer head for possible binding.

The speedometer drive pinion should also be checked. If the pinion is dry or its teeth are stripped, the speedometer may not register properly.

## VACUUM GAUGE

This gauge, **Fig. 2**, measures intake manifold vacuum. The intake manifold vacuum varies with engine operating conditions, carburetor adjustments, valve timing, ignition timing and general engine condition.

Since the optimum fuel economy is directly proportional to a properly functioning engine, a high vacuum reading on the gauge relates to fuel economy. For this reason some manufacturers call the vacuum gauge a "Fuel Economy Indicator." Most gauges have colored sectors the green sector being the "Economy" range and the red sector being the "Power" range. Therefore, the vehicle should be operated with gauge registering in the green sector or a high numerical number, **Fig. 2**, for maximum economy.

## FUEL ECONOMY WARNING SYSTEM

This system actually monitors the engine vacuum just like the vacuum gauge, but all it registers is a low vacuum. The light on the instrument panel warns the vehicle operator when engine manifold vacuum drops below the economical limit. Switch operation is similar to that of the oil pressure indicating light, except that the switch opens when vacuum, rather than oil pressure, is applied.

## TROUBLESHOOTING
### Fuel Economy Warning Light

The fuel economy warning light should go on when the ignition is turned on. If it does not light, disconnect the wire from the fuel economy vacuum switch connector and ground the wire to the frame or cylinder block. If the warning light still does not go on, check for burned out indicating bulb or an open in the harness between the vacuum switch and instrument panel. If the warning light goes on, circuit is functioning and the vacuum switch should be checked for proper ground. Remove and clean the mounting bracket screws and the mounting surfaces.

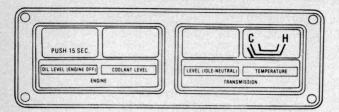

**Fig. 3  Recreational vehicle sensor package instrument cluster. 1980**

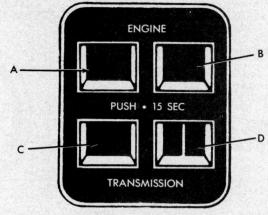

**Fig. 4  Recreational vehicle sensor package instrument cluster. 1981–82**

If system still does not operate, perform the following:

With the electrical connector and vacuum tube disconnected from the switch, connect a self-powered test light to the switch electrical connector and to the vacuum gauge mounting bracket. Attach a hand-operated vacuum pump to gauge. If the following conditions are not met the switch has to be replaced:

1. With vacuum applied test light should be "Off".
2. With no vacuum to the vacuum switch test light should be "On".
3. If the warning light remains lit when it normally should be out, check vacuum hose to vacuum switch for damage or plugged condition.

## ELECTRIC CLOCKS

Regulation of electric clocks is accomplished automatically by resetting the time. If the clock is running fast, the action of turning the hands back to correct the time will automatically cause the clock to run slightly slower. If the clock is running slow, the action of turning the hands forward to correct the time will automatically cause the clock to run slightly faster (10 to 15 seconds day).

A lock-out feature prevents the clock regulator mechanism from being reset more than once per wind cycle, regardless of the number of times the time is reset. After the clock rewinds, if the time is then reset, automatic regulation will take place. If a clock varies over 10 minutes per day, it will never adjust properly and must be repaired or replaced.

## WINDING CLOCK WHEN CONNECTING BATTERY OR CLOCK WIRING

The clock requires special attention when reconnecting a battery that has been disconnected for any reason, a clock that has been disconnected, or when replacing a blown clock fuse. It is very important that the initial wind be fully made. The procedure is as follows:

1. Make sure that all other instruments and lights are turned off.
2. Connect positive cable to battery.
3. Before connecting the negative cable, press the terminal to its post on the battery. Immediately afterward, strike

the terminal against the battery post to see if there is a spark. If there is a spark, allow the clock to run down until it stops ticking, and repeat as above until there is no spark. Then immediately make the permanent connection before the clock can again run down. The clock will run down in approximately two minutes.

4. Reset clock after all connections have been made. The foregoing procedure should also be followed when reconnecting the clock after it has been disconnected, or if it has stopped because of a blown fuse. Be sure to disconnect battery before installing a new fuse.

## TROUBLESHOOTING

If clock does not run, check for blown "clock" fuse. If fuse is blown, check for short in wiring. If fuse is not blown, check for open circuit.

With an electric clock, the most frequent cause of clock fuse blowing is voltage at the clock which will prevent a complete wind and allow clock contacts to remain closed. This may be caused by any of the following: discharged battery, corrosion on contact surface of battery terminals, loose connections at battery terminals, at junction block, at fuse clips, or at terminal connection of clock. Therefore, if in reconnecting battery or clock it is noted that the clock is not ticking, always check for blown fuse, or examine the circuits at the points indicated above to determine and correct the cause.

## RECREATIONAL VEHICLE SENSOR PACKAGE, CHRYSLER MODELS

The recreational vehicle sensor package consists of a separate instrument cluster, **Figs. 3 and 4,** which allows the driver to monitor the following conditions: engine oil level, engine coolant level, transmission fluid level and transmission fluid temperature.

## TROUBLESHOOTING
### Voltage Limiter Test

1. Connect voltmeter between temperature sending unit (locating in fitting in bottom radiator tank) and a suitable ground. Do not disconnect electrical connector from sending unit.
2. Turn ignition switch to On position and observe voltmeter.
3. If voltmeter needle fluctuates, the voltage limiter is operating properly.
4. If voltmeter does not fluctuate, replace voltage limiter. **The voltage limiter is located on the sensor panel. To gain access to the limiter, remove panel and unsnap the back cover.**

### Temperature Gauge Test

1. Disconnect electrical connector from temperature sending unit in lower radiator tank.
2. Connect tester No. C-3826 or equivalent between temperature sending unit and a suitable ground.
3. Move tester pointer to "C" position, then turn ignition switch On and observe temperature gauge. Temperature gauge should read within 1/8 inch of "C".
4. Move tester pointer to "M" position. Temperature gauge should now advance to normal range left of 1/2 position on dial.
5. Move tester pointer to "H" position. Temperature gauge should now advance to "H" position on dial.
6. If temperature gauge responds to tests described in steps 3, 4 and 5, but does not operate when sending unit electrical connector is attached, the sending unit is defective and should be replaced.
7. If temperature gauge does not respond to tests described in steps 3, 4 and 5, check for loose connections, broken wire, open printed circuit or faulty gauge.

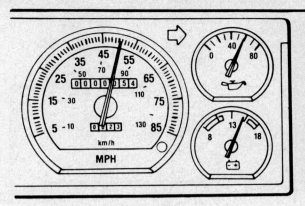  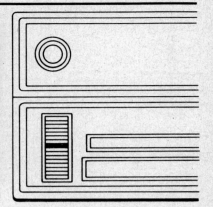

**Fig. 5 Systems Sentry System warning light display module**

### Oil Level Push Button Switch

1. Inspect switch for poor solder connections and repair or replace as necessary.
2. Test each circuit for continuity using an ohmmeter or test lamp. If any open circuits are found, the switch should be replaced. To replace switch, remove circuit board and push switch toward back of sensor housing.

### Printed Circuit Board

1. Inspect conductors for cracks or damaged circuits.
2. Test each circuit for continuity using an ohmmeter or test lamp. If any open circuits are found, the sensor panel assembly should be replaced.

## SYSTEMS SENTRY SYSTEM, JEEP MODELS

### DESCRIPTION & OPERATION

This system, available on some models, is a diagnostic warning system used to monitor vital fluid levels and disc brake pad wear.

The system consists of a warning light display module, **Fig. 5,** mounted on right side of instrument cluster, a remote module under the dash, various fluid level and wear sensors and the necessary interconnecting wiring.

The warning light display module in the instrument cluster contains three different color lights. The amber checking lights indicate that each system is being checked. The green lights indicate that fluid level or brake pads are satisfactory. The red lights indicate that fluid level or brake pads should be checked and corrected as necessary. It should be noted that disconnected fluid level sensor wires or open circuits will cause a red warning light, however,

disconnected brake pad wear sensor wires will not create any indication.

The remote module monitors and analyzes electrical current flow through the sensors connected to it. Because current varies with fluid level, the module is able to energize the appropriate warning light on the display module. The engine, transmission, transfer case and rear axle oil level sensors are connected to the remote module.

The various sensors and their locations are as follows: engine coolant, located in the coolant recovery bottle; engine oil, located in the oil pan; power steering fluid, located in the pump reservoir; manual transmission oil, located in the transmission fill plug; automatic transmission fluid, located on the transmission dipstick; windshield washer fluid, located in the washer reservoir; brake fluid, located in the master cylinder; transfer case oil, located in the rear section of the transfer case; front and rear axle oil, located in front and rear axle housings; front disc brake pads, located on each inboard brake pad.

The engine, transfer case, transmission and axle oil level sensors operate on the principle of changes in resistance in relation to contact with oil and are connected to the remote module. The power steering, brake fluid, windshield washer and engine coolant sensors are float-type sensors affected by changes in fluid level and are wired directly to the display module. The brake pad wear sensor is also wired directly to the display module and is an electromechanical device actuated by contact with the rotor surface. When the pad is worn enough to allow sensor to contact rotor, the sensor grounds against the rotor. This creates a brief current surge on the pad warning circuit and shorts the 4 amp in-line signal fuse, resulting in illumination of the red warning light.

### CHECKING FLUID LEVELS AND/OR BRAKE PAD WEAR

1. Operate vehicle until fluids reach nor-

mal operating temperature.
2. Park vehicle on a level surface.
3. Turn ignition to Off position and observe display module indicator lights, noting the following:
   a. Amber lights indicate that all systems are being checked.
   b. A green light indicates that the fluid level or pad wear is satisfactory.
   c. A red light indicates that the fluid level or pad wear should be checked.
4. To repeat warning light display, restart engine and idle for 30 seconds, then turn ignition to Off position.

### DIAGNOSIS

In a properly functioning system, a red light caused by a low fluid condition will go out when the fluid level has been corrected. If a warning light remains lit after correcting the fluid level, or if the fluid level was actually satisfactory when the warning light was energized, refer to wiring diagram, **Fig. 6,** and diagnostic charts, **Fig. 7** to pinpoint and correct the malfunction.

In the case of front disc brake pads, replacement of the pads alone will not turn off the brake pad warning light. The 4 amp signal fuse and brake pad wear sensors must also be replaced.

### TESTING

#### Engine, Front Axle, Transfer Case, Transmission & Rear Axle Sensors

These sensors may be tested while installed in vehicle.
1. Disconnect sensor electrical connectors.
2. Measure resistance across pins in sensor electrical connector using a suitable ohmmeter.
3. If ohmmeter reads 6-10 ohms resistance, sensor is satisfactory.
4. If ohmmeter indicates no resistance, sensor is defective and must be replaced.

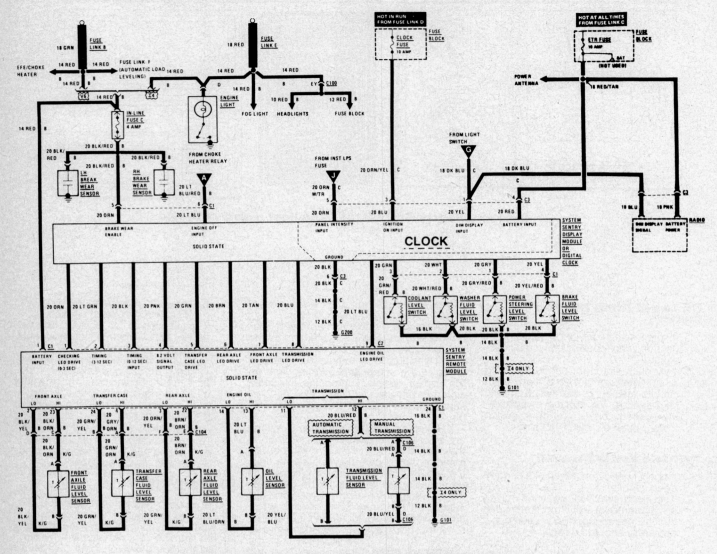

**Fig. 6  Systems Sentry System wiring diagram**

## Brake, Engine Coolant, Power Steering & Windshield Washer Sensors

These sensors must be removed from vehicle for testing.
1. Remove sensor from vehicle.
2. Connect a suitable ohmmeter to terminal pins in sensor connector.

3. Invert sensor to simulate a full reservoir condition and note ohmmeter reading. If ohmmeter does not read 2640-3960 ohms, sensor is defective and must be replaced.
4. Turn sensor right side up to simulate an empty reservoir condition and note ohmmeter reading. If any resistance is indicated, sensor is defective and

must be replaced.

## Front Disc Brake Pad Wear Sensor

This sensor cannot be tested. It is a single wire one-time use component that is activated only when grounded against the rotor surface.

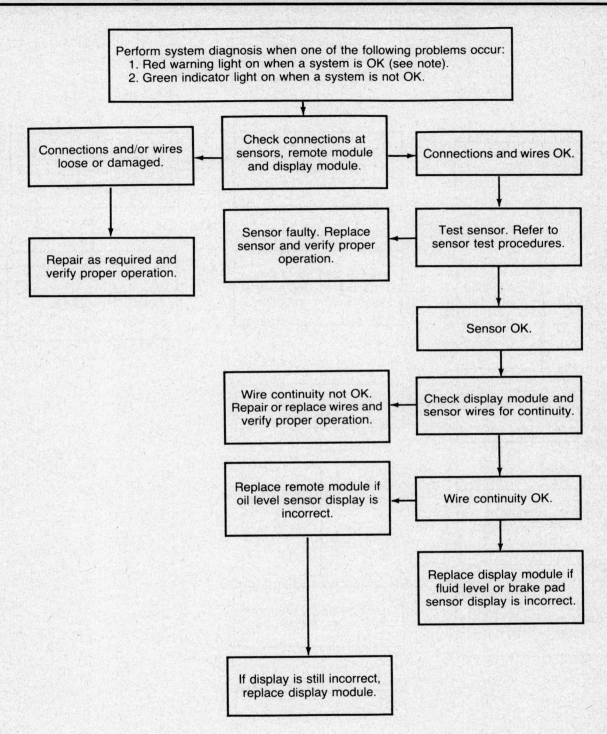

Perform system diagnosis when one of the following problems occur:
1. Red warning light on when a system is OK (see note).
2. Green indicator light on when a system is not OK.

Check connections at sensors, remote module and display module.

Connections and/or wires loose or damaged.

Repair as required and verify proper operation.

Connections and wires OK.

Test sensor. Refer to sensor test procedures.

Sensor faulty. Replace sensor and verify proper operation.

Sensor OK.

Check display module and sensor wires for continuity.

Wire continuity not OK. Repair or replace wires and verify proper operation.

Wire continuity OK.

Replace remote module if oil level sensor display is incorrect.

Replace display module if fluid level or brake pad sensor display is incorrect.

If display is still incorrect, replace display module.

**NOTE:** Front disc brake pad replacement alone will not turn off the brake wear warning light. The wear warning sensor and the 4-amp signal fuse must also be replaced.

**Fig. 7   Systems Sentry System diagnostic chart (Part 1 of 2)**

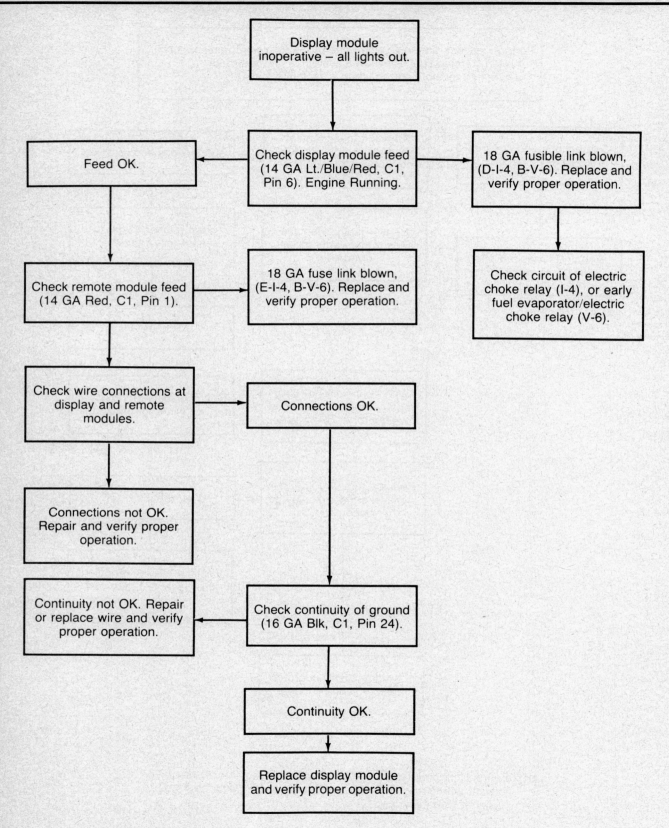

**Fig. 7   Systems Sentry System diagnostic chart (Part 2 of 2)**

# DISC BRAKES

## TABLE OF CONTENTS

# General Information

## INDEX

## TROUBLESHOOTING

### EXCESSIVE PEDAL TRAVEL

1. Worn brake lining.
2. Shoe and lining knock back after cornering or rough road travel.
3. Piston and shoe and lining assembly not properly seated or positioned.
4. Air leak or insufficient fluid in system or caliper.
5. Loose wheel bearing adjustment.
6. Damaged or worn caliper piston seal.
7. Improper booster pushrod adjustment.
8. Shoe out of flat more than .005 inch.
9. Rear brake automatic adjusters inoperative.
10. Improperly ground rear brake shoe and lining assemblies.

### BRAKE ROUGHNESS OR CHATTER; PEDAL PUMPING

1. Excessive lateral runout of rotor.
2. Rotor excessively out of parallel.

### EXCESSIVE PEDAL EFFORT

1. Frozen or seized pistons.
2. Brake fluid, oil or grease on linings.
3. Shoe and lining worn below specifications.
4. Proportioning valve malfunction.
5. Booster inoperative.
6. Leaking booster vacuum check valve.
7. Bent, broken or distorted brakeshoes.
8. Caliper, wheel cylinder or master cylinder pistons sticking or seized.
9. Brake fluid contaminated.
10. Low engine vacuum.

### PULL, UNEVEN OR GRABBING BRAKES

1. Frozen or seized pistons.
2. Brake fluid, oil or grease on linings.
3. Caliper out of alignment with rotor.
4. Loose caliper attachment.
5. Unequal front tire pressure.
6. Incorrect front end alignment.
7. Lining protruding beyond end of shoe.
8. Parking brake cables incorrectly adjusted or seized.
9. Rear height-sensing proportioning valve out of adjustment.
10. Improperly adjusted, worn or damaged wheel bearing.
11. Brake lining on one side contaminated.
12. Backing plate bent or loose on one side.
13. Brake lining improperly seated with drum or rotor.
14. Brake lining water soaked.

### BRAKE RATTLE

1. Excessive clearance between shoe and caliper or between shoe and splash shield.
2. Shoe hold-down clips missing or improperly positioned.

### HEAVY BRAKE DRAG

1. Frozen or seized pistons.
2. Operator riding brake pedal.
3. Incomplete brake pedal return due to linkage interference.
4. Faulty booster check valve holding pressure in hydraulic system.
5. Residual pressure in front brake hydraulic system.
6. Brake pedal binding at pivot.
7. Parking brake cables seized.

8. Calipers binding on slide surface or pins.
9. Rear brake adjusters reversed.

### CALIPER BRAKE FLUID LEAK

1. Damaged or worn caliper piston seal.
2. Scores in cylinder bore.
3. Corrosion build-up in cylinder bore or on piston surface.
4. Metal clip in seal groove.

### NO BRAKING EFFECT WHEN PEDAL IS DEPRESSED

1. Piston and shoe and lining assembly not properly seated or positioned.
2. Air leak or insufficient fluid in system or caliper.
3. Damaged or worn caliper piston seal.
4. Bleeder screw open.
5. Air in hydraulic system or improper bleeding.

### REAR BRAKES LOCKING ON APPLICATION

On brake system equipped with a proportioning or rear pressure regulator valve, should the valve malfunction, rear brakes may receive excess pressure, resulting in wheel lock-up.

## SERVICE PRECAUTIONS

### BRAKE LINES & LININGS

Remove one of the front wheels and inspect the brake disc, caliper and linings. (The wheel bearings should be inspected at this time and repacked if necessary).

Do not get any oil or grease on the linings. It is recommended that both front wheel sets be replaced whenever a respective shoe and lining is worn or damaged. Inspect and, if necessary, replace rear brake linings also.

If the caliper is cracked or fluid leakage through the casting is evident, it must be replaced as a unit.

## BRAKE ROUGHNESS

The most common cause of brake chatter on disc brakes is a variation in thickness of the disc. If roughness or vibration is encountered during highway operation or if pedal pumping is experienced at low speeds, the disc may have excessive thickness variation. To check for this condition, measure the disc at 8 points with a micrometer at a radius approximately one inch from edge of disc. If thickness measurements vary more than specifications allow, the disc should be replaced with a new one.

Excessive lateral runout of braking disc may cause a "knocking back" of the pistons, possibly creating increased pedal travel and vibration when brakes are applied.

Before checking the runout, wheel bearings should be adjusted. Be sure to make the adjustment according to the recommendations given in the individual truck chapters.

## BRAKE DISC SERVICE

Servicing of disc brakes is extremely critical due to the close tolerances required in machining the brake disc to insure proper brake operation.

The maintenance of these close controls on the friction surfaces is necessary to prevent brake roughness. In addition, the surface finish must be non-directional and maintained at a micro-inch finish. This close control of the rubbing surface finish is necessary to avoid pulls and erratic performance and promote long lining life and

equal lining wear of both left and right brakes.

In light of the foregoing remarks, refinishing of the rubbing surfaces should not be attempted unless precision equipment, capable of measuring in micro-inches (millionths of an inch) is available.

To check runout of a disc, mount a dial indicator on a convenient part (steering knuckle, tie rod, disc brake caliper housing) so that the plunger of the dial indicator contacts the disc at a point one inch from the outer edge. If the total indicated runout exceeds specifications, install a new disc.

## GENERAL PRECAUTIONS

1. Grease or any other foreign material must be kept off the caliper, surfaces of the disc and external surfaces of the hub, during service procedures. Handling the brake disc and caliper should be done in a way to avoid deformation of the disc and nicking or scratching brake linings.
2. If inspection reveals rubber piston seals are worn or damaged, they should be replaced immediately.
3. During removal and installation of a wheel assembly, exercise care so as not to interfere with or damage the caliper splash shield, the bleeder screw or the transfer tube (if equipped).
4. Front wheel bearings should be adjusted to specifications.
5. Be sure vehicle is centered on hoist before servicing any of the front end components to avoid bending or damaging the disc splash shield on full right or left wheel turns.
6. Before the vehicle is moved after any brake service work, be sure to obtain a firm brake pedal.
7. The assembly bolts of the two caliper housings (if equipped) should not be disturbed unless the caliper requires service.

## INSPECTION OF CALIPER

Should it become necessary to remove the caliper for installation of new parts, clean all parts in alcohol, wipe dry using lint-free cloths. Using an air hose, blow out drilled passages and bores. Check dust boots for punctures or tears. If punctures or tears are evident, new boots should be installed upon reassembly.

Inspect piston bores in both housings for scoring or pitting. Bores that show light scratches or corrosion can usually be cleaned with crocus cloth. However, bores that have deep scratches or scoring may be honed, provided the diameter of the bore is not increased more than .002 inch. If the bore does not clean up within this specification, a new caliper housing should be installed (black stains on the bore walls are caused by piston seals and will do no harm).

When using a hone, be sure to install the hone baffle before honing bore. The baffle is used to protect the hone stones from damage. Use extreme care in cleaning the caliper after honing. Remove all dust and grit by flushing the caliper with alcohol. Wipe dry with clean lint-free cloth and then clean a second time in the same manner.

## BLEEDING DISC BRAKES

The disc brake hydraulic system can be bled manually or with pressure bleeding equipment. On vehicles with disc brakes the brake pedal will require more pumping and frequent checking of fluid level in master cylinder during bleeding operation.

Never use brake fluid that has been drained from hydraulic system when bleeding the brakes. Be sure the disc brake pistons are returned to their normal positions and that the shoe and lining assemblies are properly seated. Before driving the vehicle, check brake operation to be sure that a firm pedal has been obtained.

# A.T.E. Floating Caliper, Chrysler

## INDEX

## DESCRIPTION

The single piston floating caliper disc brake assembly consists of the hub and disc brake rotor assembly, caliper, shoes and linings, splash shield and adapter, **Fig. 1.**

The caliper assembly floats on two rubber bushings riding on two steel guide pins threaded into the adapter. The bushings are inserted on the inboard portion of the caliper. Two machined abutments on the adapter position and align the caliper fore and aft. Guide pins and bushings control caliper and piston seal movement to assist in maintaining proper shoe clearance.

All braking force is taken directly by the adapter.

## BRAKE SHOE & LINING
## REPLACE
### EXC. DAKOTA

1. Raise and support front of vehicle, then remove wheel and tire assembly.
2. Remove caliper guide pins and anti-rattle spring.
3. Carefully slide caliper assembly away from disc. Support caliper assembly to prevent damage to brake hose.
4. Remove outboard shoe and lining assembly from adapter.

5. Remove rotor from drive axle flange and studs.
6. Remove inboard shoe and lining assembly from adapter.
7. Carefully push piston into caliper bore. **Remove some brake fluid from reservoir to prevent overflowing when pushing piston into caliper bore.**
8. Position inboard shoe and lining on adapter. Ensure metal portion of shoe is properly positioned in recess of adapter.
9. Install rotor over studs and drive flange.
10. While holding outboard shoe in position on adapter, carefully position adapter over disc brake rotor.
11. Carefully lower caliper over disc brake

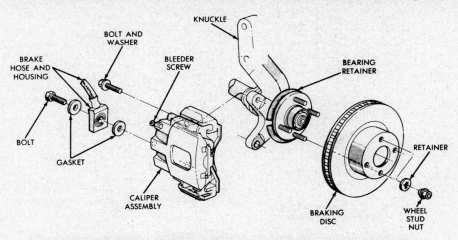

**Fig. 1 Typical exploded view of disc brake assembly**

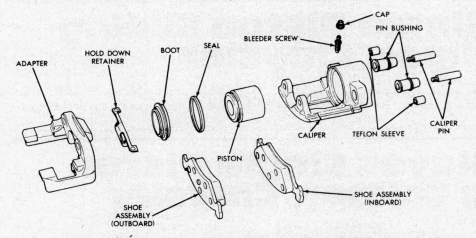

**Fig. 2 Typical exploded view of disc brake caliper assembly**

rotor and adapter.

12. Install guide pins through bushings, caliper and adapter.

13. Press in on guide pins and thread pin into adapter. Torque pins to 25 to 40 ft. lbs.

14. Install wheel and tire assembly, then lower vehicle.

## DAKOTA

1. Raise and support front of vehicle, then remove wheel and tire assembly.

2. Remove hold-down spring from caliper assembly.

3. Loosen caliper guide pins until caliper is free. Remove pins only if bushings or sleeves are to be replaced.

4. Lift caliper assembly out and away from rotor. Support caliper assembly to prevent damage to brake hose.

5. Remove outboard shoe from caliper, then the inboard shoe by pulling shoe and lining assembly away from piston.

6. Remove protective paper from noise suppression gasket on new inner and outer shoe assembly.

7. Install inboard shoe in caliper. Ensure retainer enters into bore in piston.

8. Install inboard shoe in caliper, then lower caliper assembly over rotor.

9. Install guide pins and torque to 18-26 ft. lbs. **When installing pins, use caution not to cross threads.**

10. Install holddown spring.

11. Install wheel and tire assembly, then lower vehicle.

## CALIPER OVERHAUL
### DISASSEMBLE

1. Remove caliper assembly as described under "Brake Shoe & Lining, Replace."

2. With brake hose attached to caliper, carefully depress brake pedal to push piston out of caliper bore. Prop brake pedal to any position below first inch of brake pedal travel to prevent brake fluid loss.

3. If pistons are to be removed from both calipers, disconnect brake hose at frame bracket after removing piston, then cap brake line and repeat procedure to remove piston from other caliper. **Air pressure should never be used to remove piston from bore.**

4. Disconnect brake hose from caliper.

5. Mount caliper, **Fig. 2,** in a soft jawed vise.

6. Support caliper and remove dust boot and discard.

7. Using a small wooden or plastic stick, remove seal from groove in piston bore and discard.

8. Using a suitable tool, remove bushings from caliper.

## INSPECTION

1. Clean all components using alcohol or other suitable cleaning solvent, then blow dry using compressed air. With compressed air blow out drilled passages and bores.

2. Inspect piston bore for pitting or scoring. Light scratches or corrosion can usually be cleared with crocus cloth. Bores that have deep scratches or scoring should be honed with tool No. C-4095, providing bore diameter is not increased by more than .001 inch. If scratches or scoring cannot be cleared up, or if caliper bore is increased by more than .001 inch, replace caliper housing. **When using hone C-4095, coat hone and caliper bore with clean brake fluid. After honing, carefully clean boot and seal grooves with a stiff non-metallic brush. Flush caliper with clean brake fluid and wipe dry with a clean lint free cloth, then flush and wipe caliper dry again.**

3. Replace piston if found to be scored, pitted or if plating is severely worn or if caliper bore was honed. Black stains on steel piston are caused by piston seal and are not cause for replacing piston.

## ASSEMBLE

1. Mount caliper, **Fig. 2,** in a soft jawed vise.

2. Lubricate piston seal with clean brake fluid and install seal in caliper bore groove, **Fig. 3.** Ensure seal is properly seated.

3. Position dust boot over piston.

4. Install piston into bore by pushing it evenly past piston seal until it bottoms in bore, **Fig. 4.**

5. Position dust boot in counterbore, then using a hammer and tools C-4682 and C-4171 or equivalent, drive boot into counterbore, **Fig. 5.**

6. Compress flanges of guide pin bushings and install bushings on caliper housing. Ensure that bushing flanges extend evenly over caliper housing on both sides. **Remove teflon sleeves from guide pin bushings prior to installing bushings into caliper. After bushings are installed into caliper, reinstall teflon sleeves into bushings.**

7. Connect brake hose to brake line at frame bracket.

8. Install caliper on vehicle as described under "Brake Shoe & Lining, Replace."

9. Check brake fluid level of master cylinder reservoir, then open caliper bleed screw and bleed brake system. Continue bleeding procedure until firm pedal is obtained.

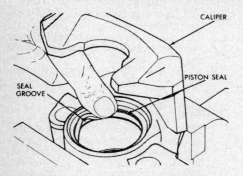

**Fig. 3   Piston seal installation**

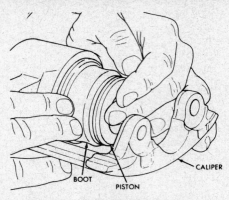

**Fig. 4   Caliper piston installation**

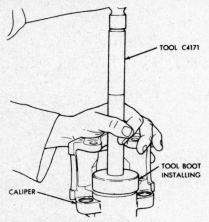

**Fig. 5   Piston dust boot installation**

# Bendix Single Piston Sliding Caliper, Chrysler

**NOTE:** For service procedures on this unit, refer to "Bendix Single Piston Sliding Caliper" section in the General Motors Chapter.

# Kelsey-Hayes Single Piston Sliding Caliper, Chrysler

## INDEX

## DESCRIPTION

This sliding caliper single piston system uses a one or two piece hub and is actuated by the hydraulic system and disc assembly, **Fig. 1.** Alignment and positioning of the caliper is achieved by two machined guides or "ways" on the adapter, while caliper retaining clips allow lateral movement of the caliper, **Fig. 2.** Outboard shoe flanges are used to position and locate the shoe on the caliper fingers, **Fig. 3,** while the inboard shoe is retained by the adapter, **Fig. 4.** Braking force applied onto the outboard shoe is transferred to the caliper, while braking force applied onto the inboard shoe is transferred directly to the adapter.

A square cut piston seal provides a hydraulic seal between the piston and the cylinder bore, **Fig. 1.** A dust boot with a wiping lip installed in a groove in the cylinder bore and piston prevents contamination in the piston and cylinder bore area. Adjustment between the disc and the shoe is obtained automatically by the outward relocation of the piston as the inboard lining wears and inward movement of the caliper as the outboard lining wears.

## CALIPER REMOVAL

1. Raise the vehicle and remove front wheel.
2. Disconnect and cap flexible brake line, then remove caliper retaining clips and anti-rattle springs, **Fig. 2.**
3. Remove caliper from disc by slowly sliding caliper assembly out and away from disc. **Use some means to support caliper. Do not let caliper hang from hydraulic line.**

## BRAKE SHOE REMOVAL

1. Remove caliper assembly as outlined above.
2. Remove outboard shoe by prying between the shoe and the caliper fingers, **Fig. 5,** since flanges on outboard shoe retain caliper firmly. **Caliper should be supported to** avoid damage to the flexible brake hose.
3. Remove inboard brake shoe from the adapter, **Fig. 4.**

## BRAKE SHOE INSTALLATION

Remove approximately 1/3 of the brake fluid out of the reservoir to prevent overflow when pistons are pushed back into the bore.

1. With care, push piston back into bore until bottomed.
2. Install new outboard shoe in recess of caliper. No freeplay should exist between brake shoe flanges and caliper fingers, **Fig. 6.** If up and down movement of the shoe shows freeplay, shoe must be removed and flanges bent to provide a slight interference fit, **Fig. 3.** Reinstall shoe after modification, if shoe can not be finger snapped into place, use light "C" clamp pressure, **Fig. 7.**

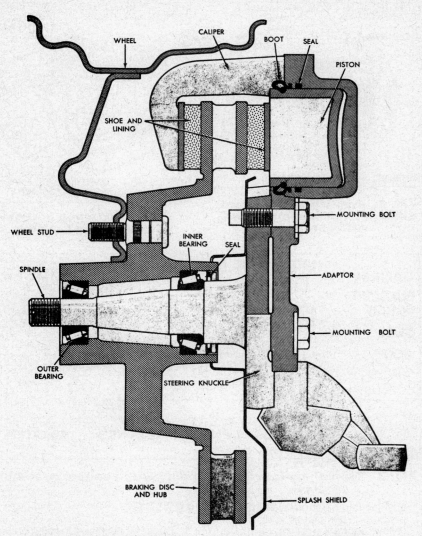

**Fig. 1   Sectional view of disc brake assembly**

**Fig. 3   Fitting outboard shoe retaining flange**

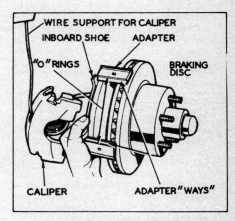

**Fig. 4   Inboard shoe replacement**

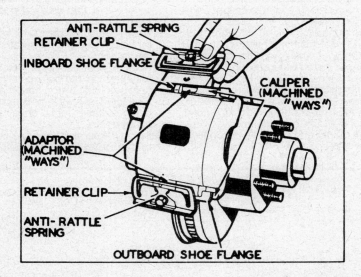

**Fig. 2   Caliper mounted "ways" & assembly retention**

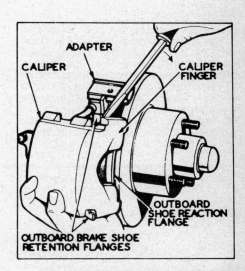

**Fig. 5   Outboard shoe removal**

3. Position inboard shoe with flanges inserted in adapter "ways," **Fig. 4.**
4. Carefully slide caliper assembly into adapter and over the disc while aligning caliper on machined "ways" of adapter. **Ensure dust boot is not pulled out from groove when piston and boot slide over the inboard shoe.**
5. Install anti-rattle springs, retaining clips and retaining screws. The inboard shoe anti-rattle spring is to be installed on top of the retainer spring plate, **Fig. 2.**

## CALIPER DISASSEMBLY

1. With caliper and shoes removed as described previously, place the caliper onto the upper control arm and slowly depress brake pedal, in turn hydraulically pushing piston out of bore.
2. Support pedal below first inch of pedal travel to prevent excessive fluid loss.
3. To remove piston from the opposite caliper, disconnect flexible brake line at frame bracket, from vehicle side where piston has been removed previously and plug tube to prevent pressure loss. By depressing brake pedal this piston can also be hydraulically pushed out. **Air pressure should never be used to remove piston from bore.**
4. Mount caliper in a vise equipped with protector jaws. **Excessive vise pressure will distort caliper bore.**
5. Remove the dust boot, **Fig. 8.**
6. Insert a suitable tool such as a small, pointed wooden or plastic object between the cylinder bore and the seal and work seal out of the groove in the piston bore. **A metal tool such as a screwdriver should not be used since it can cause damage to the piston bore or burr the edges of the seal groove.**

## CALIPER ASSEMBLY
### 1980

1. Before installing the new piston seal in groove of bore, dip seal in Ucon LB1145Y24 lubricant or equivalent. Work seal gently into the groove (using clean fingers) until seal is properly seated, making sure that seal is not twisted or rolled. **Old seals should never be reused.**
2. Lubricate new piston boot with Ucon LB1145Y24 or equivalent. Using finger pressure, install into caliper by

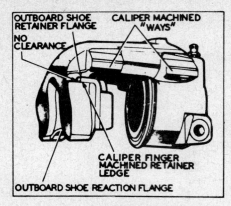

**Fig. 6  Positioning outboard shoe onto caliper machined retainer ledge**

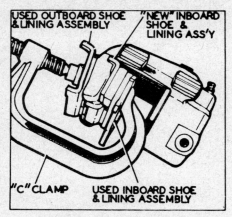

**Fig. 7  Installing outboard shoe using C-clamp**

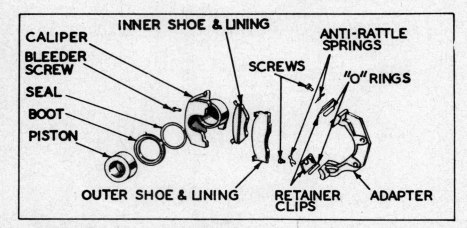

**Fig. 8  Typical exploded view of disc brake caliper assembly**

pushing into outer groove of the caliper bore. When properly positioned in groove boot will snap into place. Double check to make sure boot is properly installed and seated by running finger around the inside of the boot.
3. Plug high pressure inlet to caliper and bleeder screw hole and coat piston with a generous amount of lubricant. Spread boot with finger and work piston into boot while pressing down on piston. As piston is depressed, entrapped air below piston will force boot around piston and into its groove.
4. Remove the plug and apply uniform force to the piston (avoid cocking piston) until piston bottoms in bore.
5. Install caliper and shoes as described under "Brake Shoe Installation."

### 1981–89

1. Dip new piston seal in clean brake fluid, then work seal gently into groove (using clean fingers) until seal is properly seated, ensuring seal is not twisted or rolled. **Old seals should never be reused.**
2. Coat new piston dust boot with clean brake fluid, leaving generous amount inside boot.
3. Position dust boot over piston.
4. Install piston into bore, pushing piston past seal until piston bottoms in bore.
5. Position dust boot in counterbore, and using suitable tools, drive boot into counterbore.
6. Install caliper and shoes as described under "Brake Shoe Installation."

# Kelsey-Hayes Single Pin Floating Caliper, Chrysler

## INDEX

**Page No.**

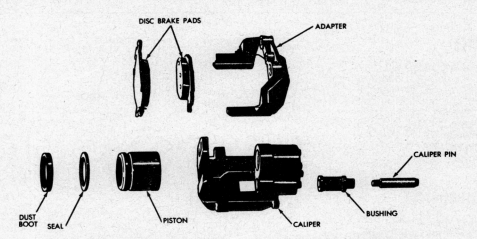

**Fig. 1  Exploded view of disc brake caliper assembly**

## DESCRIPTION

The caliper assembly consists of a rotor, caliper, shoes and linings, and adapter, **Fig. 1.** The single piston caliper assembly floats through a rubber bushing on a single pin threaded into the adapter. The bushing is inserted into the inboard portion of the caliper. Two machined abutments on the adapter position and align the caliper fore and aft. The guide pin and bushing controls the movement of the caliper and the piston seal to assist in maintaining proper shoe clearance.

This assembly has three anti-rattle clips. One is on top of the inboard shoe, one clip is on the bottom of the outboard shoe, and one clip is on top of the caliper.

All of the braking force is taken directly by the adapter. The caliper is a one-piece casting with the inboard side containing a single piston cylinder bore. The phenolic piston is 2.13 inches in diameter.

A square cut rubber piston seal is located in a machined groove in the caliper bore and provides a seal between piston and caliper bore.

A molded rubber dust boot installed in a groove in the cylinder bore and piston keeps contamination from the caliper bore and piston. The boot mounts in the caliper bore and in a groove in the piston.

## BRAKE SHOE & LINING REPLACE

### REMOVAL

1. Remove brake fluid until reservoir is half full.
2. Raise and support front of vehicle, then remove wheel and tire assembly.
3. Remove caliper guide pin and anti-rattle clips.
4. Remove caliper from disc by sliding caliper assembly out and away from braking disc. Suspend caliper with wire to avoid damaging flexible brake hose.
5. Remove outboard brake lining, then lift off rotor and remove inboard brake lining.

### INSTALLATION

1. Push piston back into cylinder bore with uniform pressure until it is bottomed.
2. Position inboard shoe and lining on adapter, then install rotor.
3. While holding outboard shoe in position on adapter, carefully position caliper over disc brake rotor.
4. Lower caliper over rotor and adapter.
5. Install guide pin through bushing caliper and adapter.
6. Press in on guide pin and thread pin into adapter. Torque pin to 25-35 ft. lbs.
7. Install wheel and tire assembly, then lower vehicle.

## CALIPER OVERHAUL

Refer to "Caliper Overhaul" under "A.T.E. Floating Caliper" for procedure.

# Kelsey-Hayes Double Pin Floating Caliper, Chrysler

## INDEX

**Page No.**

## DESCRIPTION

The double pin caliper consists of a driving hub, braking disc, caliper, pads and adapter on vehicles without an integral knuckle. The caliper is mounted through two bushings and sleeves. An anti-rattle clip is attached to the outer shoe and the inner shoe has a retainer clip. The caliper is a one piece casting with the inboard side containing a single piston and bore, **Fig. 1.**

## CALIPER, REMOVAL

1. Raise and support vehicle.
2. Remove front wheel and tire assemblies.
3. Remove two caliper-to-knuckle attaching bolts, then pull lower end of caliper from knuckle, **Fig. 2.** Shoe assemblies will remain with the caliper.
4. Remove outboard pad by prying between shoe and caliper. Remove inboard shoe from caliper by pulling shoe and lining assembly away from piston.
5. Hang assembly on a wire hook so hydraulic fluid will not get on rotor. Place a small block of wood between piston and caliper fingers.
6. Depress brake pedal to hydraulically push piston out of bore, then prop brake pedal to any position below the first inch of travel to prevent loss of fluid. **Air pressure should never be used to remove piston from bore.**

## BRAKE SHOE REMOVAL

1. Raise and support vehicle.
2. Remove front wheel and tire assemblies.
3. Remove two caliper-to-knuckle attaching bolts, then pull lower end of caliper from knuckle, **Fig. 2.** Shoe assemblies will remain with the caliper.
4. Remove outboard pad by prying between shoe and caliper. Remove inboard shoe from caliper by pulling shoe and lining assembly away from piston.
5. Hang assembly on a wire hook so hydraulic fluid will not get on rotor.

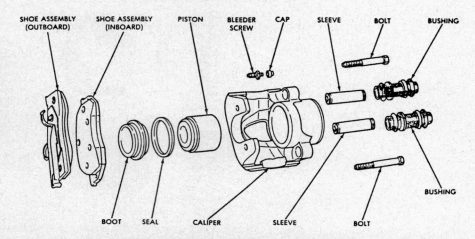

SHOE ASSEMBLY (OUTBOARD)   SHOE ASSEMBLY (INBOARD)   PISTON   BLEEDER SCREW   CAP   SLEEVE   BOLT   BUSHING

BOOT   SEAL   CALIPER   SLEEVE   BOLT   BUSHING

**Fig. 1   Double pin disc brake caliper**

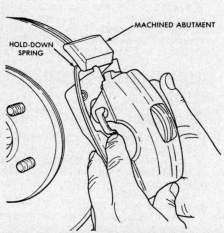

MACHINED ABUTMENT

HOLD-DOWN SPRING

**Fig. 2   Removing caliper & brake shoes**

INBOARD SHOE ASSEMBLY (RIGHT AND LEFT COMMON)

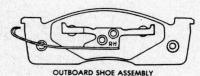

OUTBOARD SHOE ASSEMBLY (RIGHT SIDE SHOWN)

**Fig. 3   Brake pad identification**

## BRAKE SHOE INSTALLATION

1. Check piston seal for leaks and for ruptures in piston dust boot. Replace all seals, boots or bushings as necessary.
2. Lubricate adapter ways with a liberal amount of multipurpose lubricant.
3. Install new inboard pads in caliper, entering retainer into bore in piston. **Inboard pads are interchangeable. Outboard pads are marked RH or LH, Fig. 3.**
4. Remove protective paper from the noise suppression gasket, then position properly marked outboard pad

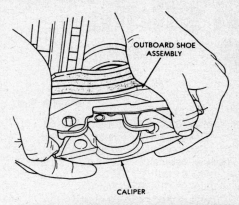

**Fig. 4    Installing outboard pad assembly**

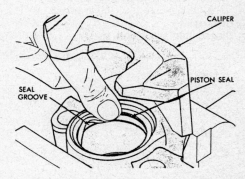

**Fig. 6    Installing piston seal**

2. Hang assembly on a wire hook so hydraulic fluid will not get on rotor. Place a small block of wood between piston and caliper fingers.
3. Depress brake pedal to hydraulically push piston out of bore, then prop brake pedal to any position below the first inch of travel to prevent loss of fluid. **Air pressure should never be used to remove piston from bore.**
4. If both caliper pistons are to be removed, disconnect flexible brake line at frame bracket after removal of first piston. Plug brake tube, then remove piston from opposite caliper.
5. Place caliper assembly in a vise equipped with protective jaws. **Excessive vise pressure will cause bore distortion and binding of piston.** Support caliper and remove dust boot, **Fig. 5.**
6. Remove piston seal using a suitable plastic tool.
7. Remove bushings from caliper, then clean and inspect for scoring or pitting of bores.

## CALIPER ASSEMBLY

1. Place caliper assembly in a vise equipped with protective jaws. **Excessive vise pressure will cause bore distortion and binding of piston.** Support caliper and remove dust boot, **Fig. 5.**
2. Dip new piston seal in clean brake fluid and install in groove of bore, **Fig. 6.**
3. Cover new piston boot with clean brake fluid, then position dust boot over piston.
4. Install piston into bore, pushing it down until it bottoms out. Force must be applied evenly to avoid binding piston in bore, **Fig. 7.**
5. Position boot in counterbore, then use seal tool C-4689 or equivalent to drive boot into counterbore.
6. Install guide pin bushings by hand, then reinstall Teflon sleeves into bushings. Ensure flanges extend evenly over caliper on both sides.

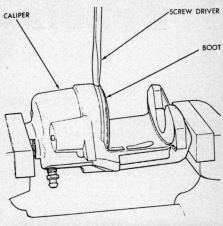

**Fig. 5    Removing piston dust boot**

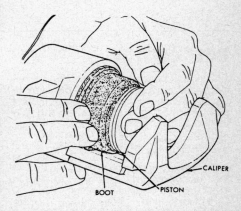

**Fig. 7    Installing piston in bore**

hold-down spring onto caliper, **Fig. 4.**
5. Lower caliper over rotor and guide hold-down spring under machined abutment on knuckle assembly.
6. Install attaching bolts and torque to 18-25 ft. lbs.
7. Install wheel and tire assembly.

## CALIPER DISASSEMBLY

1. Remove caliper as described under "Caliper, Removal."

7. Inspect caliper, ensuring all seals are in place, then reinstall on vehicle.
8. Using new seal washer, install brake hose to caliper.
9. Bleed system and check for leaks. Install hub and wheel assemblies.

# Bendix Single Piston Sliding Caliper, Jeep

## INDEX

## DESCRIPTION

The disc brake is of the sliding caliper, single piston design. On 1980-81 CJ models, the caliper is positioned on abutment surfaces machined into the leading and trailing edges of the caliper anchor bracket, **Fig. 1.** On 1980-83 Cherokee, Wagoneer and Truck and 1984-89 Grand Wagoneer and Truck models, the caliper is positioned on mounting bolts located in the caliper support bracket, **Fig. 2.** On 1982-86 CJ and Scrambler, 1984-89 Cherokee and Wagoneer models, 1986-89 Commanche and 1987-89 Wrangler, the caliper is positioned over the rotor and slides on two mounting pins which maintain caliper position relative to rotor and caliper anchor plate, **Fig. 3.** Although caliper designs differ in construction, operation and service procedures remain the same.

All models are equipped with an integral type hub and rotor. The caliper is a one-piece casting containing a piston, piston bore, bleeder screw and inlet ports. A rubber dust boot with integral metal retainer is used on all models except 1980-81 CJ models, which use a solid rubber boot. The dust boot is positioned in a counterbore machined in the upper edge of the piston bore and in a groove machined in the exterior surface of the piston.

Lining wear is compensated for by the lateral sliding movement of the caliper and by increased piston extension.

## CALIPER REMOVAL

### 1980-81 CJ

1. Drain and discard ⅔ of brake fluid from largest master cylinder reservoir.
2. Raise and support vehicle.
3. Remove front wheel and tire assemblies.
4. Press caliper piston to bottom of bore using suitable screwdriver or C-clamp.
5. Remove caliper support key retaining

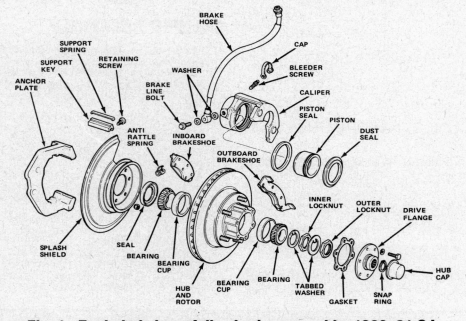

**Fig. 1 Exploded view of disc brake assembly. 1980–81 CJ**

screw using a ¼ inch hex wrench.
6. Remove caliper support key and spring using punch and hammer.
7. Lift caliper up and out of anchor plate and off rotor.

### 1980–83 CHEROKEE, TRUCK & WAGONEER; 1984–89 GRAND WAGONEER & TRUCK

1. Drain and discard ⅔ of brake fluid from master cylinder front reservoir.
2. Raise and support vehicle.
3. Remove front wheel and tire assemblies.
4. Press caliper piston to bottom of bore using suitable screwdriver or C-clamp.
5. Remove caliper mounting bolts.

6. Remove caliper by lifting upward and out of shield and support.

### 1982–86 CJ & SCRAMBLER; 1984–89 CHEROKEE & WAGONEER; 1986–89 COMMANCHE & 1987–89 WRANGLER

1. Remove and discard ⅔ of brake fluid from largest master cylinder reservoir.
2. Raise and support vehicle.
3. Remove front wheel and tire assemblies.
4. Press caliper piston to bottom of bore using suitable screwdriver or C-clamp.
5. Remove caliper mounting pins.
6. Lift caliper up and out of anchor plate and off rotor.

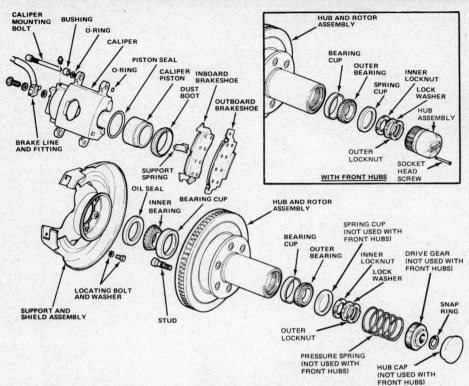

**Fig. 2 Exploded view of disc brake assembly. 1980–83 Cherokee, Truck & Wagoneer; 1984–89 Grand Wagoneer & Truck**

# BRAKE SHOE REMOVAL
## 1980–81 CJ

1. Unfasten caliper as previously described, leaving brake hose attached to caliper. **Suspend caliper from suspension spring. Do not let caliper hang by hydraulic line.**
2. Remove inboard brake shoe from anchor plate.
3. Remove anti-rattle spring from inboard shoe, noting position of spring for assembly reference.
4. Remove outboard brake shoe from caliper.
5. Clean caliper interior using clean shop cloths. Do not use compressed air, as damage to dust boot may result.

## 1980–83 CHEROKEE, TRUCK & WAGONEER; 1984–89 GRAND WAGONEER & TRUCK

1. Unfasten caliper as previously described, leaving brake hose attached to caliper. **Suspend caliper from suspension spring. Do not let caliper hang by hydraulic line.**
2. Remove inboard and outboard brake shoes from caliper.
3. Remove support spring from inboard shoe, noting position of spring for assembly reference.
4. Remove sleeves and rubber bushings from mounting bolt bores in caliper mounting ears.

5. Clean mounting bolts, bolt core and bushing grooves in caliper mounting ears with suitable solvent. **Do not use abrasives to clean or polish the mounting bolts.**
6. Clean caliper interior and dust boot using clean shop cloths. Do not use compressed air, as damage to boot may result.

## 1982–86 CJ & SCRAMBLER; 1984–89 CHEROKEE & WAGONEER; 1986–89 COMMANCHE; 1987–89 WRANGLER

1. Unfasten caliper as previously described, leaving brake hose attached to caliper. **Suspend caliper from suspension spring. Do not let caliper hang by hydraulic line.**
2. Remove outboard brake shoe from anchor plate while holding anti-rattle clip.
3. Remove inboard brake shoe and anti-rattle clip.
4. Clean caliper interior using clean shop cloths. Do not use compressed air, as damage to dust boot may result.

# BRAKE SHOE INSTALLATION
## 1980–81 CJ

1. Install inboard brake shoe anti-rattle spring on rear flange of shoe. Ensure looped section of spring faces away

from rotor.
2. Install inboard brake shoe with spring in caliper anchor plate.
3. Install outboard brake shoe in caliper.
4. Install caliper as described under "Caliper Installation."

## 1980–83 CHEROKEE, TRUCK & WAGONEER; 1984–89 GRAND WAGONEER & TRUCK

1. Apply suitable silicone lubricant to replacement bushings, sleeves, bushing grooves and small ends of mounting bolts.
2. Install new rubber bushings in caliper mounting ears.
3. Install new sleeves in inboard mounting ears of caliper. Ensure sleeve end faces shoe and lining is flush with machined surface of mounting ear.
4. Install support spring on inboard brake shoe. Position single tang end of spring over notch in shoe.
5. Install inboard shoe in caliper. Ensure shoe is flush against piston and support spring is fully seated in piston.
6. Install outboard shoe until shoe is fully seated. Ensure shoe ears rest on upper surface of caliper mounting ears and lower shoe tab fits into cutout in caliper. **Outboard shoes with formed ears are meant for original installation only and are fitted to the caliper. Shoes of this type must never be relined or reconditioned.**
7. Install caliper as described under "Caliper Installation."

## 1982–86 CJ & SCRAMBLER; 1984–89 CHEROKEE & WAGONEER; 1986–86 COMMANCHE; 1987–89 WRANGLER

1. Install anti-rattle clip on trailing edge of anchor plate, ensuring split end of clip faces away from rotor.
2. Install inboard, then the outboard shoes while holding anti-rattle clip.
3. Install caliper as described under "Caliper Installation."

# DISASSEMBLING CALIPER

1. Clean outside of caliper with suitable solvent.
2. Drain fluid from caliper and place clean shop cloths in caliper opposite piston.
3. Slowly apply compressed air to caliper inlet port until piston pops out of bore.
4. Remove and discard dust boot, using a suitable screwdriver. Use care to avoid scratching caliper piston bore.
5. Remove and discard piston seal, using a suitable wooden or plastic tool.
6. Remove bleeder screw and protective cap, if equipped.
7. Remove and discard inner and outer bushings and plastic sleeves, if equipped.
8. Clean all components with clean

brake fluid and compressed air.

## ASSEMBLING CALIPER

1. Lubricate piston bore and new piston seal with clean brake fluid.
2. Install seal in bore groove by hand and lubricate piston with clean brake fluid.
3. On 1980-81 CJ models, install bleeder screw and protective cap.
4. On 1980-81 CJ models, if piston dust boot installation tool No. J-24837 is available, install boot and piston as follows:
   a. Apply clean brake fluid to piston and new dust boot.
   b. Position dust boot on installation tool with approximately 1/4 inch of tool extending beyond small lip of dust boot.
   c. Place boot and tool assembly over piston bore, then reach through tool and work large lip of boot into boot groove in upper edge of piston bore until boot is fully seated.
   d. Apply clean brake fluid to caliper piston, then insert piston through tool and center piston in bore.
   e. Press piston half way into bore using steady pressure on a hammer handle.
   f. Remove boot installer tool, then seat dust boot rubber lip in piston groove.
   g. Press piston to bottom of bore using hammer handle.
5. On 1980-81 CJ models, if piston dust boot installation tool is not available, install boot and piston as follows:
   a. Apply clean brake fluid to piston bore.
   b. Position dry dust boot on piston bore.
   c. Reach through top of boot and work large lip of boot into boot groove at upper edge of bore until boot is fully seated.
   d. Apply clean brake fluid to piston and small lip of dust boot.
   e. Position piston over small lip of boot and apply approximately 15 psi compressed air into caliper fluid inlet port.
   f. With air pressure expanding boot, work piston into boot until boot lip seats in piston groove. When lip is fully seated, release air pressure.
   g. Press piston to bottom of bore using hammer handle.
6. On all except 1980-81 CJ models, proceed as follows:
   a. Install new dust boot on piston, sliding metal retainer portion of boot over open end of piston and pulling boot rearward until boot lip seats in piston groove.
   b. Push metal retainer portion of boot forward until retainer is flush with rim at open end of piston, then snap boot fold into place.
   c. Install piston into caliper bore, using care to avoid unseating piston seal.
   d. Press piston to bottom of bore, then using tool No. J-33028 or equivalent, seat metal retainer por-

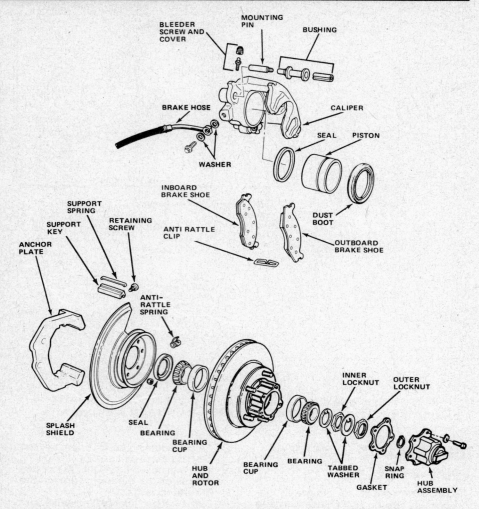

**Fig. 3   Exploded view of disc brake assembly. 1982–86 CJ & Scrambler; 1984–89 Cherokee & Wagoneer; 1986–89 Commanche; 1987–89 Wrangler**

tion of dust boot in counterbore at upper end of bore.
   e. Install bleeder screw, then new inner and outer bushings and plastic sleeves, if equipped, in caliper mounting ears.

## CALIPER INSTALLATION
### 1980–81 CJ

1. Install caliper over rotor and in anchor plate.
2. Align caliper and anchor plate, then install support key and spring between abutment surfaces at trailing edge of caliper.
3. Complete installation of support key and spring using a hammer and punch.
4. Install support key retaining screw. Ensure screw is properly seated in support key notch, then torque screw to 15 ft. lbs.
5. Install new washers on brake line connector or fitting and connect brake line to caliper. Torque brake line bolt

to 160 inch lbs. or brake line fitting to 25 ft. lbs.
6. Fill master cylinder to within 1/4 inch of reservoir rims.
7. Depress brake pedal several times to seat brake shoes, then refill master cylinder, if necessary, and bleed brakes.
8. Install wheel and tire assembly, then lower vehicle and check operation of brake system.

### 1980–83 CHEROKEE, TRUCK & WAGONEER; 1984–89 GRAND WAGONEER & TRUCK

1. Install caliper over rotor and in support shield and bracket.
2. Install caliper mounting bolts, ensuring bolts pass under inboard shoe retaining ears. Insert bolts until they enter bores in outboard shoe and caliper mounting ears, then thread bolts into support bracket and torque to 35 ft. lbs.
3. Install new copper gaskets on brake line, then connect brake line to caliper

and torque brake line bolt to 160 inch lbs.

4. Fill master cylinder to within 1/4 inch of reservoir rims, then depress brake pedal several times to seat brake shoes.

5. Clinch upper ears of outboard shoe until there is no radial clearance between shoe and caliper.

6. Install wheel and tire assemblies, then lower vehicle.

7. Check master cylinder fluid level and correct as necessary, then check operation of brake system.

## 1982–86 CJ & SCRAMBLER; 1984–89 CHEROKEE & WAGONEER; 1986–89 COMMANCHE; 1987–89 WRANGLER

1. Install caliper over rotor and in anchor plate.

2. Align caliper and anchor plate, then install caliper mounting pins and torque to 30 ft. lbs.

3. Install new washers on brake line connector or fitting and connect brake line to caliper. Torque brake line bolt to 160 inch lbs. or brake line fitting to 25 ft. lbs. on CJ and Scrambler models or 23 ft. lbs. on all other models.

4. Fill master cylinder to within 1/4 inch of reservoir rims, then depress brake pedal several times to seat brake shoes.

5. Install wheel and tire assemblies, then lower vehicle.

6. Check master cylinder fluid level and correct as necessary, then check operation of brake system.

# DRUM BRAKES

## TABLE OF CONTENTS

# General Information

## INDEX

## SERVICE PRECAUTIONS

When working on or around brake assemblies, care must be taken to prevent breathing asbestos dust, as many manufacturers incorporate asbestos fibers in the production of brake linings. During routine service operations, the amount of asbestos dust from brake lining wear is at a low level due to a chemical breakdown during use, and a few precautions will minimize exposure. **Do not sand or grind brake linings unless suitable local exhaust ventilation equipment is used to prevent excessive asbestos exposure.**

1. Wear a suitable respirator approved for asbestos dust use during all repair procedures.

2. When cleaning brake dust from brake parts, use a vacuum cleaner with a highly efficient filter system. If a suitable vacuum cleaner is not available, use a water soaked rag. **Do not use compressed air or dry brush to clean brake parts.**

3. Keep work area clean, using same equipment as for cleaning brake parts.

4. Properly dispose of rags and vacuum cleaner bags by placing them in plastic bags.

5. Do not smoke or eat while working on brake systems.

## GENERAL INSPECTION
### BRAKE DRUMS

Any time the brake drums are removed for brake service, the braking surface diameter should be checked with a suitable brake drum micrometer at several points to determine if they are within the safe oversize limit stamped on the brake drum outer surface. If the braking surface diameter exceeds specifications, the drum must be replaced. If the braking surface diameter is within specifications, drums should be cleaned and inspected for cracks, scores, deep grooves, taper, out of round and heat spotting. If drums are cracked or heat spotted, they must be replaced. Minor scores should be removed with sandpaper. Grooves and large scores can only be removed by machining with special equipment, as long as the braking surface is within specifications stamped on brake drum outer surface. Any brake drum sufficiently out of round to cause vehicle vibration or noise while braking, or showing taper should also be machined, removing only enough stock to true up the brake drum.

After a brake drum is machined, wipe the braking surface diameter with a cloth soaked in denatured alcohol. If one brake drum is machined, the other should also be machined to the same diameter to maintain equal braking forces.

### BRAKE LININGS & SPRINGS

Inspect brake linings for excessive wear, damage, oil, grease or brake fluid contamination. If any of the above conditions exists, brake linings should be replaced. Do not attempt to replace only one set of brake shoes; they should be replaced as an axle set only to maintain equal braking forces. Examine brake shoe webbing, hold-down and return springs for signs of overheating indicated by a slight blue color. If any component exhibits signs of overheating, replace hold-down and return springs with new ones. Overheated springs lose their pull and could cause brake linings to wear out prematurely. Inspect all springs for sags, bends and external damage, and replace as necessary.

Inspect hold-down retainers and pins for bends, rust and corrosion. If any of the above conditions exist, replace retainers and pins.

### BACKING PLATE

Inspect backing plate shoe contact surface for grooves that may restrict shoe movement and cannot be removed by lightly sanding with emery cloth or other suitable abrasive. If backing plate exhibits above condition, it should be replaced. Also inspect for signs of cracks, warpage and excessive rust, indicating need for replacement.

## ADJUSTER MECHANISM

Inspect all components for rust, corrosion, bends and fatigue. Replace as necessary. On adjuster mechanism equipped with adjuster cable, inspect cable for kinks, fraying or elongation of eyelet.

## PARKING BRAKE CABLE

Inspect parking brake cable end for kinks, fraying and elongation, and replace as necessary. Use a small hose clamp to compress clamp where it enters backing plate to remove.

# Chrysler Drum Brake Service

## INDEX

## 1982 MODELS w/7.87 INCH DRUMS

### REMOVAL

1. Raise and support rear of vehicle, then remove tire and wheel assembly.
2. Remove brake drum. If brake lining is dragging on brake drum, back off brake adjustment by rotating adjustment screw.
3. Disconnect parking brake cable from parking brake lever, **Fig. 1.**
4. Using suitable pliers, remove brake shoe to anchor springs and hold-down springs.
5. Fully seat adjuster nut, then spread shoes apart and remove adjuster screw assembly.
6. Raise parking brake lever, then pull trailing shoe away from support to ease return spring tension and disengage spring end from support. Remove trailing shoe.
7. Pull leading shoe away from support to ease return spring tension and disengage spring end from support. Remove leading shoe.
8. Remove parking brake lever from trailing shoe.
9. Clean dirt from brake drum, support plate and all other components. **Do not use compressed air or dry brush to clean brake parts. Many brake parts contain asbestos fibers which, if inhaled, can cause serious injury. To clean brake parts, use a water soaked rag or a suitable vacuum cleaner to minimize airborne dust.**

### INSPECTION

1. Inspect components for damage and unusual wear. Replace as necessary.
2. Inspect wheel cylinders. Any torn, cut or heat damaged boots indicate need for wheel cylinder replacement. Peel back lower edge of boot. If fluid spills out, cup leakage is indicated and

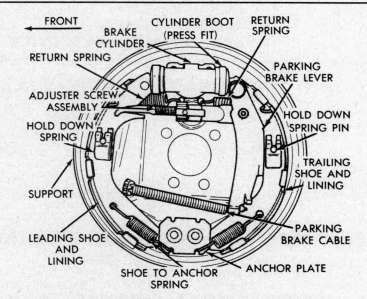

**Fig. 1  Drum brake assembly. 1982 models w/7.87 inch drums**

wheel cylinder should be replaced. **A slight amount of fluid is always present and is considered normal. Fluid acts as a lubricant for the cylinder pistons.**
3. Inspect support plate attaching bolts, and ensure they are tight.
4. Inspect adjuster screw assembly operation. If satisfactory, lightly lubricate threads with suitable brake lube. If operation is unsatisfactory, replace.
5. Using fine emery cloth or other suitable abrasive, clean rust and dirt from shoe contact surfaces on support plate.

### INSTALLATION

1. Lightly lubricate support plate shoe contact surfaces with suitable brake lube.

2. Remove brake drum hub grease seal and bearings, then clean and repack bearings and reinstall. Install new grease seal.
3. Position leading shoe return spring on shoe, then while holding shoe away from support, engage return spring in support plate, **Fig. 2,** and swing shoe end into position under anchor.
4. Install parking brake lever on trailing shoe.
5. Install trailing shoe return spring on shoe, then while holding shoe away from support, engage return spring in support plate, **Fig. 3,** and swing shoe end into position under anchor.
6. Spread shoes apart and install adjuster screw assembly. Ensure forked end enters the leading shoe with curved tines facing down, **Fig. 1.**
7. Using a suitable pair of pliers, install

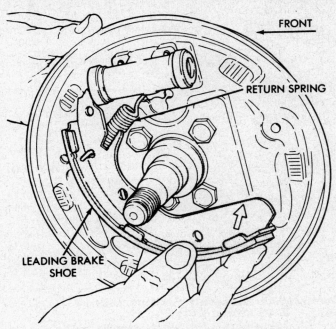

**Fig. 2 Installing trailing brake shoe**

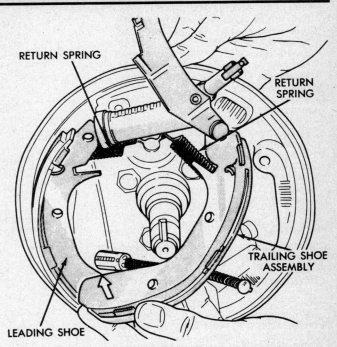

**Fig. 3 Installing leading brake shoe**

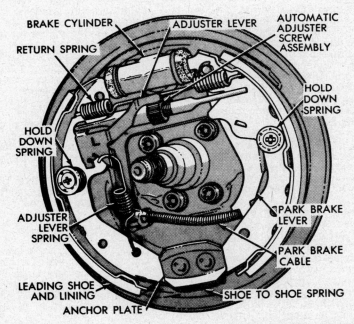

**Fig. 4 Drum brake assembly. 1983–84 models w/7.87 inch drums & all models w/8.66 inch drums**

hold-down springs and shoe to anchor springs.

8. Pull back parking brake cable return spring slightly to expose cable, then slide parking brake cable into parking brake lever and release spring.
9. Install brake drum and bearings. Refer to individual truck chapter for wheel bearing adjustment procedure.
10. Adjust brakes. Refer to individual truck chapter for procedure.
11. Install tire and wheel assembly.
12. If any hydraulic connections have been opened, bleed brake system.

13. Check master cylinder level and replenish as necessary.
14. Check brake pedal for proper feel and return.
15. Lower vehicle and road test. **Do not severely apply brakes immediately after installation of new brake linings or permanent damage may occur to linings and/or brake drums may become scored. Brakes must be used moderately during first several hundred miles of operation to ensure proper burnishing of linings.**

## 1983–84 MODELS W/7.87 INCH DRUMS & ALL MODELS W/8.66 INCH DRUMS
### REMOVAL

1. Raise and support rear of vehicle, then remove tire and wheel assembly.
2. Remove brake drum. If brake lining is dragging on brake drum, back off brake adjustment by rotating adjustment screw.
3. Using suitable pliers, remove adjuster lever spring, **Fig. 4.**
4. Remove adjuster lever.
5. Turn automatic adjuster screw out to expand shoes past wheel cylinder boot.
6. Using suitable tool, remove hold-down springs.
7. Pull brake shoe assembly down and away from anchor plate.
8. Remove "C" clip retaining parking brake lever to trailing brake shoe webbing.
9. Disassemble shoe assembly.
10. Clean dirt from brake drum, anchor plate and all other components. Do not use compressed air or dry brush to clean brake parts. Many brake parts contain asbestos fibers which, if inhaled, can cause serious injury. To clean brake parts, use a water soaked rag or a suitable vacuum cleaner to minimize airborne dust.

### INSPECTION

1. Inspect components for damage and unusual wear. Replace as necessary.
2. Inspect wheel cylinders. Any torn, cut or heat damaged boot indicates need of wheel cylinder replacement. Peel

back lower edge of boot. If fluid spills out, cup leakage is indicated and wheel cylinder should be replaced. **A slight amount of fluid is always present and is considered normal. Fluid acts as a lubricant for the cylinder pistons.**

3. Inspect anchor plate attaching bolts, and ensure they are tight.
4. Inspect automatic adjuster screw assembly operation. If satisfactory, lightly lubricate threads with suitable brake lube. If operation is unsatisfactory, replace.
5. Using fine emery cloth or other suitable abrasive, clean rust and dirt from shoe contact surfaces on anchor plate.

## INSTALLATION

1. Lightly lubricate anchor plate shoe contact surfaces with suitable brake lube.
2. Remove brake drum hub grease seal and bearings, then clean and repack bearings and reinstall. Install new grease seal.
3. Assemble automatic adjuster screw assembly, return spring and shoe-to-shoe spring to brake shoe assembly.
4. Position lining assembly near anchor plate, then assemble parking brake lever to trailing shoe webbing. Secure with C-clip.
5. Install lining assembly onto anchor plate. When positioned, back off adjuster nut to seat brake shoe ends in wheel cylinder.
6. Install hold-down springs.
7. Position adjuster lever, then using suitable pliers, install adjuster lever spring.
8. Install brake drum and bearings. Refer to individual truck chapter for wheel bearing adjustment procedure.
9. Adjust brakes. Refer to individual truck chapter for procedure.
10. Install tire and wheel assembly.
11. If any hydraulic connections have been opened, bleed brake system.
12. Check master cylinder level and replenish as necessary.
13. Check brake pedal for proper feel and return.
14. Lower vehicle and road test. **Do not severely apply brakes immediately after installation of new brake linings or permanent damage may occur to linings and/or brake drums may become scored. Brakes must be used moderately during first several hundred miles of operation to ensure proper burnishing.**

## MODELS w/9, 10 & 11 INCH DRUMS
### REMOVAL

1. Raise and support rear of vehicle, then remove tire and wheel assembly.
2. Remove brake drum. If brake lining is dragging on brake drum, back off brake adjustment by rotating adjust-

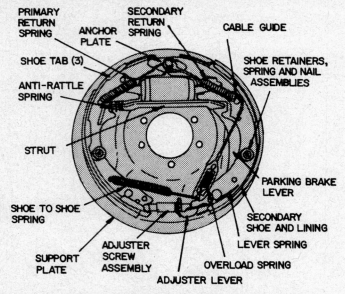

**Fig. 5   Drum brake assembly. Models w/9, 10 & 11 inch drums**

ment screw. **If brake drum is rusted or corroded to axle flange and cannot be removed, lightly tap axle flange to drum mounting surface with a suitable hammer.**

3. Using brake spring pliers or equivalent, remove primary and secondary shoe return springs, **Fig. 5.**
4. Remove automatic adjuster cable from anchor plate, then unhook from adjuster lever.
5. Remove adjuster cable, overload spring, cable guide and anchor plate.
6. Unhook adjuster lever spring from lever, then remove spring and lever.
7. Remove shoe to shoe spring from secondary shoe web, then primary shoe.
8. Spread shoes apart and remove parking brake strut and spring.
9. Using suitable tool, remove shoe retainers, then springs and nails.
10. Disconnect parking brake cable from lever, then remove brake shoes.
11. Remove parking brake lever from secondary shoe.
12. Clean dirt from brake drum, backing plate and all other components. **Do not use compressed air or dry brush to clean brake parts. Many brake parts contain asbestos fibers which, if inhaled, can cause serious injury. To clean brake parts, use a water soaked rag or a suitable vacuum cleaner to minimize airborne dust.**

## INSPECTION

1. Inspect components for damage and unusual wear. Replace as necessary.
2. Inspect wheel cylinders. Boots which are torn, cut or heat damaged indicate need for wheel cylinder replacement. Peel back lower edge of boot. If fluid spills out, cup leakage is indicated and wheel cylinder should be replaced. A

slight amount of fluid is always present and considered normal, acting as a lubricant for the cylinder pistons.

3. Inspect backing plate for evidence of seal leakage. If leakage exists, refer to individual truck chapter for axle seal replacement procedure.
4. Inspect backing plate attaching bolts, and ensure they are tight.
5. Inspect adjuster screw operation. If satisfactory, lightly lubricate adjusting screw and washer with suitable brake lube. If operation is unsatisfactory, replace.
6. Using fine emery cloth or other suitable abrasive, clean rust and dirt from shoe contact surfaces on backing plate.

## INSTALLATION

1. Lubricate parking brake lever fulcrum with suitable brake lube, then attach lever to secondary brake shoe. Ensure lever operates smoothly.
2. Lightly lubricate backing plate shoe contact surfaces with suitable brake lube.
3. Connect parking brake lever to cable, then slide secondary brake shoe into position.
4. Connect wheel cylinder link to brake shoe (if equipped).
5. Slide parking brake lever strut behind axle flange and into parking brake lever slot, then place parking brake anti-rattle spring over strut.
6. Position primary brake shoe on backing plate, then connect wheel cylinder link (if equipped) and parking brake strut.
7. Install anchor plate, then position adjuster cable eye over anchor pin.
8. Install primary shoe return spring using brake spring pliers or equivalent.
9. Place protruding hole rim of cable

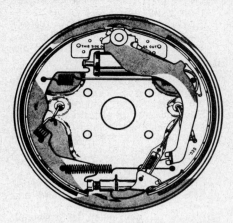

**Fig. 6 Drum brake assembly. Models w/12 & 13 inch drums**

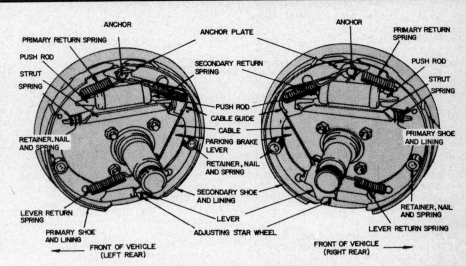

**Fig. 7 Drum brake assembly. Models w/12.12 inch drums**

guide in secondary shoe web hole, then holding guide in position, install secondary shoe return spring through cable guide and secondary shoe. Install spring on anchor pin using brake spring pliers or equivalent. **Ensure cable guide remains flat against secondary shoe web during and after return spring installation. Also ensure secondary spring end overlaps primary spring end on anchor pin.**

10. Using suitable pliers, squeeze spring ends around anchor pin until parallel.
11. Install adjuster screw assembly between primary and secondary brake shoes with star wheel on secondary shoe side. **The left side adjuster assembly stud is stamped "L" and is cadmium-plated. The right side adjuster assembly is stamped "R" and is colored black.**
12. Install shoe to shoe spring, then position adjusting lever spring over pivot pin on shoe web.
13. Install adjusting lever under spring and over pivot pin, then slide lever slightly rearward.
14. Install nails, springs and retainers.
15. Thread adjuster cable over guide and hook end of overload spring in lever. Ensure eye of cable is pulled tight against anchor and in a straight line with guide.
16. Install brake drum, tire and wheel assembly.
17. Adjust brakes. Refer to individual truck chapters for procedure.
18. If any hydraulic connections have been opened, bleed brake system.
19. Check master cylinder fluid level, and replenish as necessary.
20. Check brake pedal for proper feel and return.
21. Lower vehicle and road test. **Do not severely apply brakes immediately after installation of new brake linings or permanent damage may occur to linings, and/or brake drums may become scored. Brakes must be used moderately during first several hundred miles of operation to ensure proper burnishing of linings.**

# MODELS w/12 & 13 INCH DRUMS

## REMOVAL

1. Raise and support vehicle.
2. Remove wheel and tire assembly.
3. Remove axle shaft nuts, washers, and cones, then the axle shaft. **If cones do not release, rap axle shaft sharply at center.**
4. Remove outer hub nut, then straighten lock washer and remove washer, inner nut, and bearing.
5. Remove brake drum. If brake lining is dragging on brake drum, back off brake adjustment by rotating adjusting screw.
6. Unhook adjusting lever return spring from lever, remove lever and return spring from lever pivot pin, and unhook adjuster lever from adjuster cable assembly, **Fig. 6.**
7. Using suitable pliers, unhook upper shoe-to-shoe spring, then unhook and remove shoe hold-down springs.
8. Disconnect parking brake cable from parking brake lever.
9. Remove shoes, lower shoe-to-shoe spring and star wheel as an assembly.

## INSPECTION

1. Using suitable solvent, clean support, then inspect for burrs and remove as necessary.
2. Clean and lubricate threads of adjusting screws, then inspect for pulled or stripped threads.
3. If spring paint shows discoloration, end coils are distorted, or spring strength is questionable, replace spring.

## INSTALLATION

Pivot screw and adjusting nut have left-hand threads on left side brakes and right-hand threads on right side brakes.

1. Using suitable lubricant, lubricate and assemble star wheel assembly, then lubricate guide pads on support plates.

2. Assemble star wheel, lower shoe-to-shoe spring, and brake shoes and position assembly on support plate.
3. Connect parking brake cable to parking brake lever.
4. Install and hook hold-down springs.
5. Install upper shoe-to-shoe spring.
6. Position adjuster lever return springs on pivots.
7. Install adjuster lever and route adjuster cable and connector to adjuster.
8. Position drum on axle housing.
9. Install bearing and inner nut. Refer to individual truck chapter for bearing adjustment procedure.
10. Install lock washer and outer nut, bending washer to lock in place.
11. Place new gasket on hub and install axle shaft, cones, lock washers, and nuts.
12. Adjust brakes. Refer to individual truck chapter for procedure.
13. Install tire and wheel assembly.
14. If any hydraulic connections have been opened, bleed brake system.
15. Check fluid level in master cylinder, filling as necessary.
16. Check brake pedal for proper feel and return.
17. Lower vehicle and road test.

# MODELS w/12.12 INCH DRUMS

## REMOVAL

1. Raise and support vehicle.
2. Remove wheel and tire assemblies.
3. Remove axle shaft nuts, washers, and cones, then the axle shaft. **If cones do not release, rap axle shaft sharply at center.**
4. Using suitable tool, remove outer hub nut.
5. Straighten lock washer and remove lock washer, inner nut, and bearing, then the drum. If brake lining is dragging on brake drum, back off brake adjustment by rotating adjusting screw.

6. Using suitable tool, remove brake shoe return springs, **Fig. 7.**
7. Remove brake shoe retainers, springs, and nails.
8. Remove end of automatic adjuster cable from anchor, then other end from lever.
9. Remove automatic adjuster cable, cable guide, and anchor plate.
10. Disengage lever spring at both ends, then remove spring and lever.
11. Spread anchor ends of shoes and remove parking brake strut with spring.
12. Disconnect parking brake cable from parking brake lever and remove brake assembly.
13. Remove brake shoes with adjusting star wheel from support.

## INSPECTION

1. Using suitable solvent, clean support, then inspect for burrs and remove as necessary.
2. Clean and lubricate threads of adjusting screws, then inspect for pulled or stripped threads.

## INSTALLATION

1. Apply thin coat of suitable lubricant to shoe contact area of support platforms.
2. Attach parking brake lever to back side of secondary shoe.
3. Place brake shoes in their relative position on workbench.
4. Lubricate threads of adjusting screw and install screw between shoes with star wheel toward secondary shoe. **Star wheels are stamped with an "R" or "L" to indicate whether they go on right or left side of vehicle.**
5. Overlap anchor ends of shoes and install adjusting spring and lever.
6. Hold brake shoes in their relative position and attach parking brake cable to parking brake lever.
7. Install parking brake strut with spring between parking brake lever and primary shoe.
8. Position brake shoes on support and install retainer nails, springs, and retainers.
9. Install anchor plate.
10. Install end of adjusting cable on anchor, then install return spring between primary shoe and anchor.
11. Install cable guide in secondary shoe, then install secondary return spring. **Ensure that secondary spring overlaps primary spring and that spring does not slip between adjuster cable end and anchor.**
12. Place adjuster cable in groove of cable guide and engage hook of cable into adjusting lever, ensuring that cable guide lays flat against shoe web.
13. Position drum on axle housing.
14. Install bearing and inner nut. Refer to individual truck chapter for bearing adjustment procedure.
15. Install locking washer and outer nut, bending washer to lock in place.
16. Place new gasket on hub and install axle shaft, cones, lock washers, and nuts.
17. Adjust brakes. Refer to individual truck chapter for procedure.
18. Install tire and wheel assembly.
19. If any hydraulic connections have been opened, bleed brake system.
20. Check fluid level in master cylinder, filling as necessary.
21. Check brake pedal for proper feel and return.
22. Lower vehicle and road test.

# Jeep Drum Brake Service

## INDEX

## 1980-83 CHEROKEE & WAGONEER, 1984-89 GRAND WAGONEER & ALL J-10 & J-20

### REMOVAL

1. Raise and support vehicle.
2. Remove wheel and tire assemblies.
3. Release parking brake and loosen lock nuts at parking brake equalizer.
4. Remove rear drum-to-hub locating screws, if equipped.
5. Remove drums.
6. Remove primary return spring, then the automatic adjuster actuating spring and secondary shoe return spring, **Fig. 1.**
7. Remove hold-down springs and brake shoe assemblies.
8. On rear brakes, disengage parking brake cable from parking brake lever.
9. Place suitable clamp over ends of wheel cylinder.

### INSTALLATION

1. Using suitable lubricant, lubricate support plate edges, anchor pin, adjusting screw threads and pivot, and adjuster lever to secondary brake shoe contact surface.
2. Using suitable lubricant, lubricate parking brake lever pivot and portion of lever that contacts secondary brake shoe.
3. On rear brakes, attach parking brake cable to parking lever on secondary shoe.
4. Install secondary shoe and automatic adjuster lever and pivot as an assembly and secure assembly to support plate with hold-down spring.
5. Install actuating and adjusting levers, then the return spring on actuating lever with tang with large end of spring resting on brake shoe.
6. Install primary shoe and hold-down spring, then the guide plate onto anchor pin.
7. On rear brakes, install parking brake strut.
8. Install adjusting screw and spring.
9. Install adjuster spring, secondary shoe return spring and primary shoe return spring.
10. Turn adjusting screw until brake drum slides over shoes with slight drag, then back off adjusting screw 80 notches and install drums.
11. If any hydraulic lines were opened, bleed brake system.
12. Install wheel and tire assemblies and lower vehicle.
13. Check master cylinder fluid level, filling as necessary.
14. Check brake pedal for proper feel and return.
15. Drive vehicle and make 10-15 forward and reverse stops until satisfactory brake pedal height is obtained.

## 1984-85 SCRAMBLER, 1984-86 CJ, 1984-89 CHEROKEE & WAGONEER, 1986-89 COMANCHE & 1987-89 WRANGLER

### REMOVAL

1. Raise and support vehicle.
2. Remove wheel and tire assemblies, then the brake drums.
3. Install suitable clamps over ends of wheel cylinders.
4. Remove U-clip and washer (1) from parking brake lever pivot pin, **Fig. 2,**

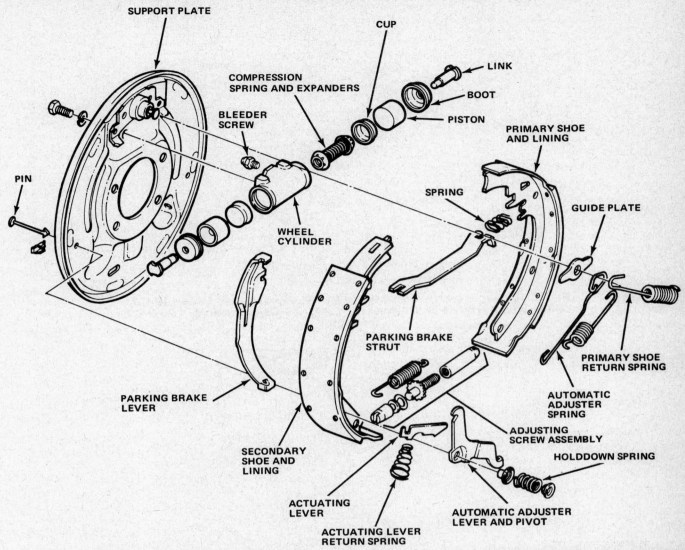

**Fig. 1 Drum brake assembly. 1980–83 Cherokee & Wagoneer; 1984–89 Grand Wagoneer; All J-10 & J-20**

and discard clip.

5. Using suitable tool, remove primary and secondary return springs (2).
6. Remove spring retainers, hold-down springs, and retaining pins (8).
7. Remove adjuster lever, adjuster screw, and spring (4) from brake shoes (5).
8. Remove brake shoes.

## INSTALLATION

1. Using suitable lubricant, lubricate support plate ledges, anchor pins, adjuster cable guides, adjuster screw and pivot, and parking brake lever and lever pivot pin.
2. Attach parking brake lever (6) to secondary brake shoe and secure with washer and new U-clip.
3. Remove clamps from wheel cylinders.
4. Install brake shoes and secure with hold-down springs, pins, and retainers.

5. Install parking brake lever strut and spring (7).
6. Install guide plate and adjuster cable (8) on anchor pin (9).
7. Install primary and secondary return springs with cable guide.
8. Install adjuster screw, spring, and lever, then connect adjuster cable at adjuster lever.
9. If any hydraulic lines were opened, bleed brake system.
10. Install drums.
11. Install wheel and tire assemblies, and lower vehicle.
12. Check master cylinder fluid level, filling as necessary.
13. Check brake pedal for proper feel and return, then road test vehicle.

## 1980–83 CJ & SCRAMBLER
### REMOVAL

1. Raise and support vehicle.

2. Remove wheel and tire assemblies, then the brake drums. If brake lining is dragging on drum, back off brake adjustment by rotating adjustment screw.
3. Using suitable pliers, grasp adjusting lever and remove lever tang from hole in secondary shoe, **Fig. 3.**
4. Place suitable clamp over ends of wheel cylinder.
5. Remove brake return springs.
6. Remove secondary return spring, adjuster cable, primary return spring, cable guide, adjuster lever, and adjuster springs.
7. Remove hold down springs and brake shoes.
8. On rear brake shoes, disengage parking brake cable from parking brake lever.

## INSTALLATION

1. Using suitable lubricant, lubricate

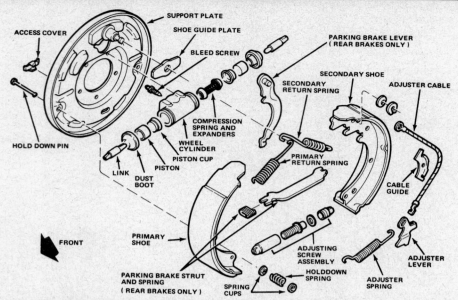

**Fig. 2   Drum brake assembly. 1984–85 Scrambler, 1984–86 CJ, 1984–89 Cherokee & Wagoneer, 1986–89 Comanche & 1987–89 Wrangler**

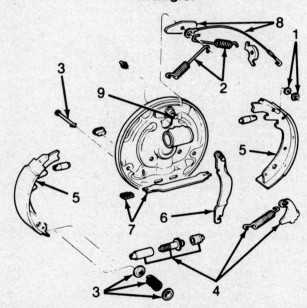

**Fig. 3   Drum brake assembly. 1980–83 CJ & Scrambler**

support plate edges, anchor pin, self-adjusting cable guide adjuster screw threads, pivot, and parking brake cable lever.

2. Position brake shoes on support plate and install hold down springs.
3. On rear brakes, install parking brake lever, then the parking brake cable on lever, and install strut and spring.
4. Install adjuster cable end on anchor pin.
5. Install primary return spring.
6. Install cable guide and secondary return spring.
7. Install adjusting screw assembly, then place small hooked end of adjuster spring in large hole in primary shoe and large hooked end in adjuster lever.
8. Place hooked end of adjuster cable over cable guide.
9. Using suitable pliers, grasp adjuster lever and hook adjuster lever tang in large hole in bottom of secondary shoe.
10. Set adjusting screws so that approximately 8/8 inch of thread is exposed between adjuster screw and adjuster

screw nut.
11. Install drums.
12. If any hydraulic lines were opened, bleed brake system.
13. Install wheel and tire assemblies and lower vehicle.
14. Check master cylinder fluid level, filling as necessary.
15. Check brake pedal for proper feel and return.
16. Drive vehicle in reverse and forward, making 10 to 15 brake applications, alternating forward and reverse stops, then road test vehicle.

# UNIVERSAL JOINTS

## INDEX

---

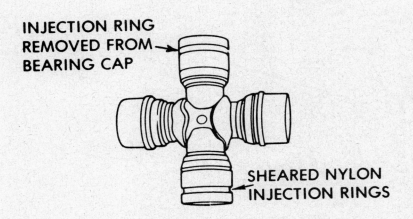

**Fig. 1   Production type universal joints which use nylon injection rings in place of snap rings**

INJECTION RING REMOVED FROM BEARING CAP

SHEARED NYLON INJECTION RINGS

BEARING CAP

SNAP RING

FLAT DELRIN WASHER

SPIDER

ROUND DELRIN WASHER

NEEDLE BEARING

SEAL

SHIELD

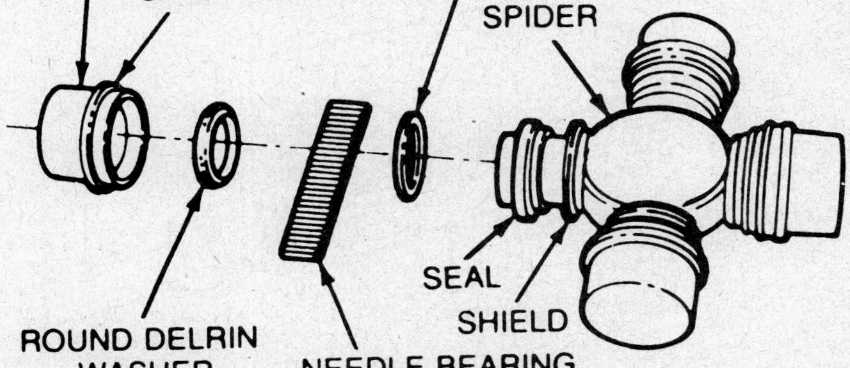

**Fig. 2   Service type universal joints (internal snap ring type)**

## SERVICE NOTES

Before disassembling any universal joint, examine the assembly carefully and note the position of the grease fitting (if used). Also, be sure to mark the yokes with relation to the propeller shaft so they may be reassembled in the same relative position. Failure to observe these precautions may produce rough vehicle operation which results in rapid wear and failure of parts, and place an unbalanced load on transmission, engine and rear axle.

When universal joints are disassembled for lubrication or inspection, and the old parts are to be reinstalled, special care must be exercised to avoid damage to universal joint spider or cross and bearing cups.

Some driveshafts use an injected nylon retainer on the universal joint bearings. When service is necessary, pressing the bearings out will sheer the nylon retainer, **Fig. 1.** Replacement with the conventional steel snap ring type is then necessary, **Fig. 2.**

## CROSS & ROLLER (SINGLE CARDAN) TYPE

**Figs. 3 and 4** illustrate typical examples of universal joints of this type. They all operate on the same principle and similar service and replacement procedures may be applied to all.

### SERVICING WITHOUT UNIVERSAL JOINT REPLACEMENT TOOL

#### Disassembly

1. Remove snap rings (or retainer plates) that retain bearings in yoke and drive shaft.
2. Place U-joint in a vise.
3. Select a wrench socket with an outside diameter slightly smaller than the U-joint bearings. Select another wrench socket with an inside diameter slightly larger than the U-joint bearings.
4. Place the sockets at opposite bearings in the yoke so that the smaller socket becomes a bearing pusher and the larger socket becomes a

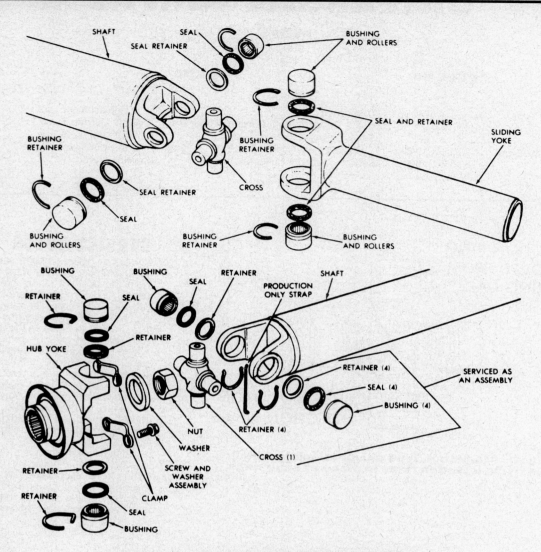

**Fig. 3  Cross & roller type universal joints**

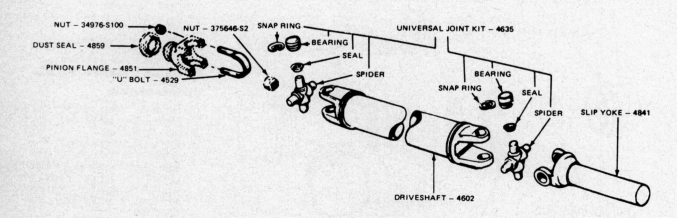

**Fig. 4  Cross & roller type universal joints & propeller shaft**

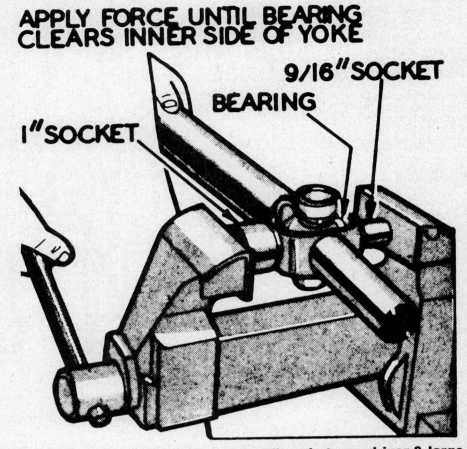

**APPLY FORCE UNTIL BEARING CLEARS INNER SIDE OF YOKE**

**9/16" SOCKET**

**BEARING**

**1" SOCKET**

**Fig. 5  Removing bearings from yoke using a small socket as a driver & large socket as a receiver**

bearing receiver when the vise jaws come together, **Fig. 5.** Close vise jaws until both bearings are free of yoke and remove bearings from the cross or spider.

5. If bearings will not come all the way out, close vise until bearing in receiver socket protrudes from yoke as much as possible without using excessive force. Then remove from vise and place that portion of bearing which protrudes from yoke between vise jaws. Tighten vise to hold bearing and drive yoke off with a soft hammer.

6. To remove opposite bearing from yoke, replace in vise with pusher socket on exposed cross journal with receiver socket over bearing cup. Then tighten vise jaws to press bearing back through yoke into receiving socket.

7. Remove yoke from drive shaft and again place protruding portion of bearing between vise jaws. Then tighten vise to hold bearing while driving yoke off bearing with soft hammer.

8. Turn spider or cross 1/4 turn and use the same procedure to press bearings out of drive shaft.

## Assembly

1. If old parts are to be reassembled, pack bearing cups with universal joint grease. Do not fill cups completely or use excessive amounts as over lubrication may damage seals during reassembly. Use new seals.

2. If new parts are being installed, check new bearings for adequate grease before assembling.

3. With the pusher (smaller) socket, press one bearing part way into drive shaft. Position spider into the partially installed bearing. Place second bearing into drive shaft. Fasten drive shaft in vise so that bearings are in contact with faces of vise jaws, **Fig. 6.** Some spiders are provided with locating lugs which must face toward drive shaft when installed.

4. Press bearings all the way into position and install snap rings or retainer plates.

5. Install bearings in yoke in same manner. When installation is completed, check U-joint for binding or roughness. If free movement is impeded, correct the condition before installation in vehicle.

## SERVICING USING UNIVERSAL JOINT REPLACEMENT TOOL

### Disassembly

1. Place driveshaft in a vise using care to avoid damaging it.

2. Remove bearing retaining snap rings. **Some universal joints use injected nylon retainers in place of snap rings. During servicing, the snap rings supplied with the replacement universal joint assembly must be used.**

3. Position tool on shaft and press bearing out of yoke, **Fig. 7.** If bearing cannot be pressed all the way out, remove it using vise grips or channel lock pliers or position driveshaft as shown and strike center yoke with hammer, **Fig. 8.** Mark yoke and shaft to make sure they will be reassembled in their same relative positions.

4. Reposition tool so that it presses on the spider in order to press other bearing from opposite side of flange.

5. If used, remove flange from spider.

## Assembly

1. Start new bearing into yoke, then position spider into yoke and press bearing until it is 1/4 inch below surface.
2. Remove tool and install a new snap ring.
3. Start new bearing in opposite side of yoke, then install tool and press on bearing until opposite bearing contacts snap ring.
4. Remove tool and install remaining snap ring.

## CONSTANT VELOCITY TYPE

This type of universal joint, **Fig. 9**, consists of two conventional cross and roller joints connected with a special link yoke. Because the two joint angles are the same, even though the usual universal joint fluctuation is present within the unit, the acceleration of the front joint (within the yoke) is always neutralized by the deceleration of the rear joint (within the yoke) and vice versa. The end result is the front and rear propeller shafts always turn at a constant velocity.

## DISASSEMBLY

### Constant Velocity Joint

To disassemble the constant velocity joint, the bearings should be removed in sequence shown in **Fig. 10**. This method requires the least amount of work.

1. Mark all yokes before disassembly as shown in **Fig. 11**, so that they can be reassembled in their original relationship to maintain driveshaft balance. The following procedure can be performed in a vise and a cross press tool, **Fig. 12**, can be used in place of the socket used to drive the bearings.
2. Support the driveshaft horizontally in line with the base plate of a press. Place rear end of coupling yoke over a 1 1/8 inch socket to accept the bearing. Place a socket slightly smaller than the bearing on the opposite side of the spider.
3. Press bearing cup out of coupling yoke ear. If bearing cup is not completely removed, insert spacer C-4365-4 or equivalent, **Fig. 13**, and complete removal of bearing cup.
4. Rotate driveshaft 180° and shear the opposite retaining ring, and press the bearing cup out of the coupling yoke as described previously, using spacer C-4365-4 or equivalent.
5. Disengage cross trunnions, still attached to flange yoke, from coupling yoke. Pull flange yoke and cross from centering ball on ball support tube yoke. The ball socket is part of the flange yoke. **The ball on some joints is not replaceable. The joints with a replaceable ball can be recognized as shown in Fig. 14. Do not attempt to remove solid ball, as removal tool may be damaged.**
6. Pry seal from ball cavity, then remove washers, spring and shoes, **Fig. 15**.

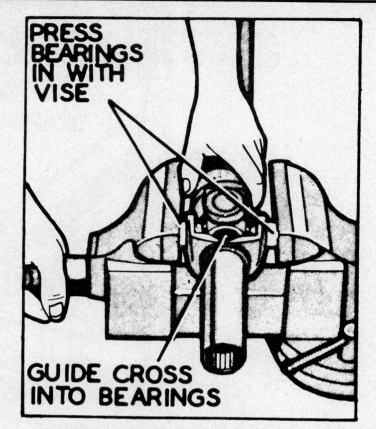

**Fig. 6   Installing bearings into driveshaft yoke**

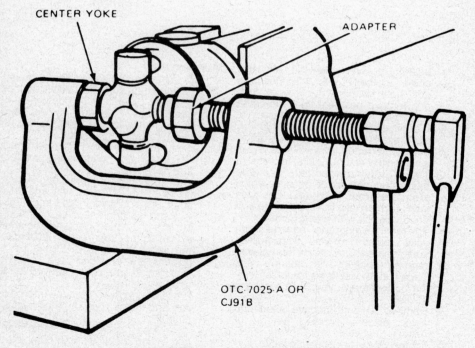

**Fig. 7   Removing bearing caps using tool & adapter**

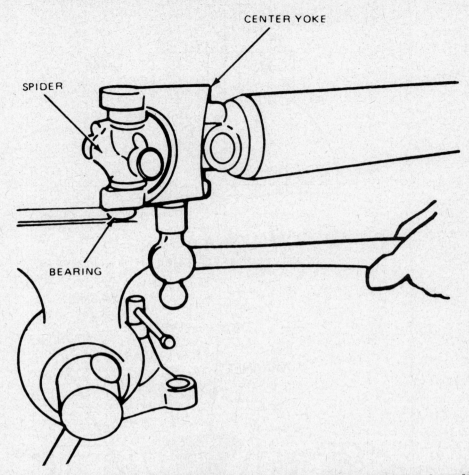

**Fig. 8  Removing bearing cap by holding cap in vise & striking center yoke with hammer**

## Ball Socket

1. To remove ball, separate universal joint between coupling yoke and flange yoke by pressing out trunnion bearing in coupling yoke. Pull flange yoke and cross with ball socket from centering ball as a unit.
2. Clean and inspect ball seat insert bushing for wear. If worn, replace flange yoke and cross assembly.
3. Pry seal from ball cavity, then remove washers, spring and ball seats.
4. Clean and inspect centering ball surface, seal, ball seats, spring and washer. If parts are worn or broken, replace with a service kit.
5. Remove centering ball as shown in **Fig. 16,** using components of tool C-4365 or equivalent. Install components as shown, and draw ball off ball stud.

## ASSEMBLY
### Ball Socket & Constant Velocity Joint

During assembly, make sure that marks made during disassembly, **Fig. 11,** are aligned to maintain balance.

1. To install centering ball onto stud, use tool C-4365 or equivalent, and drive ball until it can be seen that ball has seated firmly against shoulder at base of stud.
2. To install cross assembly, install one bearing cup part way into one side of yoke and turn this yoke to the bottom. Insert cross into yoke so that the trunnion seats into bearing, **Fig. 17.** Install opposite bearing cup part way, **Fig. 18.** Make sure that both cross journals are started straight into both bearing cups.
3. Press bearing cups, while moving cross to ensure free movement of trunnions in bearing. If any binding is felt, stop pressing and check needle bearings to make sure that needle bearings have not been trapped under the ends of the cross journals.
4. As soon as one of the retaining ring grooves clears the inside of yoke, stop pressing and install retaining ring.
5. Continue to press until opposite retaining ring can be snapped into place. If difficulty is encountered, strike the yoke firmly in locations shown in **Figs. 19, 20 and 21,** to spring the yoke ears slightly.
6. Lubricate center ball and socket, and assemble other half universal joint, if disassembled.

## LUBRICATION

Lubrication of the constant velocity joints should not be overlooked during the regular service intervals recommended by the manufacturer. During lubrication, use only the type of lubricant recommended by the manufacturer. This lubricant is usually lithium type chassis grease.

Lubrication fitting adapters and locations of the lubrication fittings are shown in **Figs. 22, 23 and 24.**

## DOUBLE CARDAN TYPE

The double cardan type joint incorporates two universal joints, a centering socket yoke, and center yoke at one end of the shaft. A single universal joint is used at the other end.

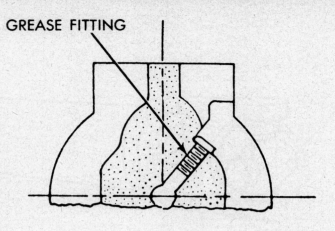

GREASE FITTING

SECTION A-A
THRU GREASE FITTING

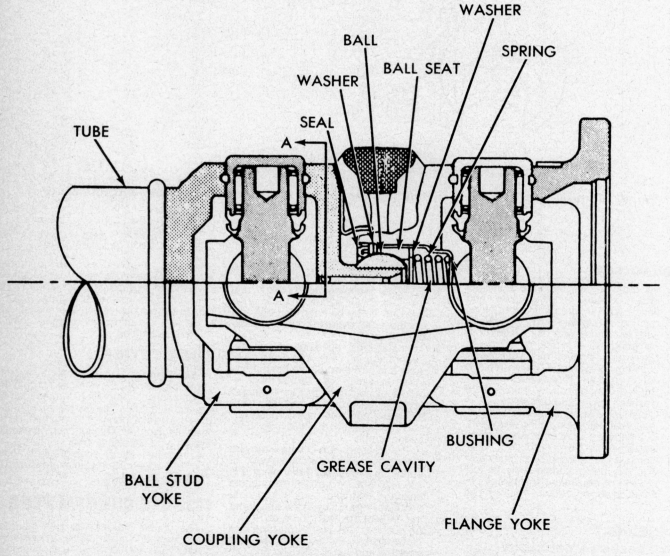

WASHER

BALL

BALL SEAT

SPRING

WASHER

SEAL

TUBE

A

A

BUSHING

GREASE CAVITY

BALL STUD
YOKE

FLANGE YOKE

COUPLING YOKE

**Fig. 9   Constant velocity (CV) universal joint**

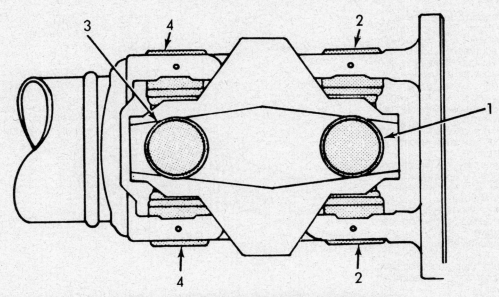

**Fig. 10   Bearing cap removal sequence**

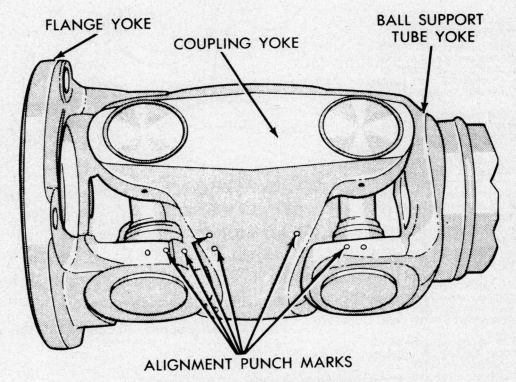

FLANGE YOKE

COUPLING YOKE

BALL SUPPORT
TUBE YOKE

ALIGNMENT PUNCH MARKS

**Fig. 11   Alignment punch marks**

## DISASSEMBLY

1. Remove all bearing cap retainers.
2. Mark bearing caps, spiders, propeller shaft yoke, link yoke and socket yoke for assembly alignment reference.
3. Remove bearing caps attaching front spider to link yoke as follows:
   a. Use a 5/8 inch socket to drive the bearing cap and a 1 1/16 inch socket to receive the opposite bearing cap as it is driven out.
   b. Place 5/8 inch socket on one bearing cap and 1 1/16 inch socket on opposite bearing.
   c. Position assembly in vise so vise jaws bear directly against sockets.
   d. Tighten vise to press first bearing cap out of link yoke.
   e. Loosen vise, reposition sockets and press opposite bearing cap out of link yoke.
4. Disengage propeller shaft yoke from link yoke.
5. Remove bearing caps attaching front spider to propeller shaft as described in step 3 above.
6. Remove front spider from yoke.
7. Remove bearing caps attaching rear spider to link yoke as outlined in step 3 above and remove spider and socket yoke from link yoke.
8. Clean all parts in solvent and wipe dry. Inspect assembly for damage or wear. If any component is worn or damaged, the entire assembly must be replaced.

## ASSEMBLY

When assembling universal joint, make sure to align spiders and yokes according to marks made during disassembly.

1. Lubricate all bearings and contact surfaces with lithium base chassis grease.
2. Install bearing caps on yoke ends of rear spider and secure caps with tape.
3. Assemble socket yoke and rear spider.
4. Position rear spider in link yoke and install bearing caps. Press caps into yoke using 5/8 inch socket until bearing cap retainer grooves are exposed.
5. Install rear spider-to-link yoke bearing cap retainers.
6. Position front spider in propeller shaft yoke and install bearing caps. Press caps into yoke using a 5/8 inch socket until bearing cap retainer grooves are exposed.
7. Install front spider-to-propeller shaft yoke bearing cap retainers.
8. Install thrust washer and socket spring in ball socket bearing bore, if removed.
9. Install thrust washer on ball socket bearing boss (located on propeller shaft yoke), if removed.
10. Align ball socket bearing boss on propeller shaft yoke with ball socket bearing bore and insert boss into bore.
11. Align front spider with link yoke bear-

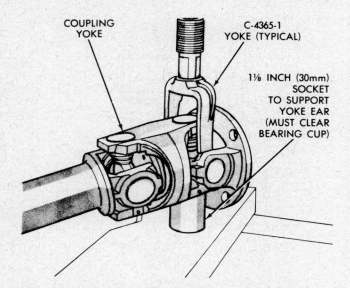

**Fig. 12 Cross press being used in place of socket**

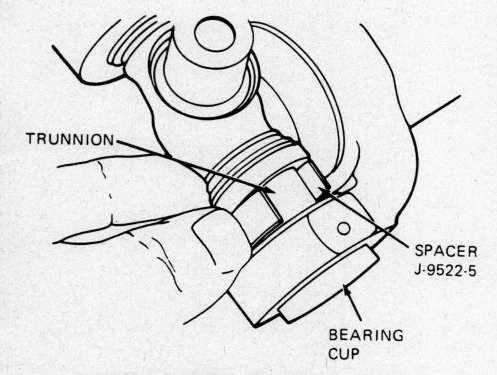

**Fig. 13 Using spacer to completely drive out bearing**

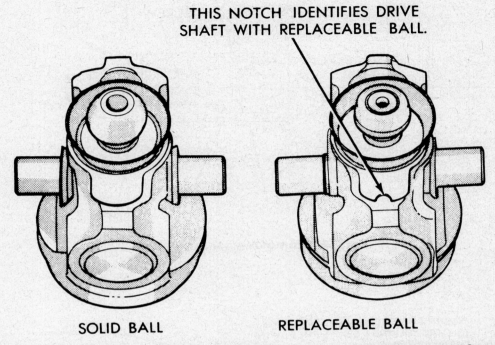

THIS NOTCH IDENTIFIES DRIVE
SHAFT WITH REPLACEABLE BALL.

SOLID BALL          REPLACEABLE BALL

**Fig. 14   Solid ball & replaceable balls. Notch identifies driveshaft w/replaceable ball**

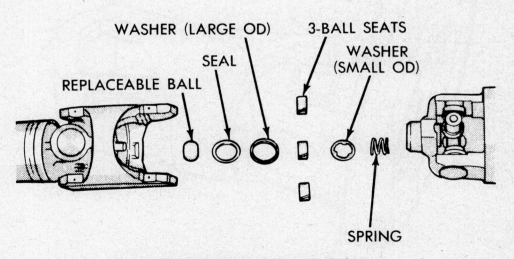

WASHER (LARGE OD)     3-BALL SEATS

SEAL          WASHER
              (SMALL OD)

REPLACEABLE BALL

SPRING

**Fig. 15   Ball & seat exploded view**

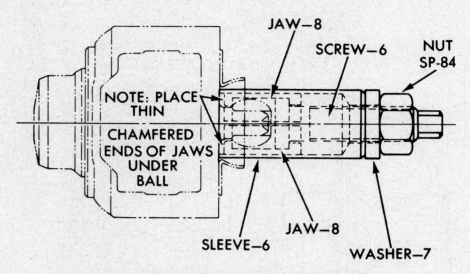

JAW—8

SCREW—6

NUT SP-84

NOTE: PLACE THIN

CHAMFERED ENDS OF JAWS UNDER BALL

SLEEVE—6

JAW—8

WASHER—7

**Fig. 16   Removing centering ball**

INSERT THE SPIDER INTO THE YOKE SO THAT JOURNAL SEATS FREELY IN THE BEARING CUP.

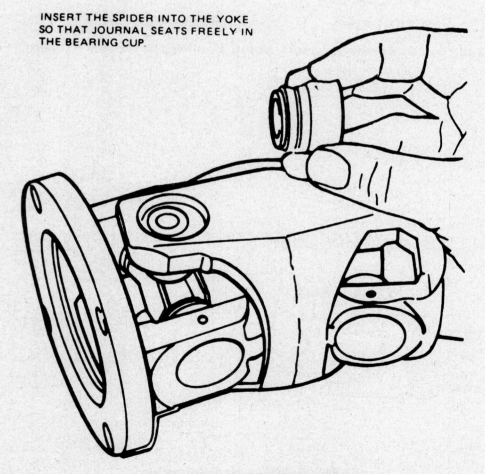

**Fig. 17   Inserting cross into yoke**

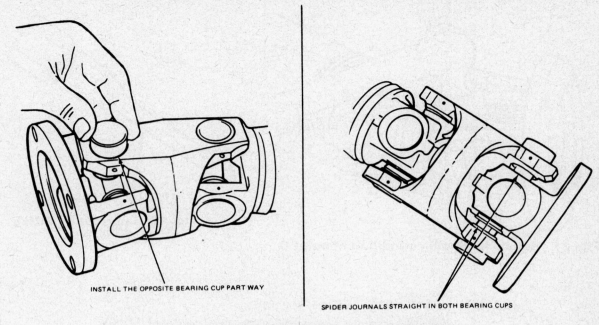

INSTALL THE OPPOSITE BEARING CUP PART WAY

SPIDER JOURNALS STRAIGHT IN BOTH BEARING CUPS

**Fig. 18   Aligning bearing cups & journals**

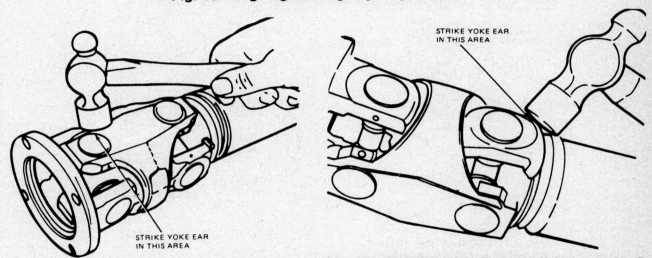

STRIKE YOKE EAR
IN THIS AREA

STRIKE YOKE EAR
IN THIS AREA

**Fig. 19   Relieving binding condition at point A**

**Fig. 20   Relieving binding condition at point B**

ing cap bores and install bearing caps. Press caps into yoke using a ⁵/₈ inch socket until bearing cap retainer grooves are exposed.

12. Install front spider-to-link yoke bearing cap retainers.

## BALL & TRUNNION TYPE

The ball and trunnion universal joint is a combination unit functioning as both a slip yoke and universal joint. It is used on some models on the transfer case end of the propeller shaft. A flange is used to connect one end while a conventional universal joint is used to connect the other.

### DISASSEMBLY

1. Straighten retainer plate lock tabs and remove plate and gasket from trunnion housing.
2. Cut and remove protective boot retaining straps.
3. Push trunnion housing and protective boot rearward to expose ball and trunnion assembly.
4. Remove trunnion cap and cap washer.
5. Remove trunnion ball, trunnion ball needle bearings and trunnion ball washer.
6. Remove trunnion pin from pin bore in shaft using an arbor press and suitable adapter.
7. Remove trunnion housing, protective boot and boot clip from shaft.
8. Clean all parts in solvent and wipe dry.

### ASSEMBLY

1. Lubricate shaft trunnion pin bore, trun-

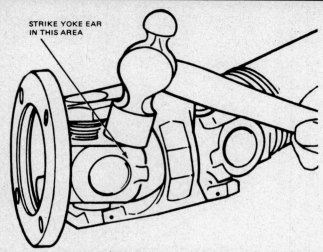

Fig. 21 Relieving binding condition at point C

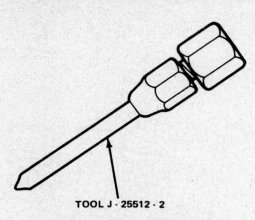

Fig. 22 Lubrication fitting adapter

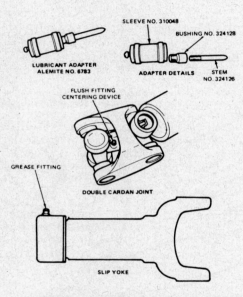

Fig. 23 Lubrication fitting adapter & fitting location

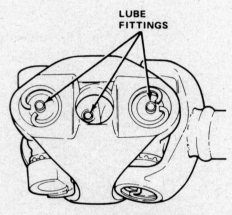

Fig. 24 Lubrication fitting locations

nion pin, trunnion ball and needle bearings and trunnion cap with chassis grease. Also, liberally apply grease to interior of trunnion housing.

2. Place boot clip on raised, semi-circular boss on shaft. Use rubber bands or string to retain clip during installation.

3. Install protective boot onto shaft and install one boot retaining strap. Make sure boot is seated on raised shaft boss and boot clip before installing strap. Also make sure strap is seated in strap groove in boot before tightening.

4. Install trunnion housing on shaft, then seat protective boot in housing and install remaining boot retaining strap. Make sure boot is fully seated in housing and strap is seated in strap groove in boot before tightening.

5. Place shaft in arbor press and start trunnion pin in bore. Carefully press pin into bore until pin is centered in shaft to within .006 inch. Pin must project an equal amount from each side of shaft pin bore. If pin is not centered within .006 inch, propeller shaft

vibration may result.

6. Install trunnion ball washer on pin and install trunnion ball and needle bearings on pin.

7. Install trunnion cap washer and trunnion cap on pin.

8. Move housing forward and over ball and trunnion assembly. Make sure assembly is properly and completely seated in housing.

9. Install gasket and plate on housing and bend plate lock tabs into housing slots to retain plate and gasket.

# AUTOMATIC TRANSMISSIONS/TRANSAXLES

## TABLE OF CONTENTS

# A-413, A-470 & A-670 Torqueflite Automatic Transaxles

## INDEX

## DESCRIPTION

These transaxles combine a torque converter, automatic 3 speed transmission, final drive gearing and differential combined into one unit. The torque converter, transaxle and differential assemblies are housed in an integral aluminum die cast housing, **Fig. 1.**

On 1982 models, the differential oil sump is separate from the transaxle pump. Be sure differential oil level is 1/8 to 3/8 inch below the oil filler hole on the differential cover. On 1983-89 models, the differential oil sump is integral with the transaxle sump, and separate filling of the differential is not necessary.

The torque converter is connected to the crankshaft through a flexible drive plate. Converter cooling is accomplished by an oil-to-water type cooler, located in the radiator side tank. The torque converter cannot be disassembled.

The transaxle consists of two multiple disc clutches, an overrunning clutch, two servos, an hydraulic accumulator, two bands and two planetary gear assemblies to provide three forward and one reverse gear. The sun gear is connected to the front clutch retainer. The hydraulic system consists of an oil pump, and a single valve body which contains all of the valves except the governor valves. Output torque from the main drive gears is transferred through helical gears to the transfer shaft. An integral ring gear on the transfer shaft drives the differential ring gear.

## TROUBLESHOOTING GUIDE

### HARSH ENGAGEMENT FROM N TO D OR R

1. High idle speed.
2. Defective or leaking valve body.
3. High hydraulic pressure.
4. Worn or damaged rear clutch.
5. Overrunning clutch inner race damaged.
6. Planetary gear sets seized or broken.
7. Insufficient clutch plate clearance.
8. Low-reverse band worn out.

### DELAYED ENGAGEMENT FROM N TO D OR R

1. Low hydraulic pressure.
2. Defective or leaking valve body.
3. Low-reverse servo, band or linkage malfunction.
4. Low fluid level.
5. Incorrect gearshift linkage adjustment.
6. Clogged transmission oil filter.
7. Faulty oil pump.
8. Worn or damaged input shaft seal rings.
9. Aerated fluid.
10. Low idle speed.
11. Worn or damaged reaction shaft support seal rings.
12. Worn or defective front clutch.
13. Worn or defective rear clutch.
14. Overrunning clutch inner race damaged.
15. Insufficient clutch plate clearance.

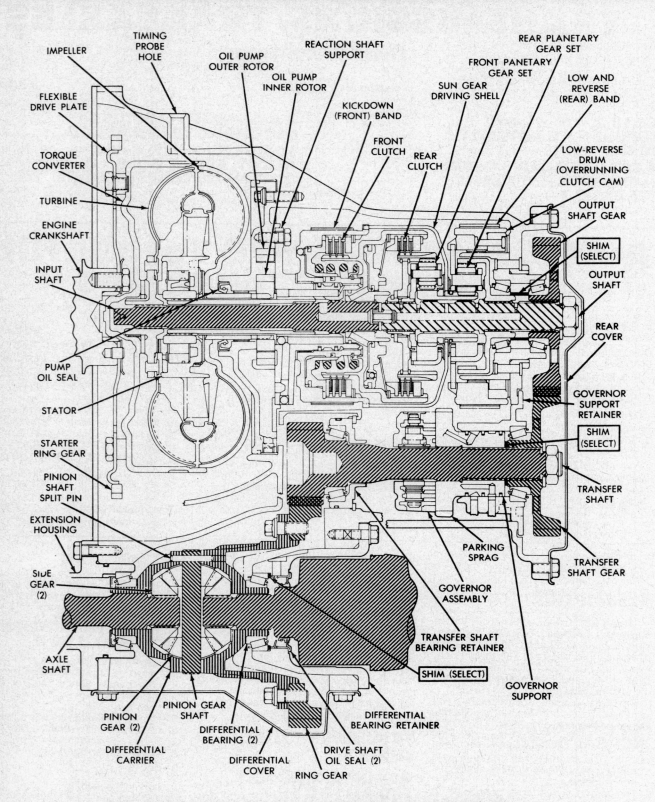

**Fig. 1  Sectional view of Torqueflite Automatic Transaxle**

16. Faulty cooling system.
17. High hydraulic pressure.
18. Governor malfunction.

## RUNAWAY UPSHIFTS

1. Low hydraulic pressure.
2. Defective or leaking valve body.
3. Low fluid level.
4. Clogged transmission oil filter.
5. Aerated fluid.
6. Incorrect throttle linkage adjustment.
7. Worn or damaged reaction shaft support seal rings.
8. Kickdown servo, band or linkage malfunction.
9. Worn or faulty front clutch.
10. Insufficient clutch plate clearance.
11. High fluid level.
12. Governor malfunction.
13. Governor support seal rings worn or broken.
14. Input shaft seal rings worn or broken.
15. Faulty oil pump.

## NO UPSHIFT

1. Low hydraulic pressure.
2. Defective or leaking valve body.
3. Low fluid level.
4. Incorrect gearshift linkage adjustment.
5. Incorrect throttle linkage adjustment.
6. Worn or damaged governor support seal rings.
7. Faulty governor.
8. Kickdown servo, band or linkage malfunction.
9. Worn or faulty front clutch.
10. Rear clutch dragging.
11. Insufficient clutch plate clearance.
12. High hydraulic pressure.
13. Aerated fluid.
14. Input shaft seals worn or broken.
15. Faulty oil pump.

## 3-2 KICKDOWN RUNAWAY

1. Low hydraulic pressure.
2. Defective or leaking valve body.
3. Low fluid level.
4. Aerated fluid.
5. Incorrect throttle linkage adjustment.
6. Kickdown band adjustment.
7. Worn or damaged reaction shaft support seal rings.
8. Kickdown servo, band or linkage malfunction.
9. Worn or faulty front clutch.
10. Rear clutch dragging.
11. Insufficient clutch plate clearance.
12. Governor malfunction.
13. Drive shaft(s) bushing(s) damaged.
14. Input shaft seal rings worn or broken.
15. Faulty oil pump.

## NO KICKDOWN OR NORMAL DOWNSHIFT

1. Defective or leaking valve body.
2. Incorrect throttle linkage adjustment.
3. Faulty governor.
4. Kickdown servo, band or linkage malfunction.
5. Insufficient clutch plate clearance.
6. Governor support seal rings worn or broken.
7. Aerated fluid.
8. Input shaft seal rings worn or broken.

## ERRATIC SHIFTS

1. Low hydraulic pressure.
2. Defective or leaking valve body.
3. Low fluid level.
4. Incorrect gearshift linkage adjustment.
5. Clogged transmission oil filter.
6. Faulty oil pump.
7. Aerated fluid.
8. Incorrect throttle linkage adjustment.
9. Worn or damaged governor support seal rings.
10. Worn or damaged reaction shaft support seal rings.
11. Faulty governor.
12. Kickdown servo, band or linkage malfunction.
13. Worn or faulty front clutch.
14. Rear clutch dragging.
15. Insufficient clutch plate clearance.
16. High hydraulic pressure.
17. High fluid level.
18. Governor support seal rings worn or broken.
19. Input shaft seal rings worn or broken.

## SLIPS IN 1, 2 OR D

1. Low hydraulic pressure.
2. Defective or leaking valve body.
3. Low fluid level.
4. Incorrect gearshift linkage adjustment.
5. Clogged transmission oil filter.
6. Faulty oil pump.
7. Worn or damaged input shaft seal rings.
8. Aerated fluid.
9. Incorrect throttle linkage adjustment.
10. Overrunning clutch not holding.
11. Worn or faulty rear clutch.
12. Overrunning clutch worn, damaged or seized.
13. Insufficient clutch plate clearance.
14. Kickdown band adjustment too tight.
15. High hydraulic pressure.
16. High fluid level.
17. Worn or faulty front clutch.
18. Kickdown servo band or linkage malfunction.
19. Governor malfunction.
20. Governor support seal rings worn or broken.
21. Low-reverse bands worn or broken.
22. Stuck switch valve.

## SLIPS IN R ONLY

1. Low hydraulic pressure.
2. Low-reverse band adjustment.
3. Defective or leaking valve body.
4. Low-reverse servo, band or linkage malfunction.
5. Low fluid level.
6. Incorrect gearshift linkage adjustment.
7. Faulty oil pump.
8. Aerated fluid.
9. Worn or damaged reaction shaft seal rings.
10. Worn or faulty front clutch.
11. Overrunning clutch inner race damaged.
12. Rear clutch dragging.
13. Worn or faulty rear clutch.
14. Faulty cooling system.
15. Kickdown band adjustment too tight.
16. High hydraulic pressure.
17. Governor malfunction.

## SLIPS IN ALL RANGES

1. Low hydraulic pressure.
2. Defective or leaking valve body.
3. Low fluid level.
4. Clogged transmission oil filter.
5. Faulty oil pump.
6. Worn or damaged input shaft seal rings.
7. Aerated fluid.
8. Rear clutch dragging.
9. Kickdown band adjustment too tight.
10. High fluid level.
11. Worn or faulty front clutch.
12. Governor malfunction.

## NO DRIVE IN ANY RANGE

1. Low hydraulic pressure.
2. Defective or leaking valve body.
3. Low fluid level.
4. Clogged transmission oil filter.
5. Faulty oil pump.
6. Planetary gear sets damaged or seized.
7. Rear clutch dragging.
8. Kickdown band adjustment too tight.
9. High fluid level.
10. Worn or faulty front clutch.
11. Engine idle speed too high.

## NO DRIVE IN 1, 2 OR D

1. Low hydraulic pressure.
2. Defective or leaking valve body.
3. Low fluid level.
4. Worn or damaged input shaft seal rings.
5. Overrunning clutch not holding.
6. Worn or faulty rear clutch.
7. Planetary gear sets damaged or seized.
8. Overrunning clutch worn, damaged or seized.
9. Rear clutch dragging.
10. Kickdown band adjustment too tight.
11. Low-reverse band worn out.
12. Engine idle speed too high.
13. Stuck switch valve.

## NO DRIVE IN R

1. Low hydraulic pressure.
2. Low-reverse band adjustment.
3. Defective or leaking valve body.
4. Low-reverse servo, band or linkage malfunction.
5. Incorrect gearshift linkage adjustment.
6. Worn or damaged reaction shaft support seal rings.
7. Worn or faulty front clutch.
8. Worn or faulty rear clutch.
9. Planetary gear sets damaged or seized.
10. Rear clutch dragging.
11. Faulty cooling system.
12. High hydraulic pressure.
13. Faulty oil pump.

## DRIVE IN NEUTRAL

1. Defective or leaking valve body.
2. Incorrect gearshift linkage adjustment.
3. Insufficient clutch plate clearance.
4. Worn or faulty rear clutch.
5. Rear clutch dragging.
6. Hydraulic pressure to high.
7. Low-reverse band worn out.
8. Hydraulic pressure too low.

## DRAGS OR LOCKS

1. Low-reverse band adjustment.
2. Kickdown band adjustment.
3. Planetary gear sets damaged or seized.
4. Overrunning clutch worn, damaged or seized.
5. Worn or faulty rear clutch.
6. Low fluid level.
7. Engine idle speed too high.
8. Stuck switch valve.

## HARD TO FILL (OIL BLOWS OUT FILLER TUBE)

1. Clogged transmission oil filter.
2. Aerated fluid.
3. High fluid level.
4. Breather clogged.
5. Governor malfunction.

## TRANSMISSION OVERHEATS

1. Stuck switch valve.
2. High idle speed.
3. Low hydraulic pressure.
4. Low fluid level.
5. Incorrect gearshift adjustment.
6. Faulty oil pump.
7. Kickdown band adjustment too tight.
8. Faulty cooling system.
9. Insufficient clutch plate clearance.
10. Overrunning clutch worn, broken or seized.
11. Planetary gear sets broken or seized.
12. Rear clutch dragging.
13. High hydraulic pressure.
14. Worn or faulty front clutch.
15. Low-reverse servo, band or linkage malfunction.
16. Defective or leaking valve body.

## HARSH UPSHIFTS

1. Low hydraulic pressure.
2. Incorrect throttle linkage adjustment.
3. Kickdown band adjustment.
4. High hydraulic pressure.
5. Rear clutch dragging.
6. Governor support seal rings worn or broken.
7. Drive shaft(s) bushing(s) damaged.

## DELAYED UPSHIFT

1. Incorrect throttle linkage adjustment.
2. Kickdown band adjustment.
3. Worn or damaged governor support seal rings.
4. Worn or damaged reaction shaft support seal rings.
5. Faulty governor.
6. Kickdown servo, band or linkage malfunction.
7. Worn or faulty front clutch.
8. Drive shaft(s) bushing(s) damaged.
9. Aerated fluid.
10. Faulty oil pump.

## GRATING, SCRAPING OR GROWLING NOISE

1. Low-reverse band out of adjustment.
2. Kickdown band adjustment.
3. Output shaft bearing or bushing damaged.

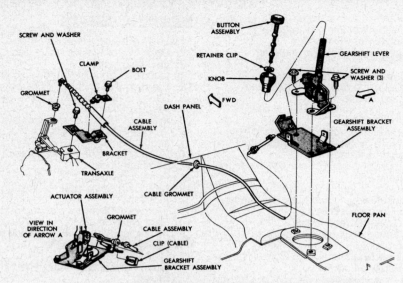

**Fig. 2   Gearshift linkage. Rampage & Scamp**

4. Planetary gear sets damaged or seized.
5. Overrunning clutch worn or damaged or seized.
6. Worn or faulty rear clutch.
7. Stuck switch valve.

## BUZZING NOISE

1. Defective or leaking valve body.
2. Low fluid level.
3. Aerated fluid.
4. Overrunning clutch inner race damaged.
5. Insufficient clutch plate clearance.
6. Kickdown band adjustment too tight.
7. Faulty governor.
8. Low-reverse band incorrectly adjusted.

## NO LOCK-UP

1. Stuck switch valve.
2. Low hydraulic pressure.
3. Defective or leaking valve body.
4. Low fluid level.
5. Faulty oil pump.
6. Worn or broken input shaft seal rings.
7. Aerated fluid.

## MAINTENANCE
### ADDING OIL

To check fluid level, apply the parking brake and operate engine at idle speed with transmission in Neutral or Park position. Add fluid as necessary.

### CHANGING OIL

Fluid and filter changes are not required for average vehicle use. Severe usage such as commercial type usage or prolonged operation in city traffic requires that fluid be changed and bands adjusted every 15,000 miles.

Whenever factory fill fluid is changed, only fluid of the type labeled Dexron II should be used.

1. Raise vehicle and place a suitable drain pan under transmission oil pan.
2. Loosen transmission oil pan attaching bolts and allow fluid to drain, then remove oil pan.
3. Replace oil filter and adjust bands, if necessary, and install oil pan and gasket.
4. Add four quarts of approved automatic transmission fluid through the filler tube.
5. Start engine and allow to idle for approximately six minutes, then with parking brake applied, move selector lever momentarily to each position. Place selector lever in Neutral or Park and check fluid level. Add fluid to bring level to Add mark.
6. Recheck fluid level after transmission has reached operating temperature. The level should be between Add and Full marks.

## IN-VEHICLE ADJUSTMENTS
### SHIFT LINKAGE, ADJUST
#### Rampage, Scamp & Mini Vans

When linkage cable must be disconnected from levers which use plastic grommets as retainers, the grommets must be replaced.

1. Place selector lever into "P" position.
2. Pull shift lever, **Figs. 2 and 3** to front detent (Park) position, then loosen cable attaching bolt.
3. While maintaining pressure on shift lever, torque attaching bolt to 90 inch lbs. on Rampage and Scamp models and 105 inch lbs. on Mini Vans.
4. Check adjustment.

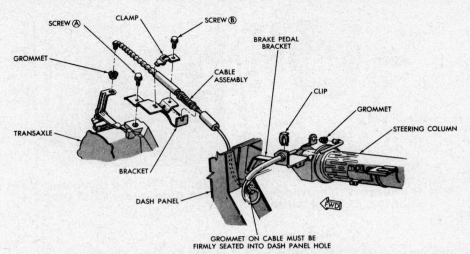

Fig. 3  Gearshift linkage. Ram Van, Caravan & Voyager Mini Van models

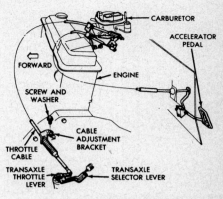

Fig. 4  Throttle cable linkage (Typical)

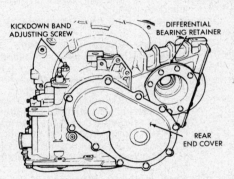

Fig. 5  Kickdown band adjusting screw location

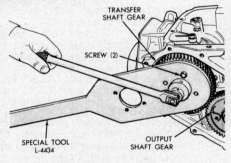

Fig. 6  Loosening transfer shaft gear retaining nut

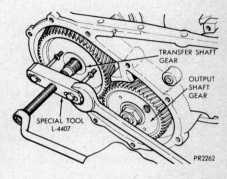

Fig. 7  Removing transfer shaft gear

## THROTTLE CABLE, ADJUST

1. Perform adjustment with engine at operating temperature, otherwise ensure carburetor is not on fast idle cam by disconnecting choke.
2. Loosen adjusting bracket lock screw, **Fig. 4.**
3. Hold transmission lever rearward against internal stop and tighten adjusting bracket lock screw to 105 inch lbs.

## KICKDOWN BAND, ADJUST

1. Loosen locknut and back off nut approximately 5 turns, **Fig. 5.**
2. Using tool No. C-3380-A and C-3705, torque band adjusting screw to 47-50 inch lbs. If tool No. C-3705 is not used, torque adjusting screw to 72 inch lbs.
3. On 1982-83 models, back off adjusting screw 2¾ turns. On 1984-89 models, back off adjusting screw 2½ turns.
4. Hold adjusting screw in this position and tighten locknut to 35 ft. lbs.

## LOW-REVERSE BAND, ADJUST

1. Loosen, then back off locknut approxi-

mately 5 turns.
2. Torque adjusting screw to 41 inch lbs.
3. Back off adjusting screw 3½ turns and torque locknut to 10 ft. lbs.

## IN-VEHICLE REPAIRS
### VALVE BODY, REPLACE

1. Loosen transmission oil pan attaching bolts and allow transmission to drain, then remove oil pan.
2. Remove oil filter attaching screws and oil filter.
3. Remove E-clip using a screwdriver, then remove parking rod.
4. Remove seven valve body attaching bolts, valve body and governor oil tubes.
5. Reverse procedure to install. Torque valve body attaching bolts to 40 inch lbs.

### GOVERNOR & TRANSFER SHAFT OIL SEAL, REPLACE

1. Remove rear cover attaching bolts and rear cover.
2. Using tool No. L-4434, remove transfer shaft gear retaining nut, **Fig. 6.**
3. Using tool No. L-4407, remove trans-

fer shaft gear and shim, **Fig. 7.**
4. Remove governor support retainer, then low-reverse band anchor pin.
5. Remove governor assembly.
6. Remove transfer shaft retainer snap ring. Using tool No. L-4512 and a suitable puller, remove transfer shaft and retainer assembly.
7. Remove transfer shaft retainer from shaft.
8. Using a screwdriver, remove oil seal from transfer shaft retainer.
9. Using tools Nos. L-4520 and C-4171, press oil seal into shaft retainer, **Fig. 8.**
10. Reverse procedure to install. Torque transfer shaft gear retaining nut to 200 ft. lbs.

## TRANSAXLE
### REPLACE

The transaxle and converter must be removed as an assembly.

### RAMPAGE & SCAMP

1. Disconnect battery ground cable.
2. Disconnect transaxle shift control and

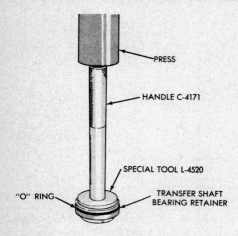

**Fig. 8  Installing oil seal into shaft retainer**

**Fig. 9  Removing speedometer adapter, cable & pinion**

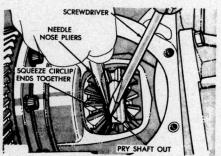

**Fig. 10  Prying drive shaft out of side gear. 1982 models**

throttle cables from transaxle and position aside.

3. On 1982 models, disconnect upper oil cooler hose. On 1983–84 models, disconnect both upper and lower oil cooler hoses.
4. On all models, support engine with suitable engine lifting equipment.
5. Remove upper bellhousing bolts.
6. Raise and support vehicle, then remove front wheels and left splash shield.
7. On 1982 models, remove differential cover.
8. On all models, remove speedometer adapter, cable and pinion as an assembly, **Fig. 9.**
9. Remove sway bar and both lower ball joint to steering knuckle bolts, then, using a suitable pry bar, remove lower ball joint.
10. Remove drive shaft from hub.
11. On 1982 models, rotate both drive shafts until circlip ends are visible. Compress circlip and pry drive shaft out of side gear, **Fig. 10.**
12. On all models, remove both drive shafts.
13. Remove dust cover, then mark position of torque converter on drive plate

and remove torque converter mounting bolts. Remove plug from access hole in right splash shield to rotate crankcase for bolt removal.
14. Disconnect Neutral/Park safety switch electrical connector and, on 1982 models, disconnect lower oil cooler hose.
15. Remove engine mount bracket from front crossmember, front mount insulator through-bolt and remaining bellhousing bolts.
16. Support transaxle with a suitable jack.
17. Remove left side engine mount.
18. Move transaxle away from engine and lower from vehicle. It may be necessary to pry transaxle away from engine between extension housing and engine block for proper clearance.
19. Reverse procedure to install. When installing differential cover on 1982 models, apply a 1/8 inch bead of RTV sealant to cover.

## MINI VANS

1. Disconnect battery ground cable.
2. Disconnect throttle linkage and shift control linkage from transaxle.
3. Remove both upper and lower oil

cooler hoses.
4. Support engine with suitable engine lifting equipment.
5. Remove bellhousing upper attaching bolts.
6. Raise and support vehicle, then remove front wheels and left splash shield.
7. Remove wheel hub nut and driveshafts.
8. Remove torque converter dust cover, then mark torque converter and drive plate for reference during reassembly.
9. Remove torque converter attaching bolts. Remove plug from access hole in right splash shield to rotate crankcase for bolt removal.
10. Remove Neutral/Park switch electrical connector.
11. Remove engine mount bracket from rear crossmember, then the front mount insulator through bolt and attaching bolts.
12. Position suitable jack under transaxle, then remove left engine mount.
13. Remove starter, then the remaining bellhousing attaching bolts.
14. Move transaxle away from engine and lower from vehicle.
15. Reverse procedure to install.

# Ultradrive A-604 4-Speed Electronic Automatic Transmission

## INDEX

## DESCRIPTION

The A-604 Ultradrive electronic four speed transaxle is a fully adaptive transmission using feedback sensors to adjust functions on a real time basis, similar to electronic antilock brake controls.

The A-604 transaxle provides four forward speeds with ratios of 2.84:1, 1.57:1, 1.00:1 and .069:1, and with torque converter lockup available in second, direct, or overdrive gear. Reverse ratio is 2.21:1. The A-604, **Fig. 1**, consists of three multiple disc input clutches, two multiple disc grounded clutches, four hydraulic accumulators and two planetary gear sets to provide four forward speeds and reverse ratio. Electrical solenoids provide the transmissions shifting control. Sensors on the transmission send control inputs to the electronic control unit located under the hood in a potted, diecast aluminum housing. The system can be diagnosed by accessing information from the electronic control unit memory. The transmission and differential sump have a common oil sump with a communicating opening between the two.

## TROUBLESHOOTING

Before attempting any repair on the A-604 EAT, general engine performance, transmission fluid level and shift linkage must first be checked and adjusted if necessary. For specific symptom diagnosis, refer to **Figs. 2, 3 and 4**.

## MAINTENANCE
### ADDING OIL

Oil level should be checked every six months. To check oil level, start engine and let idle with transaxle in park or neutral for at least one minute. Oil level, when properly filled, will read near the "Add" mark when oil is cold, (70°F), and in the "Hot" zone when oil is at normal operating temperature (180°F). Add as necessary.

### CHANGING OIL

Fluid and filter changes are not required for average passenger vehicle usage. If the vehicle is subjected to severe usage, the fluid and filter should be changed at 15,000 mile intervals. The magnet on the inside of the oil pan should also be cleaned with a clean, dry cloth at this time. Fluid and filter change procedure is as follows:

1. Raise vehicle on a suitable hoist and place a wide drain pan container under transaxle oil pan.
2. Loosen pan bolts and tap pan at one corner to break seal and allow fluid to drain, then remove pan.
3. Install new filter and O-ring an bottom of valve body, then clean the oil pan and magnet.
4. Reinstall pan using RTV sealant and torque pan bolts to 165 inch lbs.
5. Add four quarts of MOPAR ATF PLUS type 7176 fluid or DEXRON II through the fill tube.
6. Start engine and allow to idle for at least one minute, then with parking and service brakes applied, move selector lever through it's range, pausing momentarily at each position. Return lever to park or neutral position.
7. Add fluid to bring level 1/8 inch below the "Add" mark. Recheck fluid level after transaxle is at normal operating temperature.

## IN-VEHICLE ADJUSTMENTS
### GEARSHIFT LINKAGE ADJUSTMENT

When it is necessary to disassemble linkage cable from levers, plastic grommet retainers should always be replaced with new grommets.
1. Place gearshift lever in Park position, then loosen clamp bolt on gearshift cable bracket.
2. Column shift models should ensure that preload adjustment spring engages fork on transaxle bracket.
3. Pull the shift lever by hand all the way to the front detent position (Park) and torque lock screw to 100 inch lbs.

## IN-VEHICLE REPAIRS
### SPEEDOMETER PINION GEAR
### REPLACE

1. Remove bolt and washer assembly securing speedometer pinion adapter in the extension housing, then with cable housing connected, carefully work adapter and pinion out of the extension housing.
2. Remove the retainer and pinion from the adapter.
3. If transmission fluid is found in cable housing, install a new speedometer pinion and seal assembly.
4. If transmission fluid is found leaking between the cable and adapter, replace the small O-ring on the cable. Remove the adapter from the cable and replace the O-ring.
5. Clean adapter flange and mating surfaces and install the adapter on the cable, then install pinion on adapter with new large O-ring and install retainer on pinion and adapter. Be sure retainer is properly seated.
6. Install bolt and washer and torque to 60 inch lbs.

## TRANSAXLE REPLACE

1. Disconnect battery ground cable.
2. Disconnect throttle linkage and shift control linkage from transaxle.
3. Remove both upper and lower oil cooler hoses.
4. Support engine with suitable engine lifting equipment.
5. Remove bellhousing upper attaching bolts.
6. Raise and support vehicle, then remove front wheels and left splash shield.
7. Remove wheel hub nut and driveshafts.
8. Remove torque converter dust cover, then mark torque converter and drive plate for reference during reassembly.
9. Remove torque converter attaching bolts. Remove plug from access hole in right splash shield to rotate crankcase for bolt removal.
10. Remove Neutral/Park switch electrical connector.
11. Remove engine mount bracket from rear crossmember, then the front mount insulator through bolt and attaching bolts.
12. Position suitable jack under transaxle, then remove left engine mount.
13. Remove starter, then the remaining bellhousing attaching bolts.
14. Move transaxle away from engine and lower from vehicle.
15. Reverse procedure to install.

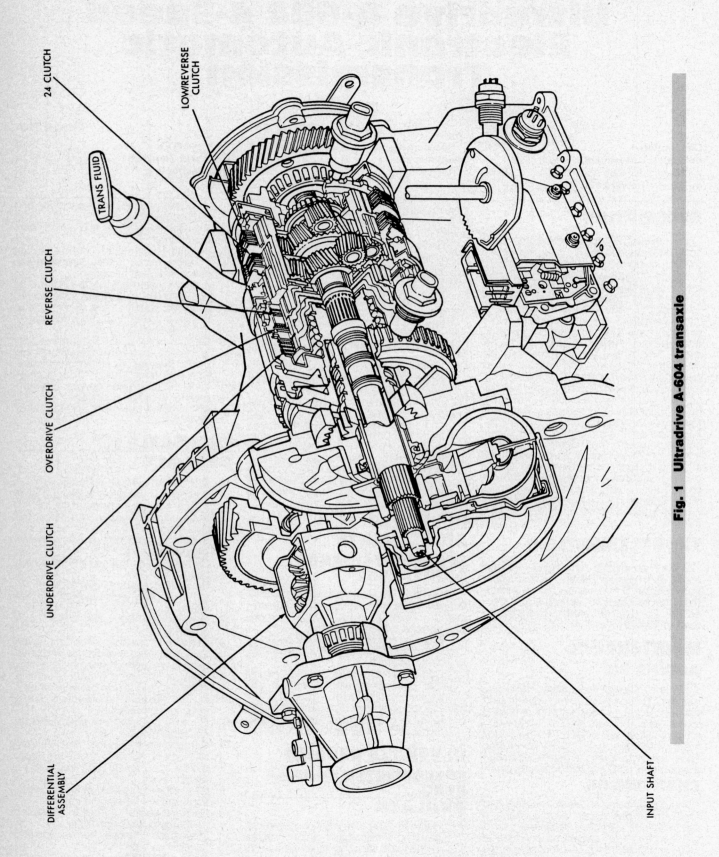

24 CLUTCH

LOW/REVERSE CLUTCH

TRANS FLUID

REVERSE CLUTCH

OVERDRIVE CLUTCH

UNDERDRIVE CLUTCH

DIFFERENTIAL ASSEMBLY

INPUT SHAFT

**Fig. 1  Ultradrive A-604 transaxle**

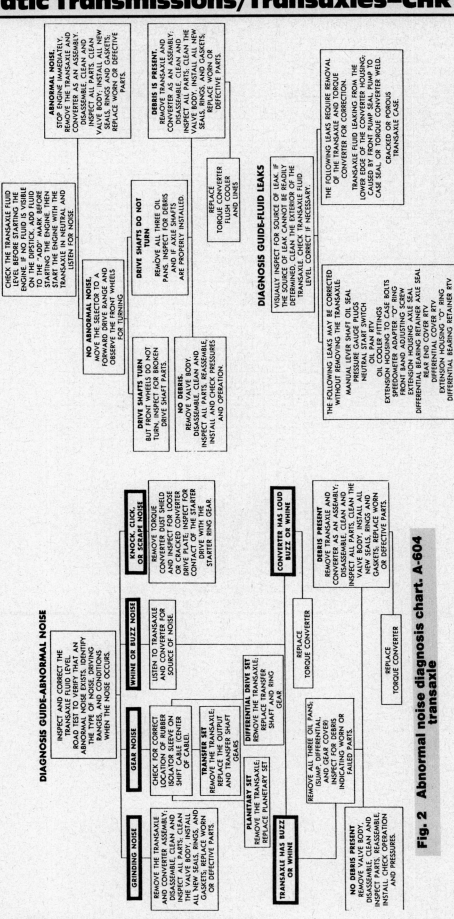

**Fig. 3  Vehicle will not move diagnosis chart. A-604 transaxle**

**Fig. 2  Abnormal noise diagnosis chart. A-604 transaxle**

DIAGNOSIS CHART "B"

| POSSIBLE CAUSE | Harsh Engagement From Neutral to D | R | Delayed Engagement From Neutral to D | R | Poor Shift Quality | Shifts Erratic | Drives in Neutral | Drags or Locks | Grating, Scraping, Growling Noise | Knocking, Noise | Buzzing Noise | Buzzing Noise During Shifts Only | Hard to Fill, Oil Blows Out Filler Tube | Transaxle Overheats | Harsh Upshift | No Upshift Into Overdrive | No Lockup | Harsh Downshifts | High Shift Efforts | Harsh Lockup Shift |
|---|---|---|---|---|---|---|---|---|---|---|---|---|---|---|---|---|---|---|---|---|
| Engine Performance | X | X | | | X | | | | | | | | | | X | | | X | | |
| Worn or faulty clutch(es) | X | X | X | X | X | X | X | | | | | | | | X | X | | X | | |
| —Underdrive clutch | X | | X | | X | X | X | | | | | | | | | | | X | | |
| —Overdrive clutch | | | | | X | X | X | | | | | | | | X | X | | | | |
| —Reverse clutch | | X | | X | | X | X | | | | | | | | | | | | | |
| —2/4 clutch | | | | | X | | X | | | | | | | | X | | | X | | |
| —Low/reverse clutch | X | X | | | X | | | | | | | | | | | | | X | | |
| Clutch(es) dragging | | | | | | X | | | | | | | | | | | | | | |
| Insufficient clutch plate clearance | | | | | | X | | | | | | | | X | | | | | | |
| Damaged clutch seals | | | X | X | | | | | | | | | | | | | | X | | |
| Worn or damaged accumulator seal ring(s) | X | X | X | X | | | | | | | | | | | | | | X | | |
| Faulty cooling system | | | | | | | | | | | | | | X | | | | | | |
| Engine coolant temp. too low | | | | | | | | | | | | | | | | X | X | | | |
| Incorrect gearshift control linkage adjustment | | | X | X | X | X | | | | | | | | X | | | | | | |
| Shift linkage damaged | | | | | | | | | | | | | | | | | | | X | |
| Chipped or damaged gear teeth | | | | | | | | | X | X | | | | | | | | | | |
| Planetary gear sets broken or seized | | | | | | | | | X | X | | | | | | | | | | |
| Bearings worn or damaged | | | | | | | | | X | X | | | | | | | | | | |
| Driveshaft(s) bushing(s) worn or damaged | | | | | | | | | X | | | | | | | | | | | |
| Worn or broken reaction shaft support seal rings | | | X | X | X | X | | | | | | | | | | | | X | | |
| Worn or damaged input shaft seal rings | | | X | X | | | | | | | | | | | | | X | | | |
| Valve body malfunction or leakage | X | X | X | X | X | X | X | | | X | | | | | | | | X | X | X |
| Hydraulic pressures too low | | | X | X | X | X | | | | | | | | | X | X | | X | | |
| Hydraulic pressures too high | X | X | | | | | | | | | | | | | | X | | | | |
| Faulty oil pump | | | X | X | X | | | | | | | | | | X | | | X | | |
| Oil filter clogged | | | X | X | X | X | | | | X | | | | | | | | | | |
| Low fluid level | | | X | X | X | X | | | | X | | | | | X | | | X | X | |
| High fluid level | | | | | | | | | | | | | | X | X | | | | | |
| Aerated fluid | | | X | X | X | X | | | | X | | | | X | X | | | X | X | |
| Engine idle speed too low | | | X | X | | | | | | | | | | | | | | | | |
| Engine idle speed too high | X | X | | | | | | | | | | | | | X | | | X | | |
| Normal solenoid operation | | | | | | | | | | | X | | | | | | | | | |
| Solenoid sound cover loose | | | | | | | | | | | X | | | | | | | | | |
| Sticking lockup piston | | | | | | | | | | | | | | | | | | | | X |

**Fig. 4   Symptom diagnosis chart. A-604 transaxle**

# Loadflite Automatic Transmission

## INDEX

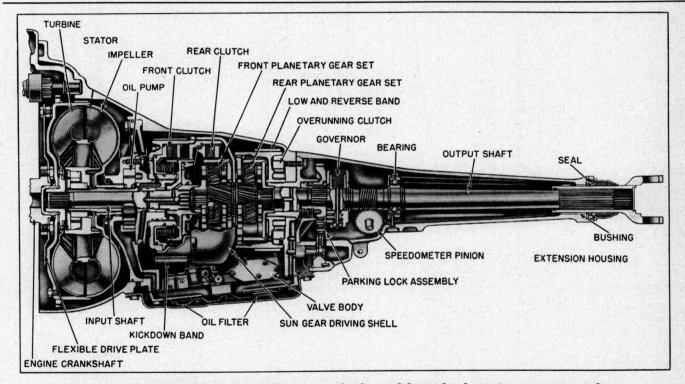

**Fig. 1   Loadflite 727 automatic transmission without lock-up torque converter**

## DESCRIPTION

These transmissions, **Figs. 1 through 3** combine a torque converter with a fully automatic three speed gear system. The converter housing and transmission case are an integral aluminum casting. **The 998 and 999 transmission is similar in appearance and operation to the 904 transmission. The service procedures for both transmissions are the same as the 904 transmission. The transmission** consists of two multiple disc clutches, an overrunning (one-way) clutch, two servos and bands and two planetary gear sets to provide three forward speeds and reverse, **Fig. 4.**

The common sun gear of the planetary gear sets is connected to the front clutch by a driving shell that is splined to the sun gear and to the front clutch retainer.

All A-904T, A-998 and A-999 transmissions, **Fig. 5**, are equipped with a wide ratio gear set. Low gear ratio is 2.74 to 1. The sun gear and front planetary gear set is unique to the wide ratio transmission.

The hydraulic system consists of a single oil pump and a valve body that contains all the valves except the governor valve.

Venting of the transmission is accomplished by a drilled passage through the upper part of the front pump housing.

The torque converter is attached to the engine crankshaft through a flexible driving plate. The converter is cooled by circu-

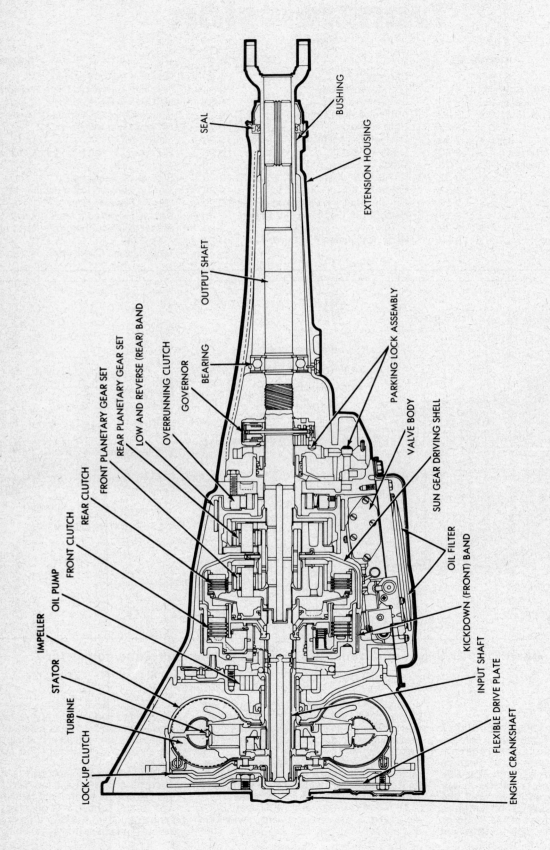

**Fig. 2 Loadflite 727 automatic transmission with lock-up torque converter**

SEAL

BUSHING

EXTENSION HOUSING

OUTPUT SHAFT

PARKING LOCK ASSEMBLY

GOVERNOR

BEARING

OVERRUNNING CLUTCH

LOW AND REVERSE (REAR) BAND

REAR PLANETARY GEAR SET

FRONT PLANETARY GEAR SET

REAR CLUTCH

FRONT CLUTCH

OIL PUMP

IMPELLER

STATOR

TURBINE

LOCK-UP CLUTCH

VALVE BODY

SUN GEAR DRIVING SHELL

OIL FILTER

KICKDOWN (FRONT) BAND

INPUT SHAFT

FLEXIBLE DRIVE PLATE

ENGINE CRANKSHAFT

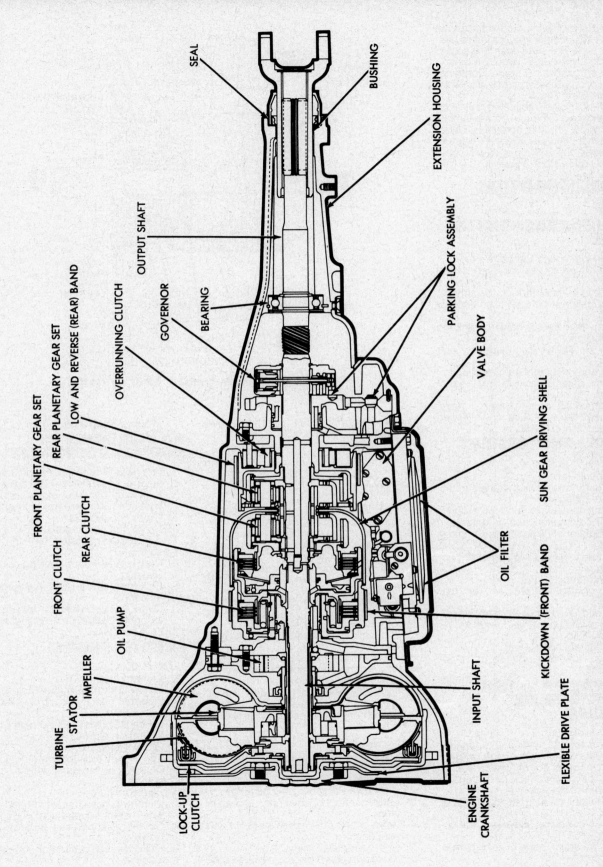

**Fig. 3 Loadflite A-904T, A-998 & A-999 automatic transmission with lock-up torque converter**

lating the transmission fluid through an oil-to-water type cooler located in the radiator lower tank. The converter is a sealed assembly that cannot be disassembled.

A lock-up clutch (torque converter clutch) is incorporated in some transmission applications, **Fig. 6.**

The lock-up mode is activated only in direct drive above a minimum preset vehicle speed. At wider throttle openings, where the 2-3 upshift occurs above the minimum lock-up speed, the lock-up shift will occur immediately after the 2-3 upshift.

# TROUBLESHOOTING GUIDE

## HARSH ENGAGEMENT IN D-1-2-R

1. Engine idle speed too high.
2. Hydraulic pressures too high or too low.
3. Low-reverse band out of adjustment.
4. Accumulator sticking, broken rings or spring.
5. Low-reverse servo, band or linkage malfunction.
6. Worn or faulty front and/or rear clutch.
7. Valve body malfunction or leakage.
8. Throttle linkage sticking or incorrect adjustment.
9. Accumulator broken seal rings, scratched bore, broken or collapsed spring, cracked piston.

## DELAYED ENGAGEMENT IN D-1-2-R

1. Lower fluid level.
2. Incorrect manual linkage adjustment.
3. Oil filter clogged.
4. Hydraulic pressures too high or low.
5. Valve body malfunction or leakage.
6. Accumulator sticking, broken rings or spring.
7. Clutches or servos sticking or not operating.
8. Faulty front oil pump.
9. Worn or faulty front and/or rear clutch.
10. Worn or broken input shaft and/or reaction shaft support seal rings.
11. Aerated fluid.
12. Incorrect idle adjustment.
13. Incorrect low and reverse band adjustment.

## RUNAWAY OR HARSH UPSHIFT AND 3-2 KICKDOWN

1. Low fluid level.
2. Incorrect throttle linkage adjustment.
3. Hydraulic pressures too high or low.
4. Kickdown band out of adjustment.
5. Valve body malfunction or leakage.
6. Governor malfunction.
7. Accumulator sticking, broken rings or spring.
8. Clutches or servos sticking or not operating.
9. Kickdown servo, band or linkage malfunction.
10. Worn or faulty front clutch.

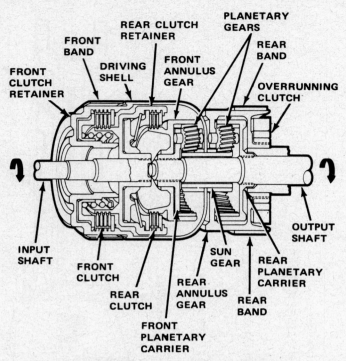

**Fig. 4   Clutch, band & gear system**

11. Worn or broken input shaft and/or reaction shaft support seal rings.
12. Aerated oil.
13. Clogged oil filter.

## NO UPSHIFT

1. Low fluid level.
2. Incorrect throttle linkage adjustment.
3. Kickdown band out of adjustment.
4. Hydraulic pressures too high or low.
5. Governor sticking.
6. Valve body malfunction or leakage.
7. Accumulator sticking, broken rings or spring.
8. Clutches or servos sticking or not operating.
9. Faulty oil pump.
10. Kickdown servo, band or linkage malfunction.
11. Worn or faulty front clutch.
12. Worn or broken input shaft and/or reaction shaft support seal rings.
13. Incorrect gear shift linkage adjustment.
14. Governor support seal rings broken or worn.

## DELAYED UPSHIFT

1. Incorrect throttle linkage adjustment.
2. Kickdown band out of adjustment.
3. Governor support seal rings broken or worn.
4. Worn or broken reaction shaft support seal rings.
5. Governor malfunction.
6. Kickdown servo band or linkage malfunction.

7. Worn or faulty front clutch.

## NO KICKDOWN OR NORMAL DOWNSHIFT

1. Incorrect throttle linkage adjustment.
2. Incorrect gearshift linkage adjustment.
3. Kickdown band out of adjustment.
4. Hydraulic pressure too high or low.
5. Governor sticking.
6. Valve body malfunction or leakage.
7. Accumulator sticking, broken rings or spring.
8. Clutches or servos sticking or not operating.
9. Kickdown servo, band or linkage malfunction.
10. Overrunning clutch not holding.
11. Incorrect control cable adjustment.
12. Low fluid level.

## ERRATIC SHIFTS

1. Low fluid level.
2. Aerated fluid.
3. Incorrect throttle linkage adjustment.
4. Incorrect gearshift control linkage adjustment.
5. Hydraulic pressures too high or low.
6. Governor sticking.
7. Oil filter clogged.
8. Valve body malfunction or leakage.
9. Clutches or servos sticking or not operating.
10. Faulty oil pump.
11. Worn or broken input shaft and/or reaction shaft support seal rings.
12. Governor support seal rings broken or worn.
13. Kickdown servo band or linkage malfunction.
14. Worn or faulty front clutch.

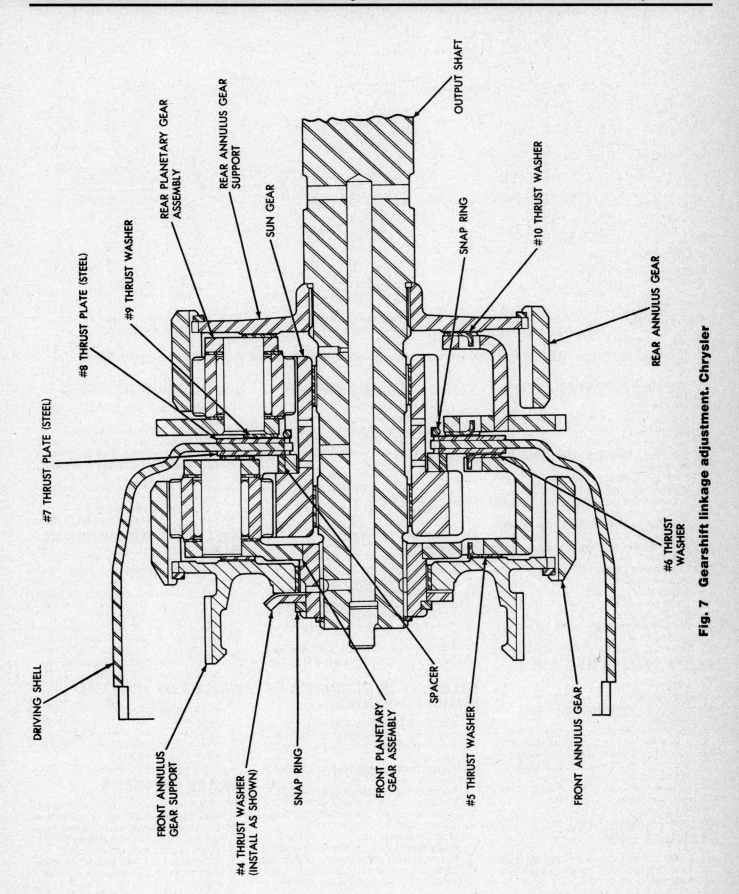

**Fig. 7 Gearshift linkage adjustment. Chrysler**

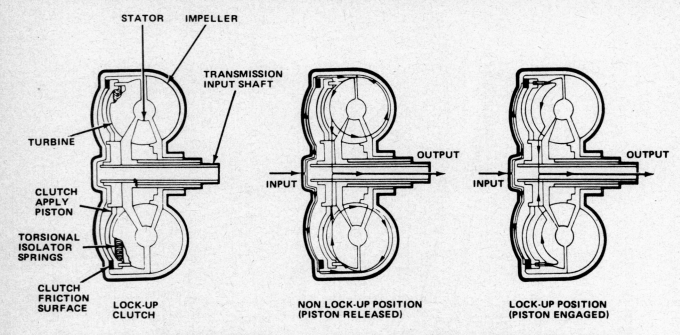

**Fig. 5 Wide ratio planetary gear set used on A-904T, A-998 & A-999 transmissions**

## SLIPS IN FORWARD DRIVE POSITIONS

1. Low oil level.
2. Aerated fluid.
3. Incorrect throttle linkage adjustment.
4. Incorrect gearshift control linkage adjustment.
5. Hydraulic pressures too low.
6. Valve body malfunction or leakage.
7. Accumulator sticking, broken rings or spring.
8. Clutches or servos sticking or not operating.
9. Worn or faulty front and/or rear clutch.
10. Overrunning clutch not holding.
11. Worn or broken input shaft and/or reaction shaft support seal rings.
12. Clogged oil filter.
13. Faulty oil pump.
14. Overrunning clutch worn, broken or seized.
15. Incorrect kickdown band adjustment.

## SLIPS IN REVERSE ONLY

1. Low fluid level.
2. Aerated fluid.
3. Incorrect gearshift control linkage adjustment.
4. Hydraulic pressures too high or low.
5. Low-reverse band out of adjustment.
6. Valve body malfunction or leakage.
7. Front clutch or rear servo sticking or not operating.
8. Low-reverse servo, band or linkage malfunction.
9. Faulty oil pump.

## SLIPS IN REVERSE OR MANUAL LOW

1. Low reverse band out of adjustment.
2. Incorrect gearshift control linkage adjustment.

## SLIPS IN ALL POSITIONS

1. Low fluid level.
2. Hydraulic pressures too low.
3. Valve body malfunction or leakage.
4. Faulty oil pump.
5. Clutches or servos sticking or not operating.
6. Worn or broken input shaft and/or reaction shaft support seal rings.
7. Oil filter clogged.
8. Aerated oil.

## NO DRIVE IN ANY POSITION

1. Low fluid level.
2. Hydraulic pressures too low.
3. Oil filter clogged.
4. Valve body malfunction or leakage.
5. Faulty oil pump.
6. Clutches or servos sticking or not operating.
7. Planetary gear sets broken or seized.
8. Incorrect gearshift linkage adjustment.

## NO DRIVE IN FORWARD DRIVE POSITIONS

1. Hydraulic pressures too low.
2. Valve body malfunction or leakage.
3. Accumulator sticking, broken rings or spring.
4. Clutches or servos, sticking or not operating.
5. Worn or faulty rear clutch.
6. Overrunning clutch not holding.
7. Worn or broken input shaft and/or reaction shaft support seal rings.
8. Low fluid level.
9. Planetary gear sets broken or seized.
10. Overrunning clutch worn, broken or seized.
11. Incorrect gearshift linkage adjustment.

## NO DRIVE IN REVERSE

1. Incorrect gearshift control linkage adjustment.
2. Hydraulic pressures too low.
3. Low-reverse band out of adjustment.
4. Valve body malfunction or leakage.
5. Front clutch or rear servo sticking or not operating.
6. Low-reverse servo, band or linkage malfunction.
7. Worn or faulty front clutch.
8. Planetary gear sets broken or seized.

## NO LOW GEAR MOVES IN D-2

1. Governor valve; burrs, nicks, scores or binding on weights, shaft and valve.Collapsed or distorted springs or distorted snap ring. Cracked or warped body. Dirty filter.
2. Valve body; nicks, scratches and burrs on valves and plugs. Rounded edges on valve lands. Scratches on bores, collapsed springs. Nicked or warped mating surfaces.

## DRIVES IN NEUTRAL

1. Incorrect gearshift control linkage adjustment.
2. Incorrect control cable adjustment.
3. Valve body malfunction or leakage.
4. Rear clutch inoperative.
5. Insufficient clutch plate clearance.

## DRAGS OR LOCKS

1. Kickdown band out of adjustment.
2. Low-reverse band out of adjustment.
3. Kickdown and/or low-reverse servo, band or linkage malfunction.
4. Front and/or rear clutch faulty.
5. Planetary gear sets broken or seized.
6. Overrunning clutch worn, broken or seized.

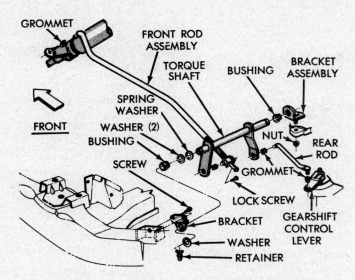

**Fig. 6  Lock-up torque converter operation**

7. Hydraulic pressures to low.
8. Valve body; nicks, scratches and burrs on valves and plugs. Rounded edges on valve lands. Scratches on bores, collapsed springs. Nicked or warped mating surfaces.
9. Accumulator, broken seal rings, scratched bore, broken or collapsed spring, cracked piston.

## GRATING, SCRAPING OR GROWLING NOISE

1. Kickdown band out of adjustment.
2. Low-reverse band out of adjustment.
3. Output shaft bearing and/or bushing damaged.
4. Governor support binding or broken seal rings.
5. Oil pump scored or binding.
6. Front and/or rear clutch faulty.
7. Planetary gear sets broken or seized.
8. Overrunning clutch worn, broken or seized.
9. Low fluid level.
10. Clogged oil filter.

## BUZZING NOISE

1. Low fluid level.
2. Pump sucking air.
3. Valve body malfunction.
4. Overrunning clutch inner race damaged.
5. Governor valve; burrs, nicks, scores or binding on weights, shaft and valve. Collapsed or distorted springs or distorted snap ring. Cracked or warped body. Dirty filter.
6. Linkage misadjusted.

## HARD TO FILL, OIL FLOWS OUT FILLER TUBE

1. High fluid level.
2. Breather clogged.
3. Oil filter clogged.
4. Aerated fluid.
5. Clogged lines to cooler.

## TRANSMISSION OVERHEATS

1. Low fluid level.
2. Kickdown band adjustment tight.
3. Low-reverse band adjustment too tight.
4. Faulty cooling system.
5. Cracked or restricted oil cooler line or fitting.
6. Faulty oil pump.
7. Insufficient clutch plate clearance in front and/or rear clutches.
8. Engine idle too low.
9. Hydraulic pressure too low.
10. Incorrect gearshift linkage adjustment.
11. Kickdown band adjustment too tight.
12. Clogged oil filter.
13. Valve body; nicks, scratches and burrs on valves and plugs. Rounded edges on valve lands. Scratches on bores, collapsed springs. Nicked or warped mating surfaces.

## STARTER WILL NOT ENERGIZE IN NEUTRAL OR PARK

1. Incorrect gearshift control linkage adjustment.
2. Faulty or incorrectly adjusted neutral starting switch.
3. Broken lead to neutral switch.
4. Incorrect control cable adjustment.

## MAINTENANCE

It has been determined that an occasional "no-drive" condition, generally occurring after making the first stop when a vehicle is cold can be caused by incorrect transmission fluid level. In cases where this condition is encountered, it is essential that the transmission fluid level be checked and corrected as outlined below.

If the no-drive condition still exists with the correct fluid level, the selector lever adjustment should be checked and/or adjusted as required.

After the above corrections have been accomplished and the no-drive condition still exists, it is suggested that the transmission be removed and the front pump disassembled for inspection before attempting any further repairs. Check pump inner rotor and front support for wear and/or damage, especially where the pinion rubs against the support.

## ADDING OIL

To check the oil level, apply the parking brake and operate the engine at idle speed. Move selector lever into each position ending in the neutral position. A properly filled transmission should read near the "add one pint" mark when the fluid temperature is 70° F, and near but not over the "full" mark at 180° F which is normal operating temperature. Then add oil as necessary to bring the oil to the prescribed level.

## CHANGING OIL

Oil should be changed every 24,000 miles. Vehicles that operate continuously with abnormal loads should have more frequent periodic maintenance. Transmission should not be idled in gear for long periods. When refilling, use only fluids labeled Dexron II.

1. Remove drain plug (if equipped) from transmission oil pan and allow oil to drain. **If the oil pan does not have a drain plug, loosen pan bolts and tap pan with a soft mallet to break it loose, permitting fluid to drain.**
2. Remove transmission oil pan, clean intake screen and pan, and reinstall.
3. Add 4 quarts of automatic transmission fluid through filler tube.
4. Start engine and add approximately one quart while engine is idling.
5. Allow engine to idle for about two minutes. Then with parking brake applied, select each range momentarily, ending with the "N" position.
6. Add oil as necessary to bring to proper level.

## IN-VEHICLE ADJUSTMENTS
### SHIFT LINKAGE, ADJUST
#### Chrysler

When linkage rod must be disconnected from levers which use plastic grommets as retainers, the grommets must be replaced.
1. Ensure adjustment swivel is free to turn on shift rod.
2. Place gearshift lever into Park position, Fig. 7.
3. With linkage assembled and adjustable swivel lock bolt loose, move transmission shift lever all the way to the rear detent (Park).
4. Tighten adjusting swivel lock bolt to 90 inch lbs.

#### Jeep

1. Loosen shift rod trunnion nuts.
2. Remove shift rod trunnion to bell

crank retaining lock pin, **Fig. 8,** then disconnect trunnion and shift rod assembly from bell crank.

3. Place gearshift lever into Park position, then lock steering column.
4. Move valve body manual lever rearward into Park.
5. Check for positive engagement of park lock by attempting to rotate drive shaft.
6. Adjust shift rod trunnion to obtain free pin fit in bell crank arm and tighten trunnion nuts. **On vehicles equipped with column shift, all gearshift linkage lash must be eliminated in order to obtain a proper adjustment. During adjustment, eliminate lash by pulling shift rod downward and pressing outer bellcrank upward.**
7. Place gearshift lever to Park and Neutral positions and ensure engine starts in these positions. If engine does not start or starts in R, D, 2 or 1, adjustment is incorrect or neutral switch is defective.
8. Check steering column lock for proper operation and lower vehicle.

## THROTTLE LINKAGE, ADJUST

### CHRYSLER

1. Support vehicle on hoist and loosen swivel lock screw, **Figs. 9, 10 and 11.** To ensure correct adjustment, swivel must be free to slide along flat end of throttle rod so that preload spring action is not restricted. If necessary, disassemble and clean or repair parts to assure free action.
2. Hold transmission lever firmly forward against its internal stop and tighten swivel lock screw to 100 inch lbs., **Figs. 9, 10 and 11.** Adjustment is now finished. Linkage backlash was automatically removed by the preload spring.
3. Lower vehicle and test linkage operation by moving throttle rod rearward and slowly releasing it making certain that it returns fully.

### JEEP

#### Six Cylinder Engines

1. Disconnect throttle rod spring, **Fig. 12,** then use throttle rod spring to hold the link forward against nylon stop.
2. On carburetors without solenoid valve, block choke open and set carburetor throttle off fast idle cam.
3. On carburetors with throttle operated solenoid valve, turn ignition switch to On position to energize solenoid, then open throttle half way to allow solenoid to lock and return carb to idle position.
4. Raise and support vehicle, then loosen the two throttle rod retainer bolts and hold throttle valve lever forward with spare spring, **Fig. 13.**
5. Pull on end of link to eliminate all lash, then slide clamp rearward until bolt retaining throttle rod to clamp bottoms against rear of slot in throttle rod, **Fig. 14.**
6. Tighten throttle rod retainer bolts se-

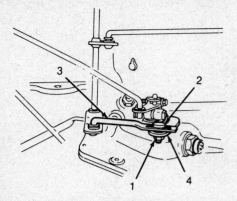

**Fig. 8  Gearshift linkage adjust. Jeep**

curely, remove holding spring from throttle valve lever, remove throttle valve spring from link, lower vehicle and connect throttle red spring to rod and bracket.

### Eight Cylinder Engine

1. Disconnect throttle rod spring from bellcrank, **Fig. 12,** then block choke open and set carburetor throttle off fast idle cam.
2. On carburetors with throttle operated solenoid valve, turn ignition switch to the On position to energize solenoid, then open throttle halfway to allow solenoid to lock and return carburetor to idle position.
3. Loosen throttle rod retainer bolt, **Fig. 15,** then remove spring clip from nylon stop.
4. Remove stop from lug and move stop to rear of link. Hold bellcrank in place, then push on end of link to eliminate lash and tighten link retaining bolt.
5. Install nylon stop and spring clip and connect throttle rod spring.

## KICKDOWN BAND, ADJUST

### Chrysler

The kickdown band adjusting screw is located on the left side of the transmission case, **Fig. 16.**

1. Loosen adjusting screw locknut, then back off nut approximately 5 turns.
2. Turn adjusting screw and check for binding. If screw binds, lubricate threads as required.
3. Torque adjusting screw to 72 inch lbs., then back off adjusting screw the number of turns listed in **Fig. 17.**
4. While holding adjusting screw in position, tighten locknut to 30-35 ft. lbs.

### Jeep

The kickdown band adjusting screw is located on the left side of the transmission case near the throttle lever shaft, **Fig. 16.**

1. Loosen adjusting screw locknut, then back off nut approximately 5 turns.
2. Turn adjusting screw and check for binding. If screw binds, lubricate threads as required.
3. Torque adjusting screw to 72 inch lbs., then back off screw 2 turns on

model 999 transmissions, or 2½ turns on all other models.

4. While holding adjusting screw in position, torque locknut to 35 ft. lbs.

## LOW & REVERSE BAND, ADJUST

### Chrysler

1. Raise vehicle, drain transmission and remove oil pan.
2. Loosen adjusting screw locknut and back off nut approximately five turns, **Fig. 18.** Check adjusting screw for free turning in the lever.
3. Using an inch-pound torque wrench, tighten band adjusting screw to a reading of 72 inch lbs.
4. Back off adjusting screw 2 turns on models except 1981-89 A-904T, A-998 and A-999 transmissions or 4 turns on 1981-89 A-904T, A-998 and A-999 transmission models, then tighten locknut.
5. Install oil pan and fill transmission with fluid.

### Jeep Except 1984—88 Cherokee & Wagoneer & 1986—88 Comanche

1. Raise vehicle, drain transmission and remove oil pan.
2. Loosen adjusting screw locknut and back off nut approximately five turns, **Fig. 18.** Check adjusting screw for free turning in the lever.
3. Using an inch-pound torque wrench, tighten band adjusting screw to a reading of 72 inch lbs.
4. On 1981 Jeep CJ-7 models with 4-151 engine (model 904 transmission) back off adjusting screw 7 turns from 41 inch lbs. On all 1980-88 vehicles except above, back off adjusting screw 2 (model 727 transmission) or 4 (model 999 transmission) turns from 72 inch lbs.
5. Install oil pan and fill transmission with fluid.

### 1984—88 Jeep Cherokee & Wagoneer & 1986—88 Comanche

1. Raise and support vehicle, then remove oil pan and drain transmission fluid.
2. Remove adjusting screw locknut.
3. Torque adjusting screw to 41 inch lbs., then back off 7 turns.
4. Install locknut and torque to 35 ft. lbs. While tightening locknut, ensure adjusting screw does not rotate.
5. Install oil pan and gasket, then lower vehicle and fill transmission to capacity.

## IN-VEHICLE REPAIRS
### EXTENSION HOUSING, REPLACE

On some models, it is necessary to unload both torsion bars and drop one side of torsion bar crossmember to provide clearance for extension housing removal.

1. Mark components for reassembly and

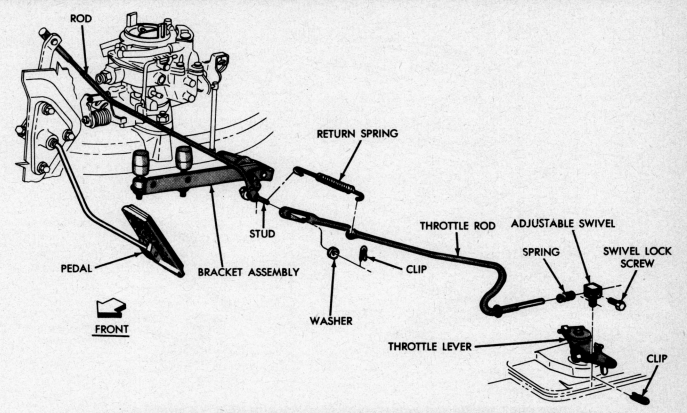

**Fig. 9 Throttle rod adjustment. Models with 6 cylinder engine & 1 barrel carburetor**

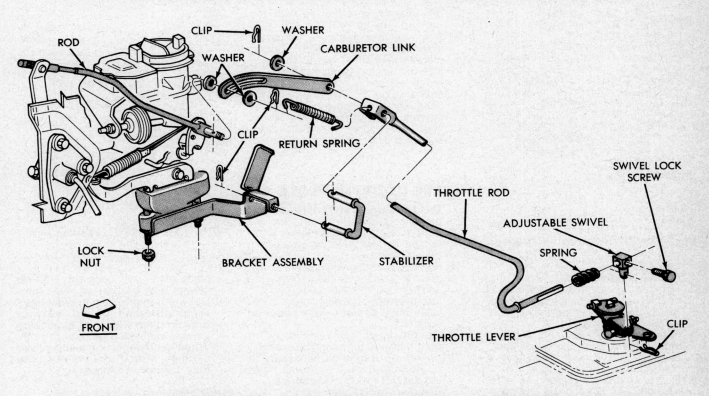

**Fig. 10 Throttle rod adjustment. Models with 6 cylinder engine & 2 barrel carburetor**

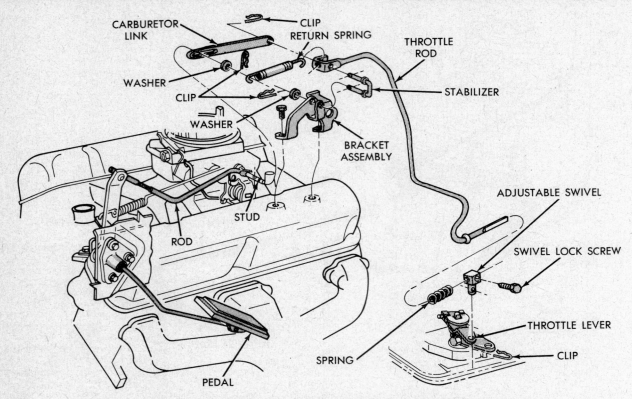

**Fig. 11  Throttle rod adjustment. Models with V6 & V8 engines**

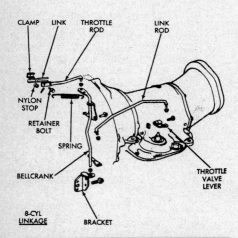

**Fig. 12  Throttle valve linkage**

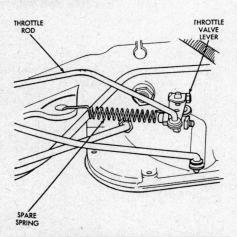

**Fig. 13  Throttle valve lever**

remove propeller shaft.

2. Remove speedometer pinion and adapter assembly, then drain approximately two quarts of transmission fluid from transmission.
3. Remove extension housing to crossmember bolts, then raise transmission with a jack and remove crossmember.
4. Remove extension housing to transmission bolts. On console shift models, remove torque shaft lower bracket to extension housing bolts. **In the following step, the gearshift must be in Low to position the parking lock control rod rearward so it can be** disengaged or engaged with the parking lock sprag.

5. Remove two screws, plate and gasket from bottom of extension housing mounting pad, then spread snap ring from output shaft bearing and carefully tap extension housing off output shaft bearing.
6. Slide extension housing off shaft to remove parking sprag and spring, then remove snap ring and slide reaction plug and pin assembly out of housing.

## VALVE BODY, REPLACE

1. Drain transmission and remove oil pan.
2. Loosen clamp bolts and remove throttle and/or gear selector levers from manual lever.
3. Remove neutral safety switch.
4. Place a drain pan under transmission and remove the ten valve body to transmission attaching bolts. Hold valve body in place while removing bolts.
5. Carefully lower valve body. Pull valve body forward to disengage parking control rod. **It may be necessary to rotate output shaft to permit parking control rod to clear sprag.**
6. Remove accumulator piston and spring from transmission case. Inspect piston for nicks, scores and wear. Inspect spring for distortion. Inspect rings for freedom in piston grooves and wear or breakage. Re-

place parts as necessary. **Never clamp any portion of the valve body or transfer plate in a vise. Any slight distortion of the body or transfer plate will result in sticking valves, excessive leakage or both. When removing or installing valves or plugs, slide them in or out carefully. Do not use force.**

## GOVERNOR, REPLACE

1. Remove extension housing.
2. Using a small screwdriver, carefully pry the snap ring from the weight end of the governor valve shaft. Slide the

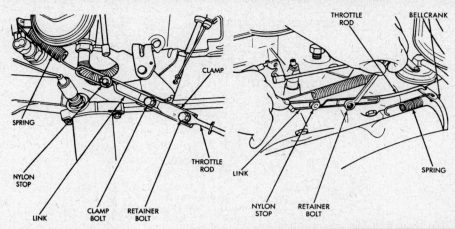

**Fig. 14  Six cylinder linkage adjustment**

**Fig. 15  Eight cylinder linkage adjustment**

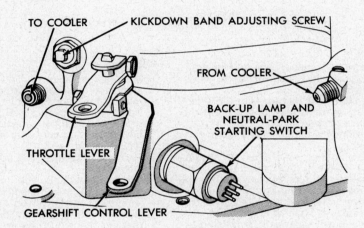

**Fig. 16  Kickdown band adjusting screw location**

| Models | Year | Engine | Number of Turns |
|---|---|---|---|
| **DODGE & PLYMOUTH** | | | |
| **Vans, Wagons & Front Sections** | 1980 | 6 Cyl. | 2½ |
| | | V8 | 2 |
| | 1981-89 | All | 2½ |
| **Ramcharger & Trail Duster** | 1980 | 6 Cyl. | 2½ |
| | | V8 | 2 |
| | 1981-89 | All | 2½ |
| **Conventional Cabs** | 1980 | 6 Cyl. | 2½ |
| | | V8 | 2 |
| | 1981-89 | All | 2½ |
| **Motor Home** | 1980 | 6 Cyl. | 2½ |
| | | V8 | 2 |
| **Dakota** | 1988-89 | All | 2½ |

**Fig. 17  Kickdown band adjustment chart**

valve and shaft out of governor housing.

3. Remove large snap ring from weight end of governor housing and lift out weight assembly.
4. Remove snap ring from inside governor weight and remove inner weight and spring from out weight.
5. Remove snap ring from behind governor housing, then slide housing and parking brake sprag assembly off input shaft. If necessary, separate governor housing from sprag (four screws).

# TRANSMISSION
## REPLACE
### CHRYSLER

1. Disconnect battery ground cable.
2. Raise and support vehicle.
3. Drain fluid from transmission.
4. Disconnect front exhaust pipe(s) from exhaust manifold(s).
5. Remove engine to transmission struts, if equipped.
6. Disconnect and cap transmission fluid lines.
7. Remove transmission fluid cooler line bracket.
8. Remove starter motor attaching bolts, then the starter motor.
9. Remove torque converter access cover.
10. Mark torque converter and drive plate for installation, then remove torque converter to drive plate attaching bolts.
11. Remove propeller shaft from vehicle.
12. Disconnect back-up light and neutral start switch electrical connector(s), then the lockup solenoid electrical connector, if equipped.
13. Disconnect gearshift rod and torque shaft assembly from transmission.
14. Disconnect throttle rod from transmission lever, then remove bell crank linkage from transmission, if equipped.
15. Remove oil filler tube, then disconnect speedometer cable from transmission.
16. Position a suitable engine holding fixture onto engine.
17. Position a suitable jack under transmission, then raise transmission slightly.
18. Remove transmission mount to crossmember and crossmember to frame attaching bolts.
19. Remove transmission to engine attaching bolts.
20. Carefully separate transmission from engine, and install a suitable C clamp onto bellhousing to secure torque converter in place.
21. Lower transmission from vehicle.
22. Reverse procedure to install.

## JEEP 4 WHEEL DRIVE MODELS

### Exc. 1984–88 Cherokee & Wagoneer & 1986–88 Comanche

1. Disconnect battery ground cable.
2. Disconnect transmission filler tube

from upper bracket.
3. Raise and support vehicle.
4. Remove inspection cover from torque converter housing.
5. On all models remove starter motor attaching bolts, then the starter motor.
6. Mark propeller shafts and axle yokes for installation.
7. Disconnect propeller shafts from transfer case yokes.
8. On models equipped with V8 engine, disconnect front exhaust pipes from exhaust manifolds.
9. Drain fluid from transfer case assembly, then disconnect speedometer cable, if applicable.
10. Disconnect gearshift, throttle linkages and transfer case shift linkages (if applicable).
11. Disconnect electrical connectors from neutral start switch.
12. Mark torque converter and drive plate for installation, then remove torque converter to drive plate bolts.
13. Position a suitable jack under transmission. Secure transmission onto jack using a safety chain.
14. Remove rear crossmember from vehicle.
15. Disconnect and cap transmission fluid lines.
16. Remove transmission to engine attaching bolts.
17. Lower transmission from vehicle.
18. Reverse procedure to install.

## 1984–88 Cherokee & Wagoneer & 1986–88 Comanche

1. Disconnect battery ground cable.
2. Raise and support vehicle.
3. Mark rear propeller shaft and yoke assembly for assembly reference.
4. Disconnect rear propeller shaft from transfer case yoke. Secure shaft to frame with wire.
5. Mark converter drive plate and converter for assembly reference, then remove converter drive plate attaching bolts.
6. On models equipped with diesel engine, remove left motor mount and starter to gain access to converter drive plate bolts through the starter opening.
7. On all models, position a suitable jack

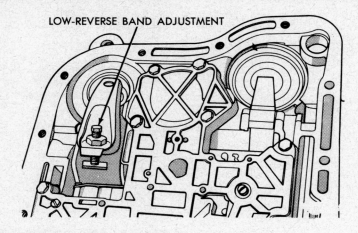

**Fig. 18  Low-reverse band adjusting screw location**

under transmission and secure transmission onto jack using a safety chain.
8. Remove rear crossmember to transmission attaching bolts, then the crossmember.
9. Disconnect exhaust pipe from converter.
10. Mark front propeller shaft for assembly reference, then disconnect front propeller at transfer case and secure shaft to frame with wire.
11. Lower transmission slightly, then disconnect and cap oil cooler lines.
12. Disconnect back-up light switch electrical connector, speedometer cable, vacuum lines and vent hose.
13. Disconnect transfer case and transmission linkage.
14. Remove bolts attaching transmission to engine.
15. Lower transmission from vehicle.
16. Reverse procedure to install.

## JEEP 2 WHEEL DRIVE MODELS

1. Disconnect battery ground cable.
2. Raise and support vehicle.
3. Mark rear propeller shaft and yoke assembly for installation reference, then remove rear propeller shaft.
4. Remove inspection cover from converter housing, then mark converter drive plate and converter for assembly reference.
5. Remove bolts attaching converter to drive plate.
6. Position a suitable jack under transmission. Secure transmission onto jack using a safety chain.
7. Remove rear crossmember to transmission attaching bolts, then the rear crossmember.
8. Disconnect exhaust pipe from converter.
9. Disconnect and cap oil cooler lines.
10. Disconnect back-up light switch electrical connector and speedometer cable.
11. Disconnect transmission linkage, then remove transmission to engine attaching bolts.
12. Lower transmission from vehicle.
13. Reverse procedure to install.

# AW-4 Automatic Transmissions

## INDEX

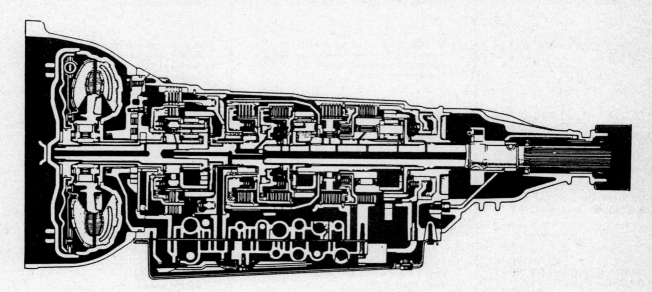

Fig. 1  AW-4 Automatic Transmission

## DESCRIPTION

The AW-4 is a four speed, electronically controlled automatic transmission, **Fig. 1.** Features include a lockup torque converter, three planetary gear sets, clutch and brake units, hydraulic accumulators and a valve body controlled by electrical solenoids and transmission computer unit (TCU). Vehicle speed and throttle position are monitored by the TCU, which then apropriately adjusts the valve body solenoids. Fourth gear is and overdrive gear having a ratio of .705:1.

## TROUBLESHOOTING

Before any troubleshooting is performed, the general engine operation, transmission shift linkage, line pressure cable, transmission fluid level, throttle cable and throttle position sensor should all be checked and adjusted if necessary. For specific symptom diagnosis, refer to **Figs. 2 and 3.**

## MAINTENANCE
### ADDING OIL

When checking oil level, the transmission fluid must be cool (85-125°F). Check fluid level with transmission in Park and the engine at curb idle speed. Shift the transmission through all gear ranges and back to Park before checking fluid level and use Mopar Mercon or equivalent Dexron II fluid to refill or top off the fluid level.

### CHANGING OIL

1. Raise and support vehicle on a suitable lift. Position a drain pan under the transmission oil pan and remove transmission oil pan drain plug and drain fluid.
2. Remove pan bolts and remove oil pan, then remove oil screen bolts and screen, **Fig. 4.**
3. Clean mating surfaces of pan and transmission. Clean oil pan and screen with solvent and dry with compresses air.

4. Install screen with a new gasket and torque bolts to 7 ft. lbs.
5. Apply a bead of RTV or equivalent sealer to the pan gasket surface, then install pan and torque bolts to 65 inch lbs. Install pan drain plug and torque to 15 ft. lbs.
6. Fill transmission with Mopar Mercon or Dexron II transmission fluid to proper level. Start engine and shift transmission through entire gear range and back to Park. Recheck fluid level.

## IN-VEHICLE REPAIRS
### NEUTRAL SWITCH, REPLACE
#### Removal

1. Raise and support vehicle, then disconnect switch wire harness connector.
2. Pry washer lock tabs up and remove switch attaching nut and washer, **Fig. 5.**

| CONDITION | POSSIBLE CAUSE | CORRECTION |
|---|---|---|
| FLUID DISCOLORED OR SMELLS BURNT | Fluid contaminated<br>Torque converter faulty<br>Transmission faulty | Replace fluid<br>Replace torque converter<br>Disassemble and repair transmission |
| VEHICLE DOES NOT MOVE IN ANY FORWARD RANGE OR REVERSE | Shift linkage out of adjustment<br>Valve body or primary regulator faulty<br>Park lock pawl faulty<br>Torque converter faulty<br>Converter drive plate broken<br>Oil pump intake screen blocked<br>Transmission faulty | Adjust linkage<br>Inspect/repair valve body<br>Repair park pawl<br>Replace torque converter<br>Replace drive plate<br>Clean screen<br>Disassemble and repair transmission |
| SHIFT LEVER POSITION INCORRECT | Shift linkage out of adjustment<br>Manual valve and lever faulty | Adjust linkage<br>Repair valve body |
| HARSH ENGAGEMENT (ALL RANGES) | Throttle cable out of adjustment<br>Valve body or primary regulator faulty<br>Accumulator pistons faulty<br>Transmission faulty | Adjust throttle cable<br>Repair valve body<br>Repair pistons<br>Disassemble and repair transmission |
| DELAYED 1-2, 2-3 OR 3-OD UP-SHIFT, OR DOWN-SHIFTS FROM 4-3 OR 3-2 AND SHIFTS BACK TO 4 OR 3 | Electronic control problem<br>Valve body faulty<br>Solenoid faulty | <br>Repair valve body<br>Repair solenoid |
| SLIPS ON 1-2, 2-3 OR 3-OD UP-SHIFT, OR SLIPS OR SHUDDERS ON TAKE-OFF | Shift linkage out of adjustment<br>LP cable out of adjustment<br>Valve body faulty<br>Solenoid faulty<br>Transmission faulty | Adjust linkage<br>Adjust cable<br>Repair valve body<br>Replace solenoid<br>Disassemble and repair transmission |
| DRAG OR BIND ON 1-2, 2-3 OR 3-OD UP-SHIFT | Shift linkage out of adjustment<br>Valve body faulty<br>Transmission faulty | Adjust linkage<br>Repair valve body<br>Disassemble and repair transmission |
| NO LOCK-UP IN 2ND, 3RD OR OD | Electronic control problem<br>Valve body faulty<br>Solenoid faulty<br>Transmission faulty | <br>Repair valve body<br>Replace solenoid<br>Disassemble and repair transmission |
| HARSH DOWN-SHIFT | Throttle cable out of adjustment<br>Throttle cable and cam faulty<br>Accumulator pistons faulty<br>Valve body faulty<br>Transmission faulty | Adjust cable<br>Replace cable and cam<br>Repair pistons<br>Repair valve body<br>Disassemble and repair transmission |
| NO DOWN-SHIFT WHEN COASTING | Valve body faulty<br>Solenoid faulty<br>Electronic control problem | Repair valve body<br>Replace solenoid |

**Fig. 2   Service diagnosis chart**

| CONDITION | POSSIBLE CAUSE | CORRECTION |
|---|---|---|
| DOWN-SHIFT LATE OR EARLY DURING COAST | Throttle cable faulty<br>Valve body faulty<br>Transmission faulty<br>Solenoid faulty<br>Electronic control problem | Replace cable<br>Repair valve body<br>Disassemble and repair transmission<br>Replace solenoid |
| NO OD-3, 3-2 OR 2-1 KICKDOWN | Solenoid faulty<br>Electronic control problem<br>Valve body faulty | Replace solenoid<br><br>Repair valve body |
| NO ENGINE BRAKING IN 1-2 POSITION | Solenoid faulty<br>Electronic control problem<br>Valve body faulty<br>Transmission faulty | Replace solenoid<br><br>Repair valve body<br>Disassemble and repair transmission |
| VEHICLE DOES NOT HOLD IN PARK | Shift linkage out of adjustment<br>Parking lock pawl cam and spring faulty | Adjust linkage<br>Replace cam and spring |

**Fig. 3   Service diagnosis chart**

3. Remove switch adjusting bolt, then slide switch off manual valve shaft.

## Installation

1. Disconnect shift linkage rod from shift lever on left side of transmission, then rotate manual shift lever all the way rearward and back forward two detent positions to Neutral.
2. Install switch on manual valve shaft and install switch adjusting bolt finger tight, then install tabbed washer on manual valve shaft and install switch attaching nut and torque to 61 inch lbs. **Do not bend washer lock tabs at this time.**
3. Verify that transmission is in Neutral, then rotate switch to align neutral standard line with vertical groove on manual valve shaft, **Fig. 6.**
4. Align switch standard line with groove or flat on manual valve shaft.
5. Torque switch adjusting bolt to 9 ft. lbs. Bend at least two washer lock tabs over switch attaching nut to secure it.
6. Connect shift linkage rod to shift lever on left side of case, connect switch wires and lower vehicle. To check switch operation, vehicle should start only in Park or Neutral.

## VALVE BODY SOLENOIDS, REPLACE

### Removal

1. Drain transmission fluid, remove oil pan and screen as outlined under "Changing Oil".
2. Disconnect solenoid wire connector, and mark or tag connectors if more than one solenoid is being removed.
3. Remove bolt attaching solenoids to valve body, then the solenoids. Use caution not to loose any valve body components when solenoids are removed.
4. Clean oil filter and pan with solvent and air dry.
5. To test the solenoid, connect an ohmmeter between the solenoid mounting bracket and th solenoid wiring terminal, **Fig. 7.**
6. If ohmmeter does not show resistance between 11-15 ohms, replace the solenoid.

### Installation

1. Position solenoids on valve body and install retaining bolts. Torque to 7 ft. lbs.
2. Connect feed wires to solenoids, install new gasket on oil screen, and install screen retaining bolts. Torque bolts to 7 ft. lbs.
3. Install oil pan and fluid as described under "Changing Oil".

## SOLENOID HARNESS ADAPTER SEAL, REPLACE

1. Remove oil pan, screen, solenoids and bracket as described under "Valve Body Solenoids, Removal".
2. Remove bracket securing solenoid harness adapter to case, **Fig. 8.**
3. Pull harness adapter and wires out of case, then remove and discard adapter O-ring.
4. Reverse procedure to install. Lubricate new O-ring before installing on adapter.

## VALVE BODY, REPLACE

### Removal

1. Remove oil pan, screen and disconnect solenoid wire connectors as outlined under "Valve Body Solenoids, Removal".
2. Remove valve body oil tubes, **Fig. 9,** by carefully prying with a screwdriver.
3. Disconnect throttle cable from throttle cam, then remove valve body bolts, **Fig. 10,** and lower valve body. Remove overdrive clutch accumulator springs, direct clutch accumulator spring and spacer, second brake accumulator spring and spacer, **Fig. 11.**
4. Remove valve body and check ball and spring, **Fig. 12.**

### Installation

1. Connect cable to throttle cam, then install check ball and spring, **Fig. 12.**
2. Position accumulator springs and spacers on valve body, then align valve body manual valve with shift sector and carefully position valve body on case, **Fig. 13.**
3. Install valve body bolts and torque evenly to 7 ft. lbs., then install valve body oil tubes as shown in **Fig. 14.**
4. Install solenoid connectors, oil screen, pan and fluid as described under "Valve Body Solenoids, Installation".

## MANUAL VALVE SHAFT SEAL, REPLACE

1. Remove neutral safety switch and disconnect transmission shift lever, then remove oil pan and valve body as outlined under "Valve Body, Replace".
2. Remove bolts attaching park rod bracket to case, **Fig. 15,** then remove park rod from shift sector, **Fig. 16.**
3. Cut spacer sleeve with chisel and remove it from manual valve shaft, **Fig. 17.** Remove pin from shaft and sector with pin punch, then remove shaft and sector from case.
4. Pry shaft seals out of case. Inspect the manual valve shaft and sector and replace either if worn of damaged.

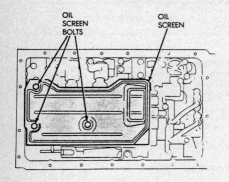

**Fig. 4   Oil screen removal**

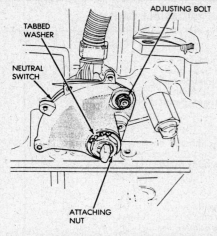

**Fig. 5   Neutral switch removal**

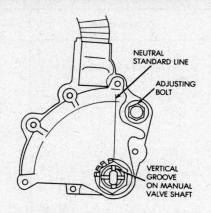

**Fig. 6   Neutral switch adjustment**

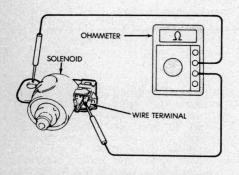

**Fig. 7   Testing valve body solenoid**

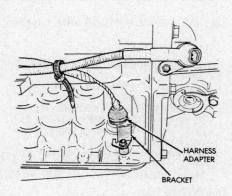

**Fig. 8   Harness adapter**

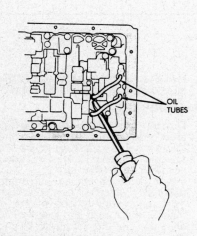

**Fig. 9   Valve body oil tubes**

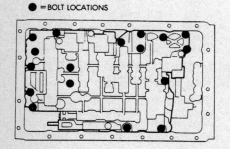

**Fig. 10   Valve body bolt location**

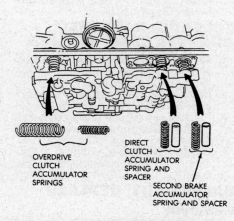

**Fig. 11   Accumulator springs**

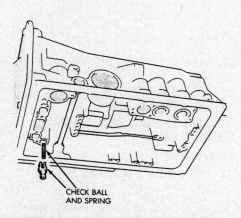

**Fig. 12   Check ball & spring**

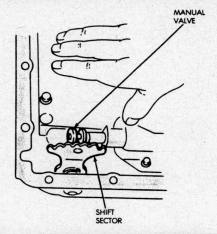

Fig. 13   Shift sector & manual valve

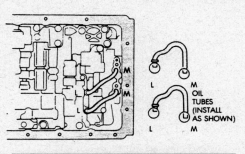

Fig. 14   Valve body oil tube installation

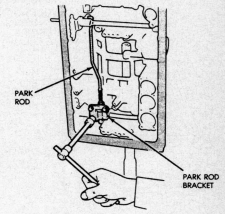

Fig. 15   Park rod bracket

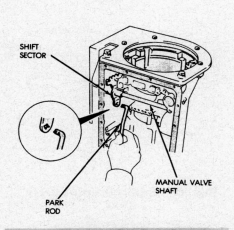

Fig. 16   Park rod

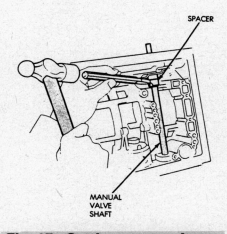

Fig. 17   Cutting spacer sleeve

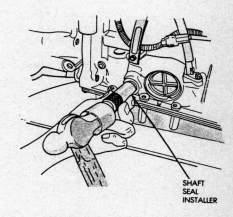

Fig. 18   Manual valve shaft seal installation

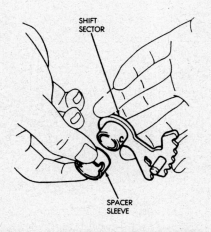

Fig. 19   Sector spacer sleeve

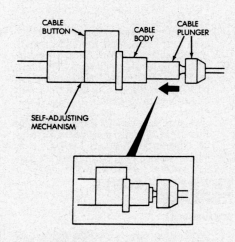

Fig. 20   Throttle cable plunger

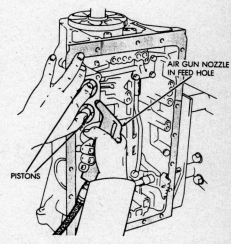

Fig. 21   Accumulator piston removal

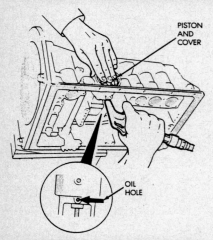

**Fig. 22  Servo cover and piston removal**

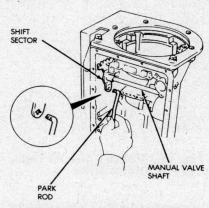

**Fig. 23  Second coast brake servo**

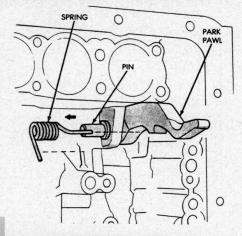

**Fig. 24  Park pawl, pin & spring**

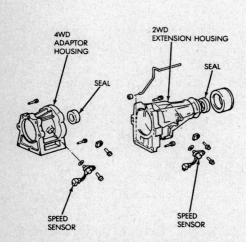

**Fig. 25  Adaptor/Extension housing seals**

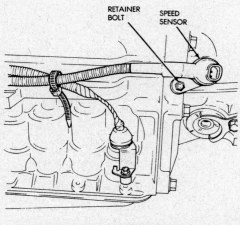

**Fig. 26  Speed sensor**

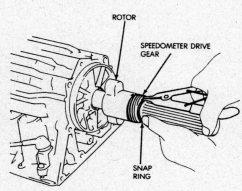

**Fig. 27  Speedometer drive gear**

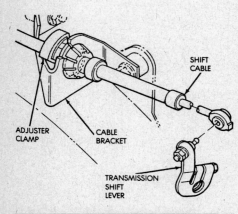

**Fig. 28  Shift cable adjustment**

5. Coat replacement shaft seals with petroleum jelly and seat them in case, **Fig. 18.** Install new spacer sleeve on sector, **Fig. 19.**
6. Lubricate manual valve shaft and install it in case, then lubricate sector and sleeve and install them on shaft.
7. Align hole in spacer sleeve with notch in sector, then install shift sector roll pin. Tap pin into sector and shaft and stake sleeve to sector and shaft securely.
8. Connect park rod to sector, **Fig. 16,** then install park rod bracket, **Fig. 15,** and torque bolts to 7 ft. lbs.
9. Install valve body, oil screen, oil pan and neutral switch.

## THROTTLE CABLE, REPLACE
### Removal

1. Working in engine compartment, disconnect cable from throttle linkage, then compress cable mounting ears and remove cable from linkage bracket.
2. Raise and support vehicle.
3. Remove transmission oil pan, disen-

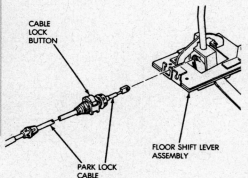

**Fig. 29  Park lock cable**

gage cable from throttle valve cam and remove cable bracket bolt.
4. Remove cable and bracket from case. Remove and discard cable seal.

### Installation

1. Lubricate and install new seal on cable, then insert cable in transmission case.
2. Attach cable to throttle cam, then install cable bracket on case and torque attaching bolt to 7 ft. lbs.
3. Remove old gasket material from oil pan and transmission case and clean pan and screen with solvent, then dry with compressed air.
4. Install screen with a new gasket, then install pan and torque bolts to 65 inch lbs.
5. Install drain plug and fill transmission with fluid to appropriate level, then adjust cable as follows:
   a. Turn ignition switch to the Off position and fully retract cable plunger, then press cable button all the way down and cable plunger inward, **Fig. 20**.
   b. Rotate primary throttle lever to wide open throttle position and hold while allowing cable plunger extend. Release lever when plunger is fully extended.

## ACCUMULATOR PISTONS & SPRINGS, REPLACE

1. Remove valve body as previously outlined, then remove accumulator pistons with compressed air, **Fig. 21**, through small feed hole next to each piston bore and catch each piston in a shop towel as it is forced out of bore. **Be sure to use only enough air pressure to remove piston, and be sure to tag each set of pistons and springs as they are removed**
2. Remove and discard piston O-ring seals. Clean pistons and springs with solvent and inspect pistons and piston bores for excessive wear or damage. Replace case if piston bores are damaged.
3. Install new O-ring seals on pistons. Lubricate each assembly with clean transmission fluid and install into appropriate bore.
4. Install screen, pan and new transmission fluid.

## SECOND COAST BRAKE SERVO, REPLACE

1. Remove valve body as previously described, then remove servo piston cover snap ring.
2. Remove servo piston and cover with compressed air, **Fig. 22**, through oil hole in servo boss; use just enough air pressure to remove piston.
3. Remove and discard seal and O-ring from cover and piston and inspect E-ring, piston, spring and retainer, piston rod and piston spring for excessive wear or damage, **Fig. 23**. Replace worn or damaged parts.
4. Install new seals on cover and piston. Lubricate servo components with

clean transmission fluid, assemble and install being sure servo piston rod is properly engaged in the second coast brake band.

## PARK ROD & PAWL, REPLACE

1. Remove valve body as previously described, then remove bolts attaching park rod bracket to case, **Fig. 15**.
2. Remove park rod from manual valve shaft sector, then remove park rod, park rod pawl, pin and spring, **Fig. 24**.
3. Examine parts for wear or damage and replace if damage is found.
4. Install pawl in case, then insert pin and install spring. Ensure spring is positioned as shown in **Fig. 24**.
5. Install park rod and bracket and torque bolts to 7 ft. lbs.
6. Install valve body, oil screen, pan and refill transmission with fluid to appropriate level.

## EXTENSION/ADAPTOR HOUSING SEAL, REPLACE

1. Raise and support vehicle.
2. Disconnect or remove components necessary to gain access to the seal.
3. On 2WD models, remove seal from adapter housing, **Fig. 25**.
4. On 4WD models, remove dust shield and remove seal from extension housing, **Fig. 25**.
5. On all models, install new seal with appropriate seal installation tool. On 4WD models, install dust shield.
6. On all models, install components removed to gain access to seal and top off transmission fluid if necessary.

## SPEED SENSOR, REPLACE

1. Disconnect sensor wire harness connector, then remove sensor retainer bolt and remove sensor, **Fig. 26**.
2. Remove and discard speed sensor O-ring and install new O-ring on speed sensor, then install sensor in transmission case.
3. Install sensor bracket and bolt and torque to 65 inch lbs. Connect sensor wire connector.

## SPEED SENSOR ROTOR-SPEEDOMETER DRIVE GEAR, REPLACE

### Removal

1. Raise and support vehicle.
2. Remove components necessary to gain access to rotor and drive gear, then disconnect speedometer cable and/or speed sensor.
3. Remove extension or adapter housing, then remove speedometer drivegear snap ring, **Fig. 27**.
4. Remove the speedometer drive gear and spacer (if equipped), then remove rotor by carefully prying it off output shaft with wood dowel or hammer handle.

### Installation

1. Clean all sealing surfaces on transmission case and extension/adapter

housing.
2. Install rotor, spacer (if equipped), and drive gear on output shaft, then install drive gear snap ring, **Fig. 27**.
3. Apply a bead of suitable RTV sealer to transmission case sealing surface and install extension/adapter housing bolts. Torque bolts to 25 ft. lbs.
4. Install components removed to gain access to rotor drive gear.

## THROTTLE POSITION SENSOR, REPLACE

1. Disconnect battery ground cable, then remove the TPS retaining screws.
2. Disconnect TPS harness connectors and remove sensor.
3. Connect new sensor to transmission TCU harness, then mount sensor on throttle body but do not tighten attaching screws at this time.
4. Check and adjust sensor output voltage as follows:
   a. Using a voltmeter, connect positive lead to terminal B and negative lead to terminal D.
   b. Rotate TPS until output voltage is approximately 4.2 volts.
   c. Tighten TPS attaching screws. If 4.2 volts cannot be attained, replace TPS.
5. Connect battery ground cable.

# IN-VEHICLE ADJUSTMENTS

## SHIFT CABLE ADJUSTMENT

1. Shift transmission into Park, then raise and support vehicle.
2. Release cable adjuster clamp to unlock cable, **Fig. 28**, then unsnap cable from cable bracket.
3. Move transmission shift lever all the way rearward into Park detent, (lever is on manual valve shaft at left side of case), then verify positive engagement of park lock by attempting to rotate propeller shaft. Shaft will not rotate when park lock is engaged.
4. Snap cable into cable bracket, then lock shaft cable by pressing cable adjuster clamp down until it snaps into place.
5. Check engine starting. Engine should start only in Park or Neutral.
6. Lower vehicle.

## PARK LOCK CABLE ADJUSTMENT

1. Shift transmission into Park, then turn ignition switch to the Lock position.
2. Remove shift lever bezel and console screws and raise bezel and console for access to cable.
3. Pull cable lock button up to release cable, **Fig. 29**, then pull cable forward. Release cable and press cable lock button down until it snaps in place.
4. Check movement of release shift handle button or shift release lever. No movement should be possible until ig-

nition is in the On position. Place shift lever into the Neutral position. If adjustment is correct you should not be able to put ignition into the Lock position when transmission shift lever is in Neutral or Drive. With transmission in the Park position, Ignition should turn freely.

## TRANSMISSION
### REPLACE

1. Raise and support vehicle, then drain transmission fluid and reinstall oil pan drain plug.
2. Remove upper half of transmission fill tube and disconnect cooler lines at transmission by pressing fitting release tabs and pulling cooler line and fittings out of case.
3. Support engine with safety stand and support transmission with jack.
4. Disconnect or remove the transmission, transfer case shift linkage, necessary exhaust components, speedometer cable, front and/or rear propeller shaft, transmission wire harnesses, transfer case vacuum and wire harnesses.
5. Remove rear crossmember, then disconnect transmission throttle cable at engine.
6. disconnect necessary vacuum and fluid hoses, then remove starter motor, converter to drive plate bolts and converter housing to engine bolts.
7. Secure transmission and transfer case assembly (if equipped), to transmission jack with safety chains, then remove transmission.
8. Remove transfer case if transmission is to be overhauled.
9. Reverse procedure to install. On 4WD models, install transfer case on transmission before installing transmission in chassis.

# ELECTRONIC IGNITION

## TABLE OF CONTENTS

# Electronic Spark Advance Specifications

## 1982 RAMPAGE

| Spark Control Computer | 5213480 | 5213481 | 5213486 |
|---|---|---|---|
| Basic Timing | 12° | 12° | 12° |
| Vacuum Advance (Range) | 0-12 | 0-12 | 1-11 |
| Accumulator Time (In Minutes) | 0 | 0 | 0 |
| Spark Advance Test @ 2000 RPM w/16" Vacuum | 45°±4° | 47°±4° | 44°±4° |

## 1983 RAMPAGE & SCAMP

| Spark Control Computer | 5213691 | 5213832 | 5213834 | 5213840 |
|---|---|---|---|---|
| Basic Timing | 10° | 10° | 10° | 6° |
| Vacuum Advance (Range) | 2-12 | 2-12 | 2-12 | 2-21 |
| Accumulator Time (In Minutes) | 0 | 0 | 0 | 0 |
| Spark Advance Test @ 2000 RPM w/16" Vacuum | 28°±4° | 28°±4° | 28°±4° | 34°±4° |
| Electronic Throttle Control | ① | ② | — | ③ |

①—30 seconds. after start. 2 seconds. after throttle closes.　②—15 seconds. after start. 2 seconds. after throttle closes.　③—0 seconds. after start. 2 seconds. after throttle closes.

## 1984 RAMPAGE

| Spark Control Computer | 5226118 | 5226122 | 5226166 |
|---|---|---|---|
| Basic Timing | 10° | 10° | 10° |
| Spark Advance Test @ 2000 RPM w/16" Vacuum | 42°±4° | 40°±4° | 38°±4° |
| Electronic Throttle Control | ① | ① | ② |

①—90 seconds. after start.
②—90 seconds. after start. 2 seconds. off idle. 1 seconds. after throttle closes.

# CHRYSLER/JEEP—Electronic Ignition

## 1984 CARAVAN, RAM VAN & VOYAGER

| Spark Control Computer | 5226118 | 5226124 | 5226166 | 5226176 | 5226178 |
|---|---|---|---|---|---|
| Basic Timing | 10° | 10° | 10° | 10° | 10° |
| Spark Advance Test @ 2000 RPM w/16" Vacuum | 42°±4° | 41°±4° | 38°±4° | 39°±4° | 40°±4° |
| Electronic Throttle Control | ① | ② | ② | ② | ② |

①—90 seconds. after start.
②—90 seconds. after start. 2 seconds. off idle. 1 seconds. after throttle closes.

## 1985 CARAVAN, RAM VAN & VOYAGER

| Spark Control Computer | 5226465 | 5226497 | 5226499 |
|---|---|---|---|
| Basic Timing | 10° | 10° | 10° |
| Spark Advance Test @ 2000 RPM w/16" Vacuum | 42°±4° | 42°±4° | 39°±4° |
| Electronic Throttle Control | ① | ② | ③ |

## 1985 CARAVAN, RAM VAN & VOYAGER—Continued

| Spark Control Computer | 5226587 | 5226589 | 5226591 |
|---|---|---|---|
| Basic Timing | 10° | 10° | 10° |
| Spark Advance Test @ 2000 RPM w/16" Vacuum | 39°±4° | 39°±4° | 42°±4° |
| Electronic Throttle Control | ② | ② | ④ |

①—300 seconds. cold. 60 seconds. after hot start. 2 seconds. off idle. 2 seconds. after throttle closes.
②—300 seconds. cold. 180 seconds. after hot start. 2 seconds. off idle. 1 seconds. after throttle closes.
③—300 seconds. cold. 90 seconds. after hot start. 2 seconds. off idle. 1 seconds. after throttle closes.
④—300 seconds. cold. 60 seconds. after hot start. 2 seconds. off idle. 1 seconds. after throttle closes.

## 1986 CARAVAN, RAM VAN & VOYAGER

| Spark Control Computer | 522782 | 5227384 | 5227386 | 5227388 |
|---|---|---|---|---|
| Basic Timing | 6° | 6° | 6° | 6° |
| Spark Advance Test @ 2000 RPM w/16" Vacuum | 22°±4° | 34°±4° | 22°±4° | 29°±4° |
| Electronic Throttle Control | ① | ② | ① | ② |

①—360 seconds. after cold. 180 seconds. after hot start. 2 seconds. off idle. ½ seconds. after throttle closes.
②—360 seconds. cold. 180 seconds. after hot start. 0 seconds. off idle. 0 seconds. after throttle closes.

## 1987 CARAVAN, RAM VAN & VOYAGER

| Spark Control Computer | 5227379 | 5227462 | 5227464 | 5227470 |
|---|---|---|---|---|
| Basic Timing | 6° | 6° | 6° | 6° |
| Spark Advance Test @ 2000 RPM w/16" Vacuum | 22°±4° | 34°±4° | 22°±4° | 29°±4° |
| Electronic Throttle Control | ① | ② | ① | ② |

①—360 seconds. cold. 180 seconds. after hot start. 2 seconds. off idle. ½ seconds. after throttle closes.
②—360 seconds. cold. 180 seconds. after hot start. 0 seconds. off idle. 0 seconds. after throttle closes.

## 1987 DAKOTA

| Spark Control Computer | 4379190 | 4379192 | 4379196 | 4379198 | 4379243 | 4379247 |
|---|---|---|---|---|---|---|
| Basic Timing | 7° | 7° | 7° | 7° | 6° | 6° |
| Spark Advance Test @ 2000 RPM w/16" Vacuum | 38°±4° | 36°±4° | 30°±4° | 26°±4° | 28°±4° | 28°±4° |
| Electronic Throttle Control | ① | ② | ② | ② | ③ | ④ |

①—120 seconds. after hot start. 1 seconds. decel hold.
②—90 seconds. after hot start.
③—120 seconds. after hot start.
④—120 seconds. after hot start. 2 seconds. decel hold.

## 1981–82 REAR WHEEL DRIVE MODELS

| Spark Control Computer | 4145472 | 4145478 | 4145747 | 4145755 |
|---|---|---|---|---|
| Basic Timing | 12° | 12° | 16° | 16° |
| Vacuum Advance (Range) | 3-10 | 3-10 | 3-10 | 3-10 |
| Accumulator Time In Minutes | 0 | 0 | 0 | 0 |
| Spark Advance Test @ 2000 RPM | 25°±4° | 25°±4° | 25°±4° | 25°±4° |
| Electronic EGR Time Delay | 60 sec. | 60 sec. | 60 sec. | 60 sec. |
| Electronic Throttle Control | Yes① | Yes① | Yes | No |

①—Federal models only.

| Spark Control Computer | 4145760 | 4145762 | 4145764 | 4289024 |
|---|---|---|---|---|
| Basic Timing | 16° | 16° | 12° | 12° |
| Vacuum Advance (Range) | 3-10 | 3-10 | 3-12 | 1-7 |
| Accumulator Time In Minutes | 0 | 0 | 0 | 0 |
| Spark Advance Test @ 2000 RPM | 25°±4° | 25°±4° | 21°±4° | 32°±4° |
| Electronic EGR Time Delay | 60 sec. | 60 sec. | 60 sec. | 0 sec. |
| Electronic Throttle Control | Yes | No | Yes | No |

①—Federal models only.

## 1983 REAR WHEEL DRIVE MODELS

| Spark Control Computer | 4289024 | 4289067 | 4289069 | 4289075 | 4289077 |
|---|---|---|---|---|---|
| Basic Timing | 12° | 12° | 16° | 16° | 16° |
| Vacuum Advance (Range) | 1-7 | 3-10 | 3-10 | 2-14 | 2-14 |
| Accumulator Time In Minutes | 0 | 1 | 1 | 0 | 0 |
| Spark Advance Test @ 1500 RPM | 25°±4° | 16°±4° | 4°±4°① | 13°±4° | 8°±4° |
| Electronic EGR Time Delay | 0 | 65 sec. | 65 sec. | 20 sec. | 20 sec. |
| Electronic Throttle Control | No | Yes | Yes | Yes | Yes |

①—At 2000 RPM.

| Spark Control Computer | 4289081 | 4289083 | 4289086 | 4289089 | 4289091 |
|---|---|---|---|---|---|
| Basic Timing | 12° | 16° | 16° | 12° | 12° |
| Vacuum Advance (Range) | 3-10 | 3-10 | 2-14 | 1-7 | 3-10 |
| Accumulator Time In Minutes | 1 | 1 | 0 | 0 | 0 |
| Spark Advance Test @ 1500 RPM | 16°±4° | 4°±4°① | 13°±4° | 28°±4° | 22°±4° |
| Electronic EGR Time Delay | 65 sec. | 60 sec. | 20 sec. | — | 6 sec. |
| Electronic Throttle Control | Yes | Yes | Yes | No | Yes |

①—At 2000 RPM.

| Spark Control Computer | 4289094 | 4289097 | 4289099 | 4289103 | 4289145 |
|---|---|---|---|---|---|
| Basic Timing | 16° | 12° | 12° | 12° | 16° |
| Vacuum Advance (Range) | 2-14 | 3-10 | 3-10 | 3-10 | 3-10 |
| Accumulator Time In Minutes | 0 | 0 | 0 | 0 | 0 |
| Spark Advance Test @ 1500 RPM | 8°±4° | 25°±4° | 21°±4° | 25°±4° | 22°±4° |
| Electronic EGR Time Delay | 20 sec. | 60 sec. | 60 sec. | 60 sec. | 60 sec. |
| Electronic THrottle Control | Yes | Yes | Yes | Yes | Yes |

## 1984 REAR WHEEL DRIVE VEHICLES

| Spark Control Computer | 4289075 | 4289077 | 4289086 | 4289094 | 4289304 |
|---|---|---|---|---|---|
| Basic Timing | 16° | 16° | 16° | 16° | 12° |
| Spark Advance Test @ 2000 RPM | 44°±4° | 42°±4° | 44°±4° | 42°±4° | 39°±4° |
| Electronic EGR Time Delay | 20 sec. | 20 sec. | 20 sec. | 20 sec. | 60 sec. |
| Electronic Throttle Control | ① | ① | ① | ① | ② |

①—20 sec. after start or 1 sec. after throttle close condition.  ②—60 sec. after start or 2 sec. after throttle close position.

# CHRYSLER/JEEP–Electronic Ignition

## 1984 REAR WHEEL DRIVE VEHICLES—Continued

| Spark Control Computer | 4289308 | 4289310 | 4289324 | 4289326 | 4289351 |
|---|---|---|---|---|---|
| Basic Timing | 16° | 16° | 12° | 16° | 12° |
| Spark Advance Test @ 2000 RPM | 43°±4° | 42°±4° | 20°±4° | 21°±4° | 39°±4° |
| Electronic EGR Time Delay | 60 sec. | 20 sec. | 65 sec. | 65 sec. | 60 sec. |
| Electronic Throttle Control | ② | ① | ③ | ③ | ② |

①—20 sec. after start or 1 sec. after throttle close condition.
②—60 sec. after start or 2 sec. after throttle close position.
③—65 sec. after start or 3 sec. after throttle close condition.

| Spark Control Computer | 4289352 | 4289356 | 4289357 | 4289364 |
|---|---|---|---|---|
| Basic Timing | 16° | 12° | 16° | 16° |
| Spark Advance Test @ 2000 RPM | 43°±4° | 20°±4° | 21°±4° | 42°±4° |
| Electronic EGR Time Delay | 60 sec. | 65 sec. | 65 sec. | 20 sec. |
| Electronic Throttle Control | ② | ③ | ③ | ① |

①—20 sec. after start or 1 sec. after throttle close condition.
②—60 sec. after start or 2 sec. after throttle close position.
③—65 sec. after start or 3 sec. after throttle close condition.

## 1985 REAR WHEEL DRIVE MODELS

| Spark Control Computer | 4289601 | 4289603 | 4289613 | 4289615 |
|---|---|---|---|---|
| Basic Timing | 16° | 12° | 12° | 16° |
| Spark Advance Test @ 2000 RPM | 38°±4° | 33°±4° | 30°±4° | 30°±4° |
| Electronic EGR Time Delay | 60 sec. | 45 sec. | 60 sec. | 28 sec. |
| Electronic Throttle Control | ① | ② | ③ | ④ |

①—90 sec. after start or 2 sec. after throttle close condition.
②—60 sec. after start or 1 sec. after throttle close condition.
③—90 sec. after start or 1 sec. after throttle close condition.
④—60 sec. after start or 2 sec. after throttle close condition.

| Spark Control Computer | 4289617 | 4289621 | 4289637 |
|---|---|---|---|
| Basic Timing | 12° | 12° | 8° |
| Spark Advance Test @ 2000 RPM | 30°±4° | 37°±4° | 34°±4° |
| Electronic EGR Time Delay | 65 sec. | 60 sec. | 25 sec. |
| Electronic Throttle Control | 60 sec. | — | ① |

①—25 sec after start or 1 sec. after throttle close position.

## 1986 REAR WHEEL DRIVE MODELS

| Spark Control Computer | 4289603 | 4289615 | 4289617 | 4289637 | 4289637 |
|---|---|---|---|---|---|
| Basic Timing | 12° | 16° | 12° | 8° | 8° |
| Spark Advance Test @ 2200 RPM | 33°±4° | 30°±4° | 30°±4° | 34°±4° | 34°±4° |
| Electronic EGR Time Delay | 45 sec. | 28 sec. | 65 sec. | 25 sec. | 25 sec. |
| Electronic Throttle Control | ① | ② | ③ | ④ | ⑤ |

①—60 sec. hot after start. 1 sec. kick.
②—60 sec. after start. 2 sec. after kick.
③—60 sec. after start.
④—25 sec. hot after start. 1 sec. kick.
⑤—25 sec. after start. 1 sec. kick.

| Spark Control Computer | 4289845 | 4289908 | 4289977 | 4289982 | 4289236 |
|---|---|---|---|---|---|
| Basic Timing | 8° | 16° | 8° | 12° | 8° |
| Spark Advance Test @ 2200 RPM | 34°±4° | 36°±4° | 45°±4° | 45°±4° | 42°±4° |
| Electronic EGR Time Delay | 25 sec. | 60 sec. | 25 sec. | 5 sec. | 25 sec. |
| Electronic Throttle Control | ① | ② | ⑤ | ③ | ④ |

①—25 sec. hot after start.
②—90 sec. hot after start. 2 sec. kick.
③—60 sec. hot after start. 10 sec. kick.
④—25 sec. hot after start. 1 sec. kick.
⑤—25 sec. after start. 1 sec. kick.

## 1987 REAR WHEEL DRIVE VEHICLES

| Spark Control Computer | 4289603 | 4289615 | 4289617 | 4289908 | 4379082 |
|---|---|---|---|---|---|
| Basic Timing | 12° | 16° | 12° | 16° | 12° |
| Spark Advance Test @ 2000 RPM | 33°±4° | 30°±4° | 30°±4° | 36°±4° | 45°±4° |
| Electronic EGR Time Delay | 45 sec. | 28 sec. | 65 sec. | 60 sec. | 5 sec. |
| Electronic Throttle Control | ① | ② | ③ | ④ | ⑤ |

①—60 sec. hot after start 1 sec. kick.    ④—90 sec. hot after start 2 sec. kick.
②—60 sec. hot after start 2 sec. kick.    ⑤—60 sec. hot after start 10 sec. kick.
③—60 sec. after start

| Spark Control Computer | 4379096 | 4379107 | 4379109 | 4379236 |
|---|---|---|---|---|
| Basic Timing | 8° | 8° | 8° | 8° |
| Spark Advance Test @ 2000 RPM | ① | 34°±4° | 34°±4° | 42°±4° |
| Electronic EGR Time Delay | 25 sec. | 25 sec. | 25 sec. | 25 sec. |
| Electronic Throttle Control | ② | ③ | ② | ④ |

①—34°±4° or 45°±4°.    ③—25 sec. hot after start.
②—25 sec. after start 1 sec. kick.    ④—25 sec. hot after start 1 sec. kick.

# Ignition Timing Adjustments

## INDEX

## JEEP

### 4 CYLINDER ENGINES

On carbureted engines, ignition timing should be checked at 30,000 mile intervals, with engine at normal operating temperature, with distributor vacuum advance hose disconnected and plugged. On 4-150/2.46L engines, disconnect three wire connector at vacuum input switches when checking ignition timing. On 4-151/2.5L California engines with EST, disconnect 4 wire Electronic Spark Timing (EST) connector at distributor when checking ignition timing.

On 4-150/2.46L engine with Throttle Body Injection (TBI), the ignition timing is not adjustable. Refer to Tune Specifications chart for ignition timing and firing order.

### IN-LINE 6 CYLINDER ENGINES

Check or adjust ignition timing with engine at normal operating temperature and with distributor vacuum advance hose disconnected and plugged. Refer to Tune Up Specifications chart for ignition timing and firing order.

### 1980–82

1. Connect timing light and tachometer following manufacturer's instructions.
2. On 1982 California and high altitude models, disconnect Yellow and Black wires from 2-wire connector at electronic ignition module, then place a suitable jumper wire across Yellow and Black wires.
3. Check ignition timing with A/C control in off position, if equipped, and engine running at specified curb idle speed.
4. Adjust as needed by rotating distributor.

### 1983–89 6-258 Engine

1. Connect timing light and tachometer following manufacturer's instructions.
2. Disconnect electrical connector from vacuum switches located on cylinder head cover.
3. Start engine and run at 1600 RPM.
4. Check and adjust ignition timing as needed, return engine to idle and ensure that curb idle speed is within specifications.

### 1987–89 6-243

Ignition timing is controlled by the ICM (Ignition Control Module), therefore no adjustment is required.

### V6 ENGINES

Check or adjust ignition timing with engine at normal operating temperature, distributor vacuum advance hose and EGR valve hose disconnected and plugged. On models equipped with EST, disconnect EST connector at distributor. Refer to Tune Up Specification chart for ignition timing setting and firing order.

### V8 ENGINES

Check or adjust ignition timing with engine at normal operating temperature and distributor vacuum advance hose disconnected and plugged. Refer to Tune Up Specifications chart for ignition timing and correct firing order.

## CHRYSLER

### 4 CYLINDER ENGINES

Check or adjust ignition timing with engine at normal operating temperature. On all 4-156 engines and 1982-83 4-135 engines, disconnect and plug vacuum line from distributor. On 1984-87 4-135 engines, disconnect and plug vacuum line from spark control computer. Connect jumper wire between carburetor switch and ground, if equipped with carburetor switch. On 1987 4-153 engines, check ignition timing with engine coolant temperature sensor disconnected. Fan should operate and instrument panel lamp should be illuminated when coolant temperature sensor is disconnected. Refer to Tune Up Specifications for ignition timing and firing order.

### INLINE 6 CYLINDER ENGINES

Check or adjust ignition timing with engine at normal operating temperature and curb idle RPM set to specifications. On models equipped with carburetor switch, connect jumper wire between switch and ground. On models equipped with Electronic Spark Control (ESC), disconnect and plug EGR vacuum hose at EGR valve and vacuum hose at the ESC computer.

On models equipped with Spark Control Computer (SCC), disconnect and plug vacuum hose at SCC. On models not equipped with SCC or ESC, disconnect and plug vacuum hose at distributor and EGR valve, if equipped.

## V6 ENGINES

Ignition timing should be checked or set with engine at operating temperature. On V6-181 engines, disconnect coolant temperature sensor electrical connector when checking ignition timing. The engine cooling fan should be operating and the instrument panel lamp should be illuminated when the coolant temperature sensor is disconnected. On V6-238 engines, the ignition timing should be checked with vacuum lines disconnected from the vacuum transducer on the spark control computer and a with jumper wire connected between connected between carburetor switch idle stop and ground. Refer to Tune Up Specifications chart for ignition timing and firing order.

## V8 ENGINES

Check or adjust ignition timing with engine at normal operating temperature and curb idle RPM set to specifications. On models equipped with carburetor switch, connect jumper wire between switch and ground. On models equipped with Electronic Spark Control (ESC), disconnect and plug EGR vacuum hose at EGR valve and vacuum hose at the ESC computer. On models equipped with Spark Control Computer (SCC), disconnect and plug vacuum hose at SCC. On models not equipped with SCC or ESC, disconnect and plug vacuum hose at distributor and EGR valve, if equipped.

# Motorcraft Solid State Ignition System

## INDEX

## DESCRIPTION

The solid state ignition system, **Figs. 1 through 3,** consist of an ignition switch, electronic control unit, ignition coil, primary resistance wire and bypass, distributor, spark plugs and on models with electronic feedback system, an electronic spark retard.

The electronic ignition control unit is a solid state , moisture resistant module. Internal components are sealed in a potting material to resist environmental conditions and vibration. Reverse polarity and transient voltage protection are incorporated into the module.

The distributor incorporates, **Fig. 4,** a sensor and trigger wheel. Current flowing through the ignition coil, creates a magnetic field in the primary windings. When the circuit is opened, the magnetic field collapses and induces a high voltage in the secondary windings. This current is electrically controlled by the electronic ignition control unit. The signal to operate the control unit is provided by the distributor sensor and trigger wheel. The trigger wheel is mounted ion the distributor shaft and has one tooth for each cylinder. The sensor, a coil of fine wire mounted to a permanent magnet, develops an electromagnetic force that is sensitive to the presence of a ferrous metal. When a trigger wheel tooth approaches the sensor pole piece, reluctance of the magnetic field is reduced, increasing field strength. As the tooth moves away from the sensor pole piece, field strength will decrease. This increase and decrease of field strength produces and alternating current which is interpreted by the electronic ignition control unit. The control unit then opens and closes the ignition primary circuit.

Since there are no contacting surfaces, no wear occurs and dwell angle requires no adjustment. Dwell angle is electronically controlled by the electronic ignition control unit. When the coil circuit is switched open, an electronic timer in the control unit keeps the circuit open only long enough for the spark to discharge. After the spark discharge, the electronic control unit will automatically close the ignition primary circuit.

## DIAGNOSIS

### SECONDARY CIRCUIT TEST

1. Disconnect coil wire from distributor cap, then using insulated pliers, hold wire approximately 1/2 inch a good engine ground. Crank engine an observe wire for spark.
   a. If spark is present, proceed to step 2.
   b. If no spark is present, proceed to step 3.
2. Connect coil wire to distributor cap, then disconnect one spark plug wire at spark plug. Do not disconnect spark plug wire form cylinder No. 3 on 4-150 engine, cylinders No. 1 and 5 on 6-258 engines or cylinders 3 and 4 on V8-360 engines. Removal of these spark plug wires may result in damage to sensor. Using insulated pliers hold spark plug wire approximately 1/2 inch from a good engine ground. While cranking engine, observe wire for spark.
   a. If spark is present, check ignition timing or fuel system problems.
   b. If no spark is present, check for defective distributor cap, rotor or spark plug wires.
3. If no spark was present at coil wire, measure coil secondary winding resistance. If resistance is more than 12,000 ohms, replace coil.
4. If problem still exist, proceed with the following test procedures.

### IGNITION COIL PRIMARY CIRCUIT TEST

1. Place ignition switch in the On position and connect a voltmeter between ignition coil positive terminal and ground.
   a. If voltage is 5.5 to 6.5 volts, proceed to step 2.
   b. If battery voltage is noted, proceed to step 4.
   c. If voltage reading is below 5.5 volts, disconnect condenser lead. If voltage reading with capacitor lead disconnected is now 5.5 to 6.5 volts, replace capacitor. If reading is still not within limits, proceed to step 7.
2. Check voltage at ignition coil positive terminal while cranking engine.
   a. If battery voltage is present, the ignition coil primary circuit is satisfactory.
   b. If less than battery voltage is present, proceed to step 3.
3. Check short or open circuit at starter motor solenoid "I"terminal or for defective starter motor solenoid and repair or replace as necessary.
4. With ignition switch in the On position, disconnect electrical lead from starter motor solenoid "I" terminal and measure voltage at ignition coil positive terminal.
   a. If voltage is now 5.5 to 6.5 volt, replace starter motor solenoid.
   b. If battery voltage is indicated, proceed to step 5.
5. With ignition switch On and electrical lead disconnected at starter motor solenoid "I" terminal disconnected, connect a jumper wire from ignition coil

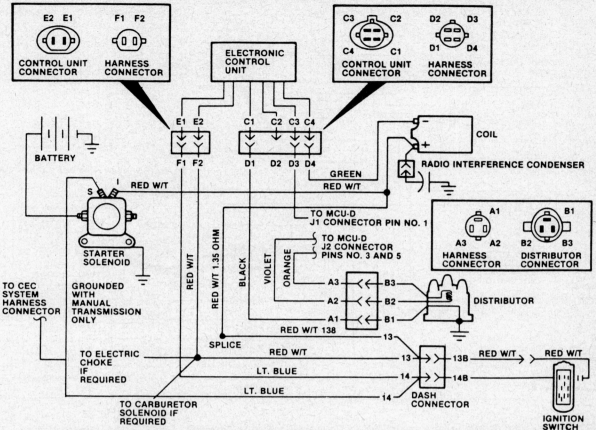

**Fig. 1  Motorcraft Solid State Ignition (SSI) System. 1980–83 6-258 & 1983–85 4-150 Engines**

negative terminal to ground and measure voltage at ignition coil positive terminal.

  a. If battery voltage is still indicated, proceed to step 7.

  b. If voltage reading is now 5.5 to 6.5 volts, proceed to step 6.

6. Check continuity between ignition coil negative terminal and electronic control unit D4, **Figs. 1 through 3.** Also check continuity between electronic control unit terminal D1 and ground.

  a. If continuity exist, replace electronic control unit.

  b. If continuity does not exist, locate and repair open circuit, then repeat step 2.

7. Place ignition switch in the Off position and measure resistance between ignition coil positive terminal and dash panel connector terminal 13 or FW depending on model, **Figs. 1 through 3.**

  a. If resistance is more than 1.4 ohms, replace resistance wire.

  b. If resistance is between 1.3 and 1.4 ohms, proceed to step 8.

8. With ignition switch in the Off position, measure resistance between dash panel connector terminal 13 or FW ,depending on model, and ignition switch terminal I1, **Figs. 1 through 3.**

  a. If resistance is less than .1 ohm, check for defective ignition switch or wiring from ignition switch to battery.

  b. If resistance is more than .1 ohm, check for faulty connection at dash

connector or ignition switch or defective wiring. After repairing, proceed to ignition coil test.

## IGNITION COIL TEST

1. Check ignition coil for oil leaks, carbon tracking and other exterior damage and replace as necessary.

2. Disconnect ignition coil electrical connector and connect an ohmmeter between coil positive and negative terminals. Ohmmeter reading should be 1.13 to 1.23 ohms at 75°F or 1.5 ohms at 200°F.

  a. If ohmmeter reading is not within limits, replace coil.

  b. If ohmmeter reading is within limits, proceed to step 3.

3. Connect ohmmeter between coil center tower and either coil positive or negative terminal. Ohmmeter reading should be 7700 to 9300 ohms at 75°F or 12000 ohms at 200°F.

  a. If ohmmeter reading is within limits, coil is satisfactory.

  b. If ohmmeter reading is not within limits, replace coil.

## CONTROL UNIT & SENSOR CHECK

### 4-150 & 6-258

1. Disconnect four wire connector at ignition control unit, then remove ignition coil wire from distributor and hold

approximately ½ inch from a good engine ground with insulated pliers. Place ignition switch in the On position and note if spark is present at coil wire.

  a. If spark is present at coil wire proceed to step 2.

  b. If spark is not present at coil wire, proceed to step 5.

2. Disconnect Microprocessor Computer Unit (MCU) electrical connector J2 and connect ohmmeter between pins 3 and 5.

  a. If ohmmeter reading is between 400 to 800 ohms, proceed to step 6.

  b. If ohmmeter reading is not between 400 to 800 ohms, proceed to step 3.

3. With ohmmeter leads still connected between MCU J2 electrical connector terminals 3 and 5. disconnect and reconnect three wire electrical connector at distributor.

  a. If ohmmeter now reads 400 to 800 ohms, proceed to step 6.

  b. If ohmmeter reading is not between 400 to 800 ohms, proceed to step 4.

4. Disconnect three wire connector at distributor and connect ohmmeter between terminals B2 and B3, **Figs. 2 and 3.**

  a. If ohmmeter now indicates 400 to 800 ohms, check for defective wiring between three wire electrical connector and four wire electrical connector.

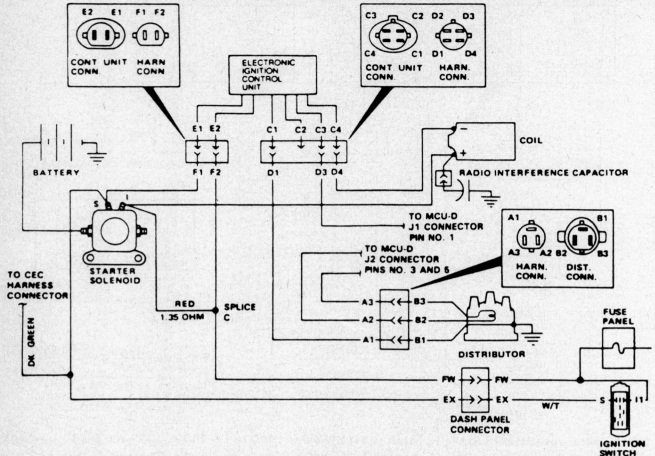

**Fig. 2   Motorcraft Solid State Ignition (SSI) System. 1984–89 6-258 engines**

b. If ohmmeter does not indicate 400 to 800 ohms, replace pick up coil.
5. Connect ohmmeter between terminal D1 and battery ground terminal.
   a. If ohmmeter indicates 0 to .002 ohms, proceed to step 2.
   b. If ohmmeter does not indicate 0 to .002 ohms, check ground cable resistance, distributor to block resistance and distributor ground screw to terminal D1 for source of faulty ground.
6. With a suitable DC voltmeter connected between MCU J2 electrical connector terminals 3 and 5, turn ignition switch to start position and note voltmeter reading.
   a. If voltmeter fluctuates, pick up coil and trigger wheel are operating properly.
   b. If voltmeter does not fluctuate, check for missing trigger wheel pin, defective trigger wheel or for cause of distributor not rotating.

## V8-360

1. Disconnect four wire connector at ignition control unit, then remove coil wire from distributor and hold approximately 1/2 inch from a good engine ground. Place ignition switch in the On position and note if spark is present at coil wire.
   a. If spark is present at coil wire, pro-

ceed to step 2.
   b If spark is not present, proceed to step 5.
2. Using a suitable ohmmeter, measure resistance between terminals D2 and D3 of ignition control unit electrical connector, **Fig. 3.**
   a. If resistance is 400 to 800 ohms, proceed to step 6.
   b. If resistance is other than 400 to 800 ohms, proceed to step 3.
3. With ohmmeter connected between ignition control unit connector terminals D2 and D3, disconnect and reconnect distributor three wire connector and note ohmmeter reading.
   a. If ohmmeter reading is now 400 to 800 ohms, proceed to step 6.
   b. If ohmmeter still reads other than 400 to 800 ohms, disconnect three wire connector at distributor and proceed to step 4.
4. Connect ohmmeter between distributor connector terminals B2 and B3 and note reading.
   a. If ohmmeter now indicates 400 to 800 ohms, check wiring between distributor three wire and ignition four wire connectors and repair or replace as necessary.
   b. If ohmmeter indicates other than 400 to 800 ohms, replace pick up coil.
5. Connect ohmmeter between terminals D1 and battery negative cable.

a. If ohmmeter indicates 0 to .02 ohms, proceed to step 2.
   b. If ohmmeter indicates above .02 ohms, check ground cable resistance, distributor to engine block resistance and distributor internal ground screw to terminal D1 for source of faulty ground.
6. Connect voltmeter between connector terminals D2 and D3, then turn ignition switch to Start position and note voltmeter needle movement.
   a. If voltmeter needle is fluctuating, pick up coil and trigger wheel are operating properly.
   b. If voltmeter needle does not fluctuate, check for missing trigger wheel pin, defective trigger wheel or other cause for distributor not rotating.

## IGNITION FEED TO ELECTRONIC IGNITION CONTROL UNIT TEST

The Ignition coil Primary Test must be performed before proceeding with the following test.
1. With ignition switch in the On position, disconnect two wire connector at control unit and connect voltmeter between terminal F2 and ground, **Figs. 1 through 3.**
   a. If voltmeter does indicate within .2 volts of battery voltage, replacer

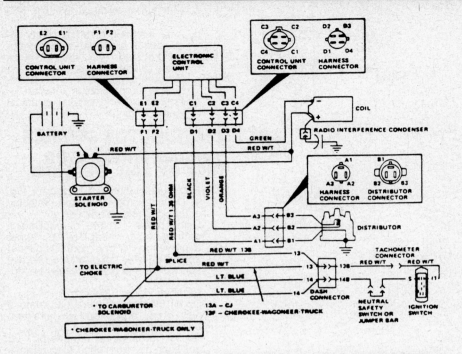

**Fig. 3  Motorcraft Solid State Ignition (SSI) System. V8-360 engines**

for defective vacuum switch or wiring from switch to Microprocessor Computer Unit (MCU). If switch and wiring are satisfactory, replace MCU and repeat test.

b. If timing did increase, proceed to step 7.

7. Allow engine to return to idle and connect electrical connector to knock sensor. Increase engine speed to 1600 RPM, while noting timing marks, knock on intake manifold in area of knock sensor. Ignition timing should retard.

a. If ignition timing did retard, system is satisfactory. allow engine to return to idle and reconnect distributor vacuum advance hose.

b. If ignition timing did not retard, check continuity of wiring between knock sensor and MCU J2 electrical connector terminal 16 on 1983 models. On 1984-89 models check continuity between knock sensor and MCU J2 electrical connector terminal 51. If wiring is faulty, repair or replace as necessary. If wiring is satisfactory, replace knock sensor and retest.

## INTERMITTENT FAILURE DIAGNOSIS

Intermittent failures are temporary. If the engine fails to start on the first try, it will eventually start on succeeding tries. If an intermittent failure occurs when the vehicle is operating, the engine may stop, but it will restart and continue operate intermittently.

## ENGINE WILL NOT START

If spark is present at spark plugs, check ignition timing or fuel system for cause. If no spark is present at spark plugs, check for the following:

1. Check for voltage to ignition system. Check battery, ignition switch and related wiring.
2. Check electronic control unit ground wires in distributor.
3. Check primary wire connectors for proper connection.
4. Check for open or shorted ignition coil.
5. Check for defective electronic control unit.
6. Check for defective distributor cap or rotor.

## ENGINE MISFIRES BUT WILL NOT START

1. Check ignition timing.
2. Check for moisture inside distributor.
3. Check for defective distributor cap.
4. Ensure spark plug wires are connected in correct firing order.

## ENGINE WILL RUN ONLY WITH IGNITION SWITCH IN START POSITION

1. Check resistance wire for excessive resistance or open circuit.

---

control unit and proceed to step 3.

b. If voltmeter does not indicate within .2 volts of battery voltage, proceed to step 2.

2. Check for corroded dash connector and ignition switch for causes of voltage reduction and repair as necessary. After completing repairs, disconnect ignition coil wire from distributor cap and check for spark.

a. If spark is present at coil wire, control unit and ignition feed are satisfactory.

b. If spark is not present at coil wire, replace control unit.

3. Connect control unit two wire connector, then disconnect control unit four wire connector and connect ammeter between terminal C1 and ground.

a. If ammeter indicates 1 amp, control unit is satisfactory.

b. If ammeter indicates other than 1 amp, replace control unit.

## CURRENT FLOW TEST

1. Remove electrical connector from ignition coil.
2. Remove positive and negative leads from coil connector by depressing plastic barbs, which are visible from coil side of connector.
3. Connect a suitable ammeter between coil positive terminal and positive lead, then connect a jumper wire coil negative terminal and a good ground. Place ignition switch in the On position and note ammeter reading.

a. Ammeter should indicate approximately 7 amps, not exceeding 7.6 amps.

b. If current flow exceeds 7.6 amps, replace ignition coil.

4. With ammeter still connected between coil positive terminal and positive lead, connect coil green wire to coil negative lead. Ammeter reading should be approximately 4 amps.

a. If ammeter reading is less than 3.5 amps, check for faulty connections at distributor three wire connector and ignition control unit four wire connector. Also check distributor internal ground screw for poor ground.

b. If ammeter reading is above 5 amps, replace ignition control unit.

5. Start engine and note ammeter reading. If ammeter reading is not between 2 to 2.4 amps, replace ignition control unit.

## ELECTRONIC SPARK RETARD TEST

1. With engine at operating temperature, disconnect vacuum switch electrical connector. The vacuum switch electrical connector is located on the wheel housing.
2. Disconnect and plug distributor vacuum advance hose.
3. Disconnect electrical connector from knock sensor and ground to engine block using a jumper wire.
4. Increase engine speed to 1600 RPM and check and adjust ignition timing as necessary.
5. Allow engine to return to idle speed, then reconnect vacuum switch electrical connector.
6. While observing timing marks, advance engine speed to 1600 RPM. Timing should advance 6° over the degree noted in step 4.

a. If timing does not advance, check

## ENGINE CONTINUES TO RUN WITH IGNITION SWITCH IN OFF POSITION

1. Check for defective starter motor solenoid.
2. Check alternator warning lamp circuit for defective diode.

## ROUGH ENGINE OPERATION &/OR ENGINE MISFIRE AT HIGH SPEED

1. Check condition of spark plugs.
2. Check condition of ignition wire, including electronic retard.
3. Check spark advance system.
4. Ensure distributor trigger wheel pin is properly installed.
5. Ensure spark plug wires are connected in correct firing order.
6. Ensure two spark plug wires of consecutive firing cylinders are not routed next to each other.
7. Check for short at S terminal at starter solenoid.

## FUEL CONSUMPTION EXCESSIVE

1. Check ignition timing,
2. Check spark advance system.
3. Check for defective microprocessor (MCU).

## TIMING ADVANCE ERRATIC

1. Check for defective vacuum advance unit.
2. Check for sticking mechanical advance weights.

## VACUUM ADVANCE NOT FUNCTIONING

1. Check for defective vacuum advance unit.
2. Ensure vacuum advance unit adjusting screw is not rotated too far counterclockwise.
3. Check for corroded or sticking pick up coil pivot.

## INTERMITTENT OPERATION

1. Check ignition system terminals for loose or corroded connections.
2. Check for defective pick up coil.
3. Check for defective electronic control unit.
4. Check distributor trigger wheel pin for proper installation.
5. Check for loose distributor ground connector.
6. Check wiring to distributor for short circuit.

# DISTRIBUTOR
## REPLACE

1. Remove distributor cap with wires attached and position aside.
2. Disconnect vacuum advance hose and primary electrical wiring from.
3. Mark position of distributor rotor to distributor housing and distributor housing to engine block.
4. Remove distributor hold down bolt and clamp, then carefully withdraw distributor from engine.
5. If engine has not been disturbed while distributor was removed from engine,

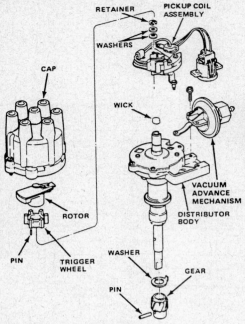

**Fig. 4  Exploded view of distributor assembly. 6-258 shown, 4-150 & V8-360 similar**

Reverse procedure to install and note the following:
a. Lubricate distributor drive gear with SAE 50 engine oil prior to installation.
b. Prior inserting distributor into engine block, position rotor 1/8 turn counterclockwise past mark made on distributor housing.
c. Distributor shaft should be fully engaged with oil pump driveshaft.
d. When distributor is installed in engine block, marks made during removal should be aligned.
e. After completing installation, adjust ignition timing.
6. If engine was disturbed while distributor was removed, proceed as follows:
a. Remove spark plug from No. 1 cylinder.
b. Place finger over spark plug hole for No. 1 cylinder and slowly crank engine until compression is felt.
c. Carefully continue to rotate engine in direction of rotation until timing mark on damper is aligned with TDC mark on timing tab. Do not rotate engine in opposite direction to align timing marks.
d. Lubricate distributor drive gear with SAE 50 engine oil.
e. Rotate distributor shaft until rotor points in direction of No. 1 cylinder in distributor cap, then turn rotor an additional 1/8 turn in the counterclockwise direction.
f. Insert distributor into engine block and ensure rotor is aligned with No. 1 cylinder terminal in distributor cap and distributor shaft is fully engaged with oil pump drive shaft. It may be necessary to rotate oil pump driveshaft with a long flat blade screwdriver to align rotor

with No. 1 terminal in distributor cap.
g. After inserting distributor into engine block, align marks on distributor housing and engine block made during removal.
h. Reverse remained of removal procedure to complete installation.
i. After completing installation, adjust ignition timing.

# DISTRIBUTOR SERVICE
## TRIGGER WHEEL &/OR PICK UP COIL, REPLACE

1. Remove distributor cap and rotor, **Fig. 4.** Do not remove silicone dielectric compound rotor blade tip.
2. Using puller J-28509 or equivalent, remove trigger wheel. Use flat washer to prevent puller from contacting inner shaft. If puller is not available, use two screwdrivers to pry alternately on trigger wheel.
3. Remove trigger wheel pin.
4. On 4-150 and 6-258 engines, remove pick up coil retainer and washers from base plate pivot pin.
5. On V8-360 engines, remove pick up coil snap ring from shaft, then remove retainer securing vacuum advance lever to pick up coil drive pin and position lever aside.
6. Remove ground screw from harness tab, then lift pick up coil assembly from distributor housing.
7. Reverse procedure to install. When installing trigger wheel, position long portion of teeth upward and install on shaft using hand pressure. Use a small hammer and suitable drift and tap trigger wheel pin into locating groove. If distributor is removed from engine, support shaft when installing trigger wheel pin. If a replacement rotor is to be installed, apply a thin coat of silicone dielectric compound to rotor blade tip prior to installation.

## VACUUM ADVANCE UNIT

1. Disconnect vacuum hose from vacuum advance unit, **Fig. 4.**
2. On 4-150 and 6-258 engines, remove attaching screws, then tilt vacuum advance unit to disengage link from pick up coil pin. On some units, it may be necessary to loosen base plate retaining screws to provide clearance for vacuum advance unit removal.
3. On V8-360 engines, remove distributor cap, then remove retainer securing vacuum advance unit to pick up coil pin. Remove vacuum advance unit attaching screws and lift unit from distributor.
4. Reverse procedure to install. If a replacement unit is to be installed, insert a suitable allen wrench into vacuum hose opening of the unit which was removed. Rotate adjusting screw clockwise, counting the number of turn necessary to bottom screw. Rotate adjusting screw of replacement vacuum advance unit clockwise unit it bottoms, then rotate adjusting screw counterclockwise the same amount of turns noted.

# Delco-Remy High Energy Ignition System

## INDEX

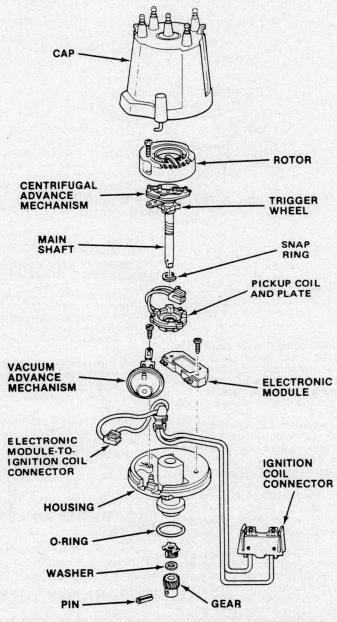

CAP

ROTOR

CENTRIFUGAL ADVANCE MECHANISM

TRIGGER WHEEL

MAIN SHAFT

SNAP RING

PICKUP COIL AND PLATE

VACUUM ADVANCE MECHANISM

ELECTRONIC MODULE

ELECTRONIC MODULE-TO-IGNITION COIL CONNECTOR

IGNITION COIL CONNECTOR

HOUSING

O-RING

WASHER

PIN

GEAR

**Fig. 1   Exploded view of high energy ignition system distributor. 4-151 model shown, V6-173 similar**

## DESCRIPTION

The High Energy Ignition (HEI) system, **Fig. 1**, used on these engines has an externally mounted ignition coil. On 4-151 and Federal V6-173 engines, centrifugal and vacuum advance is used to control spark timing. On V6-173 California engines, an Electronic Spark Timing (EST) distributor is used, **Fig. 2**, in which spark timing is controlled by the Electronic Control Module (ECM). The distributor, requires no periodic lubrications, as the lower bushing is lubricated by the engine oil and the upper bushing is lubricated by an oil filled reservoir. Dwell on HEI system is controlled by the ECM and can not be adjusted.

## DIAGNOSIS

### 4-151 & FEDERAL V6-173 ENGINES

When performing diagnostic procedures the following precautions should be noted:
1. When disconnecting electrical connector at ignition coil, do not use screwdriver or other tools, as damage to connector may result.
2. Do not connect tachometer terminal to ground, as this may cause damage to ignition coil or ECM.
3. Use care when handling spark plug wires. Also ensure spark plug wires are properly routed.
4. Ensure tachometer and other test equipment is compatible with the HEI system before using.

### ENGINE WILL NOT START

1. If equipped, disconnect tachometer electrical lead from tachometer terminal.
2. Using tool No. J-26792, check for spark at spark plug wire.
   a. If spark is present, problem is not in HEI system, check spark plugs and fuel system.
   b. If no spark is present, check another spark plug wire. If no spark is present, proceed to step 3.
3. Using a suitable voltmeter, check voltage at ignition coil B+ terminal while cranking engine.
   a. If reading is under 7 volts, check primary electrical circuit to ignition switch and repair as necessary.
   b. If 7 or more volts is present, proceed to step 4.
4. Check for voltage at Tach terminal

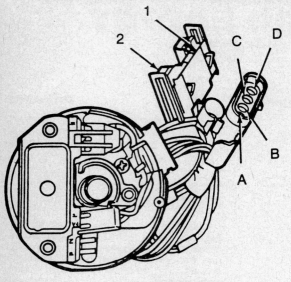

1. B+ (BATTERY)
2. C- (COIL)

A. EST SIGNAL
B. EST REF PULSE
C. EST BYPASS
D. EST DISTRIBUTOR GROUND

**49 STATE AND CALIFORNIA**

1. B+ (BATTERY)
2. C- (COIL)

**CALIFORNIA ONLY (EST)**

A. EST SIGNAL
B. EST REF PULSE
C. EST BYPASS
D. EST DISTRIBUTOR GROUND

**Fig. 2 Electronic Spark Timing (EST) distributor. California V6-173 engines**

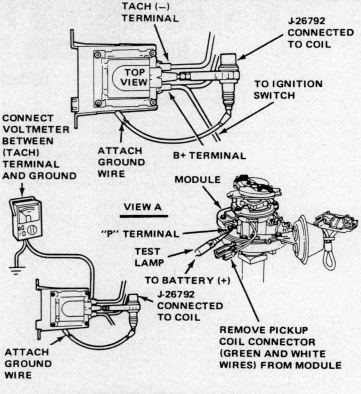

**Fig. 3 Distributor & coil diagnostic test connections**

with ignition switch in the On position.

a. If less than 1 volt is present, replace ignition coil.

b. If between 1 and 10 volts is present, replace ECM and check for spark at spark plug as described in step 2. If spark is present, HEI system is satisfactory. If spark is not present, replace ignition coil, as it is also defective.

c. If voltage reading is more than 10 volts, proceed to step 5.

5. Connect tool No. J-26792 to coil output terminal and check for spark while cranking engine, Fig. 3 (view A).

a. If spark is present, check distributor cap and rotor for damage and replace as necessary.

b. If no spark is present, proceed to step 6.

6. Remove pickup coil electrical connector from module, then place ignition switch in the On position. Connect a voltmeter with a high input impedance to Tach (-) terminal while momentarily connecting test lamp to module P terminal and note voltage reading. Do not leave test lamp connected to P terminal for longer than 5 seconds.

a. If there is no drop in voltage, check

module ground and circuit between coil and distributor. If module ground and electrical circuit between coil and distributor are satisfactory, replace module.

b. If a voltage drop is noted, proceed to step 7.

7. Using tool No. J-26792, check for spark at coil output terminal as test lamp is remove from module P terminal, Fig. 3 (view B).

a. If spark is present, replace pickup coil.

b. If a no spark is condition is encountered, proceed to step 8 if module tester is not available. If module tester is available, proceed to step 9.

8. If module tester is not available, check coil ground circuit and repair as necessary. If coil ground circuit is satisfactory, check coil as described under "Component Testing" and replace if defective. If coil is satisfactory, replace module.

9. If module tester is available, check module and replace if defective. If module is satisfactory, check coil ground circuit and repair as necessary. If coil ground circuit is satisfacto-

ry, replace coil.

## INTERMITTENT ENGINE OPERATION OR MISFIRE

1. Using tool No. J-26792, check for spark at two spark plug wires.

a. If no spark is present, refer to "Engine Will Not Start."

b. If spark is present, proceed to step 2.

2. Perform pickup coil test as described under "Component Testing."

a. If defective, replace pickup coil.

b. If pickup coil is satisfactory, refer to step 3.

3. Check for dwell increase from high RPM to low RPM.

a. If a dwell increase is noted, HEI system is satisfactory, check ignition wire, distributor cap, rotor, spark plugs and fuel system.

b. If a dwell increase was not noted, replace module.

## CALIFORNIA V6-173 ENGINES

Refer to "General Motors Corp. Section" for diagnostic procedures on models equipped with Electric Spark Timing (EST).

## COMPONENT TESTING

The following tests may be performed with distributor installed on the engine or on a work bench.

### IGNITION COIL

1. With electrical connector disconnect-

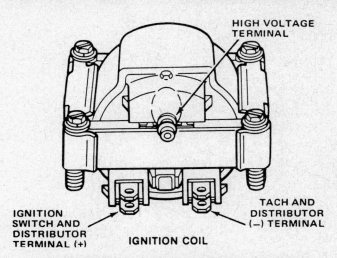

**Fig. 4   Ignition coil terminal identification**

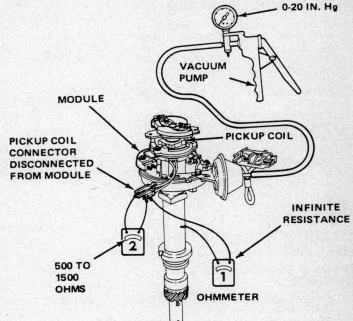

**Fig. 5   Pickup coil test connections**

ed, connect an ohmmeter set at high resistance scale between coil positive terminal and coil frame, **Fig. 4.** Ohmmeter should indicate infinite resistance, if not replace coil.

2. Connect ohmmeter set at low resistance scale between coil positive and negative terminals. Ohmmeter should read 0 or near 0 ohms, if not replace coil.

3. Connect ohmmeter set at high resistance scale between coil negative and high voltage terminals. Ohmmeter should indicate less than infinite resistance, if not replace coil.

## PICKUP COIL
### 4-151 & FEDERAL V6-173 ENGINES

During the following test, when operating the vacuum pump, the vacuum mechanism may cause the trigger wheel and pickup pole piece to align, causing the ohmmeter pointer to deflect. This deflection should not be considered as an indication of a defective pickup coil.

1. Disconnect pickup coil electrical connector.
2. Connect a suitable hand held vacuum pump to vacuum advance unit, **Fig. 5.**
3. Connect an ohmmeter set at mid scale to one of the pickup coil connector terminals and the other lead to distributor housing.
4. While operating vacuum pump, note ohmmeter reading. Ohmmeter should indicate infinite resistance at all times, if not replace pickup coil.
5. Connect ohmmeter between both pickup coil connector terminals. While flexing pickup coil wire, operate vacuum pump and note ohmmeter reading. Ohmmeter should indicate 500 to 1500 ohms at all times, if not replace pickup coil.

### CALIFORNIA V6-173 ENGINES

1. Disconnect pickup coil electrical connector.
2. Connect an ohmmeter set at mid scale to one of the pickup coil connector terminals and the other lead to distributor housing. Ohmmeter should indicate infinite resistance, if not replace pickup coil.
3. Connect ohmmeter between pickup coil terminals and note reading while flexing wires. A steady resistance reading of 500 to 1500 ohms should be obtained. If reading is not as specified, replace pickup coil.

## ELECTRONIC CONTROL MODULE

Testing of the Electronic Control Module (ECM), requires the use of tester J-24642 or equivalent. Follow tester manufacturers instructions when testing the ECM.

## DISTRIBUTOR
### REPLACE

1. Disconnect electrical connector from ignition coil.
2. Disconnect electrical leads to ignition switch and tachometer, if equipped.
3. Using a suitable screwdriver, rotate distributor cap latches counterclockwise, then remove distributor cap and position out of way.
4. Disconnect vacuum hose from vacuum advance unit, if equipped.
5. Mark position of distributor rotor to distributor housing and position of distributor housing to engine.
6. Remove distributor hold down clamp bolts and hold down clamp.
7. Carefully pull distributor upward until rotor stops turning counterclockwise and again mark position of rotor to distributor housing.
8. Remove distributor from engine.
9. Reverse procedure to install, aligning positioning marks made during removal. After completing installation, check ignition timing. If engine was disturbed while distributor was re-

moved, proceed as follows:
a. Remove spark plug from No. 1 cylinder.
b. With finger positioned over No. 1 spark plug opening, slowly rotate engine until compression is felt.
c. Align timing mark on damper with TDC mark on timing degree scale.
d. Position rotor at a point between No. 1 and No. 3 spark plug terminals on distributor cap for 4-151 engines. For V6-173 engines, position rotor at a point between No. 1 and No. 2 spark plug wire terminals on distributor cap.
e. Install distributor on engine and complete installation.

## DISTRIBUTOR SERVICE
### ELECTRONIC CONTROL MODULE, REPLACE

1. Remove distributor cap and rotor, then remove two electronic control module attaching screws, **Fig. 6.**
2. Carefully lift module upward and disconnect electrical connectors. Note position of connectors for installation. Module electrical connectors must be connected to the same terminals as removed.
3. Remove module assembly. Do not remove silicone dielectric grease compound from module or distributor face, if module is to be reinstalled. If a replacement module is to be installed, silicone dielectric grease compound must be applied to module and distributor base.
4. Reverse procedure to install. Ensure electrical connectors are installed on the corresponding module terminals as noted during removal.

# CHRYSLER/JEEP—Electronic Ignition

## PICKUP COIL, REPLACE

1. Remove distributor from engine as described under "Distributor, Replace."
2. Mark position of distributor gear to shaft for use during installation.
3. Using a suitable punch, drive roll pin from distributor shaft and remove gear, **Fig. 1.**
4. Remove distributor shaft with rotor and advance weights from distributor housing.
5. Remove pickup coil retainer ring, disconnect pickup coil electrical connector from module and remove pickup coil, **Fig. 6.** Do not remove the three screws located on the pickup coil.
6. Reverse procedure to install.

## VACUUM ADVANCE UNIT, REPLACE

### 4-151 & FEDERAL V6-173 ENGINES

1. Remove distributor as described under "Distributor, Replace."
2. Remove distributor cap and rotor, then remove two vacuum advance

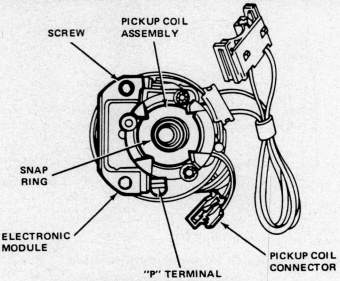

**Fig. 6   Distributor components**

unit attaching screws.
3. Rotate pickup coil assembly clockwise, then move vacuum advance unit downward to disengage from

pickup coil.
4. Remove vacuum advance unit from distributor.
5. Reverse procedure to install.

# Renix Ignition System
## INDEX

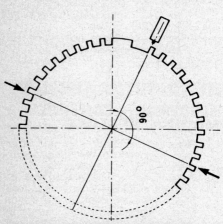

**Fig. 1   Flywheel trigger tooth locations. 4-150 engine**

## DESCRIPTION

The Ignition Control Module (ICM) incorporates a solid state ignition circuit. The ignition coil is mounted to the ICM and can be removed and serviced separately. This module electronically controls ignition advance and retard. The ICM receives input signals from the Electronic Control Unit (ECU) in the form of a 5 volt square wave.

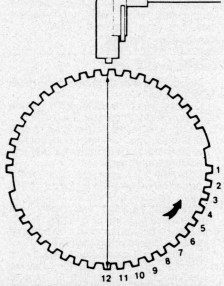

**Fig. 2   Flywheel trigger tooth locations. 6-243 engines**

When the leading edge of the 5 volt square wave contacts the ICM ignition circuitry, the ICM will charge the coil primary wind-

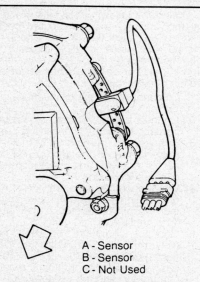

A - Sensor
B - Sensor
C - Not Used

**Fig. 3   TDC Sensor location**

ings. At a point when coil saturation occurs, the ICM circuitry will open the primary windings, causing the magnetic field to collapse. This will induce high voltage in the secondary coil windings which is routed to the spark plug through the coil wire, distributor cap, rotor and spark plug wire.

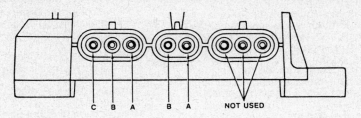

CONNECTOR 1:
A - Ignition (+)
B - Ground (−)
C - Tach Signal Diagnostic Connector
D1 - Pin 1

CONNECTOR 2:
A - Not Used
B - ECU Square Wave Output
    Ignition Coil Interface

**Fig. 4   Ignition Control Module (ICM) connectors**

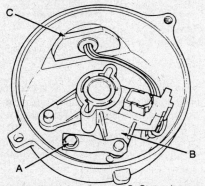

A. Stator Retaining Screw   C. Stator Harness
B. Stator

**Fig. 6   Distributor stator assembly. 6-243 engines**

The ICM also provides a Tach output signal for the diagnostic connector and tachometer.

On 4-150 engines, the flywheel, **Fig. 1**, has two teeth machined off 180° apart. These machined off teeth are position at 90° before top dead center and 90° before bottom dead center. On 6-243 engines, the flywheel, **Fig. 2**, has a large trigger tooth and notch located 70° (12 small teeth) before top dead center and 70° before bottom dead center. The TDC sensor, **Fig. 3**, which is mounted to the flywheel housing, senses TDC, BDC and engine speed from the teeth on the flywheel. Special shouldered bolts are used to secure the TDC sensor, which is non-adjustable.

# DIAGNOSIS

For additional diagnosis procedure, refer to the Throttle Body Fuel Injection Section for 4-150 engines or the Multi-Point Fuel Injection Section for 6-243 engines.

## ENGINE WILL NOT START (WEAK OR NO SPARK AT SPARK PLUGS)

1. Check for damaged or damaged ignition coil, rotor, distributor cap, ignition wires and spark plugs and repair or replace as necessary.
2. Check for loose wire connections at ignition coil.
3. Check for loose connections at ECU and ICM.

4. Check for loose or corroded ECU or ICM ground wire connections.
5. Check condition of battery and recharge or replace as necessary.
6. Check voltage between terminals A and B of ICM connector terminal 1, **Fig. 4**. With ignition switch in the Start position, voltmeter should indicate a minimum of 9.5 volts.
   a. If a minimum of 9.5 volts is indicated, proceed to step 7.
   b. If voltage is less than 9.5 volts, check continuity of ICM and ECM ground wires and repair as necessary. After repairing, recheck and proceed to step 7.
7. Check condition of ignition coil.
   a. Check ignition coil for exterior damage such as cracks and or severe dents and replace as necessary.
   b. Connect a suitable ohmmeter between ignition coil positive and negative terminals to check primary resistance. Ohmmeter should indicate .4 to .8 ohms, if not replace coil.
   c. Connect ohmmeter between positive or negative terminal and coil high voltage terminal to check secondary resistance. Ohmmeter should indicate 2500 to 4000 ohms, if not replace coil.
   d. If ignition coil is satisfactory, proceed to step 8.
8. Using Tester MS-1700 or equivalent, check ICM and ECU. Refer to instructions supplied with tester for test procedure. Replace ICM or ECU if defective.

## SECONDARY CIRCUIT TEST

1. Disconnect ignition coil wire from distributor cap.
2. Using insulated pliers, hold ignition coil wire approximately½ inch from a good engine ground.
3. Crank engine and check for spark at coil wire.
   a. If spark is present at coil wire, proceed to step 4.
   b. If spark is not present, refer to "Engine Will Not Start (No spark or Weak Spark at Spark Plugs)" and "Fuel Injection Section" for further diagnosis.

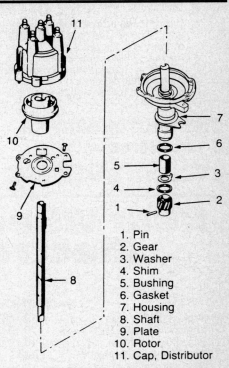

1. Pin
2. Gear
3. Washer
4. Shim
5. Bushing
6. Gasket
7. Housing
8. Shaft
9. Plate
10. Rotor
11. Cap, Distributor

**Fig. 5   Exploded view of distributor. 4-150 engines**

4. Disconnect wire from spark plug and hold approximately ½ inch from a good engine ground with insulated pliers. Crank engine and check for spark at spark plug wire.
   a. If spark occurs, refer to "Fuel Injection Section" for further diagnosis.
   b. If spark does not occur, check for defective rotor, distributor cap or spark plug wires.

# DISTRIBUTOR
# REPLACE

1. On 6-243 engines, disconnect stator electrical connector from distributor.
2. On all engines, remove distributor and position aside.
3. Mark position of distributor rotor to distributor housing and position of distributor housing to engine block.
4. Remove distributor hold down clamp, then lift distributor from engine block.
5. If engine was not disturbed while distributor was removed, reverse procedure to install. When distributor is installed on engine, alignment marks made during removal should be aligned. Torque distributor hold down bolt to 8 to 10 ft. lbs.
6. If engine was disturbed while distributor was removed, proceed as follows:
   a. Rotate engine until No. 1 cylinder is at TDC compression stroke.
   b. Using a flat blade screwdriver, position oil pump gear so that slot is slightly past the 3 o'clock position.
   c. Position distributor rotor at the 5 o'clock and install distributor on engine block.

d. When distributor is fully engaged with oil pump gear, rotor should be at the 6 o'clock position.

e. Align distributor housing to engine block marks made during removal, then install distributor hold down clamp and torque bolt to 8 to 10 ft. lbs.

## DISTRIBUTOR SERVICE
### 4-150 ENGINE

The distributor, **Fig. 5**, for the 4-150 engine incorporates no electrical components other than the distributor cap and rotor. The distributor is used only to transmit high voltage from the to the spark plugs in the correct firing order. When servicing the distributor do not remove the silicone dielectric compound from the rotor blade. If a replacement rotor is to be installed, apply a thin coat of silicone dielectric compound to rotor blade.

### 6-243 ENGINE
#### STATOR, REPLACE

1. Remove distributor as described under "Distributor, Replace".
2. Remove rotor from distributor.
3. Position distributor in a soft jawed vise to provide support for distributor gear removal.
4. Using a small punch, drive distributor gear roll pin from distributor shaft and remove gear.
5. Carefully remove distributor shaft from housing.
6. Mark location of stator so that it may be installed in the same position, **Fig. 6.**
7. Remove stator retaining screw and lift stator from distributor.
8. Reverse procedure to install.

# Rear Wheel Drive Chrysler Less Electronic Spark Control

## INDEX

## DESCRIPTION

This system, **Figs. 1 and 2**, is composed of a magnetic distributor, an electronic control unit, a wiring harness, a production coil and a single or dual ballast resistor.

The distributor is essentially the same as the conventional type except the contacts have been replaced by a pickup coil and the cam by a reluctor. With a conventional contact type system, the voltage necessary to fire the spark plugs is developed by interrupting the current flowing through the primary of the ignition coil by opening a set of contacts. With the Electronic System, the voltage is produced the same way, except that the current is interrupted by a transistor in the electronic control unit. This happens each time the control unit receives a "timing" pulse from the distributor magnetic pickup.

Since the magnetic pickup, reluctor and the control unit, which replace the contact points and cam, do not normally change or wear out with service, engine timing and dwell do not require periodic adjusting. This minimizes regular ignition maintenance of cleaning and replacing the spark plugs.

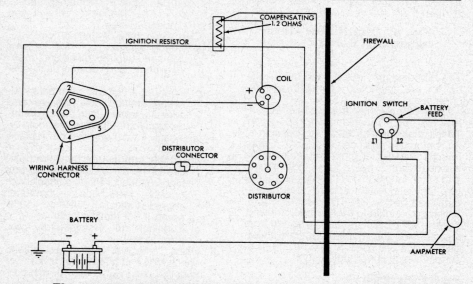

**Fig. 1   Chrysler electronic ignition system wiring. 1980**

## TROUBLESHOOTING
### ENGINE WILL NOT START—FUEL SYSTEM OK

1. Wiring harness electrical terminals covered with grease.
2. Faulty ballast resistor.
3. Faulty ignition coil.
4. Faulty pickup or improper pickup air gap.
5. Faulty wiring.
6. Faulty control unit.

### ENGINE SURGES SEVERELY—NOT LEAN CARBURETOR

1. Wiring.
2. Faulty pickup leads.
3. Ignition coil.

### ENGINE MISSES— CARBURETOR GOOD

1. Spark plugs.
2. Secondary cables.
3. Ignition coil.
4. Wiring.
5. Control unit.

## SYSTEM TESTING

To completely test components and circuits of the electronic ignition system, special testers should be used. However, in event the testers are not available, the following procedures may be utilized. A voltmeter with a 20,000 volt/ohm rating and an ohmmeter using a 1.5 volt battery on 1980 models or a 9 volt battery on 1981-87 models for power should be used for testing. Before performing any electrical tests, ensure all wiring is properly connected.

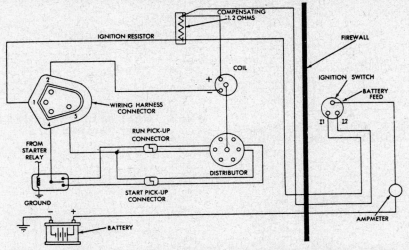

**Fig. 2   Chrysler electronic ignition system wiring. 1981–87**

**Fig. 3   Harness wiring test, No. 1 cavity. 1980 (typical)**

**Fig. 6   Pickup coil test, cavity Nos. 4 & 5. 1980 (typical)**

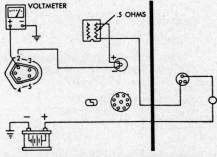

**Fig. 4   Harness wiring test, No. 2 cavity. 1980 (typical)**

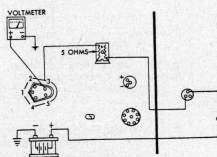

**Fig. 5   Harness wiring test, No. 3 cavity. 1980 (typical)**

## 1980 MODELS

### Harness Wiring Test

1. Check battery voltage and note reading.
2. Disconnect harness connector from control unit. **Before disconnecting or connecting harness connector, ensure ignition switch is in the "Off" position.**
3. Turn ignition switch to "On" position.
4. Connect the voltmeter between harness connector cavity No. 1 and the ground. Voltage reading should be within 1 volt of battery voltage earlier noted. If not, check circuit between cavity No. 1 and the battery, **Fig. 3.**
5. Connect voltmeter between harness connector cavity No. 2 and ground. Voltage reading should be within 1 volt of battery voltage noted in step 1. If not, check circuit between cavity No. 2 and battery, **Fig. 4.**
6. Connect voltmeter between harness connector cavity No. 3 and ground. Voltage reading should be within 1 volt of battery voltage noted in step 1. If not, check circuit between cavity No. 3 and battery, **Fig. 5.**
7. Turn ignition switch to off position.

### Distributor Pickup Coil Test

1. Connect an ohmmeter between har-

ness connector cavities numbers 4 and 5, **Fig. 6.** Resistance reading should be 150 to 900 ohms.
2. If reading is not as specified in above step, disconnect distributor dual lead connector and connect ohmmeter between the two leads on distributor side of connector, **Fig. 7.** If resistance is not between 150 and 900 ohms, replace pickup coil.
3. Connect one ohmmeter lead to a good ground and the other lead to either connector of the distributor. If ohmmeter shows a reading, the pickup coil must be replaced.

### Control Unit Ground Circuit Test

Connect an ohmmeter between control unit connector pin No. 5 and the ground, **Fig. 8.** If ohmmeter indicates infinite resistance, tighten bolts securing control unit to firewall and recheck resistance. If reading is still infinite, replace control unit.

## 1981–87 MODELS

1. Visually check all spark plug cables and spark plugs for proper installation or damage.
2. Check for proper installation of ignition coil primary wire at coil terminals and at ballast resistor.
3. If above checks are satisfactory, measure and record battery voltage.

4. Disconnect coil secondary lead from distributor cap. Turn ignition "On," then using a special jumper wire as shown in **Fig. 9,** momentarily ground distributor negative terminal while holding coil secondary lead 1/4 inch from good ground. If no spark is observed, turn ignition "Off," then disconnect four wire electrical connector at electronic control unit and proceed to next step. If spark is observed, proceed to step 10. **Before connecting or disconnecting the harness connector from the control unit, check to ensure that the ignition switch is in the Off position.**
5. Repeat step 4. If spark is observed, replace electronic control unit.
6. If no spark is observed, measure voltage at coil positive terminal. Reading obtained should be within one volt of previously recorded battery voltage.
7. If voltage reading is zero, replace starter relay and check wiring between battery positive terminal and coil, **Fig. 10.**
8. If voltage reading obtained in step 6 is not continuous, replace ignition resistor and repeat step 6.
9. Check battery voltage at coil negative terminal, **Fig. 11.** Reading obtained should be within one volt of battery voltage. If voltage reading is satisfactory, but no spark is observed when coil negative terminal is grounded, replace coil.
10. If spark was obtained in step 4 or step 9, but engine will not start, check to ensure that four-wire connector is dis-

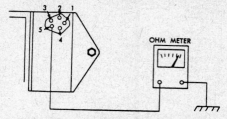

**Fig. 8 Control unit ground circuit test. 1980 (typical)**

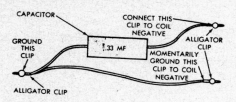

**Fig. 9 Special coil negative to ground jumper wire**

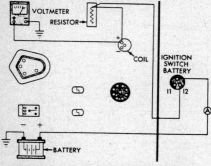

**Fig. 7 Pickup coil test, distributor lead connector. 1980 (typical)**

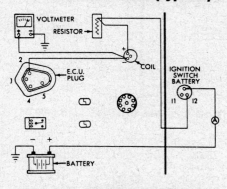

**Fig. 11 Checking battery voltage at coil negative terminal. 1981–87**

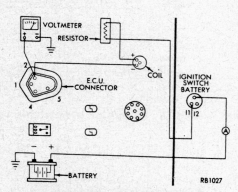

**Fig. 12 Checking battery voltage at No. 2 cavity. 1981–87**

**Fig. 10 Checking battery voltage at coil positive terminal. 1981–87**

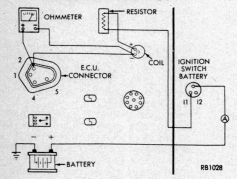

**Fig. 13 Checking continuity between coil negative terminal and No. 2 cavity. 1981–87**

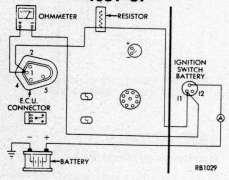

**Fig. 14 Checking continuity between ignition switch and No. 1 cavity. 1981–87**

connected from electronic control unit, then with ignition On check for battery voltage at cavity 2 of ECU harness connector. Reading obtained should be within one volt of battery voltage, **Fig. 12**.

11. If voltage reading is not satisfactory, turn ignition Off, and check for continuity between cavity 2 and coil negative terminal using suitable ohmmeter, **Fig. 13**. If continuity is not present, check for damaged wiring or loose connections and repair as necessary.

12. If voltage reading in step 10 is satisfactory, check for battery voltage at cavity 2 of ECU connector. If battery voltage is not obtained, turn ignition Off and check for continuity between cavity 1 and ignition switch using suit-

able ohmmeter, **Fig. 14**. If continuity is not present, check for damaged wiring or loose connections and repair as necessary.

13. If battery voltage is obtained at cavity 2 of ECU connector, turn ignition Off and check resistance between cavities 4 and 5 of ECU harness connector using suitable ohmmeter, **Fig. 15**. Reading of 150-900 ohms should be obtained.

14. If reading is satisfactory, check wiring between cavities 4 and 5 for open or short circuit and repair as necessary. If wiring is satisfactory, check for proper operation of dual pickup start run relay as described under "Dual Pickup Start-Run Relay Test."

15. If ohmmeter reading obtained in step 13 is not between 150-900 ohms, disconnect pickup leads and measure resistance at distributor side of pickup lead, **Fig. 16**. If reading obtained is not between 150-900 ohms, replace pickup coils as necessary.

16. Check for short circuit at each distributor side of pickup lead by connecting ohmmeter as indicated in **Fig. 17**. If ohmmeter indicates pickup is shorted, replace pickup coil and adjust air gap to .006 inch.

17. If pickup coil is satisfactory, check for proper ECU ground contact by connecting ohmmeter between pin 5 of ECU and ground. If ohmmeter indicates poor ECU ground contact, check for proper ECU installation or poor ECU electrical connections.

18. If ECU is properly grounded, reconnect all electrical connections and check again for spark. If no spark is available, replace ECU.

## Dual Pickup Start-Run Relay Test, 1981–87 Models

1. Disconnect two-way connector from pins 5 and 4 of dual pickup start-run relay, **Fig. 18**.
2. Connect suitable ohmmeter between pins 4 and 5 of relay.
3. If ohmmeter reading of 20-30 ohms cannot be obtained, replace relay.

# DISTRIBUTOR SERVICE
## DISTRIBUTOR, REPLACE
### Removal

1. Disconnect vacuum line at distributor, if equipped.
2. Disconnect distributor pickup lead(s) at wiring harness connector, then remove distributor cap.
3. Mark position of rotor on distributor body and engine block surface so that

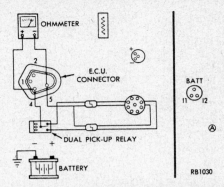

**Fig. 15 Checking resistance between cavities Nos. 4 & 5. 1981–87**

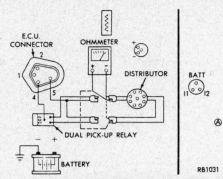

**Fig. 16 Testing pickup coil resistance. 1981–87**

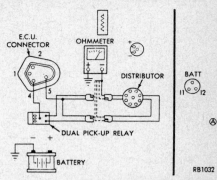

**Fig. 17 Checking for short circuit at pickup coil terminal. 1981–87**

distributor can be installed in the same position.

4. Remove hold-down and/or bolt and lift distributor from engine.

## Installation

1. If engine was cranked after distributor was removed from engine, rotate crankshaft to bring No. 1 piston up on its compression stroke and align timing mark on crankshaft pulley with "O" (TDC) mark on timing cover.
2. With distributor gasket or O-ring in place, hold distributor over mounting pad.
3. Turn rotor to a position just ahead of the No. 1 distributor cap terminal.
4. Install distributor, engaging distributor gear with camshaft drive gear on 6 cylinder engines. On V-8 engines, engage tang of distributor shaft with slot in oil pump drive gear. With distributor fully seated on engine, rotor should be under No. 1 cap terminal.
5. Install distributor hold-down and/or bolt, distributor cap, pickup lead(s) and vacuum line.
6. Adjust ignition timing to specifications found in the Tune Up section.

## DISTRIBUTOR SHAFT & BUSHING WEAR TEST

1. Remove distributor from vehicle and clamp distributor in a vise. Use extreme caution not to damage distributor.
2. Attach a dial indicator to housing so plunger rests against reluctor sleeve.
3. Place a wire loop around reluctor sleeve and hook a spring scale on the other end of the loop. Apply a 1 lb. pull toward dial indicator on 1980 models or a 1½ lb. pull toward dial indicator on 1981–87 models. On all models, apply a 1 lb. pull away from dial indicator and read movement on indicator.
4. Movement must not exceed .006 inch. If movement exceeds limit, replace either housing or shaft to bring movement back within tolerance.

## DISTRIBUTOR DISASSEMBLE

1. Remove rotor and vacuum advance unit, if equipped, **Figs. 19 thru 21.**
2. Remove reluctor by prying up from bottom of reluctor using two screw-

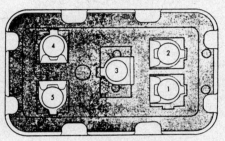

**Fig. 18 Dual pickup start run delay. 1981–87**

drivers with a maximum blade width of 7/16 in. Use care not to damage or distort reluctor teeth.

3. Remove two screws and lockwashers attaching lower plate to distributor housing, then lift out lower plate, upper plate and pickup coil as an assembly. Do not remove distributor cap clamp springs.
4. On six cylinder units, if distributor housing, or shaft and governor assembly are to be replaced, proceed as follows:
   a. If gear is worn or damaged, scribe a line on end of shaft from center to edge, so that line is centered between two gear teeth, **Fig. 22.** Do not scribe line completely across shaft. Remove distributor drive gear retaining pin and slide gear off end of shaft. Support hub of gear so that pin can be driven out without damaging shaft.
   b. If necessary, use a file to clean burrs from around pin hole area on shaft, then remove lower thrust washer.
   c. Push shaft upward and remove from distributor body.
5. On eight cylinder units, if distributor housing, shaft, reluctor sleeve or governor weights are to be replace, proceed as follows:
   a. Remove distributor shaft retaining pin and slide retainer off end of shaft.
   b. If necessary, use a file to clean burrs from around pin hole area on shaft, then remove lower thrust washer.

c. Push shaft upward and remove from distributor housing.

## DISTRIBUTOR ASSEMBLE

1. Lubricate and test operation of governor weights. Inspect weight springs for distortion and bearing surfaces and pins for damage.
2. Lubricate upper thrust washer and install onto shaft. Install shaft into housing, **Figs. 19 thru 21.**
3. On 6 cylinder units, install lower thrust washer and distributor gear and roll pin. If a replacement distributor gear is to be installed, proceed as follows:
   a. Install thrust washer and replacement gear on rotor shaft. Position pin hole in replacement gear approximately 90° from hole in distributor shaft, with scribed line made during disassembly between gear teeth, **Fig. 22.** On replacement distributor gears, the roll pin hole is located higher than the original gear roll pin hole, so that distributor shaft will not be weakened when the shaft is rotated 90° and drilled to accommodate the replacement gear.
   b. Before drilling through shaft and gear, place a .007 in. feeler gauge between gear and thrust washer and observe that center line between two gear teeth is in line with centerline of rotor electrode, **Fig. 23.** Drill a .124 to .129 in. hole and install roll pin. Support gear hub when installing roll pin so gear teeth will not be damaged.
4. On eight cylinder units, install distributor shaft retainer and pin, **Fig. 21.**
5. On all units, install lower plate, upper plate and pickup coil assembly, **Figs. 19 thru 21.**
6. Attach vacuum advance unit to pickup plate, then install vacuum advance unit attaching screws and washers.
7. Position reluctor keeper pin into place on reluctor sleeve, then slide reluctor down reluctor sleeve and press firmly into position. Install keeper pin.
8. Lubricate felt pad located in top of reluctor sleeve with one drop of light engine oil, then install rotor.

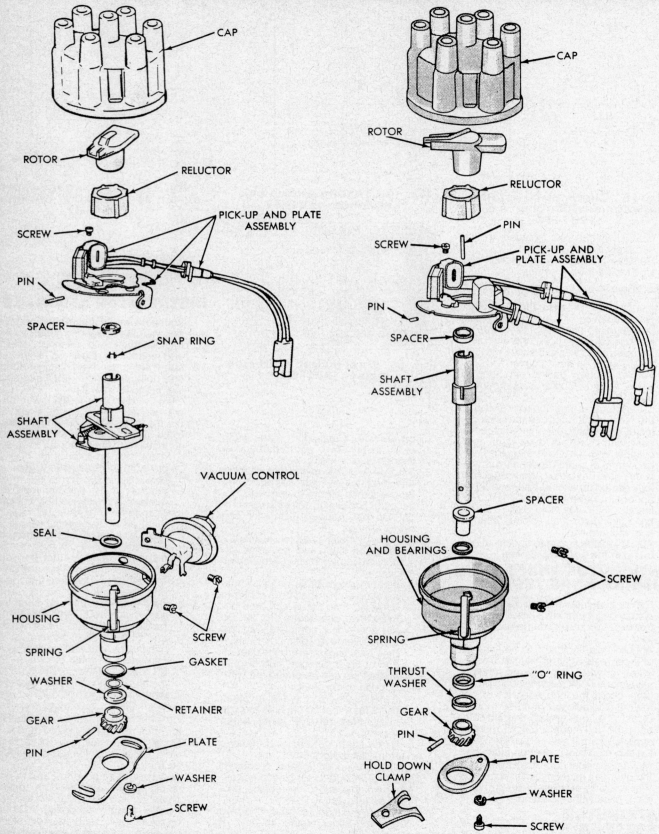

**Fig. 19 Exploded view of electronic 6 cylinder distributor with single pickup (Typical)**

**Fig. 20 Exploded view of electronic 6 cylinder distributor with dual pickup (Typical)**

*REAR WHEEL DRIVE CHRYSLER LESS ELECTRONIC SPARK CONTROL*

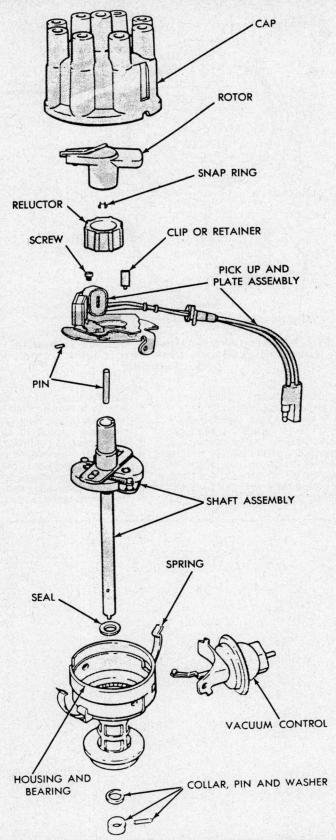

Fig. 21 Exploded view of electronic 8 cylinder distributor (Dual pickup distributor similar)

CAP

ROTOR

SNAP RING

RELUCTOR

SCREW

CLIP OR RETAINER

PICK UP AND PLATE ASSEMBLY

PIN

SHAFT ASSEMBLY

SPRING

SEAL

HOUSING AND BEARING

VACUUM CONTROL

COLLAR, PIN AND WASHER

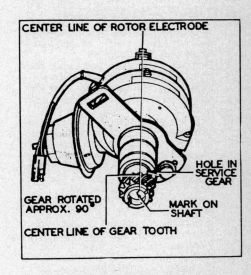

CENTER LINE OF ROTOR ELECTRODE

HOLE IN SERVICE GEAR

MARK ON SHAFT

GEAR ROTATED APPROX. 90

CENTER LINE OF GEAR TOOTH

Fig. 22 Scribe line on distributor shaft. 6 cylinder units

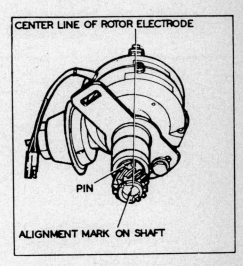

CENTER LINE OF ROTOR ELECTRODE

PIN

ALIGNMENT MARK ON SHAFT

Fig. 23 Aligning gear teeth with center line of rotor electrode. 6 cylinder units

## PICKUP REPLACEMENT & AIR GAP ADJUSTMENT

1. With distributor removed from vehicle, perform Steps 1 to 3 as outlined in Distributor Disassemble.
2. Remove pickup coil and upper plate by depressing retainer clip and moving it away from mounting stud. Pickup coil cannot be removed from upper plate.
3. Lightly lubricate upper plate pivot pin and lower plate support pins with distributor lubricant. Install upper plate pivot pin through smallest hole in lower plate and install retainer clip. **The upper plate must ride on the support pins on the lower plate.**
4. Install lower and upper plates and pickup coil as an assembly and install distributor into vehicle. On dual pickup distributors, the start pickup may be identified by a two prong male connector and the run pickup may be identified by a male-female plug, **Fig. 24.**
5. To set air gap on all single pickup distributors and start pickup of dual pickup distributors, align one reluctor tooth with pickup pole and install a .006 inch non-magnetic feeler gauge between reluctor tooth and pickup pole, **Fig. 24** . Rotate pickup coil until contact is made between reluctor tooth, feeler gauge and pickup pole. Tighten pickup coil hold down screw and remove feeler gauge. The feeler gauge should be removed without force. If it cannot, readjust gap.
6. To set air gap on run pickup of dual pickup distributors, first adjust start pickup as described in step 5, then adjust run pickup as described in step 5.

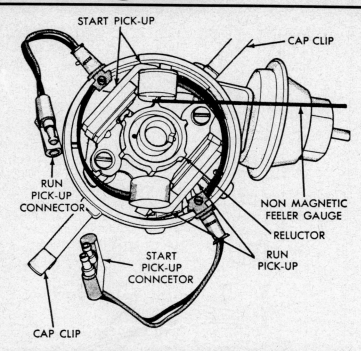

**Fig. 24  Air gap adjustment. Distributors with dual pickup shown. Distributors with single pickup similar**

Use a .012 inch non-magnetic feeler gauge to adjust run pickup air gap.

7. Perform a second gap check using a .008 inch feeler gauge on all single pickup distributors and on start pickup of dual pickup distributor or a .014 inch feeler gauge on run pickup of dual pickup distributors. Do not force feeler gauge between reluctor tooth and pickup pole as it is possible to do so. The feeler gauge should not be able to fit between the reluctor tooth and pickup pole if air gap is correctly set. Apply vacuum to vacuum control unit. Pickup should not contact reluctor tooth. Readjust air gap if contact occurs. **If pickup contacts reluctor teeth on one side of shaft only, the distributor shaft is most likely bent and shaft replacement required.**

# Rear Wheel Drive Chrysler With Electronic Spark Control, Exc. Dakota

## INDEX

## DESCRIPTION

The Electronic Spark Advance provides electronically controlled spark advance and eliminates the need for mechanical and vacuum advance controls in the distributor. The Spark Control Computer uses as many as six sensors to monitor the engines conditions so that it can fire the spark plugs at the proper time.

## SPARK CONTROL COMPUTER (SCC)

The Spark Control Computer is the heart of the entire system. It gives the capability of igniting the fuel mixture according to different modes of engine operation by delivering an infinite amount of variable advance curves. During cranking, an electrical signal from the distributor is fed into the computer. This signal will cause the computer to fire the spark plugs at a fixed amount of advance. Once the engine starts, the timing will now be controlled by the computer based on the information received from the various sensors.

The amount of spark advance is determined by three factors, coolant temperature, engine speed, and manifold vacuum. The computer determines spark advance in the following manner:

1. Coolant temperature modifies vacuum advance schedule. There is a different schedule for hot and for cold engines.
2. Advance from vacuum is programmed into computer. In a cold or warm engine spark advance depends only on amount of manifold vacuum. In a hot engine spark advance depends on both manifold vacuum and engine speed.
3. Advance from speed is programmed into computer and depends only on engine speed.

## SENSORS

The Electronic Spark Control System incorporates the following sensors:

1. The Hall Effect Pickup assembly, located in distributor, supplies basic timing signal and engine speed to computer.
2. The coolant sensor, located on thermostat housing, gives computer information on engine temperature.
3. A carburetor switch located on end of idle stop tells computer when engine

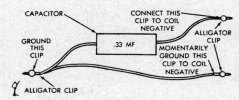

**Fig. 1  Special coil negative to ground jumper wire**

is at an idle.

4. The vacuum transducer is located on the Spark Control Computer and tells computer how much vacuum engine is producing.
5. The oxygen sensor (used with Feed Back carburetor only) is located in exhaust manifold and informs computer about oxygen in exhaust so it can alter air/fuel mixture.
6. A charge temperature switch (on 6 cyl. engines only) is located on intake manifold and monitors intake air temperature.

## SYSTEM TESTING

### IGNITION SYSTEM STARTING TEST

1. Using a suitable voltmeter, measure and record battery voltage. Battery specific gravity must be at least 1.220 temperature corrected to operate the cranking and ignition system properly.
2. Turn ignition "On," then remove coil secondary lead from distributor cap. Using a special jumper wire as shown in **Fig. 1,** momentarily ground distributor negative terminal while holding coil secondary lead 1/4 inch from good ground.
3. If a spark occurs, it must be constant and bright blue in color. If spark is proper color and constant, continue to momentarily ground coil negative with special jumper wire, **Fig. 1,** while slowly moving coil wire away from ground. If arcing occurs at the coil tower, replace coil. If the spark is weak or inconsistent or no spark at all, proceed to "Failure To Start Test." If spark is satisfactory, the ignition system is producing the proper secondary voltage. Inspect the cap, rotor, wires and plugs. If satisfactory, it will

be necessary to check the fuel system and engine mechanical components.

## FAILURE TO START TEST

Before proceeding with this test, perform "Ignition System Starting Test." Failure to do so may lead to unnecessary diagnostic time and incorrect test results.

1. Turn ignition "Off." Remove 10-way connector from base of Spark Control Computer, **Fig. 2.** Turn ignition "On," then holding end of coil wire about 1/4 inch away from a ground, momentarily short coil negative wire to ground with special jumper wire, **Fig. 1.** If a spark is obtained, replace Spark Control Computer. If no spark is obtained, proceed to step 2.
2. Using a voltmeter, check for battery voltage at coil positive terminal with the ignition "On," **Fig. 3.** If voltage is within 1 volt of battery voltage, proceed to step 4. If not, proceed to step 3.
3. Using an ohmmeter, check continuity of wiring between battery and coil positive, **Fig. 4,** repair as necessary and repeat step 2.
4. Using a voltmeter, check for battery voltage at coil negative. If within 1 volt of battery voltage, proceed to step 5. If not, replace coil.
5. If voltage is correct, but no spark is obtained when grounding coil negative, replace coil.
6. If spark is obtained, but engine will not start, place ignition switch in "On" position. Using a suitable voltmeter, measure voltage of disconnected 10-way connector cavity 1, **Fig. 2,** to ground. Voltage should be within 1 volt of battery voltage. If voltage is within 1 volt of battery voltage, proceed to step 8. If not, proceed to step 7.
7. Using an ohmmeter, check continuity of wire for opens and repair as necessary (no power between coil negative and 10-way connector). Repeat step 6.
8. Place a piece of paper between curb idle adjusting screw and carburetor switch, **Fig. 5,** or ensure curb idle adjusting screw is not contacting carburetor switch.
9. Connect negative lead of voltmeter to a good engine ground.
10. Rotate ignition switch to "On" position

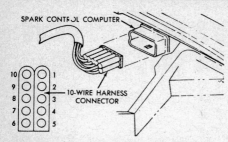

**Fig. 2   10-way connector location and cavity identification**

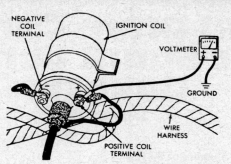

**Fig. 3   Checking ignition coil positive terminal voltage**

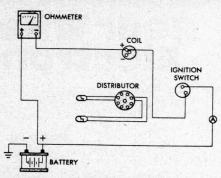

**Fig. 4   Checking battery to ignition coil positive terminal for continuity**

and measure voltage at carburetor switch terminal, **Fig. 5.** If voltage is approximately 5 volts, proceed to step 12. If voltage is not at least 5 volts, place ignition switch in "Off" position and disconnect wire connector from bottom of Spark Control Computer, **Fig. 2.** Rotate ignition switch back to the "On" position and measure voltage at wire connector terminal 2, **Fig. 2.** Voltage should be within one volt of battery voltage noted previously. If voltage is correct proceed to step 11. If voltage is incorrect check wiring between wire terminal 2 and ignition switch for open or short circuits or improper connections.

11. With ignition switch in the "Off" position, disconnect wire connector from Spark Control Computer. Using an ohmmeter, check for continuity between connector terminal 7, **Fig. 2,** and carburetor switch terminal. Continuity should exist between these two points. If not, check wiring for open or short circuit or improper connections. If continuity is noted, check for continuity between connector terminal 10 and engine ground. If continuity exists, replace Spark Control Computer. If not, check wiring for open circuit or improper connections and proceed to step 12 only if engine still fails to start.

12. Place ignition switch in the "Off" position, then using an ohmmeter, measure resistance between terminals No. 5 and 9 for run pickup coil and terminals 3 and 9 for start pickup coil, **Fig. 2.** Resistance should be between 150 and 900 ohms. If not, disconnect pickup coil leads from distributor and measure resistance at lead going into distributor. If resistance is now between 150 and 900 ohms, this would indicate an open or short circuit or improper connection between distributor connector and terminals 5 and 9 or terminals 3 and 9 of dual connector. If resistance is not within specifications, pickup coil is defective.

13. Connect one ohmmeter lead to engine ground and with the other lead check for continuity at each terminal going to the distributor. There should be no continuity. Reconnect distributor lead and proceed to step 14. If there is continuity, replace pickup coil.

14. Remove distributor cap and check air gap of pickup coil. Refer to Pickup Coil Replacement and Air Gap Adjustment and adjust gap as necessary.

15. Install distributor cap and reconnect all wiring, then start engine. If engine

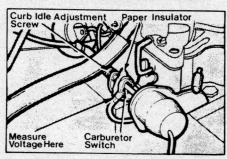

**Fig. 5   Positioning paper insulator and carburetor switch terminal location. (Typical)**

fails to start, replace spark control computer.

16. After installing new computer and engine still fails to start, reinstall original computer and repeat test procedures since one of the test procedures may have been performed incorrectly.

# POOR FUEL ECONOMY, PERFORMANCE & UNUSUALLY HIGH IDLE SPEED TESTS

## ENGINE TEMPERATURE SWITCH TESTS

Refer to figs. 6 through 9 and proceed as follows:

Turn ignition "Off." To test temperature switch, connect a suitable ohmmeter between center terminal of temperature switch and ground. To test charge temperature switch, connect ohmmeter to center terminal of charge temperature switch and switch ground terminal.

With engine cold, continuity should be present with resistance less than 100 ohms. If not, replace switch. Charge temperature switch must be cooler than 60° F in order to perform test properly.

With engine hot, continuity should not be present. If continuity is present, replace temperature switch.

## COOLANT SENSOR TEST

### 1983-87

1. Connect ohmmeter leads to coolant sensor terminals.
2. Resistance should measure 500-1100 ohms with engine cold and ambient temperature less than 90° F.
3. Resistance should measure more than 1300 ohms with engine at nor-

mal operating temperature.
4. Replace sensor if resistance readings do not meet specifications in steps 2 and 3. **Resistance of the sensor will vary as engine operating temperature changes.**

### 1988-89

1. Connect ohmmeter leads to coolant sensor terminals.
2. Resistance should measure 7000-13000 ohms with engine cold and ambient temperature AT 70° F.
3. Resistance should measure 700-1000 ohms with engine at normal operating temperature.
4. Replace sensor if resistance readings do not meet specifications in steps 2 and 3. **Resistance of the sensor will vary as engine operating temperature changes.**

## SPARK ADVANCE OF SPARK CONTROL COMPUTER TEST

1. Ensure engine is fully warmed up and the temperature sensor is connected and operating properly.
2. Set ignition timing to specifications.
3. Place a piece of paper between curb idle adjusting screw and carburetor switch, **Fig. 5,** or ensure curb idle adjusting screw is not contacting carburetor switch.
4. Remove and plug vacuum transducer line.
5. Using a suitable hand-operated vacuum pump, apply 16 inch of vacuum (10 inch on 1983-86 6-255 engine or 16 inch on 1987 6-225 engine) to vacuum transducer.
6. Increase engine speed to 2000 RPM, wait 1 minute (or specified clock up time, refer to "Electronic Spark Control Specifications"). Advance specifications are in addition to basic timing advance. On systems equipped with an accumulator the specified time must be reached with the carburetor switch ungrounded before checking the specified spark advance schedule (Refer to "Electronic Spark Control Specifications").
7. If the computer fails to obtain specified settings, replace computer.

## CARBURETOR SWITCH TEST

On most systems, grounding the carburetor switch eliminates all spark advance.

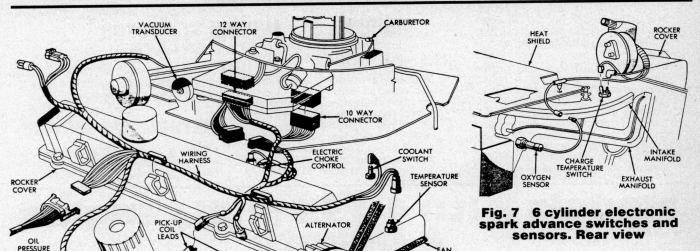

**Fig. 6  6 cylinder electronic spark advance switches and sensors. Front view**

**Fig. 7  6 cylinder electronic spark advance switches and sensors. Rear view**

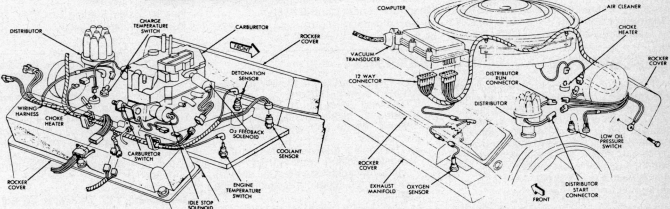

**Fig. 8  8 cylinder electronic spark advance switches & sensors. Front view**

**Fig. 9  8 cylinder electronic spark advance switches & sensors. Rear view**

1. Turn ignition Off, then disconnect 10-way connector from computer.
2. Check to ensure throttle is fully closed, then check continuity between pin 7 of harness connector and ground using suitable ohmmeter, **Fig. 2.**
3. If continuity is not present, check for open circuit in carburetor switch wiring circuit and repair as necessary.
4. Open throttle and check continuity between pin 7 of harness connector and ground. Continuity should not be present.

## EGR SYSTEM TEST

The electronic EGR control is incorporated into the Spark Control Computer. Check to ensure that engine temperature switches are operating properly before proceeding with test.

1. With engine cold and ignition Off, connect one lead of suitable voltmeter to gray wire terminal on EGR solenoid. Connect second voltmeter lead to ground.

2. Start engine and check voltmeter reading. Reading should be less than one volt. Reading will remain at this value until engine reaches normal operating temperature and electronic EGR schedule has timed out (refer to "Electronic Spark Control Specifications"). EGR Solenoid will then de-energize and voltmeter will indicate charging system voltage.
3. If system does not de-energize in specified amount of time, replace solenoid.
4. If voltmeter indicates charging system voltage before EGR schedule is complete, replace Spark Control Computer. If vehicle is started with engine at operating temperature, EGR solenoid will be energized for length of time delay schedule only and will then de-energize.

## ELECTRONIC THROTTLE CONTROL TEST

The electronic throttle control system is incorporated in the Spark Control Computer on some models (refer to "Electronic Spark Control Specifications"). A carburetor mounted solenoid is energized whenever the air conditioning, heater, electronic heated backlite or electronic timers are activated. The timers operate with an EGR time delay after an engine start condition or with a two second time delay after throttle is closed exc. on 1984-87 models. On 1984-87 models, see specifications for time delay.

1. Connect tachometer to engine, then start engine and run until operating temperature is reached.
2. Depress accelerator, then release. Curb idle speed should increase for length of time of EGR schedule (refer to "Electronic Spark Control Specifications").
3. Curb idle speed should increase when air conditioner, heater and/or electronic heated backlite are operated and return to normal when components are turned Off. **Air conditioner clutch, if equipped, will cycle on**

and off as air conditioner operates and should not be mistaken as part of electronic control system operation.

4. If curb idle speed does not increase and decrease as described above, disconnect three-way electrical connector from carburetor.
5. Connect ohmmeter between carburetor solenoid black wire terminal and ground. Resistance should be 15-35 ohms. If not, replace solenoid.
6. Start engine and measure voltage between black wire of three-way connector and ground before EGR time delay has timed out. Voltmeter reading should indicate charging system voltage. If not, replace Spark Control Computer.
7. With engine operating and voltmeter connected as described in step 6, turn on air conditioner, heater and/or electronic heated backlite. Voltmeter should read charging system voltage after time delay has timed out. If not, check wiring between three-way harness connector and instrument panel for damage and repair as necessary.

## DISTRIBUTOR REPLACE

Refer to "Rear Wheel Drive Less Electronic Spark Control System" for distributor replacement procedures.

## DISTRIBUTOR SERVICE

Refer to "Dodge/Plymouth Rear Wheel Drive Less Electronic Spark Control System" for distributor service procedures.

# Models With 4-135 (2.2L) Engine & Dakota

## INDEX

## DESCRIPTION

The Electronic Spark Advance provides electronically controlled spark advance and eliminates the need for mechanical and vacuum advance controls in the distributor. The Spark Control Computer uses as many as five sensors to monitor the engines conditions so that it can fire the spark plugs at the proper time.

### SPARK CONTROL COMPUTER (SCC)

The Spark Control Computer is the heart of the entire system. It gives the capability of igniting the fuel mixture according to different modes of engine operation by delivering an infinite amount of variable advance curves. During cranking, an electrical signal from the distributor is fed into the computer. This signal will cause the computer to fire the spark plugs with a fixed amount of advance. Once the engine starts, the timing will now be controlled by the computer based on the information received from the various sensors.

The amount of spark advance is determined by three factors, coolant temperature, engine speed, and manifold vacuum. The computer determines spark advance in the following manner:

1. Coolant temperature modifies the vacuum advance schedule. There is a different schedule for hot and for cold engines.
2. Advance from vacuum is programmed into computer. In a cold or warm engine vacuum advance depends only on amount of manifold vacuum. In a hot engine vacuum advance depends on both manifold vacuum and engine speed.
3. Advance from speed is programmed into computer and depends only on engine speed.

## SENSORS

The Electronic Control System incorporates the following sensors:

1. The Hall Effect Pickup assembly, located in distributor, supplies basic timing signal and engine speed to computer.
2. The coolant sensor, located on thermostat housing (front left side of intake manifold on V6-239 engine), gives computer information on engine temp.
3. A Carburetor Switch located on end of idle stop tells the computer when the engine is at an idle.
4. The Vacuum Transducer is located on the Spark Control Computer and tells the computer how much vacuum engine is producing.
5. The Oxygen Sensor (used with Feed Back Carburetor) is located in exhaust manifold and informs the computer about oxygen in exhaust so it can alter air/fuel mixture.

## SYSTEM TESTING

### IGNITION SYSTEM STARTING TEST

1. Remove coil wire from distributor cap and hold end of wire approximately 1/4 inch from a good engine ground. Crank engine and observe spark at coil wire.
2. The spark at the coil wire must be constant and bright blue in color. If so, continue to crank engine and slowly move coil wire away from the ground. If arcing occurs at the coil tower, replace coil. If spark is weak, not constant or there is no spark, proceed to the "Failure To Start Test."
3. If spark is satisfactory and no arcing occurs at the coil tower, the ignition system is producing the necessary high secondary voltage. However, this voltage is transmitted to the spark plugs by the distributor rotor, cap, spark plug wires and spark plugs and must also be checked. If satisfactory, the ignition system is not at fault. It will be necessary to check the fuel system and engine mechanical components.

## FAILURE TO START TEST

Before performing this test, perform the "Ignition System Starting Test." Failure to do so may lead to unnecessary diagnostic time and incorrect test results.

1. With a voltmeter, measure and note battery voltage. Battery specific gravity must be at least 1.220, temperature corrected, to deliver the necessary voltage to operate the cranking and ignition systems properly.
2. Remove coil wire from distributor cap.
3. Place ignition switch in "On" position, then using special jumper wire, **Fig. 1**, momentarily ground the ignition coil negative terminal while holding the coil wire 1/4 inch from a good engine ground. A spark should be obtained.
4. If spark was obtained, proceed to step 7. If not, turn ignition Off, then disconnect 10-way, electrical connector at Spark Control Computer, **Fig. 2**. Do not remove grease from harness connector or connector cavity since grease is used to prevent moisture from corroding the terminals. There must be at least 1/8 inch of grease on bottom of computer connector cavity. If not, apply a liberal amount of Mopar Multi-purpose grease, part number 2932524 or equivalent over end of connector plug before installation.
5. Turn ignition On, hold wire 1/4 inch

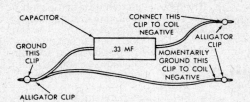

**Fig. 1 Coil negative terminal jumper wire**

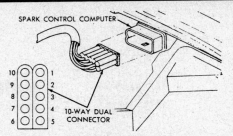

**Fig. 2 Spark control computer 10-way connector**

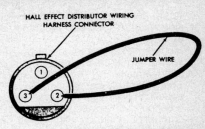

**Fig. 3 Distributor 3-wire harness connector**

from ground and momentarily ground coil negative terminal using jumper wire, **Fig. 1.** If spark is present, replace Spark Control Computer. If spark is not present, measure voltage at coil positive terminal using suitable voltmeter. Voltage reading should be within one volt of battery voltage.

6. If no voltage was obtained at coil positive terminal, check for open circuit between battery and coil and repair as necessary. If voltage was obtained, measure voltage at coil negative terminal. Reading should be within one volt of battery voltage. If no voltage is present or voltage is present but spark is not, replace coil.

7. If spark was obtained in step 2, but engine will not start, hold open carburetor switch with thin piece of paper and measure voltage at carburetor switch. Reading should be at least 5 volts on 1982-83 models or within one volt of battery voltage on 1984-89 models. If voltage reading is satisfactory, proceed to step 11. If no voltage is present, turn ignition Off, then disconnect 10-way connector from Spark Control Computer.

8. Turn ignition On and measure voltage between connector cavity 2 and ground, **Fig. 2.** Reading should be within one volt of battery voltage. If not, check for continuity between battery and cavity 2 using ohmmeter. If continuity is not present, check for open circuit between battery and cavity 2 and repair as necessary.

9. If battery voltage is present in step 8, turn ignition Off and check continuity between carburetor switch and cavity 7 on 10-way connector. If continuity is not present, check for open circuit between cavity 7 and carburetor switch and repair as necessary.

10. If continuity is present in step 9, check continuity between cavity 10 and ground. If continuity is present, replace Spark Control Computer. If continuity is not present between cavity 10 and ground, check for damaged wiring or an open circuit and repair as necessary. If wiring is satisfactory, but engine will not start, proceed to step 11.

11. Reconnect 10-way connector into Spark Control Computer, turn ignition On and hold coil wire 1/4 inch from ground. Disconnect distributor electrical connector and momentarily connect jumper wire between terminals 2 and 3 of connector, **Fig. 3.** Spark should be observed at coil wire.

12. If spark is present at coil wire, but engine will not start, replace pickup assembly and perform rotor test as described in step 18. On 4-135 engines, when replacing Hall effect pickup assembly, check to ensure rotor shutter blades are grounded, **Fig. 4.** Connect one lead of suitable ohmmeter to shutter blade and other lead to ground. If continuity is not present, press downward on rotor shaft and recheck continuity. If continuity is still not present, replace rotor. Check to ensure that new rotor is marked ESA on top. Do not start engine until continuity has been obtained.

13. If no spark is present at coil wire check voltage between cavity 1 of distributor connector and ground, **Fig. 3.** Reading obtained should be within one volt of battery voltage. If battery voltage is not present, proceed to step 15. If battery voltage is present, turn ignition off and disconnect 10-way connector from Spark Advance Computer. Check for continuity between cavity 2 of distributor connector, **Fig. 3,** and cavity 9 of 10-way connector, **Fig. 2.** Repeat procedure between cavity 3 of distributor connector and cavity 5 of 10-way connector.

14. If continuity is not present, open circuit exists in harness wiring. Repair as necessary. If continuity is present, replace Spark Advance Computer.

15. If no battery voltage is present at cavity A of distributor connector, turn ignition Off, then disconnect 10-way connector from Spark Control Computer.

16. Check for continuity between cavity 1 of distributor connector and cavity 3 of 10-way connector. If continuity is not present, repair open circuit in wire between cavities as necessary.

17. If continuity is present turn ignition On and check for voltage between cavity 2 and 10 of 10-way connector. If battery voltage is present, replace Spark Control Computer. If battery voltage is not present, check for proper computer ground circuit connection and repair as necessary.

18. To perform rotor test, check to ensure that rotor is stamped ESA on top. Turn ignition Off, then using suitable ohmmeter, check for good rotor ground contact at distributor shaft. If continuity is indicated, rotor is satisfactory. If continuity is not indicated, check to ensure that rotor is properly seated on shaft.

## POOR PERFORMANCE TESTS
### Carburetor Switch Test

1. With ignition switch in "Off" position, disconnect 10-way harness connector from "Spark Control Computer," **Fig. 2.**
2. With throttle completely closed, check continuity between terminal 7 and the engine ground, **Fig. 2.** Continuity should exist. If not, check wiring and carburetor switch.
3. With throttle opened, check continuity between terminal 7 and the engine ground, **Fig. 2.** Continuity should not exist.

### Coolant Switch Test, 1982–83 Models

1. With ignition switch in "Off" position, disconnect wire from coolant switch.
2. Check continuity between coolant switch terminal and the engine ground. The ohmmeter readings should be as follows: Engine cold—Continuity should exist. If not, replace coolant switch. Engine hot—No continuity should exist. If continuity exists, replace coolant switch.

### Coolant Sensor Test, 1984–87 Models

1. With ignition switch in "Off" position, disconnect wire from coolant sensor.
2. Connect one lead of suitable ohmmeter to one terminal of coolant sensor.
3. Connect other lead of ohmmeter to remaining connector of coolant sensor. The ohmmeter should read as follows:
   a. Engine coolant sensor hot, 200° F or above, 700 to 800 ohms.
   b. Engine coolant sensor at room temperature, approximately 70° F, 5000 to 6000 ohms.
4. If ohmmeter readings are not within specifications, replace coolant switch.

### Spark Advance Test

1. Run engine until normal operating temperature is reached, then disconnect carburetor switch electrical connector. Check to ensure that coolant sensor is operating as described under "Poor Performance Tests" under "Coolant Sensor Test."
2. Disconnect and plug vacuum transducer vacuum hose.

3. Apply 16 inches Hg vacuum from outside vacuum source to vacuum transducer.
4. Increase engine speed to 2000 RPM, wait one minute, then check amount of advance timing. Refer to "Electronic Spark Control Specification Chart" for specification. On certain models equipped with an accumulator, the accumulator must be allowed to time out with the carburetor switch disconnected before checking spark advance.
5. If spark advance specifications cannot be obtained, replace Spark Control Computer.

## Start Advance Timing Test, 1982 Models

1. Connect an adjustable timing light to engine so total timing advance can be checked.
2. Connect a jumper wire between carburetor switch and the engine ground.
3. Start engine and adjust timing light to align specified timing marks. The timing light meter should indicate the amount of advance listed in the "Rampage & Scamp Electronic Spark Control Specification Chart."

## Electronic Throttle Control Test, 1983–84 Models

The electronic throttle control system is incorporated in the Spark Control Computer system on some models. A carburetor mounted solenoid is energized whenever the air conditioning, heater, electronic heated backlite or electronic timers are activated. The timers operate with a two second time delay after the throttle is closed or after an engine start condition.
1. Connect tachometer to engine, then start engine and run until operating temperature is reached.
2. Depress accelerator, then release. Curb idle should increase for a specified time. Refer to "Electronic Spark Control Specification Chart."
3. Curb idle speed should increase when air conditioner, heater and/or electronic heated backlite are operated and return to normal when components are turned off. Air conditioner clutch, if equipped, will cycle on and off as air conditioner operates and should not be mistaken as part of electronic control system operation.
4. As the air conditioner clutch cycles on and off, the solekicker plunger should extend and retract. Also, when any of the above components are on, or during a specified time after the engine is started (refer to Electronic Spark Control Specification Chart), the solekicker should be extended. If not, check the kicker system for vacuum leaks.
5. If no vacuum leaks are found, disconnect the carburetor 3-way connector.
6. Connect a suitable ohmmeter between black wire of carburetor 3-way connector and ground. Resistance should be between 20 and 100 ohms.

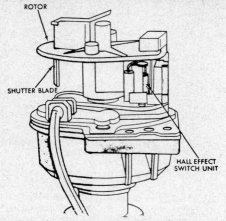

**Fig. 4   Rotor shutter blades. 4-135 engine**

If not, replace solenoid.
7. Have assistant start engine, then using a suitable voltmeter, measure voltage across vacuum solenoid terminals. Voltage should be within 2 volts of charging system voltage. If not, replace Spark Control Computer.
8. Turning on the air conditioning or electronic backlite should also produce charging system voltage after the time delay has timed out. Refer to "Electronic Spark Control Specification." If not, check wiring harness back to the instrument panel for an open circuit.

# DISTRIBUTOR SERVICE
## DISTRIBUTOR, REPLACE
### Removal

1. On 4-135 engines proceed as follows:
   a. Disconnect primary wiring connector from distributor, then remove pickup coil lead retaining screw.
   b. Remove splash shield retaining screws and the splash shield.
   c. Loosen distributor cap retaining screws, then remove distributor cap.
2. On V6-239 engines, proceed as follows:
   a. Disconnect distributor pickup lead wire electrical connectors.
   b. Disconnect distributor cap retaining clips, then lift off distributor cap.
3. On all Models, rotate crankshaft until rotor is pointing in direction of engine block, then scribe a line on block to indicate rotor position during installation.
4. Remove distributor hold-down bolt, then carefully lift distributor from engine.

### Installation

1. Position distributor into engine with gasket installed on base of distributor.
2. Engage distributor drive gear with camshaft drive gear so distributor rotor will align with scribe mark made during removal.

3. If engine was cranked while distributor was removed, proceed as follows:
   a. Rotate crankshaft until No. 1 piston is at top dead center of compression stroke. The pointer on damper, clutch housing or bellhousing should align with "0" mark on flywheel.
   b. Rotate distributor rotor to a position ahead of No. 1 distributor cap terminal.
   c. Install distributor into engine, engaging distributor drive with camshaft drive gear. The rotor should be properly positioned under distributor cap No. 1 terminal.
4. Install distributor cap, then the distributor hold-down screw or retaining clips.
5. Install splash shield, if equipped, then connect primary wiring connector to distributor.
6. Install pickup coil lead retaining screw, as required, then adjust ignition timing. Refer to "Tune Up Specifications."

## DISTRIBUTOR, DISASSEMBLE
### 4-135

1. Remove splash shield and distributor cap.
2. Remove rotor from shaft and disconnect pickup electrical connector.
3. Remove Hall Effect Pickup Assembly retaining clips.
4. Remove Hall Effect Pickup Assembly.
5. Remove distributor drive gear roll pin using punch, then remove drive gear.
6. Remove drive gear thrust washer and distributor shaft.
7. Remove distributor to block seal.

### V6-239

1. Remove distributor cap.
2. Remove ignition rotor from distributor shaft.
3. Remove two Hall Effect Pickup attaching screws on opposite sides of distributor housing, then lift Hall Effect Pickup Assembly from distributor housing.

## DISTRIBUTOR, ASSEMBLE
### 4-135

1. Lubricate distributor housing bushings with engine oil, then install engine seal onto distributor housing.
2. Install distributor shaft thrust washer onto distributor shaft, then install shaft into distributor housing.
3. Install distributor drive gear thrust washer, then install distributor drive gear onto distributor shaft.
4. Install drive gear roll pin using punch.
5. Install Hall Effect Pickup Assembly.
6. Install Hall Effect Pickup Assembly retaining clips, then rotor and distributor cap.

### V6-239

Reverse disassemble procedure to assemble.

# Models With 4-156 (2.6L) Engine

## INDEX

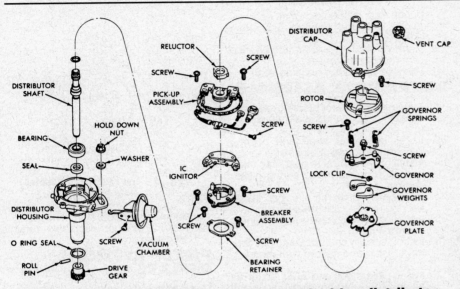

Fig. 1   Disassembled view of electronic ignition distributor

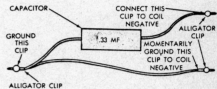

Fig. 2   Coil negative terminal jumper wire

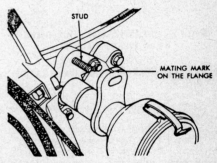

## DESCRIPTION

This system consists of the distributor, **Fig. 1**, ignition switch, ignition coil, ECU igniter and spark plugs. Primary circuit current is controlled by the ECU igniter in response to timing signals produced by the distributor pickup. The distributor consists of the power distribution section, signal generator, ECU igniter, advance mechanism and drive gear section. The signal generator is a small magneto which produces a signal that is processed by the ECU to determine the exact time to open the primary circuit and fire the spark plugs.

## SYSTEM TESTING

1. Disconnect high tension lead from distributor and hold end of cable 3/16–3/8 inch from good engine ground. Crank engine and check for spark at end of high tension lead.
2. If spark is present, continue cranking engine while slowly moving coil high tension lead away from engine ground. If arcing occurs at coil tower, replace coil. If no spark is present at coil high tension lead or spark is weak, turn ignition On and check voltage at coil negative terminal using suitable voltmeter.
3. If voltage reading obtained is the same as battery voltage, system is op-

erating satisfactorily. If reading is three volts or less, the distributor is defective and must be checked further. If zero reading is obtained, check for open circuit in ignition wiring and repair as necessary.
4. Connect special jumper wire, **Fig. 2**, to coil negative terminal. Turn ignition On, position coil high tension lead as described in step 1, then momentarily touch other end of jumper wire to a good ground.
5. If no spark is observed at coil high tension lead, check for presence of voltage at coil positive terminal. If battery voltage reading is obtained at coil positive terminal, replace coil. If proper voltage cannot be obtained, check for loose connections or damaged wiring and repair as necessary.

## DISTRIBUTOR SERVICE
## DISTRIBUTOR, REPLACE
### Removal

1. Rotate engine until No. 1 cylinder is at TDC on compression stroke.
2. Disconnect battery ground cable.
3. Remove distributor cap and mark relationship of rotor to distributor housing.
4. Remove distributor wiring harness.
5. Disconnect vacuum hose from distributor.

Fig. 3   Aligning distributor and engine mating marks

6. Remove distributor retaining nut, then the distributor.

### Installation

1. Align mating mark on distributor housing with rotor.
2. Install distributor into engine aligning mating mark on distributor mounting flange with center of distributor retaining stud, **Fig. 3**.
3. Install retaining nut, vacuum hose, secondary ignition cables and distributor wiring harness.
4. Connect battery ground cable, start engine and adjust ignition timing.

## DISTRIBUTOR, DISASSEMBLE

1. Remove distributor rotor.
2. Remove governor assembly retaining screw, **Fig. 4**, and governor assembly. **Governor springs are not interchangeable and must be installed in their original positions. Note position of each spring during disassembly for reference during assembly.**
3. Remove wire retaining clamp from side of distributor.
4. Remove pickup coil and ECU igniter retaining screws, then remove pickup

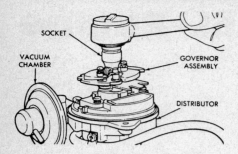

**Fig. 4  Replacing governor retaining screw**

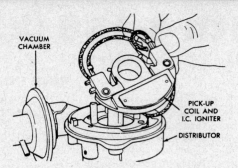

**Fig. 5  Pickup coil igniter replacement**

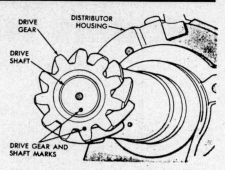

**Fig. 6  Marking driveshaft & gear**

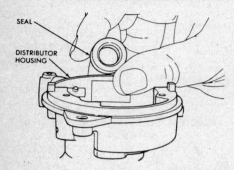

**Fig. 7  Distributor housing seal installation**

coil and ECU igniter as an assembly, **Fig. 5.**

5. Remove vacuum chamber retaining screws, then the vacuum chamber assembly.
6. Remove breaker assembly retaining screws, then the breaker assembly.
7. Remove bearing retainer plate screws, then the bearing retainer plate.
8. Mark relationship of distributor drive gear to distributor shaft, **Fig. 6,** then

punch out distributor drive gear retaining pin and remove gear from shaft.
9. Remove distributor shaft and bearing assembly from housing.
10. Remove distributor housing seal.

## DISTRIBUTOR, ASSEMBLE

1. Lubricate distributor housing seal with suitable grease and install into distributor housing, **Fig. 7.**
2. Install distributor shaft and bearing assembly into distributor housing.
3. Install distributor drive gear onto shaft and align marks made during disassembly.
4. Install drive gear roll pin, then install bearing retainer and retaining screws.
5. Install breaker assembly and retaining screws, **Fig. 8.**
6. Install vacuum chamber onto distributor housing and secure with retaining screws.
7. Install pickup coil and ECU igniter as an assembly into housing, then install retaining screws.
8. Install wire retaining clamp and governor assembly. If governor assembly was disassembled, check to ensure that governor springs are installed in

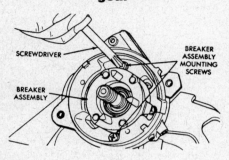

**Fig. 8  Installing breaker assembly**

original positions.
9. Install governor assembly retaining screw and rotor.

## PICKUP ASSEMBLY, REPLACE

1. Remove distributor as described under "Distributor Service."
2. Perform steps 1 through 4 as described under "Distributor Service" under "Disassembly."
3. Reverse procedure to install.

# Models With 4-153 (2.5L) & V6-181 (3.0L) Engines

## INDEX

**Fig. 1 SMEC 14-way electrical connector**

TERMINAL SIDE

## DESCRIPTION

This system provides electronically controlled spark advance and eliminates the need for mechanical and vacuum advance controls in the distributor. The Single Module Engine Controller (SMEC) uses the signals from various sensors to provide optimum driveability under all operating conditions by advancing or retarding the ignition timing.

Under cranking and starting conditions, the SMEC provides a set amount of advanced timing to ensure a quick and efficient start. The amount of electronic spark advance provided by the SMEC is determined by coolant temperature, engine RPM and available manifold vacuum.

The oxygen sensor also sends signals to the SMEC which electronically adjusts the air/fuel mixture to provide the most efficient fuel burn possible.

## HALL EFFECT PICKUP

The Hall Effect pickup, used on 4-153 engine, is located in the distributor assembly. The pickup supplies engine RPM and ignition timing data and on turbocharged engines, fuel injection synchronization to the SMEC to advance or retard ignition spark as needed.

## COOLANT TEMPERATURE SENSOR

The coolant temperature sensor, mounted near the thermostat housing, monitors coolant temperature and provides engine operating temperature data to the SMEC.

The sensor, which is a variable resistor is also used to turn on radiator fan.

## MANIFOLD ABSOLUTE PRESSURE (MAP) SENSOR

The MAP sensor monitors manifold vacuum and transmits information to the SMEC to determine the correct air/fuel mixture. The sensor is located on the right shock tower and is connected to a vacuum nipple on throttle body on non turbocharged 4-153 engine, or on the air intake on V6-181 engines.

## OPTICAL DISTRIBUTOR SYSTEM

The optical distributor, used on V6-181 engine, transmits engine speed and crankshaft position signals to the SMEC to control fuel injection, ignition timing and idle speed. The distributor also delivers firing pulses from coil to each individual cylinder through a cap and rotor. Protection against high voltage damage to the electronic circuity and optical system contamination is provided by a cover between the rotor and case.

## AUTO SHUTDOWN (ASD) RELAY

The ASD relay interrupts power to the electric fuel pump, fuel injectors and ignition coil when there is no ignition signal present with the ignition key in the Run position.

## SYSTEM TESTING

### IGNITION SYSTEM STARTING TEST

1. Remove coil secondary lead from distributor cap, then holding coil secondary lead ¼ inch from good ground, crank engine.
2. If a spark occurs, it must be constant and bright blue in color. If spark is proper color and constant, continue to momentarily ground coil negative while slowly moving coil wire away from ground. If arcing occurs at coil tower, replace coil. If the spark is weak or inconsistent or no spark at all, proceed to "Failure To Start Test." If spark is satisfactory, the ignition system is producing the proper secondary voltage. Inspect the cap, rotor, wires and plugs. If satisfactory, it will

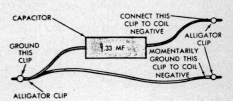

**Fig. 2 Coil negative terminal jumper wire**

be necessary to check the fuel system and engine mechanical components.

## FAILURE TO START TEST

Before proceeding with this test, perform "Ignition System Starting Test." Failure to do so may lead to unnecessary diagnostic time and incorrect test results.

1. Crank engine for 5 seconds while monitoring voltage at coil (+) terminal.
2. If voltage does not remain near battery voltage during cranking, problem is contained within the SMEC engine electronics. If voltage remains near battery voltage during cranking, turn ignition Off and remove 14-way connector from SMEC, **Fig. 1**. Check 14-way connector for any spread terminals.
3. Remove coil (+) lead, then connect suitable jumper wire between battery (+) and coil (+) terminals.
4. Momentarily ground terminal 12 of 14-way connector, using a suitable jumper, **Fig. 2**. A spark should be present when ground is removed.
5. If a spark is present, replace SMEC. If spark is not present, use special jumper to directly ground coil (−) terminal.
6. If a spark is present, check and repair wiring harness for an open circuit. If spark is not present, replace ignition coil.

## COOLANT TEMPERATURE SENSOR TEST

1. Place ignition switch in Off position, then disconnect coolant temperature sensor electrical connector.
2. Connect suitable ohmmeter to coolant temperature sensor electrical connectors.
3. Ohmmeter should read 700-1000 ohms with sensor at normal operating

temperature (200°F) or 7000-13000 ohms with sensor at room temperature (70°F). If ohmmeter reading is not as specified, replace coolant temperature sensor.

# DISTRIBUTOR
## REPLACE
### REMOVAL
#### 4-153 Engine

1. Disconnect pickup lead wires from electrical connector.
2. Remove splash shield retaining screws and splash shield.
3. Loosen distributor cap attaching screws, then remove distributor cap.
4. Rotate crankshaft until rotor is pointing in direction of engine block, then scribe a line on block for assembly reference.
5. Remove distributor hold-down bolt, then carefully lift distributor from engine.

#### V6-181 Engine

1. Disconnect distributor lead wire from electrical connector.
2. Loosen distributor cap retaining screws, then remove distributor cap.
3. Rotate crankshaft until rotor is pointing in direction of intake plenum for assembly reference.
4. Remove distributor hold-down nut, then carefully lift distributor from engine.

### INSTALLATION
#### 4-153 Engines

1. Position distributor into engine with gasket installed on base of distributor.
2. Engage distributor drive gear with auxiliary drive gear so distributor rotor aligns with scribe mark made during removal.
3. If engine was cranked while distributor was removed, proceed as follows:
   a. Rotate crankshaft until No.1 piston is at top dead center of compression stroke. The pointer on damper clutch should align with "O" mark on flywheel.
   b. Rotate distributor rotor to a position ahead of No. 1 distributor cap terminal.
   c. Install distributor into engine, engaging distributor drive with auxiliary shaft. The rotor should be properly positioned under distributor cap No. 1 terminal.
4. Install distributor cap, then the distributor hold-down screw.
5. Install splash shield, then connect

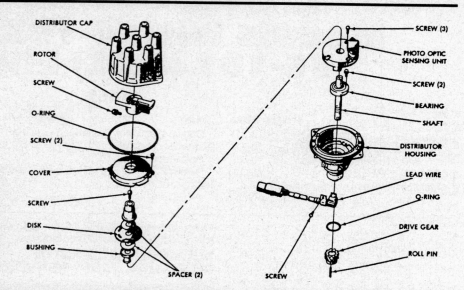

primary wiring connector to distributor.
6. Adjust ignition timing to specifications.

#### V6-181 Engine

1. Position distributor into engine with gasket installed on base of distributor.
2. Engage distributor drive gear with camshaft drive gear so distributor rotor aligns with scribe mark made during removal.
3. If engine was cranked while distributor was removed, proceed as follows:
   a. Rotate crankshaft until No. 1 piston is at top dead center of compression stroke.
   b. Rotate distributor rotor to No. 1 rotor terminal.
   c. Install distributor into engine, engaging distributor drive with camshaft. The rotor should be properly positioned under distributor cap No. 1 terminal.
4. Install distributor cap, then distributor hold-down nut.
5. Connect distributor lead wire to electrical connector.
6. Adjust ignition timing to specifications.

# DISTRIBUTOR SERVICE
## 4-153 ENGINE

1. Remove rotor from shaft and disconnect pickup electrical connector if necessary.
2. Remove Hall Effect pickup retaining screw or clips and pickup.

Fig. 3 Exploded view of optical distributor assembly. V6-181 engine

3. Remove distributor drive gear roll pin and drive gear.
4. Remove drive gear thrust washer and distributor shaft.
5. Remove distributor-to-block seal.
6. Reverse procedure to install, noting the following: 7.
   a. Lubricate distributor housing bushings with clean engine oil prior to installing engine seal onto distributor housing.
   b. Engage pickup lead wire is properly engaged in retaining slot.
   c. Ensure rotor is fully seated when pressing rotor onto shaft.

## V6-181 Engines

1. Remove distributor cap attaching screw and distributor cap, Fig. 3.
2. Remove rotor attaching screw and rotor.
3. Remove distributor housing cover, then lead wire clamp screw and lead wire.
4. Remove disk assembly attaching screw, then disk spacers and disk. Inspect disk for warpage of damage and replace as necessary.
5. Remove bushing, then photo optic sensing unit fasteners and sensing unit.
6. Remove two bearing retainer screws.
7. Mark distributor gear and shaft from assembly reference.
8. Drive roll pin out of distributor drive gear, then remove gear.
9. Remove distributor shaft and bearing assembly.
10. Reverse procedure to install.

# CARBURETORS

## TABLE OF CONTENTS

# Motorcraft 2100 & 2150 Carburetor

**NOTE:** Refer To Motorcraft 2150 Chapter In The Ford Section For Service On This Carburetor.

## ADJUSTMENT SPECIFICATIONS

| Year | Carb. Part No. ① | Float Level (Dry) | Float Level (Wet) | Choke Plate Pulldown Clearance | Fast Idle Cam | Choke Unloader Clearance | Choke Setting |
|------|------------------|-------------------|-------------------|-------------------------------|---------------|--------------------------|---------------|
| 1980 | 0DA2J | .375 | .930 | .128 | .113 | .300 | 1 Rich |
| | 0DA2J2 | .375 | .930 | .120 | .106 | .300 | 2 Rich |
| | 0DM2A | .375 | .930 | .128 | .113 | .360 | 1 Rich |
| | 0DMJ2 | .375 | .930 | .113 | .113 | .300 | 2 Rich |
| | 0DM2JC | .375 | .930 | .120 | .106 | .300 | 2 Rich |
| | 0DHA2 | .575 | .930 | .113 | .086 | .350 | 2 Rich |
| | 0DHM2 | .575 | .930 | .014 | .081 | .348 | 2 Rich |
| 1981 | DM2J | — | .930 | .125 | .113 | .300 | 2 Rich |
| | DA2J | — | .930 | .128 | .113 | .300 | 1 Rich |
| | DM2A | — | .930 | .128 | .113 | .360 | 1 Rich |
| | RHM2 | — | .930 | .104 | .081 | .348 | 2 Rich |
| | RHA2 | — | .930 | .113 | .086 | .350 | 2 Rich |
| 1982 | 2RHM2 | — | .930 | .116 | .076 | .350 | 1 Rich |
| | 2RHA2 | .328 | .930 | .116 | .076 | .350 | 1 Rich |
| 1983 | 2RHA2 | .328 | .930 | .116 | .076 | .420 | 1 Rich |
| | 1RHM2 | — | .930 | .104 | .081 | .348 | 2 Rich |
| | 1RHA2 | .575 | .930 | .113 | .086 | .350 | 2 Rich |
| 1984-88 | 4RHA2 | .575 | .930 | .113 | .086 | .350 | 2 Rich |
| | 5RHA2 | .328 | .930 | .118 | .076 | .420 | — |
| 1989 | 5RHA2 | .328 | .930 | .118 | .076 | .420 | — |

① —Located on tag attached to carburetor casting.

# Carter YFA Series 1 Bbl. Carburetor

**NOTE:** Refer to Carter YFA Carburetor Chapter In The Ford Section For Service On This Carburetor.

## ADJUSTMENT SPECIFICATIONS

| Year | Carburetor Model | Float Level | Initial Choke Valve Clearance | Choke Unloader Setting | Fast Idle Cam Setting | Choke Setting |
|---|---|---|---|---|---|---|
| 1983-84 | YFA-7700 | .600 | .240 | .280 | .175 | ① |
| | YFA-7701 | .600 | .240 | .280 | .175 | ① |
| | YFA-7702 | .600 | .240 | .280 | .175 | ① |
| | YFA-7703 | .600 | .240 | .280 | .175 | ① |
| 1985-86 | 7704, 7706 | .600 | .280 | .280 | .175 | ① |
| | 7705, 7707 | .600 | .280 | .280 | .175 | ① |

①—Tamper resistant.

# Rochester 2SE & E2SE Varajet Carburetor

**NOTE:** Refer To Rochester Varajet 2SE & E2SE Chapter In The General Motors Section For Service On This Carburetor.

## ADJUSTMENT SPECIFICATIONS

| Year | Carburetor Number | Float Level (Inches) | Pump Setting (Inches) | Fast Idle Cam Adj. | Air Valve Link | Vac. Break Pri. | Unloader | Choke | Secondary Lockout | Choke Coil Lever Gauge |
|---|---|---|---|---|---|---|---|---|---|---|
| 1980 | 17080685 | 3/16 | 1/2 | 18° | 2° | 19° | 32° | TR② | .004-.012 | .085 |
| | 17080781 | 7/32 | 1/2 | 18° | 2° | 19° | 32° | TR② | .004-.012 | .085 |
| 1981 | 17081790 | .208 | .128 | 25° | 2° | 19° | 32° | TR② | .050-.080 | .050-.080 |
| | 17081791 | .256 | .128 | 25° | 2° | 19° | 32° | TR② | .085 | .085 |
| | 17081796 | .208 | .128 | 25° | 2° | 19° | 32° | TR② | .050-.080 | .050-.080 |
| | 17081797 | .208 | .128 | 25° | 2° | 19° | 32° | TR② | .085 | .085 |
| 1982 | 17082380 | .169 | .128 | 18°① | 2° | 21° | 34° | TR② | .050-.080 | .050-.080 |
| | 17082381 | .169 | .128 | 18°① | 2° | 21° | 34° | TR② | .050-.080 | .050-.080 |
| | 17082389 | .169 | .128 | 18°① | 2° | 19° | 34° | TR② | .050-.080 | .050-.080 |
| 1983 | 17082380 | .216 | .128 | 18°① | 2° | 21° | 34° | TR② | .050-.080 | .085 |
| | 17083385 | .138 | .128 | 18°① | 2° | 19° | 34° | TR② | .050-.080 | .085 |
| 1984 | 17084581 | 5/32 | — | 22° | 1° | — | 40° | TR② | .025 | .085 |
| | 17084580 | 5/32 | — | 22° | 1° | — | 40° | TR② | .025 | .085 |
| | 17084582 | 5/32 | — | 22° | 1° | — | 40° | TR② | .025 | .085 |
| | 17084583 | 5/32 | — | 22° | 1° | — | 40° | TR② | .025 | .085 |
| | 17084584 | 1/8 | — | 22° | 1° | — | 40° | TR② | .025 | .085 |
| 1985-86 | 17085380 | 5/32 | — | 22° | 1° | 26° | 4o° | TR② | — | .085 |
| | 17085381 | 5/32 | — | 22° | 1° | 26° | 40° | TR② | — | .085 |
| | 17085382 | 5/32 | — | 22° | 1° | 26° | 40° | TR② | — | .085 |
| | 17085383 | 5/32 | — | 22° | 1° | 26° | 40° | TR② | — | .085 |
| | 17085384 | 1/8 | — | 22° | 1° | 25° | 40° | TR② | — | .085 |

①—Second step of cam.
②—Tamper resistant.

# Carter BBD 2 Bbl. Carburetor

## INDEX

## ADJUSTMENT SPECIFICATIONS, JEEP

| Year | Ident. No. | Float Level | Vacuum Piston Gap | Initial Choke Valve Clearance | Choke Unloader | Fast Idle Cam | Automatic Choke Setting |
|---|---|---|---|---|---|---|---|
| 1980 | 8253 | .250 | .035 | .128 | .280 | .095 | 2 Rich |
| | 8254 | .250 | .035 | .120 | .280 | .086 | 2 Rich |
| | 8255 | .250 | .035 | .140 | .280 | .093 | 2 Rich |
| | 8256 | .250 | .035 | .128 | .280 | .093 | 2 Rich |
| | 8257 | .250 | .035 | .128 | .280 | .095 | 2 Rich |
| | 8277 | .250 | .035 | .116 | .280 | .081 | 1 rich |
| 1981 | 8302 | .250 | .035 | .140 | .280 | .095 | 1 Rich |
| | 8303 | .250 | .035 | .140 | .280 | .095 | 1 Rich |
| | 8311 | .250 | .035 | .120 | .280 | .085 | 1 Rich |
| | 8306 | .250 | .035 | .140 | .280 | .095 | 1 Rich |
| | 8312 | .250 | .035 | .140 | .280 | .095 | 1 Rich |
| | 8307 | .250 | .035 | .140 | .280 | .095 | 1 Rich |
| 1982 | 8338 | .250 | .035 | .140 | .280 | .095 | 1 Rich |
| | 8339 | .250 | .035 | .140 | .280 | .095 | 1 Rich |
| | 8340 | .250 | .035 | .150 | .280 | .110 | 1 Rich |
| | 8341 | .250 | .035 | .150 | .280 | .150 | 1 Rich |
| | 8349 | .250 | .035 | .128 | .280 | .095 | 2 Rich |
| | 8351 | .250 | .035 | .130 | .280 | .095 | 0 Rich |
| 1983-88 | 8360, 8362 | .250 | .035 | .140 | .280 | .095 | 1 Rich |
| | 8364, 8367 | .250 | .035 | .140 | .280 | .095 | 1 Rich |
| | 8383, 8384 | .250 | .035 | .140 | .280 | .095 | 1 Rich |
| 1989 | 8383, 8384 | .250 | .035 | .140 | .280 | .095 | 1 Rich |

## ADJUSTMENT SPECIFICATIONS, CHRYSLER

| Year | Carb. Model | Float Setting | Pump Setting | Bowl Vent Adjust | Fast Idle Linkage Adjust | Choke Unloader Adjust | Choke Vacuum Kick Adjust |
|---|---|---|---|---|---|---|---|
| 1982 | 8348S | 1/4 | 1/2 | .080 | .070 | .310 | .130 |
| | 8352S | 1/4 | 1/2 | .080 | .070 | .310 | .130 |
| 1983 | 8358S | 1/4 | .470 | .080 | .070 | .280 | .130 |
| | 8359S | 1/4 | .470 | .080 | .070 | .280 | .130 |
| | 8371S | 1/4 | .470 | .080 | .070 | .280 | .130 |
| | 8374S | 1/4 | .470 | .080 | .070 | .280 | .130 |
| 1984 | 8358S | 1/4 | .470 | .080 | .070 | .280 | .130 |
| | 8359S | 1/4 | .470 | .080 | .070 | .280 | .130 |
| | 8374S | 1/4 | .470 | .080 | .070 | .280 | .130 |

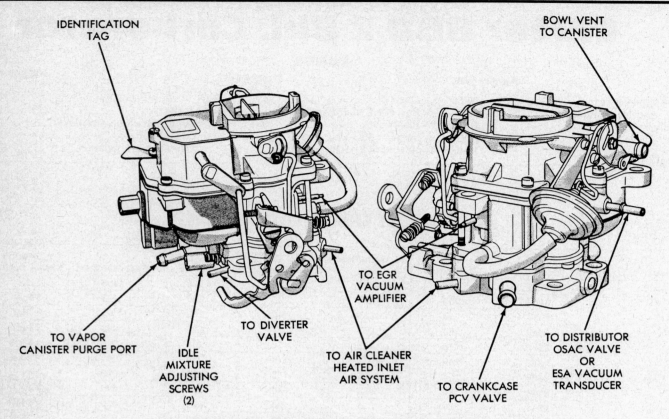

IDENTIFICATION TAG

BOWL VENT TO CANISTER

TO VAPOR CANISTER PURGE PORT

IDLE MIXTURE ADJUSTING SCREWS (2)

TO DIVERTER VALVE

TO AIR CLEANER HEATED INLET AIR SYSTEM

TO EGR VACUUM AMPLIFIER

TO CRANKCASE PCV VALVE

TO DISTRIBUTOR OSAC VALVE OR ESA VACUUM TRANSDUCER

**Fig. 1  Carter BBD carburetor assembly. 1980–81**

# IDENTIFICATION LOCATION

On 1980-83 models less Electronic Feedback Carburetor system, the carburetor identification is located on an identification tag that is located on the carburetor by one of the cover hold-down bolts. On 1984 models less Electronic Feedback Carburetor system, the identification number is stamped on the carburetor near the bowl vent nipple. On all models with Electronic Feedback Carburetor system, the identification number is stamped on the step up piston cover plate.

# DESCRIPTION

The Carter model BBD dual venturi carburetor, **Figs. 1 through 4**, uses three basic fuel metering systems. An idle system provides the correct mixture for idle and low speed performance applications, the accelerator pump system provides additional fuel during acceleration. The main metering system provides an economical fuel mixture for normal cruising conditions.

In addition to the three basic metering systems, there is a fuel inlet system that constantly supplies fuel to the basic metering system and a choke system with electric assist that temporarily enriches the mixture to aid in starting or operating a cold engine.

All BBD model carburetors have an EGR vacuum port because the EGR system is controlled by the venturi vacuum control system. Carburetors used with an Electronic Feedback Carburetor system incorporate various components to enable a computer to help control air/fuel ratio.

# ADJUSTMENTS
## FLOAT LEVEL

With carburetor body inverted so that weight of floats ONLY is forcing needle against its seat, use a T-scale or the tool shown, **Fig. 5,** and check the float level from surface of fuel bowl to crown of each float at center.

If an adjustment is necessary, hold floats on bottom of bowl and bend float lip as required to give the specified dimension.

When bending the float lip, do not allow the lip to push against the needle as the synthetic rubber tip (if used) can be compressed sufficiently to cause a false setting which will affect correct level of fuel in bowl. After being compressed, the tip is very slow to recover its original shape.

## ACCELERATOR PUMP

1. Back off curb idle adjusting screw, completely closing throttle valve, then open choke valve, allowing throttle valves to seat in bores. Ensure accelerator pump "S" link is located in outer hole or pump arm.
2. Turn curb idle adjusting screw until screw contacts, stop, then rotate screw two additional turns.
3. Measure distance between air horn surface and top of accelerator pump shaft, **Fig. 6.** Refer to BBD Specifications Chart.
4. Adjust by loosening pump arm adjusting screw and rotating sleeve until proper dimension is obtained. Tighten adjusting screw.

## BOWL VENT
### 1982–84 Models

1. Remove air cleaner, step-up piston cover plate and gasket.
2. Insert specified gauge between top of bowl vent valve and seat, **Fig. 7.**
3. If measurement is not as specified, adjust by bending bowl vent lever tab. Support bowl vent lever assembly before bending bowl vent tab.
4. Install step-up piston cover plate gasket and cover plate.

## CHOKE UNLOADER

The choke unloader is a mechanical device to partially open the choke valve at wide open throttle. It is used to eliminate choke enrichment during engine cranking. Engines that have been flooded or stalled by excessive choke enrichment can be cleared by the use of the unloader. Adjust as follows:

1. Hold throttle valve in wide open position. Insert the specified drill size or gauge between upper edge of choke valve and inner wall of air horn, **Fig. 8.**
2. With a finger lightly pressing against choke valve, a slight drag should be felt as the drill or gauge is being withdrawn.
3. If an adjustment is necessary, bend unloader tang on throttle lever until specified opening has been obtained.

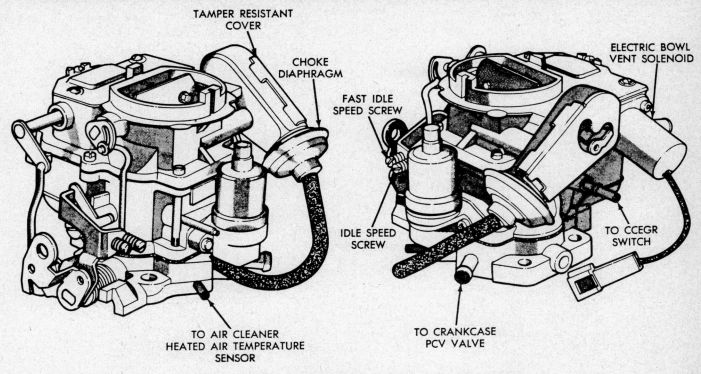

**Fig. 2   Carter BBD carburetor assembly. 1982**

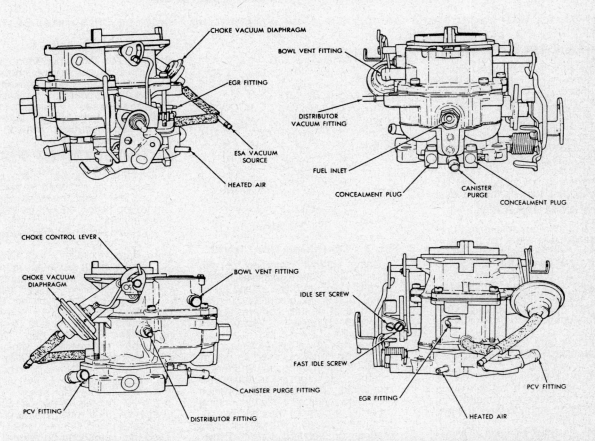

**Fig. 3   Carter BBD carburetor assembly. 1983–84 Less Electronic Feedback Carburetor System**

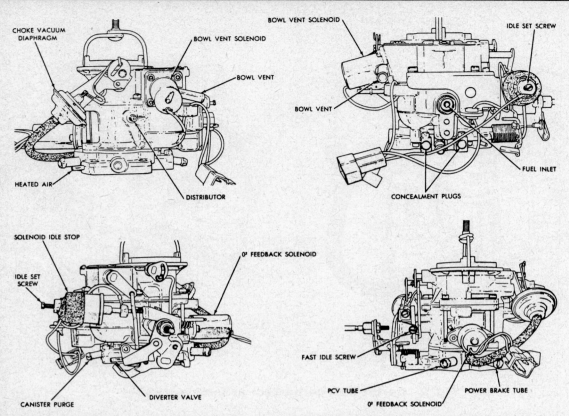

**Fig. 4  Carter BBD carburetor assembly. 1983–84 W/Electronic Feedback Carburetor System**

## FAST IDLE CAM POSITION

1. With fast idle adjusting screw contacting second highest step on fast idle cam, move choke valve toward closed position with light pressure on choke shaft lever.
2. Insert the specified size drill or gauge between choke valve and air horn wall. An adjustment will be necessary if a slight drag is not obtained as drill or gauge is being removed, **Fig. 9.**
3. If adjustment is not as specified, adjust by bending tang on throttle lever.

## CHOKE VACUUM KICK

The choke diaphragm adjustment controls the fuel delivery while the engine is running. It positions the choke valve within the air horn by action of the linkage between choke shaft and diaphragm. The diaphragm must be energized to measure the vacuum kick adjustment. Use either a distributor test machine with a vacuum source, or vacuum supplied by another vehicle.

1. Open throttle and close choke, then close throttle to place fast idle cam at closed choke position.
2. Disconnect vacuum hose from carburetor and connect to hose from auxiliary vacuum source with small length of tube, **Fig. 10.** Apply at least 15 inches of vacuum.
3. Insert the specified size drill or gauge between choke valve and wall of air horn. Apply sufficient closing pressure on lever to which choke rod attaches to provide a minimum choke valve

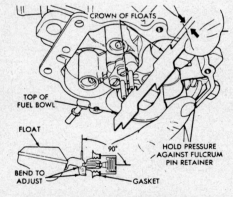

**Fig. 5  Checking float level**

opening without distortion of diaphragm link. Note that the cylindrical stem of diaphragm will extend as internal spring is compressed. This spring must be fully compressed for proper measurement of vacuum kick adjustment.

4. An adjustment will be necessary if a slight drag is not obtained as drill or gauge is being removed. Shorten or lengthen diaphragm link to obtain correct choke opening. Length changes should be made carefully by bending (opening or closing) the bend provided in the diaphragm link. Do not apply twisting or bending force to diaphragm.
5. Reinstall vacuum hose on correct carburetor fitting. Return fast idle linkage to its original condition if it has been

disturbed as in Step 1.
6. Check as follows: With no vacuum applied to diaphragm, choke valve should move freely between open and closed positions. If movement is not free, examine linkage for misalignment or interferences caused by bending operation. Repeat adjustment if necessary.

## VACUUM STEP-UP PISTON

1. On 1982-84 models, if step-up piston assembly is removed or mechanical rod lifter adjustment is disturbed, step-up piston should be readjusted as follows:
   a. Remove step-up piston cover plate and gasket.
   b. Remove rod lever lock screw, then the step-up piston assembly.
   c. Adjust gap in step-up piston by turning allen head calibration screw on top of piston, **Fig. 11.** Gap should be .035 inch. Record number of turns and direction to obtain specified gap. This gap must be reset to its original position after final vacuum step-up piston adjustment has been complete.
   d. Install step-up piston assembly and rod lifter lock screw.
2. On all models, back off curb idle screw until throttle valves are completely closed. Count number of turns so that screw can be returned to its original setting.
3. Fully depress piston and while applying moderate pressure on rod lifter, tighten rod lifter screw, **Fig. 12.**

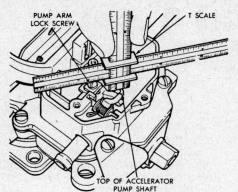

**Fig. 6   Accelerator pump setting**

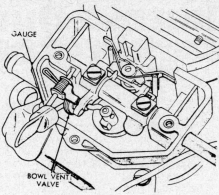

**Fig. 7   Measuring bowl vent valve. 1982–84 carburetors**

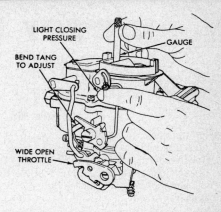

**Fig. 8   Choke unloader setting**

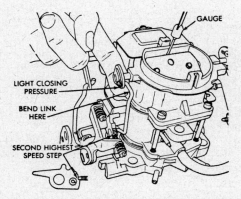

**Fig. 9   Fast idle cam position adjustment**

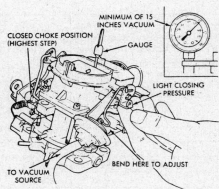
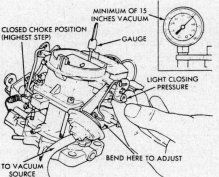

**Fig. 10   Choke vacuum kick adjustment**

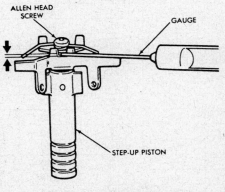

**Fig. 11   Checking step-up piston. 1982–84 carburetors**

4. Release piston and rod lifter and reset curb idle screw.
5. On 1982-84 models, reset Allen head calibration screw on top of step-up piston as recorded in step 1.

## DASHPOT
### Manual Transmission Only

To adjust the dashpot, have the curb idle speed and mixture properly adjusted, and install a tachometer. Position throttle lever so that actuating tab on lever is contacting stem of dashpot but not depressing it. Tachometer should read 2500 RPM if the setting is correct. If not correct, screw

**Fig. 12   Vacuum step-up piston adjustment**

dashpot in or out as required, then tighten lock nut on dashpot against the bracket.

## CONCEALMENT PLUG REMOVAL

1. Remove air cleaner, then disconnect hoses from front of carburetor base.
2. Center punch at a point 1/4 inch from end of mixture screw housing.
3. Drill through punch marks using a 3/16 inch drill bit.
4. Repeat steps 2 and 3 on opposite side.
5. Pry out concealment plugs and retain for reuse, then install connect hoses and install air cleaner.

# Carter Thermo-Quad 4 Bbl. Carburetor

## INDEX

## ADJUSTMENT SPECIFICATIONS

| Year | Carb. Model | Float Setting | Secondary Throttle Linkage | Secondary Air Valve Opening | Secondary Air Valve Spring | Pump Travel @ Curb Idle | Pump Travel @ Secondary Pickup | Choke Control Lever (Off Vehicle) | Choke Vacuum Kick | Choke Unloader |
|---|---|---|---|---|---|---|---|---|---|---|
| 1980 | 9251S | 29/32 | ① | 7/16 | 2 1/4 | .340 | .190 | 3 3/8 | .150 | .310 |
| | 9252S | 29/32 | ① | 7/16 | 2 1/4 | .340 | .190 | 3 3/8 | .150 | .310 |
| | 9254S | 29/32 | ① | 7/16 | 2 1/2 | .340 | .190 | 3 3/8 | .150 | .310 |
| | 9261S | 29/32 | ① | 7/16 | 2 | .340 | .190 | 3 3/8 | .130 | .310 |
| | 9265S | 29/32 | ① | 7/16 | 2 1/2 | .340 | .140 | 3 3/8 | .150 | .310 |
| | 9279S | 29/32 | ① | 3/8 | 2 | .340 | .190 | 3 3/8 | .130 | .310 |
| | 9281S | 29/32 | ① | 3/8 | 2 | .340 | .190 | 3 3/8 | .180 | .310 |
| | 9288S | 29/32 | ① | 1/2 | 2 3/4 | .340 | .190 | 3 5/16 | .120 | .310 |
| | 9292S | 29/32 | ① | 7/16 | 2 | .340 | .190 | 3 3/8 | .130 | .310 |
| | 9292S | 29/32 | ① | 3/8 | 2 1/2 | .340 | .140 | 3 3/8 | .110 | .310 |
| | 9300S | 29/32 | ① | 3/8 | 2 | .340 | .190 | 3 3/8 | .180 | .310 |
| 1981 | 9311S | 29/32 | ① | 27/64 | 2 1/2 | .340 | — | 3 3/8 | .150 | .310 |
| | 9314S | 29/32 | ① | 7/16 | 2 1/2 | .340 | — | 3 3/8 | .150 | .310 |
| | 9329S | 29/32 | ① | 27/64 | 2 1/2 | .340 | — | 3 3/8 | .130 | .310 |
| | 9330S | 29/32 | ① | 27/64 | 2 1/2 | .340 | — | 3 3/8 | .130 | .310 |
| | 9331S | 29/32 | ① | 7/16 | 2 1/2 | .340 | — | 3 3/8 | .110 | .310 |
| | 9332S | 29/32 | ① | 7/16 | 2 1/2 | .340 | — | 3 3/8 | .110 | .310 |
| | 9357S | 29/32 | ① | 27/64 | 2 | .340 | .190 | 3 3/8 | .130 | .310 |
| | 9358S | 29/32 | ① | 7/16 | 2 | .340 | — | 3 3/8 | .180 | .310 |
| | 9359S | 29/32 | ① | 7/16 | 2 | .340 | — | 3 3/8 | .130 | .310 |
| 1982 | 9342S | 29/32 | ① | 27/64 | 2 1/2 | .340 | .190 | — | .130 | .310 |
| | 9375S | 29/32 | ① | 27/64 | 2 | .340 | .190 | — | .130 | .310 |
| | 9376S | 29/32 | ① | 27/64 | 2 | .340 | .190 | — | .130 | .310 |
| | 9379S | 29/32 | ① | 27/64 | 2 | .340 | — | — | .130 | .310 |
| 1983 | 9342S | 29/32 | ① | 27/64 | 2 1/2 | .340 | .190 | — | .130 | .310 |
| | 9375S | 29/32 | ① | 3/8 | 2 1/2 | .340 | .190 | — | .130 | .310 |
| | 9376S | 29/32 | ① | 3/8 | 2 | .340 | .190 | — | .130 | .310 |
| | 9379S | 29/32 | ① | 7/16 | 2 | .340 | — | — | .130 | .310 |
| 1984 | 9376S | 29/32 | ① | 3/8 | 2 | .340 | .190 | — | .180 | .310 |
| | 9379S | 29/32 | ① | 7/16 | 2 | .340 | — | — | .130 | .310 |
| | 9386S | 29/32 | ① | 15/32 | 2 1/2 | .340 | .190 | — | .170 | .310 |
| | 9387S | 29/32 | ① | 15/32 | 2 1/2 | .340 | .190 | — | .150 | .310 |

①—Adjust link so primary & secondary stops both contact at same time.

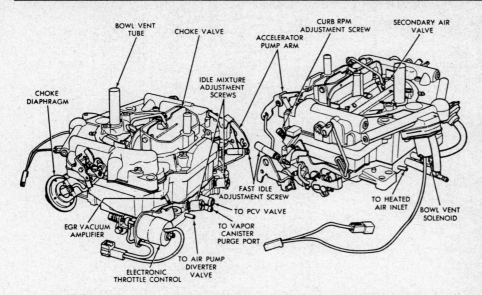

**Fig. 1   Carter Thermo-Quad carburetor assembly. 1980–81**

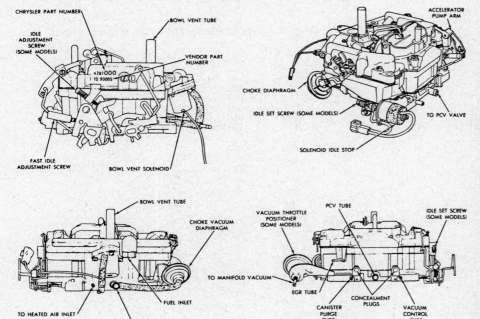

**Fig. 2   Carter Thermo-Quad carburetor assembly. 1982–84**

# IDENTIFICATION LOCATION

On 1980-81 models, the carburetor identification number is located on the driver side at lower rear corner of carburetor or on side of flange where the attaching bolt is located. On 1982-84 models, the identification number is stamped on the driver side face of the carburetor assembly.

# DESCRIPTION

The Carter TQ (Thermo-Quad) carburetor, **Figs. 1 and 2**, is unique in design in that it has a black main body or fuel bowl of molded phenolic resin. This acts as an effective heat insulator. Fuel is kept cooler by approximately 20°F than in carburetors of all metal design. Another reason for the lower operating temperatures is its suspended design metering system. All calibration points with the exception on the idle adjusting screws, are in the upper aluminum casting or air horn assembly and are in effect suspended on cavities in the plastic main body.

# ADJUSTMENTS
## FLOAT SETTING

With bowl cover inverted, gasket in-stalled and floats resting on seated needle, the dimension of each float from bowl cover gasket to bottom side of float should be as shown in the specifications chart, **Fig. 3**. If adjustment is necessary, bend lever as shown but never allow lip of float lever to be pressed against needle when adjusting.

## SECONDARY THROTTLE LINKAGE

Block choke valve in wide open position and invert carburetor, **Fig. 4**. Slowly open the primary throttle valves until it is possible to measure between lower edge of primary valve and its bore. When dimension is as shown in the specifications chart, the secondary valves should just start to open. If necessary to adjust, bend rod until correct dimension is obtained.

## SECONDARY AIR VALVE OPENING

1. With air valve in closed position, the opening along air valve at its long side must be at its maximum and parallel with air horn gasket surface, **Fig. 5**.
2. With air valve wide open, the opening of the air valve at the short side and air horn must be as shown in the specifications chart. The corner of air valve is notched for adjustment. Bend the corner with a pair of pliers to give proper opening, **Fig. 6**.

## SECONDARY AIR VALVE SPRING TENSION

Loosen air valve lock plug and allow air valve to position itself wide open. With a long screwdriver that will enter center of tool C-4152 positioned on air valve adjustment plug, turn plug counterclockwise until air valve contacts stop lightly, then turn additional turn as specified in the specifications chart. Hold plug with screwdriver and tighten lock plug securely with tool C-4152, **Fig. 7**. On 1980 light and medium duty cycle models and all 1981-84 models, use tool C-4152-B.

## ACCELERATOR PUMP STROKE
### 1980 & 1983–84

**First Stage.** Ensure throttle connector rod is in center hole on three hole pump arm or inner hole on two hole pump arm. With idle adjusting screw adjusted to the specified curb idle speed, measure distance from air horn surface to top of accelerator pump plunger. If equipped with an idle stop solenoid the ignition switch must be in the on position. Dimension should be as shown in the specifications chart. Bend throttle connector rod at lower angle to adjust, **Fig. 8**.

**Second Stage.** With choke in the open position, open throttle until secondary lockout latch is just applied. Plunger downward travel stops at this point. Measure distance from air horn surface to top of accelerator pump plunger. Dimension should be as shown in the specification chart. Bend tang on throttle to adjust, **Fig. 8**.

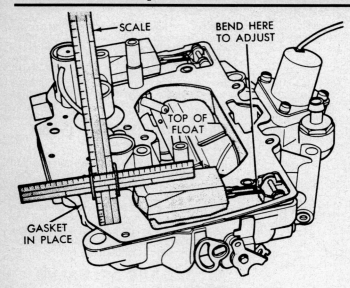

**Fig. 3   Float setting**

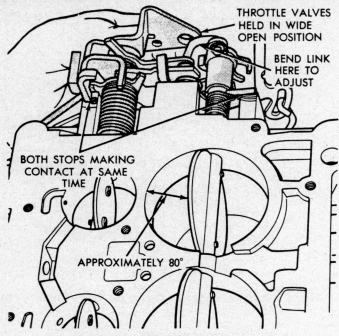

**Fig. 4   Secondary throttle adjustment**

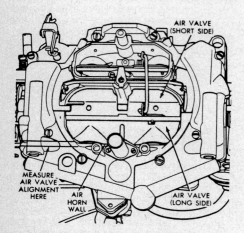

**Fig. 5   Secondary air valve alignment**

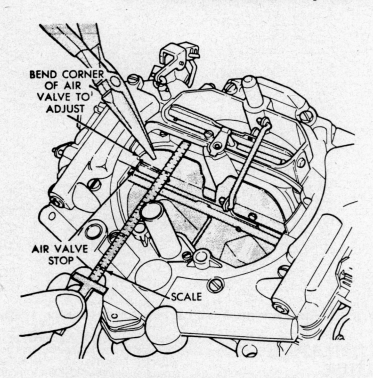

**Fig. 6   Secondary air valve opening**

## 1981—82

Accelerator pump stroke is determined by measurement of the accelerator pump plunger height above the air horn surface at curb idle.

1. Be sure throttle connector rod is in the specified hole of the pump arm.
2. Use a scale to measure height of the accelerator pump plunger stem (top) at curb idle. Pump heights are shown in specifications.
3. Adjust plunger height by bending the throttle connector rod in the proper area, **Fig. 9**.

## CHOKE CONTROL LEVER

Remove the tamper resistant cover, if equipped, by drilling out the two rivets. Place carburetor on a flat surface and disconnect choke diaphragm rod at diaphragm. Close choke by pushing on choke lever with throttle partly open. Measure vertical distance between top of rod hole in control lever and base of carburetor (flat surface). Dimension should be as shown in the specifications chart. Adjust by bending link connecting the two choke shafts. On 1983 light duty cycle models, adjust by loosening lever mounting screw and rotating lever to correct position.

If choke control lever adjustment is changed, the vacuum kick, fast idle cam position and choke unloader adjustments must also be reset.

## CHOKE DIAPHRAGM CONNECTOR ROD

Remove tamper resistant cover, if equipped, by drilling out the two rivets. Apply a vacuum of 15 or more inches of Mercury to diaphragm to fully depress dia-

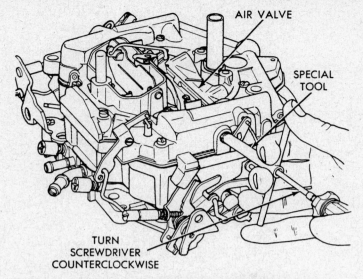

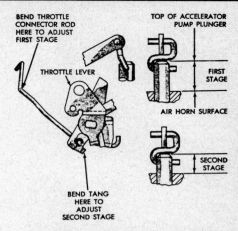

**Fig. 8  Staged accelerator pump adjustment**

**Fig. 7  Secondary air valve spring tension**

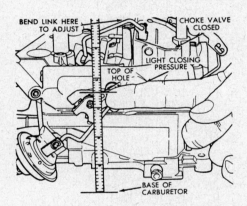

**Fig. 9  Choke control lever adjustment**

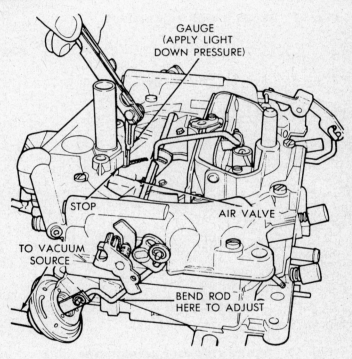

**Fig. 10  Choke diaphragm connector rod**

phragm stem. An auxiliary source like a distributor test machine can be used for this purpose. With air valve closed, adjust connector rod to give .040 inch clearance between air valve and stop, **Fig. 10.**

If choke diaphragm connector rod adjustment is changed, the vacuum kick adjustment must also be reset.

## VACUUM KICK

With engine running, back off fast idle speed screw until choke can be closed to kick position at idle. Note number of screw turns so fast idle can be turned back to original adjustment. Insert specified gauge between long side (lower edge) of choke valve and the air horn wall, **Fig. 11.** Apply sufficient pressure on choke control lever to provide a minimum choke valve opening. The spring connecting the control lever to the adjustment lever must be fully extended for proper adjustment. Bend tang as shown to change contact with end of diaphragm rod. Do not adjust diaphragm rod. A slight drag should be felt as gauge is being removed.

## FAST IDLE CAM & LINKAGE

With fast idle adjusting screw on second highest step of fast idle cam, move choke valve towards closed position with light pressure on fast idle cam lever. Clearance between choke valve and air horn wall should be as specified in "'''Adjustment Specifications" chart under "Choke Vacuum Kick." If adjustment is necessary, bend fast idle connector rod at angle, **Fig. 12.**

## CHOKE UNLOADER

Hold throttle valves in wide open position and insert specified drill or gauge between long side (lower edge) of choke valve and inner wall of air horn, **Fig. 13.** With finger lightly pressing against choke valve control lever, a slight drag should be felt as drill or gauge is withdrawn. Refer to the specification chart for proper drill or gauge size or dimension. Adjust by bending tang on fast idle control lever.

## SECONDARY THROTTLE LOCKOUT

Move choke control lever to open choke position. Measure clearance between lockout lever and stop, **Fig. 14.** Clearance should be .060-.090 inch. Adjust by bending tang on fast idle control lever.

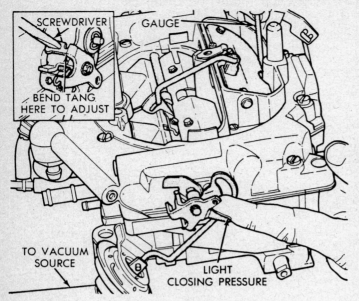

Fig. 11   Vacuum kick adjustment

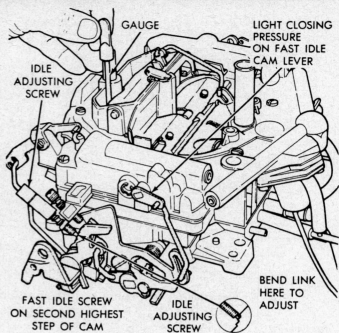

Fig. 12   Fast idle cam & linkage adjustment

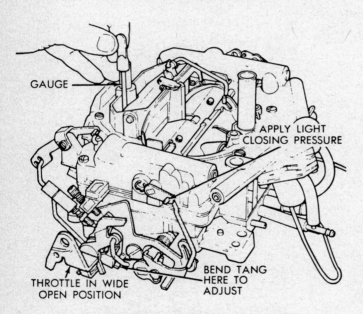

Fig. 13   Choke unloader adjustment

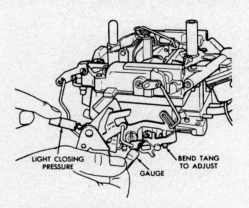

Fig. 14   Secondary throttle lockout

## BOWL VENT VALVE

Units with a solenoid bowl vent diaphragm should be tested by removing hose and applying an auxiliary vacuum source of at least 15 inches of mercury to diaphragm, **Fig. 15.** Viewed through air horn vent tube, valve should move down when vacuum is applied; if it does not, replace leaking diaphragm assembly. Turn ignition switch on and remove auxiliary vacuum source. Valve should remain in down position; if it does not, solenoid or related wiring is defective.

## VACUUM THROTTLE POSITIONER

### 1982–84 Models

1. Start engine and allow to idle in Neutral position, then accelerate engine to a speed above 2000 RPM.
2. Ensure that vacuum positioner unit operates and can withstand a hand applied load in the operating position. If operation is satisfactory proceed to step 3, if not satisfactory proceed as follows:

a. Check all wiring harness and hose connections in system.
b. Check vacuum actuator by applying vacuum from an external source, **Fig. 16.** If actuator does not operate, replace. If actuator does operate, pinch off supply hose and observe actuator. Actuator should remain in operating position for one minute or more to be satisfactory.
c. Check vacuum solenoid by applying vacuum from an external source to manifold supply hose connection on solenoid valve. Dis-

CARTER THERMO-QUAD 4 BBL. CARBURETOR

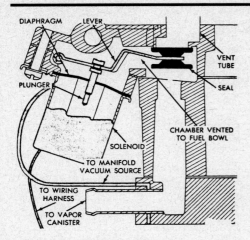

**Fig. 15  Solenoid bowl vent valve adjustment**

connect wiring harness electrical connector from solenoid and ground one terminal of solenoid. Connect 12 volts to other terminal and observe vacuum actuator operation. If actuator does not cycle as 12 volts are applied, replace solenoid. If operation is normal, replace speed switch.

3. Reduce engine speed to 2000 RPM.
4. Loosen positioner adjustment locknut, then completely rotate vacuum positioner assembly until positioner just contacts throttle lever, **Fig. 16.**
5. Release throttle, then slowly adjust positioner to decrease engine speed until a sudden drop of 1000 RPM or more occurs.
6. Continue adjusting positioner an additional 1/4 turn, then tighten locknut.
7. Accelerate engine to approximately 2300 RPM and release throttle. Engine should return to normal idle.

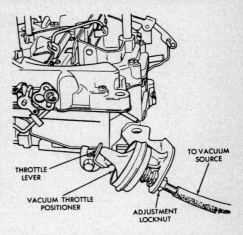

**Fig. 16  Vacuum throttle positioner adjustment**

# Holley 1945 & 6145 1 Bbl. Carburetors

## INDEX

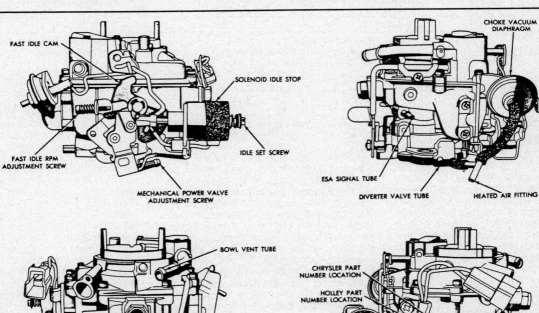

**Fig. 1  Holley model 1945 carburetor assembly. 1985 shown, others similar**

## ADJUSTMENT SPECIFICATIONS

| Year | Carb. Model | Carb. Part No. | Float Level Dry | Vacuum Kick | Fast Idle Cam Position | Bowl Vent Valve | Pump Setting |
|---|---|---|---|---|---|---|---|
| 1980 | 1945 | R-8720A | ① | .130 | .090 | .060 | — |
| | 1945 | R-8721A | ① | .130 | .090 | .060 | 1.61③ |
| | 1945 | R-8978A | ① | .130 | .080 | .060 | 1.70② |
| | 1945 | R-8979A | ① | .130 | .080 | .060 | 1.70② |
| 1981 | 1945 | R-9131A | ④ | .130 | .090 | ⑤ | 1.61③ |
| | 1945 | R-9132A | ④ | .130 | .090 | ⑤ | 1.61③ |
| | 1945 | R-9152A | ④ | .130 | .080 | ⑤ | 1.70③ |
| | 1945 | R-9153A | ④ | .130 | .080 | ⑤ | 1.70③ |
| 1982 | 1945 | R-9132A | ④ | .130 | .090 | ⑤ | 1.61③ |
| | 1945 | R-9153A | ④ | .130 | .080 | ⑤ | 1.70③ |
| | 1945 | R-9762A | ④ | .130 | .090 | ⑤ | 1.61③ |
| | 1945 | R-9765A | ④ | .130 | .080 | ⑤ | 1.70③ |
| 1983 | 1945 | R-40055A | ④ | .130 | .080 | ⑤ | 1.70③ |
| | 1945 | R-40056A | ④ | .130 | .090 | ⑤ | 1.61③ |
| | 6145 | R-40029A | ⑥ | .150 | .090 | ⑤ | 1.70③ |
| | 6145 | R-40030A | ⑥ | .150 | .090 | ⑤ | 1.61③ |
| 1984 | 1945 | R-40088A | ④ | .130 | .080 | ⑤ | 1.61③ |
| | 1945 | R-40089A | ④ | .130 | .080 | ⑤ | 1.61③ |
| | 6145 | R-40098A | ④ | .150 | .070 | ⑤ | 1.61③ |
| | 6145 | R-40099A | ④ | .150 | .070 | ⑤ | 1.61③ |
| 1985 | 1945 | R-40149 | ④ | .130 | .080 | ⑤ | 1.61③ |
| | 1945 | R-40160 | ④ | .150 | .080 | ⑤ | 1.61③ |
| | 6145 | R-40161 | ④ | .150 | .060 | ⑤ | 1.75③ |
| | 6145 | R-40162 | ④ | .150 | .070 | ⑤ | 1.75③ |
| 1986-87 | 1945 | R-40159 | ④ | .130 | .080 | ⑤ | 1.61③ |
| | 1945 | R-40160 | ④ | .150 | .080 | ⑤ | 1.61③ |
| | 6145 | R-40161 | ④ | .150 | .060 | ⑤ | 1.75③ |
| | 6145 | R-40162 | ④ | .150 | .070 | ⑤ | 1.75③ |

①—Refer to text.
②—Hole position 1.
③—Hole position 2.
④—Flush with top of bowl gasket ±1/32."
⑤—2 way electric.
⑥—Flush with top of main body casting to .050" above.

## IDENTIFICATION LOCATION

On Holley 1945 model carburetor, the identification number is located on either a tag attached to the carburetor by one of the cover hold-down bolts or is stamped on the front face of the carburetor body. On Holley 6145 model carburetor, then identification number can be found on a sticker located on the float bowl on the throttle linkage side of the carburetor where the throttle cable connects. The identification number can also be stamped on the carburetor main body or attached tag.

## DESCRIPTION

The single barrel carburetors, **Figs. 1 and 2,** utilize dual nitrophyl floats to control the fuel level, permitting high angularity operation during the most severe operating conditions. The float construction eliminates the possibility of a malfunction due to a punctured float.

An electronic choke system is incorporated to open the choke at approximately 60°F.

The accelerator pump is of the piston type and is operated by a rod and link connected to the throttle lever. The power enrichment system on all units consists of a power valve installed near the center of the carburetor body and a vacuum piston located in the bowl cover. A spring loaded modulated power valve is used. A vacuum passage in the throttle body transmits manifold vacuum to the vacuum piston chamber in the bowl cover. Under light throttle and load conditions, vacuum acting on the throttle piston is sufficient to overcome the spring tension. When the throttle valve is opened to 55°, vacuum acting on vacuum piston is bled to the atmosphere and manifold vacuum is closed off. The throttle shaft is provided with a small hole which aligns with a port in the base of the carburetor when the throttle valve is opened to 55°. This vents the vacuum piston chamber to the atmosphere, allowing the spring tension to open the power valve.

The 6145 electronic feedback carburetor incorporates a duty cycle solenoid which provides a limited regulation of air/fuel ratio in response to electrical signals from the spark control computer. The solenoid meters the main fuel system and operates in parallel with a conventional fixed main metering jet. When there is no electrical signal applied to the solenoid, the valve spring pushes upward through the main system fuel valve, fully uncovering the solenoid controlled main metering orifice so that the richest condition exists within the carburetor for any given air flow. When the electrical signal is applied to the solenoid, the field windings are energized, causing the armature to move the pushrod and main system valve downward against the valve spring. This movement will continue until the main system valve bottoms against the main system valve seat. In this position, the solenoid controlled main metering orifice is fully seated so that the leanest condition exists within the carburetor for any given airflow. This condition will remain unchanged until the signal from the spark control computer to the solenoid

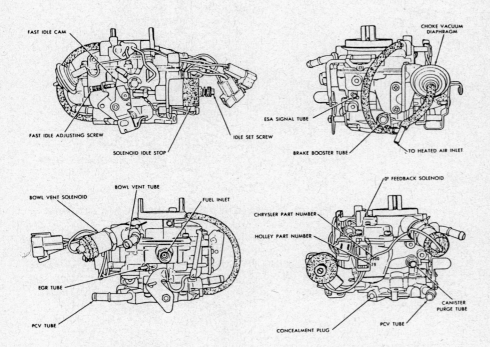

**Fig. 2  Holley model 6145 carburetor assembly.
1985 shown, others similar**

When using an auxiliary vacuum source, disconnect vacuum hose from carburetor and connect it to hose from vacuum supply with a small length of tube to act as a fitting. Removal of hose from diaphragm may require forces which damage the system. Apply a vacuum of 15 or more inches of mercury.

Insert gauge between top of choke valve and wall of air horn, **Fig. 5.** Refer to the specifications chart. Apply sufficient closing pressure on lever to which choke rod attaches to provide a minimum choke valve opening without distortion of diaphragm link.

The cylindrical stem of diaphragm extends as the internal spring is compressed. This spring must be fully compressed for proper measurement of vacuum kick adjustment.

Adjustment is necessary if slight drag is not obtained when removing the gauge. Shorten or lengthen diaphragm link to obtain correct choke valve opening. Length changes should be made by carefully opening or closing the U-bend provided in the link. Improper bending causes contact between the U-section and the diaphragm assembly. Do not apply twisting or bending force to diaphragm.

After completion of adjustment, reinstall vacuum hose on correct carburetor fitting. Return fast idle screw to its original location if disturbed. Make following check. With no vacuum applied to diaphragm, the choke valve should move freely between open and closed positions. If movement is not free, examine linkage for misalignment or interferences caused by bending operation.

On 1982-85 models, adjustment is made by means of a 5/64 inch Allen wrench inserted into vacuum diaphragm.

## CHOKE UNLOADER (WIDE OPEN KICK)

With throttle valves in wide open position, insert drill gauge between upper edge of choke valve and inner wall of air horn, **Fig. 6.** Refer to the specifications chart. With a finger lightly pressing against shaft lever, a slight drag should be felt as drill is being withdrawn. Adjust by bending unloader tang on throttle lever until correct opening has been obtained.

## ACCELERATOR PUMP SETTING

With throttle at curb idle position, measure distance from vacuum passage casting to outer edge of hole in pump operating rod, **Fig. 7.** Refer to the specifications chart. Adjust by bending link between throttle lever and pump operating rod.

## BOWL VENT VALVE
### 1980 1945 Carburetors

1. Measure distance from cover support surface down to flat on plastic bowl vent lever, **Fig. 8.**
2. If measurement is not as specified, turn bowl vent lever adjusting screw until specified measurement is obtained. If accelerator pump piston stroke is changed, this adjustment should be reset.

is switched off. The main system fuel may be regulated between richest and leanest limits by controlling the amount of time that the solenoid is in the power position. Under normal operation conditions, 12 volts at a frequency of 10Hz is applied to the field windings. By controlling duration of the voltage signal, the power on time to total time, referred to as the duty cycle, is established.

# ADJUSTMENTS

## DRY FLOAT SETTING

Hold float fulcrum retaining pin in position and invert carburetor bowl. Place a straightedge across surface of bowl, contacting float toes, **Fig. 3.** Remove straightedge and measure distance float dropped from surface of fuel bowl. Refer to the specifications chart. Adjust by bending float tang to obtain proper dimension.

## FAST IDLE CAM POSITION

With fast idle speed adjusting screw contacting second highest step on fast idle cam, move choke valve toward closed position with light pressure on choke shaft lever. Insert specified gauge between top of choke valve and wall of air horn, **Fig. 4.** Refer to the specifications chart. An adjustment will be necessary if a slight drag is not obtained as drill shank is being removed. Adjust by bending fast idle link at lower angle, until correct valve opening has been obtained.

## CHOKE VACUUM KICK

Test can be made on or off vehicle.

If adjustment is to be made with engine running, back off fast idle speed screw until choke can be closed to the kick position with engine at curb idle. (Note number of screw turns required so that fast idle can be returned to original adjustment). If an auxiliary vacuum source is to be used, open throttle valve (engine not running) and move choke to closed position. Release throttle first, then release choke.

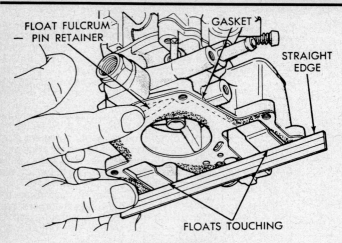

**Fig. 3 Measuring float level**

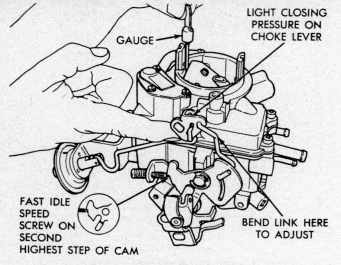

**Fig. 4 Fast idle cam position adjustment**

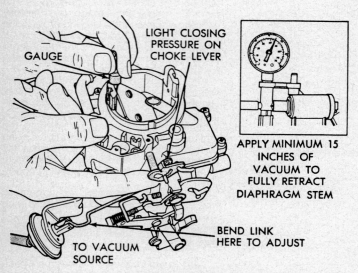

**Fig. 5 Choke vacuum kick adjustment (Typical)**

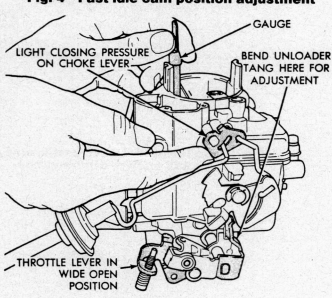

**Fig. 6 Choke unloader adjustment**

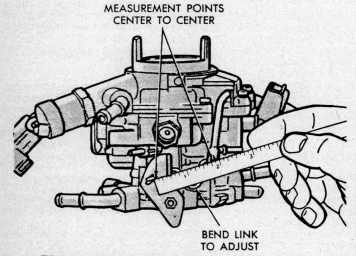

**Fig. 7 Accelerator pump adjustment**

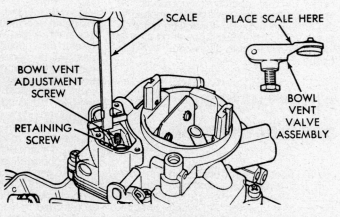

**Fig. 8 Bowl vent valve adjustment. 1980 1945 carburetor**

# Holley 2280 2 Bbl. Carburetor

## INDEX

## ADJUSTMENT SPECIFICATIONS

| Year | Carb Part No. | Float Level Dry | Vacuum Kick | Fast Idle Cam Position | Bowl Vent Valve | Pump Setting |
|---|---|---|---|---|---|---|
| 1980 | R-8999A | 1/32 | .130 | .070 | .030 | .030 ① |
| | R-9000A | 1/32 | .130 | .070 | .030 | .030 ① |
| | R-9001A | 5/16 | .150 | .070 | .030 | .030 ① |
| | R-9209A | 1/32 | .150 | .070 | .030 | .030 ① |
| 1981 | R-9135A | 9/32 | .130 | .070 | ② | ③ |
| | R-9136A | 9/32 | .110 | .070 | ② | ③ |
| | R-9151A | 9/32 | .110 | .070 | ② | ③ |
| 1982 | R-9491A | 9/32 | .140 | .052 | ② | ③ |
| | R-9493A | 9/32 | .140 | .052 | ② | ③ |
| 1983 | R-9499A | 9/32 | .140 | .052 | ② | ③ |
| | R-9951A | 9/32 | .140 | .052 | ② | ③ |
| 1984 | R-40093A | 9/32 | .140 | .070 | ② | ③ |
| 1985 | R-40164 | 9/32 | .140 | .070 | ② | ③ |
| 1986 | R-40214A | 9/32 | .140 | .070 | .035 | .210 ① |
| 1987 | R-40214A | 9/32 | .140 | .070 | .035 | .050 |

① —At idle.
② —2-way electric.
③ —Flush with top of bowl vent casting.

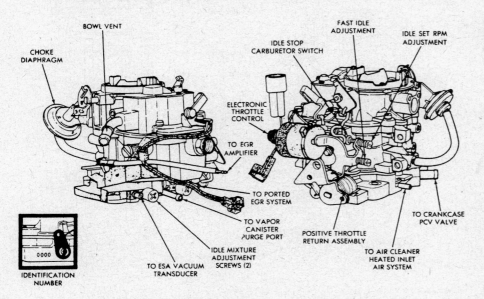

**Fig. 1   Holley 2280 2 bbl. carburetor. 1980 models**

## IDENTIFICATION LOCATION

The identification number is located at the front left side of the carburetor.

## DESCRIPTION

This carburetor, **Figs. 1 through 5,** uses four basic metering systems. The basic idle system provides the proper air/fuel mixture for idle and low speed operations. The accelerator pump system provides additional fuel during acceleration. The main metering system provides the proper air fuel mixture during normal cruising conditions. The power enrichment system, combining a mechanical and vacuum operated power valve, provides a richer mixture when higher engine power is required.

In addition to the four basic systems, there is a fuel inlet system which supplies fuel to the four basic systems and a choke system which temporarily enriches the mixture to aid in starting and running a cold engine.

## ADJUSTMENTS

### FLOAT LEVEL

Invert main body so the weight of the floats only is forcing the needle against the seat. Hold finger against hinge pin retainer to fully seat in the float hinge cradle. Using a suitable scale, **Fig. 6**, measure distance between the float bowl surface and the toe of each float. To adjust, bend the float tang. If necessary, bend either float arm to equalize individual float positions.

### ACCELERATOR PUMP

#### 1980

Remove bowl vent cover plate and vent valve spring. Do not dislodge vent valve lever retainer. Ensure that accelerator pump rod is in the inner hole of the pump operating lever and the throttle is at curb idle. Place a straightedge on bowl vent cover surface of air horn over accelerator pump lever, **Fig. 7.** Adjust until lever surface is flush with air horn surface by bending the accelerator pump connector rod. Install vent valve lever spring and bowl vent cover plate. If this adjustment is changed, the bowl vent and mechanical power valve adjustments must be reset.

#### 1981—84

Remove bowl vent cover plate and gasket. With all pump links and levers installed, adjust accelerator pump cap nut for zero clearance between pump lever and cap nut, **Fig. 8.** Check that wide open throttle can be reached without binding, then install gasket and bowl vent cover plate.

### ACCELERATOR PUMP STROKE

#### 1987

1. Remove bowl vent cover plate and vent valve lever and spring. **Do not dislodge or lose vent valve lever retainer.**
2. With levers installed, place pump link in No. 1 inner hole, then adjust throttle blades to closed position by backing out idle speed screw.
3. Adjust distance from top of pump lever to top of bowl vent cover surface to .045-.055 inch by bending pump link, **Fig. 9.** Ensure wide open throttle can be reached without binding.
4. Install vent valve lever, spring, gasket and bowl vent cover plate.
5. If adjustment was required, both bowl vent and mechanical power valve adjustments should be reset.

### CHOKE UNLOADER

Hold throttle valves in wide open position. Lightly press finger against control lever to move choke valve toward closed position. Insert .250 inch gauge between top of choke valve and air horn wall, **Fig. 10.** To adjust, bend tang on accelerator pump lever.

### CHOKE VACUUM KICK

Open throttle, close choke, then close throttle to trap fast idle cam at closed

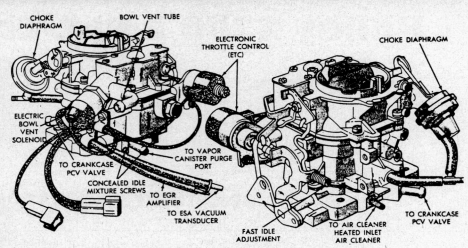

**Fig. 2   Holley 2280 2 bbl. carburetor. 1981 models**

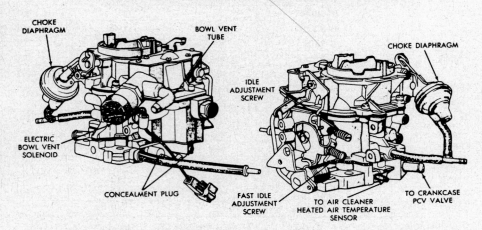

**Fig. 3   Holley 2280 2 bbl. carburetor. 1982 models**

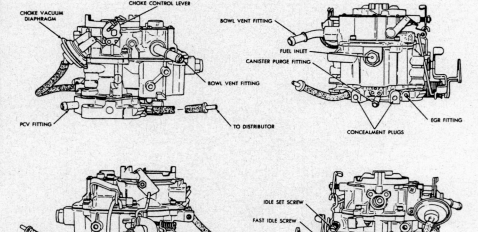

**Fig. 4   Holley 2280 2 bbl. carburetor. 1983—86 models**

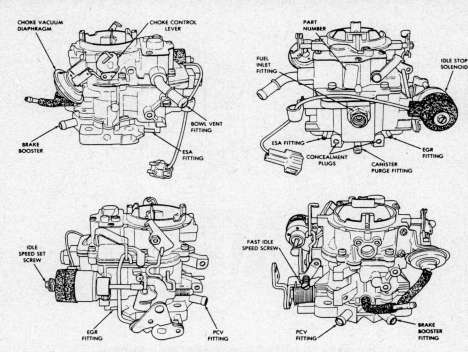

**Fig. 5  Holley 2280 2 bbl. carburetor. 1987 models**

## BOWL VENT VALVE

Remove bowl vent cover plate and vent valve lever spring. Do not dislodge vent valve lever retainer. With throttle at curb idle, press downward on vent valve lever where spring seats. Measure distance between contact surfaces of vent valve tang and vent valve lever, **Fig. 13.** Adjust by bending end of vent valve lever. Install vent valve lever spring and bowl vent cover plate.

## MECHANICAL POWER VALVE

Remove bowl vent cover plate. On 1980 models, remove vent valve lever spring and retainer, then the vent valve lever and pivot pin. On all models, hold throttle in wide open position. Insert a 5/64 inch Allen wrench in mechanical power valve adjustment screw, **Fig. 14.** Push screw downward and release to determine if clearance exists. Turn screw clockwise until zero clearance is obtained. Adjust by turning screw one turn counterclockwise. On 1980 models, install vent valve lever, pivot pin and retainer, then the vent valve lever spring. On all models, install the bowl vent cover plate.

## CONCEALMENT PLUG REMOVAL

1. Remove air cleaner, then disconnect hoses from front of carburetor base.
2. Center punch at a point 1/4 inch from end of mixture screw housing.
3. Drill through punch marks using a 3/16 inch drill bit.
4. Repeat steps 2 and 3 on opposite side.
5. Pry out concealment plugs and retain for reuse, then install connect hoses and install air cleaner.

choke position. Apply approximately 15 inches of vacuum to diaphragm with an external vacuum source, **Fig. 11.** Apply closing pressure on choke lever to completely compress spring in diaphragm stem without distorting linkage. The cylindrical stem of the diaphragm extends to a stop as the spring compresses. Insert specified gauge between top of choke valve and air horn wall. On 1980-81 and 1985-87 models, adjust by bending diaphragm link at U-bend. On 1982-84 models, adjust by inserting a 5/64 inch Allen wrench into diaphragm and turning as necessary. Check for free movement between the open and adjusted positions.

## FAST IDLE CAM POSITION

With fast idle speed adjusting screw contacting second highest step of fast idle cam, move choke valve toward closed position with light pressure on choke shaft lever. Insert specified gauge between top of choke valve and air horn wall, **Fig. 12.** To adjust, bend the U-bend in fast idle connector link to obtain proper setting.

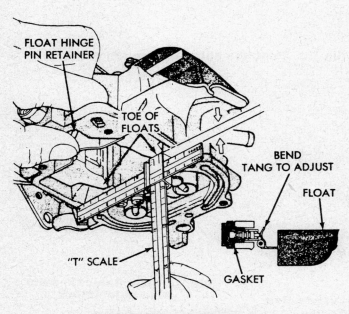

**Fig. 6  Float adjustment**

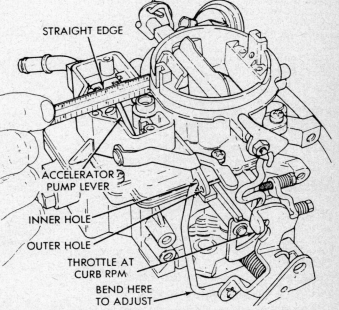

**Fig. 7  Accelerator pump adjustment. 1980 models**

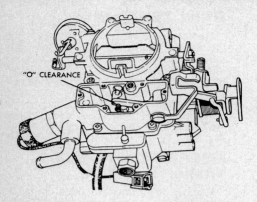

**Fig. 8   Accelerator pump adjustment. 1981–84 models**

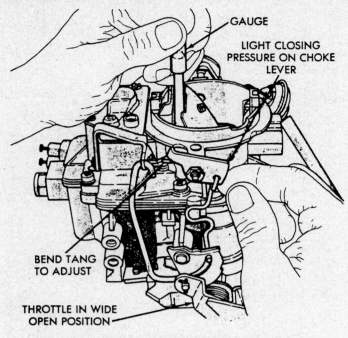

**Fig. 10   Choke unloader adjustment**

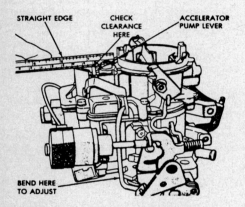

**Fig. 9   Accelerator pump stroke adjustment. 1987 models**

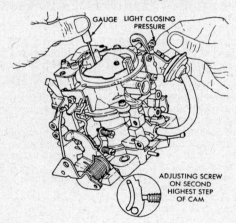

**Fig. 12   Fast idle cam position adjustment**

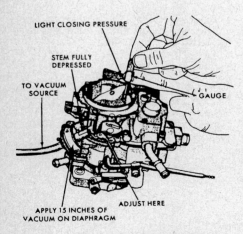

**Fig. 11   Choke vacuum kick adjustment**

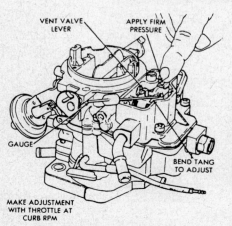

**Fig. 13   Bowl vent valve adjustment**

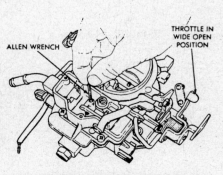

**Fig. 14   Mechanical power valve adjustment**

# Holley 5220 2 Bbl. Carburetor

## INDEX

## ADJUSTMENT SPECIFICATIONS

| Year | Model No. | Float Level | Float Drop | Acc. Pump Hole No. | Choke Vacuum Kick |
|---|---|---|---|---|---|
| 1982 | R-9582A | .480 | 1.875 | 3 | .060 |
| | R-9583A | .480 | 1.875 | 3 | .060 |
| | R-9584A | .480 | 1.875 | 3 | .060 |
| | R-9585A | .480 | 1.875 | 3 | .060 |
| 1983 | R-40020A | .480 | 1.875 | 3 | .055 |
| | R-40022A | .480 | 1.875 | 3 | .055 |
| 1984 | R-400671A | .480 | 1.875 | 3 | .070 |
| | R-400681A | .480 | 1.875 | 3 | .070 |
| | R-40069-2A | .480 | 1.785 | 3 | .070 |
| | R-40075-2A | .480 | 1.785 | 3 | .070 |
| | R-40128-2A | .480 | 1.785 | 3 | .070 |
| | R-40129-2A | .480 | 1.785 | 3 | .070 |
| 1985 | R-40136A ① | .480 | 1.785 | 3 | .075 |
| | R-40143A ① | .480 | 1.785 | 3 | .095 |
| | R-40145A ② ③ | .480 | 1.785 | 3 | .095 |
| | R-40146A ② ④ | .480 | 1.785 | 3 | .095 |
| 1986 | R-40229A ① | .480 | 1.785 | — | .130 |
| | R-40230A ② | .480 | 1.785 | — | .130 |
| | R-40231A | .480 | 1.785 | — | .130 |
| | R-40231A ① | .480 | 1.785 | — | .130 |
| 1987 | R-40234A ② ③ | .480 | 1.875 | — | .095 |
| | R-40240A ② ④ | .480 | 1.875 | — | .095 |
| | R-40303A ① | .480 | 1.875 | — | .095 |

①—Manual transmission.
②—Automatic transmission.
③—Less air conditioning.
④—W/air conditioning.

## IDENTIFICATION LOCATION

The carburetor identification number is stamped on the side of the carburetor float bowl assembly or on base of carburetor.

## DESCRIPTION

The Holley model 5220, **Figs. 1 through 4**, is a staged dual venturi carburetor. The primary bore or venturi is smaller than the secondary bore. The secondary stage is mechanically operated by linkage connecting the primary and secondary throttle levers. The primary stage includes a curb idle and transfer system, diaphragm type accelerator pump system, main metering system and power enrichment system. The secondary stage includes a main metering system and power system. Both the primary and secondary venturi draw fuel from a common fuel bowl. The electric automatic choke has a bimetal two-stage heating element. The carburetor also has an electronic solenoid and a venturi vacuum operated bowl vent.

## ADJUSTMENTS
### FLOAT LEVEL

Invert air horn and insert specified gauge between float and air horn, **Fig. 5**. To adjust, use a small screwdriver to bend tang, **Fig. 6**.

### FLOAT DROP

Using a suitable depth gauge, measure float drop, **Fig. 7**. To adjust, use a small screwdriver to bend tang, **Fig. 8**.

### CHOKE VACUUM KICK

Open throttle, close choke, then close throttle to trap fast idle system in closed choke position. Using an external vacuum source, apply 15 inches of vacuum to choke diaphragm. Apply closing pressure to position choke at smallest opening without distorting linkage. An internal spring will compress to a stop inside choke system. Insert specified gauge between upper edge of choke valve and air horn wall at primary throttle end of carburetor, **Fig. 9**. To adjust, rotate Allen head screw in center of diaphragm housing.

## CHOKE SETTING

Loosen choke coil cap retaining screws and rotate cap assembly to align mark on cap with specified mark on housing. Tighten choke coil cap retaining screws.

## CONCEALMENT PLUG REMOVAL

1. Remove air cleaner crossover assembly.
2. Remove canister purge and diverter valve vacuum hoses.
3. Center punch at a point ¼ inch from end of mixture screw housing.
4. Drill through punch marks using a 3/16 inch drill bit.
5. Pry out concealment plugs and retain for reuse.

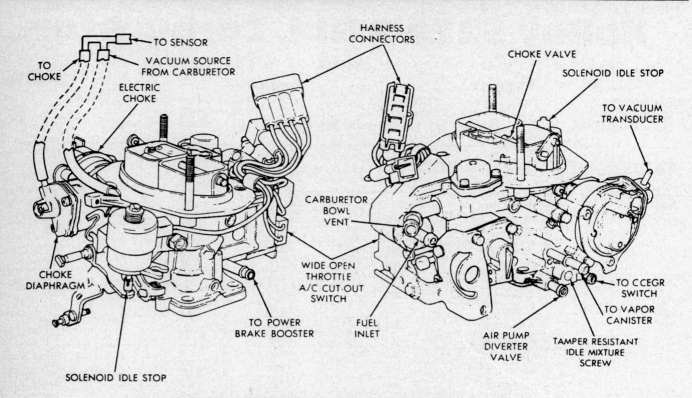

**Fig. 1   Holley 5220 carburetor. 1982 models with A/C**

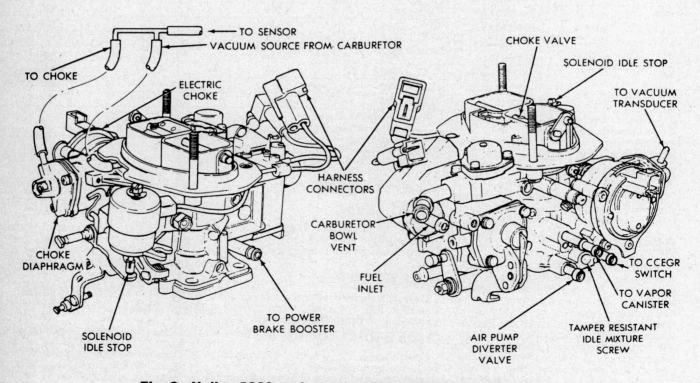

**Fig. 2   Holley 5220 carburetor. 1982 models less A/C**

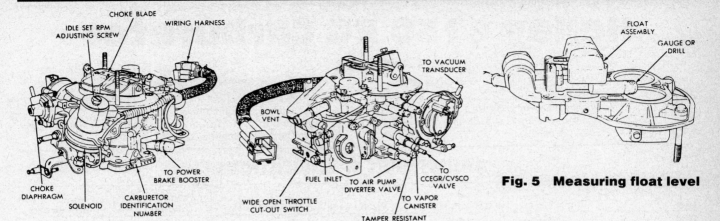

Fig. 3  Holley 5220 carburetor. 1983 models

Fig. 5  Measuring float level

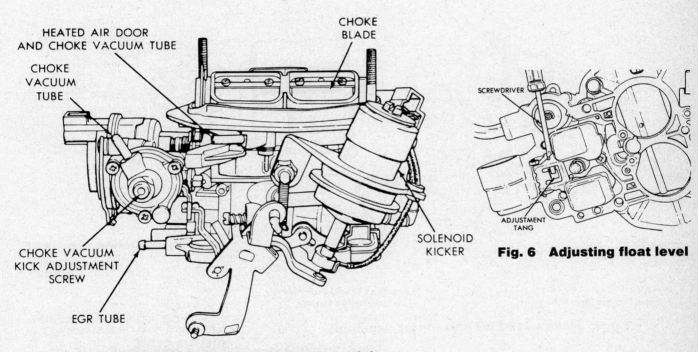

Fig. 4  Holley 5220 carburetor. 1984–87 models

Fig. 6  Adjusting float level

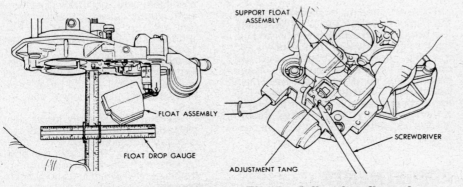

Fig. 7  Measuring float drop        Fig. 8  Adjusting float drop

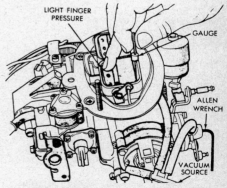

Fig. 9  Choke vacuum kick adjustment. 1982 models (1983–87 models similar)

# Holley 4150 EG Carburetor

## INDEX

## ADJUSTMENT SPECIFICATIONS

| Year | Carb. Model | Carb. Part No. | Float Level | Fuel Level | Pump Lever Setting | Pump Stroke |
|---|---|---|---|---|---|---|
| 1980 | 4150EG | All | ① | ① | .015 | ① |

①—Refer to text.

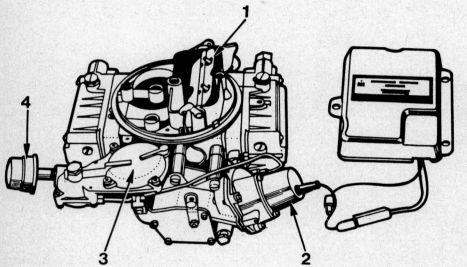

1. Screw Driver in Lock Screw
2. Wrench on Adjusting Nut
3. Sight Plug

**Fig. 2   Adjusting fuel level**

1. Choke Valve
2. Governor Solenoid Assembly
3. Secondary Control Valve Assembly
4. Control Valve Air Cleaner

**Fig. 1   Holley 4150 EG carburetor assembly**

## IDENTIFICATION LOCATION

The carburetor identification number is stamped on the carburetor air horn flange surface.

## DESCRIPTION

The Holley 4150 EG carburetor, **Fig. 1**, is a 4 barrel, two stage down draft type. This carburetor incorporates an electronic vacuum modulating governor.

The first stage (primary stage) supplies the correct air/fuel mixture throughout the entire range of engine operation. The second stage constantly supplements the fuel delivery as needed.

There are three major subassemblies of the carburetor, the main body assembly, fuel bowls and metering assembly and the throttle body assembly. The fuel bowls and metering assemblies contain the fuel chambers, fuel inlet needle valves, acceleration pump, primary and secondary main jets and the fuel metering passages. The throttle body assembly contains the primary and secondary throttle plates, throttle linkage and various fuel and vacuum passages.

## ADJUSTMENTS
### FLOAT LEVEL

With fuel bowl inverted, turn adjusting nut in or out until float lever is parallel to floor of float bowl. Tighten lock bolt.

### FUEL LEVEL

1. Start engine and allow to reach normal operating temperature, then place a suitable container below fuel level sight plug to collect any spill over of fuel.
2. Stop engine and remove air cleaner assembly.
3. Remove fuel level sight plug and gasket, then check fuel level, **Fig. 2.** Fuel level within bowl should be at lower edge of sight plug opening plus $1/32$ inch.
4. If fuel level is satisfactory, install sight plug and gasket. If fuel level is not satisfactory proceed to step 5.
5. Install sight plug, then drain fuel bowl by loosening one lower retaining bolt from fuel bowl. Drain fuel into suitable container.
6. Install retaining bolt, then start engine to fill fuel bowl. Check fuel level again before adjusting float level.

7. If fuel level is not satisfactory, loosen lock screw on top of fuel inlet seat, then turn adjusting nut in or out to correct fuel level, **Fig. 2.** 1/6 turn of adjusting nut changes fuel level approximately 3/64 inch.

8. Remove sight plug and recheck fuel level. Repeat above procedure until correct fuel level is obtained. **Do not loosen lock screw or attempt to adjust fuel level with sight plug removed and engine running.**

## ACCELERATOR PUMP LEVER SETTING

With throttle valves wide open and pump lever held down, it should be possible to insert a .015 inch gauge between adjusting nut and lever, **Fig. 3.** Adjust pump override screw to obtain correct clearance.

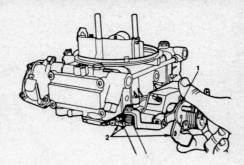

1. Location of Pump Cam
2. Clearance Between Pump Lever and Adjusting Screw With Throttle Wide Open

**Fig. 3   Accelerator pump lever adjustment**

## ACCELERATING PUMP STROKE

The bottom hole in acceleration pump cam and throttle lever provides maximum pump discharge for extreme cold weather. The top hole provides minimum pump discharge for warm weather operation. If adjustment is required, ensure correct hole in plastic accelerating pump cam, located behind throttle lever, is properly aligned with numbered hole in throttle lever before installing retaining screw, **Fig. 3.**

# Holley 6280 2 Bbl. Carburetor

## INDEX

## ADJUSTMENT SPECIFICATIONS

| Year | Carb. Part No. | Float Level Dry | Vacuum Kick | Fast Idle Cam Position | Bowl Vent Valve | Pump Setting |
|---|---|---|---|---|---|---|
| 1985 | R-40132① | 9/32 | .150 | .070 | ③ | ④ |
| | R-40133② | 9/32 | .130 | .070 | ③ | ④ |
| 1986 | R-40221A① | 9/32 | .130 | .070 | ③ | .210⑤ |
| | R-40222A② | 9/32 | .130 | .070 | ③ | .210⑤ |
| 1987 | R-40217A | 9/32 | .160 | .060 | ③ | .135 |
| | R-40218A | 9/32 | .140 | .060 | ③ | .135 |
| | R-40220A① | 9/32 | .130 | .060 | ③ | .135 |
| | R-40294A | 9/32 | .160 | .070 | ③ | — |
| | R-40221A① | 9/32 | .130 | .070 | ③ | .135 |
| | R-40222A② | 9/32 | .130 | .070 | ③ | .135 |

①—Except California models.
②—California models.
③—2-way electric.
④—Flush with top of bowl vent casting.
⑤—At idle.

## IDENTIFICATION LOCATION

The identification number is located at the front left side of the carburetor base.

## DESCRIPTION

The Holley model 6280 carburetor, **Figs. 1 and 2**, utilizes four or five basic metering systems. The idle system provides a mixture for idle and low speed conditions. The accelerator pump system provides additional fuel during acceleration. The main metering system provides an economical mixture for normal cruising conditions. The power enrichment system, which combines a mechanical and vacuum operated power valve or uses a modulated vacuum operated power valve, provides a richer mixture when a higher power output is required. Some models use an O₂ feedback solenoid that is responsive to the oxygen sensor.

In addition to the four or five basic systems, there is a fuel inlet system that constantly supplies fuel to the basic metering systems and a choke system which temporarily enriches the mixture to aid in starting and operating a cold engine.

## ADJUSTMENTS

For adjustment procedures not covered in this section, refer to "Holley Model 2280 Carburetor."

## ACCELERATOR PUMP STROKE

### 1987

1. Remove bowl vent cover plate and gasket.
2. With pump link and levers installed, adjust throttle blades to closed position by backing out idle speed screw.
3. Adjust distance from top of pump lever to top of bowl vent cover surface to specification by bending pump link. Ensure that wide open throttle can be reached without binding.
4. Install gasket and bowl vent cover plate.

## CONCEALMENT PLUG REMOVAL

Refer to Holley model 2280 for removal procedure.

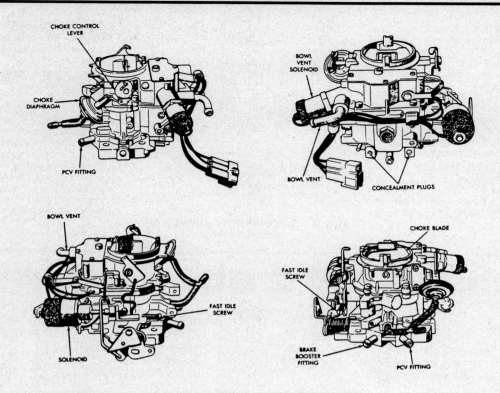

**Fig. 1   Holley 6280 carburetor assembly. Exc. Dakota**

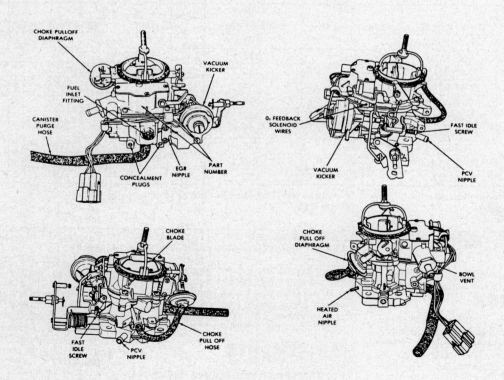

**Fig. 2   Holley 6280 carburetor assembly. Dakota**

# Holley 6520 2 Bbl. Carburetor

## INDEX

## ADJUSTMENT SPECIFICATIONS

| Year | Model No. | Float Level | Float Drop | Acc. Pump Hole No. | Choke Vacuum Kick |
|---|---|---|---|---|---|
| 1982 | R-9503A | .480 | 1.875 | 3 | .060 |
| | R-9504A | .480 | 1.875 | 3 | .070 |
| | R-9505A | .480 | 1.875 | 3 | .070 |
| | R-9506A | .480 | 1.875 | 3 | .070 |
| | R-9507A | .480 | 1.875 | 3 | .085 |
| | R-9508A | .480 | 1.875 | 3 | .085 |
| 1983 | R-40003A | .480 | 1.875 | 3 | .070 |
| | R-40004A | .480 | 1.875 | 3 | .065 |
| | R-40005A | .480 | 1.875 | 3 | .080 |
| | R-40006A | .480 | 1.875 | 3 | .080 |
| | R-40010A | .480 | 1.875 | 3 | .065 |
| | R-40014A | .480 | 1.875 | 3 | .080 |
| 1984 | R-400581A | .480 | 1.875 | 2 | .070 |
| | R-40063-2A | .480 | 1.875 | 3 | .080 |
| | R-400641A | .480 | 1.875 | 3 | .080 |
| | R-400651A | .480 | 1.875 | 3 | .080 |
| | R-40070-2A | .480 | 1.875 | 3 | .080 |
| | R-40071A | .480 | 1.875 | 3 | .080 |
| | R-40072-2A | .480 | 1.875 | 3 | .080 |
| | R-40081-1A | .480 | 1.875 | 2 | .050 |
| | R-400821A | .480 | 1.875 | 2 | .080 |
| | R-401071A | .480 | 1.875 | 2 | .055 |
| | R-40122A | .480 | 1.875 | 2 | .080 |
| 1985 | R-40137A | .480 | 1.875 | 3 | .075 |
| | R-40140A | .480 | 1.875 | 3 | .075 |
| | R-40141A | .480 | 1.875 | 3 | .075 |
| 1986 | R-40233A | .480 | 1.875 | — | .160 |
| | R-40234A | .480 | 1.875 | — | .160 |
| | R-40240A | .480 | 1.875 | — | .160 |
| 1987 | R-40234A | .480 | 1.875 | — | .095 |
| | R-40240A | .480 | 1.875 | — | .095 |
| | R-40303A | .480 | 1.875 | — | .095 |
| | R-40308A | .500 | 1.875 | — | .082 |
| | R-40309A | .500 | 1.875 | — | .082 |
| 1988 | R-4038-1 | .500 | 1.875 | — | .082 |
| | R-4039-1 | .500 | 1.875 | — | .082 |

# IDENTIFICATION LOCATION

The carburetor identification number is stamped on the carburetor body on either the driver or passenger side.

# DESCRIPTION

The Holley model 6520, **Figs. 1 through 4**, is a staged dual venturi electronic feedback carburetor. The primary bore is smaller than the secondary bore. The primary stage includes a curb idle and transfer system, diaphragm type accelerator pump system, main metering system and a fuel regulator or $O_2$ feedback solenoid responsive to oxygen sensor. The secondary stage includes a main metering system and transfer or power system. Both primary and secondary venturi draw fuel from a common fuel bowl. The electric automatic choke incorporates a two stage heating element.

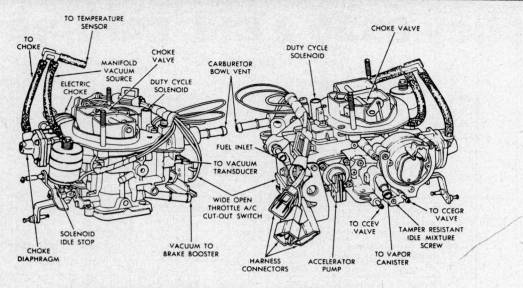

**Fig. 1   Holley 6520 Carburetor. 1982 models**

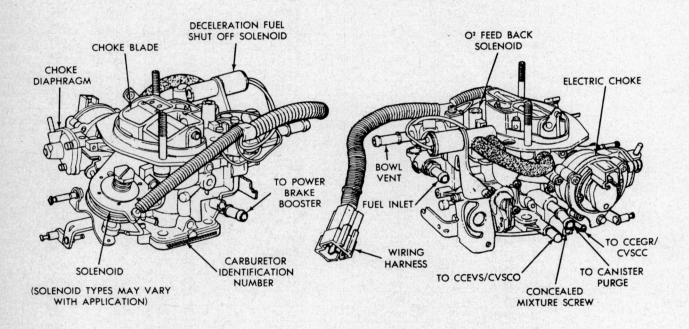

**Fig. 2   Holley 6520 carburetor. 1983 models**

# ADJUSTMENTS
## FLOAT LEVEL

Invert air horn and insert specified gauge between float and air horn, **Fig. 5**. To adjust, use a small screwdriver to bend tang, **Fig. 6**.

## FLOAT DROP

Using a suitable depth gauge measure float drop, **Fig. 7**. To adjust, use a small screwdriver to bend tang, **Fig. 8**.

## CHOKE VACUUM KICK

Open throttle and close choke valve, then close throttle to retain choke valve in the closed position. Disconnect vacuum hose from carburetor and connect an external vacuum source. Apply 15 inches Hg of vacuum or more. Apply sufficient closing pressure to choke valve, using care not to distort linkage. Note that an internal spring will compress to a stop within the choke system Insert the specified gauge in center area between top of choke valve and air horn wall at primary throttle end of carburetor, **Fig. 9**. Adjust clearance by rotating the Allen head screw in center of diaphragm housing.

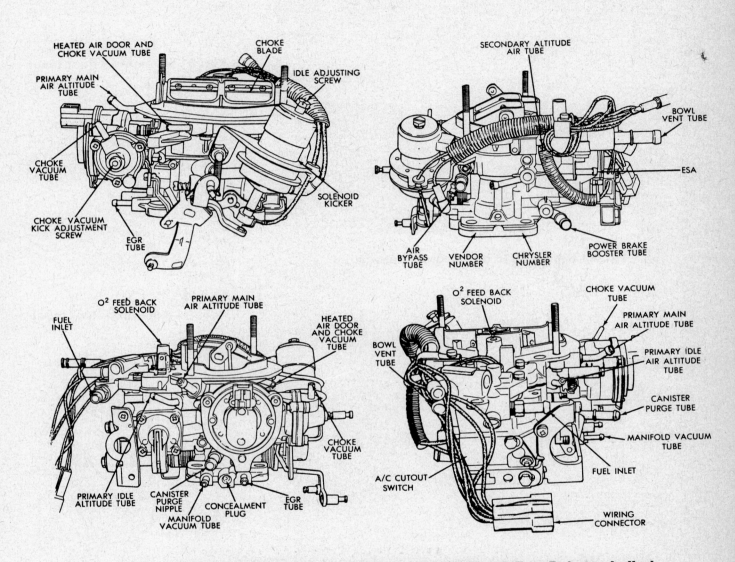

**Fig. 3  Holley 6520 carburetor. 1984 models (1985–87 Exc. Dakota similar)**

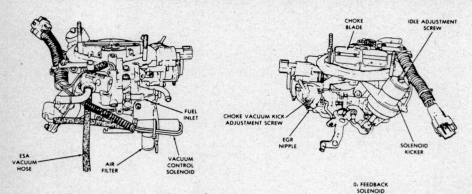

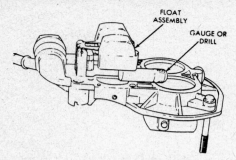

**Fig. 5  Measuring float level**

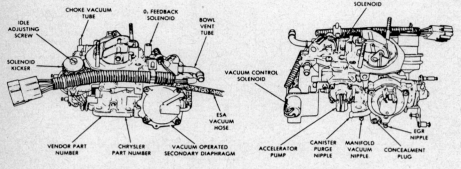

**Fig. 4  Holley 6520 carburetor. Dakota**

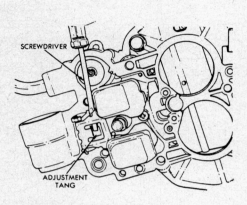

**Fig. 6  Adjusting float level**

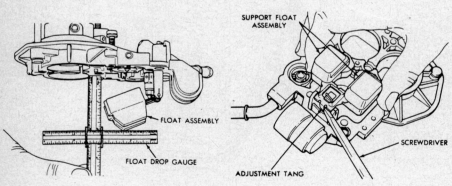

**Fig. 7  Measuring float drop**

**Fig. 8  Adjusting float drop**

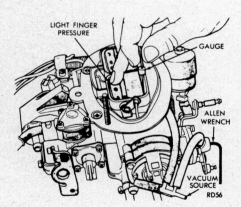

**Fig. 9  Adjusting choke vacuum kick. 1982 models (1983–87 models similar)**

# Mikuni 2 Bbl. Carburetor

## INDEX

## ADJUSTMENT SPECIFICATIONS

| Year | Model No. | Float Level | Choke Breaker Opening @ 10°C Or Less | Unloader Opening @ 0°C Or More |
|---|---|---|---|---|
| 1984-85 | All | .787 | .067 | .051 |
| 1986-87 | All | .882 | .067 | .051 |

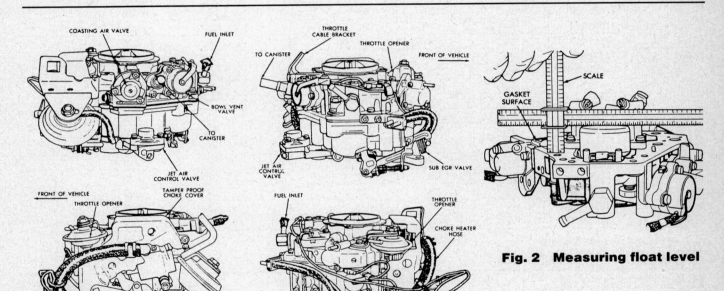

Fig. 1   Mikuni carburetor

Fig. 2   Measuring float level

## IDENTIFICATION LOCATION

The carburetor identification number is stamped on the carburetor air horn surface near the bowl vent valve assembly.

## DESCRIPTION

The Mikuni carburetor, **Fig. 1,** is a conventional downdraft two barrel compound type carburetor. The automatic choke on these units is of the thermo-wax type which is controlled by engine coolant temperature. The main body on these units consists of a black resin compound. Other features of these units include a diaphragm type accelerator pump, bowl vent, fuel cutoff solenoid, air switching valve, sub-EGR valve, coasting air valve and a air jet control valve. Some units also incorporate a high altitude compensation system.

## ADJUSTMENTS

### FLOAT LEVEL

Invert air horn, with gasket removed, and measure distance from bottom of float to surface of air horn, using a suitable depth gauge, **Fig. 2.** If reading is not within limits, the shim located under needle seat must be changed. Use shim kit MD606952 or equivalent, which has three shims with thicknesses of .012 inch, .016 inch and .020 inch. Adding or removing a shim will change float level by three times the thickness of the shim.

# Rochester Quadrajet 4 Bbl. Carburetor

## INDEX

## ADJUSTMENT SPECIFICATIONS

| Year | Carb. Production No. | Float Level | Choke Coil Lever | Choke Rod Fast Idle Cam | Choke Vacuum Kick | Choke Unloader | Air Valve Rod | Air Valve Springs (Turns) |
|---|---|---|---|---|---|---|---|---|
| 1985-86 | 17085417 ① | ¹³/₃₂ | .120 | 20° | 27° | 38° | .025 | ³/₄ |
| | 17085408 ① | ¹³/₃₂ | .120 | 20° | 27° | 38° | .025 | ¹/₂ |
| | 17085409 ② | ¹³/₃₂ | .120 | 20° | 27° | 38° | .025 | ⁵/₈ |
| | 17085415 ③ | ¹³/₃₂ | .120 | 20° | 27° | 38° | .025 | ¹/₂ |
| 1987 | 17085431 | ¹³/₃₂ | .120 | 20° | 23° | 32° | .025 | ¹/₂ |
| | 17086425 | ¹⁵/₃₂ | .120 | 20° | 23° | 38° | .025 | ¹/₂ |
| | 17087175 | ¹³/₃₂ | .120 | 20° | 26° | 30° | .025 | ³/₄ |
| | 17087176 | ¹³/₃₂ | .120 | 20° | 26° | 30° | .025 | ³/₄ |
| | 17087177 | ¹³/₃₂ | .120 | 20° | 27° | 33° | .025 | 1 |
| | 17087245 | ¹⁵/₃₂ | .120 | 20° | 23° | 32° | .025 | ⁵/₈ |
| 1988 | 17085431 | ¹³/₃₂ | .120 | 20° | 27° | 38° | .025 | ¹/₂ |
| | 17086425 | ¹⁵/₃₂ | .120 | 20° | 23° | 38° | .025 | ¹/₂ |
| | 17087175 | ¹³/₃₂ | .120 | 20° | 27° | 38° | .025 | ³/₄ |
| | 17087176 | ¹³/₃₂ | .120 | 20° | 27° | 38° | .025 | ³/₄ |
| | 17087177 | ¹³/₃₂ | .120 | 20° | 27° | 38° | .025 | 1 |
| | 17087245 | ¹⁵/₃₂ | .120 | 20° | 23° | 32° | .025 | ⁵/₈ |

① —Except California models.
② —High altitude & except California models.
③ —All models.

## IDENTIFICATION LOCATION

The carburetor identification number is a vertically stamped 8 digit number. The number can be found on the left rear corner of the float bowl casting, adjacent to the secondary pickup lever, **Fig. 1.**

## DESCRIPTION

The Rochester Quadrajet is a four barrel two stage carburetor incorporating three main carburetor assemblies, the air horn, float bowl and throttle body assembly. This carburetor incorporates six basic operating systems which are the float system, idle system, main metering system, power system, pump system and the choke system.

## ADJUSTMENTS

### FLOAT SETTING

1. Remove air horn, air horn gasket power piston assembly and plastic float bowl insert.
2. Hold float bowl retainer firmly in position.
3. Push float down lightly against needle.
4. Measure float height from top of casting to top of float at a point ³/₁₆ inch from end of float, **Fig. 2.**
5. If float level is too high, hold retainer in position and push down on center of float pontoon to obtain correct setting.
6. If float level is too low, bend float upward to obtain correct setting.
7. Install plastic float bowl insert, power piston assembly and air horn gasket.
8. Install air horn.

### AIR VALVE SPRING

1. Loosen lock screw.
2. Turn tension adjusting screw counterclockwise until air valve opens part way, **Fig. 3.**
3. Turn tension adjusting screw clockwise until air valve just closes. Then, turn adjusting screw clockwise the number of turns specified.
4. Tighten lock screw.
5. Apply lithium base grease to lubricate contact area.

### CHOKE COIL LEVER

1. Remove choke cover.
2. Place fast idle cam follower on to highest step of fast idle cam.
3. Push up on choke lever to close choke valve.
4. Insert a .120 inch plug gauge as shown in **Fig. 4.**
5. Lower edge of lever should just contact gauge.
6. Bend choke rod to adjust.

### CHOKE ROD FAST IDLE CAM

1. Attach a suitable rubber band to green tang of intermediate choke shaft as shown in **Fig. 5.**
2. Open throttle to allow choke valve to close.
3. Set up angle gauge and set angle to specifications.
4. Place cam follower on to second highest step of cam against rise of high step.
5. If cam follower does not contact cam, turn fast idle screw until it does.
6. Adjust by bending tang of fast idle cam until bubble is centered.

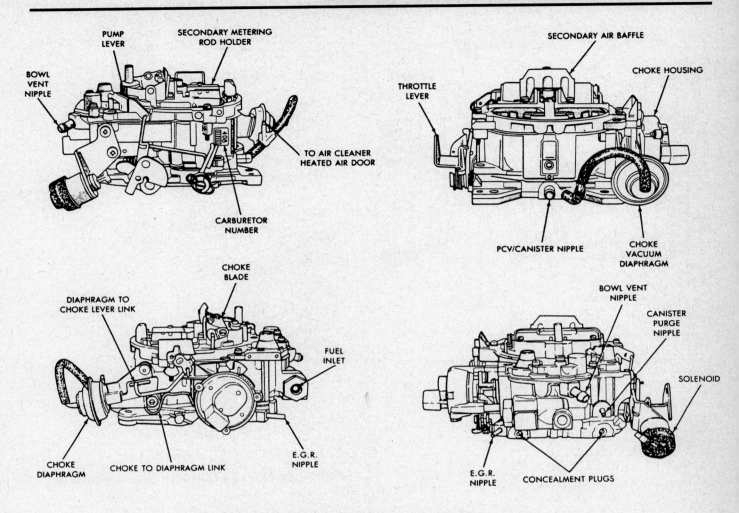

**Fig. 1  Rochester Quadrajet carburetor assembly**

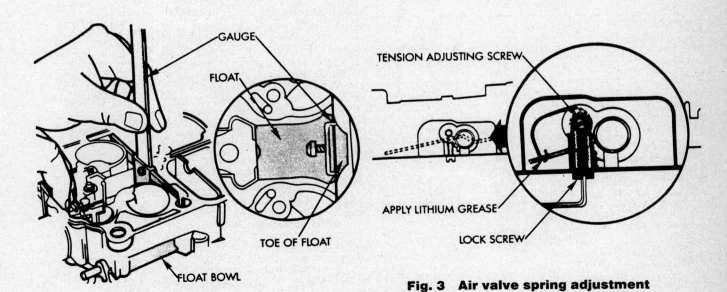

**Fig. 2  Float setting adjustment**

**Fig. 3  Air valve spring adjustment**

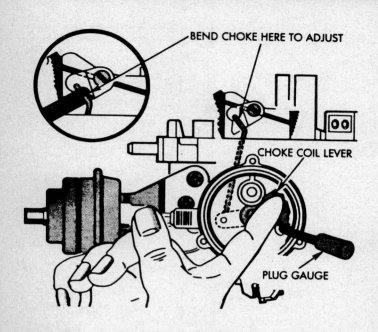

**Fig. 4   Choke coil lever adjustment**

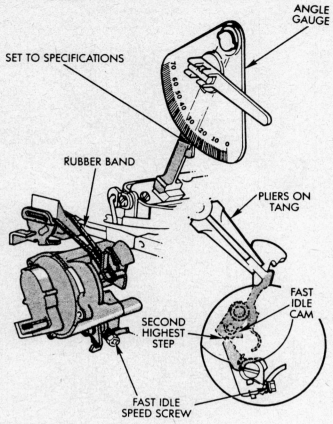

**Fig. 5   Choke rod fast idle cam adjustment**

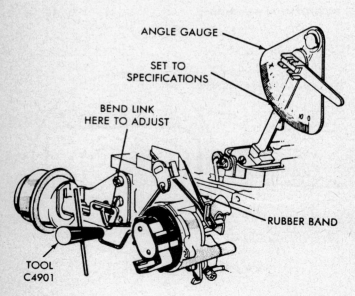

**Fig. 6   Choke vacuum kick adjustment**

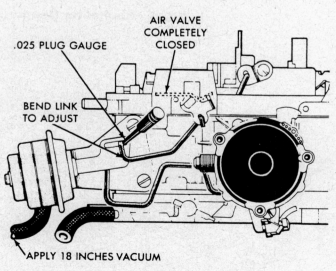

**Fig. 7   Air valve rod adjustment**

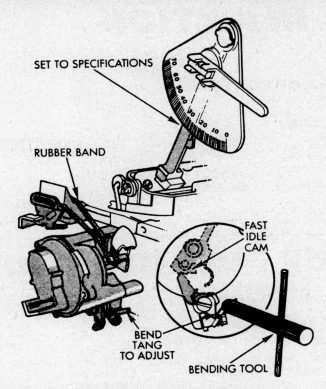

SET TO SPECIFICATIONS

RUBBER BAND

FAST
IDLE
CAM

BEND
TANG
TO ADJUST

BENDING TOOL

**Fig. 8  Choke unloader adjustment**

## CHOKE VACUUM KICK

1. Attach rubber band to green tang of intermediate choke as shown in **Fig. 6.**
2. Open throttle to allow choke valve to close.
3. Install gauge and set to specifications.
4. Using tool C-4207A or equivalent, apply 18 inches Hg to choke diaphragm nipple. The air valve rod must not restrict plunger from retracting completely. If necessary, bend rod to permit full plunger travel. Final rod clearance must be set after vacuum kick setting has been completed.
5. With at least 18 inches Hg still applied, adjust by bending link as indicated to center bubble.

## AIR VALVE ROD

1. Using tool C-4207A or equivalent, apply at least 18 inches Hg to choke vacuum diaphragm nipple.
2. Close air valve.
3. Insert a .025 inch plug gauge between rod and end of slot, **Fig. 7.**
4. Bend rod to adjust clearance to .025 inch.

## CHOKE UNLOADER

1. Attach rubber band to green tang of intermediate choke shaft.
2. Open throttle to allow choke valve to close.
3. Install angle gauge and set angle to specifications.
4. Hold secondary lock out lever away from pin.
5. Hold throttle lever in wide open position.
6. Adjust by bending tang of fast idle lever until bubble is centered, **Fig. 8.**

# CHRYSLER/JEEP FUEL INJECTION

## TABLE OF CONTENTS

# Throttle Body Fuel Injection, Jeep

## INDEX

## DESCRIPTION

The Renix Throttle Body Fuel Injection System, used on some 1986 and all later models with 4-150 engines, is a single point injection system that injects fuel into the throttle body from a injector located above the throttle plate.

The system is controlled by an electronic control unit (ECU) located under the instrument panel above the accelerator pedal. The ECU receives inputs from various sensors and switches that represent actual engine operating conditions. Based on these inputs, the ECU signals outputs that control the air/fuel mixture, ignition timing, fuel delivery, idle speed, emission controls, up-shift indicator lamp (manual transmission only) and A/C compressor clutch.

## FUEL DELIVERY SYSTEM

The fuel delivery system is comprised of an in-tank electric fuel pump, an in-line fuel filter, a fuel pressure regulator and a fuel injector.

The in-tank electric fuel pump is attached to the fuel gauge sending unit and is controlled by the ECU. It delivers and maintains fuel pressure at a standard operating pressure of 14.5 psi. The replaceable in-line fuel filter is located under the right rear floor pan. The fuel pressure regulator is an integral part of the throttle body and consists of a spring chamber that is vented to the same pressure as the tip of the injector. Since differential pressure between the injector nozzle and the spring chamber is the same, the volume of fuel delivered is only dependent on the length of time the injector solenoid is energized. Since the fuel pump delivers fuel in excess of engine requirements, the pressure regulator sends some fuel back to the fuel tank via the fuel return hose. The pressure regulator acts independently of the ECU. The fuel injector is controlled by the ECU and directs and meters fuel into the throttle bore. The fuel injector body consists of a solenoid plunger that is pulled upward by the solenoid armature. This permits the spring loaded ball valve to move from its seat, allowing fuel to pass through the injector nozzle.

## FUEL CONTROL SYSTEM

The fuel control system consists of the ECU outlined previously and various input and output components. The input components relay data to the ECU regarding engine operating conditions, while the output components change various modes of operation based on signals from the ECU.

## INPUT COMPONENTS

### Manifold Absolute Pressure(MAP)Sensor

The MAP sensor reacts to absolute pressure in the intake manifold. Manifold pressure supplies mixture density and ambient barometric pressure information to the ECU. The MAP sensor provides data to the ECU regarding this density and pressure in the form of input voltage.

### Coolant Temperature Sensor(CTS)

Located in the intake manifold coolant jacket, the CTS provides engine coolant data to the ECU. When low coolant temperature data is observed, the ECU will: enrich the air/fuel mixture, compensate for fuel condensation in the intake manifold, control warm-up idle speed, increase ignition advance and inhibit EGR system operation.

## Manifold Air/Fuel Temperature(MAT)Sensor

This sensor, located in the intake manifold, supplies air/fuel mixture temperature data to the ECU. The ECU will then compensate for air density changes during high temperature operation.

## Oxygen Sensor

This sensor, located in the exhaust pipe, supplies voltage data to the ECU depending on the oxygen content in the exhaust gas. The ECU uses this data to vary the air/fuel ratio accordingly. The sensor used on 4-150 engines is equipped with a heating element that keeps the sensor at proper operating temperatures during all operating modes. This enables the system to enter closed loop operation sooner and remain in closed loop mode during periods of extended idle. The feed circuit to the oxygen sensor is through the ignition switch.

## Battery Voltage

Battery voltage data is used by the ECM to ensure that proper voltage is applied to the fuel injector at all times. The ECU varies the voltage applied to compensate for battery voltage fluctuations.

## Speed Sensor

Attached to the flywheel/drive plate housing, this sensor provides engine speed and crankshaft angle data to the ECU. The flywheel/drive plate has a large trigger tooth and notch located 90 degrees and 12 small teeth before each top dead center(TDC)position. When a small tooth and notch pass the magnetic core of the sensor, the magnetic field collapses, causing a low voltage spike in the sensor pickup coil winding. These voltage spikes enable the ECU to count the teeth as they pass the sensor. When a large trigger tooth and notch pass the magnetic core of the sensor, the magnetic field again collapses, inducing a higher voltage spike in the sensor pickup coil winding. This higher spike indicates to the ECU that a piston will be at TDC 12 teeth later. The ignition timing is then either advanced or retarded as necessary.

## Starter Relay

The starter relay provides input data to the ECU that indicates that the starter motor is engaged.

## Closed Throttle(Idle)Switch

This switch is an integral part of the idle speed actuator(ISA)motor and provides input data to the ECU that will enable it to either increase or decrease the throttle stop angle in response to various engine operating conditions.

## Throttle Position Sensor(TPS)

Mounted on the throttle body assembly, this sensor provides an input signal of up to 5 volts to the ECU regarding throttle position. At idle speed, an input signal of approximately 1 volt is transmitted to the ECU. As throttle opening increases, a corresponding increase in the voltage signal to the ECU is observed, to a maximum of 5 volts.

## Wide Open Throttle(WOT)Switch

Attached to the side of the throttle body, this switch provides input data to the ECU regarding when a wide-open throttle condition exists. The ECU then enriches the air/fuel mixture accordingly.

## Power Steering Pressure Switch

During periods of high pump load and low engine RPM (parking maneuvers), the power steering pressure switch contacts close, transmitting this data to the ECU. The ECU then raises idle speed to accommodate the increased load on the engine from power steering pump operation.

## Load Swap Relay

Used on vehicles with air conditioning and power steering, this relay works in conjunction with the power steering pressure switch. If the compressor clutch is engaged when the pressure switch contacts close, the input signal from the switch to the ECU also activates the load swap relay. The relay contacts then open, cutting off the electrical feed to the compressor clutch. The clutch will remain disengaged until the pressure switch contacts reopen and engine idle returns to normal.

## A/C Controls

These controls indicate to the ECU that the A/C switch is in the On position. The ECU will then engage the compressor clutch and change idle speeds as required.

## Transmission Gear Position Indicator

Used on some vehicles equipped with automatic transmission, this device provides input data to the ECU indicating that the vehicle is in a driving mode.

# OUTPUT COMPONENTS

## System Power(Latch)Relay

Initially energized during engine start up, this relay remains energized 3 to 5 seconds after engine shutdown. This permits the ECU to extend the idle speed actuator for the next start up.

## Fuel Pump Control Relay

Battery voltage is applied to this relay whenever the ignition switch is turned to the On position. The ECU then completes the ground to the circuit, energizing the relay, which in turn activates the fuel pump.

## Fuel Injector

The ECU receives data from the various input sensors during all engine operating modes. Injection duration is based on these inputs and is controlled by the ECU, which energizes and de-energizes the injector solenoid as required.

## EGR Valve/Canister Purge Solenoid

This solenoid controls the vacuum source to both the EGR valve and vapor canister. When de-energized, vacuum is applied to both components. When energized by the ECU, this solenoid prevents vacuum from reaching the EGR valve and vapor canister. Conditions when this solenoid will be energized include engine warmup, curb idle, wide open throttle and rapid acceleration or deceleration.

## Idle Speed Actuator(ISA)Motor

Located on the throttle body, this device controls idle speed and deceleration throttle stop angles. The ECU controls the ISA motor by applying appropriate voltage outputs to it, thereby producing the idle speed or throttle stop angles required for specific engine operating conditions.

## Ignition Power Module

Based on input data received, the ECU triggers the ignition coil via this module.

## A/C Compressor Clutch Relay

This relay controls the engagement and disengagement of the compressor clutch based on voltage signals received from the ECU.

## Up-Shift Indicator Lamp

Used on manual transmission equipped vehicles, this lamp illuminates when the ignition switch is turned On, and is turned Off when engine start up occurs. The lamp will illuminate during driving when engine speed and load are within specified values. The ECU will turn off the lamp if a shift of gears is not performed within 3-5 seconds of lamp illumination.

# SERVICE PRECAUTIONS

Before performing any testing procedures, the following precautions should be followed:
1. Remove ECU from vehicle if it will be exposed to temperatures exceeding 175°F.
2. Never start engine when battery terminals are loose.
3. Always disconnect battery terminals before charging battery.
4. Never start any testing or repair of the fuel injection system unless the ignition system has been thoroughly checked.
5. Whenever using an ohmmeter, ensure ignition switch is in Off position, since damage to meter may result.
6. Before attempting to troubleshoot system, ensure that there are no leaks in intake system, or exhaust system above the catalytic converter.
7. Never connect or disconnect any component without turning Off the ignition switch.

# COMPONENT TESTING

Refer to diagnostic and ECU connector terminal identifications, **Figs. 1 and 2** when testing the TBFI system.

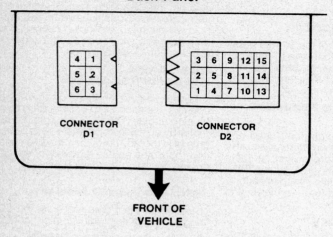

**Dash Panel**

**FRONT OF VEHICLE**

CONNECTOR D1

CONNECTOR D2

## Connector D1

1. Tach Input
2. Ignition
3. Ground
4. Start Solenoid
5. Battery
6. Fuel Pump

## Connector D2

1. Shift Lamp
2. Power Latch Relay
3. Park/Neutral
4. Power Latch Relay (B+)
5. Air Conditoning Clutch Relay
6. WOT Switch
7. Ground
8. Air/Fuel Temperature
9. M.P.A. (Ignition Output)
10. EGR/Canister Purge Solenoid
11. ISA Motor Forward
12. Coolant Temperature Sensor
13. Closed Throttle Switch
14. ISA Motor Reverse
15. Not Used.

**Fig. 1  Diagnostic connector terminal identification**

1. Ground
2. Ground
3. Ignition Switch
4. Battery
5. EGR Valve/Canister Purge
6. Fuel Pump Relay
7. System Power Relay (latch relay)
8. WOT Switch
9. Not Used
10. System Ground
11. Speed Sensor
12. Park/Neutral Switch (auto. trans. only)
13. Throttle Position Sensor Ground
14. Manifold Air/Fuel Temperature Sensor
15. Coolant Temperature Sensor
16. Manifold Absolute Pressure — Supply Voltage
17. Manifold Absolute Pressure — Ground
18. Shift Lamp (manual trans. only)
19. System Power (B+)
20. Not Used
21. Injector
22. A/C Compressor Clutch
23. ISA Motor Retract (reverse)
24. ISA Motor Extend (forward)
25. Closed Throttle (idle) Switch
26. Not Used
27. Ignition Interference
28. Speed Sensor
29. Start Signal
30. A/C Select
31. Throttle Position Sensor
32. Temperature Sensor Ground
33. MAP Sensor Output
34. A/C Request
35. O₂ Sensor Input

**Fig. 2  ECU connector terminal identification**

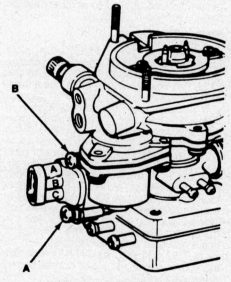

**Fig. 3  TPS terminal identification & retaining screw location**

## THROTTLE POSITION SENSOR (TPS)

Refer to pin terminal identification, **Fig. 3**, and diagnostic chart, **Fig. 4**, to test throttle position sensor.

## OXYGEN SENSOR

1. Disconnect sensor electrical connector.
2. Using suitable ohmmeter, check resistance between connector terminals A and B, **Fig. 5**.
3. Resistance should be 5-7 ohms.
4. If resistance is not as specified, replace sensor.

## MANIFOLD AIR/FUEL TEMPERATURE (MAT) SENSOR

1. Disconnect sensor electrical connector.
2. Using a suitable digital

volt-ohmmeter, measure sensor resistance.
3. Resistance should be less than 1000 ohms with engine at normal operating temperature, or approximately 3400 ohms if tested at room temperature.
4. If resistance is not as specified, replace sensor.
5. Check resistance between ECU connector terminal 32 and sensor connector, then between ECU connector terminal 14 and sensor connector. If resistance is greater than 1 ohm, repair wire harness as necessary.

## COOLANT TEMPERATURE SENSOR (CTS)

1. Disconnect sensor electrical connector.
2. Using a suitable digital volt-ohmmeter, measure sensor resistance.
3. Resistance should be less than 1000

ohms with engine at normal operating temperature, or approximately 3400 ohms if tested at room temperature.
4. If resistance is not as specified, replace sensor.
5. Check resistance between ECU connector terminal 32 and sensor connector, then between ECU connector terminal 15 and sensor connector. If a open circuit is indicated, repair wire harness as necessary.

## WIDE OPEN THROTTLE (WOT) SWITCH

1. Disconnect switch electrical connector.
2. Using a suitable digital volt-ohmmeter, measure resistance

**10-70**

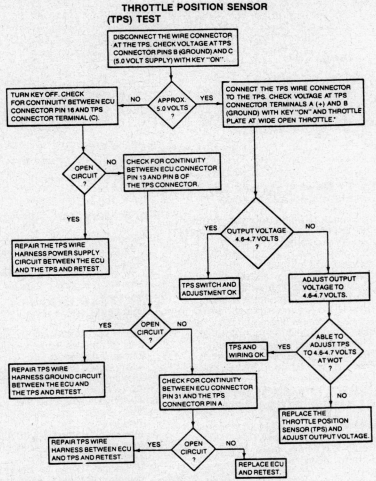

**Fig. 4  TPS diagnostic chart**

THROTTLE POSITION SENSOR (TPS) TEST

DISCONNECT THE WIRE CONNECTOR AT THE TPS. CHECK VOLTAGE AT TPS CONNECTOR PINS B (GROUND) AND C (5.0 VOLT SUPPLY) WITH KEY "ON".

APPROX. 5.0 VOLTS?

— NO → TURN KEY OFF. CHECK FOR CONTINUITY BETWEEN ECU CONNECTOR PIN 16 AND TPS CONNECTOR TERMINAL (C).

— YES → CONNECT THE TPS WIRE CONNECTOR TO THE TPS. CHECK VOLTAGE AT TPS CONNECTOR TERMINALS A (+) AND B (GROUND) WITH KEY "ON" AND THROTTLE PLATE AT WIDE OPEN THROTTLE.*

OPEN CIRCUIT? — NO → CHECK FOR CONTINUITY BETWEEN ECU CONNECTOR PIN 13 AND PIN B OF THE TPS CONNECTOR.

— YES → REPAIR THE TPS WIRE HARNESS POWER SUPPLY CIRCUIT BETWEEN THE ECU AND THE TPS AND RETEST.

OUTPUT VOLTAGE 4.6-4.7 VOLTS?

— YES → TPS SWITCH AND ADJUSTMENT OK

— NO → ADJUST OUTPUT VOLTAGE TO 4.6-4.7 VOLTS.

OPEN CIRCUIT? — YES → REPAIR TPS WIRE HARNESS GROUND CIRCUIT BETWEEN THE ECU AND THE TPS AND RETEST.

— NO → CHECK FOR CONTINUITY BETWEEN ECU CONNECTOR PIN 31 AND THE TPS CONNECTOR PIN A.

ABLE TO ADJUST TPS TO 4.6-4.7 VOLTS AT WOT? — YES → TPS AND WIRING OK.

— NO → REPLACE THE THROTTLE POSITION SENSOR (TPS) AND ADJUST OUTPUT VOLTAGE.

OPEN CIRCUIT? — YES → REPAIR TPS WIRE HARNESS BETWEEN ECU AND TPS AND RETEST.

— NO → REPLACE ECU AND RETEST.

* DO NOT UNFASTEN THE SENSOR WIRE HARNESS CONNECTOR. INSERT THE VOLTMETER TEST LEADS THROUGH THE BACK OF THE WIRE HARNESS CONNECTOR TO MAKE CONTACT WITH THE SENSOR TERMINALS. ON SOME MODELS, IT MAY ALSO BE NECESSARY TO REMOVE THE THROTTLE BODY FROM THE INTAKE MANIFOLD, TO GAIN ACCESS TO THE SENSOR WIRE HARNESS CONNECTOR.

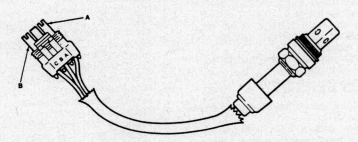

**Fig. 5  Oxygen sensor connector terminals**

while rotating switch from closed to wide open throttle position.

3. Resistance should be infinite at closed throttle, while low resistance should be obtained at wide open throttle. If operation is not as specified, replace switch.

## CLOSED THROTTLE (IDLE) SWITCH

All testing should be performed with ISA plunger in fully extended position, as it should be when engine is Off. If it is necessary to manually extend plunger, the ISA is probably defective.

1. With ignition switch On, connect voltmeter between terminals D2-13 and D2-7 of diagnostic connector. Observe voltmeter.
2. Voltmeter reading should be close to zero at closed throttle, and above 2 volts when off closed throttle position.
3. If voltage reading is zero in all positions, check for short to ground in wire harness or switch, or for open circuit between ECU connector terminal 25 and switch.
4. If voltage reading is greater than 2 volts in all positions, check for open circuit between ECU and switch connector, or between switch connector and ground.
5. Repair or replace wiring as necessary.

## MANIFOLD ABSOLUTE PRESSURE (MAP) SENSOR

1. Inspect MAP sensor vacuum hose connections at throttle body and sensor. Repair as necessary.
2. With ignition switch On and engine Off, check output voltage at sensor connector terminal B (marked on sensor body). Voltage should be 4-5 volts.
3. Test ECU connector terminal 33 for voltage. Voltage should be the same as outlined in step 2. If not, repair wire harness as necessary.
4. With ignition switch On, check supply voltage at sensor connector terminal C. Voltage should be 4.5-5.5 volts.
5. Test ECU connector 16 for voltage. Voltage should be the same as outlined in step 4. If not, repair wire harness as necessary.
6. Test MAP sensor ground circuit at sensor connector terminal A and ECU connector terminal 17. Repair wire harness as necessary.
7. Test MAP sensor ground circuit again at ECU connector terminals 17 and 2 with a suitable ohmmeter. If an open circuit is indicated, check for a defective ground connection on the flywheel/drive plate housing near the starter motor and repair as necessary. If ground connection is satisfactory, replace ECU. If ECU connector terminal 17 indicates 12 volts, repair circuit before replacing ECU.

## COMPONENT REPLACEMENT

### CANISTER PURGE & EGR VALVE SOLENOID

1. Disconnect vacuum hoses and harness connector from solenoid.
2. Remove mounting bracket and solenoid.
3. Reverse procedure to install.

### EGR VALVE

1. Disconnect vacuum hose from valve.
2. Remove the two EGR valve to intake manifold attaching bolts.
3. Remove EGR valve from intake manifold and discard old gasket.
4. Clean mating surfaces on valve and manifold, then reinstall valve using new gasket.

### ELECTRONIC CONTROL UNIT (ECU)

1. Remove retaining screws and bracket which retain ECU to lower dash panel.
2. Remove ECU, then disconnect wire harness connector.
3. Reverse procedure to install.

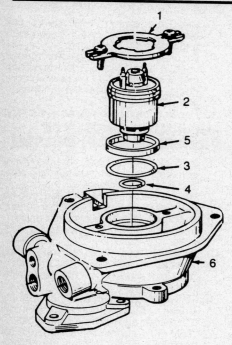

1. Retainer Clip
2. Injector
3. Upper O-Ring
4. Lower O-Ring
5. Backup Ring
6. Fuel Body

**Fig. 6   Replacing fuel injector**

## COOLANT TEMPERATURE SENSOR (CTS)

1. Disconnect harness connector from sensor. Do not attempt to remove CTS with cooling system hot and under pressure, since serious injury may result.
2. Remove CTS from intake manifold. Plug opening to prevent loss of coolant.
3. Reverse procedure to install.

## FUEL INJECTOR

1. Remove air filter, then disconnect electrical connector from injector.
2. Remove retainer clip attaching screws, then the retainer clip, **Fig. 6.**
3. Using suitable pliers, gently grasp center collar of injector between electrical terminals and carefully remove injector with a twisting/lifting motion.
4. Discard upper and lower O-rings. Note that backup ring is positioned over upper O-ring.
5. Reverse procedure to install, using new lubricated O-rings. Ensure that injector nozzle is centered in lower housing bore.

## IDLE SPEED ACTUATOR (ISA) MOTOR

The Closed Throttle (Idle) Switch is integral with the ISA motor assembly.

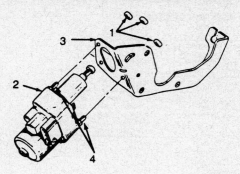

**Fig. 7   Replacing idle speed actuator(ISA)motor**

1. Disconnect throttle return spring, then the throttle cable and cruise control cable(if equipped).
2. Disconnect WOT switch and ISA motor electrical connectors.
3. Remove ISA motor and WOT switch bracket (3), **Fig. 7,** from throttle body.
4. Remove motor to bracket retaining nuts(1). Do not remove nuts from motor studs below bracket. Use a suitable wrench to hold them in position while removing retaining nuts.
5. Remove motor(2) from bracket(3).
6. Reverse procedure to install, the adjust idle speed.

## MANIFOLD ABSOLUTE PRESSURE (MAP) SENSOR

1. Disconnect sensor electrical connector and vacuum hose.
2. Remove retaining nuts.
3. Remove MAP sensor from plenum panel.
4. Reverse procedure to install.

## MANIFOLD AIR/FUEL TEMPERATURE (MAT) SENSOR

1. Disconnect harness connector from sensor.
2. Unscrew and remove MAT sensor from intake manifold.
3. Clean manifold threads, then wrap threads of replacement sensor with teflon tape.
4. Reverse removal procedure to complete installation.

## OXYGEN SENSOR

1. Disconnect electrical connector from sensor.
2. Remove sensor from exhaust pipe adapter, then clean threads in adapter.
3. Apply suitable anti-seize compound to threads of sensor, ensuring not to get any compound on any other part of sensor.
4. Hand start sensor into adapter, then torque to 20-25 ft.lbs.
5. Reconnect sensor electrical connector. Do not push rubber boot down on sensor body beyond .5 inch from base.

## PRESSURE REGULATOR

1. Remove the three pressure regulator to throttle body attaching screws.

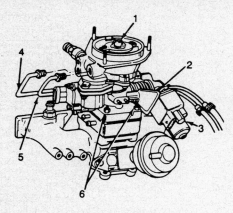

**Fig. 8   Replacing throttle body**

2. Remove pressure regulator assembly, noting location of components.
3. Discard gasket.
4. Reverse procedure to install, then start engine and check for leaks.

## THROTTLE BODY ASSEMBLY

1. Remove throttle return spring, then the throttle cable and cruise control cable, if equipped.
2. Disconnect wire harness connectors from injector (1), WOT switch (2) and ISA motor (3), **Fig. 8.**
3. Remove fuel supply and return lines, then disconnect and mark vacuum hoses.
4. Remove throttle body to intake manifold retaining nuts, then the throttle body assembly.
5. If throttle body is being replaced, transfer ISA and WOT switch and bracket to new throttle body.
6. Reverse procedure to install using new gasket.

## WIDE OPEN THROTTLE (WOT) SWITCH

1. Remove air filter, then disconnect throttle return spring.
2. Disconnect throttle cable and cruise control cable, if equipped.
3. Remove ISA bracket to throttle body attaching screws.
4. Disconnect electrical connectors from WOT switch and ISA motor.
5. Remove bracket, ISA and WOT assembly from throttle body.
6. Remove ISA motor.
7. Remove the two WOT switch to bracket attaching screws, then the switch.
8. Reverse procedure to install.

## ADJUSTMENTS

### IDLE SPEED ACTUATOR (ISA) MOTOR

Adjustment of the ISA motor is only necessary to establish the initial position of the ISA plunger after the motor has been removed and installed or replaced. Engine idle speed and deceleration throttle stop angle are controlled by an Idle Speed Actuator (ISA) motor. ISA motor operation is controlled by the ECU which provides appropriate voltage outputs to produce the idle speed or throttle angle required for engine operating conditions. Idle speed is not adjustable. However, if the ISA motor or throttle body is removed for service the initial position of the plunger should be adjusted using the following procedure.

1. Remove air filter assembly, start engine and run until it reaches normal operating temperature.
2. Ensure that A/C switch (if equipped) is in off position, then connect suitable tachometer to diagnostic connector terminals D1-1 and D1-3, **Fig. 1.**
3. Turn ignition switch to off position while observing ISA plunger. Plunger should move to fully extended position.
4. With plunger in fully extended position, disconnect electrical connector to ISA motor and start engine.
5. Adjust engine speed to 3500 RPM by rotating hex screw on end of plunger.
6. Fully retract ISA motor by pressing end of plunger inward while throttle is opened, then release throttle.
7. Ensure that clearance exists between end of plunger and throttle lever. If lever is contacting plunger, check and repair throttle linkage as needed.
8. Reconnect electrical connector to ISA motor, then turn ignition switch off for 10 seconds. ISA plunger should move to fully extended position.
9. Start engine. Engine should run at 3500 RPM for brief period, then return to normal idle speed.
10. When adjustment is correct, apply suitable thread locking compound to plunger adjuster screw threads.

## FUEL PRESSURE REGULATOR

Adjustment is only necessary after a replacement pressure regulator has been installed.

1. Remove air filter.
2. Connect tachometer between terminals D1-1 and D1-3 of diagnostic connector, **Fig. 1.**
3. Remove screw plug, then connect fuel pressure gauge to fuel body pressure test fitting.
4. Start engine and accelerate to approximately 2000 RPM.
5. Turn adjustment screw on bottom of regulator to obtain pressure of 14.5 psi. Turning screw inward increases pressure, while turning outward decreases pressure.
6. Turn ignition off, then disconnect tachometer.
7. Disconnect fuel pressure gauge, then install screw plug.
8. Install air filter.

## THROTTLE POSITION SENSOR

1. Turn ignition to On position.
2. Connect negative lead of voltmeter to B terminal of sensor and positive lead to terminal C, **Fig. 3.** Sensor wire harness should remain connected when testing voltage. Insert voltmeter test leads through back of harness connector.
3. Position throttle to wide open position, ensuring throttle linkage contacts stop.
4. Note input voltage reading, which should be 5 volts.
5. Return throttle to closed position, then attach positive lead of voltmeter to terminal A of sensor.
6. Repeat step 3 and note output voltage. Output voltage should be 4.6–4.7 volts. If output voltage is not as specified, proceed to next step.
7. Loosen sensor retaining screws(A) and (B), **Fig. 3,** then pivot sensor in adjustment slots until output voltage is as specified. Retaining screw (A) will provide coarse adjustment, while screw (B) provides fine tuning of adjustment.
8. Disconnect voltmeter, return throttle to closed position, then tighten retaining screws.

## WIDE OPEN THROTTLE (WOT) SWITCH

Adjustment of WOT switch is only necessary after replacement, to establish the initial position of switch.

1. Remove throttle body assembly as outlined previously.
2. Loosen WOT switch to bracket retaining screws, then position throttle in wide open position.
3. Attach alignment gauge J-26701 or equivalent on flat surface of throttle lever, then rotate degree scale of gauge until 15 degree mark is aligned with pointer.
4. Adjust bubble on gauge until centered, then align 0 degree mark with pointer.
5. Close throttle slightly to center bubble on gauge. Throttle is now at 15 degrees before wide open throttle position.
6. Position WOT switch lever on throttle cam so that switch plunger just closes at 15 degrees before wide open throttle position.
7. Tighten retaining screws, then remove alignment gauge.

# Multi-Point Fuel Injection System, Jeep

## INDEX

# DESCRIPTION

## ELECTRONIC CONTROL UNIT (ECU) INPUTS

### Coolant Temperature Sensor (CTS)

The coolant temperature sensor, which is located on the left hand side of the cylinder block below the exhaust manifold, provides engine temperature input to the Electronic Control Unit. The ECU will use the inputs from the CTS when coolant temperature are cold, to enrich the air/fuel mixture, control engine warm-up idle speed, increase ignition advance and inhibit the EGR system.

### Manifold Air Temperature (MAT) Sensor

The manifold air temperature sensor, which is located in the intake manifold, provides an air temperature input to the ECU. The ECU in turn will compensate for air density changes during high temperature operation.

### Manifold Absolute Pressure (MAP) Sensor

The manifold absolute pressure sensor is located on the firewall behind the engine. A hose from the intake manifold provides the input pressure for the sensor. The sensor will react to absolute pressure in the intake manifold and will provide an input voltage to the ECU. The signal from the MAP sensor supplies the ECU with mixture density information and ambient barometric pressure information.

### Oxygen Sensor

The oxygen sensor is located in the exhaust manifold. This sensor provides a voltage signal, which varies with oxygen content in the exhaust gas, to the ECU. Electrical current to the oxygen sensor is supplied through the ignition switch. The sensor is equipped with a heating element that helps maintain proper sensor operating temperature during all modes of operation. Maintaining correct sensor temperature allows the system to enter closed loop operation sooner and allows the system to remain in closed loop operation during periods of prolonged idling.

### Knock Sensor

This sensor is located at the lower left hand side of the cylinder block, just above the oil pan. This sensor provides an input to the ECU when detonation is encountered during engine operation. The ECU will retard ignition timing when the input signal from the knock sensor indicates engine detonation.

### Speed Sensor

The speed sensor is attached to the flywheel housing. This sensor detects TDC, BDC and engine speed by sensing the flywheel teeth as they pass during engine operation. The flywheel has a large trigger tooth and notch located 12 teeth before TDC and BDC, **Fig. 1.** As the small teeth on the flywheel pass the sensor magnetic core, the concentration and collapse of magnetic flux induces a low voltage spikes into the sensor pickup coil winding. These low voltage spikes allow the ECU to count the flywheel teeth as they pass the sensor. When the large trigger tooth on the flywheel passes the sensor magnetic core, a higher voltage spike is induced into the pickup coil winding, indicating to the ECU that TDC or BDC is 12 teeth away. The ignition timing will be advanced or retarded as necessary by the ECU depending on sensor input signals.

### Starter Motor Relay

The starter motor relay indicates to the ECU when starter motor is in operation.

### Throttle Position Sensor (TPS)

This sensor is mounted to the throttle plate assembly and provides the ECU with input signal indicating throttle position. At idle speed the TPS will provide the ECU with an input signal of approximately 1 volt, indicating throttle is at minimum opening. As the throttle is opened, the voltage signal to the ECU will increase. At wide open throttle the voltage signal will be approximately 5 volts. On models with automatic transmission, a dual TPS is used. The dual TPS will provide throttle opening voltage signals to the ECU and the automatic transmission control unit (TCU).

### Battery Voltage

The battery voltage input signal to the ECU is used to ensure proper voltage is being applied to the injectors. THe ECU will vary voltage applied to the injectors to compensate for battery voltage fluctuations.

### Park/Neutral Switch

This switch is used on models with automatic transmission to provide a signal to the ECU indicating when transmission is in Neutral or Park.

### A/C Controls

The A/C control inputs indicate to the ECU when A/C is in the on position and when A/C compressor clutch is engaged. When the compressor clutch is engaged, the ECU will increase engine idle speed.

### Sync Pulse

The sync pulse signal is generated by a trigger wheel located in the ignition distributor.

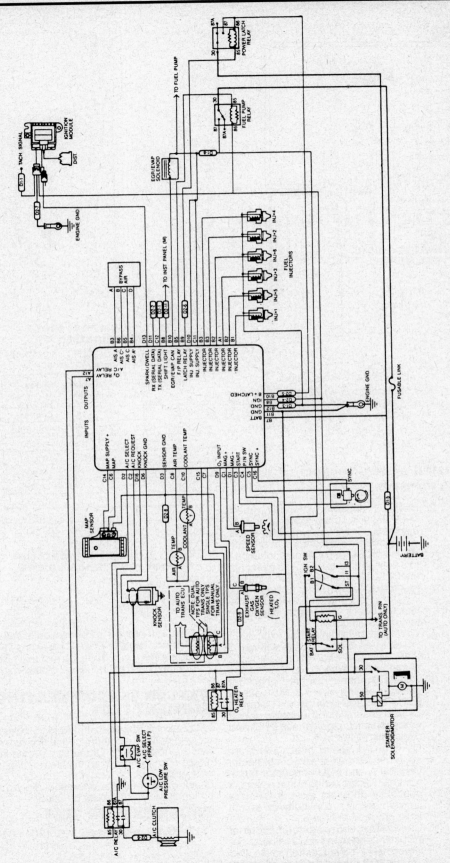

**Multi-Point Fuel Injection (MPI) system wiring circuit**

## ELECTRONIC CONTROL UNIT (ECU) OUTPUTS

### Fuel Pump Relay

This relay is located on the right hand inner fender panel. Relay is supplied battery voltage from the ignition switch and is energized by a ground provided by the ECU. When the fuel pump relay is energized, voltage is supplied to the fuel pump.

### EGR Valve Solenoid

This solenoid is energized by the ECU and controls vacuum to the EGR valve. During engine warm-up, closed or wide open throttle operation or rapid acceleration or deceleration, the solenoid will be energized, cutting off the vacuum supply to the EGR valve.

### Up-Shift Indicator Lamp

This lamp will be illuminated during engine operation according to engine speed and load. The ECU will turn off the the up-shift indicator lamp after 3 to 5 seconds if a gear shift is not performed. A switch located on the transmission will prevent the lamp from being illuminated when transmission is in high gear. The will be illuminated when the ignition switch is is placed in the on position, but the lamp should turn off as the engine is started.

### Ignition Control Module

Depending inputs received, the ECU will trigger the ignition coil by means of the ignition control module.

### Injectors

Depending on engine operating conditions provided by the input sensors, the ECU will electronically control the injection duration time. The fuel injectors are located in the intake manifold.

### Latch Relay

This relay is located on the right hand inner fender panel. The ECU will initially energize the latch relay during engine start-up. The relay will remain energized until 3 to 5 seconds after the engine has been stopped. This allows the ECU to extend the stepper motor for the next engine start-up.

### Idle Speed Stepper Motor

The stepper motor is located on the throttle plate assembly. The ECU control idle speed by providing the appropriate voltage signal to extend or retract the stepper motor plunger to maintain the proper engine idle speed.

## TESTING

## COOLANT TEMPERATURE SENSOR (CTS) TEST

1. Disconnect electrical connector from CTS.
2. Using a suitable ohmmeter, check resistance of CTS, **Fig. 2.**
3. If resistance is not within limits, replace CTS.

10-75

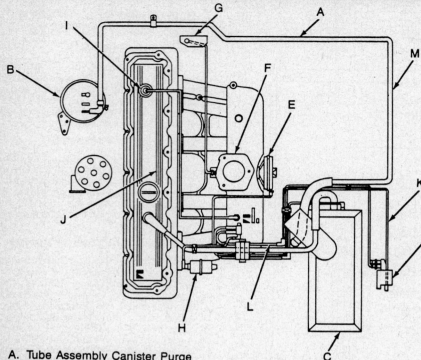

A. Tube Assembly Canister Purge
B. Canister Evaporator
C. Air Cleaner Assembly
D. Solenoid EGR
E. Valve EGR
F. Throttle Body Assembly
G. Map Sensor

H. Pressure Regulatior
I. Grommet w/2.6mm Orifice
J. Tube CCV
K. 4.0 mm O.D.
L. 6.4 mm O.D.
M. 14.3 mm O.D.

**Multi-Point Fuel Injection (MPI) system vacuum hose routing diagram**

**Fig. 1 Flywheel tooth identification**

Coolant Temperature Sensor

| Temperature-to-Resistance Values (Approximate) | | |
|---|---|---|
| °F | °C | Ohms |
| 212 | 100 | 185 |
| 160 | 70 | 450 |
| 100 | 38 | 1,600 |
| 70 | 20 | 3,400 |
| 40 | 4 | 7,500 |
| 20 | -7 | 13,500 |
| 0 | -18 | 25,000 |
| -40 | -40 | 100,700 |

**Fig. 2 Coolant temperature sensor resistance values**

4. Check CTS wiring for continuity between ECU electrical connector terminals D-3 and C-10, **Fig. 3**, and sensor electrical connector terminals. If circuit is open, repair wiring as necessary.

## MANIFOLD AIR TEMPERATURE (MAT) SENSOR TEST

1. Disconnect electrical connector from MAT sensor.
2. Using a suitable ohmmeter check MAT sensor resistance, **Fig. 4** .
3. If MAT sensor resistance is not within limits, replace sensor.
4. Using a suitable ohmmeter, check resistance between ECU electrical connector terminals D-3 and C-8 and sensor electrical connector terminals, **Fig. 3**. If resistance is greater than 1 ohm, repair wiring as necessary.

## THROTTLE POSITION SENSOR (TPS) TEST

Refer to **Fig. 5**, for TPS test procedure.

## MANIFOLD ABSOLUTE PRESSURE (MAP) SENSOR TEST

1. Check vacuum hose connectors at throttle body and sensor, and repair as necessary.

2. Using a suitable voltmeter, check MAP sensor output voltage at MAP electrical connector terminal B, **Fig. 6**, with ignition switch in the On position, engine off. Output voltage should be 4 to 5 volts. If voltage is not as indicated, check ECU terminal C-6 for a voltage reading of 4 to 5 volts to ensure wiring is satisfactory, **Fig. 3**. If wiring is satisfactory, check ECU with diagnostic tester M.S. 1700.
3. With ignition switch in the On position, check MAP sensor supply voltage at MAP electrical connector C. Voltage reading should be 4.5 to 5.5 volts. If voltage is not as indicated, check for voltage reading of 4.5 to 5.5 volts at ECU electrical connector terminal C-14 to ensure wiring is satisfactory. If wiring is satisfactory, check ECU with diagnostic tester M.S. 1700.
4. Using an ohmmeter, check MAP sensor ground circuit at sensor connector terminal A and ECU connector terminal D-3. Repair wiring a necessary, if continuity does not exist. If wiring is satisfactory, but continuity does not exist proceed to step 5.
5. Check MAP sensor ground circuit at ECU, by connecting an ohmmeter between ECU electrical terminals D-3 and B-11. If continuity does not exist, check for defective ground wire connection at right hand side of cylinder

block. If ground is connection is satisfactory, replace ECU. If terminals D-3 is shorted to 12 volts, correct this condition before installing replacement ECU.

## OXYGEN SENSOR HEATING ELEMENT TEST

Connect a suitable ohmmeter between oxygen sensor electrical connector terminals A and B, **Fig. 7**. Ohmmeter should indicate 5 to 7 ohms. If an infinite reading is obtained, replace oxygen sensor. To check oxygen sensor operation, diagnostic tester M.S. 1700 must be used.

## KNOCK SENSOR TEST

1. With diagnostic tester M.S. 1700 connected to vehicle, start engine and observe knock unit values.
2. Using a screwdriver, gently tap cylinder block in area near knock sensor and note knock valve on tester.

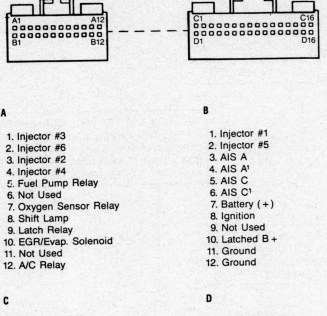

**A**

1. Injector #3
2. Injector #6
3. Injector #2
4. Injector #4
5. Fuel Pump Relay
6. Not Used
7. Oxygen Sensor Relay
8. Shift Lamp
9. Latch Relay
10. EGR/Evap. Solenoid
11. Not Used
12. A/C Relay

**B**

1. Injector #1
2. Injector #5
3. AIS A
4. AIS A¹
5. AIS C
6. AIS C¹
7. Battery (+)
8. Ignition
9. Not Used
10. Latched B +
11. Ground
12. Ground

**C**

1. Speed Sensor (+)
2. A/C Request
3. Start
4. P/N Switch
5. Sync.
6. MAP Sensor
7. TPS Sensor
8. Air Temperature Sensor
9. Not Used
10. Coolant Temperature Sensor
11. Injection Supply
12. TX (Serial Data)
13. Not Used
14. MAP Sensor Supply (+)
15. TPS Supply (+)
16. Sync. (+)

**D**

1. Speed Sensor (−)
2. A/C Select
3. Sensor Ground
4. Not Used
5. Not Used
6. Not Used
7. Not Used
8. Knock Sensor Ground
9. Oxygen Sensor Input
10. Injection Supply
11. RX (Serial Data)
12. Not Used
13. Spark/Dwell
14. Not Used
15. Not Used
16. Knock Sensor

**Fig. 3  ECU connector terminal identification**

**Manifold Air/Fuel Temperature Sensor**

| Temperature-to-Resistance Values (Approximate) | | |
|---|---|---|
| °F | °C | Ohms |
| 212 | 100 | 185 |
| 160 | 70 | 450 |
| 100 | 38 | 1,600 |
| 70 | 20 | 3,400 |
| 40 | 4 | 7,500 |
| 20 | -7 | 13,500 |
| 0 | -18 | 25,000 |
| -40 | -40 | 100,700 |

**Fig. 4  Manifold air temperature sensor resistance value chart.**

6. If battery voltage is present, but relay is not operating, proceed as follows:
   a. Place transmission in neutral and block drive wheels.
   b. With relay terminal I connected, connect a jumper wire between terminal G and ground.
   c. If starter relay does not click, replace relay.
   d. If starter relay clicks, repair ground circuit.

## SYNC PULSE TEST

1. Connect positive lead of a suitable analog voltmeter to blue wire at distributor connector. Connect negative lead of voltmeter to gray/white wire at distributor connector. Do not disconnect distributor connector. Make voltmeter connections through back of electrical connector.
2. Place ignition switch in the On position and note voltmeter reading. Voltmeter should indicate 5 volts.
3. If there is no voltage reading, check voltmeter leads for proper connection. If there is still no voltage reading, disconnect ECU electrical connector and check for voltage between connector terminal C-16 and ground. If there is still no voltage reading, check ECU with diagnostic tool M.S. 1700.
4. If voltage is present, check for continuity between blue wire at distributor connector and ECU connector terminal C-16. If continuity does not exist, repair wiring.
5. Check for continuity between gray/white wire at distributor connector and ECU connector terminal C-5. If continuity does not exist, repair wiring.
6. Check for continuity between black wire at distributor connector and ground. if continuity does not exist, repair wiring.
7. With analog voltmeter connected as described in step 1, crank engine. Voltmeter needle should fluctuate while engine is being cranked. If voltmeter does not fluctuate, replace stator located inside of distributor.

## EGR SOLENOID TEST

1. Check to ensure vacuum is present at solenoid vacuum port C, Fig. 10.

3. If knock value does not increase while tapping, check knock sensor for proper electrical connections.
4. If knock sensor electrical connections are satisfactory, replace knock sensor.

## SPEED SENSOR TEST

1. With engine at operating temperature, disconnect speed sensor electrical connector from ignition control module.
2. Connect a suitable ohmmeter between connector terminals A and B, Fig. 8.
3. Ohmmeter should indicate 125 to 275 ohms, if not replace sensor.

## RELAY TEST

1. With relay de-energized, continuity should exist between relay terminals 30 and 87A, Fig. 9.
2. Using a suitable ohmmeter, check resistance between relay terminals 85 and 86. Ohmmeter reading should be 70 to 80 ohms for resistor relays and 81 to 91 ohms for diode relays.

## STARTER MOTOR RELAY TEST

1. Disconnect electrical connectors from starter motor relay terminals G and I.
2. Using a suitable ohmmeter, check resistance between relay terminals G and I. Resistance should be approximately 22 ohms, if not replace relay.
3. Connect ohmmeter between either relay terminal G or I and battery negative post. An infinite ohmmeter reading should be obtained, if not, replace relay. If reading is satisfactory, reconnect electrical connector.
4. Disconnect electrical connector from starter motor relay terminal SOL.
5. Connect a suitable voltmeter between relay terminal SOL and battery negative post. With ignition switch in start position, voltmeter should indicate 12 battery voltage. If battery voltage is not present, check for improper bulk head wiring harness connection, defective wiring or improper ignition switch adjustment.

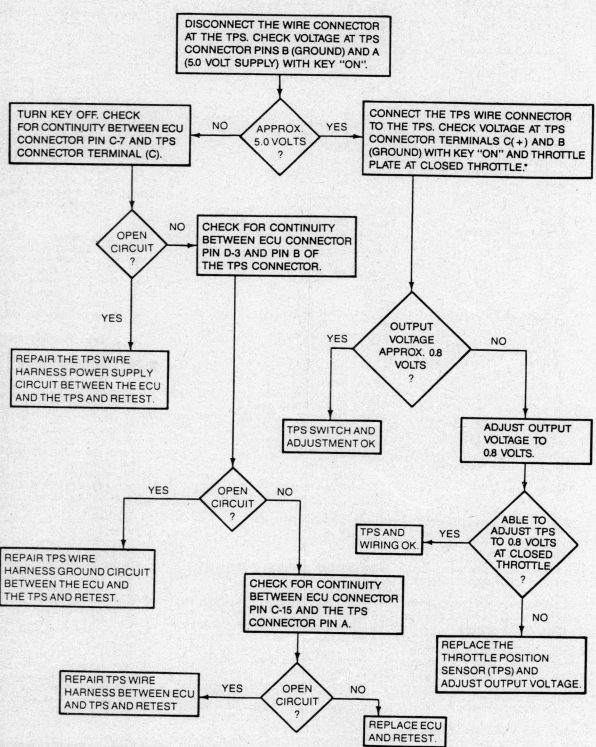

**Fig. 5  Throttle Position Sensor (TPS) test**

\* DO NOT UNFASTEN THE SENSOR WIRE HARNESS CONNECTOR. INSERT THE VOLTMETER TEST LEADS THROUGH THE BACK OF THE WIRE HARNESS CONNECTOR TO MAKE CONTACT WITH THE SENSOR TERMINALS.

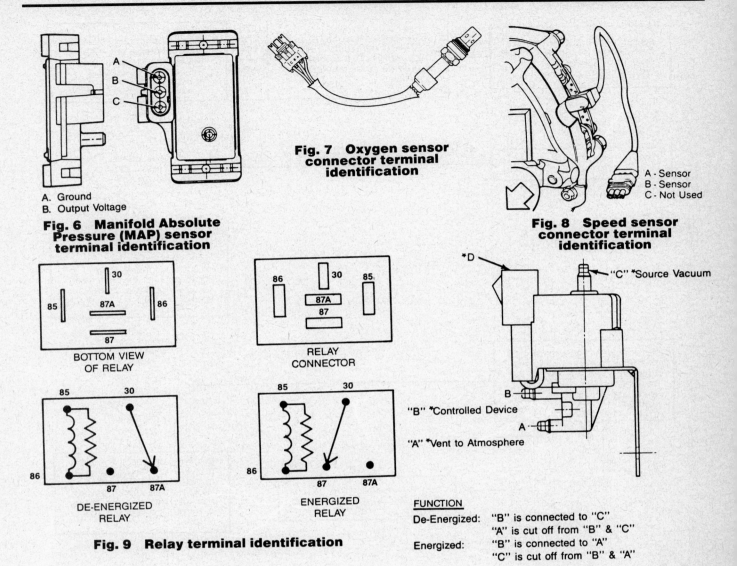

**A. Ground**
**B. Output Voltage**

**Fig. 6   Manifold Absolute Pressure (MAP) sensor terminal identification**

**Fig. 7   Oxygen sensor connector terminal identification**

A - Sensor
B - Sensor
C - Not Used

**Fig. 8   Speed sensor connector terminal identification**

BOTTOM VIEW OF RELAY

RELAY CONNECTOR

"C" *Source Vacuum

"B" *Controlled Device

"A" *Vent to Atmosphere

DE-ENERGIZED RELAY

ENERGIZED RELAY

**Fig. 9   Relay terminal identification**

FUNCTION

De-Energized:   "B" is connected to "C"
                "A" is cut off from "B" & "C"

Energized:      "B" is connected to "A"
                "C" is cut off from "B" & "A"

**Fig. 10   EGR solenoid vacuum port identification**

2. Remove vacuum hose connections at solenoid ports A and B.
3. Connect a suitable vacuum gauge to solenoid port B, then start engine and note gauge reading. N vacuum should be present at port B.
4. With engine still operating, disconnect electrical connector from solenoid and note vacuum gauge reading. Vacuum should now be present at solenoid port B.
5. If solenoid fails to operate as described above, replace solenoid. Disconnect vacuum gauge and reconnect vacuum hoses and electrical connector.

## INJECTOR TEST

Disconnect wire connector from injector. Connect a suitable ohmmeter to injector terminals and note reading. Ohmmeter should indicate approximately 16 ohms at 68°F.

If vehicle runs rough and/or misses, refer to **Fig. 11**, for diagnostic procedure.

## FUEL PUMP PRESSURE TEST

1. Remove cap from pressure test port located on fuel rail and connect a suitable fuel pressure gauge to test port, **Fig. 12**.
2. Start engine and note pressure gauge reading.
3. With vacuum hose connected to pressure regulator, pressure gauge reading should be 31 psi. With vacuum hose disconnected from fuel pressure regulator, pressure gauge reading should be 39 psi.
4. If fuel pressure is not as specified, check the following:
   a. Check fuel supply and return hoses for restrictions or kinks.

   b. Check fuel pump flow rate. Fuel pump should deliver at least 1 quart of fuel per minute. To check fuel pump flow rate, connect an old A/C gauge hose to fuel pump pressure test port. Position other end of hose into a suitable container. Pinch off fuel return hose, then operate fuel pump by connecting a jumper wire between diagnostic connector terminals D1-5 and D1-6, **Fig. 13**.

## SYSTEM SERVICE

### COOLANT TEMPERATURE SENSOR (CTS), REPLACE

1. Drain cooling system, then remove air cleaner assembly.
2. Disconnect electrical connector from CTS, then remove CTS from cylinder block.
3. Reverse procedure to install.

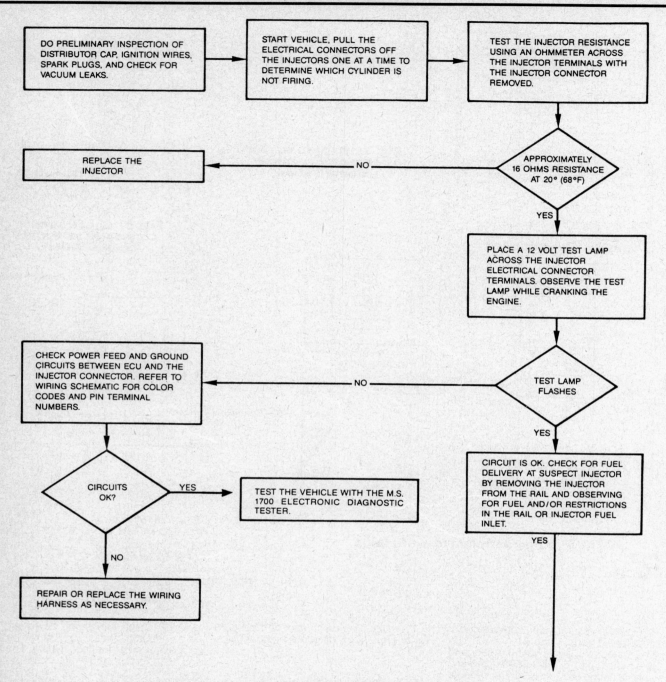

**Fig. 11   Injector diagnosis (Part 1 of 2)**

## MANIFOLD AIR TEMPERATURE (MAT) SENSOR REPLACE

1. Disconnect electrical connector from MAT sensor.
2. Using a suitable wrench, remove MAT sensor from intake manifold.
3. Reverse procedure to install.

## MANIFOLD ABSOLUTE PRESSURE (MAP) SENSOR, REPLACE

1. Disconnect electrical connector and vacuum hose from MAP sensor.
2. Remove MAP sensor retaining nuts, then remove MAP sensor from dash panel.
3. Reverse procedure to install.

## OXYGEN SENSOR, REPLACE

1. Raise and support vehicle, then disconnect electrical connector from oxygen sensor.
2. Remove oxygen sensor from exhaust manifold.
3. Reverse procedure to install. Torque oxygen sensor to 35 ft. lbs.

## KNOCK SENSOR, REPLACE

1. Raise and support vehicle, then disconnect knock sensor wire connector.
2. Remove knock sensor from cylinder block,
3. Reverse procedure to install.

## SPEED SENSOR, REPLACE

1. Disconnect speed sensor electrical connector.
2. Remove two bolts attaching speed sensor to flywheel housing, then remove speed sensor.
3. Reverse procedure to install.

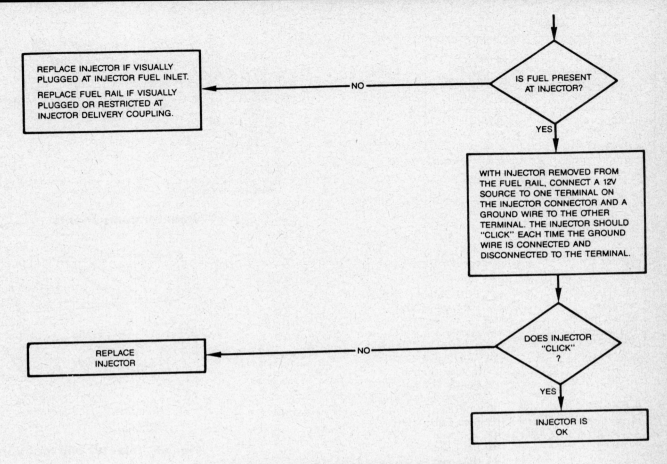

**Fig. 11  Injector diagnosis (Part 2 of 2)**

## THROTTLE POSITION SENSOR (TPS), REPLACE

1. Disconnect electrical connector from TPS.
2. Bend back locking tabs, then remove TPS attaching screws.
3. Remove TPS from throttle plate.
4. Reverse procedure to install. After completing installation, adjust TPS as described under "Throttle Position Sensor (TPS), Adjust."

## FUEL PRESSURE REGULATOR, REPLACE

1. Remove injector rail assembly as described under "Fuel Injector, Replace."
2. Remove two fuel pressure regulator attaching screws, then remove regulator and O-ring from fuel rail.
3. Reverse procedure to install.

## EGR SOLENOID, REPLACE

1. Disconnect vacuum hoses and electrical connector from EGR solenoid.
2. Remove EGR solenoid attaching screw, then remove solenoid from left hand fender apron.
3. Reverse procedure to install.

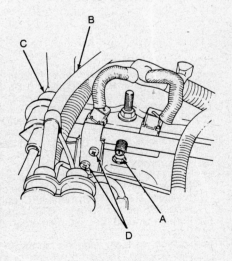

A. Pressure Test Port
B. Vacuum Hose
C. Pressure Regulator
D. Retaining Screws

**Fig. 12  Fuel pressure test port location**

## IGNITION CONTROL MODULE, REPLACE

1. Disconnect ignition coil wire from coil tower.
2. Disconnect electrical wiring from ignition control module.
3. Remove ignition control module attaching screws, then remove module.
4. Reverse procedure to install.

## INJECTORS, REPLACE

1. Disconnect fuel lines from ends of fuel rail, **Fig. 14.**
2. Mark and disconnect fuel injector electrical connectors.
3. Remove fuel rail attaching bolts, then disconnect vacuum hose from fuel pressure regulator.
4. Remove fuel rail assembly. On models equipped with automatic transmission, it may be necessary to remove throttle pressure cable and bracket to remove fuel rail assembly.
5. Remove clips (A), **Fig. 15,** retaining injectors to fuel rail, then remove injectors and O-rings.
6. Reverse procedure to install. When installing injector, brown O-rings should

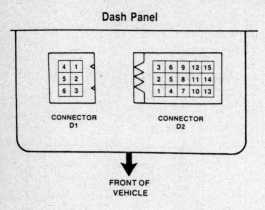

Dash Panel

CONNECTOR D1

CONNECTOR D2

FRONT OF VEHICLE

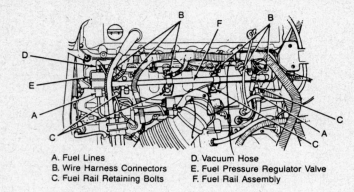

A. Fuel Lines
B. Wire Harness Connectors
C. Fuel Rail Retaining Bolts
D. Vacuum Hose
E. Fuel Pressure Regulator Valve
F. Fuel Rail Assembly

**Fig. 14  Injector components**

**Connector D1**

1. Tach Signal
2. Not Used
3. ECU Ground
4. Not Used
5. Battery (+)
6. Fuel Pump (+)

**Connector D2**

1. ECU Output (TX)
2. RX Data (ECU)
3. Latch Relay
4. Ignition
5. Latch B+
6. A/C Clutch
7. Ignition Ground
8. Sensor Ground
9. Oxygen Sensor Heater
10. Not Used
11. Shift Lamp
12. Not Used
13. Not Used
14. Not Used
15. Automatic Transmission Diagnosis

**Fig. 13  Diagnostic connector terminal identification**

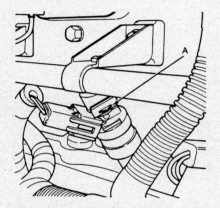

**Fig. 15  Injector clip location**

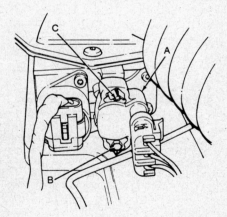

**Fig. 16  Throttle position sensor retaining screw locations**

be installed on intake manifold side of injector and black O-ring should be installed on fuel rail side of injector. Torque fuel rail attaching bolts to 20 ft. lbs.

## IDLE STEPPER MOTOR, REPLACE

1. Disconnect idle stepper motor electrical connector.
2. Remove idle stepper motor attaching screws, then remove idle stepper motor.
3. Reverse procedure to install.

## THROTTLE POSITION SENSOR (TPS)
## ADJUST
### MANUAL TRANSMISSION

1. Place ignition switch in the On position.

2. Connect positive lead of voltmeter to TPS terminal a and negative lead to terminal B. Do not disconnect electrical connector, insert voltmeter leads through back of electrical connector. On some models, it may be necessary to remove throttle body to gain access to TPS terminals.
3. With throttle plate in the closed position, TPS input voltage should be approximately 5 volts. Move voltmeter positive lead to TPS terminal C and note TPS output voltage. TPS output voltage should be approximately .8 volts.
4. Loosen sensor retaining screws(A) and (B), **Fig. 16,** then pivot sensor in adjustment slots until output voltage is as specified. Retaining screw (A) will provide coarse adjustment, while screw (B) provides fine tuning of adjustment.
5. Disconnect voltmeter, return throttle to closed position, then tighten retaining screws.

# Single Point Fuel Injection System, Chrysler

## INDEX

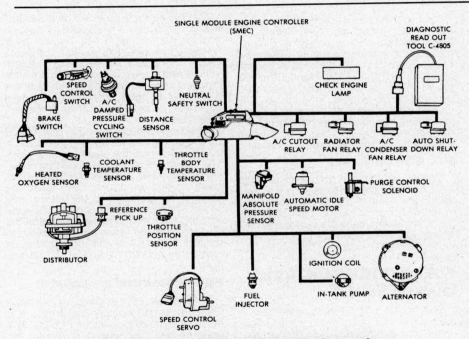

Fig. 1 Fuel injection system schematic

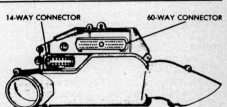

Fig. 2 Single Module Engine Controller (SMEC)

## DESCRIPTION

The electronic, single point fuel injection system uses a digital pre-programmed Single Module Engine Controller (SMEC) to control air-fuel mixtures delivered to the engine, ignition timing, idle speed, various emission control devices, the engine cooling fan and the charging system. The SMEC monitors inputs from various engine and vehicle sensors, computes ideal operating parameters for the controlled sub-systems based on these inputs, and controls operation of the subsystems. Sensors used to control system operations include: an exhaust gas oxygen sensor, Manifold Absolute Pressure (MAP) sensor, throttle position sensor, coolant and throttle body temperature sensors, vehicle distance sensor, and the neutral safety and A/C compressor clutch switches and auto shut down relay, **Fig. 1.**

All inputs to the SMEC are converted to signals. These signals cause the SMEC to alter fuel injector delivery and/or ignition

timing to maintain ideal air fuel mixtures and ignition timing for all vehicle operating conditions.

In addition, the SMEC tests many of its input and output circuits, and if a fault is found in one of the monitored circuits information relating to the malfunction is stored in the SMEC memory. Information relating to monitored circuit malfunctions can be accessed by the technician through the instrument panel mounted check engine lamp, or by connecting a diagnostic read-out instrument to the system. Both access methods provide numerical type codes which relate to specific circuit malfunctions.

## SINGLE MODULE ENGINE CONTROLLER & AUTOMATIC SHUT DOWN (ASD) RELAY

The SMEC, **Fig. 2**, is mounted in the engine compartment and contains circuits necessary to energize the ignition coil, fuel

injectors and alternator field in order to minimize electrical noise in the passenger compartment. The SMEC contains a voltage converter which converts battery voltage into a regulated 8 volt output to energize the ignition pick up coil. The externally mounted Automatic Shut Down (ASD) relay which interrupts power to the fuel pump, ignition coil and injector when necessary is controlled by the SMEC.

The ASD relay is turned on and off by the SMEC in response to distributor reference pulses. When distributor reference pulses are transmitted to the SMEC, the SMEC activates the ASD relay. However, when no reference pulse is transmitted to the SMEC, the ASD relay is deactivated and power is shut off to the fuel control system and ignition coil.

## SENSORS & SWITCHES

### Manifold Absolute Pressure (MAP) Sensor

The MAP sensor, **Fig. 3**, is mounted in the engine compartment on the dash panel and monitors intake manifold vacuum through a line connected to the throttle body. The sensor converts manifold vacuum (negative pressure) and barometric pressure into electrical signals and transmits these signals to the SMEC. The SMEC uses these signals to monitor engine load and atmospheric conditions in order to determine the correct air/fuel mixture for vehicle operating conditions.

### Oxygen Sensor

The oxygen sensor, **Fig. 4**, produces voltage signals when exposed to oxygen in the exhaust gasses. The oxygen content in the exhaust gasses is directly proportional to the air/fuel mixture entering

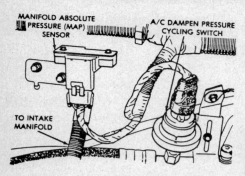

Fig. 3  Manifold Absolute Pressure (MAP) sensor location

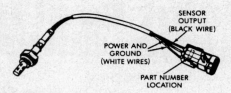

Fig. 4  Oxygen sensor

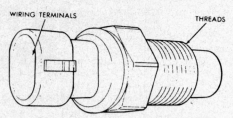

Fig. 5  Coolant temperature sensor

the engine, and the voltage signal produced by the sensor is inversely proportional to the amount of oxygen remaining in the exhaust gasses. The SMEC uses these signals to determine air/fuel mixtures entering the engine.

The oxygen sensor is mounted in the exhaust manifold, and the sensing element must be heated by exhaust gasses before the sensor begins to produce voltage signals. When exhaust gas oxygen content is high (lean mixtures), the sensor produces a low voltage. When oxygen content is low (rich mixtures), the sensor produces a higher voltage.

## Coolant Temperature Sensor

The coolant temperature sensor, **Fig. 5**, is mounted in the thermostat housing and allows the SMEC to monitor engine operating temperature in order to provide proper air/fuel mixtures. The sensor provides a variable resistance which is proportional to coolant temperature. When the engine is cold and sensor resistance is low, the SMEC provides richer air/fuel mixtures and increases engine idle speed to provide acceptable cold engine performance and allow quick warm up. When coolant temperature and sensor resistance increase, the SMEC provides leaner air/fuel mixtures and lowers engine idle speed to provide proper exhaust emission control and increased fuel economy.

## Throttle Body Temperature Sensor

The throttle body mounted temperature sensor allows the SMEC to monitor fuel temperature. The SMEC uses this information to provide the proper air/fuel mixtures for a hot restart condition.

## Throttle Position Sensor (TPS)

The TPS is mounted on the throttle body and senses the angle of the throttle plate opening. The sensor produces a voltage signal which increases and decreases according to throttle position. The SMEC uses these voltage signals to tailor air/fuel mixtures for varying conditions such as idle, wide open throttle, acceleration and deceleration.

## Vehicle Distance Sensor

The distance sensor is located in the transaxle extension housing and signals

vehicle motion to the SMEC by generating eight pulses per axle shaft revolution. The SMEC uses this signal along with signals from the throttle position sensor to determine between a closed throttle deceleration and a normal idle condition, thereby allowing the SMEC to maintain desired control of the AIS motor.

## Switch Inputs

Various switches provide information to the SMEC. These switches include the speed control, neutral safety, A/C compressor clutch and brake lamp switches. If one or more of these switches is sensed as being 'on', the SMEC signals the idle speed motor to change idle speed to a pre-set Rpm. In addition, when the A/C is on and the throttle plate is above a specified angle, the wide open throttle cut-out relay prevents the A/C clutch from being energized until throttle angle is reduced.

## A/C Clutch Relay

The A/C clutch relay is connected to the A/C damped pressure switch, the A/C switch and the A/C fan relay. The relay is in the On position during normal engine operation, but is closed when the SMEC senses low idle speeds or wide open throttle conditions, preventing A/C clutch engagement.

## FUEL SYSTEM CONTROLS
### Throttle Body

The throttle body, **Fig. 6**, assembly is mounted on the intake manifold and houses the throttle plate, fuel injector, fuel pressure regulator, temperature and position sensors, and the AIS motor. Intake air flow is controlled by the cable operated throttle plate and by a separate by-pass channel which is controlled by the AIS motor. The throttle body provides the chamber for fuel metering, atomization, and mixing atomized fuel with incoming air.

### Fuel Injector

The fuel injector, **Fig. 7**, is a solenoid operated valve which is energized and controlled by the SMEC. Fuel is supplied to the injector at a constant pressure of 14.5 psi, and excess fuel is returned to the tank. When voltage is applied to the injector solenoid, a spring loaded ball is lifted off its seat and fuel is sprayed into the throttle body through 6 spray orifices. The spray orifices and injector tip design cause the fuel to be sprayed in an even conical pattern prior to entering the intake air stream.

The amount of fuel delivered by the injector is determined by the amount of time that the injector solenoid is energized. The SMEC determines the amount of fuel necessary to maintain ideal air/fuel mixtures based upon various sensor inputs. The

SMEC then energizes the fuel injector for a sufficient amount of time to deliver the necessary amount of fuel.

## Automatic Idle Speed (AIS) Motor

The AIS motor is operated by the SMEC and controls engine idle speed by controlling air flow through the throttle body by-pass channel. The SMEC computes proper idle speed based in signals from vehicle and engine sensors and the switch inputs, and transmits voltage signals to the AIS motor to open or close the by-pass channel in order to maintain the proper engine speed.

Basic, no-load idle speed is determined by the amount of air flowing through the throttle body past the closed throttle plate. The AIS motor alters idle speed by allowing increased air flow through the by-pass channel; increasing idle speed when the channel is opened and decreasing idle speed when the channel is closed. In addition, the AIS motor is signaled to open the by-pass channel during deceleration to prevent stalling and mixture enrichment caused by sudden closing of the throttle plate.

## Fuel Pressure Regulator

The mechanical fuel pressure regulator, **Fig. 8**, is used to maintain fuel pressure at the injector tip at a constant 14.5 psi. The pressure regulator uses a spring loaded diaphragm to control the fuel return port in order to maintain constant pressure. Pressurized fuel is delivered first to the fuel injector and then flows to the pressure regulator. When fuel pressure acting on the regulator diaphragm exceeds 14.5 psi, the regulator spring is compressed and the fuel return port is opened. When fuel pressure drops below 14.5 psi spring tension causes the diaphragm to block the fuel return port. The diaphragm and spring move constantly between the open and closed positions in order to maintain constant fuel pressure at the injector tip.

## Fuel Pump & Reservoir

An electric fuel pump is located in a specially designed reservoir within the fuel tank. The reservoir ensures that fuel is available at the pump inlet during all operating conditions, particularly when little fuel remains in the tank. The fuel pump is energized by the ASD relay and operates whenever the relay is activated. Fuel is drawn into the pump through a 'sock type' filter screen, and the pump contains an integral fuel inlet check valve to prevent drain back.

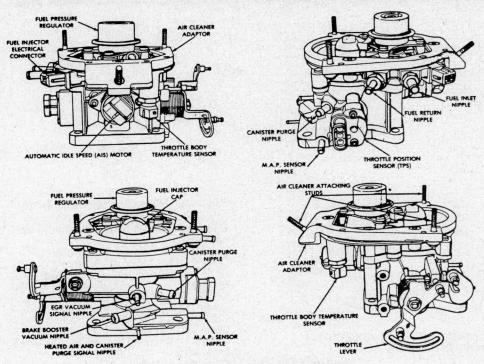

Fig. 7   Fuel injector

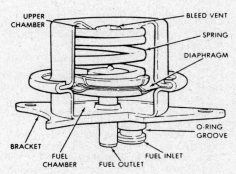

Fig. 6   Throttle body assembly

## 14 Way Single Module Engine Controller Connector

| Pin | Circuit | Color |
|---|---|---|
| 1 | N-6 | OR |
| 2 | K-5 | BK/WT |
| 3 | K-14 | DB |
| 4 | J-2 | DB |
| 6 | J-9-A | BK |
| 7 | J-9-B | BK |
| 8 | K-16 | YL/WT |
| 9 | Y-11 | WT |
| 10 | Y-12 | Tan |
| 11 | R-13 | GR/WT |
| 12 | J-5 | BK/YL |
| 13 | K-15 | BR/YL |
| 14 | R-3 | DG |

**Function**
8 Volt Output
Ground for N-5 Circuit
A.S.D.
12-Volt
Ground
Ground
Injector Control Signal (+)
Injector Ground
Injector Ground
Voltage Regulator Signal
Coil
Anti Dwell Signal
Regulator Control

Fig. 10   SMEC 14 way electrical connector terminal identification

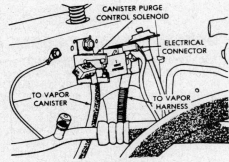

Fig. 8   Fuel pressure regulator

Fig. 9   Canister purge solenoid location

functions, or if check engine lamp remains illuminated, refer to 'System Testing' to call up fault codes stored in the SMEC memory and correct as needed.

## VISUAL INSPECTION

A visual inspection for loose, disconnected or misrouted wiring and hoses should be made prior to attempting to diagnose fuel injection system malfunctions. The visual inspection should include the following checks:

1. Ensure that vacuum connections on rear of throttle body are secure.
2. Ensure that vacuum connection and purge control solenoid and charcoal canister are secure and not leaking.
3. Inspect PCV valve and ensure that valve and hose are in satisfactory condition.
4. Inspect alternator and ensure that electrical connectors are secure and that belt is properly adjusted.
5. Ensure that MAP sensor hose is securely connected at firewall connection and at sensor.
6. Ensure that air intake heated air door vacuum hose is securely connected.
7. Inspect fuel pump and fuel lines, ensuring that pump electrical connec-

## EMISSION CONTROLS

The charcoal canister purge control solenoid, **Fig. 9**, is operated by the SMEC. When engine temperature is below 145 degrees F., the SMEC completes the purge solenoid ground circuit, the solenoid is energized and purge vacuum is prevented from being applied to the canister. When engine temperature is above 145 degrees F., the solenoid is de-energized and purge vacuum is applied from the port on the throttle body.

## DIAGNOSIS & TESTING

The SMEC has been programmed to monitor several different circuits of the fuel injection system in order to provide a self-diagnosis function. In conjunction with the self-diagnosis function, a check engine lamp is wired into the system to indicate a failure in the monitored circuits. The check engine lamp is illuminated for 3 seconds

whenever the engine is started as a 'bulb test.' However, if the SMEC detects a malfunction in one of the monitored circuits the check engine lamp will be illuminated and will remain on as long as the ignition key remains in the on position. Illumination of the check engine lamp indicates that the system has entered the 'limp-in' mode and signals an immediate need for system service.

If vehicle performance or the check engine lamp indicate fuel injection system malfunctions, certain procedures should be followed. Prior to suspecting the fuel injection service as the cause for complaints, ensure that the engine and all related systems are in proper operating condition. After checking related systems, inspect fuel injection components and connecting harnesses as outlined in 'Visual Inspection,' repair system as indicated, then road test vehicle to check system operation. If service performed during visual inspection does not correct observed mal-

| CAV | WIRE COLOR | DESCRIPTION |
|---|---|---|
| 1 | DG/RD* | MAP SENSOR |
| 2 | | |
| 3 | TN/WT* | COOLANT SENSOR |
| 4 | BK/LB* | SENSOR RETURN |
| 5 | BK/WT* | SIGNAL GROUND |
| 6 | | |
| 7 | WT/LG* | SPEED CONTROL RESUME |
| 8 | YL/RD* | SPEED CONTROL ON/OFF |
| 9 | BR/RD* | SPEED CONTROL SET |
| 10 | DG/BK* | Z1 INPUT |
| 11 | | |
| 12 | DB/WT* | FJ2 |
| 13 | VT/WT* | 5 VOLT SUPPLY |
| 14 | DG/OR* | ALTERNATOR FIELD CONTROL |
| 15 | LB/RD* | POWER GROUND |
| 16 | LB/RD* | POWER GROUND |
| 17 | BR/WT* | AIS-1 |
| 18 | YL/BK* | AIS-2 |
| 19 | GY/RD* | AIS-3 |
| 20 | VT/BK* | AIS-4 |
| 21 | BK/RD* | CHARGE TEMPERATURE SENSOR |
| 22 | OR/LB* | THROTTLE POSITION SENSOR |
| 23 | BK/DG* | OXYGEN SENSOR |
| 24 | | |
| 25 | | |
| 26 | | |
| 27 | | |
| 28 | | |
| 29 | WT/PK* | BRAKE SWITCH |
| 30 | BR/YL* | PARK/NEUTRAL SWITCH |
| 31 | LG | SCI RECEIVE |
| 32 | | |
| 33 | VT/YL* | INJECTOR CONTROL 1 |
| 34 | YL | DWELL CONTROL |
| 35 | | |
| 36 | LB/BK* | FUEL MONITOR |

| CAV | WIRE COLOR | DESCRIPTION |
|---|---|---|
| 37 | | |
| 38 | | |
| 39 | | |
| 40 | GY/YL* | EGR SOLENOID |
| 41 | RD | DIRECT BATTERY |
| 42 | | |
| 43 | | |
| 44 | | |
| 45 | BR | A/C CLUTCH INPUT |
| 46 | | |
| 47 | GY/BK* | REFERENCE PICKUP |
| 48 | WT/OR* | VEHICLE SPEED PICKUP |
| 49 | TN/YL* | HIGH DATA RATE PICKUP (EXCEPT 2.5L EFI ENGINE) |
| 50 | GY/LB* | TACHOMETER SIGNAL |
| 51 | PK | SCI TRANSMIT |
| 52 | OR | 8 VOLT INPUT |
| 53 | TN/RD* | SPEED CONTROL VACUUM SOLENOID |
| 54 | PK/BK* | PURGE SOLENOID |
| 55 | OR/BK* | LOCK-UP TORQUE CONVERTER |
| 56 | DB/OR* | A/C WIDE OPEN THROTTLE CUT-OUT |
| 57 | DB/PK* | RADIATOR FAN RELAY |
| 58 | DB/YL* | AUTO SHUT DOWN RELAY |
| 59 | BK/PK* | CHECK ENGINE |
| 60 | LG/RD* | SPEED CONTROL VENT SOLENOID |

| WIRE COLOR CODES | | | | |
|---|---|---|---|---|
| BK | BLACK | LB | LIGHT BLUE | VT | VIOLET |
| BR | BROWN | LG | LIGHT GREEN | WT | WHITE |
| DB | DARK BLUE | OR | ORANGE | YL | YELLOW |
| DG | DARK GREEN | PK | PINK | * | WITH TRACER |
| GY | GRAY | RD | RED | | |
| TN | TAN | | | | |

CONNECTOR WIRE SIDE SHOWN

RR8WH17

**Fig. 11 SMEC 60 way electrical connector terminal identification.**

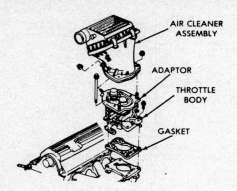

AIR CLEANER ASSEMBLY

ADAPTOR

THROTTLE BODY

GASKET

**Fig. 12 Remove throttle body**

tors and fuel hoses are securely connected.

8. Inspect back pressure transducer and EGR valve, ensuring that components are securely mounted and free from leaks.

9. Ensure that black and white 60 way connector is securely seated in proper sockets in SMEC.

10. Ensure that 14 way connector is securely seated in proper sockets in SMEC. When inspecting system electrical connectors, ensure that connector terminals are not bent or damaged, preventing proper current transfer. Do not clean conductive grease from connector cavities, where applicable, as this could adversely affect system performance.

11. Ensure that purge solenoid and distance sensor two-way connectors are secure.

12. Ensure that Fuel injector, AIS motor, throttle body sensors and temperature sensor electrical connectors are secure.

13. Ensure that coolant sensor is properly mounted in thermostat housing and that electrical connector is secure.

14. Ensure that 3 wire distributor connector and oxygen sensor lead connector are secure and free from corrosion.

15. Inspect engine harness connectors, ensuring that terminals are not bent or damaged and that connectors are properly locked.

16. Ensure that all relay electrical connectors are fully seated and that battery cable connections are clean and free from corrosion.

17. Ensure that radiator fan relay and radiator temperature sensor connectors are properly seated.

18. Inspect ignition system primary and secondary wiring, ensuring that all connections are secure and free from corrosion.

19. Ensure that neutral safety switch is operating properly and that electrical connector is secure.

20. Ensure that engine ground strap is secure at dash panel and intake manifold.

## OBTAINING FAULT CODES

If a problem is sensed by the SMEC, often enough to be considered a malfunction, a fault code is stored in the SMEC memory. If the problem is repaired, or ceases to occur, the SMEC will cancel the fault code after 20-40 engine cycles. Fault codes that remain in the SMEC memory can be called up and displayed either by using diagnostic tool C-4805 or by observing flashes of the check engine lamp. Fault codes can be obtained using the following procedures:

### Using Check Engine Lamp

If suitable tester is not available, stored fault codes and be accessed directly through the check engine lamp. To call up codes, cycle ignition switch on, off, on , off and on within 5 seconds. Stored codes will be indicated by flashes of the check engine lamp.

## FAULT CODE DIAGNOSIS

These fault codes indicate the result of a failure, but do not identify the failed component in the following areas:

Code 88—Start of test.
Code 11—Engine not cranked since battery was disconnected.
Code 12—Memory Standby power lost.
Code 13—MAP sensor pneumatic circuit.
Code 14—MAP sensor electrical circuit.
Code 15—Vehicle distance sensor.
Code 16—Loss of battery voltage sense.
Code 17—Engine running too cool.
Code 21—Oxygen sensor circuit.
Code 22—Coolant temperature sensor circuit.

Code 23—Throttle body temperature sensor circuit.
Code 24—Throttle position sensor.
Code 25—AIS motor driver circuit.
Code 26—Peak injector current not reached.
Code 27—Fuel injector control problem.
Code 31—Purge solenoid circuit.
Code 33—A/C cutout relay circuit.
Code 35—Fan control relay circuit.
Code 41—Charging system excess or no field circuit.
Code 42—ASD relay driver.
Code 43—Spark interface circuit.
Code 44—Loss of FJ2 to logic board.
Code 46—Battery voltage too high.
Code 47—Battery voltage too low.
Code 51—Oxygen feedback system stuck at lean position.
Code 52—Oxygen feedback system stuck at rich position.
Code 53—Internal SMEC problem.
Code 55—End of message.

Codes indicated by an will cause the check engine lamp to remain illuminated when set in the SMEC memory.

Test continuity of wiring in each circuit indicated by fault codes or in other circuit tests, referring to **Figs. 10 and 11**, for SMEC terminal identification. Repair wiring as needed and check operation of components as outlined in 'Description.' Replace any components that fail to perform properly, then recheck system operation.

## SYSTEM SERVICE

The electronic fuel injection system is under a constant pressure of approximately 14.5 psi. Before servicing the fuel pump, fuel lines, fuel filter, throttle body or fuel injector, the fuel system pressure must be released.

## FUEL SYSTEM PRESSURE RELEASE

1. Loosen gas cap and allow tank pressure to release.

2. Remove wiring harness connector from injector, then ground one injector terminal.

3. Connect a suitable jumper wire to a second terminal, then touch the positive post of the battery for approximately 10 seconds and release system pressure.

4. Remove jumper wires and service fuel system as required.

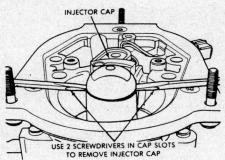

**Fig. 13  Removing fuel pressure regulator**

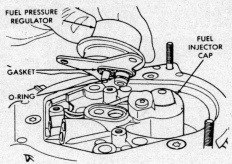

**Fig. 14  Removing fuel injector cap**

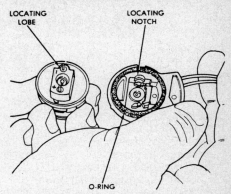

**Fig. 15  Position injector cap to fuel injector**

# THROTTLE BODY, REPLACE

1. Remove air cleaner, **Fig. 12.**
2. Perform fuel system pressure release procedures as previously described.
3. Disconnect battery ground cable.
4. Disconnect vacuum hoses, then the electrical connector.
5. Remove throttle cable, then if equipped, the speed control and transaxle kickdown cables.
6. Remove return spring, then the fuel system intake and return hoses.
7. Remove throttle body attaching bolts, then lift throttle body from vehicle.
8. Reverse procedure to install. Torque attaching bolts to 175 inch lbs.

# PRESSURE REGULATOR, REPLACE

1. Remove air cleaner assembly.
2. Perform fuel system pressure release procedures as previously described.
3. Disconnect battery ground cable.
4. Place a suitable shop towel around fuel inlet chamber as to contain any remaining fuel in system, then remove three pressure regulator to throttle body attaching screws.
5. Pull pressure regulator from throttle body, **Fig. 13.**
6. Remove O-ring from pressure regulator, then the gasket.
7. Reverse procedure to install, noting the following:
   a. Install new pressure regulator gasket and new O-ring.
   b. Torque pressure regulator to throttle body attaching screws to 40 inch lbs.
   c. Pressurize system and check for leaks after assembly.

# FUEL INJECTOR, REPLACE

1. Remove air cleaner.
2. Perform fuel system pressure release procedures as previously described.
3. Disconnect battery ground cable.
4. Remove torx screw retaining injector cap, then lift cap from injector using two suitable screwdrivers, **Fig. 14.**
5. Pry injector from pod by placing a suit-

able screwdriver into hole at side of electrical connector.
6. Remove lower O-ring from pod.
7. Place new lower O-ring on injector and new O-ring on injector cap.
8. Place injector in pod, positioning injector as to allow cap to be installed without interference, **Fig. 15.**
9. Rotate cap and injector to align attachment hold, then press down on cap to ensure proper seal.
10. Install torx screw, then torque to 35–45 inch lbs.
11. Connect battery ground cable, then pressurize system and check for leaks.
12. Reinstall air cleaner.

# THROTTLE POSITION SENSOR, REPLACE

1. Disconnect battery ground cable, then remove air cleaner.
2. Disconnect three way connector at throttle position sensor (TPS), then remove TPS to throttle body mounting screws.
3. Lift TPS from throttle shaft, then remove O-ring.
4. Reverse procedure to install. Install new O-ring and torque TPS to throttle body mounting screw to 20 inch lbs.

# THROTTLE BODY TEMPERATURE SENSOR, REPLACE

1. Remove air cleaner, then disconnect throttle cables from throttle body linkage.
2. Remove two throttle cable bracket attaching screws, then position bracket aside.
3. Disconnect electrical connector, then unscrew sensor.
4. Apply heat transfer compound to tip of new sensor.
5. Install new sensor, then torque to 80–120 inch lbs.
6. Reconnect electrical connector, then install throttle cable bracket with attaching screws.
7. Connect throttle cables to throttle body linkage, then install retaining clips.
8. Install air cleaner.

# AUTOMATIC IDLE SPEED (AIS) MOTOR ASSEMBLY, REPLACE

1. Disconnect battery ground cable, then remove air cleaner assembly.
2. Disconnect four pin connector from AIS, then remove temperature sending unit from throttle body housing.
3. Remove two AIS to throttle body torx head retaining screws.
4. Remove AIS from throttle body housing with O-ring.
5. Reverse procedure to install. Install new O-ring and torque retaining screws to 20 inch lbs.

# MANIFOLD ABSOLUTE PRESSURE SENSOR, REPLACE

1. Remove vacuum hose from sensor.
3. Remove sensor attaching screws, then the sensor.
4. Reverse procedure to install. Ensure proper installation of vacuum hose to sensor and sensor to dash panel.

# SMEC, REPLACE

1. Remove air cleaner duct from SMEC.
2. Remove battery.
3. Remove two SMEC mounting screws.
4. Remove SMEC electrical connectors.
5. Remove SMEC.
6. Reverse procedure to install.

# OXYGEN SENSOR, REPLACE

The oxygen sensor is to be removed using tool No. C-4907 or equivalent. After removal, clean threads in exhaust manifold using an 18mm x 1.5 x 6E tap. If reinstalling the same sensor, apply a suitable anti-seize to threads of sensor. New sensors are packaged with an anti-seize compound already applied to the threads and no further application is required. When installing sensor, torque to 20 ft. lbs.

# Dual Point Fuel Injection System, Chrysler

## INDEX

## DESCRIPTION

The electronic, dual point fuel injection system uses a digital pre-programmed Single Module Engine Controller (SMEC) to control air-fuel mixtures delivered to the engine, ignition timing, idle speed, various emission control devices, the engine cooling fan and the charging system. The SMEC monitors inputs from various engine and vehicle sensors, computes ideal operating parameters for the controlled sub-systems based on these inputs, and controls operation of the subsystems. Sensors used to control system operations include: an exhaust gas oxygen sensor, Manifold Absolute Pressure (MAP) sensor, throttle position sensor, coolant and throttle body temperature sensors, vehicle distance sensor, and the neutral safety and A/C compressor clutch switches and auto shut down relay, **Fig. 1.**

All inputs to the SMEC are converted to signals. These signals cause the SMEC to alter fuel injector delivery and/or ignition timing to maintain ideal air fuel mixtures and ignition timing for all vehicle operating conditions.

In addition, the SMEC tests many of its input and output circuits, and if a fault is found in one of the monitored circuits information relating to the malfunction is stored in the SMEC memory. Information relating to monitored circuit malfunctions can be accessed by the technician through the instrument panel mounted check engine lamp, or by connecting a diagnostic read-out instrument to the system. Both access methods provide numerical type codes which relate to specific circuit malfunctions.

### SINGLE MODULE ENGINE CONTROLLER & AUTOMATIC SHUT DOWN (ASD) RELAY

The SMEC, **Fig. 2,** is mounted in the engine compartment and contains circuits necessary to energize the ignition coil, fuel injectors and alternator field in order to minimize electrical noise in the passenger compartment. The SMEC contains a voltage converter which converts battery voltage into a regulated 8 volt output to energize the ignition pick up coil. The externally mounted Automatic Shut Down (ASD) re-

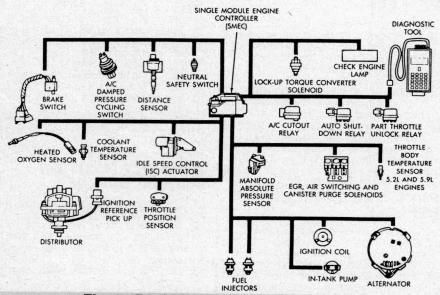

**Fig. 1   Fuel injection system schematic**

lay which interrupts power to the fuel pump, ignition coil and injector when necessary is controlled by the SMEC.

The ASD relay is turned on and off by the SMEC in response to distributor reference pulses. When distributor reference pulses are transmitted to the SMEC, the SMEC activates the ASD relay. However, when no reference pulse is transmitted to the SMEC, the ASD relay is deactivated and power is shut off to the fuel control system and ignition coil.

## SENSORS & SWITCHES

### Manifold Absolute Pressure (MAP) Sensor

The MAP sensor, **Fig. 3,** is mounted in the engine compartment on the dash panel and monitors intake manifold vacuum through a line connected to the throttle body. The sensor converts manifold vacuum (negative pressure) and barometric pressure into electrical signals and transmits these signals to the SMEC. The SMEC uses these signals to monitor engine load and atmospheric conditions in order to determine the correct air/fuel mixture for vehicle operating conditions.

### Oxygen Sensor

The oxygen sensor, **Fig. 4,** produces voltage signals when exposed to oxygen in the exhaust gasses. The oxygen content in the exhaust gasses is directly proportional to the air/fuel mixture entering the engine, and the voltage signal produced by the sensor is inversely proportional to the amount of oxygen remaining in the exhaust gasses. The SMEC uses these signals to determine air/fuel mixtures entering the engine.

The oxygen sensor is mounted in the exhaust manifold, and the sensing element must be heated by exhaust gasses before the sensor begins to produce voltage signals. When exhaust gas oxygen content is high (lean mixtures), the sensor produces a low voltage. When oxygen content is low (rich mixtures), the sensor produces a higher voltage.

### Coolant Temperature Sensor

The coolant temperature sensor, **Fig. 5,** is mounted in the thermostat housing and allows the SMEC to monitor engine operating temperature in order to provide prop-

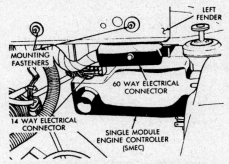

## Fig. 2 Single Module Engine Controller (SMEC)

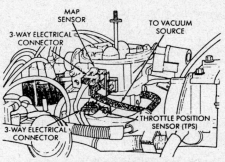

## Fig. 3 Manifold Absolute Pressure (MAP) sensor location

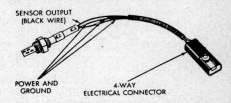

## Fig. 4 Oxygen sensor

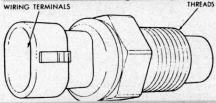

## Fig. 5 Coolant temperature sensor

er air/fuel mixtures. The sensor provides a variable resistance which is proportional to coolant temperature. When the engine is cold and sensor resistance is low, the SMEC provides richer air/fuel mixtures and increases engine idle speed to provide acceptable cold engine performance and allow quick warm up. When coolant temperature and sensor resistance increase, the SMEC provides leaner air/fuel mixtures and lowers engine idle speed to provide proper exhaust emission control and increased fuel economy.

### Throttle Body Temperature Sensor

The throttle body mounted temperature sensor allows the SMEC to monitor fuel temperature. The SMEC uses this information to provide the proper air/fuel mixtures for a hot restart condition.

### Throttle Position Sensor (TPS)

The TPS is mounted on the throttle body and senses the angle of the throttle plate opening. The sensor produces a voltage signal which increases and decreases according to throttle position. The SMEC uses these voltage signals to tailor air/fuel mixtures for varying conditions such as idle, wide open throttle, acceleration and deceleration.

### Vehicle Distance Sensor

The distance sensor is located in the transaxle extension housing and signals vehicle motion to the SMEC by generating eight pulses per axle shaft revolution. The SMEC uses this signal along with signals from the throttle position sensor to determine between a closed throttle deceleration and a normal idle condition, thereby allowing the SMEC to maintain desired control of the AIS motor.

### Switch Inputs

Various switches provide information to the SMEC. These switches include the

speed control, neutral safety, A/C compressor clutch and brake lamp switches. If one or more of these switches is sensed as being 'on', the SMEC signals the idle speed motor to change idle speed to a pre-set Rpm. In addition, when the A/C is on and the throttle plate is above a specified angle, the wide open throttle cut-out relay prevents the A/C clutch from being energized until throttle angle is reduced.

### A/C Clutch Relay

The A/C clutch relay is connected to the A/C damped pressure switch, the A/C switch and the A/C fan relay. The relay is in the On position during normal engine operation, but is closed when the SMEC senses low idle speeds or wide open throttle conditions, preventing A/C clutch engagement.

## FUEL SYSTEM CONTROLS
### Throttle Body

The throttle body, **Fig. 6**, assembly is mounted on the intake manifold and houses the throttle plate, fuel injectors, fuel pressure regulator, temperature and position sensors, and the ISC motor. Intake air flow is controlled by the cable operated throttle plate and by a separate by-pass channel which is controlled by the AIS motor. The throttle body provides the chamber for fuel metering, atomization, and mixing atomized fuel with incoming air.

### Fuel Injector

The fuel injector, **Fig. 7**, is a solenoid operated valve which is energized and controlled by the SMEC. Fuel is supplied to the injector at a constant pressure of 14.5 psi, and excess fuel is returned to the tank. When voltage is applied to the injector solenoid, a spring loaded ball is lifted off its seat and fuel is sprayed into the throttle body through 6 spray orifices. The spray orifices and injector tip design cause the fuel to be sprayed in an even conical pattern prior to entering the intake air stream.

The amount of fuel delivered by the injector is determined by the amount of time that the injector solenoid is energized. The SMEC determines the amount of fuel necessary to maintain ideal air/fuel mixtures based upon various sensor inputs. The SMEC then energizes the fuel injector for a sufficient amount of time to deliver the necessary amount of fuel.

### Idle Speed Control Actuator (ISC)

The ISC motor adjusts idle speed by physically moving the throttle lever. The SMEC computes proper idle speed based on signals from vehicle and engine sensors and the switch inputs, and transmits voltage signals to the ISC motor to open or close the throttle plates in order to maintain the proper engine speed.

Basic, no-load idle speed is determined by the amount of air flowing through the throttle body past the closed throttle plate.

### Fuel Pressure Regulator

The mechanical fuel pressure regulator, **Fig. 8**, is used to maintain fuel pressure at the injector tip at a constant 14.5 psi. The pressure regulator uses a spring loaded diaphragm to control the fuel return port in order to maintain constant pressure. Pressurized fuel is delivered first to the fuel injector and then flows to the pressure regulator. When fuel pressure acting on the regulator diaphragm exceeds 14.5 psi, the regulator spring is compressed and the fuel return port is opened. When fuel pressure drops below 14.5 psi spring tension causes the diaphragm to block the fuel return port. The diaphragm and spring move constantly between the open and closed positions in order to maintain constant fuel pressure at the injector tip.

### Fuel Pump & Reservoir

An electric fuel pump is located in a specially designed reservoir within the fuel tank. The reservoir ensures that fuel is available at the pump inlet during all operating conditions, particularly when little fuel remains in the tank. The fuel pump is energized by the ASD relay and operates whenever the relay is activated. Fuel is drawn into the pump through a 'sock type' filter screen, and the pump contains an integral fuel inlet check valve to prevent drain back.

## EMISSION CONTROLS

The charcoal canister purge control solenoid, **Fig. 9**, is operated by the SMEC. When engine temperature is below 145 degrees F., the SMEC completes the purge solenoid ground circuit, the solenoid is energized and purge vacuum is prevented from being applied to the canister. When engine temperature is above 145°F, the solenoid is de-energized and purge vacuum is applied from the port on the throttle body.

## DIAGNOSIS & TESTING

The SMEC has been programmed to monitor several different circuits of the fuel

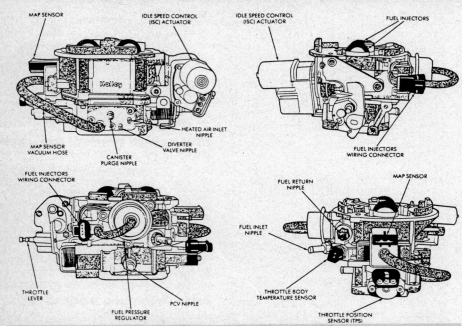

Fig. 6 Throttle body assembly

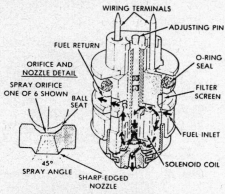

Fig. 7 Fuel injector

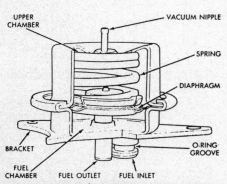

Fig. 8 Fuel pressure regulator

injection system in order to provide a self-diagnosis function. In conjunction with the self-diagnosis function, a check engine lamp is wired into the system to indicate a failure in the monitored circuits. The check engine lamp is illuminated for 3 seconds whenever the engine is started as a bulb test. However, if the SMEC detects a malfunction in one of the monitored circuits the check engine lamp will be illuminated and will remain on as long as the ignition key remains in the on position. Illumination of the check engine lamp indicates that the system has entered the limp-in mode and signals an immediate need for system service.

If vehicle performance or the check engine lamp indicate fuel injection system malfunctions, certain procedures should be followed. Prior to suspecting the fuel injection service as the cause for complaints, ensure that the engine and all related systems are in proper operating condition. After checking related systems, inspect fuel injection components and connecting harnesses as outlined in "Visual Inspection," repair system as indicated, then road test vehicle to check system operation. If service performed during visual inspection does not correct observed malfunctions, or if check engine lamp remains illuminated, refer to "System Testing" to call up fault codes stored in the SMEC memory and correct as needed.

## VISUAL INSPECTION

A visual inspection for loose, disconnected or misrouted wiring and hoses should be made prior to attempting to diagnose fuel injection system malfunctions. The visual inspection should include the following checks:
1. Ensure that vacuum connections on rear of throttle body are secure.
2. Ensure that vacuum connection and purge control solenoid and charcoal canister are secure and not leaking.
3. Inspect PCV valve and ensure that valve and hose are in satisfactory condition.
4. Inspect alternator and ensure that electrical connectors are secure and that belt is properly adjusted.
5. Ensure that MAP sensor hose is securely connected at firewall connection and at sensor.
6. Ensure that air intake heated air door vacuum hose is securely connected.
7. Inspect fuel pump and fuel lines, ensuring that pump electrical connectors and fuel hoses are securely connected.
8. Inspect back pressure transducer and EGR valve, ensuring that components are securely mounted and free from leaks.
9. Ensure that 60 way connector is securely seated in proper sockets in SMEC.
10. Ensure that 14 way connector is securely seated in proper sockets in SMEC. When inspecting system electrical connectors, ensure that connector terminals are not bent or damaged, preventing proper current transfer. Do not clean conductive grease from connector cavities, where applicable, as this could adversely affect system performance.
11. Ensure that purge solenoid and distance sensor two-way connectors are secure.
12. Ensure that Fuel injector, ISC motor, throttle body sensors and temperature sensor electrical connectors are secure.
13. Ensure that coolant sensor is properly mounted in thermostat housing and that electrical connector is secure.
14. Ensure that 3 wire distributor connector and oxygen sensor lead connector are secure and free from corrosion.
15. Inspect engine harness connectors, ensuring that terminals are not bent or damaged and that connectors are properly locked.
16. Ensure that all relay electrical connectors are fully seated and that battery cable connections are clean and free from corrosion.
17. Ensure that radiator fan relay and radiator temperature sensor connectors are properly seated.
18. Inspect ignition system primary and secondary wiring, ensuring that all connections are secure and free from corrosion.
19. Ensure that neutral safety switch is operating properly and that electrical connector is secure.
20. Ensure that engine ground strap is secure at dash panel and intake manifold.

## OBTAINING FAULT CODES

If a problem is sensed by the SMEC, often enough to be considered a malfunction, a fault code is stored in the SMEC memory. If the problem is repaired, or ceases to occur, the SMEC will cancel the fault code after 20-40 engine cycles. Fault codes that remain in the SMEC memory can be called up and displayed either by using diagnostic tool C-4805 or by observing flashes of the check engine lamp. Fault codes can be obtained using the following procedures:

### Using Check Engine Lamp

If suitable tester is not available, stored fault codes and be accessed directly through the check engine lamp. To call up codes, cycle ignition switch on, off, on, off and on within 5 seconds. Stored codes will be indicated by flashes of the check engine lamp.

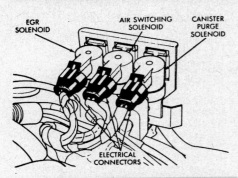

**Fig. 9  Canister purge solenoid location**

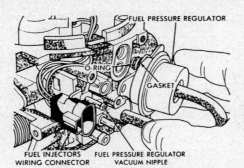

**Fig. 10  Removing fuel pressure regulator**

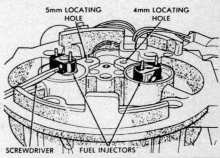

**Fig. 11  Removing fuel injector cap**

## FAULT CODE DIAGNOSIS

These fault codes indicate the result of a failure, but do not identify the failed component in the following areas:

Code 88—Start of test.
Code 11—Ignition reference signal.
Code 12—Memory Standby power lost.
Code 13—MAP sensor pneumatic circuit.
Code 14—MAP sensor electrical circuit.
Code 15—Vehicle distance sensor.
Code 16—Loss of battery voltage sense.
Code 17—Engine running too cool.
Code 21—Oxygen sensor circuit.
Code 22—Coolant temperature sensor circuit.
Code 23—Throttle body temperature sensor circuit.
Code 24—Throttle position sensor.
Code 25—ISC motor driver circuit.
Code 26—Peak injector current not reached.
Code 27—Fuel injector control problem.
Code 31—Purge solenoid circuit.
Code 32—EGR solenoid circuit.
Code 33—A/C cutout relay circuit.
Code 34—Speed Control Servo circuit.
Code 35—Idle switch.
Code 36—Air switch solenoid.
Code 37—Part throttle unlock solenoid.
Code 41—Charging system excess or no field circuit.
Code 42—ASD relay driver.
Code 43—Ignition control circuit.
Code 44—Loss of FJ2 to logic board.
Code 45—Overdrive solenoid.
Code 46—Battery voltage too high.
Code 47—Battery voltage too low.
Code 51—Oxygen feedback system stuck at lean position.
Code 52—Oxygen feedback system stuck at rich position.
Code 53—Internal SMEC problem.
Code 55—End of message.
Code 62—EMR mileage accum.
Code 63—EEPROM write denied.

Check operation of components as outlined in "Description." Replace any components that fail to perform properly, then recheck system operation.

## SYSTEM SERVICE

The electronic fuel injection system is under a constant pressure of approximately 14.5 psi. Before servicing the fuel pump, fuel lines, fuel filter, throttle body or fuel injector, the fuel system pressure must be released.

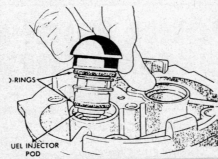

**Fig. 12  Positioning injector cap to fuel injector**

## FUEL SYSTEM PRESSURE RELEASE

1. Loosen gas cap and allow tank pressure to release.
2. Remove wiring harness connector from injector, then ground one injector terminal.
3. Connect a suitable jumper wire to a second terminal, then touch the positive post of the battery for approximately 10 seconds and release system pressure.
4. Remove jumper wires and service fuel system as required.

## THROTTLE BODY, REPLACE

1. Remove air cleaner.
2. Perform fuel system pressure release procedures as previously described.
3. Disconnect battery ground cable.
4. Disconnect vacuum hoses, then the electrical connector.
5. Remove throttle cable, then if equipped, the speed control and transaxle kickdown cables.
6. Remove fuel intake and return hoses.
7. Remove throttle body attaching bolts, then lift throttle body from vehicle.
8. Reverse procedure to install. Torque attaching bolts to 175 inch lbs.

## PRESSURE REGULATOR, REPLACE

1. Remove air cleaner assembly.
2. Perform fuel system pressure release procedures as previously described.
3. Disconnect battery ground cable.
4. Place a suitable shop towel around fuel inlet chamber as to contain any remaining fuel in system, then remove three pressure regulator to throttle

body attaching screws.
5. Pull pressure regulator from throttle body, **Fig. 10.**
6. Remove O-ring from pressure regulator, then the gasket.
7. Reverse procedure to install, noting the following:
   a. Install new pressure regulator gasket and new O-ring.
   b. Torque pressure regulator to throttle body attaching screws to 40 inch lbs.
   c. Pressurize system and check for leaks after assembly.

## FUEL INJECTOR, REPLACE

1. Remove air cleaner.
2. Perform fuel system pressure release procedures as previously described.
3. Disconnect battery ground cable.
4. Remove torx screw retaining injector cap, then lift cap from injector using two suitable screwdrivers, **Fig. 11.**
5. Pry injector from pod by placing a suitable screwdriver into hole at side of electrical connector.
6. Remove lower O-ring from pod.
7. Place new lower O-ring on injector and new O-ring on injector cap.
8. Place injector in pod, positioning injector as to allow cap to be installed without interference, **Fig. 12.**
9. Rotate cap and injector to align attachment hold, then press down on cap to ensure proper seal.
10. Install torx screw, then torque to 35 inch lbs.
11. Connect battery ground cable, then pressurize system and check for leaks.
12. Reinstall air cleaner.

## THROTTLE POSITION SENSOR, REPLACE

1. Disconnect battery ground cable, then remove air cleaner.
2. Disconnect three way connector at throttle position sensor (TPS), then remove TPS to throttle body mounting screws.
3. Lift TPS from throttle shaft.
4. Reverse procedure to install. Torque TPS to throttle body mounting screw to 20 inch lbs.

## THROTTLE BODY TEMPERATURE SENSOR, REPLACE

1. Remove air cleaner, then disconnect sensor electrical connector.

2. Remove sensor.
3. Apply heat transfer compound to tip of new sensor.
4. Install new sensor, then torque to 80-120 inch lbs.
5. Reconnect electrical connector.
6. Install air cleaner.

## IDLE SPEED CONTROL (ISC) ACTUATOR, REPLACE

1. Disconnect battery ground cable, then remove air cleaner assembly.
2. Disconnect actuator electrical connector.
3. Remove three ISC to bracket attaching nuts.
4. Remove ISC from bracket.

5. Reverse procedure to install.

## MANIFOLD ABSOLUTE PRESSURE SENSOR, REPLACE

1. Remove vacuum hose from sensor.
3. Remove sensor attaching screws, then the sensor.
4. Reverse procedure to install. Ensure proper installation of vacuum hose and electrical connections.

## SMEC, REPLACE

1. Remove air cleaner duct from SMEC.
2. Remove three SMEC mounting screws.

3. Disconnect SMEC electrical connectors.
4. Remove SMEC.
5. Reverse procedure to install.

## OXYGEN SENSOR, REPLACE

The oxygen sensor is to be removed using tool No. C-4907 or equivalent. After removal, clean threads in exhaust manifold using an 18mm x 1.5 x 6E tap. If reinstalling the same sensor, apply a suitable anti-seize to threads of sensor. New sensors are packaged with an anti-seize compound already applied to the threads and no further application is required. When installing sensor, torque to 20 ft. lbs.

# Multi-Point Fuel Injection System, Chrysler

## INDEX

## DESCRIPTION

The electronic, single point fuel injection system uses a digital pre-programmed Single Module Engine Controller (SMEC) to control air-fuel mixtures delivered to the engine, ignition timing, idle speed, various emission control devices, the engine cooling fan and the charging system. The SMEC monitors inputs from various engine and vehicle sensors, computes ideal operating parameters for the controlled sub-systems based on these inputs, and controls operation of the subsystems. Sensors used to control system operations include: an exhaust gas oxygen sensor, Manifold Absolute Pressure (MAP) sensor, throttle position sensor, coolant and charge temperature sensors, vehicle speed sensor, and the brake, speed control, neutral safety and A/C compressor clutch switches and auto shut down relay, **Fig. 1.**

All inputs to the SMEC are converted to signals. These signals cause the SMEC to alter fuel injector delivery and/or ignition timing to maintain ideal air fuel mixtures and ignition timing for all vehicle operating conditions.

In addition, the SMEC tests many of its input and output circuits, and if a fault is found in one of the monitored circuits information relating to the malfunction is stored in the SMEC memory. Information

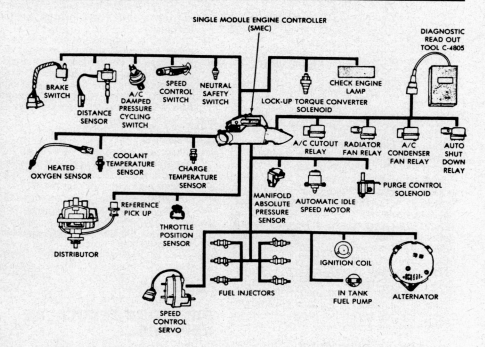

**Fig. 1   Fuel injection system schematic**

relating to monitored circuit malfunctions can be accessed by the technician through the instrument panel mounted check engine lamp, or by connecting a diagnostic read-out instrument to the system. Both access methods provide numerical type codes which relate to specific circuit malfunctions.

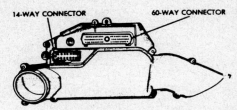

**Fig. 2  Single Module Engine Controller (SMEC)**

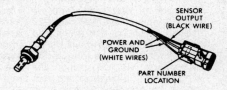

**Fig. 4  Oxygen sensor**

## SINGLE MODULE ENGINE CONTROLLER & AUTOMATIC SHUT DOWN (ASD) RELAY

The SMEC, **Fig. 2,** is mounted in the engine compartment and contains circuits necessary to energize the ignition coil, fuel injectors and alternator field in order to minimize electrical noise in the passenger compartment. The SMEC contains a voltage converter which converts battery voltage into a regulated 8 volt output to energize the ignition pick up coil. The externally mounted Automatic Shut Down (ASD) relay which interrupts power to the fuel pump, ignition coil and injector when necessary is controlled by the SMEC.

The ASD relay is turned on and off by the SMEC in response to distributor reference pulses. When distributor reference pulses are transmitted to the SMEC, the SMEC activates the ASD relay. However, when no reference pulse is transmitted to the SMEC, the ASD relay is deactivated and power is shut off to the fuel control system and ignition coil.

## SENSORS & SWITCHES

### Barometric Read Solenoid

The barometric pressure read solenoid, used on turbocharged models, is controlled by the SMEC. It is located in the MAP sensor vacuum line and decides whether manifold pressure or atmospheric pressure is sent to the MAP sensor. Atmospheric pressure is supplied to the MAP sensor once per throttle closure, but not more than once every three minutes, to measure barometric pressure and control boost.

### Manifold Absolute Pressure (MAP) Sensor

The MAP sensor, **Fig. 3,** is mounted in the engine compartment on the dash panel and monitors intake manifold vacuum through a line connected to the intake plenum. The sensor converts manifold vacuum (negative pressure) and barometric pressure into electrical signals and transmits these signals to the SMEC. The SMEC uses these signals to monitor en-

gine load and atmospheric conditions in order to determine the correct air/fuel mixture for vehicle operating conditions.

### Oxygen Sensor

The oxygen sensor, **Fig. 4,** produces voltage signals when exposed to oxygen in the exhaust gasses. The oxygen content in the exhaust gasses is directly proportional to the air/fuel mixture entering the engine, and the voltage signal produced by the sensor is inversely proportional to the amount of oxygen remaining in the exhaust gasses. The SMEC uses these signals to determine air/fuel mixtures entering the engine.

The oxygen sensor is mounted in the rear exhaust manifold, and the sensing element must be heated by exhaust gasses before the sensor begins to produce voltage signals. When exhaust gas oxygen content is high (lean mixtures), the sensor produces a low voltage. When oxygen content is low (rich mixtures), the sensor produces a higher voltage.

### Charge Temperature Sensor

The charge temperature sensor, **Fig. 5,** is mounted in the intake manifold and measures the temperature of the air/fuel mixture. This information is used by the SMEC to modify the air/fuel mixture.

### Coolant Temperature Sensor

The coolant temperature sensor, **Fig. 5,** is mounted in the thermostat housing and allows the SMEC to monitor engine operating temperature in order to provide proper air/fuel mixtures. The sensor provides a variable resistance which is proportional to coolant temperature. When the engine is cold and sensor resistance is low, the SMEC provides richer air/fuel mixtures and increases engine idle speed to provide acceptable cold engine performance and allow quick warm up. When coolant temperature and sensor resistance increase, the SMEC provides leaner air/fuel mixtures and lowers engine idle speed to provide proper exhaust emission control and increased fuel economy.

### Throttle Position Sensor (TPS)

The TPS is mounted on the throttle body and senses the angle of the throttle plate opening. The sensor produces a voltage signal which increases and decreases according to throttle position. The SMEC uses these voltage signals to tailor air/fuel mixtures for varying conditions such as idle, wide open throttle, acceleration and deceleration.

### Detonation Sensor

The detonation sensor, also called a knock sensor, is used on turbocharged models and designed to notify the SMEC when detonation occurs. Located in the intake manifold, it generates a signal when spark knock is detected in the combustion chambers.

### Vehicle Distance Sensor

The distance sensor is located in the

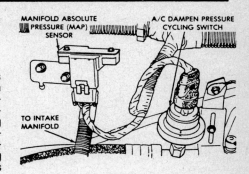

**Fig. 3  Manifold Absolute Pressure (MAP) sensor location**

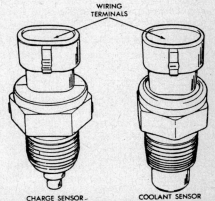

**Fig. 5  Coolant & charge temperature sensors**

transaxle extension housing and signals vehicle motion to the SMEC by generating eight pulses per axle shaft revolution. The SMEC uses this signal along with signals from the throttle position sensor to determine between a closed throttle deceleration and a normal idle condition, thereby allowing the SMEC to maintain desired control of the AIS motor.

### Switch Inputs

Various switches provide information to the SMEC. These switches include the speed control, neutral safety, A/C compressor clutch and brake lamp switches. If one or more of these switches is sensed as being 'on', the SMEC signals the idle speed motor to change idle speed to a pre-set Rpm. In addition, when the A/C is on and the throttle plate is above a specified angle, the wide open throttle cut-out relay prevents the A/C clutch from being energized until throttle angle is reduced.

### A/C Clutch Relay

The A/C clutch relay is connected to the A/C damped pressure switch and the A/C switch. This relay is in the On position during normal engine operation, but is closed when the SMEC senses low idle speeds or wide open throttle conditions, preventing A/C clutch engagement.

## FUEL SYSTEM CONTROLS

### Throttle Body

The throttle body, **Fig. 6,** assembly is lo-

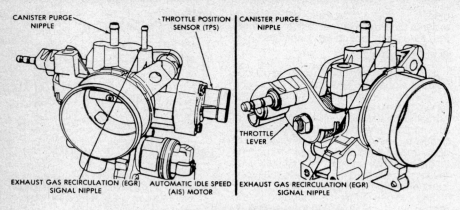

Fig. 6  Throttle body assembly

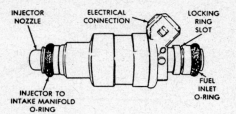

Fig. 7  Fuel injector

cated on the left end of the air intake plenum and houses the throttle plate, throttle position sensor and the AIS motor.

## Fuel Injectors

The fuel injector, **Fig. 7,** is a solenoid operated valve which is energized and controlled by the SMEC. When voltage is applied to the injector solenoid, a spring loaded ball is lifted off its seat and fuel is sprayed into the combustion chamber through spray orifices. The spray orifices and injector tip design cause the fuel to be sprayed in an even conical pattern prior to entering the intake air stream.

The amount of fuel delivered by the injector is determined by the amount of time that the injector solenoid is energized. The SMEC determines the amount of fuel necessary to maintain ideal air/fuel mixtures based upon various sensor inputs. The SMEC then energizes the fuel injector for a sufficient amount of time to deliver the necessary amount of fuel.

## Automatic Idle Speed (AIS) Motor

The AIS motor is operated by the SMEC and controls engine idle speed by controlling air flow through the throttle body by-pass channel. The SMEC computes proper idle speed based in signals from vehicle and engine sensors and the switch inputs, and transmits voltage signals to the AIS motor to open or close the by-pass channel in order to maintain the proper engine speed.

Basic, no-load idle speed is determined by the amount of air flowing through the throttle body past the closed throttle plate. The AIS motor alters idle speed by allowing increased air flow through the by-pass channel; increasing idle speed when the channel is opened and decreasing idle speed when the channel is closed. In addition, the AIS motor is signaled to open the by-pass channel during deceleration to prevent stalling and mixture enrichment caused by sudden closing of the throttle plate.

## Fuel Pressure Regulator

The mechanical fuel pressure regulator, **Fig. 8,** is used to maintain fuel pressure at the injector tip at a constant 36 psi. The pressure regulator uses a spring loaded diaphragm to control the fuel return port in order to maintain constant pressure. Pres-

surized fuel is delivered first to the fuel injector and then flows to the pressure regulator. When fuel pressure acting on the regulator diaphragm exceeds 36 psi, the regulator spring is compressed and the fuel return port is opened. When fuel pressure drops below 36 psi spring tension causes the diaphragm to block the fuel return port. The diaphragm and spring move constantly between the open and closed positions in order to maintain constant fuel pressure at the injector tip.

## Fuel Pump & Reservoir

An electric fuel pump is located in a specially designed reservoir within the fuel tank. The reservoir ensures that fuel is available at the pump inlet during all operating conditions, particularly when little fuel remains in the tank. The fuel pump is energized by the ASD relay and operates whenever the relay is activated. Fuel is drawn into the pump through a 'sock type' filter screen, and the pump contains an integral fuel inlet check valve to prevent drain back.

## Wastegate Control Solenoid

The wastegate control solenoid, controlled by the SMEC, is part of the turbocharger system. The SMEC adjusts maximum boost to varying engine conditions by varying the duty cycle of the wastegate solenoid.

## EMISSION CONTROLS

The purge solenoid, which controls both canister purge and fuel pressure regulator, **Fig. 9,** is operated by the SMEC. When energized, purge vacuum is prevented from being applied to the canister and fuel pressure is increased. Depending on data received from the charge and coolant temperature sensors at start up, the solenoid will be energized for a controlled amount of time.

## DIAGNOSIS & TESTING

The SMEC has been programmed to monitor several different circuits of the fuel injection system in order to provide a self-diagnosis function. In conjunction with the self-diagnosis function, a check engine lamp is wired into the system to indicate a failure in the monitored circuits. The check

engine lamp is illuminated for 3 seconds whenever the engine is started as a 'bulb test.' However, if the SMEC detects a malfunction in one of the monitored circuits the check engine lamp will be illuminated and will remain on as long as the ignition key remains in the on position. Illumination of the check engine lamp indicates that the system has entered the 'limp-in' mode and signals an immediate need for system service.

If vehicle performance or the check engine lamp indicate fuel injection system malfunctions, certain procedures should be followed. Prior to suspecting the fuel injection service as the cause for complaints, ensure that the engine and all related systems are in proper operating condition. After checking related systems, inspect fuel injection components and connecting harnesses as outlined in "Visual Inspection," repair system as indicated, then road test vehicle to check system operation. If service performed during visual inspection does not correct observed malfunctions, or if check engine lamp remains illuminated, refer to 'System Testing' to call up fault codes stored in the SMEC memory and correct as needed.

## VISUAL INSPECTION

A visual inspection for loose, disconnected or misrouted wiring and hoses should be made prior to attempting to diagnose fuel injection system malfunctions. The visual inspection should include the following checks:

1. Ensure that vacuum connections on throttle body are secure.
2. Ensure that throttle body electrical connections are secure.
3. Inspect alternator and ensure that electrical connectors are secure and that belt is properly adjusted.
4. Check two-way connector at each injector. Check vacuum hose connection at fuel pressure regulator and intake plenum connector.
5. Ensure that MAP sensor hose is securely connected at firewall connection and at sensor.
6. Check coolant and charge temperature sensor electrical connections.
7. Inspect fuel pump and fuel lines, ensuring that pump electrical connectors and fuel hoses are securely connected.
8. Inspect EGR valve, ensuring that components are securely mounted and free from leaks.
9. Ensure that black and white 60 way connector is securely seated in proper sockets in SMEC.
10. Ensure that 14 way connector is securely seated in proper sockets in

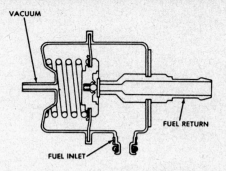

**Fig. 8    Fuel pressure regulator**

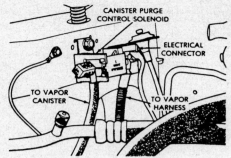

**Fig. 9    Canister purge solenoid location**

**14 Way Single Module Engine Controller (SMEC) Connector**

| CAV. | CIRCUIT | COLOR | FUNCTION |
|------|---------|-------|----------|
| 1 | N-6 | OR | 8 VOLT OUTPUT |
| 2 | K-5 | BK/WT | GROUND |
| 3 | K-14 | DB/LB | A.S.D. |
| 4 | J-2 | DB | 12-VOLT |
| 5 | IN-3 | YL/WT | INJECTOR GROUND |
| 6 | J-9-A | BK | GROUND |
| 7 | J-9-B | BK | GROUND |
| 8 | K-16 | YL/WT | INJECTOR CONTROL #1 |
| 9 | Y-11 | WT | INJECTOR GROUND |
| 10 | Y-12 | TAN | INJECTOR GROUND |
| 11 | R-13 | GR/WT | VOLTAGE REGULATOR SIGNAL |
| 12 | J-5 | BK/YL | COIL |
| 13 | K-15 | BR/YL | ANTI DWELL SIGNAL |
| 14 | R-3 | DG | REGULATOR CONTROL |

**Fig. 10    SMEC 14 way electrical connector terminal identification**

SMEC. When inspecting system electrical connectors, ensure that connector terminals are not bent or damaged, preventing proper current transfer. Do not clean conductive grease from connector cavities, where applicable, as this could adversely affect system performance.

11. Ensure that purge solenoid and distance sensor two-way connectors are secure.
12. Check oil pressure sending unit for proper connection.
13. Ensure that coolant sensor is properly mounted in thermostat housing and that electrical connector is secure.
14. Ensure that 4 wire distributor connector and oxygen sensor lead connector are secure and free from corrosion.
15. Inspect engine harness connectors, ensuring that terminals are not bent or damaged and that connectors are properly locked.
16. Ensure that all relay electrical connectors are fully seated and that battery cable connections are clean and free from corrosion.
17. Ensure that radiator fan relay and radiator temperature sensor connectors are properly seated.
18. Inspect ignition system primary and secondary wiring, ensuring that all connections are secure and free from corrosion.
19. Ensure that neutral safety switch is operating properly and that electrical connector is secure.
20. Ensure that engine ground strap is secure at dash panel and intake manifold.

## OBTAINING FAULT CODES

If a problem is sensed by the SMEC, often enough to be considered a malfunction, a fault code is stored in the SMEC memory. If the problem is repaired, or ceases to occur, the SMEC will cancel the fault code after 30 engine cycles. Fault codes that remain in the SMEC memory can be called up and displayed either by using diagnostic tool C-4805 or by observing flashes of the check engine lamp. Fault codes can be obtained using the following procedures:

### Using Check Engine Lamp

If suitable tester is not available, stored fault codes and be accessed directly through the check engine lamp. To call up codes, cycle ignition switch on, off, on , off and on within 5 seconds. Stored codes will be indicated by flashes of the check engine lamp.

## FAULT CODE DIAGNOSIS

These fault codes indicate the result of a failure, but do not identify the failed component in the following areas:
Code 88—Start of test.
Code 11—Engine not cranked since battery was disconnected.
Code 12—Memory Standby power lost.
Code 13—MAP sensor pneumatic circuit.
Code 14—MAP sensor electrical circuit.
Code 15—Vehicle distance sensor.
Code 16—Loss of battery voltage sense.
Code 17—Engine running too cool.
Code 21—Oxygen sensor circuit.
Code 22—Coolant temperature sensor circuit.
Code 23—Charge temperature sensor circuit.
Code 24—Throttle position sensor.
Code 25—AIS motor driver circuit.
Code 26—Peak injector current not reached.
Code 27—Fuel injector driver interface circuit.
Code 31—Purge solenoid circuit.
Code 32—EGR system.
Code 33—A/C cutout relay circuit.
Code 34—Speed control solenoid driver circuit.
Code 35—Fan control relay circuit.
Code 37—Torque convertor clutch circuit.
Code 41—Charging system excess or no field circuit.
Code 42—ASD relay driver.
Code 43—Ignition coil control circuit.
Code 44—Loss of FJ2 to logic board.
Code 46—Battery voltage too high.
Code 47—Battery voltage too low.
Code 51—Oxygen feedback system stuck at lean position.
Code 52—Oxygen feedback system stuck at rich position.
Code 53—Internal SMEC problem.
Code 54—Distributor high data rate pick-up.
Code 55—End of message.

Codes indicated by an   will cause the check engine lamp to remain illuminated when set in the SMEC memory.

Test continuity of wiring in each circuit indicated by fault codes or in other circuit tests, referring to **Figs. 10 and 11**, for SMEC terminal identification. Repair wiring as needed and check operation of components as outlined in 'Description.' Replace any components that fail to perform properly, then recheck system operation.

## SYSTEM SERVICE

The electronic fuel injection system is under a constant pressure of approximately 36 psi. Before servicing the fuel pump, fuel lines, fuel filter, or fuel injector, the fuel system pressure must be released.

## FUEL SYSTEM PRESSURE RELEASE

1. Loosen gas cap and allow tank pressure to release.
2. Remove wiring harness connector from any injector, then ground one injector terminal.
3. Connect a suitable jumper wire to a second terminal, then touch the positive post of the battery for approximately 10 seconds and release system pressure.
4. Remove jumper wires and service fuel system as required.

## THROTTLE BODY, REPLACE

1. Disconnect battery ground cable.
2. Remove air cleaner hose clamp, **Fig. 12.**
3. Disconnect vacuum hoses, then the electrical connector.
4. Remove throttle cable, then if equipped, the speed control and transaxle kickdown cables.
5. Remove throttle body attaching bolts, then lift throttle body from vehicle.
6. Reverse procedure to install.

## THROTTLE POSITION SENSOR, REPLACE

1. Disconnect battery ground cable.
2. Disconnect three way connector at throttle position sensor (TPS), then remove TPS to throttle body mounting screws.

| CAV | WIRE COLOR | DESCRIPTION | | CAV | WIRE COLOR | DESCRIPTION |
|---|---|---|---|---|---|---|
| 1 | DG/RD* | MAP SENSOR | | 37 | GY/PK* | EMISSION MAINTENANCE REMINDER LAMP |
| 2 | BK/LG | DETONATION (KNOCK) SENSOR | | 38 | LB | BAROMETRIC READ SOLENOID |
| 3 | TN/WT* | COOLANT SENSOR | | 39 | LG/BK | WASTEGATE SOLENOID |
| 4 | BK/LB* | SENSOR RETURN | | 40 | | |
| 5 | BK/WT* | SIGNAL GROUND | | 41 | RD | DIRECT BATTERY |
| 6 | | | | 42 | | |
| 7 | WT/LG* | SPEED CONTROL RESUME | | 43 | | |
| 8 | YL/RD* | SPEED CONTROL ON/OFF | | 44 | | |
| 9 | BR/RD* | SPEED CONTROL SET | | 45 | BR | A/C SWITCH SENSE |
| 10 | DG/BK* | Z1 INPUT | | 46 | | |
| 11 | | | | 47 | GY/BK* | DISTRIBUTOR REFERENCE PICKUP |
| 12 | DB/WT* | FJ2 | | 48 | WT/OR* | VEHICLE DISTANCE PICKUP |
| 13 | VT/WT* | 5 VOLT SUPPLY | | 49 | | |
| 14 | DG/OR* | ALTERNATOR FIELD CONTROL | | 50 | GY/LB* | TACHOMETER SIGNAL |
| 15 | LB/RD* | POWER GROUND | | 51 | PK | SCI TRANSMIT |
| 16 | LB/RD* | POWER GROUND | | 52 | OR | 8 VOLT INPUT |
| 17 | BR/WT* | AIS-1 | | 53 | TN/RD* | SPEED CONTROL VACUUM SOLENOID |
| 18 | YL/BK* | AIS-2 | | 54 | PK/BK* | PURGE SOLENOID |
| 19 | GY/RD* | AIS-3 | | 55 | OR/BK* | LOCK-UP TORQUE CONVERTER OR SHIFT INDICATOR LAMP (MANUAL ONLY) |
| 20 | VT/BK* | AIS-4 | | 56 | DB/OR* | A/C CLUTCH RELAY |
| 21 | | | | 57 | DB/PK* | RADIATOR FAN RELAY |
| 22 | OR/LB* | THROTTLE POSITION SENSOR | | 58 | DB/YL* | AUTO SHUT DOWN RELAY |
| 23 | BK/DG* | OXYGEN SENSOR | | 59 | BK/PK* | CHECK ENGINE LAMP |
| 24 | | | | 60 | LG/RD* | SPEED CONTROL VENT SOLENOID |
| 25 | | | | | | |
| 26 | TN/YL | FUEL SYNCHRONIZE PICKUP | | | | |
| 27 | | | | | | |
| 28 | | | | | | |
| 29 | WT/PK* | BRAKE SWITCH | | | | |
| 30 | BR/YL* | PARK/NEUTRAL SWITCH | | | | |
| 31 | LG | SCI RECEIVE | | | | |
| 32 | GY/WT* | INJECTOR CONTROL 2 | | | | |
| 33 | VT/YL* | INJECTOR CONTROL 1 | | | | |
| 34 | YL | DWELL CONTROL | | | | |
| 35 | | | | | | |
| 36 | LB/BK* | FUEL MONITOR | | | | |

| WIRE COLOR CODES | | | | | |
|---|---|---|---|---|---|
| BK | BLACK | LB | LIGHT BLUE | VT | VIOLET |
| BR | BROWN | LG | LIGHT GREEN | WT | WHITE |
| DB | DARK BLUE | OR | ORANGE | YL | YELLOW |
| DG | DARK GREEN | PK | PINK | * | WITH TRACER |
| GY | GRAY | RD | RED | | |
| | | TN | TAN | | |

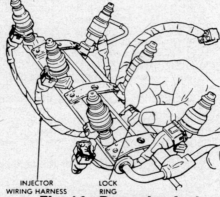

**Fig. 11   SMEC 60 way electrical connector terminal identification.**

CONNECTOR TERMINAL SIDE SHOWN

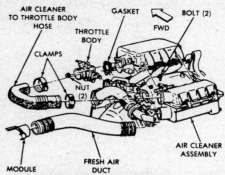

**Fig. 12   Remove throttle body**

AIR CLEANER TO THROTTLE BODY HOSE — GASKET — BOLT (2) — FWD — THROTTLE BODY — CLAMPS — NUT (2) — MODULE — FRESH AIR DUCT — AIR CLEANER ASSEMBLY

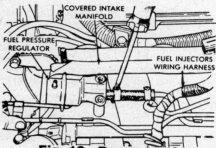

**Fig. 13   Removing fuel pressure regulator hose**

COVERED INTAKE MANIFOLD — FUEL PRESSURE REGULATOR — FUEL INJECTORS WIRING HARNESS

3. Lift TPS from throttle shaft, then remove O-ring.
4. Reverse procedure to install. Install new O-ring and torque TPS to throttle body mounting screw to 20 inch lbs.

## AUTOMATIC IDLE SPEED (AIS) MOTOR ASSEMBLY, REPLACE

1. Disconnect battery ground cable, then remove air cleaner assembly.
2. Disconnect four pin connector from AIS, then remove temperature sending unit from throttle body housing.
3. Remove two AIS to throttle body torx head retaining screws.
4. Remove AIS from throttle body housing with O-ring.
5. Reverse procedure to install. Install new O-ring and torque retaining screws to 20 inch lbs.

## MANIFOLD ABSOLUTE PRESSURE SENSOR, REPLACE

1. Remove vacuum hose from sensor.
3. Remove sensor attaching screws, then the sensor.
4. Reverse procedure to install. Ensure proper installation of vacuum hose to sensor and sensor to dash panel.

## SMEC, REPLACE

1. Remove air cleaner duct from SMEC.
2. Remove battery.
3. Remove two SMEC mounting screws.
4. Remove SMEC electrical connectors.
5. Remove SMEC.
6. Reverse procedure to install.

## OXYGEN SENSOR, REPLACE

The oxygen sensor is to be removed using tool No. C-4907 or equivalent. After removal, clean threads in exhaust manifold using an 18mm x 1.5 x 6E tap. If reinstalling the same sensor, apply a suitable

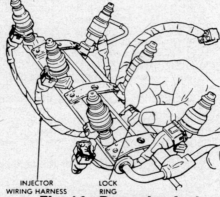

**Fig. 14   Removing fuel injector clip**

INJECTOR WIRING HARNESS — LOCK RING

anti-seize to threads of sensor. New sensors are packaged with an anti-seize compound already applied to the threads and no further application is required. When installing sensor, torque to 20 ft. lbs.

## FUEL RAIL ASSEMBLY & FUEL PRESSURE REGULATOR, REPLACE

1. Perform fuel system pressure release procedure.
2. Disconnect battery ground cable.
3. Disconnect air cleaner to throttle body hose.
4. Disconnect throttle cable and kick down linkage from throttle body.
5. Disconnect vacuum hoses and electrical connectors from throttle body.
6. Disconnect PCV and brake booster hoses from air intake plenum.
7. Remove EGR tube flange from air intake plenum.
8. Disconnect electrical connectors from charge and coolant temperature sensors.
9. Disconnect vacuum hose connections from air intake plenum.

10. Disconnect fuel hoses from fuel rail.
11. Remove eight bolts attaching air intake plenum to intake manifold, then remove air intake plenum.
12. Disconnect vacuum hoses from fuel rail and fuel pressure regulator, **Fig. 13**.
13. Disconnect fuel injector wiring harness from engine wiring harness.
14. Remove fuel pressure regulator attaching bolts, then loosen hose clamps and remove regulator.
15. Remove fuel rail attaching bolts, then carefully rail assembly from intake manifold.
16. Reverse procedure to install and note the following:
    a. Prior to installation, lubricate O-rings with clean oil.
    b. Ensure injectors are seated in receiver cup with lock ring.
    c. Ensure injectors are fully seated in ports.
    d. Torque fuel rail attaching bolts to 115 inch lbs.
    e. Torque fuel pressure regulator attaching bolts to 95 inch lbs.
    f. Prior to starting engine check all hoses and electrical connectors for proper connection.
    g. After completing installation, check system for leaks.

## FUEL INJECTOR, REPLACE

1. Remove fuel rail assembly as described under "Fuel Rail Assembly and Fuel Pressure Regulator, Replace."
2. Position fuel rail assembly so that fuel injectors are easily accessible.
3. Remove injector retaining clip, **Fig. 14**, then pull injector from fuel rail receiver cut.
4. Reverse procedure to install. Apply a drop of clean engine oil to O-rings to ease installation.

# FORD MOTOR COMPANY

## VEHICLE INFORMATION

## GENERAL SERVICE

# FORD MOTOR COMPANY

## VEHICLE INFORMATION

## GENERAL SERVICE

# FORD EXC. AEROSTAR, BRONCO II & 1983–89 RANGER

## INDEX OF SERVICE OPERATIONS

**NOTE:** Refer to the back of this manual for the manufacturer's special tool suppliers.

# SPECIFICATIONS

## GENERAL ENGINE SPECIFICATIONS

| Year | Engine Code On Truck Rating Plate | Engine Model Cid/ Liters | Fuel System | Bore & Stroke | Comp. Ratio | Horsepower @ R.P.M. | Torque Ft. Lbs. @ R.P.M. | Normal Oil Pressure Lbs. |
|---|---|---|---|---|---|---|---|---|
| 1980 | E | 6-300/4.9L | 1 Bore | 4.00 x 3.98 | 8.0 | ⑱ | ⑲ | 40-60 |
| | F | V8-302/5.0L | 2 Bore | 4.00 x 3.00 | 8.4 | ⑳ | ㉑ | 40-60 |
| | G | V8-351M/5.8L | 2 Bore | 4.00 x 3.50 | 8.0 | ㉒ | ㉓ | 50-75 |
| | W | V8-351w/5.8L | 2 Bore | 4.00 x 3.50 | 8.3 | 132 @ 3000 | 266 @ 1200 | 40-65 |
| | Z | V8-400/6.6L | 2 Bore | 4.00 x 4.00 | 8.0 | ㉔ | ㉕ | 50-75 |
| | L | V8-460/7.5L | 4 Bore | 4.36 x 3.85 | 8.0 | 212 @ 4000 | 339 @ 2400 | 40-65 |
| 1981 | E | 6-300/4.9L | 1 Bore | 4.00 x 3.98 | 8.9 | ㉖ | ㉗ | 40-60 |
| | D | V8-255/4.2L | 2 Bore | 3.68 x 3.00 | 8.2 | 118 @ 3400 | 206 @ 2000 | 40-60 |
| | F | V8-302/5.0L | 2 Bore | 4.00 x 3.00 | 8.4 | ㉘ | ㉙ | 40-60 |
| | G | V8-351/5.8L | 2 Bore | 4.00 x 3.50 | 8.3 | ㉚ | ㉛ | 40-65 |
| | Z | V8-400/6.6L | 2 Bore | 4.00 x 4.00 | 8.0 | 153 @ 3200 | 296 @ 1600 | 50-75 |
| | L | V8-460/7.5L | 4 Bore | 4.36 x 3.85 | 8.0 | 212 @ 4000 | 339 @ 2400 | 40-65 |
| 1982 | 3 | V6-232/3.8L | 2 Bore | 3.81 x 3.39 | 8.7 | 109 @ 3600 | 184 @ 1600 | 40-60 |
| | E | 6-300/4.9L | 1 Bore | 4.00 x 3.98 | 8.9 | ㉜ | ㉝ | 40-60 |
| | D | V8-255/4.2L | 2 Bore | 3.68 x 3.00 | 8.2 | 118 @ 3400 | 206 @ 2000 | 40-60 |
| | F | V8-302/5.0L | 2 Bore | 4.00 x 3.00 | 8.4 | ① | ② | 40-60 |
| | W | V8-351/5.8L | 2 Bore | 4.00 x 3.50 | 8.3 | ㉚ | ㉛ | 40-65 |
| | Z | V8-400/6.6L | 2 Bore | 4.00 x 4.00 | 8.0 | 153 @ 3200 | 296 @ 1600 | 50-75 |
| | L | V8-460/7.5L | 4 Bore | 4.36 x 3.85 | 8.0 | 212 @ 4000 | 339 @ 2400 | 40-65 |
| 1983 | 3 | V6-232/3.8L | 2 Bore | 3.81 x 3.39 | 8.7 | 109 @ 3600 | 184 @ 1600 | 40-60 |
| | Y | 6-300/4.9L | 1 Bore | 4.00 x 3.98 | 8.4 | ③ | ④ | 40-60 |
| | F | V8-302/5.0L | 2 Bore | 4.00 x 3.00 | 8.4 | 139 @ 3400 | 250 @ 2000 | 40-60 |
| | G | V8-351/5.8L | 2 Bore | 4.00 x 3.50 | 8.3 | ⑤ | ⑥ | 40-65 |
| | I | V8-420/6.9L ⑦ ⑧ | Fuel Inj. | 4.00 x 4.18 | 19.7 | 161 @ 3300 | 307 @ 1800 | 40-60 |
| | I | V8-420/6.9L ⑦ ⑨ | Fuel Inj. | 4.00 x 4.18 | 19.7 | 146 @ 3300 | 278 @ 1800 | 40-60 |
| | L | V8-460/7.5L | 4 Bore | 4.36 x 3.85 | 8.0 | 202 @ 4000 | 331 @ 2200 | 40-65 |
| 1984 | Y | 6-300/4.9L | 1 Bore | 4.00 x 3.98 | 8.4 | ⑩ | ⑪ | 40-60 |
| | F | V8-302/5.0L | 2 Bore | 4.00 x 3.00 | 8.4 | ⑫ | ⑬ | 40-60 |
| | G | V8-351/5.8L | 2 Bore | 4.00 x 3.50 | 8.3 | ⑭ | ⑮ | 40-65 |
| | G | V8-351/5.8L | 4 Bore | 4.00 x 3.50 | 8.3 | 210 @ 4000 | 305 @ 2800 | 40-65 |
| | I | V8-420/6.9L ⑦ | Fuel Inj. | 4.00 x 4.18 | 20.7 | — | — | 40-60 |
| | L | V8-460/7.5L | 4 Bore | 4.36 x 3.85 | 8.0 | ⑯ | ⑰ | 40-65 |
| 1985 | Y | 6-300/4.9L | 1 Bore | 4.00 x 3.98 | 8.4 | ⑩ | ⑪ | 40-60 |
| | F | V8-302/5.0L | 2 Bore | 4.00 x 3.00 | 8.4 | ⑫ | ⑬ | 40-60 |
| | N | V8-302/5.0L | Fuel Inj. | 4.00 x 3.00 | 8.4 | — | — | 40-60 |
| | G | V8-351/5.8L | 2 Bore | 4.00 x 3.50 | 8.3 | ⑭ | ⑮ | 40-65 |
| | H | V8-351/5.8L | 4 Bore | 4.00 x 3.50 | 8.3 | 210 @ 4000 | 305 @ 2800 | 40-65 |
| | I | V8-420/6.9L ⑦ | Fuel Inj. | 4.00 x 4.18 | 20.7 | — | — | 40-60 |
| | L | V8-460/7.5L | 4 Bore | 4.36 x 3.85 | 8.0 | ⑯ | ⑰ | 40-65 |
| 1986-87 | Y | 6-300/4.9L | 1 Bore | 4.00 x 3.98 | 8.8 | 150 @ 3400 | 260 @ 2000 | 40-60 |
| | N | V8-302/5.0L | Fuel Inj. | 4.00 x 3.00 | 9.0 | 185 @ 3800 | 270 @ 2400 | 40-60 |
| | H | V8-351/5.8L | 4 Bore | 4.00 x 3.50 | 8.3 | 190 @ 3800 | 295 @ 2600 | 40-65 |
| | I | V8-420/6.9L ⑦ | Fuel Inj. | 4.00 x 4.18 | — | — | — | 40-70 |
| | L | V8-460/7.5L | 4 Bore | 4.36 x 3.85 | 8.0 | 245 @ 4200 | 380 @ 2600 | 40-65 |
| 1988-89 | Y | 6-300/4.9L | Fuel Inj. | 4.00 x 3.98 | 8.8 | 150 @ 3400 | 260 @ 2000 | 40-60 |
| | N | V8-302/5.0L | Fuel Inj. | 4.00 x 3.00 | 9.0 | 185 @ 3800 | 270 @ 2400 | 40-60 |
| | H | V8-351/5.8L | Fuel Inj. | 4.00 x 3.50 | 8.8 | 210 @ 3800 | 315 @ 2800 | 40-65 |
| | M | V8-445/7.3L ⑦ | Fuel Inj. | 4.10 x 4.11 | 21.5 | 180 @ 3300 | 345 @ 1400 | 40-70 |
| | G | V8-460/7.5L | Fuel Inj. | 4.36 x 3.85 | 8.5 | 215 @ 3400 | 370 @ 2000 | 40-65 |

## GENERAL ENGINE SPECIFICATIONS—Continued

① —Bronco & F-100-250 exc. Calif., 132 @ 3400; E-100-250 exc. Calif., 131 @ 3600; Bronco, F-100-250 & E-100-250 Calif., 132 @ 3600.

② —Bronco & F-100-250 exc. Calif., 232 @ 1800; E-100-250 exc. Calif., 231 @ 1400; Bronco, F-100-250 & E-100-250 Calif., 239 @ 1400.

③ —Exc. F-250 over 8500 lbs, F-350 & E-350, 120 @ 3200; F-250 over 8500 lbs., F-350 & E-350, 119 @ 3200.

④ —Exc. F-250 over 8500 lbs, F-350 & E-350, 250 @ 1600; F-250 over 8500 lbs., F-350 & E-350 exc. Calif., 230 @ 2200; F-250 over 8500 lbs., F-350 & E-350 Calif., 220 @ 2200.

⑤ —Bronco & F-150-250 under 8500 lbs., 139 @ 3200; F-250 over 8500 lbs. & F-350, 147 @ 3200; E-100-150 & E-250 van, 145 @ 3200; E-250 wagon & E-350, 150 @ 3200.

⑥ —Bronco, F-150 & F-250 under 8500 lbs., 278 @ 1400; F-250 over 8500 lbs. & F-350, 276 @ 2000; E-100-150 & E-250 van, 270 @ 1400; E-250 wagon & E-350, 279 @ 2000.

⑦ —Diesel engine.

⑧ —Exc. High Alt.

⑨ —High Alt.

⑩ —120 @ 3000 or 125 @ 3200 depending on optional equipment, wheel base and/or emissions package.

⑪ —260 @ 1400, 250 @ 1600, 245 @ 1600 or 235 @ 1200 depending on optional equipment, wheel base and/or emissions package.

⑫ —145 @ 3400 or 150 @ 3600 depending on optional equipment, wheel base and/or emissions package.

⑬ —250 @ 2200, 250 @ 2600 or 255 @ 1600 depending on optional equipment, wheel base and/or emissions package.

⑭ —150 @ 3200, 160 @ 3200 or 165 @ 3200 depending on optional equipment, wheel base and/or emissions package.

⑮ —280 @ 1800, 280 @ 2000 or 295 @ 2000 depending on optional equipment, wheel base and/or emissions package.

⑯ —220 @ 4000 or 225 @ 4000 depending on optional equipment, wheel base and/or emissions package.

⑰ —360 @ 2600 or 365 @ 2800 depending on optional equipment, wheel base and/or emissions package.

⑱ —Bronco & F-100-250 exc. Calif., 119 @ 3200; E-100-250 exc. Calif., 115 @ 3200; Bronco, F-100-250 & E-150-250 Calif., 116 @ 3200; E-350 & F-350, 118 @ 3200.

⑲ —Bronco & F-150-250 exc. Calif., 243 @ 1200; E-150-250 exc. Calif., 241 @ 1200; Bronco, F-100-250 & E-150-250 Calif., 244 @ 1200; E-350 & F-350, 238 @ 1200.

⑳ —Bronco & F-100-250 exc. Calif., 137 @ 3600; E-100-250 exc. Calif., 138 @ 3600; Bronco, F-150 (4 x 4), F-250 & E-100-250, 136 @ 3600; F-100-150 (4 x 2), 133 @ 3400.

㉑ —Bronco & F-100-250 exc. Calif., 239 @ 1800; E-100-250 exc. Calif., 242 @ 1800; Bronco, F-150 (4 x 4), F-250 & E-100-250 Calif., 235 @ 1800; F-100-150 (4 x 2), 235 @ 2000.

㉒ —Bronco & F-150-250 exc. Calif., 138 @ 3400; Bronco & F-150-250 Calif., 135 @ 3200; E-250, 133 @ 3200; E-350 & F-350, 142 @ 3400.

㉓ —Bronco & F-150-250 exc. Calif., 263 @ 2000; Bronco & F-150-250 Calif., 259 @ 1600; Bronco & E-250, 133 @ 3200; E-350 & F-350, 251 @ 2400.

㉔ —F-250 (4 x 4), 136 @ 1200; E-250, 140 @ 1200; E-350 & F-350, 153 @ 3200.

㉕ —F-250 (4 x 4), 310 @ 1200; E-250, 309 @ 1200; E-350 & F-350, 296 @ 1600.

㉖ —Bronco & F-150-250 exc. Calif., 122 @ 3000; E-100-250 exc. Calif., 119 @ 3000; F-100-250, E-100-250 & F-250 under 8500 lbs. Calif., 116 @ 3200; F-250 over 8500 lbs., E-350 & F-350, 118 @ 3200.

㉗ —Bronco & F-100-250 exc. Calif., 255 @ 1400; E-100-250 exc. Calif., 253 @ 1200; F-100-250, E-100-250 & F-250 under 8500 lbs. Calif., 250 @ 1200; F-250 over 8500 lbs., E-350 & F-350, 238 @ 1200.

㉘ —Bronco & F-100-250, 133 @ 3400; E-100-250 exc. Calif., 130 @ 3400; E-100-250 Calif., 132 @ 3600.

㉙ —Bronco & F-100-250 exc. Calif., 233 @ 2000; E-150-250 exc. Calif., 230 @ 1400; Bronco, F-100-250 & E-100-250 Calif., 239 @ 1400.

㉚ —E-150-250 exc. Calif., 144 @ 3200; E-250-350, 157 @ 3400; Bronco, F-150-250 & F-250 under 8500 lbs. exc. Calif., 136 @ 3000; Bronco, F-150-250, E-150-250 & F-250 under 8500 lbs. Calif., 139 @ 3200; F-250 over 8500 lbs. & F-350, 142 @ 3400.

㉛ —E-100-250 exc. Calif., 269 @ 1200; E-250-350, 271 @ 2400; Bronco, F-150-250 & F-250 under 8500 lbs. exc. Calif., 262 @ 1600; Bronco, F-150-250, E-150-250 & F-250 under 8500 lbs. Calif., 279 @ 1400; F-250 over 8500 lbs. & F-350, 251 @ 2400.

㉜ —Bronco, F-100-250 & E-100-250 under 8500 lbs. exc. Calif., 119 @ 3000; F-100-250 under 8500 lbs. & E-100-250 Calif., 116 @ 3000; F-250 over 8500 lbs., F-350 & E-350, 117 @ 3200.

㉝ —Bronco, F-100-250 & E-100-250 under 8500 lbs. exc. Calif., 253 @ 1200; F-100-250 under 8500 lbs. & E-100-250 Calif., 250 @ 1200; F-250 over 8500 lbs. F-350 & E-350, 234 @ 1200.

## ENGINE TIGHTENING SPECIFICATIONS*

*Torque specifications are for clean and lightly lubricated threads only. Dry or dirty threads produce increased friction which prevents accurate measurement of tightness.

| Year | Engine Model | Spark Plug Ft. Lbs. | Cylinder Head Ft. Lbs. | Intake Manifold Ft. Lbs. | Exhaust Manifold Ft. Lbs. | Rocker Shaft Support Ft. Lbs. | Rocker Cover Ft. Lbs. | Conn. Rod Cap Ft. Lbs. | Main Bearing Caps Ft. Lbs. | Flywheel To Crankshaft Ft. Lbs. | Damper Or Pulley Ft. Lbs. |
|---|---|---|---|---|---|---|---|---|---|---|---|
| 1980 | 6-300 | 10-15 | ⑩ | 22-32 | 28-33 | ③ | 4-7 | 40-45 | 60-70 | 75-85 | 70-90 |
| | V8-302 | 10-15 | ⑪ | 6-25 | 18-24 | ④ | 3-5 | 19-24 | 60-70 | 75-85 | 70-90 |
| | V8-351W | 10-15 | ⑫ | 23-25 | 18-24 | ④ | 3-5 | 40-45 | 95-105 | 75-85 | 70-90 |
| | V8-351M | 10-15 | 95-105 | ⑤ | 18-24 | ⑥ | 3-5 | 40-45 | 95-105 | 75-85 | 70-90 |
| | V8-400 | 10-15 | 95-105 | ⑤ | 18-24 | ⑥ | 3-5 | 40-45 | 95-105 | 75-85 | 70-90 |
| | V8-460 | ⑦ | 130-140 | 22-32 | 28-33 | ⑥ | 5-6 | 40-45 | 95-105 | 75-85 | 70-90 |
| 1981 | V8-255 | 10-15 | 65-72 | 23-25 | 18-24 | ⑥ | 3-5 | 19-24 | 60-70 | 75-85 | 130-150 |
| | 6-300 | 10-15 | ⑩ | 22-32 | 28-33 | ③ | 4-7 | 40-45 | 60-70 | 75-85 | 70-90 |
| | V8-302 | 10-15 | ⑪ | 23-25 | 18-24 | ⑧ | 3-5 | 19-24 | 60-70 | 75-85 | 70-90 |
| | V8-351W | 10-15 | ⑫ | 23-25 | 18-24 | ⑥ | 3-5 | 40-45 | 95-105 | 75-85 | 70-90 |
| | V8-351M | 10-15 | 95-105 | ⑤ | 18-24 | ⑥ | 3-5 | 40-45 | 95-105 | 75-85 | 70-90 |
| | V8-400 | 10-15 | 95-105 | ⑤ | 18-24 | ⑥ | 3-5 | 40-45 | 95-105 | 75-85 | 70-90 |
| | V8-460 | 5-10 | 130-140 | 22-32 | 28-32 | ⑥ | 5-6 | 40-45 | 95-105 | 75-85 | 70-90 |

## ENGINE TIGHTENING SPECIFICATIONS— Continued

| Year | Engine Model | Spark Plug Ft. Lbs. | Cylinder Head Ft. Lbs. | Intake Manifold Ft. Lbs. | Exhaust Manifold Ft. Lbs. | Rocker Shaft Support Ft. Lbs. | Rocker Cover Ft. Lbs. | Conn. Rod Cap Ft. Lbs. | Main Bearing Caps Ft. Lbs. | Flywheel To Crankshaft Ft. Lbs. | Damper Or Pulley Ft. Lbs. |
|---|---|---|---|---|---|---|---|---|---|---|---|
| 1982 | V6-232 | 17-22 | 74 | 18 | 15-22 | 26 | 3-5 | 31-36 | 65-81 | 54-64 | 93-121 |
| | V8-255 | 10-15 | 65-72 | 23-25 | 18-24 | ⑥ | 3-5 | 19-24 | 60-70 | 75-85 | 70-90 |
| | 6-300 | 10-15 | ⑩ | 22-32 | 22-32 | ③ | 4-7 | 40-45 | 60-70 | 75-85 | 130-150 |
| | V8-302 | 10-15 | ⑪ | 23-25 | 18-24 | ⑥ | 3-5 | 19-24 | 60-70 | 75-85 | 70-90 |
| | V8-351W | 10-15 | ⑫ | 23-25 | 18-24 | ⑥ | 3-5 | 40-45 | 95-105 | 75-85 | 70-90 |
| | V8-351M | 10-15 | 95-105 | ⑤ | 18-24 | ⑥ | 3-5 | 40-45 | 95-105 | 75-85 | 70-90 |
| | V8-400 | 10-15 | 95-105 | ⑤ | 18-24 | ⑧ | 3-5 | 40-45 | 95-105 | 75-85 | 70-90 |
| | V8-460 | 5-10 | 130-140 | 22-32 | 28-32 | ⑧ | 5-6 | 40-45 | 95-105 | 75-85 | 70-90 |
| 1983 | V6-232 | 17-22 | 74 | 18 | 15-22 | 26 | 3-5 | 31-36 | 65-81 | 54-64 | 93-121 |
| | 6-300 | 10-15 | ⑩ | 22-32 | 22-32 | ③ | 4-7 | 40-45 | 60-70 | 75-85 | 130-150 |
| | V8-302 | 10-15 | ⑪ | 23-25 | 18-24 | ⑥ | 3-5 | 19-24 | 60-70 | 75-85 | 70-90 |
| | V8-351W | 10-15 | ⑫ | 23-25 | 18-24 | ⑥ | 3-5 | 45-50 | 95-105 | 75-85 | 70-90 |
| | V8-420⑧ | 12⑨ | 80 | 24 | 30 | ④ | 6 | 46-51 | 95 | 47 | 90 |
| | V8-460 | 5-10 | 130-140 | 22-32 | 28-32 | ⑧ | 5-6 | 40-45 | 95-105 | 75-85 | 70-90 |
| 1984 | 6-300 | 10-15 | ⑩ | 22-32 | 22-32 | ③ | 4-7 | 40-45 | 60-70 | 75-85 | 130-150 |
| | V8-302 | 10-15 | ⑪ | 23-25 | 18-24 | ⑥ | 3-5 | 19-24 | 60-70 | 75-85 | 70-90 |
| | V8-351W | 10-15 | ⑫ | 23-25 | 18-24 | ⑥ | 3-5 | 40-45 | 95-105 | 75-85 | 70-90 |
| | V8-420⑧ | 12⑨ | 80 | 24 | 30 | — | 6 | 46-51 | 95 | 47 | 90 |
| | V8-460 | 5-10 | 130-140 | 22-32 | 28-33 | ⑧ | 5-6 | 45-50 | 95-105 | 75-85 | 70-90 |
| 1985-87 | 6-300 | 10-15 | ⑩ | 22-32 | 22-32 | ③ | 70-105② | 40-45 | 60-70 | 75-85 | 130-150 |
| | V8-302 | 10-15 | ⑪ | 23-25 | 18-24 | ⑥ | 3-5 | 19-24 | 60-70 | 75-85 | 70-90 |
| | V8-351W | 10-15 | ⑫ | 23-25 | 18-24 | ⑥ | 3-5 | 40-45 | 95-105 | 75-85 | 70-90 |
| | V8-420⑧ | 12⑨ | 80 | 24 | ① | — | 6 | 48.5-53.5 | 95 | 47 | 90 |
| | V8-460 | 5-10 | 130-140 | 22-32 | 28-33 | ⑧ | 5-6 | 45-50 | 95-105 | 75-85 | 70-90 |
| 1988-89 | 6-300 | 10-15 | ⑩ | 22-32 | 22-32 | ③ | 70-105② | 40-45 | 60-70 | 75-85 | 130-150 |
| | V8-302 | 10-15 | ⑪ | 23-25 | 18-24 | ⑥ | 3-5 | 19-24 | 60-70 | 75-85 | 70-90 |
| | V8-351W | 10-15 | ⑫ | 23-25 | 18-24 | ⑥ | 3-5 | 40-45 | 95-105 | 75-85 | 70-90 |
| | V8-445⑧ | 12⑨ | ⑬ | 24 | ① | — | 6 | 51 | 95 | 47 | 90 |
| | V8-460 | 5-10 | ⑭ | ⑮ | 22-30 | ⑥ | 6-9⑯ | 45-50 | 95-105 | 75-85 | 70-90 |

①—1985, 30 ft. lbs.; 1986-89, 35 ft. lbs.
②—Inch lbs.
③—Rocker arm stud nut torque, 17-23 ft. lbs. Refer to "Valves, Adjust" procedure.
④—Rocker arm to cylinder head bolts, 20 ft. lbs.
⑤—⅜ inch bolts, 22-32 ft. lbs.; 5/16 inch bolts, 19-25 ft. lbs.
⑥—Rocker arm-to-cylinder head bolts, 18-25 ft. lbs.
⑦—5-10 ft. lbs.
⑧—Diesel engine.
⑨—Glow plug.
⑩—Progressively tighten cylinder head bolts in sequence in three steps; first, torque all bolts to 50-55 ft. lbs.,

second, torque all bolts to 60-65 ft. lbs., finally torque all bolts to 70-85 ft. lbs.
⑪—Progressively tighten all cylinder head bolts in sequence in two steps; first, torque all bolts to 55-65 ft. lbs., second, torque all bolts to 65-72 ft. lbs.
⑫—Progressively tighten cylinder head bolts in sequence in three steps; first, torque all bolts to 85 ft. lbs., second, torque all bolts to 95 ft. lbs., finally torque all bolts to 105-112 ft. lbs.
⑬—Progressively tighten cylinder head bolts in sequence in three steps; first, torque all bolts to 65 ft. lbs.,

second, torque all bolts to 90 ft. lbs., finally torque all bolts to 100 ft. lbs.
⑭—Progressively tighten cylinder head bolts in sequence in three steps; first, torque all bolts to 70-80 ft. lbs., second, torque all bolts to 100-110 ft. lbs., finally torque all bolts to 130-140 ft. lbs.
⑮—Progressively tighten intake manifold bolts in sequence in three steps; first, torque all bolts to 8-12 ft. lbs., second, torque all bolts to 12-22 ft. lbs., finally torque all bolts to 22-35 ft. lbs.
⑯On 1989 models, torque to 9-10 ft. lbs. Torque left bank bolts rear to front, then right bank bolts front to rear.

## STARTING MOTOR SPECIFICATIONS

| Year | Starter Type | Ampere Draw Normal Load | Engine Cranking Speed R.P.M. | Minimum Stall Torque @ 5 Volts Ft. Lbs. | Maximum Head Amperes | No Load Ampere @ 12 Volts | Brushes | | |
|---|---|---|---|---|---|---|---|---|---|
| | | | | | | | Length Inch | Wear Limit Inch | Spring Tension Ounces |
| 1980-89 | Ford 4" Diameter | 150-200 | 180-250 | — | — | 70 | .50 | .25 | 40 |
| | Ford 4½" Diameter | 150-180 | 150-290 | — | — | 80 | .50 | .25 | ① |
| 1983-88 | Delco Positive Engagement | 430-530 | 170-230 | — | — | 11-200 | .75 | .24 | 50 |

①—1980-83, 80 ounces; 1984-89, 40 ounces.

# FORD EXC. AEROSTAR, BRONCO II & 1983-89 RANGER
## ALTERNATOR & REGULATOR SPECIFICATIONS

| Year | Make Or Model | Current Rating | | Field Current @ 75°F | | Voltage Regulator | |
|------|---------------|----------------|-------|----------------------|-------|-------------------|----------------|
| | | Amperes | Volts | Amperes | Volts | Part No. | Voltage @ 75°F |
| 1980 | Orange ① ② | 40 | 15 | 4.00 | 12 | D9PF-AA | — |
| | Green ① ② | 60 | 15 | 4.00 | 12 | D9PF-AA | — |
| | All ③ | 70 | 15 | 4.00 | 12 | D9PF-AA | — |
| | All ③ | 100 | 15 | 4.00 | 12 | D9PF-AA | — |
| 1981-82 | Orange ① ② | 40 | 15 | 4.00 | 12 | ④ | — |
| | Green ① ② | 60 | 15 | 4.00 | 12 | ④ | — |
| | Black ① ③ | 70 | 15 | 4.00 | 12 | ④ | — |
| | Red ① ③ | 100 | 15 | 4.00 | 12 | ④ | — |
| 1983 | Orange ① ② | 40 | 15 | 4.25 | 12 | E2PF-AA | — |
| | Green ① ② | 60 | 15 | 4.25 | 12 | E2PF-AA | — |
| | Green ① ② | 65 | 15 | 4.25 | 12 | E2PF-AA | — |
| | Black ① ③ | 70 | 15 | 4.00 | 12 | E2PF-AA | — |
| | Red ① ③ | 100 | 15 | 4.00 | 12 | E2PF-AA | — |
| 1984-85 | Orange ① ② | 40 | 15 | 4.25 | 12 | — | — |
| | Green ① ② | 60 | 15 | 4.25 | 12 | — | — |
| | Black ① ③ | 70 | 15 | 4.25 | 12 | — | — |
| | Red ① ③ | 100 | 15 | 4.25 | 12 | — | — |
| 1986-88 | Orange ① ② | 40 | 15 | 4.25 | 12 | — | — |
| | Green ① ② | 60 | 15 | 4.25 | 12 | — | — |
| | Black ① ③ | 70 | 15 | 4.25 | 12 | — | — |
| | Red ① ③ | 100 | 15 | 4.25 | 12 | — | — |
| | Motorcraft ⑤ | 40 | 15 | — | — | — | — |
| | Motorcraft ⑤ | 60 | 15 | — | — | — | — |
| | Motorcraft ⑤ | 65 | 15 | — | — | — | — |
| 1989 | Ford ⑤ | 40 | 15 | — | — | — | — |
| | Ford ⑤ | 60 | 15 | — | — | — | — |
| | Ford ⑤ | 65 | 15 | — | — | — | — |
| | Ford ⑤ | 75 | 15 | — | — | — | — |

①—Stamp color code.
②—Rear terminal alternator.
③—Side terminal alternator.
④—1981, D9PF-AA; 1982, E2PF-AA.
⑤—With integral regulator.

## DRIVE AXLE SPECIFICATIONS

| Year | Make & Ring Gear Diameter | Carrier Type | Ring Gear & Pinion Backlash | | Pinion Bearing Preload | | | | Differential Bearing Preload | |
|------|---------------------------|--------------|-----------------------------|------------|------------------------|----------------------------|-----------------------------|------------------------|-------------------------|------------------------|
| | | | Method | Adjustment | Method | New Bearings Inch-Lbs. | Used Bearings Inch-Lbs. | New Bearings Inch | Used Bearings Inch |
| 1980-82 | Ford 9" | Removable | Threaded Adjuster | ④ | Collapsible Spacer | ⑤ | 8-14 | .008-.012 | .005-.008 |
| | Dana ① | Integral | Shims | .004-.009 | Shims | 1-40 | — | .015 | .015 |
| | Dana ② | Integral | Shims | .005-.009 | Shims | 20-40 | — | ⑥ | ⑥ |
| 1983-85 | Ford 8.8" | Integral | Shims | .008-.015 | Collapsible Spacer | 16-29 | 8-14 | — | — |
| | Ford 9" | Removable | Threaded Adjuster | .008-.015 | Collapsible Spacer | 16-29 | 8-14 | .008-.012 | .005-.007 |
| | Dana ① | Integral | Shims | .004-.009 | Shims | 20-40 | — | .015 | .015 |
| | Dana ② | Integral | Shims | .005-.009 | Shims | 20-40 | — | .010 | .010 |
| 1985 | Ford 10.25" | Integral | Shims | .0008-.0015 | Collapsible Spacer | 16-29 | 8-14 | ③ | ③ |
| 1986-88 | Ford 8.8" | Integral | Shims | .008-.015 | Collapsible Spacer | 16-29 | 8-14 | .006 | — |
| | Ford 9" | Removable | Threaded Adjuster | .008-.015 | Collapsible Spacer | 16-29 | 8-14 | .008-.012 | .005-.008 |
| | Ford 10.25" | Integral | Shims | .008-.015 | Collapsible Spacer | 16-29 | 8-14 | ③ | ③ |
| | Dana ① | Integral | Shims | .005-.009 | Shims | 20-40 | — | .015 | .015 |
| | Dana ② | Integral | Shims | .005-.009 | Shims | 20-40 | — | .015 | .015 |

## DRIVE AXLE SPECIFICATIONS—Continued

| Year | Make & Ring Gear Diameter | Carrier Type | Ring Gear & Pinion Backlash | | Pinion Bearing Preload | | | Differential Bearing Preload | |
|---|---|---|---|---|---|---|---|---|---|
| | | | Method | Adjustment | Method | New Bearings Inch-Lbs. | Used Bearings Inch-Lbs. | New Bearings Inch | Used Bearings Inch |
| 1989 | Ford 8.8" | Integral | Shims | .008-.015 | Collapsible Spacer | 16-29 | 8-14 | .006 | — |
| | Ford 10.25" | Integral | Shims | .008-.015 | Collapsible Spacer | 16-29 | 8-14 | .006 | .006 |
| | Dana① | Integral | Shims | .005-.009 | Shims | 20-40 | — | .015⑦ | .015⑦ |
| | Dana② | Integral | Shims | .005-.009 | Shims | 20-40 | — | .015 | .015 |

①—Rear drive axle.
②—Front drive axle.
③—Slip fit plus .004 inch clearance on each side.
④—1980-81, .008-.012 inch; 1982, .008-.015 inch.
⑤—1980, 17-27 inch lbs.; 1981-82, 16-29 inch lbs.
⑥—1980-81, .006 inch; 1982, .010 inch.
⑦—Models 70-80, .010 inch.

## BRAKE SPECIFICATIONS

| Year | Model | Rear Drum I.D. | Wheel Cyl. Bore | | Disc Brake Rotor | | | | | Master Cyl. I.D. |
|---|---|---|---|---|---|---|---|---|---|---|
| | | | Front Disc | Rear Drum | Nominal Thickness | Minimum Thickness | Thickness Variation (Parallelism) | Run Out (TIR) | Finish (Microinch) | |
| 1980 | E-100-150 | 11.031 | 2.875 | .9375 | 1.185 | 1.120 | .0007 | .003 | 15-80 | — |
| | E-250-350 | 12.000 | — | ⑬ | 1.250 | 1.180 | .0007 | ② | 15-80 | — |
| | F-100-150 | 11.031 | ⑦ | .9375 | ⑧ | ⑨ | ⑩ | .003 | 15-80 | — |
| | F-250④ | 12.000 | 2.875 | .9375 | 1.185 | 1.120 | .0007 | .003 | 15-80 | — |
| | F-250⑤ | 12.000 | — | ⑭ | 1.250 | 1.180 | ⑩ | .003 | 15-80 | — |
| | F-350 | 12.000 | — | 1.0620 | 1.250 | 1.180 | .0007 | .003 | 15-80 | — |
| | Bronco | 11.031 | 2.875 | .9375 | 1.185 | 1.120 | .0005 | .003 | 15-80 | — |
| 1981-83 | E-100-150 | 11.031 | 2.875 | .9375 | 1.185 | 1.120 | .0007 | .003 | 15-80 | ⑮ |
| | E-250-350 | 12.000 | 2.180 | ⑬ | 1.250 | 1.180 | ① | ② | 15-80 | 1.062 |
| | F-100-150 | ⑫ | ⑦ | .9375 | ⑧ | ⑨ | ① | ⑪ | 15-80 | 1.000 |
| | F-250④ | 12.000 | 2.875 | .9375 | 1.185 | 1.120 | .0007 | .003 | 15-80 | 1.000 |
| | F-250⑤ | 12.000 | 2.180 | ⑭ | 1.250 | 1.180 | ① | ⑪ | 15-80 | 1.062 |
| | F-350 | 12.000 | 2.180 | 1.0620 | 1.250 | 1.180 | ① | ② | 15-80 | 1.062 |
| | Bronco | 11.031 | 2.875 | .9375 | 1.185 | 1.120 | ① | ⑪ | 15-80 | 1.000 |
| 1984 | E-150 | 12.000 | 2.875 | — | 1.185 | 1.120 | .0007 | .003 | 15-80 | — |
| | E-250-350 | 12.000 | — | — | 1.250 | 1.180 | ① | ② | 15-80 | — |
| | F-150 | 11.031 | 2.875 | — | 1.185 | 1.120 | ① | ⑪ | 15-80 | — |
| | F-250④ | 12.000 | 2.875 | — | 1.185 | 1.120 | .0007 | .003 | 15-80 | — |
| | F-250⑤ | 12.000 | — | — | 1.250 | 1.180 | ① | ⑪ | 15-80 | — |
| | F-350 | 12.000 | — | — | 1.250 | 1.180 | ① | ② | 15-80 | — |
| | Bronco | 12.000 | 2.875 | — | 1.185 | 1.120 | ① | ⑪ | 15-80 | — |
| 1985-89 | E-150 | 11.031 | — | — | 1.190 | 1.120 | .0007 | .003 | 15-80 | — |
| | E-250-350 | 12.000 | — | — | 1.250 | 1.180 | ① | ③ | 15-80 | — |
| | F-150 | 11.031 | — | — | 1.190 | 1.120 | ① | ⑪ | 15-80 | — |
| | F-250④ | 12.000 | — | — | 1.190 | 1.120 | .0007 | .003 | 15-80 | — |
| | F-250⑤ | 12.000 | — | — | 1.250 | 1.180 | ① | ⑪ | 15-80 | — |
| | F-350 | 12.000 | — | — | 1.250 | 1.180 | ① | ③ | 15-80 | — |
| | Bronco | 11.031 | — | — | 1.190 | 1.120 | ① | ⑪ | 15-80 | — |

①—Integral hub & rotor, .0007 inch; separate hub & rotor, .0010 inch.
②—Integral hub & rotor, .0030 inch; separate hub & rotor, .0010 inch.
③—Integral hub & rotor, .003 inch; 4 x 4 vehicles w/separate hub & rotor, .005 inch; E-350 & dual rear wheel F-350 w/separate hub & rotor, .010 inch.
④—4 x 2 models under 6900 lbs. GVW.
⑤—4 x 2 models over 6900 lbs. GVW & all 4 x 4 models.
⑥—Integral hub & rotor, .003 inch; 4 x 4 vehicles w/separate hub & rotor, .005 inch; E-350 & dual rear wheel F-350 w/separate hub & rotor, .010 inch.
⑦—Exc. F-100 under 4700 lbs. GVW with power brakes, 2.875 inches; F-100 under 4700 lbs. GVW with power brakes, 2.597 inches.
⑧—Exc. F-100 under 4700 lbs. GVW with power brakes, 1.185 inches; F-100 under 4700 lbs. GVW with power brakes, .980 inch.
⑨—Exc. F-100 under 4700 lbs. GVW with power brakes, 1.120 inch; F-100 under 4700 lbs. GVW with power brakes, .810 inch.
⑩—4 x 2 models, .007 inch; 4 x 4 models, .0050 inch.
⑪—Integral hub & rotor, .003 inch; separate hub & rotor, .005 inch.
⑫—Exc. F-100 under 4700 lbs. GVW with power brakes, 11.031 inches; F-100 under 4700 lbs. GVW with power brakes, 10 inches.
⑬—E-250, .9375 inch; E-350, 1.062 inch.
⑭—Under 8500 lbs. GVW, .9375 inch; over 8500 lbs. GVW, 1.062 inch.
⑮—Exc. E-100 with manual brakes, 1.062 inches; E-100 with manual brakes, 1.000 inch.

## WHEEL ALIGNMENT SPECIFICATIONS

**NOTE:** For wheel alignment specifications, refer to "Front Suspension & Steering Section" of this chapter.

## COOLING SYSTEM & CAPACITY DATA

| Year | Model & Engine | Cooling Capacity, Qts. Less A/C | Cooling Capacity, Qts. With A/C | Radiator Cap Relief Pressure, Lbs. | Thermo. Opening Temp. | Fuel Tank Gals. [1] | Engine Oil Refill Qts. [2] | Transmission Oil 3 Speed Pts. | Transmission Oil 4 Speed Pts. | Transmission Oil Auto. Trans. Qts. [3] | Transfer Case Oil Pints | Rear Axle Oil Pints |
|---|---|---|---|---|---|---|---|---|---|---|---|---|
| 1980 | Bronco 6-300 | (28) | 14.0 | 13 | — | 25.0 | 5 | — | 7.0 | 13.4 | 6.5 | 6.5 |
| | E-100-350 6-300 | (29) | 20.0 | 13 | — | (4) | 5 | 3.5 | 4.5 | 11.9 | — | (28) |
| | F-100-350 6-300 | (28) | 14.0 | 13 | — | (30) | 5 | 3.5 | (22) | (31) | 6.5 | (32) |
| | Bronco V8-302 | (33) | 14.0 | 13 | — | 25.0 | 5 | — | 7.0 | 13.4 | 6.5 | 6.5 |
| | E-100-150 V8-302 | (34) | (35) | 13 | — | (4) | 5 | 3.5 | 4.5 | 11.9 | — | 6.5 |
| | F-100-350 V8-302 | (28) | 14.0 | 13 | — | (30) | 5 | 3.5 | (22) | (31) | 6.5 | (32) |
| | Bronco V8-351 | (19) | 16.0 | 13 | — | 25.0 | 5 | — | 7.0 | 13.4 | 6.5 | 6.5 |
| | E-100-350 V8-351 | (36) | 21.0 | 13 | — | (4) | 5 | 3.5 | 4.5 | 11.9 | — | (28) |
| | F-100-350 V8-351 | (19) | 16.0 | 13 | — | (30) | 5 | 3.5 | (22) | 13.2 | 6.5 | (32) |
| | E-250-350 V8-400 | (37) | 21.0 | 13 | — | (4) | 5 | 3.5 | 4.5 | 11.9 | — | (28) |
| | F-100-350 V8-400 | (38) | 16.0 | 13 | — | (30) | 5 | 3.5 | (22) | 13.4 | 6.5 | (32) |
| | E-350 V8-460 | 28.0 | 28.0 | 13 | — | (4) | 5 | 3.5 | 4.5 | 11.9 | — | (28) |
| 1981 | F-100 V8-255 | (33) | 14.0 | 13 | — | (30) | 5 | 3.5 | (22) | (40) | — | (32) |
| | Bronco 6-300 | (28) | 14.0 | 13 | — | 25.0 | 5 | — | (22) | 13.4 | 7.0 | 6.5 |
| | E-100-350 6-300 | (29) | 20.0 | 13 | — | (4) | 5 | 3.5 | 4.5 | 11.9 | — | (28) |
| | F-100-350 6-300 | (28) | 14.0 | 13 | — | (30) | 5 | 3.5 | (22) | (40) (41) | (42) | (32) |
| | Bronco V8-302 | (33) | 14.0 | 13 | — | 25.0 | 5 | — | (22) | 13.4 | 7.0 | 6.5 |
| | E-100-250 V8-302 | (34) | (35) | 13 | — | (4) | 5 | 3.5 | 4.5 | 11.9 | — | (26) |
| | F-100-350 V8-302 | (33) | 14.0 | 13 | — | (30) | 5 | 3.5 | (22) | (40) (41) | (42) | (32) |
| | Bronco V8-351 | (19) | 16.0 | 13 | — | 25.0 | 5 | — | (22) | 13.4 | 7.0 | 6.5 |
| | E-100-350 V8-351 | (36) | 21.0 | 13 | — | (4) | 5 | 3.5 | 4.5 | 11.9 | — | (28) |
| | F-100-350 V8-351 | (19) | 16.0 | 13 | — | (30) | 5 | 3.5 | (22) | (40) (41) | (42) | (32) |
| | E-250-350 V8-400 | (37) | 21.0 | 13 | — | (4) | 5 | 3.5 | 4.5 | 11.9 | — | (24) |
| | F-250-350 V8-400 | (38) | 16.0 | 13 | — | (30) | 5 | 3.5 | (22) | (40) (41) | (42) | (32) |
| | E-350 V8-460 | 28.0 | 28.0 | 13 | — | (4) | 5 | 3.5 | 4.5 | 11.9 | — | (28) |
| 1982 | F-100 V6-232 | (9) | 11.0 | 13 | — | (30) | 5 | 3.5 | (22) | (25) | — | 6.5 |
| | F-100 V8-255 | (33) | 14.0 | 13 | — | (30) | 5 | 3.5 | (22) | (25) | — | 6.5 |
| | Bronco 6-300 | (28) | 14.0 | 13 | — | 25.0 | 5 | — | (22) | 13.4 | 7.0 | 6.5 |
| | E-100-350 6-300 | (29) | 20.0 | 13 | — | (4) | 5 | 3.5 | (22) | 11.9 | — | (24) |
| | F-100-350 6-300 | (28) | 14.0 | 13 | — | 25.0 | 5 | 3.5 | (22) | (25) | (42) | (23) |
| | Bronco V8-302 | (33) | 14.0 | 13 | — | (30) | 5 | — | (22) | 13.4 | 7.0 | 6.5 |
| | E-100-250 V8-302 | (34) | (35) | 13 | — | (4) | 5 | 3.5 | 4.5 | 11.9 | — | (24) |
| | F-100-350 V8-302 | (33) | 14.0 | 13 | — | (30) | 5 | 3.5 | (22) | (25) | (42) | (23) |
| | Bronco V8-351 | (19) | 16.0 | 13 | — | 25.0 | 5 | — | (22) | 13.4 | 7.0 | 6.5 |
| | E-100-350 V8-351 | (36) | 21.0 | 13 | — | (4) | 5 | 3.5 | 4.5 | 11.9 | — | (24) |
| | F-100-350 V8-351 | (19) | 16.0 | 13 | — | (30) | 5 | 3.5 | (22) | (25) | (42) | (24) |
| | E-250-350 V8-400 | (37) | 21.0 | 13 | — | (4) | 5 | 3.5 | 4.5 | 11.9 | — | (24) |
| | F-250-350 V8-400 | (38) | 16.0 | 13 | — | (30) | 5 | 3.5 | (22) | (25) | 6.5 | (23) |
| | E-350 V8-460 | 28.0 | 28.0 | 13 | — | (4) | 5 | 3.5 | 4.5 | 11.9 | — | (24) |
| 1983 | F-100 V6-232 | (20) | 12.0 | 13 | — | 16.5 | 5 | 3.5 | (22) | 11 | — | 5.5 |
| | Bronco 6-300 | (28) | 14.0 | 13 | — | 25.0 | 5 | — | (22) | 13.5 | 7.0 | 5.5 |
| | E-100-350 6-300 | 15.0 | 20.0 | 13 | — | (4) | 5 | 3.5 | 4.5 | 11.8 | — | (18) |
| | F-100-350 6-300 | (28) | 14.0 | 13 | — | (30) | 5 | 3.5 | (22) | 11.8 | (42) | (17) |
| | Bronco V8-302 | (33) | 14.0 | 13 | — | 25.0 | 5 | — | (22) | 13.5 | 7.0 | 5.5 |
| | E-100-350 V8-302 | (16) | (27) | 13 | — | (4) | 5 | 3.5 | 4.5 | 11.8 | — | (18) |
| | F-100-250 V8-302 | (33) | 14.0 | 13 | — | (30) | 5 | 3.5 | (22) | 11.8 (41) | (42) | (17) |

| Year | Model & Engine | Cooling Capacity, Qts. Less A/C | Cooling Capacity, Qts. With A/C | Radiator Cap Relief Pressure, Lbs. | Thermo. Opening Temp. | Fuel Tank Gals. (1) | Engine Oil Refill Qts. (2) | Transmission Oil 3 Speed Pts. | 4 Speed Pts. | Auto. Trans. Qts. (3) | Transfer Case Oil Pints | Rear Axle Oil Pints |
|---|---|---|---|---|---|---|---|---|---|---|---|---|
| | Bronco V8-351 | (19) | 16.0 | 13 | — | 25.0 | 5 | — | (22) | 13.5 | 7.0 | 5.5 |
| | E-100-350 V8-351 | (14) | (13) | 13 | — | (4) | 5 | 3.5 | 4.5 | 11.8 | — | (18) |
| | F-100-350 V8-351 | (19) | 16.0 | 13 | — | (30) | 5 | 3.5 | (22) | 11.8(41) | (42) | (17) |
| | F-250-350 V8-420 (21) | 31.0 | 31.0 | 13 | — | (30) | 9 | 3.5 | (22) | 11.8(41) | 6.5 | (17) |
| | E-250-350 V8-460 | 28.0 | 28.0 | 13 | — | (4) | 5 | 3.5 | 4.5 | 11.8 | — | (18) |
| | F-250-350 V8-460 | (12) | 17.5 | 13 | — | (30) | 5 | 3.5 | (22) | 13.5 | 6.5 | (17) |
| 1984 | Bronco 6-300 | (28) | 14.0 | 13 | — | 32.0 | 5 | — | (22) | 13.5 | 7.0 | 5.5 |
| | E-150-350 6-300 | 15.0 | 17.5 | 13 | — | (4) | 5 | 3.5 | 4.5 | 11.8 | — | (18) |
| | F-150-350 6-300 | (28) | 14.0 | 13 | — | (30) | 5 | 3.5 | (22) | (11) | (42) | (17) |
| | Bronco V8-302 | (33) | 14.0 | 13 | — | 32.0 | 5 | — | (22) | 13.5 | 7.0 | 5.5 |
| | E-150-350 V8-302 | (34) | (10) | 13 | — | (4) | 5 | 3.5 | 4.5 | (39) | — | (18) |
| | F-150-250 V8-302 | (33) | 14.0 | 13 | — | (30) | 5 | 3.5 | (22) | (15) | (42) | (17) |
| | Bronco V8-351 | (19) | 16.0 | 13 | — | 32.0 | 5 | — | (22) | 13.5 | 7.0 | 5.5 |
| | E-150-350 V8-351 | (14) | (13) | 13 | — | (4) | 5 | 3.5 | 4.5 | 11.8 | — | (18) |
| | F-150-350 V8-351 | (19) | 16.0 | 13 | — | (30) | 5 | 3.5 | (22) | 11.8(41) | (42) | (17) |
| | E-250-350 V8-420 (21) | 31.0 | 31.0 | 13 | — | (4) | 9 | 3.5 | 4.5 | 11.8 | — | (17) |
| | F-250-350 V8-420 (21) | 31.0 | 31.0 | 13 | — | (30) | 9 | 3.5 | (22) | 11.8(41) | (42) | (17) |
| | E-250-350 V8-460 | 28.0 | 28.0 | 13 | — | (4) | 5 | 3.5 | 4.5 | 11.8 | — | (18) |
| | F-250-350 V8-460 | (12) | 17.5 | 13 | — | (30) | 5 | 3.5 | 22 | 11.8(41) | (42) | (17) |
| 1985-87 | Bronco 6-300 | (5) | (5) | 13 | — | 32.0 | 5 | — | (6) | 13.5 | 9.0 | 5.5 |
| | E-150-350 6-300 | 15.0 | 17.5 | 13 | — | (4) | 5 | 3.5 | (6) | (39) | — | (8) |
| | F-100 & F-350 6-300 | (5) | (5) | 13 | — | (30) | 5 | 3.5 | (6) | (15) | (7) | (8) |
| | Bronco V8-302 | (33) | 14.0 | 13 | — | 32.0 | 5 | — | (6) | 13.5 | 9.0 | 5.5 |
| | E-150-350 V8-302 | (34) | (10) | 13 | — | (4) | 5 | 3.5 | (6) | (39) | — | (8) |
| | F-150 & F-250 V8-302 | (33) | 14.0 | 13 | — | (30) | 5 | 3.5 | (6) | (15) | (7) | (8) |
| | Bronco V8-351 | (19) | 15.0 | 13 | — | 32.0 | 5 | — | (6) | 13.5 | 9.0 | 5.5 |
| | E-150-350 V8-351 | (14) | (13) | 13 | — | (4) | 5 | 3.5 | (6) | (39) | — | (8) |
| | F-150 & F-350 V8-351 | (19) | 15.0 | 13 | — | (30) | 5 | 3.5 | (6) | 11.8(41) | (7) | (8) |
| | E & F-250-350 V8-420 (21) | 31.0 | 31.0 | 13 | — | (4) | 9 | 3.5 | (6) | (39) | (7) | (8) |
| | Bronco V8-460 | 16.0 | 16.0 | 13 | — | 32.0 | 5 | — | (6) | 13.5 | 9.0 | 5.5 |
| | E-250 & E-350 V8-460 | 28.0 | 28.0 | 13 | — | (4) | 5 | 3.5 | (6) | (39) | — | (8) |
| | F-150 & F-350 V8-460 | 16.0 | 16.0 | 13 | — | (30) | 5 | 3.5 | (6) | 11.8(41) | (7) | (8) |
| | F-250 & F-350 V8-460 | (12) | 17.5 | 13 | — | (30) | 5 | 3.5 | (6) | 11.8(41) | (7) | (8) |
| 1988-89 | Bronco 6-300 | (5) | (5) | 13 | — | 32.0 | 5 | — | (6) | 13.5 | 9.0 | 5.5 |
| | E-150-350 6-300 | 15 | 18 | 13 | — | (4) | 5 | — | (6) | (39) | — | (8) |
| | F-100 & F-350 6-300 | (5) | (5) | 13 | — | (30) | 5 | — | (6) | (15) | (7) | (8) |
| | Bronco V8-302 | (33) | (33) | 13 | — | 32.0 | 5 | — | (6) | 13.5 | 9.0 | 5.5 |
| | E-150-350 V8-302 | (34) | (10) | 13 | — | (4) | 5 | — | (6) | (39) | — | (8) |
| | F-150 & F-250 V8-302 | (33) | (33) | 13 | — | (30) | 5 | — | (6) | (15) | (7) | (8) |
| | Bronco V8-351 | (19) | (19) | 13 | — | 32.0 | 5 | — | (6) | 13.5 | 9.0 | 5.5 |
| | E-150-350 V8-351 | 20 | 21 | 13 | — | (4) | 5 | — | (6) | (39) | — | (8) |
| | F-150 & F-350 V8-351 | (19) | (19) | 13 | — | (30) | 5 | — | (6) | 11.8(41) | (7) | (8) |
| | E-250-350 V8-445 (21) | 31.0 | 31.0 | 13 | — | (4) | 9 | — | (6) | (39) | (7) | (8) |
| | F-250-350 V8-445 (21) | 29.0 | 29.0 | 13 | — | (4) | 9 | — | (6) | (39) | (7) | (8) |
| | E-250 & E-350 V8-460 | 28.0 | 28.0 | 13 | — | (4) | 5 | — | (6) | (39) | — | (8) |
| | F-250 & F-350 V8-460 | 18 | 18 | 13 | — | (30) | 5 | — | (6) | 11.8(41) | (7) | (8) |

## COOLING SYSTEM & CAPACITY DATA—Continued

①—Standard fuel tank.

②—Add 1 qt. with filter change.

③—Approximate. Make final check with dipstick.

④—E-100-150 with 124" wheelbase, 18 gals.; E-150-350 with 138" wheelbase, 22 gals. Auxiliary tank 16 gals.

⑤—Manual trans. less A/C, 13 qts., with A/C 14 qts., with A/C & super cooling, 15 qts. Auto. trans. less A/C, 13 qts., with super cooling, 14 qts, with A/C or super cooling, 15 qts.

⑥—Ford overdrive trans & 5 speed trans., 4.5 pts.; New Process model 435 less extension, Warner model T-18 less extension & Warner model T-19, 6.5 pts.; New Process model 435 w/extension & Warner model T-18 w/extension, 7.0 pts.

⑦—Borg Warner model 1345, 6.5 pts.; New Process Gear 208, 9 pts.

⑧—Dana model 60-3 6.25 pts.; Dana model 61-1, 5.8 pts.; Dana model 70, 6.6 pts.; Dana model 70 HD, 7.4 pts.; Ford w/8.8 or 9 inch ring gear, 5.5 pts.; Ford w/10.25 inch ring gear, 7.5 pts.

⑨—Exc. models with super cooling, 10 qts.; models with super cooling, 11 qts.

⑩—Man. trans., 17.5 qts.; auto trans., 18.5 qts.

⑪—C5 units, 11 qts.; C6 units, 11.8 qts.; 4 x 4 models, 13.5 qts.

⑫—Exc. models with man. trans. & heavy duty cooling, 17.5 qts.; models with man. trans. & heavy duty cooling, 16.5 qts.

⑬—Man. trans., 15 qts.; auto. trans., 21 qts.

⑭—Exc. models with super cooling, 20 qts.; models with super cooling, 21 qts.

⑮—C5 units, 11 qts.; C6 units, 11.8 qts.; automatic overdrive units, 12 qts.; 4 x 4 models, 13.5 qts.

⑯—Models with man. trans. less super cooling, 17.5 qts.; models with super cooling, 18.5 qts.

⑰—F-100-350, 5.5 pts.; F-250 exc. Ford standard axle, 6 pts.; F-250 with Ford standard axle, 5.5 pts.; F-350 with Dana model 70 axle, 6.5 pts.; F-350 with Dana model 70 HD axle, 7.4 pts.; other F-350 models, 6 pts.

⑱—E-150-350, 5.5 pts.; E-250 exc. Ford standard axle, 6 pts.; E-250 with Ford standard axle, 5.5 pts.; E-350 exc. Dana model 70 axle, 6 pts.; E-350 with Dana model 70 axle, 6.5 pts.

⑲—Manual trans. less A/C, 15 qts.; with A/C, 16 qts.; with A/C & super cooling, 17 qts. Auto. trans. less A/C, 16 qts.; with A/C & super cooling, 17 qts.

⑳—Exc. models with super cooling, 11 qts.; models with super cooling, 12 qts.

㉑—Diesel engine.

㉒—New Process model 435 with extension & Warner model T-18(-B), 7 pts.; New Process model 435 less extension, 6.5 pts.; 4 speed overdrive units, 4.5 pts.

㉓—F-100-150, 6.5 pts.; F-250 exc. Dana model 60 axle, 6 pts.; F-250 with Dana model 60 axle, 5 pts.; F-350 with Dana model 70 axle, 6.5 pts.; F-350 with Dana model 70 HD axle, 7.4 pts.; F-350 with Dana model 61-1 axle, 6 pts.

㉔—Exc. models with dual rear wheels, 6 pts.; models with dual rear wheels, 6.5 pts.

㉕—C4 units, 9.6 qts.; C5 units, 11 qts.; C6 units, 11.9 qts.; automatic overdrive units, 12 qts.; 4 x 4 models, 14.4 qts.

㉖—E-100-150 with Ford standard or Traction-Loc axle, 6.5 pts.; E-250 with Dana model 60-2, 61-1 or 61-2 axle, 6 pts.; other models, 7 pts.

㉗—Man. trans., 15 qts.; auto. trans., 17.5 qts.

㉘—Exc. models with super cooling, 13 qts. models with super cooling, 14 qts.

㉙—Exc. models with super cooling, 15 qts.; models with super cooling, 20 qts.

㉚—Aft/Axle tank, 19 gals.; midship tank 16.5 gals exc. F-100-150 short wheelbase, 19 gals.

㉛—C4 units, 10 qts.; C6 units, 13.4 qts.

㉜—F-100-150, 6.5 pts.; F-250 exc. 4 x 2 with Dana model 61-2 axle, 5 pts.; F-250 with Dana model 61-2 axle, 6 pts.; F-350 exc. Dana 61-1 axle & 1981 F-350 with Dana 70 HD axle, 6.5 pts.; F-350 with Dana 61-1 axle & 1981 F-350 with Dana 70 HD axle, 6 pts.

㉝—Models with man. trans. less A/C, 13 quarts; auto. trans. less A/C & all models with A/C, 14 quarts; models with super cool, 15 quarts.

㉞—Models with man. trans. less super cooling, 15 qts.; models with auto. trans. less super cooling, 17.5 qts.; models with super cooling, 18.5 qts.

㉟—Exc. models with super cooling, 17.5 qts.; models with super cooling, 18.5 qts.

㊱—E-100-150 exc. super cooling & E-250-350 with standard cooling, 20 qts.; E-100-150 with super cooling & E-250-350 with heavy duty cooling, 21 qts.; E-250-350 with super cooling, 28 qts.

㊲—Models with standard cooling, 20 qts.; models with heavy duty cooling, 21 qts.; models with super cooling, 28 qts.

㊳—Models with man. trans. less super cooling, 15 qts.; models with auto. trans. and/or super cooling, 16 qts.

㊴—C6 units, 11.8 qts.; automatic overdrive units, 12 qts.

㊵—C4 units, 9.6 qts.; C6 units, 11.9 qts.; automatic overdrive units, 12 qts.

㊶—4 x 4 models, 13.4 qts.

㊷—Borg Warner model 1345, 6.5 pts.; New Process model 208, 7 pts.

# ELECTRICAL

## INDEX

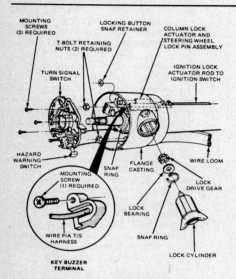

**Fig. 1   Ignition lock replacement. Fixed steering column**

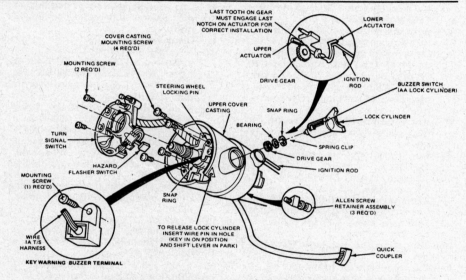

**Fig. 2   Ignition lock replacement. Tilt steering column**

## FUSE PANEL & FLASHER LOCATION

The fuse panel is located under the LH side of the instrument panel. On some vehicles, an access panel may have to be removed to facilitate service.

The hazard warning flasher on Bronco and F series vehicles is located on the back side of the fuse panel. On E series vehicles it is located under the LH side of the instrument panel. The turn signal flasher on Bronco and F series vehicles is located on the front of the fuse panel. On 1980-85 E series vehicles it is located on the lower LH side of the steering column, and on 1986-89 E series vehicles it is located under the LH side of the instrument panel.

## STARTER REPLACE

1. Disconnect battery ground cable.

2. Raise and support vehicle, if necessary.
3. Disconnect starter cable from starter motor.
4. Remove starter motor attaching bolts and the starter motor.
5. Reverse procedure to install.

## IGNITION LOCK REPLACE

1. Disconnect battery ground cable.
2. Remove steering wheel trim pad and steering wheel.
3. Shift transmission into Park on vehicles with automatic transmission, or into any gear on vehicles with manual transmission.
4. Insert a 1/8 inch diameter wire or small drift punch into retaining pin access slot and remove lock cylinder, **Figs. 1 and 2**, while depressing pin. **The lock cylinder retaining pin is located adjacent to the hazard warning button on models with tilt steering col-**

umn and inside the column near base of cylinder on models with fixed steering column.
5. To install, turn lock cylinder to On position and depress pin.
6. Install lock cylinder into housing. Turn ignition key to Off position after ensuring cylinder is fully seated and aligned into interlocking washer.
7. Turn the key to check for proper operation in all positions.
8. Install steering wheel and trim pad and reconnect battery ground cable.

## IGNITION SWITCH REPLACE

1. Disconnect battery ground cable.
2. Remove steering column shroud and lower the steering column.
3. Disconnect electrical connector from switch, then remove 2 switch attaching nuts.
4. Lift switch up to disengage actuator rod, then remove switch from vehicle,

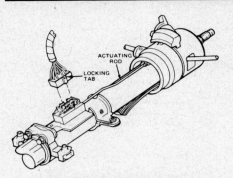

**Fig. 3   Ignition switch replacement**

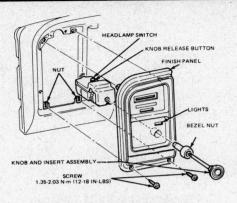

**Fig. 4   Light switch replacement. E-100–350**

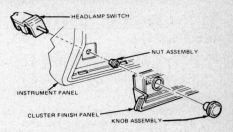

**Fig. 5   Light switch replacement. F-100–350 & Bronco**

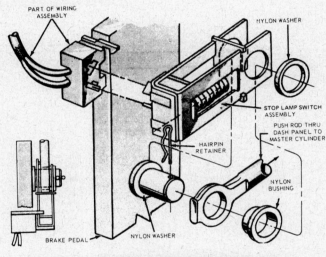

**Fig. 6   Stop light switch replacement. 1980–83 E-100 w/manual brakes.**

**Fig. 3.**
5. Reverse procedure to install.

## LIGHT SWITCH
## REPLACE
### E-100–350

1. Disconnect battery ground cable.
2. Remove knob and shaft assembly by depressing release button on switch housing and pulling straight out.
3. Remove bezel or mounting nut from switch, **Fig. 4.**
4. Disconnect electrical connector from switch and remove switch from vehicle.
5. Reverse procedure to install.

### F-100–350 & BRONCO

1. Disconnect battery ground cable.
2. Remove knobs from headlight switch, windshield wiper switch and fog light switch (if equipped). Use a suitable hook tool to release each knob lock tab.

3. Remove steering column shroud, then the cluster finish panel assembly, **Fig. 5.**
4. Remove switch attaching nut, **Fig. 5.**
5. Disconnect electrical connector from switch and remove switch from vehicle.
6. Reverse procedure to install.

## STOP LIGHT SWITCH
## REPLACE

1. Disconnect battery ground cable.
2. Disconnect electrical connector from switch, **Figs. 6 and 7.**
3. Remove hairpin retainer, then slide stop light switch, pushrod, nylon washers and bushings away from pedal and remove the switch from vehicle.
4. Reverse procedure to install. **Ensure stop light switch wires are of sufficient length to allow full travel of the brake pedal.**

## NEUTRAL SAFETY SWITCH
## REPLACE
### EXC. AUTOMATIC OVERDRIVE TRANSMISSION

1. Disconnect battery ground cable.
2. Remove downshift linkage rod return spring from low-reverse servo cover.
3. Apply penetrating oil to outer lever attaching nut, then remove transmission downshift outer lever attaching nut and lever.
4. Remove neutral safety switch attaching bolts, then disconnect electrical connectors and remove switch from vehicle.
5. To install, position switch on transmission and secure with attaching bolts. Do not tighten bolts at this time.
6. Place transmission manual lever in neutral position, then insert a .091 inch gauge pin through gauge pin holes, **Fig. 8.**
7. Tighten switch attaching bolts, then remove gauge pin.
8. Install outer downshift lever and retaining nut.
9. Install downshift linkage rod return spring between lever and retaining clip on low-reverse servo cover.
10. Reconnect electrical connectors, then check operation of switch.

### W/AUTOMATIC OVERDRIVE TRANSMISSION

1. Disconnect battery ground cable.
2. Raise and support vehicle.
3. Disconnect electrical connector at neutral safety switch, lifting connector straight up.
4. Using suitable socket, remove neutral safety switch and O-ring seal.
5. Reverse procedure to install, installing new O-ring seal.

## TURN SIGNAL SWITCH
### REPLACE

#### F-100–350 & BRONCO

1. Disconnect battery ground cable.
2. Remove horn switch, then the steering wheel.
3. Remove turn signal switch lever by unscrewing from steering column.
4. On 1981-87 models, remove lower steering column shroud. On 1989 models, remove upper and lower shrouds.
5. On all models, disconnect electrical connector from turn signal switch and remove switch attaching screws.
6. On all models with tilt column and 1980 F-100-350 and Bronco with fixed column, remove wires and terminals from steering column electrical connector, after noting color code and location of each connector. Remove plastic cover sleeve, if equipped, from wiring harness, then lift switch assembly out through opening in shift socket.
7. On all models with fixed column, except 1980 F-100-350 and Bronco, remove switch assembly by lifting out of column while guiding connector plug through opening in shift socket.
8. Reverse procedure to install.

#### E-100–350

1. Disconnect battery ground cable.
2. Remove horn switch, then the steering wheel from shaft.
3. Remove turn signal switch lever by unscrewing from steering column.
4. On 1981-88 models, remove upper and lower steering column shrouds. On 1989 models, remove steering column shrouds and instrument panel steering column opening cover.
5. On all models, disconnect electrical connector from turn signal switch and remove switch attaching screws.
6. On all models with tilt column and 1980 models with fixed column, remove wires and terminals from steering column electrical connector, after noting color code and location of each connector. Remove plastic cover sleeve, if equipped, from wiring harness, then lift switch assembly out through top of column. **On 1981-89 models equipped with tilt column and automatic transmission, disconnect transmission selector indicator light electrical connector from turn signal switch harness prior to removing the switch.**
7. On all models with fixed column, except 1980 E-100-350, remove switch assembly by lifting out of column while guiding connector plug through openings in brake and clutch support bracket and the shift socket. **On 1981-89 E-100-350 models equipped with fixed column and automatic transmission, remove transmission selector indicator light assembly with turn signal switch.**
8. Reverse procedure to install.

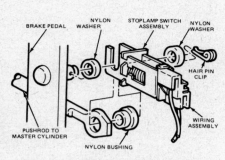

**Fig. 7 Stop light switch replacement. All models Exc. 1980–83 E-100**

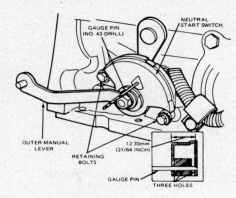

**Fig. 8 Neutral safety switch replacement. Exc. automatic overdrive transmission**

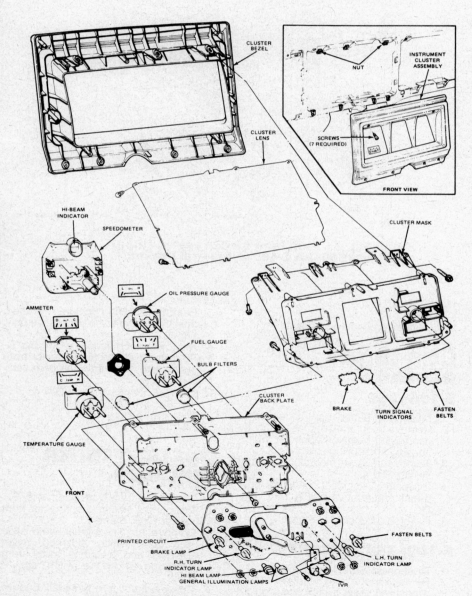

**Fig. 9 Instrument cluster replacement. E-100–350**

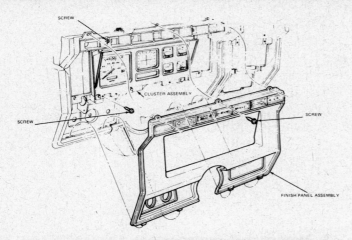

**Fig. 10 Instrument cluster replacement. F-100–350 & Bronco**

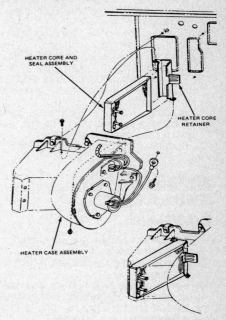

**Fig. 11 Heater core replacement. 1981–87 E-100–350 less air conditioning**

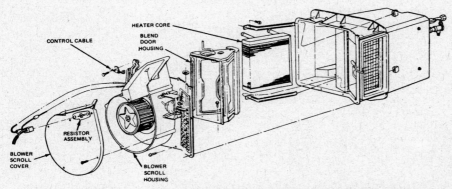

**Fig. 12 Heater core replacement. 1981–87 E-100–350 w/air conditioning**

## INSTRUMENT CLUSTER REPLACE

### E-100–350

1. Disconnect battery ground cable.
2. Remove steering column shroud.
3. On models equipped with tilt steering column, loosen column-to-band C support to provide sufficient clearance for cluster removal.
4. On all models, remove instrument cluster-to-instrument panel attaching screws.
5. Pull cluster back from panel and disconnect speedometer cable. **It may be necessary to disconnect speedometer cable from transmission to provide access to the quick disconnect on the cluster.**
6. Disconnect electrical connector from printed circuit board and remove cluster from vehicle, **Fig. 9.**
7. Reverse procedure to install.

### F-100–350 & BRONCO

1. Disconnect battery ground cable.

2. Remove wiper/washer knob, and on equipped 1980 models, the fuel gauge switch knob. Use a suitable hook tool to release each knob lock tab.
3. Remove light switch knob, windshield wiper switch knob and fog light switch knob, if equipped.
4. Remove steering column shroud, using care not to damage transmission selector indicator cables on models equipped with automatic transmission.
5. On models equipped with automatic transmission, release shift lever indicator cable retaining clip(s), then remove cable loop from retainer pin. Remove cable bracket attaching screw and slide bracket out of slot in tube.
6. On all models, remove cluster finish panel and the cluster attaching screws, **Fig. 10.**
7. Pull cluster back from panel and disconnect speedometer cable, printed circuit electrical connector and 4 x 4 indicator light electrical connector, if equipped.
8. Remove cluster from vehicle, **Fig. 10.**
9. Reverse procedure to install.

## WIPER MOTOR REPLACE

### E-100–350

1. Disconnect battery ground cable.
2. Remove fuse panel and bracket assembly.
3. Disconnect wiper motor electrical connectors from motor brush cap and gearbox cover.
4. Remove both wiper arm and blade assemblies.
5. Remove outer air inlet cowl, then the motor drive arm-to-linkage mounting arm and pivot shaft assembly retaining clip.
6. Remove wiper motor attaching bolts and the wiper motor.
7. Reverse procedure to install.

### F-100–350 & BRONCO

1. Disconnect battery ground cable.
2. Remove both wiper arm and blade assemblies.
3. Remove cowl grille attaching screws and raise the grille slightly.
4. Disconnect washer nozzle hose, then remove cowl grille assembly.
5. Remove wiper linkage clip from motor output arm.
6. Disconnect wiper motor electrical connector.
7. Remove wiper motor attaching screws and the wiper motor.
8. Reverse procedure to install.

## WIPER TRANSMISSION REPLACE

1. Disconnect battery ground cable.

2. Remove both wiper arm and blade assemblies.
3. Remove cowl grille attaching screws and raise the grille slightly.
4. Disconnect windshield washer fluid hose, then remove cowl grille.
5. Remove clip securing right and left linkage and the retaining clip from wiper motor arm.
6. Remove 3 pivot body-to-cowl panel attaching screws, then the arm and pivot shaft assembly.
7. Reverse procedure to install.

## WIPER SWITCH
### REPLACE
### E-100–350

1. Disconnect battery ground cable.
2. Remove wiper switch knob.
3. Remove ignition switch bezel from finish panel.
4. Remove light switch knob and shaft assembly by depressing release button on switch housing and pulling straight out.
5. Remove 2 lower attaching screws from finish panel, then pry the 2 upper retainers away from instrument panel.
6. Disconnect wiper switch electrical connector, then remove switch attaching screws and the switch from vehicle.
7. Reverse procedure to install.

### F-100–350 & BRONCO

1. Disconnect battery ground cable.
2. Remove wiper switch knob, bezel nut and bezel.
3. Pull switch down from under instrument panel, then disconnect electrical connector and remove switch from vehicle.
4. Reverse procedure to install.

## RADIO
### REPLACE
### E-100–350

1. Disconnect battery ground cable.
2. Remove heater and air conditioner control knobs if equipped.
3. Remove cigarette lighter, if equipped.
4. Remove radio knobs and discs from control shafts.
5. On models equipped with cigarette lighter, snap out name plate from right side of panel and remove the one accessible finish panel attaching bolt.
6. On all models, remove five finish panel attaching bolts and the finish panel.
7. Pry out cluster panel at two locations using a screwdriver.
8. Remove 4 radio-to-instrument panel attaching screws and slide radio out of panel.
9. Disconnect power, speaker and antenna leads from radio and remove radio from vehicle.
10. Remove radio mounting plate and the radio rear support nut and washer.

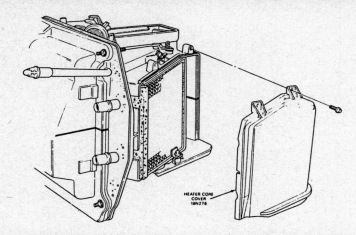

**Fig. 13   Heater core replacement. 1988–89 E-100–350**

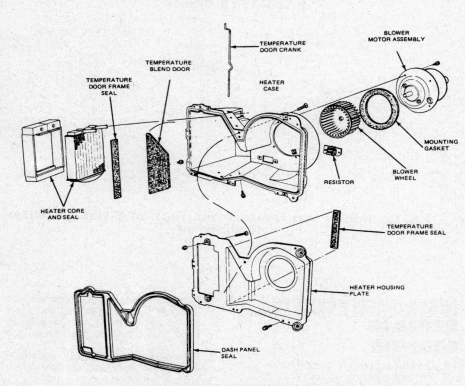

**Fig. 14   Heater core replacement. 1981–87 F-100–350 & Bronco less air conditioning**

11. Reverse procedure to install.

### F-100–350 & BRONCO

1. Disconnect battery ground cable.
2. On 1982-86 models, remove radio knobs and discs from control shafts.
3. On 1982-86 models, remove cluster bezel attaching screws or nuts and the cluster bezel. On 1987-89 models, remove bezel and retaining clips.
4. On all models, remove radio mounting plate-to-instrument panel attaching screws and slide radio out of panel.
5. Disconnect power, speaker and antenna leads from radio.
6. On 1982-86 models, remove radio rear support attaching bolt from lower edge of instrument panel.
7. On 1982-86 models, remove nuts and washers from control shafts, then remove radio front mounting plate.
8. On all models, remove radio from vehicle.
9. Reverse procedure to install.

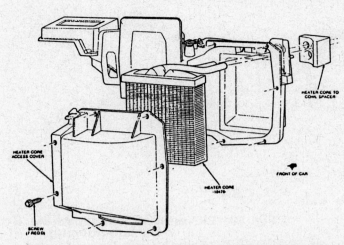

**Fig. 15   Heater core replacement. 1988-89 F-100-350 & Bronco less air conditioning**

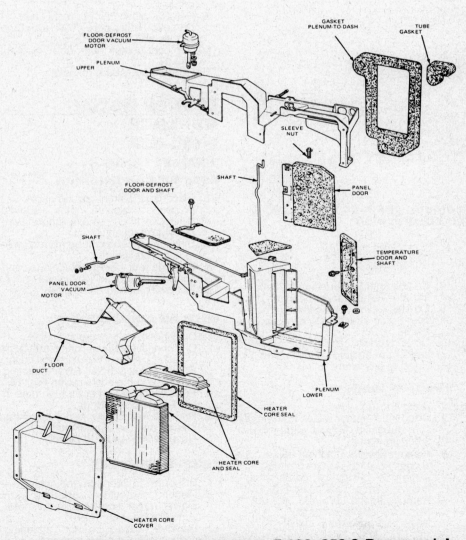

**Fig. 16   Heater core replacement. F-100-350 & Bronco w/air conditioning**

## HEATER CORE
### REPLACE
### E-100-350
### 1981-87 MODELS
#### Less Air Conditioning

1. Remove battery from vehicle. **On models equipped with diesel engine, remove righthand battery.**
2. Drain cooling system.
3. Disconnect resistor electrical connector, then the blower motor lead wire from wiring harness.
4. Remove ground wire attaching screw from dash.
5. Disconnect hoses from heater core, then remove plastic wrap securing hoses to heater assembly.
6. Remove five heater assembly attaching screws from passenger compartment, then lift heater assembly from vehicle.
7. Remove seal and retainer from front of heater core case, then slide core and seal from case, **Fig. 11.**
8. Reverse procedure to install.

#### With Air Conditioning

1. Disconnect battery ground cable.
2. Disconnect electrical connector from resistor on front of air conditioner blower scroll cover.
3. Disconnect vacuum hose from outside recirculated door vacuum motor.
4. Remove air conditioner blower cover attaching screws and the cover.
5. Remove outside-recirculated door shaft push nut and washer.
6. Remove control cable attaching screw and slide cable over bracket.
7. Remove cable clip or wire loop from blend door shaft.
8. Remove nine air conditioner blower motor housing attaching screws and the housing.
9. Remove three blend door housing attaching screws and the housing.
10. Drain cooling system, then disconnect hoses from heater core.
11. Remove two heater core retaining bracket attaching screws and the bracket.
12. Remove heater core and seal assembly, **Fig. 12.**
13. Reverse procedure to install.

#### 1988-89 MODELS

1. Drain cooling system.
2. Disconnect and plug inlet and outlet hoses from heater core.
3. Remove screws retaining panel to underside of instrument panel, then the panel.
4. Remove heater core cover attaching screws, **Fig. 13,** and the heater core cover.
5. Remove screw and retaining bracket from bottom of heater core, then slide core and seal from case.
6. Reverse procedure to install.

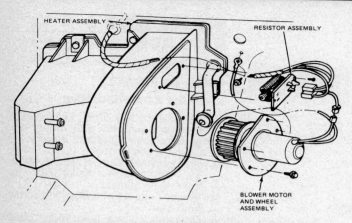

**Fig. 17  Blower motor replacement. E-100–350 less air conditioning**

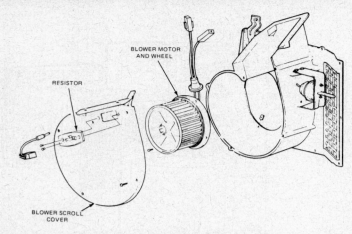

**Fig. 18  Blower motor replacement. E-100–350 w/air conditioning**

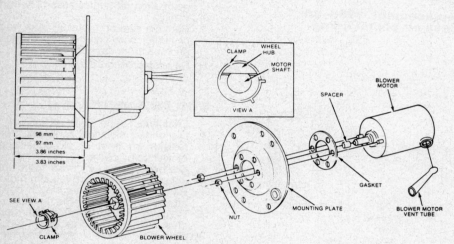

**Fig. 19  Blower motor replacement. 1980–81 F-100–350 & Bronco less air conditioning**

## F-100–350 & BRONCO

### LESS AIR CONDITIONING

#### 1980–87 Models

1. Disconnect battery ground cable.
2. Disconnect cable from temperature blend door and the mounting bracket from top of heater assembly.
3. Disconnect blower motor and resistor electrical connectors.
4. Disconnect and plug hoses from heater core.
5. Working under instrument panel, remove 2 nuts on 1980-81 models, or 3 nuts on 1982-87 models, attaching left side of heater assembly and right side of plenum to dash.
6. On 1980-81 models, remove screw attaching top center of heater assembly to dash.
7. On all models, remove 2 screws attaching right side of heater assembly to dash, then lift heater assembly out of vehicle.

8. Remove heater housing plate attaching screws, nut and bolt and the plate.
9. On 1980-82 models, remove 3 heater core frame attaching screws and the frame.
10. On all models, slide heater core and seal out of heater assembly, **Fig. 14.**
11. Reverse procedure to install.

### 1988–89 Models

1. Drain cooling system.
2. Disconnect heater hoses from heater core tubes in engine compartment and plug hoses.
3. Remove screws attaching heater core access cover to plenum chamber assembly in passenger compartment, then remove access cover **Fig. 15.**
4. Remove heater core and seal out of plenum chamber assembly.
5. Reverse procedure to install.

### WITH AIR CONDITIONING

1. Disconnect battery ground cable.

2. Disconnect and plug hoses from heater core.
3. Remove glove compartment liner.
4. Remove heater core cover attaching screws and the cover.
5. Remove heater core from plenum, **Fig. 16.**
6. Reverse procedure to install.

## BLOWER MOTOR
### REPLACE
### E-100–350
### 1980–87 MODELS
#### Less Air Conditioning

1. Disconnect battery ground cable.
2. Disconnect blower motor electrical connector, then remove ground wire screw from dash.
3. Disconnect cooling tube from blower motor, if equipped.
4. Remove four blower motor attaching screws and the blower motor, **Fig. 17.**
5. Reverse procedure to install.

#### With Air Conditioning

1. Disconnect battery ground cable.
2. Disconnect electrical connectors from resistor on front of blower scroll cover.
3. Remove blower scroll cover attaching screws and the scroll cover, **Fig. 18.**
4. Push wiring grommet through hole in blower motor housing.
5. Remove four blower motor attaching screws and the blower motor.
6. Reverse procedure to install.

#### 1988–89 MODELS

1. Disconnect battery ground cable.
2. Disconnect electrical connector from blower motor and housing to motor cooling tube.
3. Remove blower motor attaching screws, then the blower motor and wheel assembly.
4. Reverse procedure to install.

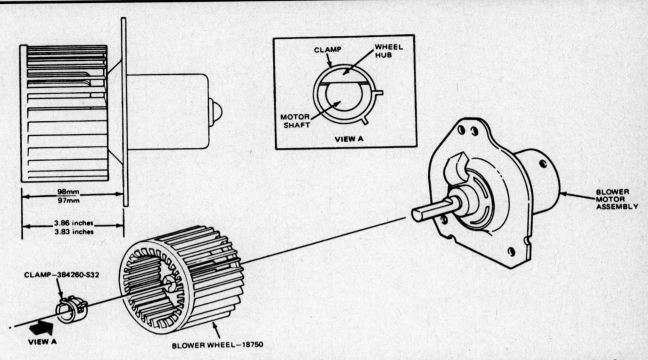

**Fig. 20   Blower motor replacement. 1982–89 F-100–350 & Bronco less air conditioning**

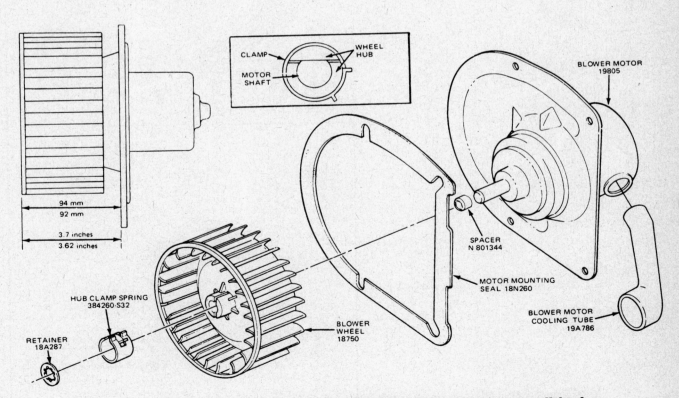

**Fig. 21   Blower motor replacement. F-100–350 & Bronco w/air conditioning**

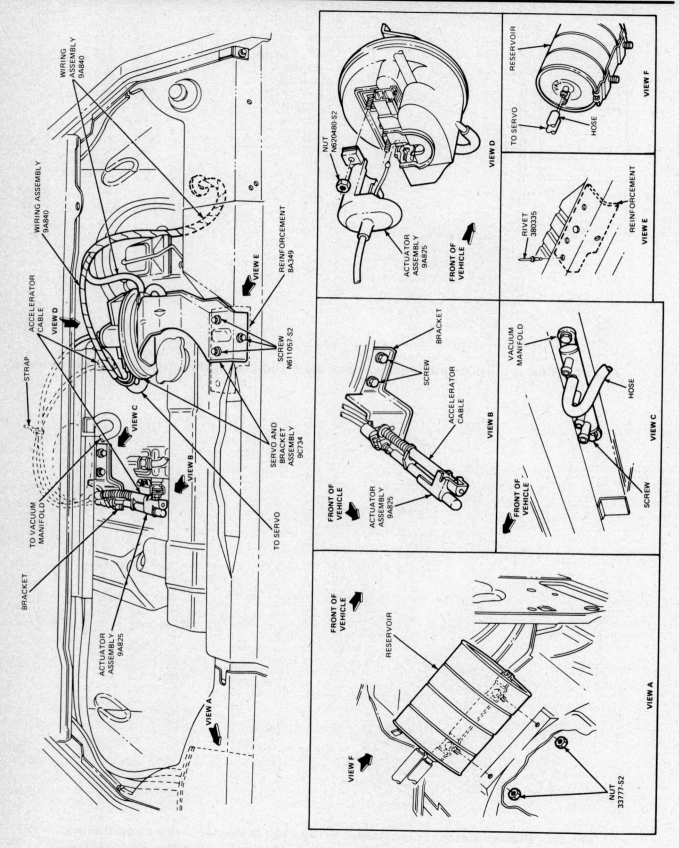

**Fig. 22  Actuator cable adjustment. 1984–89 E-250–350 w/diesel engine**

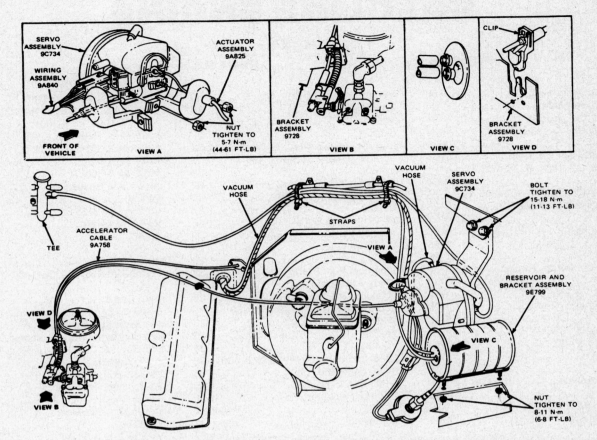

**Fig. 23   Actuator cable adjustment. 1984–89 F-250–350 w/diesel engine**

## F-100–350 & BRONCO

1. Disconnect battery ground cable.
2. Disconnect blower motor electrical connector. On 1980-81 models less air conditioning, remove ground wire screw. On 1989 models, remove electrical connector from blower motor resistor.
3. On 1989 models, remove nut (located in passenger compartment to the right of heater core access cover) from bottom of plenum assembly. Remove bolt from heater blower assembly in engine compartment.
4. On models equipped with air conditioning, disconnect air cooling tube from blower motor.
5. On all models, remove blower motor attaching screws and the blower motor, **Figs. 19, 20 and 21.**
6. Reverse procedure to install.

## SPEED CONTROL ADJUSTMENTS
### BEAD CHAIN, ADJUST

1. Adjust bead chain to obtain 1/16-1/4 inch (1980-81) or 1/16-1/8 inch (1982-87) actuator arm free travel with engine at hot idle. Make this adjustment to remove as much slack as possible from the bead chain without preventing carburetor from returning to idle. **On models equipped with a solenoid anti-diesel valve, this adjustment must be performed with ignition switch in the Off position.**
2. Cut off chain in excess of 4 beads.

## VACUUM DUMP VALVE, ADJUST
### 1981–87 All

1. Slide vacuum dump valve forward in retaining clip. With valve plunger contacting brake pedal adapter and pedal in released position until 1/8 inch or less of white plunger is exposed.
2. Ensure brake pedal contacts stop in released position after making adjustment.

## ACTUATOR CABLE, ADJUST
### 1984–87 Models w/Diesel Engine And 1988–89 models w/EFI Gas Engines

1. Snap speed control actuator cable retainer over accelerator cable end fitting attached to throttle ball stud, **Figs. 22 and 23.**
2. Remove adjuster retainer clip, if equipped, from adjuster mounting tab.
3. Insert actuator cable adjuster mounting tab in accelerator cable support bracket slot.
4. Pull cable through adjuster until a slight tension is felt without opening throttle plate or increasing idle RPM.
5. Install adjuster retainer clip slowly until it engages, then push downward until locked in position.

# GASOLINE ENGINE

## INDEX

# ENGINE MOUNTS
## REPLACE
### V6-232

1. Remove fan shroud attaching bolts and position shroud over fan.
2. Raise and support vehicle.
3. Remove insulator-to-chassis bracket attaching nut and washer, **Fig. 1.**
4. Raise engine slightly, then remove 3 insulator-to-cylinder block attaching bolts and the insulator, **Fig. 1.**
5. Reverse procedure to install. Torque insulator-to-cylinder block attaching bolts to 60-80 ft. lbs. and insulator-to-chassis bracket nut to 50-70 ft. lbs.

### 6-300
#### E-100—350

1. Raise and support vehicle.
2. Remove front insulator-to-support bracket attaching nuts and washers from both insulators, **Figs. 2 and 3.**
3. Raise engine slightly using a block of wood placed under oil pan and a suitable jack.
4. Remove support bracket attaching bolts and the brackets, if necessary.

5. Remove insulator attaching bolts and the insulator.
6. Reverse procedure to install.

### Bronco & F-100—350

1. Remove insulator-to-support bracket attaching nut and washer. **If only one insulator is being removed, loosen the opposite insulator at support bracket.**
2. Raise engine slightly using a block of wood placed under oil pan and a suitable jack.
3. Remove insulator attaching bolts and the insulator, **Figs. 4 and 5.**
4. Reverse procedure to install.

### V8-255, 302 & 351W
#### E-100—350

1. Remove fan shroud attaching bolts and the insulator-to-support nuts.
2. Raise engine assembly and remove starter motor.
3. Remove insulator attaching bolts, then the alternator splash shield and insulator, **Fig. 6.**
4. Reverse procedure to install.

#### F-100—350 & Bronco

1. Remove fan shroud attaching bolts

and position shroud over fan.
2. Remove insulator-to-chassis bracket attaching nut and washer.
3. Raise engine slightly, then remove insulator attaching bolts and the insulator, **Fig. 7.** When removing lefthand insulator, the heat shield must also be removed.
4. Reverse procedure to install.

### V8-351M & 400
#### 1980—82 F-100—350 & Bronco

1. Remove fan shroud attaching bolts and position shroud over fan.
2. Remove insulator-to-chassis bracket attaching nut and washer, **Fig. 8.**
3. Raise engine slightly, then remove insulator attaching bolts and the insulator.
4. Reverse procedure to install.

#### 1980—82 E-100—350

1. Remove fan shroud attaching bolts and the insulator-to-support nuts.
2. Raise engine slightly and remove starter motor. **When raised, the engine and transmission assembly will pivot around the rear engine mount. The engine assembly must**

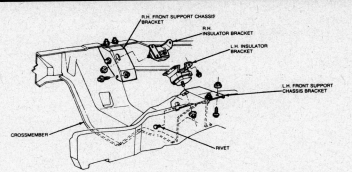

Fig. 1   Engine mounts. V6-232 engine

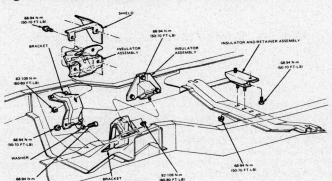

Fig. 2   Engine mounts. 1980 E-100—350 w/6-300 engine

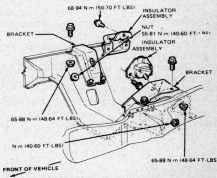

Fig. 3   Engine mounts. 1981—89 E-100—350 w/6-300 engine

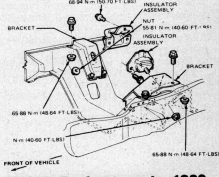

Fig. 4   Engine mounts. 1980 F-100—350 & Bronco w/6-300 engine

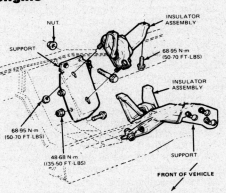

Fig. 5   Engine mounts. 1981—89 F-100—350 & Bronco w/6-300 engine

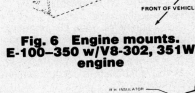

Fig. 6   Engine mounts. E-100—350 w/V8-302, 351W engine

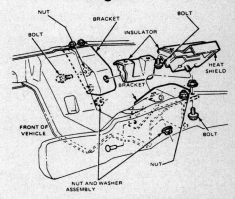

Fig. 7   Engine mounts. F-100—350 & Bronco w/V8-255, 302, 351W engine

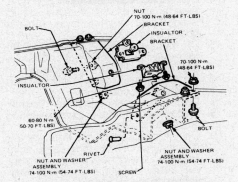

Fig. 8   Engine mounts. 1980—82 F-100—350 & Bronco w/V8-351M, 400 engine

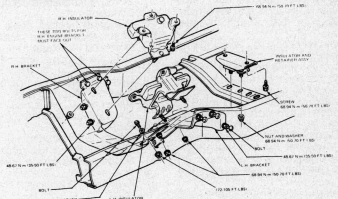

Fig. 9   Engine mounts. 1980—82 E-100—350 w/V8-351M, 400 engine

be lifted exactly two inches, measured from front mounts, and remain centered in the engine compartment. If the engine is lifted more than two inches, the A/C main and auxiliary lines will be damaged.

3. Remove insulator attaching bolts, then the alternator splash shield and insulator, **Fig. 9**.
4. Reverse procedure to install.

## V8-460

1. Support engine using a block of wood placed under oil pan and a suitable jack.
2. Remove locknuts from support bracket-to-crossmember and side rail attaching bolts.
3. Remove support bracket-to-insulator through bolts, **Fig. 10**.
4. Raise engine until insulator clears bracket, then remove insulator and bracket as an assembly.
5. Remove insulator-to-bracket attaching nuts and the insulator.
6. Reverse procedure to install.

# ENGINE
## REPLACE
### V6-232

1. Disconnect battery ground cable and drain cooling system.
2. On models equipped with an engine compartment light, disconnect electrical connector from light.
3. Mark hood hinge locations and remove hood.
4. Remove air cleaner assembly including air intake duct and heat tube.
5. Remove fan shroud attaching screws, then the fan and clutch assembly attaching bolts.
6. Remove fan and clutch assembly and fan shroud from vehicle.
7. Loosen accessory drive belt idler, then remove drive belt and water pump pulley.
8. Disconnect upper and lower hoses from radiator.
9. Disconnect Thermactor hose from downstream air tube check valve, then remove air tube bracket attaching bolt from rear of right cylinder head.
10. Remove coil secondary wire from ignition coil.
11. On models equipped with power steering, disconnect steering pump from mounting bracket and position aside with hoses connected.
12. On models equipped with A/C, disconnect A/C compressor from mounting bracket and secure to right shock tower with hoses connected.
13. On all models, remove alternator attaching bolts and position alternator aside.
14. Disconnect hoses from heater core tubes.
15. On models equipped with speed con-

trol, disconnect servo chain from carburetor, then remove servo attaching bolts and the servo.
16. On all models, disconnect necessary vacuum hoses for engine removal.
17. Remove engine ground strap attaching screw from dash, then disconnect transmission linkage from carburetor.
18. Disconnect accelerator cable from carburetor, then remove cable routing bracket attaching bolts.
19. Disconnect electrical connectors necessary for engine removal.
20. Disconnect fuel inlet line and PCV hose from carburetor, then remove carburetor from vehicle.
21. Install engine lifting plate No. T75T-6000-A or equivalent over carburetor hold down studs, leaving EGR spacer and phenolic gasket in place. Tighten nuts securely. **All studs must be used to secure the lifting plate to avoid damaging the intake manifold. When using the lifting plate, do not remove engine and transmission as an assembly.**
22. Raise and support vehicle.
23. Drain engine oil, then disconnect and plug fuel inlet line from fuel pump.
24. Remove dust shield from transmission converter housing, if equipped.
25. Remove flexplate-to-torque converter attaching nuts.
26. Disconnect battery cable from starter motor, then remove starter attaching bolts and the starter.
27. Remove transmission oil cooler line routing clip.
28. Remove exhaust pipe-to-exhaust manifold attaching nuts.
29. Remove 4 transmission-to-engine lower attaching bolts.
30. Remove engine mount-to-crossmember attaching nuts, then lower the vehicle.
31. Support transmission using a suitable jack, then remove 2 upper transmission-to-engine attaching bolts.
32. Place a piece of ¼ inch plywood between radiator and engine to protect

radiator.
33. Raise engine slightly, using a suitable lifting device, and carefully separate from transmission, then lift engine from vehicle.
34. Reverse procedure to install.

### 6-300
#### E-100—350

1. Disconnect battery ground cable and drain cooling system.
2. Install protective seat covers, then remove hood cover and air cleaner assembly. On EFI models, relieve fuel system pressure as follows:
   a. Locate, then disconnect either fuel pump, inertia switch or inline high pressure fuel pump electrical connector.
   b. Crank engine for approximately ten seconds. Engine may start and operate for a short time. If so, crank engine an additional five seconds after engine stalls.
   c. Connect electrical connector disconnected in step a.
3. Remove front bumper, then the grille and lower gravel deflector as an assembly.
4. Disconnect radiator hose from engine, then remove alternator splash shield, if equipped, and the lower radiator hose from radiator.
5. On models equipped with automatic transmission, disconnect transmission oil cooler lines from radiator.
6. On all models, remove radiator and fan shroud, if equipped.
7. Disconnect heater hoses from engine.
8. Disconnect alternator from mounting bracket and position aside.
9. On models equipped with power steering, remove steering pump drive belt, then disconnect pump and support from mounting bracket and position aside.
10. On all models, disconnect and plug fuel line from fuel rail. Label, then disconnect all EFI (if equipped) electrical connectors and vacuum lines that will

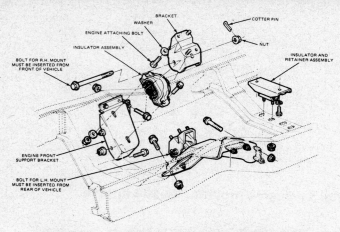

**Fig. 10   Engine mounts. V8-460 engine**

interfere with engine removal.

11. Disconnect distributor and sender unit wires and the brake booster hose from engine.
12. Disconnect electronic engine control harness from all sensors, if equipped.
13. Disconnect accelerator cable and remove bracket from engine.
14. On models equipped with automatic transmission, disconnect kickdown cable from bell crank.
15. On all models, remove exhaust manifold heat deflector, then the exhaust pipe-to-manifold attaching nuts.
16. Disconnect transmission vacuum line from intake manifold and junction.
17. Remove upper transmission-to-engine attaching bolts.
18. On models equipped with automatic transmission, remove transmission dipstick tube support bolt from intake manifold.
19. On all models, raise and support vehicle, then drain engine oil.
20. Disconnect wires from starter, then remove starter motor.
21. Remove flywheel inspection cover, then the four converter attaching nuts and front engine support nuts.
22. Remove oil filter, then the remaining transmission-to-engine nuts.
23. Lower vehicle, then remove engine assembly using suitable lifting equipment.
24. Reverse procedure to install. Torque engine to transmission bolts to 40-50 ft. lbs.

## F-100—350 & Bronco

1. Disconnect battery ground cable, then drain cooling system and engine oil.
2. Mark hood hinge locations and remove hood.
3. Remove air cleaner assembly or on vehicles with EFI remove throttle body inlet tubes. Then, on models equipped with A/C, remove A/C compressor and condenser. On EFI models, relieve fuel system pressure as follows:
   a. Locate, then disconnect either fuel pump, inertia switch or inline high pressure fuel pump electrical connector.
   b. Crank engine for approximately ten seconds. Engine may start and operate for a short time. If so, crank engine an additional five seconds after engine stalls.
   c. Connect electrical connector disconnected in step a.
4. Disconnect heater hose from water pump and coolant outlet housing.
5. Disconnect flexible fuel line from fuel pump, then remove radiator.
6. Remove cooling fan, viscous fan drive (if equipped), water pump pulley and fan drive belt **The fan clutch/water pump hub has a right hand thread.**
7. Disconnect accelerator cable, and the choke cable on 1980 models, from carburetor or throttle body and remove cable retracting spring.
8. On models equipped with power

brakes, disconnect vacuum line from intake manifold.

9. On models equipped with automatic transmission and carburetor, disconnect kickdown rod from bell crank. On models equipped with automatic transmission and EFI, disconnect kickdown cable from throttle body.
10. On all models, disconnect exhaust manifold from exhaust pipe. Label, then disconnect all EFI (if equipped) electrical connectors and vacuum lines that will interfere with engine removal.
11. Disconnect battery ground cable and body ground strap from engine.
12. Disconnect electronic engine control harness from all sensors, if equipped.
13. Disconnect engine wiring harness from ignition coil and the coolant temperature and oil pressure sending units, and position harness aside.
14. Disconnect alternator from mounting bracket and position aside, leaving wires attached.
15. On models equipped with power steering, disconnect steering pump from mounting bracket and position aside, leaving lines attached.
16. On models equipped with an air compressor, bleed air system and disconnect pressure lines from compressor.
17. On all models, raise and support vehicle.
18. Remove starter motor, and on models equipped with automatic transmission, the fluid filler tube bracket.
19. Remove engine rear plate upper right bolt.
20. On models equipped with manual transmission, remove all flywheel housing lower attaching bolts and disconnect clutch retracting spring.
21. On models equipped with automatic transmission, remove converter housing access cover, then the flywheel-to-converter nuts, and secure converter in housing. Disconnect transmission oil cooler lines from retaining clip on engine, then remove converter housing-to-engine lower attaching bolts.
22. Remove insulator-to-intermediate support bracket attaching nut from each engine front support.
23. Lower vehicle and support transmission using a suitable jack.
24. Remove remaining flywheel or converter housing-to-engine attaching bolts.
25. Raise engine slightly, using suitable lifting equipment, and carefully separate from transmission, then lift engine from vehicle.
26. Reverse procedure to install. Torque engine to transmission bolts to 40-50 ft. lbs.

## V8-255, 302 & 351W
### E-100—350

1. Remove engine cover, then disconnect battery cables and drain cooling system.
2. Remove grille assembly, including

gravel deflector.

3. Remove upper grille support bracket, hood lock support and condenser upper mounting brackets, if equipped.
4. On models equipped with A/C, discharge refrigerant from system and remove condenser. Disconnect lines from A/C compressor and remove accelerator cable bracket. On EFI models, relieve fuel system pressure as follows:
   a. Locate, then disconnect either fuel pump, inertia switch or inline high pressure fuel pump electrical connector.
   b. Crank engine for approximately ten seconds. Engine may start and operate for a short time. If so, crank engine an additional five seconds after engine stalls.
   c. Connect electrical connector disconnected in step a.
5. Disconnect speed control linkage, if equipped.
6. On all models, disconnect heater hoses from engine and radiator hoses from radiator.
7. On 1983-88 models, disconnect heater hoses from heater core and water valve.
8. On all models equipped with automatic transmission, disconnect oil cooler lines from radiator.
9. Remove fan shroud, fan and radiator, then pivot alternator inward and disconnect electrical connectors from alternator.
10. Remove air cleaner, duct and valve assembly and exhaust manifold shroud, then the flex tube from exhaust manifold stove.
11. Disconnect throttle cable from carburetor or throttle body assembly, then remove accelerator cable bracket from engine. On EFI models, label, then disconnect all EFI electrical connectors and vacuum lines.
12. Disconnect transmission shift rod, if equipped.
13. Disconnect fuel and choke lines, then remove carburetor and spacer. On models with EFI, disconnect fuel line and remove throttle body and spacer.
14. Disconnect evaporative emission hoses from front of carburetor pad and/or top of PCV valve. Disconnect vacuum line from carburetor bowl vent and evaporative canister line from vacuum harness. If equipped, also disconnect power brake booster vacuum line.
15. Raise and support vehicle.
16. Drain engine oil and remove oil filter.
17. Disconnect exhaust pipes and exhaust heat control valve (if equipped) from exhaust manifolds.
18. Remove transmission filler tube bracket attaching bolts from right cylinder head.
19. Remove engine mount attaching bolts and nuts, then the starter motor.
20. On models equipped with manual transmission, remove housing-to-engine attaching bolts.
21. On models equipped with automatic transmission, remove converter inspection cover attaching bolts. Re-

move four converter-to-flexplate nuts, three adapter plate-to-converter housing bolts and four converter housing-to-cylinder block lower bolts.

22. On all models, remove ground wire retaining bolt from cylinder block, then lower the vehicle and support transmission with a suitable jack.
23. On models equipped with power steering, remove steering pump drive belt and front bracket bolts.
24. On 1980-82 models, remove speed control servo (if equipped) and accelerator cable bracket from intake manifold and position aside.
25. On all models equipped with A/C, disconnect A/C compressor magnetic clutch lead wire.
26. On all models, install lifting bracket to intake manifold and remove two converter housing-to-cylinder block upper attaching bolts.
27. Support transmission with a suitable jack and attach lifting equipment to engine, then carefully move engine forward and lift from vehicle.
28. Reverse procedure to install. Torque engine to transmission bolts to 40-50 ft. lbs.

## F-100—250 & Bronco

1. Drain cooling system and engine oil.
2. Mark hood hinge locations and remove hood.
3. Disconnect battery and ground cables from engine block. **On EFI engines, label, then disconnect all EFI related component electrical connectors, vacuum lines and fuel lines that may interfere with engine removal. Relieve system pressure as follows:**
   a. Locate, then disconnect either fuel pump, inertia switch or inline high pressure fuel pump electrical connector.
   b. Crank engine for approximately ten seconds. Engine may start and operate for a short time. If so, crank engine an additional five seconds after engine stalls.
   c. Connect electrical connector disconnected in step a.
4. Remove air cleaner and intake duct assembly, including carbon canister hose and crankcase ventilation hose.
5. Disconnect radiator upper and lower hoses and transmission oil cooler lines (if equipped) from radiator.
6. On models equipped with A/C, discharge refrigerant from system, then remove A/C condenser and disconnect lines from compressor.
7. On all models, remove fan shroud attaching bolts and position shroud over fan.
8. Remove radiator, fan shroud, fan spacer, belts and pulley.
9. Remove alternator attaching bolts and swing alternator aside.
10. Disconnect electrical connector from oil pressure sending unit, then disconnect and plug flexible fuel line at fuel tank.
11. Disconnect vacuum hoses from evap-

orative canister.

12. On fuel injected models, disconnect chassis fuel line quick disconnects at fuel rail.
13. On all models, disconnect accelerator rod or cable from carburetor or throttle body.
14. Disconnect speed control linkages and transmission kickdown rod and remove rod retracting spring, if equipped.
15. Disconnect power brake booster vacuum hose, if equipped.
16. Disconnect heater hoses from water pump and intake manifold.
17. Disconnect electrical connector from coolant temperature sending unit.
18. Remove flywheel housing-to-engine upper attaching bolts.
19. Disconnect primary wire from ignition coil, then remove wiring harness from left rocker arm cover and position aside.
20. Disconnect ground strap from cylinder head.
21. Raise and support vehicle.
22. Remove starter motor.
23. Disconnect exhaust pipes and exhaust heat control valve (if equipped) from exhaust manifolds.
24. Disconnect engine support insulators from frame brackets.
25. On models equipped with automatic transmission, remove converter inspection plate and the converter-to-flywheel attaching bolts.
26. On all models, remove remaining flywheel housing-to-engine attaching bolts.
27. On models equipped with A/C, disconnect A/C compressor clutch electrical connector.
28. On all models, lower vehicle and support transmission with a suitable jack.
29. Install lifting brackets to intake manifold and attach suitable lifting equipment to engine.
30. Raise engine slightly and carefully separate from transmission, then lift engine from vehicle.
31. Reverse procedure to install. Torque engine to transmission bolts to 40-50 ft. lbs.

## V8-351M & 400
### E-100—350, F-100—350 & Bronco

1. Drain cooling system and engine oil.
2. Disconnect battery and alternator ground cables from cylinder block.
3. Remove air cleaner and intake duct assembly, including carbon canister hose and crankcase ventilation hose.
4. Disconnect upper and lower hoses and transmission oil cooler lines (if equipped) from radiator.
5. Remove fan shroud attaching bolts and position shroud over fan.
6. Remove radiator, fan shroud, spacer, belts and pulley.
7. Disconnect electrical connectors from alternator, then loosen mounting bolts and swing alternator down.
8. Disconnect electrical connector from oil pressure sending unit, then discon-

nect and plug fuel line at fuel tank.

9. Disconnect accelerator rod or cable from carburetor.
10. Disconnect speed control cable and transmission kickdown rod and remove rod retracting spring, if equipped.
11. Disconnect heater hoses from water pump and intake manifold.
12. Disconnect electrical connector from coolant temperature sending unit.
13. On models equipped with A/C, unfasten A/C compressor and mounting brackets and position aside.
14. On all models, remove flywheel housing-to-engine upper attaching bolts.
15. Disconnect primary wire from ignition coil, then remove wiring harness from left rocker arm cover and position aside.
16. Disconnect ground strap from cylinder block.
17. Raise and support vehicle.
18. Remove starter motor.
19. Disconnect exhaust pipes from exhaust manifolds, then the engine support insulators from frame brackets.
20. On models equipped with automatic transmission, remove converter inspection plate, then the converter-to-flywheel attaching bolts.
21. On all models, remove remaining flywheel housing-to-engine attaching bolts.
22. Lower vehicle and support transmission with a suitable jack.
23. Install lifting brackets and attach suitable lifting equipment to engine.
24. Raise engine slightly and carefully separate from transmission, then lift engine from vehicle.
25. Reverse procedure to install.

## V8-460
### E-250—350

1. Remove engine cover, then disconnect battery cables and drain cooling system.
2. Remove grille assembly, including gravel deflector.
3. On models with EFI, remove bolts that secure the air cleaner and bracket assembly, then disconnect thermactor air pump inlet hose from front of the air cleaner housing.
4. Disconnect the air outlet tube assembly from the throttle body, the air inlet tube from the air cleaner and the thermactor bypass valve hose from the air inlet tube.
5. Remove air cleaner assembly and the air inlet and outlet tubes.
6. On all models, remove upper grille support bracket, hood lock support and condenser upper mounting brackets.
7. On models equipped with A/C, discharge refrigerant from system and remove condenser. Disconnect lines from A/C compressor and remove accelerator cable bracket.
8. Disconnect heater hoses from engine.
9. Disconnect upper and lower radiator

hoses and transmission oil cooler lines (if equipped). On models equipped with oil cooler, disconnect cooling lines at oil filter adapter. **Do not attempt to remove the line at the quick disconnect fitting at the cooler as damage to the cooler or connectors may result.**

10. Remove fan shroud, fan and radiator and A/C condenser, then pivot alternator inward and disconnect electrical connectors from alternator.
11. On carbureted models, remove air cleaner, duct and valve assembly and exhaust manifold shroud, then the flex tube from exhaust manifold stove.
12. On carbureted models, disconnect throttle and transmission linkage from carburetor, then remove accelerator cable bracket from engine. On models with EFI, disconnect throttle and transmission linkage from throttle body, then remove accelerator cable bracket from upper intake manifold.
13. On models equipped with speed control, remove speed control servo vacuum line and cable.
14. On carbureted models, disconnect fuel and choke lines, then remove carburetor and spacer.
15. On models with EFI, disconnect fuel lines at quick disconnect couplings and vacuum lines to the intake manifold.
16. Disconnect EGR tube from left exhaust manifold and upper intake manifold, then plug manifold opening.
17. Raise and support vehicle.
18. Drain engine oil and remove oil filter.
19. Disconnect exhaust pipes from exhaust manifolds. On models with EFI, disconnect exhaust air supply bypass valve hose from MTA check valve, then disconnect EGR tube from left exhaust manifold and upper intake manifold, then plug manifold opening.
20. On all models, remove two transmission filler tube bracket attaching bolts from right cylinder head.
21. Remove engine mount attaching bolts and nuts, then the starter motor.
22. Remove converter inspection cover bolts, four converter-to-flex plate nuts, three adapter plate-to-converter housing bolts and four converter housing-to-cylinder block lower bolts.
23. Remove ground wire retaining bolt from cylinder block, then lower the vehicle.
24. On models equipped with power steering, remove steering pump drive belt and front bracket bolts.
25. On all models, disconnect one vacuum line from rear of intake manifold.
26. Disconnect engine wiring harness and position aside.
27. On models equipped with A/C, disconnect A/C compressor magnetic clutch electrical connector.
28. On all models, install lifting bracket to intake manifold and remove two converter housing-to-cylinder block upper attaching bolts.
29. Support transmission with a suitable jack and attach lifting equipment to engine, then carefully move engine forward and lift from vehicle.

30. Reverse procedure to install. Torque engine to transmission bolts to 40-50 ft. lbs.

## F-250–350

1. Drain cooling system and engine oil.
2. Mark hood hinge locations and remove hood.
3. Disconnect battery and ground cables from cylinder block.
4. On models with EFI, remove bolts that secure the air cleaner and bracket assembly, then disconnect thermactor air pump inlet hose from front of the air cleaner housing.
5. Disconnect the air outlet tube assembly from the throttle body, the air inlet tube from the air cleaner and the thermactor bypass valve hose from the air inlet tube.
6. On all models, remove air cleaner assembly, air inlet and outlet tubes and the intake duct assembly, including carbon canister hose and crankcase ventilation hose.
7. Disconnect upper and lower radiator hoses and transmission oil cooler lines (if equipped).
8. On models equipped with engine oil cooler, disconnect cooler lines from oil filter adapter **Do not disconnect engine oil cooler lines from fittings behind or at the cooler.**
9. On models equipped with A/C, discharge refrigerant from system, then remove A/C condenser and disconnect lines from compressor.
10. Remove fan shroud attaching bolts and position shroud over fan.
11. Remove radiator, fan shroud, fan clutch, fan blade, fan spacer, belts and pulley.
12. Remove alternator mounting bolts and swing alternator aside.
13. On models with EFI, disconnect throttle and transmission linkage at throttle body and remove accelerator cable bracket from upper intake manifold.
14. Remove speed control hardware (if equipped).
15. On all models, disconnect electrical connector from oil pressure sending unit, then disconnect vacuum hoses from evaporative canister.
16. On carbureted models, disconnect and plug flexible fuel line at fuel tank. On models with EFI, disconnect fuel lines at quick disconnect couplings and vacuum lines from intake manifold
17. On models with EFI, disconnect ERG tube from left exhaust manifold and upper intake manifold, plug manifold opening, then disconnect exhaust air supply bypass valve hose from MTA check valve.
18. On carbureted models, disconnect accelerator cable from carburetor.
19. Disconnect speed control linkages and transmission kickdown rod and remove rod retaining spring, if equipped.
20. On all models, disconnect power

brake booster vacuum hose, if equipped.
21. Disconnect heater hoses from water pump and intake manifold.
22. Disconnect electrical connector from coolant temperature sending unit.
23. Remove flywheel housing-to-engine upper attaching bolts.
24. Disconnect primary wire from ignition coil, then remove wiring harness from left rocker arm cover and position aside.
25. Disconnect ground strap from cylinder head.
26. Raise and support vehicle.
27. Remove starter motor.
28. Disconnect exhaust pipes from exhaust manifolds, then the engine support insulators from frame brackets.
29. On models equipped with automatic transmission, remove converter inspection plate, then the converter-to-flywheel attaching bolts.
30. On models equipped with manual transmission, remove rear cover plate from flywheel housing, then the remaining flywheel housing-to-engine attaching bolts.
31. On models equipped with A/C, disconnect A/C compressor magnetic clutch electrical connector.
32. On all models, lower vehicle and support transmission with a suitable jack.
33. Install lifting brackets to intake manifold and attach suitable lifting equipment to engine.
34. Raise engine slightly and carefully separate from transmission, then lift engine from vehicle.

35. Reverse procedure to install, ensuring engine to transmission bolts are torqued to 40-50 ft. lbs.

## CYLINDER HEAD
## REPLACE
### V8-460

1. Remove intake manifold, following procedures under Intake Manifold-Replace, then disconnect exhaust pipe from exhaust manifold.
2. Loosen air conditioner drive belt (if equipped), then loosen alternator bolts and remove the bolt attaching alternator bracket to cylinder head.
3. Remove thermactor air pump and alternator, then remove air pump bracket bolts and position to the side.
4. If equipped with air conditioning, shut off compressor service valves and remove valves and hoses from compressor then remove compressor and place out of way. Remove compressor and power steering pump mounting bracket from cylinder head and water pump.
5. If not equipped with air conditioning, remove bolts attaching power steering reservoir bracket to left cylinder head and position reservoir and bracket out of the way.
6. Disconnect oil filler tube (Econolines only), then remove thermactor supply manifold from exhaust manifold.

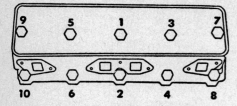

**Fig. 11 Cylinder head tightening sequence. V8 engines**

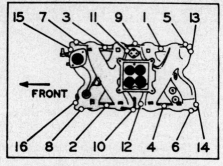

**Fig. 12 Intake manifold tightening sequence. V8-460**

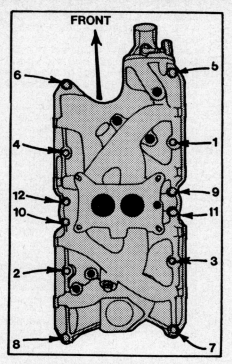

**Fig. 13 Intake manifold tightening sequence. V8-255, 302 & V8-351W**

7. Remove rocker arm covers, rocker arm bolts, rocker arms, oil deflectors, fulcrums and pushrods. **Keep all parts in sequence so that they can be reinstalled in their original locations.**
8. Remove cylinder head bolts taking note as to the length of each bolt and remove the cylinder head and exhaust manifold as an assembly. **If necessary to loosen cylinder head gasket seal, pry at forward corners of cylinder head and against casting provided on cylinder block.**
9. Install heads in the reverse order of removal and torque cylinder head bolts in three steps and in the sequence shown in **Fig. 11.** Final tightening should be to the torque listed in the "Engine Tightening Specification Chart." Torque intake manifold bolts to torque specification given in "Engine Tightening Specification Chart" and in sequence shown in **Fig. 12.**

## V8-255, 302, 351 & 400

1. Remove intake manifold, following procedures under Intake Manifold-Replace section.
2. Remove rocker arm covers.
3. If removing right cylinder head, perform the following steps:
   a. On models with V8-255, 302 and 351W engines, remove the alternator and air pump mounting bracket bolt and pivot alternator downward.
   b. On Econoline models, remove ignition coil and air cleaner inlet duct from cylinder head.
   c. On models with V8-351M and 400 engines, remove air cleaner inlet duct and ground wire from right cylinder head.
4. If removing left cylinder head, perform the following steps:
   a. On models with V8-255, 302 and 351W engines and A/C, remove A/C compressor bracket attaching bolts.
   b. On models with V8-351M and 400, unfasten power steering pump (if equipped), then remove pump drive belt and position pump aside. On models equipped with A/C, isolate and remove A/C compressor.
   c. On F series models with V8-255, 302 and 351W engines, remove oil dipstick and tube assembly and speed control bracket, if equipped.
5. Disconnect exhaust pipes from exhaust manifolds.
6. Loosen rocker arm studs or bolts and remove push rods in sequence so they may be installed in their original positions.
7. Remove exhaust valve stem caps, if equipped.
8. On Econoline models with V8-255, 302 and 351W engines, remove Thermactor air supply manifold, hose and pump valve as an assembly.
9. On Pick-up and Bronco models, disconnect Thermactor air supply hoses from check valves and plug the valves.
10. On all models, remove cylinder head attaching bolts and the cylinder head. **On 1980-81 Econoline models with V8-351M and 400 engines, it may be necessary to remove forward bolt on left side of head as a unit with cylinder head, due to a lack of clearance with body flange.**
11. Reverse procedure to install. Torque cylinder head attaching bolts to specifications in sequence shown in **Fig. 11.** Torque intake manifold attaching bolts to specifications in sequence shown in **Figs. 13 and 14.**

## 6-300

### 1980-87

1. Drain cooling system and remove air cleaner.
2. Remove PCV valve from rocker arm cover, then disconnect vent hose from intake manifold or throttle body assembly.
3. Remove carburetor or throttle body fuel inlet line and distributor line.
4. Disconnect and tag all vacuum lines from carburetor or throttle body.
5. Remove accelerator cable retracting spring and disconnect cable from carburetor or throttle body.
6. On models equipped with automatic transmission, disconnect kickdown rod from carburetor.
7. On all models, disconnect upper radiator hose and heater hose from coolant outlet elbow.
8. Disconnect exhaust pipe from exhaust manifold and discard pipe gasket.
9. Remove ignition coil bracket attaching screws and position coil aside.

10. Remove rocker arm cover and loosen rocker arm stud nuts so rocker arms can be rotated to one side.
11. Remove rocker arms in order so they may be installed in their original position.
12. Disconnect ignition wires from spark plugs, then remove cylinder head attaching bolts.
13. Remove cylinder head, using suitable lifting equipment.
14. Reverse procedure to install. Tighten cylinder head bolts in 3 steps and in sequence shown in **Fig. 15** to torque listed in the "Engine Tightening Specification Chart." Torque intake and exhaust manifold bolts to specifications in sequence shown in **Figs. 16 and 17.**

### 1988

1. Disconnect battery ground cable, then drain cooling system and engine oil.
2. Scribe hood hinge locations and remove hood, if necessary.
3. Remove throttle body inlet tubes and air conditioning compressor and condenser.
4. Disconnect heater hoses from water pump and coolant housing, then the flexible fuel line from fuel pump.
5. Remove radiator (if necessary), fan, viscous fan drive, water pump pulley and drive belt.
6. Disconnect cable retracting spring and accelerator cable from throttle body.
7. On models equipped with automatic transmission, disconnect kickdown cable from throttle body.

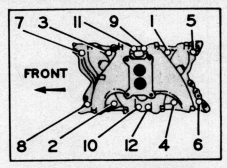

**Fig. 14 Intake manifold tightening sequence. V8-351M & 400**

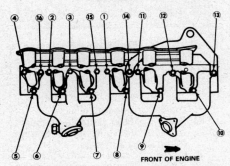

**Fig. 17 Intake & exhaust manifold tightening sequence. 1987–89 6-300**

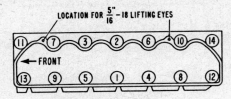

LOCATION FOR 5/16 – 18 LIFTING EYES

**Fig. 15 Cylinder head tightening sequence. 6-300**

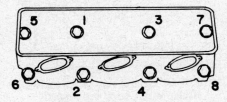

**Fig. 18 Cylinder head tightening sequence. V6-232**

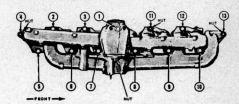

**Fig. 16 Intake & exhaust manifold tightening sequence. Exc. 1987–89 6-300**

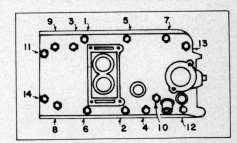

**Fig. 19 Intake manifold tightening sequence. V6-232**

8. On models equipped with power brakes, disconnect vacuum line from intake manifold.
9. On all models, disconnect exhaust pipe from exhaust manifold. Disconnect body ground strap and battery ground cable from engine.
10. Disconnect EEC harness from all sensors and the engine wiring harness from ignition coil, temperature sending unit and oil pressure sending unit. Position harnesses aside.
11. Remove alternator mounting bolts and position alternator aside.
12. On models equipped with power steering, remove power steering pump from mounting brackets and position pump aside, right side up.
13. On all models, remove coil bracket attaching bolts and position coil aside.
14. Remove rocker arm cover and loosen rocker arm stud nuts so rocker arms can be rotated to one side.
15. Remove push rods in order so they may be installed in original position.
16. Disconnect ignition wires from spark plugs, then remove cylinder head attaching bolts.
17. Remove cylinder head, intake and exhaust manifold assemblies using suitable lifting equipment. Lifting eye locations are shown in **Fig. 15.**
18. Reverse procedure to install. Tighten cylinder head bolts in three steps and in sequence shown in **Fig. 15** to specifications. Torque intake and exhaust manifold bolts to specifications in sequence shown in **Figs. 17.**

## V6-232

1. Disconnect battery ground cable, then drain cooling system.
2. Remove air cleaner, air intake duct and heat tube.
3. Loosen accessory drive belt idler and remove drive belt.
4. If left cylinder head is to be removed, proceed as follows:
   a. Remove oil filler cap.
   b. If equipped with power steering, remove pump bracket attaching bolts, then remove pump and bracket assembly and position pump aside with hoses attached.
   c. If equipped with A/C, remove compressor bracket attaching bolts, then position compressor and bracket assembly aside with refrigerant lines attached.
5. If right cylinder head is to be removed, proceed as follows:
   a. Remove Thermactor diverter valve and hose assembly.
   b. Remove accessory drive belt idler, then remove alternator.
   c. Remove Thermactor pump pulley, then remove Thermactor pump.
   d. Remove alternator mounting bracket. **On models equipped with Tripminder, the fuel supply line from the fuel pump to the fuel sensor will have to be disconnected to gain access to the upper alternator bracket bolt.**
   e. Remove PCV valve.
6. Remove intake manifold and exhaust manifolds.
7. Remove rocker arm cover attaching screws, then loosen cover by using a putty knife under cover flange and remove cover. Do not use excess force when loosening rocker arm cover as cover may become damaged.

8. Loosen rocker arm fulcrum bolt enough to allow rocker arms to be rotated to one side, then remove pushrods. **Tag pushrods so they can be installed in the same position.**
9. Remove cylinder head attaching bolts, then remove cylinder head and gasket.
10. Reverse procedure to install. Apply a thin coating of pipe sealant D8AZ-19558-A or equivalent to the shorter cylinder head bolts which are installed on the exhaust manifold side of the cylinder head. Do not apply pipe sealant to long bolts which are installed on the intake manifold side of the cylinder head. Tighten cylinder head bolts in four steps to torque listed under "Engine Tightening Specifications" using sequence shown in **Fig. 18.** Loosen cylinder bolts approximately two to three turns, then retighten bolts in four steps to specified torque in sequence, **Fig. 18.** When installing intake manifold, tighten mounting bolts to torque specified under "Engine Tightening Specifications" in sequence shown in **Fig. 19. Before installing intake manifold, apply sealer to locations shown in Fig. 19.**

## INTAKE MANIFOLD REPLACE

### V6-232

1. Drain cooling system, then remove air cleaner with air intake duct and heat tube.
2. Disconnect accelerator cable and transmission linkage (if equipped) from carburetor.
3. Remove accelerator cable mounting

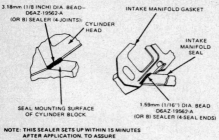

Fig. 20 Intake manifold installation. V8 engines

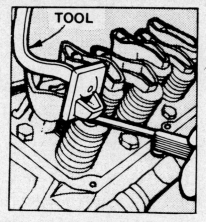

Fig. 21 Compressing valve lifter with tool to check clearance on engines with hydraulic valve lifters

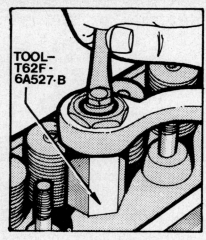

Fig. 22 Rocker arm stud removal. 1980–84 6-300

bracket attaching bolts and position bracket aside.

4. On models equipped with speed control, disconnect chain from carburetor, then remove servo bracket assembly attaching nuts and position assembly aside.

5. On all models, disconnect bowl vent hose from carburetor.

6. Disconnect Thermactor air supply hose from check valve located on back of intake manifold.

7. Disconnect fuel inlet line from carburetor.

8. Disconnect upper radiator hose from thermostat housing and the coolant bypass hose from manifold.

9. Disconnect heater tube from intake manifold and remove tube support bracket attaching nut.

10. Disconnect all vacuum lines and electrical connectors necessary for intake manifold removal.

11. On models equipped with A/C, remove A/C compressor support bracket from intake manifold.

12. On 1982 models, loosen EGR tube at EGR valve adapter.

13. On 1983 models, remove EGR tube.

14. On all models, disconnect PCV line from carburetor.

15. Remove carburetor and discard gasket.

16. On 1982 models, remove carburetor hold-down studs from manifold.

17. On all models, remove three EGR spacer attaching screws from manifold.

18. Work EGR spacer loose from manifold with EGR adapter and valve attached, then remove spacer and discard gasket. **On 1982 models, disconnect EGR tube from adapter prior to removing spacer.**

19. Remove PCV line, then the intake manifold attaching bolts and intake manifold. **It may be necessary to pry on front of manifold to break seal. If so, use care to prevent damage to machined surfaces.**

20. Reverse procedure to install. Apply sealer to gasket areas, then torque manifold attaching bolts to specifications in sequence shown in **Fig. 19.**

## 6-300

1. Remove air cleaner on carbureted

models. On models with EFI, disconnect air inlet hose from crankcase filter cap, then remove throttle body inlet hoses.

2. On carbureted models, disconnect accelerator cable or rod from carburetor and remove accelerator retracting spring. On models with EFI, disconnect accelerator and transmission cables from throttle body and remove accelerator retracting spring and cable bracket from upper intake manifold.

3. On carbureted models equipped with automatic transmission, remove kickdown rod retracting spring and accelerator rod bell crank assembly.

4. On carbureted models, disconnect fuel inlet line. On models with EFI, remove the fuel line from the fuel rail **Do not bend the fuel line.**

5. On all models, disconnect and tag all vacuum lines at carburetor or throttle body.

6. On models with EFI, remove upper intake and throttle body assembly.

7. Disconnect carburetor feedback solenoid connector or EEC connector from throttle body and the choke cap electric assist connector, if equipped.

8. Disconnect exhaust pipe from exhaust manifold.

9. Disconnect power brake vacuum line, if equipped.

10. Remove manifold attaching bolts and nuts and the intake and exhaust manifolds as an assembly.

11. Remove attaching nuts and separate intake and exhaust manifolds.

12. Reverse procedure to install. Torque manifold attaching bolts and nuts to specifications in sequence shown in **Figs. 16 and 17. The following manifold installation procedure should be used to extend exhaust manifold service life:**

a. Clean cylinder head and manifold mating surfaces.

b. Remove tube fittings from original manifold and install in replacement

manifold, as needed.

c. Apply suitable graphite grease to exhaust manifold-to-intake manifold mating surfaces.

d. Install 2 new bolts (part No. 374047-S) and a new stud (part No. 381733-S) into intake manifold.

e. Assemble intake manifold to exhaust manifold using lock washers and nuts. Tighten nuts finger tight only at this time.

f. Install a new intake manifold gasket. Do not install a combination intake/exhaust manifold gasket on a new exhaust manifold.

g. Apply suitable graphite grease to cylinder head-to-manifold mating surfaces.

h. Position manifold assemblies against cylinder head, ensuring intake manifold gaskets have not moved.

i. Install manifold attaching bolts and nuts and torque to specifications in sequence shown in **Figs. 16 and 17.**

j. Torque intake manifold-to-exhaust manifold attaching nuts to 22-32 ft. lbs.

k. Position a new gasket on exhaust pipe, then connect pipe to manifold and torque attaching bolts to 25-38 ft. lbs.

## V8-255, 302 & 351W

1. Drain cooling system, then remove air cleaner with intake duct assembly and crankcase ventilation hose.

2. Disconnect accelerator cable and speed control linkage (if equipped) from carburetor or throttle body. Remove accelerator cable bracket, then disconnect kickdown rod from carburetor or throttle body on models equipped with automatic transmission. Disconnect electric choke, carburetor solenoid electrical connectors or EEC connector, if equipped.

3. Disconnect high tension lead and

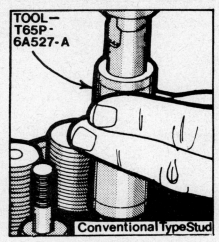

**Fig. 23 Rocker arm stud installation. 1980-84 6-300**

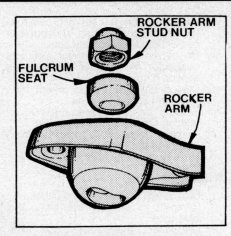

**Fig. 24 Rocker arm assembly. 1980-84 6-300**

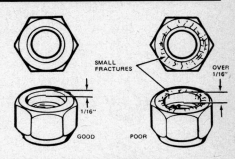

**Fig. 25 Inspection of rocker arm stud nut**

wires from ignition coil.

4. Disconnect ignition wires from spark plugs, then remove wires and bracket assembly from rocker arm cover attaching stud.
5. Remove distributor cap and ignition wires as an assembly.
6. Disconnect fuel inlet line from carburetor or throttle body.
7. Disconnect vacuum hoses from distributor, then remove distributor and disconnect evaporative hoses, if equipped.
8. Disconnect upper radiator hose from coolant outlet housing.
9. Disconnect electrical connector from coolant temperature sending unit, then remove heater hose from intake manifold.
10. Remove water pump bypass hose from coolant outlet housing, then disconnect crankcase vent hose from rocker arm cover.
11. Remove intake manifold attaching bolts, then the intake manifold and carburetor as an assembly. On models with EFI remove manifold as follows:
    a. Remove upper intake manifold and throttle body as an assembly.
    b. Remove lower intake manifold assembly.
    c. It may be necessary to carefully pry the intake manifold from the cylinder heads. Remove manifold gaskets and seals and discard intake manifold attaching bolt sealing washer.
12. Reverse procedure to install. Apply sealer as shown in **Fig. 20**. Torque manifold attaching bolts to specifications in sequence shown in **Fig. 13**.

## V8-351M & 400

1. Remove air cleaner and intake duct.
2. On models equipped with A/C, isolate and remove A/C compressor.
3. On all models, disconnect high tension lead and wires from ignition coil.
4. Disconnect ignition wires from spark

plugs, then remove wires from brackets on rocker arm covers.
5. Remove distributor cap and ignition wires as an assembly.
6. Remove Thermactor bypass valve and hose from check valve.
7. Disconnect fuel inlet line from carburetor.
8. Disconnect heater hoses from retainers and position aside.
9. Remove ignition coil, vacuum solenoid valve and bracket, then disconnect crankcase emission hose from left rocker arm cover.
10. Disconnect vacuum lines from intake manifold and distributor.
11. Remove distributor hold-down bolt and the distributor.
12. Disconnect accelerator linkage and speed control cable (if equipped) from carburetor assembly.
13. On models equipped with automatic transmission, disconnect transmission downshift linkage.
14. On all models, remove carburetor or throttle body, then the manifold attaching bolts and manifold.
15. Remove and discard manifold valley baffle and seals.
16. Reverse procedure to install. Apply sealer as shown in **Fig. 20**. Torque manifold attaching bolts to specifications in sequence shown in **Fig. 14**.

## V8-460

### 1980-87

1. Drain cooling system, then remove air cleaner and intake duct assembly.
2. Disconnect upper radiator hose from engine and the heater hose from intake manifold and water pump and position aside.
3. Loosen water pump bypass hose clamp at intake manifold.
4. Disconnect PCV valve hose from right rocker arm cover.
5. Disconnect and tag all vacuum lines at rear of intake manifold.
6. Disconnect ignition wires from spark plugs and position aside.

7. Disconnect high tension lead from ignition coil, then remove distributor cap and wires as an assembly.
8. Disconnect and tag all distributor vacuum lines at carburetor and vacuum control valve.
9. Disconnect accelerator linkage and transmission kickdown linkage (if equipped).
10. On models equipped with speed control, remove speed control linkage bracket from intake manifold and disconnect it from carburetor.
11. On all models, remove accelerator linkage cable attaching bolts and position linkage aside.
12. Disconnect fuel inlet line from carburetor.
13. Disconnect electrical connector from ignition coil battery terminal.
14. Disconnect engine temperature and oil pressure sending unit electrical connectors and any other connectors necessary for intake manifold removal.
15. Unfasten wiring harness from 3 retaining clips on left rocker arm cover and position harness aside.
16. Remove ignition coil and bracket assembly.
17. Remove intake manifold attaching bolts and nuts, then the intake manifold and carburetor as an assembly.
18. Reverse procedure to install. Apply sealer as shown in **Fig. 20** Torque manifold attaching bolts to specifications shown in **Fig. 12**.

### 1988-89

1. Disconnect battery(s).
2. Drain cooling system, then remove air cleaner and intake duct assembly.
3. Remove ignition coil mounting bracket and disconnect high tension lead from ignition coil.
4. Remove external EGR tube and both thermactor exhaust air supply manifold tubes.
5. Disconnect upper radiator hose from engine and the heater hoses from intake manifold and water pump and position aside. Loosen water pump bypass hose at intake manifold.
6. Disconnect PCV valve hose from right rocker arm cover.
7. Disconnect and tag all vacuum lines

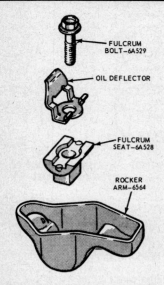

**Fig. 26   Rocker arm assembly. V8-351M, 400 & 460**

at rear of intake manifold.

8. Disconnect ignition wires from spark plugs, then remove distributor cap and wires as an assembly.
9. Remove distributor.
10. Disconnect accelerator linkage and transmission kickdown linkage from throttle body, then remove bolts holding accelerator linkage cable and position aside.
11. On models equipped with speed control, remove speed control linkage bracket from intake manifold and disconnect from throttle body
12. Disconnect fuel line from fuel rail.
13. Disconnect electrical connector from main wiring harness. **Wiring harness and manifold are to be removed as an assembly.**
14. Remove throttle body heater hose from water pump and intake manifold heater outlet connection.
15. Remove intake manifold attaching bolts and nuts, then the intake manifold and throttle body as an assembly. **If necessary, carefully pry manifold away from cylinder heads. Do not damage gasket sealing surfaces.**
16. Reverse procedure to install. Apply sealer as shown in **Fig. 20** Torque manifold attaching bolts to specifications shown in **Fig. 12**.

## EXHAUST MANIFOLD REPLACE
### V6-232
#### Left Side

1. Disconnect battery ground cable.
2. Remove oil level dipstick tube support bracket.
3. On vehicles equipped with speed control, position air cleaner assembly and disconnect servo chain at carbu-

retor, then remove servo bracket attaching bolts and nuts and position servo/bracket assembly aside.
4. On all models, disconnect electrical connector at exhaust gas oxygen sensor, if equipped.
5. Disconnect spark plug wires, then raise and support vehicle.
6. Remove exhaust pipe to manifold attaching nuts, then lower vehicle.
7. Remove exhaust manifold attaching bolts and the exhaust manifold.
8. Reverse procedure to install.

### Right Side

1. Disconnect battery ground cable.
2. Remove air cleaner assembly and heat tube.
3. Disconnect thermactor hose from downstream air tube check valve.
4. Remove downstream air tube bracket attaching bolt at rear of right side cylinder head.
5. Disconnect coil secondary wire from coil and the spark plug wires from spark plugs.
6. Remove spark plugs, then the outer heat shield.
7. Raise and support vehicle.
8. On vehicles equipped with automatic transmission, remove transmission dipstick tube.
9. Disconnect exhaust pipe at manifold.
10. Lower vehicle.
11. Remove exhaust manifold attaching bolts and the exhaust manifold, inner heat shroud and EGR tube as an assembly.
12. Reverse procedure to install.

### 6-300

Refer to "Intake Manifold, Replace".

### V8-255, 302 & 351W

1. Disconnect battery ground cable.
2. Remove air cleaner and intake duct assembly including crankcase ventilation hose.
3. Remove bolts attaching air cleaner inlet duct, if equipped.
4. Disconnect exhaust pipes at manifolds.
5. Remove exhaust manifold heat shields with attaching bolts and flat washers, if equipped.
6. Remove oil dipstick tube assembly, speed control bracket and exhaust heat control valve from left side exhaust manifold, if equipped, then remove exhaust manifold.
7. Reverse procedure to install, torquing attaching bolts to specifications from centermost bolts outward.

### V8-351M & 400

1. Disconnect battery ground cable.
2. When removing right side manifold, remove air cleaner, intake duct and heat shield.
3. When removing left side manifold, remove oil filter.
4. On 1980-82 models, remove oil dipstick and tube assembly and speed control bracket from left side exhaust manifold, if equipped.

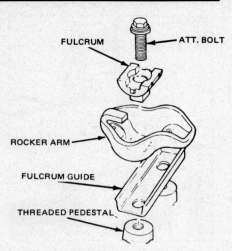

**Fig. 27   Rocker arm assembly. V8-255, 302 & 351W & 1985—89 6-300**

5. On vehicles equipped with column selector and automatic transmission, disconnect selector lever cross shaft.
6. On all models, disconnect exhaust pipe at manifold and remove spark plug heat shields.
7. Remove exhaust manifold attaching bolts and the exhaust manifold.
8. Reverse procedure to install, torquing attaching bolts to specifications from center most bolts outward.

### V8-460

1. Disconnect battery ground cable.
2. When removing right side exhaust manifold, remove air cleaner, intake duct assembly and heat shroud.
3. Remove spark plug wires, external EGR tube, power steering pump support bracket and oil dipstick tube as necessary.
4. Disconnect exhaust pipe at exhaust manifold.
5. Remove attaching bolts and washers, then the exhaust manifold, lifting bracket and spark plug wire heat shields.
6. Reverse procedure to install, torquing attaching bolts to specifications from centermost bolts outward.

## VALVE ARRANGEMENT
### FRONT TO REAR

| | |
|---|---|
| 6-300 | E-I-E-I-E-I-E-I-E-I |
| V6-232 Right | I-E-I-E-I-E |
| V6-232 Left | E-I-E-I-E-I |
| V8-255, 302 Left Bank | E-I-E-I-E-I-E-I |
| V8-255, 302 Right Bank | I-E-I-E-I-E-I-E |
| V8-351, 400 Right Bank | I-E-I-E-I-E-I-E |
| V8-351, 400 Left Bank | E-I-E-I-E-I-E-I |
| V8-460 Left Bank | E-I-E-I-E-I-E-I |
| V8-460 Right Bank | I-E-I-E-I-E-I-E |

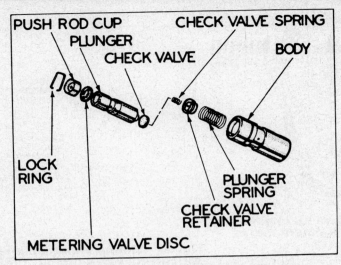

Fig. 28  Hydraulic valve lifter

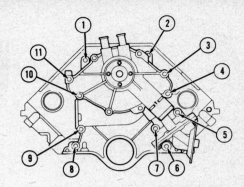

**Fig. 29  Front cover attaching bolt location. V6-232**

## VALVE CLEARANCE SPECIFICATIONS

| Engine | Year | Clearance |
|---|---|---|
| V6-232 | 1982-83 | .088-.189 |
| V8-255 | 1981-82 | .123-.173 |
| 6-300 | 1980-89 | .125-.175 |
| V8-302 | 1980-89 | .096-.165 |
| V8-351M | 1980-81 | .125 |
| V8-351W | 1980-89 | .123-.173 |
| V8-400 | 1980-82 | .175 |
| V8-460 | 1980-89 | .100-.150 |

On engines with hydraulic lifters, clearance specified is at valve stem tip with lifter collapsed.

## VALVES
### ADJUST
### 6-300

1. Crank engine with ignition Off, using an auxiliary starter switch.
2. Mark crankshaft damper at two locations, approximately 120° apart, so that, with the timing mark, the damper is divided into three equal sections.
3. Rotate crankshaft until No. 1 piston is on TDC of compression stroke.
4. Measure torque required to turn each stud nut in a counterclockwise direction (break away torque). Replace stud nuts where break away torque is not 4.5-15 ft. lbs. **If break away torque is still not within specifications after replacing stud nut, the stud must be replaced.**
5. Install stud nut and torque to 17-23 ft. lbs. with No. 1 piston at TDC of compression stroke. Using a suitable tool, **Fig. 21**, slowly apply pressure to bleed down lifter until plunger is completely bottomed. Hold lifter in this position and check clearance between rocker arm and valve. If clearance is not within specifications, install a longer or shorter pushrod as needed.
6. On all models, repeat step 5 or 6 for remaining valves. Turn crankshaft 120° at a time in normal direction of rotation and adjust valves following engine firing order.

### V6-232

A .060 inch longer or a .060 inch shorter pushrod is available to compensate for dimensional changes in the valve train. If clearance is less than specified, the .060 inch shorter pushrod should be used. If clearance is more than the maximum specified, the .060 inch longer pushrod should be used.

Using an auxiliary starter switch crankshaft until No. 1 cylinder is at TDC compression stroke, compress valve lifter using lifter bleed down tool T82C-6500-A or equivalent. At this point, the following valves can be checked:

| | |
|---|---|
| No. 1 Intake | No. 3 Intake |
| No. 1 Exhaust | No. 4 Exhaust |
| No. 2 Exhaust | No. 6 Intake |

After clearance on these valves has been checked, rotate crankshaft until No. 5 cylinder is at TDC compression stroke (1 revolution of crankshaft), and then compress valve lifter using lifter bleed down tool No. T82C-6500-A or equivalent, **Fig. 21**, and check the following valves:

| | |
|---|---|
| No. 2 Intake | No. 5 Intake |
| No. 3 Exhaust | No. 5 Exhaust |
| No. 4 Intake | No. 6 Exhaust |

### V8 ENGINES

To provide a means to compensate for dimensional changes in the valve train and provide for valve adjustment, .060 inch shorter or longer pushrods are available. If the valve clearance is less than the minimum, the .060 inch shorter pushrod should be used. If the clearance is more than the maximum, the longer pushrod should be used. To check the valve clearance, proceed as follows:

1. Mark crankshaft pulley at three locations, with No. 1 location at TDC timing mark (end of compression stroke), location No. 2 one full turn (360°) clockwise from TDC and No. 3 location one quarter turn clockwise (90°) from position No. 2.
2. Turn crankshaft to number 1 location, then compress valve lifter using tappet bleed down tool T71P-6513-A or equivalent, **Fig. 21**, and check the clearance on the following valves:

**V8-255, 302, 460**

| | |
|---|---|
| No. 1 Intake | No. 1 Exhaust |
| No. 7 Intake | No. 5 Exhaust |
| No. 8 Intake | No. 4 Exhaust |

**V8-351 & 400**

| | |
|---|---|
| No. 1 Intake | No. 1 Exhaust |
| No. 4 Intake | No. 3 Exhaust |
| No. 8 Intake | No. 7 Exhaust |

3. Turn crankshaft to number 2 location, then compress valve lifter using tool T71P-6513-A or equivalent, **Fig. 21**, and check the clearance on the following valves:

**V8-255, 302, 460**

| | |
|---|---|
| No. 5 Intake | No. 2 Exhaust |
| No. 4 Intake | No. 6 Exhaust |

**V8-351 & 400**

| | |
|---|---|
| No. 3 Intake | No. 2 Exhaust |
| No. 7 Intake | No. 6 Exhaust |

4. Turn crankshaft to number 3 location, then compress valve lifter using tool T71P-6513-A or equivalent, **Fig. 21**, and check the clearance on the following valves:

**V8-255, 302, 460**

| | |
|---|---|
| No. 2 Intake | No. 7 Exhaust |
| No. 3 Intake | No. 3 Exhaust |
| No. 6 Intake | No. 8 Exhaust |

**V8-351 & 400**

| | |
|---|---|
| No. 2 Intake | No. 4 Exhaust |
| No. 5 Intake | No. 5 Exhaust |
| No. 6 Intake | No. 8 Exhaust |

## VALVE GUIDES

Valve guides in these engines are an integral part of the head and, therefore, cannot be removed. For service, guides can be reamed oversize to accommodate one of three service valves with oversize stems (.003 inch, .015 inch and .030 inch).

Check the valve stem clearance of each valve (after cleaning) in its respective valve guide. If the clearance exceeds the

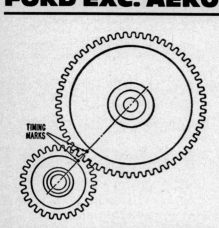

**Fig. 30   Valve timing. 6-300**

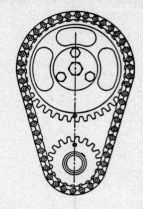

**Fig. 31   Typical V8 engine valve timing alignment marks**

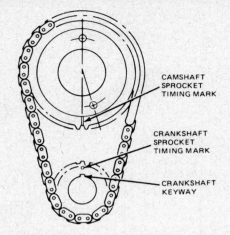

CAMSHAFT SPROCKET TIMING MARK

CRANKSHAFT SPROCKET TIMING MARK

CRANKSHAFT KEYWAY

**Fig. 32   Timing marks aligned for correct valve timing. 1982 V6-232**

service limits of .004 inch of the intake or .005 inch on the exhaust, ream the valve guides to accommodate the next oversize diameter valve.

## ROCKER ARM STUD
### 1980–84 6-300

If necessary to replace a rocker arm stud, a rocker arm stud kit is available and contains a stud remover, a stud installer, and two reamers, one .006 inch and the other .015 inch.

Rocker arm studs that are broken or have damaged threads may be replaced with standard studs. Loose studs in the head may be replaced with .006 inch, .010 inch or .015 inch oversize studs which are available for service.

When going from a standard size stud to a .015 inch oversize stud, always use a .006 inch reamer and a .010 inch reamer before reaming is finished with a .015 inch reamer.

If a stud is broken off flush with the stud boss, use an easy-out to remove the broken stud, following the instructions of the tool manufacturer.

Remove stud with tool T62F-6A527-B, **Fig. 22**, and install new stud with tool T65P-6A527-A, **Fig. 23**.

## ROCKER ARM
### REPLACE
### 1980–84 6-300

These engines use a rocker arm stud and nut. To disassemble, remove rocker arm nut, fulcrum seat and rocker arm, **Fig. 24**. Inspect condition of nut, **Fig. 25**, and replace if necessary.

## ROCKER ARM & FULCRUM BOLT
### V6-232, V8-255, 302, 351M, 351W, 400 & 460 & 1985–86 6-300

The rocker arm is supported by a fulcrum bolt which fits through the fulcrum

seat and threads into the cylinder head. To disassemble, remove the bolt, oil deflector, fulcrum seat and rocker arm, **Figs. 26 and 27**.

**1981-82 models equipped with V8-255, 302 and 351W engines with low profile rocker arm fulcrums (part No. E1TZ-6A528-A) may experience excessive oil displacement when engine is operated for extended periods during high ambient temperatures. This problem may be corrected by replacing original rocker arm fulcrums with part No. D7AZ-6A528-A.**

## HYDRAULIC VALVE LIFTERS
### REPLACE
### 6-300

1. Remove air cleaner and PCV valve on carbureted models. On models with EFI, disconnect inlet air hose from crankcase filter cap. Remove throttle body inlet tubes.
2. On 1980 models, disconnect choke cable from carburetor.
3. On carbureted models, disconnect accelerator cable from carburetor and remove retracting spring. On models with EFI, disconnect accelerator cable from throttle body and remove retracting spring. Remove accelerator cable bracket from upper intake manifold and position cable and bracket aside.
4. On 1985-87 carbureted models, remove fuel line between fuel filter and fuel pump. On models with EFI, remove fuel line from fuel rail. **Do not bend the fuel line.**
5. On models with EFI, remove upper intake manifold and throttle body assembly.
6. On all models, remove coil bracket attaching bolt or E-core assembly attaching nuts and position coil aside.
7. Remove rocker arm cover.
8. Disconnect ignition wires from spark plugs, then remove distributor cap and ignition wires as an assembly. Remove secondary high tension wire from coil.

9. Remove pushrod cover.
10. Loosen rocker arm stud nuts or bolts until rocker arms can be disengaged from pushrods.
11. Remove pushrods and valve lifters in order so they can be installed in original positions. Use a suitable magnetic rod to remove lifters, **Fig. 28**.
12. Reverse procedure to install.

### V6-232, V8-255, 302, 351, 400, & 460

1. Remove intake manifold and if necessary, disconnect thermactor air supply hose from air pump and position out of way.
2. Remove rocker arm covers. Loosen rocker arm stud nuts or bolts and rotate rocker arms to the side.
3. Remove pushrods in sequence so they can be installed in their original bores.
4. Using a magnet, or hydraulic tappet puller tool No. T70L-6500-A, remove the lifters and place them in a numbered rack so they can be installed in their original bores. If lifters are stuck in their bores, it may be necessary to use a plier-type tool to remove them.
5. The internal parts of each lifter are matched sets. Do not intermix parts.

## TIMING CASE COVER
### V6-232

1. Disconnect battery ground cable, then drain cooling system.
2. Remove air cleaner assembly and air intake duct.
3. Remove fan shroud attaching screws and fan and clutch assembly attaching bolts.
4. Remove fan and clutch assembly and fan shroud.
5. Loosen accessory drive belt idler, then remove drive belt and water pump pulley.
6. On models equipped with power steering, remove steering pump

bracket attaching bolts and position pump aside with hoses attached.

7. On models equipped with A/C, remove A/C compressor front support bracket.

8. On all models, disconnect coolant bypass hose and heater hose from water pump and the upper radiator hose from thermostat housing.

9. Disconnect coil wire from distributor cap, then remove cap with wires attached.

10. With cylinder No. 1 at TDC of compression stroke, mark position of rotor to distributor housing and position of distributor housing to front cover.

11. Remove distributor hold-down clamp, then lift distributor from front cover.

12. Raise and support vehicle.

13. Remove crankshaft damper using a suitable puller.

14. Remove fuel pump crash shield, if equipped.

15. Disconnect fuel outlet line from fuel pump.

16. Remove fuel pump attaching bolts and position pump aside with fuel line attached.

17. Remove oil filter, then disconnect lower radiator hose from water pump.

18. Remove oil pan as described under "Oil Pan, Replace".

19. Lower vehicle, then remove timing case cover attaching bolts, **Fig. 29. Ensure to remove the cover attaching bolt located behind the oil filter adapter.**

20. Remove ignition timing indicator, then the timing case cover and water pump as an assembly.

21. Reverse procedure to install. Before installing bolt at location No. 10, **Fig. 29**, coat threads of bolt with pipe sealant D8AZ-19558-A or equivalent. Torque cover attaching bolts to 15-22 ft. lbs. **If a replacement front cover is to be installed, the water pump, oil pump, oil filter adapter and intermediate shaft must be removed from the original front cover and reinstalled on the replacement cover. Also, it may be necessary to rotate crankshaft 180° from the No. 1 cylinder TDC location to position fuel pump eccentric for fuel pump installation. When installing distributor, No. 1 cylinder must be at TDC position and marks made during removal must be aligned.**

## 6-300

1. Drain cooling system.
2. Remove shroud and radiator.
3. Remove alternator adjusting arm bolt, loosen drive belt and swing the adjusting arm aside.
4. Remove fan, drive belts, spacer and pulleys.
5. Remove vibration damper.
6. Remove the front oil pan and front cover attaching screws.
7. Remove timing case cover and discard gasket. Replace crankshaft oil seal with new one.
8. Reverse procedure to install.

## V8-255, 302 & 351W
### E-100—350

1. Drain cooling system and remove fan shroud and radiator retaining bolts.
2. Remove radiator, and if equipped, A/C idler pulley, bracket and belt.
3. Remove upper radiator hose, fan and shroud.
4. Raise and support vehicle.
5. Remove alternator drive belt, then disconnect lower radiator hose from water pump.
6. Remove fuel pump, then lower vehicle.
7. Remove bypass hose, then the power steering pump drive belt (if equipped).
8. Remove pulley and disconnect heater hose from water pump.
9. On models equipped with A/C, remove A/C compressor upper bracket and (if equipped), the power steering pump mount from compressor and water pump.
10. On all models, remove crankshaft pulley and vibration damper.
11. Remove timing case cover-to-oil pan attaching bolts, then the timing case cover and water pump as an assembly.
12. Reverse procedure to install. Apply RTV sealant to oil pan-to-cylinder block mating surface.

### F-100—150 & Bronco

1. Drain cooling system, then remove fan shroud attaching bolts and position shroud over fan.
2. Disconnect hoses from water pump, then remove drive belts, fan, fan spacer and pulley.
3. Loosen alternator pivot bolt and the alternator adjusting arm-to-water pump attaching bolt.
4. Remove crankshaft pulley and vibration damper.
5. Disconnect fuel outlet line from fuel pump, then remove fuel pump attaching bolts and position pump aside.
6. On all models, remove timing case cover-to-oil pan attaching bolts.
7. Cut oil pan gasket flush with cylinder block face, then remove timing case cover and water pump as an assembly.
8. Reverse procedure to install. Apply RTV sealant to oil pan gasket surfaces.

### V8-351M & 400

1. Drain cooling system and disconnect battery cables.
2. Remove fan shroud attaching bolts and slide shroud rearward.
3. Remove fan and fan spacer from water pump shaft.
4. On models equipped with A/C, remove A/C compressor drive belt lower idler pulley and compressor mount-to-water pump bracket.
5. On all models, remove alternator drive belt, power steering pump drive belt (if equipped) and water pump pulley.
6. Remove alternator bracket and power steering pump bracket (if equipped)

from water pump and position aside.

7. Disconnect heater hose and lower radiator hose from water pump.
8. Remove crankshaft pulley, vibration damper and timing pointer.
9. Remove timing case cover-to-cylinder block attaching bolts, then the timing case cover and water pump as an assembly.
10. Reverse procedure to install. Apply suitable sealant to cylinder block and timing case cover gasket surfaces.

## V8-460

1. Drain cooling system and engine oil.
2. Remove radiator shroud and fan, then disconnect radiator hoses from engine.
3. On models equipped with automatic transmission, disconnect oil cooler lines from radiator.
4. On all models, remove radiator upper support and radiator.
5. Loosen alternator mounting bolts and, on models equipped with A/C, the A/C compressor idler pulley.
6. Remove air pump (if equipped), drive belts and water pump pulley.
7. On models equipped with A/C, remove A/C compressor support from water pump.
8. On all models, remove crankshaft pulley, then the vibration damper and woodruff key.
9. Loosen bypass hose, then disconnect heater return tube from water pump.
10. Disconnect fuel lines from fuel pump, then remove pump. Plug open lines to prevent contamination.
11. Remove timing case cover attaching bolts, then the timing case cover and water pump as an assembly.
12. Reverse procedure to install. Apply suitable sealant to cylinder block and timing case cover gasket surfaces.

## TIMING GEARS
### 6-300

When the crankshaft and camshaft lose their timing relationship through removal of timing gears, interference may occur between crankshaft and cam lobes. Therefore, to prevent possible damage to camshaft lobes, do not rotate crankshaft or camshaft without timing gears installed.

### Camshaft Gear

1. With front cover removed, crank engine until timing gear marks are aligned as shown in **Fig. 30**.
2. Install gear puller and remove gear.
3. Ensure key and spacer are properly installed. Align keyway with key and install gear on camshaft.
4. Check backlash between crank and cam gear, using a dial indicator. Hold gear firmly against block while making check. Backlash should be between .002 inch and .004 inch.

### Crankshaft Gear

1. Remove timing gear case cover as

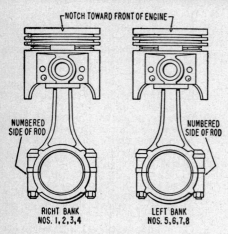

**Fig. 33   Piston & rod assembly. V8-255, 302, 351, 400 & 460**

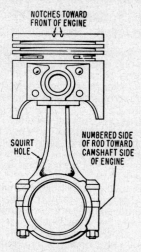

**Fig. 34   Piston & rod assembly. 6-300**

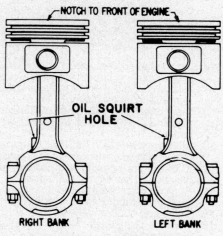

**Fig. 35   Piston & rod assembly. V6-232**

previously described.
2. Remove gear using a suitable puller.
3. Remove key from crankshaft.
4. Reverse procedure to install. Ensure timing marks are aligned, **Fig. 30.**

## TIMING CHAIN
### V6-232, V8-255, 302, 351, 400 & 460

After removing the cover as outlined previously, remove the crankshaft front oil slinger, if equipped. On V6-232 engines, remove camshaft thrust button and spring from end of camshaft. Crank the engine until the timing marks are aligned as shown in **Figs. 31 and 32.** Remove camshaft sprocket retaining bolt, washer and fuel pump eccentric. Slide sprockets and chain forward and remove them as an assembly. Reverse the order of the foregoing procedure to install the chain and sprockets, being sure the camshaft sprocket retaining bolt is torqued to 40-45 ft. lbs. and the timing marks are properly aligned.

## CAMSHAFT
## REPLACE
### 6-300

1. Disconnect battery ground cable.
2. Drain cooling system and engine oil.
3. Remove radiator, valve lifters & front cover.
4. Disconnect outlet lines at fuel pump and position fuel pump aside.
5. Remove distributor.
6. Rotate crankshaft to align timing marks, **Fig. 30.**
7. Remove camshaft thrust plate screws and the camshaft using camshaft gear puller tool No. T82T-6256-A or equivalent. Use caution not to damage the camshaft lobes when removing camshaft.
8. Reverse procedure to install.

### V6-232

1. Remove radiator.
2. If equipped with air conditioning, remove condenser.
3. Remove grille, intake manifold and tappets, then remove front cover and timing chain.
4. Remove oil pan and remove camshaft through front of engine, being careful not to damage bearing surfaces.
5. Reverse procedure to install.

### V8 ENGINES

1. On Econoline models except V8-351M and 400 engines, remove grille.
2. On all models, drain cooling system, then disconnect all lines and hoses from radiator and remove radiator.
3. Remove intake manifold, then the rocker arm covers.
4. Loosen rocker arms, then remove pushrods and valve lifters in sequence.
5. Remove timing case cover and timing chain as previously described.
6. On models equipped with A/C, remove A/C condenser attaching bolts and position condenser aside.
7. On all models, remove camshaft thrust plate and carefully slide camshaft out through front of engine.
8. Reverse procedure to install.

## PISTON & ROD ASSEMBLY

Lubricate all parts with light engine oil. Position the connecting rod in the piston and push the pin into place, **Figs. 33, 34 and 35.** Insert new piston pin retainers (when used) by spiralling them into the piston with the fingers. Do not use pliers.

**Replacement pistons for the following 6-300 equipped vehicles have an increased ring land, which raises the top compression ring .035 inch: 1980-81 E & F-100-250 & Bronco except heavy**

duty. Before installing the new piston, the cylinder ridge must be removed to ensure that the top compression ring does not contact the ridge or deposits formed at the top of the cylinder bore. When removing the ridge, do not cut into the ring travel area more than 1/32 inch.

## CRANKSHAFT REAR OIL SEAL
### EXC. 6-300 & 1984-88 V8-302 & 351W

Some 1985-87 V8-460 engines may use a one piece seal. Refer to "6-300 & 1984-88 V8-302 & 351W" for replacement procedure for one piece seal.

A new rubber split-lip rear crankshaft oil seal is released for service. This seal can be installed without removal of the crankshaft and also eliminates the necessity of seal installation tools.

1. Remove oil pan.
2. Remove rear main bearing cap.
3. Loosen remaining bearing caps, allowing crankshaft to drop down about 1/32 inch.
4. Remove old seals from both cylinder block and rear main bearing cap. Use a brass rod to drift upper half of seal from cylinder block groove. Rotate crankshaft while drifting to facilitate removal.
5. Carefully clean seal groove in block with a brush and solvent. Also clean seal groove in bearing cap. Remove the oil seal retaining pin from the bearing cap if so equipped. The pin is not used with the split-lip seal.
6. Dip seal halves in clean engine oil.
7. Carefully install upper seal half in its groove with undercut side of seal toward front of engine, **Fig. 36,** by rotating it on shaft journal of crankshaft until approximately 3/8 inch protrudes below the parting surface. Ensure no rubber has been shaved from outside

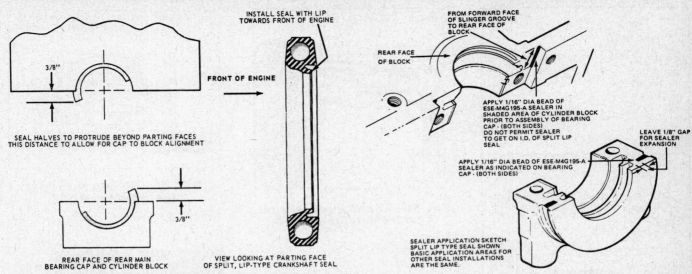

**Fig. 36  Crankshaft rear oil seal installation. All exc. 6-300 & 1984–88 V8-302 & 351W**

**Fig. 37  Applying sealer to crankshaft rear oil seal. All exc. 6-300 & 1984–88 V8-302 & 351W**

diameter of seal by bottom edge of groove.

8. Retighten main bearing caps and torque to specifications.
9. Install lower seal in main bearing cap with undercut side of seal toward front of engine, and allow seal to protrude about 3/8 inch above parting surface to mate with upper seal upon cap installation.
10. Apply suitable sealer to parting faces of cap and block, **Fig. 37**. Install cap and torque to specifications. If difficulty is encountered in installing the upper half of the seal in position, lightly lap (sandpaper the side of the seal opposite the lip side using a medium grit paper). After sanding, the seal must be washed in solvent, then dipped in clean engine oil prior to installation. A revised crankshaft rear oil seal has been released for service. This new seal may be received when ordering an oil pan gasket kit and is installed in the same manner as described previously, **Fig. 38**.

## 6-300 & 1984–88 V8-302 & 351W
### Removal

If crankshaft rear oil seal replacement is the only operation being performed, it can be done in the vehicle. If the oil seal is being replaced in conjunction with a rear main bearing replacement, the engine must be removed from the vehicle. To replace the seal only, proceed as follows:

1. Remove starting motor.
2. Disconnect transmission from engine and slide it back. On manual shift transmission, remove clutch assembly.
3. Remove flywheel and engine rear cover plate.

4. Use an awl to punch two holes in crankshaft rear oil seal. Punch holes on opposite sides of crankshaft and just above bearing cap-to-cylinder block split line. Insert a sheet metal screw in each hole.
5. Use two large screwdrivers or pry bars and pry against both screws at the same time to remove seal. It may be necessary to place small blocks of wood against cylinder block to provide a fulcrum point for pry bars. Use caution to avoid scratching or otherwise damaging crankshaft oil seal surfaces.

### Installation

1. Clean oil seal recess in cylinder block and rear main bearing cap.
2. Coat new oil seal and crankshaft with a light film of engine oil.
3. Start seal in recess and install it until it is fully seated in seal recess, **Fig. 39**.
4. Ensure seal was not damaged during installation and reverse the procedure of removal to complete the operation.

## OIL PAN
## REPLACE
### V6-232

1. Disconnect battery ground cable, then remove air cleaner.
2. Remove fan shroud attaching bolts and position shroud over fan.
3. Remove engine oil dipstick.
4. Raise and support vehicle.
5. Drain engine oil and remove oil filter.
6. Disconnect exhaust pipes from exhaust manifolds, then remove exhaust pipe-to-catalytic converter clamp and the exhaust pipe.
7. Disconnect shift linkage from transmission.
8. On models equipped with automatic

transmission, disconnect oil cooler lines from radiator.
9. On all models, remove engine support-to-chassis brackets attaching nuts.
10. Raise engine assembly using a suitable jack and position wooden blocks between engine supports and chassis brackets, then lower engine to rest on blocks and remove jack.
11. Remove oil pan attaching bolts. Separate pickup tube from oil pump and lay in oil pan, then remove oil pan from vehicle.
12. Reverse procedure to install.

## 6-300 EXC. ECONOLINE

1. Drain cooling system and engine oil.
2. On 1981-87 models, remove radiator. On 1988-89 models, remove upper intake manifold and throttle body.
3. On 1981-87 F-100-250 California models, remove combination air bypass/air control valve from rear of engine.
4. On all models, raise and support vehicle.
5. Remove starter motor.
6. Remove engine front support insulator-to-support bracket attaching nuts and washers.
7. Raise front of engine using a suitable jack and wooden block. Position 1 inch wooden blocks between front support insulators and support brackets, then lower engine to rest on blocks and remove jack.
8. Remove oil pan and inlet tube attaching bolts.
9. Remove inlet tube and screen from oil pump and lay in oil pan. Remove oil pan from vehicle.
10. Reverse procedure to install, **Figs. 40 and 41**.

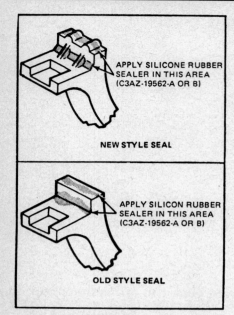

**Fig. 38   Revised crankshaft rear oil seal**

**Fig. 39   Crankshaft rear oil seal installation. 6-300**

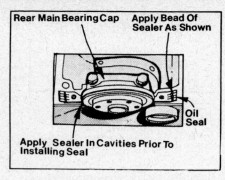

**Fig. 40   Oil pan rear seal installation. 6-300**

## 6-300 ECONOLINE

1. Remove engine cover, air cleaner and carburetor. On EFI Models, remove air cleaner, then disconnect air inlet tubes from throttle body. Remove intake and throttle body
2. On vehicles equipped with air conditioning, discharge refrigerant system, then remove compressor.
3. Remove EGR valve if equipped, then on E-250-HD and E-350 models disconnect thermactor check valve inlet hose and remove check valve.
4. Remove upper radiator hose, fan shroud and automatic transmission filler tube.
5. Remove nuts securing exhaust pipe to manifold.
6. Raise and support vehicle, then disconnect and plug fuel pump inlet hose. Remove alternator heat shield from engine support nuts.
7. Remove power steering return line clip from crossmember, then disconnect lower radiator hose and transmission cooler lines.
8. Remove starter, then raise engine and place 3 inch blocks under engine mounts. Remove oil pan dipstick tube from pan.
9. Remove oil pan bolts, then the pickup screen and tube from oil pump. Remove the pan.
10. Reverse procedure to install, **Figs. 40 and 41.**

## ECONOLINE V8-255, 302 & 351W

1. Disconnect battery ground cable.
2. Remove engine cover and air cleaner, then drain cooling system.
3. On models equipped with power steering, remove steering pump drive

belt, then unfasten pump and position aside.
4. On models equipped with A/C, unfasten A/C compressor and position aside.
5. On all models, disconnect upper radiator hose, then remove fan shroud attaching bolts, oil filler tube and oil dipstick-to-exhaust manifold attaching bolt.
6. Raise and support vehicle.
7. Remove alternator splash shield, then disconnect lower radiator hose.
8. On models equipped with automatic transmission, disconnect oil cooler lines from radiator.
9. On all models, disconnect fuel line from fuel pump, then remove engine mount attaching nuts.
10. Drain engine oil, then remove dipstick tube from oil pan.
11. Disconnect exhaust pipes from exhaust manifolds.
12. On models equipped with automatic transmission, remove transmission oil dipstick and tube.
13. On all models, disconnect manual linkage from transmission, then remove center driveshaft support and driveshaft from transmission.
14. Raise engine and transmission assembly using a suitable jack and a wooden block. Position wooden blocks to support engine at uppermost position, then lower engine to rest on blocks. **When raised, the engine and transmission assembly will pivot around the rear engine mount. The engine assembly must be lifted exactly four inches, measured from front mounts, and remain centered in the engine compartment.**
15. Remove oil pan attaching bolts and lower the pan.
16. On all except 1981-89 models equipped with V8-351W engine, remove oil pump and pickup tube assembly and lay in oil pan.
17. On all models, remove oil pan from vehicle.
18. Reverse procedure to install. Torque oil pan bolts to 9-11 ft. lbs.

## F-100—350 & BRONCO V8-255, 302, 351W, 351M & 400

1. Remove oil level dipstick and tube, then the fan shroud attaching bolts and position shroud over fan.
2. Remove engine mounts-to-chassis bracket retaining nuts.
3. If equipped with automatic transmission, disconnect oil cooler line from left side of radiator.
4. On vehicles equipped with V8-351M and 400 engines, remove starter. On 1988-89 vehicles, remove upper intake manifold.
5. On all models, raise engine and place wooden blocks between engine mounts and chassis brackets.
6. On 1988-89 models, remove exhaust system.
7. On all models, drain oil pan, then remove oil pan attaching bolts and lower oil pan onto crossmember. Support transmission with suitable jackstand and remove crossmember if necessary to facilitate oil pan removal.
8. Remove pickup tube attaching bolts, then lower pickup tube into oil pan and remove oil pan.
9. Reverse procedure to install. Torque oil pan bolts to 9-11 ft. lbs.

## 1980—82 ECONOLINE V8-351M & 400

1. Perform steps 1 thru 8 as described under "Econoline V8-255, 302 & 351W."
2. Position suitable jack under oil pan and place 1¾ inch block of wood between pan and jack. Raise engine 2 inches. **Do not raise engine more than 2 inches, as damage to the air conditioner system will result.**
3. Position wood blocks under engine mounts, then lower engine onto mounts.
4. Remove oil pan from vehicle.
5. Reverse procedure to install. Torque oil pan retaining bolts to 7-9 ft. lbs.

## V8-460

1. Remove engine cover, then disconnect battery ground cable and drain cooling system.

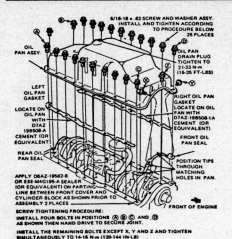

Fig. 41 Oil pan installation. 6-300 engine

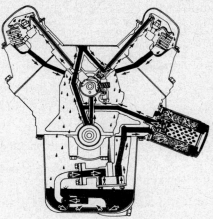

Engine oiling system. V8-302, 351, 400

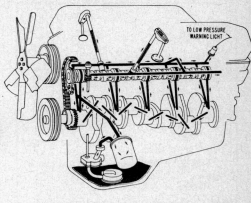

Engine oiling system. V8-460

2. Remove air cleaner, then disconnect throttle and transmission linkages from carburetor.
3. Disconnect power brake vacuum line, if equipped.
4. Disconnect fuel line and choke lines, then remove air cleaner adapter from carburetor.
5. Disconnect upper and lower radiator hoses and transmission oil cooler lines (if equipped) from radiator.
6. Remove fan shroud, fan and radiator.
7. On models equipped with power steering, unfasten steering pump and position aside.
8. On all models, remove front engine mount through bolts, then the engine oil dipstick tube.
9. On models equipped with A/C, move refrigerant lines from rear of compressor downward to clear dash, or remove lines if necessary.
10. On all models, raise and support vehicle.
11. Drain engine oil and remove oil filter.
12. Remove muffler inlet pipe assembly, then disconnect manual and kickdown linkages from transmission.
13. Remove driveshaft and coupling shaft assembly, then the transmission dipstick tube.
14. Remove dipstick and tube from oil pan, then position a suitable jack and a wooden block under oil pan. Raise engine slightly until transmission contacts floor, then block engine in place at the mounts. **The engine assembly must be raised exactly four inches and remain centered in the engine compartment to remove the oil pan.**
15. Remove oil pan attaching bolts and lower the pan.
16. Remove oil pump and pickup tube assembly and lay in oil pan, then slide oil pan rearward and remove from vehicle.
17. Reverse procedure to install. Torque 1/4 inch oil pan bolts to 7-9 ft. lbs. and 5/16 inch oil pan bolts to 8-11 ft. lbs.

## OIL PUMP
## REPLACE
### 6-300

1. After removing oil pan as outlined previously, unfasten and remove oil pump.
2. Prime pump with engine oil.
3. Coat a new pump gasket with oil resistant sealer and place it on pump.
4. Install pump and oil pan. Torque oil pump retaining bolts to 10-12 ft. lbs.

### V6-232

On these engines the oil pump is contained within the front cover.
1. If necessary remove oil filter.
2. Remove oil pump cover attaching bolts and remove cover.
3. Lift pump gears off pocket in front cover.
4. Remove cover gasket. Discard gasket.
5. If necessary, remove pump gears from cover.
6. Reverse procedure to install. If gears have been removed, pack gear pocket with petroleum jelly. Do not use chassis lubricants.

### V8 ENGINES

On some models, the oil pump must be removed when removing the oil pan. These models are indicated in the "Oil Pan, Replace" procedures.
1. Remove oil pan as previously described.
2. Remove oil pump attaching bolts and the oil pump.
3. To install, prime pump with engine oil and apply sealant to gasket.
4. Insert distributor intermediate shaft, making sure that it is properly seated, then install oil pump and torque retaining bolts to 22-32 ft. lbs. **Do not force pump into place if it will not readily seat, as the intermediate shaft may be misaligned with dis-**

tributor shaft. To align, rotate intermediate shaft until pump can be seated without applying force.
5. Install oil pan.

## OIL PUMP SERVICE
## ROTOR TYPE PUMP

1. To disassemble, **Figs. 42, 43 and 44,** remove cover, inner rotor and shaft assembly and outer race. Remove staking marks at relief valve chamber cap. Insert a self-threading sheet metal screw of proper diameter into oil pressure relief valve chamber cap and pull cap out of chamber. Then remove spring and plunger.
2. To assemble, install pressure relief valve plunger, spring and a new cap. Stake cap in place. Install outer race, inner rotor and shaft. **Be sure identification dimple mark on outer race is facing outward and on the same side as dimple on rotor. Inner rotor and shaft and outer race are furnished only as a unit. One part should not be replaced without replacing the other.**
3. Install pump cover.

## WATER PUMP
## REPLACE

All water pumps have a sealed bearing integral with the water pump shaft. The bearing requires no lubrication. A bleed hole in the pump housing allows water that may leak past the seal to be thrown out by the slinger. This is not a lubrication hole. If the pump is damaged and requires repair, replace it with a new pump or a rebuilt one.

### V6-232

1. Drain cooling system.
2. Remove air cleaner and air intake duct.
3. Remove fan and clutch assembly and the fan shroud.
4. Loosen accessory drive idler, then remove drive belt and water pump pulley.
5. On models equipped with power steering, unfasten steering pump and position aside.

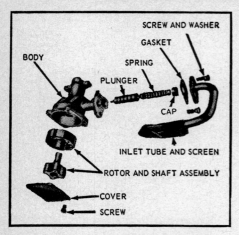

**Fig. 42  Oil pump. 6-300**

6. On models equipped with A/C, remove A/C compressor front support bracket.
7. On all models, disconnect heater hose and bypass hose from water pump.
8. Remove water pump attaching bolts and the water pump.
9. Reverse procedure to install. **Prior to installing the No. 1 bolt, Fig. 45, sealant No. D8AZ-19554-A or equivalent must be applied to the bolt threads.**

## 6-300

1. Drain cooling system, then remove alternator drive belt.
2. On models equipped with A/C, remove A/C compressor drive belt.
3. On all models, remove fan and water pump pulley.
4. Disconnect hoses from water pump.
5. Remove water pump attaching bolts and the water pump.
6. Reverse procedure to install. Torque water pump retaining bolts to 12-18 ft. lbs.

## V8-255, 302 & 351W

### E-100-350

1. Remove air cleaner and intake duct assembly, including crankcase ventilation hose.
2. Drain cooling system, then remove radiator.
3. Remove drive belts, fan, spacer and water pump pulley.
4. Disconnect heater and bypass hoses from water pump.
5. Remove water pump attaching bolts and the water pump.
6. Reverse procedure to install. Torque water pump retaining bolts to 12-18 ft. lbs.

### F-100-350 & Bronco

1. Drain cooling system.
2. Remove fan shroud attaching bolts and position shroud over fan.
3. Disconnect lower radiator hose, heater hose and bypass hose from water pump.

4. Remove drive belts, fan, spacer, water pump pulley and fan shroud.
5. Loosen alternator pivot bolt and alternator adjusting arm-to-water pump attaching bolt.
6. Remove water pump attaching bolts and the water pump.
7. Reverse procedure to install. Torque water pump retaining bolts to 12-18 ft. lbs.

## V8-351M & 400

1. Disconnect battery ground cable, then drain cooling system.
2. Remove fan shroud attaching bolts and slide shroud rearward.
3. Remove fan and fan spacer.
4. On models equipped with A/C, remove A/C compressor drive belt, lower idler pulley and compressor mount-to-water pump bracket.
5. On all models, remove alternator drive belt and power steering pump drive belt (if equipped).
6. Remove water pump pulley, then the alternator bracket from water pump.
7. On models equipped with power steering, unfasten steering pump bracket from water pump and position aside.
8. On all models, disconnect lower radiator hose and heater hose from water pump.
9. Remove water pump attaching bolts and the water pump.
10. Reverse procedure to install.

## V8-460

1. Drain cooling system, then remove fan shroud and fan.
2. On models equipped with power steering, loosen steering pump attaching bolts.
3. On models equipped with A/C, remove A/C compressor upper bracket, then the idler arm and bracket, compressor drive belt and power steering pump drive belt (if equipped).
4. On models equipped with Thermactor, remove Thermactor pump.
5. On all models, loosen alternator pivot bolt, then remove attaching bolts and spacer.
6. Remove alternator adjustment arm bolt, pivot bolt and drive belt, then the alternator and bracket as an assembly.
7. On all models equipped with power steering, remove steering pump attaching bolts and position pump aside.
8. On all models, disconnect lower radiator hose and heater hose from water pump.
9. Remove water pump attaching bolts and the water pump.
10. Reverse procedure to install. Torque water pump retaining bolts to 15-21 ft. lbs.

## BELT TENSION DATA

| | New Lbs. | Used Lbs. |
|---|---|---|
| 1980-82 Exc. 1/4 inch | 65 | 50 |

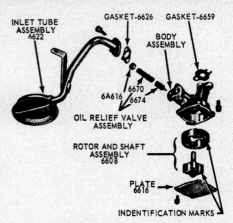

**Fig. 43  Oil pump. V8-255, 302, 351W**

| | | New Lbs. | Used Lbs. |
|---|---|---|---|
| | 1/4 inch | 140 | 105 |
| 1983 | V6-232 | 170 | 150 |
| 1983-86 | Exc. Air Pump | 140 | 120 |
| | Air Pump | | |
| | Exc. 6-300 | | |
| | Less A/C | 110 | 90 |
| | 6-300 Less | | |
| | A/C | 70 | 50 |
| 1987 | | | |
| | 6-300 | – | – |
| | V8-302 | – | – |
| | V8-351 | 140 | 100 |
| | V8-460 | 140 | 100 |
| | V8-444 Diesel | | |
| | Less A/C | 160 | 110 |
| | With A/C | 140 | 100 |
| 1988 | | | |
| | 6-300 | 90 | 90 |
| | V8-302 | 75 | 75 |
| | V8-351 | 75 | 75 |
| | V8-460 | | |
| Less Auto Trans. | | 150-190 | 140-160 |
| With Auto Trans. | | ① | ① |
| | V8-444 Diesel | | |
| | V-belt | 120 | 100 |
| | Less A/C | 140 | 100 |
| | With A/C | 160 | 115 |
| 1989 | | | |
| | 6-300 | ① | ① |
| | V8-302 | ① | ① |
| | V8-351 | ① | ① |
| | V8-460 | ① | ① |
| | V8-444 diesel | | |
| Vacuum Pump V-belt | | 90-130 | 72 |
| Exc. Vacuum Pump V-belt | | 140-180 | 104 |

①Tension is correct if belt tensioner is within marks.

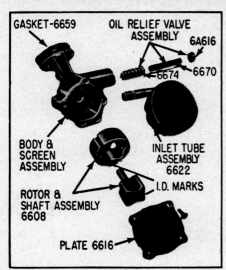

Fig. 44 Oil pump assembly. 351M & 400

## MECHANICAL FUEL PUMP
### REPLACE

1. Loosen fuel line connections, then re-tighten hand tight. Do not disconnect lines at this time.
2. Loosen fuel pump attaching bolts one or two turns. Apply hand force to break pump free from gasket.

3. Rotate engine slightly until pump cam lobe is near lowest position.
4. Disconnect inlet and outlet lines and the vapor return line, if equipped, from pump.
5. Remove fuel pump attaching bolts and the pump. Remove and discard gasket.
6. Reverse procedure to install.

## ELECTRIC FUEL PUMP
### REPLACE
### 6-300, V8-302 & V8-351W

The fuel pump system used on electronic fuel injection (EFI) engines consists of two pumps: a high pressure pump mounted on the frame rail and a low pressure mounted in the fuel tank.

#### High Pressure Pump

The high pressure fuel pump is frame mounted and can be accessed from under the vehicle.

The fuel pump assembly is retained to the frame with three bolts. Before removing the high pressure fuel pump, disconnect battery ground cable, then relieve fuel system pressure using fuel pressure gauge T80L-9974-A or equivalent on the feeler diagnostic valve, or by opening the electrical circuit to the fuel pump and cranking the engine for a minimum of 20 seconds.

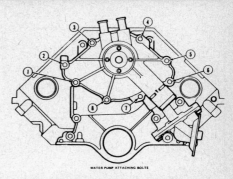

Fig. 45 Water pump installation. V6-232 engine

#### Low Pressure Pump

The low pressure pump is located in the fuel tank and may require lowering or removal of the fuel tank. With fuel tank lowered, if necessary, disconnect battery ground cable and pump electrical connector. Remove locking ring then the pump.

#### V8-460

In order to replace the fuel pump assembly, it is necessary to access the fuel tank. With fuel tank lowered or removed, disconnect battery ground cable and pump electrical connector. Remove locking ring and pump assembly.

# DIESEL ENGINE
## INDEX

## GLOW PLUG FAST START SYSTEM

The glow plug fast start system controls glow plug operation according to various operating conditions. When the ignition switch is turned on, the control switch is energized, which, in turn, energizes the power relay. The power relay contacts close and battery current is directed to the glow plugs. When the glow plugs reach a predetermined temperature, current to the plugs and the wait lamp is cut off. At this time, the engine can be started. After the engine is started, the glow plugs will cycle on and off for 40-90 seconds. This cycling of the glow plugs helps to eliminate start up exhaust smoke.

A control switch, threaded into the cylinder head coolant jacket, senses engine coolant temperature. When restarting a warm engine, the glow plug system will not be activated unless the coolant temperature falls below normal operating temperature.

When diagnosing the glow plug system, start with the Basic Test first. If the system passes the Basic Test, the problem does not exist within the glow plug system. If while doing the Basic Test a problem is found, proceed to the Pinpoint Test specified. Upon completion of any repair procedure, the Basic Test should be done again to assure proper operation of glow plug system.

Refer to **Figs. 1 through 6** for glow plug system troubleshooting procedures.

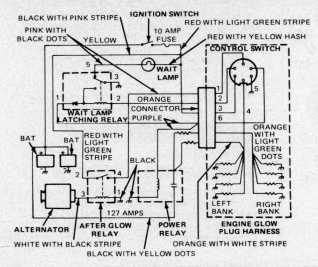

**Fig. 1  Glow plug system wiring diagram. 1983**

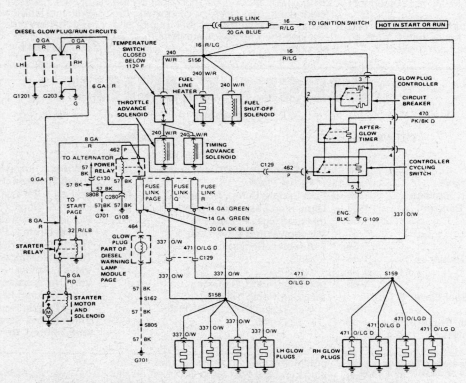

**Fig. 2  Glow plug system wiring diagram. 1984-86**

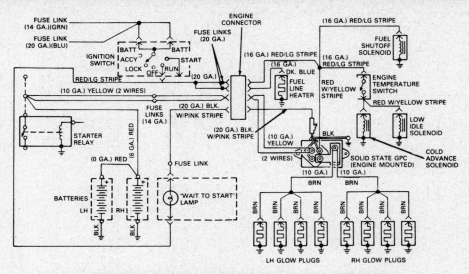

**Fig. 3   Glow plug system wiring diagram. 1987–89**

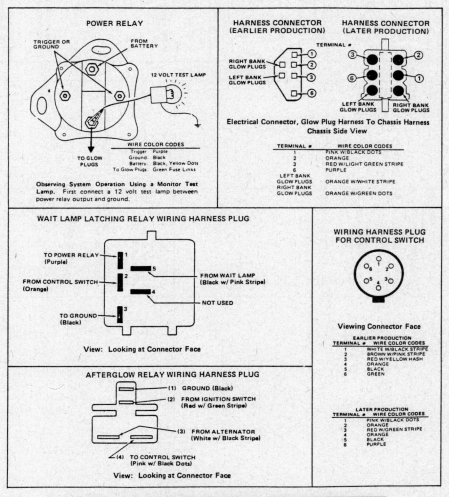

## Glow Plug System Basic Diagnostic Test

| TEST STEP | RESULT | ACTION TO TAKE |
|---|---|---|
| **1 KEY IN RUN POSITION, ENGINE OFF** | | |
| • Connect a 12-volt test lamp between the power relay output (green leads) (to glow plugs) and ground. | | |
| TEST LAMP — TO GLOW PLUGS (OUTPUT) | | |
| • Turn ignition switch to ON position. | Test lamp lights, stays lit for 4 to 10 seconds, then cycles on and off | GO to 2 |
| | Test lamp does not light | GO to Pinpoint Test C |
| | Test lamp lights, stays on continuously | GO to Pinpoint Test B |
| | Test lamp lights, stays lit for 4 to 10 seconds, then goes out and stays out | GO to Pinpoint Test E |
| **2 ENGINE STARTED** | | |
| • Leave 12-volt test lamp connected from Step 1. | | |
| • Start engine. | | |
| • Test lamp should cycle on and off for 20 to 90 seconds. | Test lamp cycles for 20 to 90 seconds, then turns off | GO to Pinpoint Test A |
| | Test lamp continues to cycle after 90 seconds | GO to Pinpoint Test D |
| | Test lamp does not light | GO to Pinpoint Test E |

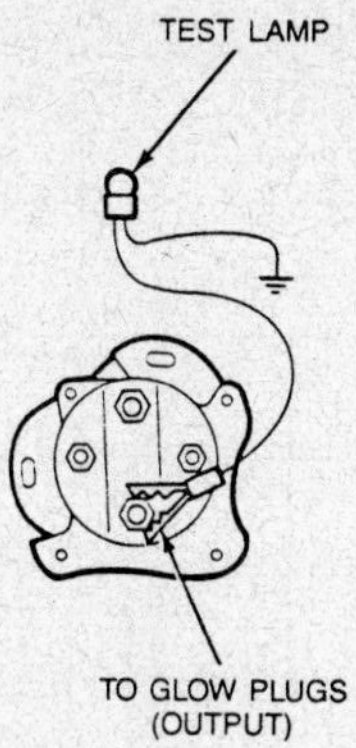

**Fig. 4 Fast start glow plug diagnosis (Part 2 of 23), 1983 6.9L diesel**

## Pinpoint Test A — Test Lamp Signal Correct

| TEST STEP | RESULT | ACTION TO TAKE |
|---|---|---|
| **A1 CHECK VOLTAGE TO EACH GLOW PLUG** | | |
| • Remove all leads from glow plugs. | Ok at all leads | GO to A4 |
| • Connect 12-volt test lamp between power relay output (green leads) (to glow plugs) and ground. 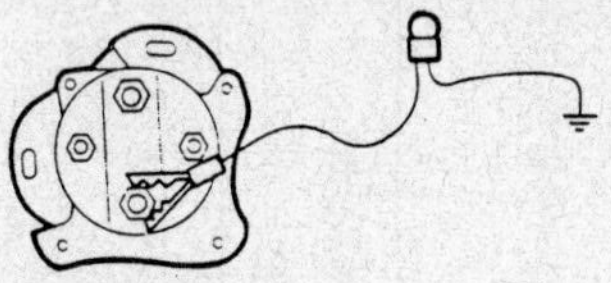 | Not OK at any or all leads | GO to A2 |
| • Turn key to ON position. | | |
| • Check voltage at each glow plug lead, with voltmeter, or equivalent, whenever test lamp is lit. | | |
| • Voltage should be minimum of 11 volts. | | |
| **A2 CHECK CHASSIS HARNESS FUSIBLE LINKS** | | |
| • Turn key to OFF position. | OK | GO to A3 |
| • Disconnect fusible links from chassis harness and engine glow plug harness. | Not OK | REPLACE fusible link(s). REPEAT Test Step A1 |
| • Check continuity of fusible links with ohmmeter. | | |
| **A3 CHECK ENGINE HARNESS FUSIBLE LINKS** | | |
| • Key in OFF position. | Less than 1 ohm | GO to A4 |
| • Disconnect engine harness from chassis connector and all glow plugs. | 1 ohm or more | REPLACE engine harness. CHECK vehicle operation. |
| • Check resistance between chassis connector left and right bank glow plug terminals (green leads) and each glow plug lead. | | |

**Fig. 4 Fast start glow plug diagnosis (Part 3 of 23), 1983 6.9L diesel**

## Test Lamp Signal Correct — Pinpoint Test — A

| TEST STEP | RESULT | ACTION TO TAKE |
|---|---|---|
| **A4 CHECK GLOW PLUG RESISTANCE**<br>• Key in OFF position.<br><br>• Remove test lamp from power relay.<br><br>• Check for resistance between glow plug terminal and metal case of glow plug.<br><br>• Resistance should be less than 2 ohms. | Less than 2 ohms at all glow plugs | Glow plug system OK. GO to Engine Performance Diagnostic Procedure if problem is hard starting. |
| | 2 ohms or greater at one or more glow plugs | REPLACE damaged glow plug(s), RECONNECT glow system leads. CHECK vehicle operation. |

**Fig. 4 Fast start glow plug diagnosis (Part 4 of 23). 1983 6.9L diesel**

## Test Lamp On Continuously — Pinpoint Test — B

| TEST STEP | RESULT | ACTION TO TAKE |
|---|---|---|
| **B1 ISOLATE DAMAGED COMPONENT**<br>CAUTION: Remove leads from all glow plugs before proceeding with this test. Do not reconnect leads to glow plugs until system has been rechecked for correct operation.<br><br>• Connect 12-volt test lamp to power relay output (green leads) (to glow plugs) and ground.<br><br>TEST LAMP<br>TO GLOW PLUGS (OUTPUT) | OK | REPLACE control switch. REPEAT Basic Test. |
| | not OK | GO to B2 . |
| • Turn key to ON position, but do not start engine.<br><br>• Disconnect harness plug from control switch.<br><br>• Test lamp should turn OFF. | | |
| **B2 CHECK ENGINE WIRING HARNESS**<br>• Test lamp connected between power relay output (green leads) (to glow plugs) and ground.<br><br>• Turn key to ON position.<br><br>• Disconnect engine harness from chassis harness.<br><br>• Does test lamp go out? | Yes | REPLACE engine harness. GO to B6 . |
| | No | GO to B3 . |

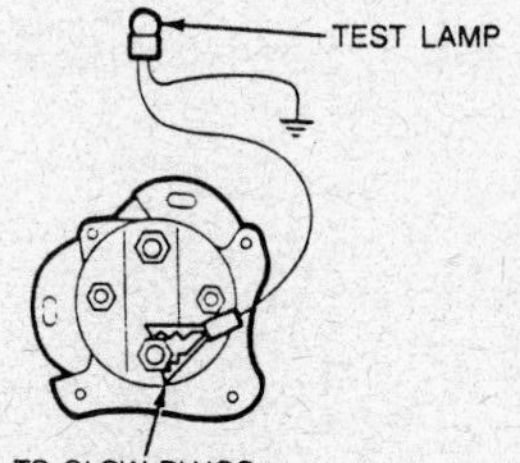

**Fig. 4 Fast start glow plug diagnosis (Part 5 of 23). 1983 6.9L diesel**

## Pinpoint Test B — Test Lamp On Continuously

| TEST STEP | RESULT | ACTION TO TAKE |
|---|---|---|
| **B6 CHECK GLOW PLUG RESISTANCE**<br>• Key in OFF position.<br><br>• Engine harness disconnected at glow plugs.<br><br>• Check resistance between glow plug terminal and metal shell of glow plug.<br>• Resistance should be less than 2 ohms. | ▲ (OK) ▲<br><br>One or more glow plugs (OK̸) ▲ | Glow plug system OK. RECONNECT engine harness leads to glow plugs. REPEAT Basic Test.<br><br>REPLACE glow plugs as necessary. RECONNECT engine harness to glow plugs. REPEAT Basic Test. |

OHMMETER / GLOW PLUG / TERMINAL / METAL SHELL

**Fig. 4  Fast start glow plug diagnosis (Part 7 of 23). 1983 6.9L diesel**

## Pinpoint Test B — Test Lamp On Continuously

| TEST STEP | RESULT | ACTION TO TAKE |
|---|---|---|
| **B3 CHECK POWER RELAY**<br>• With key in OFF position, disconnect signal lead (purple) from power relay.<br>• Turn key to ON position.<br>• Does test lamp go out? | ▲<br>Yes ▲<br><br>No ▲ | REPAIR or REPLACE chassis wiring harness. GO to B4.<br><br>REPLACE power relay. GO to B4. |
| **B4 CHECK CONTINUITY OF FUSIBLE WIRES IN ENGINE HARNESS**<br>• Key in OFF position.<br>• Remove test lamp from power relay.<br>• Glow plug leads and power relay output lead still disconnected.<br>• Check continuity between each glow plug lead and power relay output lead.<br>• Resistance should be less than 1 ohm. | All glow plug leads are less than 1 ohm ▲<br><br>One or more glow plug leads are 1 ohm or greater ▲ | GO to B6.<br><br>GO to B5. |
| **B5 CHECK CHASSIS HARNESS FUSIBLE LINKS**<br>• Key in OFF position.<br><br>• Disconnect engine harness from chassis harness.<br><br>• Disconnect chassis harness fusible links from chassis harness.<br>• Check resistance of fusible links.<br>• Resistance should be less than 1 ohm. | (OK) ▲<br><br>(OK̸) ▲ | REPLACE engine harness. GO to B6.<br><br>REPLACE fuse link(s) as necessary. REPEAT Test Step B4. |

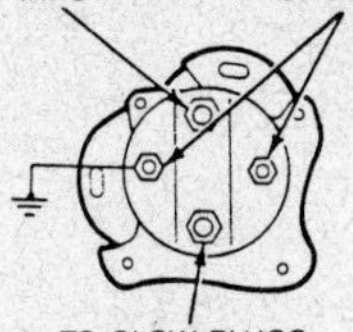

SIGNAL OR GROUND / FROM BATTERY INPUT / TO GLOW PLUGS (OUTPUT)

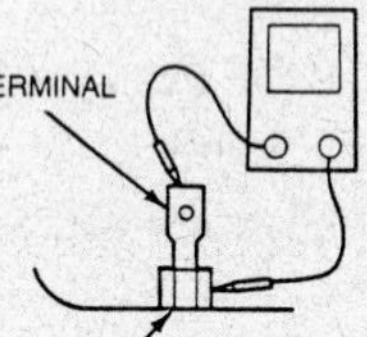

**Fig. 4  Fast start glow plug diagnosis (Part 6 of 23). 1983 6.9L diesel**

## Pinpoint Test C — Test Lamp Does Not Light

### Fig. 4 Fast start glow plug diagnosis (Part 9 of 23). 1983 6.9L diesel

| TEST STEP | RESULT | ACTION TO TAKE |
|---|---|---|
| **C4 REPLACE FUSE**<br>• Replace fusible link.<br>• Repeat Basic Test. | Fuse blows | GO to C5. |
|  | Fuse does not blow — system still not operating | GO to C8. |
|  | Fuse does not blow | System OK. |
| **C5 CHECK POWER RELAY**<br>• Remove signal lead (purple) from power relay.<br>• Replace fusible link.<br>• Turn key to ON position.<br>SIGNAL OR GROUND<br>• Turn key OFF. | Fuse blows | GO to C6. |
|  | Fuse does not blow | REPLACE power relay. REPEAT Basic Test. |
| **C6 CHECK SYSTEM WIRING**<br>• Disconnect chassis harness from engine harness.<br>• Replace fusible link.<br>• Turn key to ON position.<br>• Turn key OFF. | Fuse blows | REPAIR chassis wirings. REPEAT Basic Test. |
|  | Fuse does not blow | GO to C7. |

## Pinpoint Test C — Test Lamp Does Not Light

### Fig. 4 Fast start glow plug diagnosis (Part 8 of 23). 1983 6.9L diesel

| TEST STEP | RESULT | ACTION TO TAKE |
|---|---|---|
| **C1 VERIFY CONDITION**<br>• Connect a 12-volt test lamp between power relay output (Green leads to glow plugs) and ground.<br>• Turn key to ON position. (Do not start engine.)<br>• Observe test lamp.<br> | Test lamp lights | GO to Pinpoint Test E. |
|  | Test lamp does not light | This is normal with a warm engine (engine coolant at normal operating temperature or above.) If engine coolant is below normal operating temperature. TURN key OFF. Wait 5 minutes. TURN key to ON and observe test lamp. If lamp lights, GO to Pinpoint Test E. If it does not light, GO to C2. |
| **C2 CHECK BATTERIES**<br>• Check batteries for state of charge. (If batteries will crank engine, they will operate glow plug system.) | OK | GO to C3. |
|  | not OK | CHARGE or REPLACE batteries as necessary. REPEAT Basic Test. |
| **C3 CHECK IN-LINE FUSE**<br>• Check fusible link between ignition switch and control switch. (Circuit 16, Wht/Blk.) | OK | GO to C8. |
|  | not OK | GO to C4. |

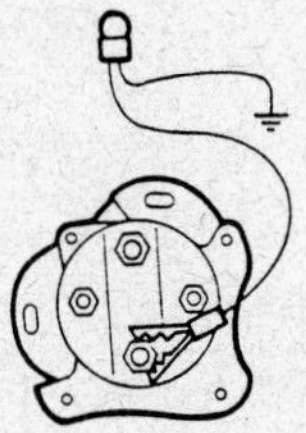

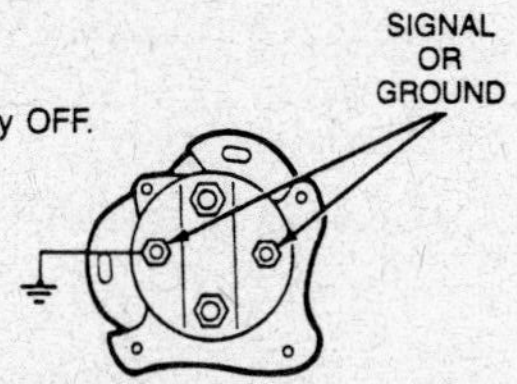

## Pinpoint Test — C

**Test Lamp Does Not Light**

| TEST STEP | RESULT | ACTION TO TAKE |
|---|---|---|
| **C9 CHECK VOLTAGE TO CONTROL SWITCH**<br>• Remove engine harness connector to control switch.<br>• Turn key to ON position.<br>• Check voltage between control switch connector Pin No. 3 and ground.<br>• Voltage should be minimum of 11 volts. | OK<br>Not OK | GO to C11.<br>GO to C10. |
| **C10 CHECK VOLTAGE TO ENGINE HARNESS**<br>• Key in OFF position.<br>• Disconnect chassis harness from engine harness.<br>• Turn key to ON position.<br>• Check voltage at Pin No. 3 on chassis side of connector.<br>• Voltage should be minimum of 11 volts. | OK<br>Not OK | REPLACE engine harness. REPEAT Basic Test.<br>REPAIR or REPLACE chassis wiring as necessary. REPEAT Basic Test. |

**Fig. 4  Fast start glow plug diagnosis (Part 11 of 23). 1983 6.9L diesel**

## Pinpoint Test — C

**Test Lamp Does Not Light**

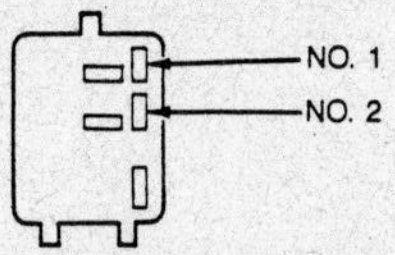

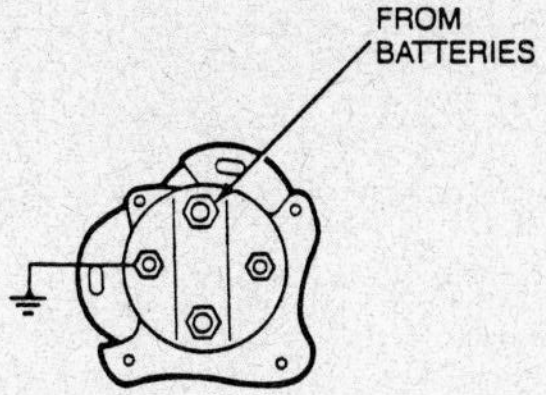

| TEST STEP | RESULT | ACTION TO TAKE |
|---|---|---|
| **C7 CHECK RESISTANCE OF LATCHING RELAY**<br>• Disconnect harness connector at latching relay.<br>• Check resistance between terminals No. 1 and No. 2 of latching relay with red probe (+) on terminal No. 2 and black probe (−) on terminal No. 1.<br>• Resistance should be minimum of 45 ohms. | 45 ohms or greater<br>Less than 45 ohms | REPLACE engine harness. REPEAT Basic Test.<br>REPLACE latching relay. REPEAT Basic Test. |
| **C8 CHECK VOLTAGE TO POWER RELAY**<br>• Key in OFF position.<br>• Connect voltmeter between power relay input terminal (from batteries) and ground.<br>• Voltage should be minimum of 11 volts. | OK<br>Not OK | GO to C9.<br>CHARGE or REPLACE batteries as necessary, and/or repair wiring from batteries to power relay. REPEAT Basic Test. |

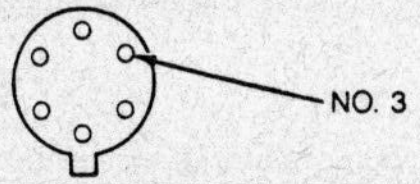

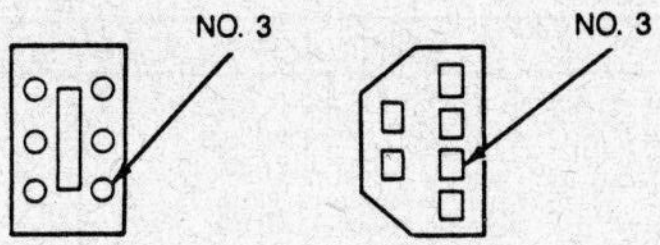

**Fig. 4  Fast start glow plug diagnosis (Part 10 of 23). 1983 6.9L diesel**

## Pinpoint Test C — Test Lamp Does Not Light

| TEST STEP | RESULT | ACTION TO TAKE |
|---|---|---|
| **C13** CHECK SIGNAL TO POWER RELAY<br>• Key in OFF position.<br>• Connect all leads, except power relay signal lead (purple).<br>• Wait 5 minutes, then turn key to ON position.<br>• Check voltage between signal lead (purple) and ground.<br>• Voltage for one cycle should be 11 volts minimum. | OK ▲ | REPAIR power relay ground connection and or REPLACE power relay. REPEAT basic test. |
| | Not OK ▲ | GO to C14 |

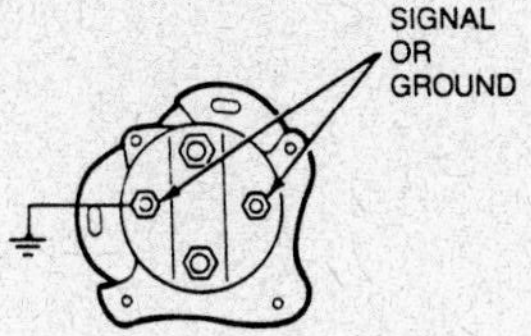

SIGNAL OR GROUND

**Fig. 4 Fast start glow plug diagnosis (Part 13 of 23). 1983 6.9L diesel**

## Pinpoint Test C — Test Lamp Does Not Light

| TEST STEP | RESULT | ACTION TO TAKE |
|---|---|---|
| **C11** CHECK RESISTANCE OF SYSTEM WIRING<br>• Key in OFF position.<br>• Disconnect power relay signal lead (purple).<br>• Disconnect engine harness at control switch.<br>• Check resistance between control switch connector Pin No. 6 and power relay signal lead (purple).<br>• Resistance should be less than 1 ohm. | OK ▲ | GO to C13 |
| | Not OK ▲ | GO to C12 |
| **C12** CHECK RESISTANCE OF CHASSIS WIRING<br>• Key in OFF position.<br>• Disconnect chassis harness from engine harness.<br>• Disconnect power relay signal lead.<br>• Check resistance between chassis side wiring connector Pin No. 2 or No. 6 (as shown) and power signal lead (purple).<br>• Resistance should be less than 1 ohm. | OK ▲ | REPLACE engine harness. REPEAT Basic Test. |
| | Not OK ▲ | REPAIR or REPLACE chassis wiring. REPEAT Basic Test. |

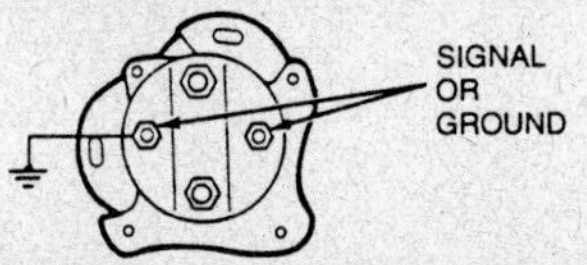

SIGNAL OR GROUND

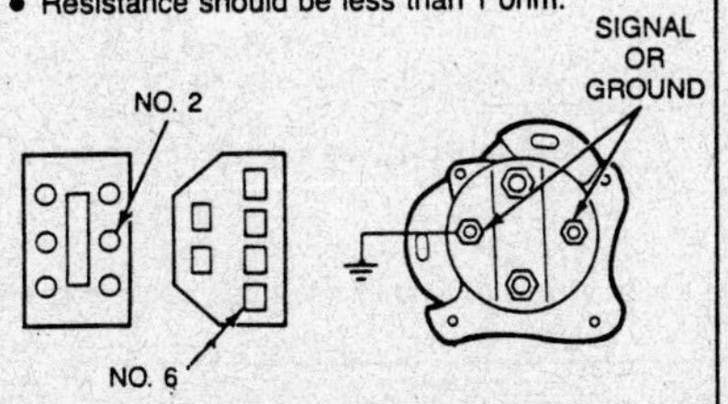

NO. 2    NO. 6

**Fig. 4 Fast start glow plug diagnosis (Part 12 of 23). 1983 6.9L diesel**

## Test Lamp Does Not Light | Pinpoint Test | C

| TEST STEP | RESULT | ACTION TO TAKE |
|---|---|---|
| **C14** CHECK FOR GLOW VOLTAGE<br>• Disconnect harness plug at control switch.<br>• Turn key to ON, but do not start engine.<br>• Check for voltage between control harness plug Pin No. 1 and ground. | Zero volts | REPLACE glow plug control switch. REPEAT Basic Test. |
| | Voltage detected | REPAIR alternator or vehicle wiring and REPLACE after-glow relay as necessary. REPEAT Basic Test. |

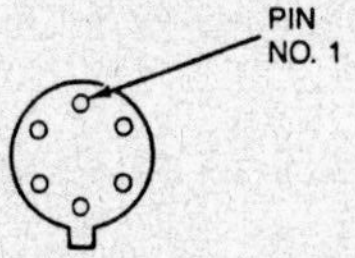

PIN NO. 1

**Fig. 4  Fast start glow plug diagnosis (Part 14 of 23). 1983 6.9L diesel**

## Test Lamp Cycles Continuously | Pinpoint Test | D

| TEST STEP | RESULT | ACTION TO TAKE |
|---|---|---|
| **D1** CHECK AFTER GLOW VOLTAGE<br>• Remove engine harness connector at control switch.<br>• Start engine.<br>• Check for voltage between control switch connector, Pin No. 1 and ground.<br>• Voltage should be 11 volts or greater. | OK | TURN engine OFF. REPLACE control switch. REPEAT Basic Test. |
| | Not OK | GO to D2. |
| **D2** CHECK AFTER GLOW RELAY FOR ADEQUATE GROUND<br>• Key in OFF position.<br>• Disconnect chassis harness connector from after glow relay.<br>• Check connector terminal No. 1 for ground. | OK | GO to D3. |
| | Not OK | REPAIR or REPLACE ground wiring as necessary. REPEAT Basic Test. |

NO. 1

NO. 1

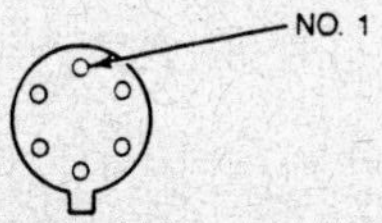

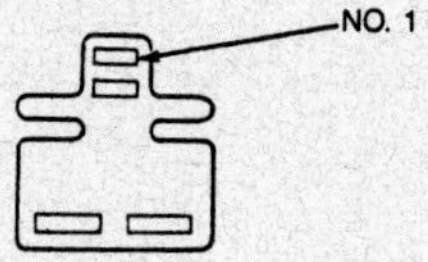

**Fig. 4  Fast start glow plug diagnosis (Part 15 of 23). 1983 6.9L diesel**

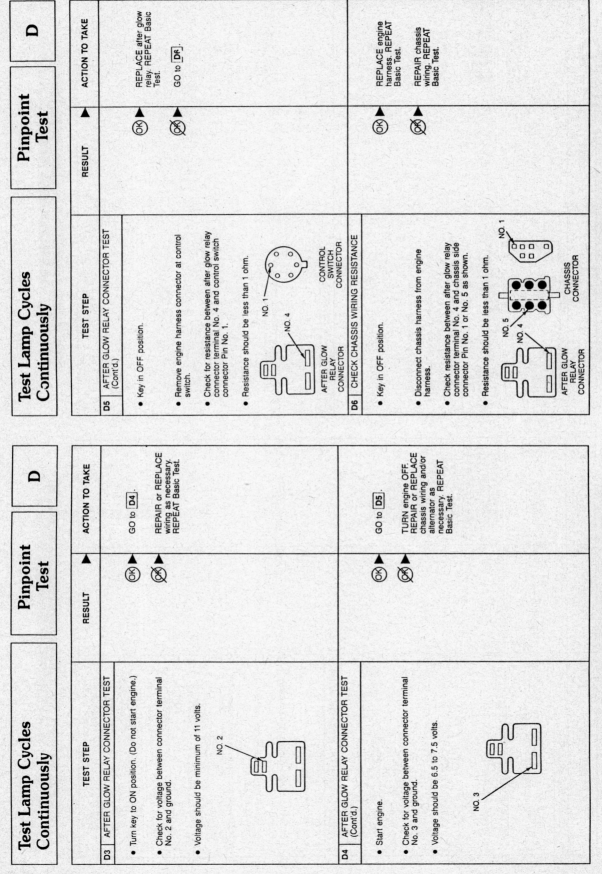

**Test Lamp Cycles Continuously**

**Pinpoint Test** — **D**

| TEST STEP | RESULT | ACTION TO TAKE |
|---|---|---|
| **D5** AFTER GLOW RELAY CONNECTOR TEST (Cont'd.) • Key in OFF position. • Remove engine harness connector at control switch. • Check for resistance between after glow relay connector terminal No. 4 and control switch connector Pin No. 1. • Resistance should be less than 1 ohm. | OK ⊗ | REPLACE after glow relay. REPEAT Basic Test. GO to D6. |
| **D6** CHECK CHASSIS WIRING RESISTANCE • Key in OFF position. • Disconnect chassis harness from engine harness. • Check resistance between after glow relay connector terminal No. 4 and chassis side connector Pin No. 1 or No. 5 as shown. • Resistance should be less than 1 ohm. | OK ⊗ | REPLACE engine harness. REPEAT Basic Test. REPAIR chassis wiring. REPEAT Basic Test. |

**Fig. 4   Fast start glow plug diagnosis (Part 17 of 23). 1983 6.9L diesel**

**Test Lamp Cycles Continuously**

**Pinpoint Test** — **D**

| TEST STEP | RESULT | ACTION TO TAKE |
|---|---|---|
| **D3** AFTER GLOW RELAY CONNECTOR TEST • Turn key to ON position. (Do not start engine.) • Check for voltage between connector terminal No. 2 and ground. • Voltage should be minimum of 11 volts. | OK ⊗ | GO to D4. REPAIR or REPLACE wiring as necessary. REPEAT Basic Test. |
| **D4** AFTER GLOW RELAY CONNECTOR TEST (Cont'd.) • Start engine. • Check for voltage between connector terminal No. 3 and ground. • Voltage should be 6.5 to 7.5 volts. | OK ⊗ | GO to D5. TURN engine OFF. REPAIR or REPLACE chassis wiring and/or alternator as necessary. REPEAT Basic Test. |

**Fig. 4   Fast start glow plug diagnosis (Part 16 of 23). 1983 6.9L diesel**

## Pinpoint Test — E

### Test Lamp Does Not Cycle

| TEST STEP | RESULT | ACTION TO TAKE |
|---|---|---|
| **E3** CHECK CHASSIS HARNESS FUSIBLE LINKS<br>• Key in OFF position.<br>• Disconnect chassis harness from engine harness.<br>• Disconnect fusible links from chassis harness.<br>• Check resistance of fusible links.<br>• Resistance should be less than 1 ohm. | (OK) | REPLACE engine harness. REPEAT Basic Test. |
| | (OK crossed out) | REPLACE fusible link(s). REPEAT Basic Test. |
| **E4** CHECK ENGINE HARNESS GROUND<br>• Key in OFF position.<br>• Check resistance between control switch connector Pin No. 5 and ground.<br>• Resistance should be less than 1 ohm. | (OK) | GO to E5. |
| | (OK crossed out) | REPAIR engine harness ground connection or REPLACE engine harness as necessary. REPEAT Basic Test. |

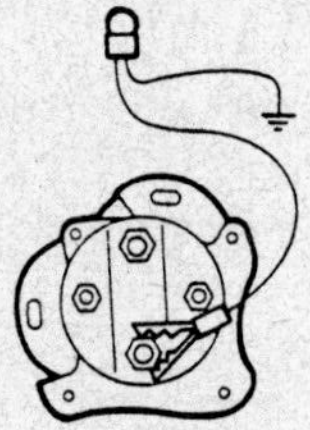

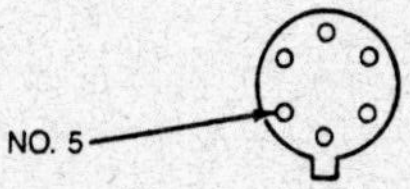

NO. 5

**Fig. 4 Fast start glow plug diagnosis (Part 19 of 23). 1983 6.9L diesel**

## Pinpoint Test — E

### Test Lamp Does Not Cycle

| TEST STEP | RESULT | ACTION TO TAKE |
|---|---|---|
| **E1** OBSERVE TEST LAMP<br>• Connect 12-volt test lamp between power relay output (green leads) (to glow plugs) and ground.<br>• Turn key to ON position. (Do not start engine.)<br>• Observe test lamp. | Lamp lights | GO to E2. |
| | Lamp does not light | This is normal and expected if engine coolant temperature is 60°C (140°F) or above. If coolant temperature is below 60°C (140°F), TURN key to OFF, WAIT 5 minutes, TURN key to ON position. If lamp lights, GO to E2.<br>If lamp does not light, GO to Pinpoint Test C. |
| **E2** CHECK WIRING HARNESS RESISTANCE<br>• Key in OFF position.<br>• Disconnect chassis harness from glow plug power relay.<br>• Disconnect engine harness from control switch and all glow plugs.<br>• Check resistance between control switch Pin No. 4 and glow plug relay power output connector.<br>• Resistance should be less than 1 ohm. | (OK) | GO to E4. |
| | (OK crossed out) | GO to E3. |

OUTPUT (GREEN LEADS) GLOW PLUG POWER RELAY

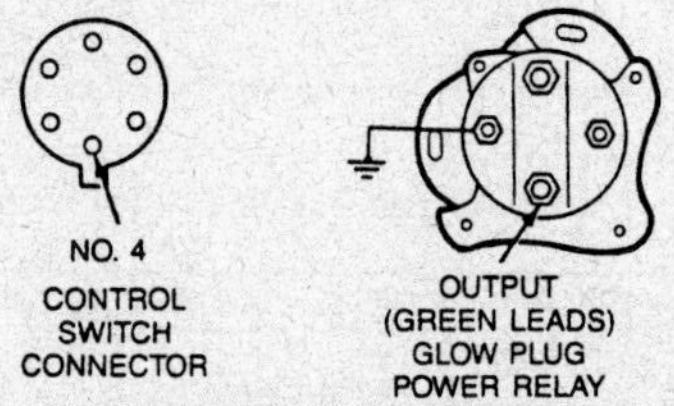

NO. 4 CONTROL SWITCH CONNECTOR

**Fig. 4 Fast start glow plug diagnosis (Part 18 of 23). 1983 6.9L diesel**

**Test Lamp Does Not Cycle**

**Pinpoint Test** | **E**

| TEST STEP | RESULT | ACTION TO TAKE |
|---|---|---|
| **E7** CHECK AFTER GLOW VOLTAGE<br>• Remove engine harness connector at control switch.<br>• Turn key to ON position. (Do not start engine.)<br>• Check for voltage between harness connector Pin No. 1 and ground. | ▲ Voltage detected | TURN key to OFF position. GO to E8 . |
| | ▲ No voltage detected | TURN key to OFF position. REPLACE control switch. REPEAT Basic Test. |
| **E8** CHECK AFTER GLOW VOLTAGE IN CHASSIS HARNESS<br>• Engine harness disconnected at control switch.<br>• Disconnect engine harness at chassis harness.<br>• Turn key to ON position. (Do not start engine.)<br>• Check for voltage on chassis side of connector at Pin No. 1 or Pin No. 5 (as shown). | ▲ Voltage detected | GO to E9 . |
| | ▲ No voltage detected | REPLACE engine harness. REPEAT Basic Test. |

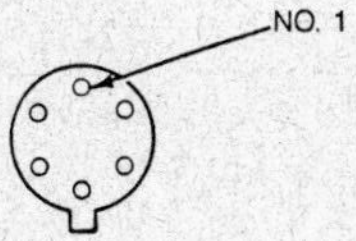

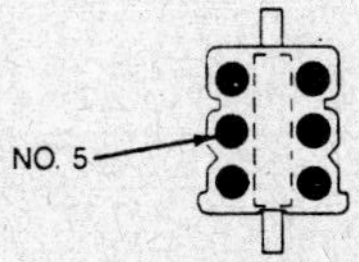

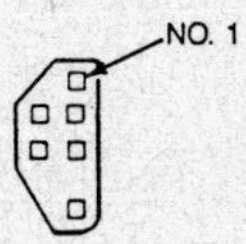

NO. 1

NO. 5

**Fig. 4  Fast start glow plug diagnosis (Part 21 of 23), 1983 6.9L diesel**

---

**Test Lamp Does Not Cycle**

**Pinpoint Test** | **E**

| TEST STEP | RESULT | ACTION TO TAKE |
|---|---|---|
| **E5** CHECK RESISTANCE OF "WAIT TO START" LAMP LATCHING RELAY<br>• Key in OFF position.<br>• Disconnect chassis harness connector at latching relay.<br>• Check resistance across latching relay terminals No. 1 and No. 2 with ohmmeter red probe (+) on terminal No. 2 and black probe (−) on terminal No. 1.<br>• Resistance should be 45 ohms or greater.<br>• Reverse leads. Resistance must be greater than 1 megaohm. | ▲ OK | GO to E6 . |
| 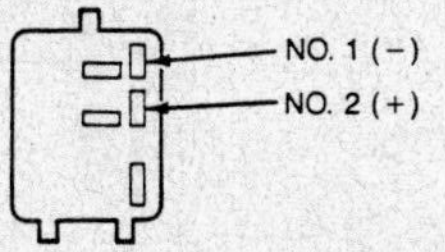 | ▲ NOT OK | REPLACE latching relay. REPEAT Basic Test. |
| **E6** CHECK POWER RELAY RESISTANCE<br>• Key in OFF position.<br>• Disconnect engine harness at control switch.<br>• Connect all other leads.<br>• Check resistance between control switch connector Pin No. 6 and ground.<br>• Resistance should be 2.5 ohms or greater. | ▲ OK | GO to E7 . |
| 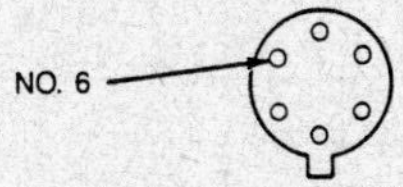 | ▲ NOT OK | REPLACE power relay. REPEAT Basic Test. |

NO. 1 (−)
NO. 2 (+)

NO. 6

**Fig. 4  Fast start glow plug diagnosis (Part 20 of 23), 1983 6.9L diesel**

## "WAIT TO START" Lamp Basic Test

| TEST STEP | RESULT | ACTION TO TAKE |
|---|---|---|
| **1 "WAIT TO START" LAMP OPERATION**<br>• Turn key to ON position.<br>• Lamp should light for 4 to 10 seconds depending on engine temperature. | Lamp lights for 4 to 10 seconds | "WAIT TO START" lamp system is OK. GO to Glow Plug System Basic Test. |
| | Lamp does not light | If engine is at or near operating temperature, lamp will not light. ALLOW engine to cool down. REPEAT [1] If lamp still does not light. GO to [2] |
| **2 GLOW PLUG SYSTEM BASIC DIAGNOSTIC TEST**<br>• Complete Glow Plug System Diagnostic Test. | Test lamp functions as required and WAIT TO START lamp did not light in [1] | GO to Pinpoint Test [A]. |
| | Test lamp functions as required and WAIT TO START lamp did not turn OFF in [1] | GO to Pinpoint Test [B]. |
| | Test lamp does not function as required | Glow Plug System is faulty. CONTINUE with Glow Plug System Diagnostic Procedure. |

**Fig. 4  Fast start glow plug diagnosis (Part 23 of 23). 1983 6.9L diesel**

## Pinpoint Test E — Test Lamp Does Not Cycle

| TEST STEP | RESULT | ACTION TO TAKE |
|---|---|---|
| **E9 CHECK FOR VOLTAGE FROM LATCHING RELAY**<br>• Engine harness disconnected at control switch and chassis connector.<br>• Turn key to ON position. (Do not start engine.)<br>• Remove connector from after glow latching relay.<br>• Check for voltage on chassis side of chassis connector at Pin No. 1 or Pin No. 5 (as shown). | Voltage detected | TURN key OFF. REPAIR or REPLACE chassis wiring between after glow relay and engine wiring harness connector. REPEAT Basic Test. |
| | No voltage detected | TURN key OFF. REPLACE after glow latching relay. GO to [E10]. |
| **E10 RETEST AFTER GLOW RELAY**<br>• Engine harness disconnected at control switch and chassis connector.<br>• Connect after glow latching relay connector.<br>• Turn key to ON position. (Do not start engine.)<br>• Check for voltage at Pin No. 1 or Pin No. 5 (as shown). | Voltage detected | REPAIR or REPLACE wiring and/or alternator as necessary. REPEAT Basic Test. |
| | No voltage detected | Problem solved. REPEAT Basic Test. |

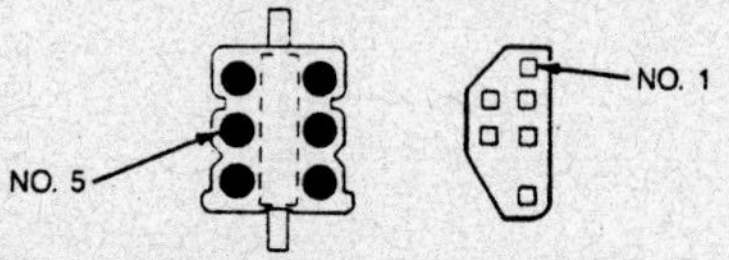

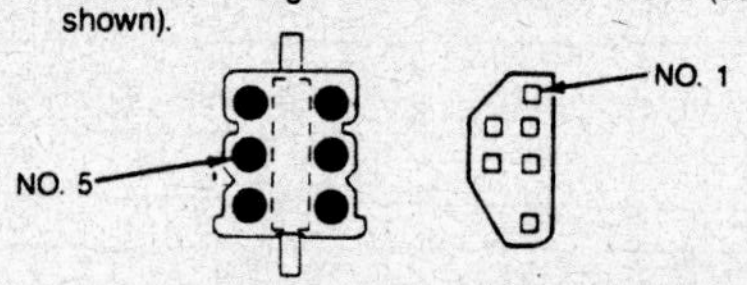

NO. 1    NO. 5

**Fig. 4  Fast start glow plug diagnosis (Part 22 of 23). 1983 6.9L diesel**

## Glow Plug System Basic Diagnostic Test

| TEST STEP | RESULT | ACTION TO TAKE |
|---|---|---|
| **1** KEY IN RUN POSITION, ENGINE OFF | | |
| • Observe Instrument Panel Glow Plug Lamp or connect a 12-volt test lamp between the power relay output (green leads) (to glow plugs) and ground. | ▲ Test lamp lights, stays lit for 4 to 10 seconds, then cycles on and off | GO to 2 |
| | ▲ Test lamp does not light | GO to Pinpoint Test C |
| 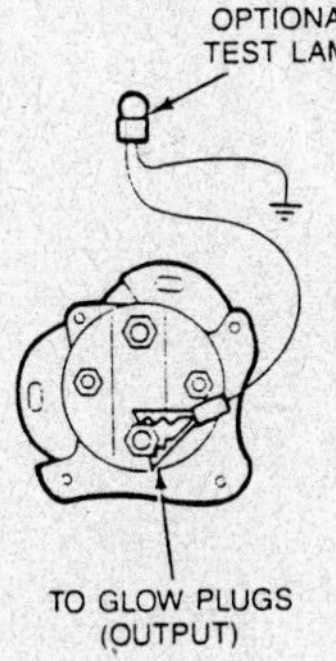 | ▲ Test lamp lights, stays on continuously | GO to Pinpoint Test B |
| | ▲ Test lamp lights, stays lit for 4 to 10 seconds, then goes out and stays out | GO to Pinpoint Test E |
| OPTIONAL TEST LAMP / TO GLOW PLUGS (OUTPUT) | | |
| • Turn ignition switch to ON position. | | |
| **2** ENGINE STARTED | | |
| • Continue to observe Instrument Panel Lamp or leave 12-volt test lamp connected from Test Step 1. | ⚠ Test lamp cycles for up to 2 minutes. then turns off | GO to Pinpoint Test A |
| • Start engine. | ⚠ Test lamp continues to cycle after 2 minutes | GO to Pinpoint Test D |
| • Test lamp should cycle on and off for up to 2 minutes. | ⚠ Test lamp does not light | GO to Pinpoint Test E |

**Fig. 5  Fast start glow plug diagnosis (Part 2 of 16). 1984–86 6.9L diesel**

## Fast Start Glow Plug System Diagnostic Procedure

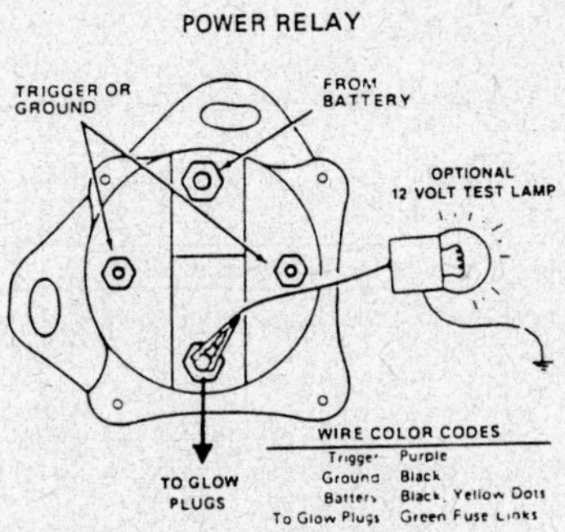

POWER RELAY

FROM BATTERY

OPTIONAL 12 VOLT TEST LAMP

WIRE COLOR CODES
Trigger — Purple
Ground — Black
Battery — Black, Yellow Dots
To Glow Plugs — Green Fusible Links

TRIGGER OR GROUND

TO GLOW PLUGS

Observing System Operation Using Instrument Panel Glow Plug Lamp or a Monitor Test Lamp. First connect a 12 volt test lamp between power relay output and ground

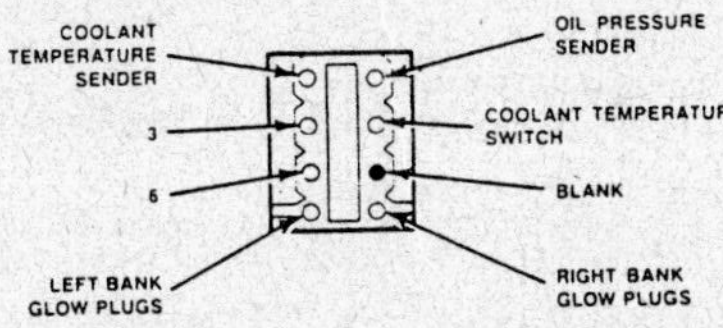

### Electrical Connector, Glow Plug Harness To Chassis Harness Chassis Side View

OIL PRESSURE SENDER
COOLANT TEMPERATURE SWITCH
BLANK
RIGHT BANK GLOW PLUGS
COOLANT TEMPERATURE SENDER
LEFT BANK GLOW PLUGS

| WIRE COLOR CODES | |
|---|---|
| 3 | RED :V LIGHT GREEN STRIPE |
| | PURPLE |
| 6 | ORANGE :V WHITE STRIPE |
| LEFT BANK GLOW PLUGS | ORANGE :V GREEN DOTS |
| RIGHT BANK GLOW PLUGS | WHITE-W. RED STRIPE |
| OIL PRESSURE SENDER | RED :V WHITE STRIPE |
| COOLANT TEMPERATURE SENDER | RED :V BLACK DOTS |
| COOLANT TEMPERATURE SWITCH | |

TERMINAL #

### WIRING HARNESS PLUG FOR CONTROL SWITCH

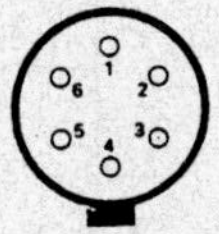

Viewing Connector Face

| TERMINAL # | WIRE COLOR CODES |
|---|---|
| 1 | RED W GREEN STRIPE |
| 3 | ORANGE-W WHITE |
| 4 | BLACK |
| 5 | PURPLE |
| 6 | |

① E-SERIES — PINK WITH BLACK DOTS
② F-SERIES — RED WITH GREEN STRIPE

*Figure 28 Glow Plug System Diagnostic Test Points*

**Fig. 5  Fast start glow plug diagnosis (Part 1 of 16). 1984–86 6.9L diesel**

## Test Lamp Signal Correct — Pinpoint Test — A

| TEST STEP | RESULT | ACTION TO TAKE |
| --- | --- | --- |
| **A4 CHECK GLOW PLUG RESISTANCE** | | |
| • Key in OFF position. | Less than 2 ohms at all glow plugs | Glow plug system OK. GO to Engine Performance Diagnostic Procedure if problem is hard starting. |
| • Remove test lamp from power relay. | 2 ohms or greater at one or more glow plugs | REPLACE damaged glow plug(s). RECONNECT glow plug system leads. CHECK vehicle operation. |
| • Check for resistance between glow plug terminal and metal case of glow plug. | | |
| • Resistance should be less than 2 ohms. | | |

**Fig. 5 Fast start glow plug diagnosis (Part 4 of 16). 1984–86 6.9L diesel**

## Test Lamp Signal Correct — Pinpoint Test — A

| TEST STEP | RESULT | ACTION TO TAKE |
| --- | --- | --- |
| **A1 CHECK VOLTAGE TO EACH GLOW PLUG** | | |
| • Remove all leads from glow plugs. | OK at all leads | GO to A4. |
| • Connect 12-volt test lamp between power relay output (green leads) (to glow plugs) and ground. | Not OK at any or all leads | GO to A2. |
| • Turn key to ON position. | | |
| • Check voltage at each glow plug lead, with voltmeter, or equivalent, whenever test lamp is lit. | | |
| • Voltage should be minimum of 11 volts. | | |
| **A2 CHECK CHASSIS HARNESS FUSIBLE LINKS** | | |
| • Turn key to OFF position. | OK | GO to A3. |
| • Disconnect fusible links from chassis harness and engine glow plug harness. | (not OK) | REPLACE fusible link(s). REPEAT Test Step A1. |
| • Check continuity of fusible links with ohmmeter. | | |
| **A3 CHECK ENGINE HARNESS FUSIBLE LINKS** | | |
| • Key in OFF position. | Less than 1 ohm | GO to A4. |
| • Disconnect engine harness from chassis connector and all glow plugs. | 1 ohm or more | REPLACE engine harness. CHECK vehicle operation. |
| • Check resistance between chassis connector left and right bank glow plug terminals (green leads), and each glow plug lead. | | |

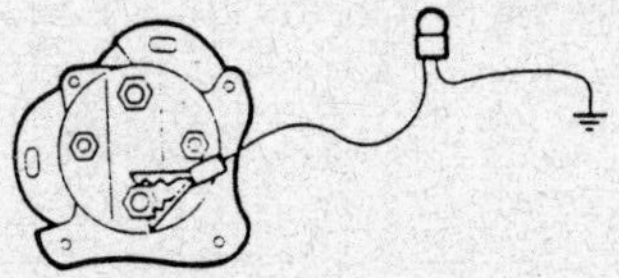

**Fig. 5 Fast start glow plug diagnosis (Part 3 of 16). 1984–86 6.9L diesel**

## Pinpoint Test B — Test Lamp On Continuously (Part 6)

| TEST STEP | RESULT | ACTION TO TAKE |
|---|---|---|
| **B3 CHECK ENGINE WIRING HARNESS**<br>• Test lamp connected between power relay output (green leads) (to glow plugs) and ground.<br>• Turn key to ON position.<br>• Disconnect engine harness from chassis harness.<br>• Does test lamp go out? | Yes | REPLACE engine harness. GO to B7. |
| | No | GO to B4. |
| **B4 CHECK POWER RELAY SIGNAL**<br>• With key in OFF position, disconnect signal lead (purple) from power relay.<br>• Turn key to ON position.<br>• Does test lamp go out? | Yes | REPAIR or REPLACE chassis wiring harness. GO to B5. |
| | No | GO to B5. |
| **B5 CHECK POWER RELAY**<br>• With key in OFF position, remove test lamp, disconnect input lead (from battery) from power relay and reconnect test lamp.<br>• Power relay signal lead still disconnected.<br>• Turn key to On position.<br>• Does test lamp go out? | No | REPAIR or REPLACE chassis wiring harness to glow plugs. GO to B6. |
| | Yes | REPLACE power relay. GO to B6. |

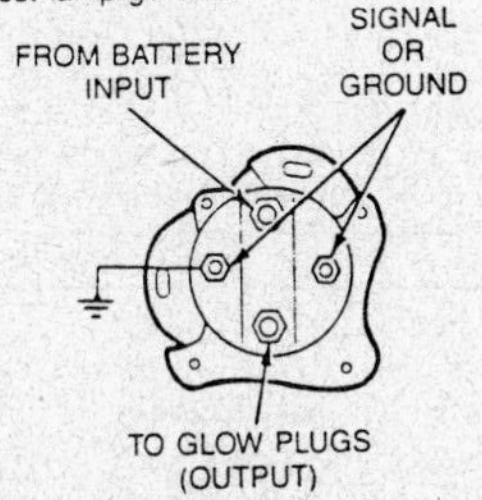

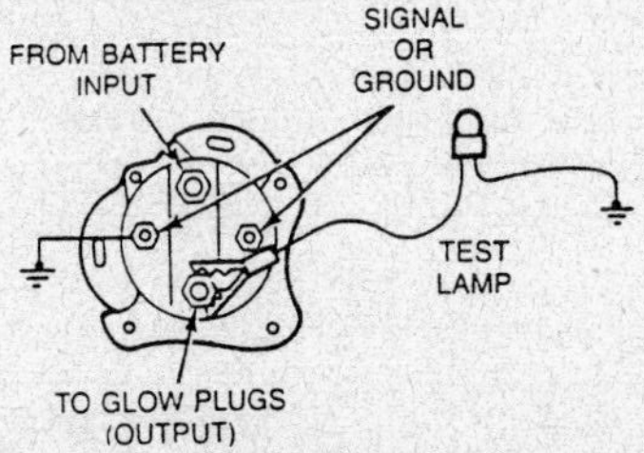

FROM BATTERY INPUT — SIGNAL OR GROUND — TO GLOW PLUGS (OUTPUT)

FROM BATTERY INPUT — SIGNAL OR GROUND — TEST LAMP — TO GLOW PLUGS (OUTPUT)

**Fig. 5  Fast start glow plug diagnosis (Part 6 of 16). 1984-86 6.9L diesel**

## Pinpoint Test B — Test Lamp On Continuously (Part 5)

| TEST STEP | RESULT | ACTION TO TAKE |
|---|---|---|
| **B1 FUNCTION TEST**<br>CAUTION: Remove leads from all glow plugs before proceeding with this test. Do not reconnect leads to glow plugs until system has been rechecked for correct operation.<br>• Key in OFF position (for a minimum of one minute).<br>• Connect a 12-volt test lamp between power relay output (green leads) (to glow plugs) and ground.<br>• Turn key to ON position. (Do not start engine.)<br>• Observe test lamp. | Test lamp cycles as expected but panel "Glow Plug" lamp did not | REPAIR or REPLACE chassis wiring to and or panel "Glow Plug" lamp. REPEAT Basic Test. |
| | Test lamp stays on | GO to B2. |
| **B2 ISOLATE DAMAGED COMPONENT**<br>• Test lamp connected between power relay output (green leads) (to glow plugs) and ground.<br>NOTE: Do not reconnect leads until directed.<br>• Turn key to ON position, but do not start engine.<br>• Disconnect harness plug from control switch.<br>• Test lamp should turn OFF. | OK | REPLACE control switch. REPEAT Basic Test. |
| | Not OK | GO to B3. |

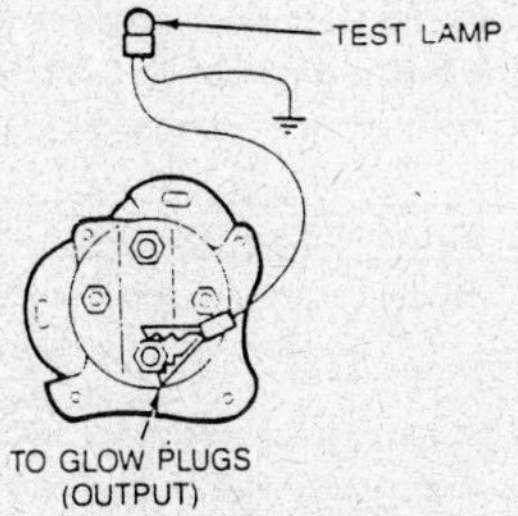

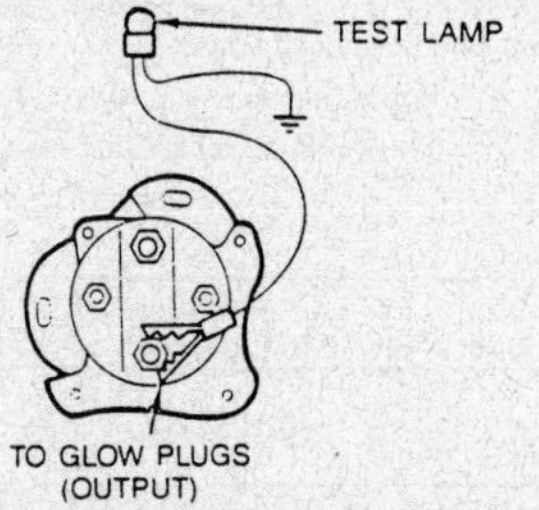

TEST LAMP — TO GLOW PLUGS (OUTPUT)

TEST LAMP — TO GLOW PLUGS (OUTPUT)

**Fig. 5  Fast start glow plug diagnosis (Part 5 of 16). 1984-86 6.9L diesel**

## Pinpoint Test C — Test Lamp Does Not Light

| TEST STEP | RESULT | ACTION TO TAKE |
|---|---|---|
| C1 VERIFY CONDITION<br>• Observe instrument panel "Glow Plug" lamp.<br>• Key in OFF position (for a minimum of 1 minute).<br>• Turn key to ON position. (Do not start engine.) | ▲ Panel lamp lights | GO to Pinpoint Test [E]. |
| | ▲ Panel lamp does not light | This is normal with a warm engine (engine coolant at normal operating temperature or above). If engine coolant is below normal operating temperature. TURN key to ON and observe panel lamp. If lamp lights. GO to Pinpoint Test [E].<br>If it does not light. GO to [C2]. |
| C2 CHECK BATTERIES<br>• Check batteries for state of charge. (If batteries will crank engine, they will operate glow plug system.) | ▲ OK | GO to [C3]. |
| | ▲ (OK crossed out) | CHARGE or REPLACE batteries as necessary.<br>REPEAT Basic Test. |
| C3 CHECK OUTPUT FROM POWER RELAY<br>• Key in ON position (for a minimum of 1 minute).<br>• Connect a 12-volt test lamp between power relay output (green leads to glow plugs) and ground.<br>• Turn key to ON position. (Do not start engine.)<br>• Observe test lamp. | ▲ Test lamp lights but panel lamp does not | GO to "Glow Plug" Lamp Basic Test Step [3]. |
| | ▲ Test lamp does not light | GO to [C4]. |

**Fig. 5 Fast start glow plug diagnosis (Part 8 of 16). 1984–86 6.9L diesel**

## Pinpoint Test B — Test Lamp On Continuously

| TEST STEP | RESULT | ACTION TO TAKE |
|---|---|---|
| B6 CHECK CONTINUITY OF FUSIBLE WIRES IN ENGINE HARNESS<br>• Key in OFF position.<br>• Remove test lamp from power relay.<br>• Reconnect all but the glow plug leads.<br>• Check continuity between each glow plug lead and power relay output lead.<br>• Resistance should be less than 1 ohm. | ▲ All glow plug leads are less than 1 ohm | GO to [B8]. |
| | ▲ One or more glow plug leads are 1 ohm or greater | GO to [B7]. |
| B7 CHECK CHASSIS HARNESS FUSIBLE LINKS<br>• Key in OFF position.<br>• Disconnect engine harness from chassis harness.<br>• Disconnect chassis harness fusible links from chassis harness.<br>• Check resistance of fusible links.<br>• Resistance should be less than 1 ohm. | ▲ OK | REPLACE engine harness. GO to [B8]. |
| | ▲ (OK crossed out) | REPLACE fuse link(s) as necessary. REPEAT Test Step [B6]. |
| B8 CHECK GLOW PLUG RESISTANCE<br>• Key in OFF position.<br>• Engine harness disconnected at glow plugs.<br>• Check resistance between glow plug terminal and metal shell of glow plug.<br>• Resistance should be less than 2 ohms. | ▲ OK | Glow plug system OK. RECONNECT engine harness leads to glow plugs. REPEAT Basic Test. |
| | ▲ One or more glow plugs | REPLACE glow plugs as necessary.<br>RECONNECT engine harness to glow plugs. REPEAT Basic Test. |

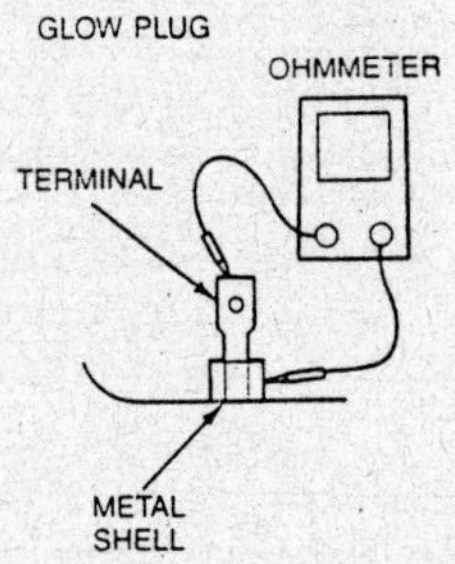

GLOW PLUG    OHMMETER

TERMINAL

METAL SHELL

**Fig. 5 Fast start glow plug diagnosis (Part 7 of 16). 1984–86 6.9L diesel**

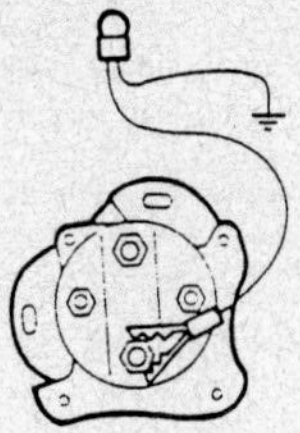

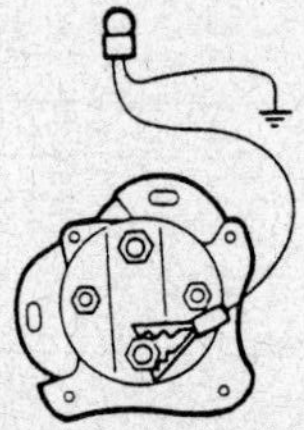

*ENGINES, DIESEL*

## Test Lamp Does Not Light — Pinpoint Test C

| TEST STEP | RESULT | ACTION TO TAKE |
|---|---|---|
| **C4 CHECK IN-LINE FUSE**<br>• Check fusible link between ignition switch and control switch. (Circuit 16, Wht/Blk.) | OK ▲ | GO to C8 |
| | not OK ▲ | GO to C5 |
| **C5 REPLACE FUSE**<br>• Replace fusible link.<br>• Repeat Basic Test. | Fuse blows ▲ | GO to C6 |
| | Fuse does not blow — system still not operating ▲ | GO to C8 |
| | Fuse does not blow ▲ | System OK. |
| **C6 CHECK POWER RELAY**<br>• Remove signal lead (purple) from power relay.<br>• Replace fusible link.<br>• Turn key to ON position.<br>• Turn key OFF.<br><br>SIGNAL OR GROUND | Fuse blows ▲ | GO to C7 |
| | Fuse does not blow ▲ | REPLACE power relay. REPEAT Basic Test. |
| **C7 CHECK SYSTEM WIRING**<br>• Disconnect chassis harness from engine harness.<br>• Replace fusible link.<br>• Turn key to ON position.<br>• Turn key OFF. | Fuse blows ▲ | REPAIR chassis wirings. REPEAT Basic Test. |
| | Fuse does not blow ▲ | GO to C8. |

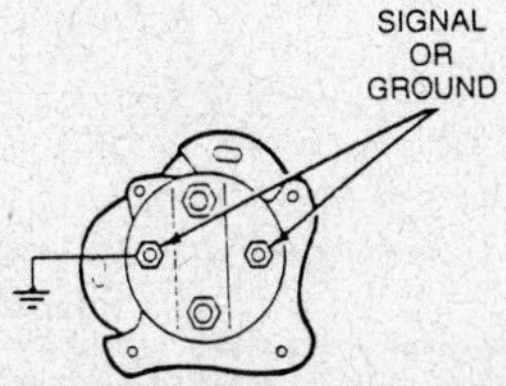

**Fig. 5  Fast start glow plug diagnosis (Part 9 of 16). 1984–86 6.9L diesel**

## Test Lamp Does Not Light — Pinpoint Test C

| TEST STEP | RESULT | ACTION TO TAKE |
|---|---|---|
| **C8 CHECK SIGNAL TO POWER RELAY**<br>• Key in OFF position (for a minimum of 1 minute).<br>• Connect all leads, including power relay signal lead (purple).<br>• Turn key to ON position.<br>• Check voltage between signal lead (purple) and ground.<br>• Voltage should be 11 volts minimum.<br><br>SIGNAL OR GROUND | OK ▲ | GO to C9 |
| | not OK ▲ | GO to C10 |
| **C9 CHECK VOLTAGE TO POWER RELAY**<br>• Key in OFF position.<br>• Connect voltmeter between power relay input terminal (from batteries) and ground.<br>• Voltage should be minimum of 11 volts.<br><br>FROM BATTERIES | OK ▲ | CHECK power relay ground connection or REPLACE power relay. REPEAT basic test. |
| | not OK ▲ | CHARGE or REPLACE batteries as necessary, and or repair wiring from batteries to power relay. REPEAT Basic Test. |

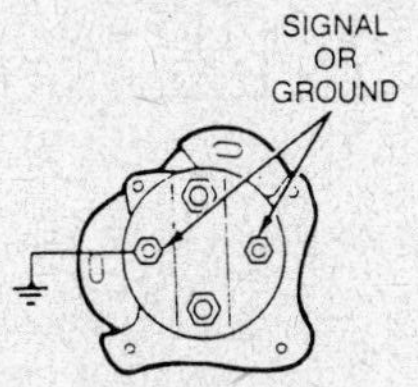

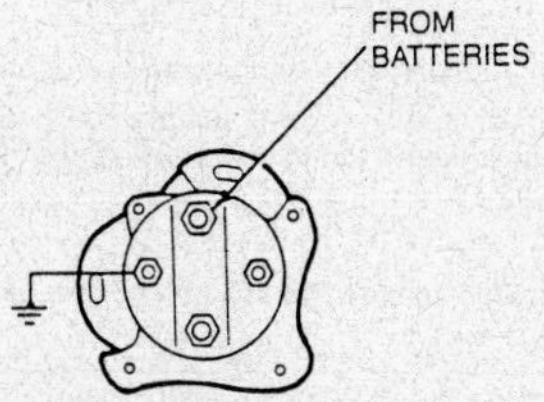

**Fig. 5  Fast start glow plug diagnosis (Part 10 of 16). 1984–86 6.9L diesel**

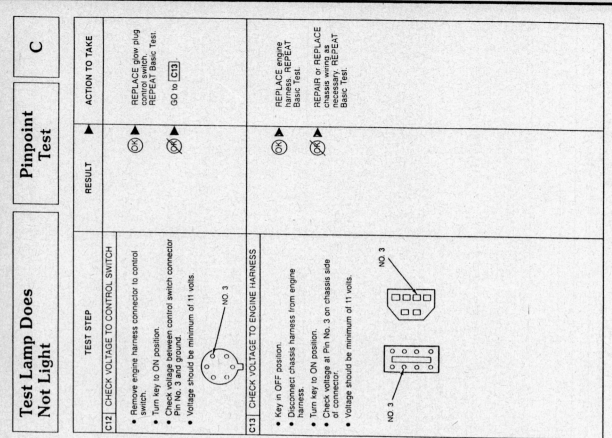

**Pinpoint Test — C**

**Test Lamp Does Not Light**

| TEST STEP | RESULT | ACTION TO TAKE |
|---|---|---|
| **C12 CHECK VOLTAGE TO CONTROL SWITCH**<br>• Remove engine harness connector to control switch.<br>• Turn key to ON position.<br>• Check voltage between control switch connector Pin No. 3 and ground.<br>• Voltage should be minimum of 11 volts. | OK | REPLACE glow plug control switch. REPEAT Basic Test. |
| | NO | GO to C13 |
| **C13 CHECK VOLTAGE TO ENGINE HARNESS**<br>• Key in OFF position.<br>• Disconnect chassis harness from engine harness.<br>• Turn key to ON position.<br>• Check voltage at Pin No. 3 on chassis side of connector.<br>• Voltage should be minimum of 11 volts. | OK | REPLACE engine harness. REPEAT Basic Test. |
| | NO | REPAIR or REPLACE chassis wiring as necessary. REPEAT Basic Test. |

NO. 3

**Fig. 5  Fast start glow plug diagnosis (Part 12 of 16). 1984–86 6.9L diesel**

---

**Pinpoint Test — C**

**Test Lamp Does Not Light**

| TEST STEP | RESULT | ACTION TO TAKE |
|---|---|---|
| **C10 CHECK RESISTANCE OF SYSTEM WIRING**<br>• Key in OFF position.<br>• Disconnect power relay signal lead (purple).<br>• Disconnect engine harness at control switch.<br>• Check resistance between control switch connector Pin No. 6 and power relay signal lead (purple).<br>• Resistance should be less than 1 ohm. | OK | GO to C12 |
| | NO | GO to C11 |
| **C11 CHECK RESISTANCE OF CHASSIS WIRING**<br>• Key in OFF position.<br>• Disconnect chassis harness from engine harness.<br>• Disconnect power relay signal lead (purple).<br>• Check resistance between chassis side wiring connector No. 6 (as shown) and power signal lead (purple).<br>• Resistance should be less than 1 ohm. | OK | REPLACE engine harness. REPEAT Basic Test. |
| | NO | REPAIR or REPLACE chassis wiring. REPEAT Basic Test. |

SIGNAL OR GROUND

NO. 6

**Fig. 5  Fast start glow plug diagnosis (Part 11 of 16). 1984–86 6.9L diesel**

## Test Lamp Does Not Cycle

**Pinpoint Test E**

| TEST STEP | RESULT | ACTION TO TAKE |
|---|---|---|
| **E1 OBSERVE TEST LAMP** <br>• Observe instrument panel Glow Plug lamp or connect 12-volt test lamp between power relay output (green leads) (to glow plugs) and ground. <br>• Turn key to ON position. (Do not start engine.) <br>• Observe test lamp. | ▲ Lamp lights | GO to E2 . |
| | ▲ Lamp does not light | This is normal and expected if engine coolant temperature is 60°C (140°F) or above. If coolant temperature is below 60°C (140°F), TURN key to OFF. WAIT 5 minutes. TURN key to ON position. If lamp lights. GO to E2 . If lamp does not light. GO to Pinpoint Test C . |
| OPTIONAL TEST LAMP | | |
| **E2 CHECK WIRING HARNESS RESISTANCE** <br>• Key in OFF position. <br>• Disconnect chassis harness from glow plug power relay. <br>• Disconnect engine harness from control switch and all glow plugs. <br>• Check resistance between control switch Pin No. 4 and glow plug relay power output connector. <br>• Resistance should be less than 1 ohm. | ⓄⓀ | GO to E4 . |
| | ⊗Ⓚ | GO to E3 . |
| 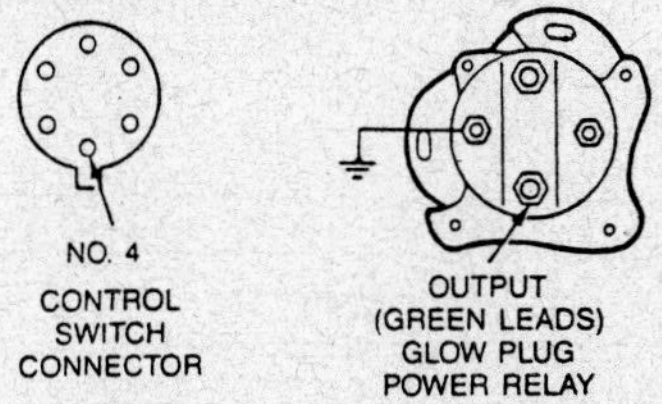 NO. 4 CONTROL SWITCH CONNECTOR <br>OUTPUT (GREEN LEADS) GLOW PLUG POWER RELAY | | |

**Fig. 5 Fast start glow plug diagnosis (Part 14 of 16). 1984-86 6.9L diesel**

## Test Lamp Cycles Continuously (Beyond 2 Minutes)

**Pinpoint Test D**

| TEST STEP | RESULT | ACTION TO TAKE |
|---|---|---|
| **D1 CHECK AFTER GLOW VOLTAGE** <br>• Remove engine harness connector at control switch. <br>• Turn key to On Position. <br>• Check for voltage between control switch connector. Pin No. 1 and ground. <br>• Voltage should be 11 volts or greater. | ▲ <br>ⓄⓀ | TURN key OFF. REPLACE control switch. REPEAT Basic Test and Pinpoint Test A4 . |
| | ⊗Ⓚ | TURN key Off. REPLACE engine wiring harness. REPEAT Basic Test and Pinpoint Test A4 . |
| NO. 1 | | |

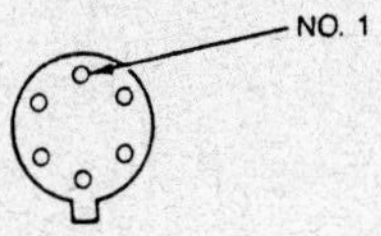

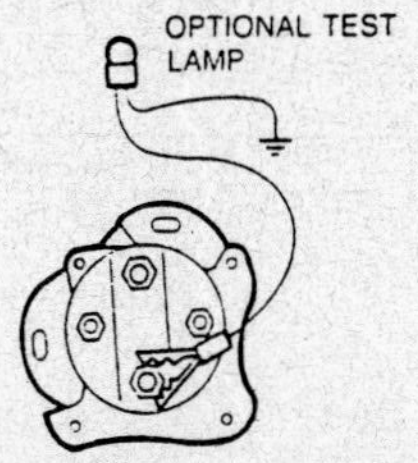

**Fig. 5 Fast start glow plug diagnosis (Part 13 of 16). 1984-86 6.9L diesel**

## Glow Plug Lamp Basic Test

| TEST STEP | RESULT | ACTION TO TAKE |
|---|---|---|
| **1** "GLOW PLUG" LAMP OPERATION<br>• Key in OFF position (for a minimum of 1 minute).<br>• Turn key to ON position.<br>• Lamp should light for 4 to 10 seconds depending on engine temperature. | ▲ Lamp lights for 4 to 10 seconds | ▲ "GLOW PLUG" lamp system is OK. GO TO Glow Plug System Basic Test. |
| | ▲ Lamp does not light | ▲ If engine is at or near operating temperature, lamp will not light. ALLOW engine to cool down. REPEAT [1]. If lamp still does not light. GO to [2]. |
| **2** GLOW PLUG SYSTEM BASIC DIAGNOSTIC TEST<br>• Complete Glow Plug System Pinpoint Test [C]. | ▲ Test lamp functions as required and GLOW PLUG lamp did not light in [1] | ▲ GO to [3]. |
| | ▲ Test lamp does not function as required | ▲ Glow Plug System is faulty. CONTINUE with Glow Plug System Diagnostic Procedure. |
| **3** CHECK LAMP BULB<br>• Remove bulb from "GLOW PLUG" indicator and test. | (OK) ▲ | ▲ REPLACE chassis wiring. REPEAT Basic Test. |
| | (OK̸) | ▲ REPLACE bulb. REPEAT Basic Test. |

**Fig. 5  Fast start glow plug diagnosis (Part 16 of 16), 1984–86 6.9L diesel**

---

## Test Lamp Does Not Cycle — Pinpoint Test — E

| TEST STEP | RESULT | ACTION TO TAKE |
|---|---|---|
| **E3** CHECK CHASSIS HARNESS RESISTANCE<br>• Key in OFF position.<br>• Disconnect chassis harness from engine harness.<br>• Check resistance between chassis harness and glow plug power relay output connector.<br>• Resistance should be less than 1 ohm.<br><br>OUTPUT (GREEN LEADS) GLOW PLUG POWER RELAY<br>LEFT BANK GLOW PLUGS | (OK) ▲ | ▲ REPLACE engine harness. REPEAT Basic Test. |
| | (OK̸) | ▲ REPLACE fusible link(s) or REPAIR chassis harness. REPEAT Basic Test. |
| **E4** CHECK ENGINE HARNESS GROUND<br>• Key in OFF position.<br>• Check resistance between control switch connector Pin No. 5 and ground.<br>• Resistance should be less than 1 ohm.<br><br>NO. 5 | (OK) ▲ | ▲ GO to [E5]. |
| | (OK̸) | ▲ REPAIR engine harness ground connection or REPLACE engine harness as necessary. REPEAT Basic Test. |
| **E5** CHECK POWER RELAY RESISTANCE<br>• Key in OFF position.<br>• Disconnect engine harness at control switch.<br>• Connect all other leads.<br>• Check resistance between control switch connector Pin No. 6 and ground.<br>• Resistance should be 2.5 ohms or greater.<br><br>NO. 6 | (OK) ▲ | ▲ REPLACE control switch. REPEAT Basic Test and Pinpoint Test [A4]. |
| | (OK̸) | ▲ REPLACE power relay. REPEAT Basic Test and Pinpoint Test [A4]. |

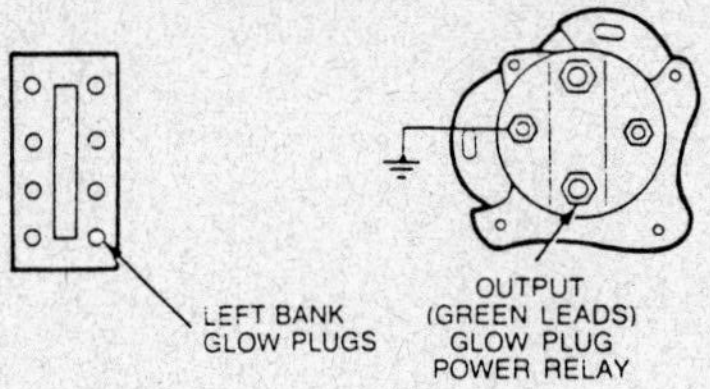

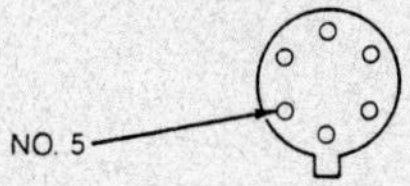

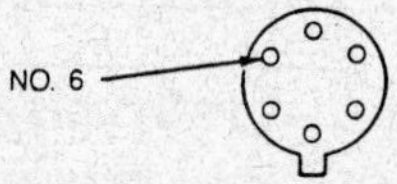

**Fig. 5  Fast start glow plug diagnosis (Part 15 of 16). 1984–86 6.9L diesel**

## Solid State Glow Plug System Diagnostic Procedure

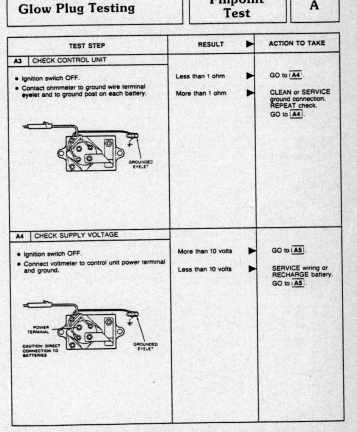

*Glow Plug System Diagnostic Test Points*

**Fig. 6   Fast start glow plug diagnosis (Part 1 of 8). 7.3L diesel & 1987 6.9L diesel**

---

| Glow Plug Testing | Pinpoint Test | A |
|---|---|---|

| TEST STEP | RESULT ▶ | ACTION TO TAKE |
|---|---|---|
| **A1   CHECK GLOW PLUGS** <br><br> • Ignition switch OFF and leads removed from glow plugs. <br> • Check continuity between glow plug terminal and a power source with glow plugs installed in engine. | (OK) ▶ <br><br> (⊘) ▶ | GO to A2. <br><br> REPLACE plug(s). GO to A2. |

**Fig. 6   Fast start glow plug diagnosis (Part 2 of 8). 7.3L diesel & 1987 6.9L diesel**

---

| Glow Plug Testing | Pinpoint Test | A |
|---|---|---|

| TEST STEP | RESULT ▶ | ACTION TO TAKE |
|---|---|---|
| **A2   CHECK HARNESS** <br><br> • Ignition switch OFF and leads removed from glow plugs. <br> • Squeeze sides of protective cover and remove. <br> • Check continuity between each glow plug lead and test terminal of control unit. | OK at all leads ▶ <br><br> Not OK at any or all leads ▶ | GO to A3. <br><br> SERVICE or REPLACE harness. GO to A3. |

**Fig. 6   Fast start glow plug diagnosis (Part 3 of 8). 7.3L diesel & 1987 6.9L diesel**

---

| Glow Plug Testing | Pinpoint Test | A |
|---|---|---|

| TEST STEP | RESULT ▶ | ACTION TO TAKE |
|---|---|---|
| **A3   CHECK CONTROL UNIT** <br><br> • Ignition switch OFF. <br> • Contact ohmmeter to ground wire terminal eyelet and to ground post on each battery. | Less than 1 ohm ▶ <br><br> More than 1 ohm ▶ | GO to A4. <br><br> CLEAN or SERVICE ground connection. REPEAT check. GO to A4. |
| **A4   CHECK SUPPLY VOLTAGE** <br><br> • Ignition switch OFF. <br> • Connect voltmeter to control unit power terminal and ground. | More than 10 volts ▶ <br><br> Less than 10 volts ▶ | GO to A5. <br><br> SERVICE wiring or RECHARGE battery. GO to A5. |

**Fig. 6   Fast start glow plug diagnosis (Part 4 of 8). 7.3L diesel & 1987 6.9L diesel**

---

*ENGINES, DIESEL*

| Glow Plug Testing | Pinpoint Test | A |
|---|---|---|

| TEST STEP | RESULT ▶ | ACTION TO TAKE |
|---|---|---|
| **A5** CHECK VOLTAGE FROM IGNITION SWITCH <br><br> • Check voltmeter to Ignition Terminal on control unit and ground. <br> • Turn ignition switch ON and ALL accessories OFF. | More than 8 volts ▶ <br><br> Less than 8 volts ▶ | GO to A6. <br><br> CHECK fusible link, SERVICE wiring or RECHARGE battery. GO to A6. |
| **A6** FUNCTIONAL TEST <br><br> • With ignition switch OFF, connect 12 volt test light to test terminal on control unit. <br> • Position test light so it can be viewed from driver's position. <br> • Turn ignition switch ON and monitor system operation. <br> • Compare test light times to Test Light Chart. | Test light times within specifications ▶ <br><br> Test light times out of specifications ▶ | System function is correct. <br><br> DISCONNECT power at both batteries. REPLACE control unit. REPEAT test. |

**Fig. 6 Fast start glow plug diagnosis (Part 5 of 8). 7.3L diesel & 1987 6.9L diesel**

| Glow Plug Testing | Pinpoint Test | A |
|---|---|---|

| TEST STEP | RESULT ▶ | ACTION TO TAKE |
|---|---|---|
| **A6** FUNCTIONAL TEST (Cont'd) | | |

**TEST LIGHT CHART**

NOTE: Total Test Light "ON" Time includes time from the begining of the initial "ON" cycle to the end of the last "ON-OFF cycle" measured in seconds.

| Control Unit Temp. °F | "Wait-to-Start" Lamp "ON" Time (Sec.) | Test Light Total Time (Sec.) |
|---|---|---|
| -20°C | 7-15 | 35-70 |
| 0°F | 7-12 | 25-60 |
| 35°F | 5-12 | 15-35 |
| 70°F | 3-5 | 7-15 |
| 105°F | 1-3 | 3-5 |
| 140°F | 1 or Less | 1-3 |

*Temperature of Control Unit, NOT ambient temperature

NOTE: The "Wait-to-Start" Lamp and/or Test Light may not illuminate if engine temperature is at or near normal operating temperature.

**Fig. 6 Fast start glow plug diagnosis (Part 6 of 8). 7.3L diesel & 1987 6.9L diesel**

| "Wait-To-Start" Lamp Testing | Pinpoint Test | B |
|---|---|---|

| TEST STEP | RESULT ▶ | ACTION TO TAKE |
|---|---|---|
| **B1** "WAIT-TO-START" LAMP STAYS ON <br><br> • Disconnect the "wait-to-start" lamp connector at control unit. <br> • Turn ignition switch ON. | Lamp On ▶ <br><br> Lamp Off ▶ | SERVICE wiring to lamp. <br><br> DISCONNECT power at both batteries. REPLACE control unit. |
| **B2** "WAIT-TO-START" LAMP DOES NOT GO ON <br><br> • Disconnect the "wait-to-start" lamp connector at control unit. <br> • Connect jumper wire from Harness side to ground. <br> • Turn ignition switch ON. | Lamp On ▶ <br><br> Lamp Off ▶ | GO to Hard Starting Checks. <br><br> REPLACE bulb or SERVICE wiring. |

**Fig. 6 Fast start glow plug diagnosis (Part 7 of 8). 7.3L diesel & 1987 6.9L diesel**

### Glow Plug Failure Analysis

The following are examples of glow plug failure. Each example gives a different clue to glow plug failure analysis.

• There is no visible damage, but glow plug is electrically open. This indicates an internal heating element failure.

• Glow plug tip that is missing can be caused by incorrect timing or poor fuel quality.

• Multiple, distorted glow plugs are usually caused by electrical overheating. A complete evaluation of the glow plug control system should be made.

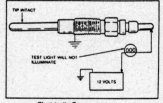

*Electrically Open*

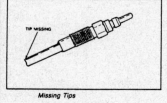

*Missing Tips*

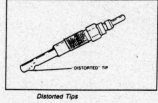

*Distorted Tips*

**Fig. 6 Fast start glow plug diagnosis (Part 8 of 8). 7.3L diesel & 1987 6.9L diesel**

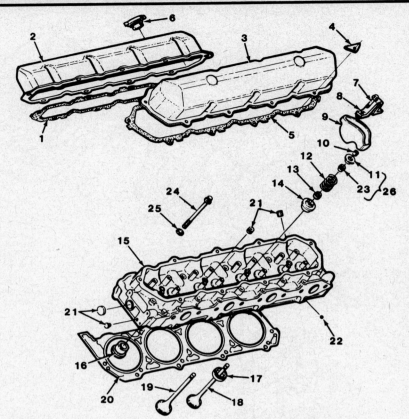

1. Valve Cover Gasket
2. Valve Cover (RH Side)
3. Valve Cover (LH Side)
4. Washer
5. Valve Cover Gasket
6. Closing Cap
7. Rocker Arm Bolt
8. Rocker Arm Post
9. Rocker Arm
10. Retainer Lock
11. Valve Spring Retainer
12. Valve Spring w/Damper
13. Valve Stem Seal (Intake Only)

14. Valve Rotator
15. Cylinder Head
16. Combustion Chamber Insert
17. Exhaust Valve Seat
18. Exhaust Valve
19. Intake Valve
20. Cylinder Head Gasket
21. Pipe Plug
22. Ball
23. Oil Shield
24. Cylinder Head Bolt
25. Washer
26. Spring Retainer Assembly

**Cylinder head assembly**

# ENGINE REPLACE
## E-250—350

1. Disconnect battery ground cables from both batteries and remove engine cover.
2. Drain cooling system, then remove front bumper, grille assembly and gravel deflector.
3. On models equipped with speed control, unfasten speed control servo bracket and position aside.
4. On all models, scribe hood latch location, then remove latch and cable assembly from grille upper support bracket.
5. Remove upper grille support.
6. On models equipped with A/C, discharge refrigerant from system, then remove A/C condenser.
7. On all models, disconnect transmission oil cooler lines from oil cooler and radiator, then remove oil cooler with mounting brackets.
8. Disconnect radiator hoses from engine, then remove fan shroud, fan and radiator. **The fan retaining nut has left hand threads.**
9. Remove vacuum pump and drive belt, then disconnect vacuum line from transmission modulation pipe.
10. Remove alternator adjusting arm, adjusting arm bracket and drive belt, then pivot alternator inward toward engine.
11. Disconnect alternator electrical connectors from alternator and fuel line heater.
12. Disconnect water temperature sender electrical connector from left front of cylinder block.
13. Disconnect water temperature overheat lamp switch electrical connector from top front of left cylinder head.
14. Remove engine ground cables from bottom front of engine.
15. On models equipped with power steering, remove steering pump and bracket, then disconnect and plug return line from steering pump and position pump aside.
16. On models equipped with A/C, disconnect refrigerant lines from A/C compressor.
17. On all models, disconnect vacuum hose between injection pump and vacuum regulator valve and position aside.
18. Disconnect and cap fuel heater inlet line from fuel filter and fuel pump.
19. Remove air cleaner and intake duct and place a suitable cover over intake manifold opening.
20. Disconnect and cap fuel filter outlet line from fuel filter and injection pump, then cover the injection pump and fuel filter openings.
21. Remove fuel filter return line, then the fuel filter and bracket as an assembly.
22. On models equipped with A/C, loosen A/C compressor mounting bolts and rotate compressor toward engine.
23. On all models, disconnect and plug fuel inlet line at fuel pump.
24. Disconnect accelerator and speed control cables, if equipped from injection pump and bracket on intake manifold and position aside. Remove cable bracket.
25. Disconnect engine wiring harnesses and position aside.
26. Remove transmission kickdown rod, then disconnect heater hose from water pump and right cylinder head.
27. On models equipped with A/C and/or auxiliary heater, remove hoses from bracket at left rear of engine.
28. On all models, disconnect oil pressure sender electrical connector from rear of engine.
29. Disconnect fuel return line from left rear of engine, then remove transmission oil dipstick tube attaching bolt from rear of right cylinder head.
30. Remove engine oil dipstick and tube.
31. Remove ground cable to cylinder block attaching bolt, then the 4 upper transmission-to-engine attaching bolts.
32. Raise and support vehicle.
33. Remove engine mount attaching nuts, then disconnect exhaust pipe from exhaust manifolds.
34. Remove converter inspection plate, then the 4 converter to flywheel at-

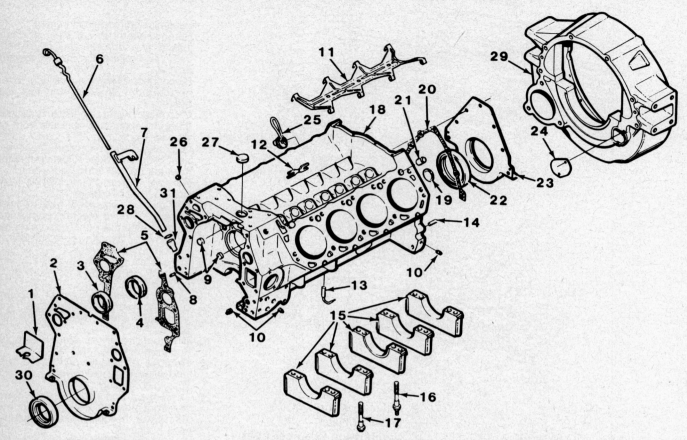

1. Timing Indicator
2. Front Cover
3. Bushing
4. Bushing
5. Front Cover Gaskets
6. Oil Level Gauge
7. Oil Level Gauge Tube, Upper
8. Dowel Pin
9. Cup Plug
10. Pipe Plug
11. Guide Retainer

12. Cam Follower Guide
13. Piston Cooling Tube
14. Dowel Pin
15. Bearing Cap
16. Bolt
17. Bolt
18. Crankcase with Plugs
19. Expansion Plugs
20. Rear Cover Gasket
21. Dowel Sleeve

22. Rear Oil Seal
23. Crankcase Rear Cover
24. Access Cover Plate
25. Block Heater
26. Ball 11/32"
27. Expansion Plug
28. "O" Ring
29. Flywheel Housing
30. Front Oil Seal
31. Oil Level Gauge Tube, Lower

**Cylinder block assembly**

taching nuts.
35. Remove starter cable, then move fuel, line on No. 1 crossmember down and aside.
36. Lower vehicle and attach suitable lifting equipment to engine.
37. Support transmission with a suitable jack and remove remaining engine to transmission attaching bolts.
38. Separate engine from transmission, then raise engine high enough to clear No. 1 crossmember. Move engine forward and remove from vehicle.
39. Reverse procedure to install.

**F-250–350**

1. Disconnect battery ground cables

from both batteries and remove hood.
2. Drain cooling system, then remove air cleaner and intake duct assembly.
3. Place a suitable cover over intake manifold opening.
4. Remove fan shroud, then the fan and clutch assembly. **The fan retaining nut has left hand threads.**
5. Disconnect upper and lower hoses and the automatic transmission cooler lines from radiator.
6. Remove radiator.
7. If equipped, remove A/C compressor drive belt, then remove and position compressor on radiator upper support.
8. Remove power steering pump drive belt and remove and position pump

aside.
9. Disconnect fuel supply line heater and alternator wiring from alternator.
10. Remove oil pressure sender from firewall and lay sender on engine.
11. Disconnect accelerator cable and speed control cable, if equipped, from injection pump.
12. Remove accelerator cable bracket, with cables, from intake manifold and position aside.
13. If equipped, disconnect transmission kickdown rod from injection pump.
14. Disconnect main wiring harness connector from right side of engine.
15. Disconnect ground strap from rear of engine.
16. Disconnect fuel return hose from left

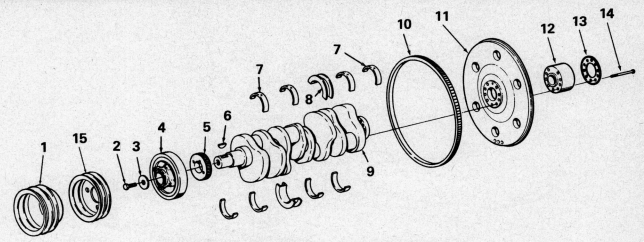

1. Pulley, Generator Drive
2. Screw
3. Crankshaft Washer
4. Vibration Damper
5. Crankshaft Gear
6. Woodruff Key
7. Bearing
8. Thrust Bearing
9. Crankshaft
10. Ring Gear
11. Flywheel
12. Flywheel Adapter
13. Reinforcement Ring
14. Bolt
15. Pulley, Crankshaft

**Crankshaft assembly**

---

rear of engine.
17. Remove two upper engine to transmission attaching bolts.
18. Disconnect heater hoses from water pump and righthand cylinder head.
19. Disconnect water temperature sender wiring from left front of cylinder block.
20. Disconnect water temperature overheat light switch from top front of lefthand cylinder head.
21. Raise and support vehicle.
22. Disconnect battery ground cables from lower front of engine and remove from vehicle.
23. Disconnect and plug fuel inlet line from supply pump.
24. Disconnect starter motor wiring.
25. Disconnect exhaust pipe from exhaust manifold.
26. Remove bolts attaching front engine mounts from front crossmember.
27. Remove flywheel cover, then the converter to flywheel attaching nuts.
28. Lower vehicle and support transmission with a suitable jack.
29. Attach suitable engine lifting equipment to engine and raise engine slightly to clear the front crossmember and pull engine forward. Move front of engine approximately 45° toward the left side of engine compartment, then lift engine from vehicle. **Use care not to damage the wiper motor when removing engine.**
30. Reverse procedure to install.

## INTAKE MANIFOLD REPLACE

1. Disconnect battery ground cables.
2. On E-250-350 models, remove engine cover.
3. On all models, remove air cleaner and place a suitable cover over intake manifold opening.
4. On E-250-350 models, disconnect fuel inlet and return lines from fuel filter, then remove fuel filter and bracket as an assembly.
5. On all models, remove injection pump as described under "Injection Pump, Replace."
6. On F-250-350 models, disconnect fuel return lines from rear injection nozzles and remove return lines to fuel tank.
7. On all models, disconnect engine harness ground wire from rear left of cylinder head, then remove engine wiring harness from engine.
8. Remove glow plug harness and controller.
9. Remove intake manifold attaching bolts and the intake manifold, **Fig. 7.**
10. Reverse procedure to install. Torque attaching bolts to specifications in sequence shown in **Fig. 8.**

## EXHAUST MANIFOLD REPLACE
### E-250-350

1. Disconnect battery ground cables, then remove engine cover.
2. If removing righthand manifold, proceed as follows:
   a. Remove fan shroud halves.
   b. Remove engine oil dipstick and tube and transmission filler tube and dipstick.
   c. Raise and support vehicle.
   d. Remove righthand engine mount insulator to frame attaching nuts.
   e. Raise right side of engine slightly until fuel filter header touches body sheet metal, then install a wooden block between insulator and frame and lower engine to rest on block.
   f. Disconnect exhaust pipe from exhaust manifold, then lower vehicle.
   g. Bend back tabs on manifold attaching bolts, then remove bolts and the manifold.
3. If removing lefthand manifold, proceed as follows:
   a. Raise and support vehicle.
   b. Disconnect exhaust pipe from exhaust manifold, then lower vehicle.
   c. Bend back tabs on manifold attaching bolts, then remove bolts and the manifold.
4. Reverse procedure to install.

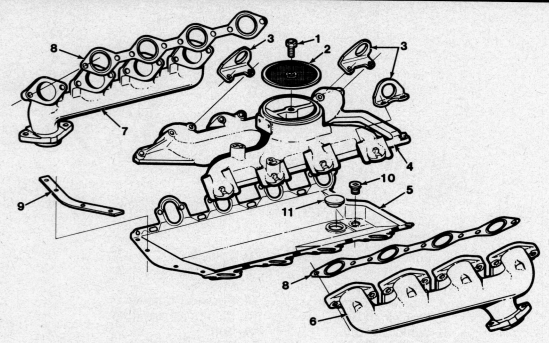

1. Stud
2. Guard
3. Lifting Bracket
4. Intake Manifold
5. Valley Pan and Gasket
6. L.H. Exhaust Manifold
7. R.H. Exhaust Manifold
8. Exhaust Manifold Gasket
9. Valley Pan Strap
10. Valley Pan Drain Plug
11. Valley Pan Closing Plug

**Fig. 7   Manifold assemblies**

## F-250–350

1. Disconnect battery ground cables.
2. Raise and support vehicle.
3. Disconnect exhaust pipe from exhaust manifold.
4. If removing left manifold, bend tabs for manifold attaching bolts, then remove bolts and the manifold.
5. If removing right manifold, lower vehicle, then bend tabs for manifold attaching bolts and remove the attaching bolts and manifold.
6. Reverse procedure to install.

## CYLINDER HEAD
## REPLACE

The procedure outlined below is for the right bank cylinder head. The left bank cylinder head is removed in a similar manner.

1. On E-250-350 models, remove engine cover.
2. On all models, disconnect battery ground cables, then drain cooling system.
3. Remove fan shroud halves, then the fan and clutch assembly. **The fan retaining nut has lefthand threads.**
4. Disconnect fuel supply line heater and alternator electrical connectors from alternator.
5. Remove alternator and vacuum pump.
6. On F-250-350 models, disconnect and plug fuel lines from fuel filter.
7. Remove alternator and vacuum pump mounting bracket, and on F-250-350 models, the fuel filter and bracket as an assembly.
8. Remove heater hose from cylinder head.
9. Remove injection pump as described under "Injection Pump, Replace."
10. Remove intake manifold as described under "Intake Manifold, Replace."
11. Raise and support vehicle.
12. Disconnect exhaust pipe from exhaust manifold.
13. Remove transmission filler tube attaching bolt, then lower vehicle and remove engine oil dipstick and tube.
14. Remove valve cover, rocker arms and pushrods.
15. Remove injection nozzles and glow plugs.
16. Remove cylinder head attaching bolts.
17. On E-250-350 models, install suitable bar through rings on lifting eyes, then lift cylinder head from engine.
18. On F-250-350 models, attach hoist to lifting eyes and lift cylinder head from engine. **Clean the precombustion chambers and inspect for cracks or burns. Some cracking and burning is acceptable, Fig. 9. When installed, the precombustion chambers may seat from .003 inch above to .001 inch below the cylinder head.**
19. Reverse procedure to install. Torque cylinder head attaching bolts in sequence to specifications as shown in **Fig. 10.** Torque intake manifold attaching bolts in sequence, **Figs. 7 and 8,** to specifications.

## ROCKER ARMS &
## PUSHRODS
## REPLACE

1. Disconnect battery ground cables.

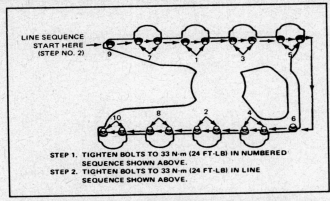

**Fig. 8  Intake manifold tightening sequence**

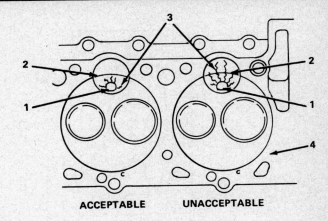

1. Throat of Pre-Combustion Chamber
2. Fire Ring Mark
3. Cracks
4. Cylinder Head (Bottom View)

**Fig. 9  Precombustion chamber inspection**

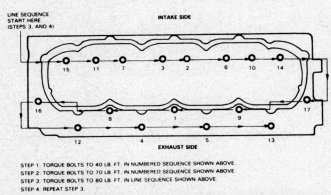

**Fig. 10  Cylinder head tightening sequence**

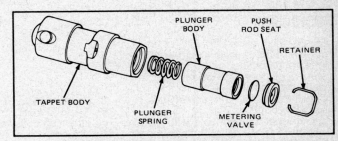

**Fig. 11  Valve lifter, disassembled**

2. On E-250-350 models, remove fan shroud halves and the engine cover.
3. If working on righthand cylinder bank on E-250-350 models, proceed as follows:
   a. Remove engine oil dipstick and tube assembly and the valve cover bracket.
   b. Remove transmission dipstick and filler tube.
   c. Raise and support vehicle.
   d. Remove righthand engine mount insulator-to-frame attaching nuts.
   e. Raise right side of engine slightly until fuel filter header touches body sheet metal, then install a wooden block between insulator and frame and lower engine to rest on block.
   f. Lower vehicle.
4. On all models, remove valve cover attaching screws and the valve cover.
5. Remove rocker arm post mounting bolts.
6. Remove rocker arms and posts, and the pushrods in order so they may be installed in their original positions.
7. Reverse procedure to install. Install rocker arm post attaching bolts with timing mark set at 11 o'clock position, as viewed from front of engine, and torque to 20 ft. lbs.

## VALVES
### ADJUST

These engines use hydraulic lifters and there is no provision for adjustment.

## VALVE ARRANGEMENT
### FRONT TO REAR

Left...................... I-E-I-E-I-E
Right .................... E-I-E-I-E-I

## VALVE GUIDES
### REPLACE

If valve guides are damaged, or are larger than specifications allow, install repair insert as follows:
1. Drill out valve guide, then ream the drilled bore to correct size for insert sleeve.
2. Chill insert in dry ice, then carefully press insert in place.
3. Finish insert with reamer to specified

valve guide diameter. **Reface valve seat after valve guide has been reamed, then, using a suitable scraping tool, break the sharp corner at top of valve guide.**

## VALVE LIFTERS
### REPLACE

1. Remove intake manifold as described under "Intake Manifold, Replace".
2. Remove Crankcase Depression Regulator (CDR) tube and grommet from valley pan.
3. Remove valley pan strap and drain plug, then the valley pan.
4. Remove rocker arms and pushrods as described under "Rocker Arms & Push Rods, Replace".
5. Remove guide retainer, then the guides and valve lifters.
6. Reverse procedure to install.

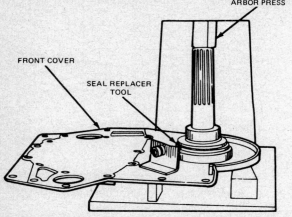

**Fig. 12   Engine front cover seal replacement**

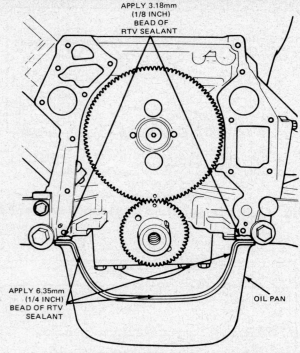

**Fig. 13   Engine front cover installation**

## VALVE LIFTERS
### SERVICE

1. Disassemble valve lifter, **Fig. 11**, then clean all parts in solvent and wipe dry.
2. If any parts of lifter are worn or damaged, or plunger is not free in body, replace entire assembly.
3. Check that roller rotates freely and is not worn or damaged.
4. Lubricate all components with clean engine oil, then assemble as shown in **Fig. 11**.

## TORSIONAL DAMPER
### REPLACE

1. Disconnect battery ground cables.
2. Remove fan shroud, then the fan and clutch assembly. **The fan retaining nut has lefthand threads.**
3. Remove drive belts.
4. Raise and support vehicle.
5. Remove crankshaft pulley.
6. Remove damper to crankshaft attaching bolt, then the damper.
7. Reverse procedure to install.

## ENGINE FRONT COVER
### REPLACE

1. Disconnect battery ground cables, then drain cooling system.
2. Remove air cleaner. Install intake air opening cap, tool T83T-9424-A.
3. Remove fan shroud, then the fan and clutch assembly. **The fan retaining nut has lefthand threads.**
4. Remove fuel injection pump, injection pump adapter and water pump.
5. Raise and support vehicle.
6. Remove torsional damper, then disconnect ground cables from front of engine.
7. Remove front cover to engine block and oil pan attaching bolts.

8. Lower vehicle.
9. Remove front cover to engine block attaching bolts, then the front cover.
10. Using seal removal tool T80T-4000-W, remove seal from front cover, **Fig. 12**.
11. Reverse procedure to install. Lubricate new oil seal with DOAZ-19584-A grease, or equivalent. Apply a bead of sealant to mating surface as shown in **Fig. 13**.

## FRONT OIL SEAL
### REPLACE

1. Remove torsional damper, then pry seal out of cover.
2. To install new seal on engines without three weldnuts on front cover, position seal into seal installation tool T83T-6700-B and install over end of crankshaft. Install tool T83T-6316-B over installation tool and tighten nut against tool and washer to seat seal.
3. To install new seal on engines with three weldnuts on front cover, position seal in installation tool T83T-6700-A and install over end of crankshaft. Attach bridge to weldnuts and draw seal into front cover by turning center screw clockwise. **Prior to installation, lubricate oil seal with DOAZ-19584-A, or equivalent.**

## TIMING GEARS
### REPLACE

1. Remove front cover.

2. Remove crankshaft drive gear, then the camshaft drive gear using tool T83T-6316-A. **When removing crankshaft drive gear, use a breaker bar to prevent crankshaft rotation.**
3. Reverse procedure to install. Align timing marks as shown in **Fig. 14. The crankshaft drive gear may be heated in an oven to 300-350° F, to ease installation.**

## CAMSHAFT
### REPLACE

1. Remove engine as described under "Engine, Replace".
2. Remove injection pump and adapter, intake manifold, valve lifters, engine front cover and fuel supply pump.
3. Remove camshaft drive gear, fuel supply pump cam, spacer and thrust plate from camshaft, **Fig. 15**.
4. Remove camshaft using camshaft bearing set tools T65L-6250-A and Rotunda 14-0314, or equivalent.
5. Reverse procedure to install. Lubricate camshaft lobes with DOAZ-19584-A grease, or equivalent, and the journals with clean engine oil. Torque camshaft Allen bolt to 15 ft. lbs.

## PISTON & ROD
## ASSEMBLY

Assemble piston to rod so that connecting rod weight pad is installed on the oppo-

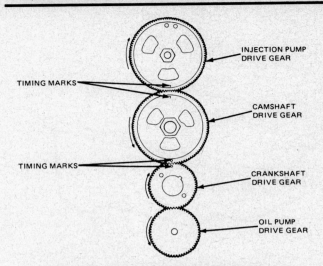

Fig. 14   Timing gear alignment

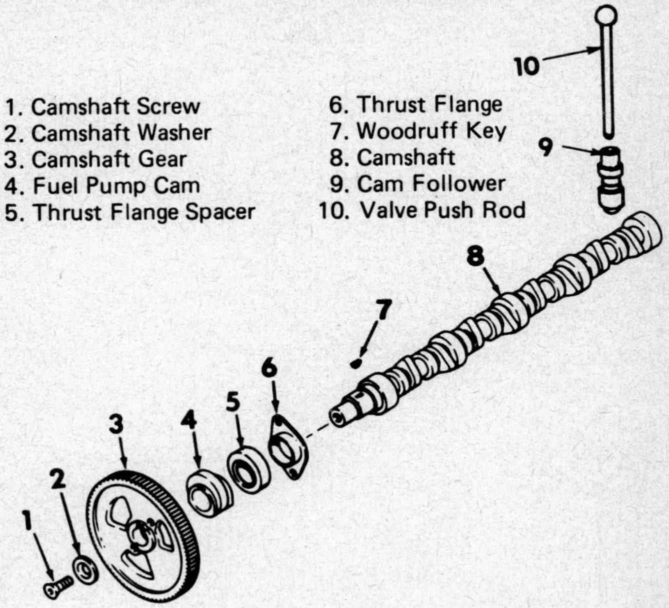

1. Camshaft Screw
2. Camshaft Washer
3. Camshaft Gear
4. Fuel Pump Cam
5. Thrust Flange Spacer
6. Thrust Flange
7. Woodruff Key
8. Camshaft
9. Cam Follower
10. Valve Push Rod

Fig. 15   Camshaft assembly

site side of the piston as the relief pocket, **Fig. 16.** Install the piston into the cylinder so the piston relief pocket is on the camshaft side of the engine and the arrow on the piston top also faces the camshaft side of the engine, **Fig. 16.**

## PISTON & RINGS

Pistons are available in standard sizes and oversize of .003 inch.

## FLYWHEEL, ENGINE REAR COVER & OIL SEAL REPLACE

1. Remove transmission, then the clutch and clutch housing.
2. Remove flywheel, then the rear cover.
3. Using an arbor press and a 4⅛ inch spacer, remove oil seal.
4. Reverse procedure to install. Lubricate new oil seal with DOAZ-19584-A grease, or equivalent. Apply suitable sealant to sealing surfaces. Torque flywheel attaching bolts to specifications.

## FLYWHEEL RING GEAR REPLACE

1. Using a blow torch, heat ring gear on engine side of gear, then knock gear off of flywheel.
2. To install gear, heat it evenly until it expands enough to press onto flywheel. **Do not allow temperature of ring gear to exceed 500° F.**

## OIL PAN & OIL PUMP REPLACE

1. Disconnect battery ground cables, then remove engine oil and transmission oil dipsticks.
2. Remove air cleaner and install intake opening cover, manifold cover T83T-9424-A.
3. Remove fan and clutch assembly. **The fan retaining nut has lefthand threads.**
4. Drain cooling system, then disconnect lower radiator hose.
5. Disconnect return hose from power steering pump, then plug pump and hose to prevent contamination.
6. Disconnect fuel line heater connector and wiring harness from alternator.
7. Raise and support vehicle.
8. Disconnect, then plug transmission oil cooler lines from radiator, if equipped.
9. Disconnect and plug fuel pump inlet line, then drain crankcase and remove oil filter.
10. Remove transmission oil filler tube.
11. Disconnect exhaust pipe from exhaust manifolds and muffler flange, then remove the inlet pipe.
12. Remove upper inlet pipe mounting stud from right exhaust manifold.
13. Remove nuts and washers securing engine insulators to No. 1 crossmember, then lower vehicle.
14. Attach suitable engine lifting equipment to engine and raise engine until transmission housing contacts body.
15. Install wood blocks between engine insulators and crossmember. Use a 2¾ inch block on left side and a 2 inch block on right side. Lower engine to rest on the blocks.
16. Raise and support vehicle.
17. Remove flywheel inspection plate.
18. Position fuel pump inlet line at rear of No. 1 crossmember and, if equipped, position transmission oil cooler lines aside.
19. Remove oil pan attaching bolts, **Fig. 17,** then remove oil pump and pickup tube, **Fig. 18,** from engine and lay in oil pan (F-250-350 only). Remove oil pan. **The crankshaft may need to be rotated to position counterweights in order to remove oil pan.**
20. Reverse procedure to install. Apply sealant to oil pan mating surface as shown in **Fig. 19.**

## ENGINE OIL COOLER REPLACE

1. Disconnect battery ground cables, then drain cooling system.
2. Remove fan shroud, then the fan and clutch assembly. The fan retaining nut has left hand threads.
3. Raise and support vehicle.
4. Drain engine oil and remove oil filter. Do not reinstall drain plug.
5. On F-250-350 models, remove left engine mount insulator to frame attaching nut, then raise left side of engine slightly and install a one inch wooden block between insulator and frame. Lower engine to rest on block.
6. On all models, remove oil cooler attaching bolts and the oil cooler, **Fig. 20.**
7. Reverse procedure to install.

## WATER PUMP REPLACE

1. Disconnect battery ground cables, then drain cooling system.
2. Remove fan shroud, then the fan and clutch assembly. **The fan retaining nut has lefthand threads.**
3. Remove all drive belts, then the water pump pulley.
4. Disconnect heater hose from water

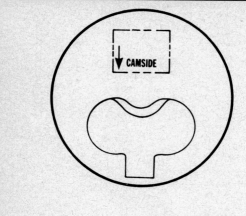

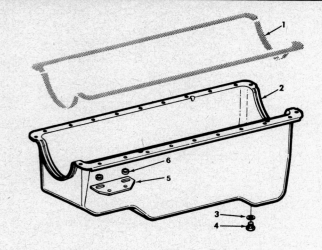

1. Oil Pan Gasket
2. Oil Pan
3. Washer
4. Drain Plug
5. Oil Pan Cover Mounting Bracket
6. Bracket Spacer

**Fig. 17   Oil pan assembly**

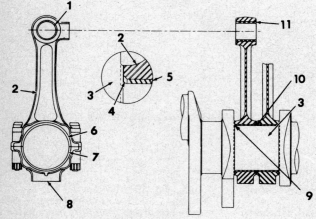

1. Split in Bushing
2. Connecting Rod
3. Crankshaft
4. Crankshaft Fillet
5. Bearing
6. Connecting Rod Bearing (Upper)
7. Connecting Rod Bearing (Lower)
8. Connecting Rod Bearing Cap
9. Large Chamfer Side
10. Small Chamfer Side
11. Bushing

**Fig. 16   Piston & rod assembly**

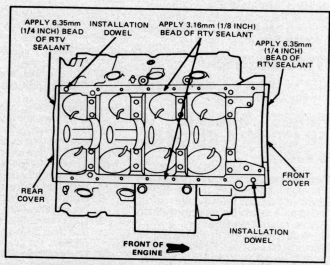

APPLY 6.35mm (1/4 INCH) BEAD OF RTV SEALANT
INSTALLATION DOWEL
APPLY 3.16mm (1/8 INCH) BEAD OF RTV SEALANT
APPLY 6.35mm (1/4 INCH) BEAD OF RTV SEALANT
REAR COVER
FRONT COVER
INSTALLATION DOWEL
FRONT OF ENGINE

**Fig. 19   Sealing oil pan mating surface**

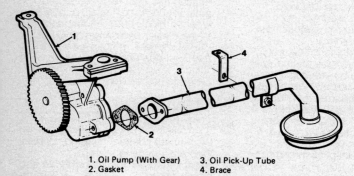

1. Oil Pump (With Gear)
2. Gasket
3. Oil Pick-Up Tube
4. Brace

**Fig. 18   Oil pump, disassembled**

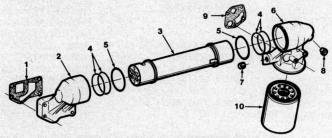

1. Front Manifold Gasket
2. Front Oil Cooler Adapter
3. Oil Cooler
4. "O" Ring
5. "O" Ring
6. Filter Header Assembly
7. Pipe Plug
8. Plug
9. Filter Header Gasket
10. Oil Filter

**Fig. 20   Oil cooler, disassembled**

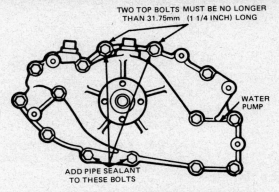

**Fig. 21 Water pump installation**

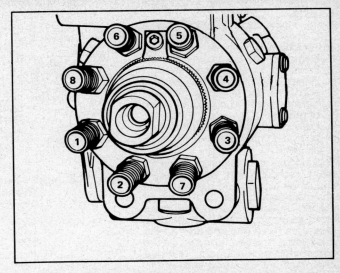

**Fig. 22 Injection pump cylinder numbering sequence**

pump, then remove heater hose fitting from pump.

5. Remove alternator adjusting arm and adjusting arm bracket.
6. Remove A/C compressor and brackets and position aside.
7. Remove power steering pump and bracket and position aside.
8. Remove water pump attaching bolts, then the pump.
9. Reverse procedure to install. Apply RTV sealer to two top and two bottom bolts, **Fig. 21.** Apply suitable pipe sealant to heater hose fitting. Torque water pump attaching bolts to 14 ft. lbs.

## FUEL SUPPLY PUMP
### REPLACE

1. Loosen fuel line connections. Do not remove fuel lines at this time.
2. Loosen fuel pump attaching bolts one to two turns. Using hand force only, loosen fuel pump to break gasket free.
3. Rotate engine by tapping starter until fuel pump cam lobe is at low position. This will reduce spring tension against pump attaching bolts.
4. Disconnect fuel pump inlet, outlet and return lines.
5. Remove fuel pump attaching bolts, then the fuel pump. Remove and discard gasket.
6. Reverse procedure to install. Run engine and check all connections for leaks.

## FUEL SUPPLY PUMP CAM, SPACER & THRUST PLATE
### REPLACE

1. Remove camshaft drive gear, then the fuel supply pump as previously described.
2. Remove fuel pump cam and spacer using suitable puller.
3. Remove thrust plate attaching bolts, then the thrust plate.
4. Reverse procedure to install.

## INJECTION PUMP
### REPLACE

Prior to removing any fuel lines, clean the exterior of lines with clean fuel oil or solvent to prevent contamination.

1. Disconnect battery ground cables.
2. On E-250-350 models, remove engine cover.
3. On all models, remove engine oil filler neck, then the injection pump to drive gear attaching bolts.
4. Disconnect electrical connectors from injection pump.
5. Disconnect accelerator cable and, if equipped, speed control cable from throttle lever.
6. Remove air cleaner and install intake opening cover, tool T83T-9424-A.
7. Remove accelerator cable bracket, with cables attached, and position aside.
8. On 1985-89 E-250-350 models, disconnect fuel inlet and return lines at fuel filter, then remove fuel filter and bracket as an assembly.
9. On all models, remove fuel filter to injection pump fuel line and cap fittings.
10. Remove and cap pump inlet elbow and fitting adapter.
11. Remove fuel return line from pump and cap fittings. It is not necessary to remove injection lines when removing injection pump. If lines are to be removed, loosen line fittings at pump before removing it from engine. Fuel lines must be removed in the following sequence, **Fig. 22,** 5-6-4-8-3-1-7-2, and installed in reverse order.
12. Remove injection lines from nozzles. Cap lines and nozzles.
13. Remove injection pump to adapter attaching nuts.

14. Loosen injection line retaining clips and injection nozzle fuel lines and cap all fittings. **Do not install injection nozzle fuel lines until pump is installed in engine.**
15. Remove injection pump, with nozzle lines attached, through passenger compartment on E-250-350 models, or from engine compartment on F-250-350 models.
16. Reverse procedure to install. Note the following:
   a. Install new O-rings on drive gear end of injection pump and pump fitting adapter.
   b. Torque pump adapter nuts to 14 ft. lbs.
   c. Torque nozzle connector nuts and pump outlet fitting nut to 22 ft. lbs.
   d. Install elbow in pump adapter and torque to a minimum of 6 ft. lbs., then tighten further to align elbow with fuel inlet line, if necessary. Do not exceed one full turn or 10 ft. lbs.
   e. Apply suitable pipe sealant to pump elbow threads and a 1/8 inch bead of RTV sealant to adapter housing mating surface.

## INJECTION PUMP DRIVE GEAR & ADAPTER
### REPLACE
#### 1983

1. Disconnect battery ground cables, then remove air cleaner and install intake opening cover, tool T83T-9424-A.
2. On E-250-350 models, remove engine cover.
3. On all models, remove injection pump as described under "Injection Pump, Replace".
4. Remove injection pump adapter

housing.

5. Crank engine until No. 1 cylinder is at TDC of compression stroke using one of the following methods:
   a. Remove right valve cover and observe No. 1 cylinder valve lever.
   b. Remove No. 1 cylinder glow plug and listen for escaping air while turning engine in normal direction of rotation.
   c. Using the timing quadrant and vibration damper, scribe a line to indicate TDC.

6. With engine at TDC compression for No. 1 cylinder, gears with chamfers should be aligned and gears without chamfers should have the "Y" marks aligned. **Injection pump and camshaft gears equipped with locating chamfers have one chamfer on the injection pump gear and two on the camshaft gear. Gears without chamfers are stamped with a "Y" on the face for proper alignment.**

7. On gears with chamfers, scribe an alignment mark on front of injection pump gear where chamfer meshes with chamfer of camshaft gear, then remove gear.

8. On gears without chamfers, slide injection pump gear back so that top of camshaft gear is exposed when observed from top of front cover. Apply a small amount of paint to tip of a long screwdriver and mark top of camshaft teeth which mesh with injection pump gear. Also, scribe an alignment mark on front face of injection pump gear, then remove gear.

9. Reverse procedure to install. On gears with chamfers, position camshaft gear chamfers in the 12 o'clock position, then install injection pump gear so that its chamfer meshes with those on camshaft gear. On gears without chamfers, mark new gear as old gear was marked in reference to "Y" mark on old gear, then install gear with marks aligned.

## 1984–89

1. Perform steps 1 through 4 as described for 1983 models.

2. Using suitable tool, remove plugs, then turn engine over by hand to TDC of compression stroke of No. 1 piston. **To determine that No. 1 piston is at TDC of compression stroke, position injection pump drive gear dowel at four o'clock position. The scribe line in vibration damper should be at TDC.**

3. Draw a line on front of injection pump drive gear at six o'clock position where the one locating chamfer meshes between the two chamfers on the camshaft gear.

4. Remove injection pump drive gear.

5. Reverse procedure to install, noting the following:
   a. With drawn line on injection pump drive gear at six o'clock position, install gear and align all drive gear timing marks, **Fig. 14.** Use extreme care to avoid disturbing injection pump drive gear after it

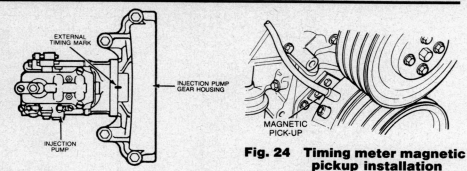

Fig. 23   **Injection pump timing marks**

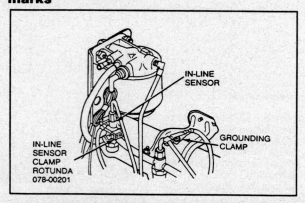

Fig. 24   **Timing meter magnetic pickup installation**

**Fig. 25   Injection pump timing tool. 1988–89**

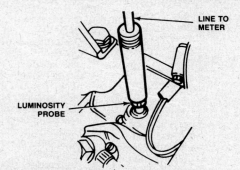

Fig. 26   **Timing meter luminosity probe installation**

is set in position.

## INJECTION NOZZLE REPLACE

Prior to removing nozzle, clean exterior of nozzle assembly with clean fuel oil or solvent to prevent contamination.

1. Remove fuel line retaining clamp from nozzle line.

2. Disconnect fuel inlet and leak-off lines from nozzle assembly. Cap all openings.

3. Remove nozzle from head by turning counterclockwise.

4. Reverse procedure to install. Note the following:
   a. Install a new copper gasket on each nozzle assembly.
   b. Apply suitable anti-seize compound to nozzle threads. Torque nozzle assembly to 33 ft. lbs.
   c. Install two new O-rings in each fuel return tee.
   d. Run engine and check for leaks. If necessary, purge air from high pressure fuel lines by loosening connector one half to one full turn and cranking engine until fuel, free of air bubbles, flows from connector.

| Fuel Cetane Value | Altitude | |
|---|---|---|
| | 0-3000 Ft* | Above 3000 Ft* |
| 38-42 | 6° ATDC | 7° ATDC |
| 43-46 | 5° ATDC | 6° ATDC |
| 47 or greater | 4° ATDC | 5° ATDC |
| *Installation or resetting tolerance for dynamic timing is ± 1°. Service limit is ± 2°. | | |

**Fig. 27 Injection pump timing specifications. 1983–84**

| Fuel Cetane Value | Calibration | |
|---|---|---|
| | 4-68J-ROD | 4-68X-ROD |
| 38-42 | 3.5° ATDC | 4.5° ATDC |
| 43-46 | 2.5° ATDC | 3.5° ATDC |
| 47 or greater | 1.5° ATDC | 2.5° ATDC |
| *Installation or resetting tolerance for dynamic timing is ± 1°. Service limit is ± 2°. | | |

**Fig. 28 Injection pump timing specifications. 1985–87**

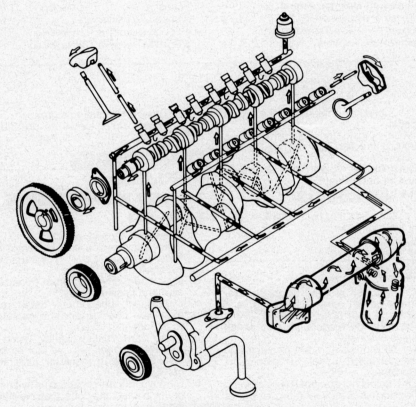

**Engine lubrication**

## INJECTION PUMP TIMING

### WITHOUT TIMING METER

1. Remove fast idle bracket and solenoid, if equipped, from injection pump.
2. Loosen 3 injection pump-to-mounting adapter attaching nuts using tool No. T83T-9000-B or equivalent.

3. Rotate injection pump, using tool No. T83T-9000-C or equivalent, to align timing marks on pump mounting flange and adapter, **Fig. 23**, to within .030 inch.
4. Remove rotating tool and torque pump attaching nuts to 14 ft. lbs.
5. Ensure timing marks are still aligned, then install fast idle bracket and solenoid, if equipped.

### WITH TIMING METER 78-0100 OR 78-00200

1. Start engine and run until normal operating temperature is reached. **Engine temperature must be stabilized between 192 and 212°F to ensure proper fuel ignition in the precombustion chambers. If temperature is less than 192°F, fuel ignition is delayed and the timing meter will record an inaccurate injection value.**
2. Shut engine off, then install timing meter by inserting magnetic pickup into timing pointer probe hole, **Fig. 24**. Insert magnetic pickup until it almost touches vibration damper.
3. On 1988-89 models, remove No. 1 injector on F Series or No. 4 injector on E Series, and install pressure sensor adapter Rotunda 78-00201, **Fig. 25**, or equivalent. On all other models, remove No. 1 glow plug, then install luminosity probe, **Fig. 26**, and torque to 12 ft. lbs. Install photocell over probe.
4. On all models connect timing meter to battery and adjust offset on meter. On 1986-89 models, dial in 20° offset on meter, then disconnect cold start advance solenoid connector from solenoid terminal. Ensure wire leads are positioned away from drive belts.
5. Start and run engine with transmission in Neutral and rear wheels raised off ground.
6. On 1988-89 models, set engine speed to 2000 RPM with no accessory load. On all other models set engine speed to 1400 RPM, using Rotunda idle adjusting tool No. 14-00302 or equivalent, with all accessories off.
7. On 1988-89 models, timing should read 6.5° BTDC at 2000 RPM. For all other models, observe injection timing on timing meter and compare to values listed in chart, **Figs. 27 and 28**. If timing is within specifications, proceed to step 14. If timing is not within specifications, proceed to step 8. **Fuel cetane is a rating of a fuel's ability to ignite under compression ignition conditions. Fuels with high cetane values will ignite faster than fuels with low cetane values. A tester is supplied with timing meter to determine cetane value of fuel.**
8. On 1986-89 models, apply battery voltage to cold start advance solenoid terminal, then readjust engine speed to appropriate test speed specified in step 6, and observe timing on meter. Timing should be advanced at lease one more degree on 1988-89 models, or advanced at least 2.5 more degrees on all other models, when compared to reading obtained in step 7. If timing is not advanced the proper amount from reading obtained in step 7, replace fuel injection pump top cover assembly.
9. For all models, shut engine off and note timing mark alignment.
10. Remove fast idle bracket and solenoid, if equipped, from injection pump.

11. Loosen 3 injection pump-to-mounting adapter attaching nuts using injection pump mounting wrench tool No. T83T-9000-B or equivalent.
12. Rotate injection pump, using injection pump rotating tool T83T-9000-C or equivalent. Rotate pump clockwise (as viewed from front of engine) to re-

tard, or counterclockwise to advance timing. **Each 2° of timing is equal to approximately .030 inch of timing mark movement.**
13. Remove rotating tool and torque pump attaching nuts to 14 ft. lbs. Start engine and recheck timing. If timing is

still not within specifications, repeat adjustment.
14. Shut engine off and remove timing meter, then install glow plug and injector and torque to specifications.
15. Install fast idle bracket and solenoid, if equipped.

# CLUTCH & MANUAL TRANSMISSION
## INDEX

## HYDRAULIC CLUTCH RELEASE
### 1984-89

When the clutch pedal is depressed, fluid is forced from the master cylinder into a slave cylinder. The slave cylinder pushrod moves the clutch release lever which in turn pivots on a trunnion in the flywheel housing, and forces the release bearing against the pressure plate release fingers.

When the clutch pedal is released, the master cylinder return spring and the release lever retracting spring force the fluid from the slave cylinder back to the master cylinder.

The fluid used in this system is the same as that used in the brake system. A bleeder fitting is installed on the slave cylinder and procedures for bleeding are the same as those for brakes. The master cylinder fluid level should be maintained at 1/2 inch below the top of the master cylinder reservoir.

## CLUTCH PEDAL
### ADJUST
#### 1980-83 MODELS

**Clutch pedal total travel is not adjustable on these models.**
1. Check clutch pedal free travel by measuring distance from clutch pedal pad to steering wheel rim, then depress clutch pedal until free travel is diminished and take a second measurement. If the difference between the two measurements is less than 1/2 inch, the clutch linkage must be adjusted.
2. Loosen and back off the two jam nuts several turns, then adjust the first jam nut until a free travel measurement of

1 1/2 inches is obtained at the clutch pedal.
3. While holding the second jam nut, tighten the first jam nut against the second one.
4. Recheck free pedal travel and readjust as necessary.

### 1984-89 MODELS

No clutch linkage or pedal travel adjustments are required.

## CLUTCH
### REPLACE

1. On 1980-83 models, disconnect release lever retracting spring and pushrod assembly from lever.
2. On 1984-89 models, remove clutch slave cylinder.
3. On all models, remove transmission as described under "Transmission, Replace."
4. On models not equipped with a clutch housing dust cover, remove starter motor and clutch housing.
5. On models equipped with a clutch housing dust cover, remove dust cover and the release lever from housing.
6. On all models, mark clutch assembly and flywheel for assembly reference.
7. Remove pressure plate and cover assembly and the clutch disc from flywheel. **Loosen attaching bolts evenly to relieve spring tension without distorting cover.**
8. Reverse procedure to install, noting the following:
   a. Apply a light coat of suitable lithium base grease to release lever fingers and lever trunnion, fulcrum or pivot ball. Do not grease the release lever pivot assembly on Econoline models.
   b. Fill release bearing hub annular

groove with suitable grease.
   c. Adjust clutch pedal as described under "Clutch Pedal, Adjust."

## TRANSMISSION
### REPLACE
#### 3 SPEED TRANSMISSION
##### E-100-350

1. Raise and support vehicle.
2. Drain transmission fluid by removing lower extension housing to transmission bolt.
3. Disconnect driveshaft from transmission and position aside.
4. Disconnect speedometer cable from extension housing and the gearshift rods from shift levers.
5. Raise transmission slightly, using a suitable jack, and remove four extension housing to insulator attaching bolts.
6. Remove four transmission to flywheel housing attaching bolts, then carefully lower transmission from vehicle.
7. Reverse procedure to install.

##### F-100-250

1. Raise and support vehicle.
2. Support engine with a suitable jack and a wooden block positioned under oil pan.
3. Drain transmission fluid by removing lower extension housing to transmission bolt.
4. Disconnect gearshift linkage and speedometer cable from transmission.
5. On 1981-88 models, disconnect back-up light electrical connector.
6. On all models, disconnect driveshaft from transmission and position aside.
7. Raise transmission and remove rear support, and on 1981-88 models, re-

move the insulator and retainer assembly.

8. Remove transmission to flywheel attaching bolts.

9. Slide transmission rearward until input shaft clears clutch housing, then carefully lower transmission from vehicle. **Do not depress clutch pedal with transmission out of vehicle.**

10. Reverse procedure to install.

## WARNER 4 SPEED TRANSMISSION

### Except 4 Wheel Drive Models

1. Disconnect battery ground cable.
2. Remove floor mat and body floor pan cover, then the shift lever and boot assembly and the weather pad.
3. Raise and support vehicle.
4. Support transmission with a suitable jack and disconnect speedometer cable.
5. Disconnect back-up lamp switch electrical connector from back of gearshift lever housing.
6. Disconnect driveshaft or coupling shaft and clutch linkage from transmission and wire to one side.
7. On 1980-82 models equipped with model T-18 transmission, remove transmission rear support, and on 1981-82 models, the upper and lower absorbers.
8. On 1983-85 models equipped with model T-19B or T-19D transmission, or 1986-87 models equipped with T-19A or T-19C transmission, remove transmission rear insulator and lower retainer, then the crossmember.
9. On all models, remove transmission attaching bolts, then slide transmission rearward and lower from vehicle.
10. Reverse procedure to install.

### 4 Wheel Drive Models

1. Remove floor mat, then the access cover attaching screws from floor pan.
2. Place gearshift lever in Reverse, then remove access cover, insulator and dust cover.
3. Remove transfer case and transmission shift lever, shift ball and boot assemblies.
4. Raise and support vehicle.
5. Drain transmission fluid, then disconnect front and rear driveshafts from transfer case and wire to one side.
6. Remove retaining ring or cotter pins from shift link, then lift shift link from transfer case.
7. Remove speedometer cable from transfer case.
8. Support transfer case with a suitable jack, then remove transfer case attaching bolts and the transfer case.
9. Remove rear support to transmission attaching bolts.
10. Support transmission with a suitable jack and remove rear support bracket and brace.
11. Remove four transmission to bellhousing attaching bolts, then lower transmission from vehicle.

12. Reverse procedure to install.

## NEW PROCESS 4 SPEED TRANSMISSION

1. Disconnect battery ground cable.
2. Remove transmission shift lever, ball and boot assembly.
3. On 4 wheel drive models, remove transfer case shift lever, ball and boot assembly.
4. On all models, remove floor pan transmission cover.
5. On F-100-350 models, remove weather pad. **It may be necessary to remove seat assembly to provide access for removal of the weather pad.**
6. On all models, remove gearshift lever and knob from housing. Use tool No. T73T-7220-A or equivalent to remove inner cap, then lift off spring seat, spring and lever.
7. Disconnect back up lamp switch electrical connector from gearshift housing cover.
8. Raise and support vehicle.
9. On 4 wheel drive models, proceed as follows:
   a. Drain transfer case, then disconnect front driveshaft from case and wire to one side.
   b. Remove shift link cotter pin and the shift link.
   c. Remove speedometer cable from transfer case.
   d. Remove three support bracket to transfer case attaching bolts.
   e. Position suitable jack under transfer case, then remove mounting bolts and the transfer case.
10. On all models, position suitable jack under transmission, then remove rear support attaching bolts and the rear support.
11. Remove transmission-to-clutch housing attaching bolts and lower transmission from vehicle.
12. Reverse procedure to install.

## 4 SPEED OVERDRIVE TRANSMISSION

### Exc. Single Rail & Top Mounted Shifter Units

1. Position a wooden block under clutch pedal to prevent it from being depressed.
2. Raise and support vehicle.
3. Mark relationship of driveshaft to flange, then disconnect driveshaft and slide off transmission output shaft. Install suitable seal installation tool into extension housing to prevent leakage.
4. Disconnect speedometer cable from extension housing.
5. Remove shift rod to shift lever retaining clips, flat washers and spring washers.
6. Remove shift control attaching bolts from extension housing and nuts from transmission case.
7. Remove crossmember support to extension housing attaching bolts from rear transmission support.

8. On 1980-81 models, support transmission with a suitable jack and remove extension housing to rear engine support attaching bolts.
9. On 1982-87 models, raise transmission, clutch and engine assembly high enough to relieve weight from No. 3 crossmember, then remove crossmember.
10. On all models, raise rear of engine high enough to relieve weight from crossmember, then remove crossmember.
11. Support transmission with a suitable jack and remove transmission to flywheel housing attaching bolts.
12. Slide transmission rearward until input shaft clears clutch housing, then carefully lower transmission from vehicle. **Do not depress clutch pedal with transmission out of vehicle.**
13. Reverse procedure to install.

### Single Rail & Top Mounted Shifter Units

1. On except 4 wheel drive models, proceed as follows:
   a. Disconnect battery ground cable.
   b. Raise and support vehicle.
   c. Mark relationship of driveshaft to flange, then disconnect driveshaft and slide off transmission output shaft. Install suitable seal installation tool into extension housing to prevent leakage.
   d. Disconnect speedometer cable from extension housing.
   e. On 1983-87 models, disconnect electrical connectors from back up lamp switch and high gear switch (if equipped).
   f. On all models, remove shift lever, ball and boot as an assembly.
   g. Support engine with a suitable jack and remove extension housing to rear engine support attaching bolts.
   h. Raise rear of engine high enough to relieve weight from crossmember, then remove crossmember.
   i. Support transmission with a suitable jack and remove transmission to flywheel housing attaching bolts.
   j. Slide transmission rearward until input shaft clears clutch housing, then carefully lower transmission from vehicle. **Do not depress clutch pedal with transmission out of vehicle.**
   k. Reverse procedure to install.
2. On 4 wheel drive models, proceed as follows:
   a. Disconnect battery ground cable.
   b. Raise and support vehicle.
   c. Drain lubricant from transmission and transfer case.
   d. Disconnect 4 wheel drive indicator switch electrical connector from transfer case, and back-up lamp switch electrical connector from transmission.
   e. Remove skid plate, if equipped, from frame.

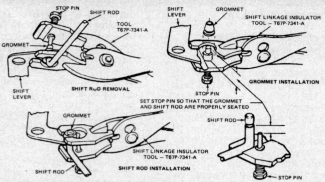

**Fig. 1 Shift lever grommet & retainer ring replacement. 1980–81 E-100–350**

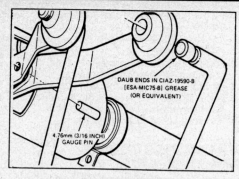

**Fig. 2 Transmission linkage adjustment. 3 speed units**

f. Mark front and rear driveshafts for assembly reference, then disconnect driveshafts from transfer case and position aside.

g. Disconnect speedometer cable from transfer case.

h. On 1983–87 models, remove retaining clips and shift rod from transfer case control lever and shift lever.

i. On all models, disconnect vent hose from transfer case.

j. On 1983–87 models, remove shift lever from transmission.

k. On all models, support transmission with a suitable jack and remove transmission housing to engine rear support bracket.

l. Raise rear of transmission to relieve weight from crossmember, then remove 2 nuts attaching upper gusset to frame on both sides of frame.

m. Remove lefthand gusset, then the transmission to crossmember support plate attaching bolts.

n. Raise transmission with a suitable jack, then remove support plate to crossmember attaching nuts and bolts. Remove support plate and righthand gusset.

o. Remove crossmember attaching nuts and bolts and the crossmember.

p. Remove heat shield from transfer case.

q. On 1981–82 models, slightly lower transmission, then remove retaining clips and shift rod from transfer case control lever and the transfer case shift lever.

r. On all models, support transfer case with a suitable jack and remove 6 transfer case to transmission adapter attaching bolts.

s. Slide transfer case rearward and remove from vehicle.

t. On 1981–82 models, remove three transmission shift lever attaching screws and the shift lever.

u. On all models, support transmission with a suitable jack and remove transmission to flywheel housing attaching bolts.

v. Slide transmission rearward until input shaft clears clutch housing, then carefully lower transmission from vehicle. It may be necessary to lower engine to provide sufficient clearance. **Do not depress clutch pedal with transmission out of vehicle.**

w. Reverse procedure to install.

## 5 SPEED OVERDRIVE TRANSMISSION

1. Shift transmission into neutral position, then remove ball from shift lever.
2. Remove floor mat or carpet, then the shift boot and bezel assembly from transmission opening cover.
3. Remove bolts, then separate upper shift lever from lower shift lever.
4. Raise and support vehicle.
5. Remove drain plug and drain oil from transmission.
6. On 2 wheel drive vehicles, proceed as follows:
   a. Disconnect speedometer cable and back-up lamp switch electrical connector.
   b. Support transmission with a suitable transmission jack.
   c. Disconnect driveshaft and clutch linkage from transmission and wire to one side.
   d. On F series super duty vehicles, remove transmission parking brake from transmission.
7. On 4 wheel drive vehicles, proceed as follows:
   a. Drain oil from transfer case.
   b. Disconnect front and rear driveshafts from transfer case and wire to one side.
   c. Disconnect back-up lamp electrical connector, then remove speedometer cable from transfer case.
   d. Remove skid pan from beneath transfer case, if equipped.
   e. Support transfer case with a suitable jack, then remove bolts holding transfer case to transmission and lower transfer case from vehicle.
   f. Support transmission with a suitable transmission jack.
8. On all models, remove transmission

rear insulator and lower retainer, then remove crossmember.
9. Remove transmission attaching bolts, then slide transmission rearward and lower from vehicle.
10. Reverse procedure to install.

## TRANSMISSION LINKAGE
## ADJUST
### 3 SPEED TRANSMISSION

1980–81 Econoline models may experience problems with hard shifting, gear disengagement or incorrect shifting functions caused by worn, damaged or missing shift linkage components. This malfunction may be corrected by replacing plastic grommets in column mounted shift lever assembly and the retainer ring attaching adjusting stud to shifter levers, using tool shown in **Fig. 1.**

1. Install a 3/16 inch diameter gauge pin through locating hole in steering column shift levers and plastic spacer, **Fig. 2.**
2. Loosen nuts "A" and "B," **Fig. 3,** and position shift levers in neutral detents.
3. Torque nuts "A" and "B" to 12-18 ft. lbs., ensuring there is no movement between stud and nut.
4. Remove gauge pin and check linkage for proper operation. **Retaining rings and insulators must be replaced when adjusting transmission linkage. The rings and plastic grommets where shift rods are attached must also be replaced if excessive wear or looseness is observed.**

### 4 SPEED OVERDRIVE TRANSMISSION

1. Disconnect 3 shift rods from shifter assembly, **Fig. 4.**
2. Insert a 1/4 diameter gauge pin through alignment hole in shifter assembly, ensuring levers are in Neutral position.
3. Align 3rd-4th (forward) lever and 1st-2nd (rearward) lever in neutral

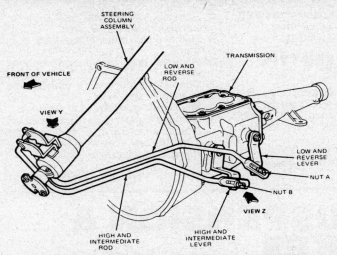

**Fig. 3   Transmission linkage. 3 speed units. E-150–350 (others similar)**

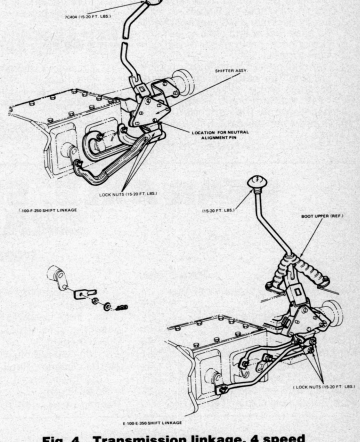

**Fig. 4   Transmission linkage. 4 speed overdrive units**

(midway) position and rotate reverse (middle) lever counterclockwise to Neutral position.

4. Rotate output shaft to ensure transmission is in neutral.
5. On 1980-81 models, attach slotted end of shift rods over slots of studs in shifter assembly. Install locknuts and torque to 15-20 ft. lbs.
6. On 1982-88 models, shift reverse lever clockwise to Reverse position, then attach 1st-2nd and 3rd-4th shift rods to corresponding levers and torque locknuts to 15-20 ft. lbs. Rotate reverse lever back to Neutral position, then install reverse shift rod and torque locknut to 15-20 ft. lbs.
7. On all models, remove gauge pin and check linkage for proper operation.

# TRANSFER CASE

## INDEX

## TRANSFER CASE
### REPLACE
#### BORG-WARNER TYPE 1345 TRANSFER CASE

1. Raise and support vehicle.
2. Drain transfer case fluid, then disconnect four wheel drive indicator switch electrical connector from transfer case.
3. Remove skid plate from frame, if equipped.
4. Disconnect front and rear driveshafts from transfer case.
5. Disconnect speedometer driven gear from transfer case rear bearing retainer.
6. Remove transfer case control lever and shift lever retaining clips and shift rod.
7. Disconnect vent hose from transfer case.
8. Remove heat shield from engine mount bracket and transfer case.
9. Support transfer case, then remove transfer case-to-transmission adapter attaching bolts.
10. Slide transfer case rearward until it clears transmission output shaft, then carefully lower transfer case from vehicle.
11. Reverse procedure to install.

#### BORG-WARNER TYPE 1356 ELECTRONIC SHIFT & 1356 MANUAL SHIFT TRANSFER CASE

1. Disconnect battery ground cable.
2. Raise and support vehicle.
3. Remove skid plate from frame, if equipped.
4. Drain fluid from transfer case.
5. Disconnect harness electrical con-

nector from transfer case, if equipped.
6. Carefully disconnect front driveshaft from front output shaft yoke.
7. Disconnect rear driveshaft from transfer case rear output shaft yoke.
8. Disconnect speedometer driven gear from transfer case.
9. Disconnect vent hose from mounting bracket. **The catalytic converter is located along side the transfer case. Extreme high temperatures generated by the converter.**
10. Support transfer case with a suitable jack.
11. Remove transfer case attaching bolts,

then slide case assembly rearward from transmission output shaft.
12. Reverse procedure to install.

## NEW PROCESS 208 TYPE TRANSFER CASE

1. Raise and support vehicle.
2. Drain transfer case fluid, then disconnect 4 wheel drive indicator switch electrical connector from transfer case.
3. Disconnect speedometer driven gear from transfer case rear bearing retainer.

4. Remove transmission shift lever to transfer case attaching nut.
5. Remove skid plate, if equipped, from frame.
6. Remove heat shield from transfer case.
7. Support transfer case with a suitable jack, then disconnect front and rear driveshafts from output shaft yokes.
8. Remove transfer case to transmission adapter attaching bolts, then carefully lower transfer case from vehicle.
9. Reverse procedure to install.

# REAR AXLE, SUSPENSION & BRAKES

## INDEX

## DANA/SPICER INTEGRAL HOUSING TYPE AXLE

This rear axle, **Fig. 1**, is a semi-floating type, while the axle shown in **Fig. 2** is of the full-floating type. The drive pinion of either axle is of the over-hung design, mounted on preloaded tapered roller bearings. Sealing of the pinion shaft is accomplished by a spring-loaded seal on the companion flange. The flange is splined and secured to the pinion shaft by a nut.

## AXLE SHAFT, BEARING & OIL SEAL, REPLACE

### Full-Floating Axle

1. Set parking brake and loosen axle shaft bolts.
2. Raise and support rear of vehicle so that axle is parallel with floor.
3. Remove axle shaft bolts.
4. Remove axle shaft and discard gasket.
5. Pry out locking wedge with screwdriver.
6. Raise wheel until weight is removed from wheel bearing.
7. Remove wheel bearing adjustment nut.
8. Remove outer bearing cone and pull wheel assembly from axle.

9. Drive inner bearing cone and seal out of wheel hub with brass drift.
10. Inspect bearings and races and replace if worn or damaged. Drive races from wheel hub with brass drift.
11. Lubricate bearing cone and roller assemblies and place inner assemblies into wheel hub. Install new hub inner seal.
12. Wrap spindle threads with tape, then slide wheel assembly onto axle housing spindle and remove tape.
13. Install outer wheel bearing and start adjuster nut. Lower wheel to ground.
14. While rotating wheel, torque adjusting nut to 120-140 ft. lbs. on 1980-86 models and 65 ft. lbs. on 1987-89 models. Back off the nut to obtain 0.001-0.010 inch endplay ($1/8$-$3/8$ turn). If nut or locking wedge are damaged or do not allow for proper endplay they should be replaced.
15. Position locking wedge in key way slot, making sure it is not bottomed against the shoulder of adjusting nut.
16. Install axle shaft and new flange gasket, then install retaining bolts and torque locking bolts to 40-50 ft. lbs.
17. Adjust brakes.
18. Remove supports and lower vehicle.

### Semi-Floating Axle

1. Raise and support vehicle.
2. Remove wheel and brake drum.
3. Remove cover plate and discard gasket.

4. Remove differential pinion shaft lock screw and the shaft.
5. Remove C-clip from button end of shaft by pushing inward on other end.
6. Pull shaft from axle tube. Do not rotate differential side gears.
7. Remove and discard oil seal from axle tube.
8. Pull bearing from axle tube.
9. Lubricate new bearing and install in axle tube.
10. Lubricate and install new oil seal.
11. Insert shaft into axle tube, making sure splines engage side gears, then install C-clip and pull shaft outward until the clip locks.
12. Install pinion mate shaft, aligning lock pin holes, and pinion gear side washers.
13. Install new lock screw and torque to 8 ft. lbs. on 1980-81 models, or 20-25 ft. lbs. on 1982-89 models.
14. Install cover plate and gasket. Torque bolts to 30-40 ft. lbs.
15. Install wheel and drum assembly.
16. Remove supports and lower vehicle.

## REAR AXLE ASSEMBLY, REPLACE

1. Raise vehicle from floor and support with stand jacks under frame side rails.
2. Remove rear wheels.
3. Split rear universal joint.

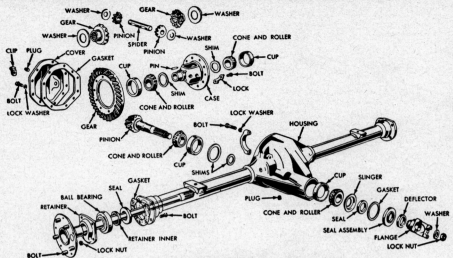

**Fig. 1   Semi-floating integral housing hypoid rear axle**

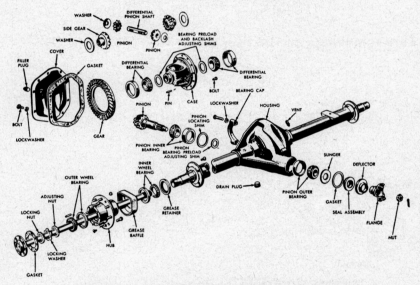

**Fig. 2   Full-floating integral housing hypoid rear axle**

to the carrier housing. Two carrier and differential cases are used to accommodate two bearing sizes. The right and left axle shafts are not interchangeable since the left shaft is shorter than the right.

## AXLE SHAFT, BEARING & OIL SEAL, REPLACE

### Removal, Units w/Ball Bearing

1. Remove wheel assembly.
2. Remove brake drum from flange.
3. Working through hole provided in axle shaft flange, remove nuts that secure wheel bearing retainer.
4. Pull axle shaft out of housing. If bearing is a tight fit in axle housing, use a slide hammer type puller.
5. Remove brake backing plate and secure to frame rail.
6. If the axle shaft bearing is to be replaced, loosen the inner retainer by nicking it deeply with a chisel in several places. The bearing will then slide off easily.
7. Press bearing from axle shaft.
8. Inspect machined surface of axle shaft and housing for rough spots that would affect sealing action of the oil seal. Carefully remove any burrs or rough spots.

### Installation

1. Press new bearing on shaft until it seats firmly against shoulder on shaft.
2. Press inner bearing retainer on shaft until it seats firmly against bearing.
3. If oil seal is to be replaced, use a hook-type tool to pull it out of housing. Wipe a small amount of oil resistant sealer on outer edge of seal before it is installed.

### Removal, Units w/Roller Bearing

1. Remove wheel assembly.
2. Remove brake drum from flange.
3. Working through hole provided in axle flange, remove nuts securing wheel bearing retainer.
4. Pull axle shaft carefully from housing to prevent damage to outer seal rubber. Use a slide hammer type puller to remove tapered bearing cup from housing. Remove brake backing plate and secure to frame rail.
5. If the axle shaft bearing or seal is to be replaced, split the inner bearing retainer.
6. Press bearing from axle shaft.
7. Inspect machined surface of axle shaft and housing for rough spots that would affect sealing action of the oil seal. Carefully remove any burrs or rough spots.
8. Install outer retainer plate on axle shaft. Press lubricated seal and bearing onto shaft until firmly seated. **Oil seal for rear drum brake equipped vehicles is different than that used on vehicles with rear disc brakes. Seals used with drum brakes have a gray metal colored outer rim, while seals used with disc brakes**

4. Disconnect parking brake cable from equalizer rod and unfasten brake cable brackets from frame crossmember.
5. Disconnect hydraulic brake line connection at rear axle housing.
6. Loosen and move shock absorbers out of the way.
7. While supporting axle housing with hydraulic jack, remove spring clips and lower axle assembly to the floor.
8. Reverse the foregoing procedure to install the rear axle assembly, being sure to bleed the brake system when the installation is completed.

## FORD REMOVABLE CARRIER TYPE AXLE

This rear axle, **Fig. 3,** is a banjo-housing hypoid in which the drive pinion is mounted 2¼ inch below the center line of the drive gear. The drive pinion is straddle-mounted in that two opposed tapered roller bearings support the pinion shaft at the front of the pinion gear and a straight roller bearing supports the pinion shaft at the rear of the pinion gear.

The pinion shaft and gear are assembled in the pinion retainer which is bolted

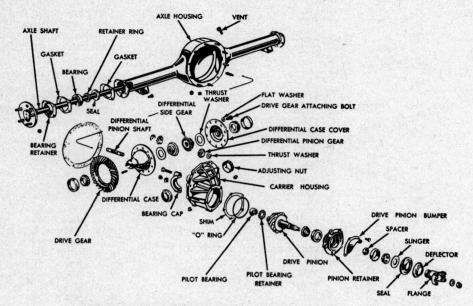

**Fig. 3   Ford removable carrier rear axle**

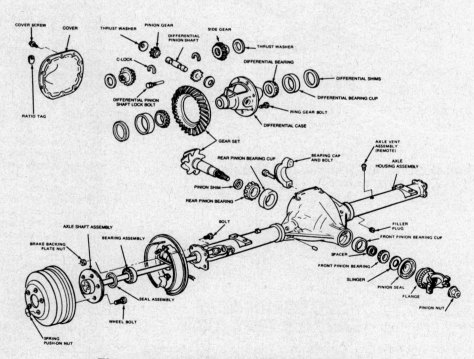

**Fig. 4   Ford integral carrier type rear axle**

**have a black or orange color.**

9. Press new bearing retainer onto shaft until seated.

### Installation

1. On 1980-84 models, place a new gasket on each side of brake carrier plate, and slide axle shaft into housing. On models with roller bearing, ensure outer seal is fully seated on bearing.
2. Start splines into differential side gear and push shaft in until bearing bottoms in housing.
3. Torque bearing retainer nuts to 20-40 ft. lbs.

## REAR AXLE ASSEMBLY, REPLACE

1. Raise and support vehicle.
2. Remove rear wheels and brake drums.
3. Remove rear wheel bearing retainer plate attaching nuts, then disconnect axle shafts from axle housing.
4. Mark driveshaft end yoke and U-joint flange for assembly reference, then disconnect driveshaft from flange. Mark position of cups to flange and remove driveshaft from transmission extension housing. Install a suitable seal installation tool into housing to prevent leakage.
5. Unfasten brake lines from retaining clips and disconnect vent tube, if equipped, from axle housing.
6. Remove brake backing plate assemblies from axle housing and wire aside.
7. Disconnect rear shock absorbers from lower mounts and position aside.
8. Lower axle slightly to reduce spring tension, then remove spring clips, U-bolt nuts and spring seat caps from each rear spring and lower axle assembly from vehicle.
9. On all models, reverse procedure to install.

## FORD INTEGRAL CARRIER TYPE AXLE

This rear axle, **Fig. 4,** is a hypoid gear design with the centerline of the pinion set below the centerline of the ring gear. The drive pinion is of the overhung design mounted on two opposed tapered roller bearings. Pinion bearing preload is adjusted by the pinion nut and a collapsible spacer maintains the seating of the inner race.

## AXLE SHAFT, REPLACE

1. Raise and support vehicle, then remove rear wheel and brake drum.
2. Loosen rear housing cover screws and allow lubricant to drain, then remove cover.
3. Remove differential pinion shaft lock bolt and differential pinion shaft.
4. Move flanged end of axle shaft inward and remove C-lock from end of shaft.
5. Remove axle shaft from housing by

pulling outward.

6. Reverse procedure to install. Apply Loctite EOAZ-19554-B to pinion shaft lock bolt threads, then torque lock bolt to 15-30 ft. lbs.

## OIL SEAL & WHEEL BEARING, REPLACE

1. Remove axle shaft as outlined in "Axle Shaft, Replace".
2. Insert tool T83T-1226-A for models with 8.8 inch ring gear, or tool T85T-1225-AH for models with 10.25 inch ring gear, and tool T50T-100-A into axle bore so tangs on tool engage bearing outer race. Remove bearing and seal as an assembly.
3. Install new bearing using tool T83T-1225-B on models with 8.8 inch ring gear, or tool T80T-4000-W on models with 10.25 inch ring gear, and new seal using tool T83T-1175-A on models with 8.8 inch ring gear, or tool T80T-4000-Y on models with 10.25 inch ring gear. Pack lips of seal with C1AZ-19590-B or equivalent.
4. Reinstall axle.

## AXLE HOUSING, REPLACE

1. Remove four backing plate nuts from each side of axle and wire backing plate aside.
2. Remove vent hose from vent and vent from brake junction block on rear axle housing.
3. Remove brake line from clips on axle housing and remove brake junction block. **Do not open brake lines when removing junction box.**
4. Support rear axle housing on suitable jack and remove U-bolt nuts and plates.
5. Disconnect lower bolts on shock absorber mounting bracket and remove housing from vehicle.
6. Reverse procedure to install. Torque U-bolt nuts to 75-100 ft. lbs. on 1983 F-100-350 and Bronco; 75-105 ft. lbs. on 1983 E-100-150 and 1984-88 E-250; 75-115 ft. lbs. on 1984-88 models exc. F-250 4 2 chassis cab and E series; 150-180 ft. lbs. on 1983 E-250 and 1983-88 E-350; and 150-210 ft. lbs. on 1983 and 1986-88 F-350 and 1984-88 F-250 4 2 chassis cab; 74-107 ft. lbs. on 1989 E-150 or E-250 Light Duty; 75-115 ft. lbs. on 1989 F-150; 150-180 on 1989 E-250-350; 150-210 on 1989 F-250 or F-350 4x2 chassis cab over 8500 lbs. GVWR; 200-270 on F-super duty. Torque shock absorber lower bolts to 40-60 ft. lbs. on Econoline models and 40-64 ft. lbs. on all other models. Torque backing brake attaching bolts to 20-40 ft. lbs. on F-100-150 models and 50-70 ft. lbs. on E-250 and F-250 models with 4050 lb. axle. **No gaskets are required on brake backing plate.**

## SERVICE BRAKES
### ADJUST

The hydraulic drum brakes are

self-adjusting and require a manual adjustment only after brake shoes have been relined or replaced. The adjustment is made as follows:

1. Determine inside diameter of brake drum using brake adjustment gauge, **Fig. 5.**
2. Reverse tool and adjust brake shoes to fit the gauge. Hold automatic adjusting lever out of engagement while rotating adjusting screw to avoid damaging screw slots.

## PARKING BRAKE
### ADJUST
### REAR WHEEL MOUNTED
#### Foot Operated Control

1. Position parking brake pedal to fully released position, then grip tension limiter housing to prevent automatic adjuster from turning and tighten equalizer nut 6 full turns past original position **Fig. 6.**
2. Depress parking brake pedal fully and measure cable tension. Cable tension should meet the following specifications: 1980 front cable with parking brake set in second notch, 120-160 lbs., and 1981-89 rear cable with parking brake fully applied, 350 lbs.
3. If cable tension is not within specifications, repeat steps 1 and 2 and recheck.
4. Release parking brake and check for rear wheel drag. **If brake drag is noted on 1983-89 E-250-350 & F-250-350 models and 1980-82 E-250-350 models after brake adjustment, remove rear drums and measure clearance between parking brake lever and cam plate. This clearance should be .015 inch with brakes fully released. If clearance is not .015 inch, repeat cable adjustment procedure.**

#### Hand Operated Control (Orschein Parking Brake Lever)
#### 1985—89 E-350

1. Place parking brake handle in ON position.
2. Grip tension limiter housing to prevent it from turning and tighten equalizer nut until front cable tension is 350 lbs.
3. Release, then reapply parking brake system and ensure front cable tension is at least 310 lbs.
4. Release parking brake and check for rear wheel drag.
5. If rear wheel drag is noted after adjustment, the rear drums must be removed after the service and parking brakes have been adjusted. Check clearance between parking brake lever and cam plate. If clearance is not .015 inch with brakes fully released, readjust parking brake cable.
6. Place parking brake in fully released position, then check slack in parking brake two rear cables. The cables should be tight enough to provide full

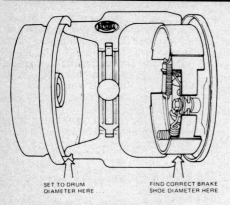

**Fig. 5  Service brake adjustment**

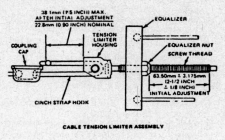

CABLE TENSION LIMITER ASSEMBLY

**Fig. 6  Rear wheel parking brake adjustment**

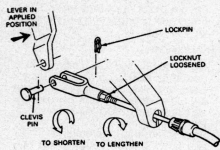

**Fig. 7  Transmission mounted parking brake adjustment**

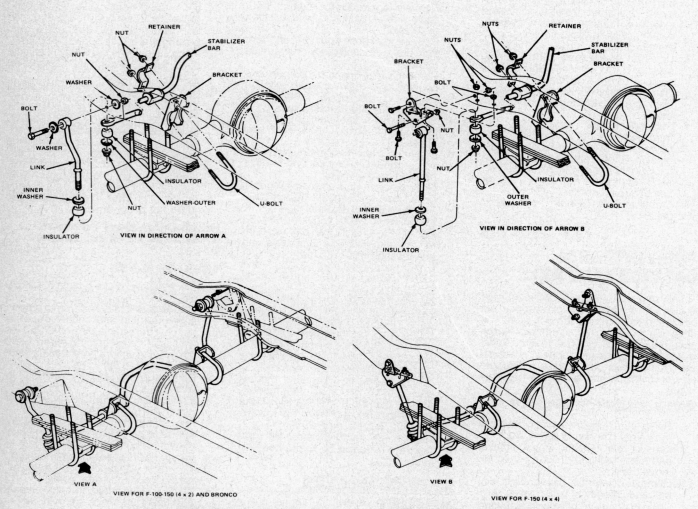

**Fig. 8  Stabilizer bar replacement. 1981–89 F-100–150 & Bronco**

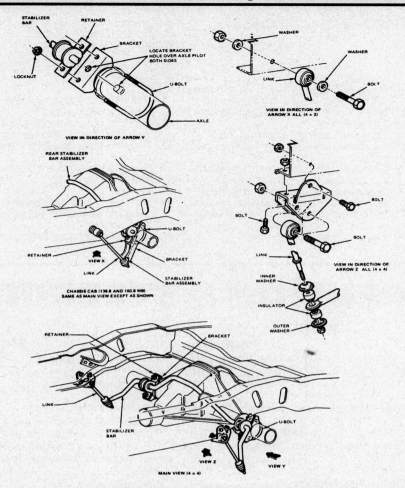

**Fig. 9   Stabilizer bar replacement. 1981–89 F-250–350**

cal connector, then disconnect brake lines from master cylinder.
3. Remove master cylinder-to-power brake unit attaching bolts, then lift master cylinder from mounting studs.
4. Reverse procedure to install.

## POWER BRAKE UNIT
### REPLACE
### VACUUM BRAKE BOOSTER

1. Disconnect battery ground cable.
2. Disconnect stop lamp switch electrical connectors.
3. Support underside of master cylinder, then remove power brake unit-to-master cylinder attaching nuts.
4. Remove vacuum hose between manifold and power brake unit, or power brake unit check valve. Remove check valve, if equipped.
5. Separate power brake unit and master cylinder, leaving master cylinder supported far enough away to allow removal of power brake unit.
6. On models equipped with push rod mounted stop lamp switch, remove retaining pin, then slide switch, push rod, spacers and bushing off brake pedal pin.
7. On models equipped with brake pedal mounted stop lamp switch, remove attaching bolt, nut and plastic bushing, then disconnect power brake unit push rod from brake pedal.
8. Remove power brake unit attaching bolts and the power brake unit.
9. Reverse procedure to install.

### HYDRO-BOOST UNIT

1. Depress brake pedal several times with engine off to discharge the accumulator.
2. Remove master cylinder from hydro-boost unit, then position master cylinder aside.
3. Disconnect three hydraulic lines from booster, then the input pushrod from the brake pedal assembly.
4. Remove booster mounting nuts, then the booster from vehicle.
5. Reverse procedure to install.

## SHOCK ABSORBER
### REPLACE

1. Raise and support rear of vehicle to a point where weight is relieved from rear springs and tires are still in contact with floor.
2. Remove lower attaching nut and bolt from shock absorber and swing lower end free of mounting bracket.
3. Remove upper attaching nut and the shock absorber.
4. Reverse procedure to install.

## LEAF SPRING
### REPLACE
### E-100–350

1. Raise rear of vehicle and support at

---

application of the rear brake shoes when the parking brake lever or foot pedal is placed in the fully applied position, yet loose enough to ensure complete release of the brake shoes when the lever is in released position.

## TRANSMISSION MOUNTED

1. Place transmission in neutral position and release parking brake, then raise and support vehicle.
2. Loosen parking brake adjusting clevis locknut several turns, then remove locking pin and clevis pin.
3. Position and hold lever in applied position, then screw the clevis clockwise onto threaded end of cable until clevis pin can be inserted into clevis and brake actuating lever **Fig. 7.**
4. Remove clevis pin, then rotate clevis counterclockwise 10 full turns. Reinstall clevis pin and lockpin and tighten locknut. Check rotation of driveshaft for freedom from drag.

## MASTER CYLINDER
### REPLACE
### LESS POWER BRAKES

1. Disconnect battery ground cable.
2. Disconnect stop lamp switch electrical connectors.
3. Remove retaining nut, shoulder bolt, spacers and bushing securing master cylinder pushrod to brake pedal.
4. Remove stop lamp switch from brake pedal.
5. Disconnect brake lines from master cylinder, then remove attaching screws or nuts and the master cylinder.
6. Remove boot from master cylinder push rod.
7. Reverse procedure to install.

### POWER BRAKES

1. Depress brake pedal, with engine off, to release vacuum from power brake unit.
2. Disconnect fluid level indicator electri-

frame. Support axle with a suitable jack.
2. Disconnect shock absorbers from lower mountings.
3. Remove two U-bolts and the U-bolt plate.
4. On E-100-150 models, lower axle assembly and remove upper and lower rear shackle bolts, then pull rear shackle assembly from bracket and spring. Remove spring mounting nut and bolt, then lower spring assembly from vehicle.
5. On E-250-350 models, lower axle assembly and remove spring front bolt from hanger. Remove two attaching bolts from rear of spring, then lower spring assembly from vehicle.
6. On all models, reverse procedure to install.

## F-100–350 & BRONCO

1. Raise and support rear of vehicle to a point where weight is relieved from rear springs and tires are still in contact with floor.
2. Remove spring U-bolts, and if equipped, the auxiliary spring and spacer.
3. Remove spring-to-bracket attaching nut and bolt from front of spring.
4. Remove upper and lower shackle attaching nuts and bolts from rear of spring, then lower spring and shackle assembly from vehicle.
5. Reverse procedure to install.

## STABILIZER BAR REPLACE
### 1981–89 F-100–350 & BRONCO

1. Remove nut from lower end of stabilizer link, **Figs. 8 and 9.**
2. Remove outer washer and insulator, then disconnect stabilizer from link.
3. Remove inner insulators and washers.
4. Remove stabilizer link attaching nuts and bolts, then disconnect link from frame.
5. Remove U-bolt, bracket and retainer attaching nuts, then the stabilizer bar from vehicle.
6. Reverse procedure to install.

# FRONT SUSPENSION & STEERING
## INDEX

# DESCRIPTION
## EXC. 4 WHEEL DRIVE MODELS
### Twin I-Beam Axle

The F-150-350 and E-150-350 vehicles use two I-beam type axles, one for each front wheel. One end of each axle is attached to the spindle and a radius arm and the other end is attached to a frame pivot bracket on the opposite side of the vehicle **Fig. 1**.

Each spindle is held in place on the axle by ball joints **Fig. 2.** or a spindle bolt which pivots in bushings pressed in the upper and lower ends of the spindle, **Figs. 3 and 4.** On models equipped with spindle bolts, a thrust bearing is installed between the lower end of the axle and the spindle to support the load on the axle. On all models, a spindle arm is installed on each spindle for attachment to the steering linkage.

The F-super duty vehicle uses a one piece solid I-beam type axle. The axle is attached by two leaf springs, which bolt to spring brackets on both frame side rails **Fig. 5**.

## 4 WHEEL DRIVE MODELS
### Bronco & F-150

The independent front suspension on these vehicles is composed of a two piece front driving axle assembly, two coil springs and two radius arms, **Fig. 6**.

The front driving axle consists of two independent yoke and tube assemblies. One end of yoke and tube assembly is anchored to the frame. The other end of each yoke and tube assembly is supported by the coil spring and radius arm.

### F-250 & F-350 EXC. F-350 W/DANA 60 MONOBEAM FRONT DRIVE AXLE

The independent front suspension on these vehicles has a two piece driving axle attached to the frame with two semi-elliptic leaf springs, **Fig. 7**. Each spring is clamped to the axle yoke with two U-bolts. The rear tube assembly of the spring rests in a rear hanger bracket. The front of the spring is attached to a shackle bracket.

### 1986–89 F-350 w/Dana 60 Monobeam Front Drive Axle

The front suspension used on these models has a one piece driving axle at-

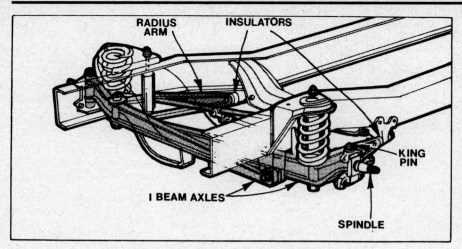

Fig. 1   Twin I-beam front axle

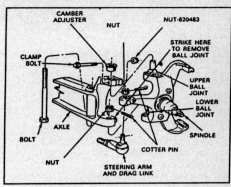

Fig. 2   Spindle used with twin
I Beam front axle. F-150–350
w/ball joints

tached to the frame with two semi-elliptic leaf springs, **Fig. 8.**Each spring is clamped to the axle assembly with two U-bolts. The rear eye of the spring is attached to the hanger bracket. The front of the spring is attached to a shackle bracket. On the right spring cap, a tracking bar is attached with the opposite end mounted on the crossmember.

## WHEEL ALIGNMENT

Prior to checking caster and camber, ensure vehicle front ride height is within 1/8 inch side to side on E-100-350. On F-100-350 models, the left side ride height should be within 0-3/8 inch higher than the right side ride height. On F-150-350 (4x4) and Bronco, the front ride heights should be within 3/16 inch side to side. Refer to **Figs. 9, 10 and 11.** If the vehicle ride heights are not within specifications, redistribute load on loaded vehicles or slightly load empty vehicles on one side. If the ride heights cannot be brought within specifications, verify correct spring installation. **The ride height variations stated, are**

for checking purposes only. The vehicle does not have to operate within these specifications.

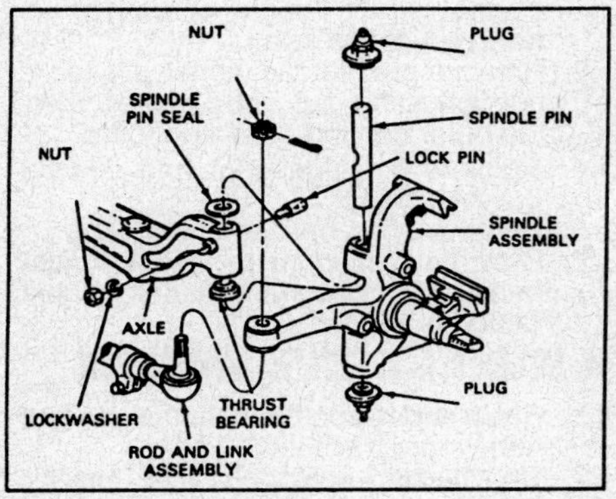

Check and correct as necessary all tire inflation pressures, then check front tires for the same size, ply rating and load range. Check front wheel bearings and adjust as necessary.

If all the above checks have been made, check wheel alignment with suitable alignment equipment. Using the ride heights obtained earlier, compare caster and camber readings to those listed in the "Wheel Alignment Specifications Chart". If the caster and camber angles exceed the specifications, inspect front end for damaged suspension components. Replace as necessary.

Alignment equipment indicates a true reading only when the vehicle's frame is horizontal. Therefore, if the frame is not level (due to tire, spring or load differences), the caster angle reading must be modified to compensate for the frame angles. If the front is higher than the rear, subtract the amount of angle from the reading. If the front is lower than the rear, add the angle. To check frame angle, use a spirit protractor, and take the frame angle measurement on the lower frame flange at the flat area immediately adjacent to the rear spring front hanger.

## 1980–85 4 X 2 MODELS EXC. 1982–85 F-100–350 W/BALL JOINTS

The camber and caster angles are designed into the front end and are not adjustable.

## F-150–350 4 X 4 & BRONCO, 1982–89 F-100–350 4 X 2 w/BALL JOINTS

The caster angle on 1981-89 F-250-350 4 x 4 models with leaf spring front suspension can be adjusted by inserting a shim between the spring and axle. Shims are available in increments of 0°, 1° and 2°. The 0° shim is used to ad-

just side to side ride height when an angled shim is installed on the opposite side of the axle. On all other models, the caster angle is designed into the axle and is not adjustable.

The camber angle may be adjusted by means of mounting sleeves placed on the upper ball joint, **Figs. 12, 13 and 14.** Four sleeves are available in 1/2° camber increments to allow a 3° range of adjustment from −1 1/2° to +1 1/2°.

## TOE-IN, ADJUST

Check the steering wheel spoke position when the front wheels are in the straight ahead position. If the spokes are not in the normal position, they can be adjusted while toe-in is being adjusted.

1. Loosen clamp bolts on each tie rod end sleeve.
2. Adjust toe-in. If steering wheel spokes are in their normal position, lengthen or shorten both rods equally to obtain specified toe-in. If spokes are not in normal position, make necessary rod adjustments to obtain specified toe-in

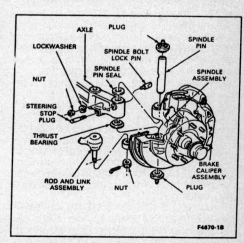

Fig. 4   Spindle used with twin
I Beam front axle. E-250–350
w/spindle pins

Fig. 3   Spindle used with twin
I Beam front axle. E-150
w/spindle pins

and steering wheel spoke alignment. Refer to applicable "'Wheel Alignment Specification Chart."

## WHEEL BEARINGS
### ADJUST
### EXCEPT 4 WHEEL DRIVE MODELS

1. Remove wheel and tire assembly, disc brake caliper and pads, dust cap, locknut, adjusting nut, washer and cotter pin.
2. Tighten wheel adjusting nut to 22-25 ft. lbs. while rotating disc brake rotor in opposite direction.
3. Back off wheel retention nut 1/8 turn and install retainer and cotter pin without any additional movement of nut.
4. Reinstall dust cap, caliper, pads and tire and wheel assembly.

### 4 WHEEL DRIVE MODELS

#### 1980 F-350, 1980–82 F-250, 1980–85 F-150 & Bronco & 1984–85 F-250 Exc. w/Dana 501FS Axle

If vehicle is equipped with free running lock-out hubs, refer to "Front Wheel Drive Section" for removal and installation procedures. On 1985 Bronco and F-150-250 4 x 4 models built after June 30, 1985, a one piece spindle bearing locknut was used, requiring a revised procedure.

When removing manual hub, use spanner wrench PN P84-171-2 or equivalent. Insert spanner wrench tangs into four slots on nut assembly, apply inward pressure to unlock bearing nut locking splines and turn counterclockwise to loosen nut.

When installing, thread the new one piece locknut onto spindle with metal stamping inboard., ensuring I. D. key on metal stamping enters spindle keyway. Insert spanner wrench tangs into four slots on locknut assembly, apply inward pressure to unlock bearing nut locking splines and torque nut to 50-60 ft. lbs. to seat wheel bearings. Back off nut approximately 180°, then torque to 15 ft. lbs.

New spindles have been released with a wider keyway. The one piece locknut can only be used with new spindles. Prior design level lock nuts will continue to be available for servicing of old spindles.

1. Raise vehicle and support with stands.
2. Remove hub assembly, then, using tool No. T59T-1197-B and a torque wrench, torque bearing inner adjusting nut to 50 ft. lbs. while rotating wheel back and forth to seat bearings.
3. Back out adjusting nut 1/4 turn on 1980 models, or 1/8 turn on 1981-85 models, and assemble lock tab and outer locknut.
4. Torque locknut to 50 ft. lbs. on 1980 models, or 150 ft. lbs. on 1981-85 models. Bend at least one tab into a slot on both the inner adjusting nut and outer locknut.
5. Final endplay of wheel when installed on spindle should be .001-.006 inch.

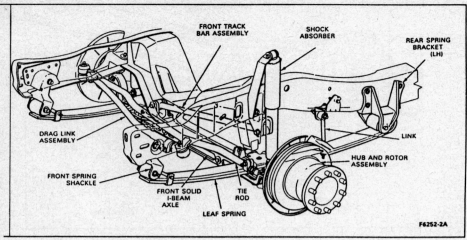

**Fig. 5   One piece Solid I-beam axle. F-super duty**

6. Install hub assembly.

#### 1981–85 F-350 & 1983–85 F-250 w/Dana 501FS Axle

1. Raise vehicle and support with stands.
2. Remove hub assembly, then using front wheel bearing spanner, D78T-1197-A and torque wrench and tighten inner locknut to 50 ft. lbs. to seat bearing.
3. Back off inner locknut and torque to 31-39 ft. lbs.
4. While rotating hub, back off locknut 3/8 turn.
5. Assemble lockwasher and outer locknut and torque to 65 ft. lbs. Bend at least one into a slot on both the inner adjusting nut and outer lock nut.
6. Final endplay of the wheel when installed on spindle should be .001-.009 inch.
7. Install hub assembly.

#### 1986–89 Bronco & F-150–250 w/Dana 44IFS Or 44IFS/HD Axle

1. Raise and support vehicle.
2. Remove hub lock assembly, then, using front wheel bearing spanner T86T-1197-A and a torque wrench, torque adjusting nut to 70 ft. lbs. while rotating wheel back and forth to seat bearing.
3. Apply inward pressure on wrench to disengage adjusting nut locking splines and back off adjusting nut approximately 45° on 1986 models, 90° on 1987 models and 180° on 1988-89 models.
4. Torque adjusting nut to 15 ft. lbs., then remove tool and torque wrench. Final endplay of the wheel on the spindle should be 0-.006 inch.
5. Install hub lock assembly.

#### 1986–89 F-250–350 w/Dana 50IFS & Dana 60 Monobeam Axle

1. Raise and support vehicle.

2. Remove hub lock assembly, then, using spanner wrench D85T-1197-A, remove outer locknut and the lock washer.
3. Torque inner locknut to 50 ft. lbs. to seat bearing, then back off inner locknut and torque to 31-39 ft. lbs.
4. Back off inner locknut 135-150° while rotating hub.
5. Install lock washer so that key is positioned in spindle groove, then rotate inner locknut so that pin is aligned into nearest lock washer hole.
6. Install outer locknut, torquing to 160-205 ft. lbs. The final endplay of spindle should be 0-.006 inch.
7. Install hub locks.

## WHEEL BEARINGS
### REPLACE
### EXC. 4 WHEEL DRIVE MODELS

1. Raise and support front of vehicle and remove front wheels.
2. Remove brake caliper and position aside, leaving brake lines attached. **Do not allow weight of caliper to hang on brake lines.**
3. Remove grease cap, cotter pin, locknut, adjusting nut and washer, then the outer bearing cone and roller.
4. Remove hub and rotor and discard grease retainer.
5. Remove inner bearing and roller.
6. Reverse procedure to install. Adjust bearings as described under "Wheel Bearings, Adjust".

### 4 WHEEL DRIVE MODELS

1. Raise and support front of vehicle and remove front wheels.
2. On models equipped with locking hubs, remove hubs as described in "Front Wheel Drive Section".
3. On 1980-81 models, remove front hub grease cap.
4. On 1980-81 models, remove driving

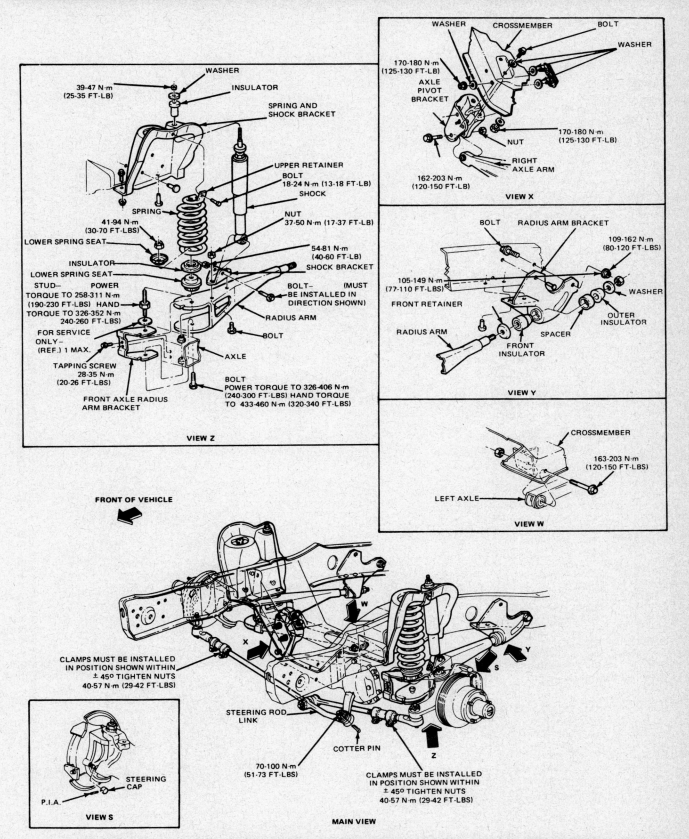

WASHER
39-47 N·m (25-35 FT-LB)
INSULATOR
SPRING AND SHOCK BRACKET
UPPER RETAINER
BOLT 18-24 N·m (13-18 FT-LB)
SHOCK
SPRING
NUT 37-50 N·m (17-37 FT-LB)
41-94 N·m (30-70 FT-LBS)
LOWER SPRING SEAT
INSULATOR
54-81 N·m (40-60 FT-LB)
SHOCK BRACKET
LOWER SPRING SEAT
STUD—POWER TORQUE TO 258-311 N·m (190-230 FT-LBS) HAND TORQUE TO 326-352 N·m 240-260 FT-LBS)
BOLT— (MUST BE INSTALLED IN DIRECTION SHOWN)
RADIUS ARM
FOR SERVICE ONLY— (REF.) 1 MAX.
BOLT
TAPPING SCREW 28-35 N·m (20-26 FT-LBS)
AXLE
FRONT AXLE RADIUS ARM BRACKET
BOLT POWER TORQUE TO 326-406 N·m (240-300 FT-LBS) HAND TORQUE TO 433-460 N·m (320-340 FT-LBS)
VIEW Z

WASHER    CROSSMEMBER    BOLT
WASHER
170-180 N·m (125-130 FT-LB)
AXLE PIVOT BRACKET
170-180 N·m (125-130 FT-LB)
NUT
RIGHT AXLE ARM
162-203 N·m (120-150 FT-LB)
VIEW X

BOLT    RADIUS ARM BRACKET
109-162 N·m (80-120 FT-LBS)
105-149 N·m (77-110 FT-LBS)
FRONT RETAINER
WASHER
RADIUS ARM
SPACER
OUTER INSULATOR
FRONT INSULATOR
VIEW Y

CROSSMEMBER
163-203 N·m (120-150 FT-LBS)
LEFT AXLE
VIEW W

FRONT OF VEHICLE

CLAMPS MUST BE INSTALLED IN POSITION SHOWN WITHIN ± 45° TIGHTEN NUTS 40-57 N·m (29-42 FT-LBS)

STEERING CAP
P.I.A.
VIEW S

W
X
Y
S
Z

STEERING ROD LINK
COTTER PIN
70-100 N·m (51-73 FT-LBS)
CLAMPS MUST BE INSTALLED IN POSITION SHOWN WITHIN ± 45° TIGHTEN NUTS 40-57 N·m (29-42 FT-LBS)
MAIN VIEW

**Fig. 6    Independent front suspension. Bronco & F-150 Four Wheel Drive. 1981–89 shown (similar to 1980)**

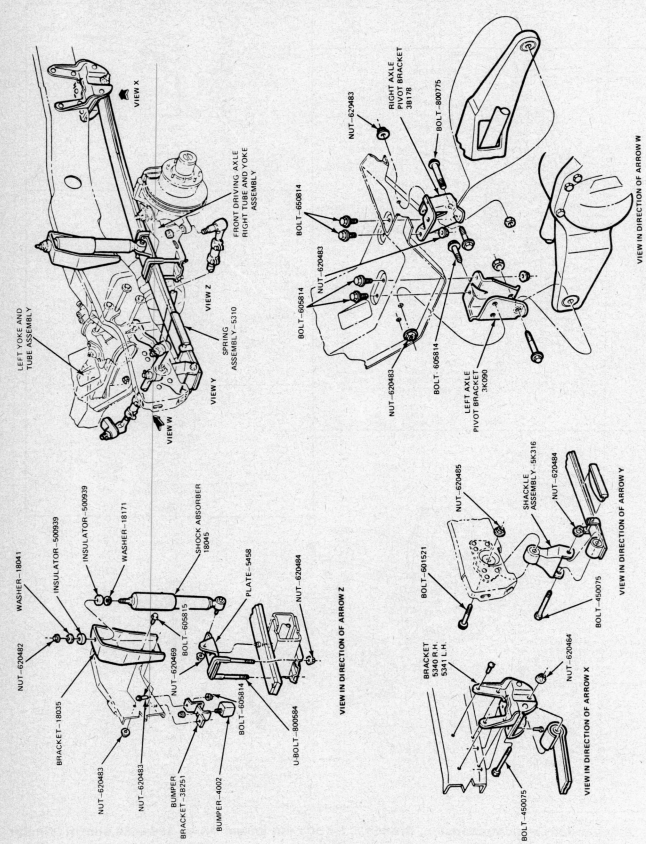

LEFT YOKE AND
TUBE ASSEMBLY

VIEW X

FRONT DRIVING AXLE
RIGHT TUBE AND YOKE
ASSEMBLY

VIEW Z

SPRING
ASSEMBLY—5310

VIEW Y

VIEW W

RIGHT AXLE
PIVOT BRACKET
3B178

NUT—620483

BOLT—800775

BOLT—650814

NUT—620483

BOLT—605814

BOLT—605814

NUT—620483

LEFT AXLE
PIVOT BRACKET
3K090

VIEW IN DIRECTION OF ARROW W

WASHER—18041

INSULATOR—500939

INSULATOR—500939

WASHER—18171

SHOCK ABSORBER
18045

NUT—620482

BRACKET—18035

NUT—620483

NUT—620483

BUMPER
BRACKET—3B251

BUMPER—4002

NUT—620469

BOLT—605815

BOLT—605814

U-BOLT—800584

PLATE—5458

NUT—620484

VIEW IN DIRECTION OF ARROW Z

NUT—620485

SHACKLE
ASSEMBLY—5K316

NUT—620484

BOLT—601521

BOLT—450075

VIEW IN DIRECTION OF ARROW Y

BRACKET
5340 R.H.
5341 L.H.

NUT—620484

BOLT—450075

VIEW IN DIRECTION OF ARROW X

**Fig. 7  Independent front suspension. F-250 & F-350 Four Wheel Drive.1980—82 shown (similar to 1983-89 exc. 1986-89 F-350 w/Dana 60 Monobeam front drive axle)**

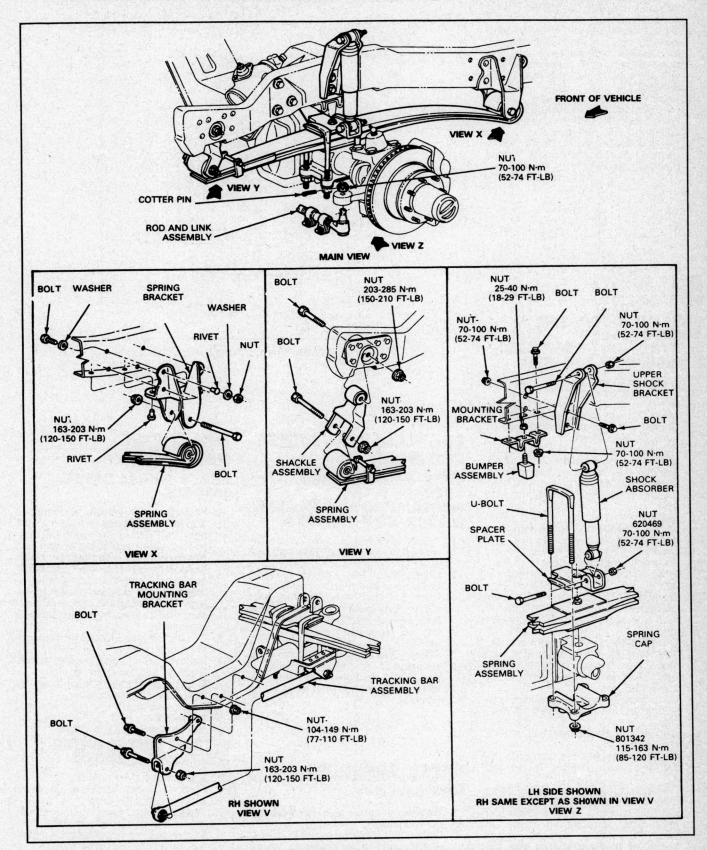

**Fig. 8  Independent front suspension. 1986–89 F-350 w/Dana 60 Monobeam front drive axle**

hub snap ring, then the splined driving hub and pressure spring.

5. On all models, remove wheel bearing locknut, lock ring and adjusting nut, then the hub and disc assembly. **The outer bearing and roller assembly will slide out when the hub is removed.**
6. Remove inner bearing and grease seal from wheel hub using a suitable driving tool on 1980-81 models or a puller on 1982-89 models.
7. Reverse procedure to install. Adjust bearings as described under "Wheel Bearings, Adjust".

## BALL JOINTS
### REPLACE
#### 1981–83 F-100–350, 1984–87 F-150 W/STAMPED FRONT AXLE & 1988–89 F-150–350

1. Raise and support front of vehicle and remove front wheels.
2. Remove brake caliper and position aside, leaving brake lines attached. **Do not allow weight of caliper to hang on brake lines.**
3. Remove dust cap, cotter pin, nut retainer, nut washer and outer bearing, then the rotor from wheel spindle.
4. Remove inner bearing and seal, then the brake dust shield. Discard bearing seal.
5. Disconnect steering linkage from spindle and spindle arm by removing cotter pin and nut.
6. On 1983-89 models, remove tie rod end from spindle arm using tie rod end remover tool No. 3290-C or equivalent.
7. On 1981-82 models, remove cotter pin from upper ball joint stud, then the nuts from upper and lower ball joint studs.
8. On 1983-89 models, remove cotter pins from upper and lower ball joint studs, then the nut from upper ball joint stud. Loosen lower nut to end of lower stud.
9. On all models, separate ball joint from spindle and remove spindle from vehicle.
10. On 1982-89 models, remove ball joint snap ring.
11. On all models, remove ball joints using tools shown in **Figs. 15, 16 and 17.**
12. Reverse procedure to install, using tools shown in **Figs. 18, 19 and 20. On 1981 models, remove lower ball joint first and install last. On 1982-89 models, remove upper ball joint first and install last. Do not heat ball joint or axle to aid in removal or installation.**

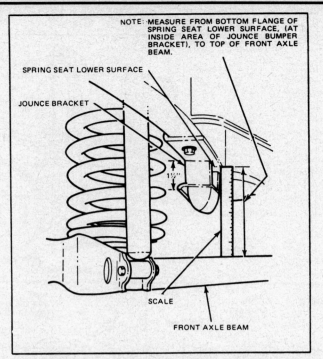

**NOTE:** MEASURE FROM BOTTOM FLANGE OF SPRING SEAT LOWER SURFACE, (AT INSIDE AREA OF JOUNCE BUMPER BRACKET), TO TOP OF FRONT AXLE BEAM.

SPRING SEAT LOWER SURFACE

JOUNCE BRACKET

1½"

SCALE

FRONT AXLE BEAM

**Fig. 9   Measuring riding height. E series**

## CHECKING BALL JOINTS FOR WEAR
#### 1981–83 F-100–350, 1984–87 F-150 W/STAMPED FRONT AXLE & 1988–89 F-150–350

1. Adjust front wheel bearings as described under "Wheel Bearings, Adjust".
2. Check lower ball joint by grasping lower edge of tire and moving wheel in and out while observing lower spindle arm and lower portion of axle jaw. If movement exceeds 1/32 inch, **Fig. 21,** the lower ball joint must be replaced.
3. Check upper ball joint by grasping upper edge of tire and moving wheel in and out. If movement exceeds 1/32 inch, the upper ball joint must be replaced.

## SHOCK ABSORBER
### REPLACE

1. Disconnect shock absorber from upper mounting.
2. Disconnect shock absorber from lower mounting, then compress shock and remove from vehicle.
3. Reverse procedure to install.

## COIL SPRING
### REPLACE
#### EXC. 4 WHEEL DRIVE MODELS

1. Raise front of vehicle and support with stands. Support axle with a suitable jack. **The axle must be supported when replacing spring and not be permitted to hang by brake hose. If length of brake hose is not sufficient to permit spring replacement, it will be necessary to remove the disc brake caliper. Do not suspend caliper by brake hose, if removed.**
2. Disconnect shock absorber from lower mounting.
3. Remove spring upper retainer attaching bolts and the retainer.
4. Remove spring lower retainer attaching nut and the retainer.
5. Lower axle slowly and remove spring from vehicle.
6. Reverse procedure to install.

#### F-150 4 WHEEL DRIVE MODELS & BRONCO

1. Raise and support vehicle.
2. Remove shock absorber to lower bracket attaching bolt.
3. Remove spring lower retainer attaching nuts from inside coil spring.
4. Remove spring upper retainer attaching screw and the upper retainer.
5. Place jack stands under frame side rails and lower axle to relieve spring

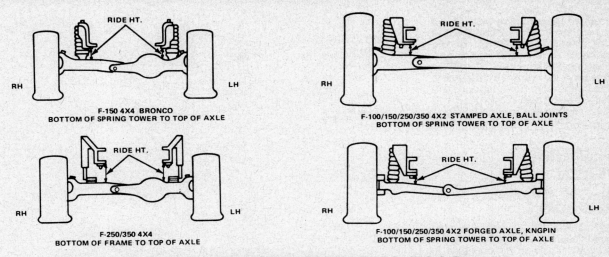

**Fig. 10  Measuring riding height. 1980–85 F-100–350 & Bronco**

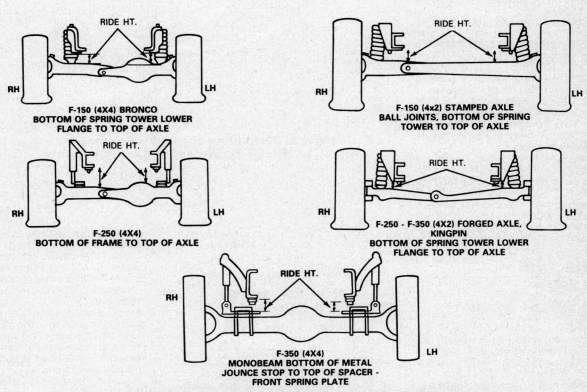

**Fig. 11  Measuring riding height. 1986–89 F-150–350 & Bronco**

tension. **The axle must be supported when replacing spring and not be permitted to hang by the brake hose. If the length of the brake hose is not sufficient to permit spring replacement, it will be necessary to remove the disc brake caliper. Do not suspend caliper by brake hose, if removed.**

6. Remove spring and lower retainer.
7. Reverse procedure to install.

## LEAF SPRING
## REPLACE

### F-250—350 4 WHEEL DRIVE MODELS

1. Raise vehicle until weight is relieved from front spring with the front wheels still contacting floor. Support axle to prevent rotation.
2. Disconnect shock absorber lower end from U-bolt spacer, then remove U-bolts, cap and spacer.
3. On 1986-87 F-350 models equipped with Dana 60 Monobeam axle, remove tracking bar to right spring cap and tracking bar mounting bracket attaching bolts.
4. Remove rear hanger bolt at rear of spring.
5. Remove front shackle bolt and remove spring.
6. Reverse procedure to install.

### F-SUPER DUTY 2 WHEEL DRIVE MODELS

1. Raise vehicle until weight is relieved from front spring with the front wheels still contacting floor. Support axle to remove weight from spring U-bolts.
2. Remove nut and bolt holding shock to spring spacer, then disconnect shock from spring spacer.
3. Remove front shackle-to-spring nut and bolt.
4. Remove rear hanger-to-spring nut and bolt.
5. Remove U-bolt nuts and jack bracket, then the U-bolts.
6. Remove spring from vehicle.
7. Reverse procedure to install.

## RADIUS ARM
## REPLACE

### EXC. 4 WHEEL DRIVE MODELS

1. Remove coil spring as described under "Coil Spring, Replace".
2. Remove spring lower seat from radius arm.
3. Remove radius arm and stabilizer bracket (if equipped) attaching nut and bolt from axle.
4. On all except 1983-89 E-100-350 models, remove nut, rear washer, insulator and spacer from rear side of radius arm rear bracket.
5. On 1980 models, disconnect tie rod end.
6. On all models, remove radius arm

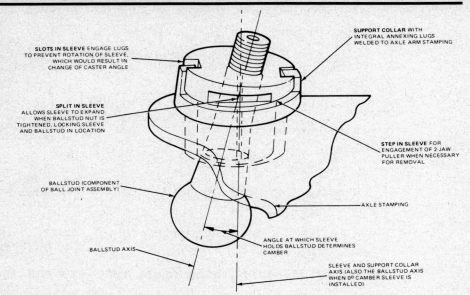

**Fig. 12   Camber adjustment. F-150—350 & Bronco**

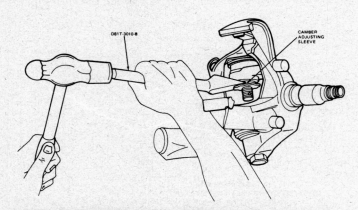

**Fig. 13   Removing camber adjustment sleeve. 1982—89 F-100—350 4 x 2 w/ball joints**

from vehicle.
7. Reverse procedure to install.

### F-150 4 WHEEL DRIVE MODELS & BRONCO

1. Raise and support vehicle under frame side rails.
2. Remove shock absorber to lower bracket attaching bolt and nut and separate shock from radius arm.
3. Remove spring lower retainer attaching bolt(s) from inside coil spring.
4. On 1983-89 models, loosen axle pivot bolt.
5. On all models, remove radius arm to frame bracket attaching nut, then the radius arm rear insulator and spacer (if equipped).
6. Lower axle and slide it forward. **The axle must be supported and not be**

**permitted to hang by brake hose. If length of brake hose is not sufficient to provide adequate clearance, it will be necessary to remove the disc brake caliper. Do not suspend caliper by brake hose, if removed.**

7. Remove axle to radius arm bracket attaching screws, then the radius arm to axle attaching bolt and stud.
8. Move axle forward and remove radius arm from axle, then pull radius arm from frame bracket.
9. Reverse procedure to install.

## STABILIZER BAR
## REPLACE

1. Disconnect both ends of stabilizer bar from link assembly on I-beam bracket.
2. On 1986-89 F-350 models equipped with Dana 60 Monobeam axle, remove nuts, washers and bolts secur-

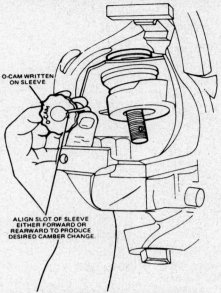

Fig. 14 Camber adjustment. 1982–89 F-100–350 4 x 2 w/ball joints

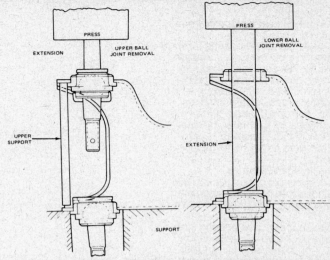

**Fig. 15 Ball joint removal. 1981 F-100–350 w/stamped front axle**

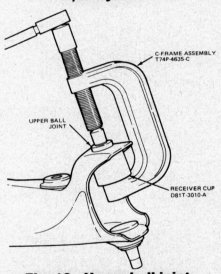

**Fig. 16 Upper ball joint removal. 1982–83 F-100–350 & 1984–89 F-150 w/stamped front axle**

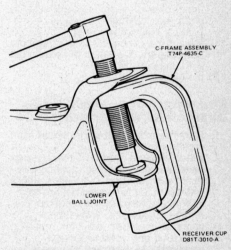

**Fig. 17 Lower ball joint removal. 1982–83 F-100–350 & 1984–89 F-150 w/stamped front axle**

ing links to mounting brackets.
3. Remove stabilizer bar attaching bolts and the stabilizer bar. **On F-150 4 4 and Bronco models, the coil spring must be removed to facilitate removal of the stabilizer bar mounting bracket.**
4. Reverse procedure to install.

## STEERING KNUCKLE REPLACE

### EXC. 4 WHEEL DRIVE MODELS

1. Raise and support front of vehicle.
2. Remove wheel and tire assembly, then unfasten brake caliper and position aside, leaving brake lines attached. **Do not allow weight of caliper to hang on brake lines.**
3. Remove dust cap, cotter pin, nut retainer, nut, washer and outer bearing, then slide hub off steering knuckle.
4. Remove inner bearing and seal and discard the seal.
5. Remove brake dust shield and caliper anchor plate, if equipped.
6. Disconnect steering linkage from knuckle.
7. On 1981-83 F-100-350 models with ball joints, remove cotter pins and nuts from upper and lower ball joint studs.
8. On 1984-89 F-150 models with ball joints, remove cotter pins from upper and lower ball joint studs. Remove nut from upper stud and loosen lower stud nut to end of stud.
9. On all models except 1981-89 with ball joints, remove lock pin nut and washer and the lock pin. Remove upper and lower steering knuckle pin plugs, then drive pin out from top of axle and remove steering knuckle and thrust bearing.
10. On 1981-89 models with ball joints, separate ball joints from steering knuckle, **Fig. 22**, and remove knuckle from vehicle.
11. Reverse procedure to install.

## 4 WHEEL DRIVE MODELS

Operation of 1982-89 F-150-250 4 x 4 and Bronco models in off-road, severe environments may result in the one piece design spindle seal and the spindle needle bearing seal allowing water and contaminants to get into the spindle needle bearings, causing premature seal and bearing wear. This condition can be remedied as follows:

1. Remove axle shaft.
2. Remove inner oil seal assembly from axle shaft.
3. Remove seal and needle bearing from spindle and inspect sealing surfaces of spindle for severely corroded, pitted, worn or galled sealing surfaces, replacing spindle as necessary.
4. Inspect outer shaft of axle shaft assembly for corroded, pitted, worn, or galled surfaces in the inner oil seal and/or needle bearing areas. If damage to this area is evident, replace outer shaft.
5. Replace axle shaft bearings.
6. Position new needle bearing No. 3123 in the spindle bore of the spindle with writing on bearing facing rear of spindle.
7. Using suitable tools, drive bearing into spindle and pack bearing with suitable lubricant, then install seal No. 1175 in bore against bearing with open end of "V" facing rear of spindle.
8. Using suitable tools, press a new slinger on axle shaft.
9. Install rubber "V" seal on slinger and axle shaft with lip of seal facing toward spindle.
10. Install plastic spacer No. 3299 on axle shaft with chamfered side of spacer inboard against axle shaft.
11. Pack thrust face of seal in spindle bore and the V-seal on the axle shaft with suitable lubricant.
12. Install axle shaft.

### Exc. 1986–89 F-350 Models w/Dana 60 Monobeam Axle

1. Remove axle shaft and spindle from steering knuckle.
2. Disconnect tie rod from steering arm.
3. Remove upper ball joint nut and loosen lower ball joint nut. Strike upper ball joint stud to loosen ball joints.
4. Remove lower ball joint nut and remove knuckle from yoke tube.
5. Remove camber adjuster bushing from tube and yoke assembly.
6. Install knuckle into vise and press out ball joints using suitable tool. **On some models, the lower ball joint is retained by a snap ring.**
7. Reverse procedure to install. Install knuckle onto tube and yoke assembly, then install camber adjusting bushing with arrow pointing outward for "positive camber" or towards center of vehicle for "negative camber". Install new lower ball joint nut and torque both upper and lower ball joint nuts to 100 ft. lbs.

### 1986–89 F-350 w/Dana 60 Monobeam Axle

1. Raise and support vehicle and remove axle shaft.
2. Loosen four spindle cap to knuckle attaching bolts alternately and evenly.
3. Remove spindle cap, compression spring and retainer, then remove and discard gasket.
4. Remove four lower kingpin and retainer to knuckle attaching bolts, then re-

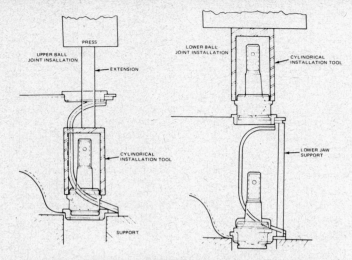

**Fig. 18  Ball joint installation. 1981 F-100–350 w/stamped front axle**

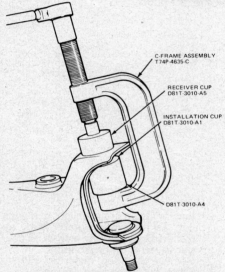

**Fig. 19  Upper ball joint installation. 1982–83 F-100–350 & 1984–89 F-150 w/stamped front axle**

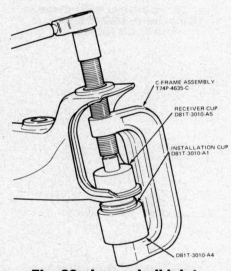

**Fig. 20  Lower ball joint installation. 1982–83 F-100–350 & 1984–89 F-150 w/stamped front axle**

move lower kingpin and retainer from knuckle.
5. Remove tapered bushing from top of upper kingpin in the knuckle, then remove knuckle from axle yoke.
6. Using suitable piece of 7/8 inch hex shaped case hardened metal stock, remove upper kingpin from axle yoke, discarding upper kingpin and seal.
7. Using suitable tools, press lower kingpin grease retainer, bearing cup, bearing and seal from axle yoke lower bore. Discard grease seal, retainer and lower bearing cup.
8. Reverse procedure to install. Coat mating surface of new lower kingpin grease retainer with suitable sealant. Install lower kingpin grease retainer so concave portion faces upper kingpin. Torque upper kingpin to 500-600 ft. lbs. Torque lower kingpin retainer

attaching bolts and the spindle cap attaching bolts to 70-90 ft. lbs.

# MANUAL STEERING GEAR
## REPLACE
### E-100–350 & F-100–350 EXC. 4 WHEEL DRIVE MODELS

1. Raise and support front of vehicle.
2. On 1983-85 F-100-350 models, loosen flex coupling shield from steering gear input shaft shield and slide it up intermediate shaft.
3. On all models, disconnect flex coupling from steering shaft flange by removing 2 attaching nuts.
4. Disconnect drag link from pitman arm using tie rod end remover tool No.

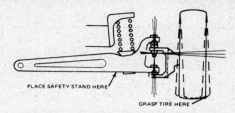

**Fig. 21 Checking lower ball joint for wear. 1981–83 F-100–350 & 1984–89 F-150 w/stamped front axle**

3290-C.

5. Remove Pitman to sector shaft attaching nut and washer, then remove pitman arm from gear sector shaft using pitman arm puller tool No. T64P-3590-F.
6. While supporting steering gear, remove bolts and washer attaching gear assembly to frame side rail and lower gear assembly from vehicle.
7. Reverse procedure to install.

## POWER STEERING GEAR REPLACE
### EXC. 1980–82 E-100–350

1. Disconnect pressure and return lines from gear. Plug open lines and fittings to prevent contamination.
2. Disconnect brake line bracket attached to gear, if necessary.
3. Remove splash shield, if equipped, from flex coupling, then disconnect flex coupling from steering gear.
4. Raise and support vehicle.
5. Remove pitman arm attaching nut

and washer.
6. Remove pitman arm from sector shaft using pitman arm puller tool No. T64P-3590-F or equivalent.
7. Support steering gear, then remove attaching bolts and lower gear from vehicle. **On models equipped with manual transmission, it may be necessary to remove clutch release lever retracting spring to provide clearance for gear removal.**

## 1980–82 ECONOLINE & E-150–350

1. Disconnect pressure and return lines from gear and plug all open lines and fittings.
2. Raise and support vehicle, then remove drag link from pitman arm.
3. Remove nuts securing flex coupling to steering column shaft assembly.
4. Support gear, then remove gear attaching bolts.
5. Remove flex coupling with pinch bolt, then the coupling from the gear.
6. Remove pitman arm from sector shaft using puller tool T64-P3590-F, or equivalent.
7. Reverse procedure to install.

## POWER STEERING PUMP REPLACE
### E-100–350

1. Disconnect pressure and return lines from pump.
2. Loosen belt tension adjusting bolt fully.
3. On models equipped with A/C, remove pump mounting bracket to A/C compressor mounting bracket attaching bolts.
4. On all models, remove pump and mounting brackets from vehicle.
5. Reverse procedure to install.

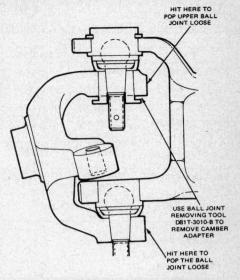

**Fig. 22 Steering knuckle removal. 4 x 2 models**

### F-100–350 & BRONCO

1. Disconnect return hose from pump reservoir and drain steering pump fluid into a suitable container.
2. Remove pressure hose from pump.
3. On models equipped with V belt, remove pump drive belt, then unfasten pump and adjusting bracket from support bracket. Remove pump pulley, then the pump attaching bolts and pump.
4. On 4.9L and 5.0L engines equipped with serpentine belt, remove the drive belt by lifting the belt tensioner out of position. Remove pump pulley, then the pump attaching bolts and pump.
5. Reverse procedure to install.

# 1980–82 Wheel Alignment Specifications Chart
## 1980–82 E SERIES

| | | Riding Height, Inches | | | | | | | Toe In |
|---|---|---|---|---|---|---|---|---|---|
| | | 3.25-3.50 | 3.50-3.75 | 4.00-4.25 | 4.25-4.50 | 4.50-4.75 | 5.00-5.25 | 5.25-5.50 | |
| E100, 150 | Camber, Deg. | −1¾ to −¼ | −1½ to +¼ | −½ to +1¼ | 0 to +1¾ | +½ to +2¼ | +1½ to +3¼ | +2 to +3¾ | ⅛ |
| | Caster, Deg. | +6¼ to +8 | +5¾ to +7¼ | +4½ to +5¾ | +4 to +5¼ | +3¼ to +4½ | +2 to +3¼ | +1½ to +2¾ | ⅛ |
| E250, 350 | Camber, Deg. | −1¾ to −¼ | −1½ to +¼ | −½ to +1¼ | 0 to +1¾ | +½ to +2¼ | +1½ to +3¼ | +2 to +3¾ | 1/32 |
| | Caster, Deg. | +9 to +10½ | +8½ to +9¾ | +7⅛ to +8½ | +6½ to +7¾ | +5¾ to +7 | +4⅝ to +6 | +4 to +5½ | 1/32 |

## 1980–82 F SERIES EXC. F-250/350 (4X4)

| | | Riding Height, Inches | | | | | | | | Toe In |
|---|---|---|---|---|---|---|---|---|---|---|
| | | 2.00-2.25 | 2.25-2.75 | 2.75-3.25 | 3.25-3.50 | 3.50-4.00 | 4.00-4.25 | 4.25-4.75 | 4.75-5.00 | |
| F100, 150 (4X2) | Camber, Deg. | — | −3 to −½ | −2 to +½ | −1¼ to +1¼ | −¼ to +2¼ | +½ to +3 | +1½ to +4 | — | 3/32 |
| | Caster, Deg. | — | +6 to +10 | +5 to +9 | +4 to +8 | +3 to +7 | +2 to +6 | +1 to +5 | — | 3/32 |
| F250/350 (4X2) | Camber, Deg. | −2½ to 0 | −1½ to +1 | +¾ to +1¾ | +¼ to +2¾ | +1 to +3½ | +2 to +4½ | — | — | ① |
| | Caster | +5¾ to +9 | +4¾ to +8 | +3¾ to +7 | +2¾ to +6 | +1¾ to +5 | +¾ to +4 | — | — | ① |
| F150 Bronco (4X4) | Camber, Deg. | — | — | −2½ to −¼ | −1¾ to +½ | −¾ to +1½ | 0 to +2¼ | +1 to +3¼ | +1¾ to +4 | ② |
| | Caster, Deg. | — | — | +6 to +9 | +5 to +8 | +4 to +7 | +3 to +6 | +2 to +5 | +1 to +4 | ② |

①—1980, 7/32; 1981-82, 3/32.
②—1980, 1/16; 1981-82, 3/32.

## 1980 F SERIES (4X4)

| | | Riding Height, Inches | | | | | | | Toe In |
|---|---|---|---|---|---|---|---|---|---|
| | | 4.25-4.75 | 4.75-5.00 | 5.00-5.50 | 5.50-6.00 | 6.00-6.25 | 6.25-6.75 | 6.75-7.00 | |
| F250-350 (4X4) | Camber, Deg. | −4 to −1¼ | −2¾ to 0 | −1½ to +1¼ | −¼ to +2½ | +1 to +3¼ | +2¼ to +5 | — | 1/16 |
| | Caster, Deg. | +3½ to +5¾ | +3¼ to +5½ | +3 to +5¼ | +2¾ to +5 | +2½ to +4¾ | +2¼ to +4½ | — | 1/16 |

## 1981–82 F SERIES (4X4)

| | | Riding Height, Inches | | | | | | | Toe In |
|---|---|---|---|---|---|---|---|---|---|
| | | 4.25-4.75 | 4.75-5.00 | 5.00-5.50 | 5.50-6.00 | 6.00-6.25 | 6.25-6.75 | 6.75-7.00 | |
| F250-350 (4X4) | Camber, Deg. | — | −2¾ to −¼ | −1¾ to +¾ | −¾ to +1¾ | +¼ to +2¾ | +1¼ to +4 | +2½ to +5 | 3/32 |
| | Caster, Deg. | — | +3 to +5 | +3⅛ to +5⅛ | +3⅛ to +5⅛ | +3¼ to +5¼ | +3⅜ to +5⅜ | +3½ to +5½ | 3/32 |

# 1983–89 Wheel Alignment Specifications

**NOTE:** Toe-in for all vehicles listed below is 1/32 inch.

| Riding Height In Inches | Caster Angle Degrees ① | | | | | | | |
|---|---|---|---|---|---|---|---|---|
| | 4 | 4¼ | 4½ | 4¾ | 5 | 5¼ | 5½ | 5¾ |
| **1983–84 E-100 & 150** | | | | | | | | |
| E-100, 150 | +4½ to +6½ | +4 to +6 | +3¼ to +5¼ | +2½ to +4½ | +2 to +4 | +1¼ to +3¼ | +¾ to +2¾ | +¼ to +2¼ |

①—Side to side caster readings must be within 1½°, when vehicle riding height is within ⅛ inch side to side.

| Riding Height In Inches | Caster Angle Degrees ① | | | | | | | |
|---|---|---|---|---|---|---|---|---|
| | 3.80 | 4.05 | 4.30 | 4.55 | 4.80 | 5.05 | 5.30 | 5.55 |
| **1985–89 E-150** | | | | | | | | |
| E-150 | +7½ to +9½ | +7 to +9 | +6¼ to +8¼ | +5½ to +7½ | +5 to +7 | +4½ to +6½ | +3¾ to +5¾ | +3¾ to +5¾ |

①—Side to side caster readings must be within 1½°, when vehicle riding height is within ⅛ inch side to side.

| Riding Height In Inches | Caster Angle Degrees ① | | | | | | | |
|---|---|---|---|---|---|---|---|---|
| | 4.00 | 4.25 | 4.50 | 4.75 | 5.00 | 5.25 | 5.50 | 5.75 |
| **1983–89 E-250 & 350** | | | | | | | | |
| E-250, 350 | +7½ to +9½ | +7 to +9 | +6¼ to +8¼ | +5½ to +7½ | +5 to +7 | +4½ to +6½ | +3¾ to +5¾ | +3¼ to +5¼ |

①—Side to side caster readings must be within 1½°, when vehicle riding height is within ⅛ inch side to side.

| Riding Height In Inches | Caster Angle Degrees ① | | | | | | | | | |
|---|---|---|---|---|---|---|---|---|---|---|
| | 3-3.2 | 3.2-3.4 | 3.4-3.6 | 3.6-3.8 | 3.8-4.0 | 4.0-4.2 | 4.2-4.4 | 4.4-4.6 | 4.6-4.8 | 4.8-5.0 |

**1983–89 F-100 & 150 (4X2)**

| | 3-3.2 | 3.2-3.4 | 3.4-3.6 | 3.6-3.8 | 3.8-4.0 | 4.0-4.2 | 4.2-4.4 | 4.4-4.6 | 4.6-4.8 | 4.8-5.0 |
|---|---|---|---|---|---|---|---|---|---|---|
| F-100, 150 | +5¼ to +7¼ | +5 to +7 | +4½ to +6½ | +4¼ to +6¼ | +3¾ to +5¾ | +3¼ to +5¼ | +2¾ to +4¾ | +2½ to +4½ | +2 to +4 | +1½ to +3½ |

①—Side to side caster readings must be within 1½°, when truck frame to axle riding height is such that right hand side is from 0 to .4 inch than left hand side.

| Riding Height In Inches | Caster Angle Degrees ① | | | | | | | | |
|---|---|---|---|---|---|---|---|---|---|
| | 2.4 | 2.6 | 2.8 | 3 | 3.2 | 3.4 | 3.6 | 3.8 | 4 |

**1983 F-250 & 350 (4X2)**

| | 2.4 | 2.6 | 2.8 | 3 | 3.2 | 3.4 | 3.6 | 3.8 | 4 |
|---|---|---|---|---|---|---|---|---|---|
| F-250, 350 | +6¼ to +7¼ | +5¾ to +7¼ | +5¼ to +7¼ | +4½ to +6½ | +4 to +6 | +3½ to +5½ | +3 to +5 | +3 to +4½ | +3 to +4 |

①—Side to side caster readings must be within 1½°, when truck frame to axle riding height is such that right hand side is from 0 to .2 inch than left hand side.

| Riding Height In Inches | Caster Angle Degrees ① | | | | | | | | | |
|---|---|---|---|---|---|---|---|---|---|---|
| | 2.4 | 2.6 | 2.8 | 3 | 3.2 | 3.4 | 3.6 | 3.8 | 4 | 4.2 |

**1984 F-250 & 350 (4X2)**

| | 2.4 | 2.6 | 2.8 | 3 | 3.2 | 3.4 | 3.6 | 3.8 | 4 | 4.2 |
|---|---|---|---|---|---|---|---|---|---|---|
| F-250, 350 | +5¼ to +7¼ | +5 to +6¾ | +4½ to +6½ | +4¼ to +6¼ | +3¾ to +5¾ | +3¼ to +5¼ | +2¾ to +4¾ | +2½ to +4½ | +2 to +4 | +1¼ to +3¼ |

①—Side to side caster readings must be within 1½°, when truck frame to axle riding height is such that right hand side is from 0 to .4 inch than left hand side.

| Riding Height In Inches | Caster Angle Degrees ① | | | | | | | | | |
|---|---|---|---|---|---|---|---|---|---|---|
| | 2.1 | 2.5 | 2.9 | 3.3 | 3.7 | 4.1 | 4.5 | 4.9 | 5.3 | 5.7 | 6.1 |

**1985 F-250 & 350 (4X2)**

| | 2.1 | 2.5 | 2.9 | 3.3 | 3.7 | 4.1 | 4.5 | 4.9 | 5.3 | 5.7 | 6.1 |
|---|---|---|---|---|---|---|---|---|---|---|---|
| F250, 350 | +5½ to +7½ | +5¼ to +7 | +4¾ to +6½ | +4½ to +6¼ | +4 to +6 | +3½ to +5½ | +3 to +5 | +2½ to +4½ | +2¼ to +4½ | +1¾ to +3¾ | +1¼ to +3¼ |

①—Side to side caster readings must be within 1½°, when truck frame to axle riding height is such that right hand side is from 0 to .4 inch than left hand side.

| Riding Height In Inches | Caster Angle Degrees ① | | | | | | | | |
|---|---|---|---|---|---|---|---|---|---|
| | 2.7 | 2.9 | 3.1 | 3.3 | 3.5 | 3.7 | 3.9 | 4.1 | 4.3 |

**1986–89 F-250 & 350 (4X2)**

| | 2.7 | 2.9 | 3.1 | 3.3 | 3.5 | 3.7 | 3.9 | 4.1 | 4.3 |
|---|---|---|---|---|---|---|---|---|---|
| F-250, 350 | +6⅛ to +7⅛ | +5½ to +7⅛ | +5⅛ to +7⅛ | +4½ to +6½ | +4⅛ to +6⅛ | +3⅝ to +5⅝ | +3⅛ to +5⅛ | +3⅛ to +4½ | +3⅛ to +4⅛ |

①—Side to side caster readings must be within 1½°, when truck frame to axle riding height is such that right hand side is from 0 to .2 inch than left hand side.

| Riding Height In Inches | Caster Angle Degrees ① | | | | | | | | |
|---|---|---|---|---|---|---|---|---|---|
| | 3.2 | 3.4 | 3.6 | 3.8 | 4 | 4.2 | 4.4 | 4.6 | 4.8 |

**1983–89 F-150 & Bronco (4X4)**

| | 3.2 | 3.4 | 3.6 | 3.8 | 4 | 4.2 | 4.4 | 4.6 | 4.8 |
|---|---|---|---|---|---|---|---|---|---|
| F-150, Bronco | +6 to +8 | +5½ to +7½ | +5 to +7 | +4½ to +6½ | +4 to +6 | +3½ to +5½ | +3 to +5 | +2½ to +4½ | +2 to +4 |

①—Side to side caster readings must be within 1½°, when vehicle riding height is within .16 inch side to side.

| Riding Height In Inches | Caster Angle Degrees ① | | | | | | | | |
|---|---|---|---|---|---|---|---|---|---|
| | 5.2 | 5.4 | 5.6 | 5.8 | 6 | 6.2 | 6.4 | 6.6 | 6.8 |

**1983–89 F-250 & 350 (4X4)**

| | 5.2 | 5.4 | 5.6 | 5.8 | 6 | 6.2 | 6.4 | 6.6 | 6.8 |
|---|---|---|---|---|---|---|---|---|---|
| F-250, 350 ② | +3 1/16 to +5 1/16 | +3 1/16 to +5 1/16 | +3⅛ to +5⅛ | +3 3/16 to +5 3/16 | +3¼ to +5¼ | +3 5/16 to +5 5/16 | +3⅜ to +5⅜ | +3 7/16 to +5 7/16 | +3½ to +5½ |

①—Side to side caster readings must be within 1½°, when vehicle riding height is within .16 inch side to side.
②—Caster angle on 1986-89 F-350 w/Dana 60 monobeam axle is 5°.

| Riding Height In Inches | Camber Angle Degrees ① | | | | | | | |
|---|---|---|---|---|---|---|---|---|
| | 4 | 4¼ | 4½ | 4¾ | 5 | 5¼ | 5½ | 5¾ |
| **1983–84 E-100 & 150** | | | | | | | | |
| E-100, 150 | −⅝ to +⅝ | 0 to +1¼ | +⅜ to +1⅝ | +⅞ to +2¼ | +1⅜ to +2⅝ | +1⅞ to +3¼ | +2⅜ to +3⅝ | +2⅞ to +4¼ |

①—Side to side camber readings must be within ⅝°, when vehicle riding height is within ⅛ inch side to side.

| Riding Height In Inches | Camber Angle Degrees ① | | | | | | | |
|---|---|---|---|---|---|---|---|---|
| | 4.25 | 4.50 | 4.75 | 5.00 | 5.25 | 5.50 | 5.75 | 6.00 |
| **1985–89 E-150** | | | | | | | | |
| E-150 | −¾ to +½ | −¼ to +1⅛ | +⅜ to +1⅝ | +⅞ to +2⅛ | +1⅜ to +2⅝ | +1¾ to +3 | +2¼ to +3⅝ | +2¾ to +4 |

①—Side to side camber readings must be within ⅝°, when vehicle riding height is within ⅛ inch side to side.

| Riding Height In Inches | Camber Angle Degrees ① | | | | | | | |
|---|---|---|---|---|---|---|---|---|
| | 3.9 | 4.15 | 4.40 | 4.65 | 4.9 | 5.15 | 5.40 | 5.65 |
| **1983–89 E-250 & 350** | | | | | | | | |
| E-250, 350 | −⅝ to +⅝ | 0 to +1¼ | +⅜ to +1⅝ | +⅞ to +2¼ | +1⅜ to +2⅝ | +1⅞ to +3¼ | +2⅜ to +3⅝ | +2⅞ to +4¼ |

①—Side to side camber readings must be within ⅝°, when vehicle riding height is within ⅛ inch side to side.

| Riding Height In Inches | Camber Angle Degrees ① | | | | | | | | | |
|---|---|---|---|---|---|---|---|---|---|---|
| | 3-3.2 | 3.2-3.4 | 3.4-3.6 | 3.6-3.8 | 3.8-4 | 4-4.2 | 4.2-4.4 | 4.4-4.6 | 4.6-4.8 | 4.8-5 |
| **1983–89 F-100 & 150 (4X2)** | | | | | | | | | | |
| F-100, 150 | −1 to +¼ | −¾ to + ¾ | −¼ to +1¼ | +¼ to +1¾ | +¾ to +2 | +1 to +2½ | +1½ to +3 | +2 to +3½ | +2½ to +4 | +3 to +4½ |

①—Side to side camber readings must be within .7°, when truck frame to axle riding height is such that right hand side is from 0–.4 inch less than left hand side.

| Riding Height In Inches | Camber Angle Degrees ① | | | | | | | | | |
|---|---|---|---|---|---|---|---|---|---|---|
| | 1.6 | 1.8 | 2 | 2.4 | 2.6 | 2.8 | 3 | 3.2 | 3.4 | 3.6 |
| **1983 F-250 & 350 (4X2)** | | | | | | | | | | |
| F-250, 350 | −½ to +½ | −½ to +¾ | −¼ to +⅞ | +¼ to +1½ | +⅝ to +1¾ | +1 to +2⅛ | +1½ to +2⅝ | +2 to +3¼ | +2½ to +3½ | +2¾ to +3½ |

①—Side to side camber readings must be within .7°, when truck frame to axle riding height is such that right hand side is from 0–.2 inch less than left hand side.

| Riding Height In Inches | Camber Angle Degrees ① | | | | | | | | | |
|---|---|---|---|---|---|---|---|---|---|---|
| | 3.1 | 3.3 | 3.5 | 3.7 | 3.9 | 4.1 | 4.3 | 4.5 | 4.7 | 4.9 |
| **1984 F-250 & 350 (4X2)** | | | | | | | | | | |
| F-250, 350 | −1 to +¼ | −¾ to +¾ | −¼ +1¼ | +¼ to +1¾ | +¾ to +2¼ | +1¼ to +2¾ | +1¾ to +3¼ | +2⅛ to +3⅝ | +2½ +4 | +3 to +4½ |

①—Side to side camber readings must be within .7°, when truck frame to axle riding height is such that right hand side is from 0–.2 inch less than left hand side.

| Riding Height In Inches | Camber Angle Degrees ① | | | | | | | | | | |
|---|---|---|---|---|---|---|---|---|---|---|---|
| | 2.1 | 2.5 | 2.9 | 3.3 | 3.7 | 4.1 | 4.5 | 4.9 | 5.3 | 5.7 | 6.1 |
| **1985 F-250 & 350 (4X2)** | | | | | | | | | | | |
| F-250, 350 | −1½ to 0 | −1 to +½ | −½ to +1 | 0 to +1½ | +½ to +2 | +¾ to +2¼ | +1¼ to +2½ | +1¾ to +3¼ | +2¼ to +3¾ | +2¾ to +4¼ | +3¼ to +4½ |

①—Side to side camber readings must be within .7°, when truck frame to axle riding height is such that right hand side is from 0–.2 inch less than left hand side.

| Riding Height In Inches | Camber Angle Degrees ① | | | | | | | | | |
|---|---|---|---|---|---|---|---|---|---|---|
| | 2.9 | 3.1 | 3.3 | 3.5 | 3.7 | 3.9 | 4.1 | 4.3 | 4.5 | 4.7 |
| **1986–89 F-250 & 350 (4X2)** | | | | | | | | | | |
| F-250, 350 | −½ to 0 | −½ to +½ | 0 to +1 | +¼ to +1¼ | +¾ to +1¾ | +1¼ to +2¼ | +1¾ to +2¾ | +2 to +3 | +2½ to +3½ | +3 to +3½ |

①—Side to side camber readings must be within .7°, when truck frame to axle riding height is such that right hand side is from 0–.2 inch less than left hand side.

| Riding Height In Inches | Camber Angle Degrees ① | | | | | | | | |
|---|---|---|---|---|---|---|---|---|---|
| | 3.1 | 3.3 | 3.5 | 3.7 | 3.9 | 4.1 | 4.3 | 4.5 | 4.7 |
| **1983–89 F-150 & Bronco (4X4)** | | | | | | | | | |
| F-150, Bronco | − 1⅝ to − ¼ | − 1 to + ¼ | − ⅝ to + ⅝ | − ¼ to + 1¼ | + ¼ to + 1⅝ | + ¾ to + 2¼ | + 1¼ to + 2⅝ | + 1⅝ to + 3¼ | + 2¼ to + 3½ |

① —Side to side camber readings must be within .7°, when truck frame to axle riding height is within 0-.16 inch of side to side.

| Riding Height In Inches | Camber Angle Degrees ① | | | | | | | | |
|---|---|---|---|---|---|---|---|---|---|
| | 5.1 | 5.3 | 5.5 | 5.7 | 5.9 | 6.1 | 6.3 | 6.5 | 6.7 | 6.9 |
| **1983–89 F-250 & 350 (4X4)** | | | | | | | | | |
| F-250, 350 ② | − 1⅝ to − ¼ | − 1⅛ to + ¼ | − ⅝ to + ¾ | − ⅛ to + 1¼ | + ⅜ to + 1¾ | + ⅞ to + 2⅜ | + 1½ to + 2⅞ | + 2 to + 3½ | + 2½ to + 4 | + 3⅛ to + 4½ |

① —Side to side camber readings must be within .7°, when truck frame to axle riding height is within 0-.16 inch of side to side.
② —Camber angle on 1986-89 F-350 w/Dana 60 monobeam axle is 1.5 degrees.

# FRONT WHEEL DRIVE

## INDEX

## FRONT AXLE ASSEMBLY REPLACE

### F-150 & BRONCO

1. Raise front of vehicle and support with safety stands under radius arm brackets.
2. On 1980 models, drain fluid from differential.
3. On all models, remove front tires and brake calipers. Position calipers aside, leaving brake lines attached. **Do not allow weight of calipers to hang on brake lines.**
4. On 1980 models, remove wheel hub and rotor assemblies, spindles, splash shields and axle shafts.
5. On all models, support axle arm assembly with a suitable jack and remove upper coil spring retainers. Carefully lower jack and remove coil springs, spring cushions and lower spring seats. **The axle must be supported when removing springs and not be permitted to hang by brake hose. If length of brake hose is not sufficient to permit spring removal,** it will be necessary to remove the disc brake caliper. Do not suspend caliper by brake hose, if removed.
6. Remove shock absorbers.
7. On 1980 models, remove upper and lower ball joint nuts and steering knuckle.
8. On all models, remove stud and spring seat from radius arm and axle arm, then the lower radius arm to axle arm attaching bolt.
9. Disconnect vent tube from left axle arm assembly on 1980 models, or from differential housing on 1981-89 models. Discard hose clamps. **On 1981-89 models, remove vent fitting from differential housing and install a ⅛ inch pipe plug.**
10. Remove right axle arm to crossmember pivot bolt.
11. On 1984-89 models, remove right axle shaft boot and discard boot clamps.
12. On all models, remove right drive axle assembly, and on 1981-89 models, slide axle shaft out of slip shaft.
13. Support differential housing with a suitable jack.
14. On 1980 models, remove differential retaining bolts.
15. On all models, remove left drive axle assembly attaching bolts and the axle assembly, **Fig. 1.**
16. Reverse procedure to install.

### F-250-350 EXC. 1986-89 F-350 w/DANA 60 MONOBEAM AXLE

1. Raise and support front of vehicle.
2. On 1980 models, drain fluid from differential.
3. On all models, remove front tires and brake calipers. Position calipers aside, leaving brake lines attached. **Do not allow weight of calipers to hang on brake lines.**
4. On 1980 models, remove hub and rotor assemblies, spindles, splash shields and axle shafts.
5. On all models, support right axle assembly with a suitable jack and remove 2 U-bolts attaching shock absorber mounting plate and leaf spring to axle assembly.
6. On 1980 models, remove upper and lower ball joint nuts and steering knuckle.

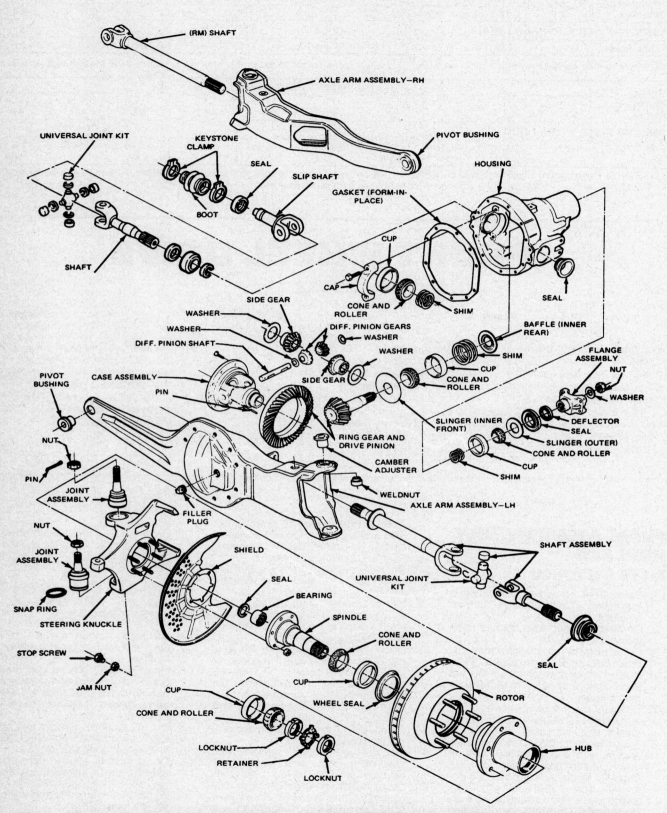

**Fig. 1   Four wheel drive front axle assembly. F-150 & Bronco (similar to other models exc. 1986–89 F-350 w/Dana 60 Monobeam axle)**

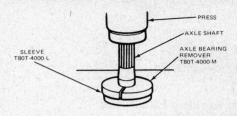

**Fig. 2 Axle shaft bearing removal. 1980–82**

7. On all models, disconnect vent tube, from left axle arm assembly on 1980 models, or from differential housing on 1981-89 models. **On 1981-89 models, remove vent fitting from differential housing and install a 1/8 inch pipe plug.**
8. Remove right axle assembly to crossmember pivot bolt and the axle assembly.
9. On 1984-89 models, remove right axle shaft boot and discard boot clamps.
10. On 1981-89 models, slide axle shaft out of slip shaft.
11. On all models, support left axle arm assembly with a suitable jack and remove 2 U-bolts attaching shock absorber mounting plate and leaf spring to axle assembly.
12. On 1980 models, remove steering knuckle from left axle arm assembly.
13. On all models, support differential housing with a suitable jack, then remove left axle assembly to crossmember pivot bolt and the axle assembly.
14. Reverse procedure to install.

## 1986–89 F-350 w/DANA 60 MONOBEAM AXLE

1. Raise and support vehicle.
2. Remove front wheels and the wheel hubs.
3. Remove brake calipers from rotors and wire out of way. **Do not let brake caliper hang by hose.**
4. Remove stabilizer bar.
5. Remove cotter pins and castellated nuts securing spindle connecting rod to steering knuckles and separate connecting rods from steering knuckles. Wire steering linkage to spring.
6. Remove two nuts and U-bolts from front axle U-joint flange, disconnect axle from front axle pinion flange and securely wire driveshaft to frame.
7. Disconnect vent tube at axle housing and plug vent fitting.
8. Remove nut and bolt and disconnect tracking bar from righthand spring cap.
9. Carefully lower vehicle until it is approximately three feet from floor, then place safety stands on front leaf springs approximately half way between front axle leaf spring and the rear mounting shackle. Lower vehicle so that springs rest on safety stands.
10. Place suitable jack under differential

carrier, then remove U-bolts and nuts securing axle to spring.
11. Carefully lower axle from vehicle.
12. Reverse procedure to install.

# AXLE SHAFT REPLACE

## EXC. 1986–89 F-350 w/DANA 60 MONOBEAM AXLE

1. Raise and support front of vehicle.
2. Remove front tire and brake caliper. Position caliper aside, leaving brake lines attached. **Do not allow weight of caliper to hang on brake lines.**
3. Remove spindle and brake splash shield, then the axle shaft, **Fig. 1.**

## 1986–89 F-350 w/DANA 60 MONOBEAM AXLE

1. Raise and support vehicle and remove front wheel and tire assemblies.
2. Remove brake caliper from rotor and wire to frame.
3. Remove six Allen head cap screws retaining cap to hub body and remove the cap.
4. Remove snap ring retaining axle shaft in hub body assembly.
5. Remove lock ring seated in groove of wheel hub.
6. Remove body assembly from hub. If body is difficult to remove, install two cap screws and pull body assembly out of hub.
7. Using suitable tool, remove outer locknut from spindle.
8. Remove lock washer from spindle.
9. Using suitable tool, remove inner locknut from spindle.
10. Remove hub and rotor assembly from spindle.
11. Remove nuts attaching spindle to knuckle, then lightly tap spindle with soft hammer to remove from knuckle.
12. Remove splash shield and caliper support from knuckle.
13. Pull axle shaft assembly out of steering knuckle.
14. Reverse procedure to install, then adjust wheel bearings.

# AXLE SHAFT BEARING REPLACE

## 1980–82

1. Remove axle shaft as described under "Axle Shaft, Replace."
2. Remove 3 bearing retainer plate to carrier attaching bolts, then slide stud shaft and slip yoke out of housing.
3. Install axle shaft in a suitable vise and drill a 1/4 inch hole 3/4 through the bearing retainer.
4. Remove bearing retainer by breaking with a chisel positioned in drilled hole.
5. Press bearing from axle shaft, **Fig. 2.**
6. Remove seal and retainer plate from stub shaft. Discard seal.
7. Reverse procedure to install. Install bearing retainer and new seal onto

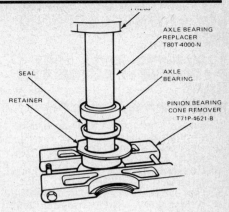

**Fig. 3 Axle shaft bearing installation. 1980–82**

shaft. Lubricate seal with wheel bearing grease. Install bearing onto axle with large radius on inner race facing yoke of axle. Press bearing, then inner bearing retainer until fully seated, **Fig. 3.** Push seal and outer retainer away from bearing and fill with grease. Wrap a piece of tape around the space, then pull retainer and seal against bearing. This will force grease into bearing. Repeat until grease is visible on small end of rollers.

## 1983–89 EXC. 1986–89 F-350 w/DANA 60 MONOBEAM AXLE

1. Remove axle shaft as described under "Axle Shaft, Replace."
2. Remove carrier to cover support arm attaching screws, then separate carrier assembly from support arm and drain lubricant into a suitable container.
3. Install carrier assembly into a suitable holding fixture and rotate axle shaft until open side of snap ring is exposed.
4. Remove snap ring, then slide slip yoke and shaft assembly from housing.
5. Remove and discard right trunnion axle shaft seal from housing.
6. Remove axle shaft bearing.
7. Reverse procedure to install. Install bearing using bearing installation tool No. T80T-4000-N or equivalent with bearing name and part number facing towards tool. Apply a light coat of suitable grease to new seal prior to installation.

## 1986–89 F-350 w/DANA 60 MONOBEAM AXLE

1. Remove axle shaft as previously described.
2. Remove bronze spacer from axle shaft assembly.
3. Using suitable tools, remove bearing from spindle.
4. Reverse procedure to install.

## FRONT WHEEL LOCKING HUB

### 1980 F-250–350 & 1981 F-150–250 w/AUTOMATIC HUBS

#### Removal & Disassembly

1. Remove capscrews and cap assembly from spindle, **Fig. 4.**
2. Remove capscrew from end of axle shaft.
3. Remove lock ring from wheel hub groove.
4. Remove body assembly from spindle. **If necessary, a puller may be used to remove body assembly.**
5. Loosen screws in spindle locknut until heads are flush with edge of locknut, then remove locknut using tool No. T80T-4000-V or equivalent.

#### Assembly & Installation

1. On 1981 models, install slotted locknut, ensuring pin on inner bearing adjusting nut enters one of the slots.
2. On all models, install spindle locknut and torque to 15-20 ft. lbs. using tool No. T80T-4000-V or equivalent.
3. Install and tighten all screws, then push body down until friction shoes are on top of spindle outer locknut, **Fig. 4.**
4. Install capscrew into axle shaft and torque to 35-50 ft. lbs.
5. Install cap assembly and torque capscrews to 30-35 inch lbs.
6. Rotate dial from stop to stop to engage dialing mechanism with body spline.

### F-150–350 & BRONCO w/MANUAL HUBS

#### Removal & Disassembly

1. Remove cap assembly capscrews and the cap assembly, **Fig. 5.**
2. Remove snap ring from end of axle shaft.
3. Remove lock ring from wheel hub groove.
4. Remove body assembly from wheel hub. If necessary, a puller may be used to remove body assembly.

#### Assembly & Installation

1. Install body assembly onto wheel hub, **Fig. 5.**
2. Install lock ring into hub groove, then the snap ring onto axle shaft.
3. Install cap assembly and torque capscrews to 35-50 inch lbs.

### 1982–89 F-150–250 & BRONCO w/AUTOMATIC HUBS

#### Removal & Disassembly

1. Remove cap assembly capscrews and the cap assembly, **Fig. 6.** Avoid dropping ball bearing, bearing race and retainer when removing cap.
2. Remove rubber seal, then the seal bridge retainer from retainer ring

space.
3. Remove retainer ring by closing ends with suitable pliers while pulling hub lock from wheel hub.
4. If wheel hub and spindle are to be removed, remove C-washer from stub shaft groove, splined spacer from shaft and the wheel bearing lock nuts and lock washer.

#### Assembly & Installation

1. Install wheel bearing locknut and lock washer. Torque locknut to 150 ft. lbs.
2. Install splined spacer and C-washer on axle shaft.
3. Install locking hub assembly into hub, ensuring large tangs are aligned with lock washer and splines align with hub and axle shaft splines, **Fig. 6.**
4. Install retainer ring by closing ends with suitable pliers while pushing locking hub assembly into wheel hub.
5. Install seal bridge retainer, narrow end first.
6. Install rubber seal, then the cap assembly. Torque cap screws alternately and evenly to 40-50 inch lbs.

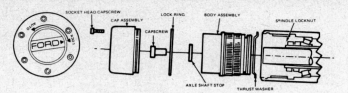

**Fig. 4   Automatic front locking hub. 1980 F-250–350 & 1981 F-150–250**

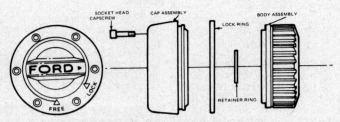

**Fig. 5   Manual front locking hub. F-150–250 & Bronco**

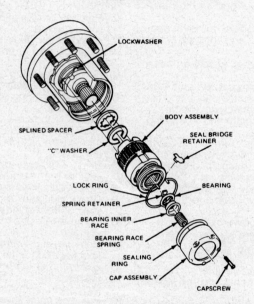

**Fig. 6   Automatic front locking hub. F-150–350 & Bronco**

**NOTE:** Refer to back of this manual for vehicle manufacturer's special service tool suppliers.

# Specifications

## GENERAL ENGINE SPECIFICATIONS

| Year | Engine CID [1]/Liter | Carburetor | Bore and Stroke | Compression Ratio | Net H.P. @ RPM | Maximum Torque Lbs. Ft. @ RPM | Normal Oil Pressure Pounds |
|---|---|---|---|---|---|---|---|
| 1983–84 | 4-11/2.0 L | YFA, 1 Bbl.[2] | 3.52 x 3.13 | 9.0 | 73 @ 4000 | 107 @ 2400 | 40-60 |
| | 4-135/2.2 L[7] | Fuel Injection | 3.50 x 3.50 | 22.0 | 59 @ 4000 | 90 @ 2500 | 57[8] |
| | 4-140/2.3 L[4] | YFA, 1 Bbl.[2][3] | 3.78 x 3.13 | 9.0 | 79 @ 3800 | 124 @ 2200 | 40-60 |
| | 4-140/2.3 L[5] | YFA, 1 Bbl.[2][3] | 3.78 x 3.13 | 9.0 | 82 @ 4200 | 126 @ 2200 | 40-60 |
| | V6-171/2.8 L | 2150, 2 Bbl.[6] | 3.65 x 2.70 | 8.7 | 115 @ 4600 | 150 @ 2600 | 40-60 |
| 1985 | 4-122/2.0 L | YFA, 1 Bbl.[2] | 3.52 x 3.13 | 9.0 | 73 @ 4000 | 107 @ 2400 | 40-60 |
| | 4-140/2.3 L | EFI | 3.78 x 3.13 | 9.0 | 82 @ 4200 | 126 @ 2200 | 40-60 |
| | 4-143/2.3 L[7][9] | Fuel Injection | 3.59 x 3.54 | 21.0 | 86 @ 4200 | 134 @ 2000 | [10] |
| | V6-171/2.8 L | 2150, 2 Bbl.[6] | 3.65 x 2.70 | 8.7 | 115 @ 4600 | 150 @ 2600 | 40-60 |
| 1986 | 4-122/2.0 L | YFA 1 Bbl.[2] | 3.52 x 3.13 | 9.0 | 74 @ 4000 | 108 @ 2600 | 40-60 |
| | 4-140/2.3 L | EFI | 3.780 x 3.126 | 9.5 | 90 @ 4000 | 134 @ 2000 | 40-60 |
| | 4-143/2.3 L[7][9] | Fuel Injection | 3.59 x 3.54 | 21.0 | 86 @ 4200 | 134 @ 2000 | [11] |
| | V6-179/2.9 L | EFI | 3.66 x 2.83 | 93 | 140 @ 4600 | 170 @ 2600 | 40-60 |
| 1987 | 4-122/2.0 L | Aisin 2 Bbl. | 3.52 x 3.13 | 9.0 | 80 @ 4200 | 106 @ 2600 | 40-60 |
| | 4-140/2.3 L | EFI | 3.78 x 3.13 | 9.5 | 90 @ 4000 | 134 @ 2000 | 40-60 |
| | 4-143/2.3 L[7][9] | Fuel Injection | 3.59 x 3.54 | 21 | 86 @ 4200 | 136 @ 2000 | [11] |
| | V6-179/2.9 L | EFI | 3.66 x 2.83 | 9.3 | 140 @ 4600 | 170 @ 2600 | 40-60 |
| 1988 | 4-122/2.0 L | Aisin 2 Bbl. | 3.52 x 3.13 | 9.0 | 80 @ 4200 | 106 @ 2600 | 40-60 |
| | 4-140/2.3 L | EFI | 3.78 x 3.13 | 9.5 | 90 @ 4000 | 134 @ 2000 | 40-60 |
| | V6-179/2.9 L | EFI | 3.66 x 2.83 | 9.3 | 140 @ 4600 | 170 @ 2600 | 40-60 |
| 1989 | 4-140/2.3 L | EFI | 3.78 x 3.13 | 9.5 | - | - | 40-60 |
| | V6-179/2.9 L | EFI | 3.66 x 2.83 | 9.0 | 140 @ 4600 | 170 @ 2600 | 40-60 |

[1]—Cubic Inch Displacement.
[2]—Carter.
[3]—Feedback carburetor, California only.
[4]—Manual trans.
[5]—Automatic trans.
[6]—Motorcraft.
[7]—Diesel engine.
[8]—At 3600 RPM.
[9]—Turbocharged engine.
[10]—11.3 psi at idle speed.
[11]—11.4 psi at idle speed.

## ENGINE TIGHTENING SPECIFICATIONS*

*Torque specifications are for clean and lightly lubricated threads only. Dry or dirty threads produce increased friction which prevents accurate measurement of tightness.

| Year | Engine | Spark Plugs Ft. Lbs. | Cylinder Head Bolts Ft. Lbs. | Intake Manifold Ft. Lbs. | Exhaust Manifold Ft. Lbs. | Rocker Arm Shaft Bracket Ft. Lbs. | Rocker Arm Cover Ft. Lbs. | Connecting Rod Cap Bolts Ft. Lbs. | Main Bearing Cap Bolts Ft. Lbs. | Flywheel To Crankshaft Ft. Lbs. | Vibration Damper Or Pulley Ft. Lbs. |
|---|---|---|---|---|---|---|---|---|---|---|---|
| 1983–84 | 4-122 | 5-10 | [1] | 14-21 | [2] | — | 6-8 | [3] | [1] | 56-64 | 100-120 |
| | 4-135[4] | [7] | 80-85 | 12-17 | 17-20 | — | 2.2-2.3 | 50-54 | 80-85 | 95-137 | 253-286 |
| | 4-140 | 5-10 | [1] | 14-21 | [2] | — | 6-8 | [3] | [1] | 56-64 | 100-120 |
| | V6-171 | 18-28 | [5] | [6] | 20-30 | — | 3-5 | 19-24 | 65-75 | 47-52 | 85-96 |
| 1985 | 4-122, 140 | 5-10 | [1] | 14-21 | [2] | — | 6-8 | [3] | [1] | 56-64 | 100-120 |
| | 4-143[4][8] | [7] | [9] | 11-14 | 11-14 | 25-28 | 4-5 | 33-34 | 55-61 | 94-101 | 123-137 |
| | V6-171 | 14-18 | [5] | [6] | 20-30 | — | 3-5 | 19-24 | 65-75 | 47-52 | 85-96 |
| 1986–87 | 4-122, 140 | 5-10 | [1] | 14-21 | [2] | — | 6-8 | [3] | [1] | 56-64 | 100-120 |
| | 4-143[4][8] | [7] | [9] | 11-14 | 11-14 | 25-28 | 4-5 | 33-34 | 55-61 | 94-101 | 123-137 |
| | V6-179 | 18-28 | [10] | [6] | 20-30 | — | 3-5 | 19-24 | 65-75 | 47-52 | 85-96 |
| 1988 | 4-122, 140 | 5-10 | [1] | 14-21 | [2] | — | 6-8 | [3] | [11] | 56-64 | 103-133 |
| | V6-179 | 18-28 | [10] | [6] | 20-30 | — | 3-5 | 19-24 | 65-75 | 47-52 | 85-96 |
| 1989 | 4-122, 140 | 5-10 | [1] | [12] | [2] | — | 6-8 | [3] | [11] | 56-64 | 103-133 |
| | V6-179 | 18-28 | [10] | [6] | 20-30 | — | 3-5 | 19-24 | 65-75 | 47-52 | 85-96 |

**Continued**

## ENGINE TIGHTENING SPECIFICATIONS—Continued

①—Torque bolts in sequence in two steps: Step 1, 50-60 ft. lbs.; Step 2, 80-90 ft. lbs.

②—Torque nuts in sequence in two steps: Step 1, 1983-84 5-7 ft. lbs.; 1985-89 15-17 ft. lbs.; Step 2, 1983-84 16-23 ft. lbs.; 1985-89 20-30 ft. lbs.

③—Torque bolts in sequence in two steps: Step 1, 25-30 ft. lbs.; Step 2, 30-36 ft. lbs.

④—Diesel engine.

⑤—Torque bolts in sequence in three steps: Step 1, 29-40 ft. lbs.; Step 2, 40-51 ft. lbs.; Step 3, 70-85 ft. lbs.

⑥—Torque nuts in sequence in four steps after hand starting all nuts and snugging nuts 3 and 4: Step 1, 3-6 ft. lbs.; Step 2, 6-11 ft. lbs.; Step 3, 11-15 ft. lbs.; Step 4, 15-18 ft. lbs.; Repeat after warm up.

⑦—Glow plugs, 11-14 ft. lbs.

⑧—Turbocharged engine.

⑨—Cold engine, 76-83 ft. lbs.; hot engine, 84-90 ft. lbs.

⑩—Torque bolts in sequence in three steps: Step 1, 22 ft. lbs.; Step 2, 51-55 ft. lbs.; Step 3, turn 90°.

⑪—Torque bolts in sequence in two steps: Step 1, 50-60 ft. lbs.; Step 2, 75-85 ft. lbs.

⑫—Torque bolts in sequence in two steps: Step 1, 5-7 ft. lbs.; Step 2, 14-21 ft. lbs.

## ALTERNATOR SPECIFICATIONS

| Year | Make Or Model | Current Rating Amperes | Current Rating Volts | Field Current At 75°F. Amperes | Field Current At 75°F. Volts |
|---|---|---|---|---|---|
| 1983-89 | Orange ①②④ | 40 | 15 | 4 | 12 |
| 1983-89 | Green ①②④ | 60 | 15 | 4 | 12 |
| 1983-89 | ②④ | 65 | 15 | — | — |
| 1985-89 | Black ①③ | 70 | 15 | 4.25 | 12 |
| 1985-89 | Red ①③ | 100 | 15 | 4.25 | 12 |

①—Color of identification tag.
②—Rear terminal alternator.
③—Side terminal alternator.
④—Integral regulator alternator.

## STARTING MOTOR SPECIFICATIONS

| Year | Starter Type | Ampere Draw Normal Load | Engine Cranking Speed RPM | No Load Ampere @ 12 Volts | Brushes Length Inch | Brushes Wear Limit Inch | Brushes Spring Tension Ounces |
|---|---|---|---|---|---|---|---|
| 1983-84 | 4" diameter/gasoline engine | 150-200 | 180-250 | 70 | .500 | .250 | 40 |
| | 4½" diameter/gasoline engine | 150-180 | 150-290 | 80 | .500 | .250 | 80 |
| | Diesel engine | 150-220 | ① | — | .669 | .452 | — |
| 1985-88 | 4" diameter/gasoline engine | 150-200 | 180-250 | 80 | .50 | .25 | 80 |
| | 4½" diameter/gasoline engine | 150-180 | 150-290 | 80 | .50 | .25 | 80 |
| | Diesel engine | ② | 150-220 | ③ | .669 | ④ | — |
| 1989 | 4" diameter | 150-200 | 180-250 | 80 | .50 | .25 | 80 |
| | 4½" diameter | 150-180 | 150-290 | 80 | .50 | .25 | 80 |

①—Less than 180 RPM.
②—Less than 500 amps.
③—Less than 50 amps.
④—Visible wear mark indicator.

## BRAKE SPECIFICATIONS

| Year | Model | Rear Drum I.D. | Wheel Cyl. Bore Front Disc | Wheel Cyl. Bore Rear Drum | Disc Brake Rotor Nominal Thickness | Disc Brake Rotor Minimum Thickness | Disc Brake Rotor Thickness Variation (Parallelism) | Disc Brake Rotor Run Out (TIR) | Disc Brake Rotor Finish (Microinch) | Master Cyl. I.D. |
|---|---|---|---|---|---|---|---|---|---|---|
| 1983-84 | All | 9.0 | — | — | .870 | .810 | — | .003 | 15-125 | — |
| 1985-89 | All | 9.0 | — | — | .980 | .810 | — | .003 | 15-125 | .9375 |

## DRIVE AXLE SPECIFICATIONS

| Year | Ring Gear Diameter | Carrier Type | Ring Gear & Pinion Backlash Inch | Pinion Bearing Preload | | Differential Bearing Preload | Pinion Nut Torque Ft. Lbs. |
|---|---|---|---|---|---|---|---|
| | | | | New Bearings With Seal Inch Lbs. | Used Bearings With Seal Inch Lbs. | | |
| 1983-84 | 6¾" | Integral | .008-.015 | 16-29 | 8-14 | .006 | 140 |
| | 7½" | Integral | .008-.015 | 16-29 | 8-14 | .006 | 170 |
| | ① | Integral | .004-.010 | 15-35 | 15-35 | .015 | 200 |
| 1985-89 | 7½" | Integral | .008-.015 | 16-29 | 8-14 | .006 | 170 |
| | ① | Integral | ② | 15-35 | 15-35 | .015 | 200 |

①—Front drive axle.
②—1985, .004-.010; 1986-89, .005-.008.

## COOLING SYSTEM & CAPACITY DATA

| Year | Model Or Engine | Cooling Capacity Qts. | | Radiator Cap Relief Pressure, Lbs. | Thermo. Opening Temp. | Fuel Tank Gals. | Engine Oil Refill Qts. ① | Transmission Oil | | | Transfer Case Pints | Rear Axle Oil Pints |
|---|---|---|---|---|---|---|---|---|---|---|---|---|
| | | Less A/C | With A/C | | | | | 4 Speed Pints | 5 Speed Pints | Auto. Trans. Qts. ② | | |
| 1983-84 | 4-122 | 6.5 | 7.2 | 13 | 192 | ③ | 4① | 3.0 | 3.0 | ⑦ | — | ⑧ |
| | 4-135 ⑤ | 10.0 | 10.7 | 13 | — | ③ | 5.5⑥ | 3.2 | 3.0 | — | — | ⑧ |
| | 4-140 | 6.5 | 7.2 | 13 | 192 | ③ | 5① | 3.0 | 3.0 | ⑦ | 3.0 | ⑧ |
| | V6-171 | 7.2 | 7.8 | 13 | 189 | ③ ④ | 4① | 3.0 | 3.0 | ⑦ | 3.0 | ⑧ ⑨ |
| 1985 | 4-122 | ⑩ | 7.8 | 13 | 192 | ③ | 4① | — | ⑭ | 9 | — | ⑧ |
| | 4-140 | ⑩ | 7.2 | 13 | 192 | ③ | 4① | — | ⑭ | 9 | 3.0 | ⑧ |
| | 4-143 ⑤ ⑪ | 12 | ⑫ | 13 | — | ③ ④ | 6.8⑬ | 3.1 | — | 9 | 3.0 | ⑧ ⑨ |
| | V6-171 | 7.2 | 7.8 | 13 | — | ③ ④ | 4① | — | ⑭ | 9 | 3.0 | ⑧ ⑨ |
| 1986 | 4-122 | 6.5 | — | 13 | — | ③ | 4① | — | ⑮ | — | — | 5 |
| | 4-140 | ⑩ | 7.2 | 13 | — | ③ | 4① | — | ⑮ | ⑯ | 3.0 | ⑧ |
| | 4-143 ⑤ ⑪ | 12 | ⑫ | 13 | — | ③ ④ | 7⑬ | — | ⑮ | — | 3.0 | ⑧ ⑨ |
| | V6-179 | 7.2 | 7.8 | 13 | — | ③ ④ | 4① | — | ⑮ | ⑯ | 3.0 | ⑧ ⑨ |
| 1987 | 4-122 | 6.5 | — | 13 | — | ③ | 4① | — | ⑮ | — | — | 5 |
| | 4-140 | 6.5 | 7.2 | 13 | — | ③ | 4① | — | ⑮ | ⑯ | 3.0 | 5 |
| | 4-143 ⑤ ⑪ | 12 | ⑫ | 13 | — | ③ | 7⑬ | — | ⑮ | — | 3.0 | 5 |
| | V6-179 | 7.2 | 7.8 | 13 | — | ③ ④ | 4① | — | ⑮ | ⑯ | 3.0 | ⑰ |
| 1988 | 4-122 | 6.5 | — | 13 | — | ③ | 4① | — | ⑮ | — | — | 5 |
| | 4-140 | 6.5 | 7.2 | 13 | — | ③ | 4① | — | ⑮ | ⑯ | 3.0 | 5 |
| | V6-179 | 7.2 | 7.8 | 13 | — | ③ ④ | 4① | — | ⑮ | ⑯ | 3.0 | ⑰ |
| 1989 | 4-140 | 6.5 | 7.2 | 13 | — | ③ | 4① | — | ⑮ | ⑯ | 3.0 | 5 |
| | V6-179 | 7.2 | 7.8 | 13 | — | ③ ④ | 4① | — | ⑮ | ⑯ | 3.0 | ⑰ |

①—Add 1 qt. with filter change.
②—Approximate. Make final check with dipstick.
③—Ranger; short wheelbase, 15.2 gals.; long wheelbase, 17.0 gals.; auxiliary tank, 13.0 gals.; Super Cab, 14.5 gals.
④—Bronco II, 23.0 gals.
⑤—Diesel engine.
⑥—Add .9 qt. for primary filter replacement & .6 qt. for bypass filter replacement.
⑦—With C-3 transmission, 8.0 qts.; 4 x 2 models with C-5 transmission, 7.5 qts.; 4 x 4 models with C-5 transmission, 7.9 qts.
⑧—Ranger with 6¾ inch ring gear, 3.0 pts.; with 7½ inch ring gear, 5.0 pts.
⑨—Bronco II with 7½ inch ring gear, 5.5 pts.
⑩—Less extra cooling system, 6.5 qts.; w/extra cooling system, 7.2 qts.
⑪—Turbocharged engine.
⑫—Standard cooling system w/AC, 13 qts.; extra cooling system w/AC 10.7 qts.
⑬—Includes oil filter change & cooler capacity.
⑭—Mazda model transmissions, 3.6 pints; Mitsubishi model transmissions, 4.8 pints.
⑮—Mazda model transmissions, 3.6 pints; Mitsubishi model transmissions, 4.8 pints.
⑯—2 WD models, 9.5 qts.; 4 WD models, 10.3 qts.
⑰—Ranger, 5.0 pts.; Bronco II, 5.5 pts.

# ELECTRICAL

## INDEX

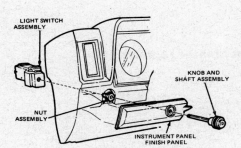

**Fig. 1 Light switch replacement**

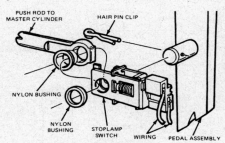

**Fig. 2 Stop light switch replacement**

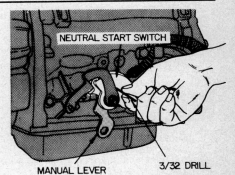

**Fig. 3 Neutral safety switch adjustment. C5 automatic transmission**

## FUSE PANEL & FLASHER LOCATION

The fuse panel is located under the lower left hand side of the instrument panel.
The hazard flasher is located on the rear of the fuse block, and the turn signal flasher is located on the front of the fuse block.

## STARTER
### REPLACE
#### EXC. DIESEL ENGINES

1. Disconnect battery ground cable.
2. Raise and support vehicle.
3. Disconnect starter cable from starter.
4. Remove starter motor attaching bolts, then disconnect ground cable and lower starter from vehicle.
5. Reverse procedure to install.

#### DIESEL ENGINES

**4-135**

1. Disconnect ground cables from both batteries.
2. Remove air intake hose between intake manifold and air cleaner.
3. Disconnect No. 1 glow plug relay from starter and position aside.
4. Disconnect starter cables, then remove starter motor attaching bolts and the starter motor.
5. Reverse procedure to install.

**4-143**

1. Disconnect battery ground cables from both battery assemblies.
2. Disconnect, then remove air intake hose between air cleaner and intake manifold.
3. Remove No. 1 glow plug relay from starter motor assembly, then position aside.
4. Mark, then disconnect starter motor solenoid electrical connectors.
5. Remove alternator reinforcement bracket attaching bolt.
6. Remove two starter motor attaching bolts, then the starter motor assembly from vehicle.
7. Reverse procedure to install.

## IGNITION LOCK
### REPLACE

1. Disconnect battery ground cable (two ground cables on diesel engines).
2. Remove steering column trim shroud, then disconnect electrical connector from key warning switch.
3. Turn lock cylinder to Run position and insert a 1/8 inch wire or pin into hole located on outer edge of lock cylinder housing. Depress retaining pin and remove lock cylinder.
4. To install, turn lock cylinder to Run position, depress retaining pin and insert assembly into housing.
5. Ensure cylinder is fully seated and

aligned into interlocking washer, then turn key to Off position to extend cylinder retaining pin into cylinder qui- thousing.
6. Turn key to check for proper operation in all positions.
7. Connect key warning switch electrical connector, install steering column trim shroud and reconnect battery ground cable(s).

## IGNITION SWITCH
### REPLACE

1. Disconnect battery ground cable (two ground cables on diesel engines).
2. Turn lock cylinder key to Lock position.
3. On models equipped with tilt steering column, remove upper extension shroud by depressing top and bottom of shroud and releasing it from retaining plate on left side.
4. On all models, remove steering column trip shroud halves.
5. Disconnect electrical connector from ignition switch.
6. Drill out bolt heads from switch attaching bolts using a 1/8 inch drill, then remove bolts using an "Easy Out" or equivalent.
7. Disengage switch from actuator pin and remove switch from vehicle.
8. Reverse procedure to install. Turn lock cylinder to Run position before installing switch.

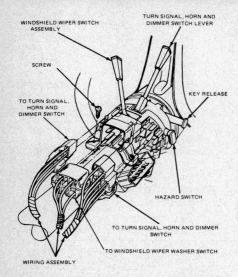

**Fig. 4   Turn signal/dimmer switch replacement**

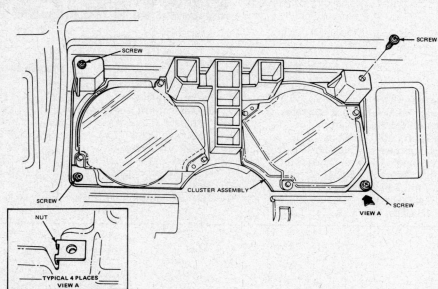

**Fig. 5   Instrument cluster replacement**

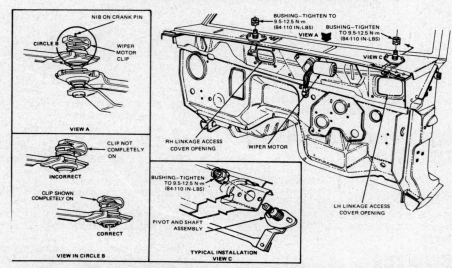

**Fig. 6   Front windshield wiper motor retaining clip removal & windshield wiper transmission replacement**

## LIGHT SWITCH
### REPLACE

1. Disconnect battery ground cable (two ground cables on diesel engines).
2. Pull light switch knob out to On position.
3. Depress shaft release button and remove knob and shaft assembly.
4. Remove instrument panel finish panel, **Fig. 1**.
5. Remove bezel nut, lower switch, disconnect electrical connector and remove switch from vehicle.
6. Reverse procedure to install.

## STOP LIGHT SWITCH
### REPLACE

1. Disconnect battery ground cable (two ground cables on diesel engines).
2. Disconnect electrical connector from switch.
3. Remove hairpin retainer, then slide switch, pushrod, nylon washers and bushings away from pedal and remove switch, **Fig. 2**.
4. Reverse procedure to install.

## NEUTRAL SAFETY SWITCH
### ADJUST
#### C5 UNITS

1. Loosen neutral safety switch attaching bolts, then position manual lever in Park position.
2. Insert a 3/32 inch drill into switch. Move switch as needed to allow drill to rest against case, **Fig. 3**.
3. Torque switch attaching bolts to 55-75 inch lbs., then remove drill from switch.

#### A4LD UNITS

1. Disconnect battery ground cable(s).

2. Disconnect neutral start switch electrical harness from switch.
3. Using a suitable tool, remove neutral start switch and O-ring.
4. Install new switch and O-ring.
5. Torque switch to 7-10 ft. lbs.
6. Connect neutral start switch electrical harness onto switch.
7. Connect battery ground cable(s) and check switch operation.

## TURN SIGNAL/DIMMER SWITCH
### REPLACE

1. Disconnect battery ground cable (two ground cables on diesel engines).
2. On models equipped with tilt steering column, remove upper extension shroud by depressing top and bottom of shroud and releasing it from retaining plate on left side.
3. On all models, remove steering column trim shroud halves.
4. Remove switch lever by grasping and using a twisting and pulling motion straight out from switch.
5. Peel back foam shield from switch, then disconnect electrical connectors, **Fig. 4**.
6. Remove 2 switch attaching screws and the switch.
7. Reverse procedure to install.

## INSTRUMENT CLUSTER
### REPLACE

1. Disconnect battery ground cable (two ground cables on diesel engines).
2. On 1989 models, proceed as follows:
   a. Remove two screws attaching ashtray assembly receptacle to instrument cluster trim panel, then

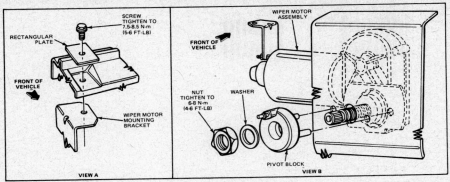

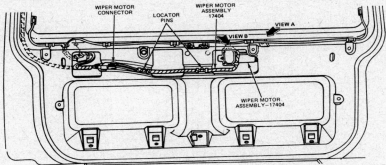

**Fig. 7   Rear windshield wiper motor assembly**

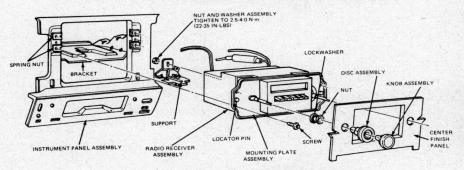

**Fig. 8   Typical radio replacement**

remove ashtray assembly receptacle.
b. Depress harzard warning switch on steering column and remove cluster trim panel.

3. On all vehicles equipped with automatic transmission, remove two screws attaching the PRNDL indicator and position aside.
4. Remove two steering column shroud attaching screws and the shroud.
5. Remove lower instrument panel trim.
6. Remove eight instrument cluster trim cover attaching screws and the trim cover.
7. Remove four instrument cluster attaching screws, then pull cluster away slightly from panel and disconnect speedometer cable and all electrical connectors. If there is not sufficient clearance to disconnect speedometer cable from speedometer, it will be necessary to disconnect cable from transmission and route cable through cowl to reach speedometer quick disconnect.

8. Remove cluster from vehicle, **Fig. 5.**
9. Reverse procedure to install.

## WINDSHIELD WIPER MOTOR
## REPLACE
### FRONT

1. Cycle windshield wipers until they are in straight up position, then turn ignition off.
2. Disconnect battery ground cable (two ground cables on diesel engines).
3. Remove right hand wiper arm and blade assembly and the pivot nut. Allow linkage to drop into cowl.
4. Remove linkage access cover from right hand side of dash panel.
5. Release wiper motor retaining clip, **Fig. 6,** then slide clip back until it clears nib on crank pin, and remove the clip. **The wiper motor retaining clip can be reached through the access cover opening.**

6. Remove wiper linkage from motor crank pin.
7. Disconnect electrical connector from wiper motor, then remove motor attaching screws and the motor.
8. Reverse procedure to install.

### REAR

1. Disconnect battery ground cable (two ground cables on diesel engines).
2. Remove wiper arm and blade assembly.
3. Remove pivot shaft attaching nut, washer and pivot block, **Fig. 7.**
4. Remove liftgate inner trim panel, then the motor bracket attaching screw and rectangular plate.
5. Disconnect motor electrical connectors, then remove motor assembly.
6. Reverse procedure to install.

## WINDSHIELD WIPER TRANSMISSION
## REPLACE
### FRONT

1. Perform steps 1 through 6 as described under "Windshield Wiper Motor, Replace."
2. Slide right hand pivot shaft and linkage assembly out through right hand access cover opening.
3. Remove left hand wiper arm and blade assembly.
4. Remove left hand linkage access cover and pivot nut, then lower linkage and slide out through access cover opening, **Fig. 6.**
5. Reverse procedure to install.

## WINDSHIELD WIPER SWITCH
## REPLACE
### FRONT

1. Disconnect battery ground cable (two ground cables on diesel engines).
2. Remove steering column trim shrouds, then disconnect electrical connector from switch.
3. Peel back foam shield, then remove wiper switch attaching screws and the switch.
4. Reverse procedure to install.

### REAR

1. Disconnect battery ground cable (two ground cables on diesel engines).
2. Remove headlight switch knob and bezel.
3. Pull finish panel away from instrument panel, then disconnect switch electrical connector.
4. Remove wiper switch to finish panel attaching screw, then the wiper switch.
5. Reverse procedure to install.

## RADIO
## REPLACE

1. Disconnect battery ground cable (two ground cables on diesel engines).
2. Remove control knobs and discs from radio shafts, **Fig. 8.**

3. Remove 2 steering column shroud attaching screws and the shroud.
4. Remove lower instrument panel trim.
5. Remove eight instrument cluster trim cover attaching screws and the trim cover.
6. Remove four radio mounting plate attaching screws, then slide radio with bracket and mounting plate out of dash.
7. Disconnect all electrical connectors from radio, then remove rear support attaching nut.
8. Remove nuts, washers and mounting plate from radio shafts.
9. Remove radio from vehicle.
10. Reverse procedure to install.

## HEATER CORE
### REPLACE

1. Drain cooling system.
2. Disconnect hoses from heater core. Plug hoses and core openings to prevent leakage of residual coolant.
3. Remove heater core access cover attaching screws and the cover, **Fig. 9.**
4. Remove heater core from passenger compartment.
5. Reverse procedure to install.

## BLOWER MOTOR
### REPLACE

1. Disconnect battery ground cable (two grounded cables on diesel engines).
2. If applicable, remove emission control module forward of blower motor.
3. Remove air cleaner and solenoid box cover in front of blower motor, if so equipped.
4. Remove vacuum reservoir and washer in front of blower motor, if so equipped.
5. On models equipped with 4-140 EFI and V6-179 EFI engines, remove air cleaner in front of blower motor.
6. On all models, disconnect electrical connector from blower motor.
7. Disconnect blower motor cooling tube at blower motor.
8. Remove blower motor attaching screws, then the blower motor from the heater blower assembly, **Fig. 10.**
9. Reverse procedure to install.

## SPEED CONTROL ADJUSTMENTS
### ACTUATOR CABLE, ADJUST

1. Remove cable retaining clip, then disengage throttle positioner.
2. Set throttle at hot idle position.
3. Pull actuator cable to remove slack, then install cable retaining clip while maintaining light tension on cable.

### VACUUM DUMP VALVE, ADJUST

1. Depress brake pedal firmly and hold in position.
2. Press in vacuum dump valve until valve collar meets retaining clip, **Fig. 11.**
3. Pull brake pedal firmly rearward to its normal position to allow valve to ratchet backwards in retaining clip.

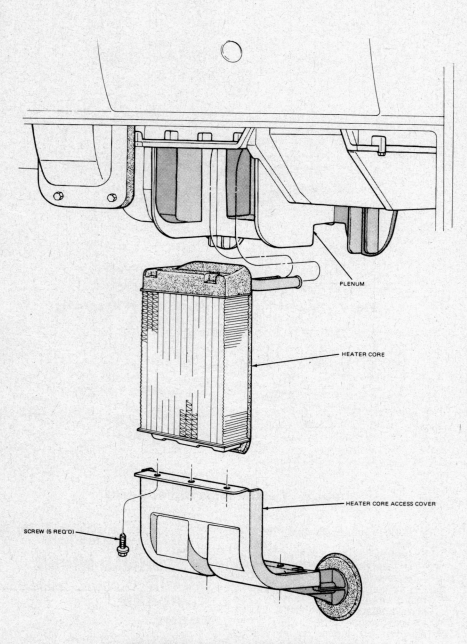

PLENUM

HEATER CORE

HEATER CORE ACCESS COVER

SCREW (5 REQ'D)

**Fig. 9   Heater core replacement**

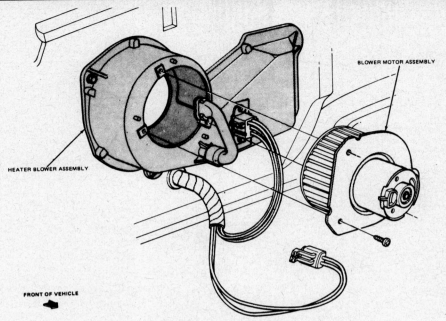

**FRONT OF VEHICLE** →

**Fig. 10  Blower motor replacement**

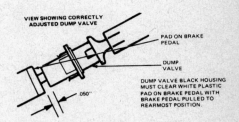

VIEW SHOWING CORRECTLY ADJUSTED DUMP VALVE

PAD ON BRAKE PEDAL

DUMP VALVE

DUMP VALVE BLACK HOUSING MUST CLEAR WHITE PLASTIC PAD ON BRAKE PEDAL WITH BRAKE PEDAL PULLED TO REARMOST POSITION.

.050"

**Fig. 11  Vacuum dump valve adjustment**

4. Ensure clearance between dump valve housing and white plastic pad on brake pedal is .050-.100 inch with brake pedal retracted to rearmost position.

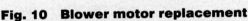

# 4-122 (2.0L) & 4-140 (2.3L) GASOLINE ENGINE
## INDEX

# ENGINE MOUNTS
## REPLACE
### FRONT

1. Remove nuts from top of insulator brackets.
2. Raise and support vehicle, then lift engine until it clears mounts.
3. Remove attaching screws and mounts.
4. Reverse procedure to install. Refer to **Figs. 1 and 2** for torque specifications.

### REAR

1. Raise and support vehicle.
2. Remove the two nuts attaching rear insulator to engine support, **Figs. 1 and 2**.
3. Using a suitable jack and wood block placed between engine and jack, raise transmission.
4. Remove bolts attaching mount to rear of engine and remove mount.
5. Reverse procedure to install. Torque bolts to 60-80 ft. lbs. and nuts to 71-94 ft. lbs.

# ENGINE
## REPLACE
### EXCEPT 1985-89 4-140 EFI ENGINE

1. Raise hood, then mark location of hood hinges and remove hood.
2. Disconnect battery ground cable at engine and battery positive cable at battery.
3. Drain coolant from radiator, then remove air cleaner and duct assembly.
4. Remove upper and lower radiator hoses, engine fan, shroud and radiator.
5. Remove oil filler cap.
6. If equipped with air conditioning, remove compressor from mounting bracket and position it aside.
7. Disconnect wires from starter, alternator, ignition coil, water temperature sending unit, and oil pressure sending unit and position aside.
8. If equipped with automatic transmission, disconnect transmission kickdown rod.
9. Disconnect heater hoses at engine, and fuel line at fuel pump.
10. Disconnect power brake vacuum hose.
11. Remove engine mount nuts.
12. Raise vehicle, then drain oil from crankcase and remove starter motor.

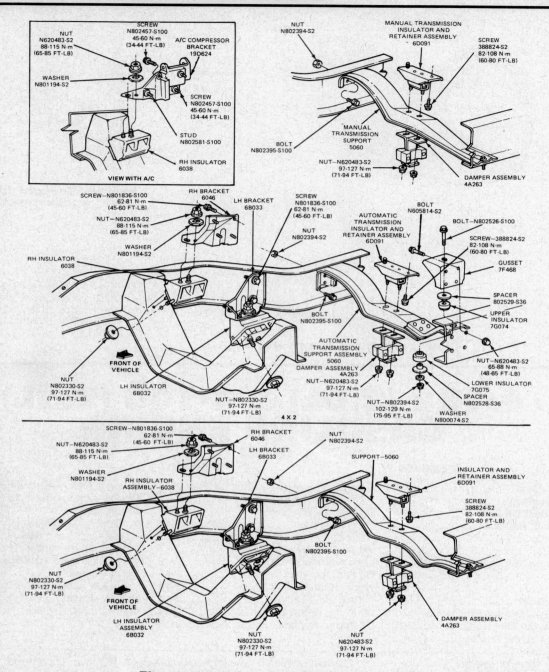

**Fig. 1  Front & rear engine mounts. 4-122**

13. Disconnect exhaust pipe from manifold.
14. Remove dust cover on manual transmission vehicles, or inspection cover on automatic transmission vehicles.
15. On vehicles with manual transmission, remove flywheel housing cover lower bolts. On vehicles with automatic transmission, remove converter-to-flywheel bolts, then remove converter housing lower bolts.
16. On manual transmission vehicles, remove slave cylinder.
17. Lower vehicle, then support transmission using a floor jack.
18. Remove flywheel housing or convert-

er housing bolts.
19. Using a suitable hoist, remove engine from vehicle.
20. Reverse procedure to install.

## 1985–89 4-140 EFI ENGINE

1. Raise hood, mark hood hinge locations, then remove hood.
2. Drain coolant from radiator.
3. Disconnect air cleaner outlet tube from throttle body, idle speed control hose and heat riser tube.
4. Disconnect battery cables.
5. Disconnect upper and lower radiator hoses from engine.

6. Remove radiator shroud attaching screws, radiator upper supports, then the shroud and fan assembly.
7. Remove radiator.
8. Remove oil filler cap.
9. Disconnect coil wire from coil.
10. Mark, then disconnect all electrical connectors and vacuum hoses from engine.
11. Disconnect accelerator cable and transmission kickdown rod, if equipped.
12. Remove A/C compressor from mounting bracket and position aside. Do not disconnect refrigerant lines from compressor.

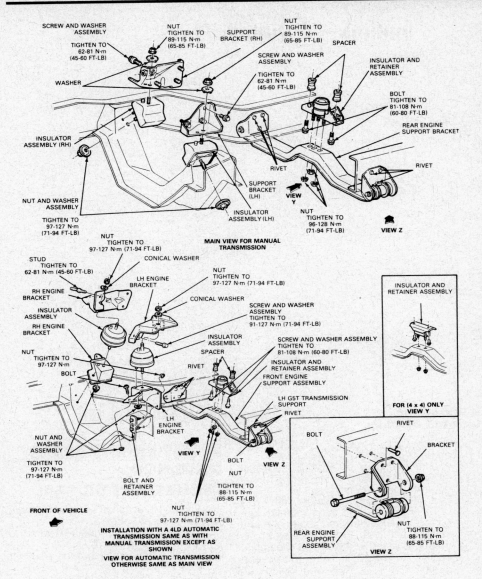

**Fig. 2  Front & rear engine mounts. 4-140**

13. Disconnect power brake vacuum hose.
14. Disconnect two push connector fittings from engine fuel rail.
15. Disconnect heater hoses from engine.
16. Remove engine mount nuts.
17. Raise and support vehicle.
18. Drain engine oil from crankcase.
19. Remove starter motor.
20. Disconnect exhaust pipe from exhaust manifold.
21. Remove dust cover or torque converter inspection plate, if equipped.
22. On vehicles equipped with manual transmission, remove flywheel housing cover attaching bolts. On vehicles equipped with automatic transmission, remove torque converter to flywheel attaching bolts.
23. Lower vehicle.
24. Support transmission and flywheel or converter housing with a suitable jack.
25. Remove flywheel housing or converter housing upper attaching bolts.
26. Install suitable engine lifting equipment onto engine, then carefully raise engine from vehicle.
27. Reverse procedure to install.

## CYLINDER HEAD
## REPLACE
### REMOVAL

1. Disconnect battery ground cable.
2. Drain cooling system, then remove air cleaner assembly.
3. Remove heater hose to rocker arm cover retaining screw.
4. Remove distributor cap and spark plug wires.
5. On 1989 models, disconnect EGO sensor from exhaust manifold.
6. On all models, remove spark plugs.
7. Disconnect vacuum hoses as necessary.
8. Remove dipstick and rocker arm cover.
9. Remove intake manifold retaining bolts.
10. Remove alternator belt and alternator bracket-to-cylinder head bolts.
11. Remove upper radiator hose.
12. Remove timing belt cover. On vehicles with power steering, remove power steering pump bracket bolts.
13. Loosen cam idler retaining bolts, then position idler in the unloaded position and tighten bolts.
14. Remove timing belt.
15. Remove heated air intake pipe and exhaust manifold bolts.
16. Remove timing cam belt idler, the two bracket bolts and idler spring from cylinder head.
17. Disconnect oil pressure sending unit lead wire.
18. Remove cylinder head bolts and cylinder head.
19. Thoroughly clean all gasket surfaces, then blow oil out of the cylinder head bolt block holes.

### INSTALLATION

1. Position cylinder head gasket onto engine block.
2. Clean rocker arm cover (cam cover).
3. Using suitable contact cement, install rocker cover gasket onto rocker cover.
4. Install cylinder head attaching bolts and torque in sequence and to specifications, **Figs. 3 and 4.**
5. Connect oil sending unit electrical connector(s).
6. Install cam belt (timing belt) idler spring stop onto cylinder head.
7. Position cam belt idler onto cylinder head and install attaching bolts.
8. Install exhaust manifold attaching bolts and/or stud bolts.
9. Install heat air intake pipe to exhaust manifold.
10. Align distributor rotor with number one plug location in the distributor cap.
11. Align cam gear with pointer.
12. Align crank pulley (TDC) with pointer on cam belt cover.
13. Position cam belt onto cam and auxiliary pulleys.
14. Loosen idler retaining bolts, rotate engine and check timing alignment.
15. Adjust belt tensioner, then tighten bolts.
16. Install cam belt cover attaching bolts.
17. Install upper radiator hose onto engine and radiator assembly, then tighten retaining clamps.
18. Position alternator bracket onto cylinder head and install retainers.
19. Position drive belt onto pulley and adjust belt tension.
20. Position intake manifold to head and install attaching bolts.
21. Install rocker arm cover and attaching bolts.
22. Install spark plugs and dipstick.
23. Connect all vacuum hoses and spark plug wires.
24. On 1989 models, install EGO sensor connector.

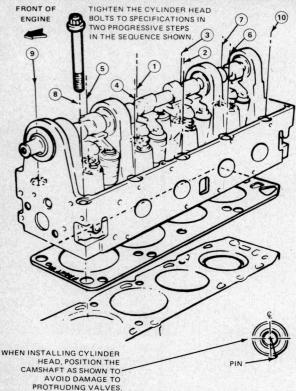

FRONT OF ENGINE

TIGHTEN THE CYLINDER HEAD BOLTS TO SPECIFICATIONS IN TWO PROGRESSIVE STEPS IN THE SEQUENCE SHOWN.

WHEN INSTALLING CYLINDER HEAD, POSITION THE CAMSHAFT AS SHOWN TO AVOID DAMAGE TO PROTRUDING VALVES.

PIN

**Fig. 3  Cylinder head bolt tightening sequence. 4-122 & 4-140 carbureted engines**

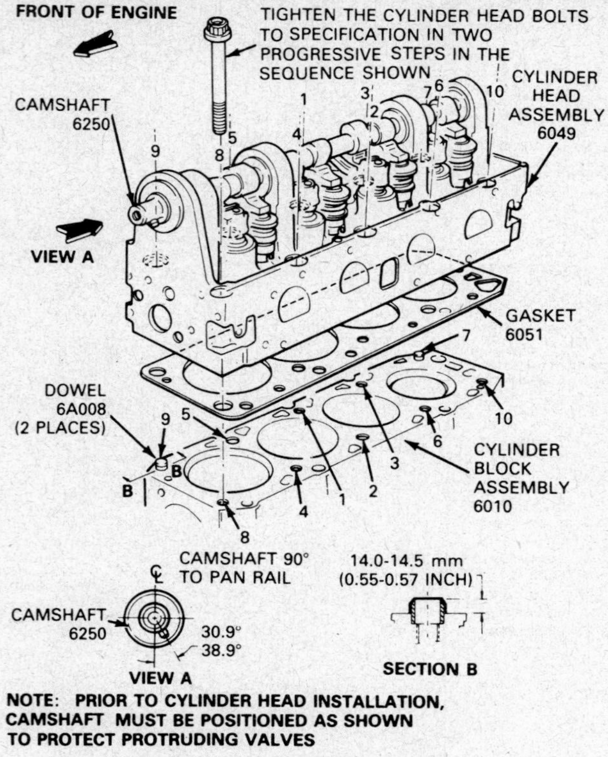

FRONT OF ENGINE

TIGHTEN THE CYLINDER HEAD BOLTS TO SPECIFICATION IN TWO PROGRESSIVE STEPS IN THE SEQUENCE SHOWN

CAMSHAFT 6250

CYLINDER HEAD ASSEMBLY 6049

VIEW A

GASKET 6051

DOWEL 6A008 (2 PLACES)

CYLINDER BLOCK ASSEMBLY 6010

CAMSHAFT 90° TO PAN RAIL

CAMSHAFT 6250

30.9°
38.9°

VIEW A

14.0-14.5 mm (0.55-0.57 INCH)

SECTION B

NOTE: PRIOR TO CYLINDER HEAD INSTALLATION, CAMSHAFT MUST BE POSITIONED AS SHOWN TO PROTECT PROTRUDING VALVES

**Fig. 4  Cylinder head bolt tightening sequence. 4-140 EFI engine**

25. On all models, install air cleaner assembly.

# VALVE ARRANGEMENT
## FRONT TO REAR

All Engines . . . . . . . . . . . . . . E-I-E-I-E-I-E-I

# VALVE LIFT SPECIFICATIONS.

Valve lift should measure .390 on all applications, except the intake valves on 1985 4-140 engines, which should measure .400 inch.

# VALVE CLEARANCE SPECIFICATIONS

Valve clearances, measured at the camshaft with hydraulic lifter collapsed, should be .035-.055 inches on intake and exhaust valves.

# VALVE GUIDES

Valve guides consist of holes bored in the cylinder head. For service, the guides can be reamed oversize to accommodate valves with oversize stems of .015 inch and .030 inch.

# VALVES
## ADJUST

The valve lash on this engine cannot be adjusted due to the use of hydraulic valve

lash adjusters. However, the valve train can be checked for wear as follows:
1. Crank engine to position camshaft with flat section of lobe facing rocker arm of valve being checked.
2. Collapse lash adjuster with tool T74P-6565A and insert correct size feeler gauge between rocker arm and camshaft lobe, **Fig. 5.** If clearance is not as listed in the "Valve Clearance Specifications," remove rocker arm and check for wear and replace as necessary. If rocker arm is found satisfactory, check valve spring assembled height and adjust as needed. If valve spring assembled height is correct, remove lash adjuster and clean or replace as necessary until desired clearance is obtained.

# ROCKER ARM SERVICE

1. Remove rocker arm cover.
2. Rotate camshaft until flat section of lobe faces rocker being removed.
3. Collapse lash adjuster and, if necessary, valve spring and slide rocker arm over lash adjuster, **Fig. 5.**
4. Reverse procedure to install.

# LASH ADJUSTERS
## REPLACE

The hydraulic valve lash adjusters can be replaced after rocker arm removal.

# FRONT ENGINE SEALS
## REPLACE
### CRANKSHAFT OIL SEAL

1. Remove crankshaft sprocket with tool T74P-6306-A, **Fig. 6.**
2. Remove crankshaft oil seal with tool T74P-6700-B, **Fig. 7.**
3. Install a new crankshaft oil seal with tool T74P-6150-A.
4. Install crankshaft sprocket.

## CAMSHAFT & AUXILIARY SHAFT OIL SEALS

1. Remove camshaft or auxiliary shaft sprocket with tool T74P-6256-B, **Fig. 8.**
2. Remove camshaft or auxiliary shaft seal with tool T74P-6700-B, **Fig. 9.**
3. Install a new oil seal with tool T74P-6150-B, **Fig. 10.**
4. Install camshaft or auxiliary shaft sprocket with tool T74P-6256-B with center arbor removed.

# TIMING BELT
## CHECKING BELT TIMING

1. Remove timing belt cover access plug, **Fig. 11.**
2. Rotate crankshaft in engine normal direction of rotation until TDC is reached. This is obtained by aligning the crankshaft pulley mark with the TC mark on the belt cover. **Never rotate engine against normal rotation, as this may cause the timing**

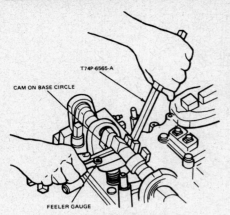

Fig. 5  Collapsing lash adjuster

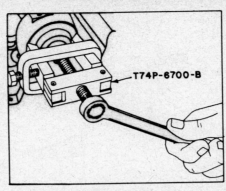

Fig. 6  Crankshaft sprocket removal

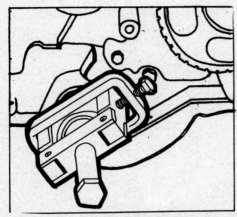

Fig. 7  Removing crankshaft front oil seal

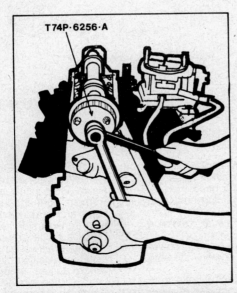

Fig. 8  Removing camshaft or auxiliary shaft sprocket

belt to jump time.

3. While looking through the belt cover access hole, ensure the timing mark on the camshaft sprocket is aligned with the pointer on the inner belt cover.
4. Remove distributor cap to ensure the distributor rotor is pointed towards the distributor cap No. 1 firing position.
5. If belt timing is satisfactory, install distributor cap and belt cover access plug. If belt timing is unsatisfactory, refer to "Adjustment or Replacement" procedure.

## ADJUSTMENT OR REPLACEMENT

1. Remove Thermactor pump drive belt, then the fan and water pump pulley.
2. Remove alternator drive belt, then drain cooling system and remove upper radiator hose.
3. Remove crankshaft pulley, then the thermostat housing and gasket.
4. On models equipped with power steering, disconnect power steering pump from bracket and position aside.
5. On all models, remove timing belt outer cover attaching bolts and the cover, **Fig. 11.**
6. Loosen belt tensioner adjustment bolt, **Fig. 12.**
7. Using tool, T74P-6254-A positioned on tension spring roll pin, retract tensioner, then tighten adjustment screw to hold tensioner in retracted position, **Fig. 13.**
8. On 1989 models, remove bolts holding the timing sensor assembly in place at the dowel pin.
9. On all models, remove crankshaft pulley and belt guide, **Fig. 11.**
10. Remove timing belt and inspect for signs of wear and damage. Replace as necessary.
11. Refer to **Fig. 14**, for proper camshaft and crankshaft sprocket position.
12. Remove distributor cap, then set distributor rotor to No. 1 firing position by turning the auxiliary shaft as necessary.
13. Install timing belt on crankshaft sprocket, then working counterclockwise, position belt on auxiliary sprocket and camshaft sprocket. Ensure timing marks do not change position.
14. Align belt on sprockets, then loosen tensioner adjustment bolt to allow tensioner to move against the belt.
15. Remove spark plugs. **Failure to remove spark plugs may result in timing belt jumping time during next step.**
16. Rotate engine in normal direction of rotation for two complete turns to remove slack from belt. Tighten tensioner adjustment and pivot bolts to specifications given in **Fig. 12.**
17. Recheck timing mark alignment, then install crankshaft pulley and belt guide (1983-89 models).
18. On 1989 models, proceed as follows:
    a. Install timing sensor onto dowel pin and tighten bolts to specification.
    b. To align timing sensor, rotate

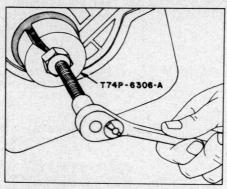

**Fig. 9  Removing camshaft or auxiliary shaft seal**

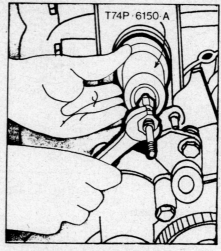

**Fig. 10  Installing camshaft seal**

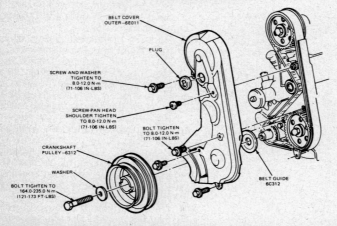

**Fig. 11  Exploded view of timing belt outer cover**

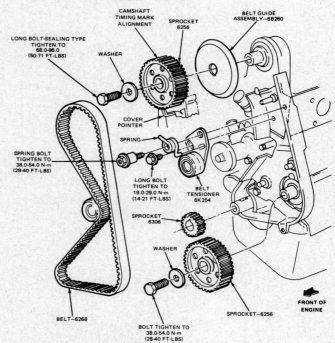

**Fig. 12  Timing belt drive train**

crankshaft ¼ turn counterclockwise and install the crankshaft pulley and hub assembly. Torque to 30-41 ft. lbs.
c. Rotate crankshaft ½ turn clockwise so vane of crankshaft pulley engages with the timing sensor positioner.
d. Rotate crankshaft ½ turn counterclockwise and remove sensor positioner.
e. Rotate crankshaft ½ turn clockwise and measure outer vane to sensor air gap. Air gap must be .018-.039 inch.
19. On all models, install timing belt cover. Refer to **Fig. 11** for torque specifications. Install spark plugs.
20. Start engine and set ignition timing to specifications.

## CAMSHAFT
## REPLACE

1. Disconnect battery ground cable, then drain cooling system and remove air cleaner.
2. Disconnect ignition wires and position aside.
3. Disconnect any vacuum hoses interfering with camshaft removal.
4. Remove rocker arm cover, then remove alternator belt.
5. Remove alternator mounting bracket retaining bolts and position aside.
6. Remove upper radiator hose, then remove fan shroud retaining bolts and fan shroud.
7. Remove cam belt cover retaining bolts and cover.
8. If vehicle is equipped with power steering, remove power steering pump bracket.
9. Loosen idler cam retaining bolts, then position idler in the unloaded position and tighten retaining bolts.
10. Remove timing belt from cam and auxiliary pulleys.
11. Remove rocker arms as described under "Rocker Arm Service," then remove gear and seal as described under "Front Engine Seals, Replace."
12. Remove camshaft rear retainer.
13. Raise and support vehicle.
14. Remove right and left engine support bolts and nuts, then position a suitable transmission jack under engine.
15. Place a block of wood on transmission jack, raise engine as high as possible and position blocks of wood between engine mounts and chassis bracket, then remove jack.
16. Carefully remove camshaft from front of head.
17. Reverse procedure to install and note the following:

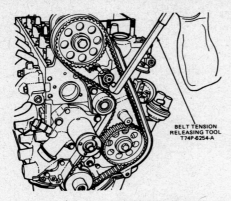

**Fig. 13 Retracting belt tensioner**

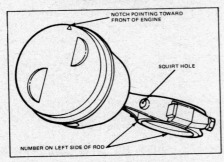

**Fig. 15 Piston & rod**

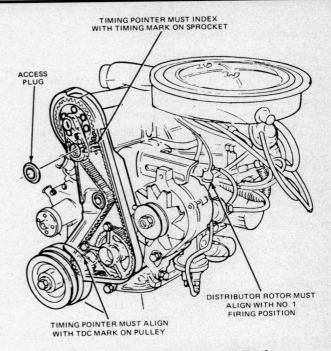

**Fig. 14 Timing belt installation**

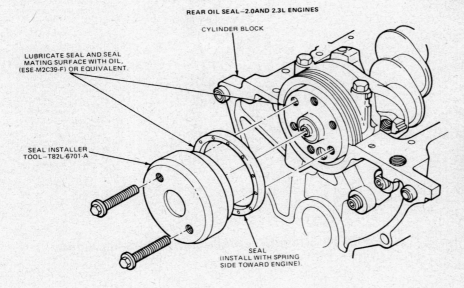

NOTE: REAR FACE OF SEAL MUST BE WITHIN 0.127mm (0.005-INCH) OF THE REAR FACE OF THE BLOCK.

**Fig. 16 Crankshaft rear oil seal replacement**

a. Ensure that threaded plug, if equipped, is positioned at rear of camshaft. If not, remove from old camshaft and install.
b. Coat camshaft lobes with grease DOAZ-19584-A or equivalent and lubricate journals with engine oil.
c. When installing timing belt, ensure timing marks are aligned as shown in **Fig. 14**.

## PISTON & ROD
### ASSEMBLE

Assemble rod to piston with arrow on top of piston facing front of engine and squirt hole on rod positioned as shown, **Fig. 15**.

## CRANKSHAFT REAR OIL SEAL

1. Remove oil pump retaining bolts, if necessary.
2. Insert small sheet metal screws into seal and pull screws to remove seal.
3. Install new seal with tool T82L-6701-A as shown, **Fig. 16**. When properly installed, rear face of seal should be within .005 inch of rear face of cylinder block.

## OIL PAN
### REPLACE
### EXC. 1986–88 4-122

The oil pan must be removed out of the front of the engine compartment on models equipped with automatic transmission, and out of the rear of the engine compartment on models equipped with manual transmission.

1. Remove air cleaner assembly, engine oil dipstick and engine mount attaching nuts.
2. On models equipped with automatic transmission, disconnect transmission oil cooler lines from radiator.
3. On all models, remove fan shroud.
4. On models equipped with automatic transmission, remove radiator attaching bolts, then lift radiator up and wire it to the hood.
5. On all models, raise and support vehicle.
6. Drain engine oil, then remove starter motor.
7. Disconnect exhaust pipe to inlet pipe bracket from Thermactor check valve.

then the catalytic converter at inlet pipe.

8. Remove transmission mount-to-crossmember attaching nuts.
9. On models equipped with automatic transmission, remove converter housing bellcrank, oil cooler lines and front crossmember.
10. On models equipped with manual transmission, disconnect right front lower shock absorber mount.
11. On all models, raise engine with a suitable jack, then place a 2½ inch block of wood under engine and remove jack.
12. On models equipped with automatic transmission, raise transmission slightly with a suitable jack.
13. On all models, remove oil pan attaching bolts and lower pan onto chassis.
14. Remove low oil level sensor, if equipped, then remove oil pump drive, pickup tube assembly and oil pan.
15. Reverse procedure to install. Refer to **Figs. 17 and 18** for torque specifications.

## 1986–88 4-122

1. Disconnect battery ground cable, then remove air cleaner assembly and dipstick.
2. Remove engine mount retainer nuts.
3. Remove fan shroud retaining bolts and shroud, then raise and support vehicle.
4. Disconnect exhaust manifold tube to inlet pipe bracket below thermactor check valve.
5. Drain engine oil, disconnect starter cable, then remove attaching bolts and starter.
6. Disconnect lower right shock absorber mount, raise engine with suitable jack, then place a 2½ inch block of wood under engine.
7. Remove oil pan retaining bolts, then lower pan onto crossmember.
8. Remove oil pump drive and pickup tube assembly, then remove oil pan through rear of vehicle.
9. Reverse procedure to install. Refer to **Fig. 17**, for torque specifications.

## OIL PUMP
### REPLACE

1. Remove oil pan as described under "Oil Pan, Replace."
2. Remove oil pump and pickup tube assembly attaching bolts.
3. Remove oil pump and pickup tube assembly from vehicle, **Fig. 19.**
4. Reverse procedure to install.

## OIL PUMP REPAIRS

If any part of pump requires replacement, the entire pump assembly must be replaced.

1. Inspect inside of pump housing, outer race and rotor for excessive wear or scoring.
2. Inspect mating surface of pump cover for excessive wear, or scoring. Either

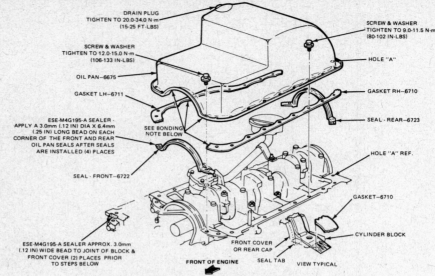

**Fig. 17   Oil pan replacement. 1983–85 All & 1986–88 4-122**

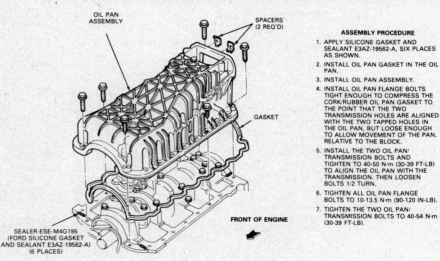

**Fig. 18   Oil pan replacement. 1986–89 4-140**

of these conditions will necessitate replacement of pump.
3. Measure inner rotor tip clearance, **Fig. 20.**
4. Measure rotor endplay, **Fig. 21.** Maximum endplay should be .004 inch on 1983-84 models and .005 inch on 1985-89 models.
5. Check driveshaft to housing bearing clearance. This measurement should be .0015-.0030 inch.
6. Check relief valve spring tension. Spring tension should be 15.2-17.2 lbs. @ 1.20 inches on 1983-86 mod-

els, or 12.6-14.5 lbs. on 1987-89 models.
7. Inspect relief valve piston for scores and free operation in bore.

## BELT TENSION DATA

Air pump drive belt tension should measure 70 lbs. for new ¼ inch belt, 110 lbs. for new ⅜ belt, 50 lbs. for used ¼ inch belt and 90 lbs. for used ⅜ inch belt. Tension on all other belts should measure 170 lbs. for new belts and 150 lbs. for used belts.

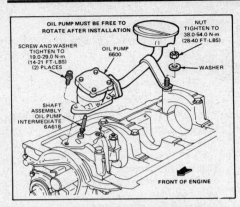

Fig. 19  Oil pump replacement (Typical)

## WATER PUMP
## REPLACE

1. Drain cooling system, then remove fan shroud attaching bolts and position shroud over fan.
2. Remove fan retaining bolts, then the fan and shroud assembly.
3. If equipped, remove A/C compressor and/or power steering pump drive belts.
4. Remove water pump pulley, then the vent tube to canister.
5. Remove heater hose to water pump, then the timing belt outer cover.
6. Remove lower radiator hose from water pump.
7. Remove water pump attaching bolts and the water pump.
8. Reverse procedure to install.

## FUEL PUMP
## REPLACE
### EXCEPT EFI ENGINES

1. Loosen fuel pump attaching bolts one or two turns and apply hand force to pump to loosen gasket.
2. Rotate engine until fuel pump cam

NOTE:  INNER TO OUTER ROTOR TIP CLEARANCE MUST NOT EXCEED 0.25mm (.012 IN) WITH FEELER GAUGE  INSERTED 13mm (1/2") MINIMUM AND ROTORS REMOVED FROM PUMP HOUSING.

Fig. 20  Checking oil pump inner rotor tip clearance

lobe is near its low position to reduce pressure on pump.
3. Disconnect fuel lines from pump.
4. Remove fuel pump attaching bolts and the pump. Remove and discard gasket.
5. Clean all gasket material from engine and fuel pump.
6. Install attaching bolts into fuel pump, then install new gasket over bolts.
7. Install bolts and torque alternately and evenly to 18 ft. lbs.
8. Connect fuel lines to fuel pump, then operate engine and check for leaks.

## EFI ENGINES
### High Pressure Pump

The high pressure fuel pump is frame mounted and can be accessed from under the vehicle. The fuel pump assembly is retained to the frame with three attaching bolts. Before removing the fuel pump, relieve fuel system pressure using either the tool on the fuel diagnostic valve or by opening the electrical circuit to the fuel

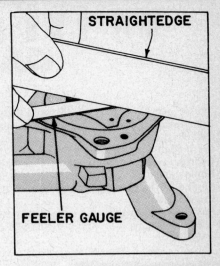

Fig. 21  Checking oil pump rotor endplay

pump and cranking the engine for a minimum of 20 seconds.

### Low Pressure Pump

The low pressure fuel pump is mounted within the fuel tank and may require fuel tank removal for fuel pump service.

## INERTIA SWITCH

The inertia switch, used on EFI engines, is located on the toe-board to the right of the transmission tunnel. Its purpose is to shut off fuel to the engine in the event of a vehicle collision. To reset switch, proceed as follows:
1. Turn ignition switch to Off position.
2. Check for leaking fuel in engine compartment, fuel lines and tank(s) and correct as necessary.
3. Push reset button on top of switch, then turn ignition switch On for several seconds.
4. Turn ignition switch Off, then check for and repair leaks as necessary.

# V6-171 (2.8L) & V6-179 (2.9L) GASOLINE ENGINE

## INDEX

## ENGINE MOUNTS
### REPLACE

1. Remove fan shroud attaching screws, then support engine using a suitable jack and block of wood under oil pan.
2. Remove insulator-to-crossmember attaching nuts and washers, then raise engine until insulator stud clears crossmember.
3. Remove fuel pump shield-to-left side engine bracket attaching bolt, if necessary.
4. Remove mount-to-cylinder block attaching bolts and the mount, Fig. 1.
5. Reverse procedure to install. Refer to Fig. 1 for torque specifications.

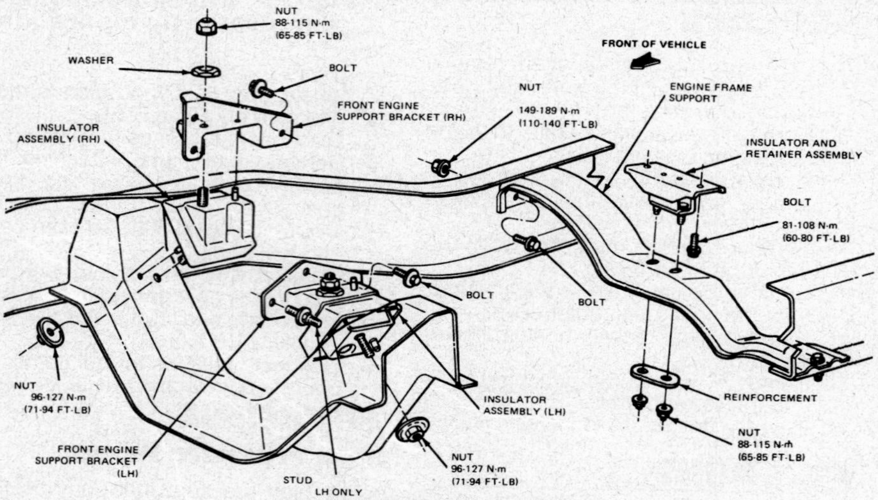

## ENGINE
### REPLACE

1. Disconnect battery ground cable.
2. Scribe hood hinge locations and remove hood from vehicle.
3. Remove air cleaner and intake duct assembly.
4. Disconnect upper and lower radiator hoses from radiator.
5. Remove fan shroud attaching bolts and position shroud over fan.
6. Remove radiator and fan shroud.
7. Remove alternator and bracket, and position aside. Disconnect alternator ground wire from engine.
8. If equipped, disconnect A/C compressor and/or power steering pump from mounting bracket and position aside.
9. Disconnect heater hoses from cylinder block and water pump.
10. Disconnect or remove Thermactor system components interfering with engine removal, if necessary.
11. Disconnect ground wires from cylinder block.
12. On models equipped with V6-171 engine, disconnect and plug fuel pump feed line at fuel pump.
13. On models equipped with V6-179 engine, disconnect fuel tank to fuel rail fuel line at the fuel rail.
14. On models equipped with V6-171 engine, disconnect throttle cable linkage from carburetor and intake manifold.
15. On models equipped with V6-179 en-

**Fig. 1 Engine mounts**

gine, disconnect throttle cable shield and linkage at throttle body and intake manifold, and all vacuum hoses from front and rear vacuum fittings at manifold.
16. On all models, disconnect primary wires from ignition coil, then the brake booster vacuum line.
17. Disconnect oil pressure sender, engine coolant temperature sender, injector harness, air charge temperature sensor, throttle position sensor and EGR pressure sensor electrical connections, as applicable.
18. Raise and support vehicle.
19. Disconnect exhaust pipes from exhaust manifolds.
20. Remove starter motor.
21. Remove engine front mount-to-crossmember attaching nuts or through bolts.
22. On vehicles equipped with automatic transmission, remove converter inspection cover, then disconnect flywheel from converter. Remove kickdown rod or cable, then the converter housing-to-cylinder block attaching bolts and adapter plate-to-converter housing bolt. Lower vehicle.
23. On 1983-84 vehicles equipped with manual transmission, remove clutch linkage, then lower the vehicle.
24. On 1985-89 vehicles equipped with manual transmission, remove clutch housing attaching bolts, then the hydraulic clutch hose.
25. On all models, attach suitable engine lifting equipment to brackets at exhaust manifolds and support transmission with a suitable jack, then carefully lift engine from vehicle.
26. Reverse procedure to install.

## CYLINDER HEAD
### REPLACE

1. Disconnect battery ground cable and drain cooling system.
2. On models equipped with V6-171 engine, remove air cleaner, then disconnect throttle linkage from carburetor.
3. On models equipped with V6-179 engine, remove intake tube from throttle body, then disconnect throttle linkage and cover.
4. On all models, remove distributor cap and wires as an assembly and disconnect distributor wiring harness.
5. Mark relationship of distributor rotor to housing for installation reference, and remove distributor from vehicle.
6. Remove radiator and bypass hoses

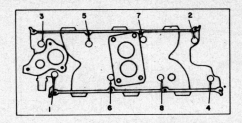

**Fig. 2  Intake manifold bolt tightening sequence. V6-171**

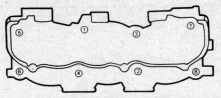

**Fig. 3  Cylinder head bolt tightening sequence. V6-171**

**Fig. 4  Cylinder head bolt tightening sequence. V6-179**

| To adjust both valves for cylinder number | 1 | 4 | 2 | 5 | 3 | 6 |
|---|---|---|---|---|---|---|
| The intake valve must be opening for cylinder number | 5 | 3 | 6 | 1 | 4 | 2 |

**Fig. 6  Valve clearance adjustment chart. V6-171**

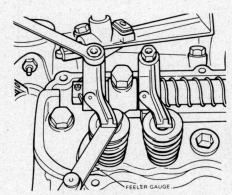

**Fig. 5  Adjusting valve clearance**

from thermostat housing and intake manifold.

7. Remove rocker arm covers and rocker arm shafts as described under "Rocker Arm Service."
8. On models equipped with V6-171 engine, disconnect fuel line from carburetor and remove carburetor from vehicle.
9. On models equipped with V6-179 engine, remove fuel line from fuel rail.
10. On all models, remove intake manifold.
11. Remove pushrods in order so they can be installed in their original positions.
12. Remove exhaust manifolds.
13. Remove cylinder head attaching bolts and the cylinder head.
14. Reverse procedure to install, noting the following:
    a. On models equipped with V6-171 engine, torque intake manifold attaching bolts to specifications in sequence shown in **Fig. 2**, and cylinder head attaching bolts to specifications in sequence shown in **Fig. 3**.
    b. On models equipped with V6-179 engine, torque cylinder head attaching bolts to specifications in sequence shown in **Fig. 4**.

## VALVE ARRANGEMENT
### FRONT TO REAR

Right Bank, V6-171 . . . . . . . . . . . I-E-I-E-E-I
Left Bank, V6-171 . . . . . . . . . . . I-E-E-I-E-I
Right Bank, V6-179 . . . . . . . . . . . E-I-E-I-E-I
Left Bank, V6-179 . . . . . . . . . . . I-E-I-E-I-E

## VALVE LIFT SPECIFICATIONS

Valve lift should measure .373 inch on all applications.

## VALVE GUIDES

Valve guides consist of holes bored in the cylinder head. For service, the guides can be reamed oversize to accommodate valves with oversize stems of .008, .016 and .032 inch.

## VALVE CLEARANCE SPECIFICATIONS

On V6-171 engines, cold valve clearance should measure .014 inch on intake valves and .016 inch on exhaust valves. On V6-179 engines, the nominal working position of the plunger is .070 inch.

## VALVES
### ADJUST
#### V6-171 ENGINE

When checking valve clearance, insert feeler gauge between valve tip and rocker arm at front or rear of valve tip and move gauge in a forward or rearward motion parallel to the crankshaft center line. If feeler gauge is inserted at outboard edge and moved perpendicular to crankshaft center line, a false indication will be given, resulting in tight valve clearance.

1. Remove rocker arm cover as described in "Rocker Arm Service."
2. Rotate engine slightly until cylinder No. 5 intake valve just begins to open. This can be verified by placing a finger on intake valve rocker arm adjusting screw for cylinder No. 5 and feeling for movement while turning engine.
3. Adjust intake and exhaust valves on No. 1 cylinder to specifications by tightening or loosening adjusting screw as necessary, **Fig. 5**.
4. Adjust remaining valves in firing order by positioning cam according to chart, **Fig. 6**.

#### V6-179 ENGINE

1. Position cams so that tappets are in the base circle area on cylinder to be adjusted.
2. Loosen adjusting screws until a distinct lash between roller arm pad and valve tip end can be noticed. Tappet plunger should now be fully extended.
3. Screw in adjustment screws until roller arms slightly touch valves.
4. Screw in adjustment screw an additional 1 1/2 turns (equivalent to .070 inch plunger travel into lifter) to achieve normal operating position.

## ROCKER ARM SERVICE

1. Remove air cleaner assembly if necessary, then disconnect ignition wires from spark plugs.
2. Remove PCV valve and vacuum hose. On V6-179 engines, disconnect fuel return and supply lines.
3. Remove carburetor choke air deflector shield, if equipped.
4. Remove rocker arm cover attaching screws and reinforcement plates. Mark washers so they can be reinstalled in their original positions.
5. On models equipped with V6-171 engine, drain transmission fluid, then remove level indicator tube and bracket from rocker arm cover.
6. On vehicles equipped with automatic transmission, disconnect kickdown linkage.
7. On models equipped with V6-171 engine, move Thermactor air hose and wiring harness away from right side rocker arm cover, then remove engine oil fill cap.
8. On models equipped with V6-171 engine, disconnect vacuum line from canister purge solenoid and the line between canister and solenoid.
9. On models equipped with power brakes, disconnect power brake booster hose.
10. On all models, remove rocker arm

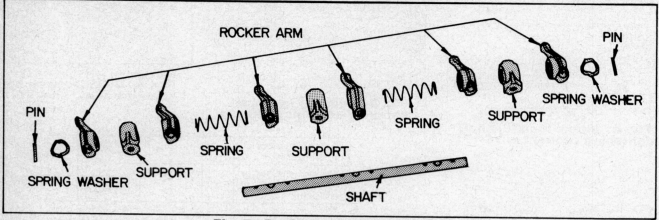

**Fig. 7   Rocker arm shaft assembly**

covers. It may be necessary to lightly tap covers with a plastic hammer to break seal.

11. Loosen rocker arm shaft attaching bolts in sequence two turns at a time, then remove bolts and the rocker arm and shaft assembly.
12. Disassemble rocker arm shaft assembly as shown in **Fig. 7**.
13. Reverse procedure to assemble and install. Refer to **Fig. 8** to install rocker arm cover reinforcement pieces.

## ENGINE FRONT COVER
## REPLACE

The front cover oil seal can be replaced without removing the front cover, using seal remover tool No. 1175-AC or equivalent and a suitable slide hammer, **Fig. 9.**

1. Remove oil pan as described under "Oil Pan, Replace."
2. Drain cooling system, then remove radiator.
3. Remove A/C compressor and power steering bracket, if equipped.
4. Remove alternator, Thermactor pump if equipped and drive belts.
5. Remove fan, then the water pump as described under "Water Pump, Replace."
6. Remove heater and radiator hoses, then the crankshaft pulley.
7. Remove front cover attaching bolts and the cover. It may be necessary to lightly tap covers with a plastic hammer to break seal.
8. Drive oil seal out of cover using tool No. T74P-6019-A or equivalent, **Fig. 10.**
9. Reverse procedure to install.

## TIMING GEARS
## REPLACE

### V6-171

1. Remove camshaft gear as described in "Camshaft, Replace."
2. Remove crankshaft gear using a suitable puller and a shaft protection sleeve. Reverse procedure to install, ensuring marks on gears are properly aligned, **Fig. 11.**

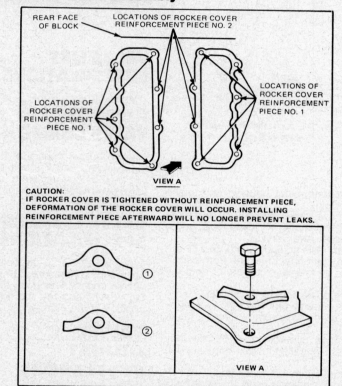

**Fig. 8   Rocker arm cover reinforcement installation**

## TIMING CHAIN
## REPLACE

### V6-179

1. Remove engine front cover as outlined previously.
2. Replace crankshaft pulley bolt, then turn crankshaft until timing marks on camshaft and crankshaft sprockets are aligned as shown, **Fig. 12.**
3. Remove camshaft sprocket retaining bolt, then slide both sprockets and chain forward and remove as an assembly.
4. Reverse procedure to install, ensuring timing marks are aligned as outlined in step 2.

## CAMSHAFT
## REPLACE

1. Disconnect battery ground cable, then drain engine oil.
2. Remove radiator, fan and spacer, drive belt and pulley.
3. Disconnect ignition wires from spark plugs.
4. Remove distributor cap and wires as an assembly, then disconnect distributor wiring harness and vacuum hose.
5. Mark relationship of distributor rotor to housing for installation reference, and remove distributor from vehicle.
6. Remove alternator and Thermactor pump.

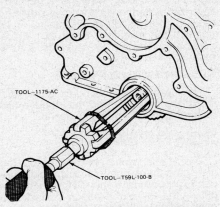

**Fig. 9   Front cover oil seal removal with cover installed**

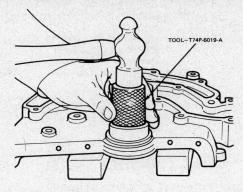

**Fig. 10   Front cover oil seal removal with cover removed**

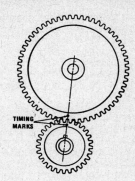

**Fig. 11   Valve timing marks. V6-171**

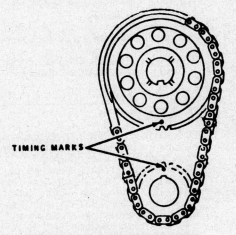

**Fig. 12   Valve timing marks. V6-179**

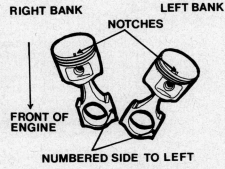

**Fig. 13   Piston & rod assembly**

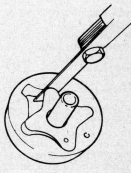

NOTE:
WITH ROTOR ASSEMBLY REMOVED FROM THE PUMP AND RESTING ON A FLAT SURFACE, THE INNER AND OUTER ROTOR TIP CLEARANCE MUST NOT EXCEED 0.30mm (0.012 IN) WITH FEELER GAUGE INSERTED 13mm (0.5 IN) MINIMUM.

**Fig. 14   Measuring oil pump inner rotor tip clearance**

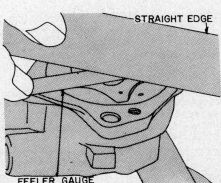

**Fig. 15   Measuring oil pump rotor endplay**

7. Disconnect fuel lines, then remove fuel filter and carburetor, if applicable.
8. Remove intake manifold.
9. Remove rocker arm covers and rocker arm shafts as described in "Rocker Arm Service."
10. Remove pushrods in order so they can be installed in their original positions.
11. Remove valve tappets, then the oil pan as described in "Oil Pan, Replace."
12. Remove crankshaft damper, then the engine front cover and water pump as an assembly.
13. Remove camshaft gear or sprocket attaching bolt, then the gear and chain, if applicable.
14. Remove camshaft thrust plate, then carefully slide camshaft out of engine block.
15. Reverse procedure to install.

## PISTON & ROD
### ASSEMBLE

Assemble rod to piston with notches on top of piston facing front of engine, **Fig. 13.**

## CRANKSHAFT REAR OIL SEAL
### REPLACE

1. Remove transmission assembly, and on models equipped with manual transmission, the clutch pressure plate and disc.
2. Remove flywheel, flywheel housing and rear plate.
3. Punch two holes in seal on opposite sides of crankshaft directly above bearing cap-to-cylinder block split line. Insert a sheet metal screw into each hole.
4. Remove oil seal by prying against

screws with two screwdrivers. Use care to avoid scratching the crankshaft oil seal surface.
5. Clean oil seal groove in main bearing cap and cylinder block.
6. Apply suitable lubricant to new seal and install using rear oil seal replacer tool No. T72C-6165-R or equivalent.

## OIL PAN
### REPLACE

1. Disconnect battery ground cable.
2. Remove air cleaner assembly or air intake tube, then the fan shroud. Place shroud over fan.
3. Disconnect distributor cap with wires and position forward of dash panel. Remove distributor and cover bore opening.
4. Remove front engine mount-to-crossmember attaching nuts.
5. Remove engine oil dipstick tube, if necessary.
6. Raise and support vehicle.
7. Drain engine oil.
8. On vehicles equipped with automatic transmission, remove transmission filler tube and plug pan hole.
9. On all models, remove oil filter, then disconnect exhaust pipes from ex-

haust manifolds, if necessary.

10. Disconnect oil cooler bracket and lower cooler, if equipped.
11. Remove starter motor.
12. On vehicles equipped with automatic transmission, disconnect transmission oil cooler lines and position aside.
13. On all models, disconnect stabilizer bar and move forward.
14. Raise engine as high as possible using a suitable jack, then place wooden blocks between front engine mounts and crossmember. Lower engine to rest on wooden blocks and remove jack.
15. Remove oil pan attaching bolts and lower pan onto crossmember.
16. On V6-179 engines, remove oil pump, baffle and pickup tube assembly and allow to drop into oil pan.
17. On all engines, remove oil pan from vehicle.
18. Reverse procedure to install, using new oil pan gaskets.

## OIL PUMP
### REPLACE

1. Remove oil pan as described in "Oil Pan, Replace."
2. Remove oil pickup screen and oil pump attaching bolts, then the oil pump and pump driveshaft.
3. Reverse procedure to install. Ensure oil pump is primed before installation.

## OIL PUMP REPAIRS

Individual oil pump components are not serviced. If any part of pump requires replacement, entire pump assembly must be replaced.

1. Inspect inside of pump housing, outer race and rotor for excessive wear or scoring.
2. Inspect mating surface of pump cover for excessive wear or scoring. Either of these conditions will necessitate replacement of pump.

3. Measure inner rotor tip clearance, **Fig. 14.**
4. Measure rotor endplay, **Fig. 15,** which should not exceed .004 inch.
5. Check driveshaft to housing bearing clearance. This measurement should be .0015-.0030 inch.
6. Measure relief valve spring tension, which should be 13.6-14.7 lbs. measured at a length of 1.39 inches.
7. Inspect relief valve piston for scores and ensure its free operation in bore.

## BELT TENSION DATA

Belt tension should measure 140 lbs. on all new belts and 120 lbs. on all uused belts.

## FUEL PUMP
### REPLACE
#### V6-171

1. Loosen fuel pump attaching bolts one or two turns. Apply hand force to pump to loosen gasket.
2. Rotate engine until fuel pump cam lobe is near its low position to reduce pressure on pump.
3. Disconnect fuel lines from pump.
4. Remove fuel pump attaching bolts and the pump. Remove and discard gasket.
5. Clean all gasket material from engine and fuel pump.
6. Install attaching bolts into fuel pump, then install new gasket over bolts.
7. Install pump and torque alternately and evenly to 18 ft. lbs.
8. Connect fuel lines to pump, then operate engine and check for leaks.

#### V6-179
##### High Pressure Pump

The high pressure fuel pump is frame mounted and can be accessed from under the vehicle. The fuel pump assembly is retained to the frame with three attaching bolts. Before removing the fuel pump, relieve fuel system pressure using either the tool on the fuel diagnostic valve or by opening the electrical circuit to the fuel pump and cranking the engine for a minimum of 20 seconds.

##### Low Pressure Pump

The low pressure fuel pump is mounted within the fuel tank and may require fuel tank removal for fuel pump service.

## INERTIA SWITCH

The inertia switch is located on the toe-board to the right of transmission tunnel. Its purpose is to shut off fuel to the engine in the event of a vehicle collision. To reset switch, proceed as follows:

1. Turn ignition switch to Off position.
2. Check for leaking fuel in engine compartment, fuel lines and tank(s) and correct as necessary.
3. Push reset button on top of switch, then turn ignition switch On for several seconds.
4. Turn ignition switch Off, then check for and repair leaks as necessary.

## WATER PUMP
### REPLACE

1. Drain cooling system, then disconnect radiator lower hose and heater return hose from water inlet housing.
2. Remove fan and clutch assembly using fan clutch nut wrench tool No. T83T-6312-A and fan clutch pulley holder tool No. T83T-6312-B. **Fan and clutch assembly retaining nut has left hand threads and is removed by turning clockwise.**
3. On all models equipped with A/C, remove alternator and mounting bracket.
4. On models less A/C, remove alternator drive belt.
5. On all models, remove water pump pulley.
6. Remove water pump attaching bolts, then the water pump assembly.
7. Reverse procedure to install.

# 4-135 (2.2L) DIESEL ENGINE

## INDEX

## QUICK START & AFTERGLOW SYSTEM

This system improves cold engine starting performance. When ignition switch is turned On, a "Wait-to-Start" light illuminates on dash panel next to cold start knob. As this happens, relay No. 1 closes and full system voltage is applied to glow plugs. If engine coolant temperature is less than 86° F, relay No. 2 also closes. The control module extinguishes "Wait-to-Start" light after 3 seconds. If ignition is left on for approximately 3 more seconds without cranking engine, No. 1 relay opens, shutting off current to glow plugs to prevent overheating. However, if engine coolant temperature is below 86° F, relay No. 2 remains closed to apply limited voltage to plugs through glow plug resistor until ignition is turned Off.

During engine cranking, relay No. 1 is cycled by control module to provide alternate voltage to glow plugs between 4 and 12 volts with relay No. 2 closed, or between 0 and 12 volts with relay No. 2 open.

With engine running, alternator output signals cause control module to prevent No. 1 relay from cycling, and afterglow function takes over. If engine coolant temperature is below 86° F, limited voltage is applied to glow plugs through relay No. 2 and glow plug resistor. When clutch and neutral switches are closed or coolant temperature exceeds 86° F, relay No. 2 opens and all current to glow plugs is cut off.

## FUEL INJECTION & GLOW PLUG SYSTEM DIAGNOSIS

### ENGINE CRANKS BUT WILL NOT START

1. Turn ignition switch to Run and check for voltage to fuel shut-off solenoid using a suitable 12 volt test lamp. If test lamp lights, proceed to step 2. If test lamp does not light, repair circuit as necessary.

2. Disconnect, then reconnect fuel shut-off solenoid electrical connector with ignition switch in Run. If solenoid clicks, proceed to step 3. If solenoid does not click, replace solenoid and repeat test.

3. Loosen one fuel injector nozzle line and crank engine. If there is no fuel flow while cranking engine, refer to "Poor Engine Performance" diagnosis. If fuel flow is observed, refer to "Glow Plug Control System" diagnosis.

### ENGINE KNOCKS

1. Check all belt-driven components for looseness. If satisfactory, proceed to step 2. If any looseness is encountered, repair or replace component(s) as necessary.

2. Perform fuel system diagnostic procedures as described in "Poor Engine Performance" diagnosis. If fuel system is satisfactory, check engine main bearing clearances. If fuel system is malfunctioning, make necessary repairs and/or adjustments. If engine continues to knock, check main bearing clearances.

### ENGINE MISSES

1. If engine misses only when cold, refer to "Glow Plug Control System" diagnosis.

2. If engine misses at operating temperature, refer to "Poor Engine Performance" diagnosis.

### EXCESSIVE ENGINE SMOKE

1. If engine smokes only when cold, refer to "Glow Plug Control System" diagnosis.

2. If engine smokes at operating temperature, refer to "Poor Engine Performance" diagnosis.

### POOR ENGINE PERFORMANCE

1. Ensure an adequate supply of fuel is available, and replenish as necessary.

If fuel supply is sufficient, proceed to step 2.

2. Check for fuel, oil and/or coolant leaks and restrictions in air cleaner, and replace or repair components as needed. If no leaks are evident and air cleaner is not restricted, proceed to step 3.

3. Inspect exhaust system for dents or other damage which could cause restrictions, and repair or replace components as necessary. If exhaust system is not restricted, proceed to step 4.

4. Disconnect fuel inlet line from injection pump and insert into a suitable container. Operate primer pump on top of fuel filter cover. If fuel flows freely from line, proceed to step 5. If there is no fuel flow, replace filter. If problem still exists, fuel tank(s) and/or fuel line(s) are faulty.

5. Examine fuel for contamination. If fuel is not contaminated, proceed to step 6. If there are contaminants in fuel, clean and/or repair fuel system components as necessary.

6. Disconnect and drain fuel line(s) from injection pump inlet and fuel tank(s). Plug tank end of line(s) and pressurize to 20-25 psi, then apply a soap and water solution to all connections. If there are no bubbles, reconnect inlet line, bleed fuel system and proceed to step 7. If any bubbles are observed, repair leaking connection(s) and repeat leak test.

7. Ensure throttle lever contacts stop with accelerator pedal fully depressed. If lever contacts stop, proceed to step 8. If lever does not contact stop, adjust or replace throttle linkage as necessary.

8. Check engine idle speed with engine at normal operating temperature, transmission in Neutral and parking brake applied. Idle speed should be 780-830 RPM. If idle speed is within specifications, proceed to step 9, otherwise adjust as necessary.

9. Check ignition pump timing as described under "Injection Pump Timing," and adjust as necessary. If pump

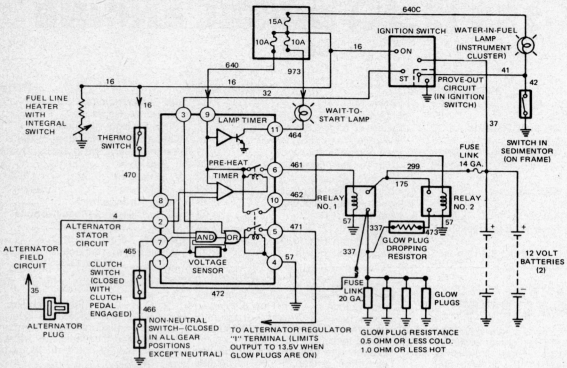

**Fig. 1  Glow plug control system**

**GLOW PLUG CONTROL SYSTEM WIRE COLOR CODE**

| | |
|---|---|
| 4 WHITE/BLACK STRIPE | 462 PURPLE BASE |
| 16 RED/LT GREEN STRIPE | 464 BLACK/PINK STRIPE |
| 32 RED/LT BLUE STRIPE | 465 WHITE/LT BLUE STRIPE |
| 35 ORANGE/LT BLUE STRIPE | 466 PINK/ORANGE DOT |
| 37 YELLOW BASE | 470 PINK/BLACK DOT |
| 41 BLACK/LT BLUE HASH | 471 ORANGE/LT GREEN DOT |
| 42 RED/WHITE DOT | 472 YELLOW/BLACK DOT ③ |
| 57 BLACK BASE | 473 LT GREEN/BLACK DOT ④ |
| 175 BLACK/YELLOW DOT | 640 RED/YELLOW HASH |
| 299 GREEN ① | 687 GRAY/YELLOW STRIPE |
| 337 ORANGE/WHITE STRIPE ② | 973 RED BASE |
| 461 ORANGE BASE | |

① WITH ES-D5ZB-14A466-DA FUSE LINK (GREEN) AT STARTER SOLENOID END.
② BLACK/WHITE STRIPE AT ENGINE END.
③ WITH ES-D5ZB-14A466-AA FUSE LINK (BLUE) AT NO. 1 RELAY END.
④ BLACK AT ENGINE END.

CAUTION: WHEN CHECKING CONTROL MODULE CIRCUITS AT THE HARNESS CONNECTOR, INSERT TESTER PROBES INTO WIRING SIDE OF CONNECTOR CAVITIES. INSERTING PROBES INTO OPEN END OF CONNECTOR CAVITIES WILL DISTORT OR DAMAGE TERMINALS.

---

is properly timed, proceed to step 10.
10. Check fuel injection nozzles for damage and ensure proper operation. If nozzles are satisfactory, proceed to step 11. If damaged or malfunctioning, clean, repair or replace as necessary.
11. Perform engine compression test. If compression is satisfactory, replace injection pump. If compression is low, inspect engine components to determine cause and repair or replace as necessary.

## "WAIT-TO-START" LAMP

Refer to wiring schematic, **Fig. 1**, when troubleshooting this system.
1. Turn ignition to Run position and observe "Wait" lamp. If lamp illuminates for 3 seconds and goes out, system is satisfactory; refer to Glow Plug Control System" diagnosis. If lamp does not light, proceed to step 2. If lamp lights and remains lit, replace glow plug control module and recheck operation.
2. Connect a suitable jumper wire between connector terminal 11 and ground, **Fig. 2**, then turn ignition to Run position and observe "Wait"

lamp. If lamp now lights, proceed to step 3. If lamp still does not light, inspect lamp bulb and its circuit and repair or replace as necessary.
3. Connect a suitable 12 volt test lamp between connector terminal 9 and ground, **Fig. 2**, then turn ignition to Run position and observe "Wait" lamp. If test lamp lights, replace glow plug control module and recheck operation. If test lamp does not light, repair or replace ignition switch or switch wiring as necessary and recheck operation.

## GLOW PLUG CONTROL SYSTEM

Refer to wiring schematic, **Fig. 1**, when troubleshooting this system.
1. Measure voltage at each glow plug lead with transmission in Neutral and ignition switch in Run position. Voltage at each lead should measure 11 volts for 6 seconds, then drop to 4.2-5.3 volts. **If engine coolant temperature is higher than 86° F, connect jumper wire between coolant thermoswitch connector terminals.**
2. If no voltage is recorded at any of the

glow plugs, proceed to step 3. If voltmeter reads 11 volts for 6 seconds, then drops to zero, proceed to step 8. If voltage is satisfactory, remove jumper wire from coolant thermoswitch and proceed to step 15. If there is no voltage at 1, 2 or 3 glow plugs, replace glow plug harness and recheck voltage.
3. Disconnect glow plug harness from engine electrical harness and glow plugs, then connect a suitable self-powered test lamp between each glow plug terminal and harness connector. If test lamp lights, reconnect harness and proceed to step 4. If test lamp does not light, repair or replace glow plug harness as necessary and recheck.
4. Connect a suitable 12 volt test lamp between glow plug control module terminal 9 and ground. Observe test lamp with ignition in Run. If test lamp lights, proceed to step 5. If test lamp does not run, repair or replace ignition switch and switch wiring as necessary and recheck.
5. Connect a suitable 12 volt test lamp between glow plug control module

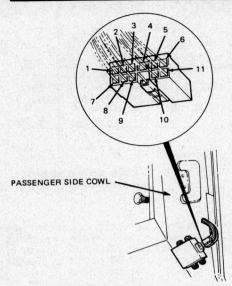

**Fig. 2  Glow plug control system electrical connector location**

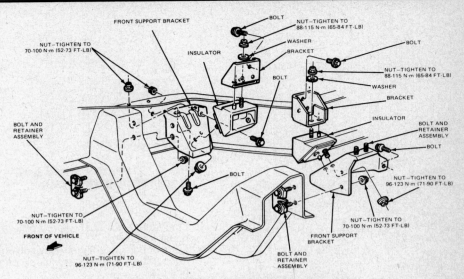

**Fig. 3  Engine mount replacement**

terminal 6 and ground. Observe test lamp with ignition in Run. If test lamp lights for 6 seconds, proceed to step 6. If test lamp does not light, replace quick start control unit and recheck.

6. Connect a suitable 12 volt test lamp between No. 1 glow plug relay signal terminal and ground. Observe test lamp with ignition in Run. If test lamp lights for 6 seconds, proceed to step 7. If test lamp does not light, repair open or short in circuit 461 and recheck.

7. Measure voltage between No. 1 glow plug relay output terminal and ground with ignition in Run. If voltmeter reads 11 volts or more for 6 seconds, proceed to step 14. If voltage is less than 11 volts, replace No. 1 glow plug relay and recheck.

8. Connect a suitable 12 volt test lamp between glow plug control module terminal 10 and ground. Observe test lamp with ignition in Run. If test lamp does not light, proceed to step 9. If test lamp lights, proceed to step 10.

9. Check operation of clutch and neutral switches using a suitable self-powered test lamp. With transmission in gear and clutch pedal released, both switches should be closed (test lamp on). With transmission in Neutral and clutch pedal depressed, both switches should be open (test lamp off). If both switches operate satisfactorily, proceed to step 10, otherwise replace defective switch and recheck.

10. Connect a suitable 12 volt test lamp between No. 2 glow plug relay signal terminal and ground. Observe test lamp with transmission in Neutral and ignition in Run. If test lamp lights, proceed to step 11. If test lamp does not light, repair open or short in circuit 462 and recheck.

11. Connect a suitable 12 volt test lamp between No. 2 glow plug relay output terminal and ground. Observe test

lamp with ignition in Run. If test lamp lights, proceed to step 12. If test lamp does not light, replace No. 2 glow plug relay and recheck.

12. Disconnect dropping resistor electrical connector and connect a suitable 12 volt test lamp between connector input terminal and ground. Observe test lamp with ignition in Run. If test lamp lights, proceed to step 13. If test lamp does not light, repair open or short in circuit 473 and recheck.

13. Measure resistance across dropping resistor connector terminals. If ohmmeter reads less than 1 ohm, reconnect dropping resistor and proceed to step 14. If resistance is 1 ohm or greater, replace dropping resistor and recheck.

14. Connect a suitable 12 volt test lamp between any glow plug terminal and ground. Observe test lamp with ignition in Run. If test lamp lights, repeat steps 1 and 2. If test lamp does not light, repair open or short in circuit 337 between No. 1 glow plug relay and glow plug harness and recheck.

15. Disconnect glow plug leads and measure resistance between each glow plug terminal and ground. If ohmmeter reads less than 1 ohm, the glow plug system is operating satisfactorily; refer to "Poor Engine Performance" diagnosis. If resistance is 1 ohm or greater, replace defective glow plug(s) and recheck.

## ENGINE MOUNTS
### REPLACE

1. Remove nuts from top of insulator bracket, Fig. 3.
2. Raise and support vehicle.
3. Raise engine sufficiently to clear insulators.
4. Remove front support bracket attaching bolts and the bracket.
5. Remove insulator attaching nut and

the insulator.
6. Reverse procedure to install.

## ENGINE
## REPLACE

1. Disconnect both battery ground cables from batteries and engine.
2. Scribe hood hinge locations and remove hood.
3. Drain cooling system.
4. Disconnect air intake hose from air cleaner and intake manifold, then the upper and lower radiator hoses from engine.
5. Remove engine cooling fan, then the radiator and fan shroud.
6. Disconnect radio ground strap, if equipped.
7. Disconnect No. 2 glow plug relay from dash and position aside with electrical connector attached.
8. Disconnect engine wiring harness from connector on left fender apron.
9. Disconnect starter cable from starter motor.
10. Disconnect accelerator cable and speed control cable, if equipped, from injector pump.
11. Disconnect cold start cable from injector pump.
12. On models equipped with A/C, discharge refrigerant from system, then disconnect A/C lines and position aside.
13. On models equipped with power steering, disconnect pressure and return lines from power steering pump.
14. On all models, disconnect vacuum fitting from vacuum pump and position fitting and hoses aside.
15. Disconnect and cap fuel return line at fuel heater and return line at air injection pump.
16. Disconnect heater hoses from engine, then loosen engine mount attaching nuts.
17. Raise and support vehicle.

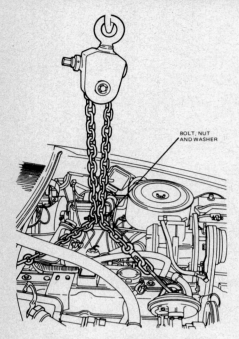

**Fig. 4  Engine removal**

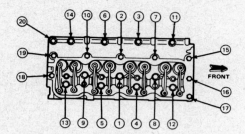

**Fig. 5  Cylinder head bolt tightening sequence**

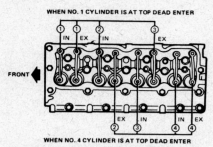

**Fig. 6  Valve adjustment sequence**

18. Drain engine oil and remove primary oil filter.
19. Disconnect oil pressure sender hose from oil filter mounting adapter.
20. Disconnect exhaust pipe from manifold, then remove lower engine mount attaching nuts.
21. Remove transmission-to-engine attaching bolts, then lower vehicle.
22. Attach suitable lifting equipment to engine. Ensure bolt, nut and washer are installed as shown, **Fig. 4**.
23. Lift engine assembly from vehicle.
24. Reverse procedure to install.

## CYLINDER HEAD
### REPLACE

1. Disconnect ground cables from both batteries.
2. Mark hood hinge locations and remove hood.
3. Drain cooling system.
4. Disconnect breather hose from valve cover, then remove intake and breather hoses from air cleaner and intake manifold.
5. Remove heater hose bracket-to-valve cover and exhaust manifold attaching nuts.
6. Disconnect heater hoses from thermostat housing and water pump, and position heater hose tube assembly aside.
7. Remove vacuum pump support brace from cylinder head and vacuum pump bracket.
8. Remove alternator and vacuum pump drive belt.
9. Remove A/C compressor and/or power steering pump drive belt, if equipped.
10. Disconnect brake booster vacuum hose, then remove vacuum pump.

11. Disconnect exhaust pipe from exhaust manifold.
12. Disconnect coolant thermoswitch and temperature sender electrical connectors.
13. Remove fuel injection lines. Cap lines and fittings.
14. Disconnect alternator, glow plug harness and dropping resistor electrical connectors and position aside.
15. Disconnect fuel lines from both sides of fuel line heater.
16. Remove fuel filter from mounting bracket and position aside with outlet line connected.
17. Loosen lower No. 3 intake port nut and "Banjo" bolt on injection pump, then disconnect lower fuel return line from intake manifold stud and upper fuel return line.
18. If equipped with power steering, remove rear power steering pump bracket attaching bolt.
19. Remove upper radiator hose from engine, then loosen clamp on water pump-to-thermostat housing bypass hose.
20. If equipped with A/C, remove A/C compressor from mounting bracket and position aside with refrigerant lines attached.
21. Remove valve cover and rocker arm shaft.
22. Remove cylinder head attaching bolts and the cylinder head.
23. Reverse procedure to install. Torque cylinder head attaching bolts to specifications in sequence shown, **Fig. 5.**

## CYLINDER SLEEVE
### REPLACE
#### REMOVAL

1. Remove cylinder head as described under "Cylinder Head, Replace."
2. Remove oil pan as described under "Oil Pan, Replace."
3. Remove connecting rod bearing caps and bearings in order so they can be installed in their original positions.
4. Remove piston assemblies from cylinder block. To remove pistons, it may be necessary to ridge ream top of cylinder sleeves.
5. Remove cylinder sleeves using sleeve remover tool No. 14-0316 or equivalent. Rotate crankshaft as necessary to avoid contact between con-

necting rod bearing journal and pilot screw on tool. **When removing sleeve from cylinder No. 4, rear of engine must be raised to provide clearance at dash panel.**

### INSTALLATION

1. Remove scratches from cylinder bores using oil soaked emery cloth.
2. Lubricate cylinder bores and outside surface of cylinder sleeves with clean engine oil.
3. Install cylinder sleeves using sleeve installer tool No. 14-0317 or equivalent. Check turning torque on tool nut when sleeve is approximately halfway installed, and again when sleeve is almost seated in block. Torque should measure 13-37 ft. lbs. at both points.
4. Reverse steps 1 through 4 as described under "Removal" to complete installation.

## VALVE ARRANGEMENT
### FRONT TO REAR

1983-84 . . . . . . . . . . . . . . . . . I-E-I-E-I-E-I-E

## VALVE LIFT SPECIFICATIONS

Valve lift should measure .257 inch.

## VALVE CLEARANCE SPECIFICATIONS

Hot valve clearance should measure .012 inch at intake and exhaust valves.

## VALVES
### ADJUST

1. Run engine until normal operating temperature is reached, then remove valve cover.
2. Torque cylinder head attaching bolts to specifications in sequence shown in **Fig. 5**.
3. Rotate crankshaft until cylinder No. 1 is at top dead center of compression stroke.
4. Check valve clearances in sequence, **Fig. 6**, using a suitable feeler gauge.

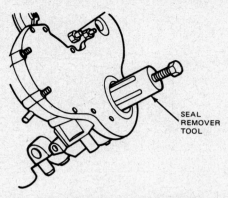

**Fig. 7   Front oil seal removal**

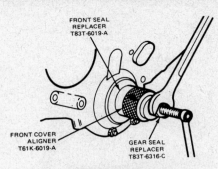

**Fig. 8   Front oil seal installation**

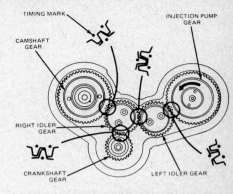

**Fig. 9   Valve timing marks**

**Fig. 10   Piston & rod assembly**

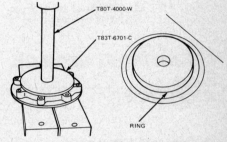

**Fig. 11   Crankshaft rear oil seal installation**

5. Adjust any valve clearances which do not meet specifications as follows:
   a. Loosen adjusting screw locknut.
   b. Rotate adjusting screw as necessary to bring clearance within specifications.
   c. Tighten locknut while holding adjusting screw in position.
   d. Recheck valve clearance.
6. Rotate crankshaft one complete revolution until cylinder No. 4 is at top dead center of compression stroke, then repeat steps 4 and 5.

## FRONT OIL SEAL
### REPLACE

1. Disconnect ground cables from both batteries.
2. Remove engine cooling fan and fan shroud.
3. Remove A/C compressor and/or power steering pump drive belt, if equipped.
4. Remove water pump and alternator drive belt.
5. Remove crankshaft pulley lock bolt using damper remover tool No. T83T-6316-D or equivalent.
6. Remove crankshaft pulley using a suitable puller.
7. Remove front oil seal using front oil seal remover tool No. T72J-6700 or equivalent, **Fig. 7**.
8. Reverse procedure to install, using tools shown in **Fig. 8**.

## TIMING GEAR CASE & TIMING GEARS
### REPLACE
#### REMOVAL

1. Disconnect ground cables from both batteries.
2. Remove engine cooling fan and fan shroud.
3. Drain cooling system and engine oil.
4. Remove A/C compressor and/or power steering pump drive belt, if equipped.
5. Remove alternator and vacuum pump drive belt.
6. Remove water pump as described under "Water Pump, Replace."
7. Remove crankshaft pulley lock bolt using damper remover tool No. T83T-6316-D or equivalent.
8. Remove timing gear case cover attaching bolts and the cover.
9. Remove oil pan as described in "Oil Pan, Replace."
10. Rotate crankshaft until timing gear marks are aligned, **Fig. 9**.
11. Remove camshaft gear and injection pump gear attaching bolts, washers and friction gears.
12. Remove camshaft and injection pump gears using a suitable puller.
13. Remove idler gear attaching bolts, thrust plates and spindles, then the idler gears. Remove gears in order so they can be reinstalled in their original positions.
14. Disconnect injection pump from timing gear case and position aside.
15. Remove timing gear case attaching bolts and the case.

#### INSTALLATION

1. Clean timing gear case, water pump, oil pan and engine block mating surfaces.
2. Install timing gear case, using a new gasket, and torque attaching bolts to 15 ft. lbs.
3. Install timing gears so all timing marks are aligned, **Fig. 9**, in the following order: right idler gear, camshaft gear, left idler gear, injection pump gear.
4. Install all friction gears, washers, nuts and bolts on gears.

5. Remove front crankshaft oil seal from timing gear case front cover.
6. Install timing gear case cover, with a new gasket, using tool No. T61K-6019-A. Torque cover attaching bolts to 15 ft. lbs.
7. Install new front oil seal, **Fig. 8**.
8. Reverse steps 1 through 7 as described under "Removal" to complete installation.

## CAMSHAFT
### REPLACE

1. Remove engine from vehicle as described under Engine, Replace."
2. Remove valve cover, rocker shaft assembly and pushrods. Remove pushrods so they can be reinstalled in their original positions.
3. Remove timing gear case cover and camshaft gear as described under "Timing Gear Case & Timing Gears, Replace."
4. Remove oil pan and oil pump from engine.
5. Remove camshaft thrust plate and the camshaft. Use care not to damage camshaft lobes during removal.
6. Reverse procedure to install.

## PISTON & ROD
### ASSEMBLE

Assemble piston to rod with bearing tang locking groove and sub-combustion chamber positioned as shown, **Fig. 10**.

NOTE: INNER TO OUTER ROTOR TIP CLEARANCE MUST NOT EXCEED 0.305mm (0.012 INCH) WITH FEELER GAUGE INSERTED 12.7mm (1/2") MINIMUM AND ROTORS REMOVED FROM PUMP HOUSING.

**Fig. 12  Measuring oil pump inner rotor tip clearance**

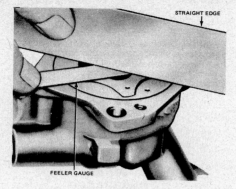

**Fig. 13  Measuring oil pump rotor endplay**

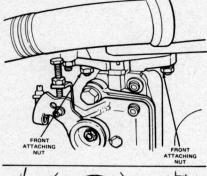

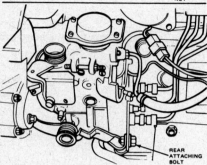

**Fig. 14  Injection pump removal**

## CRANKSHAFT REAR OIL SEAL
### REPLACE

1. Disconnect ground cables from both batteries.
2. Raise and support vehicle.
3. Remove transmission and clutch assemblies as described elsewhere in this chapter.
4. Remove flywheel, then the crankshaft rear cover assembly.
5. Remove oil seal from rear cover.
6. Reverse procedure to install, using tools shown in **Fig. 11.**

## OIL PAN
### REPLACE

1. Disconnect ground cables from both batteries.
2. Remove engine oil dipstick, then drain cooling system.
3. Disconnect air intake hose from intake manifold and air cleaner.
4. Remove engine cooling fan and fan shroud.
5. Disconnect radiator hoses, then remove radiator upper support brackets and the radiator and fan shroud.
6. Disconnect and cap fuel lines at fuel filter and return line at injection pump.
7. Remove fuel filter, then the filter mounting bracket.
8. Remove engine bracket-to-insulator attaching nuts.
9. Raise and support vehicle.
10. Loosen transmission insulator attaching bolts at rear of transmission.
11. Remove lower engine insulator attaching bolts, then drain engine oil.
12. Remove primary oil filter, then the bypass filter mounting bracket and hoses.
13. Lower vehicle.
14. Attach suitable lifting equipment to engine and raise engine until insulator studs clear insulators.
15. Slide engine forward and raise approximately 3 inches.

16. Install a 3 inch wooden block between each engine mount and bracket, then lower engine and remove engine lifting device.
17. Raise and support vehicle.
18. Remove oil pan attaching bolts and lower oil pan to rest on crossmember.
19. Disconnect oil pickup tube from oil pump and bearing cap and lay in oil pan.
20. Slide oil pan forward and up, and remove from vehicle. It may be necessary to move the A/C condenser forward to provide clearance for pan removal.
21. Reverse procedure to install. Apply a 1/8 inch bead of suitable sealer to split line between engine block and front cover along side rails and at ends of oil pan seals which contact oil pan gaskets.

## OIL PUMP
### REPLACE

1. Remove oil pan as described in "Oil Pan, Replace."
2. Disconnect oil pump outlet tube from engine.
3. Remove oil pump setscrew and the oil pump.
4. Reverse procedure to install. Apply Teflon tape to pump set screw prior to installation.

## OIL PUMP REPAIRS

Individual oil pump components are not serviced. If any part of the pump requires replacement, the entire pump assembly must be replaced.
1. Inspect inside of pump housing, outer race and rotor for excessive wear or scoring.
2. Inspect pump cover mating surface for excessive wear or scoring.
3. Measure inner rotor tip clearance, **Fig. 12.**
4. Measure rotor endplay, **Fig. 13,** which should be .0016-.0039 inch and must not exceed .0060 inch.
5. Measure driveshaft to bearing clearance, which must not exceed .0039 inch.
6. Inspect relief valve piston for scores and ensure its free operation in bore.

## WATER PUMP
### REPLACE

1. Disconnect ground cables from both batteries.
2. Remove engine cooling fan and fan shroud.
3. Remove alternator and vacuum pump drive belt.
4. Remove A/C compressor and/or power steering pump drive belt, if equipped.
5. Drain cooling system, then disconnect hoses from water pump.
6. Remove water pump attaching bolts and the pump.
7. Reverse procedure to install.

## BELT TENSION DATA

For new belts, tension should measure 170 lbs. for A/C compressor and power steering pump, 110 lbs. for vacuum pump and 140 lbs. for the alternator and water pump. For used belts, tension should measure 150 lbs. for A/C compressor and power steering pump, 90 lbs. for vacuum pump and 120 lbs. for the alternator and water pump.

|  | New Lbs. | Used Lbs. |
|---|---|---|
| A/C Compressor | 170 | 150 |
| Alternator | 140 | 120 |
| Power Steering | 170 | 150 |
| Vacuum Pump | 110 | 90 |
| Water Pump | 140 | 120 |

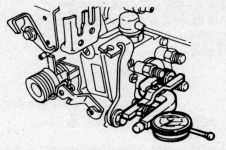

**Fig. 15    Injection pump timing**

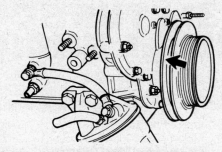

**Fig. 16    Marking crankshaft pulley for idle speed adjustment**

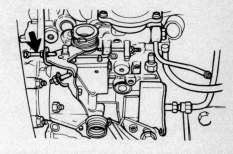

**Fig. 17    Idle speed adjustment**

# INJECTION PUMP
## REPLACE
### REMOVAL

1. Disconnect ground cables from both batteries.
2. Remove engine cooling fan and fan shroud.
3. Remove A/C compressor and/or power steering pump drive belt and idler pulley, if equipped.
4. Remove injection pump drive gear cover and gasket.
5. Rotate crankshaft until injection pump drive gear keyway is at top dead center position.
6. Remove large nut and washer from pump drive gear. Use care to avoid dropping washer into timing gear case.
7. Disconnect air intake hose from intake manifold and air cleaner.
8. Disconnect throttle cable and speed control cable, if equipped.
9. Disconnect and cap fuel inlet line at injection pump.
10. Disconnect fuel shut-off solenoid electrical connector from injection pump.
11. Remove fuel injection lines. Cap lines and fittings.
12. Disconnect lower fuel return line from injection pump and fuel lines.
13. Loosen lower No. 3 intake port nut and remove fuel return line.
14. Remove injection pump attaching nuts and bolt, Fig. 14.
15. Disconnect cold start cable, then remove injection pump using a suitable puller. **Use care to avoid dropping key into timing gear case when removing pump.**

### INSTALLATION

1. Connect cold start cable, then install injection pump in timing gear case, aligning key with keyway in drive gear in top dead center position.
2. Install injection pump attaching nuts and bolt and tighten sufficiently to draw pump into position.
3. Install injection pump drive gear washer and nut and torque to 40 ft. lbs.
4. Install injection pump gear cover with a new gasket.
5. Adjust pump timing as described under "Injection Pump Timing."

6. Install all fuel lines and clamps.
7. Connect fuel shut-off solenoid electrical connector.
8. Connect throttle cable and speed control cable, if equipped.
9. Bleed fuel system as follows:
    a. Loosen air vent plug on fuel filter.
    b. Operate priming pump on top of fuel filter adapter until clear, bubble-free fuel flows from vent plug.
    c. Close vent plug while holding priming plug in fully depressed position.
    d. Disconnect fuel return line from injection pump.
    e. Operate priming pump until fuel flows from return port on injection pump.
    f. Reconnect fuel return line to injection pump, then run engine and check for leaks.
10. Install air intake hose, drive belt and idler pulley.
11. Install engine cooling fan and fan shroud, then reconnect battery ground cables.

## INJECTION PUMP TIMING

1. Disconnect ground cables from both batteries.
2. Remove air intake hose from intake manifold and air cleaner.
3. Remove injection pump distributor head plug bolt and seal.
4. Install static timing gauge adapter (tool No. 14-0303 or equivalent) and a suitable dial indicator to injection pump, Fig. 15. Install dial indicator so pointer contacts injection pump plunger and gauge reads approximately .08 inch.
5. Align timing mark on crankshaft pulley with indicator on timing case cover, then rotate crankshaft slowly counterclockwise until dial indicator pointer stops moving.
6. Zero the dial indicator, then rotate crankshaft clockwise until crankshaft timing mark aligns with indicator pin. The dial indicator reading should be .0392-.0408 inch.
7. If reading is not within specifications, loosen injection pump nuts and bolt. Rotate pump counterclockwise past correct timing position, then rotate clockwise until timing is correct to

eliminate gear backlash and repeat steps 5 and 6.
8. Remove dial indicator and adapter, then install injection pump distributor head plug.
9. Install air intake hose and reconnect battery ground cables.
10. Run engine and check for fuel leaks.
11. Adjust idle speed as described under "Idle Speed, Adjust."

# INJECTION NOZZLE
## REPLACE

1. Disconnect ground cables from both batteries.
2. Remove fuel injection lines. Cap lines and fittings.
3. Remove fuel return line and gaskets.
4. Remove fuel line heater clamp bolts and position heater aside.
5. Remove injection nozzles using a suitable socket.
6. Remove copper washer and steel gasket using O-ring tool No. T71-P-19703-C or equivalent.
7. Reverse procedure to install. Torque nozzles to 47 ft. lbs. Install nozzle gaskets with blue side up, toward nozzle.

# IDLE SPEED
## ADJUST

1. Run engine until normal operating temperature is reached, then stop engine.
2. Wipe off crankshaft pulley and install reflective tape, Fig. 16.
3. Direct the light from photoelectric tachometer (part No. 99-0001 or equivalent) onto reflective tape and note RPM with engine running at idle.
4. If idle RPM is not within specifications listed on vehicle emissions decal, adjust idle speed as follows:
    a. Loosen idle speed adjusting bolt locknut, Fig. 17.
    b. Rotate bolt counterclockwise to decrease idle speed, or clockwise to increase idle speed.
    c. Tighten locknut when idle speed is within specifications.
    d. Depress accelerator several times to ensure engine speed returns to proper idle.

# 4-143 (2.3L) TURBOCHARGED DIESEL ENGINE

## INDEX

## SUPER-QUICK GLOW PLUG SYSTEM

This system, **Fig. 1,** is used to enable the engine to start quickly when the engine is cold. The system consists of four glow plugs, a control module, two relays, a glow plug resistor assembly, a coolant temperature switch and connecting wiring. Relay power and feedback circuits are protected by fusible links in the wiring harness. The control module is protected by a separate 10A fuse in the fuse panel assembly.

The super-quick start system eliminates the waiting time to start the engine. When the ignition switch is turned to the ON position, relay No. 1 also closes and full system voltage is applied to the glow plugs. If the ignition switch is left in the ON position approximately three seconds more without cranking, the control module opens relay No. 1 and current to the plugs stops, preventing overheating. Relay No. 2 does not close until the engine is cranked.

When the engine is cranked, the control module cycles relay No. 1 intermittently allowing the glow plug voltage to alternate between 6 and 12 volts during cranking and with the No. 2 relay closed. After the engine starts, the alternator output signals the control module to stop the No. 1 relay cycling and the afterflow function takes place. If engine coolant temperature is below 86° F, the No. 2 relay remains closed. This applies reduced voltage (6-7.6 volts) to the glow plug resistor for approximately 30 seconds.

## FUEL INJECTION & GLOW PLUG SYSTEM DIAGNOSIS

### ENGINE CRANKS BUT WILL NOT START

1. Ensure battery is fully charged and engine cranking speed is approximately 150 RPM.
2. Turn ignition switch to RUN position and check for a clicking noise at the glow plug relay. If solenoid clicks, proceed to step 3. If solenoid does not click, proceed to GLOW PLUG CONTROL SYSTEM diagnosis. **Ensure engine coolant temperature is below 86° F.**
3. Loosen one injector nozzle line nut and crank engine. If fuel discharges, proceed to GLOW PLUG CONTROL SYSTEM diagnosis. If fuel does not discharge, tighten nut and proceed to step 4.
4. Turn ignition switch to RUN position. Using a 12 volt test lamp, ensure voltage is available at fuel shut-off solenoid. If voltage is present proceed to step 5. If voltage is not present, repair circuit as necessary.
5. With ignition switch in RUN position, disconnect, then reconnect fuel shut-off solenoid electrical connector. If solenoid clicks, proceed to ENGINE PERFORMANCE DIAGNOSIS. If solenoid does not click, replace fuel shut-off solenoid and repeat step 5.

### ENGINE QUITS, STALLS OR STUMBLES

1. With engine off, ensure throttle lever contacts injection pump stop with accelerator pedal fully depressed. If satisfactory, proceed to step 2. If not satisfactory, adjust accelerator linkage as required.
2. Check Energize-To-Run (ETR) solenoid (terminal located at top rear of injection pump) for dirt, corrosion and a loose or broken electrical connection. If ETR solenoid electrical connection is satisfactory, proceed to step 3 or 4. If ETR solenoid electrical connection is not satisfactory, repair as required and repeat step. Voltage must be at least 9 volts, while cranking.

3. Ensure coolant temperature is less than 122° F, then check that cold start timing advance/fast idle device has moved lever off idle stop. If not satisfactory, replace fuel injection pump. If satisfactory, proceed to GLOW PLUG CONTROL SYSTEM diagnosis.
4. Ensure coolant temperature is greater than 122° F, then check that cold start timing advance is on idle stop. If not satisfactory, replace fuel injection pump. If satisfactory, proceed to ENGINE PERFORMANCE DIAGNOSIS.

## ENGINE KNOCKS

1. Check belt driven accessories for looseness. If belt tensions are correct, proceed to step 2. If belt tensions are incorrect, repair or replace component(s) as required.
2. Ensure engine is not overheating.
3. Loosen one injector nozzle line nut at a time while engine is running. If engine knock is isolated to a specific cylinder, proceed to step 4. If engine knock is not isolated to a specific cylinder, proceed to ENGINE PERFORMANCE DIAGNOSIS.
4. Check injection nozzle fuel lines for kinks or restrictions, then the injection nozzle for proper operation. If nozzles and lines are satisfactory, proceed to ENGINE PERFORMANCE DIAGNOSIS. If nozzles and lines are not satisfactory, replace as required.

## ENGINE MISSES

1. If engine misses only when cold, proceed to GLOW PLUG CONTROL SYSTEM diagnosis. If engine misses at normal operating temperature, proceed to step 2.
2. Loosen one injector nozzle line nut at a time while running engine. If fuel flow miss is not isolated to a specific cylinder, proceed to ENGINE PERFORMANCE DIAGNOSIS. If fuel flow miss is isolated to a specific cylinder,

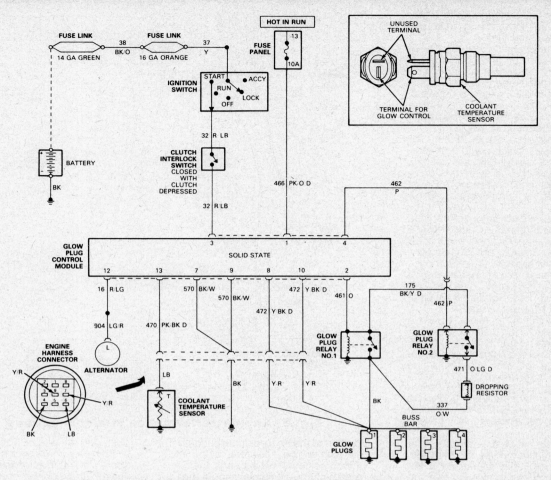

**Fig. 1  Super-Quick start glow plug control system schematic**

proceed to step 3.

3. Check injection nozzle fuel lines for kinks or restrictions, then the injection nozzle for proper operation. If nozzles and lines are satisfactory, proceed to step 4. If nozzles and lines are not satisfactory, replace as required.

4. Check crankcase pressure as follows:
   a. Install adapter tool No. 11306 and pressure test kit 019-00002 or equivalent, at the oil fill opening in the valve cover.
   b. Remove valve cover breather hose, then plug fitting on valve cover using a suitable cap.
   c. Run engine at idle and record crankcase pressure. Crankcase pressure should be a maximum of 2.96 inches of Hg. If pressure is satisfactory, problem is the result of other engine conditions. If pressure is not satisfactory, check for proper engine compression.

## BLUE/WHITE SMOKE (ENGINE AT NORMAL OPERATING TEMPERATURE)

1. Ensure engine temperature stabilizes in normal operating range. If not satisfactory, proceed to step 2. If satisfac-

tory, proceed to step 3.

2. Remove thermostat and test for proper operation. If thermostat is satisfactory, check coolant level and repeat test. If thermostat is not satisfactory, replace thermostat.

3. Check engine oil level indicator for excessive oil fill. If satisfactory, proceed to step 4. If not satisfactory, drain excess oil from oil pan. If problem still exists, proceed to step 4.

4. Check fuel return pressure as follows:
   a. Remove fuel return line at fuel injection pump.
   b. Install adapter 11301 and pressure test kit 019-00002 or equivalent.
   c. Run engine at 4000 RPM with transmission in the Neutral position, then record pressure reading. If pressure exceeds 2 psi at 4000 RPM, replace fuel return lines as required and repeat test. If pressure does not exceed 2 psi at 4000 RPM, proceed to ENGINE PERFORMANCE DIAGNOSIS.

## EXCESSIVE BLACK SMOKE

1. If black smoke occurs under light load and/or low altitude, proceed to step 2. If black smoke occurs under a heavy load, this is normal when going up

steep grades, pulling a trailer, maximum load, maximum acceleration at high altitudes or loaded with engine at low RPM.

2. Inspect exhaust system for dents or kinks which could cause restrictions. If exhaust system is satisfactory, proceed to step 3. If exhaust system is not satisfactory, repair as required and proceed to step 3.

3. Check air intake system for restrictions. If satisfactory, proceed to step 4. If not satisfactory, replace air cleaner element as required and repeat test.

4. Check injection pump timing. If timing is satisfactory, proceed to step 5. If timing is not satisfactory, adjust as required. If problem still exists, proceed to step 5.

5. Check injection nozzle fuel lines for kinks or restrictions, then the injection nozzle for proper operation. If nozzles and lines are satisfactory, replace injection pump. If nozzles and lines are not satisfactory, replace as required. If problem still exists, replace injection pump.

## ENGINE PERFORMANCE DIAGNOSIS

Refer to **Fig. 2** for proper diagnosis. Also,

ensure all tests are performed with transmission in Neutral with parking brake set, unless otherwise specified.

1. With engine operating, visually check for fuel, engine oil and coolant leakage. Ensure air cleaner is properly installed. If no leakage is detected, proceed to step 2. If leakage is detected, repair and/or replace defective component(s) as required. If problem still exists, proceed to step 2.

2. Visually inspect exhaust system for dents or kinks which could cause restrictions. If system is satisfactory, proceed to step 3. If system is damaged, repair and/or replace exhaust system and/or component(s) as required.

3. Inspect fuel supply lines, return lines and hoses for damage. Check fuel line and hose fittings for tightness. If lines, hoses and fittings are satisfactory, proceed to step 4. If lines, hoses and/or fittings are damaged, repair and/or replace damaged component(s) as required. If problem still exists, proceed to step 4.

4. Using a suitable container, obtain a fuel sample. Using cetane tester included with dynamic timing meter 078-00116 or equivalent, check cetane value of fuel. Cetane value should be a minimum of 40. If satisfactory, proceed to step 5. If not satisfactory, use different fuel supply and proceed to step 5. **Do not replace fuel pump because of a low cetane problem.**

5. With engine off, ensure throttle lever contacts injection pump stop with accelerator pedal fully depressed. If satisfactory, proceed to step 6. If not satisfactory, adjust throttle linkage as required and proceed to step 6.

6. Remove hose on air cleaner crankcase breather port, then install adapter 11308 and pressure test kit 019-00002 or equivalent. Run engine at 4000 RPM and record reading. If gauge reading is less than 1.83 inches of Hg, remove adapter and install cap on air cleaner port, then proceed to step 7. If gauge reading is greater than 1.83 inches of Hg, replace filter element and check intake system for blockage, then repeat step.

7. Install adapter 11301 and pressure test kit 019-00002 or equivalent into the fuel conditioner outlet hose. Run engine at 4000 RPM and record reading. Fuel filter outlet pressure should be a minimum of 1 psi at 4000 RPM. If satisfactory, proceed to step 9. If not satisfactory, proceed to step 8.

8. Install adapter 11302 and pressure test kit 019-00002 or equivalent into the fuel conditioner inlet hose. Run engine at 4000 RPM and record reading. Fuel supply pump outlet pressure should differ by less than 3.5 psi at 4000 RPM from pressure taken in step 7. If satisfactory, proceed to step 9. If not satisfactory, replace fuel filter and repeat test.

9. Install one end of a suitable hose on adapter 11302 and the other end in a suitable one quart fuel container. Turn

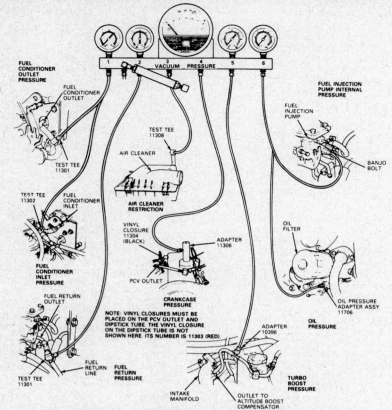

**Fig. 2   Engine performance test connections**

ignition to the Run position, but do not start the engine. Allow fuel to flow into the container for 30 seconds, then record volume. Volume should be a minimum of one pint in 30 seconds. If pressure and volume are satisfactory, proceed to step 13. If pressure is satisfactory and volume is not satisfactory, proceed to step 10. If volume is satisfactory and pressure is not satisfactory, replace fuel supply pump and repeat test. If pressure and volume are not satisfactory, proceed to step 10.

10. Disconnect fuel supply pump inlet hose and connect an auxiliary fuel supply to the inlet. Use a suitable one quart fuel container and ensure hose clamps are tight. Repeat steps 7 and 9. If pressure and volume are satisfactory, proceed to step 11. If pressure and volume are not satisfactory, replace fuel supply pump and repeat step 9.

11. Connect fuel return line removed in step 7, then install adapter 11302 and pressure test kit 019-00002 or equivalent to fuel supply pump inlet. With rear wheels off the ground and transmission in the Neutral position, run engine at 4000 RPM and record vacuum reading. Vacuum should be less than 6 inches of Hg. If vacuum is satisfactory, proceed to step 12. If vacuum is not satisfactory, replace restricted fuel lines as required and repeat step 7.

12. Disconnect fuel supply hoses from supply pump and fuel tank(s), then

plug end of hoses. Pressurize fuel system to a maximum of 15 psi and apply a solution of soapy water to all valves and connections. If bubbles are present, repair or replace component as required and repeat step 9. If bubbles are not present, check fuel tank(s) and pick up screen(s) for leaks or blockage and fuel hose ends for damage. Repair or replace as required and repeat step 9.

13. Check engine idle speed. If idle speed is satisfactory, proceed to step 14. If idle speed is not satisfactory, adjust to specifications.

14. Remove fuel return line at fuel injection pump, then install adapter 11301 and pressure test kit 019-00002 or equivalent. Run engine at 4000 RPM and record reading. Maximum fuel return pressure should not exceed 2 psi at 4000 RPM. If satisfactory, proceed to step 15. If not satisfactory, replace fuel return lines as required and repeat step.

15. Disconnect vacuum hose at fitting on base of boost compensator, then install adapter and pressure test kit 019-00002 or equivalent. Run engine at idle RPM and record reading. Constant pressure valve vacuum should be 13.8 inches of Hg, minus .84 inches Hg per 1000 feet in altitude above sea level. If vacuum reading is satisfactory, proceed to step 16. If vacuum reading is low, check vacuum pump operation. Repair or replace as required and repeat step. If vacuum reading is high, replace constant pressure valve

16. Remove banjo fitting from injection pump fuel return line, then install adapter 10356 and pressure test kit 019-00002 or equivalent. Run engine at 800 RPM and record reading, then run engine at 4400 RPM and record reading. Injection pump transfer pressure should be 27-40 psi at 800 RPM and 91-104 psi at 4400 RPM. If pressure readings are satisfactory, proceed to step 17. If pressure readings are low, replace injection pump. If problem still exists after installing new pump, proceed to step 17. If pressure readings are high, repair or replace blocked fuel return lines and repeat step.

17. Check injection pump static timing. If timing is satisfactory, proceed to step 18. If timing is not satisfactory, adjust to specifications. If performance problem still exists after adjusting timing, proceed to step 18.

18. Install adapter 10396 with pressure test kit 119-00002 or equivalent at fitting between intake and boost compensator. Road test vehicle and measure turbocharger boost pressure at wide open throttle in fourth gear from 1500-2500 RPM, then record reading. Turbocharger boost pressure should be more than 4 psi at 1500 RPM and 10 psi at 2500 RPM. If pressure is satisfactory, proceed to step 19. If pressure is not satisfactory, check boost hoses and intake system for leaks, and ensure waste gate is closed below 10 psi. Replace turbocharger if noisy. If performance problem still exists, proceed to step 19.

19. Check injection nozzle fuel lines for kinks or restrictions, then the injection nozzle for proper operation. If nozzles and lines are satisfactory, proceed to step 20. If nozzles and lines are not satisfactory, replace as required. If performance problem still exists, proceed to step 20.

20. Install adapter tool No. 11306 and pressure test kit 019-00002 or equivalent, at the oil fill opening in the valve cover. Remove valve cover breather hose, then plug fitting on valve cover using a suitable cap. Run engine at idle and record crankcase pressure. Crankcase pressure should be a maximum of 2.96 inches of Hg. If pressure is satisfactory, fuel system is satisfactory and problem is the result of other engine conditions. If pressure is not satisfactory, check for proper engine compression.

## GLOW PLUG CONTROL SYSTEM DIAGNOSIS

Refer to **Fig. 1** during system diagnosis. Also, if engine coolant temperature is above 86° F, disconnect coolant temperature sensor electrical connector during system diagnosis.

1. Turn ignition switch to the Run position, then check voltage between glow plug buss bar and engine block. Voltage should be a minimum of 10

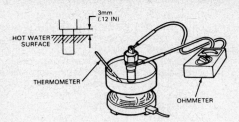

**Fig. 3 Testing coolant temperature sensor**

volts for one to six seconds after ignition is turned to the Run position. If voltage is satisfactory, proceed to step 9. If voltage is not satisfactory, proceed to step 2.

2. Check for battery voltage on battery side of glow plug relay No. 1. If battery voltage is present, proceed to step 3. If battery voltage is not present, repair circuit between battery and glow plug relay No. 1 and repeat test.

3. Connect voltmeter between Glow Plug Control Module (GPCM) pin No. 1 and ground, then turn ignition switch to the Run position. Voltage should be a minimum of 10 volts. If voltage is satisfactory, proceed to step 4. If voltage is not satisfactory, repair or replace ignition switch and/or circuit to GPCM pin No. 1 as required and repeat test.

4. Turn ignition switch to the Off position, then check for continuity of the circuit between No. 1 glow plug relay and glow plug buss bar. If continuity is present, proceed to step 5. If continuity is not present, repair circuit as required and repeat test.

5. Connect voltmeter between GPCM pin No. 2 and ground, then turn ignition switch to the Run position. Voltmeter should read a minimum of 10 volts for one to six seconds after ignition switch is turned to the Run position. If voltage is satisfactory, replace glow plug relay No. 1 and repeat test. If voltage is not satisfactory, proceed to step 6.

6. Disconnect engine coolant temperature sensor and GPCM electrical connector. Connect ohmmeter between GPCM pin No. 13 and ground. If continuity is not present, proceed to step 7. If continuity is present, repair short to ground in circuit to GPCM pin No. 13.

7. Connect GPCM electrical connector and leave engine coolant temperature sensor disconnected. Connect voltmeter between GPCM pin No. 2 and ground, then turn ignition switch to the Run position. Voltmeter should read a minimum of 10 volts for one to six seconds after ignition switch is turned to the Run position. If voltage is satisfactory, proceed to step 8. If voltage is not satisfactory, replace GPCM and repeat test.

8. Remove engine coolant temperature sensor from engine and place sensor in a container of water as shown in **Fig. 3**. Bring water to a temperature

of 68° F, then check resistance of sensor. If resistance is between 2800-3800 ohms, repair circuit between GPCM pin No. 13 and coolant temperature sensor and repeat test. If resistance is not between 2800-3800 ohms, replace sensor and repeat test.

9. Connect voltmeter between glow plug buss bar and ground, then turn ignition switch to Run position and note voltage. Voltage should be 5-8 volts for six seconds after No. 1 glow plug relay turns off. If voltage is satisfactory, proceed to step 14. If voltage is not satisfactory, proceed to step 10.

10. Check for battery voltage on circuit at glow plug relay No. 2. If battery voltage is present, proceed to step 11. If battery voltage is not present, repair circuit between battery and glow plug relay No. 2 and repeat test.

11. Check continuity of circuit between glow plug relay No. 2 and glow buss bar with ignition switch in the Off position. If continuity is present, proceed to step 13. If continuity is not present, proceed to step 12.

12. Disconnect dropping resistor electrical connector, then check continuity of resistor. If continuity is present, repair circuit as required. If continuity is not present, replace dropping resistor and repeat test. **Dropping resistor becomes extremely hot during operation of the glow plug system.**

13. Connect voltmeter between GPCM pin No. 4 and ground, then crank engine and note voltage. If voltmeter indicates 10 volts or more for seven or more seconds after ignition is cranked, replace glow plug relay No. 2 and repeat step 9. If voltmeter does not indicate 10 volts or more for seven or more seconds after ignition is cranked, replace GPCM and repeat test.

14. Connect voltmeter between GPCM pin No. 4 and ground, then crank engine and note voltage. If voltmeter indicates 9 volts or more while cranking engine, proceed to step 16. If voltmeter does not indicate 9 volts or more while cranking engine, proceed to step 15.

15. Connect voltmeter between GPCM pin No. 3 and ground, then crank engine and note voltage. If voltmeter indicates 9 volts or more while cranking engine, replace GPCM and repeat test. If voltmeter does not indicate 9 volts or more while cranking engine, repair or replace ignition switch and/or wiring to GPCM pin No. 3 and repeat test.

16. Disconnect glow plug buss bar, then remove glow plugs from engine and inspect for breakage and/or cracks. If glow plugs are satisfactory, proceed to step 17. If glow plugs are not satisfactory, check engine compression and proceed to step 17.

17. Measure resistance of each glow plug with plugs at a temperature of approximately 68°F, **Fig. 4**. Resistance should be approximately .23 ohms or less. If resistance is satisfactory, pro-

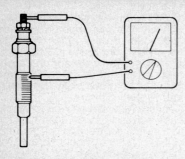

**Fig. 4  Checking glow plug resistance**

ceed to step 18. If resistance is not satisfactory, replace glow plugs as required, then install buss bar and repeat test.

18. Disconnect engine harness and GPCM electrical connectors. Check continuity between GPCM pin No. 7 and engine harness connector pin No. 4 (harness side), then check continuity between GPCM pin No. 9 and engine harness connector pin No. 4 (harness side). If continuity is present, leave engine harness connector disconnected and proceed to step 19. If continuity is not present, repair wiring between GPCM pin No. 7 and/or pin No. 9 and engine harness connector pin No. 4 and repeat test.

19. Connect ohmmeter between engine harness connect pin No. 4 (engine side) and ground. If continuity is present, connect engine harness connector and proceed to step 20. If continuity is not present, repair wiring between engine harness connector pin No. 4 and ground and repeat test.

20. Turn ignition to the Start position. If engine starts, turn ignition switch Off and proceed to step 21. If engine does not start, problem is not glow plug system. Connect coolant temperature sensor and perform Engine Performance Diagnosis."

21. Connect voltmeter between glow plug buss bar and ground, then start engine and note voltage. Voltage should be 5-8 volts for 6-30 seconds after engine starts. If voltage is satisfactory, glow plug system is satisfactory and problem is elsewhere in vehicle. If voltage is not present after engine starts, turn engine Off and proceed to step 22. If voltage is 5-8 volts for 30 seconds or more after engine starts, turn engine Off and proceed to step 24.

22. Connect voltmeter between GPCM pin No. 12 and ground, then start engine and note voltage. If voltage is approximately 14 volts, turn ignition Off and proceed to step 23. If voltage is 12 volts or less, repair wiring between GPCM pin No. 12 and alternator and repeat test.

23. Connect voltmeter between GPCM pin No. 4 and ground, then start engine. If voltmeter indicates 10 volts or more for 6-30 seconds after engine starts, steps 9 through 13 were performed incorrectly. Repeat steps 9

through 13. If voltmeter does not indicate 10 volts or more for 6-30 seconds after engine starts, replace GPCM and repeat test.

24. Connect voltmeter between glow plug buss bar and engine block. Connect coolant temperature sensor, then start engine. Note voltage while disconnecting coolant temperature sensor electrical connector. Voltage should be 5-8 volts with sensor connected and no voltage with sensor disconnected. If voltage is satisfactory, glow plug system is satisfactory and problem is elsewhere in vehicle. If voltage is not satisfactory, repeat step 21.

## ENGINE REPLACE

1. Mark locations of hood hinges, then remove hood.
2. Disconnect battery ground cables from both battery assemblies.
3. Disconnect battery ground cables from engine.
4. Drain coolant system.
5. Disconnect crankcase breather hose from rocker cover.
6. Disconnect intake hose between air cleaner and turbocharger assembly. Cap turbocharger inlet using cap set T85T-9395-A or equivalent.
7. Remove A/C compressor and position aside. Do not disconnect refrigerant lines from compressor.
8. Disconnect heater hoses from inlet and outlet fittings on heater core.
9. Remove cooling fan assembly.
10. Disconnect radiator hoses, then remove radiator assembly.
11. Disconnect electrical connector from fuel conditioner.
12. Disconnect fuel supply line from fuel conditioner and fuel return line from injection pump.
13. Mark, then disconnect all necessary vacuum lines and electrical connectors from engine assembly.
14. Disconnect coolant overflow hose from filler neck.
15. Disconnect throttle cable and speed control cable, if equipped, from injection pump.
16. Disconnect starter motor cables, then remove starter motor assembly.
17. Using a suitable jack, raise vehicle slightly and remove right hand wheel, tire and inner fender.
18. Disconnect oil pressure switch electrical connector.
19. Disconnect cooler lines from oil filter adapter.
20. Raise and support vehicle.
21. Remove nut attaching engine insulators to engine support brackets.
22. Disconnect muffler inlet pipe from turbocharger exhaust outlet pipe.
23. Disconnect and cap power steering pump lines from pump assembly.
24. Disconnect clutch servo hydraulic line (red line) from clutch housing and position aside.
25. Remove transmission attaching bolts except the top two bolts.
26. Lower vehicle.

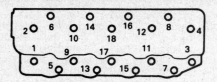

**Fig. 5  Cylinder head bolt loosening sequence**

27. Attach suitable engine lifting equipment onto engine lifting eyes.
28. Remove top two transmission attaching bolts.
29. Carefully lift engine from vehicle.
30. Reverse procedure to install.

## EXHAUST MANIFOLD REPLACE

1. Disconnect battery ground cables from both battery assemblies.
2. Remove support brace from A/C compressor bracket and inlet fitting assembly.
3. Remove A/C compressor from mounting bracket and position aside.
4. Remove inlet fitting from intake manifold.
5. Remove air inlet tube from air cleaner to turbocharger inlet.
6. Remove wastegate actuator from turbocharger and mounting bracket.
7. Raise and support vehicle, then disconnect muffler inlet pipe from turbocharger exhaust fitting.
8. Lower vehicle.
9. Disconnect turbocharger oil feed line from cylinder head and turbocharger center housing.
10. Remove nuts attaching exhaust manifold to cylinder head, then the exhaust manifold and turbocharger as an assembly.
11. Remove turbocharger from exhaust manifold, if necessary.
12. Reverse procedure to install.

## INTAKE MANIFOLD REPLACE

1. Disconnect battery ground cables, then remove support braces from A/C compressor bracket, inlet fitting and intake manifold.
2. Remove A/C compressor from mounting bracket and position compressor aside. Do not disconnect lines from compressor.
3. Remove inlet fitting from manifold, then disconnect oil feed line from cylinder head and turbocharger center housing and remove feed line clamp bolt.
4. Loosen turbocharger heat shield attaching bolts, then remove top bolt and swing shield aside.
5. Remove wastegate actuator from turbocharger and mounting bracket, then position mounting bracket aside.
6. Remove manifold attaching nuts and bolts, then the intake manifold.
7. Reverse procedure to install.

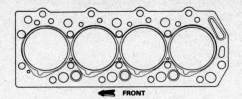

**Fig. 6   Positioning cylinder head gasket**

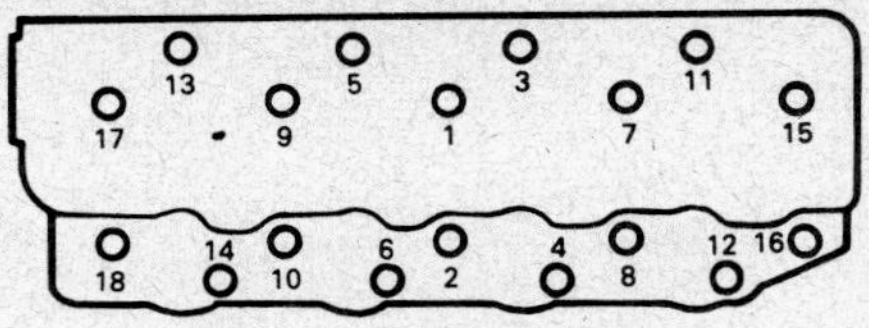

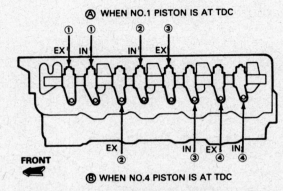

**Fig. 7   Cylinder head bolt tightening sequence**

10. Remove inlet hose between air cleaner and turbocharger inlet.
11. Raise and support vehicle, then disconnect muffler inlet pipe from turbocharger exhaust fitting. Lower vehicle.
12. Remove fuel conditioner and bracket assembly.
13. Disconnect, then remove fuel lines between injection pump and nozzles. Cap all open lines and fittings.
14. Disconnect heater hose fitting from rear left hand side of cylinder head.
15. Remove A/C compressor and mounting bracket, then position aside.
16. Disconnect electrical leads from No. 2 and 3 glow plugs.
17. Disconnect coolant temperature switch electrical connector.
18. Remove intake and exhaust manifolds.
19. Remove rocker cover.
20. Loosen cylinder head bolts in sequence shown in **Fig. 5**.
21. Remove cylinder head and gasket.
22. Reverse procedure to install. During installation of cylinder head, note the following:
    a. Clean gasket mating surface on cylinder head and block.
    b. Position new gasket onto block as shown in **Fig. 6**.
    c. Position cylinder head onto engine block and install attaching bolts.
    d. Torque bolts in two steps.
    e. First, torque bolts in sequence shown in **Fig. 7** to 38-42 ft. lbs.
    f. Second, torque bolts in sequence shown to 76-83 ft. lbs.

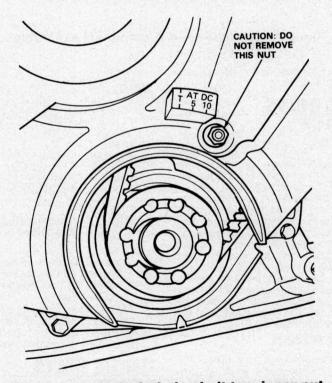

**Fig. 8   Valve adjustment sequence**

**Fig. 9   Silent shaft timing belt tensioner nut**

## VALVE ARRANGEMENT
### FRONT TO REAR

1985-88 . . . . . . . . . . . . . . . . . E-I-E-I-E-I

## VALVE CLEARANCE SPECIFICATIONS

Hot valve clearances should measure .010 inch at intake and exhaust valves.

## VALVES
### ADJUST

1. Start and operate engine until normal operating temperature is reached.
2. Remove rocker cover.
3. Rotate crankshaft until No. 1 piston is at TDC of compression stroke.
4. Using a suitable feeler gauge, check valve clearance in sequence shown in **Fig. 8**.
5. Valve clearance should be as specified.
6. To adjust valve clearance(s), proceed as follows:
   a. Loosen adjusting screw locknut.
   b. Turn adjusting screw clockwise to reduce clearance or counterclockwise to increase valve clearance.
   c. Tighten locknut while holding adjusting screw in position, then recheck valve clearance.
7. Rotate crankshaft 360° in direction of normal engine rotation until No. 4 pis-

## CYLINDER HEAD
### REPLACE

1. Mark location of hood hinges, then remove hood.
2. Disconnect battery ground cables from both battery assemblies.
3. Drain cooling system.
4. Disconnect breather hose from rocker cover.
5. Remove heater hose clamp, then position heater hose aside.
6. Remove cooling fan and shroud assembly.
7. Remove accessory drive belts.
8. Remove upper front timing belt cover.
9. Loosen, then remove camshaft/injection pump timing belt from camshaft sprocket.

ton is at TDC of compression stroke and repeat steps 4 through 6.

## FRONT UPPER TIMING BELT COVER
### REPLACE

1. Disconnect battery ground cables from both battery assemblies.
2. Remove accessory drive belts.
3. Remove front upper timing belt cover attaching bolts.
4. Remove cover and gasket from engine.
5. Reverse procedure to install.

## FRONT LOWER TIMING BELT COVER
### REPLACE

1. Disconnect battery ground cables from both battery assemblies.
2. Remove cooling fan and fan shroud.
3. Remove accessory drive belts.
4. Remove four bolts attaching water pump pulley to water pump, then the pulley.
5. Remove crankshaft pulley.
6. Remove five bolts attaching timing cover to engine. **Do not remove the nut shown in Fig. 9. This nut is for the silent shaft timing belt tensioner. Loosening this nut can alter belt tension.**
7. Remove front lower timing belt cover from engine.
8. Reverse procedure to install.

## CAMSHAFT
### REPLACE

1. Disconnect battery ground cables from both battery assemblies.
2. Remove rocker cover attaching bolts, then the rocker cover assembly from engine.
3. Remove upper front timing belt cover as described previously.
4. Rotate crankshaft until No. 1 piston is at TDC of compression stroke.
5. Loosen camshaft/injection pump drive belt tensioner and remove timing belt from camshaft sprocket.
6. Remove camshaft sprocket bolt, then the camshaft sprocket.
7. Remove rocker shaft to cylinder head attaching bolts, one turn at a time starting from front of engine and working toward the rear.
8. Remove camshaft bearing caps and camshaft assembly from engine, **Fig. 10**.
9. Remove camshaft from engine.
10. Reverse procedure to install. During installation of camshaft, note the following:
    a. Ensure bearing caps are installed in their original positions.
    b. Coat sealing lip of camshaft seal with clean engine oil. Install seal using camshaft oil seal replacer T85T-6250-A or equivalent. Ensure seal installer is positioned

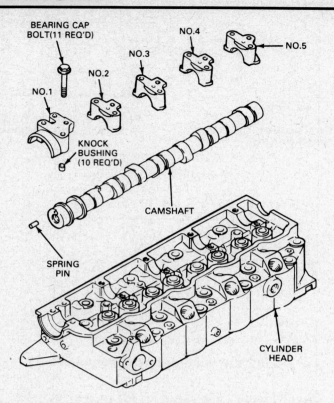

**Fig. 10   Cylinder head & camshaft assembly**

with hole over spring pin on camshaft, **Fig. 11.**

## TIMING BELTS
### REPLACE
#### REMOVAL

1. Disconnect battery ground cables, then remove engine cooling fan, fan shroud and accessory drive belts.
2. Rotate crankshaft in normal direction of rotation until No. 1 piston is at TDC of compression stroke, then remove crankshaft pulley using suitable tool.
3. Remove upper and lower timing belt covers, then mark direction of rotation on belt(s) to be removed.
4. Loosen belt tensioners, then remove timing belt(s) as required. **If injection pump/camshaft belt requires replacement, the silent shaft belt will have to be removed first.**

#### INSTALLATION

1. Align crankshaft, left hand silent shaft and right hand silent shaft sprocket timing marks with marks shown in **Fig. 12**, then pry on tensioner spring to reduce load on tensioner and install silent shaft belt.
2. Align camshaft and injection pump sprocket timing marks with marks shown, **Fig. 12**, then install injection pump/camshaft belt as follows:
    a. Release tension on tensioner spring with suitable tool, then rotate tensioner toward water pump and tighten upper bolt.
    b. Install and position timing belt onto

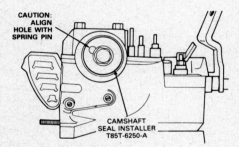

**Fig. 11   Positioning seal installer**

sprockets, then while maintaining tension on belt, loosen upper tensioner bolt to position tensioner against belt.
3. Adjust timing belt(s) as outlined under "Timing Belts, Adjust" procedure.
4. Reverse steps 1 through 3 of removal procedure to complete installation.

## TIMING BELTS
### ADJUST
#### INJECTION PUMP/CAMSHAFT

1. Remove timing belt upper cover as described previously.
2. Rotate engine until No. 1 piston is at TDC of compression stroke.
3. Check that crankshaft pulley, injection pump sprocket and camshaft sprocket are aligned properly with their timing marks, **Fig. 13**.

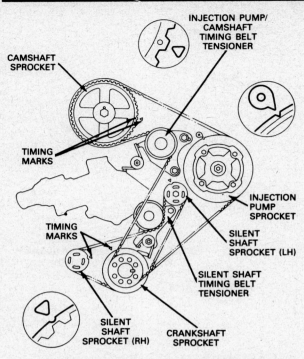

Fig. 12 Aligning sprocket timing marks

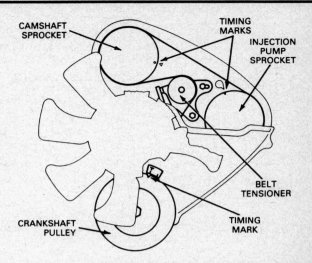

Fig. 13 Aligning injection pump sprocket & camshaft sprocket timing marks

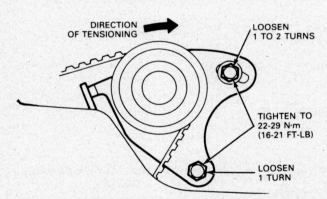
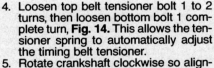

Fig. 14 Loosening top & bottom belt tensioner bolts

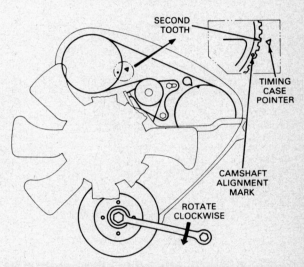

Fig. 15 Aligning pointer on timing cover with second tooth from alignment mark on camshaft sprocket

4. Loosen top belt tensioner bolt 1 to 2 turns, then loosen bottom bolt 1 complete turn, **Fig. 14**. This allows the tensioner spring to automatically adjust the timing belt tensioner.
5. Rotate crankshaft clockwise so alignment pointer on timing cover aligns with the second tooth from alignment mark on camshaft sprocket, **Fig. 15**. **Rotate crankshaft smoothly by the specified amount (two camshaft sprocket teeth). Failure to do so will result in an incorrect belt tension and possible engine damage.**
6. Tighten top belt tensioner bolt to 16-21 ft. lbs., then tighten bottom bolt also to 16-21 ft. lbs. **Tighten the top bolt first. Tightening the bottom bolt first can cause tensioner to rotate and over-tension the timing belt.**
7. Rotate crankshaft counterclockwise until timing marks are aligned, **Fig. 16**. Push belt downward halfway between

injection pump sprocket and camshaft sprocket, then check deflection. If belt is properly tensioned, belt should deflect .16-.20 inches.

## SILENT SHAFT

1. Rotate crankshaft until No. 1 piston is at TDC of compression stroke.
2. Remove access cover for top belt tensioner bolt by inserting a suitable screwdriver in slot shown in **Fig. 17** and prying outward.
3. Loosen top belt tensioner mounting bolt 1 complete turn. Then loosen bottom bolt 1 to 2 turns, **Fig. 18**. This allows tensioner spring to automatically adjust belt tension.
4. Tighten bottom tensioner bolt to 16-21 ft. lbs., then tighten top bolt to 15-19 ft. lbs. **Tighten the bottom bolt first. Tightening the top bolt first can cause the tensioner to rotate and over-tighten the timing belt.**

5. Install access cover for top tensioner bolt by sliding downward along the two guide lines embossed on the front lower cover, **Fig. 19**.

## INJECTION NOZZLES
### REPLACE

1. Disconnect battery ground cables from both battery assemblies.
2. Mark, disconnect and cap injection lines from injection nozzles and injection pump.
3. Disconnect, then remove fuel return pipe and gasket.
4. Remove injection nozzles from engine.
5. Reverse procedure to install.

## INJECTION PUMP
### REPLACE

1. Disconnect battery ground cables

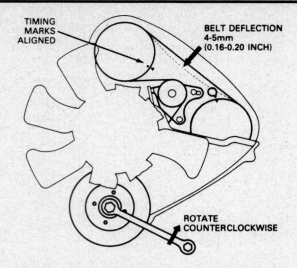

Fig. 16   Checking belt deflection

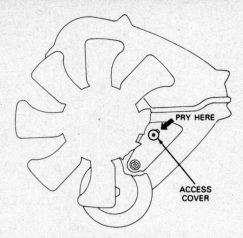

Fig. 17   Top belt tensioner bolt access cover

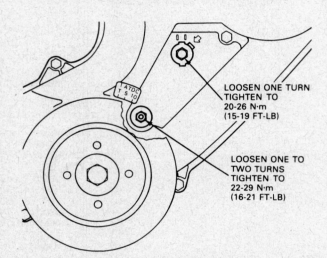

Fig. 18   Adjusting silent shaft belt tensioner

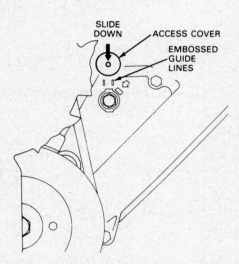

Fig. 19   Installing access cover

from both battery assemblies.
2. Remove radiator fan and shroud assembly.
3. Loosen, then remove accessory drive belts.
4. Rotate crankshaft in direction of normal engine rotation until No. 1 piston is at TDC of compression stroke.
5. Remove upper front timing cover as described previously.
6. Loosen, then remove timing belt from injection pump sprocket as described previously.
7. Remove sprocket to injection pump attaching nut.
8. Using sprocket remover tool No. T77F-4220-B1 or equivalent, remove injection pump sprocket.
9. Disconnect throttle and speed control cables, if equipped.
10. Disconnect coolant hoses from injection pump wax element.
11. Disconnect hoses from boost compensator and A/C throttle kicker.
12. Disconnect and cap fuel return line at return pipe on injection pump.
13. Disconnect chassis mounted fuel re-

turn line from injection pump assembly.
14. Disconnect and cap fuel supply line from fuel conditioner.
15. Disconnect, then remove fuel lines from injection pump and fuel nozzles. Cap all open lines and fittings.
16. Remove 2 nuts attaching injection pump to rear front case. Remove 2 injection pump bracket-to-engine bracket bolts and 2 engine bracket-to-engine block bolts, **Fig. 20.** Remove injection pump from engine assembly.
17. Reverse procedure to install.

## INJECTION PUMP TIMING
### ADJUST

1. Remove top timing belt cover.
2. Rotate engine until No. 1 piston is at TDC on compression stroke. Refer to **Fig. 21** to ensure timing marks are in proper position.

3. If engine temperature is below 122° F, bypass cold start mechanism as follows:
   a. Insert screwdriver as shown in **Fig. 22** and rotate fast idle lever.
   b. Insert a suitable spacer or wrench at least .27 inch thick between cold start advance lever and cold start device.
4. Loosen the two mounting bolts and nuts attaching injection pump to mounting bracket and front cover.
5. To prevent delivery valve holders from turning with the fuel nuts, loosen, but do not remove the nuts attaching fuel lines to injection pump using a suitable wrench.
6. Remove timing plug bolt from center of fuel injection pump hydraulic head.
7. Install timing adapter tool No. 014-00303 or equivalent into the port in hydraulic head, then mount suitable dial indicator in timing adapter with a minimum preload of .10 inch, **Fig. 23**.
8. Rotate crankshaft about 30° counterclockwise, then zero dial indicator.
9. Rotate crankshaft clockwise to 5°

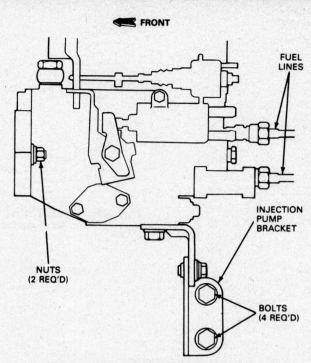

Fig. 20   Removing injection pump

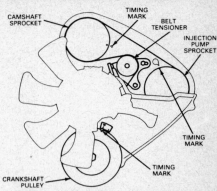

Fig. 21   Timing mark alignment

rod should be numbered to correspond with the new cylinder.

## PISTONS, PINS & RINGS

Pistons and piston rings are available in standard size and oversizes of .010, .020, .030 and .040 inch.

During installation of piston rings, position ring end gaps approximately $90^\circ$ apart from each other as shown in **Fig. 25.**

## MAIN & ROD BEARINGS

Main and rod bearings are available in standard size and undersizes of .010, .020 and .030 inch.

## FRONT OIL SEAL
### REPLACE

1. Disconnect battery ground cables from both battery assemblies.
2. Remove fan and fan shroud.
3. Remove accessory drive belts.
4. Remove crankshaft pulley, upper and lower timing belt covers and timing belts.
5. Remove crankshaft sprockets and timing plate.
6. Using a suitable punch, carefully punch a small hole in metal portion of seal. Insert oil seal remover tool No. T77L-9533-B or equivalent, then remove seal.
7. Reverse procedure to install. During installation of seal, use front seal replacer tool No. T85T-6019-A or equivalent to properly install seal.

## REAR OIL SEAL
### REPLACE

1. Disconnect battery ground cables from both battery assemblies.
2. Raise and support vehicle.
3. Remove transmission from vehicle.
4. Remove clutch assembly.
5. Remove flywheel.
6. Drain oil from engine crankcase.
7. Loosen oil pan attaching bolts.
8. Remove 2 oil pan attaching bolts from rear seal retainer.
9. Remove five bolts attaching rear seal retainer to engine block.
10. Remove retainer and gasket.
11. Remove oil separator from rear seal

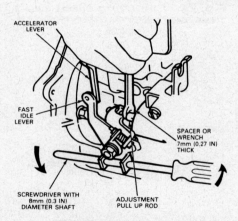

Fig. 22   Bypassing cold start device

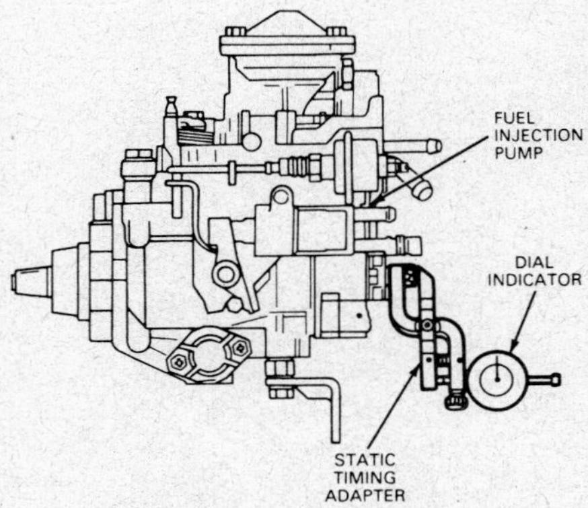

Fig. 23   Installing timing adapter & dial indicator

ATDC and check that dial indicator indicates .0383-.0405 inch.
10. If timing is not as specified in step 9, rotate injection pump body until dial indicator indicates specification. Rotate pump clockwise if reading is more than specification or counterclockwise if less than specification.
11. Torque injection pump mounting nuts to 11-15 ft. lbs. and mounting bolts to 15-19 ft. lbs. After tightening mounting nuts and bolts, repeat steps 8 and 9 to ensure injection timing has not changed.
12. Torque fuel line nuts at injection pump to 17-26 ft. lbs.
13. Install injection timing plug bolt and gasket, then torque to 10-14 ft. lbs.
14. Install upper timing belt cover, then run engine and check for fuel leaks at the injection pump.

## PISTON & ROD
### ASSEMBLE

During removal of piston and rod assemblies, mark cylinder number on connecting rod and bearing cap to facilitate installation in their original positions. If oversize pistons are required, they must be installed in sets of four. Connecting rods have the letter "D" cast into them, **Fig. 24.** Pistons should be installed with the arrow on the top of the piston and the "D" on the connecting rod toward the front of the engine. Numbers marked on the connecting rod and bearing caps during disassembly, must be on the same side when installed into their cylinder bores. If a connecting rod is ever transposed from one block or cylinder to another, new bearings should be fitted and the connecting

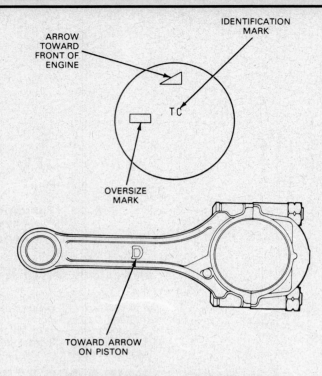

Fig. 24   Piston & rod assembly

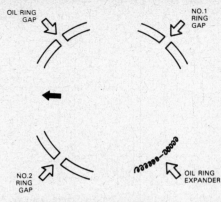

Fig. 25   Positioning piston ring end gaps

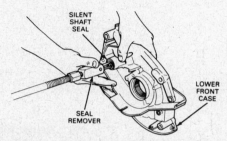

Fig. 27   Removing silent shaft reverse rotation drive gear oil seal

retainer, then remove seal from retainer using suitable drift.

12. Reverse procedure to install. During installation of seal, note the following:
   a. Position seal retainer facing downward on a suitable press. Ensure lip on seal retainer is positioned on press plate with flange over the edge.
   b. Lubricate oil seal with clean engine oil and press seal into retainer (from back side of retainer) using rear seal replacer tool No. T85T-6701-A or equivalent.
   c. During installation of oil separator, ensure oil separator is installed into seal retainer with drain hole at bottom.

## WATER PUMP
### REPLACE

1. Disconnect battery ground cables from both battery assemblies.
2. Remove cooling fan and shroud.
3. Loosen A/C compressor and power steering belt tensioner, then remove belt.
4. Remove belt tensioner.
5. Remove bolts attaching pulley to water pump, then the pulley.
6. Remove A/C compressor support bracket.
7. Drain cooling system.
8. Disconnect lower radiator hose from thermostat housing adapter.
9. Remove thermostat housing and thermostat.
10. Remove upper and lower front timing belt covers.
11. Remove water pump attaching bolts,

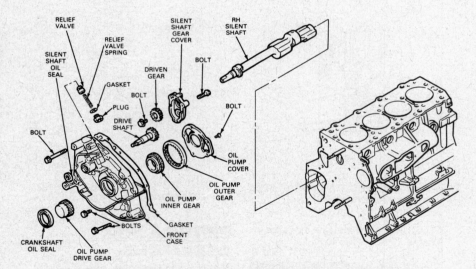

Fig. 26   Righthand silent shaft & oil pump assembly

then the water pump from engine block.

12. Reverse procedure to install.

## OIL PAN
### REPLACE

1. Disconnect battery ground cables from both battery assemblies.
2. Remove engine oil dipstick.
3. Remove cooling fan and fan shroud.
4. Drain cooling system and remove radiator.
5. Remove alternator drive belt.
6. Remove bolts attaching A/C condenser, then position condenser upward and away from radiator support.
7. Raise and support vehicle, then disconnect oil level switch wire, if applicable.
8. Drain engine oil from crankcase.
9. Remove crossmember.
10. Remove bolts attaching stabilizer bar brackets to frame, then lower stabilizer bar assembly.
11. Disconnect power steering lines from

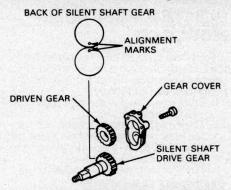

**Fig. 28 Aligning silent shaft reverse rotation gear timing marks**

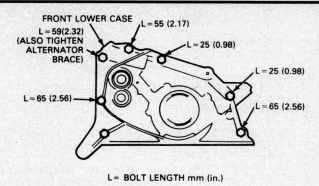

L = BOLT LENGTH mm (in.)

**Fig. 29 Installing front cover bolts**

**Fig. 30 Aligning D flat on sprocket with D flat on shaft**

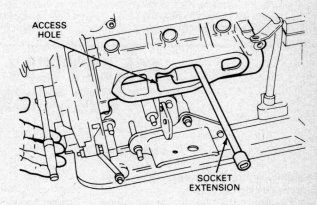

**Fig. 31 Preventing silent shaft from turning**

power steering pump.
12. Remove clamp securing power steering line to crossmember, then position line aside.
13. Remove nuts attaching engine mounts to support brackets.
14. Position a suitable jack under transmission housing and raise engine assembly. Install wooden wedges between engine mounts and crossmember assemblies.
15. Loosen, then remove oil pan attaching bolts and allow oil pan to rest on crossmember.
16. Remove 2 bolts and 1 nut securing pickup tube to engine and lower tube into oil pan.
17. Rotate crankshaft until crankshaft throws are parallel to bottom of engine, providing clearance to remove oil pan assembly.
18. Remove oil pan through the front by first raising pan up between engine and radiator support, then bring pan out through the bottom.
19. Reverse procedure to install. Torque oil pan attaching bolts to 4.5-5.5 ft. lbs.

## RIGHTHAND SILENT SHAFT & OIL PUMP REPLACE

1. Disconnect battery ground cables

from both battery assemblies.
2. Remove cooling fan and shroud assembly.
3. Remove water pump pulley, crankshaft pulley, upper and lower timing belt covers, timing belts and crankshaft sprocket.
4. Loosen oil pan attaching bolts, then remove 6 front oil pan to front case bolts.
5. Remove pipe plug from right hand side of engine block. Insert a suitable screwdriver into hole to prevent right hand silent shaft from rotating.
6. Remove nut attaching silent shaft sprocket to drive gear, then the sprocket.
7. Remove bolts attaching front case to engine block, then the front case, **Fig. 26.**
8. Remove silent shaft reverse gear cover, silent shaft and gears from engine block. Remove oil pump cover.
9. Place alignment marks on oil pump gears, then remove pump gears. Do not use a sharp tool to place alignment marks on oil pump drive, inner or outer gears.
10. Using tool No. T58L-101-B or equivalent, remove silent shaft reverse rotation drive gear oil seal from lower front case assembly, **Fig. 27.**
11. Reverse procedure to install and note the following:
 a. Using a 21 mm socket and ham-

mer, install silent shaft oil seal into lower front case assembly.
 b. Install seal protector tool No. T85T-6150-A or equivalent, onto drive gear before installation.
 c. Install silent shaft reverse rotation gears with marks properly aligned as shown in **Fig. 28.**
 d. During installation of oil pump, ensure marks placed on pump gears during removal are correctly aligned.
 e. During installation of front cover, ensure correct length bolts are installed in their original locations as shown in **Fig. 29.**
 f. During installation of silent shaft sprocket, ensure "D" flat on silent shaft sprocket aligns with "D" flat on shaft, **Fig. 30.**

## UPPER FRONT CASE COVER & LEFTHAND SILENT SHAFT REPLACE

1. Disconnect battery ground cables from both battery assemblies.
2. Remove cooling fan and shroud assembly.
3. Remove accessory drive belts.
4. Remove alternator and bracket, then position aside.

5. Remove water pump and crankshaft pulley.
6. Remove upper and lower timing belt covers, timing belts and injection pump.
7. Remove access plate on left hand side of engine, then insert a suitable socket extension tool into hole to prevent left hand silent shaft from rotating, **Fig. 31.**
8. Remove bolt attaching sprocket to silent shaft, then the sprocket.
9. Remove bolts attaching front case to engine block, then the front case.
10. Remove silent shaft and silent shaft seal.
11. Reverse procedure to install and note the following:
   a. During installation of upper front cover, ensure correct length bolts are installed in their original locations as shown in **Fig. 32.**
   b. During installation of silent shaft,

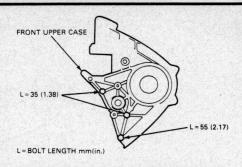

FRONT UPPER CASE
L = 35 (1.38)
L = 55 (2.17)
L = BOLT LENGTH mm(in.)

**Fig. 32  Installing correct length bolts into upper front cover**

ensure "D" flat on silent shaft sprocket aligns with "D" flat in shaft, **Fig. 30.**

## ELECTRIC FUEL PUMP
### REPLACE

Fuel from the fuel tank is delivered into the fuel lines through a frame rail mounted electric vane-type pump. To replace the pump, proceed as follows:
1. Disconnect inlet and outlet lines from pump assembly.
2. Disconnect pump electrical connector, remove pump bracket to frame rail attaching bolts, then the pump and bracket as an assembly.
3. Reverse procedure to install.

## TURBOCHARGER
### REPLACE

The turbocharger and exhaust manifold are removed from the vehicle as an assembly. Refer to "Exhaust Manifold, Replace" for procedure.

# CLUTCH & MANUAL TRANSMISSION
## INDEX

## HYDRAULIC CLUTCH

The hydraulic clutch control system consists of a fluid reservoir, a master cylinder, a slave cylinder and connective tubing. The clutch master cylinder converts mechanical clutch pedal movement into hydraulic fluid movement. The slave cylinder converts hydraulic fluid movement to mechanical movement to activate the clutch release lever. The hydraulic clutch system locates the clutch pedal and provides automatic clutch adjustment. Adjustment of clutch pedal position or clutch linkage is not required.

## BLEEDING HYDRAULIC SYSTEM

On vehicles equipped with quick-connect clutch tube, the manufacturer recommends replacing the tube whenever hydraulic system service is necessary, because the quick-connect feature tends to trap air in the system and prevents complete bleeding of the system. The replacement tube does not include the quick-connect feature. To bleed system, proceed as follows:
1. Clean area around fluid reservoir cap, remove cap, then fill reservoir with suitable brake fluid.
2. Loosen bleed screw on slave cylinder and wait until a steady stream of fluid is expelled, then tighten screw.

3. Depress clutch pedal to floor, wait 1-2 seconds, then release pedal as rapidly as possible. Repeat approximately 10 times.
4. Check fluid level in reservoir and fill as required.
5. Repeat steps 3 and 4, then reinstall reservoir cap.
6. Hold clutch pedal to floor, crack open bleed screw to allow any additional air to escape, then close screw and release clutch pedal. Check fluid level and adjust as necessary.
7. Start engine, then depress clutch pedal and shift transmission into Reverse gear. If gear clash occurs, repeat steps 3 through 6.

## CLUTCH
### REPLACE
#### 1983-84

1. Disconnect hydraulic clutch system master cylinder from clutch pedal.
2. Raise and support vehicle, then remove dust cover from clutch housing and disconnect hydraulic clutch linkage from housing and release lever. Remove starter.
3. Remove clutch housing to engine block bolts, noting direction of bolt installation, then mark alignment of driveshaft and companion flange and remove driveshaft.
4. Remove nuts which attach transmission and insulator to 2 crossmember

support, **Fig. 1**, then raise transmission with suitable jack and remove 2 crossmember support. Lower transmission and clutch housing.
5. Remove release lever, and hub and bearing, then mark assembled position of pressure plate and cover to flywheel.
6. Loosen pressure plate and cover attaching bolts evenly until pressure plate springs are expanded, then remove bolts.
7. Remove pressure plate and cover assembly and clutch disc from flywheel.
8. Position clutch disc on flywheel so that tool No. D79T-7550-A or equivalent can enter clutch pilot bearing and align disc.
9. Align pressure plate and cover assembly to flywheel and position pressure plate and cover assembly on flywheel, aligning pressure plate and disc, then install assembly to flywheel retaining bolts. Torque bolts to 15-24 ft. lbs. and remove tool.
10. Position clutch release bearing and bearing hub on release lever and install release lever on release lever seat in flywheel housing, then coat release lever fingers and lever pivot ball with suitable lubricant and fill annular groove of release bearing hub with grease.
11. Raise transmission and clutch housing into position and install 2 crossmember support to frame, then install connecting nuts, bolts and

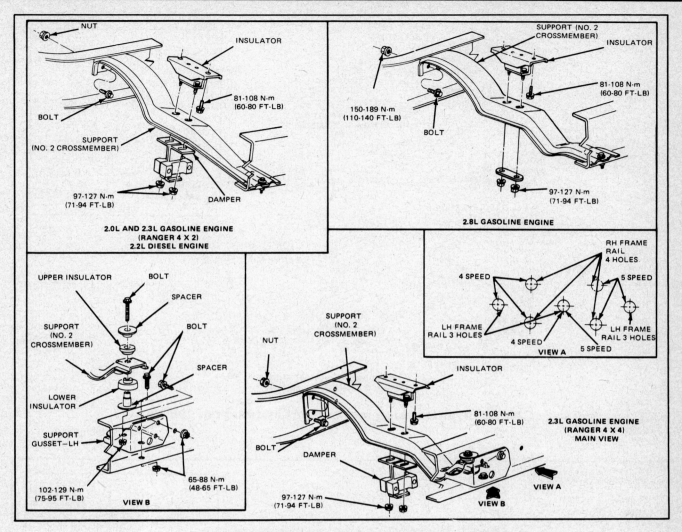

**Fig. 1   Transmission rear support installation. 1983-84**

washers, **Fig. 1.**

12. Lower transmission and insulator into support, then install nuts and torque to 71-94 ft. lbs. Remove transmission jack.
13. Install driveshaft, aligning marks on driveshaft and companion flange, and torque bolts to 70-95 ft. lbs.
14. Install housing to engine block bolts in same direction as removed and torque to 28-38 ft. lbs.
15. Install hydraulic clutch linkage, on housing in position with release lever, dust shield, and starter, then lower vehicle and check clutch for proper operation.

## 1985-89

1. Disconnect clutch hydraulic system master cylinder from clutch pedal and remove.
2. Raise and support vehicle.
3. Remove starter motor from engine.
4. Remove hydraulic hose to slave cylinder retaining clip, then disconnect hose from slave cylinder. Clean area around hose and slave cylinder to prevent fluid contamination.

5. On 1989 models, disconnect the hydraulic coupling at transmission with coupling disconnect tool No. T88T-70522-A or equivalent by sliding the white plastic sleeve toward slave cylinder and applying a slight tug on tube.
6. On all models, remove clutch housing to engine block attaching bolts. Note direction in which the bolts are installed.
7. Mark driveshaft and companion flange for installation, then remove driveshaft.
8. Remove nuts attaching transmission and insulator to No. 2 crossmember support, **Figs. 2 and 3.**
9. Raise transmission slightly, then remove No. 2 crossmember support.
10. Lower transmission and clutch housing.
11. Mark assembled position of pressure plate and cover to the flywheel for installation.
12. Loosen pressure plate and cover attaching bolts evenly until pressure plate springs are completely expanded, then remove attaching bolts.
13. Remove pressure plate, cover assem-

bly and clutch disc from flywheel. These parts can be removed through the opening in the bottom of the clutch housing on models equipped with a dust cover.
14. Remove pilot bearing, if required.
15. Install pilot bearing, if removed.
16. Install clutch disc onto flywheel, then insert clutch alignment tool No. T74P-7137-K or equivalent into clutch pilot bearing hole. Ensure clutch disc is properly aligned on flywheel.
17. If installing original pressure plate and cover assembly, align marks made during removal and position pressure plate and cover assembly onto flywheel.
18. Install pressure plate attaching bolts and torque bolts to 15-25 ft. lbs.
19. Remove clutch disc alignment tool.
20. Raise transmission and clutch housing assembly into position, then install No. 2 crossmember support onto frame.
21. Lower transmission and insulator into crossmember support, and tighten attaching nuts.
22. Remove transmission jack.

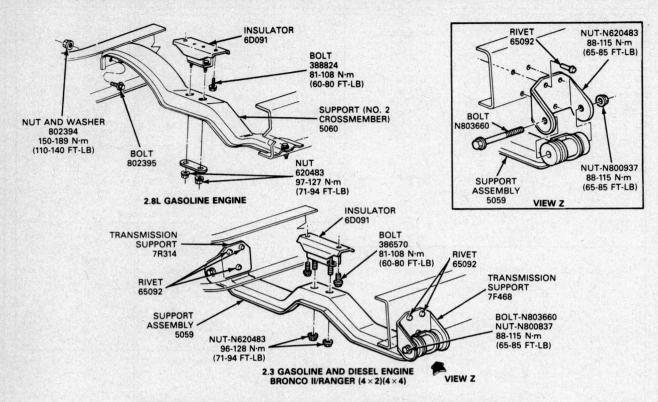

**Fig. 2   Transmission rear support installation. 1985**

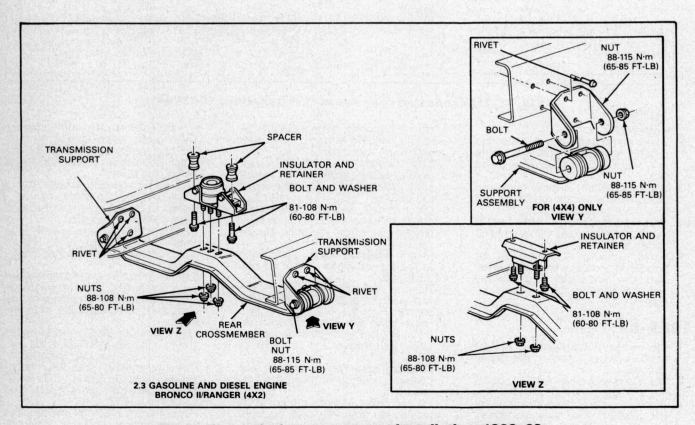

**Fig. 3   Transmission rear support installation. 1986—89**

23. Install driveshaft. Ensure marks made on driveshaft align properly with mark on companion flange. Tighten attaching nuts and bolts to 70-95 ft. lbs.
24. Install housing to engine block attaching bolts in correct position as removed. Torque attaching bolts to 28-38 ft. lbs.
25. Install slave cylinder hydraulic hose, then the hose to slave cylinder retaining clip.
26. Install starter motor onto engine.
27. Lower vehicle and connect clutch hydraulic system master cylinder to the clutch pedal and to the dash panel assembly. Check clutch for proper operation.

# TRANSMISSION
## REPLACE
### 4 SPEED UNITS

1. Disconnect battery ground cable (both battery ground cables on diesel engine).
2. Place gearshift lever in neutral position then remove boot retainer screws.
3. Remove retainer cover to gearshift lever retainer attaching bolts, then disconnect clutch master cylinder push rod from clutch pedal.
4. Pull gearshift lever assembly, shim and bushing straight up away from the gearshift lever retainer.
5. To avoid dirt entering shift tower opening in extension housing, cover with cloth.
6. Raise and support vehicle.
7. Disconnect driveshaft at rear axle drive flange, then pull driveshaft rearward and disconnect from transmission. Install suitable plug in extension housing to prevent lubricant leakage.
8. Remove clutch housing dust shield and slave cylinder and secure to the side.
9. Disconnect starter motor and all transmission electrical connectors.
10. Place suitable jack under engine using a block of wood between jack and engine to protect the oil pan.
11. Remove speedometer cable from extension housing or speed sensor unit, if equipped.
12. On four wheel drive vehicles, remove the transfer case as described in "Transfer Case."
13. Remove starter motor and position a transmission jack under transmission.
14. Remove bolts, lockwasher and flat washer attaching transmission to the engine rear plate.
15. Remove nuts and bolts attaching transmission mount to crossmember.
16. Remove nuts attaching crossmember to frame side rails and remove crossmember.
17. Lower the jack then work clutch housing from locating dowels and slide transmission rearward until input shaft spline clears clutch disc.
18. Remove transmission from vehicle.
19. Reverse procedure to install.

### 5 SPEED UNITS

1. Place gearshift lever in Neutral position, then remove boot retainer screws or bolts.
2. Remove bolts, then pull gearshift lever assembly out of retainer or transfer case adapter as applicable.
3. Cover shift lever opening with cloth to prevent dirt entry.
4. Disconnect battery ground cable, then raise and support vehicle.
5. Scribe alignment marks on driveshaft and rear axle companion flange, then disconnect driveshaft from flange.
6. Pull driveshaft rearward and disconnect from transmission or transfer case adapter. Install suitable plug to prevent lubricant leakage.
7. Disconnect hydraulic line from slave cylinder, then plug line to prevent fluid leakage.
8. Disconnect speedometer cable from extension housing or transfer case adapter as applicable.
9. Disconnect starter motor, back-up lamp, shift indicator switch and neutral position switch electrical connectors as applicable.
10. Place suitable jack under engine, using a block of wood between jack and engine to protect the oil pan, then raise jack slightly.
11. Remove transfer case, if applicable, as outlined in "Transfer Case."
12. Remove starter motor, then place a suitable jack under transmission.
13. Remove bolts, lockwashers and flat washers attaching transmission to the engine rear plate.
14. Remove nuts and bolts attaching transmission mount and damper to crossmember.
15. Remove nuts attaching crossmember to frame side rails, then remove crossmember.
16. Lower engine jack, then work clutch housing from locating dowels. Slide transmission rearward until input shaft spline clears clutch disc, then remove transmission from vehicle.
17. Reverse procedure to install.

# TRANSFER CASE

## INDEX

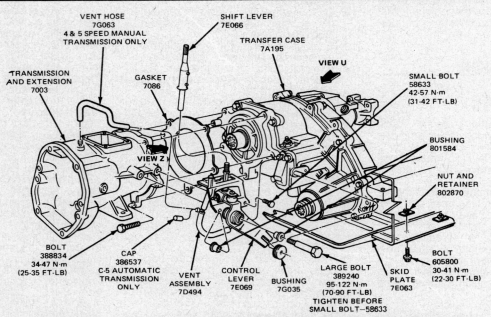

**Fig. 1   Transfer case mounting. Borg Warner Model 13-50 less electronic shift control**

## TRANSFER CASE
### REPLACE

### EXC. BORG WARNER 13-59 INLINE TRANSFER CASE

1. Raise and support vehicle.
2. Remove skid plate from frame, if equipped, then drain fluid from transfer case.
3. On models with electronic shift, squeeze electrical connector locking tabs together, then disconnect from feed wire harness at rear of transfer case.
4. On models less electronic shift, disconnect four wheel drive indicator switch electrical connector from transfer case.
5. On all models, disconnect front driveshaft from axle input yoke.
6. Loosen clamp retaining front driveshaft boot to transfer case, then remove driveshaft and front boot assembly from transfer case front output shaft.
7. Disconnect rear driveshaft from transfer case output shaft yoke, then the speedometer driven gear from transfer case rear cover.
8. Disconnect vent hose from control le-

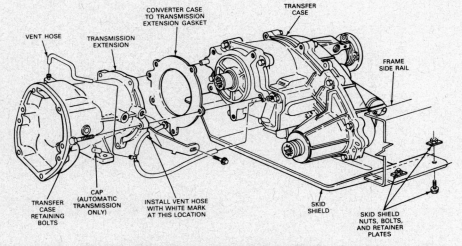

**Fig. 2   Transfer case mounting. Borg Warner Model 13-50 w/electronic shift control**

ver or mounting bracket, **Figs. 1 and 2.**
9. On models less electronic shift, remove shoulder bolt and the shifter to extension housing retaining bolt. Pull control lever out until bushing slides off shift lever pin. If necessary, remove

shift lever from control lever.
10. Remove heat shield from transfer case, if equipped.
11. On all models, support transfer case with a suitable jack, then remove retaining bolts. Slide transfer case rearward and lower from vehicle.

**Fig. 3   Transfer case retaining bolt tightening sequence. 1983-84 models**

**Fig. 4   Transfer case retaining bolt tightening sequence. 1985 models**

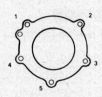

**Fig. 5   Transfer case retaining bolt tightening sequence. 1986-89 models**

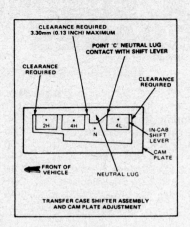

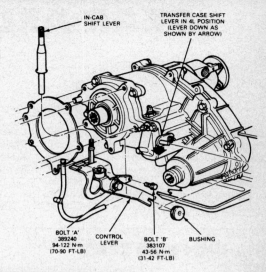

**Fig. 6   Shift linkage adjustment**

12. Reverse procedure to install. Note the following:
   a. Torque transfer case retaining bolts to 25-35 ft. lbs. on 1983-85 models or 25-43 ft. lbs. on 1986-89 models in sequence shown, **Figs. 3 through 5.**
   b. Torque heat shield retaining bolts to 27-37 ft. lbs.
   c. Torque shifter to extension housing retaining bolt to 31-42 ft. lbs. and shoulder bolt to 70-90 ft. lbs. The shifter retaining bolt must be tightened before the shoulder bolt.
   d. Torque speedometer driven gear attaching screw to 20-25 inch lbs., front and rear driveshaft retaining bolts to 12-15 ft. lbs., fill and drain plugs to 14-22 ft. lbs. and (mechanical shift) skid plate retaining bolts to 22-30 ft. lbs, (electronic shift) skid plate retaining bolts to 15-20 ft. lbs.
   e. Fill transfer case with 3 pints of Dexron II automatic transmission fluid, or equivalent.

## BORG WARNER 13-59 INLINE TRANSFER CASE

1. Raise and support vehicle, then disconnect rear driveshaft from transfer case output shaft flange.
2. Disconnect speedometer cable from case rear cover, then support case assembly with suitable jack.

3. Remove transfer case to extension housing retaining bolts.
4. Slide transfer case rearward until it clears transmission output shaft, then lower transfer case and remove vehicle.
5. Reverse procedure to install and note the following:
   a. Torque transfer case retaining bolts to 25-43 ft. lbs. in sequence shown in **Fig. 5.**
   b. Torque speedometer cable retaining screw to 20-25 inch lbs.
   c. Torque rear driveshaft to transfer case output shaft flange bolts to 61-87 ft. lbs.

## SHIFT LEVER REPLACE

### EXC. ELECTRONIC SHIFT MODELS & BORG WARNER 13-59 INLINE TRANSFER CASE

Removal of the shift ball is necessary only if the shift ball, boot, or lever is being replaced. If not, remove the ball, boot and lever as an assembly.

1. Remove plastic insert from shift ball, then warm ball to approximately 140-180° F and knock ball off lever with a hammer and a block of wood.
2. Remove rubber boot and pan cover, then disconnect vent hose from control lever.
3. Unscrew shift lever from control lever, then remove shifter to extension housing retaining bolt and the shoulder bolt. Remove control lever and bushings.
4. Reverse procedure to install. Note the

following:
   a. Torque shifter to extension housing retaining bolt to 31-42 ft. lbs. and shoulder bolt to 70-90 ft. lbs. The shifter retaining bolt must be tightened before the shoulder bolt.
   b. Torque shift lever to 27-37 ft. lbs.
   c. Install vent assembly so the white marking on housing is in line with notch in shifter. Position upper end of vent hose inside shift lever bolts.
   d. Install shift ball to the end of knurl on upper part of shift lever.

## SHIFT LINKAGE ADJUST

### EXC. ELECTRONIC SHIFT MODELS & BORG WARNER 13-59 INLINE TRANSFER CASE

1. Raise shift boot to expose cam plate, loosen bolts A and B, **Fig. 6,** approximately two turns, then place shift lever in 4L position.
2. Move cam plate rearward until bottom corner of neutral lug just contacts forward right edge of shift lever (Point C), **Fig. 6.**
3. With cam plate positioned as outlined above, torque bolt A to 70-90 ft. lbs., then bolt B to 31-42 ft. lbs.
4. Place shift lever in all shift positions and check for positive engagement.
5. Check clearance between shift lever and cam plate with shift lever positioned in 2H, 4H and 4L positions as shown, **Fig. 6.** Clearance should not exceed .130 inch. If clearance exceeds specification, repeat adjustment.

# REAR AXLE, SUSPENSION & BRAKES

## INDEX

# 6¾ INCH RING GEAR AXLE

## DESCRIPTION

This axle can be identified by the 8 cover bolts.

The axle, Fig. 1, is an integral design hypoid with the center line of the pinion set below the center line of the ring gear. The semi-floating axle shafts are retained in the housing by ball bearings and bearing retainers at axle ends.

The differential is mounted on two opposed tapered roller bearings which are retained in the housing by removable caps. Differential bearing preload and drive gear backlash is adjusted by nuts located behind each differential bearing cup.

The drive pinion assembly is mounted on two opposed tapered roller bearings. Pinion bearing preload is adjusted by a collapsible spacer on the pinion shaft. Pinion and ring gear tooth contact is adjusted by shims between the rear bearing cone and pinion gear.

## REAR AXLE ASSEMBLY, REPLACE

1. Raise vehicle and support at rear frame members.
2. Drain lubricant from axle.
3. Mark driveshaft and pinion flange for proper reassembly. Disconnect driveshaft from pinion flange.
4. Remove wheels, brake drums and both axle shafts as outlined in "Axle Shaft & Oil Seal, Replace."
5. Remove vent tube hose, then remove vent tube from axle housing.
6. Remove bolt securing hydraulic brake T-fitting from axle housing, then carefully remove the hydraulic brake hose from retaining clip. Carefully wire rear brake backing plates, hydraulic brake system and parking brake cables as one unit out of the way.
7. Using a suitable jack, support rear axle. Remove U-bolts, shock absorber lower mounting and spring plates.
8. Lower axle housing and remove from vehicle.
9. Reverse procedure to install, noting the following torques: U-bolt nuts, 55-75 ft. lbs., shock absorber lower mounts, 40-60 ft. lbs., driveshaft to

pinion flange bolts, 70-95 ft. lbs., rear axle shaft retainer plate nuts, 20-40 ft. lbs. and rear cover attaching bolts, 23-35 ft. lbs., except the ratio tag bolt which is torqued to 15-20 ft. lbs.

## AXLE SHAFT & OIL SEAL, REPLACE

1. Remove wheel and tire assembly, then remove nuts attaching brake drum to axle shaft flange and remove brake drum.
2. Working through opening in axle shaft flange, remove nuts securing axle shaft bearing retainer.
3. Using a suitable puller, pull axle shaft from housing.
4. Remove brake backing plate and attach to frame side rail with a piece of wire.
5. Using a hook type puller, remove oil seal from housing.
6. Wipe all lubricant from oil seal area of axle housing, then install oil seal using axle tube seal replacer tool No. T79P-1177-A.
7. Install gasket on housing flange, then install brake backing plate.
8. Carefully slide axle shaft into housing using care not to damage oil seal, then install bearing retainer attaching nuts and torque to 20 to 40 ft. lbs.
9. Install brake drum and retaining nuts, then install wheel and tire assembly.

## AXLE SHAFT BEARINGS, REPLACE

1. Remove axle shaft as described in "Axle Shaft & Oil Seal, Replace."
2. Loosen axle inner retainer ring by nicking deeply with a cold chisel in several places and slide off shaft.
3. Using a suitable press, remove bearing from axle. **Do not ever attempt to use heat to make bearing removal easier, as it will weaken the axle shaft bearing journal area.**
4. Position bearing retainer plate and bearing on axle, then using a suitable press, install bearing. Using the same tool, install bearing retainer ring. Do not press on the bearing and the retainer ring at the same time. They must be installed separately.
5. Reinstall axle in axle housing. Ensure new seal is installed.

# 7½ INCH RING GEAR AXLE

## DESCRIPTION

This axle can be identified by the 10 cover bolts.

The gear set, Fig. 2, consists of a ring gear and an overhung drive pinion which is supported by two opposed tapered roller bearings. The differential case is a one-piece design with openings allowing assembly of the internal parts and lubricant flow. The differential pinion shaft is retained with a threaded bolt (lock) assembled to the case.

The roller type wheel bearings have no inner race, and the rollers directly contact the bearing journals of the axle shafts. The axle shafts do not use an inner and outer bearing retainer. Rather, they are held in the axle by means of C-locks. These C-locks also fit into a machined recess in the differential side gears within the differential case. There is no retainer bolt access hole in the axle shaft flange.

## REAR AXLE ASSEMBLY, REPLACE

1. Raise vehicle and support at rear frame members.
2. Remove rear wheels and brake drums.
3. Drain rear axle lubricant by removing housing cover.
4. Remove axle shafts as described under "Axle Shafts, Seals & Bearings, Replace."
5. Remove 4 retaining nuts from each backing plate and wire the plates aside.
6. Disconnect rear axle housing vent.
7. Disconnect brake line from retaining clips on axle housing.
8. Remove hydraulic brake T-fitting from axle housing.
9. Mark driveshaft and axle flange for assembly reference, then disconnect shaft from flange.
10. Support axle with a suitable jack, then remove U-bolt nuts, U-bolts and plates.
11. Disconnect lower shock absorber studs from axle housing mounting brackets.

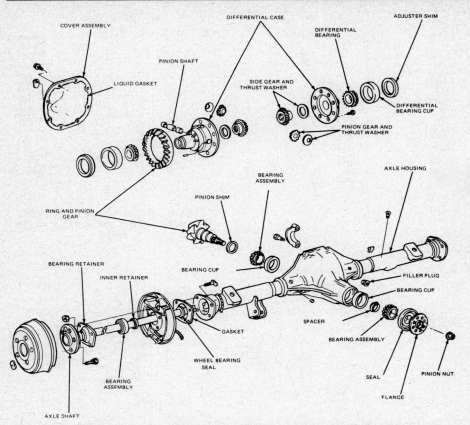

**Fig. 1   Disassembled view of Ford 6³/₄ inch ring gear axle**

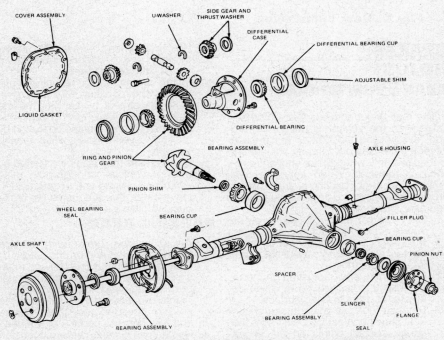

**Fig. 2   Disassembled view of Ford 7¹/₂ inch ring gear axle**

12. Lower axle housing and remove from vehicle.
13. Reverse procedure to install, noting the following torques: U-bolt nuts, 55-75 ft. lbs., shock absorber lower mounts, 40-60 ft. lbs., brake backing plate nuts, 20-40 ft. lbs., driveshaft-to-pinion flange bolts, 70-95 ft. lbs. and rear cover bolts, 25-35 ft. lbs., except ratio tag bolt, which is torqued to 15-24 ft. lbs.

## AXLE SHAFTS, SEALS & BEARINGS, REPLACE

1. Raise and support vehicle.
2. Remove rear wheels and brake drums.
3. Drain rear axle lubricant by removing housing cover.
4. On models with 3.73:1 or 4.10:1 ratio axle, remove axle shafts as follows:
   a. Remove pinion shaft lock bolt, then rotate pinion shaft until relief in shaft faces either side gear, **Fig. 3**, and remove C-lockwasher from axle shaft.
   b. Rotate pinion shaft ¹/₂ turn until relief faces opposite side gear and remove C-lockwasher from axle shafts.
   c. Carefully slide shafts out of housing.
5. On all models except those with 3.73:1 or 4.10:1 ratio axle, remove axle shafts as follows:
   a. Remove differential pinion shaft lock bolt and the shaft.
   b. Push axle shafts inward toward center of vehicle and remove C-lockwashers from shafts, **Fig. 4.**
   c. Carefully slide axle shafts out of housing.
6. Remove seal and bearing using a suitable hook-type puller.
7. Reverse procedure to install, noting the following:
   a. Apply suitable grease between lips of axle shaft seal.
   b. Install bearing using axle tube bearing replacer tool No. T78P-1225-A, and install seal and using axle tube seal replacer tool No. T78P-1177-Aor equivalent.
   c. Torque pinion shaft lock bolt to 15-22 ft. lbs.
   d. Torque differential housing cover bolts to 25-35 ft. lbs., except the ratio tag bolt which is torqued to 15-24 ft. lbs.

## SHOCK ABSORBER REPLACE

1. Raise vehicle and support rear axle.
2. Remove lower attaching bolt and nut from shock absorber, then swing lower end free from mounting bracket.
3. Disconnect shock absorber from upper mounting, then remove shock from vehicle, **Figs. 5 and 6.**
4. Reverse procedure to install.

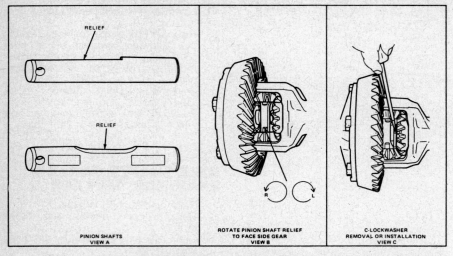

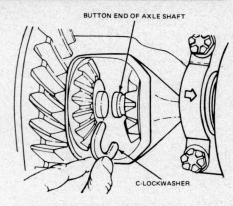

**Fig. 4 Axle shaft removal. Except 3.73:1 or 4.10:1 ratio axle**

**Fig. 3 Axle shaft removal. 3.73:1 or 4.10:1 ratio axle**

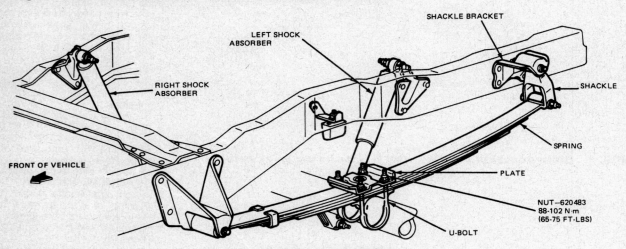

**Fig. 5 Rear suspension**

## LEAF SPRINGS
### REPLACE

1. Raise rear of vehicle until weight is relieved from spring, with tires remaining in contact with floor.
2. Remove U-bolt nuts and the U-bolts, **Fig. 7.**
3. Remove spring-to-bracket attaching nut and bolt, **Fig. 8.**
4. Remove shackle-to-bracket attaching nuts and bolts, **Fig. 9,** then the spring and shackle assembly.
5. Reverse procedure to install.

## STABILIZER BAR
### REPLACE

1. Disconnect stabilizer bar from rear link, **Fig. 10.**
2. Remove mounting bracket U-bolt, then the mounting bracket, retainer and stabilizer bar.
3. Reverse procedure to install. The "UP" marking on the mounting bracket must be positioned as shown in **Fig. 10.**

## BRAKES
### ADJUST
### REAR DRUM BRAKES

The rear brake shoes adjust automatically when the vehicle is driven forward and reverse and the brakes are applied several times sharply. Manual adjustment is required only when brake shoes are relined or replaced. When adjusting rear brake shoes, check parking brake cable for proper adjustment and be sure equalizer is operating properly.

1. With drums removed, clean areas where shoes contact backing plate, then apply suitable lubricant to these contact areas, being careful not to get lubricant on shoes.
2. Using brake shoe adjusting gauge or equivalent, adjust gauge to inside diameter of drum braking surface.
3. Reverse tool and adjust brake shoes until they touch gauge, being sure the gauge contact points on the shoes are parallel to vehicle with center line through center of axle. Holding automatic adjusting lever out of way, ro-

tate adjustment screw. Oil screw threads with suitable lubricant if screw will not turn freely.
4. Install drums, drum retaining nuts, wheels and mounting nuts, then complete adjustment by applying brakes several times while driving vehicle in reverse and check brake operation by making several stops while driving forward.
5. Drum brakes may also be adjusted by raising vehicle enough to raise wheels off ground and turning adjusting screws through holes in brake backing plate.

## PARKING BRAKE

1. Adjust parking brake with service brakes adjusted and drums cold.
2. Fully depress parking brake and measure distance between tension limiter bracket and strap hook, **Fig. 11.**
3. Tighten equalizer nut 6 full turns while holding threaded rod, then release and fully depress pedal 3 or 4 times.
4. Remeasure distance between tension limiter and strap hook. If measurement did not change by at least 1/8 inch from original measurement, tighten nut an

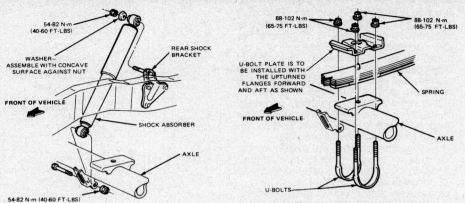

Fig. 6 Shock absorber replacement

Fig. 7 Leaf spring U-bolt removal

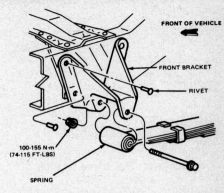

Fig. 8 Forward leaf spring mounting

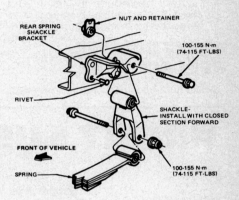

Fig. 9 Rear leaf spring mounting

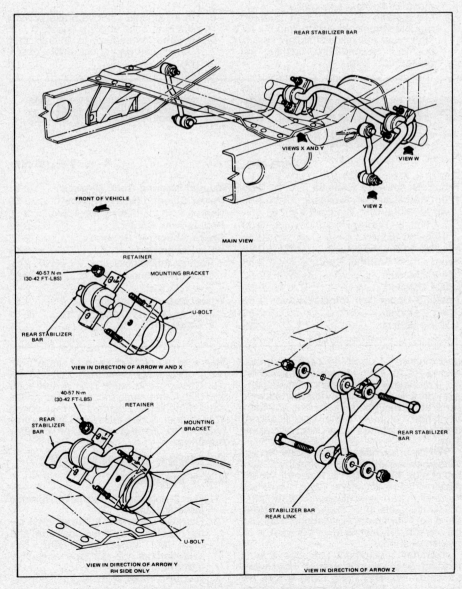

Fig. 10 Stabilizer bar replacement

additional 6 turns.
5. Release parking brake and check for rear wheel drag.

## MASTER CYLINDER
## REPLACE
## W/POWER BRAKES

1. With engine off, depress brake pedal to expel vacuum from brake booster system.
2. Disconnect hydraulic lines from master cylinder.
3. Remove brake booster to master cylinder retaining nuts and remove master cylinder from brake booster.
4. Reverse procedure to install and bleed brake system, then refill master cylinder and bleed it.

## LESS POWER BRAKES

1. Disconnect wires from stop light switch inside cab below instrument panel.
2. Remove retaining nut, shoulder bolt and spacers which secure master cylinder pushrod to brake pedal assembly, then remove stop light switch from pedal.
3. Disconnect hydraulic brake lines from master cylinder, then remove master cylinder to dash panel retaining nuts, master cylinder, and boot from master cylinder pushrod.

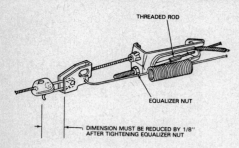

THREADED ROD

EQUALIZER NUT

DIMENSION MUST BE REDUCED BY 1/8"
AFTER TIGHTENING EQUALIZER NUT

**Fig. 11   Parking brake adjustment**

4. Reverse procedure to install and bleed brake system, then refill and bleed master cylinder.

## BRAKE BOOSTER REPLACE

Make sure booster rubber reaction disc is properly installed as shown in **Fig. 12,** if the master cylinder pushrod is removed or accidentally pulled out. A dislodged disc may cause excessive pedal travel and extreme operation sensitivity. The disc is black compared to the silver colored valve plunger that will be exposed after pushrod and front seal are removed. The booster unit is serviced as an assembly and must be replaced if the reaction disc cannot be properly installed and aligned, or if it cannot be located within the unit itself.

1. Disconnect stop light switch wiring, support master cylinder from underside, and remove master cylinder to booster retaining nuts.
2. Loosen clamp which secures manifold vacuum hose to booster check valve and remove hose, then remove booster check valve.
3. Pull master cylinder off booster and support far enough away to allow removal of booster assembly.
4. On models equipped with pushrod mounted stop light switch, remove retaining pin, then slide stop light switch, pushrod, spacer and bushing off brake pedal arm.

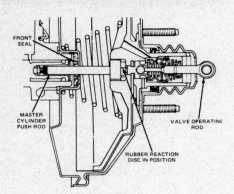

FRONT SEAL

MASTER CYLINDER PUSH ROD

VALVE OPERATING ROD

RUBBER REACTION DISC IN POSITION

**Fig. 12   Checking reaction disc installation**

5. On all models, remove brake booster attaching bolts and the booster.
6. Reverse procedure to install, then start engine and check brake operation.

# FRONT SUSPENSION & STEERING

## INDEX

## DESCRIPTION
### 4 X 2 MODELS

The twin I-beam suspension consists of coil springs, I-beam axle arms, radius arms, upper and lower ball joints, spindles, tie rods, shock absorbers and an optional stabilizer bar, **Figs. 1 and 2.**

### 4 X 4 MODELS

The independent front suspension used on four wheel drive models is comprised of a two-piece front driving axle assembly, two coil springs and two radius arms, **Fig. 3.** The front driving axle consists of two independent axle arm assemblies. One end of each axle arm assembly is mounted to the frame, with the opposite end supported by the coil spring and radius arm.

## WHEEL ALIGNMENT

Front wheel alignment specifications and method of checking caster, camber and toe-in for Twin I-beam front axles on 4 x 2 models or independent front suspension on 4 x 4 models is determined with truck at normal operating height, provided front ride height is within specifications, and tires are inflated to specified cold pressure.

To determine riding height, measure distance between bottom of spring tower and top of axle, **Figs. 4 and 5.** Refer to "Wheel Alignment Specifications Chart" to determine alignment specifications for the particular riding height of truck. If riding height does not fall within specifications, it should be corrected by installing proper springs or by use of shims.

Alignment equipment indicates a true reading only when frame is horizontal. Measure left and right hand angle as shown in **Fig. 6.** If frame is not level (due to tire, spring or load differences), the caster angle reading must be modified to compensate for frame angles. If front is higher than rear, subtract amount of angle from reading. If front is lower than rear, add angle. Check frame angle with a protractor and take frame angle measurement on flat area immediately adjacent to rear spring front hanger. **Axles are not to be bent or twisted to correct caster or camber readings.**

## CAMBER ADJUSTMENT
### 4 X 2 Models

1. Raise and support vehicle. Remove front wheels.
2. Remove upper ball joint nut, then remove cotter pin on lower ball stud and back nut down stud. Pop ball joint/camber adjuster taper assembly from mounting.
3. Wedge camber adjuster out of spindle with camber adjusting tool No. D81T-3010-B. Replace adjuster with desired camber adjuster, **Fig. 7.** Camber adjusters are available in 0°, 1/2°,

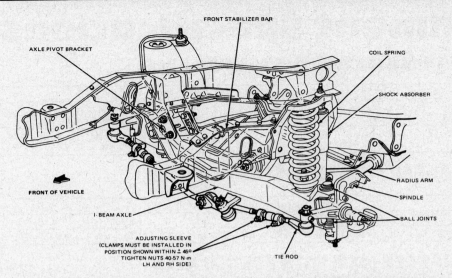

**Fig. 1   Front suspension 4 X 2 models. All 1983–85 & 1986–89 Ranger**

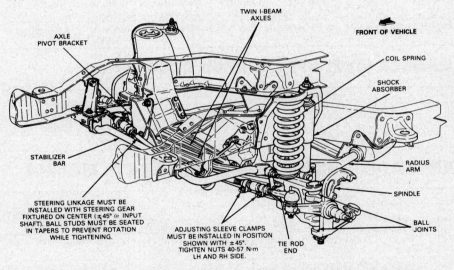

**Fig. 2   Front suspension 4 X 2 models. 1986–89 Bronco II**

1° and 1¹/₂°. To increase camber (more positive), align slot as follows: On driver's side, point slot to rear of vehicle. On passenger's side, point slot to front of vehicle. To decrease camber (more negative), align slot as follows: On driver's side point slot forward. On passenger's side, point slot rearward.

4. Remove lower ball joint stud nut and apply Loctite 242 to upper and lower ball joint studs. Hand start upper ball stud nut and torque lower ball stud nut to 35 ft. lbs. Torque upper ball stud nut to 85-110 ft. lbs. and finish torquing lower stud nut to 104-146 ft. lbs. Install cotter pin.

### 4 X 4 Models

1. Raise and support vehicle. Remove front wheels.

2. Remove upper ball joint cotter pin and nut, then back off lower ball joint nut to end of stud.
3. Break spindle loose from ball joint studs, then remove camber adjuster sleeve from spindle using pitman arm puller tool T64P-3590-F or equivalent, if necessary.
4. Install camber adjuster on top ball joint stud with arrow pointing outboard for positive camber or inboard for negative camber, **Fig. 8.** Zero camber bushings will not have an arrow and may be turned in either direction as long as the lugs on the yoke engage the slots in the bushing.
5. Remove and discard lower ball joint stud nut, then install a new nut and torque to 40 ft. lbs.
6. Install new upper ball joint stud nut and torque to 85-100 ft. lbs. Continue

to tighten nut until cotter pin hole lines up with castellation on nut, then install cotter pin. Retorque lower ball joint stud nut to 95-110 ft. lbs. **The camber adjuster will be seated at a predetermined position during the tightening sequence. Do not attempt to change this position.**

7. Reinstall wheels and lower vehicle.

## CASTER ADJUSTMENT

Caster angle is non-adjustable on 4 x 4 vehicles. On 4 x 2 models, a service kit, Part No. E4TA-3K064-AA, is available which can be used to increase caster up to 3° in ¹/₂° increments. The kit comes with complete instructions, and these instructions should be strictly followed to achieve desired results.

## TOE-IN, ADJUST

1. Loosen clamp bolts at each end of spindle connecting rod tube, then rotate the sleeve until correct toe alignment of ¹/₃₂ inch is obtained.
2. Center clamps between adjustment sleeve nibs, then position bolts horizontally with clamps nuts positioned as shown in **Fig. 9.**
3. Recheck toe-in adjustment, then check that steering wheel spokes are properly positioned and adjust as necessary.

# WHEEL BEARINGS
## ADJUST
### 4 X 2 MODELS

1. Raise and support front of vehicle.
2. Remove wheel cover, grease cap, cotter pin and locknut.
3. Loosen adjusting nut 3 turns, then rock wheel assembly in and out several times to push brake shoe and linings away from rotor.
4. Torque adjusting nut to 17-25 ft. lbs. while rotating wheel assembly.
5. Loosen adjusting nut ¹/₂ turn, then retorque to 10-15 inch lbs.
6. Install locknut and cotter pin.
7. Ensure wheel assembly rotates smoothly, then reinstall grease cap and wheel cover and lower vehicle.

### 4 X 4 MODELS
#### Manual Locking Hub

1. Raise and support front of vehicle.
2. Remove wheel and tire assembly.
3. Remove lug nut stud retainer washers, then the locking hub assembly.
4. Remove snap ring from end of spindle shaft.
5. Remove axle shaft spacer, needle thrust bearing and bearing spacer.
6. Remove outer wheel bearing locknut using a suitable spanner wrench.
7. Remove locknut washer from spindle.
8. Loosen inner wheel bearing locknut using a suitable spanner wrench, then torque locknut to 35 ft. lbs.
9. Loosen inner locknut ¹/₄ turn, retighten to 16 inch lbs., then install lockwasher on spindle. If necessary, rotate locknut slightly to align pin with closest hole in lockwasher.

# BRONCO II & 1983-89 RANGER

# Wheel Alignment Specifications

## 1983–86 RANGER (4x2) WITH STAMPED AXLE

| Riding Height in Inches | Angle Degrees | | | | | | | | |
|---|---|---|---|---|---|---|---|---|---|
| | 2.95 | 3.15 | 3.35 | 3.55 | 3.75 | 3.95 | 4.15 | 4.35 | 4.55 |
| Caster | +5⅛ to +8 | +4⅝ to +7½ | +4 to +7 | +3½ to +6½ | +3 to +6 | +2⅜ to +5⅜ | +1⅞ to +4⅞ | +1⅜ to +4¼ | +¾ to +3¾ |

## 1983–86 RANGER (4x2) WITH STAMPED AXLE

| Riding Height in Inches | Angle Degrees | | | | | | | |
|---|---|---|---|---|---|---|---|---|
| | 2.75 | 2.95 | 3.15 | 3.35 | 3.55 | 3.75 | 3.95 | 4.15 |
| Camber | −1 to −¾ | −1 to −¼ | −1 to +⅛ | −⅝ to +⅝ | −⅛ to +1⅛ | +⅜ to +1⅝ | +⅞ to +2⅛ | +1⅜ to +2¾ |

## 1985–86 RANGER (4x2) WITH FORGED AXLE

| Riding Height in Inches | Angle Degrees | | | | | | | | |
|---|---|---|---|---|---|---|---|---|---|
| | 3.28 | 3.48 | 3.68 | 3.88 | 4.08 | 4.28 | 4.48 | 4.68 | 4.88 |
| Caster | +5¼ to +8¼ | +4½ to +7½ | +4 to +7 | +3½ to +6½ | +3 to +6 | +2½ to +5½ | +1¾ to +4¾ | +1¼ to +4¼ | +¾ to +3¾ |
| Camber | −¾ to −2½ | −¼ to −1¾ | −1¼ to +¼ | −¾ to +¾ | −¼ to +1¼ | +½ to +1 | +¾ to +2¼ | +1¼ to +2¾ | +1¾ to +3¼ |

## 1987–88 RANGER (4x2) WITH FORGED AXLE

| Riding Height in Inches | Angle Degrees | | | | | | |
|---|---|---|---|---|---|---|---|
| | 3.56 | 3.68 | 3.88 | 4.08 | 4.28 | 4.48 | 4.68 |
| Caster | +4.5 to +7.5 | +4 to +7 | +3.5 to +6.5 | +3 to +6 | +2.5 to +5.5 | +1.75 to +4.75 | +1.25 to +4.25 |
| Camber | −1 to +.25 | −.75 to +.5 | 0 to +1.25 | +.5 to +1.75 | +1 to +2.25 | +1.5 to +2.75 | |

## 1983–88 BRONCO II & RANGER (4x4) EXCEPT 1988 RANGER STX MODELS

| Riding Height in Inches | Angle Degrees | | | | | | | | |
|---|---|---|---|---|---|---|---|---|---|
| | 2.75 | 2.95 | 3.15 | 3.35 | 3.55 | 3.75 | 3.95 | 4.15 | 4.35 | 4.55 |
| Caster | +5⅜ to +8⅛ | +4¾ to +7⅝ | +4¼ to +7 | +3¾ to +6½ | +3⅛ to +5⅞ | +2½ to +5⅜ | +2 to +4⅞ | +1½ to +4⅜ | +1 to +3⅞ | +1 to +3⅜ |
| Camber | −1⅞ to −⅜ | −1⅜ to +⅛ | −⅞ to +¾ | −⅜ to +1⅛ | +⅛ to +1¾ | +⅝ to +2⅛ | +1⅛ to +2⅝ | +1¾— +3⅛ | +2⅛ to +3⅝ | +2¾ to +4 |

## 1988 RANGER STX (4x4) MODELS

| Riding Height in Inches | Angle Degrees | | | | | | | | |
|---|---|---|---|---|---|---|---|---|---|
| | 4.60 | 4.68 | 4.88 | 5.08 | 5.28 | 5.48 | 5.68 | 5.88 | 6.08 | 6.28 |
| Caster | +4.5 to +7.5 | +4.25 to +7.25 | +3.5 to +6.5 | +3 to +6 | +2.5 to +5.5 | +2 to +5 | +1.5 to +4.5 | +1 to +4 | +.5 to +3.5 | +0 to +3 |
| Camber | −1 to +.5 | −.75 to +.75 | −.5 to +1 | 0 to +1.5 | +.75 to +2.25 | +1.25 to +2.75 | +1.5 to +3 | +2 to +3.5 | +2.5 to +4 | +3 to +4.5 |

## 1989 RANGER (4x2) MODELS

| Riding Height in Inches | Angle Degrees | | | | | | |
|---|---|---|---|---|---|---|---|
| | 2.76 | 3.15 | 3.55 | 4.00 | 4.33 | 4.72 | 5.12 |
| Caster ① | +9 to +11 | +7.95 to +9.95 | +6.8 to +8.8 | +4.8 to +5.8 | +4.7 to +6.7 | +3.6 to +5.6 | +2.5 to +4.5 |
| Caster ② | +8.2 to +10.2 | +7.1 to +9.1 | +6 to +8 | +4.85 to +6.85 | +3.6 to +5.6 | +2.5 to +4.5 | +1.4 to +3.4 |
| Camber ① | −4 to −2 | −2.9 to −.9 | −1.9 to +.1 | −.9 to +1.1 | +.25 to +2.25 | +1.3 to +3.3 | +2.3 to +4.3 |

①—Left side.  ②—Right side.

## 1989 BRONCO II (4x2) MODELS

| Riding Height in Inches | Angle Degrees | | | | | | |
|---|---|---|---|---|---|---|---|
| | 2.76 | 3.15 | 3.55 | 4.00 | 4.33 | 4.72 | 5.12 |
| Caster ① | +8.2 to +10.2 | +7.2 to +9.2 | +6.1 to +8.1 | +5.1 to +7.1 | +4 to +6 | +2.9 to +4.9 | +1.7 to +3.7 |
| Caster ② | +8.2 to +10.2 | +7.2 to +9.2 | +6 to +8 | +4.8 to +6.8 | +3.6 to +5.6 | +2.5 to +4.5 | +1.4 to +3.4 |
| Camber ① | −3.3 to −1.3 | −2.3 to −.3 | −1.4 to +.6 | −.4 to +1.6 | +.8 to +2.8 | +1.7 to +3.7 | +2.7 to +4.7 |
| Camber ② | −3.3 to −1.3 | −2.1 to −.1 | −1 to +1 | +.05 to +2.05 | +1.2 to +3.2 | +2.3 to +4.3 | +3.4 to +5.4 |

①—Left side.
②—Right side.

## 1989 BRONCO II & RANGER (4x4) EXCEPT RANGER STX MODELS

| Riding Height in Inches | Angle Degrees | | | | |
|---|---|---|---|---|---|
| | 2.76 | 3.15 | 3.55 | 4.00 | 4.33 |
| Caster | +6 to +8 | +4.9 to +6.9 | +3.8 to +5.8 | +2.6 to +5.6 | +1.5 to +3.5 |
| Camber | −2.1 to −.1 | −1.1 to −.9 | −.2 to +1.8 | +.8 to +2.8 | +1.7 to +3.7 |

## 1989 RANGER STX (4x4) MODELS

| Riding Height in Inches | Angle Degrees | | | | |
|---|---|---|---|---|---|
| | 4.21 | 4.61 | 5.00 | 5.40 | 5.79 |
| Caster | +6 to +8 | +4.9 to +6.9 | +3.8 to +5.8 | +2.6 to +5.6 | +1.5 to +3.5 |
| Camber | −2.1 to −.1 | −1.1 to −.9 | −.2 to +1.8 | +.8 to +2.8 | +1.7 to +3.7 |

10. Install outer bearing locknut and torque to 150 ft. lbs.
11. Install bearing thrust spacer, needle thrust bearing, axle shaft spacer and snap ring.
12. Install locking hub assembly and retainer washers, then the wheel and tire assembly.
13. Ensure wheel endplay on spindle is .001-.003 inch.

### Automatic Locking Hub

1. Perform steps 1 through 5 as described under "Manual Locking Hub."
2. Remove cam assembly, thrust washer and needle thrust bearing from wheel bearing adjusting nut.
3. Loosen adjusting nut, then torque nut to 35 ft. lbs. while rotating hub and rotor assembly.
4. Back off adjusting nut 1/4 turn, then torque nut to 16 inch lbs.
5. Align nearest hole in adjusting nut with center of spindle keyway slot. If necessary, advance nut to the next hole.
6. Install locknut needle bearing, thrust washer and cam assembly.
7. Install bearing thrust washer, needle thrust bearing, axle shaft spacer and snap ring.
8. Install locking hub assembly and retainer washers, then the wheel and tire assembly.
9. Ensure wheel endplay on spindle is .001-.003 inch.

## SHOCK ABSORBER
### REPLACE

1. Remove nut and washer from shock absorber at spring seat, Figs. 10 and 11.
2. Remove nut and bolt from shock absorber at radius arm and lower shock bracket. Slightly compress shock and remove.
3. Reverse procedure to install.

## LOWER & UPPER BALL JOINTS
### REPLACE
#### 4 X 2 MODELS

1. Remove spindle. Remove snap rings from ball joints, Fig. 12.
2. Assemble C-Frame T74P-4635-C and receiving cup D81T-3010-A on upper ball joint. Turn forcing screw clockwise until ball joint is removed. Assemble C-Frame and cup on lower ball joint and turn forcing screw clockwise until ball joint is removed. Always remove upper ball joint first.
3. Reverse procedure to install. Install lower ball joint first using ball joint receiver cup D81T-3010-A5 and installation cup D81T-3010-A1 inside adapter cup D81T-3010-A4. Turn forcing screw until ball joint is seated. Install snap ring onto lower ball joint. Install upper ball joint in same manner.

### 4 X 4 MODELS

Refer to "Front Wheel Drive" in this chapter for ball joint replacement procedure.

## COIL SPRING
### REPLACE
#### 4 X 2 MODELS

1. Raise and support front of vehicle. Support axle.
2. Remove lower retainer nut and lower retainer, Fig. 13. Lower axle until it hangs unsupported.
3. Insert pry bar between axles and force appropriate I-beam axle down far enough to allow spring to be lifted over bolt in lower spring seat. Rotate spring until retainer on upper spring seat is cleared. Remove spring. **The axle must be supported when replacing spring and not be permitted to hang by the brake hose. If the length of the brake hose is not sufficient to permit spring replacement, it will be necessary to remove the disc brake caliper. Do not suspend caliper by brake hose, if removed.**
4. Reverse procedure to install. Install bolt in axle arm and tighten nut all the way down. Install top of spring into upper spring seat and rotate into position. Raise axle until spring is seated in lower spring upper seat. Install lower retainer and nut.

## 4 X 4 MODELS

1. Raise and support front of vehicle. Support axle with a suitable jack so the spring is compressed.
2. Remove shock absorber to radius arm attaching bolt, then remove shock absorber from bracket.
3. Remove spring lower retainer attaching nut, then the retainer.
4. Lower axle until all spring tension is released, then remove spring by rotating upper coil out of tabs in upper spring seat, **Fig. 14.**
5. Remove spacer and seat from spring and the stud from axle assembly, if necessary. **The axle must be supported when replacing spring and not be permitted to hang by the brake hose. If the length of the brake hose is not sufficient to permit spring replacement, it will be necessary to remove the disc brake caliper. Do not suspend caliper by brake hose, if removed.**
6. Reverse procedure to install.

## RADIUS ARM
### REPLACE

1. Raise and support front of vehicle. Support axle.
2. Disconnect lower end of shock absorber from shock lower bracket and remove front spring as described previously.
3. Loosen axle pivot bolt. Remove spring lower seat from radius arm. Remove nut and bolt from radius arm to axle and front bracket, **Figs. 15 and 16.**
4. Remove nut, rear washer and insulator from rear side of radius arm rear bracket and remove radius arm. Remove inner insulator and retainer from radius arm stud.
5. Reverse procedure to install.

## RADIUS ARM INSULATORS
### REPLACE

1. Loosen axle pivot bolt and upper shock absorber pivot bolt and compress shock.
2. Remove nut and washer attaching radius arm to radius arm bracket. Remove outer insulator and spacer, **Figs. 15 and 16.**
3. Move radius arm and axle assembly forward out of radius arm bracket. Remove inner insulator and retainer.
4. Reverse procedure to install. Torque upper shock bolt to 25-35 ft. lbs. and axle pivot bolt and nut to 120-150 ft. lbs.

## FRONT I-BEAM AXLE
### REPLACE

1. Remove front wheel spindle and front spring.
2. Remove spring lower seat from radius arm and bolt and nut for radius arm to front axle.

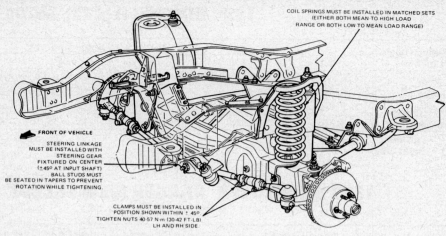

**Fig. 3   Front suspension. All 4 X 4 models**

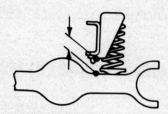

RANGER (4x4)
BOTTOM OF SPRING TOWER TO TOP OF AXLE MEASURED AT CENTER OF JOUNCE STOP IN SIDE VIEW

**Fig. 4   Ride height measurement at front end. 4 X 2 models**

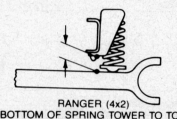

RANGER (4x2)
BOTTOM OF SPRING TOWER TO TOP OF AXLE MEASURED AT CENTER OF JOUNCE STOP IN SIDE VIEW

**Fig. 5   Ride height measurement at front end. 4 X 4 models**

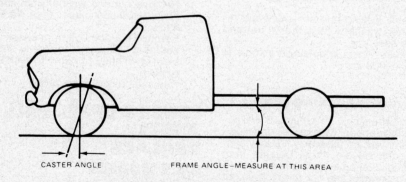

CASTER ANGLE

FRAME ANGLE—MEASURE AT THIS AREA

**Fig. 6   Ride height measurement at frame**

3. Disconnect stabilizer bar from front I-beam axle assembly, if equipped.
4. Remove axle-to-frame pivot bracket bolt and nut. Remove axle.
5. Reverse procedure to install.

## AXLE PIVOT BRACKET
### REPLACE
### 4 X 2 MODELS

1. Remove front spring, radius arm, wheel spindle and I-beam.
2. Remove four attaching nuts and two bolts and retainer assemblies. Remove axle pivot bracket, **Fig. 17 and 18.**
3. Reverse procedure to install. Position axle pivot bracket to frame and install forward and rearward bolts and retainer assemblies from inside of pivot bracket out through crossmember. Loosely install four nuts on outside of crossmember (two forward and two rearward). Torque nuts to 70-92 ft. lbs. Use nut N8802073-S2 or install one .20 inch thick hardened washer under each nut if a standard nut is used.

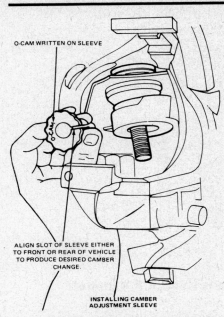

**Fig. 7 Camber adjustment. 4 X 2 models**

O-CAM WRITTEN ON SLEEVE

ALIGN SLOT OF SLEEVE EITHER TO FRONT OR REAR OF VEHICLE TO PRODUCE DESIRED CAMBER CHANGE.

INSTALLING CAMBER ADJUSTMENT SLEEVE

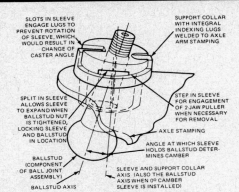

SLOTS IN SLEEVE ENGAGE LUGS TO PREVENT ROTATION OF SLEEVE, WHICH WOULD RESULT IN CHANGE OF CASTER ANGLE

SUPPORT COLLAR WITH INTEGRAL INDEXING LUGS WELDED TO AXLE ARM STAMPING

SPLIT IN SLEEVE ALLOWS SLEEVE TO EXPAND WHEN BALLSTUD NUT IS TIGHTENED, LOCKING SLEEVE AND BALLSTUD IN LOCATION

STEP IN SLEEVE FOR ENGAGEMENT OF 2-JAW PULLER WHEN NECESSARY FOR REMOVAL

AXLE STAMPING

ANGLE AT WHICH SLEEVE HOLDS BALLSTUD DETERMINES CAMBER

BALLSTUD (COMPONENT OF BALL JOINT ASSEMBLY)

SLEEVE AND SUPPORT COLLAR AXIS (ALSO THE BALLSTUD AXIS WHEN 0° CAMBER SLEEVE IS INSTALLED)

BALLSTUD AXIS

**Fig. 8 Camber adjustment. 4 X 4 models**

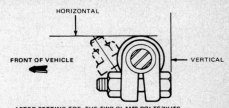

HORIZONTAL

FRONT OF VEHICLE

VERTICAL

AFTER SETTING TOE, THE TWO CLAMP BOLTS/NUTS ON EACH ADJUSTING SLEEVE MUST BE POSITIONED WITHIN A LIMIT OF ± 45 DEGREES AS SHOWN WITH THE THREADED END OF THE BOLTS ON BOTH ADJUSTING SLEEVES POINTING TOWARDS THE FRONT OF THE VEHICLE.

**Fig. 9 Toe-in adjustment**

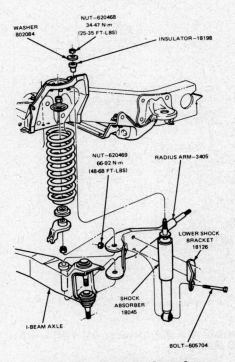

WASHER 802084

NUT—620468 34-47 N·m (25-35 FT-LBS)

INSULATOR—18198

NUT—620469 66-92 N·m (48-68 FT-LBS)

RADIUS ARM—3405

LOWER SHOCK BRACKET 18126

SHOCK ABSORBER 18045

I-BEAM AXLE

BOLT—605704

**Fig. 10 Shock absorber replacement. 4 X 2 models**

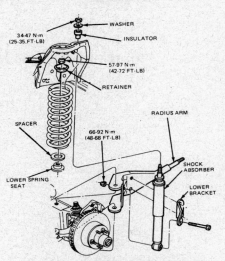

WASHER

INSULATOR

34-47 N·m (25-35 FT-LB)

57-97 N·m (42-72 FT-LB)

RETAINER

SPACER

66-92 N·m (48-68 FT-LB)

LOWER SPRING SEAT

RADIUS ARM

SHOCK ABSORBER

LOWER BRACKET

**Fig. 11 Shock absorber replacement. 4 X 4 models**

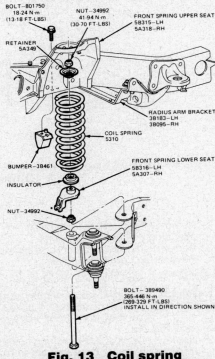

BOLT—801750 18-24 N·m (13-18 FT-LBS)

NUT—34992 41-94 N·m (30-70 FT-LBS)

FRONT SPRING UPPER SEAT 5B315—LH 5A318—RH

RETAINER 5A349

RADIUS ARM BRACKET 3B183—LH 3B095—RH

COIL SPRING 5310

BUMPER—3B461

INSULATOR

FRONT SPRING LOWER SEAT 5B316—LH 5A307—RH

NUT—34992

BOLT—389490 365-446 N·m (269-329 FT-LBS) INSTALL IN DIRECTION SHOWN

**Fig. 13 Coil spring replacement. 4 X 2 models**

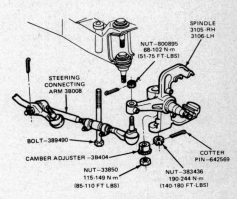

SPINDLE 3105-RH 3106-LH

NUT—800895 68-102 N·m (51-75 FT-LBS)

STEERING CONNECTING ARM 3B008

BOLT—389490

CAMBER ADJUSTER—3B404

NUT—33850 115-149 N·m (85-110 FT LBS)

COTTER PIN—642569

NUT—383436 190-244 N·m (140-180 FT-LBS)

**Fig. 12 Ball joint replacement. 4 X 2 models**

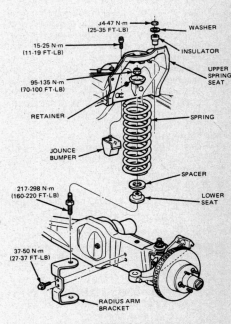

34-47 N·m (25-35 FT-LB)

WASHER

15-25 N·m (11-19 FT-LB)

INSULATOR

UPPER SPRING SEAT

95-135 N·m (70-100 FT-LB)

RETAINER

SPRING

JOUNCE BUMPER

SPACER

217-298 N·m (160-220 FT-LB)

LOWER SEAT

37-50 N·m (27-37 FT-LB)

RADIUS ARM BRACKET

**Fig. 14 Coil spring replacement. 4 X 4 models**

## 4 X 4 MODELS

1. Remove coil spring and radius arm as described previously.
2. Remove front drive axle as described in "Front Wheel Drive" of this chapter.
3. To remove right pivot bracket, remove upper bolt and retainer, then the side bolt and retainer, **Fig. 19**. Remove and discard lower bolt and retainer, then remove pivot bracket from crossmember.
4. To remove left pivot bracket, drill out rivets so that mounting holes in bracket and crossmember are 9/16 inch in diameter, then remove the bracket, **Fig. 20**.
5. Reverse procedure to install. Refer to **Figs. 19 and 20** for replacement hardware and torque specifications.

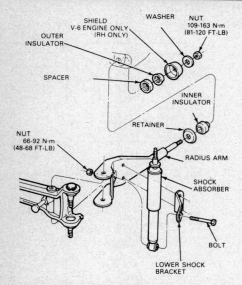

**Fig. 15   Radius arm replacement. 4 X 2 models**

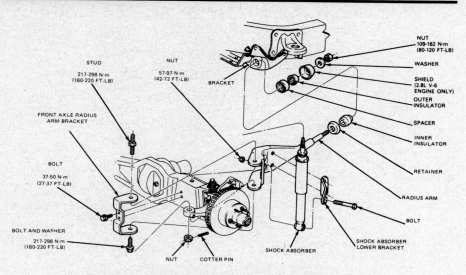

**Fig. 16   Radius arm replacement. 4 X 4 models**

## AXLE PIVOT BUSHING
### REPLACE
### 4 X 2 MODELS

1. Remove front coil spring as outlined in this chapter.
2. For left I-beam axle, remove axle pivot bolt and nut and pull left I-beam axle down until bushing is exposed. For right I-beam axle, entire right I-beam axle must be removed. Refer to "Front I-Beam Axle, Replace."
3. Install forcing screw T78P-5638-A1, bushing remover T80T-5638-A2, spacer T82T-3006-A4 and receiver cup T78P-5638-A3 onto pivot bushing. Turn forcing screw and remove pivot bushing, **Fig. 21.**
4. Reverse procedure to install. Refer to **Fig. 22.** Lower vehicle and with weight on suspension, torque pivot bushing and nut to 120-150 ft. lbs.

### 4 X 4 MODELS

Refer to "Front Wheel Drive" in this chapter for axle pivot bushing replacement procedure.

## FRONT STABILIZER BAR
### REPLACE

### ALL 1983–84, 1985 BRONCO II 4 X 2 & 1985–89 RANGER

1. Remove nuts and U-bolts retaining lower shock bracket/stabilizer bar bushing to radius arm. Remove retainers and stabilizer bar and bushings, **Fig. 23.**
2. Reverse procedure to install.

### 1985–89 BRONCO II 4 X 4

1. Remove bolts and retainers from center and right hand end of stabilizer bar, **Fig. 24.**

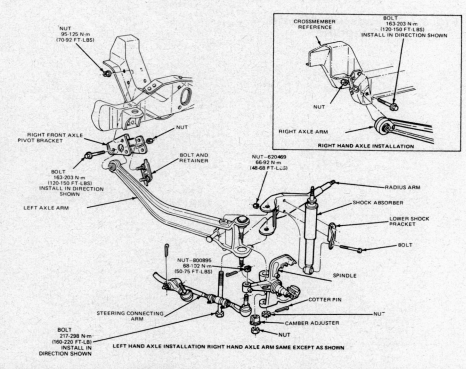

**Fig. 17   Front I-beam axle assembly 4 X 2 models. All 1983–85 & 1986–89 Ranger**

2. Remove stabilizer bar to stabilizer link attaching nut, bolt and washer.
3. Remove stabilizer bar and bushings.
4. Reverse procedure to install.

### 1986–89 BRONCO II 4 X 2

1. Remove stabilizer link assembly nut and washer, then disconnect stabilizer link assembly from front I-beam axle, **Fig. 25.**
2. Remove stabilizer bar attaching bolts, then the stabilizer bar retainers from the stabilizer bar assembly.

3. Remove stabilizer bar from vehicle.
4. Reverse procedure to install.

## FRONT WHEEL SPINDLE
### REPLACE

### 4 X 2 MODELS

1. Raise and support front of vehicle. Remove front wheel, then the brake caliper assembly. Support caliper with a length of wire.
2. Remove dust cap, cotter pin, nut re-

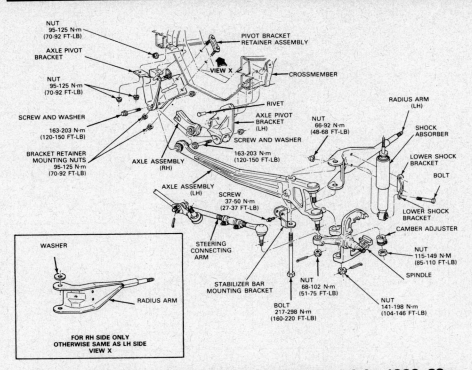

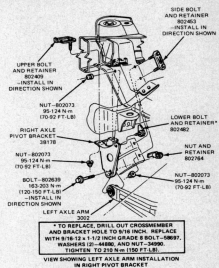

Fig. 19   Right axle pivot bracket replacement. 4 X 4 models

**Fig. 18   Front I-beam axle assembly 4 X 2 models. 1986-89 Bronco II**

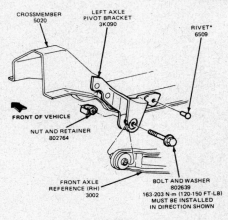

**Fig. 20   Left axle pivot bracket replacement. 4 X 4 models**

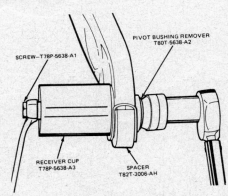

**Fig. 21   Axle pivot bushing removal. 4 X 2 models**

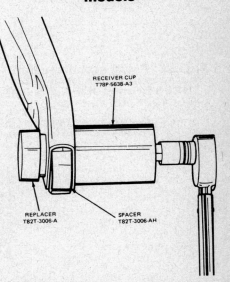

**Fig. 22   Axle pivot bushing installation. 4 X 2 models**

tainer, nut, washer, outer bearing and rotor from spindle.

3. Remove inner bearing cone and seal, then the brake dust shield. Discard the seal.

4. Disconnect steering linkage from spindle by removing cotter pin and nut.

5. Remove nut from upper ball joint stud, then the cotter pin and nut from lower ball joint stud.

6. Strike lower side of spindle to pop ball joints loose from spindle, **Fig. 26,** then

remove the spindle.

7. Reverse procedure to install. Note the following:

a. When installing ball joint stud nuts, coat studs with Loctite 242, or equivalent.

b. Install lower ball joint stud nut first and torque to 30 ft. lbs., then install upper ball joint stud nut and torque to 85-110 ft. lbs. Complete the tightening sequence by torquing lower ball joint stud nut to 104-106 ft. lbs.

c. Torque steering linkage to spindle nut to 51-75 ft. lbs.

## 4 X 4 MODELS

Refer to "Front Wheel Drive" in this chapter for front wheel spindle replacement procedure.

## POWER STEERING GEAR REPLACE

1. Disconnect pressure and return lines from steering gear and plug openings to prevent entry of dirt.

2. Remove steering gear shaft U-joint shield from flex coupling, remove bolt securing flex coupling to steering gear, and disconnect flex coupling.

3. Raise and support vehicle and remove pitman arm using a suitable puller.

4. Support steering gear and remove gear attaching bolts.

5. Work steering gear free of flex coupling and remove gear from vehicle, **Fig. 27.**

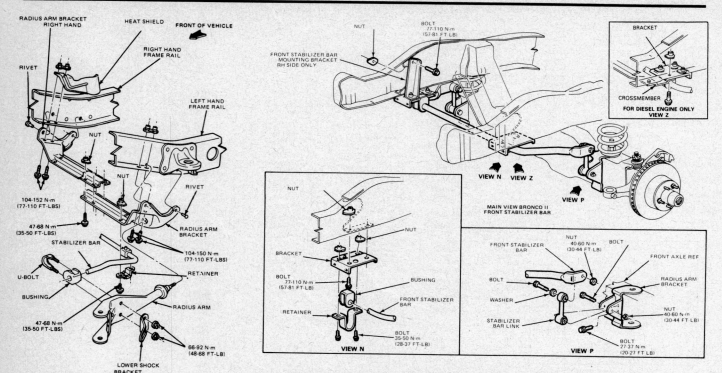

**Fig. 23 Front stabilizer bar replacement. All 1983-84, 1985 Bronco II 4 X 2 & 1985-89 Ranger**

**Fig. 24 Front stabilizer bar replacement. 1985-89 Bronco II 4 X 4**

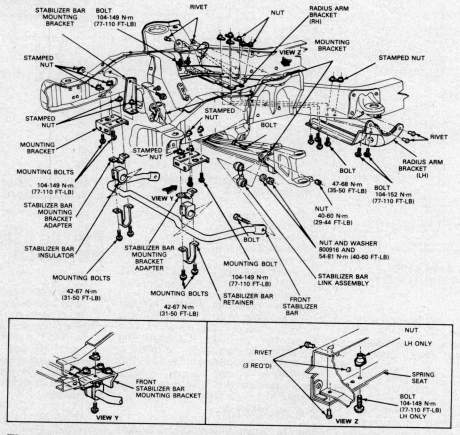

**Fig. 25 Front stabilizer bar replacement. 1986-89 Bronco II 4 X 2**

*FRONT SUSPENSION & STEERING*

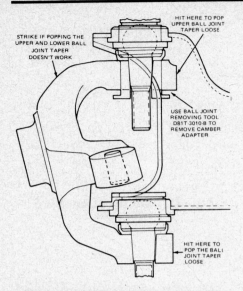

**Fig. 26  Front wheel spindle replacement. 4 X 2 models**

6. Reverse procedure to install, making sure gear is centered with index flat on input shaft pointing down, and steering wheel spokes are in horizontal position.

## MANUAL STEERING GEAR
### REPLACE

1. Disconnect flex coupling shield from

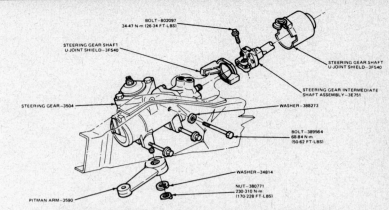

**Fig. 27  Power steering gear replacement**

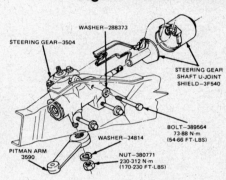

**Fig. 28  Manual steering gear replacement**

input shaft shield and slide it to upper part of intermediate shaft.
2. Remove bolt securing flex coupling to steering gear and remove steering gear input shaft shield.
3. Raise and support vehicle and remove pitman arm using a suitable puller.
4. Remove bolts securing gear to side rail and remove steering gear from vehicle, **Fig. 28.**
5. Reverse procedure to install, making sure gear is centered and flat on input shaft and is aligned with flat on flex coupling.

# FRONT WHEEL DRIVE
## INDEX

## FRONT AXLE ASSEMBLY
### REPLACE

1. Raise and support vehicle. Install jack stands under radius arm brackets.
2. Disconnect driveshaft from front axle yoke, then remove front wheels.
3. Remove disc brake calipers and position aside. Do not let caliper hang down on brake hose.
4. Disconnect steering linkage from spindle by removing the cotter pin and retaining nut.
5. Place a jack under axle arm assembly and compress the coil spring, then remove nut which retains bottom of spring to axle arm.
6. Lower axle until all spring tension is released, then remove the coil spring, spacer, seat and stud. **The axle assembly must be supported when**

removing spring and not be permitted to hang by the brake hose. If the length of the brake hose is not sufficient to provide adequate clearance for spring removal, the disc brake caliper must be removed. If so, do not suspend caliper by brake hose.
7. Disconnect shock absorber from radius arm bracket, then remove the bracket and radius arm.
8. Remove pivot bolt securing right hand axle arm to crossmember.
9. Remove clamps from axle shaft slip yoke and axle shaft, then slide rubber boot over yoke.
10. Disconnect right driveshaft from slip yoke assembly, then lower jack and remove right axle arm assembly.
11. Position another jack under differential housing, then remove bolt securing left axle arm to crossmember and

remove left axle arm assembly.
12. Reverse procedure to install. Note the following torques: pivot bracket bolts, 120-150 ft. lbs.; radius arm stud, 160-220 ft. lbs.; radius arm bracket bolts, 27-37 ft. lbs.; coil spring attaching nut, 70-100 ft. lbs.; shock absorber attaching nut, 42-72 ft. lbs.; ball joint attaching nut, 50-75 ft. lbs.; drive shaft to front axle yoke U-bolt nuts, 8-15 ft. lbs.

## SPINDLE, SHAFT & JOINT ASSEMBLY
### REPLACE

1. Raise and support vehicle. Remove front wheels.
2. Remove disc brake caliper, hub locks, wheel bearings and locknuts, then the

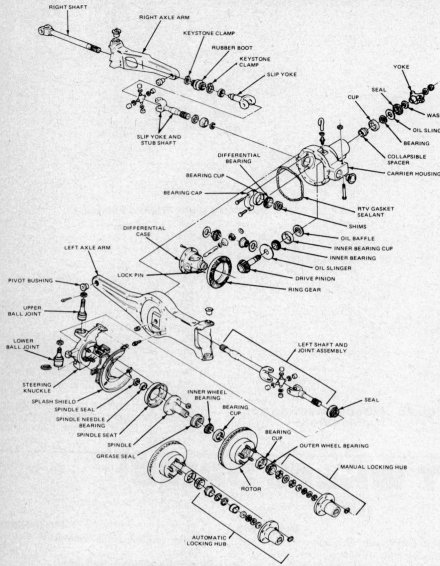

**Fig. 1   Exploded view of front axle assembly**

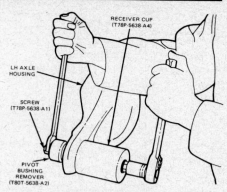

**Fig. 2   Axle pivot bushing removal**

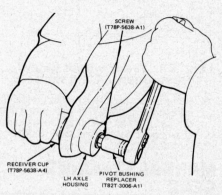

**Fig. 3   Axle pivot bushing installation**

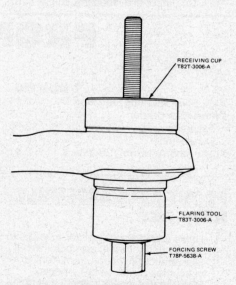

**Fig. 4   Flaring axle pivot bushing**

hub, rotor and outer wheel bearing cone, **Fig. 1.**

3. Remove and discard grease seal from rotor using grease seal remover tool No. 1175-AC.
4. Remove inner wheel bearing, then the inner and outer bearing cups.
5. Remove spindle to steering knuckle attaching nuts, then break spindle loose from knuckle and remove splash shield.
6. Remove shaft and joint assembly from right side of vehicle by pulling assembly out of carrier.
7. Remove and discard clamp from shaft and joint assembly and the stub shaft on right side of carrier. Slide rubber boot onto stub shaft, then pull shaft and joint assembly from stub shaft splines.
8. Install spindle, on second step, in suitable soft jawed vise.
9. Remove oil seal and needle bearing from spindle using bearing remover tool No. T50T-100-A and grease seal

remover tool No. 1175-AC, or equivalent. Remove oil seal from shaft, if necessary.
10. Reverse procedure to install. Torque spindle to steering knuckle attaching nuts to 35-45 ft. lbs.

# RIGHT HAND SLIP YOKE & STUB SHAFT ASSEMBLY, CARRIER, CARRIER OIL SEAL & BEARING REPLACE

1. Disconnect driveshaft from yoke. Position driveshaft aside so it will not interfere with carrier removal.
2. Remove both spindles, **Fig. 1,** then the left and right shaft and U-joint assemblies as described previously.
3. Support carrier using a suitable jack,

then remove carrier to support arm attaching bolts.
4. Remove carrier from support arm, then drain lubricant and remove carrier from vehicle.
5. Install carrier in suitable holding fixture, then rotate slip yoke and shaft assembly until open end of snap ring is exposed.
6. Remove snap ring, then the slip yoke and shaft assembly from carrier.

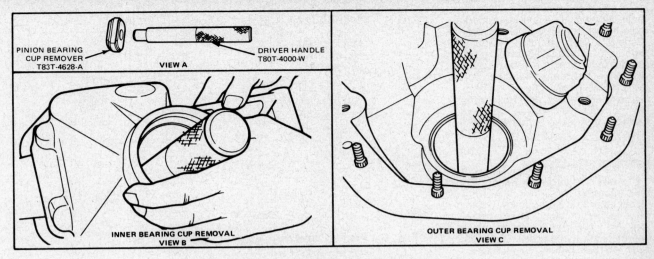

PINION BEARING CUP REMOVER T83T-4628-A

DRIVER HANDLE T80T-4000-W

VIEW A

INNER BEARING CUP REMOVAL VIEW B

OUTER BEARING CUP REMOVAL VIEW C

**Fig. 5   Bearing cup removal**

7. Remove oil seal and caged needle bearings simultaneously from carrier using tools No. T50T-100-A and D880L-100-A or equivalent. Discard seal and bearings.
8. Reverse procedure to install. Note the following:
   a. Clean mating surfaces of carrier and support arm. Apply a narrow bead of RTV sealant to mating surfaces.
   b. Install carrier attaching bolts hand tight, then torque in a clockwise or counterclockwise pattern to 40-50 ft. lbs.
   c. Torque carrier to axle arm shear bolt to 75-95 ft. lbs.
   d. Torque driveshaft to yoke U-bolt nuts to 8-15 ft. lbs.

## STEERING KNUCKLE & BALL JOINTS
### REPLACE

1. Remove spindle, **Fig. 1**, then the shaft and joint assembly as described previously.
2. If tie rod has not been removed, remove cotter pin and nut and disconnect tie rod from steering arm.
3. Remove cotter pin and loosen nut on top ball joint stud. Loosen bottom nut inside knuckle, then remove top nut.
4. Break spindle loose from ball stud, then remove camber adjuster. Mark position of adjuster for assembly reference.
5. Install steering knuckle in suitable soft jawed vise, then remove snap ring from lower ball joint socket.
6. Press ball joints from steering knuckle using C-Frame tool No. T74P-4635-C with ball joint remover tool No. T83T-3050-A, or equivalent.
7. Reverse procedure to install. The lower ball joint must be installed first. When installing ball joint stud nuts, first torque nut on lower stud to 40 ft. lbs., then torque nut on upper stud to 85-100 ft. lbs. Complete tightening sequence by torquing lower nut to

95-110 ft. lbs.

## AXLE PIVOT BUSHING
### REPLACE

1. Remove front axle assembly as described previously.
2. Remove pivot bushing from axle housing, **Fig. 2**.
3. Install bushing in axle housing, **Fig. 3**, then flare the bushing to prevent movement, **Fig. 4**. Complete installation by crimping bushing lip.

## FRONT DRIVESHAFT
### REPLACE

1. Remove nuts and U-bolts securing front driveshaft to front drive axle.
2. Remove U-joint assembly from axle yoke, then slide the splined yoke assembly out of transfer case front output shaft and remove driveshaft assembly.
3. Reverse procedure to install. Torque attaching nuts to 8-15 ft. lbs.

## DIFFERENTIAL CARRIER
### DISASSEMBLE

1. Remove left hand axle arm assembly as described previously.
2. Loosen carrier to axle arm retaining bolts, then drain fluid from differential.
3. Remove carrier retaining bolts, then the carrier.
4. Remove slip yoke and stub shaft as described previously, then install carrier in suitable holding fixture.
5. Clean gasket material from all mating surfaces, then remove bearing caps. Note location of markings on caps and carrier for assembly reference.
6. Remove differential case, then the bearing cups from carrier. Note which side of carrier bearing cups were removed from.
7. Support carrier with nose end up and hold end yoke with a suitable tool, then remove nut and washer from pin-

ion shaft.
8. Remove end yoke using tool No. T65L-4851-B, or equivalent. The yoke must be replaced if the seal contact area shows any signs of wear.
9. Remove drive pinion, drive pinion oil seal using bearing cup puller tool No. T77F-1102-A, then remove outer pinion bearing cone, oil slinger and collapsible spacer from carrier. Discard oil seal and collapsible spacer.
10. Remove inner pinion bearing cup, **Fig. 5**, then remove oil baffle from bearing cup bore.
11. Invert carrier, then remove outer pinion bearing cup, **Fig. 5**.
12. Remove differential case bearings and shims. Wire shims, bearing cup and cone together and note which side of case they were removed from.
13. Install differential case in suitable soft jawed vise. Remove ring gear attaching bolts, then the ring gear from case. **Whenever the ring gear is removed, the ring gear attaching bolts must be replaced.**
14. Remove inner pinion bearing cone and oil slinger from drive pinion using suitable tool.
15. Inspect all components for wear or damage and replace as necessary.

### Total Differential Case Endplay Check

1. Install ring gear onto differential case. Torque bolts alternately and evenly to 50-60 ft. lbs.
2. Clean trunnions on differential, then install master differential bearings on to case. Remove any burrs and nicks from hubs so bearings will rotate freely.
3. Install differential case into carrier, without drive pinion. Ensure that the case moves freely in the carrier.
4. Install suitable dial indicator on differential case flange. Position tip of indicator on a flat of one ring gear bolt.
5. Move differential case toward dial indicator as far as possible, then zero the indicator with force still applied. The dial indicator should have a mini-

mum travel of .200 inch.

6. Move differential case away from dial indicator as far as possible and record reading. This reading indicates amount of shims needed behind differential side bearings to take up total clearance between differential bearing and case.

7. Remove differential case from carrier. Do not remove master differential bearings from case at this time.

### Depth Gauge Check

1. Install oil baffle into inner bearing cup bore in carrier.

2. Install inner and outer pinion bearing cups in carrier using forcing screw tool No. T75T-1176-A and pinion bearing cup replacers tool No. T71P-4616-A, **Fig. 6.**

3. Position a new rear pinion bearing over aligning adapter T76P-4020-A1, then install into pinion bearing retainer assembly.

4. Install front pinion bearing into bearing cup in carrier. The old bearing may be reused, if serviceable. Assemble handle T76P-4020-A11 onto screw T76P-4020-A9 and hand tighten.

5. Install gauge tube T76P-4020-A7 into differential bearing bore, then install bearing caps and torque to 35-40 ft. lbs. Set bearing preload by torquing handle to 20-40 inch lbs.

6. Using a feeler gauge, measure distance between gauge tube and gauge block T76P-4020-A10.

7. If there are no markings on pinion gear, select an oil slinger with a thickness equal to the dimension measured in step 6. If pinion gear is marked with a "+" reading, this amount must be subtracted from the dimension measured in step 6. For example, if pinion is marked +2, use a slinger .002 inch thinner than measured. If pinion is marked with a "–" reading, this amount must be added to the measured dimension.

8. Measure thickness of oil slinger with a micrometer to verify correct size, then install slinger on pinion and press bearing onto pinion.

9. Apply lubricant C1AZ-19590-B, or equivalent, to ends of outer pinion bearing rollers, then install outer bearing cone in outer bearing cup.

10. Install drive pinion with inner bearing cone and oil slinger into carrier.

### Drive Pinion Preload & Final Depth Checks

1. With pinion installed in carrier, install outer bearing cone and oil slinger.

2. Install end yoke, washer, deflector and slinger on pinion shaft using alignment tool No. T80T-4000-G and flange holder T78P-4851-A.

3. Install new pinion nut and tighten to a rotating torque of 10 inch lbs. Rotate pinion several times to seal bearing.

4. Install gauge tube T76P-4020-A7 in carrier, then install the bearing caps and torque to 35-40 ft. lbs.

5. Install final check gauge block

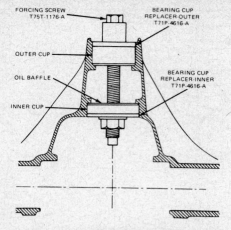

**Fig. 6 Pinion bearing cup installation**

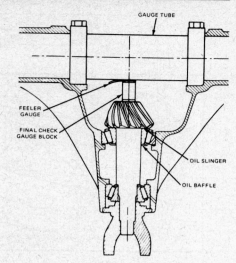

**Fig. 7 Pinion depth check**

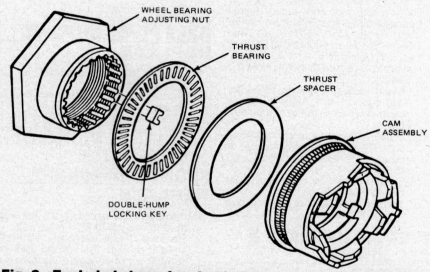

**Fig. 8 Exploded view of revised wheel bearing adjusting nut assembly**

T83T-4020-F58 on top of pinion button under gauge tube, **Fig. 7.** Press down on ends of gauge block to make sure it is level on pinion.

6. Measure clearance between gauge tube and final check block using a feeler gauge until a slight drag is felt. Clearance should be .020 inch added to the drive pinion etching, with a tolerance of ±.002 inch. For example, a pinion with an etching of "+2" will have a .022 inch clearance and a .002 inch tolerance. Therefore, shims equalling .020-.024 inch would be required.

7. When drive pinion is set at correct depth, remove yoke using tools No. T78P-4851-A and T65L-4851-B. Remove yoke, nut and washer, and outer bearing cone.

8. Install a new collapsible spacer and outer bearing cone.

9. Apply lubricant C6AZ-19580-E, or equivalent, to drive pinion oil seal,

then install the seal using tool No. T71T-3010-R. Make sure that garter spring remains in place.

10. Install yoke. Torque nut to 175 ft. lbs.

11. Using an inch-pound torque wrench, check rotational torque of pinion. Rotational torque should be 15-35 inch lbs. If rotational torque is less than 15 inch lbs., tighten the pinion nut in small increments until 15-35 inch lbs. is reached. Do not tighten nut more than 225 ft. lbs. If reading is more than 35 inch lbs., the collapsible spacer has been compressed too far and must be replaced.

### Differential Case, Service

1. Install differential case in suitable vise, then drive out lock pin which retains pinion mate shaft to case.

2. Remove drive pinion mate shaft using a suitable drift pin.

3. Rotate pinion mate gears and side gears until mate gears are exposed in

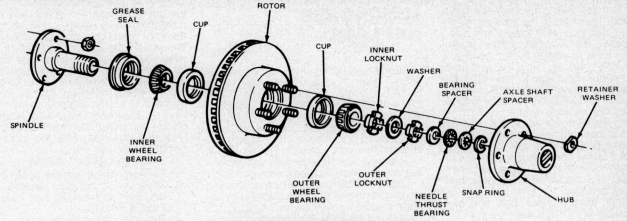

**Fig. 9  Manual locking hub**

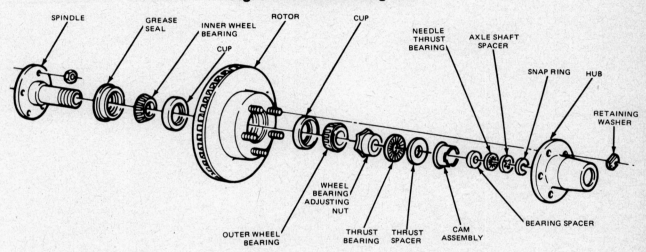

**Fig. 10  Automatic locking hub**

windows of case, then remove mate gears and spherical washers.

4. Remove side gears and thrust washers, then install lock pin in case. Set lock pin in place by peening some metal of the case over pin.

5. Apply lubricant C1AZ-19590-B, or equivalent, to all gears and washers.

6. While holding side gears in position in case, install pinion mate gears and spherical washers. Rotate side gears and pinion mate gears until holes in washers and pinion mate gears line up with holes in case, then install pinion mate shaft into case. Ensure that lock pin hole in shaft lines up with lock pin holes in case.

## ASSEMBLE

1. Install ring gear on differential case, using new bolts. Torque bolts alternately and evenly to 50-60 ft. lbs.

2. Position differential case in carrier. Move case away from drive pinion gear until it is seated against cross-bore face of carrier.

3. Install suitable dial indicator on differential so that indicator tip rests on a flat of one case bolt. Zero the dial indicator.

4. Force ring gear against pinion gear, then rock ring gear to make sure gear teeth are in contact. Move ring gear away from drive pinion gear, making sure indicator returns to zero. Repeat this procedure until reading is the same. This reading, minus .006 inch, indicates amount of shims needed between differential case and differential bearing on ring gear side.

5. Remove differential case from carrier, then the master bearings from case.

6. Install required shims, as determined in step 4, on ring gear hub of differential case.

7. Install bearing cone and bearing onto ring gear hub using differential side bearing replacer tool T80T-4000-J.

8. To determine amount of shims needed on hub of drive pinion side of differential case, subtract reading obtained in step 4 from reading obtained in "Total Differential Case Endplay" procedure, then add .003 inch to this amount.

9. Install required shims, as determined in step 8, on hub of drive pinion side of differential case.

10. Install bearing cone and bearing onto drive pinion hub using differential side

bearing replacer tool T80T-4000-J. Protect ring gear side bearing using step plate D80L-630-5, or equivalent.

11. Install bearing cone on pinion side of differential case. Protect ring gear bearing using tool No. T-53T-4621-C, or equivalent.

12. Install differential bearing cups on bearing cones, then install differential case into carrier. If ring gear and drive pinion have alignment marks, the marks must be aligned during assembly.

13. Remove dial indicator and spreader from case, then install bearing caps and bolts. Make sure that markings on caps correspond, in both position and direction, to markings on carrier. Torque bolts to 35-40 ft. lbs.

14. Install suitable dial indicator on differential case and measure ring gear and pinion backlash at three equally spaced points on ring gear. Backlash must measure .004-.010 inch on 1983-85 models, or .005-.008 inch on 1986-89 models, and cannot vary more than .003 inch between measuring points. If backlash is high, move ring gear closer to pinion by moving shims to ring gear side from opposite

side. If backlash is low, move ring gear away from pinion by moving shims from ring gear side to opposite side.

15. Apply a narrow bead of RTV sealant on carrier mounting face support arm mating surfaces. Allow the sealant at least one hour curing time after the carrier is assembled to the axle arm before filling the differential with lubricant or operating vehicle.

16. Install differential assembly onto left hand axle arm, using two guide pins. Install bolts and torque to 40-50 ft. lbs. Torque one bolt, then the bolt directly opposite it. Torque remaining bolts in a clockwise or counterclockwise direction.

17. Install carrier shear bolt and nut. Torque to 75-95 ft. lbs.

## LOCKING HUB REPLACE

Ranger and Bronco II 4 x 4 models built with front axle assembly No. E57A-3002-AFA (3.45 ratio) and E57A-3002-AGA (3.75 ratio) equipped with automatic locking hubs will incorporate (as of January 1985) a new two piece wheel bearing spindle nut locking key and engagement cam retention system, **Fig. 8.** This new retention system will replace the integral one piece key/cam design.

To prevent damage to the spindle during removal, remove adjusting nut locking key from spindle keyway under adjusting nut prior to nut removal. A slight movement of the nut will loosen the locking key so that a magnet can be used for removal. During the front wheel bearing adjustment procedure, align the closest two holes in the wheel bearing adjusting nut with the center of the spindle keyway slot. Advance the nut to the next hole if required. To ensure proper wheel retention, install adjusting nut locking key in alignment with spindle keyway and insert into locknut holes. The double humped portion must be completely seated and flush with the locknut assembly.

1. Raise and support vehicle.
2. Remove wheel and tire assembly.
3. Remove lug nut stud retainer washers, then the locking hub assembly, **Figs. 9 and 10.**
4. Reverse procedure to install.

---

**NOTE:** Refer to the back of this manual for manufacturer's special service tool suppliers.

---

**Page No.**          **Page No.**          **Page No.**

# SPECIFICATIONS
## GENERAL ENGINE SPECIFICATIONS

| Year | Engine CID ①/Liter | Carburetor | Bore & Stroke | Compression Ratio | Net H.P. @ RPM | Maximum Torque Lbs. Ft. @ RPM | Normal Oil Pressure Pounds |
|---|---|---|---|---|---|---|---|
| 1986 | 4-140/2.3L | EFI | 3.780 x 3.126 | 9.5 | 88 @ 4000 | 132 @ 2200 | 40-60 |
| | V6-171/2.8L | 2150, 2 Bbl. ② | 3.650 x 2.700 | 8.7 | 115 @ 4600 | 150 @ 2600 | 40-60 |
| | V6-182/3.0L | EFI | 3.500 x 3.1400 | 9.3 | 145 @ 4800 | 165 @ 3600 | 40-60 |
| 1987 | 4-140/2.3L | EFI | 3.780 x 3.126 | — | — | — | 40-60 |
| 1987-89 | V6-182/3.0L | EFI | 3.500 x 3.1400 | 9.3 | 145 @ 4800 | 165 @ 3600 | 40-60 |

①—Cubic Inch Displacement.
②—Motorcraft.

## ENGINE TIGHTENING SPECIFICATIONS*

*Torque specifications are for clean & lightly lubricated threads only. Dry or dirty threads produce increased friction which prevents accurate measurement of tightness.

| Year | Engine | Spark Plugs Ft. Lbs. | Cylinder Head Bolts Ft. Lbs. | Intake Manifold Ft. Lbs. | Exhaust Manifold Ft. Lbs. | Rocker Arm Shaft Bracket Ft. Lbs. | Rocker Arm Cover Ft. Lbs. | Connecting Rod Cap Bolts Ft. Lbs. | Main Bearing Cap Bolts Ft. Lbs. | Flywheel To Crankshaft Ft. Lbs. | Vibration Damper Or Pulley Ft. Lbs. |
|---|---|---|---|---|---|---|---|---|---|---|---|
| 1986 | 4-140 | 5-10 | 80-90 | 14-21 | 16-23 | — | 6-8 | 30-36 | 80-90 | 56-64 | 100-120 |
| | V6-171 | 18-28 | 70-85 | ① | 20-30 | 43-50 | 3-5 | 19-24 | 65-75 | 47-52 | 85-96 |
| | V6-182 | 5-11 | 63-80 | 16-19 | 15-22 | 18.4-25.8 ② | 6-8 | 20-25 | 65-81 | 54-64 | 103-133 |
| 1987 | 4-140 | 5-10 | 80-90 | 15-22 | 20-30 | — | 6-8 | 30-36 | 75-85 | 56-64 | 103-133 |
| | V6-182 | 5-11 | 63-80 | 16-19 | 15-22 | 18.4-25.8 ② | 6-8 | 20-25 | 65-81 | 54-64 | 103-133 |
| 1988 | V6-182 | 5-11 | ③ | ④ | 15-22 | ②⑥ | 6-8 | 21-28 | 65-81 | 54-64 | 103-133 |
| 1989 | V6-182 | 5-11 | ⑤ | ④ | 19 | ②⑥ | 6-8 | 21-28 | 66 | 54-64 | 107 |

①—Intake manifold stud to block, 10-12 ft. lbs.; intake manifold bolt or nut, 15 to 18 ft. lbs.
②—Rocker arm pivot bolt.
③—Torque in two steps; first to 50–60 ft. lbs., then to 80–90 ft. lbs.
④—Torque in two steps; first to 11 ft. lbs., then to 18 ft. lbs.
⑤—Torque in two steps; first to 37 ft. lbs., then to 68 ft. lbs.
⑥—Torque in two steps; first to 8 ft. lbs., then to 24 ft. lbs.

## ALTERNATOR SPECIFICATIONS

| Year | Make Or Model | Current Rating | |
|---|---|---|---|
| | | Amperes | Volts |
| 1986-89 | Ford | 40 | 15 |
| | Ford | 60 | 15 |
| | Ford | 65 | 15 |
| | Ford | 75 | 15 |

## STARTING MOTOR SPECIFICATIONS

| Year | Starter Type | Ampere Draw Normal Load | Engine Cranking Speed RPM | No Load Ampere @ 12 Volts | Brushes Length Inch | Brushes Wear Limit Inch | Spring Tension Ounces |
|---|---|---|---|---|---|---|---|
| 1986-89 | All | 150-200 | 180-250 | 80 | .5 | .25 | 80 |

## WHEEL ALIGNMENT SPECIFICATIONS

| Year | Caster Angle, Degrees | | Camber Angle, Degrees | | Toe-In Inch | Lateral Tilt① Inch | |
| | Limits | Desired | Limits | Desired | | Front Wheel | Rear Wheel |
|---|---|---|---|---|---|---|---|
| 1986-87 | +3 to +5 | +4 | −.3 to +.7 | +.2 | 1/32 | .6① | .8① |
| 1988-89 | +2 ½ to +4 ½ | +3 ½ | −.3 to +.7 | +.2 | 1/32 | .6① | .8① |

①—Maximum side to side height difference, measured from floor pan to top of wheel house opening.

## BRAKE SPECIFICATIONS

| Year | Model | Rear Drum I.D. | Wheel Cyl. Bore | | Disc Brake Rotor | | | | | Master Cyl. I.D. |
| | | | Front Disc | Rear Drum | Nominal Thickness | Minimum Thickness | Thickness Variation (Parallelism) | Run Out (TIR) | Finish (Microinch) | |
|---|---|---|---|---|---|---|---|---|---|---|
| 1986-87 | All | 9① | — | — | .980 | .810 | .001 | .003 | 15-125 | .9375 |
| 1988-89 | All | 9① | — | — | .980 | .810 | .001 | .002 | 15-125 | .9375 |

①—Standard model, except standard model, 10 inches.

## DRIVE AXLE SPECIFICATIONS

| Year | Make Or Model | Carrier Type | Ring Gear & Pinion Backlash Inch | Pinion Bearing Preload | | | | Differential Bearing Preload | Pinion Nut Torque Ft. Lbs. |
| | | | | New Bearings With Seal Inch Lbs. | Used Bearings With Seal Inch Lbs. | New Bearings Less Seal Inch Lbs. | Used Bearings Less Seal Inch Lbs. | | |
|---|---|---|---|---|---|---|---|---|---|
| 1986-89 | Ford 7½" | Integral | .008-.015① | 16-29 | 8-14 | — | — | .006 | 170 |
| | Dana Model 30 | Integral | .005-.009 | — | — | 20-40 | — | .015 | 200–220 |

①—.012 to .015 inch preferred.

## COOLING SYSTEM & CAPACITY DATA

| Year | Model Or Engine | Cooling Capacity Qts. | | Radiator Cap Relief Pressure, Lbs. | Thermo. Opening Temp. | Fuel Tank Gals. | Engine Oil Refill Qts. ① | Transmission Oil | | Rear Axle Oil Pints |
| | | Less A/C | With A/C | | | | | 5 Speed Pints | Auto. Trans. Qts. ② | |
|---|---|---|---|---|---|---|---|---|---|---|
| 1986 | 4-140 | ④ | ④ | 13 | 192 | 17② | 5③ | 5.9 | 9.5 | ⑤ |
| | V6-171 | 8 | 8 | 13 | 192 | 17② | 5③ | 5.9 – | 9.5 | 3.5 |
| | V6-182 | 11.8 | 11.8 | 13 | 192 | 17 | 4.5③ | 5.9 | 9.5 | ⑤ |
| 1987 | 4-140 | ④ | ④ | 13 | 192 | 17② | 5③ | 5.9 | 9.5 | ⑤ |
| | V6-182 | 11.8 | 11.8 | 13 | 192 | 17 | 4.5③ | 5.9 | 9.5 | ⑤ |
| 1988 | V6-182 | 11.8 | 11.8 | 13 | 192 | 17 | 5③ | 5.6 | 8.5 | ⑤ |
| 1989 | V6-182 | 11.8 | 11.8 | 13 | 192 | 17⑥ | 4.5③ | 4.8 | 9.5 | ⑤ |

①—Approximate, make final check with dipstick.

②—Some selected 1986 models may be equipped with a 15.2 gal. fuel tank.

③—Includes filter.

④—Man. trans. models, 6.8 qts.; auto. trans. models, 7.6 qts.

⑤—Ford 7½ inch ring gear axle, 3.5 pts.; Dana Model 30 axle, 2.5 pts.

⑥—Extended van models are equipped with a 21 gal. fuel tank

# ELECTRICAL

## INDEX

## FUSE PANEL & FLASHER LOCATION

The fuse panel is located under the LH side of the instrument panel.

The hazard warning flasher is located on the back side of the fuse panel and the turn signal flasher is located on the front side of the fuse panel.

## STARTER
### REPLACE

1. Disconnect battery ground cable, then raise and support vehicle.
2. Disconnect starter relay to starter electrical cable.
3. Remove starter mounting bolts, then starter assembly.
4. Reverse procedure to install. Torque starter mounting bolts to 15-20 ft. lbs.

## IGNITION LOCK
### REPLACE

1. Disconnect battery ground cable.
2. Remove steering column trim shroud, then disconnect electrical connector from key warning switch.
3. Place lock cylinder at Run position.
4. Position a small drift into hole in outer edge of lock cylinder, then depress retaining pin and remove lock cylinder, **Fig. 1.**
5. Lubricate lock cylinder cavity, including drive gear with lubricant No. D8AZ-19587-A or equivalent, prior to lock cylinder installation.
6. To install, turn lock cylinder to Run position, depress retaining pin and insert assembly into housing.
7. Ensure cylinder is fully seated and aligned into interlocking washer, then turn key to Off position to extend cylinder retaining pin into cylinder housing.
8. Turn key and check for proper operation in all positions.
9. Reconnect key warning switch electrical connector, then install steering column trim shroud and reconnect battery ground cable.

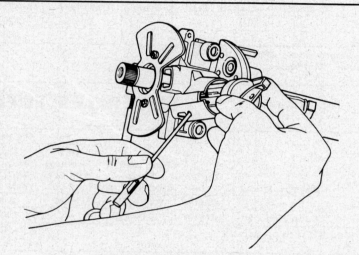

**Fig. 1   Ignition lock removal**

## IGNITION SWITCH
### REPLACE
#### 1986

1. Disconnect battery ground cable, then turn lock cylinder to Lock position.
2. On models equipped with tilt steering column, remove upper extension shroud by depressing top and bottom of shroud and releasing it from left side retaining plate.
3. On all models, remove steering column trim shroud halves.
4. Disconnect electrical connector from ignition switch.
5. Using a 1/8 inch drill bit, drill out bolt heads of switch attaching bolts, then remove bolts with a No. 3 "Easy Out" or equivalent.
6. Disengage switch from actuating pin and remove from vehicle.
7. Reverse procedure to install. Turn lock cylinder to Run position before installing switch. Tighten attaching bolts until heads shear off.

#### 1987-89

1. Disconnect battery ground cable, then

place ignition lock cylinder in the Lock position.
2. Remove steering wheel as describer under "Steering Wheel, Replace."
3. On models equipped with tilt steering column, remove upper extension shroud by depressing top and bottom of shroud to release from retaining plate.
4. On all models, remove two attaching screws from bottom of panel located to the right of the steering column, then pull panel outward to remove.
5. Remove steering column shroud as follows:
   a. Remove two screws from bottom of steering column shroud, then swing bottom portion of shroud open and remove two screws attaching shroud to retainer plate.
   b. Remove ignition lock cylinder as describer under "Ignition Lock Cylinder, Replace."
   c. Remove turn signal lever.
   d. Raise left side of shroud to clear turn signal lever receptacle, then pull upward on right side of shroud until embossment clears lock cylinder receptacle.
   e. Carefully work shroud past instru-

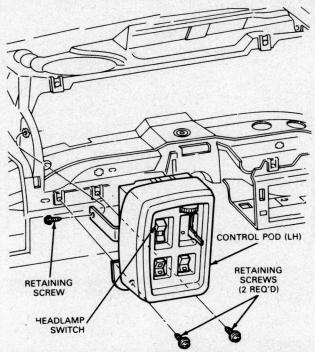

**Fig. 2 Removing control pod from instrument panel**

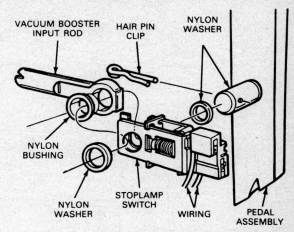

**Fig. 3 Stop light switch removal**

ment panel and remove.
6. Disconnect electrical connector from ignition switch.
7. Using a suitable hammer and chisel, rotate break-off head bolts attaching ignition switch to lock cylinder housing one turn counterclockwise, then using suitable pliers to grasp bolt head and remove bolts.
8. Disconnect ignition switch from actuator pin and remove.
9. Reverse procedure to install. Place ignition switch in the Run position prior to installation. When installing ignition lock, it also must be placed in the Run position. After completing installation, check ignition switch for proper operation.

## TURN SIGNAL/DIMMER SWITCH
### REPLACE

1. Disconnect battery ground cable.
2. Remove steering wheel as described under "Steering Wheel, Replace."
3. On models equipped with tilt column, remove upper extension shroud by depressing top and bottom of shroud to releasing retaining plate.
4. On all models, remove two screws attaching steering column trim shroud halves.
5. Remove ignition lock cylinder as described under "Ignition Lock Cylinder, Replace."
6. Grasp turn signal switch lever, then twist and pull outward to remove from switch.
7. Remove steering column shroud.
8. Peel back foam from turn signal switch, then disconnect switch electri-

cal connectors.
9. Remove turn signal switch attaching screws, then the switch.
10. Disconnect electrical connectors from turn signal switch.
11. Reverse procedure to install.

## STEERING WHEEL
### REPLACE

1. Disconnect battery ground cable.
2. Remove screws attaching horn shroud to steering wheel, disconnect horn switch/speed control electrical connectors, then remove horn shroud.
3. Remove steering wheel to steering shaft attaching bolt.
4. Remove steering wheel from steering shaft using puller tool T67L-3600-A or suitable equivalent. Do not use a knock-off type wheel puller or strike end of steering column shaft, as damage to shaft bearing may result.
5. Reverse procedure to install. Before installing steering wheel align mark on steering wheel with mark on steering shaft. Torque steering wheel attaching bolt to 23 to 33 ft. lbs. After completing installation, check steering column for proper operation.

## NEUTRAL SAFETY SWITCH
### REPLACE

1. Disconnect battery ground cable.
2. Disconnect switch electrical connector, then remove switch and O-ring using suitable tool.
3. Install new switch and O-ring and torque switch to 7-10 ft. lbs.

4. Reconnect switch electrical connector.
5. Reconnect battery ground cable, then check switch for proper operation.

## LIGHT SWITCH
### REPLACE

1. Disconnect battery ground cable.
2. Remove instrument cluster finish panel retaining screws.
3. Remove left control pod assembly retaining screws, **Fig. 2**, then pull control pod outward and disconnect electrical connector from switch.
4. Remove light switch to control pod retaining screws, then light switch.
5. Reverse procedure to install.

## STOP LIGHT SWITCH
### REPLACE

1. Disconnect battery ground cable.
2. Disconnect electrical connector from switch, **Fig. 3**.
3. Remove hairpin retainer, slide switch and pushrod.
4. Position spacers and bushing away from brake pedal and remove switch from vehicle.
5. Reverse procedure to install.

## INSTRUMENT CLUSTER
### REPLACE

1. Disconnect battery ground cable.
2. On models equipped with standard cluster, remove cluster housing to instrument panel retaining screws, then cluster housing.
3. On models equipped with electronic cluster, remove cluster binnacle.
4. On all models, remove four instrument cluster to instrument panel retaining screws, **Fig. 4**, then pull cluster outward.
5. Disconnect speedometer cable, if applicable, and wiring connectors from rear of cluster, then remove cluster from vehicle.
6. Reverse procedure to install.

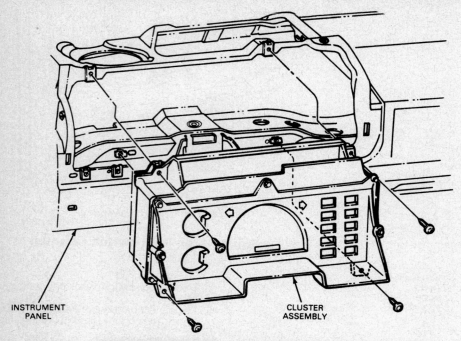

INSTRUMENT PANEL

CLUSTER ASSEMBLY

**Fig. 4 Instrument cluster replacement. Standard cluster (electronic cluster similar)**

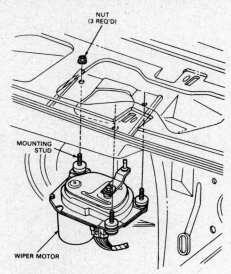

NUT (3 REQ'D)

MOUNTING STUD

WIPER MOTOR

**Fig. 5 Replacing front wiper motor**

## WIPER MOTOR
### REPLACE
#### FRONT

1. Cycle wiper motor and position wiper blades in mid-position of travel.
2. Disconnect wiper motor electrical connector, then note position of wiper arms and remove arms from pivots.
3. Remove cowl grille attaching screws, then cowl grille.
4. Remove linkage retaining clip, then disassemble linkage from motor crank arm.
5. Remove wiper motor retaining nuts, **Fig. 5**, then wiper motor.
6. Reverse procedure to install.

#### REAR

1. Disconnect battery ground cable.
2. Remove wiper arm and blade assembly.
3. Remove wiper motor shaft attaching nut and wedge block, **Fig. 6**, then remove liftgate trim panel.
4. Disconnect electrical connector from wiper motor and motor wiring pins from inner panel, then remove wiper motor from vehicle.
5. Reverse procedure to install. Before installing wiper arm and blade assembly, cycle wiper motor to park position to ensure correct installation.

## FRONT WIPER TRANSMISSION
### REPLACE

1. Perform steps 1 through 4 as outlined under "Front Wiper Motor, Replace" procedure.

2. Remove linkage pivot retaining screws and linkage from vehicle.
3. Reverse procedure to install.

## WIPER SWITCH
### REPLACE

1. Perform steps 1 through 3 as outlined under "Light Switch, Replace" procedure.
2. Remove two wiper switch to control pod assembly attaching screws, then wiper switch.
3. Reverse procedure to install.

## RADIO
### REPLACE

1. Disconnect battery ground cable.
2. Remove finish panel assembly attaching screws, then finish panel assembly.
3. Remove mounting bracket to instrument panel retaining screws, **Fig. 7**, then pull radio out from instrument panel.
4. Disconnect antenna cable, speaker wires and power feed from rear of radio.
5. Remove radio rear support, then disconnect ground cable (electronic radio) and remove radio from vehicle.
6. Reverse procedure to install.

## HEATER CORE
### REPLACE
#### EXCEPT AUXILIARY HEATER & A/C

1. Drain cooling system.
2. Disconnect hoses from heater core.

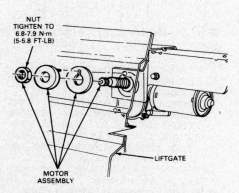

NUT TIGHTEN TO 6.8-7.9 N·m (5-5.8 FT-LB)

MOTOR ASSEMBLY

LIFTGATE

**Fig. 6 Replacing rear wiper motor**

Plug hoses and heater core to prevent spillage of coolant.
3. Working from inside passenger compartment, remove heater core access cover to plenum chamber attaching screws, then remove access cover, **Fig. 8**.
4. Depress retainer clip at top of heater core, then pull heater core rearward withdownward motion and remove from plenum chamber.
5. Reverse procedure to install.

### AUXILIARY HEATER & A/C

1. Remove first seat behind driver, if so equipped.
2. Remove auxiliary heater access cover attaching screws, then cover.
3. Remove auxiliary unit floor duct attaching screw, push downward on joint where duct connects to auxiliary unit, then rotate and remove floor duct from vehicle.
4. Remove auxiliary heater cover assembly retaining screws, **Fig. 9**, then separate cover from auxiliary heater.
5. Disconnect heater hoses from heater core, plug hoses and core to prevent

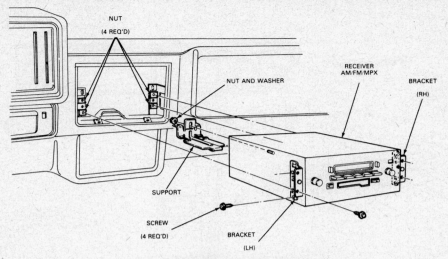

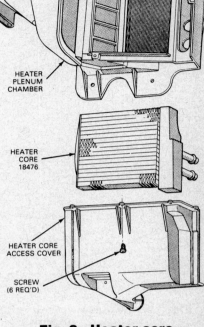

**Fig. 7  Radio replacement**

spillage of coolant, then slide core and seal assembly out through slot in housing.
6. Reverse procedure to install.

# BLOWER MOTOR REPLACE

## EXCEPT AUXILIARY HEATER & A/C

1. Disconnect battery ground cable.
2. Remove air cleaner and/or air inlet duct, if necessary.
3. Remove vacuum reservoir to blower housing attaching screws, then position reservoir aside.
4. Disconnect electrical connector and ventilation tube from blower motor.
5. Remove blower motor to housing attaching screws, position ventilation tube aside and remove blower motor from housing.
6. Reverse procedure to install, using new gasket and sealer as required.

## AUXILIARY HEATER & A/C

1. Remove first seat behind driver, if so equipped.
2. Remove access cover attaching

**Fig. 8  Heater core replacement. Except auxiliary heater**

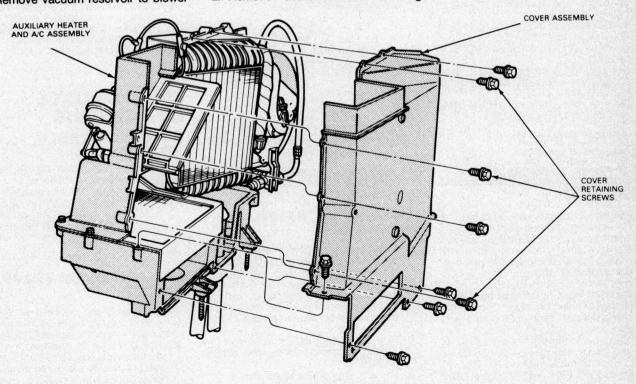

**Fig. 9  Removing auxiliary heater cover**

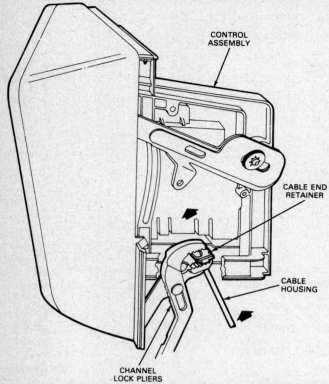

**Fig. 10 Disconnecting cables from control assembly**

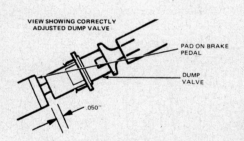

**Fig. 12 Vacuum dump valve adjustment**

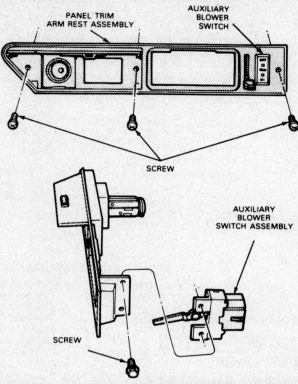

**Fig. 11 Auxiliary heater & A/C rear blower switch**

screws, then access cover.
3. Remove solenoid bracket attaching screws, then disconnect electrical connector and ventilation tube from blower motor.
4. Remove blower motor mounting plate attaching screws, then separate blower motor and wheel assembly from housing.
5. Remove wheel assembly from motor shaft, then separate blower motor from mounting plate.
6. Reverse procedure to install, using new flange seal as required.

## HEATER OR AIR CONDITIONING CONTROL ASSEMBLY
### REPLACE

1. Disconnect battery ground cable.
2. Remove instrument cluster housing cover attaching screws, then cover.
3. Remove control assembly to instrument panel retaining screws, pull control assembly outward, then disconnect electrical connectors.
4. Remove vacuum harness from function lever selector valve.
5. Using suitable pliers, compress function control cable end retainer, then pull cable in direction shown, **Fig. 10**, until cable flag can be disconnected from control assembly.
6. Disconnect temperature control cable in same manner as outlined above, then remove control assembly from vehicle.
7. Reverse procedure to install.

## BLOWER SWITCH
### REPLACE
#### INSTRUMENT PANEL MOUNTED

1. Remove heater control assembly as outlined previously, but do not disconnect control cables from assembly.
2. Using a small screwdriver, gently pry knob from blower switch.
3. Working from back of control assembly, disconnect blower switch electrical connector.
4. Remove blower switch to control assembly attaching screws, then blower switch.
5. Reverse procedure to install.

#### REAR MOUNTED

1. Disconnect battery ground cable.
2. Using a small screwdriver, gently pry

knob from blower switch, **Fig. 11**.
3. Remove ashtray bezel attaching screws, then bezel.
4. Disconnect wire harness electrical connector from blower switch.
5. Remove blower switch attaching screws, then blower switch.
6. Reverse procedure to install.

## SPEED CONTROL ADJUSTMENTS
### ACTUATOR CABLE, ADJUST

1. Remove cable retaining clip, then disengage throttle positioner.
2. Set throttle to hot idle position.
3. Pull on actuator cable to take up all slack, then while holding cable in this position, reinstall cable retaining clip.

### VACUUM DUMP VALVE, ADJUST

1. Depress brake pedal, then push inward on dump valve until valve collar bottoms against retaining clip.
2. Pull brake pedal rearward to its normal position and allow dump valve to ratchet backwards in retaining clip.
3. With pedal in this position, clearance between black housing on dump valve and white plastic pad on brake pedal should be .050-.100 inch as shown, **Fig. 12**.

# 4-140 (2.3L) GASOLINE ENGINE

**NOTE:** Refer to the 4-122 & 4-140 Gasoline Engine Section of the "Ford Bronco II & Ranger" chapter for service procedures not found in this section.

## INDEX

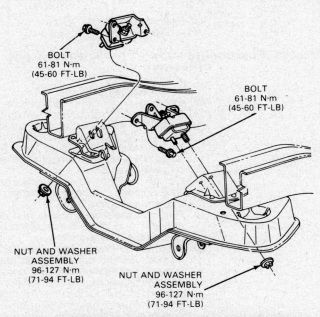

**Fig. 1    Front engine mount replacement**

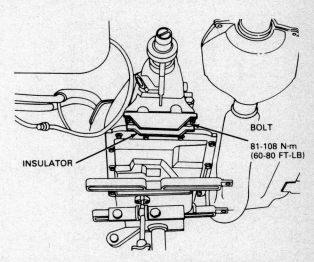

**Fig. 2    Rear engine mount replacement**

## ENGINE MOUNTS
## REPLACE
### FRONT MOUNT

1. Remove fan shroud retaining screws, then position block of wood and suitable jack under oil pan to support engine.
2. Remove insulator to frame bracket retaining nuts and washers, then loosen transmission insulator to crossmember nuts.
3. Raise engine slightly until insulator studs clear crossmember brackets.
4. Remove front mount to engine attaching nuts, then remove front mount from vehicle.
5. Reverse procedure to install. Torque all nuts and bolts to specification as shown in **Fig. 1.**

### REAR MOUNT

1. Position block of wood and suitable jack under transmission for support.
2. Remove insulator to crossmember attaching nuts, then loosen front insula-

tor to frame bracket retaining bolts.
3. Raise transmission slightly and lift insulator from transmission crossmember.
4. Remove crossmember to frame side rail bracket attaching nuts and bolts, then crossmember.
5. If applicable, remove exhaust hanger from rear engine mount.
6. Remove rear mount/insulator assembly to transmission attaching bolts, then rear mount assembly, **Fig. 2.**
7. Reverse procedure to install noting the following:
   a. When reinstalling crossmember, the positioning of the crossmember is different for manual and automatic transmission equipped vehicles. Observe notation stamped on crossmember for correct positioning, as shown in **Fig. 3.**
   b. Torque rear mount to transmission attaching bolts to 60-80 ft. lbs., crossmember to frame side rail bracket attaching nuts and bolts to 65-85 ft. lbs., and front insulator attaching nuts and bolts to 71-94 ft. lbs.

## ENGINE
## REPLACE

1. Disconnect battery ground cable, then drain cooling system.
2. Disconnect air cleaner outlet tube, idle speed control hose, upper and lower radiator hoses and heater hoses.
3. Disconnect lower intake manifold hose from heater hose T-fitting, then remove fan shroud attaching bolts and fan shroud.
4. Disconnect alternator electrical connectors, remove throttle linkage shield, then disconnect accelerator and cruise control (if applicable) cables from throttle body and position aside.
5. On models equipped with A/C, discharge refrigerant, then disconnect hoses and clutch electrical connector at compressor.
6. On all models, disconnect ignition coil electrical connector at lower left front of engine.
7. Working from beneath lower intake manifold, disconnect TFI module electrical connector at distributor.
8. Disconnect knock sensor electrical connector from upper intake manifold.

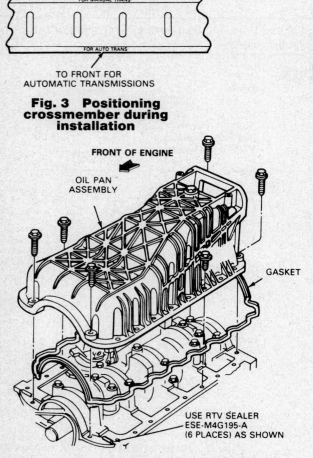

TO FRONT FOR MANUAL
TRANSMISSIONS

FOR MANUAL TRANS

FOR AUTO TRANS

TO FRONT FOR
AUTOMATIC TRANSMISSIONS

**Fig. 3  Positioning crossmember during installation**

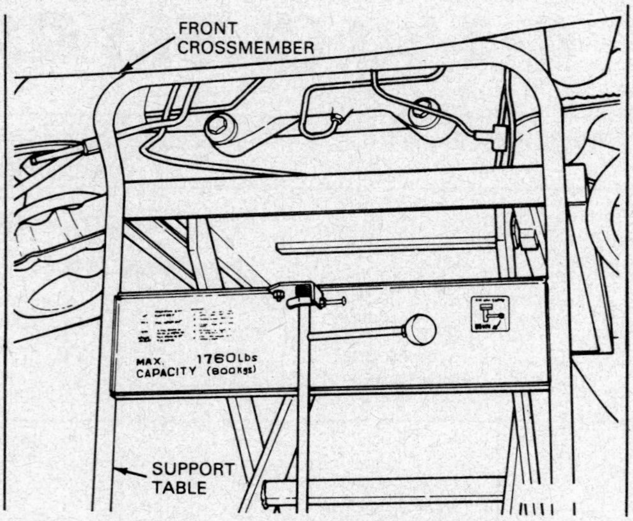

FRONT OF ENGINE

OIL PAN ASSEMBLY

GASKET

USE RTV SEALER
ESE-M4G195-A
(6 PLACES) AS SHOWN

**Fig. 5  Oil pan removal & installation**

FRONT CROSSMEMBER

MAX. 1760 Lbs
CAPACITY (800 kgs)

SUPPORT TABLE

**Fig. 4  Positioning support table under front crossmember**

9. Disconnect and mark all hoses to vacuum tree of upper intake manifold.
10. Disconnect electrical connector and vacuum hose at EGR valve.
11. Working from inside cab, remove engine cover, then disconnect throttle position sensor electrical connector at rear of throttle body.
12. Disconnect oil pressure sender electrical connector, then hoses to fuel return and supply lines.
13. Disconnect fuel injection wiring harness electrical connector.
14. Working at lower intake manifold, disconnect electrical connectors at air charge temperature (ACT) and coolant temperature sensors.
15. Remove ground strap retaining nut and ground strap at right rear of engine.
16. On manual transmission equipped vehicles, proceed as follows:
    a. Position shift lever in Neutral.
    b. Remove shift lever to floor and shift lever to transmission retaining bolts.
    c. Remove shift lever assembly from vehicle.
17. Raise and support vehicle, if equipped

with automatic transmission, disconnect fluid lines at radiator.
18. Disconnect power steering pressure switch electrical connector from steering gear, if applicable.
19. Ensuring steering wheel and front wheels are centered in travel, remove intermediate steering column shaft to steering gear retaining bolt, then disconnect shaft from gear.
20. Disconnect starter electrical cables, then route cables out from crossmember.
21. On models equipped with manual transmission, remove hydraulic hose to slave cylinder retaining pin, then disconnect and plug hose to prevent spillage.
22. On all models, disconnect oxygen sensor electrical connector.
23. Remove retaining nuts and bolts, then exhaust manifold, exhaust pipe and catalytic converter.
24. Disconnect speedometer cable, tachometer cable (if applicable) and back-up lamp switch electrical connector from transmission.
25. On models equipped with manual transmission, disconnect shift indica-

tor sensor electrical connector.
26. On models equipped with automatic transmission, disconnect electrical connector from neutral start switch, and throttle and kickdown cable from transmission lever. Route kickdown cable out of engine compartment and remove from vehicle.
27. On all models, remove driveshaft. Plug opening in extension housing to prevent spillage of fluid.
28. Remove wheel assemblies, then disconnect and remove stabilizer bar from lower control arms.
29. Disconnect brake lines at frame brackets behind spindles, then position suitable jack under lower control arm. Raise jack slightly until tension is applied to coil spring, then remove spindle to upper ball joint retaining nut and bolt. Lower jack to disconnect spindle from ball joint, then position safety chains around lower control arms and spring upper seat.
30. Position suitable jack under transmission, raise transmission slightly, then remove crossmember to frame and crossmember to transmission retaining nuts and bolts. Remove crossmember from vehicle.
31. Position engine support table 109-0002 or equivalent under front crossmember and engine assembly, **Fig. 4.**
32. Lower vehicle until front crossmember rests on support table. Position blocks of wood under front crossmember and transmission to keep assembly level, then install safety chains around crossmember and support table.
33. Remove engine and crossmember to frame retaining nuts and bolts from both sides of vehicle.
34. Disconnect any remaining wires or hoses that will interfere with engine removal, raise vehicle body until clear of engine/transmission assembly and support table, then lower support ta-

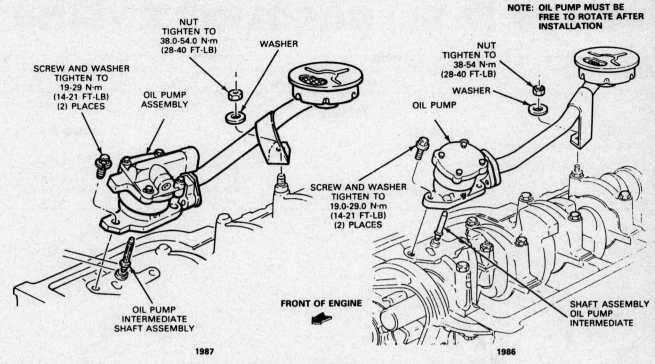

NOTE: OIL PUMP MUST BE FREE TO ROTATE AFTER INSTALLATION

NUT TIGHTEN TO 38.0-54.0 N·m (28-40 FT-LB)

WASHER

SCREW AND WASHER TIGHTEN TO 19-29 N·m (14-21 FT-LB) (2) PLACES

OIL PUMP ASSEMBLY

NUT TIGHTEN TO 38-54 N·m (28-40 FT-LB)

WASHER

OIL PUMP

SCREW AND WASHER TIGHTEN TO 19.0-29.0 N·m (14-21 FT-LB) (2) PLACES

OIL PUMP INTERMEDIATE SHAFT ASSEMBLY

FRONT OF ENGINE

SHAFT ASSEMBLY OIL PUMP INTERMEDIATE

1987

1986

**Fig. 6   Oil pump removal & installation**

ble and remove engine/transmission assembly from vehicle.

35. Reverse procedure to install.

## OIL PAN
## REPLACE

1. Disconnect battery ground cable, then remove engine oil dipstick and tube.
2. Remove engine mount attaching nuts.
3. On models with automatic transmission, disconnect oil cooler lines at radiator.
4. On all models, remove fan shroud attaching bolts and fan shroud.
5. On models with automatic transmission, remove radiator attaching bolts, then lift radiator upward and suspend from hood with wire.
6. On all models, raise and support front of vehicle, then drain engine oil from crankcase.
7. Remove starter motor, then disconnect exhaust manifold tube at Thermactor check valve.
8. Remove transmission mount to crossmember attaching nuts.
9. On models with automatic transmission, remove bell crank from converter housing, then detach oil cooler lines from retainer at engine block.

10. On models with automatic transmission, remove front crossmember assembly.
11. On models with manual transmission, remove front right hand lower shock absorber mounting.
12. On all models, position a suitable jack under engine, then raise engine slightly and position a piece of wood approximately 2½ inches to support engine in the slightly raised position. Remove jack from under engine.
13. On models with automatic transmission, position a suitable jack under transmission and raise transmission slightly.
14. On all models, remove oil pan attaching bolts, **Fig. 5,** then lower oil pan to chassis and remove oil pump drive and pickup tube assembly.
15. On models with automatic transmission, the oil pan is removed out through the front of the engine compartment. On models with manual transmission, the oil pan is removed out through the rear of the engine compartment.
16. Reverse procedure to install. Prior to installing oil pan, clean gasket surfaces, oil pump exterior and oil pump pickup tube screen. Tighten oil pan at-

taching bolts in the following sequence:
   a. Torque two oil pan to transmission attaching bolts to 29 to 40 ft. lbs., then loosen bolts ½ turn.
   b. Alternately and evenly torque oil pan to engine block attaching bolts to 7 to 10 ft. lbs.
   c. Retorque the two remaining oil pan to transmission bolts to 29 to 40 ft. lbs.
   d. Ensure oil pan is installed flush with rear face of engine block.

## OIL PUMP
## REPLACE

1. Remove oil pan as described under "Oil Pan, Replace."
2. Remove oil pump pickup tube bracket to main bearing cap bolt stud attaching nut, **Fig. 6.**
3. Remove oil pump to engine block attaching bolts, then remove oil pump.
4. Reverse procedure to install. Prior to installation, prime oil pump. Torque oil pump to engine block attaching bolts to 14 to 21 ft. lbs. Torque oil pump pickup tube bracket to main bearing cap bolt stud attaching nut to 28 to 40 ft. lbs.

# V6-171 (2.8L) GASOLINE ENGINE

**NOTE:** Refer to the V6-171 Gasoline Engine Section of the "Ford Bronco II & Ranger" chapter for service procedures not found in this section.

## INDEX

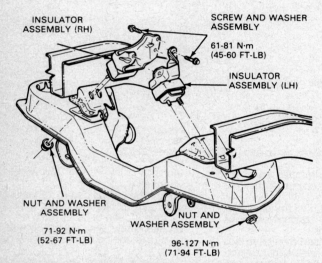

**Fig. 1   Front engine mount replacement**

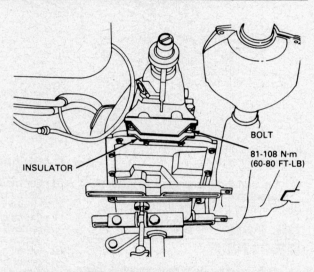

**Fig. 2   Rear engine mount replacement**

## ENGINE MOUNTS
## REPLACE
### FRONT MOUNT

1. Remove fan shroud retaining screws, then position block of wood and suitable jack under oil pan to support engine.
2. Remove insulator to frame bracket retaining nuts and washers, then loosen transmission insulator to crossmember nuts.
3. Raise engine slightly until insulator studs clear crossmember brackets.
4. Remove front mount to engine attaching nuts, then remove front mount from vehicle.
5. Reverse procedure to install. Torque all nuts and bolts to specification as shown in **Fig. 1.**

### REAR MOUNT

1. Position block of wood and suitable jack under transmission for support.
2. Remove insulator to crossmember attaching nuts, then loosen front insulator to frame bracket retaining bolts.
3. Raise transmission slightly and lift insulator from transmission crossmember.

4. Remove crossmember to frame side rail bracket attaching nuts and bolts, then crossmember.
5. If applicable, remove exhaust hanger from rear engine mount.
6. Remove rear mount/insulator assembly to transmission attaching bolts, then rear mount assembly, **Fig. 2.**
7. Reverse procedure to install noting the following:
   a. When reinstalling crossmember, position of the crossmember is different for manual and automatic transmission equipped vehicles. Observe notation stamped on crossmember for correct positioning, as shown in **Fig. 3.**
   b. Torque rear mount to transmission attaching bolts to 60-80 ft. lbs., crossmember to frame side rail bracket attaching nuts and bolts to 65-85 ft. lbs., and front insulator attaching nuts and bolts to 71-94 ft. lbs.

## ENGINE
## REPLACE

1. Disconnect battery ground cable, then drain cooling system.

2. Remove air cleaner and intake duct assembly, then disconnect upper and lower hoses at radiator.
3. Remove fan shroud attaching bolts and shroud, then disconnect MAP sensor electrical connector at dash panel.
4. On models equipped with A/C, proceed as follows:
   a. Disconnect compressor clutch electrical connector.
   b. Loosen idler pulley adjustment bolt, then remove drive belt from clutch pulley.
   c. Remove compressor retaining bolts, then position compressor aside. Do not disconnect hoses from compressor.
5. Disconnect accelerator cable and transmission kickdown cable, if applicable, from throttle lever ball stud.
6. Disconnect idle speed control (ISC) motor electrical connector at carburetor, then engine coolant temperature (ECT) and water temperature sender switch connectors at thermostat housing.
7. Disconnect EGR valve vacuum hose and EGR valve position sensor electrical connector at thermostat housing.

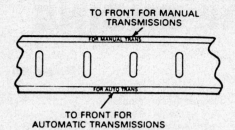

**Fig. 3 Positioning crossmember during installation**

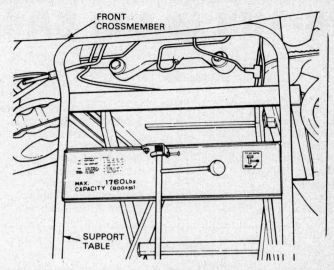

**Fig. 4 Positioning support table under front crossmember**

8. Disconnect alternator electrical connectors, then all electrical connectors and vacuum hoses at carburetor. Mark all connectors and vacuum hoses to aid installation, then position wiring harness aside.
9. Working from inside cab, remove engine cover.
10. Remove accelerator cable and transmission kickdown linkage bracket retaining bolt and bracket.
11. On models equipped with speed control, disconnect speed control cable.
12. On all models, disconnect electrical connector and supressor wire from ignition coil.
13. Disconnect air control valve to catalytic converter hose, then TFI module electrical connector at distributor.
14. Disconnect brake booster vacuum hose from retaining clip.
15. On manual transmission equipped vehicles, proceed as follows:
    a. Position shift lever in Neutral.
    b. Remove shift lever to floor and shift lever to transmission retaining bolts.
    c. Remove shift lever assembly from vehicle.
16. Raise and support vehicle, then on automatic transmission equipped vehicles, disconnect fluid lines at radiator.
17. Remove heater hoses from bracket located underneath engine at front of crossmember.
18. Remove intermediate steering column shaft to steering gear retaining bolt, then disconnect shaft from gear. Prior to disconnecting shaft, ensure steering wheel and front wheels are centered in travel.
19. Disconnect oil pressure sender electrical connector, then fuel inlet hose from fuel pump.
20. Remove ground strap to engine retaining bolt, then strap.
21. Disconnect starter electrical cables, then route cables out from crossmember.
22. On models equipped with manual transmission, remove hydraulic hose to slave cylinder retaining pin, then disconnect and plug hose to prevent spillage.
23. On all models, disconnect oxygen and knock sensor electrical connectors.
24. Remove exhaust manifold stud nuts, disconnect tube to check valve of managed Thermactor air system, then remove exhaust pipe and catalytic

converter.
25. Disconnect speedometer cable, tachometer cable (if applicable) and back-up lamp switch electrical connector from transmission.
26. On models equipped with manual transmission, disconnect shift indicator sensor electrical connector.
27. On models equipped with automatic transmission, disconnect electrical connector from neutral start switch, and throttle and kickdown cable from transmission lever. Route kickdown cable out of engine compartment and remove from vehicle.
28. On all models, remove driveshaft. Plug opening in extension housing to prevent spillage of fluid.
29. Remove wheel assemblies, then disconnect and remove stabilizer bar from lower control arms.
30. Disconnect brake lines at frame brackets behind spindles, then position suitable jack under lower control arm. Raise jack slightly until tension is applied to coil spring, then remove spindle to upper ball joint retaining nut and bolt. Lower jack to disconnect spindle from ball joint, then position safety chains around lower control arms and spring upper seat.
31. Position suitable jack under transmission, raise transmission slightly, then remove crossmember to frame and crossmember to transmission retaining nuts and bolts. Remove crossmember from vehicle.
32. Position engine support table 109-0002 or equivalent under front crossmember and engine assembly, **Fig. 4.**
33. Lower vehicle until front crossmember rests on support table. Position blocks of wood under front crossmember and transmission to keep assembly level, then install safety chains around crossmember and support table.
34. Remove engine and crossmember to frame retaining nuts and bolts from both sides of vehicle.

35. Disconnect any remaining wires or hoses that will interfere with engine removal, raise vehicle body until clear of engine/transmission assembly and support table, then lower support table and remove engine/transmission assembly from vehicle.
36. Reverse procedure to install.

## OIL PAN
### REPLACE

1. Disconnect battery ground cable, then remove starter motor.
2. Remove engine front insulator to crossmember attaching nuts.
3. Raise and support front of vehicle, then drain engine oil from crankcase.
4. Position a suitable jack under engine, then raise engine slightly and place suitable wooden blocks between front insulator mounts and No. 2 crossmember.
5. Lower engine onto wooden blocks and remove jack.
6. Remove oil pan attaching bolts, then lower oil pan from engine and remove.
7. Reverse procedure to install. Alternately and evenly, torque oil pan attaching bolts to 5 to 8 ft. lbs.

## OIL PUMP
### REPLACE

1. Remove oil pan as describer under "Oil Pan, Replace."
2. Remove oil pump attaching bolts, then remove oil pump.
3. Reverse procedure to install noting the following:
    a. When installing oil pump drive shaft into engine block, position pointed end facing inward.
    b. Torque oil pump attaching bolts to 6-10 ft. lbs.
    c. Torque oil pickup tube support to main cap to 12-15 ft. lbs.

# V6-182 (3.0L) GASOLINE ENGINE

## INDEX

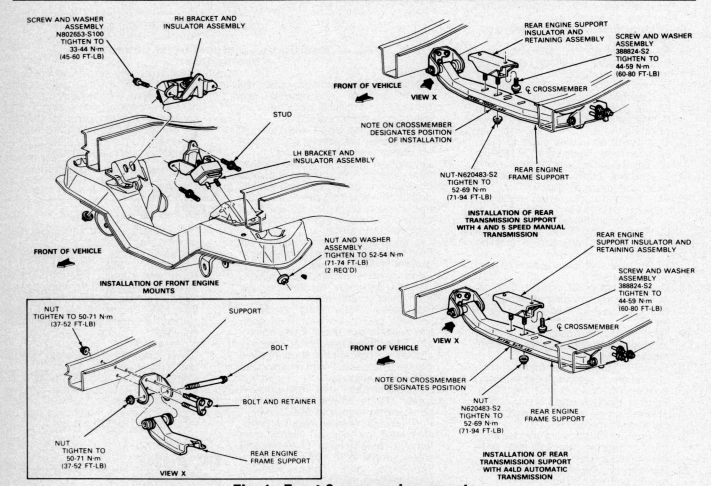

Fig. 1    Front & rear engine mounts

## ENGINE MOUNTS
### REPLACE
#### FRONT MOUNTS

1. Remove fan shroud attaching bolts.
2. Position a wooden block and suitable jack under oil pan to support engine.
3. Remove nuts and washers attaching engine insulators to frame brackets, then loosen two nuts attaching transmission insulator to crossmember, **Fig. 1.**
4. Raise engine until insulator studs clear frame brackets.
5. Remove insulator to engine attaching bolts, then remove insulator.
6. Reverse procedure to install.

### REAR MOUNT

1. Position a wooden block and suitable jack under transmission for support.
2. Remove nuts attaching insulator to crossmember, then loosen nuts retaining front insulators to frame brackets, **Fig. 1.**
3. Remove,move two bolts attaching crossmember to frame brackets, then remove crossmember.
4. On models equipped, detach exhaust hanger from rear mount.
5. Remove insulator to transmission attaching bolts, then remove insulator.
6. Reverse procedure to install. Refer to **Fig. 1,** for correct positioning of crossmember.

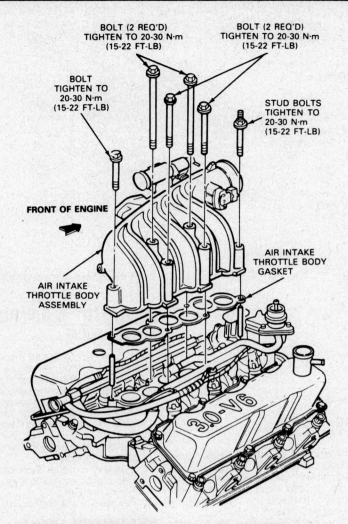

BOLT (2 REQ'D)
TIGHTEN TO 20-30 N·m
(15-22 FT-LB)

BOLT (2 REQ'D)
TIGHTEN TO 20-30 N·m
(15-22 FT-LB)

BOLT TIGHTEN TO 20-30 N·m (15-22 FT-LB)

STUD BOLTS TIGHTEN TO 20-30 N·m (15-22 FT-LB)

FRONT OF ENGINE

AIR INTAKE THROTTLE BODY GASKET

AIR INTAKE THROTTLE BODY ASSEMBLY

3.0-V6

**Fig. 2 Throttle body assembly removal & installation**

# ENGINE
## REPLACE

1. Disconnect battery ground cable.
2. Drain cooling system, then disconnect upper and lower radiator hoses.
3. Loosen clamp retaining air cleaner hose assembly to air cleaner, then disconnect hose.
4. Remove engine fan attaching bolts, then remove engine fan.
5. Disconnect barometric manifold absolute pressure sensor electrical connector and vacuum hose at dash panel.
6. Remove throttle linkage shroud, then disconnect linkage at throttle body.
7. Loosen drive belt idler arm retaining bolts, then pull injector wiring harness forward to provide clearance for disconnecting sensors.
8. Disconnect engine coolant temperature sensor and sender electrical connectors.
9. Disconnect vacuum hoses at canister purge solenoid.
10. On models equipped with power steering, disconnect power steering switch electrical connector.
11. On all models, disconnect heater hoses at engine side of ballast tube. Mark hoses so they can be installed in the same position.
12. Disconnect breather tube from air cleaner and rocker cover and remove.
13. On models equipped with automatic transmission, disconnect oil cooler lines at radiator.
14. On all models, remove radiator attaching bolts, then lift radiator from vehicle.
15. Remove alternator drive belt.
16. On models equipped with A/C, remove compressor with refrigerant lines attached and secure to frame side rail with wire.
17. On all models, remove bolt attaching oil fill tube to alternator bracket.
18. On models equipped with automatic transmission, remove bolt attaching oil fill tube to top of manifold, then carefully lift tube out from top of vehicle.
19. On all models, disconnect electrical connectors from rear of alternator.
20. Disconnect vacuum line from power brake unit.
21. Remove steering gear to steering shaft retaining bolt.
22. From inside vehicle, remove engine cover and disconnect electrical connectors from radio frequency interference supressor, TFI module and oil pressure sender.
23. On models equipped with manual transmission, place shift lever in Neutral, then remove bolts attaching shift boot to floor. Remove shift lever to transmission attaching bolts, then lift shift lever from transmission.
24. On all models, raise and support front of vehicle, then disconnect fuel lines at sender.
25. Disconnect oil level sensor electrical connector, then remove driveshaft assembly from vehicle.
26. Disconnect speedometer cable at transmission, then remove starter motor assembly.
27. On models with manual transmission, disconnect hydraulic hose from clutch slave cylinder. Cap hydraulic hose and slave cylinder openings.
28. On models with manual transmission, disconnect electrical connectors from backup lamp switch and shift indicator and neutral position senders located on transmission.
29. On models with automatic transmission, disconnect neutral safety switch electrical connector, vacuum modulator vacuum hose and shift and kickdown control cables from transmission.
30. On models with automatic transmission, remove transmission as described under "Transmission, Replace" in "Automatic Transmission." On models with manual transmissions, the engine may be removed with or without transmission.
31. On all models, remove exhaust pipe and catalytic converter.
32. Remove both front wheel and tire assemblies.
33. Disconnect engine ground straps located at cylinder head behind power steering pump and just above exhaust manifold to exhaust pipe connection.
34. Disconnect stabilizer bar from lower control arms.
35. Disconnect front brake hoses from brake lines at bracket on frame behind spindle. Cap opening at brake hoses and brake lines.
36. Position a suitable jack under lower control arm and raise arm until coil spring tension is relieved, then remove nut attaching upper ball joint to spindle. Carefully lower jack and disconnect spindle from upper ball joint.
37. Position support table No. 109-00002 or equivalent under crossmember and engine assembly, then slowly lower jack until crossmember is resting on support table.
38. Position wooden blocks under front crossmember and rear of engine block to keep assembly level, then install safety chains around crossmember and support table.
39. With engine and crossmember prop-

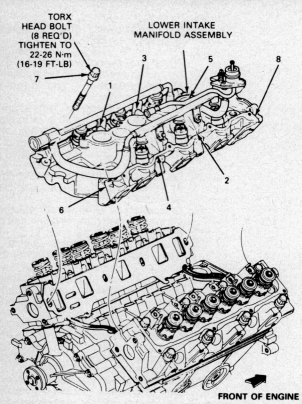

TORX HEAD BOLT (8 REQ'D) TIGHTEN TO 22-26 N·m (16-19 FT-LB)

LOWER INTAKE MANIFOLD ASSEMBLY

FRONT OF ENGINE

**Fig. 3   Intake manifold bolt tightening sequence**

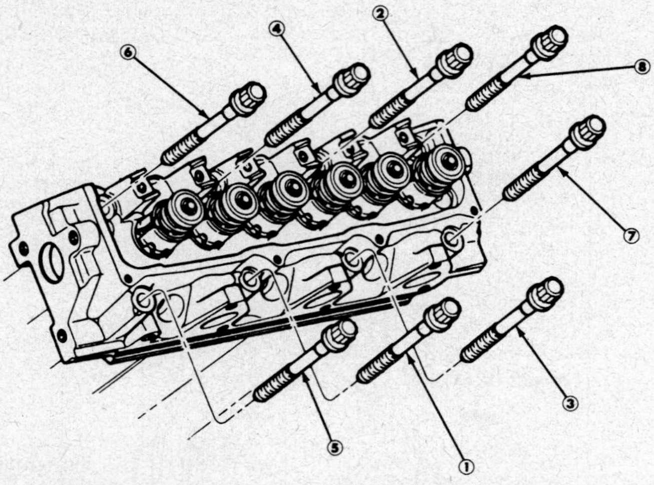

**Fig. 4   Cylinder head bolt tightening sequence**

erly supported on support table, remove nuts retaining crossmember to frame.

40. Carefully lower engine and crossmember from vehicle.
41. Reverse procedure to install.

## ROCKER COVER
### REPLACE

1. Disconnect ignition plug wires from spark plugs, then remove ignition wire separators from rocker cover.
2. If left hand rocker cover is to be replaced, remove oil filler cap and disconnect hoses from rocker cover.
3. If right hand rocker cover is to be replaced, remove PCV valve and disconnect heater hoses.
4. Remove rocker cover attaching screws and rocker cover.
5. Reverse procedure to install. Apply a bead of RTV sealant at cylinder head to intake manifold rail step.

## INTAKE MANIFOLD
### REPLACE

1. Disconnect battery ground cable, then drain cooling system.
2. Remove throttle body as follows:
   a. Disconnect air inlet hose from throttle body and air cleaner, then remove resonator and tube assembly.
   b. Tag and disconnect all vacuum hoses from throttle body.
   c. Disconnect throttle linkage from throttle body.
   d. Disconnect electrical connectors from throttle position sensor, air charge temperature sensor and idle speed control motor.
   e. Disconnect PCV valve hose, then remove alternator support brace.
   f. Remove throttle body attaching bolts and throttle body, **Fig. 2**.
3. Disconnect fuel lines as follows:
   a. Remove fuel cap to relieve fuel tank pressure.
   b. Remove cap from fuel pressure relief valve located on fuel rail assembly.
   c. Release fuel system pressure at fuel pressure relief valve using fuel pressure gauge T80L-9974-A or equivalent.
   d. Disconnect push connectors at fuel supply and return lines using suitable tool.
4. Disconnect fuel injector wiring harness from engine.
5. Disconnect upper radiator hose and heater outlet hose.
6. Remove distributor assembly and rocker covers.
7. Remove intake manifold attaching bolts, then remove intake manifold. The intake manifold can be removed with fuel rails and injectors in place.
8. Reverse procedure to install. Apply silicone sealer at the four points where the cylinder block and cylinder head intersect. Torque intake manifold bolts in sequence shown in **Fig. 3.**

## EXHAUST MANIFOLD
### REPLACE

1. If right hand exhaust manifold is to be replaced, remove engine oil dipstick tube support bracket and power steering pump pressure and return hoses.
2. If left hand exhaust manifold is to be replaced, disconnect heater hoses and remove heater hose support bracket.
3. Disconnect exhaust pipe from exhaust manifold.
4. Remove exhaust manifold to cylinder head attaching bolts, then remove exhaust manifold.
5. Reverse procedure to install.

## CYLINDER HEAD
### REPLACE

1. Disconnect battery ground cable, then drain cooling system.
2. Remove air cleaner outlet tube, then remove intake manifold as described under "Intake Manifold, Replace."
3. Loosen drive belt tensioner and remove drive belt.
4. If left hand cylinder head is to be removed, remove alternator adjusting arm to cylinder attaching bolt, ignition coil bracket and dipstick tube.
5. If right hand cylinder head is to be removed, remove drive belt tensioner, ground strap and throttle cable support bracket.
6. Remove power steering pump mounting bracket attaching bolts and position pump aside with hoses attached, if equipped.
7. Remove exhaust manifold, PCV valve and rocker arm covers.
8. Loosen rocker arm fulcrum bolts just enough to allow rocker arms to be lifted off pushrods.
9. Remove pushrods and tag for reference during installation.
10. Remove cylinder head attaching bolts, then remove cylinder head and gasket.

**Fig. 5   Checking valve clearance**

11. Reverse procedure to install. Tighten cylinder head bolts in sequence shown in **Fig. 4**, to torque listed in "Engine Tightening Specifications" table.

## VALVE ARRANGEMENT
### FRONT TO REAR

Left Bank.................... I-E-I-E-I-E
Right Bank ................... E-I-E-I-E-I

## VALVE LIFT SPECIFICATIONS

| Engine | Year | Intake | Exhaust |
|--------|------|--------|---------|
| V6-182 | 1986-89 | .419 | .419 |

## VALVE CLEARANCE CHECK

1. Position No. 1 cylinder at TDC compression stroke and check collapsed valve lifter clearance, using a suitable tappet bleed down wrench on rocker arm, **Fig. 5**. Check the following valves:
   a. No. 1 intake and exhaust.
   b. No. 2 exhaust.
   c. No. 3 intake.
   d. No. 4 exhaust.
   e. No. 6 intake.
2. Rotate crankshaft 360 degrees and check the following valves:
   a. No. 2 intake.
   b. No. 3 exhaust.
   c. No. 4 intake.
   d. No. 5 intake and exhaust.
   e. No. 6 exhaust.
3. Collapsed tappet gap should be .088 to .189 inch. If not check pushrod, valve lifter, rocker arm, fulcrum and bolt for wear and damage and replace as necessary.

## VALVE LIFTERS
### REPLACE

1. Disconnect battery ground cable, then drain cooling system.
2. Remove intake manifold as described

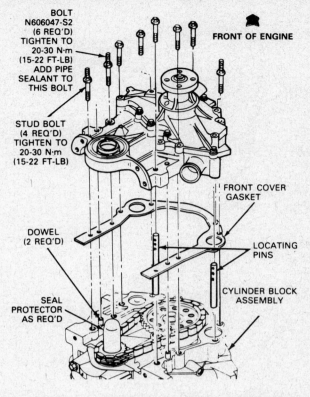

**Fig. 6   Front cover removal & installation**

under "Intake Manifold, Replace."
3. Loosen rocker arm fulcrum bolts just enough to allow rocker arms to be lifted off of pushrods, then remove pushrods. Tag pushrods for reference during installation.
4. Remove valve lifters using a suitable magnet. If lifters are stuck, use puller tool T70L-6500-A or other suitable claw type tool to remove.
5. Reverse procedure to install. Prior to installation, lubricate valve lifters, lifter bores, pushrod ends and rocker arm assemblies with a suitable oil conditioner or SAE 50 engine oil.

## FRONT OIL SEAL
### REPLACE

1. Loosen drive belts, then remove four crankshaft pulley to damper attaching bolts and remove pulley.
2. Remove crankshaft damper attaching bolts, then using a suitable puller, remove damper from crankshaft.
3. Using a suitable flat blade screwdriver, carefully remove front cover seal.
4. Check front cover and crankshaft seal surface for damage or corrosion that may cause a replacement seal to fail.
5. Lubricate seal lips with clean engine oil, then install seal with a suitable seal installer.
6. Lubricate crankshaft damper sealing surface with clean engine oil.
7. Apply RTV sealant to crankshaft damper keyway.
8. Install crankshaft damper and attaching bolt, then install crankshaft pulley and attaching bolts.

9. Install and tension drive belts, then start engine and check for oil leaks.

## VALVE GUIDES

Valves operate in guide holes bored into the cylinder head. If clearance becomes excessive, use the next oversize valve and ream bore to fit. Valve with oversize stems are available in .015 and .030 inch oversizes.

## FRONT COVER
### REPLACE

1. Drain cooling system, then disconnect lower radiator hose.
2. Remove idler pulley and bracket assembly, then remove all drive belts.
3. Remove water pump as described under "Water Pump, Replace."
4. Remove crankshaft pulley and damper.
5. Remove bolts attaching front cover to oil pan.
6. Remove bolts attaching timing cover to engine block, then remove front cover, **Fig. 6**.
7. Carefully cut and remove exposed portion of oil pan gasket. Apply a suitable sealing compound to exposed portion of oil pan. From a replacement oil pan gasket, cut and position required portion of gasket on oil pan. Apply sealing compound to corners of gasket.
8. Reverse procedure to install, applying sealing compound to surfaces of front cover, engine block and cover bolt that enters the water jacket.

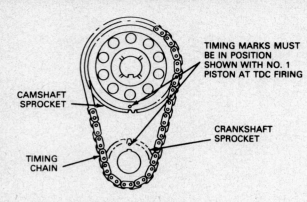

**Fig. 7   Valve timing marks**

CAMSHAFT SPROCKET

CRANKSHAFT SPROCKET

TIMING CHAIN

TIMING MARKS MUST BE IN POSITION SHOWN WITH NO. 1 PISTON AT TDC FIRING

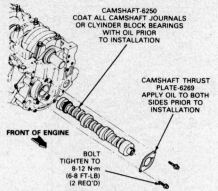

**Fig. 8   Camshaft removal & installation**

CAMSHAFT-6250 COAT ALL CAMSHAFT JOURNALS OR CYLINDER BLOCK BEARINGS WITH OIL PRIOR TO INSTALLATION

CAMSHAFT THRUST PLATE-6269 APPLY OIL TO BOTH SIDES PRIOR TO INSTALLATION

FRONT OF ENGINE

BOLT TIGHTEN TO 8-12 N·m (6-8 FT-LB) (2 REQ'D)

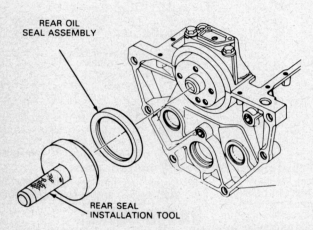

REAR OIL SEAL ASSEMBLY

REAR SEAL INSTALLATION TOOL

**Fig. 9   Crankshaft rear oil seal installation**

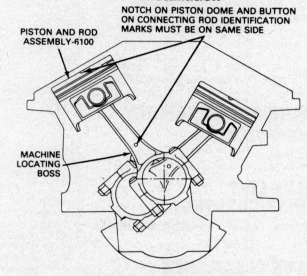

NOTCH ON PISTON DOME AND BUTTON ON CONNECTING ROD IDENTIFICATION MARKS MUST BE ON SAME SIDE

PISTON AND ROD ASSEMBLY-6100

MACHINE LOCATING BOSS

VIEWED FROM FRONT OF ENGINE

**Fig. 10   Piston & rod assembly installation**

# TIMING CHAIN
## REPLACE

1. Remove front cover as described under "Front Cover, Replace."
2. Rotate engine until No. 1 cylinder is at TDC compression stroke and timing marks are aligned, **Fig. 7.**
3. Remove attaching bolt and washer from camshaft sprocket, then remove camshaft and crankshaft sprockets with timing chain.
4. Reverse procedure to install. Align timing marks when installing timing chain, **Fig. 7.** Before installing camshaft sprocket bolt, check for damage and blockage, as this bolt has a drilled oil passage. Torque camshaft sprocket bolt to 41 to 51 ft. lbs. After installing, apply engine oil to timing chain and sprockets.

# CAMSHAFT
## REPLACE

1. Remove engine as described under "Engine, Replace" and position on a

suitable work stand.
2. Remove front cover as described under "Front Cover, Replace."
3. Remove intake manifold and valve lifter as described under "Valve Lifters, Replace."
4. Remove camshaft thrust plate, then carefully pull camshaft from front of engine, using care not to damage camshaft bearings, **Fig. 8.**
5. Reverse procedure to install. Before installing camshaft, lubricate lobes and journals with SAE 50 engine oil. Torque camshaft thrust plate attaching bolts to 6 to 8 ft. lbs.

# MAIN & ROD BEARINGS

Main and rod bearings are available in standard size and undersizes of .002, .010, and .020 inch.

# CRANKSHAFT REAR OIL SEAL
## REPLACE

1. Remove transmission from vehicle.

2. Remove flywheel attaching bolts and flywheel.
3. Remove rear cover plate.
4. Using a suitable awl, punch a hole into sheet metal portion of seal between engine and seal lip.
5. Using a suitable slide hammer type puller, remove seal from block. Use care not to damage oil seal surfaces on engine.
6. Using rear main seal installer T82L-6701-A or equivalent, install rear oil seal, **Fig. 9.**
7. Install flywheel and transmission.

# PISTON, PINS & RINGS

Pistons are available in standard size and oversizes of .003, .020, .030 and .040 inch. Piston rings are available in standard size and oversizes of .020, .030 and .040 inch. Piston pins are available in standard size only.

# PISTON & ROD ASSEMBLE

Assemble rod to piston with notch on

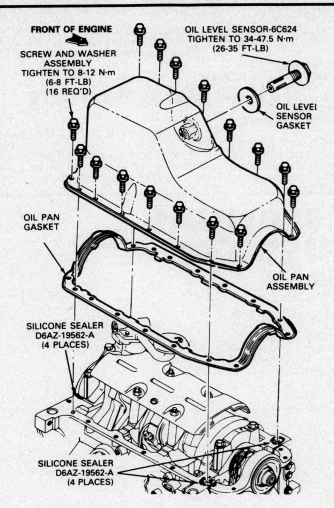

**FRONT OF ENGINE**

SCREW AND WASHER
ASSEMBLY
TIGHTEN TO 8-12 N·m
(6-8 FT-LB)
(16 REQ'D)

OIL LEVEL SENSOR-6C624
TIGHTEN TO 34-47.5 N·m
(26-35 FT-LB)

OIL LEVEL
SENSOR
GASKET

OIL PAN
GASKET

OIL PAN
ASSEMBLY

SILICONE SEALER
D6AZ-19562-A
(4 PLACES)

SILICONE SEALER
D6AZ-19562-A
(4 PLACES)

**Fig. 11  Oil pan installation**

piston dome on the same side as button on connecting rod, **Fig. 10.** When installing piston and connecting rod assembly in engine, notch on piston dome must face front.

After installing connecting and piston assembly, check connecting rod side clearance. Connecting rod side clearance should be .006 to .014 inch.

## OIL PAN
### REPLACE

1. Disconnect battery ground cable.
2. Remove engine oil dipstick and tube.
3. On models equipped with low engine oil level sensor, disconnect electrical connector at sensor.
4. Drain oil from crankcase and remove starter motor.
5. On models equipped with automatic transmission, remove flywheel dust cover from converter housing.
6. On all models, loosen transmission to engine mounting bolt and slide transmission rearward approximately ¼ inch.
7. Remove oil pan attaching bolts, then remove oil pan and gasket, **Fig. 11.**
8. Reverse procedure to install. Apply

silicone sealant to oil pan junction at rear main bearing cap and engine block and at front cover and engine block junction. Allow silicone sealant to cure for approximately 15 minutes. Torque oil pan attaching bolts to 71 to 106 inch lbs.

## OIL PUMP
### REPLACE

1. Remove oil pan as described under "Oil Pan, Replace."
2. Remove oil pump attaching bolts and lift oil pump and intermediate shaft from engine.
3. Reverse procedure to install. If intermediate shaft was removed from pump, push shaft into pump until retainer clicks.

## WATER PUMP
### REPLACE

1. Drain cooling system, then disconnect radiator and heater hoses at water pump.
2. Loosen drive belt idler pulley, then remove drive belts.
3. Remove drive belt idler pulley and

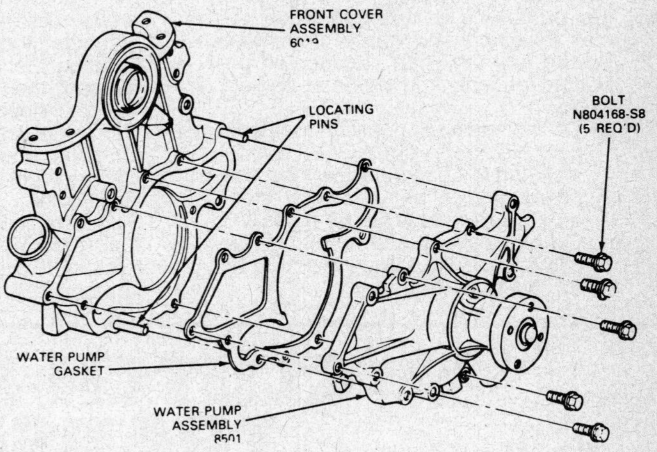

FRONT COVER
ASSEMBLY
6013

LOCATING
PINS

BOLT
N804168-S8
(5 REQ'D)

WATER PUMP
GASKET

WATER PUMP
ASSEMBLY
8501

**Fig. 12  Water pump assembly removal & installation**

bracket from engine.
4. Remove drive pulley to water pump attaching bolts.
5. Remove water pump to front cover attaching bolts, then remove water pump, **Fig. 12.**
6. Reverse procedure to install. Apply sealant to bolt that passes into water jacket on engine block. Torque water pump attaching bolts to 6 to 8 ft. lbs.

## ELECTRIC FUEL PUMP
### REPLACE

1. Depressurize fuel system by disconnecting inertia switch and cranking engine for 15 seconds. The inertia switch is located in the engine compartment.
2. Drain fuel from fuel tank into a suitable container.
3. Raise and support vehicle, then disconnect fuel filler tube.
4. Support fuel tank, then detach fuel tank support straps and lower fuel tank slightly.
5. Disconnect fuel lines, electrical connectors and vent lines from fuel tank, then remove fuel tank.
6. Clean area around fuel pump and sender assembly, then using a suitable tool rotate fuel pump lock ring in counterclockwise direction.
7. Remove fuel pump and bracket assembly from fuel tank.
8. Clean fuel pump mounting flange, fuel tank mounting surface and seal ring groove.
9. Apply suitable grease to seal ring to hold seal in position, then install in seal ring groove.
10. Position fuel pump on fuel tank, using care not to damage filter. Ensure fuel pump locating keys are in keyways and that seal ring is properly positioned.
11. On 1986 models, while holding fuel pump in place, install locking ring finger tight. Ensure locking tabs are located under fuel tank lock ring tabs.

12. On 1987-89 models, while holding fuel pump and seal ring in place, install lock ring and rotate clockwise. Locate fuel tank part No. located on bottom of tank and proceed as follows:

   a. On models equipped with fuel tank part No. E59A-9002-CAE, torque lock ring to 60 to 85 ft. lbs. Wait approximately 5 minutes and retorque lock ring to 60 to 85 ft. lbs.

   b. On models with fuel tank part No. E69A-9002-PA, torque lock ring to 80 to 113 ft. lbs.

13. On 1986 models, using a suitable tool, rotate lock ring clockwise until ring contacts stop.
14. Position fuel tank under vehicle and support, then connect fuel line, vent line and electrical connectors.
15. Raise fuel tank into position and secure with support straps.
16. Connect fuel tank filler tube, then lower vehicle.
17. Fill fuel tank with at least 10 gallons of fuel, then cycle ignition switch between Off and Run positions to pressurize system. When cycling ignition switch, leave switch in Run position for 3 seconds before returning to Off.
18. Start engine and check system for fuel leaks.

## BELT TENSION DATA

1. Tension alternator and A/C compressor belts to 120-160 lbs. for a new belt, 110-130 lbs. for a used belt. Tension power steering belt to 100-140 lbs. for a new belt, 80-100 lbs. for a used belt.

# CLUTCH & MANUAL TRANSMISSION

## INDEX

### Page No.

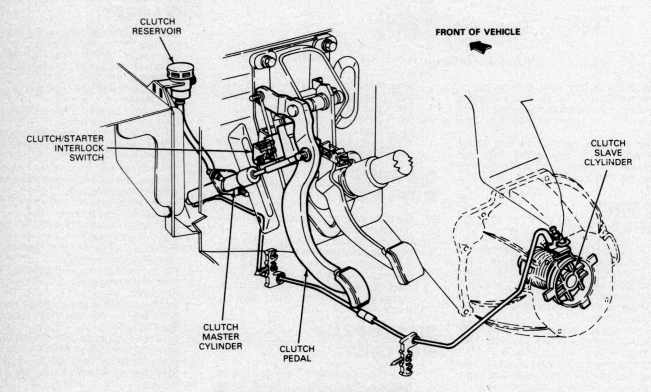

**Fig. 1   Clutch hydraulic system**

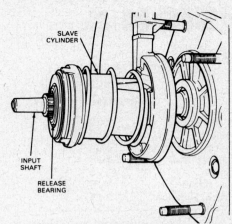

**Fig. 2 Removing clutch slave cylinder from input shaft**

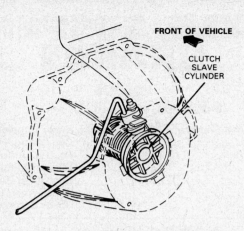

**Fig. 3 Installing clutch slave cylinder into clutch housing notches**

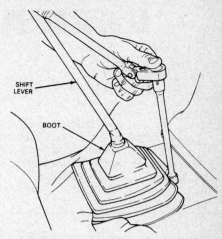

**Fig. 4 Removing shift lever boot**

# CLUTCH
## ADJUST

These models are equipped with a hydraulic clutch system, **Fig. 1.** No clutch linkage or pedal travel adjustments are required, since these adjustments are automatically taken up by the system.

# CLUTCH
## REPLACE

1. Disconnect master cylinder from clutch pedal and dash panel, then raise and support vehicle.
2. Remove starter motor.
3. Remove slave cylinder hydraulic tube by sliding the white plastic sleeve toward the slave cylinder, and applying a slight tug on the tube, then disconnect tube from cylinder.
4. Remove transmission as outlined in "Transmission, Replace" procedure.
5. Scribe alignment marks on pressure plate and flywheel to aid reassembly.
6. Evenly loosen pressure plate attaching bolts until all spring tension is removed.
7. Remove pressure plate attaching bolts, then the pressure plate and clutch disc.
8. Reverse procedure to install, ensuring that scribe marks on pressure plate and flywheel are aligned, then diagonally torque all bolts on pressure plate to 15-24 ft. lbs.

# CLUTCH SLAVE CYLINDER
## REPLACE

1. Remove transmission as outlined in "Transmission, Replace" procedure.
2. Remove clutch housing to transmission attaching bolts, then separate clutch housing from transmission.

3. Remove slave cylinder from transmission input shaft, **Fig. 2.**
4. Reverse procedure to install, noting the following:
   a. Position slave cylinder onto input shaft, ensuring that bleed screw and coupling are facing the left side of transmission.
   b. Install slave cylinder attaching bolts and torque to 13-19 ft. lbs.
   c. When installing clutch housing to transmission, ensure that slave cylinder is properly located in notches of housing, **Fig. 3.** Torque clutch housing to transmission attaching bolts to 30-40 ft. lbs.
5. Bleed hydraulic system as follows:
   a. Clean dirt and grease from around reservoir cap, then remove cap and fill to step with DOT 3 brake fluid.
   b. Loosen bleed screw, located in slave cylinder body next to inlet connection.
   c. Fluid will now begin to flow from master cylinder, down black tube and into slave cylinder. **Fluid reservoir must be kept full at all times to ensure that there will be no additional introduction of air into the system.**
   d. At this point, bubbles should appear at bleed screw outlet, indicating that air is being expelled from the system.
   e. When slave cylinder is full, a steady stream of fluid will come from the slave cylinder outlet. At this point, tighten bleed screw.
   f. Have an assistant exert a light load of pressure to the clutch pedal, then slightly loosen the bleed screw. Maintain pressure until pedal touches floor. Tighten bleed screw, then allow clutch pedal to return.
   g. After refilling reservoir, repeat above step, then install diaphragm and cap.

# TRANSMISSION
## REPLACE

1. Disconnect battery ground cable, then position shift lever in Neutral.
2. Remove boot assembly to floor retaining bolts, **Fig. 4,** then lift boot upward over shift lever.
3. Remove shift lever to shift rail adapter retaining bolts, then remove shift lever, knob and boot assembly.
4. Raise and support vehicle, disconnect starter electrical connections, then remove starter.
5. Remove hydraulic tube to slave cylinder retaining clip, then remove tube and fitting from cylinder. Cap all openings to prevent spillage of fluid.
6. Disconnect back-up lamp, shift indicator and neutral position sender electrical connectors, then speedometer cable (conventional speedometer) or wire connector (electronic speedometer) from transmission.
7. Scribe alignment marks on driveshaft and rear axle flange, then remove U-bolts, nuts and driveshaft. Cap extension housing opening to prevent loss of lubricant.
8. Remove insulator to crossmember retaining nuts, then loosen nuts attaching front insulators to crossmember brackets.
9. Position suitable transmission jack under transmission, then raise jack slightly.
10. Remove crossmember to frame attaching nuts and bolts, then crossmember.
11. Remove clutch housing to engine retaining bolts, then push transmission rearward and lower from vehicle.
12. Reverse procedure to install. Torque clutch housing to engine retaining bolts to 28-33 ft. lbs., and all crossmember related nuts and bolts to 80 ft. lbs., then bleed clutch hydraulic system as described in "Clutch Slave Cylinder, Replace".

# REAR AXLE, SUSPENSION & BRAKES

## INDEX

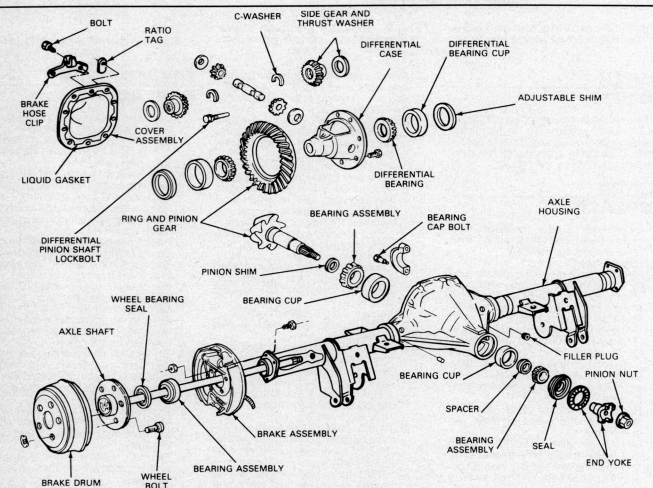

**Disassembled view of Ford 7 ½ inch ring gear rear axle**

## REAR AXLE REPLACE

1. Raise and support vehicle.
2. Working from underneath vehicle, pull rearward on front parking brake cable, clamp cable at rear of crossmember, then disconnect parking brake cables from equalizer.
3. Compress retainer tabs, then pull cables through rear crossmember.
4. Support rear axle assembly, then scribe alignment marks on driveshaft and rear axle yoke to aid installation.
5. Remove driveshaft, plug extension housing to prevent spillage of fluid, then remove rear wheels.
6. Disconnect brake jounce hose from master cylinder tube. Plug tube, then remove jounce hose and bracket from frame.
7. Disconnect axle vent tube from frame retaining clip.
8. Disconnect shock absorbers from lower control arms, then lower axle assembly until spring pressure is relieved.
9. Remove lower and upper spring retainers, then coil springs.
10. Raise axle assembly to normal load position, then disconnect lower control arms from axle.
11. Remove upper control arm to rear axle retaining nuts and bolts. Scribe alignment mark on cam adjuster and

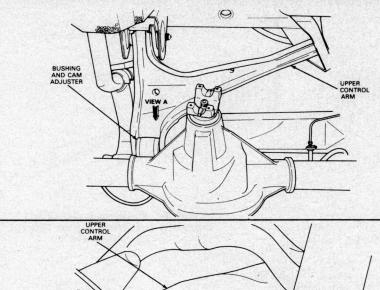

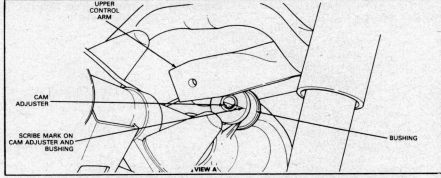

**Fig. 1   Aligning scribe marks on cam adjuster and bushing**

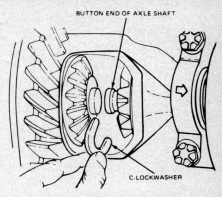

**Fig. 2   Removing C-lock from axle shaft. Ford 7½ inch rear axle w/3.45:1 ratio**

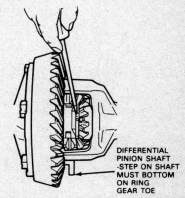

**Fig. 3   Removing C-lock from axle shaft. Ford 7½ inch rear axle w/3.73:1 or 4.10:1 ration**

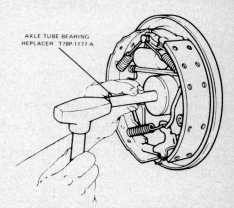

**Fig. 4   Installing axle shaft seal. Ford 7½ inch rear axle**

axle bushing, then disconnect upper control arms from axle assembly.

12. Lower axle assembly and remove from vehicle.

13. Reverse procedure to install, noting the following:
   a. When connecting upper control arms, ensure scribe marks on cam adjuster and bushing are properly aligned as shown in **Fig. 1**. Do not torque retaining nuts and bolts until springs have been installed and axle is at normal load position.
   b. When installing coil springs, ensure tapered coil (white marking) of spring faces upward.
   c. When installing lower control arm to axle retaining bolt, ensure bolts are installed with bolt heads inboard of bracket.
   d. Torque upper and lower control arm to axle retaining bolts to 115 ft. lbs., upper spring retainer attaching bolt and nut to 35 ft. lbs., and lower spring retainer and shock absorber attaching nuts and bolts to 52 ft. lbs.

## AXLE SHAFT, BEARING & SEAL
### REPLACE
#### FORD 7½ INCH REAR AXLE

1. Raise and support vehicle, then remove rear wheel and brake drum.
2. Remove housing cover and drain lubricant from axle.
3. On models with 3.45:1 ratio axle, proceed as follows:
   a. Remove differential pinion shaft lock bolt, then the pinion shaft.
   b. Push axle shaft inward toward center of vehicle, then remove C-lockwasher from end of shaft, **Fig. 2**.
   c. Carefully slide axle shaft out from housing.
4. On models with 3.73:1 or 4.10:1 ratio axle, proceed as follows:
   a. Remove pinion shaft lock bolt.
   b. Position hand behind differential case, then push outward on pinion shaft until step on shaft contacts ring gear.
   c. Remove C-lockwasher from end of axle shaft, then slide axle shaft out from housing, **Fig. 3**.
5. On all models, remove wheel bearing and seal with suitable slide hammer puller positioned into housing bore. Ensure tangs of puller are positioned behind bearing race.
6. Reverse procedure to install, noting the following:
   a. Lubricate new bearing with suitable axle lubricant, then install into housing bore using bearing installation tool T78P-1225-A or equivalent.
   b. Apply suitable grease between lips of new axle shaft seal, then install seal using tool T78P-1177-A or equivalent, **Fig. 4**.
   c. Torque pinion shaft lock bolt and housing cover retaining bolts to 18 ft. lbs.

## DANA MODEL 30 REAR AXLE

1. Remove wheel and tire assembly, then remove rear brake drum.
2. Working through hole in axle shaft flange, remove axle shaft bearing retainer plate attaching nuts.
3. Using a suitable puller, remove axle shaft from housing, **Fig. 5**. Use care when removing to prevent damage to oil seal.

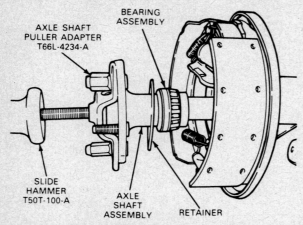

**Fig. 5 Axle shaft & bearing. Dana Model 30 rear axle**

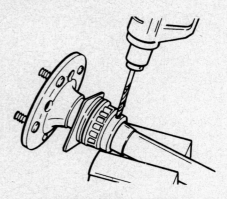

**Fig. 6 Drilling axle shaft bearing retainer. Dana Model 30 rear axle**

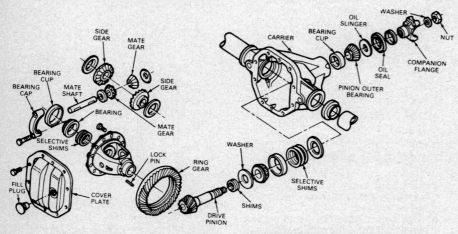

**Disassembled view of Dana Model 30 rear axle**

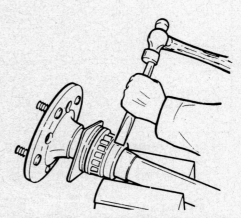

**Fig. 7 Axle shaft bearing retainer removal. Dana Model 30 rear axle**

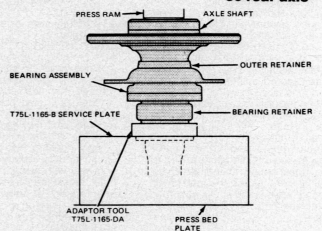

**Fig. 8 Pressing retainer bearing onto axle shaft. Dana Model 30 rear axle**

4. Using a suitable slide hammer, remove bearing outer race from axle housing.
5. Remove brake backing plate and suspend from chassis with wire.
6. If axle shaft bearing or seal are to be replaced, proceed as follows:
   a. Position axle shaft in a suitable vise.
   b. Drill a 1/4 inch diameter hole approximately 3/8 inch deep into bearing retainer, **Fig. 6**. Do not drill completely through bearing retainer, as damage to axle shaft may result.
   c. Using a hammer and suitable chisel, strike in drilled area to split retainer, **Fig. 7**, then remove retainer.
   d. Using suitable tool, press bearing and seal from axle shaft.
7. Reverse procedure to install, noting the following:
   a. Lubricate bearing and seal prior to installation.
   b. Press bearing and seal onto axle shaft using tool No. T75L-1165-DA or equivalent, then press on retainer until it is firmly positioned

against bearing, **Fig. 8**.
   c. Lubricate outer diameter of outer bearing race and seal with lubricant C1AZ-1950-E or equivalent.
   d. Ensure outer seal is properly positioned before installing axle shaft.
   e. Alternately and evenly torque

bearing retainer plate retaining nuts to 20 to 40 ft. lbs.

## SHOCK ABSORBER REPLACE

1. Raise and support rear of vehicle.

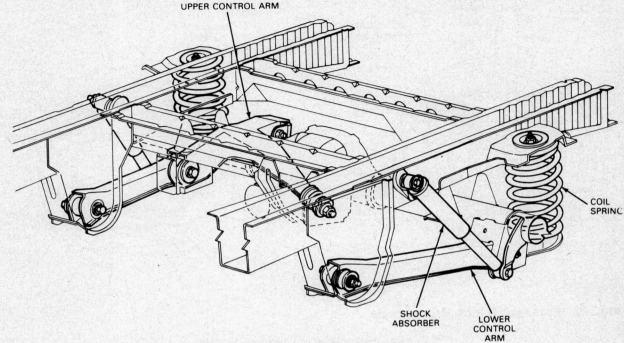

Fig. 9 Rear suspension assembly

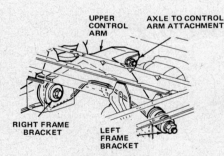

**Fig. 10 Removing upper control arm**

2. Remove lower mounting nut and bolt, then swing lower end of shock absorber out from mounting bracket.
3. Remove upper attaching bolt, washer and shock absorber, Fig. 9.
4. Reverse procedure to install. Torque upper attaching bolt to 30 ft. lbs. and lower mounting bolt and nut to 52 ft. lbs.

## COIL SPRING
### REPLACE

1. Raise and support rear of vehicle.
2. Using a suitable jack to support rear axle, disconnect shock absorber from lower mounting, then lower axle assembly until all spring pressure is relieved.
3. Remove lower and upper spring retainer attaching nuts and bolts, then spring, retainers and insulators.

4. Reverse procedure to install, noting the following:
   a. When installing coil spring, ensure tapered coil (white marking) of spring faces upward.
   b. Torque upper spring retainer attaching bolt and nut to 35 ft. lbs., and lower spring retainer and shock absorber attaching nuts and bolts to 52 ft. lbs.

## UPPER CONTROL ARM
### REPLACE

1. Raise and support rear of vehicle.
2. Using a suitable jack to support rear axle, disconnect shock absorber from lower mounting, then lower axle assembly until all spring pressure is relieved.
3. Remove control arm to rear axle retaining nuts and bolts. Scribe alignment mark on cam adjuster and axle bushing, then disconnect upper control arms from axle assembly.
4. Remove control arm to right frame bracket retaining nut and bolt, Fig. 10, then rotate arm and disengage from bracket.
5. Remove control arm to left frame bracket retaining nut, washer, outer insulator and spacer.
6. Disengage control arm from left frame bracket, then remove inner insulator, washer and control arm.
7. Reverse procedure to install, noting the following:
   a. When installing upper control arm, ensure scribe marks on cam adjuster and bushing are properly aligned as shown in Fig. 2. Do not torque retaining nuts and bolts un-

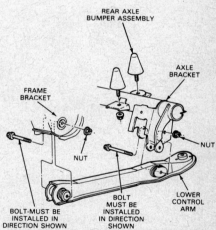

**Fig. 11 Installing lower control arm**

til springs have been installed and axle is at normal ride position.
   b. When installing coil springs, ensure tapered coil (white marking) of spring faces upward.
   c. Torque control arm to left frame bracket retaining nut to 80 ft. lbs., control arm to right frame bracket retaining nut and bolt to 115 ft. lbs., control arm to rear axle retaining nut and bolt to 115 ft. lbs. and shock absorber lower mounting bolt and nut to 52 ft. lbs.

## LOWER CONTROL ARM
### REPLACE

1. Raise and support rear of vehicle.

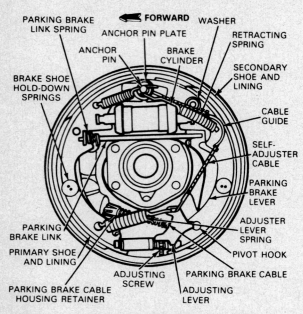

**Fig. 12   Left rear 9 inch drum brake**

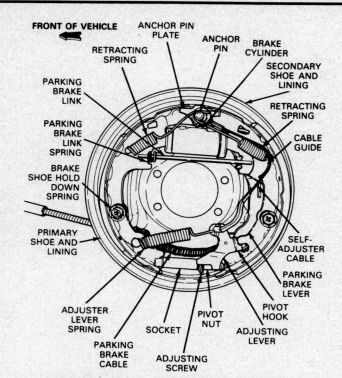

**Fig. 13   Left rear 10 inch drum brake**

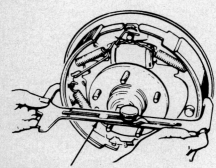

BRAKE SHOE ADJUSTMENT GAUGE

**Fig. 14   Checking brake lining clearance**

2. Using a suitable jack to support rear axle, disconnect shock absorber from lower mounting, then lower axle assembly until all spring pressure is relieved.
3. Remove coil spring lower retainer retaining nut, then remove lower retainer and insulator from control arm.
4. Remove control arm to axle housing and control arm to frame bracket retaining nuts and bolts, then the lower control arm.
5. Reverse procedure to install, noting the following:
   a. When installing control arm to frame bracket and control arm to axle housing retaining bolts, ensure that bolts are installed with heads inboard of the brackets as shown, **Fig. 11.**
   b. Do not torque retaining nuts and bolts until spring has been installed and axle is at normal ride position.

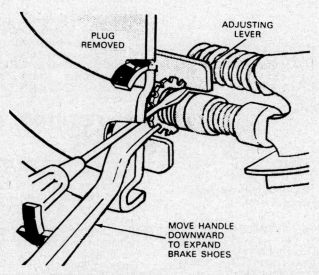

**Fig. 15   Adjusting rear drum brake**

   c. Torque control arm to frame bracket and control arm to axle housing retaining nuts and bolts to 115 ft. lbs., then the lower spring retainer and shock absorber retaining nuts and bolts to 52 ft. lbs.

# BRAKE ADJUSTMENTS
## REAR DRUM BRAKES

The rear brake shoes, **Figs. 12 and 13**, adjust automatically when the vehicle is driven forward or reverse and the brakes are applied sharply several times. Manual adjustment is required only when brake shoes are replaced. When adjusting rear brakes, ensure that parking brake is properly adjusted and that equalizer is operating freely.

## WITH DRUMS REMOVED

1. With drums removed, clean areas where shoes contact backing plate, then apply suitable lubricant to these contact areas, ensuring that lubricant does not contaminate linings.
2. Using suitable brake shoe adjusting gauge, adjust gauge to inside diame-

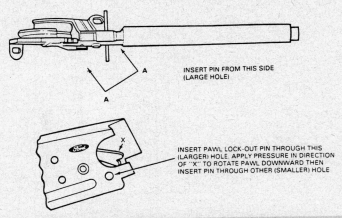

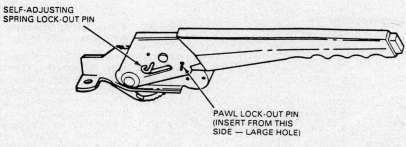

**Fig. 16 Inserting pin in pawl lock-out**

SELF-ADJUSTING
SPRING LOCK-OUT PIN

PAWL LOCK-OUT PIN
(INSERT FROM THIS
SIDE — LARGE HOLE)

INSERT PIN FROM THIS SIDE
(LARGE HOLE)

INSERT PAWL LOCK-OUT PIN THROUGH THIS
(LARGER) HOLE. APPLY PRESSURE IN DIRECTION
OF "X" TO ROTATE PAWL DOWNWARD THEN
INSERT PIN THROUGH OTHER (SMALLER) HOLE

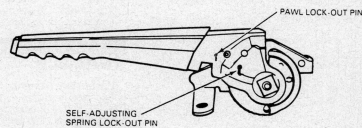

PAWL LOCK-OUT PIN

SELF-ADJUSTING
SPRING LOCK-OUT PIN

**Fig. 17 Inserting pin in self-adjusting spring lock-out**

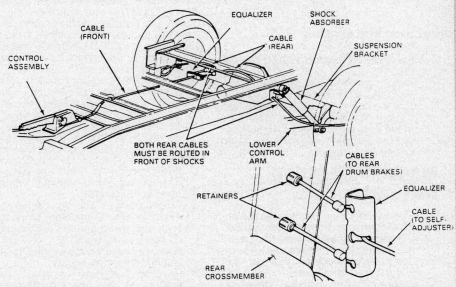

**Fig. 18 Parking brake cable assembly**

ter of brake drum.

3. Reverse tool and adjust shoes until they contact gauge, ensuring that gauge is parallel to vehicle and at centerline of axle, **Fig. 14.** Holding automatic adjusting lever aside, rotate adjusting screw as necessary.
4. Install drums, wheels and retaining nuts, then complete adjustment by applying brakes several times while driving vehicle in reverse.
5. Check brake operation by making several stops in forward gear. Repeat step 4, if necessary.

## WITH DRUMS INSTALLED

1. Raise and support rear of vehicle.
2. Remove cover from adjusting hole located at bottom of backing plate.
3. Using a small screwdriver to hold adjusting lever away from star wheel, rotate adjusting screw star wheel until brake shoes are locked against drum, **Fig. 15.**
4. Back-off brake adjusting screw approximately 10 to 12 notches so that brake drum rotates freely without drag. If brake drum does not rotate freely, remove drum and clean and inspect drum brake components.
5. After adjusting both drum brakes lower vehicle and apply brakes several times to position brake shoes.
6. Road test vehicle to ensure brakes operate properly.

## PARKING BRAKE

The parking brake system is self-adjusting and does not require adjustment.

On some models, rear brake drag that appears to be an over adjusted parking brake may be caused by parking brake cables not returning to a fully released position. This will result in a tight feel in the parking brake control and may allow the parking brake to be fully applied when parking brake control is at the first notch of handle travel. To correct this problem a new designed cable return spring must be installed. To install a new spring, proceed as follows:

1. With transmission in Neutral and parking brake off, rotate rear wheels and check for brake drag.
2. Inspect cables for any damage or kinks, then release parking brake tension as follows:
   a. Remove boot cover from parking brake control assembly, then place control in the released position.
   b. Insert a steel pin through pawl lock-out pin hole, **Fig. 16.**
   c. Pin must be inserted from inboard side of control (larger hole), at a slightly upward and forward angle then swept downward and rearward to disengage self-adjusting pawl and then insert through hole on the opposite side. This will lock out the self-adjusting pawl.
   d. With an assistant inside vehicle, raise vehicle on a hoist.
   e. While pulling down and holding front cable, have the assistant insert a pin through self-adjusting

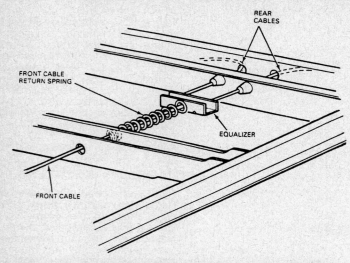

**Fig. 19   Installing front cable return spring**

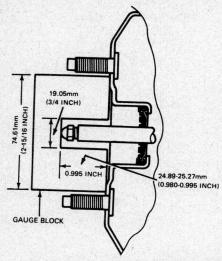

**Fig. 20   Checking master cylinder pushrod length**

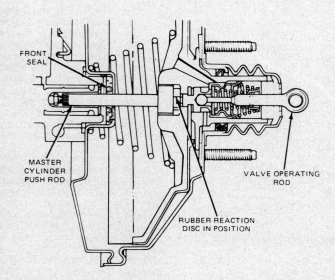

**Fig. 21   Checking reaction disc installation**

spring lock-out holes in lever and control assembly, **Fig. 17.**
3. Disconnect front and rear cables from the equalizer, **Fig. 18.**
4. By hand, push and pull each cable in its housing to ensure smooth operation.
5. Remove rear drums and clean rear brake assemblies, then grease shoe ledges with suitable lubricant.
6. Using a screwdriver, pry each shoe slightly off the anchor pin, then check for smooth action and full return to anchor pin.
7. Pull and release each rear cable by hand and check for full parking brake lever return.
8. Replace any parts that show signs of damage or do not operate freely.
9. Readjust rear brakes, then reassemble rear brakes and drums.
10. Install new front cable return spring on

the equalizer, part no. E89Z-2A651-A, **Fig. 19.**
11. Making sure that cables are connected to the equalizer, remove two steel pins from parking brake control assembly. **When removing steel pins make sure to remove pawl lock-out pin before removing self-adjusting spring lock-out pin.**

## MASTER CYLINDER REPLACE

1. Disconnect brake warning lamp electrical connector from master cylinder.
2. Disconnect hydraulic lines from master cylinder, then remove master cylinder to brake booster retaining nuts and the master cylinder.
3. Before installing cylinder, check distance from outer end of master cylin-

der pushrod to front face of booster assembly using suitable gauge block, **Fig. 20.** Pushrod length should be .980–.995 inch. Turn pushrod adjusting screw inward or outward until specified length is achieved.
4. Reinstall master cylinder and retaining nuts, reconnect hydraulic lines and brake warning lamp electrical connector, then bleed brake system and master cylinder.

## BRAKE BOOSTER REPLACE

Ensure that the brake booster rubber reaction disc is properly installed as shown, **Fig. 21,** if the master cylinder pushrod is removed or accidentally pulled out. A dislodged disc may cause excessive pedal travel and extreme operation sensitivity. The disc is black compared to the silver colored valve plunger that will be exposed after the pushrod and front seal are removed. The booster unit is serviced as an assembly and must be replaced if the reaction disc cannot be properly installed and aligned, or if it cannot be properly located within the unit itself.

1. Disconnect stop light switch wiring, support master cylinder from underneath, then remove master cylinder to booster retaining nuts.
2. Loosen manifold vacuum hose to booster check valve retaining clamp, then remove hose and check valve.
3. Pull master cylinder far enough away from booster to allow removal of booster assembly without interference from cylinder.
4. Working from inside vehicle, remove retaining pin, then slide stop light switch, pushrod, spacers and bushing off brake pedal arm.
5. Remove brake booster to firewall retaining bolts, then booster.
6. Reverse procedure to install, then start engine and check brake operation.

# FRONT SUSPENSION & STEERING

## INDEX

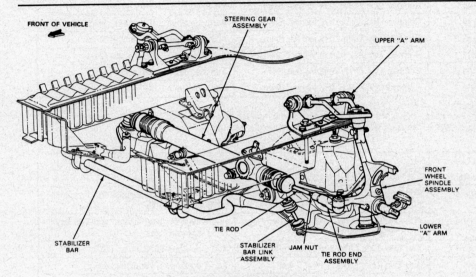

**Fig. 1  Front suspension**

## DESCRIPTION

The front coil spring suspension, **Fig. 1**, consists of spindles, unequal length control arms with integral ball joints and bushings, helical coil springs, telescopic shock absorbers and a stabilizer bar.

The lower control arm is attached to the engine crossmember through pivot bushings and to the spindle through the ball joint assembly. It provides support for the coil springs and attachments for the shock absorbers and stabilizer bar.

The upper control arm is located on top of the front longitudinal side member. It is attached to the spindle at the upper ball joint and is anchored to the body using the primary crossmember bolts and an additional bolt and washer assembly. Alignment is performed by adding or subtracting shims at the control arm to pivot shaft interface.

The telescopic, direct action-type shock absorbers are gas filled, resulting in improved damping effect and durability. Rubber bushings are provided at the upper and lower mountings to minimize road noise transmission.

The front stabilizer bar provides for both improved handling and less body sway. It is attached to both the frame, by a bracket and insulator assembly, and to the lower control arm by a link assembly.

## WHEEL ALIGNMENT
### CAMBER & CASTER ADJUSTMENTS

Caster and camber adjustments are provided for by shims on the upper control arm. Shims are to be added, subtracted or switched from the front and rear legs, as necessary, to achieve desired settings.

To adjust camber, remove or add an equal number of shims to the front and rear legs of the control arm.

To adjust caster, transfer shims between the front and rear legs of the control arm as required to achieve desired settings. If an unequal number of shims is added or subtracted to the front or rear legs of the upper control arm, both caster and camber settings will be revised. Refer to the Caster/Camber Variation Chart, **Fig. 2**, when adjusting camber and caster to specification.

### TOE-IN, ADJUST

1. Position vehicle on suitable alignment rack.
2. Start engine, turn steering wheel back and forth until centered, then turn ignition off to lock wheel.
3. Observe toe setting. If setting is not within specification, remove bellows seal clamp, if applicable, then free bellows from tie rod.
4. Loosen tie rod jam nuts, then adjust toe setting to specification.
5. Hold tie rod end with suitable wrench, then torque jam nuts to 43-50 ft. lbs.
6. Reposition bellows, then install new clamp.

## WHEEL BEARINGS
### ADJUST

1. Raise and support front of vehicle.
2. Remove wheel cover, grease cap, cotter pin and retainer.
3. Loosen adjusting nut three turns, then rock wheel assembly in and out several times to obtain sufficient clearance between rotor and brake linings.
4. Rotate wheel assembly while torquing adjusting nut to 17-25 ft. lbs.
5. Loosen adjusting nut 1/2 turn, then re-torque adjusting nut to 18-20 inch lbs.
6. Install retainer and cotter pin. Bend pin ends around castellated flange of retainer.
7. Ensure wheel rotates freely, install grease cap and wheel cover, then lower vehicle.

## SHOCK ABSORBER
### REPLACE

1. Remove upper retaining nut and washer.
2. Remove lower retaining bolts at control arm.
3. Remove shock absorber from vehicle.
4. Reverse procedure to install. Torque lower retaining bolts to 16-24 ft. lbs. and upper retaining nut to 25-35 ft. lbs.

## BALL JOINTS
### REPLACE

The ball joints are integral with the control arms and are serviced as an assembly. Refer to "Control Arm, Replace" for procedure.

## COIL SPRING
### REPLACE

1. Start engine, center steering wheel, then shut ignition off to lock wheel.
2. Raise and support vehicle, then remove wheel assembly.

**CASTER CHANGES**

| Caster Change | Notes | Shim Changes | |
|---|---|---|---|
| | | Front Leg | Rear Leg |
| Increase Caster by 2 Degrees | Note 1 | Add One 6mm (.236 inches) Shim | Remove One 6mm (.236 inches) Shim |
| Increase Caster by 1.67 Degrees | Note 2 | Add One 6mm (.236 inches) Shim | Remove Two 2mm (.078 inches) Shims |
| Increase Caster by 1.33 Degrees | Note 1 | Add Two 2mm (.078 inches) Shims | Remove Two 2mm (.078 inches) Shims |
| Increase Caster by 1 Degree | Note 2 | Add Two 2mm (.078 inches) Shims | Remove One 2mm (.078 inches) Shim |
| Increase Caster by .67 Degrees | Note 1 | Add One 2mm (.078 inches) Shim | Remove One 2mm (.078 inches) Shim |
| Increase Caster by .33 Degrees | Note 2 | Add One 2mm (.078 inches) Shim | No Change |
| 0 or Starting Position | | No Change | No Change |
| Decrease Caster by .33 Degrees | Note 3 | Remove One 2mm (.078 inches) Shim | No Change |
| Decrease Caster by .67 Degrees | Note 1 | Remove One 2mm (.078 inches) Shim | Add One 2mm (.078 inches) Shim |
| Decrease Caster by 1 Degree | Note 3 | Remove Two 2mm (.078 inches) Shims | Add One 2mm (.078 inches) Shim |
| Decrease Caster by 1.33 Degrees | Note 1 | Remove Two 2mm (.078 inches) Shims | Add Two 2mm (.078 inches) Shims |
| Decrease Caster by 1.67 Degrees | Note 3 | Remove One 6mm (.236 inches) Shim | Add Two 2mm (.078 inches) Shims |
| Decrease Caster by 2 Degrees | Note 1 | Remove One 6mm (.236 inches) Shim | Add One 6mm (.236 inches) Shim |

Note 1 — No Camber Change.
Note 2 — Slight increase in camber by .1 degree to .2 degrees since more shims were added to the front leg than the rear leg.
Note 3 — Slight decrease in camber by .1 degree to .2 degrees since more shims were removed from the front leg than added to rear leg.

**CAMBER CHANGES**

| Camber Change | Note | Shim Changes | |
|---|---|---|---|
| | | Front Leg | Rear Leg |
| Increase Camber by 1.67 Degrees | Note 1 | Add One 6mm (.236 inches) and Two 2mm (.078 inches) Shims | Add One 6mm (.236 inches) and Two 2mm (.078 inches) Shims |
| Increase Camber by 1.33 Degrees | Note 1 | Add One 6mm (.236 inches) and Two 2mm (.078 inches) Shims | Add One 6mm (.236 inches) and Two 2mm (.078 inches) Shims |
| Increase Camber by 1 Degree | Note 1 | Add One 6mm (.236 inches) Shim | Add One 6mm (.236 inches) Shim |
| Increase Camber by .66 Degrees | Note 1 | Add Two 2mm (.078 inches) Shims | Add Two 2mm (.078 inches) Shims |
| Increase Camber by .33 Degrees | Note 1 | Add One 2mm (.078 inches) Shim | Add One 2mm (.078 inches) Shim |
| 0 or Starting Position | | No Change | No Change |
| Decrease Camber by .33 Degrees | Note 1 | Remove One 2mm (.078 inches) Shim | Remove One 2mm (.078 inches) Shim |
| Decrease Camber by .67 Degrees | Note 1 | Remove Two 2mm (.078 inches) Shims | Remove Two 2mm (.078 inches) Shims |
| Decrease Camber by 1 Degree | Note 1 | Remove One 6mm (.236 inches) Shim | Remove One 6mm (.236 inches) Shim |
| Decrease Camber by 1.33 Degrees | Note 1 | Remove One 6mm (.236 inches) and One 2mm (.089 inches) Shims | Remove One 6mm (.236 inches) and One 2mm (.078 inches) Shims |
| Decrease Camber by 1.67 Degrees | Note 1 | Remove One 6mm (.236 inches) and one 2mm (.078 inches) Shims | Remove One 6mm (.236 inches) and One 2mm (.078 inches) Shims |

Note 1 — No Caster Change.

**Fig. 2  Caster/Camber variation chart**

3. Disconnect stabilizer bar link and shock absorber from lower control arm, **Fig. 3.**
4. Remove shock absorber upper retaining nut and washer, then the shock absorber.
5. Disconnect center link from pitman arm, then compress coil spring using suitable tool.
6. Loosen lower control arm pivot bolts, then remove cotter pin from lower ball joint retaining nut.
7. Loosen ball joint retaining nut several turns, then disengage ball joint from spindle using suitable tool.
8. Support lower control arm with suitable jack, remove ball joint retaining nut, then lower control arm and remove coil spring from vehicle.
9. Reverse procedure to install. Torque ball joint retaining nut to 80-120 ft. lbs. and stabilizer bar link attaching nut to 12-18 ft. lbs. Lower vehicle to normal ride height, then torque control arm pivot bolts to 187-260 ft. lbs.

# SPINDLE
## REPLACE

1. Start engine, center steering wheel, then shut ignition off to lock wheel.
2. Raise and support vehicle, then remove wheel assembly.
3. Remove brake caliper, rotor and dust shield from spindle.
4. Remove cotter pin and retaining nut, then separate tie rod end from spindle using suitable tool.
5. Support lower control arm with suitable jack, remove cotter pin, then loosen ball joint retaining nut several turns.
6. Disengage ball joint from spindle using suitable tool, remove retaining nut, then lower control arm until ball joint stud clears spindle.
7. Remove upper ball joint to spindle retaining nut and bolt, **Fig. 3,** separate ball joint from spindle, then remove spindle from vehicle.
8. Reverse procedure to install. Torque upper ball joint to spindle retaining nut and bolt to 27-37 ft. lbs., lower ball joint retaining nut to 80-120 ft. lbs., and tie rod end to spindle retaining nut to 52-74 ft. lbs.

# CONTROL ARM
## REPLACE
### UPPER ARM

1. Remove spindle as outlined previously.
2. Remove cowl drain bracket retaining

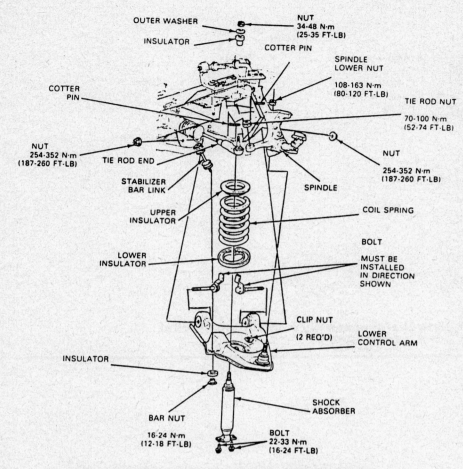

**Fig. 3 Coil spring & spindle replacement**

bolt, then bracket and retainer plate, **Fig. 4.**

3. Scribe marks on flat plate where control arm brackets are positioned, then remove front mounting bracket to flat plate retaining bolt.
4. Working from beneath frame rail, remove control arm mounting bracket to frame rail retaining nuts and bolts. To facilitate bolt removal, swing control arm aside and allow bolts to drop downward.
5. Remove upper control arm, ball joint, mounting brackets and adjusting arm as an assembly, then separate control arm from adjusting arm, noting number and position of adjusting shims.
6. Reverse procedure to install noting the following:
   a. Torque flat plate retaining bolt to 10-14 ft. lbs.
   b. Torque front mounting bracket to frame rail retaining nut and bolt to 135-145 ft. lbs.
   c. Torque center and rear mounting bracket retaining nuts and bolts to 145-155 ft. lbs.
   d. Torque cowl drain bracket retaining bolt to 10-14 ft. lbs.

**Ensure that mounting bracket to flat plate scribe marks are properly aligned. It is imperative that the mounting bracket to frame rail retaining nuts and**

bolts be torqued to the specifications above, since this is the critical joint of the front chassis area. Make sure to lubricate these nuts and bolts before assembly to ensure accurate torque readings.

## LOWER ARM

1. Remove coil spring as outlined previously.
2. Support crossmember, then remove control arm to crossmember pivot bolts and nuts, then lower control arm.
3. Reverse procedure to install. Torque ball joint retaining nut to 80-120 ft. lbs. and stabilizer bar link attaching nut to 12-18 ft. lbs. Lower vehicle to normal ride height, then torque control arm pivot bolts to 187-260 ft. lbs. Ensure that pivot bolts are installed from inside part of control arm.

## STABILIZER BAR
### REPLACE

1. Remove stabilizer bar link to lower control arm retaining nut, then disconnect link from control arm.
2. Remove mounting bracket to frame retaining bolts, then remove mounting brackets and stabilizer bar.
3. Reverse procedure to install. Torque stabilizer bar link to control arm retain-

ing nut to 12-18 ft. lbs. and mounting bracket to frame retaining bolts to 16-24 ft. lbs.

## STEERING GEAR
### REPLACE

1. Center steering system as follows:
   a. Rotate steering wheel lock-to-lock and count number of turns of rotation required.
   b. Divide the number of turns recorded in previous step by two.
   c. Rotate steering wheel to full lock position, then turn wheel the exact turns recorded in step 1b. Ensure that front wheels and steering wheel are in straight ahead position.
2. Remove intermediate shaft to steering gear pinch bolt, then disconnect shaft from gear.
3. On models equipped with power steering, disconnect pressure and return lines from steering gear. Cap lines and ports to prevent dirt entry and spillage of fluid.
4. On all models, remove tie rod end to spindle retaining nuts, then separate tie rod ends from spindle using suitable puller.
5. Support steering gear, then remove steering gear to crossmember retaining nuts, bolts and washers. Remove steering gear from vehicle.
6. Reverse procedure to install noting the following:
   a. Torque steering gear to crossmember retaining bolts and nuts to 65-90 ft. lbs.
   b. Torque pressure and return lines, if applicable, to 10-15 ft. lbs.
   c. Torque tie rod end to spindle retaining nuts to 52-73 ft. lbs.
   d. Torque intermediate shaft to steering gear pinch bolt to 30-42 ft. lbs.
   e. Check and adjust fluid in power steering pump reservoir, if applicable, then check toe setting as required.

## POWER STEERING PUMP
### REPLACE

1. Drain fluid from pump reservoir, then disconnect pressure and return lines at pump.
2. If applicable, disconnect pressure switch electrical connector, then remove switch from line fitting.
3. Loosen drive belt adjusting bolt at alternator (4-140) or idler pulley (V6-171, V6-182), then remove drive belt from pump pulley.
4. Using steering pump pulley remover T69L-10300-B or equivalent, remove pulley from pump assembly.
5. Remove pump to support bracket retaining bolts, then the pump assembly.
6. Reverse procedure to install. Fill pump reservoir, start engine, then turn steering wheel lock-to-lock to remove air from system.

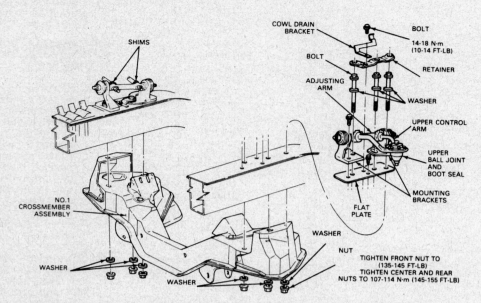

**Fig. 4   Upper control arm assembly & mounting bracket replacement**

# AIR CONDITIONING

## TABLE OF CONTENTS

# A/C System Testing

## INDEX

## GENERAL PRECAUTIONS

The Freon refrigerant used is also known as R-12 or F-12. It is colorless and odorless both as a gas and a liquid. Since it boils (vaporizes) at (−21.7° F), it will usually be in a vapor state when being handled in a repair shop. If a portion of liquid refrigerant should come in contact with the hands or face, note that its temperature momentarily will be at least (22° F) below zero.

Protective goggles should be worn when opening any refrigerant lines. If liquid coolant does touch the eyes, bathe eyes quickly in cold water, then apply a bland disinfectant oil to the eyes. See an eye doctor.

When checking a system for leaks with a torch type leak detector, do not breathe the vapors coming from the flame. Do not discharge refrigerant in the area of a live flame. A poisonous phosgene gas is produced when R-12 or F-12 is burned. While a small amount of this gas produced by a leak detector is not harmful, unless inhaled directly at the flame. The quantity of refrigerant released into the air when a system is purged can be extremely dangerous, if allowed to come in contact with an open flame. Thus, when purging a system, be sure that the discharge hose is routed to a well ventilated place where no flame is present. Under these conditions the refrigerant will be quickly dissipated into the surrounding air.

Never allow the temperature of refrigerant drums to exceed (125° F). The resultant increase in temperature will cause a corresponding increase in pressure which may cause the safety plug to release or the drum to burst.

If it is necessary to heat a drum of refrigerant when charging a system, the drum should be placed in water that is no hotter than (125° F). Never use a blowtorch, or other open flame. If possible, a pressure release mechanism should be attached before the drum is heated.

When connecting and disconnecting service gauges on A/C system, ensure that gauge hand valves are fully closed and that compressor service valves, if equipped, are in the back-seated (fully counterclockwise) position. Do not disconnect gauge hoses from service port adapters, if used, while gauges are connected to A/C system. To disconnect hoses, always remove adapter from service port. Do not disconnect hoses from gauge manifold while connected to A/C system, as refrigerant will be rapidly discharged.

After disconnecting gauge lines, check valve areas to be sure service valves are correctly seated and Schraeder valves, if used, are not leaking.

## EXERCISE SYSTEM

An important fact most owners ignore is that A/C units must be used periodically. Manufacturers caution that when the air conditioner is not used regularly, particularly during cold months, it should be turned on for a few minutes once every two or three weeks while the engine is running. This keeps the system in good operating condition.

Checking out the system for the effects of disuse before the onset of summer is one of the most important aspects of A/C servicing.

First clean out the condenser core, mounted in all cases at the front of the radiator. All obstructions, such as leaves, bugs, and dirt, must be removed, as they will reduce heat transfer and impair the efficiency of the system. Make sure the space between the condenser and the radiator also is free of foreign matter.

Make certain the evaporator water drain is open. Certain systems have two evaporators, one in the engine compartment and one toward the rear of the vehicle. The evaporator cools and dehumidifies the air before it enters the passenger compartment; there, the refrigerant is changed from a liquid to a vapor. As the core cools the air, moisture condenses on it but is prevented from collecting in the evaporator by the water drain.

## PERFORMANCE TEST

The system should be operated for at least 15 minutes to allow sufficient time for all parts to become completely stabilized. Determine if the system is fully charged by the use of test gauges and sight glass if one is installed on system. Head pressure will read from 180 psi to 220 psi or higher, depending upon ambient temperature and the type unit being tested. The sight glass should be free of bubbles if a glass is used in the system. Low side pressures should read approximately 15 psi to 30 psi, again depending on the ambient temperature and unit being tested. It is not feasible to give a definite reading for all types of systems used, as the type control and component installation used on a particular system will directly influence pressure readings on high and low sides, **Fig. 1.**

High side pressure will definitely be affected by ambient or outside air tempera-

| Evaporator Pressure Gauge Reading | Evaporator Temperature F° | High Pressure Gauge Reading | Ambient Temperature |
|---|---|---|---|
| 0 | -21° | 45 | 20° |
| 0.6 | -20° | 55 | 30° |
| 2.4 | -15° | 72 | 40° |
| 4.5 | -10° | 86 | 50° |
| 6.8 | - 5° | 105 | 60° |
| 9.2 | 0° | 126 | 70° |
| 11.8 | 5° | 140 | 75° |
| 14.7 | 10° | 160 | 80° |
| 17.1 | 15° | 185 | 90° |
| 21.1 | 20° | 195 | 95° |
| 22.5 | 22° | 220 | 100° |
| 23.9 | 24° | 240 | 105° |
| 25.4 | 26° | 260 | 110° |
| 26.9 | 28° | 275 | 115° |
| 28.5 | 30° | 290 | 120° |
| 37.0 | 40° | 305 | 125° |
| 46.7 | 50° | 325 | 130° |
| 57.7 | 60° | | |
| 70.1 | 70° | | |
| 84.1 | 80° | | |
| 99.6 | 90° | | |
| 116.9 | 100° | | |
| 136.0 | 110° | | |
| 157.1 | 120° | | |
| 179.0 | 130° | | |

**Fig. 1   A/C system pressure/temperature relationship (Typical). Equivalent to 1750 RPM (30 mph)**

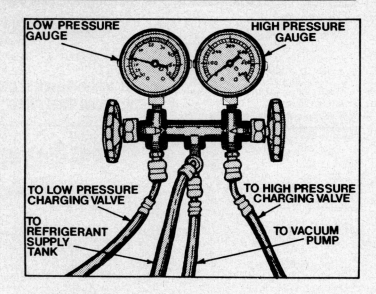

**Fig. 2   Gauge manifold hose connections**

ture. A system that is operating normally will indicate a high side gauge reading between 150-170 psi with an (80° F) ambient temperature. The same system will register 210-230 psi with an ambient temperature of (100° F). No two systems will register exactly the same, which requires that allowance for variations in head pressures must be considered. Following are the most important normal readings likely to be encountered during the season.

| Ambient Temp. Side Pressure | High |
|---|---|
| 80 | 150-170 |
| 90 | 175-195 |
| 95 | 185-205 |
| 100 | 210-230 |
| 105 | 230-250 |
| 110 | 250-270 |

## RELATIVE TEMPERATURE OF HIGH AND LOW SIDES

The high side of the system should be uniformly hot to the touch throughout. A difference in temperature will indicate a partial blockage of liquid or gas at this point.

The low side of the system should be uniformly cool to the touch with no excessive sweating of the suction line or low side service valve. Excessive sweating or frosting of the low side service valve usually indicates an expansion valve is allowing an excessive amount of refrigerant into the evaporator.

## EVAPORATOR OUTPUT

At this point, provided all other inspection tests have been performed, and components have been found to operate as they should, a rapid cooling down of the interior of the vehicle should result. The use of a thermometer is not necessary to determine evaporator output. Bringing all units to correct operating specifications will insure that evaporator performs as intended.

## LEAK TEST

Testing refrigerant system for leaks is one of the most important phases of troubleshooting. Several types of leak detectors are available that are suitable for detecting A/C system leaks. One or more of the following procedures will prove useful for detecting leaks and checking connections after service work has been performed. Prior to performing any leak test, prepare the vehicle as follows:

1. Attach a suitable gauge manifold to system and observe pressure readings.

2. If little or no pressure is indicated, system must be partially charged.
3. If gauges indicate pressure, set engine to run at fast idle and operate system at maximum cooling for 10-15 minutes, then stop engine and perform leak tests.

## FLAME TYPE (HALIDE) LEAK DETECTORS

Avoid inhaling fumes produced by burning refrigerant when using flame type detectors. Use caution when using detector near flammable materials such as interior trim components. Do not use flame-type detector where concentrations of combustible or explosive gasses, dusts or vapors may exist.

1. Light leak detector and adjust flame as low as possible to obtain maximum sensitivity.
2. Allow detector to warm until copper element is cherry-red. Flame should be almost colorless.
3. Test reaction plate sensitivity by passing end of sensor hose near an opened can of refrigerant. Flame should react violently, turning bright blue.
4. If flame does not change color, replace reaction plate following manufacturer's instructions.
5. Allow flame to clear, then slowly move sensor hose along areas suspected of leakage while observing flame. **Position sensor hose under areas of suspected leakage, as R-12 refrigerant is heavier than air.**
6. Move sensor hose under all lines, fittings and components. Insert hose into evaporator case, if possible, and check compressor shaft seal.
7. The presence of refrigerant will cause flame to change color as follows: Pale blue, no refrigerant; yellow-yellow/green, slight leak; bright blue-purple/blue, major leak or

8. If detector indicates a large leak or heavy concentration of refrigerant, ventilate area using a small fan in order to pinpoint leak.

9. Repair leaks as needed, evacuate and recharge system, then recheck system for leaks.

## ELECTRONIC LEAK DETECTORS

The procedure for using an electronic leak detector is similar to the procedure for flame-type leak detectors, except that the presence of refrigerant is indicated by an audible tone or flashing light. Refer to operating instructions for unit being used, and observe the following procedures:

1. Move detector probe 1 inch per second along areas of suspected leakage.

2. Position probe under area to be tested as refrigerant is heavier than air.

3. Check gauge manifold, hoses and service ports for leakage.

## FLUID LEAK DETECTORS

Apply leak detector solution around joints to be tested. A cluster of bubbles will form immediately if there is a leak. A white foam that forms after a short while will indicate an extremely small leak. In some confined areas such as sections of the evaporator and condenser, electronic leak detectors will be more useful.

## DISCHARGING & EVACUATING SYSTEM
### DISCHARGING

1. Ensure that all gauge manifold or charging station hand valves are closed and that compressor service valves, if equipped, are in the back-seated (fully counterclockwise) position.

2. Connect compound (low) side gauge hose to low (suction) side service port, and high pressure gauge hose to high (discharge) side port, **Fig. 2**, then open compressor service valves to mid-position, if equipped. **Refer to "Charging Valve Location" chart in "A/C System Servicing" section, for service port locations.**

3. Insert gauge manifold center hose into a suitable container that is vented to shop exhaust system.

4. If system is operational, set engine to run at fast idle and operate A/C system in maximum cooling position, with blower on high, for 10-15 minutes to return oil to compressor, then reduce idle and stop engine.

5. Slightly open low side control valve on manifold, and allow refrigerant to discharge slowly into container. **Do not allow refrigerant to discharge rapidly. Too rapid purging will draw system oil charge out with refrigerant.**

6. When system is nearly discharged, slightly open high side control valve on manifold to discharge remaining refrigerant from compressor and lines.

7. When system is completely discharged (gauges read zero), close high and low side control valves and measure amount of oil in discharge container.

8. If more than 1/2 ounce of refrigeration oil is trapped in container, perform "Oil Level Check," as outlined in "A/C System Servicing" section. **If addition of refrigeration oil is necessary, oil should be added prior to evacuating system.**

## EVACUATING SYSTEM WITH VACUUM PUMP

Vacuum pumps suitable for removing air and moisture from A/C systems are commercially available. The pump should be capable of drawing the system down to 28-29 1/2 inches Hg at sea level. For each 1000 foot increase in altitude, this specification should be decreased by 1 inch Hg. As an example, at 5000 feet elevation, only 23-24 1/2 inches Hg can be obtained.

1. Connect suitable gauge manifold and discharge system as outlined previously. **System must be completely discharged prior to evacuation. If pressurized refrigerant is allowed to enter vacuum pump, pump will be damaged.**

2. Connect hose from gauge manifold center port to vacuum pump inlet.

3. Fully open both gauge manifold hand valves.

4. Operate vacuum pump while observing low side compound gauge. If system does not "pump-down" to 28-29 1/2 inches Hg (at sea level) within approximately 5 minutes, recheck connections and leak test system.

5. Continue to operate vacuum pump for 15-30 minutes, longer if system was open for an extended period of time, then close both manifold valves and stop pump.

6. Check ability of system to hold vacuum. Watch low side compound gauge and ensure that reading does not rise at a rate faster than 1 inch Hg every 4-5 minutes.

7. If system fails to hold vacuum, recheck fittings and connections, and leak test system.

8. If system holds vacuum, charge system with refrigerant.

## CHARGING SYSTEM

Refer to "A/C Data Table" in the "A/C System Servicing" section, for refrigerant capacities.

## CHARGING WITH 14 OZ. CANS

1. Connect a suitable refrigerant valve and can adapter, such as Motorcraft YT-280 or equivalent, to refrigerant can following manufacturer's instructions.

2. Ensure that valve on can adapter is closed, then connect hose from gauge manifold center port to adapter.

3. When can is connected, charge system according to procedure under "Charging From Drum." When can is empty, close valve and remove can. Connect new can, open valve and continue charging until correct weight of refrigerant has entered system. Note capacity of refrigerant cans. When specifications require using a portion of a can, weigh it to ensure proper amount of refrigerant is installed.

## CHARGING FROM DRUM

1. With manifold gauge set valves closed to center hose, disconnect vacuum pump from manifold gauge set.

2. Connect center hose of manifold gauge set to refrigerant drum.

3. Purge air from center hose by loosening hose at manifold gauge set and open refrigerant drum valve. When refrigerant escapes from hose, tighten center hose connection at manifold gauge set.

4. On vehicles so equipped, disconnect wire harness connector at clutch cycling pressure switch. Install jumper wire across terminals of connector.

5. On all models, open manifold gauge set low side valve and allow refrigerant to enter system. Refrigerant can must be kept upright if vehicle low pressure service gauge port is not on suction accumulator/drier or suction accumulator fitting.

6. When system stops drawing refrigerant in, start engine and set control lever to A/C position and blower switch to "HI" position to draw remaining refrigerant into system.

7. When specified weight of refrigerant is in system, close gauge set low pressure valve and refrigerant supply valve.

8. On vehicles so equipped, remove jumper wire from clutch cycling pressure switch connector and connect the connector to pressure switch.

9. On all models, operate system until pressures stabilize to check operation and system pressures. **During charging, it may be necessary to use a high volume fan to blow air through the condenser in order to prevent excessive refrigerant system pressures or engine overheating.**

10. When charging is complete and system operating pressures are normal, return compressor service valves, if equipped, to the back seated position, disconnect gauge manifold hoses from system and install protective caps over service fittings.

# A/C System Servicing

## INDEX



# A/C Data Table

| Year | Model | Refrigerant Capacity Lbs. | Refrigerant Oil | | | Compressor Clutch Air Gap Inches |
|---|---|---|---|---|---|---|
| | | | Viscosity | Total System Capacity Ounces | Compressor Oil Level Check Inches | |
| 1980-82 | E100-350① | 3½ | 500 | ② | ③ | — |
| | E100-350④ | 4½ | 500 | ② | ③ | — |
| 1980-81 | Exc. E100-350 | 3½ | 500 | ② | ③ | — |
| 1982-83 | Bronco & F100-350 | 3¼ | 500 | 10 | ⑤ | .021-.036 |
| 1983 | E100-350① | 3½ | 500 | 10 | ⑤ | .021-.036 |
| | E100-350④ | 4½ | 500 | 10 | ⑤ | .021-.036 |
| 1983-86 | Ranger | 2½ | 500 | 10⑦ | ⑤ | ⑥ |
| 1984-86 | Bronco II | 2½ | 500 | 10⑦ | ⑤ | ⑥ |
| 1984-86 | Bronco & F150-350 | 3 | 500 | 10 | ⑤ | .021-.036 |
| | E150-350① | 3½ | 500 | 10 | ⑤ | .021-.036 |
| | E150-350④ | 4¼ | 500 | 10 | ⑤ | .021-.036 |
| 1986 | Aerostar | 2½ | 500 | 10 | ⑤ | .021-.042 |
| 1987-88 | Aerostar | 3½-3¾ | 500 | 10 | ⑤ | .021-.042 |
| | Bronco II & Ranger | 2½ | 500 | 10⑦ | ⑤ | .021-.036 |
| | Bronco & F150-350 | 3¼ | 500 | 10 | ⑤ | .021-.036 |
| | E150-350① | 3½-3¾ | 500 | 10 | ⑤ | .021-.036 |
| | E150-350④ | 4¼-4½ | 500 | 10 | ⑤ | .021-.036 |
| 1989 | Aerostar | 2½ | 500 | 10 | ⑤ | .021-.042⑧ |
| | Bronco II & Ranger | 2½ | 500 | 10⑦ | ⑤ | .021-.036⑧ |
| | Bronco & F150-350 | 3¼ | 500 | 10 | ⑤ | .021-.036⑧ |
| | E150-350① | 3½-3¾ | 500 | 10 | ⑤ | .021-.036⑧ |
| | E150-350④ | 4¼-4½ | 500 | 10 | ⑤ | .021-.036⑧ |

①—Models less auxiliary (rear, overhead etc.) system.
②—Tecumseh comp., 11 oz.; York comp., 10 oz.
③—Tecumseh comp.: Horizontal mount, ⅞–1⅝ inch; Vertical mount, ⅞–1⅝ inch York comp.: Horizontal mount, 13/16–1 3/16 inch; Vertical mount, ⅞–1⅝ inch.
④—Models with auxiliary (rear, overhead etc.) system.
⑤—Note that "Oil Level Inches" can not be checked. Refer to total capacity and see text for checking procedure.
⑥—Exc. Tecumseh HR-980 compressor, .021–.036 inch; Tecumseh HR-980 compressor, .009–.041 inch.
⑦—With Tecumseh HR-980 compressor, 8 oz.
⑧—With FX-15 Compressor, .018–.033 inch.

# Charging Valve Location

| Year | Model | High Pressure Fitting | Low Pressure Fitting |
|---|---|---|---|
| 1980-83 | E100-350 | Discharge Line At Condenser | Suction Line At Compressor |
| 1980-86 | Exc. E100-350 | Discharge Line At Compressor | Accumulator |
| 1984-86 | E150-350 | Compressor | Compressor |
| 1987-89 | All | High Pressure Line At Compressor | Accumulator |

## COMPRESSOR SERVICE VALVES

Most F100-350 and Bronco models are equipped with manual valves to isolate the compressor from the refrigerant system. These valves allow the compressor to be removed, or opened for oil level checks, without discharging the A/C system. Refrigerant system service access fittings, located on the manual valves, are also included on some models.

During normal system operation, the manual valves are in the back-seated (fully counterclockwise) position, **Fig. 1.** To isolate the compressor, the valves are rotated to the front-seated (fully clockwise) position, closing off the refrigerant line passage to the compressor. To allow refrigerant system service access, the valves are rotated to the mid-position, **Fig. 1,** which opens the service port while still allowing refrigerant to flow through the system. **Manual compressor service valves should be in the back-seated (fully counterclockwise) position whenever service gauges are being connected or disconnected on the A/C system. Always install protective caps over manual valve stems and service ports, if equipped, after completing A/C service.**

### ISOLATING COMPRESSOR

1. Connect suitable gauge manifold to system and remove protective caps from manual valve stems.
2. Slightly open both service valves toward mid-position, then start engine and operate air conditioning.
   a. On Tecumseh and York 2 cylinder compressors, slightly loosen oil sump filler plug.
   b. On Ford FS-6 compressors, slightly loosen flare nut securing high (discharge) side manual valve to compressor.
3. Slowly rotate suction (low) side service valve clockwise toward front-seated position.
4. When suction (low) side gauge reads zero, stop engine, then rotate both low and high side valves to the fully clockwise (front-seated) position, **Fig. 1.**
5. Relieve internal compressor pressure as follows: **A suitable face shield should be worn when relieving compressor pressure.**

### PURGING COMPRESSOR

The compressor must be purged of air whenever it has been isolated from the system for service.
1. Install oil plugs or reconnect refrigerant lines and manual valves to compressor as needed.
2. Rotate low (suction) side manual valve counterclockwise to the back-seated position.
3. Loosen flare nut securing high (discharge) side manual valve to compressor just enough to allow refrigerant to force air from compressor.

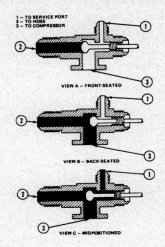

1 – TO SERVICE PORT
2 – TO HOSE
3 – TO COMPRESSOR

VIEW A – FRONT-SEATED

VIEW B – BACK-SEATED

VIEW C – MIDPOSITIONED

**Fig. 1  Compressor service valves, cross sectional view**

4. When air is completely purged, tighten high side manual valve fitting, then back seat valve to complete installation.

## OIL LEVEL CHECK

Refer to "A/C Data Table" for oil level specifications.

### TECUMSEH & YORK COMPRESSORS, EXC. TECUMSEH HR-980

**On models where compressor is mounted on an angle, reposition or remove compressor and check oil level in horizontal position.**
1. Connect suitable gauge manifold to system, set engine to operate at fast idle and operate A/C in maximum cooling position, with blower on high, for 10–15 minutes, then lower idle speed and stop engine.
2. On models with compressor service valves, isolate compressor as outlined. On models without service valves, discharge A/C system.
3. Slowly loosen, then remove oil filler plug. **A suitable face shield should be worn when removing filler plug.**
4. Insert clean dipstick, fabricated from flattened 1/8 inch rod, **Figs. 2 and 3,** through filler plug opening and measure oil level. **Ensure that dipstick is bottomed in compressor sump. Rotate crankshaft as needed to provide clearance for dipstick. On York compressors, crankshaft keyway should face compressor head.**
5. Add or remove oil, as needed, to bring oil level within specifications listed in "A/C Data Table." **If other components are being replaced, refer to "Oil Charge."**
6. Install filler plug and O-ring, then purge air from compressor or evacuate and recharge system, as needed.

## FS-6, NIPPONDENSO 6E-171 & 6P-148 & TECUMSEH HR-980 COMPRESSORS

Refer to "Oil Charge" for service procedures.

## OIL CHARGE

### OIL CHARGE— COMPONENT REPLACEMENT

**Tecumseh & York Compressor Exc. Tecumseh HR-980**
1. Discharge system as outlined, then repair or replace components as needed. **If compressor is replaced, ensure that oil level in replacement compressor is the same as the oil level in the defective compressor.**
2. Evacuate and recharge system, then operate air conditioning for approximately 10 minutes, or until pressure readings have stabilized.
3. Stop engine and perform "Oil Level Check."

### FS-6, FX-15, Nippondenso 6E-171 & 6P-148 & Tecumseh HR-980 Compressors

If there are no signs of external oil leakage, use following procedure to add oil to system during component replacement.
1. Isolate compressor or discharge system, as needed, then remove defective component.
2. Add proper amount of new refrigerant oil for each replacement component as follows:
   a. If compressor is replaced or overhauled on models except FX-15, add 6 ounces of oil to compressor prior to installation. **A factory service replacement compressor contains 10 ounces of refrigeration oil. To ensure proper oil charge, drain 4 ounces of oil from compressor prior to installation.**
   b. If FX-15 compressor is replaced, drain refrigerant oil into a calibrated container. If amount of oil drained from compressor is between 3 and 5 ounces, add same amount of oil to new compressor. If oil drained from compressor is less than 3 ounces, add 3 ounces of oil to new compressor. If oil drained from compressor is more than 5 ounces, add only 5 ounces of oil to new compressor.
   c. If accumulator is replaced, measure amount of oil remaining in defective accumulator, and add the same amount of oil to replacement accumulator plus 1 additional ounce.
   d. If condenser is replaced, add 1 ounce of oil to replacement con-

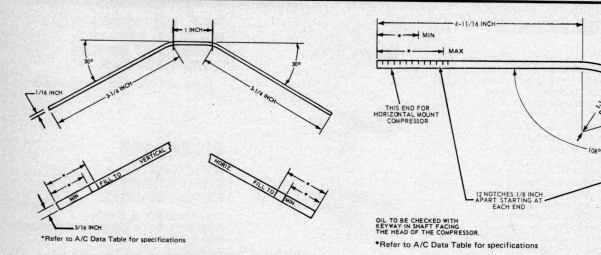

**Fig. 2   Oil level dipstick fabrication. Tecumseh compressor exc. HR-980**

**Fig. 3   Oil level dipstick fabrication. York compressor**

denser.
e. If evaporator is replaced, add 3 ounces of oil to replacement evaporator.
3. Install replacement components, then evacuate and recharge system.

## OIL CHARGE—LEAK CONDITION

### Tecumseh & York Compressor, Exc. Tecumseh HR-980

Refer to "Oil Level Check" for service procedures.

### FS-6, Nippondenso 6E-171 & 6P-148 & Tecumseh HR-980 Compressors

1. If system is operational, set engine to run at fast idle and operate A/C in maximum cooling position, with blower on high, for 10 minutes.
2. Isolate compressor or discharge system, as required, then remove compressor and drain oil into a suitable container.
3. Measure amount of oil recovered from compressor and proceed as follows:

a. If less than 3 ounces of oil are recovered from compressor, add 6 ounces of new refrigeration oil to compressor.
b. If 3-6 ounces of oil are recovered, add same amount of new refrigeration oil to compressor.
c. If more than 6 ounces of oil are recovered, add only 6 ounces of new refrigeration oil to compressor.
4. Reinstall compressor, then evacuate and recharge system as needed.

# ENGINE COOLING FANS, VARIABLE SPEED

## INDEX

Do not operate engine until fan has first been inspected for cracks and/or separations. If a fan blade is found to be bent or damaged in any way, do not attempt to repair or reuse damaged part. Proper balance is essential in fan assembly operation. Balance cannot be assured once a fan assembly has been found to be bent or damaged and failure may occur during operation, creating an extremely dangerous condition. Always replace damaged fan assembly.

## DESCRIPTION

The fan drive clutch, **Fig. 1**, is a fluid coupling containing silicone oil. Fan speed is regulated by the torque-carrying capacity of the silicone oil. The more silicone oil in the coupling, the greater the fan speed, and the less silicone oil, the slower the fan speed.

The type of fan drive clutch used, is the coiled bimetallic thermostatic spring type, Fig. 2.

The fan drive clutch uses a

heat-sensitive, coiled bimetallic spring connected to an opening plate. This units causes fan speed to increase with a rise in temperature and to decrease as temperature decreases.

## TROUBLESHOOTING
### FAN DRIVE CLUTCH TEST

Do not operate the engine until the fan has been first checked for possible

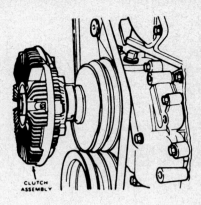

**Fig. 1  Fan drive clutch assembly (typical)**

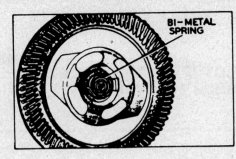

**Fig. 2  Variable speed fan w/coiled bimetallic thermostatic spring**

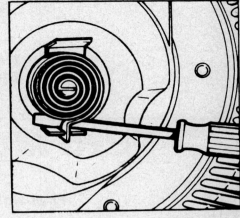

**Fig. 3  Bimetallic coiled spring removal**

cracks and separations.

Run engine at a fast idle speed (1000 RPM) until normal operating temperature is reached. This process can be done more quickly by blocking off the front of the radiator with cardboard. Regardless of temperatures, unit must be operated for at least five minutes immediately before being tested.

Stop engine and using a glove or a cloth to protect the hand, immediately check the effort required to turn the fan. If considerable effort is required, it can be assumed that coupling is operating satisfactorily. If very little effort is required to turn the fan, it is an indication that the coupling is not operating properly and should be replaced.

The clutch fan may be tested while vehicle is being driven. To check, disconnect the bimetal spring, **Fig. 3**, and rotate 90° counterclockwise. This disables the temperature-controlled, free-wheeling feature and the clutch performs like a conventional fan. If this cures the overheating condition, replace the clutch fan.

## FAN CLUTCH NOISE

Fan clutch noise can sometimes be noticed when clutch is engaged for maximum cooling. Clutch noise is also noticeable within the first few minutes after starting engine while clutch is redistributing the silicone fluid back to its normal, disengaged operating condition after settling for long periods of time (over night). However, continuous fan noise or an excessive roar indicates the clutch assembly is locked-up due to internal failure. This condition can be checked by attempting to manually rotate fan. If fan cannot be rotated manually or there is a rough, abrasive feel as fan is rotated, the clutch should be replaced.

## FAN LOOSENESS

Lateral movement can be observed at the fan blade tip under various temperature conditions because of the type bearing used. This movement should not exceed ¼ inch (6.5 mm) as measured at the fan tip. If this lateral movement does not exceed specifications, there is no cause for replacement.

## CLUTCH FLUID LEAK

Small fluid leaks do not generally affect the operation of the unit. These leaks generally occur around the area of the bearing assembly, but if the leaks appear to be excessive, engine overheating may occur. Check for clutch and fan free-wheeling by attempting to rotate fan and clutch assembly by hand five times. If no drag is felt, replace clutch.

## FAN BLADE INSPECTION

Place fan on flat surface with leading edge facing down. If there is a clearance between fan blade touching surface and opposite blade of more than .090 inch (2 mm), replace fan. **Do not operate engine until fan has first been inspected for cracks and/or separations. If a fan blade is found to be bent or damaged in any way, do not attempt to repair or re-use damaged part. Proper balance is essential in fan assembly operation. Balance cannot be assured once a fan assembly has been found to be bent or damaged and failure may occur during operation, creating an extremely dangerous condition. Always replace damaged fan assembly.**

## FAN SERVICE

**To prevent silicone fluid from draining into fan drive bearing, do not store or place drive unit on bench with rear of shaft pointing downward.**

The removal procedure for the fan clutch assembly is generally the same. Merely unfasten the unit from the water pump and remove the assembly from vehicle.

The coil spring type fan clutch cannot be disassembled, serviced or repaired. If it does not function properly it must be replaced with a new unit.

# STARTER MOTORS & SWITCHES

## TABLE OF CONTENTS

# Ford Motorcraft Starters

## INDEX

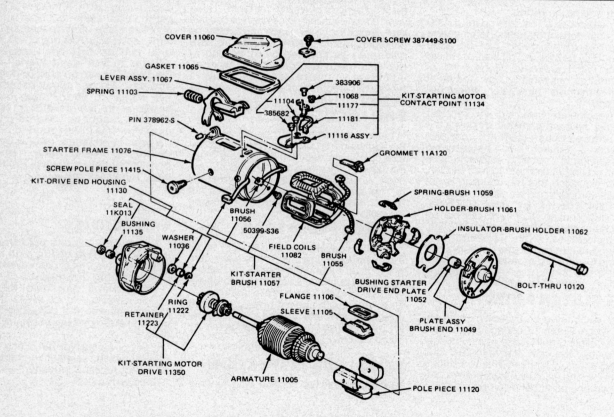

**Fig. 1  Ford Motorcraft positive engagement starting motor (Typical)**

## DESCRIPTION

This type starting motor, **Fig. 1,** is a four pole, series parallel unit with a positive engagement drive built into the starter. The drive mechanism is engaged with the flywheel by lever action before the motor is energized.

When ignition switch is turned to the start position, the starter relay is energized and supplies current to the motor. The current flows through one field coil and a set of contact points to ground. The magnetic field given off by the field coil pulls the movable pole, which is part of the lever, downward to its seat. When the pole is

pulled down, the lever moves the drive assembly into the engine flywheel, **Fig. 2.**

When the movable pole is seated, it functions as a normal field pole and opens the contact points. With the points open, current flows through the starter field coils, energizing the starter. At the same time, current also flows through a holding coil to

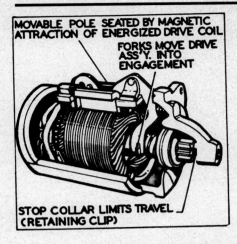

**Fig. 2   Starter drive engaged**

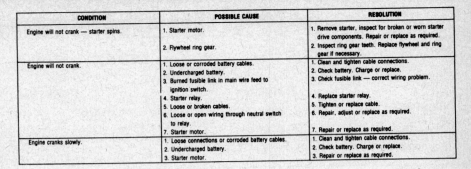

| CONDITION | POSSIBLE CAUSE | RESOLUTION |
|---|---|---|
| Engine will not crank — starter spins. | 1. Starter motor. | 1. Remove starter, inspect for broken or worn starter drive components. Repair or replace as required. |
| | 2. Flywheel ring gear. | 2. Inspect ring gear teeth. Replace flywheel and ring gear if necessary. |
| Engine will not crank. | 1. Loose or corroded battery cables. | 1. Clean and tighten cable connections. |
| | 2. Undercharged battery. | 2. Check battery. Charge or replace. |
| | 3. Burned fusible link in main wire feed to ignition switch. | 3. Check fusible link — correct wiring problem. |
| | 4. Starter relay. | 4. Replace starter relay. |
| | 5. Loose or broken cables. | 5. Tighten or replace cable. |
| | 6. Loose or open wiring through neutral switch to relay. | 6. Repair, adjust or replace as required. |
| | 7. Starter motor. | 7. Repair or replace as required. |
| Engine cranks slowly. | 1. Loose connections or corroded battery cables. | 1. Clean and tighten cable connections. |
| | 2. Undercharged battery. | 2. Check battery. Charge or replace. |
| | 3. Starter motor. | 3. Repair or replace as required. |

**Fig. 3   Diagnosis chart**

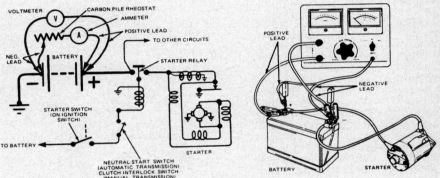

**Fig. 5   Starter load test connections**

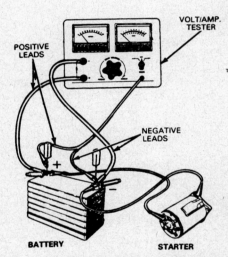

**Fig. 4   Field grounded circuit test connections**

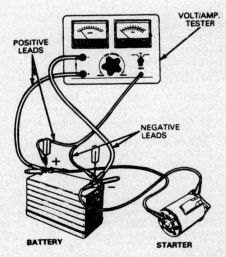

**Fig. 6   Starter no-load test connections**

hold the movable pole in its seated position.

When the ignition switch is released from the start position, the starter relay opens the circuit to the starting motor. This allows the return spring to force the lever back, disengaging the drive from the flywheel and returning the movable pole to its normal position.

# DIAGNOSIS

When diagnosing this starter motor, refer to **Fig. 3.**

# IN-VEHICLE TESTING

## ARMATURE & FIELD GROUNDED CIRCUIT TEST

1. Connect jumper lead to positive battery terminal.
2. Connect negative voltmeter lead to negative battery terminal.
3. Touch positive voltmeter lead to commutator and jumper wire to armature.
4. If voltmeter indicates voltage, armature windings are grounded.
5. Make connections as shown, **Fig. 4.** If voltmeter indicates voltage, field windings are grounded.

## ARMATURE OPEN CIRCUIT TEST

An open circuit in the armature can sometimes be detected by examining commutator for signs of burning. A spot burned on the commutator is caused by an arc formed every time the commutator segment, connected to the open circuit winding, passes under a brush.

## STARTER LOAD TEST

1. Connect test equipment as shown, **Fig. 5.**
2. Ensure that no current is flowing through ammeter and heavy duty carbon pile rheostat portion of circuit.
3. Disconnect push on connector "S" at starter relay and connect remote starter switch from positive battery terminal to "S" terminal of starter relay.
4. Crank engine with remote starter and determine exact reading on voltmeter.
5. Stop cranking engine, then reduce resistance of carbon pile until voltmeter indicates same reading as obtained while engine was cranked. Ammeter should read 150-200 amps on 4 inch diameter starter, or 150-180 amps on 4½ inch diameter starter.

## STARTER NO-LOAD TEST

1. Connect test equipment as shown, **Fig. 6.**
2. Ensure that no current is flowing through ammeter, then determine exact reading on voltmeter.
3. Disconnect starter from battery, then reduce resistance of rheostat until voltmeter indicates same reading as while starter was running. Ammeter should read 70 amps on 4 inch diameter starter, or 80 amps on 4½ inch diameter starter.

# Mitsubishi Starters

## INDEX

## DESCRIPTION

These starters, **Figs. 1 and 2,** are 12 volt units that have the solenoid mounted on the starter housing. The solenoid is energized when starter relay contacts are closed causing starter drive to engage with flywheel ring gear, thereby starting the engine. An overrunning clutch in the drive protects starter from excessive speeds once engine starts. The current flows through the solenoid energizing coil until the solenoid plunger is at full travel, at which time the plunger closes a set of contacts that bypass the energizing coil, allowing the holding coil to keep the starter drive engaged and passing starting current to the starter.

## TESTING

## ARMATURE OPEN CIRCUIT TEST

An open circuit in the armature can sometimes be detected by examining commutator for signs of burning. A spot burned on the commutator is caused by an arc formed every time a commutator segment connected to the open circuit winding passes under a brush.

## CHECKING PINION

### 4-135/2.2L Engine

1. Remove wire from M terminal on starter solenoid.
2. Connect positive lead of 12 volt source to terminal S and negative lead to starter motor body. **Do not apply power for more than 20 seconds continuously.**
3. Measure pinion travel, **Fig. 3.** If pinion travel is less than .669 inch, repair or replace as necessary.

### 4-143/2.3L Engine

1. Remove wire from M terminal on starter solenoid.
2. Connect positive lead of 12 volt source to terminal S and negative lead to terminal M.
3. Set switch to "ON", causing pinion to move outward. **Do not apply power for more than 10 seconds continuously.**
4. Lightly depress pinion, measuring length of depression. If length is less than .008 inch, adjust number of gaskets at switch area as required.

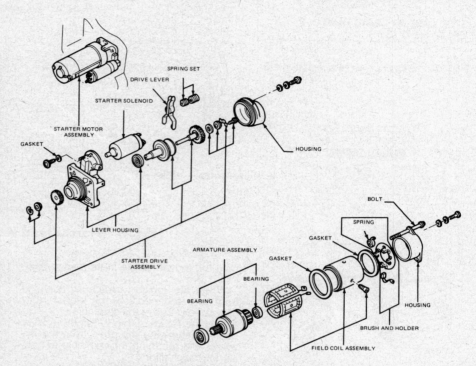

**Fig. 1   Exploded view of Mitsubishi starter. 4-135/2.2L engine**

## FIELD GROUNDED CIRCUIT TEST

1. Check insulation between yoke and field terminal using circuit tester. Circuit tester should show infinite resistance.
2. Ensure that there is continuity between lead wires.

## STARTER LOAD TEST

1. Connect test equipment as shown, **Fig. 4,** ensuring that there is no current flowing through ammeter and heavy duty carbon pile rheostat portion of circuit.
2. Disconnect push on connectors at starter solenoid and connect remote control starter switch from positive battery cable to S terminal of starter solenoid.
3. Crank engine with remote starter switch and determine exact reading on voltmeter.

4. Stop cranking engine, then reduce resistance of carbon pile until voltmeter indicates same reading as when engine was cranked. Ammeter should read less than 500 amps.

## STARTER NO-LOAD TEST

**Perform this test on test bench after removing starter from vehicle.**
1. Make test connections as shown, **Fig. 5.**
2. Ensure that no current is flowing through ammeter, then determine exact reading on voltmeter.
3. Disconnect starter from battery, then reduce resistance of rheostat until voltmeter indicates same reading as when motor was running. Ammeter should read less than 180 amps.

## STARTER SOLENOID TESTS

### 4-135/2.2L ENGINE

1. Using circuit tester, check for continu-

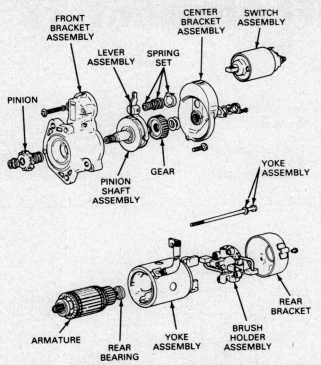

Fig. 2 Exploded view of Mitsubishi starter.
4-143/2.3L engine

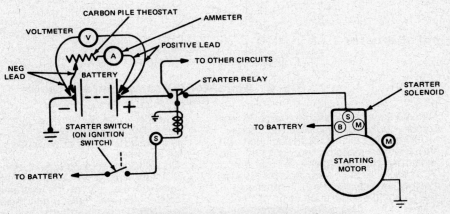

Fig. 4 Starter load test connections

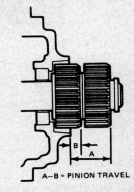

Fig. 3 Checking pinion travel.
4-135/2.2L engine

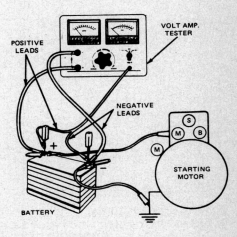

Fig. 5 Starter no-load test connections

ity between S terminal and M terminal, and between S terminal and ground.
2. If there is no continuity in either case, replace solenoid.

## 4-143/2.3L ENGINE
### Pull-In Test
1. Disconnect field coil wire from M terminal of solenoid.
2. Connect 12 volt battery between S terminal and M terminal. **Test must be performed in less than 10 seconds.**
3. If pinion does not move outward, replace solenoid.

### Hold-In Test
1. Disconnect field coil wire from M terminal of magnetic switch.
2. Connect 12 volt battery between S terminal and body.
3. If pinion moves inward, replace solenoid.

### Return Test
1. Disconnect field coil wire from M terminal of magnetic switch.
2. Connect 12 volt battery between M terminal and body. **Test must be performed in less than 10 seconds.**
3. Pull pinion outward and release. If pin-

ion does not quickly return to its original position, replace solenoid.

## TESTING ARMATURE FOR SHORT CIRCUIT
### 4-143/2.3L Engine
1. Place armature in growler.
2. Hold a thin steel blade parallel and just above armature while rotating armature slowly in growler.
3. If blade vibrates, replace armature.

## TESTING OVERRUNNING CLUTCH
### 4-143/2.3L Engine
1. Hold clutch housing and rotate pinion.
2. If pinion does not rotate clockwise or lock counterclockwise, replace overrunning clutch assembly.
3. Inspect pinion for wear or burrs, replacing overrunning clutch assembly as necessary.

# ALTERNATOR SYSTEMS
# Motorcraft Alternators
## INDEX

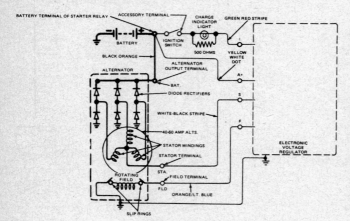

**Fig. 1  Indicator light rear terminal alternator charging circuit**

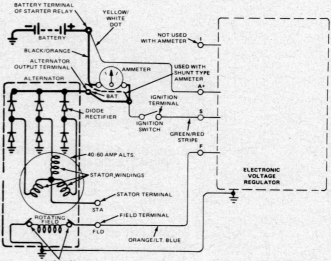

**Fig. 2  Ammeter rear terminal alternator charging circuit**

## DESCRIPTION

A charge indicator lamp or ammeter can be used in charging system.

If a charge indicator lamp is used in the charging system, **Figs. 1 through 5**, system operation is as follows: when ignition switch is turned ON, a small electrical current flows through the lamp filament (turning lamp on) and through the alternator regulator to the alternator field. When engine is started, the alternator field rotates and produces a voltage in the stator winding. When voltage at alternator stator terminal reaches about 3 volts, the regulator field relay closes. This puts the same voltage potential on both sides of the charge indicator lamp, causing it to go out. When the field relay has closed, current passes through the regulator A terminal and is metered to the alternator field.

If an ammeter is used in the charging system, **Figs. 2 and 4**, the regulator 1 terminal and the alternator stator terminal are not used. When ignition switch is turned ON, the field relay closes and electrical current passes through the regulator A terminal and is metered to the alternator field.

When engine is started, the alternator field rotates, causing the alternator to operate.

All Vehicles, except those equipped with IAR charging systems, are equipped with electronic voltage regulators, **Figs. 6 and 7**. These solid state regulators are used in conjunction with other new components in the charging system such as an alternator with a higher field current requirement, a warning indicator lamp shunt resistor (500 ohms) and a new wiring harness with a new regulator connector.

Some 1986-89 models are equipped with an Integral Alternator/Regulator (IAR) charging system. This system has a solid state voltage regulator located in the rear of the alternator. When replacing system components, note the following precautions:

1. Always use the proper alternator in the system.
2. Do not use an electro-mechanical regulator in an electronic system, as the wiring harness connector will not index properly with this type of regulator.
3. Electronic regulators are color coded for proper installation. The black color coded unit is installed in systems

equipped with a warning indicator lamp. The blue color coded regulator is installed in systems equipped with an ammeter.

4. On vehicles equipped with a warning indicator lamp a 500 ohm resistor is used on the rear of the instrument cluster . Do not replace this resistor with the 15 ohm resistance wire used on previous systems.

On electronic systems with an indicator lamp, closing the ignition switch energizes the warning lamp and turns on the regulator output stage. The alternator receives maximum field current and is ready to generate an output voltage. As alternator rotor speed increases, the output and stator terminal voltages increase from zero to system regulation level determined by the regulator setting. When ignition switch is turned off, the solid state relay circuit turns the output stage off, interrupting current flow through the regulator so there is not a current drain on the battery.

On vehicles equipped with an ammeter, the operating principle is similar. **The ammeter indicates current flow into (charge) or out of (discharge) the vehicle battery.**

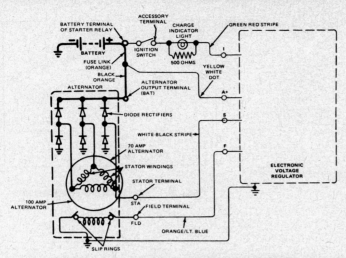

**Fig. 3 Indicator light side terminal alternator charging circuit**

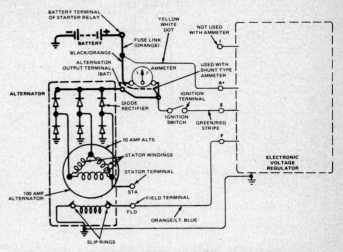

**Fig. 4 Ammeter side terminal alternator charging circuit**

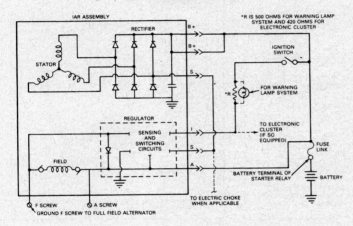

**Fig. 5 Alternator charging circuit. 1986–89 models w/integral regulator**

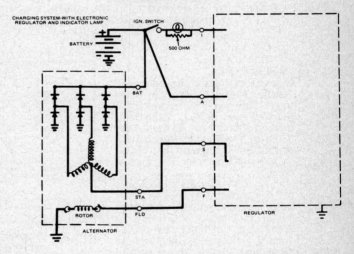

**Fig. 6 Indicator light charging system w/electronic voltage regulator**

## SYSTEM TESTING

The operations and in-vehicle test procedures for the side terminal alternator are same as for rear terminal alternator. However, the internal wiring, Figs. 3 and 7, and bench test procedures differ.

## IN-VEHICLE VOLTMETER TEST

Perform this test with all lights and electrical systems in the off position, parking brake applied, transmission in neutral and a charged battery (at least 1,200 specific gravity).

1. Connect the negative lead of the voltmeter to the negative battery cable clamp (not bolt or nut).
2. Connect voltmeter positive lead to the positive battery cable clamp (not bolt or nut).
3. Record battery voltage reading shown on voltmeter scale.

4. Connect red lead of a tachometer to the distributor terminal of the coil and the black tachometer lead to a good ground.
5. Start and operate engine at approximately 1500 RPM. With no other electrical load (foot off brake pedal and car doors closed), voltmeter reading should increase but not exceed (2 volts) above the first recorded battery voltage reading. The reading should be taken when the voltmeter needle stops moving.
6. With engine running, turn on heater and/or air conditioner blower motor to high speed and headlights to high beam.
7. Increase engine speed to 2000 RPM, voltmeter should indicate a minimum reading of .05 volts above the battery voltage, **Fig. 8. If above tests indicate proper voltage readings, charging system is operating normally. Proceed to "Test Results" if a problem still exists.**

## Test Results

1. If voltmeter reading indicates 2 volts over battery voltage (over voltage), proceed as follows:
   a. Stop engine and check ground connections between regulator and alternator and/or regulator to engine. Clean and tighten connections securely and repeat Voltmeter Test Procedures.
   b. If over voltage condition still exists, disconnect regulator wiring plug from the regulator and repeat the Voltmeter Test Procedures.
   c. If over voltage still exists with the regulator wiring plug disconnected, repair the short in the wiring harness between the alternator and regulator. Then replace the regulator and connect the regulator wiring plug to the regulator and repeat the Voltmeter Test Procedures.
2. If voltmeter does not indicate more than ½ volt above battery voltage,

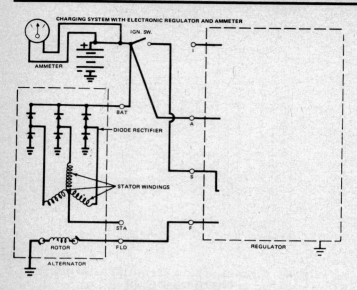

**Fig. 7   Ammeter charging system w/electronic voltage regulator**

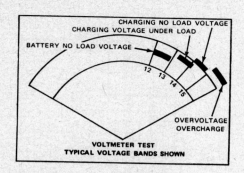

**Fig. 8   Voltmeter test scale**

proceed as follows:

a. Disconnect voltage regulator wire connector and connect an ohmmeter between wire connector F terminal and ground. Ohmmeter reading should indicate more than 3 ohms. If reading is less than 3 ohms, repair grounded field circuit and repeat Voltmeter Test procedure.

b. If ohmmeter reading is more than 3 ohms, connect a jumper wire between voltage regulator wire connector terminals A and F, **Fig. 9**, then repeat Voltmeter Test procedure. If voltmeter reading is now more than 1/2 volt above battery voltage, the voltage regulator or wiring is defective. Refer to Regulator Test.

c. If voltmeter still indicates less than 1/2 volt, disconnect jumper wire from voltage regulator wire connector and leave connector disconnected from regulator. Connect a jumper wire between alternator FLD and BAT terminals, **Figs. 10 and 11**, then repeat Voltmeter Test procedures.

d. If voltmeter reading now indicates 1/2 volt or more above battery voltage, repair alternator to regulator wiring harness.

e. If voltmeter still indicates less than 1/2 volt above battery voltage, stop engine and move voltmeter positive lead to alternator BAT terminal.

f. If voltmeter now indicates battery voltage, the alternator should be removed, inspected and repaired. If zero volts is indicated, repair BAT terminal wiring.

## FIELD CIRCUIT & ALTERNATOR TESTS

1. If field circuit is satisfactory, disconnect regulator wiring plug at regulator

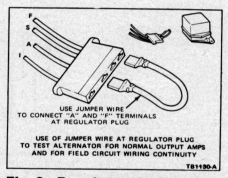

**Fig. 9   Regulator plug. Jumper wire connection**

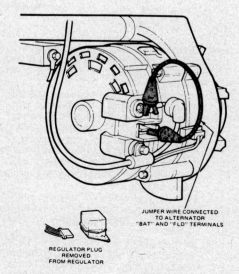

**Fig. 11   Testing stator winding**

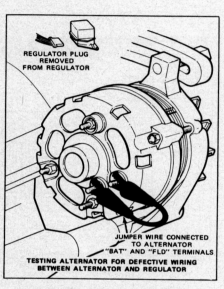

**Fig. 10   Rear terminal alternator. Jumper wire connection**

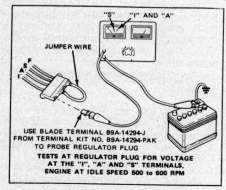

**Fig. 12   Regulator plug voltage test**

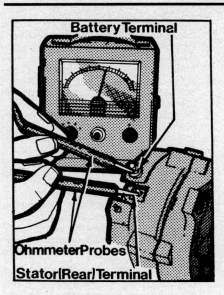

Fig. 13 Testing diode trio

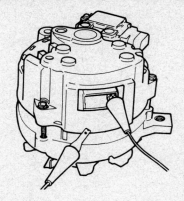

Fig. 14 Alternator w/integral regulator rectifier short or grounded & stator grounded test

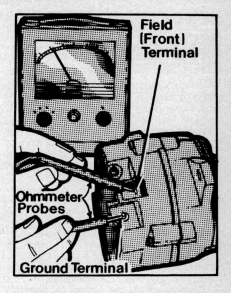

Fig. 15 Testing rectifier bridge diodes

and connect a jumper wire from the A to F terminals on regulator wiring plug, **Fig. 9.**

2. Repeat Voltmeter Test Procedures.
3. If Voltmeter Test Procedures still indicate a problem of under voltage, remove jumper wire at regulator plug and leave plug disconnected from regulator, **Figs. 10 and 11.** Connect a jumper wire to the FLD and BAT terminals on alternator, **Figs. 10 and 11.**
4. Repeat the Voltmeter Test Procedures.
5. If Voltmeter Tests are now satisfactory, repair wiring harness from alternator to regulator. Then remove jumper wire at the alternator and connect the regulator wiring plug to the regulator.
6. Repeat Voltmeter Test Procedures, to be sure charging system is operating normally.
7. If Voltmeter Test results still indicate under voltage, repair or replace alternator. With jumper wire removed, connect wiring to alternator and regulator.
8. Repeat Voltmeter Test Procedures.

## DIODE TEST

### Test Procedure

1. Disconnect electric choke, if equipped.
2. Disconnect voltage regulator wiring connector.
3. Connect a jumper wire between the "A" and "F" terminals of voltage regulator wiring connector, **Fig. 9.**
4. Connect voltmeter to battery clamps. Then start and idle engine.
5. Observe and note voltmeter reading.
6. Move voltmeter positive lead to the alternator "S" terminal and note voltage reading.

### Test Results

1. If voltmeter reading is within 1/2 of bat-

tery voltage, diodes are satisfactory.
2. If voltmeter reading is approximately 1.5 volts, the alternator has a shorted negative diode or a grounded stator winding.
3. If voltmeter reading is approximately 1.5 volts less than battery voltage, the alternator has a shorted positive diode.
4. If voltage reading is approximately 1 to 1.5 volts less than 1/2 battery voltage, the alternator has an open positive diode.
5. If voltage reading is 1 to 1.5 volts above 1/2 battery voltage, the alternator has an open negative diode.
6. Reconnect electric choke into circuit after tests are completed, if equipped.

## REGULATOR TESTS

### EXC. 4-143/2.3L TURBOCHARGED DIESEL ENGINE

#### S Circuit Test—With Ammeter

1. Connect positive lead of voltmeter to S terminal of the regulator wiring plug **Fig. 12.** Turn ignition switch to ON position, but do not start engine.
2. Voltmeter reading should indicate battery voltage.
3. If there is no voltage reading, disconnect positive voltmeter lead from positive battery clamp and repair S wire lead from ignition switch to regulator wiring plug.
4. Connect positive voltmeter lead to positive battery cable terminal and repeat the Voltmeter Test Procedures.

#### S and I Circuit Test—With Indicator Light

1. Disconnect regulator wiring plug, then install a suitable jumper wire between connector "A" and "F" terminals, **Fig. 9.**
2. With the engine idling, connect the positive lead of the voltmeter to the S

terminal and then to the I terminal of the regulator wiring plug, **Fig. 12.** The voltage of the S circuit should read approximately 1/2 of the I circuit.
3. If no voltage is present, repair the alternator or the wiring circuit at fault. Reconnect the positive voltmeter lead to the positive battery cable terminal and repeat the Voltmeter Test Procedures.
4. If the above tests are satisfactory, install a new regulator.
5. Then, remove the jumper wire from the regulator wiring plug and connect the wiring plug to regulator. Repeat Voltmeter Test Procedures.

### 4-143/2.3L TURBOCHARGED DIESEL ENGINE

#### Regulator I Circuit Test

1. Disconnect electrical connector from regulator.
2. Connect voltmeter negative lead to battery ground terminal and positive lead to electrical connector terminal I. No voltage should be indicated with ignition switch OFF. If voltage is present, service the I lead from ignition switch to identify and eliminate voltage source.
3. Turn ignition switch to ON position. Voltmeter should indicate battery voltage at connector terminal I. If there is no voltage reading, service the I lead from ignition switch to the regulator for an open or grounded circuit.
4. If voltage readings obtained in steps 2 and 3 were normal, check the resistance value of the I circuit resistor. Conduct resistance check with regulator wiring plug disconnected. Nominal value is 330 ohms for gauge systems. Replace resistor if value obtained is off by more than 50 ohms.

## BENCH TESTS

### RECTIFIER SHORT OR GROUNDED & STATOR GROUNDED TEST

Using a suitable ohmmeter, connect one probe to alternator BAT terminal, **Figs. 13 and 14**, and the other probe to the STA terminal (rear blade terminal). Then, reverse the ohmmeter probes and repeat the test. A reading of about 6.5 ohms should be obtained in one direction and no needle movement with the probes reversed. A reading in both directions indicates a bad positive diode, a grounded positive diode plate or a grounded BAT terminal.

Perform the same test using the STA and GND (ground) terminals of the alternator. A reading in both directions indicates either a bad negative diode, a grounded stator winding, a grounded stator terminal, a grounded positive diode plate, or a grounded BAT terminal.

Infinite readings (no needle movement) in all four probe positions in the proceeding tests indicates an open STA terminal lead connection inside the alternator.

### FIELD OPEN OR SHORT CIRCUIT TEST

#### Exc. Alternators W/Integral Regulators

Using a suitable ohmmeter, connect alternator field terminal with one probe and ground terminal with other probe, **Fig. 15**. Then, spin alternator pulley. The ohmmeter reading should be between 2.4 and 25 ohms on 1980 units, 2.4 and 100 ohms on all 1981–85 units and 1986–89 models less IAR system, all readings should fluctuate while the pulley is turning. An infinite reading (no meter movement) indicates an

**FIELD OPEN OR SHORT CIRCUIT TEST**

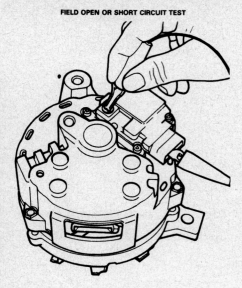

**Fig. 16   Alternator w/integral regulator field open or short circuit test**

open brush lead, worn or stuck brushes, or a bad rotor assembly. An ohmmeter reading of less than 2.4 ohms indicates a grounded brush assembly, a grounded field terminal or a bad rotor.

#### Alternators W/Integral Regulators

1. Using a suitable ohmmeter, connect regulator A blade terminal with one probe and the regulator "F" screw head with the other probe, **Fig. 16**.
2. Spin the alternator pulley and note

meter reading, then reverse probes and repeat step 1. In one probe direction ohmmeter reading should be between 2.2 and 100 ohms and may fluctuate while pulley is turning. In the other direction, reading should fluctuate between 2.2 and approximately 9 ohms.
3. An infinite reading (no meter movement) in one direction and approximately 9 ohms in the other, indicates an open brush lead, worn or stuck brushes, defective rotor or a loose regulator to brush holder attaching screw.
4. An ohmmeter reading less than 2.2 ohms in both directions indicates a shorted or defective regulator.
5. An ohmmeter reading significantly over 9 ohms in both directions indicates a defective regulator or loose "F" terminal screw.
6. Connect alternator rear housing with one ohmmeter probe and touch the other probe to the regulator "F" terminal. Reverse probes and repeat test. Ohmmeter reading should be infinite in one probe direction and approximately 9 ohms in the other.
7. If ohmmeter reads less than infinite at either point, a grounded brush lead, grounded rotor or defective regulator is indicated.

## REGULATOR ADJUSTMENTS

### ELECTRONIC REGULATORS

These regulators are factory calibrated and sealed and no adjustment is possible. If regulator calibration values are not within specifications, the regulator must be replaced.

# DASH GAUGES & GRAPHIC DISPLAYS

## INDEX

## DASH GAUGES

Gauge failures are often caused by defective wiring or grounds. The first step in locating trouble should be a thorough inspection of all wiring, terminals and printed circuits. If wiring is secured by clamps, check to see whether the insulation has been severed, thereby grounding the wire. In the case of a fuel gauge installation, rust may cause failure by corrosion at the ground connection of the tank unit.

The Constant Voltage Regulator (CVR) type indicator is a bimetal-resistance type system consisting of an Instrument Voltage Regulator (IVR), an indicator gauge, and a variable resistance sending unit. Current to the system is applied to gauge terminals by the IVR, which maintains an average-pulsating value of 5 volts.

The indicator gauge consists of a pointer which is attached to a wire-wound bimetal strip. Current passing through the coil heats the bimetal strip, causing the pointer to move. As more current passes through the coil, heat increases, moving the pointer farther.

The circuit is completed through a sending unit which contains a variable resistor. When resistance is high, less current is allowed to pass through the gauge, and the pointer moves very little. As resistance decreases due to changing conditions in system being monitored, more current passes through gauge coil, causing pointer to move farther. Do not apply battery voltage to system or ground output terminals of IVR, as damage to system components or wiring circuits may result.

### DASH GAUGE TEST

1. Disconnect battery ground cable and remove gauge from vehicle.
2. Connect ohmmeter between gauge terminals and read coil winding resistance.
3. An upward movement of ohmmeter needle from 10 ohms to 14 ohms is

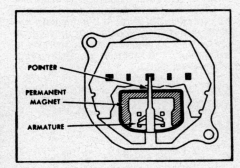

**Fig. 1  Conventional type ammeter**

normal, as test current of ohmmeter causes a temperature rise in gauge coil windings.
4. If ohmmeter reads below 10 ohms or above 14 ohms, gauge is defective.

## AMMETERS

The ammeter is an instrument used to indicate current flow into and out of the battery. When electrical accessories in the vehicle draw more current than the alternator can supply, current flows from the battery and the ammeter indicates a discharge (−) condition. When electrical loads of the vehicle are less than alternator output, current is available to charge the battery, and the ammeter indicates a charge (+) condition. If battery is fully charged, the voltage regulator reduces alternator output to meet only immediate vehicle electrical loads. When this happens, ammeter reads zero.

### CONVENTIONAL AMMETER

A conventional ammeter must be connected between battery and alternator in order to indicate current flow. This type ammeter, **Fig. 1**, consists of a frame to which a permanent magnet is attached. The frame also supports an armature and

pointer assembly. Current in this system flows from the alternator through the ammeter, then to the battery or from the battery through the ammeter into the vehicle electrical system, depending on vehicle operating conditions.

When no current flows through the ammeter, the magnet holds the pointer armature so that the pointer stands at the center of the dial. When current passes in either direction through the ammeter, the resulting magnetic field attracts the armature away from the effect of the permanent magnet, thus giving a reading proportional to the strength of the current flowing.

### Troubleshooting

When the ammeter apparently fails to register correctly, there may be trouble in the wiring which connects the ammeter to the alternator and battery or in the alternator or battery itself.

To check the connections, first tighten the two terminal posts on the back of the ammeter. Then, following each wire from the ammeter, tighten all connections on the ignition switch, battery and alternator. Chafed, burned or broken insulation can be found by following each ammeter wire from end to end.

All wires with chafed, burned or broken insulation should be repaired or replaced. After this is done, and all connections are tightened, connect the battery cable and turn on the ignition switch. The needle should point slightly to the discharge (−) side.

Start the engine and run slightly above idling speed. The needle should move slowly to the charge side (+).

If the pointer does not move as indicated, the ammeter is out of order and should be replaced.

### SHUNT TYPE AMMETER

The shunt type ammeter is actually a specifically calibrated voltmeter. It is connected to read voltage drop across a resistance wire (shunt) between the battery and alternator. The shunt is located either in the vehicle wiring or within the ammeter itself.

When voltage is higher at the alternator end of the shunt, the meter indicates a charge (+) condition. When voltage is higher at the battery end of the shunt, the meter indicates a discharge (−) condition. When voltage is equal at both ends of the shunt, the meter reads zero.

## Troubleshooting

Ammeter accuracy can be determined by comparing reading with an ammeter of known accuracy.

1. With engine stopped and ignition switch in RUN position, switch on headlamps and heater fan. Meter should indicate a discharge (−) condition.
2. If ammeter pointer does not move, check ammeter terminals for proper connection and check for open circuit in wiring harness. If connections and wiring harness are satisfactory, ammeter is defective.
3. If ammeter indicates a charge (+) condition, wiring harness connections are reversed at ammeter.

# ALTERNATOR INDICATOR LIGHT

When the ignition switch is in Start or Run position, battery current flows through the alternator warning indicator into regulator at terminal 1 and to ground through the indicator switch. The electronic control measures a low voltage at terminal A and closes the field switch. This applies battery voltage to the field through alternator terminal F. With current in the field and the rotor turning, alternator stator produces a voltage at terminals B and S.

A predetermined voltage at terminal S operates the electronic control to open indicator switch, which removes ground from alternator warning indicator.

Alternator current output is controlled by current in the field. Average field current depends on length of time field switch is closed. The electronic control closes field switch when voltage at terminal A is low and opens switch when voltage is high.

# TROUBLESHOOTING

## Exc. 4-140 Turbo Diesel Engine

1. If alternator indicator lamp does not light with ignition in On position and engine not running, check condition of indicator lamp bulb. If bulb is satisfactory, check for an open in circuit between ignition switch and regulator terminal (circuit 1).
2. If alternator indicator lamp does not light, disconnect electrical connector from regulator and connect a jumper wire between 1 terminal of regulator electrical connector and negative battery post cable clamp. With ignition turned to On position, indicator lamp should light.
3. If lamp does not light, check condition

of indicator lamp bulb. If bulb is satisfactory, repair open in circuit between ignition switch and regulator or replace 500 ohm resistor (if equipped) across indicator lamp, as necessary.

# VOLTMETER

The voltmeter is a gauge which measures the electrical flow from the battery to indicate whether the battery output is within tolerances. The voltmeter reading can range from 13.5–14.0 volts under normal operating conditions. If an undercharge or overcharge condition is indicated for an extended period, the battery and charging system should be checked.

# TROUBLESHOOTING

To check voltmeter, turn key and headlights on with engine off. Pointer should move to 12.5 volts. If no needle movement is observed, check connections from battery to circuit breaker. If connections are tight and meter shows no movement, check wire continuity. If wire continuity is satisfactory, the meter is inoperative and must be replaced.

# OIL PRESSUREINDICATOR LIGHT

Many trucks utilize a warning light on the instrument panel in place of the conventional dash indicating gauge to warn the driver when the oil pressure is dangerously low. The warning light is wired in series with the ignition switch and the engine unit—which is an oil pressure switch.

The oil pressure switch contains a diaphragm and a set of contacts. When the ignition switch is turned on, the warning light circuit is energized and the circuit is completed through the closed contacts in the pressure switch. When the engine is started, build-up of oil pressure compresses the diaphragm, opening the contacts, thereby breaking the circuit and putting out the light.

# TROUBLESHOOTING

The oil pressure warning light should go on when the ignition is turned on. If it does not light, disconnect the wire from the engine unit and ground the wire to the frame or cylinder block. Then if the warning light still does not go on with the ignition switch on, replace the bulb.

If the warning light goes on when the wire is grounded to the frame or cylinder block, the engine unit should be checked for being loose or poorly grounded. If the unit is found to be tight and properly grounded, it should be removed and a new one installed. (The presence of sealing compound on the threads of the engine unit will cause a poor ground).

If the warning light remains lit when it normally should be out, replace the engine unit before proceeding further to determine the cause for a low pressure indication.

The warning light will sometimes light up or flicker when engine is idling, even though oil pressure is adequate. However, light should go out when engine speed is increased.

# LOW OIL LEVEL WARNING LAMP

This system consists of a float-type sensor mounted to the side of the engine oil pan, an electronic control module, and an instrument panel warning lamp. The warning lamp should come on during engine starting as a bulb prove-out. When ignition switch is turned to Run or Start position, the control module determines whether sensor is grounded (oil low) or ungrounded (oil not low). If oil level is adequate, light will go out in Run. If oil level is approximately 1.5 quarts or more low, the relay turns the warning lamp on. The lamp will remain on until ignition is turned off. After ignition is turned off, module will not reset for approximately 5 minutes. This delay allows time for oil drain back before another reading is allowed to occur. If engine is restarted during this delay period, the last reading will be displayed.

# TROUBLESHOOTING

With oil level at FULL mark on oil dipstick and engine oil warm to assure that oil drains properly from oil sensor, turn ignition on and start engine. Warning lamp should come on briefly in Start for bulb test, then go out. Turn engine off. Drain 2 quarts of oil from engine. Wait approximately 5 minutes, then restart engine. Warning lamp should come on and stay on. If warning lamp does not come on check fuse, low oil level relay, low oil level sensor and lamp.

# TEMPERATURE INDICATOR LIGHT

A bimetal temperature switch located in the cylinder head controls operation of a temperature indicator light with a red lens. If engine cooling system is not functioning properly and coolant temperature exceeds a predetermined value, warning light will illuminate.

# TROUBLESHOOTING

If the red light is not lit when engine is being cranked, check for a burned out bulb, open in light circuit, or a defective ignition switch.

If red light is lit when engine is running, check wiring between light and switch for a ground, defective temperature switch, or overheated cooling system. As a test circuit to check whether the red bulb is functioning properly, a wire which is connected to the ground terminal of the ignition switch is tapped into its circuit. When the ignition is in "Start" (engine cranking) position, ground terminal is grounded inside the switch and the red bulb will be lit. When engine is started and the ignition switch is in the "On" position, test circuit is opened and bulb is then controlled by the temperature switch.

## ELECTRICAL TEMPERATURE GAUGES

This temperature indicating system consists of a sending unit, located on the cylinder head, electrical temperature gauge and an instrument voltage regulator. As engine temperature increases or decreases, the resistance of the sending unit changes, in turn controlling current flow to the gauge. When engine temperature is low, the resistance of the sending unit is high, restricting current flow to the gauge, in turn indicating low engine temperature. As engine temperature increases, the resistance of the ending unit decreases, permitting an increased current flow to the gauge, resulting in an increased temperature reading.

## TROUBLESHOOTING

A special tester is required to diagnose this type gauge. Follow instructions included with tester.

## ELECTRICAL OIL PRESSURE GAUGES

This oil pressure indicating system incorporates an instrument voltage regulator, electrical oil pressure gauge and a sending unit which are connected in series. The sending unit consists of a diaphragm, contact and a variable resistor. As oil pressure increases or decreases, the diaphragm actuates the contact on the variable resistor, which in turn controls current flow to the gauge. When oil pressure is low, resistance of the variable resistor is high, which restricts current flow to the gauge, indicating low oil pressure. As oil pressure increases, resistance of the variable resistor is lowered, permitting increased current flow to the gauge, which increases the gauge reading.

## TROUBLESHOOTING

A special tester is required to diagnose this type gauge. Follow instructions included with the tester.

## SPEEDOMETERS

The following material covers only that service on speedometers which is feasible to perform. Repairs on the units themselves are not included as they require special tools and extreme care when making repairs and adjustments that only an experienced speedometer mechanic should attempt.

The speedometer has two main parts, speedometer head and speedometer drive cable. When speedometer fails to indicate speed or mileage, cable or cable housing is probably broken.

On vehicles equipped with speed control, there is a speed sensor attached to the transmission. This is used to sense the

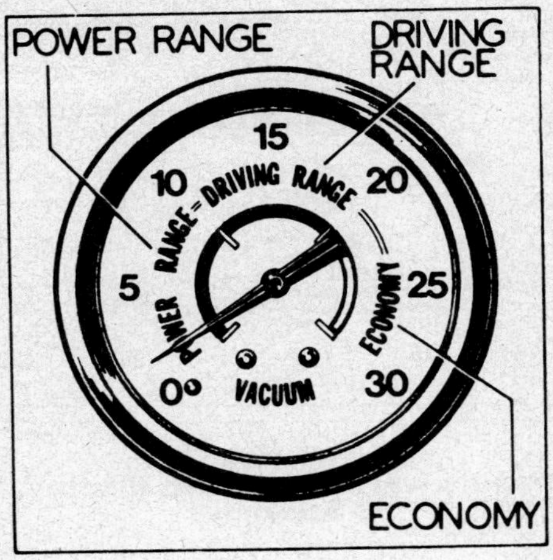

**Fig. 2   Typical vacuum gauge**

revolutions of the cable assembly and to regulate speed control.

## SPEEDOMETER CABLE

Most cables are broken due to lack of lubrication, or a sharp bend or kink in the housing.

A cable might break because of the speedometer head mechanism binds. In such cases, the speedometer head should be repaired or replaced before a new cable or housing is installed.

A "jumpy" pointer condition, together with a scraping noise, is due, in most instances, to a dry or kinked speedometer cable. The kinked cable rubs on the housing and winds up, slowing down the pointer. The cable then unwinds and the pointer "jumps."

To check for kinks, remove the cable, lay it on a flat surface and twist one end with the fingers. If it turns over smoothly the cable is not kinked. But if part of the cable flops over as it is twisted, the cable is kinked and should be replaced.

## LUBRICATION

The speedometer cable should be lubricated with special cable lubricant. Fill the ferrule on the upper end of the housing with the cable lubricant. Insert the cable in the housing, starting at the upper end. Turn the cable around carefully while feeding it into the housing. Repeat filling the ferrule except for the last six inches of cable. Too much lubricant at this point may cause the lubricant to work into the speedometer head.

## INSTALLING CABLE

During installation, if the cable sticks when inserted into the housing and will not go through, the housing is damaged inside or kinked. Be sure to check the housing from one end to the other. Straighten any sharp bends by relocating clamps or elbows. Replace housing if it is badly kinked or broken. Position the cable and housing so that they lead into the head as straight as possible.

Check the new cable for kinks before installing it. Use wide, sweeping, gradual curves where the cable comes out of the transmission and connects to the head so the cable will not be damaged during installation.

Arrange the housing so it does not lean against the engine because heat from the engine may dry out the lubricant. If inspection indicates that the cable and housing are in good condition, yet pointer action is erratic, check the speedometer head for possible binding.

The speedometer drive pinion should also be checked. If the pinion is dry or its teeth are stripped, the speedometer may not register properly.

## VACUUM GAUGE

This gauge, **Fig. 2**, measures intake manifold vacuum. The intake manifold vacuum varies with engine operating conditions, carburetor adjustments, valve timing, ignition timing and general engine condition.

Since optimum fuel economy is directly proportional to a properly functioning engine, a high vacuum reading on the gauge relates to fuel economy. Most gauges have colored sectors the green sector being the "Economy" range and the red the "Power" range. Therefore, the vehicle should be operated with gauge registering in the green sector or a high numerical number, **Fig. 2**, for maximum economy.

## FUEL ECONOMY WARNING SYSTEM

This system actually monitors engine vacuum just like the vacuum gauge, but all it registers is a low vacuum. The light on the instrument panel warns the vehicle operator when engine manifold vacuum drops below the economical limit. Switch operation is similar to that of the oil pressure indicating light, except that the switch opens when vacuum, rather than oil pressure, is applied.

## TROUBLESHOOTING
### Fuel Economy Warning Light

The fuel economy warning light should go on when ignition is turned on. If it does not light, disconnect the wire from the fuel economy vacuum switch connector and ground the wire to the frame or cylinder block. If warning light still does not go on, check for burned out indicating bulb or an open in harness between vacuum switch and instrument panel. If warning light goes on, circuit is functioning and vacuum switch should be checked for proper ground. Remove and clean mounting bracket screws and mounting surfaces.

If system still does not operate, perform the following:

With electrical connector and vacuum tube disconnected from switch, connect a self-powered test light to switch electrical connector and to vacuum gauge mounting bracket. Attach a vacuum pump to gauge. If the following conditions are not met the

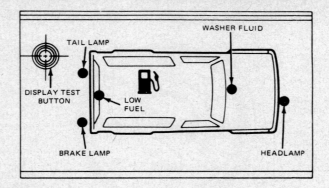

**Fig. 3  Graphic display warning system display. 1984–89 Bronco II & Ranger**

switch has to be replaced:

1. With vacuum applied, test light should be "Off."
2. Without vacuum applied, test light should be "On."
3. If warning light remains lit when it normally should be out, check vacuum hose to vacuum switch for damage or plugged condition.

## ELECTRIC CLOCKS

Regulation of electric clocks is accomplished automatically by resetting the time. If clock is running fast, turning the hands back to correct the time will automatically cause the clock to run slightly slower. If clock is running slow, turning the hands forward to correct the time will automatically cause the clock to run slightly faster, approximately 10 to 15 seconds daily.

A lockout feature prevents clock regulator mechanism from being reset more than once per wind cycle, regardless the number of times, time is reset. After clock rewinds, if time is then reset, automatic regulation will take place. If a clock varies over 10 minutes per day, it will never adjust properly and must be repaired or replaced.

## WINDING CLOCK WHEN CONNECTING BATTERY OR CLOCK WIRING

The clock requires special attention when reconnecting a battery that has been disconnected for any reason, a clock that has been disconnected, or when replacing a blown clock fuse. It is very important that the initial wind be fully made. The procedure is as follows:

1. Make sure that all other instruments and lights are turned off.
2. Connect positive cable to battery.
3. Before connecting the negative cable, press the terminal to its post on the battery. Immediately afterward, strike the terminal against the battery post to see if there is a spark. If there is spark, allow clock to run down until it stops ticking, and repeat as above until there is no spark. Then immediately make the permanent connection be-

fore the clock can again run down. The clock will run down in approximately two minutes.

4. Reset clock after all connections have been made. The foregoing procedure should also be followed when reconnecting the clock after it has been disconnected, or if it has stopped because of a blown fuse. Be sure to disconnect battery before installing a new fuse.

### TROUBLESHOOTING

If clock does not run, check for blown "clock" fuse. If fuse is blown, check for short in wiring. If fuse is not blown, check for an open circuit.

With an electric clock, the most frequent cause of a clock fuse blowing is voltage at the clock which will prevent a complete wind and allow clock contacts to remain closed. This may be caused by any of the following: discharged battery, corrosion on contact surface of battery terminals, loose connections at battery terminals, at junction block, at fuse clips, or at terminal connection of clock. Therefore, if after reconnecting battery or clock it is noted that clock is not ticking, always check for blown fuse, or examine circuits at points indicated above to determine and correct the cause.

## GRAPHIC DISPLAY WARNING SYSTEM

The graphic display warning system, **Fig. 3**, consists of a warning module equipped with 5 light-emitting diodes (LED). The module is mounted on the console and alerts the driver of the following conditions: low washer fluid, taillight failure, brake light failure, low beam headlight failure, low fuel level.

The wiring harness used with this system use special resistance wire. Do not alter wire lengths or replace bulbs with any type other than original equipment, as the system will not function properly.

### TROUBLESHOOTING

The following precautions must be taken when performing any diagnosis:

1. Check condition of system fuse before proceeding.
2. All tests must be performed with ignition switch in Run position.
3. Ambient temperature must be (60-80° F) to provide accurate test results.
4. All voltage measurements must be made using a suitable digital voltmeter. Do not touch voltmeter probes with fingers.
5. Refer to system wiring diagram, **Figs. 4 and 5,** when performing tests. The harness connectors, **Fig. 6,** are located at front of console.

### Taillight LED Illuminates or Gives False Indication

1. Measure voltage between terminals 14 and 102 with headlight switch On.
2. Voltage should measure .48 volt or more.
3. If voltage is not within specifications, check condition of bulbs and replace as necessary. If bulbs are satisfactory, check circuits for an open or short and repair as necessary.
4. If voltage is within specifications, but taillight LED remains lit, replace graphic display module.

### Headlight LED Illuminates Or Gives False Indication

1. Measure voltage between terminals 13 and 108 with headlight switch On.
2. Voltage should measure .47 volt or more.
3. If voltage is not within specifications, check condition of bulbs and replace as necessary. If bulbs are satisfactory, check circuits for an open or short and repair as necessary.
4. If voltage is within specifications, but headlight LED remains lit, replace graphic display module.

### Brake Light LED Illuminates Or Gives False Indication

1. Measure voltage between terminals 9 and 104.
2. Voltage should measure .19 volt or more.
3. If voltage is not within specifications,

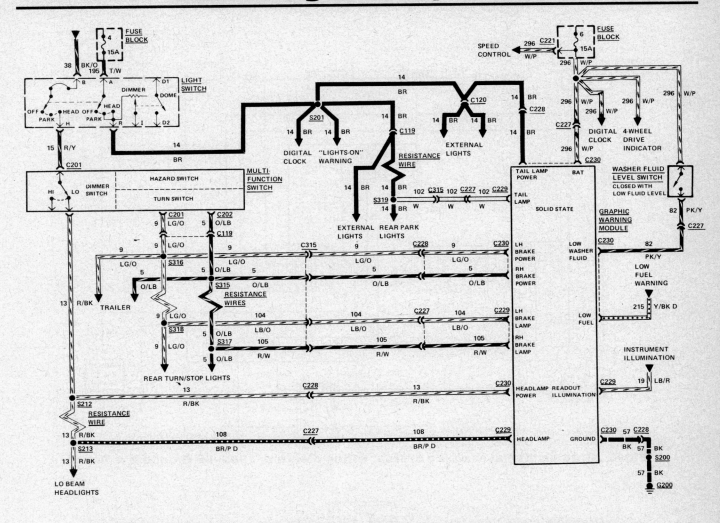

**Fig. 4   Graphic display warning system wiring diagram. 1984 Bronco II & Ranger**

check condition of left brake light bulb and replace if necessary. If bulb is satisfactory, check circuits for an open or short and repair as necessary.

4. If voltage is within specifications, but brake light LED remains lit, proceed to step 5.
5. Measure voltage between terminals 5 and 105.
6. Voltage should measure .19 volt or more.
7. If voltage is not within specifications, check condition of right brake light bulb and replace if necessary. If bulb is satisfactory, check circuits for an open or short and repair as necessary.
8. If voltage is within specifications, but brake light LED remains lit, replace graphic display module.

## Low Fuel LED Illuminates or Gives False Indication

1. Measure voltage between terminals 57 and 215 with ignition switch in Accessory or Run position and fuel level low enough to illuminate LED.
2. Voltage should be 10.5-13.5 volts.
3. If voltage is not within specifications, check circuits for an open or short and repair as necessary.

## Washer Fluid LED Illuminates Or Gives False Indication

1. Measure voltage between terminals 82 and 57 with ignition switch in Accessory or Run position and washer fluid level low enough to illuminate

LED.
2. Voltage should be 10.5-13.5 volts.
3. If voltage is not within specifications, check circuits for an open or short and repair as necessary.

## No LEDs Will Illuminate

1. Measure voltage between terminals 57 and 296 with ignition switch in Accessory or Run position.
2. Voltage should be 10.5-13.5 volts.
3. If voltage is not within specifications, check circuits for an open or short and repair as necessary.

## One Or More LEDs Will Not Illuminate

1. Replace defective LED indicator(s) located in console.

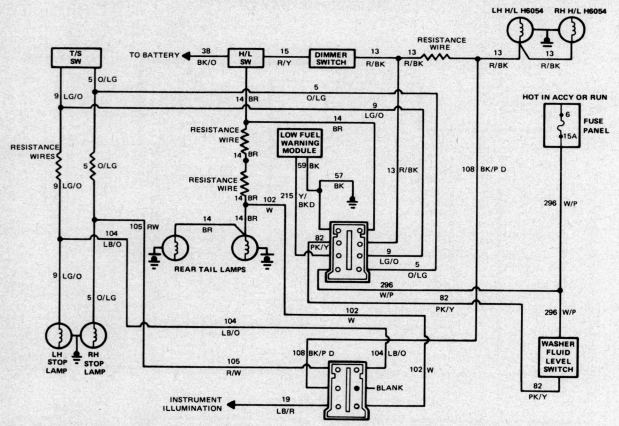

**Fig. 5 Graphic display warning system wiring diagram. 1985–89 Bronco II & Ranger**

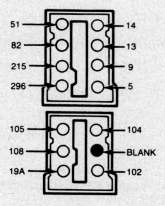

**Fig. 6 Graphic display warning system electrical connectors. 1984–89 Bronco II & Ranger**

# DISC BRAKES
## TABLE OF CONTENTS

# General Information
## INDEX

# TROUBLESHOOTING
## EXCESSIVE PEDAL TRAVEL

1. Worn brake lining.
2. Shoe and lining knock back after cornering or rough road travel.
3. Piston and shoe and lining assembly not properly seated or positioned.
4. Air leak or insufficient fluid in system or caliper.
5. Loose wheel bearing adjustment.
6. Damaged or worn caliper piston seal.
7. Improper booster pushrod adjustment.
8. Shoe out of flat more than .005 inch.
9. Rear brake automatic adjusters inoperative.
10. Improperly ground rear brake shoe and lining assemblies.

## BRAKE ROUGHNESS OR CHATTER; PEDAL PUMPING

1. Excessive lateral runout of rotor.
2. Rotor excessively out of parallel.

## EXCESSIVE PEDAL EFFORT

1. Frozen or seized pistons.
2. Brake fluid, oil or grease on linings.
3. Shoe and lining worn below specifications.
4. Proportioning valve malfunction.
5. Booster inoperative.
6. Leaking booster vacuum check valve.

## PULL, UNEVEN OR GRABBING BRAKES

1. Frozen or seized pistons.
2. Brake fluid, oil or grease on linings.
3. Caliper out of alignment with rotor.
4. Loose caliper attachment.
5. Unequal front tire pressure.
6. Incorrect front end alignment.
7. Lining protruding beyond end of shoe.

## BRAKE RATTLE

1. Excessive clearance between shoe and caliper or between shoe and splash shield.
2. Shoe hold-down clips missing or improperly positioned.

## HEAVY BRAKE DRAG

1. Frozen or seized pistons.
2. Operator riding brake pedal.
3. Incomplete brake pedal return due to linkage interference.
4. Faulty booster check valve holding pressure in hydraulic system.
5. Residual pressure in front brake hydraulic system.

## CALIPER BRAKE FLUID LEAK

1. Damaged or worn caliper piston seal.
2. Scores in cylinder bore.
3. Corrosion build-up in cylinder bore or on piston surface.
4. Metal clip in seal groove.

## NO BRAKING EFFECT WHEN PEDAL IS DEPRESSED

1. Piston and shoe and lining assembly not properly seated or positioned.
2. Air leak or insufficient fluid in system or caliper.
3. Damaged or worn caliper piston seal.
4. Bleeder screw open.
5. Air in hydraulic system or improper bleeding.

## REAR BRAKES LOCKING ON APPLICATION

On brake system equipped with a proportioning or rear pressure regulator valve, should the valve malfunction, rear brakes may receive excess pressure, resulting in wheel lock-up.

# SERVICE PRECAUTIONS
## BRAKE LINES & LININGS

Remove one of the front wheels and inspect brake disc, caliper and linings. (Wheel bearings should be inspected at this time and repacked if necessary).

Do not get any oil or grease on the linings. It is recommended that both front wheel sets be replaced whenever a respective shoe and lining is worn or damaged. Inspect and, if necessary, replace rear brake linings also.

If the caliper is cracked or fluid leakage through the casting is evident, it must be replaced as a unit.

## BRAKE ROUGHNESS

The most common cause of brake chatter on disc brakes is a variation in thickness of the disc. If roughness or vibration is encountered during highway operation or if pedal pumping is experienced at low speeds, the disc may have excessive thickness variation. To check for this condition, measure the disc at 12 points with a micrometer at a radius approximately one inch from edge of disc. If thickness measurements vary more than specifications allow, the disc should be replaced with a new one.

Excessive lateral runout of braking disc may cause a "knocking back" of the pistons, possibly creating increased pedal travel and vibration when brakes are applied.

Before checking runout, wheel bearings should be adjusted. Be sure to make adjustments according to recommendations given in the individual truck chapters.

## BRAKE DISC SERVICE

Servicing of disc brakes is extremely critical due to close tolerances required in machining the brake disc to insure proper brake operation.

Maintenance of these close controls on friction surfaces is necessary to prevent brake roughness. In addition, surface finish must be non-directional and maintained at a micro-inch finish. This close control of the rubbing surface finish is necessary to avoid pulls and erratic performance and promote long lining life and equal lining wear of both left and right brakes.

In light of the foregoing remarks, refinishing of the rubbing surfaces should not be attempted unless precision equipment, capable of measuring in micro-inches (millionths of an inch) is available.

To check runout of a disc, mount a dial indicator on a convenient part (steering knuckle, tie rod, disc brake caliper housing) so that the plunger of the dial indicator contacts the disc at a point one inch from the outer edge. If the total indicated runout exceeds specifications, install a new disc.

## GENERAL PRECAUTIONS

1. Grease or any other foreign materia must be kept off the caliper, surfaces of the disc and external surfaces of the hub, during service procedures Handling brake disc and calipers should be done in a way to avoid deformation of the disc and nicking or scratching brake linings.
2. If inspection reveals rubber piston seals are worn or damaged, they should be replaced immediately.
3. During removal and installation of a wheel assembly, exercise care so as not to interfere with or damage the caliper splash shield, the bleeder screw or the transfer tube, (if equipped).
4. Front wheel bearings should be adjusted to specifications.
5. Be sure vehicle is centered on hoist before servicing any of the front end components to avoid bending or damaging the disc splash shield on full right or left wheel turns.
6. Before the vehicle is moved after any brake service work, be sure to obtain a firm brake pedal.
7. The assembly bolts of the two caliper housings (if equipped) should not be disturbed unless the caliper requires service.

## INSPECTION OF CALIPER

Should it become necessary to remove the caliper for installation of new parts, clean all parts in alcohol, wipe dry using lint-free cloths. Using an air hose, blow out drilled passages and bores. Check dust boots for punctures or tears. If punctures or tears are evident, new boots should be installed upon reassembly.

Inspect piston bores in both housings for scoring or pitting. Bores that show light scratches or corrosion can usually be cleaned with crocus cloth. However, bores that have deep scratches or scoring may be honed, provided the diameter of the bore is not increased more than .002 inch. If the bore does not clean up within this specification, a new caliper housing should be installed (black stains on the bore walls are caused by piston seals and will do no harm).

When using a hone, be sure to install the hone baffle before honing bore. The baffle is used to protect the hone stones from damage. Use extreme care in cleaning calipers after honing. Remove all dust and grit by flushing caliper with alcohol. Wipe dry with clean lint-free cloth and then clean a second time in the same manner.

## BLEEDING DISC BRAKES

The disc brake hydraulic system can be bled manually or with pressure bleeding equipment. On vehicles with disc brakes the brake pedal will require more pumping and frequent checking of fluid level in master cylinder during bleeding operation.

Never use brake fluid that has been drained from hydraulic system when bleeding the brakes. Be sure the disc brake pistons are returned to their normal positions and that the shoe and lining assemblies are properly seated. Before driving the vehicle, check brake operation to be sure that a firm pedal has been obtained.

# Ford Single Piston Sliding Caliper, Exc. Aerostar, Bronco II & 1983–89 Ranger

## INDEX

## DESCRIPTION

The single piston sliding caliper assembly is made up of a sliding caliper housing assembly and spindle. On 2 wheel drive models, the supporting member and steering arm are cast as one piece and are combined with a wheel spindle stem to form an integral spindle assembly. On 4 wheel drive models, an integral caliper support and steering knuckle assembly contains a bolted-on spindle and dust shield.

The ends of the inner shoe and lining assembly are within the spindle assembly. An anti-rattle clip is positioned between the shoe and spindle assembly at the bottom of the caliper. The outer shoe flange bearing rests against the shoe locating and torque surfaces on the caliper housing.

The caliper is positioned either on the spindle or knuckle assembly against machined surfaces at the top end. The caliper and spindle assembly is retained by a caliper support key and spring, while a key retaining screw prevents the key from sliding out of the spindle assembly.

A square section seal fitted into a groove in the caliper cylinder bore, and a rubber boot seal the piston and caliper bore. Torque from the inner shoe is transferred directly to the spindle or knuckle assembly, while torque from the outer shoe is transferred through the caliper to the spindle or knuckle assembly.

## CALIPER REMOVAL

1. Remove a portion of brake fluid from master cylinder disc brake reservoir.
2. Raise and support vehicle and remove wheel and tire assembly.
3. Install eight inch C-clamp on caliper, **Fig. 1**, and tighten clamp to bottom piston in cylinder bore, then remove clamp. Do not use screwdriver or other edged tool to pry piston from rotor.
4. Remove key retaining screw, then using hammer and drift, drive out caliper support key and spring.
5. Remove caliper by pushing it downward against spindle assembly and rotating upper end upward and out of spindle assembly.

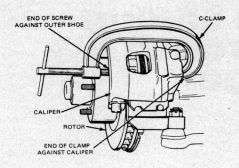

**Fig. 1  Bottoming caliper piston in cylinder bore**

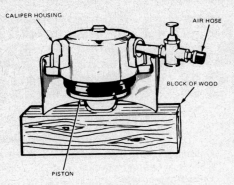

**Fig. 2  Removing caliper piston**

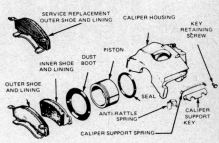

**Fig. 3  Exploded view of disc brake caliper assembly**

6. Disconnect hydraulic line from caliper.

## BRAKE SHOE REMOVAL

1. Remove caliper as previously described. If caliper is not being serviced, it is not necessary to disconnect hydraulic line from caliper.
2. Remove outer shoe from caliper, tapping shoe as necessary to loosen shoe flange.
3. Remove inner shoe, then the anti-rattle clip from lower end of shoe.

## BRAKE SHOE INSTALLATION

1. Place new anti-rattle clip on lower end of inner shoe, ensuring tabs on clip are properly positioned and that clip is fully seated.
2. Place inner shoe and anti-rattle clip in shoe abutment with anti-rattle clip tab against shoe abutment and looped spring away from rotor, then compress anti-rattle clip and slide upper end of shoe into position.
3. Ensure caliper position is fully bottomed in cylinder bore. Replacement outer shoe differs from original equipment. The replacement shoe has tabs on flange at lower edge of shoe and distance between upper tabs and low-

er flange is reduced to provide a slip-on interference fit.
4. Position outer shoe on caliper and press shoe tabs into place.
5. Install caliper.

## DISASSEMBLING CALIPER

1. Remove plug from caliper inlet port and drain fluid from caliper housing.
2. Position caliper on block of wood, **Fig. 2.**
3. Slowly and carefully apply low pressure air to caliper inlet port until piston pops out.
4. If piston is jammed or cocked and will not pop out, release air pressure and tap sharply on end of piston with soft hammer or plastic or rubber mallet to straighten piston, then apply air pressure again to remove piston.
5. Remove boot from piston and seal from caliper cylinder bore, **Fig. 3.**

## ASSEMBLING CALIPER

1. Lubricate piston seal with clean brake fluid and position seal in groove in cylinder bore.
2. Coat outside of piston and both beads of dust boot with clean brake fluid, then insert piston through dust boot until boot is around closed end of piston.

3. Hold piston and dust boot directly above caliper cylinder bore and use fingers to work bead of dust boot into groove near top of cylinder bore.
4. One bead is seated in groove, press straight down on piston until piston bottoms in bore. Ensure piston is not cocked in bore.

## CALIPER INSTALLATION

1. Position caliper on spindle assembly by pivoting caliper around support upper mounting surface, being careful not to tear or cut boot as boot slips over inner shoe.
2. Using brake adjusting tool or screwdriver, hold upper machined surface of caliper against surface of support assembly and install new caliper support spring and new caliper support key.
3. Using suitable mallet, drive key and spring assembly into position, then install key retaining screw and torque to 14-20 ft. lbs.
4. Connect hydraulic line to caliper.
5. Install wheel and tire assembly and lower vehicle to ground, then fill master cylinder as necessary with suitable brake fluid.
6. Firmly depress brake pedal several times to seat linings on rotor.
7. Bleed brakes.

# Ford Single Piston Sliding Caliper, Aerostar, Bronco II & 1983–89 Ranger

## INDEX

## DESCRIPTION

The caliper assembly consists of a pin slider caliper housing, inner and outer shoe and lining assemblies and a single piston. The assembly slides on two pins which also secure the caliper to the spindle.

The caliper housing contains a piston which has a molded rubber boot on its outer end which is pressed into a cylinder bore groove to prevent cylinder contamination. Also installed in the housing is a rubber piston seal located in the cylinder bore to provide sealing between cylinder and piston.

The outer shoe and lining assemblies are secured to the caliper by spring clips riveted to the shoe surfaces and two rectangular torque buttons on each shoe. The inner shoe and lining assemblies use a replaceable finger anti-rattle clip.

## CALIPER & LINING REMOVAL

1. Remove and discard portion of brake fluid from larger master cylinder reservoir to avoid fluid overflow when caliper piston is depressed.
2. Raise and support vehicle, then remove front wheel and tire assemblies.
3. Working on either side of vehicle, place an eight inch C-clamp or equivalent on caliper and tighten clamp to bottom caliper piston in cylinder bore, then remove clamp. Do not use a screwdriver or similar tool to pry piston away from rotor.
4. On 1983-84 models, three types of caliper pins are used: a single tang type, a double tang type, and a split-shell type. The pin removal process depends on bolt head direction of installed pin.Always remove upper caliper pin first.
5. On 1983-84 models, if bolt head is on outside of caliper, proceed as follows:
   a. Tap caliper pin bolt on inner side of caliper until there is a gap between outer bolt head and caliper pin.
   b. Using suitable cutter, remove bolt head from bolt.
   c. Using screwdriver, depress tab on bolt head end of upper caliper pin, then tap on pin with hammer until tab is depressed by V-slot.

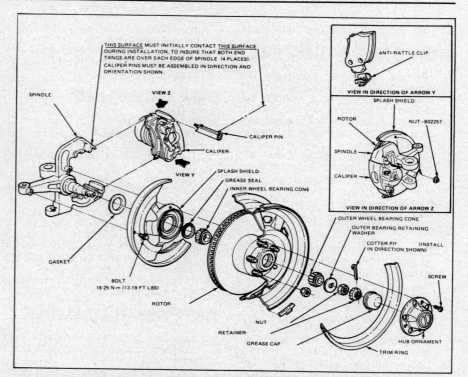

**Fig. 1   Exploded view of disc brake assembly. 4 x 2 models**

   d. Using ½ inch or smaller punch placed against end of caliper pin, drive pin out of caliper toward inside of vehicle.Do not use a screwdriver or other edged tool to drive out the pin.
6. On 1983-84 models, if nut end of bolt is on outside of caliper, proceed as follows:
   a. Remove nut from bolt.
   b. Using screwdriver, depress lead tang on end of upper caliper pin, then tap pin with hammer until lead tang is depressed by V-slot.
   c. Using ½ inch or smaller punch placed against end of caliper pin, drive pin out of caliper toward inside of vehicle. Do not use a screwdriver or other edged tool to drive out the pin.
7. On all 1985-86 models, proceed as follows:
   a. Clean all excess dirt from area

around pin tabs.
   b. Tap upper caliper pin towards inboard side until pin tabs just touch spindle face.
   c. Insert a screwdriver into slot provided behind pin tabs on inboard side of pin.
   d. Compress outboard end of pin with needle nose pliers, while simultaneously prying with screwdriver until tabs slip into spindle groove.
   e. Position one end of a 7/16 inch punch against end of caliper pin and drive caliper pin out of caliper slide groove.
8. On all models, remove lower caliper pin using procedure in step 5, 6 or 7, as applicable.
9. Remove caliper from rotor, then the brake hose from caliper, **Figs. 1, 2 and 3.**
10. Remove outer lining, then anti-rattle clips and inner lining.

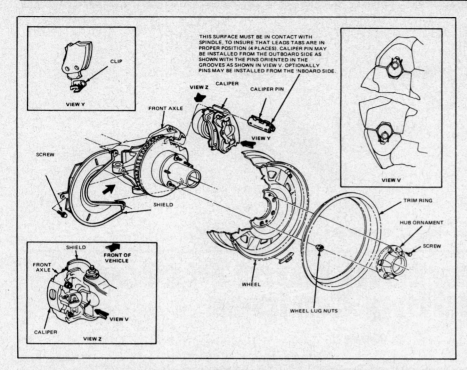

**Fig. 2 Exploded view of disc brake assembly. 4 x 4 models**

4. On 1983-84 models, clean mounting surfaces of caliper and, using suitable lubricant, lubricate caliper grooves, then install new caliper pins. Pin must be installed with lead tang in first, bolt head facing outward. Place lead tang in V-slot mounting surface and drive into caliper until drive tang is flush with caliper assembly, then install nut and torque to 32-47 ft. lbs.

5. On 1985-89 models, clean caliper mounting surfaces, then apply suitable lubricant to caliper grooves and install caliper on spindle. Position pin with pin retention tabs adjacent to spindle groove. Tap pin on outboard end with a hammer until tabs contact spindle face. Repeat procedure for lower pin. Do not install bolt and nut with new pins.

6. On all models, install brake hose on caliper.

7. Repeat steps 3-10 of removal procedure and steps 1-6 of installation procedure on opposite side of vehicle.

8. Bleed brakes, then install wheel and tire assemblies and torque nuts to 85-115 ft. lbs.

9. Lower vehicle, check brake fluid level and replenish as necessary, then check brakes for proper operation.

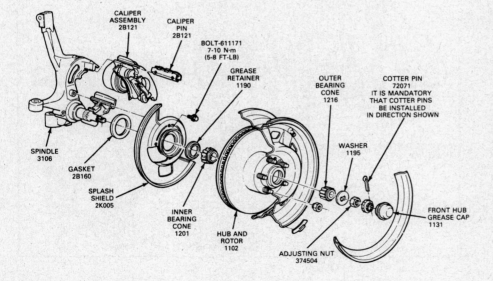

**Fig. 3 Exploded view of disc brake assembly. 1986–88 Aerostar**

## CALIPER & LINING INSTALLATION

1. Place new anti-rattle clip on lower end of inner shoe, being sure tabs on clip are properly positioned and clip is fully seated.

2. Place inner shoe and anti-rattle clip in shoe abutment with anti-rattle clip tab against shoe abutment and loop type spring away from rotor. Compress anti-rattle clip and slide upper end of shoe into position.

3. Install outer shoe, ensure that torque buttons on shoe spring clip are firmly seated in matching holes in caliper.

## CALIPER OVERHAUL

1. Remove caliper assembly as described in caliper and lining removal.

2. Placing cloth over piston to prevent damage to piston, apply air pressure to fluid port in caliper with suitable tool to remove piston. If piston is seized and cannot be forced from caliper, tap lightly around piston while applying air pressure. Piston may develop considerable force from pressure build-up.

3. Remove dust boot from caliper assembly, then remove and discard rubber piston seal of cylinder, **Fig. 4.**

4. Using suitable solvent, clean all metal parts, then clean out and dry grooves and passageways with compressed air.

5. Check cylinder bore and piston for damage or excessive wear and replace piston if it is pitted, scored, or corroded, or the plating is worn away.

6. Apply film of clean brake fluid on new caliper piston seal and install it in cylinder bore, being sure seal does not become twisted but is firmly seated in groove.

7. Install new dust boot by setting flange squarely in outer groove of caliper bore.

8. Coat piston with brake fluid and install in cylinder bore, spreading dust boot over piston as it is installed, seating dust boot in piston groove.

9. Install caliper as described in front caliper and lining installation.

*FORD SINGLE PISTON SLIDING CALIPER, AEROSTAR, BRONCO II & 1983-89 RANGER*

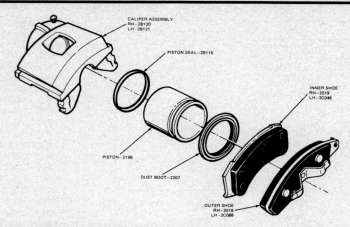

**Fig. 4 Exploded view of disc brake caliper assembly**

# Ford (Dayton) Dual Piston Sliding Caliper

## INDEX

## DESCRIPTION

### 1980

This disc brake, **Fig. 1,** is of the sliding caliper design with two pistons on one side of the rotor. The caliper which slides on the anchor plate is retained by a key and spring. A key retaining screw maintains the key and spring in proper position. Two brake shoes and lining assemblies, one on each side of the rotor, are used and are not identical. Brake shoes slide on the caliper bridge and one anti-rattle clip is used on both shoes. The cylinder housing contains two pistons. The pistons and caliper bores are protected by boot seals fitted to a piston groove and attached to the cylinder housing. The cylinder assembly is attached to the caliper with cap screws and washers. The anchor plate and shield are bolted to the spindle.

### 1981–89

The caliper, **Fig. 2,** which slides on the support assembly, is retained by a key and spring. A key retaining screw holds the key and spring in position. Each caliper contains one brake shoe and lining assembly on each side of the rotor. The shoes, which slide on the caliper bridge, are not identical. One anti-rattle clip is used on both shoes. The caliper contains two pistons. The pistons and cylinder bores are protected by boot seals fitted to a groove in the piston and a groove in the cylinder housing.

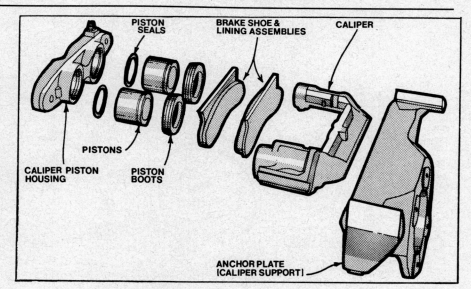

**Fig. 1 Exploded view of disc brake caliper assembly. 1980**

## BRAKE SHOE & LINING REPLACE

### REMOVAL

1. To avoid fluid overflow when pistons are pushed into caliper, remove some brake fluid from master cylinder.
2. Raise vehicle and remove wheel assembly.
3. Remove key retaining screw then, using a brass drift and hammer, drive out the key and spring.
4. Remove caliper and its support by rotating the key and spring end out and away from the rotor. Slide opposite end of caliper clear of the slide in the support and off the rotor. Place caliper on tie rod or axle. Do not allow the

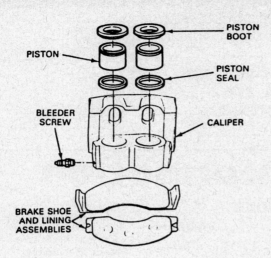

**Fig.2   Exploded view of disc brake caliper assembly 1981–88**

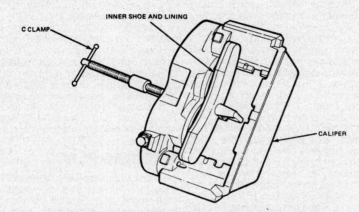

**Fig. 3   Bottoming caliper pistons**

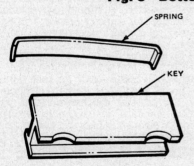

**Fig. 4   Caliper spring & key**

brake hose to support weight of caliper, as this can damage the hose.
5. Remove caliper brake shoe anti-rattle spring and inner and outer shoe and lining assemblies.
6. Clean and inspect caliper assembly. Thoroughly clean areas of caliper and support that contact during the sliding action of the caliper.

## INSTALLATION

1. Place used inner lining and shoe assembly over the pistons, then place a C-clamp on the caliper housing midway between the two pistons over the lining and shoe assembly, **Fig. 3**. Tighten the clamp until pistons are bottomed in caliper, then remove C-clamp and lining and shoe assembly.
2. Install the new inner and outer shoe and lining assemblies, and the anti-rattle spring.
3. Position caliper rail into the slide on the support and rotate the caliper onto rotor.
4. Position the key and spring, **Fig. 4**, then install the subassembly between the caliper and support. Note that the spring is between the key and caliper and that spring tangs overlap the ends of the key.
5. If necessary use a screwdriver to hold caliper against support assembly, then using a hammer, drive the key and spring into position aligning the correct notch with the existing hole in the support.
6. Install the key to support retaining screw and torque to 12–20 ft. lbs.

7. Install wheel assembly and lower vehicle. Check brake fluid level and add as necessary with heavy duty brake fluid.
8. Depress brake pedal several times to seat linings on rotor. Do not move vehicle until a firm brake pedal has been obtained.

## CALIPER
### REPLACE
#### REMOVAL

1. Perform steps 1 to 5 outlined under "Brake Shoe & Lining, Replace" removal procedure.
2. Disconnect flexible hose from caliper.
3. Remove caliper assembly.

### INSTALLATION

1. Perform steps 1 and 2 outlined under "Brake Shoe & Lining, Replace" installation procedure.
2. Connect flexible hose to caliper.
3. Perform steps 3 to 6 outlined under "Brake Shoe & Lining, Replace" installation procedure, then after bleeding brakes, proceed with the remainder of the procedure.

## CALIPER OVERHAUL
### DISASSEMBLY

1. Drain brake fluid from caliper.
2. Remove brake shoe and lining assemblies.
3. To remove pistons, apply air pressure to the caliper fluid port to ease the pistons from the bores. Use a block of wood and a shop towel to protect pistons from damage.
4. On 1980 models, remove cylinder housing to caliper attaching bolts and separate housing from caliper.
5. Remove piston seals.

### ASSEMBLY

1. Lubricate cylinder bores and new piston seals with clean brake fluid.
2. Install piston seals in cylinder bore grooves.
3. Lubricate dust boot retaining lips with clean brake fluid and install retaining lips in the boot retaining grooves in the cylinder bores.
4. Lubricate piston with clean brake fluid and insert pistons into dust boots. Start pistons into cylinders until located beyond the piston seals.
5. Place a block of wood over one piston and press piston into cylinder using caution not to damage the piston seals or piston. Press the second piston into the bore.
6. On 1980 models, place piston housing on caliper and install and torque mounting bolts to 155–185 ft. lbs.

# DRUM BRAKES

## TABLE OF CONTENTS

# General Information

## INDEX

## SERVICE PRECAUTIONS

When working on or around brake assemblies, care must be taken to prevent breathing asbestos dust, as many manufacturers incorporate asbestos fibers in the production of brake linings. During routine service operations, the amount of asbestos dust from brake lining wear is at a low level due to a chemical breakdown during use, and a few precautions will minimize exposure. Do not sand or grind brake linings unless suitable local exhaust ventilation equipment is used to prevent excessive asbestos exposure.

1. Wear a suitable respirator approved for asbestos dust use during all repair procedures.
2. When cleaning brake dust from brake parts, use a vacuum cleaner with a highly efficient filter system. If a suitable vacuum cleaner is not available, use a water soaked rag. Do not use compressed air or dry brush to clean brake parts.
3. Keep work area clean, using same equipment as for cleaning brake parts.
4. Properly dispose of rags and vacuum cleaner bags by placing them in plastic bags.
5. Do not smoke or eat while working on brake systems.

## GENERAL INSPECTION
### BRAKE DRUMS

Any time the brake drums are removed for brake service, braking surface diameter should be checked with a suitable brake drum micrometer at several points to determine if they are within the safe oversize limit stamped on the brake drum outer surface. If braking surface diameter exceeds specifications, the drum must be replaced. If braking surface diameter is within specifications, drums should be cleaned and inspected for cracks, scores, deep grooves, taper, out of round and heat spotting. If drums are cracked or heat spotted, they must be replaced. Minor scores should be removed with sandpaper. Grooves and large scores can only be removed by machining with special equipment, as long as braking surface is within specifications stamped on brake drum outer surface. Any brake drum sufficiently out of round to cause vehicle vibration or noise while braking, or showing taper should also be machined, removing only enough stock to true up the brake drum.

After a brake drum is machined, wipe braking surface diameter with a cloth soaked in denatured alcohol. If one brake drum is machined, the other should also be machined to the same diameter to maintain equal braking forces.

### BRAKE LININGS & SPRINGS

Inspect brake linings for excessive wear, damage, oil, grease or brake fluid contamination. If any of the above conditions exists, brake linings should be replaced. Do not attempt to replace only one set of brake shoes; they should be replaced as an axle set only to maintain equal braking forces. Examine brake shoe webbing, hold-down and return springs for signs of overheating indicated by a slight blue color. If any component exhibits signs of overheating, replace hold-down and return springs with new ones. Overheated springs lose their pull and could cause brake linings to wear out prematurely. Inspect all springs for sags, bends and external damage, and replace as necessary.

Inspect hold down retainers and pins for bends, rust and corrosion. If any of the above conditions exist, replace retainers and pins.

### BACKING PLATE

Inspect backing plate shoe contact surface for grooves that may restrict shoe movement and cannot be removed by lightly sanding with emery cloth or other suitable abrasive. If backing plate exhibits above condition, it should be replaced. Also inspect for signs of cracks, warpage and excessive rust, indicating need for replacement.

### ADJUSTER MECHANISM

Inspect all components for rust, corrosion, bends and fatigue. Replace as necessary. On adjuster mechanism equipped with adjuster cable, inspect cable for kinks, fraying or elongation of eyelet and replace as necessary.

### PARKING BRAKE CABLE

Inspect parking brake cable end for kinks, fraying and elongation, and replace as necessary. Use a small hose clamp to compress clamp where it enters backing plate to remove.

# Exc. E-250, 350 & F-250, 350

## INDEX

**Page No.**

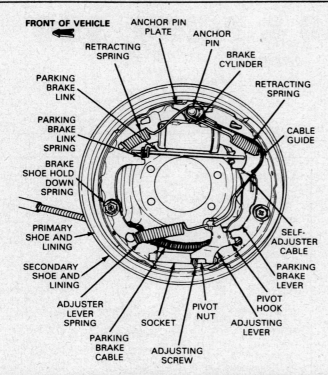

**FRONT OF VEHICLE** — ANCHOR PIN PLATE — ANCHOR PIN — BRAKE CYLINDER — RETRACTING SPRING — RETRACTING SPRING — PARKING BRAKE LINK — PARKING BRAKE LINK SPRING — CABLE GUIDE — BRAKE SHOE HOLD DOWN SPRING — PRIMARY SHOE AND LINING — SECONDARY SHOE AND LINING — SELF-ADJUSTER CABLE — PARKING BRAKE LEVER — ADJUSTER LEVER SPRING — PARKING BRAKE CABLE — SOCKET — PIVOT NUT — ADJUSTING SCREW — PIVOT HOOK — ADJUSTING LEVER

**Fig. 1   Drum brake assembly. Exc. E-250, 350 & F-250, 350**

## REMOVAL

1. Raise and support vehicle.
2. Remove hub cap, then the wheel and tire as an assembly.
3. On vehicles with full-floating axles, remove brake drum as follows:
   a. Loosen rear brake shoe adjustment screw.
   b. Remove rear axle retaining bolts and lock washers, axle shaft, and gasket.
   c. Remove wheel bearing locknut, lock washer, and adjusting nut.
   d. Remove hub and drum from axle.
   e. Remove brake drum to hub retaining screws, bolts, or bolts and nuts, then remove brake drum from hub.
4. On vehicles with semi-floating axles, remove brake drum as follows:
   a. Remove brake drum retaining nuts.
   b. Remove brake drum. If brake lining is dragging on brake drum, back off brake adjustment by rotating adjustment screw.
5. Install suitable clamp over ends of wheel cylinder.
6. Contract brake shoes as follows:
   a. Disengage adjusting lever from adjusting screw by pulling backward on adjusting lever, **Fig. 1**.
   b. Move outboard side of adjusting screw upward and back off pivot nut as far as it will go.
7. Pull adjusting lever, cable, and automatic adjuster spring down and toward rear to unhook pivot hook from large hole in secondary shoe web. Do not pry pivot hook out of hole.
8. Remove automatic adjuster spring and adjusting lever.
9. Using suitable tool, remove secondary shoe to anchor spring, then the primary shoe to anchor spring.
10. Unhook cable anchor and remove anchor pin plate, if equipped.
11. Remove cable guide from secondary shoe.
12. Remove shoe hold-down springs, shoes, adjusting screw, pivot nut, and socket. Note color and position of each hold down spring for proper assembly.
13. On rear brakes, remove parking brake link and spring, then disconnect parking brake cable from parking brake lever.
14. Remove rear brake secondary shoe and disassemble parking brake lever from shoe by removing retaining clip and spring washer.

## INSTALLATION

1. Assemble parking brake lever on secondary shoe and secure with spring washer and retaining clip.
2. Apply light coating of suitable lubricant at points where brake shoes contact backing plate.
3. Position brake shoes on backing plate, then install hold down spring pins, springs, and cups.
4. On rear brakes, install parking brake link, spring, and washer, then connect parking brake cable to parking brake lever.
5. Install anchor pin plate, if equipped, then place cable anchor over anchor pin with crimped side facing backing plate.
6. Install primary shoe to anchor spring.
7. Install cable guide on secondary shoe web with flanged holes fitted into hole in secondary shoe web, then thread cable around cable guide groove. Ensure that cable is positioned in groove and not between guide and shoe web.
8. Install secondary shoe to anchor spring. Ensure that all parts lay flat on anchor pin.
9. Remove clamp from wheel cylinder.
10. Apply suitable lubricant to threads and socket end of adjusting screw, turn adjusting screw into adjusting pivot nut to end of threads and back off 1/2 turn, then place adjusting socket on screw and install assembly between shoe ends with adjusting screw closer to secondary shoe. Socket end of each adjusting screw is stamped "R" or "L" to indicate use on right or left side of vehicle. Adjusting pivot nuts can be identified by number of lines machined around body of nut. Two lines indicate righthand nut and one line indicates lefthand nut.
11. Hook cable hook into hole in adjusting lever from outboard plate side. Adjusting levers are stamped "R" or "L" to indicate use on righthand or lefthand brake assembly.
12. Place hooked end of adjuster spring in large hole in primary shoe web and connect looped end of spring to adjuster lever hole.
13. Pull adjuster lever, cable, and automatic adjuster spring down toward rear to engage pivot hook in large hole in secondary shoe web, then ensure that adjusting mechanism works properly.
14. On vehicles with full-floating axles, install brake drums as follows:
    a. Place brake drum on hub and install attaching screws, bolts, or bolts and nuts.
    b. Place hub and drum as an assembly on axle and start adjusting nut.
    c. Adjust wheel bearing nut and install wheel bearing lock washer

and locknut. Refer to individual truck chapter for procedure.
d. Install new gasket and the bolts and lock washers.
e. Install wheel and tire assembly.
f. Adjust brakes. Refer to individual truck chapter for correct adjustment procedure.
15. On vehicles with semi-floating axles,

install brake drums as follows:
a. Adjust brakes. Refer to individual truck chapter for correct adjustment procedure.
b. Install drum.
c. Install brake drum retaining nuts and tighten securely.
d. Install wheel on axle shaft flange studs against drum, and tighten re-

taining nuts.
16. If any hydraulic connections have been opened, bleed brake system.
17. Check master cylinder fluid lever, filling as necessary.
18. Check brake pedal for proper feel and return.
19. Lower vehicle and road test.

# E-250, 350 & F-250, 350

## INDEX

## REMOVAL

1. Raise and support vehicle.
2. Remove hub cap, then wheel and tire assembly.
3. On vehicles with full-floating axles, remove brake drums as follows:
   a. Loosen rear brake shoe adjustment screw.
   b. Remove rear axle retaining bolts and lock washers, axle shaft, and gasket.
   c. Remove wheel bearing locknut, lock washer, and adjusting nut.
   d. Remove hub and drum from axle.
   e. Remove brake drum-to-hub retaining screws, bolts, or bolts and nuts, then remove brake drum from hub.
4. On vehicles with semi-floating axles, remove brake drums as follows:
   a. Remove brake drum retaining nuts.
   b. Remove brake drum. If brake lining is dragging on brake drum, back off brake adjustment by rotating adjusting screw.
5. Remove parking brake lever assembly retaining nut from behind backing plate and remove parking brake lever assembly.
6. Remove adjusting cable assembly from anchor pin, cable guide, and adjusting lever, **Fig. 1.**
7. Remove brake shoe retracting springs.
8. Remove brake shoe hold-down springs.
9. Remove brake shoes and adjusting screw assembly.
10. Disassemble adjusting screw assembly.

## INSTALLATION

1. Clean ledge pads on backing plate, sanding lightly to bare metal.
2. Apply suitable lubricant to retracting and hold-down spring contacts on brake shoes and backing plate.
3. Apply suitable lubricant to threads and socket end of adjusting screw.
4. Install upper retracting spring on primary and secondary shoes and position shoe assembly on backing plate with wheel cylinder pushrods in shoe slots.

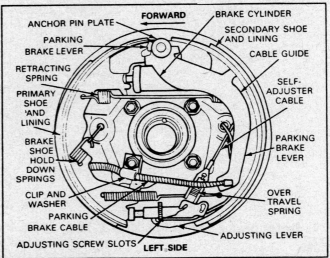

**Fig. 1   Drum brake assembly. E-250, 350 & F-250, 350**

5. Install brake shoe hold-down springs.
6. Install brake shoe adjustment screw assembly with the slot in the head of adjustment screw facing primary shoe, lower retracting spring, adjusting lever spring, and adjusting lever assembly, and connect adjusting cable to adjusting lever. Socket end of each adjusting screw is stamped "R" or "L" to indicate use on right or left side of vehicle. Adjusting pivot nuts can be identified by number of lines machined around body of nut. Two lines indicate righthand nut and one line indicates lefthand nut.
7. Position cable in cable guide and install cable anchor fitting on the anchor pin.
8. Install parking brake assembly in anchor pin and secure with retaining nut behind backing plate.
9. On vehicles with full-floating axles, install brake drums as follows:
   a. Place brake drum on hub and install attaching screws, bolts, or bolts and nuts.
   b. Place hub and drum as an assembly on axle and start adjusting nut.

   c. Adjust wheel bearing nut and install wheel bearing lock washer and lock nut. Refer to individual truck chapter for procedure.
   d. Install new gasket and the bolts and lock washers.
   e. Install wheel and tire assembly.
   f. Adjust brakes. Refer to individual truck chapter for correct adjustment procedure.
10. On vehicles with semi-floating axles, install brake drums as follows:
    a. Adjust brakes. Refer to individual truck chapter for correct adjustment procedure.
    b. Install drum.
    c. Install brake drum retaining nuts and tighten securely.
    d. Install wheel on axle shaft flange studs against drum, and tighten retaining nuts.
11. If any hydraulic connections have been opened, bleed brake system.
12. Check master cylinder fluid level, filling as necessary.
13. Check brake pedal for proper feel and return.
14. Lower vehicle and road test.

# UNIVERSAL JOINTS

## INDEX

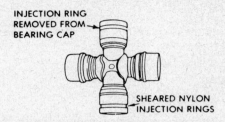

**Fig. 1 Production type universal joints which use nylon injection rings in place of snap rings**

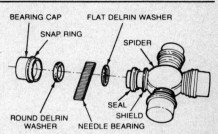

**Fig. 2 Service type universal joint (internal snap ring type)**

## SERVICE NOTES

Before disassembling any universal joint, examine the assembly carefully and note the position of the grease fitting (if used). Also, be sure to mark the yokes with relation to the propeller shaft so they may be reassembled in the same relative position. Failure to observe these precautions may produce rough vehicle operation which results in rapid wear and failure of parts, and place an unbalanced load on transmission, engine and rear axle.

When universal joints are disassembled for lubrication or inspection, and the old parts are to be reinstalled, special care must be exercised to avoid damage to universal joint spider or cross and bearing cups. Some driveshafts use an injected nylon retainer on the universal joint bearings. When service is necessary, pressing the bearings out will sheer the nylon retainer, **Fig. 1.** Replacement with the conventional steel snap ring type is then necessary, **Fig. 2.**

## CROSS & ROLLER TYPE
### SERVICING WITHOUT UNIVERSAL JOINT REPLACEMENT TOOL
#### Disassembly

1. Remove snap rings (or retainer plates) that retain bearings in yoke and drive shaft **Fig. 3**
2. Place U-joint in a vise.
3. Select a wrench socket with an outside diameter slightly smaller than the U-joint bearings. Select another wrench socket with an inside diameter slightly larger than the U-joint bearings.
4. Place the sockets at opposite bearings in the yoke so that the smaller socket becomes a bearing pusher and the larger socket becomes a bearing receiver when the vise jaws

come together, **Fig. 4.** Close vise jaws until both bearings are free of yoke and remove bearings from the cross or spider.
5. If bearings will not come all the way out, close vise until bearing in receiver socket protrudes from yoke as much as possible without using excessive force. Then remove from vise and place that portion of bearing which protrudes from yoke between vise jaws. Tighten vise to hold bearing and drive yoke off with a soft hammer.
6. To remove opposite bearing from yoke, replace in vise with pusher socket on exposed cross journal with receiver socket over bearing cup. Then tighten vise jaws to press bearing back through yoke into receiving socket.
7. Remove yoke from drive shaft and again place protruding portion of bearing between vise jaws. Then tighten vise to hold bearing while driving yoke off bearing with soft hammer.
8. Turn spider or cross 1/4 turn and use the same procedure to press bearings out of drive shaft.

### Assembly

1. If old parts are to be reassembled, pack bearing cups with universal joint grease. Do not fill cups completely or use excessive amounts as over-lubrication may damage seals during reassembly. Use new seals.
2. If new parts are being installed, check new bearings for adequate grease before assembling.
3. With the pusher (smaller) socket, press one bearing part way into drive shaft. Position spider into the partially installed bearing. Place second bearing into drive shaft. Fasten drive shaft in vise so that bearings are in contact with faces of vise jaws, **Fig. 5.** Some spiders are provided with locating lugs which must face toward drive shaft when installed.
4. Press bearings all the way into position and install snap rings or retainer plates.
5. Install bearings in yoke in same manner. When installation is completed, check U-joint for binding or roughness. If free movement is impeded, correct the condition before installation in vehicle.

### SERVICING USING UNIVERSAL JOINT REPLACEMENT TOOL
#### Disassembly

1. Place driveshaft in a vise using care

to avoid damaging it.
2. Remove bearing retaining snap rings. Some universal joints use injected nylon retainers in place of snap rings. During servicing, the snap rings supplied with the replacement universal joint assembly must be used.
3. Position tool on shaft and press bearing out of yoke, **Fig. 6.** If bearing cannot be pressed all the way out, remove it using vise grips or channel lock pliers or position driveshaft as shown and strike center yoke with hammer, **Fig. 7.** Mark yoke and shaft to make sure they will be reassembled in their same relative positions.
4. Reposition tool so that it presses on the spider in order to press other bearing from opposite side of flange.
5. If used, remove flange from spider.

### Assembly

1. Start new bearing into yoke, then position spider into yoke and press bearing until it is 1/4 inch below surface.
2. Remove tool and install a new snap ring.
3. Start new bearing in opposite side of yoke, then install tool and press on bearing until opposite bearing contacts snap ring.
4. Remove tool and install remaining snap ring.

## DOUBLE CARDAN TYPE

The double cardan type joint, **Fig. 8,** incorporates two universal joints, a centering socket yoke, and center yoke at one end of the shaft. A single universal joint is used at the other end.

### DISASSEMBLY

1. Remove all bearing cap retainers.
2. Mark bearing caps, spiders, propeller shaft yoke, link yoke and socket yoke for assembly alignment reference, **Fig. 9.**
3. Remove bearing caps attaching from

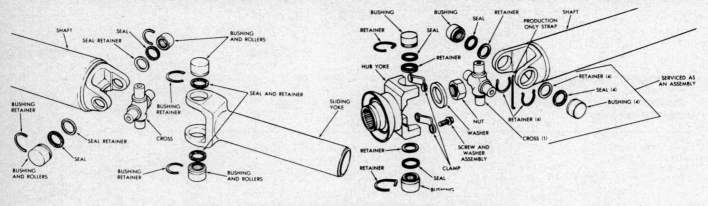

**Fig. 3   Cross & roller type universal joints**

**Fig. 4   Removing bearings from yoke using a small socket as a driver & large socket as a receiver**

spider to propeller shaft yoke as follows:

a. Use a ⅝ inch socket to drive the bearing cap and a 1 1/16 inch socket to receive the opposite bearing cap as it is driven out.

b. Place ⅝ inch socket on one bearing cap and 1 1/16 inch socket on opposite bearing.

c. Position assembly in vise so vise jaws bear directly against sockets.

d. Tighten vise to press first bearing cap out of link yoke.

e. Loosen vise, reposition sockets and press opposite bearing cap out of link yoke.

4. Disengage propeller shaft yoke from link yoke.

5. Remove bearing caps attaching front spider to propeller shaft as described in step 3 above.

6. Remove front spider from yoke.

7. Remove bearing caps attaching rear spider to link yoke as outlined in step 3 above and remove spider and socket yoke from link yoke.

8. Clean all parts in solvent and wipe dry.

Inspect assembly for damage or wear. If any component is worn or damaged, the entire assembly must be replaced.

## ASSEMBLY

When assembling universal joint, make sure to align spiders and yokes according to marks made during disassembly.

1. Lubricate all bearings and contact surfaces with lithium base chassis grease.

2. Install bearing caps on yoke ends of rear spider and secure caps with tape, **Fig. 8**.

3. Assemble socket yoke and rear spider.

4. Position rear spider in link yoke and install bearing caps. Press caps into yoke using ⅝ inch socket until bearing cap retainer grooves are exposed.

5. Install rear spider-to-link yoke bearing cap retainers.

6. Position front spider in propeller shaft yoke and install bearing caps. Press caps into yoke using a ⅝ inch socket until bearing cap retainer grooves are exposed.

7. Install front spider-to-propeller shaft yoke bearing cap retainers.

8. Install thrust washer and socket spring in ball socket bearing bore, if removed.

9. Install thrust washer on ball socket bearing boss (located on propeller shaft yoke), if removed.

10. Align ball socket bearing boss on propeller shaft yoke with ball socket bearing bore and insert boss into bore.

11. Align front spider with link yoke bearing cap bores and install bearing caps. Press caps into yoke using a ⅝ inch socket until bearing cap retainer grooves are exposed.

12. Install front spider-to-link yoke bearing cap retainers.

## CV (CONSTANT VELOCITY) TYPE

The CV type joint, **Fig. 9**, incorporates an outer bearing retainer and flange, spring, cap, circlip, inner bearing assembly and a

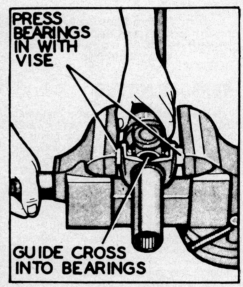

**Fig. 5   Installing bearings into drive shaft yoke**

wire ring. The inner bearing assembly incorporates a bearing cage, six ball bearings and an inner race.

## DISASSEMBLY

1. Remove clamp retaining shroud to outer bearing race and flange assembly.

2. Remove shroud taking care not to damage dust boot or outer bearing race and flange assembly, **Fig. 10**. It may be necessary to tap shroud using a plastic hammer.

3. Peel dust boot upward, **Fig. 11**, and away from outer bearing race and flange assembly.

4. Using a suitable screwdriver, remove wire ring that retains the inner race to outer race.

5. Remove inner race and shaft assembly from outer race and flange assembly, **Fig. 12**, then cap and spring from inside the outer retainer.

6. Using suitable snap ring pliers, remove circlip retaining the inner race

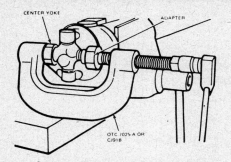

**Fig. 6   Removing bearing caps using tool & adapter**

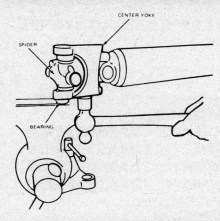

**Fig. 7   Removing bearing cap by holding cap in vise & striking center yoke with hammer**

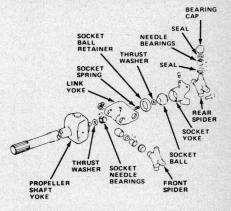

**Fig. 8   Double cardan universal joint exploded view**

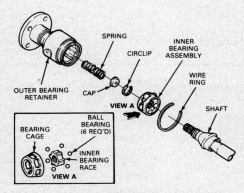

**Fig. 9   Exploded view of CV (Constant Velocity) joint**

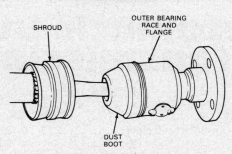

**Fig. 10   Removing shroud**

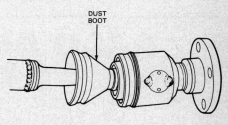

**Fig. 11   Positioning dust boot**

assembly to shaft, then inner race assembly. Discard circlip.

7. If necessary, remove clamp retaining boot to shaft, then boot.
8. Using a suitable screwdriver, pry ball bearings from cage. Do not scratch or damage cage, race or ball bearings.
9. Rotate inner race to align it with cage windows, then remove inner race through wider end of cage.

## ASSEMBLY

Individual components are not available for service. Therefore, if inspection determines component replacement, the entire CV joint must be replaced as an assembly.

1. Install inner bearing race in bearing cage with counter bore facing large end of cage.

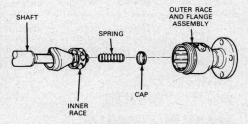

**Fig. 12   Removing inner race from outer race**

2. Push race to top of cage, then rotate race until ball slots are aligned with windows. This will lock race to top of cage.

3. Install ball bearings.
4. If removed, install dust boot on shaft using a new clamp.
5. Install inner bearing assembly on shaft, then the circlip.
6. Install spring and cap in outer bearing retainer and flange, then fill outer bearing retainer with suitable grease.
7. Install inner race and shaft assembly in the outer bearing retainer and flange, then push inner race down and install wire ring.
8. Fill top of outer bearing retainer with suitable grease. Remove excess grease from external surfaces.
9. Pull dust boot over retainer until boot is seated in groove. **Insert a suitable screwdriver blade between boot and outer bearing retainer to allow trapped air to escape from boot.**
10. Install shroud over boot and retainer, then clamp in position.

# AUTOMATIC TRANSMISSIONS

## TABLE OF CONTENTS

# A4LD Automatic Overdrive Transmission

## INDEX

## DESCRIPTION

The A4LD is a 4 speed automatic overdrive transmission and is a derivative of the C3 automatic transmission. This transmission incorporates the use of electronic controls integrated in the on-board EEC-IV system. These controls operate a piston/plate clutch in the torque converter that eliminates torque converter slip when applied.

## TROUBLESHOOTING

Refer to **Fig. 1** for troubleshooting procedures.

## MAINTENANCE

The automatic transmission fluid level should be checked as follows:
1. Place transmission in Park, then allow engine to idle with foot brake applied and vehicle on a level surface.
2. Clean all dirt from the transmission dipstick cap, before removing from the filler tube.
3. With the transmission at operating temperature (between 150-170° F), the dipstick should be hot to the touch. Fluid level should be within the cross hatched area.
4. With transmission cold (70-95° F), fluid level should be between the middle and top holes.
5. When adding fluid, use Dexron II or equivalent. **Use of a fluid other than that specified, could result in transmission malfunction and/or failure.**

## IN-VEHICLE ADJUSTMENTS

### MANUAL LINKAGE ADJUSTMENT

#### Ranger & Bronco II

1. Position transmission selector control lever in Drive position, then loosen trunnion bolt, **Fig. 2.** Do not use the overdrive position.
2. Ensure that the shift lever detent pawl is held against the rearward Drive detent stop during the linkage adjustment procedure.
3. Position transmission manual lever into Drive range by moving bellcrank lever completely rearward, then forward four detents.
4. With the transmission selector lever and manual lever in Drive position, apply light forward pressure to the shifter control lower arm while tightening trunnion bolt to 13-23 ft. lbs. Forward pressure on the shifter lower arm will ensure correct positioning within the drive detent.
5. After adjustment, check for correct Park engagement. Control lever must move to the right when engaged in Park detent. Check transmission control lever in all detent positions with the engine operating, to ensure correct detent/transmission action. Readjust, if necessary.

#### Aerostar

1. Position shift lever in Drive (Overdrive) position, then loosen shift cable adjusting screw, **Fig. 3,** and disconnect end fitting from manual lever ball stud.
2. Position manual lever in Drive (Overdrive) position by moving lever completely rearward, then forward three detents.
3. Reconnect end fitting to manual lever, then tighten cable adjusting screw to 45-60 inch lbs.
4. After adjustment, check for correct Park engagement. Control lever must move to the right when engaged in Park detent. Check transmission control lever in all detent positions with engine operating, to ensure correct detent/transmission action. Readjust, if necessary.

### KICKDOWN ROD ADJUSTMENT

The engine should be at normal operating temperature when kickdown rod adjustments are made.
1. Place a 6 lb. weight on kickdown lever, then rotate throttle lever to wide open position.

*Continued on page 6-10*

## Fig. 1 A4LD automatic overdrive transmission troubleshooting chart (Part 2 of 12)

| CONDITION | POSSIBLE SOURCE | RESOLUTION |
|---|---|---|
| Converter clutch does not engage. | 1. Converter clutch solenoid not being energized electrically. <br> a. Wires to solenoid shorted or open circuit. <br> b. Transmission case connector not seated. <br> c. Open or short circuit inside of solenoid. <br> d. Malfunctioning engine coolant temperature sensor. <br> e. Malfunctioning throttle position sensor. <br> f. Malfunctioning manifold absolute pressure sensor. <br> g. Brake switch that provides signal to processor not hooked up or malfunctioning. <br> h. Malfunctioning EEC-IV processor. <br> 2. Converter clutch solenoid is energized electrically but foreign material on hydraulic part of solenoid valve prevents valve closure. <br> 3. Converter clutch shuttle valve stuck in unlock position (against plug) or too high a load spring. <br> 4. Converter clutch shift valve stuck in downshift position (up against 4-3 T.D. sleeve assembly). | 1. <br>    Perform EEC-IV diagnostic check — key on — engine off. <br>    Perform EEC-IV diagnostic check engine running. <br>    Run diagnostic check on processor. <br> 2. Remove transmission oil pan. Remove valve body. Remove solenoid. Check operation of solenoid. NOTE: Remove any foreign material or contamination. <br> 3. Remove valve body. Check operation of converter clutch shuttle valve. Remove any contamination. Spring load is approximately 17.80 N (4.0 lb.) at 13 mm (.512 in.). <br> 4. Remove valve body. Check operation of converter clutch shift valve. Remove any contamination. Make sure valve moves freely. NOTE: 2.3L use a modulator spring and a shift spring; 2.8L just use a modulator spring. <br> 5. Remove transmission. Replace converter. |
| Converter clutch always engaged even at zero road speed. (Symptoms: engine will only run in "N" and "P" selector positions. Vehicle can only be driven away from standing start if engine rpm is brought up high and selector dropped into O.D. (D) position.) | 5. Internal problems in torque converter prevent lockup piston from coming on. <br> 1. Converter clutch shift valve stuck in lock position (away from 4-3 T.D. valve sleeve). <br> 2. Converter clutch shuttle valve stuck in locked position (away from plug). <br> 3. Lockup piston in torque converter will not disengage. | 1. Remove transmission valve body. Check to see that converter clutch shift valve moves freely. NOTE: 2.3L use a modulator spring and a shift spring; 2.8L just use a modulator spring. <br> 2. Remove valve body. Check converter clutch shuttle valve for freeness of movement. <br> 3. Remove transmission. Replace converter. |

## Fig. 1 A4LD automatic overdrive transmission troubleshooting chart (Part 1 of 12)

| CONDITION | POSSIBLE SOURCE | RESOLUTION |
|---|---|---|
| Converter clutch will not disengage on a coast down. (Symptoms: vibration on a coast down.) | 1. Malfunctioning throttle position sensor (should unlock at closed throttle). <br> 2. Converter clutch solenoid sticking. | 1. Perform EEC-IV diagnostic check — key on — engine off. <br> 2. Remove valve body. Check operation of solenoid. Remove if required. |
| Slow initial engagement. | 1. Improper fluid level. <br> 2. Damaged or improperly adjusted manual linkage. <br> 3. Contaminated fluid. <br> 4. Improper clutch and band application, or low main control pressure. | 1. Perform fluid level check. <br> 2. Service or adjust manual linkage. <br> 3. Perform fluid condition check. <br> 4. Perform control pressure test. |
| Rough initial engagement in either forward or reverse. | 1. Improper fluid level. <br> 2. High engine idle. <br> 3. Automatic choke on (warm temp). <br> 4. Looseness in the driveshaft, U-joints or engine mounts. <br> 5. Improper clutch or band application, or oil control pressure. <br> 6. Sticking or dirty valve body. <br> 7. Converter clutch not disengaging. | 1. Perform fluid level check. <br> 2. Adjust idle to specification. <br> 3. Disengage choke. <br> 4. Service as required. <br> 5. Perform control pressure test. <br> 6. Clean, service or replace valve body. <br> 7. Check converter clutch engagement/disengagement. |
| Harsh engagements (warm engine). | 1. Improper fluid level. <br> 2. Engine curb idle too high. <br> 3. Valve body bolts loose/too tight. <br> 4. Valve body dirty/sticking valves. | 1. Perform fluid level check. <br> 2. Check engine curb idle. <br> 3. Tighten to specification. <br> 4. Determine source of contamination. Service as required. |
| No/delayed forward engagement (reverse OK). | 1. Improper fluid level. <br> 2. Manual linkage misadjusted/damaged. <br> 3. Low main control pressure (leakage). Forward clutch stator support seal rings leaking. <br> 4. Forward clutch assembly burnt/damaged/leaking. Check ball in cylinder/leaking piston seal rings. <br> 5. Valve body bolts loose/too tight. <br> 6. Valve body dirty/sticking valves. <br> 7. Transmission filter plugged. <br> 8. Pump damaged, leaking. | 1. Perform fluid level check. <br> 2. Check and adjust or service as required. <br> 3. Control pressure test, note results. <br> 4. Perform air pressure test. <br> 5. Tighten to specification. <br> 6. Determine source of contamination. Service as required. <br> 7. Replace filter. <br> 8. Visually inspect pump gear. Replace pump if necessary. |

| CONDITION | POSSIBLE SOURCE | RESOLUTION |
|---|---|---|
| No engine braking in manual second gear. | 1. Intermediate band out of adjustment.<br>2. Improper band or clutch application, or oil pressure control system.<br>3. Intermediate servo leaking.<br>4. O/D clutch, O/D one-way clutch damaged.<br>5. Glazed band. | 1. Adjust intermediate band.<br>2. Perform control pressure test.<br>3. Perform air pressure test of intermediate servo for leakage. Service as required.<br>4. Replace as required.<br>5. Service or replace as required. |
| Forward engagement slips/shudders/chatters. | 1. Improper fluid level.<br>2. Manual linkage misadjusted/damaged.<br>3. Low main control pressure.<br>4. Valve body bolts loose/too tight.<br>5. Valve body dirty/sticking valves.<br>6. O.D./forward clutch piston ball — check not seating/leaking.<br>7. O.D./forward clutch piston seals cut/worn.<br>8. O.D. one-way clutch damaged.<br>9. Rear one-way clutch damaged. | 1. Perform fluid level check.<br>2. Check and adjust or service as required.<br>3. Control pressure test.<br>4. Tighten to specification.<br>5. Determine source of contamination. Service as required.<br>6. Replace O.D./forward clutch piston. Service transmission as required.<br>7. Replace seal and service clutch as required.<br>8. Replace as required.<br>9. Determine cause of condition. Service as required. |
| Reverse shudder/chatters/slips. | 1. Improper fluid level.<br>2. Low main control pressure in reverse.<br>3. Low-reverse servo leaking.<br>4. O.D. and/or rear one-way clutch damaged.<br>5. O.D. and/or reverse-high clutch drum bushing damaged.<br>6. O.D. and/or reverse-high clutch support seal rings/ring grooves worn/damaged.<br>7. O.D. and/or reverse-high clutch piston seals cut/worn.<br>8. Low-reverse servo piston damaged/worn.<br>9. Low-reverse band out of adjustment or damaged.<br>10. Looseness in the driveshaft, U-joints or engine mounts.<br>11. Servo piston/seals or bores damaged. | 1. Perform fluid level check.<br>2. Control pressure test.<br>3. Air pressure test. Visually inspect seal rings and piston bore.<br>4. Determine cause of condition. Service as required.<br>5. Determine cause of condition. Service as required.<br>6. Determine cause of condition. Service as required.<br>7. Determine cause of condition. Service as required.<br>8. Service as required.<br>9. Adjust, inspect low-reverse band.<br>10. Service as required.<br>11. Perform air pressure check. |

**Fig. 1 A4LD automatic overdrive transmission troubleshooting chart (Part 4 of 12)**

| CONDITION | POSSIBLE SOURCE | RESOLUTION |
|---|---|---|
| No/delayed reverse engagement (forward OK). | 1. Improper fluid level.<br>2. Manual linkage misadjusted/damaged.<br>3. Low main control pressure in reverse.<br>4. Reverse clutch assembly burnt/worn/leaking. Check ball in piston/leaking piston seal rings.<br>5. Valve body bolts loose/too tight.<br>6. Valve body dirty/sticking valves.<br>7. Transmission filter plugged.<br>8. Pump damaged.<br>9. Low pressure servo piston seal cut/leaking. | 1. Perform fluid level check.<br>2. Check and adjust or service as required.<br>3. Control pressure test.<br>4. Perform air pressure test.<br>5. Tighten to specification.<br>6. Determine source of contamination. Service as required.<br>7. Replace filter.<br>8. Visually inspect pump gears. Replace pump if necessary.<br>9. Perform air pressure test. Check and replace piston seal. Check and replace low reverse board. |
| No engagement or drive in forward (any position) or reverse. | 1. Improper fluid level.<br>2. Low main control pressure.<br>3. Mechanical damage. | 1. Perform fluid level check.<br>2. Control pressure test.<br>3. Check splines on turbine, input shaft and O/D carrier, O/D one-way clutch, center shaft, forward clutch, forward carrier and output shaft. Replace if necessary. |
| No engagement/drive in Ⓓ, D or 1 — (2 OK). | 1. Manual linkage misadjusted.<br>2. Rear one-way clutch damaged. | 1. Adjust manual linkage.<br>2. Replace rear one-way clutch.<br>3. Clean transmission and valve body. |
| Vehicle creeping in neutral. | 1. Forward clutch failing to disengage. | 1. Clean transmission. |
| No/delayed reverse engagement and/or no engine braking in manual low (1). | 1. Improper fluid level.<br>2. Linkage out of adjustment.<br>3. Low reverse servo piston seal leaking.<br>4. Low reverse band burnt or worn.<br>5. Overdrive clutch, overdrive one-way clutch damaged.<br>6. Polished, glazed band or drum.<br>7. Rear one-way clutch damaged.<br>8. End play clearance too tight. | 1. Perform fluid level check.<br>2. Service or adjust linkage.<br>3. Check and replace piston seal.<br>4. Perform air pressure test.<br>5. Replace as required.<br>6. Service or replace as required.<br>7. Replace.<br>8. Check and correct transmission end play clearance. |

**Fig. 1 A4LD automatic overdrive transmission troubleshooting chart (Part 3 of 12)**

| CONDITION | POSSIBLE SOURCE | RESOLUTION |
|---|---|---|
| All upshifts harsh/delayed or no upshifts. | 1. Improper fluid level. | 1. Perform fluid level check. |
| | 2. Manual linkage misadjusted/damaged. | 2. Check and adjust or service as required. |
| | 3. Governor sticking. | 3. Perform governor test. Service as required. |
| | 4. Main control pressure too high. | 4. Control pressure test. Service as required. |
| | 5. Valve body bolts loose/too tight. | 5. Tighten to specification. |
| | 6. Valve body dirty/sticking valves. | 6. Determine source of contamination. Service as required. |
| | 7. Vacuum leak to diaphragm unit. | 7. Perform vacuum supply and diaphragm test. Check vacuum lines to diaphragm unit. Service as required. |
| | 8. Vacuum diaphragm bent, sticking, leaks. | 8. Check diaphragm unit. Service as required. |
| Mushy/early all upshifts pile up/upshifts. | 1. Low main control pressure. | 1. Control pressure test. Note results. |
| | 2. Valve body bolts loose/too tight. | 2. Tighten to specification. |
| | 3. Valve body or throttle control valve sticking. | 3. Determine source of contamination. Service as required. |
| | 4. Governor valve sticking. | 4. Perform governor test. Repair as required. |
| | 5. Kickdown linkage misadjusted/sticking/damaged. | 5. Adjust linkage. Service as required. |
| No 1-2 upshift. | 1. Improper fluid level. | 1. Perform fluid level check. |
| | 2. Kickdown linkage misadjusted. | 2. Adjust linkage. |
| | 3. Manual linkage misadjusted/damaged. | 3. Check and adjust or service as required. |
| | 4. Governor valve sticking. | 4. Perform governor test. Service as required. |
| | 5. Intermediate band out of adjustment. | 5. Adjust intermediate band. |
| | 6. Vacuum leak to diaphragm unit. | 6. Check vacuum lines to diaphragm. Service as required. |
| | 7. Vacuum diaphragm bent, sticking, leaks. | 7. Check diaphragm unit. Service as necessary. |
| | 8. Valve body bolts loose/too tight. | 8. Tighten to specification. |
| | 9. Valve body dirty/sticking valves. | 9. Determine source of contamination. Service as required. |
| | 10. Intermediate band and/or servo assembly burnt. | 10. Perform air pressure test. |

**Fig. 1  A4LD automatic overdrive transmission troubleshooting chart (Part 6 of 12)**

| CONDITION | POSSIBLE SOURCE | RESOLUTION |
|---|---|---|
| No drive, slips or chatters in first gear in ① or D. All other gears normal. | 1. Damaged or worn O/D or rear one-way clutch. | 1. Service or replace. |
| No drive, slips or chatters in second gear. | 1. Intermediate band out of adjustment. | 1. Adjust intermediate band. |
| | 2. Improper band or clutch application, or control pressure. | 2. Perform control pressure test. |
| | 3. Damaged or worn intermediate servo piston and/or internal leaks. | 3. Perform air pressure test. |
| | 4. Dirty or sticking valve body. | 4. Clean, service or replace valve body. |
| | 5. Polished, glazed intermediate band or drum. | 5. Replace or service as required. |
| Starts up in 2nd or 3rd. | 1. Improper band and/or clutch application, or oil pressure control system. | 1. Perform control pressure test. |
| | 2. Damaged or worn governor. Sticking governor. | 2. Perform governor check. Replace or service governor, clean screen, check oil seals on collector body. |
| | 3. Valve body loose. | 3. Tighten to specification. |
| | 4. Dirty or sticking valve body. | 4. Clean, service or replace valve body. |
| | 5. Cross leaks between valve body and case mating surface. | 5. Service or replace valve body and/or case as required. |
| Shift points incorrect. | 1. Improper fluid level. | 1. Perform fluid level check. |
| | 2. Vacuum line damaged, clogged or leaks. | 2. Perform vacuum supply test. |
| | 3. Improper operation of EGR system. | 3. Service or replace as required. |
| | 4. Improper speedometer gear installed. | 4. Replace gear. |
| | 5. Improper clutch or band application, or oil pressure control system. | 5. Perform shift test and control pressure test. |
| | 6. Damaged or worn governor. | 6. Service or replace governor — clean screen. |
| | 7. Vacuum diaphragm bent, sticking or leaks. | 7. Service or replace as required. |
| | 8. Dirty or sticking valve body. | 8. Clean, service or replace valve body. |

**Fig. 1  A4LD automatic overdrive transmission troubleshooting chart (Part 5 of 12)**

| CONDITION | POSSIBLE SOURCE | RESOLUTION |
|---|---|---|
| Rough/harsh/delayed 1-2 upshift. | 1. Improper fluid level. | 1. Perform fluid level check. |
| | 2. Poor engine performance. | 2. Tune engine. |
| | 3. Kickdown linkage misadjusted. | 3. Adjust linkage. |
| | 4. Intermediate band out of adjustment. | 4. Adjust intermediate band. |
| | 5. Main control pressure too high. | 5. Control pressure test. Note results. |
| | 6. Governor valve sticking. | 6. Perform governor test. Service as required. |
| | 7. Damaged intermediate servo. | 7. Air pressure check intermediate servo. |
| | 8. Engine vacuum leak. | 8. Check engine vacuum lines. Check vacuum diaphragm unit. Perform vacuum supply and diaphragm test. Service as necessary. |
| | 9. Valve body bolts loose/too tight. | 9. Tighten to specifications. |
| | 10. Valve body dirty/sticking valves. | 10. Determine source of contamination. Service as required. |
| | 11. Vacuum leak to diaphragm unit. | 11. Check vacuum lines to diaphragm unit. Service as required. |
| | 12. Vacuum diaphragm bent, sticking, leaks. | 12. Check diaphragm unit. Service as necessary. |
| Mushy/early/soft/slipping 1-2 upshift. | 1. Improper fluid level. | 1. Perform fluid level check. |
| | 2. Incorrect engine performance. | 2. Tune and adjust engine idle as required. |
| | 3. Kickdown linkage misadjusted. | 3. Adjust linkage. |
| | 4. Intermediate band out of adjustment. | 4. Adjust intermediate band. |
| | 5. Low main control pressure. | 5. Control pressure test. Note results. |
| | 6. Valve body bolts loose/too tight. | 6. Tighten to specification. |
| | 7. Valve body dirty/sticking valves. | 7. Determine source of contamination. Service as required. |
| | 8. Governor valve sticking. | 8. Perform governor test. Service as required. |
| | 9. Damaged intermediate servo or band. | 9. Perform air pressure test. Service as required. |
| | 10. Polished, glazed band or drum. | 10. Service or replace as required. |

**Fig. 1  A4LD automatic overdrive transmission troubleshooting chart (Part 8 of 12)**

| CONDITION | POSSIBLE SOURCE | RESOLUTION |
|---|---|---|
| No 2-3 upshift. | 1. Low fluid level. | 1. Perform fluid level check. |
| | 2. Kickdown linkage misadjusted. | 2. Adjust linkage. |
| | 3. Low main control pressure to reverse-high clutch. | 3. Control pressure test. Note results. |
| | 4. Valve body bolts loose/too tight. | 4. Tighten to specification. |
| | 5. Valve body dirty/sticking valves. | 5. Determine source of contamination, then service as required. |
| | 6. Reverse-high clutch assembly burnt/worn. | 6. Determine cause of condition. Service as required. |
| Harsh/delayed 2-3 upshift. | 1. Incorrect engine performance. | 1. Check engine tuneup. |
| | 2. Engine vacuum leak. | 2. Check engine vacuum lines. Check vacuum diaphragm unit. Perform vacuum supply and diaphragm test. Service as necessary. |
| | 3. Kickdown linkage misadjusted. | 3. Adjust linkage. |
| | 4. Damaged or worn intermediate servo release and reverse-high clutch piston check ball. | 4. Air pressure test the intermediate servo. Apply and release the reverse-high clutch piston check ball. Service as required. |
| | 5. Valve body bolts loose/too tight. | 5. Tighten to specification. |
| | 6. Valve body dirty/sticking valves. | 6. Determine source of condition. Service as required. |
| | 7. Vacuum diaphragm bent, sticking, leaks. | 7. Check diaphragm. Replace as necessary. |
| Soft/early/mushy 2-3 upshift. | 1. Kickdown linkage misadjusted. | 1. Adjust linkage. |
| | 2. Valve body bolts loose/too tight. | 2. Tighten to specification. |
| | 3. Valve body dirty/sticking valves. | 3. Determine source of contamination. Service as required. |
| | 4. Vacuum diaphragm bent, sticking, leaks. | 4. Check diaphragm. Replace as necessary. |
| Erratic shifts. | 1. Poor engine performance. | 1. Check engine tuneup. |
| | 2. Valve body bolts loose/too tight. | 2. Tighten to specification. |
| | 3. Valve body dirty/sticking valves. | 3. Air pressure test, note results. Determine source of contamination. Service as required. |
| | 4. Governor valve stuck. | 4. Perform governor test. Service as required. |
| | 5. Output shaft collector body seal rings damaged. | 5. Service as required. |

**Fig. 1  A4LD automatic overdrive transmission troubleshooting chart (Part 7 of 12)**

| CONDITION | POSSIBLE SOURCE | RESOLUTION |
|---|---|---|
| Shifts 1-3 in Ⓓ or D. | 1. Intermediate band out of adjustment. | 1. Adjust band. |
| | 2. Damaged intermediate servo and/or internal leaks. | 2. Perform air pressure test. Service front and/or internal leaks. |
| | 3. Improper band or clutch application, or oil pressure control system. | 3. Perform control pressure test. |
| | 4. Polished glazed band or drum. | 4. Service or replace band or drum. |
| | 5. Dirty/sticky valve body, or governor. | 5. Clean, service or replace valve body or governor. |
| | 6. Governor valve stuck. | 6. Perform governor test. Service as required. |
| Engine over-speeds on 2-3 shift. | 1. Kickdown linkage out of adjustment. | 1. Service or adjust kickdown linkage. |
| | 2. Improper band or clutch application, or oil pressure control system. | 2. Perform control pressure test. |
| | 3. Damaged or worn reverse high clutch and/or intermediate servo piston. | 3. Perform air pressure test. Service as required. |
| | 4. Intermediate servo piston seals cut, leaking. | 4. Replace seals. Check for leaks. |
| | 5. Dirty or sticking valve body. | 5. Clean, service or replace valve body. |
| Rough/shudder 3-1 shift at closed throttle in D. | 1. Incorrect engine idle or performance. | 1. Tune, and adjust engine idle. |
| | 2. Improper kickdown linkage adjustment. | 2. Service or adjust kickdown linkage. |
| | 3. Improper clutch or band application or oil pressure control system. | 3. Perform control pressure test. |
| | 4. Improper governor operation. | 4. Perform governor test. Service as required. |
| | 5. Dirty or sticking valve body. | 5. Clean, service or replace valve body. |
| No 3-4 upshift. | 1. Kickdown linkage misadjusted. | 1. Adjust linkage. |
| | 2. O.D. servo damaged, leaking. | 2. Check and replace O.D. piston, seal. |
| | 3. Polished, glazed O.D. band or drum. | 3. Service or replace O.D. band or drum. |
| | 4. Dirty or sticking valve body. | 4. Clean, service or replace valve body. Check 3-4 shift valve. |
| Slipping 4th gear. | 1. O.D. servo damaged, leaking. | 1. Check and replace O.D. piston seal. |
| | 2. Polished, glazed O.D. band or drum. | 2. Service or replace O.D. band or drum. |
| Engine stall speed exceeded in Ⓓ, D or R. | 1. Vacuum system. | 1. Check and service vacuum system. |
| | 2. Low main control pressure. | 2. Control pressure test. Check and clean valve body. Replace valve body gasket. Check and service pump. |

**Fig. 1   A4LD automatic overdrive transmission troubleshooting chart (Part 9 of 12)**

| CONDITION | POSSIBLE SOURCE | RESOLUTION |
|---|---|---|
| Engine stall speed exceeded in R. OK in Ⓓ, D, 2 and 1. | 1. Low/reverse servo/band damaged. | 1. Check engine braking in 1. If not OK, check, service or replace low/reverse servo and band. |
| | 2. Reverse and high clutch damaged. | 2. If low/reverse servo OK, check and repair reverse and high clutch. |
| Engine stall speed exceeded in Ⓓ or D, OK in R. | 1. O.D. one-way clutch or rear one-way clutch damaged. | 1. Check engine stall speeds in 2 and 1. If OK, repair O.D. or rear one-way clutches. Clean transmission. |
| At moderate acceleration shift into 2nd gear is above 27 MPH. | 1. Vacuum system. | 1. Check and service hoses, vacuum diaphragm. |
| | 2. Main control pressure. | 2. Control pressure test. |
| | 3. Governor damaged or worn. | 3. Check governor and connector body oil seals. Replace if required. |
| | 4. Dirty or sticking valve body. | 4. Check 1/2 shift valve, clean or replace valve body. |
| Kickdown shift speeds low (too early) or shifts too late. | 1. Kickdown linkage misadjusted. | 1. Adjust linkage. |
| | 2. Main control pressure. | 2. Control pressure test. |
| | 3. Governor damaged or worn. | 3. Check governor and connector body oil seals. |
| No kickdown into 2nd gear between 50-70 mph in Ⓓ or D. | 1. Kickdown linkage misadjusted. | 1. Adjust linkage. |
| | 2. Main control pressure. | 2. Control pressure test. |
| | 3. Dirty or sticking valve body. | 3. Check kickdown valve, clean or replace valve body. |
| No shift to 2nd gear with accelerator 3/4 depressed at 30 mph in Ⓓ or D. | 1. Main control pressure. | 1. Control pressure test. |
| | 2. Governor damaged or worn. | 2. Check governor. |
| | 3. Dirty or sticking valve body. | 3. Clean or replace valve body. |
| When moving selector from Ⓓ/D to manual 1, at 55 mph with accelerator released, no braking felt from downshift to 2nd gear. | 1. Main control pressure. | 1. Control pressure test. |
| | 2. Intermediate band out of adjustment. | 2. Adjust band. Check intermediate servo. |
| | 3. Overdrive clutch damaged. | 3. Check and service O.D. clutch. |
| When moving selector from Ⓓ/D to manual 1, at 55 mph with accelerator released, shift into 1st gear occurs over 45 mph. | 1. Main control pressure. | 1. Control pressure test. |
| | 2. Dirty, sticking valve body. | 2. Check and clean valve body. |
| | 3. Governor damaged or worn. | 3. Check and service governor. |
| | 4. Kickdown linkage misadjusted. | 4. Check and adjust kickdown linkage. |
| When moving selector from Ⓓ/D to manual 1, at 55 mph with accelerator released, shift into 1st gear occurs under 15 mph. | 1. Main control pressure. | 1. Control pressure test. |
| | 2. Dirty, sticking valve body. | 2. Check and clean valve body. |
| | 3. Low/reverse servo damaged. | 3. Check and service as required. |
| | 4. Governor damaged or worn. | 4. Check and service governor. |
| | 5. Overdrive clutch damaged. | 5. Check and service O.D. clutch. |

**Fig. 1   A4LD automatic overdrive transmission troubleshooting chart (Part 10 of 12)**

| CONDITION | POSSIBLE SOURCE | RESOLUTION |
|---|---|---|
| No forced downshifts. | 1. Kickdown linkage out of adjustment. | 1. Service or adjust linkage. |
| | 2. Damaged internal kickdown linkage. | 2. Service internal kickdown linkage. |
| | 3. Improper clutch or band application, or oil pressure control system. | 3. Perform control pressure test. |
| | 4. Dirty or sticking governor. | 4. Service or replace governor, clean screen. |
| | 5. Dirty or sticking valve body. | 5. Clean, service, or replace valve body. |
| Engine over-speeds on 3-2 downshift. | 1. Linkage out of adjustment. | 1. Service or adjust linkage. |
| | 2. Intermediate band out of adjustment. | 2. Adjust intermediate band. |
| | 3. Improper band or clutch application, and one-way clutch, or oil pressure control system. | 3. Perform control pressure test service clutch. |
| | 4. Damaged or worn intermediate servo. | 4. Air pressure test check the intermediate servo. Service servo and/or seals. |
| | 5. Polished, glazed band or drum. | 5. Service or replace as required. |
| | 6. Dirty or sticking valve body. | 6. Clean, service or replace valve body. |
| Shift efforts high. | 1. Manual shaft linkage damaged/misadjusted. | 1. Check and adjust or service as required. |
| | 2. Inner manual lever nut loose. | 2. Tighten nut to specification. |
| | 3. Manual lever retainer pin damaged. | 3. Adjust linkage and install pin. |
| Transmission overheats. | 1. Improper fluid level. | 1. Perform fluid level check. |
| | 2. Incorrect engine idle, or performance. | 2. Tune, or adjust engine idle. |
| | 3. Improper clutch or band application, or oil pressure control system. | 3. Perform control pressure test. |
| | 4. Restriction in cooler or lines. | 4. Service restriction. |
| | 5. Seized converter one-way clutch. | 5. Replace one-way clutch. |
| | 6. Dirty or sticking valve body. | 6. Clean, service or replace valve body. |
| Transmission leaks. | 1. Case breather vent. | 1. Check the vent for free breathing. Repair as required. |
| | 2. Leakage at gasket, seals, etc. | 2. Remove all traces of lube on exposed surfaces of transmission. Check the vent for free breathing. Operate transmission at normal temperatures and perform fluid leakage check. Service as required. |

**Fig. 1   A4LD automatic overdrive transmission troubleshooting chart (Part 11 of 12)**

| CONDITION | POSSIBLE SOURCE | RESOLUTION |
|---|---|---|
| Poor vehicle acceleration. | 1. Poor engine performance. | 1. Check engine tuneup. |
| | 2. Torque converter one-way clutch locked up. | 2. Replace torque converter. |
| Transmission noisy — valve resonance. | 1. Improper fluid level. | 1. Perform fluid level check. |
| | 2. Linkage out of adjustment. | 2. Service or adjust linkage. |
| | 3. Improper band or clutch application, or oil pressure control system. | 3. Perform control pressure test. |
| NOTE: Gauges may aggravate any hydraulic resonance. Remove gauge and check for resonance level. | 4. Cooler lines grounding. | 4. Free up cooler lines. |
| | 5. Dirty or sticking valve body. | 5. Clean, service or replace valve body. |
| | 6. Internal leakage or pump cavitation. | 6. Service as required. |

**Fig. 1   A4LD automatic overdrive transmission troubleshooting chart (Part 12 of 12)**

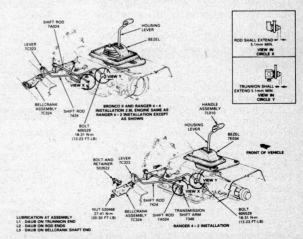

**Fig. 2   Shift control linkage adjustment. Ranger & Bronco II**

2. Insert a .060 inch spacer between throttle lever and adjusting screw, then rotate adjusting screw until it just makes contact with spacer.

3. Remove spacer and weight, then ensure that accelerator returns to idle on slow release of foot pressure, without binding or dragging. Repeat adjustment, if necessary.

## KICKDOWN CABLE ADJUSTMENT

The kickdown cable is self-adjusting and automatically adjusts to a tolerance range of 1 inch during normal operation. However, if the cable requires readjustment, depress the semi-circular metal tab on the self-adjuster, while pulling the cable toward the front of vehicle. The cable will now automatically adjust to proper length during kickdown operation.

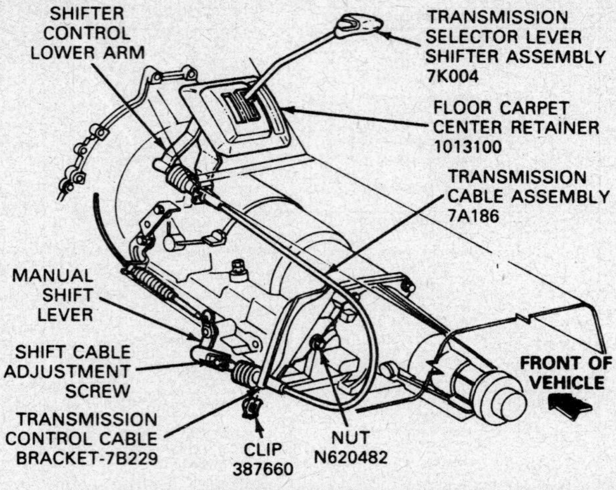

**Fig. 3   Shift control linkage adjustment. Aerostar**

## IN-VEHICLE REPAIRS

### SELECTOR HOUSING, REPLACE

#### Ranger & Bronco II

1. Loosen trunnion bolt and remove trunnion from shift control arm grommet.
2. Remove shifter handle by grasping the handle firmly with the shifter in Drive position, then pulling straight upward.
3. Remove attaching screws, disconnect electrical connectors and remove bezel assembly. On 4 x 4 models, remove transfer case shift boot to housing attaching bolts.
4. Remove selector housing to floor pan attaching bolts, then the selector housing.
5. Reverse procedure to install.

#### Aerostar

1. Working from underneath vehicle, remove cable retaining clip, then disconnect cable from selector lever.
2. Working from inside vehicle, snap off floor carpet center retainer.
3. Remove selector lever housing to floor pan retaining bolts, then the housing.
4. Reverse procedure to install.

### CONTROL VALVE BODY, REPLACE

1. Disconnect battery ground cable.
2. Raise and support vehicle.
3. Loosen pan attaching bolts and drain fluid from transmission.
4. Remove pan and gasket.
5. Remove filter screen and gasket.
6. Remove rear servo cover, piston, spring and gasket.
7. Disconnect converter clutch solenoid electrical leads, if applicable.
8. Remove control valve body attaching bolts, then the valve body.
9. Reverse procedure to install. Torque valve body attaching bolts to 71-97 inch lbs. and oil pan attaching bolts to 12-17 ft. lbs.

### REAR SERVO, REPLACE

1. Disconnect battery ground cable.
2. Starting from rear of pan and working toward front, loosen bolts and allow fluid to drain.
3. Remove all pan attaching bolts and pan.
4. Remove oil filter screen and gasket.
5. Remove rear servo cover, piston, spring and gasket.
6. Reverse procedure to install.

### EXTENSION HOUSING, REPLACE

1. Raise and support vehicle.
2. Scribe alignment marks on driveshaft end yoke and rear axle companion flange, then remove driveshaft.
3. Support transmission with suitable jack, then disconnect speedometer cable from extension housing.
4. Remove rear support to crossmember attaching nuts or bolts, then raise transmission slightly and remove rear support from extension housing.
5. Loosen extension housing attaching bolts and allow transmission to drain.
6. Remove attaching bolts and the extension housing.
7. Reverse procedure to install, noting the following:
   a. When installing housing to case, ensure that parking pawl actuating rod is correctly seated in guide cup bore of housing.
   b. Torque extension housing to case attaching bolts to 27-39 ft. lbs.

### GOVERNOR, REPLACE

1. Remove extension housing as described previously.
2. Remove governor body to oil collector body attaching bolts. Components are not retained once the governor body to oil collector body attaching bolts have been removed. It is therefore necessary to hold the governor body and components while removing or installing.
3. Remove governor body, valve, spring and weight from collector body.

4. Reverse procedure to install.

## TRANSMISSION REPLACE

1. Disconnect battery ground cable.
2. Raise and support vehicle.
3. Loosen pan attaching bolts and allow fluid to drain.
4. Remove converter access cover and adapter plate attaching bolts from lower end of converter housing.
5. Remove four flywheel to converter attaching nuts. **On belt driven overhead camshaft engines, never turn crankshaft opposite the normal direction of rotation.**
6. Remove driveshaft and install extension housing oil seal replacer tool.
7. Disconnect speedometer cable from extension housing.
8. On Ranger and Bronco II models, disconnect shift rod from transmission manual lever.
9. On Aerostar models, proceed as follows:
   a. Disconnect kickdown cable from upper selector lever.
   b. Remove retaining clip from selector cable bracket, then disconnect selector cable from lower selector lever ball stud.
   c. Depress tab on retainer, then disconnect kickdown cable from bracket.
10. On all models, remove starter to converter housing attaching bolts, then position starter aside.
11. Disconnect neutral start switch electrical connectors from switch assembly, then the solenoid connector from converter clutch solenoid, if applicable.
12. Remove vacuum line from transmission vacuum modulator.
13. Position a suitable jack under transmission and raise slightly.
14. Remove engine rear support to crossmember attaching bolts.
15. Remove crossmember to frame side support attaching bolts, then the crossmember insulator and support

damper.
16. Lower jack and allow transmission to hang.
17. Position a suitable jack under engine assembly and raise engine to gain access to the upper two converter housing to engine attaching bolts.
18. Disconnect oil cooler lines from transmission. Cap all openings.
19. Remove lower converter housing to engine attaching bolts.
20. Remove transmission filler tube.
21. Secure transmission to jack using a suitable safety chain.
22. Remove upper converter housing to engine attaching bolts.
23. Remove transmission from vehicle.
24. Reverse procedure to install.

# C3 Automatic Transmission

## INDEX

## DESCRIPTION

The main control incorporates a manually selective first and second gear range. The transmission features a drive range that provides for fully automatic upshifts and downshifts, and manually selected low and second gears.

The transmission consists essentially of a torque converter, a compound planetary gear train, two multiple disc clutches, a one-way clutch and a hydraulic control system, **Fig. 1.**

For all normal driving the selector lever is moved to the green dot under Drive on the selector quadrant on the steering column or on the floor console. As the throttle is advanced from the idle position, the transmission will upshift automatically to intermediate gear and then to high.

With the throttle closed the transmission will downshift automatically as the car speed drops to about 10 mph. With the throttle open at any position up to the detent, the downshifts will come in automatically at speeds above 10 mph and in proportion to throttle opening. This prevents engine lugging on steep hill climbing, for example.

When the selector lever is moved to Low with the transmission in high, the transmission will downshift to intermediate or to low depending on the road speed. At speeds above 25 mph, the downshift will be from high to intermediate. At speeds below 25 mph, the downshift will be from high to low. With the selector lever in the Low position the transmission cannot upshift.

## TROUBLESHOOTING GUIDE

The items to check for each trouble symptom are arranged in a logical sequence that should be followed for quickest results.

### ROUGH INITIAL ENGAGEMENT IN D1 OR D2

1. Engine idle speed.
2. Vacuum diaphragm unit or tubes restricted, leaking or improperly adjusted.
3. Check control pressure.
4. Pressure regulator.
5. Valve body.
6. Forward clutch.

### 1-2 OR 2-3 SHIFT POINTS ERRATIC

1. Check fluid level.
2. Vacuum diaphragm unit or tubes restricted, leaking or improperly adjusted.
3. Intermediate servo.
4. Manual linkage adjustment.
5. Governor.
6. Check control pressure.
7. Valve body.
8. Make air pressure check.

### ROUGH 1-2 UPSHIFTS

1. Vacuum diaphragm unit or tubes restricted, leaking or improperly adjusted.
2. Intermediate servo.
3. Intermediate band.
4. Check control pressure.
5. Valve body.
6. Pressure regulator.

### ROUGH 2-3 UPSHIFTS

1. Vacuum diaphragm unit or tubes restricted, leaking or improperly adjusted.
2. Intermediate servo.
3. Check control pressure.
4. Pressure regulator.
5. Intermediate band.
6. Valve body.
7. Make air pressure check.
8. Reverse-high clutch.
9. Reverse-high clutch piston air bleed valve.

### DRAGGED OUT 1-2 SHIFT

1. Check fluid level.
2. Vacuum diaphragm unit or tubes restricted, leaking or improperly adjusted.
3. Intermediate servo.
4. Check control pressure.
5. Intermediate band.
6. Valve body.
7. Pressure regulator.
8. Make air pressure check.
9. Leakage in hydraulic system.

### ENGINE OVERSPEEDS ON 2-3 SHIFT

1. Manual linkage.
2. Check fluid level.
3. Vacuum diaphragm unit or tubes re-

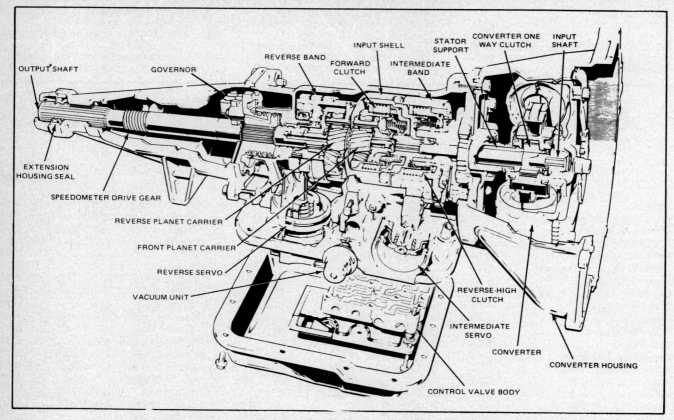

**Fig. 1  Sectional view of C3 automatic transmission**

stricted, leaking or improperly adjusted.
4. Reverse servo.
5. Check control pressure.
6. Valve body.
7. Pressure regulator.
8. Intermediate band.
9. Reverse-high clutch.
10. Reverse-high clutch piston air bleed valve.

## NO 1-2 OR 2-3 SHIFT

1. Manual linkage.
2. Downshift linkage, including inner lever position.
3. Vacuum diaphragm unit or tubes restricted, leaking or improperly adjusted.
4. Governor.
5. Check control pressure.
6. Valve body.
7. Intermediate band.
8. Intermediate servo.
9. Reverse-high clutch.
10. Reverse-high clutch piston air bleed valve.

## NO 3-1 SHIFT IN D1 OR 3-2 SHIFT IN D2

1. Governor.
2. Valve body.

## NO FORCED DOWNSHIFTS

1. Downshift linkage, including inner lever position.
2. Valve body.
3. Vacuum diaphragm or tubes restricted, leaking or improperly adjusted.

## RUNAWAY ENGINE ON FORCED 3-2 DOWNSHIFT

1. Check control pressure.
2. Intermediate servo.
3. Intermediate band.
4. Pressure regulator.
5. Valve body.
6. Vacuum diaphragm unit or tubes restricted, leaking or improperly adjusted.
7. Leakage in hydraulic system.

## ROUGH 3-2 OR 3-1 SHIFT AT CLOSED THROTTLE

1. Engine idle speed.
2. Vacuum diaphragm unit or tubes restricted, leaking or improperly adjusted.
3. Intermediate servo.
4. Valve body.
5. Pressure regulator.

## SHIFTS 1-3 IN D1 AND D2

1. Intermediate band.
2. Intermediate servo.
3. Vacuum diaphragm unit or tubes restricted, leaking or improperly adjusted.
4. Valve body.
5. Governor.
6. Make air pressure check.

## NO ENGINE BRAKING IN 1ST GEAR—MANUAL LOW

1. Manual linkage.

2. Reverse band.
3. Reverse servo.
4. Valve body.
5. Governor.
6. Make air pressure check.

## SLIPS OR CHATTERS IN 1ST GEAR—D1

1. Check fluid level.
2. Vacuum diaphragm unit or tubes restricted, leaking or improperly adjusted.
3. Check control pressure.
4. Press regulator.
5. Valve body.
6. Forward clutch.
7. Leakage in hydraulic system.
8. Planetary one-way clutch.

## SLIPS OR CHATTERS IN 2ND GEAR

1. Check fluid level.
2. Vacuum diaphragm unit or tubes restricted, leaking or improperly adjusted.
3. Intermediate servo.
4. Intermediate band.
5. Check control pressure.
6. Pressure regulator.
7. Valve body.
8. Make air pressure check.
9. Forward clutch.
10. Leakage in hydraulic system.

## SLIPS OR CHATTERS IN REVERSE

1. Check fluid level.

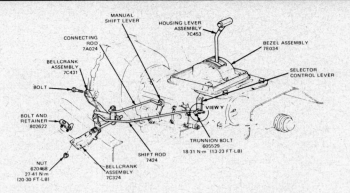

**Fig. 2  Shift linkage adjustment (Typical)**

2. Vacuum diaphragm unit or tubes restricted, leaking or improperly adjusted.
3. Reverse band.
4. Check control pressure.
5. Reverse servo.
6. Pressure regulator.
7. Valve body.
8. Make air pressure check.
9. Reverse-high clutch.
10. Leakage in hydraulic system.
11. Reverse-high piston air bleed valve.

## NO DRIVE IN D1 ONLY

1. Check fluid level.
2. Manual linkage.
3. Check control pressure.
4. Valve body.
5. Make air pressure check.
6. Planetary one-way clutch.

## NO DRIVE IN D2 ONLY

1. Check fluid level.
2. Manual linkage.
3. Check control pressure.
4. Intermediate servo.
5. Valve body.
6. Make air pressure check.
7. Leakage in hydraulic system.
8. Planetary one-way clutch.

## NO DRIVE IN LOW ONLY

1. Check fluid level.
2. Manual linkage.
3. Check control pressure.
4. Valve body.
5. Reverse servo.
6. Make air pressure check.
7. Leakage in hydraulic system.
8. Planetary one-way clutch.

## NO DRIVE IN REVERSE ONLY

1. Check fluid level.
2. Manual linkage.
3. Reverse band.
4. Check control pressure.
5. Reverse servo.
6. Valve body.
7. Make air pressure check.
8. Reverse-high clutch.
9. Leakage in hydraulic system.
10. Reverse-high clutch piston air bleed valve.

## NO DRIVE IN ANY SELECTOR POSITION

1. Check fluid level.
2. Manual linkage.
3. Check control pressure.
4. Pressure regulator.
5. Valve body.
6. Make air pressure check.
7. Leakage in hydraulic system.
8. Front pump.

## LOCKUP IN D1 ONLY

1. Reverse-high clutch.
2. Parking linkage.
3. Leakage in hydraulic system.

## LOCKUP IN D2 ONLY

1. Reverse band.
2. Reverse servo.
3. Reverse-high clutch.
4. Parking linkage.
5. Leakage in hydraulic system.
6. Planetary one-way clutch.

## LOCKUP IN LOW ONLY

1. Intermediate band.
2. Intermediate servo.
3. Reverse-high clutch.
4. Parking linkage.
5. Leakage in hydraulic system.

## LOCKUP IN REVERSE ONLY

1. Intermediate band.
2. Intermediate servo.
3. Forward clutch.
4. Parking linkage.
5. Leakage in hydraulic system.

## PARKING LOCK BINDS OR DOES NOT HOLD

1. Manual linkage.
2. Parking linkage.

## MAXIMUM SPEED TOO LOW, POOR ACCELERATION

1. Engine performance.
2. Brakes bind.
3. Converter one-way clutch.

## NOISY IN NEUTRAL OR PARK

1. Check fluid level.
2. Pressure regulator.

3. Front pump.
4. Planetary assembly.

## NOISY IN ALL GEARS

1. Check fluid level.
2. Pressure regulator.
3. Planetary assembly.
4. Forward clutch.
5. Front pump.
6. Planetary one-way clutch.

## TRUCK MOVES FORWARD IN N

1. Manual linkage.
2. Forward clutch.

# MAINTENANCE

## CHECKING OIL LEVEL

1. Make sure vehicle is on a level floor.
2. Apply parking brake firmly.
3. Run engine at normal idle speed. If transmission fluid is cold, run engine at a fast idle until fluid reaches normal operating temperature. When fluid is warm, slow engine to normal idle speed.
4. Shift selector lever through all positions, then place lever at P. Do not shut down engine during fluid level checks.
5. Clean all dirt from dipstick cap before removing dipstick from filler tube.
6. Pull dipstick out of tube, wipe it clean and push it all the way back in tube.
7. Pull dipstick out of tube again and check fluid level. If necessary, add enough fluid to raise the level to the F mark on dipstick. Do not overfill.

## DRAIN & REFILL

The Ford Motor Company recommends the use of an automatic transmission fluid with Qualification No. M2C-138-CJ or Dexron II for all models. The recommended fluid is said to have a greater coefficient of friction and greater ability to handle maximum engine torques without band or clutch slippage.

Normal maintenance and lubrication requirements do not necessitate periodic fluid changes. If a major failure has occurred in the transmission, it will have to be removed for service. At this time the converter and transmission cooler must be thoroughly flushed to remove any foreign matter.

When filling a dry transmission and converter, add five quarts of fluid. Start engine, shift the selector lever through all ranges and place in a R position. Check fluid level and add enough to raise the level in the transmission to the F (full) mark on the dipstick.

When a partial drain and refill is required due to front band adjustment or minor repair, proceed as follows:
1. Loosen and remove all but two oil pan bolts and drop one edge of the pan to drain the oil.
2. Remove and clean pan and screen.
3. Place a new gasket on pan and install pan and screen.
4. Add three quarts of fluid to transmission.

5. Run engine at idle speed for about two minutes.
6. Check oil level and add oil as necessary.
7. Run engine at a fast idle until it reaches normal operating temperature.
8. Shift selector lever through all ranges and then place it in R position.
9. Add fluid as required to bring the level to the full mark.

## IN-VEHICLE ADJUSTMENTS
### SHIFT LINKAGE, ADJUST

1. Place transmission selector control lever into Drive position, then loosen trunnion bolt, **Fig. 2.** Ensure shift lever detent pawl is held against the rearward Drive detent stop during shift linkage adjustment.
2. Place transmission manual lever into Drive range by moving bellcrank lever completely rearward, then forward three detents.
3. With transmission selector lever and manual lever in Drive position, apply a light forward pressure onto the shifter control lower arm while tightening the trunnion bolt. Torque bolt to 13-23 ft. lbs. Forward pressure on shifter lower arm will ensure correct positioning within the Drive detent.
4. After adjustment has been completed, check for proper Park engagement. Control lever must move to right when engaged in Park.

### FRONT BAND, ADJUST

1. Remove downshift rod from transmission downshift lever.
2. Clean area around band adjusting screw, then remove and discard locknut.
3. Install a new locknut onto adjusting screw.
4. Using tool kit T71P-7737-A or equivalent, tighten adjusting screw until tool handle -clicks.- The tool kit is a preset torque wrench that clicks and breaks when the torque on the adjusting screw reaches 10 ft. lbs.
5. Back off adjusting screw 2 turns, then holding the adjusting screw from turning, torque adjusting screw locknut to 35-45 ft. lbs.
6. Install downshift rod onto transmission downshift lever.

## IN-VEHICLE REPAIRS
### VALVE BODY, REPLACE

1. Disconnect battery ground cable.
2. Raise and support vehicle.
3. Loosen oil pan attaching bolts and drain fluid from transmission.
4. Remove oil pan and gasket.
5. Remove filter screen and gasket.
6. Remove rear servo cover and gasket.
7. Remove valve body attaching bolts, then the valve body from transmission. Ensure that selector lever connecting rod properly disengages from valve body.

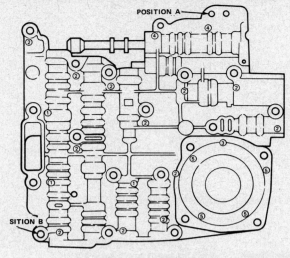

**Fig. 3   Valve body bolt hole location**

| Position | Bolt Size Metric | Length in Millimeters | Length in Inches |
|---|---|---|---|
| 1 | M6 x 45 | 45mm | 1.772 |
| 2 | M6 x 40 | 40.1mm | 1.578 |
| 3 | M6 x 35 | 35mm | 1.378 |
| 4 | M6 x 30 | 29mm | 1.141 |
| 5 | M6 x 20 | 20mm | .787 |

| Position | Quantity | Torque N-m | Torque Ft-Lb |
|---|---|---|---|
| 1 | 3 | 8-11 | 6-8 |
| 2 | 12 | 8-11 | 6-8 |
| 3 | 1 | 8-11 | 6-8 |
| 4 | 2 | 8-11 | 6-8 |
| 5 | 4 | 9.5-13.5 | 7-10 |

8. Reverse procedure to install. During installation of valve body, proceed as follows:
  a. Insert the correct length bolts finger tight in holes A and B to position valve body correctly on case, **Fig. 3.**
  b. Insert all remaining bolts, except the filter screen bolts, and tighten to specifications given in **Fig. 3.**

### REAR SERVO, REPLACE

1. Disconnect battery ground cable.
2. Raise and support vehicle.
3. Loosen oil pan attaching bolts and drain fluid from transmission.
4. Remove oil pan and gasket.
5. Remove oil filter screen and gasket.
6. Remove servo attaching bolts, then the rear servo cover, servo and gasket.
7. Reverse procedure to install.

### EXTENSION HOUSING, REPLACE

1. Disconnect battery ground cable.
2. Raise and support vehicle.
3. Remove propeller shaft from vehicle.
4. Position a suitable jack under transmission.
5. Disconnect speedometer cable from extension housing.
6. Remove rear support to crossmember bolts or nuts.
7. Raise transmission slightly, then remove rear support assembly from extension housing.
8. Loosen extension housing to transmission case attaching bolts and allow fluid to drain.
9. Remove extension housing from transmission case.
10. Reverse procedure to install. Torque extension housing to transmission case attaching bolts to 27-39 ft. lbs.

### GOVERNOR, REPLACE

1. Disconnect battery ground cable.
2. Remove extension housing as described under "Extension Housing, Replace."
3. Remove governor body to oil collector body attaching bolts, then the governor.
4. Reverse procedure to install.

## TRANSMISSION REPLACE
### EXC. RANGER & BRONCO II

1. Raise and support vehicle.
2. Place a drain pan under transmission oil pan, then, starting at rear, loosen attaching bolts and drain fluid from transmission. Leave two bolts in front and reinstall two bolts on rear of oil pan to temporarily hold it in place.
3. Remove converter drain plug access cover and adapter plate bolts from lower end of converter housing.
4. Remove converter to flywheel attaching nuts, rotating crankshaft with suitable wrench. **On engines with belt driven overhead camshaft, do not rotate crankshaft opposite normal direction of rotation.**
5. Rotate converter to gain access to converter drain plug, then remove the plug. After fluid has drained from converter, reinstall drain plug and torque to 20-30 ft. lbs.
6. Remove driveshaft, then install extension housing seal replacer tool in extension housing.
7. Remove speedometer cable from extension housing, then disconnect shift rod from transmission manual lever and the downshift rod from transmission downshift lever.
8. Remove starter to converter housing attaching bolts and position starter motor aside.
9. Disconnect neutral start switch wires from the switch, then remove vacuum line from transmission vacuum modulator.
10. Position a suitable transmission jack under transmission and raise it slightly, then remove engine rear support to crossmember attaching bolts.

11. Remove crossmember to frame side support attaching bolts, then the crossmember insulator and support and damper.
12. Lower the transmission jack, then position a suitable jack under front of engine and raise engine to gain access to the two upper converter housing to engine attaching bolts.
13. Disconnect oil cooler lines from transmission. Plug all openings to prevent contamination.
14. Remove lower converter housing to engine attaching bolts, then the transmission filler tube.
15. Install a safety chain to hold transmission on jack, then remove two upper converter housing to engine attaching bolts.
16. Move transmission rearward and lower it from vehicle.
17. Reverse procedure to install. Note the following torques: converter housing to engine bolts, 28-38 ft. lbs.; filler tube bolt, 28-38 ft. lbs.; crossmember to frame side rail bolts, 20-30 ft. lbs.; rear engine to crossmember bolt, 60-80 ft. lbs.; starter bolts, 15-20 ft. lbs.; flywheel to converter nuts, 20-34 ft. lbs.; converter drain plug access cover and adapter plate bolts, 12-16 ft. lbs.; companion flange bolts, 70-95 ft. lbs.

## RANGER & BRONCO II

1. Disconnect battery ground cable.
2. Raise and support vehicle.
3. Place a suitable fluid drain pan under transmission oil pan.
4. Starting from the rear of the pan and working toward the front, loosen transmission fluid pan attaching bolts and allow fluid to drain.
5. Remove all transmission fluid pan attaching bolts except two front bolts. After all transmission fluid has drained, temporarily install two pan rear bolts.
6. Remove converter drain plug access cover and adapter plate attaching bolts from lower end of the converter housing.
7. Remove four flywheel to converter attaching nuts. Crank engine to turn converter to gain access to the converter nuts.
8. Remove converter drain plug and drain fluid from converter. After all the fluid has drained, install plug and torque to 20-30 ft. lbs.
9. Remove drive shaft from transmission and install seal protector tool onto transmission extension housing.
10. Disconnect speedometer cable from extension housing.
11. Disconnect shift rod from transmission manual lever. Disconnect downshift rod from transmission downshift lever.
12. Remove starter to converter housing attaching bolts and position starter aside.
13. Disconnect neutral start switch electrical connectors from switch.
14. Disconnect vacuum line from transmission vacuum modulator.
15. Position a suitable jack under transmission and raise transmission assembly slightly.
16. Remove engine rear support to crossmember attaching bolts.
17. Remove engine rear support to crossmember attaching bolts.
18. Remove crossmember insulator, support and damper.
19. Lower jack supporting transmission and allow transmission to hang.
20. Position a suitable jack onto front of engine, then raise engine to gain access to the 2 upper converter housing to engine attaching bolts.
21. Disconnect and cap oil cooler lines from transmission.
22. Remove lower converter housing to engine attaching bolts.
23. Remove transmission oil filler tube.
24. Secure transmission to the jack with a safety chain.
25. Remove two upper converter housing to engine attaching bolts. Move transmission rearward and downward and remove from vehicle.
26. Reverse procedure to install. During installation of transmission, do not tilt front of transmission downward, as this will cause the converter to move forward and disengage from the pump gear. The converter must rest against the flywheel. This indicates that the converter pilot is not binding in the engine crankshaft.

# C4 Automatic Transmission

## INDEX

## DESCRIPTION

The main control incorporates a manually selective first and second gear range. The transmission features a drive range that provides for fully automatic upshifts and downshifts, and manually selected low and second gears.

The transmission consists essentially of a torque converter, a compound planetary gear train, two multiple disc clutches, a one-way clutch and a hydraulic control system, **Fig. 1.**

For all normal driving the selector lever is moved to the green dot under Drive on the selector quadrant on the steering column or on the floor console. As the throttle is advanced from the idle position, the transmission will upshift automatically to intermediate gear and then to high.

With the throttle closed the transmission will downshift automatically as the vehicle speed drops to about 10 mph. With the throttle open at any position up to the detent, the downshifts will come in automatically at speeds above 10 mph and in proportion to throttle opening. This prevents engine lugging on steep hill climbing, for example.

When the selector lever is moved to L with the transmission in high, the transmission will downshift to intermediate or to low depending on the road speed. At speed above 25 mph, the downshift will be from high to intermediate. At speeds below 25 mph, the downshift will be from high to low. With the selector lever in the L position the transmission cannot upshift.

## TROUBLESHOOTING GUIDE

The items to check for each trouble symptom are arranged in a logical sequence that should be followed for quickest results.

## ROUGH INITIAL ENGAGEMENT IN D1 OR D2

1. Engine idle speed.
2. Vacuum diaphragm unit or tubes restricted, leaking or improperly adjusted.
3. Check control pressure.
4. Pressure regulator.
5. Valve body.
6. Forward clutch.

## 1–2 OR 2–3 SHIFT POINTS ERRATIC

1. Check fluid level.
2. Vacuum diaphragm unit or tubes restricted, leaking or improperly adjusted.
3. Intermediate servo.
4. Manual linkage adjustment.
5. Governor.
6. Check control pressure.
7. Valve body.
8. Make air pressure check.

## ROUGH 1-2 UPSHIFTS

1. Vacuum diaphragm unit or tubes restricted, leaking or improperly adjusted.
2. Intermediate servo.
3. Intermediate band.
4. Check control pressure.
5. Valve body.
6. Pressure regulator.

## ROUGH 2-3 UPSHIFTS

1. Vacuum diaphragm unit or tubes restricted, leaking or improperly adjusted.
2. Intermediate servo.
3. Check control pressure.
4. Pressure regulator.
5. Intermediate band.
6. Valve body.
7. Make air pressure check.

8. Reverse-high clutch.
9. Reverse-high clutch piston air bleed valve.

## DRAGGED OUT 1-2 SHIFT

1. Check fluid level.
2. Vacuum diaphragm unit or tubes restricted, leaking or improperly adjusted.
3. Intermediate servo.
4. Check control pressure.
5. Intermediate band.
6. Valve body.
7. Pressure regulator.
8. Make air pressure check.
9. Leakage in hydraulic system.

## ENGINE OVERSPEEDS ON 2-3 SHIFT

1. Manual linkage.
2. Check fluid level.
3. Vacuum diaphragm unit or tubes restricted, leaking or improperly adjusted.
4. Reverse servo.
5. Check control pressure.
6. Valve body.
7. Pressure regulator.
8. Intermediate band.
9. Reverse-high clutch.
10. Reverse-high clutch piston air bleed valve.

## NO 1-2 OR 2-3 SHIFT

1. Manual linkage.
2. Downshift linkage, including inner lever position.
3. Vacuum diaphragm unit or tubes restricted, leaking or improperly adjusted.
4. Governor.
5. Check control pressure.
6. Valve body.
7. Intermediate band.
8. Intermediate servo.
9. Reverse-high clutch.

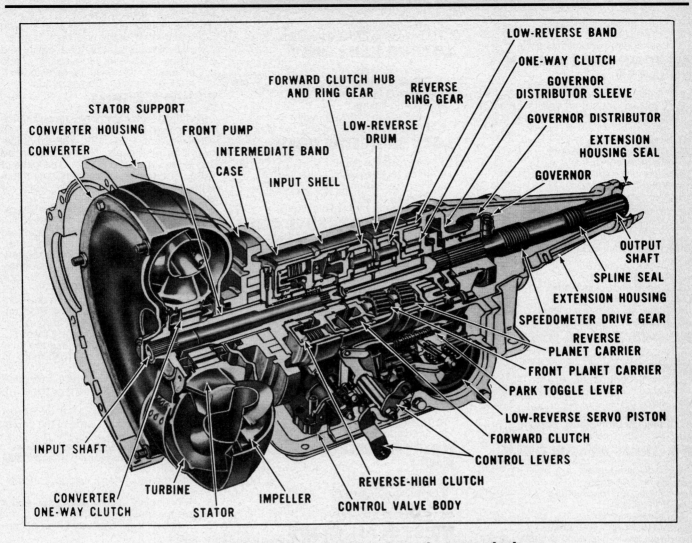

LOW-REVERSE BAND
ONE-WAY CLUTCH
GOVERNOR DISTRIBUTOR SLEEVE
GOVERNOR DISTRIBUTOR
EXTENSION HOUSING SEAL
GOVERNOR
FORWARD CLUTCH HUB AND RING GEAR
REVERSE RING GEAR
LOW-REVERSE DRUM
STATOR SUPPORT
CONVERTER HOUSING
FRONT PUMP
CONVERTER
INTERMEDIATE BAND
CASE
INPUT SHELL
OUTPUT SHAFT
SPLINE SEAL
EXTENSION HOUSING
SPEEDOMETER DRIVE GEAR
REVERSE PLANET CARRIER
FRONT PLANET CARRIER
PARK TOGGLE LEVER
LOW-REVERSE SERVO PISTON
FORWARD CLUTCH
CONTROL LEVERS
REVERSE-HIGH CLUTCH
CONTROL VALVE BODY
INPUT SHAFT
CONVERTER ONE-WAY CLUTCH
TURBINE
STATOR
IMPELLER

**Fig. 1  Sectional view of C4 automatic transmission**

10. Reverse-high clutch piston air bleed valve.

## NO 3-1 SHIFT IN D1 OR 3-2 SHIFT IN D2

1. Governor.
2. Valve body.

## NO FORCED DOWNSHIFTS

1. Downshift linkage, including inner lever position.
2. Valve body.
3. Vacuum diaphragm unit or tubes restricted, leaking or improperly adjusted.

## RUNAWAY ENGINE ON FORCED 3-2 DOWNSHIFT

1. Check control pressure.
2. Intermediate servo.
3. Intermediate band.
4. Pressure regulator.
5. Valve body.
6. Vacuum diaphragm unit or tubes restricted, leaking or improperly adjusted.
7. Leakage in hydraulic system.

## ROUGH 3-2 OR 3-1 SHIFT AT CLOSED THROTTLE

1. Engine idle speed.
2. Vacuum diaphragm unit or tubes restricted, leaking or improperly adjusted.
3. Intermediate servo.
4. Valve body.
5. Pressure regulator.

## SHIFTS 1-3 IN D1 & D2

1. Intermediate band.
2. Intermediate servo.
3. Vacuum diaphragm unit or tubes restricted, leaking or improperly adjusted.
4. Valve body.
5. Governor.
6. Make air pressure check.

## NO ENGINE BRAKING IN 1ST GEAR—MANUAL LOW

1. Manual linkage.
2. Reverse band.
3. Reverse servo.
4. Valve body.

5. Governor.
6. Make air pressure check.

## SLIPS OR CHATTERS IN 1ST GEAR—D1

1. Check fluid level.
2. Vacuum diaphragm unit or tubes restricted, leaking or improperly adjusted.
3. Check control pressure.
4. Press regulator.
5. Valve body.
6. Forward clutch.
7. Leakage in hydraulic system.
8. Planetary one-way clutch.

## SLIPS OR CHATTERS IN 2ND GEAR

1. Check fluid level.
2. Vacuum diaphragm unit or tubes restricted, leaking or improperly adjusted.
3. Intermediate servo.
4. Intermediate band.
5. Check control pressure.
6. Pressure regulator.
7. Valve body.

8. Make air pressure check.
9. Forward clutch.
10. Leakage in hydraulic system.

## SLIPS OR CHATTERS IN REVERSE

1. Check fluid level.
2. Vacuum diaphragm unit or tubes restricted, leaking or improperly adjusted.
3. Reverse band.
4. Check control pressure.
5. Reverse servo.
6. Pressure regulator.
7. Valve body.
8. Make air pressure check.
9. Reverse-high clutch.
10. Leakage in hydraulic system.
11. Reverse-high piston air bleed valve.

## NO DRIVE IN D1 ONLY

1. Check fluid level.
2. Manual linkage.
3. Check control pressure.
4. Valve body.
5. Make air pressure check.
6. Planetary one-way clutch.

## NO DRIVE IN D2 ONLY

1. Check fluid level.
2. Manual linkage.
3. Check control pressure.
4. Intermediate servo.
5. Valve body.
6. Make air pressure check.
7. Leakage in hydraulic system.
8. Planetary one-way clutch.

## NO DRIVE IN LOW ONLY

1. Check fluid level.
2. Manual linkage.
3. Check control pressure.
4. Valve body.
5. Reverse servo.
6. Make air pressure check.
7. Leakage in hydraulic system.
8. Planetary one-way clutch.

## NO DRIVE IN REVERSE ONLY

1. Check fluid level.
2. Manual linkage.
3. Reverse band.
4. Check control pressure.
5. Reverse servo.
6. Valve body.
7. Make air pressure check.
8. Reverse-high clutch.
9. Leakage in hydraulic system.
10. Reverse-high clutch piston air bleed valve.

## NO DRIVE IN ANY SELECTOR POSITION

1. Check fluid level.
2. Manual linkage.
3. Check control pressure.
4. Pressure regulator.
5. Valve body.
6. Make air pressure check.
7. Leakage in hydraulic system.
8. Front pump.

## LOCKUP IN D1 ONLY

1. Reverse-high clutch.

2. Parking linkage.
3. Leakage in hydraulic system.

## LOCKUP IN D2 ONLY

1. Reverse band.
2. Reverse servo.
3. Reverse-high clutch.
4. Parking linkage.
5. Leakage in hydraulic system.
6. Planetary one-way clutch.

## LOCKUP IN LOW ONLY

1. Intermediate band.
2. Intermediate servo.
3. Reverse-high clutch.
4. Parking linkage.
5. Leakage in hydraulic system.

## LOCKUP IN REVERSE ONLY

1. Intermediate band.
2. Intermediate servo.
3. Forward clutch.
4. Parking linkage.
5. Leakage in hydraulic system.

## PARKING LOCK BINDS OR DOES NOT HOLD

1. Manual linkage.
2. Parking linkage.

## MAXIMUM SPEED TOO LOW, POOR ACCELERATION

1. Engine performance.
2. Brakes bind.
3. Converter one-way clutch.

## NOISY IN NEUTRAL OR PARK

1. Check fluid level.
2. Pressure regulator.
3. Front pump.
4. Planetary assembly.

## NOISY IN ALL GEARS

1. Check fluid level.
2. Pressure regulator.
3. Planetary assembly.
4. Forward clutch.
5. Front pump.
6. Planetary one-way clutch.

## TRUCK MOVES FORWARD IN NEUTRAL

1. Manual linkage.
2. Forward clutch.

## MAINTENANCE

### CHECKING OIL LEVEL

1. Make sure vehicle is on a level floor.
2. Apply parking brake firmly.
3. Run engine at normal idle speed. If transmission fluid is cold, run engine at a fast idle until fluid reaches normal operating temperature. When fluid is warm, slow engine to normal idle speed.
4. Shift selector lever through all positions, then place lever at P. Do not shut down engine during fluid level checks.
5. Clean all dirt from dipstick cap before removing dipstick from filler tube.

6. Pull dipstick out of tube, wipe it clean and push it all the way back in tube.
7. Pull dipstick out of tube again and check fluid level. If necessary, add enough fluid to raise the level to the F mark on dipstick. Do not overfill.

### DRAIN & REFILL

The Ford Motor Company recommends the use of an automatic transmission fluid with Qualification No. M2C-138-CJ or Dexron II for all models. The recommended fluid is said to have a greater coefficient of friction and greater ability to handle maximum engine torques without band or clutch slippage.

Normal maintenance and lubrication requirements do not necessitate periodic fluid changes. If a major failure has occurred in the transmission, it will have to be removed for service. At this time the converter and transmission cooler must be thoroughly flushed to remove any foreign matter.

When filling a dry transmission and converter, install five quarts of fluid. Start engine, shift the selector lever through all ranges and place it a R position. Check fluid level and add enough to raise the level in the transmission to the F (full) mark on the dipstick.

When a partial drain and refill is required due to front band adjustment or minor repair, proceed as follows:

1. Loosen and remove all but two oil pan bolts and drop one edge of the pan to drain the oil.
2. Remove and clean pan and screen.
3. Place a new gasket on pan and install pan and screen.
4. Add three quarts of fluid to transmission.
5. Run engine at idle speed for about two minutes.
6. Check oil level and add oil as necessary.
7. Run engine at a fast idle until it reaches normal operating temperature.
8. Shift selector lever through all ranges and then place it in R position.
9. Add fluid as required to bring the level to the full mark.

## IN-VEHICLE ADJUSTMENTS

### SHIFT LINKAGE, ADJUST

1. Disconnect battery ground cable.
2. Place transmission selector lever on steering column into Drive position. Secure selector lever in this position.
3. Loosen shift for adjusting nut at point A, **Figs. 2 through 5.**
4. Place transmission manual lever into Drive position by moving lever completely rearward, then forward 2 detents.
5. With selector lever and transmission lever in Drive position, torque nut at point A to 12-18 ft. lbs.

### THROTTLE LINKAGE, ADJUST

1. Rotate throttle to wide open position.
2. Insert a .060 inch feeler gauge be-

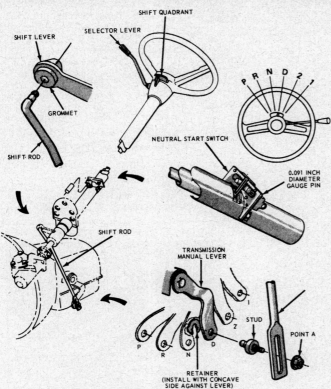

**Fig. 2   Shift linkage adjustment. F100–350 exc. 4 x 4**

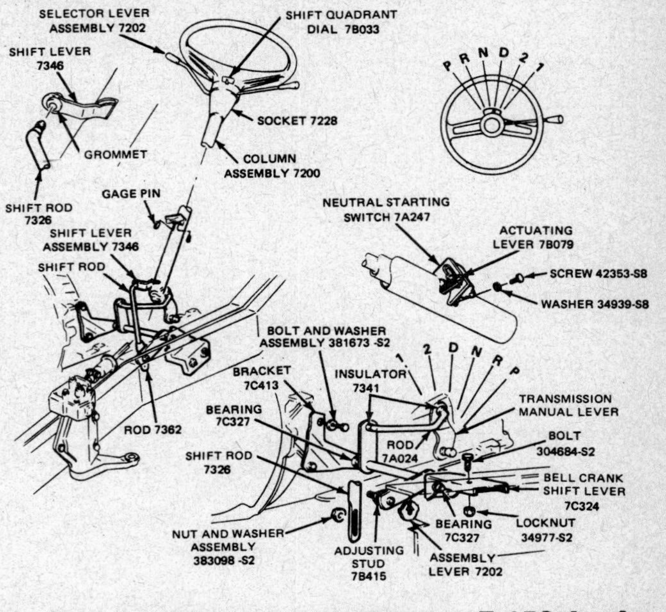

**Fig. 3   Shift linkage adjustment. F-150 4 x 4**

tween throttle lever and adjusting screw.
3. Rotate transmission kickdown lever until lever engages transmission internal stop. **Do not use kickdown rod to rotate transmission lever.**
4. Rotate adjusting screw until contact is made between adjusting screw and .060 inch feeler gauge, then tighten locknut.
5. Remove .060 inch feeler gauge.

## INTERMEDIATE BAND, ADJUST

### Transmissions Built Prior To Jan. 5, 1981

1. Loosen locknut several turns.
2. With tool shown in **Fig. 6** tighten adjusting screw until tool handle clicks. This tool is a pre-set torque wrench which clicks and overruns when the torque on the adjusting screw reaches 10 ft. lbs.
3. Back off adjusting screw exactly 1³/₄ turns.
4. Hold adjusting screw from turning and tighten locknut.

### Transmissions Built After Jan. 4, 1981

These transmissions are equipped with a new intermediate band adjuster screw and nut using a fine pitch ¹/₂-28 thread. When performing a band adjustment on these models, use the following procedure:

1. Remove and discard locknut.
2. Install new locknut on adjusting screw

and torque to 10 ft. lbs.
3. Back off adjusting screw exactly three turns.
4. Hold adjusting screw from turning, then torque locknut to 40 ft. lbs. This procedure applies to new model cases with a yellow trademark. The fine adjusting screw can be identified by an identification rib on strut end.

## LOW-REVERSE BAND

1. Loosen locknut several turns.
2. Tighten adjusting screw until tool handle clicks, **Fig. 7.** Tool shown is a pre-set torque wrench which clicks and overruns when the torque on the adjusting screw reaches 10 ft. lbs.
3. Back off adjusting screw exactly 3 full turns.
4. Hold adjusting screw from turning and tighten locknut.

# IN-VEHICLE REPAIRS
## VALVE BODY, REPLACE

1. Disconnect battery ground cable.
2. Raise and support vehicle.
3. Remove fluid filler tube from oil pan and drain fluid from transmission.
4. Remove oil pan attaching bolts, pan and gasket.
5. Place transmission manual lever into Park position, then remove 2 bolts securing detent spring to valve body and transmission case.
6. Remove remaining valve body to case attaching bolts, then while holding manual valve inward, remove

valve body from transmission. **Failure to hold manual valve inward while removing valve body, may result in damage to valve.**
7. Reverse procedure to install. Torque valve body to transmission case attaching bolts to 80-120 inch lbs.

## INTERMEDIATE SERVO, REPLACE

1. Disconnect battery ground cable.
2. Raise and support vehicle.
3. Disconnect and cap forward transmission fluid cooler line.
4. Remove 4 servo cover to transmission case bolts.
5. Disconnect vacuum line from transmission, then remove servo cover, gasket, piston and piston return spring.
6. Reverse procedure to install. Torque intermediate servo to transmission case bolts to 16-22 ft. lbs.

## LOW-REVERSE SERVO, REPLACE

1. Disconnect battery ground cable.
2. Raise and support vehicle.
3. Loosen reverse band adjusting screw locknut. Torque reverse band adjusting screw to 10 ft. lbs.
4. Remove 4 servo cover to transmission case attaching bolts. Remove vent tube retaining clip, servo cover and seal from transmission case.
5. Remove servo piston from transmission case.
6. Reverse procedure to install. Torque low-reverse servo cover to transmission case bolts to 12-20 ft. lbs.

## EXTENSION HOUSING, REPLACE

### E-100, 150, F-100—250 Models

1. Disconnect battery ground cable.

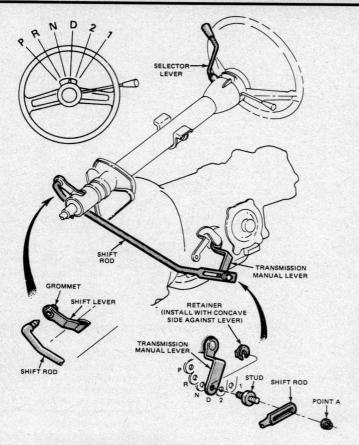

**Fig. 4  Shift linkage adjustment. Bronco**

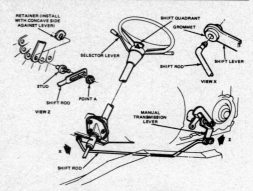

**Fig. 5  Shift linkage adjustment. E100–350**

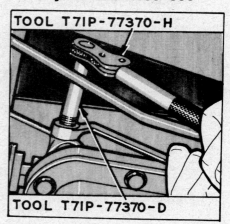

**Fig. 6  Intermediate band adjustment**

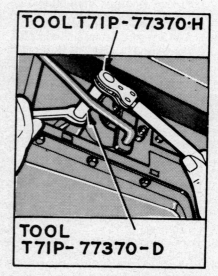

**Fig. 7  Low-reverse band adjustment**

2. Raise and support vehicle.
3. Remove propeller shaft from vehicle. Scribe alignment marks on propeller shaft yoke and companion flange to ensure proper positioning during assembly.
4. Position a suitable jack under transmission.
5. Disconnect speedometer cable from extension housing.
6. Remove crossmember to extension housing attaching bolts.
7. Loosen extension housing to transmission case attaching bolts and drain fluid from transmission.
8. Remove 6 extension housing to transmission case attaching bolts, then the extension housing and gasket.
9. Reverse procedure to install. Torque extension housing to transmission case attaching bolts to 28-40 ft. lbs.

## GOVERNOR, REPLACE

### E100, 150, F100–250 Models

1. Disconnect battery ground cable.
2. Raise and support vehicle.
3. Remove extension housing as described under "Extension Housing, Replace."
4. Remove governor housing to governor distributor attaching bolts.
5. Remove governor housing from distributor.
6. Reverse procedure to install. Torque

governor housing to governor distributor bolts to 80-120 inch lbs.

### Bronco Models

1. Disconnect battery ground cable.
2. Remove fan shroud from radiator.
3. Raise and support vehicle.
4. Remove transfer case shield, if equipped.
5. Remove drain plug from transfer case and drain lubricant.
6. Disconnect front and rear driveshafts from transfer case assembly and position aside.
7. Disconnect speedometer cable from transfer case assembly.
8. Disconnect shift rod from transfer case shift lever bracket.
9. Remove bolts, washers, plates and insulators securing crossmember to transfer case adapter.
10. Remove crossmember to frame side support attaching bolts.
11. Position a suitable jack under transmission and transfer case assemblies.
12. Raise transmission and transfer case assembly slightly, then remove 4 bolts securing left side support bracket to frame. Remove side support bracket, crossmember and upper crossmember insulators from vehicle.
13. Remove bolts securing shift lever bracket to transfer case adapter. Allow assembly to hang by the shift lever.

14. Remove transfer case to transmission case attaching bolts. Remove transfer case from vehicle.
15. Remove governor housing to governor distributor attaching bolts. Remove governor housing from distributor.
16. Reverse procedure to install.

# TRANSMISSION REPLACE

## EXC. BRONCO & ECONOLINE

1. Drain transmission and converter.
2. Remove drive shaft.
3. Disconnect oil cooler lines from transmission.
4. Remove downshift lever return spring from low-reverse servo cover.
5. Disconnect shift rods from transmission levers.
6. Disconnect neutral start switch wiring harness and back-up wires at connectors, then retaining clips and retainer.
7. Remove speedometer gear from extension housing.
8. Remove four converter to flywheel bolts.
9. Remove starter.
10. Disconnect vacuum line from diaphragm unit.
11. Support transmission with a jack.
12. Remove crossmember from under extension housing.
13. Remove transmission to engine bolts.
14. Move transmission away from engine, then lower and remove transmission from under truck.
15. Reverse procedure to install.

## BRONCO

1. Remove fan shroud and raise vehicle.
2. Remove transfer case shield, if used, and drain transmission, converter and transfer case.
3. Disconnect rear drive shaft from transfer case and remove front drive shaft from vehicle.
4. Disconnect exhaust system and position aside.
5. Remove speedometer gear from transfer case.
6. Disconnect oil cooler lines, shift linkage and neutral start switch wires from transmission.
7. Remove starter.
8. Disconnect vacuum lines from modulator and retaining clip.
9. Remove crossmember to transfer case adapter and crossmember to frame side support attaching bolts.
10. Raise transmission and transfer case with a suitable jack and remove left side support bracket to frame bolts, side support bracket, crossmember and upper crossmember insulators.
11. Raise transmission and transfer case slightly and disconnect shift rod and shift lever bracket from transfer case.
12. Remove converter housing to engine bolts, slide transmission and transfer case rearward and lower assembly from vehicle.
13. Remove transfer case adapter to transmission bolts and slide transmission from transfer case.
14. Reverse procedure to install.

## ECONOLINE

1. Working from inside the truck, remove engine cover and disconnect neutral start switch wires.
2. On V8 engines, remove air cleaner heat tube flex hose.
3. On all models, remove upper converter housing to engine bolts.
4. On V8 engines, disconnect exhaust pipe from manifold.
5. On all models, raise vehicle and drain transmission and converter.
6. Remove converter cover and remove converter to flywheel bolts.
7. Disconnect drive shaft.
8. Remove transmission filler tube.
9. Remove starter.
10. Install suitable engine support bar.
11. Disconnect vacuum and cooler lines, shift linkage and speedometer cable.
12. Support transmission with suitable jack and remove crossmember.
13. Remove remaining converter housing to engine bolts and lower transmission away from vehicle.
14. Reverse procedure to install.

# C5 Automatic Transmission

## INDEX

## DESCRIPTION

The C5 transmission, **Fig. 1,** is a fully automatic transmission with three speeds and one reverse. It consists of a welded torque converter assembly, a two unit planetary gear train, and a hydraulic system to control gear selection and automatic shift. The 12 inch torque converter, used with larger displacement engine, has a converter clutch. The planetary gear train is a Simpson design with two gear sets in series and a common sun gear. It is the same gear train used in model C4 with minor changes. Two friction clutches and two bands are used to control the gear operation.

The torque converter is coupled to the engine crankshaft, and transmits engine power into the gear train. The output shaft drives the rear wheels through a conventional driveshaft and rear axle. Gear reductions needed to match the engine to the axle take place in the planetary gear train and in the torque converter.

The C5 transmission is closest in resemblance to the C4 which it replaced in production. Some major differences from the C4 transmission are in the hydraulic system. Several new valves are incorporated along with a new timing valve body. Also the converter relief valve is moved from the reactor support (in the pump assembly) to the timing valve body. Thus, C4 oil pump assemblies must not be used to service the C5. The C5 12 inch converter with the converter clutch is also different than the C4 conventional converter.

In general, C4 special tools will service the C5. One new seal protector tool is needed to install the reverse and high clutch piston. The tool number is T82L-77404-A.

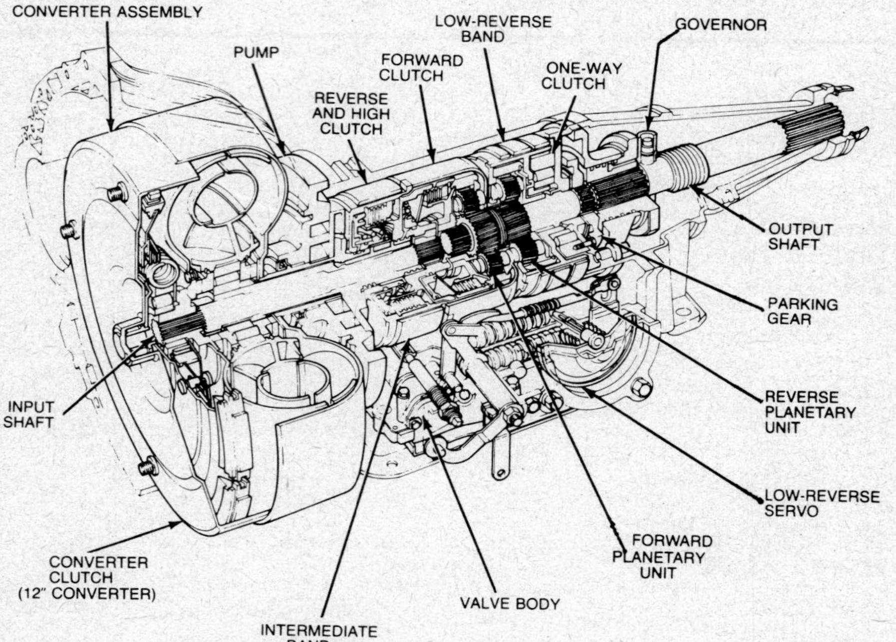

Fig. 1  C5 automatic transmission

## TROUBLESHOOTING GUIDE

### SLOW INITIAL ENGAGEMENT

1. Improper fluid level.
2. Damaged or improperly adjusted linkage.
3. Contaminated fluid.
4. Improper clutch and band application or low main control pressure.

### ROUGH INITIAL ENGAGEMENT IN EITHER FORWARD OR REVERSE

1. Improper fluid level.
2. High engine idle.
3. Automatic choke on (warm temp.).
4. Looseness in the driveshaft U-joint or

engine mount.
5. Incorrect linkage adjustment.
6. Improper clutch or band application, or oil control pressure.

## DELAYED OR NO FORWARD ENGAGEMENT

1. Improper fluid level.
2. Manual linkage, improperly adjusted or damaged.
3. Low main control pressure.
4. Valve body bolts, loose or too tight.
5. Valve body, dirty or sticking valve.
6. Forward clutch assembly burnt or damaged.
7. Forward clutch assembly piston seals worn or cut.
8. Forward clutch assembly cylinder ball check not seating.
9. Forward clutch assembly stator support seal ring grooves, damaged or worn.

## DELAYED OR NO REVERSE ENGAGEMENT

1. Improper fluid level.
2. Low main control pressure in reverse.
3. Manual linkage improperly adjusted or damaged.
4. Valve body, dirty or sticking valve.
5. Valve body bolts loose or too tight.
6. Reverse clutch assembly, burnt or worn.
7. Reverse clutch assembly piston seals, worn or cut.
8. Reverse clutch assembly piston ball not seating.
9. Reverse clutch assembly stator support seal rings or ring grooves, worn or damaged.

## DELAYED OR NO REVERSE ENGAGEMENT AND/OR NO ENGINE BRAKING IN MANUAL LOW (1)

1. Low reverse band or servo piston burnt or worn.
2. Low reverse servo seal worn or cut.
3. Low reverse servo bore damaged.
4. Low reverse servo piston sticking in bore.
5. Low reverse band, line pressure low.
6. Low reverse bands out of adjustment.
7. Polished or glazed band or drum.

## NO ENGINE BRAKING IN MANUAL SECOND GEAR

1. Improper fluid level.
2. Linkage out of adjustment.
3. Intermediate band out of adjustment.
4. Improper band or clutch application, or oil pressure control system.
5. Intermediate servo leaking.
6. Polished or glazed band or drum.

## DELAYED OR NO FORWARD & REVERSE ENGAGEMENT

1. Pump gear damaged (no engagement).
2. Output shaft broken (no engagement only).
3. Turbine shaft or input shaft broken (no engagement only).

## FORWARD ENGAGEMENT SLIP, SHUDDERS OR CHATTERS

1. Improper fluid level.
2. Manual linkage improperly adjusted or damaged.
3. Low main control pressure.
4. Valve body bolts, loose or too tight.
5. Valve body dirty or sticking valve.
6. Forward clutch piston ball check not sealing.
7. Forward clutch piston seal cut or worn.
8. Contamination blocking forward clutch feed hole.
9. Low (planetary) one-way clutch damaged.

## REVERSE ENGAGEMENT SLIP, SHUDDERS OR CHATTERS

1. Improper fluid level.
2. Low main control pressure in reverse.
3. Reverse servo or servo bore damaged.
4. Low (planetary) one-way clutch damaged.
5. Reverse clutch drum bushing damaged.
6. Reverse clutch stator support seal rings or ring grooves worn or damaged.
7. Reverse clutch piston seal cut or worn.
8. Reverse band out of adjustment or damaged.
9. Looseness in the driveshaft U-joints or engine mounts.

## NO DRIVE, SLIPS OR CHATTERS IN FIRST GEAR D

1. Damaged or worn one-way clutch.

## NO DRIVE, SLIPS OR CHATTERS IN SECOND

1. Improper fluid level.
2. Damaged or improperly adjusted linkage.
3. Intermediate band out of adjustment.
4. Improper band or clutch application, or oil pressure control.
5. Damaged or worn servo and/or internal leaks.
6. Dirty or sticking valve body.
7. Polished or glazed intermediate band or drum.

## START UP IN SECOND OR THIRD

1. Improper fluid level.
2. Damaged or improperly adjusted linkage.
3. Improper band and/or clutch application, or oil pressure control system.
4. Damaged or worn governor, governor sticking.
5. Valve body loose.
6. Dirty or sticking valve body.
7. Cross leaks between valve body and case mating surface.

## SHIFT POINTS INCORRECT

1. Improper fluid level.
2. Improper vacuum hose routing or leaks.
3. Improper operation of EGR system.
4. Throttle out of adjustment.
5. Improper clutch or band application, or oil pressure control system.
6. Damaged or worn governor.
7. Dirty or sticking valve body.

## ALL UPSHIFTS HARSH, DELAYED OR NO UPSHIFTS

1. Improper fluid level.
2. Manual linkage improperly adjusted or damaged.
3. Governor sticking.
4. Main control pressure too high.
5. Valve body bolts loose or too tight.
6. Valve body dirty or valves sticking.
7. Vacuum leak to diaphragm unit.

## ALL UPSHIFTS EARLY OR SLUGGISH

1. Improper fluid level.
2. Low main control pressure.
3. Valve body loose or too tight.
4. Valve body valve sticking.
5. Governor valve sticking.

## NO LOW TO SECOND UPSHIFT

1. Improper fluid level.
2. Manual linkage improperly adjusted or damaged.
3. Governor valve sticking.
4. Valve body bolts loose or too tight.
5. Valve body dirty or sticking valves.
6. Intermediate clutch or band and/or servo assembly burnt.
7. Intermediate piston seals worn or cut.
8. Intermediate piston not positioned properly.
9. Intermediate clutch improper stack up.
10. Low line pressure in intermediate clutch or band.

## ROUGH, HARSH, OR DELAYED UPSHIFT LOW TO SECOND

1. Governor valve sticking.
2. Improper fluid level.
3. Poor engine performance.
4. Main control pressure too high.
5. Valve body bolts loose or too tight.
6. Valve body dirty or valves sticking.
7. Intermediate band out of adjustment.
8. Damaged intermediate servo.
9. Engine vacuum leak.

## EARLY, SOFT OR SLIPPING LOW TO SECOND UPSHIFT

1. Improper fluid level.
2. Low main control.
3. Valve body bolts loose or too tight.
4. Valve body dirty or valves sticking.
5. Governor valve sticking.
6. Incorrect engine performance.
7. Intermediate band out of adjustment.
8. Damaged intermediate servo or band.
9. Polished or glazed band or drum.

# FORD—Automatic Transmissions

## NO SECOND TO THIRD UPSHIFT

1. Low fluid level.
2. Low main control pressure to direct clutch.
3. Valve body bolts too loose or too tight.
4. Valve body dirty or valves sticking.
5. Converter damper hub weld broken.

## HARSH OR DELAYED SECOND TO THIRD UPSHIFT

1. Low fluid level.
2. Valve body bolts loose or too tight.
3. Valve body dirty or valves sticking.
4. Damaged or worn intermediate servo release and high clutch piston check ball.
5. Incorrect engine performance.
6. Engine vacuum leak.

## EARLY OR SOFT SECOND TO THIRD UPSHIFT

1. Improper fluid level.
2. Valve body bolts loose or too tight.
3. Valve body dirty or valves sticking.

## ERRATIC SHIFTS

1. Improper fluid level.
2. Throttle linkage binding or sticking.
3. Valve body bolts loose or too tight.
4. Valve body dirty or valves sticking.
5. Governor valve sticking.
6. Output shaft collector body seal rings (large cast iron) worn or cut.

## SHIFTS FROM LOW TO THIRD IN DRIVE

1. Improper fluid level.
2. Intermediate band out of adjustment.
3. Damaged intermediate servo and/or internal leaks.
4. Polished or glazed band or drum.
5. Improper band or clutch application, or oil pressure control system.
6. Valve body dirty or valves sticking.

## ENGINE OVER SPEEDS ON SECOND TO THIRD UPSHIFT

1. Improper fluid level.
2. Linkage out of adjustment.
3. Improper band or clutch application, or oil pressure control system.
4. Damaged or worn high clutch and/or intermediate servo.
5. Valve body dirty or valves sticking.

## ROUGH OR SHUDDER THIRD TO LOW SHIFT AT CLOSED THROTTLE

1. Improper fluid level.
2. Incorrect engine idle or performance.
3. Improper linkage adjustment.
4. Improper clutch or band application, or oil pressure control system.
5. Improper governor operation.
6. Valve body dirty or valves sticking.

## NO FORCED DOWNSHIFT

1. Improper fluid level.
2. Kickdown linkage out of adjustment.
3. Damaged internal kickdown linkage.

4. Damaged or improperly adjusted (short) throttle linkage.
5. Valve body dirty or valves sticking.
6. Dirty or sticking governor.

## ENGINE OVER SPEEDS ON THIRD TO SECOND SHIFT

1. Improper fluid level.
2. Linkage out of adjustment.
3. Intermediate band out of adjustment.
4. Improper band or clutch application, or oil pressure control system.
5. Damaged or worn intermediate servo.
6. Polished or glazed band or drum.
7. Valve body dirty or valves sticking.

## SHIFT EFFORTS HIGH

1. Manual shift linkage damaged or improperly adjusted.
2. Inner manual lever nut loose.
3. Manual lever retainer pin damaged.

## NO START IN PARK

1. Manual linkage improperly adjusted.
2. Plug connector for the neutral start switch does not fit properly.
3. Neutral start switch plunger travel, inadequate.

## NO START IN PARK & NEUTRAL

1. Plug connector for the neutral start switch does not fit properly.

## TRANSMISSION OVERHEATS

1. Improper fluid level.
2. Incorrect engine idle or performance.
3. Improper band or clutch application, or oil pressure control system.
4. Restriction in cooler or lines.
5. Seized converter one-way clutch.
6. Valve body dirty or valves sticking.

# MAINTENANCE
## CHECKING OIL LEVEL

1. With engine idling, foot brake applied and vehicle on level surface, move selector lever through each range, pausing in each position.
2. Place selector in Park and apply parking brake. Leave engine running during fluid level check.
3. Clean dirt from transmission fluid dipstick cap and remove dipstick. Wipe dipstick and push back into tube making sure it is fully seated.
4. Pull dipstick out and check fluid level. With transmission at operating temperature, fluid level should be between arrows. With transmission cool, fluid level should read between inner holes. Use only Type H fluid, Ford spec. ESP M2C166-H. Do not overfill.
5. Insert dipstick, making sure it is fully seated. If transmission fluid is at operating temperature, the fluid level on the dipstick should be between the arrows. If fluid level is checked at room temperature, the fluid level on the dipstick should be between the middle and top holes.

## DRAIN & REFILL

Normal maintenance and lubrication requirements do not necessitate periodic fluid changes. If a major failure has occurred in the transmission, it will have to be removed for service. At this time, the converter, transmission cooler and cooler lines must be thoroughly flushed to remove any foreign matter. If vehicle is operated under continuous or severe conditions, the transmission and torque converter should be drained and refilled every 20,000 miles.

When a partial drain and refill is required due to an in-vehicle repair operation, proceed as follows:
1. On all except Ranger models, disconnect fluid filler tube from transmission oil pan and drain fluid.
2. On Ranger models, loosen oil pan bolts and lower one edge of pan to drain fluid.
3. Remove and clean pan and screen.
4. Place new gasket on pan and install pan and screen. Torque bolts to 12-16 ft. lbs.
5. Connect filler tube to pan and tighten fitting.
6. Add three quarts of fluid to transmission through the filler tube.
7. Check oil level and add fluid as necessary.

# IN-VEHICLE ADJUSTMENTS
## SHIFT LINKAGE
### Exc. Ranger & Bronco II

1. Disconnect battery ground cable.
2. Place transmission selector lever on steering column in Drive position. Secure selector lever in this position.
3. Loosen shift rod adjusting nut at point A, **Fig. 2.**
4. Place transmission shift lever into Drive position by moving lever completely rearward, then forward 2 detents.
5. With selector lever and transmission manual lever in Drive position, torque nut at point A to 12-18 ft. lbs.

### Ranger & Bronco II

1. Disconnect battery ground cable.
2. Position transmission selector lever in Drive position, then loosen trunnion bolt, **Figs. 3 and 4.**
3. Position transmission manual lever into Drive position by moving bell crank lever completely rearward, then forward 3 detents.
4. With transmission selector lever and manual lever in Drive position, apply a light forward pressure on shifter control lower arm and torque trunnion bolt to 13-23 ft. lbs.

## KICKDOWN ROD

1. Install a suitable weight onto transmission kickdown lever.
2. Rotate throttle to wide open throttle position.
3. Insert a .060 inch feeler gauge be-

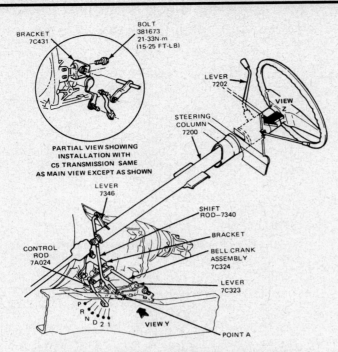

**Fig. 2  Shift linkage adjustment. Except Ranger & Bronco II**

tween throttle lever and adjusting screw.
4. Rotate adjusting screw until contact is made between screw and feeler gauge, then tighten locknut.
5. Remove feeler gauge.
6. After removing feeler gauge a gap of .010 inch on all except Ranger and Bronco II models is acceptable. On Ranger and Bronco II models, a gap of .001-.008 inch is acceptable.
7. Remove weight from kickdown lever.

## INTERMEDIATE BAND

1. Clean all dirt from the band adjusting screw area. Remove and discard the locknut.
2. Install a new locknut on the adjusting screw.
3. Tighten adjusting screw using Band Adjusting Ratchet T71P-77370-H and Socket T71P-77370-D or equivalent, **Fig. 5.** Tool T71P-77370-H or equivalent, is a pre-set torque wrench which will click when the torque on the adjusting screw reaches 10 ft. lbs.
4. Back off adjusting screw exactly 4¼ turns.
5. Hold the adjusting screw from turning and tighten locknut to 40 ft. lbs.

## LOW REVERSE BAND

1. Clean all dirt from the band adjusting screw area. Remove and discard the locknut.
2. Install a new locknut on the adjusting screw.
3. Tighten adjusting screw using Band Adjusting Ratchet T71P-77370-H and Socket T71P-77370-D or equivalent, **Fig. 6.** Tool T71P-77370-H or equivalent, is a pre-set torque wrench which will click when the torque on the ad-

justing screw reaches 10 ft. lbs.
4. Back off adjusting screw exactly three full turns. Hold adjusting screw from turning and tighten locknut to 40 ft. lbs.

## NEUTRAL START SWITCH

1. Loosen neutral start switch attaching bolts.
2. On 1980-82 models, proceed as follows:
   a. Set manual lever in park position, then insert a ³/₃₂ inch drill bit through switch hole.
   b. Move switch as necessary to allow drill bit to fully seat, then torque switch attaching bolts to 8 ft. lbs.
   c. Remove drill bit.
3. On 1982-85 models, proceed as follows:
   a. Set manual lever in neutral position, then insert a No. 43 drill bit into the three switch holes.
   b. Move switch as necessary to allow drill bit to fully seat, then torque switch attaching bolts to 65 inch lbs.
   c. Remove drill bit.

## IN-VEHICLE REPAIRS

### EXTENSION HOUSING SEAL, REPLACE

1. Raise and support vehicle.
2. Remove the driveshaft.
3. Remove extension housing seal using Seal Remover T74P-77248-A and Slide Hammer T50T-100-A or equivalent.
4. Reverse procedure to install using Seal Installer T61L-7657-A or equivalent.

## EXTENSION HOUSING, REPLACE

### 4 x 2 Models

1. Raise vehicle and remove driveshaft.
2. Using suitable jack, support transmission.
3. Remove speedometer cable from extension housing.
4. Remove engine rear support to crossmember nuts.
5. Raise transmission and remove rear support bolts. Remove crossmember.
6. Loosen extension housing bolts and let transmission drain.
7. Remove the six extension housing bolts and vacuum tube clip and remove extension housing.
8. Reverse procedure to install, noting the following torques: extension housing bolts, 28-40 ft. lbs.; crossmember nuts, 35-50 ft. lbs.; rear support bolts, 25-35 ft. lbs.

### 4 x 4 Models

1. Disconnect battery ground cable.
2. Remove transfer case assembly from vehicle.
3. Position a suitable jack under transmission assembly.
4. Remove engine rear support to crossmember nuts.
5. Raise transmission slightly, then remove rear support to body bracket attaching bolts.
6. Loosen extension housing attaching bolts and allow transmission fluid to drain.
7. Remove extension housing bolts, extension housing and vacuum tube clip.
8. Disconnect transmission vent fitting line.
9. Reverse procedure to install. Torque extension housing to transmission case bolts to 28-40 ft. lbs. Torque crossmember attaching nuts to 75-95 ft. lbs. Torque engine rear support to crossmember attaching nuts to 71-94 ft. lbs.

## GOVERNOR, REPLACE

1. Refer to "Extension Housing, Replace" and remove extension housing.
2. Remove bolts holding governor housing to governor distributor.
3. Slide governor away from distributor body and off output shaft.
4. Reverse procedure to install. Torque governor bolts to 80-120 inch lbs.

## LOW-REVERSE SERVO, REPLACE

1. Raise and support vehicle.
2. Loosen low-reverse band adjusting screw locknut. Torque band adjusting screw to 10 ft. lbs. to prevent band strut from falling when reverse servo piston assembly is removed.
3. Disengage neutral switch harness from clips on servo cover.
4. Remove servo cover bolts, servo cover, and seal from case.
5. Remove servo piston from case. If seal is bad, piston must be replaced.

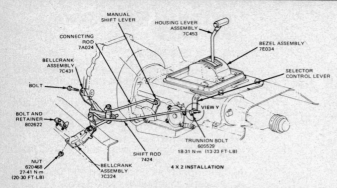

**Fig. 3   Shift linkage adjustment. Ranger & Bronco II 4 x 2 models**

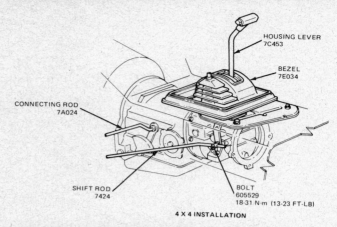

**Fig. 4   Shift linkage adjustment. Ranger & Bronco II 4 x 4 models**

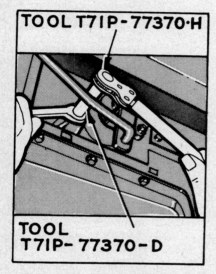

**Fig. 5   Intermediate band adjustment**

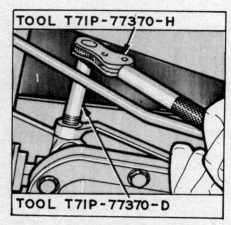

**Fig. 6   Low-reverse band adjustment**

6. Install piston in case. Install cover with new seal. Use two ⁵/₁₆-18 x 1¹/₄ bolts to position cover against case. Install two cover bolts, remove two locating bolts and install remaining bolts. Torque to 12-20 ft. lbs.
7. Position neutral switch harness in clips.
8. Adjust low-reverse band. If band cannot be adjusted properly, low-reverse band struts are not in position. Remove oil pan and valve body, reposition struts and install valve body and pan, then adjust band.
9. Lower vehicle and check transmission fluid level.

## INTERMEDIATE SERVO, REPLACE

1. Remove the four servo cover to case attaching bolts, together with the transmission identification tag.
2. Remove the servo cover, gasket and piston return spring from case, then remove servo piston from cover.
3. Position new gasket onto servo cover, ensuring notch in gasket aligns with case fluid passage.
4. Install piston return spring and servo

cover/piston assembly into case. Use two ⁵/₁₆-18 x 1¹/₄ bolts to position cover against case. Install two cover bolts, remove locating bolts and install remaining cover bolts. Torque cover bolts to 16-22 ft. lbs.
5. Adjust intermediate band. If band cannot be properly adjusted, the intermediate band strut is incorrectly positioned. Remove oil pan and valve body, reposition strut, then adjust band as outlined previously.

## TRANSMISSION REPLACE

1. On 4 x 4 models, remove filler tube to valve cover bracket attaching bolt.
2. On all models, raise and support vehicle.
3. Position a drain pan under transmission oil pan, then, starting at rear, loosen attaching bolts and drain fluid from transmission. Leave 2 bolts in front and reinstall 2 bolts in rear of oil pan to temporarily hold it in place.
4. Remove converter drain plug access

cover from lower end of converter housing.
5. Remove converter to flywheel attaching nuts. Rotate converter to gain access to nuts using a suitable wrench on crankshaft pulley attaching bolt.
6. Rotate converter to gain access to converter drain plug, then remove the plug to drain converter. After fluid has been drained, reinstall plug.
7. On 4 x 2 models, mark relationship between rear driveshaft yoke and axle flange, then disconnect driveshaft from rear axle and slide shaft rearward from transmission. Install a suitable seal installation tool in extension housing to prevent fluid leakage.
8. On all models, disconnect starter cables, then remove starter motor from vehicle.
9. Disconnect neutral start switch electrical connector.
10. Remove rear engine mount to crossmember attaching nuts.
11. Remove 2 crossmember to frame attaching bolts, then the right and left gussets.
12. Remove 2 rear engine mount to extension housing attaching bolts.
13. Disconnect manual and downshift

linkage rods from transmission control levers.

14. On 4 x 4 models, disconnect vacuum hose from vacuum diaphragm unit and remove from retaining clip.
15. On all models, remove 2 bell crank bracket to converter housing attaching bolts.
16. On 4 x 4 models, remove transfer case.
17. On all models, raise transmission using a suitable jack, then remove rear engine mount and crossmember.
18. Lower transmission and disconnect oil cooler lines from transmission.
19. Disconnect speedometer cable from extension housing.
20. On 4 x 2 models, remove filler tube to cylinder block attaching bolt, then the filler tube with dipstick.
21. On all models, install a safety chain to secure transmission to jack, then remove converter housing to cylinder block attaching bolts.
22. Move transmission and converter assembly away from engine, then lower assembly and remove from vehicle.
23. Reverse procedure to install. Torque converter housing to engine attaching bolts to 22-32 ft. lbs. and converter attaching nuts to 20-34 ft. lbs. **Ensure converter rests squarely against flywheel, indicating converter pilot is not binding in crankshaft.**

# C6 Automatic Transmission

## INDEX

# DESCRIPTION

As shown in **Fig. 1**, the transmission consists essentially of a torque converter, a compound planetary gear train controlled by one band, three disc clutches and a one-way clutch, and a hydraulic control system.

# TROUBLESHOOTING GUIDE

## NO DRIVE IN FORWARD SPEED

1. Manual linkage adjustment.
2. Check control pressure.
3. Valve body.
4. Make air pressure check.
5. Forward clutch.
6. Leakage in hydraulic system.

## ROUGH INITIAL ENGAGEMENT IN D, D1, D2 OR 2

1. Engine idle speed too high.
2. Vacuum diaphragm unit or tubes restricted, leaking or improperly adjusted.
3. Check control pressure.
4. Valve body.
5. Forward clutch.

## 1-2 OR 2-3 SHIFT POINTS INCORRECT OR ERRATIC

1. Check fluid level.
2. Vacuum diaphragm unit or tubes restricted, leaking or improperly adjusted.
3. Downshift linkage, including inner lever position.
4. Manual linkage adjustment.
5. Governor defective.
6. Check control pressure.
7. Valve body.
8. Make air pressure check.

## ROUGH 1-2 UPSHIFTS

1. Vacuum diaphragm unit or tubes restricted, leaking or improperly adjusted.
2. Intermediate servo.
3. Intermediate band.
4. Check control pressure.
5. Valve body.

## ROUGH 2-3 SHIFTS

1. Vacuum diaphragm or tubes restricted leaking or improperly adjusted.
2. Intermediate servo.
3. Check control pressure.
4. Intermediate band.
5. Valve body.
6. Make air pressure check.
7. Reverse-high clutch.

8. Reverse-high clutch piston air bleed valve.

## DRAGGED OUT 1-2 SHIFT

1. Check fluid level.
2. Vacuum diaphragm unit or tubes restricted, leaking or improperly adjusted.
3. Intermediate servo.
4. Check control pressure.
5. Intermediate band.
6. Valve body.
7. Make air pressure check.
8. Leakage in hydraulic system.

## ENGINE OVERSPEEDS ON 2-3 SHIFT

1. Manual linkage adjustment.
2. Check fluid level.
3. Vacuum diaphragm unit or tubes restricted, leaking or improperly adjusted.
4. Intermediate servo.
5. Check control pressure.
6. Valve body.
7. Intermediate band.
8. Reverse-high clutch.
9. Reverse-high clutch piston air bleed valve.

## NO 1-2 OR 2-3 SHIFT

1. Manual linkage adjustment.
2. Downshift linkage including inner le-

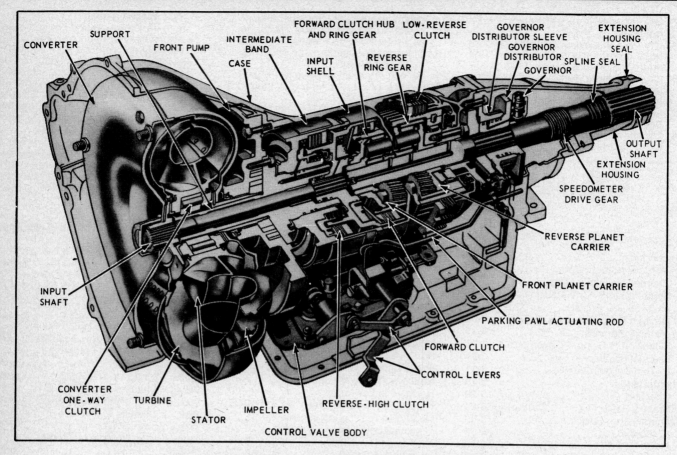

**Fig. 1  C6 dual range automatic transmission**

ver position.
3. Vacuum diaphragm unit or tubes restricted, leaking or improperly adjusted.
4. Governor.
5. Check control pressure.
6. Valve body.
7. Intermediate band.
8. Intermediate servo.
9. Reverse-high clutch.
10. Leakage in hydraulic system.

## NO 3-1 SHIFT IN D1, 2 OR 3-2 SHIFT IN D2 OR DRIVE

1. Governor.
2. Valve body.

## NO FORCED DOWNSHIFTS

1. Downshift linkage, including inner lever position.
2. Check control pressure.
3. Valve body.

## RUNAWAY ENGINE ON FORCED 3-2 SHIFT

1. Check control pressure.
2. Intermediate servo.
3. Intermediate band.
4. Valve body.
5. Vacuum diaphragm unit or tubes restricted, leaking or improperly adjusted.
6. Leakage in hydraulic system.

## ROUGH 3-2 SHIFT OR 3-1 SHIFT AT CLOSED THROTTLE

1. Engine idle speed.
2. Vacuum diaphragm unit or tubes restricted, leaking or improperly adjusted.
3. Intermediate servo.
4. Check control pressure.
5. Valve body.

## SHIFTS 1-3 IN DRIVE, D1, 2, D2

1. Intermediate band.
2. Intermediate servo.
3. Valve body.
4. Governor.
5. Make air pressure check.

## NO ENGINE BRAKING IN 1ST GEAR—MANUAL LOW RANGE

1. Manual linkage adjustment.
2. Low-reverse clutch.
3. Valve body.
4. Governor.
5. Make air pressure check.
6. Leakage in hydraulic system.

## CREEPS EXCESSIVELY

1. Engine idle speed too high.

## SLIPS OR CHATTERS IN 1ST GEAR, D1

1. Check fluid level.
2. Vacuum diaphragm unit or tubes restricted, leaking or improperly adjusted.
3. Check control pressure.
4. Valve body.
5. Forward clutch.
6. Leakage in hydraulic system.
7. Planetary one-way clutch.

## SLIPS OR CHATTERS IN 2ND GEAR

1. Check fluid level.
2. Vacuum diaphragm unit or tubes restricted, leaking or improperly adjusted.
3. Intermediate servo.
4. Intermediate band.
5. Check control pressure.
6. Valve body.
7. Make air pressure check.
8. Forward clutch.
9. Leakage in hydraulic system.

## SLIPS OR CHATTERS IN REVERSE

1. Check fluid level.
2. Vacuum diaphragm unit or tubes restricted, leaking or improperly adjusted.

3. Manual linkage adjustment.
4. Low-reverse clutch.
5. Check control pressure.
6. Valve body.
7. Make air pressure check.
8. Reverse-high clutch.
9. Leakage in hydraulic system.
10. Reverse-high clutch piston air bleed valve.

## NO DRIVE IN D1 OR 2

1. Manual linkage adjustment.
2. Check control pressure.
3. Valve body.
4. Planetary one-way clutch.

## NO DRIVE IN DRIVE, D2

1. Check fluid level.
2. Manual linkage adjustment.
3. Check control pressure.
4. Intermediate servo.
5. Valve body.
6. Make air pressure check.
7. Leakage in hydraulic system.

## NO DRIVE IN LOW OR 1

1. Check fluid level.
2. Check control pressure.
3. Valve body.
4. Make air pressure check.
5. Leakage in hydraulic system.

## NO DRIVE IN REVERSE ONLY

1. Check fluid level.
2. Manual linkage adjustment.
3. Low-reverse clutch.
4. Check control pressure.
5. Valve body.
6. Make air pressure check.
7. Reverse-high clutch.
8. Leakage in hydraulic system.
9. Reverse-high clutch piston air bleed valve.

## NO DRIVE IN ANY SELECTOR POSITION

1. Check fluid level.
2. Manual linkage adjustment.
3. Check control pressure.
4. Valve body.
5. Make air pressure check.
6. Leakage in hydraulic system.
7. Front pump.

## LOCKUP IN D1 OR 2

1. Valve body.
2. Parking linkage.
3. Leakage in hydraulic system.

## LOCKUP IN D2 OR DRIVE

1. Low-reverse clutch.
2. Valve body.
3. Reverse-high clutch.
4. Parking linkage.
5. Leakage in hydraulic system.
6. Planetary one-way clutch.

## LOCKUP IN LOW OR 1

1. Valve body.
2. Parking linkage.
3. Leakage in hydraulic system.

## LOCKUP IN REVERSE ONLY

1. Valve body.
2. Forward clutch.
3. Parking linkage.
4. Leakage in hydraulic system.

## PARKING LOCK BINDS OR DOES NOT HOLD

1. Manual linkage adjustment.
2. Parking linkage.

## TRANSMISSION OVERHEATS

1. Oil cooler and connections.
2. Valve body.
3. Vacuum diaphragm unit or tubes restricted, leaking or improperly adjusted.
4. Check control pressure.
5. Converter one-way clutch.
6. Converter pressure check valves.

## MAXIMUM SPEED TOO LOW, POOR ACCELERATION

1. Engine performance.
2. Car brakes.
3. Forward clutch.

## TRANSMISSION NOISY IN NEUTRAL & PARK

1. Check fluid level.
2. Valve body.
3. Front pump.

## NOISY IN 1ST, 2ND, 3RD OR REVERSE

1. Check fluid level.
2. Valve body.
3. Planetary assembly.
4. Forward clutch.
5. Reverse-high clutch.
6. Planetary one-way clutch.

## VEHICLE MOVES FORWARD IN NEUTRAL

1. Manual linkage adjustment.
2. Forward clutch.

## FLUID LEAK

1. Check fluid level.
2. Converter drain plugs.
3. Oil pan gasket, filler tube or seal.
4. Oil cooler and connections.
5. Manual or downshift lever shaft seal.
6. 1/8 inch pipe plugs in case.
7. Extension housing to case gasket.
8. Extension housing rear oil seal.
9. Speedometer driven gear adapter seal.
10. Vacuum diaphragm unit or tubes.
11. Intermediate servo.
12. Engine rear oil seal.

# MAINTENANCE
## CHECKING OIL LEVEL

1. Make sure vehicle is on a level floor.
2. Apply parking brake firmly.
3. Run engine at normal idle speed. If transmission fluid is cold, run engine at a fast idle until fluid reaches normal operating temperature. When fluid is warm, slow engine to normal idle speed.
4. Shift selector lever through all positions, then place lever at P. Do not shut down engine during fluid level checks.
5. Clean all dirt from dipstick cap before removing dipstick from filler tube.
6. Pull dipstick out of tube, wipe it clean and push it all the way back in tube.
7. Pull dipstick out of tube again and check fluid level. If necessary, add enough fluid to raise the level to the F (full) mark on dipstick. Do not overfill.

## DRAIN & REFILL

The Ford Motor Company recommends the use of an automatic transmission fluid M2C-138-CJ or Dexron II for all models. The recommended fluid is said to have a greater coefficient of friction and greater ability to handle maximum engine torques without band or clutch slippage.

Normal maintenance and lubrication requirements do not necessitate periodic fluid changes. If a major failure has occurred in the transmission, it will have to be removed for service. At this time the converter and transmission cooler must be thoroughly flushed to remove any foreign matter.

1. To drain the fluid, loosen pan attaching bolts and allow fluid to drain.
2. After fluid has drained to the level of the pan flange, remove pan bolts working from rear and both sides of pan to allow it to drop and drain slowly.
3. When fluid has stopped draining, remove and clean pan and screen. Discard pan gasket.
4. Using a new gasket, install pan.
5. Add 3 quarts of recommended fluid to transmission through filler tube.
6. Run engine at idle speed for 2 minutes, and then run it at a fast idle until it reaches normal operating temperature.
7. Shift selector lever through all positions, place it at P and check fluid level.
8. If necessary, add enough fluid to transmission to bring it to the F (full) mark on the dipstick.

# IN-VEHICLE ADJUSTMENTS
## SHIFT LINKAGE, ADJUST

1. Disconnect battery ground cable.
2. Place transmission selector lever on steering column into Drive position. Secure lever in this position.
3. Loosen shift rod adjusting nut at point A, **Figs. 2 and 3.**
4. Place transmission manual lever into Drive position by moving lever completely rearward, then forward 2 detents.
5. With selector lever and transmission manual lever in Drive (D) position, tighten nut at point A to 12-18 ft. lbs.

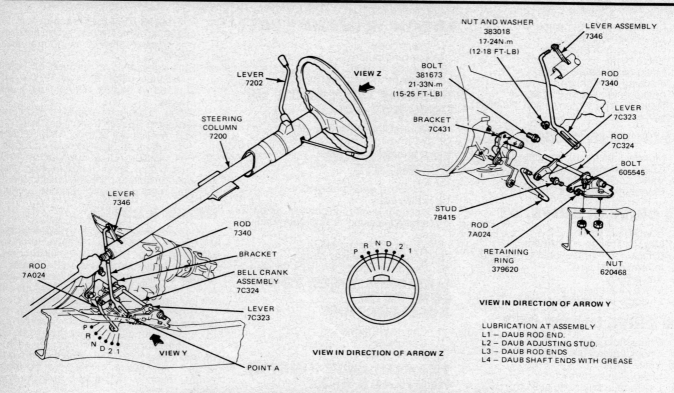

**Fig. 2    Shift linkage adjustment. Bronco & F Series**

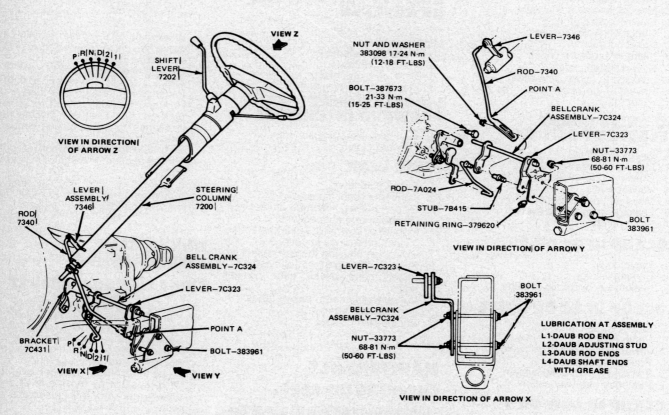

**Fig. 3    Shift linkage adjustment. E Series**

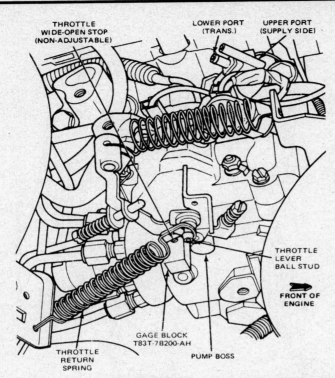

THROTTLE WIDE-OPEN STOP (NON-ADJUSTABLE)

LOWER PORT (TRANS.)

UPPER PORT (SUPPLY SIDE)

THROTTLE LEVER BALL STUD

FRONT OF ENGINE

GAGE BLOCK T83T-7B200-AH

PUMP BOSS

THROTTLE RETURN SPRING

**Fig. 4    VRV gauge block installation. V8-420 6.9L diesel engine**

## NEUTRAL START SWITCH, ADJUST

1. Apply parking brake.
2. Loosen 2 switch attaching bolts.
3. Position transmission selector lever into Neutral. Rotate switch, then insert a 3/32 inch drill shank end into gauge pin holes of switch.
4. Completely seat drill shank end into hole, then tighten switch attaching bolts to 65 inch lbs.
5. Remove drill shank end from switch.

## INTERMEDIATE BAND, ADJUST

When making the intermediate band adjustment, the locknut must be discarded and a new one installed each time the band is adjusted.
1. Raise truck on hoist and support on suitable jack stands.
2. Loosen the locknut on the adjusting screw several turns.
3. Torque the screw to 10 ft. lbs., or until the adjuster wrench overruns.
4. Back the screw off exactly 1 1/2 turns.
5. Hold the adjustment and torque the locknut to 22-29 ft. lbs. on 1980 vehicles, 40 ft. lbs. on 1981 vehicles, or 35-40 ft. lbs. on 1982-89 vehicles.

## VACUUM REGULATOR VALVE, ADJUST

### Models With V8-420 (6.9L) Diesel Engine

1. Disconnect 2 port vacuum connector from VRV located on left side of fuel

injection pump.
2. Disconnect throttle cable from throttle lever located on right side of fuel injection pump.
3. Remove throttle return spring. Install one end of spring over throttle lever ball stud and other end of spring over throttle cable support bracket. Insert gage block T83T-7B200-AH or equivalent, **Fig. 4**, between pump and throttle wide open stop.
4. Install a suitable vacuum pump onto upper port of VRV (vacuum supply side).
5. Install a vacuum gauge to lower port of VRV marked TRANS.
6. Apply and maintain 20 inches Hg vacuum to VRV. Vacuum gauge should indicate 7 inches Hg vacuum. If gauge does not indicate specified amount, proceed as follows:
   a. Loosen the adjustment screws attaching VRV to the fuel injection pump.
   b. Rotate VRV until correct vacuum reading on gauge is obtained.
   c. Torque adjustment screws to 75-90 inch lbs. If correct vacuum reading cannot be obtained, replace VRV.
7. Remove gauge block, then reconnect throttle return spring and throttle cable.
8. Again apply 20 inches Hg vacuum to VRV, and while maintaining vacuum, cycle throttle five times from idle to wide open position. Vacuum gauge should indicate at least 13 inches Hg vacuum with throttle in idle position. If gauge indication is less than specified, replace VRV.

## IN-VEHICLE REPAIRS
### OIL PAN & CONTROL VALVE

#### Removal

1. Raise truck on hoist or jack stands.
2. Loosen and remove all but two oil pan bolts from front of case and drop rear edge of pan to drain fluid. Remove and clean pan and screen.
3. Unfasten and remove valve body.

#### Installation

1. Position valve body to case, making sure that selector and downshift levers are engaged, then install and torque attaching bolts to 95-125 inch lbs.
2. Using a new pan gasket, secure pan to case and torque bolts to 12 ft. lbs.
3. Lower truck and fill transmission to correct level with specified fluid.

### INTERMEDIATE SERVO
#### Removal

1. Raise truck and remove engine rear support to extension housing bolts.
2. Raise transmission high enough to relieve weight from support.
3. Remove support.
4. Lower transmission.
5. Disconnect muffler inlet pipe from exhaust manifolds and let pipe hang free.
6. Place drain pan beneath servo.
7. Remove servo cover to case bolts.
8. Loosen band adjusting screw locknut.
9. Remove servo cover, piston, spring and gasket from case, screwing band adjusting screw inward as piston is removed. This insures that there will be enough tension on the band to keep the struts properly engaged in the band end notches while the piston is removed.

#### Replacing Seal

1. Apply air pressure to port in servo cover to remove piston and stem.
2. Remove seals from piston.
3. Remove seal from cover.
4. Dip new seals in transmission fluid.
5. Install seals in piston and cover.
6. Dip piston in transmission fluid and install in cover.

#### Installation

1. Position new gasket on servo cover and spring on piston stem.
2. Insert piston stem in case. Secure cover with bolts, taking care to back off band adjusting screw while tightening cover bolts. Make sure that vent tube retaining clip is in place.
3. Connect muffler inlet pipe to exhaust manifolds.
4. Raise transmission high enough to install engine rear support. Secure support to extension housing. Lower transmission as required to install support to crossmember bolt.
5. Remove jack and adjust band.
6. Lower truck and replenish fluid as required.

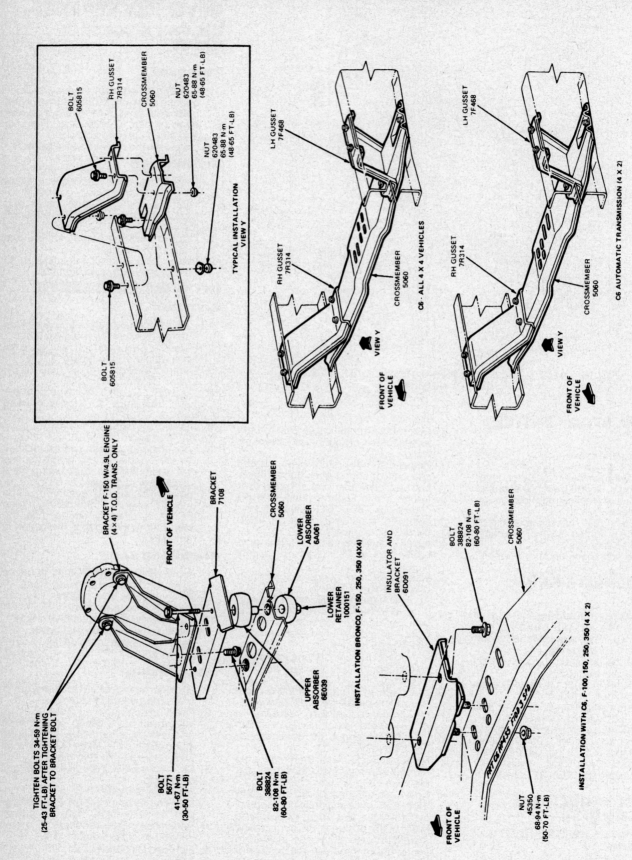

**Fig. 5  Crossmember installation. Bronco & F Series**

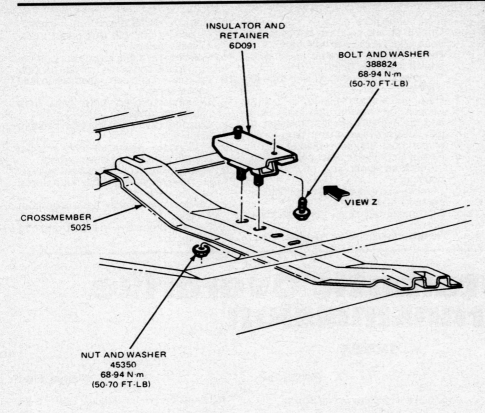

INSULATOR AND
RETAINER
6D091

BOLT AND WASHER
388824
68-94 N·m
(50-70 FT-LB)

VIEW Z

CROSSMEMBER
5025

NUT AND WASHER
45350
68-94 N·m
(50-70 FT-LB)

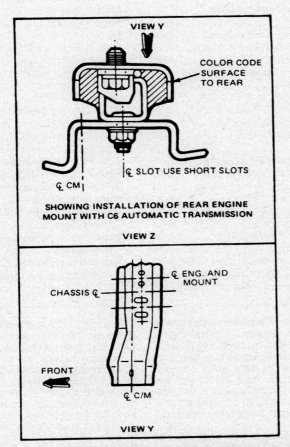

VIEW Y

COLOR CODE
SURFACE
TO REAR

₵ SLOT USE SHORT SLOTS

₵ CM

**SHOWING INSTALLATION OF REAR ENGINE MOUNT WITH C6 AUTOMATIC TRANSMISSION**

VIEW Z

₵ ENG. AND
MOUNT

CHASSIS ₵

FRONT

₵ C/M

VIEW Y

**Fig. 6   Crossmember installation. E Series**

## EXTENSION HOUSING & GOVERNOR
### Removal

1. Raise truck and drain transmission.
2. Disconnect drive shaft from rear axle flange and remove from transmission. On 4 x 4 models, the transfer case must be removed.
3. Disconnect speedometer cable from extension housing.
4. Remove two nuts that secure engine rear mount to crossmember.
5. Raise transmission with a jack just high enough to relieve weight from crossmember. Remove crossmember.
6. Remove engine rear support.
7. Lower transmission to permit access to extension housing bolts. Remove bolts and slide housing off output shaft.
8. Disconnect governor from distributor (4 bolts) and slide governor off output shaft.

### Installation

1. Secure governor to distributor flange and torque attaching bolts to 90-120 inch lbs.
2. Position new gasket on transmission.
3. Secure extension housing to case.
4. Secure engine rear support to case.
5. Install crossmember.
6. Lower transmission and remove jack. Then install and torque engine rear support to extension housing bolts.
7. Install speedometer cable and install drive shaft.
8. Replenish transmission fluid.

## TRANSMISSION
## REPLACE
### F150-350 & BRONCO

1. Drive vehicle onto a suitable hoist.
2. Disconnect battery ground cable.
3. Remove 2 upper converter housing to engine attaching bolts.
4. Raise and support vehicle.
5. Loosen transmission pan drain plug and drain fluid from transmission. If pan does not have a drain plug, loosen pan bolts and allow fluid to drain.
6. Remove converter drain plug access cover from lower end of converter housing.
7. Remove converter to flywheel attaching bolts and/or nuts, then drain converter.
8. On 4 x 2 models, disconnect driveshaft from axle and slide driveshaft rearward from transmission. Install a suitable seal tool into transmission extension housing.
9. Disconnect speedometer cable from extension housing.
10. Disconnect and cap transmission fluid cooler lines.
11. Disconnect downshift and manual linkage rods from transmission levers.
12. Disconnect vacuum line from vacuum diaphragm.
13. Remove starter motor from vehicle.

14. On 4 x 4 models, remove transfer case assembly from vehicle.
15. Remove 2 engine rear support to insulator attaching bolts.
16. Position a suitable jack under transmission, then raise transmission slightly.
17. Remove crossmembers from vehicle.
18. Remove remaining converter housing to engine attaching bolts.
19. Lower transmission from vehicle.
20. Reverse procedure to install, referring to **Fig. 5**.

## E150-350

1. Disconnect battery ground cable.
2. Working from inside of vehicle, remove engine compartment cover.
3. Disconnect neutral start switch elec-

trical connectors.
4. On V8 engine models, remove flex hose from air cleaner heat tube.
5. Remove upper converter housing to engine attaching bolts.
6. Remove bolt securing oil filler tube to engine.
7. Raise and support vehicle.
8. Loosen transmission pan drain plug and drain fluid from transmission. If pan does not have a drain plug, loosen pan bolts and allow fluid to drain.
9. Remove converter drain plug access cover from lower end of converter housing.
10. Remove converter to flywheel attaching bolts and/or nuts.
11. Disconnect driveshaft from transmission.
12. Remove transmission fluid filler tube.

13. Remove starter motor from vehicle.
14. Position a suitable jack under transmission assembly.
15. Position a suitable engine support bar onto frame and engine oil pan flanges.
16. Disconnect and cap transmission fluid cooler lines.
17. Disconnect speedometer cable from extension housing.
18. Disconnect vacuum line from vacuum diaphragm.
19. Disconnect downshift and manual linkage from transmission levers.
20. Remove crossmembers from vehicle.
21. Remove remaining converter housing to flywheel bolts.
22. Lower transmission assembly from vehicle.
23. Reverse procedure to install, referring to **Fig. 6**.

# Ford Automatic Overdrive Transmission

## INDEX

## DESCRIPTION

This unit is a 4 speed automatic transmission incorporating an integral overdrive feature. With selector lever in 1 position, the transmission will start and remain in first gear until the selector lever is moved to another position. In 3 position, the transmission will automatically shift through 1-2-3 range, but will not engage overdrive. In D position, the transmission will automatically select the appropriate time to shift into overdrive (4th gear). The design

of the transmission features a split torque path in third gear, where 40% of the engine torque is transmitted hydraulically through the torque converter and 60% is transmitted mechanically through solid connections (direct drive input shaft) to the driveshaft. When transmission is in overdrive (4th gear), 100% of engine torque is transmitted through the direct drive input shaft.

The transmission consists essentially of a torque converter assembly, compound planetary gear train and an hydraulic control system, **Fig. 1**. For gear control the

transmission has four friction clutches, two one-way roller clutches and two bands. Overdrive is accomplished by the addition of a band to lock the reverse sun gear while driving the planet carrier. The torque converter operation is similar to other types of automatic transmissions, but has an added damper assembly and input shaft for 3rd gear and overdrive. The direct drive input shaft couples the engine directly to the clutch. This shaft is driven by the torque converter cover through the damper assembly which cushions engine shock to the transmission.

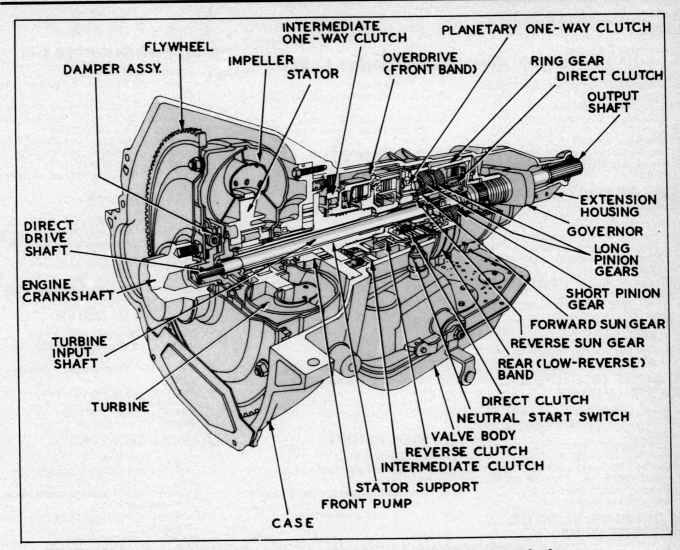

**Fig. 1 Sectional view of Ford automatic overdrive transmission**

# TROUBLESHOOTING GUIDE

## ROUGH INITIAL ENGAGEMENT IN FORWARD OR REVERSE

1. Improper fluid level.
2. High engine idle.
3. Loose driveshaft, engine mounts or U-joints.
4. Sticking or dirty valve body.
5. Improper clutch or band application, or low oil control pressure.

## SLOW INITIAL ENGAGEMENT

1. Improper fluid level.
2. Damaged or improperly adjusted linkage.
3. Contaminated fluid.
4. Low main control pressure or improper clutch and band application.

## HARSH ENGAGEMENTS WITH WARM ENGINE

1. Improper fluid level.
2. Damaged or improperly adjusted linkage.
3. High engine idle.
4. Sticking or dirty valve body.

## SLOW FORWARD ENGAGEMENT

1. Improper fluid level.
2. Damaged or improperly adjusted linkage.
3. Low main control pressure.
4. Sticking or dirty valve body.
5. Blocked filter.
6. Damaged pump.

## SLOW REVERSE ENGAGEMENT

1. Improper fluid level.
2. Damaged or improperly adjusted linkage.

3. Low main control pressure.
4. Damaged forward clutch assembly.
5. Sticking or dirty valve body.
6. Blocked filter.
7. Damaged pump.

## NO ENGINE BRAKING IN MANUAL LOW

1. Improper fluid level.
2. Damaged or improperly adjusted linkage.
3. Damaged low reverse servo piston band.
4. Damaged planetary low one-way clutch.

## NO ENGINE BRAKING IN MANUAL 2ND

1. Improper fluid level.
2. Damaged or improperly adjusted linkage.
3. Improper clutch or band application.
4. Improper control system pressure.
5. Leaking intermediate servo.
6. Damaged intermediate one-way clutch.

## SLIPS OR CHATTERS IN DRIVE

1. Improper fluid level.
2. Improper throttle valve rod adjustment.
3. Damaged or improperly adjusted linkage.
4. Low main control pressure.
5. Sticking or dirty valve body.
6. Open forward clutch check valve.
7. Damaged forward clutch piston seal.
8. Blocked forward clutch feed hole.
9. Damaged planetary low one-way clutch.

## SLIPS OR CHATTERS IN REVERSE

1. Improper fluid level.
2. Low main control pressure in reverse.
3. Damaged reverse servo bore.
4. Damaged planetary low one-way clutch.
5. Damaged reverse clutch drum bushing.
6. Worn reverse clutch stator support seal rings or grooves.
7. Reverse clutch piston seal.
8. Reverse band adjustment.
9. Loosen driveshaft, engine mounts or U-joints.

## NO DRIVE OR SLIPS OR CHATTERS IN D2

1. Improper fluid level.
2. Damaged or improperly adjusted linkage.
3. Intermediate friction or one-way clutch.
4. Blocked intermediate bleed hole or bleed hole not at 12 o'clock position.
5. Sticking or dirty valve body.
6. Damaged or worn servo.

## NO DRIVE OR SLIPS OR CHATTERS IN D1

1. Damaged planetary low one-way clutch.

## STARTS IN 2ND OR 3RD

1. Improper fluid level.
2. Damaged or improperly adjusted linkage.
3. Improper clutch or band application.
4. Improper control system pressure.
5. Sticking governor valve.
6. Sticking or dirty valve body.
7. Leaking valve body mating surface.

## IMPROPER SHIFT POINTS

1. Improper fluid level.
2. Damaged or improperly adjusted linkage.
3. Improper speedometer gear installed.
4. Improper clutch or band application.
5. Improper control system pressure.
6. Damaged or worn governor.
7. Sticking or dirty valve body.

## HARSH, DELAYED OR NO UPSHIFTS

1. Improper fluid level.
2. Damaged or improperly adjusted linkage.
3. Governor sticking.

4. High main control pressure.
5. Sticking or dirty valve body.
6. Throttle return spring disconnected.

## ALL UPSHIFTS EARLY

1. Improper fluid level.
2. Damaged or improperly adjusted linkage.
3. Low main control pressure.
4. Sticking throttle control valve or valve body.
5. Sticking governor valve.

## NO 1-2 UPSHIFT

1. Improper fluid level.
2. Damaged or improperly adjusted linkage.
3. Low main control pressure to intermediate friction clutch.
4. Sticking, leaking or bent diaphragm unit.
5. Sticking or dirty valve body.
6. Burnt intermediate clutch, band or servo.

## EARLY OR SLIPPING UPSHIFT IN 1-2

1. Improper fluid level.
2. Improperly tuned engine.
3. Damaged or improperly adjusted linkage.
4. High main control pressure.
5. Sticking governor valve.

## NO 2-3 UPSHIFT

1. Improper fluid level.
2. Damaged or improperly adjusted linkage.
3. Low main control pressure to direct clutch.
4. Sticking or dirty valve body.
5. Burnt or worn direct clutch.
6. Broken weld on converter damper hub.

## EARLY OR SLIPPING 2-3 UPSHIFT

1. Improper fluid level.
2. Improperly tuned engine.
3. Damaged or improperly adjusted linkage.
4. Cut or worn 2-3 accumulator piston seals.
5. Plugged 2-3 accumulator piston drain hole.
6. Damaged accumulator.
7. Dirty or sticking valve body.
8. Leaking vacuum diaphragm.
9. Worn governor seal ring or counterbore in case.

## NO 3-4 UPSHIFT

1. Low fluid level.
2. Damaged or improperly adjusted linkage.
3. Low pressure to overdrive band servo.
4. Sticking or dirty valve body.
5. Burnt or worn overdrive band assembly.
6. Blocked case passage.

7. Broken converter damper hub.
8. Direct clutch circuit leakage.

## EARLY OR SLIPPING 3-4

1. Improper fluid level.
2. Damaged or improperly adjusted linkage.
3. Low main control pressure to overdrive band servo.
4. Sticking or dirty valve body.
5. Burnt overdrive band assembly.
6. Damaged or glazed reverse clutch drum or overdrive band.
7. Worn governor seal ring or counterbore in case.

## ERRATIC SHIFTS

1. Improper fluid level.
2. Improperly tuned engine.
3. Damaged or improperly adjusted linkage.
4. Dirty or sticking valve body.
5. Sticking governor valve.
6. Damaged output shaft collector body seal rings.

## SHIFTS 1-3 IN DRIVE

1. Improper fluid level.
2. Damaged or burnt intermediate friction clutch.
3. Damaged intermediate one-way clutch.
4. Improper control system pressure or clutch application.
5. Sticking or dirty valve body.
6. Sticking governor valve.

## LATE 2-3 SHIFTING

1. Improper fluid level.
2. Damaged or improperly adjusted linkage.
3. Improper control system pressure or clutch application.
4. Damaged or worn high clutch or intermediate servo.
5. Sticking or dirty valve body.
6. Broken converter damper hub.
7. Plugged or missing 2-3 accumulator apply passage.
8. Cut or worn 2-3 accumulator piston seals.
9. Sticking 2-3 capacity modulator valve.

## SHIFT HUNTING 3-4 OR 4-3

1. Improperly tuned engine.
2. Damaged or improperly adjusted linkage.
3. Worn or damaged EGR solenoid.

## NO FORCED DOWNSHIFTS

1. Improper fluid level.
2. Damaged or improperly adjusted linkage.
3. Improper control system pressure or clutch application.
4. Sticking or dirty valve body.
5. Sticking or dirty governor.

## 3-1 SHIFT AT CLOSED THROTTLE IN DRIVE

1. Improper fluid level.
2. Improperly tuned engine.
3. Damaged or improperly adjusted linkage.
4. Improper control system pressure or

clutch application.
5. Improper governor operation.
6. Sticking or dirty valve body.

## HARSH OR SLIPPING 4-2 OR 3-1 SHIFT

1. Improper fluid level.
2. Improperly tuned engine.
3. Damaged or improperly adjusted linkage.
4. Improper application of intermediate friction and one-way clutch.
5. Sticking or dirty valve body.
6. Worn governor seal ring or counterbore in case.

## HIGH SHIFT EFFORT

1. Damaged or improperly adjusted linkage.
2. Loose manual lever nut.
3. Damaged manual lever retainer pin.

## TRANSMISSION OVERHEATS

1. Improper fluid level.
2. Improperly tuned engine.
3. Improper control system pressure or clutch application.
4. Restricted cooler or lines.
5. Seized converter one-way clutch.
6. Sticking or dirty valve body.

## CLUNK OR SQUAWK IN 1-2 OR 2-3

1. Blocked intermediate bleed hole or bleed hole not at 12 o'clock position.
2. Misaligned anti-clunk spring.
3. Converter damper spring brake.

## HARSH DOWNSHIFT COASTING CLUNK

1. Improperly seated anti-clunk spring.
2. Damaged or improperly adjusted linkage.

## POOR VEHICLE ACCELERATION

1. Improperly tuned engine.
2. Seized torque converter one-way clutch.

## SLIPPING SHIFT FOLLOWED BY SUDDEN ENGAGEMENT

1. Throttle valve linkage set too short.

## TRANSMISSION NOISY (VALVE RESONANCE)

1. Improper fluid level.
2. Damaged or improperly adjusted linkage.
3. Improper control system pressure or clutch application.
4. Cooler lines contacting frame, floor pan or other components.
5. Sticking or dirty valve body.
6. Internal leakage or pump cavitation.

## TRANSMISSION NOISY (OTHER THAN VALVE RESONANCE)

1. Improper fluid level.
2. Damaged or improperly adjusted linkage.

3. Contaminated fluid.
4. Loose converter to flywheel housing bolts or nuts.
5. Loose or worn speedometer driven gear.
6. Damaged or worn extension housing bushing seal or driveshaft.
7. Damaged or worn front or rear planetary and/or one-way clutch.

## THROTTLE VALVE LINKAGE DIAGNOSIS

Refer to the following for TV linkage conditions which may result in shifting abnormalities.

### T.V. CONTROL LINKAGE ADJUSTED TOO SHORT

1. Early or soft upshifts.
2. Harsh light throttle shift into and out of overdrive.
3. No forced downshift at proper speeds.

### T.V. LINKAGE ADJUSTED TOO LONG

1. Harsh idle engagement after engine warm up.
2. Clunking when throttle is released after heavy acceleration.
3. Harsh coasting downshifts out of overdrive.

### INTERFERENCE PREVENTING RETURN OF T.V. CONTROL ROD

1. Delayed or harsh upshifts.
2. Harsh idle engagement.

### BINDING GROMMETS PREVENTING T.V. LINKAGE RETURN

1. Delayed or harsh upshifts.
2. Harsh idle engagement.

### T.V. CONTROL ROD DISCONNECTED

1. Delayed or harsh upshifts.
2. Harsh idle engagement.

### CLAMPING BOLT ON TRUNNION AT LOWER END OF T.V. CONTROL ROD LOOSE

1. Delayed or harsh upshifts.
2. Harsh idle engagement.

### LINKAGE LEVER RETURN SPRING BROKEN OR DISCONNECTED

1. Delayed or harsh upshifts.
2. Harsh idle engagements.

## MAINTENANCE

### CHECKING OIL LEVEL

1. With transmission at operating temperature, park vehicle on level surface.
2. Operate engine at idle speed with parking brake applied and move selector lever through each detent posi-

tion. Return selector lever to Park.
3. With engine idling, remove dipstick and check fluid level. Fluid level should be between arrows on dipstick.
4. Add fluid as necessary to bring fluid to proper level. Use only fluid meeting Ford Qualification No. M2C-138-CJ or Dexron II.

### DRAIN & REFILL

1. Raise the vehicle and place a drain pan under the transmission.
2. Loosen the pan attaching bolts and drain the fluid.
3. Remove and clean the pan discarding the filter, filter gasket, oil pan gasket, and valve body gasket.
4. Install new gaskets and the pan.
5. Add three quarts of fluid to the transmission through the filler tube.
6. Run the engine and move the selector lever through the detents checking the fluid level as described above.

## IN-VEHICLE ADJUSTMENTS

### SHIFT LINKAGE, ADJUST

1. Place transmission selector lever on steering column into Drive (Overdrive) position. Secure lever in this position.
2. Loosen shift rod adjusting nut at point A, **Figs. 2 and 3.**
3. Place manual lever on transmission into Drive (Overdrive) position by moving lever completely rearward, then forward 2 detents.
4. With selector lever and transmission manual lever in Drive (Overdrive) position, torque adjusting nut at point A to 12-18 ft. lbs.

### T.V. CONTROL ROD LINKAGE, ADJUST

#### V8 ENGINES

#### Adjustment At Carburetor

1. Ensure engine idle speed is set to specification.
2. Disconnect fast idle cam from carburetor so throttle lever is at its idle stop.
3. Turn adjusting screw on linkage lever completely counterclockwise.
4. Turn adjusting screw clockwise until a .005 feeler gauge can be installed with minimum friction, **Fig. 4.**
5. Turn adjusting screw an additional 4 turns.

#### Adjustment At Transmission

1. Ensure engine idle speed is set to specification.
2. Disconnect fast idle cam from carburetor so throttle lever is at its idle stop.
3. Position linkage lever screw at approximately the midpoint.
4. Raise and support vehicle.
5. Using a suitable tool, loosen bolt on sliding trunnion block on T.V. control rod assembly, **Fig. 5.**
6. Push up on the lower end of the control rod, **Fig. 5,** to ensure linkage lever

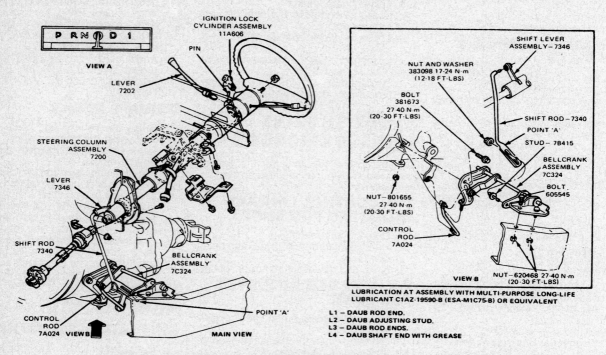

**Fig. 2 Shift linkage adjustment. F-150-250 4 x 2 models**

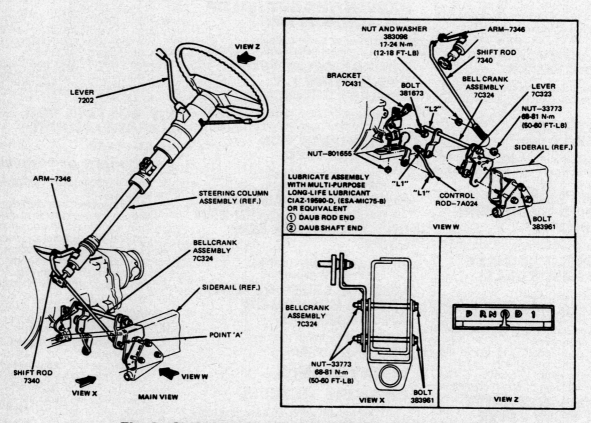

**Fig. 3 Shift linkage adjustment. E-150-250 models**

at carburetor is firmly against the throttle lever.

7. Push T.V. control lever on the transmission up against internal stop, then tighten bolt on trunnion block, **Fig. 5.**

## T.V. CONTROL CABLE, ADJUST

### V8-302 w/Fuel Injection & All 6 Cylinder Engines

On 1985-89 V8-302 fuel injected engines, proceed directly to step 6. On 6 cylinder engines, the ISC plunger must first be retracted before adjusting T.V. cable. To retract ISC plunger, follow steps 1 through 5.

1. Working inside of engine compartment, locate Self Test Connector and Self Test Input Connector. These two connectors are next to each other, **Fig. 6.**
2. Connect a jumper wire between the Self Test Input Connector and the Signal Return (ground) of the Self Test Connector, **Figs. 7 and 8.**
3. Turn ignition key to Run position but do not start engine.
4. Ensure that ISC plunger retracts, **Fig. 9.** Wait approximately 10 seconds for plunger to fully retract.
5. Shut off key, then remove jumper wire and air cleaner.
6. Apply parking brake and place selector lever in N.
7. Ensure that throttle lever is at idle stop. If not, check for binding or interference in throttle system. Do not attempt to adjust idle stop.
8. Ensure that cable routing is free of sharp bends or pressure points and that cable operates freely. Lubricate T.V. lever ball stud with suitable lubricant as necessary.
9. Unlock locking tab at end by pushing up from below, then pry up the rest of the way to free cable, **Figs. 10 and 11.**
10. Install retention spring on T.V. control lever to hold lever in idle position. If suitable single spring is not available, two V8 T.V. return springs may be used. Attach retention spring(s) to transmission T.V. lever and hook rear end of spring to transmission case, **Fig. 12.**
11. On 6 cylinder engine, de-cam carburetor, **Fig. 13.** The carburetor throttle lever must be in the anti-diesel idle position. Ensure that take up spring properly tensions cable and that there is no binding or sticking in sliding adjusting mechanism. If spring is loose or bottomed out, check for bent cable brackets.
12. Press down on locking key until flush, **Fig. 14.**
13. Remove retention springs from transmission T.V. lever.

## T.V. CONTROL PRESSURE, ADJUST

### Exc. 1986-89 Models

1. Ensure engine idle speed is set to specification.

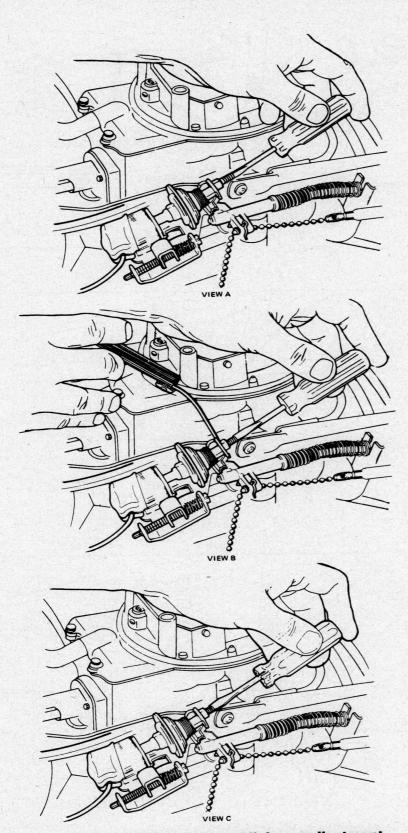

VIEW A

VIEW B

VIEW C

**Fig. 4   Throttle valve control linkage adjustment**

2. Connect a 0-100 psi pressure gauge with adapter fitting D80L-77001 or equivalent onto transmission T.V. port, **Fig. 15.**
3. Operate engine until normal operating temperature is obtained and throttle lever is off of fast idle.
4. Apply parking brake, place transmission selector lever into Neutral and remove air cleaner assembly from carburetor.
5. With engine idling in Neutral, insert a 1/16 inch drill bit, T.V. control pressure gauge block or fabricated block between carburetor throttle lever and adjusting screw on T.V. linkage lever at carburetor, **Figs. 16 and 17.**
6. The T.V. pressure should be between 30 and 40 psi, as close to 33 psi as possible. If not, turn adjusting screw inward to raise T.V. pressure or outward to lower T.V. pressure. If harsh or delayed shifting is evident on 1985 Bronco, E Series and F Series models with with V8-305 (5.0L) engines, adjust T.V. pressure to 29 psi in neutral. This will result in a T.V. pressure of approximately 31 psi when the selector is placed in drive.

## 1986—89 Models

1. Attach TV pressure gauge and hose, tool T86L-70002-A or equivalent, to TV pressure port on transmission.
2. On V8 engines, remove protective cover from cable linkage.
3. Install tapered end of TV control cable pressure gauge tool T86L-70332-A or equivalent, between crimped slug on end of cable and the plastic cable fitting that attaches to the throttle lever, **Fig. 18.**
4. Push gauge tool fully inward, until crimped slug is forced away from plastic fitting.
5. Run engine until normal operating temperature is reached and temperature of transmission fluid is 100-150 degrees F.
6. Apply parking brake, place shift selector in Neutral and observe pressure gauge. TV pressure should be between 30 and 40 psi, with optimum setting at 33 psi. If pressure is not as specified, proceed as follows:
   a. Using suitable tool, pry upward on locking tab of cable adjuster located at carburetor or throttle body. The adjuster preload spring should cause the adjusting slider to move away from the throttle body, causing TV pressure to increase.
   b. Push on slider from behind bracket until pressure is as specified, hold in this position, then push downward on locking tab to lock slider in position.
7. Remove gauge tool, allow cable to return to normal idle position, then observe pressure gauge.
8. Pressure should be at or near zero, and not greater than 5 psi. If pressure is greater than 5 psi, reinstall gauge block and readjust pressure to less than 35 psi, but not less than 30 psi, following procedure outlined in step 6,

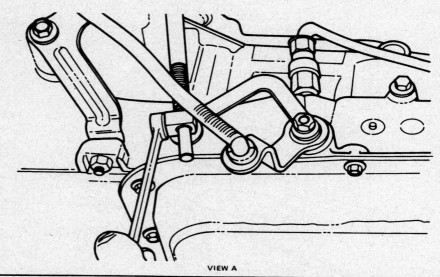

VIEW A

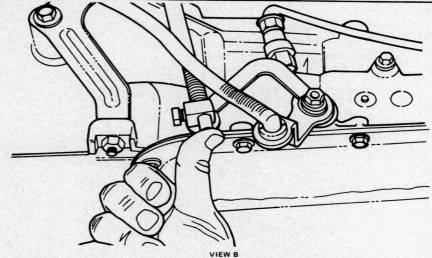

VIEW B

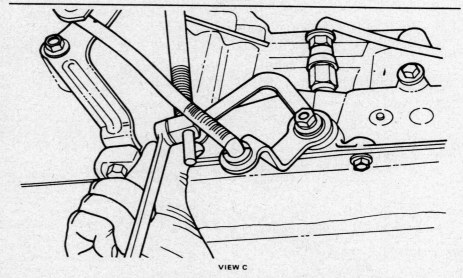

VIEW C

**Fig. 5  Transmission linkage adjustment**

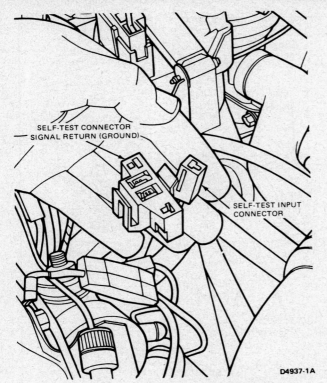

Fig. 6   Self-test connector location

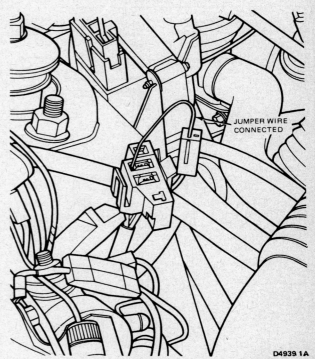

Fig. 7   Connecting jumper wires between self-test connectors

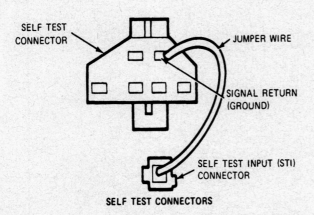

Fig. 8   Connecting self test connector ground circuit

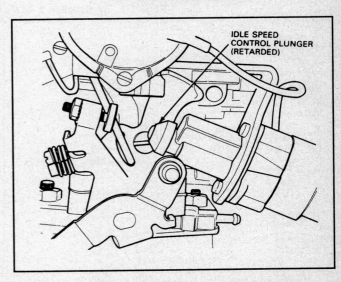

Fig. 9   ISC plunger in retracted position

then repeat step 7. If harsh or delayed shifting is evident on Bronco, E Series and F Series models with with V8-305 (5.0L) engines, adjust T.V. pressure to 29 psi in neutral. This will result in a T.V. pressure of approximately 31 psi when the selector is placed in drive.

# IN-VEHICLE REPAIRS
## CONTROL VALVE BODY

1. Raise and support vehicle, drain transmission fluid, then remove transmission pan, gasket and filter.
2. Remove detent spring attaching bolt, then the spring.
3. Remove valve body to case attaching bolts noting installation position, then remove valve body.
4. Reverse procedure to install. Use suitable guide pins to align valve body to case. On 1987–89 models, 2 special shouldered bolts are used to align and attach the valve body. **These bolts must be installed in the same locations noted during removal, Fig. 19. Installing these bolts in any other position may damage the valve body or cause misalignment that can result in transmission failure.**

## OVERDRIVE SERVO ASSEMBLY

1. Remove valve body as previously described.
2. Compress overdrive servo piston cover with a suitable tool, then remove snap ring retainer.
3. Apply compressed air to servo piston release passage and remove the overdrive servo piston cover and spring. Remove piston from cover, then the rubber seal from piston and cover.
4. Install new servo piston and cover seals on the servo piston and cover.

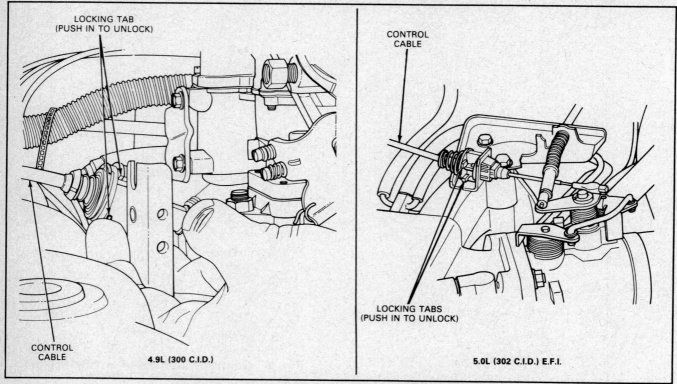

**Fig. 10   Unlocking T.V. control cable locking tab**

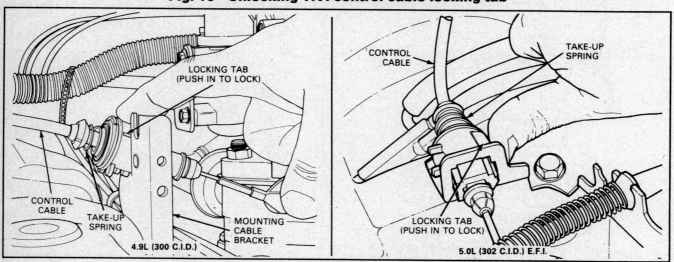

**Fig. 11   Prying up T.V. control cable locking tab**

5. Lubricate all seals, piston and piston bore with transmission fluid.
6. Install servo piston into cover, then the return spring into servo piston.
7. Install overdrive piston assembly into overdrive servo bore.
8. Compress overdrive piston using suitable tool, then install snap ring retainer.
9. Install valve body, filter, pan and gasket. Refill transmission to proper fluid level.

## REVERSE SERVO ASSEMBLY

Refer to "Overdrive Servo Assembly"

procedure for replacement. Apply compressed air to the servo piston release passage to remove servo piston from case. **Reverse servo piston is under spring pressure. Use caution when removing servo piston cover.**

## 3-4 ACCUMULATOR PISTON

1. Remove valve body as previously described.
2. Compress 3-4 accumulator piston cover, then remove snap ring retainer.

3. Release cover slowly, then remove piston cover, return spring and piston. Some models do not use a spring.
4. Remove seal from 3-4 accumulator cover and piston and inspect for damage and wear.
5. Install new seals on 3-4 accumulator cover, if necessary. Lubricate cover pocket of case with transmission fluid.
6. Install 3-4 accumulator piston and return spring into case, then the cover.
7. Compress cover using suitable tool, then install snap ring. Ensure cover is reseated snugly against snap ring.
8. Install valve body, filter, pan and gasket. Refill transmission pan to proper fluid level.

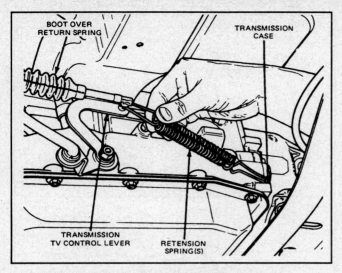

**Fig. 12   T.V. lever retention spring**

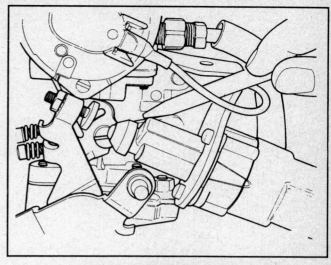

**Fig. 13   De-camming carburetor**

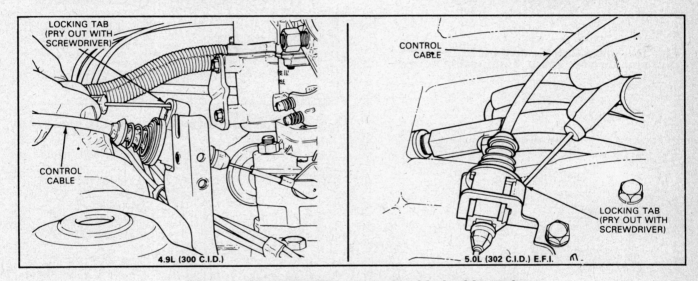

**Fig. 14   Installing T.V. control cable locking tab**

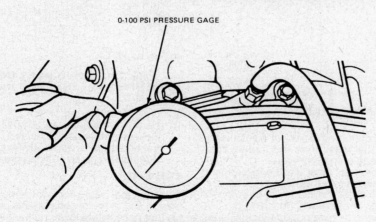

**Fig. 15   Install 0-100 pressure gauge**

## 2-3 ACCUMULATOR PISTON

Refer to "3-4 Accumulator Piston" for replacement procedure.

## EXTENSION HOUSING

1. Raise and support vehicle.
2. Disconnect parking brake cable from equalizer, if necessary.
3. Disconnect drive shaft from rear axle flange, then remove drive shaft from transmission.
4. Disconnect speedometer cable from extension housing.
5. Remove engine rear support to extension housing attaching bolts.
6. Support transmission with suitable jack and raise transmission enough to remove weight from rear engine support.
7. Remove engine rear support from crossmember, then lower transmission and remove extension housing attaching bolts. Slide extension housing from output shaft and allow fluid to drain.
8. Reverse procedure to install.

## GOVERNOR

1. Remove extension housing as described above. If governor body only is being removed, proceed to step 4.
2. Remove governor to output shaft retaining snap ring.

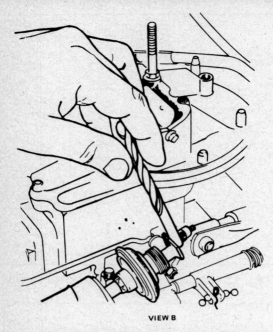

VIEW B

**Fig. 16  Installing 1/16 drill bit between carburetor throttle lever & adjusting screw**

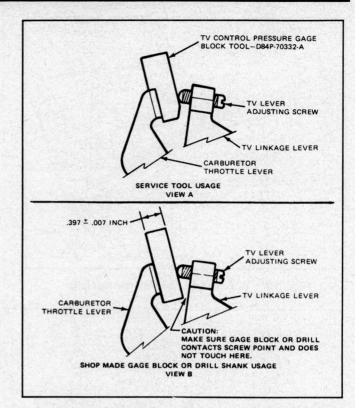

TV CONTROL PRESSURE GAGE BLOCK TOOL—D84P-70332-A

TV LEVER ADJUSTING SCREW

TV LINKAGE LEVER

CARBURETOR THROTTLE LEVER

SERVICE TOOL USAGE
VIEW A

.397 ± .007 INCH

TV LEVER ADJUSTING SCREW

TV LINKAGE LEVER

CARBURETOR THROTTLE LEVER

CAUTION:
MAKE SURE GAGE BLOCK OR DRILL CONTACTS SCREW POINT AND DOES NOT TOUCH HERE.

SHOP MADE GAGE BLOCK OR DRILL SHANK USAGE
VIEW B

**Fig. 17  T.V. control pressure gauge block tool**

TV CONTROL PRESSURE CHECK AND ADJUSTMENT

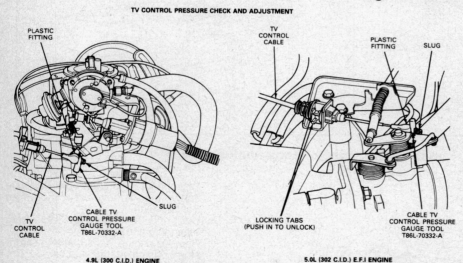

PLASTIC FITTING

TV CONTROL CABLE

PLASTIC FITTING

SLUG

CABLE TV CONTROL PRESSURE GAUGE TOOL T86L-70332-A

SLUG

LOCKING TABS (PUSH IN TO UNLOCK)

CABLE TV CONTROL PRESSURE GAUGE TOOL T86L-70332-A

4.9L (300 C.I.D.) ENGINE

5.0L (302 C.I.D.) E.F.I ENGINE

**Fig. 18  Installing tool T86L-70332-A onto throttle lever**

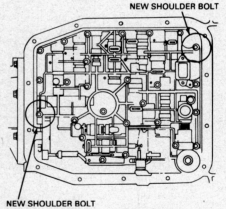

NEW SHOULDER BOLT

NEW SHOULDER BOLT

**Fig. 19  Valve body bolt identification. 1987—89 models**

3. Remove governor assembly from output shaft using suitable tool. Remove governor drive ball.
4. Remove governor to counterweight attaching screws. Remove governor from counterweight.
5. Reverse procedure to install.

## INTERNAL & EXTERNAL SHIFT LINKAGE

### 1981—83

1. Raise and support vehicle.
2. Drain transmission fluid from pan, then remove pan and gasket.

3. Disconnect shift rod at transmission manual lever, then the throttle valve linkage at transmission.
4. Disconnect inner throttle lever spring. Remove detent spring.
5. Hold outer throttle lever, then loosen outer throttle lever attaching nut. Remove attaching nut and lock washer.
6. Remove outer throttle lever seal, then the manual lever roll pin.
7. Remove outer manual lever attaching bolt, then the outer manual lever.
8. Remove inner throttle lever and spring.
9. Remove inner manual lever and park

pawl actuating rod.
10. Remove manual lever oil seal.
11. Reverse procedure to install. Adjust transmission manual linkage and throttle linkage as outlined previously.

### 1984—89

It may be necessary to remove fan shroud and exhaust components on models that necessitate lowering transmission to gain access to manual lever.
1. Raise and support vehicle.
2. Apply penetrating oil to outer throttle lever attaching nut to prevent breaking inner throttle lever.
3. Grasp outer throttle lever and hold firmly, then remove outer throttle lever

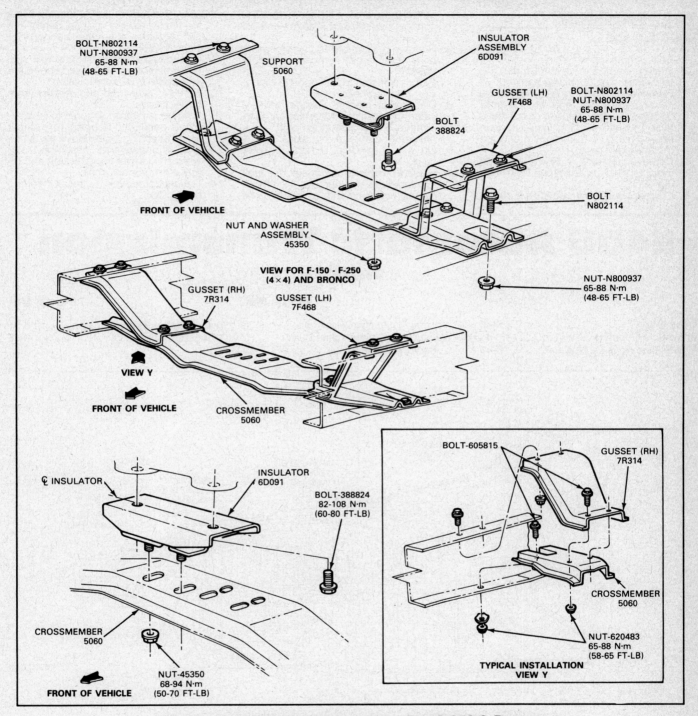

**Fig. 20  Crossmember installation. F-150-250 & Bronco**

attaching nut and lock washer and position lever and TV rod or cable assembly aside.

4. Carefully disconnect shift rod from transmission manual lever at transmission using shift linkage grommet removal tool T84P-7341-A or equivalent.
5. Remove oil pan, gasket and filter.
6. Remove manual lever detent spring and roller assembly.
7. Remove manual lever retaining pin by carefully prying with sharp narrow screwdriver.
8. Note assembled position of TV lever torsion spring, then remove spring.
9. Slide a 5/8 inch box wrench over inner manual lever close to bottom of lever, ensuring wrench does not contact rooster comb area, then using a 21 mm wrench, remove manual lever attaching nut. Hold inner manual lever securely with box wrench while applying break torque to attaching nut.
10. Remove outer manual lever from case.
11. Remove inner throttle lever and shaft assembly.
12. Remove inner manual lever and park pawl actuating rod assembly, then disconnect actuating rod from inner manual lever.
13. Remove and discard manual lever oil seal.
14. Reverse procedure to install, then adjust manual and throttle linkages.

## TRANSMISSION REPLACE

1. Raise and support vehicle.
2. Drain transmission fluid from pan. After fluid is drained, install pan.
3. Remove converter drain plug access cover from lower end of converter housing. Rotate engine to gain access to converter drain plug. Remove drain plug, drain fluid from converter, then replace drain plug.
4. Remove converter to flywheel attaching nuts, then the driveshaft from vehicle.
5. Disconnect battery cable from starter motor, then remove starter motor. Disconnect neutral start switch electrical connector.
6. Remove rear mount to crossmember bolts and crossmember to frame bolts.
7. Remove engine rear support to extension housing bolts.
8. Disconnect manual linkage and TV cable or rod from transmission, then remove bolts securing bell crank bracket to converter housing.
9. On 4 x 4 models, remove transfer case.
10. Raise transmission with suitable jack and remove crossmember. 4 x 4 models are equipped with a deep well oil pan. Ensure that jack used will allow for the increased oil pan depth and still provide adequate support for transmission.
11. Lower transmission slightly and disconnect oil cooler lines and speedometer cable from transmission.
12. Remove filler tube and dipstick from transmission.
13. With transmission secured to jack, remove converter housing to cylinder block attaching bolts. Move transmission and converter assembly rearward, then lower transmission and remove from under vehicle.
14. Reverse procedure to install, referring to **Fig. 20**.

# E4OD Automatic Transmission

## INDEX

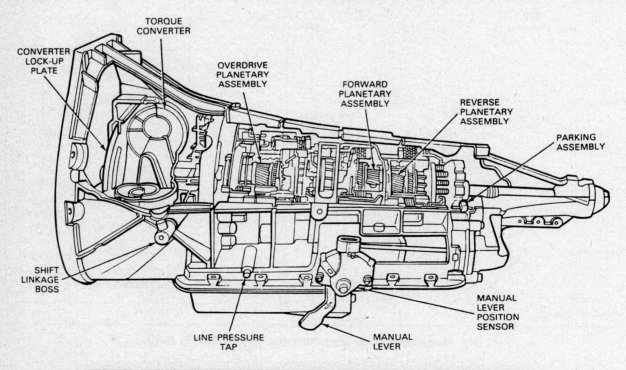

**Fig. 1   Cross-sectional view of E4OD automatic transmission**

## DESCRIPTION

This unit is a fully automatic, electronically controlled four-speed with a three element locking torque converter. It consists of a converter clutch, six multiple disc friction clutches, one band, two sprag one way clutches and a roller one way clutch,

**Fig. 1.** The roller one way clutch provides for desired function of three planetary gear sets.

## TROUBLESHOOTING

Refer to **Fig. 2** for troubleshooting procedures.

## IN-VEHICLE REPAIRS
### EXTENSION HOUSING, REPLACE
#### 4 x 4 Models

1. Raise and support vehicle.

*Continued on page 6-53*

## Fig. 2 E4OD automatic transmission troubleshooting chart (Part 2 of 12)

| CONDITION | POSSIBLE SOURCE | ACTION |
|---|---|---|
| Transmission overheats | 1. Excessive tow loads | 1. Check owner's manual for tow restriction. |
| | 2. Check fluid level — Fluid level high or low | 2. Drain or fill transmission to proper level. |
| | 3. Check electronic engine control operation | 3. EEC IV system malfunction. |
| | 4. Inspect transmission cooler and cooler lines — Restricted or blocked | 4. Service as required. |
| | 5. Test converter clutch — Converter clutch does not apply | 5. Service as required. |
| | 6. Inspect valve body — Dirty or sticky valves | 6. Clean, service or replace valve body. |
| | 7. Inspect torque converter one-way clutch — One-way clutch locked up | 7. Service as required. |
| No 1st gear, starts in higher gear | 1. Check line pressure — Low line pressure | 1. Perform line pressure test. |
| | 2. Check solenoid operation | 2. Service as required. |
| | 3. Inspect D2 valve, 2-3 shift valve and 3-4 shift valve — Springs missing or tangled — Dirty or sticky valves | 3. Determine source of contamination or damage. Service as required. |
| No 1-2 upshift | 1. Check fluid level — Fluid level high or low | 1. Drain or fill transmission to the proper level. |
| | 2. Check manual linkage — Misadjusted/damaged | 2. Service as required. |
| | 3. Test line pressure — Low to intermediate friction clutch | 3. Perform line pressure test. |
| | 4. Check solenoid operation — (S2 solenoid suspected) | 4. Service as required. |
| | 5. Inspect valve body bolts — Bolts loose or light | 5. Tighten bolts to 80-100 ft. lbs. |
| | 6. Inspect valve body — Dirty/sticky valves | 6. Determine source of contamination. Service as required. |
| | 7. Inspect 1-2 shift valve — Stuck, nicked or damaged | 7. Determine source of contamination. Service as required. |
| | 8. Inspect D2 valve — Spring missing or damaged — Dirty or sticky valves | 8. Determine source of contamination. Service as required. |

## Fig. 2 E4OD automatic transmission troubleshooting chart (Part 1 of 12)

| CONDITION | POSSIBLE SOURCE | ACTION |
|---|---|---|
| Fluid Leaks | 1. Case breather valve — Transmission fluid foaming | 1. Service as required. |
| | 2. Leakage at gasket, seals etc. | 2. Service as required. |
| Fluid venting or foaming | 1. Check fluid level (venting) — Transmission overfilled | 1. Drain transmission to proper level. |
| | 2. Inspect transmission fluid — Contaminated with anti-freeze or engine overheating | 2. Determine source of leak. Service as required. |
| | 3. Inspect transmission fluid filter — Damaged seal — Misassembly to pump | 3. Replace filter seals or reassemble fluid filter. |
| Stalls when stopping | 1. Poor engine performance | 1. Check engine and service as required. |
| | 2. Check fluid level | 2. Drain or fill transmission to proper level. |
| | 3. Check electronic engine control operation | 3. EEC IV system malfunction. |
| | 4. Test converter clutch — Converter clutch does not release | 4. Service as required. |
| Shift efforts high | 1. Inspect manual shift linkage — Damaged or misadjusted | 1. Service as required. |
| | 2. Inspect manual lever retainer pin — Damaged | 2. Adjust linkage and install new pin. |
| | 3. Check detent spring | 3. Service as required. |
| | 4. Inspect inner manual lever nut | 4. Tighten nut to 30-40 ft. lbs. |
| Poor vehicle performance | 1. Poor engine performance | 1. EEC IV system malfunction. |
| | 2. Test converter clutch — Converter clutch does not release | 2. Service as required. |
| | 3. Inspect torque converter one-way clutch — One-way clutch locked up | 3. Replace converter. |
| Vehicle will not start | 1. Inspect ignition switch — Misadjusted or defective | 1. Adjust or replace as required. |
| | 2. Check fluid level — Fluid level high or low | 2. Drain or fill transmission to proper level. |
| | 3. Check electronic engine control operation | 3. EEC IV system malfunction. |

## Fig. 2 E4OD automatic transmission troubleshooting chart (Part 4 of 12)

| CONDITION | POSSIBLE SOURCE | ACTION |
|---|---|---|
| 2-3 Shift harsh or soft (Cont'd) | 5. Inspect intermediate clutch accumulator<br>— Plunger stuck or damaged<br>— Springs missing or tangled | 5. Determine source of contamination or damage. Service as required. |
| | 6. Inspect valve body<br>— Dirty or sticky valves | 6. Determine source of contamination. Service as required. |
| | 7. Inspect pump air bleed check valve<br>— Valve leaking or damaged | 7. Determine source of contamination or damage. Service as required. |
| | 8. Inspect intermediate clutch assembly<br>— Clutch plates damaged/missing<br>— Piston or seals damaged<br>— Ball check stuck or missing<br>— Feedbolt loose/missing sealant leak<br>— Clutch hub damaged | 8. Determine source of contamination or damage. Service as required. |
| No 2-3 upshift | 1. Check fluid level<br>— Fluid level high or low | 1. Drain or fill transmission to the proper level. |
| | 2. Check line pressure<br>— Low to direct clutch | 2. Perform line pressure test. |
| | 3. Check solenoid operation<br>— (S1 solenoid suspected) | 3. Service as required. |
| | 4. Inspect valve body bolts<br>— Loose or tight | 4. Tighten bolts to 80-100 ft. lbs. |
| | 5. Inspect valve body<br>— Dirty or sticky valves | 5. Determine source of contamination. Service as required. |
| | 6. Inspect 2-3 shift valve<br>— Valve stuck, nicked or damaged | 6. Determine source of contamination. Service as required. |
| | 7. BS5 check ball missing<br>— Plate seat damaged | 7. Service as required. |
| | 8. Inspect direct clutch assembly<br>— Clutch plates damaged/missing<br>— Piston or seals damaged<br>— Ball check assembly stuck or missing | 8. Determine source of contamination. Service as required. |
| | 9. Inspect direct clutch cylinder<br>— Seals damaged or missing or holes blocked | 9. Determine source of contamination. Service as required. |
| | 10. Inspect center support<br>— Damaged<br>— Feedbolts loose or missing<br>— Center support O.D. or case bore damaged/leaking<br>— Teflon seal damaged | 10. Service as required. |

## Fig. 2 E4OD automatic transmission troubleshooting chart (Part 3 of 12)

| CONDITION | POSSIBLE SOURCE | ACTION |
|---|---|---|
| No 1-2 upshift (Cont'd) | 9. Inspect intermediate clutch accumulator regulator valve<br>— Stuck, nicked or damaged | 9. Determine source of contamination. Service as required. |
| | 10. Inspect intermediate clutch accumulator<br>— Plunger stuck or damaged<br>— Springs missing or damaged | 10. Determine source of contamination. Service as required. |
| | 11. Inspect intermediate clutch assembly<br>— Clutch plates damaged/missing<br>— Piston or seals damaged<br>— Ball check stuck/missing<br>— Feedbolt loose/missing/sealant leak<br>— Clutch hub damaged | 11. Determine source of contamination or damage. Service as required. |
| | 12. Inspect intermediate one-way clutch assembly<br>— Damaged cage/sprags<br>— Misassembled on inner race | 12. Disassemble and inspect. Service as required. |
| 1-2 Shift harsh or soft | 1. Check line pressure<br>— High or low line pressure | 1. Perform line pressure test. |
| | 2. Service line modulator pressure<br>— High or low | 2. Service as required. |
| | 3. Inspect valve body bolts<br>— Loose or tight | 3. Tighten bolts to 80-100 ft. lbs. |
| | 4. Inspect intermediate clutch accumulator regulator valve<br>— Valve stuck, nicked or damaged<br>— Spring missing or tangled | 4. Determine source of contamination or damage. Service as required. |
| | 5. Inspect valve body<br>— Dirty or sticky valves | 5. Determine source of contamination. Service as required. |
| | 6. Inspect intermediate clutch accumulator<br>— Plunger stuck or damaged<br>— Springs missing or tangled | 6. Determine source of contamination or damage. Service as required. |
| 2-3 Shift harsh or soft | 1. Check line pressure<br>— High or low line pressure | 1. Perform line pressure test. |
| | 2. Service line modulator pressure<br>— High or low | 2. Service as required. |
| | 3. Inspect valve body bolts<br>— Loose or tight | 3. Tighten bolts to 80-100 ft. lbs. |
| | 4. Inspect intermediate clutch accumulator regulator valve<br>— Valve stuck, nicked or damaged<br>— Spring missing or tangled | 4. Determine source of contamination or damage. Service as required. |

## Fig. 2 E4OD automatic transmission troubleshooting chart (Part 6 of 12)

| CONDITION | POSSIBLE SOURCE | ACTION |
|---|---|---|
| No 3-4 upshift (Cont'd) | 8. Inspect overdrive clutch assembly<br>— Clutch plates burnt or worn<br>— Overdrive clutch cylinder damaged/feedbolt loose or missing/sealant leaking<br>— Cylinder ball check assembly stuck or missing | 8. Service as required. |
| 3-4 Shift harsh or soft | 1. Check line pressure<br>— Line pressure high or low | 1. Perform line pressure test. |
| | 2. Service line modulator pressure<br>— High or low | 2. Refer to service procedure in this section if necessary. |
| | 3. Inspect valve body bolts<br>— Bolts loose or tight | 3. Tighten bolts to 80-100 ft. lbs. |
| | 4. Inspect valve body<br>— Dirty or sticky valves | 4. Determine source of contamination. Service as required. |
| | 5. Inspect overdrive accumulator regulator valve<br>— Valve stuck, nicked/damaged<br>— Spring missing or tangled | 5. Determine source of contamination. Service as required. |
| | 6. Inspect overdrive accumulator<br>— Accumulator plunger stuck or damaged<br>— Springs missing or tangled | 6. Determine source of contamination. Service as required. |
| | 7. Inspect overdrive clutch assembly<br>— Clutch plates burnt or worn<br>— Overdrive clutch cylinder damaged or feedbolt loose or missing<br>— Cylinder ball check assembly stuck or missing | 7. Service as required. |
| Shifts 1-3 | 1. Check fluid level<br>— Fluid level high or low | 1. Drain or fill transmission to the proper level. |
| | 2. Check solenoid operation<br>— (S1 solenoid suspected) | 2. Service as required. |
| | 3. Inspect D2 shift valve<br>— Dirty or sticky<br>— Spring missing or damaged | 3. Determine source of contamination. Service as required. |
| | 4. Inspect intermediate clutch accumulator regulator valve<br>— Valve sticky or dirty | 4. Determine source of contamination. Service as required. |
| | 5. Inspect intermediate friction clutch<br>— Burnt or worn | 5. Service as required. |

## Fig. 2 E4OD automatic transmission troubleshooting chart (Part 5 of 12)

| CONDITION | POSSIBLE SOURCE | ACTION |
|---|---|---|
| 2-3 Shift harsh or soft | 1. Check line pressure<br>— High or low line pressure | 1. Perform line pressure test. |
| | 2. Service line modulator pressure<br>— High or low | 2. Service as required. |
| | 3. Inspect valve body bolts<br>— Bolts tight or loose | 3. Tighten bolts to 80-100 ft. lbs. |
| | 4. Inspect valve body<br>— Dirty or sticky valves | 4. Determine source of contamination. Service as required. |
| | 5. Inspect direct clutch accumulator regulator valve<br>— Valve stuck, nicked or damaged<br>— Spring missing or tangled | 5. Determine source of contamination or damage. Service as required. |
| | 6. Inspect direct clutch accumulator<br>— Springs missing or tangled<br>— Plunger nicked or damaged | 6. Determine source of contamination. Service as required. |
| | 7. Inspect direct clutch assembly<br>— Clutch plates damaged/missing<br>— Piston or seals damaged<br>— Ball check assembly stuck or missing | 7. Determine source of contamination or damage. Service as required. |
| | 8. Inspect direct clutch cylinder<br>— Seals damaged, missing or holes blocked | 8. Determine source of contamination. Service as required. |
| | 9. Inspect center support<br>— Damaged<br>— Feedbolts loose or missing<br>— Center support O.D. or case bore damaged/leaking<br>— Teflon seal damaged | 9. Service as required. |
| No 3-4 upshift | 1. Check fluid level<br>— Fluid level high or low | 1. Drain or fill transmission to the proper level. |
| | 2. Check line pressure<br>— High or low line pressure | 2. Perform line pressure test. |
| | 3. Check solenoid operation<br>— (S2 solenoid suspected) | 3. Service as required. |
| | 4. Inspect valve body bolts<br>— Bolts tight or loose | 4. Tighten bolts to 80-100 ft. lbs. |
| | 5. Inspect valve body<br>— Dirty or sticky valves | 5. Determine source of contamination. Service as required. |
| | 6. Inspect 3-4 shift valve<br>— Valve stuck, nicked or damaged<br>— Springs missing or tangled | 6. Determine source of contamination. Service as required. |
| | 7. Inspect overdrive accumulator regulator valve<br>— Valve stuck, nicked or damaged<br>— Spring missing or tangled | 7. Determine source of contamination or damage. Service as required. |

**Fig. 2 E4OD automatic transmission troubleshooting chart (Part 8 of 12)**

| CONDITION | POSSIBLE SOURCE | ACTION |
|---|---|---|
| No drive in drive range (Cont'd) | 9. Inspect reverse one-way clutch<br>— Improperly assembled<br>— Damaged rollers | 9. Determine source of damage. Service as required. |
| | 10. Inspect front sun gear/shell<br>— Damaged | 10. Determine source of damage. Service as required. |
| | 11. Inspect front and rear carrier<br>— Damaged pinions/lugs to rear ring gear | 11. Determine source of damage. Service as required. |
| | 12. Inspect reverse ring gear<br>— Damaged gears/lugs to forward carrier | 12. Determine source of damage. Service as required. |
| | 13. Inspect output shaft<br>— Damaged splines | 13. Determine source of damage. Service as required. |
| No reverse | 1. Check fluid level<br>— Fluid level low | 1. Fill transmission to the proper level. |
| | 2. Inspect manual linkage<br>— Misadjusted, disconnected, damaged, broken or bent | 2. Service as required. |
| | 3. Check line pressure<br>— Line pressure low | 3. Perform line pressure test. |
| | 4. Check transmission filter inside oil pan | 4. Replace filter if plugged. |
| | 5. Inspect valve body and pump control body bolts<br>— Loose or tight | 5. Tighten bolts to 80-100 ft. lbs. |
| | 6. Inspect pump control body and valve body<br>— Dirty or sticky valves | 6. Determine source of contamination. Service as required. |
| | 7. Inspect direct clutch accumulator regulator valve<br>— Valve stuck, nicked/damaged<br>— Spring missing or tangled | 7. Determine source of contamination or damage. Service as required. |
| | 8. BS5 checkball missing<br>— Plate seat damaged | 8. Service as required. |
| | 9. Inspect direct clutch assembly (if 3rd gear inoperative)<br>— Damaged piston or seals<br>— Burnt or missing clutch plates<br>— Direct clutch ball check<br>— Direct clutch assembly missing or damaged<br>— Center support seals damaged or missing or holes blocked<br>— Direct clutch hub damaged | 9. Disassemble and inspect clutch assembly. Service as required. |
| | 10. Inspect coast clutch assembly for leakage | 10. Disassemble and inspect clutch assembly. Service as required. |

**Fig. 2 E4OD automatic transmission troubleshooting chart (Part 7 of 12)**

| CONDITION | POSSIBLE SOURCE | ACTION |
|---|---|---|
| Shifts 1-3 (Cont'd) | 6. Inspect intermediate one-way clutch assembly<br>— Damaged cage/sprags<br>— Misassembled on inner race | 6. Disassemble and inspect. Service as required. |
| Shift speed high or low | 1. Check fluid level<br>— Fluid level high or low | 1. Drain or fill transmission to the proper level. |
| | 2. Check electronic engine control operation | 2. EEC IV system malfunction. |
| | 3. Inspect vehicle speed sensor<br>— Wrong gear/damaged gear | 3. Repair or replace as necessary. |
| 4-3 Downshift harsh | 1. CB7 check ball missing<br>— Plate seat damaged | 1. Service as required. |
| 3-2 Downshift harsh | 1. CB6 check ball missing<br>— Plate seat damaged | 1. Service as required. |
| 2-1 Downshift harsh | 1. CB14 check ball missing<br>— Plate seat damaged | 1. Service as required. |
| No drive in drive range | 1. Check fluid level<br>— Fluid level low | 1. Fill transmission to the proper level. |
| | 2. Check line pressure<br>— Line pressure low | 2. Perform line pressure test. |
| | 3. Inspect manual linkage (internal and external)<br>— Misadjusted, disconnected, damaged, broken or bent | 3. Service as required. |
| | 4. Check transmission filter inside oil pan | 4. Replace filter if plugged. |
| | 5. Inspect valve body and pump control body bolts<br>— Loose or tight | 5. Tighten bolts to 80-100 ft. lbs. |
| | 6. Inspect pump control body and valve body<br>— Dirty or sticky valves | 6. Determine source of contamination. Service as required. |
| | 7. Inspect overdrive one-way clutch<br>— Improperly assembled/damaged<br>— Damaged sprags or races | 7. Service as required. |
| | 8. Inspect forward clutch assembly<br>— Burnt or missing clutch plates<br>— Damaged piston or seals<br>— Forward clutch ball check<br>— Forward clutch assembly missing or damaged<br>— Center support seals damaged or missing/holes blocked/feedbolt loose or missing<br>— Forward clutch hub damaged | 8. Determine source of contamination or damage. Service as required. |

| CONDITION | POSSIBLE SOURCE | ACTION |
|---|---|---|
| No forced downshifts | 1. Check fluid level<br> — Fluid level high or low<br>2. Check electronic engine control operation<br>3. Inspect valve body bolts<br> — Bolts loose or tight<br>4. Inspect valve body<br> — Dirty or sticky valves | 1. Drain or fill transmission to the proper level.<br>2. EEC IV system malfunction.<br><br>3. Tighten bolts to 80-100 ft. lbs.<br>4. Determine source of contamination. Service as required. |
| No engine braking in manual one | 1. Check fluid level<br> — Fluid level low<br>2. Check line pressure<br> — Line pressure low<br>3. Check solenoid operation<br> — (S1 solenoid suspected)<br>4. Inspect for dirty or sticky valves<br> — Reverse clutch modulator, D2 4-3-2 timing or 2-3 or coast clutch shift valves<br>5. Check ball missing<br> — BS1, BS3 or CB1<br> — Plate seat damaged<br>6. Inspect coast clutch<br> — Worn or burnt<br> — Piston or seals damaged<br> — Stator support damaged or holes blocked<br> — Coast clutch hub damaged or holes blocked<br>7. Inspect reverse clutch<br> — Worn or burnt<br> — Piston or seals damaged | 1. Fill transmission to the proper level.<br>2. Perform line pressure test.<br><br>3. Service as required.<br><br>4. Determine source of contamination. Service as required.<br><br>5. Service as required.<br><br>6. Service as required.<br><br><br><br><br>7. Service as required. |
| No engine braking in manual second | 1. Check fluid level<br> — Fluid level low<br>2. Check line pressure<br> — Line pressure low<br>3. Inspect for dirty or sticky valves<br> — 4-3-2 timing, D2, 2-3 or coast clutch shift valve<br>4. Check ball missing<br> — BS1, BS3 or CB1<br> — Plate seat damaged<br>5. Check intermediate servo<br>6. Inspect intermediate band or drum<br> — Worn or burnt | 1. Fill transmission to the proper level.<br>2. Perform line pressure test.<br><br>3. Determine source of contamination. Service as required.<br><br>4. Service as required.<br><br>5. Perform air pressure test of servo for leakage. Service as required.<br>6. Service as required. |

**Fig. 2 E4OD automatic transmission troubleshooting chart (Part 10 of 12)**

| CONDITION | POSSIBLE SOURCE | ACTION |
|---|---|---|
| No reverse (Cont'd) | 11. Inspect reverse clutch<br> — Burnt or missing clutch plates<br> — Damaged piston or seals<br>12. Inspect front and rear carrier<br> — Damaged pinions/lugs to rear ring gear | 11. Determine source of damage. Service as required.<br><br>12. Determine source of damage. Service as required. |
| No park range | 1. Inspect manual shift linkage<br> — Damaged or misadjusted<br>2. Damage park mechanism<br> — Chipped or broken parking pawl or parking gear<br> — Broken park pawl return spring<br> — Bent or broken actuating rod | 1. Service as required.<br><br>2. Determine source of damage. Service as required. |
| Harsh neutral to drive or neutral to reverse engagements | 1. Check fluid level<br> — Fluid level low<br>2. Check electronic engine control operation<br>3. Worm/damaged/loose U-joint, slip yoke, rear axle or rear suspension<br>4. Inspect valve body bolts<br> — Loose or tight<br>5. Engagement control valve<br> — Valve stuck, nicked or damaged<br>6. CB13 check ball missing<br> — Plate seat damaged<br>7. Inspect direct clutch accumulator regulator valves<br> — Valve sticking or dirty<br> — Spring missing or tangled<br>8. Inspect direct clutch accumulator<br> — Accumulator plunger stuck<br> — Accumulator seal damaged or missing<br> — Springs missing or tangled<br>9. Inspect forward clutch assembly<br> — Burnt or missing clutch plates<br> — Damaged piston or seals<br> — Forward clutch ball check assembly missing or damaged<br> — Center support seals damaged or missing/holes blocked/ feedbolt loose or missing<br> — Forward clutch hub damaged<br>10. Inspect reverse clutch for leakage.<br>11. Excessive transmission end play | 1. Fill transmission to the proper level.<br>2. EEC IV system malfunction.<br><br>3. Service as required.<br><br>4. Tighten bolts to 30-40 ft. lbs.<br><br>5. Determine source of contamination. Service as required.<br>6. Service as required.<br><br>7. Determine source of contamination. Service as required.<br><br>8. Determine source of contamination. Service as required.<br><br><br>9. Determine source of contamination or damage. Service as required.<br><br><br><br><br><br>10. Identify source of leakage. Service as required.<br>11. Check transmission end play. Replace selective thrust washer if necessary. |

**Fig. 2 E4OD automatic transmission troubleshooting chart (Part 9 of 12)**

| CONDITION | POSSIBLE SOURCE | ACTION |
|---|---|---|
| No engine braking in manual second (Cont'd) | 7. Inspect coast clutch<br>— Worn or burnt<br>— Piston or seals damaged<br>— Stator support damaged or holes blocked<br>— Coast clutch hub damaged or holes blocked | 7. Service as required. |
| Erratic shifts | 1. Check fluid level<br>— Fluid level high or low<br><br>2. Check electronic engine control operation<br><br>3. Inspect vehicle speed sensor<br>— Damaged or defective<br>4. Inspect valve body bolts<br>— Bolts loose or tight<br>5. Inspect valve body<br>—Dirty or sticky valves | 1. Drain or fill transmission to the proper level.<br>2. EEC IV system malfunction.<br><br>3 Service as required.<br><br>4. Tighten bolts to 80-100 ft. lbs.<br>5. Determine source of contamination. Service as required. |
| Shift hunting | 1. Check fluid level<br>— Fluid level high or low<br>2. Check electronic engine control operation | 1. Drain or fill transmission to the proper level.<br>2. EEC IV system malfunction. |
| High or low line pressure | 1. Check fluid level<br>— Fluid level high or low<br>2. Electronic pressure control solenoid malfunction<br><br>3. Main regulator valve or spring<br>— Dirty or sticky valve<br>— Damaged spring<br>4. Pump assembly<br>— Gears damaged, broken or worn | 1. Drain or fill transmission to the proper level.<br>2. EEC IV system malfunction.<br><br>3. Determine source of damage or contamination. Service as required.<br>4. Determine source of damage. Service as required. |
| No converter clutch apply | 1. Check fluid level<br>— Fluid level high or low<br>2. Electrical system or electronic engine control<br>— No lock-up signal<br>— S3 solenoid malfunction<br>— Bulkhead connector damaged<br>— Pinched wires<br>3. Inspect stator shaft Teflon seal<br>— Damaged seal<br>4. Converter clutch control valve<br>— Dirty or sticky | 1. Drain or fill transmission to the proper level.<br>2. EEC IV system malfunction.<br><br><br>3. Determine source of contamination. Service as required.<br>4. Determine source of contamination. Service as required. |

**Fig. 2   E4OD automatic transmission
troubleshooting chart (Part 11 of 12)**

| CONDITION | POSSIBLE SOURCE | ACTION |
|---|---|---|
| Converter clutch does not release | 1. Check fluid level<br>— Fluid level high or low<br>2. Electrical system or electronic engine control<br>— No unlock signal<br>— S3 solenoid malfunction<br>— Bulkhead connector damaged<br>— Pinched wires<br>3. Converter clutch control valve<br>— Dirty or stuck valve | 1. Drain or fill transmission to the proper level.<br>2. EEC IV system malfunction.<br><br><br>3. Determine source of contamination. Service as required. |
| Line modulator pressure high or low | 1. Check line pressure<br>— High or low line pressure<br><br>2. Inspect line pressure modulator valve<br>— Valve stuck or damaged<br>— Plunger or sleeve stuck or damaged | 2. Perform line pressure test.<br><br>2. Determine source of contamination or damage. Service as required. |

**Fig. 2   E4OD automatic transmission
troubleshooting chart (Part 12 of 12)**

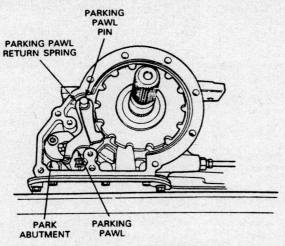

**Fig. 3   Removing parking pawl pin**

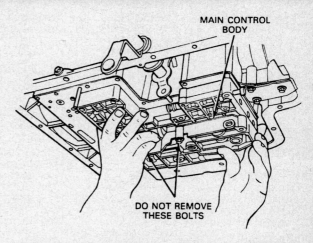

**Fig. 4   Removing main control body**

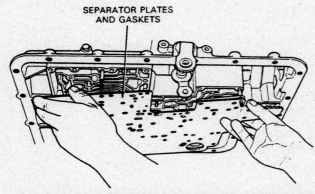

**Fig. 5   Removing separator plate & gaskets**

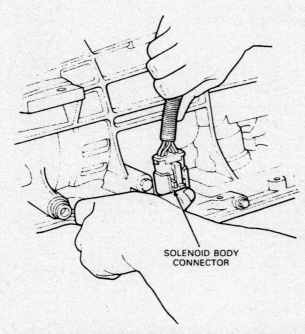

**Fig. 6   Removing solenoid body connector**

2. Remove front and rear driveshafts.
3. Remove transmission mounting pad attaching nuts and bolts.
4. Remove transfer case shift linkage to shift lever.
5. Remove four-wheel drive switch connector from transfer case. Do not overextend tabs.
6. Disconnect wire harness locators from left side of crossmember.
7. Disconnect speedometer cable and remove transfer case vent hose.
8. Position a suitable jack under transfer case.
9. Remove nine bolts securing extension housing, then slide transfer case to gain clearance and remove housing.
10. Reverse procedure to install.

## PARKING MECHANISM, REPLACE

1. Remove two attaching bolts from park rod guide plate.
2. Remove parking pawl, return spring and pin from case.
3. Remove Torx head bolt and parking pawl abutment, **Fig. 3.**
4. Reverse procedure to install, noting the following:
   a. Ensure return spring end rests on inside surface of case.
   b. Torque Torx head bolt to 16-20 ft. lbs.
   c. Ensure plate dimple is facing inward.

## VALVE BODY & INTERMEDIATE BAND SERVO, REPLACE

1. Disconnect battery ground cable.
2. Raise and support vehicle.
3. Loosen oil pan attaching bolts and drain fluid from transmission.
4. Remove filter and gasket.
5. Remove accumulator body and main control body attaching bolts, **Do not remove two bolts, as shown in Fig. 4,** from main control body.
6. Remove solenoid attaching bolts, then the solenoid and screen by turning counterclockwise.
7. Remove three plate attaching bolts,

then carefully lower separator plate and gasket so check balls, EPC ball and spring are retained, **Fig. 5.**
8. Remove servo snap ring and retaining plate, piston, rod assembly and servo spring.
9. Reverse procedure to install.

## TRANSMISSION
## REPLACE

1. Disconnect battery ground cable.
2. Remove transmission dipstick, then place selector in Neutral position.
3. Raise and support vehicle.
4. Remove driveshaft.
5. On 4 x 4 models, remove front driveshaft.
6. On F-Super Duty vehicles, remove transmission mounted parking brake.
7. On all models, disconnect shift linkage.
8. On 4 x 4 models, remove shift linkage from transfer case shift lever.
9. On all models, remove manual lever position sensor connector. **Do not pry tab with screwdriver.**
10. Remove solenoid heat shield, then disconnect solenoid body connector, **Fig. 6.**
11. On 4 x 4 models, remove switch connector from transfer case.
12. On all models, pry wire harness locators from extension housing wire bracket.
13. On 4 x 4 models, remove wire harness locators from LH side of crossmember.
14. On all models, disconnect speedometer cable, then remove lower converter cover attaching bolts.
15. Remove rear engine mount attaching bolts.
16. Disconnect starter cables, then remove starter from vehicle.
17. Rotate crankshaft bolt to gain access to converter nuts, then remove four converter retaining nuts.
18. Raise transmission using a suitable jack and safety chain.
19. Remove rear engine mount and crossmember, then disconnect oil cooler lines from transmission.
20. Remove bell housing attaching bolts, then back out converter from flywheel and lower transmission from vehicle.
21. Remove converter housing and transmission filler tube.
22. On 4 x 4 models, remove transfer case vent hose from detent bracket and transfer case from transmission.
23. On all models, reverse procedure to install.

# ELECTRONIC IGNITION

## TABLE OF CONTENTS

# Ignition Timing Adjustments

## INDEX

## IGNITION TIMING ADJUST

Refer to Tune Up Specifications chart for timing specifications only in the absence of a decal affixed in the engine compartment. Ignition timing should be checked and, if necessary, adjusted every 30,000 miles.

1. Place transmission in Park or Neutral position.
2. Turn A/C and heater systems Off.
3. Connect suitable tachometer and timing light to engine following manufacturers instructions.
4. On 1981-82 models with V8-460 engine, remove air cleaner assembly.
5. On all models, disconnect and plug vacuum advance hoses, if equipped, from distributor.
6. On 1981 models with V8-351W engine over 8500 lbs. gross vehicle weight, V8-351M or V8-400 engine, disconnect and plug vacuum hose to Thermactor bypass valve. If bypass hose is equipped with two hoses, disconnect hose nearest front of vehicle, then install a slave vacuum hose from a manifold vacuum source to bypass valve.
7. On models so equipped, disconnect single wire inline "spout" connector or remove shorting bar from double wire "spout" connector. Up to mid-year 1985 production vehicles, a single wire inline "spout" connector was installed near the distributor on all EEC applications. On 1985 4-140 engines, the connector was relocated between the engine and right side fender apron. Beginning with all 1986 models, the inline connector is replaced by a double wire "spout" connector with a shortening bar.
8. On 1982–83 models with 6-300 engine (calibration codes 2-51P and 3-51P), disconnect MCU electrical connector from ignition module and connect a jumper wire across module connector terminals.
9. On models equipped with barometric pressure switch, disconnect switch electrical connector from ignition module and connect a jumper wire across module connector terminals.
10. On all models, start engine and run until normal operating temperature is reached.
11. Set engine idle speed to specification, then check and adjust ignition timing as required.
12. Remove test equipment and restore all original connections.

# 1980 Dura Spark II Ignition System

## INDEX

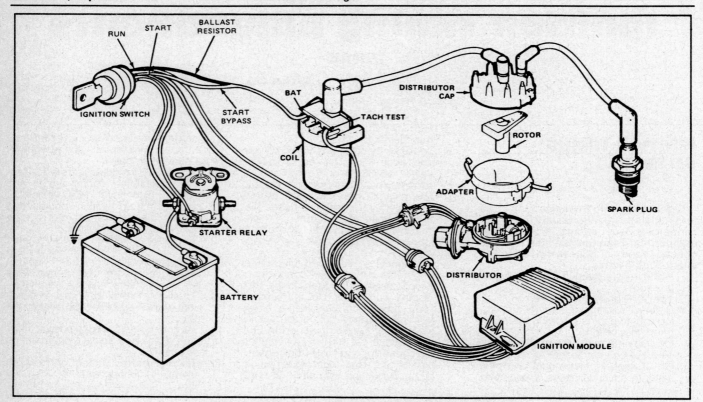

**Fig. 1   Dura Spark II Ignition System**

## DESCRIPTION

The Dura Spark II ignition system, **Fig. 1**, is controlled by an electronic module. Also incorporated into this system, is a low rated ballast resistor, which generates higher voltage to create a hotter spark. Centrifugal and vacuum advance units are utilized in the distributor, **Fig. 2**,

The ignition system consists of the following: A primary circuit containing an ignition switch, ballast resistor with bypass start wires, battery, primary coil winding, distributor stator assembly and ignition module. A secondary circuit containing an ignition switch, battery, secondary coil winding, distributor cap and rotor, ignition wires, ballast resistor with bypass start wires and spark plugs.

Current from the battery flows through the ignition switch, ballast resistor, ignition coil primary winding, ignition module, distributor ground and returns to the battery. The flow of current creates a magnetic field in the ignition coil. When the distributor armature rotates past the stator assembly, fluctuations occur in the stator assembly magnetic field. The fluctuations induce voltage in the stator assembly pickup coil, the voltage is sent through a wiring harness, to the ignition module. The ignition module stops primary current when armature and stator poles line up. This collapses the magnetic field in the coil inducing high voltage in the secondary coil winding. The high voltage is sent, through the coil wire, distributor cap and rotor, then through the ignition wires to the spark plugs.

## SYSTEM DIAGNOSIS

If the ignition system is suspected of a malfunction inspect for loose connections and check for spark at the spark plug.

If no spark is observed during the above test, check the ignition coil high tension wire, replace if damaged.

A condition of intermittent vehicle operation may be diagnosed as follows:

1. With engine running at idle, move all primary wires, connectors and battery cables by pushing, pulling and twisting by hand. If vehicle stalls, make necessary repairs to wire or connector.
2. With engine off, disconnect secondary wire from ignition coil. Inspect coil for cracks or carbon tracings, and the wires for cracks. If any damage is found, replace components as needed.
3. Inspect distributor cap for damage or carbon tracings. If any damage is

found, replace cap and/or rotor as needed.

4. On models equipped with stator, remove distributor cap and position a 250 watt heat lamp 1-2 inches away from stator for 5-10 minutes. Measure resistance between orange and purple wires located at inner left hand fender apron. Lightly tap pickup coil with a screwdriver. If resistance is less than 400 ohms or greater than 1000 ohms, replace stator.

5. With engine running at idle, heat ignition module with a 250 watt heat lamp positioned 1-2 inches from module. Do not allow temperature of module to exceed 212 degrees F. If engine stalls, replace module with a known good unit. If this corrects malfunction, recheck original module by reconnecting it to circuit.

6. Measure primary circuit ground resistance at ignition module connector black wire. If resistance is not zero ohms, remove distributor cap and inspect retaining screw at rubber plug where wires enter distributor. If screw or connection is loose or corroded, an intermittent high resistance or complete loss of ground may be causing ignition problem.

7. Start engine several times and jiggle ignition switch with engine idling. If engine stalls, repair or replace ignition switch and/or connectors as needed. If engine does not stall, replace ignition module.

8. If engine malfunction occurs only at extreme low ambient temperature conditions, check for an open in feed to white lead to module.

## SECONDARY CIRCUIT TESTS

### Rotor Air Gap

1. Connect an oscilloscope with voltage pickup on coil to distributor cable. Set oscilloscope to 30 KV parade pattern.

2. Disconnect any spark plug wire (except no. 1) and ground it firmly to engine block. **While engine is running, do not disconnect spark plug wires 1, 3, or 5 on inline 6 cylinder engine, or 1 or 8 on V8 engine. These contacts in the distributor cap are above the stator and arcing may result when the circuit is open.**

3. Run engine at 1000 RPM and observe height of firing spike of disconnected cylinder. Firing spike should be 8 KV or less.

4. If firing spike is 8000 volts or less, air gap resistance is within acceptable limits. If firing spike is greater than 8000 volts, replace rotor and repeat test. If still too high, replace distributor cap. **White deposits on rotor are normal and should not be removed. If rotor is replaced, coat new rotor with silicone grease.**

### Spark Plug Firing Voltage Test

1. Reconnect spark plug lead, then run engine at 2000 RPM and set oscillo-

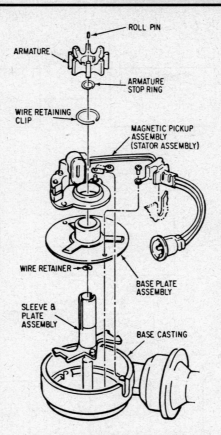

**Fig. 2   Exploded view of distributor**

scope to 30 KV parade pattern.

2. Check for firing spikes which are appreciably lower or higher (50 percent) than the other cylinders.

3. Normal firing spikes should be 6-20 KV.

4. Expand pattern to inspect individual firing spikes. If all spikes are below or above specifications, check rotor, distributor cap or coil to distributor cable.

5. To check low firing voltage, disconnect spark wire from spark plug and hold it so that spark cannot arc to ground:
   a. If spike does not increase to 28,000 volts or more (coil output), check for a cracked distributor cap with a grounded terminal.
   b. If spike does not rise, replace affected spark plug.

6. To check high firing voltage, disconnect spark plug wire from spark plug and ground the wire:
   a. If high spike drops, replace spark plug.
   b. If high spike remains, check spark plug wire and its connection at distributor cap.

### Spark Plug Wires Continuity Test

1. Remove distributor cap and disconnect suspected wire from spark plug or coil.

2. Using an ohmmeter, check wire resistance through distributor cap. Resis-

tance should be 5,000 ohms or less.

3. If resistance of wire is greater than 5,000 ohms, replace wire.

### Spark Plug Wire Inspection

1. Clean off any deposits of road salt, dirt, etc. from wires, boots, distributor cap and coil using water and a mild soap solution.

2. Inspect wires and boots for cuts, punctures, scrapes and burns. Replace as required.

3. Inspect wire terminals for corrosion. Remove corrosion with fine sandpaper.

4. Coat inside of all boots with silicone grease before reinstalling.

## PRIMARY CIRCUIT TESTS

The flow chart in **Fig. 3**, and test procedures provide a sequence for testing which should locate most problems in the primary ignition circuit. It is important to perform these tests in the exact order listed to check all portions of the system. A volt/ohmmeter, 16 inch jumper wire, straight pin, modified spark plug and ballast resistor, **Fig. 4**, are required to check the system.

### Test 1, Tap Test

1. Remove distributor cap and rotor. Crank engine to align one tooth of armature with magnet in pickup coil, **Fig. 5**.

2. Remove coil wire from distributor cap and connect to a well grounded modified spark plug, **Fig. 4**, or hold wire 1/4 inch from engine. Turn ignition switch to Run and tap distributor body with a screwdriver handle.

3. If there are sparks, proceed to test 2. If there are no sparks, proceed to Test 4.

### Test 2, Voltage Drop On Module White Wire

1. Connect positive lead of voltmeter to positive battery terminal and negative lead of voltmeter to pin in white wire. Crank engine and observe voltmeter reading. Reading should not exceed 1 volt.

2. If reading is above 1 volt, repair circuit feeding white wire, then repeat Test 1. If reading is less than 1 volt, perform Test 3.

### Test 3, Crank Test

1. Crank engine while checking for sparks.

2. If there are no sparks, perform Test 6. If there are sparks, ignition system is functioning properly. Remove pin and ballast resistor. Check fuel system and refer to "Testing for Intermittent Conditions."

### Test 4, Voltage Drop On Module Red Wire

1. Insert pin into red wire to make contact, **Fig. 6**.

2. Measure voltage drop on red wire of ignition module with key in On position. Connect positive lead of voltmeter to positive terminal and negative

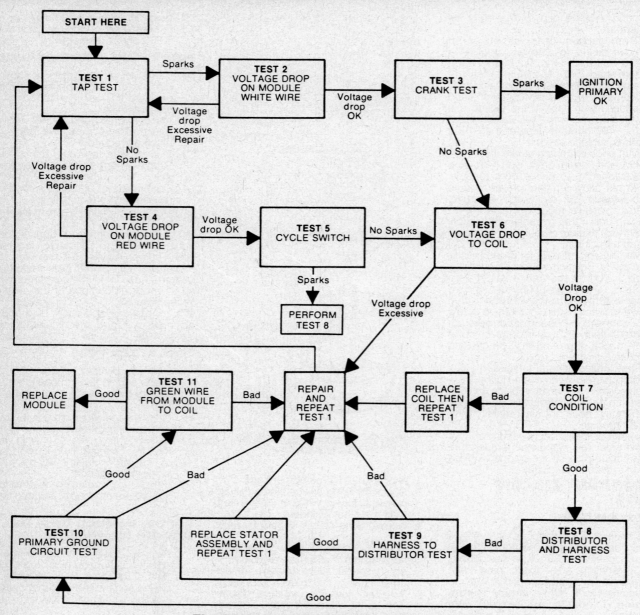

**Fig. 3   System diagnosis flow chart**

lead to red wire.
3. If reading is above 1 volt, repair circuit feeding red wire, then repeat Test 1. If reading is below 1 volt, perform Test 5.

## Test 5, Cycle Switch

1. Cycle ignition switch On and Off or turn ignition switch On and disconnect and reconnect distributor connector. A spark should be seen at the modified spark plug each time the ignition switch is cycled, or each time the connector is disconnected.
2. If there are no sparks, perform Test 6. If there are sparks, perform Test 8.

## Test 6, Voltage Drop to Coil

1. Connect jumper wire from "Dec" terminal to ground, **Fig. 7**. Turn ignition switch to Start and then Run positions.
2. Measure voltage drop to "Bat" terminal of coil:
   a. While cranking engine, voltage drop should be no more than 1 volt.
   b. With ignition switch at Run, voltage drop should be less than 6.5 volts.
3. If voltage drop is within specifications, perform Test 7. If voltage drop is not within specifications, perform repairs as necessary and repeat test.

## Test 7, Coil Condition

Refer to **Fig. 8**, for ohmmeter connections to check coil primary and secondary resistance. Resistance values should be as specified. If resistance values are within specifications, perform Test 8. If not, re-

place coil and repeat Test 1.

## Test 8, Distributor & Harness Test

1. Disconnect module connector with purple and orange wires, **Fig. 9**. Test distributor by connecting a voltmeter to orange and purple wires at harness side of male connector. Do not use a voltmeter combined with a dwell meter, as slight needle oscillations of 1/2 volt may not be detectable on this type of test equipment. Also, a digital volt-ohmmeter will not function on this test. **If vehicle is equipped with a catalytic converter, disconnect air supply line between bypass valve and manifold before cranking engine with ignition off. This will prevent damage to the catalytic**

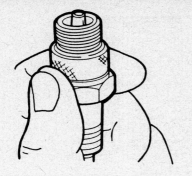

MODIFIED SPARK PLUG WITH THE SIDE
ELECTRODE REMOVED

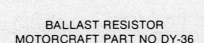

BALLAST RESISTOR
MOTORCRAFT PART NO DY-36

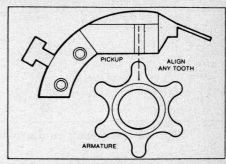

**Fig. 5   Aligning armature with magnet in pickup coil**

**Fig. 4   Test Equipment**

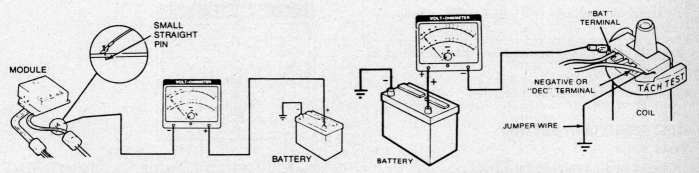

**Fig. 6   Checking voltage drop on module red wire**

**Fig. 7   Checking voltage drop to coil**

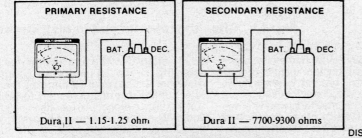

**Fig. 8   Checking coil condition**

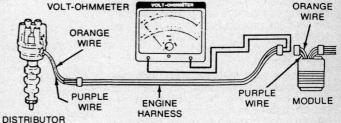

**Fig. 9   Distributor & harness test**

converter. Also, after testing, run engine for at least three minutes before reconnecting air supply line, to clear excess fuel from exhaust system.
2. Set voltmeter to its lowest scale and crank engine. Meter needle should oscillate slightly (about 1/2 volt). Refer to "Distributor Testing" for additional information.
3. If voltmeter indications are as specified, perform Test 10. If not, perform Test 9.

## Test 9, Harness To Distributor Test

1. Check for open or shorted condition in orange and purple wires from module connector (harness side) to distributor connector (harness side), **Fig. 10**.
2. If wires are not open or shorted, replace stator assembly and repeat test. If a shorted or open condition exists, make necessary repairs and repeat test.

## Test 10, Primary Ground Circuit Test

1. Connect an ohmmeter to black lead at harness side of module connector and a good ground, **Fig. 11**.
2. With ohmmeter at its lowest scale, there should be no measurable resistance.
3. If there is no measurable resistance, perform Test 11. If resistance can be measured, check ground in distributor and wire from module to distributor.

Repair or replace as necessary and repeat test.

## Test 11, Green Wire From Module To Coil

1. Check green wire, **Fig. 12**, from module to coil for open or shorted condition.
2. If wires are open or shorted, repair or replace as necessary and repeat test. If shorted or open condition does not exist, refer to "Testing For Intermittent Conditions." If problem cannot be found, replace module.

## COIL TESTING

If an oscilloscope is available, connect oscilloscope and disconnect one spark plug wire not allowing it to arc to ground.

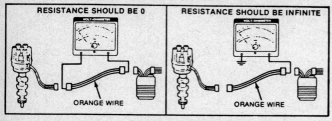

**Fig. 10   Harness to distributor test**

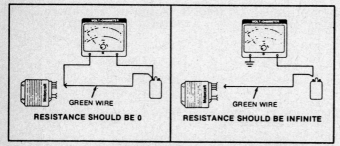

**Fig. 12   Checking green wire from module to coil**

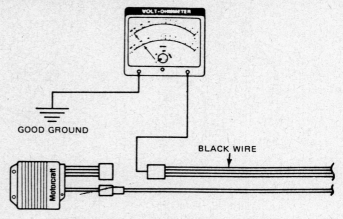

**Fig. 11   Primary ground circuit test**

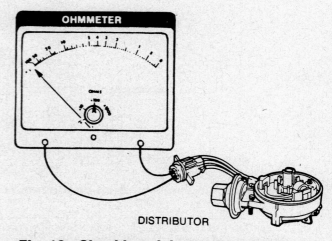

**Fig. 13   Checking pickup coil in distributor**

Crank engine while observing coil reserve voltage. Voltage spike should be 28 KV or more.

## DISTRIBUTOR TESTING

### Test 1

Connect an ohmmeter to parallel blade of distributor connector, **Fig. 13**. Resistance should be 400-1000 ohms. A reading of less than 400 ohms indicates a short while an infinity reading indicates an open. With ignition switch off, check resistance between orange wire and ground and purple wire and ground. Reading at each wire should be greater than 70,000 ohms.

### Test 2

Remove distributor cap and check that roll pin retaining armature on distributor shaft is in place, **Fig. 14**. If roll pin is missing, armature can rotate in relation to distributor shaft causing timing to be out of specifications. Check for correct connection of orange and purple wires between distributor and module. If wires are reversed, distributor timing will be 22½ degrees out of phase.

### Test 3

If a known good distributor is available, connect it to harness, turn ignition switch On and spin distributor by hand while checking for sparks.

## TESTING FOR INTERMITTENT CONDITIONS

If the ignition system becomes operative while performing diagnosis and a repair has not been made, it indicates that a malfunctioning component has become operative. The following procedures may locate the malfunctioning components:

With engine running, try to recreate the problem by moving wires at the coil, mod-ule, distributor and other harness connectors. Start with connectors disturbed originally. Also check ground connection in distributor. Also, disconnecting and reconnecting connectors may locate an intermittent condition. **Do not clean compound from connectors as it is required to prevent terminal corrosion.**

### Pickup Coil

With engine off, remove distributor cap, rotor and adapter, if used. Heat stator pickup coil using a 250 watt heat lamp placed about 1 to 2 inches from its top surface. Apply heat for 5 to 10 minutes while observing pickup coil continuity between the parallel blades of the disconnected distributor connector. Resistance should be 400-1000 ohms. Less than 400 ohms indicates a short while infinity indicates an open. Lightly tapping distributor with a screwdriver may reveal an intermittent condition.

### Ignition Module

With engine running, heat module using a 250 watt heat lamp placed about 1 to 2 inches from module. Tapping with a screwdriver may reveal an intermittent condition. **Do not allow module temperature to exceed 212 degrees. This can** be checked after the first 10 minutes by applying drops of water to module housing. Repeat every 2 minutes thereafter until water droplets start to boil.

If the above procedure results in an ignition malfunction, substitute a known good module. If substitution corrects the malfunction, recheck old module by reconnecting it into the circuit. Refer to "Test 1" under "Primary Circuit Test" to functionally check the original and the substitute modules.

## TROUBLESHOOTING INTERMITTENT CONDITIONS

### Engine Starts & Runs OK But Quits When Normal Operating Temperature Is Reached

1. Run engine until normal operating temperature is reached or engine quits, whichever occurs first.
2. Crank engine while checking voltage between orange and purple wires at ignition module. With voltmeter set at lowest scale, only a slight needle movement (about ½ volt) should be observed.
3. With ignition switch "Off," check resistance between purple and orange

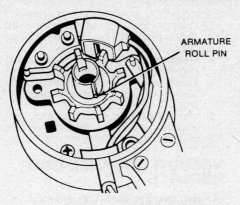

Fig. 14   Armature roll pin

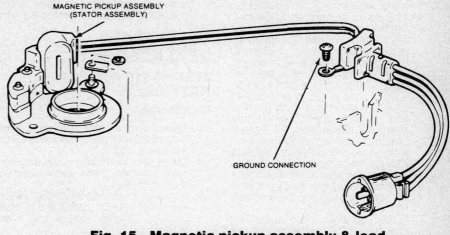

Fig. 15   Magnetic pickup assembly & lead

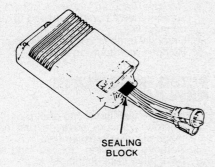

Fig. 16   Module identification

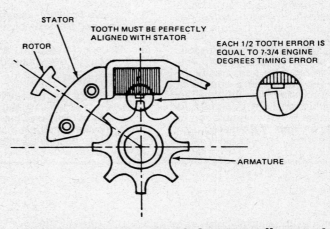

Fig. 17   Armature tooth & stator alignment

wires at distributor. Resistance should be 400-1000 ohms.
4. With ignition switch Off check resistance between purple wire at distributor and ground and between orange wire and ground. Resistance should be greater than 70,000 ohms at each wire.
5. If resistance values in step 3 and 4 are not within specifications, replace pickup assembly.

### Engine Starts Normally At Moderate Temperature But Starts Hard Or Will Not Start In Extremely Cold Temperature

1. Check for open in feed to white lead to module.

### Engine Quits Intermittently With Complete Loss Of Ignition

1. Check primary circuit ground resistance at ignition module connector black wire. Resistance should be zero ohms.
2. If resistance is not zero ohms, remove distributor cap and inspect retaining screw at rubber plug where wires enter distributor, **Fig. 15**. A loose or cross threaded screw or a dirty or corroded connection at this screw can cause an intermittent high resistance or a complete loss of ground.

## MODULE IDENTIFICATION

The ignition module can be identified as to type of ignition system by the color of the sealing block, **Fig. 16**.

| Sealing Block Color | Type Of Ignition System |
| --- | --- |
| White | Dura Spark II (With Cranking Retard) |
| Blue | Dura Spark II |
| Yellow | Dura Spark II (Dual Mode) |
| Brown | EEC System |

## DISTRIBUTOR
## REPLACE
### REMOVAL

On some six cylinder models, it will be necessary to position thermactor air pump aside to gain access to distributor. It may also be necessary to disconnect the thermactor air pump.

1. Disconnect distributor electrical connector from engine wiring harness.
2. Disconnect vacuum advance hose, then remove distributor cap and position aside.
3. Remove rotor and adapter, then reinstall rotor.
4. Mark position of distributor in engine and position of rotor on distributor housing for installation reference.
5. Remove distributor hold-down bolt and clamp, then lift distributor out of engine. Do not crank engine after distributor has been removed.

### INSTALLATION

1. If engine was not cranked after distributor was removed, proceed as follows:
   a. Position distributor in engine, aligning housing to block marks and rotor to housing marks made during removal.
   b. Install distributor hold-down bolt and clamp. Do not tighten at this time.
   c. Install distributor cap and wire, then connect distributor electrical connector to engine wiring harness and attach vacuum advance hose.
   d. Adjust ignition timing to specifications.

2. If engine was cranked after distributor was removed, proceed as follows:

   a. Remove No. 1 spark plug and crank engine until compression pressure is felt in No. 1 cylinder. Slowly rotate engine until correct initial timing mark on crankshaft damper aligns with timing pointer.

   b. Position distributor in engine with rotor at number one firing position and armature tooth aligned with starter as shown, **Fig. 17.** Ensure oil pump intermediate shaft properly engages the distributor shaft. It may be necessary to crank engine with starter after distributor drive gear is partially engaged in order to engage the oil pump intermediate shaft.

   c. Install distributor hold down bolt and clamp. Do not tighten at this time.

   d. Install distributor cap and wires, then connect distributor electrical connector to engine wiring harness and attach vacuum advance hose.

3. Adjust ignition timing to specifications. **Due to higher ignition system voltage, a timing light specifically designed for this system should be used when checking ignition timing. If a timing light designed for this system is not available, an inductive pickup type timing light may operate satisfactorily if a** piece of split vacuum hose is first placed around the spark plug wire.

# COMPONENT REPLACEMENT

## MAGNETIC PICKUP ASSEMBLY

### Removal

1. Remove distributor cap and rotor, then disconnect distributor wiring harness plug, **Fig. 1.**
2. Using two screwdrivers, pry armature from advance plate sleeve and remove roll pin.
3. Remove snap ring securing pickup assembly to base plate. On 6 cylinder models, remove washer and wave washer.
4. On all models, remove snap ring securing vacuum advance link to pickup assembly.
5. Remove pickup assembly ground screw and lift assembly from distributor.
6. Disconnect vacuum advance link from pickup assembly post.

### Installation

1. Position pickup assembly over base plate and slide wiring harness into slot on side of distributor housing, **Fig. 2.**
2. On 6 cylinder models, install washers. On all models, install snap ring securing pickup assembly to base plate.
3. Position vacuum advance link on pickup assembly post and install snap ring.
4. Insert ground screw through wiring harness tab and install on base plate.
5. Install armature on advance plate sleeve, ensure roll pin is engaged in slot.
6. Install distributor rotor and cap, then connect distributor wiring harness plug to vehicle wiring harness.

## VACUUM ADVANCE UNIT, REPLACE

1. Remove distributor cap and rotor.
2. Disconnect vacuum lines, then remove snap ring that secures vacuum advance link to pickup assembly.
3. Remove vacuum advance attaching screws, then tilt unit downward to disconnect link.
4. Carefully remove unit from distributor.
5. Reverse procedure to install.

## FIXED BASE PLATE, REPLACE

1. Remove distributor cap and rotor.
2. Remove vacuum advance unit and magnetic pickup assembly.
3. Remove attaching screws and lift base plate from distributor.
4. Reverse procedure to install.

# 1981–89 Dura Spark II Ignition System

## INDEX

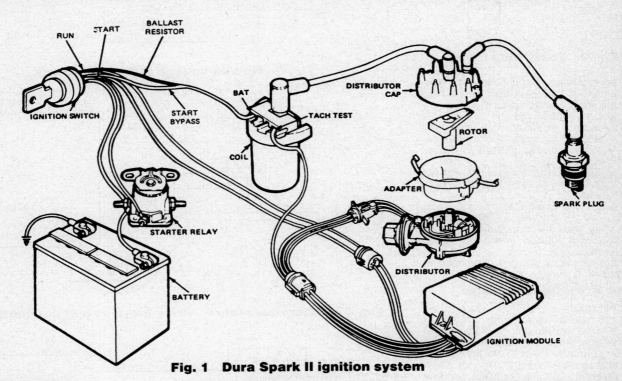

**Fig. 1   Dura Spark II ignition system**

## DESCRIPTION

This system, **Fig. 1**, is described under "1980 Dura Spark II Ignition System."

## SYSTEM DIAGNOSIS

When performing diagnostic or service procedures on models equipped with Dura Spark II, the ignition switch should remain in the Off position unless otherwise stated in the procedure. On these units, a spark will be generated when the ignition switch is placed from the On position to "Off," which may inadvertently cause the engine to rotate, resulting in personal injury.

Refer to "1980 Dura Spark Ignition System" for an intermittent vehicle operation diagnostic procedure under "System Diagnosis" procedure.

## SPARK PLUG FIRING VOLTAGE TEST

1. Connect an oscilloscope with voltage pickup on coil to distributor cable.
2. Check for firing spikes which are appreciably lower or higher (5 KV) than the other cylinders

3. Normal firing spikes should be approximately 15 KV.
4. Expand pattern to inspect individual firing spikes. If all spikes are above or below specifications, check rotor, distributor cap, or coil to distributor cable.

## SPARK PLUG WIRE CONTINUITY TEST

1. Remove distributor cap and disconnect suspected wire from spark plug or coil.
2. Using an ohmmeter, check wire resistance through distributor cap. Resistance should be 5000 ohms per inch on 1981-85 models, or 7000 ohms per foot on 1986-89 models. If reading is greater than as specified, replace wire.

## SPARK PLUG WIRE INSPECTION

1. Clean off any deposits of dirt from wires, boots, distributor cap and coil using mild soap and water solution.
2. Inspect wires and boots for cuts, punctures or other damage.
3. Inspect wire terminals for corrosion

and clean with fine sandpaper.
4. Coat all boots with silicone grease before installing.

## CIRCUIT TESTS
### Test 1, Start Circuit

1. Connect a suitable spark tester between coil wire and a suitable ground, **Fig. 2**.
2. While cranking engine, check for sparks.
3. If spark is observed, start circuit is satisfactory. If spark does not occur, measure coil wire resistance. If resistance exceeds 5000 ohms per inch on 1981-85 models, or 7000 ohms per foot on 1986-89 models, replace wire.
4. If coil wire is satisfactory, inspect coil for signs of carbon tracking or external damage and inspect distributor shaft with engine cranking to ensure distributor shaft rotation. Proceed to test 5.

### Test 2, Run Circuit

1. While observing spark tester, cycle ignition switch from Off to Run position

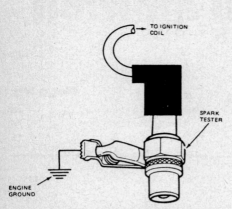

**Fig. 2  Spark plug tester**

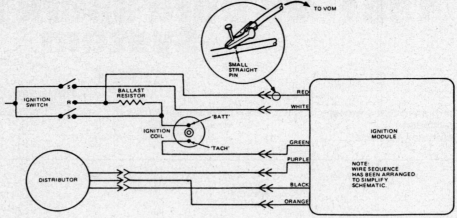

**Fig. 3  Module voltage test connections**

several times (a spark should be generated at the spark tester each time the ignition switch is turned Off).

2. If spark is observed:
   a. Inspect distributor cap, rotor and adapter for signs of carbon tracking and cracks, replace as necessary.
   b. Ensure armature to sleeve roll pin is correctly installed, repair as necessary.
   c. Ensure orange and purple wires are not crossed between distributor and ignition module.
   d. Check ignition timing, adjust as necessary.
3. If spark does not occur, proceed to test 3.

## Test 3, Module Voltage

1. With ignition "Off," install a straight pin into module red wire, **Fig. 3.** Connect a suitable voltmeter positive lead to straight pin and ground negative lead to distributor base. Turn ignition On and measure voltage. **Do not allow straight pin to contact engine ground.**
2. If reading obtained is 90% of battery voltage or greater, module voltage is satisfactory. Proceed to test 4.
3. If reading obtained is less than 90% of battery voltage, inspect ignition switch and wiring between ignition switch and module, repair as necessary.

## Test 4, Ballast Resistor

1. Disconnect module connector with red and white wires then, ignition coil connector.
2. Using a suitable ohmmeter, measure resistance between Batt. terminal of ignition coil connector and wiring harness connector wire that joins red wire in module connector.
3. If resistance is 0.8-1.6 ohms, ballast resistor is satisfactory. If resistance is less than 0.8 ohms or greater than 1.6 ohms, replace ballast resistor.

## Test 5, Supply Voltage Circuit

1. Reconnect coil wire to distributor cap (if still removed).
   a. If starter relay is equipped with a I

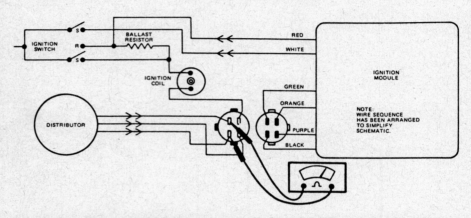

**Fig. 4  Stator assembly & wiring harness test connections**

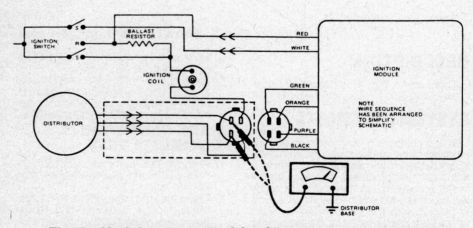

**Fig. 5  Module to stator wiring harness test connections**

terminal, disconnect starter cable from starter relay.
   b. If starter relay is equipped with a S terminal, disconnect S wire from relay.
2. With ignition "Off," install straight pins into module red and white wires. **Do not allow straight pins to contact engine ground.**
3. Using a suitable voltmeter, connect negative lead to ground at distributor base.
   a. With ignition in On position, measure voltage at red wire pin.
   b. Place ignition in "Start" position, measure voltage at white wire pin and at coil Batt. terminal. When measuring voltages, wiggle wires to simulate any open circuits that might exist.

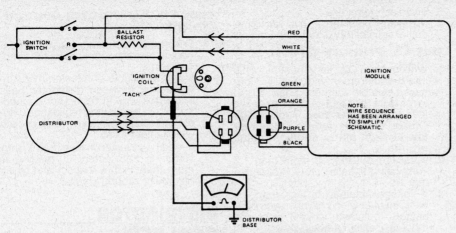

**Fig. 6   Coil tach terminal circuit test connections**

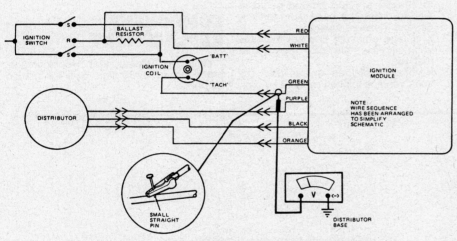

**Fig. 7   Coil primary circuit test connections**

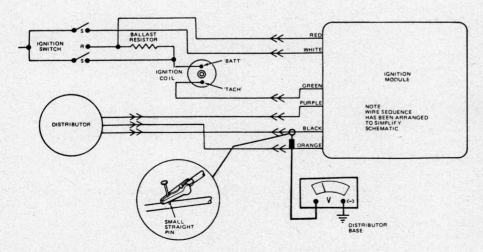

**Fig. 8   Ground circuit test connections**

4. If readings obtained are 90% of battery voltage or greater, supply circuits are satisfactory. Proceed to test 6.
5. If readings obtained are less than 90% of battery voltage:
   a. Defective wiring harness or connectors in supply voltage circuits.
   b. Defective ignition switch.
   c. Defective radio interference capacitor on ignition coil.

## Test 6, Ignition Coil Supply Voltage

1. Connect positive lead of voltmeter to coil Batt. terminal and negative lead to ground at distributor base.
2. Turn ignition switch to On position.
3. Observe voltmeter reading. If 6-8 volts, proceed to test 7. If less than 6 volts or more than 8 volts, proceed to test 12.

## Test 7, Distributor Stator Assembly & Wiring Harness

1. Disconnect module 4 wire connector. Inspect connectors for dirt and corrosion.
2. Using a suitable ohmmeter, measure resistance of stator and wiring harness between wiring harness terminals joining orange and purple wires of module connector, **Fig. 4.** When measuring resistance, wiggle wires to simulate any open circuits that might exist.
3. If resistance is 400-1300 ohms, test results are satisfactory. Proceed to test 8. If resistance is less than 400 ohms or more than 1300 ohms, proceed to test 11.

## Test 8, Ignition Module To Distributor Stator Assembly Wiring Harness

1. Disconnect module 4 wire connector. Inspect connectors for dirt and corrosion.
2. Using a suitable ohmmeter, connect one lead to ground at distributor base. Using other lead, alternately measure resistance of harness wiring which connects to orange and purple wires of module connector and ground, **Fig. 5.**
3. If test results are greater than 70,000 ohms, circuits are satisfactory. If test results are less than 70,000 ohms, inspect and repair as necessary wiring harness between module connector and distributor. Also inspect distributor grommet.

## Test 9, Ignition Coil Secondary Resistance

1. Disconnect and inspect ignition coil electrical connector.
2. Using a suitable ohmmeter, measure resistance between coil Batt. terminal and high tension lead terminal.
3. If resistance is between 7,700-10,500 ohms, coil is satisfactory. If not between limits, replace coil.

## Test 10, Module To Coil Wire

1. Disconnect module 4 wire connector. Inspect connectors for dirt and corrosion.

2. Using a suitable ohmmeter, measure resistance between coil connector tach wire and ground, **Fig. 6.**

3. If resistance is greater than one ohm on 1981-85 models, or greater than 100 ohms on 1986-89 models, replace ignition module. If resistance is one ohm or less on 1981-85 models, or 100 ohms or less on 1986-89 models, inspect wiring harness between ignition coil and module and repair as necessary.

### Test 11, Distributor Stator Assembly

1. Disconnect distributor electrical connector. Inspect connections for dirt or corrosion.

2. Using a suitable ohmmeter, measure resistance across orange and purple wires in distributor connector.

3. If readings obtained are within 400-1000 ohms, circuit is satisfactory. If readings are less than 400 or more than 1000 ohms, replace stator assembly.

### Test 12, Ignition Coil Primary Resistance

1. Disconnect ignition coil electrical connector.

2. Using a suitable ohmmeter, measure resistance between coil Batt. terminal and Tach terminal.

3. If reading obtained is 0.8-1.6 ohms, coil is satisfactory. If not, replace coil.

### Test 13, Primary Circuit

1. With ignition "Off," install a straight pin into module green wire, **Fig. 7.** Connect a suitable voltmeter positive lead to straight pin and ground negative lead to distributor base. Turn ignition On and measure voltage. **Do not allow straight pin to contact engine ground.**

2. If voltage obtained is more than 1.5 volts, circuit is satisfactory. Proceed to test 14.

3. If voltage obtained is less than 1.5 volts, inspect wiring harness and connectors between ignition coil and module. Repair as necessary.

### Test 14, Ground Circuit

1. With ignition "Off," install a straight pin into module black wire, **Fig. 8.** Connect a suitable voltmeter positive lead to straight pin and ground negative lead to distributor base. Turn ignition On and measure voltage.

2. If voltage obtained is more than 0.5 volts, circuit is satisfactory. Proceed to test 15.

3. If voltage obtained is less than 0.5 volts, replace ignition module.

### Test 15, Distributor Ground Circuit

1. Disconnect distributor electrical connector. Inspect connections for dirt or corrosion.

2. Using a suitable ohmmeter, measure resistance between distributor base and black wire in distributor connector. When measuring resistance, wiggle wires to simulate any open circuits which might exist.

3. If reading obtained is less than 1 ohm, circuit is satisfactory. If reading is more than 1 ohm, inspect and repair distributor ground screw.

## DISTRIBUTOR REPLACE

Refer to "Distributor, Replace" procedure in "1980 Dura Spark II Ignition Systems."

## COMPONENT REPLACEMENT

Refer to "Component Replacement" procedure in "1980 Dura Spark II Ignition Systems."

# Dura Spark III Solid State Ignition System

## INDEX

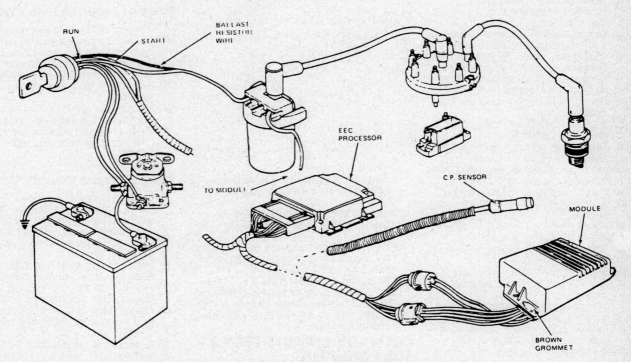

**Fig. 1   Typical Dura Spark III ignition system**

## DESCRIPTION

The Dura Spark III system, **Fig. 1**, is used on vehicles equipped with Electronic Engine Control (EEC). The system consists of a primary side consisting of the battery, ignition switch, primary circuit, EEC system input and ignition module and a secondary side consisting of distributor cap, rotor, spark plug wires and spark plugs. When the ignition switch is in the On position, the primary circuit and the ignition coil are energized. The EEC system provides a signal which tells the ignition module to turn off the coil primary circuit. The off and on times of the primary circuit are controlled by the EEC computer. When the circuit is turned Off, the magnetic field built up in the ignition coil collapses, inducing a high voltage into the coil secondary windings. This high voltage is then delivered to the spark plugs by the secondary ignition wires.

## SYSTEM DIAGNOSIS

Before proceeding with system diagnosis, ensure battery is fully charged and all accessories are "Off." Inspect all vacuum hoses and spark plug wires for proper routing and secure connections. Inspect engine compartment ignition wiring harness and connectors for signs of insulation damage, burning, overheating and loose or broken connections. Repair as necessary.

## SECONDARY CIRCUIT TESTS

### Spark Plug Firing Voltage Test, 1981 Models

1. Connect an oscilloscope with voltage pickup on coil to distributor cable. Set oscilloscope to 30 KV parade pattern.
2. Connect timing light to No. 1 spark plug, then start engine and operate at 2000 RPM.

3. Apply 25 inches Hg of vacuum from outside source to BP port of MAP sensor.
4. Check oscilloscope for highest firing spikes. If highest spikes are between 6 and 20 KV, system is operating properly.
5. If reading is greater than 20 KV or highest spike is 50% greater than lowest, refer to "Primary Circuit Test" under "Test 3, Ignition Coil Primary Voltage."
6. If voltage reading is less than 6 KV, refer to "Spark Plug Wires Continuity Test."
7. Check ignition timing at 2000 RPM. If reading is not between 27 and 30° BTDC, EEC system is malfunctioning and must be repaired.

### Spark Plug Firing Voltage Test, 1982-83 Models

1. Connect an oscilloscope with voltage pickup on coil to distributor wire. Set

oscilloscope to parade pattern.

2. Start engine, then while slowly increasing engine RPM from idle to 2000 RPM, observe scope pattern. If the average spark plug firing voltage is 15 KV and the spark plug firing voltages do not vary more than 5 KV, the system is operating properly.

3. If the spark plug firing voltages do not vary more than 5 KV and the average spark plug firing voltage is more than 15 KV, check:
   a. Ignition coil wire for proper installation and resistance. Resistance should be less than 5000 ohms per inch. If more, replace.
   b. Spark plugs for wide gaps.
   c. Distributor cap and rotor for excessive clearance.
   d. Distributor cap and rotor for lack of silicone compound on rotor.
   e. Distributor rotor alignment. See Distributor Rotor, Replace.

4. If the spark plug firing voltages vary more than 5 KV, check:
   a. Spark plug gap(s) or worn electrodes.
   b. Correct distributor cap, adapter and rotor installation.
   c. Distributor rotor alignment. See Distributor Rotor, Replace.

5. If one or more spark plug firing voltages are unusually high, check:
   a. Disconnected spark plug wire(s).
   b. Spark plug gap(s) or open plug wire(s).

6. If one or more spark plug firing voltages are unusually low, check:
   a. Spark plug(s) for fouling or narrow gap(s).
   b. Spark plug wires for grounding.
   c. Distributor cap and adapter for tracking.

7. If spark plug firing voltages are inverted, check:
   a. Ignition coil primary connector for improper installation. If installation is satisfactory, replace coil.

## Spark Plug Wire Continuity Test, All Models

1. Remove distributor cap and disconnect suspected wire from spark plug or coil.
2. Using an ohmmeter, check wire resistance through distributor cap.
3. Resistance should be 5000 ohms per inch. If reading is greater than specified, replace wire.

## Spark Plug Wire Inspection, All Models

1. Clean off any deposits of dirt from wires, boots, distributor cap and coil using mild soap and water solution.
2. Inspect wires, boots for cuts, punctures or other damage.
3. Inspect wire terminals for corrosion and clean with fine sandpaper.
4. Coat all boots with silicone grease before installing.

## Secondary Circuit Voltage Drop, 1981 Models

1. Connect an oscilloscope with voltage pickup on coil to distributor cable.
2. Disconnect a spark plug wire and

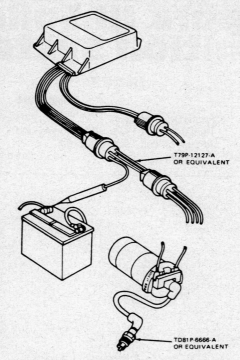

**Fig. 2 Installing ignition diagnostic test adapter**

ground firmly to engine block.
3. Start engine and operate at idle speed.
4. If oscilloscope indicates reading of 8 KV, distributor cap voltage drop is satisfactory.
5. If reading is greater than 8 KV, check for damaged cap or rotor and replace.
6. If an abnormal scope pattern is obtained, check for worn or damaged distributor parts.

## PRIMARY CIRCUIT TESTS, 1981 MODELS

### Test 1, Ignition Coil Output

1. Disconnect spark plug wire and ground firmly to engine block.
2. Crank engine while checking for spark.
3. If spark is observed, system is operating properly.
4. If no spark is observed, remove cap and crank engine to verify rotor movement.
5. If rotor does not move when engine is cranked, repair distributor as necessary.

### Test 2, Trigger Test

1. Disconnect ignition module connector and install ignition diagnostic test adapter into wiring circuit, **Fig. 2**.
2. Disconnect ignition coil secondary wire at distributor and ground firmly to engine block. Turn ignition to Run position.
3. Touch diagnostic adapter lead to battery positive terminal. Spark should occur every time lead touches battery.
4. If spark occurs, system is operating properly. If not, refer to "Test 3, Ignition Coil Primary Voltage."

### Test 3, Ignition Coil Primary Voltage

1. Turn ignition to Run position. Connect voltmeter between BATT terminal of ignition coil and ground.
2. If reading is between 5 and 8 volts, ignition system is satisfactory. If reading is greater than 8 volts, refer to "Test 7, Ground Circuit Check." If reading is less than 6 volts, refer to "Test 6, Wiring Harness Short Circuit" and to "Test 8, Ignition Coil Circuit."
3. In addition, check for open circuit in power supply circuit such as battery lead to ignition coil.

### Test 4, Module Run Circuit

1. Turn ignition key to Run position.
2. Measure voltage between red module wire and engine ground by connecting straight pin to voltmeter positive lead and inserting into red wire. **Do not allow straight pin to contact ground.**
3. If reading is within 90% of battery voltage, system is operating properly.
4. If not, check for open circuit in run circuit wiring harness and repair as necessary.

### Test 5, Start Circuit Voltage

1. On starter relays equipped with 1 terminal, disconnect cable between starter relay and starter motor.
2. On starter relays without I terminal, disconnect electrical connector at relay S terminal.
3. Hold ignition switch in Start position and measure voltage between coil BATT terminal and ground and between white module wire and ground. Connect straight pin to voltmeter lead and insert into white wire to perform test.
4. If reading is greater than 90% of battery voltage, system is satisfactory.
5. If reading is less than 90% of battery voltage, check for open circuit in ballast resistor bypass wire or module start wire and repair as necessary. Also check for defective ignition switch.

### Test 6, Wiring Harness Short Circuit

1. Disconnect ignition module, ignition coil and EEC computer connectors and inspect for damage.
2. Check for damaged primary circuit wiring and repair as necessary.
3. Place transmission in Park and set parking brake. Check resistance between module connector orange wire terminal and ground, **Fig. 3.**
4. Measure resistance between the following connector wire terminals:
   a. Red to white wire terminals.
   b. Red to green wire terminals.
   c. Red to orange wire terminals.
   d. White to green wire terminals.
   e. White to orange wire terminals.
5. If any resistance reading obtained is less than 70,000 ohms, repair damaged wire in that circuit as necessary.

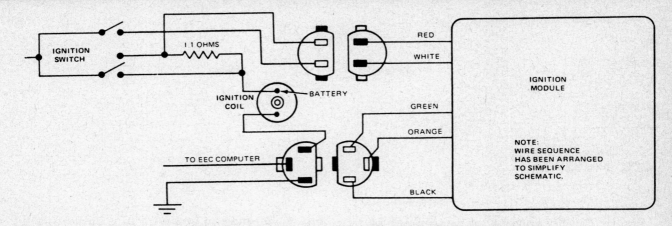

**Fig. 3 Dura Spark III ignition system electrical schematic**

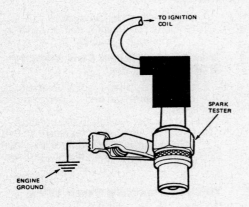

**Fig. 4 Spark tester**

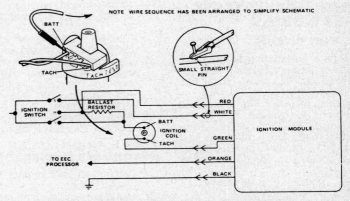

**Fig. 5 Start voltage test connections. 1982-83**

## Test 7, Ground Circuit Check

1. Disconnect ignition module connector containing black wire and check for damage.
2. Check resistance between black wire terminal in module connector and ground.
3. If resistance is less than one ohm,
4. If resistance is greater than one ohm, check for open circuit at battery ground strap connection and repair as necessary.

## Test 8, Ignition Coil Circuit

1. Disconnect ignition coil and module connectors and inspect for damage.
2. Measure resistance between green wire terminal of module connector and TACH terminal on ignition coil.
3. If resistance is greater than 2 ohms, check for open circuit in TACH wire and repair as necessary.
4. If resistance is less than 2 ohms, check resistance of ballast resistor by connecting ohmmeter between BATT terminal on coil and red wire terminal in ignition module connector.
5. If resistance is less than 2 ohms, system is operating satisfactorily. If not, check for an open circuit or replace ballast resistor as necessary.

## Test 9, Module Output Check

1. Connect any connectors that were previously disconnected.
2. Connect voltmeter between coil TACH terminal and ground.
3. Set voltmeter on highest scale, then firmly ground ignition coil high tension lead to engine block.
4. Crank engine, then switch voltmeter to lowest scale.
5. If meter needle fluctuates, module is operating satisfactorily. If not, refer to "Test 10, Module Check." If difficulty is encountered in performing this test using a voltmeter, a test light may be substituted in its place. The light flashing would correspond to the voltmeter needle fluctuating.

## Test 10, Module Check

1. Disconnect module connector containing green wire.
2. Connect voltmeter between green wire terminal of module connector and ground.
3. Turn ignition to Run position and check voltage.
4. If reading is more than 90% of battery voltage, replace ignition module.
5. If reading is less than 90% of battery voltage, refer to "Test 11, Continuity Check."

## Test 11, Continuity Check

1. Check resistance between green wire terminal in harness side module connector and coil TACH terminal.
2. If ohmmeter indicates less than one ohm, system is operating satisfactorily.
3. If reading is greater than one ohm, check for open circuit in wire between coil TACH terminal and ignition module and repair as necessary.

## Test 12, Coil Primary Circuit Check

1. Disconnect ignition coil electrical connector.
2. Measure resistance between coil BATT and TACH terminals.
3. If reading is between 1 and 2 ohms, primary circuit is satisfactory.
4. If not, replace coil.

## Test 13, Coil Secondary Circuit Check

1. Check resistance between coil TACH terminal and high tension lead terminal.
2. If reading is between 7700 and 9600 ohms, secondary circuit is satisfactory.
3. If not, replace ignition coil.

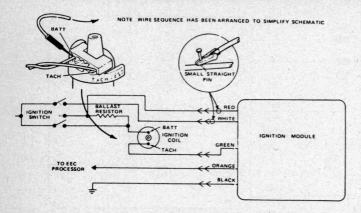

**Fig. 6   Supply voltage test connections. 1982-83**

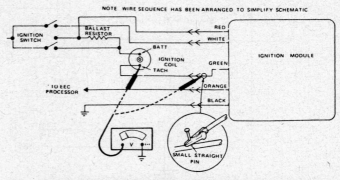

**Fig. 7   Module to coil wire test connections. 1982-83**

## PRIMARY CIRCUIT TESTS, 1982-83 MODELS

### Test 1, Run Circuit

1. Disconnect ignition module three wire connector and install ignition diagnostic test adapter into wiring circuit, **Fig. 2.**
2. Connect spark tester, **Fig. 4**, between ignition coil and ground.
3. Turn ignition "On," then while observing spark tester, touch diagnostic test lead to battery positive terminal. Spark should occur every time lead touches battery.
4. If spark occurs, circuit is satisfactory. If not, proceed to test 2.

### Test 2, Start Circuit

1. Remove diagnostic test adapter installed in test 1 but, leave spark tester attached.
2. While cranking over engine with ignition switch, observe spark tester for sparks.
3. If sparks occur, circuit is satisfactory. If not, proceed to test 3.

### Test 3, Start Voltage

1. Reconnect coil wire to distributor cap.
   a. If starter relay is equipped with a I terminal, disconnect starter cable from starter relay.
   b. If starter relay is equipped with S terminal, disconnect S wire from relay.
2. With ignition "Off," install straight pin into module white wire, **Fig. 5.**
3. Connect a suitable voltmeter between ground and straight pin.
4. Turn ignition switch to "Start" position and note voltage.
5. Move voltmeter positive lead to coil Batt. connector and note voltage with ignition switch in start "position."
6. If voltage obtained is 90% of battery voltage, circuit is satisfactory. If voltage obtained is less than 90% of battery voltage, a defective ignition switch or wiring harness is indicated.

### Test 4, Ignition Coil Primary Circuit Switching

1. Disconnect ignition module three wire connector and install ignition diagnostic test adapter into wiring circuit, **Fig. 2.**
2. Connect a suitable test light between coil Tach terminal and engine ground.
3. Turn ignition "On," then while observing test light, touch diagnostic test lead to battery positive terminal. Test light should flash every time lead touches battery.
4. If test light flashes, circuit is satisfactory. If not, Proceed to test 6.

### Test 5, Ignition Coil Secondary Resistance

1. Disconnect and inspect ignition coil electrical lead.
2. Using a suitable ohmmeter, measure resistance between coil Batt. terminal and high tension lead terminal.
3. If resistance is between 7700-10,500 ohms, coil is satisfactory. If not between limits, replace coil.

### Test 6, Supply Voltage Circuits

1. Remove diagnostic test adapter installed in test 4 and test light, then:
   a. If starter relay is equipped with a I terminal, disconnect starter cable from starter relay.
   b. If starter relay is equipped with S terminal, disconnect S wire from relay.
2. With ignition "Off," install straight pins into module red and white wires, **Fig. 6. Do not allow straight pins to contact engine ground.**
3. Using a suitable voltmeter, connect negative lead to ground.
   a. With ignition in On position, measure voltage at red wire pin.
   b. Place ignition in "Start" position, measure voltage at white wire pin and at coil Batt. terminal. When measuring voltages, wiggle wires to simulate any open circuits that might exist.
4. If readings obtained are 90% of battery voltage, supply circuits are satisfactory. Proceed to test 7.
5. If readings obtained are less than 90% of battery voltage:
   a. Defective wiring harness or connectors in supply voltage circuits.

b. Defective ignition switch.
c. Defective ignition coil or radio interference capacitor.

### Test 7, Ignition Coil Supply Voltage

1. Connect positive lead of voltmeter to coil Batt. terminal and negative lead to ground.
2. Turn ignition switch to On position.
3. Observe voltmeter reading. If 6-8 volts, circuit is satisfactory. If less than 6 volts or more than 8 volts, proceed to test 9.

### Test 8, Testing Tach Wire

1. Disconnect and inspect module three wire connector and coil connector.
2. Using a suitable ohmmeter, connect one lead to ground and the other to the coil connector Tach. terminal. Measure resistance.
3. If readings obtained are one ohm or less, circuit is satisfactory. If readings are more than one ohm, repair short in tach wire.

### Test 9, Ignition Coil Primary Resistance

1. Disconnect and inspect ignition coil connector.
2. Using a suitable tachometer, measure resistance between coil Batt. and Tach. terminals.
3. If readings are 0.8-1.6 ohms, circuit is satisfactory. If readings are out of specifications, replace coil.

### Test 10, Module to Coil Wire

1. With ignition "Off," insert straight pin in module green wire, **Fig. 7. Do not allow straight pin to contact engine ground.**
2. Using a suitable voltmeter, connect negative lead to ground.
3. Turn ignition "On," then measure voltage at green wire pin and Tach. terminal of ignition coil, **Fig. 7.**
4. If voltmeter shows less than 1/2 volt difference, circuit is satisfactory. If more than 1/2 volt difference, inspect and repair wiring harness between coil and module.

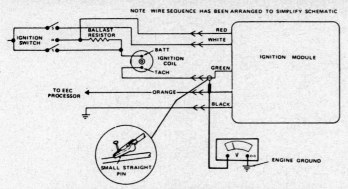

**Fig. 8  Primary circuit continuity test connections. 1982–83**

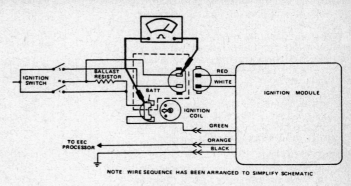

**Fig. 9  Ballast resistor test connections. 1982–83**

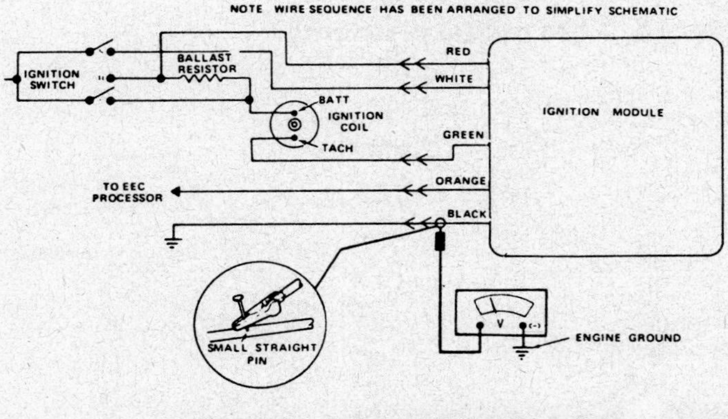

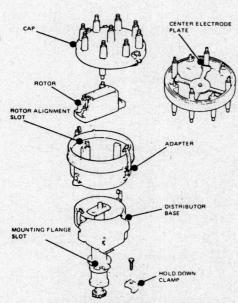

**Fig. 10  Ground circuit test connections. 1982–83**

**Fig. 11  Early model distributor**

## Test 11, Primary Circuit Continuity

1. Leave straight pin in green wire as outlined in test 10.
2. Turn ignition "On," then using a suit-able voltmeter connected to ground measure voltage at green wire pin, **Fig. 8.**
3. If voltage exceeds 1½ volts, proceed to test 13. If voltage obtained is 1½ volts or less, proceed to test 12.

## Test 12, Ballast Resistor

1. Disconnect and inspect module two wire connector and ignition coil connector, **Fig. 9.**
2. Using a suitable ohmmeter, measure resistance between coil connector Batt. terminal and wiring harness connector which mates with module red wire, **Fig. 9.**
3. If reading is 0.8-1.6 ohms, circuit is satisfactory. If reading is less than 0.8 ohms or more than 1.6 ohms, replace ballast resistor.

## Test 13, Ground Circuit

1. With ignition "Off," install straight pin in module black wire, **Fig. 10.** Do not allow straight pin to touch engine ground.
2. Using a suitable ohmmeter, correct negative lead to engine ground and positive lead to black wire pin.
3. Turn ignition "On," measure voltage.
4. If voltage obtained was more than 1½ volts, proceed to test 14. If voltage obtained was less than 1½ volts, replace ignition module.

## Test 14, Wiring Harness Ground Circuit

1. Disconnect module three wire connector, inspect connector for dirt and corrosion.
2. Using a suitable ohmmeter, connect one lead to engine ground. Connect other lead to wiring harness terminal which mates with black module wire terminal. Measure resistance. When measuring resistances, wiggle wires to simulate any open circuits that might exist.
3. If resistance is less than one ohm, inspect wiring harness connector and module black wire. If no problem is found, it is either intermittent or not in ignition system.
4. If resistance is greater than one ohm, inspect and repair wiring harness between ignition module and ground connection.

## TESTING FOR INTERMITTENT CONDITIONS

Refer to "1980 Dura Spark II Solid State Ignition Systems" under "Testing For Intermittent Conditions" for procedure.

## TROUBLESHOOTING INTERMITTENT CONDITIONS

Refer to "1980 Dura Spark II Solid State Ignition Systems" under "Troubleshooting Intermittent Conditions" for procedures.

## COMPONENT REPLACEMENT

### DISTRIBUTOR, REPLACE
#### Early Models

1. Remove distributor cap, **Fig. 11.** Install rotor alignment tool T78P-12200-A and remove rotor. Refer to Distributor Rotor, Replace.
2. With rotor alignment tool in position, remove distributor hold-down bolt and clamp. Remove alignment tool.
3. Carefully remove distributor from engine block, noting position of rotor blades in relation to distributor housing as distributor drive gear is felt to disengage with cam gear. Do not ro-

tate engine after distributor has been removed.

4. Install distributor in engine block. Ensure the distributor hold-down flange slot is aligned with the clamp bolt hole and rotor upper blade slot is aligned with the slot in the distributor cap adapter.
5. Install distributor hold-down bolt and clamp. Torque to 17 ft. lbs.
6. Align rotor and install distributor cap, refer to "Distributor Rotor, Replace."

### Late Models

1. Remove distributor cap and rotor, **Fig. 12**. Position crankshaft as outlined in Distributor Rotor, Replace. The alignment slot in the adapter should be aligned with the alignment slot in the sleeve assembly.
2. Remove distributor hold-down bolt and clamp.
3. Carefully remove distributor from engine block, noting position of the large slot in the sleeve in relation to the adapter alignment slot as distributor drive gear is felt to disengage with cam gear. Do not rotate engine after distributor has been removed.
4. Install distributor in engine block. Ensure the distributor hold-down flange slot is aligned with the clamp bolt hole and adapter alignment slot is aligned with the large sleeve alignment slot.
5. Install distributor hold-down bolt and clamp. Torque to 17 ft. lbs.

## DISTRIBUTOR ROTOR, REPLACE

### Early Models

1. Remove distributor cap, **Fig. 11**.
2. Position the crankshaft to align the rotor upper blade slot with the distributor cap adapter slot to enable the rotor alignment tool T78P-12200-A to fall into place. **Fig. 13.** If alignment of rotor and adapter is not possible due to damage, position No. 1 cylinder at TDC on compression stroke with timing marks aligned at O.
3. Remove rotor alignment tool, then remove rotor retaining screws and rotor.
4. Position rotor on distributor shaft with upper rotor blade slot facing adapter slot. Install, but do not tighten rotor retaining screws.
5. Position rotor alignment tool as shown in **Fig. 13**, then tighten rotor retaining screws to 15-20 inch lbs.
6. Remove rotor alignment tool and install distributor cap.

### Late Models

1. Remove distributor cap and rotor, **Fig. 12**.
2. Position No. 1 piston on compression stroke, then rotate crankshaft until rotor alignment tool, T79P-12200-A or equivalent, can be inserted into alignment slots, **Fig. 14**.
3. Check vibration damper and timing pointer alignment marks. If timing pointer is within ±4° of TDC, alignment is satisfactory. If alignment is out of specifications, position vibration damper at TDC with cylinder No. 1 at TDC. Loosen sleeve assembly adjust-

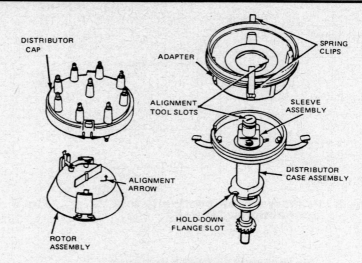

**Fig. 12   Late model distributor**

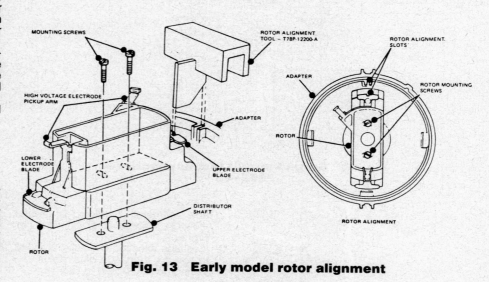

**Fig. 13   Early model rotor alignment**

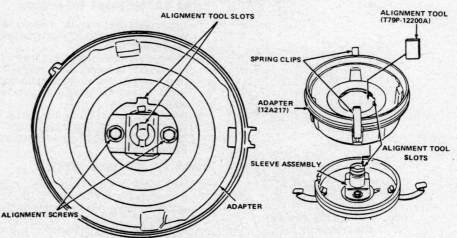

**Fig. 14   Late model rotor alignment**

ment screws and rotate sleeve until rotor alignment tool can be inserted into alignment slots. **Fig. 14**. Torque

adjustment screws to 25-35 inch lbs. and remove tool.
4. Replace rotor and distributor cap.

# Thick Film Integrated (TFI-IV) Ignition System

## INDEX

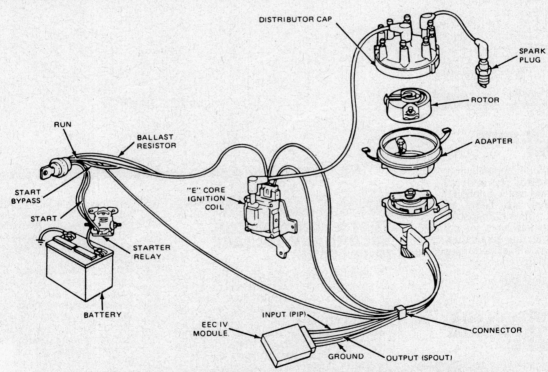

**Fig. 1   Thick Film Integrated (TFI-IV) ignition system**

## DESCRIPTION

The TFI-IV ignition system, **Fig. 1,** is used with the Electronic Engine Control (EEC-IV) system and features a universal distributor design. This distributor, **Fig. 2,** uses no mechanical or vacuum advance since spark is controlled by the EEC-IV microprocessor. On some applications, security-type hold-down bolts are used to secure the distributor. The distributor uses an integrally mounted ignition module, a "Hall Effect" vane switch stator assembly, and a provision for fixed octane adjustment. Initial timing is not a normal adjustment on this unit.

## SYSTEM DIAGNOSIS

### SPARK PLUG FIRING VOLTAGE TEST

1. Connect an oscilloscope with voltage pick up on coil to distributor coil.
2. Check for firing spikes which are appreciably lower or higher (5 kv) than the other cylinders.
3. Normal firing spikes should be approximately 15 kv.
4. Expand pattern to inspect individual firing spikes. If all spikes are above or below specifications, check rotor, distributor cap and coil-to-distributor cable.

### SPARK PLUG WIRE CONTINUITY TEST

1. Remove distributor cap and disconnect suspected wire from spark plug or coil.
2. Measure wire resistance through distributor cap using a suitable ohmmeter. Resistance should measure 5000 ohms per inch on 1984-85 models or 7000 ohms per foot on 1986-89 models. If resistance is greater than specified, replace wire.

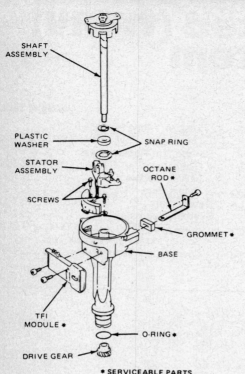

**Fig. 2   Typical universal distributor exploded view**

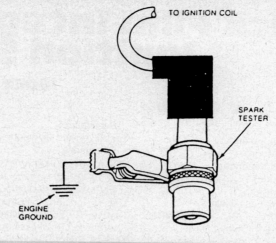

**Fig. 3   Spark tester**

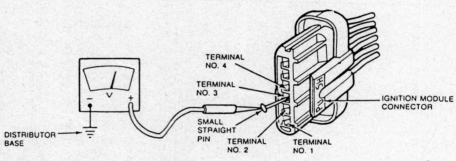

**Fig. 4   Checking ignition module wiring harness voltage**

## SPARK PLUG WIRE INSPECTION

1. Clean off any dirt deposits from wires, boots, distributor cap and coil using mild soap and water solution.
2. Inspect wires and boots for cuts, punctures or other damage.
3. Inspect wire terminals for corrosion and clean with fine sandpaper.
4. Coat all boots with silicone grease before reinstalling.

## CIRCUIT TESTS

### TEST 1, IGNITION COIL SECONDARY VOLTAGE (CRANK MODE)

1. Connect spark plug tester, **Fig. 3**, between ignition coil wire and ground.
2. Crank engine.
3. If spark is present, inspect distributor cap and rotor for damage or carbon tracking. If engine starts, check pattern on oscilloscope. If engine does not start, proceed to Test 2.
4. If no spark is present, proceed as follows:
   a. Check that resistance of coil wire is not greater than 7,000 ohms per foot. If resistance is greater than specified, replace wire.
   b. Check ignition coil for damage or carbon tracking.
   c. Crank engine to verify distributor rotation.
   d. On units less closed bowl distributor, proceed to Test 4.
   e. On units with closed bowl distributor, proceed to Test 5.

### TEST 2, IGNITION COIL SECONDARY VOLTAGE (RUN MODE)

1. Connect spark plug tester, **Fig. 3**, between ignition coil wire and ground.
2. Place shift lever in Park (manual transmission in Neutral), then set parking brake.
3. Disconnect "S" terminal wire from starter relay, attach remote starter switch, then turn ignition switch to Run position.
4. Crank engine with remote starter switch and check for spark at tester.
5. If spark is evident, ignition system is functioning properly. If no spark is evident, proceed to Test 3.

### TEST 3, WIRING HARNESS

1. Disconnect wiring harness connector from ignition module and check for dirt, corrosion, or damage. Push connector tabs to separate.
2. Disconnect wire from "S" terminal of starter relay.
3. Connect negative lead of volt-ohmmeter to distributor base.
4. Check battery voltage.
5. Check connector terminal voltage by connecting a volt-ohmmeter to small straight pin inserted into connector terminal, **Fig. 4**. Check voltage with ignition switch in following positions: check connector terminal 3 with ignition switch in Run and Start positions; and terminal 4 with switch in Start position.
6. If voltage readings are within 90 percent of battery voltage, replace TFI module.
7. If any voltage readings are less than 90 percent of battery voltage, check the following:
   a. Check wiring harness and connectors for damage or shorts.
   b. Check for damaged or worn ignition switch.

### TEST 4, STATOR (UNITS LESS CLOSED BOWL DISTRIBUTOR)

1. Place shift lever in Park (manual transmission in Neutral), then set parking brake.
2. Disconnect TFI module harness connector. Attach TFI tester, Rotunda No. 105-00003 or equivalent, to battery positive and TFI harness connector.
3. Disconnect "S" terminal wire from starter relay, and connect remote starter switch.
4. Crank engine with remote starter switch, noting the tester LED lights.
5. If PIP light blinks, proceed to Test 6.
6. If PIP light does not blink, remove dis-

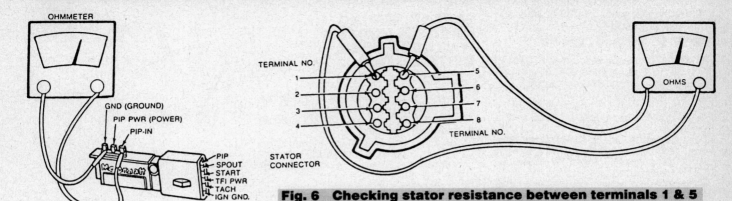

**Fig. 5  Checking TFI module resistance**

**Fig. 6  Checking stator resistance between terminals 1 & 5**

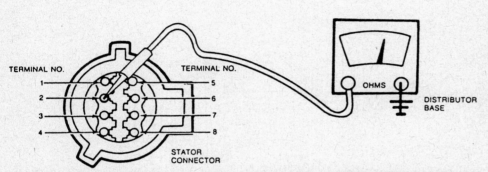

**Fig. 7  Checking stator resistance between terminal 2 & ground & between terminal 6 & ground**

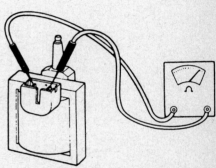

**Fig. 8  Checking ignition coil primary resistance**

tributor cap and verify distributor rotation, then proceed to step 7.

7. Remove distributor from engine and separate TFI module from distributor.

8. With TFI module removed, measure and record resistance values between module terminals, **Fig. 5**, and compare values as follows:
   a. Resistance between terminals GND and PIP-in should be greater than 500 ohms.
   b. Resistance between terminals PIP PWR and PIP-in should be less than 2000 ohms.
   c. Resistance between terminals PIP PWR and TFI PWR should be less than 200 ohms.
   d. Resistance between terminals GND and IGN GND should be less than 2 ohms.
   e. Resistance between terminals PIP-in and PIP should be less than 200 ohms.

9. If Resistance values recorded in previous step are within specified limits, replace stator. If values are not within specified limits, replace TFI module.

## TEST 5, STATOR (UNITS W/CLOSED BOWL DISTRIBUTOR)

1. Disconnect wiring harness connector from distributor and check for dirt, cor-

rosion and damage.

2. Using a volt-ohmmeter, measure resistance at the following connector terminals:
   a. Resistance between connector terminals 1 and 5, **Fig. 6**. If resistance is greater than than 5 ohms, replace stator.
   b. If resistance measures less than 5 ohms, proceed to step 3.
   c. Resistance between connector terminal 2 and distributor base, and terminal 6 and distributor base, **Fig. 7**.
   d. If resistance is less than 1 ohm for either terminal, inspect stator retaining screws in distributor bowl. If satisfactory, replace stator.

3. Place shift lever in Park (manual transmission in Neutral), then set parking brake.

4. Disconnect TFI module harness connector.

5. Attach TFI tester Rotunda No. 105-00003 or equivalent, to battery positive and harness connector.

6. Disconnect "S" terminal wire from starter relay and connect remote starter switch.

7. Crank engine with remote starter switch, noting the tester LED lights.

8. If PIP light blinks, proceed to Test 6.

9. If PIP light does not blink, replace stator.

## TEST 6, TFI MODULE

1. If Tach light blinked in Test 4 or 5, proceed to Test 7.

2. If Tach light did not blink, proceed as follows:
   a. Replace TFI module.
   b. Check for spark, using procedures in Test 1.
   c. If spark is not evident, replace coil.

## TEST 7, IGNITION COIL PRIMARY RESISTANCE

1. Turn ignition switch off.

2. Disconnect ignition coil connector and check for dirt, corrosion and damage.

3. Check resistance between positive and negative terminal of ignition coil, **Fig. 8**.

4. If resistance measures 0.3-1.0 ohm, proceed to Test 8.

5. If resistance measures less than 0.3 ohms or greater than 1.0 ohm, replace ignition coil.

## TEST 8, IGNITION COIL SECONDARY RESISTANCE

1. Check resistance between negative terminal and high voltage terminal of ignition coil, **Fig. 9**.

2. If resistance measures 6,500-11,500 ohms, proceed to Test 9.

3. If resistance measures less than 6,500 ohms, or greater than 11,500, replace ignition coil.

*THICK FILM INTEGRATED (TFI-IV)*

4. Reconnect ignition coil connector and secondary connector.

## TEST 9, EEC-IV/TFI-IV

1. Connect spark tester between ignition coil wire and ground, **Fig. 3**, and disconnect pin-in-line connector near distributor or TFI module.
2. Crank engine and check for spark.
3. If no spark is present, proceed as follows:
   a. On units less closed bowl distributor, proceed to Test 11.
   b. On units with closed bowl distributor, proceed to Test 10.
4. If spark is present, check PIP and IGN GND wires for continuity and repair as necessary. If ground wires are satisfactory, the EEC-IV system must be diagnosed.

## TEST 10, WIRING HARNESS (UNITS W/CLOSED BOWL DISTRIBUTOR)

1. Disconnect TFI module and distributor harness connectors.
2. Insert a straight pin into TFI module connector terminal 6.
3. Using a volt-ohmmeter, measure resistance between distributor connector terminal 5 and TFI module terminal 6. **Fig. 10**.
4. If resistance is less than 5 ohms, proceed to Test 11.
5. If resistance is greater than 5 ohms, check wiring between TFI module and distributor.

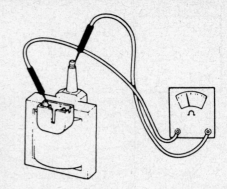

**Fig. 9  Checking ignition coil secondary resistance**

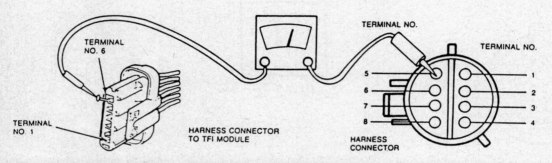

**Fig. 10  Checking distributor to TFI module resistance**

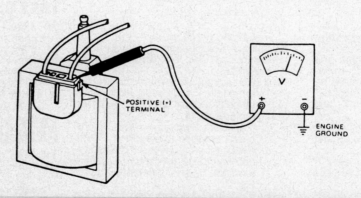

**Fig. 11  Checking ignition coil supply voltage**

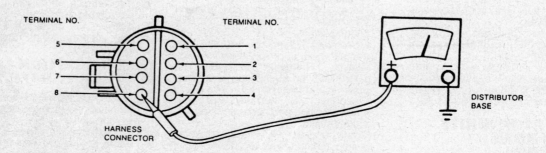

**Fig. 12  Checking stator supply voltage**

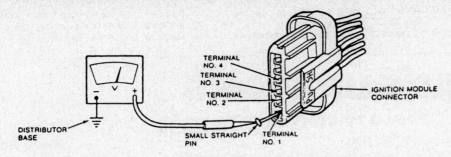

**Fig. 13   Checking ignition module wiring harness resistance**

## TEST 11, IGNITION COIL SUPPLY VOLTAGE

1. Connect volt-ohmmeter negative lead to distributor base.
2. Check battery voltage.
3. Turn ignition switch to Run position.
4. Check voltage at positive terminal of ignition coil, **Fig. 11.**
5. If voltage is at least 90 percent of battery voltage, proceed as follows:
   a. On units less closed bowl distributor, proceed to Test 3.
   b. On units with closed bowl distributor, check ignition coil harness connector and terminals for damage, corrosion and dirt. If satisfactory, proceed to Test 12.
6. If voltage is less than 90 percent of battery voltage, proceed as follows:
   a. Check wiring between ignition switch and ignition coil.
   b. Check worn or damaged ignition switch.

## TEST 12, TFI SUPPLY VOLTAGE (UNITS W/CLOSED BOWL DISTRIBUTOR)

1. Disconnect wiring harness connector from ignition module and check for dirt, corrosion and damage. Push connector tabs to separate.
2. Disconnect wire from "S" terminal of starter relay.
3. Connect volt-ohmmeter negative lead to distributor base.
4. Check battery voltage.
5. Check connector terminal voltage by connecting a volt-ohmmeter to small straight pin inserted into connector terminal, **Fig. 4.** Check voltage with ignition switch in following positions: check connector terminal 3 with ignition switch in Run and Start positions; and terminal 4 with switch in Start position.
6. If voltage readings are greater than 90 percent of battery voltage, proceed to Test 13.
7. If any voltage readings are less than 90 percent of battery voltage, check the following:
   a. Check wiring harness and connectors for damage or shorts.
   b. Check for damaged or worn ignition switch.

## TEST 13, STATOR SUPPLY VOLTAGE (UNITS W/CLOSED BOWL DISTRIBUTOR)

1. Connect voltmeter negative lead to distributor base.
2. Check battery voltage.
3. Turn ignition switch to the Run position. Measure voltage at stator harness connector terminal 8. **Fig. 12.**
4. If voltage is greater than 90 percent of battery voltage, proceed to Test 14.
5. If voltage is less than 90 percent of battery voltage, check the following:
   a. Check wiring harness and connectors for damage or shorts.
   b. Check for damaged or worn ignition switch.

## TEST 14, WIRING HARNESS (UNITS W/CLOSED BOWL DISTRIBUTOR)

1. Ensure distributor wiring harness is connected.
2. Using a volt-ohmmeter, measure resistance between distributor base and terminal 1 of ignition module harness connector. **Fig. 13.**
3. If resistance is less than 1 ohm, proceed as follows:
   a. Check all wiring and components, between TFI module and coil.
   b. Check wiring between ignition module and distributor GND circuit.

## COMPONENT REPLACEMENT

### DISTRIBUTOR, REPLACE

1. Disconnect primary wiring connector from distributor.
2. Mark position of No. 1 wire tower on distributor base.
3. Remove distributor cap and adapter and position aside leaving wiring attached.
4. Remove rotor to prevent damage.
5. Remove TFI connector.
6. Remove distributor hold-down bolt and clamp. Remove distributor. On vehicles equipped with security-type hold-down bolt, use tool T82L-12270-A or equivalent to re-

move hold-down bolt.
7. Turn engine until No. 1 piston is on compression stroke.
8. Align timing marks to proper initial timing.
9. Turn distributor shaft so rotor tip is pointing toward mark made in step 2 on distributor base.
10. Continue turning distributor shaft slightly so leading edge of vane is centered in switch stator assembly.
11. Rotate distributor in engine block to align leading edge of vane and vane switch and verify that rotor is pointing at No. 1 cap terminal. If vane and vane switch stator cannot be aligned by rotating distributor in engine block, pull distributor out of block enough to disengage distributor and to engage a different distributor gear tooth. Repeat steps 9, 10, and 11 as necessary.
12. Install distributor hold-down bolt and clamp without tightening.
13. Connect distributor TFI and primary wiring harnesses.
14. Install distributor rotor, cap adapter, and cap.
15. Using timing light, set initial timing according to specification given on Vehicle Emission Control Information Decal.
16. Torque distributor hold-down bolt to 17-25 ft. lbs.
17. Recheck timing and adjust, if necessary.

### IGNITION MODULE, REPLACE

1. Remove distributor cap and adapter. Position cap and wires aside.
2. Disconnect TFI wiring.
3. Remove distributor from engine using tool T82L-12270-A or equivalent to remove security-type hold-down bolt, if equipped.
4. Place distributor on workbench and remove 2 TFI module screws, **Fig. 2.**
5. Pull right side of module down distributor mounting flange and then back up to disengage module terminals from connector in distributor base. Module may then be pulled toward flange and away from distributor. **Do not attempt to lift module from mounting surface before moving entire TFI module toward distributor flange, as pins at distributor/module connector will break otherwise.**
6. Coat metal base plate of TFI ignition module with 1/32 inch thick layer of silicone grease D7AZ-19A331-A, or equivalent.
7. Place TFI module on distributor base mounting flange. Carefully position TFI module assembly toward distributor bowl and securely engage 3 distributor connector pins.
8. Install 2 TFI module mounting screws and torque to 9-16 inch lbs. on 1984-85 models, or 15-35 inch lbs. on 1986-89 models.
9. Install distributor on engine.
10. Install distributor cap and adapter.
11. Connect TFI wiring.
12. Check and, if necessary adjust engine timing according to decal.

## OCTANE ROD, REPLACE

1. Remove distributor cap, adapter, and rotor.
2. Remove octane rod retaining screw, **Fig. 2.**
3. Slide octane rod grommet out so rod can be disengaged from stator retaining post, and remove octane rod.
4. Reverse procedure to install.

# CARBURETORS
## TABLE OF CONTENTS
### Page No.

# Carter YFA 1 Barrel Carburetor
## INDEX
### Page No.

## ADJUSTMENT SPECIFICATIONS

| Year | Carb. Model | Float Level | Fast Idle Cam Setting | Dechoke or Unloader Setting | Pulldown Setting | Choke Setting |
|------|-------------|-------------|-----------------------|-----------------------------|------------------|---------------|
| 1980 | E0TE-ABA | 11/16 | .140 | .280 | .290 | — |
|      | E0TE-ACA | 11/16 | .140 | .280 | .320 | — |
|      | E0TE-AEA | 11/16 | .140 | .280 | .230 | — |
|      | E0TE-AFA | 11/16 | .140 | .280 | .230 | — |
|      | E0TE-AHA | 11/16 | .140 | .280 | .230 | — |
|      | E0TE-AKA | 11/16 | .140 | .280 | .230 | — |
|      | E0TE-ALA | 11/16 | .140 | .280 | .230 | — |
|      | E0TE-ATA | 11/16 | .140 | .280 | .320 | — |
|      | E0TE-CA | 11/16 | .140 | .280 | .230 | — |
|      | E0TE-FA | 11/16 | .140 | .280 | .290 | — |
|      | E0TE-GA | 11/16 | .140 | .280 | .230 | — |
|      | E0TE-LA | 11/16 | .140 | .280 | .230 | — |
|      | E0TE-ARA | 11/16 | .140 | .280 | .320 | — |
|      | E0UE-KA | 11/16 | .140 | .280 | .230 | — |

## ADJUSTMENT SPECIFICATIONS-Continued

| Year | Carb. Model | Float Level | Fast Idle Cam Setting | Dechoke or Unloader Setting | Pulldown Setting | Choke Setting |
|------|-------------|-------------|----------------------|----------------------------|------------------|---------------|
| 1981 | D5TE-AGB | — | .375 | .110 | .280 | 1 Rich |
| | D9TE-CA | — | .690 | .140 | .280 | Index |
| | D9TE-VA | — | .690 | .140 | .280 | Index |
| | E0TE-AMA | — | .690 | .140 | .280 | Index |
| | E0TE-FA | — | .690 | .140 | .280 | Index |
| | E1TE-ANA | — | .780 | .140 | .280 | Index |
| | E1TE-ARA | — | .780 | .140 | .280 | Index |
| | E1TE-AUA | — | .780 | .140 | .280 | 2 Rich |
| | E1TE-AZA | — | .780 | .140 | .330 | 2 Rich |
| | E1TE-DA | — | .780 | .140 | .280 | Index |
| | E1TE-EA | — | .780 | .140 | .280 | Index |
| | E1TE-GA | — | .780 | .140 | .330 | 2 Rich |
| | E1TE-TA | — | .780 | .140 | .280 | Index |
| | E1TE-UA | — | .780 | .140 | .280 | Index |
| | E1TE-VA | — | .780 | .140 | .280 | 2 Rich |
| | E1TE-ANB | — | .780 | .140 | .280 | Index |
| | E1TE-EB | — | .780 | .140 | .280 | Index |
| 1982 | E2TE-BZA,BVA | .780 | — | .280 | .270 | Index |
| | E2TE-AMA | .780 | — | .280 | .230 | Index |
| | E2UE-EA | .780 | — | .280 | .230 | Index |
| | E2TE-CEA | .780 | — | .330 | .320 | 2 Rich |
| | E2TE-JA | .780 | — | .330 | .320 | 2 Rich |
| | E2TE-YA | .780 | — | .280 | .300 | Index |
| | E2TE-AAA | .780 | — | .280 | .300 | Index |
| | E2TE-MA | .780 | — | .280 | .300 | 2 Rich |
| | E2TE-ANA | .780 | — | .280 | .300 | 2 Rich |
| | E2TE-KA | .780 | — | .330 | .320 | 2 Rich |
| | E2UE-DA | .780 | — | .330 | .320 | 2 Rich |
| 1983 | D5TE-AGB | ⅜ | .110 | .280 | .290 | — |
| | E0TE-FB | .690 | .140 | .280 | .290 | — |
| | E0TE-AMB | .690 | .140 | .280 | .290 | — |
| | E2TE-ZA | .690 | .140 | .280 | .290 | — |
| | E3TE-FA | .780 | .140 | .330 | .320 | — |
| | E3TE-GA | .780 | .140 | .330 | .320 | — |
| | E3TE-YA | .780 | .140 | .280 | .270 | — |
| | E3TE-ZA | .780 | .140 | .280 | .300 | — |
| | E3TE-AAA | .780 | .140 | .280 | .300 | — |
| | E3TE-ABA | .780 | .140 | .280 | .300 | — |
| | E3TE-AFA | .780 | .140 | .280 | .270 | — |
| | E3TE-AGA | .780 | .140 | .280 | .270 | — |
| | E3TE-AHA | .780 | .140 | .280 | .270 | — |
| | E3TE-AJA | .780 | .140 | .280 | .270 | — |
| | E3TE-AKA | .780 | .140 | .280 | .300 | — |
| | E3TE-ALA | .780 | .140 | .330 | .320 | — |
| | E3TE-AMA | .780 | .140 | .280 | .270 | — |
| | E3TE-ANA | .780 | .140 | .280 | .270 | — |
| | E3TE-APA | .780 | .140 | .280 | .300 | — |
| | E3TE-ARA | .780 | .140 | .280 | .270 | — |
| | E3TE-ASA | .780 | .140 | .280 | .270 | — |
| | E3TE-BDA | .780 | .140 | .330 | .320 | — |

*CARTER YFA 1 BARREL*

## ADJUSTMENT SPECIFICATIONS-Continued

| Year | Carb. Model | Float Level | Fast Idle Cam Setting | Dechoke or Unloader Setting | Pulldown Setting | Choke Setting |
|---|---|---|---|---|---|---|
| 1983 | E3TE-BKA | .780 | .140 | .330 | .320 | — |
| | E3TE-BNA | .780 | .140 | .330 | .320 | — |
| | E3TE-BRA | .780 | .140 | .280 | .300 | — |
| | E27E-BB | .650 | .140 | .220 | .320 | — |
| | E27E-CB | .650 | .140 | .220 | .320 | — |
| | E27E-CC | .650 | .140 | .220 | .320 | — |
| | E27E-EB | .650 | .140 | .220 | .320 | — |
| | E27E-FB | .650 | .140 | .220 | .320 | — |
| | E27E-GB | .650 | .140 | .220 | .320 | — |
| | E27E-HB | .650 | .140 | .220 | .320 | — |
| 1984 | E37E-BB | .650 | .140 | .270 | .320 | — |
| | E37E-EB | .650 | .140 | .270 | .320 | — |
| | E37E-FB | .650 | .140 | .270 | .320 | — |
| | E37E-LB | .650 | .140 | .270 | .320 | — |
| | E37E-NB | .650 | .140 | .270 | .320 | — |
| | E37E-RB | .650 | .140 | .270 | .320 | — |
| | E37E-TB | .650 | .140 | .270 | .320 | — |
| | E4TE-AAA | .780 | .140 | .330 | .360 | — |
| | E4TE-EA | .780 | .140 | .330 | .360 | — |
| | E4TE-FA | .780 | .140 | .330 | .360 | — |
| | E4TE-GA | .780 | .140 | .330 | .360 | — |
| | E4TE-HA | .780 | .140 | .330 | .360 | — |
| | E4TE-UA | .780 | .140 | .330 | .360 | — |
| | E4TE-VA | .780 | .140 | .330 | .360 | — |
| | E4TE-ZA | .780 | .140 | .330 | .360 | — |
| 1985 | E57E-DA | .650 | .140 | .270 | .320 | — |
| 1985–86 | E5TE-BA | .780 | .140 | .330 | .360 | — |
| | E5TE-CA | .780 | .140 | .330 | .360 | — |
| | E5TE-DA | .780 | .140 | .330 | .360 | — |
| | E5TE-FA | .780 | .140 | .330 | .340 | — |
| | E5TE-HA | .780 | .140 | .330 | .320 | — |
| | E5TE-JA | .780 | .140 | .330 | .360 | — |
| | E5TE-MA | .780 | .140 | .330 | .360 | — |
| | E5TE-RA | .780 | .140 | .330 | .360 | — |
| | E5TE-SA | .780 | .140 | .330 | .360 | — |
| | E5TE-TA | .780 | .140 | .330 | .360 | — |
| | E5TE-UA | .780 | .140 | .330 | .360 | — |
| | E5TE-VA | .780 | .140 | .330 | .360 | — |

## IDENTIFICATION LOCATION

The carburetor identification number is located on a tag attached to the carburetor by one of the fuel bowl cover attaching screws.

## DESCRIPTION

The Carter YF Series carburetor is a single-barrel down draft unit combining the fundamental features of other Carter carburetors. In addition, it features a diaphragm type accelerating pump. It also has a diaphragm operated metering rod, both vacuum and mechanically controlled.

## ADJUSTMENTS

### FLOAT LEVEL

Invert the air horn assembly, and check the clearance from the top of the float to the bottom of the air horn with the float level gauge, **Fig. 1.** Hold the air horn at eye level when gauging the float level. The float arm (lever) should be resting on the needle pin. Do not load the needle when adjusting the float. Bend the float arms as necessary to adjust the float level (clearance). Do not bend the tab at the end of the float arm. It prevents the float from striking the bottom of the fuel bowl when empty.

## ACCELERATOR PUMP

With throttle valve seated in bore of carburetor, press down on upper end of diaphragm shaft until it reaches its bottom position. The metering rod arm should now contact the pump lifter link at the outer end nearest the springs. Adjust by bending the pump connector link at its lower angle.

### METERING ROD

Back out the idle speed adjusting screw until the throttle plate is closed tight in the throttle bore. Press down on upper end of diaphragm shaft until diaphragm bottoms in vacuum chamber. Metering rod should contact bottom of metering rod well, and

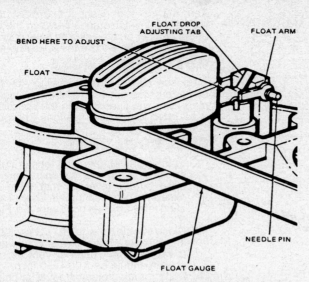

**Fig. 1   Float level adjustment (typical)**

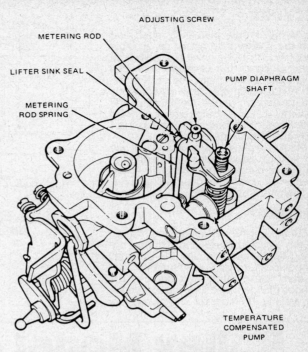

**Fig. 2   Metering rod adjustment**

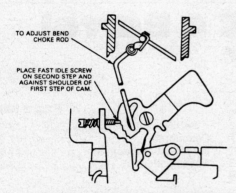

**Fig. 3   Fast idle cam linkage adjustment**

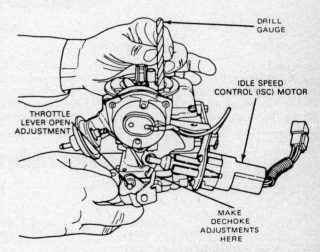

**Fig. 4   Dechoke adjustment**

metering rod should contact lifter link at the outer end, nearest the springs and at supporting lug. For models not equipped with metering rod adjusting screw, adjust by bending lip of metering rod arm to which metering rod is attached, up or down as required. For models equipped with a metering rod adjusting screw, turn the adjusting screw until metering rod just bottoms in the body casting, **Fig. 2.** For final adjustment turn metering rod adjusting screw in (clockwise) one additional turn.

## FAST IDLE CAM LINKAGE

Position fast idle screw on second step of fast idle cam and against shoulder of highest step. Using a drill of specified size, check clearance between lower edge of choke plate and bore. Refer to the Specifications Chart. To adjust, bend choke connector rod as required, **Fig. 3.**

## CHOKE PLATE PULLDOWN

### Models w/Piston Type Choke

Bend a 0.026 inch diameter wire gauge at a 90 degree angle approximately 1/8-inch from one end. Insert the bent end of the gauge between the choke piston slot and the right hand slot in choke housing. Rotate the choke piston lever counterclockwise until gauge is snug in the piston slot. Exert a light pressure on choke piston lever to hold the gauge in place, then use a drill with a diameter equal to the specified edge of choke plate and carburetor bore to check clearance.

To adjust the choke plate pulldown clearance, bend the choke piston lever as required to obtain specified setting.

When bending the lever, be careful not to distort the piston link. Install the choke thermostatic spring housing and gasket. Set the housing to specifications.

### Models w/Diaphragm Type Choke

1. On 1981-82 models, remove choke thermostat housing, then reinstall using two screws in place of rivets.
2. Temporarily rotate choke housing rich to lightly close choke plate, then increase an additional 90 degrees.
3. On all models, activate pulldown motor by applying external vacuum source.
4. On 1983-86 models, close choke plate as far as possible without forcing it.
5. On all models, using drill of specified size, check clearance between lower edge of choke plate and the air horn wall.
6. Adjust as necessary by bending choke diaphragm link.
7. Reconnect pulldown motor vacuum tube.

## DECHOKE

Hold the throttle plate fully open and close the choke plate as far as possible without forcing it. Use a drill of specified diameter to check the clearance between choke plate and air horn, **Fig. 4**. If clearance is not within specification, adjust by bending arm on choke trip lever of the throttle lever. Bending the arm downward will decrease the clearance, bending it upward will increase the clearance.

If the choke plate clearance and fast idle cam linkage adjustment was performed with the carburetor on the engine, adjust the engine idle speed and fuel mixture. Adjust dashpot, if equipped.

## DASHPOT

With the engine idle speed and mixture properly adjusted, the engine at normal operating temperature, loosen the anti-stall dashpot locknut, **Fig. 4**. Hold the throttle in the curb idle position and depress the dashpot plunger. Measure the clearance between the throttle lever and plunger tip.

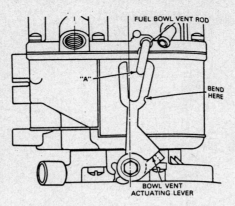

**Fig. 5 Fuel bowl vent adjustment**

Turn the anti-stall dashpot to provide 7/64 inch ± 1/64 inch clearance between the tip of the plunger and the throttle lever. Tighten the locknut to secure the adjustment.

## AUTOMATIC CHOKE

Loosen choke cover retaining screws and turn choke cover so that line or index mark on cover lines up with the specified mark listed in the Specifications Chart on choke housing.

## FUEL BOWL VENT

1. With engine at operating temperature and idle RPM set to specification, open throttle lever so that there is clearance between throttle lever actuating lever and fuel bowl vent rod, **Fig. 5**.
2. Close throttle lever to idle set position and measure travel of fuel bowl vent rod at point A. Travel of vent rod at point A should be .100-.150 inch.
3. Bend throttle actuating lever at point indicated in **Fig. 5** to adjust as necessary.

# Holley Model 4180-C 4 Barrel Carburetor

## INDEX

## ADJUSTMENT SPECIFICATIONS

| Year | Carb. Model | Float Level (Dry) | Float Level (Wet) | Pump Cam Position | Pump Override Spring Adjustment | Pulldown Setting | Choke Unloader | Choke Setting |
|---|---|---|---|---|---|---|---|---|
| 1980 | D9TE-BKA | ① | ② | 1 | .015 | .210 | .315 | 5 Rich |
| | D9TE-AGA | ① | ② | 1 | .015 | .210 | .315 | 5 Rich |
| | D9TE-AEA | ① | ② | 1 | .015 | .210 | .315 | 5 Rich |
| 1981-82 | D9TE-EBA | — | ② | 1 | — | .210 | — | — |
| | D9TE-EUA | — | ② | 1 | — | .210 | — | — |
| | E0TE-RA | — | ② | 1 | — | .210 | — | — |
| | E1UE-RA | — | ② | 1 | — | .210 | — | — |
| | E2TE-AGA | — | ② | 1 | — | .210 | — | — |
| | E2TE-AJA | — | ② | 1 | — | .210 | — | — |
| | E2TE-AKA | — | ② | 1 | — | .210 | — | — |
| | E2TE-NA | — | ② | 1 | — | .210 | — | — |
| 1983 | E3TE-PC | ① | ② | 1 | — | .220 | .315 | 3 Rich |
| | E3TE-RC | ① | ② | 1 | — | .220 | .315 | 3 Rich |
| | E3TE-SB | ① | ② | 1 | — | .220 | .315 | 3 Rich |
| | E3TE-TB | ① | ② | 1 | — | .220 | .315 | 3 Rich |

## ADJUSTMENT SPECIFICATIONS-Continued

| Year | Carb. Model | Float Level (Dry) | Float Level (Wet) | Pump Cam Position | Pump Override Spring Adjustment | Pulldown Setting | Choke Unloader | Choke Setting |
|---|---|---|---|---|---|---|---|---|
| 1984-85 | E4TE-ARA | ① | ② | 1 | — | .185 | .300 | Index |
| 1986 | E6HE-AC | ① | ② | 1 | — | .140 | — | — |
| | E6HE-GA | ① | ② | 1 | — | .150 | — | — |
| | E6JL-AA | ① | ② | 1 | — | .170 | — | — |
| | E6JL-BA | ① | ② | 1 | — | .170 | — | — |
| 1987 | E5TE-ZB | ① | ② | 1 | — | .157 | — | — |
| | E6HE-AC | ① | ② | 1 | — | .157 | — | — |
| | E6HE-GA | ① | ② | 1 | — | .150 | — | — |
| | E6HE-GB | ① | ② | 1 | — | .150 | — | — |

①—Parallel with float bowl floor (inverted).
②—Lower edge of sight plug.

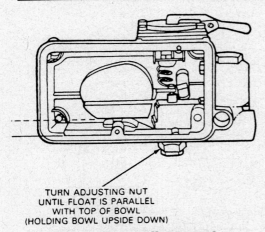

TURN ADJUSTING NUT UNTIL FLOAT IS PARALLEL WITH TOP OF BOWL (HOLDING BOWL UPSIDE DOWN)

**Fig. 1    Float adjustment**

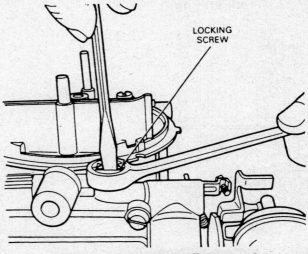

LOCKING SCREW

**Fig. 2    Fuel level adjustment**

## IDENTIFICATION LOCATION

The carburetor identification number is located on a tag attached to the carburetor at the choke shield screw.

## DESCRIPTION

The Holley Model 4180-C is a four barrel, down draft two-stage carburetor. This unit can be considered as two dual carburetors, one which supplies an air/fuel mixture throughout the entire engine operating range (primary stage), and the other which functions only when a greater quantity of air/fuel mixture is needed (secondary stage).

The primary stage contains a fuel bowl, metering body and accelerating pump assembly. Each primary barrel contains a primary and booster venturi, throttle plate, main fuel discharge nozzle and idle fuel passage.

The secondary stage contains a fuel bowl, metering body and secondary throttle operating diaphragm assembly. The secondary barrels each contain a primary and booster venturi, throttle plate, idle fuel passages, main secondary fuel discharge nozzle and a transfer system fuel passage from the primary fuel bowl.

A constant fuel supply is provided to fuel metering systems by a fuel inlet system for both primary and secondary stages.

## ADJUSTMENTS

### FLOAT LEVEL (DRY)

The dry float adjustment is a preliminary fuel level adjustment only. The final adjustment must be performed after the carburetor is installed on the engine.

With fuel bowl and float removed, adjust the float so that it is parallel to the fuel bowl with the top of the fuel bowl inverted, **Fig. 1.** Adjust both sides in the same manner.

### FUEL LEVEL (WET)

1. With vehicle resting on a flat surface, operate engine until normal operating temperature is reached.
2. Remove air cleaner, then operate engine at approximately 1000 RPM for 30 seconds to stabilize fuel level.
3. Stop engine, then remove sight plug from side of primary carburetor bowl.
4. Fuel level should be at bottom of sight plug hole. If fuel level is below sight plug hole, raise fuel level. If fuel overflows when plug is removed, lower fuel level. **Never loosen lock screw or nut or attempt to adjust fuel level with sight plug removed or engine running, as this will create a potential fire hazard.**
5. Adjust fuel level as necessary by loosening lock screw, then turning adjusting nut clockwise to lower fuel level or counterclockwise to raise fuel level, **Fig. 2.** Tighten lock screw and install sight plug, using old gasket, then run engine at 1000 RPM for approximately 30 seconds to stabilize fuel level. Each 1/8 turn of the adjusting nut will change fuel level approximately 1/32 inch.
6. Stop engine, remove sight plug and recheck fuel level. Repeat step 5 until fuel level is at bottom of sight plug

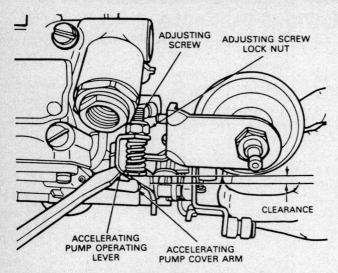

**Fig. 3  Checking accelerator pump lever clearance**

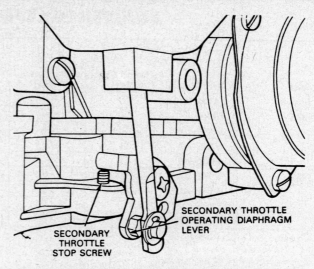

**Fig. 4  Secondary throttle plate adjustment**

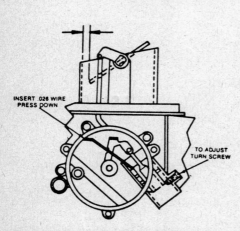

**Fig. 5  Choke plate pulldown adjustment. Exc. 1985–87 models w/electric choke**

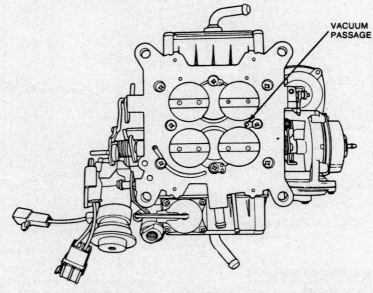

**Fig. 6  Choke plate pulldown vacuum passage. 1985–87 models w/electric choke**

hole, then reinstall sight plug using a new gasket.

7. Perform steps 3 through 6 for secondary fuel bowl. To stabilize fuel level in the secondary fuel bowl, the secondary throttle must be used.

## ACCELERATOR PUMP LEVER

1. Using a feeler gauge and with throttle plates wide open, there should be the specified clearance (minimum) between pump operating lever adjustment screw and pump arm when pump arm is depressed manually, **Fig. 3.**
2. If adjustment is required, loosen locknut and turn adjusting screw in to increase clearance and out to decrease clearance. One-half turn of screw is equal to approximately .015 inch.

3. When proper adjustment has been made, hold screw in position with a wrench and tighten locknut.

## ACCELERATOR PUMP STROKE

To satisfy the requirements in various climates, the pump discharge can be adjusted. The bottom hole (No. 2) in the pump cam and throttle lever provides the maximum pump discharge for extreme cold weather, and the top hole (No. 1) provides the minimum pump discharge for warm weather operation.

If a change in the adjustment is required, make certain the proper hole in plastic pump cam, located behind throttle lever, is

properly indexed with the numbered hole in the throttle lever before installing the retaining screw.

## SECONDARY THROTTLE PLATE

With secondary throttle plates closed, rotate secondary throttle shaft lever adjusting screw counterclockwise until the secondary throttle plates seat in the bores. On all units rotate adjusting screw clockwise until it contacts the secondary lever, **Fig. 4,** then an additional 1/4 turn on 1982–84 models or 3/8 turn on 1985–87 models.

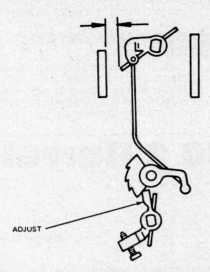

**Fig. 7 Dechoke adjustment**

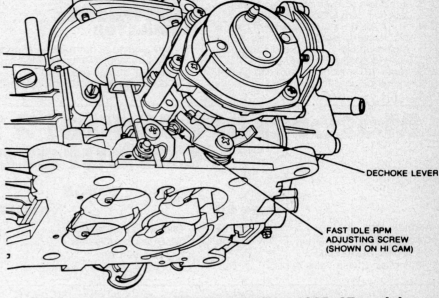

**Fig. 8 Fast idle cam adjustment. Exc. 1985–87 models w/electric choke**

## CHOKE PLATE PULLDOWN

### Exc. 1985–87 Models w/Electric Choke

1. Remove thermostat housing, gasket and retainer.
2. Insert a piece of wire, **Fig. 5**, into choke piston bore to move the piston down against the stop screw. Maintain light closing pressure on choke plate and measure the gap between the lower edge of the choke plate and air horn wall.
3. To adjust, remove the putty covering the adjustment screw and turn clockwise to decrease or counterclockwise to increase gap setting.
4. Reinstall choke thermostatic housing, gasket and retainer. Do not tighten screws until Fast Idle Cam Set adjustment has been performed.

### 1985–87 Models w/Electric Choke

1. Remove carburetor from vehicle and cover intake manifold.
2. Place carburetor on workstand suitable to allow access to pulldown diaphragm vacuum passage on underside of throttle body, **Fig. 6**.
3. Scribe alignment marks on choke cap and choke housing, then remove choke cap, gasket and retainer.
4. Temporarily install choke cap with standard choke cap gasket and align scribe marks, then rotate cap 90° counterclockwise and secure with one screw.
5. Ensuring that choke plate is in fully closed position, actuate choke pulldown motor using an outside vacuum source of at least 17 inches Hg
6. Using drill gauge of specified size, check clearance between upper edge of choke plate and air horn wall. Gauge should fit in such a manner that it contacts air horn and choke plate but does not move plate.

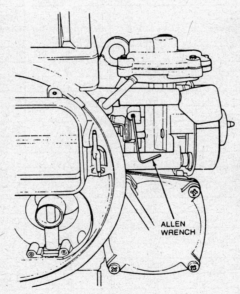

**Fig. 9 Fast idle cam adjustment. 1985–87 models w/electric choke**

7. If adjustment is necessary, carefully remove diaphragm adjustment screw cap using suitable tool.
8. Using 5/64 inch Allen wrench, turn adjustment screw clockwise to decrease setting or counterclockwise to increase setting. Maintain a minimum of 17 inches Hg to pulldown diaphragm during adjustment. Cycle vacuum from 0 to 17 inches Hg. to verify setting.
9. Apply suitable sealant to adjustment screw cavity and check fast idle cam adjustment.

## DECHOKE CLEARANCE

1. Hold throttle in wide open throttle position.
2. Apply a light closing pressure on the choke plate and measure the gap between the lower edge of the choke plate and air horn wall.
3. To adjust, bend the pawl on the fast idle lever, **Fig. 7**, forward to increase or backward to decrease the clearance.

## FAST IDLE CAM

### Exc. 1985–87 Models w/Electric Choke

1. Rotate choke cap 45 degrees counterclockwise to close the choke plate. Tighten screws.
2. Open and close throttle to place fast idle screw on top step of cam, **Fig. 8**.
3. Place a pull down gauge between lower edge of choke plate and air horn wall, then open and close the throttle to allow fast idle cam to drop.
4. Press upward on fast idle cam. There should be little or no movement indicating that the fast idle screw is on the kickdown step of the cam, against the first step.
5. To adjust, use a suitable tool and bend choke control rod to ensure proper fast idle location on the cam, **Fig. 8**.
6. Loosen screws and set choke thermostatic housing to the proper index mark, then tighten screws.

### 1985–87 Models w/Electric Choke

1. Perform choke plate pulldown adjustment as previously described.
2. With choke cap still wrapped and with

vacuum applied to diaphragm, cycle the throttle.

3. If fast idle screw rests on No. 2 step of fast idle cam, proceed to step 5.
4. Turn Allen head adjustment screw clockwise to position fast idle screw higher on No. 2 step or counterclockwise to position it lower, **Fig. 9.**
5. Remove temporary choke cap gasket, install original locking gasket, choke cap and choke cap retainer and secure with breakaway screws.

## DECEL THROTTLE MODULATOR

1. With engine at normal operating temperature, apply 19 inches Hg vacuum to decel throttle modulator.
2. Loosen decel throttle modulator lock nut and rotate modulator to achieve 1800 RPM.

## CHOKE THERMOSTATIC SPRING

1. Loosen thermostatic spring housing clamp retaining screws.
2. Rotate spring housing to align index mark on spring housing with center index mark on choke housing.

# Motorcraft Model 2150 2 Barrel Carburetor

## INDEX

## ADJUSTMENT SPECIFICATIONS

| Year | Carb. Model | Float Level (Dry) | Fuel Level (Wet) | Pump Setting Hole No. | Choke Plate Clearance (Pull Down) | Dechoke Clearance | Choke Setting |
|---|---|---|---|---|---|---|---|
| 1980 | E0TE-BEA | — | 13/16 | 2 | .140 | .250 | — |
| | E0TE-BGA | — | 13/16 | 2 | .135 | .250 | — |
| | E0TE-BHA | — | 13/16 | 2 | .135 | .250 | — |
| | E0TE-BRA | — | 7/8 | 3 | .128 | .115 | — |
| | E0TE-BSA | — | 7/8 | 2 | .140 | .115 | — |
| | E0TE-BYA | — | 7/8 | 2 | — | .115 | — |
| | E0TE-CFA | — | 13/16 | 2 | .128 | .250 | — |
| | E0TE-CLA | — | 7/8 | 2 | .140 | .200 | — |
| | E0TE-CVA | — | 7/8 | 2 | .105 | .250 | — |
| | E0TE-CYA | — | 13/16 | 2 | .140 | .250 | — |
| | E0TE-CZA | — | 13/16 | 2 | .140 | .250 | — |
| | E0TE-DBA | — | 7/8 | 3 | .130 | .250 | — |
| | E0TE-DCA | — | 7/8 | 3 | .130 | .250 | — |
| | E0TE-DDA | — | 7/8 | 3 | .128 | .115 | — |
| | E0TE-EAA | — | 13/16 | 2 | .128 | .250 | — |
| | EQUE-AA | — | 13/16 | 3 | .105 | .250 | — |
| | EQUE-ABA | — | 13/16 | 2 | .140 | .250 | — |
| | E0UE-AAA | — | 13/16 | 3 | .195 | .250 | — |
| | E0TE-BLA | — | 7/8 | 3 | .148 | .250 | — |
| | E0TE-BFA | — | 7/8 | 3 | .148 | .250 | — |
| | E0TE-BZA | — | 7/8 | 3 | .148 | .250 | — |
| | E0TE-CCA | — | 7/8 | 3 | .159 | .250 | — |
| | E0TE-CBA | — | 7/8 | 3 | .159 | .250 | — |
| | E0TE-EDA | — | 7/8 | 4 | .155 | .250 | — |
| | E0TE-DGA | — | 7/8 | 4 | .155 | .250 | — |
| | E0TE-EEA,EFA | — | 7/8 | 4 | .160 | .250 | — |
| | E0UE-NA | — | 13/16 | 3 | .105 | .250 | — |
| | E0UE-PN,RA | — | 13/16 | 4 | .185 | .250 | — |
| | E0UE-SA,TA | — | 13/16 | 3 | .195 | .250 | — |
| | E0UE-VA | — | 13/16 | 4 | .185 | .250 | — |

## ADJUSTMENT SPECIFICATIONS-Continued

| Year | Carb. Model | Float Level (Dry) | Fuel Level (Wet) | Pump Setting Hole No. | Choke Plate Clearance (Pull Down) | Dechoke Clearance | Choke Setting |
|------|-------------|-------------------|------------------|----------------------|-----------------------------------|-------------------|---------------|
| 1980 | E0TE-DEA | — | 7/8 | 4 | .170 | .250 | — |
|      | E0TE-DFA | — | 7/8 | 4 | .180 | .250 | — |
|      | E0TE-ECA | — | 7/8 | 4 | .175 | .250 | — |
| 1981 | E1TE-BFA | .484 | .875 | 2 | .140 | .200 | V-Notch |
|      | E1TE-BGA | .484 | .875 | 3 | .148 | .250 | V-Notch |
|      | E1TE-BHA | .484 | .875 | 2 | .140 | .200 | 3 Rich |
|      | E1TE-BJA | .484 | .875 | 3 | .148 | .250 | V-Notch |
|      | E1TE-BSA | .484 | .875 | 3 | .130 | .250 | V-Notch |
|      | E1TE-BTA | .484 | .875 | 3 | .130 | .250 | V-Notch |
|      | E1TE-BVA | .438 | .810 | 2 | .130 | .200 | V-Notch |
|      | E1TE-BYA | .484 | .875 | 4 | .175 | .250 | V-Notch |
|      | E1TE-BZA | .484 | .875 | 4 | .180 | .250 | V-Notch |
|      | E1TE-CAA | .484 | .875 | 4 | .175 | .250 | V-Notch |
|      | E1TE-CBA | .484 | .875 | 4 | .180 | .250 | V-Notch |
|      | E1TE-CCA | .484 | .875 | 4 | .155 | .250 | V-Notch |
|      | E1TE-CDA | .484 | .875 | 4 | .155 | .250 | V-Notch |
|      | E1TE-CEA | .484 | .875 | 4 | .160 | .200 | V-Notch |
|      | E1TE-CFA | .484 | .875 | 4 | .160 | .200 | V-Notch |
|      | E1TE-CHA | .484 | .875 | 3 | .148 | — | — |
|      | E1TE-CKA | .438 | .810 | 2 | .125 | .200 | V-Notch |
|      | E1TE-CLA | .438 | .810 | 2 | .125 | .200 | V-Notch |
|      | E1TE-CMA | .438 | .810 | 2 | .125 | .200 | V-Notch |
|      | E1TE-CNA | .438 | .810 | 2 | .125 | .200 | V-Notch |
|      | E1TE-CPA | .438 | .810 | 2 | .125 | .200 | V-Notch |
|      | E1TE-CRA | .438 | .810 | 2 | .125 | .200 | V-Notch |
|      | E1TE-CSA | .438 | .810 | 2 | .125 | .200 | V-Notch |
|      | E1UE-GA | .438 | .810 | 2 | .130 | .200 | V-Notch |
|      | E1UE-HA | .484 | .875 | 2 | .125 | .200 | V-Notch |
|      | E1UE-KA | .484 | .875 | 3 | .180 | .250 | V-Notch |
|      | E1VE-CA | .484 | .875 | 3 | .120 | .200 | V-Notch |
|      | E1VE-FA | .484 | .875 | 3 | .120 | .200 | Index |
|      | E1VE-JA | .484 | .875 | 3 | .120 | .200 | V-Notch |
| 1982 | E1UE-JA | 31/64 | .875 | 3 | .120 | .200 | V-Notch |
|      | E2TE-AYA | 7/16 | .810 | 2 | .130 | .200 | V-Notch |
|      | E2TE-BAA | 7/16 | .810 | 2 | .125 | .200 | V-Notch |
|      | E2TE-BBA | 7/16 | .810 | 2 | .125 | .200 | V-Notch |
|      | E2TE-BEA | 7/16 | .810 | 2 | .130 | Dechoke .200 | V-Notch |
|      | E2TE-BFA | 7/16 | .810 | 2 | .125 | .200 | V-Notch |
|      | E2TE-BGA | 31/64 | .875 | 4 | .180 | .250 | V-Notch |
|      | E2TE-BHA | 31/64 | .875 | 4 | .180 | .250 | V-Notch |
|      | E2TE-BJA | 31/64 | .875 | 4 | .175 | .250 | V-Notch |
|      | E2TE-BKA | 31/64 | .875 | 4 | .175 | .250 | V-Notch |
|      | E2TE-BLA | 7/16 | .810 | 2 | .125 | .200 | V-Notch |
|      | E2TE-BMA | 7/16 | .810 | 2 | .125 | .250 | V-Notch |
|      | E2TE-BNA | 7/16 | .810 | 2 | .125 | .200 | V-Notch |
|      | E2TE-CFA | 7/16 | .810 | 2 | .125 | .250 | V-Notch |
|      | E2TE-CGA | 7/16 | .810 | 2 | .125 | .200 | V-Notch |
|      | E2TE-CJA | 7/16 | .810 | 2 | .130 | .200 | V-Notch |
|      | E2TE-CKA | 7/16 | .810 | 2 | .120 | .200 | V-Notch |
|      | E2UE-FA | 31/64 | .875 | 3 | .120 | .200 | V-Notch |
|      | E2UE-JA | 31/64 | .875 | 2 | .130 | .200 | V-Notch |
|      | E2UE-KA | 31/64 | .875 | 2 | .120 | .200 | V-Notch |

*MOTORCRAFT MODEL 2150 2 BARREL*

## ADJUSTMENT SPECIFICATIONS-Continued

| Year | Carb. Model | Float Level (Dry) | Fuel Level (Wet) | Pump Setting Hole No. | Choke Plate Clearance (Pull Down) | Dechoke Clearance | Choke Setting |
|------|-------------|-------------------|------------------|----------------------|-----------------------------------|-------------------|---------------|
| 1983 | E2TE-BPA | 31/64 | .875 | 3 | .130 | .250 | V-Notch |
| | E2TE-BRA | 31/64 | .875 | 3 | .130 | .250 | V-Notch |
| | E2UE-FA | 31/64 | .875 | 3 | .120 | .200 | V-Notch |
| | E2UE-KA | 31/64 | .875 | 2 | .120 | .200 | V-Notch |
| | E2UE-AKA | 31/64 | .875 | 3 | .180 | .250 | V-Notch |
| | E2UE-ANA | 31/64 | .875 | 3 | .180 | .250 | V-Notch |
| | E3UE-BA | 31/64 | .875 | 2 | .120 | .200 | V-Notch |
| | E3UE-CA | 31/64 | .875 | 3 | .120 | .200 | V-Notch |
| | E3UE-DA | 31/64 | .875 | 3 | .180 | .250 | V-Notch |
| | E3UE-EA | 31/64 | .875 | 3 | .180 | .250 | V-Notch |
| | E3TE-AUA | 7/16 | .810 | 3 | .142 | .200 | V-Notch |
| | E3TE-AVA | 7/16 | .810 | 3 | .149 | .250 | V-Notch |
| | E3TE-AYA | 7/16 | .810 | 4 | .137 | .250 | V-Notch |
| | E3TE-AZA | 31/64 | .875 | 3 | .130 | .250 | V-Notch |
| | E3TE-BAA | 31/64 | .875 | 3 | .130 | .250 | V-Notch |
| | E3TE-BBA | — | .810 | 3 | .125 | .250 | V-Notch |
| | E3TE-BCA | — | .810 | 3 | .125 | .250 | V-Notch |
| | E3TE-BEA | 7/16 | .810 | 3 | .149 | .200 | V-Notch |
| | E3TE-BFA | — | .810 | 3 | .125 | .250 | V-Notch |
| | E3TE-BGA | — | .810 | 3 | .125 | .250 | V-Notch |
| | E3TE-BHA | 7/16 | .810 | 3 | .152 | .200 | V-Notch |
| | E3TE-BJA | 7/16 | .810 | 4 | .157 | .200 | V-Notch |
| | E3TE-BLA | 7/16 | .810 | 3 | .157 | .200 | V-Notch |
| | E3TE-BMA | 7/16 | .810 | 4 | .150 | .200 | V-Notch |
| | E3TE-BPA | 7/16 | .810 | 3 | .157 | .200 | V-Notch |
| 1984 | E37E-AAA | 7/16 | .810 | 4 | .136 | .200 | V-Notch |
| | E37E-ABA | 7/16 | .810 | 4 | .136 | .200 | V-Notch |
| | E37E-ACA | 7/16 | .810 | 4 | .136 | .200 | V-Notch |
| | E37E-ADA | 7/16 | .810 | 4 | .136 | .200 | V-Notch |
| | E37E-AEA | 7/16 | .810 | 4 | .136 | .200 | V-Notch |
| | E47E-TA | 7/16 | .810 | 4 | .136 | .200 | V-Notch |
| | E47E-UA | 7/16 | .810 | 4 | .136 | .200 | V-Notch |
| | E47E-VA | 7/16 | .810 | 4 | .136 | .200 | V-Notch |
| | E4TE-ACA | 7/16 | .810 | 4 | .155 | .200 | V-Notch |
| | E4TE-ADA | 7/16 | .810 | 4 | .152 | .200 | V-Notch |
| | E4TE-AEA | 31/64 | .875 | 3 | .142 | .200 | V-Notch |
| | E4TE-AFA | 31/64 | .075 | 3 | .144 | .200 | V-Notch |
| | E4TE-AHA | 31/64 | .875 | 4 | .150 | .200 | V-Notch |
| | E4TE-AJA | 31/64 | .875 | 3 | .150 | .200 | V-Notch |
| | E4TE-AKA | 31/64 | .875 | 3 | .137 | .200 | V-Notch |
| | E4TE-ALA | 31/64 | .875 | 3 | .125 | .200 | V-Notch |
| | E4TE-AMA | 31/64 | .875 | 3 | .140 | .200 | V-Notch |
| | E4TE-APA | 31/64 | .875 | 3 | .145 | .200 | V-Notch |
| 1985 | E57E-BA | 1/16 | .810 | 4 | .136 | .250 | V-Notch |
| | E57E-CA | 1/16 | .810 | 4 | .136 | .250 | V-Notch |
| | E5TE-PA | 1/4 | .810 | 4 | .152 | .200 | V-Notch |
| | E5TE-YA | 9/32 | .875 | 4 | .150 | .200 | V-Notch |
| | E5TE-AAA | 1/4 | .810 | 4 | .155 | .200 | V-Notch |
| | E5TE-ACA | 9/32 | .875 | 4 | .150 | .200 | V-Notch |
| 1986 | E69E-AA | 1/16 | .810 | 4 | .136 | .250 | V-Notch |
| | E69E-BA | 1/16 | .810 | 4 | .136 | .250 | V-Notch |
| | E69E-CA | 1/16 | .810 | 4 | .136 | .250 | V-Notch |
| | E69E-DA | 1/16 | .810 | 4 | .136 | .250 | V-Notch |

**Fig. 1   Float adjustment**

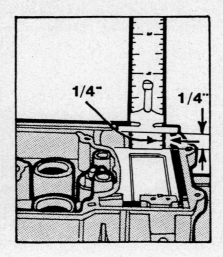

**Fig. 2   Fuel level adjustment**

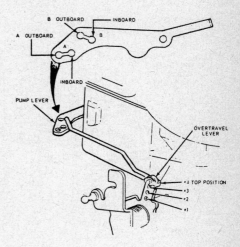

**Fig. 3   Pump stroke adjustment. 1980**

## IDENTIFICATION LOCATION

The carburetor identification number is located on a tag attached to the carburetor by one of the fuel bowl cover attaching screws.

## DESCRIPTION

The Motorcraft 2150 carburetor has two main bodies, the air horn and throttle body. The air horn assembly, which serves as a cover for the throttle body, contains a choke plate and vents for the fuel bowl. On 2150 units installed on V6 engines, the air horn assembly contains a fuel deceleration system which consists of a metered pickup orifice in the fuel bowl and air/fuel mixing orifices and bleeds.

An electric choke system is incorporated which opens a choke plate within 1-1½ minutes when under hood temperatures are above approximately 55°F to 60°F. The electronic choke system is supplied current to open the choke when under hood temperatures are between 54°F and 74°F.

Some 2150 units are equipped with an altitude compensation aneroid to improve high altitude emission control and driveability. Intake air entering the bypass valve is metered into the air flow above the throttle plates, leaning the mixture for high altitude operation. Air flow is controlled by a valve activated by an aneroid attached to the rear of the carburetor main body. Also, these units are equipped with a choke in

the bypass air intake, linked to the main choke.

The throttle plate, accelerating pump, power (enrichment) valve and fuel bowl are in the throttle body. The choke housing is attached to the throttle body.

The two bodies each contain a main and booster venturi, main fuel discharge, accelerating pump discharge, idle fuel discharge and a throttle plate. On some units, an anti-stall dash pot is attached to the carburetor when the vehicle is equipped with an automatic transmission.

Some 1983-86 vehicles use a feedback carburetor. The air horn assembly used on the feedback carburetor has an auxiliary fresh air intake for the duty cycle solenoid/altitude compensator.

The main body used on feedback carburetors has a provision at the back to attach the duty cycle solenoid/altitude compensator as well as an opening that accepts auxiliary fresh air from the horn and channels that link up to the bleed circuits to the booster support assembly. There is also a throttle angle potentiometer mounted on the throttle at the choke side.

The booster support assembly has cast in channels that flow bleed air to the idle and main system vacuum circuit.

## ADJUSTMENTS
### FLOAT LEVEL (DRY)

The dry float fuel level adjustment is a preliminary adjustment only. The final adjustment must be made after the carburetor is mounted on the engine.

Remove the air horn. With float raised and fuel inlet needle seated, check dis-

tance between top surface of main body and top surface of float. Take measurement at a point ⅛ inch from the free end of the float and ⅛ inch (5/16 inch metal float) in from side of float adjacent to inside wall of air horn.

If cardboard gauge is used, place gauge in corner of the enlarged end section of fuel bowl as shown. The gauge should touch float near the end but not on the end radius, **Fig. 1**.

Depress the float tab to seat the fuel inlet needle. The float height is measured from the gasket surface of the main body with gasket removed. If necessary, bend float tab to bring setting within specified limits. This should provide the correct fuel level setting.

### FUEL LEVEL (WET)

1. Operate engine to normalize engine temperatures, and place vehicle on a flat surface as near level as possible. Stop the engine.
2. Remove air cleaner and carburetor air horn assembly and gasket.
3. Temporarily place air horn gasket in position on carburetor main body and start engine. Let engine idle for a few minutes, then remove air horn and gasket to provide accessibility to float assembly.
4. While engine is idling, use a standard depth scale to measure vertical distance from top machined surface of carburetor main body to level of fuel in bowl, **Fig. 2**. Measurement must be made at least ¼ inch away from any vertical surface to insure an accurate reading, because the surface of the fuel is higher at the edges than in the center.

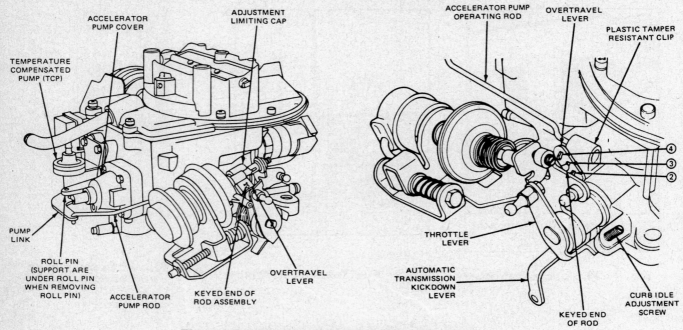

**Fig. 4   Pump stroke adjustment. 1981–86**

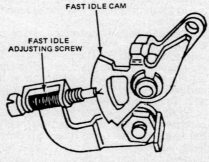

CONVENTIONAL ONE-PIECE FAST IDLE LEVER

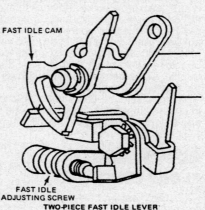

TWO-PIECE FAST IDLE LEVER

**Fig. 5   Fast idle cam assemblies**

5. If an adjustment is required, stop the engine and bend the float tab as necessary to bring the fuel level within specifications.

## ACCELERATING PUMP

The primary throttle shaft lever (over travel lever) has 4 holes on 1980 models or three holes on 1981-86 models and the accelerating pump link has 2 or 4 holes to control the pump stroke for various atmospheric temperatures, operating conditions and specific engine applications, **Figs. 3 and 4.** Adjustment holes are not provided on the temperature compensated accelerator pump carburetors. The stroke should not be changed from the specified setting.

1. To release rod from retainer clip, press tab end of clip toward rod. Then, at the same time, press rod away from clip until it is disengaged.
2. Position clip over specified hole in over travel lever. Press ends of clip together and insert operating rod through clip and lever. Release clip to engage rod.

## CHOKE PLATE CLEARANCE

1. Set throttle on fast idle cam top step, **Fig. 5**, then loosen choke thermostatic housing retaining screws and set housing 90° in rich direction.
2. Activate pulldown motor by manually

forcing pulldown control diaphragm link in direction of applied vacuum or by applying vacuum to external vacuum tube.

3. Check clearance between choke plate and center of carburetor air horn wall nearest fuel bowl, **Fig. 6.** Refer to the Specifications Chart. If clearance is not as specified, reset by adjusting diaphragm stop on end of choke pulldown diaphragm.

## FAST IDLE CAM CLEARANCE

1. Open and close throttle slightly and observe where fast idle screw contacts cam. The fast idle screw should be set to approximate high cam speed and should strike the second highest step on fast idle cam.
2. After adjusting fast idle cam with fast idle screw, allow choke plate to close. Choke plate should close tightly in air horn.
3. If choke plate is loose, an additional adjustment must be made to pulldown diaphragm rod assembly, by loosening locknut and tightening turnbuckle until choke plate is tight on air horn.

## AUTOMATIC CHOKE VALVE TENSION

Turn thermostatic spring cover against spring tension until index mark on cover is aligned with mark specified in the Specifications Chart on choke housing, **Fig. 7.**

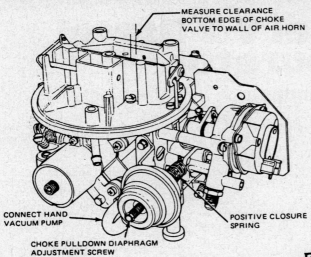

Fig. 6  Choke plate clearance

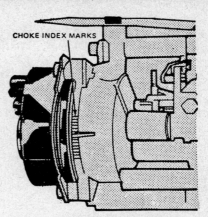

Fig. 7  Automatic choke adjustment

## ANTI-STALL DASH POT

With air cleaner removed, and with engine idle speed and mixture properly adjusted, loosen anti-stall dash pot locknut, **Fig. 8.** Hold throttle in closed position and depress plunger with a screwdriver. Check clearance between throttle lever and plunger tip with a feeler gauge of the specified clearance dimension. Then turn dash pot in its bracket in a direction to provide the specified clearance.

Fig. 8  Dash pot adjustment

# Aisin Model Y 2 Barrel Carburetor

## INDEX

## ADJUSTMENT SPECIFICATIONS

| Year | Carb. Model (Code 9510) | Float Level (Dry) | Float Drop | Fast Idle Cam Setting | Choke Pulldown | |
|---|---|---|---|---|---|---|
|  |  |  |  |  | 1st Stage | 2nd Stage |
| 1987 | E77E-AA | .787 | 1.854 | 14.5° | 17° TO 19° | 40° TO 44° |
| 1988 | E87E-AA | .787 | 1.854 | 14.5° | 17° TO 19° | 40° TO 44° |

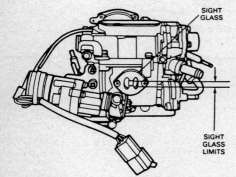

**Fig. 1 Checking float level through sight glass**

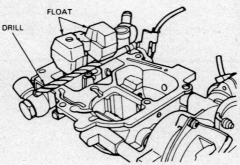
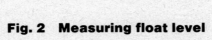

**Fig. 2 Measuring float level**

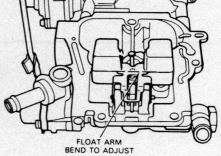

**Fig. 3 Adjusting float level**

## IDENTIFICATION LOCATION

he carburetor identification number is located on a tag attached to the carburetor.

## DESCRIPTION

The Aisin model Y two barrel carburetor incorporates three major assemblies, the air horn, main body and throttle body. The air horn contains the choke plate, choke pulldown system, electric choke cap, fast idle cam breaker, fuel bowl internal vent, inlet needle and seat, inlet fitting and solenoid bowl vent assembly. The air horn also acts as a cover for the main body. The main body contains the idle system, main metering system, power enrichment system, accelerator pump system and the auxiliary accelerator pump. An idle speed motor is also mounted to the main body. The throttle body contains the idle mixture screws, which are concealed by tamper resistance plugs, and the throttle shaft and lever assembly.

The auxiliary accelerator pump is used to improve driveability during engine warm up. This pump will supply additional fuel to the pump discharge, providing engine coolant temperature is below the calibrated value.

## ADJUSTMENTS

### FLOAT LEVEL

The float level can be checked with the carburetor installed on the vehicle. With vehicle parked on a level surface and engine at normal operating temperature, fuel level should be within sight glass limits, **Fig. 1.** If fuel level is not within sight glass limits, perform the following float level adjustment:

1. Remove carburetor air horn.
2. Remove power valve piston and spring, then invert air horn assembly an insert a drill bit of the specified diameter between top of float and air horn surface, **Fig. 2.** Float lever should be resting on needle when checking clearance.
3. Bend float arm, as necessary, to obtain specified clearance, **Fig. 3.** Do not bend tab at end of float arm, as this tab is used to adjust float drop.
4. Install power valve piston, spring and air horn.

### FLOAT DROP

1. Remove carburetor air horn.

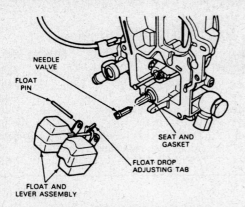

Fig. 4  Adjusting float drop

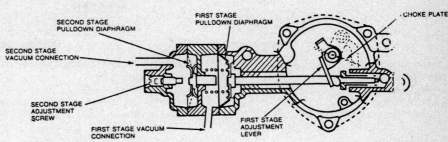

Fig. 5  Adjusting choke plate pulldown angle

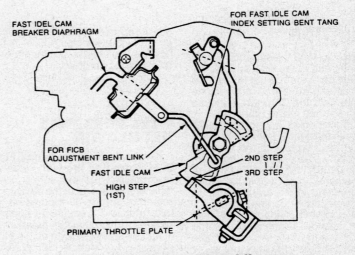

Fig. 6  Adjusting fast idle cam

2. While holding carburetor air horn upright, measure distance from toe end of float to air horn casting with vernier calipers or other suitable measuring device.
3. If float drop is not within specifications, adjust by bending float drop adjusting tab, **Fig. 4.**
4. Install carburetor air horn.

## CHOKE PULLDOWN

### First Stage

1. Depress throttle lever and place choke plate in the fully closed position.
2. Using a suitable hand held vacuum pump, apply a minimum of 16 inches Hg of vacuum to first stage vacuum fitting and check choke plate angle with a suitable choke plate angle gauge. Apply a light closing pressure to choke plate when checking choke plate angle.
3. If necessary, remove choke cap and bend first stage adjustment lever to obtain specified angle, **Fig. 5.**

### Second Stage

1. With choke plate in fully closed position, apply a minimum of 16 inches Hg

of vacuum to the first and second stage vacuum fittings.
2. Check choke plate angle using a suitable choke plate angle gauge. Apply light closing pressure to choke plate when checking choke plate angle.
3. If necessary, adjust by turning second stage adjusting screw, **Fig. 5.**

## FAST IDLE CAM

1. With fast idle screw positioned on second step of fast idle cam, check choke plate angle with suitable choke plate angle gauge.
2. If not within limits, adjust by bending fast idle cam tang, **Fig. 6.**

# FUEL INJECTION

## INDEX

## DESCRIPTION

The Electronic Fuel Injection (EFI) system is a multi-point, pulse time, speed density fuel injection system. Fuel is metered into the air intake stream in accordance with engine demand through injectors mounted on a tuned intake manifold.

An electronic engine control computer (EEC IV) receives signals from various engine sensors and computes the required rate of fuel flow to maintain an optimum air/fuel ratio throughout the entire range of engine operation. The computer then sends a command to the fuel injectors to meter the appropriate quantity of fuel.

The fuel charging manifold assembly houses the injectors which are mounted directly above each of the engine's intake ports. When energized, the injectors spray a metered quantity of fuel into the intake air stream.

## SYSTEM COMPONENTS
### AIR INTAKE MANIFOLD

The air intake manifold is a two-piece aluminum casting which provides mounting flanges for the throttle body assembly, fuel supply manifold, accelerator control brackets and the EGR valve and supply tube. Runner lengths are precisely tuned to optimize engine torque and power output. Vacuum taps in the manifold are provided to support various engine accessories. Cutouts for the fuel injectors are specially machined to prevent both air and fuel leakage.

### FUEL INJECTORS

The fuel injectors, **Fig. 1**, are electro-mechanical devices which meter and atomize fuel for combustion. The injectors, located in the lower intake manifold, are installed so fuel is directed just ahead of the intake valves. The injector solenoid receives an electrical control signal from the electronic control unit which causes the pintle to move off its seat, allowing fuel to flow. Because the fuel pressure drop across the injector tip is constant and the injector orifice is fixed, fuel flow is regulated by the length of time the solenoid is energized.

## FUEL PRESSURE REGULATOR

The fuel pressure regulator, **Figs. 2 and 3**, is located on the fuel supply manifold and regulates fuel pressure supplied to the injectors. One side of the diaphragm in the regulator senses fuel pressure, while intake manifold pressure is applied to the other side. Nominal fuel pressure is established by spring tension applied to the diaphragm. A constant fuel pressure drop across the injectors is maintained by balancing one side of the diaphragm with manifold pressure. Excess fuel is bypassed through the regulator and returned to the fuel tank.

## FUEL SUPPLY MANIFOLD
### 4-140 & 6-300 Engines

The fuel supply manifold delivers high pressure fuel from the fuel supply line to the injectors. The assembly consists of two preformed tubes or stampings, one for fuel supply and one for fuel return. The fuel pressure manifold assembly has four injector connectors, a mounting flange to the fuel pressure regulator and mounting attachments which locate the fuel manifold assembly and retain fuel injectors. The manifold is also equipped with a fuel pressure relief valve on the fuel supply tube.

### V6-177, 183 & V8-302, 351 Engines

The fuel supply manifold delivers high pressure fuel from the fuel supply line to the injectors. The assembly consists of two banks of stamped fuel rails connected by a crossover connection, six or eight injection connectors, a mounting flange to the fuel pressure regulator and mounting attachments which locate the fuel manifold assembly and retain fuel injectors.

### V8-460 Engine

The fuel supply manifold delivers high pressure fuel from the fuel supply line to the injectors. The assembly consists of two banks of stamped fuel rails connected by two permanent crossmver connections, eight injection connectors, a mounting flange to the fuel pressure regulator and mounting attachments which locate the fuel manifold assembly and retain fuel injectors.

## THROTTLE BODY

Air flow to the engine is controlled by the throttle body through a single butterfly-type valve on 4-140 and V6-177 engines, **Fig. 4,** or a double butterfly-type valve on 6-300, V8-302, V8-351 and V8-460 engines, **Figs. 5 and 6.** On V6-183 engine, the throttle body and air intake assembly is a single piece aluminum casting. Throttle position is controlled by multi-link, progressive opening, throttle linkage. The throttle body has a single bore on 4-140, V6-177 and 183 engines and a dual bore on 6-300, V8-302 and V8-351 engines with an air bypass channel around the throttle plate. The bypass channel controls both cold and warm engine idle air flow which is regulated by an air bypass valve assembly mounted on the air cleaner on 4-140 engines, the upper intake manifold on V6-177 and 183 engines and on the throttle body on 6-300, V8-302 and V8-351 engines. The air bypass valve is controlled by the EEC computer and incorporates a linear actuator which positions a variable area metering valve.

## SELF-DIAGNOSTIC SYSTEM
### ACCESSING SERVICE CODES

Service codes can be accessed from the EEC-IV system memory through the diagnostic connector, Fig. 7 through 10, using an analog voltmeter and jumper wire. The proper set-up is as follows:
1. Turn ignition switch to Off position,

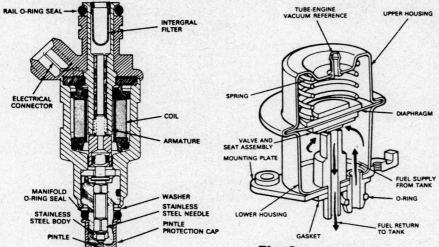

**Fig. 1   Fuel injector**

**Fig. 2   Fuel pressure regulator. Except V6-177 engines**

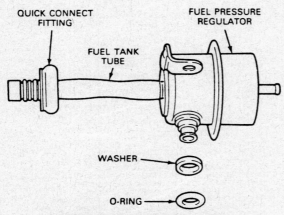

**Fig. 7   Fuel pressure regulator. V6-177 engine**

then set the VOM on a DC voltage range to read from 0 to 15 volts.

2. Insert one end of jumper wire into the No. 4 pin on the self-test connector.
3. Clamp negative lead from the voltmeter on to the other end of jumper wire, **Fig. 11.**
4. Clamp positive lead from voltmeter on to positive battery terminal, **Fig. 12.**
5. Insert one end of the second jumper wire into No. 2 pin on the self-test connector, and other end into the self-test input connector, **Fig. 13.** The final connection also activates the ECA self-test sequence when the ignition switch is turned to the ON position.

## SERVICE CODE FORMAT

The EEC-IV system transmits its information by the use of the self-test service codes. These service codes are two digit

numbers representing the results of the self-test. The service codes are transmitted on the self-test output (found in the self-test electrical connector) in the form of time pulses, and read by the use of a analog volt-ohmmeter.

The pulse format, **Figs. 14, 15 and 16** is as follows:

1. One-half second on-time for each digit.
2. Two seconds off-time between digits.
3. Four seconds off-time between codes.
4. Six to nine seconds off-time before and after the half-second separator pulse.

## CODE INTERPRETATION

When a service code is reported on the analog voltmeter for a functional test, it will represent itself as a pulsing or sweeping

movement of the voltmeter's needle across the dial face, **Fig. 17.** A single digit of three will be reported by three needle pulses (sweeps). However as previously stated, a service code is represented by a two digit number, such as 2-3. The self-test service code of 2-3 will appear on the voltmeter as two needle pulses (sweeps), then after a two second pause, the needle will pulse (sweep) three times. The continuous testing codes are separated from the functional codes by a six-second delay, a single half-second sweep and another six-second delay. They are produced on the voltmeter in the same manner as the functional codes.

## SELF-TEST SERVICE CODES

The following listed self-test service codes may not all be used on one particular engine or group of engines. These codes are transmitted on the self-test output (found in the self-test connector) in the form of timed pulses (as stated previously) and can be read with the use of an analog voltmeter.

The numerals 20, 30 or 40 are always (and only) displayed at the beginning of the engine running test, and always refer to the number of cylinders in the engine. A code 11 (system pass) will always indicate that the system checked out satisfactorily during any phase of the self-test conducted at that time. All other service codes will refer to a specific problem area or component within the EEC-IV system.

CODE 11 System "Pass"
CODE 12 RPM out of spec (extended idle)
CODE 13 RPM out of spec (normal idle)
CODE 14 PIP was erratic (continuous test)
CODE 15 RPM test failed
CODE 16 RPM too low (fuel lean test)
CODE 17 RPM too low (upstream/lean test)
CODE 18 No tach
CODE 21 ECT out of range
CODE 22 MAP out of range
CODE 23 TPS out of range
CODE 24 ACT out of range
CODE 25 Knock not sensed in test
CODE 26 MAF (VAF) out of range
CODE 31 EVP out of limits
CODE 32 EGR not controlling
CODE 33 EVP not closing properly
CODE 34 No EGR flow
CODE 35 RPM too low (EGR test)
CODE 36 Fuel always lean (at idle)
CODE 37 Fuel always rich (at idle)
CODE 41 System always lean
CODE 42 System always rich
CODE 43 EGO cooldown occurred
CODE 44 Air management system inoperative
CODE 45 Air always upstream
CODE 46 Air not always bypassed
CODE 47 Up air/lean test always rich
CODE 48 Injectors unbalanced
CODE 51 ECT input too high
CODE 53 TPS input too high
CODE 54 ACT (VAT) input too high

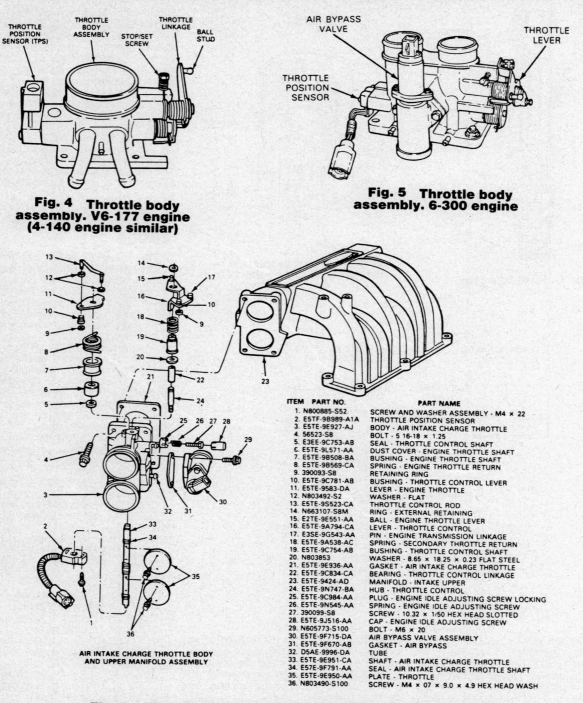

**Fig. 4** Throttle body assembly. V6-177 engine (4-140 engine similar)

**Fig. 5** Throttle body assembly. 6-300 engine

AIR INTAKE CHARGE THROTTLE BODY AND UPPER MANIFOLD ASSEMBLY

| ITEM | PART NO. | PART NAME |
|------|----------|-----------|
| 1. | N800885-S52 | SCREW AND WASHER ASSEMBLY - M4 × 22 |
| 2. | E5TF-9B989-A1A | THROTTLE POSITION SENSOR |
| 3. | E5TE-9E927-AJ | BODY - AIR INTAKE CHARGE THROTTLE |
| 4. | 56523-S8 | BOLT - 5 16-18 × 1.25 |
| 5. | E3EE-9C753-AB | SEAL - THROTTLE CONTROL SHAFT |
| 6. | E5TE-9L571-AA | DUST COVER - ENGINE THROTTLE SHAFT |
| 7. | E5TE-9B508-BA | BUSHING - ENGINE THROTTLE SHAFT |
| 8. | E5TE-9B569-CA | SPRING - ENGINE THROTTLE RETURN |
| 9. | 390093-S8 | RETAINING RING |
| 10. | E5TE-9C781-AB | BUSHING - THROTTLE CONTROL LEVER |
| 11. | E5TE-9583-DA | LEVER - ENGINE THROTTLE |
| 12. | N803492-S2 | WASHER - FLAT |
| 13. | E5TE-9S523-CA | THROTTLE CONTROL ROD |
| 14. | N663107-S8M | RING - EXTERNAL RETAINING |
| 15. | E2TE-9E551-AA | BALL - ENGINE THROTTLE LEVER |
| 16. | E5TE-9A794-CA | LEVER - THROTTLE CONTROL |
| 17. | E3SE-9G543-AA | PIN - ENGINE TRANSMISSION LINKAGE |
| 18. | E5TE-9A538-AC | SPRING - SECONDARY THROTTLE RETURN |
| 19. | E5TE-9C754-AB | BUSHING - THROTTLE CONTROL SHAFT |
| 20. | N803853 | WASHER - 8.65 × 18.25 × 0.23 FLAT STEEL |
| 21. | E5TE-9E936-AA | GASKET - AIR INTAKE CHARGE THROTTLE |
| 22. | E5TE-9C834-CA | BEARING - THROTTLE CONTROL LINKAGE |
| 23. | E5TE-9424-AD | MANIFOLD - INTAKE UPPER |
| 24. | E5TE-9N747-BA | HUB - THROTTLE CONTROL |
| 25. | E5TE-9C984-AA | PLUG - ENGINE IDLE ADJUSTING SCREW LOCKING |
| 26. | E5TE-9N545-AA | SPRING - ENGINE IDLE ADJUSTING SCREW |
| 27. | 390099-S8 | SCREW - 10.32 × 1/50 HEX HEAD SLOTTED |
| 28. | E5TE-9J516-AA | CAP - ENGINE IDLE ADJUSTING SCREW |
| 29. | N605773-S100 | BOLT - M6 × 20 |
| 30. | E5TE-9F715-DA | AIR BYPASS VALVE ASSEMBLY |
| 31. | E5TE-9F670-AB | GASKET - AIR BYPASS |
| 32. | D5AE-9996-DA | TUBE |
| 33. | E5TE-9E951-CA | SHAFT - AIR INTAKE CHARGE THROTTLE |
| 34. | E57E-9F791-AA | SEAL - AIR INTAKE CHARGE THROTTLE SHAFT |
| 35. | E5TE-9E950-AA | PLATE - THROTTLE |
| 36. | N803490-S100 | SCREW - M4 × 07 × 9.0 × 4.9 HEX HEAD WASH |

**Fig. 6** Throttle body assembly. V8-302 & V8-351 engines

CODE 55 Electrical charging under voltage

CODE 56 MAF (VAF) input too high

CODE 58 Idle tracking switch input too high (engine running test)

CODE 61 ECT Input too low

CODE 63 TPS input too low

CODE 64 ACT (VAT) input too low

CODE 65 Electrical charging over voltage

CODE 66 MAF (VAF) input too low

CODE 67 Neutral drive switch-drive or accellerator on (engine off)

CODE 68 ITS open or AC on (engine-off test)

CODE 72 No MAP change in "goose test"

CODE 73 No TPS change in "goose test"

CODE 76 No MAF (VAF) change in "goose test"

CODE 77 Operator did not do "goose test"

CODE 81 Thermactor air bypass (TAB) circuit fault

CODE 82 Thermactor air deverter (TAD) circuit fault

CODE 83 EGR control (EGRC) circuit fault

CODE 84 EGR vent (EGRV) circuit fault

CODE 85 Canister purge (CANP) circuit fault

CODE 86 WOT A/C cut-off circuit fault

CODE 87 Fuel pump circuit fault

CODE 88 Throttle kicker circuit fault (5.0L)

CODE 89 Exhaust heat control valve circuit fault

CODE 91 Right EGO always lean

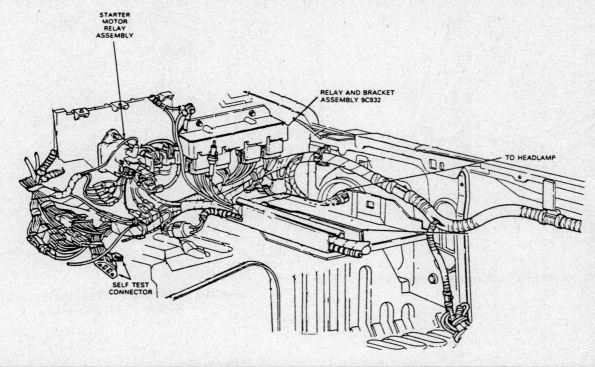

**Fig. 7 Self-test connector location. Aerostar**

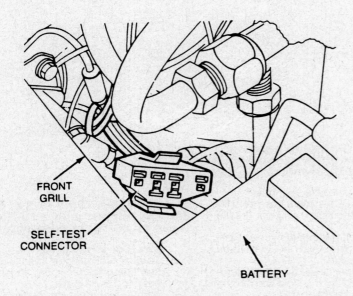

**Fig. 8 Self-test connector location. Econoline**

CODE 92 Right EGO always rich
CODE 93 Right EGO cooldown occurred
CODE 94 Right secondary air inoperative
CODE 95 Right air always upstream
CODE 96 Right air always not bypassed
CODE 97 RPM drop (with fuel lean) but right EGO lean

**Each code has only one interpretation, wherever it appears. The same code will never mean two different things on two different engines.**

## UNIT REPLACEMENT

If any sub-assemblies of the system are to be serviced and/or replaced with the fuel charging assembly installed on the engine, or the entire assembly is to be removed, the following steps should be taken:

1. On 4-140, V6-183 and 6-300 engines proceed as follows:
   a. Disconnect battery ground cable.
   b. On 4-140 engines, drain engine coolant from radiator.
   c. On all engines, remove gas cap to release residual fuel pressure from tank.
   d. Remove valve cap from fuel pressure relief valve, located on the fuel line in the upper right hand corner of engine compartment, then using tool No. T801-9974-A or equivalent release fuel system pressure at the valve.
2. On V6-177 engine, proceed as follows:
   a. Disconnect battery ground cable, then remove air inlet tube from air cleaner to throttle body.
   b. Remove gas cap to relieve fuel tank pressure.
   c. Disconnect vacuum hose from fuel pressure regulator on engine fuel rail.
   d. Apply approximately 25 inches Hg vacuum to pressure regulator using a suitable hand vacuum pump.
3. On V8-302, V8-351 and V8-460 engines proceed as follows:
   a. Remove gas cap to release residual fuel pressure from tank.
   b. Disconnect electrical connector to either the fuel pump relay, inertia switch or in-line high pressure fuel pump.
   c. Crank engine for approximately ten seconds. Engine may start and run for a short time, if so, crank engine an additional five seconds after engine stalls.
   d. Connect electrical connector that was disconnected in step b, then disconnect battery ground cable.

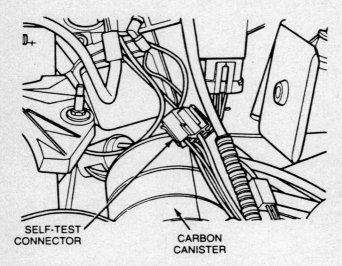

**Fig. 9   Self-test connector location. F series**

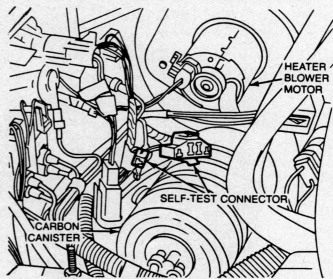

**Fig. 10   Self-test connector location. Bronco II & Ranger**

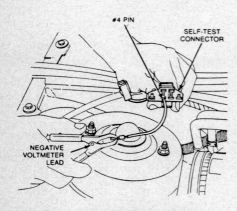

**Fig. 11   Clamping negative lead from voltmeter on to other end of jumper wire**

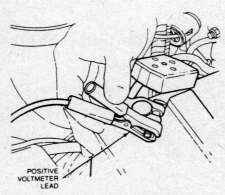

**Fig. 12   Clamping positive lead from voltmeter on to battery terminal**

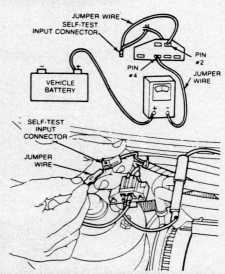

**Fig. 13   Inserting 1 end of the second jumper wire into No. 2 pin on self-test connector**

## FUEL CHARGING ASSEMBLY, REPLACE

### 4-140 Engine

1. Disconnect battery ground cable.
2. Disconnect the following electrical connectors:
   a. Throttle Position Sensor (TPS).
   b. Injector wiring harness.
   c. Knock sensor.
   d. Air charge temperature sensor.
   e. Engine coolant temperature sensor.
3. Disconnect vacuum lines at upper intake manifold vacuum tree. Label vacuum hose locations using suitable tape to facilitate installation.
4. Disconnect vacuum line from EGR valve and fuel pressure regulator.
5. Remove throttle linkage shield, then disconnect throttle linkage, cruise control and kickdown cable.
6. Remove accelerator cable from bracket and position to one side.
7. Disconnect air intake hose, air bypass hose and crankcase vent hose.
8. Disconnect PCV system hose from fitting on underside of upper intake manifold.
9. Disconnect lower intake manifold water bypass line, then the EGR tube from EGR valve.
10. Remove upper intake manifold retaining nuts, then the manifold and throttle body as an assembly.
11. Disconnect manifold fuel supply and fuel return lines.
12. Remove engine oil dipstick bracket attaching bolt.
13. Disconnect fuel injector electrical connectors and position harness to one side.
14. Remove two fuel supply manifold attaching bolts, then the fuel supply manifold and injectors.
15. Remove lower manifold attaching bolts, then the lower manifold.
16. Reverse procedure to install, noting the following:
    a. Torque lower intake manifold attaching bolts to 12-15 ft. lbs. in the sequence shown in **Fig. 18.**
    b. Torque fuel injector manifold to fuel charging assembly attaching bolts to 15-22 ft. lbs.
    c. Torque fuel pressure regulator attaching bolts to 27-40 inch lbs.
    d. Torque upper intake manifold attaching bolts to 14-21 ft. lbs. in the sequence shown in **Fig. 19.**
    e. Torque air throttle body attaching bolts to 12-15 ft. lbs.
    f. Replace fuel pressure cap, then without starting the engine build up fuel pressure by turning key back and forth at least six times from "ON" to "OFF" position, leaving key on for 15 seconds each time.

### 6-300 Engines

1. Disconnect electrical connectors from throttle position sensor, air bypass

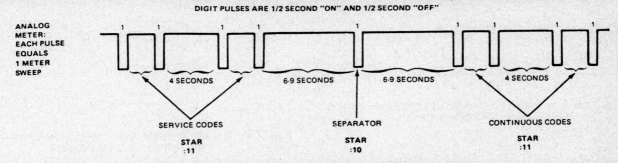

DIGIT PULSES ARE 1/2 SECOND "ON" AND 1/2 SECOND "OFF"

ANALOG METER: EACH PULSE EQUALS 1 METER SWEEP

4 SECONDS — SERVICE CODES — STAR :11

6-9 SECONDS — 6-9 SECONDS — SEPARATOR — STAR :10

4 SECONDS — CONTINUOUS CODES — STAR :11

**Fig. 14    Service code format**

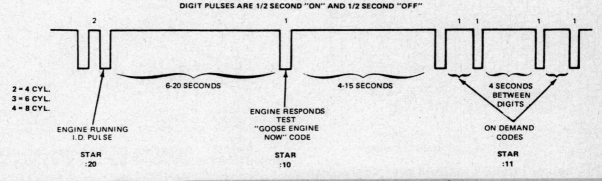

DIGIT PULSES ARE 1/2 SECOND "ON" AND 1/2 SECOND "OFF"

2 = 4 CYL.
3 = 6 CYL.
4 = 8 CYL.

ENGINE RUNNING I.D. PULSE — STAR :20

6-20 SECONDS

ENGINE RESPONDS TEST "GOOSE ENGINE NOW" CODE — STAR :10

4-15 SECONDS

4 SECONDS BETWEEN DIGITS — ON DEMAND CODES — STAR :11

**Fig. 15    Time pulse format. Except V6-171 engine**

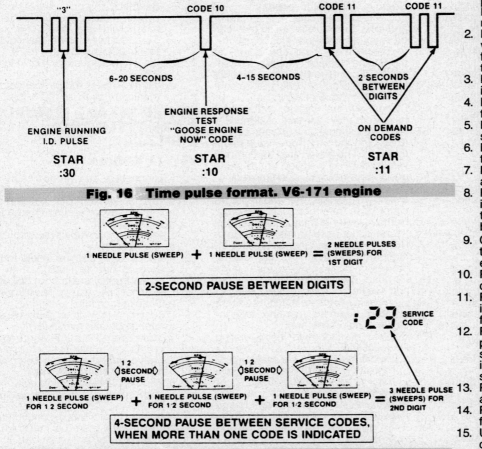

Digit Pulses are ½ second "on" and ½ second "off"

"3" — CODE 10 — CODE 11 — CODE 11

6-20 SECONDS — 4-15 SECONDS — 2 SECONDS BETWEEN DIGITS

ENGINE RUNNING I.D. PULSE — STAR :30

ENGINE RESPONSE TEST "GOOSE ENGINE NOW" CODE — STAR :10

ON DEMAND CODES — STAR :11

**Fig. 16    Time pulse format. V6-171 engine**

1 NEEDLE PULSE (SWEEP) + 1 NEEDLE PULSE (SWEEP) = 2 NEEDLE PULSES (SWEEPS) FOR 1ST DIGIT

**2-SECOND PAUSE BETWEEN DIGITS**

1 NEEDLE PULSE (SWEEP) FOR 1 2 SECOND + 1 2 SECOND PAUSE + 1 NEEDLE PULSE (SWEEP) FOR 1 2 SECOND + 1 2 SECOND PAUSE + 1 NEEDLE PULSE (SWEEP) FOR 1 2 SECOND = 3 NEEDLE PULSE (SWEEPS) FOR 2ND DIGIT

: 2 3 SERVICE CODE

**4-SECOND PAUSE BETWEEN SERVICE CODES, WHEN MORE THAN ONE CODE IS INDICATED**

**Fig. 17    Code interpretation using analog volt-ohmmeter**

valve, EGR valve, engine coolant temperature sensor and injector wiring harness to main engine harness connector.

2. Disconnect vacuum lines from EGR valve, Thermactor air bypass valve, fuel pressure regulator and evaporative lines from throttle body.

3. Disconnect and tag vacuum line from intake manifold tree.

4. Disconnect PCV hose from upper intake manifold.

5. Disconnect accelerator linkage and speed control cables, if equipped.

6. Disconnect air inlet hoses from throttle body.

7. Remove EGR tube from EGR valve and cylinder block.

8. Remove Thermactor tube from lower intake manifold, then remove nut attaching Thermactor bypass valve bracket.

9. On E Series models, remove nut attaching transmission filler tube bracket.

10. Remove two heat shield retaining clips, then remove heat shield.

11. Remove seven studs retaining upper intake manifold to lower intake manifold.

12. Remove upper intake manifold support bracket to manifold attaching screws, then carefully remove upper intake manifold and throttle body assembly from lower intake manifold.

13. Position vacuum harness assembly away from lower intake manifold.

14. Remove injector cooling manifold from eye bracket attachment.

15. Using tool No. T81P-19623-G, disconnect fuel supply and return lines.

16. Remove sixteen bolts attaching lower

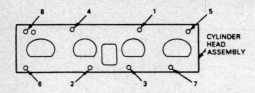

**Fig. 18   Lower intake manifold bolt tightening sequence. 4-140 engine**

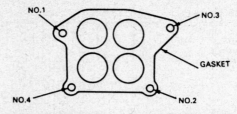

**Fig. 19   Upper intake manifold bolt tightening sequence. 4-140 engine**

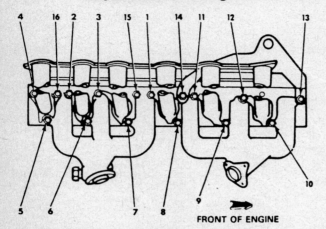

FRONT OF ENGINE

**Fig. 20   Lower intake manifold bolt tightening sequence. 6-300 engine**

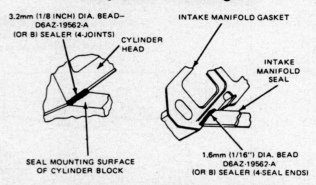

3.2mm (1/8 INCH) DIA. BEAD— D6AZ-19562-A (OR B) SEALER (4-JOINTS)

CYLINDER HEAD

INTAKE MANIFOLD GASKET

INTAKE MANIFOLD SEAL

SEAL MOUNTING SURFACE OF CYLINDER BLOCK

1.6mm (1/16") DIA. BEAD D6AZ-19562-A (OR B) SEALER (4-SEAL ENDS)

**Fig. 21   Applying RTV sealer for intake manifold installation. V8-302 & V8-351 engines**

intake manifold and exhaust manifold to cylinder head. Remove lower intake manifold and exhaust manifold as an assembly. Do not remove exhaust manifold to lower intake manifold attaching bolts.

17. Reverse procedure to install, Torque lower intake manifold and exhaust manifold to cylinder head attaching bolts to 22 to 32 ft. lbs. in sequence shown in **Fig. 20**. Torque upper intake manifold to lower intake manifold attaching bolts to 12 to 18 ft. lbs.

## V8-302, 351 Engines

1. Disconnect battery ground cable.
2. Disconnect air bypass valve, throttle position sensor and EGR position sensor electrical connector.
3. Disconnect throttle linkage at throttle ball and automatic overdrive transmission linkage from throttle body.
4. Remove throttle linkage bracket attaching bolts, then position bracket with cables to one side.
5. Disconnect upper intake manifold vacuum lines from vacuum tree, then the vacuum lines from EGR valve and fuel pressure regulator.
6. Disconnect PCV system hose from fitting on rear of upper manifold.
7. Remove two canister purge lines from throttle body.
8. Disconnect water heater lines from throttle body, if applicable
9. On all models, disconnect EGR tube from EGR valve.
10. Remove upper intake manifold attaching bolts, then the upper intake manifold and throttle body as an assembly.

11. Remove distributor assembly, cap and wires. Mark position of distributor and rotor prior to removal so they can be installed in their original position.
12. Disconnect electrical connectors at the Engine Coolant Temperature sensor (ECT), engine temperature sending unit, Air Charge Temperature sensor (ACT), and knock sensor.
13. Disconnect fuel injector wiring harness from main harness assembly.
14. Remove Exhaust Gas Oxygen sensor (EGO) ground wire from intake manifold stud. The plated stud and ground wire should be installed in the same position as which it was removed.
15. Disconnect fuel supply and return lines from fuel rails, then the upper radiator hose from thermostat housing.
16. Remove water bypass hose, then the heater outlet hose at intake manifold.
17. Remove three air cleaner bracket attaching nuts, then the air cleaner bracket.
18. Remove coil bracket attaching nut and position bracket to one side.
19. Remove lower intake manifold attaching studs and bolts, then the lower intake manifold assembly.
20. Reverse procedure to install, noting the following:
   a. Before installing lower intake manifold, apply 1/8 inch bead of silicone rubber sealer DAZ-19562-A or equivalent at mating surfaces of intake manifold, cylinder heads and cylinder block, **Fig. 21**. Also apply a 1/16 inch bead of sealer to the outer end of intake manifold seal for the full width of the seal.
   b. Install new end seals on the cylin-

der block and new gaskets on the cylinder heads. Ensure gaskets interlock with seal tabs.
   c. Torque lower intake manifold attaching bolts and studs to 23-25 ft. lbs. in the sequence shown in **Fig. 22**.
   d. Torque upper intake manifold attaching bolts to 15-22 ft. lbs.

## UPPER INTAKE MANIFOLD & THROTTLE BODY, REPLACE

### V6-177 Engine

1. Disconnect battery ground cable.
2. Disconnect electrical connectors from air bypass valve, throttle position sensor, EGR sensor and air charge temperature sensor.
2. Remove air inlet tube from air cleaner to throttle body.
3. Remove snow and ice shield to gain access to throttle linkage, then disconnect throttle cable from ball stud.
4. Disconnect all vacuum lines from upper intake manifold.
5. Disconnect PCV lines from beneath throttle body and manifold.
6. Remove canister purge line from fitting adjacent to power steering pump.
7. Remove flange nut and disconnect vacuum line from EGR valve.
8. Loosen A/C line retaining bolt on top rear of upper manifold and unfasten retainer.
9. Remove upper intake manifold attaching bolts, then the manifold and throttle body as an assembly.
10. Reverse procedure to install, noting the following:

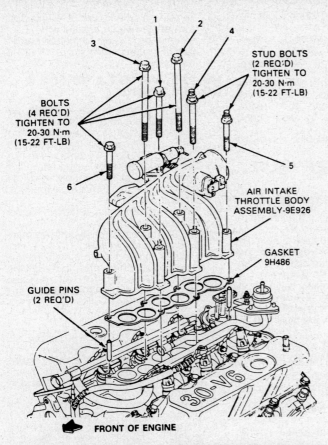

**Fig. 22 Lower intake manifold bolt tightening sequence. V8-302 & V8-351 engines**

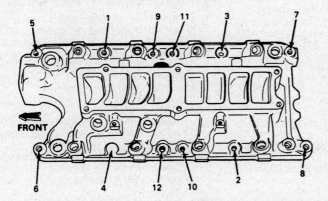

**Fig. 23 Air intake/throttle body assembly bolt tightening sequence. V6-183 engine**

a. Install new gasket on lower manifold mating surface.
b. Torque upper intake manifold attaching bolts to 11-15 ft. lbs.

## V8-460 Engine

1. Disconnect battery ground cable.
2. Disconnect air bypass valve, throttle position sencor and EGR position sensor electrical connectors.
3. Disconnect throttle linkage from throttle ball and automatic overdrive transmission linkage from throttle body.
4. Remove throttle linkage bracket at-

taching bolts, then position bracket with cables aside.
5. Remove two canister purge lines from throttle body.
6. Disconnect upper intake manifold vacuum lines from vacuum tree, then the vacuum lines from EGR valve, MAP sensor and fuel pressure regulator.
7. Disconnect PCV system hose from fitting on rear of upper manifold.
8. Disconnect EGR valve flange nut.
9. Disconnect water heater lines from throttle body.

10. Remove upper intake manifold attaching bolts, then the upper manifold and throttle body as an assembly.
11. Reverse procedure to install. Torque manifold attaching bolts to 12-18 ft. lbs.

## AIR INTAKE/THROTTLE BODY ASSEMBLY, REPLACE

### V6-183

1. Disconnect battery ground cable.
2. Disconnect fuel supply and return lines using tool No. T81P-19623-G.
3. Disconnect wiring harness from fuel injectors, throttle position sensor, air bypass valve and air charge temperature sensor.
4. Remove engine air cleaner outlet tube, then remove snow shield retaining nut and bolts and remove snow shield.
5. Disconnect vacuum hoses from intake manifold vacuum fittings. Tag hoses and fitting for installation.
6. Disconnect accelerator and speed control (if equipped) cables.
7. On models equipped with automatic transmission, disconnect transmission throttle valve linkage from throttle lever.
8. On all models, remove attaching bolts and air intake/throttle body assembly and gasket.
9. Reverse procedure to install. Torque air intake/throttle body assembly attaching bolts to 15 to 22 ft. lbs. in sequence shown in **Fig. 23**.

## THROTTLE BODY, REPLACE

### 4-140 Engine

1. Remove throttle linkage shield, throttle cable, cruise control and kickdown cable.
2. Disconnect throttle position sensor electrical connector, air bypass hose, crankcase vent hose and air intake hose.
3. Remove throttle body attaching bolts, then separate throttle body from upper intake manifold.
4. Remove and discard gasket between throttle body and intake manifold.
5. Reverse procedure to install. Torque throttle body attaching bolts to 12-15 ft. lbs.

### V6-177 Engine

1. Disconnect battery ground cable.
2. Disconnect electrical connector from throttle positioner sensor.
3. Remove air inlet duct.
4. Remove snow and ice shield to gain access to throttle linkage, then disconnect throttle cable from ball stud.
5. Disconnect air bypass, PCV and canister purge hoses from fitting beneath throttle body.
6. Remove throttle body-to-upper intake manifold attaching bolts and the throttle body.
7. Remove and discard throttle body gasket from manifold.
8. Reverse procedure to install. Torque

throttle body attaching bolts to 71-102 inch lbs.

### 6-300, V8-302 & V8-351 Engines

1. Disconnect throttle position sensor and air bypass valve electrical connectors, then disconnect and plug any water heater lines at throttle body.
2. Remove throttle body attaching bolts, the separate throttle body from upper intake manifold.
3. Remove and discard gasket between throttle body and intake manifold.
4. Reverse procedure to install. On 6-300, torque throttle body attaching bolts to 14 top 20 ft. lbs. On V8-302 and V8-351, torque throttle body attaching bolts to 12-15 ft. lbs. on 1985 models, or 12-18 ft. lbs. on 1986—89 models.

### V8-460

1. Disconnect throttle position sensor electrical connector.
2. Disconnect water heater lines from throttle body.
3. Remove four throttle body attaching bolts.
4. Remove throttle body from upper intake manifold, then discard gasket between throttle body and manifold.
5. Reverse procedure to install. Torque throttle body-to-manifold attaching bolts to 12-18 ft. lbs.

## AIR BYPASS VALVE, REPLACE

1. Disconnect battery ground cable.
2. Disconnect air bypass valve electrical connector.
3. On models with 4-140 engine, remove air cleaner assembly.
4. On all models, remove air bypass valve attaching bolts, then the air bypass valve and gasket.
5. Reverse procedure to install. Torque air bypass valve attaching bolts to 71-102 inch lbs.

## THROTTLE POSITION SENSOR, REPLACE

1. Disconnect battery ground cable.
2. Disconnect throttle position sensor electrical connector.
3. Scribe a reference mark across edge of sensor and to throttle body to en-

sure correct position during installation.
4. Remove two sensor attaching screws, then the sensor and gasket.
5. Reverse procedure to install, noting the following:
   a. Slide the throttle position sensor rotary tangs into position over throttle shaft blade, then rotate sensor clockwise to align scribe marks.
   b. Torque sensor attaching screws to 11-16 inch lbs.

## PRESSURE RELIEF VALVE, REPLACE

### 4-140 & V6-183 Engines

1. Remove fuel tank cap, if fuel charging assembly is mounted to the engine, then release pressure from system by opening the pressure relief valve on the fuel line using a suitable tool. Cap on relief valve must be removed.
2. Remove pressure relief valve from fuel line using a suitable wrench.
3. Reverse procedure to install. Torque valve to 48-84 inch lbs. and cap to 4-6 inch lbs.

## FUEL PRESSURE REGULATOR, REPLACE

1. Remove vacuum line at pressure regulator, then the regulator housing attaching screws.
2. Remove pressure regulator assembly, gasket and O-ring.
3. Reverse procedure to install, noting the following:
   a. Lubricate fuel pressure regulator O-ring with suitable oil before installation.
   b. Torque regulator housing attaching screws to 27-40 inch lbs. on 4-140, V6-183, 6-300, V8-302, 351 & 460 engines, or 71-102 inch lbs. on V6-177 engine.

## FUEL MANIFOLD, REPLACE

### 4-140 Engine

1. Remove fuel supply and return lines from manifold.
2. Disconnect injector electrical connectors.
3. Remove two fuel manifold attaching bolts.

4. Remove manifold and fuel injectors from engine as an assembly.
5. Reverse procedure to install. Torque manifold attaching bolts to 15-22 ft. lbs.

### V6-177, V6-183 & V8-302 & V8-351 Engines

1. Remove upper intake manifold assembly as previously described.
2. Disconnect fuel crossover hose from fuel supply manifold using tool No. T81P-19623-G or G1 or equivalent.
3. Disconnect fuel supply and return line connections at fuel supply manifold, then remove two fuel supply manifold attaching bolts.
4. On 6-300 engines, remove injector cooling manifold.
5. On all engines, carefully remove manifold and fuel injectors.
6. Reverse procedure to install. Torque manifold attaching bolts to 6-8 ft. lbs. on V6-177 and V6-183 engines, 15-22 ft. lbs. on 6-300, V8-302 and V8-351 engines.

### V8-460 Engine

1. Remove upper intake manifold assembly as previously described.
2. Disconnect fuel supply and return line connections from fuel supply manifold, then remove four fuel supply manifold attaching bolts.
3. Carefully remove manifold and fuel injectors.
4. Reverse procedure to install. Torque manifold attaching bolts to 15-22 ft. lbs.

## FUEL INJECTOR, REPLACE

1. Remove fuel supply manifold, refer to "Fuel Manifold, Replace" procedure.
2. Disconnect fuel injector electrical connectors.
3. Remove injector from fuel manifold by gently rocking injector from side to side while pulling upward.
4. Reverse procedure to install, noting the following:
   a. Install two new O-rings on each injector. Use suitable oil to facilitate installation.
   b. Use a light twisting and pushing motion to install injectors into the fuel supply manifold.

# GENERAL MOTORS CORPORATION

# GENERAL MOTORS CORPORATION

# CHEVROLET & GMC FULL SIZE TRUCKS & VANS EXC. 1988–89 C & K SERIES

## INDEX OF SERVICE OPERATIONS

---

**NOTE:** Refer to back of this manual for vehicle manufacturer's special service tool suppliers.

---

Page No.        Page No.        Page No.

# SPECIFICATIONS
## GENERAL ENGINE SPECIFICATIONS

| Year | Engine Model | Carb. Type | Bore & Stroke | Comp. Ratio | Horsepower @ R. P.M. ① | Torque Ft. Lbs. @ R.P.M. ② | Normal Oil Pressure Lbs. |
|------|--------------|-----------|---------------|-------------|------------------------|----------------------------|--------------------------|
| 1980 | V6-229/3.8L | 2 Bore | 3.736 x 3.48 | 8.6 | 115 @ 4000 | 175 @ 2000 | 45 |
| | V6-231/3.8L | 2 Bore | 3.80 x 3.4 | 8.0 | 110 @ 3800 | 190 @ 1600 | 37 |
| | 6-250/4.1L | 2 Bore | 3.876 x 3.53 | 8.25 | 130 @ 4000 | 210 @ 2000 | 40–60 |
| | V8-267/4.4L | 2 Bore | 3.50 x 3.48 | 8.3 | 120 @ 3600 | 215 @ 2000 | 45 |
| | 6-292/4.8L ⑮ | 1 Bore | 3.876 x 4.12 | 7.8 | 115 @ 3400 | 215 @ 1600 | 50 |
| | V8-305/5.0L ⑫ | 4 Bore | 3.74 x 3.48 | 8.6 | 155 @ 4000 | 230 @ 2400 | 45 |
| | V8-305/5.0L ㉒ | 4 Bore | 3.74 x 3.48 | 8.6 | 155 @ 4000 | 240 @ 1600 | 45 |
| | V8-350/5.7L | 4 Bore | 4.00 x 3.48 | 8.5 | — | — | 45 |
| | V8-350/5.7L ⑦ | — | 4.057 x 3.385 | 22.5 | 125 @ 3600 | 225 @ 1600 | 35 |
| | V8-400/6.6L | 4 Bore | 4.125 x 3.750 | 8.5 | — | — | 40 |
| | V8-454/7.4L | 4 Bore | 4.25 x 4.00 | 7.6 | 225 @ 4000 | 365 @ 2400 | 40–55 |
| 1981 | V6-229/3.8L ㉒ | 2 Bore | 3.736 x 3.48 | 8.6 | 110 @ 4200 | 170 @ 2000 | 45 |
| | V6-231/3.8L ⑫ | 2 Bore | 3.80 x 3.40 | 8.0 | 110 @ 3800 | 190 @ 1600 | 37 |
| | 6-250/4.1L ⑩ | 2 Bore | 3.88 x 3.53 | 8.3 | 115 @ 3600 | 200 @ 2000 | 40–60 |
| | 6-250/4.1L ⑪ | 2 Bore | 3.88 x 3.53 | 8.3 | 105 @ 3600 | 195 @ 1600 | 40–60 |
| | 6-292/4.8L ⑮ | 1 Bore | 3.88 x 4.12 | 7.8 | 115 @ 3400 | 215 @ 1600 | 40–60 |
| | V8-267/4.4L ㉒ | 2 Bore | 3.50 x 3.48 | 8.3 | 115 @ 4000 | 200 @ 2400 | 45 |
| | V8-305/5.0L ⑯ ㉒ | 4 Bore | 3.74 x 3.48 | 8.6 | 145 @ 3800 | 240 @ 2400 | 45 |
| | V8-305/5.0L ⑩ | 4 Bore | 3.74 x 3.48 | 9.2 | 165 @ 4400 | 240 @ 2000 | 45 |
| | V8-350/5.7L ⑦ ㉒ | — | 4.057 x 3.385 | 22.5 | 125 @ 3600 | 225 @ 1600 | 35 |
| | V8-350/5.7L ⑦ ⑫ | — | 4.057 x 3.385 | 22.5 | 105 @ 3200 | 200 @ 1600 | 35 |
| | V8-350/5.7L ⑩ | 4 Bore | 4.00 x 3.48 | 8.2 | 165 @ 3800 | 275 @ 1600 | 45 |
| | V8-350/5.7L ⑪ | 4 Bore | 4.00 x 3.48 | 8.2 | 150 @ 3600 | 255 @ 1600 | 45 |
| | V8-350/5.7L ⑧ ㉒ | 4 Bore | 4.00 x 3.48 | 8.3 | 165 @ 3800 | 255 @ 2800 | 45 |
| | V8-350/5.7L ⑧ ㉒ | 4 Bore | 4.00 x 3.48 | 8.3 | 155 @ 4000 | 240 @ 2800 | 45 |
| | V8-454/7.4L ⑧ | 4 Bore | 4.25 x 4.00 | 7.9 | 210 @3800 | 340 @ 2800 | 40 |
| 1982 | V6-229/3.8L ㉒ | 2 Bore | 3.74 x 3.48 | 8.6 | 110 @ 4200 | 170 @ 2000 | 50 |
| | V6-231/3.8L ⑫ | 2 Bore | 3.8 x 3.4 | 8.0 | 110 @ 3800 | 190 @ 1600 | 37 |
| | 6-250/4.1L ⑩ | 2 Bore | 3.88 x 3.53 | 8.3 | 120 @ 3600 | 200 @ 2000 | 40–60 |
| | 6-250/4.1L ⑪ | 2 Bore | 3.88 x 3.53 | 8.3 | 110 @ 3600 | 195 @ 2000 | 40–60 |
| | 6-292/4.8L ⑮ | 1 Bore | 3.88 x 4.12 | 7.8 | 115 @ 3400 | 215 @ 1600 | 40–60 |
| | V8-267/4.4L ㉒ | 2 Bore | 3.50 x 3.48 | 8.3 | 115 @ 4000 | 205 @ 2400 | 45 |
| | V8-305/5.0L ⑯ | 4 Bore | 3.74 x 3.48 | 8.6 | 150 @ 3800 | 240 @ 2400 | 45 |
| | V8-305/5.0L ⑰ ⑲ ㉒ | 4 Bore | 3.74 x 3.48 | 9.2 | 160 @ 4400 | 235 @ 2000 | 45 |
| | V8-305/5.0L ⑫ ⑰ ⑳ | 4 Bore | 3.74 x 3.48 | 9.2 | 165 @ 4400 | 240 @ 2000 | 45 |
| | V8-305/5.0L ⑫ ⑰ | 4 Bore | 3.74 x 3.48 | 8.6 | 155 @ 4000 | 245 @ 1600 | 45 |
| | V8-350/5.7L ⑨ | 4 Bore | 4.0 x 3.48 | 8.2 | 165 @ 3800 | 275 @ 1600 | 45 |
| | V8-350/5.7L ⑱ ㉒ | 4 Bore | 4.0 x 3.48 | 8.3 | 160 @ 3800 | 250 @ 2800 | 45 |
| | V8-350/5.7L ⑫ ⑱ | 4 Bore | 4.0 x 3.48 | 8.3 | 155 @ 4000 | 240 @ 2800 | 45 |
| | V8-379/6.2L ③ ⑦ | — | 3.98 x 3.80 | 21.5 | 130 @ 3600 | 240 @ 2000 | 35 |
| | V8-379/6.2L ④ ⑦ | — | 3.98 x 3.80 | 21.5 | 135 @ 3600 | 240 @ 2000 | 35 |
| | V8-454/7.4L | 4 Bore | 4.25 x 4.00 | 7.9 | 210 @ 3800 | 340 @ 2800 | 40 |

## GENERAL ENGINE SPECIFICATIONS—Continued

| Year | Engine Model | Carb. Type | Bore & Stroke | Comp. Ratio | Horsepower @ R.P.M. [1] | Torque Ft. Lbs. @ R.P.M. [2] | Normal Oil Pressure Lbs. |
|---|---|---|---|---|---|---|---|
| 1983 | V6-229/3.8L [19] [22] | 2 Bore | 3.74 x 3.48 | 8.6 | 110 @ 4200 | 170 @ 2000 | 50 |
| | V6-231/3.8L [12] [16] | 2 Bore | 3.80 x 3.40 | 8.0 | 110 @ 3800 | 190 @ 1600 | 37 |
| | 6-250/4.1L [10] | 2 Bore | 3.88 x 3.53 | 8.3 | 120 @ 3600 | 200 @ 2000 | 40–60 |
| | 6-250/4.1L [11] | 2 Bore | 3.88 x 3.53 | 8.3 | 110 @ 3600 | 195 @ 2000 | 40–60 |
| | 6-292/4.8L [8] | 1 Bore | 3.88 x 4.12 | 7.8 | 115 @ 3400 | 215 @ 1600 | 40–60 |
| | V8-305/5.0L [16] | 4 Bore | 3.74 x 3.48 | 8.6 | 150 @ 3800 | 240 @ 2400 | 45 |
| | V8-305/5.0L [20] [22] | 4 Bore | 3.74 x 3.48 | 9.2 | 165 @ 4400 | 240 @ 2000 | 45 |
| | V8-305/5.0L [19] [22] | 4 Bore | 3.74 x 3.48 | 9.2 | 160 @ 4400 | 235 @ 2000 | 45 |
| | V8-305/5.0L [3] [12] | 4 Bore | 3.74 x 3.48 | 8.6 | 155 @ 4000 | 245 @ 1600 | 45 |
| | V8-350/5.7L [3] [9] | 4 Bore | 4.00 x 3.48 | 8.2 | 165 @ 3800 | 275 @ 1600 | 45 |
| | V8-350/5.7L [8] [18] [22] | 4 Bore | 4.00 x 3.48 | 8.3 | 160 @ 3800 | 250 @ 2800 | 45 |
| | V8-350/5.7L [8] [12] [18] | 4 Bore | 4.00 x 3.48 | 8.3 | 155 @ 4000 | 240 @ 2800 | 45 |
| | V8-350/5.7L [7] [16] | — | 4.057 x 3.385 | 22.1 | 105 @ 3200 | 200 @ 1600 | 35 |
| | V8-379/6.2L [3] [7] [9] | — | 3.98 x 3.80 | 21.3 | 130 @ 3600 | 240 @ 2000 | 35 |
| | V8-379/6.2L [4] [7] [18] | — | 3.98 x 3.80 | 21.3 | 135 @ 3600 | 240 @ 2000 | 35 |
| | V8-454/7.4L [8] | 4 Bore | 4.25 x 4.00 | 7.9 | 230 @ 3800 | 360 @ 2800 | 40 |
| 1984 | V6-229/3.8L [16] [22] | 2 Bore | 3.74 x 3.48 | 8.6 | 110 @ 4000 | 190 @ 1600 | 50–65 |
| | V6-231/3.8L [12] [16] | 2 Bore | 3.80 x 3.40 | 8.0 | 110 @ 3800 | 190 @ 1600 | 50–65 |
| | 6-250/4.1L [10] | 2 Bore | 3.88 x 3.53 | 8.3 | 115 @ 3600 | 200 @ 2000 | 40–60 |
| | 6-250/4.1L [11] | 2 Bore | 3.88 x 3.53 | 8.3 | 110 @ 3600 | 200 @ 1600 | 40–60 |
| | 6-292/4.8L [8] | 1 Bore | 3.88 x 4.12 | 7.8 | 115 @ 3600 | 215 @ 1600 | 40–60 |
| | V8-305/5.0L [16] | 4 Bore | 3.74 x 3.48 | 8.6 | 150 @ 4000 | 240 @ 2400 | 50–65 |
| | V8-305/5.0L [10] | 4 Bore | 3.74 x 3.48 | 9.2 | 160 @ 4400 | 235 @ 2000 | 45 |
| | V8-305/5.0L [3] [12] | 4 Bore | 3.74 x 3.48 | 8.6 | 155 @ 4000 | 245 @ 1600 | 45 |
| | V8-350/5.7L [3] [9] | 4 Bore | 4.00 x 3.48 | 8.2 | 165 @ 3800 | 275 @ 1600 | 45 |
| | V8-350/5.7L [8] [18] [22] | 4 Bore | 4.00 x 3.48 | 8.3 | 160 @ 3800 | 250 @ 2800 | 45 |
| | V8-350/5.7L [8] [12] [18] | 4 Bore | 4.00 x 3.48 | 8.3 | 155 @ 4000 | 240 @ 2800 | 45 |
| | V8-350/5.7L [7] [16] | — | 4.057 x 3.385 | 22.1 | 105 @ 3200 | 200 @ 1600 | 35 |
| | V8-379/6.2L [3] [7] [9] | — | 3.98 x 3.80 | 21.3 | 130 @ 3600 | 240 @ 2000 | 35 |
| | V8-379/6.2L [4] [7] [18] | — | 3.98 x 3.80 | 21.3 | 135 @ 3600 | 240 @ 2000 | 35 |
| | V8-454/7.4L [8] | 4 Bore | 4.25 x 4.00 | 7.9 | 230 @ 3800 | 360 @ 2800 | 40 |
| 1985 | V6-262/4.3L [16] | [21] | 4.00 x 3.48 | 9.3 | 130 @ 3600 | 210 @ 2000 | 35 |
| | V6-262/4.3L [17] | 4 Bore | 4.00 x 3.48 | 9.3 | [13] | [14] | 50 |
| | 6-292/4.8L [8] [22] | 1 Bore | 3.88 x 4.12 | 7.8 | 115 @ 4000 | 210 @ 800 | 50 |
| | 6-292/4.8L [8] [12] | 1 Bore | 3.88 x 4.12 | 7.8 | 115 @ 3600 | 215 @ 1600 | 50 |
| | V8-305/5.0L [16] | 4 Bore | 3.74 x 3.48 | 8.6 | 150 @ 4000 | 240 @ 2400 | 50–65 |
| | V8-305/5.0L [17] [22] | 4 Bore | 3.74 x 3.48 | 9.2 | 160 @ 4400 | 235 @ 2000 | 45 |
| | V8-305/5.0L [12] [17] | 4 Bore | 3.74 x 3.48 | 8.6 | 155 @ 4000 | 245 @ 1600 | 45 |
| | V8-350/5.7L [3] | 4 Bore | 4.00 x 3.48 | 8.2 | 165 @ 3800 | 275 @ 1600 | 45 |
| | V8-350/5.7L [9] [22] | 4 Bore | 4.00 x 3.48 | 8.3 | 185 @ 4000 | 285 @ 2400 | 45 |
| | V8-350/5.7L [9] [12] | 4 Bore | 4.00 x 3.48 | 8.3 | 155 @ 4000 | 240 @ 2800 | 45 |
| | V8-379/6.2L [3] [7] | — | 3.98 x 3.82 | 21.3 | 130 @ 3600 | 240 @ 2000 | 35 |
| | V8-379/6.2L [4] [7] | — | 3.98 x 3.82 | 21.3 | 148 @ 3600 | 246 @ 2000 | 35 |
| | V8-454/7.4L [8] [22] | 4 Bore | 4.25 x 4.00 | 7.9 | 240 @ 3800 | 375 @ 3200 | 40 |
| | V8-454/7.4L [8] [12] | 4 Bore | 4.25 x 4.00 | 7.9 | 230 @ 3800 | 360 @ 2800 | 40 |

## GENERAL ENGINE SPECIFICATIONS—Continued

| Year | Engine Model | Carb. Type | Bore & Stroke | Comp. Ratio | Horsepower @ R.P.M. [1] | Torque Ft. Lbs. @ R.P.M. [2] | Normal Oil Pressure Lbs. |
|------|-------------|-----------|--------------|------------|------------------------|------------------------------|--------------------------|
| 1986 | V6-262/4.3L [16] | [21] | 4.00 x 3.48 | 9.3 | 140 @ 4000 | 225 @ 2000 | 35 |
|  | V6-262/4.3L [17] | 4 Bore | 4.00 x 3.48 | 9.3 | [13] | [14] | 50 |
|  | 6-292/4.8L [9] [22] | 1 Bore | 3.88 x 4.12 | 7.8 | 115 @ 4000 | 210 @ 800 | 50 |
|  | 6-292/4.8L [9] [12] | 1 Bore | 3.88 x 4.12 | 7.8 | 115 @ 3600 | 215 @ 1600 | 50 |
|  | V8-305/5.0L [16] | 4 Bore | 3.74 x 3.48 | 9.5 | 150 @ 4000 | 240 @ 2000 | 50–65 |
|  | V8-305/5.0L [10] | 4 Bore | 3.74 x 3.48 | 9.2 | 160 @ 4400 | 235 @ 2000 | 45 |
|  | V8-305/5.0L [11] | 4 Bore | 3.74 x 3.48 | 8.6 | 155 @ 4000 | 245 @ 1600 | 45 |
|  | V8-350/5.7L [3] | 4 Bore | 4.00 x 3.48 | 8.2 | 165 @ 3800 | 275 @ 1600 | 45 |
|  | V8-350/5.7L [9] [22] | 4 Bore | 4.00 x 3.48 | 8.3 | 185 @ 4000 | 285 @ 2400 | 45 |
|  | V8-350/5.7L [9] [12] | 4 Bore | 4.00 x 3.48 | 8.3 | 155 @ 4000 | 240 @ 2800 | 45 |
|  | V8-379/6.2L [3] [7] | — | 3.98 x 3.82 | 21.3 | 130 @ 3600 | 240 @ 2000 | 35 |
|  | V8-379/6.2L [7] [9] | — | 3.98 x 3.82 | 21.3 | [5] | [6] | 35 |
|  | V8-454/7.4L | 4 Bore | 4.25 x 4.00 | 7.9 | 240 @ 3800 | 375 @ 3200 | 40 |
| 1987 | V6-262/4.3L | [21] | 4.00 x 3.48 | 9.3 | 160 @ 4000 | 235 @ 2400 | 30–35 |
|  | 6-292/4.8L [22] | 1 Bore | 3.88 x 4.12 | 7.8 | 115 @ 4000 | 210 @ 800 | 30–45 |
|  | V8-305/5.0L [16] | 4 Bore | 3.74 x 3.48 | 9.3 | 150 @ 4000 | 240 @ 2000 | 50–65 |
|  | V8-305/5.0L [17] | [21] | 3.74 x 3.48 | 9.3 | 170 @ 4000 | 255 @ 2400 | 45 |
|  | V8-350/5.7L [3] | [21] | 4.00 x 3.48 | 9.3 | [23] | [24] | 30–55 |
|  | V8-350/5.7L [4] [25] | [21] | 4.00 x 3.48 | 9.3 | 195 @ 4000 | 300 @ 2800 | 30–55 |
|  | V8-350/5.7L [4] [26] | [21] | 4.00 x 3.48 | 9.3 | 185 @ 4000 | 295 @ 2400 | 30–55 |
|  | V8-379/6.2L [7] | — | 3.98 x 3.82 | — | — | — | 4–45 |
|  | V8-454/7.4L [22] | 4 Bore | 4.25 x 4.00 | 7.9 | 230 @ 3800 | 370 @ 2800 | 40–60 |
|  | V8-454/7.4L [12] | 4 Bore | 4.25 x 4.00 | 7.9 | 230 @ 3800 | 360 @ 2800 | 40–60 |
|  | V8-454/7.4L | [21] | 4.25 x 4.00 | 7.9 | 230 @ 3600 | 385 @ 1600 | 40–60 |
| 1988 | V6-262/4.3L | [21] | 4.00 x 3.48 | 9.3 | 150 @ 4000 | 230 @ 2400 | 30–35 |
|  | 6-292/4.8L [22] | 1 Bore | 3.88 x 4.12 | 7.8 | 115 @ 4000 | 210 @ 800 | 30–45 |
|  | V8-305/5.0L [17] | [21] | 3.74 x 3.48 | 9.3 | 170 @ 4000 | 255 @ 2400 | [27] |
|  | V8-350/5.7L [3] | [21] | 4.00 x 3.48 | 9.3 | [23] | [24] | [27] |
|  | V8-350/5.7L [9] [25] | [21] | 4.00 x 3.48 | 9.3 | 195 @ 4000 | 300 @ 2800 | [27] |
|  | V8-350/5.7L [9] [26] | [21] | 4.00 x 3.48 | 9.3 | 185 @ 4000 | 295 @ 2400 | [27] |
|  | V8-350/5.7L [4] [22] [32] | 4 Bore | 4.00 x 3.48 | 8.3 | 185 @ 4000 | 285 @ 2800 | [27] |
|  | V8-379/6.2L [28] [30] | — | 3.98 x 3.82 | 21.3 | 126 @ 3600 | 240 @ 2000 | 40–45 @ 2000 |
|  | V8-379/6.2L [29] | — | 3.98 x 3.82 | 21.3 | 126 @ 3600 | 240 @ 2000 | 40–45 @ 2000 |
|  | V8-454/7.4L [32] | 4 Bore | 4.25 x 4.00 | 7.9 | 230 @ 3800 | 370 @ 2800 | 40–60 |
|  | V8-454/7.4L [12] | [21] | 4.25 x 4.00 | 8.3 | 230 @ 3600 | 385 @ 1600 | 40–60 |
|  | V8-454/7.4L | [21] | 4.25 x 4.00 | 7.9 | 230 @ 3600 | 385 @ 1600 | 40–60 |
| 1989 | V6-262/4.3L | [21] | 4.00 x 3.48 | 9.3 | 150 @ 4000 | 230 @ 2400 | 40–60 @ 2000 |
|  | 6-292/4.8L [22] | 1 Bore | 3.88 x 4.12 | 8.0 | 115 @ 4000 | 210 @ 800 | 30–45 |
|  | V8-305/5.0L [17] | [21] | 3.74 x 3.48 | 9.3 | 170 @ 4000 | 255 @ 2400 | [27] |
|  | V8-350/5.7L [3] | [21] | 4.00 x 3.48 | 9.3 | [23] | [24] | [27] |
|  | V8-350/5.7L [9] [25] | [21] | 4.00 x 3.48 | 8.6 | 195 @ 4000 | 300 @ 2800 | [27] |
|  | V8-350/5.7L [9] [26] | [21] | 4.00 x 3.48 | 8.6 | 185 @ 4000 | 295 @ 2400 | [27] |
|  | V8-350/5.7L [4] [22] [32] | 4 Bore | 4.00 x 3.48 | 8.2 | 185 @ 3600 | 285 @ 2400 | [27] |
|  | V8-379/6.2L [28] | — | 3.98 x 3.82 | 21.3 | 130 @ 3600 | 240 @ 2000 | 40–45 @ 2000 |
|  | V8-379/6.2L [29] | — | 3.98 x 3.82 | 21.3 | 148 @ 3600 | 259 @ 2000 | 40–45 @ 2000 |
|  | V8-454/7.4L [32] | 4 Bore | 4.25 x 4.00 | 7.9 | 230 @ 3800 | 370 @ 2800 | 40–60 @ 2000 |
|  | V8-454/7.4L [4] [31] | [21] | 4.25 x 4.00 | 7.9 | 230 @ 3600 | 385 @ 1600 | 40–60 @ 2000 |

[1]—Horsepower ratings may vary slightly depending on model application.
[2]—Torque ratings may vary slightly depending on model application.
[3]—Except heavy duty emissions.
[4]—Heavy duty emissions.

[5]—Exc. G series, 148 @ 3600; G series, 145 @ 3600.
[6]—Exc. G series, 246 @ 2000; G series 248 @ 2000.
[7]—Diesel engine.
[8]—Heavy duty emissions (G.V.W.R. 8501 lbs. or above).

[9]—Exc. C6P heavy duty chassis.
[10]—Light duty emissions G.V.W.R. 8500 lbs. or under) exc. Calif.
[11]—California light & medium duty emissions (G.V.W.R. 8500 lbs. or under).
[12]—California.

⑬—Exc. G series, 155 @ 4000; G series, 145 @ 4000.
⑭—Exc. G series, 230 @ 2400; G series, 225 @ 2400.
⑮—P-10/1500-30/3500 & C, K-30/3500.
⑯—Caballero & El Camino.
⑰—Exc. Caballero & El Camino.
⑱—With C6P heavy duty chassis.
⑲—All models exc. C-10/1500.

⑳—C-10/1500.
㉑—Electronic fuel injection.
㉒—Exc. Calif.
㉓—Exc. G Series, 210 @ 4000; G Series, 195 @ 4000.
㉔—Exc. G Series, 300 @ 2800; G Series, 290 @ 2400.
㉕—Federal Suburban models.
㉖—Exc. Federal Suburban models.

㉗—Greater than 18 psi @ 2000 RPM & 24 psi @ 4000 RPM.
㉘—Up to 8500 GVWR.
㉙—Above 8500 GVWR.
㉚—With auto. trans., H.P. 140 @ 3600, torque 247 @ 2000.
㉛—Up to 10,000 GVWR.
㉜—10,001 and above GVWR.

## ALTERNATOR SPECIFICATIONS

| Year | Model ① | Field Current @ 80°F 12 Volts | Rated Hot Output Amperes |
|---|---|---|---|
| 1980 | 1101016 | 4–4.5 | 80 |
| | 1101028 | 4–4.5 | 80 |
| | 1102394 | 4–4.5 | 37 |
| | 1102480 | 4–4.5 | 61 |
| | 1102485 | 4–4.5 | 37 |
| | 1102486 | 4–4.5 | 61 |
| | 1102491 | 4–4.5 | 37 |
| | 1102841 | 4–4.5 | 42 |
| | 1102886 | 4–4.5 | 61 |
| | 1102887 | 4–4.5 | 42 |
| | 1102888 | 4–4.5 | 61 |
| | 1102889 | 4–4.5 | 37 |
| | 1101044 | 4–4.5 | 70 |
| | 1101066 | 4–4.5 | 70 |
| | 1101071 | 4–4.5 | 70 |
| | 1103043 | 4–4.5 | 42 |
| | 1103044 | 4–4.5 | 63 |
| | 1103085 | 4–4.5 | 55 |
| | 1103088 | 4–4.5 | 55 |
| | 1103091 | 4–4.5 | 63 |
| | 1103092 | 4–4.5 | 55 |
| | 1103100 | 4–4.5 | 55 |
| | 1103118 | 4–4.5 | 37 |
| | 1103161 | 4–4.5 | 37 |
| | 1103162 | 4–4.5 | 37 |
| | 1103169 | 4–4.5 | 63 |
| 1981–82 | 1101016 | 4–4.5 | 80 |
| | 1101028 | 4–4.5 | 80 |
| | 1102394 | 4–4.5 | 37 |
| | 1102480 | 4–4.5 | 61 |
| | 1102485 | 4–4.5 | 42 |
| | 1102486 | 4–4.5 | 61 |
| | 1102491 | 4–4.5 | 37 |
| | 1102841 | 4–4.5 | 42 |
| | 1102886 | 4–4.5 | 61 |
| | 1102887 | 4–4.5 | 42 |
| | 1102888 | 4–4.5 | 61 |
| | 1102889 | 4–4.5 | 37 |
| | 1103161 | 4–4.5 | 37 |
| | 1103162 | 4–4.5 | 37 |

## ALTERNATOR SPECIFICATIONS— Continued

| Year | Model ① | Field Current @ 80°F 12 Volts | Rated Hot Output Amperes |
|---|---|---|---|
| 1982 | 1101044 | 4.0–4.5 | 70 |
| | 1101066 | 4.0–4.5 | 70 |
| | 1101071 | 4.0–4.5 | 70 |
| | 1103043 | 4.0–4.5 | 42 |
| | 1103044 | 4.0–4.5 | 63 |
| | 1103085 | 4.0–4.5 | 55 |
| | 1103088 | 4.0–4.5 | 55 |
| | 1103091 | 4.0–4.5 | 63 |
| | 1103092 | 4.0–4.5 | 55 |
| | 1103118 | 4.0–4.5 | 37 |
| | 1103169 | 4.0–4.5 | 63 |
| 1983–84 | 1100200 | 4.0–4.5 | 78 |
| | 1100203 | 4.0–4.5 | 37 |
| | 1100204 | 4.0–5.0 | 37 |
| | 1100207 | 4.5–5.0 | 66 |
| | 1100208 | 4.5–5.0 | 66 |
| | 1100209 | 4.5–5.0 | 66 |
| | 1100217 | 4.5–5.0 | 78 |
| | 1100225 | 4.5–5.0 | 37 |
| | 1100226 | 4.0–5.0 | 37 |
| | 1100228 | 4.0–5.0 | 37 |
| | 1100229 | 4.0–5.0 | 42 |
| | 1100230 | 4.0–5.0 | 42 |
| | 1100231 | 4.0–5.0 | 42 |
| | 1100237 | 4.5–5.0 | 55 |
| | 1100239 | 4.5–5.0 | 55 |
| | 1100241 | 4.5–5.0 | 66 |
| | 1100242 | 4.5–5.0 | 66 |
| | 1100247 | 4.5–5.0 | 63 |
| | 1100259 | 4.5–5.0 | 78 |
| | 1100263 | 4.5–5.0 | 78 |
| | 1100264 | 4.5–5.0 | 78 |
| | 1100270 | 4.5–5.0 | 78 |
| | 1100293 | 4.0–4.6 | 85 |
| | 1100297 | 4.0–5.0 | 42 |
| | 1100300 | 4.5–5.0 | 63 |
| | 1101063 | 4.4–4.9 | 80 |
| | 1101064 | 4.4–4.9 | 80 |
| | 1105022 | 4.5–5.0 | 78 |
| | 1105025 | 4.5–5.0 | 63 |
| | 1105041 | 4.5–5.0 | 78 |

## ALTERNATOR SPECIFICATIONS— Continued

| Year | Model ① | Field Current @ 80°F 12 Volts | Rated Hot Output Amperes |
|---|---|---|---|
| 1985 | 1100204 | 4.0–5.0 | 37 |
| | 1100207 | 4.5–5.0 | 66 |
| | 1100208 | 4.5–5.0 | 66 |
| | 1100209 | 4.5–5.0 | 66 |
| | 1100217 | 4.5–5.0 | 78 |
| | 1100223 | 4.0–4.6 | 37 |
| | 1100225 | 4.0–5.0 | 37 |
| | 1100229 | 4.0–5.0 | 42 |
| | 1100231 | 4.0–5.0 | 42 |
| | 1100237 | 4.5–5.0 | 56 |
| | 1100241 | 4.5–5.0 | 66 |
| | 1100242 | 4.5–5.0 | 66 |
| | 1100246 | 4.5–5.0 | 66 |
| | 1100259 | 4.5–5.0 | 78 |
| | 1100293 | 4.0–4.6 | 85 |
| | 1101063 | 4.4–4.9 | 80 |
| | 1101064 | 4.4–4.9 | 80 |
| | 1105521 | 4.5–5.0 | 78 |
| | 1105523 | 4.5–5.0 | 56 |
| | 1105652 | — | 78 |
| 1986 | 1100203 | 4.0–5.0 | 37 |
| | 1100204 | 4.0–5.0 | 37 |
| | 1100207 | 4.0–5.0 | 66 |
| | 1100208 | 4.0–5.0 | 66 |
| | 1100209 | 4.0–5.0 | 66 |
| | 1100217 | 4.0–5.0 | 78 |
| | 1100225 | 4.0–5.0 | 37 |
| | 1100229 | 4.0–5.0 | 42 |
| | 1100231 | 4.0–5.0 | 42 |
| | 1100241 | 4.0–5.0 | 66 |
| | 1100242 | 4.0–5.0 | 66 |
| | 1100259 | 4.0–5.0 | 78 |
| | 1100293 | 4.0–4.6 | 85 |
| | 1101063 | 4.4–4.9 | 80 |
| | 1101064 | 4.4–4.9 | 80 |
| | 1105651 | 4.0–5.0 | 94 |
| | 1105652 | 4.0–5.0 | 78 |
| | 1105673 | 4.0–5.0 | 56 |
| | 1105674 | 4.0–5.0 | 66 |
| | 1105676 | 4.0–5.0 | 56 |
| 1987 | 1100200 | — | 78 |
| | 1100207 | 4.5–5.0 | 66 |
| | 1100239 | — | 56 |
| | 1101205 | 1.7–2.1 | 120 |
| | 1101240 | 4.2–5.0 | 94 |
| | 1101241 | 4.2–5.0 | 94 |
| | 1101242 | 4.5–5.0 | 66 |
| | 1101243 | 4.2–5.0 | 66 |
| | 1101244 | 4.0–5.0 | 66 |
| | 1101245 | 4.2–5.0 | 94 |
| | 1105197 | — | 70 |
| | 1105628 | 4.5–5.0 | 78 |
| | 1105632 | 4.5–5.0 | 66 |
| | 1105651 | 4.0–5.0 | 94 |

## ALTERNATOR SPECIFICATIONS— Continued

| Year | Model ① | Field Current @ 80°F 12 Volts | Rated Hot Output Amperes |
|---|---|---|---|
| | 1105652 | 4.0–5.0 | 78 |
| | 1105661 | 6.0–7.5 | 105 |
| | 1105673 | — | 56 |
| | 1105674 | 4.0–5.0 | 66 |
| | 1105676 | 4.0–5.0 | 56 |
| | 1105688 | 6.0–7.5 | 100 |
| | 1105710 | 4.8–5.7 | 85 |
| | 1105711 | 6.0–7.5 | 100 |
| | 1105712 | 4.8–5.7 | 85 |
| | 1105718 | 6.0–7.5 | 85 |
| | 1105720 | 6.0–7.5 | 105 |
| 1988 | 1100207 | 4.5–5.0 | 66 |
| | 1101240 | 4.2–5.0 | 94 |
| | 1101243 | 4.2–5.0 | 66 |
| | 1101244 | 4.0–5.0 | 66 |
| | 1101245 | 4.2–5.0 | 94 |
| | 1101299 | — | 94 |
| | 1101300 | — | 78 |
| | 1105628 | 4.5–5.0 | 78 |
| | 1105632 | 4.5–5.0 | 66 |
| | 1105661 | 6.0–7.5 | 105 |
| | 1105688 | 6.0–7.5 | 100 |
| | 1105710 | 4.8–5.7 | 85 |
| | 1105711 | 6.0–7.5 | 100 |
| | 1105712 | 4.8–5.7 | 85 |
| | 1105718 | 6.0–7.5 | 85 |
| | 1105720 | 6.0–7.5 | 105 |
| | 1101157 | 4.2–5.0 | 78 |
| | 1101215 | 5.7–7.1 | 120 |
| | 1101263 | 5.7–7.1 | 120 |
| | 1105716 | 6.0–7.5 | 105 |
| 1989 | 1100207 | 4.5–5.0 | 66 |
| | 1101240 | 4.2–5.0 | 94 |
| | 1101243 | 4.2–5.0 | 66 |
| | 1101244 | 4.0–5.0 | 66 |
| | 1101245 | 4.2–5.0 | 94 |
| | 1101317 | 4.8–5.7 | 85 |
| | 1101318 | 6.0–7.5 | 105 |
| | 1101571 | 6.0–7.5 | 105 |
| | 1105628 | 4.5–5.0 | 78 |
| | 1105632 | 4.5–5.0 | 66 |
| | 1105661 | 6.0–7.5 | 105 |
| | 1105688 | 6.0–7.5 | 100 |
| | 1105710 | 4.8–5.7 | 85 |
| | 1105711 | 6.0–7.5 | 100 |
| | 1105712 | 4.8–5.7 | 85 |
| | 1105714 | 6.0–7.5 | 100 |
| | 1105716 | 6.0–7.5 | 105 |
| | 1105718 | 6.0–7.5 | 85 |
| | 1105720 | 6.0–7.5 | 105 |
| | 1101215 | 5.7–7.1 | 120 |
| | 1105716 | 6.0–7.5 | 105 |
| | 1101561 | 5.7–7.1 | 120 |

①—Part number.

## STARTING MOTOR SPECIFICATIONS

| Year | Engine | Starter Model | Free Speed Test | | |
|---|---|---|---|---|---|
| | | | Amperes ② | Volts | R.P.M. |
| 1980 | V6-229 ③ ⑥ | 1109524 | 50–80 | 10.6 | 7500–11400 |
| | V6-231 ③ | 1109061 | 60–85 | 9 | 6800–10300 |
| | 6-250 ④ | 1108778 | 50–80 | 9 | 5500–10500 |
| | 6-250 ⑤ | 1108779 | 50–80 | 9 | 5500–10500 |
| | 6-292 | 1108780 | 50–80 | 9 | 3500–6000 |
| | V8-267, 305 ③ | 1109524 | 50–80 | 10.6 | 7500–11400 |
| | V8-305 | 1109056 | 50–80 | 9 | 5500–10500 |
| | V8-305 ⑤ | 1109798 | 50–80 | 9 | 5500–10500 |
| | V8-350 ③ ⑦ | 1109061 | 65–95 | 10.6 | 7500–10500 |
| | V8-350 | 1109052 | 65–95 | 9 | 7500–10500 |
| | V8-350 ⑧ | 1109216 | 100–230 | 9 | 8000–14000 |
| | V8-400 | 1108776 | 65–95 | 9 | 7500–10500 |
| | V8-454 | 1108776 | 65–95 | 9 | 7500–10500 |
| 1981 | V6-229 ③ ⑥ | 1109524 | 50–80 | 10.6 | 7500–11400 |
| | V6-231 ③ | 1109061 | 60–85 | 9 | 6800–10300 |
| | 6-250 ④ | 1108778 | 50–80 | 9 | 5500–10500 |
| | 6-250 ⑤ | 1108779 | 50–80 | 9 | 5500–10500 |
| | 6-292 | 1108780 | 50–80 | 9 | 3500–6000 |
| | V8-267, 305 ③ | 1109524 | 50–80 | 10.6 | 7500–11400 |
| | V8-305 | 1109056 | 50–80 | 9 | 5500–10500 |
| | V8-305 ⑤ | 1109798 | 50–80 | 9 | 5500–10500 |
| | V8-350 | 1109052 | 65–95 | 9 | 7500–10500 |
| | V8-350 ⑧ | 1109216 | 100–230 | 9 | 8000–14000 |
| | V8-454 | 1108776 | 65–95 | 9 | 7500–10500 |
| 1982 | V6-229 ③ | 1109534 | 50–80 | 10.6 | 7500–11400 |
| | V6-231 ③ | 1998236 ① | 60–85 | 9 | 6800–10300 |
| | 6-250 ④ | 1108778 | 50–80 | 9 | 5500–10500 |
| | 6-250 ⑤ | 1108779 | 50–80 | 9 | 5500–10500 |
| | 6-292 | 1108780 | 50–80 | 9 | 3500–6000 |
| | V8-267, 305 ③ | 1109534 | 50–80 | 10.6 | 7500–11400 |
| | V8-305 | 1109056 | 50–80 | 9 | 5500–10500 |
| | V8-305 ⑤ | 1109798 | 50–80 | 9 | 5500–10500 |
| | V8-350 | 1109052 | 65–95 | 9 | 7500–10500 |
| | V8-379 ⑧ | 1109219 | — | — | — |
| | V8-454 | 1108776 | 65–95 | 9 | 7500–10500 |
| 1983 | V6-229 ③ | 1109534 | 50–80 | 10.6 | 7500–11400 |
| | V6-231 ③ | 1998236 ① | 60–85 | 9 | 6800–10300 |
| | 6-250 ⑨ | 1998244 ① | 60–85 | 10 | 6800–10300 |
| | 6-250 ⑩ | 1998396 ① | 70–110 | 10 | 6500–10700 |
| | 6-292 ⑪ ⑫ | 1998244 ① | 60–85 | 10 | 6800–10300 |
| | 6-292 ⑩ | 1998396 ① | 70–110 | 10 | 6500–10700 |
| | V8-305 ③ | 1109534 | 45–70 | 10 | 7000–11900 |
| | V8-305 ⑫ | 1109535 | 45–70 | 10 | 7000–11900 |
| | V8-305 ⑩ | 1998396 ① | 70–110 | 10 | 6500–10700 |
| | V8-305 ⑤ | 1998244 ① | 65–95 | 10 | 7500–10500 |
| | V8-350 ⑪ ⑫ | 1998241 ① | 65–95 | 10 | 7500–10500 |
| | V8-350 ⑤ | 1998244 ① | 65–95 | 10 | 7500–10500 |
| | V8-350 ⑩ | 1998396 ① | 70–110 | 10 | 6500–10700 |
| | V8-350 ③ ⑧ | 1998554 ① | 140–160 | 10 | 4400–6300 |
| | V8-379 ⑧ ⑨ ⑩ ⑪ | 1109563 | 120–210 | 10 | 9000–13400 |
| | V8-454 ⑪ ⑫ | 1998243 ① | 65–95 | 10 | 7500–10500 |
| | V8-454 ⑩ | 1998397 ① | 70–110 | 10 | 6500–10700 |

## STARTING MOTOR SPECIFICATIONS—Continued

| Year | Engine | Starter Model | Free Speed Test | | |
|------|--------|---------------|---------|-------|--------|
| | | | Amperes ② | Volts | R.P.M. |
| 1984 | V6-229 ③ | 1998452 ① | 50–75 | 10 | 6000–11900 |
| | V6-231 ③ | 1998236 ① | 60–85 | 9 | 6800–10300 |
| | 6-250 ⑨ | 1998437 ① | 60–90 | 10 | 6500–10500 |
| | 6-250 ⑦ ⑩ | 1998437 ① | 60–90 | 10 | 6500–10500 |
| | 6-250 ⑥ ⑩ | 1998438 ① | 70–110 | 10 | 6500–10700 |
| | 6-292 ⑫ | 1998437 ① | 60–90 | 10 | 6500–10500 |
| | 6-292 ⑦ ⑩ | 1998437 ① | 60–90 | 10 | 6500–10700 |
| | 6-292 ⑥ ⑩ | 1998438 ① | 70–110 | 10 | 6500–10700 |
| | 6-292 ⑪ | 1998437 ① | 60–90 | 10 | 6500–10500 |
| | V8-305 ③ | 1998430 ① | 50–75 | 10 | 6000–11900 |
| | V8-305 ⑫ | 1998427 ① | 50–75 | 10 | 6000–11900 |
| | V8-305 ⑦ ⑩ | 1998427 ① | 50–75 | 10 | 6000–11900 |
| | V8-305 ⑥ ⑩ | 1998438 ① | 70–110 | 10 | 6500–10700 |
| | V8-305 ⑤ | 1998439 ① | 70–110 | 10 | 6500–10700 |
| | V8-350 ⑨ | 1998439 ① | 70–110 | 10 | 6500–10700 |
| | V8-350 ⑦ ⑩ | 1998439 ① | 70–110 | 10 | 6500–10700 |
| | V8-350 ⑥ ⑩ | 1998438 ① | 70–110 | 10 | 6500–10700 |
| | V8-350 ⑪ | 1998444 ① | — | — | — |
| | V8-350 ③ ⑧ | 1998554 ① | 160–240 | 10 | 4400–6300 |
| | V8-379 ⑧ ⑨ ⑩ ⑪ | — | — | — | — |
| | V8-454 ⑪ ⑫ | 1998441 ① | 70–110 | 10 | 6500–10700 |
| | V8-454 ⑥ ⑩ | 1998443 ① | 70–110 | 10 | 6500–10700 |
| | V8-454 ⑦ ⑩ | 1998441 ① | 70–110 | 10 | 6500–10700 |
| 1985 | V6-262 ③ | 1998435 ① | 50–75 | 10 | 6000–11900 |
| | V6-262 ⑤ ⑩ ⑫ | — | — | — | — |
| | 6-292 ⑫ | 1998437 ① | 60–90 | 10 | 6500–10500 |
| | 6-292 ⑦ ⑩ | 1998437 ① | 60–90 | 10 | 6500–10500 |
| | 6-292 ⑪ | 1998437 ① | 60–90 | 10 | 6500–10500 |
| | 6-292 ⑥ ⑩ | 1998438 ① | 70–110 | 10 | 6500–10700 |
| | V8-305 ③ | 1998435 ① | 50–75 | 10 | 6000–11900 |
| | V8-305 ⑫ | 1998427 ① | 50–75 | 10 | 6000–11900 |
| | V8-305 ⑦ ⑩ | 1998427 ① | 50–75 | 10 | 6000–11900 |
| | V8-305 ⑥ ⑩ | 1998438 ① | 70–110 | 10 | 6500–10700 |
| | V8-305 ⑤ | 1998439 ① | 70–110 | 10 | 6500–10700 |
| | V8-350 ⑥ ⑩ | 1998438 ① | 70–110 | 10 | 6500–10700 |
| | V8-350 ⑦ ⑩ | 1998439 ① | 70–110 | 10 | 6500–10700 |
| | V8-350 ⑨ | 1998439 ① | 70–110 | 10 | 6500–10700 |
| | V8-379 ⑧ ⑨ ⑩ ⑪ | — | — | — | — |
| | V8-454 ⑪ ⑫ | 1998441 ① | 70–110 | 10 | 6500–10700 |
| | V8-454 ⑦ ⑩ | 1998441 ① | 70–110 | 10 | 6500–10700 |
| | V8-454 ⑥ ⑩ | 1998443 ① | 70–110 | 10 | 6500–10700 |
| 1986 | V6-262 ③ | 1998557 ① | 70–120 | 10 | 5500–10700 |
| | V6-262 ⑬ | 1998441 ① | 70–110 | 10 | 6500–10700 |
| | 6-292 ⑭ | 1998437 ① | 60–90 | 10 | 6500–10500 |
| | 6-292 ⑮ | 1998438 ① | 70–110 | 10 | 6500–10700 |
| | V8-305 ③ | 1998557 ① | 70–120 | 10 | 5500–10700 |
| | V8-305 ⑫ ⑯ | 1998427 ① | 50–75 | 10 | 6000–11900 |
| | V8-305 ⑮ | 1998438 ① | 70–110 | 10 | 6500–10700 |
| | V8-305 ⑤ | 1998439 ① | 70–110 | 10 | 6500–10700 |
| | V8-350 ⑨ ⑯ | 1998439 ① | 70–110 | 10 | 6500–10700 |
| | V8-350 ⑮ | 1998438 ① | 70–110 | 10 | 6500–10700 |
| | V8-350 ⑪ | 1998444 ① | 70–110 | 10 | 6500–10700 |

| Year | Engine | Starter Model | Free Speed Test Amperes [2] | Volts | R.P.M. |
|---|---|---|---|---|---|
| | V8-379 [8] [14] | 1998442 [1] | 120–210 | 10 | 9000–13400 |
| | V8-379 [8] [15] | 1998401 [1] | 120–210 | 10 | 9000–13400 |
| | V8-454 [14] | 1998441 [1] | 70–110 | 10 | 6500–10700 |
| | V8-454 [15] | 1998443 [1] | 70–110 | 10 | 6500–10700 |
| 1987 | V6-262 [17] | 1998562 [1] | 70–110 | 10 | 6500–11070 |
| | V6-262 [3] | 1998557 [1] | 70–120 | 10 | 5500–10700 |
| | V6-262 [18] | 1998565 [1] | 70–110 | 10 | 6500–10700 |
| | 6-292 [11] | 1998559 [1] | 60–90 | 10 | 6500–10500 |
| | V8-305 [18] | 1998560 [1] | 70–110 | 10 | 6500–10700 |
| | V8-305 [18] | 1998565 [1] | 70–110 | 10 | 6500–10700 |
| | V8-305 [11] [16] | 1998561 [1] | 70–110 | 10 | 6500–10700 |
| | V8-305 [17] | 1998562 [1] | 70–110 | 10 | 6500–10700 |
| | V8-350 [18] | 1998560 [1] | 70–110 | 10 | 6500–10700 |
| | V8-350 [11] [17] | 1998561 [1] | 70–110 | 10 | 6500–10700 |
| | V8-350 [11] [17] | 1998562 [1] | 70–110 | 10 | 6500–10700 |
| | V8-350 [11] [18] | 1998565 [1] | 70–110 | 10 | 6500–10700 |
| | V8-379 [8] [11] [17] | 1113589 [1] | 120–210 | 10 | 9000–13400 |
| | V8-379 [8] [18] | 1113590 [1] | 120–210 | 10 | 9000–13400 |
| | V8-454 [19] | 1998562 [1] | 70–110 | 10 | 6500–10700 |
| | V8-454 [18] | 1998565 [1] | 70–110 | 10 | 6500–10700 |
| 1988 | V6-262 [5] | 1998584 | 70–110 | 10 | 6500–10700 |
| | V6-262 [3] | 1998591 | 70–110 | 10 | 6500–10700 |
| | 6-292 [19] | 1998559 | 60–90 | 10 | 6500–10500 |
| | 6-292 [20] | 1998588 | 70–110 | 10 | 6500–10700 |
| | V8-305 [3] | 1998580 | 70–110 | 6500–10700 | |
| | V8-305 [5] | 1998583 | 70–110 | 10 | 6500–10700 |
| | V8-305 [5] | 1998584 | 70–110 | 10 | 6500–10700 |
| | V8-350 [5] [19] | 1998583 | 70–110 | 10 | 6500–10700 |
| | V8-350 [17] | 1998584 | 70–110 | 10 | 6500–10700 |
| | V8-350 [20] | 1998588 | 70–110 | 10 | 6500–10700 |
| | V8-350 [20] | 1998589 | 70–110 | 10 | 6500–10700 |
| | V8-350 [3] | 1998591 | 70–110 | 10 | 6500–10700 |
| | V8-379 [8] [5] [17] | 1113589 | 120–210 | 10 | 9000–13400 |
| | V8-379 [8] [20] | 1113590 | 120–210 | 10 | 9000–13400 |
| | V8-454 [20] | 1998589 | 70–110 | 10 | 6500–10700 |
| | V8-454 [5] [19] | 1998584 | 70–110 | 10 | 6500–10700 |
| 1989 | V6-262 [5] | 1998590 | 70–110 | 10 | 6500–10700 |
| | 6-292 [19] | 1998559 | 60–90 | 10 | 6500–10500 |
| | 6-292 [20] | 1998588 | 70–110 | 10 | 6500–10700 |
| | V8-305 [5] | 1998583 | 70–110 | 10 | 6500–10700 |
| | V8-305 [5] | 1998584 | 70–110 | 10 | 6500–10700 |
| | V8-350 [5] [20] | 1998583 | 70–110 | 10 | 6500–10700 |
| | V8-350 [5] [19] | 1998584 | 70–110 | 10 | 6500–10700 |
| | V8-350 [20] | 1998588 | 70–110 | 10 | 6500–10700 |
| | V8-350 [19] | 1998598 | 70–110 | 10 | 6500–10700 |
| | V8-379 [8] [20] | 1113269 | 125–190 | 10 | 3500–5600 |
| | V8-379 [8] [19] [5] | 1113270 | 125–190 | 10 | 3500–5600 |
| | V8-454 [5] [20] | 1998584 | 70–110 | 10 | 6500–10700 |
| | V8-454 [11] | 1998584 | 70–110 | 10 | 900–13400 |
| | V8-454 [20] | 1998588 | 70–110 | 10 | 6500–10700 |
| | V8-454 [20] | 1998589 | 70–110 | 10 | 6500–10700 |

①—Part No.
②—Includes solenoid.
③—Cabellero & El Camino.
④—C, K-10.
⑤—G series.
⑥—With auto. trans.
⑦—With manual trans.
⑧—Diesel engine.
⑨—C & G series.

[10] —K series.
[11] —P series.
[12] —C series.
[13] —Exc. Caballero & El Camino.
[14] —Exc. K series with auto. trans.
[15] —K series with auto trans.
[16] —K series with manual trans.
[17] —R, V & G series.
[18] —V series.
[19] —R, V & P series.
[20] —R,V series.

## ENGINE TIGHTENING SPECIFICATIONS

| Engine | Year | Spark Plugs Ft. Lbs. | Cylinder Head Bolts Ft. Lbs. | Intake Manifold Ft. Lbs. | Exhaust Manifold Ft. Lbs. | Rocker Arm Stud Ft. Lbs. | Rocker Arm Cover Ft. Lbs. | Connecting Rod Cap Bolts Ft. Lbs. | Main Bearing Cap Bolts Ft. Lbs. | Flywheel To Crankshaft Ft. Lbs. | Vibration Damper Or Pulley Ft. Lbs. |
|---|---|---|---|---|---|---|---|---|---|---|---|
| V6-229 | 1980–84 | 22 | 65 | 30 | 20 | — | 45[1] | 45 | 70 | 60 | 60 |
| V6-231 | 1980–84 | 15 | 80 | 45 | 25 | 30[2] | 4 | 40 | 100 | 60 | 225 |
| 6-250 | 1980–84 | 17–27 | 95[6] | — | 30 | — | 45[1] | 35 | 65 | 60 | — |
| V6-262[3] | 1985–88 | 22 | 60–75 | 25–45 | 30[22] | — | 50–65[1] | 45 | 70–85 | 50–70 | 65–75 |
| V6-262[4] | 1985 | 22 | 65 | 30 | 20 | — | 45[1] | 45 | 70 | 60 | 60 |
| V6-262[4] | 1986–88 | 22 | 65 | 35 | [19] | — | [20] | 45 | 75[21] | 75 | 70 |
| V6-262 | 1989 | 22 | 65 | 35 | [19] | — | 90[1] | 45 | 80 | 75 | 70 |
| V8-267 | 1980–82 | 22 | 65 | 30 | 20 | — | 45[1] | 45 | 70 | 60 | 60 |
| 6-292 | 1980–85 | 17–27 | 95[6] | 40 | 45 | — | 45[1] | 40 | 65 | 110 | 60 |
| 6-292 | 1986–89 | 15 | 95[6] | 44 | 38 | — | [15] | 44 | 65 | 110 | 50 |
| V8-305[3] | 1980–84 | 22 | 65 | 30 | 20 | — | 45[1] | 45 | 70 | 60 | 60 |
| V8-305[4] | 1980–82 | 17–27 | 65 | 30 | 20 | — | 45[1] | 45 | 80 | 60 | 60 |
| V8-305[4] | 1983–85 | 22 | 65 | 30 | 20 | — | 45[1] | 45 | 70 | 60 | 60 |
| V8-305[3] | 1985–88 | 22 | 60–75 | 25–45 | 30 | — | 50–65[1] | 45 | 70–85 | 50–70 | 65–75 |
| V8-305[4] | 1986–88 | 22 | 65 | 35 | [16] | — | [17] | 45 | [18] | 75 | 65[23] |
| V8-305 | 1989 | 22 | 65 | 35 | [16] | — | [17] | 45 | [18] | 75 | 70 |
| V8-350[4] | 1980–82 | 17–27 | 65 | 30 | 20[7] | — | 45[1] | 45 | 80[10] | 60 | 60 |
| V8-350[4] | 1983–85 | 22 | 65 | 30 | 20 | — | 45[1] | 45 | 70 | 60 | 60 |
| V8-350[14] | 1980–81 | 12[9] | 130[8] | 40[8] | 25 | 28[11] | 15[1] | 42 | 120 | 60 | 200–310 |
| V8-350[14] | 1983–84 | 12[9] | 130[8] | 40[8] | 25 | 28[11] | [12] | 42 | 120 | 60 | 200–310 |
| V8-350[4] | 1986–88 | 22 | 65 | 35 | [16] | — | [17] | 45 | [18] | 75 | 65[23] |
| V8-350 | 1989 | 22 | 65 | 35 | [16] | — | [17] | 45 | [18] | 75 | 70 |
| V8-379[14] | 1982–83 | 10[9] | [5] | 31 | 22 | 34[2] | 17 | 48 | [13] | 60 | 151[25] |
| V8-379[14] | 1984–86 | 10[9] | [5] | 31 | 25 | 41[2] | 17 | 48 | [13] | 60 | 151[25] |
| V8-379[14] | 1987–89 | 10[9] | [5] | 31 | 26 | 40[2] | 16 | 48 | [13] | 65 | 200[25] |
| V8-400 | 1980 | 17–27 | 65 | 30 | 20 | — | 45[1] | 45 | 80[10] | 60 | 60 |
| V8-454 | 1980–86 | 17–27 | 80 | 30 | 20 | 50 | 50[1] | 50 | 110 | 65 | 85 |
| V8-454 | 1987–89 | 22 | 80 | 30 | 40 | 40 | 115[1] | 48 | 110[24] | 65 | 85 |

[1] —Inch lbs.
[2] —Rocker arm shaft.
[3] —Caballero & El Camino.
[4] —Series 10-30 & 15-3500.
[5] —Torque bolts in sequence in three steps: Step 1, 20 ft. lbs.; Step 2, 50 ft. lbs.; Step 3, turn each bolt an additional ¼ turn.
[6] —Torque lefthand front bolt to 85 ft. lbs.
[7] —Inside bolts, 30 ft. lbs.
[8] —Clean & dip entire bolt in engine oil before tightening to obtain a correct specified torque reading.
[9] —Glow plugs.
[10] —Intermediate (2, 3, 4) outer bolts, 70 ft. lbs.
[11] —Rocker arm pivot bolt.
[12] —Fully driven, seated & not stripped.
[13] —Inner, 111 ft. lbs; outer, 100 ft. lbs.
[14] —Diesel engine.
[15] —1986 models with cork gasket, 58 inch lbs.; 1986 models with rubber gasket & 1987-89 models, 38 inch lbs.
[16] —Stainless steel manifold, 26 ft. lbs.; cast manifold: two center bolts, 26 ft. lbs.; all others, 20 ft. lbs.
[17] —Carbureted engine, 65 inch lbs.; fuel injected engine, 100 inch lbs.
[18] —Outer bolts on caps 2, 3 & 4, 70 ft. lbs.; all others, 80 ft. lbs.
[19] —Two center bolts, 26 ft. lbs.; all others, 20 ft. lbs.
[20] —1986, 88 inch lbs.; 1987, 100 inch lbs.
[21] —1988, 80 ft. lbs.
[22] —Two center bolts, 25 ft. lbs., all others 20 ft. lbs.
[23] —1988, 70 ft. lbs.
[24] —1989, 100 ft. lbs.
[25] —On 1982-85 models, torque crankshaft pulley bolts, to 15-20 ft. lbs.; On 1986-89 models to 30 ft. lbs.

1988-89 TBI model, 90 inch lbs.

## WHEEL ALIGNMENT SPECIFICATIONS

| Year | Model | Caster Deg. | Camber Deg. | Toe-In Inch |
|---|---|---|---|---|
| **CABALLERO & EL CAMINO** | | | | |
| 1980–85 | Man. Steer. | +½ to +1½ | 0 to +1 | 1/16 to 3/16 |
| | Power Steer. | +2½ to +3½ | 0 to +1 | 1/16 to 3/16 |
| 1986–87 | Man. Steer. | 0 to +2 | −.3 to +1.3 | +.05 to +.25③ |
| | Power Steer. | +2 to +4 | −.3 to +1.3 | +.05 to +.25③ |
| 1988 | Man. Steer. | -.2 to +1.8 | -.3 to +1.3 | -.05 to +.15③ |
| | Power Steer. | +1.8 to +3.8 | -.3 to +1.3 | -.05 to +.15③ |
| **SERIES 10 THRU 30 & 1500 THRU 3500** | | | | |
| 1980 | C, P | ① | +.2 | 3/16 |
| | G-10, 20/1500, 2500 | ① | +.5 | 3/16 |
| | G-30/3500 | ① | +.2 | 3/16 |
| | K-10, 20/1500, 3500 | ① | +1② | 0 |
| | K-30/3500 | ① | +.5② | 0 |
| | Motor Home (32) | ① | +.2 | 5/16 |
| 1981 | C, P | ① | +.2 | 3/16 |
| | G-10, 20/1500, 2500 | ① | +.5 | 3/16 |
| | G-30/3500 | ① | +.2 | 3/16 |
| | K-10, 20/1500, 2500 | ① | +1② | 3/16 |
| | K-30/3500 | ① | +.5② | 3/16 |
| | Motor Home (32) | ① | +.2 | 5/16 |
| 1982–84 | C-10/1500 | ① | +.7 | 3/16 |
| | C-20, 30/2500, 3500 | ① | +.2 | 3/16 |
| | G-10, 20/1500, 2500 | ① | +.5 | 3/16 |
| | G-30/3500 | ① | +.2 | 3/16 |
| | K-10, 20/1500, 2500 | ① | +1② | 3/16 |
| | K-30/3500 | ① | +.5② | 3/16 |
| | P | ① | +.2 | 3/16 |
| | Motor Home (32) | ① | +.2 | 5/16 |
| 1985–86 | C-10/1500 | ① | +.70 | .18 |
| | C-20, 30/2500, 3500 | ① | +.25 | .36 |
| | G-10, 20/2500, 3500 | ① | +.50 | .18 |
| | G-30/3500 | ① | +.25 | .18 |
| | K-10, 20, 30/1500, 2500, 3500 | +8② | +1.5② | 0 |
| | P-20, 30/2500, 3500 | ① | +.25 | .18 |
| | Motor Home (32) | ① | +.25 | .25 |
| 1987–88 | G-100/200 | ① | +.50 | .18 |
| | G-300 | ① | +.25 | .18 |
| | P-200, 300 | ① | +.25 | ⑤ |
| | P-30/3500 | ① | +1.5② | .12 |
| | R-100 | ① | +.70 | .18 |
| | R-200, 300 | ① | +.25 | .18 |
| | V-100, 200, 300 | ① | +1.5② | 0④ |
| 1989 | G-100/200 | ① | +.50 | 0 |
| | G-300 | ① | +.25 | 0 |
| | P-200, 300 | ① | +.25 | ⑤ |
| | P-30/3500 | ① | +1.5② | .12 |
| | R-100 | ① | +.70 | .09 |
| | R-200, 300 | ① | +.25 | .09 |
| | V-100, 200, 300 | ① | +1.5② | .07 |

①—Refer to "Front Suspension & Steering" section of this chapter.
②—No adjustment provision.
③—Degrees.
④—For 1988 models, .12.
⑤—P-200 & 300 Less I-Beam Front Axle .18; P-300 w/I-Beam Front Axle .25

## BRAKE SPECIFICATIONS

| Year | Model | Rear Drum I.D. | Wheel Cyl. Bore | | Disc Brake Rotor | | | | Master Cyl. I.D. | |
|---|---|---|---|---|---|---|---|---|---|---|
| | | | Front Disc | Rear Drum | Nominal Thickness | Minimum Thickness | Thickness Variation (Parallelism) | Run Out (TIR) | Manual Brakes | Power Brakes |
| 1980 | C10/1500[2] | [3] | 2.940 | [4] | 1.280 | 1.215 | .0005 | .004 | 1.00 | 1.125 |
| | G10/1500 | [3] | 2.940 | [4] | 1.280 | 1.215 | .0005 | .004 | 1.00 | 1.125 |
| | C10/1500[5] | 11.15 | 2.940 | .937 | 1.280 | 1.215 | .0005 | .004 | — | 1.125 |
| | C10/1500[6][7] | 11.15 | 2.940 | .937 | 1.280 | 1.215 | .0005 | .004 | — | 1.125 |
| | P10/1500 | 11.15 | 2.940 | .937 | 1.280 | 1.215 | .0005 | .004 | — | 1.125 |
| | K10/1500[7] | 11.15 | 2.940 | .937 | 1.280 | 1.215 | .0005 | .004 | — | 1.125 |
| | C10/1500[8][9] | 11.00 | 2.940 | 1.00 | 1.280 | 1.215 | .0005 | .004 | — | 1.125 |
| | K10/1500[2][8] | 11.00 | 2.940 | 1.00 | 1.280 | 1.215 | .0005 | .004 | — | 1.125 |
| | G10/1500[10] | 11.00 | 2.940 | 1.00 | 1.280 | 1.215 | .0005 | .004 | — | 1.125 |
| | C10/1500[2][11] | [3] | 2.940 | [4] | 1.280 | 1.215 | .0005 | .004 | — | 1.125 |
| | C, K20/2500[2][5][6] | [12] | 2.940 | [13] | 1.280 | 1.215 | .0005 | .004 | — | [14] |
| | P20/2500 | [12] | 2.940 | [13] | 1.280 | 1.215 | .0005 | .004 | — | [14] |
| | C20/2500[2][15] | 13.00 | 2.940 | 1.062 | 1.280 | 1.215 | .0005 | .004 | — | 1.250 |
| | G20/2500[10] | 11.15 | 2.940 | 1.00 | 1.280 | 1.215 | .0005 | .004 | — | 1.125 |
| | C30/3500[2][5] | 13.00 | [16] | [17] | [18] | [19] | .0005 | .004 | — | [20] |
| | C30/3500[15] | 13.00 | 3.380 | 1.187 | 1.530 | 1.465 | .0005 | .004 | — | 1.312 |
| | K30/3500[2][5] | 13.00 | 3.380 | 1.187 | 1.530 | 1.465 | .0005 | .004 | — | 1.312 |
| | G30/3500[10] | [12] | 2.940 | [13] | 1.280 | 1.215 | .0005 | .004 | — | [14] |
| | G30/3500[21][22] | 13.00 | 2.940 | 1.062 | 1.280 | 1.215 | .0005 | .004 | — | 1.250 |
| | G30/3500[21][23] | 13.00 | 3.380 | 1.187 | 1.530 | 1.465 | .0005 | .004 | — | 1.312 |
| | P30/3500[24][25] | 13.00 | [16] | [17] | [18] | [19] | .0005 | .004 | — | [20] |
| | P30/3500[24][25] | — | 3.380 | 3.380[27] | 1.530 | 1.465 | .0005 | .004 | — | 1.336 |
| | P30/3500[25][28] | 13.00 | 3.380 | 1.187 | 1.530 | 1.465 | .0005 | .004 | — | 1.312 |
| | P30/3500[26][28] | — | 3.380 | 3.380[27] | 1.530 | 1.465 | .0005 | .004 | — | 1.336 |
| 1980–88 | [1] | 9.50 | 2.50 | .750 | 1.043 | .965 | .0005 | .004 | — | .940 |
| 1981–82 | C10/1500[2] | [3] | 2.940 | 1.00 | [30] | [39] | .0005 | .004 | 1.00 | 1.125 |
| | C10/1500[2][11] | [3] | 2.940 | [4] | 1.280 | 1.215 | .0005 | .004 | — | 1.125 |
| | G10/1500 | [3] | 2.940 | [4] | 1.280 | 1.215 | .0005 | .004 | 1.00 | 1.125 |
| | K10/1500[2] | 11.15 | 2.940 | .937 | 1.280 | 1.215 | .0005 | .004 | — | 1.125 |
| | C,K10/1500[6][8] | 11.15 | 2.940 | .937 | 1.280 | 1.215 | .0005 | .004 | — | 1.125 |
| | G20/2500[10] | 11.15 | 2.940 | .937 | 1.280 | 1.215 | .0005 | .004 | — | 1.125 |
| | C, K20/2500[2] | [12] | [31] | [13] | 1.280 | 1.215 | .0005 | .004 | — | [14] |
| | P20/2500 | [12] | [31] | [13] | 1.280 | 1.215 | .0005 | .004 | — | [14] |
| | C, K20/2500[5][6] | 13.00 | 3.150 | 1.062 | 1.280 | 1.215 | .0005 | .004 | — | 1.250 |
| | C20/2500[2][15] | 13.00 | 3.150 | 1.062 | 1.280 | 1.215 | .0005 | .004 | — | 1.250 |
| | G30/3500[10] | 13.00 | 3.150 | 1.062 | 1.280 | 1.215 | .0005 | .004 | — | 1.250 |
| | G30/3500[21][22] | 13.00 | 3.150 | 1.062 | 1.280 | 1.215 | .0005 | .004 | — | 1.250 |
| | G30/3500[21][23] | 13.00 | 3.380 | 1.190 | 1.530[35] | 1.465 | .0005 | .004 | — | 1.340[37] |
| | C, K30/3500[2][5] | 13.00 | 3.380 | 1.190 | 1.530[35] | 1.465 | .0005 | .004 | — | 1.340[37] |
| | P30/3500[24][25] | 13.00 | [32] | [33] | [18][36] | [19] | .0005 | .004 | — | [34][38] |
| | P30/3500[24][26] | — | 3.380 | 3.380[27] | 1.530[35] | 1.465 | .0005 | .004 | — | 1.336 |
| | P30/3500[25][28] | 13.00 | 3.380 | 1.190 | 1.530[35] | 1.465 | .0005 | .004 | — | 1.340[37] |
| | P30/3500[26][28] | — | 3.380 | 3.380[27] | 1.530[35] | 1.465 | .0005 | .004 | — | 1.336 |

## BRAKE SPECIFICATIONS—Continued

| Year | Model | Rear Drum I.D. | Wheel Cyl. Bore | | Disc Brake Rotor | | | | Master Cyl. I.D. | |
|---|---|---|---|---|---|---|---|---|---|---|
| | | | Front Disc | Rear Drum | Nominal Thickness | Minimum Thickness | Thickness Variation (Parallelism) | Run Out (TIR) | Manual Brakes | Power Brakes |
| 1983–86 | C10/1500 [2] | [3] | 2.940 | [4] | [30] | [39] | .0005 | .004 | 1.00 | 1.125 |
| | C10/1500 [2] [11] | [3] | 2.940 | [4] | [30] | [39] | .0005 | .004 | — | 1.250 |
| | K10/1500 [2] | 11.15 | 2.940 | .937 | 1.280 | 1.215 | .0005 | .004 | — | 1.125 |
| | K10/1500 [2] [11] | 11.15 | 2.940 | .937 | 1.280 | 1.215 | .0005 | .004 | — | 1.250 |
| | C, K10/1500 [6] | 11.15 | 2.940 | .937 | 1.280 | 1.215 | .0005 | .004 | — | 1.125 |
| | C,K10/1500 [6] [11] | 11.15 | 2.940 | .937 | 1.280 | 1.215 | .0005 | .004 | — | 1.250 |
| | K10/1500 [8] | 11.15 | 2.940 | .937 | 1.280 | 1.215 | .0005 | .004 | — | 1.125 |
| | K10/1500 [8] [11] | 11.15 | 2.940 | .937 | 1.280 | 1.215 | .0005 | .004 | — | 1.250 |
| | G10/1500 [40] | [3] | 2.940 | [4] | 1.280 | 1.215 | .0005 | .004 | 1.00 | 1.125 |
| | G10/1500 [41] | [3] | 2.940 | [4] | 1.280 | 1.215 | .0005 | .004 | — | 1.125 |
| | G20/2500 [10] | 11.15 | 2.940 | .937 | 1.280 | 1.215 | .0005 | .004 | — | 1.125 |
| | G20/2500 [10] [11] | 11.15 | 2.940 | .937 | 1.280 | 1.215 | .0005 | .004 | — | 1.250 |
| | C, K20/2500 [2] [42] | 11.15 | 2.940 | 1.00 | 1.280 | 1.215 | .0005 | .004 | — | 1.125 |
| | C, K20/2500 [2] [11] [42] | 11.15 | 2.940 | .937 | 1.280 | 1.215 | .0005 | .004 | — | 1.250 |
| | C, K20/2500 [2] [43] | 13.00 | 3.150 | 1.062 | 1.280 | 1.215 | .0005 | .004 | — | 1.250 |
| | C20/2500 [5] | 13.00 | 3.150 | 1.062 | 1.280 | 1.215 | .0005 | .004 | — | 1.250 |
| | C20/2500 [2] [15] | 13.00 | 3.150 | 1.062 | 1.280 | 1.215 | .0005 | .004 | — | 1.250 |
| | C, K20/2500 [6] | 13.00 | 3.150 | 1.062 | 1.280 | 1.215 | .0005 | .004 | — | 1.250 |
| | P20/2500 | [12] | [31] | [13] | 1.280 | 1.215 | .0005 | .004 | — | [14] |
| | P20/2500 [11] [44] | 11.15 | 2.940 | .937 | 1.280 | 1.215 | .0005 | .004 | — | 1.250 |
| | P20/2500 [11] [29] | 13.00 | 3.150 | 1.062 | 1.280 | 1.215 | .0005 | .004 | — | 1.250 |
| | G30/3500 [2] [5] | 13.00 | 3.380 | 1.190 | 1.530 | 1.465 | .0005 | .004 | — | 1.312 |
| | G30/3500 [10] | 13.00 | 3.150 | 1.062 | 1.280 | 1.215 | .0005 | .004 | — | 1.250 |
| | G30/3500 [21] [22] | 13.00 | 3.150 | 1.062 | 1.280 | 1.215 | .0005 | .004 | — | 1.250 |
| | G30/3500 [23] | 13.00 | 3.380 | 1.190 | 1.530 | 1.465 | .0005 | .004 | — | 1.336 |
| | P30/3500 [24] [25] | 13.00 | [32] | [33] | [18] | [19] | .0005 | .004 | — | [20] |
| | P30/3500 [24] [26] | — | 3.380 | 3.380 [27] | 1.530 | 1.465 | .0005 | .004 | — | 1.336 |
| | P30/3500 [25] [28] | 13.00 | 3.380 | 1.190 | 1.530 | 1.465 | .0005 | .004 | — | 1.312 |
| | P30/3500 [26] [28] | — | 3.380 | 3.380 [27] | 1.530 | 1.465 | .0005 | .004 | — | 1.336 |
| 1987 | R10/1500 [2] | [3] | 2.940 | [4] | [30] | [39] | .0005 | .004 | 1.00 | 1.125 |
| | R10/1500 [2] [11] | [3] | 2.940 | [4] | [30] | [39] | .0005 | .004 | — | 1.250 |
| | V10/1500 [2] | 11.15 | 2.940 | .937 | 1.280 | 1.215 | .0005 | .004 | — | 1.125 |
| | V10/1500 [2] [11] | 11.15 | 2.940 | .937 | 1.280 | 1.215 | .0005 | .004 | — | 1.250 |
| | R, K10/1500 [6] | 11.15 | 2.940 | .937 | 1.280 | 1.215 | .0005 | .004 | — | 1.125 |
| | R,V10/1500 [6] [11] | 11.15 | 2.940 | .937 | 1.280 | 1.215 | .0005 | .004 | — | 1.250 |
| | V10/1500 [8] | 11.15 | 2.940 | .937 | 1.280 | 1.215 | .0005 | .004 | — | 1.125 |
| | V10/1500 [8] [11] | 11.15 | 2.940 | .937 | 1.280 | 1.215 | .0005 | .004 | — | 1.250 |
| | G10/1500 [40] | [3] | 2.940 | [4] | 1.280 | 1.215 | .0005 | .004 | 1.00 | 1.125 |
| | G10/1500 [41] | [3] | 2.940 | [4] | 1.280 | 1.215 | .0005 | .004 | — | 1.125 |
| | G20/2500 [10] | 11.15 | 2.940 | .937 | 1.280 | 1.215 | .0005 | .004 | — | 1.125 |
| | G20/2500 [10] [11] | 11.15 | 2.940 | .937 | 1.280 | 1.215 | .0005 | .004 | — | 1.250 |
| | R, V20/2500 [2] [42] | 11.15 | 2.940 | 1.00 | 1.280 | 1.215 | .0005 | .004 | — | 1.125 |
| | R, V20/2500 [2] [11] [42] | 11.15 | 2.940 | .937 | 1.280 | 1.215 | .0005 | .004 | — | 1.250 |
| | R, V20/2500 [2] [43] | 13.00 | 3.150 | 1.062 | 1.280 | 1.215 | .0005 | .004 | — | 1.250 |
| | R20/2500 [5] | 13.00 | 3.150 | 1.062 | 1.280 | 1.215 | .0005 | .004 | — | 1.250 |
| | R20/2500 [2] [15] | 13.00 | 3.150 | 1.062 | 1.280 | 1.215 | .0005 | .004 | — | 1.250 |
| | R, V20/2500 [6] | 13.00 | 3.150 | 1.062 | 1.280 | 1.215 | .0005 | .004 | — | 1.250 |
| | P20/2500 | [12] | [31] | [13] | 1.280 | 1.215 | .0005 | .004 | — | [14] |
| | P20/2500 [11] [44] | 11.15 | 2.940 | .937 | 1.280 | 1.215 | .0005 | .004 | — | 1.250 |
| | P20/2500 [11] [29] | 13.00 | 3.150 | 1.062 | 1.280 | 1.215 | .0005 | .004 | — | 1.250 |

## BRAKE SPECIFICATIONS—Continued

| Year | Model | Rear Drum I.D. | Wheel Cyl. Bore | | Disc Brake Rotor | | | | Master Cyl. I.D. | |
|---|---|---|---|---|---|---|---|---|---|---|
| | | | Front Disc | Rear Drum | Nominal Thickness | Minimum Thickness | Thickness Variation (Parallelism) | Run Out (TIR) | Manual Brakes | Power Brakes |
| | G30/3500 ② ⑤ | 13.00 | 3.380 | 1.190 | 1.530 | 1.465 | .0005 | .004 | — | 1.312 |
| | G30/3500 ⑩ | 13.00 | 3.150 | 1.062 | 1.280 | 1.215 | .0005 | .004 | — | 1.250 |
| | G30/3500 ㉑ ㉒ | 13.00 | 3.150 | 1.062 | 1.280 | 1.215 | .0005 | .004 | — | 1.250 |
| | G30/3500 ㉓ | 13.00 | 3.380 | 1.190 | 1.530 | 1.465 | .0005 | .004 | — | 1.336 |
| | P30/3500 ㉔ ㉕ | 13.00 | ㉜ | ㉝ | ⑱ | ⑲ | .0005 | .004 | — | ⑳ |
| | P30/3500 ㉔ ㉖ | — | 3.380 | 3.380 ㉗ | 1.530 | 1.465 | .0005 | .004 | — | 1.336 |
| | P30/3500 ㉕ ㉘ | 13.00 | 3.380 | 1.190 | 1.530 | 1.465 | .0005 | .004 | — | 1.312 |
| | P30/3500 ㉖ ㉘ | — | 3.380 | 3.380 ㉗ | 1.530 | 1.465 | .0005 | .004 | — | 1.336 |
| 1988 | R, 10/1500 ⑥ ⑧ | 11.15 | 2.940 | .937 | 1.280 | 1.215 | .0005 | .004 | — | 1.125 |
| | R,V10/1500 ⑧ ⑪ ⑧ | 11.15 | 2.940 | .937 | 1.280 | 1.215 | .0005 | .004 | — | 1.250 |
| | G10/1500 ⑩ | ③ | 2.940 | ④ | 1.280 | 1.215 | .0005 | .004 | 1.00 | 1.125 |
| | G10/1500 ㊶ | ③ | 2.940 | ④ | 1.280 | 1.215 | .0005 | .004 | — | 1.125 |
| | G20/2500 ⑩ | 11.15 | 2.940 | .937 | 1.280 | 1.215 | .0005 | .004 | — | 1.125 |
| | G20/2500 ⑩ ⑪ | 11.15 | 2.940 | .937 | 1.280 | 1.215 | .0005 | .004 | — | 1.250 |
| | R20/2500 ② | 13.00 | 3.150 | 1.062 | 1.280 | 1.215 | .0005 | .004 | — | 1.250 |
| | R, V20/2500 ⑧ | 13.00 | 3.150 | 1.062 | 1.280 | 1.215 | .0005 | .004 | — | 1.250 |
| | P20/2500 | ⑫ | ㉛ | ⑬ | 1.280 | 1.215 | .0005 | .004 | — | ⑭ |
| | P20/2500 ⑪ ㊹ | 11.15 | 2.940 | .937 | 1.280 | 1.215 | .0005 | .004 | — | 1.250 |
| | P20/2500 ⑪ ㉙ | 13.00 | 3.150 | 1.062 | 1.280 | 1.215 | .0005 | .004 | — | 1.250 |
| | R,V30,3500 ② ⑤ | 13.00 | 3.380 | 1.190 | 1.530 | 1.465 | .0005 | .004 | — | 1.31 |
| | G30/3500 ⑩ | 13.00 | 3.150 | 1.062 | 1.280 | 1.215 | .0005 | .004 | — | 1.250 |
| | G30/3500 ㉒ | 13.00 | 3.150 | 1.062 | 1.280 | 1.215 | .0005 | .004 | — | 1.250 |
| | G30/3500 ㉓ | 13.00 | 3.380 | 1.190 | 1.530 | 1.465 | .0005 | .004 | — | 1.336 |
| | P30/3500 ㉔ ㉕ | 13.00 | ㉜ | ㉝ | ⑱ | ⑲ | .0005 | .004 | — | ⑳ |
| | P30/3500 ㉔ ㉖ | 13.75 | 3.380 | 3.380 ㉗ | 1.530 | 1.465 | .0005 | .004 | — | 1.336 |
| | P30/3500 ㉕ ㉘ | 13.00 | 3.380 | 1.190 | 1.530 | 1.465 | .0005 | .004 | — | 1.312 |
| | P30/3500 ㉖ ㉘ | 13.75 | 3.380 | 3.380 ㉗ | 1.530 | 1.465 | .0005 | .004 | — | 1.336 |
| 1989 | V10/1500 ⑧ | 11.15 | 2.94 | .937 | 11.86 | — | .0005 | .004 | — | 1.12 |
| | R,V10/1500 ⑧ | 11.15 | 2.94 | .937 | 11.86 | — | .0005 | .004 | — | 1.12 |
| | V10/1500 ⑧ ⑪ | 11.15 | 2.94 | .937 | 11.86 | — | .0005 | .004 | — | 1.25 |
| | R,V10/1500 ⑧ ⑪ | 11.15 | 2.94 | .937 | 11.86 | — | .0005 | .004 | — | 1.25 |
| | G10/1500 ㊽ | 11.0 | 2.94 | 1.06 | 11.86 | — | .0005 | .004 | 1.0 | — |
| | G10/1500 ㊽ ㊺ | 11.0 | 2.94 | 1.06 | 11.86 | — | .0005 | .004 | — | 1.12 |
| | G10/1500 ㊽ ㊻ | 11.15 | 2.94 | .937 | 11.86 | — | .0005 | .004 | — | 1.12 |
| | G10/1500 ㊶ | 11.0 | 2.94 | 1.06 | 11.86 | — | .0005 | .004 | — | 1.12 |
| | G10/1500 ㊶ ㊻ | 11.15 | 2.94 | .937 | 11.86 | — | .0005 | .004 | — | 1.12 |
| | G20/2500 ⑩ | 11.15 | 2.94 | .937 | 11.86 | — | .0005 | .004 | — | 1.12 |
| | G20/2500 ⑩ ⑪ | 11.15 | 2.94 | .937 | 11.86 | — | .0005 | .004 | — | 1.25 |
| | R20/2500 ③ | 13.0 | 3.15 | 1.06 | 12.50 | — | .0005 | .004 | — | 1.25 |
| | R,V20/2500 ⑧ | 13.0 | 3.15 | 1.06 | 12.50 | — | .0005 | .004 | — | 1.25 |
| | P20/2500 ㊹ | 11.15 | 2.94 | 1.0 | 12.50 | — | .0005 | .004 | — | 1.12 |
| | P20/2500 ㊹ ⑪ | 11.15 | 2.94 | .937 | 11.86 | — | .0005 | .004 | — | 1.25 |
| | P20/2500 ㊼ | 13.0 | 3.15 | 1.06 | 12.50 | — | .0005 | .004 | — | 1.25 |
| | P20/2500 ㉙ ⑪ | 13.0 | 3.15 | 1.06 | 12.50 | — | .0005 | .004 | — | 1.25 |
| | R30/3500 ② | 13.0 | 3.38 | 1.19 | 12.54 | — | .0005 | .004 | — | 1.31 |
| | V30/3500 ② | 13.0 | 3.38 | 1.19 | 12.88 | — | .0005 | .004 | — | 1.33 |
| | G30/3500 ⑩ | 13.0 | 3.15 | 1.06 | 12.50 | — | .0005 | .004 | — | 1.25 |

## BRAKE SPECIFICATIONS—Continued

| Year | Model | Rear Drum I.D. | Wheel Cyl. Bore | | Disc Brake Rotor | | | | Master Cyl. I.D. | |
|---|---|---|---|---|---|---|---|---|---|---|
| | | | Front Disc | Rear Drum | Nominal Thickness | Minimum Thickness | Thickness Variation (Parallelism) | Run Out (TIR) | Manual Brakes | Power Brakes |
| | G30/3500 [22] | 13.0 | 3.15 | 1.06 | 12.50 | — | .0005 | .004 | — | 1.25 |
| | G30/3500 [23] [46] | 13.0 | 3.38 | 1.19 | 12.50 | — | .0005 | .004 | — | 1.33 |
| | P30/3500 | 13.0 | 3.15 | 1.06 | 12.50 | — | .0005 | .004 | — | 1.25 |
| | P30/3500 [46] | 13.0 | 3.38 | 1.19 | 12.50 | — | .0005 | .004 | — | 1.31 |
| | P30/3500 [46] [48] | 13.0 | 3.38 | 1.19 | 12.50 | — | .0005 | .004 | — | 1.31 |
| | P30/3500 [29] | 13.0 | 3.38 | 1.19 | 12.50 | — | .0005 | .004 | — | 1.31 |
| | P30/3500 [29] [46] | 13.75 | 3.38 | 3.38 | 14.25 | — | .0005 | .004 | — | 1.33 |
| | P30/3500 [29] [46] [48] | 13.75 | 3.38 | 3.38 | 14.25 | — | .0005 | .004 | — | 1.33 |
| | P30/3500 [28] [29] | 13.75 | 3.38 | 3.38 | 14.25 | — | .0005 | .004 | — | 1.33 |
| | P30/3500 [28] [29] [50] | 13.75 | 3.38 | 3.38 | 14.25 | — | .0005 | .004 | — | 1.33 |

① —Caballero & El Camino.
② —Pickup.
③ —Exc. heavy duty power brakes, 11.00; heavy duty power brakes, 11.15.
④ —Exc. heavy duty power brakes, 1.060; heavy duty power brakes, .937.
⑤ —Chassis cab.
⑥ —Suburban.
⑦ —With V8 engine.
⑧ —Blazer & Jimmy.
⑨ —Suburban with 6 cylinder engine.
⑩ —Sportvan, Rally, Vandura & Chevy van.
⑪ —With diesel engine.
⑫ —Exc. heavy duty power brakes, 11.15; heavy duty power brakes, 13.00.
⑬ —Exc. heavy duty power brakes, 1.00; heavy duty power brakes, 1.062.
⑭ —Exc. heavy duty power brakes, 1.125; heavy duty power brakes, 1.250.
⑮ —Bonus & Crew cab.
⑯ —Exc. heavy duty power brakes, 2.940; heavy duty power brakes, 3.380.
⑰ —Exc. heavy duty power brakes, 1.062; heavy duty power brakes, 1.187.

⑱ —Exc. heavy duty power brakes, 1.280; heavy duty power brakes, 1.530.
⑲ —Exc. heavy duty power brakes, 1.215; heavy duty power brakes, 1.465.
⑳ —Exc. heavy duty power brakes, 1.250; heavy duty power brakes, 1.312.
㉑ —Cutaway & Hi-cube van.
㉒ —Single rear wheels.
㉓ —Dual rear wheels.
㉔ —Exc. motor home chassis.
㉕ —Less 4 wheel disc brakes.
㉖ —With 4 wheel disc brakes.
㉗ —Rear caliper.
㉘ —Motor home chassis.
㉙ —Gross vehicle weight rating, 8600 lbs.
㉚ —Exc. heavy duty power brakes, 1.040; heavy duty power brakes, 1.280.
㉛ —Exc. heavy duty power brakes, 2.940; heavy duty power brakes, 3.150.
㉜ —Exc. heavy duty power brakes, 3.150; heavy duty power brakes, 3.380.
㉝ —Exc. heavy duty power brakes, 1.062; heavy duty power brakes, 1.190.

㉞ —Exc. heavy duty power brakes, 1.250; heavy duty power brakes, 1.340.
㉟ —1982 models, 1.540.
㊱ —1982 models with heavy duty power brakes, 1.540.
㊲ —1982 models.
㊳ —1982 models with heavy duty power brakes, 1.312.
㊴ —Exc. heavy duty power brakes, .965; heavy duty power brakes, 1.215.
㊵ —Chevy Van & Vandura.
㊶ —Sportvan & Rally.
㊷ —Less C6P heavy duty chassis.
㊸ —With C6P heavy duty chassis.
㊹ —Gross vehicle weight rating, 6800 lbs.
㊺ —Gross vehicle weight rating, 4900–5600 lbs.
㊻ —Heavy duty power brakes
㊼ —Gross vehicle weight rating, 6800–8000 lbs.
㊽ —School bus equipment
㊾ —11000 lb axle
㊿ —10000 lb axle

## DRIVE AXLE SPECIFICATIONS

| Year | Make & Application | Ring Gear Size | Carrier Type | Ring Gear & Pinion Backlash | | Pinion Bearing Preload | | | Differential Bearing Preload | | |
|---|---|---|---|---|---|---|---|---|---|---|---|
| | | | | Method | Adjustment | Method | New Bearings Inch Lbs. | Used Bearings Inch Lbs. | Method | New Bearings Inch Lbs. | Used Bearings Inch Lbs. |
| 1980 | Chevrolet ① | 7½ | Integral | Shims | .005–.008 | Spacer | 20–25 | 10–15 | Shims | ③ | ③ |
| | Chevrolet ⑤ ㉑ | 8½ | Integral | Shims | .005–.008 | Spacer | 20–25 | 10–15 | Shims | ③ | ③ |
| | Chevrolet ④ ⑤ | 8⁷⁻⁸ | Integral | Shims | .005–.008 | Spacer | 20–25 | 10–15 | Shims | ③ | ③ |
| | Spicer ⑥ ⑦ | 8½ | Integral | Shims | .005–.010 | Shims | 20–40 | 10–20 | Shims | .015⑧ | .015⑧ |
| | Chevrolet ⑥ ⑦ | 8½ | Integral | Shims | .005–.008 | Spacer | 20–25 | 10–15 | Shims | ③ | ③ |
| | Spicer ⑥ ⑨ | 9¾ | Integral | Shims | .004–.009 | Shims | 20–40 | 10–20 | Shims | .015⑧ | .015⑧ |
| | Chevrolet ⑩ ⑪ | 10½ | Integral | Adj. Nut | .005–.008 | Spacer | 25–35 | 5–15 | Adj. Nut | ⑫ | ⑬ |
| | Chevrolet ⑭ | 10½ | Integral | Adj. Nut | .005–.008 | Spacer | 25–35 | 5–15 | Adj. Nut | ⑫ | ⑬ |
| | Spicer ⑮ | 9¾ | Integral | Shims | .004–.009 | Shims | 20–40 | 10–20 | Shims | .015⑧ | .015⑧ |
| | Spicer ⑯ | 10½ | Integral | Shims | .004–.009 | Shims | 20–40 | 10–20 | Shims | .006⑧ | .006⑧ |
| | Chevrolet ⑰ | 12¼ | Integral | Adj. Nut | .005–.008 | — | — | — | Adj. Nut | ⑱ | ⑱ |
| 1981 | Chevrolet ① | 7½ | Integral | Shims | .005–.008 | Spacer | 20–25 | 10–15 | Shims | ③ | ③ |
| | Chevrolet ⑤ ㉒ | 8½ | Integral | Shims | .005–.008 | Spacer | 20–25 | 10–15 | Shims | ③ | ③ |
| | Chevrolet ④ ⑤ | 8⁷⁄₈ | Integral | Shims | .005–.008 | Spacer | 20–25 | 10–15 | Shims | ③ | ③ |
| | Chevrolet ⑥ ⑦ | 8½ | Integral | Shims | .005–.008 | Spacer | 20–25 | 10–15 | Shims | ③ | ③ |
| | Spicer ⑥ ⑨ | 9¾ | Integral | Shims | .004–.009 | Shims | 20–40 | 10–20 | Shims | .015⑧ | .015⑧ |
| | Chevrolet ㉓ ㉔ | 9½ | Integral | Shims | .005–.008 | Spacer | 20–25 | 10–15 | Adj. Nut | ② | ② |
| | Chevrolet ⑪ ⑭ ⑲ | 10½ | Integral | Adj. Nut | .005–.008 | Spacer | 25–35 | 5–15 | Adj. Nut | ⑫ | ⑬ |
| | Spicer ⑮ | 9¾ | Integral | Shims | .004–.009 | Shims | 20–40 | 10–20 | Shims | .015⑧ | .015⑧ |
| | Spicer ⑯ | 10½ | Integral | Shims | .004–.009 | Shims | 20–40 | 10–20 | Shims | .006⑧ | .006⑧ |
| | Chevrolet ⑰ | 12¼ | Integral | Adj. Nut | .005–.008 | — | — | — | Adj. Nut | ⑱ | ⑱ |
| 1982 | Chevrolet ① | 7½ | Integral | Shims | .005–.009 | Spacer | 24–32 | 8–12 | Shims | ③ | ③ |
| | Chevrolet ⑤ ㉒ | 8½ | Integral | Shims | .005–.008 | Spacer | 20–25 | 10–15 | Shims | ③ | ③ |
| | Chevrolet ④ ⑤ | 8⁷⁄₈ | Integral | Shims | .005–.008 | Spacer | 20–25 | 10–15 | Shims | ③ | ③ |
| | Chevrolet ⑥ ⑦ | 8½ | Integral | Shims | .005–.008 | Spacer | 20–25 | 10–15 | Shims | ③ | ③ |
| | Spicer ⑥ ⑨ | 9¾ | Integral | Shims | .004–.009 | Shims | 20–40 | 10–20 | Shims | .015⑧ | .015⑧ |
| | Chevrolet ㉓ ㉔ | 9½ | Integral | Shims | .005–.008 | Spacer | 20–25 | 10–15 | Adj. Nut | ② | ② |
| | Chevrolet ⑪ ⑭ ⑲ | 10½ | Integral | Adj. Nut | .005–.008 | Spacer | 25–35 | 5–15 | Adj. Nut | ⑫ | ⑬ |
| | Spicer ⑮ | 9¾ | Integral | Shims | .004–.009 | Shims | 20–40 | 10–20 | Shims | .015⑧ | .015⑧ |
| | Spicer ⑯ | 10½ | Integral | Shims | .004–.009 | Shims | 20–40 | 10–20 | Shims | .006⑧ | .006⑧ |
| | Timken ⑰ | 12 | Removable | Adj. Ring | .010 | Spacer | 5–15 | — | Adj. Nut | ⑳ | ⑳ |
| 1983–86 | Chevrolet ① | 7½ | Integral | Shims | .005–.009 | Spacer | 24–32 | 8–12 | Shims | ③ | ③ |
| | Chevrolet ⑤ ㉒ | 8½ | Integral | Shims | .005–.008 | Spacer | 20–25 | 10–15 | Shims | ③ | ③ |
| | Chevrolet ⑥ ⑦ | 8½ | Integral | Shims | .005–.008 | Spacer | 20–25 | 10–15 | Shims | ③ | ③ |
| | Spicer ⑥ ⑨ | 9¾ | Integral | Shims | .004–.009 | Shims | 20–40 | 10–20 | Shims | .015⑧ | .015⑧ |
| | Chevrolet ㉓ ㉔ | 9½ | Integral | Shims | .005–.008 | Spacer | 20–25 | 10–15 | Adj. Nut | ② | ② |
| | Chevrolet ⑪ ⑭ ⑲ | 10½ | Integral | Adj. Nut | .005–.008 | Spacer | 25–35 | 5–15 | Adj. Nut | ⑫ | ⑬ |
| | Spicer ⑮ | 9³⁻⁴ | Integral | Shims | .004–.009 | Shims | 20–40 | 10–20 | Shims | .015⑧ | .015⑧ |
| | Spicer ⑯ | 10½ | Integral | Shims | .004–.009 | Shims | 20–40 | 10–20 | Shims | .006⑧ | .006⑧ |
| | Timken ⑰ | 12 | Removable | Adj. Ring | .010 | Spacer | 5–15 | — | Adj. Nut | ⑳ | ⑳ |
| 1987–89 | Chevrolet | 8½ | Integral | Shims | .005–.009 | Spacer | 20–25 | 10–15 | Shims | ③ | ③ |
| | Chevrolet | 9½ | Integral | Shims | .005–.008 | Spacer | 20––25 | 10–15 | Adj. Nut | ② | ② |
| | Chevrolet | 10½ | Integral | Adj. Nut | .005–.008 | Spacer | 25–35 | 5–15 | Adj. Nut | ⑫ | ⑬ |
| | Dana | 9¾ | Integral | Shims | ㉕ | Shims | 20–40 | 20–40 | Shims | .015⑧ | .015⑧ |
| | Dana | 10½ | Integral | Shims | ㉕ | Shims | 20–40 | 20–40 | Shims | .015⑧ | .015⑧ |
| | Rockwell | 12 | Removable | Adj. Ring | .010 | Spacer | 5–15 | — | Adj. Nut | ⑳ | ⑳ |

① —Caballero & El Camino.
② —Tighten adjusting nut until it contacts bearing, then tighten an additional 3 slots.
③ —Slip fit plus .004 inch clearance on each side.
④ —Series 10/1500.
⑤ —G20/2500.
⑥ —Front axle.
⑦ —K, V10-20/1500-2500.
⑧ —Inch.
⑨ —K, V30/3500.
⑩ —C, K, P20/2500.
⑪ —C, G, K, R, V30/3500 less dual rear wheels.
⑫ —Tighten adjusting nut until it contacts bearing, then tighten an additional 3 slots.

⑬—Tighten adjusting nut until it contacts bearing, then tighten an additional 2 slots.

⑭—P30/3500 exc. 5.43 & 6.17 rear axle ratio.

⑮—G30/3500 with dual rear wheels.

⑯—C, G, K, R, V30/3500 with dual rear wheels.

⑰—P30/3500 with 5.43 & 6.17 rear axle ratio.

⑱—Tighten adjusting nut until it contacts bearing, then tighten an additional 1-2 notches.

⑲—C, R20/2500 Bonus & Crew cab.

⑳—Tighten adjusting nut to obtain zero endplay, then tighten nut one

additional notch.

㉑—C, G10/1500.

㉒—C, G, K, R, V10/1500.

㉓—K, P, V20/2500.

㉔—C, R20/2500 exc. Bonus & Crew cab.

㉕—1987 models .004–.009; 1988–89 models .005–.009

## COOLING SYSTEM & CAPACITY DATA

| Year | Model | Engine | Cooling Capacity, Qts. Less A/C | With A/C | Radiator Cap Relief Pressure, Lbs. | Thermo. Opening Temp. | Fuel Tank Gals. | Engine Oil Refill Qts. ① | Transmission Oil 3 Speed Pints | 4 Speed Pints | Auto. Trans. Qts. ㉒ | Transfer Case Pints | Rear Axle Oil Pints |
|---|---|---|---|---|---|---|---|---|---|---|---|---|---|
| 1980 | ② | V6-229 | 18.5 | 18.5 | 15 | 195 | 17.7 | 4㉓ | 3 | — | ㉖ | — | 3.5 |
| | | V6-231 | 15.5 | 15.5 | 15 | 195 | 17.7 | 4㉓ | — | — | ㉖ | — | 3.5 |
| | | V8-267 | 21 | 21 | 15 | 195 | 17.7 | 4 | — | — | ㉖ | — | 3.5 |
| | | V8-305 | 19 | 19 | 15 | 195 | 17.7 | 4 | — | 3 | ㉖ | — | 3.5 |
| | C10/1500 | 6-250 | 14.4 | 14.4 | 15 | 195 | ③④ | 4 | ⑤ | 8 | ⑥ | — | ⑧ |
| | | V8-305 | 17.2 | 17.2 | 15 | 195 | ③④ | 4 | ⑤ | 8 | ⑥ | — | ⑧ |
| | | V8-350 | 17.2 | 17.2 | 15 | 195 | ③④ | 4 | ⑤ | 8 | ⑥ | — | ⑧ |
| | | V8-350㉔ | 18 | 19.6 | 15 | 195 | — | 7㉓ | — | — | ⑥ | — | ⑧ |
| | G10/1500 | 6-250 | 14.4 | 14.8 | 15 | 195 | 22 | 4 | ⑤ | — | 10 | — | ⑧ |
| | | V8-305 | 16.8 | 17.2 | 15 | 195 | 22 | 4 | ⑤ | — | 10 | — | ⑧ |
| | | V8-350 | 17.2 | 17.2 | 15 | 195 | 22 | 4 | ⑤ | — | 10 | — | ⑧ |
| | K10/1500 | 6-250 | 14.4 | 14.4 | 15 | 195 | ③④ | 4 | ⑤ | 8 | ⑥ | ⑨ | 3.5⑩ |
| | | V8-305 | 17.2 | 17.2 | 15 | 195 | ③④ | 4 | ⑤ | 8 | ⑥ | ⑨ | 3.5⑩ |
| | | V8-350 | 17.2 | 17.2 | 15 | 195 | ③④ | 4 | ⑤ | 8 | ⑥ | ⑨ | 3.5⑩ |
| | | V8-400 | 18.4 | 20.4 | 15 | 195 | ③④ | 4 | — | — | ⑥ | ⑨ | 3.5⑩ |
| | P10/1500 | 6-292 | 13.6 | — | 15 | 195 | 21 | 5 | 3 | 8 | ⑥ | — | 3.5 |
| | C20/2500 | 6-250 | 14.4 | 14.4 | 15 | 195 | ⑪ | 4 | 3 | 8 | ⑥ | — | 5.4 |
| | | 6-292 | 15.2 | 15.2 | 15 | 195 | ⑪ | 5 | — | 8 | ⑥ | — | 5.4 |
| | | V8-305 | 17.2 | 17.2 | 15 | 195 | ⑪ | 4 | 3 | 8 | ⑥ | — | 5.4 |
| | | V8-350 | 17.2 | 17.2 | 15 | 195 | ⑪ | 4 | — | 8 | ⑥ | — | 5.4 |
| | | V8-454 | 21.6 | 24.8 | 15 | 195 | ⑪ | 6 | — | 8 | ⑥ | — | 5.4 |
| | G20/2500 | 6-250 | 17.2 | — | 15 | 195 | 22 | 4 | ⑤ | — | 10 | — | ⑧ |
| | | V8-350 | 20 | 20.4 | 15 | 195 | 22 | 4 | ⑤ | — | 10 | — | ⑧ |
| | | V8-400 | 20 | 20 | 15 | 195 | 22 | 4 | — | — | 10 | — | ⑧ |
| | K20/2500 | 6-292 | 15.2 | 15.2 | 15 | 195 | ⑪ | 5 | — | 8 | ⑥ | ⑨ | 5.4⑩ |
| | | V8-350 | 17.6 | 18.4 | 15 | 195 | ⑪ | 4 | 3 | 8 | ⑥ | ⑨ | 5.4⑩ |
| | | V8-400 | 18.4 | 20.4 | 15 | 195 | ⑪ | 4 | — | 8 | ⑥ | ⑨ | 5.4⑩ |
| | P20/2500 | 6-292 | 13.6 | — | 15 | 195 | 31 | 5 | 3 | 8 | ⑥ | — | 5.4 |
| | | V8-350 | ⑬ | — | 15 | 195 | 31 | 4 | 3 | 8 | ⑥ | — | 5.4 |
| | C30/3500 | 6-292 | 15.2 | 15.2 | 15 | 195 | 20 | 5 | — | 8 | ⑥ | — | ⑭ |
| | | V8-350 | 17.2 | 17.2 | 15 | 195 | 20 | 4 | — | 8 | ⑥ | — | ⑭ |
| | | V8-454 | 21.6 | 24.8 | 15 | 195 | 20 | 6 | — | 8 | ⑥ | — | ⑭ |
| | G30/3500 | 6-250 | 17.2 | — | 15 | 195 | 22 | 4 | ⑤ | — | 10 | — | ⑮ |
| | | V8-350 | 20 | 20.4 | 15 | 195 | 22 | 4 | ⑤ | — | 10 | — | ⑮ |
| | | V8-400 | 20 | 20.4 | 15 | 195 | 22 | 4 | — | — | 10 | — | ⑮ |
| | K30/3500 | 6-292 | 14.8 | — | 15 | 195 | 20 | 5 | — | 8 | ⑥ | ⑨ | ⑩⑭ |
| | | V8-350 | 17.6 | 18.4 | 15 | 195 | 20 | 4 | — | 8 | ⑥ | ⑨ | ⑩⑭ |
| | | V8-400 | 18.4 | 20.4 | 15 | 195 | 20 | 4 | — | — | ⑥ | ⑨ | ⑩⑭ |
| | P30/3500⑯ | 6-292 | 13.6 | — | 15 | 195 | 31 | 5 | — | 8 | ⑥ | — | ⑰ |
| | | V8-350 | 17.2 | — | 15 | 195 | 31 | 4 | — | 8 | ⑥ | — | ⑰ |
| | | V8-454 | 24.8 | — | 15 | 195 | 31 | ㉕ | — | — | ⑥ | — | ⑰ |
| | P30/3500⑱ | V8-350 | 20 | 20 | 15 | 195 | 40 | 4 | — | — | ⑥ | — | ⑰ |
| | | V8-454 | 24.8 | 24.8 | 15 | 195 | 40 | 6 | — | — | ⑥ | — | ⑰ |

## COOLING SYSTEM & CAPACITY DATA—Continued

| Year | Model | Engine | Cooling Capacity, Qts. Less A/C | With A/C | Radiator Cap Relief Pressure, Lbs. | Thermo. Opening Temp. | Fuel Tank Gals. | Engine Oil Refill Qts. [1] | Transmission Oil 3 Speed Pints | 4 Speed Pints | Auto. Trans. Qts. [22] | Transfer Case Pints | Rear Axle Oil Pints |
|---|---|---|---|---|---|---|---|---|---|---|---|---|---|
| 1981 | [2] | V6-229 | 18.5 | 18.5 | 15 | 195 | 17.7 | 4[23] | 3.5 | — | [26] | — | 3 |
| | | V6-231 | 15.5 | 15.5 | 15 | 195 | 17.7 | 4[23] | — | — | [26] | — | 3 |
| | | V8-267 | 21 | 21 | 15 | 195 | 17.7 | 4 | — | — | [26] | — | 3 |
| | | V8-305 | 19 | 19 | 15 | 195 | 17.7 | 4 | — | 3.5 | [26] | — | 3 |
| | C10/1500 | 6-250 | 14.4 | 14.4 | 15 | 195 | [3][4] | 4 | [5] | 8 | [6] | — | [8] |
| | | V8-305 | 17.2 | 17.2 | 15 | 195 | [3][4] | 4 | [5] | 8 | [6] | — | [8] |
| | | V8-350 | 17.2 | 17.2 | 15 | 195 | [3][4] | 4 | [5] | 8 | [6] | — | [8] |
| | | V8-350[24] | 18 | 19.6 | 15 | 195 | — | 7[23] | — | — | [6] | — | [8] |
| | G10/1500 | 6-250 | 14.4 | 14.8 | 15 | 195 | 22 | 4 | [5] | — | [6] | — | [8] |
| | | V8-305 | 16.8 | 17.2 | 15 | 195 | 22 | 4 | [5] | — | [6] | — | [8] |
| | | V8-350 | 17.2 | 17.2 | 15 | 195 | 22 | 4 | [5] | — | [6] | — | [8] |
| | K10/1500 | 6-250 | 14.4 | 14.4 | 15 | 195 | [3][4] | 4 | [5] | 8 | [6] | [9] | [8][10] |
| | | V8-305 | 17.2 | 17.2 | 15 | 195 | [3][4] | 4 | [5] | 8 | [6] | [9] | [8][10] |
| | | V8-350 | 17.2 | 17.2 | 15 | 195 | [3][4] | 4 | — | 8 | [6] | [9] | [8][10] |
| | C20/2500 | 6-250 | 14.4 | 14.4 | 15 | 195 | [11] | 4 | [5] | 8 | [6] | — | 5.4 |
| | | 6-292 | 15.2 | 15.2 | 15 | 195 | [11] | 5 | — | 8 | [6] | — | 5.4 |
| | | V8-305 | 17.2 | 17.2 | 15 | 195 | [11] | 4 | [5] | 8 | [6] | — | 5.4 |
| | | V8-350 | 17.2 | 17.2 | 15 | 195 | [11] | 4 | — | 8 | [6] | — | 5.4 |
| | | V8-454 | 21.6 | 24.8 | 15 | 195 | [11] | 6 | — | 8 | [6] | — | 5.4 |
| | G20/2500 | 6-250 | 14.4 | 14.8 | 15 | 195 | 22 | 4 | [5] | — | [6] | — | [8] |
| | | V8-305 | 16.8 | 17.2 | 15 | 195 | 22 | 4 | [5] | — | [6] | — | [8] |
| | | V8-350 | 17.2 | 17.2 | 15 | 195 | 22 | 4 | [5] | — | [6] | — | [8] |
| | K20/2500 | 6-292 | 15.2 | 15.2 | 15 | 195 | [11] | 5 | — | 8 | [6] | [9] | 5.4[10] |
| | | V8-350 | 17.2 | 17.2 | 15 | 195 | [11] | 4 | — | 8 | [6] | [9] | 5.4[10] |
| | P20/2500 | 6-292 | 14 | — | 15 | 195 | 31 | 5 | [5] | 8 | [6] | — | 5.4 |
| | | V8-350 | 15.6 | — | 15 | 195 | 31 | 4 | [5] | 8 | [6] | — | 5.4 |
| | C30/3500 | 6-292 | 15.2 | 15.2 | 15 | 195 | 20 | 5 | — | 8 | [6] | — | [14] |
| | | V8-350 | 17.2 | 17.2 | 15 | 195 | 20 | 4 | — | 8 | [6] | — | [14] |
| | | V8-454 | 21.6 | 24.8 | 15 | 195 | 20 | 6 | — | 8 | [6] | — | [14] |
| | G30/3500 | V8-350 | 17.2 | 17.6 | 15 | 195 | 22 | 4 | [5] | — | [6] | — | [15] |
| | K30/3500 | 6-292 | 15.2 | 15.2 | 15 | 195 | 20 | 5 | — | 8 | [6] | [9] | [10][14] |
| | | V8-350 | 17.2 | 17.2 | 15 | 195 | 20 | 4 | — | 8 | [6] | [9] | [10][14] |
| | | V8-454 | 21.6 | 24.8 | 15 | 195 | 20 | 5 | — | 8 | [6] | [9] | [10][14] |
| | P30/3500 [16] | 6-292 | 14 | — | 15 | 195 | 31 | 5 | — | 8 | [6] | — | [17] |
| | | V8-350 | 15.6 | — | 15 | 195 | 31 | 4 | — | 8 | [6] | — | [17] |
| | P30/3500 [18] | V8-350 | 19.2 | — | 15 | 195 | 40 | 4 | — | — | [6] | — | [17] |
| | | V8-454 | 24.4 | — | 15 | 195 | 40 | 6 | — | — | [6] | — | [17] |
| 1982 | [2] | V6-229 | 15 | 15 | 15 | 195 | 17.7 | 4[23] | — | — | [27] | — | 3 |
| | | V6-231 | 12 | 12 | 15 | 195 | 17.7 | 4[23] | — | — | [27] | — | 3 |
| | | V8-267 | 18.6 | 18.6 | 15 | 195 | 17.7 | 4 | — | — | [27] | — | 3 |
| | | V8-305 | 16.3 | 16.3 | 15 | 195 | 17.7 | 4 | — | — | [27] | — | 3 |
| | C10/1500 | 6-250 | 14.4 | 14.4 | 15 | 195 | [3][4] | 4 | 3 | 8 | [12] | — | [8] |
| | | V8-305 | 17.2 | 17.2 | 15 | 195 | [3][4] | 4 | 3 | 8 | [12] | — | [8] |
| | | V8-350 | 17.2 | 17.2 | 15 | 195 | [3][4] | 4 | — | — | [12] | — | [8] |
| | | V8-379[24] | 25.2 | 25.2 | 15 | 195 | [7] | 7[23] | — | 8 | [12] | — | [8] |
| | G10/1500 | 6-250 | 14.4 | 14.8 | 15 | 195 | 22 | 4 | 3 | — | [12] | — | [8] |
| | | V8-305 | 16.8 | 17.2 | 15 | 195 | 22 | 4 | 3 | — | [12] | — | [8] |
| | | V8-350 | 17.2 | 17.2 | 15 | 195 | 22 | 4 | 3 | — | [12] | — | [8] |

## COOLING SYSTEM & CAPACITY DATA—Continued

| Year | Model | Engine | Cooling Capacity, Qts. Less A/C | With A/C | Radiator Cap Relief Pressure, Lbs. | Thermo. Opening Temp. | Fuel Tank Gals. | Engine Oil Refill Qts. [1] | Transmission Oil 3 Speed Pints | 4 Speed Pints | Auto. Trans. Qts. [22] | Transfer Case Pints | Rear Axle Oil Pints |
|---|---|---|---|---|---|---|---|---|---|---|---|---|---|
| | K10/1500 | 6-250 | 14.4 | 14.4 | 15 | 195 | [3][4] | 4 | 3 | 8 | [12] | [9] | [8][10] |
| | | V8-305 | 17.2 | 17.2 | 15 | 195 | [3][4] | 4 | 3 | 8 | [12] | [9] | [8][10] |
| | | V8-350 | 17.2 | 17.2 | 15 | 195 | [3][4] | 4 | — | — | [12] | [9] | [8][10] |
| | | V8-379 [24] | 25.2 | 25.2 | 15 | 195 | [7] | 7 [23] | — | 8 | [12] | [9] | [8][10] |
| | C20/2500 | 6-250 | 14.4 | 14.4 | 15 | 195 | [11] | 4 | 3 | 8 | [12] | — | 5.4 |
| | | 6-292 | 15.2 | 15.2 | 15 | 195 | [11] | 5 | 3 | 8 | [12] | — | 5.4 |
| | | V8-305 | 17.2 | 17.2 | 15 | 195 | [11] | 4 | 3 | 8 | [12] | — | 5.4 |
| | | V8-350 | 14.4 | 14.4 | 15 | 195 | [11] | 4 | — | — | [12] | — | 5.4 |
| | | V8-379 [24] | 25.2 | 25.2 | 15 | 195 | [19] | 7 [23] | — | 8 | [12] | — | 5.4 |
| | | V8-454 | 21.6 | 24.4 | 15 | 195 | [11] | 6 | — | 8 | [12] | — | 5.4 |
| | G20/2500 | 6-250 | 14.4 | 14.8 | 15 | 195 | 22 | 4 | 3 | — | [12] | — | [8] |
| | | V8-305 | 16.8 | 17.2 | 15 | 195 | 22 | 4 | 3 | — | [12] | — | [8] |
| | | V8-350 | 17.2 | 17.2 | 15 | 195 | 22 | 4 | 3 | — | [12] | — | [8] |
| | K20/2500 | 6-292 | 15.2 | 15.2 | 15 | 195 | [11] | 5 | 3 | 8 | [12] | [9] | 5.4 [10] |
| | | V8-350 | 17.2 | 17.2 | 15 | 195 | [11] | 4 | — | — | [12] | [9] | 5.4 [10] |
| | | V8-379 [24] | — | — | 15 | 195 | [19] | 7 [23] | — | 8 | [12] | [9] | 5.4 [10] |
| | P20/2500 | 6-292 | 14 | | 15 | 195 | 40 | 5 | — | 8 | — | — | 5.4 |
| | | V8-350 | 15.6 | | 15 | 195 | 40 | 4 | — | 8 | [12] | — | 5.4 |
| | | V8-379 [24] | — | — | 15 | 195 | 40 | 7 [23] | — | 8 | [12] | — | 5.4 |
| | C30/3500 | 6-292 | 15.2 | 15.2 | 15 | 195 | 20 | 5 | — | 8 | — | — | [14] |
| | | V8-350 | 17.2 | 17.2 | 15 | 195 | 20 | 4 | — | 8 | [12] | — | [14] |
| | | V8-379 [24] | 25.2 | 25.2 | 15 | 195 | 20 | 7 [23] | — | 8 | [12] | — | [14] |
| | | V8-454 | 21.6 | 24.4 | 15 | 195 | 20 | 6 | — | 8 | [12] | — | [14] |
| | G30/3500 | 6-250 | 14.4 | 14.8 | 15 | 195 | 22 | 4 | 3 | — | [12] | — | [15] |
| | | V8-350 | 17.2 | 17.2 | 15 | 195 | 22 | 4 | 3 | — | [12] | — | [15] |
| | K30/3500 | 6-292 | 15.2 | 15.2 | 15 | 195 | 20 | 5 | — | 8 | — | [9] | [10][14] |
| | | V8-350 | 17.2 | 17.2 | 15 | 195 | 20 | 4 | — | 8 | [12] | [9] | [10][14] |
| | | V8-379 [24] | 25.2 | 24.8 | 15 | 195 | 20 | 7 [23] | — | 8 | [12] | [9] | [10][14] |
| | | V8-454 | 21.6 | 24.4 | 15 | 195 | 20 | 6 | — | 8 | [12] | [9] | [10][14] |
| | P30/3500 [16] | 6-292 | 14 | — | 15 | 195 | 40 | 5 | — | 8 | — | — | [21] |
| | | V8-350 | 15.6 | — | 15 | 195 | 40 | 4 | — | 8 | [12] | — | [21] |
| | P30/3500 [18] | V8-350 | 19.2 | — | 15 | 195 | 40 | 5 | — | — | [12] | — | [21] |
| | | V8-454 | 24.4 | — | 15 | 195 | 40 | 6 | — | — | [12] | — | [21] |
| 1983–84 | [2] | V6-229 | 15 | 15 | 15 | 195 | 17.7 | 4 [23] | — | — | [27] | — | 3 |
| | | V6-231 | 12 | 12 | 15 | 195 | 17.7 | 4 [23] | — | — | [27] | — | 3 |
| | | V8-305 | 16.3 | 16.3 | 15 | 195 | 17.7 | 4 | — | — | [27] | — | 3 |
| | | V8-350 [24] | 18.3 | 18.3 | 15 | 195 | 22 | 7 [23] | — | — | [27] | — | 3 |
| | C10/1500 | 6-250 | 14.4 | 14.4 | 15 | 195 | [3][4] | 4 | 3 | 8 [20] | [12] | — | 4.2 |
| | | V8-305 | 17.2 | 17.2 | 15 | 195 | [3][4] | 4 | 3 | 8 [20] | [12] | — | 4.2 |
| | | V8-350 | 17.2 | 17.2 | 15 | 195 | [3][4] | 4 | — | 8 [20] | [12] | — | 4.2 |
| | | V8-379 [24] | 24.8 | 24.8 | 15 | 195 | [7] | 7 [23] | — | 8 [20] | [12] | — | 4.2 |
| | G10/1500 | 6-250 | 14.4 | 14.8 | 15 | 195 | 22 | 4 | 3 | 8 [20] | [12] | — | 4.2 |
| | | V8-305 | 16.8 | 17.2 | 15 | 195 | 22 | 4 | 3 | 8 [20] | [12] | — | 4.2 |
| | | V8-350 | 16.8 | 16.8 | 15 | 195 | 22 | 4 | — | — | [12] | — | 4.2 |
| | K10/1500 | 6-250 | 14.4 | 14.4 | 15 | 195 | [3][4] | 4 | 3 | 8 [20] | [12] | [9] | 4.2 [10] |
| | | V8-305 | 17.2 | 17.2 | 15 | 195 | [3][4] | 4 | 3 | 8 [20] | [12] | [9] | 4.2 [10] |
| | | V8-350 | 17.2 | 17.2 | 15 | 195 | [3][4] | 4 | — | 8 [20] | [12] | [9] | 4.2 [10] |
| | | V8-379 [24] | 24.8 | 24.8 | 15 | 195 | [7] | 7 [23] | — | 8 [20] | [12] | [9] | 4.2 [10] |

## COOLING SYSTEM & CAPACITY DATA—Continued

| Year | Model | Engine | Cooling Capacity, Qts. Less A/C | With A/C | Radiator Cap Relief Pressure, Lbs. | Thermo. Opening Temp. | Fuel Tank Gals. | Engine Oil Refill Qts. ① | Transmission Oil 3 Speed Pints | 4 Speed Pints | Auto. Trans. Qts. ㉒ | Transfer Case Pints | Rear Axle Oil Pints |
|---|---|---|---|---|---|---|---|---|---|---|---|---|---|
| | C20/2500 | 6-250 | 14.4 | 14.4 | 15 | 195 | ⑪ | 4 | — | 8 | ⑫ | — | 5.4 |
| | | 6-292 | 15.2 | 15.6 | 15 | 195 | ⑪ | 5 | — | 8 | ⑫ | — | 5.4 |
| | | V8-305 | 17.2 | 17.2 | 15 | 195 | ⑪ | 4 | — | 8 | ⑫ | — | 5.4 |
| | | V8-350 | 17.2 | 17.2 | 15 | 195 | ⑪ | 4 | — | 8 | ⑫ | — | 5.4 |
| | | V8-379 ㉔ | 24.8 | 24.8 | 15 | 195 | ⑱ | 7 ㉓ | — | 8 ⑳ | ⑫ | — | 5.4 |
| | | V8-454 | 21.6 | 24.8 | 15 | 195 | ⑪ | 6 | — | 8 | ⑫ | — | 5.4 |
| | G20/2500 | 6-250 | 14.4 | 14.8 | 15 | 195 | 22 | 4 | 3 | 8 | ⑫ | — | 4.2 |
| | | V8-305 | 16.8 | 17.2 | 15 | 195 | 22 | 4 | — | 8 | ⑫ | — | 4.2 |
| | | V8-350 | 16.8 | 16.8 | 15 | 195 | 22 | 4 | — | — | ⑫ | — | 4.2 |
| | | V8-379 ㉔ | 25.2 | 25.2 | 15 | 195 | 22 | 7 ㉓ | — | 8 | ⑫ | — | 4.2 |
| | K20/2500 | 6-292 | 15.2 | 15.6 | 15 | 195 | ⑪ | 5 | — | 8 | ⑫ | ⑨ | 5.4 ⑩ |
| | | V8-350 | 17.2 | 17.2 | 15 | 195 | ⑪ | 4 | — | 8 | ⑫ | ⑨ | 5.4 ⑩ |
| | | V8-379 ㉔ | 24.8 | 24.8 | 15 | 195 | ⑲ | 7 ㉓ | — | 8 ⑳ | ⑫ | ⑨ | 5.4 ⑩ |
| | P20/2500 | 6-292 | 14 | — | 15 | 195 | 40 | 5 | — | 8 | — | — | 5.4 |
| | | V8-350 | 15.6 | — | 15 | 195 | 40 | 4 | — | 8 | ⑫ | — | 5.4 |
| | | V8-379 ㉔ | 24.8 | — | 15 | 195 | 40 | 7 ㉓ | — | 8 | ⑫ | — | 5.4 |
| | C30/3500 | 6-292 | 15.2 | 15.6 | 15 | 195 | 20 | 5 | — | 8 | ⑫ | — | ⑭ |
| | | V8-350 | 17.2 | 17.2 | 15 | 195 | 20 | 4 | — | 8 | ⑫ | — | ⑭ |
| | | V8-379 ㉔ | 24.8 | 25.2 | 15 | 195 | 20 | 7 ㉓ | — | 8 | ⑫ | — | ⑭ |
| | G30/3500 | 6-250 | 14.4 | 14.8 | 15 | 195 | 22 | 4 | 3 | — | ⑫ | — | ⑮ |
| | | V8-350 | 17.2 | 16.8 | 15 | 195 | 22 | 4 | — | 8 | ⑫ | — | ⑮ |
| | | V8-379 ㉔ | 24.8 | 24.8 | 15 | 195 | 22 | 7 ㉓ | — | 8 | ⑫ | — | ⑮ |
| | K30/3500 | 6-292 | 15.2 | 15.6 | 15 | 195 | 20 | 5 | — | 8 | ⑫ | ⑨ | ⑩ ⑭ |
| | | V8-350 | 17.2 | 17.2 | 15 | 195 | 20 | 4 | — | 8 | ⑫ | ⑨ | ⑩ ⑭ |
| | | V8-379 ㉔ | 24.8 | 25.2 | 15 | 195 | 20 | 7 ㉓ | — | 8 | ⑫ | ⑨ | ⑩ ⑭ |
| | | V8-454 | 21.6 | 24.8 | 15 | 195 | 20 | 6 | — | 8 | ⑫ | ⑨ | ⑩ ⑭ |
| | P30/3500 ⑯ | 6-292 | 14.0 | — | 15 | 195 | 40 | 5 | — | 8 | ⑫ | — | ㉑ |
| | | V8-350 | 15.6 | — | 15 | 195 | 40 | 4 | — | 8 | ⑫ | — | ㉑ |
| | | V8-379 ㉔ | 24.8 | — | 15 | 195 | 40 | 7 ㉓ | — | 8 | ⑫ | — | ㉑ |
| | P30/3500 ⑲ | V8-379 ㉔ | 27.6 | — | 15 | 195 | 40 | 7 ㉓ | — | — | ⑫ | — | ㉑ |
| | | V8-454 | 22.8 | — | 15 | 195 | 40 | 6 | — | — | ⑫ | — | ㉑ |
| 1985–86 | ② | V6-262 | 13.1 | 13.1 | 15 | 195 | 17.7 | 4 ㉓ | — | — | ㉗ | — | 3.5 |
| | | V8-305 | 15.6 | 15.6 | 15 | 195 | ㉘ | 5 ㉓ | — | — | ㉗ | — | 3.5 |
| | C10/1500 | V6-262 | 13.6 | 13.6 | 15 | 195 | ③④ | 5 ㉓ | 3 | 8 ⑳ | ⑫ | — | 4.2 |
| | | V8-305 | 17.2 | 17.2 | 15 | 195 | ③④ | 5 ㉓ | 3 | 8 ⑳ | ⑫ | — | 4.2 |
| | | V8-350 | 17.2 | 17.2 | 15 | 195 | ③④ | 5 ㉓ | — | 8 ⑳ | ⑫ | — | 4.2 |
| | | V8-379 ㉔ | 24.8 | 24.8 | 15 | 195 | ⑦ | 7 ㉓ | — | 8 ⑳ | ⑫ | — | 4.2 |
| | G10/1500 | V6-262 | 13.6 | 13.6 | 15 | 195 | 22 | 5 ㉓ | 3 | — | ⑫ | — | 4.2 |
| | | V8-305 | 16.8 | 16.8 | 15 | 195 | 22 | 5 ㉓ | 3 | 8 ⑳ | ⑫ | — | 4.2 |
| | | V8-350 | 16.8 | 16.8 | 15 | 195 | 22 | 5 ㉓ | — | — | ⑫ | — | 4.2 |
| | K10/1500 | V6-262 | 13.6 | 13.6 | 15 | 195 | ③④ | 5 ㉓ | — | 8 ⑳ | ⑫ | ⑨ | 4.2 ⑩ |
| | | V8-305 | 17.2 | 17.2 | 15 | 195 | ③④ | 5 ㉓ | — | 8 ⑳ | ⑫ | ⑨ | 4.2 ⑩ |
| | | V8-350 | 17.2 | 17.2 | 15 | 195 | ③④ | 5 ㉓ | — | 8 ⑳ | ⑫ | ⑨ | 4.2 ⑩ |
| | | V8-379 ㉔ | 24.8 | 24.8 | 15 | 195 | ⑦ | 7 ㉓ | — | 8 ⑳ | ⑫ | ⑨ | 4.2 ⑩ |

## COOLING SYSTEM & CAPACITY DATA—Continued

| Year | Model | Engine | Cooling Capacity, Qts. Less A/C | Cooling Capacity, Qts. With A/C | Radiator Cap Relief Pressure, Lbs. | Thermo. Opening Temp. | Fuel Tank Gals. | Engine Oil Refill Qts. ① | 3 Speed Pints | 4 Speed Pints | Auto. Trans. Qts. ㉒ | Transfer Case Pints | Rear Axle Oil Pints |
|---|---|---|---|---|---|---|---|---|---|---|---|---|---|
|  | C20/2500 | V6-262 | 13.6 | 13.6 | 15 | 195 | ⑪ | 5 ㉓ | — | 8 | ⑫ | — | 5.4 |
|  |  | 6-292 | 15.2 | 15.6 | 15 | 195 | ⑪ | 6 ㉓ | — | 8 | ⑫ | — | 5.4 |
|  |  | V8-305 | 17.2 | 17.2 | 15 | 195 | ⑪ | 5 ㉓ | — | 8 | ⑫ | — | 5.4 |
|  |  | V8-350 | 17.2 | 17.2 | 15 | 195 | ⑪ | 5 ㉓ | — | 8 | ⑫ | — | 5.4 |
|  |  | V8-379 ㉔ | 24.8 | 24.8 | 15 | 195 | ⑲ | 7 ㉓ | — | 8 | ⑫ | — | 5.4 |
|  |  | V8-454 | 21.6 | 24.8 | 15 | 195 | ⑪ | 7 ㉓ | — | 8 | ⑫ | — | 5.4 |
|  | G20/2500 | V6-262 | 13.6 | 13.6 | 15 | 195 | 22 | 5 ㉓ | 3 | — | ⑫ | — | 4.2 |
|  |  | V8-305 | 16.8 | 17.2 | 15 | 195 | 22 | 5 ㉓ | — | 8 ⑳ | ⑫ | — | 4.2 |
|  |  | V8-350 | 16.8 | 17.2 | 15 | 195 | 22 | 5 ㉓ | — | — | ⑫ | — | 4.2 |
|  |  | V8-379 ㉔ | 25.2 | 25.2 | 15 | 195 | 22 | 7 ㉓ | — | 8 ⑳ | ⑫ | — | 4.2 |
|  | K20/2500 | 6-292 | 15.2 | 15.6 | 15 | 195 | ⑪ | 6 ㉓ | — | 8 ⑳ | ⑫ | ⑨ | 5.4 ⑩ |
|  |  | V8-350 | 17.2 | 17.2 | 15 | 195 | ⑪ | 5 ㉓ | — | 8 ⑳ | ⑫ | ⑨ | 5.4 ⑩ |
|  |  | V8-379 ㉔ | 24.8 | 24.8 | 15 | 195 | ⑲ | 7 ㉓ | — | 8 ⑳ | ⑫ | ⑨ | 5.4 ⑩ |
|  | P20/2500 | 6-292 | 14.0 | 14.0 | 15 | 195 | 40 | 5 ㉓ | — | 8 | ⑫ | — | 5.4 |
|  |  | V8-350 | 16.0 | 16.0 | 15 | 195 | 40 | 5 ㉓ | — | 8 | ⑫ | — | 5.4 |
|  |  | V8-379 ㉔ | 24.8 | — | 15 | 195 | 40 | 7 ㉓ | — | 8 | ⑫ | — | 5.4 |
|  | C30/3500 | 6-292 | 15.2 | 15.6 | 15 | 195 | 20 | 6 ㉓ | — | 8 | ⑫ | — | ⑭ |
|  |  | V8-350 | 17.2 | 17.2 | 15 | 195 | 20 | 5 ㉓ | — | 8 | ⑫ | — | ⑭ |
|  |  | V8-379 ㉔ | 24.8 | 24.8 | 15 | 195 | 20 | 7 ㉓ | — | 8 | ⑫ | — | ⑭ |
|  |  | V8-454 | 21.6 | 21.6 | 15 | 195 | 20 | 7 ㉓ | — | 8 | ⑫ | — | ⑭ |
|  | G30/3500 | V6-262 | 13.6 | 13.6 | 15 | 195 | 22 | 5 ㉓ | — | — | ⑫ | — | ⑮ |
|  |  | V8-350 | 17.2 | 17.2 | 15 | 195 | 22 | 5 ㉓ | — | — | ⑫ | — | ⑮ |
|  |  | V8-379 ㉔ | 24.8 | 24.8 | 15 | 195 | 22 | 7 ㉓ | — | — | ⑫ | — | ⑮ |
|  | K30/3500 | 6-292 | 15.2 | 15.2 | 15 | 195 | 20 | 6 ㉓ | — | 8 | ⑫ | ⑨ | ⑩ ⑭ |
|  |  | V8-350 | 17.2 | 17.2 | 15 | 195 | 20 | 6 ㉓ | — | 8 | ⑫ | ⑨ | ⑩ ⑭ |
|  |  | V8-379 ㉔ | 24.8 | 24.8 | 15 | 195 | 20 | 7 ㉓ | — | 8 | ⑫ | ⑨ | ⑩ ⑭ |
|  |  | V8-454 | 21.6 | 24.8 | 15 | 195 | 20 | 7 ㉓ | — | 8 | ⑫ | ⑨ | ⑩ ⑭ |
|  | P30/3500 ⑯ | 6-292 | 14.0 | 14.0 | 15 | 195 | 40 | 5 ㉓ | — | 8 | ⑫ | — | ㉑ |
|  |  | V8-350 | 16.0 | 16.0 | 15 | 195 | 40 | 5 ㉓ | — | 8 | ⑫ | — | ㉑ |
|  |  | V8-379 ㉔ | 24.8 | — | 15 | 195 | 40 | 7 ㉓ | — | 8 | ⑫ | — | ㉑ |
|  | P30/3500 ⑱ | V8-379 ㉔ | 28.0 | — | 15 | 195 | 40 | 7 ㉓ | — | — | ⑫ | — | ㉑ |
|  |  | V8-454 | 22.8 | — | 15 | 195 | 40 | 7 ㉓ | — | — | ⑫ | — | ㉑ |
| 1987 | ② | V6-262 | 13.2 | 13.2 | 15 | 195 | 17.7 | 4 ㉓ | — | — | ㉗ | — | 3.5 |
|  |  | V8-305 | 15.6 | 15.6 | 15 | 195 | ㉘ | 5 ㉓ | — | — | ㉗ | — | 3.5 |
|  | G-10/1500 | V6-262 | 11 | 11 | 15 | 195 | ㉚ | 5 ㉓ | 3.2 | 8.4 | ㉞ | — | ㊱ |
|  |  | V8-305 | 17 | 17 | 15 | 195 | ㉚ | 5 ㉓ | 3.2 | 8.4 | ㉞ | — | ㊱ |
|  |  | V8-350 | 17 | 17 | 15 | 195 | ㉚ | 5 ㉓ | — | 8.4 | ㉞ | — | ㊱ |
|  | R-10/1500 | V6-262 | 10.9 | 10.9 | 15 | 195 | ㉜ | 5 ㉓ | 3.2 | 8.4 | ㉞ | — | ㊲ |
|  |  | V8-305 | 17.5 | 17.5 | 15 | 195 | ㉝ | 5 ㉓ | — | 8.4 | ㉞ | — | ㊲ |
|  |  | V8-350 | 17.5 | 17.5 | 15 | 195 | ㉝ | 5 ㉓ | — | 8.4 | ㉞ | — | ㊲ |
|  |  | V8-379 ㉔ | 25 | 25 | 15 | 195 | ㉝ | 7 ㉓ | — | 8.4 | ㉞ | — | ㊲ |
|  | V-10/1500 | V6-262 | 10.9 | 10.9 | 15 | 195 | ㉜ | 5 ㉓ | — | 8.4 | ㉞ | 10 | ㊲ |
|  |  | V8-305 | 17.5 | 17.5 | 15 | 195 | ㉝ | 5 ㉓ | — | 8.4 | ㉞ | 10 | ㊲ |
|  |  | V8-350 | 17.5 | 17.5 | 15 | 195 | ㉝ | 5 ㉓ | — | 8.4 | ㉞ | 10 | ㊲ |
|  |  | V8-379 ㉔ | 25 | 25 | 15 | 195 | ㉝ | 7 ㉓ | — | 8.4 | ㉞ | 10 | ㊲ |
|  | G-20/2500 | V6-262 | 11 | 11 | 15 | 195 | ㉚ | 5 ㉓ | 3.2 | 8.4 | ㉞ | — | ㊱ |
|  |  | V8-305 | 17 | 17 | 15 | 195 | ㉚ | 5 ㉓ | — | 8.4 | ㉞ | — | ㊱ |
|  |  | V8-350 | 17 | 17 | 15 | 195 | ㉚ | 5 ㉓ | — | 8.4 | ㉞ | — | ㊱ |
|  |  | V8-379 ㉔ | ㉙ | ㉙ | 15 | 195 | ㉚ | 7 ㉓ | — | 8.4 | ㉞ | — | ㊱ |

## COOLING SYSTEM & CAPACITY DATA—Continued

| Year | Model | Engine | Cooling Capacity, Qts. Less A/C | Cooling Capacity, Qts. With A/C | Radiator Cap Relief Pressure, Lbs. | Thermo. Opening Temp. | Fuel Tank Gals. | Engine Oil Refill Qts. ① | 3 Speed Pints | 4 Speed Pints | Auto. Trans. Qts. ㉒ | Transfer Case Pints | Rear Axle Oil Pints |
|---|---|---|---|---|---|---|---|---|---|---|---|---|---|
|  | P-20/2500 | 6-292 | 13.8 | 13.8 | 15 | 195 | 40 | 6㉓ | — | 8.4 | ㉞ | — | ㉟ |
|  |  | V8-350 | 15.5 | 15.5 | 15 | 195 | 40 | 5㉓ | — | 8.4 | ㉞ | — | ㉟ |
|  |  | V8-379㉔ | 25 | 25 | 15 | 195 | 40 | 7㉓ | — | 8.4 | ㉞ | — | ㉟ |
|  | R20/2500 | V6-262 | 10.9 | 10.9 | 15 | 195 | ㉜ | 5㉓ | — | 8.4 | ㉞ | — | ㊲ |
|  |  | V8-305 | 17.5 | 17.5 | 15 | 195 | ㉝ | 5㉓ | — | 8.4 | ㉞ | — | ㊲ |
|  |  | V8-350 | 17.5 | 17.5 | 15 | 195 | ㉝ | 5㉓ | — | 8.4 | ㉞ | — | ㊲ |
|  |  | V8-379㉔ | 25 | 25 | 15 | 195 | ㉝ | 7㉓ | — | 8.4 | ㉞ | — | ㊲ |
|  |  | V8-454 | 23 | 24.5 | 15 | 195 | ㉛ | 6㉓ | — | 8.4 | ㉞ | — | ㊲ |
|  | V20/2500 | 6-292 | 15.2 | 15.6 | 15 | 195 | ⑪ | 6㉓ | — | — | ㉞ | 10 | ㊲ |
|  |  | V8-350 | 17.5 | 17.5 | 15 | 195 | ㉝ | 5㉓ | — | 8.4 | ㉞ | 10 | ㊲ |
|  |  | V8-379㉔ | 25 | 25 | 15 | 195 | ㉝ | 7㉓ | — | 8.4 | ㉞ | 10 | ㊲ |
|  | G-30/3500 | V6-262 | 11 | 11 | 15 | 195 | ㉚ | 5㉓ | — | — | ㉞ | — | ㊱ |
|  |  | V8-350 | 17 | 17 | 15 | 195 | ㉚ | 5㉓ | — | — | ㉞ | — | ㊱ |
|  |  | V8-379㉔ | ㉙ | ㉙ | 15 | 195 | ㉚ | 7㉓ | — | — | ㉞ | — | ㊱ |
|  | P-30/3500 | 6-292 | 13.8 | 13.8 | 15 | 195 | 40 | 6㉓ | — | 8.4 | ㉞ | — | ㉟ |
|  |  | V8-350 | 15.5 | 15.5 | 15 | 195 | 40 | 5㉓ | — | 8.4 | ㉞ | — | ㉟ |
|  |  | V8-379㉔ | 25 | 25 | 15 | 195 | 40 | 7㉓ | — | 8.4 | ㉞ | — | ㉟ |
|  |  | V8-454 | 22.5 | 22.5 | 15 | 195 | 40 | 7㉓ | — | 8.4 | ㉞ | — | ㉟ |
|  | P-30/3500 | V8-379㉔ | 24.7 | 24.7 | 15 | 195 | ㉘ | 7㉓ | — | — | ㉞ | — | ㉟ |
|  |  | V8-454 | 22.5 | 22.5 | 15 | 195 | ㉘ | 7㉓ | — | — | ㉞ | — | ㉟ |
|  | R30/3500 | 6-292 | 15.2 | 15.6 | 15 | 195 | 20 | 6㉓ | — | 8.4 | ㉞ | — | ㊲ |
|  |  | V8-350 | 17.5 | 17.5 | 15 | 195 | ㉝ | 5㉓ | — | 8.4 | ㉞ | — | ㊲ |
|  |  | V8-379㉔ | 25 | 25 | 15 | 195 | ㉝ | 7㉓ | — | 8.4 | ㉞ | — | ㊲ |
|  |  | V8-454 | 23 | 24.5 | 15 | 195 | ㉛ | 6㉓ | — | 8.4 | ㉞ | — | ㊲ |
|  | V30/3500 | 6-292 | 15.2 | 15.6 | 15 | 195 | 20 | 6㉓ | — | 8.4 | ㉞ | 10 | ㊲ |
|  |  | V8-350 | 17.5 | 17.5 | 15 | 195 | ㉝ | 5㉓ | — | 8.4 | ㉞ | 10 | ㊲ |
|  |  | V8-379㉔ | 25 | 25 | 15 | 195 | ㉝ | 7㉓ | — | 8.4 | ㉞ | 10 | ㊲ |
|  |  | V8-454 | 23 | 24.5 | 15 | 195 | ㉛ | 6㉓ | — | 8.4 | ㉞ | 10 | ㊲ |
| 1988 | ② | V6-262 | 12.2 | 12.2 | 15 | 195 | 17.6 | 4㉓ | — | — | ㉗ | — | 3.5 |
|  |  | V8-305 | 16.8 | 16.7 | 15 | 195 | 12.1 | 5㉓ | — | — | ㉗ | — | 3.5 |
|  | G-10/1500 | V6-262 | 10.5 | 10.5 | 15 | 195 | ㉚ | 5㉓ | — | — | ㉞ | — | ㊲ |
|  |  | V8-350 | 17 | 17 | 15 | 195 | ㉚ | 5㉓ | — | — | ㉞ | — | ㊲ |
|  | R-10/1500 | V6-262 | 10.9 | 10.9 | 15 | 195 | ㊵ | 5㉓ | — | 8.4 | ㉞ | — | ㊲ |
|  |  | V8-350 | 17.5 | 17.5 | 15 | 195 | ㊵ | 5㉓ | — | 8.4 | ㉞ | — | ㊲ |
|  |  | V8-379㉔ | 25 | 25 | 15 | 195 | ㊵ | 7㉓ | — | 8.4 | ㉞ | — | ㊲ |
|  | V-10/1500 | V6-262 | 10.9 | 10.9 | 15 | 195 | ㉜ | 5㉓ | — | 8.4 | ㉞ | 10.4 | ㊲ |
|  |  | V8-350 | 17.5 | 17.5 | 15 | 195 | ㉝ | 5㉓ | — | 8.4 | ㉞ | 10.4 | ㊲ |
|  |  | V8-379㉔ | 25 | 25 | 15 | 195 | ㉝ | 7㉓ | — | 8.4 | ㉞ | 10.4 | ㊲ |
|  | G-20/2500 | V6-262 | 10.5 | 10.5 | 15 | 195 | ㉚ | 5㉓ | — | 8.4 | ㉞ | — | ㊲ |
|  |  | V8-350 | 17 | 17 | 15 | 195 | ㉚ | 5㉓ | — | 8.4 | ㉞ | — | ㊲ |
|  |  | V8-379㉔ | ㉙ | ㉙ | 15 | 195 | ㉚ | 7㉓ | — | 8.4 | ㉞ | — | ㊲ |
|  | P-20/2500 | 6-292 | 13.8 | 13.8 | 15 | 195 | 40 | 6㉓ | — | 8.4 | ㉞ | — | ㊲ |
|  |  | V8-350 | 15.5 | 15.5 | 15 | 195 | 40 | 5㉓ | — | 8.4 | ㉞ | — | ㊲ |
|  |  | V8-379㉔ | 25 | 25 | 15 | 195 | 40 | 7㉓ | — | 8.4 | ㉞ | — | ㊲ |
|  | R20/2500 | V6-262 | 10.9 | 10.9 | 15 | 195 | ㊵ | 5㉓ | — | 8.4 | ㉞ | — | ㊲ |
|  |  | V8-350 | 17.5 | 17.5 | 15 | 195 | ㊵ | 5㉓ | — | 8.4 | ㉞ | — | ㊲ |
|  |  | V8-379㉔ | 25 | 25 | 15 | 195 | ㊵ | 7㉓ | — | 8.4 | ㉞ | — | ㊲ |
|  |  | V8-454 | 23 | 24.5 | 15 | 195 | ㊵ | 6㉓ | — | 8.4 | ㉞ | — | ㊲ |
|  | V20/2500 | 6-292 | 13.8 | 13.8 | 15 | 195 | ㉝ | 6㉓ | — | — | ㉞ | 10 | ㊲ |
|  |  | V8-350 | 17.5 | 17.5 | 15 | 195 | ㉝ | 5㉓ | — | 8.4 | ㉞ | 10 | ㊲ |
|  |  | V8-379㉔ | 25 | 25 | 15 | 195 | ㉝ | 7㉓ | — | 8.4 | ㉞ | 10 | ㊲ |

## COOLING SYSTEM & CAPACITY DATA—Continued

| Year | Model | Engine | Cooling Capacity, Qts. Less A/C | Cooling Capacity, Qts. With A/C | Radiator Cap Relief Pressure, Lbs. | Thermo. Opening Temp. | Fuel Tank Gals. | Engine Oil Refill Qts. [1] | Transmission Oil 3 Speed Pints | Transmission Oil 4 Speed Pints | Transmission Oil Auto. Trans. Qts. [22] | Transfer Case Pints | Rear Axle Oil Pints |
|---|---|---|---|---|---|---|---|---|---|---|---|---|---|
| | G-30/3500 | V6-262 | 11 | 11 | 15 | 195 | [30] | 5 [23] | — | — | [34] | — | [37] |
| | | V8-350 | 17 | 17 | 15 | 195 | [30] | 5 [23] | — | — | [34] | — | [37] |
| | | V8-379 [24] | [29] | [29] | 15 | 195 | [30] | 7 [23] | — | — | [34] | — | [37] |
| | P-30/3500 | 6-292 | 13.8 | 13.8 | 15 | 195 | 40 | 6 [23] | — | 8.4 | [34] | — | [37] |
| | | V8-350 | 15.5 | 15.5 | 15 | 195 | 40 | 5 [23] | — | 8.4 | [34] | — | [37] |
| | | V8-379 [24] | 25 | 25 | 15 | 195 | 40 | 7 [23] | — | 8.4 | [34] | — | [37] |
| | | V8-454 | 22.5 | 22.5 | 15 | 195 | 40 | 7 [23] | — | 8.4 | [34] | — | [37] |
| | P-30/3500 | V8-379 [24] | 24.7 | 24.7 | 15 | 195 | [38] | 7 [23] | — | — | [34] | — | [37] |
| | | V8-454 | 22.5 | 22.5 | 15 | 195 | [38] | 7 [23] | — | — | [34] | — | [37] |
| | R30/3500 | 6-292 | 13.8 | 13.8 | 15 | 195 | 20 | 6 [23] | — | 8.4 | [34] | — | [37] |
| | | V8-350 | 17.5 | 18.0 | 15 | 195 | [33] | 5 [23] | — | 8.4 | [34] | — | [37] |
| | | V8-379 [24] | 25 | 25 | 15 | 195 | [33] | 7 [23] | — | 8.4 | [34] | — | [37] |
| | | V8-454 | 23 | 24.5 | 15 | 195 | [31] | 6 [23] | — | 8.4 | [34] | — | [37] |
| | V30/3500 | 6-292 | 13.8 | 13.8 | 15 | 195 | 20 | 6 [23] | — | 8.4 | [34] | 10.4 | [37] |
| | | V8-350 | 17.5 | 18.0 | 15 | 195 | [33] | 5 [23] | — | 8.4 | [34] | 10.4 | [37] |
| | | V8-379 [24] | 25 | 25 | 15 | 195 | [33] | 7 [23] | — | 8.4 | [34] | 10.4 | [37] |
| | | V8-454 | 23 | 24.5 | 15 | 195 | [31] | 6 [23] | — | 8.4 | [34] | 10.4 | [37] |
| 1989 | R10/1500 | V8-350 | 17.2 | — | 15 | 195 | 31 | 5 [23] | — | 8.4 | [34] | — | [37] |
| | | V8-379 | 24.8 | — | 15 | 195 | 32 | 7 [23] | — | 8.4 | [34] | — | [37] |
| | V10/1500 | V8-350 | 17.2 | [47] | 15 | 195 | 31 | 5 [23] | — | 8.4 | [34] | 2.8 | [37] |
| | | V8-379 | 24.8 | 24.8 | 15 | 195 | 32 | 7 [23] | — | 8.4 | [34] | 2.8 | [37] |
| | R20/2500 | 6-292 | 15.2 | — | 15 | 195 | 31 | 6 [23] | — | 8.4 | [34] | — | [37] |
| | | V8-350 | 17.2 | 17.2 | 15 | 195 | 31 | 5 [23] | — | 8.4 | [34] | — | [37] |
| | | V8-454 | 21.6 | [48] | 15 | 195 | 31 | [52] | — | 8.4 | [34] | — | [37] |
| | | V8-379 | 24.8 | 24.8 | 15 | 195 | 32 | 7 [23] | — | 8.4 | [34] | — | [37] |
| | V20/2500 | 6-292 | 15.2 | — | 15 | 195 | 31 | 6 [23] | — | 8.4 | [34] | 2.8 | [37] |
| | | V8-350 | 17.2 | 17.2 | 15 | 195 | 31 | 5 [23] | — | 8.4 | [34] | 2.8 | [37] |
| | | V8-454 | 21.6 | — | 15 | 195 | 31 | [52] | — | 8.4 | [34] | 2.8 | [37] |
| | | V8-379 | 24.8 | 24.8 | 15 | 195 | 32 | 7 [23] | — | 8.4 | [34] | 2.8 | [37] |
| | G10/1500 | V6-262 | 13.6 | 13.2 | 15 | 195 | 22 | 5 [23] | — | 8.4 | [34] | — | [37] |
| | | V8-305 | 16.8 | [46] | 15 | 195 | 22 | 5 [23] | — | 8.4 | [34] | — | [37] |
| | | V8-350 | 16.8 | 16.8 | 15 | 195 | 22 | 5 [23] | — | 8.4 | [34] | — | [37] |
| | | V8-379 | 25.2 | — | 15 | 195 | 22 | 7 [23] | — | 8.4 | [34] | — | [37] |
| | G20/2500 | V6-262 | 13.6 | 13.2 | 15 | 195 | 22 | 5 [23] | — | 8.4 | [34] | — | [37] |
| | | V8-305 | 16.8 | [46] | 15 | 195 | 22 | 5 [23] | — | 8.4 | [34] | — | [37] |
| | | V8-350 | 16.8 | 16.8 | 15 | 195 | 22 | 5 [23] | — | 8.4 | [34] | — | [37] |
| | | V8-379 | 25.2 | [49] | 15 | 195 | 22 | 7 [23] | — | 8.4 | [34] | — | [37] |
| | P20/2500 | 6-292 | 14 | — | 15 | 195 | 40 | 6 [23] | — | 8.4 | [34] | — | [37] |
| | | V8-350 | 16 | 15.6 | 15 | 195 | 40 | 5 [23] | — | 8.4 | [34] | — | [37] |
| | | V8-379 | 24.8 | — | 15 | 195 | 40 | 7 [23] | — | 8.4 | [34] | — | [37] |
| | R30/3500 | 6-292 | 15.2 | [50] | 15 | 195 | 20 | 6 [23] | — | 8.4 | [34] | — | [37] |
| | | V8-350 | 17.2 | 17.2 | 15 | 195 | 20 | 5 [23] | — | 8.4 | [34] | — | [37] |
| | | V8-454 | 21.6 | [48] | 15 | 195 | 20 | [52] | — | 8.4 | [34] | — | [37] |
| | | V8-379 | 24.8 | 24.8 | 15 | 195 | 20 | 7 [23] | — | 8.4 | [34] | — | [37] |
| | V30/3500 | 6-292 | 15.2 | [50] | 15 | 195 | 20 | 6 [23] | — | 8.4 | [34] | 5.2 | [37] |
| | | V8-350 | 17.2 | 17.2 | 15 | 195 | 20 | 5 [23] | — | 8.4 | [34] | 5.2 | [37] |
| | | V8-454 | 21.6 | [51] | 15 | 195 | 20 | [52] | — | 8.4 | [34] | 5.2 | [37] |
| | | V8-379 | 24.8 | 24.8 | 15 | 195 | 20 | 7 [23] | — | 8.4 | [34] | 5.2 | [37] |

## COOLING SYSTEM & CAPACITY DATA—Continued

| Year | Model | Engine | Cooling Capacity, Qts. Less A/C | Cooling Capacity, Qts. With A/C | Radiator Cap Relief Pressure, Lbs. | Thermo. Opening Temp. | Fuel Tank Gals. | Engine Oil Refill Qts. ① | Transmission Oil 3 Speed Pints | Transmission Oil 4 Speed Pints | Transmission Oil Auto. Trans. Qts. ㉒ | Transfer Case Pints | Rear Axle Oil Pints |
|---|---|---|---|---|---|---|---|---|---|---|---|---|---|
| | G30/3500㊴ ㊵ | V6-262 | 13.6 | 13.2 | 15 | 195 | 22 | 5㉓ | — | 8.4 | ㉞ | — | ㊲ |
| | ㊴ ㊶ | V8-350 | 16.8 | 16.8 | 15 | 195 | 22 | 5㉓ | — | 8.4 | ㉞ | — | ㊲ |
| | ㊹ ㊵ ㊶ | V8-350 | 16.8 | 16.8 | 15 | 195 | 22 | 5㉓ | — | 8.4 | ㉞ | — | ㊲ |
| | ㊹ ㊵ ㊶ | V8-454 | 23.2 | — | 15 | 195 | 22 | (52) | — | 8.4 | ㉞ | — | ㊲ |
| | ㊹ ㊵ ㊶ | V8-379 | 24.8 | 24.8 | 15 | 195 | 22 | 7㉓ | — | 8.4 | ㉞ | — | ㊲ |
| | ㊷ ㊺ | V8-350 | 17.2 | 16.8 | 15 | 195 | 22 | 5㉓ | — | 8.4 | ㉞ | — | ㊲ |
| | ㊷ ㊺ | V8-379 | 24.8 | 24.8 | 15 | 195 | 22 | 7㉓ | — | 8.4 | ㉞ | — | ㊲ |
| | P30/3500⑯ | 6-292 | 14 | — | 15 | 195 | 40 | 6㉓ | — | 8.4 | ㉞ | — | ㊲ |
| | ⑯ | V8-350 | 16 | 15.6 | 15 | 195 | 40 | 5㉓ | — | 8.4 | ㉞ | — | ㊲ |
| | ⑯ | V8-379 | 24.8 | — | 15 | 195 | 40 | 7㉓ | — | 8.4 | ㉞ | — | ㊲ |
| | ⑱ | V8-454 | 22.8 | — | 15 | 195 | 40 | (52) | — | 8.4 | ㉞ | — | ㊲ |
| | ⑱ | V8-379 | 28 | — | 15 | 195 | 40 | 7㉓ | — | 8.4 | ㉞ | — | ㊲ |

①—Add one quart with filter change.
②—Caballero & El Camino.
③—Exc. Suburban, Jimmy & Blazer, 20 gals.; Suburban, Jimmy & Blazer, 25 gals.
④—Chassis cab, 16 gals.
⑤—Exc. Muncie, 3 pts.; Muncie, 4 pts.
⑥—THM 350, 10 qts.; THM 400, 475, 11 qts.
⑦—Exc. Suburban, Jimmy & Blazer, 20 gals.; Suburban, Jimmy & Blazer, 27 gals.
⑧—With 8½ inch ring gear, 4.2 pts.; with 8⅞ inch ring gear, 3.5 pts.
⑨—New Process 203, 8.2 pts.; New Process 205, 5.2 pts.; New Process 208, 10 pts.
⑩—Front axle, 5.0 pts.
⑪—Exc. Suburban, 20 gals.; Suburban, 25 gals.
⑫—THM 350C, 10 qts.; THM 400, 11 qts.; THM 700-R4, 11.5 qts.; THM 475, 9.5 qts.
⑬—Exc. heavy duty cooling, 16.8 qts.; heavy duty cooling, 17.2 qts.
⑭—Less dual rear wheels, 5.4 pts.; with dual rear wheels, 7.2 pts.
⑮—Less dual rear wheels, 5.4 pts.; with dual rear wheels and 9¾ inch ring gear, 6.0 pts.; with dual rear wheels and 10½ inch ring gear, 7.2 pts.
⑯—Exc. motor home.
⑰—With 10½ inch ring gear, 5.4 pts.; with 12¼ inch ring gear, 14.0 pts.
⑱—Motor home.
⑲—Exc. Suburban, 20 gals; Suburban, 27 gals.
⑳—With overdrive, 7.5 pts.
㉑—With 10½ inch ring gear, 5.4 pts.; with 12 inch ring gear, 14 pts.
㉒—Approximate, make final check with dipstick.
㉓—Includes filter.
㉔—Diesel engine.
㉕—Exc. Step van, 6 qts.; Step van, 4 qts.
㉖—THM 200, 5 qts.; THM 350, 10 qts.
㉗—THM 200C, 9.5 qts.; THM 200-4R, 11 qts.; THM 250C, 10.5 qts.; THM 350C, 10 qts.; THM 700-R4, 11.5 qts.
㉘—Standard, 18.1 gals.; optional, 22 gals.
㉙—VIN code C, 24 qts.; VIN code J, 25.5 qts.
㉚—Standard, 22 gals.; optional, 33 gals.
㉛—Pickups: standard, 20 gals.; optional, 40 gals. Exc. Pickup: standard, 27 gals.; optional, 32 or 41 gals.
㉜—Standard, 20 gals.; optional, 32 gals.
㉝—Pickups: standard, 20 gals.; optional, 32 gals. Exc. Pickups: standard, 25 gals.; optional, 31 or 40 gals.
㉞—THM 400/475, 11 qts.; THM 700-R4, 11.5 qts.
㉟—With 10½ inch ring gear, 7.2 pts.; with 12 inch ring gear, 14 pts.
㊱—With 8½ inch ring gear, 4.2 pts.; with 9¾ or 10½ inch ring gear, 5.5 pts.
㊲—With 8½ inch ring gear, 4.2 pts.; with 10½ inch Chevrolet ring gear, 7.2 pts.; with 12 inch ring gear 14 pts.; others, 5.5 pts.
㊳—Standard, 40 gals.; optional, 60 gals.
㊴—Exc. heavy duty chasis
㊵—Van
㊶—Suburban
㊷—Conventional cab
㊸—Forward control chasis
㊹—Heavy duty chasis
㊺—Motor home chasis & RV cutaway van
㊻—Manual trans. 17.2; Automatic trans. 16.8
㊼—Manual trans. 17.2; Automatic trans. 18
㊽—Manual trans. 21.6; Automatic trans. 24.4
㊾—Manual trans. 25.2; Automatic trans. 24.8
㊿—Manual trans. 15.6; Automatic trans. 15.2
(51)—Manual trans. 24.8; Automatic trans. 24.4
(52)—V8-454/7.4L VIN N engine, 6 quarts w/filter; 2 wheel drive V8-454/7.4L VIN W engine, 7 quarts w/filter; 4 wheel drive w/V8-454/7.4L VIN W engine, 6 quarts w/filter.

# ELECTRICAL

## INDEX

## FUSE PANEL & FLASHER LOCATION

The fuse panel is located under the left hand side of the instrument panel. The turn signal and hazard warning flashers are located in the fuse panel.

## STARTER REPLACE

A clashing or grinding condition may exist due to improper engagement of the starter to flexplate on some 1985-88 models equipped with V6-262/4.3L, V8-305/5.0L and V8-350/5.7L engines with automatic transmission. To correct this condition, replace the starter drive assembly, with new drive assembly P/N 10456422, which utilizes a stiffer jump spring allowing for proper engagement. During starter drive assembly replacement, all ring gear teeth should be inspected. If three or more consecutive teeth are damaged, the flexplate should be replaced. Use flexplate No. 10128414.

1. Disconnect battery ground cable.
2. Raise and support vehicle.
3. Remove starter to engine brace and heat shields, if equipped.
4. Remove starter mounting bolts and lower starter. Note position of shims, if used.
5. Disconnect wires from solenoids, then remove starter from vehicle.
6. Reverse procedure to install.

Starter whining or a no-start condition on 1982-83 vehicles equipped with V8-379 diesel engines, may be due to insufficient flywheel ring gear to starter pinion clearance. To correct the above mentioned complaint, proceed as follows:

1. Disconnect battery ground cable, then raise and support vehicle.
2. Remove flywheel inspection cover and inspect flywheel teeth for damage. If teeth are excessively worn, replace flywheel.
3. Loosen both starter mounting bolts, then remove outside bolt and shim pack.
4. Measure shim pack thickness. If shim pack is less than .120 inch thick, add shims until total thickness is as stated above. If shim pack is already .120 inch thick, add an additional .040 inch shim to pack. Shim pack thickness should not exceed .160 inch.
5. Reposition shims, install outside mounting bolt, then torque both bolts to 30-40 ft. lbs.
6. Install flywheel inspection cover, then lower vehicle and reconnect battery ground cable.

## HORN SOUNDER & STEERING WHEEL REPLACE

### CABALLERO & EL CAMINO

Scribe alignment marks on steering wheel and shaft to ensure correct installation.

#### Standard Wheel

1. Disconnect battery ground cable.
2. Remove attaching screws on underside of steering wheel.
3. Lifting steering wheel shroud and pull horn wires from cancelling cam tower.
4. Remove steering wheel retaining nut, washer and snap ring.
5. Using a suitable puller, remove steering wheel.
6. Reverse procedure to install.

#### Cushioned Rim Wheel

1. Disconnect battery ground cable.
2. Pry off horn button cap.
3. Remove three spacer screws, spacer, plate and belleville spring.
4. Remove steering wheel retaining nut, washer and snap ring.
5. Using a suitable puller, remove steering wheel.
6. Reverse procedure to install.

### C, K, R & V MODELS; 1987-89 G & P MODELS

Scribe alignment marks on steering wheel and shaft to ensure correct installation.

1. Disconnect battery ground cable.
2. Remove horn button cap.
3. Remove snap ring and steering wheel retaining nut, then if equipped, the horn lead assembly.
4. Using a suitable puller, remove steering wheel.
5. Reverse procedure to install, ensuring turn signal switch is in neutral position.

### 1980-86 G & P MODELS

1. Disconnect battery ground cable.
2. Remove horn button or shroud, then the receiving cup, belleville spring and bushing.

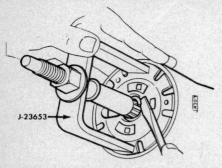

**Fig. 1 Lock plate retaining ring removal. Caballero, El Camino, C, K, R, V & 1986–88 G models**

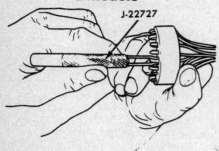

**Fig. 4 Removing wires from connector. 1980–85 G & 1980–88 P models**

3. Remove snap ring and steering wheel retaining nut.
4. Using a suitable puller, remove steering wheel.
5. Reverse procedure to install, ensuring turn signal switch is in neutral position.

## TURN SIGNAL SWITCH
### REPLACE
#### CABALLERO, EL CAMINO, C, K, R, V & 1986–89 G MODELS

1. Disconnect battery cable, then remove steering wheel and column to instrument panel trim cover.
2. On models with telescoping column, remove bumper spacer and snap ring retainer. On all other models, remove cover from lock plate.
3. Using a suitable tool, compress lock plate (horn contact carrier on tilt models) and remove snap ring (C-ring on tilt models), **Fig. 1.**
4. Remove lock plate, cancelling cam, upper bearing preload spring, thrust washer and signal lever.
5. Remove turn signal lever or actuating arm screw, if equipped, or on models with column mounted wiper switch, pull lever straight out of detent. Depress hazard warning button, then unscrew button.
6. Pull connector from bracket and wrap upper part of connector with tape to prevent snagging the wires during removal. On Tilt models, position shifter

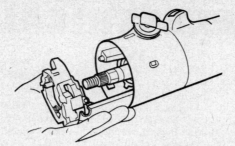

**Fig. 2 Turn signal switch replacement. Caballero, El Camino, C, K, R, V & 1986–8? G models**

housing in "Low" position. Remove harness cover.
7. Remove retaining screws and remove switch, **Fig. 2.**
8. Reverse procedure to install.

### 1980–85 G & 1980–89 P MODELS

1. Remove steering wheel as outlined previously.
2. Remove cancelling cam and spring, then the instrument panel trim plate, if equipped.
3. Disconnect turn signal switch wiring harness at half moon connector.
4. Pry wiring harness protector from column retaining slots, **Fig. 3.**
5. Mark location of each wire in half moon connector, then disconnect wires from connector using tool J-22727 or equivalent, **Fig. 4.**
6. Remove turn signal lever screw and lever.
7. Push hazard warning knob inward, then unscrew knob from plunger.
8. On tilt column models:
   a. If equipped with automatic transmission, remove PRNDL dial screws, then the dial and indicator needle. Remove cap and dial bulb from housing cover.
   b. Unscrew, then remove tilt release lever.
   c. Using tool J-22708 or equivalent, remove turn signal housing cover from housing as shown, **Fig. 5.**
9. On all models, remove turn signal switch mounting screws, then carefully remove switch assembly from column by guiding wiring harness through opening in shift lever housing.
10. Reverse procedure to install.

## IGNITION LOCK
### REPLACE
#### 1980–85 G & 1980–89 P MODELS

1. Disconnect battery ground cable.
2. Position lock cylinder in "Acc" position.
3. Insert a stiff wire into hole in cylinder face, then depress plunger while turning ignition key counterclockwise.
4. Remove lock cylinder from vehicle.
5. Reverse procedure to install.

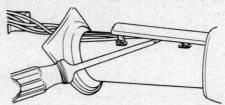

**Fig. 3 Removing wiring harness protector. 1980–85 G & 1980–88 P models**

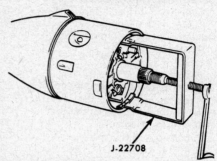

**Fig. 5 Removing turn signal housing cover. 1980–85 G & 1980–88 P models**

### EXC. 1980–85 G & 1980–89 P MODELS

1. Remove steering wheel as outlined previously.
2. Remove turn signal switch as outlined in "Turn Signal Switch, Replace" procedure.
3. Place ignition switch in "Run" position, then remove lock cylinder retaining screw and lock cylinder.
4. To install, rotate lock cylinder to stop, while holding housing as shown, **Fig. 6.** Align cylinder key with keyway in housing, then push lock cylinder assembly into housing until fully seated.
5. Install lock cylinder retaining screw. Torque screw to 40 inch lbs. for standard columns, or 22 inch lbs. for adjustable columns.
6. Install buzzer switch, turn signal switch and steering wheel.

## IGNITION SWITCH
### REPLACE
#### CABALLERO, EL CAMINO, C, K, R, V & 1986–89 G MODELS

The ignition switch is mounted on top of the mast jacket inside the brake pedal support and is actuated by a rod and rack assembly.
1. Disconnect battery ground cable.
2. Disconnect and lower steering column. **On some models, it may be necessary to remove the upper column mounting bracket if it hinders servicing of switch. Use extreme care when lowering steering column to prevent damage to column assembly. Only lower steering column a sufficient distance to perform ignition switch service.**

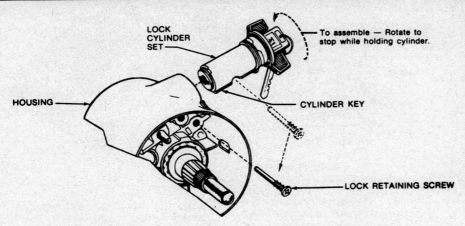

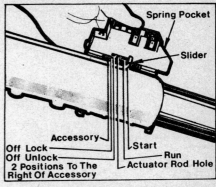

**Fig. 7   Positioning ignition switch**

**Fig. 6   Ignition lock installation. Exc. 1980–85 G & all P models**

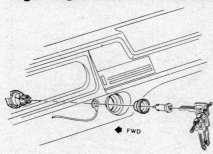

**Fig. 8   Ignition switch replacement. 1980–85 G & 1980–88 P models**

3. On Caballero and El Camino, rotate ignition lock to "Off" unlocked position.
4. On C, K, R and V models, rotate ignition lock to "Off" locked position.
5. If lock cylinder has been removed, pull switch actuator rod up to stop, then pushrod down to second (Caballero or El Camino) or first (C, K, R and V models) detent as shown, **Fig. 7.**
6. Remove column mounted dimmer switch, if equipped, then remove switch retaining screws and switch.
7. Reverse procedure to install, noting the following:
   a. Place gear shift lever in neutral.
   b. Place lock cylinder and switch in positions noted in steps 3 and 4.
   c. Fit actuator rod into hole in switch slider and secure switch with retaining screws, ensuring switch does not move out of detent.
   d. Install and adjust dimmer switch, if equipped, as outlined in "Column Mounted Dimmer Switch, Replace" procedure.
   e. Torque retaining screws to 35 inch lbs., then check switch operation.

## 1980–85 G & 1980–89 P MODELS

1. Disconnect battery ground cable.
2. Remove ignition lock as outlined previously.
3. Remove metallic nut from ignition switch.
4. Pull ignition switch away from instru-

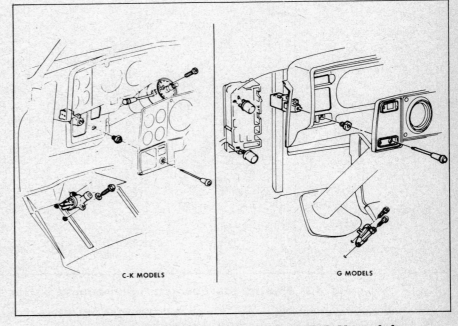

**Fig. 9   Headlamp switch. C, G, K, R & V models**

ment panel, then using a screwdriver or equivalent, unsnap locking tangs from theft resistant connector.
5. Remove ignition switch.
6. To install, snap connector onto switch, position grounding ring, **Fig. 8**, then install ignition switch and metallic nut.
7. Install ignition lock, then connect battery ground cable.

## LIGHT SWITCH
## REPLACE
### C, K, R & V MODELS

1. Disconnect battery ground cable.
2. Reaching behind instrument cluster, depress shaft retaining button and remove switch knob and rod.
3. Remove left side instrument cluster bezel screws, then pull outward on bezel and hold switch retaining nut with wrench, **Fig. 9.**

4. Disconnect wiring connector, then rotate switch counterclockwise and remove from vehicle.
5. Reverse procedure to install.

### G MODELS

1. Disconnect battery ground cable.
2. Reaching from behind instrument panel, depress shaft retaining button and remove switch knob and shaft.
3. Remove switch retaining nut from front of instrument panel, **Fig. 9**, then push switch from panel opening, disconnect wiring connector and remove from vehicle.
4. Reverse procedure to install.

### CABALLERO & EL CAMINO

1. Disconnect battery ground cable.
2. Remove instrument panel bezel.
3. Pull switch knob to "On" position.
4. Remove three screws attaching windshield wiper/light switch mounting

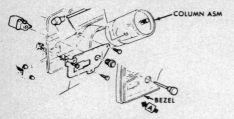

**Fig. 10   Headlamp switch removal. Caballero & El Camino**

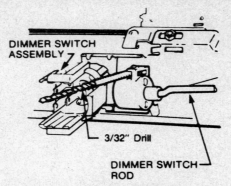

**Fig. 11   Column mounted dimmer switch installation**

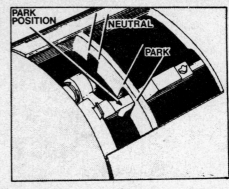

**Fig. 12   Mechanical neutral start system, shown in Park position**

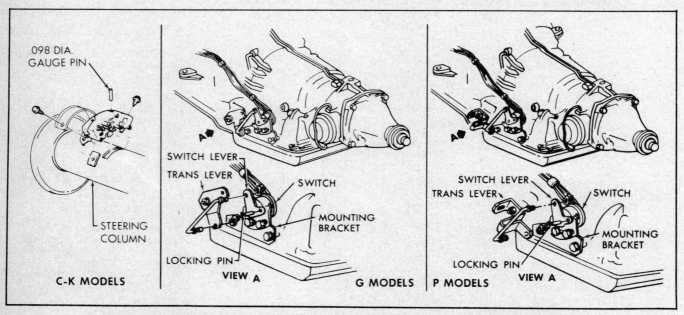

**Fig. 13   Neutral start switch replacement. Series 10–30/1500–3500**

plate to cluster and pull assembly rearward.

5. Depress shaft retainer button on switch and pull knob and shaft assembly from switch, **Fig. 10.**
6. Remove ferrule nut and switch assembly from mounting plate.
7. Reverse procedure to install.

## STOP LIGHT SWITCH
### REPLACE

1. Disconnect wiring connector at switch.
2. Remove retaining nut, if equipped, then unscrew switch from mounting bracket.
3. To install, depress brake pedal and push new switch into clip until shoulder bottoms out.
4. Plug connector onto switch and check operation. Electrical contact should be made when pedal is depressed .500 inch (Caballero and El Camino), 0.45-0.95 inch (G and P models) or 1.0-1.25 inch (C, K, R and

V models) from its fully released position.

## COLUMN MOUNTED DIMMER SWITCH
### REPLACE
#### 1980–87

1. Disconnect battery ground cable.
2. Remove instrument panel lower trim and on models with A/C, remove A/C duct extension at column.
3. Disconnect shift indicator from column and remove toe-plate cover screws.
4. Remove two nuts from instrument panel support bracket studs and lower steering column, resting steering wheel on front seat.
5. Remove dimmer switch retaining screws and the switch. Tape actuator rod to column and separate switch from rod.
6. Reverse procedure to install. To adjust switch, depress dimmer switch

slightly and install a 3/32 inch twist drill to lock the switch to the body, **Fig. 11.** Force switch upward to remove lash between switch and pivot. Torque switch retaining screw to 35 inch lbs. and remove tape from actuator rod. Remove twist drill and check for proper operation.

#### 1988–89

1. Disconnect battery ground cable.
2. Remove steering wheel as described under, "Horn Sounder & Steering Wheel Replace."
3. Disconnect dimmer switch connector, then pry switch up away from steering column.
4. Reverse procedure to install.

## FLOOR MOUNTED DIMMER SWITCH
### REPLACE

1. Disconnect battery ground cable.
2. Fold back carpeting in area of switch,

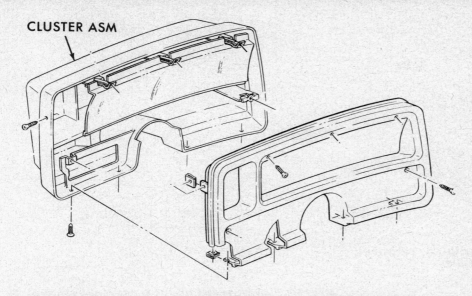

CLUSTER ASM

**Fig. 14 Instrument cluster bezel removal. Caballero & El Camino**

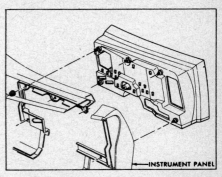

INSTRUMENT PANEL

**Fig. 15 Instrument cluster removal. 1982–88 Caballero & El Camino**

then disconnect electrical connector from switch.
3. Remove switch retaining screws and the switch.
4. Reverse procedure to install.

## NEUTRAL START/MECHANICAL LOCKOUT SYSTEM

On some automatic transmission equipped vehicles, the actuation of the ignition switch is prevented by a mechanical lockout system, **Fig. 12**, which prevents the lock cylinder from rotating when the selector lever is out of Park or Neutral. When the selector lever is in Park or Neutral, the slots in the bowl plate and the finger on the actuator rod align, allowing the finger to pass through the bowl plate, in turn actuating the ignition switch, **Fig. 12**. If the selector lever is in any position other than Park or Neutral, the finger contacts the bowl plate when the lock cylinder is rotated, thereby preventing full travel of the lock cylinder.

## NEUTRAL START SWITCH
## REPLACE

On some automatic transmission equipped vehicles, the back-up light switch is integral with the neutral start switch.

### C, K, R & V MODELS

1. Disconnect battery ground cable.
2. Disconnect electrical connector at switch.
3. Remove switch mounting screws, then the switch.
4. Position shift lever in neutral gate notch.
5. Insert a .098 inch gauge pin into switch gauge hole as shown, **Fig. 13**, then assemble switch to column by

inserting carrier tang into shift tube slot.
6. Install switch mounting screws into retainers. **If retainers strip, they must be replaced.**
7. Remove gauge pin, then position shift lever into Park to shear internal plastic pin in switch.
8. Return shift lever to neutral gate notch, then ensure switch gauge hole will accept .080 inch gauge pin. If not, loosen mounting screws, then rotate switch on column until .098 inch gauge pin can be reinserted into gauge hole.
9. Reconnect electrical connector and battery ground cable.

### G & P MODELS

1. Raise and support vehicle, then disconnect battery ground cable.
2. Disconnect electrical harness from switch.
3. Remove switch to mounting bracket retaining bolts and the switch, **Fig. 13**.
4. Loosely install new switch to mounting bracket, then align .093-.097 inch hole in transmission lever with hole in switch assembly. Insert pin to hold in neutral position, **Fig. 13**.
5. Set transmission lever in neutral position by moving lever counterclockwise to L1 detent, then move clockwise three detents.
6. Install rod into transmission and switch levers and secure with clips.
7. Tighten switch retaining bolts, lower vehicle and check switch for proper operation.

## BACK-UP LIGHT SWITCH
## REPLACE
### MANUAL TRANSMISSION MODELS
#### Column Mounted Type

1. Disconnect battery ground cable.

2. Disconnect switch wiring harness.
3. Remove switch retaining screws and switch.
4. Assemble new switch onto column, then install retaining screws.
5. Reconnect battery ground cable, then check switch for proper operation.

#### Transmission Mounted Type

1. Disconnect battery ground cable.
2. Raise and support vehicle.
3. Disconnect switch wiring harness, then remove switch from transmission.
4. Reverse procedure to install, then check switch for proper operation.

## MODELS WITH NEUTRAL START/MECHANICAL LOCKOUT

1. Disconnect battery ground cable.
2. Disconnect wiring harness connectors at switch.
3. Remove switch retaining screws and switch from mast jacket.
4. Place gear selector in neutral, then align actuator on new switch with hole in shift tube.
5. Position connector side of switch into cutout in lower jacket, then push down on front of switch until tangs snap into holes in jacket. Install retaining screws.
6. Reconnect wiring harness connectors, then place shift lever in Park.
7. Reconnect battery ground cable, then check switch for proper operation.

## INSTRUMENT CLUSTER
## REPLACE
### CABALLERO & EL CAMINO
#### 1980–81

1. Disconnect battery ground cable.
2. Remove clock set stem knob, if equipped.
3. Remove instrument bezel retaining screws, **Fig. 14**.
4. Pull bezel from panel slightly and disconnect rear defogger switch, if equipped.
5. Remove bezel, **Fig. 14**.
6. Remove two screws at transmission selector indicator and lower indicator assembly to disconnect cable.

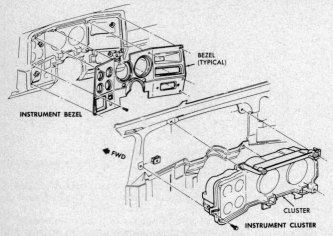

**Fig. 16 Instrument bezel & cluster removal. C, K, R & V models**

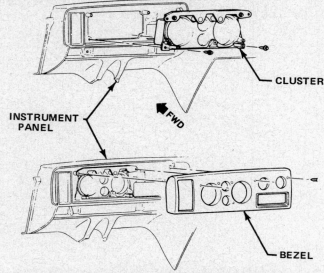

**Fig. 17 Instrument bezel & cluster removal. G models**

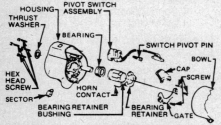

**Fig. 18 Windshield wiper switch replacement. 1983–88 Caballero & El Camino w/standard column**

7. Remove three screws at windshield wiper/light switch mounting plate and pull assembly rearward for access to lower left cluster attaching bolt and nut.
8. Remove nuts attaching cluster to instrument panel.
9. Pull cluster rearward and disconnect the speedometer cable and all wiring and cables.
10. Remove cluster from vehicle.
11. Reverse procedure to install.

### 1982–88

1. Disconnect battery ground cable.
2. Remove radio knobs and clock set stem knob.
3. Remove instrument bezel retaining screws, **Fig. 14**.
4. Pull bezel rearward slightly and disconnect the rear defogger switch and remote control mirror control, if equipped.
5. Remove bezel, **Fig. 14**.
6. Remove speedometer retaining screws, then the speedometer.
7. Remove fuel gauge or tachometer retaining screws, disconnect electrical connectors and remove fuel gauge or tachometer.
8. Remove clock or voltmeter retaining screws, disconnect electrical connectors and remove clock or voltmeter.
9. Disconnect transmission shift indicator cable from steering column.
10. Disconnect all wiring connectors and

speedometer cable, then remove cluster case, **Fig. 15**.
11. Reverse procedure to install.

### C, K, R & V MODELS

1. Disconnect battery ground cable.
2. Remove headlight switch knob as outlined in "Light Switch, Replace" procedure.
3. Remove radio control knobs.
4. Remove steering column cover, if necessary.
5. Remove the eight instrument panel bezel attaching screws, **Fig. 16**, then the bezel.
6. Working from behind instrument cluster, disconnect speedometer cable.
7. Disconnect all lines and electrical connectors that will interfere with cluster removal.
8. Remove instrument cluster attaching screws, **Fig. 16**, then the instrument cluster.
9. Reverse procedure to install.

### G MODELS

1. Disconnect battery ground cable.
2. Working from behind instrument cluster, disconnect speedometer cable.
3. Remove clock set stem knob, if equipped.
4. Remove instrument cluster bezel attaching screws, then the bezel, **Fig. 17**.
5. Remove two lower cluster attaching screws, then pull top of cluster outward.
6. Disconnect instrument panel harness connector from printed circuit, then remove cluster from vehicle.
7. Reverse procedure to install.

### 1988–89 P MODELS

1. Disconnect battery ground cable.
2. Working from behind instrument cluster, disconnect speedometer cable.
3. Remove instrument cluster bezel retaining screws.
4. Disconnect electrical connector and remove instrument cluster.

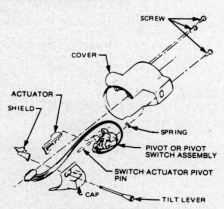

**Fig. 19 Windshield wiper switch replacement. 1983–88 Caballero & El Camino w/tilt steering column**

5. Reverse procedure to install.

# WIPER MOTOR
## REPLACE
### C, K, R & V MODELS

1. Ensure wiper motor is in Park position, then disconnect battery ground cable.
2. Disconnect electrical connector from wiper motor.
3. If washer motor is integral, disconnect hoses from washer pump.
4. Loosen wiper drive rod attaching screws, then remove drive rod from motor crank arm.
5. Remove wiper motor to dash panel attaching screws, then the wiper motor.
6. Reverse procedure to install.

### G MODELS

1. Ensure wiper motor is in Park position, then disconnect battery ground cable.
2. Remove wiper arms from wiper transmission linkage.
3. Remove cowl panel cover attaching screws, then the cowl panel cover.

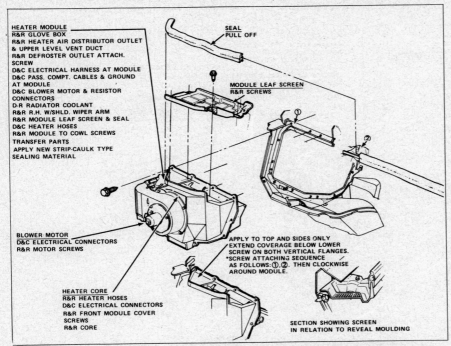

HEATER MODULE
R&R GLOVE BOX
R&R HEATER AIR DISTRIBUTOR OUTLET
& UPPER LEVEL VENT DUCT
R&R DEFROSTER OUTLET ATTACH.
SCREW
D&C ELECTRICAL HARNESS AT MODULE
D&C PASS. COMPT. CABLES & GROUND
AT MODULE
D&C BLOWER MOTOR & RESISTOR
CONNECTORS
D-R RADIATOR COOLANT
R&R R.H. W/SHLD. WIPER ARM
R&R MODULE LEAF SCREEN & SEAL
D&C HEATER HOSES
R&R MODULE TO COWL SCREWS
TRANSFER PARTS
APPLY NEW STRIP-CAULK TYPE
SEALING MATERIAL

SEAL
PULL OFF

MODULE LEAF SCREEN
R&R SCREWS

BLOWER MOTOR
D&C ELECTRICAL CONNECTORS
R&R MOTOR SCREWS

APPLY TO TOP AND SIDES ONLY
EXTEND COVERAGE BELOW LOWER
SCREW ON BOTH VERTICAL FLANGES.
*SCREW ATTACHING SEQUENCE
AS FOLLOWS:①,②. THEN CLOCKWISE
AROUND MODULE.

HEATER CORE
R&R HEATER HOSES
D&C ELECTRICAL CONNECTORS
R&R FRONT MODULE COVER
SCREWS
R&R CORE

SECTION SHOWING SCREEN
IN RELATION TO REVEAL MOULDING

**Fig. 20  Blower motor & heater core. Caballero & El Camino less A/C**

4. Loosen transmission linkage to motor crank arm retaining nuts, then disconnect linkage from crank arm.
5. Disconnect wiper motor electrical connector, then remove left dash defroster duct flex hose to gain access to wiper motor retaining screws.
6. Remove left heater duct to engine cover shroud attaching screw, then pull heater duct downward and out of vehicle.
7. If washer motor is integral, disconnect hoses from washer pump.
8. Remove wiper motor retaining screws, then the wiper motor.
9. Reverse procedure to install.

## CABALLERO & EL CAMINO

1. Raise hood and remove cowl screen or grille.
2. Disconnect wiring and washer hoses.
3. Reaching through cowl opening, loosen transmission drive link attaching nuts to motor crankarm.
4. Disconnect drive link from motor crankarm.
5. Remove motor attaching screws.
6. Remove motor while guiding crankarm through hole.
7. Reverse procedure to install.

## WIPER TRANSMISSION
### REPLACE
### C, K, R & V MODELS

1. Remove wiper arms from pivot shafts.
2. Remove cowl ventilator grille, if necessary.
3. Working from plenum access hole, remove connector link to motor drive arm retaining nuts and washers.
4. Remove transmission pivot shaft as-

sembly to windshield frame attaching screws.
5. Remove wiper linkage and transmission assembly from vehicle.
6. Reverse procedure to install.

## G MODELS

1. Remove wiper arms from pivot shafts.
2. Remove ventilator grille to cowl attaching screws, then the ventilator grille.
3. Working from center of cowl, remove link rod to motor drive attaching nuts, then disconnect link rods from pins.
4. Remove transmission pivot shaft assembly to cowl retaining screws.
5. Remove transmission pivot shaft assembly with link rods through opening in plenum chamber.
6. Reverse procedure to install.

## CABALLERO & EL CAMINO

1. Raise hood and remove cowl vent screen.
2. Remove wiper arms from pivot shafts.
3. Loosen drive link to motor crank arm attaching nuts, then disconnect transmission drive link from crank arm.
4. Remove transmission to body attaching screws.
5. Remove transmission and linkage through opening in cowl.
6. Reverse procedure to install.

## WINDSHIELD WIPER/WASHER SWITCH
### REPLACE
### CABALLERO & EL CAMINO
#### 1980–82

1. Disconnect battery ground cable.

2. Remove instrument panel bezel.
3. Remove screws securing wiper switch mounting plate to cluster and pull assembly rearward.
4. Disconnect electrical connector and remove wiper switch.
5. Reverse procedure to install.

### 1983–88

1. Disconnect battery ground cable.
2. Remove turn signal switch, ignition lock, ignition switch and dimmer switch as outlined previously.
3. Remove parts, then the switch as shown, **Figs. 18 and 19.**
4. Reverse procedure to install.

### 1980–85 C & K MODELS

1. Disconnect battery ground cable.
2. Remove instrument panel bezel screws, then the bezel.
3. Remove switch to instrument panel attaching screws, then pull switch assembly outward and disconnect electrical connector.
4. Remove wiper/washer switch.
5. Reverse procedure to install.

### 1980–85 G MODELS

1. Disconnect battery ground cable.
2. Working from behind left side of instrument panel, disconnect electrical connector from switch, then remove switch to bezel mounting screws.
3. Remove wiper/washer switch.
4. Reverse procedure to install, ensuring ground wires are attached properly to switch.

### 1986–89 C, G, K, R & V MODELS

1. Disconnect battery ground cable.
2. Remove turn signal switch, ignition lock, ignition switch and dimmer switch as previously described.
3. Remove switch pin and the switch.
4. Reverse procedure to install.

## RADIO
### REPLACE

When installing radio, be sure to adjust antenna trimmer for peak reception.

### CABALLERO & EL CAMINO

1. Disconnect battery ground cable.
2. Remove control knobs from control shafts.
3. Remove trim plate attaching screws and trim plate.
4. Disconnect antenna lead and wire connector from radio.
5. Remove stud nut at right side of bracket attachment.
6. Remove control shaft nuts and washers.
7. Remove instrument panel bracket screws and bracket.
8. Remove radio through opening in instrument panel.
9. Reverse procedure to install.

### C, K, R & V MODELS

1. Disconnect battery ground cable.
2. Remove radio control knobs and bezels.

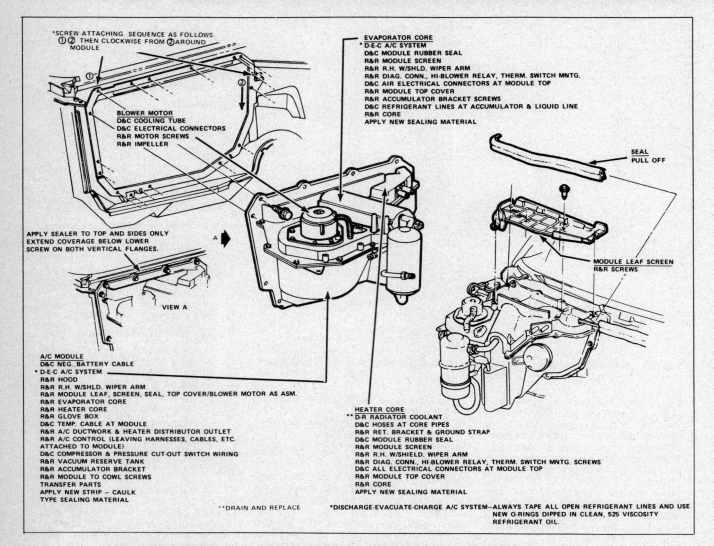

**Fig. 21   Blower motor & heater core. Caballero & El Camino with A/C**

3. Remove nuts and washers from control shafts.
4. On AM radio equipped vehicles, remove radio support bracket stud nut and washer.
5. On AM-FM equipped vehicles, remove radio support bracket to instrument panel attaching screws.
6. Lift upward on rear edge of radio, then push radio forward until control shafts clear instrument panel.
7. Disconnect power feed, speaker and antenna lead, then remove radio.
8. Reverse procedure to install.

## G MODELS
1. Disconnect battery ground cable.
2. Remove engine cover.
3. Remove air cleaner cover and filter element. On some models, it may be necessary to remove the air cleaner stud to gain sufficient clearance to remove radio.
4. Remove control knobs, washers and retaining nuts from control shafts.
5. Remove mounting bracket retaining screw, then the bracket.
6. Push radio forward, then lower as-

sembly until electrical connector and antenna lead can be disconnected.
7. Remove radio from vehicle.
8. Reverse procedure to install.

# BLOWER MOTOR
## REPLACE
### CABALLERO & EL CAMINO
1. Disconnect battery ground cable.
2. Disconnect blower motor lead wire.
3. If equipped with A/C, disconnect cooling tube from motor.
4. Remove blower motor attaching screws, then the blower motor, **Figs. 20 and 21.**
5. Reverse procedure to install.

### C, G, K, R & V MODELS
#### Front Unit
1. Disconnect battery ground cable. On some G model vehicles, it may be necessary to remove the battery, coolant recovery tank and power antenna, if equipped, to gain access to the blower motor.

2. On G models equipped with A/C and diesel engine, proceed as follows:
   a. Remove parking lamp assembly, then the coolant recovery tank.
   b. Remove retaining screws, then the blower insulation through the hood opening.
3. On all models, disconnect blower motor electrical connections.
4. If equipped with A/C, remove blower motor cooling tube.
5. Remove blower motor attaching screws, then pry blower motor from case.
6. Reverse procedure to install.

#### Overhead Unit
1. Disconnect battery ground cable.
2. Remove rear duct drain tube, duct to header bracket and roof panel screws, then rear duct assembly, **Fig. 22.**
3. Disconnect blower motor harness lead and ground wire.
4. While supporting lower case to prevent damage to motor or case assemblies, remove case mounting screws, then lower case from vehicle roof.
5. Remove motor retaining strap, then lift

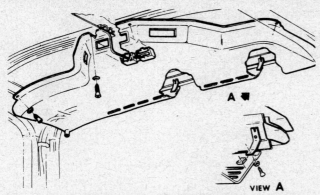

**Fig. 22 Rear duct assembly. C, G, K, R & V models w/overhead system**

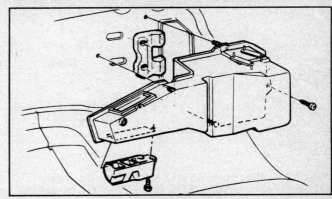

**Fig. 23 Heater distributor assembly. C, K, R & V models less A/C**

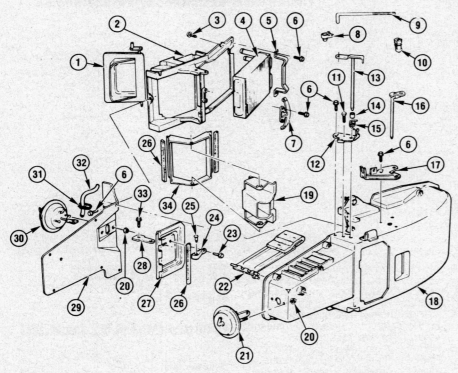

**Fig. 24 A/C & heater assembly. C, K, R & V models**

1. BAFFLE
2. TEMPERATURE VALVE HOUSING
3. SCREW
4. HEATER CORE
5. MOUNTING STRAP
6. SCREW
7. CLAMP
8. CONNECTOR
9. DIVERTER VALVE LINK
10. CONNECTOR
11. SCREW
12. DIVERTER VALVE ADJ. BRACKET
13. PIVOT SHAFT
14. SPACER
15. SPRING
16. PIVOT SHAFT
17. CABLE ADJ. BRACKET
18. CASE
19. BI-LEVEL VALVE
20. NUT
21. DEFROSTER VALVE VACUUM ACTUATOR
22. DEFROSTER VALVE
23. SCREW
24. LINK
25. PIN
26. SEAL
27. DIVERTER VALVE
28. CONNECTOR
29. FRONT CASE PLATE
30. AIR DIST. VACUUM ACTUATOR
31. GROMMET
32. HOSE
33. SCREW
34. SLAVE VALVE YOKE

2. Disconnect heater hoses at core, then plug core tubes to prevent coolant spillage.
3. Working from engine compartment, remove distributor duct stud attaching nuts.
4. Remove glove box and door assembly.
5. Disconnect air-defrost and temperature door cables.
6. Remove floor outlet, then the defroster duct to heater distributor duct attaching screw.
7. Remove heater distributor to dash panel attaching screws, **Fig. 23**.
8. Pull distributor rearward, then disconnect all harnesses that will interfere with distributor removal.
9. Remove heater distributor from vehicle.
10. Remove heater core retaining straps, then the heater core.
11. Reverse procedure to install.

## With A/C

1. Disconnect battery ground cable, then drain cooling system.
2. Disconnect heater hoses at core and plug core tubes.
3. Remove glove box assembly.
4. Remove screws at center duct to selector duct/instrument panel. Remove center upper and lower ducts.
5. Disconnect bowden cable at temperature door.
6. Remove nuts at selector duct studs (projecting through firewall). Remove selector duct to firewall screw.
7. Draw selector duct assembly rearward so core tubes clear firewall. Lower assembly sufficiently to remove vacuum lines and harness connections.
8. Remove selector duct assembly. Disconnect core mounting straps and remove core, **Fig. 24**.
9. Reverse procedure to install.

motor and cage assembly from case. Remove cages by removing shaft retaining nuts.

6. Reverse procedure to install. When installing cages on motor shaft, tension springs must be installed on motor shafts. Cages should be mounted so leading edges of blades face lower evaporator case (thin edge first). After installing blower assembly in case, check to ensure there is no interference with rotating cages.

# HEATER CORE
## REPLACE
### C, K, R & V MODELS
#### Less A/C

1. Disconnect battery ground cable, then drain cooling system.

# CABALLERO & EL CAMINO
## Less A/C

1. Disconnect battery ground cable, then drain cooling system.
2. Disconnect hoses from heater core, then plug outlets to prevent coolant spillage.

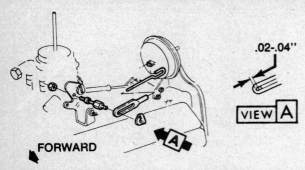

**Fig. 25  Servo unit rod adjustment. 1980 Series 10–30/1500–3500 & 1980–83 Caballero & El Camino**

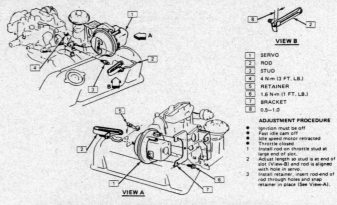

**Fig. 26  Servo unit rod adjustment. 1984 Caballero & El Camino w/V6-231 engine**

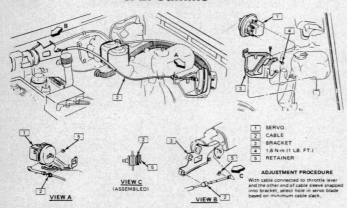

**Fig. 27  Servo unit cable adjustment. 1984 Caballero & El Camino w/V6-229 engine**

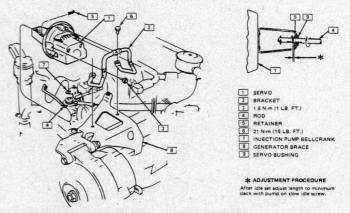

**Fig. 28  Servo unit rod adjustment. 1984 Caballero & El Camino w/V8-350 diesel engine**

3. Disconnect wire connectors, then remove front module cover attaching screws and cover.
4. Remove heater core from module, **Fig. 20.**
5. Reverse procedure to install.

## With A/C

1. Disconnect battery ground cable, then drain cooling system.
2. Disconnect heater hoses at core.
3. Remove retaining bracket and ground strap.
4. Remove module rubber seal and module screen, **Fig. 21.**
5. Remove righthand wiper arm.
6. Remove high blower relay and thermostatic switch mounting screws.
7. Disconnect wire connector at top of module, then remove module top cover.
8. Remove heater core from module.
9. Reverse procedure to install.

## G MODELS

1. Disconnect battery ground cable.
2. Remove coolant recovery tank, and place to side.

3. After placing suitable drain pan under vehicle, disconnect heater hoses at core, plug hose ends, and allow core to drain.
4. Remove heater air distributor duct to air distributor case retaining screws. Remove duct.
5. Remove engine housing cover.
6. Remove upper (at windshield) and all lower instrument panel retaining screws. Remove right lower instrument panel support bracket.
7. Lower steering column. Raise right side of instrument panel, and place on suitable support.
8. Remove air distributor case to defroster duct retaining screw. Remove 2 air distributor to heater case retaining screws.
9. Disconnect temperature door cable. Fold cable away from work area to provide access.
10. Remove air distributor case retaining nuts in engine compartment. Remove retainer screw in vehicle interior.
11. Remove core and case from vehicle as assembly by tilting case assembly rearward at top. Lift case assembly up at same time, until core tubes clear openings in dash.
12. Remove core retaining strap screws and core.
13. Reverse procedure to install, replacing sealer where needed.

# SPEED CONTROLS

## ADJUST

### CABALLERO & EL CAMINO

#### 1980–83

#### Servo Unit Adjustment

Adjust the bead chain cable or rod so that it is as tight as possible without holding the throttle open when the carburetor is set at its lowest idle throttle position. The cable is adjusted by turning the hex portion of servo. The bead chain or cable is adjusted so there is 1/16 inch of lost motion in servo cable. The rod is adjusted by turning link onto rod. With rod hooked through tab, on power unit, turn link onto rod until dimension in **Fig. 25** is obtained, then install link and retainer. This adjustment should be made with ignition off and fast idle cam in off position with throttle completely closed.

When connecting the bead chain or cable (engine stopped) manually set the fast idle cam at its lowest step and connect the chain so that it does not hold the idle screw off the cam. If the chain needs to be cut, cut it three beads beyond the bead that pulls the linkage.

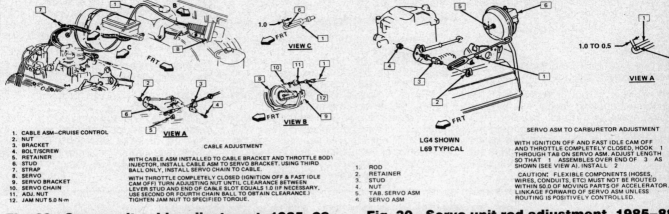

1. CABLE ASM—CRUISE CONTROL
2. NUT
3. BRACKET
4. BOLT/SCREW
5. RETAINER
6. STUD
7. STRAP
8. SERVO
9. SERVO BRACKET
10. SERVO CHAIN
11. ADJ. NUT
12. JAM NUT 5.0 N·m

**CABLE ADJUSTMENT**

WITH CABLE ASM INSTALLED TO CABLE BRACKET AND THROTTLE BODY/ INJECTOR, INSTALL CABLE ASM TO SERVO BRACKET. USING THIRD BALL ONLY, INSTALL SERVO CHAIN TO CABLE.

WITH THROTTLE COMPLETELY CLOSED (IGNITION OFF & FAST IDLE CAM OFF) TURN ADJUSTING NUT UNTIL CLEARANCE BETWEEN LEVER STUD AND END OF CABLE SLOT EQUALS 1.0 (IF NECESSARY, USE SECOND OR FOURTH CHAIN BALL TO OBTAIN CLEARANCE.) TIGHTEN JAM NUT TO SPECIFIED TORQUE.

**Fig. 29  Servo unit cable adjustment. 1985–88 Caballero & El Camino w/V6-262 engine**

LG4 SHOWN
L69 TYPICAL

1. ROD
2. RETAINER
3. STUD
4. NUT
5. TAB. SERVO ASM
6. SERVO ASM

**SERVO ASM TO CARBURETOR ADJUSTMENT**

WITH IGNITION OFF AND FAST IDLE CAM OFF AND THROTTLE COMPLETELY CLOSED, HOOK 1 THROUGH TAB ON SERVO ASM. ADJUST LENGTH SO THAT 1 ASSEMBLES OVER END OF 3 AS SHOWN (SEE VIEW A). INSTALL 2

CAUTION: FLEXIBLE COMPONENTS (HOSES, WIRES, CONDUITS, ETC) MUST NOT BE ROUTED WITHIN 50.0 OF MOVING PARTS OF ACCELERATOR. LINKAGE FORWARD OF SERVO ASM UNLESS ROUTING IS POSITIVELY CONTROLLED.

**Fig. 30  Servo unit rod adjustment. 1985–88 Caballero & El Camino w/V8-305 engine**

## Regulator Unit Adjustment

To remove any difference between engagement and cruising speed, one adjustment is possible. However, no adjustment should be made until the following items have been checked or serviced.
1. Bead chain or cable properly adjusted.
2. All hoses in good condition, properly attached, not leaking, pinched or cracked.
3. Regulator air filter cleaned and properly oiled.
4. Electric and vacuum switches properly adjusted.

## Engagement-Cruising Speed Zeroing

If the cruising speed is lower than the engagement speed, loosen the orifice tube locknut and turn the tube outward; if higher turn the tube inward. Each 1/4 turn will alter the engagement-cruising speed difference one mph. Tighten locknut after adjustment and check the system operation at 50 mph.

## Brake Release Switch

The electric brake switch is actuated when the brake pedal is depressed .38-.64 inch. The vacuum release switch is actuated when brake pedal is moved 5/16 inch on all units.

## 1984–88
### Brake Release Switches

The brake electric and vacuum release switches are both mounted on the brake pedal support bracket and are self-adjusting. If either switch is replaced, pull brake pedal rearward against stop until audible clicks are no longer heard. Release brake pedal, then repeat operation. Release switches are now adjusted.

## Servo Unit Adjustment

Refer to **Figs. 26 through 30** for servo unit adjustments.

## SERIES 10–30/1500–3500
## 1980
### Servo Unit Adjustment

With throttle closed and ignition and fast idle cam off, adjust linkage length by turning link onto rod until dimension shown in **Fig. 25** is obtained. Reinstall link and link retainer.

### Engagement-Cruising Speed Zeroing

The only transducer adjustment possible is engagement-cruising speed zeroing. No adjustment should be performed unless the servo unit and brake release switches are properly adjusted and all vacuum lines are checked for kinks, leaks or punctures.

If cruising speed is lower than engagement speed, loosen orifice tube locknut and turn tube counterclockwise. If cruising speed is greater than engagement speed, turn orifice tube clockwise. Each 1/4 turn of orifice tube will alter engagement-cruising speed approximately one mph. After adjustment is completed, tighten locknut and test system at 55 mph.

### Brake Release Switches

The brake release electrical switch should be adjusted so that the switch contacts are open when the brake pedal is depressed .38-.64 inch.

The brake release vacuum switch should be adjusted so that the valve plunger clears the pedal arm when the arm is moved 1.17-1.36 (less Hydro-Boost) or 1.23-1.49 (with Hydro-Boost) inch.

## 1981–82
### Power Unit Adjustment

With air conditioner off and idle speed solenoid disconnected (if equipped), set curb hot idle speed to 500 RPM, then shut engine off. Unsnap swivel from ball stud, then hold chain taught. Center of swivel should extend 1/8 inch beyond center of ball stud. If not, remove swivel and chain assembly retainer, then position chain into swivel cavities which will give adjustment stated above. Reinstall retainer.

## Engagement-Cruising Speed Zeroing

The only transducer adjustment possible is engagement-cruising speed zeroing. No adjustment should be performed unless the servo unit and brake release switches are properly adjusted and all vacuum lines are checked for kinks, leaks or punctures.

If cruising speed is lower than engagement speed, loosen orifice tube locknut and turn tube counterclockwise. If cruising speed is greater than engagement speed, turn orifice tube clockwise. Each 1/4 turn of orifice tube will alter engagement-cruising speed approximately one mph. After adjustment is completed, tighten locknut and test system at 50 mph.

## Brake Release Switch & Valve

With brake pedal fully depressed, push switch and valve fully forward against bracket or arm. Pull pedal rearward with a force of 15-20 lbs. to automatically adjust switch and valve.

## Clutch Release Switch & Valve

With clutch pedal at rest, push switch and valve assembly forward against bracket or arm. Pull pedal rearward with a force of 15-20 lbs. to automatically adjust switch and valve.

## 1983–84
### Servo Unit Adjustment

To adjust servo on six cylinder engines, use second (6-292) or third (6-250) ball on servo chain. With throttle closed and ignition and fast idle off, adjust jam nuts until .040 inch clearance exists between lever pin and cable assembly end slots. Tighten jam nuts.

To adjust servo on V8 gasoline engines, close throttle, then with ignition and fast idle off, adjust rod assembly length to give .007-.015 inch clearance between rod and stud.

To adjust servo on V8 diesel engines, position idle screw against stop, then with engine off, assemble lower end of rod link to throttle lever and upper end to hole closest servo which will provide .040 inch slack minimum.

## Engagement-Cruising Speed Zeroing

There is no provision for engagement-cruising speed zeroing. If cruising speed is too high or low, check vacuum hoses for improper routing, restrictions or leaks and servo linkage for proper adjustment. If cruising speed is still too high or low, replace the electronic controller.

## 1985–89
### Servo Unit Adjustment

To adjust servo on V6 and V8 gasoline engines, close throttle, then with ignition and fast idle off, adjust rod assembly length to give .020-.040 (Exc. C, K, R and V models with V6 engine) or .007-.015 (C, K, R and V models with V6 engine) inch clearance between rod and stud.

To adjust servo on G models with diesel engines, use third ball on servo chain. With ignition off, adjust cable jam nuts until cable sleeve at throttle lever is tight, without holding throttle open. To adjust servo on C, K, R and V models with diesel engines, po-sition idle screw against stop, then with ig-nition off, assemble lower end of rod link to throttle lever and upper end to hole closest servo which will provide .040 inch slack maximum.

## Engagement-Cruising Speed Zeroing

There is no provision for engagement-cruising speed zeroing. If cruising speed is too high or low, check vacuum hoses for improper routing, restrictions or leaks and servo linkage for proper adjustment. If cruising speed re-mains too high or low, replace the elec-tronic controller.

# GASOLINE ENGINE
## INDEX

# ENGINE MOUNTS
## REPLACE

### CABALLERO & EL CAMINO
#### V6-231

1. Raise and support front of vehicle.
2. Support engine at front edge of oil pan, then remove mount to engine at-taching bolts.
3. Raise engine slightly, then remove mount to mount bracket retaining bolt and nut. Remove mount from vehicle.
4. Reverse procedure to install.

### V6-229, 262 & All V8 Engines

1. Remove mount retaining bolt from be-low frame mounting bracket, **Fig. 1.**
2. Raise front of engine and remove mount to engine bolts and mount. On models equipped with V6 engine, the righthand mount may be removed by loosening the through bolt. **Raise en-gine only enough to provide suffi-cient clearance for mount removal. Check for interferance between rear of engine and cowl panel which could result in distributor damage.**
3. Reverse procedure to install.

### SERIES 10–30/1500–3500
#### L-6 Engines

1. Remove engine mount through bolt, **Figs. 2 and 3.**
2. Raise engine, then remove mount to frame bracket attaching bolts and mount. **Raise engine only enough to gain sufficient clearance for re-moval. Check for interference be-tween rear of engine and cowl pan-el.**
3. Install new engine mount to frame bracket, then install and tighten at-taching bolts.

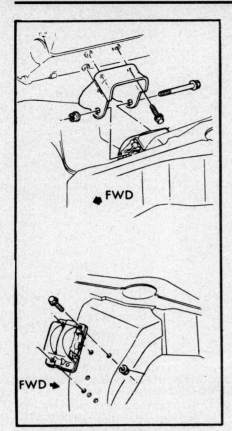

**Fig. 1 Engine mount replacement. Caballero & El Camino w/V6-229, 262 & all V8 engines**

4. Install engine mount through bolt and torque bolt to 30 ft. lbs. On 1988-89 models, torque mount-to-engine/frame bolts to 36 ft. lbs. and through bolt to 85 ft. lbs., or nut to 54 ft. lbs.

### V6 & V8 Engines

1. Working from below frame mounting bracket, remove engine mount through bolt, **Figs. 4 through 7. When replacing right side mount on some models with V6-262 engine it is only necessary to loosen the through bolt.**
2. Raise and support engine, then remove mount attaching bolts and the mount. **Raise engine only enough to gain sufficient clearance for removal. Check for interference between rear of engine and cowl panel.**
3. Install new engine mount to engine, then tighten attaching bolts.
4. Install and tighten engine mount through bolt.

# ENGINE
# REPLACE
## CABALLERO & EL CAMINO
### 1980-84

1. Disconnect battery ground cable and remove air cleaner.

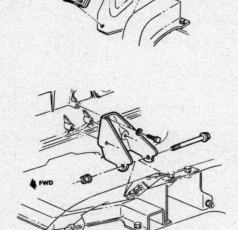

**Fig. 2 Engine mount replacement. C, K, P, R & V models w/inline 6 cylinder engine**

2. Mark position of hinges for reassembly, then remove hood.
3. Drain cooling system, remove radiator hoses, and disconnect heater hoses from engine.
4. On models with A/C, disconnect electrical connector from compressor clutch and ground wire from bracket, remove compressor and secure aside.
5. On V6-231 engines, remove fan blade, pulleys and shroud. On all other engines, remove fan shroud and radiator. On models with automatic transmission, disconnect and plug cooler lines.
6. Remove power steering pump retaining bolts, if equipped, and secure pump aside.
7. Disconnect accelerator linkage at throttle lever and bracket. Disconnect vacuum hoses to body mounted accessories and fuel hoses at fuel pump, then plug fuel hoses.
8. Disconnect battery and chassis ground straps from engine.
9. Disconnect electrical connectors from alternator, distributor or remote mounted coil and all engine mounted switches and accessories.
10. Remove engine harness from retaining clips and secure aside.
11. Raise and support vehicle and drain crankcase.
12. Disconnect exhaust pipes and AIR pipe from manifolds, and remove front exhaust and cruise control brackets, if equipped.
13. Disconnect electrical connectors and battery cable from starter, or remove starter.

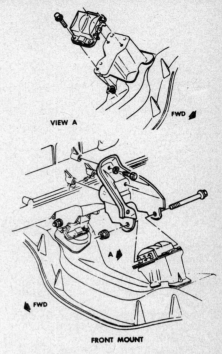

**Fig. 3 Engine mount replacement. G models w/inline 6 cylinder engine**

14. Remove flywheel shield and remove bolts securing torque converter to flex plate, if equipped. Mark position of converter in relation to flex plate for reassembly.
15. Remove motor mount through bolts and bolts securing bellhousing to engine.
16. Lower vehicle and support transmission with suitable floor jack.
17. Attach suitable lifting equipment to engine lifting brackets, raise engine and transmission, and remove motor mount to engine brackets.
18. Separate engine and transmission while supporting transmission with jack. **On automatic transmission models, ensure converter remains with transmission during engine removal and is properly seated prior to engine installation.**
19. Lift and remove engine after disconnecting any remaining harness connectors.
20. Reverse procedure to install.

### 1985-88 V8-305

1. Disconnect battery ground cable, remove air cleaner and drain cooling system.
2. Disconnect radiator and heater hoses, then remove upper fan shroud and fan assembly.
3. Remove power steering pump bracket bolts and secure pump assembly aside.
4. Disconnect electrical connectors to A/C compressor. Remove mounting bolts and secure compressor aside.
5. Disconnect accelerator, cruise control and throttle valve cables.

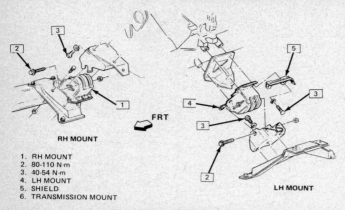

RH MOUNT

1. RH MOUNT
2. 80-110 N·m
3. 40-54 N·m
4. LH MOUNT
5. SHIELD
6. TRANSMISSION MOUNT

FRT

LH MOUNT

**Fig. 4 Engine mount replacement. C, K, R & V models w/V6-262 engine**

RH MOUNT

FRT

LH MOUNT

1. RH MOUNT
2. 90-110 N·m
3. 40-54 N·m
4. LH MOUNT
5. POWER STEERING BRACKET
7. 60-75 N·m

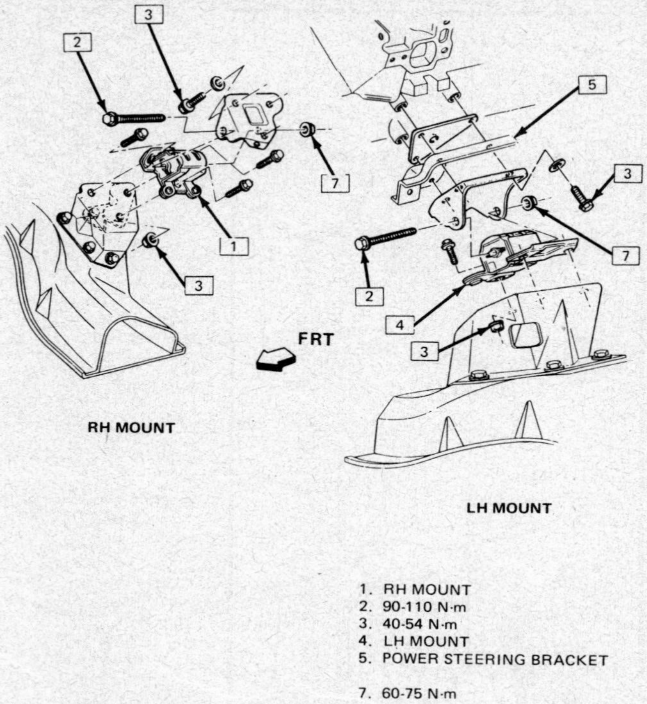

**Fig. 5 Engine mount replacement. G models w/V6-262 engine**

6. Disconnect transmission cooling lines, plug lines and open fittings, then remove radiator.
7. Disconnect C3 system harness connectors, noting position for installation.
8. Remove windshield washer reservoir and disconnect AIR system hose from converter pipe.
9. Disconnect engine harness at bulkhead connector, then disconnect necessary electrical connectors and vacuum hoses, noting position for installation.
10. Mark position of hood hinges, disconnect hood lamp if equipped, then remove hood.
11. Remove distributor cap.
12. Disconnect positive cable from battery and frame, and battery negative cable from retaining brackets.
13. Raise and support vehicle, then remove crossover pipe and catalytic converter as an assembly.
14. Remove flywheel dust shield and torque converter to flywheel bolts.
15. Disconnect and plug fuel supply hose, disconnect torque converter clutch wiring from transmission, and remove transmission cooler lines from clip on oil pan.
16. Remove motor mount through bolts and bolts securing bellhousing to engine, then lower vehicle.
17. Attach suitable lifting equipment, support transmission with suitable jack, then remove engine assembly.
18. Reverse procedure to install.

## 1985—88 V6-262

1. Disconnect battery ground cable, then raise and support vehicle.
2. Disconnect exhaust pipe from manifold, then remove flywheel dust shield.
3. Remove torque converter to flywheel bolts, disconnect cooling lines from transmission, then plug lines and open fittings.
4. Loosen right motor mount through bolt, and remove left through bolt and bolts securing transmission to engine.
5. Disconnect C3 harness connectors from transmission and electrical connector from knock sensor.
6. Disconnect fuel hoses at frame.
7. Remove lower fan shroud.

8. Remove starter motor, then lower vehicle.
9. Disconnect ECM harness connectors from engine mounted connectors, and all other necessary electrical connectors and vacuum hoses, noting position for installation.
10. Remove air cleaner assembly and the upper fan shroud.
11. Disconnect accelerator and throttle valve cables.
12. Drain cooling system, then disconnect radiator and heater hoses.
13. Disconnect necessary electrical connectors, remove A/C compressor and power steering pump mounting bolts, then secure pump and compressor aside.
14. Disconnect and plug transmission cooling lines.
15. Remove fan and pulleys.
16. Disconnect hood lamp electrical connector, mark position of hood hinges and remove hood.
17. Disconnect battery cables from frame and ground straps from rear of each cylinder head.
18. Disconnect AIR converter pipe from manifold and AIR hose from converter pipe.
19. Attach suitable lifting equipment to engine, support transmission and remove engine.
20. Reverse procedure to install.

## SERIES 10—30/1500—3500

### L-6 ENGINES

### C, K, R, V & 1985—89 G Models

1. Disconnect battery ground cable, then drain cooling system.
2. Remove air cleaner.

3. Disconnect accelerator cable and detent cable (automatic transmission models) from carburetor throttle lever.
4. Disconnect all engine wiring that will interfere with engine removal.
5. Disconnect radiator hoses from radiator and heater hoses from engine.
6. Remove radiator attaching bolts, then the radiator.
7. Remove fan and water pump pulley, then disconnect fuel line from fuel pump.
8. Remove hood.
9. Raise and support vehicle, then remove starter motor.
10. Remove flywheel or torque converter splash shield.
11. Disconnect exhaust pipe from exhaust manifold and wire pipe aside.
12. Remove engine mount through bolts.
13. On automatic transmission equipped vehicles, remove torque converter to flex plate attaching bolts.
14. On K and V models, remove strut rods at motor mounts.
15. On all models, support transmission, then remove bellhousing to engine retaining bolts.
16. Lower vehicle.
17. Attach a suitable engine lifting device and remove engine from vehicle.
18. Reverse procedure to install.

## 1980—84 G Models

1. Disconnect battery ground cable, then drain cooling system.
2. Remove engine cover and air cleaner assembly.
3. Evacuate A/C system, then remove A/C compressor, if equipped.
4. Disconnect accelerator linkage, then remove carburetor mounting bolts and carburetor.

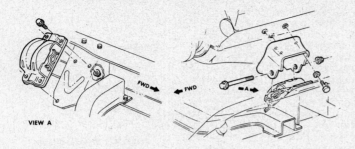

**Fig. 6   Engine mount replacement. C, K, P, R & V models w/V8 engines**

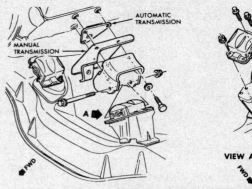

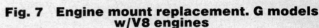

**Fig. 7   Engine mount replacement. G models w/V8 engines**

5. Remove grille and grille cross brace.
6. Remove windshield washer reservoir and A/C vacuum reservoir, if equipped.
7. Disconnect hoses from radiator.
8. On automatic transmission equipped vehicles, disconnect cooling lines from radiator.
9. If equipped with A/C, remove A/C condenser to radiator support attaching bolts, then position condenser aside.
10. Remove radiator to radiator support attaching brackets, then the radiator.
11. Disconnect heater hoses from engine.
12. Disconnect all wiring that will interfere with engine removal.
13. Raise and support vehicle.
14. Disconnect fuel line from fuel pump, then drain crankcase.
15. Remove propeller shaft, then plug transmission housing to prevent fluid leakage.
16. Disconnect exhaust pipe from exhaust manifold.
17. Disconnect shift linkage and speedometer cable from transmission.
18. Remove transmission mount retaining bolts.
19. On manual transmission equipped vehicles, disconnect clutch linkage, then remove clutch cross shaft.
20. Remove engine mount through bolts, then lower vehicle.
21. Attach a suitable engine lifting device, then raise engine and remove right hand engine mount from engine.
22. Remove engine/transmission assembly.
23. Reverse procedure to install.

## V6 ENGINES
### 1980–87 C, K, R & V Models

1. Disconnect battery ground cable, then drain cooling system.
2. Remove air cleaner assembly.
3. Remove accessory drive belts, then the fan and water pump pulley.
4. Disconnect all hoses from engine.
5. If equipped with automatic transmission, disconnect cooling lines from radiator.
6. Remove radiator and fan shroud.
7. Disconnect accelerator linkage and detent cable (automatic transmission models) from carburetor or TBI unit.
8. If equipped with A/C, remove A/C compressor from mounting bracket and position aside. Do not disconnect lines from compressor.

9. Remove power steering pump, if equipped, and position aside.
10. Disconnect wiring harness from engine, then the fuel line from fuel pump.
11. Disconnect vacuum lines from intake manifold, then raise and support vehicle.
12. Drain crankcase, then disconnect exhaust pipes from exhaust manifolds.
13. On K and V models with automatic transmission, remove strut rods from motor mounts.
14. Remove flywheel or converter splash shield, then disconnect wiring along right pan rail.
15. Disconnect starter wiring and remove starter.
16. Disconnect wiring from gas gauge.
17. If equipped with automatic transmission, remove converter to flex plate attaching bolts.
18. Support transmission with a suitable transmission jack, then remove bellhousing to engine attaching bolts.
19. Remove lower engine mount bracket to frame attaching bolts, then lower vehicle.
20. Remove hood.
21. Attach a suitable engine lifting device and remove engine from vehicle.
22. Reverse procedure to install.

### G & 1988–89 R, V Models

1. Disconnect battery ground cable, then remove glove box.
2. Remove engine cover, then drain cooling system.
3. Remove outside air duct and power steering reservoir bracket, if applicable.
4. Disconnect hood release cable, then remove upper fan shroud bolts and overflow hoses.
5. Disconnect transmission cooler lines, then remove radiator.
6. Remove upper fan shroud, then the fan and pulley.
7. Remove air cleaner assembly, then the cruise control servo, if equipped.
8. On carbureted models, disconnect brake vacuum line, cables and fuel line from carburetor.
9. On fuel injected models, disconnect vacuum hoses from intake manifold, then the accelerator, cruise control and TVS cables, as equipped.

10. On all models, remove carburetor or TBI unit and distributor cap, then disconnect AIR hoses from diverter valve. Remove diverter valve.
11. Disconnect coolant hoses, PCV valve, and all vacuum hoses and electrical harnesses that will interfere with engine removal.
12. Discharge A/C system, if equipped, then remove compressor brace and position compressor aside.
13. Remove upper oil dipstick, oil filler and transmission dipstick tubes, then disconnect accelerator cable at dipstick.
14. Disconnect fuel hoses from fuel pump, then remove power steering pump, if equipped, and position aside.
15. If equipped with A/C, remove idler pulley.
16. Remove headlamp bezels, grille and upper radiator support, then the lower fan shroud and filler panel.
17. Remove hood latch support.
18. If equipped with A/C, disconnect lines, then remove condenser from vehicle.
19. Raise and support vehicle, then drain crankcase.
20. Disconnect exhaust pipe from manifolds.
21. Disconnect strut rods at flywheel cover, then remove cover.
22. Disconnect starter electrical wires, then remove attaching bolts and starter.
23. On automatic transmission equipped vehicles, remove flex plate to torque converter attaching bolts.
24. On all vehicles, remove transmission to engine attaching bolts, then the motor mount through bolts.
25. Lower vehicle, then support transmission with suitable jack.
26. Attach suitable engine lifting device, then remove engine from vehicle.
27. Reverse procedure to install.

## V8 ENGINES EXC. V8-454
## C, K, R & V Models

1. Disconnect battery ground cable, then drain cooling system.
2. Remove air cleaner assembly.
3. Remove accessory drive belts, then the fan and water pump pulley.
4. Disconnect all hoses from engine.

**Fig. 8 Intake manifold tightening sequence. V6-231**

5. If equipped with automatic transmission, disconnect cooling lines from radiator.
6. Remove radiator and fan shroud.
7. Disconnect accelerator linkage and detent cable (automatic transmission models) from carburetor throttle lever.
8. If equipped with A/C, remove A/C compressor from mounting bracket and position aside. Do not disconnect lines from compressor.
9. Remove power steering pump, if equipped, and position aside.
10. Disconnect wiring harness from engine, then the fuel line from fuel pump.
11. Disconnect vacuum lines from intake manifold, then raise and support vehicle.
12. Drain crankcase, then disconnect exhaust pipes from exhaust manifolds.
13. On K and V models with automatic transmission, remove strut rods from motor mounts.
14. Remove flywheel or converter splash shield, then disconnect wiring along right pan rail.
15. Disconnect starter wiring and remove starter.
16. Disconnect wiring from gas gauge.
17. If equipped with automatic transmission, remove converter to flex plate attaching bolts.
18. Support transmission with a suitable transmission jack, then remove bellhousing to engine attaching bolts.
19. Remove lower engine mount bracket to frame attaching bolts, then lower vehicle.
20. Remove hood.
21. Attach a suitable engine lifting device and remove engine from vehicle.
22. Reverse procedure to install.

## G Models

1. Disconnect battery ground cable, then drain cooling system.
2. Remove coolant reservoir, then the grille, upper radiator support and lower grille valence.
3. Disconnect hoses from radiator.
4. If equipped with automatic transmission, disconnect cooling lines from radiator.
5. If equipped with A/C, evacuate system, then remove A/C condenser and vacuum reservoir.
6. Remove washer reservoir and bracket.

7. Remove radiator to radiator support mounting brackets, then the radiator and shroud.
8. Remove power steering pump, if equipped, and position aside.
9. Remove engine cover.
10. Remove air cleaner stove pipe.
11. Disconnect accelerator cable, then remove carburetor or TBI unit.
12. Disconnect engine wiring harness from firewall connection.
13. Disconnect heater hoses from engine, then remove thermostat housing.
14. Remove oil filler pipe.
15. If equipped with cruise control, remove servo, servo bracket and transducer.
16. Raise and support vehicle.
17. Disconnect exhaust pipes from exhaust manifolds.
18. Remove propeller shaft, then plug transmission housing to prevent fluid leakage.
19. Disconnect shift linkage and speedometer cable from transmission.
20. Disconnect fuel line from fuel pump, then remove transmission mount retaining bolts.
21. Remove engine mount bracket to frame retaining bolts, then drain crankcase.
22. Remove engine mount through bolts, then raise engine slightly and remove engine mounts.
23. Position a piece of wood between oil pan and front crossmember, then lower vehicle.
24. Attach a suitable engine lifting device, then remove engine/transmission assembly.
25. Reverse procedure to install.

## V8-454 EXC. 1988–89 G MODELS

1. Remove hood.
2. Disconnect battery ground cable, then remove air cleaner.
3. Drain cooling system.
4. Disconnect radiator and heater hoses, then remove radiator and fan shroud.
5. Disconnect wires at starter solenoid, alternator, TRC speed switch, TRC solenoid, temperature and oil pressure switches, and the distributor.
6. Disconnect accelerator linkage from intake manifold.
7. Disconnect fuel line from fuel pump and fuel vapor hose from vapor storage canister, if applicable.
8. Disconnect brake booster vacuum line from intake manifold, if equipped.
9. Remove power steering pump and A/C compressor, if equipped. Do not disconnect hoses from pump or compressor.
10. Raise and support vehicle, then drain crankcase.
11. Disconnect exhaust pipes from manifolds and converter bracket from transmission mount, if equipped.
12. Disconnect wires, then remove starter motor.
13. Remove flywheel splash shield or converter housing cover.
14. On automatic transmission equipped vehicles, remove converter to flex plate attaching bolts.

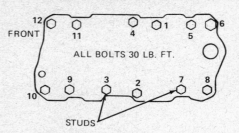

ALL BOLTS 30 LB. FT.

STUDS

**Fig. 9 Intake manifold tightening sequence. V6-229**

15. Lower vehicle, then attach a suitable engine lifting device.
16. Remove engine mount through bolts, then the bellhousing to engine attaching bolts.
17. Support transmission, then disconnect motor mounts from engine brackets.
18. Remove engine from vehicle.
19. Reverse procedure to install.

### 1988–89 G MODELS

1. Disconnect battery ground cable, then drain cooling system.
2. Remove vacuum and electrical lines from cruise control servo, if equipped.
3. Remove grille, grille valence and upper radiator support.
4. Remove A/C compressor (if equipped), then the radiator and fan shroud.
5. Remove power steering pump and A/C compressor and position aside.
6. Disconnect any wiring necessary to remove engine, then remove air cleaner and ducts.
7. Scribe hood hinge locations and remove hood.
8. Disconnect vacuum lines, fuel lines, accelerator, cruise control and throttle linkages.
9. Remove heater hoses, thermostat housing, oil filler tube and TBI.
10. Remove cruise transducer and bracket, then raise and support vehicle.
11. Drain crankcase oil, then remove transmission shift linkage and speedometer cable.
12. Remove exhaust pipes from manifolds.
13. Remove propeller shaft at transmission and plug transmission.
14. Remove rear engine mount bolts while supporting engine with a suitable jack.
15. Remove front engine mount bracket bolts from frame, then the front mount through bolts.
16. Remove front engine mount frame brackets. **Lift engine only enough to remove brackets. Block engine in place with wood blocks.**
17. Lower vehicle, then carefully remove engine and transmission.

## INTAKE MANIFOLD
## REPLACE
### 1980–85 6-250, 292

On some 6-250 engines, the intake manifold is an integral part of the cylinder head. The procedure outlined below ap-

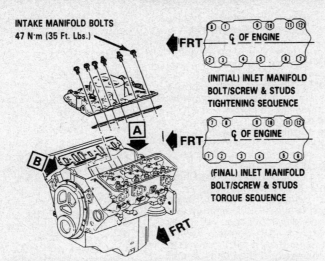

**Fig. 10   Intake manifold tightening sequence. V6-262**

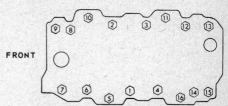

**Fig. 11   Intake manifold tightening sequence. V8-267, 305, 350 & 400**

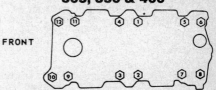

**Fig. 12   Intake manifold tightening sequence. 1980–85 V8-454**

plies to engines with non-integrated cylinder heads. The exhaust manifold is removed together with the intake manifold. Refer to "Exhaust Manifold, Replace" procedure for removal of exhaust manifold on integrated cylinder heads.

1. Disconnect battery ground cable, then remove air cleaner assembly.
2. Disconnect throttle controls at bellcrank, then remove throttle control spring.
3. Disconnect fuel and vacuum lines at carburetor and crankcase ventilation hose at valve cover.
4. Disconnect vapor hose at canister.
5. Disconnect exhaust pipe at manifold flange, then remove manifold attaching bolts and clamps and the manifold assembly.
6. Remove bolts and nut at center of assembly, then separate manifolds.
7. Reverse procedure to install using new gasket. Torque bolts to specification, working from center of cylinder head outward.

## 1986–89 6-250

1. Disconnect battery ground cable, then remove air cleaner assembly.
2. Disconnect throttle controls at bellcrank, then if necessary remove the carburetor.
3. Disconnect fuel and vacuum lines from the manifold and remove the PCV hose. If equipped, disconnect vacuum lines from EGR and EFE valves.
4. Remove air pump and bracket.
5. Disconnect exhaust pipe from manifold flange, then remove manifold heat stove.
6. Remove manifold attaching bolts and clamps, then the manifold assembly and gasket.
7. Remove bolts and nut at center of assembly, then separate manifolds.
8. Reverse procedure to install using new gasket, and torque bolts to specification. The manifold to cylinder head nuts and bolts should always be tightened prior to tightening manifold center nuts and bolt.

## V6-231

1. Disconnect battery ground cable.
2. Drain cooling system, then remove air cleaner.
3. Disconnect upper radiator and heater hose at manifold.
4. Disconnect accelerator, downshift or throttle valve cables at carburetor.
5. Disconnect brake booster vacuum line from manifold, if applicable.
6. Disconnect fuel line from carburetor.
7. Disconnect all remaining vacuum hoses and electrical connections that will interfere with manifold removal.
8. Remove distributor cap and rotor to gain access to left side torx bolt.
9. Remove A/C compressor and alternator mounting brackets, if applicable.
10. Remove spark plug wires, if necessary, then the accelerator linkage springs.
11. Remove intake manifold attaching bolts, then the intake manifold.
12. Reverse procedure to install using new gasket(s) and seals. Coat seal surface with RTV sealant. Torque manifold bolts to specification in sequence shown in **Fig. 8.**

## V6-229

1. Disconnect battery ground cable.
2. Remove air cleaner, then drain cooling system.
3. Remove AIR crossover hose, if applicable.
4. Remove alternator upper mounting bracket.
5. Disconnect all vacuum hoses and electrical connections that will interfere with manifold removal.
6. Disconnect fuel line and linkage from carburetor.
7. Disconnect spark plug wires, if necessary, then remove distributor.
8. If equipped with A/C, remove compressor and mounting bracket and position aside.
9. Remove attaching bolts, then the EGR valve.
10. Remove intake manifold attaching bolts, then the intake manifold.

11. Reverse procedure to install, using new gaskets and seals. Coat front and rear ridges of cylinder case with a $3/16$ inch bead of RTV sealant. Extend bead $1/2$ inch up each cylinder head to retain side gaskets, then seal around all water passages. Torque manifold bolts to specification in sequence shown in **Fig. 9.**

## V6-262
### Caballero & El Camino

1. Disconnect battery ground cable.
2. Remove air cleaner, then drain cooling system.
3. Disconnect heater and radiator hoses, and the dipstick tube, then remove upper alternator bracket.
4. Disconnect all remaining hoses and electrical connections that will interfere with manifold removal.
5. Disconnect fuel pipes from AIR control valve bracket, then disconnect fuel line clips and lines at TBI unit.
6. Disconnect accelerator and T.V. cables, if applicable.
7. Disconnect spark plug wires, if necessary, then remove distributor.
8. Remove ignition coil.
9. If equipped with A/C, remove compressor bracket and position compressor aside.
10. Remove intake manifold attaching bolts, then the intake manifold.
11. Reverse procedure to install, using new gaskets and seals. Coat front and rear ridges of cylinder case with a $3/16$ inch bead of RTV sealant. Extend bead $1/2$ inch up each cylinder head to retain side gaskets, then seal around all water passages. Torque manifold bolts to specification in sequence shown in **Fig. 10.**

## Series 10–30/1500–3500

1. Disconnect battery ground cable.
2. Remove necessary access covers.
3. Remove air cleaner and if equipped, the heat stove tube.

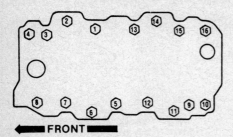

**Fig. 12A   Intake manifold tightening sequence. 1986 V8-454**

4. Drain cooling system.
5. Remove distributor cap and wires, then disconnect ESC connector, if applicable.
6. Remove distributor.
7. Disconnect detent and accelerator cables.
8. Disconnect cruise control transducer, cable and bracket, if equipped.
9. On all 1985-86 models, and 1987 R and V models, remove rear A/C compressor brace. On 1987 G models and all 1988-89 models, remove A/C compressor and position aside.
10. On 1985-86 models, remove transmission and engine oil filler tubes from alternator brace.
11. On all models, remove A/C idler pulley, if equipped.
12. Remove alternator brace, then on carbureted models, disconnect fuel line from carburetor.
13. Disconnect all vacuum hoses and electrical connections from the manifold and carburetor or TBI unit.
14. On 1985-86 models, remove AIR hoses and brackets, then disconnect heater hose from intake manifold and remove carburetor.
15. On 1987-89 models, remove power brake vacuum pipe, and the upper radiator hose.
16. Remove heater pipe, coil wires and the EGR vacuum line.
17. Remove right hand sensors with bracket, and the right hand wiring harness.
18. Remove transmission dipstick tube, if equipped.
19. On all models, remove intake manifold attaching bolts, then the intake manifold and gasket.
20. Reverse procedure to install, using new gaskets and seals. Coat front and rear ridges of cylinder case with a $3/16$ inch bead of RTV sealant. Extend bead $1/2$ inch up each cylinder head to retain side gaskets, then seal around all water passages. Torque manifold bolts to specification in sequence shown in **Fig. 10.**

## V8 ENGINES EXC. V8-454
### Caballero & El Camino

1. Disconnect battery ground cable, then drain cooling system.
2. Remove air cleaner.
3. If applicable, disconnect C3 wiring harness and position aside.

4. Remove heater and radiator hoses, then the upper alternator bracket.
5. Disconnect all vacuum hoses and electrical connections that will interfere with manifold removal.
6. Disconnect accelerator linkage, cables and fuel line from carburetor.
7. If necessary, remove spark plug wires from right cylinder head.
8. Remove distributor.
9. Remove carburetor, if necessary.
10. If equipped with A/C, remove compressor brace and bracket, then position compressor aside.
11. Remove intake manifold attaching bolts, then the intake manifold.
12. Reverse procedure to install, using new gaskets and seals. Coat front and rear ridges of cylinder case with a $3/16$ inch bead of RTV sealant. Extend bead $1/2$ inch up each cylinder head to retain side gaskets, then seal around all water passages. Torque manifold bolts to specification in sequence shown in **Fig. 11.**

### Series 10–30/1500–3500

1. Disconnect battery ground cable, then drain cooling system.
2. Remove air cleaner.
3. On G models, remove engine cover.
4. Remove AIR crossover hose, if applicable.
5. Disconnect heater and radiator hoses, then remove upper alternator bracket.
6. Disconnect all vacuum hoses and electrical connections that will interfere with manifold removal.
7. Disconnect fuel line, linkage and cables from carburetor or TBI unit.
8. Remove spark plug wires, if necessary.
9. Remove distributor.
10. On all except G models with fuel injected engine, if equipped with A/C, remove compressor and bracket and position aside.
11. On fuel injected models, disconnect ignition coil wires, then remove emission control sensors and bracket on right side. Remove cruise control transducer and bracket, then the fuel line bracket at rear of manifold. On G models, remove bracket at rear of belt idler.
12. On all models, remove carburetor or TBI unit, if necessary.
13. Remove intake manifold attaching bolts, then the intake manifold.
14. Reverse procedure to install, using new gaskets and seals. Coat front and rear ridges of cylinder case with a $3/16$ inch bead of RTV sealant. Extend bead $1/2$ inch up each cylinder head to retain side gaskets, then seal around all water passages. Torque manifold bolts to specification in sequence shown in **Fig. 11.**

### V8-454
#### 1980–86

1. Disconnect battery ground cable, then drain cooling system.
2. Remove air cleaner.
3. Disconnect upper radiator hose and water pump bypass hose.

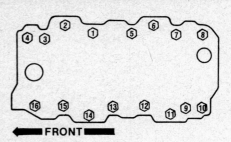

**Fig. 12B   Intake manifold tightening sequence. 1987–89 V8-454**

4. Disconnect fuel line, accelerator linkage and cables from carburetor.
5. Remove distributor.
6. If equipped with A/C, remove compressor and front bracket and position aside.
7. Remove alternator upper mounting bracket.
8. Remove rear A/C bracket, if equipped.
9. Remove intake manifold attaching bolts, then the intake manifold.
10. Reverse procedure to install, using new gaskets and seals. Torque manifold bolts to specification in sequence shown in **Figs. 12 and 12A.**

#### 1987–89

1. Disconnect battery ground cable, then remove air cleaner assembly.
2. Drain cooling system, then disconnect upper radiator hose and water pump bypass hose.
3. On carbureted engines, disconnect heater hose from intake manifold.
4. On fuel injected engines, disconnect heater hose and pipes, then the wire sensor from front if intake manifold.
5. On all engines, disconnect accelerator cable, cruise control cable and TVS cable, as equipped.
6. Disconnect wiring harness from clips on intake manifold, then remove cruise control transducer, if equipped.
7. Disconnect fuel line from carburetor or fuel lines from TBI unit.
8. Disconnect crankcase ventilation hoses and any other vacuum hoses necessary for intake manifold removal.
9. Remove distributor assembly.
10. On fuel injected engines, disconnect wires from ignition coil, then remove EGR solenoid and MAP sensor with brackets.
11. On models equipped with A/C, remove A/C compressor rear bracket.
12. On models equipped with fuel injected engine, remove front alternator/AIR pump bracket.
13. On models equipped with carbureted engine, remove upper alternator bracket.
14. On all models, remove intake manifold attaching bolts and the manifold.
15. Reverse procedure to install, using new gaskets and seals. Torque manifold attaching bolts to specification in sequence shown in **Fig. 12B.**

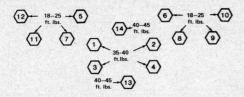

**Fig. 13 Exhaust manifold tightening sequence. 6-250**

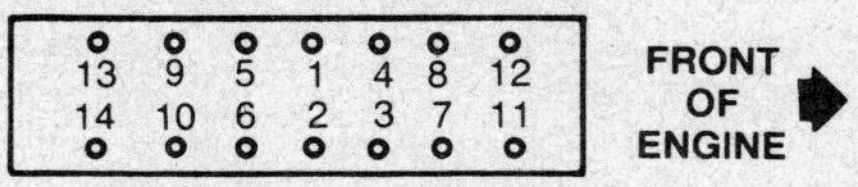

**Fig. 14 Cylinder head tightening sequence. 6-250 & 292**

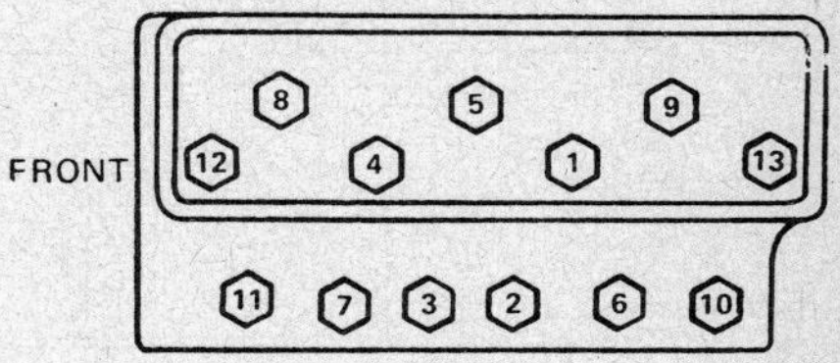

**Fig. 15 Cylinder head tightening sequence. V6-229 & 262**

## EXHAUST MANIFOLD
## REPLACE
### 6-250 WITH INTEGRATED CYLINDER HEAD

1. Disconnect battery ground cable, then remove air cleaner.
2. Remove power steering and/or AIR pump brackets, if equipped.
3. If equipped with Pulsair, remove pipes as necessary.
4. Raise and support vehicle, then disconnect exhaust pipe from manifold and, if equipped, the converter bracket from transmission mount.
5. Lower vehicle and, if applicable, remove rear heat shield and accelerator cable bracket.
6. Remove exhaust manifold attaching bolts, then the exhaust manifold.
7. Reverse procedure to install, using new gasket. Torque bolts to specification in sequence shown in **Fig. 13.**

## V6 ENGINES
### CABALLERO & EL CAMINO
#### V6-229

1. Disconnect battery ground cable, then remove air cleaner.
2. If removing right side manifold, disconnect heat stove pipe.
3. Remove spark plug wires and heatshield, if necessary, then raise and support vehicle.
4. Disconnect exhaust pipe from manifold, then lower vehicle.
5. If removing right side manifold, disconnect EFE valve vacuum hose, if equipped, then remove oil dipstick tube retainer, if necessary.
6. If removing left side manifold, remove A/C compressor and power steering pump brackets, if equipped.
7. Remove exhaust manifold attaching bolts, then the exhaust manifold.
8. Reverse procedure to install, using new gasket.

#### V6-231

1. Raise and support vehicle.
2. Disconnect crossover pipe from manifolds.
3. Disconnect EFE pipe from manifold, if applicable.
4. Remove exhaust manifold attaching bolts, then the exhaust manifold.
5. Reverse procedure to install, using new gasket.

#### V6-262

1. Disconnect battery ground cable, then raise and support vehicle.

2. On 1985 models, if removing right side manifold, proceed as follows:
   a. Disconnect exhaust pipe from manifold, then lower vehicle.
   b. Disconnect air management valve bracket and AIR hoses.
   c. Disconnect AIR pipes from converter, cylinder head and manifold.
   d. Disconnect spark plug wires, then remove exhaust manifold attaching bolts and manifold.
3. On 1986-88 models, if removing right side manifold, proceed as follows:
   a. Remove air cleaner assembly.
   b. Raise and support vehicle.
   c. Remove exhaust pipe attaching bolts, then disconnect air pipe from left of block.
   d. Lower vehicle, then disconnect fuel lines from AIR control bracket.
   e. Disconnect converter AIR pipe from exhaust manifold.
   f. Disconnect spark plug wires from plugs and manifold retainer.
   g. Disconnect AIR pipe from cylinder heads and manifold.
   h. Disconnect AIR lines from converter and manifold check valve, then remove the check valve.
   i. Remove exhaust manifold attaching bolts and the manifold.
4. On all models, if removing left side manifold, proceed as follows:
   a. Disconnect exhaust pipe from manifold, then remove A/C compressor, if equipped, and position aside.
   b. Remove power steering pump, if equipped, then the rear A/C compressor adjusting brace, if applicable.
   c. If equipped, remove rear power steering pump adjusting brace.
   d. Disconnect spark plug wires, then remove exhaust manifold attaching bolts and manifold.
5. Reverse procedure to install, using new gasket.

### SERIES 10—30/1500—3500
#### V6-262

1. Disconnect battery ground cable.
2. Remove necessary access covers.
3. Raise and support vehicle.
4. Disconnect exhaust pipe from manifold, then lower vehicle.
5. Disconnect AIR hose from check valve.
6. If removing left side manifold, proceed as follows:
   a. Disconnect oxygen sensor connector.
   b. On 1986 models, remove AIR pipe bracket at the head.
   c. On 1987 R and V models, remove A/C compressor rear bracket, if equipped.

   d. On 1987 G models and all 1988-89 models, remove power steering pump bracket from the manifold.
7. If removing right side manifold, proceed as follows:
   a. On 1985-86 models, disconnect AIR pipe, from the diverter valve.
   b. On 1987 R and V models, disconnect AIR pipe from the diverter valve, and the diverter valve bracket from the manifold.
   c. On 1987 G models and all 1988-89 models, disconnect dipstick tube bracket from the manifold.
   d. On all 1987-89 models, remove heat stove pipe.
8. On all models, remove exhaust manifold attaching bolts, washers and tab washers, then remove manifold.
9. Reverse procedure to install, using new gaskets.

## V8 ENGINES
### 1980—84 CABALLERO & EL CAMINO

1. Disconnect battery ground cable, then remove air cleaner.
2. If removing right side manifold, disconnect heat stove pipe.
3. Remove spark plug wires and heatshield, if necessary, then raise and support vehicle.
4. Disconnect exhaust pipe from manifold, then lower vehicle.
5. If removing right side manifold, disconnect EFE vacuum hose and all emission components that will interfere with manifold removal.
6. If removing left side manifold, remove A/C compressor and power steering pump brackets, if equipped.
7. Remove exhaust manifold attaching bolts, then the exhaust manifold.
8. Reverse procedure to install, using new gasket.

### 1985—88 CABALLERO & EL CAMINO

1. Disconnect battery ground cable, then raise and support vehicle.
2. If removing right side manifold, proceed as follows:
   a. Disconnect exhaust pipe from manifold, then lower vehicle.
   b. Remove air cleaner, then disconnect spark plug wires.
   c. Disconnect vacuum hose from EFE valve.
   d. Disconnect AIR hose, loosen alternator drive belt, then remove lower alternator bracket and AIR valve.

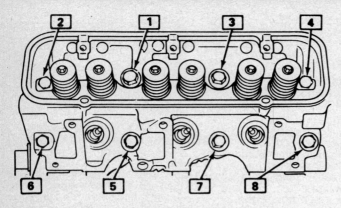

**Fig. 16 Cylinder head tightening sequence. 1980-83 V6-231**

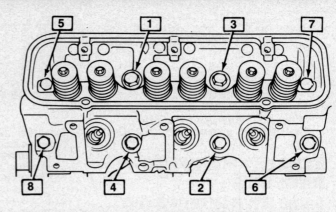

**Fig. 17 Cylinder head tightening sequence. 1984 V6-231**

e. Disconnect converter AIR pipe from rear of manifold.
f. Remove exhaust manifold attaching bolts, then the exhaust manifold.
3. If removing left side manifold:
a. Disconnect exhaust pipe from manifold and electrical connector from oxygen sensor, if applicable.
b. Lower vehicle, then disconnect AIR hose.
c. Remove power steering pump, then loosen front A/C compressor bracket, if equipped, from cylinder head.
d. Remove rear A/C compressor bracket, if equipped, then position compressor aside.
e. Remove lower power steering pump adjusting bracket, if equipped.
f. Remove wire loom holder from valve cover.
g. Remove exhaust manifold attaching bolts, then the exhaust manifold.
4. Reverse procedure to install, using new gasket.

### SERIES 10-30/1500-3500

#### 1980-85

1. Remove air cleaner and carburetor heat stove pipe.
2. Remove spark plugs and spark plug wiring heat shields.
3. Disconnect exhaust pipe from manifold, then remove manifold attaching bolts and the manifold.
4. Reverse procedure to install, using new gasket.

### 1986-89 V8-305 & V8-350

1. Disconnect battery ground cable.
2. On G models, remove engine cover.
3. On all models, raise and support vehicle.
4. Disconnect exhaust pipe from manifold, then lower vehicle.
5. Disconnect oxygen sensor wire from left side manifold, if applicable.
6. Disconnect AIR hose from check valve.
7. On 1987-89 models, remove heat stove pipe from right side manifold.

8. On 1987-89 R and V models, proceed as follows:
a. Remove A/C compressor rear bracket from left side manifold.
b. Remove diverter valve and bracket from right side manifold.
9. On 1987-89 G models with fuel injected engine, proceed as follows:
a. Remove power steering pump rear bracket from left side manifold.
b. Remove dipstick tube bracket from right side manifold.
10. On all 1986 engines and carbureted 1987-89 engines, remove AIR pipe bracket from left side manifold stud.
11. On all models, remove exhaust manifold attaching bolts, washers, tab washers and spark plug heat shields, as equipped, then the exhaust manifold.
12. Reverse procedure to install, using a new gasket.

### 1986 V8-454

1. Disconnect battery ground cable.
2. Remove air cleaner assembly and heat stove pipe.
3. Disconnect AIR hose from check valve.
4. Remove spark plugs, then disconnect exhaust pipe from manifold.
5. Remove exhaust manifold attaching bolts and spark plug heat shields, if equipped.
6. Remove exhaust manifold.
7. Reverse procedure to install, using a new gasket.

### 1987-89 V8-454

1. Disconnect battery ground cable.
2. On G models, remove engine cover.
3. Remove heat stove pipe and dipstick tube from right side manifold.
4. On fuel injected engines, disconnect oxygen sensor wire from left side manifold.
5. On all engines, disconnect AIR hose from check valve.
6. Remove spark plugs, then disconnect exhaust pipe from manifold.
7. Remove exhaust manifold attaching bolts and spark plug heat shields.
8. Remove exhaust manifold.
9. Reverse procedure to install, using a new gasket.

## CYLINDER HEAD
### REPLACE
### 1980-85 6-250, 292

1. Remove necessary access covers depending on vehicle being serviced.
2. Drain cooling system and remove air cleaner and air compressor.
3. Disconnect choke cable, accelerator pedal rod at bell crank on manifold, and fuel and vacuum lines at carburetor.
4. Disconnect exhaust pipe at manifold flange, then remove manifolds and carburetor as an assembly.
5. Disconnect wire harness from temperature sending unit and coil, leaving harness clear of clips in rocker arm cover.
6. Disconnect radiator hose at water outlet housing and battery ground strap at cylinder head.
7. Remove spark plugs and ignition coil.
8. Remove rocker arm cover. Back off rocker arm nuts, pivot rocker arms to clear pushrods and remove pushrods.
9. Unfasten and remove cylinder head.
10. Reverse removal procedure to install and tighten head bolts to the specified torque and in the sequence shown in **Fig. 14**.

### 1986-89 6-250

1. Remove necessary access covers.
2. Disconnect battery ground cable.
3. Remove manifolds as previously described.
4. Disconnect fuel line, wire and vacuum harness from clips in rocker arm cover.
5. Remove air check valve.
6. Remove spark plug wires from spark plugs.
7. Remove rocker arm cover, then back off rocker arm nuts, pivot rocker arms to clear pushrods and remove pushrods. Store pushrods in order of removal for proper installation.
8. Drain cooling system, then disconnect upper radiator hose, heater hose and water pump bypass hoses.
9. Remove battery ground strap from cylinder head.

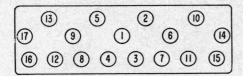

**Fig. 18 Cylinder head tightening sequence. V8-267, 305, 350 & 400**

10. Remove cylinder head attaching bolts, then the cylinder head and gasket.
11. Reverse procedure to install and tighten head bolts to the specified torque and in the sequence shown in **Fig. 14.**

## V6-229

1. Drain cooling system and engine block.
2. Remove intake and exhaust manifolds.
3. Remove alternator lower mounting bolt and position alternator aside.
4. If equipped with A/C, remove compressor and forward mounting bracket and position aside.
5. Remove rocker arm cover, rocker arms and pushrods. Keep rocker arm, rocker arm balls and pushrods in order so they can be installed in the same position.
6. Remove cylinder head bolts and cylinder head.
7. Reverse procedure to install. Tighten cylinder head and intake manifold bolts in sequence shown in **Figs. 9 and 15.**

## V6-231

1. Drain coolant and disconnect battery.
2. Remove intake manifold.
3. When removing right cylinder head, remove Delcotron and/or A/C compressor with mounting bracket and move out of the way. Do not disconnect hoses from A/C compressor.
4. When removing left cylinder head, remove oil dipstick, power steering pump and move out of the way with hoses attached.
5. Disconnect exhaust manifold from head to be removed.
6. Remove rocker arm shaft and lift out pushrods.
7. Remove cylinder head.
8. Reverse procedure to install and tighten bolts gradually and evenly in the sequence shown in **Figs. 16 and 17.** When installing intake manifold, refer to **Fig. 8** for bolt tightening sequence.

## V6-262

### Caballero & El Camino

1. Remove intake manifold.
2. Remove alternator lower mounting bolt, then position alternator aside.
3. Remove exhaust manifold.
4. Remove rocker arm cover, rocker arms and pushrods.
5. Drain coolant from cylinder block, then remove diverter valve, if equipped.
6. Remove cylinder head attaching

bolts, then the cylinder head. **Before installing cylinder head, check gasket surfaces on both head and block for nicks or heavy scratches. Bolt threads in block and threads on head bolts must be clean as dirt will affect bolt torque.**
7. On engines using steel gasket, coat both sides of gasket using suitable sealer. On engines equipped with steel/asbestos type gasket, no sealer should be used.
8. Place gasket in position over dowel pins, then carefully lower cylinder head into place.
9. Coat threads of cylinder head bolts with suitable sealer, then install bolts finger tight.
10. Tighten each bolt a little at a time in sequence shown in **Fig. 15** until specified torque is reached.
11. Install intake manifold, then torque bolts to specification in sequence shown in **Fig. 10.**
12. Install exhaust manifold.
13. Install valve train, then adjust valves as outlined in "Valves, Adjust" procedure.

### 1985 Series 10–30/1500–3500

1. Disconnect battery ground cable, then remove intake manifold.
2. Raise and support vehicle, then disconnect exhaust pipe from manifold.
3. Lower vehicle, then disconnect AIR hose from check valve.
4. If removing right side cylinder head, proceed as follows:
   a. Remove exhaust manifold, then disconnect AIR pipe at cylinder head and diverter valve.
   b. Disconnect oil filler tube and PCV valve.
   c. Disconnect wiring harness, then remove valve cover.
   d. Remove alternator mounting bolt, then disconnect spark plug wires and remove spark plugs.
   e. Remove rocker arms and pushrods.
   f. Remove cylinder head attaching bolts, then the cylinder head.
5. If removing left side cylinder head:
   a. Remove exhaust manifold, then disconnect power steering pump and A/C compressor, if equipped, and position aside.
   b. Remove valve cover, then disconnect spark plug wires and remove spark plugs.
   c. Remove rocker arms and pushrods.
   d. Remove cylinder head attaching bolts, then the cylinder head. **Before installing cylinder head, check gasket surfaces on both head and block for nicks or heavy scratches. Bolt threads in block and threads on head bolts must be clean as dirt will affect bolt torque.**
6. On engines using steel gasket, coat both sides of gasket using suitable sealer. On engines equipped with steel/asbestos type gasket, no sealer should be used.

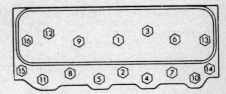

**Fig. 19 Cylinder head tightening sequence V8-454**

7. Place gasket in position over dowel pins, then carefully lower cylinder head into place.
8. Coat threads of cylinder head bolts with suitable sealer, then install bolts finger tight.
9. Tighten each bolt a little at a time in sequence shown in **Fig. 15** until specified torque is reached.
10. Install intake manifold, then torque bolts to specification in sequence shown in **Fig. 10.**
11. Install exhaust manifold.
12. Install valve train, then adjust valves as outlined in "Valves, Adjust" procedure.

### 1986–89 Series 10–30/1500–3500

1. Disconnect battery ground cable and remove engine cover.
2. Remove intake and exhaust manifolds as previously described.
3. If working on the right side cylinder head, remove the following:
   a. Air pipe.
   b. Air pump mounting bolt with spacer.
   c. Engine wiring harness, clip and ground strap.
4. If working on the left side cylinder head, remove the following:
   a. Air pipe.
   b. Fuel pipes and bracket.
   c. Coolant sensor wire.
   d. Cruise control transducer bracket.
5. On either head, remove any other engine accessory brackets, bolts and studs that may interfere with head removal.
6. Remove valve cover, then disconnect spark plug wires and remove spark plugs.
7. Remove rocker arms and pushrods.
8. Remove cylinder head attaching bolts, then the cylinder head. **Before installing cylinder head, check gasket surfaces on both head and block for nicks or heavy scratches. Bolt threads in block and threads on head bolts must be clean as dirt will affect bolt torque.**
9. On engines using steel gasket, coat both sides of gasket using suitable sealer. On engines equipped with steel/asbestos type gasket, no sealer should be used.
10. Place gasket in position over dowel pins, then carefully lower cylinder head into place.
11. Coat threads of cylinder head bolts with suitable sealer, then install bolts finger tight.
12. Tighten each bolt a little at a time in sequence shown in **Fig. 15** until specified torque is reached.

13. Install intake manifold, then torque bolts to specifications in sequence shown in **Fig. 10**.
14. Install exhaust manifold.
15. Install valve train, then adjust valves as outlined in "Valves, Adjust" procedure.

## V8-267, 305, 350, 400 & 454

### EXC. 1987–89 SERIES 10–30/1500–3500

### Removal

1. Remove intake and exhaust manifolds and A/C compressor, if equipped.
2. Remove valve mechanism.
3. Drain coolant from block.
4. Unfasten and remove cylinder head.

### Installation

The gasket surfaces on both head and block must be clean of any foreign material and free of nicks or heavy scratches. Cylinder bolt threads in the block and threads on the head bolts must be clean as dirt will affect bolt torque.
1. On engines using a steel gasket, coat both sides of a new gasket with a good sealer. One method of applying the sealer that will assure the proper coat is with the use of a paint roller. Too much sealer may hold the gasket away from the head or block. **Use no sealer on engines using a composition steel asbestos gasket.**
2. Place gasket in position over the dowel pins with the head up.
3. Carefully guide cylinder head into place over dowel pins and gasket.
4. Coat threads of cylinder head bolts with sealing compound and install bolts finger tight.
5. Tighten each bolt a little at a time in the sequence shown in **Figs. 18 and 19** until the specified torque is reached.
6. Install and tighten intake manifold bolts in sequence shown in **Figs. 11 and 12**.
7. Install and adjust valve mechanism as outlined further on.

### 1987–89 SERIES 10–30/1500–3500

### V8-305, 350

1. Disconnect battery ground cable.
2. On G models, remove engine cover.
3. On all models, drain cooling system, then remove intake and exhaust manifolds as previously described.
4. If removing right side cylinder head on R and V models, proceed as follows:
   a. Disconnect ground strap from rear of cylinder head.
   b. Remove AIR pipe from rear of cylinder head.
   c. Disconnect spark plug wires from support brackets.
   d. Unfasten alternator and position aside.
5. If removing left side cylinder head on R and V models, proceed as follows:
   a. On models equipped with A/C compressor, unfasten compressor

and front bracket and position aside.
   b. On models equipped with power steering, unfasten power steering pump and position aside.
   c. On all models, disconnect coolant sensor electrical connector.
   d. Disconnect spark plug wires from support brackets.
   e. Disconnect AIR pipe from rear of cylinder head.
6. If removing right side cylinder head on G models with fuel injected engine, proceed as follows:
   a. Disconnect ground strap from rear of cylinder head.
   b. Remove AIR pump bolt and spacer from cylinder head.
   c. On models equipped with A/C, remove A/C compressor nut and stud from cylinder head.
   d. Disconnect fuel pipe and plug wire, then remove wiring harness brackets from rear of cylinder head.
7. If removing left side cylinder head on G models with fuel injected engine, proceed as follows:
   a. Remove main accessory bracket nut and stud from cylinder head. **Remaining studs and bolts may need to be loosened to move bracket forward to allow removal removal of cylinder head.**
   b. Disconnect coolant sensor electrical connector.
   c. Remove cruise control transducer, if equipped, and spark plug wire brackets from rear of cylinder head.
8. On models equipped with carbureted engine, proceed as follows:
   a. If removing left side cylinder head, unfasten A/C compressor and bracket, if equipped, and position aside.
   b. If removing right side cylinder head, unfasten alternator and position aside.
9. On all models, remove rocker arm cover, then the spark plugs and pushrods.
10. Remove cylinder head attaching bolts and the cylinder head.
11. Reverse procedure to install, noting the following:
   a. Thoroughly clean block and head mating surfaces.
   b. Install new head gasket over block dowel pins with bead up. **If using a steel gasket, apply a thin, even**

coat of sealer to both sides of gasket. **If using a composition gasket, do not use any sealer.**
   c. Coat cylinder head bolt threads with a suitable sealing compound.
   d. Install head bolts finger tight, then torque in sequence, **Fig. 18**, to specifications.

### V8-454

1. Remove intake manifold as previously described.
2. Unfasten alternator and position aside.
3. On models equipped with fuel injected engine, remove AIR pump, then the AIR pump/alternator bracket.
4. If equipped, remove power steering pump with bracket, and position aside.
5. Remove exhaust manifold as previously described.
6. On models equipped with A/C, unfasten A/C compressor and bracket and position aside.
7. On all models, remove rocker arm cover, then the spark plugs.
8. On models equipped with fuel injected engine, remove AIR pipe bolts from rear of cylinder head.
9. On all models, disconnect ground strap from rear of cylinder head.
10. Remove pushrods, then the cylinder head attaching bolts and cylinder head.
11. Reverse procedure to install, noting the following:
   a. Thoroughly clean block and head mating surfaces.
   b. Install new head gasket over block dowel pins with bead up. **If using a steel gasket, apply a thin, even coat of sealer to both sides of gasket. If using a composition gasket, do not use any sealer.**
   c. Coat cylinder head bolt threads with a suitable sealing compound,
   d. Install head bolts finger tight, then torque in sequence, **Fig. 19**, to specifications.

## VALVE ARRANGEMENT
### FRONT TO REAR

| | |
|---|---|
| 6-250, 292 | E-I-I-E-E-I-I-E-E-I-I-E |
| V6-231 | E-I-I-E-I-E |
| V6-262 | |
|   Left Side | E-I-E-I-I-E |
|   Right Side | E-I-I-E-I-E |
| V8-267, 305, 350, 400 | E-I-I-E-E-I-I-E |
| V8-454 | E-I-E-I-E-I-E-I |

**Fig. 20   Valve rotator & retaining components**

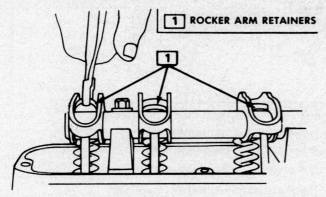

**Fig. 21   Removing rocker arm nylon retainer. V6-231**

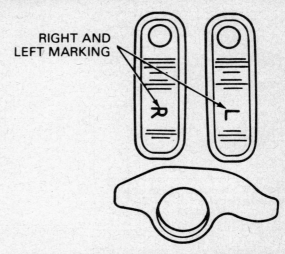

RIGHT AND LEFT MARKING

**Fig. 22   Service rocker arm identification. V6-231**

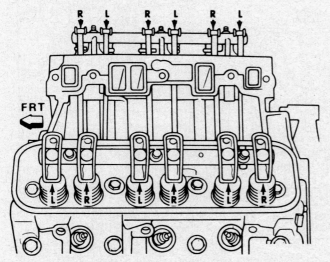

**Fig. 23   Service rocker arm installation. V6-231**

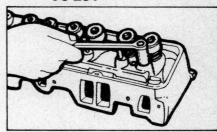

**Fig. 24   Rocker arm stud removal. Exc. V6-231 & V8-454**

## VALVES
## ADJUST
### EXC. V6-231
#### Initial adjustment

1. With engine in position to fire No. 1 cylinder, adjust the following valves: V6-229 and 262 engines, Exhaust Nos. 1, 5 and 6; Intake Nos. 1, 2 and 3. 6-250 and 292 engines, Exhaust Nos. 1, 3 and 5; Intake Nos. 1, 2 and 4. V8 engines, Exhaust Nos. 1, 3, 4 and 8; Intake Nos. 1, 2, 5 and 7.
2. To properly adjust valves back off adjusting nut until lash is felt, (when push rod can be rotated by hand), then tighten nut until lash is eliminated.
3. When zero lash is aqquired, tighten adjusting nuts additionally as follows: All exc. V8-454/7.4L engine, tighten nut one full additional turn from zero lash. On V8-454/7.4L engine tighten nut ¾ additional turn from zero lash.
4. Turn crankshaft one complete revolution, which will bring engine in position to fire cylinders 4 (V6) or 6 (Inline 6 and V8).

5. With engine in this position, adjust the following valves: V6-229 and 262 engines, Exhaust Nos. 2, 3 and 4; Intake Nos. 4, 5 and 6. 6-250 and 292, Exhaust Nos. 2, 4 and 6; Intake Nos. 3, 5 and 6. V8 engines, Exhaust Nos. 2, 5, 6 and 7; Intake Nos. 3, 4, 6 and 8.
6. When zero lash is aqquired, tighten adjusting nuts additionally as specified in step 3.

#### Readjustment

1. After engine has been warmed to operating temperature, remove valve cover.
2. With engine running at idle speed, back off valve rocker arm nut until rocker arm starts to clatter.
3. Turn rocker arm nut down slowly until the clatter just stops. This is the zero lash position.
4. Turn nut down ¼ additional turn and pause 10 seconds until engine runs smoothly. Repeat additional ¼ turns, pausing 10 seconds each time, until nut has been turned down as specified: All exc. V8-454/7.4L engine, tighten rocker nut one full additional turn from zero lash; On V8-454/7.4L engine tighten rocker nut ¾ additional

turn from zero lash. **This preload adjustment must be done slowly to allow the lifter to adjust itself to prevent the possibility of interference between the intake valve head and top of piston, which might result in internal damage and/or bent pushrods. Noisy lifters should be replaced.**
5. Install valve cover, with new gasket.

### V6-231

These engines use hydraulic valve lifters. No provision for adjustment is provided.

## VALVE ROTATORS

The parts involved in the rotating mechanism, **Fig. 20**, are a special spring seat retainer, a pair of flat half-moon keys, a close fitting cap located on the valve stem and a specially constructed valve stem.

In order to accommodate valve expansion, the valve lash must be maintained. When camshaft rotation causes this lash or clearance to be taken up, the cap on the valve stem causes the valve keys to raise the spring retainer, removing the load on the valve springs from the valve before the valve is moved from its seat. A clearance of .002–.004 inch should be maintained between the end face of the valve stem and cap. This is the distance the spring retainer is moved before the valve is moved. The slow valve rotating motion is caused by the vibration of the valve, the flowing of exhaust gases around the valve head, and

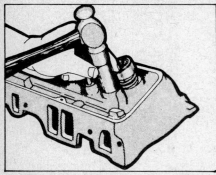

**Fig. 25   Rocker arm stud installation. Exc. V6-231 & V8-454**

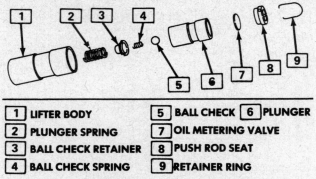

| | | |
|---|---|---|
| **1** LIFTER BODY | **5** BALL CHECK | **6** PLUNGER |
| **2** PLUNGER SPRING | **7** OIL METERING VALVE | |
| **3** BALL CHECK RETAINER | **8** PUSH ROD SEAT | |
| **4** BALL CHECK SPRING | **9** RETAINER RING | |

**Fig. 26   Hydraulic valve lifter (Typical)**

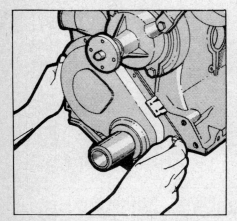

**Fig. 27   Timing case cover installation. 6-250 & 292**

REMOVE BOLTS MARKED ➡ FOR COMPLETE REMOVAL

SEAL THREADS

FUEL PUMP MUST BE REMOVED

**Fig. 28   Timing case cover installation. V6-231**

CAMSHAFT GEAR

SUPPORT SLEEVE

CAMSHAFT

**Fig. 29   Camshaft gear removal. 6-250 & 292**

a slight rotating motion imparted to the valve by the valve spring.

Whenever valve work is being done, a check for clearance should be made by holding the assembled valve and rotating mechanism in the hands. With one hand, press down on the valve cap and turn the valve with the other hand. If the valve turns readily, it indicates that there is clearance present.

A special gauge is available to check this clearance. If the gauge indicates no clearance, grind off the end of the valve stem. If the clearance is too great, grind off the open end of the valve cap.

## VALVE GUIDES

Valve guides in these engines are an integral part of the head and, therefore, cannot be removed. For service, guide holes can be reamed oversize to accommodate one of several service valves with oversize stems.

Check the valve stem clearance of each valve (after cleaning) in its respective valve guide. If the clearance exceeds the service limits of .004 inch on the intake or .005 inch on the exhaust, ream the valve guide to accommodate the next oversize diameter valve stem.

Select the reamer for the smallest oversize which will provide a clean straight bore through the valve guide. After reaming, a new seat should be cut into the head to assure perfect seating of the new valve.

## ROCKER ARM SERVICE
### V6-231

A nylon retainer is used to retain the rocker arm. Break them below their heads with a chisel or pry out with channel locks, **Fig. 21.** Production rocker arms can be installed in any sequence since the arms are identical.

Replacement rocker arms for all engines are identified with a stamping, right (R) and left (L), **Fig. 22** and must be installed as shown in **Fig. 23.**

## ROCKER ARM STUDS
### REPLACE
#### EXC. V6-231

Rocker arm studs that have damaged threads may be replaced with standard studs. Loose studs should be replaced with .003 inch or .013 inch oversize studs which are available for replacement.

Remove the old stud by placing a suitable spacer over the stud, **Fig. 24.** Install a nut and flat washer on the stud and pull out the stud by turning the nut. After reaming the hole for an oversize stud, coat the press-fit area of the new stud with rear axle lubricant. Install the stud using stud

driver tool J6880 or equivalent, by driving it in until tool bottoms on the head, **Fig. 25.** On V8-454, the rocker arm studs are threaded into the cylinder head. Coat threads on cylinder head end of stud with sealer before assembling to head.

## PUSHRODS

When a replacement pushrod has a paint stripe at one end, this painted end must be installed in contact with the rocker arm. To provide durability a hardened insert is incorporated in the rocker arm end of these pushrods.

## HYDRAULIC LIFTERS

Hydraulic valve lifters, **Fig. 26,** do not normally require periodic adjustment. However, if the cylinder head or valve train requires service and/or valve noise is excessive, adjust valves as outlined previously. Servicing the lifters requires that care and cleanliness be exercised in the handling of parts.

### DISASSEMBLE & ASSEMBLE

1. Hold plunger down with pushrod and, using a small screw driver or awl, remove plunger retainer.
2. Remove parts from lifter body.
3. Clean all parts and inspect for damage. If any parts are damaged, the en-

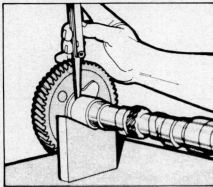

**Fig. 30   Checking camshaft endplay. 6-250 & 292**

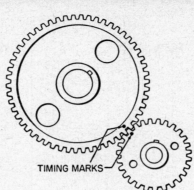

**Fig. 31   Valve timing marks. 6-250 & 292**

**Fig. 32   Checking timing gear backlash. 6-250 & 292**

**Fig. 33   Checking timing gear runout. 6-250 & 292**

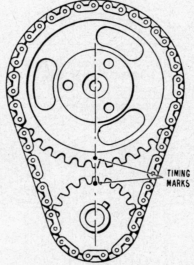

**Fig. 34   Valve timing marks. V6-229, 262, V8-267, 305, 350, 400 & 454**

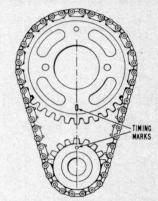

**Fig. 35   Valve timing marks. V6-231**

tire lifter assembly should be replaced. The inertia valve in the plunger for rocker arm lubrication should move when the plunger is shaken.

4. To reassemble, invert plunger and set ball into hole in plunger. Place ball check valve retainer over ball and on plunger. Place check valve retainer spring over retainer. Assemble body over plunger assembly. Turn assembly over and install pushrod seat. Compress plunger with pushrod and install retainer.
5. Compress plunger to open oil holes and fill plunger with engine oil. Work plunger up and down and refill.

## TIMING CASE COVER
### REPLACE
### 6-250 & 6-292

1. Remove radiator, accessory drive belt(s) and pulley as equipped.
2. Remove vibration damper.
3. Remove two oil pan-to-front cover attaching bolts.
4. Remove front cover-to-cylinder block attaching bolts.
5. On 6-292 engines, pull cover slightly forward, then using a sharp knife, cut oil pan front seal flush with cylinder block at both sides of cover.
6. On 6-292 engines, remove cover and attached portion of oil pan front seal.

7. On 6-250 engines, remove cover from cylinder block.
8. On all engines, clean gasket surfaces.
9. Pry oil seal out of cover with a large screwdriver. Install new seal with open side of seal inside of cover and drive or press seal into place.
10. On 6-292 engines, cut tabs from new oil pan front seal, then install seal on cover, pressing tips into cover holes.
11. On 6-292 engines, apply a 1/8 inch bead of RTV sealant to the joint formed at oil pan and cylinder block.
12. On 6-250 engine, apply a 3/16 bead of RTV sealant to the cover gasket surface.
13. On all engines, position a suitable centering tool in crankcase front cover seal.
14. Install cover with centering tool, **Fig. 27**, to cylinder block and install cover bolts. Torque front cover-to-engine block attaching bolts to 80 inch lbs. Torque oil pan-to-front cover attaching bolts to 50 inch lbs. on 1980-84 6-250 and 1980-86 6-292 engines and 45 inch lbs. on 1987-89 6-292 engine. It is important that the centering tool be used to align the cover so

the vibration damper installation will not damage the seal. Position seal evenly around damper hub surface.
15. Install vibration damper and torque attaching bolt to 60 ft. lbs. on 1980-86, 6-292 engine and 50 ft. lbs. on 1987-89 6-292 engine.
16. Install accessory drive belt(s) and pulley, as equipped.

### V6-229, 262, V8-267, 305, 350, 400 & 454

1. Remove vibration damper and water pump, then the oil pan, if necessary.
2. Remove cover retaining bolts and cover.
3. Clean gasket surface of block and timing case cover.
4. Remove any excess oil pan gasket material that may be protruding at the oil pan to engine block junction.
5. Apply a thin bead of RTV 1052366 sealer or equivalent to the joint formed at oil pan and block.
6. Coat new gasket with sealer and position it on cover, then install cover to oil pan seal on cover and coat bottom of seal with engine oil.
7. Position cover on engine and loosely install the upper bolts.
8. Tighten bolts alternately and evenly while pressing downward on cover so that dowels are aligned with holes in cover. Do not force cover over dowels as cover can be distorted.

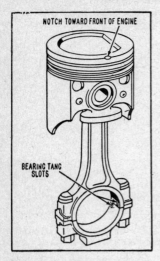

**Fig. 36 Piston & rod assembly. 6-250**

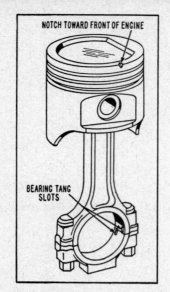

**Fig. 37 Piston & rod assembly. 6-292**

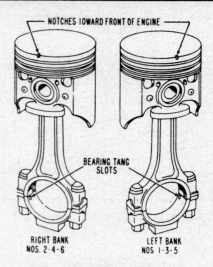

**Fig. 38 Piston & rod assembly. V6-229 & 262**

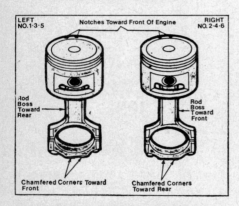

**Fig. 39 Piston & rod assembly. V6-231**

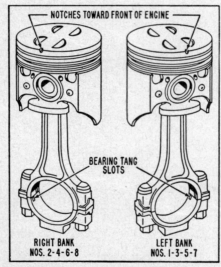

**Fig. 40 Piston & rod assembly. V8-267, 305, 350 & 400**

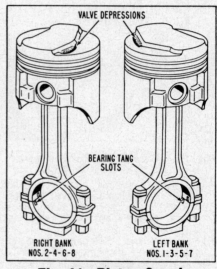

**Fig. 41 Piston & rod assembly. V8-454**

9. Install remaining cover bolts and torque to specifications as follows:On V6-262 engine, torque front cover-to-engine block attaching bolts to 80 inch lbs. on 1985 models, 92 inch lbs. on 1986 models, 100 inch lbs. on 1987 models and 120 inch lbs. on 1988-89 models. On V8-305 and V8-350 engines, torque front cover-to-engine block attaching bolts to 80 inch lbs. on 1980-85 models and 100 inch lbs. on 1986-89 models. On 1980-84 V6-229 and 1980-82 V8-267 engines, torque front cover-to-engine block attaching bolts to 80 inch lbs. On V8-454 engine, torque front cover-to-engine block attaching bolts to 80 inch lbs. on 1980-85 models and 96 inch lbs. on 1986-89 models. Torque oil-pan-to front cover attaching bolts to 55 inch lbs. on 1980-85 models and 70 inch lbs. on 1986-89 models.

10. Install oil pan and torque attaching bolts to specifications as follows: On 1980-84 V6-229, 1985 V6-262, 1980-82 V8-267, 1980-85 V8-305 nd V8-350 engines, torque oil pan-to-engine block attaching bolts to 80 inch lbs. with 1/4 bolts and 265 inch lbs. with 5/16 bolts. On 1986-89 V6-262, V8-305 and V8-350 engines, torque attaching bolts to 100 inch lbs. and attaching nuts to 200 inch lbs. On V8-454 engine, torque oil pan-to-engine block attaching bolts to 135 inch lbs. on 1980-86 models and 160 inch lbs. on 1987-89 models.

11. Install water pump and torque attaching bolts to 30 ft. lbs.

12. Install vibration damper and torque attaching bolt to specifications as follows:On 1980-84 V6-229, 1985 V6-262, 1980-82 V8-267, 1980-85 V8-305 and V8-350 engines, torque vibration damper attaching bolt to 60 ft. lbs. On 1986-89 V6-262, V8-305 and V8-350 engines, torque vibration damper attaching bolt to 70 ft. lbs. On V8-454 engine, torque vibration damper attaching bolt to 85 ft. lbs.

## V6-231

1. Drain cooling system and remove radiator.

2. Remove fan, pulleys and belts.

3. Remove crankshaft pulley and reinforcement.

4. If equipped with power steering, remove any pump bracket bolts attached to timing chain cover and loosen and remove any other bolts necessary that will allow pump and brackets to be moved out of the way.

5. Remove fuel pump.

6. Remove alternator and brackets.

7. Remove distributor cap and pull spark plug wire retainers off brackets on rocker arm cover. Swing distributor cap with wires attached out of the way. Disconnect distributor primary lead.

8. Remove distributor. If chain and sprockets are not to be disturbed, note position of distributor rotor for installation in the same position.

9. Loosen and slide clamp on thermostat bypass hose rearward.

10. Remove bolts attaching chain cover to block.

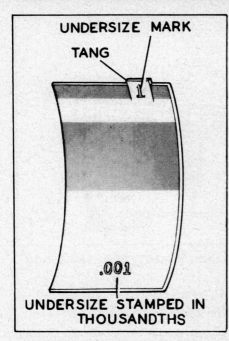

**Fig. 42 Location of main & rod bearing undersize markings. V6-231**

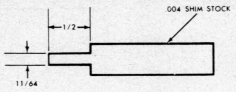

**Fig. 43 Fabricated seal starting tool for helix type seal.**

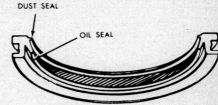

**Fig. 44 Crankshaft rear oil seal. Helix type**

is disturbed. If the pump is not packed it may not pump oil as soon as the engine is started.

13. Torque attaching bolts to specifications as follows:
   a. Torque front cover attaching bolts to 30 ft. lbs.
   b. Torque oil pump cover attaching bolts to 10 ft. lbs.
   c. Torque vibration damper attaching bolt to 175 ft. lbs. on 1980-81 models, and 225 ft. lbs on 1982-84 models.
   d. Torque oil pan attaching bolts to 14 ft. lbs.
   e. Torque water pump attaching bolts to 30 ft. lbs.

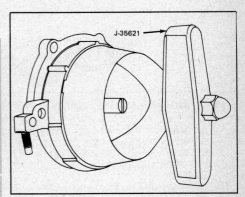

**Fig. 46 Rear oil seal installation. 1986-88 V6-262,**

## TIMING GEARS
### REPLACE
### 6-250, 292

When necessary to install a new camshaft gear, the camshaft will have to be removed as the gear is a pressed fit on the shaft. The camshaft is held in position by a thrust plate which is fastened to the crankcase by two capscrews which are accessible through two holes in the gear web.

Use an arbor press to remove the gear and when doing so, a suitable sleeve, **Fig. 29**, should be employed to support the gear properly on its steel hub. **If old thrust plate is to be used, position it so the key won't cause damage during removal.**

Before installing a new gear, assemble the key, then the spacer with it's champhered end facing the journal radius. Lubricate the thrust plate, and install it to the shaft. Press the gear on until it bottoms against the spacer. The correct camshaft to thrustplate clearance is from .001 inch to .005 inch. on 1980-85 models and .003 inch to .008 inch on 1986-89 models **Fig. 30**.

The crankshaft gear can be removed by utilizing the two tapped holes in conjunction with a gear puller.

When the timing gears are installed, be sure the punch-marks on both gears are in mesh, **Fig. 31**. Backlash between the gears should be from .004 inch to .006 inch, **Fig. 32**. Check the runout of the gears, **Fig. 33**, and if the camshaft gear runout exceeds .004 inch or the crank gear runout is in excess of .003 inch, remove the gear (or gears) and examine for burrs, dirt or some other fault which may cause the runout. If these conditions are not the cause, replace the gear (or gears).

## TIMING CHAIN
### REPLACE
### V6-229, 262, V8-267, 305, 350, 400 & 454

1. Remove timing case cover as outlined previously.
2. Remove crankshaft oil slinger.
3. Position timing marks on sprockets as shown **Fig. 34**.
4. Remove three camshaft-to-sprocket bolts.
5. Remove camshaft sprocket and timing chain together. Sprocket is a light press fit on camshaft for approximately 1/8 inch. If sprocket does not come off easily, a light blow with a plastic hammer on the lower edge of the sprocket should dislodge it.
6. If crankshaft sprocket is to be replaced, remove it with a suitable gear puller. Install new sprocket, aligning key and keyway.
7. Install chain onto camshaft sprocket. Hold sprocket with chain hanging vertically, then align marks on sprockets as shown, **Fig. 34**. The valve timing marks shown in Fig. 34, do not indicate TDC compression stroke for No. 1 cylinder, which is used during distributor installation. If distributor was removed, install timing chain and sprockets, aligning timing marks, Fig. 34, then rotate engine until No. 1 cylinder is on compression and crankshaft timing mark is 180° from valve timing position shown in Fig. 34. Install distributor.
8. Align dowel in camshaft with dowel hole in sprocket and install sprocket on camshaft. Do not attempt to drive

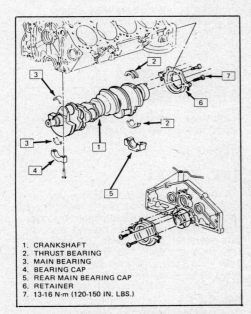

1. CRANKSHAFT
2. THRUST BEARING
3. MAIN BEARING
4. BEARING CAP
5. REAR MAIN BEARING CAP
6. RETAINER
7. 13-16 N·m (120-150 IN. LBS.)

**Fig. 45 Rear crankshaft oil seal. 1986-88 V6-262, V8-305 & V8-350**

11. Remove two oil pan-to-chain cover bolts and remove cover.
12. Reverse procedure to install, noting data shown in Fig. 28. **Remove the oil pump cover and pack the space around the oil pump gears completely with petroleum jelly. There must be no air space left inside the pump. Reinstall the cover using a new gasket. This step is very important as the oil pump may lose its prime whenever the pump, pump cover or timing chain cover**

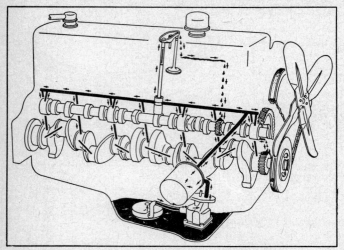

**Engine oiling system. 6-250 & 292**

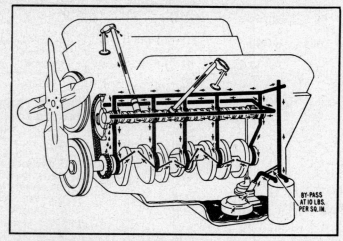

**Engine oiling system. V8-267, 305, 350 & 400**

sprocket on camshaft as welch plug at rear of engine can be dislodged.

9. Draw sprocket onto camshaft, using the three mounting bolts. Torque to 20 ft. lbs.

10. Lubricate timing chain and install cover.

## V6-231

1. With the timing case cover removed as outlined previously, temporarily install the vibration damper bolt and washer in end of crankshaft.

2. Turn crankshaft so sprockets are positioned as shown in **Fig. 35**. Use a sharp rap on a wrench handle to start the vibration damper bolt out, without disturbing the position of the sprockets.

3. Remove oil slinger.

4. Remove camshaft sprocket retaining bolt.

5. Use two large screwdrivers to alternately pry the camshaft sprocket then the crankshaft sprocket forward until the camshaft sprocket is free. Then remove camshaft sprocket and chain, and the crankshaft sprocket.

6. To install, assemble chain on sprockets and slide sprockets on their respective shafts with the "O" marks on the sprockets lined up as shown, **Fig. 35**.

7. Complete the installation in the reverse order of removal. Torque sprocket bolts to 22 ft. lbs.

## CAMSHAFT
### REPLACE
#### 6-250, 292
##### 1980–86

It is recommended that the engine be removed from the vehicle for camshaft removal. Remove rocker arms and pushrods, engine front cover, fuel pump and distributor, and the side cover and lifters, noting position of components for installation. Remove camshaft thrust plate screws and pull camshaft from cylinder block. During installation, coat cam lobes and lifters

with suitable break-in lubricant. If the camshaft is replaced, it is recommended that the lifters be replaced also. If components are reused, they should be installed in original positions. Torque thrust plate bolts to 80 inch lbs.

##### 1987–89

1. Remove necessary front end components.

2. Drain cooling system, then remove radiator, fan shroud, fan and pulley.

3. Remove air cleaner and fuel pump.

4. Remove rocker arm cover, then the distributor assembly.

5. Remove pushrod cover, then the hydraulic valve lifters.

6. Remove torsional damper, then the timing case cover.

7. Align timing marks, **Fig. 31**, then remove thrust plate bolts and the camshaft. **Support camshaft during removal to prevent damage to bearings. On some models, it may be necessary to disconnect front engine mounts and raise engine slightly to provide clearance for camshaft removal.**

8. Reverse procedure to install. Torque thrust plate bolts to 80 inch lbs. **During installation, coat cam lobes and lifters with suitable break-in lubricant. If the camshaft is replaced, it is recommended that the lifters be replaced also. If components are reused, they should be installed in original positions.**

#### V6-229, 262, V8-267, 305, 350, 400 & 454

Depending on vehicle and engine application, the grille, radiator and condenser (if equipped) must be removed to facilitate camshaft removal.

1. Remove intake manifold as outlined previously.

2. Remove pushrods and valve lifters.

3. Remove timing case cover and timing chain as outlined previously.

4. Install two ⁵⁄₁₆-18 x 4 inch bolts into camshaft bolt holes, then pull camshaft out of cylinder block.

5. Reverse procedure to install.

#### V6-231

If engine is in the vehicle, the radiator, grille and A/C components will have to be removed. If engine is out, proceed as follows:

1. To remove camshaft, remove intake manifold, rocker arm shaft assemblies, pushrods and valve lifters.

2. Remove timing chain and sprockets.

3. Slide camshaft out of engine, using care not to mar the bearing surfaces.

4. Reverse procedure to install.

## PISTON & ROD
### ASSEMBLE

Assemble pistons to connecting rods as shown in **Figs. 36 through 41**.

## PISTONS
### EXC. V6-231

A .001 inch oversize piston is available for service use so that proper clearances can be obtained for slightly worn cylinder bores requiring only light honing. In addition, oversizes of .020 inch, .030 inch and .040 inch are available. If the cylinders have less than .005 inch taper or wear, they can be reconditioned with a hone and fitted with the .001 inch oversize piston.

### V6-231

Pistons are available in standard sizes and oversizes of .005, .010 and .030 inch.

## ROD BEARINGS
### 6-250, 292, V6-229, 262, V8-267, 305, 350, 400 & 454

Connecting rod bearing inserts are available in standard size and undersizes of .001 inch, .002 inch, .010 inch and .020 inch. The bearings can be replaced without removing the rod assembly by removing the cap and replacing the upper and lower halves of the bearing.

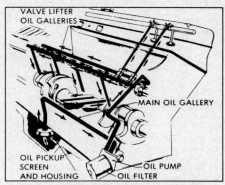

**Engine oiling system. V6-231**

## V6-231

Rod bearings are available in standard sizes and undersizes of .001, .002 and .010 inch. Refer to **Fig. 42,** for undersize markings on bearing.

## MAIN BEARINGS

### 6-250, 292

The rear main bearing journal has no oil hole drilling. To remove the upper bearing half (bearing half with oil hole) proceed as follows after cap is removed:

1. Use a small drift punch and hammer to start the bearing rotating out of the block.
2. Use a pair of pliers (tape jaws) to hold the bearing thrust surface to the oil slinger and rotate the crankshaft to pull the bearing out.
3. To install, start the bearing (side not notched) into side of block by hand, then use pliers as before to turn bearing half into place.
4. The last 1/4 inch movement may be done by holding just the slinger with the pliers or tap in place with a drift punch.

Main bearings are available in standard and undersizes of .001, .002, .009, .010 and .020 inch.

### V6-229, 262, V8-267, 305, 350, 400 & 454

Shell type bearings are used, and if worn excessively, should be replaced. No attempt should be made to shim, file or otherwise take up worn bearings.

Main bearings are available in standard and undersizes of .001, .002, .009, .010 and .020 inch.

### V6-231

Main bearings are available in standard sizes and undersizes of .001, .002, and .010 inch. Refer to **Fig. 42** for undersize markings.

## CRANKSHAFT REAR OIL SEAL

### REPLACE

### EXC. V6-231 & 1986–89 V6-262, V8-305 & V8-350

These engines are equipped with a two-piece, helix type rear seal. A seal starting tool, **Fig. 43,** must be used to prevent the upper seal half from coming into contact with the sharp edge of the block.

When necessary to correct an oil leak due to a defective seal, always replace the upper and lower seal halves as a unit, **Fig. 44.** When installing either half, lubricate the lip portion only with engine oil, keeping oil off the parting line surface as this is treated with glue. Always clean crankshaft surface before installing a new seal.

1. To replace the lower seal, remove seal from groove in bearing cap, using a small screwdriver.
2. Insert new seal and roll it in place with finger and thumb.
3. To replace the upper seal (with engine in car) use a small hammer and tap a brass pin punch on one end of the seal until it protrudes far enough to be removed with pliers.
4. Position tip of tool, **Fig. 43,** between crankshaft and seal seat in cylinder block.
5. Position seal between crankshaft and tip of tool with seal bead contacting tip of tool. Ensure oil seal lip is facing toward front of engine.
6. Roll seal around crankshaft, using tool as a "shoehorn" to protect seal bead from sharp corner of seal seat surface in cylinder block. **Tool must remain in position until seal is properly seated with both ends flush with block.**
7. Remove tool, using care not to dislodge seal.
8. Install new seal into bearing cap with tool as outlined previously.
9. Install bearing cap with sealant applied to the cap to case interface. Do not apply sealant to seal ends. Torque rear main bearing cap bolts to specifications as listed in the "Engine Tightening Specification Chart."

### V6-231

Since the braided fabric seal used on these engines can be replaced only when the crankshaft is removed, the following repair procedure is recommended.

1. Remove oil pan and bearing cap.
2. Drive end of old seal gently into groove, using a suitable tool, until

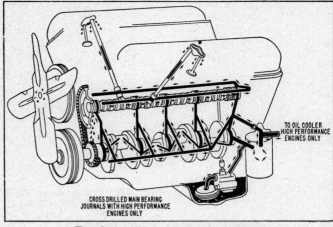

**Engine oiling system. V8-454**

packed tight. This may vary between 1/4 and 3/4 inch depending on amount of pack required.

3. Repeat previous step for other end of seal.
4. Measure and note amount that seal was driven up on one side. Using the old seal removed from bearing cap, cut a length of seal the amount previously noted plus 1/16 inch.
5. Repeat previous step for other side of seal.
6. Pack cut lengths of seal into appropriate side of seal groove. A guide tool, J-21526-1, and packing tool, J-21526-2, may be used since these tools have been machined to provide a built-in stop.
7. Install new seal in bearing cap.

### 1986–89 V6-262, V8-305 & V8-350

The rear main seal used on these engines is a one-piece type, and is mounted in a special seal retainer, **Fig. 45.** Use the following procedure to replace the rear oil seal on these models.

1. Raise and support vehicle, then remove transmission and flex plate.
2. Pry out seal with screwdriver, using notches provided in retainer. **Take care not to mar crankshaft sealing surface when removing seal.**
3. Lubricate inner and outer diameter of replacement seal with engine oil, then install seal on tool J-35621 or equivalent, **Fig. 46.**
4. Thread screws of installation tool into rear of crankshaft, snugly tightening screws to ensure seal is seal is square with crankshaft.
5. Tighten wing nut on tool until it bottoms.
6. Remove installation tool, torque flex plate attaching bolts to 75 ft. lbs. and bellhousing bolts to 32 ft. lbs.

## OIL PAN

### REPLACE

### 6-250, 292

### Exc. 1980–84 G Models

1. Disconnect battery ground cable.

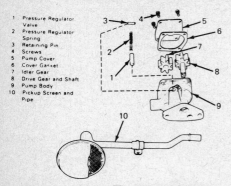

1. Pressure Regulator Valve
2. Pressure Regulator Spring
3. Retaining Pin
4. Screws
5. Pump Cover
6. Cover Gasket
7. Idler Gear
8. Drive Gear and Shaft
9. Pump Body
10. Pickup Screen and Pipe

**Fig. 47   Oil pump. 6-250 & 292**

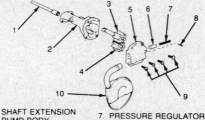

1. SHAFT EXTENSION
2. PUMP BODY
3. DRIVE GEAR AND SHAFT
4. IDLER GEAR
5. PUMP COVER
6. PRESSURE REGULATOR VALVE
7. PRESSURE REGULATOR SPRING
8. RETAINING PIN
9. SCREWS
10. PICKUP SCREEN AND PIPE

**Fig. 48   Oil pump. V6-229, 262, V8-267, 305, 350 & 400**

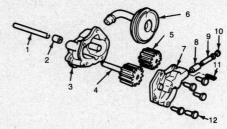

1. Shaft Extension
2. Shaft Coupling
3. Pump Body
4. Drive Gear and Shaft
5. Idler Gear
6. Pickup Screen and Pipe
7. Pump Cover
8. Pressure Regulator Valve
9. Pressure Regulator Spring
10. Washer
11. Retaining Pin
12. Screws

**Fig. 49   Oil pump. V8-454**

2. Raise and support vehicle. Drain oil pan and remove starter.
3. Remove flywheel splash shield or converter under pan, as applicable.
4. Remove front engine mount through bolts, raise front of engine and reinstall bolts, then lower engine.
5. Remove oil pan bolts and oil pan.
6. Reverse procedure to install. Torque oil pan-to-engine block attaching bolts from 75-80 inch lbs.

### 1980–84 G Models

1. Disconnect battery ground cable. Remove engine cover.
2. Remove air cleaner and studs. Remove fan shroud and radiator upper support brackets.
3. Raise and support vehicle.
4. On models equipped with a manual transmission:
   a. Disconnect clutch cross shaft from motor mount bracket.
   b. Remove transmission to bellhousing upper bolt.
   c. Remove transmission rear mount bolts and install two 7/16 x 3 inch bolts.
   d. Raise transmission and install 2 inch block between mount and crossmember.
5. On all models, remove starter and drain oil.
6. Remove front engine mount through bolts, raise engine and install wood blocks between engine mounts and crossmember brackets.
7. Remove flywheel splash shield or converter cover, as applicable.
8. Remove oil pan bolts and lower pan.
9. Reverse procedure to install. Torque oil pan-to-engine block attaching bolts from 75-80 inch lbs.

### V6-229, 262, V8-267, 305, 350 & 400

#### 1980–84

1. Drain engine oil and remove dipstick and tube.
2. If equipped, remove exhaust crossover pipe.
3. With automatic transmission, remove converter housing under pan.
4. Remove starter brace and inboard bolt and swing starter aside.
5. On K models, remove strut rods, if equipped.

6. On El Camino and Caballero with V6-229, remove upper half of fan shroud. Loosen left engine front mount through bolt and remove right bolt. Raise engine and reinstall bolt. Do not tighten.
7. Remove oil pan and discard gaskets and seals.
8. Reverse procedure to install. Torque oil pan attaching bolts to specifications as follows: On V6-229/3.8L VIN K & 9 and V8-267/4.4L engines, torque oil pan attaching bolts to 80 inch lbs. with 1/4-20 bolts; and 265 inch lbs. with 5/16-18 bolts. On V8-305/5.0L and V8-350/5.7L engines, torque oil pan attaching bolts to 80 inch lbs w/1/4 20 bolts; and 165 inch lbs. w/5/16-18 bolts.

#### 1985–89

Late production 1985 and all 1986-89 models with V6-262 engines are equipped with a one-piece oil pan gasket that replaces the four-piece gasket previously used. The one-piece gasket (P/N14081222) can be installed on all V6-262 engines and should be used during installation whenever the oil pan is removed.

#### Caballero & El Camino

1. Disconnect battery ground cable, then remove air cleaner.
2. Remove upper fan shroud.
3. Raise and support vehicle, then drain oil pan.
4. On V8 engines, disconnect AIR pipes from converter and exhaust manifold.
5. On all models, remove exhaust crossover pipe and converter as an assembly.
6. Remove starter and flywheel cover.
7. Disconnect transmission cooler lines at oil pan.
8. On V8 engines, remove engine mount through bolts. On V6 engines, loosen right bolt and remove left through bolt.
9. Remove oil pan attaching bolts, then lower oil pan. **If crankshaft counterweights are blocking oil pan removal, turn crankshaft as necessary to facilitate removal.**
10. Raise engine and reinstall engine mount through bolts to provide necessary clearance, then remove oil pan.

11. Reverse procedure to install. Torque oil pan attaching bolts to specifications as follows: On 1985 V6-262/4.3L, 1985 V8-305/5.0L and V8-350/5.7L engines, torque oil pan-to-engine block attaching bolts to 80 inch lbs. with 1/4-20 bolts; and to 265 inch lbs. with 5/16-18 bolts. On 1986-89 V6-262/4.3L, V8-305/5.0L and V8-350/5.7L engines, torque attaching bolts to 100 inch lbs.; and attaching nuts to 200 inch lbs.

### Series 10–30/1500–3500

1. Disconnect battery ground cable and drain oil pan.
2. Raise and support vehicle, then remove exhaust crossover pipe.
3. On vehicles equipped with automatic transmission, remove converter housing under pan.
4. If equipped with V6 engine, remove strut rods at flywheel cover, then remove starter.
5. On K and V models with automatic transmission, remove strut rods at motor mounts.
6. Remove oil pan attaching bolts, then the oil pan.
7. Reverse procedure to install. Torque oil pan attaching bolts to specifications as follows: On 1985 V6-262/4.3L, 1985 V8-305/5.0L and V8-350/5.7L engines, torque oil pan-to-engine block attaching bolts to 80 inch lbs. with 1/4-20 bolts; and to 265 inch lbs. with 5/16-18 bolts. On 1986-89 V6-262/4.3L, V8-305/5.0L and V8-350/5.7L engines, torque attaching bolts to 100 inch lbs.; and attaching nuts to 200 inch lbs.

### V6-231

1. Support vehicle on hoist and drain oil.
2. Remove flywheel cover and exhaust crossover pipe, then raise engine.
3. Remove oil pan bolts and allow pan to drop. **To remove oil pan, front wheels must be turned to the left, also the crankshaft may have to be turned to provide clearance.**
4. Reverse procedure to install. Torque oil pan attaching bolts to 14 ft. lbs. **Some 1981-84 engines use R.T.V. silicone sealer instead of a cork gasket for oil pan to crankcase**

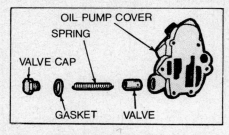

**Fig. 50   Oil pump cover & bypass valve. V6-231**

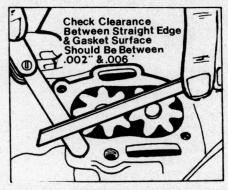

Check Clearance Between Straight Edge & Gasket Surface Should Be Between .002" & .006"

**Fig. 51   Checking clearance between oil pump gear & housing gasket surface. V6-231**

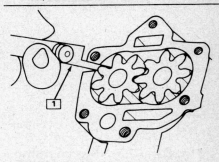

1  CHECK CLEARANCE BETWEEN GEAR TEETH AND SIDE WALL, CLEARANCE SHOULD BE BETWEEN .002" & .005"

**Fig. 52   Checking oil pump side clearance. V6-231**

sealing. When replacing the oil pan or sealing material on these engines, either R.T.V. sealer or a cork gasket can be used during reassembly. If R.T.V. sealer is used, the pan rail and block sealing surfaces should be cleaned thoroughly and a ¼ inch bead of sealant applied evenly to the pan rail, avoiding any breaks or gaps in the sealer during application.

## V8-454

1. Disconnect battery ground cable.
2. Loosen fan shroud, then remove air cleaner assembly.
3. Remove distributor cap.
4. Raise and support vehicle, then drain oil pan.
5. On manual transmission equipped vehicles, remove starter.
6. Remove torque converter or clutch cover as applicable.
7. Remove oil filter.
8. If equipped with oil pressure gauge, disconnect oil pressure line from side of cylinder block to prevent damaging line.
9. Remove engine mount through bolts, then raise engine.
10. Remove oil pan attaching bolts, then the oil pan.
11. Reverse procedure to install. Torque oil pan-to-engine block attaching bolts to 135 inch lbs. on 1985-86 models; and to 160 inch lbs. on 1987-89 models.

# REAR OIL SEAL RETAINER
## REPLACE
### 1986—89 V6-262, V8-305 & V8-350

1. Disconnect battery ground cable, raise and support vehicle, and drain oil pan.
2. Remove transmission and flex plate.
3. Remove oil pan retaining bolts and lower oil pan.
4. Remove screws securing retainer, retainer and gasket, **Fig. 45**, then remove seal from retainer. **Whenever the retainer is removed, the retainer gasket and rear oil seal should be replaced.**
5. Clean retainer, pan and engine block mating surfaces.
6. Position retainer gasket on block studs, then install retainer and torque

fasteners to 120-150 inch lbs. on 1985-87 models or 135 inch lbs. on 1988-89 models.
7. Install rear oil seal as outlined.
8. Reverse remaining procedure to complete installation, using new oil pan gaskets as needed. Torque oil pan-to-engine block attaching bolts to 100 inch lbs., and attaching nuts to 200 inch lbs. Torque flex plate attaching bolts to 75 ft. lbs. and bellhousing bolts to 32 ft. lbs.

# OIL PUMP SERVICE
## 6-250, 292, V6-229, 262, V8-267, 305, 350, 400 & 454
### Removal & Installation

1. Remove oil pan as described previously.
2. On 1980-85 6-250 and 6-292 engines, remove the two flange mounting bolts, then the pickup pipe bolt and oil pump assembly.
3. On all except 1980-85 6-250 and 6-292 engines, remove pump to rear main bearing cap nut, then the pump and extension shaft.
4. Reverse procedure to install. Torque oil pump attaching bolt(s) to 65 ft. lbs on all exc. 6-250 and 6-292 engines; and to 115 inch lbs. on all 6-250 and 6-292 engines.

### Disassembly, Inspection & Assembly

1. Remove oil pump as described previously.
2. Remove pump cover screws and pump cover, **Figs. 47 through 49**. On 6-250 and 292 engines, remove pump cover gasket.
3. Mark gear teeth so they can be reassembled with same teeth indexing, then remove drive gear, idler gear and shaft.
4. Remove pressure regulator valve retaining pin, pressure regulator valve and related parts.
5. If pickup screen and pipe require replacement, mount pump in a soft-jawed vise and extract pipe from pump.

6. Wash all parts in cleaning solvent and dry with compressed air.
7. Inspect pump body and cover for cracks and excessive wear.
8. Inspect pump gears for damage or excessive wear.
9. Check drive gear shaft for looseness in pump body.
10. Inspect inside of pump cover for wear that would allow oil to leak past the ends of the gears.
11. Inspect pickup screen and pipe assembly for damage to screen, pipe or relief grommet.
12. Check pressure regulator valve for proper fit in pump housing.
13. Reverse procedure to assemble. Turn driveshaft by hand to check for smooth operation. **The pump gears and body are not serviced separately. If the pump gears or body are damaged or worn, the pump assembly should be replaced. Also, if the pickup screen was removed, it should be replaced with a new one as loss of the press fit condition could result in an air leak and loss of oil pressure.**

## V6-231
### Removal & Disassembly

1. Remove oil filter.
2. Disconnect wire from oil pressure indicator switch in filter bypass valve cap (if so equipped).
3. Remove screws attaching oil pump cover to timing chain cover. Remove cover and slide out pump gears. Replace any parts not serviceable.
4. Remove oil pressure relief valve cap, spring and valve, **Fig. 50**.
5. Check relief valve in its bore in cover. Valve should have no more clearance than an easy slip fit. If any perceptible side shake can be felt, the valve and/or cover should be replaced.
6. The filter bypass valve should be flat and free of nicks and scratches.

### Assembly & Installation

1. Lubricate and install pressure relief valve and spring in bore of pump cover. Install cap and gasket. Torque cap to 30-35 ft. lbs.
2. Install pump gears and shaft in pump body section of timing chain cover to check gear end clearance. Check

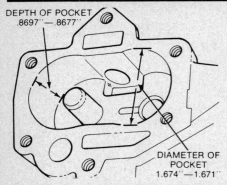

**Fig. 53 Checking oil pump gear pocket for wear. V6-231**

clearance as shown in **Fig. 51.** If clearance is less than .0020 inch, check timing chain cover for evidence of wear.

3. Check oil pump side clearance as shown in **Fig. 52.** Clearance should be .002-.005 inch. If clearance is not as specified, measure gears and pocket to determine which is at fault, **Figs. 53 and 54.**
4. Check oil pump cover for wear with straightedge and feeler gauge. If clearance is greater than .001 inch, replace cover.
5. If clearances are as specified, remove gears and pack gear pocket with petroleum jelly.
6. Reinstall gears so petroleum jelly is forced into every cavity of gear pocket and between teeth of gears. Unless pump is packed with petroleum jelly, it may not prime itself when engine is started.
7. Install cover and tighten screws alternately and evenly. Final tightening is

10-15 ft. lbs. torque. Install filter on nipple.

## FUEL PUMP
## REPLACE
### MECHANICAL PUMP

1. Disconnect fuel lines and vapor return hose, if equipped, from fuel pump.
2. Remove fuel pump attaching bolts.
3. Remove fuel pump, pushrod, gasket and mounting plate, if equipped.
4. Reverse procedure to install, using a new gasket.

### ELECTRIC PUMP

1. Disconnect battery ground cable.
2. Raise and support vehicle.
3. Remove fuel tank.
4. Turn pump cam lock ring counterclockwise and remove fuel lever sending unit and pump assembly.
5. Pull fuel pump up into hose while pulling away from bottom support, then remove pump from rubber connector.
6. Reverse procedure to install, using a new O-ring.

## WATER PUMP
## REPLACE
### EXC. V6-231

1. Drain cooling system.
2. Remove accessory drive belts as equipped and the fan.
3. Disconnect all hoses from water pump.
4. Remove alternator upper and lower mounting braces, if necessary.
5. Remove pump attaching bolts and remove water pump. On 6-250 engines,

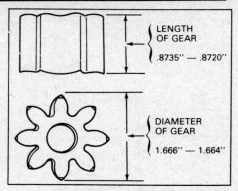

**Fig. 54 Checking oil pump gears for wear. V6-231**

pull pump straight out of block to prevent damage to impeller.

6. Reverse procedure to install. On in-line 6 cylinder engines torque water pump attaching bolts to 15 ft. lbs. On all other engines torque to 30 ft. lbs.

### V6-231

1. Disconnect battery ground cable, then drain cooling system.
2. Remove drive belts, then remove fan and pulley from water pump shaft hub. **On some models, it may be necessary to remove the alternator upper and lower mounting braces, and if equipped, the lower power steering pump brace.**
3. Disconnect radiator hose and heater hose from water pump fittings.
4. Remove bolts attaching water pump to timing case cover, then remove water pump assembly.
5. Reverse procedure to install. Torque water pump attaching bolts to 30 ft. lbs.

## INDEX

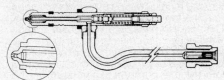

**Fig. 1 Fuel injection nozzle. 1980 all & 1981 exc. Calif.**

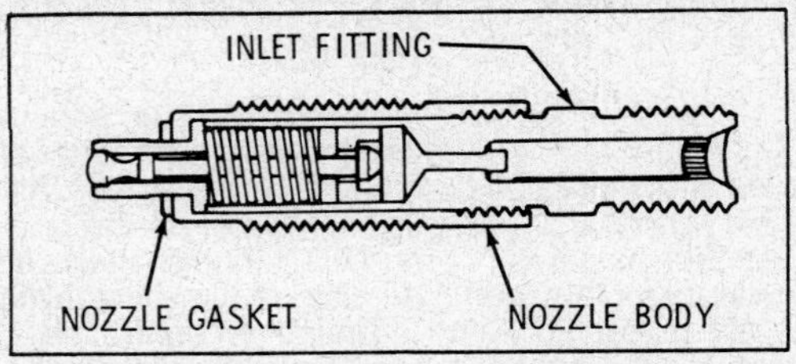

**Fig. 2 Fuel injection nozzle. 1981 Calif. & all 1983-84**

INLET FITTING

NOZZLE GASKET    NOZZLE BODY

# DESCRIPTION
## ENGINE CONSTRUCTION

The Oldsmobile four stroke cycle diesel V8-350 engine is basically the same in construction as the Oldsmobile gasoline V8-350 engine. The cylinders are numbered 1, 3, 5, 7 on the left bank and 2, 4, 6, 8 on the right bank. The firing order is 1-8-4-3-6-5-7-2. The major differences between the diesel and gasoline versions is in the cylinder heads, combustion chamber, fuel distribution system, air intake manifold and method of ignition. The cylinder block, crankshaft, main bearings, connecting rods, pistons and pins are of heavy construction due to the high compression ratio required to ignite the diesel fuel. The diesel fuel is ignited when the heat developed in the combustion chamber during the compression stroke reaches a certain temperature.

The valve train operates the same as in the gasoline engine, but are of special design and material for diesel operation. The stainless steel pre-chamber inserts in the cylinder head combustion chambers are serviced separately from the cylinder head. With the cylinder head removed, these pre-chamber inserts can be driven from the cylinder head after removing the glow plugs or injection nozzles.

On 1980 models and 1981 models except California, the glow plugs are threaded into the cylinder head and the injection nozzles are retained by a bolt and clamp. On 1981 California and all 1983-84 models, the glow plugs and the injection nozzles are both threaded into the cylinder head. The injection nozzles are spring loaded and calibrated to open at a specified fuel pressure.

## FUEL SYSTEM

The fuel injection pump is mounted on top of the engine and is gear driven by the camshaft and rotates at camshaft speed. This high pressure rotary pump injects a metered amount of fuel to each cylinder at the proper time. Eight high pressure fuel delivery pipes from the injection pump to the injection nozzles, **Figs. 1 and 2,** are the same length to prevent any difference in timing from cylinder to cylinder. The fuel injection pump provides the required timing advance under all operating conditions. Engine speed is controlled by a rotary fuel metering valve, **Fig. 3.** When the accelerator is depressed, the throttle cable opens the metering valve and allows more fuel to be delivered to the engine. The injection pump also incorporates a low pressure transfer pump to deliver fuel to the fuel line to the high pressure pump, **Fig. 3.**

The fuel filter is located between the mechanical fuel pump and the injection pump. The diaphragm type mechanical fuel pump is mounted on the right side of the engine and is driven by a cam on the crankshaft. The fuel tank at the rear of the vehicle is connected by fuel pipes to the mechanical fuel pump. Excess fuel returns from the fuel injection pump and injection nozzles to the fuel tank through pipes and hoses.

Injection nozzles used on 1981 California models and all 1983-84 models do not use a fuel return line.

## WATER IN FUEL SYSTEM

This system is available on some 1980 and all 1981 and 1983-84 models. These vehicles have a "Water in Fuel" light mounted in the instrument panel. The "Water in Fuel" light has a bulb check feature and should light for 2 to 2½ seconds when the ignition is turned on. If not, the bulb is burned out or there is an open in the wiring circuit. When there is water in the fuel, the light will come back on and remain on after a 15 to 20 second delay.

A water sensing probe, mounted on the fuel sender, actuates the instrument panel light when it is partially covered with water. About 1 to 2½ gallons of water must be present in the fuel tank to cause the sensor light to activate.

If the "Water in Fuel" lamp goes on while the vehicle is being driven, the fuel system should be checked for water. If the lamp goes on immediately after refueling and before the vehicle is moved, there is a large quantity of water in the tank and should be removed immediately.

The water may be removed from the tank with a pump or by siphoning. The pump or siphon hose should be connected to the quarter inch fuel return hose (the smaller of the two hoses), located under the hood near the fuel pump. Refer to "Purging Water From Fuel Tank" procedure.

## FUEL HEATER

This cold weather device is installed on some 1981 and 1983-84 vehicles. This thermostatically controlled fuel heater reduces the possibility of wax plugging the filter when temperatures are below 20°F. Battery voltage is directed to the heater whenever the ignition is in the "Run" position.

The heater consists of a strip spiral wound around the fuel pipe and a bimetal thermal switch which closes and completes the circuit when fuel temperatures are approximately 20°F. When fuel temperatures reach 50°F the thermal switch opens and deactivates the circuit.

The fuel tank filter sock is equipped with a bypass valve which opens when the filter is covered with wax, allowing fuel to flow to the heater.

## HOUSING PRESSURE COLD ADVANCE (HPCA)

This feature is used on all 1981 and 1983-84 engines and advances the injection timing 3° during cold operation. This circuit is actuated by a temperature switch calibrated to open the circuit at 125°F. Below the switching point, housing pressure is decreased from 10 to 0 psi which advances the injection timing 3°. Above the switching point, the switch opens, de-energizing the solenoid and the hous-

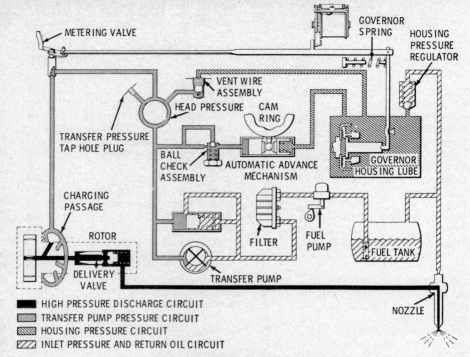

**Fig. 3   Fuel injection pump circuit**

ing pressure is returned to 10 psi. The fast idle solenoid is energized by the same switch and closes when the temperature falls below 95°F.

## HOUSING PRESSURE ALTITUDE ADVANCE (HPAA)

Used on 1984 engines, the HPAA is used to meet emission standards at both low and high altitudes. Altitude compensation is achieved through timing changes and EGR modification and is controlled by an altitude sensitive switch.

Timing is controlled by two pressure regulators, the Housing Pressure Cold Advance, located in the injection pump, and the Housing Pressure Altitude Advance solenoid in the fuel return line.

The HPAA solenoid regulates housing pressure according to altitude. When the solenoid is activated, the glass check ball seats, regulating pressure at its calibrated value. When the solenoid is de-activated, the check ball moves off its seat, opening the fuel return line and preventing pressure regulation. It is possible for both the HPCA and the HPAA to regulate housing pressure at the same time. Likewise, it is also possible to have just the HPCA or the HPAA regulate pressure singularly. The HPCA must be energized and not regulating to allow the HPAA solenoid to regulate at its calibrated value.

## ENGINE LUBRICATION SYSTEM

On 1980 engines, the recommended diesel engine oil designation is SE/CC. On 1981 engines, the recommended diesel engine oil is SF/CC, SF/CD or SE/CC. On 1983-84 engines, the recommended die-

sel engine oil is SF/SC or SF/CD, it is also recommended that the oil be a fuel saving product.

The diesel engine lubrication system is basically the same as the gasoline engine. The fuel injection pump driven gear is lubricated by oil directed through a passage from the top of the camshaft bearing, **Fig. 4.** An angled passage in the shaft portion of the driven gear directs the oil to the rear driven gear bearing. At the front of the right oil gallery, a small orifice sprays oil to lubricate the fuel pump eccentric cam on the crankshaft and timing chain.

## ENGINE COOLING SYSTEM

The diesel engine cooling system is the same as the gasoline engine except the radiator incorporates two oil coolers. One cooler is used to cool the transmission fluid and the other cooler is used to cool the engine oil.

## ENGINE ELECTRICAL SYSTEM

### 1980—81 & 1983

Eight glow plugs are used to pre-heat the pre-chamber to aid in starting. The type 1 glow plugs are 12 volt heaters and are activated when the ignition switch is turned to the "Run" position. The type 1 system uses steady current applied to 12 volt glow plugs. The type 2 system uses 6 volt glow plugs with a controlled pulsating current applied to them for starting. The type 2 glow plug system uses an electromechanical controller for glow plug temperature, pre glow time, wait/start lights and after glow time. The 6 and 12 volt plugs are not interchangeable and can be identified by the wire connector spade. The 6 volt glow plugs have a 5/16 inch wire

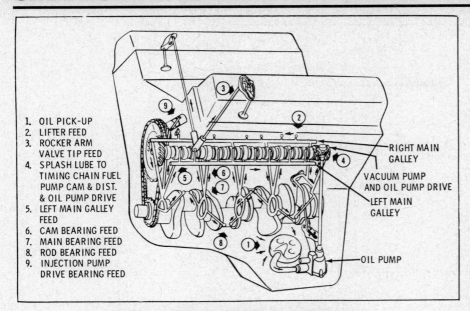

1. OIL PICK-UP
2. LIFTER FEED
3. ROCKER ARM VALVE TIP FEED
4. SPLASH LUBE TO TIMING CHAIN FUEL PUMP CAM & DIST. & OIL PUMP DRIVE
5. LEFT MAIN GALLEY FEED
6. CAM BEARING FEED
7. MAIN BEARING FEED
8. ROD BEARING FEED
9. INJECTION PUMP DRIVE BEARING FEED

RIGHT MAIN GALLEY

VACUUM PUMP AND OIL PUMP DRIVE

LEFT MAIN GALLEY

OIL PUMP

**Fig. 4   Engine lubricating system**

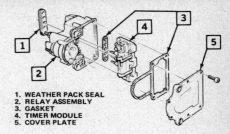

1. WEATHER PACK SEAL
2. RELAY ASSEMBLY
3. GASKET
4. TIMER MODULE
5. COVER PLATE

**Fig. 5   Glow plug control module. 1984**

connector spade, while the 12 volt plugs have a ¼ inch wide spade. The glow plug remains activated for a short time after starting then is automatically turned "Off." Two 12 volt batteries, connected in parallel, are required for the higher electrical load due to the glow plugs and starting motor. The diesel starter motor is larger than the gasoline starter motor. It is designed to crank the engine at least the 100 RPM required for starting. An alternator supplies charging current to both batteries at the same time and there are no switches or relays in the charging circuit.

## 1984

A new glow plug system is used for 1984 diesel engines. A self-limiting feature regulates maximum temperature, while the glow plugs are programmed to shut off automatically should the vehicle not be started within the specified time period.

### System Components

The glow plug control module, **Fig. 5**, is an integral assembly that includes the timer functions, lamp switch and glow plug relay. The control module serves the following functions:
1. Controls wait lamp operation, which varies according to system voltage and/or ambient temperature.
2. Controls system shutdown timing depending on voltage and ambient temperature.
3. An overvoltage function that protects the glow plugs from failure, should higher than normal voltages be incurred.
4. A thermal cutout function that disengages the glow plug system when module temperatures are greater than 113°F.
5. A power relay function that switches the voltage applied to the glow plugs.
6. A quick reset function that permits the module to recycle quickly, after initial shutdown time.

This control module can only be used with glow plugs that regulate their own temperature. The new glow plugs used have positive temperature coefficient properties, which mean they have low resistance values at low temperatures and high resistance values at high temperatures. The new plugs offer a fast temperature rise similar to past fixed resistance plugs, plus improved and simpler glow plug control.

### System Operation

The glow plug control circuit, **Fig. 6**, operates the glow plug system in three steps: pre glow, after-glow and off. During pre-glow, the circuit activates the wait lamp and heats the glow plugs until they are sufficiently warm to start the engine. During after-glow, the circuit deactivates the wait lamp, but continues to apply power to the glow plugs. During the Off cycle, the circuit removes power from the glow plugs and keeps it off until the engine is restarted.

As stated previously, the glow plug control module controls all circuit functions. The thermal controls open the pre glow and after-glow switches to end the respective cycles, and are responsive to engine temperature. When the system is energized with the engine cold, both switches are in the "Cold" position. As time passes, current flow heats the thermal controls, moving both switches toward their "Hot" position. The time needed for each switch to reach its "Hot" position is dependent upon how cold the engine and control module were when the system was first energized. As the pre glow switch reaches the "Hot" position, the wait lamp deactivates and the engine may now be started. The control module continues to operate, whether the engine is started or not, since the after-glow switch has not yet reached its "Hot" position. Current flow continues to heat the thermal control. When the thermal control reaches full temperature, the after-glow switch moves to "Hot," opening

the path to ground from the coil of the glow plug relay. This allows current flow to bypass the coil of the reset relay. With the path to ground now open, current must flow to bypass the coil of the reset relay. With the path to ground now open, current must flow to ground through the reset relay coil. The glow plug relay de-energizes, removing power to the glow plugs. The reset relay now energizes, opening the contact of the relay and locking off the thermal controls. When the ignition switch is turned off, the reset relay contact closes, and the glow plug module is ready to repeat the cycle. If the engine is above 140°F when restarted, the thermal controls will be "Hot," energizing the reset relay and preventing glow plug operation.

The over-voltage protector protects the glow plugs should battery voltage rise above 14 volts. When the protector senses over 14 volts, it opens the circuit to the glow plug relay coil and prevents current from flowing to the glow plugs. After a short time, the protector closes the circuit. If battery voltage is still above 14 volts, it will reopen the circuit again. The protector continues to cycle in this way as long as the over-voltage condition exists and as long as glow plug operation is needed.

## DIESEL ENGINE DIAGNOSIS

Refer to **Fig. 6A** to diagnose engine malfunctions.

## GLOW PLUG SYSTEM TROUBLESHOOTING & DIAGNOSIS
### 1984

Refer to wiring diagram, **Fig. 7**, then use the following procedures for troubleshooting and diagnosis of glow plug system. When troubleshooting system, the glow plug controller must be operated with engine below 122°F. If it is necessary to remove or test glow plug controller, ensure that battery ground cable is disconnected, since damage to electrical components may result.

### No Wait Lamp-Engine Cold

1. With ignition switch in "Run" position and engine off, check wait lamp operation. Wait lamp should be on. If not, proceed to next step.

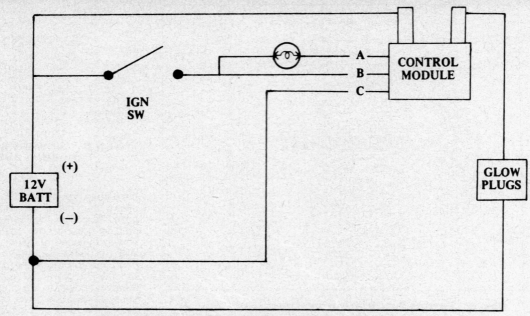

**Fig. 6  Glow plug control circuit schematic. 1984**

## DIESEL ENGINE DIAGNOSIS

| Condition | Possible Cause | Correction |
|---|---|---|
| **ENGINE WILL NO CRANK** | 1. Loose or corroded battery cables | 1. Check connections at battery, engine block and starter solenoid. |
| | 2. Discharged batteries | 2. Check charging system. |
| | 3. Starter inoperative | 3. Check starting system. |
| **ENGINE CRANKS SLOWLY—WILL NOT START (Minimum Engine Crank Speed—100 RPM)** | 1. Battery cable connections loose or corroded | 1. Check connections at battery, engine block and starter. |
| | 2. Batteries undercharged. | 2. Check charging system. |
| | 3. Wrong engine oil | 3. Drain and refill with recommended oil. |
| **ENGINE CRANKS NORMALLY—WILL NOT START** | 1. Incorrect starting procedure. | 1. Use recommended starting procedure. |
| | 2. Incorrect or contaminated fuel | 2. Flush fuel system and install correct fuel. |
| | 3. No fuel to nozzles | 3. Loosen injection line at a nozzle. Do not disconnect. Use care to direct fuel away from sources of ignition. Wipe connection to be sure it is dry. Crank 5 seconds. Fuel should flow from injection line. Tighten connection. If fuel does not flow, check fuel solenoid operation as follows: |
| | | Connect a 12 volt test lamp from wire at injection pump solenoid to ground. Turn ignition to "On". Lamp should light. |
| | | If lamp does not light, check wiring to solenoid. |
| | 4. No fuel to injection pump | 4. Remove line at inlet to injection pump fuel filter. Connect hose from line to metal container. Crank engine. If no fuel is discharged, test the fuel supply pump. |
| | | If lamp does not light, check wiring to solenoid. |
| | | If the pump is OK, check the injection pump fuel filter and replace if plugged. If filter and inlet line to injection pump are OK, replace injection pump. |

**Fig. 6A  Diesel engine diagnostic chart (Part 1 of 4)**

| Condition | Possible Cause | Correction |
|---|---|---|
| **ENGINE CRANKS NORMALLY—WILL NOT START (Continued)** | 5. Plugged fuel return system | 5. Disconnect fuel return line at injection pump and route hose to a metal container. Connect a hose to the injection pump connection and route it to the metal container. Crank the engine; if engine starts and runs, correct restriction in fuel return system. |
| | 6. Pump timing incorrect | 6. Make certain that pump timing mark is aligned with mark on adapter. |
| | 7. Glow plug control system inoperative | 7. Refer to Glow Plug System Trouble-Shooting & Diagnosis. |
| | 8. Glow plugs inoperative | 8. Refer to Glow Plug System Trouble-Shooting & Diagnosis. |
| | 9. Internal engine problems | 9. Correct as necessary. |
| | 10. No voltage to fuel solenoid | 10. Connect a 12 volt test lamp from injection pump solenoid to ground. Turn ignition to "On"; lamp should light. If lamp lights, remove test lamp and connect and disconnect solenoid connector and listen for solenoid operation. If solenoid does not operate, remove injection pump for repairs. If lamp does not light, refer to Glow Plug System Trouble-Shooting & Diagnosis. |
| | 11. Restricted fuel tank filter. | 11. Remove fuel tank and check filter. |
| **ENGINE STARTS BUT WILL NOT CONTINUE TO RUN AT IDLE** | 1. No fuel in tank | 1. Install correct fuel in tank. |
| | 2. Incorrect or contaminated fuel | 2. Flush fuel system and install correct fuel. |
| | 3. Limited fuel to injection pump | 3. Test the fuel supply pump. Replace as necessary. |
| | 4. Fuel solenoid disengaged with ignition switch in the "ON" position | 4. Connect a 12 volt test lamp from wire at injection pump solenoid to ground. Turn ignition to "ON". Lamp should light. Turn ignition to "START". Lamp should light. If lamp does not light in both positions, check wiring to solenoid. |
| | 5. Restricted fuel return system | 5. Disconnect fuel return to a metal container. Connect a hose to injection pump connection and route to metal container. Crank engine; if engine starts and runs, correct restriction in fuel system. |
| | 6. Fast idle solenoid inoperative | 6. With engine cold, start car; solenoid should move to support injection pump lever in "Fast idle position" for about 5 seconds. If solenoid does not move, refer to Electrical System Diagnosis. |
| | 7. Low idle incorrectly adjusted | 7. Adjust idle screw to specification. |
| | 8. Pump timing incorrect. | 8. Make certain that timing mark, on injection pump, is aligned with mark on adapter. |
| | 9. Glow plug control system malfunction | 9. Refer to Glow Plug System Trouble-Shooting & Diagnosis. |
| | 10. Injection pump malfunction | 10. Install replacement pump. |
| | 11. Internal engine problems | 11. Correct as necessary. |
| **ENGINE STARTS, IDLES ROUGH, WITHOUT ABNORMAL NOISE OR SMOKE** | 1. Low idle incorrectly adjusted | 1. Adjust idle screw to specification |
| | 2. Injection line leaks | 2. Wipe off injection lines and connections. Run engine and check for leaks. Correct leaks. |
| | 3. Restricted fuel return system | 3. Disconnect fuel return line at injection pump and route hose to a metal container. Connect a hose to the injection pump container. Crank the engine; if engine starts and runs, correct restriction in fuel return system. |

**Fig. 6A   Diesel engine diagnostic chart (Part 2 of 4)**

| Condition | Possible Cause | Correction |
|---|---|---|
| **ENGINE STARTS, IDLES ROUGH, WITHOUT ABNORMAL NOISE OR SMOKE, continued** | 4. Incorrect or contaminated fuel | 4. Flush fuel system and install correct fuel. |
| | 5. Nozzle(s) inoperative | 5. With engine running, loosen injection line fitting at each nozzle in turn. Use care to direct fuel away from sources of ignition. Each nozzle should contribute to rough running. If nozzle is found that does not change idle quality, it should be replaced. |
| | 6. Internal fuel leak at nozzle(s) | 6. Disconnect fuel return system from nozzles on one bank at a time. With the engine running, observe the normal fuel seepage at the nozzles. Replace any nozzle with excessive fuel leakage. |
| | 7. Fuel supply pump malfunctions | 7. Test the fuel supply pump. Replace if necessary. |
| | 8. Uneven fuel distribution to cylinders | 8. Install new or reconditioned nozzles, one at a time, until condition is corrected as indicated by normal idle. |
| **ENGINE STARTS AND IDLES ROUGH WITH EXCESSIVE NOISE AND/OR SMOKE** | 1. Injection pump timing incorrect | 1. Be sure timing mark on injection pump is aligned with mark on adapter. |
| | 2. Nozzle(s) inoperative | 2. With engine running, crank injection line at each nozzle, one at a time. Use care to direct fuel away from sources of ignition. Each nozzle should contribute to rough running. If a nozzle is found that does not affect idle quality or changes noise and/or smoke, it should be replaced. |
| | 3. High pressure lines incorrectly installed | 3. Check routing of each line. Correct as required. |
| **ENGINE MISFIRES BUT IDLES CORRECTLY** | 1. Plugged fuel filter | 1. Replace filter. |
| | 2. Incorrect injection pump timing | 2. Be sure that timing mark on injection pump and adapter are aligned. |
| | 3. Incorrect or contaminated fuel | 3. Flush fuel system and install correct fuel. |
| **ENGINE WILL NOT RETURN TO IDLE** | 1. External linkage misadjustment or failure | 1. Reset linkage or replace as required. |
| | 2. Internal injection pump malfunction | 2. Install replacement injection pump. |
| **FUEL LEAKS ON GROUND—NO ENGINE MALFUNCTION** | 1. Loose or broken fuel line or connection | 1. Examine complete fuel system, including tank, supply, injection and return system. Determine source and cause of leak and repair. |
| | 2. Internal injection pump failure | 2. Install replacement injection pump. |
| **SIGNIFICANT LOSS OF POWER** | 1. Incorrect or contaminated fuel | 1. Flush fuel system and install correct fuel. |
| | 2. Pinched or otherwise restricted return system | 2. Examine system for restriction and correct as required. |
| | 3. Plugged fuel tank vent | 3. Remove fuel cap. If "hissing" noise is heard, vent is plugged and should be cleaned. |
| | 4. Restricted fuel supply | 4. Examine fuel supply system to determine cause of restriction. Repair as required. |
| | 5. Plugged fuel filter | 5. Remove and replace filter. |
| | 6. External compression leaks | 6. Check for compression leaks at all nozzles and glow plugs, using "Leak-Tec" or equivalent. If leak is found, tighten nozzle clamp or glow plug. If leak persists at a nozzle, remove it and reinstall with a new carbon stop seal and compression seal. |
| | 7. Plugged nozzle(s) | 7. Remove nozzles, check for plugging and have repaired or replaced. |
| | 8. Internal engine problem | 8. Correct as necessary. |
| | 9. EGR malfunction | 9. Correct as necessary |

| Condition | Possible Cause | Correction |
|---|---|---|
| NOISE—"RAP" FROM ONE OR MORE CYLINDERS | 1. Air in fuel system<br>2. Air in high pressure line(s)<br><br><br><br><br>3. Nozzle(s) sticking open or with very low blowoff pressure<br>4. Internal engine problem | 1. Check for leaks and correct.<br>2. Crack line at nozzle(s) and bleed air at each cylinder determined to be causing noise. Use care to direct fuel away from sources of ignition and be sure to carefully retighten lines.<br>3. Replace the nozzle(s) causing the problem.<br>4. Correct as necessary. |
| NOISE—SIGNIFICANT OVERALL COMBUSTION NOISE INCREASE WITH EXCESSIVE BLACK SMOKE | 1. Timing not set to specification<br><br>2. Internal engine problem<br><br><br>3. Injection pump housing pressure out of specifications.<br>4. Internal injection pump problem<br>5. EGR malfunction | 1. Align timing marks on adapter and injection pump.<br>2. Check for presence of oil in the air crossover. If present, determine cause and correct.<br>3. Check housing pressure. If incorrect, replace fuel return line connector assembly.<br>4. Replace pump.<br>5. Correct as necessary. |
| NOISE—INTERNAL OR EXTERNAL | 1. Fuel supply pump, alternator, water pump, valve train, vacuum pump, bearings, etc. | 1. Inspect and correct as necessary. |
| ENGINE OVERHEATS | 1. Coolant system leak or oil cooler system leak<br>2. Belt failure or slippage<br>3. Thermostat malfunction, head gasket failure or internal engine problem | 1. Check for leaks and correct as required.<br>2. Replace or adjust as required.<br>3. Inspect and correct as necessary. |
| INSTRUMENT PANEL OIL WARNING LAMP "ON" AT IDLE | 1. Oil cooler or oil cooler line restricted<br>2. Internal engine problem | 1. Remove restriction in cooler or cooler line.<br>2. Correct as necessary. |
| ENGINE WILL NOT SHUT OFF WITH KEY<br><br>**NOTE:** With engine at idle, pinch the fuel return line at the injection pump to shut off engine. | 1. Injection pump solenoid does not drop out<br><br><br><br>2. Injection pump solenoid return spring failed | 1. Refer to electrical diagnosis. If problem is determined to be internal with the injection pump, replace the injection pump.<br>2. Replace injection pump. |

**Fig. 6A  Diesel engine diagnostic chart (Part 4 of 4)**

2. Check gauge fuse. If fuse is blown, replace fuse and repeat step 1. If fuse is good, check pink and pink/black wires between ignition switch and S203 for opens.
3. Disconnect connector of glow plug controller. Connect a jumper wire at connector pin A (dark blue wire) to ground. If wait lamp does not go on, check for burned out bulb. If bulb is not burned out, check for opens in dark blue wire between controller connector and wait lamp, and also in pink/black wire between wait lamp and S203. If wires are not open, proceed to next step.
4. Connect one end of test lamp BT-7905 or equivalent to red wire terminal of glow plug relay and other end to ground, then touch lead to glow plug controller connector pin C (black wire). If wait lamp comes on, replace glow plug controller.

### Wait Lamp Stays On More Than 15 Seconds

1. With ignition switch "Off," check bat-

tery voltage. Charge battery if voltage is below 10.5 volts.
2. Connect one end of test lamp BT-7905 or equivalent to ground, and the other lead to red wire post of glow plug relay. Turn ignition switch "On," then touch test lead to green wire post of relay. If test lamp comes on, the glow plug relay should operate. If relay operates, replace controller. If relay does not operate, proceed to next step.
3. Check diesel fuse. If fuse is good, separate connector at glow plug controller. Connect test light between pins B (pink/black wire) and C (black wire) at harness connector. Turn ignition switch to "Run" and observe test lamp. If test lamp does not come on, check continuity of pink/black wires. If test lamp comes on proceed to next step.
4. Check continuity (less than 75 ohms) between pins B and C at controller. If no continuity is evident, remove glow plug controller, disconnect glow plug relay and replace thermal controller.

### Engine Does Not Start—Wait Lamp OK

1. Ensure cranking speed is greater than 100 RPM. If not, check battery voltage and charge battery if necessary.
2. With ignition switch in "Run," use test lamp mentioned previously and check for voltage at pink wire of injection pump fuel solenoid. If no voltage is evident, repair wire. If voltage is present, proceed to next step.
3. Turn ignition switch "Off." Using a self-powered test lamp, check for continuity from fuel control solenoid to ground. If no continuity exists, replace solenoid.
4. Connect one end of test lamp BT-7905 or equivalent to ground, and the other end to red wire post of glow plug relay. With ignition switch "On," touch test lead to green wire post of relay. Test lamp should come on and relay should operate.
5. If relay operates, turn ignition switch "Off," then disconnect glow plug harness connectors at glow plugs. Con-

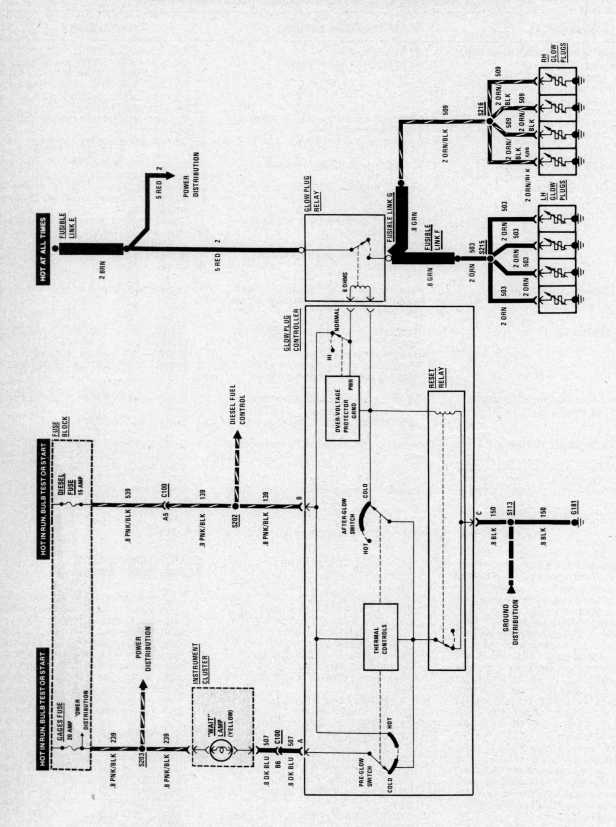

Fig. 7 Glow plug system wiring diagram, 1984

nect self-powered test lamp between green wire post of relay and ground. At each glow plug, momentarily connect harness connector to glow plug spade terminal. Observe test lamp. If lamp comes on, glow plug and harness lead are OK. If test lamp does not come on, ground harness connector and observe test lamp. If test lamp comes on, replace glow plug. If test lamp does not come on, replace harness connector.

6. If glow plug relay does not operate, remove controller and relay. Check for continuity of both parts. Replace controller or relay as necessary.

### 1983

Refer to wiring diagram, **Fig. 8 and Figs. 9 through 15,** for troubleshooting and diagnosis procedures for the 1983 glow plug system.

### 1980-81

Refer to wiring diagram, **Fig. 16 and Figs. 17 through 21,** for troubleshooting and diagnosis procedures for the 1980-81 glow plug system.

## ROUGH IDLE DIAGNOSIS

Check for mechanical malfunctions such as incorrect idle speed or injection pump timing, or leaking nozzles or high pressure lines. If rough idle is still evident, refer to "Glow Plug Resistance Check."

## GLOW PLUG RESISTANCE CHECK

### 1981 & 1983-84

1. Using multi-meter J-29125 (1981 and 1983) or J-29125A (1984), set left selector switch to "Ohms," right selector switch to 200 ohms and center slide switch to "D.C. Lo." **If another ohmmeter is used, different values will result. Tools J-29125 and J-29125A were used in the development of this procedure. Their use is required if similar readings are to be obtained.**
2. Start engine, allow it to reach normal operating temperature, then disconnect all feed wires from glow plugs. Turn heater to "On" position.
3. Disconnect alternator two wire connector.
4. Using tachometer J-26925, or equivalent, adjust idle speed screw to obtain worst engine idle roughness condition. Do not exceed 900 RPM.
5. Allow engine to run at worst idle speed for approximately one minute, then attach an alligator clip to black test lead of meter. Ground black test lead to fast idle solenoid (1983-84) or engine lift strap (1981).
6. Write down the engine firing order on a piece of paper, then with engine idling, probe each glow plug terminal and record the resistance values on each cylinder in the firing sequence. **If vehicle is equipped with an electric cooling fan, record resistance values with cooling fan inoperative. Do not disconnect cooling fan cir-**

cuitry. **The resistance values are dependent on the temperature in each cylinder, and therefore, can indicate cylinder output.**

7. If a resistance reading on any cylinder is 1.3-1.4 ohms for 1984 vehicles, or 1.2-1.3 for 1981 and 1983 vehicles, check engine for a mechanical problem. Make a compression check of the lowest reading cylinder and the cylinders which fire before and after. Correct cause of low compression before proceeding to fuel system.
8. On 1984 vehicles, install glow plug luminosity probe, from tool J-33075, into cylinder with lowest resistance value. Observe combustion light flashes of probe. The flashes will usually be erratic and in sequence with the misfire. If not, move to the next lowest reading cylinder, until the misfire is found.
9. On all vehicles, observe the results of all glow plug resistance readings, looking for differences between cylinders. Rough engines will normally have a difference of .4 ohms or more between cylinders in the firing sequence. To correct rough engine idle, it will be necessary to raise or lower the resistance values on one or more of the offending cylinders by replacing the injection nozzles.
10. Remove nozzle from the cylinder(s) affecting idle performance. Determine the pop off pressure of the nozzle and check the nozzle for leakage and spray pattern. Refer to tool manufacturer for proper testing procedures. Install nozzles with higher pop off pressures to lower resistance values, and nozzles with lower pop off pressures to raise values. A change of 30 psi nozzle pressure will result in a .1 ohm difference in resistance. Use new nozzles on new vehicles and broken in nozzles on vehicles with 1500 or more miles, if possible. **Whenever a nozzle is cleaned or replaced, crank the engine and watch for air bubbles at the nozzle inlet before connecting the injection pipe. If bubbles are evident, clean or replace the nozzle.**
11. Connect injection pipe, restart engine and check idle quality. If idle quality is still not acceptable, repeat steps 6 through 10.
12. After making additional nozzle changes, check idle quality again.
13. If problem moves from cylinder to cylinder and resistance values do not change as nozzles are changed, the injection pump may be defective. Always recheck cylinder at same engine RPM. Sometimes cylinder readings may not indicate that an improvement has been made, even though the engine may idle better. A nozzle with a tip leak can allow more fuel than required into a cylinder, raising the glow plug resistance value. This will steal fuel from the next nozzle in the firing order and will result in that glow plug having a lower resistance value. If this is evident, remove and check the nozzle with the high reading. If it is leak-

ing, it may be responsible for the rough idle. If low readings are evident on a glow plug and it does not change with a nozzle change, switch glow plugs between the good and bad cylinder. If the reading of each cylinder is not the same as before the switch, then the glow plug cannot be used for rough idle diagnosis.

## WATER IN FUEL SYSTEM DIAGNOSIS

### WATER IN FUEL LAMP DOES NOT GO ON

If the likelihood of water in the fuel tank exists and the Water In Fuel lamp is off, siphon the fuel tank to check for water by connecting a pump to the fuel return line. If at least 3 gallons of water are siphoned from the tank, proceed as follows:

1. Disconnect Water In Fuel electrical lead at fuel tank and ground the lead. If lamp does not go on, proceed to step 4. If it does, check for at least 8 volts at the electrical lead. If no voltage is present, replace the Water In Tank light bulb.
2. Ground the Water In Tank electrical lead. If lamp does not go on, check for open circuit in wiring.
3. Remove fuel level sender and Water in Fuel detector unit from fuel tank.
4. Check connections to "Water In Fuel." If satisfactory, check detector unit as follows:
   a. Remove detector from fuel sender unit.
   b. Connect the detector to a bulb and power source. The lamp should go on when the detector probe is lowered into the container of water $3/8$ inch or less. Make sure water is grounded to negative side of battery.

### WATER IN FUEL LAMP STAYS ON

Under this condition, siphon the tank to check for water by connecting a pump to the fuel line. If no water is present, proceed as follows:

1. Disconnect the Water In Fuel electrical lead near the fuel tank. If lamp does not go off, proceed to step 2. If lamp goes off, remove fuel level sender and check detector as described previously under "Water In Fuel Lamp Does Not Go On."
2. Check for short circuit in wire between the "Water In Fuel" connection at the fuel tank and the dash indicator lamp.

## ENGINE MOUNTS
### REPLACE

1. Raise and support vehicle.
2. Support engine, then remove engine mount through bolts.
3. Raise engine slightly, then remove engine mount attaching bolts as shown, **Fig. 22.**
4. Reverse procedure to install, torquing bolts to specifications.

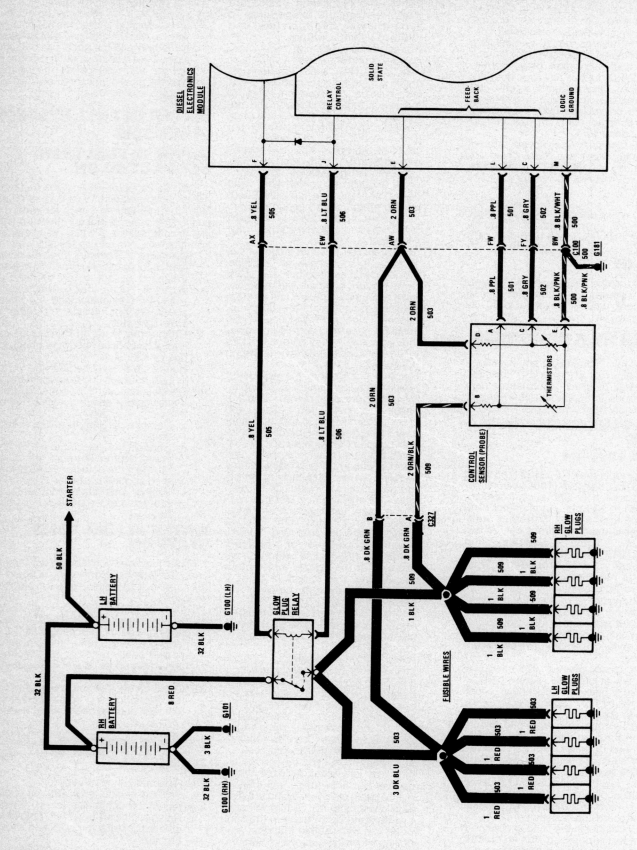

**Fig. 8 Glow plug system wiring diagram (Part 1 of 2). 1983**

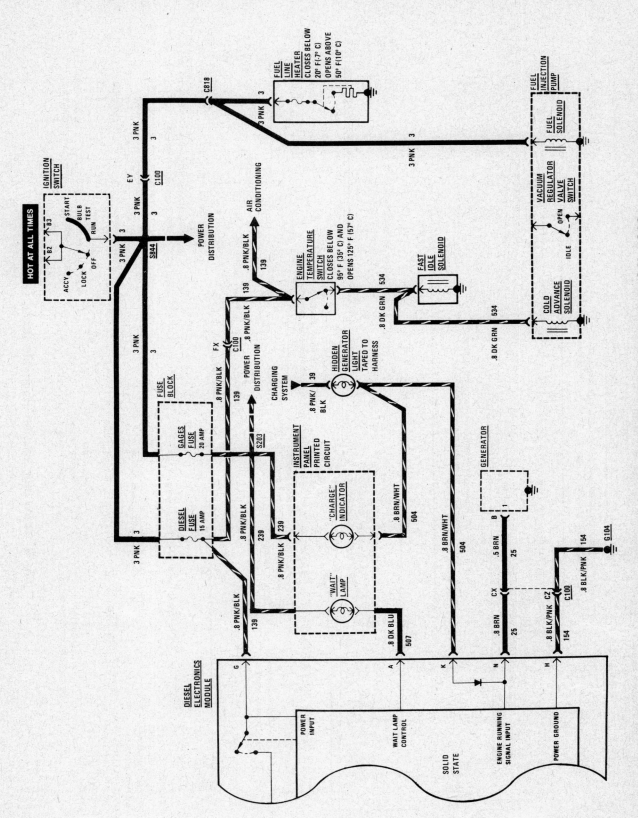

**Fig. 8 Glow plug system wiring diagram (Part 2 of 2). 1983**

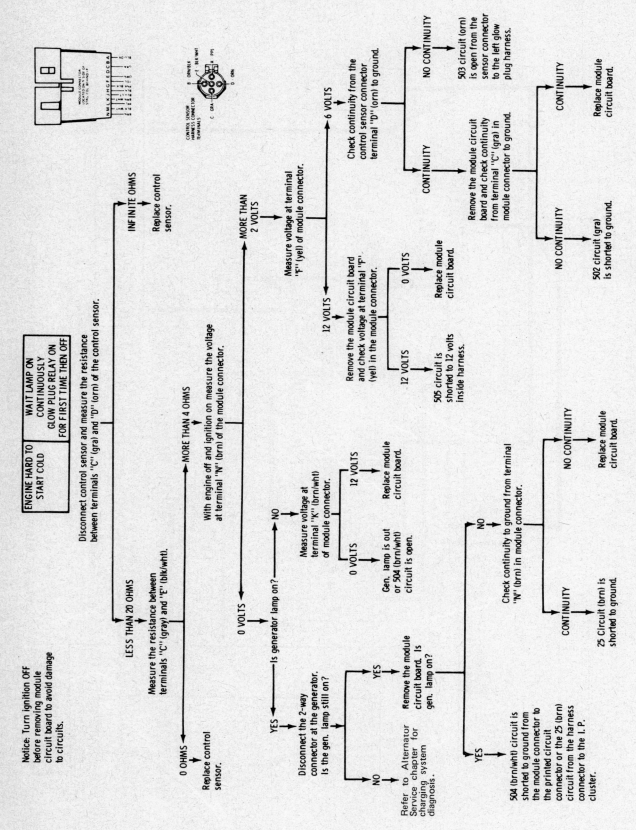

**Fig. 9 Glow plug system diagnosis chart. 1983**

Notice: Turn ignition OFF before removing module circuit board to avoid damage to circuits.

| ENGINE HARD TO START COLD | WAIT LAMP ON CONTINUOUSLY GLOW PLUG RELAY ON FOR FIRST TIME THEN OFF |

Disconnect control sensor and measure the resistance between terminals "C" (gra) and "D" (orn) of the control sensor.

LESS THAN 20 OHMS

INFINITE OHMS → Replace control sensor.

Measure the resistance between terminals "C" (gray) and "E" (blk/wht).

0 OHMS → Replace control sensor.

MORE THAN 4 OHMS

With engine off and ignition on measure the voltage at terminal "N" (brn) of the module connector.

0 VOLTS

MORE THAN 2 VOLTS

Measure voltage at terminal "F" (yel) of module connector.

12 VOLTS

6 VOLTS → Check continuity from the control sensor connector terminal "D" (orn) to ground.

NO CONTINUITY → 503 circuit (orn) is open from the sensor connector to the left glow plug harness.

CONTINUITY → Remove the module circuit board and check continuity from terminal "C" (gra) in module connector to ground.

CONTINUITY → Replace module circuit board.

NO CONTINUITY → 502 circuit (gra) is shorted to ground.

Remove the module circuit board and check voltage at terminal "F" (yel) in the module connector.

0 VOLTS → Replace module circuit board.

12 VOLTS → 505 circuit is shorted to 12 volts inside harness.

Is generator lamp on?

NO → Measure voltage at terminal "K" (brn/wht) of module connector.

12 VOLTS → Replace module circuit board.

0 VOLTS → Gen. lamp or 504 (brn/wht) circuit is open.

YES → Disconnect the 2-way connector at the generator. Is the gen. lamp still on?

YES → Remove the module circuit board. Is gen. lamp on?

NO → Refer to Alternator Service chapter for charging system diagnosis.

YES → Check continuity to ground from terminal "N" (brn) in module connector.

NO CONTINUITY → Replace module circuit board.

CONTINUITY → 25 Circuit (brn) is shorted to ground.

YES → 504 (brn/wht) circuit is shorted to ground from the module connector to the printed circuit connector or the 25 (brn) circuit from the harness connector to the I.P. cluster.

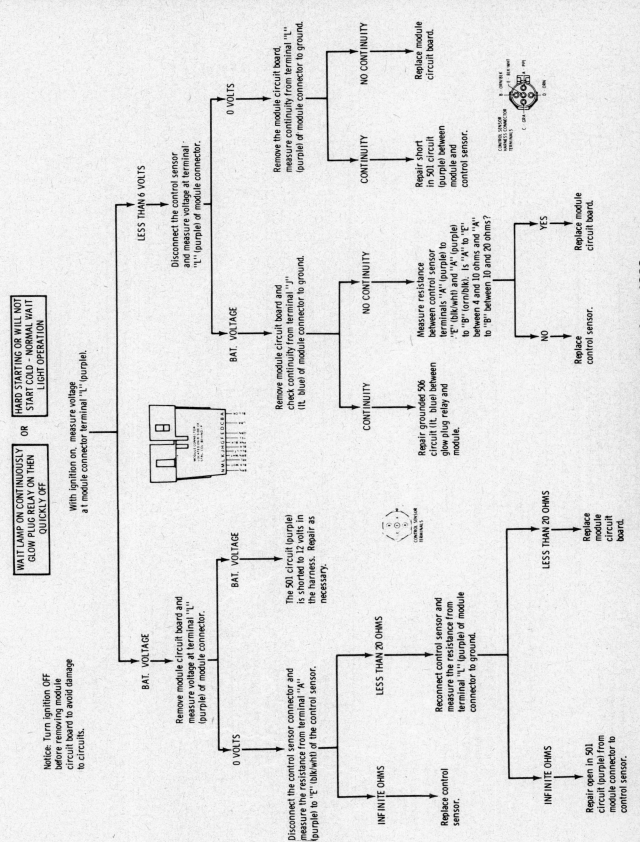

**Fig. 10 Glow plug system diagnosis chart. 1983**

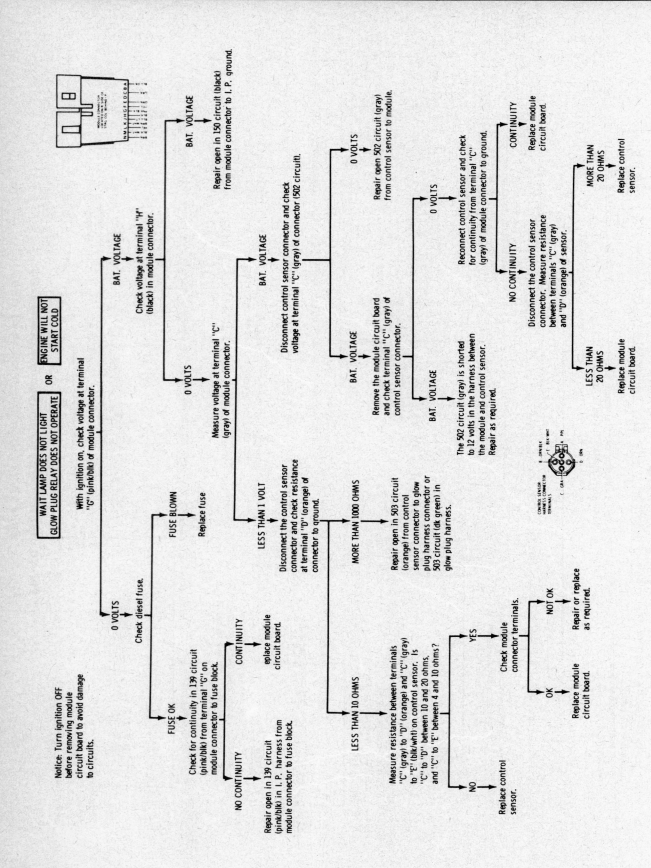

**Fig. 11 Glow plug system diagnosis chart. 1983**

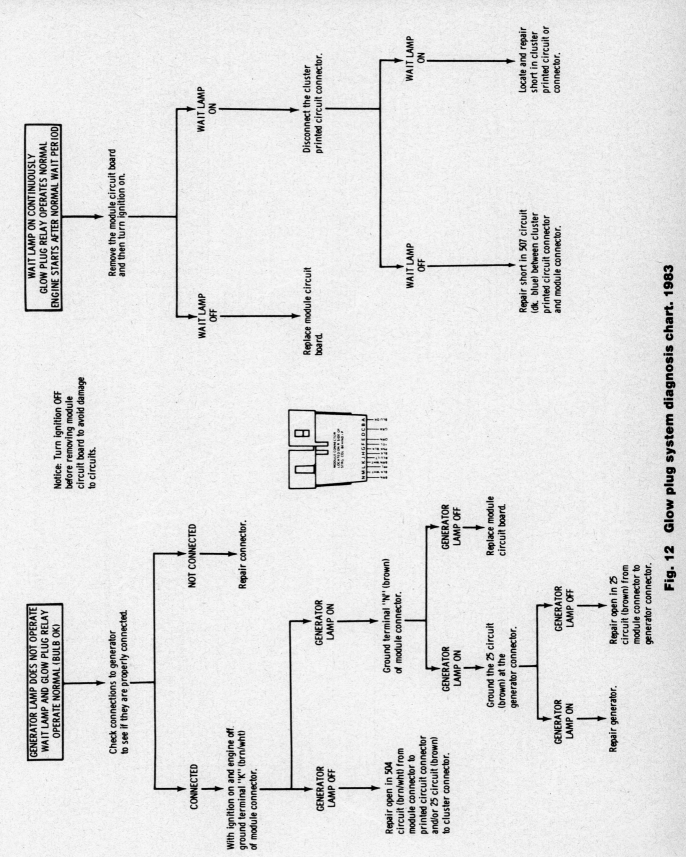

Fig. 12 Glow plug system diagnosis chart. 1983

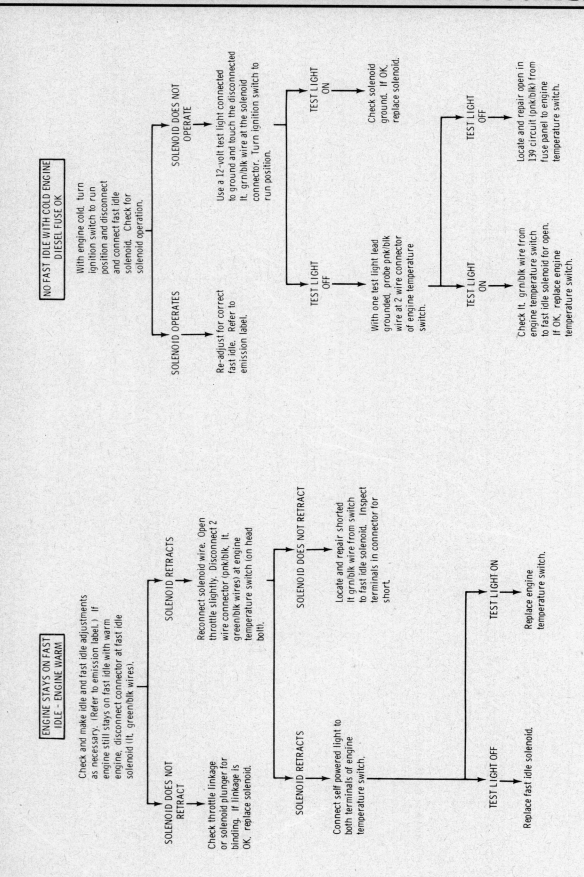

**Fig. 13  Glow plug system diagnosis chart. 1983**

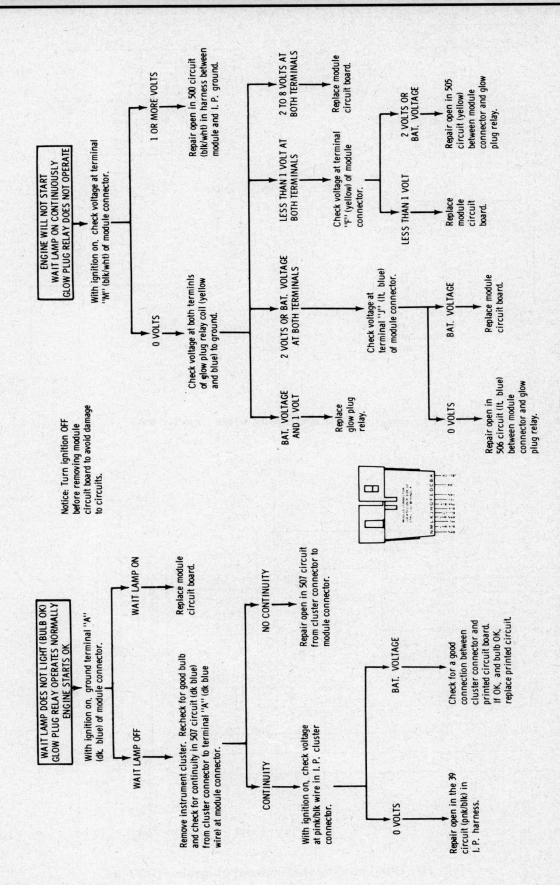

**Fig. 14  Glow plug system diagnosis chart. 1983**

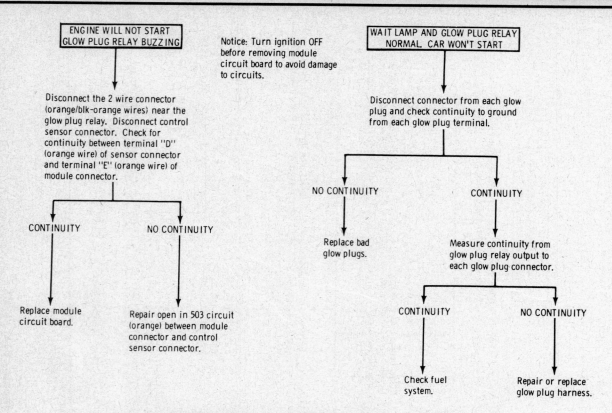

**Fig. 15   Glow plug system diagnosis chart. 1983**

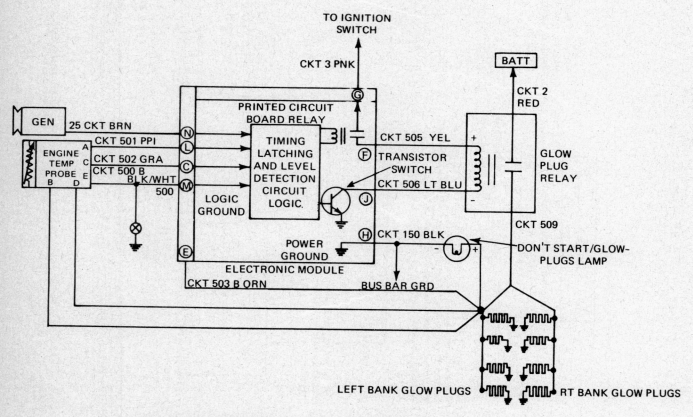

**Fig. 16   Glow plug system wiring diagram. 1980—81**

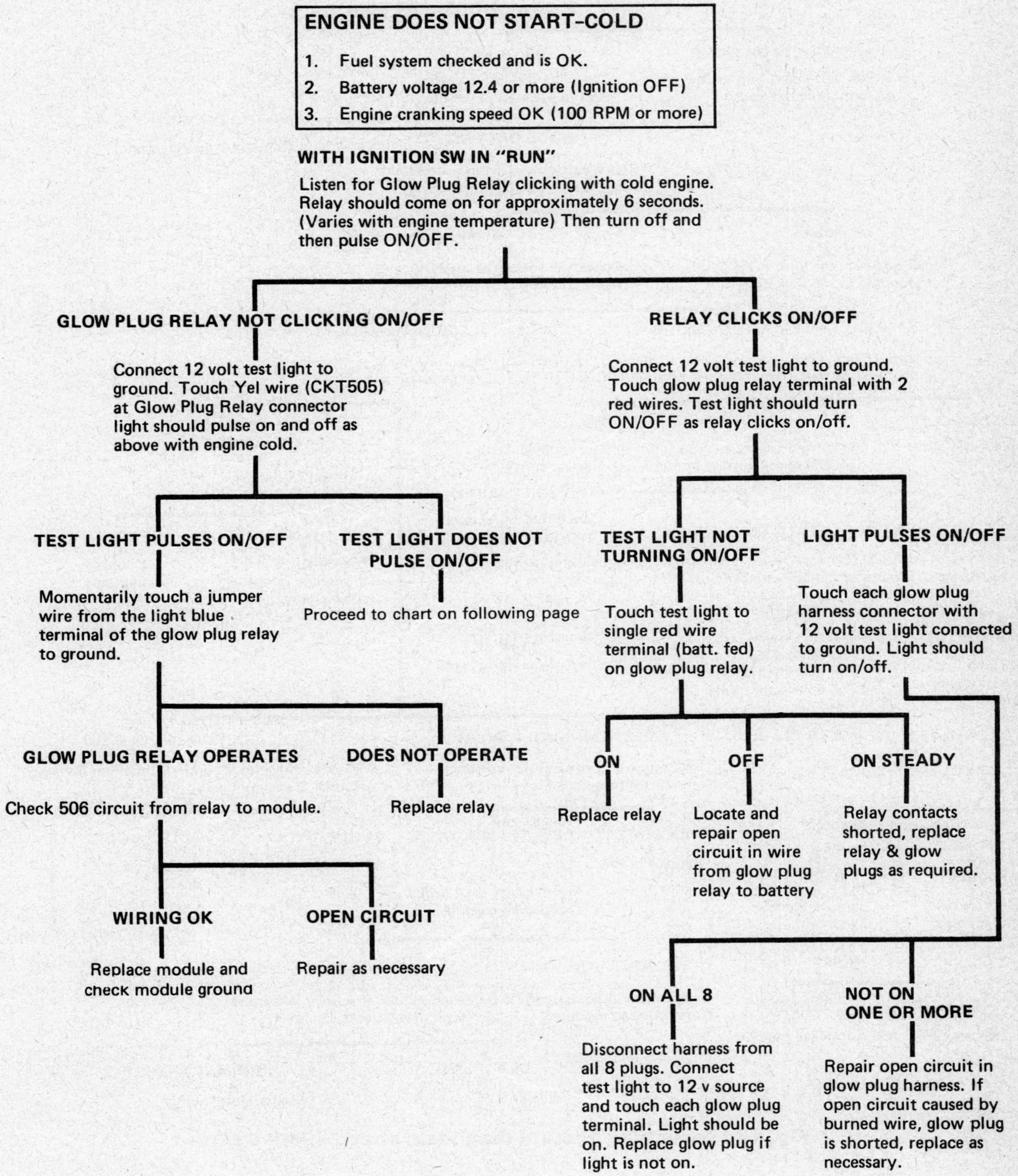

**ENGINE DOES NOT START–COLD**

1. Fuel system checked and is OK.
2. Battery voltage 12.4 or more (Ignition OFF)
3. Engine cranking speed OK (100 RPM or more)

**WITH IGNITION SW IN "RUN"**

Listen for Glow Plug Relay clicking with cold engine. Relay should come on for approximately 6 seconds. (Varies with engine temperature) Then turn off and then pulse ON/OFF.

**GLOW PLUG RELAY NOT CLICKING ON/OFF**

Connect 12 volt test light to ground. Touch Yel wire (CKT505) at Glow Plug Relay connector light should pulse on and off as above with engine cold.

**TEST LIGHT PULSES ON/OFF**

Momentarily touch a jumper wire from the light blue terminal of the glow plug relay to ground.

**TEST LIGHT DOES NOT PULSE ON/OFF**

Proceed to chart on following page

**GLOW PLUG RELAY OPERATES**

Check 506 circuit from relay to module.

**DOES NOT OPERATE**

Replace relay

**WIRING OK**

Replace module and check module ground

**OPEN CIRCUIT**

Repair as necessary

**RELAY CLICKS ON/OFF**

Connect 12 volt test light to ground. Touch glow plug relay terminal with 2 red wires. Test light should turn ON/OFF as relay clicks on/off.

**TEST LIGHT NOT TURNING ON/OFF**

Touch test light to single red wire terminal (batt. fed) on glow plug relay.

**LIGHT PULSES ON/OFF**

Touch each glow plug harness connector with 12 volt test light connected to ground. Light should turn on/off.

**ON**

Replace relay

**OFF**

Locate and repair open circuit in wire from glow plug relay to battery

**ON STEADY**

Relay contacts shorted, replace relay & glow plugs as required.

**ON ALL 8**

Disconnect harness from all 8 plugs. Connect test light to 12 v source and touch each glow plug terminal. Light should be on. Replace glow plug if light is not on.

**NOT ON ONE OR MORE**

Repair open circuit in glow plug harness. If open circuit caused by burned wire, glow plug is shorted, replace as necessary.

**Fig. 17  Glow plug system diagnosis chart. 1980–81**

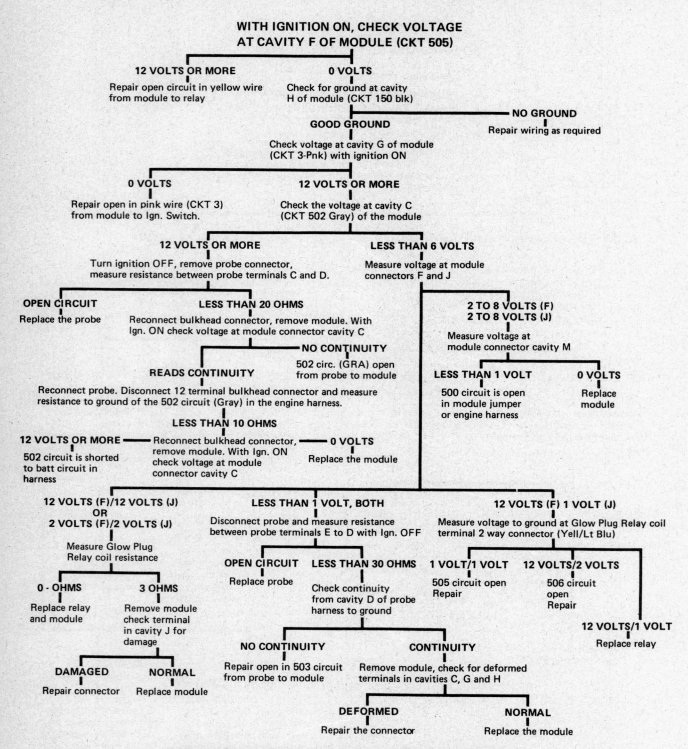

**WITH IGNITION ON, CHECK VOLTAGE AT CAVITY F OF MODULE (CKT 505)**

**12 VOLTS OR MORE**
Repair open circuit in yellow wire from module to relay

**0 VOLTS**
Check for ground at cavity H of module (CKT 150 blk)

**NO GROUND**
Repair wiring as required

**GOOD GROUND**
Check voltage at cavity G of module (CKT 3-Pnk) with ignition ON

**0 VOLTS**
Repair open in pink wire (CKT 3) from module to Ign. Switch.

**12 VOLTS OR MORE**
Check the voltage at cavity C (CKT 502 Gray) of the module

**12 VOLTS OR MORE**
Turn ignition OFF, remove probe connector, measure resistance between probe terminals C and D.

**LESS THAN 6 VOLTS**
Measure voltage at module connectors F and J

**OPEN CIRCUIT**
Replace the probe

**LESS THAN 20 OHMS**
Reconnect bulkhead connector, remove module. With Ign. ON check voltage at module connector cavity C

**NO CONTINUITY**
502 circ. (GRA) open from probe to module

**2 TO 8 VOLTS (F)**
**2 TO 8 VOLTS (J)**
Measure voltage at module connector cavity M

**READS CONTINUITY**
Reconnect probe. Disconnect 12 terminal bulkhead connector and measure resistance to ground of the 502 circuit (Gray) in the engine harness.

**LESS THAN 1 VOLT**
500 circuit is open in module jumper or engine harness

**0 VOLTS**
Replace module

**LESS THAN 10 OHMS**

**12 VOLTS OR MORE**
502 circuit is shorted to batt circuit in harness

**Reconnect bulkhead connector, remove module. With Ign. ON check voltage at module connector cavity C**

**0 VOLTS**
Replace the module

**12 VOLTS (F)/12 VOLTS (J)**
**OR**
**2 VOLTS (F)/2 VOLTS (J)**
Measure Glow Plug Relay coil resistance

**LESS THAN 1 VOLT, BOTH**
Disconnect probe and measure resistance between probe terminals E to D with Ign. OFF

**12 VOLTS (F) 1 VOLT (J)**
Measure voltage to ground at Glow Plug Relay coil terminal 2 way connector (Yell/Lt Blu)

**0 - OHMS**
Replace relay and module

**3 OHMS**
Remove module check terminal in cavity J for damage

**OPEN CIRCUIT**
Replace probe

**LESS THAN 30 OHMS**
Check continuity from cavity D of probe harness to ground

**1 VOLT/1 VOLT**
505 circuit open Repair

**12 VOLTS/2 VOLTS**
506 circuit open Repair

**12 VOLTS/1 VOLT**
Replace relay

**DAMAGED**
Repair connector

**NORMAL**
Replace module

**NO CONTINUITY**
Repair open in 503 circuit from probe to module

**CONTINUITY**
Remove module, check for deformed terminals in cavities C, G and H

**DEFORMED**
Repair the connector

**NORMAL**
Replace the module

**Fig. 18   Glow plug system diagnosis chart. 1980–81**

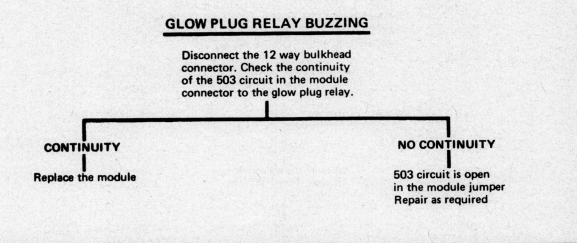

**GLOW PLUG RELAY BUZZING**

Disconnect the 12 way bulkhead connector. Check the continuity of the 503 circuit in the module connector to the glow plug relay.

**CONTINUITY**

Replace the module

**NO CONTINUITY**

503 circuit is open in the module jumper Repair as required

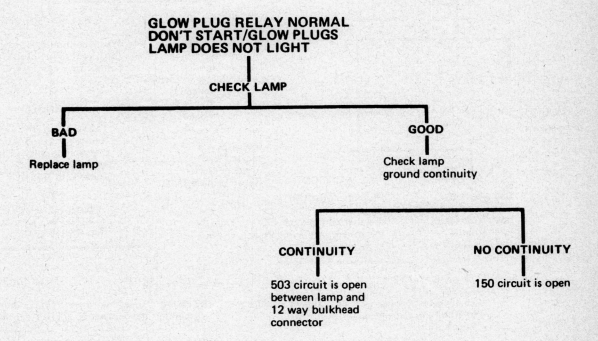

**GLOW PLUG RELAY NORMAL DON'T START/GLOW PLUGS LAMP DOES NOT LIGHT**

**CHECK LAMP**

**BAD**

Replace lamp

**GOOD**

Check lamp ground continuity

**CONTINUITY**

503 circuit is open between lamp and 12 way bulkhead connector

**NO CONTINUITY**

150 circuit is open

**Fig. 19  Glow plug system diagnosis chart. 1980–81**

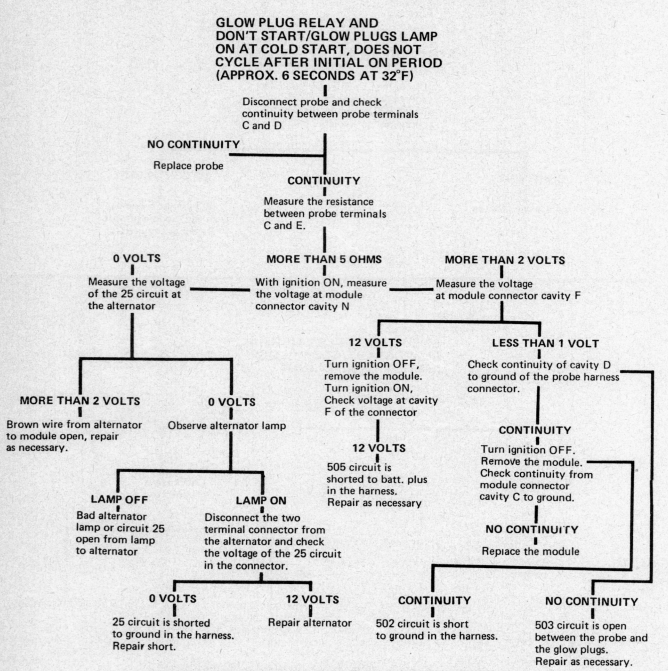

**GLOW PLUG RELAY AND DON'T START/GLOW PLUGS LAMP ON AT COLD START, DOES NOT CYCLE AFTER INITIAL ON PERIOD (APPROX. 6 SECONDS AT 32°F)**

Disconnect probe and check continuity between probe terminals C and D

**NO CONTINUITY**

Replace probe

**CONTINUITY**

Measure the resistance between probe terminals C and E.

**0 VOLTS**

Measure the voltage of the 25 circuit at the alternator

**MORE THAN 5 OHMS**

With ignition ON, measure the voltage at module connector cavity N

**MORE THAN 2 VOLTS**

Measure the voltage at module connector cavity F

**MORE THAN 2 VOLTS**

Brown wire from alternator to module open, repair as necessary.

**0 VOLTS**

Observe alternator lamp

**12 VOLTS**

Turn ignition OFF, remove the module. Turn ignition ON, Check voltage at cavity F of the connector

**LESS THAN 1 VOLT**

Check continuity of cavity D to ground of the probe harness connector.

**12 VOLTS**

505 circuit is shorted to batt. plus in the harness. Repair as necessary

**CONTINUITY**

Turn ignition OFF. Remove the module. Check continuity from module connector cavity C to ground.

**LAMP OFF**

Bad alternator lamp or circuit 25 open from lamp to alternator

**LAMP ON**

Disconnect the two terminal connector from the alternator and check the voltage of the 25 circuit in the connector.

**NO CONTINUITY**

Replace the module

**0 VOLTS**

25 circuit is shorted to ground in the harness. Repair short.

**12 VOLTS**

Repair alternator

**CONTINUITY**

502 circuit is short to ground in the harness.

**NO CONTINUITY**

503 circuit is open between the probe and the glow plugs. Repair as necessary.

**Fig. 20 Glow plug system diagnosis chart. 1980–81**

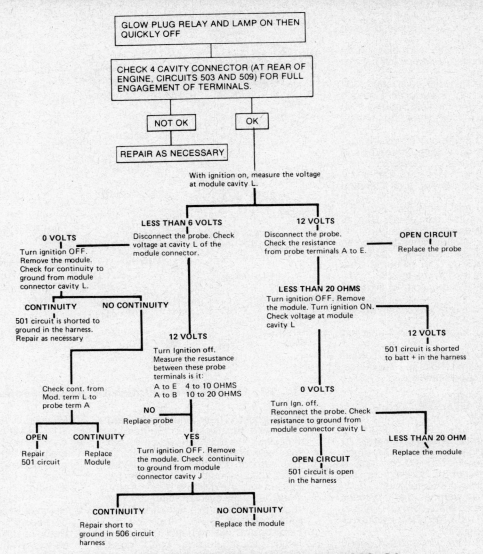

**Fig. 21  Glow plug system diagnosis chart. 1980–81**

# ENGINE
## REPLACE

1. Disconnect ground cable from batteries and drain cooling system.
2. Remove air cleaner.
3. Scribe hood hinge locations and remove hood.
4. Disconnect ground wires at inner fender and the engine ground strap at right cylinder head.
5. Disconnect radiator hoses, oil cooler lines, heater hoses, vacuum hoses, power steering hoses from gear, A/C attached, fuel pump hose from fuel pump and the wiring.
6. Remove hairpin clip from bell crank.
7. Remove throttle and throttle valve cables from intake manifold brackets and position cables aside.
8. Remove upper radiator support and the radiator.
9. Raise and support vehicle.
10. Disconnect exhaust pipes from exhaust manifold.
11. Remove torque converter cover and the three bolts securing torque converter to flywheel.
12. Remove engine mount bolts or nuts.
13. Remove three engine to transmission bolts on the right side.
14. Disconnect starter wiring and remove starter.
15. Lower vehicle.
16. Attach suitable engine lifting equipment to engine. Support transmission with a suitable jack.
17. Remove the three engine to transmission bolts on the left side.
18. Remove engine from vehicle.
19. Reverse procedure to install.

# EXHAUST MANIFOLD
## REPLACE
### LEFT SIDE

1. Remove air cleaner and cover carburetor.
2. Remove lower generator bracket.
3. Raise and support vehicle.
4. Remove crossover or exhaust pipe.
5. Lower vehicle, then remove exhaust manifold from above.

6. Reverse procedure to install, torquing bolts to 25 ft. lbs.

## RIGHT SIDE

1. Raise and support vehicle.
2. Remove crossover pipe and/or exhaust pipe as necessary.
3. On 1983-84 vehicles, remove right front wheel.
4. Remove exhaust manifold.
5. Reverse procedure to install, torquing attaching bolts to 25 ft. lbs.

# INTAKE MANIFOLD
## REPLACE

1. Disconnect ground cables from batteries.
2. Remove air cleaner assembly.
3. Drain cooling system, then disconnect upper radiator hose and thermostat bypass hose from water pump outlet. Disconnect heater hose and vacuum hose from water control valve.

4. Remove breather pipes from valve covers and air crossover, **Fig. 23.**
5. Remove air crossover and cap intake manifold, **Fig. 24.**
6. Disconnect throttle rod and return spring. If equipped with cruise control, remove servo.
7. Remove hairpin clip from bell crank and disconnect the cables. Remove throttle and throttle valve cables from intake manifold brackets and position cables aside.
8. Disconnect wiring as necessary.
9. Disconnect or remove alternator and A/C compressor as necessary.
10. Disconnect fuel line from fuel pump and filter and remove fuel filter and bracket.
11. Disconnect lines from injector nozzles and remove injection pump. Cap all open fuel lines and fittings.
12. Disconnect vacuum lines at vacuum pump. Remove vacuum pump, if equipped with A/C, or oil pump drive assembly, if less A/C, **Fig. 25.**
13. Remove intake manifold drain tube, **Fig. 26.**
14. Remove intake manifold bolts and the intake manifold.
15. Remove adapter seal and injection pump adapter.
16. Reverse procedure to install. Torque intake manifold bolts in sequence, **Fig. 27,** to specifications.

## CYLINDER HEAD REPLACE

If a cylinder head is being removed to correct a head gasket problem on these engines, a few checks should be made to ensure the cause of the condition is corrected. The checks are as follows:

a. Cylinder head warpage. If any cylinder head is warped more than .010 inch, it should be replaced. Resurfacing is not recommended.
b. Cylinder head to cylinder block dowel pin interference. With the head properly positioned on the block, without the head gasket installed, run a .005 inch feeler gauge around the perimeter of the area where the head and

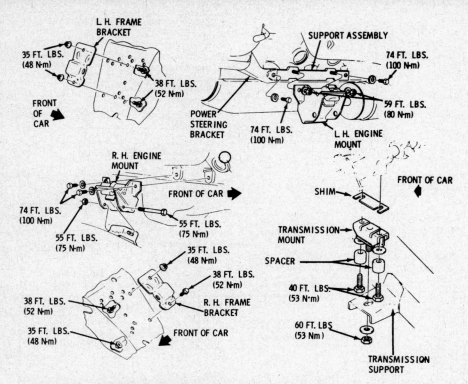

**Fig. 22   Engine & transmission mount replacement (typical)**

block meet. There should be zero clearance, thus ensuring the head is flush with the block and no dowel pin interference exists.
c. Prechamber location. The cylinder head prechambers must not be recessed into the cylinder head or protrude out of the cylinder head by more than .004 inch as this will affect head gasket sealing.
d. Head gasket sealing bead. Ensure the head gasket sealing bead goes around all core holes in the block and head. If the sealing bead crosses a raised, depressed or stamped area, the raised area should be filed and the depressed or stamped area filled with

RTV sealer and assembled before the RTV sealer cures.
e. Cylinder head cracks. Minor surface cracks in the cylinder head valve port area between the intake and exhaust ports are considered a normal condition and does not warrant replacement of the heads.

1. Remove intake manifold as outlined previously.
2. Remove valve cover. It may be necessary to remove any interfering accessory brackets.
3. Disconnect glow plug wiring.
4. If right side head is to be removed, remove ground strap from head.
5. Remove rocker arm bolts, pivots, rocker arms and pushrod. Note locations of valve train components so they can be installed in original locations.
6. Remove fuel return lines from injection nozzles.
7. Remove exhaust manifold.

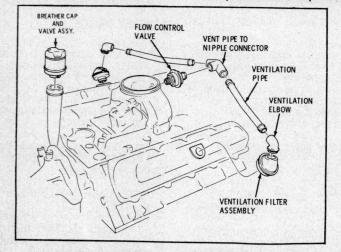

**Fig. 23   Crankcase ventilation system**

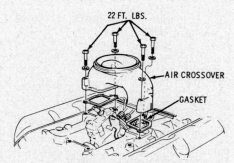

**Fig. 24   Air crossover installation**

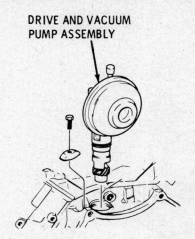

**Fig. 25  Vacuum pump & oil pump drive assembly**

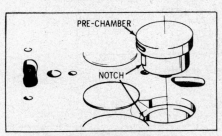

**Fig. 28  Pre-chamber installation**

8. Remove engine block drain plug on side of block that cylinder head is being removed.
9. Remove cylinder head bolts, then cylinder head.
10. If necessary to remove pre-chamber, remove glow plug and injection nozzle, then tap out pre-chamber with a suitable drift, **Fig. 28.**
11. Reverse procedure to install. Do not use any sealing compound on cylinder head gasket. Torque cylinder head bolts in sequence, **Fig. 29,** to 100 ft. lbs., then 130 ft. lbs.

New head bolts with increased torque capacity were introduced into production during March 1980 and are now available, **Fig. 30.**

When replacing a cylinder head, it is recommended new head bolts be used if they have not already been installed in the engine. When installing later production model head bolts, be sure to clean and oil the threads. Before installation of the cylinder head ensure bolt holes are tapped deep enough into the block. Blow out any chips or liquid in the bolt holes. Then position cylinder head on cylinder block without the cylinder head gasket. Install bolt and tighten by hand until bolt head contacts the cylinder head. This will indicate that the holes are tapped deep enough into the block, allowing for proper torque. For cylinder head bolt location, refer to **Fig. 31.**

A new designed head gasket went into production in March 1981, and is available for service replacement. It can be identified by the use of blue print O sealer instead of orange. This gasket is of the slotted and shim design.

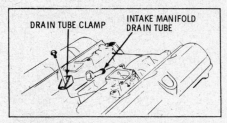

**Fig. 26  Intake manifold drain tube installation**

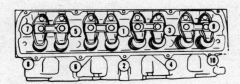

**Fig. 29  Cylinder head tightening sequence**

No sealer should be used on the gasket during installation. Also the prechamber shield on the cylinder head gasket must be installed toward the cylinder head.

## ROCKER ARMS

This engine uses valve rotators, **Fig. 32.** The rotator operates on a sprag clutch principle utilizing the collapsing action of a coil spring to give rotation to the rotor body which turns the valve.

Some 1980-83 engines may experience valve train ticking noise and/or exhaust backfire. This condition may be caused by premature wear of the rocker arm pivots. Two types of rocker arm pivots were used on these engines. Type 1 pivot assemblies, **Fig. 33,** are the only ones showing premature wear. It is therefore recommended that only Type 2 pivot assemblies, **Fig. 34,** be used when servicing the engine for the above mentioned condition.

1. Remove valve cover.
2. Remove flanged bolts, rocker arm pivot and rocker arms, **Fig. 32.**
3. When installing rocker arm assemblies, lubricate wear surfaces with suitable lubricant. Torque flanged bolts to 25 ft. lbs. on 1980 models and 28 ft. lbs. on 1981 and 1983-84 models.

## VALVE ROTATORS

The rotator operates on a sprag clutch principle utilizing the collapsing action of coil spring to give rotation to the rotor body which turns the valve, **Fig. 32.**

To check rotator action, draw a line across rotator body and down the collar. Operate engine at 1500 RPM. Rotator body should move around collar. Rotator action can be in either direction. Replace rotator if no movement is noted.

When servicing valves, valve stem tips should be checked for improper wear pattern which could indicate a defective valve rotator, **Fig. 35.**

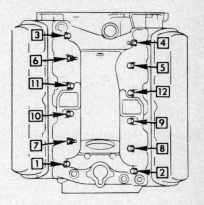

**Fig. 27  Intake manifold tightening sequence**

| LOCATION NUMBER | PART NUMBER | SIZE |
|---|---|---|
| 1 | 22510580 | 1/2 - 13 x 3.10 |
| 2 | 22510582 | 1/2-13 x 3.10 stud end |
| 3 | 22510579 | 1/2 - 13 x 4.30 |
| 4 | 22510585 | 1/2 - 13 x 4.30 stud end |

**Fig. 30  Cylinder head bolt identification**

## VALVES
### ADJUST

These engines are equipped with hydraulic valve lifters. No provision for adjustment is provided.

## VALVE ARRANGEMENT

V8-350 Diesel . . . . . . . . . . . I-E-I-E-E-I-E-I

## VALVE LIFT SPECIFICATIONS.

Valve lift should measure .375 inch on intake valves and .376 inch on exhaust valves.

## VALVE TIMING
### INTAKE OPENS BEFORE TDC

V8-350 Diesel. . . . . . . . . . . . . .16  Degrees

## VALVES
### REPLACE

Whenever a new valve is installed or after grinding valves, it is necessary to measure the valve stem height with the special tool as shown in **Fig. 36.**

There should be at least .015 inch clearance between the gauge and end of valve stem. If clearance is less than .015 inch, remove valve and grind end of valve stem as required.

Check valve rotator height, **Fig. 37.** If valve stem end is less than .005 inch above rotator, the valve is too short and a new valve must be installed.

## VALVE GUIDES

Valve stem guides are not replaceable, due to being cast in place. If valve guide

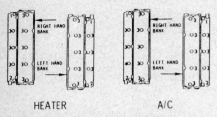

**Fig. 31 Cylinder head bolt locations**

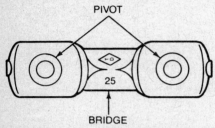

**Fig. 33 Type 1 rocker arm pivot. 1980-83**

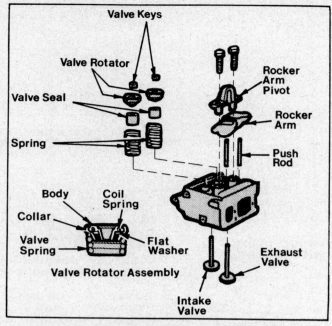

**Fig. 32 Cylinder head exploded view**

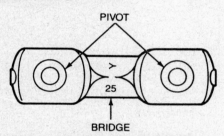

**Fig. 34 Type 2 rocker arm pivot. 1980-83**

bores are worn excessively, they can be reamed oversize.

If a standard valve guide bore is being reamed, use a .003 inch or .005 inch oversize reamer. For the .010 inch oversize valve guide bore, use a .013 inch oversize reamer. If too large a reamer is used and the spiraling is removed, it is possible that the valve will not receive the proper lubrication.

Occasionally a valve guide will be oversize as manufactured. These are marked on the cylinder head as shown in **Fig. 38**. If no markings are present, the guide bores are standard. If oversize markings are present, any valve replacement will require an oversize valve. Service valves are available in standard diameters as well as .003 inch, .005 inch, .010 inch and .013 inch oversize.

## VALVE LIFTERS
## REPLACE

1981 and 1983-84 engines are equipped with roller lifters. These are the same internally as in the past. However, the lifter cannot be "leak down" tested at this time as a tester adapter is not available. On this type lifter, a guide holds the lifters from rotating, **Fig. 39**. A spring steel retainer holds the guide in place.

In addition, some engines have both standard and .010 inch oversize valve lifters. The .010 inch oversize valve lifters are etched with a "0" on the side of the lifter. Also, the cylinder block will be marked if an oversize lifter is used, **Fig. 40**.

1. Remove intake manifold as outlined previously.
2. Remove valve covers, rocker arm assemblies and pushrods. On 1981 and 1983-84 models, remove the lifter retainer and lifter guides. Note location of valve train components so they can be installed in original position.

3. Remove valve lifters.
4. Reverse procedure to install.

## VALVE LIFTER SERVICE

1. Remove valve lifters, refer to "Valve Lifters, Replace."
2. Using a small screwdriver, remove retainer ring, **Figs. 41 and 42**.
3. Remove pushrod seat, oil metering valve, plunger and plunger spring.
4. Remove check ball retainer from plunger, then remove ball and spring.
5. Clean parts in a suitable solvent. **Do not interchange parts between lifters. If any parts are worn, replace lifter.**
6. Inspect all parts for nicks, burrs or scoring. If any parts are defective, replace lifter.
7. On 1981 and 1983-84 roller lifters, inspect roller. It should rotate freely, but without excessive play, also check for missing or broken needle bearing. If any parts are defective, replace lifter.
8. Apply a coating of light engine oil to all lifter surfaces.
9. Install ball check spring and retainer into plunger. Ensure retainer flange is pressed tight against bottom of recess in plunger.
10. Install plunger spring over check retainer.
11. Hold plunger with spring up and insert in lifter body. Hold plunger vertically to prevent cocking spring.
12. Submerge lifter assembly in clean diesel fuel or kerosene, then install oil metering valve and pushrod seat into lifter and install retaining ring.

## VALVE LIFTER BLEED DOWN

If the intake manifold has been removed and if any rocker arms have been removed

or loosened, it will be necessary to remove those lifters, disassemble them, drain the oil from them and reassemble. Refer to "Valve Lifters, Service."

If the intake manifold has not been removed, but rocker arms have been loosened or removed, the valve lifters must be bled down to prevent possible valve to piston interference by using the following procedure:

1. Prior to installing rocker arms, rotate crankshaft pulley to a position 32° BTDC (before top dead center). This is approximately 2 inches counterclockwise from 0° pointer.
2. If the right side valve cover was removed only, remove cylinder No. 1 glow plug and determine if No. 1 piston is in the correct position. This can be determined by compression pressure.
3. If the left side valve cover was removed only, rotate crankshaft until No. 5 cylinder intake valve pushrod is .28 inch above the No. 5 cylinder exhaust valve pushrod.
4. If removed, install cylinder No. 5 pivot and rocker arms. Alternately torque the bolts until the intake valve begins to open and stop tightening. **When torquing rocker arms, use only**

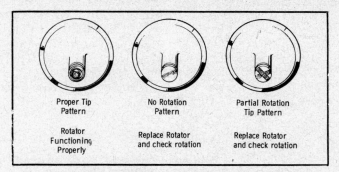

**Fig. 35 Checking valve stem for rotator malfunction**

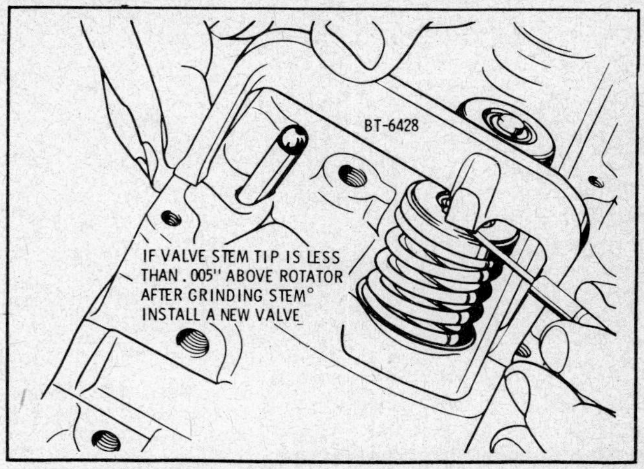

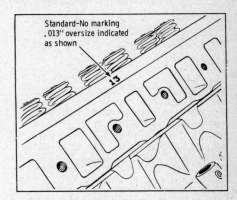

**Fig. 36 Measuring valve stem height**

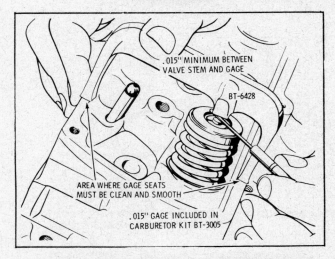

**Fig. 37 Measuring valve rotator height**

**Fig. 38 Valve guide bore marking**

hand wrenches to prevent engine damage.

5. Install remaining rocker arms except No. 3 exhaust valve. Torque bolt to 25 ft. lbs. on 1980 models and 28 ft. lbs. on 1981 and 1983-84 models.
6. If removed, install No. 3 exhaust rocker arm and pivot, but do not torque beyond the point that the valve would be fully opened. This is indicated by a strong resistance while turning the pivot retaining bolt. Going beyond this point would bend the pushrod. **While performing step 6, torque bolt slowly allowing the lifter to bleed down.**
7. Finish torquing No. 5 rocker arm pivot bolt slowly, allowing valve lifter to bleed down. Do not torque beyond the point that the valve would be fully opened. This is indicated by a strong resistance while turning the pivot retaining bolt. Going beyond this point would bend the pushrod.
8. Do not turn the crankshaft for at least 45 minutes while lifters bleed down. **Do not rotate the engine until the valve lifters have bled down, otherwise engine damage might occur.**

## FRONT OIL SEAL
### REPLACE

1. Disconnect ground cables from batteries.

2. Remove accessory drive belts.
3. Remove crankshaft pulley and harmonic balancer.
4. Using tool BT-6406, remove front oil seal, **Fig. 43.**
5. Apply suitable sealer to outside diameter of new oil seal.
6. File .020 inch from flange of tool No. BT-6405 **Fig. 44,** to prevent tool from contacting oil slinger before seal is properly seated in front cover.
7. Using tool BT-6611 and BT-6405, install new oil seal, **Fig. 45.**
8. Install harmonic balancer and crankshaft pulley.
9. Install and tension accessory drive belts.

## ENGINE FRONT COVER
### REPLACE

1. Disconnect ground cables from batteries.
2. Drain cooling system and disconnect radiator hoses and bypass hose.
3. Remove all drive belts, fan and pulley, crankshaft pulley and harmonic balancer, and accessory brackets.
4. Remove front cover to block attaching bolts, then remove front cover, timing indicator and water pump assembly.
5. Remove front cover alignment dowel pins. It may be necessary to grind a flat on the dowel pins to provide a rough surface for gripping.

6. Grind a chamfer on one end of each dowel pin, **Fig. 46.**
7. Cut excess material from front end of oil pan gasket on each side of cylinder block.
8. Trim approximately 1/8 inch from each end of new front pan seal, **Fig. 47.**
9. Install new front cover gasket and apply suitable sealer to gasket around coolant holes.
10. Apply RTV sealer to mating surfaces of cylinder block, oil pan and front cover.
11. Place front cover on cylinder block and press downward to compress seal. Rotate cover right and left and guide oil pan seal into cavity with a small screwdriver.
12. Apply engine oil to bolts.
13. Install two bolts finger tight to retain cover.
14. Install the two dowel pins, chamfered end first.
15. Install timing indicator and water pump and torque bolts as shown in **Fig. 48.**
16. Install harmonic balancer and crankshaft pulley.
17. Install accessory brackets.
18. Install fan and pulley and drive belts.
19. Connect radiator hoses and bypass hose.
20. Connect ground cables to batteries.

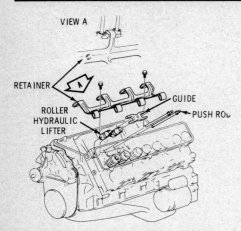

Fig. 39   Oversize valve lifter bore marking

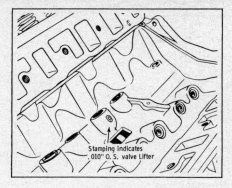

Fig. 40   Valve lifters & guide. 1981 & 1983–84

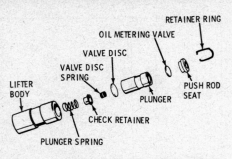

Fig. 41   Valve lifter exploded view. 1980

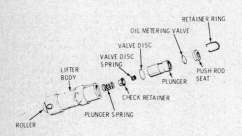

Fig. 42   Valve lifter exploded view. 1981 & 1983–84

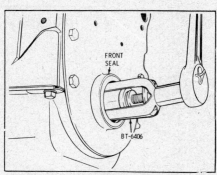

Fig. 43   Front oil seal removal

Fig. 44   Modifying tool for front seal installation

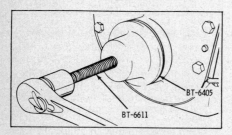

Fig. 45   Front oil seal installation

Fig. 46   Dowel pin chamfer

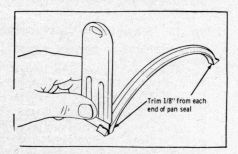

Fig. 47   Trimming oil pan seal

## TIMING CHAIN & GEARS REPLACE

1. Remove front cover as outlined previously.
2. Remove oil slinger, cam gear, crank gear and timing chain.
3. Remove fuel pump eccentric from crankshaft, if necessary.
4. Install key in crankshaft, if removed.
5. Install fuel pump eccentric, if removed.
6. Install cam gear, crank gear and timing chain with timing marks aligned, **Fig. 49**. With the timing marks aligned as shown in Fig. 49. No. 6 cylinder is in the firing position. To place No. 1 cylinder in the firing position, rotate crankshaft one complete revolution. This will bring the camshaft gear mark to top and No. 1 cylinder will be in the firing position.
7. Install oil slinger.

## CAMSHAFT & INJECTION PUMP DRIVE & DRIVEN GEARS REPLACE

1. Disconnect ground cables from batteries.
2. Drain cooling system.
3. Remove radiator upper baffle.
4. Disconnect upper radiator hose at water outlet and hose support clamp.
5. Disconnect cooler lines at radiator.
6. Remove fan shroud and radiator.
7. Remove intake manifold as outlined previously.
8. Remove engine front cover as outlined previously.
9. Remove valve covers.
10. Remove rocker arm bolts, pivots, rocker arms and pushrod. Note valve train component locations to install components in original locations.

8. Install front cover. Whenever timing chain and gears are replaced, it will be necessary to re-time the engine. Refer to "Injection Pump Timing" procedure.

11. If equipped with A/C, discharge refrigerant system and remove condenser.
12. On all models, remove timing chain and gears as outlined previously.
13. Position camshaft dowel pin at 3 o'clock position.
14. While holding the camshaft rearward and rocking the injection pump driven gear slide, slide the injection pump drive gear from camshaft.
15. Remove injection pump adapter, snap ring, selective washer, injection pump driven gear and spring, **Fig. 50.**
16. Slide camshaft from front of engine.
17. Reverse procedure to install. Check injection pump driven gear endplay. If endplay is not .002-.006 inch, replace selective washer, **Fig. 50**. Selective washers are available from .080 to .115 inch in increments of .003 inch.

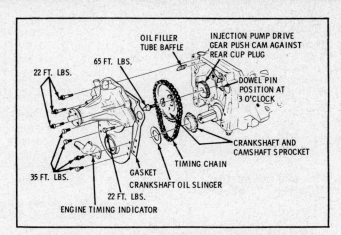

**Fig. 48   Engine front cover installation**

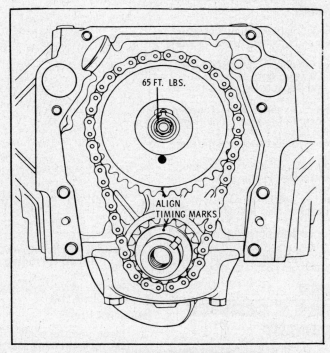

**Fig. 49   Valve timing marks**

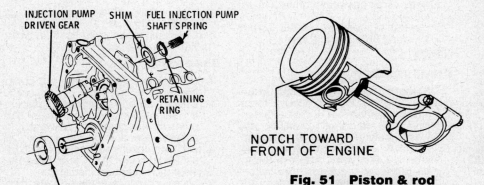

**Fig. 50   Fuel injection pump driven gear installation**

**Fig. 51   Piston & rod installation. 1983-84**

## PISTON & ROD ASSEMBLE

### 1983-84

Install piston and rod assembly so that notch at top of piston is facing toward front of engine, **Fig. 51.**

### 1980-81

Assemble piston to rod and install into cylinder block. The piston is installed with the valve depression facing toward the crankshaft. Also, there are two different pistons used in this engine. In cylinder numbers 1, 2, 3 and 4, the large valve depression faces the front of the engine, **Fig. 52.** In cylinder numbers 5, 6, 7 and 8 the large valve depression faces the rear of the engine, **Fig. 52.** The pistons are interchangeable between cylinder numbers 1, 3, 6 and 8 and 2, 4, 5 and 7.

## PISTONS, RINGS & PINS

Some engines may exhibit excessive oil consumption, low compression and/or excessive blowby. These conditions may be caused by stuck or frozen piston rings. To correct the above mentioned problem, proceed as follows:

1. With engine warm, remove all glow plugs from cylinders.
2. Using top engine cleaner Part No. 1050002 or equivalent, divide contents of can equally into each cylinder. Allow engine to soak for 24 hours.
3. Crank engine with glow plugs removed to expel excess cleaner.
4. Install glow plugs and start engine.

Pistons are available in standard sizes and oversizes of .010 and .030 inch. Rings are available in standard sizes and oversizes of .010 and .030 inch.

## MAIN & ROD BEARINGS

Main bearing inserts are available in standard sizes and undersizes of .0005, .0010 and .0015 inch. On 1983-84 models, a letter stamped on the bearing tang identifies the size of the bearing, **Fig. 53.** The undersize is also stamped on the bearing insert on the other side of the insert tang, **Fig. 53.** On 1980-81 models, the amount of undersize and part number is stamped on the bearing shell, **Fig. 54.**

Rod bearings are available in standard sizes and an undersize of .010 inch.

Beginning in the 1981 model year, a 1/4 inch longer main bearing cap bolt entered production. The new part number is 22511818, replacing 392190. All 1981 and newer diesel engine main bearing bolt holes have a 1/4 inch deeper tap and 1/4 inch longer counterbore.

## REAR CRANKSHAFT SEAL SERVICE

Since the braided fabric seal used on these engines can be replaced only when the crankshaft is removed, the following repair procedure is recommended.

1. Remove oil pan and bearing cap.

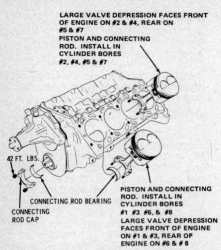

LARGE VALVE DEPRESSION FACES FRONT OF ENGINE ON #2 & #4, REAR ON #5 & #7
PISTON AND CONNECTING ROD. INSTALL IN CYLINDER BORES #2, #4, #5 & #7

42 FT. LBS.

CONNECTING ROD BEARING
CONNECTING ROD CAP

PISTON AND CONNECTING ROD. INSTALL IN CYLINDER BORES #1 #3 #6, & #8
LARGE VALVE DEPRESSION FACES FRONT OF ENGINE ON #1 & #3, REAR OF ENGINE ON #6 & #8

**Fig. 52 Piston & rod installation. 1980–81**

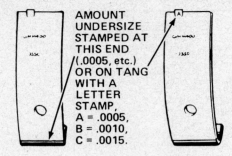

AMOUNT UNDERSIZE STAMPED AT THIS END (.0005, etc.) OR ON TANG WITH A LETTER STAMP, A = .0005, B = .0010, C = .0015.

**Fig. 53 Main bearing identification. 1983–84**

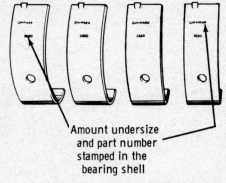

Amount undersize and part number stamped in the bearing shell

**Fig. 54 Main bearing identification. 1980–81**

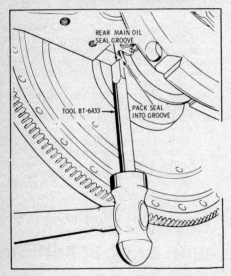

REAR MAIN OIL SEAL GROOVE

TOOL BT-6433
PACK SEAL INTO GROOVE

**Fig. 55 Packing upper rear main bearing seal**

2. Drive end of old seal gently into groove, using a suitable tool, until packed tight. This may vary between 1/4 and 3/4 inch depending on amount of pack required.
3. Repeat previous step for other end of seal.
4. Measure and note amount that seal was driven up on one side. Using the old seal removed from bearing cap, cut a length of seal the amount previously noted plus 1/16 inch.
5. Repeat previous step for other side of seal.
6. Pack cut lengths of seal into appropriate side of seal groove. A packing tool, BT-6433, **Fig. 55**, may be used since the tool has been machined to provide a built-in stop. Use tool BT-6436 to trim the seal flush with block, **Fig. 56.**
7. Install new seal in lower bearing cap.

## OIL PAN
### REPLACE

1. Disconnect battery ground cables.
2. Remove oil pump drive and vacuum pump.
3. Remove fan shroud attaching screws and pull upward from clips.
4. Raise and support vehicle. Drain oil pan.
5. Disconnect exhaust and crossover pipes, then remove oil cooler lines from filter base.
6. Remove flywheel cover and the starter motor.
7. Remove both engine mount through bolts and raise engine with suitable equipment.
8. Loosen the righthand engine mount and remove the lefthand engine mount.
9. Remove oil pan attaching bolts and the oil pan.
10. Reverse procedure to install. Torque oil pan attaching bolts to 10 ft. lbs.

## OIL PUMP
### REPLACE & SERVICE
#### REPLACEMENT

1. Remove oil pan as outlined previously.
2. Remove oil pump to rear main bearing cap attaching bolts, **Fig. 57.**
3. Remove oil pump and driveshaft extension.
4. Reverse procedure to install. Torque attaching bolts to 35 ft. lbs.

### SERVICE
#### Disassembly

1. Remove oil pump driveshaft extension, **Fig. 58.** Do not attempt to remove washers from driveshaft extension. The driveshaft extension and washers are serviced as an assembly.
2. Remove cotter pin, spring and pressure regulator valve. **Apply pressure on pressure regulator bore before removing cotter pin since the spring is under pressure.**
3. Remove oil pump cover attaching screws and the oil pump cover and gasket.

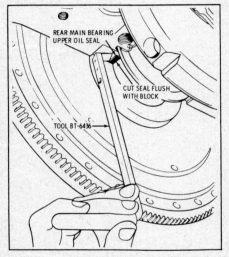

REAR MAIN BEARING UPPER OIL SEAL
CUT SEAL FLUSH WITH BLOCK
TOOL BT-6436

**Fig. 56 Trimming upper rear main bearing seal**

4. Remove drive gear and idler gear from pump body.

#### Inspection

1. Check gears for scoring or other damage, replace if necessary.
2. Proper end clearance is .0005-.0075 inch.
3. Check pressure regulator valve, valve spring and bore for damage. Proper bore to valve clearance is .0025-.0050 inch.
4. Check extension shaft ends for wear, **Fig. 59.**

#### Assembly

1. Install gears and shaft in oil pump body.
2. Check gear end clearance by placing a straightedge over the gears and measure the clearance between the straightedge and gasket surface. If end clearance is excessive, check for scores in cover that would bring the clearance over specified limits.
3. Install cover and torque attaching screws to 8 ft. lbs.
4. Install pressure regulator valve, closed end first, into bore, then the valve spring and cotter pin.

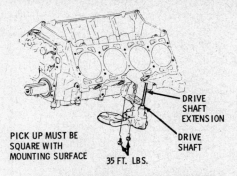

**Fig. 57  Oil pump installation**

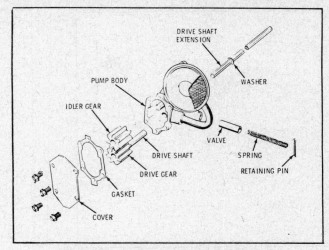

**Fig. 58  Oil pump disassembled**

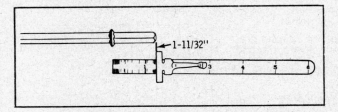

**Fig. 59  Oil pump driveshaft extension**

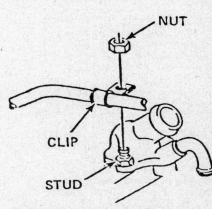

**Fig. 60  Installing fuel line stud & clip assembly**

# WATER PUMP
## REPLACE

1. Disconnect ground cables from batteries.
2. Drain cooling system.
3. Loosen drive belts and remove fan and pulley assembly.
4. Disconnect all hoses from water pump.
5. Remove alternator bracket, then the power steering pump and air conditioning compressor brackets, if equipped.
6. Remove water pump attaching screws and the water pump.
7. Reverse procedure to install.

# MECHANICAL FUEL PUMP
## REPLACE

Some diesel engines may exhibit a condition of hard cold starts. If this condition exists, check the fuel pump housing for a crack in the area where the fuel line is connected to the fuel pump, which may allow air to enter the system. The cracked fuel pump housing could be caused by the fuel line vibrating.

To correct this condition, remove the righthand thermostat housing bolt and install stud, part No. 6270979. Disconnect fuel line at the fuel pump and install clip, part No. 343463 onto fuel line as shown in **Fig. 60**. Install washer face nut, part No. 10008001. Replace the fuel pump and connect the fuel line.

1. Disconnect fuel lines from pump.
2. Remove fuel pump mounting bolts and the fuel pump.
3. Remove all gasket material from the pump and block gasket surfaces. Apply sealer to both sides of new gasket.
4. Position gasket on pump flange and hold pump in position against its mounting surface. Make sure rocker arm is riding on crankshaft eccentric.
5. Press pump tight against its mounting. Install retaining screws and tighten them alternately.
6. Connect fuel lines. Then operate engine and check for leaks. **Before installing the pump, it is good practice to crank the engine so that the nose of the crankshaft eccentric is out of the way of the fuel pump rocker arm when the pump is installed. In this way there will be the least amount of tension on the rocker arm, thereby easing the installation of the pump.**

# INJECTION PUMP TIMING
## LESS TIMING METER

1. The mark on the injection pump adapter must be aligned with the mark on the injection pump flange, **Fig. 61.**
2. To adjust:
   a. Loosen the injection pump retaining nuts with tool J-26987.
   b. Align the mark on the injection pump flange with the mark on the injection pump adapter, **Fig. 61.**
   c. Torque injection pump retaining nuts to 18 ft. lbs.

## WITH TIMING METER J-33075

Certain engine malfunctions can cause inaccurate timing readings. Engine malfunctions should be corrected before adjusting pump timing. The marks on the pump and pump adapter will normally be aligned within .030 inch.

1. Place transmission in Park, apply parking brake and block drive wheels.
2. Start engine and allow to reach normal operating temperature.

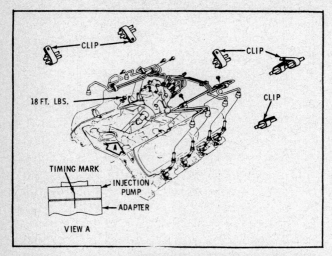

**Fig. 61    Fuel injection pump timing marks**

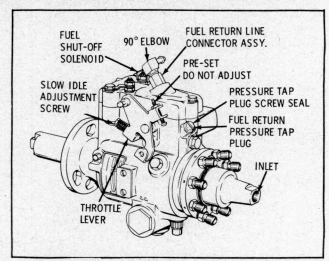

**Fig. 62    Fuel injection pump connections. 1980**

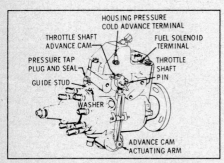

**Fig. 63    Fuel injection pump housing right side view. 1981 & 1983–84**

3. Shut engine off.
4. Remove air cleaner assembly, install cover J-26996-1, then disconnect EGR valve hose.
5. Clean dirt from engine probe holder and crankshaft balancer rim.
6. Clean lens on both ends of glow plug probe. Look through probe to ensure that it is clean.
7. Remove glow plug from No. 3 cylinder. Insert glow plug probe into glow plug opening and torque probe to 8 ft. lbs.
8. Set timing meter selector to B, then connect meter battery leads.
9. Disconnect generator two lead connector, then start engine and adjust idle speed to specifications.
10. Observe timing meter, wait approximately two minutes, then observe timing meter again. When meter stabilizes, compare timing reading to specifications. If timing is as specified, proceed to step 16. If timing is not as specified, proceed to next step.
11. Turn timing off and note relative position of marks on pump flange and adapter.
12. Loosen nuts or bolts holding pump to adapter, then rotate pump to the left (advance) or right (retard) as necessary. Torque retaining nuts or bolts to 18 ft. lbs. **Move pump gradually when adjusting timing. On V8 en-**

gines, the width of the adapter timing mark is equal to approximately 1°.
13. Start engine and recheck timing. Reset timing, if necessary.
14. On V8 engines, adjust pump rod, then reset curb and fast idle speeds.
15. Disconnect timing meter and install removed glow plug. Torque glow plug to 12 ft. lbs.
16. Connect generator two lead connector, install air cleaner assembly and reconnect EGR-valve hose.

The timing marks on the injection pump and adapter should be close to being lined up after timing the engine. If they are not, and the engine still exhibits poor performance, the timing may still be incorrect. A misfiring cylinder can result in incorrect timing. When this occurs, it is necessary that timing be checked in an alternate cylinder. Timing can be checked in cylinders 2 or 3. If a difference exists between cylinders, try both positions to determine which timing performs best.

If the engine continues to run poorly and excessive exhaust smoke is evident, check the housing pressure cold advance (1981-84) for proper operation. If the advance is operating properly, a stuck or frozen injection pump advance piston may be at fault. This piston is used on 1980-84 vehicles and can be checked by pushing in on the bottom of the face cam lever on the right side of the injection pump. If the piston is free, the timing will retard and cause the engine to run roughly. If no change is evident, the piston is sticking and must be repaired.

## FUEL INJECTION PUMP HOUSING FUEL PRESSURE CHECK

1. With engine thoroughly warmed up, remove air crossover and install screened covers, tool J-26996-2 or equivalent.

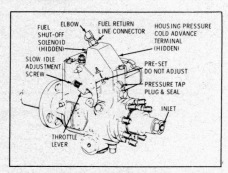

**Fig. 64    Fuel injection pump housing left side view. 1981 & 1983–84**

2. Remove fuel return pressure tap plug or torque screw, **Figs. 62, 63 and 64.** If equipped with torque screw, add a second nut to the locknut and back out screw to avoid disturbing the adjustment.
3. Remove the seal from the pressure tap plug or torque screw and place seal on pressure tap adapter J-29382. Screw pressure tap adapter into pressure tap hole in pump, then screw adapter J-28526 into J-29382 adapter.
4. Attach a suitable low pressure gauge to J-28526 adapter.
5. Connect magnetic pickup tachometer, tool J-26925, to engine.
6. With engine running at 1000 RPM in park, check fuel pressure. Pressure should be 8-12 psi with no more than 2 psi fluctuation. If vehicle is equipped with Housing Pressure Cold Advance (HPCA) and housing pressure is zero, disconnect electrical connector from housing pressure cold advance terminal, **Figs. 63 and 64.** If pressure remains zero, remove injection pump cover and check advance solenoid operation. If binding or not operating, free up or replace parts as necessary. If pressure is normal after electrical lead is disconnected, check for proper

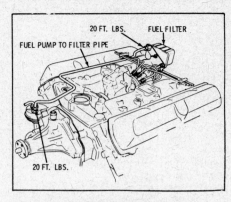

**Fig. 65   Fuel filter & lines**

operation of temperature switch located on the cylinder head bolt.

7. If fuel pressure is too low, replace the fuel return line connector assembly. If fuel pressure is too high, the fuel return system may be restricted. Remove the fuel return line at the injection pump, then install a fitting and short piece of hose to discharge the return line fuel into a suitable container.
8. Recheck fuel injection pump housing fuel pressure. If fuel pressure is lower than in previous step, correct fuel restriction in fuel return line. If pressure is still too high, replace fuel return line connector assembly. **Whenever the fuel return line connector assembly is replaced, the injection pump timing should be checked and reset as necessary. Refer to "Injection Pump Timing."**
9. Recheck fuel injection pump housing fuel pressure. If still too high, remove injection pump for repair.
10. Remove tachometer, pressure gauge and adapters.
11. Install new pressure tap plug screw seal on the pressure tap plug or torque screw and replace in pump.
12. Remove screened covers and install crossover.

## INJECTION PUMP REPLACE
### REMOVAL

1. Disconnect battery ground cables and remove air cleaner assembly.
2. Remove crankcase ventilation filters and pipes from valve covers and air crossover, **Fig. 23.**
3. Remove air crossover, then install screened covers J-26996-2 or equivalent.
4. Disconnect throttle rod and throttle return spring.
5. Remove bell crank.
6. Remove throttle and T.V. detent cables from intake manifold brackets and position aside.
7. Remove fuel lines to fuel filter, then the fuel filter and bracket, **Fig. 65.** If equipped with A/C, remove rear compressor base.
8. Disconnect fuel return line from injection pump.

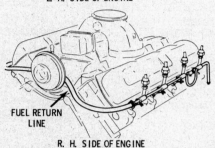

**Fig. 66   Fuel return lines. 1980 all & 1981 exc. Calif.**

9. To remove injection pump only:
   a. Disconnect injection line clips.
   b. Disconnect injection lines from injection pump and plug all open lines.
   c. Reposition injection lines to gain access for pump removal.
   d. Using tool J-26987, remove 3 pump retaining nuts, then remove pump.
10. To remove injection pump with injection lines attached:
   a. On 1980 models and 1981 models except California, slide clamp from fuel return lines at injector nozzles, **Fig. 66,** and remove fuel return lines from each bank.
   b. On all models, disconnect injection pump lines at injector nozzles, **Figs. 67 and 68.** It is necessary to use two wrenches.
   c. Remove three nuts retaining injection pump with tool J-26987.
   d. Remove injection pump and lines. Cap all lines and fittings.

### INSTALLATION

1. With cylinder No. 1 at TDC, align offset tang on pump driveshaft with pump driven gear, **Fig. 69.**
2. Install new pump to adapter O-ring, then install the pump or pump and lines, fully seating pump by hand. Loosely install 3 retaining nuts.
3. Align mark on injection pump with line on adapter, **Fig. 61,** then torque retaining nuts to 18 ft. lbs.
4. To install injection pump with injection lines attached:
   a. Connect injector lines at injector nozzles. Using a back-up wrench on upper nozzle hex, torque line nuts to 25 ft. lbs., **Figs. 67 and 68.**
   b. On 1980 (all) and 1981 except California, install fuel return lines to injectors on each bank, **Fig. 66.**
5. To install injection pump only:

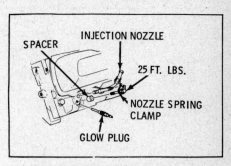

**Fig. 67   Injection nozzle installation. 1980 all & 1981 exc. Calif.**

   a. Position injector lines in proper position and connect injector lines to injection pump. Torque line nuts to 25 ft. lbs.
   b. Install injection line clips.
6. Connect fuel return line to injection pump.
7. Install fuel filter and bracket, then install fuel line. Return to **Fig. 65,** for torque specifications.
8. Install throttle and T.V. detent cables. Adjust T.V. cable.
9. Install bell crank, then install throttle rod and throttle return spring. If equipped with A/C, install rear compressor brace.
10. Remove screened covers, then install air crossover.
11. Install crankcase ventilation filters and pipes to valve covers and air crossover, **Fig. 23.**
12. Install air cleaner assembly. Connect battery ground cables.
13. Start engine and allow to idle for several minutes. Turn ignition "Off," for approximately two minutes, then restart to allow air to bleed off within pump.

## INJECTION PUMP ADAPTER, ADAPTER SEAL & NEW TIMING MARK
### ADAPTER SEAL, REPLACE

1. Remove injection pump. Refer to "Injection Pump, Replace."
2. Using a suitable probe, pry out adapter seal. **When prying out adapter seal, use caution not to nick or gouge adapter.**
3. Loosen bolts securing adapter to engine block, **Fig. 70.**
4. Lubricate new adapter seal inside and outside diameter with chassis lube.
5. Using seal installer J-28425, install seal on adapter, **Fig. 71.**
6. Remove seal installer tool and inspect seal for proper installation.
7. Torque adapter bolts to 25 ft. lbs.
8. Refer to "Marking Injection Pump Adapter" for remaining procedure.

### ADAPTER, REPLACE

1. Remove injection pump. Refer to "Injection Pump, Replace."

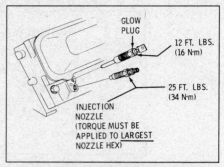

**Fig. 68   Injection nozzle installation. 1981 Calif. & all 1983-84**

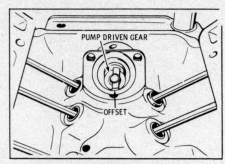

**Fig. 69   Offset on fuel injection pump driven gear**

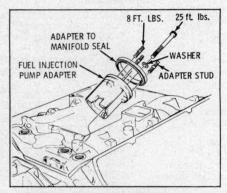

**Fig. 70   Fuel injection pump adapter installation**

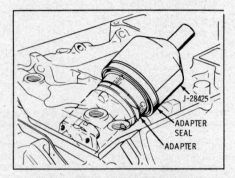

**Fig. 71   Fuel injection pump adapter seal installation**

2. Remove bolts securing adapter into engine block, **Fig. 70,** then remove adapter.
3. Install replacement adapter in engine block and install bolts. Do not tighten.
4. Refer to "Adapter Seal, Replace" steps 4 through 8, for remaining procedure.

## MARKING INJECTION PUMP ADAPTER

1. Using a suitable file, remove original timing mark from adapter. Do not remove timing mark from injection pump.
2. With cylinder No. 1 approaching TDC, align timing mark on balancer with zero mark on indicator. The injection pump driven gear should be slightly offset to the right when cylinder No. 1 is at TDC, **Fig. 69.**
3. Install timing tool J-26896, into pump adapter, **Fig. 72.** Using a suitable torque wrench, torque tool towards cylinder No. 1 to 50 ft. lbs. While holding torque steady, mark pump adapter, **Fig. 72.** Remove tool.
4. Reinstall injection pump. Refer to "Injection Pump, Replace."

## INJECTION NOZZLE
### REPLACE
#### 1981 CALIF. MODELS & 1983-84 ALL

Injection nozzle body leaks may be corrected by loosening the inlet fitting and re-

torquing to 45 ft. lbs. on DED type injection nozzles, and 25 ft. lbs. on CAV type injection nozzles, **Fig. 73.** In the event this does not correct the leak, remove the inlet fitting. Using a piece of crocus cloth, press and rotate the end of the inlet fitting against the crocus cloth back and forth about six times. After polishing has been performed, flush inlet fitting using diesel fuel and install fitting onto pump.

1. Remove fuel lines, using a back-up wrench on upper injection nozzle hex.
2. Remove nozzle by applying torque to largest nozzle hex, **Fig. 68.**
3. Cap nozzle and lines to prevent entry of dirt. Also remove copper gasket from cylinder head if gasket did not remain with nozzle.
4. Reverse procedure to install. Torque nozzle to 25 ft. lbs. When tightening nozzle, torque must be applied to largest nozzle hex. Torque fuel line to 25 ft. lbs. using a back-up wrench on upper injection nozzle hex.

### 1980 MODELS & 1981 EXC. CALIF.

1. Remove fuel line from injector nozzle.
2. Remove fuel line clamps from all nozzles on bank where nozzle is being removed. Remove fuel return line from nozzle being replaced.
3. Remove nozzle hold-down clamp and spacer, **Fig. 67,** then the nozzle with tool J-26952.
4. Cap nozzle inlet line and tip of nozzle.
5. Reverse procedure to install. Install new seals on injection nozzles, **Fig. 74.** Torque nozzle hold-down clamp

bolt to 25 ft. lbs.

## THROTTLE SHAFT SEAL REPLACE

1. Disconnect battery ground cables, then remove the air cleaner and crossover, and install screened covers, J-26996-2 or equivalent.
2. Disconnect injection pump fuel solenoid wire and fuel return line. On 1981 and 1983-84 models, disconnect housing pressure cold advance (HPCA) wires, **Fig. 63.**
3. On 1980 models, remove the transmission vacuum regulator valve. On 1981 and 1983-84 models, scribe a line on the vacuum regulator valve and pump body to aid in reassembly, and remove the vacuum regulator. Refer to "Transmission Vacuum Regulator Valve, Replace."
4. Remove the throttle rod, return spring and throttle cable bracket.
5. Position tool J-29601 over throttle shaft with tool slots engaging pin. Place the tool spring clip over the throttle shaft advance cam and tighten the wing nut, **Fig. 75.** Without loosening the wing nut, pull tool from throttle shaft. This will maintain proper alignment during reassembly. Drive pin from throttle shaft, loosen the clamp screw and remove the throttle shaft advance cam and fiber washer.
6. Remove any burrs on throttle shaft with shaft still installed in pump.

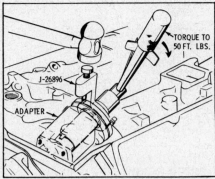

**Fig. 72   Marking fuel injection pump adapter with new timing mark**

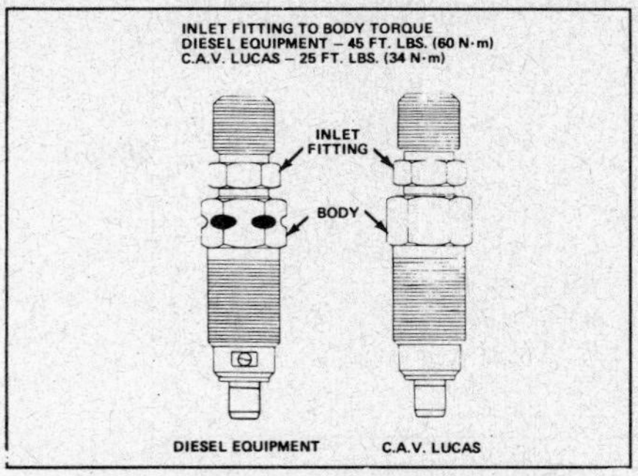

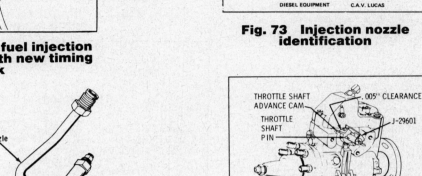

**Fig. 73   Injection nozzle identification**

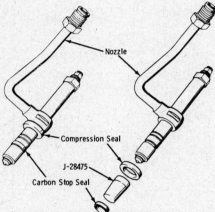

**Fig. 74   Injection nozzle seal installation**

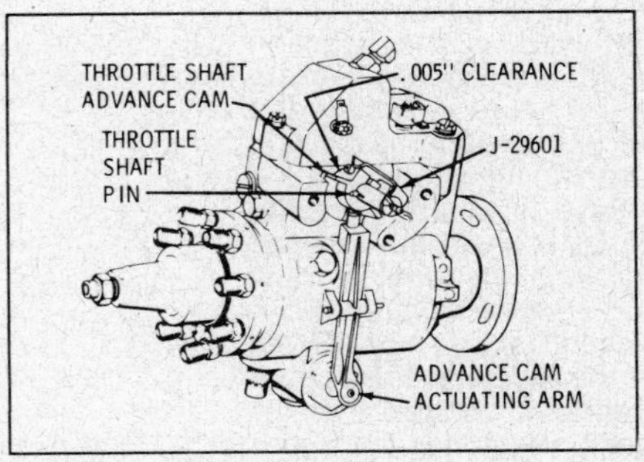

**Fig. 75   Injection pump with tool J-29601 installed**

7. Thoroughly clean the injection pump cover, the upper portion of the pump and the throttle shaft and guide stud area. Place shop towels in the engine valley to catch spilled fuel.
8. Remove injection pump top cover, then remove screws from cover. **When the injection pump top cover is removed, extreme care must be taken to keep foreign materials out of the pump. If any objects are dropped in the injection pump, they must be removed before the engine is started to prevent engine or injection pump damage.**
9. Note position of metering valve spring over top of guide stud. This position must be duplicated exactly during reassembly.
10. Remove guide stud and washer, **Fig. 63.** Note part location prior to removal.
11. Rotate min-max governor assembly upwards to provide clearance, then remove from throttle shaft, **Fig. 76.**
12. Remove throttle shaft assembly and examine shaft for unusual wear or damage. Replace if necessary. When removing throttle shaft assembly, it may be necessary to loosen the injection pump mounting nuts and rotate pump slightly to provide clearance for shaft removal.
13. Examine pump housing bushings for unusual wear or damage. If wear is evident, the pump should be removed and sent to manufacturer for repairs.
14. Remove throttle shaft seals. Do not attempt to cut seals to remove, as nicks in the seat will cause fuel leakage.
15. Install replacement shaft seals taking care not to cut seals on shaft edges. Apply chassis lube lightly to the seals.
16. Slide the throttle shaft assembly carefully into the pump body to the point the min-max governor assembly will slide back onto the throttle shaft assembly, **Fig. 76.**
17. Rotate the min-max governor assembly downward into the pump body, then while holding in position, slide the throttle shaft and governor assembly into position.
18. Install new mylar washer, throttle shaft advance cam (do not tighten screw at this time) and throttle shaft drive pin. Align the throttle shaft advance cam so tool J-29601 can be re-installed over the throttle shaft, pin in the slots and the spring clip over the advance cam, **Fig. 75.** Insert a .005 inch feeler gauge between the mylar washer on the throttle shaft and the pump housing. Squeeze the cam and throttle shaft together and tighten the cam screw. Torque to 30 inch lbs. Secure with suitable locking compound.
19. Install guide stud with new washer, **Fig. 63.** Ensure the metering valve spring upper extension rides on top of the guide stud. Torque guide stud to 85 inch lbs. Do not overtorque.
20. Hold throttle in idle position.
21. Install new pump cover seal. Ensure the securing screws are not in the cover and position the cover approximately 1/4 inch forward and 1/8 inch above the pump.
22. Move cover rearward and downward into proper position, using caution not to cut the seal, then install pump cover screws, **Fig. 77.** Torque screws to 35 inch lbs. **Use caution not to drop and lose flat washer and internal lock washer with each screw. Flat washers must be against pump cover.**
23. On 1980 models, install vacuum regulator valve. On 1981 and 1983-84 models, install vacuum regulator valve aligning marks made previously.
24. Connect battery ground cables.

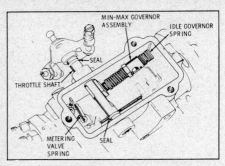

**Fig. 76   Min-max governor removal**

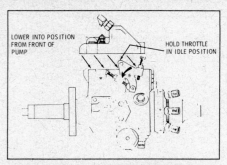

**Fig. 77   Installing injection pump cover**

25. Turn ignition to "Run" position. Touch pink solenoid wire to the injection pump solenoid terminal. A clicking noise should be heard indicating the fuel solenoid is operating. If clicking noise is heard, proceed to step 28. If no clicking noise is heard, the solenoid linkage may be jammed in a wide open position and the engine must not be started. Proceed to step 26.
26. Remove injection pump top cover, then ground the solenoid lead opposite the hot lead and connect the pink wire. With ignition switch in the "Run" position, the solenoid should move the linkage. If not, replace the solenoid. **The minimum voltage across the solenoid terminals must be 12 volts.**
27. Reinstall cover and repeat step 25.
28. Install throttle cable bracket and throttle rod, then install throttle cable and return spring. Connect solenoid wire and on 1981 and 1983-84 models housing pressure cold advance (HPCA) wire.
29. Install fuel return line. Ensure the timing mark on the pump is aligned with the adapter timing mark. Also ensure the injection pump retaining bolts are tight.
30. Start engine and check for leaks. If engine roughness is observed, it may be due to air in the pump. To purge air, let engine idle for several minutes. It may be necessary to shut engine down for several minutes to allow air bubbles to rise to top of pump where they will be purged.
31. Remove intake manifold screens, then reinstall air crossover and air cleaner.

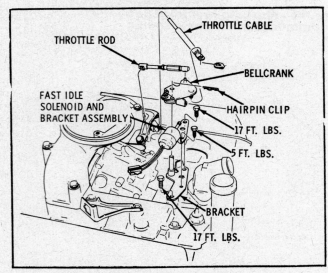

**Fig. 78   Throttle linkage**

## TRANSMISSION VACUUM REGULATOR VALVE
### REPLACE

1. Note location of the valve vacuum hoses, then disconnect the vacuum hoses.

2. Remove the two valve attaching bolts and the valve.
3. Reverse procedure to install.
4. Adjust vacuum valve. Refer to "Transmission Vacuum Regulator Valve, Adjust."

## THROTTLE ROD
### ADJUST

1. If equipped with cruise control, remove clip from cruise control rod, then the rod from bell crank.
2. Remove throttle valve cable from bell crank, **Fig. 78.**
3. Loosen the throttle rod locknut and shorten the rod several turns.

4. Rotate the bell crank to the full throttle stop, then lengthen the throttle rod until the injection pump lever contacts the injection pump full throttle stop. Release the bell crank.
5. Tighten the throttle rod locknut.
6. Connect the throttle valve cable and cruise control rod, if equipped, to bellcrank.

## THROTTLE VALVE OR DETENT CABLE
### ADJUST

1. Remove throttle rod from bell crank, **Fig. 79.**
2. Push snap lock to disengaged position.

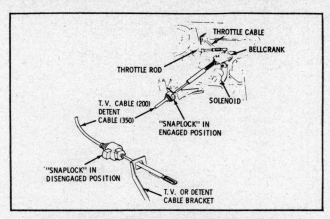

**Fig. 79   Throttle valve or detent cable adjustment**

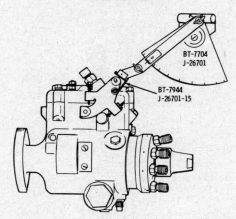

**Fig. 80   Transmission vacuum regulator valve adjustment. 1980–83 Turbo Hydra-Matic 350**

## PURGING WATER FROM FUEL TANK
### 1980—84 MODELS WITH WATER IN FUEL DETECTOR
#### Single Tank Models

Water in the fuel tank may be purged by siphoning or using a pump. The pump or siphon hose should be connected to the 1/4 inch fuel return hose (smaller of the two hoses) under the hood near the fuel pump. Purging should continue until all water is removed from the fuel tank. Also, remove fuel filler cap while purging, and replace cap when completed. **Use all safety precautions while handling the fuel/water mixture.**

#### Dual Tank Models

Water in the dual fuel tanks is purged in much the same way as single tank models, except that the fuel selector control should be switched to the main tank position. Siphoning should continue until all water is removed from the main tank. Place ignition switch in the "On" position, and move the fuel selector control to the auxiliary position. Turn ignition "Off" and continue to siphon water from auxiliary tank until all water is removed. **Auxiliary tank must be siphoned within twenty minutes. If water cannot be siphoned within twenty minutes, cycle ignition switch "Run" and back to "Off" to obtain another twenty minute siphon period.**

When siphoning water from tanks, fuel filler caps should be removed and reinstalled when siphoning is completed. **Use all safety precautions while handling the fuel/water mixture.**

3. Rotate bell crank to full throttle stop position and push in snap lock until flush with cable end fitting. Release bell crank.
4. Connect the throttle rod.

## TRANSMISSION VACUUM REGULATOR VALVE
### ADJUST

1. Remove air crossover, then install screen covers J26996-2.
2. Remove throttle rod from throttle lever, then loosen transmission regulator vacuum valve injection pump bolts.
3. Install carburetor angle gauge adapter, J-26701-15 on injection pump throttle lever, then place angle gauge, J-26701 on adapter, **Fig. 80.**

4. Rotate throttle lever to wide open position and set angle gauge to zero degrees.
5. Center bubble in level, then set angle gauge to 50° on 1980 units or 58° on 1981-84 units.
6. Rotate throttle lever so level bubble is centered.
7. Attach a suitable vacuum pump to center port of vacuum regulator valve, then install a vacuum gauge to outside port of vacuum regulator valve. Apply 18-22 inches of vacuum.
8. Rotate vacuum regulator valve clockwise to obtain 10.6 inches of vacuum on 1983-84 models, 8½ to 9 inches of vacuum on 1981 models and 7 to 8 inches of vacuum on 1980 models.
9. Tighten vacuum regulator to injection pump retaining bolts, then remove vacuum gauge and pump.
10. Install throttle rod to bell crank, then remove screened covers and install air crossover and air cleaner.

## VACUUM PUMPS

On engines equipped with gear driven type vacuum pump, do not operate engine unless vacuum pump and drive assembly are installed, as the drive gear of the vacuum pump also drives the engine lubricating oil pump.

On these engines, a vacuum pump is required to provide vacuum for accessory operation. The vacuum pump may be either gear driven or belt driven, depending on vehicle application. The gear driven pump has a drive gear located at the lower end of the shaft which meshes with a gear on the engine camshaft. This vacuum pump drive gear also drives the engine lubricating oil pump. The belt driven pump has a pulley attached to the lower end of the shaft and is driven by an accessory belt.

When servicing the vacuum pump, refer to **Fig. 81** for service procedures.

## 1. REMOVE AND INSTALL

### REMOVE

1. Remove hose from pump inlet.
2. Remove bolt and bracket holding pump to engine block.
3. Remove pump.

### INSTALL

1. Insert pump in engine, making sure the gears on the pump mesh with the gears on the engine cam shaft.
2. Rotate the pump into position so the bracket and bolt can be installed.
3. Install vacuum hose.

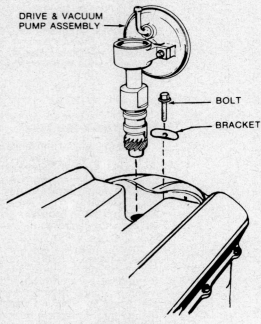

VACUUM HOSE

DRIVE & VACUUM PUMP ASSEMBLY

BOLT

BRACKET

Removing assembly from engine.

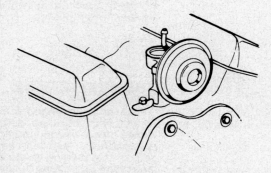

View showing assembly from rear of engine.

## 2. DISASSEMBLE AND ASSEMBLE

**CAUTION:** *Take extreme care when clamping the vacuum pump in vise.*

### DISASSEMBLE

1. Remove hex head tapping screws.
2. Remove "O" Ring Seal.

### ASSEMBLE

1. Install "O" Ring Seal in cavity of drive assembly.
2. Connect drive assembly to vacuum pump with hex head tapping screws.

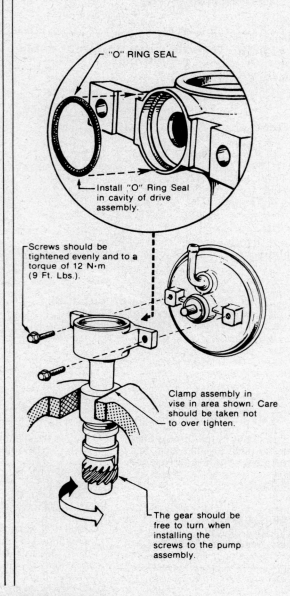

"O" RING SEAL

Install "O" Ring Seal in cavity of drive assembly.

Screws should be tightened evenly and to a torque of 12 N·m (9 Ft. Lbs.).

Clamp assembly in vise in area shown. Care should be taken not to over tighten.

The gear should be free to turn when installing the screws to the pump assembly.

**Fig. 81   Vacuum pump service**

# V8-379 (6.2L) DIESEL ENGINE

## INDEX

# DESCRIPTION

The V8-379 (6.2L) diesel engine is similar in many ways to gasoline engines, however, in the diesel engine air alone is compressed in cylinder; then after the air has been compressed, a charge of fuel is sprayed into the cylinder and ignition occurs due to the heat of compression. Due to the increased compression and resultant increase in combustion temperatures, major differences are evident in the cylinder heads, combustion chambers, fuel distribution system, intake manifold and engine mechanical components.

The cylinder block, crankshaft, main bearings, connecting rods, pistons and wrist pins are all heavy duty designs, due to the higher compression ratios, and the main bearing caps are 4 bolt design to provide rigid crankshaft support, while minimizing stress. Roller hydraulic lifters are used to minimize wear on the forged steel camshaft, and intake and exhaust valves are of special alloy material to combat the higher internal operating temperatures. Steel alloy pre-chamber inserts are installed in the combustion chambers and are serviced separately from the cylinder head. Injector nozzles and glow plugs are threaded into the cylinder head to allow direct fuel delivery and to provide chamber pre-heating.

The injector nozzles are spring loaded and designed to open and deliver fuel at specifically calibrated fuel pressures. Fuel is delivered into the high swirl pre-combustion chambers which mix fuel and air to provide an efficient fuel burn and low emissions. The glow plugs are used to heat the pre-chambers, and assist starting. In addition, a block heater is used to aid starting in cold climates. Because the intake manifold is always open to atmospheric pressures no engine vacuum supply is available, and a vacuum pump is installed to supply vacuum to components such as A/C and cruise control.

## LUBRICATION SYSTEM

The gear-type oil pump is attached to the bottom side of the rear main bearing cap and is driven by the camshaft through an intermediate shaft. Oil flows through the pump outlet tube to the cooler located in the radiator. A bypass valve is incorporated into the system, which allows oil to bypass the cooler and continue to feed the engine should the cooler become clogged. From the cooler, the oil then flows through a cartridge type oil filter. A bypass valve is incorporated into the system to prevent oil starvation should the filter become clogged.

From the oil filter, oil then flows through the drilled galleries in the cylinder block. The rear crankshaft bearing is fed by a hole drilled from the rear main bearing bore to the main oil gallery. Oil is also pumped through the main gallery to a gallery which has been drilled the full length of the left side of the block. Oil from the left side gallery feeds the camshaft bearings and a gallery which runs the full length of the right side of the block. All other engine components are lubricated through these left and right main galleries.

Oil is supplied to lifters on the right bank from the right side main gallery, and to lifters on the left bank from the left side main gallery. The lifters contain disc valves which meter oil to the hollow pushrods and provide valve train lubrication. Holes drilled from the camshaft bearing bores to the crankshaft bearing bores supply oil to main bearings 1-4. Oil flows onto the crankshaft bearings providing lubrication for the crankshaft to rotate freely in its bearings, and cross drilling provides lubrication to the crankpins. As the crankshaft rotates, oil slings off the crankpins to lubricate cylinder walls, pistons and piston pins, and the piston rings.

## FUEL SYSTEM
### COMPONENTS

The fuel system consists of a tank, fuel pickup assembly, fuel filters, mechanical fuel pump, fuel line heater, and an injection pump, injector lines and individual fuel injectors for each cylinder. On 1982-83 models, the fuel pickup incorporates a water in fuel detector, **Fig. 1**, primary and secondary fuel filters are used, and a water drain siphon valve is included in the system, **Fig. 2**. On 1984-89 models, a single fuel filter assembly is used, which includes the water in fuel sensor, water separator and drain, and the fuel heater, **Figs. 3 and 4**. In addition, 1984-89 models are equipped with a low pressure switch which illuminates a warning lamp should the fuel filter become clogged.

### SYSTEM OPERATION
### 1982-83

Fuel is drawn from the fuel tank through the primary fuel filter and by the camshaft driven mechanical fuel pump. It then flows

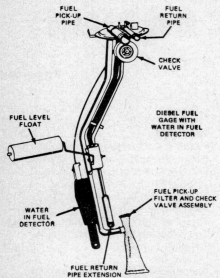

**Fig. 1   Water in fuel detector, strainer & pickup tube assembly. 1982–83 models**

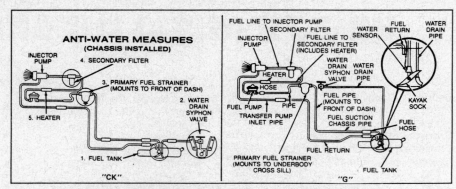

**Fig. 2   Fuel filter system. 1982–83 models**

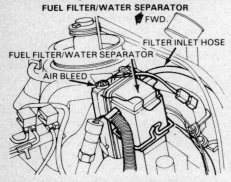

**Fig. 3   Fuel filter/water separator. 1984–89 G & P models**

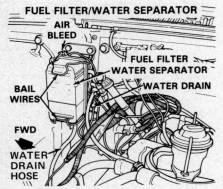

**Fig. 4   Fuel filter/water separator. 1984–89 C, K, R & V models**

through the fuel line heater, which prevents fuel waxing, to the secondary fuel filter, which again strains contaminants from the fuel. The fuel is then directed to the high pressure rotary vane type injection pump. The injection pump meters and pressurizes the fuel, then directs it through the equal length high pressure lines to the injector nozzles.

### 1984–89

Fuel is drawn from the tank by the camshaft drive mechanical mechanical pump. Fuel is then pumped through the fuel filter and heater assembly mounted on the front of the dash on C, K, R and V models or under the air cleaner on G and P models. In the filter, contaminants are strained out of the fuel, water is separated and the fuel is heated to prevent formation of wax deposits. From the filter fuel is delivered to the high pressure rotary vane type injection pump. The injection pump meters and pressurizes the fuel, then directs it through the injector lines to the injector nozzles. The eight high pressure injector lines are

all of equal length, although their shapes may be different, in order to prevent any difference in injection timing between cylinders.

## WATER IN FUEL WARNING SYSTEM
### 1982–83

The fuel tank is equipped with a filter and water in fuel detector, **Fig. 1**. The filter prevents water from entering the pickup tube, allowing it instead to lay at the bottom of the fuel tank, below the tube. When the water level reaches a point where it may enter the fuel system, the detector activates a warning lamp on the dash panel, alerting the driver. A siphoning system starting at the tank and going to the rear spring hanger (C and K models) or to the midpoint of the right frame rail (G models), **Fig. 2**, allows the driver to attach a hose to the shut-off valve and drain the system.

### 1984–89

The water separation system on these models is incorporated into the fuel filter assembly, **Figs. 3 and 4**. The fuel filter separates and traps water contained in the fuel, and when the water level reaches a point where it could be drawn into the system, the "WATER IN FUEL" lamp on the instrument panel is illuminated. In addition, the low pressure sensor on the filter outlet will also illuminate the lamp if the fuel filter becomes clogged.

## GLOW PLUG CONTROL SYSTEM
### DESCRIPTION
#### 1982–84 Models

The glow plug control system consists of a thermal controller, a glow plug relay, 6 volt glow plugs and a glow plug warning lamp, **Fig. 5**.

The thermal controller is mounted in the water passage at the rear of the engine. Glow plug operation is controlled by thermostatic elements within the controller which open or close the ground circuit to the glow plug relay as necessary. The relay is located on the left inner fender panel and provides current to the glow plugs as long as the thermal controller completes the ground circuit. Glow plugs used in this

system are 6 volt plugs operated at the system voltage (12 volts). They are not designed to burn continuously, and are pulsed on and off by the glow plug relay in response to messages received by the controller. The glow plug warning lamp, mounted in the instrument cluster, is wired across the glow plugs and is illuminated whenever the glow plugs are heating.

Initially, during cold starting, the glow plugs are activated continuously for 7½–9 seconds at 0°F. The glow plugs then pulse on and off at a rate determined by the thermal characteristics of the controller, to provide stable engine warm-up. As the engine warms up, the controller turned off all current to the relay, de-energizing the glow plugs completely. In addition the controller is capable of varying glow plug operation, as needed, to allow proper operation during cold starting when little or no heating is required. In the event of controller failure, as in the case of prolonged preheat, a circuit breaker within the controller opens and current to the glow plugs is cut off completely.

#### 1985–89 Models

The glow plug control system consists of an integral electronic control/glow plug relay assembly, eight 6-volt glow plugs, a glow plug inhibit temperature switch and a glow plug indicator lamp, **Fig. 6**. The controller assembly is mounted at the rear of

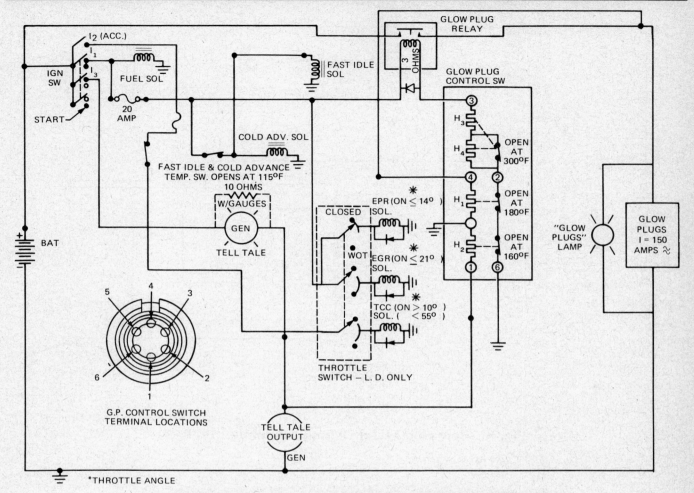

**Fig. 5 Engine control system wiring schematic. 1982–84**

the left cylinder head, and contains the circuitry to monitor and control glow plug operation.

On 1987 R and V and 1988–89 models, the inhibit switch is installed in the water cross-over near the front of the engine. On all other models the inhibit temperature switch is threaded into the rear of the right cylinder head. The switch is calibrated to open when temperature exceeds approximately 125°F to prevent glow plug operation above this temperature. The glow plug warning lamp, mounted in the instrument cluster, is wired across the glow plugs and is illuminated whenever the glow plugs are heating.

Battery voltage is applied at all times to the relay input stud on the controller, and the glow plugs are connected to the relay output stud. Inputs at terminals B and C of the module, **Fig. 6,** provide information to determine glow plug operating requirements, while terminals D and E respectively provide battery voltage and a ground path for the relay. Terminal B at the controller receives the cranking voltage signal from the starter motor, while terminal C senses glow plug voltage through the inhibit switch which is wired in series with the glow plug voltage feed.

A normally functioning system operates as follows: With the key on and the engine stopped and at room temperature, the

glow plugs will be energized for 4–6 seconds, then off for approximately 4.5 seconds. After this initial sequence, the glow plugs will be cycled on for approximately 1.5 seconds and off for approximately 4.5 seconds for a total duration (including the initial 4–6 seconds) of approximately 20 seconds. If the engine is cranked either during or after the above sequence, the glow plugs will cycle on and off for approximately 25 seconds after the key is returned from the crank position to the on position, whether the engine starts or not. The engine does not have to be running to terminate glow plug cycling.

The duration of the glow plug cycling sequence is dependent upon engine temperature with lower temperatures producing longer cycling duration. In addition, the initial on time and the cycling on/off times vary with system voltage. That is, lower system voltage causes longer on times during each cycle.

## GLOW PLUG RESISTANCE CHECK

### 1982

1. Use Kent-Moore High Impedance Digital Multimeter (J-29125) for resistance measurements.

2. Select scales as follows: LH switch to OHMS, RH switch to full counter-clockwise, 200 OHMS, slide center switch to left DC.LO.

3. Start engine, turn on heater and allow engine to warm up. Remove all feed wires from glow plugs.

4. Turn engine idle speed screw on side of injector pump to worst engine idle roughness. Do not exceed 900 RPM. Allow engine to run for a minimum of one minutes.

5. Attach alligator clip to black test lead of multimeter and grounded to engine lift strap on left hand side of intake manifold.

6. Probe each glow plug terminal and record resistance values on each cylinder in firing sequence (1-8-7-2-6-5-4-3) with engine idling. Readings should be between 1.8 and 3.4 OHMS. If these readings are not obtained, turn engine off for several minutes and recheck glow plugs. Resistance should be .7-.9 OHMS. Readings of 1.2-1.3 OHMS would indicate an engine mechanical problem.

## THERMAL CONTROLLER CHECK

### 1982–84

1. Disconnect electrical connector from

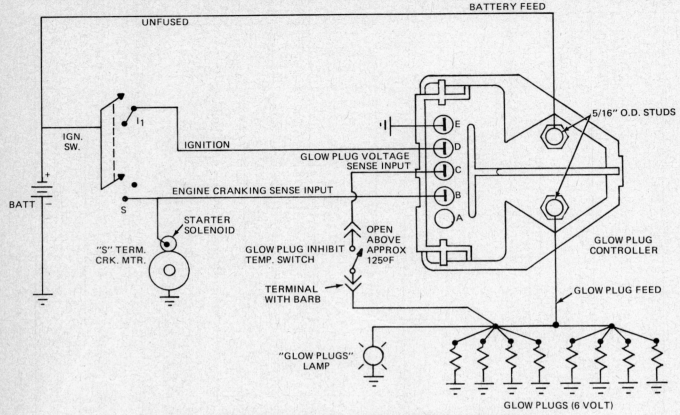

**Fig. 6   Glow plug system wiring schematic. 1985-89**

thermal controller.
2. Measure resistance between controller terminals using high impedance, digital ohmmeter set on 200 ohms scale.
3. Resistance should be as follows:
   Pins 2 to 3............ 0.40-0.75ohms
   Pins 4 to 5.............. 24-30ohms
   Pins 1 to 5........... 117-143ohms
   Pins 2 to 6 ....... Continuity(0)ohms
4. If resistance values are not as specified, controller is defective.
5. If resistance values are within specifications, reconnect electrical connector and observe controller operation with ignition key in on position and engine stopped.
6. If controller cycles more than one time, controller is satisfactory.
7. If controller cycles only once, check for a short or open in harness as outlined in "System Diagnosis."
8. If all other components are satisfactory, but controller cycles only once in step 5, replace controller and recheck system operation.

## SYSTEM DIAGNOSIS

The glow plug relays are automatically controlled. Do not attempt to bypass either the separate glow plug relay used on 1982-84 models or the relay terminals of the controller used on 1985-89 models, as the glow plugs will be damaged.

1. Inspect all system electrical connectors and ensure terminals are free from corrosion and that connectors are fully seated.
2. Inspect engine harness ground stud, ensuring wire end terminals are free from corrosion and that stud nut is properly tightened.
3. On 1985-89 models, inspect relay terminal lugs on controller, ensuring wire end terminals are free from corrosion and that nut is torqued to 35-45 inch lbs. on 1985-87 models, or 48 inch lbs. on 1988-89 models.
4. On all models, if glow plugs function normally but glow plug lamp fails to light, inspect connections and bulb in instrument panel jumper harness and repair as needed.
5. If system fails to operate properly refer to wiring schematic and diagnostic charts, **Figs. 5 and 7** for 1982-84 models, **Figs. 6 and 8** for 1985 models, **Figs. 6 and 9** for 1986-89 models.

On early 1982 vehicles, the engine wiring harness connector at the glow plug controller, has an open hole at the No. 2 pin connection. Accumulated moisture and dirt in this hole may cause controller malfunction. If the engine is hard to start, or has burned glow plugs, remove the connector and clean the pin area on the controller and connector, then reconnect the connector. Apply a small amount of RTV

sealant, or equivalent, over the No. 2 pin hole to prevent further contamination. Check operation of controller. If the controller does not cycle and/or the pins are excessively corroded, the controller must be replaced.

## ENGINE MOUNTS
### REPLACE

1. Raise and support vehicle.
2. Support engine, then working from below frame mounting bracket, remove engine mount retaining bolt.
3. Raise engine slightly, then remove mount to engine retaining bolts and mount.
4. Reverse procedure to install.

## ENGINE
### REPLACE
#### EXC. VAN

1. Disconnect batteries and raise vehicle.
2. Remove transmission dust cover and disconnect torque converter and exhaust.
3. Disconnect wires from starter and remove starter.
4. Remove transmission bellhousing bolts and motor mount bolts.

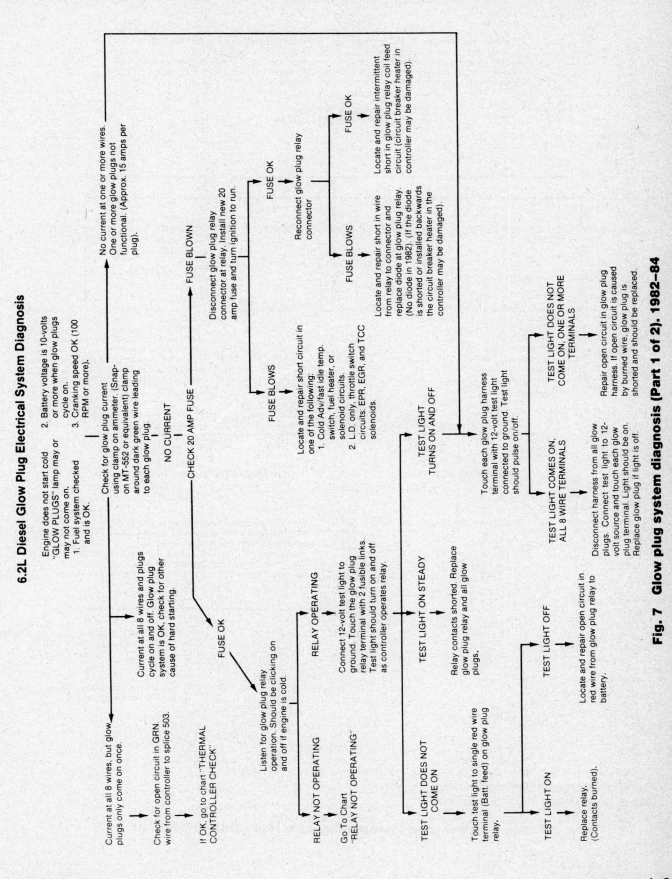

**6.2L Diesel Glow Plug Electrical System Diagnosis**

Engine does not start cold "GLOW PLUGS" lamp may or may not come on.
1. Fuel system checked and is OK.
2. Battery voltage is 10-volts or more when glow plugs cycle on.
3. Cranking speed OK (100 RPM or more).

Check for glow plug current using clamp on ammeter. (Snap-on MT-552 or equivalent) clamp around dark green wire leading to each glow plug.

**NO CURRENT** → **CHECK 20 AMP FUSE**

No current at one or more wires. One or more glow plugs not functional. (Approx. 15 amps per plug).

Current at all 8 wires and plugs cycle on and off. Glow plug system is OK, check for other cause of hard starting.

Current at all 8 wires, but glow plugs only come on once.

Check for open circuit in GRN. wire from controller to splice 503.

If OK, go to chart "THERMAL CONTROLLER CHECK".

**FUSE OK** → Listen for glow plug relay operation. Should be clicking on and off if engine is cold.

**RELAY OPERATING** → Connect 12-volt test light to ground. Touch the glow plug relay terminal with 2 fusible links. Test light should turn on and off as controller operates relay.

**RELAY NOT OPERATING** → Go To Chart "RELAY NOT OPERATING"

**TEST LIGHT ON STEADY** → Relay contacts shorted. Replace glow plug relay and all glow plugs.

**TEST LIGHT DOES NOT COME ON** → Touch test light to single red wire terminal (Batt. feed) on glow plug relay.

**TEST LIGHT OFF** → Locate and repair open circuit in red wire from glow plug relay to battery.

**TEST LIGHT ON** → Replace relay. (Contacts burned).

**FUSE BLOWN** → Disconnect glow plug relay connector at relay. Install new 20 amp fuse and turn ignition to run.

**FUSE BLOWS** → Locate and repair short circuit in one of the following:
1. Cold Adv/fast idle temp. switch, fuel heater, or solenoid circuits.
2. L.D. only, throttle switch circuits: EPR, EGR, and TCC solenoids.

**FUSE OK** → Reconnect glow plug relay connector

**FUSE BLOWS** → Locate and repair short in wire from relay to connector and replace diode at glow plug relay. (No diode in 1982). (If the diode is shorted or installed backwards the circuit breaker heater in the controller may be damaged).

**FUSE OK** → Locate and repair intermittent short in glow plug relay coil feed circuit (circuit breaker heater in controller may be damaged).

**TEST LIGHT TURNS ON AND OFF** → Touch each glow plug harness terminal with 12-volt test light connected to ground. Test light should pulse on/off.

**TEST LIGHT COMES ON, ALL 8 WIRE TERMINALS** → Disconnect harness from all glow plugs. Connect test light to 12-volt source and touch each glow plug terminal. Light should be on. Replace glow plug if light is off.

**TEST LIGHT DOES NOT COME ON, ONE OR MORE TERMINALS** → Repair open circuit in glow plug harness. If open circuit is caused by burned wire, glow plug is shorted and should be replaced.

**Fig. 7  Glow plug system diagnosis (Part 1 of 2). 1982–84**

Connect an ammeter in series (induction type meter may also be used)* with DK red or orange wire leading from the Glow Plug Relay to the LH bank of glow plugs. Operate the system and note the ammeter reading. Repeat the procedure for the red or orange wire leading from the Glow Plug Relay to the RH bank of glow plugs. Operate the system and note the reading.

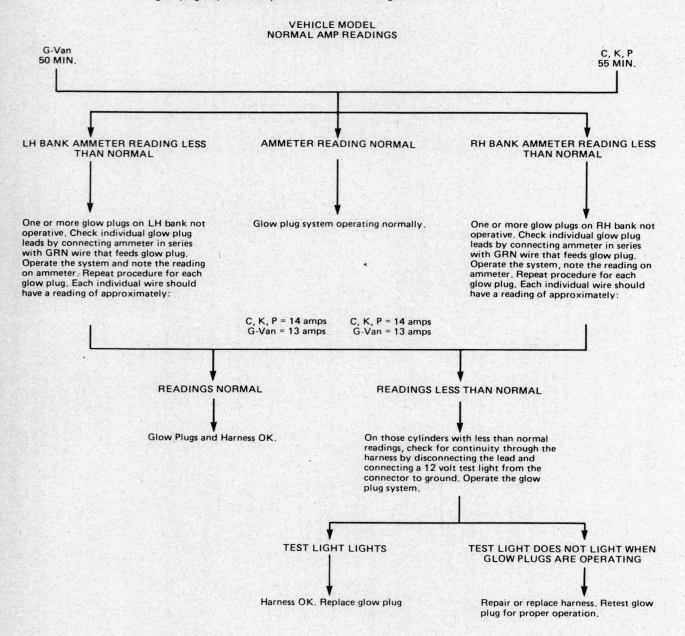

**VEHICLE MODEL**
**NORMAL AMP READINGS**

G-Van
50 MIN.

C, K, P
55 MIN.

**LH BANK AMMETER READING LESS THAN NORMAL**

**AMMETER READING NORMAL**

**RH BANK AMMETER READING LESS THAN NORMAL**

One or more glow plugs on LH bank not operative. Check individual glow plug leads by connecting ammeter in series with GRN wire that feeds glow plug. Operate the system and note the reading on ammeter. Repeat procedure for each glow plug. Each individual wire should have a reading of approximately:

Glow plug system operating normally.

One or more glow plugs on RH bank not operative. Check individual glow plug leads by connecting ammeter in series with GRN wire that feeds glow plug. Operate the system, note the reading on ammeter. Repeat procedure for each glow plug. Each individual wire should have a reading of approximately:

C, K, P = 14 amps
G-Van = 13 amps

C, K, P = 14 amps
G-Van = 13 amps

**READINGS NORMAL**

**READINGS LESS THAN NORMAL**

Glow Plugs and Harness OK.

On those cylinders with less than normal readings, check for continuity through the harness by disconnecting the lead and connecting a 12 volt test light from the connector to ground. Operate the glow plug system.

**TEST LIGHT LIGHTS**

**TEST LIGHT DOES NOT LIGHT WHEN GLOW PLUGS ARE OPERATING**

Harness OK. Replace glow plug

Repair or replace harness. Retest glow plug for proper operation.

*If using an in line ammeter read both banks at once. Do not cut wire.

(Snap-on meter MT552, VAT-40, or equivalent)

**Fig. 7    Glow plug system diagnosis (Part 2 of 2). 1982–84**

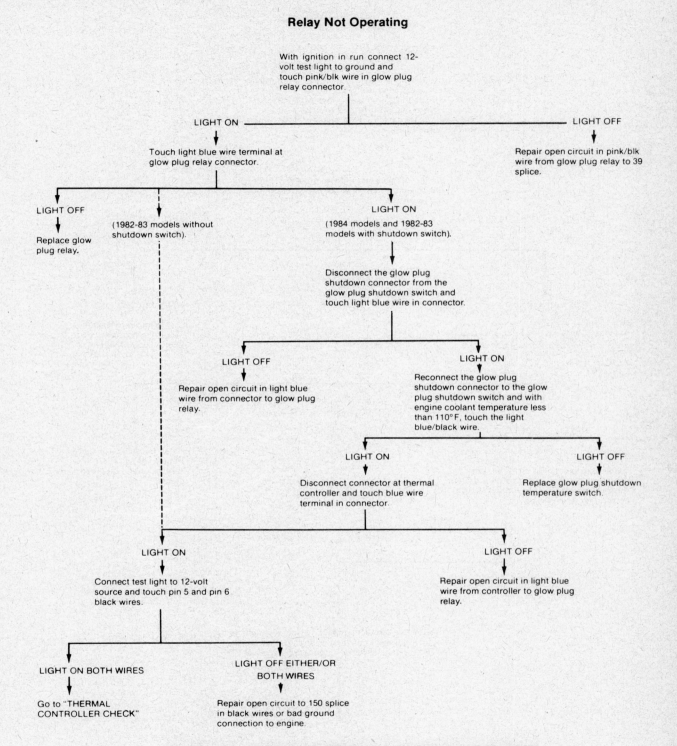

**Fig. 8   Glow plug system diagnosis (Part 1 of 3). 1985**

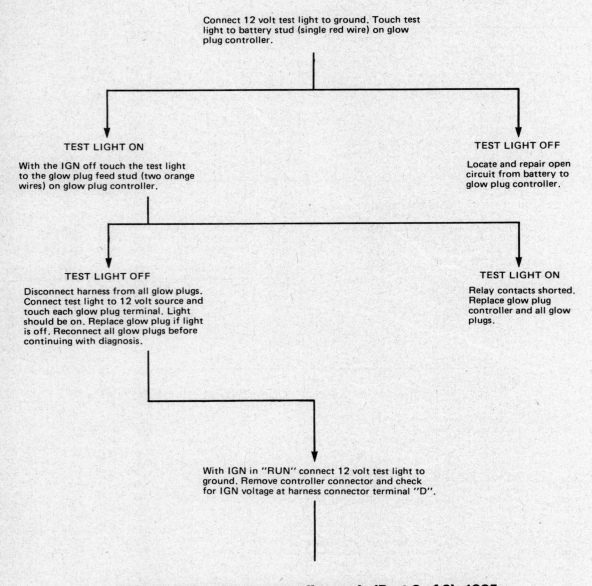

Engine does not start cold — "GLOW PLUGS" lamp may or may not come on
1. Fuel system checked and is OK.
2. Battery voltage is 12.4 volts or more with IGN off.
3. Cranking speed OK (100 RPM or more).
4. Reference electronic glow plug system figure for wiring harness terminal identification.

Connect 12 volt test light to ground. Touch test light to battery stud (single red wire) on glow plug controller.

**TEST LIGHT ON**

With the IGN off touch the test light to the glow plug feed stud (two orange wires) on glow plug controller.

**TEST LIGHT OFF**

Locate and repair open circuit from battery to glow plug controller.

**TEST LIGHT OFF**

Disconnect harness from all glow plugs. Connect test light to 12 volt source and touch each glow plug terminal. Light should be on. Replace glow plug if light is off. Reconnect all glow plugs before continuing with diagnosis.

**TEST LIGHT ON**

Relay contacts shorted. Replace glow plug controller and all glow plugs.

With IGN in "RUN" connect 12 volt test light to ground. Remove controller connector and check for IGN voltage at harness connector terminal "D".

**Fig. 8 Glow plug system diagnosis (Part 2 of 3). 1985**

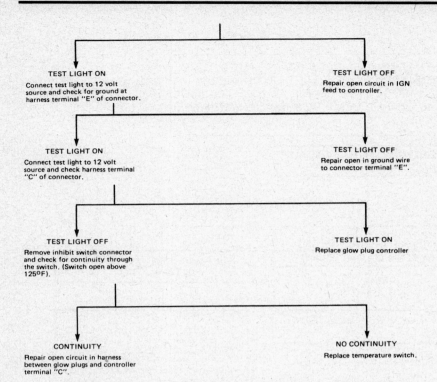

**TEST LIGHT ON**
Connect test light to 12 volt source and check for ground at harness terminal "E" of connector.

**TEST LIGHT OFF**
Repair open circuit in IGN feed to controller.

**TEST LIGHT ON**
Connect test light to 12 volt source and check harness terminal "C" of connector.

**TEST LIGHT OFF**
Repair open in ground wire to connector terminal "E".

**TEST LIGHT OFF**
Remove inhibit switch connector and check for continuity through the switch. (Switch open above 125°F).

**TEST LIGHT ON**
Replace glow plug controller

**CONTINUITY**
Repair open circuit in harness between glow plugs and controller terminal "C".

**NO CONTINUITY**
Replace temperature switch.

**Fig. 8  Glow plug system diagnosis (Part 3 of 3). 1985**

5. Disconnect block heaters, then remove wiring harness, transmission cooler lines and front battery cable clamp at oil pan.
6. Disconnect fuel return lines and oil cooler lines from engine, remove lower fan shroud bolts and lower vehicle.
7. Scribe hood hinge locations and remove hood.
8. Drain cooling system, remove air cleaner with resonator attached and primary filter from cowl, if equipped.
9. Disconnect ground cable at alternator bracket and remove alternator wires and clips.
10. Disconnect TPS, EGR-EPR and fuel cut-off electrical connectors at injection pump.
11. Remove harness from clips at rocker covers and disconnect glow plugs.
12. Disconnect EGR-EPR solenoids, glow plugs, controller and temperature sender. Move harness aside.
13. Disconnect ground strap from left side.
14. Remove fan, upper radiator hoses from engine, fan shroud, power steering pump and belt, and power steering reservoir, and secure pump assembly aside.
15. Disconnect vacuum at cruise servo and accelerator cable at injection pump.
16. Disconnect heater hose and lower radiator hose from engine and oil cooler lines from radiator.
17. Disconnect heater hose and overflow at radiator, automatic transmission cooler lines, upper radiator cover and radiator.
18. Remove detent cable.
19. Support transmission and remove engine.
20. Reverse procedure to install. If fuel filters were removed, they must be filled with clean diesel fuel.

## VAN

1. Disconnect batteries.
2. Remove headlight bezels, then the grille.
3. Remove bumper, then the lower valence.
4. Remove hood latch assembly.
5. Remove coolant recovery bottle and upper fan shroud.
6. Remove upper tie bar, then engine cover.
7. If vehicle is equipped with A/C, discharge system, then disconnect A/C condenser inlet and outlet lines and remove condenser. Plug A/C lines and condenser fittings to prevent entry of dirt and moisture.
8. Disconnect low coolant sensor wire and drain radiator.
9. Disconnect transmission and engine oil cooler lines from radiator.
10. Remove radiator upper and lower hose, then remove radiator and fan assembly.
11. Remove fuel injection pump. Refer to "Injection Pump, Replace."
12. Raise and support vehicle.
13. Disconnect exhaust pipes from manifolds.
14. Remove inspection cover, then remove torque converter to flex plate bolts.
15. Remove motor mount through bolt nuts.
16. Disconnect block heater electrical

connector from heating element and the ground wire from block.
17. Remove bellhousing-to-cylinder case attaching bolts.
18. Disconnect starter wiring, then remove starter.
19. Lower vehicle.
20. If equipped with cruise control, remove cruise control transducer.
21. If equipped with A/C, disconnect A/C compressor suction and discharge lines, then remove rear compressor brace, brackets and compressor. Plug A/C lines and compressor fittings to prevent entry of dirt and moisture.
22. Remove power steering pump and position aside.
23. Remove oil filler tube upper bracket.
24. Remove glow plug relay, then disconnect oil pressure sender and loom.
25. Remove air cleaner resonator and bracket.
26. Remove transmission filler tube bracket nut and position bracket aside.
27. Disconnect radiator, heater and bypass hoses at air crossover.
28. Remove generator upper bracket.
29. Remove coolant crossover.
30. Disconnect fuel lines from fuel pump.
31. Install engine lifting adapter J-33888 or equivalent.
32. Position suitable engine lifting device and connect to engine lifting adapter. Remove engine.
33. Reverse procedure to install.

## INTAKE MANIFOLD
## REPLACE
### 1982-85
#### Exc. Van

1. Disconnect batteries, remove air cleaner, crankcase ventilator tubes, secondary filter lines and secondary filter and adapter, if equipped.
2. Loosen vacuum pump bolts and rotate pump for access to manifold bolts.
3. Remove EGR/EPR valve bracket and A/C bracket, if equipped.
4. Remove intake manifold bolts, then the manifold. Injection line clips are retained by intake manifold bolts.
5. Reverse procedure to install. Refer to **Fig. 10** for bolt torque and tightening sequence and **Fig. 11** for fuel line installation. **Gasket has opening for EGR on light duty application and insert to cover opening for heavy duty applications.**

#### Van

1. Disconnect batteries, then remove engine cover.
2. Remove air cleaner assembly.
3. Disconnect necessary electrical connectors and hoses, and remove EGR/EPR switches.
4. Remove crankcase depression regulator valve hoses from intake manifold.
5. If equipped with A/C, remove rear compressor bracket.

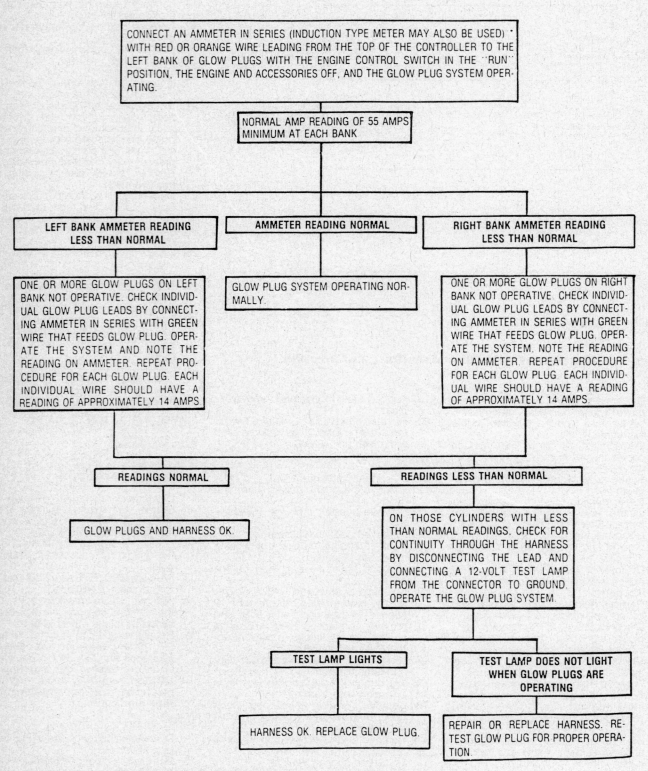

CONNECT AN AMMETER IN SERIES (INDUCTION TYPE METER MAY ALSO BE USED) • WITH RED OR ORANGE WIRE LEADING FROM THE TOP OF THE CONTROLLER TO THE LEFT BANK OF GLOW PLUGS WITH THE ENGINE CONTROL SWITCH IN THE "RUN" POSITION, THE ENGINE AND ACCESSORIES OFF, AND THE GLOW PLUG SYSTEM OPERATING.

NORMAL AMP READING OF 55 AMPS MINIMUM AT EACH BANK

LEFT BANK AMMETER READING LESS THAN NORMAL

AMMETER READING NORMAL

RIGHT BANK AMMETER READING LESS THAN NORMAL

ONE OR MORE GLOW PLUGS ON LEFT BANK NOT OPERATIVE. CHECK INDIVIDUAL GLOW PLUG LEADS BY CONNECTING AMMETER IN SERIES WITH GREEN WIRE THAT FEEDS GLOW PLUG. OPERATE THE SYSTEM AND NOTE THE READING ON AMMETER. REPEAT PROCEDURE FOR EACH GLOW PLUG. EACH INDIVIDUAL WIRE SHOULD HAVE A READING OF APPROXIMATELY 14 AMPS.

GLOW PLUG SYSTEM OPERATING NORMALLY.

ONE OR MORE GLOW PLUGS ON RIGHT BANK NOT OPERATIVE. CHECK INDIVIDUAL GLOW PLUG LEADS BY CONNECTING AMMETER IN SERIES WITH GREEN WIRE THAT FEEDS GLOW PLUG. OPERATE THE SYSTEM. NOTE THE READING ON AMMETER. REPEAT PROCEDURE FOR EACH GLOW PLUG. EACH INDIVIDUAL WIRE SHOULD HAVE A READING OF APPROXIMATELY 14 AMPS.

READINGS NORMAL

READINGS LESS THAN NORMAL

GLOW PLUGS AND HARNESS OK.

ON THOSE CYLINDERS WITH LESS THAN NORMAL READINGS. CHECK FOR CONTINUITY THROUGH THE HARNESS BY DISCONNECTING THE LEAD AND CONNECTING A 12-VOLT TEST LAMP FROM THE CONNECTOR TO GROUND. OPERATE THE GLOW PLUG SYSTEM.

TEST LAMP LIGHTS

TEST LAMP DOES NOT LIGHT WHEN GLOW PLUGS ARE OPERATING

HARNESS OK. REPLACE GLOW PLUG.

REPAIR OR REPLACE HARNESS. RETEST GLOW PLUG FOR PROPER OPERATION.

• IF USING AN IN LINE AMMETER READ BOTH BANKS AT ONCE. DO NOT CUT WIRE. (SNAP-ON METER MT552, VAT-40, OR EQUIVALENT)

**Fig. 9   Glow plug system diagnosis (Part 1 of 2). 1986–89**

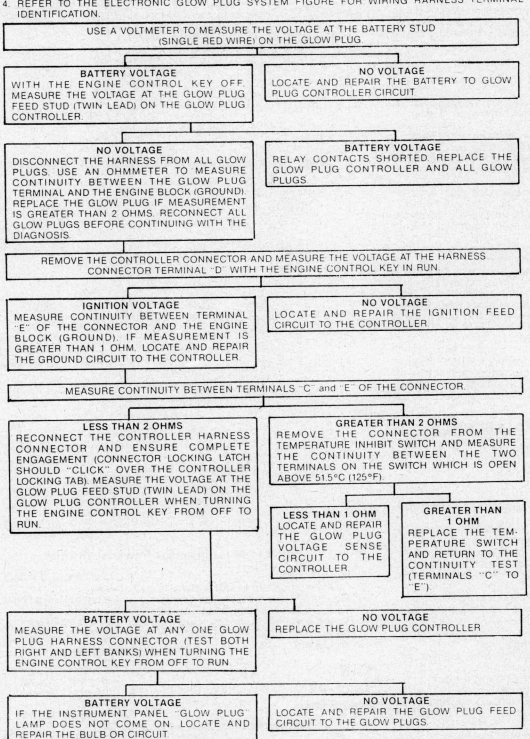

6.2L DIESEL ELECTRICAL SYSTEM DIAGNOSIS

ENGINE DOES NOT START COLD - "GLOW PLUG" LAMP MAY OR MAY NOT COME ON

1. FUEL SYSTEM CHECKED AND IS OK.
2. BATTERY VOLTAGE IS 12.4 VOLTS OR MORE WITH ENGINE CONTROL SWITCH OFF.
3. CRANKING SPEED OK (100 RPM OR MORE).
4. REFER TO THE ELECTRONIC GLOW PLUG SYSTEM FIGURE FOR WIRING HARNESS TERMINAL IDENTIFICATION.

USE A VOLTMETER TO MEASURE THE VOLTAGE AT THE BATTERY STUD (SINGLE RED WIRE) ON THE GLOW PLUG.

**BATTERY VOLTAGE**
WITH THE ENGINE CONTROL KEY OFF, MEASURE THE VOLTAGE AT THE GLOW PLUG FEED STUD (TWIN LEAD) ON THE GLOW PLUG CONTROLLER.

**NO VOLTAGE**
LOCATE AND REPAIR THE BATTERY TO GLOW PLUG CONTROLLER CIRCUIT.

**NO VOLTAGE**
DISCONNECT THE HARNESS FROM ALL GLOW PLUGS. USE AN OHMMETER TO MEASURE CONTINUITY BETWEEN THE GLOW PLUG TERMINAL AND THE ENGINE BLOCK (GROUND). REPLACE THE GLOW PLUG IF MEASUREMENT IS GREATER THAN 2 OHMS. RECONNECT ALL GLOW PLUGS BEFORE CONTINUING WITH THE DIAGNOSIS.

**BATTERY VOLTAGE**
RELAY CONTACTS SHORTED. REPLACE THE GLOW PLUG CONTROLLER AND ALL GLOW PLUGS.

REMOVE THE CONTROLLER CONNECTOR AND MEASURE THE VOLTAGE AT THE HARNESS CONNECTOR TERMINAL "D" WITH THE ENGINE CONTROL KEY IN RUN.

**IGNITION VOLTAGE**
MEASURE CONTINUITY BETWEEN TERMINAL "E" OF THE CONNECTOR AND THE ENGINE BLOCK (GROUND). IF MEASUREMENT IS GREATER THAN 1 OHM, LOCATE AND REPAIR THE GROUND CIRCUIT TO THE CONTROLLER.

**NO VOLTAGE**
LOCATE AND REPAIR THE IGNITION FEED CIRCUIT TO THE CONTROLLER.

MEASURE CONTINUITY BETWEEN TERMINALS "C" and "E" OF THE CONNECTOR.

**LESS THAN 2 OHMS**
RECONNECT THE CONTROLLER HARNESS CONNECTOR AND ENSURE COMPLETE ENGAGEMENT (CONNECTOR LOCKING LATCH SHOULD "CLICK" OVER THE CONTROLLER LOCKING TAB). MEASURE THE VOLTAGE AT THE GLOW PLUG FEED STUD (TWIN LEAD) ON THE GLOW PLUG CONTROLLER WHEN TURNING THE ENGINE CONTROL KEY FROM OFF TO RUN.

**GREATER THAN 2 OHMS**
REMOVE THE CONNECTOR FROM THE TEMPERATURE INHIBIT SWITCH AND MEASURE THE CONTINUITY BETWEEN THE TWO TERMINALS ON THE SWITCH WHICH IS OPEN ABOVE 51.5°C (125°F).

**LESS THAN 1 OHM**
LOCATE AND REPAIR THE GLOW PLUG VOLTAGE SENSE CIRCUIT TO THE CONTROLLER.

**GREATER THAN 1 OHM**
REPLACE THE TEMPERATURE SWITCH AND RETURN TO THE CONTINUITY TEST (TERMINALS "C" TO "E").

**BATTERY VOLTAGE**
MEASURE THE VOLTAGE AT ANY ONE GLOW PLUG HARNESS CONNECTOR (TEST BOTH RIGHT AND LEFT BANKS) WHEN TURNING THE ENGINE CONTROL KEY FROM OFF TO RUN.

**NO VOLTAGE**
REPLACE THE GLOW PLUG CONTROLLER

**BATTERY VOLTAGE**
IF THE INSTRUMENT PANEL "GLOW PLUG" LAMP DOES NOT COME ON, LOCATE AND REPAIR THE BULB OR CIRCUIT.

**NO VOLTAGE**
LOCATE AND REPAIR THE GLOW PLUG FEED CIRCUIT TO THE GLOW PLUGS.

**Fig. 9   Glow plug system diagnosis (Part 2 of 2). 1986—89**

6. Remove fuel filter to intake manifold bracket.
7. Remove vacuum pump. After removal, place a rag or cover over hole to prevent foreign material from entering engine.
8. Remove intake manifold bolts and fuel line clips, then remove intake manifold.
9. Reverse procedure to install. Refer to **Fig. 10** for bolt torque and tightening sequence, and **Fig. 11** for fuel line installation.

## 1986–89

1. Disconnect cables from both batteries.
2. On Van models, remove engine cover.
3. On all models, remove air cleaner.
4. Remove EGR/EPR solenoids with bracket from intake manifold studs.
5. On Van models, remove CDR valve.
6. On all models, disconnect crankcase ventilation and EGR hoses from manifold.
7. On models equipped with A/C, remove rear A/C compressor bracket.
8. On all models, remove fuel line bracket and disconnect ground strap from manifold.
9. On Van models, remove fuel filter bracket from manifold.
10. On all models, remove intake manifold attaching bolts and fuel line clips. **On models equipped with gear-driven vacuum pump, loosen pump clamp bolt and pivot pump aside to gain access to all manifold bolts.**
11. Remove intake manifold and gasket.
12. Reverse procedure to install. Refer to **Fig. 10** for bolt torque and tightening sequence. On 1988-89 models, torque manifold attaching bolts to 32 ft. lbs.

## EXHAUST MANIFOLD
## REPLACE
### EXC. VAN
#### Right Side

1. Disconnect batteries and raise vehicle.
2. Disconnect exhaust pipe from manifold and lower vehicle.
3. Disconnect glow plug wires and remove air cleaner duct bracket.
4. Remove glow plugs and manifold bolts.
5. Reverse procedure to install. Refer to **Fig. 12** for bolt locations and torque.

#### Left Side

1. Disconnect batteries.
2. Remove dipstick tube bracket nut, then the dipstick tube.
3. Disconnect glow plug wires, then remove glow plugs.
4. On 1986-89 models equipped with A/C, remove rear A/C compressor bracket.
5. On all models, remove manifold bolts, then raise vehicle.
6. Disconnect exhaust pipe from manifold, then remove manifold from bot-

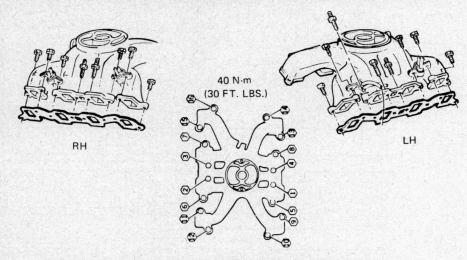

40 N·m (30 FT. LBS.)

RH

LH

**Fig. 10  Intake manifold tightening sequence**

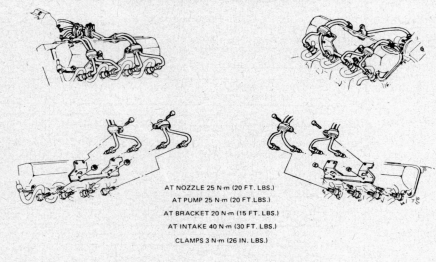

AT NOZZLE 25 N·m (20 FT. LBS.)
AT PUMP 25 N·m (20 FT. LBS.)
AT BRACKET 20 N·m (15 FT. LBS.)
AT INTAKE 40 N·m (30 FT. LBS.)
CLAMPS 3 N·m (26 IN. LBS.)

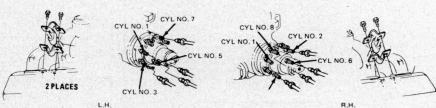

CYL NO. 7
CYL NO. 1
CYL NO. 5
CYL NO. 3
2 PLACES
L.H.

CYL NO. 8
CYL NO. 1
CYL NO. 2
CYL NO. 6
R.H.

**Fig. 11  Fuel injector line installation**

tom of vehicle.
7. Reverse procedure to install. Refer to **Fig. 12** for bolt location and torque. Torque 1988-89 models to 26 ft. lbs. **To aid installation, install manifold bolts hand tight while vehicle is still raised.**

## VAN
### 1982–85
#### Right Side

1. Disconnect batteries and raise vehicle.
2. Disconnect exhaust pipe at manifold flange.
3. Lower vehicle and remove engine

cover, then disconnect glow plug wires.
4. Remove manifold bolts, then the manifold.
5. Reverse procedure to install. Refer to **Fig. 12** for bolt locations and torque.

#### Left Side

1. Disconnect batteries, remove engine cover and raise vehicle.
2. Disconnect glow plug wires, then lower vehicle.
3. Disconnect exhaust pipe at manifold flange.
4. Remove manifold bolts, then the manifold.
5. Reverse procedure to install. Refer to **Fig. 12** for bolt locations and torque.

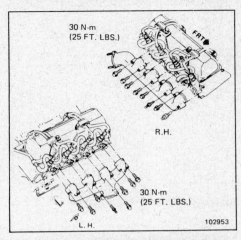

**Fig. 12  Exhaust manifold bolt location**

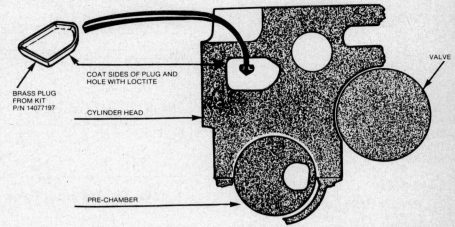

**Fig. 13  Installing brass plug into cylinder head**

## 1986–89

1. Disconnect batteries.
2. Raise and support vehicle.
3. Disconnect exhaust pipe from manifold, then lower vehicle.
4. Remove engine cover, then disconnect glow plug wires.
5. If removing left side manifold on models equipped with A/C, remove A/C compressor rear bracket.
6. Remove exhaust manifold attaching bolts and the exhaust manifold.
7. Reverse procedure to install. Refer to **Fig. 12** for bolt locations and torque. Torque 1988-89 models to 26 ft. lbs.

## CYLINDER HEAD
## REPLACE

External coolant loss from the rear lower corner of the left cylinder head and front lower corner of the right cylinder head is the result of a sealing condition around the core clean-out hole in the cylinder head. This condition can be corrected by installing a brass plug kit (part No. 14077197), consisting of two brass plugs and one driver. To install plugs, remove cylinder head as outlined below, then proceed as follows:

1. Clean inside edge of plug hole, **Fig. 13**, with a wire brush and suitable solvent.
2. Apply suitable sealant to sides of brass plug and hole.
3. Install plug slowly and squarely using an arbor press and plug driver, until plug is flush with head surface. If the plug deforms or pulls away from side of hole, lightly tap sides of plug to move back into contact with side of hole while sealant is still wet.
4. Remove all old sealant from cylinder head bolt holes in block using an M12 1.75 tap.
5. Clean block mating surfaces and remove any sheared brass or excessive sealant from cylinder head.
6. Install cylinder head as outlined below.

## EXC. VAN

1. Remove injection lines, then the intake manifold and rocker arm covers.
2. Drain coolant, remove dipstick tube and disconnect ground wire at cowl.
3. Raise vehicle, disconnect exhaust pipe from manifold, and lower vehicle.
4. Remove A/C compressor (if equipped).
5. Remove generator and disconnect glow plug wires. Remove rocker arm assemblies and pushrods. **Mark rocker arms and pushrods so they can be reinstalled in same location.**
6. Disconnect radiator, bypass, heater hoses and ground strap.
7. Remove thermostat housing/crossover at cylinder head.
8. Remove cylinder head bolts and cylinder head. **Whenever removing a cylinder head on 1982-83 models, the original head bolts should be discarded and new bolts (part No. 14077193) installed. These new type bolts are standard equipment on 1984 and later production engines.**
9. Reverse procedure to install, noting the following:
   a. Position cylinder head gasket over dowel pins. Do not use any sealer on cylinder head gasket, as sealer is "printed" onto gaskets during manufacture, and any additional sealer will increase the possibility of leakage.
   b. Coat cylinder head bolts with sealing compound 1052080, or equivalent.
   c. Install left rear cylinder head bolt through bolt hole and carefully guide cylinder head onto block.
   d. Torque cylinder head bolts in 3 steps, using torque sequence shown in **Fig. 14**. Refer to "Engine Tightening Specifications" chart for torque specifications.

## VAN
### Right Side

1. Remove intake manifold. Refer to "Intake Manifold, Replace."

2. Remove injection lines.
3. If equipped with cruise control, remove cruise control transducer.
4. If equipped with A/C, remove upper fan shroud and A/C compressor belt.
5. Raise vehicle, then disconnect exhaust pipe at manifold flange.
6. If equipped with A/C, remove A/C compressor brace from exhaust manifold.
7. Disconnect glow plug wires and lower vehicle.
8. If equipped with A/C, discharge system, disconnect A/C compressor suction and discharge lines, then remove A/C compressor from brackets and remove.
9. Loosen dipstick tube front bracket and remove from stud.
10. Remove upper bracket from oil fill tube.
11. Remove wire loom bracket, rocker cover bolts and rocker cover.
12. Remove rocker arm assemblies, then remove pushrods. **Prior to removing pushrods, mark upper end as an aid during reassembly. Failure to identify pushrods could result in incorrect installation, leading to premature wear or damage.**
13. Drain cooling system, then remove air cleaner resonator and bracket.
14. Remove transmission fill tube bracket nut and position tube aside.
15. Disconnect heater, radiator and bypass hoses at coolant crossover, then remove crossover.
16. Remove generator upper bracket.
17. Remove cylinder head bolts.
18. Remove transmission dipstick at rear of head and remove tube.
19. Remove cylinder head. **Whenever removing a cylinder head on 1982-83 models, the original head bolts should be discarded and new bolts (part No. 14077193) installed. These new type bolts are standard equipment on 1984 and later production engines.**
20. Reverse procedure to install, noting the following:
   a. Position cylinder head gasket over dowel pins. Do not use any sealer on cylinder head gasket, as sealer

is "printed" onto gaskets during manufacture, and any additional sealer will increase the possibility of leakage.

b. Coat cylinder head bolts with sealing compound 1052080, or equivalent.

c. Install left rear cylinder head bolt through bolt hole and carefully guide cylinder head onto block.

d. Torque cylinder head bolts in 3 steps, using torque sequence shown in **Fig. 14**. Refer to "Engine Tightening Specifications" chart for torque specifications.

## Left Side

1. Remove intake manifold. Refer to "Intake Manifold, Replace."
2. Remove fuel injection lines from injection pump.
3. If equipped with cruise control, remove cruise control transducer.
4. If equipped with A/C, remove upper fan shroud and A/C compressor belt.
5. Raise vehicle, then disconnect exhaust pipe at manifold flange.
6. If equipped with A/C, remove A/C compressor brace from exhaust manifold.
7. Remove exhaust manifold.
8. Remove power steering pump lower adjusting bolts.
9. Disconnect glow plug wiring and temperature switch.
10. Remove injection lines from nozzles, then cap all openings. Lower vehicle.
11. If equipped with A/C, discharge system, disconnect A/C compressor suction and discharge lines, then remove A/C compressor.
12. Remove power steering pump upper attaching bolt and position pump aside.
13. Remove stud from dipstick tube front bracket, then remove oil filler tube upper bracket.
14. Remove glow plug controller and bracket, then remove glow plug relay.
15. Disconnect T.V. cable.
16. Disconnect oil pressure switch and loom, then remove loom bracket.
17. Remove vacuum line clip attaching bolt from head.
18. Remove rocker cover bolts, then disconnect fuel return line bracket.
19. Remove rocker cover, then remove rocker arm assemblies and pushrods. **Prior to removing pushrods, mark upper end as an aid during reassembly. Failure to identify pushrods could result in incorrect installation, leading to premature wear or damage.**
20. Drain cooling system, then remove air cleaner resonator and bracket.
21. Remove transmission fill tube bracket nut, then position tube aside.
22. Disconnect heater, radiator and bypass hoses at coolant crossover, then remove crossover.
23. Remove generator upper mounting bracket.
24. Remove cylinder head bolts, then the cylinder head. **Whenever removing a cylinder head on 1982-83 models, the original head bolts should be**

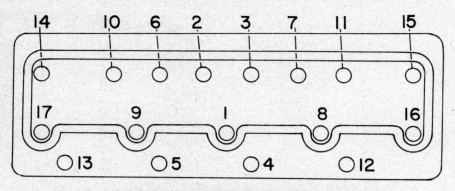

**Fig. 14  Cylinder head bolt tightening sequence**

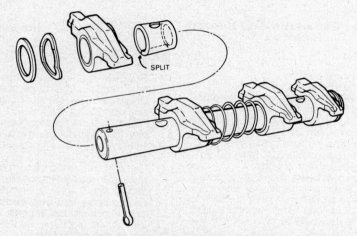

**Fig. 15  Rocker arm shaft assembly. 1982-84**

discarded and new bolts (part No. 14077193) installed. **These new type bolts are standard equipment on 1984 and later production engines.**

25. Reverse procedure to install, noting the following:

a. Position cylinder head gasket over dowel pins. Do not use any sealer on cylinder head gasket, as sealer is "printed" onto gaskets during manufacture, and any additional sealer will increase the possibility of leakage.

b. Coat cylinder head bolts with sealing compound 1052080, or equivalent.

c. Install left rear cylinder head bolt through bolt hole and carefully guide cylinder head onto block.

d. Torque cylinder head bolts in 3 steps, using torque sequence shown in **Fig. 14**. Refer to "Engine Tightening Specifications" chart for torque specifications.

## ROCKER ARMS & PUSHRODS
### REPLACE

1. Remove valve cover.
2. Remove rocker arm and shaft assembly.

3. On 1982-84 engines, remove cotter pin, then remove rocker arms from shaft noting position for installation, **Fig. 15**.
4. On 1985-89 engines, proceed as follows:
   a. Insert screwdriver into bore of rocker shaft and break off ends of nylon rocker arm retainers.
   b. Remove tops of retainers, **Fig. 16**, then remove rockers, noting position for installation.
5. Remove pushrods, noting position for installation. Pushrods are identified with a paint stripe on the on the upper end, and the hardened upper ball is darker in color than the lower ball. Failure to install pushrods in proper position may result in premature wear or damage.
6. Reinstall pushrods, if removed.
7. On 1982-84 engines, install rockers and springs on shaft in proper order, then secure assembly with new cotter pins.
8. On 1985-89 engines, install rockers on shaft, centering each rocker over hole in shaft, then install new retainers using suitable drift.
9. Before installing rocker arm shafts, align TDC mark on engine with mark on engine balancer, then rotate crankshaft 3½ inches counterclockwise, or to first lower water pump bolt, **Fig. 17**. This will position engine so that all

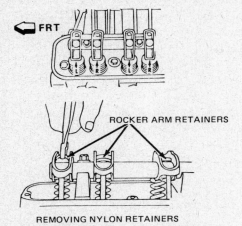

**Fig. 16 Rocker arm shaft assembly. 1985–89**

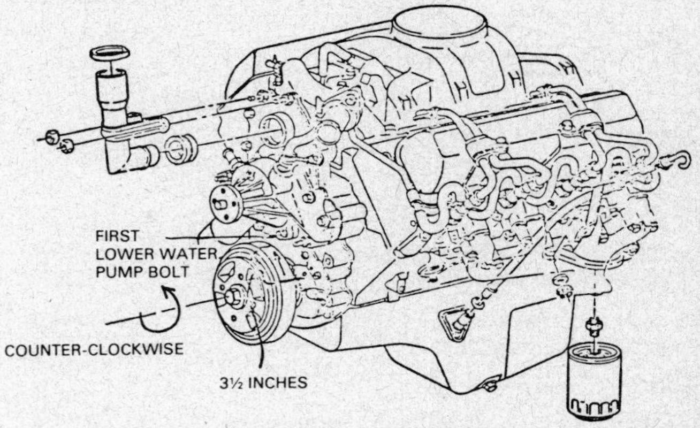

**Fig. 17 Positioning engine for rocker arm shaft installation**

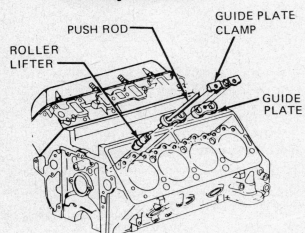

**Fig. 18 Valve lifter exploded view**

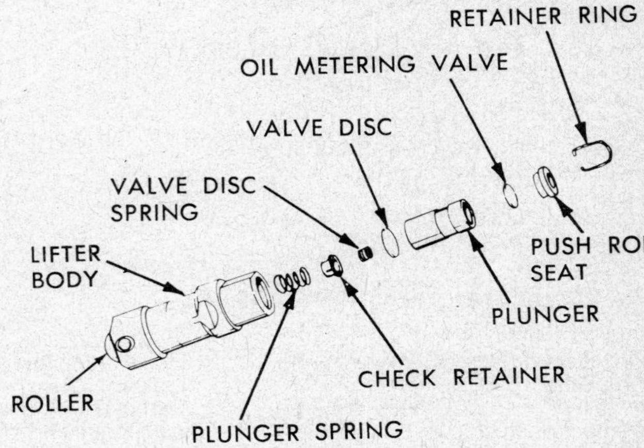

**Fig. 19 Valve lifter installation**

valves are closed. Torque rocker arm shaft bolts to specifications, tightening bolts slowly to allow lifters to bleed down. **The rocker arm shaft must be installed with the split in the ring around the shaft at bottom.**

# VALVES
## ADJUST

These engines are equipped with hydraulic valve lifters. No provision for adjustment is provided.

## VALVE ARRANGEMENT

V8-379 Diesel . . . . . . . . . . . . I-E-I-E-I-E-I-E

## VALVE TIMING
### INTAKE OPENS BEFORE TDC

V8-379 Diesel . . . . . . . . . . . . . 13 Degrees

## VALVE GUIDES

The valve guides are an integral part of the cylinder head and are not replaceable. Check valve stem to guide clearance and compare to specifications. If clearance is

excessive, ream valve guides using tool set J-7049 and install oversize valves.

# VALVE LIFTERS
## REPLACE

Roller hydraulic lifters are used to reduce friction between valve lifter and camshaft lobe. Guides keep the lifters from rotating on the camshaft lobes, **Figs. 18 and 19.**

### EXC. VAN

1. Remove rocker arm covers and rocker arms.
2. Remove guide clamps and guide plates.
3. Remove valve lifters through access hole in cylinder head using hydraulic lifter removal Tool J-29834 and a magnet.
4. Reverse procedure to install. **Crankshaft must be manually rotated 720° after assembly of lifter guide plate clamp to insure free movement of lifters.**

### VAN

1. Remove cylinder head as described under "Cylinder Head, Replace."

2. Remove valve guide clamps and guide plates.
3. Remove valve lifters through holes in cylinder head.
4. Reverse procedure to install.

When diagnosing the cause of lifter noise, the following checks should be performed after the noise has been isolated to a specific cylinder:

1. Remove suspected cylinder's rocker arm assembly and pushrods.
2. Move each lifter up and down in bore using hydraulic lifter removal tool J-29834 or suitable magnet. Lifter must move up and down freely.
3. Remove clamp and guide as outlined.
4. Rotate lifter in bore. Lifter must rotate freely, without binding or sticking.
5. Remove lifter assembly, as outlined, check for wear and damage and replace as needed.
6. Inspect inner (contact) surface of lifter guide, **Fig. 20,** for burrs or sharp edges contacting lifter, and replace as needed.
7. Inspect outer surface of lifter guide for burrs or sharp edges that could contact engine block. Burrs or sharp edges on outer surfaces should be filed or ground off.
8. When reinstalling guide, use 2 long screwdrivers to lightly pry the paired

*ENGINE, V8-379 (6.2L) DIESEL*

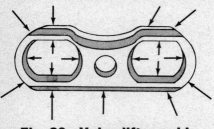

**Fig. 20  Valve lifter guide plate inspection**

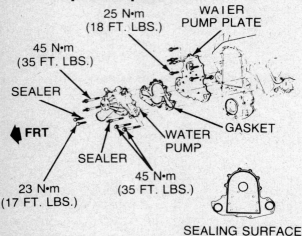

**Fig. 22  Water pump installation**

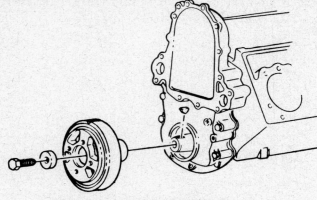

**Fig. 21  Torsional damper**

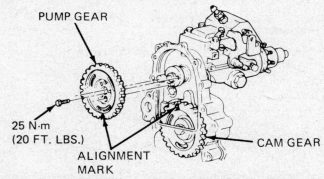

**Fig. 23  Injection pump & cam gear alignment**

guides toward each other while tightening clamp.
9. Reinstall lifters and check for free movement as in step 2.
10. Reassemble engine as outlined in appropriate procedure.

## CRANKSHAFT PULLEY
### REPLACE

1. Disconnect batteries.
2. On Van models, remove upper fan shroud. On all models, remove generator belt.
3. Remove power steering belt.
4. If equipped with A/C, remove A/C compressor belt.
5. On Van models, raise vehicle.
6. Remove crankshaft pulley.
7. Reverse procedure to install.

## TORSIONAL DAMPER
### REPLACE

1. Disconnect batteries, then remove crankshaft pulley as described under "Crankshaft Pulley, Replace."
2. Remove torsional damper, using torsional damper removal tool J-23523 and suitable pilot.
3. Reverse procedure to install. Torque bolt to 150 ft. lbs. on 1982-84 models, or 200 ft. lbs. on 1985-88 models, **Fig. 21.**

## WATER PUMP
### REPLACE

1. Disconnect batteries.

2. Remove fan and fan shroud and, drain radiator.
3. Remove A/C hose bracket nuts (if equipped). Remove oil fill tube generator pivot bolt and generator belt.
4. Remove generator lower bracket, power steering pump and belt, and A/C belt.
5. Disconnect bypass hose and lower radiator hose. Remove water pump plate and water pump, **Fig. 22.**
6. Reverse procedure to install. **Before installing attaching bolts, apply anaerobic sealer 1052357 or equivalent to sealing surface as shown, Fig. 22. Sealer should be wet to touch before installing bolts.**
7. Torque bolts to specifications as follows:
   a. Torque water pump-to-front cover attaching bolts, exc. M8-1.25 x 35 bolts, to 25-37 ft. lbs., With M8-1.25 x 35 bolts, to 15-20 ft. lbs.
   b. Torque water pump plate-to-front cover attaching bolts to 13--20 ft. lbs.
   c. Torque water pump plate-to-water pump attaching bolts to 13-20 ft. lbs.

## ENGINE FRONT COVER
### REPLACE

1. Drain engine block and remove water pump.
2. Align marks on pump gear and camshaft gear, **Fig. 23,** then scribe mark aligning injection pump flange and front cover.

3. Remove crank pulley, torsional damper, front cover to oil pan bolts, fuel return line clips and injection pump driven gear.
4. Remove injection pump retaining nuts from front cover.
5. Remove baffle, remaining cover bolts and front cover, **Fig. 24.**
6. Reverse procedure to install. Apply a bead of anerobic sealant 1052357 or equivalent around sealing surface as shown in **Fig. 24.** Use RTV sealant around bottom portion of front cover which attaches to oil pan. Make sure scribe marks on injection pump and front cover are aligned and marks on cam gear and pump gear are aligned. Torque bolts to specifications shown in **Figs. 23 and 24.**

## FRONT OIL SEAL
### REPLACE

1. Remove front cover and pry seal out of cover.
2. Install new seal, using seal installer Tool J-22102.

## TIMING CHAIN
### INSPECT

The timing chain on these engines has an allowable deflection of up to 0.80 inch. However, if timing chain deflection exceeds 0.80 inch, due to component wear or chain stretch, the engine may experience rough idle, low power, poor fuel econ-

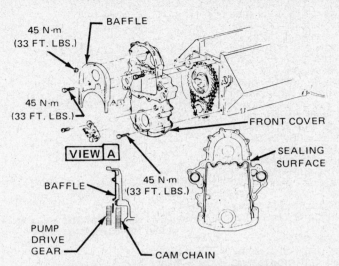

Fig. 24  Front cover installation

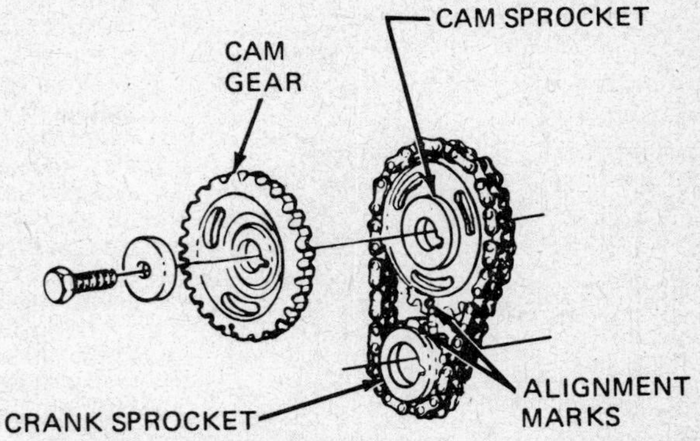

**Fig. 25  Timing chain alignment marks**

omy and/or excessive emission of white smoke. It is recommended that timing chain deflection be measured whenever the front cover is removed, and any time the above symptoms cannot be traced to a fuel system malfunction. To check timing chain deflection, proceed as follows:

1. Remove front cover as outlined.
2. Mount suitable dial indicator on left front of block positioning indicator so that plunger contacts timing chain at the mid-point between the two timing gears.
3. Press timing chain outward (parallel to engine block) as far as possible by hand, then zero indicator.
4. Press chain inward as far as possible, then read deflection from dial indicator.
5. Deflection should not exceed 0.80 inch for used chain or 0.50 inch for new chain.
6. If deflection is excessive, replace chain and/or timing gears as needed.

## TIMING CHAIN & GEARS
### REPLACE

1. Remove front cover.
2. Remove camshaft and injection pump gears.
3. Remove cam sprocket, chain and crank sprocket.
4. Reverse procedure to install. Install cam sprocket and crank sprocket so that timing marks are aligned. Next, rotate crankshaft 360° so that camshaft gear and injection pump gear timing marks will align. Torque cam gear bolt to 65 ft. lbs. on 1982-83 models, 77 ft. lbs. on 1984-87 models, 75 ft. lbs. on 1988-89 models, **Fig. 25.**

## CAMSHAFT
### REPLACE

Whenever camshaft is replaced, it is recommended that the valve lifters and oil filter be replaced and that the oil be changed. When installing replacement camshaft, coat camshaft lobes with suit-

able molybdenum based assembly lubricant.

## EXC. VAN

1. Disconnect batteries, raise vehicle and drain radiator and block.
2. Disconnect exhaust pipe from engine and remove fan shroud attaching bolts.
3. Lower vehicle and remove radiator, fan, vacuum pump and intake manifold.
4. Remove injector pump lines. Cap injector nozzles and identify lines for installation.
5. Remove water pump and injection pump gear.
6. Scribe a mark on front cover and injection pump flange for realignment. Remove injection pump from front cover.
7. Remove power steering pump, generator and (if equipped) A/C compressor.
8. Remove rocker arm covers, rocker arm shaft assemblies and pushrods. Mark valve train components so parts may be reinstalled in original location.
9. Remove thermostat housing/crossover from cylinder head, then the cylinder head.
10. Remove valve lifter clamps, guide plates and valve lifters. Mark location of parts so they can be reinstalled in same position.
11. Remove front cover, timing chain, fuel pump and cam retainer plate.
12. Remove condenser mounting bolts, if equipped, then raise condenser to provide clearance for camshaft removal.
13. Remove camshaft.
14. Reverse procedure to install. Camshaft retainer plate should be torqued to 20 ft. lbs. on 1982-85 models, or 17 ft. lbs. on 1986-89 models.

## VAN

1. Disconnect batteries, then remove headlight bezels, grille and front bumper.
2. Remove lower valence panel and

hood latch mechanism.
3. Remove coolant recovery bottle, then the upper tie bar.
4. On models equipped with A/C, disconnect refrigerant lines and remove condenser on 1982-85 models, or compressor on 1986-89 models.
5. On all models, drain coolant, and disconnect low coolant sensor electrical connector.
6. Disconnect all hoses and lines from radiator, then remove radiator and fan assembly.
7. Remove oil pump drive unit.
8. Remove cylinder heads, then the alternator lower bracket.
9. Remove water pump, crankshaft pulleys and torsional damper.
10. Remove timing cover plate and water pump.
11. Rotate crankshaft to align timing marks, then remove injection pump driven gear and inner baffle.
12. Mark relationship between injection pump and front cover for assembly reference, then remove front cover, fuel pump and valve lifters.
13. Remove injection pump drive gear, timing chain and crankshaft gear.
14. Remove camshaft retainer plate and the camshaft.
15. Reverse procedure to install. Torque camshaft retainer plate bolts to 20 ft. lbs. On 1988-89 models, to 17 ft. lbs.

## PISTON & ROD ASSEMBLY

Assemble piston to rod and install into cylinder block. Install with depression on top of piston toward outside of engine, **Fig. 26.** Install connecting rod bearing with tang slots positioned on side opposite camshaft.

## PISTON & RINGS

Pistons are available in standard sizes and oversize of .030 inch. Rings are available in standard sizes and oversize of .030 inch.

## MAIN & ROD BEARINGS

Main bearings are available in standard sizes and undersizes of .005 and .010 inch. Rod bearings are available in standard

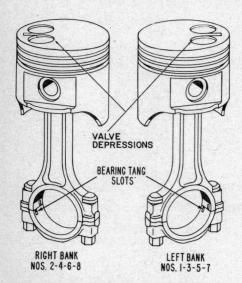

**Fig. 26   Piston & rod assembly**

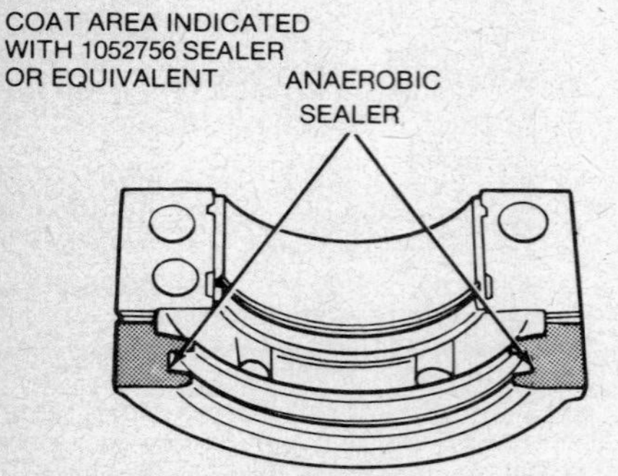

COAT AREA INDICATED WITH 1052756 SEALER OR EQUIVALENT    ANAEROBIC SEALER

**Fig. 28   Rear bearing cap sealing areas**

sizes and undersizes of .010 inch and .020 inch.

## CRANKSHAFT REAR OIL SEAL SERVICE

A revised two-piece lip seal (part No. 23500417, two required) should be used to replace the rope seal installed during production whenever oil leak conditions or engine service call for oil seal replacement. The new seal can be installed without removing the crankshaft using the following procedure:

1. Raise and support vehicle, drain engine oil, then remove oil pan and oil pump.
2. Remove rear main bearing cap, then the upper and lower rope seals, taking care not to mar the crankshaft.
3. Clean upper and lower seal grooves, bearing cap slot, cylinder block and oil pan rails with chlorinated solvent such as carburetor cleaner. **Do not use cleaners such as mineral spirits that leave a film, as RTV sealer will not bond properly. All surfaces must be clean and dry before applying sealer.**
4. Check rear main bearing clearance using plastigauge. If clearance is not .0022-.0037 inch, correct as needed.

5. Apply thin coat of oil to crankshaft contact lips of seal, then roll one piece of the seal into the cylinder block upper seal groove until one end of seal projects $1/2$ inch from block, **Fig. 27.**
6. Insert second half of seal into a $1/2$ inch recess in upper cylinder block groove. Contact ends of seals should be located at 4 and 10 or 8 and 2 o'clock positions, with seal ring snug against crankshaft, **Fig. 27. Ensure seals are installed with "outside" marking facing flywheel.**
7. Apply thin coat of suitable anerobic sealer to bearing cap contact surface, **Fig. 28,** keeping sealer out of cap oil relief slot.
8. Apply two drops of Loctite 414 sealer or equivalent to center of lower bearing cap seal groove.
9. Install bearing cap as follows:
   a. Position bering cap on cylinder block, ensuring cap groove and seal are properly aligned, then tap seal into place using suitable mallet.
   b. Lubricate cap bolts with oil, install bolts, then torque inner bolts to 110 ft. lbs. and outer bolts to 100 ft. lbs. **Do not draw cap into place with retaining bolts, as cap may be damaged.**
10. Install oil pump and torque bolts to 66 ft. lbs.
11. Apply $3/16$ inch bead of RTV sealer to top and bottom surfaces of new rear pan seal and to each end of seal where it contacts block, and apply $3/16$ inch bead of RTV sealer along pan rail inner edge and around all bolt holes, **Fig. 29.**
12. Install pan and rear seal while sealer is still wet. On 1982-85 models, torque oil pan bolts to 6 ft. lbs. On 1986-89 models, torque two rear bolts to 17 ft. lbs. and all other bolts to 84 inch lbs.
13. Reverse remaining procedure to complete installation.
14. Allow 30 minutes for sealer to cure, fill crankcase to specified capacity and check for leaks.

## OIL PAN
## REPLACE
### EXC. VAN

1. Disconnect batteries and raise vehicle.
2. Drain oil and remove transmission dust cover, oil pan bolts and engine mount through bolt (left side).
3. Raise engine and remove oil pan.
4. Reverse procedure to install. On 1982-85 models, torque oil pan bolts to 6 ft. lbs., **Fig. 29.** On 1986-89 models, torque two rear bolts to 17 ft. lbs. and all other bolts to 84 inch lbs.

### VAN

1. Disconnect batteries and remove engine cover.
2. Remove engine and transmission oil dipsticks and tubes.

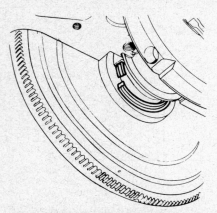

**Fig. 27   Crankshaft rear oil seal installation tool**

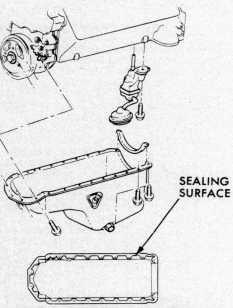

SEALING SURFACE

**Fig. 29   Oil pan installation**

3. Disconnect T.V. cable at injection pump rod and remove upper routing clips if used.
4. Remove upper bellhousing to engine retaining bolts.
5. Remove vacuum pump assembly.
6. Raise and support vehicle.
7. Remove driveshaft, then disconnect speedometer cable from transmission.
8. Disconnect torque converter clutch connector from transmission.
9. Disconnect transmission shift linkage.
10. Disconnect transmission cooler lines from transmission.
11. Remove transmission flex plate inspection cover, then remove torque converter to flex plate retaining bolts.
12. Support transmission with a suitable jack.
13. Remove transmission mount, then remove crossmember.
14. Remove transmission to engine block retaining bolts, then remove transmission.
15. Remove flex plate.
16. Drain oil into a suitable container.

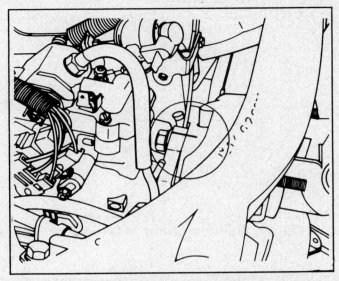

**Fig. 30   Front cover to injection pump timing mark**

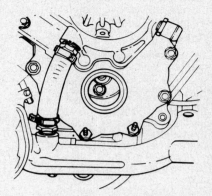

**Fig. 31   Injection pump drive gear bolt removal**

17. Disconnect engine oil cooler lines from engine block.
18. Remove starter.
19. Remove oil pan bolts, then lower pan from engine block. It may be necessary to rotate the crankshaft so number one and two crankshaft throws are up, to gain additional clearance for oil pan removal.
20. Remove oil pump retaining bolt and allow oil pump assembly to fall into oil pan.
21. Remove oil pan.
22. Reverse procedure to install. On 1982-85 models, torque oil pan bolts to 6 ft. lbs., **Fig. 29**. On 1986-89 models, torque two rear bolts to 17 ft. lbs. and all other bolts to 84 inch lbs.

## OIL PUMP SERVICE
### REMOVAL

1. Remove oil pan as outlined previously.
2. On 1987-89 G models, rotate crankshaft to position numbers one and two connecting rod journals and the forward crankshaft throw upward.
3. On all models, remove oil pump to rear main bearing cap attaching bolts and remove pump and extension shaft.

### SERVICE
#### Disassembly

1. Remove pump cover attaching screws and pump cover.
2. Remove drive gear and idler gear and shaft from pump body. **Mark gear teeth so that they can be reassembled with same teeth indexing.**
3. Remove retaining pin, pressure regulator valve and related parts.

#### Inspection

1. Inspect pump body and pump gears for damage or excessive wear. If either pump body or pump gears are damaged or worn, entire oil pump assembly must be replaced.
2. Check pressure regulator valve for fit and drive gear shaft for looseness in pump body.

#### Assembly

1. Install pressure regulator valve and related parts. **Install idler gear with smooth side of gears toward pump cover opening.**
2. Install gears and shaft in oil pump body.
3. Install pump cover.

### INSTALLATION

Reverse removal procedures to install. Align hex on lower end of vacuum pump driveshaft with hex on top of pump drive extension shaft. Install oil pump to bearing cap bolts and torque to 67 ft. lbs.

## MECHANICAL FUEL PUMP
### REPLACE

1. Disconnect fuel lines and hoses from fuel pump.
2. Remove fuel pump attaching bolts, then the fuel pump and gasket.
3. Remove fuel pump mounting plate attaching bolts, then the mounting plate and gasket.
4. Remove pushrod, if necessary.
5. Reverse procedure to install.

## INJECTION PUMP TIMING

1. Check marks on top of engine front cover and injection pump flange. These marks must be aligned for engine to be properly timed, **Fig. 30**. Engines used in California have been timed with a microwave process.

After timing with the microwave, an additional timing mark consisting of two half circles is stamped over the pump flange/housing interface. When checking pump timing on these models, the half-moon marks should form a circle.
2. To adjust:
   a. Loosen three pump retaining nuts.
   b. Align mark on injection pump with mark on front cover. Torque nuts to 30 ft. lbs.
   c. Adjust throttle rod.

## INJECTION PUMP
### REPLACE

When installing injection pump on California models, ensure half circles align to form a complete circle. Any deviation in timing will result in the two half circles not matching. If a new injection pump is being installed, use the conventional timing marks, **Fig. 30**.

### ALL 1989 MODELS, & 1980—88 MODELS EXC. VAN
#### Removal

1. Disconnect batteries and remove fan and fan shroud.
2. Remove intake manifold and fuel lines.
3. Disconnect accelerator cable at injection pump. On models equipped with 700-4R auto. trans. also disconnect detent cable.
4. Disconnect fuel return line and remove wires and hoses from injection pump.
5. Remove fuel line from pump.
6. Remove A/C hose retainer bracket, if equipped.
7. Remove oil fill tube and PCV or CDRV vent hose assembly.
8. Scribe a mark on front cover and pump for alignment at reinstallation.
9. Rotate engine, as needed, to gain access to pump drive gear retaining bolts through oil filler opening, **Fig. 31**, then remove bolts.

10. Remove front cover to injection pump attaching nuts and remove pump. Cap all open lines and nozzles.

## Installation

1. Install new gasket. Align locating pin on pump hub with slot in injection pump gear, **Fig. 32.** Align scribe mark on front cover and pump and torque attaching nuts to 35 ft. lbs. on 1982-85 models, 30 ft. lbs. on 1986, 1987 and 1989 models, or 31 ft. lbs. on 1988 models.**Figs. 30 and 33.**
2. Install pump driven gear to pump and torque bolts to 20 ft. lbs on 1982-87 and 1989 models, or 17 ft. lbs. on 1988 models.
3. Install oil fill tube and PCV vent hose assembly. Install A/C hose retainer bracket (if equipped).
4. Install fuel line at pump and torque to 20 ft. lbs.
5. Connect fuel return line, accelerator cable, injection lines and necessary wires and hoses.
6. Install intake manifold, fan shroud and fan. Connect batteries.

## 1980-88 VAN

### Removal

1. Remove intake manifold. Refer to "Intake Manifold, Replace."
2. Rotate air cleaner snorkel up to gain clearance.
3. Remove hood latch, then the windshield washer bottle.
4. Remove upper fan shroud.
5. Remove oil fill tube and grommet.
6. Working through oil fill tube hole, remove injection pump drive gear bolts, **Fig. 31.** It may be necessary to rotate engine to gain access to injection pump drive gear bolts.
7. Remove fuel filter, bracket and injection pump feed line.
8. Disconnect wire looms from injection lines.
9. Disconnect fuel injection lines from brackets, then disconnect engine oil dipstick.
10. Disconnect injection pump electrical connectors.
11. Disconnect T.V. cable (if equipped).
12. Disconnect throttle cable.

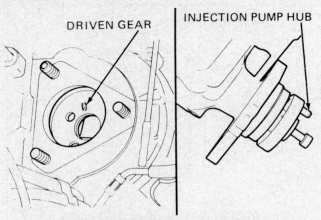

**Fig. 32   Injection pump locating pin**

13. On 1982-85 models, proceed as follows:
    a. Disconnect injection lines 2, 4, 5, 6, 7 and 8.
    b. Raise and support vehicle.
    c. Disconnect injection lines 1 and 3.
    d. Cap injectors and lines to prevent entry of dirt.
    e. Identify injection lines at pump and remove. Cap line and pump openings.
14. On 1986-88 models, disconnect injection lines.
15. On all models, disconnect fuel return line.
16. Scribe a mark on front cover and pump flange to aid during reassembly.
17. Remove injection pump retaining bolts, then remove injection pump.

### Installation

1. Install new gasket. Align locating pin on pump hub with slot in injection pump gear, **Fig. 32.** Align scribe mark on front cover and pump flange, then torque attaching nuts to 35 ft. lbs. on 1982-85 models, or 30 ft. lbs. on 1986-88 models, **Figs. 30 and 33.**
2. Install pump driven gear into injection pump and torque bolts to 20 ft. lbs. on 1982-878 models, or 17 ft. lbs. on

1988 models.
3. Reverse remaining removal procedure to install.

## INJECTION PUMP ON-TRUCK SERVICE

### PUMP COVER SEAL AND/OR GUIDE STUD SEAL, REPLACE

1. Disconnect battery ground cables.
2. Remove air cleaner and intake, then install protective screens J-29664.
3. Disconnect injection pump fuel solenoid and housing pressure cold advance electrical leads, then the fuel return pipe.
4. Remove fast idle solenoid upper attaching bolt, then loosen lower bolt and position solenoid aside.
5. Clean injection pump cover, upper portion of pump and guide stud area.
6. Remove injection pump cover attaching screws and cover. Ensure no dirt or foreign material enters pump, since damage to pump or engine may result.
7. Observe metering valve spring to top of guide position, **Fig. 34,** to aid reassembly.

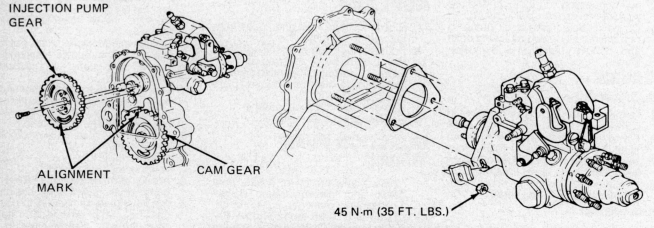

**Fig. 33   Injection pump installation**

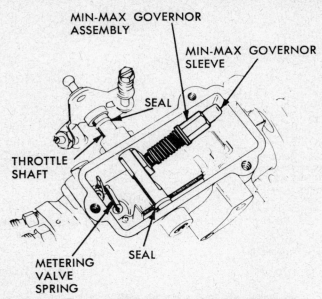

Fig. 34  Injection pump cover removed

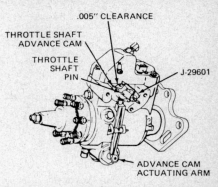

**Fig. 35   Installing tool J-29601 onto injection pump**

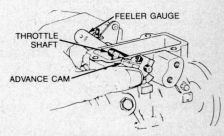

**Fig. 36   Adjusting throttle shaft advance cam**

8. Remove guide stud and washer, noting location of parts.
9. Install guide stud and new washer ensuring upper extension of metering valve spring is positioned over guide stud. Torque guide stud to 85 inch lbs.
10. Install new seal onto pump cover.
11. Proceed as follows for pump cover installation: **When installing pump cover, ensure shutdown solenoid pivot arm is positioned to correct side of linkage hook tab. Improper installation could cause engine to go to full run operation, causing severe damage to vehicle.**
   a. Hold throttle rod in the idle position.
   b. Position cover 1/8 inch above the pump and 1/4 inch forward of the shaft end.
   c. Move cover rearward and down carefully so as not to tear the seal.
   d. Install cover screws with washers, ensure flat washers are against pump cover, and torque screws to 33 inch lbs.
12. Reconnect battery ground cables.
13. Turn ignition switch to "Run" position, then momentarily connect pink wire to solenoid. A clicking noise should be heard whenever wire contacts solenoid. If clicking noise is evident, connect fuel solenoid and housing pressure cold advance electrical leads and proceed to Step 14. If clicking noise is not evident, proceed to next step.
14. Remove cover. With ignition switch in "Run" position, ground solenoid lead and connect pink wire. The solenoid should activate and move the linkage. If solenoid does not activate, replace it. Repeat Steps 11 and 12.
15. Reinstall fuel return pipe, throttle cable and return springs, then reposition fast idle solenoid.
16. Start engine and check for leaks. Engine may idle roughly due to air in the injection system. Allowing engine to idle for several moments will usually purge system of air. If not, shut engine off and allow air bubbles to rise to the top of the injection pump, then restart engine.
17. Remove intake manifold screens, then reinstall intake and air cleaner.

## THROTTLE SHAFT SEAL, REPLACE

1. Disconnect battery ground cables.
2. Remove air cleaner and intake, then install protective screens J-29664.
3. Disconnect injection pump fuel solenoid and housing pressure cold advance electrical leads, then the fuel return pipe.
4. Mark position of TPS switch or vacuum regulator valve to aid in reassembly, then remove throttle rod and return springs.
5. Loosen, then position fast idle solenoid aside.
6. Remove throttle cable bracket.
7. Install tool J-29601 over throttle shaft, with slots of tool engaging shaft pin, **Fig. 35.** Position spring clip over throttle shaft advance cam, then tighten wing nut. Pull tool off throttle shaft without loosening wing nut, to provide proper alignment for reassembly. Loosen face cam screw.
8. Drive pin from throttle shaft, then remove throttle shaft advance cam and fiber washer. Remove any burrs from shaft.
9. Clean injection pump cover, upper portion of pump, throttle shaft and guide stud area.
10. Remove injection pump cover attaching screws and cover. Ensure no dirt or foreign material enters pump, since damage to pump or engine may result.
11. Observe metering valve spring to top of guide position, **Fig. 34,** to aid reassembly.

12. Remove guide stud and washer, noting location of parts.
13. Rotate min-max governor assembly, **Fig. 34,** then remove from throttle shaft. If idle governor spring becomes disengaged from throttle block, reinstall spring with tightly wound coils facing toward throttle block.
14. Remove throttle shaft assembly and examine for wear or damage. Replace if necessary.
15. Examine pump housing throttle shaft bushings. If bushings are worn or show signs of leakage, remove pump and send to authorized Stanadyne distributor for bushing replacement.
16. Remove seals from throttle shaft. Do not cut seals from shaft, since nicks in seal seat can cause leakage.
17. Coat new seals with chassis grease or equivalent, and install seals onto throttle shaft.
18. Slide throttle shaft into pump housing until min-max governor assembly can be installed onto throttle shaft.
19. Rotate min-max governor assembly downward, hold in this position, then slide throttle shaft and governor into position.
20. Install new washer, throttle shaft advance cam and a new throttle shaft drive pin. Do not tighten cam screw at this time.
21. Align throttle shaft advance cam so tool J-29601 can be installed as outlined in Step 7.
22. Insert a .005 inch feeler gauge between throttle shaft white washer and pump housing, then squeeze throttle shaft and torque cam screw to 30 inch lbs., **Fig. 36.** Apply Loctite 290 or equivalent to secure screw, then remove tool.

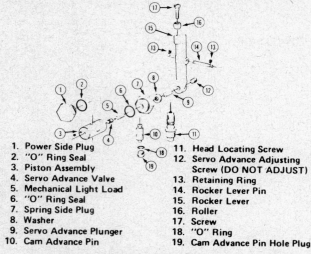

1. Power Side Plug
2. "O" Ring Seal
3. Piston Assembly
4. Servo Advance Valve
5. Mechanical Light Load
6. "O" Ring Seal
7. Spring Side Plug
8. Washer
9. Servo Advance Plunger
10. Cam Advance Pin
11. Head Locating Screw
12. Servo Advance Adjusting Screw (DO NOT ADJUST)
13. Retaining Ring
14. Rocker Lever Pin
15. Rocker Lever
16. Roller
17. Screw
18. "O" Ring
19. Cam Advance Pin Hole Plug

**Fig. 37   Automatic advance group**

1. Return Line Connector
2. Cover, Governor Control
3. Screw
4. Lockwasher or Plain Washer
5. Governor Cover Gasket
6. Vent Screw Assembly
7. Head Locking Screw
8. Pressure Tap Screw
9. Seal
10. Housing
11. Screw
12. Timing Line Cover
13. Timing Line Cover Gasket

**Fig. 38   Side housing & drive group**

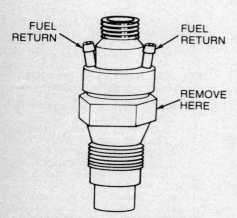

FUEL RETURN

FUEL RETURN

REMOVE HERE

**Fig. 39   Injection nozzle**

23. Install guide stud and new washer, ensuring upper extension of metering valve spring is positioned over guide stud. Torque guide stud to 85 inch lbs.
24. Install new seal onto pump cover.
25. Proceed as follows for pump cover installation: **When installing pump cover, ensure shutdown solenoid pivot arm is positioned to correct side of linkage hook tab. Improper installation could cause engine to go to full run operation, causing severe damage to vehicle.**
    a. Hold throttle rod in the idle position.
    b. Position cover 1/8 inch above the pump and 1/4 inch forward of the shaft end.
    c. Move cover rearward and down carefully so as not to tear the seal.
    d. Install cover screws with washers, ensure flat washers are against pump cover, and torque screws to 33 inch lbs.
26. Install vacuum regulator valve or TPS switch, then reconnect battery ground cables.
27. Turn ignition switch to "Run" position, then momentarily connect pink wire to solenoid. A clicking noise should be heard whenever wire contacts solenoid. If clicking noise is evident, con-

nect fuel solenoid and housing pressure cold advance electrical leads and proceed to Step 28. If clicking noise is not evident, proceed to next step.
28. Remove cover. With ignition switch in "Run" position, ground solenoid lead and connect pink wire. The solenoid should activate and move the linkage. If solenoid does not activate, replace it. Repeat steps 26 and 27.
29. Reinstall throttle cable bracket, detent cable and fast idle solenoid.
30. Reinstall throttle cable and return springs.
31. Ensure timing marks on injection pump and housing are aligned, then tighten attaching nuts. Reconnect fuel return line.
32. Start engine and check for leaks. Engine may idle roughly due to air in the injection system. Allowing engine to idle for several moments will usually purge system of air. If not, shut engine off and allow air bubbles to rise to the top of the injection pump, then restart engine.
33. Remove intake manifold screens, then reinstall intake and air cleaner.

# INJECTION PUMP OFF-TRUCK SERVICE
## ADVANCE PIN HOLE PLUG SEAL, REPLACE
1. Loosen advance pin hole plug seal by tapping with hammer.
2. Remove plug and seal, **Fig. 37**.
3. Reverse procedure to install. Torque plug to 75-100 inch lbs. on 1982-87 models, or 90 inch lbs. on 1988-89 models.

## AUTO ADVANCE SEALS, REPLACE
1. Remove advance pin hole plug.
2. Remove spring side advance piston hold plug, plug, piston, spring and slide washer.

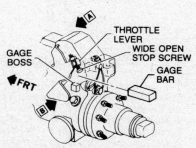

THROTTLE LEVER

WIDE OPEN STOP SCREW

GAGE BOSS

GAGE BAR

FRT

**Fig. 40   Installing vacuum regulator valve gauge bar**

3. Remove power side advance piston hole plug, plug, piston, and slide washer, **Fig. 37**.
4. Disassemble both plugs and pistons.
5. Reverse procedure to install. Torque plugs to 20 ft. lbs.

## HYDRAULIC HEAD SEAL O-RING, REPLACE
### Removal
1. Remove throttle shaft and seals.
2. Remove metering valve, **Fig. 34**.
3. Remove housing vent screw assembly, **Fig. 38**.
4. Remove advance pin hole plug and advance pin, **Fig. 37**.
5. Remove head locating screws and seal.
6. Remove hydraulic head assembly and O-ring.

### Installation
1. Install hydraulic head seal and place head assembly into pump housing.
2. Install two head locking screws finger tight and turn pump upside down.
3. Install head-locating screw and torque to 15-18 ft. lbs., **Fig. 37**.
4. Torque head-locking screws to 15-18 ft. lbs.
5. Install advance pin and advance pin plug.
6. Turn pump so cover opening is up, and install metering valve.
7. Install throttle shaft, seals and pump cover.

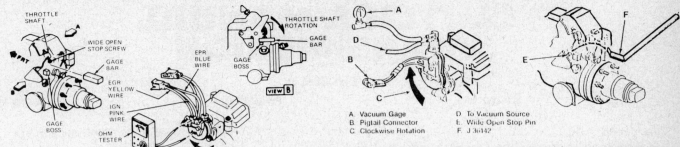

Fig. 41 Throttle position switch adjustment.
1982–85

Fig. 42 Throttle position switch adjustment.
1986–89

A. Vacuum Gage
B. Pigtail Connector
C. Clockwise Rotation
D. To Vacuum Source
E. Wide Open Stop Pin
F. J 36142

## INJECTION NOZZLE REPLACE

The fuel injection nozzles used on some models have a different thread pitch size and are shorter than those used on other models. If replacement becomes necessary, make certain the correct nozzle is used.

1. Disconnect batteries, fuel return clip, fuel return hose and fuel injection line.
2. Remove injection nozzle by applying torque to largest nozzle hex, with nozzle socket tool J-36142, **Fig. 39**.
3. Reverse procedure to install. Torque nozzle to 50 ft. lbs. Torque fuel injection line to 20 ft. lbs.

## TRANSMISSION VACUUM REGULATOR VALVE

### ADJUST
#### 1982–85

1. Attach vacuum regulator valve to injection pump. **Vacuum regulator valve should be attached snugly without being over-tightened.**
2. Attach vacuum gauge to outboard vacuum nipple on 1982 models, or top vacuum nipple on 1983-85 models.
3. Attach vacuum source to inboard vacuum nipple on 1982 models, or bottom vacuum nipple on 1983-85 models, then apply 9.0-10.4 inches Hg vacuum on 1982 models, or 18.5-21.5 inches Hg vacuum on 1983-85 models, to nipple.
4. Open stop screw on throttle lever to fully open position, then insert 0.646 inch vacuum regulator gage bar between gage boss on pump and stop

screw, **Fig. 40**.
5. Rotate and hold throttle shaft against gage bar, then slowly rotate regulator body clockwise until vacuum gauge reads 5.3-5.9 inches Hg on 1982 models, 7.4-8.6 inches Hg on 1983-85 models. Hold body in this position, then torque mounting screws to 4 ft. lbs.
6. Allow throttle shaft to return to idle position, then repeat Step 5. Readjust valve if necessary.

## THROTTLE POSITION SWITCH

### ADJUST
#### 1982–85

1. Place throttle position switch on fuel injector pump with throttle lever in closed position. **Throttle position switch should be attached snugly. Do not tighten.**
2. Attach continuity meter across terminals or wires as shown, **Fig. 41**.
3. Turn stop screw on throttle shaft to wide open position and insert "switch closed" gage block between gage boss on injection pump and stop screw.
4. Rotate and hold throttle lever against gage block.
5. Rotate throttle switch clockwise (facing throttle switch) until continuity just occurs across terminals or wires. Hold switch body in this position and tighten mounting screws. **Switch point must be set only while rotating switch body in clockwise direction.**
6. Check by allowing throttle lever to return to idle position. Remove "switch closed" gage bar and install "switch open" gage bar. Rotate throttle lever against it. There should be no continuity between terminals or wires.

## VACUUM REGULATOR VALVE/THROTTLE POSITION SWITCH

### ADJUST
#### 1986–89

1. Loosen vacuum regulator valve, then attach vacuum gauge to the top vacuum nipple.
2. Attach vacuum source to bottom vacuum nipple, then apply 18.5-21.5 inches Hg vacuum to nipple.
3. Insert a .646 inch vacuum regulator gage bar between gauge boss on pump and stop screw, **Fig. 40**.
4. Rotate and hold throttle shaft against gauge bar, then slowly rotate regulator body clockwise until vacuum gauge reads 7.4-8.6 inches Hg on 1986 models, or 10.9-12.1 inches Hg on 1987-89 models. Hold body in this position, then torque mounting screws to 4 ft. lbs.
5. Allow throttle shaft to return to idle position, then repeat step 4. Readjust valve if necessary.
6. Attach ohmmeter across terminals as shown, **Fig. 42**.
7. Insert switch gauge tool J-29873, between wide open stop pin and wide open stop screw.
8. Rotate throttle lever against gauge tool. There should be no continuity reading.
9. Release throttle lever and remove gauge tool.
10. Rotate throttle lever to wide open throttle position, (so the stop screw and stop pin touch). A reading of 1-ohms must be present before the throttle reaches wide open throttle position. If reading is not as specified, repeat procedure.

# CLUTCH & MANUAL TRANSMISSION

## INDEX

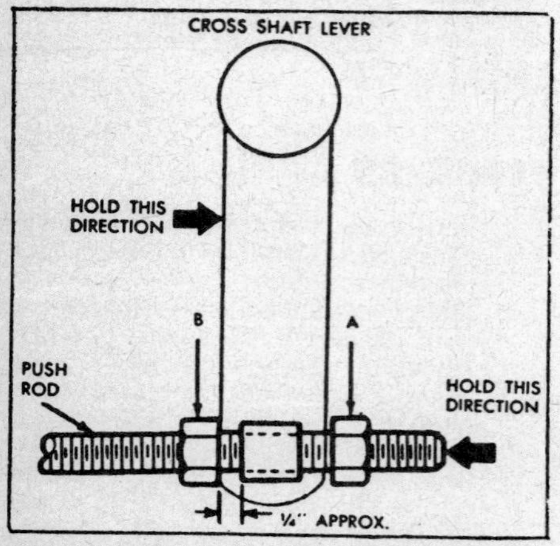

**Fig. 1 Clutch pedal free travel adjustment. G models**

# CLUTCH PEDAL
## ADJUST
### G MODELS

1. Disconnect clutch fork return spring at fork.
2. Loosen nut "A," **Fig. 1**, and back off from swivel about $1/2$ inch.
3. Hold clutch fork push rod against fork to move clutch release bearing against clutch fingers (push rod will slide through swivel at cross-shaft).
4. Adjust nut "B" to obtain $3/16$ to $1/4$ inch clearance between nut "B" and swivel.
5. Release pushrod, connect return spring and tighten nut "A" to lock swivel against nut "B."
6. Check free pedal travel which should be $1 1/4$ to $1 1/2$ inch.

### 1980-84 C & K MODELS & 1980-89 P MODELS EXC. 157 INCH WHEEL BASE P30/3500 & MOTOR HOME

1. Disconnect return spring at clutch fork.
2. Position clutch lever firmly against rubber bumper on brake pedal bracket.
3. Push outer end of fork rearward until

release bearing lightly contacts pressure plate.
4. Loosen locknut and adjust rod length so that swivel slips freely into gauge hole, **Fig. 2**. Increase length until all lash is removed from linkage.
5. Reinstall rod into lower hole on lever. Install two washers and cotter pin. Tighten locknut without changing rod length.
6. Reinstall return spring and check pedal travel. Pedal travel should be $1 3/8$ to $1 5/8$ inch on C-K models; and $1 1/4$ to $1 1/2$ inch on P models.

### 157 INCH WHEEL BASE P30/3500

1. Disconnect return spring from clutch fork.
2. Loosen nut "G" at swivel, **Fig. 2**.
3. Move clutch fork rod against fork to eliminate play between release bearing and clutch.
4. Position clutch lever against rubber stop on brake pedal bracket.
5. Rotate fork rod until a clearance of $1/4$ to $5/16$ inch is obtained between shoulder fork rod and the adjustment nut.
6. Tighten nut "G" against swivel and install return spring.
7. Check free pedal clearance at pedal. Pedal clearance should be $1 3/8$ to $1 5/8$ inch.

### 1980-81 CABALLERO & EL CAMINO

1. Disconnect return spring at clutch fork.
2. Rotate clutch lever and shaft assembly until pedal is against rubber bumper on dash brace.
3. Push outer end of clutch fork rearward until throwout bearing lightly contacts pressure plate fingers.
4. Install pushrod in gauge hole and increase length until all lash is removed, **Fig. 3**.
5. Remove swivel or rod from gauge hole and insert into lower hole on lever. Install retainer and tighten locknut using care not to change rod length.
6. Install return spring and check clutch pedal free travel. Free travel should be $3/4$ to $1 5/16$ inch.

# HYDRAULIC CLUTCH CONTROL SYSTEM

The clutch control system used on 1985-86 C and K models and 1987-88 R and V models consists of a clutch master cylinder, slave cylinder and a connecting hose. Pressure applied to the master cylinder pushrod from the clutch pedal forces the master cylinder plunger and seal assembly along the cylinder bore. As the plunger moves, the seal closes off the cylinder bore fluid inlet and hydraulic pressure is created which operates the slave cylinder. The slave cylinder, in turn, operates the clutch release fork through a short pushrod.

When the clutch pedal is released, the combination of fluid and return spring pressure moves the piston and seal assembly back until it reaches a stop in the bore. When the piston contacts the stop, the seal is behind the cylinder bore inlet (recuperation hole) and pressure is released from the system.

## SYSTEM CHECK

1. Inspect slave cylinder and clutch pedal travel.
2. Clutch pedal travel should be approximately 8.3 inches, and slave cylinder rod should have a minimum of 1 inch travel, measured at the clutch fork.
3. Inspect pedal bushings for binding and excessive wear, and the fork for damage, wear and proper lubrication. Replace components that are damaged or worn.
4. With engine running at normal operating temperature, hold clutch pedal approximately $1/2$ from floor mat, wait approximately 9 seconds and move shift lever between first and reverse several times.
5. If shift is not smooth, bleed system and recheck operation.
6. If shift is still not smooth, inspect clutch components and repair or replace as needed.

## BLEEDING CLUTCH SYSTEM

1. Fill master cylinder, as needed with

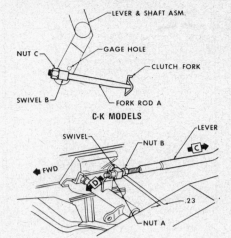

C-K MODELS

G MODELS

P10-30 ( EXC. MOTOR HOME & 157" WB )

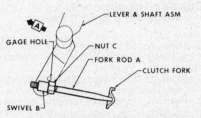

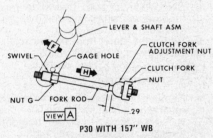

P30 WITH 157" WB

**Fig. 2 Clutch pedal adjustment. 1980-84 C & K models & 1980-88 P models**

new brake fluid conforming to DOT 3 specification.

2. Raise and support vehicle and remove slave cylinder attaching bolts.
3. Hold slave cylinder at approximately 45° angle with bleed valve at highest point.
4. Fully depress clutch pedal, then open bleed valve.
5. Close bleed valve, then release clutch pedal. **Do not release clutch pedal with bleed valve open as air will be drawn into hydraulic system.**
6. Repeat steps 4 and 5 until all air is evacuated from system. Check and refill master cylinder at regular intervals during procedure to prevent air from being drawn into system through master cylinder.

# CLUTCH
## REPLACE
### CABALLERO & EL CAMINO

1. Remove transmission as outlined in

---

"Transmission, Replace" procedure.

2. Disconnect clutch fork pushrod and return spring.
3. Remove flywheel housing.
4. Slide clutch fork from ball stud and remove fork from dust boot.
5. Look for "X" mark on flywheel and clutch cover. If no marks are present, scribe marks on flywheel and cover to aid reassembly.
6. Loosen clutch to flywheel attaching bolts evenly one turn at a time until spring pressure is released.
7. Remove attaching bolts and clutch assembly.
8. Reverse procedure to install.

### SERIES 10–30/1500–3500

1. Remove transmission as outlined in "Transmission, Replace" procedure.
2. On all except 1985-86 C and K models and 1987-89 R and V models, disconnect clutch fork pushrod and return spring. On 1985-86 C and K models and 1987-89 R and V models, remove slave cylinder from flywheel housing and secure aside.
3. Remove flywheel housing.
4. Press clutch fork away from ball mounting, then remove clutch fork, retainer and throwout bearing.
5. Support clutch assembly with suitable tool, then scribe alignment marks on flywheel and clutch cover.
6. Loosen clutch to flywheel attaching bolts evenly one turn at a time until spring pressure is released. **On coil spring type pressure plates, it may be helpful to install 3/8 inch spacers between clutch levers and cover.**
7. Remove support tool, then the attaching bolts and clutch assembly.
8. Reverse procedure to install.

# TRANSMISSION
## REPLACE
### CABALLERO & EL CAMINO

It may be necessary to disconnect the catalytic converter to provide adequate clearance for transmission removal.

1. Disconnect battery ground cable.
2. Remove shift lever knob and, on four speed models, the spring and "T" handle.
3. Raise and support vehicle.
4. Disconnect speedometer cable and TCS wiring at transmission.
5. Remove propeller shaft.
6. Remove transmission mount to crossmember bolts and the crossmember to frame bolts.
7. Remove shift lever attaching bolts and shift levers from transmission. Disconnect back drive rod at bellhousing crank on floor shift models.
8. On floor shift models, remove bolts attaching shift control assembly to support on transmission. Carefully pull unit downward until shift lever clears rubber boot and remove assembly from vehicle.
9. On all models, remove transmission to clutch housing upper retaining bolts and install guide pins in holes and remove the lower retaining bolts.

---

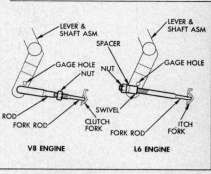

**Fig. 3 Clutch pedal adjustment. 1980-81 Caballero & El Camino**

10. Slide transmission rearward until clutch drive gear clears the clutch assembly and remove transmission from vehicle.
11. Reverse procedure to install.

### SERIES 10–30/1500–3500 EXC. K & V MODELS

1. On 4 speed models with internal shift linkage, proceed as follows:
   a. Remove shift lever boot retaining screws, then slide boot up lever.
   b. Depress collar securing shift lever and rotate collar counterclockwise, then remove shift lever. On some models it may be necessary to remove center console and/or floor mat, and the transmission access panel in vehicle floor in order to gain clearance for transmission removal.
2. On all models, raise and support vehicle, then drain transmission lubricant.
3. Disconnect speedometer cable.
4. On models with external shift linkage, disconnect shift levers and linkage from transmission, noting position for installation.
5. Disconnect parking brake lever and controls, if necessary, then the back-up light switch wiring.
6. Disconnect propeller shaft from transmission, then the exhaust pipes from exhaust manifolds, if necessary.
7. Support transmission with a suitable jack.
8. Remove any lines or brackets that will interfere with transmission removal.
9. Remove transmission mount and rear crossmember, if applicable.
10. Remove transmission to clutch housing attaching bolts.
11. Slide transmission rearward, lower and remove from vehicle.
12. Reverse procedure to install.

### K & V MODELS
#### 3 SPEED UNITS

1. Raise and support vehicle.
2. Drain transfer case and transmission, then disconnect speedometer cable.
3. Remove propeller shafts.
4. Remove shift lever control assembly to adapter attaching bolt, then the shift lever rod to transfer case connector link.

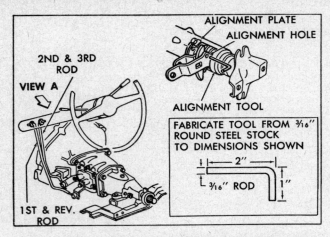

**Fig. 4  Three speed column shift linkage adjustment. 1980–81 Caballero & El Camino**

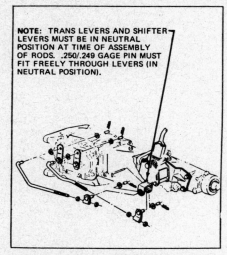

**Fig. 5  Three speed floor shift linkage adjustment. 1980–81 Caballero & El Camino**

5. Remove transfer case to engine support strut.
6. Support transfer case, then remove transfer case to adapter attaching bolts and the transfer case.
7. Disconnect shift linkage from transmission, then support rear of engine and remove adapter mount bolts.
8. Remove the top two transmission to clutch housing attaching screws, then install guide pins in holes.
9. Remove the two lower transmission to clutch housing attaching screws.
10. Slide transmission and adapter assembly rearward and remove from vehicle.
11. Separate adapter from transmission.
12. Reverse procedure to install.

## 4 SPEED UNITS
### 1980–81 Models

1. Remove transfer case shift lever boot retainer.
2. Remove transmission shift lever boot, retainer and shift lever.
3. Remove carpeting or floor mat from cab.
4. Remove heater distributor duct center floor outlet, if necessary.
5. Remove center console, if equipped.
6. Remove transmission floor cover, then disconnect shift lever rod assembly from transfer case connecting link.
7. Remove shift lever control attaching bolt and shift lever from adapter.
8. Raise and support vehicle, then drain transfer case and transmission.
9. Disconnect speedometer cable and propeller shafts.
10. Remove transmission mount to crossmember attaching bolts.
11. Support transmission and transfer case, then remove crossmember.
12. Remove exhaust crossover pipe, if equipped.
13. Remove upper transmission to clutch housing attaching bolts, then install guide pins in holes.
14. Remove lower transmission to clutch housing attaching bolts.
15. Slide transmission rearward, lower, then remove transmission/transfer case assembly.

16. Separate transfer case from transmission.
17. Reverse procedure to install.

### 1982 Models

1. Remove transmission shift lever boot, retainer and shift lever.
2. On vehicles equipped with New Process 208 transfer case, raise and support vehicle, then disconnect transfer case shift lever from control rod. Lower vehicle.
3. On vehicles equipped with New Process 205 transfer case, remove transfer case shift lever boot retainer.
4. On all vehicles, remove floor mat or carpeting, then the center console, if equipped.
5. Remove transmission floor cover.
6. On vehicles equipped with New Process 205 transfer case, disconnect shift lever rod assembly from connecting link, then remove shift lever to adapter attaching bolt.
7. Raise and support vehicle, then drain transmission and transfer case.
8. Disconnect speedometer cable and propeller shafts.
9. Support transfer case, then remove transfer case to adapter attaching bolts and the transfer case.
10. Remove transmission mount attaching bolts, then support transmission and remove crossmember.
11. Remove upper transmission to clutch housing attaching bolts, then install guide pins in holes.
12. Slide transmission rearward, then lower and remove from vehicle. Remove adapter.
13. Reverse procedure to install.

### 1983–89 Exc. 117 mm Transmission

1. Raise and support vehicle, then drain transmission and transfer case.
2. Disconnect propeller shafts and speedometer cables.
3. Disconnect shift lever from transfer case.
4. Support transfer case, then remove transfer case to adapter attaching bolts and the transfer case.

5. Remove all lines and brackets that will interfere with transmission removal.
6. Remove attaching bolts, then remove crossmember.
7. Remove upper transmission to clutch housing attaching bolts, then install guide pins in holes.
8. Remove lower bolts, then slide transmission rearward and remove from vehicle.
9. Remove adapter from transmission.
10. Reverse procedure to install.

### 1983–89 117 mm Transmission

1. Remove transmission shift lever boot, retainer and shift lever.
2. Raise and support vehicle, then drain transfer case and transmission.
3. Disconnect speedometer cable and propeller shafts.
4. Support transfer case, then remove transfer case to adapter attaching bolts and the transfer case.
5. Disconnect exhaust pipes from manifolds, then remove transmission mount to crossmember attaching bolts.
6. Support transmission, then remove crossmember.
7. Remove upper transmission to clutch housing attaching bolts, then install guide pins in holes.
8. Remove lower bolts, slide transmission rearward and remove from vehicle.
9. Remove adapter from transmission.
10. Reverse procedure to install.

## 3 SPEED SHIFT LINKAGE ADJUST
## CABALLERO & EL CAMINO
### Column Shift

1. Place shift lever in "Reverse" position and ignition switch in "Lock."
2. Raise vehicle on a hoist.

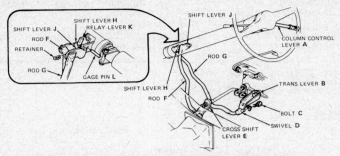

**Fig. 6   Three speed column shift linkage adjustment. C, K, R & V models**

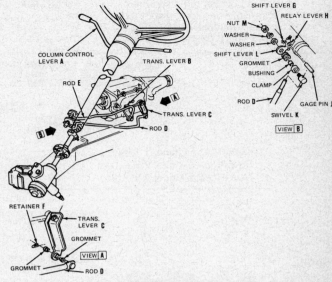

**Fig. 7   Three speed column shift linkage adjustment. G & P models**

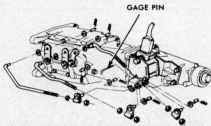

**Fig. 8   Four speed floor shift linkage adjustment. 1980—81 Caballero & El Camino**

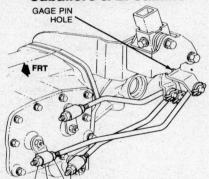

**Fig. 9   Four speed shift linkage adjustment. Series 10—30/1500-3500**

3. Loosen shift control rod swivel lock nuts. Pull down slightly on 1/R rod attached to column lever to remove any slack and then tighten clevis locknut at transmission lever, **Fig. 4.**
4. Unlock ignition switch and shift column lever to "Neutral." Position column lower levers in "Neutral," align gauge holes in levers and insert gauge pin.
5. Support rod and swivel to prevent movement and tighten 2-3 shift control rod locknut.
6. Remove alignment tool from column lower levers and check operation. Then place column lever in "Reverse" and check interlock control.

### Floor Shift

1. Place ignition switch in "Off" position and raise vehicle.

2. Loosen locknuts at shift rod swivels, **Fig. 5.** The rods should pass freely through the swivels.
3. Place transmission shift levers in neutral position.
4. Move shift control lever into the neutral detent position, align control assembly levers and insert gage pin into lever alignment slot.
5. Tighten locknuts at shift rod swivels and remove gage pin.
6. Place transmission control lever in reverse position and the ignition switch in "Lock" position. Loosen lock nut at back-drive control rod swivel, then pull rod downward slightly to remove slack in the column mechanism, then tighten the locknut.
7. Check interlock control. The ignition switch should move freely to and from the "Lock" position.
8. Check transmission shift operation and if satisfactory, lower vehicle.

### SERIES 10—30/1500-3500
#### Column Shift

1. Position transmission lever B (C, K, R and V models) or C (G and P models) clockwise to forward detent, **Figs. 6 and 7**, then turn ignition switch to "Lock."
2. Remove column lash by rotating lever J (C, K, R and V models) or L (G and P models) downward and tightening bolt C (C, K, R and V models) or M (G and P models).
3. Turn ignition switch to "Unlock," then position transmission levers in Neutral. To position levers in Neutral, move levers B and E (C, K, R and V models) or B and C (G and P models) to forward detent, then turn counterclockwise one detent, **Figs. 6 and 7.**
4. Align gage pin holes in levers H, J and K (C, K, R and V models) or G, H, and

L (G and P models), then insert gage pin.
5. Repeat Step 2 for rod F (C, K, R and V models) or E (G and P models) and levers E and H (C, K, R and V models) or B and G (G and P models).
6. Remove gage pin.
7. Place column lever in Reverse and check interlock control. Ignition should lock only when in Reverse.

### 4 SPEED SHIFT LINKAGE ADJUST
#### CABALLERO & EL CAMINO

Refer to **Fig. 8,** then follow the same procedure as outlined under "3 Speed Floor Shift Linkage, Adjust."

#### SERIES 10—30/1500-3500

Transmission and shifter levers must be in Neutral position at time of rod assembly. A .250 inch gage pin must fit freely into gage pin hole when shifter levers are positioned as outlined above, **Fig. 9.**

Some 1982-83 C, K and P models equipped with V8-379 diesel engine and four speed 117 mm transmission may exhibit hard shifting, bearing or gear noise, or improper clutch operation. The above mentioned complaints may be caused by the transmission top cover protruding beyond the front face of the transmission, resulting in transmission to engine misalignment. If the vehicle exhibits any of the complaints noted, proceed as follows:

1. Raise and support vehicle.
2. Using a .005 inch feeler gauge or shim, check for gaps between transmission and clutch housing.
3. If a gap or separation is noted, check for interference between top cover and clutch housing. If interference exists, proceed to next step.

4. Loosen, but do not remove, transmission to clutch housing attaching bolts.
5. Remove transmission top cover, then grind excess material from forward side of cover until proper transmission to clutch housing clearance is obtained. Remove burrs from ground edges.
6. Wash cover with suitable solvent, then torque transmission to clutch housing attaching bolts to 100 ft. lbs.
7. Install reworked top cover, using a new gasket.
8. Torque top cover attaching bolts to 20 ft. lbs., then lower vehicle.

# TRANSFER CASE

## INDEX

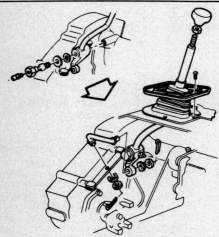

**Fig. 1  Transfer case shift linkage. New Process Model 205**

## TRANSFER CASE
### REPLACE
#### NEW PROCESS MODEL 205 & 241

1. Raise and support vehicle.
2. Drain transfer case, then disconnect speedometer cable, back-up light switch connector and TCS switch, if equipped.
3. Remove skidplate and crossmember supports, if necessary.
4. Disconnect front and rear propeller shafts from case and position aside.
5. Disconnect shift lever rod from shift rail link.
6. Support transfer case, then remove case to adapter attaching bolts.
7. Slide transfer case rearward until input shaft clears adapter and remove from vehicle.
8. Reverse procedure to install.

### NEW PROCESS MODEL 208

1. Place transfer case shift lever in 4H position.
2. Raise and support vehicle, then drain transfer case.
3. Remove cotter pin from shift lever swivel.
4. Scribe alignment marks on front and rear output shaft yokes and propeller shafts to aid reassembly.
5. Disconnect speedometer cable and indicator switch wiring.
6. Disconnect propeller shafts from yokes.
7. Disconnect parking brake cable guide from right frame rail pivot, if necessary.
8. On automatic transmission equipped vehicles, disconnect engine strut rod from transfer case.
9. Support transfer case, then remove case to adapter attaching bolts.
10. Slide transfer case rearward until free of transmission output shaft and remove from vehicle. Remove gasket from adapter housing.
11. Reverse procedure to install using new gasket on adapter housing.

## TRANSFER CASE LINKAGE
### ADJUST
#### NEW PROCESS MODEL 205

The control linkage for New Process Model 205 transfer cases is shown in **Fig. 1**. Inspect linkage system periodically for freedom of operation, proper engagement or loose attaching bolts. Adjust, clean and tighten as necessary.

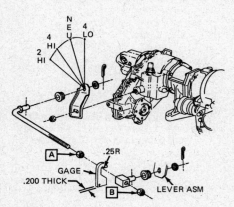

**Fig. 2  Transfer case shift linkage adjustment. New Process Model 208 & 241**

### NEW PROCESS MODEL 208 & 241

1. Position transfer case shift lever in 4 Hi detent.
2. Push lower shifter lever forward to 4 Hi stop, then install rod swivel into shift lever hole.
3. Install .200 inch gage behind swivel as shown, **Fig. 2**.
4. With shifter against 4 Hi stop, tighten rod nut (A) until it contacts gage.
5. Remove gage, then push swivel rearward against nut (A) and tighten nut (B).

# REAR AXLE, SUSPENSION & BRAKES

## INDEX

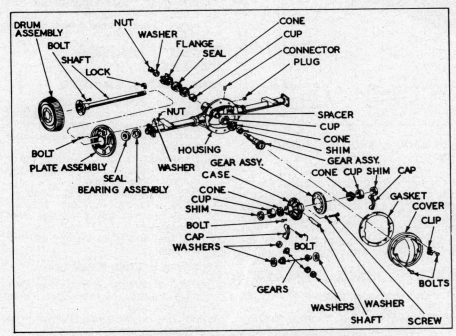

**Fig. 1 Salisbury type semi-floating rear axle**

## CHEVROLET SALISBURY TYPE SEMI-FLOATING AXLE

In these rear axles, **Figs. 1 and 2,** the rear axle housing and differential carrier are cast into an integral assembly. The drive pinion assembly is mounted in two opposed tapered roller bearings. The pinion bearings are preloaded by a spacer behind the front bearing. The pinion is positioned by a washer between the head of the pinion and the rear bearing.

The differential is supported in the carrier by two tapered roller side bearings. These bearings are preloaded by spacers located between the bearings and carrier housing. The differential assembly is positioned for proper ring gear and pinion backlash by varying these spacers. The differential case houses two side gears in mesh with two pinions mounted on a pinion shaft which is held in place by a lock pin. The side gears and pinions are backed by thrust washers.

## AXLE HOUSING, REPLACE
### Caballero & El Camino

1. Raise vehicle and support at frame rails, then raise and support rear axle with suitable jack.
2. Disconnect shock absorbers from lower mountings.
3. Remove propeller shaft.

4. Disconnect upper control arms from axle housing attachments.
5. Disconnect brake line from axle housing junction block.
6. Disconnect parking brake cable, then the lower control arms from axle housing.
7. Lower axle slowly until spring tension is relieved, then roll axle housing out from underneath vehicle.
8. Reverse procedure to install.

### Series 10–30/1500–3500

Construction of the axle assembly is such that service operations may be performed with the housing installed in the vehicle or with the housing removed and installed in a holding fixture. The following procedure is necessary only when the housing requires replacement.

1. Raise vehicle and place jackstands under frame side rails.
2. Remove rear wheels and drums.
3. Support rear axle assembly with a suitable jack so that tension is relieved in springs and tie rod, if equipped.
4. Disconnect tie rod at axle housing bracket, if equipped.
5. Remove trunnion bearing U-bolts from rear yoke, split universal joint, position propeller shaft to one side and tie it to frame side rail.
6. Remove axle U-bolt nuts and allow shock absorbers to hang freely so that they do not interfere with axle. On K and V Series trucks, remove spacer from axle housing.
7. Disconnect hydraulic brake hose at connector on axle housing.
8. Remove brake drum and disconnect parking brake cable at lever and at flange plate.
9. Lower axle and remove from vehicle.
10. Reverse foregoing procedure to install axle assembly.

## AXLE SHAFT, REPLACE

1. Raise vehicle and remove wheel and brake drum.

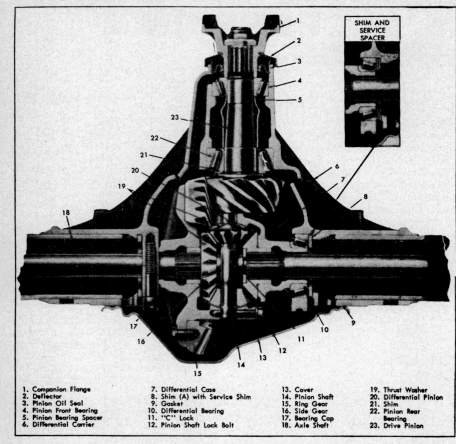

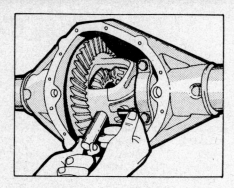

**Fig. 3   Removing differential pinion shaft**

**Fig. 2   Semi-floating rear axle of 3300 & 3500 lbs. rated capacity**

1. Companion Flange
2. Deflector
3. Pinion Oil Seal
4. Pinion Front Bearing
5. Pinion Bearing Spacer
6. Differential Carrier
7. Differential Case
8. Shim (A) with Service Shim
9. Gasket
10. Differential Bearing
11. "C" Lock
12. Pinion Shaft Lock Bolt
13. Cover
14. Pinion Shaft
15. Ring Gear
16. Side Gear
17. Bearing Cap
18. Axle Shaft
19. Thrust Washer
20. Differential Pinion
21. Shim
22. Pinion Rear Bearing
23. Drive Pinion

2. Drain lube from carrier and remove cover.
3. Remove differential pinion shaft lock screw and remove differential pinion shaft, **Fig. 3.**
4. Pull flanged end of axle shaft toward center of vehicle and remove C-lock from button end of shaft.
5. Remove axle shaft from housing, being careful not to damage seal.
6. Reverse foregoing procedure to install the axle shaft.

## WHEEL BEARING/OIL SEAL, REPLACE

1. Remove axle shaft as previously described.
2. Use a suitable puller to remove bearing and oil seal.
3. Lubricate wheel bearing and cavity between seal lips with wheel bearing lubricant before installation.
4. Reverse procedure to install.

## CHEVROLET FULL FLOATING AXLE

The straddle mounted drive pinion is supported at the front by two opposed tapered roller bearings. The pinion gear roller bearing consists of an outer race and roller assembly and a precision ground diameter on the pinion pilot functions as an inner race.

On units with 10½ inch ring gear, **Fig. 4,** side bearing preload and ring gear to pinion backlash are controlled by side bearing adjusting rings threaded into the carrier. Pinion depth is controlled by a shim located between the pinion bearing retainer assembly and axle housing.

## AXLE HOUSING, REPLACE

1. Raise and support vehicle, then remove rear wheels.
2. Remove the two trunnion bearing U-bolts, then split universal joint and position propeller shaft aside.
3. Remove hub and drum assembly, then disconnect parking brake cable at lever and flange plate.
4. Disconnect brake hose at axle connector, then the shock absorbers at axle brackets.
5. Support axle housing with a suitable jack, remove spring plate U-bolts and remove axle housing from vehicle.
6. Reverse procedure to install.

## AXLE SHAFT, REPLACE

1. Remove bolts that attach axle shaft flange to wheel hub.
2. Tap on flange with a rawhide mallet to loosen axle shaft, then remove axle shaft by twisting shaft with locking pliers.
3. Thoroughly clean both axle shaft flange and end of wheel hub. Any lu-

bricant on these surfaces tends to loosen axle shaft flange bolts.
4. Place a new gasket over axle shaft and position axle shaft in housing so that shaft splines enter differential side gear. Position gasket so that holes are in alignment and install flange-to-hub attaching bolts. Torque bolts to 115 ft. lbs.

## WHEEL BEARINGS, REPLACE

### Hub & Drum, Remove

1. Remove wheel and axle shaft.
2. Disengage tang of locknut from slot or flat of locknut, then remove locknut from housing tube, using appropriate tool, **Fig. 5.**
3. Disengage tang of locknut from slot or flat of adjusting nut and remove locknut from housing tube.
4. Use appropriate tool, **Fig. 5,** to remove adjusting nut from housing tube. Remove thrust washer from housing tube.
5. Pull hub and drum straight off axle housing.

### Bearing & Cup, Replace

1. Using a hammer and suitable drift, drive inner bearing, cup and seal from hub assembly.
2. Remove outer bearing snap ring using suitable pliers.
3. Using tools J-24426 and J-8092, **Fig. 6,** drive outer bearing and cup from hub assembly.
4. Install new outer bearing into hub assembly.
5. Install outer bearing cup using tools mentioned in Step 3. Drive cup beyond snap ring groove. **Install outer bearing cup with tool J-8092 positioned upside down to prevent chamfer on tool from damaging cup.**
6. Install snap ring into groove using suitable pliers.
7. Using tool J-24426, drive cup against snap ring.
8. Install inner bearing cup using tools J-24427 and J-8092. Drive cup into position until it seats against shoulder of hub bore.
9. Install new oil seal.

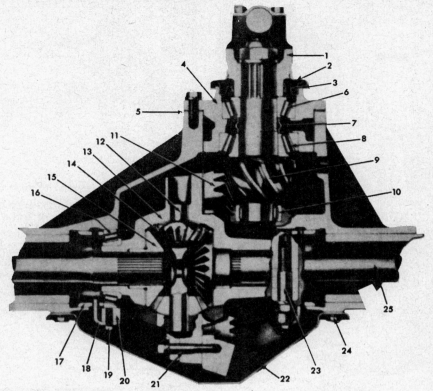

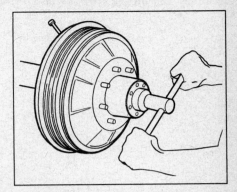

**Fig. 5 Removing bearing adjusting nut locknut**

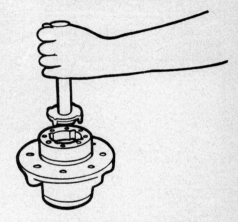

**Fig. 6 Removing outer bearing & cup**

| | | |
|---|---|---|
| 1. Companion Flange | 10. Straddle Bearing | 19. Retainer Screw |
| 2. Oil Deflector | 11. Ring Gear | 20. Bearing Cap |
| 3. Oil Seal | 12. Differential Spider | 21. Case-to-Ring Gear Bolt |
| 4. Bearing Retainer | 13. Differential Case | 22. Differential Cover |
| 5. Shim | 14. Differential Pinion | 23. Bearing Cap Bolt |
| 6. Pinion Front Bearing | 15. Differential Side Gear | 24. Cover Screw |
| 7. Collapsible Spacer | 16. Side Bearing | 25. Axle Shaft |
| 8. Pinion Rear Bearing | 17. Side Bearing Adjusting Nut | |
| 9. Drive Pinion | 18. Adjusting Nut Retainer | |

**Fig. 4 Full floating rear axle**

## WHEEL BEARINGS, ADJUST

Before checking wheel bearing adjustment, make sure brakes are fully released and do not drag. Check bearing play by grasping tire at top and pulling back and forth or by using a pry bar under tire. If bearings are properly adjusted, movement of brake drum in relation to brake flange plate will be barely noticeable and wheel will turn freely. If movement is excessive, adjust bearings as follows:

1. Raise vehicle until wheel is free to rotate, then remove axle shaft.
2. Disengage retainer tang and remove retainer from axle housing tube.
3. Tighten adjusting nut to 50 ft. lbs. while rotating hub assembly. Ensure bearing cones are seated and in contact with spindle shoulder.
4. Back off adjusting nut until just loose.
5. Insert key into adjusting nut slot, if equipped. Install snap ring to retain key in position.
6. Lower vehicle, then install axle shaft.

## GMC SINGLE SPEED AXLE

This axle, **Fig. 7**, is a full floating type and enables removal of the axle shafts

without removing the truck load or raising the rear axle. The drive pinion is straddle mounted and supported at the rear end by a straight roller bearing and at the front end by a double row ball bearing.

## AXLE HOUSING, REPLACE

Refer to "Chevrolet Full Floating Axles" for axle housing replacement procedures, since procedures are identical for both axles.

## AXLE SHAFT, REPLACE

1. Remove hub cap retaining cap screws and hub cap.
2. Install a slide hammer adapter into tapped hole in axle flange.
3. Attach slide hammer onto adapter and remove axle shaft from housing, **Fig. 8**.
4. Reverse procedure to install. Lubricate small end of axle shaft and install into housing using a new gasket. Torque axle flange cap screws on 15 ft. lbs.

## WHEEL BEARINGS, REPLACE

1. Remove wheel and axle shaft.

2. Disengage tang of retainer from slot or flat of locknut, then remove locknut from housing tube, **Fig. 5**.
3. Disengage tang of retainer from slot or flat of adjusting nut, then remove retainer.
4. Using tool shown in **Fig. 5**, remove adjusting nut from housing tube. Remove thrust washer.
5. Pull hub and drum assembly off axle housing. Remove oil seal and discard.
6. Using a suitable steel bar and an arbor press, press inner bearing cup from hub.
7. Using a suitable pliers, remove outer bearing retaining ring, **Fig. 9**.
8. Using an old axle shaft or equivalent, drive on axle shaft spacer to remove outer bearing assembly from hub.
9. Position axle shaft spacer and outer bearing into hub, ensuring larger side of bearing faces outer end of hub.
10. Position outer bearing cup into hub with thin edge facing toward outer end of hub, then press cup into hub.
11. Install retaining ring, then press cup into contact with ring.
12. Drive inner bearing cup into hub, then install new oil seal.
13. Reverse Steps 1 through 5 to complete installation, then adjust wheel bearings as outlined in "Wheel Bearing, Adjust" procedure.

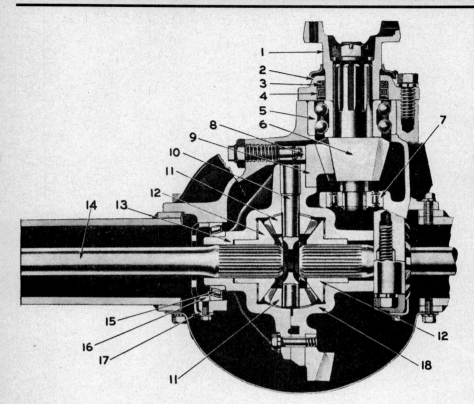

1. Universal Joint Yoke
2. Pinion Bearing Retainer and Oil Seal
3. Oil Seal Packing
4. Oil Seal
5. Front Pinion Bearing
6. Drive Pinion
7. Rear Pinion Bearing
8. Ring Gear Thrust Pad
9. Ring Gear
10. Differential Spider
11. Differential Pinion (Spider) Gear
12. Differential Side Gear
13. Differential Case—Left Half
14. Axle Shaft
15. Differential Bearing
16. Differential Bearing Adjusting Nut
17. Adjusting Nut Lock
18. Differential Case—Right Half

**Fig. 7 GMC single speed rear axle of 11,000 lbs. rated capacity**

**Fig. 8 Removing axle shaft. GMC single speed axle**

**Fig. 9 Removing bearing retainer ring**

## WHEEL BEARINGS, ADJUST

1. Raise and support rear axle.
2. Remove axle shaft as outlined previously. Release brakes.
3. Disengage retainer tang from locknut, then remove locknut and retainer from axle housing tube.
4. Torque inner adjusting nut to 50 ft. lbs. while rotating wheel, then back off nut 1/8 of a turn.
5. Install retainer so that short tang engages nearest slot on adjusting nut.
6. Install outer locknut and torque to 250 ft. lbs., then bend long tang of retainer into slot of outer nut.

## SPICER AXLES

These axles, **Figs. 10 and 11**, are similar to Salisbury type units. They are different, however, in that the axle shafts are full floating and the drive pinion incorporates two shim packs. The inner shim pack controls pinion depth, while the outer pack controls pinion bearing preload.

### SERVICE

Refer to "Chevrolet Full Floating Axle" for axle housing and shaft replacement, hub and drum components and wheel bearing service, since procedures are identical for both types of axles.

## TIMKEN (ROCKWELL) AXLE

This axle, **Fig. 12**, employs a heavy duty hypoid drive pinion and ring gear. The differential and gear assembly is mounted on tapered roller bearings. The straddle mounted pinion has two tapered roller bearings in front of the pinion teeth which take the forward and reverse thrust, while a third bearing behind the pinion teeth carries the radial load.

### AXLE HOUSING, REPLACE

Refer to "Chevrolet Full Floating Axles" for axle housing replacement procedures, since procedures are identical for both axles.

### AXLE SHAFT, REPLACE

1. Remove hub cap, then install slide hammer adapter into tapped hole in axle flange.
2. Attach slide hammer onto adapter, then remove axle shaft from housing.
3. Install axle shaft, ensuring flange and hub splines align.
4. Install new gasket, position flange to hub, then install attaching bolts and tighten to specifications.

### WHEEL BEARINGS, ADJUST

1. Remove axle shaft as outlined previ-

ously.
2. Raise and support vehicle.
3. Disengage retainer tang from locknut, then remove locknut and retainer from axle housing tube.
4. While rotating wheel, torque inner adjusting nut to 50 ft. lbs., then back off nut 1/8 of a turn.
5. Install retainer so that short tang engages nearest slot on adjusting nut.
6. Install outer locknut and torque to 250 ft. lbs., then bend long tang of retainer into slot of outer nut.

## SHOCK ABSORBER
### REPLACE
### CABALLERO & EL CAMINO

1. Raise and support vehicle, then the rear axle.
2. Remove retaining bolts, then disconnect shock absorber from upper mounting bracket.
3. Disconnect shock absorber from lower mounting bracket.
4. Remove shock absorber from vehicle.
5. Reverse procedure to install.

### SERIES 10–30/1500–3500

1. Raise and support vehicle, then the rear axle.
2. On models equipped with air lift shock absorbers, bleed air from lines, then disconnect line from shock.
3. Remove upper retaining nut or bolt, then the lower retaining bolt, nut and washer.
4. Remove shock absorber from vehicle.
5. Reverse procedure to install.

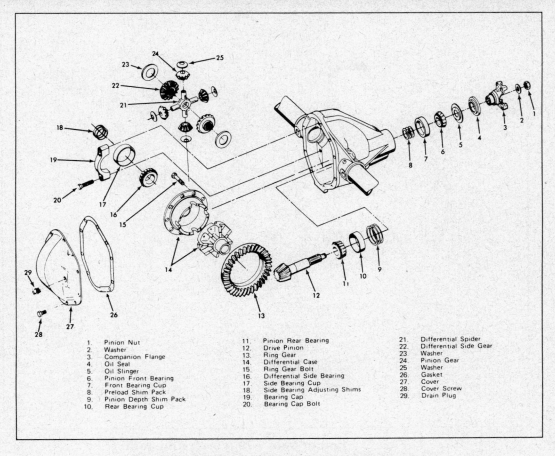

| | | | | | |
|---|---|---|---|---|---|
| 1. | Pinion Nut | 11. | Pinion Rear Bearing | 21. | Differential Spider |
| 2. | Washer | 12. | Drive Pinion | 22. | Differential Side Gear |
| 3. | Companion Flange | 13. | Ring Gear | 23. | Washer |
| 4. | Oil Seal | 14. | Differential Case | 24. | Pinion Gear |
| 5. | Oil Slinger | 15. | Ring Gear Bolt | 25. | Washer |
| 6. | Pinion Front Bearing | 16. | Differential Side Bearing | 26. | Gasket |
| 7. | Front Bearing Cup | 17. | Side Bearing Cup | 27. | Cover |
| 8. | Preload Shim Pack | 18. | Side Bearing Adjusting Shims | 28. | Cover Screw |
| 9. | Pinion Depth Shim Pack | 19. | Bearing Cap | 29. | Drain Plug |
| 10. | Rear Bearing Cup | 20. | Bearing Cap Bolt | | |

**Fig. 10   Spicer axle w/10½ inch ring gear**

# COIL SPRING
## REPLACE
## CABALLERO & EL CAMINO

1. Support vehicle at frame and rear axle.
2. Disconnect shock absorbers at lower mountings.
3. Disconnect upper control arms from axle housing.
4. If equipped with a stabilizer bar, disconnect bar from either right or left hand side of control arm.
5. Remove brake hose support bolt and support without disconnecting the brake lines.
6. Lower axle until it reaches end of its travel and using a suitable tool, pry lower pigtail over retainer on axle bracket. Remove spring and insulator.
7. Reverse procedure to install. Springs must be installed with an insulator between upper seat and spring and positioned properly, **Fig. 13.**

# LEAF SPRING & BUSHING
## REPLACE
## SERIES 10-30/1500-3500

1. Raise and support vehicle and allow axle to hang freely.
2. Loosen, but do not remove, spring to

shackle retaining nut.
3. Remove shackle to spring hanger retaining nut and bolt.
4. Remove spring to front hanger retaining nut and bolt.
5. Remove U-bolt retaining nuts, then the U-bolt and spring plate.
6. Remove leaf spring from vehicle.
7. To replace bushing, position spring on an arbor press and press bushing from spring using a suitable rod or pipe. **On some vehicles equipped with heavy duty leaf springs, the front bushing is staked in place. Before attempting to remove these bushings, the staked locations must be straightened with a suitable drift. After installation of bushing, re-stake bushing in three equally spaced locations.**
8. Reverse procedure to install, installing U-bolts as follows:
   a. Install four attaching nuts uniformly on U-bolts to retain and position anchor plate in proper position.
   b. Torque four nuts to 18 ft. lbs. in diagonal sequence.
   c. Torque four nuts to specifications in diagonal sequence, **Fig. 14.**

# CONTROL ARM
## REPLACE
## CABALLERO & EL CAMINO

1. Raise and support vehicle.

2. Support nose of axle housing with suitable jack to prevent assembly from twisting when control arm is removed.
3. If lower control arm is being replaced, remove stabilizer bar attaching bolts, if equipped.
4. Remove control arm to chassis and control arm to axle housing retaining bolts, then the control arm.
5. Reverse procedure to install. Tighten attaching bolts with vehicle at curb height.

# STABILIZER BAR
## REPLACE
## CABALLERO & EL CAMINO

1. Raise and support vehicle, then the rear axle.
2. Remove stabilizer bar to lower control arm attaching bolts, then the stabilizer bar, **Fig. 15.**
3. Reverse procedure to install. Use spacer shims, if needed, placed equally on each side of stabilizer bar. Tighten attaching bolts with vehicle at curb height.

## SERIES 10-30/1500-3500

1. Raise and support vehicle, then the rear axle.
2. Remove link bolt to frame attaching nut, washer and grommet at each side of vehicle. Remove link bolts.

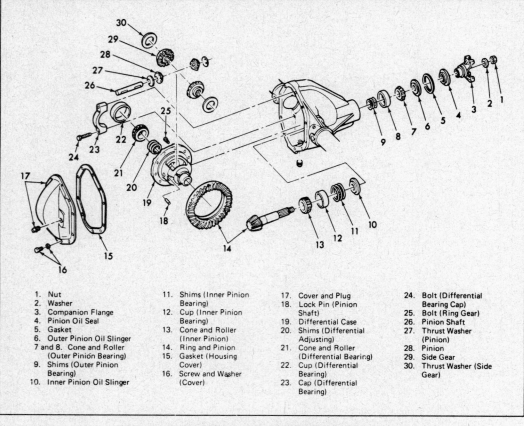

1. Nut
2. Washer
3. Companion Flange
4. Pinion Oil Seal
5. Gasket
6. Outer Pinion Oil Slinger
7 and 8. Cone and Roller (Outer Pinion Bearing)
9. Shims (Outer Pinion Bearing)
10. Inner Pinion Oil Slinger

11. Shims (Inner Pinion Bearing)
12. Cup (Inner Pinion Bearing)
13. Cone and Roller (Inner Pinion)
14. Ring and Pinion
15. Gasket (Housing Cover)
16. Screw and Washer (Cover)

17. Cover and Plug
18. Lock Pin (Pinion Shaft)
19. Differential Case
20. Shims (Differential Adjusting)
21. Cone and Roller (Differential Bearing)
22. Cup (Differential Bearing)
23. Cap (Differential Bearing)

24. Bolt (Differential Bearing Cap)
25. Bolt (Ring Gear)
26. Pinion Shaft
27. Thrust Washer (Pinion)
28. Pinion
29. Side Gear
30. Thrust Washer (Side Gear)

**Fig. 11   Spicer axle w/9³/₄ inch ring gear**

3. Remove support bracket to anchor plate attaching screws, then withdraw stabilizer bar and remove from vehicle.
4. Reverse procedure to install. Ensure parking brake cable is positioned over stabilizer bar.

## MASTER CYLINDER
### REPLACE

1. Disconnect and plug brake lines from master cylinder.
2. Remove attaching nuts, then the master cylinder.
3. Reverse procedure to install.

## POWER BRAKE UNIT
### REPLACE
## CABALLERO & EL CAMINO
### Exc. Hydro-Boost

1. Remove vacuum hose from check valve and master cylinder retaining nuts.
2. Pull master cylinder forward so it clears mounting studs and move to one side. Support cylinder to avoid stress on hydraulic lines.
3. Remove power unit to dash nuts.
4. Remove brake pedal pushrod retainer and disconnect pushrod from pin.
5. Remove power brake unit from vehicle.
6. Reverse procedure to install.

### Hydro-Boost

Pump brake pedal several times with engine off to deplete accumulator of fluid.
1. Remove two nuts attaching master cylinder to booster, then move master cylinder away from booster with brake lines attached.
2. Remove three hydraulic lines from booster. Plug and cap all lines and outlets.
3. Remove retainer and washer securing booster pushrod to brake pedal arm.
4. Remove four nuts attaching booster unit to dash panel.
5. From engine compartment, loosen booster from dash panel and move booster pushrod inboard until it disconnects from brake pedal arm. Remove spring washer from brake pedal arm.
6. Remove booster unit from vehicle.
7. Reverse procedure to install. To purge system, disconnect feed wire from injection pump. Fill power steering pump reservoir, then crank engine for several seconds and recheck power steering pump fluid level. Connect injection pump feed wire and start engine, then cycle steering wheel from stop to stop twice and stop engine. Discharge accumulator by depressing brake pedal several times, then check fluid level. Start engine, then turn steering wheel from stop to stop and turn engine off. Check fluid level and add fluid as necessary. If foaming oc-

curs, stop engine and wait approximately one hour for foam to dissipate, then recheck fluid level.

### SERIES 10–30/1500–3500
### Exc. Hydro-Boost

1. Remove master cylinder attaching nuts and position master cylinder aside. Do not disconnect brake lines from cylinder.
2. Disconnect power brake unit pushrod from brake pedal.
3. Remove attaching nuts, then the power brake unit.
4. Reverse procedure to install.

### Hydro-Boost

Before disconnecting lines from power unit, depress and release brake pedal several times to allow pressure to discharge from accumulator.
1. On P30 motor home, raise and support vehicle, if necessary.
2. On all vehicles, remove master cylinder to power brake unit attaching nuts, then position master cylinder aside. Do not disconnect brake lines from master cylinder.
3. Disconnect hydraulic lines from power brake unit. Plug all lines and ports to prevent fluid loss and dirt entry.
4. On all models except P30 motor home, remove pedal pushrod cotter pin and washer, then disconnect pushrod from brake pedal or pivot lever. Lower steering column or remove support brackets as necessary. Re-

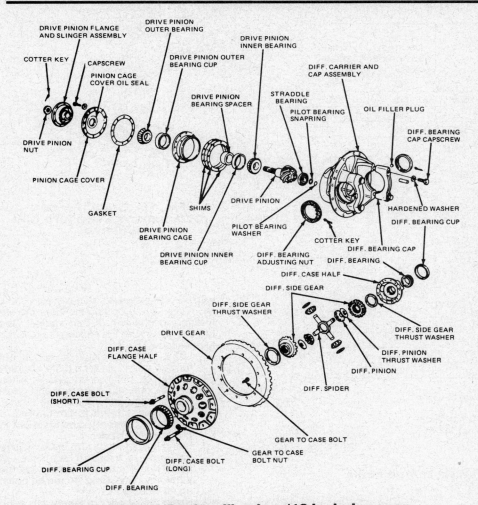

**Fig. 12   Timken (Rockwell) axle w/12 inch ring gear**

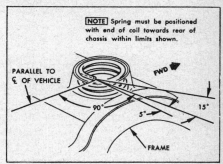

**Fig. 13   Coil spring installation**

move power brake unit bracket to dash panel or support bracket attaching nuts, then the power brake unit.

5. On P30 motor home, remove operating lever to vertical brake rod cotter pin, nut, bolt and washers. Remove power brake unit linkage bracket to front and rear support bracket attaching nuts, washers and bolts, then remove power brake unit from vehicle. Remove operating lever to pedal rod cotter pin, nut, washer and bolt. Remove brake pedal rod lever nut and bolt, then the lever, sleeve and bushing.

6. Reverse procedure to install, then bleed hydraulic system as follows:
   a. Fill power steering reservoir to proper level and allow vehicle to sit for approximately two minutes.
   b. Start engine and allow to run for several minutes, then shut engine off. Correct fluid level as necessary. Do this several times until fluid level becomes constant.
   c. Raise and support front of vehicle, then turn wheels lock to lock. Shut engine off and add fluid as necessary.
   d. Lower vehicle, then start engine and depress brake pedal several times while turning steering wheel lock to lock.
   e. Shut engine off, then depress brake pedal 4 to 5 times to allow accumulator to deplete.
   f. Check reservoir and refill as required. If fluid is extremely foamy, allow vehicle to sit for several minutes, then repeat procedure above.

## PARKING BRAKE
### ADJUST
#### CABALLERO & EL CAMINO

1. Raise and support rear of vehicle.
2. Apply parking brake two clicks on 1980-85 models, or three clicks on 1986-88 models.
3. Tighten adjusting nut until left rear wheel can just be rotated rearward, but is locked when forward rotation is attempted.
4. Release parking brake and check to ensure rear wheels rotate freely in either direction with no brake drag.

#### SERIES 10–30/1500–3500
**Pedal Type**

1. Raise and support rear of vehicle.

2. Loosen equalizer adjusting nut, then apply parking brake four clicks from fully released position.
3. Tighten equalizer nut until moderate drag is felt when rear wheels are rotated forward.
4. Release parking brake and rotate rear wheels. No drag should be present.
5. Lower vehicle.

#### Lever Type

1. Turn parking brake lever adjusting knob fully counterclockwise.
2. Apply parking brake, then raise and support rear of vehicle.
3. Loosen nut at intermediate cable equalizer, then adjust nut to give light drag at rear wheels.
4. Fine tune adjustment with adjusting knob on parking brake lever.
5. Release parking brake lever and rotate rear wheels. No drag should be present.
6. Lower vehicle.

#### Propeller Shaft Type

1. Raise and support rear of vehicle.
2. Remove cotter and clevis pins connecting pull rod and relay lever.
3. Rotate brake drum to bring access holes in alignment with adjusting screw.
4. Expand shoes by rotating adjusting screws with a screwdriver. Continue adjustment until shoes are tight against drum and drum cannot be rotated by hand. Back off adjustment ten notches and check drum for free rotation.
5. Ensure parking brake lever is in fully released position.
6. Take up slack in brake linkage by pulling rearward on cable just enough to overcome spring tension. Adjust clevis of pull rod or front cable to align with hole in relay levers, then insert clevis and cotter pins. Tighten clevis locknut.
7. Install new metal plug in drum, then lower vehicle.

## SERVICE BRAKES
### ADJUST

These brakes have self-adjusting shoe mechanisms that assure correct lining-to-drum clearances at all times. The automatic adjusters operate only when the brakes are applied as the vehicle is moving rearward or when the car comes to an uphill stop.

| Year | Model | Bolts Located Above Axle ① | Bolts Located Below Axle |
|------|-------|:---:|:---:|
| 1980-81 | C & K | 140 | 140 |
| | G10-20/1500-2500 | 120 | 120 |
| | G30/3500 | 150 | 150 |
| 1980-85 | P10-20/1500-2500 | 140 | 140 |
| | P30/3500 | ② | ② |
| 1982-83 | C & K | 148 | 170 |
| | G10-20/1500-2500 | 125 | 177 |
| | G30/3500 | 177 | 177 |
| 1984-85 | C & K | 148 | 170 |
| | G | 114 | 151 |
| 1986 | C & K | 125 | 147 |
| | G10-20/1500-2500 | 114 | — |
| | G30/3500 | 151 | 151 |
| | P20/2500 | 125 | — |
| | P30/3500 | — | ③ |
| 1987-89 | G10-20/1500-2500 | 114 | — |
| | G30/3500 | 151 | 151 |
| | P20/2500 | 125 | — |
| | P30/3500 | — | 147 |
| | R & V | 125 | ③ |

① —Ft. lbs.
② —¾ inch bolt, 200 ft. lbs.; exc. ¾ inch bolt, 170 ft. lbs.
③ —Four wheel disc brakes, 177 ft. lbs.; exc. four wheel disc brakes, 147 ft. lbs.

**Fig. 14   U-bolt nuts torque chart**

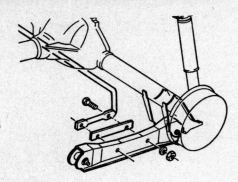

**Fig. 15   Stabilizer bar replacement. Caballero & El Camino**

will be necessary to remove the brake drum, clean, free up and lubricate the adjusting mechanism. Then adjust the brakes, being sure the parking brake is fully released.

1. Using a suitable punch, knock out lanced area in backing plate or drum. If drum is installed on vehicle when this is done, remove drum and clean brake compartment of all metal. **When adjustment is completed, a new hole cover must be installed in the backing plate.**
2. Using suitable tool, turn brake adjusting screw to expand brake shoes at each wheel until wheel can just be turned by hand. Drag should be equal on all wheels.
3. Back off adjusting screw at each wheel 30 notches.
4. If shoe still drags slightly on drum, back off adjusting screw an additional one or two notches.
5. When adjusting screw has been backed off approximately 12 notches, brakes should be free of drag. Heavy drag at this point indicates tight parking brake cables.
6. Install adjusting hole cover in brake backing place.
7. Check parking brake for proper adjustment.

Although the brakes are self-adjusting, an initial adjustment is necessary after the brake shoes have been relined or replaced, or when the length of the adjusting screw has been changed during some other service operation.

Frequent usage of an automatic transmission forward range to halt reverse vehicle motion may prevent the automatic adjusters from functioning, thereby inducing low pedal heights. Should low pedal heights be encountered, it is recommended that numerous forward and reverse stops be made until satisfactory pedal height is obtained.

If a low pedal condition cannot be corrected by making numerous reverse stops (provided the hydraulic system is free of air) it indicates that the self-adjusting mechanism is not functioning. Therefore it

# FRONT SUSPENSION & STEERING

## INDEX

**NOTE:** Steering linkage relay rod assemblies use crimped nuts. Whenever a crimped nut is loosened or removed, it must be replaced with a prevailing torque nut, Fig. 1.

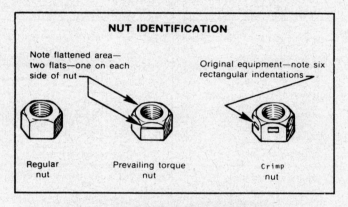

**NUT IDENTIFICATION**

Note flattened area—two flats—one on each side of nut

Original equipment—note six rectangular indentations

Regular nut

Prevailing torque nut

Crimp nut

**Fig. 1 Crimp nut identification**

## COIL SPRING SUSPENSION

This suspension, **Fig. 2,** consists of upper and lower control arms pivoting on steel threaded bushings on upper and lower control arm shafts which are bolted to the front suspension crossmember and bracket assembly. These control arms are connected to the steering knuckle through pivoting ball joints. A coil spring is located between the lower control arm and a formed seat in the suspension crossmember, thus the lower control arm is the load-carrying member. The double-acting shock absorbers are also attached to the lower control arms and connect with the frame to the rear of the suspension on the upper end.

## WHEEL ALIGNMENT
### EXC. CABALLERO & EL CAMINO

Caster and camber adjustments are made by means of shims located between upper control arm shaft and mounting bracket attached to suspension crossmember. A series of convex and concave spacers with flat opposite sides are used. These spacers allow a positive cross shaft-to-bracket attachment regardless of the number of shims used. Shims may be changed at either front or rear to vary caster, or at both points to vary camber.

### Caster

1. Measure frame angle at "B," **Fig. 3.**
2. Check caster on alignment machine.
3. Using frame angle measurement and measured caster angle, determine actual (corrected) caster angle as follows:
   a. Subtract a "down in rear" frame angle from a positive caster angle reading, **Fig. 4 (A).**
   b. Add an "up in rear" frame angle to a positive caster angle reading, **Fig. 4 (B).**
   c. Add a "down in rear" frame angle to a negative caster angle reading, **Fig. 4 (C).**
   d. Subtract an "up in rear" frame angle from a negative caster angle reading, **Fig. 4 (D).**

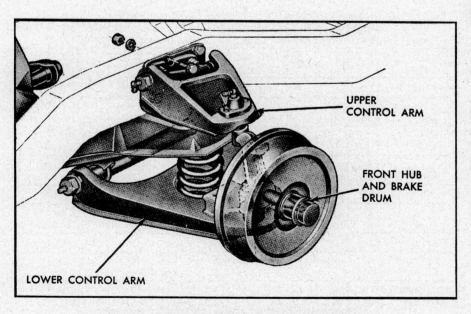

UPPER CONTROL ARM

FRONT HUB AND BRAKE DRUM

LOWER CONTROL ARM

**Fig. 2 Coil spring suspension (typical)**

4. Measure dimension "A" **Fig. 3.**
5. Using dimension "A," and Caster Specification Chart, **Figs. 5 through 7,** find the recommended caster angle.
6. The frame corrected angle should correspond to the recommended angle on the chart within plus or minus $1/4°$. Make necessary changes to bring caster angle within limits.

## Camber

1. Determine camber angle using suitable equipment.
2. Add or subtract shims from both front and rear bolts to adjust camber as required.

## Toe-In

Toe-in can be increased or decreased by changing the length of the tie rods. A threaded sleeve is provided for this purpose. When tie rods are mounted ahead of the steering knuckle, decrease the length to increase toe-in. When tie rods are mounted behind the steering knuckle, increase the length to increase toe-in.

## CABALLERO & EL CAMINO

Caster and camber adjustments are made by means of shims between the upper control arm inner support shaft and the support bracket attached to the frame. Shims may be added, subtracted or transferred to change the readings as follows.

## Caster

Transfer shims from front to rear or rear to front. The transfer of one shim to the front bolt from the rear bolt will decrease positive caster. One shim ($1/32$ inch) transferred from the rear bolt to the front bolt will change caster about $1/2°$.

## Camber

Change shims at both the front and rear of the shaft. Adding an equal number of shims at both front and rear of the support shaft will decrease positive camber. One shim ($1/32$ inch) at each location will move camber approximately $1/5°$.

## Toe-In

Toe-in can be increased or decreased by changing the length of the tie rods. A threaded sleeve is provided for this purpose. When tie rods are mounted ahead of the steering knuckle, decrease the length to increase toe-in. When tie rods are mounted behind the steering knuckle, increase the length to increase toe-in.

## COIL SPRINGS, REPLACE

1. Raise front of vehicle and place jack stands under frame, allowing control arms to hang free.
2. Disconnect shock absorber and stabilizer bar from lower control arm.
3. Install tool J-23028 or similar tool onto a suitable jack, **Fig. 8,** place jack under cross shaft so cross shaft seats in grooves of tool.
4. Place a safety chain through coil spring and lower control arm, then raise jack, relieving tension from coil spring. On models with air bag sus-

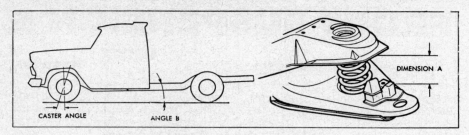

**Fig. 3   Caster-camber adjustment**

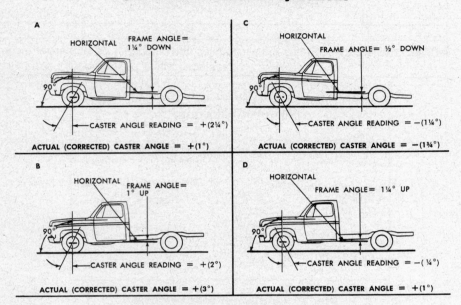

**Fig. 4   Determining actual (corrected) caster angle**

| MODELS (mm) | 2½'' 63.5 | 2¾'' 69.8 | 3'' 76.2 | 3¼'' 82.5 | 3½'' 89.0 | 3¾'' 95.2 | 4'' 102.0 | 4¼'' 107.9 | 4½'' 114.3 | 4¾'' 121.6 | 5'' 127.0 |
|---|---|---|---|---|---|---|---|---|---|---|---|
| C10 | 2.4° | 2.1° | 1.8° | 1.5° | 1.2° | 1.0° | 0.7° | 0.5° | 0.2° | 0.1° | 0.3° |
| C20, 30 | 1.5° | 1.2° | 0.9° | 0.6° | 0.3° | 0.1° | 0° | -0.1° | -0.7° | -1.0° | -1.2° |
| K10,20,30 | (8°)   (NO ADJUSTMENT PROVISION) | | | | | | | | | | |
| (mm) | 1½'' 38.0 | 1¾'' 44.4 | 2'' 51.0 | 2¼'' 57.1 | 2½'' 63.5 | 2¾'' 69.8 | 3'' 76.2 | 3¼'' 82.5 | 3½'' 89.0 | 3¾'' 95.2 | 4'' 102.0 | 4¼'' 107.9 |
| G10, 20 | 3.5° | 3.3° | 3.1° | 2.9° | 2.7° | | 2.4° | 2.2° | 2.1° | 1.9° | 1.8° | 1.6° |
| G30 | 2.8° | 2.5° | 2.2° | 1.9° | 1.6° | | 1.0° | .7° | .5° | .2° | 0° | -0.2° |
| (mm) | 2½'' 63.5 | 2¾'' 69.8 | 3'' 76.2 | 3¼'' 82.5 | 3½'' 89.6 | 3¾'' 95.2 | 4'' 102.0 | 4¼'' 107.9 | 4½'' 114.3 | 4¾'' 120.6 | 5'' 127.0 |
| P10 | 2.3° | 2.0° | 1.7° | 1.5° | 1.2° | 0.9° | 0.6° | 0.4° | 0.1° | -0.1° | -0.3° |
| (mm) | 2'' 51.0 | 2¼'' 57.1 | 2½'' 63.5 | 2¾'' 69.8 | 3'' 76.2 | 3¼'' 82.5 | 3½'' 89.0 | 3¾'' 95.2 | 4'' 102.0 | 4¼'' 107.9 | 4½'' 114.3 | 4¾'' 120.6 |
| *P20, 30 | 2.9° | 2.6° | 2.3° | 2.0° | 1.7° | 1.4° | 1.2° | 0.9° | 0.6° | 0.4° | 0.2° | 0.1° |
| * Add .3 degrees on vehicles equipped with Hydro-Boost Subtract .4 degrees on vehicles with dual rear wheels | | | | | | | | | | | |
| MOTOR HOME (32) (mm) | 2½'' 63.5 | 2¾'' 69.8 | 3'' 76.2 | 3¼'' 82.5 | 3½'' 89.0 | 3¾'' 95.2 | 4'' 102.0 | 4¼'' 107.9 | 4½'' 114.3 | 4¾'' 120.6 | 5'' 127.0 |
| | 5.5° | 5.3° | 5.0° | 4.7° | 4.4° | 4.1° | 3.8° | 3.6° | 3.3° | 3.1° | 2.9° |

**Fig. 5   Caster specification chart. 1980-81 exc. Caballero & El Camino**

| MODELS (mm) | 2½" 63.5 | 2¾" 69.8 | 3" 76.2 | 3¼" 82.5 | 3½" 89.0 | 3¾" 95.2 | 4" 102.0 | 4¼" 107.9 | 4½" 114.3 | 4¾" 121.6 | 5" 127.0 | |
|---|---|---|---|---|---|---|---|---|---|---|---|---|
| C10 | 3.6° | 3.4° | 3.1° | 2.8° | 2.6° | 2.4° | 2.0° | 1.8° | 1.5° | 1.2° | 1.0° | |
| C20, 30 | 1.5° | 1.2° | 0.9° | 0.6° | 0.3° | 0.1° | 0° | -0.1° | -0.7° | -1.0° | -1.2° | |
| K10,20,30 | (8°) (NO ADJUSTMENT PROVISION) | | | | | | | | | | | |
| (mm) | 1½" 38.0 | 1¾" 44.4 | 2" 51.0 | 2¼" 57.1 | 2½" 63.5 | 2¾" 69.8 | 3" 76.2 | 3¼" 82.5 | 3½" 89.0 | 3¾" 95.2 | 4" 102.0 | 4¼" 107.9 |
| G10, 20 | 3.5' | 3.3' | 3.1' | 2.9' | 2.7' | | 2.4' | 2.2' | 2.1' | 1.9' | 1.8' | 1.6' |
| G30 | 2.8' | 2.5' | 2.2' | 1.9' | 1.6' | | 1.0' | .7' | .5' | .2' | 0' | -0.2' |
| (mm) | 2½" 63.5 | 2¾" 69.8 | 3" 76.2 | 3¼" 82.5 | 3½" 89.6 | 3¾" 95.2 | 4" 102.0 | 4¼" 107.9 | 4½" 114.3 | 4¾" 120.6 | 5" 127.0 | |
| P10 | 2.3° | 2.0° | 1.7° | 1.5° | 1.2° | 0.9° | 0.6° | 0.4° | 0.1° | -0.1° | -0.3° | |
| (mm) | 2" 51.0 | 2¼" 57.1 | 2½" 63.5 | 2¾" 69.8 | 3" 76.2 | 3¼" 82.5 | 3½" 89.0 | 3¾" 95.2 | 4" 102.0 | 4¼" 107.9 | 4½" 114.3 | 4¾" 120.6 |
| *P20, 30 | 2.9° | 2.6° | 2.3° | 2.0° | 1.7° | 1.4° | 1.2° | 0.9° | 0.6° | 0.4° | 0.2° | 0.1° |
| * Add .3 degrees on vehicles equipped with Hydro - Boost. Subtract .4 degrees on vehicles with dual rear wheels | | | | | | | | | | | | |
| MOTOR HOME (32) (mm) | 2½" 63.5 | 2¾" 69.8 | 3" 76.2 | 3¼" 82.5 | 3½" 89.0 | 3¾" 95.2 | 4" 102.0 | 4¼" 107.9 | 4½" 114.3 | 4¾" 120.6 | 5" 127.0 | |
| | 5.5° | 5.3° | 5.0° | 4.7° | 4.4° | 4.1° | 3.8° | 3.6° | 3.3° | 3.1° | 2.9° | |

**Fig. 6   Caster specification chart. 1982–84 exc. Caballero & El Camino**

pension, remove valve core from air bag, and force air from bag. Reinstall valve cap to retain collapsed condition.

5. Remove cross shaft to crossmember U-bolts, lower jack slowly and remove spring.
6. Reverse procedure to install.

## BALL JOINT INSPECTION
### UPPER
#### Exc. Caballero & El Camino

The upper ball joint is spring loaded in its socket. This minimizes looseness at this point and compensates for normal wear. If upper stud has any perceptible lateral shake, or if it can be manually twisted in its socket, the upper ball joint should be replaced.

#### Caballero & El Camino

1. Ensure wheel bearings are properly adjusted.
2. Raise vehicle and position supporting devices under lower control arms as near as possible to lower ball joints, ensuring vehicle is stable and does not rock on supporting devices.
3. Position dial indicator against wheel rim, **Fig. 9**.
4. Grasp front wheel and push in on bottom of tire while pulling out at top and read gauge, then reverse push pull procedure.

| Dimension "A" (inch) | 2½ | 2¾ | 3 | 3¼ | 3½ | 3¾ | 4 | 4¼ | 4½ | 4¾ | 5 | 5¼ | 5½ | 5¾ | 6 |
|---|---|---|---|---|---|---|---|---|---|---|---|---|---|---|---|
| C, R10 (deg.) | 3.65 | 3.45 | 3.15 | 2.85 | 2.60 | 2.35 | 2.05 | 1.75 | 1.50 | 1.25 | 1.00 | .75 | .50 | .25 | 0 |
| C, R20, 30 (deg.) | 1.507 | 1.224 | .928 | .612 | .328 | .114 | -.011 | -.152 | -.746 | -.999 | -1.246 | -1.440 | -1.638 | -1.849 | — |
| K, V10, 20, 30 ① | — | — | — | — | — | — | — | — | — | — | — | — | — | — | — |

① —8° (no adjustment provision).

| Dimension "A" (inch) | 1½ | 1¾ | 2 | 2¼ | 2½ | 2¾ | 3 | 3¼ | 3½ | 3¾ | 4 | 4¼ | 4½ |
|---|---|---|---|---|---|---|---|---|---|---|---|---|---|
| G10, 20 (deg.) | 3.417 | 3.217 | 3.00 | 2.85 | 2.667 | 2.48 | 2.33 | 2.15 | 2.00 | 1.80 | 1.687 | 1.53 | 1.40 |
| G30 (deg.) | 3.094 | 2.967 | 2.667 | 2.367 | 2.100 | 1.833 | 1.500 | 1.233 | .967 | .700 | .450 | .200 | -.033 |

| Dimension "A" (inch) | 2 | 2¼ | 2½ | 2¾ | 3 | 3¼ | 3½ | 3¾ | 4 | 4¼ | 4½ | 4¾ | 5 | 5¼ | 5½ | 5¾ |
|---|---|---|---|---|---|---|---|---|---|---|---|---|---|---|---|---|
| P20, 30① (deg.) | 2.950 | 2.583 | 2.266 | 2.000 | 1.733 | 1.433 | 1.166 | .933 | .633 | .400 | .166 | -.100 | — | — | — | — |
| P20, 30② (deg.) | 2.516 | 2.183 | 1.866 | 1.600 | 1.316 | 1.050 | .800 | .516 | .266 | 0 | -.216 | -.433 | — | — | — | — |
| P30③ (deg.) | 3.233 | 2.933 | 2.600 | 2.350 | 2.066 | 1.766 | 1.500 | 1.233 | .983 | .700 | .450 | .200 | -.066 | -.316 | -.533 | -.733 |
| P30④ | — | — | — | — | — | — | — | — | — | — | — | — | — | — | — | — |

① —With single rear wheels, less hydro-boost.
② —With dual rear wheels, less hydro-boost.
③ —With hydro-boost.
④ —With I-beam front suspension, 5° (no provision for adjustment).

| Dimension "A" (inch) | 2½ | 2¾ | 3 | 3¼ | 3½ | 3¾ | 4 | 4¼ | 4½ | 4¾ | 5 | 5¼ | 5½ | 5¾ | 6 |
|---|---|---|---|---|---|---|---|---|---|---|---|---|---|---|---|
| Motor Home | 5.533 | 5.283 | 5.000 | 4.716 | 4.400 | 4.133 | 3.833 | 3.566 | 3.333 | 3.100 | 2.866 | 2.633 | 2.400 | 2.200 | 2.000 |

**Fig. 7   Caster specification chart. 1985–89 exc. Caballero & El Camino**

**Fig. 8  Coil spring removal (typical)**

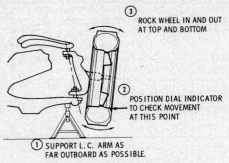

③ ROCK WHEEL IN AND OUT AT TOP AND BOTTOM

② POSITION DIAL INDICATOR TO CHECK MOVEMENT AT THIS POINT

① SUPPORT L. C. ARM AS FAR OUTBOARD AS POSSIBLE.

**Fig. 9  Checking upper ball joint. Caballero & El Camino**

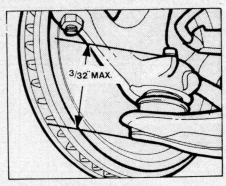

3/32" MAX.

**Fig. 10  Checking lower ball joint for wear**

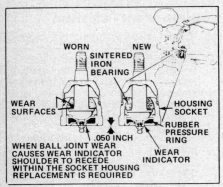

WORN    NEW

SINTERED IRON BEARING

WEAR SURFACES

HOUSING SOCKET

RUBBER PRESSURE RING

.050 INCH

WEAR INDICATOR

WHEN BALL JOINT WEAR CAUSES WEAR INDICATOR SHOULDER TO RECEDE WITHIN THE SOCKET HOUSING REPLACEMENT IS REQUIRED

**Fig. 11  Lower ball joint wear indicator**

5. If dial indicator reading exceeds .125 inch or if ball stud has been disconnected from knuckle assembly and any looseness is detected or the stud can be manually twisted in its socket, replace ball joint.

## LOWER

Lower ball joints are a loose fit when not connected to the steering knuckle. Wear may be checked without disassembling the ball stud as follows:
1. Support weight of control arms at wheel hub and drum.
2. Measure distance between tip of ball stud and tip of grease fitting below ball joint, **Fig. 10.**
3. Move support to control arm to allow wheel hub and drum to hang free. Measure distance as in Step 2. If difference in measurements exceeds 1/16 inch for Caballero and El Camino and 3/32 inch for all other models, ball joint is worn and should be replaced. Caballero and El Camino models have lower ball joints that incorporate wear indicators. Refer to **Fig. 11** to check for wear.

## BALL JOINT, REPLACE
### Upper

1. Raise vehicle, then support lower control arm with suitable jack.
2. Remove cotter pin from upper ball stud, then loosen stud nut approximately two turns.

3. Separate ball joint from steering knuckle using suitable tool, then remove stud nut.
4. Center punch rivet heads, then drill out rivets and remove ball joint from control arm.
5. Reverse procedure to install. Torque stud nut to 50 ft. lbs. on 1980-89 10/1500 Series and 1985-89 G20/2500 Series, 65 ft. lbs. on 1980-84 Caballero and El Camino, 52 ft. lbs. on 1985-87 Caballero and El Camino, 60 ft. lbs. on 1988 Caballero and El Camino, or 90 ft. lbs. on all other models. If cotter pin does not align with stud nut, tighten nut an additional amount until cotter pin can be installed. Never loosen stud nut when installing cotter pin.

### Lower

1. Raise and support front of vehicle.
2. Support lower control arm with a suitable jack, then remove wheel and tire.
3. Remove cotter pin from lower ball stud, then loosen stud nut approximately two turns.
4. Separate ball joint from steering knuckle using suitable tool, then remove stud nut.
5. Lift knuckle assembly from ball stud, then position knuckle aside to allow clearance for joint removal.
6. Press ball joint from control arm using suitable tool, **Fig. 12.**
7. Press new joint into control arm by reversing removal tool.
8. Install ball joint to steering knuckle.
9. Install stud nut and torque to 90 ft. lbs. Install cotter pin. **If cotter pin does not align with stud nut, tighten nut an additional amount until cotter pin can be installed. Never loosen stud nut when installing cotter pin.**
10. Install wheel and tire assembly, then lower vehicle.

## WHEEL BEARINGS, ADJUST

1. While rotating wheel forward, torque spindle nut to 12 ft. lbs.
2. Back off nut until "just loose" then hand tighten nut and back it off again until either hole in spindle lines up with hole in nut. **Do not back off nut more than 1/2 flat.**
3. Install new cotter pin. With wheel bearing properly adjusted, there will be .001-.005 inch endplay.

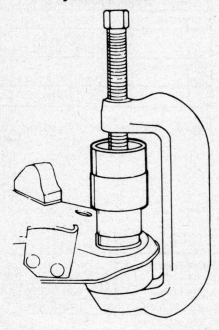

**Fig. 12  Pressing lower ball joint from control arm**

## WHEEL BEARINGS, REPLACE

1. Raise and support vehicle, then remove wheel and tire assembly.
2. Remove hub cap and cotter pin.
3. Remove brake caliper. Do not allow caliper to hang from brake hose.
4. Remove retaining nut, then the hub and disc assembly.
5. Remove outer wheel bearing.
6. To remove inner bearing, pry out grease seal, then remove seal and inner bearing.
7. Reverse procedure to install, then adjust wheel bearings as previously described.

## SHOCK ABSORBER, REPLACE

1. Raise and support vehicle.
2. Remove wheel and tire assembly.
3. Remove upper retaining nuts or bolts.
4. Remove lower retaining bolts, then the shock absorber.
5. Reverse procedure to install.

## LEAF SPRING SUSPENSION

For information on leaf spring front suspensions used on four wheel drive vehicles, refer to "Front Wheel Drive Section."

A leaf spring type front suspension is available on P Series vehicles. The suspension is centered around a solid I-beam axle and includes leaf springs, shock absorbers and a stabilizer bar.

### LEAF SPRINGS, REPLACE

1. Raise and support front of vehicle. Support axle assembly with a separate jack to relieve load from springs.
2. Remove wheel and tire assembly.
3. Remove lower shock absorber attaching bolt and nut.
4. Remove stabilizer link-to-bar attaching nut, then separate the link from bar using a suitable tool.
5. Remove stabilizer link, nut and retainer from axle, then pull link away from axle. **Use care to avoid losing inner insulator and retainer.**
6. Remove leaf spring retaining nuts, washers, U-bolts and spacers, then separate leaf spring from axle.
7. Remove leaf spring-to-rear shackle attaching nut and bolt, then separate spring from the shackle.
8. Remove leaf spring-to-front hanger attaching nut and bolt, then separate spring from the hanger and remove assembly from vehicle.
9. Reverse procedure to install, noting the following:
   a. Torque leaf spring-to-frame attaching nut to 92 ft. lbs.
   b. Torque leaf spring-to-axle attaching nuts in a diagonal sequence first to 18 ft. lbs. then to 80 ft. lbs.

c. Tighten stabilizer link-to-axle attaching nut until distance between each retainer is .82 inch.
d. Torque stabilizer bar-to-link attaching nut to 50 ft. lbs.
e. Torque lower shock absorber attaching nut to 37 ft. lbs.

## SHOCK ABSORBER, REPLACE

1. Raise and support front of vehicle.
2. Remove wheel and tire assembly.
3. Remove lower shock absorber attaching bolt and nut.
4. Unfasten shock absorber from upper attachment at frame and remove from vehicle.
5. Reverse procedure to install. On 1980-87 models, torque upper nut to 136 ft. lbs. and lower nut to 37 ft. lbs. On 1988-89 models, torque upper nut to 80 ft. lbs. and lower nut to 33 ft. lbs. On models with four wheel drive front suspension, torque upper nut to 65 ft. lbs. and lower nut to 65 ft. lbs. On models with quad shock set-up, torque upper nut to 65 ft. lbs. and lower nut to 89 ft. lbs.

## WHEEL BEARINGS, ADJUST

1. Raise front of vehicle and support under lower control arms.
2. Remove retainer and cotter pin, then torque spindle nut to 12 ft. lbs. while rotating wheel forward.
3. Back off spindle nut one flat, then install cotter pin. **If cotter pin holes do not align, back off nut no more than an additional 1/2 flat more as necessary.**
4. Ensure hub and rotor assembly endplay measures .0005-.0080 inch, then install retainer and lower vehicle.

## MANUAL STEERING GEAR
### REPLACE

1. Place front wheels in straight ahead position.
2. Remove flexible coupling to steering shaft bolts, or the lower universal joint pinch bolts, as equipped, and mark position of universal yoke to worm shaft.
3. Mark position of pitman arm to pitman shaft and remove pitman shaft nut or pinch bolt, then pitman arm from shaft with a puller.
4. Unfasten steering gear and remove.
5. If equipped, remove flexible coupling pinch bolt, then the flexible coupling from steering gear worm shaft.
6. Reverse procedure to install.

## POWER STEERING GEAR
### REPLACE

To remove gear assembly, disconnect pressure and return hoses from gear housing and cap both hoses and steering gear outlets to prevent foreign material from entering system, then follow procedure as outlined under "Manual Steering Gear, Replace."

## POWER STEERING PUMP
### REPLACE

1. Disconnect hoses at power steering pump, then plug pump ports and hoses to prevent dirt entry.
2. Loosen pump adjusting bolt and remove pump drive belt.
3. Remove pump to support bracket retaining bolts, then the pump.
4. Reverse procedure to install.

# FRONT WHEEL DRIVE

## INDEX

## DESCRIPTION

The front axles on these vehicles, **Figs. 1 and 2,** are hypoid gear units equipped with steering knuckles retained by either ball joints (K10-20/1500-2500) or king pins (K30/3500). The axle shafts drive the front wheels through yoke and trunnion type universal joints.

## AXLE HOUSING
### REPLACE

1. Disconnect propeller shaft from differential.
2. Raise front of vehicle, then support behind front springs.
3. Disconnect drag link or connecting rod from steering arm.

4. Remove brake calipers. Do not allow calipers to hang from brake hose.
5. Disconnect shock absorbers from spring clamp plate or axle bracket.
6. Disconnect axle vent tube clip from differential housing, and front stabilizer bar if equipped.
7. Remove U-bolts, then separate leaf springs from axle housing.
8. Roll axle housing assembly out from

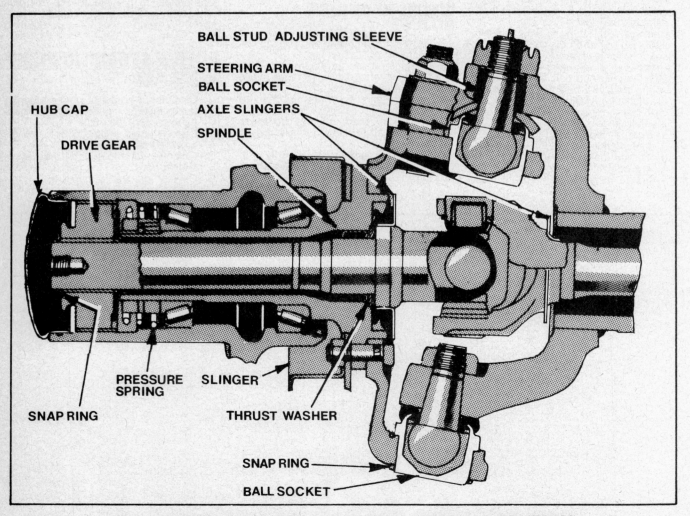

**Fig. 1   Sectional view of front driving axle. K10/K1500, K20/K2500**

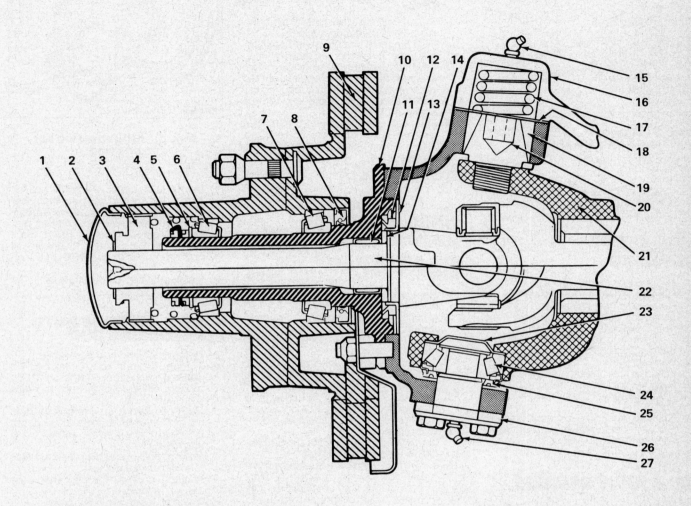

| | | |
|---|---|---|
| 1. HUB CAP | 11. SPINDLE BEARING | 24. LOWER BEARING |
| 2. SNAP RING | 12. SEAL | 25. SEAL |
| 3. HUB DRIVE GEAR | 13. DEFLECTOR | 26. BEARING CAP |
| 4. ADJUSTING NUT ASM | 14. SPACER | 27. LUBE FITTING |
|    LOCK NUT | 15. LUBE FITTING | |
|    LOCK TANG | 16. UPPER BEARING CAP | |
|    ADJUSTING NUT | 17. PRESSURE SPRING | |
| 5. WASHER | 18. GASKET | |
| 6. OUTER WHEEL BEARING | 19. BUSHING, KING-PIN | |
| 7. INNER WHEEL BEARING | 20. KING-PIN | |
| 8. SEAL | 21. YOKE | |
| 9. HUB-AND-DISC ASM | 22. OUTER AXLE SHAFT | |
| 10. SPINDLE | 23. GREASE RETAINER | |

**Fig. 2 Sectional view of front driving axle. K30/K3500 series**

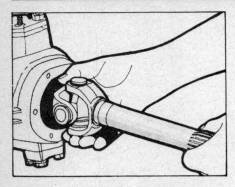

**Fig. 3 Removing & installing axle shaft & U-joint**

1. Raise vehicle and support with jack stands placed just inside front springs.
2. Disconnect drag link or connecting rod, then the tie rod to permit independent movement of each steering knuckle.
3. Attach a spring scale to tie rod mounting hole of steering knuckle.
4. With wheel in straight ahead position, measure the force required to keep knuckle assembly turning after initial breakaway. The force required should not exceed 25 lbs. If force required exceeds specifications, proceed to next step.
5. Remove upper ball stud nut, then loosen adjusting sleeve as required. Retighten ball stud nut, then recheck turning effort.

**Fig. 4 Adjusting wheel bearing**

### AXLE SHAFT
### REPLACE

underneath vehicle.
9. Reverse procedure to install.

1. Raise and support vehicle.
2. Remove wheel and tire assembly.
3. Remove brake caliper and position aside. Do not allow caliper to hang from brake hose.
4. Remove hub lock mechanism, then the gears and snap rings.
5. Remove rotor.
6. Remove inner bearing and seal.
7. Remove spindle and backing plate.
8. Withdraw axle shaft from housing, **Fig. 3.**
9. Reverse procedure to install, then adjust wheel bearings as outlined under "Wheel Bearings, Adjust."

### AXLE JOINT REPAIRS

1. Remove lock rings from trunnion bearings.
2. Support shaft yoke in a suitable vise.
3. With a brass drift and a hammer, tap on one end of trunnion bearing to drive the opposite bearing from yoke. Then, support other side of yoke and drive out remaining bearing.
4. Remove trunnion. Inspect and replace bearings if necessary, then lubricate with wheel bearing grease.
5. Replace trunnion and press bearings into yoke and over trunnion hubs far enough to install lock rings.
6. Gently tap yoke to seat bearings against lock rings.

### BALL JOINT
### ADJUSTMENT

Ball joint adjustment is generally required only when excessive play exists in steering, tires wear irregularly, or tie rods continually loosen. If any of the above mentioned complaints are evident, proceed as follows:

### WHEEL BEARINGS
### ADJUST
### EXC. HUBS W/MONROE AUTO. TYPE LOCKING HUB

1. Remove dust cap or locking hub, lockwasher and outer locknut.
2. Using suitable spanner wrench, torque inner adjusting nut to 50 ft. lbs. while rotating hub. Back off adjusting nut and torque to 50 ft. lbs. on 1985-89 models with manual hubs, or 35 ft. lbs. on all other models, while rotating hub, **Fig. 4.**
3. Back off adjusting nut just enough to free bearing on 1986-89 models with manual hubs, or 3/8 of a turn on all other models.
4. On 1980-84 K10-20/1500-2500 vehicles, proceed as follows:
   a. On 1980 models, assemble adjusting nut lock by aligning nearest hole in lock with adjusting nut pin. Install outer locknut and torque to 80 ft. lbs.
   b. On 1981-84 models, assemble drag sleeve retainer washer over the axle shaft and against bearing adjusting nut. The tang on the inside diameter of this washer is assembled in the keyway of the spindle. Assemble and tighten outer locknut to 160-205 ft. lbs.
5. On 1980-84 K30/3500 vehicles, proceed as follows:
   a. On 1980-81 models, assemble lockwasher and locknut, then torque locknut to 65 ft. lbs. Bend one ear of lockwasher at least 30° over inner adjusting nut, and the other ear at least 60° over outer locknut.
   b. On 1982-84 models, assemble drag sleeve retainer washer over axle shaft and against bearing adjusting nut. The tang on the inside diameter of this washer is assembled in the keyway of the spindle. Assemble and tighten outer locknut to 160-205 ft. lbs.
6. On 1985-88 models, assemble drag sleeve retainer washer. Ensure tang

on inside diameter of washer passes onto slot in spindle and hole in washer aligns with locknut pin. **Move adjustment nut as necessary to align pin, then torque locknut to 160 ft. lbs.**
7. On all vehicles, check to ensure all hub assemblies have .001-.010 inch endplay.
8. Install dust cap or locking hub.

### HUBS W/MONROE AUTO. TYPE LOCKING HUB

1. Remove locking hub assembly.
2. Torque locknut to 70 ft. lbs. on 1980-87 models, or 50 ft. lbs. on 1988 models, while rotating hub and disc assembly.
3. Back off locknut, then torque to 25 ft. lbs. on 1980-87 models, or 35 ft. lbs. on 1988 models, while rotating hub and disc.
4. Back off locknut to align nearest slot, then install locknut key.
5. Measure endplay. Endplay should be .001-.010 inch.
6. Reinstall locking hub assembly.

### STEERING KNUCKLE
### REPLACE
### EXC. K30/3500 & V30/3500

1. Remove hub and spindle.
2. Disconnect tie rod from steering arm. **If steering arm is removed from knuckle, discard the self-locking nuts and replace with new ones during installation. Tighten nuts to 90 ft. lbs.**
3. Remove cotter pin from upper ball joint stud nut, and remove retaining nuts from both ball joints.
4. Separate stud from yoke using suitable ball joint fork at lower joint and repeat at upper joint is required. **Do not remove upper ball joint adjusting sleeve from yoke unless ball joint is being replaced. If it is necessary to loosen the sleeve to remove the knuckle, only loosen the**

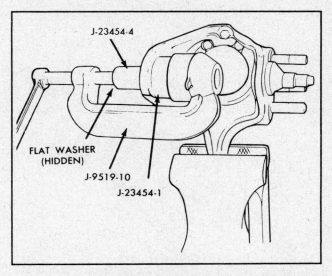

**Fig. 5  Pressing lower ball joint from steering knuckle**

sleeve two threads. The non-hardened threads in the yoke can be easily damaged by the adjusting sleeve.
5. Reverse procedure to install.
6. Torque lower ball joint to 70 ft. lbs., adjusting sleeve to 50 ft. lbs., and upper ball joint to 100 ft. lbs. Tighten tie rod nut to 45 ft. lbs.

## K30/3500 & V30/3500

1. Remove hub and spindle.
2. Remove upper king pin cap by alternately loosening nuts to unload the compression spring. Withdraw the spring and gasket.
3. Remove the lower bearing cap and king pin.
4. Remove upper king pin tapered bushing and knuckle from yoke. Remove felt king pin seal.
5. Remove upper king pin from yoke using a large breaker bar.
6. Drive lower king pin bearing cup, cone, grease retainer, and seal through bottom of knuckle using suitable tool.
7. Reverse procedure to install.
8. Torque upper king pin to 500-600 ft. lbs., and upper and lower bearing cap nuts to 70-90 ft. lbs.

## BALL JOINT
## REPLACE

1. Remove steering knuckle as previously described.
2. Remove lower ball joint snap ring.

The lower ball joint must be removed before servicing the upper joint.
3. Using a suitable C-clamp and service tools as shown, **Fig. 5,** press lower ball joint from steering knuckle.
4. Press upper joint from steering knuckle in the same manner as stated in Step 3.
5. Reverse procedure to install.

## KING PIN
## REPLACE

Follow the procedure under "Steering Knuckle, Replace" for king pin service.

## HUB & BEARING
## REPLACE

1. Raise and support vehicle.
2. Remove dust cap, if equipped.
3. Remove locking hub as outlined under "Locking Hub Service."
4. Remove disc brake caliper and position aside. Do not allow caliper to hang from brake hose.
5. Remove wheel bearing outer locknut, lock ring and wheel bearing inner adjusting nut.
6. Remove hub and disc assembly, and outer wheel bearing.
7. Remove oil seal, inner wheel bearing and inner and outer bearing cups using a suitable drift.

8. Reverse procedure to install. Adjust wheel bearings as outlined under "Wheel Bearings, Adjust" procedure.

## LOCKING HUB SERVICE
## WARNER AUTO. LOCKING HUB

### Description

The Automatic Locking Hub, shown in **Fig. 6,** engages or disengages to lock the front axle shaft to the hub of the front wheel. Engagement occurs whenever the vehicle is operated in 4WD. Disengagement occurs whenever 2WD has been selected and the vehicle is moving rearward. Disengagement will not occur when the vehicle is moved rearward if 4WD is selected and the hub has already been engaged.

Before disassembling a unit for a complaint of abnormal noise, note the following:
1. To obtain all-wheel drive, the transfer case lever must be placed in 4L or 4H, at which time the hub locks will automatically engage.
2. To unlock the hubs, shift the transfer case lever to 2H, then slowly reverse the vehicle direction approximately 10 feet.
3. An incomplete shift from 2WD to 4WD, or disengagement of only one hub lock may cause an abnormal sound from the front axle. Shift to 4WD to stop the noise, then unlock the hubs as previously stated.

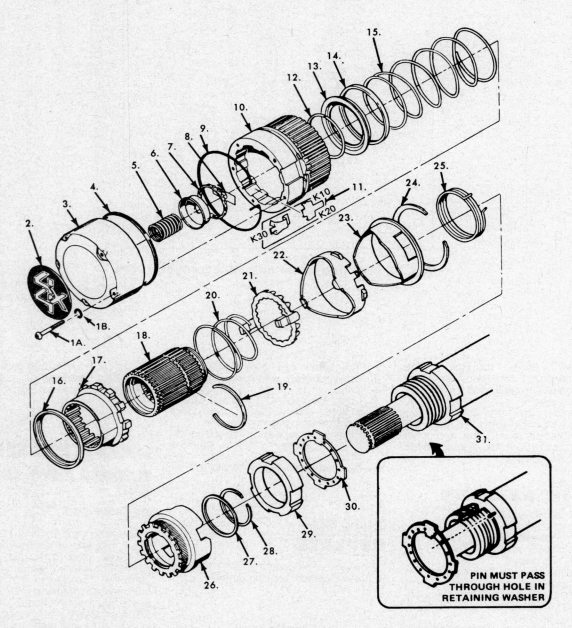

**K10**
**K20**
**K30**

**PIN MUST PASS THROUGH HOLE IN RETAINING WASHER**

1A. Machine Screw
1B. O-Ring Seal
2. Cover Plate
3. Cover
4. Sealing Ring
5. Bearing Race Spring
6. Bearing Inner Race
7. Bearing
8. Bearing Retainer Clip
9. Wire Retaining Ring
10. Outer Clutch Housing

11. (K10-20) Seal Bridge-Retainer
    (K30) Assembly Aid-Retainer
12. Retaining Ring
13. Spring Support Washer
14. Spring Retainer
15. Return Spring
16. Spring Retainer
17. Clutch Gear
18. Hub Sleeve
19. "C" Type Retaining Ring
20. Conical Spring

21. Cam Follower
22. Outer Cage
23. Inner Cage
24. Snap Ring
25. Brake Band
26. Drag Sleeve and Detent
27. Small Spacer
28. Retaining Ring
29. Lock Nut
30. Drag Sleeve Retainer Washer
31. Adjusting Nut, Wheel Bearing

**Fig. 6   Exploded view of Warner automatic locking hub**

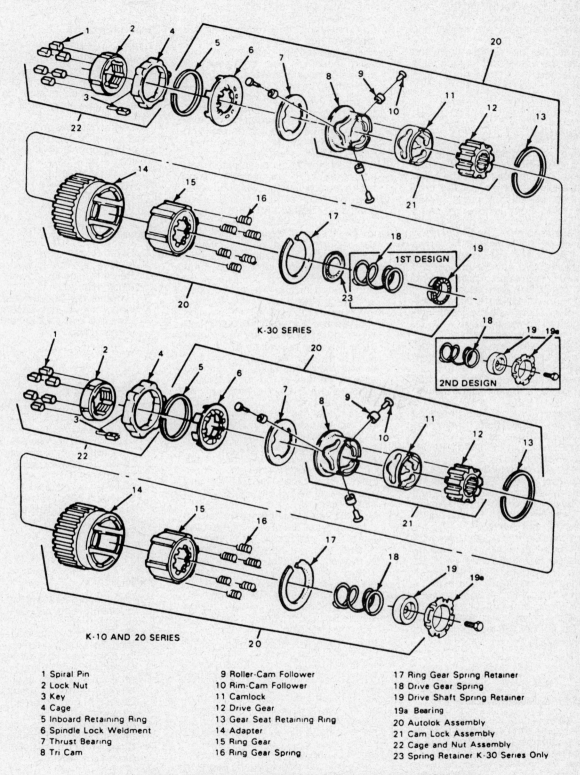

**Fig. 7   Exploded view of Monroe automatic locking hub**

| | | |
|---|---|---|
| 1 Spiral Pin | 9 Roller-Cam Follower | 17 Ring Gear Spring Retainer |
| 2 Lock Nut | 10 Rim-Cam Follower | 18 Drive Gear Spring |
| 3 Key | 11 Camlock | 19 Drive Shaft Spring Retainer |
| 4 Cage | 12 Drive Gear | 19a Bearing |
| 5 Inboard Retaining Ring | 13 Gear Seat Retaining Ring | 20 Autolok Assembly |
| 6 Spindle Lock Weldment | 14 Adapter | 21 Cam Lock Assembly |
| 7 Thrust Bearing | 15 Ring Gear | 22 Cage and Nut Assembly |
| 8 Tri Cam | 16 Ring Gear Spring | 23 Spring Retainer K-30 Series Only |

## Removal

1. Remove 5 screws retaining the cover to outer clutch housing.
2. Remove cover, seal, seal bridge and bearing components.
3. Compress the wire retaining ring and remove the remaining components from the hub.

## Disassembly

1. Remove snap ring from groove in hub sleeve, then turn clutch gear until it falls into engagement with the outer clutch housing. Lift and tilt the drag sleeve to unlock the tangs of the brake band from window of inner cage, then remove the drag sleeve and brake assembly. **The brake band must never be removed from the drag sleeve. The spring tension of the brake band can be changed if the coils are overexpanded and could affect hub operation.**
2. Remove snap ring from groove in outer clutch housing, then pry plastic outer cage free from inner cage while inner cage is being removed.
3. Pry plastic outer cage tabs free from groove in outer clutch housing, then remove outer cage.
4. Remove clutch sleeve and attached components from outer clutch housing.
5. Compress return spring and hold the spring with clamps, then position the assembly in a vise so that the vise holds both ends of the clutch sleeve. Remove retaining spring.
6. Remove clamps holding the return spring, then slowly open the vise to permit the release of the return spring in a safe manner. Remove retainer seat, spring and spring support washers from the hub sleeve.
7. Remove C-ring from clutch sleeve. It is necessary to position sleeve assembly so that the C-ring ends are aligned with legs of cam follower, allowing removal between the legs.
8. Remove conical spring from between cam follower and clutch gear, then separate cam follower from clutch gear. Do not pry the legs of the cam follower apart.

## Assembly & Installation

1. Install tangs of cam follower over flats of clutch gear, then compress conical spring and position with large diameter located against clutch gear.
2. Position clutch gear assembly over splines of hub sleeve. The teeth of the cam follower should be located at the end of the hub sleeve with no splines, and the clutch gear and spring should slide freely over splines of hub sleeve.
3. Install C-ring into groove of hub sleeve, then install a spring retainer over each end of return spring.

4. Position one end of return spring with retainer against shoulder of clutch gear, then place support washer on end of the return spring. Compress return spring and install retainer ring into groove of hub sleeve.
5. Place assembled components into outer housing. The cam follower should be positioned with legs facing outward.
6. Install 3 of the cover screws into 3 holes of the outer clutch housing. These screws will support the component to permit the clutch hub to drop down so that the tangs of the brake band can be assembled.
7. Carefully install the plastic outer cage into outer clutch housing with ramps facing toward cam follower. The small external tabs of the plastic cage should be located in wide groove of outer clutch housing.
8. Install steel inner cage into the outer cage, aligning tab of outer cage with window of the inner cage, then install retaining ring into groove of outer clutch housing above outer cage.
9. The brake band and drag are serviced as a complete assembly. Install one of the 2 tangs of the brake band on each side of the lug of the outer cage, located in the window of the steel inner cage. It will be necessary to tilt these parts to engage the tangs in this position as the drag sleeve is positioned against the face of the cam follower.
10. Remove the 3 screws and rest the end of the hub sleeve on a suitable support, then install washer and snap ring above drag sleeve. **The following steps may be completed as the hub is installed into vehicle.**
11. Install wire retaining ring into groove of end of clutch housing without spline. The tangs of retainer ring should point away from splined end of clutch housing.
12. Hold the tangs together and install the 2 bent down tabs of seal bridge over tangs. The seal bridge holds the wire retainer ring in a clamped position in groove of outer clutch housing. Install O-ring into groove of outer clutch housing and over the seal bridge.
13. Lubricate and install the bearing over the inner race. The steel ball bearing should be visible when the bearing is properly installed.
14. Install bearing retainer clip into hole in outer race, then install bearing and retainer assembly in end of hub sleeve. Install seal ring over outer clutch housing.
15. Install bearing race spring into bore of cover, then install cover and spring assembly. Align holes in cover to holes in outer clutch housing and install 5 screws.
16. Install O-ring over seal bridge to prevent it from dislodging during handling prior to the hub bearing being installed into the vehicle.
17. The hub and attached parts should turn freely after installation. The 5 cover screws must be loosened to install the hub into the vehicle. After installation, torque the cover screws to 40-50 inch lbs.

## MONROE AUTO. LOCKING HUB

### Description

This automatic locking hub, **Fig. 7**, when placed in four wheel drive, directs power to the front wheels. The front axle turns the axle shaft, activating the tri-cam mechanism, which then moves the drive gear outward into engagement with the ring gear.

When two wheel drive is selected, disengagement is accomplished by the reverse movement of the wheels, which causes the drive gear and tri-cam to rotate to the disengaged position, moving the drive gear out of mesh with the ring gear.

### Removal

1. Remove tire and wheel assembly, hubcap and hub lock.
2. Remove spring retainer, then the loose spring.
3. Carefully pull hub lock assembly from wheel. If hub lock assembly will not slide out freely, rotate wheel to facilitate removal.

### Disassembly

1. Position hub lock assembly with plastic bearing side facing downward.
2. Pry inboard spring from assembly, then remove spindle lock, thrust bearing and tri-cam assembly.
3. Clean adapter housing assembly. If any part of this assembly is worn, replace as necessary.
4. Slide ring gear from adapter housing, then remove the six ring gear springs.
5. Remove ring gear spring retainer.

### Assembly

1. Install ring gear spring retainer.
2. Position the six ring gear springs into adapter housing.
3. Grease outside surface of ring gear, then install into adapter housing. Ensure gear teeth are closest to springs.
4. Insert and install ring gear retaining ring. Ensure ring gear springs are properly seated in adapter housing.
5. Grease tri-cam assembly, then install into adapter housing.
6. Install thrust bearing, spindle lock and inboard snap ring. Rotate spindle lock tangs in both directions to check for free movement.

### Installation

1. Install hub lock by first sliding hub onto axle shaft spline, then guide hub into wheel hub spline. When hub lock

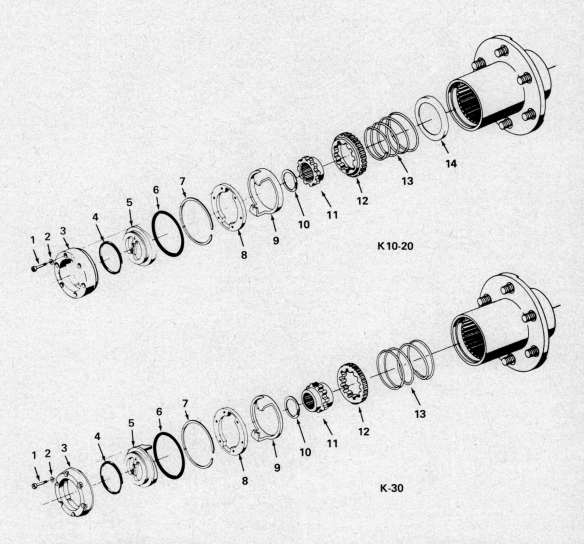

K 10-20

K-30

1.  RETAINING PLATE BOLTS
2.  WASHER
3.  HUB RING RETAINING KNOB
4.  ACTUATOR KNOB "O" RING
5.  ACTUATOR KNOB
6.  "O" RING
7.  INTERNAL SNAP RING

8.  OUTER CLUTCH RETAINING RING
9.  ACTUATING CAM BODY
10. AXLE SHAFT SNAP RING
11. AXLE SHAFT SLEEVE AND RING
12. INNER CLUTCH RING
13. PRESSURE SPRING
14. SPRING RETAINER PLATE

**Fig. 8   Exploded view of Spicer manual locking hub**

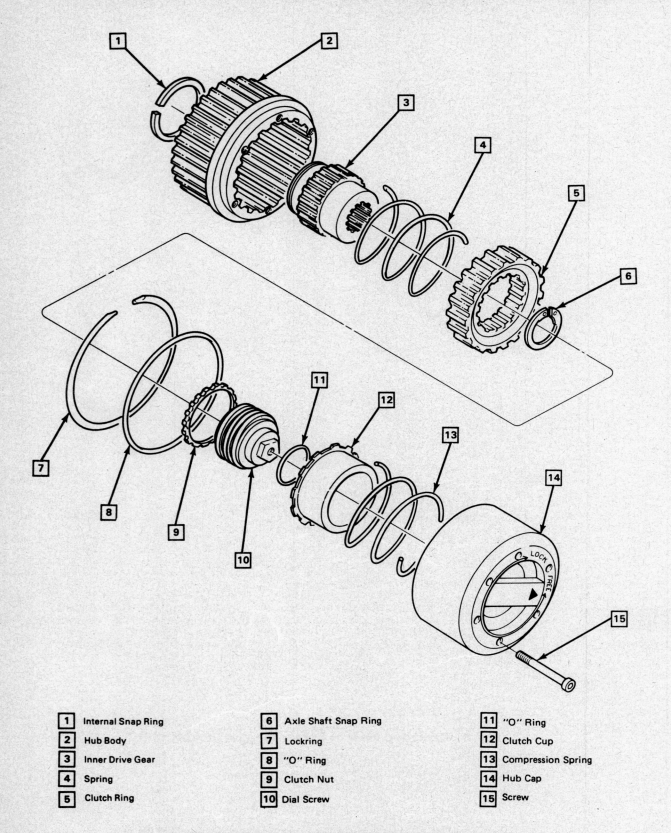

| 1 | Internal Snap Ring | 6 | Axle Shaft Snap Ring | 11 | "O" Ring |
|---|---|---|---|---|---|
| 2 | Hub Body | 7 | Lockring | 12 | Clutch Cup |
| 3 | Inner Drive Gear | 8 | "O" Ring | 13 | Compression Spring |
| 4 | Spring | 9 | Clutch Nut | 14 | Hub Cap |
| 5 | Clutch Ring | 10 | Dial Screw | 15 | Screw |

**Fig. 9  Exploded view of Warner manual locking hub**

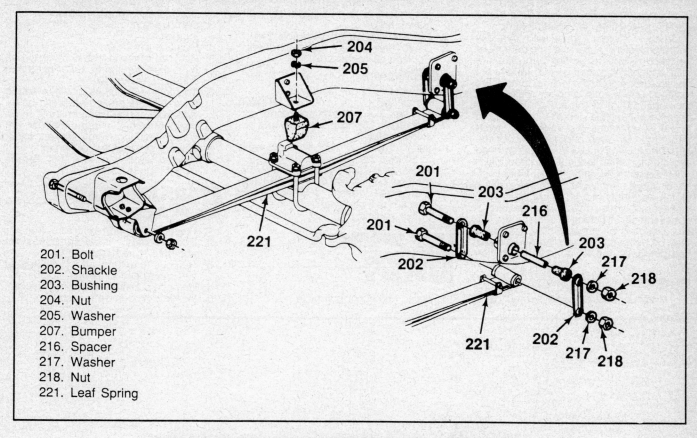

201. Bolt
202. Shackle
203. Bushing
204. Nut
205. Washer
207. Bumper
216. Spacer
217. Washer
218. Nut
221. Leaf Spring

**Fig. 10 Exploded view of leaf springs and bushings**

bottoms out, rotate entire wheel while pressing inward on hub until hub lock tangs engage wheel bearing locknut. Allow hub lock to seat itself. **Hub lock should not protrude more than 3/8 inch from face of wheel hub.**

2. Install spring, then unlock hub lock by rotating wheel hub while applying force to drive gear spring.
3. Install spring retainer and spring.
4. Install hub cap.

## SPICER MANUAL LOCKING HUB

### Description

As shown in **Fig. 8,** the splines on the inside diameter of the axle shaft sleeve and ring assembly mesh with the axle shaft splines. The assembly is retained on the axle shaft with a snap ring. The splines on the outside diameter of the inner clutch ring assembly mesh with the wheel hub splines. Therefore, when the actuator knob is turned towards the "L" position, the actuating cam body is forced outward towards the hub end, allowing the inner clutch to be forced under spring tension towards the axle shaft sleeve and ring assembly until the inner clutch assembly teeth are engaged in the axle shaft sleeve and ring assembly teeth, locking the axle and hub.

### Operation

When the transfer case is shifted into

the position for driving the front axle, turn the actuating knob so that it is aligned with the letter L. If the clutch teeth do not engage with the knob turned to this position, the clutch teeth are butted and a slight movement of the wheel in either direction will complete the lock. The front axle will now drive the wheel.

When the transfer case is to be shifted into the position for driving the rear axle only, turn the actuating knob so that it is aligned with the letter F. This will disengage the clutch teeth and thus unlock the wheel hub from the axle shaft. The wheel will now turn free on the axle. **Be certain that the transfer case is shifted into two wheel drive position before disengaging the Hub-Lok.**

### Removal

1. Position actuator knob in "Lock," then raise and support vehicle. Rotate tire to ensure engagement of hub lock.
2. Remove retaining plate attaching bolts, then the retaining plate, actuating knob and O-rings.
3. Remove internal snap ring, outer clutch retaining ring, actuating cam body, outer clutch gear and pressure spring, **Fig. 8.**
4. Remove axle shaft snap ring, then the inner clutch ring.
5. Remove spring retainer plate, if equipped.

### Installation

1. Install spring retainer plate, if equipped, over spindle nuts and against wheel bearing outer cup. Ensure flanged side of plate faces toward wheel bearing.
2. Install inner clutch ring onto axle shaft, press ring inward, then install snap ring.
3. Install pressure spring with larger side facing inward.
4. Install outer clutch gear, actuating cam body, outer clutch retaining ring and the internal snap ring. Ensure actuating cams face outward.
5. Install O-ring, actuating knob, actuating knob O-ring and the retaining plate.
6. Install retaining plate attaching bolts and torque to 38 inch lbs.

## WARNER MANUAL LOCKING HUB

### Description

Turning the locking hub clutch control to the "L" or "4" position connects the wheel hubs to the axle shafts. Therefore, when the transfer case is driving the front axle and the locking hubs are in the "L" or "4" position, the wheels are driven by the axle shafts. When the transfer case is not driving the front axle, the locking hub clutch controls are turned to the "F" or "2" position to disconnect the wheel hubs from the axle shafts. The wheels now rotate freely, but the axle shafts remain stationary.

On any vehicle equipped with manually operated locking hubs, extreme care must be taken to ensure locking hub dials are fully engaged or disengaged, to prevent possible damage to the locking hubs. If the locking hubs are not properly maintained, full engagement of the control dials may become impossible due to excessive dirt and dust. Any time the vehicle is driven through water deep enough to cover the hubs, the locking hubs should be removed and cleaned, then lubricated thoroughly.

These hubs are serviced as an assembly or subassembly only (hub body or hub clutch assembly only). Do not attempt to disassemble these units. If an entire hub or subassembly is defective, replace the entire assembly or subassembly. The hubs may be removed for cleaning and inspection purposes and for periodic lubrication only.

### Removal

1. Remove socket head screws, axle hub retaining ring and axle shaft retaining ring.
2. Remove hub clutch assembly, **Fig. 9.**
3. Clean and inspect all components. Replace as necessary.

### Installation

1. Lubricate all hub components.
2. Install hub clutch, axle hub retaining ring and axle shaft retaining ring.
3. Install new O-ring in hub body and position in clutch.
4. Install socket head screws and torque to 30 inch lbs.
5. Raise and support front of vehicle, then set control dial to "Free" position and rotate wheels. If wheels drag, check hub installation.
6. Lower vehicle.

## LEAF SPRINGS & BUSHINGS
### REPLACE

1. Raise and support vehicle.
2. Support axle with suitable jack.
3. Remove spring shackle upper retaining bolt.
4. Remove eye bolt.
5. Remove spring to axle housing U-bolt nuts, then the spring, lower plate and spring pads **Fig. 10.**
6. To replace bushings, position spring on a suitable press and press bushings from spring using suitable tools. Install bushings in same manner, ensuring bushings protrude an equal amount at each side of spring.
7. Reverse procedure to install. Torque U-bolt nuts to 150 ft. lbs.

## STABILIZER BAR
### REPLACE

1. Raise and support vehicle.
2. Remove stabilizer bar attaching bolts and nuts at frame locations.
3. Remove brackets and bushings at leaf spring anchor plates.
4. Remove stabilizer bar from vehicle.
5. Reverse procedure to install.

# 1988–89 CHEVROLET & GMC C & K SERIES

## INDEX OF SERVICE OPERATIONS

---

**NOTE:** Refer to the rear of this manual for vehicle manufacturer's special tool suppliers.

---

# SPECIFICATIONS
## GENERAL ENGINE SPECIFICATIONS

| Year | Engine Code | Engine Model | Fuel System | Bore & Stroke | Comp. Ratio | Horsepower @ RPM | Torque Ft. Lbs. @ RPM | Normal Oil Pressure Lbs. |
|------|-------------|--------------|-------------|---------------|-------------|------------------|----------------------|--------------------------|
| 1988-89 | Z | V6-262/4.3L | TBI① | 4.00 x 3.48 | 9.3 | 160 @ 4000 | 235 @ 2400 | 30-35 |
| | H | V8-305/5.0L | TBI① | 3.73 x 3.48 | ② | 175 @ 4000 | 270 @ 2400 | 30-55 |
| | K, M | V8-350/5.7L | TBI① | 4.00 x 3.48 | ③ ④ | 210 @ 4000 | 300 @ 2800 | 30-55 |
| | C, J⑤ | V8-379/6.2L | Fuel Inj. | 3.98 x 3.82 | 21.3 | 143 @ 3600 | 247 @ 2400 | 40-45 |
| | N | V8-454/7.4L | TBI① | 4.25 x 4.00 | 7.9 | 230 @ 3600 | 385 @ 1600 | 40-60 |

①—TBI: throttle body injection.
②—Light duty emissions, 9.3; heavy duty emissions, 8.6.
③—Engine code K with light duty emissions, 9.3; heavy duty emissions, 8.6.
④—Engine code M, 8.3.
⑤—Engine code C, light duty emissions; engine code J, heavy duty emissions.

## ALTERNATOR SPECIFICATIONS

| Year | Part No. | Field Current @ 80°F, 12 Volts | Rated Hot Output Amperes |
|------|----------|-------------------------------|--------------------------|
| 1988-89 | 1101110 | 4.8-5.7 | 85 |
| | 1101111 | 6.0-7.5 | 100 |
| | 1105688 | 6.0-7.5 | 100 |
| | 1105710 | 4.8-5.7 | 85 |
| | 1105711 | 6.0-7.5 | 100 |
| | 1105712 | 4.8-5.7 | 85 |

## STARTING MOTOR SPECIFICATIONS

| Year | Engine | Starter Part No. | Free Speed Test Amperes① | Volts | RPM |
|------|--------|------------------|--------------------------|-------|-----|
| 1988-89 | V6-262 | 9000719 | — | 10 | — |
| | V8-305 | 1998583 | 70-110 | 10 | 6500-10700 |
| | V8-305 | 1998584 | 70-110 | 10 | 6500-10700 |
| | V8-305 | 1998588 | 70-110 | 10 | 6500-10700 |
| | V8-305 | 1998589 | 70-110 | 10 | 6500-10700 |
| | V8-350 | 1998583 | 70-110 | 10 | 6500-10700 |
| | V8-350 | 1998584 | 70-110 | 10 | 6500-10700 |
| | V8-350 | 1998588 | 70-110 | 10 | 6500-10700 |
| | V8-350 | 1998589 | 70-110 | 10 | 6500-10700 |
| | V8-379② | 1113589 | 120-210 | 10 | 9000-13400 |
| | V8-379② | 1113590 | 120-210 | 10 | 9000-13400 |
| | V8-454 | 1998584 | 70-110 | 10 | 6500-10700 |
| | V8-454 | 1998589 | 70-110 | 10 | 6500-10700 |

①—Includes solenoid.
②—Diesel engine.

# 1988-89 CHEVROLET/GMC C & K SERIES

## ENGINE TIGHTENING SPECIFICATIONS

| Engine | Year | Spark Plugs Ft. Lbs. | Cylinder Head Bolts Ft. Lbs. | Intake Manifold Ft. Lbs. | Exhaust Manifold Ft. Lbs. | Rocker Arm Stud Ft. Lbs. | Rocker Arm Cover Ft. Lbs. | Connecting Rod Cap Bolts Ft. Lbs. | Main Bearing Cap Bolts Ft. Lbs. | Flywheel To Crankshaft Ft. Lbs. | Vibration Damper Or Pulley Ft. Lbs. |
|---|---|---|---|---|---|---|---|---|---|---|---|
| V6-262 | 1988-89 | 22 | 65 | 35 | ② | — | 100③ | 45 | 75 | 75 | 70 |
| V8-305 | 1988-89 | 22 | 65 | 35 | ② | — | 100③ | 45 | ④ | 75 | 70 |
| V8-350 | 1988-89 | 22 | 65 | 35 | ② | — | 100③ | 45 | ④ | 75 | 70 |
| V8-379① | 1988-89 | ⑤ | ⑥ | 31 | 26 | 40 | 16 | 48 | ⑦ | 65 | 200 |
| V8-454 | 1988-89 | 22 | 80 | 30 | 40 | — | 115③ | 48 | 110 | 65 | 85 |

①—Diesel engine.
②—Center two bolts, 26 ft. lbs.; all other bolts, 20 ft. lbs.
③—Inch lbs.
④—Outer bolts on cap Nos. 2, 3 & 4, 70 ft. lbs. All others 80 ft. lbs.
⑤—Glow plugs, 10 ft. lbs.
⑥—Torque bolts in sequence in three steps: first, torque all bolts to 20 ft. lbs.; second, torque all bolts to 50 ft. lbs.; finally, torque all bolts an additional 90° (¼ turn).
⑦—Inner bolts, 110 ft. lbs.; outer bolts, 100 ft. lbs.

## WHEEL ALIGNMENT SPECIFICATIONS

| Year | Model | Caster Deg. Checking① | Caster Deg. Setting② | Camber, Deg. Checking① | Camber, Deg. Setting② | Toe-In, Deg. Checking | Toe-In, Deg. Setting |
|---|---|---|---|---|---|---|---|
| **1500 Thru 3500** | | | | | | | |
| 1988-89 | C | +1.75 to +5.75 | +2.75 to +4.75 | −.5 to +1.5 | 0 to +1 | +.02 to +.22 | +.02 to +.22 |
| **1500 Thru 2500** | | | | | | | |
| 1988-89 | K | +2 to +6① | +3 to +5① | −.1 to +1.9 | +.4 to +1.4 | −.03 to +.17 | −.03 to +.17 |
| **3500** | | | | | | | |
| 1988-89 | K | +2 to +6① | +3 to +5① | −.25 to +1.75 | +.25 to +1.25 | −.03 to +.17 | −.03 to +.17 |

①—Maximum left to right should not exceed +1.0.
②—Maximum left to right should not exceed +.5.

## BRAKE SPECIFICATIONS

| Year | Model | Rear Drum I.D. | Wheel Cyl. Bore Front Disc | Wheel Cyl. Bore Rear Drum | Disc Brake Rotor Nominal Thickness | Disc Brake Rotor Minimum Thickness | Disc Brake Rotor Thickness Variation (Parallelism) | Disc Brake Rotor Run Out (TIR) | Master Cyl. I.D. Manual Brakes | Master Cyl. I.D. Power Brakes |
|---|---|---|---|---|---|---|---|---|---|---|
| 1988-89 | ① | 9.9 | — | — | 1 | — | .0005 | .004 | — | — |
| | ② | 11.15④ | — | — | 1.25 | — | .0005 | .004 | — | — |
| | ③ | 13.00 | — | — | 1.26 | — | .0005 | .004 | — | — |

①—With brake systems JN1 & JN3.
②—With brake system JN6.
③—With brake systems JN7 & JN8.
④—With brake system JN5, drum I.D. 9.9

## DRIVE AXLE SPECIFICATIONS

| Year | Make & Application | Ring Gear Size | Carrier Type | Ring Gear & Pinion Backlash Method | Ring Gear & Pinion Backlash Adjustment | Pinion Bearing Preload Method | Pinion Bearing Preload New Bearings Inch Lbs. | Pinion Bearing Preload Used Bearings Inch Lbs. | Differential Bearing Preload Method | Differential Bearing Preload New Bearings Inch Lbs. | Differential Bearing Preload Used Bearings Inch Lbs. |
|---|---|---|---|---|---|---|---|---|---|---|---|
| 1988-89 | Chevrolet | 8½① | Integral | Shims | — | Shims | — | — | Shims | — | — |
| | Chevrolet | 9½① | Integral | Shims | — | Shims | — | — | Shims | — | — |
| | Dana/Spicer | 10½① | Integral | Shims | — | Shims | — | — | Shims | — | — |

①—Rear axle.

## COOLING SYSTEM & CAPACITY DATA

| Year | Model | Engine | Cooling Capacity Less A/C | Cooling Capacity With A/C | Radiator Cap Relief Pressure Lbs. | Thermo. Opening Temp. | Fuel Tank Gals. | Engine Oil Refill Qts. ① | Transmission Oil 5 Speed Pints | 4 Speed Pints | Auto. Trans. Qts. | Transfer Case Pts. | Rear Axle Oil Pints |
|------|-------|--------|------|------|------|------|------|------|------|------|------|------|------|
| 1988-89 | C, K | V6-262 | 10.9 | 10.9 | 15 | 195 | — | 5③ | 3.6 | ④ | ⑤ | ⑥ | ⑦ |
| | C, K | V8-305 | 17.5 | 18 | 15 | 195 | — | 5③ | 3.6 | ④ | ⑤ | ⑥ | ⑦ |
| | C, K | V8-350 | 17.5 | 18 | 15 | 195 | — | 5③ | 3.6 | ④ | ⑤ | ⑥ | ⑦ |
| | C, K | V8-379② | 25 | 25 | 15 | 195 | — | 6③ | 3.6 | ④ | ⑤ | ⑥ | ⑦ |
| | C, K | V8-454 | 23 | 25 | 15 | 195 | — | 7③ | 3.6 | ④ | ⑤ | ⑥ | ⑦ |

①—Add one qt. with filter change.
②—Diesel engine.
③—Includes filter.
④—85 mm 3.6 pts.; 117 mm 8.4 pts.
⑤—THM 400, 10.6 qts.; THM 700-R4, 11.5 qts.
⑥—Four wheel drive models, 4.6 pts.
⑦—8½, 4.2 pts.; 9½, 10½, 5.5 pts.

# ELECTRICAL

## INDEX

## FUSE PANEL & FLASHER LOCATION

The fuse panel is located behind a pull cover in the dash to the left of the steering column.

The hazard and turn signal flashers are mounted in the convenience center under the lefthand side of the instrument panel.

## STARTER
### REPLACE

A clashing or grinding condition, may exist, due to improper engagement of the starter to flexplate on some vehicles equipped with V8-305/5.0L & V8-350/5.7L engines with automatic transmission. To correct this condition, replace the starter drive assembly with new drive assembly (part No. 10456422), which utilizes a stiffer jump spring allowing for proper engagement. During starter drive assembly replacement, all ring gear teeth should be inspected. If three or more consecutive teeth are damaged, the flexplate should be replaced with flexplate No. 10128414.

1. Disconnect battery ground cable.
2. Remove starter braces or heat shields, if equipped.
3. Disconnect starter solenoid electrical connectors.
4. Raise and support vehicle.
5. Remove attaching bolts, nuts and washers from starter motor.
6. Remove starter motor from engine.
7. Reverse procedure to install.

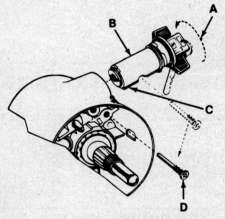

A. Hold the lock cylinder sleeve and rotate the knob clockwise against the stop.
B. Lock Cylinder Set
C. Cylinder Key
D. Lock Retaining Screw

**Fig. 1 Lock cylinder installation**

## STEERING WHEEL
### REPLACE

1. Disconnect battery ground cable.
2. Remove horn button cap.
3. Remove steering wheel retainer and nut.
4. Remove horn lead assembly, if equipped.
5. Mark relationship of steering wheel to the steering shaft.

6. Using a suitable puller, remove steering wheel.
7. Reverse procedure to install.

## TURN SIGNAL SWITCH
### REPLACE

1. Disconnect battery ground cable.
2. Remove steering wheel.
3. Remove instrument panel trim cover.
4. Remove lock plate.
5. Remove turn signal lever screw and lever.
6. Remove hazard warning knob.
7. Remove turn signal switch attaching screws.
8. Disconnect electrical connector from turn signal switch.
9. Remove wire protector.
10. Position turn signal and shifter housing in the low position. Remove harness cover by pulling toward the lower end of the column. Ensure not to damage the wires on tilt column models.
11. Remove turn signal switch.
12. Reverse procedure to install.

## LOCK CYLINDER
### REPLACE

1. Disconnect battery ground cable.
2. Place lock cylinder in the "Run" position.
3. Remove steering wheel.
4. Remove turn signal switch. **It is not necessary to completely remove the turn signal switch from the col-**

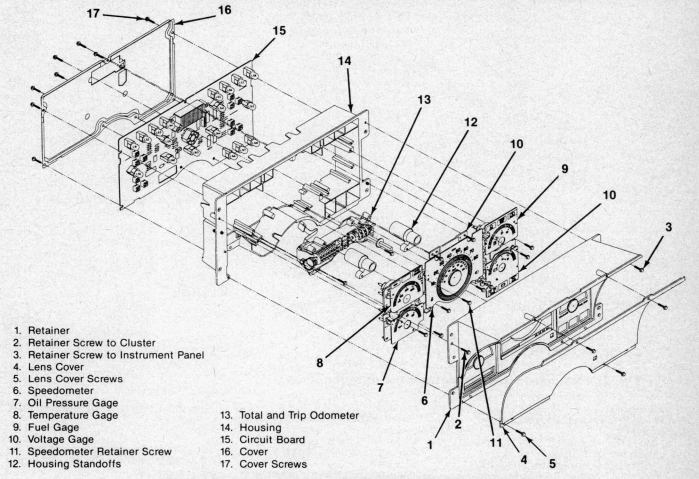

1. Retainer
2. Retainer Screw to Cluster
3. Retainer Screw to Instrument Panel
4. Lens Cover
5. Lens Cover Screws
6. Speedometer
7. Oil Pressure Gage
8. Temperature Gage
9. Fuel Gage
10. Voltage Gage
11. Speedometer Retainer Screw
12. Housing Standoffs
13. Total and Trip Odometer
14. Housing
15. Circuit Board
16. Cover
17. Cover Screws

**Fig. 2  Exploded view of instrument cluster assembly**

umn. **Pull switch rearward enough to slip it over the end of the shaft. Do not pull the harness out of the column.**
5. Remove attaching screw and lock cylinder set. **Do not drop the screw into the column.**
6. To install, align cylinder key with keyway in housing, as shown in **Fig. 1.** Push the lock completely inward, install attaching screw and torque to 40 inch lbs. on except tilt columns or 22 inch lbs. on tilt columns.

# IGNITION SWITCH
## REPLACE

1. Disconnect battery ground cable.
2. Carefully loosen attaching bolts, then lower steering column.
3. Place ignition switch into the "Lock" position.
4. Remove two attaching screws from ignition switch.
5. Remove ignition switch assembly.
6. Reverse procedure to install.

# INSTRUMENT CLUSTER
## REPLACE

1. Disconnect battery ground cable.
2. Remove radio and heater control

units.
3. Remove instrument cluster attaching screws.
4. Remove trim plate, if equipped. **A periodic grounding is recommended prior to handling the instrument cluster.**
5. Remove instrument cluster, **Fig. 2.**
6. Reverse procedure to install.

# WINDSHIELD WIPER MOTOR
## REPLACE

1. Disconnect battery ground cable.
2. Remove wiper arms.
3. Remove cowl vent grille.
4. Disconnect wiring harness connector from wiper motor.
5. Remove drive link sockets from the motor crank arm. **Do not remove crank arm.**
6. Remove wiper bolts and motor from vehicle.
7. Reverse procedure to install.

# BLOWER MOTOR
## REPLACE

1. Disconnect battery ground cable.
2. Disconnect electrical connector from blower motor.

3. Remove blower motor flange screws.
4. Remove blower motor, **Fig. 3.**
5. Reverse procedure to install.

# HEATER CORE
## REPLACE

1. Disconnect battery ground cable.
2. Remove coolant bottle.
3. Remove heater hoses from core tubes.
4. Remove attaching screws, **Fig. 3.**
5. Disconnect antenna cable from mast for access.
6. Remove instrument panel.
7. Disconnect electrical connector from computer, then remove computer bracket.
8. Remove kick pad.
9. Remove right side lower dash panel attaching bolt and nut.
10. Remove heater case mounting bolts.
11. Remove heater case from vehicle.
12. Remove heater core from heater case.
13. Reverse procedure to install.

# SPEED CONTROLS
## ADJUST

### CONTROL CABLE ADJUSTMENT

1. Unlock the cable conduit engine fit-

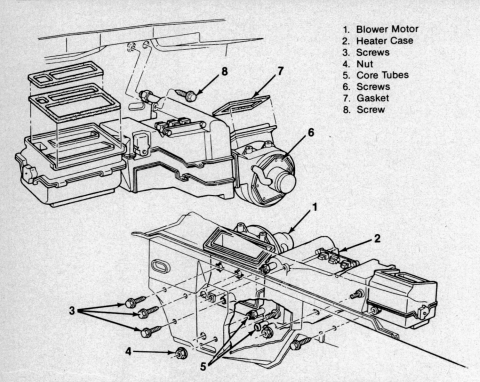

1. Blower Motor
2. Heater Case
3. Screws
4. Nut
5. Core Tubes
6. Screws
7. Gasket
8. Screw

**Fig. 3   Exploded view of heater case components**

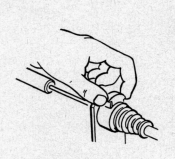

A. Unlocked Position

**Fig. 4   Unlocking cable conduit**

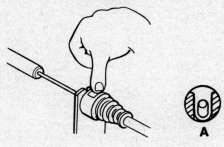

A. Locked Position

**Fig. 5   Locking cable conduit**

ting, **Fig. 4.**

2. On gasoline engine models, proceed as follows:
   a. Move cable conduit until throttle plate begins to open.
   b. In this position, move conduit in the opposite direction enough to close the throttle plate.
   c. Do not release hand grip from the cable until the cable conduit lock is in place.
3. On diesel engine models, proceed as follows:
   a. Move cable conduit until the injection pump lever moves off the idle stop screw.
   b. In this position, move the conduit in the opposite direction enough to return the lever to the idle stop screw.
   c. Do not release hand grip from the cable until the cable conduit lock is in place.
4. While holding the cable conduit, firmly push down on the cable conduit until it snaps in place, **Fig. 5.**

# GASOLINE ENGINE

## INDEX

## ENGINE MOUNTS
### REPLACE
#### FRONT MOUNTS

When raising or supporting the engine for any reason, do not use a jack under the oil pan, any sheet metal or crankshaft pulley. Due to the small clearance between the oil pan and oil pump screen, jacking against the oil pan may cause it to be bent against the pump screen, resulting in a damaged oil pickup unit.

1. Using a suitable jack, support engine.
2. Remove engine mount through bolt and nut, **Fig. 1.** Raise engine only enough for sufficient clearance. **Check for interference between rear of engine and the dash panel which could cause distributor damage.**
3. Remove engine mount assembly bolts, nuts and washers.
4. Remove mount assembly.
5. Reverse procedure to install.

#### REAR MOUNTS

When raising or supporting the engine for any reason, do not use a jack under the oil pan, any sheet metal or crankshaft pulley. Due to the small clearance between the oil pan and oil pump screen, jacking against the oil pan may cause it to be bent against the pump screen, resulting in a damaged oil pickup unit.

1. Support rear of engine to relieve the weight on the rear mounting.
2. Remove mount to crossmember nuts and washers.
3. Remove mount to transmission attaching bolts and washers. **Raise rear of engine only enough to permit removal of the mount.**
4. Reverse procedure to install.

## ENGINE
### REPLACE
#### V6-262

1. Disconnect battery ground cable.
2. Mark hood hinge locations, then remove hood.
3. Drain cooling system.
4. Remove air cleaner.
5. Remove accessory drive belt, fan and water pump pulley.
6. Remove radiator and shroud.
7. Disconnect heater hoses from engine.
8. Disconnect accelerator cruise control and detent linkage, if equipped.
9. Loosen air conditioning compressor and position aside, if equipped.
10. Remove power steering pump and position aside, if equipped.
11. Disconnect engine wiring harness from engine.
12. Disconnect and cap fuel line.
13. Label, then disconnect vacuum lines from intake manifold.
14. Raise and support vehicle.
15. Drain oil from engine.
16. Disconnect front exhaust pipes from exhaust manifolds.
17. Remove strut rods from engine mounts, if equipped.
18. Remove flywheel or torque converter cover.
19. Disconnect engine wiring attaching brackets from oil pan rail.
20. On automatic transmission models, remove converter to flex plate attaching bolts.
21. Lower vehicle and support transmission assembly.
22. Install suitable engine lifting equipment onto engine.
23. Remove bellhousing to engine attaching bolts.
24. Remove engine mount to frame attaching bolts.

25. Remove engine from vehicle.
26. Raise and support vehicle.

#### V8-305 & 350

1. Disconnect battery ground cable.
2. Mark hood hinge locations, then remove hood.
3. Drain cooling system.
4. Remove air cleaner and accessory drive belt, fan and water pump pulley.
5. Remove radiator and shroud.
6. Disconnect heater hoses from engine.
7. Disconnect accelerator, cruise control and detent linkage, if equipped from TBI unit.
8. Loosen air conditioning compressor, if equipped and position aside.
9. Loosen power steering pump, if equipped and position aside.
10. Disconnect engine wiring harness from engine.
11. Disconnect and cap fuel lines.
12. Label, then disconnect vacuum lines from engine.
13. Raise and support engine.
14. Drain oil from engine.
15. Disconnect front exhaust pipes from exhaust manifold.
16. Remove strut rods from engine mounts, if equipped.
17. Remove flywheel or torque converter under cover.
18. Remove engine wiring attaching brackets from oil pan rail.
19. Remove starter motor.
20. Remove converter to flex plate attaching bolts, if equipped.
21. Lower vehicle and support transmission.
22. Attach suitable engine lifting equipment onto engine.
23. Remove bellhousing to engine attaching bolts.
24. Remove front engine mount to frame bolts.
25. Remove engine from vehicle.

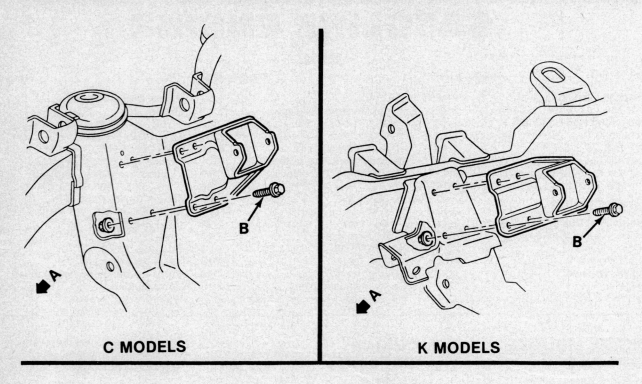

C MODELS       K MODELS

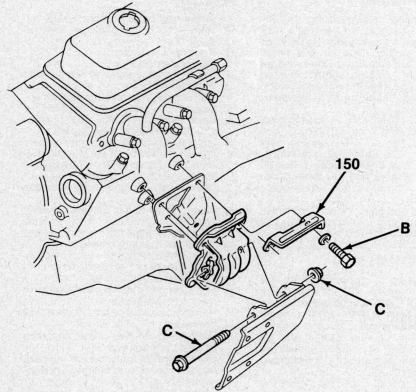

A. Forward
B. 60 N·m (45 ft. lbs.)
C. Torque Bolt to 95 N·m (70 Ft. Lbs.) or, Torque Nut to 70 N·m (50 Ft. Lbs.)
150. Bracket (C15 Models)

**Fig. 1 Front engine mounts**

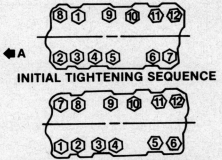

**INITIAL TIGHTENING SEQUENCE**

**FINAL TIGHTENING SEQUENCE**

A. Front Of Engine

**Fig. 2  Intake manifold bolt tightening sequence. V6-262**

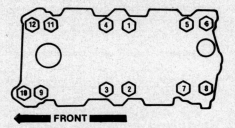

**Fig. 3  Intake manifold bolt tightening sequence. V8-305 & 350**

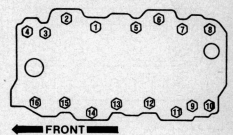

**Fig. 4  Intake manifold bolt tightening sequence. V8-454**

26. Reverse procedure to install.

## V8-454

1. Disconnect battery ground cable.
2. Mark hood hinge locations, then remove hood.
3. Remove air cleaner, radiator and fan shroud.
4. Label, then disconnect all electrical connectors and vacuum lines from engine.
5. Disconnect accelerator, cruise control and TVS linkage from engine, if equipped.
6. Disconnect and cap fuel lines.
7. Loosen power steering pump and position aside, if equipped.
8. Loosen air conditioning compressor and position aside, if equipped.
9. Raise and support vehicle.
10. Disconnect front exhaust pipes from exhaust manifold.
11. Remove starter motor from engine.
12. Remove flywheel or torque converter under cover.
13. Remove flex plate to torque converter attaching bolts, if equipped.
14. Lower vehicle and support transmission.
15. Attach suitable engine lifting equipment onto engine.
16. Remove bellhousing to engine attaching bolts.
17. Remove front engine mount through bolts.
18. Remove engine from vehicle.
19. Reverse procedure to install.

## INTAKE MANIFOLD
## REPLACE

### V6-262

1. Disconnect battery ground cable.
2. Remove air cleaner and heat stove tube then drain cooling system.
3. Disconnect heater and radiator hoses, and the dipstick tube, then remove upper alternator bracket.
4. Disconnect all remaining hoses and electrical connections that will interfere with manifold removal.
5. Disconnect fuel and vacuum lines and electrical connectors from TBI unit and manifold assembly.
6. Disconnect accelerator, cruise control

and TVS cables, if equipped.
7. Disconnect spark plug wires, if necessary, then remove distributor.
8. Remove ignition coil.
9. If equipped with A/C, remove compressor bracket and position compressor aside.
10. Remove intake manifold attaching bolts, then the intake manifold.
11. Reverse procedure to install, using new gaskets and seals. Coat front and rear ridges of cylinder case with a 3/16 inch bead of RTV sealant. Extend bead 1/2 inch up each cylinder head to retain side gaskets, then seal around all water passages. Torque manifold bolts to specification in sequence shown in **Fig. 2.**

## V8-305 & 350

1. Disconnect battery ground cable, then drain cooling system.
2. Remove air cleaner.
3. Remove heater and radiator hoses, then the rear alternator bracket.
4. Disconnect all vacuum hoses and electrical connectors from TBI unit and EGR valve.
5. Disconnect accelerator, cruise control and TSV cables, if equipped.
6. Remove spark plug wires and distributor, if necessary.
7. Disconnect fuel lines from TBI unit.
8. Remove air conditioning compressor rear bracket.
9. Remove emission control sensors and bracket.
10. Remove fuel line bracket from rear of manifold, then place fuel lines aside. Remove bracket from rear of belt idler.
11. Remove TBI unit, if necessary.
12. Remove intake manifold attaching bolts, then the intake manifold.
13. Reverse procedure to install, using new gaskets and seals. Coat front and rear ridges of cylinder case with a 3/16 inch bead of RTV sealant. Extend bead 1/2 inch up each cylinder head to retain side gaskets, then seal around all water passages. Torque manifold bolts to specification in sequence shown in **Fig. 3.**

## V8-454

1. Disconnect battery ground cable, then drain cooling system.
2. Remove air cleaner.
3. Disconnect upper radiator and heater hoses at manifold and bypass hose at water pump.
4. Disconnect all electrical connectors

and vacuum lines from TBI unit. Disconnect fuel lines from TBI unit.
5. Remove distributor.
6. Remove air conditioning compressor and front bracket, then position aside.
7. Remove alternator right rear bracket.
8. Remove rear air conditioning compressor bracket, if equipped.
9. Remove emission sensors and bracket.
10. Remove intake manifold attaching bolts, then the intake manifold.
11. Reverse procedure to install, using new gaskets and seals. Torque manifold bolts to specification in sequence shown in **Fig. 4.**

## EXHAUST MANIFOLD
## REPLACE

### V6-262, V8-305 & V8-350

1. Disconnect battery ground cable, then raise and support vehicle.
2. Raise and support vehicle.
3. Disconnect exhaust pipe from manifold.
4. Lower vehicle.
5. Disconnect oxygen sensor electrical connector from left side manifold. Do not remove oxygen sensor from the manifold unless it is to be replaced. Remove dipstick tube bracket from right side manifold, if equipped.
6. Remove power steering pump bracket from left side manifold.
7. Remove heat stove pipe from right side manifold.
8. Disconnect AIR hose from check valve.
9. Remove manifold attaching bolts, washers, heat shield and tab washers.
10. Remove exhaust manifold.
11. Reverse procedure to install using a new gasket.

### V8-454

1. Disconnect battery ground cable.
2. Remove heat stove and dipstick tube from right side manifold.
3. Remove oxygen sensor wire from left side manifold.
4. Disconnect AIR hose from check valve.
5. Remove spark plugs.
6. Remove exhaust pipe from manifold.
7. Remove exhaust manifold attaching bolts and spark plug heat shields.
8. Remove exhaust manifold.
9. Reverse procedure to install using a new gasket.

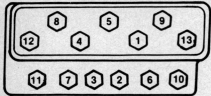

**FRONT**

**Fig. 5   Cylinder head bolt tightening sequence. V6-262**

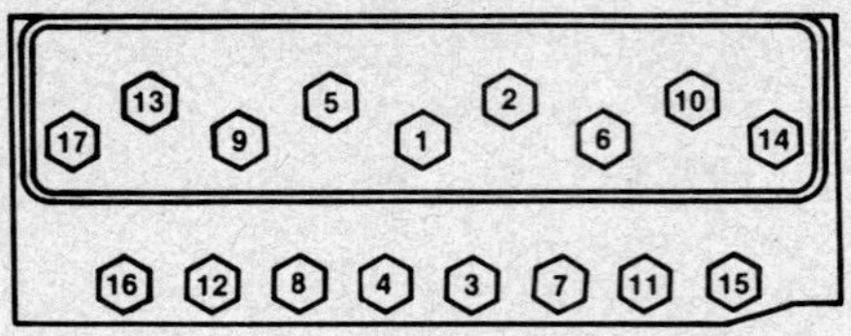

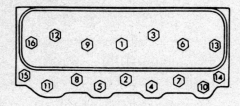

**Fig. 6   Cylinder head bolt tightening sequence. V8-305 & 350**

**Fig. 7   Cylinder head bolt tightening sequence. V8-454**

# CYLINDER HEAD
## REPLACE
### V6-262

1. Disconnect battery ground cable.
2. Remove intake manifold.
3. Remove exhaust manifold(s).
4. Remove AIR pipe from rear of cylinder head.
5. Remove air pump mounting bolt and spacer from right side cylinder head.
6. Remove engine accessory attaching bolts and studs from cylinder head. For the left side cylinder head assembly, it may be necessary to loosen the remaining bracket bolts to provide clearance for head removal.
7. Remove spark plug wires from plug brackets.
8. Remove ground strap from right side cylinder head.
9. Disconnect coolant sensor electrical connector from left side cylinder head.
10. Remove rocker arm cover.
11. Remove spark plugs.
12. Remove pushrods. **Keep pushrods in order removed on a clean workbench. Ensure to install pushrods into cylinder from which they were removed.**
13. Remove cylinder head bolts, cylinder head and gasket.
14. Reverse procedure to install. Coat cylinder head bolt threads with suitable sealer. Torque cylinder head bolts to specifications in sequence shown in **Fig. 5.** Adjust valves.

### V8-305 & V8-350

1. Disconnect battery ground cable.
2. Drain cooling system.
3. Remove intake manifold.
4. Remove exhaust manifold.
5. Remove ground strap from rear of right side cylinder head.
6. Remove AIR pipe from rear of cylinder head.
7. Remove the following components from the right side cylinder head:
   a. Remove AIR pump bolt and spacer from cylinder head.
   b. Remove air conditioning compressor attaching bolt and nut from cylinder head.
   c. Remove fuel pipe, plug wire(s) and wiring harness brackets from rear of cylinder head.

8. Remove the following components from the left side cylinder head:
   a. Remove attaching nut and stud securing main accessory bracket to cylinder head. It may be necessary to loosen the remaining attaching bolts and studs to move the bracket forward slightly for clearance to remove the cylinder head.
   b. Disconnect coolant sensor electrical connector.
   c. Remove spark plug wires from brackets.
9. Remove rocker arm cover.
10. Remove spark plugs.
11. Remove pushrods. **Keep pushrods on a clean workbench. Ensure to install pushrods into the cylinder from which they were removed.**
12. Remove cylinder head attaching bolts, cylinder head and gasket.
13. Reverse procedure to install. Coat cylinder head bolt threads with suitable sealer. Torque cylinder head bolts to specifications in sequence shown in **Fig. 6.** Adjust valves.

### V8-454

1. Disconnect battery ground cable.
2. Remove intake manifold.
3. Loosen air conditioning compressor and bracket, then position aside.
4. Remove AIR pump and bracket.
5. Remove alternator and brackets and position aside.
6. Remove power steering pump and bracket and position aside.
7. Remove exhaust manifold.
8. Remove rocker arm cover.
9. Remove spark plugs.
10. Remove AIR pipe bolts from cylinder head.
11. Remove ground strap from rear of cylinder head.
12. Remove sensor electrical connector from cylinder head.
13. Remove pushrods from cylinder head. **Keep pushrods on a clean workbench. Ensure to install pushrods in order removed into cylinder from which they were removed.**
14. Remove cylinder head bolts, cylinder head and gasket.
15. Reverse procedure to install. Coat cylinder head bolts with suitable sealer. Torque cylinder head bolts to specifications in sequence shown in **Fig. 7.**

# VALVE ARRANGEMENT
## FRONT TO REAR

V6-262
   Left Side . . . . . . . . . . . . . . . . . . E-I-E-I-I-E
   Right Side . . . . . . . . . . . . . . . E-I-I-E-I-E
V8-305 & 350. . . . . . . . . . . . E-I-I-E-E-I-I-E
V8-454. . . . . . . . . . . . . . . . . . E-I-E-I-E-I-E-I

# VALVE CLEARANCE SPECIFICATIONS

Turn rocker arm stud nut until all lash is eliminated, then tighten nut an additional $\frac{3}{4}$ turn on V8-454 engines, or 1 turn on all other engines.

# VALVES
## ADJUST
### V6-262

1. Remove rocker arm cover.
2. Crank engine until mark on the torsional damper aligns with the "0" mark on the timing tab and the engine is in the number one firing position.
3. This may be determined by placing fingers on the number one valve as the mark on the damper comes near the "0" mark on the timing tab. If the rocker arms are not moving, the engine is in the number one firing position. If the rocker arms move as the mark comes up to the timing tab, the engine is in the number four firing position and should be turned over one more time to reach the number one firing position.
4. With the engine in the number one firing position as determined in step 3, exhaust valves 1, 5 and 6 and intake valves 1, 2 and 3 can be adjusted. **Even numbered cylinders are in the right bank, odd numbered cylinders are in the left bank when viewed from the rear of the engine.**
5. Back off the adjusting nut until lash is felt at the pushrod, then turn adjusting until all lash is removed. This can be determined by rotating the pushrod while turning the adjusting nut. When play has been removed, turn adjusting nut one full turn (to center the lifter plunger).
6. Crank engine one complete revolution until the timing tab "0" mark and vibration damper mark are again in align-

ment. This is the number four firing position.

7. With the engine in this position, exhaust valves 2, 3 and 4 and intake valves 4, 5 and 6 can be adjusted.

8. With valves properly adjusted, install rocker arm cover.

## V8-305, 350 & 454

1. Remove rocker arm cover.
2. Crank engine until the mark on the vibration damper aligns with the "0" mark on the timing tab and the engine is in the number one firing position. This may be determined by placing fingers on valves of number one cylinder as the mark on the damper comes near the "0" mark on the timing tab. If the rocker arms are not moving, the engine is in the number one firing position. If the rocker arms move as the marks comes up to the timing tab, the engine is in the number six firing position and should be turned over one more time to reach the number one firing position.
3. With the engine in this position, exhaust valves 1, 3, 4 and 8 and intake valves 1, 2, 5 and 7 can be adjusted. **Even numbered cylinders are in the right bank, odd numbered cylinders are in the the left bank when viewed from the rear of the engine.**
4. Back off the adjusting nut until lash is felt at the pushrod, then turn in the adjusting nut until all lash is removed. This can be determined by rotating the pushrod while turning the adjusting nut. When play has been removed, turn the adjusting nut in one full additional turn on V8-305 and 350 engines or 3/4 turn on V8-454 engines (to center the lifter plunger).
5. Crank engine one complete revolution until the timing tab "0" mark and vibration damper mark are aligned. This is the number six firing position.
6. With the engine in this position, exhaust valves 2, 5, 6 and 7 and intake valves 3, 4, 6 and 8 can be adjusted.
7. With valves properly adjusted, install rocker arm cover.

## VALVE GUIDES

Valve guides in these engines are an integral part of the head and, therefore, cannot be removed. For service, guide holes can be reamed oversize to accommodate one of several service valves with oversize stems.

Check the valve stem clearance of each valve (after cleaning) in its respective valve guide. If the clearance exceeds the service limits of .004 inch on the intake or .005 inch on the exhaust, ream the valve guide to accommodate the next oversize diameter valve stem.

Select the reamer for the smallest oversize which will provide a clean straight bore through the valve guide. After reaming, a new seat should be cut into the head to assure perfect seating of the new valve.

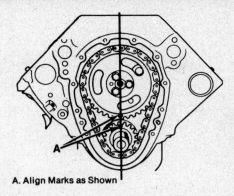

A. Align Marks as Shown

**Fig. 8   Aligning timing marks**

## ROCKER ARM STUDS
### REPLACE

Rocker arm studs that have damaged threads may be replaced with standard studs. Loose studs should be replaced with .003 inch or .013 inch oversize studs which are available for replacement.

Remove the old stud by placing a suitable spacer over the stud. Install a nut and flat washer on the stud and pull out the stud by turning the nut. After reaming the hole for an oversize stud, coat the press fit area of the new stud with rear axle lubricant. Install the stud by driving it in until it protrudes from the head the same distance as the other studs. On V8-454, the rocker arm studs are threaded into the cylinder head. Coat threads on cylinder head end of stud before assembling to head.

## PUSHRODS

When a replacement pushrod has a paint stripe at one end, this painted end must be installed in contact with the rocker arm. To provide durability a hardened insert is incorporated in the rocker arm end of these pushrods.

## HYDRAULIC LIFTERS

The hydraulic valve lifters are simple in design. Readjustments are not necessary and servicing them requires that care and cleanliness be exercised in the handling of parts.

### DISASSEMBLE & ASSEMBLE

1. Hold plunger down with pushrod and, using a small screwdriver or awl, remove plunger retainer.
2. Remove parts from lifter body.
3. Clean all parts and inspect for damage. If any parts are damaged, the entire lifter assembly should be replaced. The inertia valve in the plunger for rocker arm lubrication should move when the plunger is shaken.
4. To reassemble, invert plunger and set ball into hole in plunger. Place ball check valve retainer over ball and on plunger. Place check valve retainer spring over retainer. Assemble body

over plunger assembly. Turn assembly over and install pushrod seat. Compress plunger with pushrod and install retainer.

5. Compress plunger to open oil holes and fill plunger with engine oil. Work plunger up and down and refill.

## TIMING CASE COVER
### REPLACE
### V6-262, V8-305, 350 & 454

1. Remove vibration damper and water pump.
2. Remove cover retaining screws and cover.
3. Clean gasket surface of block and timing case cover.
4. Remove any excess oil pan gasket material that may be protruding at the oil pan to engine block junction.
5. Apply a thin bead of RTV 1052366 sealer or equivalent to the joint formed at oil pan and block.
6. Coat new gasket with sealer and position it on cover, then install cover to oil pan seal on cover and coat bottom of seal with engine oil.
7. Position cover on engine and install cover mounting flange reinforcement, if equipped.
8. Install cover screws and torque to 100 inch lbs. alternately and evenly while pressing downward on cover so that dowels are aligned with holes in cover. Do not force cover over dowels as cover can be distorted.
9. Install remaining cover screws, vibration damper and water pump.

## TIMING CHAIN
### REPLACE
### V6-262, V8-305, 350 & 454

1. Remove timing case cover.
2. Remove crankshaft oil slinger.
3. Crank engine until "O" marks on sprockets are in alignment, **Fig. 8.**
4. Remove three camshaft to sprocket bolts.
5. Remove camshaft sprocket and timing chain together. Sprocket is a light press fit on camshaft for approximately 1/8 inch. If sprocket does not come off easily, a light blow with a plastic hammer on the lower edge of the sprocket should dislodge it.
6. If crankshaft sprocket is to be replaced, remove it with a suitable gear puller. Install new sprocket, aligning key and keyway.
7. Install chain onto camshaft sprocket. Hold sprocket with chain hanging vertically, then align marks on sprockets as shown, **Fig. 8. The valve timing marks shown in Fig. 8, do not indicate TDC compression stroke for No. 1 cylinder, which is used during distributor installation. If distributor was removed, install timing chain and sprockets, aligning timing marks, Fig. 8, then rotate engine until No. 1 cylinder is on compression and camshaft timing mark**

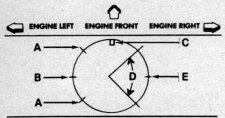

A. Oil Ring Rail Gaps
B. 2nd Compression Ring Gap
C. Notch In Piston
D. Oil Ring Spacer Gap
   (Tang In Hole Or Slot With Arc)
E. Top Compression Ring Gap

**Fig. 9  Piston & ring end gap positioning**

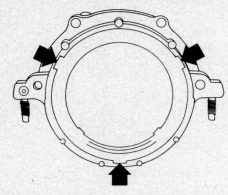

**Fig. 10  Seal removal notches. V6-262, V8-305 & 350**

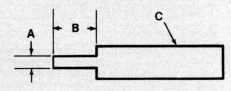

A. 4 mm (¹¹/₆₄-inch)
B. 13 mm (¹/₂-inch)
C. 0.10 mm (0.004-inch) shim stock

**Fig. 12  Oil seal installation tool. V8-454**

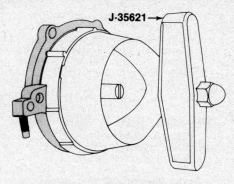

**Fig. 11  Installing rear crankshaft oil seal. V6-262, V8-305 & 350**

is 180° from valve timing position shown in Fig. 8. Install distributor.
8. Align dowel in camshaft with dowel hole in sprocket and install sprocket on camshaft. Do not attempt to drive sprocket on camshaft as welch plug at rear of engine can be dislodged.
9. Draw sprocket onto camshaft, using the three mounting bolts. Tighten to 20 ft. lbs. torque.
10. Lubricate timing chain and install cover.

## CAMSHAFT
## REPLACE
## V6-262, V8-305, 350 & 454

Depending on vehicle and engine application, the grille, radiator and condenser (if equipped) must be removed to facilitate camshaft removal.
1. Remove intake manifold as described previously.
2. Remove pushrods and valve lifters.
3. Remove timing case cover.
4. Remove camshaft sprocket bolts and timing chain.
5. Remove camshaft sprocket.
6. Install two ⁵/₁₆ 18 x 4-5 inch bolts into camshaft bolt holes, then pull camshaft out of cylinder block.
7. Reverse procedure to install.
8. Torque camshaft sprocket bolts to 17 ft. lbs.

## PISTON & ROD ASSEMBLY

Assemble pistons to connecting rods, locating piston ring end gaps as shown in **Fig. 9.** Lubricate piston rings with clean engine oil. Without disturbing the piston ring end gap location, install piston using a suitable tool. Piston must be installed with notch in piston facing front of engine.

## PISTONS

A .001 inch oversize piston is available for service use so that proper clearances can be obtained for slightly worn cylinder bores requiring only light honing. In addition, oversizes of .020 inch, .030 inch and .040 inch are available. If the cylinders have less than .005 inch taper or wear,

they can be reconditioned with a hone and fitted with the .001 inch oversize piston.

## CONNECTING ROD BEARINGS

Connecting rod bearing inserts are available in standard size and undersizes of .001 inch, .002 inch, .010 inch and .020 inch. The bearings can be replaced without removing the rod assembly by removing the cap and replacing the upper and lower halves of the bearing.

## MAIN BEARINGS

Shell type bearings are used, and if worn excessively, should be replaced. No attempt should be made to shim, file or otherwise take up worn bearings.

Main bearings are available in standard and undersizes of .001, .002, .009, .010 and .020 inch.

## CRANKSHAFT REAR OIL SEAL
## REPLACE
## V6-262, V8-305 & 350
### Removal

1. Disconnect battery ground cable.
2. Remove transmission assembly.
3. Remove clutch, flywheel or flex plate, if equipped.
4. Using a suitable screwdriver, insert screwdriver into notches provided in the seal retainer, **Fig. 10,** and remove

rear oil seal. **Carefully remove seal as not to nick the crankshaft sealing surface.**

### Installation

1. Using rear crankshaft seal installer J-35621 or equivalent, install crankshaft rear oil seal as follows:
   a. Using clean engine oil, lubricate inner and outer diameter of seal.
   b. Install new seal onto tool, **Fig. 11.**
   c. Thread attaching screws into the tapped holes in the crankshaft.
   d. Using a suitable screwdriver, tighten attaching screws. **This will ensure that the seal is installed properly over crankshaft assembly.**
   e. Turn tool handle until it bottoms out.
   f. Remove tool.

## V8-454
### Removal

The rear main bearing oil seal can be replaced (both halves) without removal of the crankshaft assembly. Always replace the upper and lower seal as an assembly. Install the seal with the lip facing front of engine. Extreme care should be exercised when installing this seal to protect the sealing bead located in the seal outer diameter channel. An installation tool should be used to protect the seal bead when positioning the seal.
1. Disconnect battery ground cable.
2. Remove oil pan and oil pump assemblies.
3. Remove rear main bearing cap.
4. Remove lower seal half, then the upper seal half. Using a suitable drift and hammer, tap upper seal half, then remove upper seal using pliers.

### Installation

1. Install new upper seal half as follows. **An oil seal installation tool, Fig. 12, should be fabricated (if not provided with the seal kit) to prevent seal damage during installation:**
   a. Coat seal lips lightly with clean engine oil. Keep oil off of seal mating surface.
   b. Position tip of tool between crank-

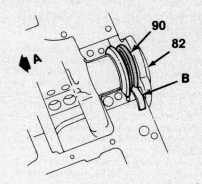

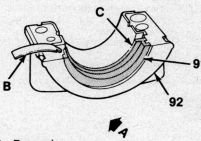

A. Forward
B. Fabricated Tool
C. Oil Seal Lip
82. Crankshaft
90. Upper Seal Half
91. Lower Seal Half
92. Main Bearing Cap

**Fig. 13 Installing rear crankshaft oil seal. V8-454**

shaft and seal seat in the engine block, **Fig. 13.**

c. Position seal half between crankshaft and tip of tool.
d. Ensure oil seal lip is positioned toward front of engine.
e. Roll seal around crankshaft using the tool as a "shoe horn" to protect the seal bead from block seal surface sharp corner. The installation tool must remain in position until the seal half is properly positioned with both ends flush with the block.
f. Remove tool carefully as not to withdraw the seal half.
2. Install lower seal half as follows:
a. Coat seal lips lightly with engine oil. Keep oil off of the seal mating surface.
b. Insert seal half into rear main bearing cap. Use tool to protect the seal half from the sharp edges. Feed seal half into the rear main bearing cap, using light finger pressure. Ensure oil seal lip faces front of engine, **Fig. 13.**
3. Install rear main bearing cap and lower main bearing cap as follows:
a. Apply a brush on type oil sealing compound to the mating surface on the engine block and cap as shown in **Fig. 14.** Do not allow sealant to contact either the crankshaft or rear oil seal.
b. Apply engine oil to the lower main bearing.

Apply Sealant to Shaded Areas Only

**Fig. 14 Applying sealer to engine block. V8-454**

c. Position cap onto the block. Install cap attaching bolts.
d. Tighten rear main bearing cap attaching bolts temporarily to 10 ft. lbs.
e. Tap end of crankshaft first rearward, then forward with a suitable hammer. This will align the rear main bearing and crankshaft thrust surfaces.

## OIL PAN
## REPLACE
### V6-262, V8-305, 350

A one piece type oil pan gasket is used on these engines.
1. Disconnect battery ground cable.
2. Raise and support vehicle.
3. Drain oil from engine.
4. Disconnect exhaust crossover pipe.
5. Remove torque converter cover, if equipped.
6. Remove strut rods from flywheel cover, if equipped.
7. Remove strut rods from front engine mounts, if equipped.
8. Remove oil pan attaching bolts, nuts and reinforcements.
9. Remove oil pan and gasket.
10. Reverse procedure to install. Apply suitable sealant to front cover block joint and to the rear crankshaft seal to block joint. Apply sealant approximately 1 inch in both directions from each of the four corners.
11. Torque oil pan attaching bolts to 100 inch lbs. and oil pan nuts in corners to 200 inch lbs.

### V8-454

1. Disconnect battery ground cable.
2. Loosen fan shroud, then remove air cleaner assembly.
3. Remove distributor cap.
4. Raise and support vehicle, then drain oil pan.
5. On vehicles equipped with manual transmission, remove starter.
6. Remove torque converter or clutch cover as applicable.
7. Remove oil filter.
8. If equipped with oil pressure gauge, disconnect oil pressure line from side

of cylinder block to prevent damaging line.
9. Remove engine mount through bolts, then raise engine.
10. Remove oil pan attaching bolts, then the oil pan.
11. Reverse procedure to install. Apply suitable sealant to front and rear corners of gaskets. Torque oil pan attaching bolts to 160 inch lbs.

## REAR OIL SEAL RETAINER
## REPLACE
### V6-262, V8-305 & 350

1. Disconnect battery ground cable, raise and support vehicle, and drain oil pan.
2. Remove transmission and flex plate.
3. Remove oil pan retaining bolts and lower oil pan.
4. Remove screws securing retainer, retainer and gasket, then remove seal from retainer. **Whenever the retainer is removed, the retainer gasket and rear oil seal should be replaced.**
5. Clean retainer, pan and engine block mating surfaces.
6. Position retainer gasket on block studs, install retainer and torque fasteners to 135 inch lbs.
7. Install rear oil seal as outlined.
8. Reverse remaining procedure to complete installation, using new oil pan gaskets as needed.

## OIL PUMP SERVICE
## REMOVAL & INSTALLATION

1. Remove oil pan as described previously.
2. Remove pump to rear main bearing cap bolt, then the pump and extension shaft.
3. Reverse procedure to install. Ensure bottom edge of oil pump screen is parallel to bottom edge of oil pan rails. Torque oil pump to rear main bearing cap bolt to 65 ft. lbs.

## DISASSEMBLY, INSPECTION & ASSEMBLY

1. Remove oil pump as described previously.
2. Remove pump cover screws and pump cover.
3. Mark gear teeth so they can be reassembled with same teeth indexing, then remove drive gear, idler gear and shaft.
4. Remove pressure regulator valve retaining pin, pressure regulator valve and related parts.
5. If pickup screen and pipe require replacement, mount pump in a soft-jawed vise and extract pipe from pump.
6. Wash all parts in cleaning solvent and dry with compressed air.

7. Inspect pump body and cover for cracks and excessive wear.
8. Inspect pump gears for damage or excessive wear.
9. Check drive gear shaft for looseness in pump body.
10. Inspect inside of pump cover for wear that would allow oil to leak past the ends of the gears.
11. Inspect pickup screen and pipe assembly for damage to screen, pipe or relief grommet.
12. Check pressure regulator valve for proper fit in pump housing.
13. Reverse procedure to assemble. Turn driveshaft by hand to check for smooth operation. **The pump gears and body are not serviced separately. If the pump gears or body are damaged or worn, the pump assembly should be replaced. Also, if the pickup screen was removed, it should be replaced with** a new one as loss of the press fit condition could result in an air leak and loss of oil pressure.

## WATER PUMP
## REPLACE

1. Disconnect battery ground cable.
2. Drain coolant from radiator.
3. Remove upper fan shroud.
4. Remove fan assembly from engine.
5. Lower radiator and heater hose from the water pump.
6. On V8-454 engine, remove bypass hose.
7. Remove water pump attaching bolts and water pump.
8. Reverse procedure to install. Torque water pump attaching bolts to 30 ft. lbs.

## ELECTRIC FUEL PUMP
## REPLACE

Prior to removing the electric fuel pump, fuel pressure must be relieved by disconnecting the fuel line fittings. A small amount of fuel may still be released when the fuel line is disconnected. To reduce the chance of injury, cover the fitting(s) to be disconnected with a shop towel. Place towel in an approved container when the disconnect is complete.

1. Allow fuel pressure to bleed off.
2. Disconnect battery ground cable.
3. Raise and support vehicle.
4. Disconnect fuel lines from pump.
5. Remove pump support bracket attaching screws and support bracket from brake lines.
6. Remove fuel pump and bracket from frame rail.
7. Reverse procedure to install.

# DIESEL ENGINE

## INDEX

## DESCRIPTION

The diesel engine used on 1988-89 full-size pickup trucks is the V8-379 (6.2L) diesel engine, which is similar in many ways to gasoline engines, however, in the diesel engine air alone is compressed in the cylinder. After the air has been compressed, a charge of fuel is sprayed into the cylinder and ignition occurs due to the heat of compression. Due to the increased compression and resultant increase in combustion temperatures, major differences are evident in the cylinder heads, combustion chambers, fuel distribution system, intake manifold and engine mechanical components.

The cylinder block, crankshaft, main bearings, connecting rods, pistons and wrist pins are all heavy duty designs, due to the higher compression ratios, and the main bearing caps are 4 bolt design to provide rigid crankshaft support, while mini-

mizing stress. Roller hydraulic lifters are used to minimize wear on the forged steel camshaft, and intake and exhaust valves are of special alloy material to combat the higher internal operating temperatures. Steel alloy prechamber inserts are installed in the combustion chambers and are serviced separately from the cylinder head. Injector nozzles and glow plugs are threaded into the cylinder head to allow direct fuel delivery and to provide chamber preheating.

The injector nozzles are spring loaded and designed to open and deliver fuel at specifically calibrated fuel pressures. Fuel is delivered into the high swirl precombustion chambers which mix fuel and air to provide an efficient fuel burn and low emissions. The glow plugs are used to heat the prechambers, and assist starting. In addition, a block heater is used to aid starting in cold climates. Because the intake manifold is always open to atmo-

spheric pressures no engine vacuum supply is available, and a vacuum pump is installed to supply vacuum to components such as A/C and cruise control.

## LUBRICATION SYSTEM

The gear type oil pump is attached to the bottom side of the rear main bearing cap and is driven by the camshaft through an intermediate shaft. Oil flows through the pump outlet tube to the cooler located in the radiator. A bypass valve is incorporated into the system, which allows oil to bypass the cooler and continue to feed the engine should the cooler become clogged. From the cooler, the oil then flows through a cartridge type oil filter. A bypass valve is incorporated into the system to prevent oil starvation should the filter become clogged.

From the oil filter, oil then flows through the drilled galleries in the cylinder block.

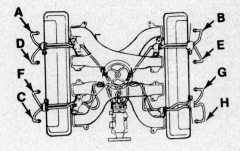

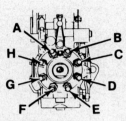

A. Cylinder Number 8
B. Cylinder Number 7
C. Cylinder Number 2
D. Cylinder Number 6
E. Cylinder Number 5
F. Cylinder Number 4
G. Cylinder Number 3
H. Cylinder Number 1

**Fig. 1   Fuel injection line routing**

The rear crankshaft bearing is fed by a hole drilled from the rear main bearing bore to the main oil gallery. Oil is also pumped through the main gallery to a gallery which has been drilled the full length of the left side of the block. Oil from the left side gallery feeds the camshaft bearings and a gallery which runs the full length of the right side of the block. All other engine components are lubricated through these left and right main galleries.

Oil is supplied to lifters on the right bank from the right side main gallery, and to lifters on the left bank from the left side main gallery. The lifters contain disc valves which meter oil to the hollow pushrods and provide valve train lubrication. Holes drilled from the camshaft bearing bores to the crankshaft bearing bores supply oil to main bearings 1-4. Oil flows onto the crankshaft bearings providing lubrication for the crankshaft to rotate freely in its bearings, and cross drilling provides lubrication to the crankpins. As the crankshaft rotates, oil slings off the crankpins to lubricate cylinder walls, pistons and piston pins, and the piston rings.

## FUEL SYSTEM COMPONENTS

The fuel system consists of a fuel tank, electric fuel pump, fuel filter with water sensor and heater, fuel filter restricter switch, injection distributor pump, high pressure lines and fuel injection nozzles.

## SYSTEM OPERATION

Fuel is drawn from the fuel tank by an electric fuel pump which is located on the left side of the frame rail. Fuel is then pumped through the filter/water separator. The filter/water separator is located under the rear of the air cleaner. The fuel is then transferred to the injection pump.

The injection pump is mounted on top of the engine under the intake manifold. The pump is driven by the camshaft through two gears, one attached to the front of the camshaft and the other attached to the end of the injection pump shaft. These gears are the same size and have the same number of teeth, therefore, the injection pump shaft turns at the same RPM as the camshaft. The pump rotates in the opposite direction of the camshaft and crankshaft.

The injection pump is a high pressure rotary type pump that meters, pressurizes and distributes fuel to the eight injector nozzles.

The eight high pressure lines, **Fig. 1** are all the same length although their shape may be different. This prevents timing differences between cylinders. Injection lines should not be bent to ease removal.

## GLOW PLUG CONTROL SYSTEM

### DESCRIPTION

Two glow plug control system are used on the V8-379 diesel engine, one system for heavy duty emissions (LL4 designation) and one for light duty emissions (LH6 designation).

The system used for heavy duty emission versions consists of an integral electronic control/glow plug relay assembly, 6 volt glow plugs, a glow plug inhibit temperature switch and a Wait lamp.

The system used for light duty emission versions, incorporates the same glow plugs, glow plug controller and "Wait" lamp. However, there is no temperature inhibit switch. Instead, the glow plug cycle is controlled by the ECM computer which receives temperature information from the coolant temperature sensor, located in the water crossover on the engine. The computer transmits a voltage signal to the cold advance relay in the ignition circuit to the glow plug controller. The relay is located at the junction block in the engine compartment on the right hand side of the cowl.

### SYSTEM COMPONENTS

#### Glow Plugs

The glow plugs used are 6 volt heaters (operated at 12 volts) that energize when the engine control (ignition) switch is turned to the Run position prior to starting the engine. They remain pulsing a short time after the engine starts, then automatically turns off.

#### Instrumentation

Vehicles equipped with the V8-379 diesel engine incorporate special instrumentation indicators to permit the operator to properly apply the starting procedure. A Wait lamp on the instrument panel provides this information on engine starting conditions. In addition, a Water In Fuel

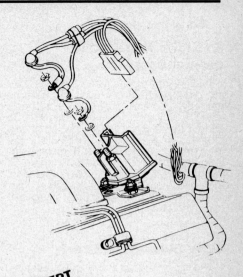

◀FRT

**Fig. 2   Glow plug controller**

lamp and "Low Coolant lamp are used.

### Electronic Controller/Glow Plug Relay Assembly

This assembly, **Figs. 2 and 3**, contains the circuitry which monitors and controls glow plug relay operation. Information received at pins B and C is used by the controller to determine glow plug operating requirements. Pin B senses voltage at the starting motor solenoid. Pin C senses glow plug voltage through the glow plug inhibit switch (if used) which is wired in series with the glow plug voltage sense lead to the glow plugs. The controller is mounted at the rear of the left cylinder head on two .393 inch (10 mm) studs.

### SYSTEM OPERATION

Normal system function operation is as follows:
1. Key-On/Engine Not Running and at room temperature:
   a. The glow plugs energize (turn On) for approximately 4-6 seconds, then de-energize for approximately 4.5 seconds.
   b. The glow plugs cycle On for approximately 1.5 seconds, Off for approximately 4.5 seconds and continue to cycle 1.5 seconds On/4.5 seconds Off for a total duration (including the initial 4-6 seconds) of approximately 20 seconds.
2. If the engine is cranked during or after the above sequence, the glow plugs will cycle On/Off for a total duration of 25 seconds after the engine control switch is returned from the crank position, whether the engine starts or not. The engine does not have to be operating to terminate the glow plug cycling. **The times indicated here are approximate because they vary with initial engine temperature. The initial On time and cycling On/Off times vary also with system voltage and/or temperature. Lower temperatures will cause a longer**

duration of cycling.

## SYSTEM DIAGNOSIS
### Glow Plug System

If all system connections are intact, but the glow plug system does not operate properly, conduct preliminary diagnosis using a suitable ammeter and refer to chart **Fig. 4**. The preliminary diagnosis provides a fast way to determine if the glow plug system is operating properly. Use this procedure whenever there is doubt about correct system operation, then refer to diesel electrical system diagnosis chart, **Fig. 5**, to pinpoint a specific operating condition.

### Glow Plug After Start

The glow plug controller provides glow plug operation after starting a cold engine. This after start operation is initiated when the engine control (ignition) switch is returned to the Run from the Start position. While loss of this function may not cause a cold start problem, it may result in excessive white smoke and/or poor idle after start. To check for proper operation, proceed as follows:

1. With engine temperature at approximately 80°F, turn engine control (ignition) switch to the Run position and allow glow plug to cycle.
2. After approximately two minutes, crank engine for 1 second (it is not important that the engine start). Return ignition switch to the Run position. Glow plugs should cycle at least once after cranking.
3. If the plugs do not energize (turn On), disconnect electrical connector from glow plug controller and check connector harness terminal B with a grounded 12 volt test lamp. The test lamp should be Off with the engine control (ignition) switch in the Run position and should light when the engine is cranked.
4. If the lamp does not operate as described, repair short or open circuit in the engine harness purple wire.
5. If the operates as described, but the glow plug after start feature does not, replace controller.

## ENGINE MOUNTS
## REPLACE
### FRONT MOUNT

1. Disconnect battery ground cable.
2. Using a suitable jack, support engine. **Do not allow engine weight to rest on mount.**
3. Remove engine mount through bolt and nut.
4. Raise engine only enough to allow mount removal.
5. Remove mount assembly bolts, nuts and washers.
6. Remove mount.
7. Reverse procedure to install.

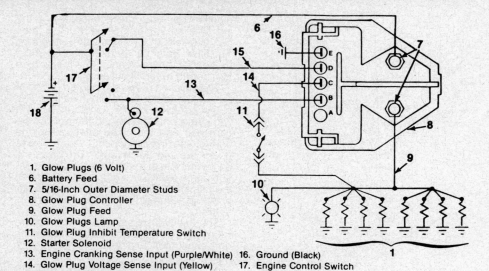

1. Glow Plugs (6 Volt)
6. Battery Feed
7. 5/16-Inch Outer Diameter Studs
8. Glow Plug Controller
9. Glow Plug Feed
10. Glow Plugs Lamp
11. Glow Plug Inhibit Temperature Switch
12. Starter Solenoid
13. Engine Cranking Sense Input (Purple/White)
14. Glow Plug Voltage Sense Input (Yellow)
15. Engine Control (Pink)
16. Ground (Black)
17. Engine Control Switch
18. Battery

**Fig. 3   Electronic glow plug system wiring circuit**

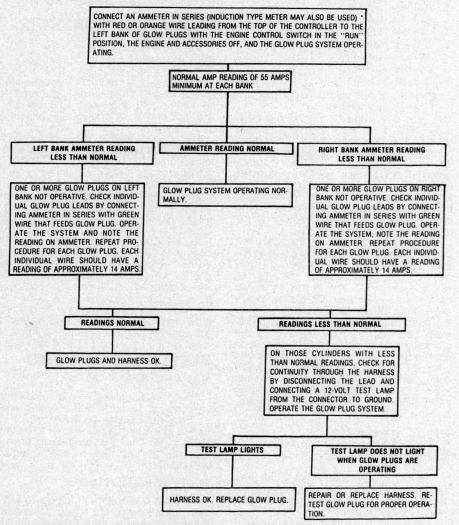

CONNECT AN AMMETER IN SERIES (INDUCTION TYPE METER MAY ALSO BE USED) WITH RED OR ORANGE WIRE LEADING FROM THE TOP OF THE CONTROLLER TO THE LEFT BANK OF GLOW PLUGS WITH THE ENGINE CONTROL SWITCH IN THE "RUN" POSITION, THE ENGINE AND ACCESSORIES OFF, AND THE GLOW PLUG SYSTEM OPERATING.

NORMAL AMP READING OF 55 AMPS MINIMUM AT EACH BANK

| LEFT BANK AMMETER READING LESS THAN NORMAL | AMMETER READING NORMAL | RIGHT BANK AMMETER READING LESS THAN NORMAL |

ONE OR MORE GLOW PLUGS ON LEFT BANK NOT OPERATIVE. CHECK INDIVIDUAL GLOW PLUG LEADS BY CONNECTING AMMETER IN SERIES WITH GREEN WIRE THAT FEEDS GLOW PLUG. OPERATE THE SYSTEM AND NOTE THE READING ON AMMETER. REPEAT PROCEDURE FOR EACH GLOW PLUG. EACH INDIVIDUAL WIRE SHOULD HAVE A READING OF APPROXIMATELY 14 AMPS.

GLOW PLUG SYSTEM OPERATING NORMALLY.

ONE OR MORE GLOW PLUGS ON RIGHT BANK NOT OPERATIVE. CHECK INDIVIDUAL GLOW PLUG LEADS BY CONNECTING AMMETER IN SERIES WITH GREEN WIRE THAT FEEDS GLOW PLUG. OPERATE THE SYSTEM, NOTE THE READING ON AMMETER. REPEAT PROCEDURE FOR EACH GLOW PLUG. EACH INDIVIDUAL WIRE SHOULD HAVE A READING OF APPROXIMATELY 14 AMPS.

READINGS NORMAL

READINGS LESS THAN NORMAL

GLOW PLUGS AND HARNESS OK.

ON THOSE CYLINDERS WITH LESS THAN NORMAL READINGS, CHECK FOR CONTINUITY THROUGH THE HARNESS BY DISCONNECTING THE LEAD AND CONNECTING A 12-VOLT TEST LAMP FROM THE CONNECTOR TO GROUND. OPERATE THE GLOW PLUG SYSTEM.

TEST LAMP LIGHTS

TEST LAMP DOES NOT LIGHT WHEN GLOW PLUGS ARE OPERATING

HARNESS OK. REPLACE GLOW PLUG.

REPAIR OR REPLACE HARNESS. RETEST GLOW PLUG FOR PROPER OPERATION.

\* IF USING AN IN LINE AMMETER READ BOTH BANKS AT ONCE. DO NOT CUT WIRE. (SNAP-ON METER MT552, VAT-40, OR EQUIVALENT)

**Fig. 4   Preliminary diagnosis using an ammeter**

**6.2L DIESEL ELECTRICAL SYSTEM DIAGNOSIS**

ENGINE DOES NOT START COLD - "GLOW PLUG" LAMP MAY OR MAY NOT COME ON.

1. FUEL SYSTEM CHECKED AND IS OK.
2. BATTERY VOLTAGE IS 12.4 VOLTS OR MORE WITH ENGINE CONTROL SWITCH OFF.
3. CRANKING SPEED OK (100 RPM OR MORE).
4. REFER TO THE ELECTRONIC GLOW PLUG SYSTEM FIGURE FOR WIRING HARNESS TERMINAL IDENTIFICATION.

---

USE A VOLTMETER TO MEASURE THE VOLTAGE AT THE BATTERY STUD (SINGLE RED WIRE) ON THE GLOW PLUG.

**BATTERY VOLTAGE**
WITH THE ENGINE CONTROL KEY OFF, MEASURE THE VOLTAGE AT THE GLOW PLUG FEED STUD (TWIN LEAD) ON THE GLOW PLUG CONTROLLER.

**NO VOLTAGE**
LOCATE AND REPAIR THE BATTERY TO GLOW PLUG CONTROLLER CIRCUIT.

**NO VOLTAGE**
DISCONNECT THE HARNESS FROM ALL GLOW PLUGS. USE AN OHMMETER TO MEASURE CONTINUITY BETWEEN THE GLOW PLUG TERMINAL AND THE ENGINE BLOCK (GROUND). REPLACE THE GLOW PLUG IF MEASUREMENT IS GREATER THAN 2 OHMS. RECONNECT ALL GLOW PLUGS BEFORE CONTINUING WITH THE DIAGNOSIS.

**BATTERY VOLTAGE**
RELAY CONTACTS SHORTED. REPLACE THE GLOW PLUG CONTROLLER AND ALL GLOW PLUGS.

REMOVE THE CONTROLLER CONNECTOR AND MEASURE THE VOLTAGE AT THE HARNESS CONNECTOR TERMINAL "D" WITH THE ENGINE CONTROL KEY IN RUN.

**IGNITION VOLTAGE**
MEASURE CONTINUITY BETWEEN TERMINAL "E" OF THE CONNECTOR AND THE ENGINE BLOCK (GROUND). IF MEASUREMENT IS GREATER THAN 1 OHM, LOCATE AND REPAIR THE GROUND CIRCUIT TO THE CONTROLLER.

**NO VOLTAGE**
LOCATE AND REPAIR THE IGNITION FEED CIRCUIT TO THE CONTROLLER.

MEASURE CONTINUITY BETWEEN TERMINALS "C" AND "E" OF THE CONNECTOR.

**LESS THAN 2 OHMS**
RECONNECT THE CONTROLLER HARNESS CONNECTOR AND ENSURE COMPLETE ENGAGEMENT (CONNECTOR LOCKING LATCH SHOULD "CLICK" OVER THE CONTROLLER LOCKING TAB). MEASURE THE VOLTAGE AT THE GLOW PLUG FEED STUD (TWIN LEAD) ON THE GLOW PLUG CONTROLLER WHEN TURNING THE ENGINE CONTROL KEY FROM OFF TO RUN.

**GREATER THAN 2 OHMS**
REMOVE THE CONNECTOR FROM THE TEMPERATURE INHIBIT SWITCH AND MEASURE THE CONTINUITY BETWEEN THE TWO TERMINALS ON THE SWITCH WHICH IS OPEN ABOVE 51.5°C (125°F).

**LESS THAN 1 OHM**
LOCATE AND REPAIR THE GLOW PLUG VOLTAGE SENSE CIRCUIT TO THE CONTROLLER.

**GREATER THAN 1 OHM**
REPLACE THE TEMPERATURE SWITCH AND RETURN TO THE CONTINUITY TEST (TERMINALS "C" TO "E").

**Fig. 5  Diesel electrical system diagnosis (Part 1 of 2)**

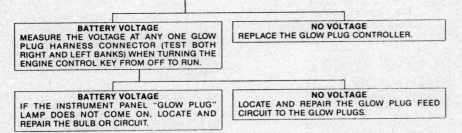

**BATTERY VOLTAGE**
MEASURE THE VOLTAGE AT ANY ONE GLOW PLUG HARNESS CONNECTOR (TEST BOTH RIGHT AND LEFT BANKS) WHEN TURNING THE ENGINE CONTROL KEY FROM OFF TO RUN.

**NO VOLTAGE**
REPLACE THE GLOW PLUG CONTROLLER.

**BATTERY VOLTAGE**
IF THE INSTRUMENT PANEL "GLOW PLUG" LAMP DOES NOT COME ON, LOCATE AND REPAIR THE BULB OR CIRCUIT.

**NO VOLTAGE**
LOCATE AND REPAIR THE GLOW PLUG FEED CIRCUIT TO THE GLOW PLUGS.

**Fig. 5  Diesel electrical system diagnosis (Part 2 of 2)**

## REAR MOUNT

1. Disconnect battery ground cable.
2. Using a suitable jack, support rear of engine.
3. Remove mount to crossmember nuts and washers.
4. Remove mount to transmission attaching bolts and washers.
5. Raise engine only enough to allow mount removal.
6. Remove mount.
7. Reverse procedure to install.

## ENGINE
## REPLACE

1. Disconnect battery cables, then raise

and support vehicle.
2. Remove flywheel cover.
3. Disconnect electrical connectors from starter, then remove starter. Disconnect exhaust pipes from manifolds.
4. Remove transmission bellhousing bolts and front mount bolts.
5. Disconnect block heaters, then remove wiring harness, transmission cooler lines and front battery cable clamp at oil pan.
6. Disconnect fuel return lines and oil cooler lines from engine, remove lower fan shroud bolts and lower vehicle.
7. Scribe hood hinge locations and remove hood.
8. Drain cooling system, remove air cleaner with resonator attached and primary filter from cowl, if equipped.
9. Disconnect ground cable at alternator bracket and remove alternator wires and clips.
10. Disconnect EGR-EPR solenoids, glow plug controller and temperature sensor electrical connectors. Move harness aside.
11. Remove left side ground strap. Remove fan and shroud.
12. Remove power steering pump and reservoir, then position aside.
13. Remove vacuum hose at cruise control cables at the injection pump.
14. Disconnect accelerator, detent and cruise control cables from injection pump.
15. Disconnect heater hose from engine.
16. Remove radiator.
17. Support transmission and remove engine.
18. Reverse procedure to install.

## INTAKE MANIFOLD
## REPLACE

1. Disconnect battery cables.
2. Remove air cleaner.
3. Remove alternator rear attaching bracket.
4. Remove EGR/EPR solenoids and bracket from the intake manifold.
5. Disconnect CDR line from manifold.
6. Remove EGR and crankcase vent hoses.
7. Remove fuel line bracket and ground strap.
8. Remove fuel line bracket from intake manifold, if equipped.
9. Remove intake manifold bolts and fuel line clips.
10. Remove manifold and gasket.
11. Reverse procedure to install. Torque intake manifold attaching bolts to specification in sequence shown in Fig. 6.

## EXHAUST MANIFOLD
## REPLACE
## LEFT SIDE

1. Disconnect battery cables, then raise and support vehicle.
2. Disconnect exhaust pipe from manifold and lower vehicle.
3. Disconnect glow plug wires, then re-

LEFT SIDE

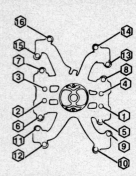

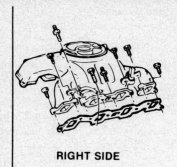

RIGHT SIDE

**Fig. 6  Intake manifold tightening sequence**

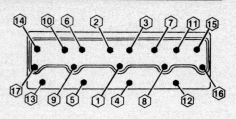

**Fig. 7  Cylinder head bolt tightening sequence**

move air cleaner duct bracket.
4. Remove glow plugs and manifold bolts.
5. Reverse procedure to install.

## RIGHT SIDE

1. Disconnect battery cables.
2. Remove dipstick tube bracket nut, then the dipstick tube.
3. Disconnect glow plug wires, then remove glow plugs.
4. Remove oil cooler pipes and clip. Remove manifold bolts, then raise and support vehicle.
5. Disconnect exhaust pipe from manifold, then remove manifold from bottom of vehicle.
6. Reverse procedure to install.

## CYLINDER HEAD
### REPLACE

1. Disconnect battery ground cable.
2. Remove intake manifold.
3. Label, then remove injection lines.
4. Remove rocker arm covers.
5. Drain cooling system, then raise and support vehicle.
6. Disconnect exhaust pipe from manifold.
7. Lower vehicle. Remove A/C compressor from right side cylinder head, then disconnect ground strap.
8. Remove following components from the left cylinder head:
   a. Remove power steering pump and position aside.
   b. Remove alternator and rear bracket and position aside.
   c. Remove left side engine accessory bracket.
   d. Remove wiring harness attaching clips and position aside.
   e. Remove glow plug relay and dipstick tube.
9. Disconnect coolant sensor electrical connector from cylinder head.
10. Disconnect and remove glow plug wires.
11. Remove rocker arm assemblies and pushrods. **Place components on a suitable workbench in order removed for installation in cylinders from which they were removed.**
12. Disconnect radiator, bypass and heater hoses.
13. Remove ground straps.
14. Remove water crossover pipe and

17. Hydraulic Lifter
18. Pushrod
30. Bolt
31. Rocker Arm Assembly
32. Clamp
33. Guide Plate

**Fig. 8  Valve train components**

thermostat housing assembly.
15. Remove cylinder head attaching bolts. **The rear bolt in the left side cylinder head may have to remain in the head during removal.**
16. Remove cylinder head.
17. Reverse procedure to install, noting the following:
   a. Ensure cylinder head bolt threads are clean.
   b. Apply suitable sealant to the cylinder head bolt threads and under bolt heads.
   c. Torque cylinder head bolts in sequence shown in **Fig. 7**, in three steps. First torque all bolts to 20 ft. lbs. Then torque all bolts to 50 ft. lbs. Finally torque all bolts an additional 90° (1/4 turn).

## ROCKER ARMS & PUSHRODS
### REPLACE

1. Remove rocker arm cover.
2. Remove rocker arm and shaft assembly, **Fig. 8.**
3. Insert screwdriver into bore of rocker shaft and break off ends of nylon rocker arm retainers.
4. Remove tops of retainers, then the rockers, noting position for installation.
5. Remove pushrods, noting position for installation.
6. Reinstall pushrods, if removed.
7. Install rockers on shaft, centering each rocker over hole in shaft, then install new retainers using suitable drift.

8. Before installing rocker arm shafts, align TDC mark on engine with mark on engine balancer, then rotate crankshaft 3½ inches counterclockwise, or to first lower water pump bolt, **Fig. 9.** This will position engine so that all valves are closed. Torque rocker arm shaft bolts to specifications, tightening bolts slowly to allow lifters to bleed down. **The rocker arm shaft must be installed with the split in the ring around the shaft at bottom.**

## VALVE ARRANGEMENT

V8-379 Diesel . . . . . . . . . . . . I-E-I-E-I-E-I-E

## VALVE TIMING
### INTAKE OPENS BEFORE TDC

V8-379 Diesel . . . . . . . . . . . . . . . . . . . . .13°

## VALVES, ADJUST

Hydraulic valve lifters are used, no adjustment is required.

## VALVE GUIDES

The valve guides are an integral part of the cylinder head and are not replaceable. Check valve stem to guide clearance and compare to specifications. If clearance is excessive, ream valve guides using valve guide set J-7049 and install oversize valves.

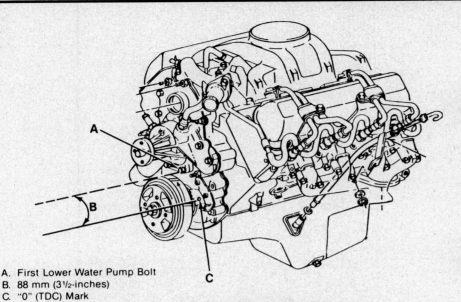

A. First Lower Water Pump Bolt
B. 88 mm (3½-inches)
C. "0" (TDC) Mark

**Fig. 9   Aligning timing marks**

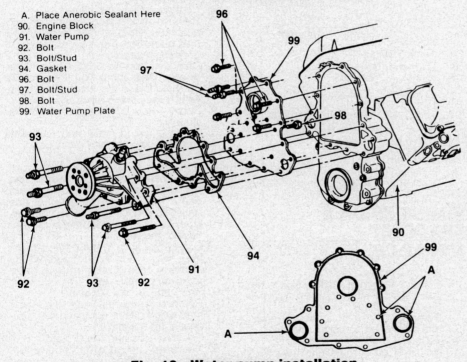

A. Place Anerobic Sealant Here
90. Engine Block
91. Water Pump
92. Bolt
93. Bolt/Stud
94. Gasket
96. Bolt
97. Bolt/Stud
98. Bolt
99. Water Pump Plate

**Fig. 10   Water pump installation**

# HYDRAULIC VALVE LIFTERS
## REPLACE

Roller hydraulic lifters are used to reduce friction between valve lifter and camshaft lobe. Guides keep the lifters from rotating on the camshaft lobes, **Fig. 8.**
1. Remove rocker arm covers and rocker arms.
2. Remove guide clamps and guide plates.
3. Remove valve lifters through access hole in cylinder head using hydralic lifter remover J-29834 and a magnet.

4. Reverse procedure to install, noting the following:
   a. Some engines will have both standard and/or .010 inch oversize hydraulic lifters. The oversize lifter(s) will have a "10" etched on the side of the lifter. The block will be stamped "O.S." on the cast pad adjacent to the lifter bore and on the top rail of the cylinder case above the lifter bore.
   b. New hydraulic lifters must be primed before installation.
   c. After guide plate clamp bolts are installed, turn the crankshaft manually 720° (two complete revolu-

tions), to ensure free movement of the lifters in the guide plates. If the engine will not turn by hand, one or more of the lifters may be binding in the guide plate.

# TORSIONAL DAMPER
## REPLACE

1. Disconnect battery cables, then remove accessory drive belt and crankshaft pulley.
2. Remove torsional damper using torsional damper puller J-23523 and suitable pilot.
3. Reverse procedure to install. Torque bolt to 200 ft. lbs. Torque pulley attaching bolts to 30 ft. lbs.

# WATER PUMP
## REPLACE

1. Disconnect battery cables.
2. Remove fan and fan shroud and, drain radiator.
3. Remove A/C hose bracket nuts, if equipped. Remove oil fill tube alternator pivot bolt and alternator drive belt.
4. Remove alternator lower bracket, power steering pump and belt, and A/C belt.
5. Disconnect bypass hose and lower radiator hose. Remove water pump plate and water pump.
6. Reverse procedure to install. **Before installing attaching bolts, apply anaerobic sealer 1052357 or equivalent to sealing surface as shown, Fig. 10. Sealer should be wet to touch before installing bolts. Torque attaching bolts to 30 ft. lbs.**

# ENGINE FRONT COVER
## REPLACE

1. Drain engine block and remove water pump.
2. Align marks on injection pump gear and camshaft gear, **Fig. 11,** then scribe mark aligning injection pump flange and front cover.
3. Remove crank pulley, torsional damper, front cover to oil pan bolts, fuel return line clips and injection pump driven gear.
4. Remove injection pump retaining nuts from front cover.
5. Remove baffle, remaining cover bolts and front cover, **Fig. 12.**
6. Reverse procedure to install. Apply a ³/₃₂ bead of anerobic sealant 1052357 or equivalent around sealing surface as shown in **Fig. 12.**. Apply a ³/₁₆ bead of RTV sealant around bottom portion of front cover which attaches to oil pan. Ensure scribe marks on injection pump and front cover are aligned and marks on cam gear and pump gear are aligned. Torque the following bolts to the following values, noting the following:
   a. Torque front cover to block attaching bolts to 33 ft. lbs.
   b. Torque oil pan to front cover at-

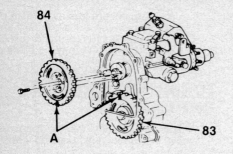

A. Timing Marks
83. Camshaft Gear
84. Injection Pump Gear

**Fig. 11  Injection pump gear & gear timing marks**

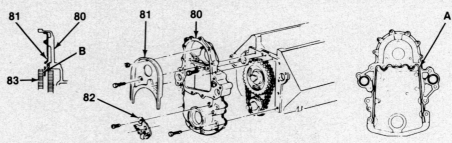

A. Apply Anaerobic Sealer
B. Minimum Clearance 1.0 mm (0.040-inch)
80. Front Cover
81. Baffle
82. Probe Holder
83. Camshaft Gear

**Fig. 12  Front cover & components**

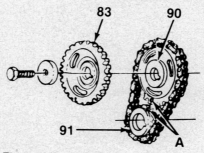

A. Timing Marks
83. Camshaft Gear
90. Camshaft Sprocket
91. Crankshaft Sprocket

**Fig. 13  Timing chain & sprockets**

taching bolts to 84 inch lbs.
c. Torque baffle attaching bolts and nut to 33 ft. lbs.
d. Torque injection pump nuts to 31 ft. lbs.
e. Torque injection pump gear attaching bolts to 17 ft. lbs.
f. After torquing bolts and nuts, measure clearance between injection pump gear and baffle. It is necessary to maintain a minimum of .040 inch between the gear and baffle or noise may result.

## FRONT OIL SEAL
### REPLACE

1. Remove front cover and pry seal out of cover.
2. Lubricate new seal. Using seal installer J-22102 or equivalent, install new seal.

## TIMING CHAIN INSPECTION

The timing chain on these engines has an allowable deflection of up to 0.80 inch. However, if timing chain deflection exceeds 0.80 inch, due to component wear or chain stretch, the engine may experience rough idle, low power, poor fuel economy and/or excessive emission of white smoke. It is recommended that timing chain deflection be measured whenever the front cover is removed, and any time the above symptoms cannot be traced to a fuel system malfunction. To check timing chain deflection, proceed as follows:

1. Remove front cover as outlined.
2. Mount suitable dial indicator on left front of block positioning indicator so that plunger contacts timing chain at the midpoint between the two timing gears.
3. Press timing chain outward (parallel to front face engine block) as far as possible by hand, then zero indicator.
4. Press chain inward as far as possible, then read deflection from dial indicator.
5. Deflection should not exceed 0.80 inch for used chain or 0.50 inch for

new chain.
6. If deflection is excessive, replace chain and/or timing gears as needed.

## TIMING CHAIN & SPROCKET
### REPLACE

1. Remove front cover.
2. Remove camshaft and injection pump gears. Align timing marks as shown in Fig. 13.
3. Remove camshaft sprocket, chain and crankshaft sprocket.
4. To install, proceed as follows:
   a. Install crankshaft and camshaft sprockets.
   b. Install chain.
   c. Align timing marks.
   d. Install camshaft gear, bolt and washer. Torque bolt to 75 ft. lbs.
   e. Install injection pump gear and bolts. Align timing marks.
   f. Torque bolts to 17 ft. lbs.
   g. Install front cover.
   h. Adjust injection pump timing, if new gears, sprockets or timing chain were installed.

## CAMSHAFT
### REPLACE

1. Disconnect battery cables.

2. Drain cooling system.
3. Remove radiator, shrouds and fan.
4. Remove oil pump drive.
5. Remove power steering pump, alternator, air conditioning compressor and position aside.
6. Remove rocker arm covers.
7. Remove rocker arm assemblies and pushrods. **Rocker arm assemblies and pushrods must be marked for proper assembly.**
8. Remove hydraulic lifters. **Place lifters in a suitable rack. The lifters must be installed in the same bore from which they were removed.**
9. Remove front cover as described previously.
10. Remove timing chain and camshaft sprocket as described previously.
11. Remove fuel pump.
12. Remove front engine mount through bolts. **When raising or supporting the engine for any reason, do not use a jack under the oil pan, any sheet metal or crankshaft pulley. Due to the small clearance between the oil pan and oil pump screen, jacking against the oil pan may cause it to be bent against the pump screen, resulting in a damaged oil pickup unit.**
13. Raise and support engine.
14. Remove air conditioning condenser mounting bolts, if equipped. Lift condenser from vehicle.
15. Remove bolts and thrust plate.
16. Remove camshaft as described previously. Pull camshaft from engine block carefully to avoid damage to camshaft bearings.
17. Remove spacer, if necessary.
18. Reverse procedure to install, noting the following:
    a. If a new camshaft is installed, the hydraulic lifters, engine oil and oil filter should be replaced.
    b. Install spacer, with I.D. chamfer facing towards the camshaft.
    c. Coat camshaft lobes with Molykote.
    d. Torque camshaft sprocket, thrust plate and bolt. Torque bolts to 17 ft. lbs.
    e. When installing timing chain and sprockets, properly align timing marks.

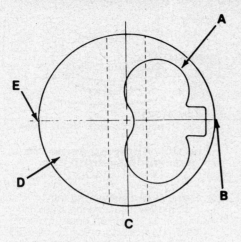

A. Oil Control Ring Expander Gap
B. Second Compression Ring Gap
C. Centerline Of Piston Pin
D. Oil Control Ring Gap
E. Top Compression Ring Gap

**Fig. 14   Piston & piston ring end gap positioning**

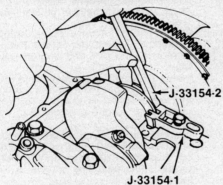

**Fig. 17   Installing rope seal piece**

## PISTON & ROD ASSEMBLY

Assemble piston to rod and install into cylinder block. Install with depression on top of piston toward outside of engine, **Fig. 14.** Install connecting rod bearing with tang slots positioned on side opposite camshaft.

## PISTON & RINGS

Pistons are available in standard sizes and oversize of .030 inch. Rings are available in standard sizes and oversize of .030 inch. When installing piston rings, stagger piston rings as shown in **Fig. 14.**

## MAIN & ROD BEARINGS

Main bearings are available in standard sizes and undersizes of .005 and .010 inch. Rod bearings are available in standard sizes and undersizes of .010 inch and .020 inch.

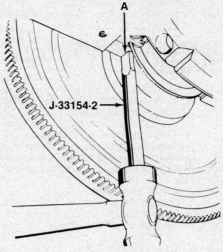

A. Upper Seal Groove

**Fig. 15   Packing upper rear crankshaft rope seal**

## CRANKSHAFT REAR OIL SEAL SERVICE

The production rear crankshaft oil seal is a rope type seal. The rope seal can be replaced with a two piece type seal, if desired. The CDR and crankcase ventilation system should be thoroughly inspected and crankcase pressure should be checked before a new seal is installed.
1. Remove oil pan and oil pump.
2. Remove rear main bearing cap.
3. Remove old rope seal from main bearing cap. Do not discard.
4. To install seal onto upper seal groove, proceed as follows:
   a. Using rear oil seal packer J-33154-2 or equivalent, gently drive upper seal into groove approximately 1/4 inch. Do this on both side, **Fig. 15.**
   b. Measure the amount the seal was driven up on one side. Add 1/16 inch. Cut this length from the old seal removed from the old seal removed from the main bearing cap. Use the main bearing cap as a holding tool when cutting the seal, **Fig. 16.** Use a sharp tool, repeat this procedure for the other side.
   c. Install rear oil seal packer J-33154-2 or equivalent, onto the cylinder block as shown in **Fig. 17.**
   d. Use rear oil seal packer J-33154-2 or equivalent, to work the short pieces of the seal cut previously onto the guide tool and into the seal groove in the block. It may help to use clean engine oil on the seal pieces. repeat this procedure for the other side.
5. To install a new rope seal to the main bearing cap, proceed as follows:
   a. Apply suitable adhesive part No. 1052621 or equivalent, to seal groove.
   b. Position rope seal onto bearing cap.

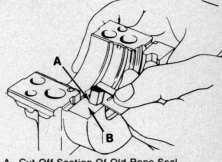

A. Cut Off Section Of Old Rope Seal
B. Use Bearing Cap As Holding Fixture

**Fig. 16   Cutting rope seal**

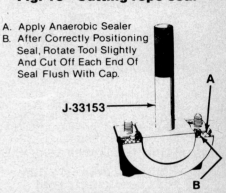

A. Apply Anaerobic Sealer
B. After Correctly Positioning Seal, Rotate Tool Slightly And Cut Off Each End Of Seal Flush With Cap.

**Fig. 18   Installing lower rope seal piece**

   c. Using rear oil seal installer J-33153 or equivalent, install seal as shown in **Fig. 18.**
   d. After correctly positioning the seal, rotate rear oil seal installer J-33153 slightly and cut the seal ends flush with the bearing cap surface.
   e. Measure rear main bearing clearance, using Plastigage. **The main bearing caps are to be tapped into place with a suitable mallet before attaching bolts are installed.**
6. To install a two piece type seal in place of the rope seal, proceed as follows:
   a. Apply a light coat of clean engine oil to the seal lips where they contact the crankshaft.
   b. Roll one seal half into the engine block seal groove until 1-2 of seal end is extending out of the block, **Fig. 19.**
   c. Insert other seal half into the opposite side of the seal groove in the block.
   d. The contact ends of the seal halves should now be at the four and ten o'clock positions, or at the eight and two o'clock positions. This is necessary to align the rear main bearing cap and seal lips.
7. To install main bearing cap, proceed as follows:
   a. Apply a thin film of suitable sealant to the bearing cap as shown in **Fig. 20.** Do not place sealant in the

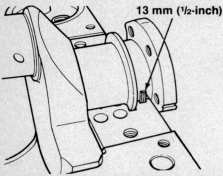

**INSTALLING THE UPPER SEAL HALF**

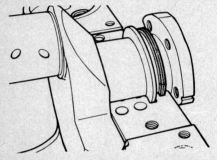

**INSTALLING THE LOWER SEAL HALF**

**Fig. 19  Installing two piece rear crankshaft seal**

bearing cap oil relief slot.
b. Apply a light coat of clean engine oil to the crankshaft surface that will contact the seal.
c. Apply clean engine oil to the main bearing cap bolt threads.
d. Tap main bearing cap into place with a suitable mallet.
e. Torque inner cap bolts to 110 ft. lbs. Torque outer bolts to 100 ft. lbs. Then, tighten all bolts again in the same sequence.

## OIL PAN
### REPLACE

1. Disconnect batteries and raise vehicle.
2. Drain oil and remove transmission or flywheel dust cover, oil pan bolts and left front engine mount through bolt.
3. Carefully raise and support engine, then remove oil pan.
4. Reverse procedure to install. Apply a 3/32 inch bead of RTV sealant or equivalent, to the oil pan sealing surfaces, inboard of the bolt holes. The sealer must be wet to the touch when oil pan is installed. Torque all attaching bolts except the two rear bolts to 84 inch lbs. Torque the two rear bolts to 17 ft. lbs.

## OIL PUMP
### REPLACE

1. Remove oil pan as described previously.
2. Remove oil pump to rear main bearing cap attaching bolts and remove pump

and extension shaft.
3. Reverse procedure top install. Torque attaching bolts to 65 ft. lbs.

## INJECTION PUMP TIMING

1. Check marks on top of engine front cover and injection pump flange, **Fig. 21**. These marks must be aligned for engine to be properly timed. **The ignition switch must be Off when adjusting timing. On except California models, align the scribe marks on California models align the half circles.**
2. To adjust, proceed as follows:
   a. Loosen three pump retaining nuts.
   b. Align mark on injection pump with mark on front cover. Torque nuts to 30 ft. lbs.
   c. Adjust throttle rod.

## INJECTION PUMP REPLACE
### REMOVAL

1. Disconnect battery ground cable.
2. Remove intake manifold.
3. Disconnect injection lines.
4. Disconnect accelerator cable from injection pump.
5. Disconnect detent cable, if equipped.
6. Disconnect and cap fuel return line from top of injection pump.
7. Disconnect and cap fuel supply line from injection pump.
8. Disconnect all electrical connectors and vacuum lines from injection pump.
9. Remove air conditioning hose retainer bracket, if equipped.
10. Remove oil fill tube.
11. Place a paint mark on the front cover and injection pump flange as a reference.
12. Turn crankshaft to gain access to the bolts attaching driven gear to injection pump.
13. Remove bolts, nuts and injection pump.

### INSTALLATION

1. Install a new gasket.
2. Install injection pump onto front cover.
3. Align locating pin on pump hub with slot in the injection pump driven gear.
4. Install and torque attaching nuts to 30 ft. lbs. Check to ensure timing marks are properly aligned before torquing nuts.
5. Install drive gear to injection pump. Torque bolts to 20 ft. lbs.
6. Reverse removal procedure to complete installation.

## INJECTION PUMP IN-VEHICLE SERVICE

### PUMP COVER SEAL AND/OR GUIDE STUD SEAL, REPLACE

1. Disconnect battery cables.

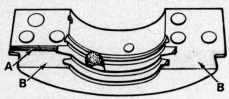

A. Oil Relief Slot
B. Apply Anaerobic Sealer to Shaded Area

**Fig. 20   Applying sealer to rear main bearing cap**

2. Remove air cleaner and intake, then install protective screens J-29664.
3. Disconnect injection pump fuel solenoid and housing pressure cold advance electrical leads, then the fuel return pipe.
4. Remove fast idle solenoid upper attaching bolt, then loosen lower bolt and position solenoid aside.
5. Clean injection pump cover, upper portion of pump and guide stud area.
6. Remove injection pump cover attaching screws and cover. Ensure that no dirt or foreign material enters pump, since damage to pump or engine may result.
7. Observe metering valve spring to top of guide position to aid reassembly.
8. Remove guide stud and washer, noting location of parts.
9. Install guide stud and new washer ensuring that upper extension of metering valve spring is positioned over guide stud. Torque guide stud to 85 inch lbs.
10. Hold throttle in idle position, then install new seal onto pump cover. Install cover onto injection pump, then torque cover attaching screws to 33 inch lbs.
11. Connect battery cables.
12. Turn ignition switch to Run position, then momentarily connect pink wire to solenoid. A clicking noise should be heard whenever wire contacts solenoid. If clicking noise is evident, connect fuel solenoid and housing pressure cold advance electrical leads and proceed to Step 14. If clicking noise is not evident, proceed to next step.
13. Remove cover. With ignition switch in Run position, ground solenoid lead and connect pink wire. The solenoid should activate and move the linkage. If solenoid does not activate, do not start engine and replace solenoid. Repeat Steps 11 and 12.
14. Install fuel return pipe, throttle cable and return springs, then position fast idle solenoid.
15. Start engine and check for leaks. **Engine may idle roughly due to air in the injection system. Allowing engine to idle for several moments will usually purge system of air. If not, shut engine off and allow air bubbles to rise to the top of the injection pump, then restart engine.**
16. Remove intake manifold screens, then install intake and air cleaner.

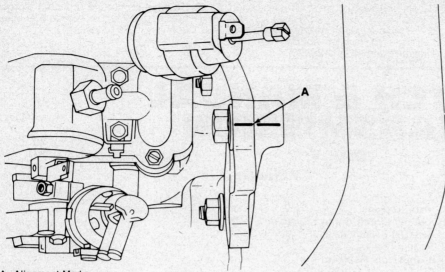

A. Alignment Marks

### Fig. 21 Timing alignment marks

## THROTTLE SHAFT SEAL, REPLACE

1. Disconnect battery cables.
2. Remove air cleaner and intake, then install protective screens J-29664.
3. Disconnect injection pump fuel solenoid and housing pressure cold advance electrical leads, then the fuel return pipe.
4. Mark position of TPS switch or vacuum regulator valve to aid in reassembly, then remove throttle rod and return springs.
5. Loosen, then position fast idle solenoid aside.
6. Remove throttle cable bracket.
7. Install injection pump timing adapter J-29601 over throttle shaft, with slots of tool engaging shaft pin. Position spring clip over throttle shaft advance cam, then tighten wing nut. Pull tool off throttle shaft without loosening wing nut, to provide proper alignment for reassembly. Loosen face cam screw.
8. Drive pin from throttle shaft, then remove throttle shaft advance cam and fiber washer. Remove any burrs from shaft.
9. Clean injection pump cover, upper portion of pump, throttle shaft and guide stud area.
10. Remove injection pump cover attaching screws and cover. Ensure that no dirt or foreign material enters pump, since damage to pump or engine may result.
11. Observe metering valve spring to top of guide position to aid assembly.
12. Remove guide stud and washer, noting location of parts.
13. Rotate min-max governor assembly, then remove from throttle shaft. **If idle governor spring becomes disengaged from throttle block, install spring with tightly wound coils facing toward throttle block.**
14. Remove throttle shaft assembly and examine for wear or damage. Replace if necessary.
15. Examine pump housing throttle shaft bushings. If bushings are worn or show signs of leakage, remove pump and send to authorized Stanadyne distributor for bushing replacement.
16. Remove seals from throttle shaft. Do not cut seals from shaft, since nicks in seal seat can cause leakage.
17. Coat new seals with chassis grease or equivalent, and install seals onto throttle shaft.
18. Slide throttle shaft into pump housing until min-max governor assembly can be installed onto throttle shaft.
19. Rotate min-max governor assembly downward, hold in this position, then slide throttle shaft and governor into position.
20. Install new washer, throttle shaft advance cam and a new throttle shaft drive pin. Do not tighten cam screw at this time.
21. Align throttle shaft advance cam so injection pump timing adapter J-29601 can be installed as outlined in Step 7.
22. Insert a .005 inch feeler gauge between throttle shaft white washer and pump housing, then squeeze throttle shaft and torque cam screw to 30 inch lbs. Apply Loctite 290 or equivalent to secure screw, then remove tool.
23. Install guide stud and new washer. Ensure that upper extension of metering valve spring is positioned over guide stud. Torque guide stud to 85 inch lbs.
24. Hold throttle in idle position, then install new seal onto pump cover. Install cover onto injection pump, then torque attaching screws to 33 inch lbs.
25. Install vacuum regulator valve or TPS switch, then reconnect battery ground cables.
26. Turn ignition switch to Run position, then momentarily connect pink wire to solenoid. A clicking noise should be heard whenever wire contacts solenoid. If clicking noise is evident, connect fuel solenoid and housing pressure cold advance electrical leads and proceed to Step 28. If clicking noise is not evident, proceed to next step.
27. Remove cover. With ignition switch in Run position, ground solenoid lead and connect pink wire. The solenoid should activate and move the linkage. If solenoid does not activate, replace it. Repeat steps 26 and 27.
28. Install throttle cable bracket, detent cable and fast idle solenoid.
29. Install throttle cable and return springs.
30. Ensure that timing marks on injection pump and housing are aligned, then tighten attaching nuts. Connect fuel return line.
31. Start engine and check for leaks. **Engine may idle roughly due to air in the injection system. Allowing engine to idle for several moments will usually purge system of air. If not, shut engine off and allow air bubbles to rise to the top of the injection pump, then restart engine.**
32. Remove intake manifold screens, then install intake and air cleaner.

## INJECTION PUMP OFF-VEHICLE SERVICE

### ADVANCE PIN HOLE PLUG SEAL, REPLACE

1. Loosen advance pin hole plug seal by tapping with hammer.
2. Remove plug and seal.
3. Reverse procedure to install. Torque plug to 90 inch lbs.

### HYDRAULIC HEAD SEAL O-RING, REPLACE

#### Removal

1. Remove throttle shaft and seals.
2. Remove metering valve.
3. Remove housing vent screw assembly.
4. Remove advance pin hole plug and advance pin.
5. Remove head locating screws and seal.
6. Remove hydraulic head assembly and O-ring.

#### Installation

1. Install hydraulic head seal and place head assembly into pump housing.
2. Install two head locking screws finger tight and turn pump upside down.
3. Install head locating screw and torque to 17 ft. lbs.
4. Install advance pin and advance pin plug.
5. Turn pump so cover opening is up, and install metering valve.
6. Install throttle shaft, seals and pump cover.

## INJECTION NOZZLE
### REPLACE

1. Disconnect battery cables, fuel return clip, fuel return hose and fuel injection line.
2. Remove injection nozzle by applying torque to largest nozzle hex with switch gage tool J-29873.
3. Reverse procedure to install. Torque nozzle to 50 ft. lbs. Torque fuel injection line to 20 ft. lbs.

# CLUTCH & MANUAL TRANSMISSION

## INDEX

### Page No.

## HYDRAULIC CLUTCH CONTROL SYSTEM

The clutch control system consists of a clutch master cylinder, slave cylinder and a connecting hose. Pressure applied to the master cylinder pushrod from the clutch pedal forces the master cylinder plunger and seal assembly along the cylinder bore. As the plunger moves, the seal closes off the cylinder bore fluid inlet and hydraulic pressure is created which operates the slave cylinder. The slave cylinder, in turn, operates the clutch release fork through a short pushrod.

When the clutch pedal is released, the combination of fluid and return spring pressure moves the piston and seal assembly back until it reaches a stop in the bore. When the piston contacts the stop, the seal is behind the cylinder bore inlet (recuperation hole) and pressure is released from the system.

### SYSTEM CHECK

1. Inspect slave cylinder and clutch pedal travel.
2. Clutch pedal travel should be approximately 8.3 inches, and slave cylinder rod should have a minimum of 1 inch travel, measured at the clutch fork.
3. Inspect pedal bushings for binding and excessive wear, and the fork for damage, wear and proper lubrication. Replace components that are damaged or worn.
4. With engine running at normal operating temperature, hold clutch pedal approximately 1/2 from floor mat, wait approximately 9 seconds and move shift lever between first and reverse several times.
5. If shift is not smooth, bleed system and recheck operation.
6. If shift is still not smooth, inspect clutch components and repair or replace as needed.

### BLEEDING CLUTCH SYSTEM

1. Fill master cylinder as needed with new brake fluid conforming to DOT 3 specification.
2. Raise and support vehicle and remove slave cylinder attaching bolts.
3. Hold slave cylinder at approximately 45° angle with bleed valve at highest point.
4. Fully depress clutch pedal, then open bleed valve.
5. Close bleed valve, then release clutch pedal. **Do not release clutch pedal with bleed valve open as air will be drawn into hydraulic system.**
6. Repeat steps 4 and 5 until all air is evacuated from system. Check and refill master cylinder at regular intervals during procedure to prevent air from being drawn into system through master cylinder.

## CLUTCH
### REPLACE

1. Remove transmission as outlined in "Transmission, Replace" procedure.
2. Disconnect hydraulic line from secondary cylinder, then the clutch fork pushrod and return spring.
3. Remove flywheel housing.
4. Slide clutch fork from ball stud and remove fork from dust boot. **Look for "X" mark on flywheel and clutch cover. If no marks are present, scribe marks on flywheel and cover to aid assembly.**
5. Loosen clutch to flywheel attaching bolts evenly one turn at a time until spring pressure is released.
6. Remove attaching bolts and clutch assembly.
7. Reverse procedure to install.

## TRANSMISSION
### REPLACE

1. Disconnect battery ground cable.
2. Remove shift control lever and boot.
3. Raise and support vehicle.
4. Drain fluid from transmission.
5. Disconnect driveshaft from transmission.
6. Remove transfer case, if equipped.
7. Disconnect parking brake cable.
8. Disconnect exhaust pipes from exhaust manifolds.
9. Disconnect electrical connectors from transmission.
10. Remove clutch slave cylinder and position aside.
11. Remove transmission cover.
12. Support transmission using a suitable jack.
13. Remove hydraulic lines attaching clips from transmission.
14. Remove crossmember.
15. Remove transmission attaching bolts, then the transmission.
16. Reverse procedure to install. Torque transmission attaching bolts to 50 ft. lbs.

# TRANSFER CASE

## INDEX

## TRANSFER CASE
### REPLACE

1. Disconnect battery ground cable.
2. Place transfer case in "4H" position.
3. Raise and support transmission.
4. Drain fluid from transfer case.
5. Remove skid shield and plate.
6. Remove shift lever swivel.
7. Disconnect speed sensor electrical connector.
8. Remove indicator switch electrical connector.
9. Mark driveshafts and flanges, then remove front and rear driveshafts.
10. Support transfer case with a suitable jack.
11. Remove transfer case to transmission

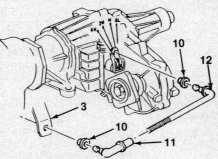

3. Shift Lever  11. Swivel
10. Insulator   12. Rod

**Fig. 1   Transfer case shift linkage adjustment**

adapter attaching bolts.
12. Remove transfer case and gasket.
13. Reverse procedure to install. Torque adapter attaching bolts to 29 ft. lbs. on 1988 models and 24 ft. lbs. on 1989 models. Torque front driveshaft flange attaching bolts to 75 ft. lbs. Torque skid plate attaching bolts to 46 ft. lbs.

## TRANSFER CASE LINKAGE
### ADJUST

1. Remove swivel (11) from shift lever (3), **Fig. 1.**
2. Turn swivel (11) inward or outward to determine shift detent.
3. Install swivel (11) to shift lever (3).

# REAR AXLE, SUSPENSION & BRAKES

## INDEX

## CHEVROLET SALISBURY TYPE SEMI-FLOATING AXLE

In this rear axle, **Fig. 1**, the rear axle housing and differential carrier are cast into an integral assembly. The drive pinion assembly is mounted in two opposed tapered roller bearings. The pinion bearings are preloaded by a spacer behind the front bearing. The pinion is positioned by a washer between the head of the pinion and the rear bearing.

The differential is supported in the carrier by two tapered roller side bearings. These bearings are preloaded by spacers located between the bearings and carrier housing. The differential assembly is positioned for proper ring gear and pinion backlash by varying these spacers. The differential case houses two side gears in mesh with two pinions mounted on a pinion shaft which is held in place by a lock pin. The side gears and pinions are backed by thrust washers.

### AXLE ASSEMBLY, REPLACE

1. Raise and support vehicle. Using a suitable jack, support rear axle assembly.
2. Drain fluid from axle assembly.
3. Mark driveshaft to flange, then disconnect driveshaft and tie driveshaft to side rail or crossmember.
4. Tape bearing cups to prevent loss of the rollers.
5. Remove wheel and brake drum or hub and drum assembly.
6. Disconnect parking brake cable from lever and brake flange plate.
7. Disconnect and cap hydraulic brake lines from connectors.
8. Remove shock absorbers from axle brackets.
9. Disconnect vent line from vent fitting.
10. Remove height sensing and brake proportional valve brackets.
11. Remove nuts and washers from U-bolts.
12. Carefully remove U-bolts, spring plates and spacers from axle assembly.
13. Lower axle assembly from vehicle.
14. Reverse procedure to install.

### AXLE SHAFT, OIL SEAL & BEARING, REPLACE

1. Raise and support vehicle.
2. Remove wheel and tire assembly.
3. Remove brake drum.
4. Remove carrier cover and drain fluid from axle. Remove gasket.
5. Remove locking screw.
6. Remove pinion shaft as follows:

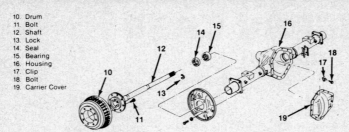

10. Drum
11. Bolt
12. Shaft
13. Lock
14. Seal
15. Bearing
16. Housing
17. Clip
18. Bolt
19. Carrier Cover

**Fig. 1   Axle shaft & housing components. Chevrolet semi-floating axle**

a. On models without locking differential, remove pinion shaft from case.
b. On models with locking differential, remove pinion shaft partially and rotate case until pinion shaft touches the housing, **Fig. 2.**
c. Using a suitable screwdriver, rotate lock until it aligns with thrust block.
7. Push axle shaft flange toward differential. **Do not hammer the shaft to move.**
8. Remove lock (13), **Fig. 1,** from button end of axle shaft.
9. Slide axle shaft out from housing. Do not damage seal.
10. Using axle shaft bearing remover J-23689 or equivalent, remove oil seal.
11. Remove bearing as follows:
    a. Using axle shaft bearing remover, J-23689 (for 8½ ring gear) or axle shaft bearing remover J-29712 (for 9½ ring gear), carefully pull bearing from axle.
    b. Insert appropriate tool into axle bore so it grasps behind the bearing. Tighten nut and washer against bearing face, then pull bearing out using slide hammer with adapter J-2619-01 or equivalent.
12. Reverse procedure to install.

## DANA/SPICER FULL FLOATING AXLE

This axle, **Fig. 3,** is similar to Salisbury type units. However, in the axle shafts are full floating and the drive pinion incorporates two shim packs. The inner shim pack controls pinion depth, while the outer pack controls pinion bearing preload.

### AXLE ASSEMBLY, REPLACE

Refer to "Chevrolet Salisbury Type Semi-Floating Axle" for axle assembly replace procedure.

### AXLE SHAFT, REPLACE

1. Using a soft faced mallet, tap axle shaft flange lightly to loosen shaft.
2. Remove axle shaft attaching bolts, **Fig. 3,** then grip axle shaft rib with pliers and twist to start shaft removal.
3. Remove axle shaft from axle tube.
4. Reverse procedure to install.

### WHEEL BEARING, REPLACE

1. Raise and support vehicle.

2. Remove axle shaft.
3. Remove hub and drum.
4. Remove oil seal, inner bearing and retaining ring.
5. Remove outer bearing.
6. Reverse procedure to install.

## WHEEL BEARINGS, ADJUST

Ensure the brakes are completely released and do not drag. Check wheel bearing play by grasping the tire at the top and pulling and pushing back and forth, or by using a pry bar under the tire. If the wheel bearings are properly adjusted, movement of the brake drum in relation to the brake flange plate will be barely noticeable and the wheel will turn freely. If the movement is excessive, adjust the bearings as follows:

1. Back off attaching nut until just loose, but not more than one slot of the lock or the axle spindle using wheel bearing nut wrench J-2222-C or equivalent.
2. Align adjusting nut slot with keyway in the axle spindle.

## SHOCK ABSORBER REPLACE

1. Raise and support vehicle, then the rear axle.
2. Remove retaining bolts, then disconnect shock absorber from upper mounting bracket.
3. Disconnect shock absorber from lower mounting bracket.
4. Remove shock absorber from vehicle.
5. Reverse procedure to install.

## LEAF SPRING REPLACE

1. Raise and support vehicle, then the rear axle assembly.
2. Remove U-bolt nuts and washers.
3. Remove anchor plate, **Fig. 4.**
4. Remove U-bolts and spacer.
5. Loosen shackle to spring nut.
6. Remove shackle to rear bracket attaching nut, washer and bolt.
7. Remove spring to front bracket, nut, washers and bolt.
8. Remove spring assembly from vehicle.
9. Reverse procedure to install. Torque leaf spring to bracket attaching nuts to 80 ft. lbs. Torque leaf spring to shackle nuts to 80 ft. lbs. Torque shackle to bracket nuts to 80 ft. lbs. Torque up-

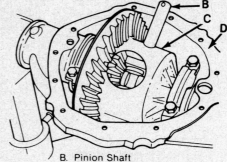

B. Pinion Shaft
C. Differential Case
D. Housing

**Fig. 2   Position case for clearance**

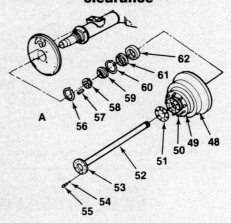

| | |
|---|---|
| A. Dana | 55. Bolt |
| 48. Drum | 56. Retaining Ring |
| 49. Hub | 57. Key |
| 50. Stud | 58. Adjusting Nut |
| 51. Gasket | 59. Outer Bearing |
| 52. Shaft | 60. Retaining Ring |
| 53. Axle Shaft Flange | 61. Inner Bearing |
| 54. Washer | 62. Oil Seal |

**Fig. 3   Axle, hub & drum components. Dana/Spicer full floating axle**

per shock absorber nuts to 52 ft. lbs. Torque lower shock absorber nuts to 17 ft. lbs. Torque U-bolt nuts as follows:
a. On 100 and 200 models, torque nuts to 80 ft. lbs.
b. On 300 models without dual rear wheels or V8-454 engine, torque nuts to 80 ft. lbs.
c. On 300 models with dual rear wheels or V8-454 engine without dual rear wheels, torque nuts to 109 ft. lbs. **Ensure to torque bolts and nuts as specified to assure proper retention of the components.**

## SHACKLE REPLACE

1. Raise and support vehicle, then the axle.
2. Loosen shackle to spring attaching

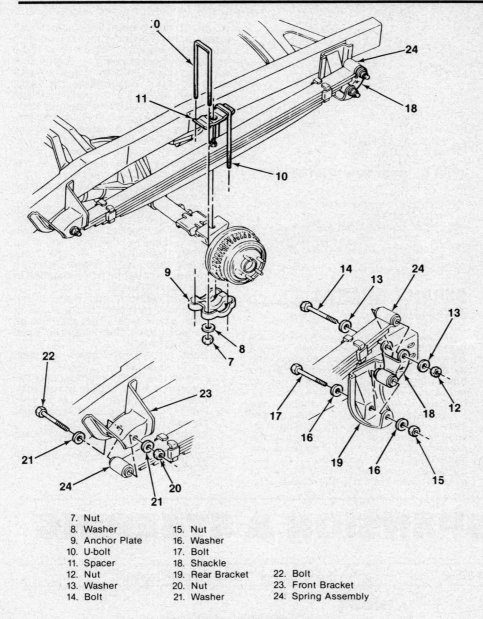

**Fig. 4 Axle components**

| | |
|---|---|
| 7. Nut | |
| 8. Washer | 15. Nut |
| 9. Anchor Plate | 16. Washer |
| 10. U-bolt | 17. Bolt |
| 11. Spacer | 18. Shackle |
| 12. Nut | 19. Rear Bracket |
| 13. Washer | 20. Nut |
| 14. Bolt | 21. Washer |

22. Bolt
23. Front Bracket
24. Spring Assembly

bolt.
3. Remove shackle to rear bracket bolt, nut and washers.
4. Remove shackle to spring nut, washers and bolt.
5. Remove shackle from vehicle.
6. Reverse procedure to install. To adjust spring height, proceed as follows:
   a. Adjust spring height to obtain a measurement of 7.17 inches (182 mm) between top surface of axle jounce pad and bottom surface of the frame jounce bracket, **Fig. 5.**
   b. After adjustment, torque front and rear spring nuts and shackle nut to 80 ft. lbs.

## MASTER CYLINDER REPLACE

1. Disconnect and plug brake lines from master cylinder.
2. Remove attaching nuts, then the master cylinder.
3. Reverse procedure to install.

## POWER BRAKE UNIT REPLACE
### EXC. HYDRO-BOOST

1. Remove vacuum hose from check valve and master cylinder retaining nuts.
2. Pull master cylinder forward so it clears mounting studs and move to one side. Support cylinder to avoid stress on hydraulic lines.
3. Remove power unit to dash nuts.
4. Remove brake pedal pushrod retainer and disconnect pushrod from pin.
5. Remove power brake unit from vehicle.
6. Reverse procedure to install.

## HYDRO-BOOST

Pump brake pedal several times with engine off to deplete accumulator of fluid.
1. Remove two nuts attaching master cylinder to booster, then move master cylinder away from booster with brake lines attached.
2. Remove hydraulic lines from booster. Plug and cap all lines and outlets.
3. Remove retainer and washer securing booster pushrod to brake pedal arm.
4. Remove nuts attaching booster unit to dash panel.
5. Loosen booster from dash panel and move booster pushrod inboard until it disconnects from brake pedal arm. Remove spring washer from brake pedal arm.
6. Remove booster unit from vehicle.
7. Reverse procedure to install. To fill the Hydro-Boost system, proceed as follows: **The power steering fluid and brake fluid cannot be intermixed. If the brake seals contact power steering fluid or steering seals contact brake fluid, seal damage will result.**
   a. Fill power steering pump reservoir to the proper level and allow fluid to remain undisturbed for at least two minutes.
   b. Start and operate engine momentarily. Add fluid, if necessary.
   c. Repeat steps a and b until the fluid level remains constant after operating engine.
   d. Raise and support front of engine enough so front wheels do not contact floor.
   e. Turn steering wheel from stop to stop, lightly contacting the stops. Add fluid, if necessary.
   f. Lower vehicle.
   g. Start engine and depress brake pedal several times while rotating the steering wheel from stop to stop.
   h. Switch ignition to Off position, then pump brake pedal 4-5 times.
   i. Check fluid level, add fluid if necessary.
   j. If fluid is extremely foamy, allow vehicle to stand for a few minutes with the engine not operating. Then, repeat steps g through i.
   k. Check for presence of air in the oil. Air in the oil will have a milky appearance. Air in the system will also cause the fluid level in the pump to rise when the ignition switch is turned to the Off position. If the pump will not bleed the air after a few attempts, check power steering system.

## PARKING BRAKE ADJUST
### LEAD/TRAILING DRUM BRAKES

1. Raise and support vehicle. Mark relationship of wheel to axle flange.
2. Remove wheel and tire assembly.

Mark relationship of drum to axle flange.

3. Remove brake drum.
4. Using drum to brake shoe clearance gage J-21177-A or equivalent, measure brake drum inside diameter.
5. Turning the adjuster nut, adjust shoe and lining diameter to .010-.020 inch, less than the inside drum diameter for each rear wheel.
6. Ensure stops on park brake levers are against the edge of the brake shoe web. If the parking brake cable is holding the stops off the edge of shoe web, loosen the parking brake cable adjustment.
7. Tighten parking brake cable at adjuster nut until the lever stops begin to move off the shoe webs. Loosen adjustment nut until the lever stops moving back, barely touching the shoe webs. There should be no more than .019 inch clearance between stops and either web.
8. Install drums and wheels, aligning marks made previously.
9. Apply and release service brake pedal 30-35 times with normal pedal force. Pause approximately one second between pedal applications.
10. Depress parking brake six ratchet clicks. Rear wheels should not rotate.
11. Release parking brake and check for free wheel rotation.
12. Lower vehicle.

## DUO-SERVO DRUM BRAKES

1. Raise and support vehicle. Support rear axle using suitable safety stands.
2. Loosen equalizer nut.

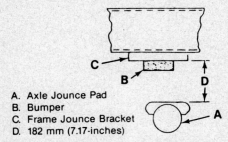

A. Axle Jounce Pad
B. Bumper
C. Frame Jounce Bracket
D. 182 mm (7.17-inches)

**Fig. 5  Rear axle trim height**

3. Depress parking brake pedal four ratchet clicks.
4. Adjust equalizer nut until wheels rotate forward with moderate drag.
5. Release parking brake and check for free wheel rotation.
6. Lower vehicle.

## SERVICE BRAKES
## ADJUST

These brakes, have self-adjusting shoe mechanisms that assure correct lining-to-drum clearances at all times. The automatic adjusters operate only when the brakes are applied as the car is moving rearward or when the car comes to an uphill stop. Although the brakes are self-adjusting, an initial adjustment is necessary after the brake shoes have been relined or replaced, or when the length of the adjusting screw has been changed during some other service operation.

Frequent usage of an automatic transmission forward range to halt reverse vehicle motion may prevent the automatic adjusters from functioning, thereby inducing low pedal heights. Should low pedal heights be encountered, it is recommended that numerous forward and reverse stops be made until satisfactory pedal height is obtained. If a low pedal condition cannot be corrected by making numerous reverse stops (provided the hydraulic system is free of air) it indicates that the self-adjusting mechanism is not functioning. Therefore it will be necessary to remove the brake drum, clean, free up and lubricate the adjusting mechanism. Then adjust the brakes, being sure the parking brake is fully released.

1. Using a suitable punch, knock out lanced area in backing plate or drum. If drum is installed on vehicle when this is done, remove drum and clean brake compartment of all metal. **When adjustment is completed, a new hole cover must be installed in the backing plate.**
2. Using suitable tool, turn brake adjusting screw to expand brake shoes at each wheel until wheel can just be turned by hand. Drag should be equal on all wheels.
3. Back off adjusting screw at each wheel 33 notches.
4. Brakes should have no drag after the screw has been backed off approximately 15 notches.
5. Heavy drag at this point indicates tight parking brake cables.
6. Install adjusting hole cover in brake backing place.
7. Check parking brake for proper adjustment.

---

# FRONT SUSPENSION & STEERING

**NOTE:** Refer to "Front Wheel Drive" for service procedures on four wheel drive models.

## INDEX

## FRONT SUSPENSION

The front suspension system is designed to allow each wheel to compensate for changes in the road surface level without appreciably affecting the opposite wheel. Each wheel is independently connected to the frame by a steering knuckle, ball joint assemblies and upper/lower control arms. The front wheel are held in

proper relationship to each other by two tie rods which are connected to steering arms on the knuckles and to an intermediate rod.

Coil chassis springs are mounted between the spring housings on the frame and the lower control arms. Shock absorbers are mounted inside the coil springs and attached to the lower control arms.

Four wheel drive models incorporate a front suspension consisting of control

arms, stabilizer bar, shock absorber and a right and left torsion bar. **Front suspension attaching nuts and bolts are an important part of the front suspension assembly. Never replace an attaching bolt and/or nut with a lesser quality or substitute design attaching bolt and/or nut. Torque values must be used as specified during assembly to assure proper retention of the front suspension components.**

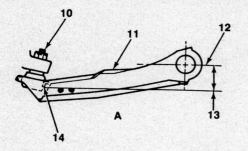

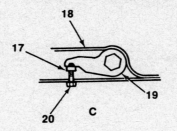

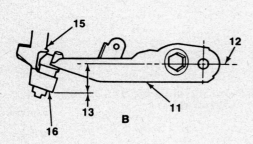

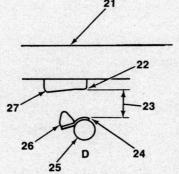

A. "C" Model
B. "K" Model
C. "K" Model Torsion Bar Adjuster
D. "CK" Model Rear Suspension
10. Lower Ball Joint
11. Lower Control Arm
12. Pivot Bolt Center Line
13. "Z" Height
14. Lower Ball Joint Extrusion
15. Steering Knuckle
16. Steering Knuckle Lower Corner

17. Nut
18. Torsion Bar Support Asm.
19. Torsion Bar Adjustment Arm
20. Bolt — One Turn Equals 6 mm Height Change
21. Frame
22. Bottom Surface of Jounce Bracket
23. "D" Height — 182.0 ± 6.0 mm
24. Jounce Bumper Bracket — Top Surface
25. Rear Axle
26. Jounce Bumper
27. Jounce Bracket

**Fig. 1    Vehicle trim heights**

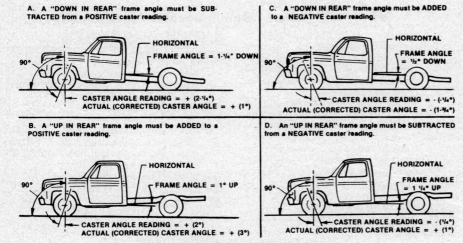

**Fig. 2    Caster measurements**

# FRONT WHEEL ALIGNMENT

## "Z" HEIGHT ADJUSTMENT

1. Lift front bumper of vehicle up approximately 1.5 inches (38 mm).
2. Gently remove hands and allow vehicle to settle on its own.
3. Repeat this operation twice more for a total of three times.
4. Measure "Z" height, **Fig. 1.**
5. Push front bumper on vehicle down approximately 1.5 inches (38 mm).
6. Gently remove hands and allow vehicle to rise on its own.
7. Repeat this operation twice more for a total of three times.
8. Measure "Z" height.
9. Find the average of the high and low measurements. This is the "Z" height. "Z" height should be as follows: C Series, 3.74 inches, K1500 and 2500 less heavy duty front springs, 5.31 inches, K1500 and 2500 with heavy duty front springs, 6.33 inches, K3500 less heavy duty front springs, 4.84 inches, K3500 with heavy duty front springs, 5.94 inches.

## "D" HEIGHT ADJUSTMENT

Use the same procedure used in determining the "Z" height.

## CAMBER ADJUSTMENT

1. Determine the camber from the alignment equipment.
2. Install adjustment kit No. 15538596.
3. Reset camber to specifications.

## CASTER ADJUSTMENT

All caster specifications are given with the vehicle frame level (zero angle).

1. Position vehicle on a smooth level surface.
2. If necessary, correct "Z" height.
3. Using a bubble protractor or inclinometer, measure frame angle, **Figs. 1 and 2.**
4. Note frame angle as being up in the rear or down in the rear.
5. Determine caster angle from alignment equipment.
6. Determine actual (corrected) caster reading, **Fig. 2.**
7. When measuring caster, note the following:
   a. A down in rear frame angle must be subtracted from a positive caster reading.
   b. An up in rear frame angle must be added to a positive caster reading.
   c. A down in rear frame angle must be added to a negative caster reading.
   d. An up in rear frame angle must be subtracted from a negative caster reading.
8. If the caster angle is incorrect, correct the caster angle by turning the adjustment cam bolts.

## TOE-IN ADJUSTMENT

1. Determine toe-in from the alignment equipment.
2. Change length of both tie rod sleeves to effect a toe change.
3. Toe-in can be increased or decreased by changing the length of the tie rod ends. A threaded sleeve is provided for this purpose. When the tie rod ends are mounted ahead of the steering knuckle they must be decreased in length in order to increase toe-in. When the tie rod ends are mounted behind the steering knuckle they must be lengthened in order to increase toe-in.

## CAMBER & CASTER ADJUSTMENT KIT INSTALLATIOn

As originally installed, the upper control arm cannot be adjusted for camber or caster. However, if the camber or caster is measured and found to be out of specifica-

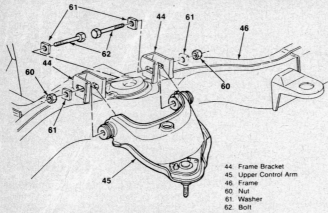

**44.** Frame Bracket
**45.** Upper Control Arm
**46.** Frame
**60.** Nut
**61.** Washer
**62.** Bolt

### Fig. 3   Upper control arm removal

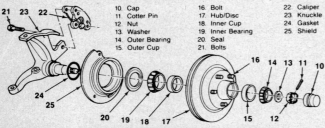

| | | |
|---|---|---|
| **10.** Cap | **16.** Bolt | **22.** Caliper |
| **11.** Cotter Pin | **17.** Hub/Disc | **23.** Knuckle |
| **12.** Nut | **18.** Inner Cup | **24.** Gasket |
| **13.** Washer | **19.** Inner Bearing | **25.** Shield |
| **14.** Outer Bearing | **20.** Seal | |
| **15.** Outer Cup | **21.** Bolts | |

### Fig. 5   Hub, knuckle & bearing components. 2 wheel drive models

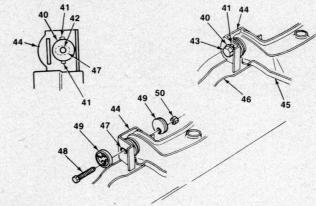

**40.** Flat Washer
**41.** Weld
**42.** Round Hole in Washer
**43.** Bolt
**44.** Frame Bracket
**45.** Upper Control Arm
**46.** Frame
**47.** Slot in Bracket
**48.** Bolt with Flat Side
**49.** Cam
**50.** Nut

### Fig. 4   Alignment service kit 15538596 installation

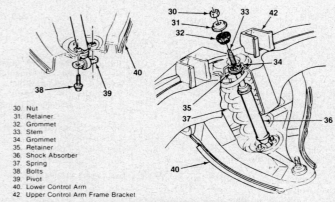

**30.** Nut
**31.** Retainer
**32.** Grommet
**33.** Stem
**34.** Grommet
**35.** Retainer
**36.** Shock Absorber
**37.** Spring
**38.** Bolts
**39.** Pivot
**40.** Lower Control Arm
**42.** Upper Control Arm Frame Bracket

### Fig. 6   Shock absorber attachment

tion, the camber and caster can be set to proper specifications using adjustment kit 15538596. To install, proceed as follows:

1. Raise and support vehicle and lower control arms, then remove nut (60), washer (61) and bolt (62) from upper control arm bracket (44). Discard nut, washer and bolt.
2. Remove large washers (40), **Figs. 3 and 4,** which are welded to the upper control arm frame brackets.
3. Remove weld beads from the upper control arm bracket. Grind area smooth.
4. Install adjusting cams (49) to bracket (44).
5. Install bolt (48) and nut (50).
6. Adjust camber and caster to specifications by rotating bolt head. Torque nuts to 75-90 ft. lbs.

## HUB, BEARING & SEAL
### REPLACE

1. Disconnect battery ground cable.
2. Raise and support vehicle, then remove brake caliper.
3. Remove cap from hub/disc assembly, **Fig. 5.**
4. Remove cotter pin, nut and washer.
5. Remove hub/disc from spindle.
6. Remove outer bearing, seal, inner bearing and cup.
7. Reverse procedure to install. Note the following:
   a. Clean all components before installing.
   b. Apply an approved high temperature front wheel bearing grease to the spindle at the inner and outer bearing seat, shoulder and seal seat. Also finger apply a small amount of grease inboard of each

bearing cup in the hub/disc assembly. Pressure pack the bearings with a grease machine or hand pack them. Ensure grease is worked thoroughly into the rollers, cone and cage.
   c. When installing inner bearing, apply an additional quantity of grease outboard of the inner bearing.
   d. Torque nut (12) to 12 ft. lbs. while turning the wheel assembly forward by hand. Apply grease to the outboard side of the outer bearing. Adjust wheel bearings.

## WHEEL BEARINGS
### ADJUST

1. Raise and support vehicle.
2. Remove wheel cover, if equipped.
3. Remove cap from hub/disc assembly.
4. Remove cotter pin.
5. Tighten nut (12), **Fig. 5,** to 12 ft. lbs., while turning wheel forward by hand. This will seat the bearing.
6. Loosen nut (12) to a just loose position, then back nut off until hole in the spindle aligns with a slot in the nut. Do not back the nut off more than 1/2 flat.

## SHOCK ABSORBER
### REPLACE

1. Raise and support vehicle.
2. Remove shock absorber attaching nut, **Fig. 6.**
3. Remove retainer, grommet and attaching bolts.
4. Remove shock absorber.
5. Reverse procedure to install. Torque attaching nut to 8 ft. lbs. Torque attaching bolts to 20 ft. lbs.

## STABILIZER SHAFT
### REPLACE

1. Raise and support vehicle.
2. Remove nut from link bolt, **Fig. 7.**
3. Remove link bolt.
4. Remove spacer, attaching bolts, bracket and stabilizer shaft.
5. Remove bushing.
6. Reverse procedure to install. Torque bracket attaching bolts to 24 ft. lbs. Torque link bolt assembly attaching bolt to 13 ft. lbs.

## LOWER BALL JOINT
### REPLACE

1. Raise and support vehicle.

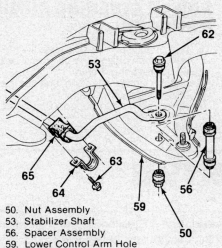

50. Nut Assembly
53. Stabilizer Shaft
56. Spacer Assembly
59. Lower Control Arm Hole
62. Link Bolt Assembly
63. Bolts
64. Bracket
65. Rubber Bushing

**Fig. 7   Stabilizer shaft components**

2. Remove wheel and tire assembly.
3. Place a suitable jack under control arm spring seat and raise it until it supports the control arm. The jack must remain under the control arm spring seat during removal and installation to retain the spring and control arm in position.
4. Remove caliper.
5. Remove cotter pin and nut.
6. Remove lower control arm from knuckle, **Fig. 8**.
7. Block knuckle assembly out of way by placing a wooden block between frame and upper control arm.
8. Using a suitable tool, remove lower ball joint from lower control arm.
9. Reverse procedure to install. Torque stub attaching nut to 90 ft. lbs. and align the slot in the stud nut with hole in the stud for cotter pin installation.

## UPPER BALL JOINT
### REPLACE

1. Raise and support vehicle.
2. Using a suitable jack support control arm. The jack must remain under the control arm spring seat during removal and installation to retain the spring and control arm in position.
3. Remove wheel and tire assembly.
4. Remove caliper.
5. Remove rivets from upper ball joint.
6. Remove cotter pin.
7. Remove stud nut from upper ball joint.
8. Remove upper ball joint.
9. Reverse procedure to install. Torque ball joint attaching nuts to 8 ft. lbs. on 1988 models, 17 ft. lbs. on 1989 C1500/2500 models and 52 ft. lbs. on 1989 C3500 models. Torque stud nut to 90 ft. lbs.

## STEERING KNUCKLE
### REPLACE

1. Raise and support front of vehicle. Do

37. Coil Spring
40. Lower Control Arm
42. Upper Control Arm
66. Upper Ball Joint
67. Nut
68. Cotter Pin
69. Lower Ball Joint
71. Nut
72. Screw
73. Insulator
74. Bumper
75. Bushing
76. Bushing
77. Screw
78. Nut
79. Screw
80. Nut
82. Nut
83. Washer
84. Bushing
85. Nut
86. Bracket
87. Screw

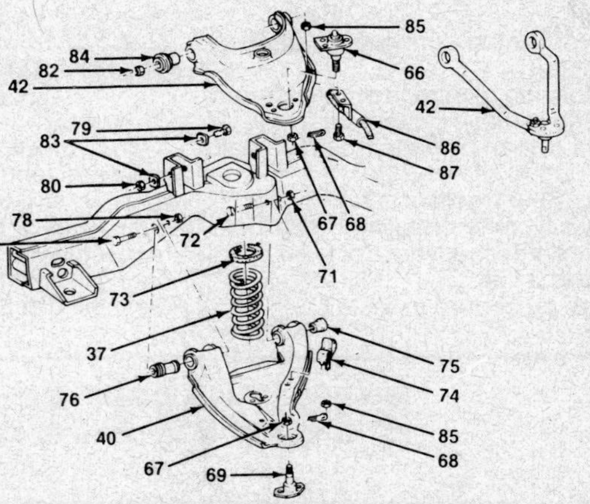

**Fig. 8   Control arms & components**

not place jacks under lower control arm.
2. Remove wheel and tire assembly.
3. Remove tie rod from steering knuckle.
4. Remove caliper.
5. Remove hub/disc assembly.
6. Remove splash to knuckle attaching bolts.
7. Remove knuckle seal from knuckle, if necessary.
8. Remove ball studs from knuckle. **Jack must remain under control arm spring seat during removal and installation to retain the spring and control arm position.**
9. Remove knuckle.
10. Reverse procedure to install. Torque splash shields bolts to 12 ft. lbs.

## COIL SPRING
### REPLACE

1. Raise and support vehicle. Allow control arms to hang.
2. Remove wheel and tire assembly.
3. Remove shock absorber.
4. Cradle lower control arm using coil spring remover and installer J-23028-01 or equivalent, secured to the end of a suitable jack.
5. Remove stabilizer shaft from lower control arm. Raise jack to remove tension from lower control arm pivot bolts. Secure spring with a chain placed through spring and control arm.
6. Remove pivot bolts and nuts.
7. Remove coil spring and insulator.
8. Reverse procedure to install. Install coil spring with tape at the lowest position and facing front of vehicle with gripper notch at the top. Ensure drain holes, one of which must be covered by the end of the spring and one must be open, are properly positioned. Tighten attaching nuts to 96 ft. lbs.

## UPPER CONTROL ARM & BUSHING
### REPLACE

1. Raise front of vehicle and support lower control arms. Jacks must remain under control arm spring seat

during removal and installation to retain spring and control arm position.
2. Remove wheel and tire assembly.
3. Disconnect battery ground cable.
4. Remove air cleaner extension, if necessary.
5. Remove brake hose.
6. Remove upper ball joint as described previously.
7. Remove upper ball joint from steering knuckle. Remove upper control arm attaching bolts and nuts. Note location of shims, if used.
8. Remove upper control arm and bushings. The bushings on C1500 and 2500 models are welded in position and are not serviceable.
9. Reverse procedure to install. Torque attaching nuts to 88 ft. lbs.

## LOWER CONTROL ARM & BUSHING
### REPLACE

Some 1988 C models vehicles may experience a condition where the brake rotor comes in contact with the lower control arm. This occurs only when the steering wheel is turned to the full lock position and most often on left hand turns. The interference between the lower control arm and brake rotor will cause a screeching noise as metal contacts metal. A gouge on the inner brake rotor is evidence that an interference condition exists. If this condition exists, the nose area of the lower control arm should be ground away to provide additional clearance. If a gouge is found on the inside of the brake rotor, replacement of the rotor will be necessary.

1. Remove coil spring as described previously.
2. Remove cotter pin and nut.
3. Separate ball joint from control arm.
4. Remove control arm from knuckle.
5. Remove bushings.
6. Reverse procedure to install. Torque attaching nut to 95 ft. lbs.

## MANUAL STEERING GEAR
### REPLACE

1. Place front wheels in straight ahead

position.
2. Remove flexible coupling to steering shaft bolts.
3. Mark position of pitman arm to pitman shaft and remove pitman shaft nut or pinch bolt, then pitman arm from shaft with a puller.
4. Loosen steering gear and remove.
5. Remove flexible coupling pinch bolt, then flexible coupling from steering gear wormshaft.
6. Reverse procedure to install.

## POWER STEERING GEAR
### REPLACE

To remove gear assembly, disconnect pressure and return hoses from gear housing and cap both hoses and steering gear outlets to prevent foreign material from entering system, then follow procedure as outlined under "Manual Steering Gear, Replace."

## POWER STEERING PUMP
### REPLACE

1. Disconnect hoses at power steering pump, then plug pump ports and hoses to prevent dirt entry.
2. Loosen pump adjusting bolt and remove pump drive belt.
3. Remove pump to support bracket retaining bolts, then the pump.
4. Reverse procedure to install.

# FRONT WHEEL DRIVE

**NOTE:** The following procedures are for four wheel drive models. Refer to "Front Suspension & Steering" for front suspension wheel alignment procedures. All front suspension fasteners are important attaching components in that they could affect the performance of vital components and systems. They must be replaced with one of the same part number or with an equivalent part if replacement is necessary. Do not use a replacement part of lesser quality or substitute design. Torque values must be used as specified during assembly to assure proper retention.

## INDEX

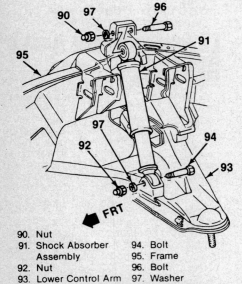

90. Nut
91. Shock Absorber Assembly
92. Nut
93. Lower Control Arm
94. Bolt
95. Frame
96. Bolt
97. Washer

**Fig. 1  Shock absorber attachment**

93. Lower Control Arm
95. Frame
103. Nut Assembly
104. Spacer Assembly
105. Bolt Assembly
107. Stabilizer Shaft
108. Clamp
109. Bolt
110. Insulator

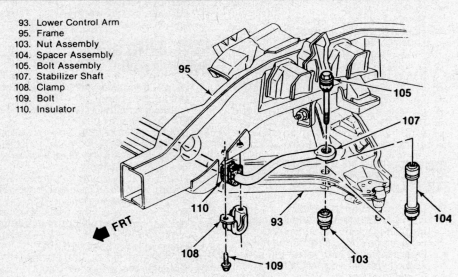

**Fig. 2  Stabilizer shaft components**

## SHOCK ABSORBER
### REPLACE

1. Raise and support vehicle.
2. Remove nut, washer and bolt, **Fig. 1.**
3. Collapse shock absorber, then remove nut, washer and attaching bolt.
4. Remove shock absorber.
5. Reverse procedure to install. Torque attaching nuts to 48 ft. lbs.

## STABILIZER SHAFT
### REPLACE

1. Raise and support vehicle.
2. Remove nuts, bolts and spacers, **Fig. 2.**
3. Remove attaching bolts, clamp, stabilizer shaft and insulators.
4. Reverse procedure to install. Torque frame bolts to 24 ft. lbs. Torque attaching nuts to 12 ft. lbs.

## HUB, BEARING, KNUCKLE & SEAL
### REPLACE

1. Raise and support vehicle.
2. Remove wheel and tire assembly.
3. Remove caliper.
4. Remove disc.

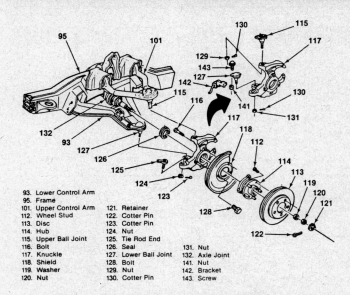

93. Lower Control Arm
95. Frame
101. Upper Control Arm
112. Wheel Stud
113. Disc
114. Hub
115. Upper Ball Joint
116. Bolt
117. Knuckle
118. Shield
119. Washer
120. Nut

121. Retainer
122. Cotter Pin
123. Cotter Pin
124. Nut
125. Tie Rod End
126. Seal
127. Lower Ball Joint
128. Bolt
129. Nut
130. Cotter Pin

131. Nut
132. Axle Joint
141. Nut
142. Bracket
143. Screw

**Fig. 3   Hub, knuckle & ball joints assembly**

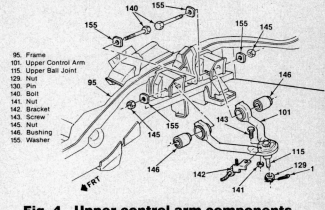

95. Frame
101. Upper Control Arm
115. Upper Ball Joint
129. Nut
130. Pin
140. Bolt
141. Nut
142. Bracket
143. Screw
145. Nut
146. Bushing
155. Washer

**Fig. 4   Upper control arm components**

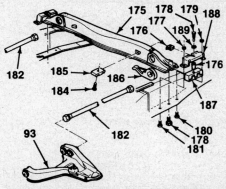

93. Lower Control Arm
175. Support
176. Spacer
177. Nut
178. Bolt/Screw
179. Nut
180. Bolt
181. Bolt

182. Torsion Bar(s)
184. Adjusting Bolt
185. Nut
186. Adjusting Arm
187. Insulator
188. Retainer
189. Nut

**Fig. 6   Torsion bar & support assembly**

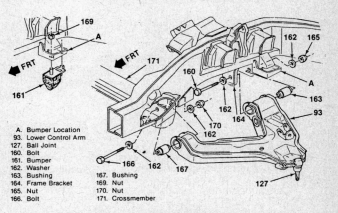

A. Bumper Location
93. Lower Control Arm
127. Ball Joint
160. Bolt
161. Bumper
162. Washer
163. Bushing
164. Frame Bracket
165. Nut
166. Bolt

167. Bushing
169. Nut
170. Nut
171. Crossmember

**Fig. 5   Lower control arm components**

5. Remove pin, retainer, nut and washer, **Fig. 3.**
6. Remove pin, nut and tie rod end from knuckle.
7. Remove bolts, hub and bearing assembly.
8. Remove bolts and splash shield.
9. Remove pins and ball joints from knuckle.
10. Remove nuts and knuckle.
11. Remove spacer from knuckle.
12. Remove seal from knuckle.
13. Reverse procedure to install. Torque nuts (129 and 131) to 94 ft. lbs., tighten nuts to align cotter pin holes. Do not tighten more than $1/16$ of a turn. Torque bolts (128) to 12 ft. lbs. Torque bolts (116) to 66 ft. lbs. Torque nut (124) to 35 ft. lbs. Torque nut (120) to 173 ft. lbs.

## BALL JOINT REPLACE

1. Raise and support vehicle.
2. Remove wheel and tire assembly.
3. Remove rivets from ball joint, pin, nut and ball joint.
4. Reverse procedure to install. Torque ball joint attaching nuts to 15 ft. lbs. Torque nut (129), **Fig. 3,** to 94 ft. lbs.

## UPPER CONTROL ARM & BUSHING REPLACE

1. Raise and support vehicle.
2. Remove wheel and tire assembly.
3. Disconnect battery ground cable.
4. Remove air cleaner extension, if necessary.
5. Remove brake hose.
6. Remove pin, nut and upper control arm from knuckle, **Fig. 4.**
7. Remove nuts, bolts and upper control arm.
8. Remove bushings.
9. Reverse procedure to install. Torque nuts (145) to 88 ft. lbs. Torque nut (129) to 94 ft. lbs.

## LOWER CONTROL ARM & BUSHING REPLACE

1. Raise and support vehicle.
2. Remove wheel and tire assembly.
3. Remove stabilizer shaft.
4. Remove shock absorber.
5. Remove inner tie rod end from relay rod.
6. Remove outer axle shaft nut and washer from hub assembly.
7. Remove output shaft-to-drive axle attaching bolts and drive axle.
8. Unload torsion bar and remove adjuster arm.
9. Remove lower ball joint nut and separate ball joint from steering knuckle.
10. Remove nuts (170) (165), washer (162) and bolts (166) (160), **Fig. 5.**
11. Remove lower control arm and torsion bar as a unit.
12. Separate the lower control arm from the torsion bar.
13. Remove lower control arm bushings.
14. Reverse procedure to install. Torque nuts (170 and 165) to 135 ft. lbs.

## TORSION BAR & SUPPORT ASSEMBLY REPLACE

1. Raise and support vehicle.

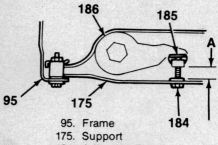

95. Frame
175. Support
184. Adjusting Bolt
185. Nut
186. Adjusting Arm
A. 34 mm (1.3-inch)

**Fig. 7   Torsion bar adjusting height**

2. Remove adjusting bolt, **Fig. 6.** Record number of turns when removing adjusting bolt.
3. Remove bolt/screw, nuts, bolts, retainer, spacer, insulator and torsion bar(s).
4. Remove support, adjusting arm, adjusting bolt and nut.
5. To install, proceed as follows:
   a. Lubricate top of adjusting arm, then install adjusting arm.
   b. Install nut onto support.
   c. Install adjusting screw onto nut loosely. Lubricate adjusting screw.
   d. Install insulator onto support end.
   e. Install support onto frame.
   f. Install nut onto retainer.
   g. Install retainer and spacer.
   h. Install bolts onto retainer.
   i. Install nuts onto bolts.
   j. Install bolt/screw into retainer.
   k. Torque bolts (180, 181) to 35 ft. lbs. Torque bolt/screw (178) to 33 ft. lbs.
   l. Install torsion bar(s) (182) onto lower control arm. Slide torsion bar into lower control arm. Raise and slide torsion bar into the adjusting arm. Ensure adjusting arm has a 1.3 inch (34 mm) clearance, **Fig. 7,** at the support.
   m. Thread adjusting screw in the recorded amount of turns.
   n. Lower vehicle.
   o. Check front wheel alignment.

# DRIVE AXLE
## REPLACE

1. Raise and support vehicle.
2. Remove skid plate.

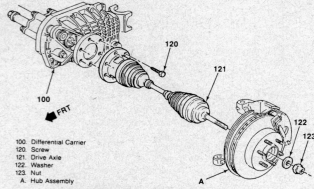

100. Differential Carrier
120. Screw
121. Drive Axle
122. Washer
123. Nut
A. Hub Assembly

**Fig. 8   Drive axle assembly**

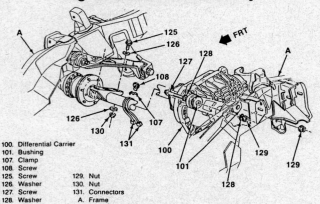

100. Differential Carrier
101. Bushing
107. Clamp
108. Screw
125. Screw
126. Washer
127. Screw
128. Washer
129. Nut
130. Nut
131. Connectors
A. Frame

**Fig. 9   Differential carrier assembly**

3. Remove stabilizer bar clamp.
4. Remove inner tie rod from steering relay rod.
5. Remove stabilizer bar bolt, spacer and bushings.
6. Remove hub nut and washer.
7. Remove drive axle flange bolts.
8. Remove drive axle from vehicle.
9. Reverse procedure to install. Torque nut (123) to 175 ft. lbs. Torque attaching screws (120) to 60 ft. lbs., **Fig. 8.**

# DIFFERENTIAL CARRIER
## REPLACE

1. Raise and support vehicle.
2. Remove skid plate, if equipped.
3. Remove idler arm from frame.
4. Remove drive axles.
5. Disconnect front driveshaft.
6. Disconnect vent hose.
7. Disconnect electrical connector from differential.

8. Remove bolts (125), nuts (130) and washers (126), **Fig. 9.**
9. Remove carrier lower mounting bolt and right side inner tie rod end from relay rod.
10. Support differential assembly with a jack.
11. Remove upper washers and attaching screw.
12. Remove upper carrier mounting bolt, then differential carrier, **Fig. 9.**
13. To install, proceed as follows:
    a. Install differential carrier.
    b. Install attaching bolts, washers and nuts.
    c. Install and torque attaching screws (127) to 80 ft. lbs.
    d. Install nuts (130). On K 1500/2500 models, torque nuts to 75 ft. lbs. On K 3500 models, torque nuts to 110 ft. lbs.
    e. Reverse removal procedure to complete assembly.

# CHEVROLET S/T 10 & GMC S/T 15

## INDEX OF SERVICE OPERATIONS

# SPECIFICATIONS
## GENERAL ENGINE SPECIFICATIONS

| Year | Engine Model | Carburetor Type | Bore & Stroke | Compression Ratio | Net Horsepower @ R.P.M. | Torque Ft. Lbs. @ R.P.M. | Normal Oil Press. Lbs. |
|------|-------------|-----------------|---------------|-------------------|-------------------------|--------------------------|------------------------|
| 1982 | 4-119/1.9L | 2 Bore | 3.43 x 3.23 | 8.4 | 82 @ 4600 | 101 @ 3000 | 57 |
|      | V6-173/2.8L | 2 Bore | 3.50 x 3.00 | 8.5 | 110 @ 4800 | 145 @ 2400 | 30-50② |
| 1983 | 4-119/1.9L | 2 Bore | 3.42 x 3.23 | 8.4 | 82 @ 4600 | 101 @ 3000 | 57 |
|      | 4-121/2.0L | 2 Bore | 3.50 x 3.15 | 9.3 | 83 @ 4600 | 108 @ 2400 | 45③ |
|      | V6-173/2.8L | 2 Bore | 3.50 x 3.00 | 8.5 | 110 @ 4800 | 145 @ 2100 | 30-50② |
| 1984 | 4-119/1.9L | 2 Bore | 3.42 x 3.23 | 8.4 | 82 @ 4600 | 101 @ 3000 | 57 |
|      | 4-121/2.0L | 2 Bore | 3.50 x 3.15 | 9.3 | 83 @ 4600 | 108 @ 2400 | 45③ |
|      | 4-137/2.2L① | Fuel Injection | 3.46 x 3.62 | 21.0 | 62 @ 4300 | 96 @ 2200 | 60 |
|      | V6-173/2.8L | 2 Bore | 2.99 x 3.50 | 8.5 | 110 @ 4800 | 145 @ 2100 | 30-50② |
| 1985 | 4-119/1.9L | 2 Bore | 3.43 x 3.23 | 8.4 | 82 @ 4600 | 101 @ 3000 | 57 |
|      | 4-137/2.2L① | Fuel Injection | 3.46 x 3.62 | 21.0 | 62 @ 4300 | 96 @ 2200 | 60 |
|      | 4-151/2.5L | Fuel Injection | 4.00 x 3.00 | 9.0 | 92 @ 4400 | 134 @ 2800 | 37.5 |
|      | V6-173/2.8L | 2 Bore | 2.99 x 3.50 | 8.5 | 115 @ 4800 | 150 @ 2100 | 30-50② |
| 1986 | 4-151/2.5L | Fuel Injection | 4.00 x 3.00 | 9.0 | 92 @ 4400 | 134 @ 2800 | 45③ |
|      | V6-173/2.8L | Fuel Injection | 3.50 x 2.99 | 8.5 | 125 @ 4800 | 150 @ 2200 | 50② |
| 1987 | 4-151/2.5L | Fuel Injection | 4.00 x 3.00 | 8.3 | 92 @ 4400 | 130 @ 3200 | 36-41② |
|      | V6-173/2.8L | Fuel Injection | 3.50 x 2.99 | 8.5 | 125 @ 4800 | 150 @ 2400 | 50-55② |
| 1988 | 4-151/2.5L | Fuel Injection | 4.00 x 3.00 | 8.3 | 92 @ 4400 | 130 @ 3200 | 36-41② |
|      | V6-173/2.8L | Fuel Injection | 3.50 x 2.99 | 8.9 | 125 @ 4800 | 150 @ 2400 | 30-55② |
|      | V6-262/4.3L | Fuel Injection | 4.00 x 3.48 | 9.3 | 160 @ 4000 | 230 @ 2800 | 30-35② |
| 1989 | 4-151/2.5L | Fuel Injection | 4.00 x 3.00 | 8.3 | 92 @ 4400 | 130 @ 3200 | 36-41② |
|      | V6-173/2.8L | Fuel Injection | 3.50 x 2.99 | 8.9 | 125 @ 4800 | 150 @ 2400 | 30-55② |
|      | V6-262/4.3L | Fuel Injection | 4.00 x 3.48 | 9.3 | 160 @ 4000 | 230 @ 2800 | 40-60② |

①—Diesel engine.
②—At 2000 RPM.
③—At 2200 RPM.

## ALTERNATOR & REGULATOR SPECIFICATIONS

| Year | Model | Alternator | | | | Regulator |
|------|-------|------------|---|---|---|-----------|
|      |       | Field Current @ 80°F. 12 Volts | Cold Output @ 14 Volts | | Rated Hot Output Amperes | Type |
|      |       |            | Amperes At 2000 R.P.M. | Amperes At 5000 R.P.M | | |
| 1982 | 1100140 | 4.0-5 | 22 | 33 | 37 | Integral |
|      | 1100146 | 4.0-5 | 32 | 60 | 63 | Integral |
|      | 1100201 | 4.0-5 | 22 | 33 | 37 | Integral |
|      | 1100202 | 4.0-5 | 32 | 60 | 63 | Integral |
| 1983-84 | 1100204 | 4.0-5 | 22 | 33 | 37 | Integral |
|      | 1100207 | 4.5-5 | 38 | 70② | 66 | Integral |
|      | 1100209 | 4.5-5 | 51 | 81② | 78 | Integral |
|      | 1100227 | 4.0-5 | 22 | 33 | 37 | Integral |
|      | 1100249 | 4.5-5 | 38 | 70② | 66 | Integral |
|      | 1100273 | 4.5-5 | 51 | 81② | 78 | Integral |
|      | 1100275 | — | — | — | 66 | Integral |
|      | 1100276 | — | — | — | 78 | Integral |
|      | 1105185 | 4.0-5 | 22 | 33 | 37 | Integral |
| 1984 | 1105370① | 4.5-5 | 51 | 81② | 78 | Integral |

## ALTERNATOR & REGULATOR SPECIFICATIONS—Continued

| Year | Model | Alternator Field Current @ 80°F. 12 Volts | Cold Output @ 14 Volts Amperes At 2000 R.P.M. | Cold Output @ 14 Volts Amperes At 5000 R.P.M | Rated Hot Output Amperes | Regulator Type |
|------|-------|------|------|------|------|------|
| 1985 | 1100207 ① | 4.5-5 | 38 | 70 ② | 66 | Integral |
| | 1100250 ③ | 4.5-5 | 51 | 81 ② | 78 | Integral |
| | 1105368 ③ | 4.5-5 | 51 | 81 ② | 78 | Integral |
| | 1105370 ① ③ | 4.5-5 | 51 | 81 ② | 78 | Integral |
| | 1105492 ③ | 4.5-5 | 56 | 103 ② | 94 | Integral |
| | 1105504 | 4.5-5 | 38 | 70 ② | 66 | Integral |
| | 1105516 | 4.5-5 | 38 | 70 ② | 66 | Integral |
| | 1105575 | 4.5-5 | 37 | 60 ② | 56 | Integral |
| | 1105621 | — | — | — | 66 | Integral |
| | 1105623 | — | — | — | 78 | Integral |
| | 1105624 | — | — | — | 56 | Integral |
| | 1105627 | — | — | — | 78 | Integral |
| | 1105633 | — | — | — | 56 | Integral |
| | 1105635 | — | — | — | 66 | Integral |
| | 1105647 ③ | — | — | — | 78 | Integral |
| 1986 | 1105627 | 4.5-5.0 | 51 | 81 ② | 78 | Integral |
| | 1105663 | 5.4-6.4 | 30 ④ | — | 85 | Integral |
| 1987-89 | 1101259 | 4.8-5.7 | 30 ④ | — | 85 | Integral |
| | 1101317 | 5.7-7.1 | 30 ④ | — | 85 | Integral |
| | 1105722 | 4.8-5.7 | 30 ④ | — | 85 | Integral |
| 1989 | 1101346 | 6.0-7.5 | 26 ④ | — | 96 | Integral |

①—Alternator used on diesel engine models.
②—At 7000 RPM.
③—Service replacement part.
④—At 1600 RPM.

## STARTING MOTOR SPECIFICATIONS

| Year | Engine | Starter Model | Brush Spring Tension Oz. ① | Free Speed Test Amperes | Free Speed Test Volts | Free Speed Test R.P.M. |
|------|--------|---------------|------|------|------|------|
| 1982 | 4-119 | 94241705 | 56.5 | — | — | — |
| | V6-173 | 1109535 | — | 50-80 ② | 10.6 | 7500-11400 |
| 1983-84 | 4-119 | 94241705 | 56.5 | — | — | — |
| | 4-121 | 1109561 | — | 50-75 | 9.0 | 6000-11900 |
| | V6-173 | 1109535 | — | 45-70 | 9.0 | 7000-11900 |
| 1984-85 | 4-137 ③ | — | — | 120 ② | 11.5 | 4000 ④ |
| 1985 | 4-119 | — | 56.5 | — | — | — |
| | 4-151 | 1998431 | — | 50-75 | 10 | 6000-11900 |
| | 4-151 | 1998482 | — | 50-75 | 10 | 6000-11900 |
| | V6-173 | 1998427 | — | 50-75 | 10 | 6000-11900 |
| 1986-88 | 4-151 | 1998532 | — | 50-75 | 10 | 6000-11900 |
| | V6-173 | 1998524 | — | 50-75 | 10 | 6000-11900 |
| 1988-89 | V6-262 | 9000735 | — | 50-90 | 10 | 2330-2660 ⑤ |
| 1989 | 4-151 | 10455018 | — | 50-75 | 10 | 6000-11900 ⑤ |
| | V6-173 | 10455016 | — | 50-75 | 10 | 6000-11900 ⑤ |

①—Minimum.
②—Includes solenoid.
③—Diesel engine.
④—Minimum speed.
⑤—Drive speed.

## ENGINE TIGHTENING SPECIFICATIONS*

*Torque specifications are for clean and lightly lubricated threads only. Dry or dirty threads produce increased friction which prevents accurate measurement of tightness.

| Year | Engine | Spark Plugs Ft. Lbs. | Cylinder Head Bolts Ft. Lbs. | Intake Manifold Ft. Lbs. | Exhaust Manifold Ft. Lbs. | Rocker Arm Shaft Bracket Ft. Lbs. | Rocker Arm Cover Ft. Lbs. | Connecting Rod Cap Bolts Ft. Lbs. | Main Bearing Cap Bolts Ft. Lbs. | Flywheel To Crankshaft Ft. Lbs. | Vibration Damper Or Pulley Ft. Lbs. |
|---|---|---|---|---|---|---|---|---|---|---|---|
| 1982-85 | 4-119 | 18-22 | 72 | 16 | 16 | 16 | 4 | 43 | 72 | 76 | 87 |
| 1982 | V6-173 | 7-15 | 65-75 | 20-25 | 22-28 | 43-49 ① | 6-9 | 34-40 | 63-74 | 45-55 | 66-84 |
| 1983-84 | 4-121 | 7-19 | 65-75 | 22-29 | 19-29 | 43-49 ① | 3 | 34-42 | 63-77 | 45-59 | 66-88 |
| 1983-85 | V6-173 | 7-15 | 55-77 | 13-25 | 20-30 | 43-53 ① | 6-12 | 34-44 | 63-83 | 45-59 | 48-55 |
| 1984-85 | 4-137 ② | — | ③ | 10-17 | 10-17 | 9-17 | 9-13 | 58-65 | 116-130 | 70 | 124-151 |
| 1985-86 | 4-151 | 7-15 | ⑤ | ④ | 44 | 20 | 6 | 32 | 70 | 44 | 160 |
| 1986-89 | V6-173 | 22 | ⑧ | 23 | 25 | — | 6 | 39 | 70 | 52 | 70 |
| 1987 | 4-151 | 7-15 | ⑤ | 25 | ⑥ | 24 | 4 | 32 | 70 | ⑦ | 160 |
| 1988 | 4-151 | 7-15 | ⑤ | 25 | ⑥ | 22 | 4 | 32 | 70 | ⑦ | 160 |
|  | V6-262 | 22 | 65 | 35 | ⑨ | — | 90 ⑩ | 45 | 80 | 75 | 70 |
| 1989 | 4-151 | 715 | ⑤ | 25 | ⑥ | 22 | 6.5 | 30 | 65 | ⑦ | 160 |
|  | V6-262 | 22 | 65 | 35 | ⑨ | — | 90 ⑩ | 45 | 80 | 75 | 70 |

① —Rocker arm stud.
② —Diesel engine.
③ —Torque to 40-47 ft. lbs., then retorque new bolts to 54-61 ft. lbs. or used bolts to 61-69 ft. lbs.
④ —Lower rear, upper center (2) & upper & lower front, 25 ft. lbs.; upper rear, 37 ft. lbs.; lower center (2), 28 ft. lbs.
⑤ —Refer to text for procedure.
⑥ —Front & rear exhaust tubes, 32 ft. lbs.; center exhaust tube, 36 ft. lbs.
⑦ —Automatic trans., 55 ft. lbs.; manual trans., 65 ft. lbs.
⑧ —1986-87, 70 lbs.; 1988-89, refer to text for procedure.
⑨ —Torque center two bolts to 26 ft. lbs., all others 20 ft. lbs.
⑩ —Inch lbs.

## WHEEL ALIGNMENT SPECIFICATIONS

| Year | Truck Model | Caster Deg. | Camber Deg. | Toe-In (Inches) | King Pin Angle Deg. |
|---|---|---|---|---|---|
| 1982-89 | S/T-10, 15 | +2.0 to +0.50 | +0.8 to +0.5 | ① | — |

① —Toe-in, +0.15 to +0.05° per wheel.

## BRAKE SPECIFICATIONS

| Year | Model | Rear Drum I.D. | Wheel Cyl. Bore Front Disc | Wheel Cyl. Bore Rear Drum | Disc Brake Rotor Nominal Thickness | Disc Brake Rotor Minimum Thickness | Disc Brake Rotor Thickness Variation (Parallelism) | Run Out (TIR) | Finish (Microinch) | Master Cyl. I.D. |
|---|---|---|---|---|---|---|---|---|---|---|
| 1982-84 | All | 9.45 | — | .874 | — | .978 | .0005 | .004 | 30-80 | .945 ① |
| 1985 | All | 9.45 | — | ② | — | .978 | .0005 | .004 | 30-80 | .945 ① |
| 1986-89 | All | 9.50 | — | — | 1.030 | .980 | .0005 | .004 | — | — |

① —Piston diameter.
② —Exc. power brakes, .875 inch; power brakes, .750 inch.

## DRIVE AXLE SPECIFICATIONS

| Year | Model | Carrier Type | Ring Gear & Pinion Backlash | | Pinion Bearing Preload | | | Differential Bearing Preload | | |
|------|-------|--------------|--------|------------|--------|-----------------------------|------------------------------|--------|-----------------------------|------------------------------|
| | | | Method | Adjustment | Method | New Bearings Inch-Lbs. | Used Bearings Inch-Lbs. | Method | New Bearings Inch-Lbs. | Used Bearings Inch-Lbs. |
| 1982-89 | All ③ | Integral | Shim | .005-.009 | Spacer | 24-32 ① | 8-12 ① | Shim | ② | ② |
| 1983-89 | All ④ | Split | Sleeve | .005-.007 | Spacer | 15-25 ① | — | — | — | — |

①—Measured with torque wrench at pinion flange nut.
②—Slip fit plus .004 inch preload on each side.
③—Rear axle.
④—Front axle (four wheel drive).

## COOLING SYSTEM & CAPACITY DATA

| Year | Model Or Engine | Cooling Capacity, Qts. | | Radiator Cap Relief Pressure, Lbs. | Thermo. Opening Temp. | Fuel Tank Gals. | Engine Oil Refill Qts. | Transmission Oil | | | | Rear Axle Oil Pints |
|------|-----------------|-----------|----------|----------|-------|-------|--------|---------|---------|-------|-------|------|
| | | Less A/C | With A/C | | | | | 4 Speed Pints | 5 Speed Pints | Auto. Trans. ② | Trans. Case Pints | |
| 1982 | 4-119 | 9.4 | 9.5 | 15 | 180° | 13 | 4① | ⑦ | ⑦ | ⑥ | — | 3.5 |
| | V6-173 | 12.0 | 12.0 | 15 | 195° | 13⑧ | 4① | ⑦ | ⑦ | ⑥ | — | 3.5 |
| 1983 | 4-119 | 9.3 | 9.5 | 15 | 180° | ③⑧ | 4① | ⑦ | ⑦ | ⑥ | 4.5 | 3.5⑤ |
| | 4-121 | 9.5 | 9.6 | 15 | 195° | ③⑧ | 4① | ⑦ | ⑦ | ⑥ | 4.5 | 3.5⑤ |
| | V6-173 | 12.0 | 12.0 | 15 | 195° | ③⑧ | 4① | ⑦ | ⑦ | ⑥ | 4.5 | 3.5⑤ |
| 1984 | 4-119 | 9.5 | 9.5 | 15 | 180° | ③⑧ | 4① | ⑦ | ⑦ | ⑥ | 4.5 | 3.5⑤ |
| | 4-121 | 9.5 | 9.5 | 15 | 195° | ③⑧ | 4① | ⑦ | ⑦ | ⑥ | 4.5 | 3.5⑤ |
| | 4-137④ | 11.5 | 12.0 | 15 | 180° | 14⑧ | 5.5① | ⑦ | ⑦ | ⑥ | 4.5 | 3.5⑤ |
| | V6-173 | 12.0 | 12.0 | 15 | 195° | ③⑧ | 4① | ⑦ | ⑦ | ⑥ | 4.5 | 3.5⑤ |
| 1985 | 4-119 | 9.5 | 9.5 | 15 | 180° | 13⑧ | 4① | ⑨ | 4.1 | ⑥ | 4.5 | 3.5⑤ |
| | 4-137④ | 11.5 | 12 | 15 | 180° | 14⑧ | 5.5① | ⑨ | 4.1 | — | 4.5 | 3.5⑤ |
| | 4-151 | 12 | 12 | 15 | 195° | ③⑧ | 3① | ⑨ | 4.1 | ⑥ | 4.5 | 3.5⑤ |
| | V6-173 | 12 | 12 | 15 | 195° | ③⑧ | 4① | ⑨ | 4.1 | ⑥ | 4.5 | 3.5⑤ |
| 1986 | 4-151 | 12 | 12 | 15 | 195° | 13.2 | 3① | ⑨ | 4.1 | ⑧ | 4.5 | 3.5⑤ |
| | V6-173 | 12 | 12 | 15 | 195° | 13.2 | 4① | ⑨ | 4.1 | ⑥ | 4.5 | 3.5⑤ |
| 1987 | 4-151 | 10.5 | 10.5 | 15 | 195° | ③⑧ | 3① | ⑪ | 3.2 | ⑩ | 4.5 | 3.9⑤ |
| | V6-173 | 11.5 | 11.5 | 15 | 195° | ③⑧ | 4① | ⑪ | 3.2 | ⑩ | 4.5 | 3.9⑤ |
| 1988-89 | 4-151 | 11.5 | 11.5 | 15 | 195° | ③⑧ | 3① | 4.4 | 4.4 | ⑩ | ⑫ | 3.9⑤ |
| | V6-173 | 10.5 | 10.5 | 15 | 195° | ③⑧ | 4① | 4.4 | 4.4 | ⑩ | ⑫ | 3.9⑤ |
| | V6-262 | 13.5 | 13.5 | 15 | 195° | ③⑧ | 4① | 4.4 | 4.4 | ⑩ | ⑫ | 3.9⑤ |

①—Additional oil may be required with filter change.
②—Approximate, make final check with dipstick.
③—All models exc. Blazer & Jimmy, 13.0; Blazer & Jimmy, 13.5.
④—Diesel engine.
⑤—Front drive axle, 2.6 pts.
⑥—THM 200C: total 9.5 qts.; pan only, 3.5 qts. THM 7004R: total, 11.5 qts.; pan only, 5 qts.
⑦—Fill to bottom of oil filler plug.
⑧—Optional tank, 20 gals.
⑨—77 mm trans., 4.1 pts.; 77.5 mm trans., 4.8 pts.
⑩—THM 180C: total, 2.3 qts.; pan only, 1.5 qts. THM700-R4: total, 11.5 qts.; pan only, 5 qts.
⑪—77 mm trans., 3.2 pts.; 77.5 mm trans., 5.0 pts.
⑫—Model 207, 4.6 pts.; 231, 2.2 pts.

# ELECTRICAL

## INDEX

## FUSE BLOCK & FLASHER LOCATION

The fuse block is located at the far left side of the dash panel. On some 1983-85 models, the fuse block as accessed through an opening in the glove box.

The hazard and turn signal flashers are located under the left side of the dash panel on the convenience center.

## STARTER
### REPLACE
#### 4-119

1. Disconnect battery ground cable.
2. Disconnect EGR pipe from EGR valve and exhaust manifold, then remove.
3. Disconnect starter solenoid wiring.
4. Remove starter mounting bolts and nuts.
5. Remove starter motor assembly.
6. Reverse procedure to install.

#### 4-121, 4-151, V6-173 & V6-262

Upon removal of starter, note if any shims are used. If shims are used, they should be reinstalled in their original location during replacement. If starter is noisy during cranking, remove one .015 inch double shim or add one .015 inch single shim to the outer bolt. If starter makes a high pitched whine after firing, add .015 inch double shims until noise ceases.

1. Disconnect battery ground cable.
2. Raise and support front of vehicle.
3. Remove any shields or braces blocking access to the starter, on V6-262 raise vehicle half way to gain access to starter.
4. On 4-wheel drive vehicles remove skid plate if equipped
5. Remove bolts and brackets holding brake line to crossmember.
6. Remove crossmember.
7. On all models remove starter mounting bolts, then allow starter to drop down.
8. Remove solenoid wiring and battery

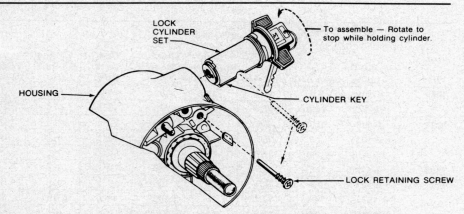

**Fig. 1 Ignition lock removal & installation**

cable, then the starter assembly.
6. Reverse procedure to install.

#### 4-137 DIESEL

1. Disconnect battery ground cable.
2. Disconnect starter motor wiring.
3. Remove starter mounting bolts and nuts.
4. Remove starter motor assembly.
5. Reverse procedure to install.

## IGNITION LOCK
### REPLACE

1. Disconnect battery ground cable.
2. Remove steering wheel. Refer to "Horn Sounder & Steering Wheel, Replace."
3. Remove turn signal switch. Refer to "Turn Signal Switch, Replace."
4. Place ignition switch in "Run" position, then remove lock cylinder retaining screw and lock cylinder.
5. To install, rotate lock cylinder to stop while holding housing, **Fig. 1**. Align cylinder key with keyway in housing, then push lock cylinder assembly into housing until fully seated.
6. Install lock cylinder retaining screw, turn signal switch and steering wheel.

## IGNITION & DIMMER SWITCHES
### REPLACE
#### 1982–85

1. Disconnect battery ground cable.
2. Remove lower instrument panel trim and nuts securing steering column bracket, then lower column enough to gain access to switches. **Use care when lowering steering column to prevent damage to column assembly. If necessary remove bracket from column to gain access to switches.**
3. Rotate ignition lock to the "ACC" position on models with key release lever, or to the "Off" unlocked position on models less release lever.
4. If lock cylinder has been removed, pull actuator rod back to stop, on models without key release lever, push actuator rod down to second detent.
5. Remove nut and screw securing dimmer switch, disconnect electrical connector, then disengage and remove dimmer switch, **Figs. 2 and 3.** If ignition switch is not being replaced, proceed to step 10.

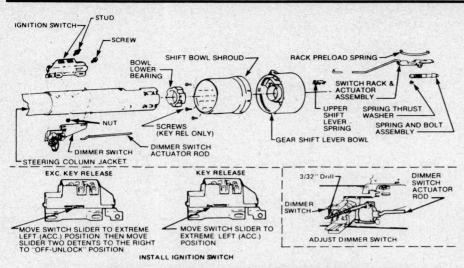

**Fig. 2   Ignition & dimmer switch removal & installation. 1982–85 exc. tilt column**

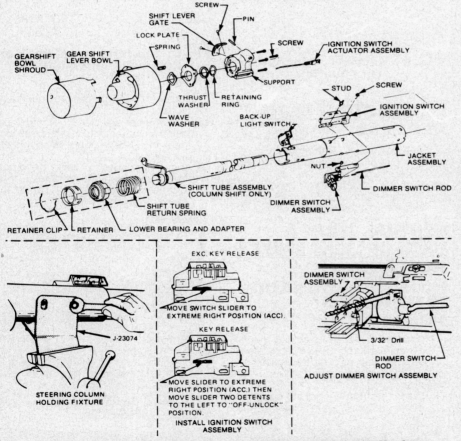

**Fig. 3   Ignition & dimmer switch removal & installation. 1982–85 w/tilt column**

6. Remove stud screw securing ignition switch, disconnect electrical connector, then disengage and remove switch.
7. Position slider on replacement switch in "ACC" position for models with key release, or in "Off" unlocked position for models less key release as shown in **Figs. 2 and 3.**
8. Mount ignition switch over actuator rod and install stud screw finger tight.
9. Apply slight rearward pressure to switch body, ensuring that switch remains in proper detent position, then torque screw to 35 inch lbs. to secure adjustment.
10. Depress dimmer switch plunger slightly and insert 3/32 inch drill or

rod to lock plunger to switch body, **Figs. 2 and 3.**
11. Engage actuator rod in switch and install retaining nut and screw finger tight.
12. Apply slight rearward pressure to switch to take up slack, then torque mounting nut and screw to 35 inch lbs.
13. Connect electrical connectors to ignition and dimmer switches, align steering column and bracket on mounting studs and torque retaining nuts to 20 ft. lbs.
14. Reverse remaining procedure to complete installation and ensure switches operate properly in all positions.

## IGNITION SWITCH
## REPLACE
### 1986–89

1. Disconnect battery ground cable.
2. Remove lower instrument panel trim, then unfasten and carefully lower steering column to gain access to ignition switch. **Support steering column to prevent damage.**
3. Place ignition switch in "Lock" position. If lock cylinder has been removed, pull switch actuator rod up to stop, then move down one detent to the "Lock" position.
4. Remove ignition switch attaching screws then the switch.
5. Reverse procedure to install. **Place ignition switch in "Lock" position prior to installation.**

## LIGHT SWITCH
## REPLACE
### 1982–83

1. Disconnect battery ground cable.
2. Pull headlight switch knob to "On" position.
3. Reach up under instrument panel and depress headlight switch shaft retaining button while gently pulling on switch control shaft knob to remove control shaft.
4. Remove three headlight switch trim plate retaining screws, then the trim plate.
5. Using a suitable screwdriver, remove switch ferrule nut.
6. Working behind instrument panel, remove switch wiring connector, then the switch.
7. Reverse procedure to install.

### 1984–85

1. Disconnect battery ground cable and remove hush panel over fuse box.
2. Remove hood release handle retaining screws, then the lower steering column cover.
3. Remove cruise control module.
4. Remove delay wiper switch knob and locknut, if equipped.
5. Pull light switch to full on position, depress retainer on frame of switch, then remove shaft and knob assembly.
6. Disconnect parking brake release cable, depress tabs on release handle

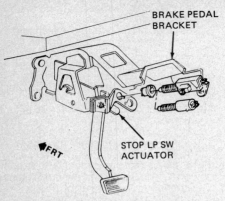

Fig. 4 Stop light switch installation

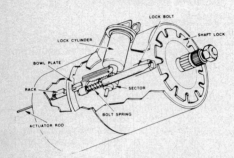

**Fig. 7 Mechanical lockout. Exc. tilt column**

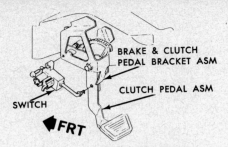

**Fig. 5 Clutch start switch installation**

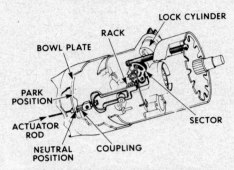

**Fig. 8 Mechanical lockout. Tilt column**

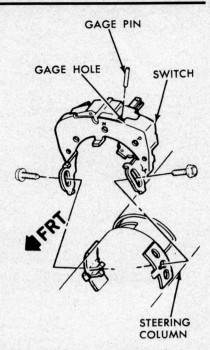

**Fig. 6 Neutral start & back-up light switch installation**

and remove cable assembly.
7. Remove headlamp switch bezel and retaining nut.
8. Disconnect headlamp switch electrical connector and remove switch.
9. Reverse procedure to install.

## 1986–89

1. Disconnect battery ground cable.
2. Remove headlamp switch trim plate and switch assembly attaching screws.
3. Disconnect electrical connectors from headlamp switch, then remove switch assembly from dash panel.
4. Reverse procedure to install.

## STOP LIGHT SWITCH REPLACE

1. Disconnect battery ground cable.
2. Disconnect wiring connector from brake light switch located on brake pedal bracket.
3. Pull switch from mounting bracket.
4. Depress brake pedal, then push new switch into clip until shoulder bottoms out, **Fig. 4.**
5. Pull brake pedal rearward against pedal stop to adjust switch. Switch is properly adjusted when brake lights operate when brake pedal is depressed .53 inch from normal position. If further adjustment of switch is necessary, switch can be rotated or pulled in clip.

## CLUTCH START SWITCH REPLACE

1. Remove lower I/P trim panel.
2. Remove clutch start switch electrical connector.
3. Remove clutch start switch from clutch pedal.
4. Reverse procedure to install, **Fig. 5.**

## NEUTRAL START & BACK-UP LIGHT SWITCH REPLACE
### MODELS w/AUTOMATIC TRANSMISSION
#### 1982–85

The following procedure applies to automatic transmission equipped models only. On vehicles with manual transmission, a transmission mounted back-up light switch is used.
1. Disconnect battery ground cable.
2. Place gear selector in "Neutral" position.
3. Remove screws securing switch to steering column, then the switch.
4. Disconnect wiring connectors. Connect wiring connectors to new switch.
5. Insert .096 inch gage pin into switch gage hole to a depth of 3/8 inch, **Fig. 6. The switch is fixed in neutral position by a plastic shear pin installed during production.**
6. Position the switch on the steering column. Ensure switch carrier tang is inserted in shift tube slot, then install switch retaining screws and tighten.
7. Remove gage pin, then place gear se-

lector in "Park" position to shear plastic pin.
8. Return gear selector to "Neutral" position and attempt to insert a .089 inch gage pin in gage hole. Pin should enter freely.
9. If gage pin does not enter gage hole freely, switch should be reset.
10. Connect battery ground cable and check switch operation.

#### 1986–89
1. Remove battery ground cable.
2. Remove lower insulator panel.
3. Remove neutral start switch electrical connector.
4. Remove neutral start switch.
5. Reverse procedure to install, noting the following:
   a. Align actuator on the switch with holes in shift tube.
   b. Press down on front of switch until tangs snap into rectangular holes in the steering column jacket.
   c. Adjust switch by moving the gear selector to park.

### MODELS w/MANUAL TRANSMISSION
1. Disconnect battery ground cable.
2. Disconnect back-up lamp switch electrical connector.
3. Disconnect switch wiring from transmission bracket, four-wheel drive vehicles only.
4. Remove switch from transmission.
5. Reverse procedure to install.

## NEUTRAL START MECHANICAL LOCKOUT

Actuation of the ignition switch is pre-

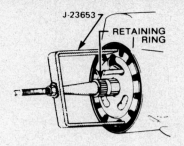

**Fig. 9   Compressing lock plate**

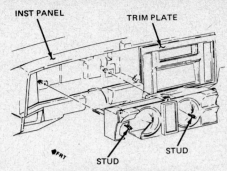

**Fig. 10   Instrument cluster removal. 1982–85**

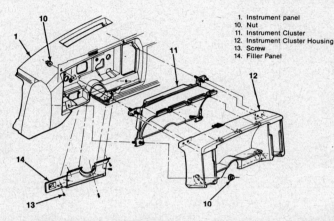

1. Instrument panel
10. Nut
11. Instrument Cluster
12. Instrument Cluster Housing
13. Screw
14. Filler Panel

**Fig. 11   Instrument cluster removal. 1986–89**

vented by a mechanical lockout system, **Figs. 7 and 8,** which prevents the lock cylinder from rotating when the selector lever is out of Park or Neutral. When the selector lever is in Park or Neutral, the slots in the bowl plate and the finger on the actuator rod align, allowing the finger to pass through the bowl plate in turn actuating the ignition switch. If the selector lever is in any position other than Park or Neutral, the finger contacts the bowl plate when the lock cylinder is rotated, thereby preventing full travel of the lock cylinder.

## HORN SOUNDER & STEERING WHEEL
### REPLACE

1. Disconnect battery ground cable.
2. Remove steering wheel trim pad retaining screws from underside of steering wheel spokes, then lift off trim pad and remove wiring connector, if equipped.
3. Remove snap ring and nut from steering shaft.
4. Remove steering wheel using steering wheel puller tool J-1859-03 or equivalent.
5. Reverse procedure to install.

## TURN SIGNAL SWITCH
### REPLACE

1. Disconnect battery ground cable.
2. Remove steering wheel as outlined under "Horn Sounder & Steering Wheel, Replace" procedure.
3. Using a screwdriver, pry cover from lock plate.
4. Using lock plate compressing tool J-23653, compress lock plate and pry retaining ring from groove on shaft, **Fig. 9.** Slowly release lock plate compressing tool, remove tool and lock plate from shaft end.
5. Slide canceling cam and upper bearing preload spring from end of shaft.
6. Remove turn signal (multi-function) lever.
7. Remove hazard warning knob retaining screw, button, spring and knob.
8. Remove pivot arm.
9. Remove switch retaining screws and pull switch up from column, guiding wire harness through column.
10. Reverse procedure to install.

## INSTRUMENT CLUSTER
### REPLACE
### 1982–85

1. Disconnect battery ground cable.
2. Remove five instrument cluster trim plate retaining screws, then trim plate.
3. Lift off instrument cluster face plate and lens.
4. Disconnect speedometer cable.
5. Disconnect electrical connector from instrument cluster, then remove cluster, **Fig. 10.**
6. Reverse procedure to install.

### 1986–89

1. Disconnect battery ground cable.
2. Remove headlamp switch assembly as previously described.
3. Remove A/C and heater control assembly retaining screws, then disconnect electrical connectors and remove control assembly from dash panel.
4. Remove filler panel retaining screws then the panel, **Fig. 11.**
5. Remove instrument cluster housing retaining nuts then the housing.
6. Remove instrument cluster retaining nuts.
7. Disconnect speedometer cable and electrical connectors from instrument cluster, then remove cluster from vehicle.
8. Reverse procedure to install.

## WINDSHIELD WIPER SWITCH
### REPLACE

1. Remove turn signal switch. Refer to "Turn Signal Switch, Replace" procedure.
2. Refer to **Figs. 12 and 13** for wiper switch replacement. **Some 1986 models use a spun-in housing bearing in place of a bearing retainer and bushing. On these models, the complete housing assembly must be replaced if repair is necessary.**

## WINDSHIELD WIPER MOTOR
### REPLACE

1. Disconnect battery ground cable.
2. Remove windshield wiper arms.
3. Remove cowl vent and grille.
4. Loosen, but do not remove transmission drive link to motor crank arm attaching nuts, then disconnect drive link from motor crank arm.
5. Disconnect motor electrical connector and remove attaching bolts.
6. Remove motor by rotating up and outward.
7. Reverse procedure to install. Torque motor attaching bolts to 49 to 75 inch lbs.

## W/S WIPER TRANSMISSION
### REPLACE

1. Disconnect battery ground cable.
2. Remove windshield wiper arms.
3. Remove cowl vent and grille.
4. Remove motor assembly to wiper linkage retaining nut.
5. Remove screws securing wiper linkage to cowl panel and lift out linkage.
6. Reverse procedure to install. Torque all attaching fasteners to 49 to 80 inch lbs.

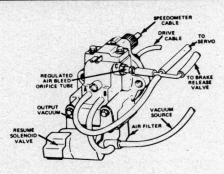

**Fig. 14  Cruise control transducer assembly**

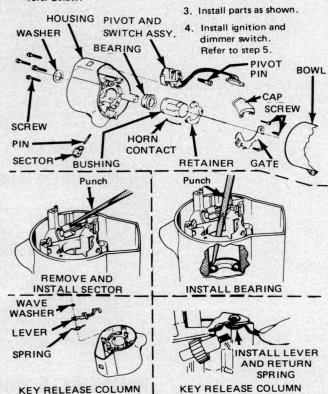

**REMOVE**

1. Remove ignition and dimmer switch. Refer to step 5.
2. Remove parts as shown.
3. For KEY RELEASE refer below.

**INSTALL**

1. For KEY RELEASE refer below.
2. Assemble rack so that first rack tooth engages between first and second tooth of sector.
3. Install parts as shown.
4. Install ignition and dimmer switch. Refer to step 5.

**Fig. 12  Windshield wiper switch removal. Exc. tilt column**

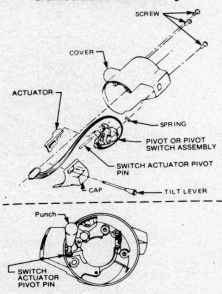

**Fig. 13  Windshield wiper switch removal. Tilt column**

# RADIO
## REPLACE
### 1982–85

1. Disconnect battery ground cable.
2. Remove screws securing center instrument panel bezel, then the bezel.
3. Remove four screws securing radio bracket, then pull radio outward.
4. Disconnect radio electrical connectors, then unplug antenna lead and remove radio.
5. Reverse procedure to install.

### 1986–89

1. Disconnect battery ground cable.
2. Remove ashtray, then disconnect any wires necessary to provide access for radio removal.
3. Remove radio trim plate attaching screws and the trim plate.
4. Remove radio support clip retaining nuts, then the support bracket attaching screws.
5. Pull radio assembly back from dash panel, then disconnect antenna lead and electrical connectors and remove

radio from vehicle.
6. Reverse procedure to install.

# BLOWER MOTOR
## REPLACE

1. Disconnect battery ground cable.
2. On 1982-85 models equipped with A/C, remove vacuum tank.
3. On all models, disconnect blower motor electrical connections.
4. Remove blower motor retaining screws, then the blower motor.
5. Reverse procedure to install.

# HEATER CORE
## REPLACE

1. Disconnect battery ground cable.
2. Drain radiator coolant.
3. Disconnect heater hoses at heater core and plug core tubes.
4. Working inside vehicle, remove core cover.
5. Remove four heater core retaining screws, then the heater core.
6. Reverse procedure to install.

# SPEED CONTROLS
## ADJUST
### BRAKE RELEASE SWITCH & VACUUM RELEASE VALVE

With brake or clutch pedal depressed, push valve or switch fully into tubular clip until seated. Pull brake or clutch pedal rearward until pedal is against stop. Valve or switch will travel in tubular clip to provide proper adjustment.

### SERVO LINKAGE, ADJUST
#### 1982 Models

With carburetor throttle completely closed (ignition "Off" and fast idle cam off), loosen cable adjustment jam nuts. Position cable so chain is almost tight (some slack), and tighten jam nuts.

#### 1983–84 Models

With carburetor throttle completely closed (ignition "Off" and fast idle cam off), loosen cable adjustment jam nuts. On 4-122 models, position cable so cable sleeve at carburetor is tight but not holding throttle open. On 4-119 and V6-173 models, position cable so a 1.0 mm clearance exists between throttle lever stud and end of cable slot. On all models, tighten jam nuts.

### 1985 Models w/4-119 Engine & All 1986–89 Models

Ensure throttle is completely closed, ignition and fast idle cam, if equipped, off. With cable properly secured and connected at throttle lever end, install cable in bracket at servo. Pull on cable just enough to remove slack, then connect cable to hole in servo actuator that will provide approximately .15 inch slack in cable. Do not

stretch cable to make connection at servo, as engine will not return to idle.

### 1985 Models w/4-151 Engine

Ensure throttle is completely closed and ignition and fast idle cam are off. With cable properly connected and secured at throttle lever end, pull servo end of cable toward servo without moving throttle body lever. If one of the six holes in servo assembly tab aligns with cable stud, connect stud to tab with retainer. If no hole aligns with stud, move cable away from servo assembly until next closest hole lines up and connect stud to tab with retainer. Do not stretch cable to make connection, as engine will not return to idle.

## CRUISE SPEED, ADJUST
### 1982 Models

The cruise speed adjustment is made at the transducer, **Fig. 14,** as follows: If vehicle cruises below engagement speed, loosen regulated air bleed orifice tube locknut, **Fig. 14,** and turn orifice tube outward. If cruising speed is higher than engagement speed, turn orifice tube inward. Turning the orifice tube 90° (1/4 turn) changes the engagement-cruising speed difference one MPH. After adjustment is completed, tighten locknut.

### 1983–89 Models

There is no provision for adjusting cruise speed on these models.

# 4-119 (1.9L) GASOLINE ENGINE
## INDEX

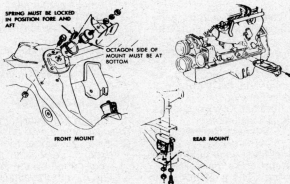

SPRING MUST BE LOCKED IN POSITION FORE AND AFT

OCTAGON SIDE OF MOUNT MUST BE AT BOTTOM

FRONT MOUNT  REAR MOUNT

**Fig. 1  Engine mount**

## ENGINE
### REPLACE

1. Disconnect battery ground cable.
2. Scribe reference marks in the hood hinge area, then remove hood.
3. Drain cooling system, then remove radiator hoses, overflow hose, transmission cooler lines (if equipped), upper radiator shroud and radiator.
4. Remove cooling fan, then disconnect heater hoses.
5. Remove air cleaner assembly.
6. Identify, then disconnect vacuum hoses from engine.
7. Disconnect necessary engine wiring from bulkhead.
8. Disconnect throttle linkage as necessary, then remove distributor cap.
9. Raise and support vehicle.
10. Remove converter to exhaust pipe bolts, then disconnect exhaust pipe at manifold.
11. Remove strut rods at bellhousing (if equipped).
12. Remove flywheel cover bolts, then the cover.
13. On models equipped with automatic transmission, remove torque converter bolts.
14. On all models, disconnect shield at

rear of catalytic converter, then remove converter hanger.
15. Remove lower radiator fan shroud.
16. Disconnect fuel lines from fuel pump.
17. Remove two outer bolts from front air deflector.
18. Remove left side body mount bolts, then raise body using suitable lifting equipment.
19. Remove bellhousing bolts, then lower body to frame.
20. Remove motor mount through bolts, then lower vehicle.
21. If equipped with A/C or power steering disconnect A/C compressor and/or power steering pump.
22. Install suitable lifting device on engine.
23. Support transmission with suitable jack.
24. Remove engine assembly.
25. Reverse procedure to install.

## ENGINE MOUNTS
### REPLACE
#### FRONT

1. Disconnect battery ground cable.
2. Remove air cleaner, duct and upper fan shroud.
3. Remove engine mount nuts and retaining wire.
4. With vehicle raised, raise engine to take weight off mounts.

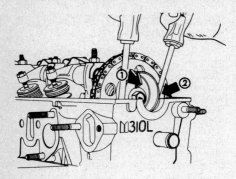

**Fig. 2 Depressing adjusting lock lever**

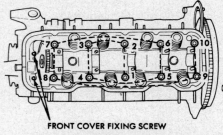

**Fig. 3 Cylinder head hold-down bolt torque sequence**

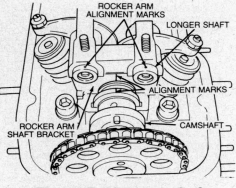

**Fig. 4 Rocker arm shaft installation**

5. Remove engine mount to engine bracket.
6. Remove engine mount using tool J-25510, or equivalent, **Fig. 1.**
7. Reverse procedure to install.

## REAR

1. Disconnect battery ground cable.
2. Remove mount nut and bolts.
3. Support, and slightly raise, transmission at extension housing and remove engine mount, **Fig. 1.**
4. Reverse procedure to install.

## CYLINDER HEAD
### REPLACE

1. Remove cam cover.
2. Remove EGR pipe clamp at rear of cylinder head.
3. Raise and support vehicle.
4. Disconnect exhaust pipe at manifold.
5. Lower vehicle, drain cooling system and disconnect heater hoses.
6. Remove A/C compressor and/or power steering pump, and position aside.
7. Disconnect accelerator linkage and fuel line at carburetor, all necessary electrical connections, spark plug wires and necessary vacuum lines.
8. Rotate crankshaft until No. 4 cylinder is in firing position. Remove distributor cap and mark rotor to housing relationship, then remove distributor.
9. Remove fuel pump.
10. Lock shoe on timing chain automatic adjuster in fully retracted position by depressing the adjuster lock lever with a screwdriver or equivalent in direction as indicated, **Fig. 2.**
11. Remove timing sprocket to camshaft bolt. Remove sprocket and fuel pump drive cam from the camshaft. Do not remove the sprocket from the chain.
12. Disconnect AIR hose and check valve at air manifold.
13. Remove cylinder head to timing cover bolts.
14. Remove cylinder head bolts using tool J-24239-01, or equivalent. Remove outer bolts first.
15. With an assistant, remove cylinder head, intake and exhaust manifold as an assembly.
16. Clean all gasket material from cylinder head and block surfaces. **Gasket sur-**

faces on both head and block must be clean of all foreign matter and free of nicks or heavy scratches. Cylinder bolt threads in the block and threads on the bolts must be cleaned, as dirt will affect bolt torque.
17. Reverse procedure to install and tighten head bolts to specifications in sequence, **Fig. 3.**

## INTAKE MANIFOLD
### REPLACE

1. Drain engine cooling system. **Before removing intake manifold, check that the cooling system is completely drained. Any coolant left in the engine will flow into the cylinder when the manifold is removed.**
2. Remove air cleaner assembly.
3. Disconnect radiator upper hose from intake manifold.
4. Disconnect vacuum hose from manifold.
5. Disconnect heater hoses from manifold and from connector under the dashboard.
6. Disconnect accelerator control cable from carburetor.
7. Disconnect distributor vacuum hose from distributor and the thermo-unit wiring at the connector.
8. Disconnect automatic choke and solenoid wiring at connectors.
9. Disconnect PCV hose from the rocker arm cover.
10. Disconnect oil level gage guide tube fixing bolt at the intake manifold.
11. Disconnect the EGR pipe from the EGR valve adapter and the AIR vacuum hose from the 3-way joint.
12. Remove EGR valve and adapter.
13. Remove the eight attaching nuts and remove the intake manifold.
14. Using a new gasket, reverse procedure to install.

## EXHAUST MANIFOLD
### REPLACE

1. Disconnect battery ground cable.
2. Raise and support vehicle.
3. Disconnect exhaust pipe from exhaust manifold.
4. Disconnect E.G.R pipe at exhaust manifold.
5. Lower vehicle, remove bolts attaching air cleaner and loosen clamp bolts.

6. Raise air cleaner slightly, then remove air cleaner hot air inlet hose.
7. If equipped with A/C or power steering, remove A/C compressor and/or power steering pump.
8. Remove the four attaching bolts and remove the manifold cover.
9. Remove the seven mounting nuts from the manifold and remove the exhaust manifold.
10. Using a new gasket, reverse procedure to install. Torque manifold stud nuts to 16 ft. lbs. in a sequence beginning with the inner nuts and working outward.

## ROCKER ARMS & SHAFTS
### REPLACE
#### REMOVAL

1. Remove cam cover.
2. Alternately loosen rocker arm shaft bracket nuts and remove nuts from brackets.
3. Remove springs from rocker arm shaft, then the rocker arm brackets and arms, keeping components in order.

#### INSTALLATION

1. Lubricate rocker arms, shafts and valve stems with engine oil.
2. Install the longer rocker shaft on the exhaust valve side and the shorter rocker shaft on the intake valve side, **Fig. 4,** with the aligning marks facing front.
3. Install rocker arm shaft brackets and rocker arms on the rocker arm shafts with the cylinder number on the upper face of the brackets facing toward front of engine.
4. Align the mark on the No. 1 rocker arm shaft bracket with the mark on the rocker arm shafts.
5. The exhaust side rocker arm shaft should project a greater distance from the face of the No. 1 rocker shaft bracket outer face than the intake side rocker arm shaft when the rocker arm shaft stud holes are aligned with the rocker arm shaft bracket stud holes.
6. Position rocker arm shaft springs between rocker arm shaft bracket and rocker arm.

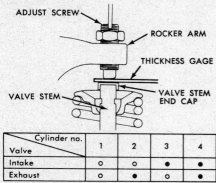

| Cylinder no. Valve | 1 | 2 | 3 | 4 |
|---|---|---|---|---|
| Intake | o | o | ● | ● |
| Exhaust | o | ● | o | ● |

Note: o When piston in No. 1 cylinder is at TDC on compression stroke.
● When piston in No. 4 cylinder is at TDC on compression stroke.

**Fig. 5   Valve adjustment**

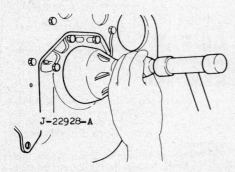

**Fig. 8   Installing rear main oil seal**

7. Ensure punch mark on rocker arm shaft is facing upward. Install rocker arm shaft bracket assembly onto cylinder head studs. Align mark on camshaft with mark on No. 1 rocker arm shaft bracket.
8. Torque rocker arm shaft stud nuts to 16 ft. lbs. **Hold the rocker arm springs in position while torquing the stud nuts to prevent spring damage.**
9. Adjust valves and install cam cover.

## VALVES
### ADJUST

1. Before adjusting valve clearances, check the rocker arm shaft bracket nuts for looseness and retighten as necessary.
2. Bring either No. 1 or No. 4 piston to top dead center on the compression stroke by turning the crankshaft to align timing mark on crankshaft pulley with pointer.
3. Hold crankshaft in above position and adjust clearance of the valves indicated, **Fig. 5**, to specifications. Take measurement at the clearance between rocker arm and valve stem.
4. Turn crankshaft one full turn and adjust clearance of remaining valves to specifications.

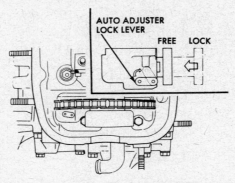

**Fig. 6   Locking timing chain adapter**

## VALVE CLEARANCE SPECIFICATIONS

Cold valve clearance should measure .006 inch at the intake valves and .010 inch at the exhaust valves.

## VALVE ARRANGEMENT
### FRONT TO REAR

All . . . . . . . . . . . . . . . . . . . . . . . E-I-I-E-E-I-I-E

## VALVE TIMING

Intake valves open at 21° before TDC.

## CAMSHAFT
### REPLACE
#### REMOVAL

1. Remove cam cover.
2. Rotate camshaft until No. 4 cylinder is in firing position. Remove distributor cap and mark rotor to housing position, then remove distributor.
3. Remove the fuel pump.
4. Lock the shoe on timing chain automatic adjuster in fully retracted position by depressing the adjuster lock lever with a screwdriver or equivalent in direction as indicated, **Figs. 2 and 6**. After locking the automatic adjuster, check that the chain is loose.
5. Remove timing sprocket to camshaft bolt. Remove sprocket and fuel pump drive cam from camshaft. Do not remove sprocket from chain.
6. Remove rocker arm, shaft and bracket assembly.
7. Remove camshaft assembly.

#### INSTALLATION

1. Lubricate camshaft and journals of cylinder head with engine oil.
2. Install camshaft assembly.
3. Install rocker arm, shaft and bracket assembly.
4. Align mark on the No. 1 rocker arm shaft bracket with the mark on the camshaft. Also, ensure crankshaft pulley groove is aligned with TDC mark on front cover.
5. Assemble timing sprocket to camshaft by aligning sprocket with pin on

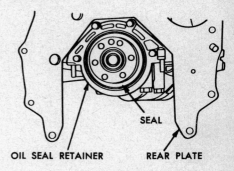

**Fig. 7   Rear main oil seal**

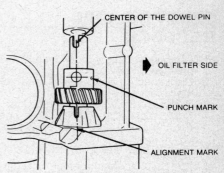

**Fig. 9   Oil pump alignment**

camshaft. Use caution not to remove chain from sprocket.
6. Install fuel pump drive cam and sprocket retaining bolt and washer. Remove the half-moon seal at front of head, then torque retaining bolt to 60 ft. lbs. Then install the half-moon seal in cylinder head.
7. Install distributor.
8. Release lock by depressing shoe on timing chain automatic adjuster and check timing chain for proper tension.
9. Check that distributor rotor and mark on distributor housing are aligned with No. 4 piston firing position in distributor cap, then install distributor. Timing mark on crank pulley should also be aligned with TDC mark on front cover.
10. Install distributor cap.
11. Install cam cover.

## REAR MAIN SEAL
### REPLACE

1. Remove starter motor and position aside.
2. Remove transmission.
3. On vehicles equipped with manual transmission, remove clutch cover and pressure plate assembly, then the flywheel and flywheel cover.
4. On vehicles equipped with automatic transmission, remove flex plate.
5. On all vehicles, pry seal from retainer, **Fig. 7**.
6. Install new seal using tool J-22928-A, **Fig. 8**. Prior to installation, fill clearance between lips of seal with suitable grease and lubricate seal lip with clean engine oil.

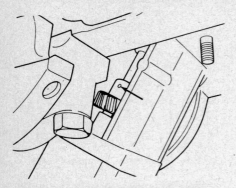

**Fig. 10 Checking alignment**

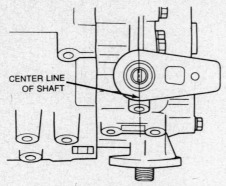

**Fig. 11 Oil pump shaft alignment**

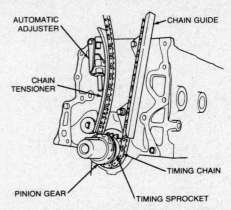

**Fig. 12 Timing chain removal**

## FRONT OIL SEAL
### REPLACE

1. Disconnect battery ground cable and drain cooling system.
2. Disconnect radiator hoses and remove radiator assembly.
3. Remove drive belts and engine fan.
4. Remove crankshaft pulley center bolt and the pulley and balancer assembly.
5. Pry seal from timing cover with a suitable screwdriver.
6. Using tool J-26587, install new seal.

## FRONT COVER
### REPLACE
#### REMOVAL

1. Disconnect battery ground cable.
2. Remove oil pan as described under "Oil Pan, Replace."
3. Remove cylinder head.
4. Remove oil pickup tube from oil pump.
5. Remove harmonic balancer and the AIR pump drive belt.
6. On air conditioned vehicles, remove A/C compressor and position aside. Remove compressor mounting brackets.
7. On models equipped with power steering, remove power steering pump and bracket and position aside.
8. On all models, remove distributor assembly.
9. Remove front cover attaching bolts and the front cover.

#### INSTALLATION

1. Install new gasket onto cylinder block.
2. Align oil pump drive gear punch mark with oil filter side of cover, **Fig. 9,** then align the center of dowel pin with alignment mark on oil pump case.
3. Rotate crankshaft until Nos. 1 and 4 cylinders are at top dead center.
4. Install front cover by engaging pinion gear with oil pump drive gear on crankshaft.
5. Ensure punch mark on oil pump drive gear is turned to the rear, viewed through the clearance between front cover and cylinder block, **Fig. 10.**
6. Ensure slit at the end of oil pump shaft is parallel with front face of cylinder block and is offset forward, **Fig. 11.**

7. Install front cover and tighten front cover bolts.
8. Reverse steps 1 thru 7 under "Front Cover, Replace."
9. Check engine timing.
10. Check for leaks.

## TIMING CHAIN
### REPLACE

1. Remove front cover assembly. Refer to steps under "Front Cover, Replace" procedure.
2. Lock automatic adjuster shoe in fully retracted position.
3. Remove timing chain from crankshaft sprocket, **Fig. 12.**
4. Remove E-clip and the chain adjuster and tensioner, **Fig. 13.** Inspect components for wear or damage. Also, inspect chain guide and oil jet. View "A," **Fig. 13.**
5. Install timing sprocket and pinion gear with groove side toward front cover. Align key grooves with key on crankshaft, then drive into position with tool J-26587.
6. Turn crankshaft so key is turned toward cylinder head side with Nos. 1 and 4 pistons at top dead center.
7. Install timing chain by aligning mark plate on chain with the mark on crankshaft timing sprocket. The side of the chain with mark plate is located on the front side and the side of chain with the most links between mark plates is located on the chain guide side, **Fig. 14.**
8. Install the camshaft timing sprocket so marked side of sprocket faces forward and the triangular mark aligns with the chain mark plate. **Keep the timing chain engaged with camshaft timing sprocket until the camshaft timing sprocket is installed on camshaft.**
9. Install automatic chain adjuster, then release lock by depressing the adjusting shoe.
10. Install front cover assembly as outlined previously.

## PISTONS & RODS

Assemble piston to rod so the mark on the piston is facing toward front of engine,

**Fig. 15,** and the face of the connecting rod with the cylinder number mark is facing toward the starter side of the engine.

Pistons are available in oversizes of .020 and .030 inch.

## OIL PAN
### REPLACE
#### REMOVAL

1. Remove engine as outlined under "Engine, Replace."
2. Remove nuts and bolts attaching oil pan to cylinder block and remove oil pan.
3. Remove oil level gage guide tube from the intake manifold and oil pan.

#### INSTALLATION

1. Apply a thin coat of Permatex No. 2, or equivalent, to locations indicated by arrows, **Fig. 16.**
2. Install new oil pan gasket aligning holes and install oil pan on cylinder block.
3. Install nuts and bolts and torque evenly to 4 ft. lbs. **Check edge of gasket to check proper positioning. If projection of gasket edge beyond the oil pan flange is uneven, remove and reinstall, Fig. 17.**
4. Install engine into vehicle as outlined under "Engine, Replace."

## OIL PUMP
### REPLACE
#### REMOVAL

1. Remove cam cover, distributor assembly and oil pan.
2. Remove bolt securing oil pickup tube to engine block and the tube from the oil pump.
3. Remove oil pump mounting bolts, then the oil pump.
4. Remove rubber hose and relief valve assembly from the pump.

#### INSPECTION

1. Measure clearance between drive rotor and driven rotor with a feeler gauge, **Fig. 18.** If clearance is greater than .0079 inch, replace oil pump assembly.

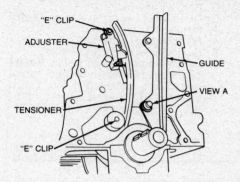

**Fig. 13 Timing chain guide, tensioner & adjuster**

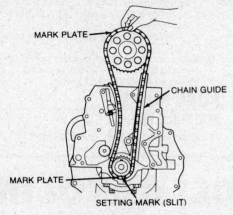

**Fig. 14 Timing chain alignment**

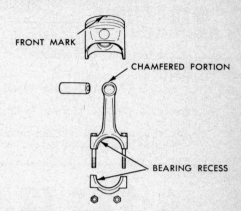

**Fig. 15 Piston & connecting rod assembly**

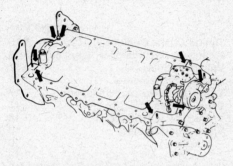

**Fig. 16 Sealer locations on oil pan gasket surface**

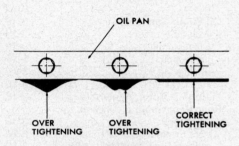

**Fig. 17 Oil pan gasket installation**

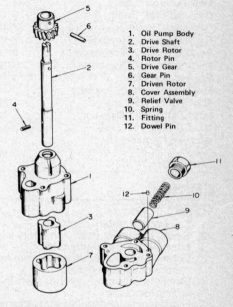

1. Oil Pump Body
2. Drive Shaft
3. Drive Rotor
4. Rotor Pin
5. Drive Gear
6. Gear Pin
7. Driven Rotor
8. Cover Assembly
9. Relief Valve
10. Spring
11. Fitting
12. Dowel Pin

**Fig. 18 Oil pump assembly**

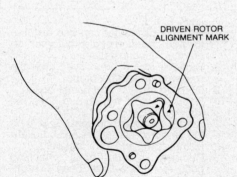

**Fig. 19 Aligning drive & driven rotors**

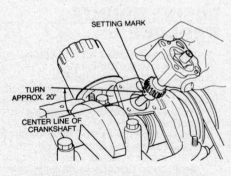

**Fig. 20 Oil pump installation**

2. Measure clearance between driven rotor and inner wall of pump body, **Fig. 18.** If clearance is greater than .0098 inch, replace oil pump assembly.
3. Measure clearance between drive rotor, driven rotor and oil pump cover with a feeler gauge and a straightedge, **Fig. 18.** If clearance is greater than .0079 inch, replace oil pump assembly.
4. Determine clearance between drive shaft and drive shaft hole in pump cover. Measure the inside diameter of the shaft hole in the cover and the diameter of the drive shaft. Subtract the drive shaft diameter from the inside diameter of the shaft hole. If the clearance is greater than .0098 inch, replace oil pump.
5. Inspect components for wear or damage.

## INSTALLATION

1. Align mark on camshaft with mark on No. 1 rocker arm shaft bracket. Align notch on crankshaft pulley with "Ō" mark on front cover. When these two sets of marks are properly aligned, No. 4 piston is at top dead center, compression stroke.
2. Install driven rotor with alignment mark aligned with mark on drive rotor. **Fig. 19.**
3. Engage oil pump drive gear with pinion gear on crankshaft so alignment mark on drive gear is turned rearward and approximately 20° from the crankshaft in a clockwise direction, **Fig. 20.**
4. Ensure oil pump drive gear is turned

rearward as viewed from clearance between front cover and cylinder block and the slit at the end of the oil pump drive shaft is parallel with the front face of the cylinder block and is offset forward as viewed through the distributor fitting hole, **Fig. 11.**
5. Install oil pump cover and mounting bolts.
6. Install relief valve assembly and rubber hose on cover.
7. Connect oil pickup tube to rubber hose and secure tube to cylinder block.
8. Install oil pan and cam cover.
9. Install distributor so boss on shaft is fitted into slit at end of oil pump drive shaft.
10. Refill engine oil and check for leaks.

## WATER PUMP
### REPLACE

1. Disconnect battery ground cable.
2. Remove lower cover.
3. Drain cooling system.
4. On models less A/C, remove engine fan.
5. On models with A/C, proceed as follows:
   a. Remove air pump and alternator mounting bolts and the fan and air pump drive belt.
   b. Remove engine fan and pulley assembly.
   c. Remove fan set plate and fan pulley.
6. On all models, remove water pump attaching bolts and the water pump.
7. Reverse procedure to install.

## FUEL PUMP
### REPLACE

1. Disconnect battery ground cable.
2. Remove distributor.
3. Disconnect fuel pump inlet and outlet hoses.
4. Remove engine lift hook.
5. Remove fuel pump and gasket.
6. Reverse procedure to install. **Rotate camshaft to "down stroke" position before installing pump. Lubricate rod with engine oil.**
7. Adjust timing and check for leaks.

# 4-121 (2.0L) GASOLINE ENGINE

## INDEX

## ENGINE
### REPLACE

1. Disconnect battery cables.
2. Scribe alignment marks on hood and hood hinge, then remove hood.
3. Drain cooling system, then remove radiator hoses from radiator.
4. Remove upper fan shroud, then the radiator and fan.
5. Disconnect heater hoses from engine.
6. Disconnect wiring harness at bulkhead, then remove air cleaner.
7. Disconnect accelerator cable from carburetor, then the fuel line from frame.
8. Disconnect battery ground cable from engine block, then remove the ground strap from bulkhead.
9. Raise and support vehicle.
10. Remove clutch bell crank, then disconnect exhaust pipe from manifold.
11. Remove motor mount through bolt, left hand body mount bolts and left air dam bolts.
12. Raise body to gain access to upper bell housing bolts, then remove the bolts.
13. Lower body, then remove flywheel dust shield.
14. Lower vehicle and support transmission with suitable jack.
15. If equipped, disconnect power steering pump and/or A/C compressor and position aside.
16. Install suitable lifting device, then remove engine from vehicle.
17. Reverse procedure to install.

## ENGINE MOUNTS
### REPLACE

1. Disconnect battery ground cable.
2. Remove upper fan shroud.
3. Raise and support vehicle.
4. Remove engine mount through bolt. On left mount, remove mount-to-engine upper bracket attaching nuts.
5. Raise front of engine and remove mount-to-engine attaching bolts, then the mount. **Raise engine only enough to provide sufficient clearance to remove mount. Check for interference between rear of engine and cowl panel which could cause damage to the distributor or EGR.**
6. Reverse procedure to install. Torque mount-to-engine attaching bolts to 29-39 ft. lbs. and mount-to-frame bolt to 35-47 ft. lbs.

## CYLINDER HEAD
### REPLACE

1. Disconnect battery ground cable.
2. Remove air cleaner and drain cooling system.
3. Raise and support vehicle.
4. Disconnect exhaust pipe from exhaust manifold, then lower vehicle.
5. Disconnect accelerator linkage and any necessary wires and vacuum lines.
6. Remove fuel vapor canister harness lines, **Fig. 1.**
7. Remove distributor cap and distributor. Mark position of distributor for reference during installation.
8. Remove rocker arm cover, then the rocker arms and pushrods.
9. Remove radiator and heater hoses.
10. Remove upper fan shroud, then the fan.
11. Remove air management valve, then the air pump and upper AIR bracket.
12. Remove fuel line from fuel pump.
13. Remove cylinder head attaching bolts, then the cylinder head. Disconnect wires from rear of head.
14. Reverse procedure to install. Coat cylinder head gasket and bolts with suitable sealant and install bolts finger tight. Torque bolts to specifications in sequence shown in **Fig. 2.**

## INTAKE MANIFOLD
### REPLACE

1. Disconnect battery ground cable.
2. Remove air cleaner and distributor cap.
3. Raise and support vehicle.
4. Remove middle right bell housing-to-engine block attaching bolt, then move wiring harness aside.
5. Remove distributor hold down nut and clamp, then disconnect primary wires from coil.
6. Remove fuel pump attaching bolts and position pump aside, then lower vehicle.
7. Disconnect accelerator cable, fuel in-

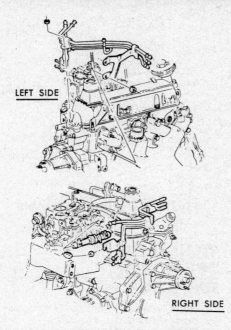

LEFT SIDE

RIGHT SIDE

**Fig. 1   Fuel vapor canister harness**

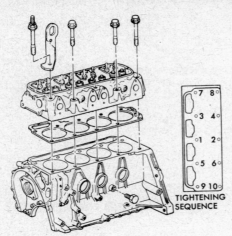

**Fig. 2   Cylinder head bolt tightening sequence**

TIGHTENING SEQUENCE

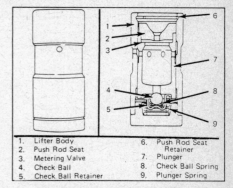

1. Lifter Body
2. Push Rod Seat
3. Metering Valve
4. Check Ball
5. Check Ball Retainer
6. Push Rod Seat Retainer
7. Plunger
8. Check Ball Spring
9. Plunger Spring

**Fig. 3   Sectional view of hydraulic valve lifter**

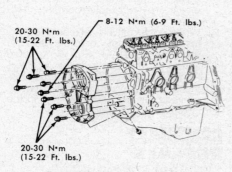

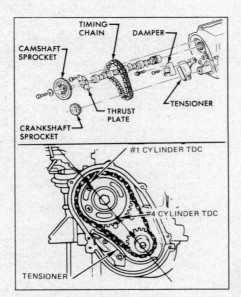

TIMING CHAIN
CAMSHAFT SPROCKET
DAMPER
TENSIONER
THRUST PLATE
CRANKSHAFT SPROCKET

#1 CYLINDER TDC
#4 CYLINDER TDC
TENSIONER

**Fig. 5   Valve timing marks**

20-30 N•m (15-22 Ft. lbs.)
8-12 N•m (6-9 Ft. lbs.)
20-30 N•m (15-22 Ft. lbs.)

**Fig. 4   Engine front cover replacement**

let line and any necessary wires and vacuum lines.
8. Remove carburetor, then drain cooling system.
9. Disconnect fuel vapor canister harness lines, **Fig. 1**.
10. Disconnect hoses and wires from manifold.
11. Remove intake manifold attaching bolts, then the manifold.
12. Reverse procedure to install. Clean mating surface and install a new gasket. Torque bolts to specifications.

## EXHAUST MANIFOLD
### REPLACE

1. Disconnect battery ground cable.
2. Remove air cleaner.
3. Raise and support vehicle.
4. Remove exhaust pipe from manifold.
5. Remove AIR hose and pipe bracket bolt, then the dipstick tube bracket.
6. Remove fuel vapor canister harness pipes, **Fig. 1**.
7. Remove exhaust manifold attaching bolts, then the manifold.

8. Reverse procedure to install. Torque attaching bolts to specifications. **If exhaust manifold is being replaced, remove AIR manifold and exhaust manifold seal.**

## ROCKER ARM STUDS

Rocker arm studs that have stress cracks or damaged threads should be replaced. If threads in cylinder head are damaged, the head can be retapped and a helical type insert installed. When installing a new rocker arm stud, torque stud to 43–49 ft. lbs.

## VALVES
### ADJUST

1. Crank engine until mark on crankshaft pulley is aligned with "O" mark on timing tab. Check to ensure engine is in the No. 1 cylinder firing position by placing fingers on No. 1 cylinder rock-

er arms as mark on pulley comes near "O" mark on timing tab. If valves are not moving, the engine is in the No. 1 firing position. If valves are moving, engine is on No. 4 cylinder firing position and should be rotated one revolution to reach the No. 1 cylinder firing position.
2. With engine in No. 1 cylinder firing position, adjust the following valves: exhaust, 1 and 3: intake 1 and 2. To adjust valves, back off adjusting nut until lash is felt at pushrod, then tighten nut until all lash is removed. This can be determined by rotating pushrod while tightening adjusting nut. When all lash has been removed, turn adjusting nut in an additional 1½ turns.
3. Crank one full revolution until mark on crankshaft pulley and "O" mark are aligned. This is the No. 4 cylinder firing position. With engine in this position, adjust the following valves: exhaust, 2 and 4: intake 3 and 4.
4. Install rocker arm cover, then start engine and check timing and idle speed.

## VALVE CLEARANCE SPECIFICATIONS

Turn rocker arm stud nut until all lash is eliminated, then tighten nut an additional 1½ turns.

## VALVE ARRANGEMENT

All . . . . . . . . . . . . . . . . . . . . . . E-I-I-E-E-I-I-E

## CAMSHAFT LIFT SPECS.

Camshaft lift should measure .26 inch at intake and exhaust valves.

## VALVE TIMING

Intake valves open at 14° before TDC.

## VALVE GUIDES

Valve guides are an integral part of the cylinder head and are not removable. If valve stem clearance becomes excessive, the valve guide should be reamed to the next oversize and the appropriate oversize valves installed. Valves are available in .003, .006 and .012 inch oversizes.

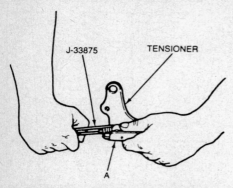
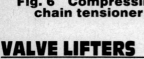

**Fig. 6   Compressing timing chain tensioner spring**

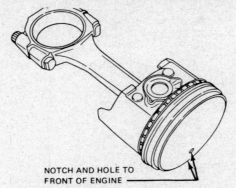

NOTCH AND HOLE TO FRONT OF ENGINE

**Fig. 7   Piston & rod assembly**

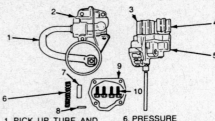

1. PICK UP TUBE AND SCREEN.
2. PUMP COVER.
3. DRIVE GEAR AND SHAFT.
4. IDLER GEAR.
5. PUMP BODY.
6. PRESSURE REGULATOR SPRING.
7. PRESSURE REGULATOR VALVE.
8. RETAINING PIN.
9. GASKET.
10. ATTACHING BOLTS.

**Fig. 8   Oil pump assembly**

## VALVE LIFTERS
### REPLACE

1. Remove rocker arm cover and push-rod.
2. Remove rocker arm studs and push-rod guide.
3. Using tool J-29834, or equivalent, remove valve lifter.
4. Reverse procedure to install. Coat foot of valve lifters with Molykote, or equivalent. Following installation, adjust valve as described under - Valves, Adjust. -

## VALVE LIFTER SERVICE
### DISASSEMBLY

1. Depress plunger with a pushrod, then remove pushrod seat retainer using a small screwdriver, **Fig. 3.**
2. Remove pushrod seat, metering valve, plunger, ball check valve assembly and plunger spring.
3. Pry ball retainer loose from plunger and remove ball check valve and spring.

### CLEANING & INSPECTION

1. Clean all parts in suitable solvent.
2. Inspect all lifter components for wear or damage. If any one part is worn or damaged, that entire assembly must be replaced.
3. If lifter body wall is worn, inspect cylinder block lifter bore.
4. If bottom of lifter is worn, inspect camshaft lobe.
5. If pushrod seat is worn, inspect pushrod.

### ASSEMBLY

1. Position check ball on small hole in bottom of plunger, then install spring and ball retainer.
2. Install plunger spring over ball retainer, then slide lifter body over spring and plunger. Make sure oil holes in lifter body and plunger are aligned.
3. Fill assembly with SAE 10 oil, then depress plunger with a 1/8 inch drift pin. Insert a 1/16 inch drift pin through both oil holes to hold plunger down against spring tension.
4. Remove the 1/8 inch drift pin and refill

assembly with SAE 10 oil, then install the metering valve and pushrod seat.
5. Install pushrod seat retainer, then push down on the pushrod seat and remove the 1/16 inch drift pin from oil holes.

## ENGINE FRONT COVER
### REPLACE

1. Disconnect battery ground cable.
2. Drain cooling system.
3. Remove upper fan shroud, accessory drive belts, fan and pulley.
4. Remove radiator and heater hoses.
5. Remove water pump as described under "Water Pump, Replace."
6. Remove crankshaft pulley retaining bolts, then the pulley.
7. Using tool J-24420, or equivalent, remove crankshaft hub .
8. Remove front cover attaching bolts, then the front cover, **Fig. 4.**
9. Reverse procedure to install. Apply a continuous bead of sealant 1052357, or equivalent to front cover sealing surface and 1052366, or equivalent to oil pan surface of front cover.

## TIMING CHAIN
### REPLACE

1. Remove engine front cover as previously described.
2. Align timing marks on camshaft and crankshaft sprockets, then remove timing chain tensioner as described under "Timing Chain Tensioner, Replace."
3. Remove camshaft sprocket and timing chain, **Fig. 5.**
4. If crankshaft sprocket is to be replaced, remove sprocket using a suitable puller.
5. Reverse procedure to install, noting the following:
   a. Lubricate thrust surface of sprockets with Molykote, or equivalent.
   b. Align timing marks on sprockets.
   c. Align dowel in camshaft with dowel hole in camshaft sprocket.
   d. Lubricate timing chain with clean engine oil.
   e. Torque camshaft sprocket attaching bolts to 66-88 ft. lbs.

## TIMING CHAIN TENSIONER
### REPLACE

1. Remove engine front cover as previously described.
2. Remove tensioner attaching bolts, then the tensioner.
3. Using tool J33875 to install tensioner, position tangs under tensioner sliding blocks, then pull tool to compress tensioner spring.
4. While compressing tensioner spring, insert a cotter pin or other suitable tool into hole "A," **Fig. 6,** to hold spring in the compressed position. Remove tool J-33875 from tensioner.
5. Install tensioner on engine, then remove cotter pin holding spring in the compressed position.

## CAMSHAFT
### REPLACE

1. Remove rocker arm cover, then the timing chain and camshaft sprocket as previously described.
2. Drain cooling system, then remove radiator.
3. Mark position of rotor to distributor body for assembly reference.
4. Raise and support vehicle.
5. Remove fuel pump, then the distributor hold down nut and clamp.
6. Lower vehicle, then remove distributor.
7. Remove rocker arm studs and push-rod guides.
8. Remove valve lifter, then the camshaft.
9. Reverse procedure to install. Align timing marks on crankshaft and camshaft sprockets, **Fig. 5.**

## PISTONS & RODS
### ASSEMBLE

Install piston to rod with notch and hole on piston facing toward front of engine, **Fig. 7.**

## MAIN & ROD BEARINGS

Main bearings are available in standard

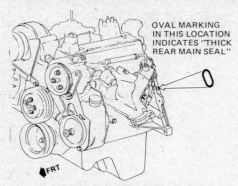

**Fig. 9 Rear main oil seal installation. 1983 & early production 1984**

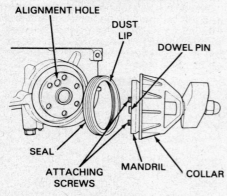

**Fig. 11 Rear main oil seal installation. Late production 1984**

size and undersizes of .016 and .032 inch. Connecting rod bearings are available in standard size and undersizes of .005 and .010 inch.

## OIL PAN
## REPLACE
### 4 X 2

1. Remove engine as described under "Engine, Replace."
2. Drain engine oil, then remove oil pan attaching bolts and the oil pan.
3. Reverse procedure to install. Also, refer to step 12 under 4 X 4 oil pan replacement procedure.

### 4 X 4

1. Disconnect battery ground cable.
2. Remove starter motor front brace bolt.
3. Remove engine mount through bolts.
4. Raise and support vehicle.
5. Remove splash shield, then the brake and fuel line clip retaining bolts.
6. Remove crossmember attaching bolts, then the crossmember.
7. Drain crankcase, then remove starter motor and position aside.
8. Disconnect steering damper from frame.
9. Mark location of pitman arm, then disconnect pitman arm and steering gear from frame.
10. Disconnect front axle from frame, then the front propeller shaft from front dif-

ferential. Slide differential forward.
11. Remove oil pan attaching bolts, then raise engine slightly and remove the oil pan.
12. Reverse procedure to install, noting the following:
    a. Apply a thin coat of RTV sealant to both ends of new rear oil pan seal prior to installing seal in rear main bearing cap. The sealant must not extend beyond tabs of seal.
    b. Apply a continuous bead of RTV sealant on oil pan side rails. The bead of sealant should circle inboard at each bolt hole location.
    c. Do not apply sealant to rear oil pan seal mating surface.
    d. Apply RTV sealant to oil pan-to-front cover mating surface. This sealant must meet the two side rail beads.
    e. Torque oil pan-to-cover bolts to 6-9 ft. lbs., oil pan-to-side rail bolts to 4-9 ft. lbs. and oil pan-to-rear rail bolts to 11-17 ft. lbs. All bolts must be torqued before sealant dries.

## OIL PUMP SERVICE
### REMOVAL

1. Drain crankcase, then remove oil pan as previously described.
2. Remove pump to rear main bearing attaching bolt, then remove pump and extension shaft.

### DISASSEMBLY

1. Remove four pump cover to body attaching bolts, then remove cover, idler and drive gears and shaft, **Fig. 8. Place alignment marks on oil pump drive and idler gear teeth so they can be installed in the same position.**
2. Remove pressure regulator valve retaining pin, spring and the valve from pump body.

### INSPECTION

Inspect pump components and should any of the following conditions exist, the oil pump assembly should be replaced.
1. Inspect pump body, gears and cover for cracks or excessive wear.
2. Check drive gear shaft for looseness in housing.
3. Check inside of pump cover for wear that would allow oil to leak past ends of gears.
4. Check oil pickup screen assembly for damage to screen or pickup tube.
5. Check pressure regulator valve for fit in pump body.

### ASSEMBLY

1. Install a replacement pickup screen and tube assembly, if removed. Position pump in a soft jawed vise then apply sealer to end of tube and tap into position using tool No. J8369 and a plastic hammer. Use care not to damage inlet screen and tube assembly when installing on pump housing.
2. Place pressure regulator valve, spring and retaining pin into pump body, then install drive gear and shaft.

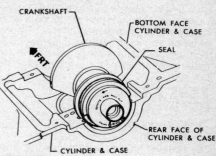

**Fig. 10 Rear main seal identification stamping**

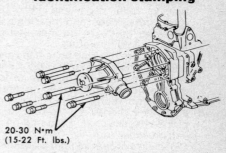

**Fig. 12 Water pump replacement**

3. Install idler gear into pump body, then the pump cover gasket, **Fig. 8.**
4. Install pump cover and cover retaining bolts, then torque bolts to 6-9 ft. lbs.

### INSTALLATION

1. Align oil pump extension shaft to distributor drive gear socket and pump housing with dowels on cap, then install shaft retainer and pump assembly.
2. Install oil pump assembly retaining bolt to rear main bearing cap and torque bolt to 26-38 ft. lbs.
3. Install oil pan as previously described.

## REAR MAIN BEARING OIL SEAL
### REPLACE

A new, one piece, rear crankshaft oil seal has been introduced for 1984 4-121 engines. As this new seal has been proven effective in correcting rear main seal oil leaks, this seal should be used to replace the two piece seal on 1983 4-121 engines. Use of the two piece seal should be discontinued when servicing these engines.

Early production 4-121 engines installed in 1984 vehicles were assembled with a thin, one piece rear main oil seal, service P/N 14081761, which is also suitable for installation in 4-121 engines used in 1983 vehicles. Beginning with December 1983 production, 4-121 engines are equipped with a thick one piece seal, service P/N 14085829. As these seals are not interchangeable, 4-121 engines installed in 1984 vehicles must be inspected for an identification mark stamped on the left rear engine block boss, **Fig. 9.** Engines without an oval stamping in this area must be serviced with the thin, one piece seal, while engines with an oval stamping in this area must be serviced with the thick seal. Service replacement procedures for the two types of rear main oil seals are outlined below.

## 1983 & EARLY PRODUCTION 1984

1. Drain cooling and lubrication systems, then remove engine assembly.
2. Install engine in suitable engine stand in inverted position, then remove oil pan and oil pump.
3. Remove timing chain. Refer to "Timing Chain, Replace" for procedure.
4. Rotate crankshaft to horizontal position, then remove connecting rod bearing nuts, caps and bearings. **Keep nuts, caps and bearings in order so they can be installed in their original positions.**
5. Remove main bearing bolts, caps and bearings, then the crankshaft. **Keep bolts, caps and bearings in order so they can be installed in their original positions.**
6. Remove old seal and sealant from cylinder block grooves and rear main cap grooves.
7. Clean excess sealant from crankshaft using suitable solvent.
8. Apply a light coating of sealant 1052357 or equivalent to outside diameter of seal included in kit 14081761.
9. Place seal tool assembly on rear area of crankshaft, then position tool so arrow points towards cylinders and crankcase, **Fig. 10.**
10. Install crankshaft in engine with tool installed, then remove tool and discard.
11. Lightly lubricate crankshaft journals.
12. Seal rear main bearing split-line surface with sealant 1052357 or equivalent, then install rear main bearing and cap.
13. Install remaining main bearings, caps and bolts. Torque to specifications.
14. Install connecting rod bearings, caps and bolts. Torque to specifications.
15. Install oil pump.
16. Install timing chain.
17. Install oil pan, then the engine assembly.

## LATE PRODUCTION 1984

1. Disconnect battery ground cable, raise and support vehicle, and place suitable support under engine.
2. Remove transmission assembly, clutch assembly if equipped, and flywheel or flex plate.
3. Insert screwdriver or suitable puller through dust lip of seal and pull seal from cavity, taking care not to mar crankshaft.
4. Inspect seal bore and crankshaft surface for nicks, burrs and excessive wear, and correct as needed.
5. Lubricate seal lip and bore contact surface with engine oil, then slide seal onto mandrel of J-34686 until dust lip is bottomed against collar of tool, **Fig. 11.**
6. Align dowel pin on tool with dowel pin hole in crankshaft, then mount tool on shaft and tighten bolts hand tight (2-4 ft. lbs.).
7. Rotate "T" handle of tool clockwise to press seal into place, turning handle until collar is tight against case to ensure seal is seated.
8. Rotate "T" handle of tool counterclockwise to stop to set collar in proper position for next repair, then remove tool from crankshaft.
9. Inspect seal ensuring that seal is seated squarely in bore.
10. Reverse remaining procedure to complete installation.

## WATER PUMP
## REPLACE

1. Disconnect battery ground cable.
2. Remove accessory drive belts.
3. Remove upper fan shroud, then drain cooling system.
4. Remove radiator and heater hoses.
5. Remove water pump attaching bolts, then the water pump, **Fig. 12.**
6. Reverse procedure to install. Apply a narrow bead of sealant 10523357, or equivalent to sealing surfaces. Torque attaching bolts to 15-22 ft. lbs.

## BELT TENSION DATA

New drive belt tension should measure 145 lbs. for the A/C compressor belt and 130 lbs. for all other belts. Used drive belt tension should measure 65-100 lbs. for the A/C compressor belt and 50-80 lbs. for all other belts.

|  | New Lbs. | Used Lbs. |
|---|---|---|
| Air Cond. | 145 | 65-100 |
| Alternator | 130 | 50-80 |
| Power Steer. | 130 | 50-80 |
| Air Pump | 130 | 50-80 |

## FUEL PUMP
## REPLACE

1. Disconnect battery ground cable.
2. Remove distributor, then disconnect inlet and outlet lines from fuel pump.
3. Remove engine lift hook, then the fuel pump attaching bolts and fuel pump.
4. Reverse procedure to install. Install pump with camshaft on down stroke.
5. Adjust timing and check for fuel leaks.

# 4-151 (2.5L) GASOLINE ENGINE

## INDEX

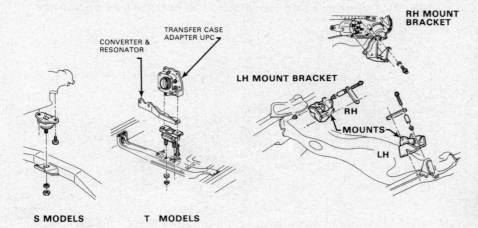

**Fig. 1  Engine mount installation**

## ENGINE
## REPLACE

1. Disconnect battery ground cable, mark position of hood hinges and remove hood.
2. Disconnect power steering reservoir from fan shroud, then remove upper shroud and fan.
3. Drain coolant, then disconnect radiator hoses and overflow hose from radiator.
4. Disconnect transmission cooling lines from radiator, if equipped, then plug lines.
5. Remove radiator.
6. Remove A/C compressor and power steering pump from brackets and position aside, if equipped.
7. Remove air cleaner and disconnect fuel line bracket by filter.
8. Disconnect fuel lines and vacuum hoses, accelerator cable, and TV and cruise control cables, as equipped, then secure aside. **To reduce risk of fire and injury, it is necessary to allow fuel system pressure to bleed off prior to disconnecting lines.**
9. Disconnect heater hoses from engine.
10. Disconnect electrical connector to oxygen sensor and other engine mounted components, release engine harness from retainers and secure harness aside.
11. Raise and support vehicle.
12. On 2 wheel drive models, disconnect strut rods.
13. On 4 wheel drive models, proceed as follows:
    a. Remove clips securing brake lines to crossmember, then the crossmember.
    b. Disconnect transmission cooler lines at flywheel cover, if equipped.
    c. Disconnect propeller shaft at front axle.
14. On all models, disconnect exhaust pipe at converter hanger and manifold, and secure aside.
15. Remove flywheel cover and drive belt splash shield, as equipped.
16. Remove starter motor.
17. Remove bolts securing torque converter to flex plate if equipped.
18. Remove 2 outer (left side) air dam bolts and the lower fan shroud.
19. Remove left body mount bolts, then position suitable jacks under body.
20. Carefully raise body and insert suitable block of wood between body and frame.
21. Remove upper bellhousing to engine bolts, then lower body.
22. Remove remaining bellhousing to engine bolts and motor mount through bolts, then lower vehicle.
23. Place suitable support under transmission and attach suitable lifting equipment to engine.
24. Raise engine and disconnect remaining wires, wire loom brackets at side cover and rear of head, and ground straps.
25. Separate engine from transmission and remove engine assembly from vehicle.
26. Reverse procedure to install.

## ENGINE MOUNTS
## REPLACE
## FRONT MOUNTS

1. Disconnect battery ground cable, then raise and support vehicle.
2. Remove mount center bolt(s), then raise and support engine to take weight off mount.
3. Remove mount retaining nuts from underside of crossmember, then remove mount, bolts and spacers, **Fig. 1.**
4. Reverse procedure to install.

## REAR MOUNT

1. Raise and support vehicle.
2. Remove nut(s) securing mount to crossmember, **Fig. 1**, then raise and support rear of transmission to take weight off mount.
3. Remove bolts securing mount to transmission tail housing, then the mount.
4. Reverse procedure to install, ensuring converter bracket, if equipped, is properly positioned.

## CYLINDER HEAD
## REPLACE
## 1985-86

1. Disconnect battery ground cable, drain cooling system and remove air cleaner.

2. Remove A/C compressor, if equipped, and secure aside.
3. Disconnect wires from spark plugs and disconnect PCV hose and plug wires from rocker cover.
4. Remove EGR valve.
5. Disconnect vacuum line hold down at thermostat housing and vacuum hoses from throttle body and studs on intake manifold.
6. Remove bolts securing rocker cover and the cover.
7. Disconnect necessary electrical connectors and harness clips, and secure wiring harness aside.
8. Disconnect accelerator, TV and cruise control cables, as equipped, from throttle levers and brackets.
9. Disconnect bypass and heater hoses from intake manifold, and remove upper radiator hose.
10. Remove alternator brace and A/C compressor bracket, disconnect A/C line hold down, then remove alternator and secure aside.
11. Disconnect exhaust pipe from manifold.
12. Disconnect fuel line bracket near filter and remove dipstick tube.
13. Disconnect fuel and vacuum hoses at fuel filter. **To avoid possibility of fire or injury, allow fuel system pressure to bleed off before servicing fuel system components.**
14. Remove cylinder head bolts, noting position for installation.
15. Disconnect harness bracket and ground from rear of head and remove coil bracket.
16. Remove brace between engine block and intake manifold.
17. Remove rocker arms and pushrods, keeping components in order for assembly.
18. Remove cylinder head as an assembly with intake and exhaust manifolds.
19. Thoroughly clean gasket from head and block mating surfaces.
20. Install new head gasket, then the cylinder head, ensuring that both gasket and head are seated over dowel pins in block.
21. Clean threads of head bolts, coat threads with suitable sealing compound, then install head bolts finger tight.
22. Gradually torque head bolts to specified torque in sequence shown in **Fig. 2**, then reverse remaining steps to complete installation.

## 1987–89

1. Disconnect battery ground cable, then drain cooling system and remove air cleaner assembly.
2. On models equipped with A/C, unfasten A/C compressor and brackets and position aside.
3. On all models, disconnect PCV hose, then remove EGR valve.
4. Disconnect spark plug wires from rocker arm cover.
5. Disconnect vacuum line and wiring harness from water outlet stud and position aside.
6. Disconnect vacuum lines from intake manifold stud, then remove rocker

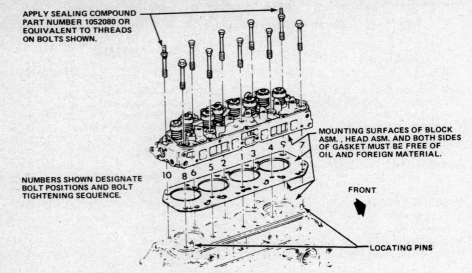

APPLY SEALING COMPOUND PART NUMBER 1052080 OR EQUIVALENT TO THREADS ON BOLTS SHOWN.

MOUNTING SURFACES OF BLOCK ASM., HEAD ASM. AND BOTH SIDES OF GASKET MUST BE FREE OF OIL AND FOREIGN MATERIAL.

NUMBERS SHOWN DESIGNATE BOLT POSITIONS AND BOLT TIGHTENING SEQUENCE.

FRONT

LOCATING PINS

**Fig. 2   Cylinder head installation & bolt torque sequence**

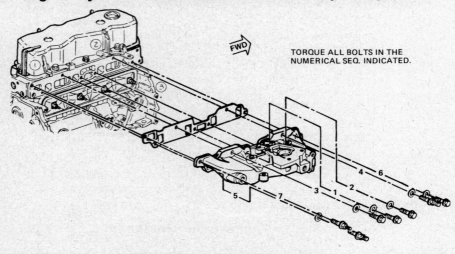

FWD

TORQUE ALL BOLTS IN THE NUMERICAL SEQ. INDICATED.

**Fig. 3   Intake manifold installation & bolt torque sequence**

arm cover attaching bolts and the cover.
7. Remove rocker arms and pushrods.
8. Disconnect electrical connectors, fuel and vacuum lines from throttle body unit.
9. Disconnect vacuum lines from intake manifold.
10. Disconnect accelerator, TV and cruise control cables, as equipped, from throttle levers and brackets.
11. Remove alternator and mounting brackets and position aside.
12. Disconnect water pump bypass and heater hoses from intake manifold.
13. Disconnect exhaust pipe from manifold.
14. Disconnect upper radiator hose, then remove fuel filter and fuel line brackets from rear of cylinder head.
15. Remove dipstick tube.
16. Remove wiring harness bracket, then disconnect ground strap from rear of cylinder head.

17. Disconnect electrical connectors from rear of cylinder head and thermostat housing.
18. Disconnect spark plug and ignition coil wires.
19. Disconnect oxygen sensor electrical connector.
20. Remove cylinder head attaching bolts, then the cylinder head and manifolds as an assembly.
21. Thoroughly clean gasket from head and block mating surfaces.
22. Install new head gasket, then the cylinder head, ensuring gasket and head are seated over dowel pins in block.
23. Apply suitable sealant to threads of bolts indicated in **Fig. 2.**
24. Tighten bolts in three steps using sequence shown, **Fig. 2.** On 1985-87 models, torque all bolts to 18 ft. lbs., then torque all bolts except No. 9 to 29 ft. lbs. Finally, tighten all bolts except No. 9 an additional 120° and bolt No. 9 an additional 90°. On 1988-89

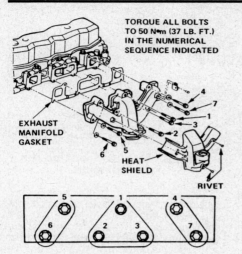

TORQUE ALL BOLTS TO 50 N·m (37 LB. FT.) IN THE NUMERICAL SEQUENCE INDICATED

EXHAUST MANIFOLD GASKET

HEAT SHIELD

RIVET

BOLT LOCATIONS

**Fig. 4  Exhaust manifold installation & bolt torque sequence**

RETAINER

GUIDE

**Fig. 5  Lifter & guide plate removal**

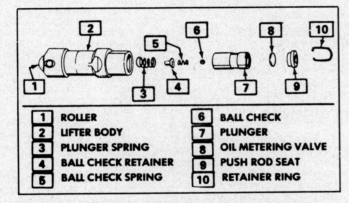

| 1 | ROLLER | 6 | BALL CHECK |
|---|---|---|---|
| 2 | LIFTER BODY | 7 | PLUNGER |
| 3 | PLUNGER SPRING | 8 | OIL METERING VALVE |
| 4 | BALL CHECK RETAINER | 9 | PUSH ROD SEAT |
| 5 | BALL CHECK SPRING | 10 | RETAINER RING |

**Fig. 6  Hydraulic roller lifter exploded view**

models, torque all bolts to 18 ft. lbs., then retorque all bolts except No. 9 to 27 ft. lbs. Finally, tighten all bolts an additional 90°.

25. Reverse remaining steps to complete installation.

## INTAKE MANIFOLD
### REPLACE

1. Disconnect battery ground cable, drain cooling system and remove air cleaner.
2. Disconnect necessary electrical connectors from injector assembly, sensors and solenoids.
3. Disconnect accelerator, TV and cruise control cables, as equipped.
4. Disconnect fuel and vacuum pipes at injector and manifold. **To prevent possibility of fire or injury, allow fuel system pressure to bleed off before servicing fuel system components.**
5. Disconnect bypass and heater hoses from manifold.
6. Remove alternator rear adjusting bracket, then disconnect alternator

brace and position aside.
7. Disconnect necessary vacuum hoses and remove vacuum pipe from brace at thermostat housing.
8. Disconnect coil from manifold.
9. Remove manifold retaining bolts then the manifold and gasket.
10. Ensure manifold and cylinder head mating surfaces are clean, position new gasket and manifold on head, then install retaining bolts hand tight.
11. Torque intake manifold bolts to specifications in sequence shown in **Fig. 3.**
12. Reverse remaining procedure to complete installation.

## EXHAUST MANIFOLD
### REPLACE

1. Disconnect battery ground cable.
2. Release A/C compressor belt tension, remove compressor from bracket and secure aside, then remove rear adjusting bracket.
3. Raise and support vehicle, disconnect exhaust pipe from manifold, then lower vehicle.
4. Remove air cleaner and disconnect

electrical connector to oxygen sensor.
5. Remove exhaust manifold bolts and the manifold.
6. Position new gasket and manifold on cylinder head, then install bolts hand tight.
7. Torque exhaust manifold bolts to specifications in sequence shown in **Fig. 4.**
8. Reverse remaining procedure to complete installation.

## HYDRAULIC ROLLER VALVE LIFTERS
### LIFTERS, REPLACE

1. Remove rocker and side covers.
2. Loosen rocker arms and remove pushrods, noting position for installation.
3. Remove guide plate and clamp, **Fig. 5,** then the lifter.
4. Reverse procedure to install, torquing side cover nuts to 90 inch lbs.

### SERVICE
#### Disassembly

1. Depress pushrod seat with pushrod, remove seat retainer, **Fig. 6,** then slowly release spring tension.
2. Remove pushrod seat and metering valve.
3. Invert lifter and tap on flat surface to remove plunger. **If plunger cannot be removed, clean with suitable solvent and repeat step 3.**
4. Remove ball check valve assembly using small screwdriver.
5. Remove plunger spring from lifter body.
6. Clean lifter components in suitable solvent, keeping components for each lifter separate.

#### Inspection

1. Inspect lifter body for internal and external wear and scuffing, and inspect bottom for wear grooves and flat spots.
2. Inspect roller for free operation, flat spots and pitting. Replace lifter if roller is worn, pitted, or if roller cannot be freed-up.
3. Inspect pushrod seat, and replace lifter and pushrod if seat is scored or excessively worn.
4. Inspect check ball and replace lifter if ball is pitted or scored. **Do not attempt to recondition lifter assembly by interchanging components from other lifters. If components are damaged or worn, lifter assembly should be replaced.**

#### Assembly

Ensure lifter components are kept clean during assembly, as small particles of dirt or lint can cause lifter to fail.
1. Position check ball on small hole in bottom of plunger.
2. Install check ball spring and retainer, **Fig. 6,** over check ball, then press retainer into position in plunger with small screwdriver.
3. Install plunger spring over check ball

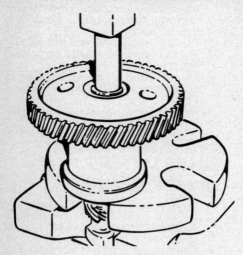

**Fig. 7  Camshaft timing gear removal**

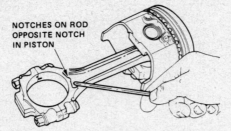

**Fig. 8  Piston & connecting rod assembly**

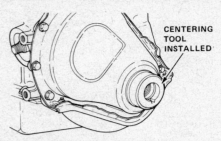

**Fig. 9  Engine front cover installation**

retainer, align oil holes in lifter body with plunger, then slide body over spring and plunger.

4. Fill lifter with SAE 10 engine oil and proceed as follows:
   a. Using a 1/8 inch drift, press plunger into lifter body until oil holes in plunger and body are aligned.
   b. Insert 1/16 inch pin through oil holes to lock plunger into body.
   c. Remove 1/8 inch drift and fill lifter with SAE 10 engine oil.
5. Install metering valve, pushrod seat and seat retainer.
6. Depress pushrod seat to relieve spring tension, then remove 1/16 inch pin holding plunger.

## NOISE DIAGNOSIS
### Momentary Noise When Engine Is Started

Condition normal. Oil drains from lifters which are holding valves open when engine is not running.

### Intermittent Noise At Idle, Disappears As Engine Speed Is Increased

1. Dirt in lifter.
2. Pitted check ball.

### Noise At Slow Idle Or With Hot Oil; Quiet With Cold Oil Or Increased Engine Speed

Excessive lifter leak down. Lifter should be replaced.

### Noise At Idle, Becomes Louder As Engine Speed Increased To 1500 RPM

1. Excessive valve stem to guide clearance.
2. Off square valve spring.
3. Scuffed or worn valve tip/rocker arm pad.
4. Excessive valve seat or face runout.
5. Damper spring clicking on rotator.

### Valves Noisy At All Speeds

1. Rotate crankshaft until piston of af-

fected cylinder is at TDC of firing stroke.
2. Hold rocker arm against valve spring and check for valve lash by moving pushrod up and down.
3. If no lash is present, check for dirt in lifter or pitted check ball.
4. If valve lash is present, inspect pushrod and rocker arm for excessive wear and replace as needed.
5. If valve lash is present, and pushrod and rocker arm are satisfactory, lifter should be replaced.

### Quiet At Low Speeds, Noisy At High Speeds

1. Incorrect oil level, oil foaming.
2. Clogged oil pump screen, bent pan or oil pump pickup.
3. Incorrect oil pressure.

## VALVE GUIDES

Measure valve stem diameter in 3 places, top, center and bottom, noting that exhaust valve stems are approximately .001 inch larger at top of stem than at the bottom. Measure valve guide bore with suitable gauge and compare with valve stem diameter to obtain clearance. If clearance is not within specifications, replace valves and/or ream valve guide bores as needed. Valves are available in standard size and .003 inch and .005 inch oversize.

## VALVES
## ADJUST

This engine uses hydraulic lifters that are not adjustable.

## VALVE ARRANGEMENT

All . . . . . . . . . . . . . . . . . . . . . . I-E-I-E-E-I-E-I

## VALVE LIFT SPECS

Camshaft lobe lift should measure .232 inch on intake and exhaust valves.

## CAMSHAFT & TIMING GEAR SERVICE

Some models may experience engine knocking due to loose or improperly seated camshaft gears. This condition is affected by engine speed, rather than loads imposed on the engine. To diagnose this condition, remove all drive belts and listen to engine with a stethoscope placed

against timing gear cover while accelerating slowly between 700 and 1000 RPM. Timing gear noise is most noticeable at approximately 800 RPM and can be heard at the oil pan between cylinders 3 and 4 as well as at the timing gear cover. If gears are determined to be at fault, proceed as follows:

1. Remove valve cover, rocker arms and engine front cover.
2. Check camshaft end clearance, which should measure .0015-.0050 inch.
3. Install crankshaft pulley and torque retaining bolt to 160 ft. lbs.
4. Position a magnetic dial indicator on front of engine block with probe contacting one tooth of camshaft gear.
5. Check backlash at four points on camshaft gear by rotating gear back and forth. Backlash should measure .0005-.0095 inch.
6. If camshaft end clearance exceeds .0050 inch, or backlash exceeds .0095 inch, the timing gears and/or cam gear thrust plate must be replaced.
7. If gear backlash exceeds .0095 inch, both the camshaft and crankshaft gears must be replaced.

## REMOVAL

1. Disconnect battery ground cable and drain cooling system.
2. Remove side cover as described under "Side Cover, Replace."
3. Disconnect power steering reservoir and set aside, then remove upper fan shroud, drive belts, fan and pulley.
4. Remove crankshaft pulley and hub.
5. Remove front cover.
6. Rotate crankshaft until timing marks on crank and camshaft timing gears are aligned.
7. Remove distributor cap and plug wire assembly, mark position of rotor and distributor body, disconnect electrical connectors and remove distributor.
8. Remove oil pump driveshaft cover and driveshaft.
9. Remove air cleaner and EGR valve.
10. Disconnect vacuum hoses at intake manifold and thermostat housing, then remove rocker cover.
11. Remove valve lifters as described under "Hydraulic Roller Valve Lifters."
12. Disconnect hoses and transmission cooler lines from radiator, as equipped, plug cooler lines, then remove radiator.
13. On models equipped with A/C, proceed as follows:

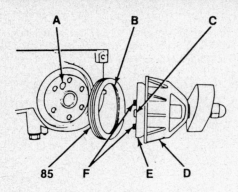

A. Alignment Hole In Crankshaft
B. Dust Lip
C. Dowel Pin
D. Collar
E. Mandrel
F. Screws
85 Crankshaft Rear Oil Seal

### Fig. 10   Rear main bearing oil seal installation.

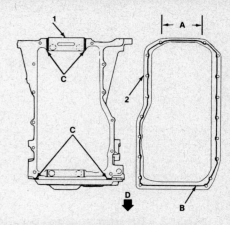

A. 10 mm (³/₈-Inch) Wide x 5 mm (³/₁₆-Inch) Thick

B. 5 mm (³/₁₆-Inch) Wide x 3 mm (¹/₈-Inch) Thick

C. 3 mm (¹/₈-Inch) Bead In Areas Shown

D. Front Of Engine

1. Rear Main Bearing Cap
2. Oil Pan

### Fig. 11   Oil pan sealant application. 1986

a. Remove A/C condenser baffles.
b. Discharge A/C system.
c. Disconnect A/C refrigerant hoses from A/C condenser.
d. Remove condenser mounting bolts, then the condenser.
14. On all models, remove headlamp bezel, grille and bumper filler panel.
15. Remove bolts securing camshaft thrust plate, then withdraw camshaft from engine, taking care not to damage cam bearings.
16. Inspect timing gear on crankshaft and replace as needed.

## CAMSHAFT DISASSEMBLY

1. Position adapter J-971 or equivalent on suitable press.
2. Insert camshaft through adapter with timing gear facing up, **Fig. 7.**
3. Secure adapter in press, then press shaft out of gear using suitable spacer. **Align thrust plate so that plate is not damaged by Woodruff key as camshaft is pressed out of gear.**

## CAMSHAFT ASSEMBLY

1. Support rear of front camshaft journal in press using suitable adapters.
2. Install gear spacer ring and thrust plate/retainer over end of camshaft, then seat Woodruff key in shaft keyway.
3. Mount timing gear on shaft ensuring that keyway is aligned with Woodruff key, then press gear onto shaft until it bottoms against spacer ring.
4. Measure clearance between thrust plate and front camshaft journal. If clearance is not .0015–.005 inch, thrust plate should be replaced.

## INSTALLATION

1. Coat camshaft journals and lobes with suitable assembly lubricant.
2. Insert camshaft into bearing bores, taking care not to damage bearings.
3. Rotate crankshaft and/or camshaft

as needed to ensure stamped timing marks are aligned when camshaft is fully seated in block.
4. Install thrust plate/retainer bolts, and torque bolts to 75 inch lbs.
5. Align and install front cover assembly as outlined in "Front Cover, Replace."
6. Reverse remaining procedure to complete installation. **With cam and crankshaft timing gear marks aligned, engine should be in number 4 cylinder firing position and distributor can be indexed to marks made during removal procedure. However, if crankshaft is rotated during reassembly, rotate crankshaft until engine is in firing position for number 1 cylinder, with timing mark on balancer indexed at TDC on timing pad, then install distributor with body in original position but with rotor arm pointing toward number 1 cylinder spark plug contact in cap.**

## PISTON & ROD ASSEMBLY

There are 2 notches in the piston crown. When assembling pistons onto connecting rods, position rod so that raised notch side of rod at bearing end, **Fig. 8,** is opposite notch in piston crown. Install piston and rod assemblies in engine block with notches in piston crowns facing front of engine. After installation, check connecting rod side clearance. If clearance is not .006–.022 inch, connecting rod should be replaced.

## SIDE COVER

### REPLACE

1. Disconnect battery ground cable and drain cooling system.
2. Remove alternator and bracket and secure alternator aside.
3. Remove spark plug and ignition coil wires and bracket. On 1989 models, disconnect fuel lines and remove clips from pushrod cover.
4. Disconnect lower radiator and heater hoses.

5. Remove oil pressure sending unit and disconnect wiring harness brackets from side cover.
6. Remove side cover retaining nuts and the cover.
7. Ensure old sealant is removed from cover and block mating surfaces, then apply a continuous bead of RTV sealant, ³/₁₆ inch wide, to cover sealing surface.
8. Install side cover and torque retaining nuts to 90 inch lbs., then reverse remaining procedure to complete installation.

## FRONT COVER
### REPLACE

1. Disconnect battery ground cable.
2. Disconnect power steering pump reservoir from fan shroud and position aside.
3. Release drive belt tension, then remove upper fan shroud, fan and water pump pulley.
4. Remove alternator, brackets, brace and front bracket.
5. Remove crankshaft pulley, hub bolt and the hub.
6. Loosen lower radiator hose clamp at water pump and reposition as needed.
7. Remove front cover bolts and the front cover.
8. Remove front crankshaft seal.
9. Thoroughly clean front cover and block sealing surfaces, then apply a continuous bead of RTV sealer, ³/₁₆ inch wide, to cover sealing surface and oil pan joint.
10. Position centering tool J-34995, or equivalent, in front cover seal, mount front cover on block, **Fig. 9,** then install and partially tighten 2 oil pan to front cover bolts.
11. Torque front cover attaching bolts to 90 inch lbs.
12. Reverse remaining procedure to complete installation.

## FRONT OIL SEAL
### REPLACE

1. Remove drive belts.

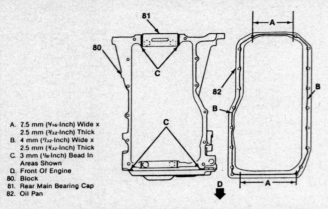

A. 7.5 mm (⁹⁄₁₆-Inch) Wide x
   2.5 mm (³⁄₃₂-Inch) Thick
B. 4 mm (⁷⁄₃₂-Inch) Wide x
   2.5 mm (³⁄₃₂-Inch) Thick
C. 3 mm (⅛-Inch) Bead In
   Areas Shown
D. Front Of Engine
80. Block
81. Rear Main Bearing Cap
82. Oil Pan

**Fig. 12   Oil pan sealant application. 1987–89**

2. Remove center bolt, then slide hub and pulleys off crankshaft.
3. Carefully pry seal from front cover, taking care not to damage or distort cover.
4. Install seal with helical lip toward rear of engine, using tool No. J-23042 or equivalent on 1985 models, or tool No. J-34995 on 1986-89 models, **Fig. 9**, to seat seal in cover.
5. Coat seal lip with clean engine oil, then reverse remaining procedure to complete installation.

## REAR MAIN BEARING OIL SEAL
### REPLACE

1. Raise and support vehicle and place suitable supports under engine.
2. Remove transmission assembly.
3. Remove clutch and pressure plate, if equipped, then the flywheel or flex plate.
4. Pry seal from bore with suitable tool, taking care not to mar crankshaft.
5. Thoroughly clean seal bore in block, inspect bore and crankshaft surface for nicks, burrs and wear, and correct as needed.
6. Apply light coat of clean engine oil to inner and outer surfaces of seal, install seal using J-34924 or equivalent, **Fig. 10**, then reverse remaining procedure to complete installation.

## OIL PAN
### REPLACE
#### 4 X 2
**1985–86**

1. Disconnect battery ground cable, raise and support vehicle, and drain oil pan.
2. Remove strut rods.
3. Disconnect exhaust pipe at converter bracket and manifold and secure aside.
4. Remove torque converter or flywheel dust cover.
5. Disconnect starter brace from engine block and remove starter motor.
6. Disconnect transmission cooler lines,

if equipped, and plug lines and open fittings.
7. Remove oil pan bolts and the oil pan.
8. Thoroughly clean oil pan and block mating surfaces, ensuring that sealer is removed from pan bolt holes.
9. Apply a continuous bead of RTV sealer, ³⁄₁₆ inch wide, to entire pan sealing surface on 1985 models, or sealant as indicated in **Fig. 11** on 1986 models.
10. Install oil pan, torque retaining bolts to 75 inch lbs. on 1985 models, or 90 inch on 1986 models, and reverse remaining procedure to complete installation.

**1987–89**

1. Disconnect battery ground cable, then remove power steering pump reservoir, if equipped, from fan shroud.
2. Remove radiator shroud, then drain engine oil into a suitable container.
3. Remove strut rods, then disconnect exhaust pipe from manifold.
4. Remove catalytic converter and exhaust pipe.
5. Remove flywheel cover, then the starter motor and bracket.
6. Disconnect brake line from crossmember.
7. Raise and support engine and remove front engine mount bolts.
8. Remove oil pan attaching bolts and the oil pan.
9. Thoroughly clean oil pan and block mating surfaces, ensuring sealer is removed from pan bolt holes.
10. Apply RTV sealant to mating surfaces as indicated in **Fig. 12**.
11. Install oil pan, torque retaining bolts to 90 inch lbs. and reverse remaining procedure to complete installation.

#### 4 X 4

1. Disconnect battery ground cable.
2. Disconnect power steering pump reservoir from upper fan shroud, secure reservoir aside and remove upper shroud.
3. Remove dipstick.
4. Raise and support vehicle and drain oil pan.
5. Disconnect brake line clips from crossmember and remove crossmember.
6. Disconnect cooler lines from trans-

mission, if equipped, then plug lines and open fittings.
7. Disconnect exhaust pipe from manifold.
8. Disconnect catalytic converter hanger, removing one bolt and loosening the other.
9. Remove flywheel cover and driveshaft splash shield.
10. Mark position of idler arm for installation, then remove idler arm retaining bolts.
11. Remove steering gear retaining bolts, then pull gear and linkage forward.
12. Remove differential housing bolts at bracket on right side and at frame on left side, then move housing forward.
13. Remove starter motor bolts, position starter aside and loosen brace.
14. Disconnect front propeller shaft at drive pinion.
15. Remove motor mount through bolts and oil pan retaining bolts.
16. Raise engine to provide clearance, then remove oil pan.
17. Clean pan and block sealing surfaces, ensuring that sealer is removed from pan bolt holes.
18. Apply continuous bead of RTV sealer, ³⁄₁₆ inch wide, to entire sealing surface of pan on on 1985 models, or sealant as indicated in **Fig. 11** on 1986 models, or Fig. 12 on 1987-89 models.
19. Raise engine, position pan on block and secure with bolts, then lower engine.
20. Install remaining pan bolts and torque to 75 inch lbs. on 1985 models, or 90 inch lbs. on 1986-89 models, then reverse remaining procedure to complete installation.

---

1  PUMP BODY
2  PICKUP TUBE
3  PICKUP SCREW ASSEMBLY
4  PRESSURE REGULATOR VALVE
5  PRESSURE REGULATOR SPRING
6  SPRING RETAINER
7  COVER SCREWS
8  COVER
9  IDLER GEAR
10  DRIVE GEAR AND SHAFT

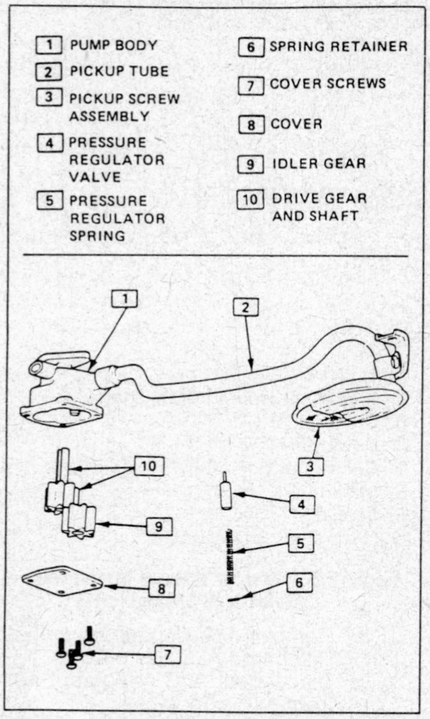

**Fig. 13   Oil pump exploded view**

## OIL PUMP SERVICE
### REMOVAL

1. Remove oil pan as outlined.
2. Remove bolts securing pump to block and the oil pump and screen assembly.

### DISASSEMBLY

1. Remove 4 cover retaining bolts and the cover, **Fig. 13.**
2. Mark position of drive gear and rotor to ensure proper assembly.
3. Remove drive gear and rotor from body.
4. Remove pin, spring and pressure regulator valve.**Do not remove oil pump pickup and screen assembly. If pickup tube is loose, or if tube or screen are damaged or clogged, oil pump should be replaced.**

### INSPECTION

1. Inspect pump body for cracks, scoring and excessive wear.
2. Inspect gears for cracks, excessive wear and damage, and check shaft for looseness in housing.
3. Inspect inside of cover for wear and scoring that would allow oil to leak past ends of gears.
4. Check fit of relief valve in bore, checking for looseness or binding.
5. If any components are damaged or excessively worn, or if pickup assembly is loose or damaged, oil pump assembly should be replaced.

### ASSEMBLY

1. Install pressure relief valve, spring, and spring retaining pin.
2. Install drive gear and shaft.
3. Install idler gear in pump body with smooth side toward pump cover opening.
4. Align marks made during disassembly.
5. Install gasket, cover and retaining screws and torque to 10 ft. lbs.

## INSTALLATION

1. Prime pump with engine oil or pack with petroleum jelly.
2. Align slot in pump shaft with tang on drive shaft.
3. Install pump on block, positioning flange over oil pump driveshaft lower bushing, and torque mounting bolts to 22 ft. lbs.
4. Reinstall oil pan as outlined.

## WATER PUMP
### REPLACE
#### 1982–88

1. Disconnect battery ground cable and drain cooling system.
2. Disconnect power steering pump reservoir from upper fan shroud and remove upper shroud.
3. Remove necessary drive belts, fan and pulley.
4. Disconnect radiator and heater hose and position aside.
5. Remove bolts securing water pump then the pump.
6. Thoroughly clean old sealant from block sealing surface, retaining bolts and bolt holes.
7. Apply a continuous bead of RTV sealer, 1/8 inch wide, to pump sealing surface and apply suitable sealer to retaining bolt threads.
8. Install pump, torque retaining bolts to 15 ft. lbs. on 1985 models, or 22 ft. lbs. on 1986-88 models, then reverse remaining procedure to complete installation.

#### 1989

1. Disconnect battery ground cable and drain coolant from radiator.
2. Remove serpentine drive belt.
3. Remove upper fan shroud, fan and clutch assembly.
4. Remove water pump pulley.
5. Remove clamps and hoses from water pump.
6. Remove water pump mounting bolts and one water pump retaining nut.
7. Remove water pump and water pump gasket.
8. Reverse procedure to install. Torque water pump retaining bolts to 17 ft. lbs.

## BELT TENSION DATA

On 1985-86 models, new drive belt tension should measure 146 lbs. for the power steering pump and vacuum pump belts, 169 lbs. for the A/C compressor and alternator belts on models with A/C, and 90 lbs. for the alternator belt on models less A/C. Used drive belt tension should measure 67 lbs. for the power steering pump and vacuum pump belts, 90 lbs. for the A/C compressor, 145 lbs. for the alternator belt on models with A/C, and 67 lbs. for the alternator belt on models less A/C.

1989 models are equipped with a Serpentine type drive belt which adjusts automatically.

## FUEL PUMP
### REPLACE

1. Allow fuel system pressure to bleed off through orifice in pressure regulator, disconnect battery ground cable, then raise and support vehicle.
2. Drain fuel tank, support tank and remove bolts securing tank retaining straps, lower tank enough to disconnect ground and harness connectors, then remove tank from under vehicle.
3. Turn fuel sender unit cam lock ring counterclockwise, then lift sending unit/pump assembly from tank.
4. Pull fuel pump up into hose while pulling out from bottom and remove pump from sending unit.
5. Reverse procedure to install, using new O-ring when installing sending unit in tank.

# V6-173 (2.8L) GASOLINE ENGINE

## INDEX

# ENGINE
# REPLACE

## 4 X 2

1. Disconnect battery ground cable.
2. Scribe reference marks in the hood hinge area, then remove hood.
3. Drain cooling system, then remove radiator hoses, overflow hose, transmission cooler lines (if equipped), upper radiator shroud and radiator.
4. Remove cooling fan, then disconnect heater hoses.
5. Remove air cleaner assembly.
6. Identify, then disconnect vacuum hoses from engine.
7. Disconnect necessary engine wiring from bulkhead.
8. Disconnect throttle and cruise control cables as equipped, then remove distributor cap.
9. Raise and support vehicle.
10. Remove converter to exhaust pipe bolts, then disconnect exhaust pipes at manifolds.
11. Remove strut rods at bellhousing.
12. Remove flywheel cover bolts, then the cover (if equipped).
13. On models equipped with automatic transmission, remove torque converter bolts.
14. On all models, disconnect shield at rear of catalytic converter, then remove converter hanger.
15. Remove lower radiator fan shroud.
16. Disconnect fuel lines.
17. Remove two outer bolts from front air deflector.
18. Remove left side body mount bolts, then raise body using suitable lifting equipment.
19. Remove bellhousing bolts, then lower body to frame.
20. Remove motor mount through bolts, then lower vehicle.
21. Remove A/C compressor and power steering pump, if equipped and position aside.
22. Install suitable lifting device on engine.
23. Support transmission with suitable jack.
24. Remove engine assembly.
25. Reverse procedure to install.

## 4 X 4

### Man. Trans.

1. Disconnect battery ground cable.
2. Scribe reference marks in hood hinge area, then disconnect under hood light and remove hood.
3. Remove air cleaner assembly.
4. Drain cooling system, then remove radiator hoses, overflow hose, upper fan shroud, radiator, cooling fan and fan clutch.
5. Remove A/C compressor (if equipped) and position aside.
6. Remove power steering pump (if equipped) and position aside.
7. Disconnect fuel lines.
8. Identify, then disconnect vacuum hoses from engine.
9. Disconnect throttle and cruise control cables as necessary, then remove heater hoses.
10. Disconnect engine wiring harness at bulkhead connector, then the ground strap at bulkhead.
11. On 1982-83 models, disconnect clutch cable, then remove clutch cross shaft. On 1984-89 models, remove hydraulic clutch slave cylinder and position aside.
12. On all models, remove lower radiator fan shroud.
13. Disconnect battery ground cable from engine, then the main feed wire from bulkhead.
14. Remove distributor cap, then the AIR system diverter valve.
15. Remove console cover, shifter boot, transfer case shifter, transmission shift lever and shifter.
16. Raise and support vehicle, then remove front and rear skid plates and front splash shield.
17. Drain transmission and transfer case, then remove rear driveshaft.
18. Disconnect speedometer cable, then the front driveshaft from transfer case.
19. Disconnect shift linkage and vacuum hoses from transfer case.
20. Disconnect parking brake cable, then remove rear mount.
21. Remove catalytic converter bracket, then support transfer case.
22. Remove transfer case to transmission retaining bolts, then the transfer case.
23. Remove transmission crossmember, then disconnect back-up light switch wire and clip.
24. Remove transmission to bellhousing retaining bolts, then the transmission.
25. Remove clutch release bearing and inspection cover from bellhousing.
26. Remove left hand body mount bolts, then loosen radiator support to frame mount bolt.
27. Raise left side of body using suitable lifting equipment, then install a block of wood between frame and body.
28. On 1982-83 models, disconnect remaining clutch linkage.
29. On all models, remove bellhousing to engine block retaining bolts, then the bellhousing.
30. Disconnect exhaust pipes from manifolds, then from the catalytic converter.
31. Remove starter motor.
32. Remove motor mount through bolts.
33. Lower vehicle.
34. Install suitable lifting device on engine.
35. Remove engine assembly.
36. Reverse procedure to install.

### Auto. Trans.

1. Disconnect battery ground cable.
2. Scribe reference marks in the hood hinge area, then disconnect under hood light and remove hood.
3. Raise and support vehicle.
4. Remove front end air dam end bolts.
5. Remove body mount bolts as necessary to enable body to be raised to gain access to top transmission mounting bolts.
6. Remove top transmission mounting bolts, then lower body.
7. Remove remaining transmission mounting bolts, then the second

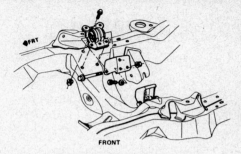

**Fig. 1 Engine mount installation**

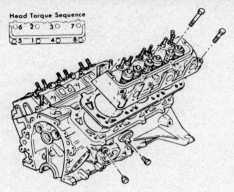

**Fig. 2 Cylinder head installation**

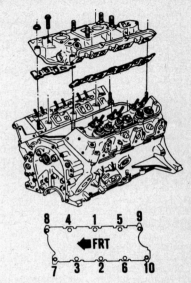

**Fig. 3 Intake manifold tightening sequence. 1982–85**

crossmember.

8. Disconnect exhaust pipes at manifolds, then the catalytic converter hanger.
9. Disconnect front driveshaft from differential.
10. Remove torque converter cover bolts, then the cover.
11. Disconnect transmission cooler lines from clips on engine.
12. Remove motor mount through bolts.
13. Remove torque converter to flex plate bolts.
14. Remove front splash shield, then the lower radiator fan shroud mounting bolts.
15. Lower vehicle.
16. Drain cooling system, then remove upper fan shroud, radiator hoses, transmission cooler lines at radiator, radiator and cooling fan.
17. Remove air cleaner assembly.
18. Remove A/C compressor (if equipped) and position aside.
19. Remove power steering pump (if equipped) and position aside.
20. Disconnect fuel lines.
21. Identify, then disconnect all necessary vacuum lines, wires and emission hoses.
22. Disconnect throttle and cruise controls as equipped.
23. Disconnect engine wiring harness at bulkhead.
24. Disconnect heater hoses at engine.
25. Support transmission with suitable jack.
26. Install suitable lifting device on engine.
27. Remove engine assembly.
28. Reverse procedure to install.

## ENGINE MOUNTS
### REPLACE

**1982–87**

1. Disconnect battery ground cable.
2. Remove top half of fan shroud.
3. Raise and support vehicle.
4. Remove mount through bolt, then raise front of engine and remove mount, **Fig. 1. Do not raise engine any more than is needed to provide sufficient clearance. Also, check for interference between rear of engine and cowl panel which could damage the distributor.**
5. Reverse procedure to install.

## 1988–89
### 4 X 2

1. Remove fan shroud.
2. Raise and support vehicle.
3. Remove right wheel, then the engine mounting bolts on both sides.
4. Raise engine using suitable lifting equipment and block in place.
5. Remove tie rod from drag link and stabilizer link from control arm.
6. Remove lower shock absorber bolts.
7. Remove lower control arm pivot bolts, then the lower control arm.
8. Remove engine mount-to-frame attaching bolts, then the mount.
9. Reverse procedure to install. Torque engine mount to frame bolts to 41 ft. lbs., engine mount through bolts to 85 ft. lbs. and nuts to 53 ft. lbs.

### 4 X 4

1. Raise and support vehicle.
2. Remove front shield and skid plate, if equipped.
3. Remove front axle assembly attaching bolts and lower out of the way.
4. Remove engine mounting through bolts and engine mounting-to-frame bolts.
5. Raise engine using suitable lifting equipment and block engine in place.
6. Remove engine mounting.
7. Reverse procedure to install. Torque engine mounting-to-frame bolts to 41 ft. lbs., engine mounting through bolts to 85 ft. lbs. and nuts to 53 ft. lbs.

## CYLINDER HEAD
### REPLACE

1. Remove intake manifold.
2. Raise and support vehicle.
3. Drain engine block.
4. Disconnect exhaust pipe.
5. Lower vehicle.
6. If removing left cylinder head, remove dipstick tube attachment, ground strap at rear of head and sensor connector at front of head.
7. If removing right cylinder head, remove drive belt, alternator bracket and air pump.
8. Loosen rocker arm retaining nuts until pushrods can be removed.

9. Remove pushrods. **Keep pushrods in order so they can be installed in their original positions.**
10. Remove head bolts and cylinder head. **The gasket surfaces on both head and cylinder case deck must be clean of any foreign matter and free of nicks or heavy scratches. Cylinder bolt threads in the case and threads on the cylinder head bolts must be clean. Dirt will affect bolt torque.**
11. Reverse procedure to install. **Coat cylinder head bolt threads with sealer, 1052080 or equivalent, and install bolts. On 1982-87 models, torque bolts in proper sequence to specifications, Fig. 2. On 1988-89 models, torque bolts in proper sequence to 40 ft. lbs., then tighten all bolts an additional 90°.**

## INTAKE MANIFOLD
### REPLACE

1. Disconnect battery ground cable.
2. Remove air cleaner, then drain cooling system.
3. Disconnect all vacuum hoses, electrical connectors, linkages and fuel line from carburetor or throttle body unit.
4. On 1985-87 models, proceed as follows:
   a. Disconnect ignition wires from spark plugs.
   b. Disconnect ignition coil wiring, then remove distributor cap with spark plug wires.
   c. Mark distributor position for installation reference, then remove hold-down bracket and the distributor.
5. On all models, disconnect air management hose and the emission canister hoses and remove pipe bracket from left hand valve cover.
6. Remove left hand valve cover, then the air management bracket and right

hand valve cover.
7. Disconnect coolant hoses from intake manifold.
8. Disconnect electrical connectors from intake manifold.
9. Remove intake manifold attaching bolts and the manifold.
10. Reverse procedure to install, using new gaskets. **Ensure no oil or water is present on surface when new RTV is applied. Place a (³/₁₆ inch) bead of RTV, 1052917 or equivalent, on each ridge. Install manifold retaining bolts and nuts and torque in the sequence shown in Figs. 3 and 4 to 23 ft. lbs.**

## EXHAUST MANIFOLDS
### REPLACE

1. Disconnect battery ground cable.
2. Raise and support vehicle, then disconnect exhaust pipe.
3. If removing left manifold, remove rear manifold bolts and nut, then lower vehicle. Disconnect air management hoses and wires, remove power steering bracket, if equipped, and remove manifold.
4. If removing right manifold on 1982-87 models, lower vehicle, remove manifold attaching bolts, alternator bracket and air pump, disconnect air management hose and remove manifold.
5. If removing right manifold On 1988-89 models lower vehicle, remove diverter valve and heat shield, manifold attaching bolts, alternator bracket and air pump, disconnect air management hose and remove manifold.
6. Reverse procedure to install. **Clean mating surfaces on manifold and head, then install manifold in position and torque manifold bolts to 25 ft. lbs.**

## ROCKER ARM STUDS

Rocker arm studs that are cracked or have damaged threads can be replaced. If threads in cylinder head are damaged or stripped, the head can be retapped and a helical type insert added. When installing a new rocker arm stud, torque stud to 43 to 53 ft. lbs.

## VALVES
### ADJUST

1. Crank engine until mark on torsional damper is aligned with TDC mark on timing tab. Check to ensure engine is in the No. 1 cylinder firing position by placing fingers on No. 1 cylinder rocker arms as mark on damper comes near TDC mark on timing tab. If valves are not moving, the engine is in the No. 1 firing position. If valves move as damper mark nears TDC mark on timing tab, engine is in the No. 4 cylinder firing position and should be rotated one revolution to reach the No. 1 cylinder firing position.
2. With engine in the No. 1 cylinder firing position, adjust the following valves:

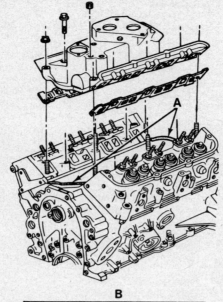

**B**

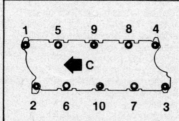

A. Apply RTV Sealant
B. Nut And Bolt Tightening Sequence
C. Front

**Fig. 4  Intake manifold tightening sequence. 1986–89**

Exhaust- 1, 2, 3; Intake- 1, 5, 6. To adjust valves, back off adjusting nut until lash is felt at pushrod, then tighten adjusting nut until all lash is removed. This can be determined by rotating the pushrod while tightening the adjusting nut. When all lash has been eliminated, turn adjusting nut the specified additional number of turns.
3. Crank engine one revolution until mark on torsional damper and TDC mark are again aligned. This is the No. 4 cylinder firing position. With engine in this position, the following valve can be adjusted: Exhaust- 4, 5, 6; Intake- 2, 3, 4.
4. Install rocker arm covers, then start engine and check timing and idle speed.

## VALVE CLEARANCE SPECIFICATIONS

Turn rocker arm stud nut until all lash is eliminated, then tighten nut additional 1½ turns.

## VALVE GUIDES

Valve guides are an integral part of the

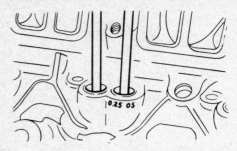

**Fig. 5  Oversize valve lifter marking**

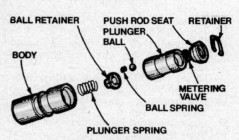

**Fig. 6  Hydraulic valve lifter**

cylinder head and are not removable. If valve stem clearance becomes excessive, the valve guide should be reamed to the next oversize and the appropriate oversize valves installed. Valves are available in .0035 inch, .0155 inch and .0305 inch oversizes.

## VALVE LIFTERS

Some engines will be equipped with both standard and .25 mm oversize valve lifters. The cylinder case will be marked where the oversize valve lifters are installed with a daub of white paint and .25 mm O.S. will be stamped on the valve lifter boss, **Fig. 5.**

Failure of a hydraulic valve lifter, **Fig. 6,** is generally caused by an inadequate oil supply or dirt. An air leak at the intake side of the oil pump or too much oil in the engine will cause air bubbles in the oil supply to the lifters causing them to collapse. This is a probable cause of trouble if several lifters fail to function, but air in oil is an unlikely cause of failure of a single unit.

Valve lifters can be removed after removing rocker arm covers, intake manifold, rocker arm nuts, rocker arm balls, rocker arms and pushrods.

## VALVE ARRANGEMENT

All . . . . . . . . . . . . . . . . . . . . . . . . E-I-I-E-I-E

## VALVE TIMING

Intake valves open at 7° before TDC.

## CAMSHAFT LIFT SPECIFICATIONS

Camshaft lift at intake valves should measure .231 inch on 1982-87 models and .262 inch on 1988-89 models. At the exhaust valves, lift should measure .262

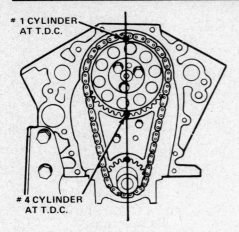

**Fig. 7   Valve timing marks**

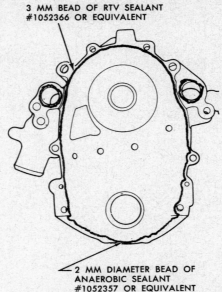

**Fig. 8   Engine front cover sealant application. 1982–83**

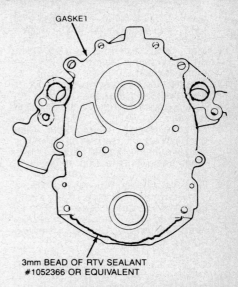

**Fig. 9   Engine front cover sealant application. 1984–86**

inch on 1982-87 models and .273 inch on 1988-89 models.

## CAMSHAFT
### REPLACE

1. Remove valve lifters and engine front cover as previously described.
2. On 1982-85 models, remove fuel pump and pushrod.
3. On 1986-89 models, remove radiator.
4. On models with A/C, discharge A/C system and remove A/C condenser.
5. On all models, remove timing chain and sprocket as described under "Timing Chain, Replace."
6. Withdraw camshaft from engine, using care not to damage camshaft bearings.
7. Reverse procedure to install. When installing timing chain, align valve timing marks as shown in **Fig. 7**. Whenever a new camshaft is installed, coat lobes with GM Engine Oil Supplement or equivalent. It is also recommended that valve lifters be replaced to ensure durability of camshaft lobes and lifter feet.

## TIMING CHAIN
### REPLACE

1. Remove front cover as described under "Front Cover, Replace."
2. Place No. 1 piston at top dead center with marks on camshaft and crankshaft sprockets aligned, **Fig. 7**.
3. Remove camshaft sprocket bolts, then remove sprocket and timing chain. If sprocket does not come off easily, tap lower edge of sprocket with a plastic mallet.
4. Install timing chain on camshaft sprocket. Hold sprocket vertically with chain hanging down and align marks on camshaft and crankshaft sprockets.
5. Align dowel pin hole in sprocket with dowel pin on camshaft, then install sprocket on camshaft.
6. Using camshaft sprocket attaching bolts, draw sprocket on camshaft. Torque bolts to 15 to 20 ft. lbs.

7. Lubricate timing chain with engine oil, then install front cover as outlined previously.

## FRONT COVER
### REPLACE

1. Remove water pump as described under "Water Pump, Replace."
2. On 1982-86 models, remove A/C compressor and bracket, if equipped, and position aside. On 1987-89 models, remove power steering pump bracket.
3. Remove torsional damper, then disconnect lower radiator hose from front cover and the heater hose from water pump.
4. Remove remaining front cover attaching bolts and stud, then the front cover.
5. Reverse procedure to install. On 1982-83 models, clean engine block and front cover mating surfaces of oil, water and old gasket sealer. Apply RTV and anaerobic sealer as shown in **Fig. 8**. On 1984-86 models, clean engine block and front cover mating surfaces of oil, water and old gasket. Install new gasket and apply RTV sealant as shown in **Fig. 9**. On 1987-89 models, clean engine block and front cover mating surfaces of oil, water and old gasket. Apply anaerobic sealer to both sides of new gasket and install gasket. On 1982 models, torque M8 x 1.25 bolts to 13-18 ft. lbs. and M10 x 1.5 bolts to 20-30 ft. lbs. On 1983-87 models, torque front cover bolts to 13-22 ft. lbs. and front cover studs to 19-24 ft. lbs. On 1988-89 models, torque bolts to 18 ft. lbs.

## PISTON & ROD ASSEMBLY

Assemble pistons to connecting rods as shown in **Fig. 10**.

## OIL PAN
### REPLACE
#### 4 X 2

1. Disconnect battery ground cable.
2. Remove engine as described under "Engine, Replace."
3. Remove oil pan.
4. Reverse procedure to install. **Before installing oil pan, thoroughly clean all sealing surfaces, then apply a 1/8 inch bead of RTV sealant, or equivalent, to the entire oil pan sealing flange.**

#### 4 X 4

1. Disconnect battery ground cable and remove dipstick.
2. Raise and support vehicle.
3. Remove drive belt splash shield, front axle shield and transfer case shield.
4. Disconnect brake line clips from No. 2 crossmember, then remove the crossmember.
5. On models equipped with automatic transmission, remove catalytic converter hanger bolts, then disconnect exhaust pipe clamp from converter.
6. On models equipped with automatic transmission, disconnect exhaust pipes from manifolds, then slide exhaust rearward.
7. On all models, disconnect front driveshaft from axle drive pinion.
8. Disconnect engine braces from flywheel cover and loosen braces at the block.
9. Remove flywheel cover.
10. Remove starter motor retaining bolts and position starter aside.

11. Disconnect steering shock absorber from frame bracket, then remove steering gear bolts.
12. Mark position of idler arm for reference during installation, then remove attaching bolts.
13. Pull steering gear and linkage forward, then remove differential housing attaching bolts and move the housing forward.
14. Remove motor mount bolts, then drain oil pan and remove oil pan bolts.
15. Install suitable engine lifting equipment, raise engine and remove oil pan.
16. Reverse procedure to install. **Before installing oil pan, thoroughly clean all sealing surfaces, then apply a 1/8 inch bead of RTV sealant, or equivalent to entire oil pan sealing flange.**

## OIL PUMP SERVICE
### REMOVAL

1. Remove oil pan as described under "Oil Pan, Replace."
2. Remove pump to rear main bearing cap bolt and remove pump and extension shaft.

### DISASSEMBLY

1. Remove pump cover attaching bolts and pump cover, **Fig. 11.**
2. Mark drive and idler gear teeth so they can be installed in the same position, then remove idler and drive gear and shaft from pump body.
3. Remove pin, spring and pressure regulator valve from pump cover.
4. If pickup tube and screen assembly are to be replaced, mount pump cover in a soft jawed vise and remove pickup tube from cover. Do not remove screen from pickup tube, these components are serviced as an assembly.

### INSPECTION

1. Inspect pump body and cover for excessive wear and cracks.
2. Inspect pump gear for damage or excessive wear. If pump gears are damaged or worn, the entire pump assembly must be replaced.
3. Check drive gear shaft for looseness in pump body.
4. Inspect pump cover for wear that would allow oil to leak past gear teeth.
5. Inspect pickup tube and screen assembly for damage.
6. Check pressure regulator valve for fit in pump cover.

### ASSEMBLY

1. If pickup tube and screen were removed, apply sealer to end of pickup tube, then mount pump cover in a soft jawed vise and using tool No. J-8369, 82-85 models, or tool J-21882, 86-89 models, **Fig. 12,** tap pickup tube into position using a plastic mallet. **Whenever the pickup tube and screen assembly have been removed, a new pickup tube and screen assembly should be installed. Use**

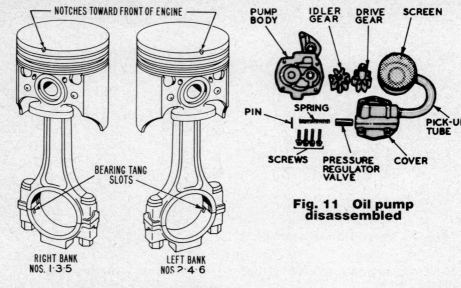

Fig. 10   Piston & rod assembly

**Fig. 11   Oil pump disassembled**

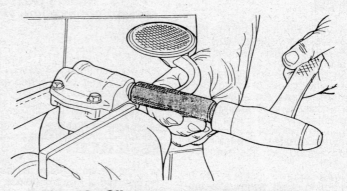

**Fig. 12   Oil pump screen installation.**

care when installing pickup tube and screen assembly so that tube does not twist, shear or collapse. Loss of a press fit condition could result in an air leak and a loss of oil pressure.
2. Install pressure regulator valve, spring and pin, **Fig. 11.**
3. Install drive gear and shaft in pump body.
4. Align marks made during disassembly, then install idler gear.
5. Install pump cover gasket, cover and attaching bolts. Torque bolts to 6-9 ft. lbs.
6. Rotate pump drive shaft by hand and check pump for smooth operation.

### INSTALLATION

1. Assemble pump and extension shaft with retainer to rear main bearing cap, aligning top end of hexagon extension shaft with hexagon socket on lower end of distributor shaft.
2. Install pump to rear main bearing cap bolt.
3. Install oil pan as described under "Oil Pan, Replace."

## FUEL PUMP
### REPLACE
#### 1982-85

1. Disconnect battery ground cable.
2. Disconnect inlet and outlet hoses from fuel pump.
3. Remove fuel pump attaching bolts, then the fuel pump and gasket.
4. Reverse procedure to install. **Before installing pump, rotate camshaft to "downstroke" position. Also, when installation is completed, start engine and check for fuel leaks.**

#### 1986-89

1. Drain fuel tank, then support tank and remove bolts securing tank retaining straps.
2. Lower tank slightly and disconnect ground and harness connectors, then remove tank from under vehicle.
3. Turn fuel sender unit cam counterclockwise, then lift pump assembly from tank.
4. Pull fuel pump up into hose while pulling out from bottom and remove

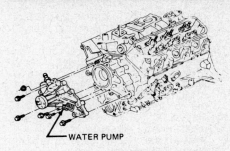

**Fig. 13 Water pump removal**

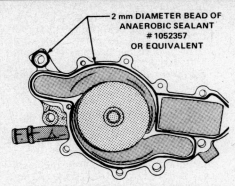

2 mm DIAMETER BEAD OF ANAEROBIC SEALANT # 1052357 OR EQUIVALENT

**Fig. 14 Water pump sealer application**

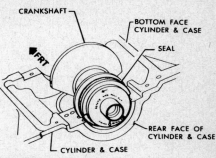

CRANKSHAFT — BOTTOM FACE CYLINDER & CASE — SEAL — REAR FACE OF CYLINDER & CASE — CYLINDER & CASE — FRT

CAUTION RETAINER SPRING SIDE OF SEAL MUST FACE TOWARD FRONT OF CYLINDER & CASE.

**Fig. 15 Rear main oil seal installation. 1982–84 models & 1985 models w/engine coded K (thin seal)**

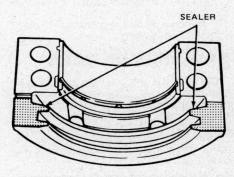

SEALER

**Fig. 16 Sealing rear main bearing cap**

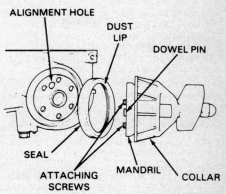

ALIGNMENT HOLE — DUST LIP — DOWEL PIN — SEAL — ATTACHING SCREWS — MANDRIL — COLLAR

**Fig. 17 Rear main oil seal installation. 1985 models w/engine coded A or T & 1986–89 models (thick seal)**

pump from sending unit.
5. Reverse procedure to install, using a new O-ring.

# WATER PUMP
## REPLACE
### 1982–88

1. Disconnect battery ground cable.
2. Drain cooling system then remove the fan and the heater hose and drive belts from the pump.
3. Remove water pump attaching bolts and nut, then the pump, **Fig. 13.**
4. Reverse procedure to install. On 1982-85 models, torque M6 x 1.0 bolts to 6-9 ft. lbs., M8 x 1.25 bolts to 13-18 ft. lbs. and on 1982 models, M10 x 1.5 bolts to 20-30 ft. lbs. On 1986-88 models, torque attaching bolts to 22 ft. lbs. **Prior to installing water pump, thoroughly clean sealing surfaces. 1982-84 models apply a 3/32 inch bead of sealant 1052357, or equivalent, to the pump sealing surface, Fig. 14.** All models, coat bolt threads with sealant 1052080, or equivalent.

### 1989

1. Disconnect battery ground cable and drain coolant from radiator.
2. Remove serpentine drive belt.
3. Remove upper fan shroud, fan and clutch assembly.
4. Remove water pump pulley.
5. Remove clamps and hoses.
6. Remove water pump mounting bolts and one water pump retaining nut.
7. Remove water pump and water pump

gasket.
8. Reverse procedure to install. Torque water pump to engine retaining bolts to 22 ft. lbs.

# REAR MAIN BEARING OIL SEAL
## REPLACE

When rear main oil seal replacement is required on 1982-84 models, the existing seal should be replaced with the thin, one piece, lip type seal used on 1985 models with engine coded K. This seal, available as kit part No. 14081761, should be used to replace the rope type seal used on early production engines and the two piece rubber seal released for service on 1982-84 models, both for oil leak correction and during engine service. In addition, a redesigned crankshaft has been recommended for use on 1982-84 engines where installation of the one piece seal alone does not correct oil leakage at the rear main seal. This new crankshaft, part No. 14089826, has had the knurled portion removed from the rear seal area to improve sealing and oil retention.

Engines installed in 1985 models with engine coded K use the early lip seal designated for service on 1982-84 engines (part No. 14081761, thin seal), while 1985 models with engine coded A or T and all 1986-89 models have been modified to use a thicker lip type seal (part No. 14077817). Models that use the thin type rear seal require engine and crankshaft removal for seal replacement, while the crankshaft need not be removed for seal replacement on models using the thick type seal.

Some models use an O-ring (part No. 14083381) to seal oil pump transfer passage from rear main bearing cap to cylinder block. The O-ring fits into a machined groove in the cylinder block and must be replaced whenever the rear main bearing cap is removed. In addition to the O-ring, the rear main bearing cap must also be sealed to the block using suitable sealing compound.

## 1982–84 & 1985 W/ENGINE CODED K (THIN SEAL)

1. Remove engine as outlined previously.

2. Remove clutch assembly, if equipped, and flywheel or flex plate, drain engine oil and mount engine in suitable holding fixture.
3. Remove crankshaft as follows:
   a. Remove spark plugs, crankshaft pulley and damper.
   b. Remove oil pan and oil pump.
   c. Remove water pump, front cover, camshaft sprocket and timing chain, referring to "Timing Chain, Replace" procedure.
   d. Note position of connecting rod caps, remove caps and place in order for assembly, then push pistons to tops of bores, taking care not to mar crankshaft.
   e. Note installation position of main bearing caps, loosen main bearing bolts and remove main caps, keeping them in order for assembly.
   f. Lift crankshaft from block and set aside, taking care not to damage bearing surfaces.
4. Remove old oil seal and clean all sealant and foreign material from seal groove, engine case and bearing cap, and crankshaft sealing surface.
5. Inspect seal groove and crankshaft for wear, nicks, burrs and machining defects, and repair as needed.
6. Leaving seal on installation tool, coat

outer diameter of seal with anaerobic sealer such as Loctite 515 or equivalent.

7. Push seal and tool assembly onto crankshaft as far as it will go, positioning tool so that arrow points toward cylinder case as shown in **Fig. 15.**
8. Ensure main bearings in block are properly positioned and lubricated, then set crankshaft into engine, aligning oil seal with case groove.
9. Lightly lubricate crankshaft journals, and ensure bearing shells are properly installed in main caps and that rear main cap sealing surfaces are clean and free from oil.
10. Apply a 1-2 mm bead of anaerobic sealer (Loctite 515 or equivalent) to rear main cap as shown in **Fig. 16,** install cap and torque retaining bolts to specifications. **It is important that cap joint be properly sealed to prevent oil leakage. Do not substitute RTV sealer for the specified anaerobic sealer, and do not apply an excessive amount of sealer to the cap, as this will cause oil leaks.**
11. Install remaining main bearing caps and torque to specifications.
12. Ensure connecting rod bearings are properly seated in rods and caps, lightly lubricate bearings and crankpin journals, then reconnect rods to crankpins, install caps and torque cap nuts to specifications.
13. Complete engine reassembly and installation as outlined in appropriate service procedures.

## 1985 w/ENGINE CODED A OR T & 1986-89 (THICK SEAL)

Engines with this type rear main oil seal can be identified by the date code stamping located on the horizontal pad above the left upper water pump bolt.
1. Raise and support vehicle.
2. Support engine as needed, then remove transmission.
3. Remove clutch and pressure plate, if equipped, then remove flywheel or flex plate.
4. Insert screwdriver through seal lip and pry seal from bore, taking care not to damage crankshaft.
5. Clean seal bore and crankshaft, then inspect for burrs, nicks and wear, and repair as needed.
6. Lightly lubricate replacement seal lip, mount seal on installer J-34686 or equivalent, **Fig. 17,** and seat dust lip of seal squarely against collar.
7. Lubricate outer diameter of seal, align dowel pin of tool with dowel pin hole in crankshaft, mount tool on crankshaft and torque retaining bolts to 2-5 ft. lbs. on 88-89 models torque retaining bolt to 36 in. lbs.
8. Rotate "T" handle of tool clockwise, pressing seal into bore until collar is tight against engine case to ensure seal is fully seated.
9. Rotate "T" handle of tool counterclockwise to stop, then remove tool and ensure seal is seated squarely in bore.
10. Reverse remaining procedure to complete installation.

## BELT TENSION DATA

On 1982-88 models, new belt tension should measure 146 lbs. for the A/C compressor and alternator belts and 135 lbs. at all other belts. Used belt tension should measure 67 lbs. at all belts.

1989 models are equipped with a Serpentine type drive belt which adjusts automatically.

# V6-262 (4.3L) GASOLINE ENGINE

## INDEX

# ENGINE REPLACE

## 4 X 2

1. Disconnect battery ground cable.
2. Scribe hood hinge location, then remove hood.
3. Drain cooling system, then remove radiator hoses, heater hoses and overflow hose.
4. Remove upper fan shroud, then disconnect transmission and oil cooler lines, if equipped.
5. Remove radiator and fan.
6. Remove air cleaner and disconnect vacuum hoses.
7. Disconnect necessary wiring at the bulkhead, then disconnect ground wires and main feed wires.
8. Remove distributor cap, then disconnect throttle and cruise control cables, if equipped

9. Raise and support vehicle.
10. Remove converter-to-exhaust pipe bolts.
11. Disconnect exhaust pipes from manifolds.
12. Disconnect strut rods from bell housing.
13. Remove flywheel cover attaching bolts, then the cover, if equipped.
14. Remove torque converter bolts.
15. Remove shield at rear of catalytic converter.
16. Disconnect converter hanger from exhaust pipe.
17. Remove lower fan shroud, then disconnect fuel lines and hoses.
18. Remove two outer air dam bolts.
19. Remove left body mount bolts and raise the body using suitable jackstands.
20. Remove bell housing bolts, then lower body.
21. Remove engine mount through bolts.

22. Remove jackstands and lower vehicle.
23. Remove A/C compressor and power steering pump, if equipped.
24. Support transmission and remove engine.
25. Reverse procedure to install.

## 4 X 4

1. Disconnect battery ground cable.
2. Scribe hood hinge locations, then disconnect underhood light and remove hood.
3. Raise and support vehicle.
4. Remove body mounts on utility vehicles. Loosen front and remove two body mounts on cab and chassis models.
5. Remove front air dam end bolts and raise body.
6. Remove top transmission-to-engine attaching bolts and lower body.
7. Remove remaining

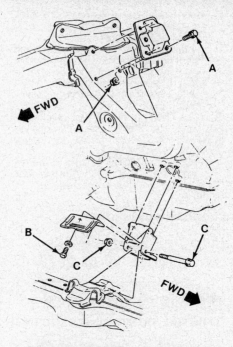

A. Torque Bolt to 57 N·m (42 ft. lbs.) or. Torque Nut to 47 N·m (35 ft. lbs.)
B. 47 N·m (35 ft. lbs.)
C. 70 N·m (52 ft. lbs.)

**Fig. 1   Front engine mount installation**

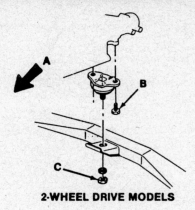

**2-WHEEL DRIVE MODELS**

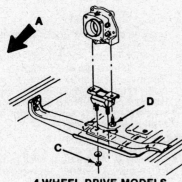

**4-WHEEL DRIVE MODELS**

A. Forward
B. 60 N·m (45 Ft. Lbs.)
C. 32 N·m (24 Ft. Lbs.)
D. 55 N·m (40 Ft. Lbs.)
E. 30 N·m (22 Ft. Lbs.)

**Fig. 2   Rear engine mount installation**

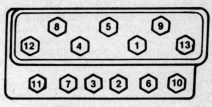

**FRONT**

**Fig. 3   Cylinder head tightening sequence**

transmission to engine attaching bolts.
8. Remove second crossmember, then disconnect catalytic converter hanger.
9. Disconnect exhaust pipes from manifolds.
10. Disconnect front propeller shaft from front differential.
11. Remove torque converter cover bolts, then the cover.
12. Remove transmission cooler lines from engine clips.
13. Remove engine mount bolts.
14. Remove flexplate-to-torque converter attaching bolts.
15. Remove front splash shield.
16. Remove lower fan shroud bolts, then lower vehicle and drain cooling system.
17. Remove upper fan shroud and radiator hoses.
18. Remove oil filter pipe from remote oil filter.
19. Remove radiator, fan and air cleaner.
20. Remove A/C compressor and power steering pump, if equipped.
21. Disconnect necessary wiring, fuel lines, vacuum and emission hoses.
22. Disconnect throttle, cruise control and TV cables as equipped.
23. Disconnect engine wiring harness at bulkhead.
24. Remove heater hoses from engine, then support transmission.
25. Remove engine from vehicle.
26. Reverse procedure to install.

# ENGINE MOUNTS
## REPLACE
### FRONT

1. Support engine using suitable lifting equipment.
2. Remove engine mount through bolt and nut.
3. Raise engine and remove mount-to-engine attaching bolts, **Fig. 1.**
4. Remove engine mount.
5. Reverse procedure to install

### REAR

1. Raise and support vehicle.
2. Support rear of engine using suitable equipment.
3. Remove mount to crossmember attaching nuts and washers.
4. Remove mount to transmission attaching bolts, then the mount.
5. Reverse procedure to install. Torque bolts to specifications shown in **Fig. 2.**

# CYLINDER HEAD
## REPLACE

1. Disconnect battery ground cable.

2. Remove rocker arm cover.
3. Remove intake manifold, then the exhaust manifold.
4. If removing right cylinder head, disconnect electrical connector from sensor and dipstick tube bracket from cylinder head, then remove A/C compressor and belt tensioner bracket and position aside.
5. If removing left cylinder head, remove power steering pump, brackets and alternator and position aside.
6. Remove spark plugs.
7. Remove pushrods.
8. Remove cylinder head bolts and cylinder head.
9. Reverse procedure to install. **The gasket surfaces on both head and cylinder block must be clean of any foreign matter and free of nicks or heavy scratches. Cylinder head bolt threads in the block and on the bolts must be clean as dirt will affect bolt torque. Coat cylinder head bolt threads with sealer, No. 1052080 or equivalent, and install bolts. Torque bolts to specification in sequence shown in Fig. 3.**

# INTAKE MANIFOLD
## REPLACE

1. Disconnect battery ground cable.
2. Remove air cleaner and heat stove tube.
3. Remove two braces from rear of fan belt tensioner.
4. Drain cooling system, then remove upper radiator hose.
5. Remove emission relays and bracket.
6. Remove wiring harnesses from retainers and position aside.
7. Remove power brake vacuum pipe, then ground cable from manifold stud.
8. Disconnect heater hose pipe from manifold.
9. Disconnect fuel pipes from throttle body.
10. Remove electrical connectors from sensors on manifold, then the ignition coil.
11. Remove distributor.
12. Remove electrical connectors and hoses from throttle body.
13. Remove throttle, TVS and cruise control cables, as equipped.
14. Remove EGR hose, then the manifold bolts.
15. Remove intake manifold.
16. Reverse procedure to install, noting

the following:

a. Ensure gaskets are installed with port blocking plates facing the rear.
b. Apply a 3/16 bead of sealer to front and rear of block, **Fig. 4**. Extend bead 1/2 inch up each cylinder head to seal gaskets.
c. Install manifold retaining bolts and torque to specification in proper sequence shown in **Fig. 5**.

## EXHAUST MANIFOLD
### REPLACE

1. Disconnect battery ground cable.
2. Raise and support vehicle.
3. Disconnect exhaust pipe from manifold.
4. Lower vehicle, then remove spark plug wires from spark plugs.
5. Remove power steering and alternator rear bracket from left manifold.
6. Remove air cleaner with heat stove pipe and cold air intake pipe.
7. Remove exhaust manifold bolts and washers, then the manifold.
8. Reverse procedure to install.

## ROCKER ARMS & PUSHRODS
### REPLACE

1. Disconnect battery ground cable.
2. Remove air cleaner assembly, then the emission relays and bracket.
3. Remove wiring harnesses and spark plug wires from clips and position aside.
4. Disconnect dipstick tube from cylinder head and position tube aside.
5. Remove rocker arm cover.
6. Remove rocker arm nut, then rocker arm and ball.
7. Remove pushrod.
8. Reverse procedure to install. Adjust valves as described under "Valves, Adjust."

## ROCKER ARM STUDS

Rocker arm studs that have damaged threads or are loose should be replaced with oversize studs. Oversize studs are available in .003 and .013 inch and can be installed after properly reaming the holes as follows:

1. Remove stud using tool No. J-5802-01, **Fig. 6** or equivalent with a nut and flat washer placed over the tool.
2. Ream hole to proper size using tool No. J-5715, **Fig. 7** for .003 inch oversize or tool No. J-6036 for .013 inch oversize. **Do not install oversize stud without reaming hole since cylinder head damage could occur.**
3. Apply axle lubricant to press fit area of stud and install using tool No. J-6880 or equivalent, **Fig. 8**.

## VALVE LIFTER SERVICE
### REMOVAL

1. Remove rocker arm cover and push-

rods as described under "Rocker Arm & Pushrods, Replace."
2. Remove intake manifold as described under "Intake Manifold, Replace."
3. Remove retainer-to-engine attaching bolts, retainer and restrictors, **Fig. 11**.
4. Remove lifters. **Note lifter location when removing. Lifters must be installed in same bore.**

### DISASSEMBLY

1. Depress pushrod seat with pushrod, remove seat retainer, then slowly release spring tension.
2. Remove pushrod seat and metering valve.
3. Invert lifter and tap on flat surface to remove plunger and plunger spring.
4. Remove check ball retainer by prying from plunger with small screwdriver.
5. Remove check ball spring and check ball.
6. Clean lifter components in suitable solvent, keeping components for each lifter separate

### INSPECTION

1. Inspect lifter body for internal and external wear. Also inspect bottom for wear grooves and flat spots.
2. Inspect roller for free operation, flat spots and pitting. Replace lifter if roller is worn, pitted or cannot be freed up.
3. Inspect pushrod seat and replace lifter and pushrod if seat is scored or excessively worn.
4. Inspect check ball and replace lifter if ball is pitted or scored. **Do not attempt to recondition lifter assembly by interchanging components from other lifters. If components are damaged or worn, lifter assembly should be replaced.**

### ASSEMBLY

Ensure lifter components are kept clean during assembly, as small particles of dirt or lint can cause lifter to fail.

1. Install check ball to the small hole in bottom of plunger.
2. Install check ball spring and retainer, over check ball, then press retainer into position in plunger with small screwdriver.
3. Install plunger spring to check ball retainer.

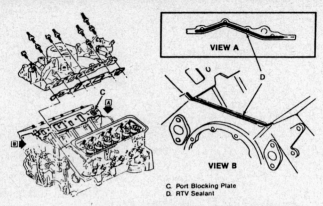

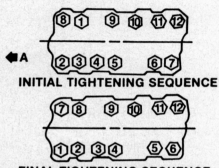

C. Port Blocking Plate
D. RTV Sealant

**Fig. 4 Intake manifold sealant application**

**INITIAL TIGHTENING SEQUENCE**

**FINAL TIGHTENING SEQUENCE**
A. Front Of Engine

**Fig. 5 Intake manifold tightening sequence**

4. Align oil feed holes in lifter body and plunger, then install plunger into lifter body.
5. Fill lifter with SAE 10 oil and proceed as follows:
   a. Insert a 1/8 inch punch into plunger and press down solidly, then using a 1/16 inch punch, insert punch through oil holes to retain plunger down against plunger spring tension.
   b. Remove 1/8 inch punch and fill lifter with SAE 10 oil.
6. Install metering valve, pushrod seat and seat retainer.
7. Depress pushrod seat with pushrod and remove 1/16 inch punch from lifter body.

## VALVES
### ADJUST

1. Remove rocker arm covers as described in "Rocker Arms & Pushrods, Replace."
2. Crank engine until mark on torsional damper is aligned with "0" mark on timing tab and engine is in No. one cylinder firing position. Ensure engine is in No. 1 firing position by placing fingers on rocker arms of No. 1 cylinder as timing mark approaches "0" mark. If rocker arms are not moving engine is at the No. 1 firing position. If rocker arms are moving, engine is in the No.

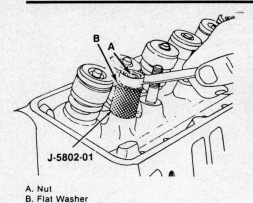

A. Nut
B. Flat Washer

**Fig. 6 Rocker arm stud removal.**

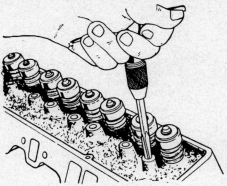

**Fig. 7 Reaming of rocker arm stud bore.**

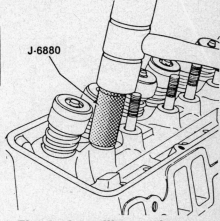

**Fig. 8 Installing rocker arm stud.**

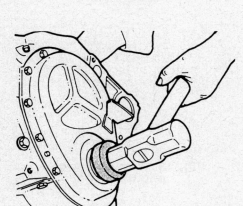

**Fig. 9 Installing front oil seal.**

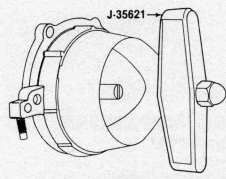

**Fig. 10 Installing rear main oil seal.**

4 firing position and should be rotated one revolution to the No. 1 position.

3. Adjust the following valves with the engine in the No. 1 firing position: exhaust 1, 5 and 6; intake 1, 2 and 3. Adjust valves by backing off nut until lash is felt at the pushrod, then tightening nut until all lash is removed. This can be determined by rotating pushrod while tightening nut. **Fig. 12.** When all lash is removed, tighten nut one full turn to center pushrod in lifter plunger.

4. Crank engine one full revolution until mark on torsional damper and "0" mark on timing tab are aligned. This is the No. 4 cylinder firing position. Adjust the following valves: exhaust 2, 3 and 4; intake 4, 5 and 6.

5. Install valve covers and related components.

## VALVE ARRANGEMENT

All . . . . . . . . . . . . . . . . . . . . . . . . . . E-I-E-I-I-E

## CAMSHAFT LIFT SPECIFICATIONS

Camshaft lift should measure .357 inch at intake valves and .390 inch at exhaust valves.

## CAMSHAFT
### REPLACE

1. Disconnect battery ground cable.
2. Remove air cleaner assembly and drain cooling system.
3. Remove rocker arm covers and pushrods as described under "Rocker Arm & Pushrods, Replace."
4. Remove distributor.
5. Remove intake manifold as described under "Intake Manifold, Replace."
6. Remove valve lifters as described under "Valve Lifters, Replace."
7. Remove radiator, fan and pulley.
8. Remove water pump and torsional damper.
9. Remove timing cover as described under "Timing Cover, Replace."
10. Remove camshaft sprocket bolts, then the sprocket and timing chain.
11. Remove thrust plate attaching bolts, then the thrust plate.
12. Remove camshaft.
13. Reverse procedure to install. **Ensure timing marks are properly aligned after installation of sprockets and chain, Fig. 13.**

## FRONT COVER
### REPLACE

1. Remove torsional damper.

2. Remove water pump, then the upper radiator hose.
3. Remove oil pan as described under "Oil Pan, Replace."
4. Remove A/C compressor and position aside.
5. Remove right side engine accessory bracket.
6. Remove front cover attaching bolts and reinforcements.
7. Remove front cover.
8. Reverse procedure to install, torquing cover bolts to 10 ft. lbs.

## FRONT OIL SEAL
### REPLACE

1. Disconnect battery ground cable.
2. Remove fan belt, fan and pulley.
3. Remove fan shroud, then the accessory drive pulley.
4. Remove torsional damper.
5. Remove front crankshaft seal by prying out with large screwdriver. **Ensure not to distort front cover.**
6. Remove crankshaft key, if necessary.
7. Coat seal lips with engine oil and install using tool No. J-35468 or equivalent **Fig. 9.**
8. Reverse steps 1 through 6 to complete installation.

## REAR MAIN OIL SEAL
### REPLACE

1. Remove transmission.
2. Remove clutch and flywheel, if equipped.
3. Remove rear crankshaft oil seal by placing screwdriver in notches provided and pry the seal out.
4. Lubricate seal with engine oil and install using tool No. J-35621 or equivalent, **Fig. 10.**
5. Reverse steps 1 and 2 to complete installation.

## OIL PAN
### REPLACE
### 4 X 2

1. Drain oil, then remove engine as de-

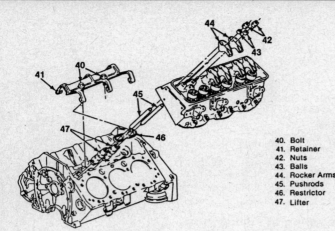

40. Bolt
41. Retainer
42. Nuts
43. Balls
44. Rocker Arms
45. Pushrods
46. Restrictor
47. Lifter

**Fig. 11  Hydraulic lifters & retainer**

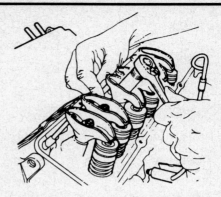

**Fig. 12  Valve adjustment**

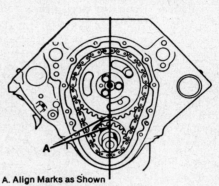

A. Align Marks as Shown

**Fig. 13  Timing mark alignment**

scribed under "Engine, Replace."

2. Remove oil pan attaching bolts, nuts and reinforcements.
3. Remove oil pan. Clean sealing surfaces on pan and block.
4. Apply sealer No. 1052080 or equivalent to front cover-to-block joint and rear crankshaft oil seal retainer-to-block joint, extend sealer one inch in both on all four corners. Install pan gasket.
5. Reverse procedure to install. Torque bolts to 100 inch lbs., and nuts to 200 inch lbs.

## 4 X 4

1. Disconnect battery ground cable.
2. Remove dipstick, then the drive belt splash shield.
3. Raise and support vehicle.
4. Remove front axle shield and transfer case shield.
5. Disconnect brake line clips from crossmember and remove second crossmember.
6. Remove converter hanger attaching bolts and exhaust pipe clamp from converter.
7. Disconnect front propshaft from drive pinion.
8. Remove flywheel cover.
9. Remove starter attaching bolts and position starter aside.
10. Disconnect steering shock absorber from frame bracket.
11. Remove steering gear attaching bolts.
12. Mark position of idler arm and remove idler arm attaching bolts.
13. Remove differential housing mounting bolts from the bracket on the right side and the frame on the left side.
14. Pull steering gear and linkage forward, then move differential housing forward.
15. Remove engine mount through bolts, then raise engine and block in position.
16. Drain oil, then remove oil pan attaching bolts, nuts and reinforcements.
17. Remove oil pan. Clean pan and block sealing surfaces.
18. Apply sealer No. 1052080 or equivalent to front cover-to-block joint and rear crankshaft oil seal

retainer-to-block joint, extend sealer one inch in both directions on all four corners.

19. Install gasket and oil pan. Torque bolts to 100 inch lbs. and nuts to 200 inch lbs.
20. Reverse steps 1 to 17 to complete installation.

## OIL PUMP SERVICE

### REMOVAL

1. Remove oil pan as described under "Oil Pan, Replace."
2. Remove oil pump-to-main bearing cap attaching bolt.
3. Remove oil pump.

### DISASSEMBLY

1. Remove pump cover attaching bolts and pump cover, **Fig. 14.**
2. Mark drive and idler gear teeth so they can be installed in same position, then remove drive and idler gears and shaft from pump body.
3. Remove pin, spring and pressure regulator valve from pump cover.
4. If pickup tube and screen are to be replaced, mount pump cover in soft jawed vise and remove pickup tube from cover. Do not remove screen from pickup tube, as these components are serviced as an assembly.

### INSPECTION

1. Inspect pump body and cover for excessive wear and cracks.
2. Inspect pump gears for damage or excessive wear. If pump gears are damaged or worn, the entire pump assembly must be replaced.
3. Check drive gear shaft for looseness in pump body.
4. Inspect pump cover for wear that would allow oil to leak past teeth.
5. Inspect pickup tube and screen for damage.
6. Check pressure regulator valve for fit in pump cover.

### ASSEMBLY

1. If pickup tube and screen were removed, apply sealer to end of pickup

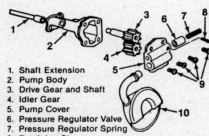

1. Shaft Extension
2. Pump Body
3. Drive Gear and Shaft
4. Idler Gear
5. Pump Cover
6. Pressure Regulator Valve
7. Pressure Regulator Spring
8. Retaining Pin
9. Screws
10. Pickup Screen and Pipe

**Fig. 14  Oil pump exploded view**

tube, then mount pump cover in a soft jawed vise and using tool No. J-21882, tap pickup tube into place with a hammer. **Whenever the pickup tube and screen have been removed, a new pickup tube and screen assembly should be installed. Ensure tube does not twist, shear or collapse when installing pickup tube and screen. Loss of a press fit condition could result in an air leak and loss of oil pressure.**

2. Install pressure regulator valve, spring and pin, **Fig. 14.**
3. Install drive gear and shaft in body.
4. Align marks made during disassembly, then install idler gear.
5. Install pump cover gasket, cover and attaching bolts. Torque bolts to 7 ft. lbs.
6. Rotate pump drive shaft by hand and ensure smooth operation.

## INSTALLATION

1. Align oil pump shaft with oil pump driveshaft.
2. Install oil pump attaching bolts and torque to 65 ft. lbs.
3. Install oil pan.

## MAIN & ROD BEARINGS

Main bearings are available in standard size and undersizes of .001, .002, .009, .010 and .020 inch. Connecting rod bearings are available in standard size and .001 and .002 inch undersize for use with new and used standard size crankshafts and .010 and .020 inch undersize for use with reconditioned crankshafts.

## FUEL PUMP
### REPLACE

1. Disconnect battery ground cable.
2. Raise and support vehicle.
3. Remove fuel tank.
4. Remove fuel pump/sender unit by turning cam lock counterclockwise.
5. Remove fuel pump/sender from tank, then pump from sender.
6. Reverse procedure to install, using new O-ring when installing fuel pump/sender unit in tank.

## WATER PUMP
### REPLACE

1. Drain cooling system.
2. Remove serpentine drive belt, then the upper fan shroud.
3. Remove fan, fan clutch assembly and water pump pulley.
4. Remove hoses from pump.
5. Remove water pump attaching bolts, then pump.
6. Reverse procedure to install. Torque bolts to 22 ft. lbs.

# 4-137 (2.2L) DIESEL ENGINE

## INDEX

## DIESEL ENGINE TROUBLESHOOTING
### HARD STARTING

1. Check fuel level and replenish if necessary.
2. Check notched line on injection pump flange and reset timing as necessary.
3. Check to ensure fuel is reaching injection nozzles. If fuel is reaching injectors:
   a. Check connections of fuse, glow plugs, Q.O.S. controller and glow plug relays.
   b. Check fuel spray pattern and ensure injection starting pressure is 1493 psi.
   c. Ensure valve clearances are satisfactory. Refer to specifications.
   d. Check compression pressure in each cylinder. Standard value should be 441 psi.
   e. Ensure proper installation of timing belt and camshaft.
4. If fuel is not reaching injectors:
   a. Check for air in fuel filter.
   b. Check if air is being drawn into fuel line through leakage in the pipe joints.
   c. Check operation of fuel cut out solenoid.
   d. Check fuel filter for restrictions.
   e. Check fuel pipes for restrictions.
   f. Check delivery valve for possible sticking.
5. Replace or readjust setting of injection pump.

### ENGINE IDLING ROUGH

1. Check if idle speed is within specifications.
2. Ensure accelerator control cable is not binding or twisting.
3. Check accelerator lever setting for looseness.
4. Check for air or water in fuel filter.
5. On models with A/C, check that Fast Idle Control Device (FICD) is operating properly.
6. Check for proper alignment on injection pump flange.

7. Check engine mounting for cracks or looseness.
8. Check fuel spray valve pattern and ensure injection starting pressure is 1493 psi.
9. Ensure valve clearances are satisfactory. Refer to specifications.
10. Check compression pressure in each cylinder. Standard valve should be 441 psi.
11. Ensure proper installation of timing belt and camshaft.
12. Check delivery valve for sticking.
13. Replace or readjust setting of injection pump.

### LACK OF POWER

1. Check intake system for restrictions.
2. Ensure accelerator control cable is not twisted or binding.
3. Check seals on full load adjustment bolt and maximum speed stop bolt.
4. Ensure accelerator control lever is in contact with maximum speed stop bolt.
5. Check exhaust system for restrictions.

6. Ensure all air has been removed from fuel filter.
7. Check fuel lines to ensure all connections are secure and no lines are collapsed.
8. Check fuel tank breather for restrictions.
9. Check fuel quality.
10. Check notched line on injection pump flange, and reset timing as necessary.
11. Check fuel spray pattern and ensure injection starting pressure is 1493 psi.
12. Ensure valve clearances are satisfactory. Refer to specifications.
13. Check compression pressure in each cylinder. Standard value should be 441 psi.
14. Check delivery valve for sticking.
15. Replace or readjust setting of injection pump.

## EXCESSIVE EXHAUST SMOKE

1. Ensure engine is thoroughly warmed up.
2. Check intake system for restrictions.
3. Ensure all air and water has been removed from fuel filter.
4. Check seal on full load adjust bolt.
5. Check exhaust system for restrictions.
6. Check fuel quality.
7. Check notched line on injection pump flange, and reset timing as necessary.
8. Check fuel spray pattern and ensure injection starting pressure is 1493 psi.
9. Ensure valve clearances are satisfactory. Refer to specifications.
10. Check compression pressure in each cylinder. Standard value should be 441 psi.
11. Ensure proper installation of timing belt and camshaft.
12. Check delivery valve for sticking.
13. Check condition of valve guides and seals.
14. Replace or readjust setting of injection pump.

## ENGINE OVERHEATING

1. Check coolant level in radiator.
2. Check condition of coolant for contamination, anti-freeze concentration and leakage of oil into coolant.
3. Check hoses and clamps for signs of leakage.
4. Check water pump and thermostat housing for leakage.
5. Check cylinder head gasket for leakage.
6. Check fan belt tension. Belt deflection should not exceed .4 inch.
7. Check fan clutch operation.
8. Check radiator cap operation.
9. Check thermostat operation. Thermostat opening temperature is approximately 192°F.
10. Check notched line on injection pump flange, and reset timing as necessary.
11. Check fuel spray pattern and ensure injector starting pressure is 1493 psi.
12. Check water pump impeller condition.
13. Check combustion chambers for excessive combustion deposits.
14. Replace or readjust setting of injection pump.

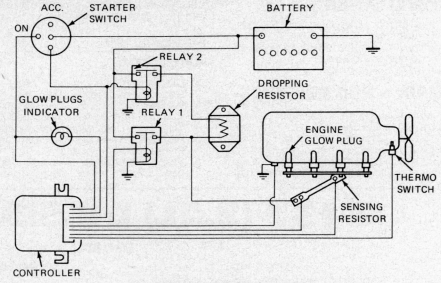

**Fig. 1   Glow plug system**

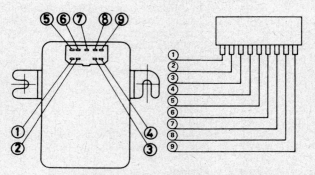

Position to which connector terminal is connected

1. Starter switch (ON position)
2. Sensing resistor
3. Thermo switch
4. Starter switch (ST position)
5. Sensing resistor
6. Glow plug relay No. 1
7. Ground
8. Glow indicator lamp
9. Not used

**Fig. 2   Controller wiring connections**

## ENGINE KNOCKING

1. Ensure engine has been thoroughly warmed up.
2. Check injection timing.
3. Check fuel spray pattern, and ensure injection starting pressure is 1493 psi.
4. Check compression pressure in each cylinder. Standard value should be 441 psi.
5. Ensure proper quality of fuel is being used.
6. Replace or readjust setting of injection pump.

## NOISE INDICATING ABNORMAL LEAKAGE

1. Check exhaust system for loose connections or leakage.
2. Ensure proper installation of nozzles and glow plugs.
3. Check for damaged cylinder head gasket.
4. Ensure valve clearances are satisfactory. Refer to specifications.
5. Check compression pressure in each cylinder. Standard value should be 441 psi.

## CONTINUOUS NOISE

1. Check fan belt tension. Deflection of

fan belt should be no more than .4 inch.
2. Ensure cooling fan is secure.
3. Check water pump bearing for wear and damage.
4. Check operation of alternator and vacuum pump.
5. Ensure valve clearances are satisfactory. Refer to specifications.

## SLAPPING NOISE

1. Ensure valve clearances are satisfactory. Refer to specifications.
2. Check rocker arms for damage.
3. Check to ensure flywheel bolts are secure.
4. Check crankshaft and thrust bearing for wear and/or damage.
5. Check main bearing oil clearances.
6. Check connecting rod bearing and bushing oil clearances.
7. Ensure clearance between pistons and cylinder walls is satisfactory. Refer to specifications.

## EXCESSIVE OIL CONSUMPTION

1. If oil is leaking:
   a. Check oil level.
   b. Ensure drain plug is secure.
   c. Check oil pipes for leakage.
   d. Check oil seal retainer and oil filter

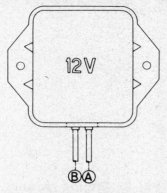

**Fig. 3 Dropping resistor test connections**

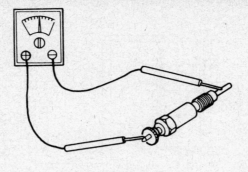

**Fig. 4 Testing glow plug**

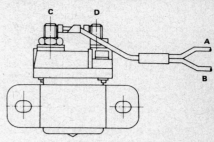

**Fig. 5 Glow plug relay test connections**

gasket for leakage.
  e. Check cylinder head cover, oil pan and oil pump for leakage.
  f. Check cylinder head gasket for leakage.
  g. Check oil seal for leakage.
2. If oil is burning:
  a. Ensure proper quality of oil is being used.
  b. Check valve stem oil seals.
  c. Check valve guides and valve stems for wear and damage.
  d. Check for damaged cylinder head gasket.
  e. Ensure proper setting of piston rings.
  f. Check piston rings for wear and damage.
  g. Check cylinder walls for wear and damage.

## EXCESSIVE FUEL CONSUMPTION

1. Check air cleaner for restrictions.
2. Check full load adjustment bolt seal for leakage.
3. Check fuel pipes for leakage.
4. Check exhaust system for restrictions.
5. Ensure idle speed is within specifications.
6. Ensure proper quality of fuel.
7. Check injection timing.
8. Check fuel spray pattern, and ensure injection starting pressure is 1493 psi.
9. Ensure valve clearances are satisfactory. Refer to specifications.
10. Check compression pressure in each cylinder. Standard value should be 441 psi.
11. Check delivery valve for sticking.
12. Replace or readjust setting of injection pump.

## GLOW PLUG SYSTEM ELECTRICAL DIAGNOSIS

### COLD ENGINE

With a normally operating Q.O.S. (Quick On System) with coolant temperature below 140°F and ignition turned to "On" position, glow plug indicator turns on for about 3.5 seconds and No. 1 relay (quick pre-heat) turns on for a few seconds, then off. When ignition switch is turned to "Start" position, glow plug indicator and

No. 2 relay (constant heat) will go on and remain on until ignition is returned to "On" position.

### IGNITION IN "ON" (PRE-HEAT) POSITION

#### Relay No. 1 & Glow Indicator Are Both Inoperative

1. Starter circuit fuse is burnt out or fusible link wire is open.
2. Starter wire circuit is open or not properly connected.
3. Controller is defective or not properly connected.
4. Starter switch is inoperative.

#### Relay No. 1 Inoperative

1. Relay No. 1 is open.
2. Relay coil in relay No. 1 is open.
3. Controller to No. 1 relay circuitry is open or not properly connected.
4. Grounding circuit for No. 1 relay is open or not properly connected.
5. Controller is inoperative.
6. Circuit from controller to signal feed wire of sensing resistor is open or not properly connected.
7. Terminals of sensing resistor are not connected.
8. Main terminal of No. 1 relay is not connected.
9. Main contact is open in No. 1 relay.
10. Terminals in quick preheat circuit are not connected.
11. Engine harness ground is not properly connected.
12. Quick preheating wiring is not properly connected or circuit is open.

#### Glow Indicator Light Inoperative

Light bulb is burnt out.

#### Relay No. 1 Turns Off Within 2 Seconds

1. Controller is damaged.
2. One or more glow plugs are defective.
3. Wiring at connector is poorly connected.

#### Relay No. 1 Will Not Turn Off After A Few Seconds

Controller is damaged.

#### Relay No. 1 Operates When Coolant Temperature Is Above 140°F

1. Thermostat switch is inoperative.
2. Circuit has a short.

### IGNITION IN "START" (CONSTANT HEAT) POSITION

#### Relay No. 2 & Glow Indicator Inoperative

Starter switch "R" circuit is not properly connected or open.

#### Relay No. 2 Inoperative

1. Relay No. 2 terminals are not connected.
2. Circuit between R terminal and No. 2 relay is not properly connected or open.
3. No. 2 relay coil is open.

#### Glow Indicator Light Inoperative

Controller is damaged.

### WARM ENGINE

With a normally operating Q.O.S. (Quick On System) with coolant temperature above 140°F and ignition turned to "On" position, glow plug indicator turns on for about .3 second, then off. When ignition switch is turned to "Start" position, glow plug indicator and No. 2 relay (constant heat) turn on and remain on until ignition switch is returned to "On" position.

### IGNITION IN "ON" POSITION

#### Glow Plug Light Remains On For 3.5 Seconds & Causes Relay No. 1 To Turn On

1. Thermo-switch circuit is not properly connected or open.
2. Thermostat switch is inoperative.

### IGNITION IN "START" POSITION

#### Relay No. 2 & Glow Plug Indicator Inoperative

Starter switch "R" terminal not properly connected or open.

#### Relay No. 2 Inoperative

1. Relay No. 2 terminals not connected.

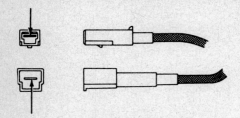

**Fig. 6  Fusible link connections**

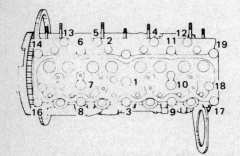

**Fig. 9  Cylinder head tightening sequence**

2. Circuit between "R" terminal and No. 2 relay not properly connected or open.
3. No. 2 relay coil is open.

### Glow Indicator Light Inoperative

Controller damaged.

# DIESEL ENGINE ELECTRICAL DIAGNOSIS & TESTING

## CONTROLLER

The controller in this system, **Fig. 1**, has four functions. As engine coolant temperature changes, it controls the glow plug relay. For determining glow plug heating requirements, it monitors differences between sensing resistance and glow plug resistance. It controls rapid preheat circuit to 1652°F of glow plug temperature and, during pre-heat cycle, controls glow plug pre-heat indicator lamp (3.5 sec.). Refer to **Fig. 2** for wiring connections.

## DROPPING RESISTOR

During stabilized heating, this fixed value resistor is used to lower voltage of glow plugs. Check dropping resistor by performing continuity check across the terminals. Replace resistor if no continuity is found. Refer to **Fig. 3**.

## GLOW PLUGS

The glow plugs used in this system are the fast warm up type. Check glow plugs by performing continuity test across plug terminals and body. If no continuity is found, heater wire is damaged and glow plug should be replaced. Refer to **Fig. 4**.

## GLOW PLUG RELAY NO. 1

This is the main relay for stabilized heat-

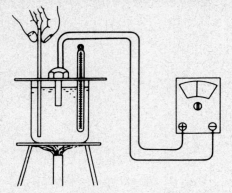

**Fig. 7  Testing thermo switch**

ing circuit and rapid pre-heat cycle. Check glow relay by performing continuity test across terminals C and D while battery voltage is applied to terminals A and B. If no continuity is found, replace glow plug relay. Refer to **Fig. 5**.

## GLOW PLUG RELAY NO. 2

During starting, this relay is used to provide stabilized heating. To check this relay use same procedure as for glow plug relay No. 1.

## FUSIBLE LINKS

These two in-line fusible links are used to protect the glow plug electrical wiring. To check fusible links, perform continuity check across terminals. If no continuity is found, fusible link should be replaced. Refer to **Fig. 6**.

## SENSING RESISTOR

Used in series with the glow plugs, this shunt type sensing resistor causes a small voltage drop which is monitored by the controller.

## THERMO SWITCH

This thermo switch is used to provide a ground circuit to controller circuitry when engine temperature is above 140°F To check thermo switch, perform continuity check across terminal and body while end of thermal switch is submerged in water. Gradually bring temperature of water to 140°F Replace thermal switch if continuity is not found at this temperature. Refer to **Fig. 7**.

# ENGINE
## REPLACE

1. Disconnect battery ground cable.
2. Disconnect exhaust pipe from manifold.
3. Disconnect power steering reservoir from upper fan shroud and position aside, then remove upper shroud.
4. Drain cooling system and disconnect hoses from radiator.
5. Remove radiator and cooling fan, then lower fan shroud.
6. Disconnect heater hoses from engine, then PCV valve at cylinder head cover.
7. Disconnect positive cable from bat-

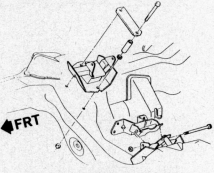

**Fig. 8  Engine mounts**

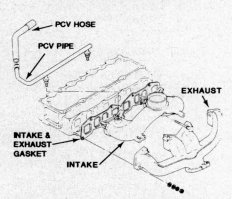

**Fig. 10  Exhaust & Intake manifold removal**

tery, and remove air cleaner and bracket.
8. If equipped with air conditioning, evacuate system and remove manifold at compressor.
9. If equipped with power steering, disconnect power steering pump.
10. Disconnect necessary vacuum hoses, wiring, fuel hoses and throttle linkage.
11. Remove starter.
12. Scribe alignment marks in hood hinge area, then remove hood.
13. Remove shifter assembly, then raise and support vehicle.
14. Remove right side motor mount through bolt, **Fig. 8**, then disconnect lower clutch cable.
15. Disconnect clutch bell crank at frame.
16. Disconnect back-up light switch wires and speedometer cable and position aside.
17. Remove driveshaft and transmission mount nut, then support transmission.
18. Remove transmission crossmember, then transmission to bellhousing mounting bolts.
19. Remove transmission, then engine to bellhousing mounting bolts.
20. Remove bellhousing, then lower vehicle.
21. Disconnect upper clutch cable, then remove bell crank.
22. Install suitable engine lifting device.
23. Remove left side motor mount through bolt, **Fig. 8**, then disconnect battery ground cable at engine block.
24. Remove engine.
25. Reverse procedure to install.

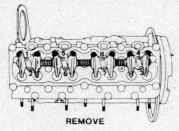

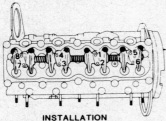

**Fig. 11   Rocker arm shaft assembly mounting bolts removal & installation**

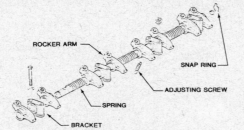

**Fig. 12   Rocker arm shaft assembly**

**Fig. 13   Valve guide removal**

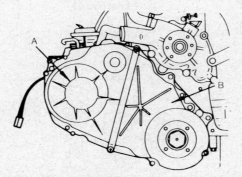

**Fig. 15   Timing pulley housing upper & lower covers**

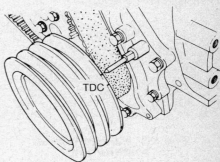

**Fig. 16   Crankshaft pulley at TDC**

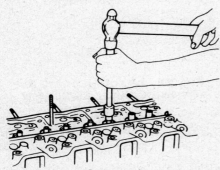

**Fig. 14   Valve guide installation**

## CYLINDER HEAD
### REPLACE

1. Disconnect battery ground cable.
2. Remove rocker arms and pushrods. Refer to "Rocker Arms, Replace."
3. Drain radiator coolant, then disconnect radiator hose from cylinder head.
4. Remove heater tube.
5. Disconnect exhaust pipe from manifold, then remove vacuum pump.
6. If equipped with air conditioning, remove A/C compressor and bracket and position aside.
7. Disconnect heater hose and bracket.
8. Disconnect PCV hose and position aside, then the oil dipstick and dipstick tube.
9. Disconnect necessary electrical wiring from engine and accessories.
10. Disconnect injection lines. **Cover all open injection lines to prevent entry of dirt.**
11. Disconnect breather pipe and the oil jet pipe.
12. Disconnect fuel return hose.
13. Remove cylinder head bolts, then the cylinder head.
14. Position new gasket on engine block with "TOP" side of gasket facing up.
15. Apply engine oil to sealing faces and

threads of cylinder head bolts, then install cylinder head and bolts. Torque bolts in sequence shown in **Fig. 9** to values given in specifications at beginning of chapter.

## ROCKER ARM COVER
### REPLACE

1. Disconnect battery ground cable.
2. Remove PCV valve from rocker arm cover.
3. Remove air cleaner assembly.
4. Disconnect PCV hose.
5. Remove rocker arm cover bolts, then the cover.
6. Reverse procedure to install. Torque rocker arm cover bolts to value given in specifications at beginning of chapter.

## EXHAUST MANIFOLD
### REPLACE

1. Disconnect battery ground cable.
2. Disconnect PCV valve from rocker arm cover.
3. Remove air cleaner assembly.
4. Disconnect exhaust pipe from manifold.
5. Remove exhaust manifold retaining nuts and washers, then the manifold, **Fig. 10.** If exhaust manifold gasket replacement is required, the intake manifold must be removed. Refer to "Intake Manifold, Replace" for procedure.
6. Reverse procedure to install. Torque exhaust manifold nuts to value given in specifications at beginning of chapter.

## INTAKE MANIFOLD
### REPLACE

1. Disconnect battery ground cable.
2. Remove air cleaner assembly.
3. Disconnect heater pipe bracket, then the PCV pipe hose, **Fig. 10.**
4. Disconnect clips and wires from intake manifold.
5. Remove intake manifold retaining bolts, then the manifold. If intake manifold gasket replacement is required, the exhaust manifold must be removed. Refer to "Exhaust Manifold, Replace" for procedure.
6. Reverse procedure to install. Torque intake manifold bolts to values given in specifications at beginning of chapter.

## ROCKER ARMS
### REPLACE

1. Disconnect battery ground cable.
2. Remove rocker arm cover. Refer to "Rocker Arm Cover, Replace."
3. Loosen rocker arm shaft assembly bracket bolts in sequence shown in **Fig. 11.**
4. Remove rocker arm shaft assembly and pushrods.
5. Mark rocker arms and pushrods to ensure they are reinstalled in the same position.
6. Remove snap ring, then the rocker arms, springs and brackets, **Fig. 12.**
7. Apply clean engine oil to rocker arm shaft, rocker arms, springs and brackets.
8. Assemble rocker arm shaft assembly, **Fig. 12. When assembling rocker**

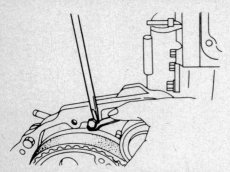

**Fig. 17  Belt tensioner spring removal**

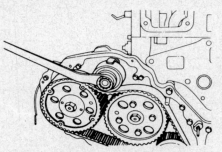

**Fig. 18  Belt tensioner pulley nut removal**

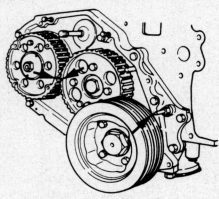

**Fig. 19  Pulley alignment**

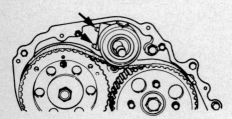

**Fig. 20  Belt tensioner installation**

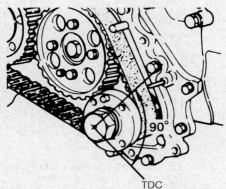

**Fig. 21  Crankshaft hub positioning**

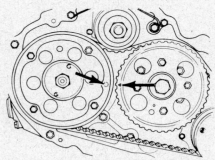

**Fig. 22  Injection pump & camshaft pulley alignment**

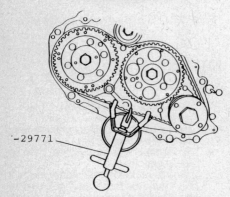

**Fig. 23  Measuring belt tension**

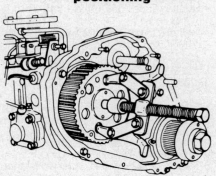

**Fig. 24  Injection pump pulley removal**

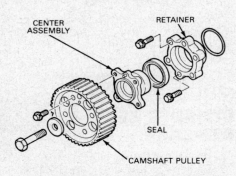

**Fig. 25  Camshaft pulley & center assembly**

arm shaft assembly, position brackets with "F" mark facing front of engine.
9. Install pushrods, then rocker arm shaft bracket.
10. Torque rocker arm shaft retaining bolts in sequence shown in **Fig. 11** to values given in specifications at beginning of chapter.
11. Adjust valves. Refer to "Valves, Adjust" for procedure.
12. Install rocker arm cover.

## VALVES
### ADJUST

1. Rotate crankshaft until cylinder No. 1 is at T.D.C.
2. Remove rocker arm cover. Refer to "Rocker Arm Cover, Replace."
3. Ensure rocker arm bracket bolts are torqued to specifications.
4. Adjust cylinder No. 1 intake and ex-

haust, cylinder No. 2 intake and cylinder No. 3 exhaust to specifications.
5. Rotate crankshaft one revolution and adjust remaining valves to specifications.
6. Install rocker arm cover.

## VALVE CLEARANCE SPECIFICATIONS

Cold valve clearances should measure .016 inch at both intake and exhaust valves.

## VALVE TIMING

Intake valves open at 16° before TDC.

## VALVE GUIDE
### REPLACE

1. Using tool J-26512, drive out valve guide from lower face of cylinder head, **Fig. 13.**
2. Apply engine oil to outer circumference of valve guide. Using tool J-26512, drive guide into position from upper face of cylinder head, **Fig. 14. Always replace valve guides and valve as a set.**

## CRANKSHAFT PULLEY
### REPLACE

1. Disconnect battery ground cable.

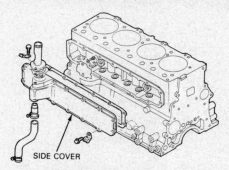

**Fig. 26   Side cover removal**

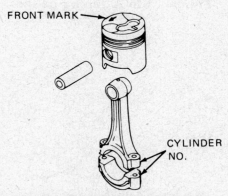

**Fig. 29   Piston & connecting rod assembly**

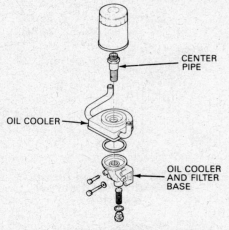

**Fig. 27   Oil cooler assembly**

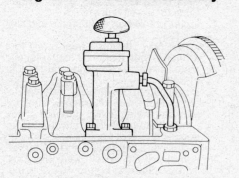

**Fig. 30   Oil pump assembly**

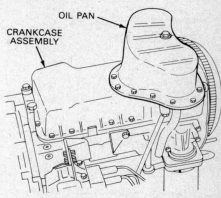

**Fig. 28   Oil pan & crankcase assembly**

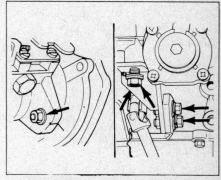

**Fig. 31   Injection pump bracket bolts**

2. Loosen accessory drive belts.
3. Remove crankshaft pulley retaining bolts, then the pulley.
4. Reverse procedure to install.

# TIMING PULLEY HOUSING COVER
## REPLACE
### UPPER

1. Disconnect battery ground cable.
2. If equipped with power steering, remove P/S pump reservoir.
3. Remove upper fan shroud and cooling fan.
4. Loosen accessory drive belts, then remove fan drive pulley.
5. Remove timing pulley housing upper cover, **Fig. 15,** view A.
6. Reverse procedure to install.

### LOWER

1. Remove timing pulley housing upper cover as described above.
2. Remove alternator belt.
3. Align crankshaft pulley TDC mark with pointer, **Fig. 16,** then remove crankshaft pulley. Refer to "Crankshaft Pulley, Replace."
4. Remove timing pulley housing lower cover, **Fig. 15,** view B.
5. Reverse procedure to install.

# TIMING BELT
## REPLACE

1. Disconnect battery ground cable.
2. Remove timing pulley housing covers.

Refer to "Timing Pulley Housing Cover, Replace" for procedure.
3. Remove injection pump timing pulley flange retaining bolts.
4. Remove tension spring, **Fig. 17. When removing tension spring, use care to avoid distorting spring.**
5. Remove tension pulley nut, **Fig. 18,** then the pulley and tension center.
6. Remove timing belt. **Avoid twisting or kinking belt. Keep the belt free of water, oil, dust and other foreign material.**
7. Ensure crankshaft pulley TDC mark is still aligned with timing pointer, **Fig. 16.**
8. Rotate injection pump timing pulley and camshaft timing pulley as necessary to bring them into alignment, **Fig. 19.**
9. Install timing belt over crankshaft timing pulley, then the camshaft timing pulley and the injection timing pulley.
10. Install tension center and tension pulley. Ensure tension center end is in proper contact with two pins on timing pulley housing, **Fig. 20.**
11. Loosely install tension pulley nut, then install tension pulley spring.
12. Semi-tighten tension pulley nut.
13. Rotate crankshaft two complete revolutions in normal direction of rotation to seat timing belt, then rotate an additional 90° beyond TDC to settle injection pump, **Fig. 21. Do not attempt to rotate crankshaft in opposite direction of normal crankshaft rotation.**

14. Loosen tension pulley nut, allowing the tension pulley assembly to take up belt slack. Torque tension pulley nut to 78–95 ft. lbs.
15. Install injection pump pulley flange. The hole in the flange outer circumference should be aligned with injection pump timing mark.
16. Again rotate engine in normal direction of rotation and bring cylinder No. 1 to TDC on compression stroke. Check injection pump and camshaft pulley alignment marks to ensure proper installation, **Fig. 22.**
17. Check timing belt tension between crankshaft and injection pump pulley with tool J-29771, **Fig. 23.** Tension should be 213–356 psi.
18. Install upper and lower timing pulley housing covers.
19. Install crankshaft pulley and drive belts.

# TIMING PULLEY HOUSING
## REPLACE
### REMOVAL

1. Disconnect battery ground cable.
2. Drain radiator coolant, then remove radiator hoses and radiator.
3. Remove timing pulley housing covers. Refer to "Timing Pulley Housing Cover, Replace" for procedure.
4. Remove timing belt. Refer to "Timing

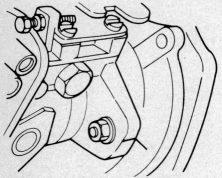

**Fig. 32 Injection pump alignment**

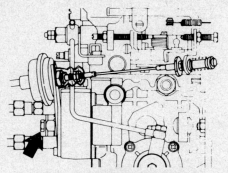

**Fig. 33 Injection pump distributor head screw location**

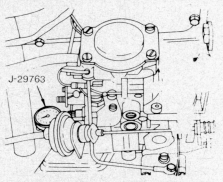

**Fig. 34 Static timing gauge installed**

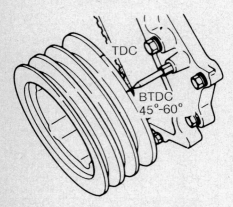

**Fig. 35 Crankshaft pulley alignment**

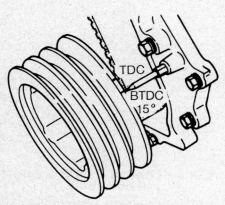

**Fig. 36 Crankshaft pulley at 15° BTDC**

Belt, Replace" for procedure.
5. Install a 6 mm bolt through injection pump pulley hole into threaded hole in timing pulley housing to prevent pulley from turning, then remove injection pump pulley nut.
6. Remove injection pump pulley using puller J-22888-D, **Fig. 24.**
7. Remove camshaft pulley retaining bolt.
8. Remove camshaft pulley and center assembly using puller J-22888-D, **Fig. 25.**
9. Remove camshaft center assembly oil seal.
10. Remove crankshaft hub bolt, then crankshaft pulley hub and pulley using puller J-24420-A. If crankshaft front seal requires replacement, it may be replaced at this time.
11. Disconnect fuel shut-off solenoid and vacuum line.
12. Remove injection lines.
13. Disconnect fuel and return lines.
14. Disconnect throttle return spring, then remove injection pump bracket to injection pump mounting bolts.
15. Remove timing pulley housing bolts, then remove housing and injection pump as an assembly.

## INSTALLATION

1. Clean timing pulley housing and engine block mounting surfaces, then install new gasket.
2. Position timing pulley housing on engine block and install bolts. Torque bolts to 10-17 ft. lbs.
3. Install crankshaft front seal using tool J-24250.
4. Install new camshaft seal using tool J-24254, then install oil seal retainer.
5. Install injection pump mounting bracket bolts.
6. Install all removed wires and hoses.
7. Using tool J-26587, or equivalent, install crankshaft pulley hub and pulley, then install hub bolt and torque to specifications at beginning of chapter.
8. Install camshaft pulley and center assembly, then install retaining bolt. Torque retaining bolt to 42-52 ft. lbs.
9. Remove injection pump pulley locking bolt.
10. Install timing belt.
11. Install timing pulley cover.
12. Install crankshaft pulley.
13. Install radiator and hoses.
14. Refill cooling system and connect battery ground cable.

## ENGINE SIDE COVER
### REPLACE

1. Disconnect battery ground cable.
2. Remove injection pump lines and cap all open lines to prevent entry of dirt.
3. Disconnect crankcase breather hoses.
4. Disconnect dipstick tube bracket from dipstick, then remove dipstick.
5. Disconnect bus bar input lead.
6. Remove oil filter.
7. Remove side cover bolts, then the side cover, **Fig. 26.**
8. Reverse procedure to install.

## REAR MAIN OIL SEAL
### REPLACE

1. Remove transmission.
2. Remove clutch assembly and flywheel.
3. Remove rear main bearing oil seal using a suitable screwdriver.
4. Apply clean engine oil to lipped portion and fitting face of new seal.
5. Using tool J-29818, or equivalent, install new seal.
6. Install flywheel and clutch assembly.
7. Install transmission.

## OIL COOLER
### REPLACE

1. Disconnect battery ground cable.
2. Disconnect cooler hoses, **Fig. 27.**
3. Remove oil filter and center pipe.
4. Remove oil cooler. If oil cooler and filter base are to be removed, raise and support vehicle to gain access to retaining bolts.
5. Reverse procedure to install.

## CAMSHAFT
### REPLACE

1. Remove engine assembly. Refer to "Engine, Replace" for procedure.
2. Remove rocker arm cover. Refer to "Rocker Arm Cover, Replace" for procedure.
3. Remove rocker arm shaft. Refer to "Rocker Arms, Replace" for procedure.
4. Remove timing belt. Refer to "Timing Belt, Replace" for procedure.
5. Remove camshaft gear and hub, then the oil seal retainer.
6. Remove oil pan and oil pump. Refer to "Crankcase & Oil Pump, Replace" for procedure.
7. Carefully withdraw camshaft from engine block to avoid damaging camshaft bearings.
8. Remove valve lifters.
9. Reverse procedure to install.

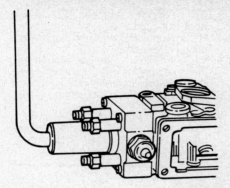

**Fig. 37    High pressure plug removal**

## OIL PAN
### REPLACE

1. Disconnect battery ground cable.
2. Raise and support vehicle.
3. Drain crankcase, then remove oil pan bolts and oil pan, **Fig. 28.**
4. Reverse procedure to install. Torque oil pan mounting bolts to 2-4 ft. lbs.

## VALVE LIFTERS
### REPLACE

To replace valve lifters, the camshaft must be removed. Refer to "Camshaft, Replace."

## PISTON & ROD ASSEMBLY

Assemble piston to rod so combustion chamber on piston head is positioned on side of connecting rod with cylinder No. stamp, **Fig. 29.**

Install piston and rod assembly in cylinder with arrow on piston head facing front of engine.

## CRANKCASE & OIL PUMP
### REPLACE

1. Remove engine. Refer to "Engine, Replace."
2. Disconnect crankcase end of PCV hose.
3. Remove dipstick tube, then the oil pan, **Fig. 28.**
4. Remove crankcase retaining bolts, then the crankcase.
5. Remove oil pump sleeve nut, retaining bolts and pump, **Fig. 30.**
6. Reverse procedure to install.

## INJECTION PUMP
### REPLACE

1. Disconnect battery ground cable.
2. Remove timing belt. Refer to "Timing Belt, Replace."
3. Remove injection pump pulley using

tool J-22888-D, **Fig. 24.**
4. Remove fuel input and return lines.
5. Remove injection pump electrical wiring, then the throttle cable.
6. Remove injection lines, then the throttle return spring.
7. Raise and support vehicle.
8. Remove injection pump bracket bolts, **Fig. 31,** then lower vehicle. If injection pump bracket is removed, injection timing must be reset. Refer to "Injection Pump Timing" for procedure.
9. Remove injection pump.
10. Reverse procedure to install.

## INJECTION PUMP TIMING

1. Ensure notched line on injection pump flange is aligned with notched line on injection pump front bracket, **Fig. 32.**
2. Rotate crankshaft in normal direction of rotation until cylinder No. 1 is at TDC compression stroke, **Fig. 16.**
3. Remove upper radiator fan shroud.
4. Remove timing pulley housing upper cover. Refer to "Timing Pulley Housing Cover, Replace" for procedure.
5. Check timing belt for proper tension, then check timing mark alignment, **Fig. 19. If timing marks are not properly aligned, timing belt must be removed and reinstalled properly.**
6. Remove injection pump lines, then the distributor head screw and washer, **Fig. 33.**
7. Install static timing gauge J-29763 in distributor head screw threaded hole. Set gauge lift approximately .004 inch from the plunger, **Fig. 34.**
8. Rotate crankshaft to bring cylinder No. 1 to a point 45-60° BTDC, **Fig. 35.** Calibrate dial on gauge to zero. Rotate crankshaft slightly in either direction to ensure gauge needle is stable.
9. Rotate crankshaft in normal direction of rotation until timing pointer is aligned with 13° BTDC mark for California models or 15° BTDC for non-California models, **Fig. 36,** then observe dial indicator.
10. If indicator reading is not .020 inch, maintain crankshaft position, loosen injection pump flange nuts and rotate pump, as needed, until indicator reading is .020 inch.
11. Tighten pump flange nuts, recheck indicator reading and readjust as needed.
12. Remove dial gauge, reinstall distributor head and screw, and reinstall remaining components in reverse order of removal.

## INJECTION NOZZLE
### REPLACE

1. Disconnect battery ground cable.
2. Remove fuel return pipe at injection nozzle.
3. Disconnect injection line at injection nozzle.
4. Remove nozzle.

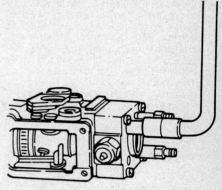

**Fig. 38    Delivery valve removal**

5. Reverse procedure to install.

## INJECTION PUMP IN-VEHICLE SERVICE
### FUEL INLET & RETURN PIPE GASKETS, REPLACE

1. Disconnect battery ground cable.
2. On models equipped with A/C, remove A/C compressor drive belt, then unfasten compressor and position aside.
3. On all models, if removing fuel inlet hose, disconnect hose, then remove fuel inlet pipe and gaskets. If removing fuel return hose, disconnect hose, then remove fuel return pipe and gaskets.
4. Replace gaskets, then reverse procedure to install.

### TACHOMETER PLUG O-RING, REPLACE

1. Disconnect battery ground cable.
2. On models equipped with A/C, remove A/C compressor drive belt, then unfasten compressor and position aside.
3. On all models, remove "Tach" plug and replace O-ring.
4. Reverse procedure to install. Torque "Tach" plug to 8 ft. lbs.

### HIGH PRESSURE PLUG O-RING, REPLACE

1. Disconnect battery ground cable.
2. On models equipped with A/C, remove A/C compressor drive belt, then unfasten compressor and position aside.
3. On all models, remove fuel injection lines as an assembly.
4. Remove high pressure plug using tool J-33309, **Fig. 37.** Remove O-ring.
5. Reverse procedure to install. Torque high pressure plug to 50 ft. lbs.

### DELIVERY VALVE HOLDER GASKET, REPLACE

1. Disconnect battery ground cable.
2. If equipped with air conditioning, remove A/C belt, then compressor and position aside.
3. Remove fuel injection lines as an assembly.

4. Using a suitable 14 mm wrench, remove delivery valve holder(s), **Fig. 38.**
5. Remove delivery valve and seat assembly. The delivery valve and seat assembly are match ground and should not be interchanged with other delivery valve and seat assemblies. **The letters A, B, C, & D are engraved on each cylinder of the distributor head. Remove each delivery valve in proper sequence to ensure correct assembly.**
6. Remove delivery valve gasket.

7. Reverse procedure to install. Torque delivery valve holder(s) to 28 ft. lbs.

## MAXIMUM FUEL ADJUSTMENT SCREW/LOAD SCREW O-RING, REPLACE

1. Disconnect battery ground cable.
2. On models equipped with A/C, remove A/C compressor drive belt, then unfasten compressor and position aside.

3. On all models, remove fuel return hose and pipe.
4. Remove staking wire, then disconnect accelerator cable.
5. Install an M8 x 1 jam nut against adjusting screw locknut. Tighten the two nuts together to preserve adjustment.
6. Remove full load adjusting screw, then O-ring.
7. Install new O-ring.
8. Reverse procedure to install. Torque full load adjusting screw locknut to 6 ft. lbs. and remove jam nut.

# CLUTCH & MANUAL TRANSMISSION

## INDEX

# CLUTCH
## ADJUST
### 1982-83

1. Clutch is adjusted by lifting clutch pedal up to allow mechanism to adjust cable. Depress pedal several times to set pawl into mesh with detent teeth.
2. Check clutch linkage for lost motion caused by loose or worn swivels, deflection of mounting brackets or damaged cordon shaft.

### 1984-89

These models are equipped with a hydraulic clutch. No adjustment of the clutch pedal or linkage is provided.

# CLUTCH
## REPLACE

On 1985-89 models, the hydraulic clutch system uses a constant running throw-out bearing which rides against the diaphragm fingers on the pressure plate. After a period of time, the ball stud in which the fork pivots will become dry from lack of lubrication and cause noisy operation.

To repair this condition it will be necessary to replace the clutch plate, (part No. 15608692), ball stud (part No. 14036046), clutch fork (part No. 1407374) and disc (part No. 15608690 on 4-151 engine, or 15608691 on V6-173 engine.

1. On 1984-89 models, remove slave cylinder mounting bolts and position cylinder aside. On 1982-83 models, disconnect clutch fork cable.
2. On all models, remove transmission assembly as outlined under "Transmission, Replace."
3. On 82-85, remove left body mounting bolts, loosen radiator support bolt and

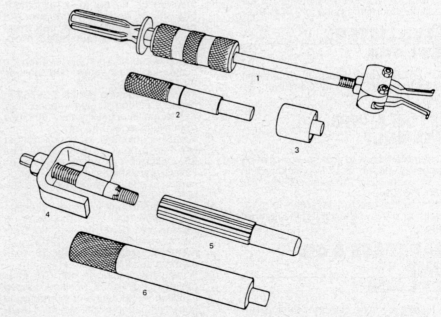

| | | | | | | |
|---|---|---|---|---|---|---|
| 1. J-2307 | BEARING PULLER | (2.2L – 1.9L) | 4. J-1448 | PILOT BEARING REMOVER | (2.5L – 2.8L) |
| 2. J-33034 | CLUTCH DISC ALIGNER | (2.2L – 1.9L) | 5. J-33169 | CLUTCH DISC ALIGNER | (2.5L – 2.8L) |
| 3. J-26516-A | PILOT BEARING INSTALLER | (2.2L – 1.9L) | 6. J-1522 | PILOT BEARING INSTALLER | (2.5L – 2.8L) |

**Fig. 1  Clutch assembly support tool**

raise the cab to gain access to upper bellhousing mounting bolts. After cab is raised, a suitable block of wood should be installed between frame and cab for support.
4. On all models remove bellhousing.
5. Slide clutch fork from ball stud and remove fork from dust boot.
6. On 83-85 models install tool J-33169 or tool J-33034 to support clutch assembly. On 86-87 models use tool J-33034 or J-1448 and 88-89 models

use tool J-33034 or J-23907, **Fig. 1.** Look for "X" mark on flywheel and on clutch cover or white painted letter on clutch cover. If marks are not evident, mark flywheel and clutch cover for proper alignment during assembly.
6. Loosen clutch-to-flywheel attaching bolts evenly, **Fig. 2,** one turn at a time, until spring pressure is released. Then remove bolts, clutch and pressure plate assembly.
7. Clean pressure plate and flywheel

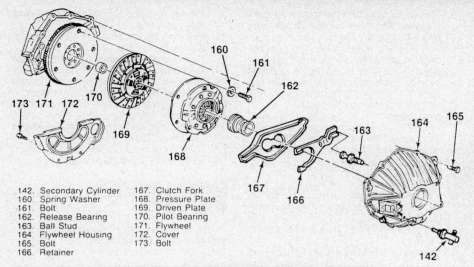

.142. Secondary Cylinder
160. Spring Washer
161. Bolt
162. Release Bearing
163. Ball Stud
164. Flywheel Housing
165. Bolt
166. Retainer
167. Clutch Fork
168. Pressure Plate
169. Driven Plate
170. Pilot Bearing
171. Flywheel
172. Cover
173. Bolt

**Fig. 2   Clutch-to-flywheel attaching bolts**

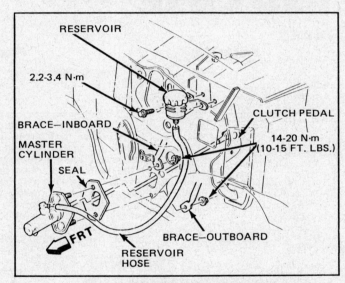

**Fig. 3   Clutch master cylinder**

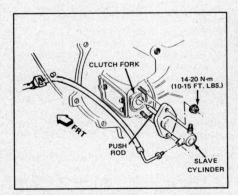

**Fig. 4   Clutch slave cylinder**

mating surfaces and inspect flywheel for defects. Replace or repair as needed.
8. Reverse procedure to install.

## CLUTCH MASTER CYLINDER
### REPLACE
#### 1984–89
**Removal**

1. Disconnect battery ground cable.
2. Remove sound absorbing panel from upper left side foot well.
3. On 89 models, remove lower left side air conditioning duct if needed.
4. Disconnect master cylinder pushrod from clutch pedal.
5. Remove master cylinder retaining nuts, **Fig. 3.**
6. Disconnect reservoir hose and slave cylinder hydraulic line from master cylinder.
7. Remove clutch master cylinder.

**Installation**

1. Position master cylinder at front of

dash, then install retaining nuts and torque to 10-15 ft. lbs., **Fig. 3.**
2. Connect master cylinder pushrod to clutch pedal and install retaining clip.
3. Install sound absorbing panel.
4. Install lower left air conditioning duct if removed.
5. Connect reservoir hose and slave cylinder hydraulic line to master cylinder.
6. Connect battery ground cable.
7. Bleed system.

## CLUTCH SLAVE CYLINDER
### REPLACE
#### 1984–89
**Removal**

1. Raise and support vehicle.
2. Disconnect hydraulic line from slave cylinder, **Fig. 4.**
3. Remove slave cylinder retaining nuts, then the slave cylinder.

**Installation**

1. Connect hydraulic line to slave cylinder, **Fig. 4.**
2. Bleed system.
3. Position slave cylinder on bellhousing, then install retaining nuts and torque to 10-15 ft. lbs.

## CLUTCH SYSTEM
### BLEED
#### 1984–89

When refilling or bleeding system, use only new brake fluid conforming to DOT 3 specifications.
1. Raise and support vehicle.
2. Remove slave cylinder retaining nuts, then the slave cylinder.
3. While holding slave cylinder at approximately 45° with bleeder at highest point, have an assistant depress clutch pedal while opening bleeder valve.
4. With clutch pedal held at end of stroke, close bleeder valve and release clutch pedal.
5. Repeat steps 3 and 4 until all air has been expelled from system. **While bleeding clutch system, constantly check master cylinder reservoir fluid level and replenish as necessary to prevent master cylinder running out of fluid.**

## TRANSMISSION
### REPLACE
#### 1983–86 4 SPEED (77 mm) & 5 SPEED

On 4 x 4 models, prior to removing transmission, transfer case must be removed. Refer to Transfer Case Section for procedures.
1. Disconnect battery ground cable.
2. Remove upper starter motor retaining nut.
3. Remove attaching screws and slide shift lever boot up shift lever.

4. Remove shift lever attaching bolts at transmission.
5. Disconnect electrical connection and clip at transmission shift tower.
6. Raise and support vehicle.
7. Remove propeller shaft.
8. Disconnect exhaust pipe at manifold.
9. Disconnect speedometer cable and electrical connector, if equipped, at transmission.
10. Disconnect clutch cable or hydraulic clutch slave cylinder from transmission.
11. With transmission supported, remove transmission mount attaching bolts.
12. Remove catalytic converter hanger.
13. Remove crossmember attaching bolts and crossmember.
14. Remove lower dust cover bolts.
15. Remove lower starter motor attaching bolt.
16. Remove transmission-to-engine

mounting bolts and the transmission. It may be necessary to remove left body mounting bolts, loosen radiator support bolt and raise the cab to gain access to upper transmission mounting bolts. After cab is raised, a suitable block of wood should be installed between frame and cab for support.
17. Reverse procedure to install.

## 1987-89

1. Disconnect battery ground cable.
2. Shift transmission into neutral and remove shift lever boot.
3. Remove transmission shift lever.
4. Raise and support vehicle.
5. Disconnect parking brake cable for removal clearance, then remove propeller shaft.
6. Remove skid plate and transfer case if used.
7. Disconnect vehicle speed sensor and

electrical wiring harnesses as needed.
8. Remove exhaust pipes.
9. Remove slave cylinder from transmission.
10. Remove transmission mount retaining bolts and support transmission.
11. Remove catalytic converter hanger and any support braces if needed.
12. Remove transmission crossmember.
13. Remove transmission-to-bellhousing retaining bolts and support the clutch release bearing.
14. Remove transmission.
15. Reverse procedure to install.

## SHIFT LINKAGE
### ADJUST

The shift mechanism does not require adjustment and may be serviced independently of the transmission.

# TRANSFER CASE

## INDEX

## SHIFT LEVER
### REPLACE
#### REMOVAL

1. Disconnect battery ground cable.
2. Remove console, then the shift boot.
3. Loosen shift lever jam nut, then unscrew shift lever.
4. Remove transfer case selector switch.
5. Raise and support vehicle.
6. Disconnect shift rod at shifter assembly, then remove pivot and adjusting bolt, **Fig. 1.**
7. Remove shifter.

#### INSTALLATION

1. Position shifter at bracket, then install pivot and adjusting bolt, **Fig. 1.**
2. Connect shift rod, then adjust shift linkage.
3. Lower vehicle.
4. Install shift lever on shifter, then screw lever down until pawl just clears bracket, then tighten shift lever an additional 1 1/2 turns and tighten jam nut.
5. Install selector switch, shift boot and console.
6. Install battery ground cable.

## SHIFT LINKAGE
### ADJUST

1. Remove console, then pull shift boot up shift lever.
2. Loosen small bolt and washer (A) and pivot bolt (B), **Fig. 2.**
3. Position transfer case shift lever at 4 Hi position.
4. Install a 8 mm gage pin or 5/16 inch drill bit through shifter into bracket (C),

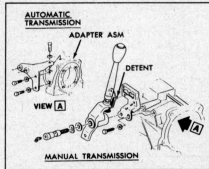

**Fig. 1   Shifter & shift lever mounting**

**Fig. 2.**
5. Install a suitable bolt at the transfer case lever to lock transfer case in 4 Hi, **Fig. 3.**
6. Torque small bolt and washer (A) to 25-35 ft. lbs., then pivot bolt (B) to 88-103 ft. lbs., **Fig. 2.**
7. Remove bolt installed at transfer case lever, then gage pin or drill bit from shifter and bracket.
8. Place shift boot in proper position, then install console.

## SELECTOR SWITCH
### REPLACE

1. Disconnect battery ground cable.
2. Remove console, then disconnect console wiring harness.
3. Remove shifter boot retaining screws and slide boot up shift lever.
4. Remove switch attaching screw, then

the switch and harness, **Fig. 2.**
5. Position new switch on mounting bracket and install attaching screw. **Ensure shift lever assembly pawl is on the switch contact carrier.**
6. Route wiring as shown in **Fig. 4.**
7. Place shifter boot in proper position, then install retaining screws.
8. Connect console wiring harness, then install console.
9. Connect battery ground cable.

## TRANSFER CASE
### REPLACE
#### REMOVAL

1. Position transfer case shift lever at 4 Hi.
2. Disconnect battery ground cable.
3. Raise and support vehicle.
4. Remove skid plate, if equipped and drain transfer case.
5. Remove front and rear propeller shafts.
6. Remove speedometer cable and shift linkage at transfer case.
7. Remove catalytic converter front bracket bolts and loosen front converter clamp.
8. Remove rear transmission mounting bolts.
9. Support transmission with a suitable jack then raise transmission and transfer case.
10. Remove catalytic converter front bracket.
11. Lower transmission and transfer case.
12. Support transfer case with a suitable jack.
13. Remove transmission-to-transfer case retaining bolts. On models

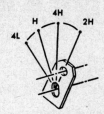

Fig. 3 **Transfer case shift lever positioning**

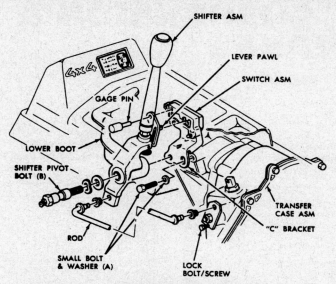

Fig. 2 **Transfer case shift linkage**

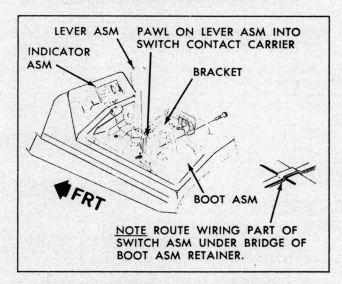

Fig. 4 **Selector switch installation**

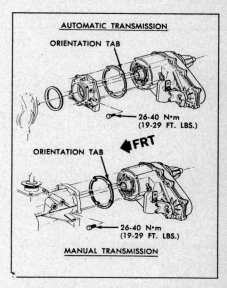

Fig. 5 **Transfer case installation**

hanger bolts and front clamp.
7. Install shift lever to transfer case, then connect speedometer cable.
8. Install front and rear driveshafts.
9. Install skid plate.
10. Fill transfer case with suitable lubricant and lower vehicle.
11. Connect battery ground cable.

# TRANSFER CASE ADAPTER REPLACE

1. Remove transfer case, as outlined in "Transfer Case. Replace."
2. Remove transfer case adapter-to-transfer case retaining bolts.
3. Remove transfer case adapter-to-transfer case gasket.
4. Reverse procedure to install.

equipped with automatic transmission, remove shift lever bracket mounting bolts, **Fig. 1**, to gain access to upper left side transfer case mounting bolt.
14. Separate transfer case from transmission then remove gasket.

## INSTALLATION

1. Position new gasket on transfer case as shown in **Fig. 5**.
2. Position transfer case near end of transmission, then align transfer case input shaft splines with transmission splines and slide transfer case forward until seated against transmission.
3. Install transfer case attaching bolts. Torque bolts to 19-29 ft. lbs. On models equipped with automatic transmission, install shift lever bracket mounting bracket bolts.
4. Raise transmission and transfer case assembly with a suitable jack, then install mount and catalytic converter hanger bracket. Lower transmission and transfer case assembly.
5. Install transmission rear mounting bolts and torque to 23 ft. lbs.
6. Install and tighten catalytic converter

# REAR AXLE, SUSPENSION & BRAKES

## INDEX

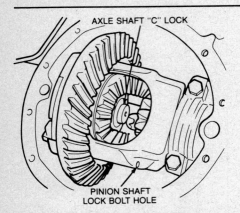

**Fig. 1 Removing differential pinion shaft**

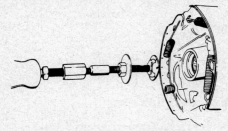

**Fig. 2 Axle shaft bearing removal**

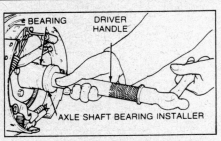

**Fig. 3 Axle shaft bearing installation**

## AXLE SHAFT
### REPLACE

1. Raise and support rear of vehicle, then remove wheel and brake drum on side axle is to be replaced.
2. Loosen carrier cover bolts and allow lubricant to drain, then remove bolts and carrier cover.
3. Remove rear axle pinion shaft lock screw, then the pinion shaft, **Fig. 1.** Discard the lock screw.
4. Push flanged end of axle shaft toward center of vehicle, then remove "C" lock from button end of shaft.
5. Withdraw axle shaft from housing using caution not to damage seal.
6. Reverse procedure to install, noting the following: torque new pinion shaft lock screw to 20 ft. lbs. on 1982 models or 25 ft. lbs. on 1983-89 models. Torque carrier cover bolts to 20 ft. lbs. on all models.

## WHEEL BEARING & AXLE SEAL
### REPLACE

1. Remove axle shaft as described under "Axle Shaft, Replace."
2. Remove axle seal by prying behind seal steel case with a suitable pry bar. Use caution to avoid damaging axle housing.
3. Using a suitable puller and slide hammer, remove axle bearing, **Fig. 2.**

4. Lubricate new bearing with gear lubricant, then install bearing in axle housing with tool J-23765, or equivalent, until bearing is seated in housing, **Fig. 3.**
5. Lubricate seal lips with gear lubricant, then position seal on tool J-23771 or equivalent, and install in axle housing, tapping into place until seal is flush with axle housing, **Fig. 4.**
6. Reinstall axle shaft.

## AXLE ASSEMBLY
### REPLACE

Construction of the axle assembly is such that service operations may be performed with the housing installed in the vehicle or with the housing removed and installed in a holding fixture. The following procedure is necessary only when the housing requires replacement.

1. Raise vehicle and place jack stands under frame side rails. Position a suitable jack under the rear axle housing and raise slightly to support axle assembly.
2. Remove rear wheels and drums then disconnect shock absorbers from anchor plates.
3. Scribe reference marks between drive shaft and pinion flange for use during reassembly, then disconnect drive shaft and position aside.
4. Disconnect brake lines from junction block and backing plates, then remove junction block attaching bolt and position aside.
5. Remove backing plates.
6. Remove U-bolts and anchor plates, **Fig. 5.**
7. On 1988-89 models disconnect vent hose from axle housing.
8. Lower rear axle assembly, then remove lower spring shackle bolts.

9. Remove rear axle assembly.
10. Reverse procedure to install. Torque shock absorber nut to 50 ft. lbs., U-bolt nuts to 85 ft. lbs. and lower spring shackle bolts to 88 ft. lbs.

## SHOCK ABSORBER
### REPLACE

1. Raise vehicle and place jack stands under frame side rails. Position a suitable jack under the rear axle housing and raise slightly to support axle assembly.
2. Disconnect shock absorber from upper mounting location, **Fig. 6.**
3. Disconnect shock absorber attaching nut from spring anchor plate.
4. Remove shock absorber.
5. Reverse procedure to install. Torque upper mount to 15 ft. lbs. and lower mount nut to 50 ft. lbs.

## LEAF SPRING ASSEMBLY SERVICE
### REMOVAL

1. Raise vehicle and place jack stands under frame side rails to relieve spring load. Support axle assembly.
2. On 1988-89 models remove shock absorber.
3. Loosen, but do not remove, spring to shackle attaching nut, **Fig. 5.**
4. Remove U-bolt attaching nuts, then the U-bolts.
5. Remove shackle to frame attaching nut and bolt. **After removal of shackle to frame attaching nut and bolt, spring is free to rotate on front hanger bolt. Use suitable restraining device to prevent rotation.**
6. Remove front spring hanger nut and

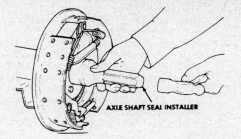

**Fig. 4  Axle shaft seal installation**

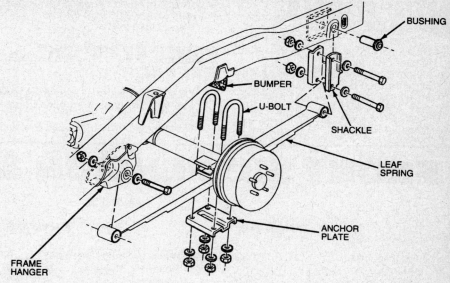

**Fig. 5  Rear suspension (left side)**

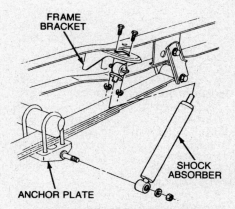

**Fig. 6  Shock absorber mounting**

bolt, then the spring.

## BUSHING, REPLACE

1. Remove spring assembly.
2. Place spring in suitable press and press out bushing.

## INSTALLATION

1. Clean axle spring pad and apply a rubber lubricant to the bushing and the spring eye.
2. Using a suitable press install bushing to spring assembly.
3. Install spring assembly to vehicle.

## DRUM BRAKE ADJUSTMENTS

These brakes have self adjusting shoe mechanisms that ensure correct lining-to-drum clearances at all times. The automatic adjusters operate only when brakes are applied as vehicle is moving rearward.

Although the brakes are self-adjusting, an initial adjustment is necessary after brake shoes have been relined or replaced, or when length of star wheel adjuster has been changed during some other service operation.

Frequent usage of an automatic transmission forward range to halt reverse vehicle motion may prevent automatic adjusters from functioning, thereby inducing low pedal heights. Should low pedal heights be encountered, it is recommended that nu-

merous forward and reverse stops be made until satisfactory pedal height is obtained.

If a low pedal height condition cannot be corrected by making numerous reverse stops (provided hydraulic system is free of air), the self-adjusting mechanism is not functioning. Therefore it will be necessary to remove brake drum, clean, free up and lubricate adjusting mechanism. Then adjust brakes as follows, being sure parking brake is fully released.

Upon initial adjustment, a lanced area in the brake backing plate must be removed prior to adjusting brakes. To remove lanced area, knock out with a suitable hammer and punch, then remove brake drum to clear any metal particles caught inside the brake compartment. Install brake drum and proceed with adjustment. After adjustment is complete, install brake adjustment hole cover to prevent entry of water and dirt.

1. Turn brake adjusting screw to expand shoes until wheel can just be turned by hand.
2. Using a suitable tool to hold actuator lever off adjuster, back adjuster off 30 notches on 1982-84 models or 24 notches on 1985-89 models. If shoes still drag, back off one or two additional notches. **Brakes should be free of drag when adjuster has been backed off approximately 12 notches. Heavy drag at this point indicates tight parking brake cables.**
3. Install adjusting hole cover on brake drum or backing plate.
4. Check parking brake adjustment.

## PARKING BRAKE
### ADJUST
### 1982-84

1. Depress parking brake pedal 10 clicks

on all models except 4 x 2 Pickup. On 4 x 2 Pickup, depress parking brake pedal 8 clicks.
2. Raise and support vehicle.
3. Place a cable tension gauge on right hand side cable on all except 4 x 2 Pickup. On 4 x 2 Pickup, place tension gauge on left hand side cable. On all models, place tension gauge as close as possible to cable equalizer.
4. Tighten or loosen adjusting nut as necessary to provide 140-150 lbs. of tension on all except 4 x 2 Pickup. On 4 x 2 Pickup, adjust nut to provide 200-220 lbs. of tension. **Do not over adjust parking brake.**
5. Remove tension gauge and lower vehicle.

### 1985-89

1. Block front wheels, ensure brake pedal is fully released, then raise and support rear of vehicle.
2. Loosen adjusting nut at rear cable equalizer until rear wheels spin freely and ensure cables do not bind or stick over operating range. **On Pickup models with intermediate cable bracket, remove bracket before performing any parking brake adjustments.**
3. Depress parking brake pedal 2 clicks on 2 wheel drive models or 3 clicks on 4 wheel drive models.
4. Tighten equalizer adjusting nut until rear wheels will not rotate forward without applying excessive force.
5. Loosen adjusting nut until moderate drag is felt when rotating wheels forward, ensuring drag at each wheel is approximately equal.
6. Reinstall cable guide, if removed, release parking brake pedal, and ensure little or no brake drag is felt when rotating rear wheels.

# CHEVROLET S/T 10 & GMC S/T 15

## MASTER CYLINDER
### REPLACE

1. Disconnect hydraulic brake lines from master cylinder.
2. Remove two master cylinder attaching nuts, then the master cylinder.
3. Install master cylinder and attaching nuts. Torque nuts to 22-33 ft. lbs. on 1982-85 models, or 20 ft. lbs. on 1986-89 models.

4. Attach hydraulic brake lines. Torque nuts to 120-180 inch lbs.
5. Bleed brake system.

## POWER BRAKE UNIT
### REPLACE

1. Disconnect master cylinder assembly and vacuum hose from power brake unit.
2. Disconnect power brake unit pushrod from brake pedal.
3. Remove power brake unit attaching nuts from inside of vehicle.
4. Remove power brake unit.
5. Reverse procedure to install. On 1982-85 models, torque power brake unit attaching nuts and master cylinder attaching nuts to 22-33 ft. lbs. On 1986-89 models, torque power brake unit attaching nuts to 15 ft. lbs. and master cylinder attaching nuts to 20 ft. lbs.

# FRONT SUSPENSION & STEERING

## INDEX

## WHEEL ALIGNMENT

Before checking or adjusting caster and camber angles, jounce vehicle at least 3 times to prevent false geometric readings.

### 4 X 2 MODELS

Caster and camber adjustments are made by shims inserted between upper control arm shaft and frame bracket, **Fig. 1.** Add, subtract, or transfer shims to change readings as noted below.

To adjust caster and/or camber, loosen upper control arm shaft to frame nuts, then add or subtract shims as necessary and torque upper control arm shaft to frame nuts to 45 ft. lbs. After adjustment, the shim pack should have at least two threads of bolt exposed beyond the nut. The difference between front and rear shim packs must not exceed 0.40 inches.

### Caster, Adjust

Transfer shims from front to rear, or rear to front. The transfer of one shim from rear to front bolt will decrease positive caster.

### Camber, Adjust

Change shims at both front and rear of shaft. Adding an equal amount of shims at both front and rear locations will decrease positive camber.

### 4 X 4 MODELS

Caster and camber adjustments are made by cam mounted upper control arm attaching bolts.

To adjust caster and/or camber, loosen upper control arm to frame attaching bolt nut, then rotate cam by turning bolt head. When proper alignment settings are established, torque upper control arm to frame attaching bolt nut to 70 ft. lbs.

### Caster, Adjust

To increase positive caster, move front cam lobe inward and rear cam lobe outward.

### Camber, Adjust

To increase positive camber, move both front and rear cam lobes inward.

## TOE-IN
### ADJUST

To adjust, loosen clamp bolts at each end of steering tie rod adjustable sleeves. With steering wheel in straight ahead position, turn tie rod adjusting sleeves to obtain proper adjustment. After adjusting, check that number of threads showing on each end of sleeve are equal and that the tie rod end housings are at the right angles to steering arm. Position tie rod clamps and sleeves, **Figs. 2 and 3,** and torque nuts to 15 ft. lbs.

## WHEEL BEARINGS
### ADJUST
### 4 X 2 MODELS

1. Raise and support front of vehicle.
2. Remove hub dust cover, then the cotter pin.
3. While rotating wheel assembly in forward direction, torque spindle nut to 12 ft. lbs. to fully seat the bearings.
4. Loosen nut to the "just loose" position, then tighten the spindle nut finger tight.
5. If either spindle hole does not line up with a spindle nut slot, back off spindle nut not more than 1/2 nut flat.
6. Install new cotter pin, then measure hub endplay. End play should be .001-.005 inches when properly adjusted.
7. Install hub dust cover and lower vehicle.

### 4 X 4 MODELS

These vehicles use sealed front wheel bearings which require no lubrication or adjustment.

## COIL SPRING
### REPLACE
### 4 X 2 MODELS

1. Raise and support vehicle.

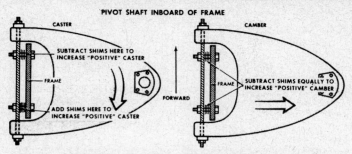

**Fig. 1   Caster & camber adjustment. 4 x 2 models**

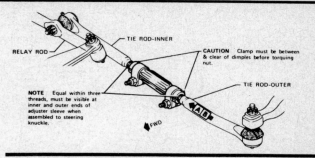

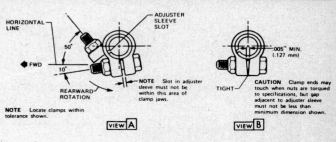

**Fig. 2   Tie rod clamp & sleeve positioning. 1982–85**

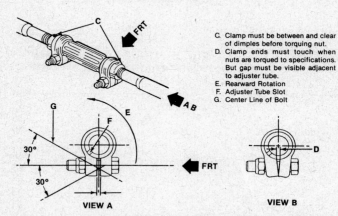

C. Clamp must be between and clear of dimples before torquing nut.
D. Clamp ends must touch when nuts are torqued to specifications. But gap must be visible adjacent to adjuster tube.
E. Rearward Rotation
F. Adjuster Tube Slot
G. Center Line of Bolt

**Fig. 3   Tie rod clamp & sleeve positioning. 1986–89**

2. Remove the two shock absorber screws and push shock up through control arm and into spring.
3. Support vehicle so that control arms hang free.
4. Place Tool J-23028, or equivalent, into position cradling the inner bushings, **Fig. 4.** Tool should be secured to a suitable jack.
5. Remove stabilizer to lower control arm attachment.
6. Raise the jack to remove tension on lower control arm pivot bolts, then install a chain around spring and through control arm and remove the nuts and bolts.
7. Lower control arm by slowly lowering jack.
8. With all pressure removed from spring, remove safety chain and spring. **Do not apply force to lower control arm and ball joint to remove spring. Proper maneuvering of spring will allow for easy removal.**
9. Reverse procedure to install, noting the following:
   a. Ensure coil spring is installed with flat coiled end with gripper notch on top and the lower coil covering all or part of one drain hole in lower control arm and with other hole exposed.
   b. Install both lower control arm bolts from front to rear to ensure adequate steering linkage clearance.
   c. Torque stabilizer link nuts to 13 ft. lbs., lower vehicle and torque lower

control arm bolt nuts to 65 ft. lbs. after suspension had been weighted.

## UPPER CONTROL ARM
### REPLACE
#### 4 X 2 MODELS

1. Raise vehicle and support the lower control arms with floor stands.
2. Remove wheel and tire assembly.
3. Disconnect upper ball joint from from steering knuckle and support the brake rotor to prevent damage to the brake hose.
4. Remove upper control arm attaching nuts and bolts, **Fig. 5.** noting location of any shims removed.
5. Remove upper control arm.
6. Reverse procedure to install, noting the following:
   a. Install shims in their original position.
   b. Torque control arm pivot nuts to 65 ft. lbs.

#### 4 X 4 MODELS

1. Raise vehicle and support at frame, raise lower control arm to relieve spring tension, placing jack as far outboard on lower control arm as possible.
2. Remove front wheel.
3. Remove and install control arm as shown in **Fig. 6**, supporting spindle to prevent damaging brake hoses.

## UPPER CONTROL ARM BUSHING
### REPLACE
#### 4 X 2 MODELS

1. Remove upper control arm as described in "Upper Control Replace".
2. Remove nuts from end of pivot shaft, then remove bushings, **Fig. 7.**
3. Install bushings by installing pivot shaft in control arm and pressing new bushings into control arm, **Fig. 8.** Torque pivot shaft nuts to 85 ft. lbs. on 1982-85 models, or 65 ft. lbs. on 1986-89 models with weight of vehicle resting on wheels. **Both bushings must be installed .48-.52 inch from face of control arm to bushing outer sleeve.**

#### 4 X 4 MODELS

1. Remove upper control arm as previously outlined in "Upper Control Arm Replace".
2. Refer to **Fig. 7-8**, for bushing removal and installation.

## LOWER CONTROL ARM
### REPLACE
#### 4 X 2 MODELS

1. Remove coil spring as described previously in "Coil Spring replace".
2. Remove lower ball joint stud, then remove lower control arm through opening in splash shield.
3. Reverse procedure to install.

#### 4 X 4 MODELS

Refer to **Fig. 9** for lower control arm replacement procedure on 4 x 4 vehicles.

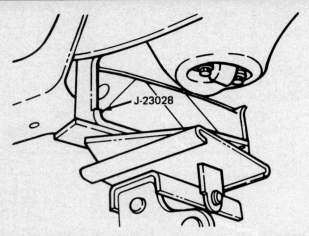

**Fig. 4    Removing spring with adapter J-23028.**
**4 x 2 models**

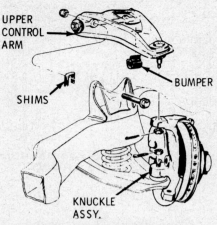

**Fig. 5    Upper control arm replacement. 4 x 2 models**

## LOWER CONTROL ARM BUSHINGS
### REPLACE
#### 4 X 2 MODELS

1. Remove coil spring as outlined in "Coil spring replace".
2. Remove lower control arm pivot bolts, refer to "Coil spring replace".
3. Drive bushing flare down flush with rubber of front bushing, then remove front and rear bushings from control arm, **Figs. 10 and 11.**
4. Install front bushing, **Fig. 12,** then flare the bushing, **Fig. 13.**
5. Install rear bushings, **Fig. 14,** then the lower control arm as described previously.

#### 4 X 4 MODELS

1. Raise and support vehicle.
2. Remove wheel and tire assembly.
3. Unload torsion bar.
4. Remove stabilizer shaft, refer to "Stabilizer Shaft Replace".
5. Remove shock absorber as outlined in "Shock Absorber Replace".
6. Remove control arm pivot bolts then the lower control arm.
7. Remove lower control arm front and rear bushings, refer to **Fig. 15.**
8. Reverse procedure to install.

## LOWER BALL JOINT
### REPLACE
#### 4 X 2 MODELS

1. Raise vehicle and support with jack stands under frame side rails.
2. Remove front wheel, then support control arm spring seat with a suitable jack.
3. Using tool J-23742, or equivalent, re-move cotter pin and stud nut, then break ball joint loose from steering knuckle. Inspect and clean the ta-pered hole in steering knuckle. If hole is out of round, or damaged in any way, the steering knuckle must be re-

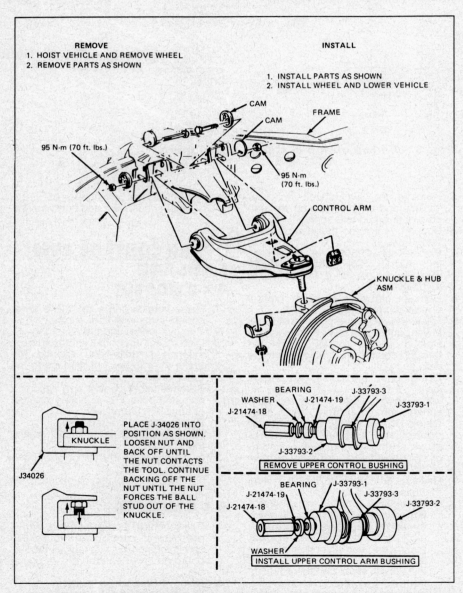

**Fig. 6    Upper control arm & bushing replacement. 4 x 4 models**

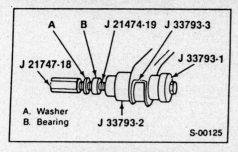

**Fig. 7 Upper control arm bushing removal. 4 x 2 models**

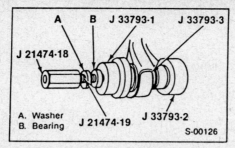

**Fig. 8 Upper control arm bushing installation. 4 x 2 models**

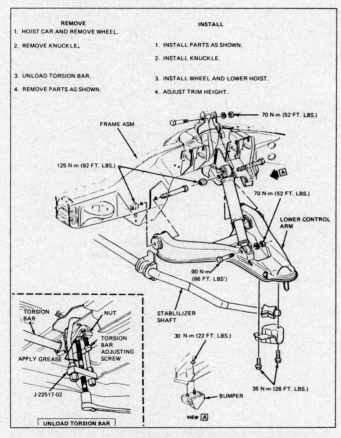

**Fig. 9 Lower control arm replacement. 4 x 4 models**

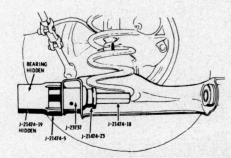

**Fig. 10 Lower control arm front bushing removal. 4 x 2 models**

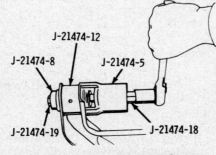

**Fig. 11 Lower control arm rear bushing removal. 4 x 2 models**

placed.

4. Guide lower control arm out of opening in splash shield. **Block the knuckle assembly out of the way by placing a wooden block between the frame and upper control arm.**

5. Remove grease fittings, then press ball joint from lower control arm.

6. Reverse procedure to install. Torque stud nut to 90 ft. lbs.

## 4 X 4 MODELS

Refer to **Fig. 16** for lower ball joint replacement procedure on 4 x 4 vehicles.

## UPPER BALL JOINT
### REPLACE
### 4 X 2 MODELS

1. Raise vehicle and support at lower control arm with suitable jacks. **Jack must be positioned between coil spring seat and ball joint of lower control arm to obtain maximum leverage against coil spring pressure.**

2. Remove wheel, then remove cotter pin and stud nut from ball joint.

3. Using tool J-23742, or equivalent, break stud loose from steering knuckle . Support knuckle assembly to avoid damaging brake line.

4. With control arm in raised position, drill rivets 1/4 inch deep with a 1/8 inch drill, then drill off rivet heads with a 1/2 inch drill.

5. Punch out rivets, then remove ball joint.

6. Reverse procedure to install. Replace rivets with attaching bolts and nuts. Torque attaching nuts to 17 ft. lbs. and the stud nut to 65 ft. lbs.

### 4 X 4 MODELS

Refer to **Fig. 16** for upper ball joint replacement procedure on 4 x 4 vehicles.

## SHOCK ABSORBER
### REPLACE
### 4 X 2 MODELS

1. Raise and support vehicle.

2. Hold shock upper stem from turning with a suitable wrench and remove nut, retainer and grommet.

3. Remove lower shock pivot bolts, then remove shock absorber from vehicle.

4. Reverse procedure to install. Torque upper attaching nut to 8 ft. lbs. and lower attaching bolts to 20 ft. lbs.

### 4 X 4 MODELS

Refer to **Fig. 17** for shock absorber replacement procedure on 4 4 vehicles.

## STEERING KNUCKLE
### REPLACE
### 4 X 2 MODELS

1. Raise and support front of vehicle, then support lower control arm with suitable jack. **Jack must be positioned between coil spring seat**

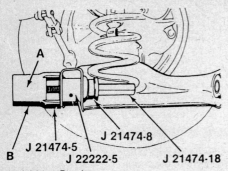

A. Hidden Bearing
B. J 221474-19, Bolt, Hidden

**Fig. 12 Lower control arm front bushing installation. 4 x 2 models**

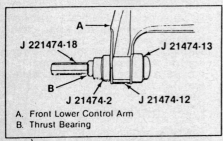

A. Front Lower Control Arm
B. Thrust Bearing

**Fig. 13 Flaring lower control arm front bushing. 4 x 2 models**

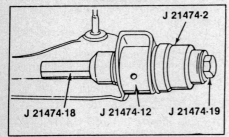

**Fig. 14 Lower control arm rear bushing installation. 4 x 2 models**

and ball joint of lower control arm to obtain maximum leverage against coil spring pressure.
2. Remove wheel and tire assembly.
3. Remove brake caliper, then the hub and rotor assembly.
4. Remove splash shield to steering knuckle attaching bolts.
5. Using tool J-6627, or equivalent, remove tie rod end from steering knuckle.
6. If steering knuckle is to be replaced, remove knuckle seal.
7. Using tool J-23742, or equivalent, remove ball joint studs from steering knuckle.
8. Raise upper control arm to disengage upper ball joint stud from knuckle.
9. Remove knuckle from lower ball joint stud.
10. After removal, inspect tapered holes. If holes are out of round, or deformation or damage is observed, replace steering knuckle.
11. Reverse procedure to install. Torque splash shield attaching bolts to 10 ft. lbs. Install tie rod end using tool

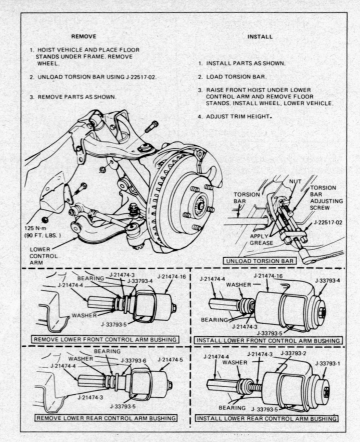

**Fig. 15 Lower control arm bushing replacement. 4 x 4 models**

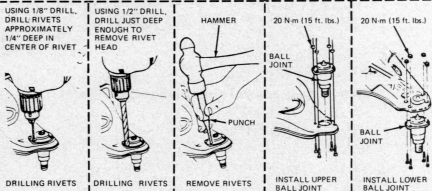

**Fig. 16 Ball joint replacement. 4 x 4 models**

J-29193 and torque to 15 ft. lbs., then remove tool and torque to 40 ft. lbs.

## 4 X 4 MODELS

Refer to **Fig. 18** for steering knuckle replacement procedure on 4 x 4 vehicles.

## STABILIZER BAR
### REPLACE
### 4 X 2 MODELS

1. Raise and support front of vehicle.

**REMOVE**

1. HOIST VEHICLE
2. REMOVE PARTS AS SHOWN

**INSTALL**

1. INSTALL PARTS AS SHOWN.
2. LOWER VEHICLE

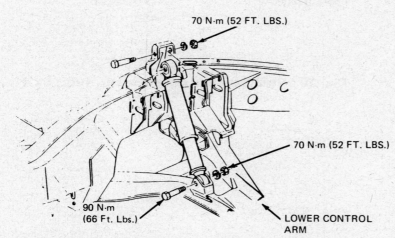

70 N·m (52 FT. LBS.)

70 N·m (52 FT. LBS.)

90 N·m (66 Ft. Lbs.)

LOWER CONTROL ARM

**Fig. 17 Shock absorber replacement. 4 x 4 models**

**REMOVE**

1. REMOVE PARTS AS SHOWN.

**INSTALL**

1. INSTALL PARTS AS SHOWN.

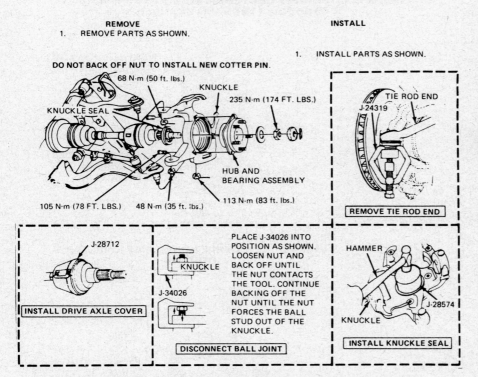

DO NOT BACK OFF NUT TO INSTALL NEW COTTER PIN.

68 N·m (50 ft. lbs.)

KNUCKLE

235 N·m (174 FT. LBS.)

KNUCKLE SEAL

HUB AND BEARING ASSEMBLY

105 N·m (78 FT. LBS.)   48 N·m (35 ft. lbs.)   113 N·m (83 ft. lbs.)

TIE ROD END
J-24319

REMOVE TIE ROD END

J-28712

INSTALL DRIVE AXLE COVER

KNUCKLE

J-34026

PLACE J-34026 INTO POSITION AS SHOWN. LOOSEN NUT AND BACK OFF UNTIL THE NUT CONTACTS THE TOOL. CONTINUE BACKING OFF THE NUT UNTIL THE NUT FORCES THE BALL STUD OUT OF THE KNUCKLE.

DISCONNECT BALL JOINT

HAMMER

KNUCKLE

J-28574

INSTALL KNUCKLE SEAL

**Fig. 18 Steering knuckle replacement. 4 x 4 models**

2. Remove stabilizer link bolt nuts from both sides, then pull link bolt from linkage and remove retainers, grommets and spacers, **Fig. 19.**
3. Remove stabilizer bracket to frame or body attaching bolts, then the stabilizer bar, bushings and brackets.
4. Reverse procedure to install, noting the following: install stabilizer bar so the identification stamping appears on the right side of vehicle. Position the rubber bushings squarely in the brackets with the slit facing the front of vehicle. Torque link nuts to 13 ft. lbs. and bracket bolts to 24 ft. lbs.

## 4 X 4 MODELS

Refer to **Figs. 20 and 21** for stabilizer bar replacement procedure on 4 x 4 vehicles.

## TORSION BAR
### REPLACE
#### 4 X 4 MODELS

Refer to **Fig. 22** for torsion bar replacement procedure on 4 x 4 vehicles.

## BALL JOINT INSPECTION
### 4 X 2 MODELS
#### Upper Ball Joint

Before checking ball joints, wheel bearings must be properly adjusted.
1. Raise vehicle and position floor stands under right and left lower control arms near each lower ball joint.
2. Position dial indicator against wheel rim, **Fig. 23.**
3. Shake wheel, **Fig. 23,** and read gauge. Horizontal deflection should not exceed .125 in.
4. If reading exceeds .125 in., or if ball stud has been disconnected from knuckle assembly and any looseness is detected or stud is loose, replace ball joint.

#### Lower Ball Joint

The lower ball joint has a visual wear indicator, **Fig. 24.** To check, vehicle weight must rest on wheels to properly load ball joints.

### 4 X 4 MODELS

Refer to **Fig. 25** for ball joint inspection procedure on 4 x 4 vehicles.

## STEERING GEAR
### REPLACE

1. On models equipped with power steering, disconnect pressure and return hoses from steering gear housing, then plug hose ends and gear housing ports to prevent entry of dirt.
2. On all models, disconnect battery ground cable and remove coupling shield if so equipped.
3. Remove retaining nuts, lock washers and bolts at steering coupling to steering shaft flange.
4. Remove pitman arm nut and washer from pitman shaft and mark relation of arm position to shaft, then remove pitman arm using a suitable puller.
5. Remove screws securing steering gear to frame and remove gear from vehicle.
6. Reverse procedure to install.

## POWER STEERING PUMP
### REPLACE

1. Disconnect pressure and return hoses from power steering pump or steering gear housing, then secure ends in raised position to prevent oil drainage. Cap all open lines and fittings.
2. Remove power steering pump belt, then power steering pump attaching bolts.
3. Remove power steering pump assembly, **Fig. 26.**

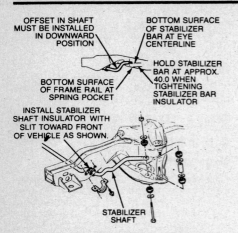

OFFSET IN SHAFT MUST BE INSTALLED IN DOWNWARD POSITION

BOTTOM SURFACE OF STABILIZER BAR AT EYE CENTERLINE

HOLD STABILIZER BAR AT APPROX. 40.0 WHEN TIGHTENING STABILIZER BAR INSULATOR

BOTTOM SURFACE OF FRAME RAIL AT SPRING POCKET

INSTALL STABILIZER SHAFT INSULATOR WITH SLIT TOWARD FRONT OF VEHICLE AS SHOWN.

STABILIZER SHAFT

**Fig. 19  Stabilizer bar replacement. 4 x 2 models**

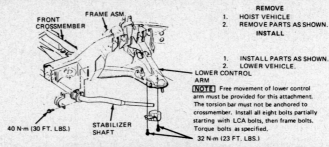

FRONT CROSSMEMBER

FRAME ASM.

REMOVE
1. HOIST VEHICLE
2. REMOVE PARTS AS SHOWN.

INSTALL

1. INSTALL PARTS AS SHOWN.
2. LOWER VEHICLE.

LOWER CONTROL ARM

40 N·m (30 FT. LBS.)

STABILIZER SHAFT

NOTE  Free movement of lower control arm must be provided for this attachment. The torsion bar must not be anchored to crossmember. Install all eight bolts partially starting with LCA bolts, then frame bolts. Torque bolts as specified.

32 N·m (23 FT. LBS.)

**Fig. 20  Stabilizer bar replacement. 1983 4 x 4 models**

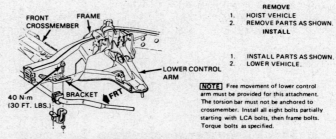

FRONT CROSSMEMBER

FRAME

REMOVE
1. HOIST VEHICLE
2. REMOVE PARTS AS SHOWN.

INSTALL

1. INSTALL PARTS AS SHOWN.
2. LOWER VEHICLE.

LOWER CONTROL ARM

40 N·m (30 FT. LBS.)

BRACKET  FRT

NOTE  Free movement of lower control arm must be provided for this attachment. The torsion bar must not be anchored to crossmember. Install all eight bolts partially starting with LCA bolts, then frame bolts. Torque bolts as specified.

**Fig. 21  Stabilizer bar replacement. 1984–85 4 x 4 models (1986–89 similar)**

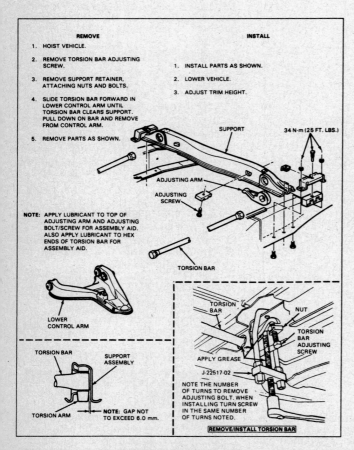

REMOVE

1. HOIST VEHICLE.
2. REMOVE TORSION BAR ADJUSTING SCREW.
3. REMOVE SUPPORT RETAINER, ATTACHING NUTS AND BOLTS.
4. SLIDE TORSION BAR FORWARD IN LOWER CONTROL ARM UNTIL TORSION BAR CLEARS SUPPORT. PULL DOWN ON BAR AND REMOVE FROM CONTROL ARM.
5. REMOVE PARTS AS SHOWN.

INSTALL

1. INSTALL PARTS AS SHOWN.
2. LOWER VEHICLE.
3. ADJUST TRIM HEIGHT.

SUPPORT

34 N·m (25 FT. LBS.)

ADJUSTING ARM

ADJUSTING SCREW

NOTE: APPLY LUBRICANT TO TOP OF ADJUSTING ARM AND ADJUSTING BOLT/SCREW FOR ASSEMBLY AID. ALSO APPLY LUBRICANT TO HEX ENDS OF TORSION BAR FOR ASSEMBLY AID.

TORSION BAR

LOWER CONTROL ARM

TORSION BAR

SUPPORT ASSEMBLY

TORSION ARM

NOTE: GAP NOT TO EXCEED 6.0 mm.

TORSION BAR

NUT

TORSION BAR ADJUSTING SCREW

APPLY GREASE

J-22517-02

NOTE THE NUMBER OF TURNS TO REMOVE ADJUSTING BOLT. WHEN INSTALLING TURN SCREW IN THE SAME NUMBER OF TURNS NOTED.

REMOVE/INSTALL TORSION BAR

**Fig. 22  Torsion bar replacement. 4 x 4 models**

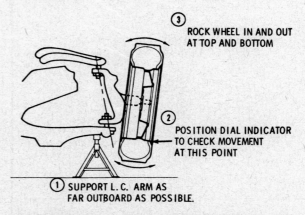

③ ROCK WHEEL IN AND OUT AT TOP AND BOTTOM

② POSITION DIAL INDICATOR TO CHECK MOVEMENT AT THIS POINT

① SUPPORT L.C. ARM AS FAR OUTBOARD AS POSSIBLE.

**Fig. 23  Checking upper ball joint. 4 x 2 models**

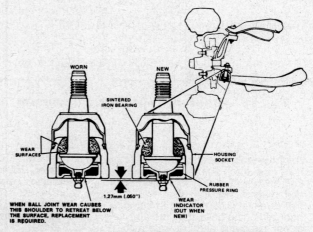

WORN

NEW

SINTERED IRON BEARING

WEAR SURFACES

HOUSING SOCKET

RUBBER PRESSURE RING

WEAR INDICATOR (OUT WHEN NEW)

1.27mm (.050")

WHEN BALL JOINT WEAR CAUSES THIS SHOULDER TO RETREAT BELOW THE SURFACE, REPLACEMENT IS REQUIRED.

**Fig. 24  Lower ball joint wear indicator. 4 x 2 models**

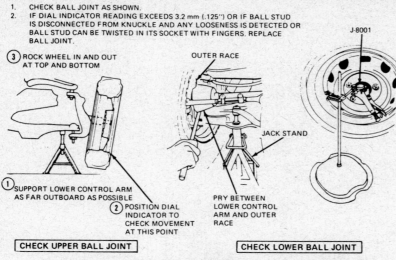

1. CHECK BALL JOINT AS SHOWN.
2. IF DIAL INDICATOR READING EXCEEDS 3.2 mm (.125") OR IF BALL STUD IS DISCONNECTED FROM KNUCKLE AND ANY LOOSENESS IS DETECTED OR BALL STUD CAN BE TWISTED IN ITS SOCKET WITH FINGERS. REPLACE BALL JOINT.

③ ROCK WHEEL IN AND OUT AT TOP AND BOTTOM

OUTER RACE

J-8001

JACK STAND

① SUPPORT LOWER CONTROL ARM AS FAR OUTBOARD AS POSSIBLE

② POSITION DIAL INDICATOR TO CHECK MOVEMENT AT THIS POINT

PRY BETWEEN LOWER CONTROL ARM AND OUTER RACE

CHECK UPPER BALL JOINT

CHECK LOWER BALL JOINT

**Fig. 25 Checking ball joints. 4 x 4 models**

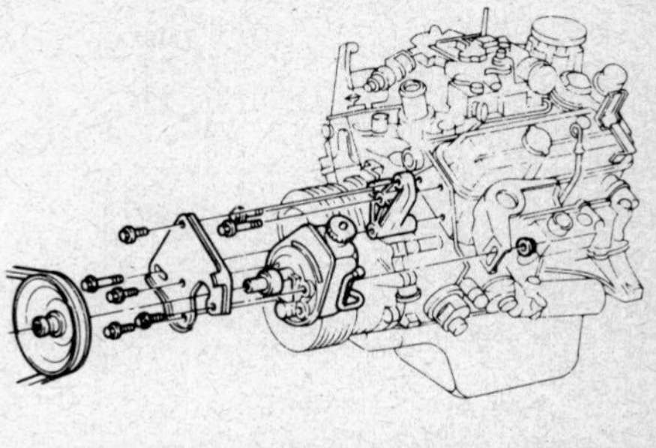

**Fig. 26 Power steering pump assembly mounting (typical)**

# FRONT WHEEL DRIVE

## INDEX

## DESCRIPTION

The front suspension is independent with torsion bars attached to the lower control arms. The front differential, **Fig. 1**, is mounted to the frame, with universal joints mounted on the inner and and outer ends of the axle shafts. The front axle utilizes a center disconnect system which makes shifting in or out of four-wheel drive possible at any vehicle speed. When the transfer case is shifted, a vacuum diaphragm locks or unlocks the center disconnect. This system replaces automatic-locking front hubs.

## TUBE & SHAFT ASSEMBLY
### REPLACE
#### REMOVAL

1. Disconnect battery ground cable.
2. Disconnect shift cable from vacuum actuator. Disengage locking spring, then push actuator diaphragm into release cable, **Fig. 2.**

3. Unlock steering wheel so linkage is free to move.
4. Raise vehicle and place jack stands under frame side rails.
5. Remove front wheels, drive belt shield and the axle skid plate, if equipped.
6. Support right hand lower control arm with a suitable jack, then disconnect right upper ball joint and remove support so that control arm hangs free.
7. Disconnect right hand drive axle shaft from tube assembly, **Fig. 3.** Insert a drift through opening in top of brake caliper and into corresponding vane of brake rotor to prevent axle from turning.
8. Disconnect four-wheel drive indicator light electrical connector from switch.
9. Remove the three shift cable and switch housing-to-carrier attaching bolts and pull housing out to gain access to cable locking spring. Do not remove cable coupling nut unless cable is being replaced.
10. Disconnect shift cable from fork shaft by lifting spring over slot in shift fork.
11. Remove tube bracket bolts from frame and tube assembly attaching bolts from carrier.
12. Remove tube assembly from axle.

Use care not to allow sleeve, thrust washers, connector and output shaft to fall from carrier or be damaged when removing tube.

## INSTALLATION

1. Install sleeve, thrust washers, connector and output shaft in carrier. The thrust washer notch must align with tab on washer, **Fig. 4.**
2. Coat the tube to carrier mating surface with Loctite 514 sealant or equivalent.
3. Install tube and shaft assembly to carrier using only one bolt installed finger tight at the one o'clock position. Pull assembly down, then install cable and switch housing and four remaining bolts. Torque bolts to 30-40 ft. lbs.
4. Install the two tube to frame attaching bolts and torque to 45-60 ft. lbs.
5. Check four wheel drive mechanism for proper operation by inserting tool J-33799 into shift fork and checking for rotation of axle shaft, **Fig. 5.**
6. Remove tool and install shift cable switch housing, then guide cable through housing into fork shaft hole and push cable in by sliding cable

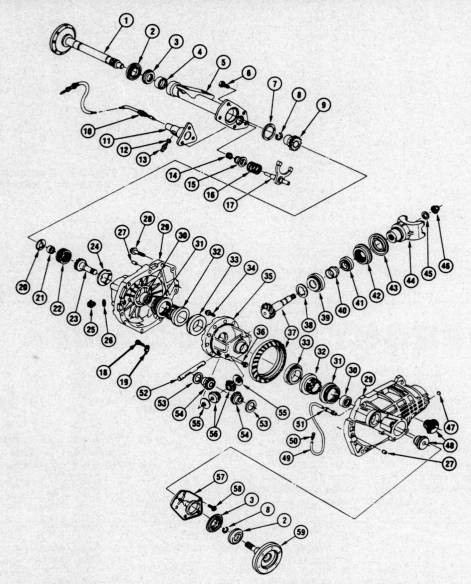

1. SHAFT, Differential Output — Right Hand (Including #2, 8)
2. DEFLECTOR, Differential Output Shaft
3. SEAL, Differential Output Shaft Tube
4. BEARING, Differential Output Shaft Tube
5. TUBE, Differential Carrier Output Shaft
6. BOLT, Tube to Carrier
7. WASHER, Carrier Thrust
8. RING, Shaft Retainer
9. CONNECTOR, Differential Carrier
10. CABLE, Differential Lock
11. HOUSING, Differential Shifter Cable
12. GASKET, Four Wheel Drive Indicator Switch
13. SWITCH, Four Wheel Drive Indicator
14. SPRING, Differential Shifter
15. SEAL, Differential Shifter
16. SPRING, Differential Shifter
17. SHAFT, w/Fork, Differential Shifter
18. BOLT, Hex Flange Head (M6 x 1 x 14)
19. LOCK, Differential Adjuster
20. WASHER, Differential Output Shaft Thrust
21. BEARING, Differential Output Shaft Pilot
22. SLEEVE, Differential
23. SHAFT, Differential Output — Left Hand
24. WASHER, Differential Thrust
25. PLUG, Differential Carrier (M20 x 1.5)
26. WASHER, Differential Carrier Plug
27. PIN, Differential Carrier Alignment
28. BOLT, Differential Carrier (10 Required)
29. CARRIER, Differential (Including #27, 28, 47, 51) (Carrier halves not serviced separately)

30. BEARING, Differential Output Shaft
31. INSERT, Differential Carrier Bearing Adjuster
32. SLEEVE, Differential Carrier Bearing Adjuster
33. BEARING, Differential Side
34. BOLT, Hypoid Drive Gear to Case
35. CASE, Differential
36. SCREW, Differential Pinion Shaft Lock
37. GEAR KIT, Ring and Pinion (Gear Kits also Include #34, 40)
38. SHIM KIT
39. BEARING, Pinion Inner
40. SPACER, Pinion Bearing
41. BEARING, Pinion Outer
42. SEAL, Differential Carrier Pinion
43. DEFLECTOR, Differential Carrier Flange
44. FLANGE, Prop Shaft Pinion (Including #43)
45. WASHER, Prop Shaft Pinion Flange
46. NUT, Prop Shaft Pinion Flange
47. PLUG, Cup Expansion (3/8")
48. BUSHING, Differential Carrier
49. HOSE, Bulk (5/16" ID)
50. VENTILATOR, Front Axle
51. CONNECTOR, Front Axle Vent Hose
52. SHAFT, Differential Pinion
53. WASHER, Differential Side Gear Thrust
54. GEAR, Differential Side
55. WASHER, Differential Carrier Pinion Thrust
56. GEAR, Differential Pinion
57. COVER, Differential Carrier
58. BOLT, Differential Carrier Cover
59. SHAFT, Differential (Including #2, 8)

**Fig. 1   Exploded view of front drive axle**

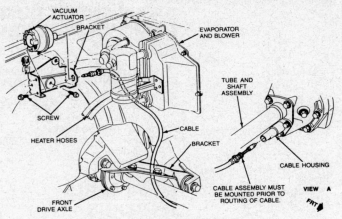

Fig. 2   Vacuum actuator

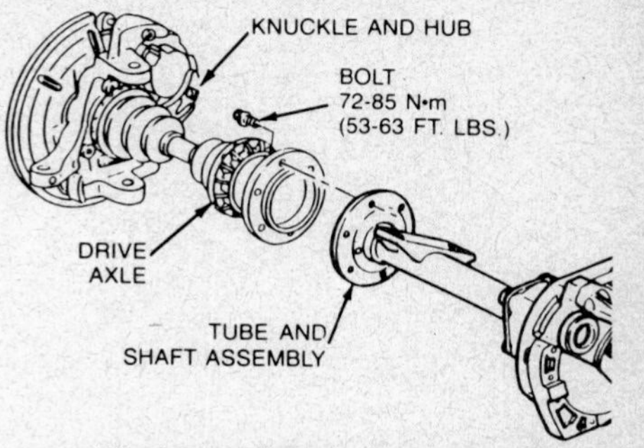

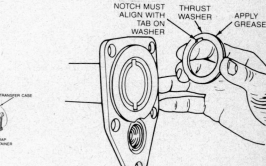

Fig. 3   Drive axle & tube assembly

Fig. 4   Thrust washer installation

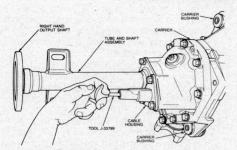

Fig. 5   Checking operation of four wheel drive mechanism

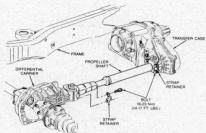

Fig. 6   Front propeller shaft

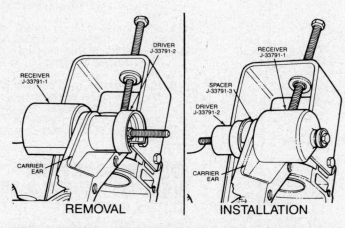

REMOVAL          INSTALLATION

Fig. 7   Differential carrier bushing replacement

through into fork shaft hole.
7. Connect four wheel drive indicator light electrical connector to switch.
8. Support and raise right hand lower control arm using a suitable jack and connect upper ball joint.
9. Install right hand drive axle to axle tube. Install one bolt first, then rotate axle to install five remaining bolts. Torque bolts to 53-63 ft. lbs.
10. Install front axle skid plate, if equipped, drive belt shield and front wheels. Torque skid plate bolts to 20-28 ft. lbs.
11. Connect shift cable to vacuum actuator by pushing cable end into actuator shaft hole.

## DIFFERENTIAL CARRIER REPLACE

1. Raise vehicle and place jack stands under frame side rails.
2. Remove tube and shaft assembly as described under "Tube & Shaft Assembly, Replace."
3. Remove steering stabilizer to frame attaching bolt.
4. Mark position of steering idler arm for reference during installation, then remove idler arm-to-frame attaching bolts.
5. Push steering linkage towards front of vehicle, then remove axle vent hose

from carrier fitting.
6. Disconnect left hand drive axle shaft from carrier. When removing bolts, insert a drift through opening in top of brake caliper and into corresponding vane of brake rotor to prevent axle from turning.
7. Disconnect front propeller shaft, **Fig. 6.**
8. Remove carrier-to-frame attaching bolts, then the carrier.
9. Reverse procedure to install. On 1983-85 models, torque carrier-to-frame attaching bolts to 60-74 ft. lbs. and axle shaft-to-carrier bolts to 53-63 ft. lbs. On 1986-89 models, torque carrier attaching bolts to 65 ft. lbs. and nuts to 55 ft. lbs.

## DIFFERENTIAL CARRIER BUSHING REPLACE

1. Remove tube and shaft assembly as described under "Tube & Shaft Assembly, Replace."
2. Remove differential carrier as described under "Differential Carrier, Replace."
3. Remove bushing from carrier ear using tool J-33791, **Fig. 7.**
4. Install new bushing using tool J-33791, **Fig. 7.** Ensure tool J-33791-3 is positioned properly between bushing and carrier ear to prevent bushing from being pressed in too far.

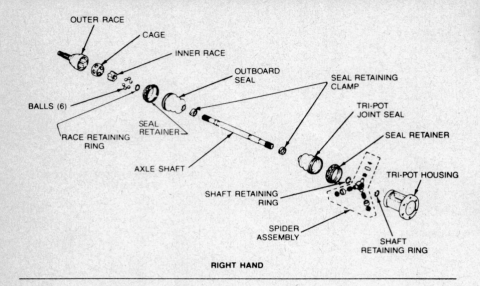

RIGHT HAND

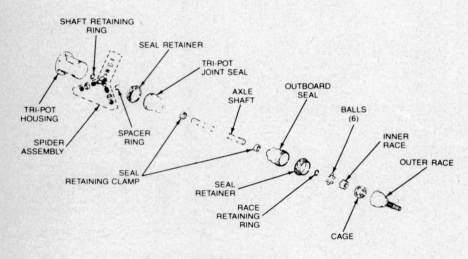

LEFT HAND

**Fig. 8  Exploded view of front axle. 1983–84**

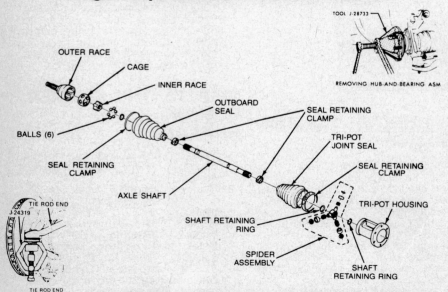

**Fig. 9  Exploded view of front axle. 1985–89**

## DIFFERENTIAL OUTPUT SHAFT PILOT BEARING REPLACE

1. Remove tube and shaft assembly as described under -Tube & Shaft Assembly, Replace.-
2. Remove bearing. Refer to **Fig. 1** for bearing location.
3. Install new bearing.
4. Reverse procedure to complete installation.

## SHIFT CABLE REPLACE

1. Remove shift cable from vacuum actuator by disengaging locking spring and pushing actuator diaphragm in to release cable. Compress cable locking fingers with pliers, then remove cable from bracket.
2. Raise and support vehicle.
3. Remove switch housing mounting bolts and pull housing away from axle tube flange to gain access to cable locking spring.
4. Disconnect cable from shaft fork by lifting spring over slot in shift fork, then unscrew cable from housing and remove from vehicle.
5. Install cable following proper routing, **Fig. 2.**
6. Install cable and switch housing to carrier. Torque mounting bolts to 36 ft. lbs.
7. Slide cable through switch housing into fork shaft hole and push cable in. The cable will snap in place automatically. Torque coupling nut to 90 inch lbs.
8. Lower vehicle, then connect shift cable to vacuum actuator by pressing cable into bracket hole. The cable will snap in place automatically.
9. Check cable for proper operation.

## OUTER CONSTANT VELOCITY JOINT & SEAL REPLACE

For removal and installation procedures, refer to **Figs. 8 through 12.**

## INNER TRI-POT SEAL REPLACE

For removal and installation procedures, refer to **Figs. 13 and 14.**

## DIFFERENTIAL CARRIER RIGHT HAND OUTPUT SHAFT & TUBE SERVICE

### DISASSEMBLE

1. Remove output shaft from tube by

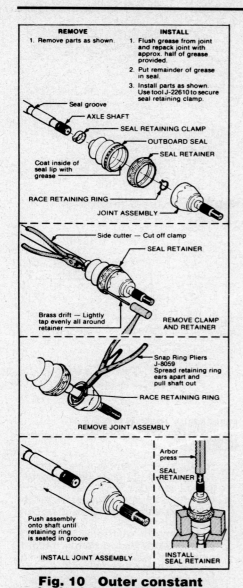

**Fig. 10 Outer constant velocity joint seal removal & installation. 1983–84**

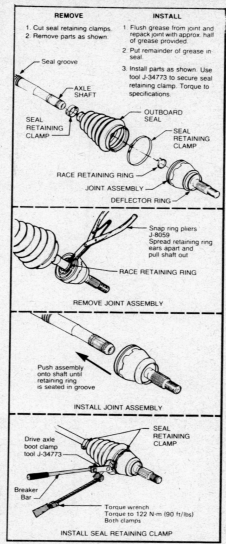

**Fig. 11 Outer constant velocity joint seal removal & installation. 1985–89**

**Fig. 12 Outer constant velocity joint disassembly & assembly**

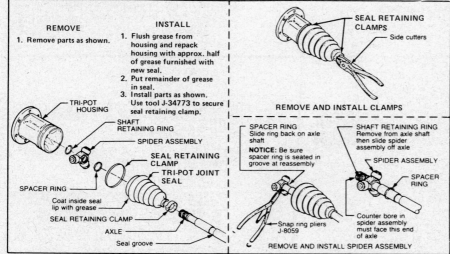

**Fig. 13 Inner tri-pot seal removal & installation. 1983–85 (1986–89 similar)**

tapping inside of flange with a rubber mallet.
2. Pry tube seal from tube, then remove bearing from tube.
3. Drive differential shift cable housing seal out of tube using a suitable punch.

## ASSEMBLE

1. Install output shaft tube bearing.
2. Install tube seal. Flange of seal must be flush with tube outer surface.
3. Install output shaft into tube by tapping flange with a rubber mallet.
4. Install differential shift cable housing seal.

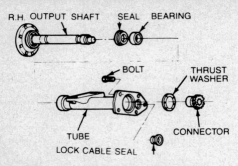

**Fig. 14   Right hand output shaft & tube**

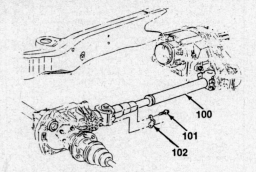

100. Front Prop Shaft
101. Bolt
102. Clamp

**Fig. 15   Pinion flange retaining bolts**

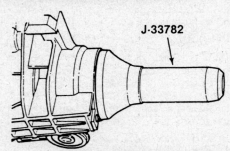

**Fig. 17   Pinion seal installation**

## PINION OIL SEAL REPLACE

1. Remove crossmember if necessary.
2. Remove pinion flange bolts and retainers, **Fig. 15.**
3. Remove propeller shaft from pinion shaft and tape bearing caps to hold in place.
4. Remove pinion shaft retaining nut and washer. **Mark pinion flange, pinion shaft, and pinion retaining nut to ensure proper bearing preload.**
5. Using tool No. J-8614-01, remove pinion flange, **Fig. 16.**
6. Remove pinion seal using a suitable seal puller.
7. Reverse procedure to install, using tool No. J-33782 to install pinion oil seal, **Fig. 17.**

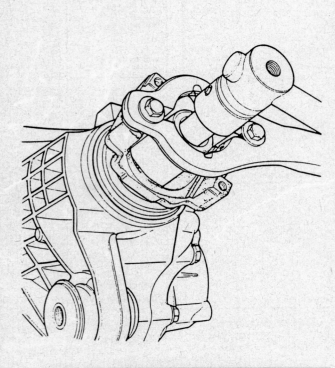

**Fig. 16   Pinion flange removal**

# CHEVROLET ASTRO VAN & GMC SAFARI VAN

## INDEX OF SERVICE OPERATIONS

**NOTE:** Refer to rear of this manual for vehicle manufacturer's special service tool suppliers.

# SPECIFICATIONS
## GENERAL ENGINE SPECIFICATIONS

| Year | Engine Model | Carb. Type | Bore & Stroke | Comp. Ratio | Net Horsepower @ RPM | Torque Ft. Lbs. @ RPM | Normal Oil Press. Lbs. |
|------|-------------|-----------|---------------|-------------|---------------------|----------------------|------------------------|
| 1985 | 4-151/2.5L | T.B.I.① | 4.00 x 3.00 | 9.0 | 92 @ 4400 | 134 @ 2800 | 45 |
| | V6-262/4.3L | 4 Bore | 4.00 x 3.48 | 9.3 | 145 @ 4000 | 225 @ 2400 | 50 |
| 1986 | 4-151/2.5L | T.B.I.① | 4.00 x 3.00 | 9.0 | 92 @ 4400 | 134 @ 2800 | 45 |
| | V6-262/4.3L | T.B.I.① | 4.00 x 3.48 | 9.3 | 145 @ 4000 | 230 @ 2400 | 30–40 |
| 1987 | 4-151/2.5L | T.B.I.① | 4.00 x 3.00 | 8.3 | 96 @ 4400 | 135 @ 3200 | 36–41 |
| | V6-262/4.3L | T.B.I.① | 4.00 x 3.48 | 9.3 | 150 @ 4000 | 230 @ 2400 | 30–35 |
| 1988 | 4-151/2.5L | T.B.I.① | 4.00 x 3.00 | 8.3 | 96 @ 4400 | 150 @ 2400 | 36–41 |
| | V6-262/4.3L | T.B.I.① | 4.00 x 3.48 | 9.3 | 160 @ 4000 | 235 @ 2400 | 30–35 |
| 1989 | 4-151/2.5L | T.B.I.① | 4.00 x 3.00 | 8.3 | 96 @ 4400 | 135 @ 3200 | 36–41 |
| | V6-262/4.3L | T.B.I.① | 4.00 x 3.48 | 9.3 | 150 @ 4000 | 230 @ 2400 | ② |

①—Throttle body fuel injection.
②—Minimum Pressures: 6 lbs. @ 1000 RPM; 18 lbs. @ 2000 RPM; 24 lbs. @ 4000 RPM.

## ALTERNATOR SPECIFICATIONS

| Year | Model | Field Current @ 80°F 12 volts | Rated Hot Output Amperes | Cold Output Amperes @ 2000 RPM | Cold Output Amperes @ 7000 RPM |
|------|-------|-------------------------------|--------------------------|--------------------------------|--------------------------------|
| 1985 | 1100206 | 4.5–5 | 37 | 60 | 56 |
| | 1100217 | 4.5–5 | 51 | 81 | 78 |
| | 1100250 | 4.5–5 | 51 | 81 | 78 |
| | 1100259 | 4.5–5 | 51 | 81 | 78 |
| | 1100287 | 4.5–5 | 37 | 60 | 56 |
| | 1105492 | 4.5–5 | 56 | 103 | 94 |
| | 1105507 | 4.5–5 | 56 | 103 | 94 |
| | 1105582 | 4.5–5 | 56 | 103 | 94 |
| 1986 | 1105612 | 5.4–6.4 | 100 | 36① | — |
| | 1105662 | 5.4–6.4 | 85 | 30① | — |
| | 1105664 | 5.4–6.4 | 85 | 30① | — |
| | 1105665 | 5.4–6.4 | 100 | 36① | — |
| 1987 | 1105710 | 4.8–5.7 | 85 | 30① | — |
| | 1105711 | 6.0–7.5 | 100 | 36① | — |
| | 1105722 | 4.8–5.7 | 85 | 30① | — |
| 1988-89 | 1101346 | 6.0–7.5 | 96 | 26① | — |
| | 1105710 | 4.8–5.7 | 85 | 30① | — |
| | 1105711 | 6.0–7.5 | 100 | 36① | — |

①—Amperes @ 1600 RPM.

## STARTING MOTOR SPECIFICATIONS

| Year | Engine | Starter Model | Brush Spring Tension ① | Free Speed Test Amperes ② | Free Speed Test Volts | Free Speed Test RPM |
|------|--------|---------------|------------------------|---------------------------|-----------------------|---------------------|
| 1985 | 4-151/2.5L | 1998450 | — | 50–75 | 10 | 6000–11900 |
| | V6-262/4.3L | 1998441 | — | 70–110 | 10 | 6500–10700 |
| 1986-87 | 4-151/2.5L | 1998530 | — | 50–75 | 10 | 6000–11900 |
| | V6-262/4.3L | 1998574 | — | 70–110 | 10 | 6500–10700 |
| 1988 | 4-151/2.5L | 1998530 | — | 50–75 | 10 | 6000–11900 |
| | V6-262/4.3L | 1998590 | — | 70–110 | 10 | 6500–10700 |
| 1989 | 4-151/2.5L | 10455017 | — | 50–75 | 10 | 6000–11900 |
| | V6-262/4.3L | 1998590 | — | 70–110 | 10 | 6500–10700 |

①—Minimum.
②—Includes solenoid.

## ENGINE TIGHTENING SPECIFICATIONS*

*Torque specifications are for clean and lightly lubricated threads only. Dry or dirty threads produce increased friction which prevents accurate measurement of tightness.

| Year | Engine | Spark Plug Ft. Lbs. | Cylinder Head Bolts Ft. Lbs. | Intake Manifold Ft. Lbs. | Exhaust Manifold Ft. Lbs. | Rocker Arm Shaft Bracket Ft. Lbs. | Rocker Arm Cover Ft. Lbs. | Connecting Rod Cap Bolts Ft. Lbs. | Main Bearing Cap Bolts Ft. Lbs. | Flywheel To Crankshaft Ft. Lbs. | Vibration Damper Or Pulley Ft. Lbs. |
|---|---|---|---|---|---|---|---|---|---|---|---|
| 1985 | 4-151/2.5L | 7–15 | ② | ② | ② | 20① | 6 | 32 | 70 | 44 | 160 |
| | V6-262/4.3L | 22 | 65 | 30 | ④ | — | 4 | 45 | 70 | 65 | 60 |
| 1986 | 4-151/2.5L | 7–15 | ② | ② | ② | 20① | 6 | 32 | 70 | ③ | 160 |
| | V6-262/4.3L | 22 | 65 | 36 | ④ | — | 7 | 45 | 75 | 75 | 70 |
| 1987 | 4-151/2.5L | 7–15 | ② | 25 | ② | 24① | 4 | 32 | 70 | ③ | 160 |
| | V6-262/4.3L | 22 | 65 | 35 | ④ | — | 8 | 45 | 75 | 75 | 70 |
| 1988 | 4-151/2.5L | 7–15 | ② | ② | ② | 22① | 4 | 32 | 70 | ③ | 160 |
| | V6-262/4.3L | 22 | 65 | 35 | ④ | — | 8 | 45 | 80 | 75 | 70 |
| 1989 | 4-151/2.5L | 7–15 | ② | 25 | ⑤ | 22① | 6 | 30 | 65 | ③ | 160 |
| | V6-262/4.3L | 22 | 65 | 35 | ④ | — | 8 | 45 | 80 | 75 | 70 |

①—Rocker arm bolt.
②—Refer to text for procedure.
③—Auto. Trans., 55 ft. lbs.; man. trans., 65 ft. lbs.
④—Two center bolts, 26 ft. lbs.; others, 20 ft. lbs.
⑤—Center tube, 36 ft. lbs.; front and rear tubes, 32 ft. lbs.

## BRAKE SPECIFICATIONS

| Year | Model | Rear Drum I.D. | Wheel Cyl. Bore Front Disc | Wheel Cyl. Bore Rear Drum | Disc Brake Rotor Nominal Thickness | Disc Brake Rotor Minimum Thickness | Disc Brake Rotor Thickness Variation (Parallelism) | Disc Brake Rotor Run Out (TIR) | Disc Brake Rotor Finish (Microinch) | Master Cyl. I.D. |
|---|---|---|---|---|---|---|---|---|---|---|
| 1985-86 | All | 9.5 | 2.94 | .812 | 1.04 | .980 | .0005 | .004 | — | ① |
| 1987 | All | — | — | .812 | 1.04 | .980 | .0005 | .004 | — | — |
| 1988 | All | — | — | — | 1.04 | .980 | .0005 | .004 | — | — |
| 1989 | All | 9.5 | — | — | 1.04 | .980 | .0005 | .004 | — | — |

①—Manual brakes, 1.00; power brakes, 1.25.

## DRIVE AXLE SPECIFICATIONS

| Year | Model | Carrier Type | Ring Gear & Pinion Backlash Method | Ring Gear & Pinion Backlash Adjustment | Pinion Bearing Preload Method | Pinion Bearing Preload New Bearings Inch Lbs. | Pinion Bearing Preload Used Bearings Inch Lbs. | Differential Bearing Preload Method | Differential Bearing Preload New Bearings Inch Lbs. | Differential Bearing Preload Used Bearings Inch Lbs. |
|---|---|---|---|---|---|---|---|---|---|---|
| 1985-89 | All | Integral | Shim | .005–.009 | Collapsible Spacer | 24–32① | 8–12① | Shim | ② | ② |

①—Measured with torque wrench at pinion flange nut.
②—Slip fit plus .004 inch preload on each side.

## WHEEL ALIGNMENT SPECIFICATIONS

| Year & Model | Caster Degrees | Camber Degrees | Toe In Degrees |
|---|---|---|---|
| 1985-86 All | +2.2 to +3.2 | +.44 to +1.44 | +.10 to +.20 |
| 1987-89 All | +2.2 to +3.2 | +.30 to +1.30 | +.05 to +.15 |

## COOLING SYSTEM & CAPACITY DATA

| Year | Model Or Engine | Cooling Capacity, Qts. | | Radiator Cap Relief Pressure, Lbs. | Thermo. Opening Temp. | Fuel Tank Gals. | Engine Oil Refill Qts. | Transmission Oil | | | | Rear Axle Oil Pts. |
|---|---|---|---|---|---|---|---|---|---|---|---|---|
| | | Less A/C | With A/C | | | | | 4 Speed Pts. | 5 Speed Pts. | Auto. Trans.① | Trans. Case Pts. | |
| 1985 | 4-151/2.5L | 9.2 | 9.2 | 15 | 195 | 17 | 3② | 2.4 | 4.1 | ④ | — | 4 |
| | V6-262/4.3L | 13.5 | 13.5 | 15 | 195 | 17 | 4③ | 2.4 | 4.1 | ④ | — | 4 |
| 1986-87 | 4-151/2.5L | 10⑤ | 10⑤ | 15 | 195 | 17 | 3② | 5 | 4.4 | ④ | — | 4 |
| | V6-262/4.3L | 13.5 | 13.5 | 15 | 195 | 17 | 4③ | 5 | 4.4 | ④ | — | 4 |
| 1988-89 | 4-151/2.5L | 10⑥ | 10⑥ | 15 | 195 | 17 | 3⑦ | — | 4.4 | ⑧ | — | 4 |
| | V6-262/4.3L | 13.5⑥ | 13.5⑥ | 15 | 195 | 17 | 4③ | — | 4.4 | ⑧ | — | 4 |

①—Approximate, make final check with dipstick.
②—With or without filter.
③—Add one quart with filter change.
④—Total, 11.5 qts.; pan only, 5 qts.
⑤—Add 2.8 qts. if equipped w/rear heater.
⑥—Add 3.0 qts. if equipped w/rear heater.
⑦—Add .5 qts. with new filter.
⑧—Total, 10.5 qts.; pan only, 5 qts.

# ELECTRICAL
## INDEX

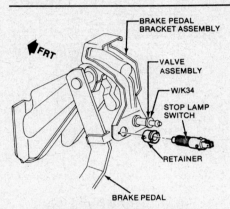

**Fig. 1   Stop lamp switch replacement**

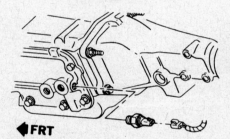

**Fig. 3   Back-up light switch replacement. Manual transmission**

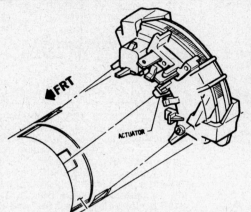

**Fig. 2   Neutral start/back-up light switch replacement. Automatic transmission**

INSTALLATION PROCEDURE

1. PLACE GEAR SELECTOR IN NEUTRAL.
2. ALIGN ACTUATOR ON SWITCH WITH HOLE IN SHIFT TUBE.
3. POSITION REARWARD PORTION OF SWITCH (CONNECTOR SIDE) TO FIT INTO CUTOUT IN LOWER JACKET.
4. PUSH DOWN ON FRONT OF SWITCH: THE TWO TANGS ON HOUSING BACK WILL SNAP INTO PLACE IN RECTANGULAR HOLES IN JACKET.
5. ADJUST SWITCH BY MOVING GEAR SELECTOR TO PARK. THE MAIN HOUSING AND THE HOUSING BACK SHOULD RATCHET, PROVIDING PROPER SWITCH ADJUSTMENT.

READJUSTMENT PROCEDURE

1. WITH SWITCH INSTALLED, MOVE THE HOUSING ALL THE WAY TOWARD "LOW GEAR" POSITION.
2. REPEAT STEP 5.

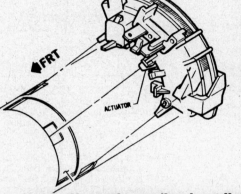

**Fig. 4   Turn signal switch replacement**

## FUSE PANEL & FLASHER LOCATION

The fuse block is located under the left-hand side of the instrument panel, above the kick panel. The hazard flasher is located at the convenience center, on the left side of the steering column, behind the instrument panel. The turn signal flasher is located to the right of the steering column behind the instrument panel.

## STARTER REPLACE

A clashing or grinding condition may exist, due to improper engagement of the starter to flexplate on some 1985-88 vehicles equipped with V6-262/4.3L engines with automatic transmission. To correct this condition, replace the starter drive assembly with new drive assembly (part No. 10456422), which utilizes a stiffer jump spring allowing for proper engagement.

During starter drive assembly replacement, all ring gear teeth should be inspected. If three or more consecutive teeth are damaged, the flexplate should be replaced. Use flexplate No. 10128414.

1. Disconnect battery ground cable.
2. Remove starter braces or shields if equipped.
3. Remove wires from starter solenoid.
4. Raise and support vehicle.
5. Remove two starter motor-to-engine attaching bolts and shims if present.
6. Remove starter from vehicle.
7. Reverse procedure to install.

## STOP LAMP SWITCH REPLACE

1. Disconnect battery ground cable.
2. Disconnect electrical connector from switch by reaching up under right side of instrument panel at brake pedal support.
3. Pull switch from mounting bracket, **Fig. 1**, then remove from bracket.
4. To install new switch, depress brake pedal and push switch into clip until shoulder on switch bottoms out against clip. Audible clicks can be heard while pushing switch through clip.
5. Adjust stop lamp switch by pulling the brake pedal up against the pedal stop until the audible clicks can no longer be heard. **Electrical contact should be made when the brake pedal is depressed .53 inch from the fully released position. If further adjustment is necessary, the switch may be pulled or rotated in the clip.**

## NEUTRAL START & BACK-UP LIGHT SWITCH REPLACE

Refer to **Fig. 2** when replacing the combination neutral start/back-up light switch on automatic transmission vehicles and **Fig. 3** when replacing the back-up light switch on manual transmission vehicles.

## STEERING WHEEL REPLACE

1. Disconnect battery ground cable.
2. Remove steering wheel shroud attaching screws, if equipped, from underside of steering wheel.
3. Remove cap or lift steering wheel

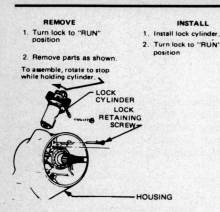

**REMOVE**
1. Turn lock to "RUN" position
2. Remove parts as shown.
To assemble, rotate to stop while holding cylinder.

**INSTALL**
1. Install lock cylinder.
2. Turn lock to "RUN" position

LOCK CYLINDER
LOCK RETAINING SCREW
HOUSING

**Fig. 5   Ignition lock replacement. Exc. tilt column**

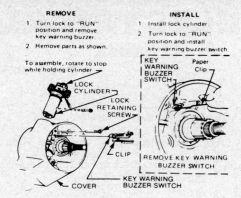

**REMOVE**
1. Turn lock to "RUN" position and remove key warning buzzer.
2. Remove parts as shown.
To assemble, rotate to stop while holding cylinder.

**INSTALL**
1. Install lock cylinder.
2. Turn lock to "RUN" position and install key warning buzzer switch.

LOCK CYLINDER
LOCK RETAINING SCREW
CLIP
COVER
KEY WARNING BUZZER SWITCH
KEY WARNING BUZZER SWITCH
Paper Clip
REMOVE KEY WARNING BUZZER SWITCH

**Fig. 6   Ignition lock replacement. Tilt column**

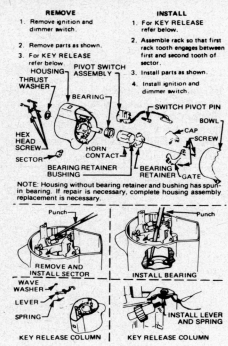

**REMOVE**
1. Remove ignition and dimmer switch.
2. Remove parts as shown.
3. For KEY RELEASE refer below.

**INSTALL**
1. For KEY RELEASE refer below.
2. Assemble rack so that first rack tooth engages between first and second tooth of sector.
3. Install parts as shown.
4. Install ignition and dimmer switch.

HOUSING
THRUST WASHER
HEX HEAD SCREW
SECTOR
BEARING RETAINER BUSHING
PIVOT SWITCH ASSEMBLY
BEARING
HORN CONTACT
SWITCH PIVOT PIN
BOWL
CAP SCREW
BEARING RETAINER
GATE

NOTE: Housing without bearing retainer and bushing has spun-in bearing. If repair is necessary, complete housing assembly replacement is necessary.

Punch
REMOVE AND INSTALL SECTOR
INSTALL BEARING
WAVE WASHER
LEVER
SPRING
INSTALL LEVER AND SPRING
KEY RELEASE COLUMN
KEY RELEASE COLUMN

**Fig. 7   Windshield wiper switch replacement. Exc. tilt column**

shroud and horn contact lead assembly from steering wheel.
4. Remove retainer, then the steering wheel nut.
5. Remove steering wheel using puller J-1859-03 or equivalent.
6. Reverse procedure to install.

## TURN SIGNAL SWITCH REPLACE

1. Disconnect battery ground cable.
2. Remove steering wheel as described under "Steering Wheel, Replace."
3. Refer to **Fig. 4** to replace turn signal switch. On 1989 models, remove instrument panel trim cover.
4. Position a screwdriver blade into the steering shaft lock plate cover slot.

Pry up and out to free the cover from the lock plate.
5. Screw the center post of puller J 23653-A (or substitute) onto the steering shaft as far as it will go. Compress the lock plate by turning the center post nut clockwise. Pry the retaining ring out of the shaft, then remove the puller. **If the column is being disassembled on a bench, the shaft could slide out of the end of the mast jacket when the snap ring is removed.**
6. Remove the lock plate.
7. Remove the turn signal lever screw and lever.
8. Remove the hazard warning knob by pressing the knob inward, then unscrew.
9. Remove the turn signal mounting screws.
10. Pull the switch connector from the bracket on the jacket and feed switch connector through the column support bracket, then pull the switch straight up. guide the wiring harness through the column housing and protector.

11. Remove the wire protector by pulling tab down and out of the column with pliers.
12. Remove the turn signal switch.
13. Reverse procedure to install.

## IGNITION LOCK REPLACE

1. Remove turn signal switch as described under "Turn Signal Switch, Replace." It is not necessary to completely remove the switch from the

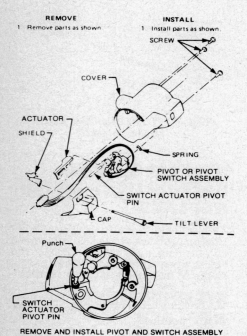

**REMOVE**
1 Remove parts as shown.

**INSTALL**
1. Install parts as shown.

SCREW
COVER
ACTUATOR
SHIELD
SPRING
PIVOT OR PIVOT SWITCH ASSEMBLY
SWITCH ACTUATOR PIVOT PIN
CAP
TILT LEVER

Punch
SWITCH ACTUATOR PIVOT PIN
REMOVE AND INSTALL PIVOT AND SWITCH ASSEMBLY

**Fig. 8   Windshield wiper switch replacement. Tilt column**

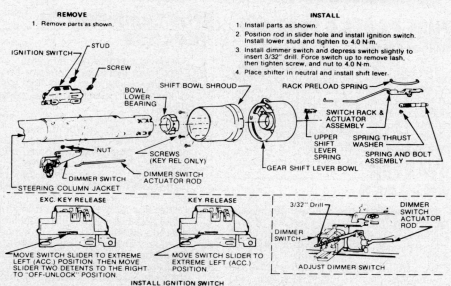

**REMOVE**
1. Remove parts as shown.

IGNITION SWITCH
STUD
SCREW
BOWL LOWER BEARING
SHIFT BOWL SHROUD
NUT
SCREWS (KEY REL ONLY)
DIMMER SWITCH
STEERING COLUMN JACKET
DIMMER SWITCH ACTUATOR ROD

**INSTALL**
1. Install parts as shown.
2. Position rod in slider hole and install ignition switch. Install lower stud and tighten to 4.0 N·m.
3. Install dimmer switch and depress switch slightly to insert 3/32" drill. Force switch up to remove lash, then tighten screw, and nut to 4.0 N·m.
4. Place shifter in neutral and install shift lever.

RACK PRELOAD SPRING
SWITCH RACK & ACTUATOR ASSEMBLY
UPPER SHIFT LEVER SPRING
SPRING THRUST WASHER
SPRING AND BOLT ASSEMBLY
GEAR SHIFT LEVER BOWL

EXC. KEY RELEASE
MOVE SWITCH SLIDER TO EXTREME LEFT (ACC) POSITION, THEN MOVE SLIDER TWO DETENTS TO THE RIGHT TO "OFF-UNLOCK" POSITION.

KEY RELEASE
MOVE SWITCH SLIDER TO EXTREME LEFT (ACC.) POSITION

INSTALL IGNITION SWITCH

3/32" Drill
DIMMER SWITCH
DIMMER SWITCH ACTUATOR ROD
ADJUST DIMMER SWITCH

**Fig. 9   Ignition & dimmer switch replacement. Exc. tilt column**

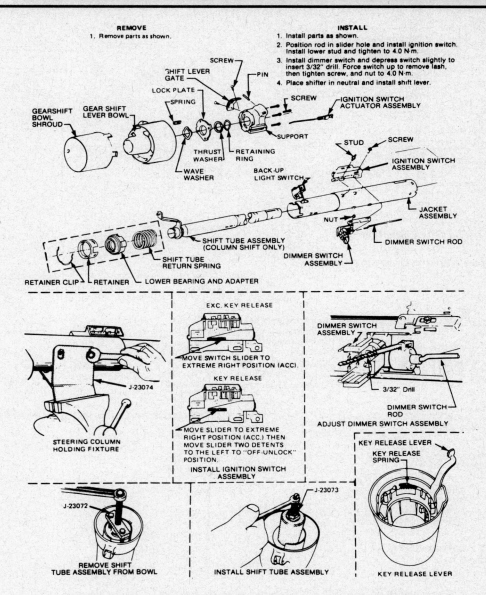

**Fig. 10  Ignition & dimmer switch replacement. Tilt column**

column. Pull it rearward just far enough to slip it over the shaft.
2. Turn lock cylinder to Run position and remove key warning buzzer switch, if equipped.
3. Remove retaining screw and the lock cylinder, **Figs. 5 and 6.**
4. Reverse procedure to install. **Turn lock cylinder to Run position prior to installation.**

## WINDSHIELD WIPER SWITCH
### REPLACE

1. Remove ignition lock as described under "Ignition Lock, Replace."
2. Refer to **Figs. 7 and 8** to replace wiper switch.

## IGNITION & DIMMER SWITCHES
### REPLACE
#### 1985–88

1. Remove turn signal switch as described under "Turn Signal Switch, Replace."
2. Refer to **Figs. 9 and 10** to replace ignition and dimmer switches.

#### 1989

1. Lower the steering column as described under "Steering Column, Replace," then properly support the column. There is no need to remove the steering wheel.
2. Put the ignition switch in the Lock po-

sition. If the lock cylinder was removed, the actuating rod to the switch should be pulled up until there is a definite stop, then moved down one detent. This is the Lock position **Fig. 11.**
3. Remove two ignition switch screws, then the switch assembly.
4. Reverse procedure to install.

## INSTRUMENT CLUSTER
### REPLACE

Use care in handling the exchange unit and the inoperative cluster. Hands must be free of dirt and grease. Avoid touching electronic components, as electro-static discharge can degrade performance or cause failure.
1. Disconnect battery ground cable.
2. Remove steering column lower trim

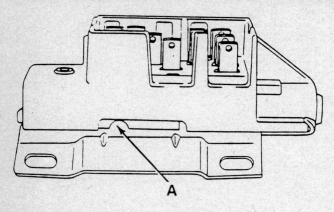

A. Switch In The Lock Position

**Fig. 11   Ignition switch in lock position**

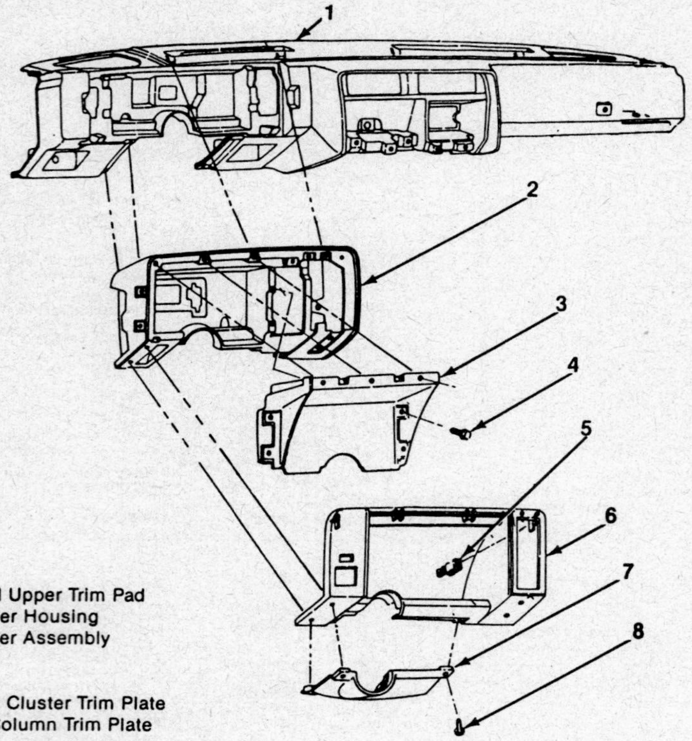

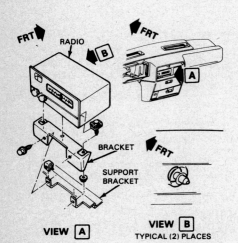

**VIEW** [A]

**VIEW** [B]
TYPICAL (2) PLACES

**Fig. 13   Radio replacement.
1985–87**

1. Instrument Panel Upper Trim Pad
2. Instrument Cluster Housing
3. Instrument Cluster Assembly
4. Screw
5. Retainer
6. Instrument Panel Cluster Trim Plate
7. Lower Steering Column Trim Plate
8. Screw

**Fig. 12   Instrument cluster replacement**

plate.
3. Remove instrument cluster trim plate attaching screws and allow panel to hang to left side by wiring.
4. Remove A/C control assembly attaching screws and position assembly to one side, on 1985-88 models only.
5. Remove alarm assembly, then the instrument panel cluster trim panel, on 1985-88 models only.
6. Remove instrument panel-to-cluster attaching screws.
7. Disconnect speedometer cable and all electrical connectors from rear of cluster, then remove cluster, **Fig. 12**, from vehicle.
8. Reverse procedure to install.

# RADIO
## REPLACE

1. Disconnect battery ground cable.
2. Refer to **Figs. 13 and 14** to replace radio assembly.

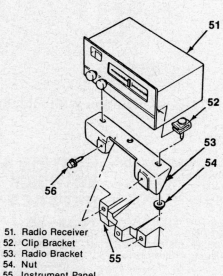

51. Radio Receiver
52. Clip Bracket
53. Radio Bracket
54. Nut
55. Instrument Panel
56. Screw

**Fig. 14   Radio replacement.
1988–89**

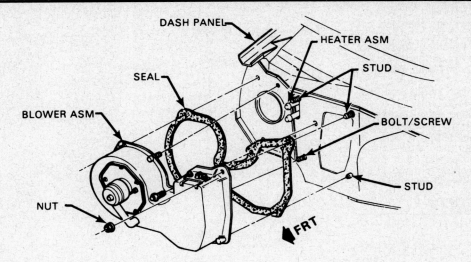

**Fig. 15  Blower motor replacement**

## BLOWER MOTOR
### REPLACE

1. Disconnect battery ground cable.
2. Disconnect electrical connectors from blower motor, then remove coolant overflow bottle.
3. Remove windshield washer fluid bottle attaching bolts and position bottle aside.
4. Remove blower motor attaching screws and the blower motor, Fig. 15.
5. Reverse procedure to install.

## HEATER CORE
### REPLACE

1. Disconnect battery ground cable.
2. Drain cooling system, then remove coolant overflow bottle.
3. Remove windshield washer fluid bottle attaching bolts and position bottle aside.
4. Disconnect heater core hose from core and plug tubes to prevent contamination.
5. Remove core cover attaching screws and the cover.
6. Remove upper and lower air distribution ducts.
7. Remove attaching screws from rear of heater core.
8. Remove heater core from vehicle.
9. Reverse procedure to install.

# 4-151 (2.5L) ENGINE
## INDEX

## ENGINE
### REPLACE

1. Disconnect battery ground cable.
2. Drain cooling system, then remove engine cover.
3. Remove headlamp bezel and grille, then the radiator lower close-out panel and radiator support brace.
4. Remove lower tie bar and cross braces.
5. Remove hood latch mechanism, then the upper radiator core support.
6. Disconnect coolant hoses and transmission cooler lines from radiator, as required, then remove radiator filler panels.
7. Remove radiator and fan shroud as an assembly.
8. Disconnect engine harness from bulkhead connector.
9. Disconnect electrical connector from ECM and pull through bulkhead.
10. Disconnect heater hoses from heater core, then plug heater core tubes to prevent contamination.
11. Disconnect accelerator, cruise control and detent cables, as required, then the battery ground cable from cylinder head.
12. Disconnect canister purge hose, then remove air cleaner and air cleaner adapter.
13. Raise and support vehicle.
14. Disconnect exhaust pipe from exhaust manifold.
15. Disconnect wiring harness from transmission and frame, then the starter

16. Remove starter motor, then the flywheel shield.
17. Disconnect fuel lines from fuel pump.
18. Remove engine mount through bolts, then remove transmission bellhousing bolts.
19. Lower vehicle, then remove oil filler neck and thermostat outlet.
20. Install engine lifting device and support transmission with a suitable jack, then remove engine from vehicle.
21. Reverse procedure to install. Torque the bellhousing bolts to 55 ft. lbs. if equiped with an automatic and 34.5 if equiped with a manual transmission.

## ENGINE MOUNTS
### REPLACE

Refer to **Fig. 1** to replace engine mounts.

## CYLINDER HEAD
### REPLACE

1. Disconnect battery ground cable.
2. Remove glove box assembly, if necessary, then the engine cover.
3. Remove air cleaner assembly, then disconnect wires from the spark plugs.
4. Remove accelerator, cruise control and TVS cables, if equipped.
5. Remove PCV hose and EGR valve.
6. Remove engine oil filler tube, then disconnect vacuum line and harness from the water outlet stud, then move aside.
7. Remove valve cover attaching bolts and the valve cover.
8. Drain cooling system and remove necessary hoses.
9. Disconnect front coolant hose from intake manifold.
10. Remove alternator bracket from intake manifold.
11. Remove rear alternator bracket and position alternator aside.
12. On models equipped with A/C, unfasten A/C compressor and position aside, leaving refrigerant lines attached.
13. On all models, remove thermostat outlet from cylinder head.
14. Disconnect remaining vacuum, fuel and electrical lines necessary for cylinder head removal.
15. Remove ignition coil, then disconnect wires from spark plugs.
16. Raise and support vehicle.
17. Disconnect exhaust pipe from exhaust manifold.
18. Disconnect electrical connector from oxygen sensor, then lower vehicle.
19. Remove pushrods, then the cylinder head attaching bolts.
20. Remove cylinder head with intake and exhaust manifolds as an assembly.
21. On 1985—87 models reverse procedure to install, noting the following:
    a. Ensure cylinder head attaching bolts are clean and dry, then apply suitable sealer to threads of bolts 9 and 10, **Fig. 2.**
    b. Apply engine oil to underside of remaining bolts, then install bolts and

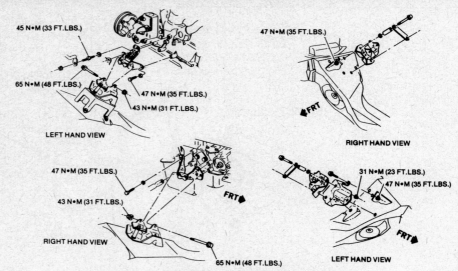

**Fig. 1   Engine mount replacement**

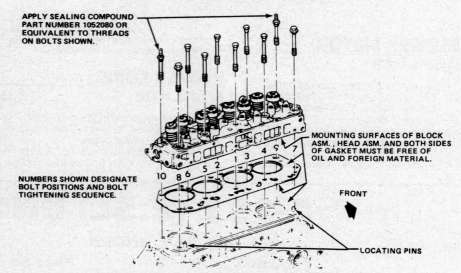

**Fig. 2   Cylinder head bolt tightening sequence**

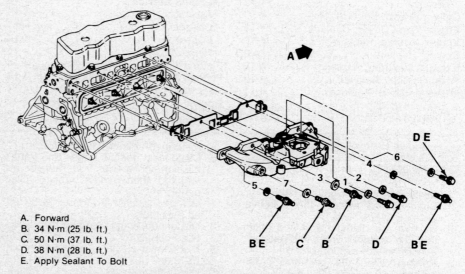

A. Forward
B. 34 N·m (25 lb. ft.)
C. 50 N·m (37 lb. ft.)
D. 38 N·m (28 lb. ft.)
E. Apply Sealant To Bolt

**Fig. 3   Intake manifold bolt tightening sequence. 1985—86**

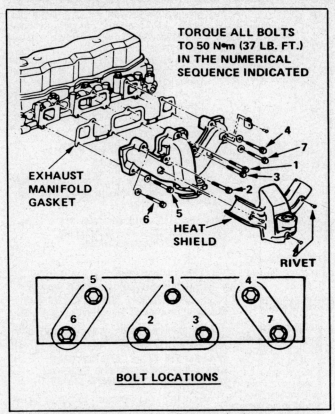

**TORQUE ALL BOLTS TO 50 N•m (37 LB. FT.) IN THE NUMERICAL SEQUENCE INDICATED**

EXHAUST MANIFOLD GASKET

HEAT SHIELD

RIVET

BOLT LOCATIONS

**Fig. 4 Exhaust manifold bolt tightening sequence. 1985**

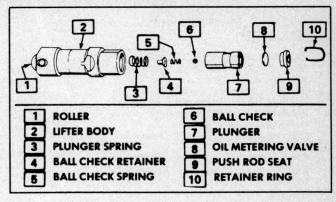

| 1 | ROLLER | 6 | BALL CHECK |
|---|---|---|---|
| 2 | LIFTER BODY | 7 | PLUNGER |
| 3 | PLUNGER SPRING | 8 | OIL METERING VALVE |
| 4 | BALL CHECK RETAINER | 9 | PUSH ROD SEAT |
| 5 | BALL CHECK SPRING | 10 | RETAINER RING |

**Fig. 6 Hydraulic valve lifter**

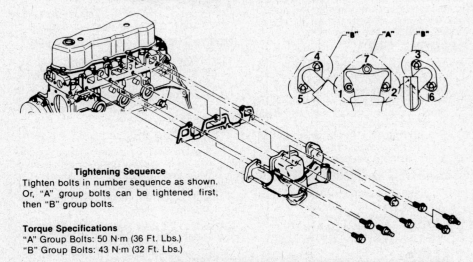

**Tightening Sequence**

Tighten bolts in number sequence as shown. Or, "A" group bolts can be tightened first, then "B" group bolts.

**Torque Specifications**
"A" Group Bolts: 50 N·m (36 Ft. Lbs.)
"B" Group Bolts: 43 N·m (32 Ft. Lbs.)

**Fig. 5 Exhaust manifold bolt tightening sequence. 1986–89**

torque to 18 ft. lbs. in sequence shown in **Fig. 2.**

c. Repeat sequence torquing all bolts except No. 9 to 22 ft. lbs. Torque bolt No. 9 to 30 ft. lbs.

d. Repeat sequence, tightening all bolts except No. 9 120° (2 flats). Tighten bolt No. 9 90° (¼ turn).

22. On 1988-89 models reverse procedure to install, noting the following:

a. Ensure cylinder head bolts are clean and dry, then apply suitable sealer to threads of bolt 9 only, **Fig. 2.**

b. Install and torque all bolts to 18 ft. lbs. in sequence, **Fig. 2.**

c. Torque all bolts in sequence to 26 ft. lbs., except No. 9. Torque No. 9 to 18 ft. lbs.

d. Tighten bolts in sequence an additional 90° (¼ turn).

## INTAKE MANIFOLD REPLACE
### 1985–86

1. Disconnect battery ground cable.

2. Remove glove box assembly, as required, then the engine cover.

3. Remove air cleaner assembly, then drain cooling system.

4. Disconnect vacuum pipe rail from exhaust manifold and thermostat housing.

5. Disconnect all electrical and vacuum connectors necessary for intake manifold removal.

6. Disconnect accelerator, TVS and cruise control cables, as required.

7. Disconnect vacuum and fuel lines and the coolant hoses from intake manifold.

8. Unfasten alternator and position aside.

9. Remove ignition coil attaching bolts from cylinder head and intake manifold.

10. Remove intake manifold attaching bolts and the intake manifold.

11. Reverse procedure to install. Torque intake manifold attaching bolts to specifications in sequence, **Fig. 3.**

### 1987–89

1. Disconnect battery ground cable.

2. Remove engine cover and air cleaner assembly.

3. Disconnect wire harness electrical connectors from intake manifold.

4. Disconnect accelerator, TVS and cruise control cables and bracket.

5. Remove cruise control transducer, if equipped.

6. Disconnect EGR vacuum line, then remove emissions sensor bracket from the manifold.

7. Remove fuel lines, vacuum lines and wiring from TBI unit, then drain cooling system.

8. Remove coolant hoses from manifold.

9. Remove alternator rear bracket.

10. Disconnect vacuum hoses and lines from the manifold, then the vacuum line clips from the thermostat and manifold.

11. Disconnect spark plug and coil wires.

12. Remove intake manifold attaching bolts and washers, then the intake manifold.

13. Reverse procedure to install. Torque intake manifold attaching bolts to 25 ft. lbs.

## EXHAUST MANIFOLD
### REPLACE

1. Disconnect battery ground cable.
2. Remove glove box assembly, if necessary, then the engine cover.
3. Remove exhaust stove pipe from manifold, then disconnect electrical connector from oxygen sensor.
4. Raise and support vehicle.
5. Disconnect exhaust pipe from exhaust manifold.
6. On models equipped with A/C, remove rear A/C compressor bracket.
7. On all models, remove exhaust manifold attaching bolts and the exhaust manifold.
8. Reverse procedure to install. Torque exhaust manifold attaching bolts to specifications in sequence, **Figs. 4 and 5.**

## ROCKER ARMS & PUSHRODS
### REPLACE

1. Disconnect battery ground cable.
2. Remove glove box assembly, if necessary, then the engine cover.
3. Remove air cleaner assembly, then disconnect spark plug wires from valve cover.
4. Remove PCV hose and EGR valve.
5. Remove engine oil filler tube, then disconnect vacuum pipe rail from intake manifold and thermostat housing.
6. Remove valve cover attaching bolts and the valve cover.
7. **If only pushrods are being replaced, loosen rocker bolt and swing arm away from pushrod, then remove pushrod through hole in cylinder head.** Remove rocker arm bolt and ball, then the rocker arm(s) and pushrod(s).
8. Reverse procedure to install.

## VALVES
### ADJUST

This engine uses hydraulic lifter. No provision for adjustment is provided.

## VALVE ARRANGEMENT
### FRONT TO REAR

All ..................... I-E-I-E-E-I-E-I

## VALVE LIFT SPECIFICATIONS

| Engine | Year | Intake | Exhaust |
|---|---|---|---|
| 4-151 | 1985-88 | .398① | .398① |
| 4-151 | 1989 | .232① | .232① |

①Measured at camshaft lobe.

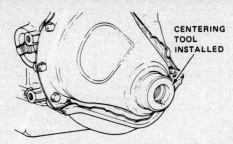

**Fig. 7  Engine front cover installation**

CENTERING TOOL INSTALLED

## VALVE TIMING
### INTAKE OPENS BEFORE TDC

| Engine | Year | Degrees |
|---|---|---|
| 4-151 | 1985-89 | 33 |

## VALVE LIFTER SERVICE

Failure of a hydraulic valve lifter, **Fig. 6,** is generally caused by an inadequate oil supply or dirt. An air leak at the intake side of the oil pump or too much oil in the engine will cause air bubbles in the oil supply to the lifters causing them to collapse. This is a probable cause of trouble if several lifters fail to function, but air in the oil is an unlikely cause of failure of a single unit.

Valve lifters can be removed after removing rocker arm cover and pushrod cover. Loosen rocker arm stud nut and rotate rocker arm so that pushrod can be removed, then remove valve lifter.

### DISASSEMBLY

1. Depress plunger with a pushrod, then remove pushrod seat retainer, **Fig. 6,** using a suitable screwdriver.
2. Remove pushrod seat, metering valve, plunger, plunger spring and ball check valve assembly.
3. Pry ball retainer loose from plunger and remove ball check valve and spring using a small screwdriver.

### CLEANING & INSPECTION

1. Clean all lifter components in suitable solvent.
2. Inspect all parts for wear or damage. If any one component is worn or damaged, the entire assembly must be replaced.
3. If lifter body wall is worn, inspect cylinder block lifter bore.
4. If bottom of lifter is worn, inspect camshaft lobe.
5. If pushrod seat is worn, inspect pushrod.

### ASSEMBLY

1. Position check ball on small hole in bottom of plunger, then install spring and ball retainer.
2. Install plunger spring over ball retainer, then slide lifter body over spring and plunger. Ensure oil holes in lifter body and plunger are aligned.
3. Fill assembly with SAE 10 oil, then de-

press plunger with a 1/8 inch drift pin. Insert a 1/16 inch drift pin through both oil holes to hold plunger down against spring tension.
4. Remove the 1/8 inch drift pin and refill assembly with SAE 10 oil, then install metering valve and pushrod seat.
5. Install pushrod seat retainer, then push down on pushrod seat and remove 1/16 inch drift pin from oil holes.

## NOISE DIAGNOSIS
### Momentary Noise When Engine Is Started

Condition normal. Oil drains from lifters which are holding valves open when engine is not running.

### Intermittent Noise at Idle, Disappears As Engine Speed Is Increased

1. Dirt in lifter.
2. Pitted check ball.

### Noise At Slow Idle Or With Hot Oil; Quiet With Cold Oil Or Increased Engine Speed

1. Excessive lifter leak down, lifter should be replaced.

### Noise At Idle, Becomes Louder As Engine Speed Increased To 1500 RPM

1. Excessive valve stem to guide clearance.
2. Off square valve spring.
3. Scuffed or worn valve tip/rocker arm pad.
4. Excessive valve seat or face runout.
5. Damper spring clicking on rotator.

### Valves Noisy At All Speeds

1. Rotate crankshaft until piston of affected cylinder is at TDC of firing stroke.
2. Hold rocker arm against valve spring and check for valve lash by moving pushrod up and down.
3. If no lash is present, check for dirt in lifter or pitted check ball.
4. If valve lash is present, inspect pushrod and rocker arm for excessive wear and replace as needed.
5. If valve lash is present, and pushrod and rocker arm are satisfactory, lifter should be replaced.

### Quiet At Low Speeds, Noisy At High Speeds

1. Incorrect oil level, oil foaming.
2. Clogged oil pump screen, bent pan or oil pump pickup.
3. Incorrect oil pressure.

## CAMSHAFT
### REPLACE
#### REMOVAL

1. Disconnect battery ground cable.
2. On 1985-86 models, proceed as follows:
   a. Remove alternator and bracket.
   b. Remove brace between intake manifold and block.
   c. Drain cooling system and oilpan,

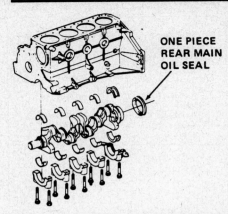

**Fig. 8  Rear main seal removal**

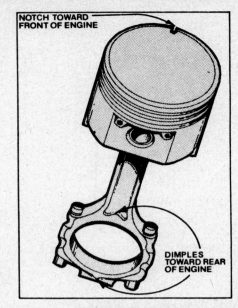

**Fig. 9  Piston & rod assembly**

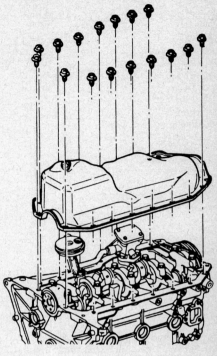

**Fig. 10  Oil pan replacement**

then disconnect lower radiator and heater hoses.

d. Remove oil sender, then the wiring harness brackets from pushrod side cover.

e. Remove pushrod side cover attaching nuts and the side cover.

3. On 1987–89 models, proceed as follows:

a. Remove engine cover, then drain cooling system and oilpan.

b. Remove coil wires, then the spark plug wires and bracket from intake manifold.

c. Disconnect fuel pipes and clips from pushrod cover.

d. Remove two pushrod cover outboard attaching nuts, then loosen two inboard nuts.

e. Install one 6 mm hex nut on each of the two inboard studs, then jam nuts together.

f. Using a suitable wrench on inner nut, unscrew studs until cover breaks loose.

g. After breaking cover loose, remove jammed nuts from each stud, then remove pushrod cover from studs.

4. On models equipped with power steering, remove power steering reservoir from the fan shroud.

5. On all models, remove upper fan shroud.

6. Remove accessory drive belt, as required.

7. Remove fan and pulley, crankshaft pulley and crankshaft hub.

8. Remove timing gear front cover attaching bolts and the front cover.

9. Remove distributor cap and distributor.

10. Remove oil pump driveshaft and cover, then the air cleaner assembly and EGR valve.

11. Disconnect vacuum lines from intake manifold and thermostat housing.

12. Disconnect spark plug wires from rocker arm cover, as required.

13. Remove rocker arm cover, then the pushrods, lifter guides and lifters.

14. On models equipped with automatic transmission, disconnect transmission cooler lines from radiator.

15. On all models, disconnect hoses from radiator and remove radiator from vehicle.

16. On models equipped with A/C, re-move A/C condenser baffles, then unfasten compressor, raise and block in position.

17. On all models, remove headlamp bezel, grille, then the bumper filler panel.

18. Remove cam thrust plate bolts, then plate.

19. Carefully remove camshaft from engine. Support the camshaft carefully to avoid damage to the camshaft bearings.

## INSTALLATION

Reverse procedure to install, noting the following:

1. Lubricate camshaft journals with suitable engine oil supplement.

2. Slide camshaft into engine block, using care to avoid damaging bearings or cam.

3. Rotate crankshaft and camshaft until valve timing marks on gear teeth are aligned, then install camshaft thrust plate-to-block attaching screws and torque to 75 inch lbs. on 1985 models or 90 inch lbs. on 1986–89 models.

4. Slide hub onto crankshaft with key-way in hub and key on crankshaft aligned, then install center bolt and torque to 160 ft. lbs.

5. Install valve lifters, pushrods, pushrod side cover, oil pump shaft and gear assembly.

6. Rotate crankshaft 360°F to firing position of No. 1 cylinder, then install distributor in original position, aligning shaft so rotor arm points toward No. 1 cylinder spark plug contact.

7. Pivot rocker arms over pushrods, then torque rocker arm bolt to specifications with lifters on base circle of camshaft.

8. Install water pump pulley and fan assembly, A/C condenser (if equipped) and radiator. Torque water pump to 25 ft. lbs. on 1985–88 models and 17 ft. lbs. on 1989 models.

9. Refill cooling system and crankcase.

## ENGINE FRONT COVER
### REPLACE

1. Disconnect battery ground cable.

2. On models equipped with power steering, remove power steering pump fan shroud.

3. On all models, remove upper fan shroud, then the fan and pulley.

4. Loosen drive belts, then remove alternator, alternator brackets, brace and front bracket.

5. Remove crankshaft pulley, hub bolt, then hub.

6. Disconnect lower radiator hose clamp from water pump.

7. Remove front cover attaching bolts and the front cover.

8. Reverse procedure to install, noting the following:

a. Apply a continuous bead of RTV sealant on cover prior to installation.

b. Install front cover with centering tool J-34995 positioned in seal, **Fig. 7**. Torque front cover to 90 inch lbs.

## FRONT OIL SEAL
### REPLACE

1. Disconnect battery ground cable.

2. Remove all drive belts.

3. Remove center bolt, then slide hub and pulleys from shaft.

4. Pry seal out of front cover using a suitable screwdriver.

5. Reverse procedure to install, using seal installer J-23042 or equivalent to drive seal into position.

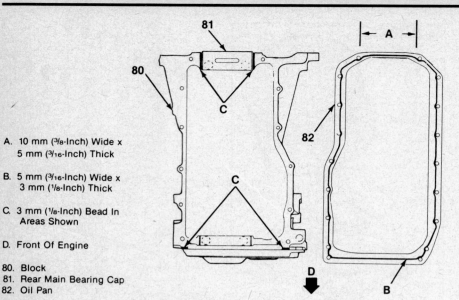

A. 10 mm (³/₈-Inch) Wide x
   5 mm (³/₁₆-Inch) Thick

B. 5 mm (³/₁₆-Inch) Wide x
   3 mm (¹/₈-Inch) Thick

C. 3 mm (¹/₈-Inch) Bead In
   Areas Shown

D. Front Of Engine

80. Block
81. Rear Main Bearing Cap
82. Oil Pan

**Fig. 11   Applying sealant to oil pan & block**

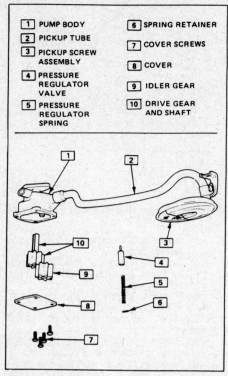

| 1 | PUMP BODY | 6 | SPRING RETAINER |
| 2 | PICKUP TUBE | 7 | COVER SCREWS |
| 3 | PICKUP SCREW ASSEMBLY | 8 | COVER |
| 4 | PRESSURE REGULATOR VALVE | 9 | IDLER GEAR |
| 5 | PRESSURE REGULATOR SPRING | 10 | DRIVE GEAR AND SHAFT |

**Fig. 12   Typical oil pump assembly**

## REAR MAIN OIL SEAL
### REPLACE

1. Remove transmission as described elsewhere in this manual.
2. On models equipped with manual transmission, remove flywheel, pressure plate and disc.
3. On models equipped with automatic transmission, remove flexplate.
4. On all models, remove seal, **Fig. 8**, using a suitable screwdriver.
5. Install new seal using seal installer J-34924 or equivalent.

## TIMING GEARS

When necessary to install a new camshaft gear, the camshaft will have to be removed as the gear is press fit on the camshaft. The camshaft is held in place by a thrust plate which is retained to the engine by two capscrews, accessible through the two holes in the gear web.

To remove gear, use an arbor press and a suitable sleeve to properly support gear on its steel hub.

Before installing gear, assemble thrust plate and gear spacer ring, then press gear onto shaft until it bottoms against spacer ring. The thrust plate end clearance should be .0015-.0050 inch. If clearance is less than .0015 inch, the spacer ring must be replaced. If clearance is greater than .0050 inch, the thrust plate must be replaced.

The crankshaft gear can be removed using a puller and two bolts in the tapped holes of the gear.

## PISTONS & RODS
### ASSEMBLE

Assemble piston to rod with notch on piston facing toward front of engine and the raised dimples on the side of rod and rod cap facing toward rear of engine, **Fig. 9.**

## PISTONS & RINGS

Pistons and rings are available in standard size and oversizes of .005, .010, .020 and .030 inch.

## MAIN & ROD BEARINGS

Main and rod bearings are available in standard size and undersizes of .001, .002 and .010 inch. The 4-151/2.5L engine uses a fillet type crankshaft which can not be ground. If clearances are not within proper specifications, replace the crankshaft.

## OIL PAN
### REPLACE

1. Disconnect battery ground cable.
2. Raise and support vehicle.
3. Drain oil pan, then disconnect starter wiring.
4. Remove flywheel shield, then the starter motor.
5. Disconnect exhaust pipe from exhaust manifold.
6. Disconnect all exhaust hangers.
7. Remove oil pan attaching bolts and the oil pan, **Fig. 10.**
8. Reverse procedure to install, noting the following:
   a. Prior to installation, ensure sealing surfaces on pan, cylinder block and front cover are clean and free of oil.
   b. If reinstalling old pan, ensure all RTV has been removed, paying particular attention to the blind attaching holes.
   c. Apply a ¹/₈ inch bead of RTV sealant to entire oil pan sealing flange, as shown in **Fig. 11.**
   d. Torque oil pan bolts to 75 inch lbs.

for 1985 models and 90 inch lbs. for 1986-89 models.

## OIL PUMP SERVICE
### REMOVAL

1. Remove oil pan as previously described.
2. Remove oil pump attaching bolts, pump, then screen as an assembly.

### DISASSEMBLY

1. Remove four pump cover attaching screws, cover and gasket.
2. Mark the gear teeth prior to removal so the pump gears can be installed with the same gear teeth indexed.
3. Remove idler gear, drive gear, then the shaft, **Fig. 12.**
4. Remove pressure regulator valve and valve components. **Do not remove the oil pickup tube in relation to the pump body or screen.**

### INSPECTION

Inspect oil pump components. Should any of the following conditions be found, the pump assembly should be replaced.

1. Inspect pump body for cracks or excessive wear.
2. Inspect pump gears for damage, cracks or excessive wear.
3. Check drive gear and shaft for looseness in housing.
4. Check interior of cover for wear that would allow oil to leak past ends of gears.
5. Inspect oil pickup screen and relief grommet for damage. Also, remove

6. Ensure proper fit of pressure relief valve plunger in bore. Valve should slide freely in bore without sticking.
7. Check pickup tube for looseness causing an air leak and loss of oil pressure.

## ASSEMBLY

1. Position drive gear and shaft in pump body using index marks made prior to disassembly, then install idler gear with smooth side of gear toward cover

opening.
2. Install pump cover and gasket if necessary. Torque attaching screws to 105 inch lbs. on 1985 models or 10 ft. lbs. on 1986-89 models. Ensure shaft turns freely.
3. Install regulator valve plunger, spring, retainer and pin.

## WATER PUMP
## REPLACE

1. Disconnect battery ground cable.

2. Drain cooling system.
3. Remove drive belt and upper fan shroud.
4. Remove fan and clutch assembly, then the water pump pulley.
5. Remove all hoses from the water pump.
6. Remove water pump attaching bolts and the water pump.
7. Reverse procedure to install. Torque water pump to 25 ft. lbs. for 1985 models and 17 ft. lbs. for 1986-89 models.

# V6-262 (4.3L) ENGINE

## INDEX

## ENGINE
## REPLACE

1. Disconnect battery ground cable.
2. Drain cooling system.
3. Raise and support vehicle.
4. Disconnect exhaust pipe from exhaust manifold.
5. Disconnect strut rods from flywheel inspection cover, then remove flywheel cover.
6. Remove torque converter attaching bolts, if necessary.
7. Disconnect starter wires from starter, then remove starter motor from vehicle.
8. Remove oil filter, then disconnect electrical connectors from transmission and frame.
9. On models equipped with automatic transmission, disconnect lower transmission cooler line from radiator.
10. Disconnect lower engine oil cooler lines from radiator, if used.
11. Remove lower fan shroud attaching bolts, then the engine mount thru bolts.
12. On 1985-88 models, remove bellhousing attaching bolts.
13. On all models, lower vehicle. Remove headlamp bezel and grille, then the radiator lower close-out panel.
14. Remove radiator support brace, then the core support cross brace.
15. Remove lower tie bar, then the hood latch mechanism.
16. Unfasten master cylinder and position aside.
17. Remove upper fan shroud, then the radiator upper core support.
18. Disconnect remaining hoses and lines from radiator, then remove radiator from vehicle.
19. On models equipped with A/C, discharge refrigerant from A/C system.
20. On all models, remove radiator filler panels, then the engine cover.
21. On models equipped with A/C, remove brace from back of A/C compressor, then disconnect refrigerant hose from accumulator and remove compressor and bracket.
22. On models equipped with power steering, remove power steering pump.
23. On all models, disconnect all vacuum hoses necessary for engine removal.
24. Disconnect engine harness from bulkhead, then remove right kick panel.
25. Disconnect electrical connector from ESC module and push connector through bulkhead.
26. Remove distributor cap, then, if equipped, the A/C accumulator.
27. Disconnect fuel line from carburetor, then remove diverter valve.
28. Disconnect transmission oil dipstick tube.

29. Disconnect heater hoses from heater core and plug heater core tubes to prevent contamination.
30. Remove horn assembly, then the air injection system check valves.
31. Install engine lifting device and support transmission with a suitable jack. On 1989 models, remove bellhousing bolts.
32. Remove engine from vehicle.
33. Reverse procedure to install. Torque bellhousing bolts to 32 ft. lbs.

## ENGINE MOUNTS
## REPLACE
### FRONT

1. Remove mount retaining bolt from below frame mounting bracket.
2. Raise front of engine to remove weight from mount and to place a slight tension on the rubber cushion, remove mount attaching bolts, then the mount, **Fig. 1**. Check for interference between rear of engine and cowl panel. **Raise engine only enough to provide sufficient clearance for mount removal.**
3. Reverse procedure to install.

### REAR

1. Support transmission to relieve weight from rear mounts.

2. Remove crossmember-to-mount attaching nuts.
3. Remove mount attaching bolts, then raise transmission and remove mount, **Fig. 1.**
4. Reverse procedure to install. **Align mount to crossmember when lowering transmission into position.**

# CYLINDER HEAD
## REPLACE
### RIGHT SIDE
#### 1985—86

1. Remove intake manifold as described under "Intake Manifold, Replace."
2. Raise and support vehicle.
3. Disconnect exhaust pipe from exhaust manifold, then lower vehicle.
4. Remove spark plug wires, PCV hose and oil filler tube.
5. Disconnect air injection pipe and electrical connector from rear of cylinder head.
6. Remove engine ground wire from rear of cylinder head.
7. Remove valve cover, then the spark plugs.
8. Remove alternator lower mounting bolt, then remove alternator and position aside.
9. Remove pushrods, then the cylinder head attaching bolts and cylinder head.
10. Reverse procedure to install, noting the following:
    a. On engine using a steel gasket, apply a suitable sealant to both sides of gasket.
    b. On engines using a steel asbestos gasket, do not use any sealant on gasket.
    c. Apply suitable sealant to cylinder head bolt threads prior to installation.
    d. Torque cylinder head attaching bolts to specifications in sequence shown, **Fig. 2.**

#### 1987—89

1. Disconnect battery ground cable.
2. Remove intake manifold as described under "Intake Manifold, Replace."
3. Remove exhaust manifold as described under "Exhaust Manifold, Replace."
4. Remove AIR pipe from rear of cylinder head.
5. Remove AIR pump attaching bolt and spacer from cylinder head.
6. Remove engine accessory bracket bolts and studs from cylinder head.
7. Remove wiring harness and clip from rear of cylinder head.
8. Disconnect spark plug wires and remove spark plugs.
9. Remove valve cover and pushrods.
10. Remove cylinder head attaching bolts, then the cylinder head and gasket.
11. Reverse procedure to install, noting the following:
    a. On engine using a steel gasket, apply a suitable sealant to both sides of gasket.
    b. On engines using a steel asbestos

gasket, do not use any sealant on gasket.
c. Apply suitable sealing compound to cylinder head bolt threads prior to installation.
d. Torque cylinder head attaching bolts to specifications in sequence shown, **Fig. 2.**

### LEFT SIDE
#### 1985—86

1. Remove intake manifold as described under "Intake Manifold, Replace."
2. Disconnect electrical harness from valve cover, then remove the valve cover and pushrods.
3. Raise and support vehicle.
4. Disconnect exhaust pipe from exhaust manifold.
5. Disconnect air injection hoses and exhaust manifold from cylinder head, then lower vehicle.
6. On models equipped with power steering, remove power steering pump.

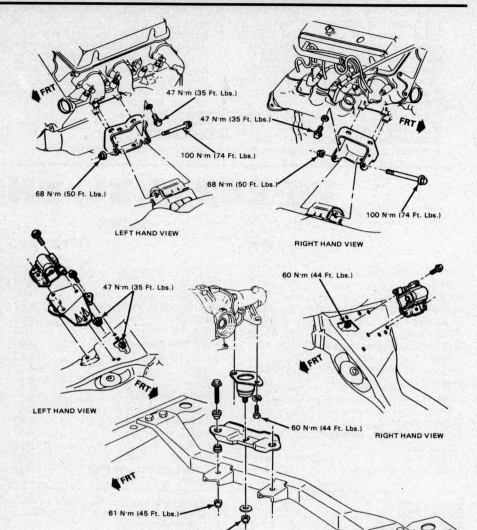

**Fig. 1  Engine mount replacement**

7. On models equipped with A/C, remove A/C compressor idler pulley and compressor mounting bracket.
8. On all models, disconnect spark plug wires from cylinder head and remove spark plugs.
9. Remove cylinder head attaching bolts and the cylinder head.
10. Reverse procedure to install, noting the following:
    a. On engines using a steel gasket, apply a suitable sealant to both sides of gasket.
    b. On engines using a steel asbestos gasket, do not use any sealant on gasket.
    c. Apply suitable sealant to cylinder head bolt threads prior to installation.
    d. Torque cylinder head attaching bolts to specifications in sequence shown, **Fig. 2.**

#### 1987—89

1. Disconnect battery ground cable.
2. Remove intake manifold as described

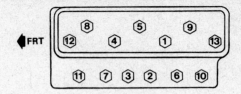

**Fig. 2  Cylinder head bolt tightening sequence**

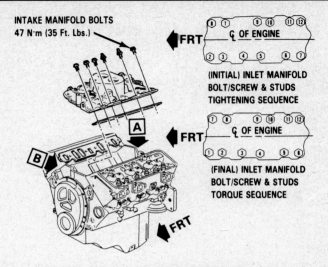

**Fig. 3  Intake manifold bolt tightening sequence**

under "Intake Manifold, Replace."

3. Remove exhaust manifold as described under "Exhaust Manifold, Replace."
4. Remove AIR pipe from rear of cylinder head.
5. Remove engine accessory bracket bolts and studs from cylinder head. **It may be necessary to loosen remaining bracket bolts to provide clearance for head removal.**
6. Remove fuel pipes and brackets from rear of cylinder head.
7. Disconnect coolant sensor electrical connector, then remove cruise control transducer bracket, if equipped.
8. Disconnect spark plug wires and remove spark plugs.
9. Remove valve cover and pushrods.
10. Remove cylinder head attaching bolts, then the cylinder head and gasket.
11. Reverse procedure to install, noting the following:
    a. On engine using a steel gasket, apply a suitable sealant to both sides of gasket.
    b. On engines using a steel asbestos gasket, do not use any sealant on gasket.
    c. Apply suitable sealing compound to cylinder head bolt threads prior to installation.
    d. Torque cylinder head attaching bolts to specifications in sequence shown, **Fig. 2.**

# INTAKE MANIFOLD
## REPLACE
### 1985–86

1. Disconnect battery ground cable.
2. Remove engine cover and air cleaner, then drain cooling system.
3. Remove distributor cap and spark plug wires.
4. Disconnect ESC electrical connector, then remove distributor.
5. Remove detent and accelerator cables, then the A/C compressor rear brace, if equipped.
6. Remove transmission and engine oil filler tubes from alternator brace.
7. On models equipped with A/C, remove A/C idler pulley from alternator brace.
8. On all models, remove alternator brace, then disconnect fuel line from carburetor.
9. Disconnect necessary vacuum lines and electrical connectors from carburetor.

10. Remove air injection hoses and brackets from manifold.
11. Disconnect heater hose from manifold, then remove manifold attaching bolts and the manifold.
12. Reverse procedure to install, noting the following:
    a. Remove all traces of old sealant from cylinder head, block and manifold.
    b. Install gaskets on cylinder heads and apply a 3/16 inch bead of RTV sealant to front and rear ridges of cylinder case. Extend sealant 1/2 inch up each cylinder head to seal and retain side gaskets.
    c. Apply suitable sealant at water passages.
    d. Torque manifold attaching bolts to specifications in sequence shown, **Fig. 3.**

### 1987–89

1. Disconnect battery ground cable.
2. Remove engine cover, air cleaner and heat stove tube.
3. Drain cooling system, then remove distributor assembly.
4. Remove cruise control transducer, if equipped.
5. Disconnect cruise control, TVS and accelerator cables, as required.
6. On models equipped with A/C, disconnect A/C compressor and position aside.
7. On all models, remove engine oil filler tube from the alternator bracket.
8. Remove transmission dipstick tube from manifold, if equipped.
9. Remove idler pulley bracket and alternator brackets from manifold.
10. Disconnect fuel and vacuum lines and all electrical connectors from manifold and TBI unit.
11. Remove heater pipe, upper radiator hose, then the power brake vacuum pipe.
12. Disconnect coil wires, then the EGR vacuum line.

13. Disconnect sensors with bracket and wire harness form right side.
14. Remove intake manifold attaching bolts, then the intake manifold.
15. Reverse procedure to install, noting the following:
    a. Remove all traces of old sealant from cylinder head, block and manifold.
    b. Install gaskets on cylinder heads and apply a 3/16 inch bead of RTV sealant to front and rear ridges of cylinder case. Extend sealant 1/2 inch up each cylinder head to seal and retain side gaskets.
    c. Torque manifold attaching bolts to specifications in sequence shown, **Fig. 3.**

# EXHAUST MANIFOLD
## REPLACE
### RIGHT SIDE
#### 1985–86

1. Disconnect battery ground cable.
2. Raise and support vehicle.
3. Disconnect exhaust pipe from manifold, then lower vehicle.
4. Remove engine cover, then disconnect air injection hose from check valve.
5. Remove exhaust manifold attaching bolts, then disconnect air injection hose from diverter valve and remove exhaust manifold, **Figs. 4 and 5.**
6. Reverse procedure to install.

#### 1987–89

1. Disconnect battery ground cable.
2. Remove engine cover, then raise and support vehicle.
3. Remove exhaust pipe from exhaust manifold, then lower vehicle.
4. Remove heat stove pipe.
5. Remove dipstick tube bracket from manifold.
6. Remove AIR hoses from check valve.

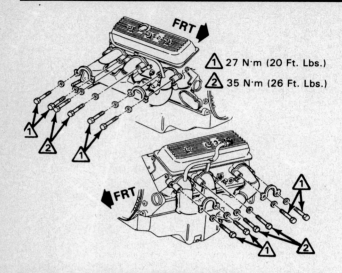

① 27 N·m (20 Ft. Lbs.)
② 35 N·m (26 Ft. Lbs.)

**Fig. 4  Exhaust manifold replacement. 1985**

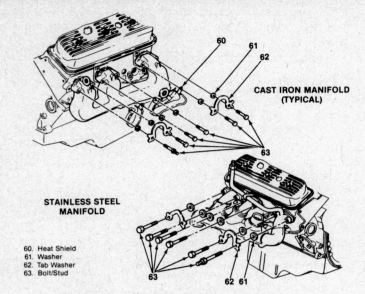

CAST IRON MANIFOLD (TYPICAL)

STAINLESS STEEL MANIFOLD

60. Heat Shield
61. Washer
62. Tab Washer
63. Bolt/Stud

**Fig. 5  Exhaust manifold replacement. 1987–89 (1986 similar)**

7. Remove exhaust manifold attaching bolts, washers and tab washers, then the exhaust manifold, **Fig. 5.**
8. Reverse procedure to install. Bend tab washers over heads of all bolts.

## LEFT SIDE
### 1985–86

1. Disconnect battery ground cable.
2. Raise and support vehicle.
3. Disconnect exhaust pipe from manifold.
4. Disconnect air injection hose bracket from cylinder head.
5. Remove manifold attaching bolts and the manifold, **Figs. 4 and 5.**
6. Reverse procedure to install.

### 1987–89

1. Disconnect battery ground cable.
2. Remove engine cover, then raise and support vehicle.
3. Remove exhaust pipe from exhaust manifold, then lower vehicle.
4. Disconnect oxygen sensor electrical connector. **Do not remove sensor unless it must be replaced.**
5. Remove power steering pump and alternator brackets from manifold.
6. Remove AIR hoses from check valve.
7. Remove exhaust manifold attaching bolts, washers and tab washers, then the heat shield and exhaust manifold, **Fig. 5.**
8. Reverse procedure to install. Bend tab washers over heads of all bolts.

## ROCKER ARMS & PUSHRODS
## REPLACE
### 1985–86

1. Disconnect battery ground cable.
2. Remove engine cover and the air cleaner assembly.
3. To remove right side valve cover, proceed as follows:
   a. Disconnect air injection hoses from diverter valve.

b. Disconnect diverter valve bracket from intake manifold.
   c. Remove engine and transmission oil filler tubes from alternator bracket.
   d. Remove PCV valve, then disconnect air injection hoses from rear of right cylinder head and position aside.
   e. Remove distributor cap and wires, then the valve cover attaching bolts and valve cover.
4. To remove left side valve cover, proceed as follows:
   a. Disconnect vacuum pipe from carburetor.
   b. Disconnect electrical harness from valve cover, then remove valve cover attaching bolts.
   c. Disconnect detent and accelerator cables from carburetor.
   d. Remove detent and accelerator cable bracket from intake manifold.
   e. Remove valve cover.
5. Remove rocker arm nuts and balls, then the rocker arms and pushrods, **Fig. 6.**

### 1987–89

1. Disconnect battery ground cable.
2. Remove engine cover, then the air cleaner assembly.
3. To remove right side valve cover, proceed as follows:
   a. Remove heat stove tube.
   b. Remove diverter valve, bracket and hoses.
   c. Disconnect spark plug wire brackets, then the spark plug wires and clip.
   d. Disconnect dipstick tube bracket from cylinder head.
   e. Remove PCV valve, then move wire harness away from valve cover.
   f. Remove valve cover attaching bolts, then the valve cover and gasket.

4. To remove left side valve cover, proceed as follows:
   a. Remove air cleaner, oil filler tube, then the AIR pipe and check valve.
   b. Disconnect alternator rear brackets, then the crankcase ventilation pipe.
   c. Remove valve cover attaching bolts, then the valve cover and gasket.
5. Remove rocker arm attaching nuts, then the rocker arms with balls.
6. Remove pushrods.

## VALVES
## ADJUST

1. Remove valve covers as described under "Rocker Arms & Pushrods, Replace."
2. Crank engine until mark on torsional damper is aligned with "0" mark on timing tab fastened to crankcase front cover. To ensure engine is at No. 1 cylinder firing position, place fingers on No. 1 cylinder valves as the mark on damper approaches the "0" mark on timing tab. If valves are not moving, engine is in the No. 1 cylinder firing position. If valves are moving, engine is in the No. 4 cylinder firing position and should be rotated one revolution.
3. With engine in No. 1 cylinder firing position, adjust the following valves: exhaust valves 1, 5 and 6; intake valves 1, 2 and 3. (Even numbered cylinders are in the right bank and odd numbered cylinders are in the left bank, when viewed from rear of engine.) To adjust valves, back off adjusting nut until lash is felt at pushrod, then tighten nut until all lash is removed. This can be determined by rotating pushrod while turning adjusting nut, **Fig. 7.** When all lash is removed, tighten adjusting nut one full turn to center lifter plunger.
4. Crank engine one full revolution until

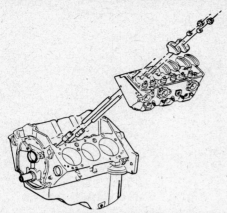

**Fig. 6   Rocker arm & pushrod replacement**

mark on torsional damper and "0" mark on timing tab are aligned. This is the No. 4 cylinder firing position. With engine in this position, adjust the following valves: exhaust valves 2, 3 and 4; intake valves 4, 5 and 6.
5. Install valve covers and related components, then start engine and check timing and idle speed.

## VALVE CLEARANCE SPECIFICATIONS

This engine uses hydraulic lifters. To properly set lifter plunger, turn rocker arm stud nut until valve lash is eliminated, then tighten one additional turn.

## VALVE ARRANGEMENT
### FRONT TO REAR

Right . . . . . . . . . . . . . . . . . . . . . . . E-I-I-E-I-E
Left . . . . . . . . . . . . . . . . . . . . . . . . E-I-E-I-I-E

## VALVE LIFT SPECIFICATIONS

### Engine Year Intake Exhaust

| Engine | Year | Intake | Exhaust |
|---|---|---|---|
| V6-262 | 1985-88 | .398 | .398 |
| V6-262 | 1989 | .355-.359① | .389-.392① |

① measured at camshaft lobe.

## VALVE TIMING
### INTAKE OPENS BEFORE TDC

| Engine | Year | Degrees |
|---|---|---|
| V6-262 | 1985-88 | 22 |

## VALVE LIFTERS
### REPLACE

1. Remove intake manifold as described under "Intake Manifold, Replace."
2. Remove valve cover, rocker arm and pushrods on cylinder(s) to be serviced.
3. Remove retainer and restrictors, if equipped, then the valve lifter.
4. Place lifters in organizing rack after removal. Lifters must be installed in same from which they were removed.

5. Reverse procedure to install. Coat foot of valve lifters with Molykote or equivalent. Following installation, lubricate lifter roller and body with Engine Oil Supplement or equivalent. If new lifter(s) are installed, change engine oil and filter. Adjust valves as described under "Valves, Adjust."

## VALVE LIFTERS SERVICE
### DISASSEMBLY

1. Depress plunger with a pushrod, then remove pushrod seat retainer, **Fig. 8**, using a suitable screwdriver.
2. Remove pushrod seat, metering valve, plunger, ball check valve assembly and plunger spring.
3. Pry ball retainer loose from plunger and remove ball check valve and spring.

### CLEANING & INSPECTION

1. Clean all lifter components in suitable solvent.
2. Inspect all parts for wear or damage. If any one component is worn or damaged, the entire assembly must be replaced.
3. If lifter body wall is worn, inspect cylinder block lifter bore.
4. If bottom of lifter is worn, inspect camshaft lobe.
5. If pushrod seat is worn, inspect pushrod.
6. Check roller for flat spots, pits, and missing or broken needle bearings. If damaged, also check mating camshaft lobe.
7. Check roller for freedom of movement.

### ASSEMBLY

1. Position check ball on small hole in bottom of plunger, then install spring and ball retainer.
2. Install plunger spring over ball retainer, then slide lifter body over spring and plunger. Ensure oil holes in lifter body and plunger are aligned.
3. Turn the assembly has open end up. Fill assembly with SAE 10 oil, then depress plunger with a 1/8 inch drift pin. Insert a 1/16 inch drift pin through both oil holes to hold plunger down against spring tension.
4. Remove the 1/8 inch drift pin and refill assembly with SAE 10 oil, then install metering valve and pushrod seat.
5. Install pushrod seat retainer, then push down on pushrod seat and remove 1/16 inch drift pin from oil holes.

## ROCKER ARM STUDS

Rocker arm studs that have damaged threads or are loose in cylinder head should be replaced with oversize studs. Studs are available in oversizes of .003 and .013 inch and can be installed after reaming holes as follows:
1. Remove stud using stud remover J-5802-01 or equivalent with a nut

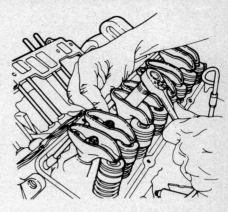

**Fig. 7   Valve adjustment**

and flat washer placed over the tool.
2. Ream hole for oversize stud using reamer J-5715 for .003 inch oversize or J-6036 for .013 inch oversize.
3. Apply hypoid axle lubricant to press fit area of stud, then install new stud using stud installer J-6880 or equivalent.

## CAMSHAFT
### REPLACE
### 1985–86

1. Disconnect battery ground cable.
2. Remove engine cover and air cleaner, then drain cooling system.
3. Remove distributor, then the carburetor.
4. On models equipped with A/C, remove A/C compressor rear brace.
5. On all models, remove transmission and engine oil filler tubes from alternator bracket.
6. Disconnect A/C idler pulley, if equipped.
7. Unfasten alternator adjusting bracket and position aside.
8. Remove diverter valve bracket, then disconnect air injection hoses from diverter valve.
9. Remove intake manifold attaching bolts and the intake manifold.
10. Remove upper fan shroud, then the power steering pump, if equipped.
11. Remove air injection pump and bracket, then the fan and pulley.
12. Remove water pump, torsional damper and engine front cover.
13. Align timing marks, **Fig. 9**, then remove timing chain and camshaft gear.
14. Remove fuel pump, then disconnect engine and transmission cooler lines, as equipped.
15. Remove lower fan shroud, then disconnect brake master cylinder from power brake unit.
16. Remove valve lifters, then carefully remove camshaft using two 5/16 x 18 x 4 inch bolts installed in camshaft bolt holes.
17. Reverse procedure to install. When installing camshaft, align marks on camshaft and crankshaft sprockets, **Fig. 9.** Torque specifications: Water pump; 30 ft. lbs., front cover; 92 inch lbs. and camshaft sprocket; 18 ft. lbs.

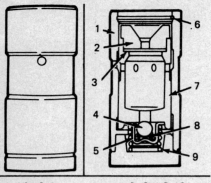

| | |
|---|---|
| I. Lifter Body | 6. Push Rod Seat |
| 2. Push Rod Seat | Retainer |
| 3. Metering Valve | 7. Plunger |
| 4. Check Ball | 8. Check Ball Spring |
| 5. Check Ball Retainer | 9. Plunger Spring |

**Fig. 8   Sectional view of hydraulic valve lifter**

## 1987–89

1. Disconnect battery ground cable.
2. Remove engine cover and air cleaner, then drain cooling system.
3. Remove valve cover, rocker arm and pushrods, refer to "Rocker Arms & Pushrods, Replace" procedure.
4. Remove valve lifters, refer to "Valve Lifters, Replace" procedure.
5. Remove distributor.
6. Remove intake manifold, refer to "Intake Manifold, Replace" procedure.
7. Remove radiator, fan and pulley, then the water pump.
8. Remove torsional damper using a suitable tool, then the engine front cover.
9. Align timing marks, **Fig. 9**, then remove timing chain and camshaft gear. **Tap sprocket on its lower edge, using a suitable mallet, to facilitate removal.**
10. Install two or three 5/16 x 18 x 4 inch bolts into in camshaft bolt holes, then using these bolts as a handle, carefully pull camshaft from block. **Use caution not to damage camshaft bearings.**
11. Reverse procedure to install. When installing camshaft, align marks on camshaft and crankshaft sprockets, **Fig. 9.** Torque specifications: Water pump; 30 ft. lbs., front cover, 1987; 92 inch lbs., 1988-89; 120 inch lbs. and camshaft sprocket, 1887; 18 ft. lbs., 1988-89; 21 ft.lbs. If a new camshaft is being installed, replace all valve lifters.

## ENGINE FRONT COVER
## REPLACE
### 1985
#### Removal

1. Remove drive belts and pulley.
2. Raise and support vehicle.
3. Remove crankshaft pulley, then the damper retaining bolt.
4. Remove torsional damper using torsional damper remover J-23523-1 or equivalent.

5. Remove water pump as described under "Water Pump, Replace."
6. Remove front cover attaching bolts, then the front cover and gasket. Discard gasket.

#### Installation

1. Clean gasket surface on front cover and block.
2. Remove any excess gasket material protruding at oil pan-to-engine block junction using a suitable cutting tool.
3. Apply a 1/8 inch bead of RTV sealant to joint formed at oil pan and block.
4. Apply suitable gasket sealant to gasket and place in position on cover.
5. install cover-to-oil pan seal, then lightly coat bottom of seal with clean engine oil.
6. Position cover over crankshaft end, then loosely install cover-to-block attaching bolts.
7. Tighten attaching screws alternately and evenly while pressing down on cover so dowels in block align with holes in cover. **Do not force cover over dowels so that cover flange or holes are distorted.**
8. Install remaining screws and torque to 92 inch lbs.
9. Install torsional damper and water pump. Torque water pump to 30 ft. lbs.

## 1986–89
### Removal

1. Remove fan belt, then crankshaft pulley.
2. Raise and support vehicle.
3. Remove torsional damper attaching bolt, then the torsional damper using puller J-23523.
4. Remove water pump, refer to "Water Pump, Replace" procedure.
5. Remove oil pan, refer to "Oil Pan, Replace" procedure.
6. Remove front cover attaching bolts, then the front cover and gasket. Discard gasket.

### Installation

1. Install front cover gasket, then the front cover and cover attaching bolts. Torque bolts to 92 inch lbs. on 1986-87 models, and 120 inch lbs. on 1988-89 models.
2. Install oil pan, torquing to nuts to 200 inch lbs. and bolts to 100 inch lbs.
3. Install water pump, torquing to 30 ft. lbs.
4. Install the torsional damper.

## FRONT OIL SEAL
## REPLACE

1. Remove engine front cover, refer to "Engine Front Cover, Replace" procedure.
2. Pry seal out of front cover using a suitable screwdriver, using caution not to scar the surface.
3. Drive new seal into position using seal installer J-23042 for 1985-88 models, J-35468 for 1989 models, or equivalent.

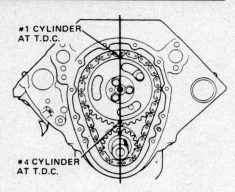

**Fig. 9   Valve timing marks**

## REAR MAIN OIL SEAL
## REPLACE
### 1985

1. Remove oil pan as described under "Oil Pan, Replace."
2. Remove oil pump as described under "Oil Pump, Service."
3. Remove rear main bearing cap, then pry seal out of cap using a suitable screwdriver, being careful not to scar the surface.
4. Remove upper half of seal using a small hammer and punch to tap seal far enough until it may be removed with pliers.
5. Clean all sealant and debris from cylinder case bearing cap and crankshaft using a suitable non-abrasive cleaner.
6. Apply clean engine oil to seal lips and bead, keeping seal mating ends dry.
7. Position tip of fabricated tool, **Fig. 10,** between crankshaft and seal seat in cylinder case.
8. Insert seal between crankshaft and tip of tool so seal bead contacts tip of tool. Ensure oil seal lip is positioned toward front of engine.
9. Roll seal around crankshaft using tool to protect seal from sharp corner of seal seat surface in cylinder case. **Installation tool must remain in place until seal is properly positioned with both ends flush with block.**
10. Remove installation tool, being careful not to disturb seal.
11. Install seal half in bearing cap, using installation tool to feed seal into cap.
12. Apply sealant to bearing cap and case mating surfaces, then install bearing cap. **Avoid getting any sealant on seal split line.**
13. Install rear main bearing cap and torque to 11 ft. lbs. Tap end of crankshaft rearward, then forward to align thrust surfaces, then retorque bearing cap to specifications.

### 1986–89

1. Remove transmission from vehicle.
2. Remove clutch and flywheel, if equipped.
3. Insert suitable screwdriver into notches in seal retainer, then pry out oil seal. **Use caution not to damage crankshaft sealing surface.**

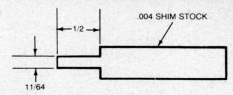

**Fig. 10 Rear main oil seal installation tool. 1985**

4. Clean sealing surface of crankshaft using non-abrasive cleaner.
5. Apply engine oil to inner and outer diameter of oil seal.
6. Install seal using seal installer J-35621, or equivalent.
7. Install clutch and flywheel, as required.
8. Install transmission, torquing transmission-to-engine bolts to 32 ft. lbs.

## MAIN & ROD BEARINGS

Main bearings are available in standard size and undersizes of .001, .002, .009, .010 and .020 inch. Connecting rod bearings are available in standard size and .001 and .002 inch undersize for use with new and used standard size crankshafts and .010 and .020 inch undersize for use with reconditioned crankshafts.

## OIL PAN
### REPLACE
### 1985

1. Disconnect battery ground cable.
2. Raise and support vehicle.
3. Drain oil pan, then disconnect exhaust pipes from exhaust manifolds.
4. Disconnect engine struts from inspection cover, then remove inspection cover.
5. Disconnect starter motor and position aside.
6. Remove engine mount trim bolts, then raise and support engine using a suitable jack.
7. Remove oil pan attaching bolts and the oil pan.
8. Reverse procedure to install, using new seals and gaskets. Torque 5/16 inch oil pan bolts to 14 ft. lbs. and 1/2 inch oil pan bolts to 7 ft. lbs.

### 1986–89

1. Disconnect battery ground cable.
2. Raise and support vehicle.
3. Drain engine oil, then disconnect exhaust pipes from exhaust manifolds.
4. Disconnect engine struts from flywheel cover, then remove flywheel cover.
5. Disconnect starter motor and position aside.
6. Remove oil pan attaching bolts, nuts and reinforcements.
7. Remove oil pan and gasket.
8. Reverse procedure to install. Apply suitable sealant to front cover to block joints and to rear crankshaft seal to block joints. Torque oil pan nuts to 200 inch lbs. and oil pan bolts to 100 inch lbs.

## OIL PUMP SERVICE
### REMOVAL

1. Remove oil pan as previously described.
2. Remove pump-to-rear main bearing cap bolt, then the pump and extension shaft, **Fig. 11.**

### DISASSEMBLY

1. Remove pump cover attaching bolts, then the pump cover, **Fig. 11.**
2. Mark drive and idler gear teeth for assembly reference, then remove idler and drive gear and shaft from pump body.
3. Remove pin, spring and pressure regulator valve from pump cover.
4. If pickup tube and screen assembly are to be replaced, mount pump cover in a soft jawed vise and remove pickup tube from cover. **Do not remove screen from pickup tube, as these components are serviced as an assembly.**

### INSPECTION

1. Inspect pump body and cover for excessive wear or cracks.
2. Inspect pump gears for damage or excessive wear. **If pump body or gears are damaged or worn, the entire oil pump assembly must be replaced.**
3. Check drive gear shaft for looseness in pump body.
4. Inspect interior of cover for wear that would allow oil to leak past ends of gears.
5. Inspect pickup tube, screen and relief grommet for damage.
6. Check pressure regulator valve for fit in pump cover.

### ASSEMBLY

1. If pickup tube and screen were removed, apply suitable sealant to end of tube, then mount pump cover in a soft jawed vise and tap tube into position with a rubber mallet and a pickup tube and screen installer J-8369 or equivalent.
2. Install pressure regulator valve, spring and pin.
3. Install drive gear and shaft in pump body.
4. Install idler gear in pump body with smooth side of gear towards pump cover opening.
5. Install pump cover and torque attaching screws to 7 ft. lbs.
6. Rotate pump driveshaft by hand to ensure smooth operation.

### INSTALLATION

1. Position pump and extension shaft in rear main bearing cap, aligning slot on top of extension shaft with drive tang on lower end of distributor drive shaft. Oil pump should slide easily into place. No gasket is used.
2. Install pump-to-rear main bearing cap bolt and torque to 65 ft. lbs.
3. Install oil pan as previously described. For 1985 models, torque 5/16 inch oil pan bolts to 14 ft. lbs. and 1/2 inch oil

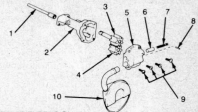

1. SHAFT EXTENSION
2. PUMP BODY
3. DRIVE GEAR AND SHAFT
4. IDLER GEAR
5. PUMP COVER
6. PRESSURE REGULATOR VALVE
7. PRESSURE REGULATOR SPRING
8. RETAINING PIN
9. SCREWS
10. PICKUP SCREEN AND PIPE

**Fig. 11 Exploded view of oil pump**

pan bolts to 7 ft. lbs. For 1986–89 models, torque oil pan nuts to 200 inch lbs. and oil pan bolts to 100 inch lbs.

## WATER PUMP
### REPLACE

1. Disconnect battery ground cable.
2. Drain cooling system.
3. Remove the serpentine drive belt.
3. Remove upper fan shroud, fan and fan clutch assembly, then the water pump pulley.
4. Remove water pump attaching bolts, then disconnect the heater hose from pump.
5. Remove the water pump, **Fig. 12.**
6. Remove old gasket material.
7. Reverse procedure to install, using suitable pipe sealant on bolt threads. Torque water pump bolts to 30 ft. lbs.

## FUEL PUMP
### REPLACE
### 1985

1. Disconnect fuel inlet line, outlet line and vapor return hose, if equipped, from fuel pump.
2. Remove fuel pump attaching bolts, then the fuel pump, pushrod, gasket and mounting plate.
3. Reverse procedure to install. Following installation, start engine and check for leaks. **If it is difficult to start fuel outlet line fitting, disconnect upper end of line from carburetor and tighten fitting while holding fuel pump nut with a wrench.**

### 1986–89

1. Disconnect battery ground cable.
2. Drain fuel from tank, then disconnect fuel tank attaching straps.
3. Disconnect all electrical connectors, ground strap and hoses from fuel tank, then lower fuel tank from vehicle.
4. Remove sender unit and pump assembly by turning lock ring counterclockwise using cam lock removal tool J-36608, J-24187, or equivalent.
5. Remove pump from sending unit, using caution not to damage the rubber insulator or the strainer.
6. Reverse procedure to install.

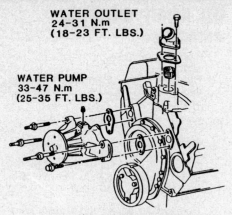

WATER OUTLET
24–31 N.m
(18–23 FT. LBS.)

WATER PUMP
33–47 N.m
(25–35 FT. LBS.)

**Fig. 12  Water pump replacement**

# CLUTCH & MANUAL TRANSMISSION

## INDEX

# CLUTCH
## ADJUST

These models are equipped with a hydraulic clutch. No adjustment of the clutch pedal or linkage is provided.

# CLUTCH
## REPLACE
### 1985

1. Disconnect battery ground cable.
2. Raise and support vehicle.
3. Remove slave cylinder attaching bolts from bellhousing.
4. Remove transmission as described under "Transmission, Replace."
5. Remove bellhousing, then slide clutch fork from ball stud. **Ball stud is threaded in housing and can be easily removed, if necessary.**
6. Install alignment tool J-33169, **Fig. 1**, to support clutch assembly. **Look for "X" mark on flywheel and on clutch cover, or white painted letter on clutch cover. If marks are not evident, mark flywheel and clutch cover for proper alignment during assembly.**
7. Loosen clutch-to-flywheel attaching bolts evenly, one at a time, until spring pressure is released, then remove bolts, clutch and pressure plate as-

sembly, **Fig. 1**.
8. Clean pressure plate and flywheel mating surfaces and inspect flywheel for defects. Replace or repair as necessary.
9. Reverse procedure to install. Torque bellhousing bolts to 32 ft. lbs.

### 1986–89

1. Disconnect battery ground cable.
2. Raise and support vehicle.
3. Remove transmission, refer to "Transmission, Replace" procedure.
4. Remove secondary slave cylinder.
5. Remove flywheel housing cover attaching screws, then the flywheel housing cover, **Fig. 2**.
6. Remove flywheel housing attaching screws, then the flywheel housing.
7. Remove boot, then pry clutch fork off ball stud. Pry retainer from clutch fork, if worn or damaged.
8. Remove release bearing, then the ball stud, if worn or damaged.
9. Install clutch alignment tool J-33169 or equivalent to support clutch assembly.
10. Place alignment marks on flywheel, clutch cover and pressure plate lug.
11. Remove pressure plate attaching screws and lock washers. **Loosen each screw one turn at a time to prevent damaging clutch cover.**
12. Remove clutch cover assembly and driven plate, then the clutch alignment

tool.
13. Remove pilot bearing using pilot bearing puller J-1448, as required.
14. Reverse procedure to install. Torque bellhousing bolts to 32 ft. lbs.

# CLUTCH MASTER CYLINDER SERVICE
## REMOVAL

1. Disconnect battery ground cable.
2. Remove hush panel from passenger compartment, then disconnect pushrod from clutch pedal.
3. Disconnect slave cylinder hydraulic line from master cylinder.
4. Remove master cylinder retaining nuts and the master cylinder, **Fig. 3**.

## DISASSEMBLY

1. Remove reservoir and seal from master cylinder.
2. Remove rubber dust cover from cylinder, **Fig. 4**.
3. Remove snap ring and pushrod, then shake out plunger and spring assembly.
4. Remove reservoir adapter and seal, as required.
5. Remove spring, seal support, recuperation seal and shim from plunger.

## INSPECTION

1. Replace seals and clean all compo-

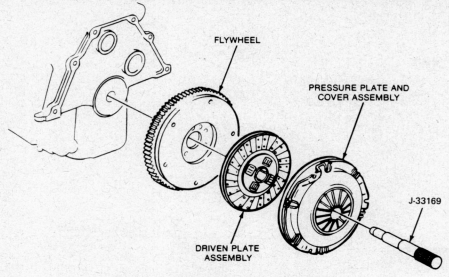

Fig. 1 Clutch assembly. 1985

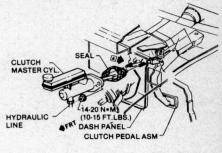

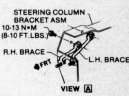

Fig. 3 Clutch master cylinder replacement

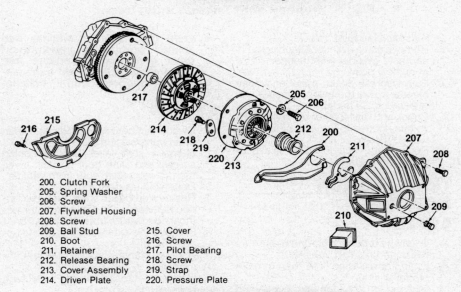

200. Clutch Fork
205. Spring Washer
206. Screw
207. Flywheel Housing
208. Screw
209. Ball Stud
210. Boot
211. Retainer
212. Release Bearing
213. Cover Assembly
214. Driven Plate
215. Cover
216. Screw
217. Pilot Bearing
218. Screw
219. Strap
220. Pressure Plate

Fig. 2 Clutch assembly. 1986–89

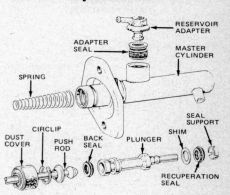

Fig. 4 Exploded view of clutch master cylinder

nents in clean brake fluid.
2. Inspect cylinder bore for visible scores and ridges. Ensure it is smooth to the touch. Replace master cylinder if defective.

## ASSEMBLY

1. Apply clean brake fluid to seals and cylinder bore. Install back seal, shim, recuperation seal, seal support and spring on plunger.
2. Carefully slide plunger assembly into master cylinder bore.
3. Position pushrod into plunger, then depress plunger and install snap ring.
4. Apply suitable grease to inside of rubber dust cover, then install the dust cover.
5. Install reservoir adapter seal, then press in the adapter.

## INSTALLATION

1. Install master cylinder assembly and

torque retaining nuts to 10-15 ft. lbs.
2. Connect pushrod to clutch pedal and install retaining clip.
3. Install hush panel, then connect slave cylinder hydraulic line to master cylinder.
4. Fill master cylinder reservoir with new brake fluid, then bleed system as described under "Clutch System, Bleed."
5. Connect battery ground cable.

## CLUTCH SLAVE CYLINDER SERVICE

### REMOVAL

1. Disconnect battery ground cable.
2. Raise and support vehicle.
3. Disconnect hydraulic line from slave cylinder.
4. Remove slave cylinder attaching nuts and the slave cylinder, Fig. 5. Cover all hydraulic line openings to keep

dirt and moisture out of braking system.

## DISASSEMBLY

1. Remove pushrod and rubber dust cover from slave cylinder, Fig. 6.
2. Remove snap ring, then shake out plunger and spring assembly.
3. Remove seal from plunger, using care to avoid damaging plunger surfaces.

## INSPECTION

1. Replace seal and clean all components in clean brake fluid.
2. Inspect cylinder bore for visible scores and ridges. Ensure it is smooth to the touch. Replace slave cylinder if defective.
3. Ensure dust cover is not worn or cracking.

## ASSEMBLY

1. Lubricate with clean brake fluid, then install seal and spring on plunger.
2. Lubricate seal and cylinder bore with clean brake fluid, then slide plunger and spring assembly into cylinder bore.
3. Depress plunger and install snap ring.
4. Apply suitable grease to inside of rubber dust cover, then install the dust

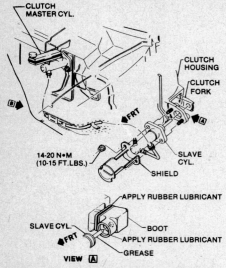

**Fig. 5  Clutch slave cylinder replacement**

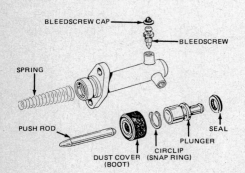

**Fig. 6  Exploded view of clutch slave cylinder**

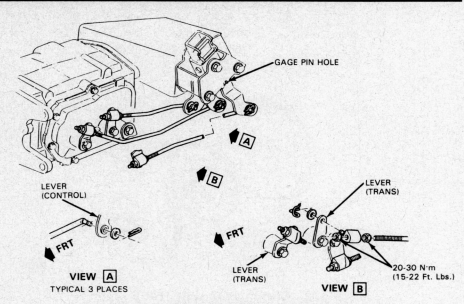

**Fig. 7  4-speed shift linkage adjustment**

cover and pushrod.

## INSTALLATION

1. Connect hydraulic line to slave cylinder, then install slave cylinder to bellhousing and torque retaining nuts to 10-15 ft. lbs.
2. Fill reservoir with new brake fluid and bleed system as described under "Clutch System, Bleed."

## CLUTCH SYSTEM
### BLEED

When refilling or bleeding system, use only new brake fluid conforming to DOT 3 specifications. Never use fluid which has been bled from a system to fill the reservoir, as it may be aerated or otherwise contaminated.

1. Fill master cylinder reservoir with new brake fluid.

2. Raise and support vehicle.
3. Remove slave cylinder attaching bolts and hold cylinder with bleeder screw at highest point.
4. Fully depress clutch pedal and open bleeder valve, then close bleeder and release clutch pedal.
5. Check and refill master cylinder reservoir as needed to prevent air from entering system.
6. Repeat sequence until all air is evacuated from system.

## TRANSMISSION
### REPLACE
#### 4 SPEED

1. Disconnect battery ground cable.
2. Raise and support vehicle.
3. Drain transmission fluid, then remove propeller shaft.
4. Disconnect speedometer cable and electrical connectors from transmission.
5. Disconnect shift linkage from shifter.
6. Remove shifter support attaching bolts from transmission.
7. Remove transmission mount attaching bolts.
8. Support transmission and remove crossmember attaching bolts and the crossmember.
9. Remove transmission attaching bolts and the transmission.
10. Reverse procedure to install. Torque transmission-to-clutch housing bolts to 48 ft. lbs. on 1985 models, 50 ft. lbs. on 1986-88 models and 46 ft. lbs. on 1989 models. **Apply a light coating of high temperature grease to main**

drive gear bearing retainer and splined portion of transmission drive gear shaft to ensure free movement of clutch and transmission components during installation.

#### 5 SPEED

1. Disconnect battery ground cable, then drain transmission oil.
2. Remove shift lever boot attaching screws and slide boot up shift lever, then remove shift lever from vehicle.
3. Raise and support vehicle.
4. Remove propeller shaft, then disconnect speedometer cable and all electrical connectors from transmission.
5. Remove the exhaust pipes, then support transmission.
6. Remove transmission mount attaching bolts.
7. Remove crossmember attaching bolts and the crossmember.
8. Remove transmission support braces.
9. Remove transmission-to-engine attaching bolts and the transmission.
10. Reverse procedure to install. Torque transmission-to-clutch housing bolts to 55 ft. lbs. on 1985 models, 50 ft. lbs. on 1986-88 models and 46 ft. lbs. on 1989 models.

## 4 SPEED SHIFT LINKAGE
### ADJUST

Transmission and shifter levers must be in Neutral position at time of rod assembly. A ¼ inch gage pin must fit freely into gage pin hole when levers are positioned as outlined above, Fig. 7.

# REAR AXLE, SUSPENSION & BRAKE

## INDEX

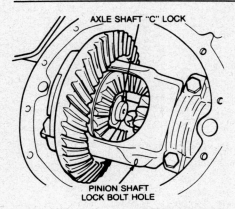

**Fig. 1  Removing differential pinion shaft**

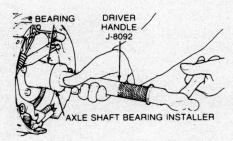

**Fig. 4  Axle shaft bearing installation**

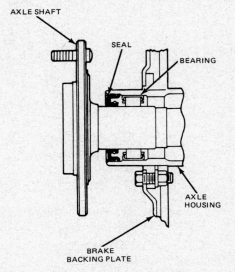

**Fig. 2  Cross sectional view of axle shaft & seal**

a. Torque new pinion shaft lock bolt to 25 ft. lbs.
b. Torque carrier cover attaching bolts to 20 ft. lbs.
c. Fill axle to bring lubricant level within 3/8 inch of filler hole.

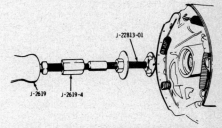

**Fig. 3  Axle shaft bearing removal**

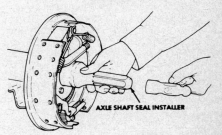

**Fig. 5  Axle shaft seal installation**

Install in axle housing, tapping into place until seal is flush with housing, Fig. 5.

## AXLE SHAFT
### REPLACE

1. Raise and support rear of vehicle, then remove wheel and brake drum on side axle is to be replaced.
2. Loosen carrier cover attaching bolts and allow lubricant to drain, then remove the bolts and carrier cover.
3. Remove rear axle pinion shaft lock bolt and the pinion shaft, **Fig. 1.**
4. Push flanged end of axle shaft toward center of vehicle, then remove C-lock from button end of shaft.
5. Remove axle shaft from housing, using care to avoid damaging seal, **Fig. 2.**
6. Reverse procedure to install, noting the following:

## WHEEL BEARING & AXLE SEAL
### REPLACE

1. Remove axle shaft as described under "Axle Shaft, Replace."
2. Remove axle seal by prying behind seal steel case with a suitable pry bar. Use care to avoid damaging axle housing.
3. Remove axle bearing using slide hammer J-2619, adapter J-2619-4, or axle bearing puller J-22813-01. The tangs of the axle bearing puller should engage the bearing outer race, **Fig. 3.**
4. Lubricate new bearing with gear lubricant, then install bearing in axle housing with axle shaft bearing installer J-23765 or equivalent until bearing is seated in housing, **Fig. 4.**
5. Apply suitable gear lubricant to seal lips, then position seal on axle shaft seal installer J-23771 or equivalent.

## AXLE ASSEMBLY
### REPLACE

Construction of the axle assembly is such that service operations may be performed with the housing installed in the vehicle or with the housing removed and installed in a holding fixture. The following procedure is necessary only when the housing requires replacement.

1. Raise vehicle and support at the frame.
2. Position a suitable jack under rear axle housing and raise slightly to support axle assembly.
3. Remove rear wheels and drums, then disconnect shock absorbers from anchor plates.
4. Scribe reference marks between driveshaft and the pinion flange for assembly reference, then disconnect driveshaft and position aside.
5. Remove brake lines from axle housing, then disconnect brake lines from backing plate.

6. If equipped with a stabilizer bar refer to "Rear Stabilizer, Replace," then proceed.
7. Remove U-bolts and anchor plates.
8. Remove vent hose from axle housing, move the axle clear of springs, then lower axle from vehicle.
9. Reverse procedure to install. Torque shock absorber nuts to 74 ft. lbs., inner U-bolt nuts to 74 ft. lbs., and outer U-bolt nuts to 48 ft. lbs.

## STABILIZER BAR
## REPLACE

1. Raise and support vehicle.
2. Remove the bolts and washers from the link brackets, **Fig. 6**.
3. Remove the nuts, washers and clamp from the anchor block studs. At this point, the stabilizer bar assembly will be clear from the vehicle. Proceed only if a new stabilizer bar will be installed.
4. Remove the insulator from the stabilizer bar.
5. Remove the upper link nuts, washers and bolts from the assembly.
6. Remove the link bracket from the link assembly.
7. Remove the link nuts, washers and bolts, then pry open lower link to obtain clearance from the link insulator.
8. Remove the link insulator from the stabilizer bar.
9. Reverse procedure to install, noting the following torques; link bracket bolts, 25 ft. lbs., lower link bolts, 12 ft. lbs., upper link bolts, 33 ft. lbs. and cap nuts, 38 ft. lbs.

## SHOCK ABSORBER
## REPLACE

1. Raise vehicle and place jackstands under frame side rails.
2. Position a suitable jack under rear axle housing and raise slightly to support axle assembly.
3. Disconnect parking brake bracket from right shock absorber.
4. Disconnect shock absorber from upper mounting, **Fig. 7**.
5. Disconnect shock absorber from lower mounting, then remove from vehicle.
6. Reverse procedure to install. Torque retaining nuts to 75 ft. lbs.

## LEAF SPRING
## ASSEMBLY
## REPLACE
### 1985–88

1. Raise vehicle and place jackstands under frame side rails. Support axle assembly separately to relieve spring load.
2. Remove wheel and tire assembly.
3. Loosen, but do not remove, spring-to-shackle and shackle-to-body retaining nuts, **Fig. 8**.
4. Disconnect shock absorber from lower mounting.
5. Remove U-bolt retaining nuts, spring retainer and spring plate, then lower

| | |
|---|---|
| 12. Lower Plate | 35. Link Assembly |
| 21. Washer | 36. Bolt |
| 22. Nut | 37. Washer |
| 23. Anchor Plate | 38. Nut |
| 24. Nut | 39. Rivnuts |
| 28. Anchor Block | 40. Link Bracket |
| 29. Insulator | 41. Bolt |
| 30. Clamp | 42. Washer |
| 31. Washer | 43. Nut |
| 32. Nut | 44. Washer |
| 33. Stabilizer Bar | 45. Bolt |
| 34. Link Insulator | |

**Fig. 6   Rear Stabilizer assembly**

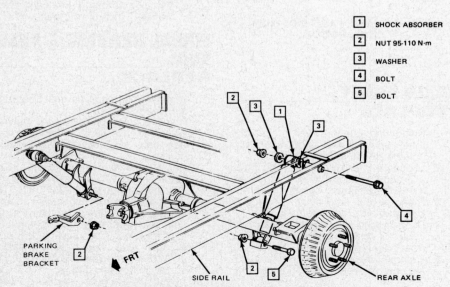

| | |
|---|---|
| 1 | SHOCK ABSORBER |
| 2 | NUT 95-110 N·m |
| 3 | WASHER |
| 4 | BOLT |
| 5 | BOLT |

PARKING BRAKE BRACKET

FRT

SIDE RAIL

REAR AXLE

**Fig. 7   Shock absorber replacement**

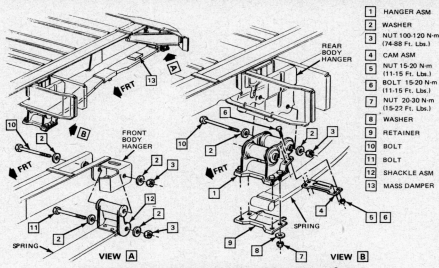

| | |
|---|---|
| 1 | HANGER ASM |
| 2 | WASHER |
| 3 | NUT 100-120 N·m (74-88 Ft. Lbs.) |
| 4 | CAM ASM |
| 5 | NUT 15-20 N·m (11-15 Ft. Lbs.) |
| 6 | BOLT 15-20 N·m (11-15 Ft. Lbs.) |
| 7 | NUT 20-30 N·m (15-22 Ft. Lbs.) |
| 8 | WASHER |
| 9 | RETAINER |
| 10 | BOLT |
| 11 | BOLT |
| 12 | SHACKLE ASM |
| 13 | MASS DAMPER |

**Fig. 8  Leaf spring & shackle mounting**

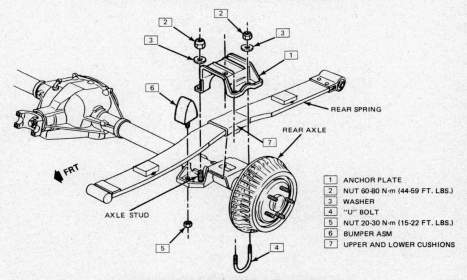

| | |
|---|---|
| 1 | ANCHOR PLATE |
| 2 | NUT 60-80 N·m (44-59 FT. LBS.) |
| 3 | WASHER |
| 4 | "U" BOLT |
| 5 | NUT 20-30 N·m (15-22 FT. LBS.) |
| 6 | BUMPER ASM |
| 7 | UPPER AND LOWER CUSHIONS |

**Fig. 9  Leaf spring removal**

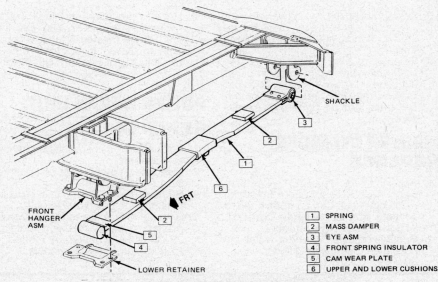

| | |
|---|---|
| 1 | SPRING |
| 2 | MASS DAMPER |
| 3 | EYE ASM |
| 4 | FRONT SPRING INSULATOR |
| 5 | CAM WEAR PLATE |
| 6 | UPPER AND LOWER CUSHIONS |

**Fig. 10  Leaf spring assembly. 1985–88**

axle. **Do not allow weight of axle to hang on brake hoses. Always support axle and body separately.**

6. Remove nuts, washers and retainer from front spring hanger.
7. Slide spring forward to gain access to spring-to-shackle bolt through rear bumper bracket, then remove nut, washer, bolt and spring assembly, **Fig. 9.**
8. If necessary, drill out rivets and remove leaf spring eye, **Fig. 10.**
9. Reverse procedure to install. If eye assembly was removed, replace rivets with 10 mm bolts and nuts.

## 1989

1. Raise the vehicle and support at the frame rails. Support the rear axle separately to relieve the load on rear springs.
2. Remove shock absorbers, **Fig. 11.**
3. Remove the U-bolt and lower plate nuts, then the flat washers. **On models equipped with a stabilizer bar, it will be necessary to remove the lower nuts, washers and anchor blocks, then swing the stabilizer bar down to obtain clearance.**
4. Loosen, but do not remove the shackle nuts.
5. Remove the anchor plate, then lower the axle away from the spring. **Do not let the axle hang by the brake hose or damage may occur.**
6. Remove the retainer nuts and washers, then the retainer.
7. Remove the spring-to-shackle nut, washers and bolt.
8. Remove the spring from vehicle.
9. Reverse procedure to install, noting the following:
   a. Torque retainer nuts to 28 ft. lbs., U-bolt nuts to 48 ft. lbs., and the lower plate nuts to 41 ft. lbs.
   b. Adjust the rear suspension trim height by raising the rear axle until the top of the axle is 5.5–6.3 inches from the bottom of the frame. **Damage to the spring and axle could result if the axle supports are not in complete contact with the axle and resting firmly on the floor.**
   c. After trim height has been adjusted, torque leaf spring rear anchor nuts to 81 ft. lbs. and front anchor nuts to 103 ft. lbs.
   d. Install shock absorbers, then lower vehicle.

## SHACKLE
## REPLACE

1. Remove leaf spring as previously described.
2. Remove shackle nut, washers and bolt, then the shackle, **Fig. 8.**
3. Press center sleeve and bushing out of shackle, if necessary.
4. Reverse procedure to install. Press in new center sleeve and bushing, if removed.

## DRUM BRAKE
### ADJUSTMENTS

These brakes have self adjusting shoe mechanisms that ensure correct lining-to-drum clearances at all times. The automatic adjusters operate only when brakes are applied as vehicle is moving in reverse.

Although the brakes are self-adjusting, an initial adjustment is necessary after brake shoes have been relined or replaced, or when length of star wheel adjuster has been changed during some other service operation.

Frequent usage of an automatic transmission forward range to halt reverse vehicle motion may prevent automatic adjusters from functioning, thereby inducing low pedal heights. Should low pedal heights be encountered, it is recommended that numerous forward and reverse stops be made until satisfactory pedal height is obtained.

If a low pedal height condition cannot be corrected by making numerous reverse stops (provided hydraulic system is free of air), the self-adjusting mechanism is not functioning. Therefore it will be necessary to remove brake drum, clean, free up and lubricate adjusting mechanism, then adjust brakes as follows, being sure parking brake is fully released.

### ADJUSTMENTS

Upon initial adjustment, a lanced area in the brake backing plate must be removed prior to adjusting brakes. To remove lanced area, knock out with a suitable hammer and punch, then remove brake drum to clear any metal particles caught inside the brake compartment. Install brake drum and proceed with adjustment. After adjustment is complete, install brake adjustment hole cover to prevent entry of water and dirt.

1. Turn brake adjusting screw to expand shoes until wheel can just be turned by hand.
2. Using a suitable tool to hold actuator from adjuster, back off adjuster 24 notches. If shoes still drag, back off one or two additional notches. **Brakes should be free of drag when adjuster has been backed off approximately 12 notches. Heavy drag at this point indicates tight parking brake cables.**
3. Install adjusting hole cover on brake backing plate.
4. Check parking brake adjustment.

## PARKING BRAKE
### ADJUST

1. Ensure service brakes have been properly adjusted, then depress parking brake pedal exactly 2 clicks.
2. Raise and support vehicle.

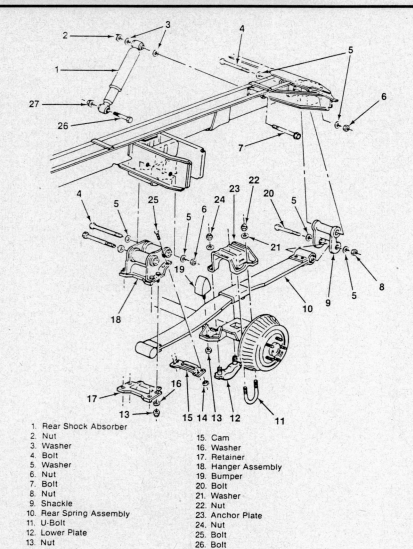

| | |
|---|---|
| 1. Rear Shock Absorber | |
| 2. Nut | |
| 3. Washer | 15. Cam |
| 4. Bolt | 16. Washer |
| 5. Washer | 17. Retainer |
| 6. Nut | 18. Hanger Assembly |
| 7. Bolt | 19. Bumper |
| 8. Nut | 20. Bolt |
| 9. Shackle | 21. Washer |
| 10. Rear Spring Assembly | 22. Nut |
| 11. U-Bolt | 23. Anchor Plate |
| 12. Lower Plate | 24. Nut |
| 13. Nut | 25. Bolt |
| 14. Nut | 26. Bolt |
| | 27. Nut |

**Fig. 11   Leaf spring assembly, 1989**

3. Adjust equalizer nut until left rear wheel can just be turned rearward using two hands, but cannot be turned forward.
4. Release parking brake and ensure both rear wheels turn freely in either direction, then lower vehicle. **To avoid brake drag, the parking brake cable must not be tightened excessively.**

## MASTER CYLINDER
### REPLACE

1. Apply the vehicle parking brakes, then disconnect hydraulic brake lines from master cylinder. **Cap all open lines to prevent dirt or moisture contamination of braking system.**
2. Remove master cylinder retaining nuts, then the master cylinder.

3. Reverse procedure to install. Torque hydraulic line nuts to 120-180 inch lbs. Torque master cylinder retaining nuts to 22-33 ft. lbs. on 1985-87 models or 21 ft. lbs. on 1988-89 models.

## POWER BRAKE UNIT
### REPLACE

1. Disconnect master cylinder from power brake unit.
2. Disconnect power brake unit pushrod from brake pedal.
3. Remove power brake unit retaining nuts and the power brake unit.
4. Reverse procedure to install. Torque master cylinder retaining nuts to 22-33 ft. lbs. on 1985-87 models, or 21 ft. lbs. on 1988-89 models.

## INDEX

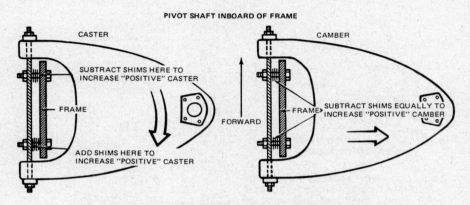

Fig. 1   Caster & camber adjustment

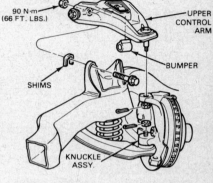

Fig. 3   Upper control arm replacement

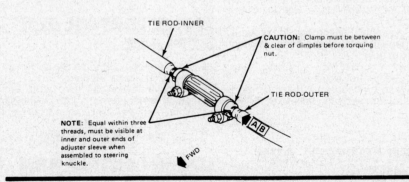

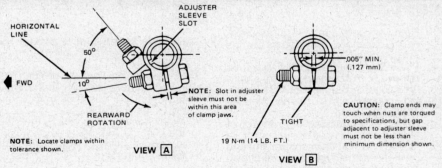

Fig. 2   Tie rod clamp & sleeve positioning

## WHEEL ALIGNMENT
### CASTER & CAMBER, ADJUST

Before checking and adjusting caster and camber angles, jounce front bumper at least three times, to allow vehicle to return to normal "trim height." This will prevent false readings.

Caster and camber adjustments are made by add, subtract or transfer shims inserted between upper control arm shaft and frame bracket, **Fig. 1.** as noted below.

To adjust caster and/or camber, loosen upper control arm shaft-to-frame nuts, then the add or subtract shims as necessary, adjust, then retorque nuts to 66 ft. lbs. After adjustment, the shim pack should have at least two threads of bolt exposed beyond the nut. The difference between front and rear shim packs must not exceed .40 inch.

When adjusting caster, transfer shims from front to rear or rear to front. The transfer of one shim from rear to front bolt will decrease positive caster.

When adjusting camber, change shims equally at both front and rear of shaft. Adding an equal number of shims at front and rear will decrease positive camber.

When performing either caster or camber adjustment, always tighten nut on thinner shim pack first to improve shaft-to-frame clamping force and torque retention.

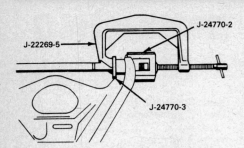

**Fig. 4  Upper control arm bushing removal**

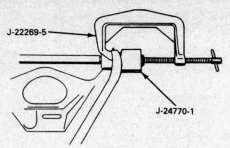

**Fig. 5  Upper control arm bushing installation**

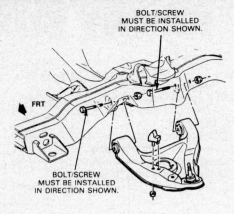

**Fig. 6  Lower control arm replacement**

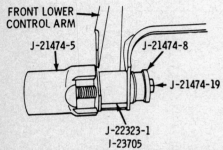

**Fig. 7  Lower control arm front bushing removal**

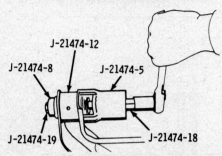

**Fig. 8  Lower control arm rear bushing removal**

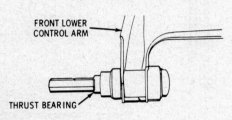

**Fig. 9  Lower control arm front bushing installation**

## TOE-IN, ADJUST

To adjust toe-in, loosen clamp bolts at each end of steering tie rod adjusting sleeves. Replace the clamp bolts if the clamp bolt breakaway exceeds 80 inch lbs. With steering wheel in straight ahead position, turn tie rod adjusting sleeves to obtain proper adjustment. Decrease the length of the tie rod to increase toe-in. Increase the length of the tie rod to decrease the toe-in. After adjustment, check that number of threads showing on the inside of the adjusting sleeves are equal to within three and that the tie rod end stud lines up with steering knuckle. Position tie rod clamps and sleeves as shown in **Fig. 2**, then torque nuts to 14 ft. lbs.

## WHEEL BEARINGS
### ADJUST

1. Raise and support front of vehicle.
2. While rotating wheel assembly in forward direction, torque spindle nut to 12 ft. lbs. to fully seat the bearings.
3. Back off spindle nut until just loose, then hand tighten spindle nut.
4. Loosen nut until hole in spindle aligns with a spindle nut slot, then install new cotter pin.
5. When properly adjusted, endplay should measure .001-.005 inch.
6. Install rotor/hub cap, then lower vehicle.

## UPPER CONTROL ARM
### REPLACE

1. Note location of shims for assembly reference. Remove retaining nuts and shims, **Fig. 3**.
2. Raise vehicle and support lower con-

trol arm with suitable jackstands. **Jack must be positioned between coil spring seat and ball joint of lower control arm to obtain maximum leverage against coil spring pressure.**
3. Remove front wheel, then loosen upper ball joint from steering knuckle as described under "Upper Ball Joint, Replace."
4. Support hub assembly to prevent damage to brake line when removing control arm.
5. Remove control arm attaching bolts and the control arm, **Fig. 3**.
6. Reverse procedure to install. Torque control arm retaining nuts to 66 ft. lbs.

## UPPER CONTROL ARM BUSHING
### REPLACE

1. Remove upper control arm as previously described in "Upper Control Arm, Replace."
2. Place upper control arm in a vise, then remove nuts from end of pivot shaft.
3. Press bushings out of control arm, using control arm bushing installer J-22269, **Fig. 4**.
4. Remove the bushing from the pivot shaft.
5. Position pivot shaft in control arm and press new bushings into control arm and over pivot shaft, **Fig. 5**. Both bushings must be installed .48-.52 inch from face of control arm to bushing outer sleeve.
6. Install pivot shaft retaining nuts and torque to 85 ft. lbs.

## LOWER CONTROL ARM
### REPLACE

1. Remove coil spring as described under "Coil Spring, Replace."
2. Remove lower ball joint stud, then guide control arm through opening in splash shield and remove from vehicle, **Fig. 6**.
3. Reverse procedure to install.

## LOWER CONTROL ARM BUSHINGS
### REPLACE

1. Remove lower control arm as described in "Lower Control Arm, Replace."
2. Drive bushing flare down flush with rubber of front bushing, then remove front and rear bushings from control arm, **Figs. 7** and **8**.
3. Install front bushing, **Fig. 9**, then flare the bushing, **Fig. 10**.
4. Install rear bushing, **Fig. 11**, then the lower control arm.

## COIL SPRING
### REPLACE

1. Raise and support vehicle so control

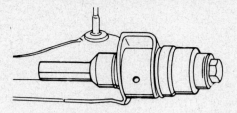

**Fig. 10 Flaring lower control arm front bushing**

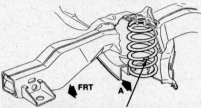

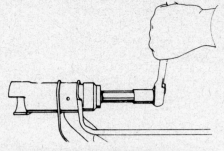

**Fig. 11 Lower control arm rear bushing installation**

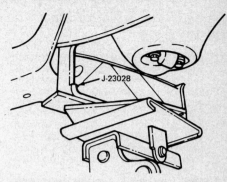

**Fig. 12 Coil spring removal**

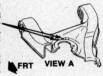

SPRING TO BE INSTALLED WITH TAPE AT LOWEST POSITION. BOTTOM OF SPRING IS COILED HELICAL, AND THE TOP IS COILED FLAT WITH A GRIPPER NOTCH NEAR END OF SPRING COIL.

AFTER ASSEMBLY, END OF SPRING COIL MUST COVER ALL OR PART OF ONE IN-SPECTION DRAIN HOLE. THE OTHER HOLE MUST BE PARTLY EXPOSED OR COM-PLETELY UNCOVERED. ROTATE SPRING AS NECESSARY.

**Fig. 13 Coil spring installation**

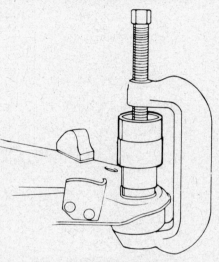

**Fig. 14 Lower ball joint removal**

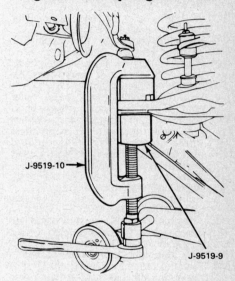

**Fig. 15 Lower ball joint installation**

arms hang free.
2. Remove two shock absorber nuts and push shock up through control arm and into spring.
3. Secure spring remover J-23028 to a suitable jack and position tool to cradle inner bushings, **Fig. 12.**
4. Remove stabilizer-to-lower control arm attachment.
5. Raise jack to relieve tension from lower control arm pivot bolts, then install a chain around spring and through control arm.
6. Remove attaching nuts and bolts, then slowly lower jack and control arm and remove spring. **Do not apply force to lower control arm and ball joint to remove spring. Proper maneuvering of spring will allow for easy removal.**
7. Reverse procedure to install. Refer to **Figs. 6 and 13** for proper assembly of coil spring and pivot ball.

## UPPER BALL JOINT
### REPLACE

1. Raise and support vehicle. Support lower control arm with suitable jackstands. **Jack must be positioned between coil spring seat and ball joint of lower control arm to obtain maximum leverage against coil spring pressure.**
2. Remove wheel and tire assembly, then the ball joint cotter pin, stud nut and grease fitting.
3. Break stud loose from steering knuckle using ball joint separator J-23742 or equivalent. Apply pressure on stud

by expanding tool until stud breaks free.
4. Support the steering knuckle to prevent damage to brake hoses.
5. With control arm in raised position, drill rivets 1/4 inch deep with a 1/8 inch drill, then drill off rivet heads with a 1/2 inch drill.
6. Punch out rivets, then remove ball joints.
7. Reverse procedure to install. Replace rivets with attaching bolts and nuts. For 1985-87 models, torque retaining nuts to 8 ft. lbs. and the stud nut to 52 ft. lbs. For 1988-89 models, torque retaining nuts to 17 ft. lbs. and the ball joint stud nut to 65 ft. lbs. For all models, torque lug nuts to 90 ft. lbs.

## LOWER BALL JOINT
### REPLACE

1. Raise vehicle and support with jack stands under frame side rails.
2. Remove wheel and tire assembly, then support control arm spring seat with a suitable jack.
3. Remove ball joint cotter pin and stud nut, then break ball joint loose from steering knuckle using ball joint separator J-23742 or equivalent. **Inspect and clean the tapered hole in steering knuckle. If hole is out of round or damaged in any way, the steer-**

ing knuckle must be replaced.
4. Position a wooden block between frame and upper control arm to block steering knuckle/hub assembly out of the way. Make sure there is no tension on the brake hoses.
5. Press ball joint out of lower control arm using ball joint removal and installation set J-9519-D. Remove rubber grease seal, then the grease fitting, **Fig. 14.**
6. Reverse procedure to install. Refer to **Fig. 15** and torque stud nut to 81 ft. lbs. Tighten nut to align cotter pin slot.

## SHOCK ABSORBER
### REPLACE

1. Raise and support vehicle.
2. Hold shock upper stem from turning with a suitable wrench and remove nut, retainer and grommet.
3. Remove lower shock pivot bolts, then the shock absorber through the hole in the lower control arm, **Fig. 16.**
4. Reverse procedure to install. Torque upper attaching nut to 15 ft. lbs. for 1985-87 models, 11 ft. lbs. for 1988-89 models. For all models, torque lower attaching bolts to 18 ft. lbs.

## STEERING KNUCKLE
### REPLACE

1. Raise front of vehicle and support with jackstands under front lift points, then remove wheel and tire assembly. **Do not support vehicle under lower control arm at this time, as vehicle may slip off stands during knuckle removal. Spring tension will also aid in breaking ball joint studs loose from steering knuckle.**
2. Remove brake caliper, then the brake and hub assembly.
3. Remove splash shield-to-steering knuckle attaching bolts.
4. Remove tie rod end from steering knuckle using tie rod end puller J-6627 or equivalent.
5. If steering knuckle is to be repaired or replaced, remove knuckle seal.
6. Remove ball joint studs from steering knuckle using ball joint remover J-23742 or equivalent.
7. Position a suitable jack under lower control arm near spring seat, then raise jack until it just supports control arm. **Jack must remain in position under control arm during removal and installation to hold spring and control arm in position.**
8. Raise upper control arm to disengage upper ball joint stud from knuckle.
9. Remove steering knuckle from lower ball joint stud, **Fig. 17.**
10. After removal, inspect and clean tapered hole in steering knuckle. If hole is out of round or damaged in any way, then knuckle must be replaced.
11. Reverse procedure to install. Torque upper ball joint nut to 65 ft. lbs., lower ball joint nut to 90 ft. lbs., splash shield attaching bolts to 10 ft. lbs. and tie rod end to 33 ft. lbs.

## STABILIZER BAR
### REPLACE

1. Raise and support front of vehicle.
2. Remove nuts from both sides to disconnect linkage. Pull the bolts down through the retainers, grommets and spacers. These components will come free with the ends of the stabilizer.
3. Remove bracket-to-frame or body bolts, then the stabilizer bar, rubber bushings and brackets, **Fig. 18.**
4. Reverse procedure to install, noting the following:
    a. Install stabilizer bar insulators with the slit toward the front of the vehicle, stabilizer bar identification stamping appears on right side of vehicle and the offset in the bar is in the downward position.
    b. Position rubber bushings squarely in brackets with slit in bushings facing front of vehicle.
    c. For 1985-87 models, torque stabilizer bar retaining nuts to 13 ft. lbs. and bracket bolts to 22 ft. lbs. For 1988-89 models, torque stabilizer bar retaining nuts to 13 ft. lbs. and bracket bolts to 27 ft. lbs.

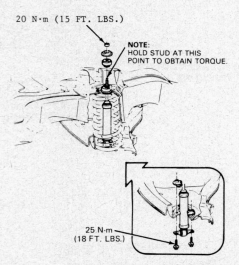

20 N·m (15 FT. LBS.)

**NOTE:** HOLD STUD AT THIS POINT TO OBTAIN TORQUE.

25 N·m (18 FT. LBS.)

**Fig. 16   Shock absorber replacement**

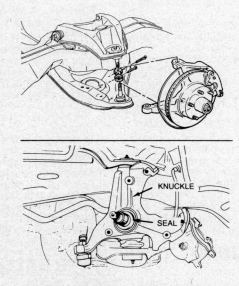

KNUCKLE

SEAL

**Fig. 17   Steering knuckle replacement**

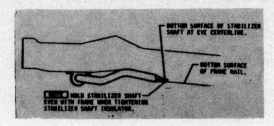

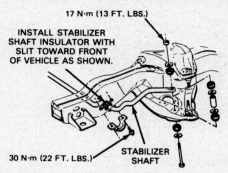

**Fig. 18  Stabilizer bar replacement**

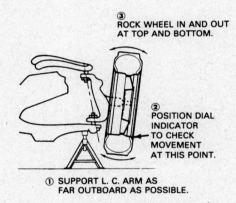

**Fig. 19  Checking upper ball joint**

# BALL JOINT INSPECTION

Prior to inspecting ball joints, ensure wheel bearings are properly adjusted.

## UPPER BALL JOINT

1. Raise vehicle and position stands under right and left lower control arms near each lower ball joint. Vehicle should not rock while on stands and the upper control arm bumper must not contact frame.
2. Clean and inspect ball joint seals for cuts or tears. If seal is cut or torn, the ball joint must be replaced.
3. Position dial indicator against the lowest outboard point on the wheel rim, **Fig. 19.**
3. Rock the wheel in and out and observe gauge. Horizontal deflection should not exceed .125 inch.

4. If reading exceeds specification, or if ball stud had been disconnected from knuckle assembly and any looseness is evident, or if stud can be turned by hand, replace ball joint.

## LOWER BALL JOINT

The lower ball joint is equipped with a visual wear indicator, **Fig. 20.** Check ball joint with vehicle weight resting on wheels.

# STEERING GEAR
## REPLACE

1. Disconnect battery ground cable.
2. On models equipped with power steering, disconnect pressure and return lines from steering gear housing, then plug hose ends and gear housing ports to prevent contamination.
3. On all models, remove pinch bolt from

intermediate shaft.
4. On models equipped with power steering, remove the universal yoke from the stub shaft.
5. Remove pitman arm nut and washer from pitman shaft, then mark relationship between shaft and arm for assembly reference.
6. Remove pitman arm using pitman arm remover J-29107 for models equipped with power steering and J-6632 or J-5504-D for models equipped with manual steering. or equivalent.
7. Remove steering gear frame bolts and washers, then the steering gear.
8. Reverse procedure to install. Torque steering gear frame bolts to 70 ft. lbs. on 1985 models or 55-60 ft. lbs. on 1986-89 models. On all models torque the intermediate shaft pinch bolt to 30 ft. lbs. If equipped with manual steering, torque the pitman shaft nut to 177-180 ft. lbs. on 1985 models or 185 ft. lbs. on 1986-89 models.

# POWER STEERING PUMP
## REPLACE
### 1985

1. Disconnect battery ground cable.
2. Disconnect return line, then the pressure line from steering gear. Plug hose ends and gear housing ports to prevent contamination.
3. Disconnect drive belt from power steering pump, then remove pump attaching bolts and the pump.
4. Reverse procedure to install.

### 1986

1. Disconnect battery ground cable, then place suitable drain pan under pump.
2. Disconnect and cap pressure and return hoses.
3. Loosen adjusting bolt, adjusting nut and pivot bolt or pivot nut.
4. Remove belt, then the adjusting bolt, washer and pivot bolt.
5. Remove pulley, using pump pulley remover J-29785-A or equivalent.
6. Remove pump attaching bolts, mounting bracket and pump.
7. Reverse procedure to install.

### 1987-89

1. Disconnect battery ground cable, then place suitable drain pan under pump.
2. Loosen belt tensioner, then remove belt.
3. On V6-262 engines, remove rear brace attaching nuts, then the rear brace.
4. On all models, remove pulley, using puller J-29785-A or equivalent.
5. Disconnect and cap pressure and return hoses.
6. Remove pump attaching bolts, then the pump.
7. Reverse procedure to install. Torque mounting bolts to 37 ft. lbs. If equipped with a V6-262 engine, torque the rear brace-to-stud nut to 37 ft. lbs. and the brace-to-pump nut to 26 ft. lbs.

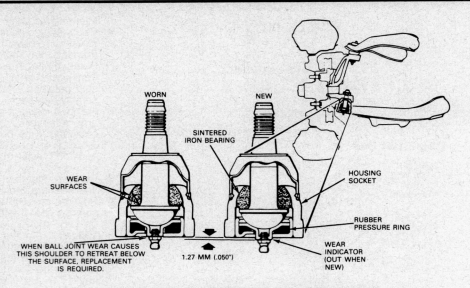

**Fig. 20   Lower ball joint wear indicators**

# AIR CONDITIONING
## TABLE OF CONTENTS

# A/C System Testing
## INDEX

## GENERAL PRECAUTIONS

The Freon refrigerant used is also known as R-12 or F-12. It is colorless and odorless both as a gas and a liquid. Since it boils (vaporizes) at −21.7°F, it will usually be in a vapor state when being handled in a repair shop. If a portion of the liquid coolant should come in contact with the hands or face, note that momentarily, its temperature will be at least 22°F below zero.

Protective goggles should be worn and fittings should be wrapped with a clean cloth when opening any refrigerant lines. If liquid coolant touches the skin, treat as if it were frost bitten or frozen. If liquid coolant touches the eyes, bathe the eyes quickly in cold water, then apply a bland disinfectant oil to the eyes. **Never rub the eyes. See an eye doctor.**

When checking a system for leaks with a torch type leak detector, do not breathe the vapors coming from the flame. Do not discharge refrigerant in the area of a live flame. A poisonous phosgene gas is produced when R-12 or F-12 is burned. While the small amount of this gas produced by a leak detector is not harmful unless inhaled directly at the flame, the quantity of refrigerant released into the air when a system is purged can be extremely dangerous if allowed to come in contact with an open flame. Thus, when purging a system, be sure that the discharge hose is routed to a well ventilated place where no flame is present. Under these conditions the refrigerant will be quickly dissipated into the surrounding air.

Never allow the temperature of refrigerant drums to exceed 125°F. The resultant increase in temperature will cause a corresponding increase in pressure which may cause the safety plug to release or the drum to burst.

If it is necessary to heat a drum of refrigerant when charging a system, the drum should be placed in water that is no hotter than 125°F. Never use a blow torch, or other open flame. If possible, a pressure release mechanism should be attached before the drum is heated.

When connecting and disconnecting service gauges on A/C system, ensure gauge hand valves are fully closed and that compressor service valves, if equipped, are in the back-seated (fully counterclockwise) position. Do not disconnect gauge hoses from service port adapters, if used, while gauges are connected to A/C system. To disconnect hoses, always remove adapter from service port. Do not disconnect hoses from gauge manifold while connected to A/C system, as refrigerant will be rapidly discharged.

After disconnecting gauge lines, check the valve areas to be sure service valves are correctly seated and schraeder valves, if used, are not leaking.

## EXERCISE SYSTEM

An important fact most owners ignore is that A/C units must be used periodically. Manufacturers caution that when the air conditioner is not used regularly, particularly during cold months, it should be turned on for a few minutes once every two or three weeks while the engine is running.This keeps the system in good operating condition.

Checking out the system for the effects of disuse before the onset of summer is one of the most important aspects of A/C servicing.

First clean out the condenser core, mounted in all cases at the front of the radiator. All obstructions, such as leaves, bugs, and dirt, must be removed, as they will reduce heat transfer and impair the efficiency of the system. Make sure the space between the condenser and the radiator also is free of foreign matter.

Make certain the evaporator water drain is open. Certain systems have two evaporators, one in the engine compartment and one toward the rear of the vehicle. The evaporator cools and dehumidifies the air before it enters the passenger compartment; there, the refrigerant is changed from a liquid to a vapor. As the core cools the air, moisture condenses on it but is prevented from collecting in the evaporator by the water drain.

## PERFORMANCE TEST

**When performing air conditioning diagnosis on vehicles equipped with a catalytic converter, warm the engine to a normal operating temperature before attempting to idle the engine for more than five minutes.**

1. Open all doors or windows.
2. Position the right lever to the "Norm" mode, the left lever in the "Cold" position and the blower switch in the "Hi" position.
3. Install a J-21213-A four jack-dual range temperature tester at the instrument panel right outlet, then take perature reading.
4. Start the engine and run at 2,000 RPM.
5. After one minute, take temperature reading at the right outlet. The minimum drop in temperature should correspond to **Fig. 1.**

## RELATIVE TEMPERATURE OF HIGH & LOW SIDES

The high side of the system should be uniformly hot to the touch throughout. A difference in temperature will indicate a partial blockage of liquid or gas at this point.

The low side of the system should be uniformly cool to the touch with no excessive sweating of the suction line or low side service valve. Excessive sweating or frosting of the low side service valve usually indicates an expansion valve is allowing an excessive amount of refrigerant into the evaporator.

## EVAPORATOR OUTPUT

At this point, provided all other inspection tests have been performed, and components have been found to operate as they should, a rapid cooling down of the interior of the vehicle should result. The use of a thermometer is not necessary to determine evaporator output. Bringing all units to the correct operating specifications will insure that the evaporator performs as intended.

## LEAK TEST

Testing the refrigerant system for leaks is one of the most important phases of troubleshooting. Several types of leak detectors are available that are suitable for detecting A/C system leaks. One or more of the following procedures will prove useful for detecting leaks and checking connections after service work has been performed. Prior to performing any leak test, prepare the vehicle as follows:

1. Attach a suitable gauge manifold to system and observe pressure readings.
2. If little or no pressure is indicated, the system must be partially charged.
3. If gauges indicate pressure, set engine to run at fast idle and operate system at maximum cooling for 10-15 minutes, then stop engine and perform leak tests.

### FLAME TYPE (HALIDE) LEAK DETECTORS

**Avoid inhaling fumes produced by burning refrigerant when using flame-type detectors. Use caution when using detector near flammable materials such as interior trim components. Do not use flame-type detector where concentrations of combustible or explosive gasses, dusts or vapors may exist.**

1. Light leak detector and adjust flame as low as possible to obtain maximum sensitivity.
2. Allow detector to warm until copper element is cherry-red. Flame should be almost colorless.
3. Test reaction plate sensitivity by passing end of sensor hose near an opened can of refrigerant. Flame should react violently, turning bright blue.
4. If flame does not change color, replace reaction plate following manufacturer's instructions.
5. Allow flame to clear, then slowly move sensor hose along areas suspected of leakage while observing flame. **Position sensor hose under areas of suspected leakage, as R-12 refrigerant is heavier than air.**
6. Move sensor hose under all lines, fittings and components. Insert hose into evaporator case, if possible, and check compressor shaft seal.
7. The presence of refrigerant will cause flame to change color as follows: pale

blue, no refrigerant; yellow-yellow/green, slight leak; bright blue-purple/blue, major leak or concentration of refrigerant.
8. If detector indicates a large leak or heavy concentration of refrigerant, ventilate area using a small fan in order to pinpoint leak.
9. Repair leaks as needed, evacuate and recharge system, then recheck system for leaks.

### ELECTRONIC LEAK DETECTORS

The procedure for using an electronic leak detector is similar to the procedure for flame-type leak detectors, except that the presence of refrigerant is indicated by a change in the audible tone or flashing light. Refer to operating instructions for unit being used, and observe the following procedures:

1. Move detector probe 1 inch per second along areas of suspected leakage.
2. Position probe under area to be tested as refrigerant is heavier than air.
3. Check gauge manifold, hoses and service ports for leakage.
4. After repairs have been made, recheck entire A/C system

### FLUID TYPE LEAK DETECTORS

Apply leak detector solution around joints to be tested. A cluster of bubbles will form immediately if there is a leak. A white foam that forms after a short while will indicate an extremely small leak. In some confined areas such as sections of the evaporator and condenser, electronic leak detectors will be more useful.

## DISCHARGING & EVACUATING SYSTEM

### DISCHARGING

Never remove a gauge line from its adapter when the line is connected to the A/C system. Always remove the line adapter from the service fitting to disconnect a line. Do not remove charging hose at gauge set while attached to service "Low" side fitting. This will discharge the system due to the depressed schrader valve in service "Low" side fitting. May also cause personal injury due to the release of refrigerant.

1. With the ignition turned off, disconnect the protective cap from the "Low" side service fitting.
2. If a charging station is to be used, ensure all valves are closed, connect

charging station gauge set J-23500-01 to the "Low" side service fitting. then slowly discharge system, **Fig. 2. Rapidly purging will draw the system oil charge out with the refrigerant.**

a. If a charging station is not being used, discharge the system by slowly connecting a gauge hose to the "Low" side service fitting on the accumulator, then discharge into a suitable container. **Rapidly purging will draw the system oil charge out with the refrigerant.**

b. As the hose is slowly tightened onto the schrader valve, refrigerant will discharge from the system into the container. If no discharge occurs, check for missing or defective schrader depressor in the hose fitting.

3. With the "Low" pressure side discharged, check the "High" side system fitting (on the liquid line or muffler) for remaining pressure.
4. If pressure is found, discharge in the same manner as the "Low" pressure side. The presence of pressure indicates a restriction in the "High" side. This restriction must be corrected before evacuation and charging of system.
5. After discharging is complete, measure the amount of oil. If 1/2 ounce or more is recovered, add same amount of 525 viscosity refrigerant oil plus any amount remaining in parts which were removed. Refer to "A/C System Servicing" for quantities. **If addition of refrigeration oil is necessary, oil should be added prior to evacuating system.**
6. To add refrigerant oil, remove the suction hose from the accumulator outlet pipe connection, then pour in correct amount.

### EVACUATING SYSTEM WITH VACUUM PUMP

Vacuum pumps suitable for removing air and moisture from A/C systems are commercially available. The pump should be capable of drawing the system down to 28-29 inches Hg at sea level. For each 1000 foot increase in altitude, this specification should be decreased by 1 inch Hg. As an example, at 5000 feet elevation, only 23-24 inches Hg can be obtained.

1. Connect suitable gauge manifold and discharge system as outlined previously. **System must be completely discharged prior to evacuation. If pressurized refrigerant is allowed to enter vacuum pump, pump will be damaged.**

| Condenser Inlet Temperature | 21°C (70°F) | 26°C (80°F) | 32-43°C (90-110°F) |
|---|---|---|---|
| Instrument Panel Right Outlet Temperature (Minimum Drop) | -7°C (20°F) | -4°C (25°F) | -1°C (30°F) |

**Fig. 1   A/C system performance test specifications**

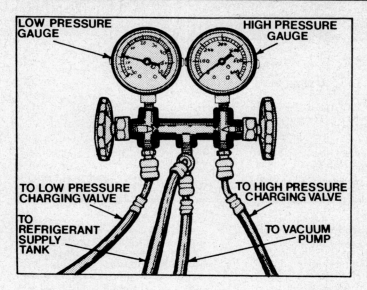

**LOW PRESSURE GAUGE**

**HIGH PRESSURE GAUGE**

**TO LOW PRESSURE CHARGING VALVE**

**TO REFRIGERANT SUPPLY TANK**

**TO HIGH PRESSURE CHARGING VALVE**

**TO VACUUM PUMP**

**Fig. 2   Gauge manifold hose connections**

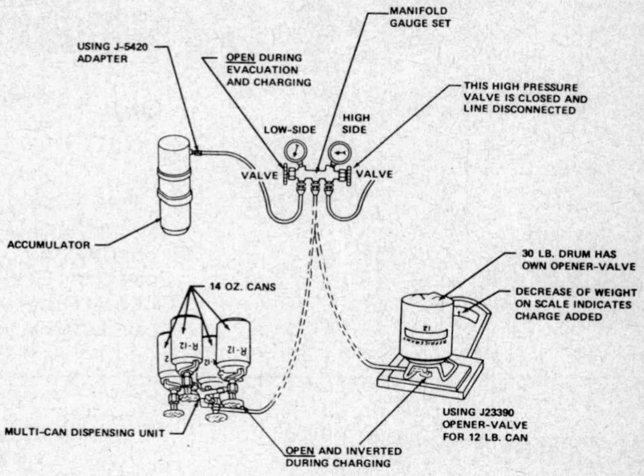

**Fig. 3   A/C system charging. Chevrolet & GMC with C.C.O.T. system**

2. Connect hose from gauge manifold center port to vacuum pump inlet.
3. Fully open both gauge manifold hand valves.
4. Operate vacuum pump while observing low side compound gauge. If system does not "pump-down" to 28-29 inches Hg (at sea level) within approximately 5 minutes, recheck connections and leak test system.
5. Continue to operate vacuum pump for 15-30 minutes, longer if system was open for an extended period of time, then close both manifold valves and stop pump.
6. Check ability of system to hold vacuum. Watch low side compound gauge and ensure reading does not rise at a rate faster than 1 inch Hg every 4-5 minutes.
7. If system fails to hold vacuum, recheck fittings and connections, and leak test system.
8. If system holds vacuum, charge system with refrigerant.

## EVACUATING SYSTEM WITH CHARGING STATION

A vacuum pump is built into the charging station that is constructed to withstand repeated and prolonged use without damage. Complete moisture removal from the A/C system is possible only with a pump of this type.

1. Connect charging station J-23500-01, then discharge system as outlined previously. **System must be completely discharged prior to evacuation. If pressurized refrigerant is allowed to enter vacuum pump, pump will be damaged.**
2. Reconnect vacuum hose to vacuum pump and ensure vacuum control valve is closed.

3. Fully open low pressure control valve only.
4. Connect station to a suitable voltage source and operate vacuum pump.
5. Slowly open vacuum control valve and observe low side compound gauge. If system does not "pump down" to 28-29½ inches Hg (at sea level) within approximately 5 minutes, recheck connections and leak test system.
6. Continue to operate vacuum pump for 15-30 minutes, longer if system was open for an extended period of time, then close all control valves and stop pump.
7. Check ability of system to hold vacuum. Watch low side compound gauge and ensure reading does not rise at a rate faster than 1 inch Hg every 4-5 minutes.
8. If system fails to hold vacuum, recheck fittings and connections, and leak test system.
9. If system holds vacuum, charge system with refrigerant.

## CHARGING THE SYSTEM

Refer to A/C Data Table in the "A/C System Servicing" section for refrigerant capacities.

### J-23500-01 CHARGING STATION METHOD

Use instructions provided with charging station with the following exceptions:
1. Do not connect high pressure line to A/C system.
2. Always keep high pressure valve closed on charging station.
3. Perform all evacuation and charging through low-side pressure service fitting. **Use of these procedures will**

prevent charging station from being accidentally exposed to high-side system pressure.

## DISPOSABLE CAN OR REFRIGERANT DRUM METHOD

If R-12 drum is used, place on scale and note total weight before charging. During charging, watch scale to determine amount of R-12 used. If 14 ounce R-12 cans are used, close tapping valve, then attach cans following instructions included with manifold adapter.

1. Start engine and allow to warm up (choke open, normal idle). Set A/C control lever to "Off."
2. With R-12 drum or cans inverted, open R-12 supply valve and allow 1 lb. or more of liquid R-12 to flow into system through low-side service fitting, **Fig. 3.**
3. When 1 lb. of refrigerant has entered system, engage compressor by setting A/C lever to NORM and blower switch to HI to draw in remainder of charge. Cooling the condenser with a fan will speed up charging procedure by maintaining condenser temperature below that of the charging cylinder temperature.
4. Close refrigerant supply valve and run engine for 30 seconds to clear lines and gauges.
5. With engine running, remove charging low-side hose adapter from accumulator service fitting. Unscrew rapidly to avoid excessive refrigerant loss.
6. Replace protective cap on accumulator fitting and turn engine off.
7. Check system for leaks.
8. Start engine and check for proper system operation.

# A/C System Servicing

## INDEX

### Page No.

## OIL LEVEL CHECK

Refer to "A/C Data Table" for oil level specifications.

The Frigidaire/Delco Air axial 6 cylinder and radial 4 cylinder compressors must be removed from vehicle and drained to check the oil level. Refer to "Oil Charge" for service procedures.

## OIL CHARGE

Compressor oil level need only be checked when there is evidence of major oil loss from the system as in the case of a broken hose, severely leaking fitting, defective compressor seal or collision damage to the system.

## COMPONENT, REPLACE

If there are no external signs of oil leakage from the A/C system, maintain the proper system oil charge by adding new refrigeration oil during component replacement as follows:
1. Discharge system as outlined, then measure amount of oil collected in discharge container. **If more than 1/2 ounce of oil is collected when discharging system, an equal amount of new refrigeration oil must be added to the system.**
2. Remove defective components. Drain and measure oil remaining in compressor or accumulator, if removed.
3. Add the proper amount of oil to each replacement component as follows:
   a. If accumulator is being replaced, add the same amount of oil that was drained from the defective accumulator plus 1 additional ounce on 1980 models or 2 additional ounces on 1981-89 models.
   b. If compressor is replaced, add the same amount of oil that was

drained from defective compressor plus 3.5 additional ounces in the HR-6 model and 1 additional ounce in all other models.
   c. If condenser is replaced, add 1 ounce of oil to replacement condenser.
   d. If evaporator is replaced, add 1 ounce of oil to the V-5 model evaporator and 3 ounces of oil to all other model replacement evaporators.
   e. If receiver/drier is replaced, add 1 ounce of oil to replacement receiver/drier.

## OIL LEVEL CHECK—LEAK CONDITION

If external oil leakage is evident, check compressor oil level using the following procedures.
1. Discharge system as outlined, then measure amount of oil collected in discharge container. **If more than 1/2 ounce of oil is collected when discharging system, an equal amount of new refrigeration oil must be added to the system.**
2. On models with A-6 axial compressor, proceed as follows:
   a. Remove compressor and accumulator, drain oil from components into a suitable container and measure amount of oil recovered.
   b. If more than 4 ounces are recovered for 1980-87 models, or 6 ounces for 1988-89 models, add the same amount of new refrigeration oil to system.
   c. If less than 4 ounces are recovered for 1980-87 models, add 4 additional ounces. If less than 6 ounces are recovered for 1988-89 models, add 6 additional ounces.
3. On models with R-4 radial compressor, proceed as follows:
   a. Remove accumulator, drain oil remaining in accumulator into a suit-

able container and measure amount of oil recovered. **The R-4 radial compressor does not have an oil sump, therefore it is unnecessary to drain this compressor to check system oil level.**
   b. If the amount of oil recovered is 2 ounces or more for 1980 models, or 3 ounces or more for 1981-89 models, add the same amount of new refrigeration oil to system.
   c. If less than 2 ounces of oil are recovered on 1980 models, add 2 ounces of new refrigeration oil to system.
   d. If less than 3 ounces of oil are recovered on 1981-89 models, add 3 ounces of new refrigeration oil to system.
4. On models with DA-6 axial compressors, proceed as follows:
   a. Remove accumulator, drain oil into suitable container, then measure amount of oil recovered.
   b. If amount of oil recovered is less than 3 ounces for 1980-87 models, add 3 ounces to system. If less than 6 ounces are recovered from 1988-89 models, add 6 ounces to system.
   c. If amount of oil recovered is more than 3 ounces for 1980-87 models, or 6 ounces for 1988-89 models, add the same amount to system.
5. Add refrigeration oil, as needed, to compressor sump or accumulator, reinstall components, then evacuate and recharge system.

## CHARGING VALVE LOCATION

The high pressure fitting is located either in the high pressure vapor line or muffler, while the low pressure fitting is located on the accumulator.

# A/C Data Table

| Year | Model | Refrigerant Capacity Lbs. | Refrigeration Oil | | | Compressor Clutch Air Gap Inches |
| --- | --- | --- | Viscosity | Total System Capacity Ounces | Compressor Oil Level Check Inches | |
| 1980 | Caballero & El Camino | 3.75 | 525 | ① | ② | ③ |
| 1980-83 | C & K Series ④ | 3.75 | 525 | ① | ② | ③ |
| | C & K Series ⑤ | 5.25 | 525 | ① | ② | ③ |
| | G Series ④ | 3 | 525 | ① | ② | ③ |
| | G Series ⑤ | 5 | 525 | ① | ② | ③ |
| 1981-82 | Caballero & El Camino | 3.25 | 525 | ① | ② | ③ |
| 1982-89 | S/T-10 & 15 | 2.50 | 525 | 10 | ② | .020-.040 |
| 1983 | Caballero & El Camino | 3.25 | 525 | ⑥ | ② | ⑦ |
| 1984-85 | Caballero & El Camino | 3.25 | 525 | 6 | ② | .020-.040 |
| | C & K Series ④ | 3 | 525 | ① | ② | ③ |
| | C & K Series ⑤ | 5.33 | 525 | ① | ② | ③ |
| | G Series ④ | 3 | 525 | ① | ② | ③ |
| | G Series ⑤ | 4.50 | 525 | ① | ② | ③ |
| 1985-86 | Astro & Safari Vans, 4-151 ④ | 2 | 525 | 8 | ② | .015-.025 |
| | Astro & Safari Vans, V6-262 ④ | 2 | 525 | 6 | ② | .020-.040 |
| | Astro & Safari Vans ⑤ | 3 | 525 | 9 | ② | .020-.040 |
| 1986 | Caballero & El Camino | 3.25 | 525 | 6 | ② | .020-.040 |
| | C & K Series ④ | 3.50 | 525 | ⑥ | ② | ⑦ |
| | C & K Series ⑤ | 5.25 | 525 | ⑥ | ② | ⑨ |
| | G Series ④ | 3.50 | 525 | ① | ② | ③ |
| | G Series ⑤ | 4.50 | 525 | ① | ② | ③ |
| 1987-88 | Astro & Safari Vans, 4-151 ④ | 2 | 525 | 8 | ② | .015-.025 |
| | Astro & Safari Vans, V6-262 ④ | 2 | 525 | 6 | ② | .020-.040 |
| | Astro & Safari Vans ⑤ | 3 | 525 | 9 | ② | .020-.040 |
| 1987 | Caballero & El Camino | 3.25 | 525 | 6 | ② | .020-.040 |
| | R & V Series ④ | 3.50 | 525 | ⑥ | ② | ⑦ |
| | R & V Series ⑤ | 5.25 | 525 | ⑥ | ② | ⑦ |
| | G Series ④ | 3.50 | 525 | ① | ② | ③ |
| | G Series ⑤ | 4.50 | 525 | ① | ② | ③ |
| 1988 | Caballero & El Camino | 3.25 | 525 | 6 | ② | .020-.040 |
| 1988-89 | C & K Series | 2.50 | 525 | 6 | ② | .020-.040 |
| | R & V Series ④ | 3.25 | 525 | ⑧ | ② | ③ |
| | R & V Series ⑤ | 5.25 | 525 | ⑨ | ② | ③ |
| | G Series ④ | ⑩ | 525 | ⑧ | ② | ③ |
| | G Series ⑤ | ⑪ | 525 | ⑨ | ② | ③ |
| 1989 | Astro & Safari Vans, 4-151 ④ | 2.25 | 525 | 8 | ② | .015-.025 |
| | Astro & Safari Vans, V6-262 ④ | 2.25 | 525 | 6 | ② | .020-.040 |
| | Astro & Safari Vans ⑤ | 3.75 | 525 | 9 | ② | .020-.040 |

① —A-6 axial 6 cyl., comp. 10 oz.; R-4 radial 4 cyl. comp., 6 oz.

② —Note that "Oil Level Inches" cannot be checked. Refer to total capacity and see text for checking procedure.

③ —A-6 axial 6 cyl. comp., .022-.057 in.; R-4 radial 4 cyl. comp., .020-.040 in.; HR-6 axial 6 cyl. comp., .015-.025 in.

④ —Models less auxiliary (rear, overhead etc.) system.

⑤ —Models with auxiliary (rear, overhead etc.) system.

⑥ —DA-6 axial 6 cyl. comp., 8 oz.; R-4 radial 4 cyl. comp., 6 oz.

⑦ —DA-6 axial 6 cyl. comp., .015-.025 in.; R-4 radial 4 cyl. comp., .020-.040 in.

⑧ —A-6 axial 6 cyl. comp., 10 oz.; R-4 radial 4 cyl. comp., 6 oz.; HR-6 axial 6 cyl. comp., 8 oz.

⑨ —A-6 axial 6 cyl. comp., 13 oz.; R-4 radial 4 cyl. comp., 9 oz.; HR-6 axial 6 cyl. comp., 11 oz.

⑩ —With V8-454 EFI engine, 2.75 lbs.; Less V8-454 EFI engine, 3.50 lbs.

⑪ —With V8-454 EFI engine, 4.0 lbs.; Less V8-454 EFI engine, 4.50 lbs.

# ENGINE COOLING FANS

## TABLE OF CONTENTS

# Electric Fans

## INDEX

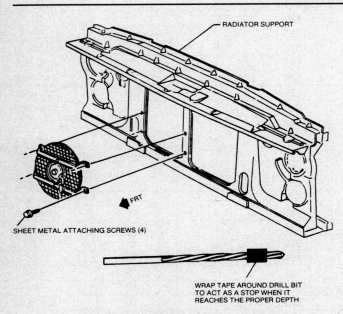

**Fig. 1  Electric cooling fan installation**

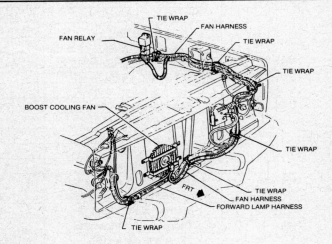

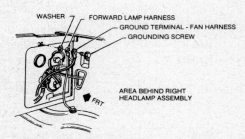

**Fig. 2  Electric cooling fan wiring harness installation**

## ELECTRIC COOLING FAN MODIFICATION

As of January 1, 1985, all C, K, R and V-20/2500-30/3500 models equipped with the V8-454 engine and heavy duty emissions systems are equipped with an auxiliary electric engine cooling fan. Similar 1982-85 truck models not equipped with the fan may have one installed using the following procedure:

1. Disconnect battery ground cable.
2. Remove grille assembly.
3. Drill mounting holes and install fan assembly (part No. 15593566), **Fig. 1.**
4. Drain cooling system, then install fan relay (part No. 14078902), **Fig. 2.**
5. Install fan wiring harness (part No. 12064526), **Fig. 2. Secure harness to fender and radiator support away from sharp edges.**
6. Install temperature sender (part No. 14080661) in right cylinder head, **Fig. 3.**

7. Route and secure fan wiring harness as shown in **Figs. 4 and 5.**
8. Fill cooling system and connect battery ground cable.
9. Run engine and check for proper fan operation. Fan should be energized when engine temperature reaches approximately 225-240°F. **Ensure fan blows air through radiator. If fan blows in opposite direction, reverse wires in fan electrical connector at motor.**

## ELECTRIC COOLING FAN REPLACE

1. Disconnect battery ground cable.
2. Remove grille assembly.
3. Disconnect electrical connector from cooling fan.
4. Remove fan assembly attaching bolts and the fan.
5. Reverse procedure to install.

*ELECTRIC FANS*

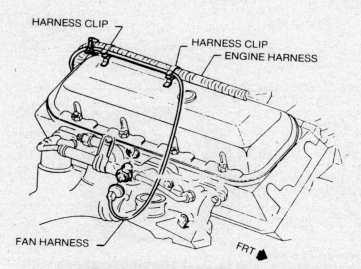

**Fig. 3   Electric cooling fan temperature sender installation**

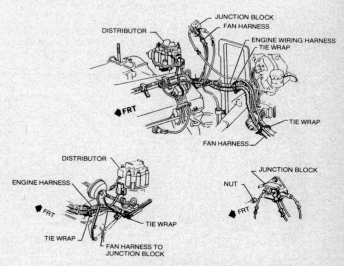

**Fig. 4   Electric cooling fan wiring harness routing**

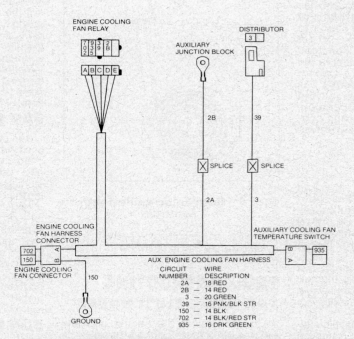

**Fig. 5   Electric cooling fan wiring circuit**

# Variable Speed Fans

### INDEX

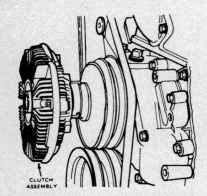

**Fig. 1 Fan drive clutch assembly. 1984–89 (1980–83 similar)**

Do not operate engine until fan has first been inspected for cracks and/or separations. If a fan blade is found to be bent or damaged in any way, do not attempt to repair or reuse damaged part. Proper balance is essential in fan assembly operation. Balance cannot be assured once a fan assembly has been found to be bent or damaged and failure may occur during operation, creating an extremely dangerous condition. Always replace damaged fan assembly.

## DESCRIPTION

The fan drive clutch, **Fig. 1,** is a fluid coupling containing silicone oil. Fan speed is regulated by the torque-carrying capacity of the silicone oil. The more silicone oil in the coupling, the greater the fan speed, and the less silicone oil, the slower the fan speed.

There are two types of fan drive clutches in use, one with a flat bimetallic thermostatic spring, **Fig. 2,** and the second with a coiled bimetallic thermostatic spring, **Fig. 3.**

The fan drive clutch with the flat bimetallic spring works with a control piston on front of the fluid coupling to regulate the amount of silicone oil entering the coupling. The bimetallic strip bows outward with an increase in ambient temperature and allows a piston to move outward. This piston opens a valve regulating the flow of silicone oil into the coupling from a reserve chamber. The silicone oil is returned to the reserve chamber through a bleed hole when the valve is closed.

The second fan drive clutch uses a heat-sensitive, coiled bimetallic spring connected to an opening plate which brings about similar results. Both units

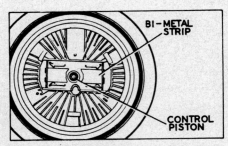

**Fig. 2 Variable speed fan with flat bimetallic thermostatic spring**

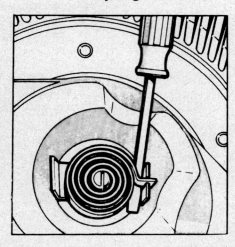

**Fig. 4 Bimetallic coiled spring removal**

cause the fan speed to increase with a rise in temperature and to decrease as temperature decreases.

## TROUBLESHOOTING
## FAN DRIVE CLUTCH TEST

Do not operate the engine until the fan has been first checked for possible cracks and separations.

Run the engine at a fast idle speed (1000 RPM) until normal operating temperature is reached. This process can be speeded up by blocking off the front of the radiator with cardboard. Regardless of temperatures, the unit must be operated for at least five minutes immediately before being tested.

Stop the engine, then using a glove or a cloth to protect the hand, immediately check the effort required to turn the fan. If considerable effort is required, it can be assumed that the coupling is operating

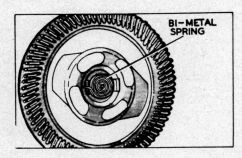

**Fig. 3 Variable speed fan with bimetallic coiled thermostatic spring**

satisfactorily. If very little effort is required to turn the fan, it is an indication that the coupling is not operating properly and should be replaced.

If the clutch fan is the coiled bimetallic spring type, it may be tested while the vehicle is being driven. To check, disconnect the bimetal spring, **Fig. 4,** and rotate 90° counterclockwise. This disables the temperature-controlled, free-wheeling feature and the clutch performs like a conventional fan. If this cures the overheating condition, replace the clutch fan.

## FAN CLUTCH NOISE

Fan clutch noise can sometimes be noticed when clutch is engaged for maximum cooling. Clutch noise is also noticeable within the first few minutes after starting engine while clutch is redistributing the silicone fluid back to its normal, disengaged operating condition after settling for long periods of time (overnight). However, continuous fan noise or an excessive roar indicates the clutch assembly is locked-up due to internal failure. This condition can be checked by attempting to manually rotate the fan. If fan cannot be rotated manually or there is a rough, abrasive feel as fan is rotated, the clutch should be replaced.

## FAN LOOSENESS

Lateral movement can be observed at the fan blade tip under various temperature conditions because of the type bearing used. This movement should not exceed 1/4 inch (6.5 mm) as measured at the fan tip. If this lateral movement does not exceed specifications, there is no cause for replacement.

## CLUTCH FLUID LEAK

Small fluid leaks do not generally affect the operation of the unit. These leaks generally occur around the area of the bearing assembly, but if the leaks appear to be excessive, engine overheating may occur. Clutch and fan free-wheeling can cause overheating. To check for clutch and fan free-wheeling, turn the motor off. Spin the fan and clutch assembly by hand. If the fan spins five or more times before it stops, replace the clutch.

## FAN BLADE INSPECTION

Place fan on flat surface with leading edge facing down. If there is a clearance between fan blade touching surface and opposite blade of more than .090 inch (2 mm), replace fan. (See caution at beginning of chapter.)

## FAN SERVICE

**To prevent silicone fluid from draining into fan drive bearing, do not store** or place drive unit on bench with rear of shaft pointing downward.

The removal procedure for either type of fan clutch assembly is generally the same. Remove the radiator fan shroud, unfasten the unit from the water pump, then remove the assembly from vehicle.

The type of unit shown in **Fig. 2**, may be partially disassembled for inspection and cleaning. Remove capscrews that hold the assembly together and separate the fan from the drive clutch. Next, remove metal strip on front of clutch assembly by pushing one end of it toward the fan clutch body so it clears the retaining bracket. Push the strip to the side so that its opposite end will spring out of place. Now remove the small control piston underneath it.

Check the piston for free movement of the coupling device. If piston sticks, clean it with emery cloth. If the bimetal strip is damaged, replace the entire unit. These strips are not interchangeable.

When reassembling, install the control piston so that the projection on the end of it will contact the metal strip. Next install metal strip with any identification number or letters facing the clutch. After reassembly, clean the clutch drive assembly with a cloth soaked in a suitable solvent. Avoid dipping the clutch assembly in any type liquid. Install the assembly in the reverse order of removal, torquing the fan bolts to 18 ft. lbs.

The coil spring type fan clutch cannot be disassembled, serviced or repaired. If it does not function properly, it must be replaced with a new unit.

# ALTERNATOR SYSTEMS

## TABLE OF CONTENTS

# Delcotron 10, 12, 15, 17 & 27 SI (Type 100) Integral Charging Systems

## INDEX

## DESCRIPTION

These units, **Figs. 1 through 5**, feature a solid state regulator mounted inside the alternator slip ring end frame along with the brush holder assembly. All regulator components are enclosed in a solid mold with no need or provision for adjustment of the regulator voltage. The alternator bearings contain enough grease to eliminate periodic lubrication. Two brushes carry current through two slip rings to the field coil. The stator windings are assembled on the inside of a laminated core that forms part of the alternator frame. A rectifier bridge, containing six diodes and connected to the stator windings, changes A.C. voltage to D.C. voltage which is available at the "Bat" output terminal. Alternator field current is supplied through a diode trio connected to the stator windings. A capacitor, or condenser mounted to the end frame protects the diodes and rectifier bridge from high voltages and also suppresses radio noise. **Some units incorpo-**

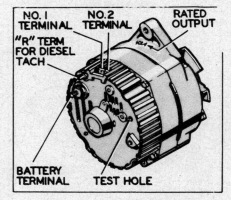

**Fig. 1 Delcotron type 10 SI alternator**

rate a resistor in the warning indicator circuit, **Fig. 6**

Some alternators used on diesel engines are equipped with an R terminal for the tachometer. On these units, if the alter-

nator pulley is to be replaced, a pulley of the same diameter as the one removed must be installed, or tachometer may provide inaccurate readings.

No maintenance or adjustments of any kind are required on this unit.

## TROUBLESHOOTING

### UNDERCHARGED BATTERY

#### Preliminary Checks

1. Disconnect battery ground cable.
2. Disconnect wire at BAT terminal of alternator, connect ammeter positive lead to BAT terminal and negative lead to wire.
3. Connect the battery ground cable.
4. Turn on all accessories, then connect a carbon pile regulator across battery.
5. Operate engine at moderate speed, adjust carbon pile regulator to obtain maximum current output.

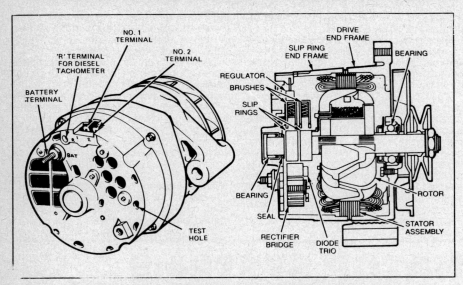

**Fig. 2    Cross sectional view of 12 SI alternator**

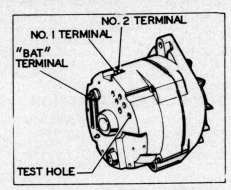

**Fig. 3    Delcotron type 15 SI alternator**

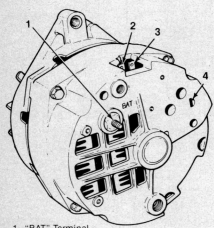

1. "BAT" Terminal
2. No. 1 Terminal
3. No. 2 Terminal
4. Field Ground Hole

**Fig. 4    Delcotron type 17 SI alternator**

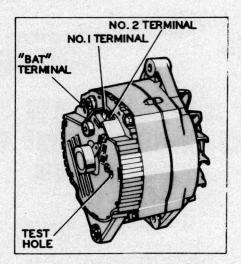

**Fig. 5    Delcotron type 27 SI alternator**

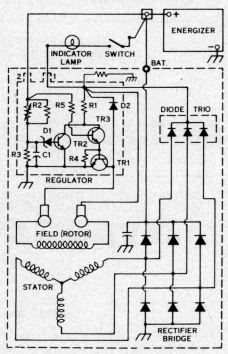

**Fig. 6    Wiring diagram of charging circuit**

6. If ammeter reading is within 10 amps of rated output, the alternator is not at fault. **Alternator rating is stamped on alternator frame.**
7. If ammeter reading is not within 10 amps of rated output, ground field winding by inserting screwdriver in end frame hole, contacting tab, **Fig. 7. Do not insert screwdriver deeper than one inch, as tab is usually located within 3/4 inch of casing surface.**
8. If reading is within 10 amps of rated output, regulator must be replaced. If reading is not within limits, check field winding, diode trio, rectifier bridge and stator.
9. Turn off all accessories, disconnect ammeter then carbon pile regulator.

## IN-VEHICLE VOLTAGE REGULATOR TEST

1. Connect a suitable voltmeter and fast charger to 12 volt battery.

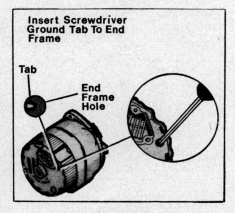

**Fig. 7    Grounding field windings**

2. Connect regulator and test light, observing battery polarity. Test Light should be on.

3. Turn on the fast charger and slowly increase charge rate. Observe the voltmeter and test light.
4. Test light should go out at voltage regulator setting of 13.5-16.0 volts.
   The test light is connected into the circuit exactly as the rotor is when the regulator is inside the alternator. The regulator shuts off the current to the test light when the regulator setting is reached. This voltage will vary with changes in temperature.

## ALTERNATOR NOISE

Alternator noise may be caused by a loose drive pulley, loose mounting bolts, worn or dirty bearings, defective diodes or a defective stator. Inspect all components and replace as necessary.

## CHARGING SYSTEM DIAGNOSIS

For charging system diagnosis, refer to "Charging System Diagnosis Chart," **Fig. 8.**

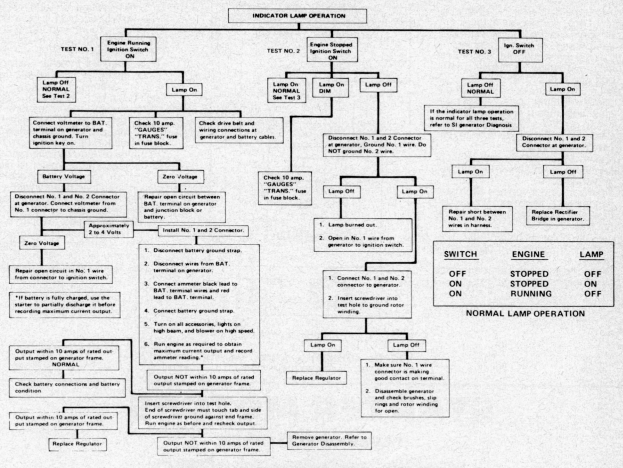

**Fig. 8 Charging system diagnosis chart**

---

# Delcotron CS-130 & CS-144 Integral Charging System

## INDEX

## DESCRIPTION

These units, **Fig. 1**, features a high ampere output-to-weight ratio. The Delcotron CS-130 & CS-144 alternators are electrically similar to standard units, however, they do not contain a diode trio. The voltage setting of the integral regulator varies with temperature and limits system voltage by controlling rotor field current.

The regulator has four terminals; P, L, I and S. The P terminal is wired to the stator and may be used to connect a tachometer or other device. The S terminal may be connected to the battery to sense the voltage to be controlled. The L and I terminals activate the regulator, allowing field current to flow when the switch is closed. The

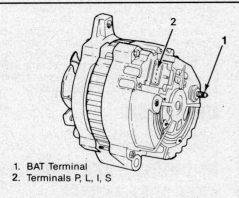

1. BAT Terminal
2. Terminals P, L, I, S

**Fig. 1 Delcotron type CS-130 and CS-144 alternators**

I terminal may be connected either through a resistor or directly to the switch. The I circuit may be used with or without anything connected to the L circuit.

## DIAGNOSIS

During normal system operation, the indicator lamp, if equipped, will illuminate until the engine is started. If the indicator lamp operates abnormally, or an overcharged or undercharged battery condition exists, the following procedure should be used to diagnose the charging system. **Refer to charging circuit wiring diagram, Fig. 2 when diagnosing the system.**

1. Ensure alternator drive belt is in good condition and properly tentioned.

2. On models equipped with a charge indicator lamp, proceed as follows:
   a. Observe indicator lamp with ignition on and engine not running.
   b. If lamp does not light, disconnect electrical connector from alternator and ground L terminal.
   c. If lamp lights, replace alternator assembly. If lamp does not light, locate and repair open circuit between ground and ignition switch.
   d. Observe indicator lamp with engine running at idle.
   e. If lamp lights, disconnect electrical connector from alternator and observe lamp.
   f. If lamp goes out, replace alternator assembly. If lamp remains lit, locate and repair ground in L terminal wire.
3. On all models, if battery is overcharged or undercharged, proceed as follows:
   a. Disconnect electrical connector from alternator.

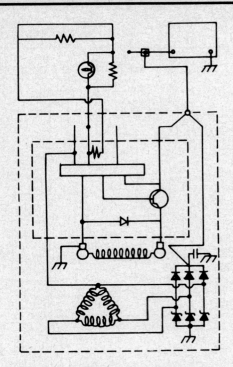

**Fig. 2  Charging circuit wiring diagram**

b. With ignition on and engine not running, connect a voltmeter between ground and terminal L, then terminal I (if used), measuring voltage at each terminal.
c. If voltmeter indicates zero voltage at either terminal, locate, then correct open in circuit.
d. Reconnect alternator electrical connector, then measure voltage across battery with engine running at idle and all accessories off.
e. If voltage reading is more than 16 volts, replace the alternator.
f. Connect an ammeter to alternator output terminal, turn accessories on, then load battery with a carbon pile to obtain maximum amperage.
g. While maintaining 13 volts or more, note amperage reading. If reading is within 15 amps of rated output, the alternator is satisfactory. If reading is not within 15 amps of rated output, replace the alternator.

# STARTER MOTORS
## TABLE OF CONTENTS

# Delco-Remy Starters
## INDEX

## DESCRIPTION

The Delco-Remy starter motor, **Figs. 1 through 6**, has the solenoid shift lever mechanism and the solenoid plunger enclosed in the drive housing to protect them from exposure to road dirt, icing conditions and splash. They have an extruded field frame and an overrunning clutch type drive. The overrunning clutch is operated by a solenoid switch mounted to a flange on the drive housing. The permanent magnet gear reduction starter has a gear reduction assembly to achieve free speed of up to 7000 RPM. The diesel starters, 25MT and 27MT, have a center bearing.

The solenoid, **Fig. 7**, is attached to the drive end housing by two screws. The cover can be removed to inspect the contacts and contact disc, but the switch is serviced as an assembly only.

Most motors of this type have graphite and oil impregnated bronze bearings which ordinarily require no added lubrication except at time of overhaul when a few drops of light engine oil should be placed on each bearing before reassembly.

## DIAGNOSIS

When diagnosing Delco-Remy starter motors, refer to **Fig. 8**.

## IN-VEHICLE TESTING
### FREE SPEED CHECK

With the circuit connected as shown in **Fig. 9**, use a tachometer to measure armature revolutions per minute. Failure of the motor to perform to specifications may be due to light or dry bearings, or high resistance connections.

### PINION CLEARANCE

There is no provision for adjusting pinion clearance on this type motor, but should be checked after motor reassembly on all models except the 28 MT, which is not serviceable. When the shift lever mechanism is correctly assembled, the pinion clearance should fall within the limits of .010 to .140 inch on 1980-87 models and .010-.160 inch on 1988-89 models. When the clearance is not within these limits, it may indicate excessive wear of the solenoid linkage or shift lever yoke buttons. Pinion clearance should be checked as

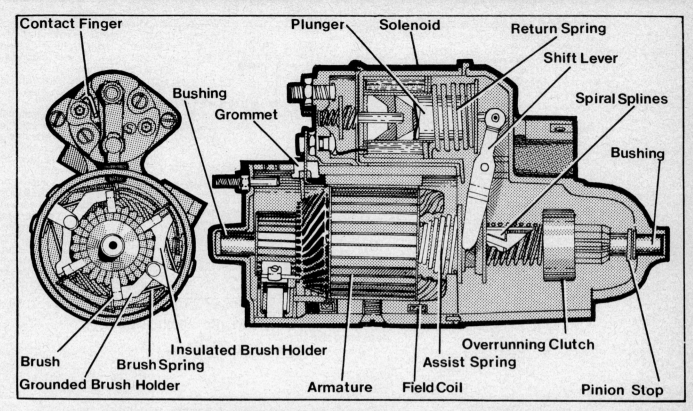

**Fig. 1  Delco Remy 5MT & 10MT (SD-200 & SD-300) standard duty starter. 1984 shown, others similar**

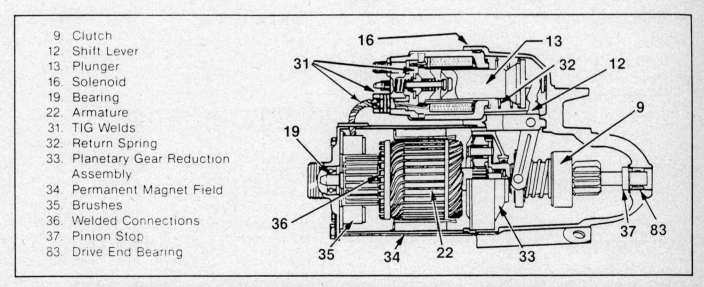

9. Clutch
12. Shift Lever
13. Plunger
16. Solenoid
19. Bearing
22. Armature
31. TIG Welds
32. Return Spring
33. Planetary Gear Reduction Assembly
34. Permanent Magnet Field
35. Brushes
36. Welded Connections
37. Pinion Stop
83. Drive End Bearing

**Fig. 2  PG-200 (PMGR) permanent magnet gear reduction starter. 1988–89 S/T-10 & 15 models w/V6-262 engine**

follows:

1. Disconnect motor field coil connector from solenoid motor terminal, then insulate end carefully.
2. Connect one battery lead to solenoid switch terminal, then the other lead to the solenoid frame, **Fig. 10.**
3. Using a jumper lead connected to the solenoid motor terminal. Momentarily flash the lead to the solenoid frame. This will shift the pinion into the cranking position until the battery is disconnected.
4. Push the pinion back toward the commutator end as far as possible to take up any slack movement, then check the clearance with feeler gauge, **Fig. 11.**

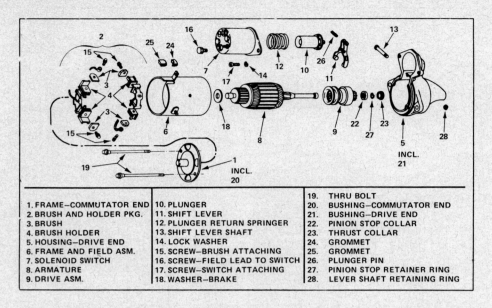

| | | |
|---|---|---|
| 1. FRAME—COMMUTATOR END | 10. PLUNGER | 19. THRU BOLT |
| 2. BRUSH AND HOLDER PKG. | 11. SHIFT LEVER | 20. BUSHING—COMMUTATOR END |
| 3. BRUSH | 12. PLUNGER RETURN SPRINGER | 21. BUSHING—DRIVE END |
| 4. BRUSH HOLDER | 13. SHIFT LEVER SHAFT | 22. PINION STOP COLLAR |
| 5. HOUSING—DRIVE END | 14. LOCK WASHER | 23. THRUST COLLAR |
| 6. FRAME AND FIELD ASM. | 15. SCREW—BRUSH ATTACHING | 24. GROMMET |
| 7. SOLENOID SWITCH | 16. SCREW—FIELD LEAD TO SWITCH | 25. GROMMET |
| 8. ARMATURE | 17. SCREW—SWITCH ATTACHING | 26. PLUNGER PIN |
| 9. DRIVE ASM. | 18. WASHER—BRAKE | 27. PINION STOP RETAINER RING |
| | | 28. LEVER SHAFT RETAINING RING |

**Fig. 3    Disassembled view of Delco-Remy 5MT (SD-200) series starting motor**

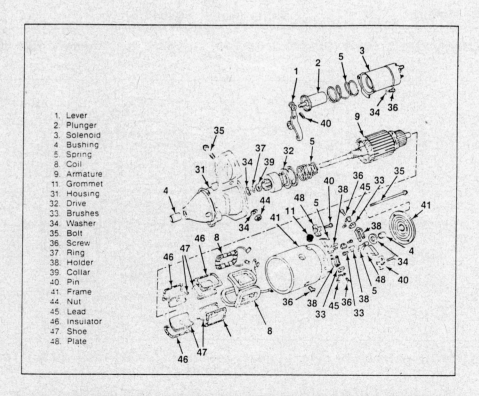

1. Lever
2. Plunger
3. Solenoid
4. Bushing
5. Spring
8. Coil
9. Armature
11. Grommet
31. Housing
32. Drive
33. Brushes
34. Washer
35. Bolt
36. Screw
37. Ring
38. Holder
39. Collar
40. Pin
41. Frame
44. Nut
45. Lead
46. Insulator
47. Shoe
48. Plate

**Fig. 4    Disassembled view of Delco-Remy 10MT (SD-300) series starting motor**

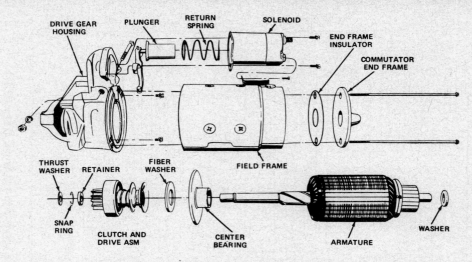

**Fig. 5   Disassembled view of Delco-Remy 25MT & 27MT series starting motor**

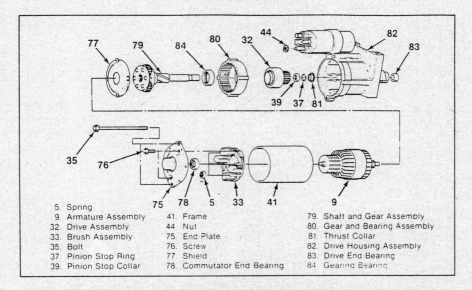

| | | |
|---|---|---|
| 5. Spring | 41. Frame | 79. Shaft and Gear Assembly |
| 9. Armature Assembly | 44. Nut | 80. Gear and Bearing Assembly |
| 32. Drive Assembly | 75. End Plate | 81. Thrust Collar |
| 33. Brush Assembly | 76. Screw | 82. Drive Housing Assembly |
| 35. Bolt | 77. Shield | 83. Drive End Bearing |
| 37. Pinion Stop Ring | 78. Commutator End Bearing | 84. Gearing Bearing |
| 39. Pinion Stop Collar | | |

**Fig. 6   Disassembled view of Delco-Remy PG-200 starting motor**

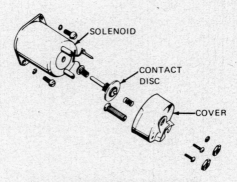

**Fig. 7   Solenoid contact assembly**

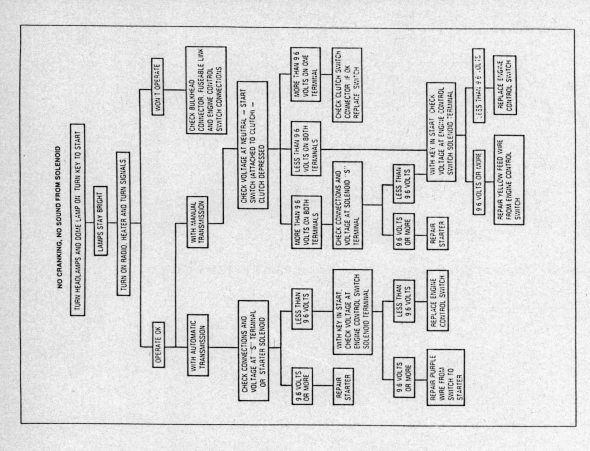

**Fig. 8  Diagnosis chart. All 1989 models (Part 2 of 6)**

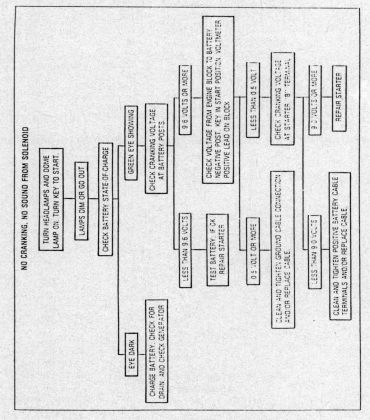

**Fig. 8  Diagnosis chart. All 1986–89 models (Part 1 of 6)**

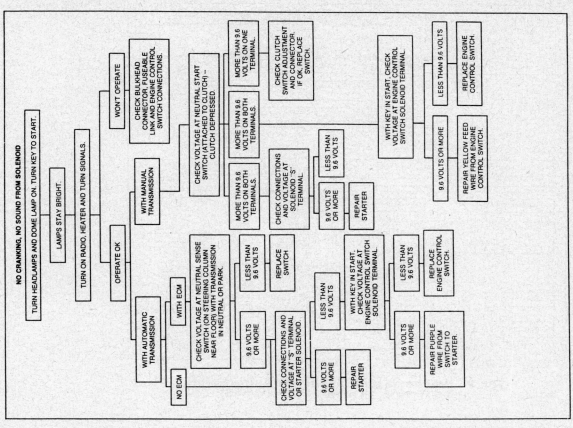

**Fig. 8   Diagnosis chart. 1988 C & K, R-V-G-P, 10-30 models and all 1986-87 models (Part 4 of 6)**

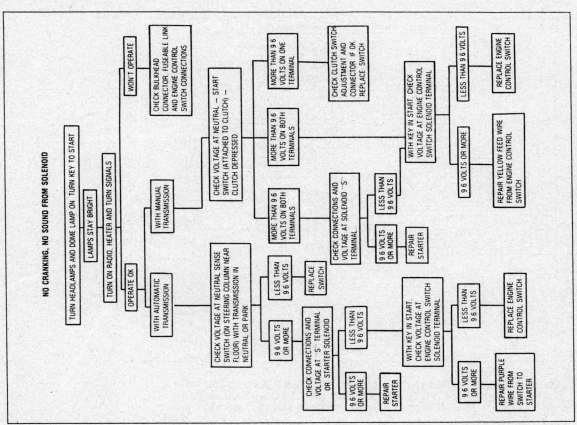

**Fig. 8   Diagnosis chart. 1988 Astro/Safari and S/T 10 & 15 models (Part 3 of 6)**

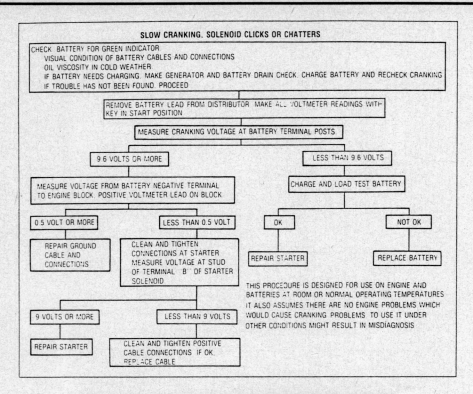

**Fig. 8   Diagnosis chart. 1988–89 Astro/Safari and S/T 10 & 15 models (Part 5 of 6)**

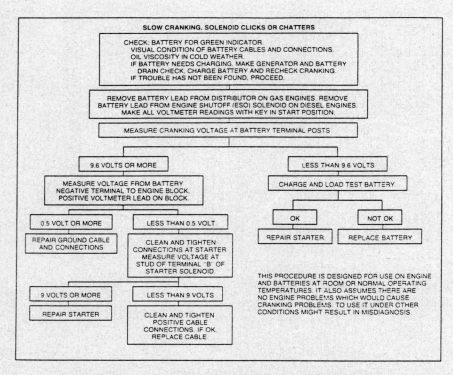

**Fig. 8   Diagnosis chart. 1986–87 Astro/Safari and S/T 10 & 15 models and 1986–89 C & K, R-V-G-P and 10-30 models (Part 6 of 6)**

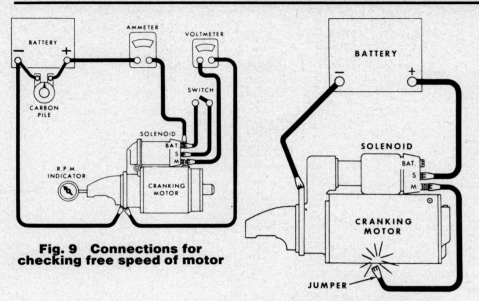

Fig. 9   Connections for checking free speed of motor

Fig. 10   Connections for checking pinion clearance

JUMPER

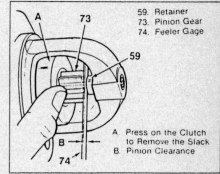

59. Retainer
73. Pinion Gear
74. Feeler Gage

A. Press on the Clutch to Remove the Slack
B. Pinion Clearance

Fig. 11   Checking pinion clearance

# Hitachi Starters

## INDEX

Page No.

## DIAGNOSIS

When diagnosing Hitachi starters, refer to **Figs. 1 and 2.**

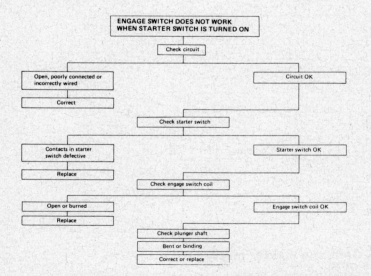

Fig. 1   Diagnosis chart. Gasoline starter motor (Part 1 of 4)

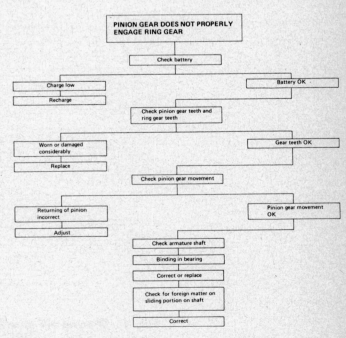

Fig. 1   Diagnosis chart. Gasoline starter motor (Part 2 of 4)

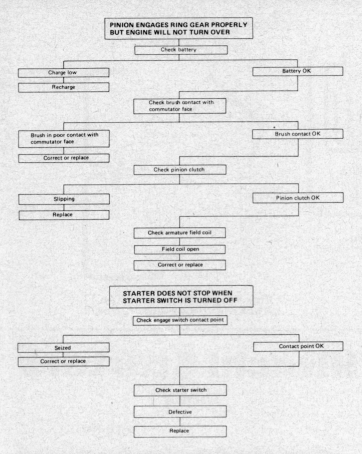

**Fig. 1    Diagnosis chart. Gasoline starter motor (Part 3 of 4)**

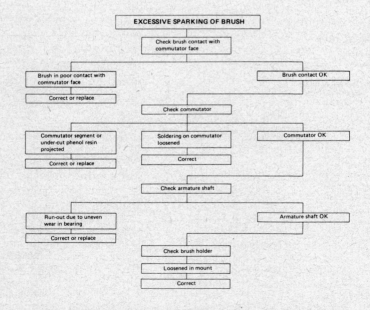

**Fig. 1    Diagnosis chart. Gasoline starter motor (Part 4 of 4)**

| Complaint | Faulty parts | Cause | Correction |
|---|---|---|---|
| Pinion does not jump out when starter switch is turned on | Wiring | Circuit open, battery or switch terminals loosened, or poor connections at connector | Correct and retighten |
| | Starter switch | Current not flowing due to poor contact | Correct or replace |
| | Starter | 1. Helical splines on pinion shaft damaged preventing smooth movement of pinion | Correct or replace |
| | | 2. Torsion spring or shift lever broken | Replace |
| | Solenoid | Plunger operation sluggish, coil open or shorted | Correct or replace |
| | Battery | Under-charged | Recharge |
| Pinion engages ring gear but starter does not turn over | Wiring | 1. Cable connecting solenoid to battery broken | Correct, retighten or replace |
| | | 2. Lead wire between solenoid and motor poorly connected. | |
| | Starter | 1. Incorrectly installed. | Remove and reinstall correctly |
| | | 2. Brushes worn beyond limit | Replace |
| | | 3. Commutator face fouled | Correct |
| | | 4. Armature or field coil(s) shorted | Replace |
| | | 5. Brushes not properly connected to field coils | Correct |
| | | 6. Ball bearing locked | Replace |
| | Solenoid | Contact points defective | Replace |
| Motor operates before pinion engages ring gear | Starter | 1. Torsion spring weakened or shift lever distorted | Replace |
| | | 2. Pinion shaft sticking or binding | Replace |
| | | 3. Pinion gear teeth worn | Correct |
| | | 4. Pinion setting incorrect | Replace |
| | Engine | Ring gear worn | Replace |
| Pinion engages ring gear and motor operates but power is not carried to engine | Starter | 1. Clutch defective | Replace |
| | | 2. Reduction gear broken | Replace |
| Motor continues to spin even when starter switch is turned off after engine starting. | Starter switch | Contact point returning action poor | Replace |
| | Solenoid | Contact point returning action poor | Replace |

**Fig. 2   Diagnosis chart. Diesel starter**

# DASH GAUGES & GRAPHIC DISPLAYS

## INDEX

## DASH GAUGES

Gauge failures are often caused by defective wiring or grounds. The first step in locating trouble should be a thorough inspection of all wiring, terminals and printed circuits. If wiring is secured by clamps, check to see whether the insulation has been severed, thereby grounding the wire. In the case of a fuel gauge installation, rust may cause failure by corrosion at the ground connection of the tank unit.

## VARIABLE VOLTAGE TYPE

The variable voltage type dash gauge consists of two magnetic coils to which battery voltage is applied. The coils act on the gauge pointer and pull in opposite directions. One coil is grounded directly to the chassis, while the other coil is grounded through a variable resistor within the sending unit. Resistance through the sending unit determines current flow through its coil, and therefore pointer position.

When resistance is high in the sending unit, less current is allowed to flow through its coil, causing the gauge pointer to move toward the directly grounded coil. When resistance in the sending unit decreases, more current is allowed to pass through its coil, increasing the magnetic field. The gauge pointer is then attracted toward the coil which is grounded through the sending unit.

A special tester is required to diagnose this type gauge. Follow instructions included with the tester.

## AMMETERS

The ammeter is an instrument used to indicate current flow into and out of the battery. When electrical accessories in the vehicle draw more current than the alternator can supply (output), current flows from the battery and the ammeter indicates a discharge (−) condition. When electrical loads of the vehicle are less than alternator output, current is available to charge the battery, and the ammeter indicates a charge (+) condition. If battery is fully charged, the voltage regulator reduces alternator output to meet only immediate vehicle electrical loads. When this happens, the ammeter reads zero.

A conventional ammeter must be connected between the battery and alternator in order to indicate current flow. This type ammeter, **Fig. 1**, consists of a frame to which a permanent magnet is attached. The frame also supports an armature and pointer assembly. Current in this system flows from the alternator through the ammeter, then to the battery or from the battery through the ammeter into the vehicle electrical system, depending on vehicle operating conditions.

When no current flows through the ammeter, the magnet holds the pointer armature so that the pointer stands at the center of the dial. When current passes in either direction through the ammeter, the resulting magnetic field attracts the armature away from the effect of the permanent magnet, thus giving a reading proportional to the strength of the current flowing.

## TROUBLESHOOTING

When the ammeter fails to register correctly, there may be trouble in the wiring between the ammeter, alternator and battery or the components themselves.

To check the connections, first clean then tighten the two terminal posts on the back of the ammeter. Following each wire from the ammeter, clean and tighten all connections on the ignition switch, battery and alternator. Chafed, burned or broken insulation can be located by following each ammeter wire from end to end. All wires abnormal insulation should be repaired or replaced. Tighten all connec-

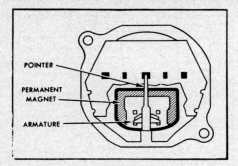

**Fig. 1    Conventional type ammeter**

tions, connect the battery cable, then turn the ignition switch on. The ammeter needle should point slightly to the discharge (−) side.

Start the engine and run slightly above idling speed. The needle should move slowly to the charge side (+).

If the pointer does not move as indicated, the ammeter is out of order and should be replaced.

## ALTERNATOR INDICATOR LIGHT
### DELCOTRON SI INTEGRAL CHARGING SYSTEM

This system features an integral solid state regulator mounted inside the alternator slip ring end frame. The alternator indicator lamp is installed in the field wire circuit connected between the ignition "Ign." terminal and alternator No. 1 terminal, **Fig. 2.** The resistance provided by the alternator warning light circuit is needed to protect the diode trio. The alternator indicator lamp should light when the ignition switch is turned on before engine is started. If lamp does not light, either lamp is burned out or indicator lamp wiring has an open circuit. After engine is started, the indicator lamp should be out at all times. If indicator lamp comes on, alternator belt may be loose, alternator or regulator may be defective, charging circuit may be defective or fuse may be blown.

### Troubleshooting

1. Switch Off, lamp On:
   a. Disconnect electrical connector from alternator terminals 1 and 2.
   b. If indicator light remains lit, repair short circuit between leads.
   c. If indicator light goes out, replace alternator rectifier bridge.
2. Switch On, lamp Off, engine not running:
   a. Perform tests described in step 1.
   b. If problem still exists, check for an open circuit.
   c. When locating an open circuit, check for blown fuse or fusible link, burned out bulb, defective bulb socket or an open in No. 1 lead circuit between alternator and ignition switch.
   d. If no faults are found, check charging system for proper operation.

3. Switch On, lamp On, engine running:
   a. Check condition of fuse between indicator light and ignition switch and fuse in A/C circuit, if equipped.
   b. Check charging system for proper operation.

## VOLTMETER

The voltmeter is a gauge which measures the electrical flow from the battery to indicate whether the battery output is within tolerances. The voltmeter reading can range from 13.5-14.0 volts under normal operating conditions. If an undercharge or overcharge condition is indicated for an extended period, the battery and charging system should be checked.

## TROUBLESHOOTING

To check voltmeter, turn ignition switch and headlights on with engine off. Pointer should move to 12.5 volts. If no needle movement is observed, check connections from battery to circuit breaker. If connections are tight and and clean but check wire continuity. If wire continuity is satisfactory, replace the voltmeter.

## OIL PRESSURE INDICATOR LIGHT

Many trucks utilize a warning light on the instrument panel in place of the conventional dash indicating gauge to warn the driver when the oil pressure is dangerously low. The warning light is wired in series with the ignition switch and the engine unit—which is an oil pressure switch.

The oil pressure switch contains a diaphragm and a set of contacts. When the ignition switch is turned on, the warning light circuit is energized and the circuit is completed through the closed contacts in the pressure switch. When the engine is started, build-up of oil pressure compresses the diaphragm, opening the contacts, thereby breaking the circuit causing the light to go out.

## TROUBLESHOOTING

**On some models, the oil pressure indicator light also serves as the electric choke defect indicator. If Oil or Eng. indicator light does not light, check to ensure electric choke is not disconnected at carburetor. Also check for defect in electric choke heater, blown gauge fuse or defect in lamp or wiring circuit. If indicator light stays on with engine running possible causes are: low oil pressure, switch to indicator light open circuit, disconnected oil pressure switch connector or oil pressure gauge or radio fuse has blown.**

The oil pressure warning light should go on when the ignition is turned on. If it does not light, disconnect the wire from the engine unit and ground the wire to the frame or cylinder block. Then if the warning light still does not go on, replace the bulb.

If the warning light goes on when the wire is grounded, check the engine unit for a poor ground, or improper installation. (The presence of sealing compound on the threads of the engine unit will cause a

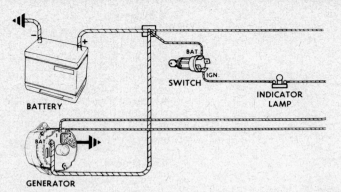

**Fig. 2   Charge indicator lamp wiring system. Delco S1 type charging system**

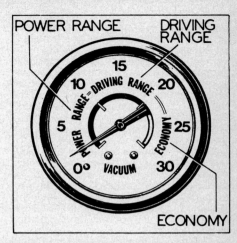

**Fig. 3   Typical vacuum gauge**

poor ground.) If the unit is found to be properly grounded and installed, replace the unit.

If the warning light remains lit when it normally should be out, replace the engine unit before proceeding to determine the cause for low pressure indication.

The warning light will sometimes light or flicker when the engine is idling, even if oil pressure is adequate. However, the light should go out when the engine speed is increased.

# TEMPERATURE INDICATOR LIGHT

A bimetal temperature switch located in the cylinder head controls the operation of a temperature indicator light. If the engine cooling system is not functioning properly and/or coolant temperature exceeds a predetermined value, the warning light will illuminate.

## TROUBLESHOOTING

If the light is not lit when the engine is being cranked, check for a burned out bulb, an open in the light circuit, or a defective ignition switch.

If the light is lit when the engine is running, check the wiring between light and switch for a ground, defective temperature switch, or overheated cooling system.

As a test circuit to check whether the bulb is functioning properly, connect a wire from the ground terminal of the ignition switch to the temperature indicator light circuit. When the ignition is in the "Start" (engine cranking) position, the ground terminal is grounded inside the switch and the bulb will be lit. When the engine is started and the ignition switch is in the "On" position, the test circuit is opened and the bulb is then controlled by the temperature switch.

# SPEEDOMETERS

The following material covers only that service on speedometers which is feasible to perform. Repairs on the units themselves are not included as they require special tools and extreme care when making repairs and adjustments that only an experienced speedometer technician should attempt.

The speedometer has two main parts—the speedometer head and the speedometer drive cable. When the speedometer fails to indicate speed or mileage, check the cable or cable housing for cracks or breaks.

## SPEEDOMETER CABLE

Most cables are broken due to lack of lubrication, or a sharp bend or kink in the housing.

A cable might break because of the speedometer head mechanism binds. In such cases, the speedometer head should be repaired or replaced before a new cable or housing is installed.

A "jumpy" pointer condition, together with a scraping noise, is due, in most instances, to a dry or kinked speedometer cable. The kinked cable rubs on the housing and winds up, slowing down the pointer. The cable then unwinds and the pointer "jumps."

To check for kinks, remove the cable, lay it on a flat surface and twist one end with the fingers. If it turns over smoothly the cable is not kinked. But if part of the cable flops over as it is twisted, the cable is kinked and should be replaced.

## LUBRICATION

The speedometer cable should be lubricated with special cable lubricant. Fill the ferrule on the upper end of the housing with the cable lubricant. Insert the cable in the housing, starting at the upper end. Turn the cable around carefully while feeding it into the housing. Repeat filling the ferrule except for the last six inches of cable. Too much lubricant at this point may cause the lubricant to work into the speedometer head.

## INSTALLING CABLE

During installation, if the cable sticks when inserted in the housing and will not go through, the housing is damaged inside or kinked. Be sure to check the housing from end to end. Straighten any sharp bends by relocating clamps or elbows. Replace housing if badly kinked or broken. Position the cable and housing so that they lead into the head as straight as possible.

Check the new cable for kinks before installing it. Use wide, sweeping, gradual curves where the cable comes out of the transmission and connects to the head so the cable will not be damaged during installation.

Arrange the housing so it does not lean against the engine because heat from the engine may dry out the lubricant.

If inspection indicates that the cable and housing are in good condition, yet pointer action is erratic, check the speedometer head for possible binding.

The speedometer drive pinion should also be checked. If the pinion is dry or its teeth are stripped, the speedometer may not register properly.

# VACUUM GAUGE

This gauge, **Fig. 3**, measures intake manifold vacuum. The intake manifold vacuum varies with engine operating conditions, carburetor adjustments, valve timing, ignition timing and general engine condition.

Since the optimum fuel economy is directly proportional to a properly functioning engine, a high vacuum reading on the gauge relates to fuel economy. Most gauges have colored sectors, the green sector being the "Economy" range and the red the "Power" range. Therefore, the vehicle should be operated with gauge registering in the green sector or a high numerical number, **Fig. 3**, for maximum economy.

# FUEL ECONOMY WARNING SYSTEM

This system actually monitors the engine vacuum just like the vacuum gauge, but registers only low vacuum readings. The light on the instrument panel warns the vehicle operator when engine manifold vacuum drops below the economical limit. Switch operation is similar to that of the oil pressure indicating light, except that the switch opens when vacuum pressure, rather than oil pressure, is applied.

## TROUBLESHOOTING
### Fuel Economy Warning Light

The fuel economy warning light should go on when the ignition is turned on. If it does not light, disconnect the wire from the fuel economy vacuum switch connector and ground the wire to the frame or cylinder block. If the warning light still does not go on, check for burned out indicating bulb or an open in the harness between the vacuum switch and instrument panel. If the warning light goes on, circuit is functioning and the vacuum switch should be checked for proper ground. Remove and clean the mounting bracket screws and the mounting surfaces.

If system still does not operate, perform the following:

With the electrical connector and vacuum tube disconnected from the switch, connect a self-powered test light to the switch electrical connector and to the vacuum gauge mounting bracket. Attach a vacuum pump to the gauge. If the following conditions are not met, the switch has to be replaced:

1. With vacuum applied, test light should be "Off."
2. With no vacuum to the vacuum switch, test light should be "On."

If the warning light remains lit when it normally should be out, check vacuum hose to vacuum switch for damage or plugged condition.

## ELECTRIC CLOCKS

Regulation of electric clocks is accomplished automatically by resetting the time. If the clock is running fast, the action of turning the hands back to correct the time will automatically cause the clock to run slightly slower. If the clock is running slow, the action of turning the hands forward to correct the time will automatically cause the clock to run slightly faster (10 to 15 seconds per day).

A lock-out feature prevents the clock regulator mechanism from being reset more than once per wind cycle, regardless of the number of times the time is reset. After the clock rewinds, if the time is then reset, automatic regulation will take place. If a clock varies over 10 minutes per day, it will never adjust properly and must be repaired or replaced.

## WINDING CLOCK WHEN CONNECTING BATTERY OR CLOCK WIRING

The clock requires special attention when reconnecting the battery, the clock or replacing the clock fuse. It is very important that the initial wind be fully made. The procedure is as follows:

1. Make sure that all other instruments and lights are turned off.
2. Connect positive cable to battery.
3. Before connecting the negative cable, press the terminal to its post on the battery. Immediately afterward, strike the terminal against the battery post to see if there is a spark. If there is a spark, allow the clock to run down until it stops ticking, and repeat as above until there is no spark. Then immediately make the permanent connection before the clock can again run down. The clock will run down in approximately two minutes.
4. Reset clock after all connections have been made. The foregoing procedure should also be followed when reconnecting the clock after it has been dis-

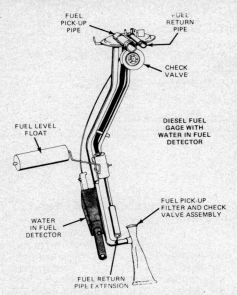

**Fig. 4  Water in fuel detector & tank purge procedure. 1980–84**

connected, or if it has stopped because of a blown fuse. Be sure to disconnect battery before installing a new fuse.

## TROUBLESHOOTING

If clock does not run, check for blown "clock" fuse. If fuse is blown, check for short in wiring. If fuse is not blown, check for open circuit.

With an electric clock, the most frequent cause of a blown fuse, is voltage at the clock which will prevent a complete wind and allow clock contacts to remain closed. This may be caused by any of the following: discharged battery, corrosion on contact surface of battery terminals, loose connections at battery terminals, junction block, fuse clips, or terminal connection of clock. Therefore, if in reconnecting battery or clock it is noted that the clock is not ticking, always check for blown fuse, or examine the circuits at the points indicated above to determine and correct the cause.

## WATER IN FUEL INDICATOR

### DESCRIPTION & OPERATION

#### 1980–84

The Water In Fuel warning system employs an electronic water detector mounted inside the fuel tank on the fuel gauge sending unit. The detector provides a warning when 1-2½ gallons of water are present in the fuel tank by lighting a warning lamp on the instrument panel. The sending unit assembly also contains a provision for siphoning off water in the fuel tank through the fuel return line, **Fig. 4.**

The Water In Fuel lamp will come on for 2-5 seconds each time ignition is switched to Run position to ensure lamp is operating. If water is present in fuel, the lamp will come on after a 15-20 second delay and remain on.

#### 1985–89

The Water In Fuel warning system employs a fuel detector integral with the fuel filter and fuel heater and mounted on the engine. When 2.2 ounces of water more has collected in the filter, the Water In Fuel lamp on the instrument panel will light. After the light comes on, the filter should be drained as soon as possible and must be drained within 2 hours of operation.

## TROUBLESHOOTING

### 1980–84

1. If warning indicator fails to light during bulb check, proceed as follows:
   a. Disconnect electrical connector from fuel gauge sensing unit.
   b. Ground yellow/black wire in connector, then turn ignition to Run position.
   c. If indicator lamp lights, remove fuel gauge tank unit and check yellow wire for opens. Also, check connections to Water In Fuel detector and mounting screws. If connections and attachments are satisfactory, replace detector.
   d. If indicator lamp fails to light, check indicator lamp bulb. If bulb is satisfactory, check for open in yellow wire between lamp socket and sending unit and repair as necessary.
2. If warning indicator is lit at all times, proceed as follows:
   a. Disconnect electrical connector from fuel gauge sending unit, then turn ignition to Run position.
   b. If light remains lit, repair short to ground in yellow/black wire between sender and warning lamp.
   c. If light goes out, drain water from fuel tank, then recheck circuit. If lamp remains on with harness connected to sending unit, wiring to water detector or the detector itself is at fault.

### 1985–89

1. If warning lamp lights intermittently, drain water from fuel filter.
2. If warning lamp remains lit with engine running and ambient temperature above 32°F, drain fuel filter immediately. If lamp remains lit, replace filter.
3. If warning lamp remains lit with engine running and ambient temperature 32°F or below, drain fuel filter immediately. If water is frozen and cannot be drained, open air bleed to check for fuel pressure. If no fuel pressure is present, replace filter.
4. If warning lamp lights at high speed or under heavy acceleration, the fuel filter is plugged and must be replaced.
5. If warning lamp remains lit and engine stalls, then will not restart after initial start-up, then fuel filter or fuel lines may be plugged. Repair or replace as necessary.
6. If warning lamp remains lit and engine stalls and will not restart immediately after refueling, a large quantity of water has likely been pumped into the fuel tank and the tank should be purged.

# DISC BRAKES

## TABLE OF CONTENTS

# General Information

## INDEX

## TROUBLESHOOTING

### EXCESSIVE PEDAL TRAVEL

1. Worn brake linings.
2. Disc pads knock back after cornering or rough road travel.
3. Piston and linings not properly seated or positioned.
4. Insufficient fluid in system.
5. Loose wheel bearing adjustment.
6. Damaged or worn caliper piston seal.
7. Improper booster pushrod adjustment.
8. Pads out of flat more than .005 inch.
9. Rear brake automatic adjusters inoperative.
10. Improperly ground rear brake shoes.

### BRAKE ROUGHNESS OR CHATTER; PEDAL PUMPING

1. Excessive lateral runout of rotor.
2. Rotor excessively out of parallel.

### EXCESSIVE PEDAL EFFORT

1. Frozen or seized pistons.
2. Brake fluid, oil or grease on linings.
3. Linings worn below specifications.
4. Proportioning valve malfunction.
5. Booster inoperative.
6. Leaking booster vacuum check valve.

### PULL, UNEVEN OR GRABBING BRAKES

1. Frozen or seized pistons.
2. Brake fluid, oil or grease on linings.
3. Caliper out of alignment with rotor.
4. Loose caliper attachment.
5. Front tire pressure not equalized.

6. Incorrect front end alignment.
7. Linings improperly bonded.

### BRAKE RATTLE

1. Excessive clearance between pad and caliper.
2. Hardware missing or improperly positioned.

### HEAVY BRAKE DRAG

1. Frozen or seized pistons.
2. Operator riding brake pedal.
3. Incomplete brake pedal return due to linkage interference.
4. Faulty booster check valve holding pressure in hydraulic system.
5. Residual pressure in front brake hydraulic system.

### CALIPER BRAKE FLUID LEAK

1. Damaged or worn caliper piston seal.
2. Scores in cylinder bore.
3. Corrosion build-up in cylinder bore or on piston surface.

### NO BRAKING EFFECT WHEN BRAKE PEDAL IS DEPRESSED

1. Piston and linings not properly seated or positioned.
2. Insufficient fluid in system.
3. Damaged or worn caliper piston seal.
4. Bleeder screw open.
5. Air in hydraulic system.

### REAR BRAKES LOCKING ON APPLICATION

On brake system equipped with a proportioning or rear pressure regulator valve, should the valve malfunction, rear brakes may receive excess pressure, resulting in wheel lock-up.

## SERVICE PRECAUTIONS

### BRAKE LINES & LININGS

Remove one of the front wheels and inspect the brake disc, caliper and linings.

Do not get any oil or grease on the linings. It is recommended that all linings be replaced in sets when worn or damaged.

If the caliper is cracked or fluid leakage through the casting is evident, it must be replaced as a unit.

### BRAKE ROUGHNESS

The most common cause of brake chatter on disc brakes is a variation in thickness of the disc. If roughness or vibration is encountered during highway operation or if pedal pumping is experienced at low speeds, the disc may have excessive thickness variation. To check for this condition, measure the disc at 12 points with a micrometer at a radius approximately one inch from edge of disc. If thickness measurements vary more than specifications allow, the disc should be replaced with a new one.

Excessive lateral runout of braking disc may cause a "knocking back" of the pistons, possibly creating increased pedal travel and vibration when brakes are applied.

Before checking the runout, wheel bearings should be adjusted. Be sure to make the adjustment according to the recommendations given in the individual truck chapters.

## BRAKE DISC SERVICE

Servicing of disc brakes is extremely critical due to the close tolerances required in machining the brake disc to insure proper brake operation.

The maintenance of these close controls on the friction surfaces is necessary to prevent brake roughness. In addition, the surface finish must be non-directional and maintained at a micro-inch finish. This close control of the rubbing surface finish is necessary to avoid pulls and erratic performance and promote long lining life and equal lining wear of both left and right brakes.

In light of the foregoing remarks, refinishing of the rubbing surfaces should not be attempted unless precision equipment, capable of measuring in micro-inches is available.

To check runout of a disc, mount a dial indicator on a convenient part (steering knuckle, tie rod, disc brake caliper housing) so that the plunger of the dial indicator contacts the disc at a point one inch from the outer edge. If the total indicated runout exceeds specifications, install a new disc.

When refacing rotors on 1988 K1-2 models it is extremely important that the rotor is mounted on the lathe exactly as it is mounted on the vehicle. To accomplish this, rotor adaptor tool No. J-37620, or equivalent must be used. Failure to use this tool can result in unparallel rotor surfaces. This condition can cause brake pedal vibration or pulsation.

## GENERAL PRECAUTIONS

1. Grease or any other foreign material must be kept off the caliper, surfaces of the disc and external surfaces of the hub, during service procedures. Handling the brake disc and caliper should be done in a way to avoid deformation of the disc and nicking or scratching of the brake linings.
2. If inspection reveals rubber piston seals are worn or damaged, they should be replaced immediately.
3. During removal and installation of a wheel assembly, exercise care so as not to interfere with or damage the caliper splash shield or bleeder screw.
4. Front wheel bearings should be adjusted to specifications.
5. Be sure vehicle is centered on hoist before servicing any of the front end components to avoid bending or damaging the disc splash shield on full right or left wheel turns.
6. Before the vehicle is moved after any brake service work, be sure to obtain a firm brake pedal.
7. The assembly bolts of the two caliper housings (if equipped) should not be disturbed unless the caliper requires service.

## INSPECTION OF CALIPER

Should it become necessary to remove the caliper for installation of new parts, clean all parts in denatured alcohol, wipe dry using lint-free cloths. Using compressed air, blow out drilled passages and bores. Check dust boots for punctures or tears. If punctures or tears are evident, new boots should be installed upon reassembly.

Inspect piston bores in both housings for scoring or pitting. Bores that show light scratches or corrosion can usually be cleaned with crocus cloth. However, bores that have deep scratches or scoring may be honed, provided the diameter of the bore is not increased more than .002 inch. If the bore does not clean up within this specification, a new caliper housing should be installed (black stains on the bore walls are caused by piston seals and will do no harm).

When using a hone, be sure to install the hone baffle before honing bore. The baffle is used to protect the hone stones from damage. Use extreme care in cleaning the caliper after honing. Remove all dust and grit by flushing the caliper with denatured alcohol. Wipe dry with clean lint-free cloth and then clean a second time in the same manner.

## BLEEDING DISC BRAKES

The braking system can be bled manually or with pressure bleeding equipment. If manually bleeding, check fluid level frequently.

Brake fluid should never to be reused. Before driving the vehicle, check brake operation to be sure that a firm pedal has been obtained.

# Delco-Moraine Single Piston Caliper

## INDEX

## DESCRIPTION

The caliper assembly, **Fig. 1,** slides on its mounting surfaces. Upon brake application, hydraulic pressure against the piston forces the inboard pad against the inboard side of the disc. This action causes the caliper assembly to slide until the outboard pad comes into contact with the disc, which in turn creates a slowing or stopping action.

## CALIPER REMOVAL

1. Siphon enough brake fluid out of the master cylinder to bring fluid level to 1/3 full to avoid fluid overflow when the caliper piston is pushed back into its bore.
2. Raise and support vehicle, remove front wheels.
3. Using a C-clamp, as illustrated in **Fig.**

**2,** push piston back into its bore.
4. Remove two mounting bolts and lift caliper away from disc.

## BRAKE PAD REMOVAL

1. Remove caliper assembly as outlined above.
2. Remove inboard pad with retainer spring. Dislodge outboard pad and position caliper on the front suspension so the brake hose will not support the weight of the caliper.
3. Remove two sleeves from inboard ears of the caliper.
4. Remove four rubber bushings from the grooves in each of the caliper ears.

## BRAKE PAD INSTALLATION

1. Lubricate new sleeves, rubber bushings, bushing grooves and mounting bolt ends with Delco Silicone Lube or equivalent.
2. Install new bushings and sleeves in caliper ears. Position the sleeve so that the end toward the pad is flush with the machined surface of the ear.
3. Install retainer spring on back of inboard pad.
4. Position inboard pad with ears up and retainer spring facing the piston then press pad into piston bore until seated.
   a. Some inboard pads contain a wear sensor, the sensor should be toward the rear of the caliper when installed properly.
5. Position outboard pad to caliper interior with pad ears over caliper ears and tab at bottom of pad seated in caliper cutout.
6. With pads installed, install caliper as described under caliper installation

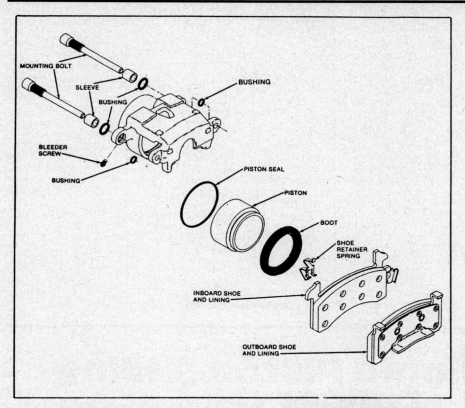

Fig. 1 Typical exploded view of disc brake caliper assembly

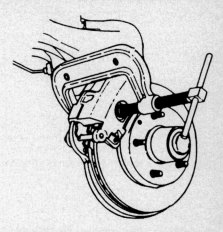

Fig. 2 Compressing piston & pad with C-clamp

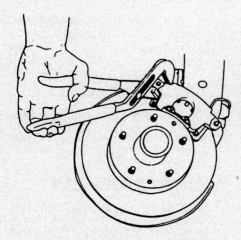

Fig. 3 Fitting pad to caliper

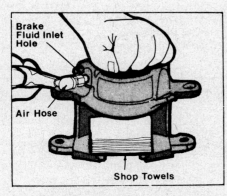

Fig. 4 Removing piston from caliper

7. Seat the outboard pad to the caliper by grasping the ears with channel locks and pressing together firmly, **Fig. 3.**

## DISASSEMBLING CALIPER

1. Disconnect hose from the caliper being careful not to lose copper washers.
2. Remove caliper as outlined above.

3. Drain brake fluid from caliper.
4. Pad caliper interior with clean shop towels and apply compressed air to remove piston, **Fig. 4.** Use just enough air pressure to ease piston out of bore. **When applying compressed air do not place fingers in front of piston in an attempt to catch or protect it as this could result in serious injury.**
5. Carefully pry dust boot out of bore.
6. Using a small piece of wood or plastic, remove piston seal from bore. **Do not use a metal tool of any kind to remove seal as it may damage bore.**

7. Remove bleeder valve.

## ASSEMBLING CALIPER

1. Lubricate caliper piston bore and new piston seal with clean brake fluid. Position seal in bore groove.
2. Lubricate piston with clean brake fluid and assemble a new boot into the groove in the piston so the fold faces the open end of the piston, **Fig. 5.**
3. Using care not to unseat the seal, insert piston into bore and force the piston to the bottom of the bore.
4. Position dust boot in caliper counterbore and install, **Fig. 6.** Check the boot installation to be sure the retaining ring molded into the boot is not bent and that the boot is installed below the caliper face and evenly all around. If the boot is not fully installed, dirt and moisture may enter the bore and cause corrosion.
5. If available, use new copper washers discarding the old washers and install the brake hose to the caliper.
6. Install pads and caliper assembly.

## CALIPER INSTALLATION

1. Position caliper over disc, lining up mounting holes in caliper with holes in mounting bracket. If brake hose was not disconnected during removal, be sure not to kink it during installation.
2. Start mounting bolts through sleeves in inboard caliper ears and the mounting bracket, making sure ends of bolts pass under ears on inboard shoe. **Right and left calipers must not be interchanged.**
3. Push mounting bolts through to engage holes in the outboard ears. Then thread mounting bolts into bracket.
4. Torque mounting bolts to 30-40 ft. lbs.
5. If brake hose was removed, reconnect it and bleed the calipers.

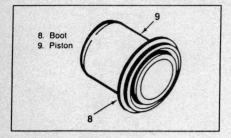

8. Boot
9. Piston

**Fig. 5   Installing boot to piston**

6. Replace front wheels, lower vehicle and add brake fluid to master cylinder to bring level to 1/4 inch from top. **Before moving vehicle, pump brake pedal several times to be sure it is firm. Do not move vehicle until a firm pedal is obtained.**

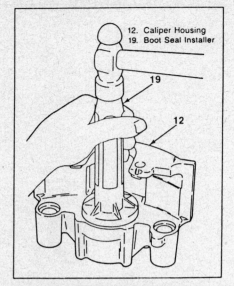

12. Caliper Housing
19. Boot Seal Installer

**Fig. 6   Installing boot to caliper**

# Bendix Single Piston Sliding Caliper

## INDEX

## DESCRIPTION

The Bendix single piston sliding caliper disc brake is standard equipment on some truck applications, while on other trucks it is used only in Hydro-Boost power brake applications with both front disc brakes and 4 wheel disc brakes. On 4 wheel disc brakes, the front and rear systems are identical.

The sliding caliper attaches to and slides on the steering knuckle. The caliper assembly is held in place with a support key and spring **Fig. 1.** A screw prevents the key from sliding on the steering knuckle. The friction material is bonded with rivets. The inboard and outboard brake pads are not interchangeable.

## CALIPER REMOVAL

1. Siphon two-thirds of brake fluid from master cylinder reservoir serving front disc brakes.
2. Raise vehicle, support on jack stands and remove front wheels.
3. Bottom the caliper piston in bore. Insert a screwdriver between inboard shoe and piston, then pry piston back into bore. The piston can also be bottomed in the bore with a large C-clamp, **Fig. 2.**
4. Remove support key retaining screw.
5. Drive caliper support key and spring from steering knuckle with a suitable drift and hammer, **Fig. 3.**
6. Lift caliper from anchor plate and off rotor, **Fig. 4.** Hang caliper from coil spring with wire. Do not allow caliper to hang from brake hose.
7. Remove inboard pad from steering knuckle, then the anti-rattle spring from the pad.
8. Remove outboard pad from caliper. It may be necessary to loosen the pad with a hammer to permit removal.

## CALIPER DISASSEMBLY

1. Drain brake fluid from caliper.
2. Position caliper with shop cloths, **Fig. 5,** and apply compressed air to fluid inlet port to ease piston from bore. **Do not attempt to catch piston or to protect it when applying compressed air, since personal injury is possible.**
3. Remove dust boot, then the piston seal from bore, **Fig. 6.** Use wooden or plastic tool to remove piston seal since metal tools may damage piston.
4. Remove bleeder screw.

## CALIPER ASSEMBLY

1. Coat square cut piston seal with clean brake fluid, then install seal into piston bore. Work seal into groove with clean fingers.
2. Install and torque bleeder screw to 100 inch lbs.
3. Lubricate boot and tool J-24548 with clean brake fluid, then place dust seal on tool, allowing 1/4 inch of tool to extend past small lip of boot, **Fig. 7.**
4. Place dust seal and tool over piston bore, then work large lip of boot into seal groove, **Fig. 8.** Ensure dust seal is fully seated.
5. Lubricate caliper piston and insert through tool. Center piston in bore and use a hammer handle to apply pressure to install piston halfway into bore, **Fig. 8.**
6. Remove tool J-24548 and seat small lip of boot in caliper piston groove, then bottom piston in bore.

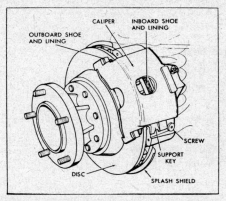

**Fig. 1  Disc brake assembly**

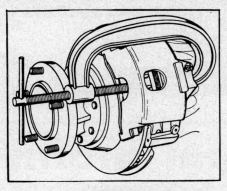

**Fig. 2  Bottoming position in bore**

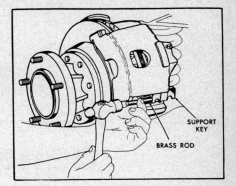

**Fig. 3  Removing caliper support key**

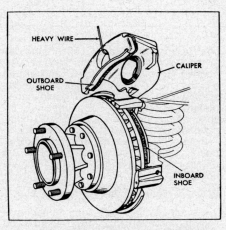

**Fig. 4  Removing caliper from disc**

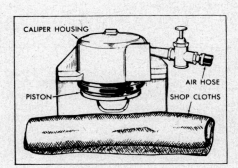

**Fig. 5  Removing caliper piston**

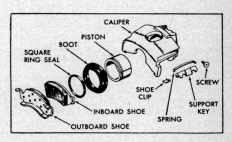

**Fig. 6  Exploded view of disc brake caliper assembly**

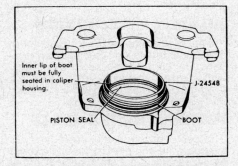

**Fig. 7  Installing caliper piston boot**

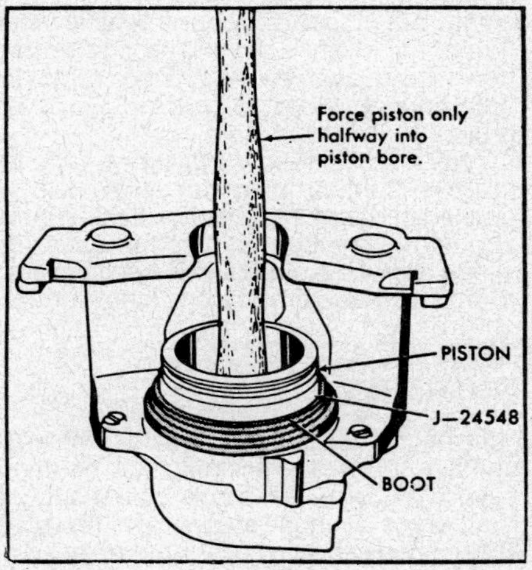

**Fig. 8  Installing piston in caliper**

# BRAKE PADS
## REPLACE

The procedures to remove & install the brake pads are outlined under "Caliper Removal" and "Caliper Installation." It is not necessary to disconnect the brake hose, however, use caution not to twist or kink hose.

# CALIPER INSTALLATION

1. Clean and lubricate sliding surfaces of caliper and the anchor plate with Delco Silicone Lube, P/N 5459912, or equivalent.
2. Install anti-rattle spring on inboard pad, and ensure looped section of clip is facing away from rotor.
3. Install inboard pad in steering knuckle.
4. Install outboard pad in caliper. Ensure pad is seated fully into outboard arms of caliper. It may be necessary to tap the ears and bottom tab with a hammer to seat the pad being careful not to hit the friction material.
5. Place caliper assembly over rotor and position in steering knuckle. Ensure dust boot is not torn or improperly positioned by inboard pad during caliper installation.
6. Align caliper with steering knuckle abutment surfaces, then insert support key and spring between abutment surfaces at the trailing end of caliper and steering knuckle. With a hammer and brass drift, drive caliper support key and spring into position, then install and torque support key retaining screw to 12-18 ft. lbs.
7. Refill master cylinder to within one inch of rim. Press brake pedal several times to seat pads.
8. Install front wheels and lower vehicle.

# DRUM BRAKES

## TABLE OF CONTENTS

# General Information

## INDEX

## SERVICE PRECAUTIONS

When working on or around brake assemblies, care must be taken to prevent breathing asbestos dust, as many manufacturers incorporate asbestos fibers in the production of brake linings. During routine service operations, the amount of asbestos dust from brake lining wear is at a low level due to a chemical breakdown during use, and a few precautions will minimize exposure. **Do not sand or grind brake linings unless suitable local exhaust ventilation equipment is used to prevent excessive asbestos exposure.**

1. Wear a suitable respirator approved for asbestos dust use during all repair procedures.
2. When cleaning brake dust from brake parts, use a vacuum cleaner with a highly efficient filter system or denatured alcohol. **Do not use compressed air or dry brush to clean brake parts.**
3. Keep work area clean, using same equipment as for cleaning brake parts.
4. Properly dispose of rags and vacuum cleaner bags by placing them in plastic bags.
5. Do not smoke or eat while working on brake systems.

## GENERAL INSPECTION
### BRAKE DRUMS

Any time the brake drums are removed for brake service, the braking surface diameter should be checked with a suitable brake drum micrometer at several points to determine if they are within the safe oversize limit stamped on the brake drum outer surface. If the braking surface diameter exceeds specifications, the drum must be replaced. If the braking surface diameter is within specifications, drums should be cleaned and inspected for cracks, scores, deep grooves, taper, out of round and heat spotting. If drums are cracked or heat spotted, they must be replaced. Grooves and large scores can only be removed by machining with special equipment, as long as the braking surface is within specifications stamped on brake drum outer surface. Any brake drum sufficiently out of round to cause vehicle vibration or noise while braking, or showing taper should also be machined, removing only enough stock to true up the brake drum.

After a brake drum is machined, wipe the braking surface diameter with a cloth soaked in denatured alcohol. Brake drums should always be machined in pairs and within allowable side to side specifications to maintain equal braking forces.

### BRAKE LININGS & SPRINGS

Inspect brake linings for excessive wear, damage, oil, grease or brake fluid contamination. If any of the above conditions exists, brake linings should be replaced. Brake shoes should always be replaced as an axle set to maintain equal braking forces. Examine brake shoe webbing, hold-down and return springs for signs of overheating indicated by a slight blue color. If any component exhibits signs of overheating, replace hold-down and return springs with new ones. Overheated springs lose their pull and could cause brake linings to wear out prematurely. Inspect all springs for sags, bends and external damage, and replace as necessary.

Inspect hold-down retainers and pins for bends, rust and corrosion. If any of the above conditions exist, replace retainers and pins.

### BACKING PLATE

Inspect backing plate shoe contact surface for grooves that may restrict shoe movement and cannot be removed by lightly sanding with emery cloth or other suitable abrasive. If backing plate exhibits above condition, it should be replaced. Also inspect for signs of cracks, warpage and excessive rust, indicating need for replacement.

### ADJUSTER MECHANISM

Inspect all components for rust, corrosion, bends and fatigue. Replace as necessary. On adjuster mechanism equipped with adjuster cable, inspect cable for kinks, fraying or elongation of eyelet and replace as necessary.

### PARKING BRAKE CABLE

Inspect parking brake cable end for kinks, fraying and elongation, and replace as necessary. Use a small hose clamp to compress clamp where it enters backing plate to remove.

# Drum Brake Service

## INDEX

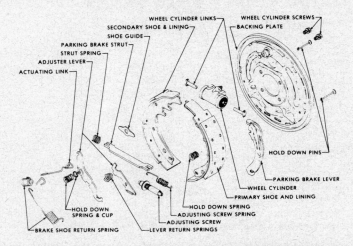

**Fig. 1   Typical exploded view of drum brake assembly. Exc. Caballero, El Camino & 1985-87 S/T 10-15**

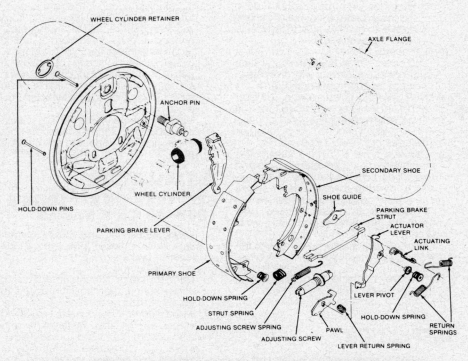

**Fig. 2   Typical exploded view of drum brake assembly. Caballero, El Camino & 1985-87 S/T 10-15**

## REMOVAL

### EXC. 1982-84 S/T 10-15 & 1988-89 C & K SERIES

1. Raise and support vehicle, then remove tire and wheel assembly.
2. Remove brake drum. If brake lining is dragging on brake drum, back off brake adjustment by rotating adjustment screw. Refer to individual truck chapter for procedure. If brake drum is rusted or corroded to axle flange and cannot be removed, lightly tap flange to drum mounting surface with a suitable hammer.
3. Using brake spring pliers or equivalent, unhook primary and secondary return springs, **Figs. 1 and 2.** Observe location of brake parts being removed to aid during installation.
4. Remove brake hold-down springs with suitable tool.
5. Lift actuating lever, then unhook actuator link from anchor pin and remove.
6. Remove actuating lever(s) and return spring.
7. Spread shoes apart and remove parking brake strut and spring.
8. Disconnect parking brake cable from lever, then remove brake shoes from backing plate.
9. Separate brake shoes by removing adjusting screw and spring, then unhook parking brake lever from shoe assembly
10. Clean dirt from brake drum, backing plate and all other components. **Do not use compressed air or dry brush to clean brake parts. which, if inhaled, can cause serious injury. Clean brake parts with a denatured alcohol or a suitable vacuum cleaner to minimize airborne dust.**

### 1982-84 S/T 10-15

1. Raise and support rear of vehicle, then remove tire and wheel assembly.
2. Remove brake drum. If brake lining is dragging on brake drum, back off brake adjustment by rotating adjustment screw. If brake drum is rusted or corroded to axle flange and cannot be removed, lightly tap flange to drum mounting surface with a suitable hammer.
3. Using brake spring pliers or equivalent, unhook primary and secondary return springs, **Fig. 3.**
4. Remove hold-down springs with suitable tool, then lift off lever pivot.

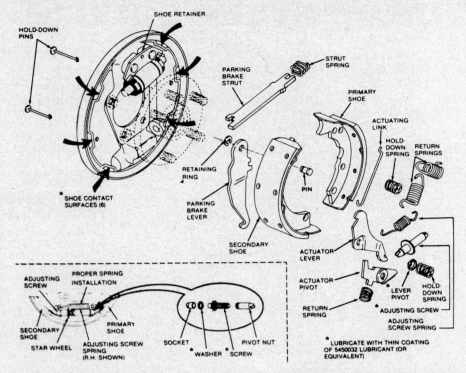

**Fig. 3   Exploded view of drum brake assembly. 1982–84 S/T 10-15**

5. Remove hold-down pins, then lift actuator lever and remove actuator link.
6. Remove actuator lever, pivot and return spring.
7. Spread shoes apart and remove parking brake strut and spring.
8. With brake shoes spread, disconnect parking brake spring from lever then lift brake shoes, adjusting screw and spring from backing plate.
9. Note position of adjusting screw and spring, then remove from shoe assemblies.
10. Remove parking brake lever from secondary shoe.
11. Clean dirt from brake drum, backing plate and all other components. **Do not use compressed air or dry brush to clean brake parts. Many brake parts will be covered with asbestos fibers from the friction material which, if inhaled, can cause serious injury. Clean brake parts with a denatured alcohol or a suitable vacuum cleaner to minimize airborne dust.**

## 1988–89 C & K SERIES

1. Raise and support rear of vehicle, then remove tire and wheel assembly.
2. Mark relationship of brake drum to axle for installation reference, then remove the drum. If drum is difficult to remove, proceed as follows:
   a. Ensure parking brake is fully released, then back off parking brake cable adjustment.
   b. Remove plug from access hole in backing plate, then push parking brake lever off its stop using a suitable screwdriver.
3. Lift actuator lever arm up until upper end clears slot in adjuster screw, then slide actuator off pin and disconnect actuator spring from shoe, **Fig. 4.**
4. Remove hold-down springs and pins.
5. Separate lower ends of shoes, then lift lower return spring over anchor plate. Allow ends of shoes to come together, then remove lower return spring.
6. Remove shoe and lining assemblies together with upper return spring and adjusting screw assembly. **If necessary, overlap lower ends of shoes so upper shoe ends clear wheel cylinder boots, then spread bottom of assembly to clear axle flange.**
7. Remove upper return spring and adjusting screw assembly from brake shoes.
8. Remove retaining ring, pin, spring washer and parking brake lever.
9. Remove parking brake lever from shoe.

## INSPECTION

1. Inspect components for damage or unusual wear. Replace as necessary.
2. Inspect backing plate attaching bolts, and ensure they are tight.
3. Inspect wheel cylinders. Excessive fluid indicates cup leakage and need for wheel cylinder replacement. A slight amount of fluid is always present and is considered normal, acting as a lubricant for the cylinder pistons.
4. Check adjuster screw operation. If satisfactory, lightly lubricate adjusting screw and washer with suitable brake lube. If operation is unsatisfactory, replace.
5. Using fine emery cloth or other suitable abrasive, clean rust and dirt from shoe contact surfaces on backing plate.

## INSTALLATION
### EXC. 1982–84 S/T 10-15 & 1988–89 C & K SERIES

1. Lubricate parking brake lever fulcrum with suitable brake lube, then attach lever to brake shoe. Ensure lever operates smoothly.
2. Connect brake shoes with adjusting screw spring, then position adjusting screw. Ensure adjusting screw star wheel does not contact adjusting screw spring after installation, and also ensure right hand thread adjusting screw is installed on left side of vehicle and lefthand thread adjusting screw is installed on right side of vehicle. When brake shoe installation is completed, ensure star wheel lines up

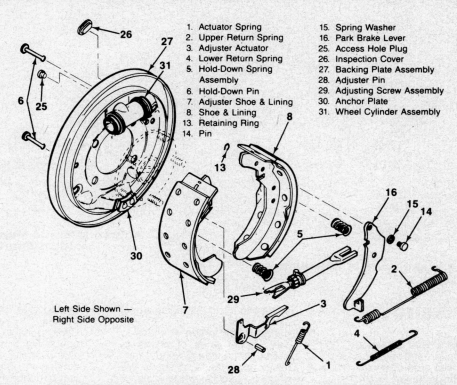

| | | | |
|---|---|---|---|
| 1. | Actuator Spring | 15. | Spring Washer |
| 2. | Upper Return Spring | 16. | Park Brake Lever |
| 3. | Adjuster Actuator | 25. | Access Hole Plug |
| 4. | Lower Return Spring | 26. | Inspection Cover |
| 5. | Hold-Down Spring Assembly | 27. | Backing Plate Assembly |
| 6. | Hold-Down Pin | 28. | Adjuster Pin |
| 7. | Adjuster Shoe & Lining | 29. | Adjusting Screw Assembly |
| 8. | Shoe & Lining | 30. | Anchor Plate |
| 13. | Retaining Ring | 31. | Wheel Cylinder Assembly |
| 14. | Pin | | |

Left Side Shown —
Right Side Opposite

**Fig. 4   Exploded view of drum brake assembly. 1988–89 C & K Series**

with adjusting hole in backing plate.

3. Lightly lubricate backing plate shoe contact surfaces with suitable brake lube, then the area where parking brake cable contacts backing plate.
4. Install brake shoes on backing plate while engaging wheel cylinder links (if equipped) with shoe webbing. Connect parking brake cable to parking brake lever. The primary shoe (short lining) faces towards front of vehicle.
5. Install actuating levers, actuating link and return spring, **Figs. 1 and 2.**
6. Install hold-down springs with suitable tool.
7. Install primary and secondary shoe return springs using brake spring pliers or equivalent.
8. Using suitable brake drum to shoe gauge, **Fig. 5,** measure brake drum inside diameter. Adjust brake shoes to dimension obtained on outside portion of gauge, **Fig. 6.**
9. Install brake drum, wheel and tire assembly.
10. If any hydraulic connections have been opened, bleed brake system.
11. Adjust parking brake. Refer to individual truck chapters for procedures.
12. Inspect all hydraulic lines and connections for leakage, and repair as necessary.
13. Check master cylinder fluid level and replenish as necessary.
14. Check brake pedal for proper feel and return.
15. Lower vehicle and road test. **Do not**

severely apply brakes immediately after installation of new brake linings or permanent damage may occur to linings. Brakes must be applied moderately during first several hundred miles of operation to ensure proper burnishing of linings.

## 1982–84 S/T 10-15

1. Lightly lubricate backing plate shoe contact surfaces with suitable brake lube.
2. Install parking brake lever on secondary shoe.
3. Connect primary and secondary brake shoes with adjusting screw spring, then position adjusting screw in same position from which it was removed. Ensure star wheel does not contact adjusting screw spring after installation, and also ensure righthand thread adjusting screw is installed on left side of vehicle and lefthand thread adjusting screw is installed on right side of vehicle.
4. Spread brake shoes apart to clear axle flange, then install parking brake cable on lever. Position brake assembly on backing plate.
5. Spread brake shoes slightly, then install parking brake strut and spring. Spring end of strut engages the primary shoe, while the other end engages the parking brake lever and secondary shoe.

6. Install actuator lever, pivot and return spring, then hook actuating link in shoe retainer.
7. Lift actuator lever and hook actuating link to lever.
8. Install hold-down pins, lever pivot and hold-down springs.
9. Install primary and secondary return springs using suitable brake spring pliers.
10. Using suitable brake drum to shoe gauge, **Fig. 5,** measure brake drum inside diameter. Adjust brake shoes to dimension obtained on outside portion of gauge, **Fig. 6.**
11. Install brake drum, tire and wheel assembly.
12. If any hydraulic connections have been opened, bleed brake system.
13. Adjust parking brake. Refer to individual truck chapters for procedures.
14. Inspect all hydraulic lines and connections for leakage, and repair as necessary.
15. Check master cylinder fluid level, and replenish as necessary.
16. Check brake pedal for proper feel and return.
17. Lower vehicle and road test. **Do not severely apply brakes immediately after installation of new brake linings or permanent damage may occur to linings. Brakes must be applied moderately during first several hundred miles of operation to ensure proper burnishing of linings.**

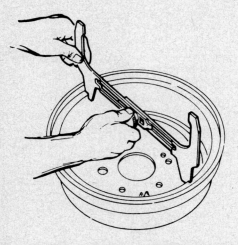

**Fig. 5   Measuring brake drum inside diameter**

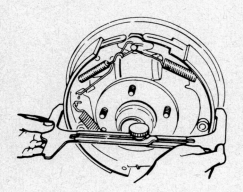

**Fig. 6   Adjusting brake shoes to brake drum inside diameter**

## 1988–89 C & K SERIES

1. Install parking brake lever to shoe with spring washer, pin and retaining ring. **Ensure concave side of washer faces parking brake lever, Fig. 4.**
2. Install adjuster pin into shoe. **Pin must project .268-.276 inch from side of shoe where adjuster actuator is installed.**
3. Apply suitable lubricant to threads of adjuster screw, inside diameter of socket and socket face.
4. Position brake shoes on a clean, flat surface, then install upper return spring to shoes. **The spring must not be stretched to a length exceeding 8.04 inches.**
5. Install adjusting screw assembly between shoes. Ensure screw properly engages adjuster shoe and parking brake lever. **The spring clip must be installed toward the backing plate.**
6. Apply a thin coat of white lithium grease or equivalent to shoe pads.
7. Install shoe and lining assemblies, upper return spring and adjusting screw assembly over axle and behind axle flange, then into backing plate, noting the following:
   a. Use care to avoid damaging wheel cylinder boots.
   b. Overlap lower portion of shoes to enable upper ends of shoes to clear boots on wheel cylinder.
   c. Ensure upper ends of shoes are resting on ends of wheel cylinder pistons.
   d. Do not position lower ends of shoes under anchor plate until lower return spring is installed.
   e. Do not stretch lower return spring to a length exceeding 4.22 inches.
8. Position ends of shoe and lining assemblies together over anchor plate, then hook lower return spring into shoe web holes.
9. Spread lower ends of shoe and lining assemblies until they clear anchor plate, then position shoes against backing plate and release them.
10. Engage spring in groove at bottom of anchor plate.
11. Install hold-down springs and spring assemblies.
12. Position adjuster actuator over end of adjuster pin, ensuring top leg properly engages notch in adjuster screw.
13. Install actuator spring, ensuring free end of actuator engages notch in adjuster nut. **Do not stretch actuator spring to a length exceeding 3.27 inches.**
14. Using suitable brake drum to shoe gauge, **Fig. 5,** measure brake drum inside diameter. Adjust brake shoes to dimension obtained on outside portion of gauge, **Fig. 6.**
15. Connect parking brake cable to brake lever.
16. Install brake drum, tire and wheel assembly.
17. If any hydraulic connections have been opened, bleed brake system.
18. Adjust parking brake. Refer to individual truck chapters for procedures.
19. Inspect all hydraulic lines and connections for leakage and repair as necessary.
20. Check master cylinder fluid level and replenish as necessary.
21. Check brake pedal for proper feel and return.
22. Lower vehicle and road test. **Do not severely apply brakes immediately after installation of new brake linings or permanent damage may occur to linings. Brakes must be applied moderately during first several hundred miles of operation to ensure proper burnishing of linings.**

# UNIVERSAL JOINTS

## INDEX

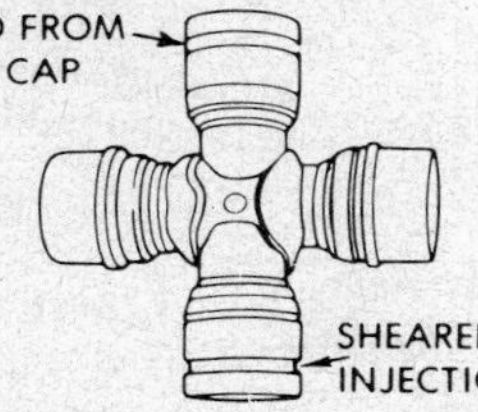

Fig. 1 Production type universal joints which use nylon injection rings in place of snap rings

## SERVICE NOTES

Before disassembling any universal joint, examine the assembly carefully and note the position of the grease fitting (if used). Also, be sure to mark the yokes with relation to the propeller shaft so they may be reassembled in the same relative position. Failure to observe these precautions may produce rough vehicle operation which results in rapid wear and failure of parts, and place an unbalanced load on transmission, engine and rear axle.

When universal joints are disassembled for lubrication or inspection, and the old parts are to be reinstalled, special care must be exercised to avoid damage to universal joint spider or cross and bearing cups.

Some driveshafts use an injected nylon retainer to hold the bearing cups. When service is necessary, pressing the cups out will sheer the nylon retainer, Fig. 1. Replacement with the conventional steel snap ring type is then necessary, Fig. 2.

## CROSS & ROLLER TYPE

Figs. 3 and 4 illustrate typical examples of universal joints of this type. They all operate on the same principle and similar service and replacement procedures may be applied to all.

### SERVICING WITHOUT UNIVERSAL JOINT REPLACEMENT TOOL

#### Disassembly

1. Place driveshaft into a vise using care not to damage it.
2. Remove snap rings (or retainer plates) that retain bearing cups in yoke and driveshaft.
3. Select a socket with an outside diameter slightly smaller than the bearing cup. Select another socket with an in-

side diameter slightly larger than the bearing cup.
4. Place the sockets at opposite ends of the yoke so that the smaller socket becomes a cup pusher and the larger socket becomes a cup receiver and reposition in vise as shown Fig. 5. Close vise jaws until both cups are free of yoke. Remove cups from the cross or spider and remove yoke.
5. If bearing cups will not come all the way out, close the vise until the cup in receiver socket protrudes from yoke as much as possible without using excessive force. Then remove from vise and place that portion of the cup which protrudes from yoke between vise jaws. Tighten vise to hold cup and drive yoke off with a soft hammer.
6. To remove opposite bearing cup from yoke, replace in vise with pusher socket in exposed cross journal and receiver socket over bearing cup, then tighten vise jaws to press cup through yoke into receiving socket. **If bearing cup will not come all the way out, place protruding portion of cup between vise jaws, then tighten vise to hold cup while driving yoke off cup with soft hammer.**
7. Turn spider or cross 1/4 turn and repeat procedure to press cups out of driveshaft.

#### Assembly

1. If old parts are to be reassembled, pack bearing cups with universal joint grease. Do not fill cups completely or use excessive amounts as over-lubrication may damage seals during reassembly. Use new seals if available.
2. If new parts are being installed, check new bearings for adequate grease before assembling.
3. With the pusher (smaller) socket, press one bearing cup part way into driveshaft. Position spider into the partially installed cup. Place second bearing cup into driveshaft. Fasten driveshaft in vise so that cups are in contact with faces of vise jaws, Fig. 6. Some spiders are provided with locating lugs which must face toward driveshaft when installed.
4. Press bearing cups all the way into position and install snap rings or retainer plates.
5. Install bearing cups in yoke in same manner. When installation is completed, check U-joint for binding or roughness. If free movement is impeded, correct the condition before installation in vehicle.

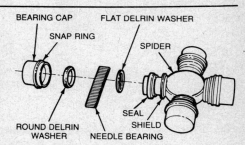

Fig. 2 Service type universal joints (internal snap ring type)

## SERVICING WITH UNIVERSAL JOINT REPLACEMENT TOOL

### Disassembly

1. Place driveshaft in a vise using care to avoid damaging it.
2. Remove bearing cup retaining snap rings. Some universal joints use injected nylon retainers in place of snap rings. During servicing, the snap rings supplied with the replacement universal joint assembly must be used.
3. Mark relationship between yoke and shaft for assembly reference.
4. Position tool on shaft and press bearing cup out of yoke, Fig. 7. If the cup cannot be pressed all the way out, remove it using vise grips or channel lock pliers or position driveshaft as shown and strike center yoke with hammer, Fig. 8.
5. Reposition tool so that it presses on the spider in order to press other bearing cup from opposite side of flange.
6. Remove tool, then the flange from spider.

### Assembly

1. Start new bearing cup into yoke, then position spider into yoke and press cup until it is 1/4 inch below surface.
2. Remove tool and install a new snap ring.
3. Start new bearing cup in opposite side of yoke, then install tool and press until cup is fully seated.
4. Remove tool and install remaining snap ring.

## DOUBLE CARDAN TYPE

The double cardan type joint, Fig. 9, incorporates two universal joints, a centering socket yoke, and center yoke at one end of the shaft. A single universal joint is used at the other end.

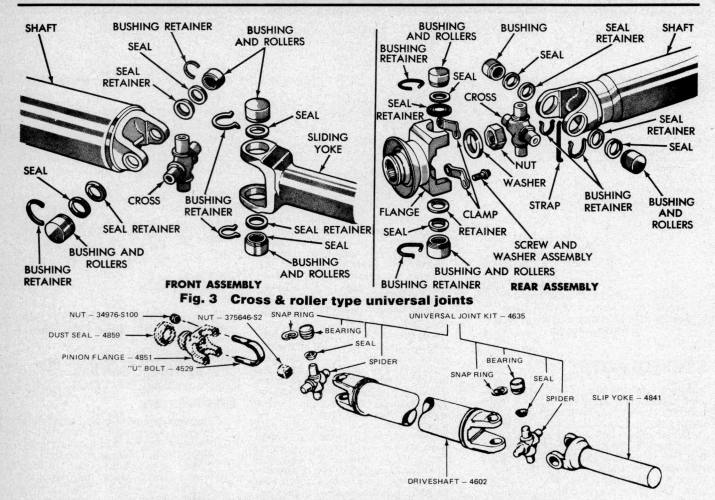

**Fig. 3  Cross & roller type universal joints**

FRONT ASSEMBLY — SHAFT, BUSHING RETAINER, SEAL, SEAL RETAINER, BUSHING AND ROLLERS, SEAL, SLIDING YOKE, CROSS, BUSHING RETAINER, SEAL RETAINER, SEAL, BUSHING AND ROLLERS, SEAL, SEAL RETAINER, BUSHING AND ROLLERS, BUSHING RETAINER

REAR ASSEMBLY — BUSHING AND ROLLERS, BUSHING RETAINER, SEAL, BUSHING, SEAL, SEAL RETAINER, SHAFT, CROSS, SEAL RETAINER, SEAL, NUT, WASHER, STRAP, BUSHING RETAINER, BUSHING AND ROLLERS, FLANGE, CLAMP, RETAINER, SEAL, SCREW AND WASHER ASSEMBLY, BUSHING AND ROLLERS, BUSHING RETAINER

**Fig. 4  Cross & roller type universal joints & propeller shaft**

NUT – 34976-S100, DUST SEAL – 4859, PINION FLANGE – 4851, "U" BOLT – 4529, NUT – 375646-S2, SNAP RING, BEARING, SEAL, SPIDER, UNIVERSAL JOINT KIT – 4635, BEARING, SNAP RING, SEAL, SPIDER, SLIP YOKE – 4841, DRIVESHAFT – 4602

---

APPLY FORCE UNTIL BEARING CLEARS INNER SIDE OF YOKE — 9/16" SOCKET, BEARING, 1" SOCKET

**Fig. 5  Removing bearing cups from yoke**

## DISASSEMBLY

1. Remove all bearing cup retainers.
2. Mark bearing cups, spiders, propeller shaft yoke, link yoke and socket yoke for assembly alignment reference, **Fig. 9.**
3. Remove bearing cups attaching from spider to propeller shaft yoke as follows:
   a. Use a 5/8 inch socket to drive the bearing cup and a 1 1/16 inch socket to receive the opposite bearing cup as it is driven out.
   b. Place 5/8 inch socket on one bearing cup and 1 1/16 inch socket on opposite bearing cup.
   c. Position assembly in vise so vise jaws bear directly against sockets.
   d. Tighten vise to press first bearing cup out of link yoke.
   e. Loosen vise, reposition sockets and press opposite bearing cup out of link yoke.
4. Disengage propeller shaft yoke from link yoke.
5. Remove bearing cups attaching front spider to propeller shaft as described in step 3 above.
6. Remove front spider from yoke.
7. Remove bearing cups attaching rear spider to link yoke as outlined in step 3 above and remove spider and socket yoke from link yoke.
8. Clean and inspect assembly for damage or wear. If any component is worn

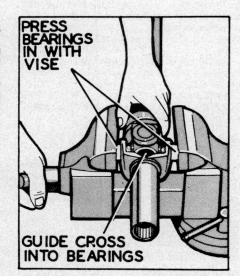

PRESS BEARINGS IN WITH VISE — GUIDE CROSS INTO BEARINGS

**Fig. 6  Installing bearing cups into driveshaft yoke**

or damaged, the entire assembly must be replaced.

## ASSEMBLY

When assembling universal joint, make

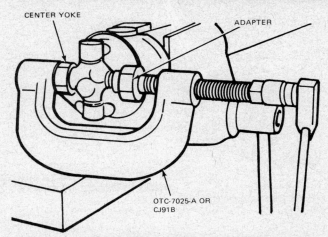

**Fig. 7  Removing bearing cups using tool & adapter**

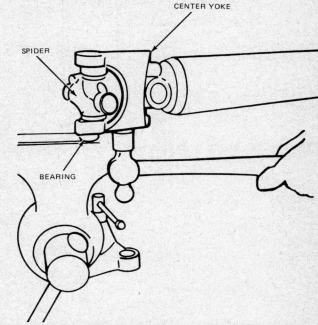

**Fig. 8  Removing bearing cup by holding cup in vise & striking center yoke with hammer**

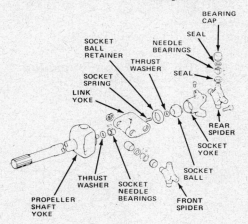

**Fig. 9  Double cardan universal joint exploded view**

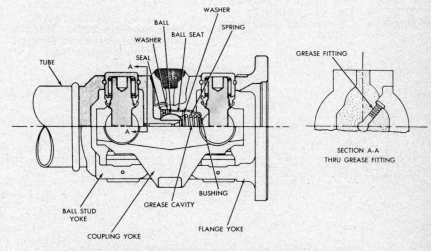

**Fig. 10  Constant velocity (CV) universal joint**

sure to align spiders and yokes according to marks made during disassembly.

1. Lubricate all bearings and contact surfaces with lithium base chassis grease.
2. Install bearing cups on yoke ends of rear spider and secure cups with tape, **Fig. 9.**
3. Assemble socket yoke and rear spider.
4. Position rear spider in link yoke and install bearing cups. Press cups into yoke using 5/8 inch socket until bearing cup retainer grooves are exposed.
5. Install rear spider-to-link yoke bearing cup retainers.
6. Position front spider in propeller shaft yoke and install bearing cups. Press cups into yoke using a 5/8 inch socket until bearing cup retainer grooves are exposed.
7. Install front spider-to-propeller shaft yoke bearing cup retainers.
8. Install thrust washer and socket spring in ball socket bearing bore, if removed.
9. Install thrust washer on ball socket bearing boss (located on propeller shaft yoke), if removed.
10. Align ball socket bearing boss on propeller shaft yoke with ball socket

bearing bore and insert boss into bore.
11. Align front spider with link yoke bearing cup bores and install bearing cups. Press cups into yoke using a 5/8 inch socket until bearing cup retainer grooves are exposed.
12. Install front spider-to-link yoke bearing cup retainers.

# CONSTANT VELOCITY TYPE

This type of universal joint, **Fig. 10,** consists of two conventional cross and roller joints connected with a special link yoke. Because the two joint angles are the same, even though the usual universal joint fluctuation is present within the unit, the acceleration of the front joint (within the yoke) is

always neutralized by the deceleration of the rear joint (within the yoke) and vice versa. The end result is the front and rear propeller shafts always turn at a constant velocity.

# DISASSEMBLY
## Constant Velocity Joint

To disassemble the constant velocity joint, the bearing cups should be removed in sequence shown in **Fig. 11.** This method requires the least amount of work.

1. Mark all yokes before disassembly as shown in **Fig. 12,** so that they can be reassembled in their original relationship to maintain driveshaft balance. The following procedure can be performed in a vise. A cross press tool, **Fig. 13,** can be used in place of the socket used to drive the bearing cups.

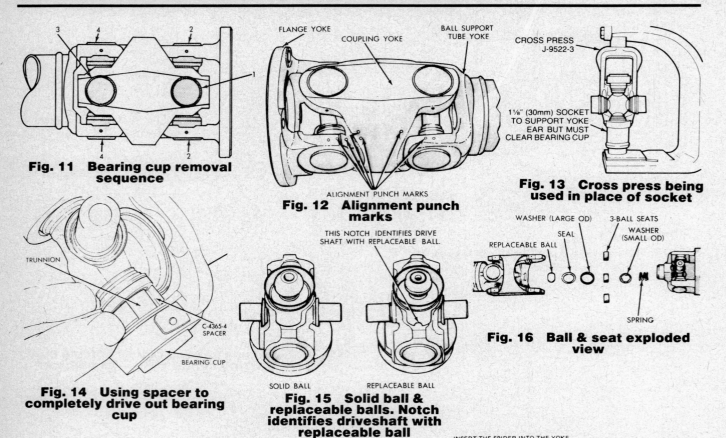

**Fig. 11   Bearing cup removal sequence**

**Fig. 12   Alignment punch marks**

**Fig. 13   Cross press being used in place of socket**

**Fig. 14   Using spacer to completely drive out bearing cup**

**Fig. 15   Solid ball & replaceable balls. Notch identifies driveshaft with replaceable ball**

**Fig. 16   Ball & seat exploded view**

**Fig. 17   Removing centering ball**

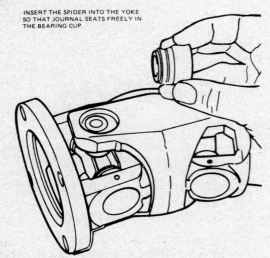

**Fig. 18   Inserting cross into yoke**

2. Support the driveshaft horizontally in line with the base plate of a press. Place rear end of coupling yoke over a 1⅛ inch socket to accept the bearing cup. Place a socket slightly smaller than the bearing cup, on the opposite side of the spider.
3. Press bearing cup out of coupling yoke ear. If bearing cup is not completely removed, insert spacer C-4365-4 or equivalent, **Fig. 14,** and complete removal of bearing cup.
4. Rotate driveshaft 180° and shear the opposite retaining ring, and press the bearing cup out of the coupling yoke as described previously, using spacer C-4365-4 or equivalent.
5. Disengage cross trunnions, still attached to flange yoke, from coupling yoke. Pull flange yoke and cross from centering ball on ball support tube yoke. The ball socket is part of the flange yoke. **The ball on some joints is not replaceable. The joints with a replaceable ball can be recognized as shown in Fig. 15.** Do not attempt to remove solid ball, as removal tool may be damaged.
6. Pry seal from ball cavity, then remove washers, spring and shoes, **Fig. 16.**

## Ball Socket

1. To remove ball, separate universal joint between coupling yoke and flange yoke by pressing out trunnion bearing in coupling yoke. Pull flange yoke and cross with ball socket from centering ball as a unit.
2. Clean and inspect ball seat insert bushing for wear. If worn, replace flange yoke and cross assembly.

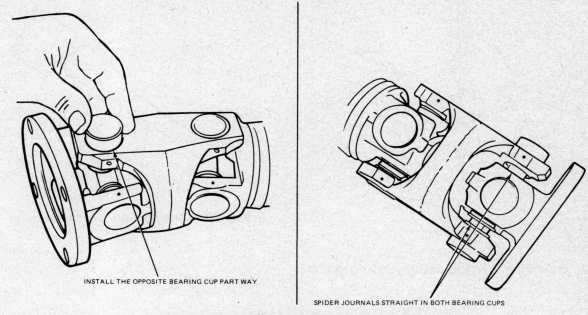

INSTALL THE OPPOSITE BEARING CUP PART WAY

SPIDER JOURNALS STRAIGHT IN BOTH BEARING CUPS

**Fig. 19  Aligning bearing cups & journals**

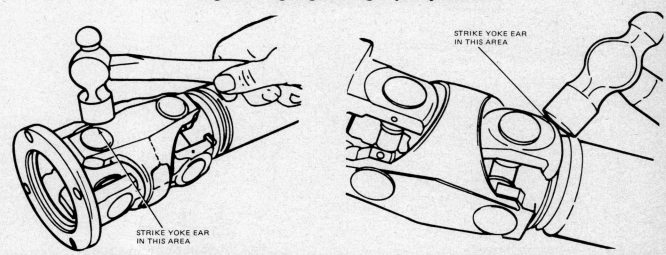

STRIKE YOKE EAR IN THIS AREA

STRIKE YOKE EAR IN THIS AREA

**Fig. 20  Relieving binding condition at point A  Fig. 21  Relieving binding condition at point B**

3. Pry seal from ball cavity, then remove washers, spring and ball seats.
4. Clean and inspect centering ball surface, seal, ball seats, spring and washer. If parts are worn or broken, replace with a service kit.
5. Remove centering ball as shown in **Fig. 17**, using components of tool C-4365 or equivalent. Install components as shown, and draw ball off ball stud.

## ASSEMBLY

### Ball Socket & Constant Velocity Joint

During assembly, make sure that marks made during disassembly, **Fig. 12**, are aligned to maintain balance.

1. To install centering ball onto stud, use tool C-4365 or equivalent, and drive ball until it can be seen that ball has seated firmly against shoulder at base

of stud.
2. To install cross assembly, install one bearing cup part way into one side of yoke and turn this yoke to the bottom. Insert cross into yoke so that the trunnion seats into bearing, **Fig. 18**. Install opposite bearing cup part way, **Fig. 19**. Make sure that both cross journals are started straight into both bearing cups.
3. Press bearing cups, while moving cross to ensure free movement of trunnions in bearing. If any binding is felt, stop pressing and check needle bearings to make sure that needle bearings have not been trapped under the ends of the cross journals.
4. As soon as one of the retaining ring grooves clears the inside of yoke, stop pressing and install retaining ring.
5. Continue to press until opposite re-

taining ring can be snapped into place. If difficulty is encountered, strike the yoke firmly in locations shown in **Figs. 20, 21 and 22**, to spring the yoke ears slightly.
6. Lubricate center ball and socket, and assemble other half universal joint, if disassembled.

## LUBRICATION

Lubrication of the constant velocity joints should not be overlooked during the regular service intervals recommended by the manufacturer. During lubrication, use only the type of lubricant recommended by the manufacturer. This lubricant is usually lithium type chassis grease.

Lubrication fitting adapters and locations of the lubrication fittings are shown in **Figs. 23, 24 and 25**.

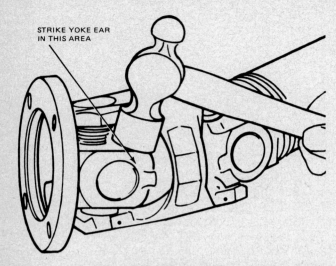

Fig. 22 Relieving binding condition at point C

STRIKE YOKE EAR IN THIS AREA

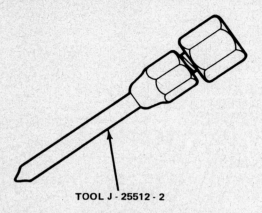

TOOL J - 25512 - 2

Fig. 23 Lubrication fitting adapter

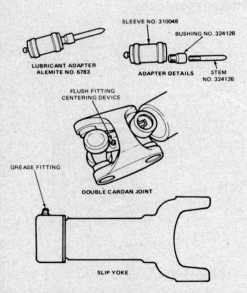

LUBRICANT ADAPTER ALEMITE NO. 6783

SLEEVE NO. 310048

BUSHING NO. 324128

ADAPTER DETAILS

STEM NO. 324126

FLUSH FITTING CENTERING DEVICE

DOUBLE CARDAN JOINT

GREASE FITTING

SLIP YOKE

Fig. 24 Lubrication fitting adapter & fitting location

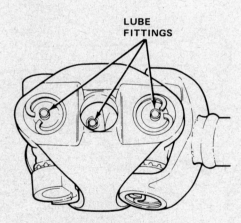

LUBE FITTINGS

Fig. 25 Lubrication fitting locations

# AUTOMATIC TRANSMISSIONS

## TABLE OF CONTENTS

# Turbo Hydra-Matic 180C Automatic Transmission

## INDEX

## DESCRIPTION

The 180C transmission is a fully automatic unit consisting primarily of four-element hydraulic torque converter with a lock-up clutch and a compound planetary gear set, **Fig. 1**. Three multiple disc clutches, a roller clutch, and a band provide the friction elements required to obtain the desired function of the compound planetary gear set.

The clutch type converter consists of a cover, pressure plate, pump, spring, stator, thrust bearing, thrust spacer and a turbine. The turbine and lock-up clutch are splined together. When used, it is directed against the converter cover creating a direct mechanical coupling of the planetary gears and engine. When released, it reverts back to a basic torque converter.

The torque converter couples the engine to the planetary gears through oil and provides torque multiplication. It consists of a pump or driving member, a turbine or driven member and a stator assembly. The stator is mounted on a one-way roller clutch which allows the stator to turn clockwise but not counterclockwise.

The torque converter housing is filled with oil and rotates at engine speed. The converter pump is an integral part of the converter housing, therefore the pump blades rotating at engine speed set the oil within the converter into motion and direct it to the turbine causing the turbine to rotate. As the oil passes through the turbine it travels in such a direction that if it were not redirected by the stator it would strike the rear of the converter pump blades and impede its pumping action. Therefore at low turbine speeds, the oil is redirected by the stator to the converter pump in such a

manner that it actually assists the converter pump to deliver power or multiply engine torque. As turbine speed increases the direction of the oil leaving the turbine changes and flows against the rear side of the stator vanes in a clockwise direction. Since the stator is now impeding the smooth flow of oil, its roller clutch releases and it revolves freely in its shaft.

Once the stator becomes inactive, there is no further multiplication of torque within the converter. At this point the converter is acting as a fluid coupling since the converter pump and turbine are being driven at about the same speed, or at a one-to-one ratio.

The hydraulic system in this transmission is pressurized by a gear type pump to provide the working pressures required to operate the friction elements and automatic controls.

*TURBO HYDRA-MATIC 180C TRANSMISSION*

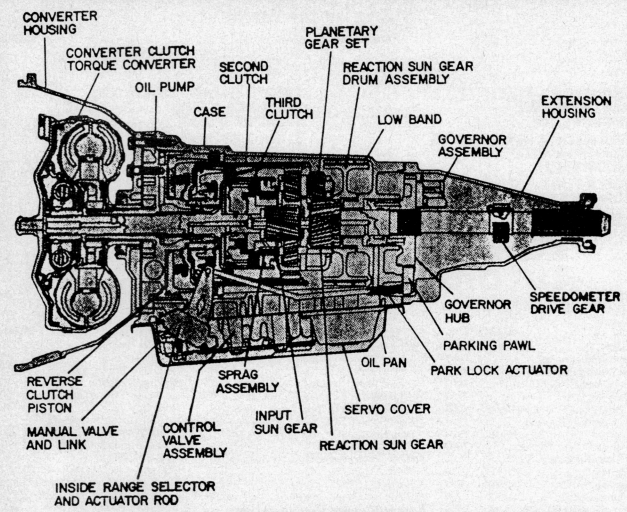

**Fig. 1  Sectional view of Turbo Hydra-Matic 180C automatic transmission**

## MAINTENANCE
### FLUID LEVEL CHECK

Check fluid at regular intervals. Noticing a change in color, odor or fluid level can serve as a warning of possible transmission problems.

To check fluid level, bring fluid to operating temperature of 200° F. With vehicle on a level surface and engine idling in Park and parking brake applied, the level on the dipstick should be at the Full mark. To bring the fluid level from the Add mark to the Full mark requires one pint of fluid. If additional fluid is required, use only Dexron II automatic transmission fluid.

When adding fluid, do not overfill, as foaming and loss of fluid through the vent may occur as the fluid heats up. Also, if fluid level is too low, complete loss of drive may occur especially when cold, which can cause transmission failure. The oil should be drained, the oil pan removed, the screen cleaned and fresh fluid added every 30,000 miles for trucks under 8600 lbs. GVWR or every 24,000 miles for vehicles over 8600 GVWR. For vehicles subjected to more severe use such as heavy city traffic especially in hot weather, prolonged periods of idling or as a tow vehicle this maintenance should be performed every 15,000 miles for trucks under 8600 GVWR, or every 12,000 miles for trucks over 8600 GVWR.

### DRAINING BOTTOM PAN

1. Raise and support vehicle.
2. Position a suitable drain pan below transmission oil pan.
3. Remove front and side oil pan bolts.
4. Loosen rear bolts and gently pry the pan down to allow fluid to drain.
5. Remove remaining bolts and pull pan away from case carefully, as there will still be fluid contained in the pan.
6. Drain remaining fluid from pan, then remove gasket, oil filter retaining bolts, oil filter and seal.
7. Using solvent, thoroughly clean oil pan and gasket surfaces, then air dry.
8. Install new oil seal and filter into case. Torque attaching bolts to 13-15 ft. lbs.
9. Install oil pan with new gasket and torque bolts to 7-10 ft. lbs.
10. Add transmission fluid, then with engine idling and brakes applied, move selector lever through each gear range and return selector lever to Park.
11. Bring fluid to proper operating temperature and check fluid level, adding as required to bring level to the Full mark.

### ADDING FLUID TO A DRY TRANSMISSION

1. Add transmission fluid.
2. With transmission in Park, start engine and let engine idle (carburetor off fast idle cam.)
3. Apply brakes and move shifter lever through each gear range, then with transmission in Park, add additional fluid as required to bring the level up to Full mark on dipstick.

## TROUBLESHOOTING
### LOW FLUID LEVEL

1. Fluid coming out of filler tube.
2. External fluid leak.
3. Defective vacuum modulator.

### FLUID COMING OUT OF THE FILLER TUBE

1. High fluid level.

2. Engine coolant in transmission fluid.
3. Clogged external vent.
4. Leak in pump suction circuit.

## LOW FLUID PRESSURE

1. Low fluid level.
2. Clogged screen.
3. Leak in oil pump suction or pressure circuit.
4. Missing sealing ball in valve body.

## HIGH FLUID PRESSURE

1. Modulator vacuum line leaking.
2. Defective vacuum modulator.
3. Leak in vacuum system.
4. Defective pressure regulator valve.

## NO DRIVE

1. Low fluid level.
2. clogged screen.
3. Manual valve linkage or inner transmission selector lever disconnected.
4. Broken input shaft.
5. Pressure regulator valve stuck in open position.
6. Defective oil pump.

## DELAYED ENGAGEMENT

1. Manual valve position does not coincide with valve body channels:
   a. Missing selector lever shaft retaining pin.
   b. Loose connecting rod to manual valve connection.
   c. Loose selector lever shaft nut.

## NO DRIVE WHEN SHIFTING FORM P TO D, L2 OR L1

1. Parking pawl does not disengage.

## HARSH ENGAGEMENT

1. Band servo piston jamming.
2. Low fluid level.
3. Defective oil pump.
4. Missing screen.
5. Missing sealing ball in valve body.

## SHUDDER ON ACCELERATION

1. Low fluid pressure
2. Wrong modulator valve installed.
3. Stuck pressure regulator valve.
4. Missing sealing ball in valve body.

## DRIVE IN L1 & R BUT NOT IN D OR L2

1. Input sprag installed backwards
2. Failed input sprag.

## DRIVE IN R BUT NOT IN D, L2 OR L1

1. Worn band, slipping.
2. Band servo piston jamming.
3. Excessive leak in band servo.
4. Parking pawl does not disengage.

## DRIVE IN D, L2 & L1 BUT NOT IN R

1. Failed reverse clutch.

## DRIVE IN NUTRAL POSITION

1. Linkage improperly adjusted.
2. Broken planetary gear set.
3. band improperly adjusted.

## NO 1-2 UPSHIFT IN D & L2

1. Stuck governor valves.
2. 1-2 shift valve stuck in first gear position.
3. Leaking seal rings in oil pump hub.
4. Excessive leak in governor pressure circuit.
5. Clogged governor screen.

## NO 2-3 UPSHIFT IN D

1. 2-3 shift valve stuck.
2. Excessive leak in governor pressure circuit.

## UPSHIFTS IN D & L2 ONLY AT FULL THROTTLE

1. Faulty vacuum modulator.
2. Modulator vacuum line leaking.
3. Leak in vacuum system.
4. Stuck detent valve or cable.

## UPSHIFTS IN D OR L2 ONLY AT PART THROTTLE NO DETENT UPSHIFT

1. Stuck detent pressure regulator valve.
2. Detent cable broken or adjusted improperly.

## DRIVE IN 1ST GEAR OF D OR L2

1. L1 and R control valve stuck in L1 or R position.

## NO PART THROTTLE 3-2 DOWNSHIFT AT LOW SPEEDS

1. Stuck 3-2 downshift control valve.

## NO FORCED DOWNSHIFTS

1. Detent cable broken or improperly adjusted.
2. Stuck detent pressure regulator valve.

## IMMEDIATE DOWNSHIFT AFTER THROTTLE UPSHIFT & RELEASING ACCELERATOR

1. Detent valve stuck in open position.
2. Detent cable stuck.
3. Clogged or leaking vacuum modulator line.

## TRANSMISSION DOWNSHIFTS AT HIGH VEHICLE SPEEDS

1. Missing selector lever shaft retaining pin.
2. Loose selector lever linkage to manual valve connection.
3. Pressure Leak at governor.

## HARD DISENGAGEMENT FROM PARK POSITION

1. Missing steel guide bushing from parking pawl actuating rod.
2. Stuck manual valve selector lever.

## SLIPPING 1-2 SHIFT

1. Low fluid pressure.
2. Missing sealing ball in valve body.
3. Leaking second clutch piston seals.
4. Second clutch piston centrifugal ball stuck open.

5. Second clutch piston cracked or broken.
6. Second clutch plates worn.
7. Leaking oil pump hub sealing rings.

## SLIPPING 2-3 SHIFT

1. Low fluid pressure.
2. Improper band adjustment.
3. Third clutch piston seals leaking.
4. Third clutch piston centrifugal ball stuck open.
5. Third clutch piston cracked or broken.
6. Worn input shaft bushing.
7. Missing sealing ball in valve body.

## HARSH 1-2 SHIFT

1. High fluid pressure.
2. 1-2 accumulator valve stuck.
3. Second clutch spring cushion broken.
4. Second gear ball valve missing.

## HARSH 2-3 SHIFT

1. High fluid pressure.
2. Improper band adjustment.

## HARSH 3-2 DETENT DOWNSHIFT AT HIGH VEHICLE SPEEDS

1. High speed downshift valve stuck open.
2. Improper band adjustment.

## HARSH 3-2 COAST DOWNSHIFT

1. Low speed downshift timing valve stuck open.

## ENGINE FLARE ON HIGH SPEED FORCED DOWNSHIFT

1. Low fluid pressure
2. Loose band adjustment.

## ENGINE FLARE ON LOW SPEED FORCED DOWNSHIFT

1. Low fluid pressure.
2. loose band adjustment.
3. High speed downshift timing valve stuck in closed position.
4. Sprag race does not engage on 3-1 downshift.

## NO ENGINE BRAKING IN L1

1. Selector level linkage improperly adjusted.
2. Stuck low manual control valve.

## NO ENGINE BRAKING IN L2

1. Selector lever linkage improperly adjusted.

## NO PARK

1. Selector lever linkage improperly adjusted.
2. Parking lock actuator spring broken.
3. Damaged parking pawl.
4. Governor hub.

## EXCESSIVE NOISES IN ALL DRIVE RANGES

1. Excessive backlash between sun

gear and planetary gears.
2. Lock plate on planetary carrier loose.
3. defective thrust bearing.
4. Worn bearing bushings.
5. Excessive transmission axial play.
6. Unhooked parking pawl spring contacting governor hub.
7. Converter balancing weights loose.
8. Converter housing attaching bolts loose and contacting converter.

## SCREECHING NOISE ON ACCELERATION

1. Converter failure.

## SHORT VIBRATING HISSING NOISE BEFORE 1-2 UPSHIFT

1. Reverse clutch dampening cushion wearing into transmission case.

## IN-VEHICLE ADJUSTMENTS
## MANUAL LINKAGE
## ADJUST

1. Apply parking brake.
2. Loosen screw (242), **Fig. 2.**
3. Place column selector lever in Neutral position.
4. Place transmission in neutral by moving shift lever (A) to the forward position, then back to second detent.
5. Hold rod (240) tightly in swivel (232) and torque screw (242) to 17 Ft. lbs.
6. Place column selector in Park position and check adjustment. Column selector lever must go into all positions and engine should start in Park and Neutral positions only. Adjust as necessary. **With selector lever in Park position, parking pawl should freely engage within rear (reaction) internal gear lugs or output ring gear lugs and prevent vehicle from rolling.**
7. Align indicator as necessary.
8. Release parking brake.

## DETENT DOWNSHIFT CABLE
## ADJUST

1. Depress and hold readjust tab on cable, **Fig. 3.**
2. Move slider back through fitting, in direction away from throttle lever, until slider contacts fitting.
3. Release readjust tab, then move throttle to wide open position. Slider will ratchet automatically to correct position.

## IN-VEHICLE REPAIRS
## VALVE BODY
## REPLACE

1. Raise and support vehicle.
2. Drain transmission fluid by removing oil pan attaching bolts, then the oil pan and gasket.
3. Remove oil strainer attaching bolts, then the strainer and gasket.

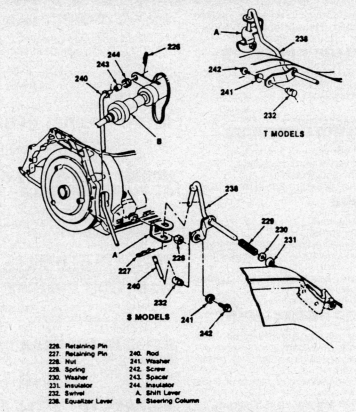

**T MODELS**

**S MODELS**

| | | | |
|---|---|---|---|
| 226. | Retaining Pin | 240. | Rod |
| 227. | Retaining Pin | 241. | Washer |
| 228. | Nut | 242. | Screw |
| 229. | Spring | 243. | Spacer |
| 230. | Washer | 244. | Insulator |
| 231. | Insulator | A. | Shift Lever |
| 232. | Swivel | B. | Steering Column |
| 238. | Equalizer Lever | | |

**Fig. 2   Manual linkage adjustment**

4. Remove manual detent roller and spring assembly.
5. Disconnect electrical connections from governor pressure switch.
6. Remove solenoid from transfer plate reinforcement.
7. Remove solenoid from solenoid tubes.
8. Remove solenoid tubes from valve body and case.
9. Remove governor pressure switch.
10. Remove transfer plate reinforcement attaching bolts, then the reinforcement.
11. Remove servo cover attaching bolts, then the cover and gasket.
12. Remove valve body attaching bolts, then the valve body and manual link valve, being careful not to lose check balls.

## SERVO ASSEMBLY
## REPLACE

1. Remove valve body from transmission as outlined previously.
2. Compress servo piston with tool J-23075.
3. With suitable pliers, remove servo piston snap ring and slowly loosen the tool. Remove tool, servo piston return spring and apply rod from transmission.
4. Install apply rod, return spring and piston into case.
5. Use tool J-23075 to compress spring and install ring. Remove tool.
6. With a 3/16 inch wrench on servo adjusting bolt, adjust apply rod by torqu-

ing bolt to 40 inch lbs. then back off bolt exactly 5 turns. tighten locknut, while holding apply rod in position.
7. Install valve body.

## SPEEDOMETER DRIVEN GEAR
## REPLACE

1. Remove bolt securing driven gear housing retainer, then the retainer.
2. Pull speedometer driven gear from housing.
3. Install speedometer driven gear into housing, then the retainer into slot of driven gear housing.
4. Install retainer attaching bolt.

## REAR EXTENSION OIL SEAL
## REPLACE

1. Remove propeller shaft.
2. Remove oil seal with a screwdriver or suitable tool.
3. Lubricate new seal lip with transmission fluid and install seal into extension housing using a suitable driver.
4. Install propeller shaft.

## VACUUM MODULATOR
## REPLACE

1. Raise and support vehicle.
2. Remove vacuum line from modulator.
3. Using vacuum modulator wrench J-23100 remove modulator, seal and modulator plunger.
4. Then remove modulator valve and

sleeve.
5. Clean all parts with soapy water and air dry.
6. Check modulator and vacuum line for kinks, cracks and dry rot damage.
7. Reverse procedure to install using new seal. Add transmission fluid as necessary.

## TRANSMISSION REPLACE

1. Disconnect battery ground cable and remove air cleaner.
2. Raise and support vehicle.
3. Drain transmission fluid, then disconnect shift linkage and propeller shaft.
4. Disconnect support bracket from catalytic converter.
5. Disconnect or remove components necessary to obtain clearance for removal.
6. Support transmission with suitable jack.
7. Remove transmission crossmember.
8. Remove dipstick tube and seal and cover opening in transmission.
9. Disconnect speedometer cable, modulator vacuum line, electrical connectors and cooler lines. **Cap all openings in transmission and the lines.**
10. Remove dampener and support, if applicable.
11. Remove transmission support braces. Notice location of braces for installa-

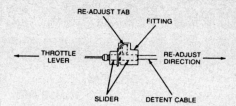

**Fig. 3   Detent downshift cable adjustment.**

tion reference.
12. Remove converter housing cover and mark relationship between flywheel and torque converter.
13. Remove flywheel-to-torque converter attaching screws. **Support engine with suitable jack before disconnecting transmission.**
14. Remove remaining transmission-to-engine attaching screws. Note location of any brackets or clips before moving them aside.
15. Slide transmission straight back off locating pins and install converter holding strap J-21366 or equivalent. **Do not stretch or damage any cables, wires or other components when lowering transmission.**
16. Reverse procedure to install.

## SERVICE BULLETIN
### SLIPPING OR NO UPSHIFT—BURNED SECOND CLUTCH

THM 180C transmission may exhibit a slipping or no upshift condition due to a burned second clutch. This condition may be caused by distortion of the valve body spacer plate, resulting in loss of second clutch apply pressure. This distortion may be caused by carbon blockage of the modulator vacuum line fitting at the engine intake manifold. As the fitting becomes blocked, the second clutch check ball vibrates back and forth against the spacer plate causing the distortion. To correct this condition, proceed as follows:
1. Inspect and replace, as necessary, second clutch plates, third clutch plates, valve body spacer plates and gasket.
2. Using tool J-24466 or equivalent, check vacuum modulator.
3. Remove vacuum line fitting from intake manifold and clean orifice with a 7/16 inch drill bit, turning bit by hand. Carburetor cleaner may be used to loosen carbon deposits, if necessary.
4. To prevent a vacuum leak when reinstalling fitting, use a suitable sealant around the threads. Whenever transmission service is performed on these transmissions, the vacuum line fitting should be inspected and cleaned.

# Turbo Hydra-Matic 200 & 200C Automatic Transmission

## INDEX

## DESCRIPTION

The Turbo Hydra-Matic 200 transmission, **Fig. 1**, is fully automatic and consists of a three element torque converter and a compound planetary gear set. Three multiple disc clutches, a roller clutch and a band provide the required friction elements to obtain the desired function of the planetary gear set.

The Turbo Hydra-Matic 200C incorporates a converter clutch assembly consisting of a three element torque converter, and a converter clutch, **Fig. 2**. The converter clutch is splined to the turbine assembly and when operated, applies against the converter cover providing a mechanical direct drive coupling of the engine to the planetary gears. When the converter clutch is released, the assembly operates as a normal torque converter. The converter clutch is applied only when transmission is in third gear, vehicle speed is above 30 mph, engine coolant temperature is above 130° F, engine vacuum is above 3 inches Hg and brake pedal is released.

## TROUBLESHOOTING

### NO DRIVE IN DRIVE RANGE

1. Low oil level.
2. Manual linkage improperly adjusted.
3. Low oil pressure due to:
   a. Restricted or plugged oil screen.
   b. Oil screen gasket improperly installed.
   c. Oil pump pressure regulator.
   d. Pump drive gear tangs damaged by converter.
   e. Case porosity in intake bore.
4. Forward clutch malfunctioning due to:
   a. Forward clutch not applying due to cracked piston, damaged or missing seals, burned clutch plates, snap ring not in groove.
   b. Forward clutch seal rings damaged or missing on turbine shaft, leaking feed circuits due to damaged or improperly positioned gasket.
   c. Clutch housing check ball stuck or missing.
   d. Cup plug leaking or missing from rear of turbine shaft in clutch apply passage.
   e. Incorrect forward clutch piston assembly or incorrect number of clutch plates.
5. Roller clutch malfunctioning due to missing rollers or springs or possibly galled rollers.

### OIL PRESSURE HIGH OR LOW

1. Throttle valve cable improperly adjusted, binding, disconnected or broken.
2. Throttle lever and bracket improperly installed, disconnected or binding.
3. Throttle valve shift valve, throttle valve or plunger binding.
4. Pressure regulator valve and spring malfunctioning due to:
   a. Binding valve.
   b. Incorrect spring.
   c. Oil pressure control orifice in pump cover plugged, causing high oil pressure.
   d. Pressure regulator bore plug leaking.
5. Manual valve disconnected.
6. Intermediate boost valve binding, causing oil pressures to be incorrect in 2nd and low ranges.
7. Orifice in spacer plate at end of intermediate boost valve plugged.
8. Reserve boost valve binding, causing pressure to be incorrect in reverse only.
9. Orifice in spacer plate at end of reverse boost valve plugged.

### 1-2 SHIFT AT FULL THROTTLE ONLY

1. Throttle valve cable improperly adjusted, binding, disconnected or broken.
2. Throttle lever and bracket assembly binding or disconnected.
3. Throttle valve exhaust ball lifter or number 5 check ball binding, improperly positioned or disconnected. If number 5 ball is fully seated, it will cause full throttle valve pressure regardless of throttle valve position.
4. Throttle valve and plunger binding.
5. Valve body gaskets leaking, damaged or incorrectly installed.
6. Porous control valve assembly.

### FIRST SPEED ONLY, NO 1-2 SHIFT

1. Due to governor and governor feed passages:
   a. Plugged governor oil feed orifice in spacer plate.
   b. Plugged orifice in spacer plate that feeds governor oil to the shift valves.
   c. Balls missing in governor assembly.
   d. Governor cover O-ring missing or leaking. If governor cover O-ring leaks, an external oil leak will be present and there will be no upshift.
   e. Governor shaft seal missing or damaged.
   f. Governor driven gear stripped.
   g. Governor weights binding.
   h. Governor assembly missing.
2. Control valve assembly 1-2 shift valve or 1-2 throttle valve stuck in downshift position.
3. Porosity in case channels or 2nd speed feed holes.
4. Excessive leakage between case bore and intermediate band apply ring.

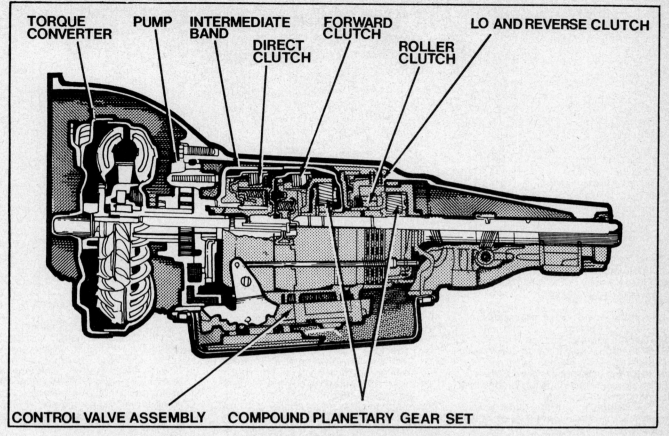

**TORQUE CONVERTER** **PUMP** **INTERMEDIATE BAND** **DIRECT CLUTCH** **FORWARD CLUTCH** **ROLLER CLUTCH** **LO AND REVERSE CLUTCH**

**CONTROL VALVE ASSEMBLY** **COMPOUND PLANETARY GEAR SET**

**Fig. 1 Sectional view of Turbo Hydra-Matic 200 & 200C automatic transmission**

5. Intermediate band anchor pin missing or disconnected from band.
6. Missing or broken intermediate band.
7. Due to intermediate servo assembly:
   a. Servo to cover oil seal ring damaged or missing.
   b. Porous servo cover or piston.
   c. Incorrect intermediate band apply pin.
   d. Incorrect cover and piston.

## 1ST & 2ND ONLY, NO 2-3 SHIFT

1. 2-3 shift valve or 2-3 throttle valve stuck in downshift position.
2. Direct clutch feed orifice in spacer plate plugged.
3. Valve body gaskets leaking, damaged or incorrectly installed.
4. Porosity between case passages.
5. Pump passages plugged or leaking.
6. Pump gasket incorrectly installed.
7. Rear seal on pump cover leaking or missing.
8. Direct clutch oil seals missing or damaged.
9. Direct clutch piston or housing cracked.
10. Direct clutch plates damaged or missing.
11. Direct clutch backing plate snap ring out of groove.
12. Intermediate servo to case oil seal broken or missing on intermediate servo piston.
13. Intermediate servo exhaust hole in

case between servo piston seals plugged or undrilled.

## MOVES FORWARD IN NEUTRAL

1. Manual linkage improperly adjusted.
2. Forward clutch does not release.
3. Cross leakage between pump passages.
4. Cross leakage to forward clutch through clutch passages.

## NO DRIVE IN REVERSE OR SLIPS IN REVERSE

1. Throttle valve cable binding or improperly adjusted.
2. Manual linkage improperly adjusted.
3. Throttle valve binding.
4. Reverse boost valve binding in bore.
5. Low overrun clutch valve binding in bore.
6. Reverse clutch piston cracked, broken or has missing seals.
7. Reverse clutch plates burned.
8. Reverse clutch has incorrect selective spacer ring.
9. Porosity in passages to direct clutch.
10. Pump to case gasket improperly installed or missing.
11. Pump passages cross leaking or restricted.
12. Pump cover seals damaged or missing.
13. Direct clutch piston or housing cracked.

14. Direct clutch piston seals cut or missing.
15. Direct clutch housing ball check, stuck, leaking or missing.
16. Direct clutch plates burned.
17. Incorrect direct clutch piston.
18. Direct clutch orifices plugged in spacer plate.
19. Intermediate servo to case seal cut or missing.

## SLIPS 1-2 SHIFT

1. Aerated oil due to low level.
2. 2nd speed feed orifice in spacer plate partially blocked.
3. Improperly installed or missing spacer plate gasket.
4. 1-2 accumulator valve stuck, causing low 1-2 accumulator pressure.
5. Weak or missing 1-2 accumulator valve spring.
6. 1-2 accumulator piston seal leaking or spring missing or broken.
7. Leakage between 1-2 accumulator piston and pin.
8. Incorrect intermediate band apply pin.
9. Excessive leakage between intermediate band apply pin and case.
10. Porous intermediate servo piston.
11. Servo cover to servo seal damaged or missing.
12. Incorrect servo and cover.
13. Throttle valve cable improperly adjusted.
14. Shift throttle valve or throttle valve binding.

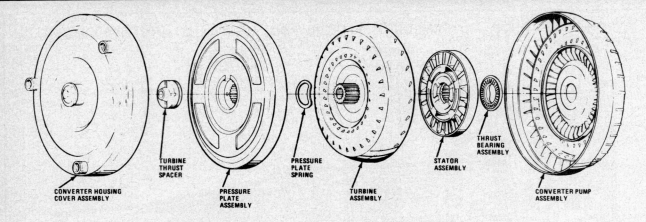

**Fig. 2    Torque converter clutch. 200C transmission**

15. Intermediate band worn or burned.
16. Case porosity in 2nd clutch passages.

## ROUGH 1-2 SHIFT

1. Throttle valve cable improperly adjusted or binding.
2. Throttle valve or plunger binding.
3. Shift throttle or 1-2 accumulator valve binding.
4. Incorrect intermediate servo pin.
5. Intermediate servo piston to case seal damaged or missing.
6. 1-2 accumulator oil ring damaged piston stuck, bore damaged or spring broken or missing.

## SLIPS 2-3 SHIFT

1. Low oil level.
2. Throttle valve cable improperly adjusted.
3. Throttle valve binding.
4. Direct clutch orifice in spacer plate partially blocked.
5. Spacer plate gaskets improperly installed or missing.
6. Intermediate servo to case seal damaged.
7. Porous direct clutch feed passages in case.
8. Pump to case gasket improperly installed or missing.
9. Pump passages cross feeding, leaking or restricted.
10. Pump cover oil seal rings damaged or missing.
11. Direct clutch piston or housing cracked.
12. Direct clutch piston seals cut or missing.
13. Direct clutch plates burned.

## ROUGH 2–3 SHIFT

1. Throttle valve cable improperly installed or missing.
2. Throttle valve or throttle valve plunger binding.
3. Shift throttle valve binding.
4. Intermediate servo exhaust hole undrilled or plugged between intermediate servo piston seals.
5. Direct clutch exhaust valve number 4 check ball missing or improperly installed.

## NO ENGINE BRAKING IN 2ND SPEED

1. Intermediate boost valve binding in valve body.
2. Intermediate-Reverse number 3 check ball improperly installed or missing.
3. Shift throttle valve number 3 check ball improperly installed or missing.
4. Intermediate servo to cover seal missing or damaged.
5. Intermediate band off anchor pin, broken or burned.

## NO ENGINE BRAKING IN 1ST SPEED

1. Low overrun clutch valve, binding in valve body.
2. The following conditions will also cause no reverse:
   a. Low-reverse clutch piston seals broken or missing.
   b. Porosity in low-reverse piston or housing.
   c. Low-reverse clutch housing snap ring out of case.
   d. Cup plug or rubber seal missing or damaged between case and low-reverse clutch housing.

## NO PART THROTTLE DOWNSHIFT

1. Throttle plunger bushing passages obstructed.
2. 2-3 throttle valve bushing passages obstructed.
3. Valve body gaskets improperly installed or damaged.
4. Spacer plate hole obstructed or undrilled.
5. Throttle valve cable improperly adjusted.
6. Throttle valve or shift throttle valve binding.

## LOW OR HIGH SHIFT POINTS

1. Throttle valve cable binding or disconnected.
2. Throttle valve or shift throttle valve binding.
3. Number 1 throttle shift check ball improperly installed or missing.
4. Throttle valve plunger, 1-2 or 2-3 throttle valves binding.
5. Valve body gaskets improperly installed or missing.
6. Pressure regulator valve binding.
7. Throttle valve exhaust number 5 check ball and lifter, improperly installed, disconnected or missing.
8. Throttle lever binding, disconnected or loose at valve body mounting bolt or not positioned at the throttle valve plunger bushing pin locator.
9. Governor shaft to cover seal broken or missing.
10. Governor cover O-rings broken or missing. Outer ring will leak externally and the inner ring will leak internally.
11. Case porosity.

## WILL NOT HOLD IN PARK

1. Manual linkage improperly adjusted.
2. Parking pawl binding in case.
3. Actuator rod or plunger damaged.
4. Parking pawl damaged.
5. Parking bracket loose or damaged.
6. Detent lever nut loose.
7. Detent lever hole worn or damaged.
8. Detent roller to valve body bolt loose.
9. Detent roller or pin damaged, incorrectly installed or missing.

## CONVERTER CLUTCH APPLIED IN ALL RANGES, ENGINE STALLS WHEN TRANSMISSION IS PUT IN GEAR (T.H.M. 200C)

1. Converter clutch valve in pump sticking in apply position.

## CONVERTER CLUTCH APPLIES ERRATICALLY (T.H.M. 200C)

1. Vacuum switch malfunction.
2. Release orifice at pump blocked or restricted.
3. Damaged turbine shaft O-ring.
4. Converter malfunctioning, clutch pressure plate warped.
5. O-ring damaged at solenoid.
6. Solenoid bolts loose.

## CONVERTER CLUTCH APPLIES AT A VERY LOW OR HIGH 3RD SPEED GEAR (T.H.M. 200C)

1. Governor switch malfunction.
2. Governor malfunction.
3. High line pressure.
4. Converter clutch valve sticking or binding.
5. Solenoid inoperative or shorted to case.

## THROTTLE VALVE SYSTEM DIAGNOSIS

T.V. pressure controls the shift pattern and the hydraulic line pressure used to apply clutches and bands. If proper line pressure is not available to apply clutch elements and bands, excess slippage may occur during shifting, and the components will be damaged. A T.V. cable which is damaged, disconnected or improperly adjusted, will cause high or low line pressure which can in turn cause the following conditions: Delayed or harsh upshifts, early upshifts and clutch slippage during shifting, no upshift, chatter on takeoff, 1-2 upshift at full throttle only, no full throttle or part throttle detent downshift, and intermittent second gear starts.

Do not attempt to correct a condition by changing the T.V. cable setting from its proper adjustment. If the T.V. cable is adjustment is "tailored" to modify the transmission shift pattern, line pressure may be adversely affected and can cause transmission failure. To diagnose T.V. system related complaints and ensure proper T.V. cable adjustment, proceed as follows:

1. Ensure that the engine and all related systems are in proper operating condition.
2. Inspect the T.V. cable for kinked, binding, disconnected or broken conditions, and replace cable as needed. Also ensure that the proper T.V. cable is installed.
3. Connect suitable line pressure gauge to transmission and connect tachometer to engine.
4. Run engine until it reaches normal operating temperature. Perform the following tests with engine speed at 1000 rpm.
5. Place gear selector in Park and record line pressure.
6. Place gear selector in drive and note line pressure reading. Line pressure should be equal to or not more than 10 psi greater than the pressure recorded with selector in park.
7. Manually pull the T.V. cable to its full length, taking care not to increase the throttle opening and note pressure readings.
8. Pressure should gradually increase as the cable is pulled out and gradually decrease as the cable is returned to its original position, and approximate line pressures should be 65-80 psi minimum and 120-145 psi maximum.
9. Check the T.V system "fail-safe" system by disconnecting the T.V. cable from the throttle lever with the engine running at idle. Line pressure should increase to maximum.
10. Stop engine for at least 30 seconds to take the T.V. system out of the "fail-safe" mode.
11. Connect and adjust the T.V. cable as outlined in the appropriate service section, then repeat line pressure checks with selector lever in park and drive. Line pressure should return to normal range.
12. If the T.V. system fails to operate as outlined in the preceding tests, check the following components:
    a. Inspect the throttle lever and bracket on the control valve assembly and repair as needed.
    b. Check that the T.V. exhaust valve lifter rod is not distorted or binding in the control valve or spacer plate.
    c. Ensure that the T.V. exhaust check ball moves freely up and down as the lifter is moved.
    d. Ensure that the lifter spring holds the lifter rod against the bottom of the control valve assembly.
    e. Ensure that the T.V. plunger does not stick at any position in its range of travel.

## MAINTENANCE

Check fluid at regular intervals. Noticing a change in color, odor or fluid level can serve as a warning of possible transmission problems.

To check fluid level, bring fluid to operating temperature of 200° F. With vehicle on a level surface and engine idling in Park and parking brake applied, the level on the dipstick should be at the Full mark. To bring the fluid level from the Add mark to the Full mark requires one pint of fluid. If additional fluid is required, use only Dexron II automatic transmission fluid.

When adding fluid, do not overfill, as foaming and loss of fluid through the vent may occur as the fluid heats up. Also, if fluid level is too low, complete loss of drive may occur especially when cold, which can cause transmission failure. The oil should be drained, the oil pan removed, the screen cleaned and fresh fluid added every 30,000 miles for trucks under 8600 lbs. GVWR or every 24,000 miles for vehicles over 8600 GVWR. For vehicles subjected to more severe use such as heavy city traffic especially in hot weather, prolonged periods of idling or as a tow vehicle this maintenance should be performed every 15,000 miles for trucks under 8600 GVWR, or every 12,000 miles for trucks over 8600 GVWR.

## DRAINING BOTTOM PAN

1. Remove front and side oil pan attaching bolts, then loosen the rear bolts.
2. Carefully pry oil pan loose and allow fluid to drain into a suitable container.
3. Remove oil pan and gasket, then the screen attaching bolts, screen and gasket.
4. Thoroughly clean oil pan and gasket surfaces with solvent.
5. Install new oil screen and gasket and torque attaching bolts to 6-10 ft. lbs., then install oil pan using a new gasket and torque attaching bolts to 10-13 ft.

lbs.
6. Add 3½ quarts of fluid, then with engine idling and brakes applied, move selector lever through each range and return selector lever to Park.
7. Bring fluid to proper operating temperature, check fluid and add as required to bring level to Full mark on dipstick.

## ADDING FLUID TO DRY TRANSMISSION & CONVERTER

1. Add 5 quarts of fluid to transmission.
2. With transmission in Park and brakes applied, start the engine.
3. Move shifter lever through each gear range, then with transmission in Park, add additional fluid as required to bring level to Full mark on dipstick.

## IN-VEHICLE ADJUSTMENTS

### SHIFT LINKAGE, ADJUST

#### Exc. S-10 & S-15 Series

1. Position transmission shift lever in Neutral.
2. Position transmission manual valve lever in Neutral.
3. With clamp spring washer and screw assembled into equalizer lever and control rod, hold clamp against equalizer lever, then snug tighten clamp screw against control rod, **Fig. 3**.

#### S-10 & S-15 Series

1. Position the steering column shift lever in neutral gate notch.
2. Set transmission lever (A) in neutral detent, **Fig. 4**.
3. Assemble clamp spring washer and screw to transmission control lever (B) and control rod, **Fig. 4**.
4. Hold clamp flush against transmission control lever (B) and finger tighten clamping screw against rod. No force should be exerted in either direction on the rod or transmission control lever (B) while tightening the clamping screw.
5. Tighten screw securely.

### T.V. CABLE, ADJUST

#### Gasoline Engine

1. Depress and hold metal readjust tab. Move slider back through fitting in direction away from throttle body until slider stops against fitting, **Fig. 5**.
2. Release metal readjust tab.
3. Open carburetor lever to full throttle stop position to automatically adjust cable and release carburetor lever.
4. Check cable for proper operation. If sticking or binding occurs, refer to "Throttle Valve System Diagnosis."

#### Diesel Engine

1. On vehicles equipped with cruise control, remove cruise control rod.
2. Disconnect T.V. cable from throttle assembly, then loosen locknut on pump rod and shorten several turns.
3. Rotate lever assembly to full throttle stop and hold in this position.

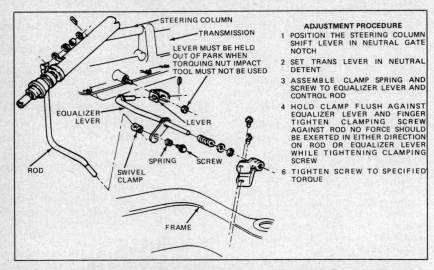

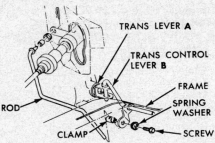

**Fig. 4 Shift linkage adjustment. S-10 & S-15 models**

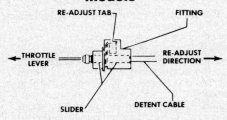

**Fig. 3 Shift linkage adjustment. Exc. S-10 & S-15 models**

**Fig. 5 T.V. cable adjustment**

4. Adjust pump rod until injection pump lever contacts full throttle stop.
5. Release the lever assembly and tighten pump rod locknut, then remove pump rod from the lever assembly.
6. Reconnect T.V. cable to throttle assembly, then depress and hold metal readjust tab. Move slider back through fitting in direction away from lever assembly until slider stops against fitting.
7. Release the readjust tab, then rotate lever assembly to full throttle stop and release the lever.
8. Reconnect pump rod and, if equipped, the cruise control throttle rod.
9. On vehicles equipped with cruise control, adjust the servo throttle rod to minimum slack position, then install clip into the servo bail in first free hole closest to the bell crank.

# IN-VEHICLE REPAIRS
## VALVE BODY ASSEMBLY, REPLACE

1. Drain transmission fluid, then remove oil pan and screen.
2. Remove detent cable retaining bolt and disconnect cable.
3. Remove throttle lever and bracket assembly. Use care to avoid bending throttle lever link.
4. Remove detent roller and spring assembly.
5. Support valve body and remove retaining bolts, then while holding manual valve, remove valve assembly, spacer plate and gaskets as an assembly to prevent dropping the five check balls. After removing valve body assembly, the intermediate band anchor pin, and reverse cup plug may be removed.
6. To install, control valve reverse removal procedure and torque all valve body bolts to 8 ft. lbs. **Failure to ensure that the intermediate band anchor pin is located on intermediate band prior to installation of valve body may damage transmission.**

## GOVERNOR, REPLACE

1. Disconnect battery ground cable and remove air cleaner.
2. If necessary, on vehicles with air conditioning, remove the five heater core cover screws, then disconnect the electrical connectors and position heater core aside.
3. Disconnect exhaust pipe and allow to hang down.
4. Support transmission, then remove transmission rear support bolts and propeller shaft and lower transmission until enough clearance is obtained to remove governor.
5. Remove governor retainer ring and cover, then remove governor and washer. If governor to case washer falls into transmission, use a small magnet to remove it. If it cannot be easily removed, replace the washer with a new one.
6. To install governor, reverse removal procedure. **Do not attempt to hammer governor assembly into case, as damage to governor, case or cover may result.**

## PRESSURE REGULATOR VALVE, REPLACE

1. Drain transmission fluid, then remove oil pan and screen.
2. Using a small screwdriver or tool J-24684, **Fig. 6,** compress regulator spring.
3. Remove retaining ring and slowly release spring tension.
4. Remove pressure regulator bore plug, valve, spring and guide.
5. To assemble, install pressure regulator spring, guide and valve with stem end first and bore plug with hole side out.
6. Using a small screwdriver or tool J-24684, **Fig. 6,** compress regulator spring and install retaining ring.

**Fig. 6 Removing or installing pressure regulator**

# TRANSMISSION
## REPLACE
### EXC. S-10 & S-15

1. Disconnect battery ground cable and detent cable from bracket and carburetor.
2. On models equipped with air conditioning, remove heater core cover from heater assembly.
3. Raise and support vehicle.
4. Disconnect driveshaft, then the speedometer cable from transmission.
5. Disconnect and cap fluid lines from transmission.
6. Disconnect shift control linkage from transmission.
7. Position a suitable jack under transmission, then remove rear transmission support bolts.
8. Remove nuts attaching catalytic converter to rear support.
9. Disconnect exhaust pipe from exhaust manifold, then remove exhaust pipe, catalytic converter and bracket as an assembly.
10. Remove torque converter cover bolts, then the cover.

11. Remove torque converter-to-flexplate attaching bolts.
12. Remove transmission-to-engine mounting bolts.
13. Place a suitable jack under engine.
14. Remove transmission from vehicle.
15. Reverse procedure to install.

## S-10 & S-15 MODELS

1. Open hood and place fender covers on both fenders.
2. Remove air cleaner assembly.
3. Disconnect T.V. cable at its upper end.
4. On vehicles equipped with 4-119 engine, remove starter motor upper retaining nut.
5. Raise and support vehicle.
6. Remove propeller shaft.
7. Disconnect speedometer cable at the transmission.
8. Disconnect shift linkage at transmission.

9. Disconnect all electrical leads at the transmission and any clips that retain the leads to the transmission case.
10. If equipped, remove transmission support brace attaching bolts at converter cover.
11. Remove converter cover attaching bolts and cover, mark flywheel and torque converter to maintain original balance.
12. Remove exhaust crossover pipe with catalytic converter.
13. Remove torque converter to flywheel bolts and/or nuts.
14. Disconnect the catalytic converter support bracket.
15. Position a transmission jack under the transmission and raise slightly.
16. Remove transmission support to transmission mount bolt and transmission support to frame bolts (and insulators if used).
17. Slide the transmission support rearward.

18. Lessen pressure on the jack. Disconnect the oil cooler lines and T.V. cable and cap all openings.
19. Support engine and remove the transmission to engine mounting bolts.
20. Disconnect the transmission assembly, being careful not to damage any cables, lines or linkage.
21. Install torque converter holding tool J-21366 and remove the transmission assembly from the vehicle.
22. To install, reverse the removal procedure, and note the following:
    a. Before installing the flex plate to converter bolts, make certain that the weld nuts on the converter are flush with the flex plate and the converter rotates freely by hand in this position.
    b. Hand start the bolts and tighten finger tight, then torque to 35 ft. lbs. This will ensure proper converter alignment. Install new oil filler tube gasket before installing tube.

# Turbo Hydra-Matic 200-4R Automatic Transmission

## INDEX

## DESCRIPTION

This transmission is a fully automatic unit consisting primarily of a three element hydraulic torque converter with a converter clutch, a compound planetary gear set and an overdrive unit, Fig. 1. Five multiple disc clutches and a band provide the friction elements required to obtain the desired function of the compound planetary gear set and the overdrive unit.

The torque converter couples the engine to the overdrive unit and planetary gears through oil and provides torque multiplication. The combination of the compound planetary gear set and the overdrive unit provides four forward ratios and one reverse. Fully automatic changing of the gear ratios is determined by vehicle speed and engine torque.

The hydraulic system in this transmission is pressurized by a variable capacity vane type pump to provide the working pressure required to operate the friction elements and automatic controls.

## TROUBLESHOOTING

### NO DRIVE

1. Low fluid level.
2. Manual linkage improperly adjusted.
3. Low fluid pressure:
   a. Plugged or restricted oil filter.
   b. Cut or missing oil filter O-ring seals.
   c. Faulty pressure regulator valve.
   d. Damaged pump rotor tangs.
   e. Porosity in oil filter to pump intake bore.
4. Springs missing in overdrive unit roller clutch.
5. Overdrive unit roller galled or missing.
6. Forward clutch malfunctions:
   a. Forward clutch does not apply—piston cracked, seals missing, damaged; clutch plates burned; snap ring out of groove.
   b. Missing or damaged forward clutch oil seal rings; leak in feed circuits; pump to case gasket im-

properly positioned or damaged.
   c. Stuck or missing clutch housing ball check.
   d. Cup plug leaking or missing in the rear of the forward clutch shaft in the clutch apply passage.
7. Low and reverse roller clutch springs missing.
8. Low and reverse roller clutch rollers galled or missing.

### HIGH OR LOW OIL PRESSURE

1. Throttle valve cable improperly adjusted, binding, unhooked, broken, or wrong link.
2. Damaged or leaking throttle valve assembly:
   a. Throttle lever and bracket assembly binding, unhooked or improperly positioned. Refer to "Throttle Valve System Diagnosis."
   b. Binding throttle valve or plunger valve.

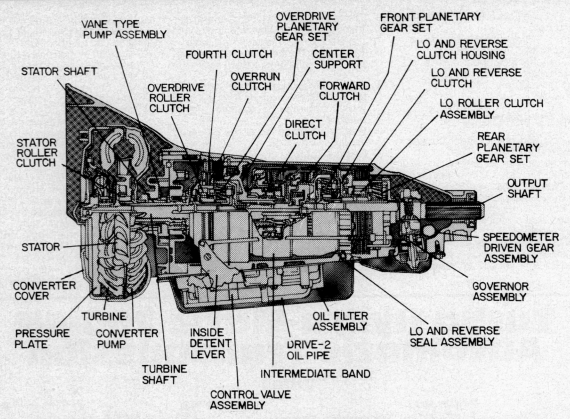

VANE TYPE
PUMP ASSEMBLY

STATOR SHAFT

OVERDRIVE
ROLLER
CLUTCH

FOURTH CLUTCH

OVERRUN
CLUTCH

OVERDRIVE
PLANETARY
GEAR SET

CENTER
SUPPORT

FORWARD
CLUTCH

DIRECT
CLUTCH

FRONT PLANETARY
GEAR SET

LO AND REVERSE
CLUTCH HOUSING

LO AND REVERSE
CLUTCH

LO ROLLER CLUTCH
ASSEMBLY

REAR
PLANETARY
GEAR SET

STATOR
ROLLER
CLUTCH

STATOR

CONVERTER
COVER

PRESSURE
PLATE

TURBINE

CONVERTER
PUMP

INSIDE
DETENT
LEVER

TURBINE
SHAFT

CONTROL VALVE
ASSEMBLY

DRIVE-2
OIL PIPE

INTERMEDIATE BAND

OIL FILTER
ASSEMBLY

LO AND REVERSE
SEAL ASSEMBLY

OUTPUT
SHAFT

SPEEDOMETER
DRIVEN GEAR
ASSEMBLY

GOVERNOR
ASSEMBLY

**Fig. 1   Sectional view of Turbo Hydra-Matic 200-4R automatic transmission**

3. Pressure regulator valve binding.
4. Throttle valve boost valve:
   a. Valve binding.
   b. Wrong valve (causing low oil pressure only).
5. Reverse boost valve binding.
6. Manual valve unhooked or improperly positioned.
7. Pressure relief valve ball missing or spring damaged.
8. Pump:
   a. Slide stuck.
   b. Slide seal damaged or missing.
   c. Decrease air bleed orifice missing or damaged causing high oil pressure.
   d. Decrease air bleed orifice plugged causing low oil pressure.
9. Throttle valve limit valve binding.
10. Line bias valve binding in open position causing high oil pressure.
11. Line bias valve binding in closed position causing high oil pressure.
12. Incorrect orifices or passages in control valve assembly spacer plate or case.

## 1-2 SHIFT ONLY AT FULL THROTTLE

1. Throttle valve cable binding, unhooked, broken, or improperly adjusted.
2. Throttle lever and bracket assembly binding or unhooked.
3. Throttle valve exhaust ball lifter or No. 5 check ball binding, improperly positioned, or unhooked.
4. No. 5 check ball sealed causing full

throttle valve pressure regardless of throttle valve position.
5. Throttle valve and plunger binding.
6. Control valve body gaskets leaking, damaged, or incorrectly installed.
7. Porous case assembly.

## NO 1-2 SHIFT

1. Governor and governor feed passages:
   a. Plugged governor oil feed orifice in spacer plate.
   b. Governor balls missing in governor assembly.
   c. Missing or leaking inner governor assembly.
   d. Governor shaft seal missing or damaged.
   e. Stripped governor driven gear.
   f. Governor weights binding on pin.
   g. Governor driven gear not engaged with governor shaft.
2. Control valve assembly:
   a. 1-2 shift—Lo/1st detent, or 1-2 throttle valve stuck in downshift position.
   b. Spacer plate gaskets improperly positioned.
3. Case:
   a. Case channels porous or 2nd oil feed hole undrilled.
   b. Excessive leakage between case bore and intermediate band apply rings.
   c. Intermediate band anchor pin missing or unhooked from band.
   d. Broken or missing band.
4. Intermediate servo assembly:

   a. Missing servo cover oil seal.
   b. Porosity in serve; cover, inner piston, or outer piston.
   c. Incorrect intermediate band apply pin.
   d. Incorrect usage of cover and piston.
5. 1-2 accumulator:
   a. Loose 1-2 accumulator housing bolts.
   b. Damaged 1-2 accumulator housing face.
   c. Missing or damaged accumulator plate.

## NO 2-3 SHIFT

1. Control valve assembly and spacer plate:
   a. 2-3 shift valve or 2-3 throttle valve stuck in the downshift position.
   b. Leaking, damaged or incorrectly installed valve body gaskets.
   c. Reverse/3rd check ball not seating, damaged or missing.
2. Case channels porous.
3. Center support:
   a. Plugged or undrilled center support.
   b. Damaged steel oil seal rings on center support.
4. Direct clutch:
   a. Inner oil seal ring on piston damaged or missing.
   b. Center oil seal ring on direct clutch hub damaged or missing.
   c. Check ball and/or retainer damaged or missing from direct clutch piston.

d. Damaged or missing direct clutch piston or housing.
e. Damaged or missing direct clutch plates.
f. Direct clutch backing plate snap ring not in groove.
g. Release spring guide improperly located, preventing piston check ball from seating in retainer.
5. Intermediate servo assembly (third clutch accumulator oil passages):
   a. Broken or missing servo to case oil seal ring on intermediate servo piston.
   b. Intermediate servo and/or capsule missing or damaged.
   c. Plugged or undrilled exhaust hole in case between servo piston seal rings.
   d. Bleed orifice cup plug missing from intermediate servo pocket in case.

## NO MOVEMENT IN R OR SLIPS IN R

1. Binding or improperly adjusted throttle valve cable.
2. Improperly adjusted manual linkage.
3. Binding throttle valve.
4. Throttle valve limit valve binding.
5. Binding line bias valve.
6. Reverse boost valve binding in pressure regulator bore.
7. Reverse/3rd or Lo/Reverse check ball missing or seat in spacer plate damaged.
8. Reverse clutch:
   a. Cracked piston, or missing inner or outer seals.
   b. Clutch plates burned.
   c. Missing or damaged reverse oil seal in case.
   d. Missing clutch plate or valve plate.
9. Center support:
   a. Loose or missing center support attaching bolts.
   b. Blocked or undrilled passages.
   c. Porosity.
10. Direct clutch housing:
    a. Cracked housing or piston.
    b. Missing or damaged inner or outer piston seal.
    c. Missing or damaged check ball in either the direct clutch housing or the piston.
    d. Plates burned.
11. Plugged Lo/Reverse overrun clutch orifice in spacer plate.

## DRIVE IN NEUTRAL

1. Manual linkage improperly adjusted or disconnected.
2. Forward clutch:
   a. Clutch does not release.
   b. Sticking exhaust check ball.
   c. Plates burned together.
3. Case cross leaking to forward clutch passage (D4).

## SLIPPING 1-2 SHIFT

1. Low fluid level.
2. Spacer plate gaskets damaged or incorrectly installed.
3. Accumulator valve:
   a. Valve sticking in valve body causing low 1-2 accumulator pressure.
   b. Weak or missing spring.

4. 1-2 accumulator piston:
   a. Leaking seal, broken or missing spring.
   b. Leak between piston and pin.
   c. Binding 1-2 accumulator piston.
   d. Damaged 1-2 accumulator piston bore.
5. Intermediate band apply pin:
   a. Incorrect selection of apply pin.
   b. Excessive leakage between apply pin and case.
   c. Apply pin feed hole not completely drilled.
6. Intermediate servo assembly:
   a. Porosity in piston.
   b. Damaged or missing cover to servo oil seal ring.
   c. Leak between servo apply pin and case.
7. Improperly adjusted throttle valve cable.
8. Throttle valve binding, causing low throttle valve pressure.
9. Binding throttle valve limit valve.
10. Line bias valve sticking, causing low line pressure.
11. Worn or burned intermediate band.
12. Case porosity in 2nd clutch passage.

## ROUGH 1-2 SHIFT

1. Throttle valve cable binding or improperly adjusted.
2. Binding throttle valve to throttle valve plunger.
3. Binding throttle valve limit valve.
4. Binding accumulator valve.
5. Binding line bias valve.
6. Intermediate servo assembly:
   a. Incorrect selection apply pin.
   b. Damaged or missing servo piston to case oil seal ring.
   c. Bleed cup plug missing in case.
7. 1-2 accumulator:
   a. Oil ring damaged.
   b. Piston stuck.
   c. Broken or missing spring.
   d. Damaged bore.
8. 1-2 shift check ball No. 8 missing or sticking.

## SLIPPING 2-3 SHIFT

1. Low fluid level.
2. Improperly adjusted throttle valve cable.
3. Binding throttle valve.
4. Spacer plate and gaskets:
   a. Direct clutch orifice partially blocked in spacer plate.
   b. Gaskets out of position or damaged.
5. Intermediate servo assembly:
   a. Damaged or missing servo to case oil seal ring.
   b. Damaged piston or servo bore.
   c. Intermediate servo orifice bleed cup plug in case missing.
   d. Case porous in the servo bore area.
6. Direct clutch feed:
   a. Direct clutch feed channels porous.
   b. Loose case to support bolts causing leakage.
   c. Cracked direct clutch piston or housing.
   d. Cut or missing piston seals.
   e. Burned direct clutch plates.

f. Check ball in piston and/or housing missing, damaged, or leaking.
g. Check ball capsule damaged.
h. Release spring guide improperly located preventing check ball from seating in piston.
7. Center support:
   a. Channels cross feeding, leaking, or restricted.
   b. Damaged or missing oil seal rings.

## ROUGH 2-3 SHIFT

1. Missing or improperly positioned throttle valve cable.
2. Throttle valve plunger binding.
3. Throttle valve binding.
4. Throttle valve limit valve binding.
5. Intermediate servo assembly exhaust hole undrilled or plugged between intermediate servo piston seals, preventing intermediate servo piston from completing its stroke.
6. 3-2 exhaust check ball No. 4 missing or improperly positioned.
7. 3rd accumulator check ball No. 2 missing or improperly positioned.

## SLIPPING 3-4 SHIFT

1. Low fluid level.
2. Control valve assembly and spacer plate gaskets damaged or incorrectly installed.
3. Accumulator valve sticking causing low 3-4 accumulator pressure.
4. Weak or missing accumulator valve spring.
5. 3-4 accumulator piston stuck.
6. Damaged 3-4 accumulator bore or oil ring.
7. Center support porosity.
8. Loose center support attaching bolts.
9. Fourth clutch piston surface or seals damaged.
10. Improper clutch plate usage.
11. Burned fourth clutch plate.
12. Case:
    a. Porosity.
    b. 1-2 accumulator housing bolts loose.
    c. 3-4 accumulator piston seal damaged.
    d. 3-4 accumulator leaking between the piston and pin.
    e. 3-4 accumulator bore damaged.

## ROUGH 3-4 SHIFT

1. Throttle valve cable improperly positioned or missing.
2. Throttle valve plunger binding.
3. Throttle valve binding.
4. Throttle valve limit valve binding.
5. 3-4 accumulator piston stuck.
6. 3-4 accumulator bore damaged.
7. Fourth clutch piston binding.

## NO CONVERTER CLUTCH APPLICATION

1. Electrical malfunctions:
   a. 12 volts not being supplied to clutch solenoid.
   b. Defective solenoid.
   c. Damaged electrical connector.
   d. Defective pressure switch.
   e. Wire grounded.
2. Converter clutch shift valve or throttle valve stuck.

3. Pump assembly:
   a. Plugged converter signal oil orifice in pump.
   b. Damaged or missing solenoid O-ring.
   c. Orifice cup plug missing in oil cooler passage in pump.
   d. Damaged or improperly positioned pump to case gasket.
   e. Converter clutch application valve stuck.
   f. Cup plug missing from application passage.

## ROUGH CONVERTER CLUTCH APPLICATION

1. Damaged converter clutch pressure plate.
2. Damaged or missing check ball in end of turbine shaft.

## CONVERTER CLUTCH DOES NOT RELEASE

1. Converter clutch apply valve stuck.
2. Damaged converter.
3. Missing cup plug in pump release passage.
4. Missing or damaged turbine shaft end seal.
5. Hole not drilled through turbine shaft.

## FIRST, SECOND & THIRD SPEED ONLY, NO 3-4 SHIFT

1. Control valve assembly and spacer plate, loose, damaged.
2. 3-4 shift valve or 3-4 throttle valve stuck.
3. Plugged spacer plate orifice.
4. Center support:
   a. Plugged or undrilled oil passages.
   b. Loose or missing center support attaching bolts.
   c. Cracked or damaged fourth clutch piston.
   d. Damaged, missing or improperly assembled fourth clutch piston seals.
   e. Improper plate usage.
   f. Burned fourth clutch plates.
   g. Binding overrun clutch plates.
5. Case porous.
6. Orifice cup plug missing in 3-4 accumulator passage in case.
7. Leakage between accumulator piston and pin.
8. 3-4 accumulator bore damaged.

## NO ENGINE BRAKING IN L1

1. Improperly adjusted manual linkage.
2. D-3 orifice in space plate plugged.
3. Control valve body gaskets leaking, damaged, or incorrectly installed.
4. D-2 oil pipe leaking or out of position.
5. L1 overrun clutch valve binding in valve body.
6. L1/Detent check ball No. 10 improperly positioned or missing.
7. L1/Detent check ball No. 9 improperly positioned or missing.
8. PT/D-3 check ball No. 3 improperly positioned or missing.
9. Turbine shaft and overrun clutch. No manual 3rd or 2nd should also be a complaint with the following:

a. Plugged or undrilled D-3 oil passage in turbine shaft.
b. D-3 oil passage not drilled through in overrun clutch hub.
c. Missing or damaged oil seals in the overrun clutch piston.
d. Burned overrun clutches.
e. Overrun clutch backing plate snap ring out of groove.
10. Case porosity.
11. L1/Reverse clutch assembly. No reverse should also be a complaint with any of the following conditions:
    a. Broken or missing piston seals.
    b. Clutch housing snap ring out of case.
    c. Cracked/porous piston or housing.
    d. Missing or damaged cup plug or rubber seal between case and L1/Reverse clutch housing.

## NO ENGINE BRAKING IN L2

1. Manual linkage improperly adjusted.
2. Valve body gaskets leaking, damaged, or improperly installed.
3. Leaking or out of position D-2 oil pipe.
4. Plugged D-3 orifice in spacer plate.
5. PT/D-3 check ball No. 3 improperly positioned or missing.
6. Porous case.
7. Missing or damaged intermediate servo cover to case oil seal ring.
8. Intermediate band off anchor pin.
9. Broken or burned intermediate band.
10. D-3 oil passage not drilled through in overrun clutch hub.
11. Missing or damaged oil seals in the overrun clutch piston.
12. Undrilled or plugged D-3 oil hole in turbine shaft.
13. Burned overrun clutches.
14. Overrun clutch backing plate snap ring out of groove.

## NO ENGINE BRAKING IN D

1. Manual linkage improperly adjusted.
2. Plugged D-3 orifice in spacer plate.
3. Leaking, damaged, or incorrectly installed valve body gaskets.
4. PT/D-3 check ball No. 3 improperly positioned or missing.
5. Undrilled or plugged D-3 oil passage in turbine shaft.
6. D-3 oil hole not drilled through in overrun clutch hub.
7. Missing or damaged oil seals in the overrun clutch piston.
8. Burned overrun clutches.
9. Overrun clutch backing plate snap ring out of groove.

## LOW OR HIGH SHIFT POINT

1. Binding or improperly adjusted throttle valve cable.
2. Throttle valve limit valve binding.
3. Throttle valve binding.
4. Throttle valve modulator upshift valve binding.

## THROTTLE VALVE SYSTEM DIAGNOSIS

T.V. pressure controls the shift pattern and the hydraulic line pressure used to apply clutches and bands. If proper line pressure is not available to apply clutch ele-

ments and bands, excess slippage may occur during shifting, and the components will be damaged. A T.V. cable which is damaged, disconnected or improperly adjusted, will cause high or low line pressure which can in turn cause the following conditions: Delayed or harsh upshifts, early upshifts and clutch slippage during shifting, no upshift, chatter on take-off, 1-2 upshift at full throttle only, no full throttle or part throttle detent downshift, and intermittent second gear starts.

Do not attempt to correct a condition by changing the T.V. cable setting from its proper adjustment. If the T.V. cable is adjustment is "tailored" to modify the transmission shift pattern, line pressure may be adversely affected and can cause transmission failure. To diagnose T.V. system related complaints and ensure proper T.V. cable adjustment, proceed as follows:

1. Ensure that the engine and all related systems are in proper operating condition.
2. Inspect the T.V. cable for kinked, binding, disconnected or broken conditions, and replace cable as needed. Also ensure that the proper T.V. cable is installed.
3. Connect suitable line pressure gauge to transmission and connect tachometer to engine.
4. Run engine until it reaches normal operating temperature, perform the following tests with engine speed at 1000 rpm.
5. Place gear selector in Park and record line pressure.
6. Place gear selector in Drive and note line pressure reading. Line pressure should be equal to or not more than 10 psi greater than the pressure recorded with selector in Park.
7. Manually pull the T.V. cable to its full length, taking care not to increase the throttle opening and note pressure readings.
8. Pressure should gradually increase as the cable is pulled out and gradually decrease as the cable is returned to its original position, and approximate line pressures should be 50-75 psi minimum and 110-170 psi maximum.
9. Check the T.V system "fail-safe" system by disconnecting the T.V. cable from the throttle lever with the engine running at idle. Line pressure should increase to maximum.
10. Stop engine for at least 30 seconds to take the T.V. system out of the "fail-safe" mode.
11. Connect and adjust the T.V. cable as outlined in the appropriate service section, then repeat line pressure checks with selector lever in park and drive. Line pressure should return to normal range.
12. If the T.V. system fails to operate as outlined in the preceding tests, check the following components:
    a. Inspect the throttle lever and bracket on the control valve assembly and repair as needed.
    b. Check that the T.V. exhaust valve lifter rod is not distorted or binding in the control valve or spacer plate.
    c. Ensure that the T.V. exhaust check

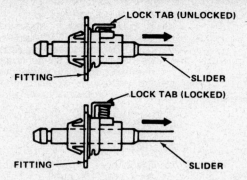

**Fig. 2   Self adjusting throttle valve linkage**

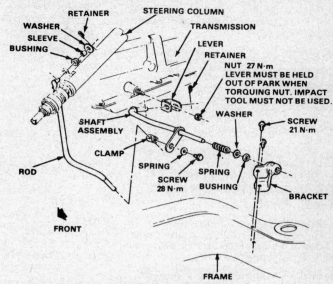

**Fig. 3   Column mounted shift linkage adjustment**

ball moves freely up and down as the lifter is moved.
d. Ensure that the lifter spring holds the lifter rod against the bottom of the control valve assembly.
e. Ensure that the T.V. plunger does not stick at any position in its range of travel.

## MAINTENANCE
### OIL LEVEL CHECK

Check fluid at regular intervals. Noticing a change in color, odor or fluid level can serve as a warning of possible transmission problems.

To check fluid level, bring fluid to operating temperature of 200° F. With vehicle on a level surface and engine idling in Park and parking brake applied, the level on the dipstick should be at the Full mark. To bring the fluid level from the Add mark to the Full mark requires one pint of fluid. If additional fluid is required, use only Dexron II automatic transmission fluid.

When adding fluid, do not overfill, as foaming and loss of fluid through the vent may occur as the fluid heats up. Also, if fluid level is too low, complete loss of drive may occur especially when cold, which can cause transmission failure. The oil should be drained, the oil pan removed, the screen cleaned and fresh fluid added every 30,000 miles for trucks under 8600 lbs. GVWR or every 24,000 miles for vehicles over 8600 GVWR. For vehicles subjected to more severe use such as heavy city traffic especially in hot weather, prolonged periods of idling or as a tow vehicle this maintenance should be performed every 15,000 miles for trucks under 8600 GVWR, or every 12,000 miles for trucks over 8600 GVWR.

### DRAINING BOTTOM PAN

1. Remove front and side oil pan attaching bolts, then loosen the rear oil pan attaching bolts.
2. Carefully pry oil pan loose and allow fluid to drain into a suitable container.
3. Remove oil pan and gasket, then remove screen attaching bolts and the screen.
4. Thoroughly clean and oil pan and gasket surfaces with solvent.
5. Install new oil screen and seal, then the oil pan using a new gasket and torque attaching bolts to 10-13 ft. lbs.

6. Add approximately 3 quarts of fluid, then with engine idling and brakes applied, move selector lever through each range and return selector lever to Park.
7. Bring fluid to proper operating temperature, then check fluid and add as required to bring level to the Full mark on the dipstick.

## IN-VEHICLE ADJUSTMENTS
### THROTTLE VALVE LINKAGE, ADJUST
#### MODELS EQUIPPED WITH DIESEL ENGINE

1. Remove cruise control rod on vehicles equipped with cruise control.
2. Disconnect throttle valve linkage from throttle assembly.
3. Loosen locknut on pump rod, then shorten rod by rotating several turns.
4. Rotate throttle lever assembly to full throttle position and secure in this position.
5. Lengthen pump rod by rotating in opposite direction as described in step 3 until injection pump lever contacts full throttle stop.
6. Release throttle lever assembly and tighten pump rod locknut.
7. Disconnect pump rod from throttle lever assembly.
8. Connect throttle valve linkage to throttle assembly.
9. Depress metal locking tab on upper end of cable and hold in this position.
10. Position slider through fitting and away from lever assembly until slider contacts metal fitting.
11. Release metal tab, then rotate throttle lever assembly to full throttle position and release.
12. Connect pump rod to lever assembly, then connect cruise control throttle rod, if equipped.

13. On models equipped with cruise control, adjust servo throttle rod until minimum amount of slack is present. Install clip into first hole closest to bell crank that is within servo ball.

### MODELS EQUIPPED WITH GASOLINE ENGINE
#### Manual Type Linkage

1. With engine static, disconnect throttle valve linkage retaining lock.
2. Rotate throttle lever to wide open position and hold in this position.
3. Connect throttle valve linkage retaining lock.

#### Self Adjusting Linkage

1. With engine static, depress locking tab and move slider rearward through fitting until slider contacts fitting, **Fig. 2.**
2. Release locking tab, then move carburetor throttle lever to wide open position and release.
3. Check cable for sticking or binding, then test vehicle for proper operation.
4. If transmission does not shift properly, refer to "Throttle Valve System Diagnosis."

### MANUAL LINKAGE, ADJUST
#### Column Shift

1. Position transmission shift lever in Neutral.
2. Position transmission manual valve lever in Neutral detent.
3. With clamp spring washer and screw assembled into equalizer lever and control rod, hold clamp against equalizer lever, then snug tighten clamp screw against control rod, **Fig. 3.**

#### Floor Shift

1. Position console shift lever in Park position.
2. Position transmission in manual valve lever in Park detent.

3. Position pin, **Fig. 4**, until pin fits loosely in transmission lever, then tighten attaching nut.

## IN-VEHICLE REPAIRS
### INTERMEDIATE SERVO, REPLACE

1. Remove intermediate servo cover retaining ring, using a small screwdriver.
2. Remove servo cover and discard seal ring.
3. Remove servo piston and band apply pin assembly.
4. Reverse procedure to install.

### SPEEDOMETER DRIVEN GEAR, REPLACE

1. Disconnect speedometer cable.
2. Remove bolt, retainer, speedometer driven gear and the O-ring seal.
3. Reverse procedure to install.

### REAR OIL SEAL, REPLACE

1. Remove propeller shaft.
2. Pry seal from extension housing with a suitable tool.
3. Drive new oil seal into extension housing, using a suitable tool.
4. Install propeller shaft.

### VALVE BODY, REPLACE

1. Drain transmission oil pan.
2. Remove oil pan and filter.
3. Remove screw and washer securing T.V. cable to transmission and disconnect the cable.
4. Remove throttle lever and bracket assembly. Use caution not to bend throttle lever link.
5. Disconnect electrical connectors at the 4-3 pressure switch and the 4th clutch pressure switch.
6. Remove solenoid attaching bolts, clips and solenoid assembly.
7. Remove manual detent roller and spring assembly.
8. Remove valve body retaining bolts while supporting valve body. Secure manual valve and remove valve body.

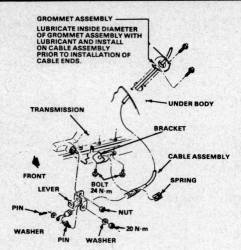

**Fig. 4   Console mounted shift linkage adjustment**

Use caution not to lose the three check balls.
9. Reverse procedure to install. Torque valve body bolts to 12 ft. lbs.

### 1-2 & 3-4 ACCUMULATOR, REPLACE

1. Remove valve body.
2. While supporting 1-2 accumulator housing, remove housing retaining bolts. Then, remove housing and gasket.
3. Support valve body spacer plate, gaskets and accumulator plate to prevent loss of the eight check balls and the 3-4 accumulator spring piston and pin located in the case. Remove remaining retaining bolt on accumulator plate. The intermediate band anchor pin may become dislodged after removing spacer plate and gaskets.
4. Reverse procedure to install.

### GOVERNOR, REPLACE

1. Drain transmission oil pan.
2. Remove oil pan and filter.
3. Remove governor attaching bolts, cover and gasket. The governor may come out with the cover. Also, it may be necessary to rotate output shaft counterclockwise while removing governor.
4. Reverse procedure to install.

## TRANSMISSION
### REPLACE

1. Disconnect battery ground cable and remove air cleaner.
2. Disconnect throttle valve cable.
3. Remove upper bolt on dipstick tube.
4. Raise and support vehicle.
5. Mark driveshaft and companion flange for reference during installation, then remove driveshaft.
6. Disconnect speedometer cable and manual shift linkage from transmission.
7. Disconnect torque converter clutch solenoid electrical connector.
8. Remove flywheel under cover. Mark flywheel and converter for reference during installation. Remove three flywheel to converter attaching bolts.
9. Remove catalytic converter support bracket bolts and the tunnel strap.
10. Remove transmission crossmember to transmission mount bolts. Remove transmission crossmember to frame bolts.
11. Support transmission with suitable jack, then move crossmember rearward.
12. Lower transmission slightly and disconnect throttle valve cable and oil cooler lines.
13. Support engine with suitable jack, then remove engine to transmission mounting bolts.
14. Lower jack and remove transmission from vehicle. Use caution not to drop torque converter as transmission is removed. Install suitable converter holding tool to secure converter.
15. Reverse procedure to install.

# Turbo Hydra-Matic 250, 250C, 350 & 350C

## INDEX

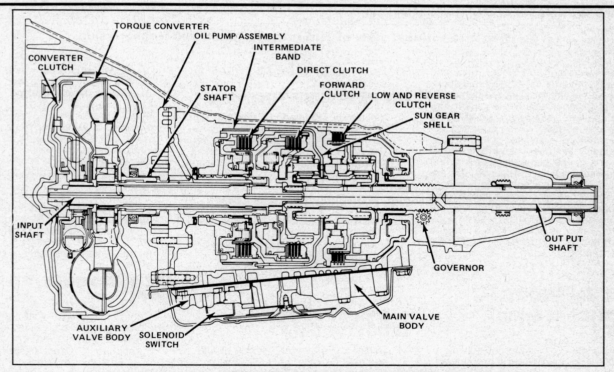

**Fig. 1 Sectional view of Turbo Hydra-Matic 250C transmission**

## DESCRIPTION

The Turbo Hydra-Matic 250, 350, **Figs. 1 and 2,** are fully automatic three speed transmissions consisting of a three element torque converter and a compound planetary gear set. The Turbo Hydra-Matic 250C and 350C, also incorporate a torque converter clutch, **Fig. 3.** The turbo Hydra-Matic 350 transmission has four multiple disc clutches, two roller clutches and a band to provide the required friction elements to obtain the desired function of the planetary gear set. The Turbo Hydra-Matic 250 transmission uses an adjustable intermediate band in place of the intermediate clutch found in the Turbo Hydra-Matic 350. Also, the Turbo Hydra-Matic 250 has three multiple-disc clutches and one roller clutch. The friction elements couple the engine to the planetary gears through oil pressure, providing three forward speeds and one reverse.

The three element torque converter is of welded construction and is serviced as an assembly. The unit consists of a pump or driving member, a turbine or driven member and a stator assembly. When required, the torque converter supplements the gears by multiplying engine torque.

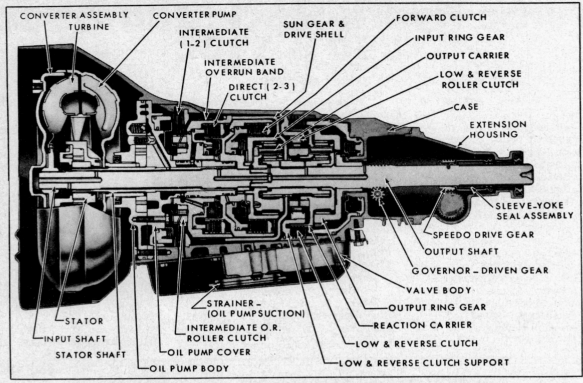

**Fig. 2   Sectional view of Turbo Hydra-Matic 350 transmission**

On the Turbo Hydra-Matic 250C and 350C, the converter clutch assembly consists of a three element torque converter, with the addition of a converter clutch, **Fig. 3.** The converter clutch is splined to the turbine assembly and when operated applies against the converter cover, providing a mechanical direct drive coupling of the engine to the planetary gears. When the converter clutch is released, the assembly operates as a normal torque converter. The converter clutch is applied only when the transmission is in third gear, vehicle speed is above 30 mph, engine coolant temperature is above 130° F, engine vacuum is above 3 inches Hg and brake pedal is released.

## TROUBLESHOOTING
### NO DRIVE IN DRIVE RANGE

1. Low oil level (check for leaks).
2. Manual control linkage improperly adjusted.
3. Low oil pressure due to blocked strainer, defective pressure regulator, pump assembly or pump drive gear. See that tangs have not been damaged by converter. Check case for porosity in intake bore.
4. Check control valve assembly to be sure manual valve has not been disconnected from inner lever.
5. Forward clutch may be stuck or damaged. Check pump feed circuits to forward clutch, including clutch drum ball check.

6. Roller clutch assembly broken or damaged.

### OIL PRESSURE TOO HIGH

1. Incorrectly adjusted T.V. cable, see "Throttle Valve System Diagnosis."
2. Vacuum line or fittings leaking.
3. Vacuum modulator.
4. Modulator valve.
5. Pressure regulator.
6. Oil pump.

### OIL PRESSURE TOO LOW

1. Incorrectly adjusted T.V. cable, see "Throttle Valve System Diagnosis."
2. Vacuum line or fittings obstructed.
3. Vacuum modulator.
4. Modulator valve.
5. Pressure regulator.
6. Governor.
7. Oil pump.

### 1–2 SHIFT AT FULL THROTTLE ONLY

1. Detent valve may be sticking or linkage may be improperly adjusted.
2. Vacuum line or fittings leaking.
3. Control valve body gaskets leaking, damaged or incorrectly installed. Detent valve train or 1-2 valve stuck.
4. Check case for porosity.

### FIRST SPEED ONLY, NO 1-2 SHIFT
#### T.H.M. 250 & 350

1. Governor valve sticking.
2. Driven gear in governor assembly loose, worn or damaged. If driven gear shows damage, check output shaft

drive gear for nicks or rough finish.
3. Control valve governor feed channel blocked or gaskets leaking. 1-2 shift valve train stuck closed.
4. Check case for blocked governor feed channels or for scored governor bore which will allow cross pressure leak. Check case for porosity.
5. Intermediate clutch or seals damaged.
6. Intermediate roller clutch damaged.

#### T.H.M. 250

1. Intermediate servo piston seals damaged, missing or installed improperly.
2. Intermediate band improperly adjusted.
3. Intermediate servo apply rod broken.

### 1ST & 2ND ONLY, NO 2-3 SHIFT

1. Control valve 2-3 shift train stuck. Valve body gaskets leaking, damaged or improperly installed.
2. Pump hub to direct clutch oil seal rings broken or missing.
3. Direct clutch piston seals damaged. Piston ball check stuck or missing.

### NO FIRST SPEED
#### T.H.M. 250

1. Intermediate band adjusted too tightly.
2. 1-2 shift valve stuck in upshift position.

#### T.H.M. 350

1. Excessive number of clutch plates in intermediate clutch pack.
2. Incorrect intermediate clutch piston.

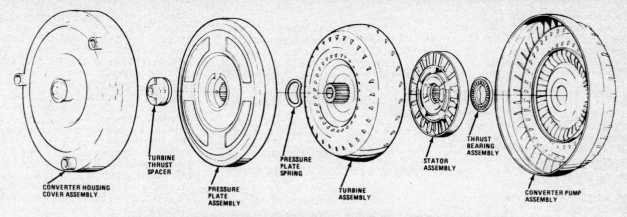

**Fig. 3   Torque converter clutch 250C & 350C transmission**

## MOVES FORWARD IN NEUTRAL

1. Manual linkage improperly adjusted.
2. Forward clutch not releasing.

## NO MOVEMENT IN REVERSE OR SLIPS IN REVERSE

1. Low oil level.
2. Manual linkage improperly adjusted.
3. Modulator valve stuck.
4. Modulator and reverse boost valve stuck.
5. Pump hub to direct clutch oil seal rings broken or missing.
6. Direct clutch piston seal cut or missing.
7. Low and reverse clutch piston seal cut or missing.
8. No. 1 check ball missing.
9. Control valve body gaskets leaking or damaged.
10. 2-3 valve train stuck in upshifted position.
11. 1-2 valve train stuck in upshifted position.
12. Intermediate servo piston or pin stuck so intermediate overrun band is applied.
13. Low and reverse clutch piston out or seal damaged.
14. Direct clutch plates burned—may be caused by stuck ball check in piston.
15. Forward clutch not releasing.

## SLIPS IN ALL RANGES

1. Low oil level.
2. Vacuum modulator valve defective or sticking.
3. Filter assembly plugged or leaking.
4. Pressure regulator valve stuck.
5. Pump to case gasket damaged.
6. Check case for cross leaks or porosity.
7. Forward clutch slipping.

## SLIPS 1-2 SHIFT

### T.H.M. 250 & 350

1. Low oil level.
2. Vacuum modulator assembly defective.
3. Modulator valve sticking.
4. Pump pressure regulator valve defec-

tive.
5. 2-3 accumulator oil ring damaged or missing. 1-2 accumulator oil ring damaged or missing. Case bore damaged.
6. Pump to case gasket improperly positioned or damaged.
7. Check for case porosity.
8. Intermediate clutch piston seals damaged. Clutch plates burned.

### T.H.M. 250

1. Intermediate servo piston seals damaged or missing.
2. Burned intermediate band.

### T.H.M. 350

1. 2-3 accumulator oil ring damaged or missing.

## ROUGH 1-2 SHIFT

### T.H.M. 250 & 350

1. Vacuum modulator, check for loose fittings, restrictions in line or defective modulator assembly.
2. Modulator valve stuck.
3. Valve body regulator or boost valve stuck.
4. Pump to case gasket improperly positioned or damaged.
5. Check case for porosity.
6. Check 1-2 accumulator assembly for damaged oil rings, stuck piston, broken or missing spring, or damaged case bore.

### T.H.M. 250

1. Intermediate band improperly adjusted.
2. Improper or broken servo spring.

### T.H.M. 350

1. Burned intermediate clutch plates.
2. Improper number of intermediate clutch plates.

## SLIPS 2-3 SHIFT

1. Low oil level.
2. Modulator valve or vacuum modulator assembly defective.
3. Pump pressure regulator valve or boost valve; pump to case gasket improperly positioned.
4. Check case for porosity.

5. Direct clutch piston seals or ball check leaking.

## ROUGH 2-3 SHIFT

1. High oil pressure. Vacuum leak, modulator valve sticking or pressure regulator or boost valve inoperative.
2. 2-3 accumulator piston stuck, spring broken or missing.

## NO ENGINE BRAKING IN 2ND SPEED

1. Intermediate servo or 2-3 accumulator oil rings or bores leaking or accumulator piston stuck.
2. Intermediate overrun band burned or broken.
3. Low oil pressure: Pressure regulator and/or boost valve stuck.

## NO ENGINE BRAKING IN 1ST SPEED

1. Manual low control valve assembly stuck.
2. Low oil pressure: Pressure regulator and/or boost valve stuck.
3. Low and reverse clutch piston inner seal damaged.

## NO PART THROTTLE DOWNSHIFT

1. Incorrect oil pressure caused by vacuum modulator assembly, modulator valve or pressure regulator valve train malfunctioning.
2. Detent valve and linkage sticking, disconnected or broken.
3. 2-3 shift valve stuck.

## NO DETENT DOWNSHIFTS

1. 2-3 valve stuck.
2. Detent valve and linkage sticking, disconnected or broken.

## LOW OR HIGH SHIFT POINTS

1. Incorrect oil pressure. Check engine vacuum at transmission end of modulator pipe.
2. Vacuum modulator assembly vacuum line connections at engine and transmission, modulator valve, pressure regulator valve train.

3. Check governor for sticking valve, restricted or leaking feed holes, damaged pipes or plugged feed line.
4. Detent valve stuck open.
5. 1-2 or 2-3 valve train sticking.
6. Check case for porosity.

## WILL NOT HOLD IN PARK

1. Manual linkage improperly adjusted.
2. Parking brake lever and actuator assembly defective.
3. Parking pawl broken or inoperative.

## BURNED FORWARD CLUTCH PLATES

1. Check ball in clutch drum damaged, stuck or missing.
2. Clutch piston cracked, seals damaged or missing.
3. Low line pressure.
4. Pump cover oil seal rings missing, broken or undersize; ring groove oversize.
5. Transmission case valve body face not flat or porosity between channels.

## BURNED INTERMEDIATE CLUTCH PLATES

### T.H.M. 350

1. Intermediate clutch piston seals damaged or missing.
2. Low line pressure.
3. Transmission case valve body face not flat or porosity between channels.

## BURNED INTERMEDIATE BAND

### T.H.M. 250

1. Intermediate servo piston seals damaged or missing.
2. Low line pressure.
3. Transmission case valve body face not flat or porosity between channels.

## BURNED DIRECT CLUTCH PLATES

1. Restricted orifice in vacuum line to modulator.
2. Check ball in clutch drum damaged, stuck or missing.
3. Defective modulator.
4. Clutch piston cracked, seals damaged or missing.
5. Transmission case valve body face not flat or porosity between channels.

## NOISY TRANSMISSION

Before checking transmission for noise, ensure noise is not coming from water pump, alternator or any belt driven accessory.

### Park, Neutral & All Driving Ranges

1. Low fluid level.
2. Plugged or restricted screen.
3. Damaged screen to valve body gasket.
4. Porosity in valve body intake area.
5. Transmission fluid contaminated with water.
6. Porosity at transmission case intake port.
7. Improperly installed case to pump

gasket.
8. Pump gears are damaged.
9. Driving gear assembled backwards.
10. Crescent interference in pump.
11. Damaged or worn oil pump seals.
12. Loose converter to flywheel bolts.
13. Damaged converter.

### 1st, 2nd And/Or Reverse Gear

1. Planetary gears or thrust bearings damaged.
2. Damaged input or output ring gear.

### Acceleration In Any Gear

1. Transmission case or transmission oil cooler lines contacting underbody.
2. Broken or loose engine mounts.

### Squeal At Low Vehicle Speed

1. Speedometer driven gear shaft seal requires lubrication or replacement.
2. Defective torque converter.
3. Dried or contaminated extension housing seal.

## CONVERTER CLUTCH APPLIED IN ALL RANGES; ENGINE STALLS WHEN TRANSMISSION IS PUT IN GEAR

### T.H.M. 250C & 350C

1. Converter clutch valve in pump sticking in apply position.

## CONVERTER CLUTCH APPLIES ERRATICALLY

### T.H.M. 250C & 350C

1. Vacuum switch malfunction.
2. Release orifice at pump blocked or restricted.
3. Damaged turbine shaft O-ring.
4. Converter malfunctioning, clutch pressure plate warped.
5. O-ring damaged at solenoid.
6. Solenoid bolts loose.

## CONVERTER CLUTCH APPLIES AT A VERY LOW OR HIGH 3RD SPEED GEAR

### T.H.M. 250C & 350C

1. Governor switch malfunction.
2. Governor malfunction.
3. High line pressure
4. Converter clutch valve sticking or binding.
5. Solenoid inoperative or shorted to case.

## T.V. SYSTEM DIAGNOSIS

T.V. pressure controls the shift pattern and the hydraulic line pressure used to apply clutches and bands. If proper line pressure is not available to apply clutch elements and bands, excess slippage may occur during shifting, and the components will be damaged. A T.V. cable which is damaged, disconnected or improperly adjusted, will cause high or low line pressure

which can in turn cause the following conditions: Delayed or harsh upshifts, early upshifts and clutch slippage during shifting, no upshift, chatter on take-off, 1-2 upshift at full throttle only, no full throttle or part throttle detent downshift, and intermittent second gear starts.

Do not attempt to correct a condition by changing the T.V. cable setting from its proper adjustment. If the T.V. cable adjustment is "tailored" to modify the transmission shift pattern, line pressure may be adversely affected and can cause transmission failure. To diagnose T.V. system related complaints and ensure proper T.V. cable adjustment, proceed as follows:

1. Ensure that the engine and all related systems are in proper operating condition.
2. Inspect the T.V. cable for kinked, binding, disconnected or broken conditions, and replace cable as needed. Also ensure that the proper T.V. cable is installed.
3. Connect suitable line pressure gauge to transmission and connect tachometer to engine.
4. Run engine until it reaches normal operating temperature. Perform the following tests with engine speed at 1000 RPM.
5. Place gear selector in park and record line pressure.
6. Place gear selector in drive and note line pressure reading. Line pressure should be equal to or not more than 10 psi greater than the pressure recorded with selector in park.
7. Manually pull the T.V. cable to its full length, taking care not to increase the throttle opening and note pressure readings.
8. Pressure should gradually increase as the cable is pulled out and gradually decrease as the cable is returned to its original position.
9. Check the T.V system "fail-safe" system by disconnecting the T.V. cable from the throttle lever with the engine running at idle. Line pressure should increase to maximum.
10. Stop engine for at least 30 seconds to take the T.V. system out of the "fail-safe" mode.
11. Connect and adjust the T.V. cable as outlined, then repeat line pressure checks with selector lever in park and drive. Line pressure should return to normal range.
12. If the T.V. system fails to operate as outlined in the preceding tests, check the following components:
   a. Inspect the throttle lever and bracket on the control valve assembly and repair as needed.
   b. Check that the T.V. exhaust valve lifter rod is not distorted or binding in the control valve or spacer plate.
   c. Ensure that the T.V. exhaust check ball moves freely up and down as the lifter is moved.
   d. Ensure that the lifter spring holds the lifter rod against the bottom of the control valve assembly.
   e. Ensure that the T.V. plunger does not stick at any position in its range of travel.

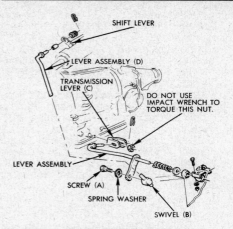

**Fig. 4   Column shift linkage adjustment. 1980–81 C & K models**

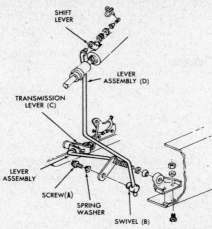

**Fig. 5   Column shift linkage adjustment. 1980–81 P models**

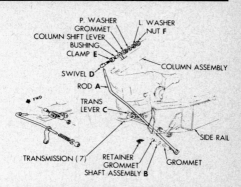

**Fig. 6   Column shift linkage adjustment. 1980–81 G models**

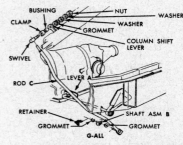

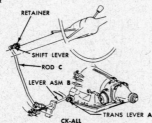

**Fig. 7   Column shift linkage adjustment. 1982–85 C, G & K models**

## MAINTENANCE

Check fluid at regular intervals. Noticing a change in color, odor or fluid level can serve as a warning of possible transmission problems.

Fluid should be checked with engine idling, selector lever in neutral position, parking brake set and transmission at operating temperature. Use only General Motors Dexron transmission fluid when adding oil. Do not overfill.

Under normal service, fluid should be changed every 100,000 miles. If vehicle is operated under severe conditions, such as frequent trailer towing, fluid should be changed at the every 12,000 miles on models with heavy duty emissions and/or diesel engine, or every 15,000 miles on models with light duty emissions.

## IN-VEHICLE ADJUSTMENTS

### SHIFT LINKAGE, ADJUST

#### 1980–81 C, K & P Series

1. Remove screw (A) and spring washer from swivel (B), **Figs. 4 and 5.**
2. Place transmission lever (C) into Neutral position by moving lever counterclockwise to L1 detent, then clockwise 3 detent positions to Neutral.
3. Place transmission selector lever into Neutral.
4. Assemble swivel, spring washer and screw onto shift lever assembly. Tighten screw to 20 ft. lbs.

#### 1980–81 G Series

1. Move transmission lever (C) counterclockwise to L1 detent, then clockwise 3 detent positions to Neutral or obtain Neutral by moving transmission lever (C) clockwise to the Park detent, then counterclockwise 2 detent positions to Neutral, **Fig. 6.**
2. Position column shift lever into Neutral.
3. Connect rod (A) to shaft assembly (B).
4. Slide swivel (D) and clamp (E) onto rod (A).
5. Hold column lever against Neutral stop Park position side.
6. Tighten nut (F) to 18 ft. lbs.

#### 1982–85 C, G & K Series

1. Position transmission shift lever into Neutral by moving shift lever (A) clockwise to the Park detent, then counterclockwise 2 detents to Neutral, **Fig. 7.**
2. Position column shift lever into Neutral.
3. Connect rod (C) to transmission shaft assembly (B).
4. Align column shift lever with transmission shaft assembly (B), then slide swivel and clamp onto rod (C).
5. Hold column lever against Neutral stop Park position side.
6. Tighten nut to 20 ft. lbs.

#### 1986 C, G, K & P Series

1. Loosen nut (11) or screw (17), **Fig. 8,** then place column selector lever in Neutral position.
2. Move shift lever (A) to forward position, then back to second detent (neutral).
3. Hold rod (15) securely in swivel (7), then torque nut or screw to 17 ft. lbs.

#### 1980–81 Caballero & El Camino w/Console Shift

1. Loosen swivel screw so rod is free to move in swivel, **Fig. 9.**
2. Place transmission control lever in Drive and loosen pin in transmission, so it moves in slot.
3. Move transmission lever counterclockwise to L1 detent, then 3 detents clockwise to Drive position. Tighten nut on transmission lever to 20 ft. lbs.
4. Place transmission control lever in Park and ignition switch in the lock position and pull lightly against lock stop, then tighten swivel screw to 20 ft. lbs.

#### 1980–81 Caballero & El Camino w/Column Shift

1. Place transmission lever into Neutral by moving lever counterclockwise to L1 detent, then clockwise 3 detent positions to Neutral.
2. Place selector lever in Neutral as determined by mechanical stop on steering column. Do not use indicator as reference.
3. Assemble swivel, spring washer and screw to lever assembly, then tighten screw to 20 ft. lbs., **Fig. 10.**

#### 1982–84 Caballero & El Camino w/Column Shift

1. Position steering column shift lever into Neutral.
2. Position transmission lever into Neutral.
3. Assemble clamp spring and screw onto equalizer lever and control rod, **Fig. 11.**
4. Hold clamp flush against equalizer lever and finger tighten clamping screw against rod. **No force should be exerted in either direction on rod or equalizer lever while tightening clamping screw.**

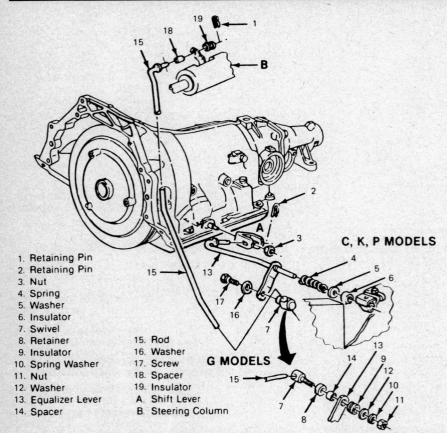

1. Retaining Pin
2. Retaining Pin
3. Nut
4. Spring
5. Washer
6. Insulator
7. Swivel
8. Retainer
9. Insulator
10. Spring Washer
11. Nut
12. Washer
13. Equalizer Lever
14. Spacer
15. Rod
16. Washer
17. Screw
18. Spacer
19. Insulator
A. Shift Lever
B. Steering Column

**Fig. 8 Column shift linkage adjustment. 1986 C, G, K & P models**

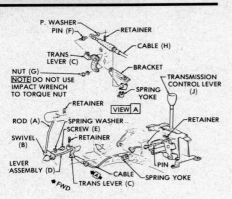

**Fig. 9 Console shift adjustment. 1980–81 Caballero & El Camino**

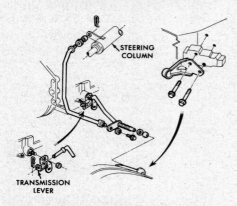

**Fig. 10 Column shift linkage adjustment. 1980–81 Caballero & El Camino**

5. Torque screw to 20 ft. lbs.

## T.V. OR DETENT CABLE, ADJUST

### 1980–81 C, G, K & P SERIES

1. Push up on bottom end of snap lock, then disconnect detent cable, **Figs. 12 and 13.**
2. With snap lock disconnected, cable installed onto support bracket and connected to transmission lever, position carburetor to wide open throttle.
3. With carburetor lever in wide open throttle position, push snap lock downward until snap lock top is flush with cable.

### 1980–84 CABALLERO, EL CAMINO & 1982–86 C, G, K & P MODELS

#### Diesel Engine

1. Remove cruise control rod, if equipped.
2. Disconnect throttle valve linkage from throttle assembly.
3. Loosen locknut on pump rod, then shorten rod by rotating several turns.
4. Rotate throttle lever assembly to full throttle position and secure in this position.
5. Lengthen pump rod by rotating in opposite direction as described in step 3 until injection pump lever contacts full throttle stop.
6. Release throttle lever assembly and

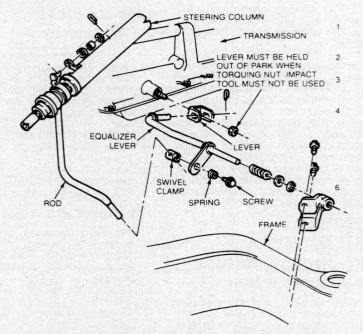

**Fig. 11 Column shift linkage adjustments. 1982–84 Caballero & El Camino models**

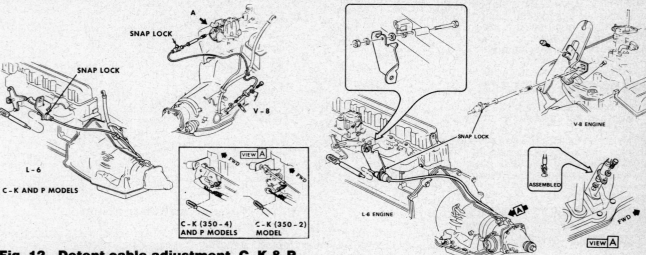

**Fig. 12   Detent cable adjustment. C, K & P models**

**Fig. 13   Detent cable adjustment. G models**

tighten pump rod locknut.
7. Disconnect pump rod from throttle lever assembly.
8. Connect throttle valve linkage to throttle assembly.
9. Depress metal locking tab on upper end of cable and hold in this position.
10. Position slider through fitting and away from lever assembly until slider contacts metal fitting.
11. Release metal tab, then rotate throttle lever assembly to full throttle position and release.
12. Connect pump rod to lever assembly, then connect cruise control throttle rod, if equipped.
13. On models equipped with cruise control, adjust servo throttle rod until minimum amount of slack is present. Install clip into first hole closest to bell crank that is within servo bail.

### Gasoline Engine

1. With engine off, depress locking tab and move slider rearward through fitting until slider contacts fitting, **Fig. 14**.
2. Release locking tab, then move carburetor throttle lever to wide open position and release.
3. Check cable for sticking or binding, then test vehicle for proper operation.
4. If transmission does not shift properly, refer to "Throttle Valve System Diagnosis."

## INTERMEDIATE BAND, ADJUST

### Turbo Hydra-Matic 250

The Turbo Hydra-Matic 250 transmission uses an intermediate band instead of a clutch to control the operation of the planetary gear sets. To adjust the intermediate band proceed as follows:
1. Loosen adjusting screw locknut, located on case right side, 1/2 turn.
2. Torque adjusting screw to 30 inch pounds, then back off screw 3 turns.
3. Torque adjusting screw locknut to 15 foot pounds while holding adjusting screw in position.

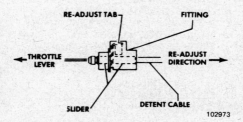

**Fig. 14   Self adjusting T.V. cable. Gasoline engine models**

## TORQUE CONVERTER CLUTCH SWITCH ADJUSTMENTS

### T.H.M. 250C & 350C

### Low Vacuum Switch

1. Disconnect vacuum and electrical connectors from low vacuum switch, **Fig. 15**.
2. Connect a suitable test light to either terminal of vacuum switch. Connect a suitable jumper cable from the other terminal to a good ground.
3. Connect remaining lead of test light to power side of removed vacuum switch connector.
4. Attach suitable vacuum pump to vacuum port of switch.
5. Turn ignition on, then actuate vacuum pump. On V6 engines, test light should remain off until vacuum gauge reads 5.5-6.5 inches Hg. On V8 gas engines, test light should remain off until vacuum gauge reads 7.5-8.5 inches Hg. On V8 diesel engines, test light should remain off until vacuum gauge reads 5-6 inches Hg.
6. Decrease vacuum slowly. Light should remain on until vacuum drops to .3-1.3 inches Hg on V6 engines, 1.5-2.5 inches Hg on V8 gas engines and 3.5-4.5 inches Hg on V8 diesel engines. Decreasing vacuum beyond above value should cause light to go

out.
7. Ensure that there is at least 4 inches Hg difference between the point at which light comes on and the point at which light goes out.
8. If above results cannot be obtained, switch is defective and must be replaced.

### High Vacuum Switch

The high vacuum switch must be adjusted anytime the throttle rod, transmission vacuum valve and high idle speed adjustments are changed.
1. Disconnect high vacuum switch electrical connector, **Fig. 15**.
2. Connect the leads of a suitable test light across the terminals of the high vacuum switch.
3. Energize fast idle solenoid by disconnecting pink and green wire from coolant switch and operate engine at high idle speed, then remove cap from back of high vacuum switch.
4. Before adjustment is performed, the test light must be on, indicating that the switch contacts are closed. If test light is off, close the switch contacts by turning switch adjusting screw clockwise until contacts close.
5. Adjust vacuum switch by turning adjusting screw counterclockwise until switch contact just opens and test light goes off. Turn adjusting screw counterclockwise an additional 1/8-3/16 turn.
6. Reinstall cap on back of vacuum switch and reconnect high vacuum switch and coolant switch electrical connectors.

## IN-VEHICLE REPAIRS

## VALVE BODY ASSEMBLY, REPLACE

1. Remove oil pan and strainer.
2. Remove retaining pin to disconnect downshift actuating lever bracket, remove valve body attaching bolts and detent roller and spring assembly.

3. Remove valve body assembly while disconnecting manual control valve link from range selector inner lever. **Do not drop valve.**
4. Remove manual valve and link from valve body assembly.
5. Reverse procedure to install.

## GOVERNOR, REPLACE

1. Where necessary, remove shift linkage and transmission to crossmember bolts.
2. Raise transmission with jack and remove crossmember. Lower transmission enough to remove governor.
3. Remove governor cover retainer and cover.
4. Remove governor.

## INTERMEDIATE CLUTCH ACCUMULATOR PISTON ASSEMBLY, REPLACE

1. Remove two oil pan bolts adjacent to accumulator piston cover, install compressor on oil pan lip and retain with these two bolts.
2. Compress intermediate clutch accumulator piston cover and remove retaining ring piston cover and O-ring from case.
3. Remove spring and intermediate clutch accumulator piston.

## VACUUM MODULATOR & MODULATOR VALVE ASSEMBLY, REPLACE

1. Disconnect vacuum hose from modulator stem and remove vacuum modulator screw and retainer.
2. Remove modulator and its O-ring.
3. Remove modulator valve from case.

## EXTENSION HOUSING OIL SEAL & BUSHING, REPLACE

1. Remove propeller shaft.
2. Pry out lip seal with screwdriver or small chisel.
3. Remove and install slip yoke bushing using suitable tool. Tool sets depth of bushing in extension housing.
4. Install replacement seal with suitable driver and coat seal lip with grease.

## MANUAL SHAFT, RANGE SELECTOR INNER LEVER & PARKING LINKAGE ASSEMBLIES, REPLACE

1. Remove oil pan and strainer.
2. Remove manual shaft to case retainer and unthread jam nut holding range selector inner lever to manual shaft.
3. Remove jam nut and remove manual shaft from range selector inner lever and case. Do not remove manual shaft lip seal unless replacement is

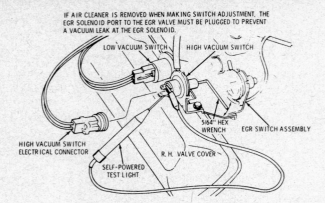

IF AIR CLEANER IS REMOVED WHEN MAKING SWITCH ADJUSTMENT, THE EGR SOLENOID PORT TO THE EGR VALVE MUST BE PLUGGED TO PREVENT A VACUUM LEAK AT THE EGR SOLENOID.

LOW VACUUM SWITCH — HIGH VACUUM SWITCH

5/64" HEX WRENCH — EGR SWITCH ASSEMBLY

HIGH VACUUM SWITCH ELECTRICAL CONNECTOR

SELF-POWERED TEST LIGHT

R.H. VALVE COVER

**Fig. 15   Vacuum switch location**

required.
4. Disconnect parking pawl actuating rod from range selector inner lever and remove bolt from case.
5. Remove bolts and parking lock bracket.
6. Remove pawl disengaging spring.
7. If necessary to replace pawl or shaft, clean up bore in case and remove shaft retaining plug, shaft and pawl.

## TRANSMISSION
### REPLACE
#### 4 x 2 MODELS

1. Disconnect battery ground cable.
2. Remove air cleaner assembly from engine.
3. Disconnect T.V. or detent cable from throttle lever.
4. Remove transmission oil dipstick tube.
5. Raise and support vehicle.
6. Disconnect propeller shaft and shift linkage from transmission.
7. Disconnect speedometer cable and electrical connectors from transmission.
8. Remove transmission braces and flywheel cover.
9. Mark flywheel and torque converter for installation.
10. Remove torque converter to flywheel bolts and/or nuts.
11. Remove catalytic converter support bracket, if equipped.
12. Remove transmission mount attaching bolts.
13. Position a suitable jack under transmission, then raise transmission slightly.
14. Remove transmission crossmember to frame attaching bolts, then slide crossmember rearward from vehicle.
15. Lower transmission, then disconnect

fluid cooler lines, T.V. or detent cable from transmission.
16. Position a suitable jack under engine, then remove transmission to engine attaching bolts.
17. Carefully separate transmission from engine.
18. Install torque converter holding tool No. J-21366 or equivalent, and remove transmission from vehicle.
19. Reverse procedure to install.

#### 4 x 4 MODELS

1. Disconnect battery ground cable.
2. Remove air cleaner assembly from engine.
3. Disconnect T.V. or detent cable at upper end.
4. Remove transfer case shift lever knob and boot.
5. Raise and support vehicle.
6. Remove propeller shafts from vehicle.
7. Disconnect speedometer cable.
8. Disconnect electrical connectors from transmission and transfer case.
9. Disconnect shift linkage assemblies from transmission and transfer case.
10. Remove transmission support strut rods and flywheel cover.
11. Mark torque converter and flywheel for installation.
12. Remove torque converter to flywheel attaching bolts and/or nuts.
13. Disconnect transmission fluid cooler lines from transmission.
14. Position a suitable jack under transmission and transfer case assemblies.
15. Remove transfer case to frame bracket attaching bolts.
16. Remove crossmember mounting bolts, then the crossmember from vehicle.
17. Remove transmission to engine attaching bolts.
18. Carefully separate transmission and transfer case assembly from engine and remove from vehicle.
19. Reverse procedure to install.

# Turbo Hydra-Matic 400 (3L80) & 475 (3L80-HD) Automatic Transmission

## INDEX

## DESCRIPTION

This transmission, **Fig. 1,** is a fully automatic unit consisting primarily of a three element hydraulic torque converter and a compound planetary gear set. Three multiple disc clutches, two one-way clutches, and two bands provide the friction elements required to obtain the desired functions of the planetary gear set. The two one-way clutches, each consist of two roller clutches.

The torque converter, the multiple disc clutches and the one-way clutches couple the engine to the planetary gears through oil pressure, providing three forward speeds and reverse. The torque converter, when required, supplements the gears by multiplying engine torque.

### TORQUE CONVERTER

The torque converter is of welded construction and is serviced as an assembly. The unit is made up of two vained sections, or halves, that face each other in an oil filled housing. The pump half of the converter is connected to the engine and the turbine half is connected to the transmission.

When the engine makes the converter pump revolve, it sends oil against the turbine, making it revolve also. The oil then returns in a circular flow back to the converter pump, continuing this flow as long as the engine is running.

### STATOR

The convertor also has a smaller vained section, called a stator, that funnels the oil back to the converter pump through smaller openings, at increased speed. The speeded up oil directs additional force to the engine driven converter pump, thereby multiplying engine torque. Without the sta-

tor, the torque converter would only provide a fluid coupling.

## TROUBLESHOOTING

### OIL PRESSURE HIGH

1. Vacuum line or fittings clogged or leaking.
2. Improper engine vacuum.
3. Vacuum leak in vacuum operated accessory.
4. Vacuum modulator.
5. Modulator valve.
6. Water in modulator.
7. Pressure regulator.
8. Oil pump.
9. Governor.
10. Malfunction in detent downshift system. Check for shorted detent wiring, detent solenoid stuck open, detent feed orifice in spacer plate blocked or restricted, loose detent solenoid, damaged detent valve bore plug or detent regulator valve pin too short.

### OIL PRESSURE LOW

1. Low oil level.
2. Defective vacuum modulator.
3. Filter blocked or restricted, or incorrect filter assembly.
4. O-ring seal on intake pipe and/or grommet omitted or damaged.
5. Split or leaking oil intake pipe.
6. Malfunction in oil pump. Check for stuck pressure regulator and/or boost valve, weak pressure regulator valve spring, insufficient spacers in pressure regulator, excessive gear clearance, gears damaged, worn or incorrectly installed, pump cover gasket improperly positioned or defective, or mismatched pump body and pump cover.

7. Internal circuit leakage.
8. Case porosity.
9. Intermediate clutch cup plug leaking or improperly positioned.
10. Low-reverse check ball improperly positioned or missing. This will cause no reverse and no overrun braking in low range.

### NO DRIVE IN DRIVE RANGE

1. Low oil level (check for leaks).
2. Manual control linkage not adjusted properly.
3. Low oil pressure. Check for blocked strainer, defective pressure regulator, pump assembly or pump drive gear. Ensure tangs have not been damaged by converter.
4. Check control valve assembly to see if manual valve has been disconnected from manual lever pin.
5. Forward clutch may be stuck or damaged. Check pump feed circuits to forward clutch, including clutch drum ball check.
6. Roller clutch assembled incorrectly.

### 1-2 SHIFT AT FULL THROTTLE ONLY

1. Detent switch sticking or defective.
2. Detent solenoid may be stuck open, loose or have leaking gasket.
3. Control valve assembly may be leaking, damaged or incorrectly installed.
4. 3-2 shift valve stuck.
5. Case porous.

### 1ST SPEED ONLY—NO 1-2 SHIFT

1. Governor valve sticking.
2. Driven gear in governor assembly loose, worn or damaged.

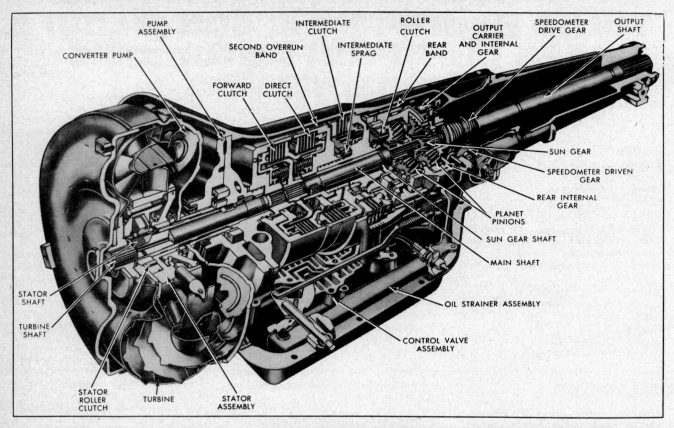

**Fig. 1   Cutaway view of Turbo Hydra-Matic 400 (3L80) & 475 (3L80-HD) automatic transmission**

3. The 1-2 shift valve in control valve assembly stuck closed. Check governor feed channels for blocks, leaks, and position. Also check control valve body gaskets for leaks and damage.
4. Intermediate clutch plug in case may be leaking or blown out.
5. Check for porosity between channels and for blocked governor feed channels in case.
6. Center support oil rings missing, or damaged. Orifice plug missing.
7. Intermediate clutch piston seals missing, incorrectly installed or damaged.

## NO 2-3 SHIFT—1ST & 2ND ONLY

1. Detent solenoid may be stuck open.
2. Detent switch improperly adjusted.
3. Control valve assembly may be stuck, leaking, damaged, or incorrectly installed.
4. Control valve body gaskets leaking, damaged or incorrectly installed.
5. Check direct clutch case center support for broken, leaking or missing oil rings.
6. Check clutch piston seals and piston ball check in clutch assembly.

## MOVES FORWARD IN NEUTRAL

1. Manual control linkage improperly adjusted.
2. Manual valve disconnected or broken.
3. Inside detent lever pin broken.

4. Transmission oil pressure leaking into forward clutch apply passage.
5. Burned forward clutch plates.
6. Forward clutch does not release.

## NO MOVEMENT IN REVERSE OR SLIPS IN REVERSE

1. Check oil level.
2. Manual control linkage improperly adjusted.
3. Vacuum modulator assembly may be defective.
4. Vacuum modulator valve sticking.
5. Strainer may be restricted or leaking at intake.
6. Regulator or boost valve in pump assembly may be sticking.
7. Low oil pressure.
8. Rear servo and accumulator may have damaged or missing servo piston seal ring.
9. Reverse band burned out or damaged. Determine that apply pin or anchor pins engage properly.
10. Direct clutch may be damaged or may have stuck ball check in piston.
11. Forward clutch does not release.
12. Low-reverse ball check missing from case.
13. Control valve body malfunctioning. Check for leaking, damaged or incorrectly installed gaskets, 2-3 shift valve stuck open, or restricted reverse feed passage.

## SLIPS IN ALL RANGES & ON STARTS

1. Check oil level.
2. Vacuum modulator defective.
3. Modulator valve sticking.
4. Strainer assembly plugged or leaking at neck.
5. Pump assembly regulator or boost valve sticking.
6. Leaks from damaged gaskets or cross leaks from porosity of case.
7. Forward and direct clutches burned.
8. Low oil pressure.

## SLIPS 1-2 SHIFT

1. Incorrect oil level.
2. Vacuum modulator valve sticking.
3. Vacuum modulator defective.
4. Pump pressure regulator valve defective.
5. Porosity between channels in case.
6. Control valve assembly.
7. Pump to case gasket improperly positioned.
8. Intermediate clutch plug in case missing or leaking excessively.
9. Intermediate clutch piston seal missing or damaged.
10. Intermediate clutch plates burned.
11. Front or rear accumulator oil ring damaged.
12. Leak in center support feed circuit, excessive leak between center support tower and bushing, blocked center support orifice bleed plug hole, center

support bolt not properly seated.
13. Raised ridge around case center support bolt not allowing control valve assembly to seat properly.
14. Low oil pressure.

## SLIPS 2-3 SHIFT

1. Items 1 through 6 under Slips 1-2 Shift will also cause 2-3 shift slips.
2. Direct clutch plates burned.
3. Oil seal rings on direct clutch damaged, permitting excessive leaking between tower and bushing.

## ROUGH 1-2 SHIFT

1. Modulator valve sticking.
2. Modulator assembly defective.
3. Pump pressure regulator or boost valve stuck or inoperative.
4. Control valve assembly loosened from case, damaged or mounted with wrong gaskets.
5. Intermediate clutch ball missing or not sealing.
6. Porosity between channels in case.
7. Rear servo accumulator assembly may have oil rings damaged, stuck piston, broken or missing spring or damaged bore.

## ROUGH 2-3 SHIFT

1. Items 1, 2 and 3 under Rough 1-2 Shift will also cause rough 2-3 shift.
2. Front servo accumulator spring broken or missing. Accumulator piston may be sticking.

## NO ENGINE BRAKING IN 2ND SPEED

THM 400 (3L80)/475 (3L80-HD) transmissions contain a plastic front accumulator piston, if broken or cracked, can cause a no engine braking in drive 2 (D2) condition. The piston should be replaced with an aluminum front accumulator piston, part number 8626883.

1. Front servo or accumulator oil rings leaking.
2. Front band broken or burned.
3. Front band not engaged on anchor pin and/or servo pin.

## NO ENGINE BRAKING IN LOW RANGE

1. Low-reverse check ball may be missing from control valve assembly.
2. Rear servo may have damaged oil seal ring, bore or piston; leaking, apply pressure.
3. Rear band broken, burned or not engaged on anchor pins or servo pin.

## NO PART THROTTLE DOWNSHIFTS

1. Vacuum modulator assembly.
2. Modulator valve.
3. Regulator valve train.
4. Control valve assembly has stuck 3-2 valve or broken spring.

## NO DETENT DOWNSHIFTS

1. Detent switch needs fuse, connections tightened or adjustment.
2. Detent solenoid may be inoperative.
3. Detent valve train in control valve assembly malfunctioning.

## LOW OR HIGH SHIFT POINTS

1. Oil pressure. Check vacuum modulator assembly, vacuum line connections, modulator valve, and pressure regulator valve train.
2. Governor may have sticking valve or feed holes that are leaking, plugged or damaged.
3. Detent solenoid may be stuck open or loose.
4. Control valve assembly. Check detent, 3-2, and 1-2 shift valve trains, and check spacer plate gaskets for positioning.
5. Check case for porosity, missing or leaking intermediate plug.

## WIll Not HOLD IN PARK

1. Manual control linkage improperly adjusted.
2. Internal linkage defective; check for chamfer on actuator rod sleeve.
3. Parking pawl broken or inoperative.
4. Parking pawl return spring missing, broken or incorrectly installed.

## NOISY TRANSMISSION

1. Pump noises caused by high or low oil level.
2. Cavitation due to plugged strainer, porosity in intake circuit or water in oil.
3. Pump gears damaged.
4. Gear noise in low gear of drive range—transmission grounded to body.
5. Defective planetary gear set.
6. Clutch noises during application can be worn or burned clutch plates.

## FORWARD CLUTCH PLATES BURNED

1. Check ball in clutch housing damaged, stuck or missing.
2. Clutch piston cracked, seals damaged or missing.
3. Low line pressure.
4. Manual valve improperly positioned.
5. Restricted oil feed to forward clutch.
6. Pump cover oil seal rings missing, broken or undersize; ring groove oversize.
7. Case valve body face not flat or porosity between channels.
8. Manual valve bent and center land not properly ground.

## INTERMEDIATE CLUTCH PLATES BURNED

1. Constant bleed orifice in center support missing.
2. Rear accumulator piston oil ring damaged or missing.
3. 1-2 accumulator valve stuck in control valve assembly.
4. Intermediate clutch piston seal damaged or missing.
5. Center support bolt loose.
6. Low line pressure.
7. Intermediate clutch plug in case missing.
8. Case valve body face not flat or porosity between channels.
9. Manual valve bent and center land not ground properly.

## DIRECT CLUTCH PLATES BURNED

1. Restricted orifice in vacuum line to modulator.
2. Check ball in direct clutch piston damaged, stuck or missing.
3. Defective modulator bellows.
4. Center support bolt loose.
5. Center support oil rings or grooves damaged or missing.
6. Clutch piston seals damaged or missing.
7. Front and rear servo pistons and seals damaged.
8. Manual valve bent and center land not cleaned up.
9. Case valve body face not flat or porosity between channels.
10. Intermediate sprag clutch installed backwards.
11. 3-2 valve, 3-2 spring or 3-2 spacer pin installed in wrong location in 3-2 valve bore.

## MAINTENANCE
### CHECKING & ADDING FLUID

Check fluid at regular intervals. Noticing a change in color, odor or fluid level can serve as a warning of possible transmission problems.

To check fluid level, bring fluid to operating temperature of 200°F. With vehicle on a level surface, engine idling in park and parking brake applied, the level on the dipstick should be at the Full mark. To bring the fluid level from the Add mark to the Full mark requires one pint of fluid. If additional fluid is required, use only Dexron II automatic transmission fluid. When adding fluid, do not overfill, as foaming and loss of fluid through the vent may occur as the fluid heats up. Also, If fluid level is too low, complete loss of drive may occur especially when cold, Which can cause transmission failure.

The drain interval is 100,000 miles under normal service and 15,000 miles under severe operating conditions on light duty emissions vehicles, or 12,000 miles on diesel and/or heavy duty emissions vehicles.

### CHANGING FLUID

1. Raise and support vehicle.
2. Place a suitable container under transmission oil pan, then remove attaching bolts from front and sides of oil pan.
3. Loosen rear attaching bolts approximately four turns, then carefully pry oil pan loose and allow fluid to drain.
4. Remove remaining bolts and separate oil pan from transmission.
5. Drain remaining fluid from pan, then clean pan and gasket surfaces with a suitable solvent and thoroughly dry with compressed air.
6. On 1980-81 vehicles, remove oil filter and the O-ring from intake pipe. Install new O-ring and filter, then torque filter retaining bolt to 10 ft. lbs.
7. On 1982-88 vehicles, remove screen/filter, gasket and intake pipe.

Clean screen in solvent and dry with compressed air. If applicable, paper or felt filter should be replaced. Install screen/filter assembly, using a new intake pipe O-ring, and torque retaining bolt to 10 ft. lbs.

8. On 1989 vehicles, remove the filter, spacer and intake pipe. Install filter assembly with spacer, using a new intake pipe O-ring and torque retaining bolt to 8 ft. lbs.
9. Install oil pan with a new gasket. Torque attaching bolts to 12 ft. lbs.
10. Lower vehicle and add 5 pints of Dexron II or equivalent transmission fluid through filler tube.
11. With transmission in Park, start engine and run at idle.
12. With brakes applied, Move transmission through each gear range and return to Park position, then recheck fluid level. Add additional fluid to bring level to full mark on dipstick.

## ADDING FLUID TO FILL DRY TRANSMISSION & CONVERTER

1. Add 9 pints of transmission fluid through filler tube.
2. Start engine and let run at fast idle in Park.
3. Return engine speed to idle. With brakes applied, move transmission lever through each gear range then return to park.
4. After 1-3 minutes of idle operation with transmission in Park, recheck fluid level. Add additional fluid to bring level to Full mark on dipstick.

# IN-VEHICLE ADJUSTMENTS

## SHIFT LINKAGE, ADJUST

### 1980-81 Models

1. Loosen shift rod clamp nut.
2. Remove screw (A) and spring washer from swivel (B), **Figs. 2 and 3.**
3. Place transmission lever (C) into neutral by moving lever counterclockwise to L1 detent, then clockwise 3 detent positions to neutral.
4. Position transmission selector lever into neutral as determined by mechanical stop in steering column assembly. Do not use indicator pointer as a reference to position selector lever into neutral.
5. Assemble swivel, spring washer and screw to lever assembly (D). Tighten screw to 20 ft. lbs.

### 1982-85 Models

1. Loosen shift rod clamp nut.
2. Place transmission lever (A) into neutral by moving lever (A) clockwise to the park detent, then counterclockwise 2 detent positions into neutral.
3. Place column shift lever rod (C) into Neutral, **Fig. 4.** Do not use indicator pointer as a reference to position selector lever into neutral.
4. Connect rod (C) onto transmission shaft lever assembly (B).
5. Slide swivel and clamp onto rod (C).

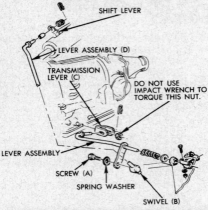

**Fig. 2 Column shift linkage adjustment. 1980-81 C & K models**

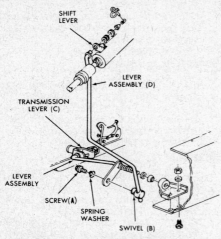

**Fig. 3 Column shift linkage adjustment. 1980-81 P models**

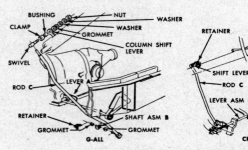

**Fig. 4 Column shift linkage adjustment. 1982-85 models**

6. Hold column lever against neutral stop on the park position side.
7. Tighten nut to 20 ft. lbs.

### 1986-89 Models Exc. 1988-89 C & K Series

1. Loosen nut (11) or screw (17), **Fig. 5,** then place column selector lever in neutral position.
2. Move shift lever (A) to forward position, then back to second detent (neutral).
3. Hold rod (15) securely in swivel (7), then torque nut or screw to 17 ft. lbs.

### 1988-89 C & K Series

1. Apply parking brake, then loosen screw securing selector rod in clamp at lower steering column lever, **Fig. 6.**
2. Place column selector lever in neutral position, using shifter gate to find position. Do not use shift indicator to find neutral position.
3. Place column selector manual lever in neutral by pushing lever fully forward to park stop, then pushing lever back 2 detents into neutral position.
4. Hold selector rod and swivel securely to prevent them from moving out of position, then torque retaining screw to 17 ft. lbs.
5. Place column selector lever in park, then check adjustment as follows:
   a. Ensure column selector moves into all positions.
   b. Ensure starter engages in neutral and park only. Check and adjust neutral safety switch, as needed.
   c. Ensure that parking pawl freely engages the reaction internal gear lugs or output ring gear lugs when column selector lever is moved into park position.

## DOWNSHIFT SWITCH

### C, G, K & P Series

All except 1988-89 models with diesel engine, or 1989 models with throttle body injection, install switch as shown in **Fig. 7.** After installing switch, press switch plunger as far forward as possible. This switch will then adjust itself the first time the accelerator pedal is pushed to the floor.

On 1988-89 models with diesel engines, the detent downshift switch is part of the vacuum regulator valve.

On 1989 models with throttle body injection, the detent downshift is controlled by the ECM.

# IN-VEHICLE REPAIRS

## PRESSURE REGULATOR VALVE, REPLACE

A solid type pressure regulator valve must be used only in a pump cover with a

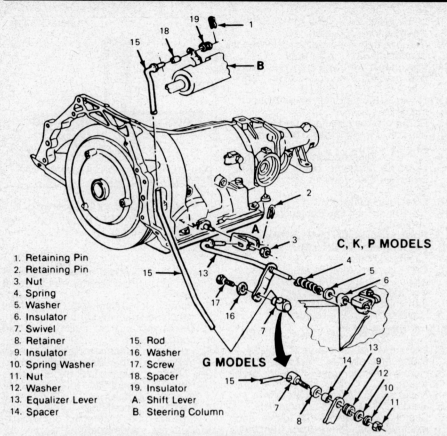

**Fig. 5   Column shift linkage adjustment. 1986–89 models exc. 1988–89 C & K Series**

1. Retaining Pin
2. Retaining Pin
3. Nut
4. Spring
5. Washer
6. Insulator
7. Swivel
8. Retainer
9. Insulator
10. Spring Washer
11. Nut
12. Washer
13. Equalizer Lever
14. Spacer
15. Rod
16. Washer
17. Screw
18. Spacer
19. Insulator
A. Shift Lever
B. Steering Column

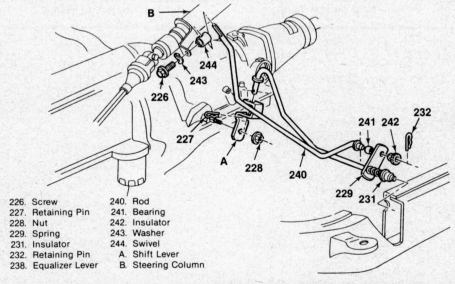

**Fig. 6   Column shift linkage adjustment. 1988–89 C & K Series**

226. Screw
227. Retaining Pin
228. Nut
229. Spring
231. Insulator
232. Retaining Pin
238. Equalizer Lever
240. Rod
241. Bearing
242. Insulator
243. Washer
244. Swivel
A. Shift Lever
B. Steering Column

"squared off" (machined) pressure regulator boss, **Fig. 8.** A pressure regulator valve with oil holes and an orifice cup plug may be used with either type pump.

1. Remove bottom pan and strainer.
2. Using a screwdriver or steel rod, compress regulator boost valve bushing against pressure regulator spring, re-

move snap ring, then gradually release pressure on valve bushing until spring tension is released. **Pressure regulator spring is under extreme pressure and will force bushing out of bore when snap ring is removed if bushing is not held securely.**

3. Carefully remove regulator boost valve bushing and valve, and pressure regulator spring. Be careful not to drop parts as they will fall out if they are not held.
4. Remove pressure regulator valve, spring retainer and spacers, as equipped.
5. Reverse procedure to install.

## CONTROL VALVE BODY, REPLACE

1. Remove bottom pan and strainer.
2. Disconnect pressure switch lead wire.
3. Remove control valve body attaching screws and detent roller spring assembly. Do not remove solenoid attaching screws.
4. Remove control valve body and governor pipes. If care is used in removing control valve body, the six check balls will stay in place above spacer plate.
5. Remove governor pipes and manual valve from control valve body.
6. Reverse procedure to install.

## GOVERNOR, REPLACE

1. Remove governor cover and discard gasket.
2. Withdraw governor from case.
3. Reverse procedure to install, using a new gasket.

## MODULATOR & MODULATOR VALVE, REPLACE

1. Remove modulator attaching screw and retainer.
2. Remove modulator assembly from case and discard O-ring seal.
3. Remove modulator valve from case.
4. Reverse procedure to install, using a new O-ring seal.

## PARKING LINKAGE, REPLACE

1. Remove bottom pan and oil strainer.
2. Unthread jam nut holding detent lever to manual shaft.
3. Remove manual shaft retaining pin from case.
4. Remove manual shaft and jam nut from case.
5. Remove O-ring seal from manual shaft.
6. Remove parking actuator rod and detent lever assembly.
7. Remove parking pawl bracket, pawl return spring and pawl shaft retainer.
8. Remove parking pawl shaft, O-ring seal and parking pawl.
9. Reverse procedure to install, using new seals and gasket.

## REAR SEAL, REPLACE

1. Remove propeller shaft.
2. Pry out seal with screwdriver.
3. Install new seal with a suitable seal driver.
4. Install propeller shaft.

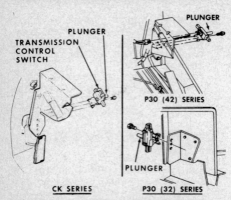

**Fig. 7   Detent switch location. Exc. 1988–89 models w/diesel engine and throttle body injection**

# TRANSMISSION
## REPLACE
### 4 X 2 MODELS

1. Disconnect battery ground cable.
2. Remove air cleaner assembly.
3. Remove transmission fluid dipstick tube.
4. Raise and support vehicle.
5. Remove drive shaft from vehicle.
6. Disconnect speedometer cable and electrical connectors from transmission.
7. Disconnect shift linkage assembly from transmission.
8. Remove transmission support braces and flywheel cover.

9. Mark position of torque converter and flywheel for installation.
10. Remove torque converter to flywheel attaching bolts and/or nuts.
11. Disconnect catalytic converter support bracket, if equipped from transmission.
12. Remove transmission mount attaching bolts.
13. Position a suitable jack under transmission, then raise transmission slightly.
14. Remove transmission crossmember to frame attaching bolts, then slide crossmember rearward and out of vehicle.
15. Lower transmission.
16. Disconnect and cap transmission fluid cooler lines.
17. Position a suitable jack under engine, then remove transmission to engine attaching bolts.
18. Carefully separate transmission from engine. Install torque converter holding tool No. J-21366 and remove transmission from vehicle.
19. Reverse procedure to install.

### 4 X 4 MODELS

1. Disconnect battery ground cable.
2. Remove air cleaner assembly.
3. Remove transfer case shift lever knob and boot.
4. Raise and support vehicle.
5. Remove drive shafts from vehicle.
6. Disconnect speedometer cable and electrical connectors from transmission.
7. Disconnect shift linkage assembly from transfer case.
8. Remove transmission support strut

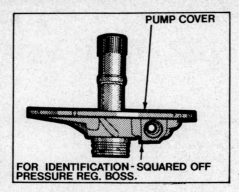

**Fig. 8   Solid type pressure regulator**

rods and flywheel cover. Mark position of torque converter and flywheel for installation.
9. Remove torque converter to flywheel attaching bolts/and or nuts.
10. Disconnect and cap transmission fluid cooler lines.
11. Position a suitable jack under transmission and transfer case assembly.
12. Position a suitable jack under engine.
13. Remove transfer case to frame bracket attaching bolts.
14. Remove mounting bolts and crossmember assembly from vehicle.
15. Remove transmission to engine attaching bolts, then carefully separate transmission from engine.
16. Remove transmission from vehicle.
17. Reverse procedure to install.

# Turbo Hydra-Matic 700-R4 (4L-60) Automatic Transmission

## INDEX

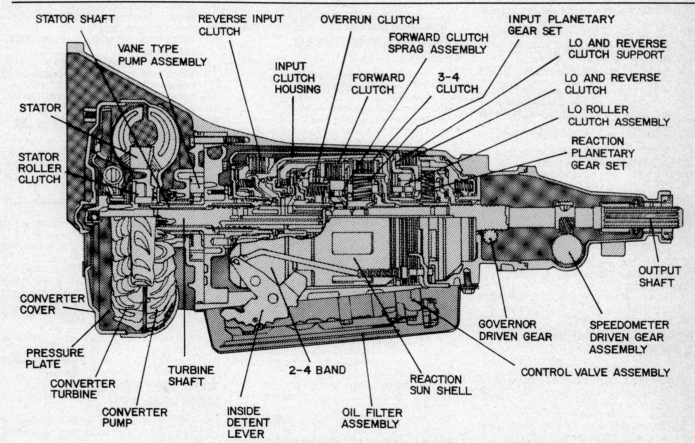

**Fig. 1  Sectional view of Turbo Hydra-Matic 700-R4 (4L-60) automatic transmission**

## DESCRIPTION

The model 700-R4 (4L-60) **Fig. 1**, is fully automatic transmission consisting of a 3-element hydraulic torque converter with the addition of a converter clutch, Two planetary gear sets, five multiple disc type clutches, two roller or one-way clutches and a band are used to provide the friction elements which produce four forward speeds, the last of which is overdrive. A hydraulic system pressurized by a variable capacity vane type pump provides the pressure required for the operation of the friction elements and automatic controls. The gear ratio changes are fully automatic in relation to the vehicle speed and engine torque. Vehicle speed and engine torque are directed to the transmission providing the proper gear ratio for maximum efficiency and performance at all throttle openings.

The torque converter hydraulically couples the engine power to the gear sets and provides additional torque multiplication whenever the converter clutch operates in the unlocked mode. The converter clutch, **Fig. 2**, allows converter drive and driven members to operate as one unit when applied, providing a mechanical coupling between the engine and transmission.

## TROUBLESHOOTING

Always check oil level, T.V. cable and oil pressure prior to following trouble shooting procedures.

### OIL PRESSURE HIGH OR LOW

1. Improperly adjusted or malfunctioning T.V. system. Refer to "Throttle Valve System Diagnosis."
2. Pump pressure regulator valve binding, dirty or damaged spring.
3. T.V. and reverse boost plug and bushing are dirty, sticking, damaged or incorrectly assembled.
4. Pump assembly pressure relief ball not seated or damaged.
5. Pump assembly slide sticking.
6. Pump assembly not regulating.
7. Excess rotor clearance in pump assembly.
8. Manual valve not engaged or damaged.
9. T.V. exhaust valve binding or damaged.
10. Throttle lever and bracket assembly, improperly assembled, binding, damaged or check valve missing.
11. Valve body throttle valve or plunger sticking.
12. Valve body T.V. limit valve sticking.
13. Throttle link, not engaged, damaged, incorrect, burr on upper end or hanging on T.V. sleeve.
14. Filter, restricted, has missing O-ring or hole in intake pipe.

### HIGH OR LOW SHIFT POINTS

1. T.V. cable binding or not adjusted properly.
2. Improper external linkage travel.
3. Binding throttle valve or plunger.
4. T.V. modulator up or down valve sticking.
5. Valve body gaskets or spacer plate improperly positioned or damaged.
6. T.V. limit valve sticking.
7. Pump assembly, sticking pressure regulator valve, T.V. boost valve.
8. Pump slide sticking.

### FIRST SPEED ONLY—NO UPSHIFT

1. Sticking governor valve.
2. Governor driven gear is damaged.
3. Governor driven gear retainer pin missing.
4. Nicks or burrs on output shaft.
5. Correct governor retainer pin in case (longer or shorter).
6. Burrs on governor sleeve.
7. Burrs on governor case.
8. Governor weights and springs damaged.
9. 1-2 shaft valve sticking.
10. Valve body gaskets or spacer plate are improperly positioned.
11. Valve body pad—porosity and or damaged lands.
12. Restricted or damaged governor screen.
13. 2-4 servo apply passages, servo apply pin and pin hole in case, restricted or damaged.

14. Damaged or missing servo piston seals.
15. 2-4 band assembly burned, band anchor pin not engaged.
16. 2-4 band assembly apply end broken.

### SLIPS IN FIRST GEAR

1. Forward clutch plates burned.
2. Porosity—forward clutch piston.
3. Forward clutch seals, cut or damaged.
4. Damaged forward clutch housing.
5. Forward clutch internal leak.
6. Forward clutch housing check ball damage.
7. Low oil or oil pressure.
8. Accumulator valve sticking.
9. Valve body lands or interconnected passages damaged.
10. Valve body gasket, spacer plate damaged or improperly positioned.
11. Binding internal T.V. linkage.
12. 1-2 accumulator piston assembly, piston or bore porous.
13. 1-2 accumulator piston assembly seals, cut or damaged.
14. Leak between piston and pin.
15. Missing or broken accumulator spring.

### 1-2 FULL THROTTLE SHIFTS ONLY

1. T.V. cable not connected.
2. T.V. cable too long or short.
3. Throttle lever bracket assembly improperly assembled or binding.
4. Missing exhaust check valve.
5. Throttle link not connected, burr on upper end or hanging on T.V. sleeve.
6. Throttle valve or plunger hanging or sticking in full open position.
7. Inter connected passages—pump, case or valve body restricted or damaged.

### SLIPPING OR ROUGH 1-2 SHIFT

1. Throttle lever and bracket assembly, damaged or incorrectly installed.
2. Throttle valve or bushing, sticking.
3. Sticking 1-2 shift valve train.
4. Valve body gasket or spacer plate, improperly positioned.
5. Sticking line bias valve.
6. Sticking accumulator valve.
7. Sticking T.V. limit valve.
8. Incorrect 2-4 servo apply pin.
9. 2-4 servo oil seal rings or seals, damaged.
10. 2-4 servo bores, damaged.
11. 2-4 servo oil passages, restricted or missing.
12. 2nd accumulator piston seal, damaged.
13. Accumulator spring, missing.
14. 2nd accumulator bores, damaged.
15. 2nd accumulator piston, porous.
16. 2nd accumulator oil passages, restricted or missing.
17. Burned 2-4 band.

### SLIPPING OR ROUGH 2-3 SHIFT

1. 2-3 shift valve train sticking.
2. Accumulator valve sticking.
3. Valve body gasket or spacer plate improperly positioned.
4. Throttle valve sticking.

5. T.V. limit valve sticking.
6. 3-4 clutch plates burned or excessive clutch plate travel.
7. 3-4 piston seals, cut or damaged.
8. 3-4 piston porosity.
9. 3-4 piston exhaust ball open.
10. Apply passages restricted.
11. 3-4 clutch check ball capsule, damaged or improperly assembled.

### SLIPPING OR ROUGH 3-4 SHIFT

1. 3-4 accumulator spring, missing.
2. 3-4 piston porosity.
3. Accumulator feed passages, restricted.
4. 3-4 accumulator piston oil seal ring, broken.
5. Accumulator case bore damaged.
6. Servo band apply incorrect.
7. Servo piston seals damaged or missing.
8. Servo piston bores damaged.
9. Servo piston porosity.
10. 3-4 Clutch burned. (Refer to 2-3 slip for other clutch diagnosis.)
11. 2-4 band burned.
12. Valve body 2-3 shift valve train, sticking.
13. Accumulator valve sticking.
14. Valve body gaskets or spacer plate improperly positioned.
15. Valve body throttle valve sticking.
16. T.V. limit valve sticking.

### NO REVERSE OR SLIPS IN REVERSE

1. Forward clutch will not release.
2. Manual linkage improperly adjusted.
3. Pump assembly reverse boost plug sticking.
4. Valve body gaskets or saucer plate improperly positioned.
5. Low reverse clutch piston seals cut or damaged.
6. Low reverse clutch apply passages restricted or missing.
7. Low reverse clutch plates burned.
8. Low reverse clutch cover plate loose or cover plate gasket damaged.
9. Reverse input clutch plates burned.
10. Reverse input clutch piston seals cut or damaged.
11. Reverse input clutch apply passage restricted or missing.
12. Reverse input clutch housing exhaust ball and capsule, damaged.

### NO PART THROTTLE DOWNSHIFTS

1. Binding external or internal linkage.
2. Valve body T.V. modulator downshift valve binding.
3. Valve body throttle valve binding.
4. Valve body throttle valve bushing, feed hole restricted or missing.
5. Valve body check ball No. 3 improperly positioned.

### NO OVERRUN BRAKING MANUAL 3-2-1

1. External manual linkage not properly adjusted.
2. Overrun clutch plates burned.
3. Overrun clutch inner or outer piston seals damaged.

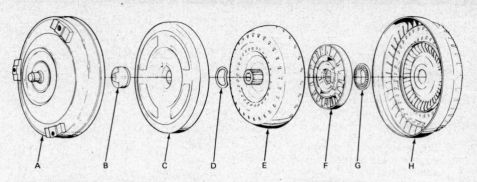

A  HOUSING COVER ASSEMBLY, CONVERTER
B  SPACER, TURBINE THRUST
C  PRESSURE PLATE ASSEMBLY
D  SPRING, PRESSURE PLATE

E  TURBINE ASSEMBLY
F  STATOR ASSEMBLY
G  THRUST BEARING ASSEMBLY
H  CONVERTER PUMP ASSEMBLY

*THE TORQUE CONVERTER CLUTCH ASSEMBLY CANNOT BE DISASSEMBLED. SHOWN HERE FOR INFORMATION ONLY. SEE SECTION 7A FOR MORE INFORMATION.

**Fig. 2   Lockup torque converter**

4. Overrun clutch piston exhaust ball sticking or missing.
5. Overrun clutch piston porosity.
6. Valve body gaskets or spacer plate improperly positioned or orifice holes plugged.
7. Valve body 4-3 sequence valve sticking.
8. Valve body check balls 3, 9 or 10 improperly positioned.
9. Turbine shaft oil feed passages restricted or missing.
10. Turbine shaft oil seal ring damaged.
11. Turbine shaft plug missing.

## NO CONVERTER CLUTCH APPLY

1. 12 volts not being supplied to the transmission.
2. Defective transmission outside electrical connector.
3. Defective inside electrical connectors, wiring harness, solenoid.
4. Defective electrical ground inside transmission.
5. Defective pressure switch or improper connection.
6. Solenoid not grounded.
7. Valve body converter clutch shift or throttle valve sticking.
8. Valve body casting or spacer plate in converter clutch valve area are improperly positioned or damaged.
9. Converter clutch apply valve, stuck or installed backwards.
10. Pump assembly signal oil orifice, restricted or missing.
11. Pump assembly O-ring on solenoid damaged or missing.
12. Pump to case gasket, damaged or improperly positioned.
13. Pump assembly cup plug missing from apply passage.
14. Pump assembly orifice plug missing from the cooler input passage.
15. High or uneven bolt torque on cover to body.
16. Converter clutch stop valve or retainer ring not installed properly.

## CONVERTER SHUDDER

1. Converter clutch pressure plate damaged.
2. Check ball on end of turbine shaft damaged.
3. Sticking converter clutch shift valve in valve body.
4. Sticking converter clutch apply valve in valve body.
5. Restricted converter clutch apply passage.
6. Low oil or oil pressure.
7. Engine not tuned properly.

## NO CONVERTER RELEASE

1. Converter clutch apply valve stuck in the open position.
2. O-ring or check ball in the end of the turbine shaft damaged.
3. Internal converter damage.

## DRIVES IN NEUTRAL

1. Forward clutch burned or not releasing.
2. Manual linkage or manual valve incorrectly set, or disconnected internal linkage.
3. Case interconnected passage.

## NO PARK OR WILL NOT HOLD IN PARK

1. Actuator rod assembly bent or damaged.
2. Actuator rod spring, binding or improper crimp.
3. Parking lock pawl return spring, damaged or not assembled properly.
4. Actuator rod is not attached to inside detent lever.
5. Parking brake bracket damaged or bolts not torqued.
6. Inside detent lever nut, not torqued.
7. Detent roller improperly installed or damaged.
8. Parking lock pawl, binding or damaged.
9. Parking lock pawl interference with the low reverse piston.

## T.V. SYSTEM DIAGNOSIS

T.V. pressure controls the shift pattern and the hydraulic line pressure used to apply clutches and bands. If proper line pressure is not available to apply clutch elements and bands, excess slippage may occur during shifting, and the components will be damaged. A T.V. cable which is damaged, disconnected or improperly adjusted, will cause high or low line pressure which can in turn cause the following conditions: Delayed or harsh upshifts, early upshifts and clutch slippage during shifting, no upshift, chatter on take-off, 1-2 upshift at full throttle only, no full throttle or part throttle detent downshift, and intermittent second gear starts.

Do not attempt to correct a condition by changing the T.V. setting from its proper adjustment. If the T.V. cable adjustment is "tailored" to modify the transmission shift pattern, line pressure may be adversely affected and can cause transmission failure. To diagnose T.V. system related complaints and ensure proper T.V. cable adjustment, proceed as follows:

1. Ensure that the engine and all related systems are in proper operating condition.
2. Inspect the T.V. cable for kinked, binding, disconnected or broken conditions, and replace cable as needed. Also ensure that the proper T.V. cable is installed.
3. Connect suitable line pressure gauge to transmission and connect tachometer to engine.
4. Run engine until it reaches normal operating temperature, perform the following tests with engine speed at 1000 RPM.
5. Place gear selector in park and record line pressure.
6. Place gear selector in drive and note line pressure reading. Line pressure should be equal to or not more than 10 psi greater than the pressure recorded with selector in park.
7. Manually pull the T.V. cable to its full length, taking care not to increase the throttle opening and note pressure readings.
8. Pressure should gradually increase as the cable is pulled out and gradually decrease as the cable is returned to its original position, and approximate line pressures should be 55-75 psi minimum and 115-200 psi maximum.
9. Check the T.V system "fail-safe" system by disconnecting the T.V. cable from the throttle lever with the engine running at idle. Line pressure should increase to maximum.
10. Stop engine for at least 30 seconds to take the T.V. system out of the "fail-safe" mode.
11. Connect and adjust the T.V. cable as outlined, then repeat line pressure checks with selector lever in park and drive. Line pressure should return to normal.
12. If the T.V. system fails to operate as outlined in the preceding tests, check the following components:
   a. Inspect the throttle lever and bracket on the control valve as-

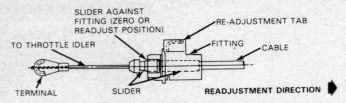

**Fig. 3   Typical T.V. cable adjuster**

sembly and repair as needed.

b. Check that the T.V. exhaust valve lifter rod is not distorted or binding in the control valve or spacer plate.

c. Ensure that the T.V. exhaust check ball moves freely up and down as the lifter is moved.

d. Ensure that the lifter spring holds the lifter rod against the bottom of the control valve assembly.

e. Ensure that the T.V. plunger does not stick at any position in its range of travel.

## MAINTENANCE
### CHECKING & ADDING FLUID

Check fluid at regular intervals. Noticing a change in color, odor or fluid level can serve as a warning of possible transmission problems.

To check fluid level, bring fluid to operating temperature of 200°F. With vehicle on a level surface, engine idling in park and parking brake applied, the level on the dipstick should be at the Full mark. To bring the fluid level from the Add mark to the Full mark requires one pint of fluid. If additional fluid is required, use only Dexron II automatic transmission fluid. When adding fluid, do not overfill, as foaming and loss of fluid through the vent may occur as the fluid heats up. Also, If fluid level is too low, complete loss of drive may occur especially when cold, Which can cause transmission failure.

Every 100,000 miles, the oil should be drained, the pan removed, the screen should be cleaned or replaced if applicable, and fresh fluid added. For vehicles subjected to more severe use such as heavy city traffic especially in hot weather, prolonged periods of idling or use as a tow vehicle, this maintenance should be performed every 15,000 miles.

### CHANGING OIL

1. Raise vehicle and position drain pan under transmission pan.
2. Remove front and side attaching bolts form the oil pan.
3. Loosen rear attaching bolts approximately four turns.
4. Carefully pry transmission pan loose and allow fluid to drain.
5. Remove rear attaching bolts, pan and pan gasket.
6. Drain remaining fluid from pan, then clean pan and gasket surfaces with solvent and dry with compressed air.
7. Remove transmission screen. Remove O-ring seal from intake pipe or case bore.

8. Replace screen if applicable, or thoroughly clean screen assembly with solvent and dry with compressed air.
9. Install O-ring on intake pipe, then install screen assembly.
10. Install gasket on pan, then install pan and torque attaching bolts to 12 ft. lbs.
11. Lower vehicle and add approximately 5 qts. of Dexron II type transmission fluid through filler tube.
12. Start engine and let run at idle, then with brakes applied move selector lever through each gear range.
13. Place transmission in Park position and check fluid level.

## IN-VEHICLE ADJUSTMENTS
### T.V. CABLE, ADJUST
#### Gasoline Engine

1. Depress and hold metal readjust tab. Move slider back through fitting in direction away from throttle body until slider stops against fitting, **Figs. 3 through 6.**
2. Release metal readjust tab.
3. Open throttle lever to full throttle stop position to automatically adjust cable, then release throttle lever.
4. Check cable for proper operation. If sticking or binding occurs, check system as outlined in "Throttle Valve System Diagnosis."

#### Diesel Engine

1. On vehicles equipped cruise control, remove cruise control rod.
2. Disconnect T.V. cable from throttle assembly, then loosen locknut on pump rod and shorten several turns.
3. Turn lever assembly to full throttle stop and hold in this position.
4. Adjust pump rod until injection pump lever contacts full throttle stop.
5. Release lever assembly and tighten pump rod locknut, then remove pump rod from lever assembly.
6. Connect T.V. cable to throttle assembly, then depress and hold metal readjusting tab. Move slider back through fitting in direction away from lever assembly until slider stops against fitting, **Fig. 7.**
7. Release readjust tab, then rotate lever assembly to full throttle stop and release the lever.
8. Connect pump rod and, if equipped, the cruise control throttle rod.
9. On vehicles equipped with cruise control, adjust servo throttle rod to minimum slack position. Install clip into servo ball in first free hole closest to the bell crank.

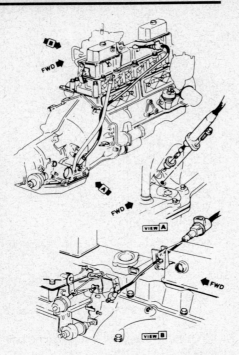

**Fig. 4   T.V. cable adjustment. Models w/6-292/4.9L engine**

## MANUAL LINKAGE ADJUSTMENT
### 1982–85 C, G & K Series

1. Position transmission lever (A), **Fig. 8,** in neutral position by moving lever clockwise to the park detent, then counterclockwise two detents to neutral.
2. Place column shift lever in neutral gate notch by rotating lever until it drops into neutral gate notch. Do not use indicator pointer as a reference to position shift lever.
3. Attach rod (C), **Fig. 8,** to transmission shaft assembly.
4. Slide swivel and clamp onto rod, (C), **Fig. 8,** then attach to column shift lever.
5. Hold column shift lever against neutral stop, park position side, then tighten attaching nuts.

### 1986–89 Exc. Astro, Safari, S/T-10/15 & 1988–89 C & K Series

1. Loosen nut (11) or screw (17), **Fig. 9,** then place column selector lever in Neutral position.
2. Move shift lever (A) to forward position, then back to second detent (neutral).
3. Hold rod (15) securely in swivel (7), then torque nut or screw to 17 ft. lbs.

### 1988–89 C & K Series

1. Apply parking brake, then loosen screw securing selector rod in clamp at lower steering column lever, **Fig. 10.**
2. Place column selector lever in neutral position, using shifter gate to find position. Do not use shift indicator to find

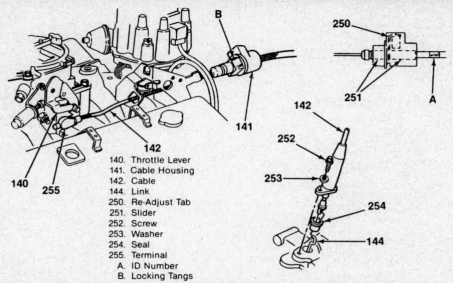

140. Throttle Lever
141. Cable Housing
142. Cable
144. Link
250. Re-Adjust Tab
251. Slider
252. Screw
253. Washer
254. Seal
255. Terminal
A. ID Number
B. Locking Tangs

**Fig. 5 T.V. cable adjustment. Models w/V6 and V8 gasoline engines exc. Astro, Safari & S/T-10/15**

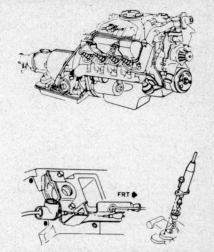

**Fig. 7 T.V. cable adjustment. Models w/diesel engine**

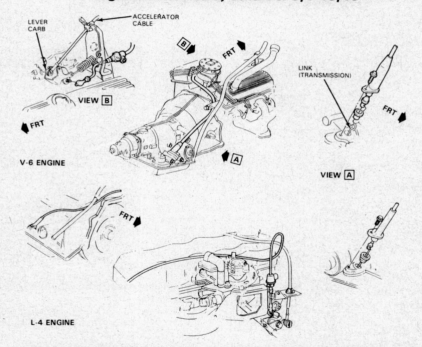

**Fig. 6 T.V. cable adjustment. Astro, Safari & S/T-10/15**

neutral position.
3. Place transmission manual lever in neutral by pushing lever fully forward to park stop, then pushing lever back 2 detents into neutral position.
4. Hold selector rod and swivel securely to prevent them from moving out of position, then torque retaining screw to 17 ft. lbs.
5. Place column selector lever in park, then check adjustment as follows:
   a. Ensure column selector moves into all positions.
   b. Ensure starter engages in neutral and park only. Check and adjust neutral safety switch, as needed.
   c. Ensure that parking pawl freely engages the reaction internal gear lugs or output ring gear lugs when column selector lever is moved into park position.

### Astro & Safari Vans

1. Position transmission lever (J), **Fig. 11**, to neutral position by one of the following methods:
   a. Obtain neutral position by moving transmission lever counterclockwise to L1 detent, then three detent positions to neutral.
   b. Obtain neutral position by moving transmission lever clockwise to the park detent, then counterclockwise two detents to neutral.
2. Place column shift lever in neutral gate notch by rotating lever until it drops into neutral gate notch. Do not use indicator pointer as a reference to position shift lever.
3. Attach rod to column shift lever.
4. Slide swivel (A), retainer (B), spacer (C), washer (D), and insulator (E), onto rod (K), then align with lever (H), and complete attachment, **Fig. 11**, Torque nut (F) to 9-12 ft. lbs.

### S/T-10/15

1. Place steering column shift lever in neutral gate notch.
2. Place transmission lever (A), **Fig. 12**, in neutral detent.
3. Install clamp spring washer and screw on transmission control lever (B), **Fig. 12**, and control rod.
4. Hold clamp flush against transmission control lever (B), **Fig. 12**, then finger tighten clamping screw against rod. No force should be exerted in either direction on the rod or transmission control lever (B), **Fig. 12**, while tightening the clamp screw.
5. Tighten control rod attaching screw.

# IN-VEHICLE REPAIRS
## SERVO ASSEMBLY, REPLACE

1. Disconnect battery ground cable, then raise and support vehicle.
2. Install servo cover compressor tool No. J-29714, then remove 2-4 servo cover retaining ring using a small screwdriver.
3. Remove servo cover and O-ring using suitable tool.
4. Remove fourth gear apply piston and O-ring, then the second servo piston assembly.
5. Remove inner servo piston assembly oil seal and spring.
6. Reverse procedure to install.

BUSHING
NUT
WASHER
CLAMP
WASHER
GROMMET
COLUMN SHIFT LEVER
SWIVEL
LEVER A
ROD C
RETAINER
SHAFT ASM B
GROMMET
GROMMET
G-ALL
RETAINER
SHIFT LEVER
ROD C
LEVER ASM B
TRANS LEVER A
CK-ALL

LINKAGE ADJUSTMENT

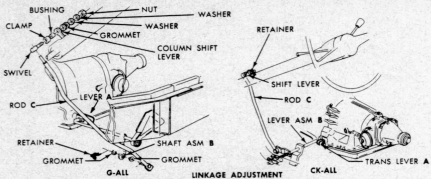

1. SET TRANS LEVER (A) IN "NEUTRAL" POSITION BY MOVING TRANS LEVER (A) CLOCKWISE TO THE "PARK" DETENT THEN COUNTERCLOCKWISE TWO DETENTS TO "NEUTRAL".
2. SET THE COLUMN SHIFT LEVER IN "NEUTRAL" GATE NOTCH. THIS IS OBTAINED BY ROTATING UNTIL SHIFT LEVER DROPS INTO "NEUTRAL" GATE NOTCH. NOTE DO NOT USE INDICATOR POINTER AS A REFERENCE TO POSITION THE SHIFT LEVER.
3. ATTACH ROD (C) TO TRANS SHAFT ASM (B) AS SHOWN.
4. SLIDE SWIVEL AND CLAMP ONTO ROD (C) ALIGN WITH COLUMN SHIFT LEVER AND COMPLETE ATTACHMENT.
5. HOLD COLUMN LEVER AGAINST NEUTRAL STOP "PARK POSITION SIDE".
6. TIGHTEN NUT USING RECOMMENDED TORQUE.

**Fig. 8 Shift linkage adjustment. 1982–85 Exc. Astro, Safari & S/T-10/15**

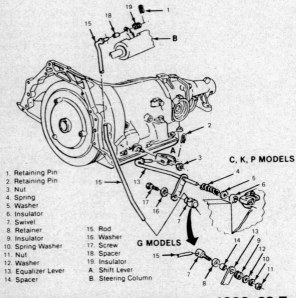

C, K, P MODELS
G MODELS
1. Retaining Pin
2. Retaining Pin
3. Nut
4. Spring
5. Washer
6. Insulator
7. Swivel
8. Retainer
9. Insulator
10. Spring Washer
11. Nut
12. Washer
13. Equalizer Lever
14. Spacer
15. Rod
16. Washer
17. Screw
18. Spacer
19. Insulator
A. Shift Lever
B. Steering Column

**Fig. 9 Shift linkage adjustment. 1986–89 Exc. Astro, Safari, S/T-10/15 & 1988–89 C & K Series**

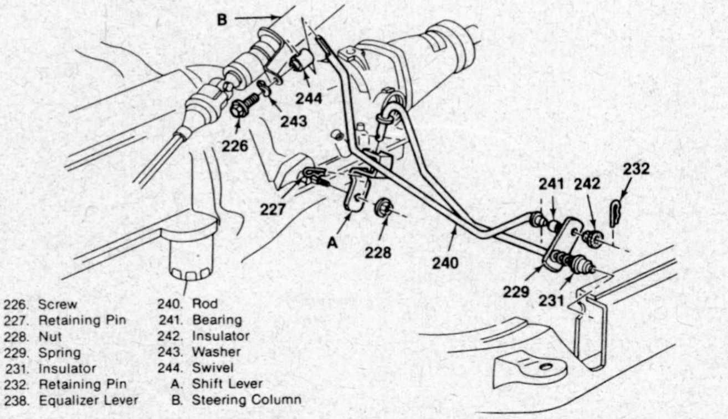

226. Screw
227. Retaining Pin
228. Nut
229. Spring
231. Insulator
232. Retaining Pin
238. Equalizer Lever
240. Rod
241. Bearing
242. Insulator
243. Washer
244. Swivel
A. Shift Lever
B. Steering Column

**Fig. 10 Shift linkage adjustment. 1988–89 C & K Series**

## SPEEDOMETER DRIVEN GEAR, REPLACE

1. Disconnect speedometer cable.
2. Remove retainer bolt, retainer, speedometer driven gear, and O-ring seal.
3. Reverse procedure to install, using new O-ring and adjusting fluid level.

## REAR OIL SEAL, REPLACE

1. Remove driveshaft, and tunnel strap, as equipped.
2. Using suitable tool, pry out lip oil seal.
3. Coat outer casting of new oil seal with suitable sealer and drive into place with installer J-21426.
4. Install tunnel strap if used, then install driveshaft.

## GOVERNOR, REPLACE

1. Raise and support vehicle.
2. Remove governor cover from case using extreme care not to damage cover. If cover is damaged, it must be replaced.
3. Remove governor.
4. Reverse procedure to install and check fluid level.

## CONTROL VALVE ASSEMBLY, REPLACE

1. Drain and remove oil pan and remove filter and gasket.
2. Disconnect electrical connectors at valve body.
3. Remove detent spring and roller assembly from valve body and remove valve body to case bolts.
4. Remove valve body assembly while disconnecting manual control valve link from range selector inner lever and removing throttle lever bracket from T.V. link.
5. Reverse procedure to install. Torque bolts to 8 ft. lbs. and replenish fluid.

## TRANSMISSION REPLACE

### 4 X 2 MODELS

1. Disconnect battery ground cable.
2. Remove air cleaner assembly.

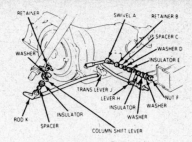

**TRANSMISSION CONTROL LINKAGE ADJUSTMENT**

1. STEERING COLUMN ATTACHMENT TO BODY MUST BE COMPLETE AND ALL BODY BOLT SCREWS MUST BE SECURED BEFORE ADJUSTING TRANS CONTROL LINKAGE

2. SET TRANS LEVER (J) IN "NEUTRAL" POSITION BY ONE OF THE FOLLOWING OPTIONAL METHODS

   A   OBTAIN "NEUTRAL" POSITION BY MOVING TRANS LEVER (J) COUNTER CLOCKWISE TO "L1" DETENT. THEN CLOCKWISE THREE DETENT POSITIONS TO "NEUTRAL" OR OBTAIN

   B   "NEUTRAL" POSITION BY MOVING TRANS LEVER (J) CLOCKWISE TO THE "PARK" DETENT THEN COUNTER-CLOCKWISE TWO DETENTS TO "NEUTRAL"

3. SET THE COLUMN SHIFT LEVER IN "NEUTRAL GATE NOTCH" THIS IS OBTAINED BY ROTATING UNTIL SHIFT LEVER DROPS INTO "NEUTRAL" GATE NOTCH NOTE DO NOT USE INDICATOR POINTER AS A REFERENCE TO POSITION THE SHIFT LEVER

4. ATTACH ROD (K) TO COLUMN SHIFT LEVER AS SHOWN

5. SLIDE SWIVEL (A), RETAINER (B), SPACER (C), WASHER (D) AND INSULATOR (E) ONTO ROD (K) ALIGN WITH LEVER (H) AND COMPLETE ATTACHMENT

6. TIGHTEN NUT (F) USING RECOMMENDED TORQUE 12-17 N·m (9-12 Ft Lbs)

**Fig. 11   Shift linkage adjustment. Astro & Safari Vans**

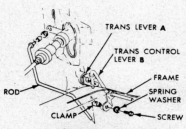

**ADJUSTMENT PROCEDURE**

1. POSITION THE STEERING COLUMN SHIFT LEVER IN NEUTRAL GATE NOTCH.

2. SET TRANS LEVER (A) IN NEUTRAL DETENT.

3. ASSEMBLE CLAMP SPRING WASHER AND SCREW TO TRANS CONTROL LEVER (B) & CONTROL ROD.

4. HOLD CLAMP FLUSH AGAINST TRANS CONTROL LEVER (B) & FINGER TIGHTEN CLAMPING SCREW AGAINST ROD. NO FORCE SHOULD BE EXERTED IN EITHER DIRECTION ON THE ROD OR TRANS CONTROL LEVER (B) WHILE TIGHTENING THE CLAMPING SCREW.

5. TIGHTEN SCREW TO SPECIFIED TORQUE.

**Fig. 12   Shift linkage adjustment. S/T-10/15**

Transmission to engine attaching bolts. Astro Van & Safari

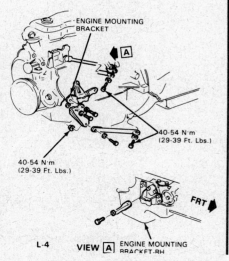

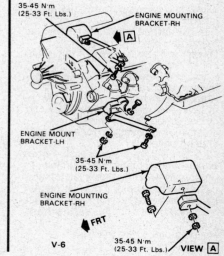

Transmission support braces. Astro Van & Safari

3. Disconnect T.V. cable at its upper end.
4. On vehicles equipped with 4-119/1.9L engine, remove starter motor upper retaining nut.
5. Raise and support vehicle.
6. Remove propeller shaft from vehicle.
7. Disconnect speedometer cable, shift linkage assembly and electrical connectors from transmission.
8. Remove transmission support brace attaching bolts from converter cover, if equipped.
9. Remove converter cover, then mark flywheel and torque converter for installation.
10. Remove exhaust crossover pipe and catalytic converter attaching bolts from vehicle.
11. Remove torque converter to flywheel bolts and/or nuts.
12. Disconnect catalytic converter support bracket.
13. Position a suitable jack under transmission and raise slightly.
14. Remove transmission crossmember to transmission mount bolt.
15. Remove transmission crossmember to frame bolts and/or insulators, if equipped.
16. Slide crossmember rearward and remove from vehicle.
17. Lower transmission.
18. Disconnect and cap transmission fluid cooler lines.
19. Disconnect T.V. cable from transmission.
20. Position a suitable jack under engine, then remove transmission to engine attaching bolts.
21. Carefully separate transmission from engine. Install torque converter holding tool No. J-21366.

*Turbo Hydra-Matic 700-R4 (4L60) Transmission*

22. Remove transmission from vehicle.
23. To install transmission, reverse removal procedure.

## 4 X 4 MODELS

1. Disconnect battery ground cable.
2. Remove air cleaner assembly.
3. Disconnect T.V. cable at its upper end.
4. Remove transfer case shift lever knob and boot.
5. Raise and support vehicle.
6. Remove skid plate, then drain lubricant from transfer case.
7. Place an alignment mark between transfer case front output shaft yoke and propeller shaft. Disconnect front propeller shaft from transfer case.
8. Place an alignment mark between rear axle yoke and propeller shaft. Remove rear propeller shaft.
9. Disconnect speedometer cable, shift linkage assembly and electrical connectors from transmission. Remove catalytic converter hanger, if necessary.
10. Disconnect shift linkage from transfer case assembly.
11. Remove transmission support strut rods and flywheel cover. Mark flywheel and torque converter for installation.
12. Remove torque converter to flywheel attaching bolts and/or nuts.
13. Disconnect and cap transmission fluid cooler lines.
14. Position a suitable jack under transmission and transfer case assembly.
15. Remove transfer case to frame bracket bolts. Remove mounting bolts and crossmember from vehicle.
16. Remove transmission to engine attaching bolts.
17. Carefully separate transmission from engine and remove from vehicle. In order to remove the upper left transfer case attaching bolts, it may be necessary to remove the shift lever bracket mounting bolts from the transfer case adapter.
18. Reverse procedure to install.

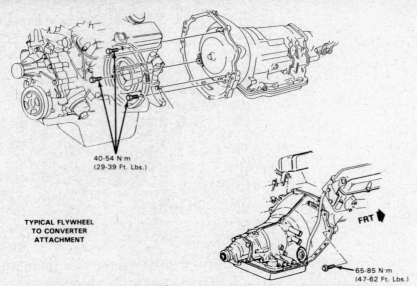

40-54 N·m
(29-39 Ft. Lbs.)

TYPICAL FLYWHEEL
TO CONVERTER
ATTACHMENT

65-85 N·m
(47-62 Ft. Lbs.)

**Transmission to engine attaching bolts. S/T-10/15**

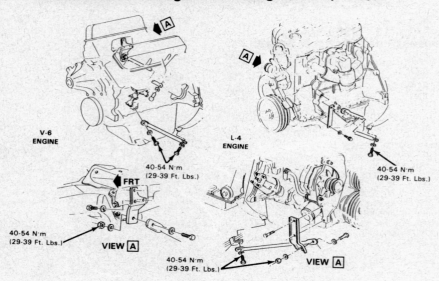

V-6
ENGINE

L-4
ENGINE

40-54 N·m
(29-39 Ft. Lbs.)

40-54 N·m
(29-39 Ft. Lbs.)

40-54 N·m
(29-39 Ft. Lbs.)

VIEW A

40-54 N·m
(29-39 Ft. Lbs.)

VIEW A

**Transmission support braces. S/T-10/15**

# ELECTRONIC IGNITION SYSTEMS

## TABLE OF CONTENTS

# Ignition Timing Adjustments

## INDEX

## IGNITION TIMING ADJUST

On vehicles with light duty emissions, check ignition timing every 30,000 miles. On vehicles with heavy duty emissions, check ignition timing every 12,000 miles. Refer to Tune Up Specifications chart for firing order and specified ignition timing.

### 4-119/1.9L ENGINE

Adjust ignition timing with engine at operating temperature. Disconnect and plug vacuum hose at distributor, canister purge hose at canister and vacuum hose at EGR valve. Connect a suitable timing light to No. 1 spark plug wire, as per timing light manufacturer's instructions. Check ignition timing with engine at idle speed and adjust as necessary.

### 4-121/2.0L & 4-151/2.5L ENGINES

Adjust ignition timing with engine at normal operating temperature. Disconnect EST 4 wire connector at distributor to place system in bypass mode. Connect a suitable timing light to No. 1 spark plug wire, as per timing light manufacturer's instructions, then check ignition timing. On 4-151 engines, ignition timing must also be checked at No. 4 cylinder. Add ignition timing figures obtained at No. 1 and No. 4 cyl-

inders to obtain an average ignition timing. Adjust ignition timing as necessary, then reconnect EST wire connector at distributor.

### V6-173/2.8L, V6-229/3.8L, V6-231/3.8L & V6-262/4.3L ENGINES

Adjust ignition timing with engine at operating temperature. On V6-173, 231 and 262 carbureted engines, disconnect EST 4 wire connector at distributor to place system in bypass mode. On V6-173 and 262 TBI engines, disconnect timing connector, which is a single wire sealed connector with a tan wire with black stripes. The timing connector is located below the heater case in the passenger compartment for V6-173 engines. On V6-262 engines, the timing connector breaks out of the engine wiring harness conduit. On V6-229 engines, connect a jumper wire between ALCL connector terminals A and B. The ALCL connector is located under the instrument panel to the right of the steering column. Connect a suitable timing light to No. 1 spark plug wire, as per timing light manufacturer's instructions, then check ignition timing. Adjust ignition timing as necessary.

### 6-250/4.1L & 6-292/4.8L ENGINES

Adjust ignition timing with engine at operating temperature. On engines equipped with EST, disconnect EST 4 wire connector at distributor to place system in bypass mode. On engines less EST, disconnect and plug distributor vacuum advance hose. Connect a suitable timing light to No. 1 spark plug wire, as per timing light manufacturer's instructions, then check ignition timing. Adjust ignition timing as necessary.

### V8-267/4.4L, V8-305/5.0L, V8-350/5.7L, V8-400/6.6L & V8-454/7.4L ENGINES

Adjust ignition timing with engine at normal operating temperature. On carbureted engines with EST, disconnect EST 4 wire connector at distributor to place system in bypass mode. On 1987-89 TBI engines, disconnect timing connector, which is a single wire sealed connector with tan wire with black stripes. The timing connector breaks out of the engine wiring harness conduit. On engine less EST, disconnect and plug distributor vacuum advance hose. On all engines, connect a suitable timing light to No. 1 spark plug wire, as per timing light manufacturer's instructions, then check ignition timing. Adjust ignition timing as necessary.

# Delco-Remy High Energy Ignition (HEI) System

## INDEX

## DESCRIPTION

The HEI system utilizes an all electronic module, pickup coil and timer core in place of the conventional breaker points, condenser and distributor cam. In addition, a specially designed ignition coil, distributor cap, rotor and high tension leads are used to provide and distribute high intensity secondary system voltages to the spark plugs. Typical HEI system components are illustrated in **Figs. 1 and 2.**

The magnetic pickup consists of a rotating timer core attached to the distributor shaft, a stationary pole piece, permanent magnet and pickup coil. When the distributor shaft rotates, the teeth of the timer core line up and pass the teeth of the pole piece inducing voltage in the pickup coil which signals the electronic module to open the ignition coil primary circuit. Since this is a full 12 volt system that does not use a resistance wire, high current saturation occurs in the coil primary windings. Maximum inductance occurs at the moment the timer core teeth are lined up with the teeth on the pole piece. At the instant the timer core teeth start to pass the pole teeth, the module opens the primary circuit, and the current decay causes a high voltage to be induced in the ignition coil secondary winding. The high secondary voltage is directed through a specially designed cap, rotor and high voltage leads to fire the spark plugs.

HEI systems use conventional vacuum and centrifugal advance mechanisms. The vacuum diaphragm is connected by linkage to the pole piece. When the diaphragm moves against spring pressure it rotates the pole piece allowing the poles to advance relative to the timer core. The timer core is rotated about the shaft by conventional advance weights, thus providing centrifugal advance.

Some models are equipped with and Electronic Spark Control (ESC) system that controls spark timing in order to provide maximum engine performance while preventing detonation. The ESC system consists of an engine mounted knock sensor and an electronic controller, **Fig. 3.** ESC is a closed loop system that monitors engine detonation through a sensor and constantly adjusts ignition timing to provide the maximum usable spark advance while preventing prolonged detonation.

Th ESC knock sensor monitors the

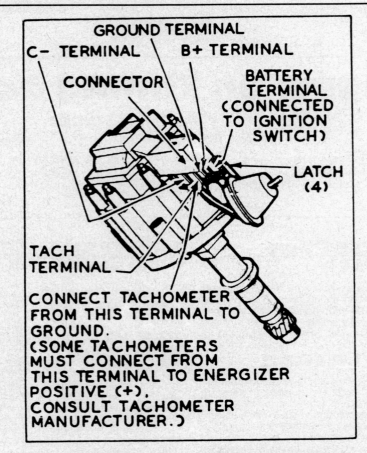

presence and intensity of engine detonation by sensing the resultant vibrations. The sensor produces a voltage signal which is proportional to the intensity of the detonation and this voltage signal is transmitted to the controller. The ESC controller is a hard wired signal processor/amplifier that operates in the 6-16 volt range, and has no memory storage provisions. The controller monitors knock sensor voltage output, processes these signals and controls the amount of spark advance through a special circuit in the HEI ignition module.

In addition, 1982-86 models with automatic transmissions include an ESC vacuum switch. The vacuum switch provides a

**Fig. 1  High Energy Ignition (HEI) distributor. Internal coil unit shown**

signal to the ESC controller during throttle tip-in which causes the module to momentarily retard spark timing to prevent detonation on acceleration.

## SYSTEM DIAGNOSIS
### ELECTRONIC SPARK TIMING (ESC) SYSTEM DIAGNOSIS

Use the following procedures to diagnose ESC system malfunctions only. To diagnose general ignition system malfunctions, refer to "High Energy Ignition (HEI) System Diagnosis."

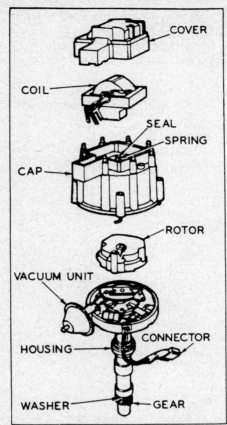

**Fig. 2   High Energy Ignition (HEI) distributor internal components. Internal coil unit shown**

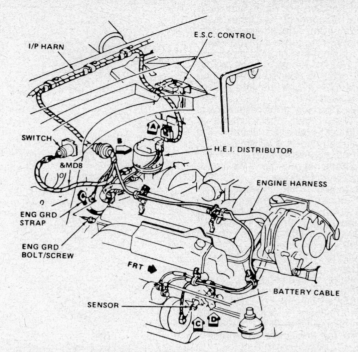

**Fig. 3   Typical Electronic Spark Control (ESC) system**

## 1980–83 MODELS

### Engine Cranks But Will Not Start

1. Inspect ESC harness for damage, shorts and opens. Inspect controller connector, distributor connectors and ignition switch connectors for corrosion, damage and deformed terminals, **Fig. 4**. Repair connectors and wiring as needed.
2. Disconnect distributor 4 pin connector, connect pins A and C on distributor side of connector with jumper wire, then attempt to start engine. If engine fails to start, refer to HEI system diagnosis; if engine starts, proceed to next step.
3. Remove jumper wire and reconnect connector to distributor. Turn on ignition, then measure voltage between pins F and K in the ESC controller 10 pin connector. If reading is less than 7 volts, check circuit between controller and ignition switch and repair as needed. If voltage is greater than 7 volts, proceed to next step.
4. Inspect wiring from ESC controller terminals G, H, J and K, and repair if damaged shorted or open. If wiring is satisfactory, but engine still will not start, ESC controller is defective.

### Poor Engine Performance

1. Disconnect distributor 4 pin connec-

tor, connect pins A and C on distributor side of connector with jumper wire, **Fig. 4**, and road test vehicle.
2. If engine performance is still poor, cause is not in ESC system. If proper engine performance is restored by disconnecting ESC controller from distributor, remove jumper wire, reconnect 4 pin connector and proceed to next step.
3. Connect pins A and B on ESC controller connector , leaving connector in place, then road test vehicle. If proper engine performance is restored, proceed to step 5 or 6.
4. If engine performance is still poor with jumper between controller terminals A and B, proceed as follows:
   a. Remove jumper wire from controller terminals A and B.
   b. Start engine and measure voltage between between pins F and K of ESC controller. If reading is less than 11.6 volts, check charging system and repair as needed.
   c. If voltage between terminals F and K is greater than 11.6 volts, check wiring to ESC controller and repair as needed. If wiring is satisfactory, ESC controller is defective.
5. On 1980-82 models, proceed as follows:
   a. Remove jumper wire from controller terminals A and B.
   b. Disconnect 10 pin connector from ESC controller and measure resistance between pins B and K in connector. Resistance should be 175-375 ohms
   c. If resistance is within specifications, check engine and related components for conditions caus-

ing sensor to pickup false detonation readings.
   d. If resistance is not within specifications, disconnect electrical connector from knock sensor and measure resistance between sensor terminal and ground. If reading is 175-375 ohms, check wiring and repair as needed. If resistance is not 175-375 ohms, knock sensor is defective.
6. On 1983 models, proceed as follows:
   a. Remove jumper wire from controller terminals A and B.
   b. Set engine to run at approximately 2000 RPM, disconnect electrical connector from knock sensor and measure voltage between sensor terminal and ground.
   c. If voltage is not .08 volt or greater, knock sensor is defective. If voltage is .08 volt or greater, inspect wiring to pins A, B and K of controller and repair as needed. If wiring is satisfactory, controller is defective.

### Engine Detonation

1. Connect suitable timing advance tester to engine, run engine until it reaches normal operating temperature and set engine to run at 1000 RPM, then repeatedly tap on exhaust manifold while observing ignition timing. If timing retards while tapping on manifold, system is operating normally.
2. If timing does not retard on 1980-82 models, proceed as follows:
   a. Stop engine, disconnect 10 pin connector from ESC controller and measure resistance between terminals B and K in connector. Resistance should be 175-375 ohms.

b. If resistance is not within specifications, disconnect electrical connector from knock sensor and measure resistance between sensor terminal and ground. If reading is 175-375 ohms, check wiring and repair as needed. If resistance is not 175-375 ohms, knock sensor is defective.

c. If knock sensor circuit resistance is 175-375 ohms, check wiring to controller terminals A, B and K and repair as needed. If wiring is satisfactory, proceed to step 4.

3. If timing does not retard on 1983 models, proceed as follows:

a. Disconnect 10 pin connector from ESC controller and measure voltage between connector terminals B and K with engine running at 2000 RPM. Voltage reading should be .08 volt or greater.

b. If voltage is as specified, proceed to step 4.

c. If voltage is not as specified, repeat voltage check at knock sensor. If voltage is .08 volt or greater, repair wiring between knock sensor and controller. If voltage is not .08 volt or greater, knock sensor is defective.

4. With 10 pin ESC controller disconnected, attempt to start engine. If engine starts, replace HEI module; if engine does not start, proceed to next step.

5. Reconnect 10 pin connector to ESC controller, connect suitable spark advance tester to engine and disconnect electrical connector from knock sensor.

6. Run engine at fast idle and jump terminals of knock sensor connector while observing ignition timing. If timing retards, knock sensor is defective.

7. If timing does not retard when sensor connector is jumped, measure voltage between terminals H and K at controller with ignition on. If reading is less than .2 volt check wiring top controller terminal H and repair as needed. If voltage is greater than .2 volt, controller is defective.

## 1984–86 MODELS
### Engine Cranks But Will Not Start

1. Check for spark at at the ends of at least 2 spark plug wires using tester ST-125 or equivalent. If spark is observed, malfunction is not in ignition system.

2. If no spark is observed, disconnect 4 pin connector to distributor, connect jumper wire between pins A and C on distributor side of connector, **Figs. 5, 6 and 7**, and attempt to start engine. If engine starts, proceed to step 3. If engine does not start, proceed as follows:

a. Remove jumper wire and reconnect 4 pin connector to distributor. Turn on ignition and measure voltage at pins F and K of controller 10 pin connector. If voltage is less than 11.6 volts, check feed circuit and repair as needed.

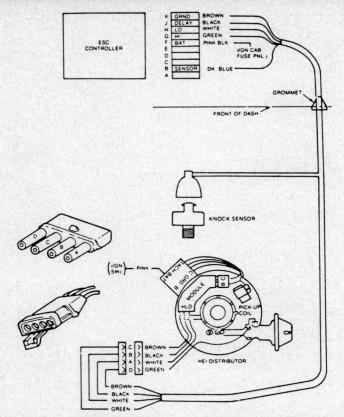

**Fig. 4   ESC system wiring schematic. 1980–83**

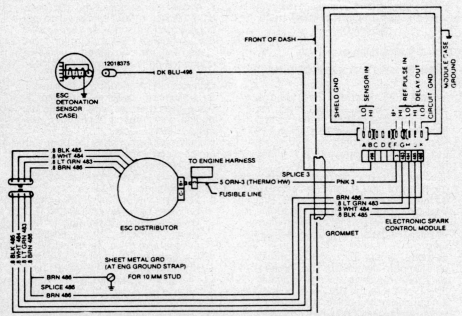

**Fig. 5   ESC system wiring schematic. 1984–86 models w/manual 4 speed top loader transmission**

b. Set voltmeter on 2 volt scale and measure voltage between pins J and K of 10 pin connector while cranking engine. If reading is .75 volts or greater, ESC system is satisfactory.

c. Set voltmeter on 2 volt scale and measure voltage between pins G and H of 10 pin connector while cranking engine. If reading is .20 volt or greater, controller is defective. If reading is less than .20 volt, pole piece is defective.

3. Stop engine and remove jumper wire

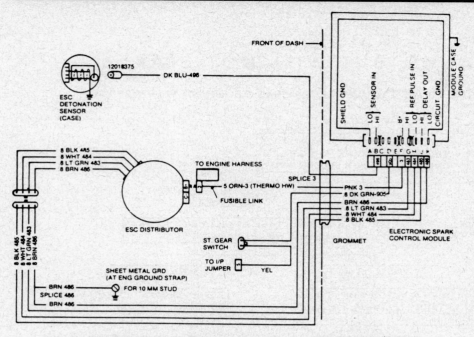

**Fig. 6   ESC system wiring schematic. 1984–86 models w/manual 3 & 4 speed side loader transmission**

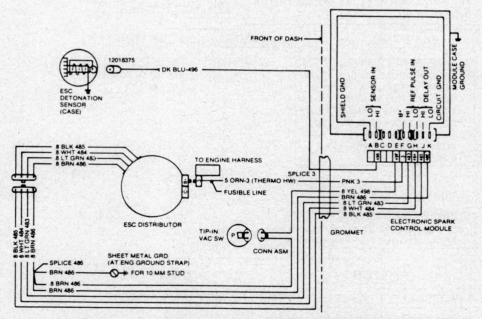

**Fig. 7   ESC system wiring schematic. 1984–86 models w/auto. trans.**

tion module is defective.

## Poor Engine Performance

1. Disconnect distributor 4 pin connector, connect pins A and C on distributor side of connector with jumper wire, and road test vehicle.
2. If engine performance is still poor, cause is not in ESC system. If proper engine performance is restored by disconnecting ESC controller from distributor, remove jumper wire, reconnect 4 pin connector and proceed to next step.
3. Disconnect 10 pin connector from ESC controller, inspect terminals for proper contact, shots and opens, repair as needed, then recheck system operation.
4. If problem persists, disconnect 10 pin connector and measure resistance between pins B and K in connector. Reading should be 98-99 ohms.
5. If resistance is not as specified, disconnect electrical connector from knock sensor and measure resistance between sensor terminal and ground. If resistance is 98-99 ohms, repair wiring between knock sensor and controller.If resistance is not 98-99 ohms, knock sensor is defective.
6. Reconnect 10 pin connector to controller and measure voltage between pins F and K with ignition on. If voltage reading is less than 11.6 volts repair feed circuit as needed.
7. Set voltmeter on 20 volt AC scale and measure voltage between connector pins H and K with ignition on. If reading is less than .20 volt, inspect system wiring and repair as needed. If reading is greater than .20 volt, ensure all connectors are properly seated, then road test vehicle. If problem persists, replace ESC controller.

## Engine Detonation

1. Inspect connector and wiring to knock sensor and repair as needed.
2. Connect suitable spark advance tester to engine, run engine until it reaches normal operating temperature and set engine to run at a minimum of 1200 RPM, then observe ignition timing while tapping on exhaust manifold. If ignition timing retards when manifold is tapped, ESC system is operating properly.
3. Stop engine, disconnect 10 pin connector from ESC controller and measure resistance between pins B and K of connector. If resistance is not 98-99 ohms, proceed to step 5.
4. Measure resistance between pins H and K in connector. If resistance is 14-16 ohms, replace controller. If resistance is not 14-16 ohms, repair wiring to controller.
5. Disconnect electrical connector from knock sensor and measure voltage at sensor terminal with engine running at 2000 RPM. If reading is not .08 volt or more, knock sensor is defective.
6. Stop engine. If knock sensor voltage output is satisfactory, check wiring between knock sensor and terminal B of controller and between controller ter-

from distributor.
4. Connect suitable high resistance test lamp between distributor TACH terminal and ground, then turn on ignition. If test lamp lights, proceed to step 6.
5. If lamp does not light at TACH terminal, connect lamp between BAT terminal and ground and turn on ignition. If lamp does not light, repair feed circuit to ignition.
6. Crank engine with test lamp connected between distributor TACH terminal

and ground. If test lamp flickers, system is satisfactory.
7. If test lamp does not flicker as engine is cranked, connect lamp between BAT terminal and pin A on distributor side of 4 pin ESC connector, then tap on coil. If coil makes a clicking noise when tapped, pole piece is defective.
8. If coil does not click, remove distributor cap an disconnect and reconnect pole piece electrical connector. If coil still does not click when tapped, igni-

# ENGINE CRANKS, BUT WILL NOT START

IF A TACHOMETER IS CONNECTED TO THE TACHOMETER TERMINAL, DISCONNECT IT BEFORE PROCEEDING WITH THE TEST.

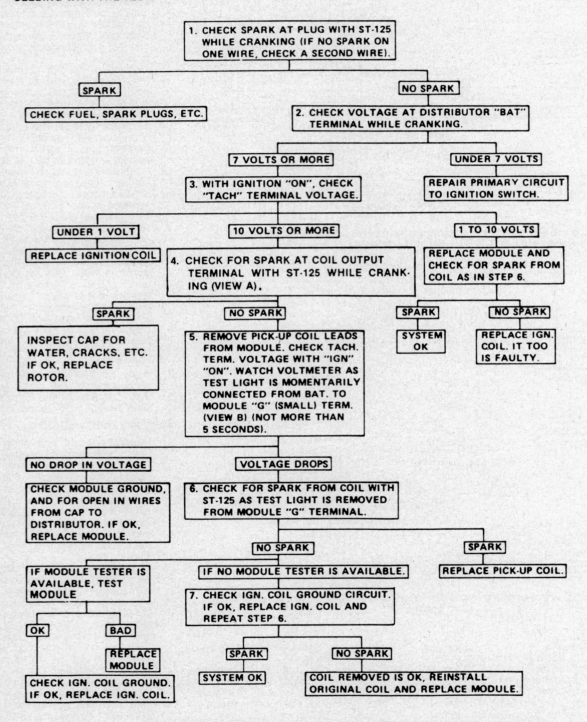

**Fig. 8   High Energy Ignition (HEI) system "No Start" condition diagnosis**

## INTERMITTENT OPERATION OR MISS

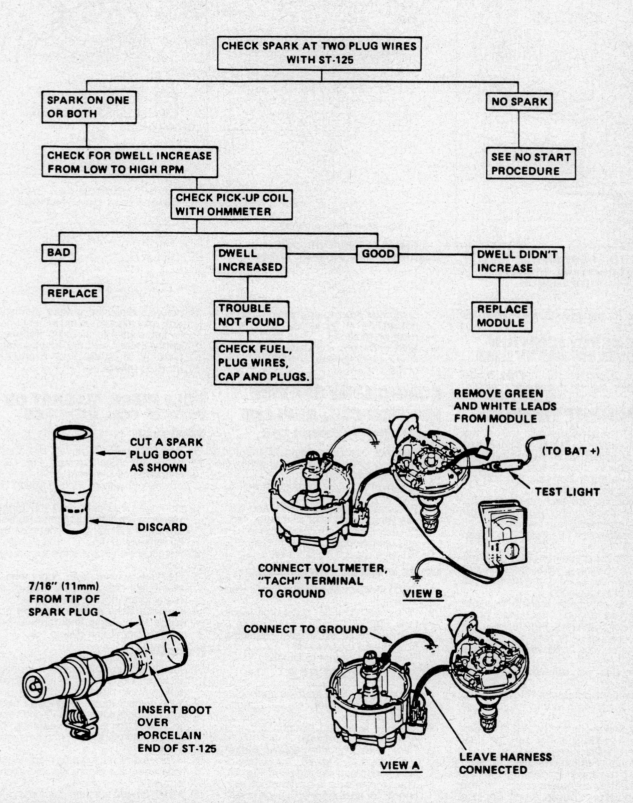

**Fig. 9   High Energy Ignition (HEI) system "Intermittent Operation or Misfire" condition diagnosis**

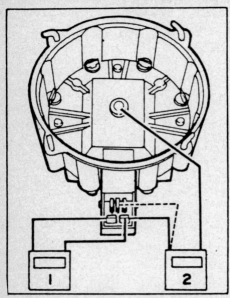

**Fig. 10   Ignition coil test connections. Models w/internal coil**

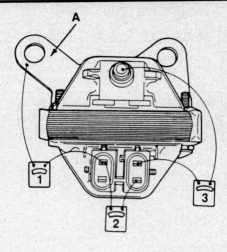

A. Scrape clean metal ground.

**Fig. 11   Ignition coil test connections. Models w/remote coil**

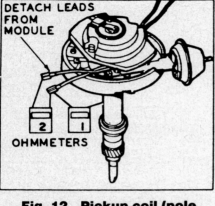

**Fig. 12   Pickup coil (pole piece) test connections**

minal K and ground and repair as needed.

## HIGH ENERGY IGNITION (HEI) SYSTEM DIAGNOSIS

Refer to diagnostic charts, **Figs. 8 and 9**, for ignition system diagnosis.

## COMPONENT TESTING

Tester J-24624 is required to test the module. If this tester is not available, and malfunction still exists after performing the following checks, replace module.

1. Remove distributor cap and coil assembly, as equipped.
2. Inspect cap, coil and rotor for arcing, carbon tracking and damage, and replace as needed.
3. On models with integral coil, proceed as follows:
   a. Connect ohmmeter, **Fig. 10**, step 1. If reading is other than zero or very near to zero, the ignition coil must be replaced.
   b. If no ohmmeter reading was observed in step 1, reconnect ohmmeter both ways, **Fig. 10**, step 2. If both ohmmeter readings are infinite on high scale, replace ignition coil.
4. On models with remote coil, proceed as follows:
   a. Connect ohmmeter, **Fig. 11**, step 1. If reading is not infinite, replace coil.
   b. Connect ohmmeter, **Fig. 11**, step 2. If reading is not zero or near zero, replace coil.
   c. Connect ohmmeter, **Fig. 11**, step 3. If reading is infinite, replace coil.
5. Connect an external vacuum source to the vacuum advance unit. Replace vacuum unit if inoperative.
6. If vacuum unit is operating properly, connect ohmmeter, **Fig. 12**, step 1. If

ohmmeter reading on middle scale is not infinite at all times, pickup coil must be replaced.
7. With ohmmeter connected, **Fig. 12**, step 2, reading should be 500 to 1500 ohms.

## COMPONENT SERVICE
### IGNITION COIL, REPLACE
#### Units With Internal Coil

1. Remove screws holding distributor cover to distributor cap and remove distributor cover, **Fig. 2**.
2. Remove four screws holding coil to cap.
3. Remove harness connector and battery wire from side of distributor cap.
4. Push coil leads out of position in cap and remove coil.
5. Reverse procedure to install.

#### Units With External Coil

1. Disconnect ignition switch to coil lead from coil.
2. Disconnect coil to distributor leads from coil.
3. Remove coil to engine retaining screws and remove coil.
4. Reverse procedure to install.

### MODULE, REPLACE

1. Disconnect wiring harness connector at side of distributor cap and remove distributor cap.
2. Remove rotor and disconnect wires from module terminals.
3. Remove two mounting screws and remove module, **Fig. 13**. Two types of H.E.I. wiring harness are used, **Fig. 14**. The second type is a wiring harness, connector and capacitor which is serviced as an assembly.
4. Reverse procedure to install. Prior to installation, coat bottom of new mod-

ule with dielectric grease (furnished with new module) to aid in heat transfer into distributor housing. **Failure to apply grease will cause excessive heat at module and premature module failure.**

## POLE PIECE, MAGNET OR PICKUP COIL REPLACE
### Removal

1. With distributor removed, disconnect wires at module terminals, **Fig. 13**.
2. Remove roll pin from drive gear by driving out with 1/8 inch diameter drift punch.
3. Remove gear, shim and the tanged washer from distributor shaft. Remove any burrs that may have been caused by removal of pin.
4. Remove distributor shaft from housing.
5. Remove washer from upper end of distributor housing. Bushings in the housing are not serviceable.
6. Remove three screws securing pole piece to housing and remove pole piece, magnet and pickup coil.

### Installation

1. Install pickup coil, magnet and pole piece and loosely install three screws holding pole piece.
2. With washer installed at top of housing, install distributor shaft and rotate to check for proper clearance between pole piece teeth and timer core teeth.
3. If necessary, realign pole piece to provide adequate clearance and secure properly.
4. Install tanged washer, shim and drive gear (teeth up) to bottom of shaft. Align drive gear and install new roll pin.

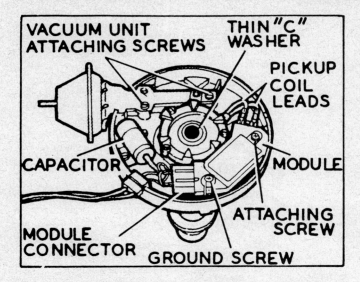

**Fig. 13  Distributor component identification**

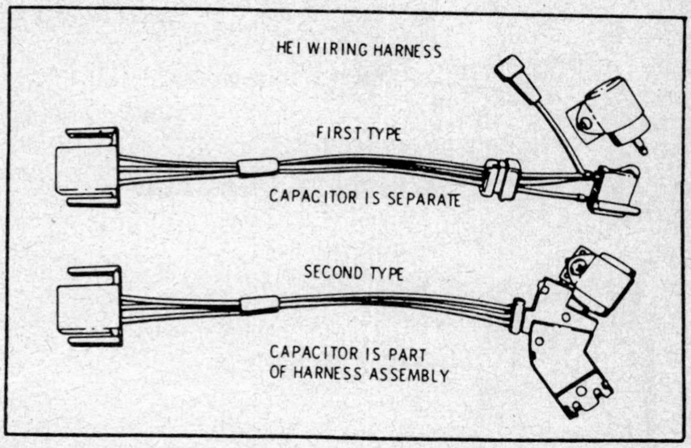

Fig. 14  Ignition module harness identification

## DISTRIBUTOR
## REPLACE
### REMOVAL

1. Disconnect vacuum advance hose and electrical connectors from distributor cap (models with internal coil), then remove cap and position aside.
2. Remove No. 1 spark plug, crank engine until compression pressure can be felt in No. 1 cylinder, then slowly rotate crankshaft until timing marks are aligned at TDC on compression stroke for No. 1 cylinder.
3. Disconnect battery ground cable, then mark position of distributor body in relation to engine and position of rotor contact in relation to distributor body.
4. Remove distributor hold-down bolt, raise distributor noting rotor rotation, place second mark on distributor housing to indicate position where rotor stops moving, then remove distributor. **Do not rotate crankshaft with distributor removed from engine.**

### INSTALLATION

1. Ensure No. 1 cylinder is at TDC on compression stroke as outlined in removal procedure.
2. Align rotor with second mark made in step 4 of removal procedure.
3. Insert distributor into engine, aligning body with mark made on engine prior to removal, then seat distributor in engine. With distributor fully seated, marks made in step 3 of removal procedure should be aligned. If distributor will not seat against boss on engine, oil pump driveshaft may have to be

rotated slightly to allow proper installation.
4. Install hold down clamp and hand tighten retaining bolt.
5. Reverse remaining procedure to complete installation, then adjust ignition timing as outlined.

## DISTRIBUTOR SERVICE
### DISASSEMBLY

1. Remove distributor as outlined, then remove rotor, **Fig. 15.**
2. Remove advance springs and weights (if equipped).
3. Remove module retaining screws and move module to a position where connector may be removed.
4. Remove wires from module terminals.
5. Support distributor gear so that distributor shaft will not be damaged, then remove roll pin by driving it out with a punch.
6. Remove gear, shim and tanged washer from shaft. Remove any burrs that may have been caused by removal of roll pin. Some distributors do not use a shim or tanged washer.
7. Remove distributor shaft and magnet assembly.
8. Remove pole piece retaining screws, pole piece, magnet and pickup coil.
9. Remove lock ring from top of housing, pickup coil retainer and felt washer.
10. Remove vacuum advance unit (if equipped).
11. Remove capacitor and wiring harness from distributor housing.

## ASSEMBLY

1. Install vacuum advance unit (if used) and secure with two screws, **Fig. 15.**
2. Place felt washer over lubricant reservoir at top of housing.
3. Position pick up coil retainer onto housing with vacuum advance arm over actuating pin of vacuum advance mechanism and secure with lock ring.
4. Install pick up coil magnet and pole piece. Loosely install the three retaining screws.
5. Install distributor shaft and rotate to check for even clearance all around between pole piece and shaft projections.
6. Move pole piece to provide even clearance and secure with three retaining screws.
7. Install drive onto shaft with teeth facing up. Drive gear has a dimple on one side next to drive pin hole. Align drive gear so that dimple is on same side of shaft as the rotor pointer. Temporarily install rotor to ensure correct alignment.
8. Install tanged washer, shim and drive gear, then retain with a new roll pin.
9. Install capacitor and loosely install retaining screw.
10. Install connector on module with tab on top, then liberally apply silicone grease to bottom of module and install screws. **Failure to apply silicone grease to module will cause excessive heat build up of module and premature failure.**
11. Position wiring harness with grommet in housing notch, then connect pink wire to capacitor stud and black wire to capacitor retaining screw. Tighten screw.
12. Reconnect wires to module, then install centrifugal advance weights and springs.

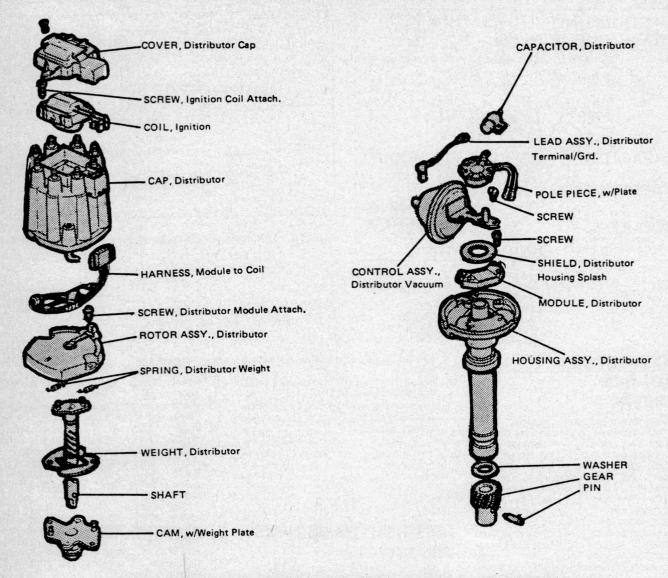

**Fig. 15   Typical High Energy Ignition (HEI) distributor exploded view**

COVER, Distributor Cap

SCREW, Ignition Coil Attach.

COIL, Ignition

CAP, Distributor

HARNESS, Module to Coil

SCREW, Distributor Module Attach.

ROTOR ASSY., Distributor

SPRING, Distributor Weight

WEIGHT, Distributor

SHAFT

CAM, w/Weight Plate

CAPACITOR, Distributor

LEAD ASSY., Distributor
Terminal/Grd.

POLE PIECE, w/Plate

SCREW

SCREW

SHIELD, Distributor
Housing Splash

MODULE, Distributor

CONTROL ASSY.,
Distributor Vacuum

HOUSING ASSY., Distributor

WASHER
GEAR
PIN

# Delco-Remy High Energy Ignition/Electronic Spark Timing (HEI/EST) System Less Sealed Module Connector

## INDEX

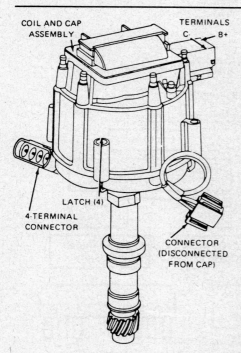

**Fig. 1 Typical HEI/EST distributor. Models w/integral coil**

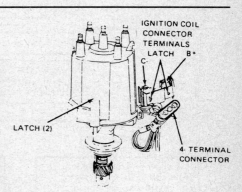

**Fig. 2 Typical HEI/EST distributor. Models w/remote coil**

## DESCRIPTION

The HEI/EST is used on models with Computer Command Control (C-3) or Electronic Fuel Injection systems. The system utilizes a distributor similar to the unit used with conventional HEI systems that has been modified to allow spark advance to be controlled by the fuel control system Electronic Control Module (ECM). Modifications to the distributor include a revised ignition module, with additional terminals to receive signals from the ECM, and the elimination of the conventional centrifugal and vacuum advance mechanisms. In addition, some models use a Hall effect switch mounted above the pickup coil in the distributor to provide a reference pulse to the ECM. The ignition coil on HEI/EST systems is mounted either integral with the distributor, **Fig. 1,** or remotely mounted, **Fig. 2,** depending upon engine and application.

Primary current switching in the HEI/EST system is performed by the ignition module based on reference pulses from the pickup coil as in conventional HEI systems. However, all spark timing changes in the HEI/EST system are performed electronically by the Electronic Control Module (ECM). The ECM monitors information from various engine and vehicle sensors, determines the correct spark timing and signals the distributor to change timing as necessary. An EST bypass circuit is incorporated into the ignition module to allow ignition in case of ECM failure and to allow base timing adjustment.

On some HEI-EST systems, Electronic Spark Control (ESC) is used to retard ignition timing when detonation occurs. The ESC system consists of a knock sensor, distributor module and controller. The knock sensor is an accelerometer or magneto-strictive device, mounted on the engine block. It detects the presence and intensity of detonation by vibration characteristics of the engine. The sensor's output is an electrical signal which is sent to the controller. The controller is a hard-wired signal processor and amplifier which operates from 6 to 16 volts. The ESC controller processes the sensor signal into a command signal to the distributor to adjust spark timing. This is a continuous process monitoring and controlling detonation.

When detonation is detected the spark advance command is delayed, providing the level of retard required. The spark is retarded for 20 seconds, then the spark control returns to EST. The amount of retard is determined by the controller based on the severity of detonation. A failure of the sensor would allow no retard, while controller failure would be indicated by no ignition, no retard or full retard.

## SYSTEM DIAGNOSIS

Refer to diagnostic charts, **Figs. 3 through 5,** for system diagnosis.

Note the following when testing system or system components:

1. Since this is a full 12 volt system, no resistance wire is used. Also, a diagnostic connector is used on some models. This connector is located in the engine compartment on the left side front fender skirt. On vehicles equipped with this connector, a tachometer may be connected between terminals 6 and G.
2. A tachometer connection is incorporated in the wiring connector on the side of the distributor on models with integral coil, or next to the coil battery terminal on models with remote coil.
3. Never connect a wire directly between the Tach terminal of the distributor connector and ground as this will damage the electronic circuitry of the module.
4. When using a timing light to adjust ignition timing, the connection should be made at the No. 1 spark plug using a suitable adapter or inductive pickup. Piercing the plug wire or boot will cause engine misfire.

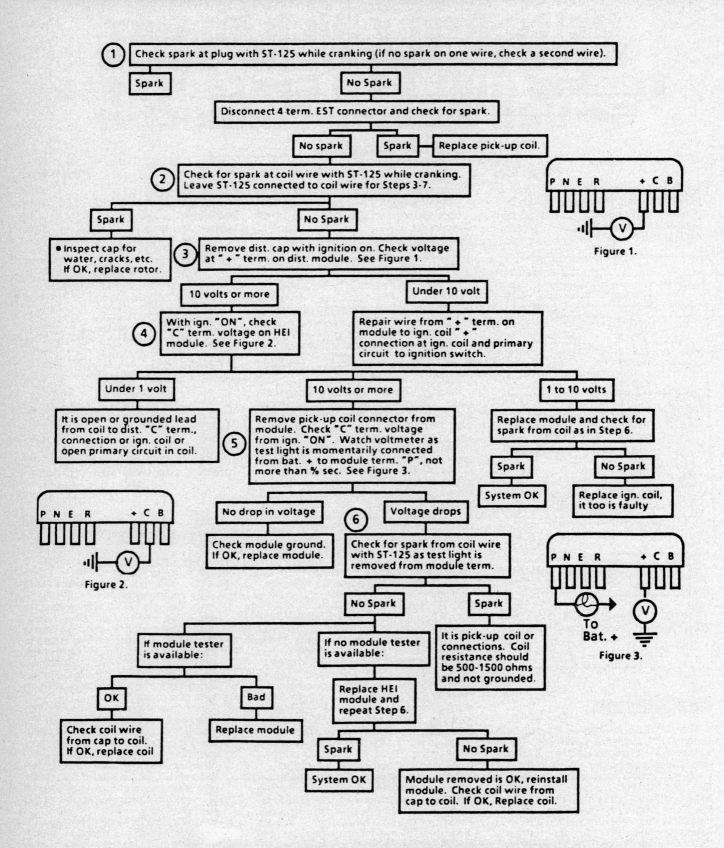

**Fig. 3   HEI/EST ignition system diagnosis. Models w/remote coil**

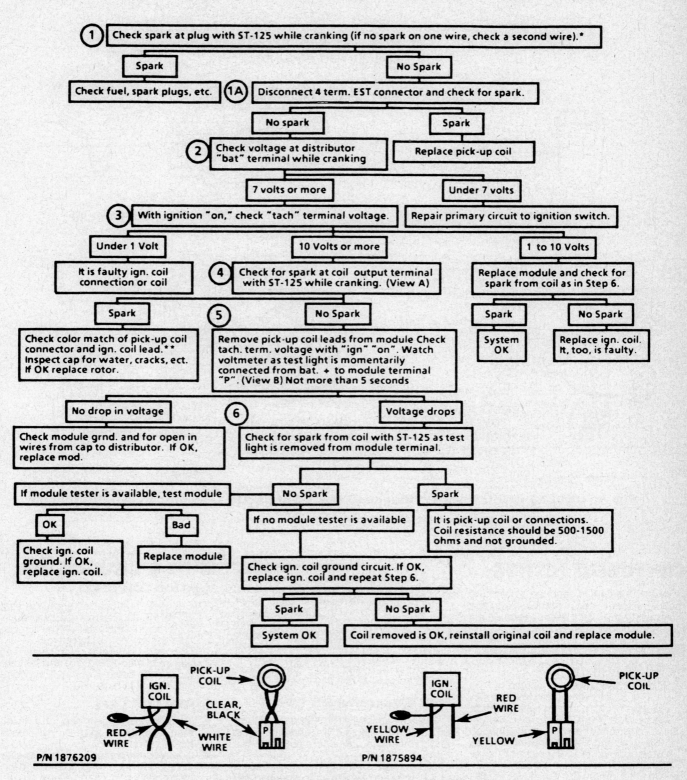

**① Check spark at plug with ST-125 while cranking (if no spark on one wire, check a second wire).***

| Spark | No Spark |

Check fuel, spark plugs, etc.　　**①A** Disconnect 4 term. EST connector and check for spark.

| No spark | Spark |

**② Check voltage at distributor "bat" terminal while cranking**　　Replace pick-up coil

| 7 volts or more | Under 7 volts |

**③ With ignition "on," check "tach" terminal voltage.**　　Repair primary circuit to ignition switch.

| Under 1 Volt | 10 Volts or more | 1 to 10 Volts |

It is faulty ign. coil connection or coil　　**④ Check for spark at coil output terminal with ST-125 while cranking. (View A)**　　Replace module and check for spark from coil as in Step 6.

| Spark | **⑤** No Spark | Spark | No Spark |

Check color match of pick-up coil connector and ign. coil lead.** Inspect cap for water, cracks, ect. If OK replace rotor.　　Remove pick-up coil leads from module Check tach. term. voltage with "ign" "on". Watch voltmeter as test light is momentarily connected from bat. + to module terminal "P". (View B) Not more than 5 seconds　　System OK　　Replace ign. coil. It, too, is faulty.

| No drop in voltage | **⑥** Voltage drops |

Check module grnd. and for open in wires from cap to distributor. If OK, replace mod.　　Check for spark from coil with ST-125 as test light is removed from module terminal.

| No Spark | Spark |

If module tester is available, test module　　If no module tester is available　　It is pick-up coil or connections. Coil resistance should be 500-1500 ohms and not grounded.

| OK | Bad |

Check ign. coil ground. If OK, replace ign. coil.　　Replace module　　Check ign. coil ground circuit. If OK, replace ign. coil and repeat Step 6.

| Spark | No Spark |

System OK　　Coil removed is OK, reinstall original coil and replace module.

PICK-UP COIL
IGN. COIL
CLEAR, BLACK
RED WIRE
WHITE WIRE
P
P/N 1876209

IGN. COIL
RED WIRE
YELLOW WIRE
PICK-UP COIL
YELLOW
P
P/N 1875894

*A few sparks and then nothing, is considered no spark.

**Fig. 4   HEI/EST ignition system diagnosis (Part 1 of 2). 1981–89 models w/integral coil**

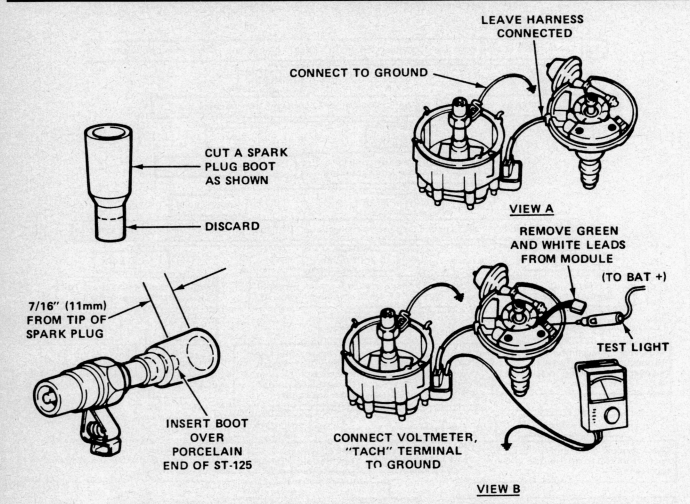

**CUT A SPARK PLUG BOOT AS SHOWN**

**DISCARD**

**LEAVE HARNESS CONNECTED**

**CONNECT TO GROUND**

**VIEW A**

**7/16″ (11mm) FROM TIP OF SPARK PLUG**

**INSERT BOOT OVER PORCELAIN END OF ST-125**

**REMOVE GREEN AND WHITE LEADS FROM MODULE**

**(TO BAT +)**

**TEST LIGHT**

**CONNECT VOLTMETER, "TACH" TERMINAL TO GROUND**

**VIEW B**

**Fig. 4   HEI/EST ignition system diagnosis (Part 2 of 2). 1981—89 models w/integral coil**

# COMPONENT TESTING

Tester J-24624 is required to test the module. If this tester is not available, and malfunction still exists after performing the following checks, replace module.

## UNITS W/REMOTE COIL
### Ignition Coil Test

1. Connect ohmmeter as shown in step 1, **Fig. 6,** and set meter in high scale. Meter should read very high to infinite resistance. If not, coil is defective.
2. Connect ohmmeter as shown in step 2, **Fig. 6,** and set meter on low scale. Meter should read very low or no resistance. If not, coil is defective.
3. Connect ohmmeter as shown in step 3, **Fig. 6,** and set meter on high scale. If meter indicates infinite resistance, coil is defective.

### Pickup Coil Test

1. Remove distributor cap and rotor, then disconnect pickup coil leads from ignition module.

2. Connect ohmmeter as shown in step 1,**Fig. 7,** and flex pickup coil leads while observing meter. Meter should indicate infinite resistance at all times. If not, pickup coil is defective.
3. Connect ohmmeter as shown in step 2, **Fig. 7,** and flex pickup coil leads while observing ohmmeter. Meter should indicate a constant value between 500 and 1500 ohms. If not, pickup coil is defective.

### Hall Effect Switch Test

The Hall effect switch, **Fig. 8,** is mounted above the pickup coil on some models and provides a reference pulse to the ECM.
1. Carefully observing polarity, connect battery and ohmmeter to switch terminals as shown in **Fig. 9.**
2. If meter reading exceeds 0.5 volt, Hall effect switch is defective.
3. Insert knife blade straight down against magnet, **Fig. 7,** while observing voltmeter. Meter should read within 0.5 volts of battery voltage. If not, Hall effect switch is defective.

## UNITS W/INTEGRAL COIL
### Ignition Coil Test

1. Connect ohmmeter as shown in step 1, **Fig. 10,** and set meter on low scale. Meter should indicate low or no resistance. If not, coil is defective.
2. Connect ohmmeter both ways as shown in step 2, **Fig. 10,** and set meter on high scale. If both readings are infinite, coil is defective.

### Pickup Coil Test

1. Remove distributor cap and rotor, then disconnect pickup coil leads from ignition module.
2. Connect ohmmeter as shown in step 1, **Fig. 11,** and flex pickup coil leads while observing meter. Meter should indicate infinite resistance at all times. If not, pickup coil is defective.
3. Connect ohmmeter as shown in step 2, **Fig. 11,** and flex pickup coil leads while observing ohmmeter. Meter should indicate a constant value between 500 and 1500 ohms. If not, pickup coil is defective.

ELECTRONIC SPARK CONTROL (ESC) CHECK
ENGINE KNOCK, POOR PERFORMANCE OR POOR ECONOMY
This chart should only be used after all other causes of Spark Knock have been checked, i.e. Timing,
EGR, MAP, Engine Temperature or Excessive Engine Noise, etc.

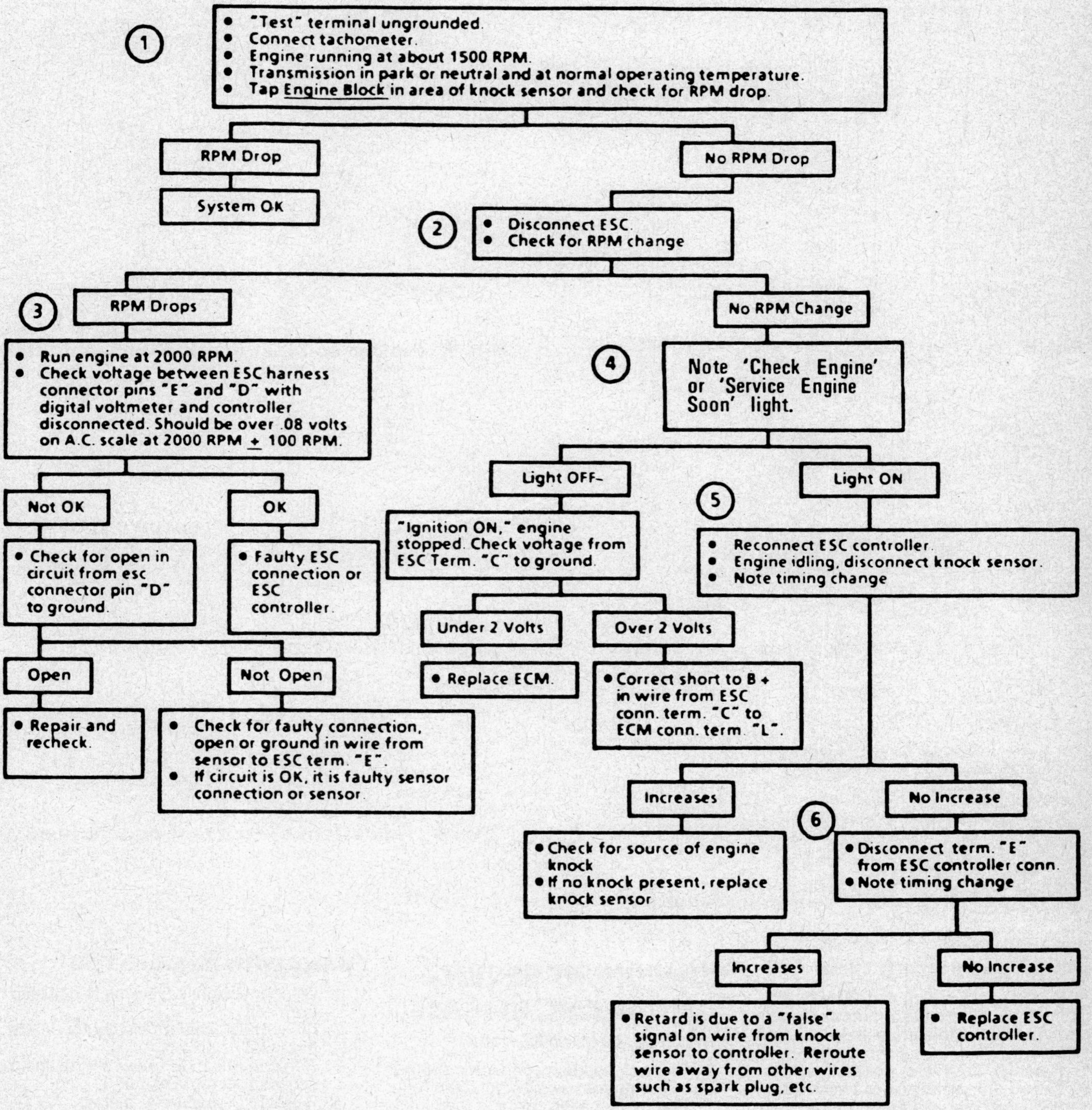

**①**
- "Test" terminal ungrounded.
- Connect tachometer.
- Engine running at about 1500 RPM.
- Transmission in park or neutral and at normal operating temperature.
- Tap <u>Engine Block</u> in area of knock sensor and check for RPM drop.

**RPM Drop**

**System OK**

**No RPM Drop**

**②**
- Disconnect ESC.
- Check for RPM change

**③ RPM Drops**
- Run engine at 2000 RPM.
- Check voltage between ESC harness connector pins "E" and "D" with digital voltmeter and controller disconnected. Should be over .08 volts on A.C. scale at 2000 RPM ± 100 RPM.

**No RPM Change**

**④** Note 'Check Engine' or 'Service Engine Soon' light.

**Not OK**
- Check for open in circuit from esc connector pin "D" to ground.

**OK**
- Faulty ESC connection or ESC controller.

**Light OFF–**
"Ignition ON," engine stopped. Check voltage from ESC Term. "C" to ground.

**Light ON**

**⑤**
- Reconnect ESC controller.
- Engine idling, disconnect knock sensor.
- Note timing change

**Open**
- Repair and recheck.

**Not Open**
- Check for faulty connection, open or ground in wire from sensor to ESC term. "E".
- If circuit is OK, it is faulty sensor connection or sensor.

**Under 2 Volts**
- Replace ECM.

**Over 2 Volts**
- Correct short to B + in wire from ESC conn. term. "C" to ECM conn. term. "L".

**Increases**
- Check for source of engine knock
- If no knock present, replace knock sensor

**No Increase**

**⑥**
- Disconnect term. "E" from ESC controller conn.
- Note timing change

**Increases**
- Retard is due to a "false" signal on wire from knock sensor to controller. Reroute wire away from other wires such as spark plug, etc.

**No Increase**
- Replace ESC controller.

**Fig. 5   Electronic Spark Control (ESC) system check**

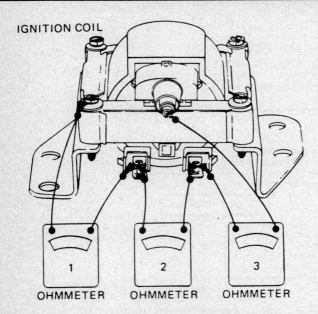

Fig. 6  Ignition coil test connections. Models w/remote coil

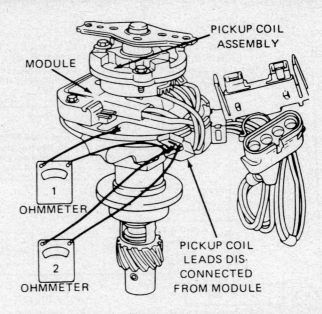

Fig. 7  Pickup coil test connections. Models w/remote coil

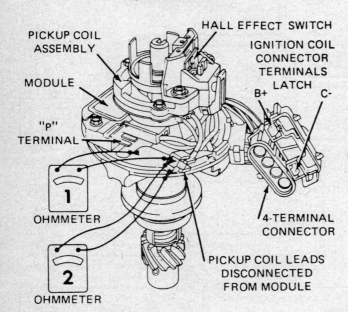

Fig. 8  Hall effect switch installation

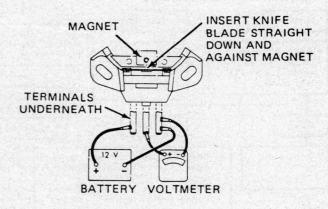

Fig. 9  Hall effect switch test connections

## Hall Effect Switch Test

The Hall effect switch, **Fig. 8**, is mounted above the pickup coil on some models and provides a reference pulse to the ECM.

1. Carefully observing polarity, connect battery and ohmmeter to switch terminals as shown in **Fig. 9**.
2. If meter reading exceeds 0.5 volt, Hall effect switch is defective.
3. Insert knife blade straight down against magnet, **Fig. 7**, while observing voltmeter. Meter should read within 0.5 volts of battery voltage. If not, Hall effect switch is defective.

## COMPONENT SERVICE
### IGNITION COIL, REPLACE
#### Units W/Integral Coil

1. Remove harness connector and battery wire from side of distributor cap.
2. Remove screws holding distributor cover to distributor cap and remove distributor cover.
3. Remove four screws holding coil to cap, **Fig. 12.**
4. Push coil leads out of position in cap and remove coil.
5. Reverse procedure to install.

### Units With Remote Coil

1. Disconnect ignition switch to coil lead from coil.
2. Disconnect coil to distributor leads from coil.
3. Remove coil to engine retaining screws and remove coil.
4. Reverse procedure to install.

### IGNITION MODULE, REPLACE

1. Disconnect wiring harness connector at side of distributor cap, if equipped, then remove distributor cap and rotor.
2. Remove two mounting screws, then

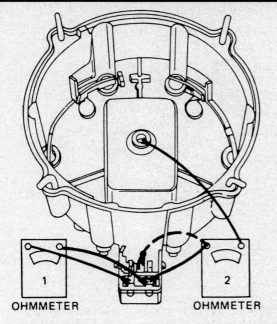

**Fig. 10  Ignition coil test connections. Models w/integral coil**

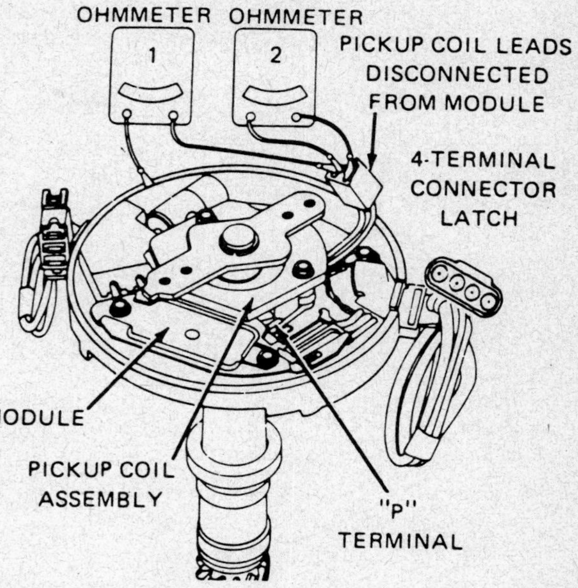

**Fig. 11  Pickup coil test connections. Models w/integral coil**

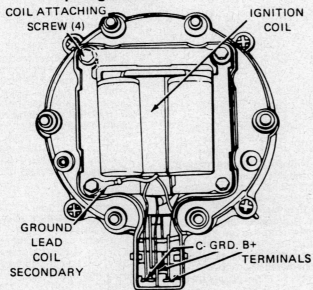

**Fig. 12  Ignition coil installation. Models w/integral coil**

lift module upward.

3. Disconnect electrical connectors from module noting installation position, then remove module.
4. Reverse procedure to install. Prior to installation, coat bottom of new module with dielectric grease (furnished with new module) to aid in heat transfer into distributor housing. **Failure to apply grease will cause excessive heat at module and premature module failure.**

## PICKUP COIL REPLACE
### Removal

1. With distributor removed, disconnect pickup coil leads from module terminals.
2. Remove roll pin from drive gear by driving out with 1/8 inch diameter drift punch.
3. Remove gear, shim and the tanged washer from distributor shaft, as equipped. Remove any burrs that may have been caused by removal of pin.
4. Remove distributor shaft from housing.
5. Remove washer from upper end of distributor housing. Bushings in the housing are not serviceable.
6. Remove pickup coil shield, if equipped, then remove retaining screws and the pile piece, magnet and pick-up coil, **Figs. 13 and 14.**

### Installation

1. Install pick-up coil, magnet and pole piece and loosely install three screws holding pole piece.
2. With washer installed at top of housing, temporarily install distributor shaft and rotate to check for proper clearance between pole piece teeth and timer core teeth.
3. If necessary, realign pole piece to provide adequate clearance and secure properly.
4. Install pickup coil shield, if equipped, then install washer and distributor shaft.
5. Install tanged washer, shim and drive gear (teeth up) to bottom of shaft. Align drive gear and install new roll pin.

## HALL EFFECT SWITCH, REPLACE

1. Disconnect battery ground cable, then remove distributor cap and rotor.
2. Remove switch retaining screws.
3. Disconnect electrical connector while pulling switch away from distributor.
4. Reverse procedure to install. After switch is installed, carefully rotate distributor shaft and check for interference with pole piece. If pole piece contacts switch, loosen switch retaining screws and realign switch as needed.

## DISTRIBUTOR REPLACE
### UNITS W/INTEGRAL COIL
#### Removal

1. Disconnect electrical connectors from distributor cap and disconnect 4 wire

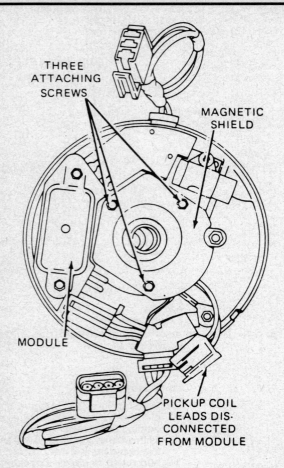

**Fig. 13   Distributor shield installation**

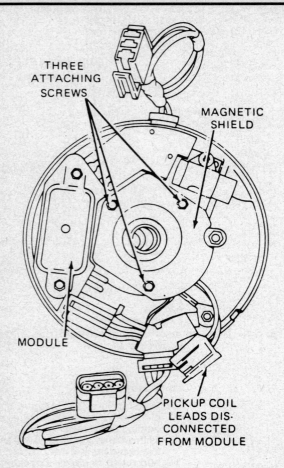

**Fig. 14   Typical pickup coil assembly**

EST connector. **Carefully bend connector locking tabs away from housing by hand to prevent damage to locking tabs.**
2. Remove distributor cap assembly leaving plug wires connected and position cap aside.
3. Remove No. 1 spark plug, crank engine until compression pressure can be felt in No. 1 cylinder, then slowly rotate crankshaft until timing marks are aligned at TDC on compression stroke for No. 1 cylinder.
4. Disconnect battery ground cable, then mark position of distributor body in relation to engine and position of rotor contact in relation to distributor body.
5. Remove distributor hold-down bolt, raise distributor noting rotor rotation, place second mark on distributor housing to indicate position where rotor stops moving, then remove distributor. **Do not rotate crankshaft with distributor removed from engine.**

## Installation

1. Ensure No. 1 cylinder is at TDC on compression stroke as outlined in removal procedure.

2. Align rotor with second mark made in step 5 of removal procedure.
3. Insert distributor into engine, aligning body with mark made on engine prior to removal, then seat distributor in engine. With distributor fully seated, marks made in step 4 of removal procedure should be aligned. If distributor will not seat against boss on engine, oil pump driveshaft may have to be rotated slightly to allow proper installation.
4. Install hold-down clamp and hand tighten retaining bolt.
5. Reverse remaining procedure to complete installation, then adjust ignition timing as outlined.

## UNITS W/REMOTE COIL
### Removal

1. Disconnect distributor harness and feed wire connectors from ignition coil and disconnect EST connector.
2. Remove distributor cap leaving plug wires connected and position cap aside.
3. Remove No. 1 spark plug, crank engine until compression pressure can

be felt in No. 1 cylinder, then slowly rotate crankshaft until timing marks are aligned at TDC on compression stroke for No. 1 cylinder.
4. Disconnect battery ground cable, then mark position of distributor body in relation to engine and position of rotor contact in relation to distributor body.
5. Remove distributor hold-down bolt, raise distributor noting rotor rotation, place second mark on distributor housing to indicate position where rotor stops moving, then remove distributor. **Do not rotate crankshaft with distributor removed from engine.**

## Installation

1. Ensure No. 1 cylinder is at TDC on compression stroke as outlined in removal procedure.
2. Align rotor with second mark made in step 5 of removal procedure.
3. Insert distributor into engine, aligning body with mark made on engine prior to removal, then seat distributor in engine. With distributor fully seated, marks made in step 4 of removal procedure should be aligned. If distributor will not seat against boss on engine, oil pump driveshaft may have to be rotated slightly to allow proper installation.
4. Install hold-down clamp and hand tighten retaining bolt.
5. Reverse remaining procedure to complete installation, then adjust ignition timing as outlined.

## DISTRIBUTOR SERVICE
**Refer to "Component Service" procedures.**

# Delco-Remy High Energy Ignition/Electronic Spark Timing (HEI/EST) System w/Sealed Module Connector

## INDEX

## DESCRIPTION

This system utilizes a distributor similar to the unit used with conventional HEI systems that has been modified to allow spark advance to be controlled by the fuel control system Electronic Control Module (ECM). Modifications to the distributor, **Fig. 1,** include a revised ignition module and sealed module connector, with additional terminals to receive signals from the ECM, and the elimination of the conventional centrifugal and vacuum advance mechanisms. In addition, some models use a Hall effect switch mounted above the pickup coil in the distributor to provide a reference pulse to the ECM. The ignition coil on HEI/EST systems with a sealed module connector is remotely mounted.

Primary current switching in the HEI/EST system is performed by the ignition module based on reference pulses from the pickup coil as in conventional HEI systems. However, all spark timing changes in the HEI/EST system are performed electronically by the Electronic Control Module (ECM). The ECM monitors information from various engine and vehicle sensors, determines the correct spark timing and signals the distributor to change timing as necessary. An EST bypass circuit is incorporated into the ignition module to allow ignition in case of ECM failure and to allow base timing adjustment.

## SYSTEM DIAGNOSIS

Refer to diagnostic chart 2, **Fig 2,** for ignition system diagnosis procedures.

## COMPONENT TESTING

Tester J-24624 is required to test the module. If this tester is not available, and malfunction still exists after performing the following checks, replace module.

## IGNITION COIL TEST

1. Connect ohmmeter as shown in step 1, **Fig. 3,** and set meter on high scale. Meter should indicate very high or infinite resistance. If not, coil is defective.

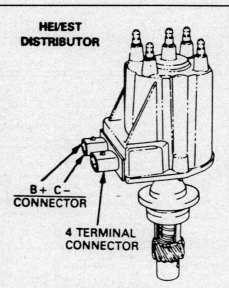

**HEI/EST DISTRIBUTOR**

**B + C −**
**CONNECTOR**

**4 TERMINAL CONNECTOR**

**Fig. 1   Typical sealed module connector distributor**

2. Connect ohmmeter as shown in step 2, **Fig. 3,** and set meter on low scale. Meter should indicate low or no resistance. If not, coil is defective.
3. Connect ohmmeter as shown in step 3, **Fig. 3,** and set meter on high scale. If meter indicates infinite resistance, coil is defective.

## PICKUP COIL TEST

1. Remove distributor cap and rotor, and disconnect pickup coil leads from module.
2. Connect ohmmeter as shown in step 1, **Fig. 4,** and flex pickup coil leads while observing meter. Meter should indicate infinite resistance at all times. If not, pickup coil is defective.
3. Connect ohmmeter as shown in step 2, **Fig. 4,** and flex pickup coil leads while observing meter. Meter reading should remain constant between 500 and 1500 ohms. If not, replace pickup coil.

## COMPONENT SERVICE
### IGNITION COIL

1. Disconnect electrical connectors and high tension lead from coil.
2. Remove coil attaching screws and the coil
3. Reverse procedure to install.

### MODULE

1. Remove distributor cap and rotor.
2. Remove mounting screws, then lift module upward.
3. Disconnect electrical connectors from module noting installation position, then remove module.
4. Reverse procedure to install. Prior to installation, coat bottom of new module with dielectric grease, **Fig. 5,** (furnished with new module) to aid in heat transfer into distributor housing. **Failure to apply grease will cause excessive heat at module and premature module failure.**

### PICKUP COIL, REPLACE
**Removal**

1. Remove distributor as outlined, mark installation position of rotor, then remove rotor by pulling it straight up from distributor shaft.
2. Remove Hall effect switch, if equipped.
3. Remove roll pin from drive gear by driving out with 1/8 inch diameter drift punch.
4. Remove gear, spring and the tanged washer from distributor shaft, **Fig. 6.** Remove any burrs that may have been caused by removal of pin.
4. Remove distributor shaft from housing.
5. Remove thin C-washer from inside pickup coil, pry off retainer, then remove pickup coil. Bushings in the housing are not serviceable.

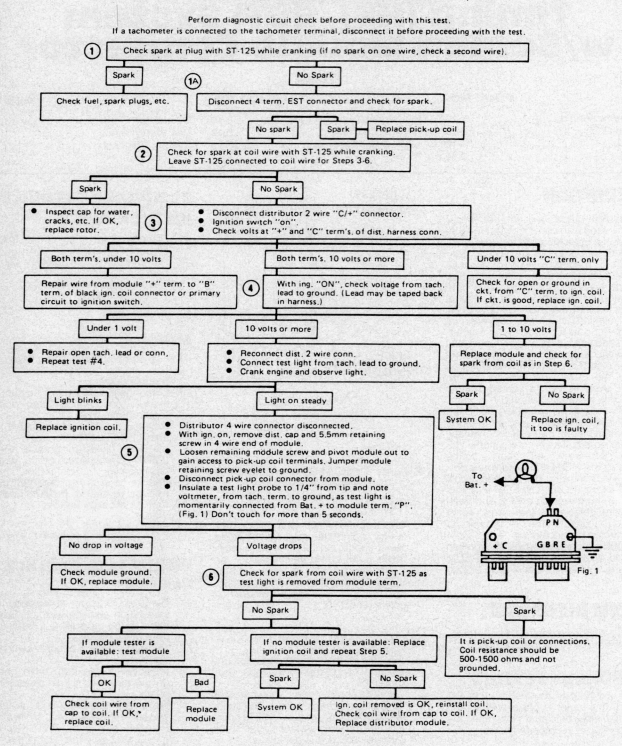

## IGNITION SYSTEM CHECK (REMOTE COIL)
## (SEALED MODULE CONNECTOR DISTRIBUTOR)

Perform diagnostic circuit check before proceeding with this test.
If a tachometer is connected to the tachometer terminal, disconnect it before proceeding with the test.

**①** Check spark at plug with ST-125 while cranking (if no spark on one wire, check a second wire).

**Spark** → Check fuel, spark plugs, etc.

**①A**

**No Spark** → Disconnect 4 term. EST connector and check for spark.

No spark

Spark → Replace pick-up coil

**②** Check for spark at coil wire with ST-125 while cranking. Leave ST-125 connected to coil wire for Steps 3-6.

**Spark** → • Inspect cap for water, cracks, etc. If OK, replace rotor.

**③** **No Spark** → • Disconnect distributor 2 wire "C/+" connector. • Ignition switch "on". • Check volts at "+" and "C" term's. of dist. harness conn.

**Both term's. under 10 volts** → Repair wire from module "+" term. to "B" term. of black ign. coil connector or primary circuit to ignition switch.

**Both term's. 10 volts or more** → **④** With ing. "ON", check voltage from tach. lead to ground. (Lead may be taped back in harness.)

**Under 10 volts "C" term. only** → Check for open or ground in ckt. from "C" term. to ign. coil. If ckt. is good, replace ign. coil.

**Under 1 volt** → • Repair open tach. lead or conn. • Repeat test #4.

**10 volts or more** → • Reconnect dist. 2 wire conn. • Connect test light from tach. lead to ground. • Crank engine and observe light.

**1 to 10 volts** → Replace module and check for spark from coil as in Step 6.

Spark → System OK

No Spark → Replace ign. coil, it too is faulty

**Light blinks** → Replace ignition coil.

**Light on steady** →

**⑤** • Distributor 4 wire connector disconnected. • With ign. on, remove dist. cap and 5.5mm retaining screw in 4 wire end of module. • Loosen remaining module screw and pivot module out to gain access to pick-up coil terminals. Jumper module retaining screw eyelet to ground. • Disconnect pick-up coil connector from module. • Insulate a test light probe to 1/4" from tip and note voltmeter, from tach. term. to ground, as test light is momentarily connected from Bat. + to module term. "P". (Fig. 1) Don't touch for more than 5 seconds.

To Bat. +

P N
+ C    G B R E

Fig. 1

**No drop in voltage** → Check module ground. If OK, replace module.

**Voltage drops** → **⑥** Check for spark from coil wire with ST-125 as test light is removed from module term.

**No Spark**

**Spark** → It is pick-up coil or connections. Coil resistance should be 500-1500 ohms and not grounded.

If module tester is available: test module

If no module tester is available: Replace ignition coil and repeat Step 5.

OK → Check coil wire from cap to coil. If OK, replace coil.

Bad → Replace module

Spark → System OK

No Spark → Ign. coil removed is OK, reinstall coil. Check coil wire from cap to coil. If OK, Replace distributor module.

**Fig. 2   HEI/EST ignition system diagnosis chart**

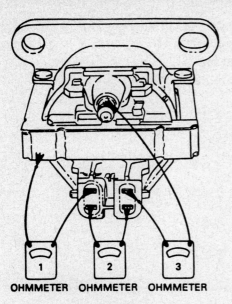

**Fig. 3   Ignition coil test connections**

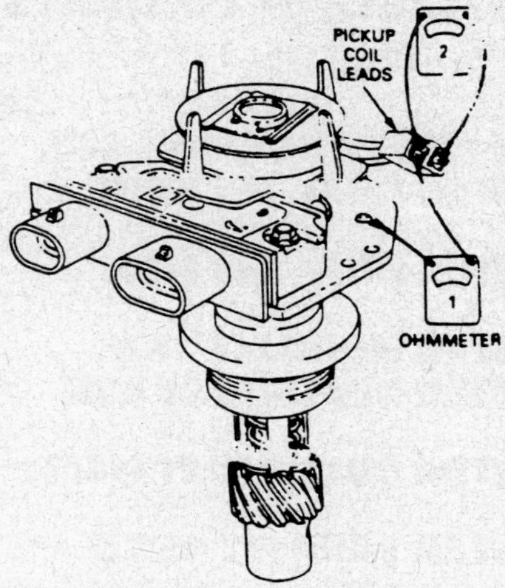

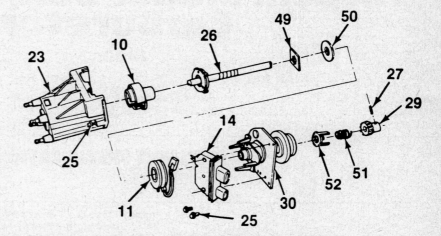

**Fig. 4   Pickup coil test connections**

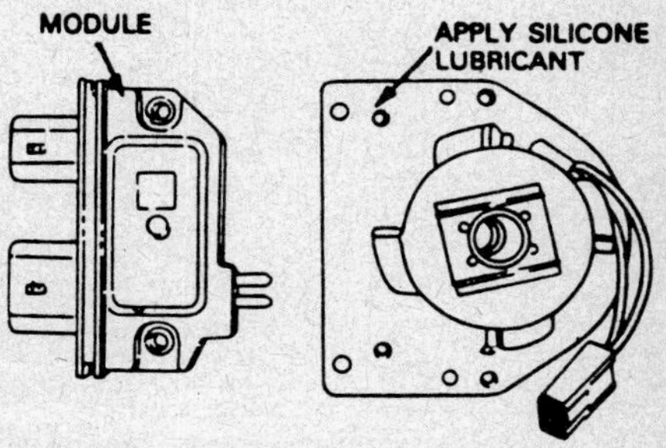

**Fig. 5   Ignition module installation**

10. Rotor
11. Pickup Coil
14. Module
23. Cap
25. Screw
26. Shaft Assembly
27. Pin
29. Gear
30. Housing
49. Retainer
50. Shield
51. Spring
52. Spring Retainer

**Fig. 6   Sealed module connector distributor exploded view**

## Installation

1. Install pickup coil, aligning tab on bottom of coil with anchor hole in housing.
2. Install C-washer and/or retainer, as equipped, then install distributor shaft and rotate to check for proper clearance between pole piece teeth and timer core teeth.
3. Install tanged washer, spring and drive gear (teeth up) to bottom of shaft. Align drive gear and install new roll pin.
4. Reverse remaining procedure to complete installation.

## DISTRIBUTOR
## REPLACE
### REMOVAL

1. Disconnect harness connectors from distributor.

2. Remove distributor cap leaving plug wires connected and position cap aside.
3. Remove No. 1 spark plug, crank engine until compression pressure can be felt in No. 1 cylinder, then slowly rotate crankshaft until timing marks are aligned at TDC on compression stroke for No. 1 cylinder.
4. Disconnect battery ground cable, then mark position of distributor body in relation to engine and position of rotor contact in relation to distributor body.
5. Remove distributor hold-down bolt, raise distributor noting rotor rotation, place second mark on distributor housing to indicate position where rotor stops moving, then remove distributor. **Do not rotate crankshaft with distributor removed from engine.**

### Installation

1. Ensure No. 1 cylinder is at TDC on compression stroke as outlined in re-

moval procedure.
2. Align rotor with second mark made in step 5 of removal procedure.
3. Insert distributor into engine, aligning body with mark made on engine prior to removal, then seat distributor in engine. With distributor fully seated, marks made in step 4 of removal procedure should be aligned. If distributor will not seat against boss on engine, oil pump driveshaft may have to be rotated slightly to allow proper installation.
4. Install hold-down clamp and hand tighten retaining bolt.
5. Reverse remaining procedure to complete installation, then adjust ignition timing as outlined.

## DISTRIBUTOR SERVICE
### Refer to "Component Service" procedures.

# CARBURETORS

## TABLE OF CONTENTS

# Hitachi Model DCH/DFP 340 Carburetor

## INDEX

## ADJUSTMENT SPECIFICATIONS

| Year | Model | Float Level, Inch | Primary Throttle Valve Opening, Degrees | Primary throttle valve opening Clearance, Inch | Secondary Throttle Valve Linkage, Inch | Kick Lever |
|---|---|---|---|---|---|---|
| 1982-85 | DCH/DFP 340 | .059 | ① | ② | .240-.300③ | ③ |

①—Auto. trans., 18°; manual trans., 16°.
②—Auto. trans., .059-.069 inch; manual trans., .050-.059 inch.
③—Refer top text.

## DESCRIPTION

This carburetor is a two barrel, down-draft type unit comprised of a low speed or primary side, and a high speed or secondary side, both integrated into a single unit.

An electric choke is used and incorporates a thermostatic spring which automatically works in response to changes in ambient temperatures, controlling the choke valve and facilitating easier starts. The choke valve is positioned by the action of the thermostatic spring which is activated when the accelerator pedal is depressed. When the engine starts, manifold vacuum is applied to the choke breaker diaphragm unit. The diaphragm unit contains two springs, one of which offsets bi-metal spring tension, balancing the opening of the choke valve with tension of the bi-metal. The bi-metal spring senses engine and ambient temperatures, thereby varying the choke opening and allowing a slightly richer or leaner mixture depending on the temperatures previously mentioned.

## ADJUSTMENTS
### FLOAT LEVEL

If fuel level is within the mark on window of float chamber, with engine stationary, a normal fuel level is indicated. If fuel level is outside the line, adjust by bending float seat. The effective stroke of the needle valve should be about 0.059 inches. To check stroke, hold carburetor bottom side up and fully raise the float. Normal needle valve stroke is indicated by a clearance of 0.059 inches between valve stem and float seat, **Fig. 1.** If necessary, adjust needle valve seat by bending the float stopper.

### PRIMARY THROTTLE VALVE

Check that the primary throttle valve is opened by fast idle adjusting screw to an angle of 16°, with manual transmission or 18°, with automatic transmission when choke valve is completely closed. To

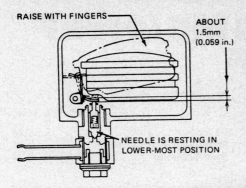

**Fig. 1   Float level adjustment**

check opening angle of primary throttle valve, close choke valve completely and measure clearance between throttle valve and wall of throttle valve chamber at center part of throttle valve, **Fig. 2**. Standard clearances are 0.050 to 0.059 inches with manual transmission and 0.059 to 0.069 with automatic transmission. If needed, throttle valve opening angle may be adjusted with the fast idle adjusting screw. Before measuring the clearance, be certain to turn throttle stop screw in completely.

## SECONDARY THROTTLE VALVE

With primary throttle valve opened to an angle of 47°, the adjust plate is brought into contact with portion (A) of kick lever. With primary throttle valve opened further, the return plate is pulled away from stopper (B), allowing secondary throttle valve to open. To measure secondary throttle valve opening point, measure clearance between primary throttle valve and wall of throttle chamber at center of throttle valve when adjust plate is brought into contact with point (A) of kick lever, **Fig. 3**. Standard clearance (G2) is 0.24 to 0.30 inches, and may be adjusted by bending portion (A) of kick lever.

## KICK LEVER

Turn out throttle adjustment screw until primary side throttle valve is completely closed. Loosen locknut on kick lever screw and turn screw until contact is made with return plate, **Fig. 4**, then tighten locknut.

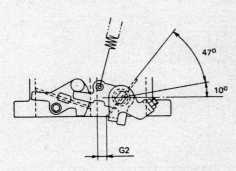

**Fig. 3   Secondary throttle valve linkage adjustment**

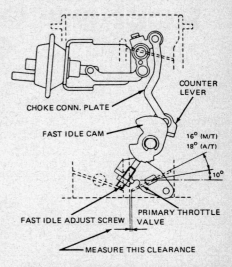

**Fig. 2   Primary throttle valve adjustment**

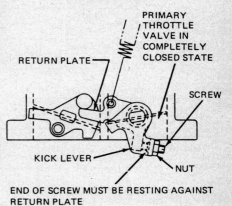

**Fig. 4   Kick lever adjustment**

# Rochester Monojet 1ME/1MEF Carburetors

## INDEX

## ADJUSTMENT SPECIFICATIONS

| Year | Carburetor Number ① | Float Level | Metering Rod | Choke Fast Idle Link | Vacuum Break | Unloader |
|---|---|---|---|---|---|---|
| 1980 | 17058011 | 5/16 | .065 | .150 | — | — |
| | 17080009 | 11/32 | .090 | .275 | .400 | .520 |
| | 17080309 | 11/32 | .090 | .275 | .400 | .520 |
| | 17080358 | 11/32 | .090 | .275 | .400 | .520 |
| 1981–82 | 17081009 | 11/32 | .090 | .275 | .400 | .520 |
| | 17081309 | 11/32 | .090 | .275 | .400 | .520 |
| | 17081329 | 11/32 | .090 | .275 | .400 | .520 |
| 1983–85 | All | 11/32 | .090 | .275 | .400 | .520 |
| 1986–89 | 17086101 | 11/32 | .090 | .275 | .200 | .520 |
| 1987–88 | 17086096 | 11/32 | .090 | .275 | .200 | .520 |
| | 17086102 | 11/32 | .090 | .275 | .200 | .520 |

—Not Available.
① —Refer to "Identification Location."

## IDENTIFICATION LOCATION

The carburetor model identification is stamped on a vertical portion of the float bowl, next to the fuel inlet nut. If the float bowl is to be replaced, follow instructions contained in service package for transferring identification number to replacement float bowl.

## DESCRIPTION

The Monojet 1ME is a single barrel, downdraft carburetor using a triple venturi and plain fuel tube nozzle to draw fuel from an integral float bowl. Fuel enters the carburetor through a pleated paper type fuel filter with an integral check valve. Fuel level within the float bowl is maintained by a plastic composition float acting on a viton tipped needle valve.

Fuel flow in the main metering circuit is controlled by a main well air bleed and variable orifice main jet. Power enrichment is provided by a mechanically operated metering rod connected to the throttle linkage, which varies the opening of the main jet depending upon throttle position.

1MEF carburetors include a metering rod adjusting screw located in the air horn that controls the position of the metering rod in the jet. This screw provides wide open throttle mixture adjustment and is preset at the factory. During normal service the position of this screw should not be altered, as increased exhaust emissions and engine damage may result.

Compensation enrichment during rapid throttle opening is provided by an acceleration pump plunger which draws fuel into the pump bore from the main float bowl. When the throttle is opened, the pump plunger pressurizes fuel within the pump bore, overcoming check ball spring tension and causing a stream of fuel to be delivered into the intake air stream. When pressure in the pump bore decreases, spring tension forces the pump check ball into its seat, preventing further injection of fuel. Then, as the throttle is closed, the pump plunger is raised and additional fuel is drawn into the pump bore through a slot milled into the side of the bore.

The idle/transition circuit consists of upper and lower idle air bleeds, idle and off idle discharge ports and an adjustable metering needle. At idle, vacuum created at the idle discharge port below the throttle plate draws air into the circuit through the upper idle air bleed. Vacuum created by air passing through the idle circuit draws fuel into the circuit from the main jet well through an idle tube. Fuel drawn into the circuit is further emulsified by the lower idle air bleed, and the emulsified mixture is regulated by the metering needle and discharged through the idle discharge port.

As the throttle is opened, vacuum at the idle discharge port decreases and vacuum at the transition discharge port increases. Emulsified fuel is then drawn into the intake air stream through the transition port and regulated by the idle channel restriction.

An integral automatic choke mechanism is used which includes an electrically heated choke coil, linkage actuated fast idle cam and externally mounted choke pull-off. When the engine is cold, the choke blade is closed and fast idle cam set by choke coil tension after fully depressing, then releasing the accelerator pedal. If properly adjusted, this mechanism allows the engine to start and run at fast idle without further modulation of the accelerator pedal. When the engine starts, the vacuum operated pull-off opens the choke blade slightly to allow sufficient air into the carburetor to prevent flooding. As the engine runs, battery voltage applied to the choke coil warms the coil, which then expands and opens the choke blade. Once the choke blade begins to open, quickly depressing, then releasing the accelerator pedal will release the fast idle cam and allow the engine to run at normal curb idle speed.

## ADJUSTMENTS
### FLOAT LEVEL

1. Remove air horn and gasket.

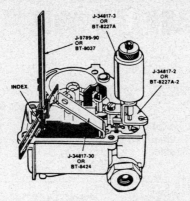

**Fig. 1   Float level adjustment**

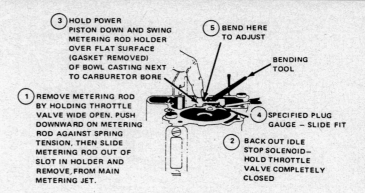

**Fig. 2   Metering rod adjustment**

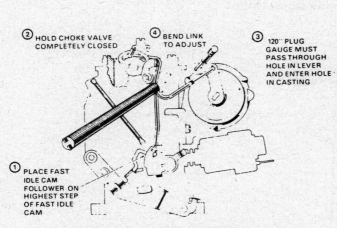

**Fig. 3   Choke coil lever adjustment**

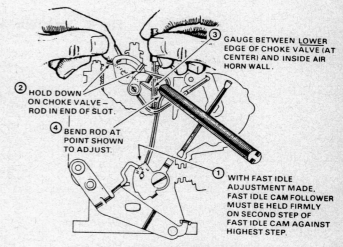

**Fig. 4   Choke rod adjustment**

2. Attach base tool J-34817-2 or BT-8227A-2 to float bowl and retain with air horn attaching screw, **Fig. 1.**
3. Position tool J-34817-3 or BT-8227A into base, ensuring contact point rests against outer edge of float lever.
4. Using adjustable T-scale, measure distance from top of casting to top of index at float toe.
5. If float adjustment is not within 2/32 inch from specification, bend lever up or down as required with tool shown, **Fig. 1.**
6. Remove bending tool, then repeat steps 2 through 4.
7. Check float alignment, then reassemble carburetor.

## METERING ROD

1. Remove metering rod by holding throttle valve wide open. Push downward on metering rod against spring tension, then slide metering rod out of slot in holder and remove from main metering jet.
2. To check adjustment, back out idle stop solenoid and rotate fast idle cam so that fast idle cam follower is not contacting steps on cam.

3. With throttle valve completely closed, apply pressure to top of power piston and hold piston down against its stop, **Fig. 2.**
4. While holding downward pressure on power piston, swing metering rod holder over flat surface of bowl casting next to carburetor bore.
5. Insert specified size gauge between bowl casting sealing bead and lower surface of metering rod holder. Gauge should have a slide fit between both surfaces as shown.
6. To adjust, carefully bend metering rod holder up or down at point shown.
7. After adjustment, install metering rod.

## CHOKE COIL LEVER

1. With fast idle adjusting screw on fast idle cam high step, close choke valve.
2. Insert a .120 inch gauge pin through hole in lever and into casting, **Fig. 3.** If holes do not align, bend link to adjust.

## CHOKE ROD

1. With fast idle adjustment made, place fast idle cam follower on second step of fast idle cam and hold firmly against the rise to the high step.

2. Rotate choke towards direction of closed choke by applying force to choke coil lever, **Fig. 4.**
3. Bend choke rod at point shown to give specified opening between lower edge of choke valve (at center of valve) and inside air horn wall.

## VACUUM BREAK

1. With fast idle screw on fast idle cam high step, seat diaphragm using an outside vacuum source. Cover purge hole with a piece of tape, if equipped.
2. Close choke valve to compress plunger bucking spring and seat plunger stem.
3. Place specified size gauge between lower edge of choke valve and air horn wall. Bend link to adjust, **Fig. 5.**

## UNLOADER

1. With throttle valve wide open, hold choke valve closed with specified gauge between lower edge of choke valve and air horn wall, **Fig. 6.**
2. If distance is not within specifications, bend unloader tang to adjust.

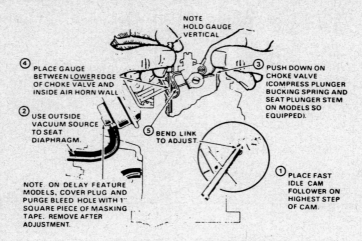

**Fig. 5   Vacuum break adjustment**

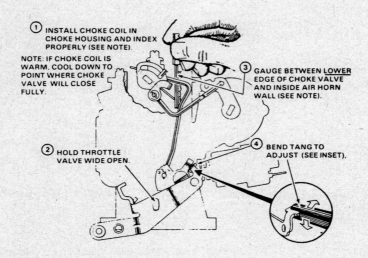

**Fig. 6   Unloader adjustment**

# Rochester Varajet 2SE & E2SE Series Carburetors

## INDEX

## ADJUSTMENT SPECIFICATIONS, 4-121/2.0L & V6-173/2.8L ENGINES

| Year | Carb. Production No. | Float Level | Choke Coil Lever | | Vacuum Break Primary | Vacuum Break Secondary | Air Valve Rod | Unloader | Secondary Lockout | Air Valve Spring (Turns) |
|---|---|---|---|---|---|---|---|---|---|---|
| 1982 | 17082348 | 7/16 | — | 22° | 30° | 32° | 1° | 40° | .025 | 1 |
| | 17082349 | 7/16 | — | 22° | 30° | 32° | 1° | 40° | .025 | 1 |
| | 17082350 | 7/16 | — | 22° | 30° | 32° | 1° | 40° | .025 | 1 |
| | 17082351 | 7/16 | — | 22° | 30° | 32° | 1° | 40° | .025 | 1 |
| | 17082353 | 7/16 | — | 22° | 30° | 35° | 1° | 40° | .025 | 1 |
| | 17082355 | 7/16 | — | 22° | 30° | 35° | 1° | 40° | .025 | 1 |
| | 17082356 | 13/16 | .085 | 22° | 25° | 30° | 1° | 30° | .025 | 1 |
| | 17082357 | 13/16 | .085 | 22° | 25° | 32° | 1° | 30° | .025 | 1 |
| | 17082358 | 13/16 | .085 | 22° | 25° | 30° | 1° | 30° | .025 | 1 |
| | 17082359 | 13/16 | .085 | 22° | 25° | 32° | 1° | 30° | .025 | 1 |
| 1983 | 17083348 | 7/16 | .085 | 22° | 30° | 32° | 1° | 40° | .025 | 1 |
| | 17083349 | 7/16 | .085 | 22° | 30° | 32° | 1° | 40° | .025 | 1 |
| | 17083350 | 7/16 | .085 | 22° | 30° | 32° | 1° | 40° | .025 | 1 |
| | 17083351 | 7/16 | .085 | 22° | 30° | 32° | 1° | 40° | .025 | 1 |
| | 17083352 | 7/16 | .085 | 22° | 30° | 35° | 1° | 40° | .025 | 1 |
| | 17083353 | 7/16 | .085 | 22° | 30° | 35° | 1° | 40° | .025 | 1 |
| | 17083354 | 7/16 | .085 | 22° | 30° | 35° | 1° | 40° | .025 | 1 |
| | 17083355 | 7/16 | .085 | 22° | 30° | 35° | 1° | 40° | .025 | 1 |
| | 17083360 | 7/16 | .085 | 22° | 30° | 32° | 1° | 40° | .025 | 1 |
| | 17083361 | 7/16 | .085 | 22° | 28° | 32° | 1° | 40° | .025 | 1 |
| | 17083362 | 7/16 | .085 | 22° | 30° | 32° | 1° | 40° | .025 | 1 |
| | 17083363 | 7/16 | .085 | 22° | 28° | 32° | 1° | 40° | .025 | 1 |
| | 17083364 | 7/16 | .085 | 22° | 30° | 35° | 1° | 40° | .025 | 1 |
| | 17083365 | 7/16 | .085 | 22° | 30° | 35° | 1° | 40° | .025 | 1 |
| | 17083366 | 7/16 | .085 | 22° | 30° | 35° | 1° | 40° | .025 | 1 |
| | 17083367 | 7/16 | .085 | 22° | 30° | 35° | 1° | 40° | .025 | 1 |
| | 17083391 | 13/16 | .085 | 28° | 30° | 35° | 1° | 38° | .025 | 1¼ |
| | 17083392 | 13/16 | .085 | 28° | 30° | 35° | 1° | 38° | .025 | 1¼ |
| | 17083393 | 13/16 | .085 | 28° | 30° | 35° | 1° | 38° | .025 | 1¼ |
| | 17083394 | 13/16 | .085 | 28° | 30° | 35° | 1° | 38° | .025 | 1¼ |
| | 17083395 | 13/16 | .085 | 28° | 30° | 35° | 1° | 38° | .025 | 1¼ |
| | 17083396 | 13/16 | .085 | 28° | 30° | 35° | 1° | 38° | .025 | 1¼ |
| | 17083397 | 13/16 | .085 | 28° | 30° | 35° | 1° | 38° | .025 | 1¼ |

## ADJUSTMENT SPECIFICATIONS, 4-121/2.0L & V6-173/2.8L ENGINES— Continued

| Year | Carb. Production No. | Float Level | Choke Coil Lever | | Vacuum Break | | Air Valve Rod | Unloader | Secondary Lockout | Air Valve Spring (Turns) |
|------|------|------|------|------|------|------|------|------|------|------|
| | | | | | Primary | Secondary | | | | |
| 1984 | 17084348 | 11/32 | .085 | 22° | 30° | 32° | 1° | 40° | .025 | 1 |
| | 17084349 | 11/32 | .085 | 22° | 30° | 32° | 1° | 40° | .025 | 1 |
| | 17084350 | 11/32 | .085 | 22° | 30° | 32° | 1° | 40° | .025 | 1 |
| | 17084351 | 11/32 | .085 | 22° | 30° | 32° | 1° | 40° | .025 | 1 |
| | 17084352 | 11/32 | .085 | 22° | 30° | 35° | 1° | 40° | .025 | 1 |
| | 17084353 | 11/32 | .085 | 22° | 30° | 35° | 1° | 40° | .025 | 1 |
| | 17084354 | 11/32 | .085 | 22° | 30° | 35° | 1° | 40° | .025 | 1 |
| | 17084355 | 11/32 | .085 | 22° | 30° | 35° | 1° | 40° | .025 | 1 |
| | 17084356 | 9/32 | .085 | 22° | 25° | 30° | 1° | 30° | .025 | ¾ |
| | 17084357 | 9/32 | .085 | 22° | 25° | 30° | 1° | 30° | .025 | ¾ |
| | 19084358 | 9/32 | .085 | 22° | 25° | 30° | 1° | 30° | .025 | ¾ |
| | 17084359 | 9/32 | .085 | 22° | 25° | 30° | 1° | 30° | .025 | ¾ |
| | 17084360 | 5/32 | .085 | 22° | 30° | 32° | 1° | 40° | .025 | 1 |
| | 17084362 | 5/32 | .085 | 22° | 30° | 32° | 1° | 40° | .025 | 1 |
| | 17084364 | 5/32 | .085 | 22° | 30° | 35° | 1° | 40° | .025 | 1 |
| | 17084366 | 5/32 | .085 | 22° | 30° | 35° | 1° | 40° | .025 | 1 |
| | 17084368 | 4/32 | .085 | 22° | 25° | 30° | 1° | 30° | .025 | ¾ |
| | 17084370 | 4/32 | .085 | 22° | 25° | 30° | 1° | 30° | .025 | ¾ |
| | 17084390 | 7/16 | .085 | 28° | 30° | 38° | 1° | 38° | .025 | 1½ |
| | 17084391 | 7/16 | .085 | 28° | 30° | 38° | 1° | 38° | .025 | 1½ |
| | 17084392 | 7/16 | .085 | 28° | 30° | 38° | 1° | 38° | .025 | 1½ |
| | 17084393 | 7/16 | .085 | 28° | 30° | 38° | 1° | 38° | .025 | 1½ |
| | 17084410 | 11/32 | .085 | 15° | 23° | 38° | 1° | 42° | .025 | — |
| | 17084412 | 11/32 | .085 | 15° | 23° | 38° | 1° | 42° | .025 | — |
| | 17084425 | 11/32 | .085 | 15° | 26° | 36° | 1° | 40° | .025 | — |
| | 17084427 | 11/32 | .085 | 15° | 26° | 36° | 1° | 40° | .025 | — |
| | 17084430 | 11/32 | .085 | 15° | 26° | 38° | 1° | 42° | .025 | 1 |
| | 17084431 | 11/32 | .085 | 15° | 26° | 38° | 1° | 42° | .025 | 1 |
| | 17084434 | 11/32 | .085 | 15° | 26° | 38° | 1° | 42° | .025 | 1 |
| | 17084435 | 11/32 | .085 | 15° | 26° | 38° | 1° | 42° | .025 | 1 |
| | 17084534 | 5/32 | .085 | 28° | 25° | 35° | 1° | 45° | .025 | ½ |
| | 17084535 | 5/32 | .085 | 28° | 25° | 35° | 1° | 45° | .025 | ½ |
| | 17084537 | 5/32 | .085 | 28° | 25° | 35° | 1° | 45° | .025 | ½ |
| | 17084538 | 5/32 | .085 | 28° | 25° | 35° | 1° | 45° | .025 | ½ |
| | 17084540 | 5/32 | .085 | 28° | 25° | 35° | 1° | 45° | .025 | ½ |
| | 17084542 | 4/32 | .085 | 28° | 25° | 35° | 1° | 45° | .025 | ½ |
| | 17084560 | 11/32 | .085 | 15° | 24° | 34° | 1° | 38° | .025 | — |
| | 17084562 | 11/32 | .085 | 15° | 24° | 34° | 1° | 38° | .025 | — |
| | 17084569 | 11/32 | .085 | 15° | 24° | 34° | 1° | 38° | .025 | — |
| | 17084632 | 9/32 | .085 | 28° | 25° | 35° | 1° | 45° | .025 | ½ |
| | 17084633 | 9/32 | .085 | 28° | 25° | 35° | 1° | 45° | .025 | ½ |
| | 17084635 | 9/32 | .085 | 28° | 25° | 35° | 1° | 45° | .025 | ½ |
| | 17084636 | 9/32 | .085 | 28° | 25° | 35° | 1° | 45° | .025 | ½ |

## ADJUSTMENT SPECIFICATIONS, 4-121/2.0L & V6-173/2.8L ENGINES— Continued

| Year | Carb. Production No. | Float Level | Choke Coil Lever | | Vacuum Break | | Air Valve Rod | Unloader | Secondary Lockout | Air Valve Spring (Turns) |
|------|------|------|------|------|------|------|------|------|------|------|
| | | | | | Primary | Secondary | | | | |
| 1985 | 17084534 | 5/32 | .085 | 28° | 25° | 35° | 1° | 45° | .025 | 1/2 |
| | 17084535 | 5/32 | .085 | 28° | 25° | 35° | 1° | 45° | .025 | 1/2 |
| | 17084540 | 5/32 | .085 | 28° | 25° | 35° | 1° | 45° | .025 | 1/2 |
| | 17084542 | 4/32 | .085 | 28° | 25° | 35° | 1° | 45° | .025 | 1/2 |
| | 17085348 | 5/32 | .085 | 22° | 32° | 36° | 1° | 40° | .025 | 1 |
| | 17085350 | 5/32 | .085 | 22° | 32° | 36° | 1° | 40° | .025 | 1 |
| | 17085351 | 11/32 | .085 | 22° | 32° | 36° | 1° | 40° | .025 | 1 |
| | 17085352 | 5/32 | .085 | 22° | 30° | 34° | 1° | 40° | .025 | 1 |
| | 17085354 | 5/32 | .085 | 22° | 30° | 34° | 1° | 40° | .025 | 1 |
| | 17085355 | 11/32 | .085 | 22° | 30° | 34° | 1° | 40° | .025 | 1 |
| | 17085356 | 4/32 | .085 | 22° | 25° | 30° | 1° | 30° | .025 | 1 |
| | 17085357 | 9/32 | .085 | 22° | 25° | 30° | 1° | 30° | .025 | 1 |
| | 17085358 | 4/32 | .085 | 22° | 25° | 30° | 1° | 30° | .025 | 1 |
| | 17085359 | 9/32 | .085 | 22° | 25° | 30° | 1° | 30° | .025 | 1 |
| | 17085360 | 5/32 | .085 | 22° | 32° | 36° | 1° | 40° | .025 | 1 |
| | 17085362 | 5/32 | .085 | 22° | 32° | 36° | 1° | 40° | .025 | 1 |
| | 17085363 | 11/32 | .085 | 22° | 32° | 36° | 1° | 40° | .025 | 1 |
| | 17085364 | 5/32 | .085 | 22° | 30° | 34° | 1° | 40° | .025 | 1 |
| | 17085366 | 5/32 | .085 | 22° | 30° | 34° | 1° | 40° | .025 | 1 |
| | 17085367 | 11/32 | .085 | 22° | 30° | 34° | 1° | 40° | .025 | 1 |
| | 17085368 | 4/32 | .085 | 22° | 25° | 30° | 1° | 30° | .025 | 1 |
| | 17085369 | 9/32 | .085 | 22° | 25° | 30° | 1° | 30° | .025 | 1 |
| | 17085370 | 4/32 | .085 | 22° | 25° | 30° | 1° | 30° | .025 | 1 |
| | 17085371 | 9/32 | .085 | 22° | 25° | 30° | 1° | 30° | .025 | 1 |
| | 17075372 | 5/32 | .085 | 22° | 32° | 36° | 1° | 40° | .025 | 3/4 |
| | 17085374 | 5/32 | .085 | 22° | 32° | 36° | 1° | 40° | .025 | 3/4 |
| | 17085452 | 5/32 | .085 | 28° | 25° | 35° | 1° | 45° | .025 | 1/2 |
| | 17085453 | 5/32 | .085 | 28° | 25° | 35° | 1° | 45° | .025 | 1/2 |
| | 17085458 | 5/32 | .085 | 28° | 25° | 35° | 1° | 45° | .025 | 1/2 |

## ADJUSTMENT SPECIFICATIONS, 6-250/4.1L ENGINES

| Year | Carb. Production No. | Float Level | Accel. Pump | Choke Coil Lever | Choke Rod | Vacuum Break Primary | Vacuum Break Secondary | Air Valve Rod | Unloader | Secondary Lockout | Air Valve Spring (Turns) |
|------|---------------------|-------------|-------------|------------------|-----------|---------|-----------|--------------|----------|-------------------|--------------------------|
| 1980 | 17059774 | 3/16 | 15/32 | .085 | 18° | 18° | — | 2° | 32° | .025 | — |
|      | 17059775 | — | — | .085 | — | — | — | — | — | .025 | — |
|      | 17059776 | 3/16 | 15/32 | .085 | 18° | 18° | — | 2° | 32° | .025 | — |
|      | 17059777 | — | — | .085 | — | — | — | — | — | .025 | — |
|      | 17080621 | 1/8 | 9/16 | .085 | 17° | 22° | 35° | 2° | 41° | .025 | — |
|      | 17080622 | 1/8 | 9/16 | .085 | 17° | 22° | 35° | 2° | 41° | .025 | — |
|      | 17080623 | 1/8 | 9/16 | .085 | 17° | 22° | 35° | 2° | 41° | .025 | — |
|      | 17080626 | 1/8 | 9/16 | .085 | 17° | 22° | 35° | 2° | 41° | .025 | — |
|      | 17080674 | 3/16 | 1/2 | .085 | 18° | 19° | — | 2° | 32° | .025 | — |
|      | 17080675 | 3/16 | 1/2 | .085 | 18° | 21° | — | 2° | 32° | .025 | — |
|      | 17080676 | 3/16 | 1/2 | .085 | 18° | 19° | — | 2° | 32° | .025 | — |
|      | 17080677 | 3/16 | 1/2 | .085 | 18° | 21° | — | 2° | 32° | .025 | — |
|      | 17080720 | 1/8 | 9/16 | .085 | 17° | 20° | 35° | 2° | 41° | .025 | — |
|      | 17080721 | 1/8 | 9/16 | .085 | 17° | 23.5° | 35° | 2° | 41° | .025 | — |
|      | 17080722 | 1/8 | 9/16 | .085 | 17° | 20° | 35° | 2° | 41° | .025 | — |
|      | 17080723 | 1/8 | 9/16 | .085 | 17° | 23.5° | 35° | 2° | 41° | .025 | — |
| 1981 | 17081621 | 3/16 | — | .085 | 15° | 26° | 38° | 1° | 38° | .025 | — |
|      | 17081622 | 3/16 | — | .085 | 15° | 26° | 38° | 1° | 38° | .025 | — |
|      | 17081623 | 3/16 | — | .085 | 15° | 26° | 38° | 1° | 38° | .025 | — |
|      | 17081624 | 3/16 | — | .085 | 15° | 26° | 38° | 1° | 38° | .025 | — |
|      | 17081625 | 3/16 | — | .085 | 15° | 26° | 38° | 1° | 38° | .025 | — |
|      | 17081626 | 3/16 | — | .085 | 15° | 26° | 38° | 1° | 38° | .025 | — |
|      | 17081627 | 3/16 | — | .085 | 15° | 26° | 38° | 1° | 38° | .025 | — |
|      | 17081629 | 3/16 | — | .085 | 15° | 26° | 38° | 1° | 41° | .025 | — |
|      | 17081630 | 3/16 | — | .085 | 15° | 26° | 38° | 1° | 38° | .025 | — |
|      | 17081633 | 3/16 | — | .085 | 15° | 26° | 38° | 1° | 38° | .025 | — |
|      | 17081720 | 3/16 | — | .085 | 15° | 30° | 37° | 1° | 41° | .025 | — |
|      | 17081721 | 3/16 | — | .085 | 15° | 30° | 37° | 1° | 41° | .025 | — |
|      | 17081725 | 3/16 | — | .085 | 15° | 30° | 37° | 1° | 41° | .025 | — |
|      | 17081726 | 3/16 | — | .085 | 15° | 30° | 37° | 1° | 41° | .025 | — |
|      | 17081727 | 3/16 | — | .085 | 15° | 30° | 37° | 1° | 41° | .025 | — |

## ADJUSTMENT SPECIFICATIONS, 6-250/4.1L ENGINES—Continued

| Year | Carb. Production No. | Float Level | Accel. Pump | Choke Coil Lever | Choke Rod | Vacuum Break | | Air Valve Rod | Unloader | Secondary Lockout | Air Valve Spring (Turns) |
|------|------|------|------|------|------|------|------|------|------|------|------|
| | | | | | | Primary | Secondary | | | | |
| 1982 | 17082334 | 3/16 | — | .085 | 15° | 26° | 38° | 1° | 42° | .025 | — |
| | 17082335 | 3/16 | — | .085 | 15° | 26° | 38° | 1° | 42° | .025 | — |
| | 17082336 | 3/16 | — | .085 | 15° | 26° | 38° | 1° | 42° | .025 | — |
| | 17082337 | 3/16 | — | .085 | 15° | 26° | 38° | 1° | 42° | .025 | — |
| | 17082338 | 3/16 | — | .085 | 15° | 26° | 38° | 1° | 42° | .025 | — |
| | 17082339 | 3/16 | — | .085 | 15° | 26° | 38° | 1° | 42° | .025 | — |
| | 17082341 | 3/16 | — | .085 | 15° | 30° | 37° | 1° | 42° | .025 | — |
| | 17082342 | 3/16 | — | .085 | 15° | 30° | 37° | 1° | 42° | .025 | — |
| | 17082344 | 3/16 | — | .085 | 15° | 30° | 37° | 1° | 42° | .025 | — |
| | 17-82345 | 3/16 | — | .085 | 15° | 30° | 37° | 1° | 42° | .025 | — |
| | 17082431 | 3/16 | — | .085 | 15° | 24° | 38° | 1° | 42° | .025 | — |
| | 17082433 | 3/16 | — | .085 | 15° | 24° | 38° | 1° | 42° | .025 | — |
| | 17082480 | 3/16 | — | .085 | 15° | 26° | 38° | 1° | 42° | .025 | — |
| | 17082481 | 3/16 | — | .085 | 15° | 26° | 38° | 1° | 42° | .025 | — |
| | 17082482 | 3/16 | — | .085 | 15° | 23° | 38° | 1° | 42° | .025 | — |
| | 17082483 | 3/16 | — | .085 | 15° | 26° | 38° | 1° | 42° | .025 | — |
| | 17082484 | 3/16 | — | .085 | 15° | 26° | 38° | 1° | 42° | .025 | — |
| | 17082485 | 3/16 | — | .085 | 15° | 26° | 38° | 1° | 42° | .025 | — |
| | 17082486 | 3/16 | — | .085 | 15° | 28° | 38° | 1° | 42° | .025 | — |
| | 17082487 | 3/16 | — | .085 | 15° | 28° | 38° | 1° | 42° | .025 | — |
| | 17082488 | 3/16 | — | .085 | 15° | 28° | 38° | 1° | 42° | .025 | — |
| | 17042489 | 3/16 | — | .085 | 15° | 28° | 38° | 1° | 42° | .025 | — |
| 1983 | 17083410 | 3/16 | — | .085 | 15° | 23° | 38° | 1° | 42° | .025 | — |
| | 17083411 | 3/16 | — | .085 | 15° | 26° | 38° | 1° | 42° | .025 | — |
| | 17083412 | 3/16 | — | .085 | 15° | 23° | 38° | 1° | 42° | .025 | — |
| | 17083413 | 3/16 | — | .085 | 15° | 26° | 38° | 1° | 42° | .025 | — |
| | 17083414 | 3/16 | — | .085 | 15° | 23° | 38° | 1° | 42° | .025 | — |
| | 17083415 | 3/16 | — | .085 | 15° | 26° | 38° | 1° | 42° | .025 | — |
| | 17083416 | 3/16 | — | .085 | 15° | 23° | 38° | 1° | 42° | .025 | — |
| | 17083417 | 3/16 | — | .085 | 15° | 26° | 38° | 1° | 42° | .025 | — |
| | 17083419 | 3/16 | — | .085 | 15° | 26° | 38° | 1° | 42° | .025 | — |
| | 17083421 | 3/16 | — | .085 | 15° | 26° | 38° | 1° | 42° | .025 | — |
| | 17083423 | 3/16 | — | .085 | 15° | 28° | 38° | 1° | 42° | .025 | — |
| | 17083425 | 3/16 | — | .085 | 15° | 26° | 38° | 1° | 42° | .025 | — |
| | 17083427 | 3/16 | — | .085 | 15° | 26° | 38° | 1° | 42° | .025 | — |
| | 17083429 | 3/16 | — | .085 | 15° | 28° | 38° | 1° | 42° | .025 | — |
| | 17083430 | 11/32 | — | .085 | 15° | 26° | 38° | 1° | 42° | .025 | 1 |
| | 17083431 | 11/32 | — | .085 | 15° | 26° | 38° | 1° | 42° | .025 | 1 |
| | 17083434 | 11/32 | — | .085 | 15° | 26° | 38° | 1° | 42° | .025 | 1 |
| | 17083435 | 11/32 | — | .085 | 15° | 26° | 38° | 1° | 42° | .025 | 1 |
| | 17083460 | 3/16 | — | .085 | 15° | 28° | 38° | 1° | 42° | .025 | — |
| | 17083562 | 3/16 | — | .085 | 15° | 28° | 38° | 1° | 42° | .025 | — |
| | 17083565 | 3/16 | — | .085 | 15° | 28° | 38° | 1° | 42° | .025 | — |
| | 17023569 | 3/16 | — | .085 | 15° | 28° | 38° | 1° | 45° | .025 | — |

## ADJUSTMENT SPECIFICATIONS, 6-250/4.1L ENGINES—Continued

| Year | Carb. Production No. | Float Level | Accel. Pump | Choke Coil Lever | Choke Rod | Vacuum Break | | Air Valve Rod | Unloader | Secondary Lockout | Air Valve Spring (Turns) |
|---|---|---|---|---|---|---|---|---|---|---|---|
| | | | | | | Primary | Secondary | | | | |
| 1984 | 17072683 | 9/32 | — | .085 | 28° | 15° | 35° | 1° | 45° | .025 | — |
| | 17074812 | 9/32 | — | .085 | 28° | 15° | 35° | 1° | 45° | .025 | — |
| | 17084348 | 11/32 | — | .085 | 22° | 30° | 32° | 1° | 40° | .025 | 1 |
| | 17084349 | 11/32 | — | .085 | 22° | 30° | 32° | 1° | 40° | .025 | 1 |
| | 17084350 | 11/32 | — | .085 | 22° | 30° | 32° | 1° | 40° | .025 | 1 |
| | 17084351 | 11/32 | — | .085 | 22° | 30° | 32° | 1° | 40° | .025 | 1 |
| | 17084352 | 11/32 | — | .085 | 22° | 30° | 35° | 1° | 40° | .025 | 1 |
| | 17084353 | 11/32 | — | .085 | 22° | 30° | 35° | 1° | 40° | .025 | 1 |
| | 17084354 | 11/32 | — | .085 | 22° | 30° | 35° | 1° | 40° | .025 | 1 |
| | 17084355 | 11/32 | — | .085 | 22° | 30° | 35° | 1° | 40° | .025 | 1 |
| | 17084356 | 9/32 | — | .085 | 22° | 25° | 35° | 1° | 40° | .025 | ¾ |
| | 17084357 | 9/32 | — | .085 | 22° | 25° | 35° | 1° | 40° | .025 | ¾ |
| | 17084358 | 9/32 | — | .085 | 22° | 25° | 35° | 1° | 40° | .025 | ¾ |
| | 17084359 | 9/32 | — | .085 | 22° | 25° | 35° | 1° | 40° | .025 | ¾ |
| | 17084360 | 5/32 | — | .085 | 22° | 30° | 32° | 1° | 40° | .025° | 1 |
| | 17084362 | 5/32 | — | .085 | 22° | 30° | 32° | 1° | 40° | .025° | 1 |
| | 17084364 | 5/32 | — | .085 | 22° | 30° | 35° | 1° | 40° | .025° | 1 |
| | 17084366 | 5/32 | — | .085 | 22° | 30° | 35° | 1° | 40° | .025° | 1 |
| | 17084368 | 1/8 | — | .085 | 22° | 25° | 30° | 1° | 30° | .025 | ¾ |
| | 17084370 | 1/8 | — | .085 | 22° | 25° | 30° | 1° | 30° | .025 | ¾ |
| | 17084390 | 7/16 | — | .085 | 28° | 30° | 38° | 1° | 38° | .025 | 1½ |
| | 17084391 | 7/16 | — | .085 | 28° | 30° | 38° | 1° | 38° | .025 | 1½ |
| | 17084392 | 7/16 | — | .085 | 28° | 30° | 38° | 1° | 38° | .025 | 1½ |
| | 17084393 | 7/16 | — | .085 | 28° | 30° | 38° | 1° | 38° | .025 | 1½ |
| | 17084410 | 11/32 | — | .085 | 15° | 23° | 38° | 1° | 42° | .025 | — |
| | 17084412 | 11/32 | — | .085 | 15° | 23° | 38° | 1° | 42° | .025 | — |
| | 17084425 | 11/32 | — | .085 | 15° | 26° | 36° | 1° | 40° | .025 | — |
| | 17084427 | 11/32 | — | .085 | 15° | 26° | 36° | 1° | 40° | .025 | — |
| | 17084430 | 11/32 | — | .085 | 15° | 26° | 38° | 1° | 42° | .025 | 1 |
| | 17084431 | 11/32 | — | .085 | 15° | 26° | 38° | 1° | 42° | .025 | 1 |
| | 17084434 | 11/32 | — | .085 | 15° | 26° | 38° | 1° | 42° | .025 | 1 |
| | 17084435 | 11/32 | — | .085 | 15° | 26° | 38° | 1° | 42° | .025 | 1 |
| | 17084452 | 5/32 | — | .085 | 28° | 25° | 35° | 1° | 45° | .025 | — |
| | 17084453 | 5/32 | — | .085 | 28° | 25° | 35° | 1° | 45° | .025 | — |
| | 17084455 | 5/32 | — | .085 | 28° | 25° | 35° | 1° | 45° | .025 | — |
| | 17084456 | 5/32 | — | .085 | 28° | 25° | 35° | 1° | 45° | .025 | — |
| | 17084458 | 5/32 | — | .085 | 28° | 25° | 35° | 1° | 45° | .025 | — |
| | 17084532 | 5/32 | — | .085 | 28° | 25° | 35° | 1° | 45° | .025 | — |
| | 17084534 | 5/32 | — | .085 | 28° | 25° | 35° | 1° | 45° | .025 | ½ |
| | 17084535 | 5/32 | — | .085 | 28° | 25° | 35° | 1° | 45° | .025 | ½ |
| | 17084537 | 5/32 | — | .085 | 28° | 25° | 35° | 1° | 45° | .025 | ½ |
| | 17084538 | 5/32 | — | .085 | 28° | 25° | 35° | 1° | 45° | .025 | ½ |
| | 17084540 | 5/32 | — | .085 | 28° | 25° | 35° | 1° | 45° | .025 | ½ |
| | 17084542 | 1/8 | — | .085 | 28° | 25° | 35° | 1° | 45° | .025 | ½ |
| | 17084560 | 11/32 | — | .085 | 15° | 24° | 34° | 1° | 38° | .025 | — |
| | 17084569 | 11/32 | — | .085 | 15° | 24° | 34° | 1° | 38° | .025 | — |
| | 17085632 | 9/32 | — | .085 | 28° | 25° | 35° | 1° | 45° | .025 | — |
| | 17084633 | 9/32 | — | .085 | 28° | 25° | 35° | 1° | 45° | .025 | ½ |
| | 17084635 | 9/32 | — | .085 | 28° | 25° | 35° | 1° | 45° | .025 | ½ |
| | 17084636 | 9/32 | — | .085 | 28° | 25° | 35° | 1° | 45° | .025 | ½ |

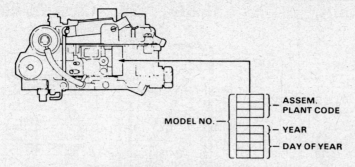

MODEL NO.—
ASSEM. PLANT CODE
YEAR
DAY OF YEAR

**Fig. 1   Carburetor identification number location**

## IDENTIFICATION LOCATION

The carburetor model identification is stamped vertically on the float bowl in the flat area adjacent to the vacuum tube, **Fig. 1.**

## DESCRIPTION

The Varajet models 2SE and E2SE, **Figs. 2 and 3,** are two barrel, two stage, down draft design carburetors. Aluminum die castings are used for the air horn, float bowl and throttle body. A heat insulator gasket is used between the throttle body and float bowl to reduce heat transfer to the float bowl.

The primary stage has a triple venturi, with a small 35 mm bore, resulting in good fuel metering control during idle and part throttle operation. The secondary stage has a 46 mm bore, providing sufficient air capacity for engine power requirements. An air valve is used in the secondary stage with a single tapered metering rod.

The float chamber is internally vented through a vertical vent cavity in the air horn. The float chamber is also externally vented through a tube in the air horn. A hose connects this tube directly to a vacuum operated vapor vent valve located in the vapor canister. When the engine is not running, the canister vapor vent valve is open, allowing fuel vapor from the float chamber to pass into the canister where the vapor is stored until normally purged.

An adjustable part throttle screw is used in the float bowl to aid emission control. This screw is factory preset and a plug is installed to prevent further adjustment or fuel leakage. The plug should not be removed or the screw setting disturbed. If float bowl replacement is required, the service float bowl will include a factory preset and plugged adjustable part throttle screw.

A hot idle compensator is used on some models and is located in the air horn. The opening and closing of the hot idle compensator valve is controlled by a bi-metal strip that is calibrated to a specific temperature. When the valve opens, additional air is allowed to bypass the throttle valves

and enter the intake manifold to prevent rough idle during periods of hot engine operation.

The idle mixture screw is recessed in the throttle body and is sealed with a hardened steel plug to prevent alteration of the factory preset mixture setting. The plug should not be removed and the mixture screw readjusted unless required by major carburetor overhaul or throttle body replacement.

The E2SE carburetor includes special design features for use with the Computer Controlled Catalytic Converter (C4) System or the Computer Command Control (C3) System. An electrically operated mixture control solenoid, mounted in the air horn, controls air and fuel metered to the idle and main metering systems of the carburetor. The plunger located at the end of the solenoid is submerged in fuel in the fuel chamber of the float bowl. This plunger is controlled by an electrical signal from the Electronic Control Module (ECM). The Electronic Control Module responding to signals from the oxygen sensor in the exhaust and other engine operating condition signals, energizes the solenoid to move the plunger down to the lean position or de-energizes the solenoid to move the plunger up to the rich position to control fuel delivery to the idle and main metering systems. When the plunger is in the lean position, fuel metering is controlled by a lean mixture screw located in the float bowl. When the plunger is in the rich position, the additional fuel is metered to the main fuel well through a rich mixture screw located at the end of the fuel supply channel in the float bowl. Air metered to the idle system is controlled by the up and down movement of the mixture control solenoid plunger. The plunger increases or decreases air supplied to the idle system which is further metered by the idle air

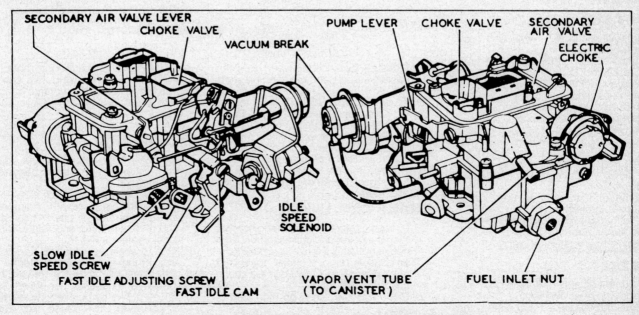

SECONDARY AIR VALVE LEVER
CHOKE VALVE
VACUUM BREAK
PUMP LEVER
CHOKE VALVE
SECONDARY AIR VALVE
ELECTRIC CHOKE
IDLE SPEED SOLENOID
SLOW IDLE SPEED SCREW
FAST IDLE ADJUSTING SCREW
FAST IDLE CAM
VAPOR VENT TUBE (TO CANISTER)
FUEL INLET NUT

**Fig. 2   Rochester Varajet 2SE Carburetor**

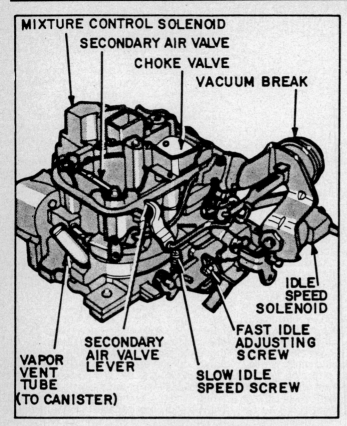

Fig. 3   Rochester Varajet E2SE Carburetor

Labels in Fig. 3:
MIXTURE CONTROL SOLENOID
SECONDARY AIR VALVE
CHOKE VALVE
VACUUM BREAK
IDLE SPEED SOLENOID
FAST IDLE ADJUSTING SCREW
SLOW IDLE SPEED SCREW
SECONDARY AIR VALVE LEVER
VAPOR VENT TUBE (TO CANISTER)

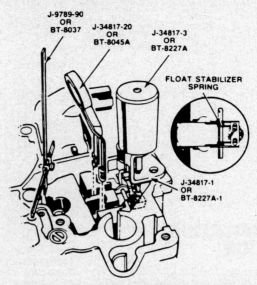

Fig. 4   Float level adjustment

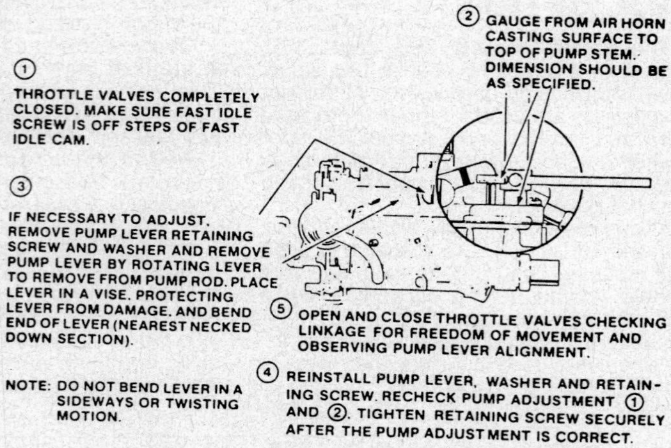

Labels in Fig. 4:
J-9789-90 OR BT-8037
J-34817-20 OR BT-8045A
J-34817-3 OR BT-8227A
FLOAT STABILIZER SPRING
J-34817-1 OR BT-8227A-1

bleed screw. The plunger cycles up and down approximately 10 times per second, controlling air and fuel mixtures.

# ADJUSTMENTS
## FLOAT LEVEL

1. Remove air horn, gasket and upper float bowl insert, if equipped.
2. Attach base tool J-34817-1 or BT-8227A-1 to float bowl, **Fig. 4**.
3. Position tool J-34817-3 or BT-8227A into base, ensuring contact pin rests on outer edge of float lever.
4. Using adjustable T-scale, measure distance from top of casting to top of float, at point farthest from float hinge.
5. If float adjustment is not within 2/32 inch from specification, bend lever up or down as required with tool shown, **Fig. 4**.
6. Remove bending tool, then repeat steps 2 through 4.
7. Check float alignment, then reassemble carburetor.

## ACCELERATOR PUMP
### 1980 2SE

The pump adjustment should not be altered from the specified setting.
1. Close throttle valves and ensure that fast idle screw is not contacting fast idle cam steps.

Fig. 5 notes:
① THROTTLE VALVES COMPLETELY CLOSED. MAKE SURE FAST IDLE SCREW IS OFF STEPS OF FAST IDLE CAM.
② GAUGE FROM AIR HORN CASTING SURFACE TO TOP OF PUMP STEM. DIMENSION SHOULD BE AS SPECIFIED.
③ IF NECESSARY TO ADJUST, REMOVE PUMP LEVER RETAINING SCREW AND WASHER AND REMOVE PUMP LEVER BY ROTATING LEVER TO REMOVE FROM PUMP ROD. PLACE LEVER IN A VISE, PROTECTING LEVER FROM DAMAGE, AND BEND END OF LEVER (NEAREST NECKED DOWN SECTION).
④ REINSTALL PUMP LEVER, WASHER AND RETAINING SCREW. RECHECK PUMP ADJUSTMENT ① AND ②. TIGHTEN RETAINING SCREW SECURELY AFTER THE PUMP ADJUSTMENT IS CORRECT.
⑤ OPEN AND CLOSE THROTTLE VALVES CHECKING LINKAGE FOR FREEDOM OF MOVEMENT AND OBSERVING PUMP LEVER ALIGNMENT.

NOTE: DO NOT BEND LEVER IN A SIDEWAYS OR TWISTING MOTION.

Fig. 5   Pump adjustment. 1980 2SE

2. Measure distance between air horn casting surface and top of pump stem, **Fig. 5**.
3. To adjust, remove pump lever retaining screw and the pump lever. Place the lever in a vise and bend lever end. Do not bend lever in a twisting motion.
4. Install pump lever and retaining screw. Recheck pump adjustment.
5. Operate throttle valves to check for freedom of movement and pump lever alignment.

## CHOKE COIL LEVER

1. Loosen choke cover retaining screws, then the cover and coil assembly from choke housing. If a riveted choke cover is used, remove choke cover and coil assembly as outlined in the choke cover retainer kit.
2. Place fast idle screw on high step of cam.
3. Push the intermediate choke lever until the choke valve closes, **Fig. 6**.

4. Insert specified gauge into hole provided in choke housing. The edge of the lever should just contact gauge.
5. To adjust, bend intermediate choke rod.

## CHOKE ROD

The choke coil lever and fast idle adjustments must be made before performing this adjustment.
1. Rotate degree scale until zero is opposite pointer, then with choke valve completely closed, place magnet on top of choke valve and rotate bubble until centered, **Fig. 7**.
2. Rotate scale so specified degree for adjustment is opposite pointer.
3. Place fast idle screw on second step of cam against shoulder of high step.
4. Close choke by pushing intermediate choke lever. On 1983-85 units, attach rubber band to intermediate choke lever to hold choke valve closed.

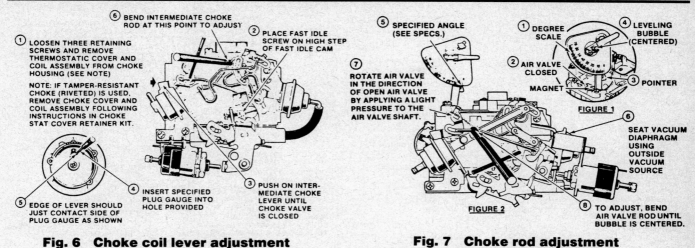

**Fig. 6  Choke coil lever adjustment**

**Fig. 7  Choke rod adjustment**

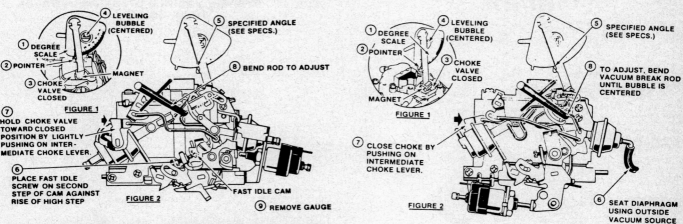

**Fig. 8  Air valve rod adjustment. 1980–85 All**

**Fig. 9  Primary vacuum break adjustment. 1980 2SE**

5. Push vacuum break lever toward open choke position until lever contacts rear tang on choke lever.
6. To adjust, bend fast idle cam rod until bubble is centered.

## AIR VALVE ROD

1. Rotate gauge scale until pointer is opposite zero.
2. With air valve completely closed, place magnet on top of air valve and rotate bubble until centered.
3. Rotate scale so that specified degree for adjustment is opposite pointer.
4. Seat vacuum diaphragm using an external vacuum source.
5. Rotate air valve toward the open position by applying light pressure to the air valve shaft, **Fig. 8.**
6. To adjust, bend air valve rod until bubble is centered.

## PRIMARY VACUUM BREAK

### 1980 2SE

1. Rotate degree scale until zero is opposite pointer, then with choke valve completely closed, place magnet on top of choke valve and rotate bubble until it is centered.

2. Rotate degree scale so specified degree for adjustment is opposite pointer, **Fig. 9.**
3. Seat vacuum diaphragm with an external vacuum source.
4. Hold choke valve toward closed position by pushing on intermediate choke lever.
5. To adjust, bend vacuum break rod until bubble is centered.

### 1981–82 All

Before performing adjustment procedure, remove primary vacuum break from carburetor and position bracket in vise, then grind off adjusting screw cap, if applicable, and reinstall vacuum break.

1. Rotate degree scale until zero is opposite pointer, then with choke valve completely closed and fast idle screw on high step of fast idle cam, place magnet squarely on top of choke valve and rotate bubble until it is centered.
2. Rotate scale so that specified adjustment angle is opposite pointer, **Fig. 10.**
3. Seat choke diaphragm using a vacuum source with over 5 inches Hg of vacuum. Check to ensure that air

valve rod is not restricting the vacuum diaphragm from being seated. It may be necessary to bend air valve rod to obtain a slight clearance between rod and end of slot in air valve lever. If the air valve rod adjustment is disturbed, refer to the Air Valve Rod Adjustment procedure after completing the primary vacuum break adjustment.

4. Hold choke valve toward the closed position by lightly pushing on intermediate lever and note angle gauge reading.
5. If adjustment is necessary, use a $1/8$ inch hex wrench to rotate adjusting screw in rear cover until bubble is centered.
6. After completing adjustment, apply a suitable sealer over adjusting screw head.

### 1983–85 All

1. Attach rubber band to intermediate choke shaft to hold choke valve closed.
2. Install angle gauge and set angle to specifications.
3. Using outside vacuum source, retract vacuum break plunger with a minimum of 18 inches Hg of vacuum.

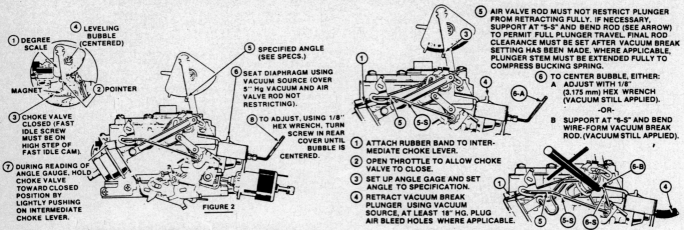

**Fig. 10 Primary vacuum break adjustment. 1981–82 All**

① DEGREE SCALE

④ LEVELING BUBBLE (CENTERED)

MAGNET

② POINTER

③ CHOKE VALVE CLOSED (FAST IDLE SCREW MUST BE ON HIGH STEP OF FAST IDLE CAM).

⑦ DURING READING OF ANGLE GAUGE, HOLD CHOKE VALVE TOWARD CLOSED POSITION BY LIGHTLY PUSHING ON INTERMEDIATE CHOKE LEVER.

⑤ SPECIFIED ANGLE (SEE SPECS.)

⑥ SEAT DIAPHRAGM USING VACUUM SOURCE (OVER 5" Hg VACUUM AND AIR VALVE ROD NOT RESTRICTING).

⑧ TO ADJUST, USING 1/8" HEX WRENCH, TURN SCREW IN REAR COVER UNTIL BUBBLE IS CENTERED.

FIGURE 2

**Fig. 11 Primary vacuum break adjustment. 1983–85 All**

⑤ AIR VALVE ROD MUST NOT RESTRICT PLUNGER FROM RETRACTING FULLY. IF NECESSARY, SUPPORT AT "5-S" AND BEND ROD (SEE ARROW) TO PERMIT FULL PLUNGER TRAVEL. FINAL ROD CLEARANCE MUST BE SET AFTER VACUUM BREAK SETTING HAS BEEN MADE. WHERE APPLICABLE, PLUNGER STEM MUST BE EXTENDED FULLY TO COMPRESS BUCKING SPRING.

⑥ TO CENTER BUBBLE, EITHER:
A ADJUST WITH 1/8" (3.175 mm) HEX WRENCH (VACUUM STILL APPLIED).
-OR-
B SUPPORT AT "6-S" AND BEND WIRE-FORM VACUUM BREAK ROD. (VACUUM STILL APPLIED).

① ATTACH RUBBER BAND TO INTERMEDIATE CHOKE LEVER.

② OPEN THROTTLE TO ALLOW CHOKE VALVE TO CLOSE.

③ SET UP ANGLE GAGE AND SET ANGLE TO SPECIFICATION.

④ RETRACT VACUUM BREAK PLUNGER USING VACUUM SOURCE, AT LEAST 18" HG. PLUG AIR BLEED HOLES WHERE APPLICABLE.

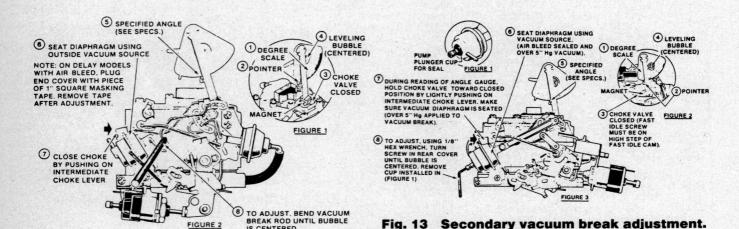

**Fig. 12 Secondary vacuum break adjustment. 1980 2SE**

⑥ SEAT DIAPHRAGM USING OUTSIDE VACUUM SOURCE

NOTE: ON DELAY MODELS WITH AIR BLEED, PLUG END COVER WITH PIECE OF 1" SQUARE MASKING TAPE. REMOVE TAPE AFTER ADJUSTMENT.

⑦ CLOSE CHOKE BY PUSHING ON INTERMEDIATE CHOKE LEVER

⑤ SPECIFIED ANGLE (SEE SPECS.)

① DEGREE SCALE

② POINTER

④ LEVELING BUBBLE (CENTERED)

③ CHOKE VALVE CLOSED

MAGNET

FIGURE 1

⑧ TO ADJUST, BEND VACUUM BREAK ROD UNTIL BUBBLE IS CENTERED.

FIGURE 2

**Fig. 13 Secondary vacuum break adjustment. 1981–82 All**

⑥ SEAT DIAPHRAGM USING VACUUM SOURCE. (AIR BLEED SEALED AND OVER 5" Hg VACUUM).

PUMP PLUNGER CUP FOR SEAL

FIGURE 1

⑦ DURING READING OF ANGLE GAUGE, HOLD CHOKE VALVE TOWARD CLOSED POSITION BY LIGHTLY PUSHING ON INTERMEDIATE CHOKE LEVER. MAKE SURE VACUUM DIAPHRAGM IS SEATED (OVER 5" Hg APPLIED TO VACUUM BREAK).

⑧ TO ADJUST, USING 1/8" HEX WRENCH, TURN SCREW IN REAR COVER UNTIL BUBBLE IS CENTERED. REMOVE CUP INSTALLED IN (FIGURE 1)

④ LEVELING BUBBLE (CENTERED)

① DEGREE SCALE

⑤ SPECIFIED ANGLE (SEE SPECS.)

MAGNET

② POINTER

③ CHOKE VALVE CLOSED (FAST IDLE SCREW MUST BE ON HIGH STEP OF FAST IDLE CAM).

FIGURE 2

FIGURE 3

**Fig. 14 Secondary vacuum break adjustment. 1983–85 All**

① ATTACH RUBBER BAND TO INTERMEDIATE CHOKE LEVER.

② OPEN THROTTLE TO ALLOW CHOKE VALVE TO CLOSE.

③ SET UP ANGLE GAGE AND SET ANGLE TO SPECIFICATION.

④ RETRACT VACUUM BREAK PLUNGER USING VACUUM SOURCE, AT LEAST 18" HG. PLUG AIR BLEED HOLES WHERE APPLICABLE. WHERE APPLICABLE, PLUNGER STEM MUST BE EXTENDED FULLY TO COMPRESS PLUNGER BUCKING SPRING.

⑤ TO CENTER BUBBLE, EITHER:
A. ADJUST WITH 1/8" (3.175 mm) HEX WRENCH (VACUUM STILL APPLIED)
-OR-
B. SUPPORT AT "5-S", BEND WIRE-FORM VACUUM BREAK ROD (VACUUM STILL APPLIED)

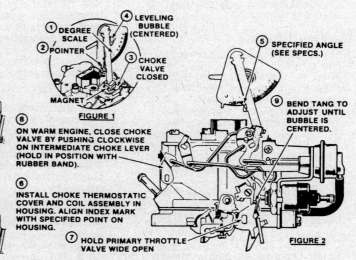

**Fig. 15 Unloader adjustment**

① DEGREE SCALE

④ LEVELING BUBBLE (CENTERED)

② POINTER

③ CHOKE VALVE CLOSED

MAGNET

FIGURE 1

⑥ ON WARM ENGINE, CLOSE CHOKE VALVE BY PUSHING CLOCKWISE ON INTERMEDIATE CHOKE LEVER (HOLD IN POSITION WITH RUBBER BAND).

⑧ INSTALL CHOKE THERMOSTATIC COVER AND COIL ASSEMBLY IN HOUSING. ALIGN INDEX MARK WITH SPECIFIED POINT ON HOUSING.

⑦ HOLD PRIMARY THROTTLE VALVE WIDE OPEN

⑤ SPECIFIED ANGLE (SEE SPECS.)

⑨ BEND TANG TO ADJUST UNTIL BUBBLE IS CENTERED.

FIGURE 2

① HOLD CHOKE VALVE WIDE OPEN BY PUSHING DOWN ON INTERMEDIATE CHOKE LEVER.

② OPEN THROTTLE LEVER UNTIL END OF SECONDARY ACTUATING LEVER IS OPPOSITE TOE OF LOCKOUT LEVER.

③ GAGE CLEARANCE - DIMENSION SHOULD BE .025".

④ IF NECESSARY TO ADJUST, BEND LOCKOUT LEVER TANG CONTACTING FAST IDLE CAM.

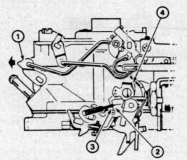

**Fig. 16   Secondary lockout adjustment**

① IF NECESSARY, REMOVE INTERMEDIATE CHOKE ROD, TO GAIN ACCESS TO LOCK SCREW.

② LOOSEN LOCK SCREW USING 3/32" (2.381mm) HEX WRENCH.

③ TURN TENSION-ADJUSTING SCREW CLOCKWISE UNTIL AIR VALVE OPENS SLIGHTLY.
TURN ADJUSTING SCREW COUNTERCLOCKWISE UNTIL AIR VALVE JUST CLOSES. CONTINUE COUNTERCLOCKWISE SPECIFIED NUMBER OF TURNS.

④ TIGHTEN LOCK SCREW.

⑤ APPLY LITHIUM BASE GREASE TO LUBRICATE PIN AND SPRING CONTACT AREA.

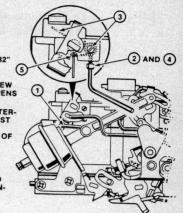

**Fig. 17   Air valve spring adjustment. 1982–85 All**

4. Ensure that air valve rod does not restrict plunger from full retraction. If necessary, bend rod as shown to permit full plunger travel, **Fig. 11.**
5. Make adjustment with vacuum still applied by rotating adjusting screw with a 1/8 inch Allen wrench, or bending rod as shown until bubble is centered.

## SECONDARY VACUUM BREAK

### 1980 2SE

1. Rotate degree scale until zero is opposite pointer, then with choke valve completely closed, place magnet on top of choke valve and rotate bubble until centered.
2. Rotate scale so specified adjustment angle is opposite pointer, **Fig. 12.**
3. Seat vacuum diaphragm with an external vacuum source.
4. Hold choke valve toward closed position by pushing on intermediate choke lever. Ensure that bucking spring, if used is compressed and seated.
5. To adjust, bend vacuum break rod as shown until bubble is centered.

### 1981–82 All

Before performing adjustment procedure, remove secondary vacuum break from carburetor and position bracket in a vise, then grind off adjusting screw cap, if applicable, and reinstall vacuum break.
1. Rotate degree scale so that zero is inside pointer, then with choke valve completely closed and fast idle screw on high step of fast idle cam, place magnet on top of choke valve and rotate until bubble is centered.
2. Rotate scale so that specified adjustment angle is opposite pointer.
3. Seat vacuum diaphragm using a vacuum source with over 5 inches Hg of vacuum, **Fig. 13.**
4. Hold choke valve toward the closed position by lightly pushing on intermediate choke lever and note angle

gauge reading. When noting reading check to ensure that vacuum diaphragm is seated.
5. Rotate adjusting screw in rear cover until bubble is centered. After completing adjustment, apply a suitable sealer over adjusting screw head.

### 1983–85 All

1. Attach rubber band to intermediate choke lever to hold choke valve closed, **Fig. 14.**
2. Install angle gauge to set angle to specifications. Refer to Specifications Chart.
3. Using outside vacuum source, retract vacuum break plunger with a minimum of 18 inches Hg of vacuum, then plug air bleed holes if applicable.
4. Make final adjustment with vacuum still applied by rotating adjusting screw with a 1/8 inch Allen wrench, or bending rod as shown until bubble is centered.

## UNLOADER

1. Rotate degree scale until zero is opposite pointer, then with choke valve completely closed, place magnet on top of choke valve and rotate bubble until centered.
2. Rotate degree scale so specified adjustment angle is opposite pointer, **Fig. 15.**
3. With choke setting properly adjusted, hold primary throttle valve wide open.
4. On warm engines and all 1983-85 units, close choke valve by pushing on intermediate choke lever, then hold in position with a rubber band.
5. To adjust, bend tang on throttle lever until bubble is centered.

## SECONDARY LOCKOUT

1. Hold choke valve wide open by pulling on intermediate choke lever.
2. Position throttle lever until end of secondary actuating lever is opposite toe of lockout lever, **Fig. 16.**

3. Insert specified gauge between throttle lever and secondary lockout lever toe.
4. To adjust, bend lockout lever tang contacting fast idle cam.

## AIR VALVE SPRING

### 1982–85 All

1. Loosen lock screw, then turn adjusting screw clockwise until air valve is partially open, **Fig. 17.** On 1983-85 models, it may be necessary to remove the intermediate choke rod to gain access to the lock screw.
2. Turn adjusting screw counterclockwise until air valve just closes, then continue turning counterclockwise the specified number of turns. Tighten lock screw.
3. Lubricate air valve shaft pin and closing spring with lithium base grease.

## THROTTLE POSITION SENSOR (TPS)

### 1982–85 E2SE Carburetor

Do not remove plug sealing TPS adjustment or adjust TPS unless carburetor is overhauled or "Computer Command Control (C3)" system diagnosis indicates a problem with the switch.
1. Drill a 5/64 inch hole, 1/16 to 1/8 inch deep, in plug covering TPS adjustment screw.
2. Thread a small slide hammer or equivalent into plug and remove plug from air horn.
3. Disconnect TPS connector and jumper all three terminals.
4. Connect digital voltmeter J-29125-A or equivalent to center and bottom terminals of connector.
5. With ignition On and engine Off, turn TPS adjusting screw to obtain .26 volts.
6. Turn ignition Off and install a new plug over TPS adjusting screw or seal opening with RTV sealer.

# Rochester Dual-Jet M2M Series Carburetor

## INDEX

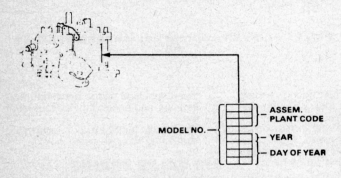

**Fig. 1   Carburetor identification location**

## IDENTIFICATION LOCATION

The carburetor model identification is stamped vertically on the rear left edge of the float bowl, **Fig. 1.**

## DESCRIPTION

The M2M Series (M2ME, M2MC) Duel Jet carburetor is a two barrel, single stage unit, incorporating the design features of the primary side of the Quadrajet (four barrel) carburetor. The triple venturi stack up, plus the smaller 1³/₈ inch bores results in good fuel metering control during all phases of operation.

The main metering system has a separate main well for each main nozzle for good fuel flow through the venturi. An adjustable part throttle screw is used in the float bowl to aid in controlling fuel mixtures for good emission control. This screw is factory preset and should not be adjusted in service. However, if it becomes necessary to replace the float bowl, the new service float bowl will include the adjustable part throttle screw which has been preset.

## ADJUSTMENTS

### FLOAT LEVEL

1. Remove air horn, gasket, power piston/metering rod assembly and float bowl.
2. Attach base tool J-34817-1 or BT-8227A-1 to float bowl, **Fig. 2.**
3. Position tool J-34817-3 or BT-8227A into base, ensuring contact pin rests on outer edge of float lever.

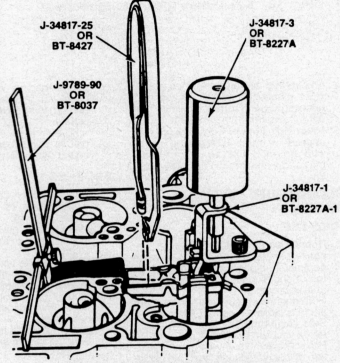

**Fig. 2   Float level adjustment**

4. Using T-scale shown, measure distance from top of casting to top of float at a point ³/₁₆ inch from large end of float.
5. If float level is not within ²/₃₂ inch from specification, bend float lever as required using tool shown, **Fig. 2.**
6. Repeat steps 2 through 4.
7. Check float alignment, then reassemble carburetor.

### PUMP ROD

With throttle valves completely closed and pump rod in specified hole in pump lever, measure from top of choke valve wall (next to vent stack) to top of pump stem, **Fig. 3.** Dimension should be as listed in the Specifications Chart. To adjust, bend pump lever as required.

### CHOKE COIL LEVER

With thermostatic coil assembly removed, push upward on coil tang until choke valve closes. Insert gauge specified in the Specifications Chart into choke housing hole. The lower edge of choke coil lever should just contact gauge. To adjust, bend choke rod as required, **Fig. 4.**

### CHOKE ROD

Choke coil lever and fast idle adjustment must be performed before making the following adjustment. Do not remove choke cover and rivets, if equipped, to perform this adjustment. If necessary, hold vacuum break lever tang with rubber band to keep choke valve closed.

Rotate degree scale until zero is opposite pointer, then with choke valve completely closed, position magnet on top of valve. Rotate bubble until centered, then rotate degree scale until specified angle adjustment is opposite pointer. Position cam follower on second step of fast idle cam against high step, then close choke valve fully. To adjust, bend tang on fast idle cam until bubble is centered, **Fig. 5.**

### VACUUM BREAK

Choke coil lever and fast idle adjustment must be performed before making the following adjustment. Do not remove choke

## ADJUSTMENT SPECIFICATIONS

| Year | Carb. Production No. | Float Level | Pump Rod Hole | Pump Rod Adj. | Choke Coil Lever | Choke Rod | Vacuum Break Front | Vacuum Break Rear | Choke Unloader |
|---|---|---|---|---|---|---|---|---|---|
| 1980 | 17080100 | 7/16 | Inner | 9/32 | .120 | 38° | 29° | — | 38° |
| | 17080102 | 7/16 | Inner | 9/32 | .120 | 38° | 29° | — | 38° |
| | 17080108 | 3/8 | Inner | 5/16 | .120 | 20° | 25° | — | 38° |
| | 17080110 | 3/8 | Inner | 5/16 | .120 | 20° | 25° | — | 38° |
| | 17080130 | 3/8 | Inner | 5/16 | .120 | 20° | 25° | — | 38° |
| | 17080131 | 3/8 | Inner | 5/16 | .120 | 20° | 25° | — | 38° |
| | 17080132 | 3/8 | Inner | 5/16 | .120 | 20° | 25° | — | 38° |
| | 17080133 | 3/8 | Inner | 5/16 | .120 | 20° | 25° | — | 38° |
| | 17080138 | 3/8 | Inner | 5/16 | .120 | 20° | 25° | — | 38° |
| | 17080140 | 3/8 | Inner | 5/16 | .120 | 20° | 25° | — | 38° |
| | 17080142 | 7/16 | Inner | 9/32 | .120 | 38° | 29° | — | 38° |
| | 17080143 | 7/16 | Inner | 9/32 | .120 | 38° | 29° | — | 38° |
| | 17080144 | 7/16 | Inner | 9/32 | .120 | 38° | 29° | — | 38° |
| | 17080145 | 7/16 | Inner | 9/32 | .120 | 38° | 29° | — | 38° |
| | 17080190 | 9/32 | Inner | 1/4 | .120 | 24.5° | 22° | 20° | 38° |
| | 17080191 | 11/32 | Inner | 1/4 | .120 | 24.5° | 18° | 18° | 38° |
| | 17080192 | 9/32 | Inner | 1/4 | .120 | 24.5° | 22° | 20° | 38° |
| | 17080195 | 9/32 | Inner | 1/4 | .120 | 24.5° | 19° | 17° | 38° |
| | 17080197 | 9/32 | Inner | 1/4 | .120 | 24.5° | 19° | 17° | 38° |
| | 17080490 | 5/16 | — | — | .120 | 24.5° | 30° | 28° | 38° |
| | 17058492 | 5/16 | — | — | .120 | 24.5° | 30° | 28° | 38° |
| | 17058496 | 5/16 | — | — | .120 | 24.5° | 21° | 30° | 38° |
| | 17058498 | 5/16 | — | — | .120 | 24.5° | 21° | 30° | 38° |
| 1981 | 17080185 | 9/32 | Inner | 1/4 | .120 | 24.5° | 19° | 14° | 38° |
| | 17080187 | 9/32 | Inner | 1/4 | .120 | 24.5° | 19° | 14° | 38° |
| | 17080491 | 5/16 | — | — | .120 | 24.5° | 21° | 35° | 38° |
| | 17080496 | 5/16 | — | — | .120 | 24.5° | 21° | 33° | 38° |
| | 17080498 | 5/16 | — | — | .120 | 24.5° | 21° | 33° | 38° |
| | 17081101 | 13/32 | Inner | 5/16 | .120 | 38° | 25° | — | 38° |
| | 17081103 | 13/32 | Inner | 5/16 | .120 | 38° | 25° | — | 38° |
| | 17081130 | 3/8 | Inner | — | .120 | 20° | 25° | — | 38° |
| | 17081131 | 3/8 | Inner | — | .120 | 20° | 25° | — | 38° |
| | 17081132 | 3/8 | Inner | — | .120 | 20° | 25° | — | 38° |
| | 17081133 | 3/8 | Inner | — | .120 | 20° | 25° | — | 38° |
| | 17081138 | 3/8 | Inner | — | .120 | 20° | 25° | — | 40° |
| | 17081140 | 3/8 | Inner | — | .120 | 20° | 25° | — | 40° |
| | 17081142 | 13/32 | Inner | 5/16 | .120 | 38° | 25° | — | 38° |
| | 17081143 | 13/32 | Inner | 5/16 | .120 | 38° | 25° | — | 38° |
| | 17081144 | 13/32 | Inner | 5/16 | .120 | 38° | 25° | — | 38° |
| | 17081145 | 13/32 | Inner | 5/16 | .120 | 38° | 25° | — | 38° |
| | 17081191 | 5/16 | — | — | .120 | 24.5° | 28° | 24° | 38° |
| | 17081192 | 5/16 | — | — | .120 | 24.5° | 28° | 24° | 38° |
| | 17081194 | 5/16 | — | — | .120 | 24.5° | 21° | 24° | 38° |
| | 17081196 | 5/16 | — | — | .120 | 24.5° | 28° | 24° | 38° |
| | 17081197 | 5/16 | — | — | .120 | 18° | 28° | 24° | 38° |
| | 17081198 ① | 3/8 | — | — | .120 | 24.5° | 28° | 24° | 38° |
| | 17081198 ② | 3/8 | — | — | .120 | 18° | 28° | 24° | 38° |
| | 17081199 | 3/8 | — | — | .120 | 18° | 28° | 24° | 38° |
| | 17081496 | 3/8 | — | — | .120 | 18° | 28° | 24° | 38° |

①—Models w/code letters AH stamped on fast idle cam.  ②—Models w/code letter T stamped on fast idle cam.

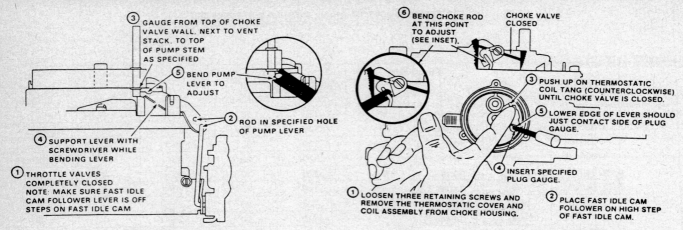

**Fig. 3  Pump rod adjustment**

**Fig. 4  Choke coil lever adjustment**

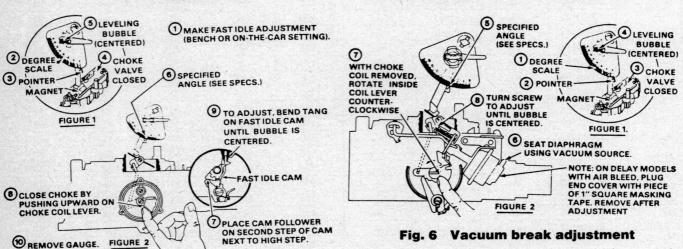

**Fig. 5  Choke rod adjustment**

**Fig. 6  Vacuum break adjustment**

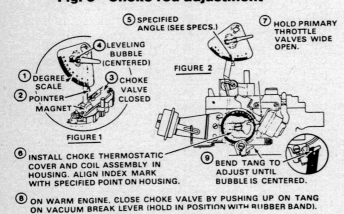

**Fig. 7  Choke unloader adjustment**

**Fig. 8  Choke coil adjustment**

cover and rivets, if equipped, to perform this adjustment. If necessary, hold vacuum break lever tang with rubber band to keep choke valve closed.

Rotate degree scale until zero is opposite pointer, then position magnet on top of choke valve. With choke valve completely closed, rotate bubble until centered. Rotate degree scale until degree specified for adjustment is opposite pointer. Using an external vacuum source, seat choke vacuum diaphragm, then close choke valve. To adjust, turn adjustment screw inward or outward until bubble is centered, Fig. 6.

On delay models with air bleed, remove rubber cover over filter element and plug small bleed hole in vacuum tube with tape. On models with air bleed in end cover, plug cover with tape. On some models, a protective cover is used over the adjusting screw. To gain access to adjusting screw, remove vacuum break from carburetor, then grind off cover weld. Remove cover, reinstall vacuum break and proceed with adjustment.

## CHOKE UNLOADER

Choke coil lever and fast idle adjustment must be performed before making the following adjustment. Do not remove choke cover and rivets, if equipped, to perform this adjustment. If necessary, hold vacuum break lever tang with rubber band to keep choke valve closed.

Rotate degree scale until zero is opposite pointer, then with choke valve completely closed, position magnet on top of valve. Rotate bubble until centered, then rotate degree scale until degree specified for adjustment is opposite pointer. Reinstall choke cover and coil assembly, if removed, then hold primary throttle valves wide open and close choke valve. To adjust, bend fast idle cam lever until bubble is centered, **Fig. 7.**

## CHOKE COIL

Some carburetors are equipped with tamper proof choke covers. On these models, no adjustment is possible or necessary.

Position fast idle cam follower on high step of fast idle cam. Rotate choke cover and coil assembly counterclockwise until choke valve just closes, then align mark on cover with specified point on housing, **Fig. 8.**

# Rochester Dual-Jet E2MC & E2ME Carburetors

## INDEX

## ADJUSTMENT SPECIFICATIONS

| Year | Carb. Production No. | Float Level | Choke Coil Lever | Choke Rod | Vacuum Break Front | Vacuum Break Rear | Unloader |
|---|---|---|---|---|---|---|---|
| 1980 | 17080493 | 5/16 | .120 | 24.5° | 21° | 30° | 38° |
| | 17080495 | 5/16 | .120 | 24.5° | 21° | 30° | 38° |
| | 17080496 | 5/16 | .120 | 24.5° | 21° | 33° | 38° |
| | 17080498 | 5/16 | .120 | 24.5° | 21° | 33° | 38° |
| 1981 | 17080491 | 5/16 | .120 | 24.5° | 21° | 35° | 38° |
| | 17080496 | 5/16 | .120 | 24.5° | 21° | 33° | 38° |
| | 17080498 | 5/16 | .120 | 24.5° | 21° | 33° | 38° |
| | 17081191 | 5/16 | .120 | 24.5° | 28° | 24° | 38° |
| | 17081192 | 5/16 | .120 | 24.5° | 28° | 24° | 38° |
| | 17081194 | 5/16 | .120 | 24.5° | 21° | 24° | 38° |
| | 17081196 | 5/16 | .120 | 24.5° | 28° | 24° | 38° |
| | 17081197 | 5/16 | .120 | 18° | 28° | 24° | 38° |
| | 17081198 | 3/8 | .120 | 24.5° | 28° | 24° | 38° |
| | 17081199 | 3/8 | .120 | 18° | 28° | 24° | 38° |
| 1982 | 17082130 | 3/8 | .120 | 20° | 27° | — | 38° |
| | 17082132 | 3/8 | .120 | 20° | 27° | — | 38° |
| | 17082138 | 3/8 | .120 | 20° | 27° | — | 38° |
| | 17082140 | 3/8 | .120 | 20° | 27° | — | 38° |
| | 17082497 | 3/8 | .120 | 24.5° | 28° | 24° | 38° |
| 1983 | 17082130 | 3/8 | .120 | 20° | 27° | — | 38° |
| | 17082132 | 3/8 | .120 | 20° | 27° | — | 38° |
| | 17083130 | 3/8 | .120 | 20° | 27° | — | 38° |
| | 17083132 | 3/8 | .120 | 20° | 27° | — | 38° |
| | 17083190 | 3/8 | .120 | 20° | 28° | 24° | 38° |
| | 17083192 | 3/8 | .120 | 20° | 28° | 24° | 38° |
| | 17083193 | 3/8 | .120 | 20° | 23° | 28° | 38° |
| 1984 | 17082130 | 3/8 | .120 | 20° | 27° | — | 38° |
| | 17082132 | 3/8 | .120 | 20° | 27° | — | 38° |
| | 17084191 | 5/16 | .120 | 18° | 28° | 24° | 32° |

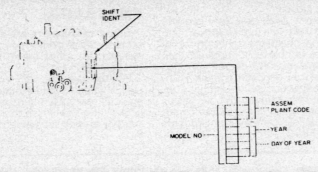

**Fig. 1   Carburetor identification location**

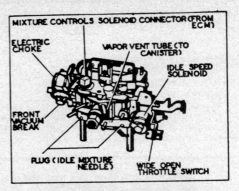

**Fig. 2   Rochester Dual-Jet model E2M carburetor**

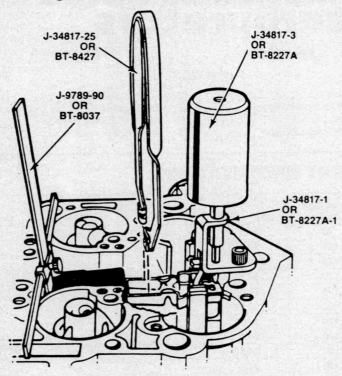

**Fig. 3   Float level adjustment**

## IDENTIFICATION LOCATION

The carburetor model identification is stamped vertically on the rear left edge of the float bowl, **Fig. 1.**

## DESCRIPTION

The dual jet carburetor, **Fig. 2,** is a two barrel, single stage unit, incorporating the design features of the primary side of the Quadrajet (four barrel) carburetor. These E2M carburetors are used with the Computer Controlled Catalytic Converter (C4) System or the Computer Command Control (C3) System. The triple venturi stack, plus small bores, results in precise fuel metering control during all periods of engine operation.

The main metering system has a separate main well for each main nozzle for good fuel flow through the venturi. An electrically operated mixture control solenoid, mounted in the fuel bowl, is used to control the fuel/air mixture metered to the idle and main metering systems. Fuel metering is controlled by two stepped metering rods positioned by a plunger in the mixture control solenoid. The solenoid plunger is controlled by an electric output signal from the Electronic Control Module (ECM). The ECM, responding from a signal from the Oxygen Sensor, energizes the solenoid to move the plunger and metering rods to control fuel delivery to the idle and main metering systems. At the same time, air metering to the idle system is controlled by an idle air bleed valve, located in the air horn, which follows the movement of the mixture control solenoid plunger to control the amount of air bleed into the idle system, to lean or enrich the mixture. The movement or cycling of the solenoid plunger occurs approximately ten times per second, thereby controlling the fuel/air mixture to achieving optimum mixture ratios.

On some 1981-84 units, an idle speed control (ISC), located on the float bowl, is used to control idle speed. On these units, the curb idle speed is programmed and controlled by the ECM. On some 1981-82 units, an idle load compensator (ILC), located on the float bowl, is used to control idle speed. The compensator uses manifold vacuum to sense changes in engine load and compensates by adjusting curb idle speed. These units should not be adjusted, unless during diagnosis, curb idle speed is not within specifications.

## ADJUSTMENTS
### FLOAT LEVEL

1. Remove air horn and gasket, then the solenoid plunger, metering rods and float bowl insert. If necessary, remove solenoid (lean mixture) adjusting screw, counting the number of turns it takes to bottom screw to aid in reassembly.
2. Attach base tool J-34817-1 or BT-8227A-1, **Fig. 3,** to float bowl.
3. Position tool J-34817-3 or BT-8227-A into base, ensuring contact pin rests on outer edge of float lever.
4. Using T-scale shown, measure distance from top of casting to top of float, at a point 3/16 inch from large end of float. If adjustment is greater than 2/32 inch from specification, bend float lever up or down as required with bending tool shown, **Fig. 3.**
5. Repeat measurement and check float alignment.
6. Reinstall solenoid adjusting screw, if removed. Adjust screw to measurement recorded during removal, then reassemble carburetor.

### CHOKE COIL LEVER

The choke coil cover is retained to the choke housing by three rivets. If remove is necessary, properly support float bowl and throttle body, then carefully center a suitable drill on rivet head. Drill only deep enough to remove rivet head, then drive remainder of rivet from choke housing using a suitable drift.

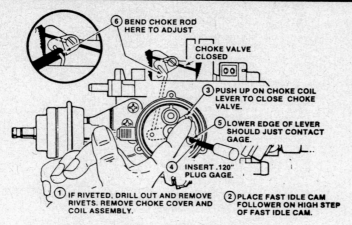

**Fig. 4   Choke coil lever adjustment**

A service kit is available for choke cover installation. The choke cover should be removed only during major carburetor overhaul or if choke coil is damaged.

1. Remove thermostatic coil assembly, then push upward on coil tang until choke valve closes.
2. Insert gauge specified in Specifications Chart into choke coil housing hole. The lower edge of choke coil lever should just contact gauge.
3. To adjust, bend choke rod as required, **Fig. 4.**

## CHOKE ROD

**Do not remove rivets or choke cover to place choke valve in the closed position.**

1. Use a rubber band on vacuum break lever tang to hold choke valve closed.
2. Rotate degree scale until zero is opposite pointer, **Fig. 5,** then with choke valve completely closed, place magnet squarely on top of choke valve and rotate bubble until centered.
3. Rotate degree scale until specified adjustment setting is opposite pointer. Refer to Specifications Chart for proper adjustment settings.
4. Place cam follower on second step of fast idle cam and next to high step. Close choke by pushing upward on choke coil lever. To adjust, bend tang on fast idle lever until bubble is centered.

## VACUUM BREAK

### FRONT (GAUGE METHOD)

#### 1980–82

Do not remove rivets or choke cover to place choke valve in the closed position. Use a rubber band on the vacuum break lever tang to hold choke valve closed. Prior to adjustment, remove vacuum break and place in vise, then grind off adjusting screw cover and reinstall vacuum break. After completing adjustment, apply a suitable sealer to adjusting screw head.

1. Rotate degree scale until zero is opposite pointer, then with choke valve completely closed, place gauge on top of choke valve and rotate bubble until centered, **Fig. 6.**

**FIGURE 1**

1. CHOKE COIL LEVER ADJUSTMENT MUST BE CORRECT AND FAST IDLE ADJUSTMENT MUST BE MADE BEFORE PROCEEDING.
2. USE CHOKE VALVE MEASURING GAUGE J-26701 OR BT-7704. TOOL MAY BE USED WITH CARBURETOR ON OR OFF ENGINE. IF OFF ENGINE, PLACE CARBURETOR ON HOLDING FIXTURE SO THAT IT WILL REMAIN IN SAME POSITION WHEN GAUGE IS IN PLACE.
3. ROTATE DEGREE SCALE UNTIL ZERO (0) IS OPPOSITE POINTER.
4. WITH CHOKE VALVE COMPLETELY CLOSED, PLACE MAGNET SQUARELY ON TOP OF CHOKE VALVE.
5. ROTATE BUBBLE UNTIL IT IS CENTERED.

**FIGURE 2**

6. ROTATE SCALE SO THAT DEGREE SPECIFIED FOR ADJUSTMENT IS OPPOSITE POINTER.
7. PLACE CAM FOLLOWER ON SECOND STEP OF CAM AGAINST RISE OF HIGH STEP.
8. CLOSE CHOKE BY PUSHING UPWARD ON CHOKE COIL LEVER OR VACUUM BREAK LEVER TANG (HOLD IN POSITION WITH RUBBER BAND).
9. TO ADJUST, BEND TANG ON FAST IDLE CAM UNTIL BUBBLE IS CENTERED.
10. REMOVE GAUGE.

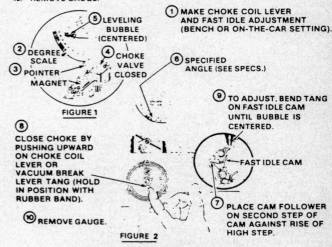

**Fig. 5   Choke rod adjustment**

2. Rotate gauge to degree indicated on Specifications Chart.
3. Seat choke vacuum diaphragm using an external vacuum source, then remove choke coil and rotate inside coil lever counterclockwise.
4. To make final adjustment, turn screw in or out, until bubble is centered.

### 1983–84

1. Attach a rubber band to green tang of intermediate choke shaft to hold choke valve closed.
2. Install angle gauge and rotate scale to degree indicated on Specifications Chart.
3. Retract vacuum break plunger using an external vacuum source, then plug air bleed holes, if applicable.
4. Make final adjustment with vacuum still applied by turning screw in or out until bubble is centered, **Fig. 7.**

### REAR (GAUGE METHOD)

#### 1980–82

Do not remove rivets or choke cover to place choke valve in closed position. Use a rubber band on vacuum break lever tang to hold choke valve closed. Prior to adjustment, remove vacuum break from carburetor and place bracket in a vise, then grind

off weld holding adjusting screw cover. Remove adjusting screw cover, then reinstall vacuum break and proceed with adjustment.

1. Rotate degree scale, **Fig. 8,** until zero is opposite pointer, then with choke valve completely closed, place a magnet on top of choke valve and rotate bubble until centered.
2. Rotate gauge to degree indicated on Specification Chart.
3. Seat choke vacuum diaphragm using an external vacuum source, then remove choke coil and rotate inside coil lever counterclockwise ensuring bucking spring is compressed and seated.
4. To make final adjustment, bend link until bubble is centered.

### 1983–84

1. Attach rubber band to green tang of intermediate choke shaft to hold choke valve closed.
2. Install angle gauge, then rotate scale to degree indicated on Specifications Chart.
3. Retract vacuum break plunger using an external vacuum source, then plug air bleed holes, if applicable.

**FIGURE 1**

1. USE CHOKE VALVE MEASURING GAUGE J-26701 OR BT-7704. TOOL MAY BE USED WITH CARBURETOR ON OR OFF ENGINE. IF OFF ENGINE, PLACE CARBURETOR ON HOLDING FIXTURE SO THAT IT WILL REMAIN IN SAME POSITION WHEN GAUGE IS IN PLACE.
2. ROTATE DEGREE SCALE UNTIL ZERO (0) IS OPPOSITE POINTER.
3. WITH CHOKE VALVE COMPLETELY CLOSED, PLACE MAGNET SQUARELY ON TOP OF CHOKE VALVE.
4. ROTATE BUBBLE UNTIL IT IS CENTERED.

**FIGURE 2**

5. ROTATE SCALE SO THAT DEGREE SPECIFIED FOR ADJUSTMENT IS OPPOSITE POINTER.
6. SEAT CHOKE VACUUM DIAPHRAGM USING VACUUM SOURCE.
7. HOLD CHOKE VALVE TOWARDS CLOSED POSITION, PUSHING UPWARD ON CHOKE COIL LEVER OR VACUUM BREAK LEVER TANG (HOLD IN POSITION WITH RUBBER BAND).
8. TO ADJUST, TURN SCREW IN OR OUT UNTIL BUBBLE IS CENTERED.
9. REMOVE GAUGE.

① ATTACH RUBBER BAND TO GREEN TANG OF INTERMEDIATE CHOKE SHAFT
② OPEN THROTTLE TO ALLOW CHOKE VALVE TO CLOSE
③ SET UP ANGLE GAGE AND SET TO SPECIFICATION
④ RETRACT VACUUM BREAK PLUNGER USING VACUUM SOURCE, AT LEAST 18" HG. PLUG AIR BLEED HOLES WHERE APPLICABLE

ON QUADRAJETS, AIR VALVE ROD MUST NOT RESTRICT PLUNGER FROM RETRACTING FULLY. IF NECESSARY, BEND ROD (SEE ARROW) TO PERMIT FULL PLUNGER TRAVEL. FINAL ROD CLEARANCE MUST BE SET AFTER VACUUM BREAK SETTING HAS BEEN MADE.

⑤ WITH AT LEAST 18" HG STILL APPLIED, ADJUST SCREW TO CENTER BUBBLE

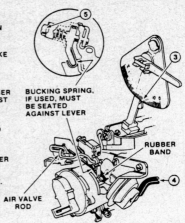

BUCKING SPRING, IF USED, MUST BE SEATED AGAINST LEVER

RUBBER BAND

AIR VALVE ROD

**Fig. 7 Front vacuum break adjustment. 1983–84**

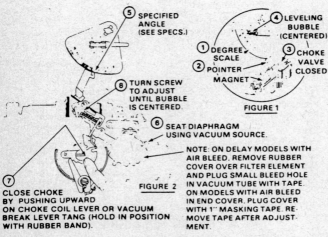

⑤ SPECIFIED ANGLE (SEE SPECS.)

⑧ TURN SCREW TO ADJUST UNTIL BUBBLE IS CENTERED.

⑦ CLOSE CHOKE BY PUSHING UPWARD ON CHOKE COIL LEVER OR VACUUM BREAK LEVER TANG (HOLD IN POSITION WITH RUBBER BAND).

⑥ SEAT DIAPHRAGM USING VACUUM SOURCE.

④ LEVELING BUBBLE (CENTERED)

① DEGREE SCALE
② POINTER MAGNET
③ CHOKE VALVE CLOSED

**FIGURE 1**

**FIGURE 2**

NOTE: ON DELAY MODELS WITH AIR BLEED, REMOVE RUBBER COVER OVER FILTER ELEMENT AND PLUG SMALL BLEED HOLE IN VACUUM TUBE WITH TAPE. ON MODELS WITH AIR BLEED IN END COVER, PLUG COVER WITH 1" MASKING TAPE. REMOVE TAPE AFTER ADJUSTMENT.

**Fig. 6 Front vacuum break adjustment. 1980–82**

**FIGURE 1**

1. USE CHOKE VALVE MEASURING GAUGE J-26701 OR BT-7704. TOOL MAY BE USED WITH CARBURETOR ON OR OFF ENGINE. IF OFF ENGINE, PLACE CARBURETOR ON HOLDING FIXTURE SO THAT IT WILL REMAIN IN SAME POSITION WHEN GAUGE IS IN PLACE.
2. ROTATE DEGREE SCALE UNTIL ZERO (0) IS OPPOSITE POINTER.
3. WITH CHOKE VALVE COMPLETELY CLOSED, PLACE MAGNET SQUARELY ON TOP OF CHOKE VALVE.
4. ROTATE BUBBLE UNTIL IT IS CENTERED.

**FIGURE 2**

5. ROTATE SCALE SO THAT DEGREE SPECIFIED FOR ADJUSTMENT IS OPPOSITE POINTER.
6. SEAT CHOKE VACUUM DIAPHRAGM USING VACUUM SOURCE.
7. HOLD CHOKE VALVE TOWARDS CLOSED POSITION, PUSHING UPWARD ON CHOKE COIL LEVER OR VACUUM BREAK LEVER TANG (HOLD IN POSITION WITH RUBBER BAND).
8. TO ADJUST, BEND LINK UNTIL BUBBLE IS CENTERED.
9. REMOVE GAUGE.

⑥ SEAT DIAPHRAGM USING VACUUM SOURCE.

NOTE: ON DELAY MODELS WITH AIR BLEED, REMOVE RUBBER COVER OVER FILTER ELEMENT AND PLUG SMALL BLEED HOLE IN VACUUM TUBE WITH TAPE. ON MODELS WITH AIR BLEED IN END COVER, PLUG COVER WITH 1" SQUARE MASKING TAPE. REMOVE TAPE AFTER ADJUSTMENT.

⑧ TO ADJUST, BEND CHOKE LINK UNTIL BUBBLE IS CENTERED.

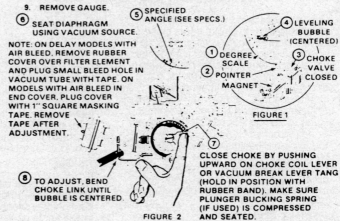

⑤ SPECIFIED ANGLE (SEE SPECS.)

④ LEVELING BUBBLE (CENTERED)

① DEGREE SCALE
② POINTER MAGNET
③ CHOKE VALVE CLOSED

**FIGURE 1**

**FIGURE 2**

⑦ CLOSE CHOKE BY PUSHING UPWARD ON CHOKE COIL LEVER OR VACUUM BREAK LEVER TANG (HOLD IN POSITION WITH RUBBER BAND). MAKE SURE PLUNGER BUCKING SPRING (IF USED) IS COMPRESSED AND SEATED.

**Fig. 9 Rear vacuum break adjustment. 1983–84**

4. Make final adjustment with vacuum still applied by turning adjusting screw with a suitable Allen wrench or by bending vacuum break rod until bubble is centered, **Fig. 9**.

## CHOKE UNLOADER
### 1980–82 Units

1. Rotate degree scale until zero is opposite pointer, **Fig. 10**, then with choke valve completely closed, place magnet squarely on top of choke valve and rotate bubble until centered.

① ATTACH RUBBER BAND TO GREEN TANG OF INTERMEDIATE CHOKE SHAFT.
② OPEN THROTTLE TO ALLOW CHOKE VALVE TO CLOSE.
③ SET UP ANGLE GAGE AND SET ANGLE TO SPECIFICATION.
④ RETRACT VACUUM BREAK PLUNGER, USING VACUUM SOURCE, AT LEAST 18" HG. PLUG AIR BLEED HOLES WHERE APPLICABLE.
④A ON QUADRAJETS, AIR VALVE ROD MUST NOT RESTRICT PLUNGER FROM RETRACTING FULLY. IF NECESSARY, BEND ROD HERE TO PERMIT FULL PLUNGER TRAVEL. WHERE APPLICABLE, PLUNGER STEM MUST BE EXTENDED FULLY TO COMPRESS PLUNGER BUCKING SPRING.
⑤ TO CENTER BUBBLE, EITHER:
   A. ADJUST WITH 1/8" HEX WRENCH (VACUUM STILL APPLIED)
   -OR-
   B. SUPPORT AT "S" AND BEND VACUUM BREAK ROD (VACUUM STILL APPLIED)

**Fig. 8 Rear vacuum break adjustment. 1980–82**

FIGURE 1

1. USE CHOKE VALVE MEASURING GAUGE J-26701 TOOL MAY BE USED WITH CARBURETOR ON OR OFF ENGINE. IF OFF ENGINE, PLACE CARBURETOR ON HOLDING FIXTURE SO THAT IT WILL REMAIN IN SAME POSITION WHEN GAUGE IS IN PLACE.
2. ROTATE DEGREE SCALE UNTIL ZERO (0) IS OPPOSITE POINTER.
3. WITH CHOKE VALVE COMPLETELY CLOSED, PLACE MAGNET SQUARELY ON TOP OF CHOKE VALVE.
4. ROTATE BUBBLE UNTIL IT IS CENTERED.

FIGURE 2

5. ROTATE DEGREE SCALE SO THAT DEGREE SPECIFIED FOR ADJUSTMENT IS OPPOSITE POINTER.
6. INSTALL CHOKE THERMOSTATIC COVER AND COIL ASSEMBLY IN HOUSING. ALIGN INDEX MARK WITH SPECIFIED POINT ON HOUSING.
7. HOLD THROTTLE VALVES WIDE OPEN.
8. ON WARM ENGINE, CLOSE CHOKE VALVE BY PUSHING UP ON TANG ON VACUUM BREAK LEVER (HOLD IN POSITION WITH RUBBER BAND).
9. TO ADJUST, BEND TANG ON FAST IDLE LEVER UNTIL BUBBLE IS CENTERED.
10. REMOVE GAUGE.

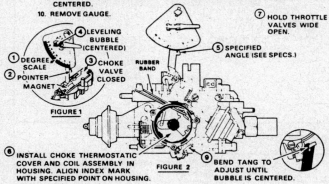

Fig. 10   Choke unloader adjustment. 1980–82

① ATTACH RUBBER BAND TO GREEN TANG OF INTERMEDIATE CHOKE SHAFT
② OPEN THROTTLE TO ALLOW CHOKE VALVE TO CLOSE
③ SET UP ANGLE GAGE AND SET ANGLE TO SPECIFICATION
④ ON QUADRAJET, HOLD SECONDARY LOCKOUT LEVER AWAY FROM PIN
⑤ HOLD THROTTLE LEVER IN WIDE OPEN POSITION
⑥ ADJUST BY BENDING TANG OF FAST IDLE LEVER UNTIL BUBBLE IS CENTERED

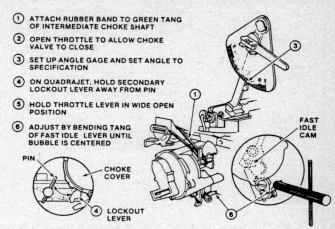

Fig. 11   Choke unloader adjustment. 1983–84

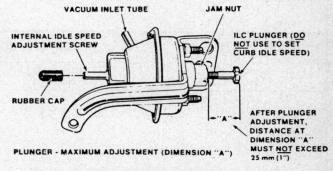

Fig. 12   Idle load compensator (ILC) assembly

2. Rotate scale until degree indicated on Specification Chart is opposite pointer.
3. Install choke cover and coil assembly, then align index mark with specified point on housing.
4. Hold throttle valve wide open. With engine warm, close choke valve by pushing upward on vacuum break lever tang, then retain using a rubber band.
5. To adjust, bend fast idle lever tang until bubble is centered.

## 1983–84 Units

1. Attach rubber band to green tang of intermediate choke shaft, **Fig. 11**, then open throttle to allow choke valve to close.
2. Install angle gauge, then rotate scale until degree indicated on Specification Chart is opposite pointer.
3. Hold secondary lockout lever away from pin, if applicable, then place throttle lever in wide open position.
4. To adjust, bend fast idle lever tang until bubble is centered.

## IDLE LOAD COMPENSATOR (ILC)

This adjustment should not be performed unless during diagnosis, curb idle speed is not within specifications. This adjustment should be performed with engine at normal operating temperature and with choke and A/C off.

1. Remove air cleaner assembly and plug vacuum hose to thermal vacuum valve.

2. Disconnect and plug hoses to EGR valve, canister purge port and idle load compensator.
3. Apply parking brake and block wheels, then back throttle screw out 3 turns.
4. With engine operating, place transmission selector lever in drive (neutral on vehicles with manual transmissions).
5. With ILC plunger fully extended, adjust plunger to obtain 750 RPM. Jam nut on plunger must be held in position to prevent damage to guide tabs. If a replacement idle load compensator is to be installed, the plunger should be set to obtain a clearance of $61/64$ inch from jam nut to tip of plunger, **Fig. 12**.
6. Reconnect hose to idle load compensator and note idle speed. If idle speed requires adjustment, stop engine and remove idle load compensator, then the rubber and metal plug from center outlet tube, **Fig. 12**.
7. Start engine, then adjust center outlet tube adjusting screw to obtain 550 RPM on 1981 models or 500 RPM on 1982 models, using a suitable Allen wrench. Turning adjusting screw counterclockwise increases RPM, while turning clockwise decreases RPM.
8. Reinstall rubber plug on center outlet tube, then install idle load compensator on carburetor. If final adjustment is necessary, repeat steps 6, 7 and 8.

9. Retract ILC plunger using a suitable external vacuum source, then adjust throttle body idle stop screw to obtain 550 RPM on 1981 models or 500 RPM on 1982 models. Reconnect vacuum hoses and install air cleaner.

## IDLE SPEED CONTROL (ISC)

Do not use ISC plunger to adjust curb idle speed, as idle speed is controlled by the Electronic Control Module (ECM). When a new ISC is installed or when indicated by the "System Performance Check," a base (minimum authority) and a high (maximum authority) RPM check must be made and adjustments performed as needed. When making low and high speed adjustments, low speed adjustment must be performed first.

### Preliminary Check

1. Check ISC plunger for an identification letter as shown, **Fig. 13**. If letter appears, proceed to "Adjustment Procedure."
2. If letter does not appear, remove plunger using tool No. J-29607 or equivalent, then measure distance from back of plunger head to plunger end (dimension A), **Fig. 13**. Record dimension for use during "Adjustment Procedure."
3. Reinstall plunger to a dimension less than dimension B, **Fig. 13**.

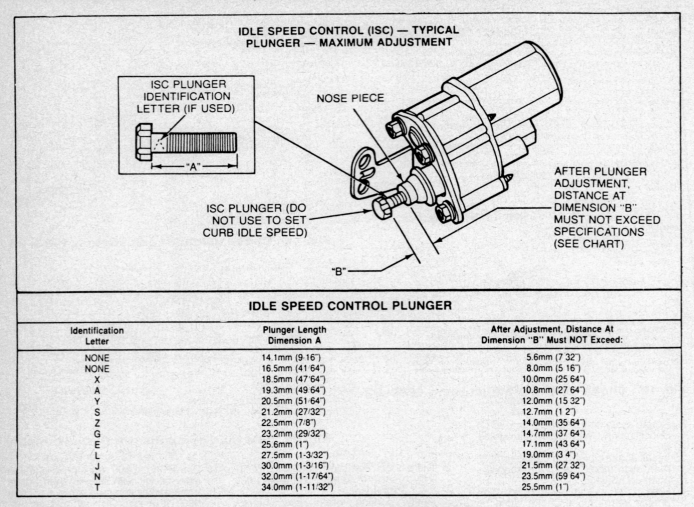

IDLE SPEED CONTROL (ISC) — TYPICAL
PLUNGER — MAXIMUM ADJUSTMENT

ISC PLUNGER
IDENTIFICATION
LETTER (IF USED)

NOSE PIECE

"A"

ISC PLUNGER (DO
NOT USE TO SET
CURB IDLE SPEED)

AFTER PLUNGER
ADJUSTMENT,
DISTANCE AT
DIMENSION "B"
MUST NOT EXCEED
SPECIFICATIONS
(SEE CHART)

"B"

### IDLE SPEED CONTROL PLUNGER

| Identification Letter | Plunger Length Dimension A | After Adjustment, Distance At Dimension "B" Must NOT Exceed: |
|---|---|---|
| NONE | 14.1mm (9 16") | 5.6mm (7 32") |
| NONE | 16.5mm (41 64") | 8.0mm (5 16") |
| X | 18.5mm (47 64") | 10.0mm (25 64") |
| A | 19.3mm (49 64") | 10.8mm (27 64") |
| Y | 20.5mm (51 64") | 12.0mm (15 32") |
| S | 21.2mm (27/32") | 12.7mm (1 2") |
| Z | 22.5mm (7/8") | 14.0mm (35 64") |
| G | 23.2mm (29/32") | 14.7mm (37 64") |
| E | 25.6mm (1") | 17.1mm (43 64") |
| L | 27.5mm (1-3/32") | 19.0mm (3 4") |
| J | 30.0mm (1-3/16") | 21.5mm (27 32") |
| N | 32.0mm (1-17/64") | 23.5mm (59 64") |
| T | 34.0mm (1-11/32") | 25.5mm (1") |

**Fig. 13  Idle speed control (ISC) plunger
adjustment specifications**

## Adjustment Procedure

1. Connect a tachometer to engine. If vehicle is equipped with tachometer, connect remote tachometer to distributor side of tach filter.
2. Connect dwell meter to MC solenoid dwell lead, then set meter to 6 cylinder scale.
3. Start engine and run at fast idle until engine reaches normal operating temperature and dwell readings start to fluctuate.
4. Turn off ignition, then disconnect ISC motor connector.
5. Apply battery voltage to terminal C of ISC motor connector to retract plunger, **Fig. 14**, then ground terminal D. **Do not leave battery voltage connected to ISC motor longer than necessary to retract plunger. Do not connect battery voltage to terminals A or B on motor. ISC motor will be damaged if connections are improperly made.**
6. Start engine and run until dwell reading begins to fluctuate, then place automatic transmissions in Drive (manual transmission in Neutral).

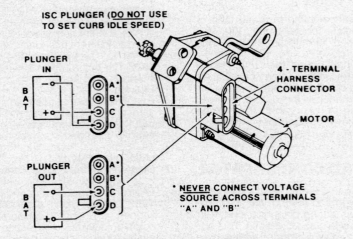

ISC PLUNGER (<u>DO NOT USE</u>
TO SET CURB IDLE SPEED)

PLUNGER
IN

BAT

A*
B*
C
D

4 - TERMINAL
HARNESS
CONNECTOR

MOTOR

PLUNGER
OUT

BAT

A*
B*
C
D

* <u>NEVER</u> CONNECT VOLTAGE
SOURCE ACROSS TERMINALS
"A" AND "B"

**Fig. 14  Idle speed control (ISC) motor test
connections**

| Year | Engine (VIN Code) | Carburetor Number | Minimum Authority ① | Maximum Authority ② |
|------|-------------------|-------------------|---------------------|---------------------|
| 1981–82 | V6-229/3.8L (K) | 17082130, 17082132 | 475D | 800D |
| | V6-231/3.8L (A) | 17082180, 17082184, 17082192, 17082194 | 450D | 900D |
| 1983 | V6-229/3.8L (9) | 17082130 | 475D | 750D |
| | | 17082132 | 475D | 800D |
| | V6-231/3.8L (A) | All | 450D | 900D |
| 1984 | V6-229/3.8L (9) | 17082130, 17082132, 17084191 | 475D | ③ |
| | V6-231/3.8L (A) | 17082130, 17082132, 17084191 | 450D | 1000D |

①—Plunger retracted.
②—Plunger Extended.
③—Less A/C, 750D RPM; with A/C, 800D RPM.

**Fig. 15   Idle speed control (ISC) adjustment specifications**

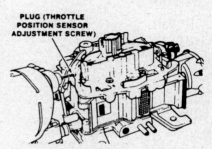

**Fig. 16   Throttle Position Sensor (TPS) adjustment screw plug removal**

| Year | Engine (VIN Code) | Voltage | Throttle Position |
|------|-------------------|---------|-------------------|
| 1981–82 | V6-229/3.8L (K) | .51 | ISC Retracted At Slow Idle |
| | V6-231/3.8L (A) | .77 | High Step Of Fast Idle Cam |
| 1983 | V6-229/3.8L (9) | .51 | ISC Retracted At Slow Idle |
| | V6-231/3.8L (A) | .77 | High Step Of Fast Idle Cam |
| 1984 | V6-229/3.8L (9) | .28 | ISC Retracted At Base Idle |
| | V6-231/3.8L (A) | .39 | High Step Of Fast Idle Cam |

**Fig. 17   Throttle Position Sensor (TPS) adjustment specifications**

7. With ISC plunger fully retracted, adjust idle speed to specified minimum authority RPM, **Fig. 15**, using throttle stop screw.
8. Place automatic transmission in Park, manual transmission in Neutral, then reverse jumper wire connections. Apply battery voltage to terminal D, then ground terminal C. **Only leave jumper wires connected long enough to extend ISC plunger.**
9. On vehicles with manual transmission, adjust idle speed to specified maximum authority RPM, **Fig. 15**, by turning ISC plunger using tool No. J-29607 or equivalent.
10. On vehicles with automatic transmission, adjust idle speed to specified maximum authority RPM, **Fig. 15**, by turning ISC plunger using tool No. J-29607 or equivalent.
11. On all vehicles, recheck ISC maximum authority adjustment RPM with battery voltage applied to motor. Motor will ratchet at full extension with power applied.
12. Measure distance from back of plunger head to ISC nose piece, dimension B, **Fig. 13**. Dimension must not exceed specification shown in chart.
13. Fully retract ISC plunger, then place automatic transmission in Park, manual transmission in Neutral and turn off ignition. Disconnect 12 volt power source, ground lead, tachometer and dwell meter. Connect four terminal harness to ISC motor. This procedure will cause the Check Engine lamp to light and an ISC motor trouble code to be set. Restoring the system to normal operation will cause the lamp to go out, but the trouble code will continue to be stored as an intermittent problem. To clear diagnostic trouble code, remove ECM fuse from fuse panel or disconnect battery ground cable for approximately 10 seconds.

## THROTTLE POSITION SENSOR (TPS)

Do not remove plug sealing TPS adjustment or adjust TPS unless carburetor is overhauled or "Computer Command Control (C3)" system diagnosis indicates a problem with the switch.

1. Drill a .078 (5/64) inch hole, 1/16–1/8 inch deep in plug covering TPS adjustment, **Fig. 16**.
2. Thread a No. 8 sheet metal screw into hole and pry out plug using a suitable lever.
3. Remove TPS adjusting screw using tool J-28696 or equivalent.
4. Leaving electrical connector in place, connect a digital voltmeter between TPS center terminal (B) and bottom terminal (C), using jumper wires if necessary. Only a digital voltmeter with 10 megohm input impedance or higher can be used. Conventional voltmeters do not have sufficient resistance to obtain accurate readings.
5. With ignition on, engine stopped and A/C off, install TPS screw and adjust quickly to obtain specified TPS idle voltage, **Fig. 17**.
6. Turn ignition off and install new plug over TPS adjusting screw or seal opening with RTV sealer.

# Rochester Quadrajet E4M Series Carburetor

## INDEX

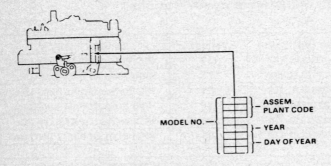

**Fig. 1   Identification number location**

## IDENTIFICATION LOCATION

The carburetor identification number is stamped on the left rear corner of the float bowl casting, adjacent to the secondary throttle lever, **Fig. 1.**

## DESCRIPTION

The E4M series (E4MC, E4ME, E4MED) carburetors are used on vehicles equipped with the Computer Command Control (C3) System. An electrically operated mixture control solenoid, mounted in the float bowl, is used to control the air and fuel metered to the idle and main metering systems of the carburetor. Fuel metering is controlled by two special stepped or tapered primary metering rods operating in removable jets. The metering rods are positioned by a plunger in the solenoid, which is controlled by an electrical signal from the electronic control module. Air metering to the idle system is controlled by an idle air bleed valve located in the air horn, which follows the movement of the mixture control solenoid plunger and thereby controls the amount of bleed air into the idle system. A throttle position sensor, mounted in the float bowl, is used to electrically signal the electronic control module as to the various changes in throttle position.

On E4MED models, a dual capacity pump valve and combined mixture control/dual capacity pump solenoid assembly is used. These assemblies provide a smoother transition from idle to part throttle operation during cold engine operation.

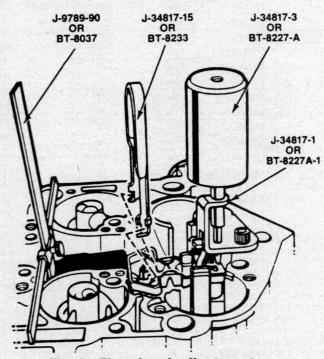

**Fig. 2   Float level adjustment**

An idle speed solenoid or a throttle kicker assembly, depending on engine and application, is used to control curb idle speed. The throttle kicker is vacuum operated and controlled by the electronic control module. It maintains primary throttle position during deceleration, above a specified RPM. The idle speed solenoid, used primarily on air conditioned vehicles, maintains correct curb idle speed whenever the compressor clutch is engaged.

All carburetors use electrically heated choke coils. The heated coils provide choke valve closing force for cold starts, as well as correct opening timing during warm-up. Vacuum break assemblies control initial choke valve opening during starting and warmup periods.

## ADJUSTMENTS
### FLOAT LEVEL

1. Remove air horn and gasket, then the solenoid plunger, metering rods and float bowl insert, if equipped. If lean mixture screw requires removal, count number of turns it takes to seat screw. Return to exact position when reassembling carburetor.
2. Attach base tool BT-8227A-1 or equivalent to float bowl, **Fig. 2.** Position tool BT-8233 or equivalent into base, ensuring contact pin rests on outer edge of float lever.
3. Using adjustable T-scale as shown, measure distance from top of casting to top of float, at a point 3/16 inch from large end of float.
4. If float level is more than 2/32 inch from specification, bend float lever up or down as required with bending tool shown, **Fig. 6.**
5. Remove bending tool, then recheck float level. Check float alignment, then reassemble carburetor.

### FAST IDLE (BENCH)
#### 1982 Units

With cam follower on highest step of

## ADJUSTMENT SPECIFICATIONS

| Year | Carb. Production No. | Float Level | Choke Coil Lever | Choke Rod | Vacuum Break Front | Vacuum Break Rear | Air Valve Rod | Choke Unloader | Air Valve Spring (Turns) |
|---|---|---|---|---|---|---|---|---|---|
| 1982 | 17082202 | 11/32 | .120 | 20° | — | — | .015 | 38° | 7/8 |
| | 17082204 | 11/32 | .120 | 20° | — | — | .015 | 38° | 7/8 |
| 1983 | 17083202 | 11/32 | .120 | 20° | — | 27° | .025 | 38° | 7/8 |
| | 17083203 | 11/32 | .120 | 38° | — | 27° | .025 | 38° | 7/8 |
| | 17083204 | 11/32 | .120 | 20° | — | 27° | .025 | 38° | 7/8 |
| | 17083207 | 11/32 | .120 | 38° | — | 27° | .025 | 38° | 7/8 |
| | 17083216 | 11/32 | .120 | 20° | — | 27° | .025 | 38° | 7/8 |
| | 17083218 | 11/32 | .120 | 20° | — | 27° | .025 | 38° | 7/8 |
| | 17083236 | 11/32 | .120 | 20° | — | 27° | .025 | 38° | 7/8 |
| | 17083506 | 7/16 | .120 | 20° | 27° | 36° | .025 | 36° | 7/8 |
| | 17083508 | 7/16 | .120 | 20° | 27° | 36° | .025 | 36° | 7/8 |
| | 17083524 | 7/16 | .120 | 20° | 25° | 36° | .025 | 36° | 7/8 |
| | 17083526 | 7/16 | .120 | 20° | 25° | 36° | .025 | 36° | 7/8 |
| 1984 | 17084201 | 11/32 | .120 | 20° | 27° | — | .025 | 38° | 7/8 |
| | 17084205 | 11/32 | .120 | 38° | 27° | — | .025 | 38° | 7/8 |
| | 17084208 | 11/32 | .120 | 20° | 27° | — | .025 | 38° | 7/8 |
| | 17084209 | 11/32 | .120 | 38° | 27° | — | .025 | 38° | 7/8 |
| | 17084210 | 11/32 | .120 | 20° | 27° | — | .025 | 38° | 7/8 |
| | 17084507 | 7/16 | .120 | 20° | 27° | 36° | .025 | 36° | 1 |
| | 17084509 | 7/16 | .120 | 20° | 27° | 36° | .025 | 36° | 1 |
| | 17084525 | 7/16 | .120 | 20° | 25° | 36° | .025 | 36° | 1 |
| | 17084527 | 7/16 | .120 | 20° | 25° | 36° | .025 | 36° | 1 |
| 1985 | 17085202 | 11/32 | .120 | 20° | 27° | — | .025 | 38° | 7/8 |
| | 17085203 | 11/32 | .120 | 20° | 27° | — | .025 | 38° | 7/8 |
| | 17085204 | 11/32 | .120 | 20° | 27° | — | .025 | 38° | 7/8 |
| | 17085207 | 11/32 | .120 | 38° | 27° | — | .025 | 38° | 7/8 |
| | 17085218 | 11/32 | .120 | 20° | 27° | — | .025 | 38° | 7/8 |
| | 17085502 | 7/16 | .120 | 20° | 26° | 36° | .025 | 39° | 7/8 |
| | 17085503 | 7/16 | .120 | 20° | 26° | 36° | .025 | 39° | 7/8 |
| | 17085506 | 7/16 | .120 | 20° | 27° | 36° | .025 | 36° | 1 |
| | 17085508 | 7/16 | .120 | 20° | 27° | 36° | .025 | 36° | 1 |
| | 17085524 | 7/16 | .120 | 20° | 25° | 36° | .025 | 36° | 1 |
| | 17085526 | 7/16 | .120 | 20° | 25° | 36° | .025 | 36° | 1 |
| 1986 | 17080212 | 3/8 | .120 | 46° | 24° | 30° | .025 | 40° | 3/4 |
| | 17080213 | 3/8 | .120 | 37° | 23° | 30° | .025 | 40° | 1 |
| | 17081298 | 3/8 | .120 | 37° | 23° | 30° | .025 | 40° | 1 |
| | 17082213 | 3/8 | .120 | 37° | 23° | 30° | .025 | 40° | 1 |
| | 17083298 | 3/8 | .120 | 37° | 23° | 30° | .025 | 40° | 1 |
| | 17084500 | 3/8 | .120 | 37° | 23° | 30° | .025 | 40° | 1 |
| | 17084501 | 3/8 | .120 | 37° | 23° | 30° | .025 | 40° | 1 |
| | 17084502 | 3/8 | .120 | 46° | 24° | 30° | .025 | 40° | 7/8 |
| | 17085000 | 3/8 | .120 | 46° | 24° | 30° | .025 | 40° | 7/8 |
| | 17085001 | 3/8 | .120 | 46° | 23° | 30° | .025 | 40° | 1 |
| | 17085003 | 13/32 | .120 | 46° | 23° | — | .025 | 35° | 7/8 |
| | 17085004 | 13/32 | .120 | 46° | 23° | — | .025 | 35° | 7/8 |
| | 17085202 | 11/32 | .120 | 20° | 27° | — | .025 | 38° | 7/8 |
| | 17085203 | 11/32 | .120 | 20° | 27° | — | .025 | 38° | 7/8 |
| | 17085204 | 13/32 | .120 | 20° | 27° | — | .025 | 38° | 7/8 |
| | 17085205 | 13/32 | .120 | 20° | 26° | 38° | .025 | 39° | 7/8 |
| | 17085206 | 13/32 | .120 | 46° | — | 26° | .025 | 39° | 7/8 |
| | 17085207 | 11/32 | .120 | 38° | 27° | — | .025 | 38° | 7/8 |
| | 17085208 | 13/32 | .120 | 20° | 26° | 38° | .025 | 39° | 7/8 |
| | 17085209 | 13/32 | .120 | 20° | 26° | 38° | .025 | 39° | 7/8 |

## ADJUSTMENT SPECIFICATIONS—Continued

| Year | Carb. Production No. | Float Level | Choke Coil Lever | Choke Rod | Vacuum Break | | Air Valve Rod | Choke Unloader | Air Valve Spring (Turns) |
|------|------|------|------|------|------|------|------|------|------|
| | | | | | Front | Rear | | | |
| | 17085210 | 13/32 | .120 | 20° | 26° | 38° | .025 | 39° | 7/8 |
| | 17085211 | 13/32 | .120 | 20° | 26° | 38° | .025 | 39° | 7/8 |
| | 17085212 | 13/32 | .120 | 46° | 23° | — | .025 | 35° | 7/8 |
| | 17085213 | 13/32 | .120 | 46° | 23° | — | .025 | 35° | 7/8 |
| | 17085215 | 13/32 | .120 | 46° | — | 26° | .025 | 32° | 7/8 |
| | 17085216 | 13/32 | .120 | 20° | 26° | 38° | .025 | 39° | 7/8 |
| | 17085217 | 13/32 | .120 | 20° | 26° | 38° | .025 | 39° | 1/2 |
| | 17085218 | 11/32 | .120 | 20° | 27° | | .025 | 38° | 7/8 |
| | 17085219 | 13/32 | .120 | 20° | 26° | 38° | .025 | 39° | 1/2 |
| | 17085220 | 13/32 | .120 | 20° | — | 26° | .025 | 32° | 7/8 |
| | 17085221 | 13/32 | .120 | 20° | — | 26° | .025 | 32° | 7/8 |
| | 17085222 | 13/32 | .120 | 20° | 26° | 36° | .025 | 39° | 7/8 |
| | 17085223 | 13/32 | .120 | 20° | 26° | 36° | .025 | 39° | 1/2 |
| | 17085224 | 13/32 | .120 | 20° | 26° | 36° | .025 | 39° | 1/2 |
| | 17085225 | 13/32 | .120 | 20° | 26° | 36° | .025 | 39° | 1/2 |
| | 17085226 | 13/32 | .120 | 20° | — | 24° | .025 | 32° | 7/8 |
| | 17085227 | 13/32 | .120 | 20° | — | 24° | .025 | 32° | 7/8 |
| | 17085228 | 13/32 | .120 | 46° | — | 24° | .025 | 39° | 7/8 |
| | 17085229 | 13/32 | .120 | 46° | — | 24° | .025 | 39° | 7/8 |
| | 17085230 | 13/32 | .120 | 20° | — | 26° | .025 | 32° | 7/8 |
| | 17085231 | 13/32 | .120 | 20° | — | 26° | .025 | 32° | 7/8 |
| | 17085235 | 13/32 | .120 | 46° | — | 26° | .025 | 39° | 7/8 |
| | 17085238 | 13/32 | .120 | 20° | — | 26° | .025 | 32° | 7/8 |
| | 17085239 | 13/32 | .120 | 20° | — | 26° | .025 | 32° | 7/8 |
| | 17085290 | 13/32 | .120 | 46° | — | 24° | .025 | 39° | 7/8 |
| | 17085291 | 13/32 | .120 | 46° | — | 26° | .025 | 39° | 7/8 |
| | 17085292 | 13/32 | .120 | 46° | — | 24° | .025 | 39° | 7/8 |
| | 17085293 | 13/32 | .120 | 46° | — | 26° | .025 | 39° | 7/8 |
| | 17085294 | 13/32 | .120 | 46° | — | 26° | .025 | 39° | 7/8 |
| | 17085298 | 13/32 | .120 | 46° | — | 26° | .025 | 39° | 7/8 |
| | 17085502 | 7/16 | .120 | 20° | 26° | 36° | .025 | 39° | 7/8 |
| | 17085503 | 7/16 | .120 | 20° | 26° | 36° | .025 | 39° | 7/8 |
| | 17085506 | 7/16 | .120 | 20° | 27° | 36° | .025 | 36° | 1 |
| | 17085508 | 7/16 | .120 | 20° | 27° | 36° | .025 | 36° | 7/8 |
| | 17085524 | 7/16 | .120 | 20° | 25° | 36° | .025 | 36° | 7/8 |
| | 17085526 | 7/16 | .120 | 20° | 25° | 36° | .025 | 36° | 7/8 |
| | 17086057 | 15/00032 | .120 | — | 26° | 36° | .025 | 39° | 7/8 |
| | 17086058 | 15/32 | .120 | — | 26° | 36° | .025 | 39° | 7/8 |
| 1987 | 17087129 | 11/32 | .120 | 20° | 27° | — | .025 | 38° | 7/8 |
| | 17087130 | 11/32 | .120 | 20° | 27° | — | .025 | 38° | 7/8 |
| | 17087132 | 11/32 | .120 | 20° | 27° | — | .025 | 38° | 7/8 |

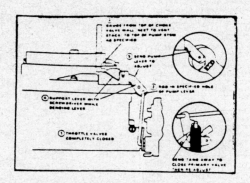

**Fig. 3  Fast idle adjustment (Bench). 1982 Units**

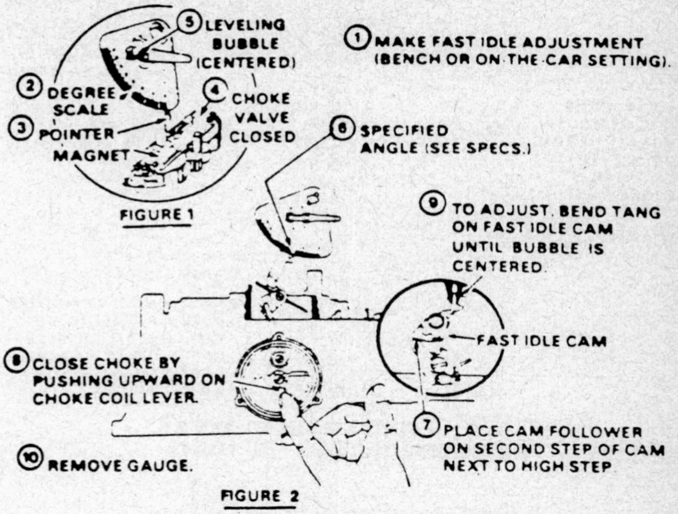

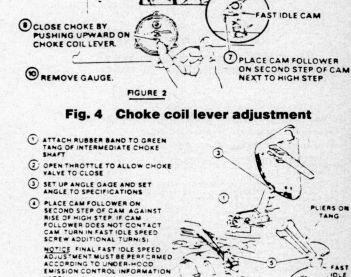

**Fig. 4  Choke coil lever adjustment**

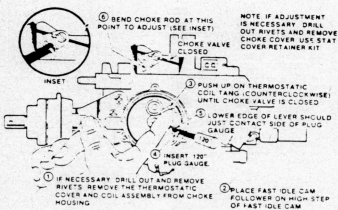

**Fig. 5  Choke rod adjustment**

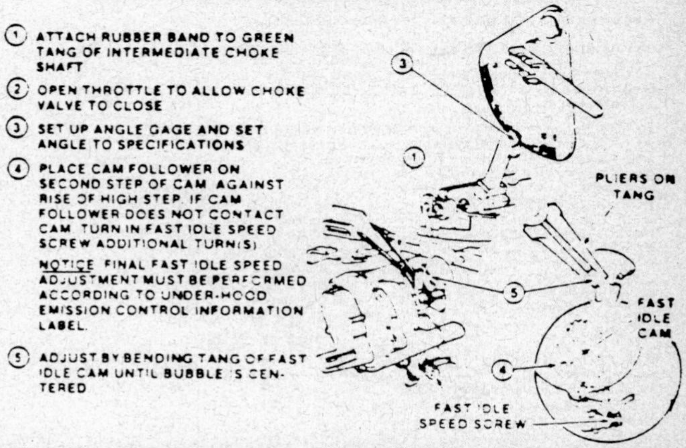

**Fig. 6  Front vacuum break adjustment. 1982 Units**

cam, **Fig. 3,** turn fast idle screw out until primary throttle valve is completely closed. Turn screw in to contact lever, then turn screw in an additional 4½ turns.

## CHOKE COIL LEVER

With thermostatic coil assembly removed from choke housing, push upward on coil tang to close choke valve. Insert gauge specified in the Specification Chart into hole in choke housing. The choke coil lever should contact the gauge. If not, bend choke rod to adjust, **Fig. 4.**

## CHOKE ROD

Perform fast idle adjustment before making this adjustment. Do not remove rivets and choke cover to perform this adjustment. Use a rubber band on the vacuum break lever tang to hold the choke valve in the closed position.
1. Rotate degree scale until zero is opposite pointer, then with choke valve completely closed, place magnet squarely on top of choke valve and rotate bubble until centered.
2. Rotate scale so the specified degree for adjustment is opposite pointer. Re-

fer to Specification Chart for proper setting.
3. Place cam follower on second step of cam next to high step. Close choke by pushing upward on choke coil lever.
4. To adjust, bend tang on fast idle cam until bubble is centered, **Fig. 5.** Remove gauge.

## FRONT VACUUM BREAK

Do not remove rivets or choke cover to place choke valve in the closed position. Use a rubber band on vacuum break lever tang to hold choke valve in the closed position.

### 1982 Units
1. Rotate degree scale until zero is opposite pointer, then with choke valve completely closed, place magnet squarely on top of choke valve and rotate bubble until centered.
2. Rotate scale so the specified degree for adjustment is opposite pointer. Refer to Specification Chart to obtain proper setting for adjustment.
3. Seat choke diaphragm using an external vacuum source. On some models, it will be necessary to plug air bleed with a piece of masking tape.

4. Hold choke valve toward closed position, pushing counterclockwise on inside coil lever. To adjust, rotate screw until bubble is centered, **Fig. 6.** Remove gauge.

### 1983–88 Units
1. Attach rubber band to green tang of intermediate choke shaft, then open throttle lever to allow choke valve to close.
2. Position magnet on top of choke valve, then rotate degree scale until zero is opposite pointer.
3. Center leveling bubble, then rotate degree scale until specified adjustment angle is opposite pointer.
4. Seat vacuum break plunger using external vacuum source of at least 18 inches Hg vacuum. On some models, it will be necessary to plug air bleed with a piece of masking tape.
5. With vacuum still applied, rotate adjustment screw until bubble is centered, **Fig. 7.** On units equipped with bucking spring, spring must be seated against lever before adjusting screw. Also, the air valve rod must not restrict the vacuum plunger from retracting fully. If necessary, bend rod at arrow, **Fig. 7,** to permit full plunger travel.

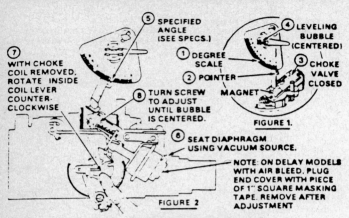

**Fig. 7 Front vacuum break adjustment.1983–88 Units**

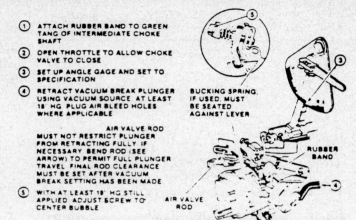

**Fig. 8 Rear vacuum break adjustment.1982 Units**

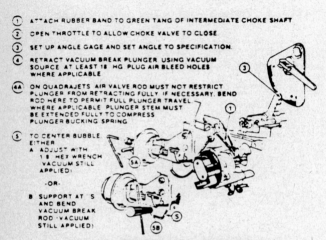

**Fig. 9 Rear vacuum break adjustment.1983–88 Units**

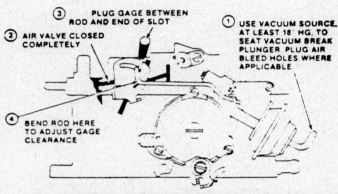

**Fig. 10 Choke unloader adjustment. 1982 Units**

## REAR VACUUM BREAK

### 1982 Units

1. Rotate degree scale until zero is opposite pointer, then with choke valve completely closed, place magnet squarely on top of choke valve and rotate bubble until centered.
2. Rotate scale so specified degree for adjustment is opposite pointer. Refer to Specification Chart for proper setting for adjustment.
3. Seat choke diaphragm using an external vacuum source. On some models, it will be necessary to plug air bleed with a piece of masking tape.
4. Hold choke valve toward closed position, pushing counterclockwise on inside coil lever. On units equipped with an adjusting screw, turn adjusting screw in rear cover until bubble is centered using a 1/8 inch hex wrench, **Fig. 8.**

### 1983–88 Units

1. Attach rubber band to green tang intermediate choke shaft, then open throttle lever to allow choke valve to close.

2. Position magnet on top of choke valve, then rotate degree scale until zero is opposite pointer.
3. Center leveling bubble, then rotate degree scale until specified adjustment angle is opposite pointer.
4. Seat vacuum break plunger using external vacuum source of at least 18 inches Hg vacuum. On some models, it will be necessary to plug air bleed with a piece of masking tape.
5. With vacuum still applied, either rotate adjustment screw or bend vacuum break rod at S until bubble is centered, **Fig. 9.** On units equipped with bucking spring, plunger stem must be fully extended to compress spring on plunger. Also, the air valve rod must not restrict the vacuum plunger from retracting fully. If necessary, bend rod at arrow, **Fig. 9,** to permit full plunger travel.

## CHOKE UNLOADER

### 1982 Units

1. Rotate degree scale until zero is opposite pointer, then with choke valve completely closed, place magnet

squarely on top of choke valve, then rotate bubble until centered.
2. Rotate scale so specified adjustment angle is opposite pointer. Refer to Specification Chart for proper setting for adjustment.
3. Install choke cover and coil assembly and align index mark with specified point on housing. Hold primary throttle valve wide open and close choke valve by pushing upward on vacuum break lever tang. Hold in position with a rubber band.
4. To adjust, bend tang on fast idle lever until bubble is centered, **Fig. 10,** then remove gauge.

### 1983–88 Units

1. Attach rubber band to green tang of intermediate choke shaft, then open throttle lever to allow choke valve to close.
2. Position magnet on top of choke valve, then rotate degree scale until zero is opposite pointer.
3. Center leveling bubble, then rotate degree scale until specified adjustment angle is opposite pointer.
4. Hold secondary lockout lever away from pin, **Fig. 11,** then bend fast idle lever tang until bubble is centered.

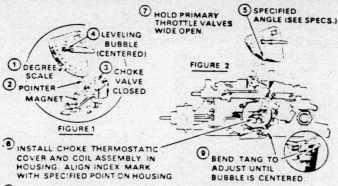

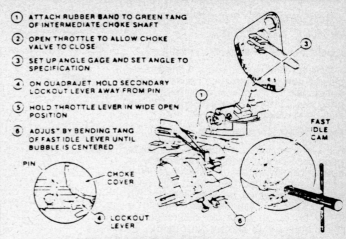

**Fig. 11 Choke unloader adjustment. 1983–88 Units**

**Fig. 12 Secondary throttle valve lockout adjustment**

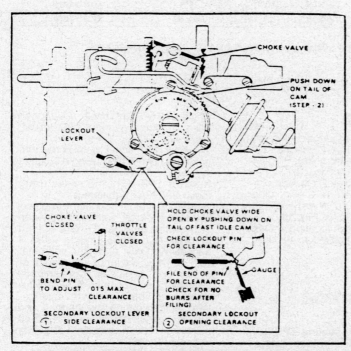

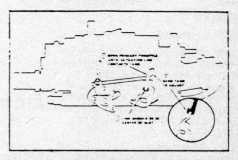

**Fig. 14 Secondary throttle valve opening. 1982 Units**

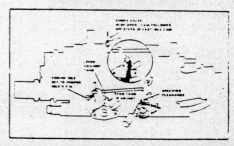

**Fig. 13 Secondary throttle valve closing adjustment. 1982 Units**

**Fig. 15 Air valve spring wind-up adjustment**

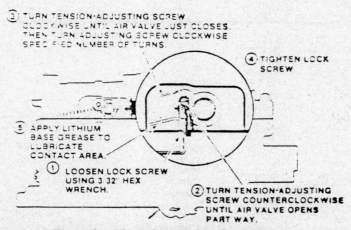

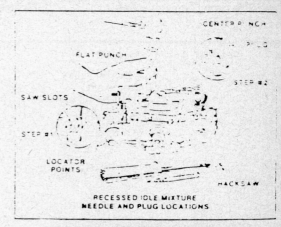

**Fig. 16 Air valve rod adjustment**

**Fig. 17 Throttle position sensor adjustment screw cover removal**

## SECONDARY THROTTLE VALVE LOCKOUT

### Lockout Pin Clearance

With choke and throttle valves fully closed, measure clearance between lockout pin and lockout lever. Maximum clearance should not exceed .015 inch. To adjust, bend lockout pin, **Fig. 12.**

### Opening Clearance

Push downward on fast idle cam tail to open choke valve, then push lockout lever counterclockwise so upper end of lever contacts the round pin in fast idle cam. Measure clearance between lockout pin and lockout lever toe. Clearance should be .015 inch. To obtain proper clearance, file metal from end of lockout pin, **Fig. 12.**

## SECONDARY THROTTLE VALVES

### 1982 UNITS

### Throttle Closing

With curb idle speed set, hold choke valve open with cam follower lever off fast idle cam steps. Measure clearance between forward edge of slot in the secondary throttle valve pickup lever and the secondary actuating rod. Clearance should be .020 inch. To adjust, bend secondary closing tang on primary throttle lever, **Fig. 13.**

### Throttle Opening

Open primary throttle lever until link lightly contacts secondary lever tang. The bottom end of the link should be in the center of the slot in secondary lever. To adjust, bend tang on secondary lever, **Fig. 14.**

## AIR VALVE SPRING WIND-UP

Loosen lock screw using suitable hex wrench, then turn adjusting screw counterclockwise until air valve partially opens, **Fig. 15.** Turn adjusting screw clockwise until air valve just closes, then continue turning screw clockwise the number of turns listed in the Specification Chart. After adjustment is complete, apply lithium base grease to contact area of spring.

| Year | Engine (VIN Code) | Voltage | Throttle Position |
|------|-------------------|---------|-------------------|
| 1983 | V8-305/5.0L (H) | .51 | Curb Idle |
| | V8-305/5.0L (F) | .40 | Curb Idle |
| | V8-350 5.7L (L) | .40 | Curb Idle |
| 1984 | V8-305/5.0L (H) | .48 | Curb Idle |
| | V8-305/5.0L (F) | .41 | Curb Idle |
| | V8-350 5.7L (L) | .41 | Curb Idle |
| 1985 | V6-262/4.3L (N) | .25 | Curb Idle |
| | V8-305/5.0L (H) | .48 | Curb Idle |
| | V8-305/5.0L (F) | .41 | Curb Idle |
| | V8-350 5.7L (L) | .41 | Curb Idle |
| 1986 | V6-262/4.3L (N) | .25 | Curb Idle |
| | V8-305/5.0L (H) | .48 | Curb Idle |
| | V8-305/5.0L (F) | .41 | Curb Idle |
| | V8-350 5.7L (L) | .41 | Curb Idle |
| 1987 | V8-305.5.0L (G) | .50-.58 | Curb Idle |

**Fig. 18   Throttle position sensor specifications**

## AIR VALVE ROD

1. Seat vacuum break plunger using external vacuum source (18 inches Hg minimum on 1983-88 units). Plug air bleed holes where applicable.
2. With air valve completely closed, position gauge specified in Specification Chart between air valve rod and end of slot in air valve lever, **Fig. 16.**
3. To adjust, bend rod in location shown with vacuum still applied to vacuum break plunger.

## THROTTLE POSITION SENSOR (TPS)

**Do not remove plug sealing TPS adjustment or adjust TPS unless carburetor is overhauled or "Computer Command Control (C3)" system diagnosis indicates a problem with the switch.**

1. Drill a .078 (5/64) inch hole, 1/16-1/8 inch deep, in plug covering TPS adjustment, **Fig. 17.**
2. Thread a No. 8 sheet metal screw into hole and pry out plug using a suitable lever.
3. Remove TPS adjusting screw using tool J-28696 or equivalent.
4. Leaving electrical connector in place, connect a digital voltmeter between TPS center terminal (B) and bottom terminal (C), using jumper wires if necessary. Only a digital voltmeter with 10 megohm input impedance or higher can be used. Conventional voltmeters do not have sufficient resistance to obtain accurate readings.
5. With ignition on, engine stopped and A/C off, install TPS screw and adjust quickly to obtain specified TPS idle voltage, **Fig. 18.**
6. Turn ignition off and install new plug over TPS adjusting screw or seal opening with RTV sealer.

# Rochester Quadrajet M4M Series

## INDEX

## ADJUSTMENT SPECIFICATIONS

| Year | Carb. Production No. | Float Level | Pump Rod Hole | Pump Rod Adj. | Choke Coil Lever | Choke Rod | Vacuum Break Front | Vacuum Break Rear | Air Valve Dashpot | Choke Unloader | Air Valve Spring (Turns) |
|---|---|---|---|---|---|---|---|---|---|---|---|
| 1980 | 17080201 | 15/32 | Inner | 9/32 | — | 46° | — | 23° | .025 | 42° | 7/8 |
| | 17080202 | 13/32 | Inner | 1/4 | .120 | 20° | 27° | — | .025 | 38° | 7/8 |
| | 17080204 | 13/32 | Inner | 1/4 | .120 | 20° | 27° | — | .025 | 38° | 7/8 |
| | 17080205 | 15/32 | Inner | 9/32 | — | 46° | — | — | .025 | 42° | 7/8 |
| | 17080206 | 15/32 | Inner | 9/32 | — | 46° | — | 23° | .025 | 42° | 7/8 |
| | 17080207 | 13/32 | Inner | 1/4 | — | 20° | 27° | — | .025 | 38° | 7/8 |
| | 17080211 | 13/32 | Inner | 9/32 | — | 20° | 28° | — | .025 | 38° | 1 |
| | 17080212 | 3/8 | Inner | 9/32 | .120 | 46° | 24° | 30° | .025 | 40° | 3/4 |
| | 17080213 | 3/8 | Inner | 9/32 | .120 | 37° | 23° | 30° | .025 | 40° | 1 |
| | 17080215 | 3/8 | Inner | 9/32 | .120 | 37° | 23° | 30° | .025 | 40° | 1 |
| | 17080224 | 15/32 | Inner | 9/32 | .120 | 46° | — | 23° | .025 | 42° | 7/8 |
| | 17080225 | 15/32 | Inner | 9/32 | .120 | 46° | — | 23° | .025 | 42° | 7/8 |
| | 17080226 | 15/32 | Inner | 9/32 | .120 | 46° | — | 23° | .025 | 42° | 7/8 |
| | 17080227 | 15/32 | Inner | 9/32 | .120 | 46° | — | 23° | .025 | 42° | 7/8 |
| | 17080228 | 13/32 | Inner | 9/32 | .120 | 20° | 25° | — | .025 | 38° | 1 |
| | 17080229 | 3/8 | Inner | 9/32 | .120 | 37° | 23° | 30° | .025 | 40° | 1 |
| | 17080240 | 13/16 | Inner | 9/32 | .120 | 14.5° | 16° | 16° | .025 | 30° | 9/16 |
| | 1708024 | 13/16 | Inner | 9/32 | .120 | 14.5° | 15° | 18° | .025 | 35° | 9/16 |
| | 17080243 | 13/16 | Inner | 9/32 | .120 | 14.5° | 16° | 16° | .025 | 30° | 9/16 |
| | 17080274 | 7/16 | Outer | 11/32 | — | 16° | 24° | 32° | .025 | 35° | 5/8 |
| | 17080290 | 15/32 | Inner | 9/32 | — | 46° | — | 26° | .025 | 42° | 7/8 |
| | 17080291 | 15/32 | Inner | 9/32 | — | 46° | — | 26° | .025 | 42° | 7/8 |
| | 17080292 | 15/32 | Inner | 9/32 | — | 46° | — | 26° | .025 | 42° | 7/8 |
| | 17080293 | 15/32 | Inner | 9/32 | — | 46° | — | 26° | .025 | 42° | 7/8 |
| | 17080295 | 15/32 | Inner | 9/32 | — | 46° | — | 23° | .025 | 42° | 7/8 |
| | 17080297 | 15/32 | Inner | 9/32 | — | 46° | — | 23° | .025 | 42° | 7/8 |
| | 17080502 | 19/32 | — | 3/8 | .120 | 20° | 26° | 30° | .025 | 38° | 7/8 |
| | 17080503 | 15/32 | Inner | 9/32 | .102 | 46° | — | 26° | .025 | 42° | 7/8 |
| | 17080504 | 19/32 | — | 3/8 | .120 | 20° | 26° | 30° | .025 | 38° | 7/8 |
| | 17080505 | 15/32 | Inner | 9/32 | .102 | 46° | — | 26° | .025 | 42° | 7/8 |
| | 17080506 | 15/32 | Inner | 9/32 | .102 | 46° | — | 26° | .025 | 42° | 7/8 |
| | 17080508 | 15/32 | Inner | 9/32 | .102 | 46° | — | 26° | .025 | 42° | 7/8 |
| | 17080509 | 15/32 | Outer | 11/32 | — | 46° | 30° | — | .025 | 42° | 7/8 |
| | 17080510 | 15/32 | Outer | 11/32 | .120 | 46° | 30° | — | .025 | 42° | 7/8 |
| | 17080512 | 3/8 | Inner | 9/32 | .120 | 46° | 24° | 30° | .025 | 40° | 3/4 |
| | 17080513 | 3/8 | Inner | 9/32 | .120 | 37° | 23° | 30° | .025 | 40° | 1 |
| | 17080515 | 3/8 | Inner | 9/32 | .120 | 37° | 23° | 30° | .025 | 40° | 1 |
| | 17080523 | 15/32 | Inner | 9/32 | .120 | 46° | — | 23° | .025 | 42° | 7/8 |
| | 17080524 | 15/32 | Inner | 9/32 | .120 | 46° | — | 23° | .025 | 42° | 7/8 |

## ADJUSTMENT SPECIFICATIONS—Continued

| Year | Carb. Production No. | Float Level | Pump Rod Hole | Pump Rod Adj. | Choke Coil Lever | Choke Rod | Vacuum Break Front | Vacuum Break Rear | Air Valve Dashpot | Choke Unloader | Air Valve Spring (Turns) |
|------|------|------|------|------|------|------|------|------|------|------|------|
| 1980 | 17080525 | 15/32 | Inner | 9/32 | .120 | 46° | — | 23° | .025 | 42° | 7/8 |
| | 17080526 | 15/32 | Inner | 9/32 | .120 | 46° | — | 23° | .025 | 42° | 7/8 |
| | 17080527 | 15/32 | Inner | 9/32 | .120 | 46° | — | 23° | .025 | 42° | 7/8 |
| | 17080528 | 15/32 | Inner | 9/32 | .120 | 46° | — | 23° | .025 | 42° | 7/8 |
| | 17080529 | 3/8 | Inner | 9/32 | .120 | 37° | 23° | 30° | .025 | 40° | 1 |
| | 17080540 | 3/8 | — | 3/8 | .120 | 14.5° | 19° | 23° | .025 | 38° | 9/16 |
| | 17080542 | 3/8 | — | 3/8 | .120 | 14.5° | 19° | 23° | .025 | 38° | 9/16 |
| | 17080543 | 3/8 | — | 3/8 | .120 | 14.5° | 19° | 23° | .025 | 38° | 9/16 |
| 1981 | 17080212 | 3/8 | Inner | 9/32 | .120 | 46° | 24° | 30° | .025 | 40° | 3/4 |
| | 17080213 | 3/8 | Inner | 9/32 | .120 | 37° | 23° | 30° | .025 | 40° | 1 |
| | 17080215 | 3/8 | Inner | 9/32 | .120 | 37° | 23° | 30° | .025 | 40° | 1 |
| | 17080298 | 3/8 | Inner | 9/32 | .120 | 37° | 23° | 30° | .025 | 40° | 1 |
| | 17080507 | 3/8 | Inner | 9/32 | .120 | 37° | 23° | 30° | .025 | 40° | 1 |
| | 17080512 | 3/8 | Inner | 9/32 | .120 | 46° | 24° | 30° | .025 | 40° | 3/4 |
| | 17080513 | 3/8 | Inner | 9/32 | .120 | 37° | 23° | 30° | .025 | 40° | 3/4 |
| | 17081200 | 15/32 | Inner | 9/32 | .120 | 46° | 24° | 23° | .025 | 42° | 7/8 |
| | 17081201 | 15/32 | Inner | 9/32 | .120 | 46° | 23° | 23° | .025 | 42° | 7/8 |
| | 17081205 | 15/32 | Inner | 9/32 | .120 | 46° | 23° | 23° | .025 | 42° | 7/8 |
| | 17081206 | 15/32 | Inner | 9/32 | .120 | 46° | 23° | 23° | .025 | 42° | 7/8 |
| | 17081220 | 15/32 | Inner | 9/32 | .120 | 46° | 23° | 23° | .025 | 42° | 7/8 |
| | 17081226 | 15/32 | Inner | 9/32 | .120 | 46° | 24° | 23° | .025 | 42° | 7/8 |
| | 17081227 | 15/32 | Inner | 9/32 | .120 | 46° | 24° | 23° | .025 | 42° | 7/8 |
| | 17081290 | 13/32 | Inner | 9/32 | .120 | 46° | 23° | 24° | .025 | 42° | 7/8 |
| | 17081291 | 13/32 | Inner | 9/32 | .120 | 46° | 23° | 24° | .025 | 42° | 7/8 |
| | 17081292 | 13/32 | Inner | 9/32 | .120 | 46° | 23° | 24° | .025 | 42° | 7/8 |
| | 17081506 | 13/32 | Inner | 9/32 | .120 | 46° | 23° | 36° | .025 | 36° | 7/8 |
| | 17081508 | 13/32 | Inner | 9/32 | .120 | 46° | 23° | 36° | .025 | 36° | 7/8 |
| | 17081524 | 13/32 | Outer | 5/15 | .120 | 46° | 25° | 36° | .025 | 38° | 7/8 |
| | 17081526 | 13/32 | Outer | 5/16 | .120 | 46° | 25° | 36° | .025 | 38° | 7/8 |
| 1982 | 17080212 | 3/8 | Inner | 9/32 | .120 | 46° | 24° | 30° | .025 | 40° | 3/4 |
| | 17080213 | 3/8 | Inner | 9/32 | .120 | 37° | 23° | 30° | .025 | 40° | 1 |
| | 17080215 | 3/8 | Inner | 9/32 | .120 | 37° | 23° | 30° | .025 | 40° | 1 |
| | 17080298 | 3/8 | Inner | 9/32 | .120 | 37° | 23° | 30° | .025 | 40° | 1 |
| | 17080507 | 3/8 | Inner | 9/32 | .120 | 37° | 23° | 30° | .025 | 40° | 1 |
| | 17080512 | 3/8 | Inner | 9/32 | .120 | 46° | 24° | 30° | .025 | 40° | 3/4 |
| | 17080513 | 3/8 | Inner | 9/32 | .120 | 37° | 23° | 30° | .025 | 40° | 3/4 |
| | 17082213 | 3/8 | Inner | 9/32 | .120 | 37° | 23° | 30° | .025 | 40° | 1 |
| | 17082220 | 13/32 | Inner | 9/32 | .120 | 46° | 24° | 34° | .025 | 39° | 7/8 |
| | 17082221 | 13/32 | Inner | 9/32 | .120 | 46° | 24° | 34° | .025 | 39° | 7/8 |
| | 17082222 | 13/32 | Inner | 9/32 | .120 | 46° | 24° | 34° | .025 | 39° | 7/8 |
| | 17082223 | 13/32 | Inner | 9/32 | .120 | 46° | 24° | 34° | .025 | 39° | 7/8 |
| | 17082224 | 13/32 | Inner | 9/32 | .120 | 46° | 24° | 34° | .025 | 39° | 7/8 |
| | 17082225 | 13/32 | Inner | 9/32 | .120 | 46° | 24° Y° 34° | .025 | 39° | 7/8 | |
| | 17082226 | 13/32 | Inner | 9/32 | .120 | 46° | 24° | 34° | .025 | 39° | 7/8 |
| | 17082227 | 13/32 | Inner | 9/32 | .120 | 46° | 24° | 34° | .025 | 39° | 7/8 |
| | 17082230 | 13/32 | Inner | 9/32 | .120 | 46° | 26° | 34° | .025 | 39° | 7/8 |
| | 17082231 | 13/32 | Inner | 9/32 | .120 | 46° | 26° | 34° | .025 | 39° | 7/8 |
| | 17082234 | 13/32 | Inner | 9/32 | .120 | 46° | 26° | 34° | .025 | 39° | 7/8 |
| | 17082235 | 13/32 | Inner | 9/32 | .120 | 46° | 26° | 34° | .025 | 39° | 7/8 |
| | 17082290 | 13/32 | Inner | 9/32 | .120 | 46° | 24° | 34° | .025 | 39° | 7/8 |
| | 17082291 | 13/32 | Inner | 9/32 | .120 | 46° | 24° | 34° | .025 | 39° | 7/8 |

## ADJUSTMENT SPECIFICATIONS—Continued

| Year | Carb. Production No. | Float Level | Pump Rod | | Choke Coil Lever | Choke Rod | Vacuum Break | | Air Valve Dashpot | Choke Unloader | Air Valve Spring (Turns) |
| | | | Hole | Adj. | | | Front | Rear | | | |
|---|---|---|---|---|---|---|---|---|---|---|---|
| 1982 | 17082292 | 13/32 | Inner | 9/32 | .120 | 46° | 24° | 34° | .025 | 39° | 7/8 |
| | 17082293 | 13/32 | Inner | 9/32 | .120 | 46° | 24° | 34° | .025 | 39° | 7/8 |
| | 17082506 | 13/32 | Inner | 9/32 | .120 | 46° | 23° | 36° | .025 | 39° | 7/8 |
| | 17082508 | 13/32 | Inner | 9/32 | .120 | 46° | 23° | 36° | .025 | 39° | 7/8 |
| | 17082513 | 13/32 | Inner | 9/32 | .120 | 37° | 23° | 30° | .025 | 40° | 7/8 |
| | 17082524 | 13/32 | Outer | 5/15 | .120 | 46° | 25° y °36° | .025 | 39° | 7/8 | |
| | 17082526 | 13/32 | Outer | 5/16 | .120 | 46° | 25° | 36° | .025 | 39° | 7/8 |
| 1983 | 17080201 | 15/32 | Inner | 9/32 | .120 | 46° | — | 23° | .025 | 42° | 7/8 |
| | 17080205 | 15/32 | Inner | 9/32 | .120 | 46° | — | 23° | .025 | 42° | 7/8 |
| | 17080206 | 15/32 | Inner | 9/32 | .120 | 46° | — | 23° | .025 | 42° | 7/8 |
| | 170802012 | 3/8 | Inner | 9/32 | .120 | 46° | 24° | 30° | .025 | 40° | 3/4 |
| | 17080213 | 3/8 | Inner | 9/32 | .120 | 37° | 23° | 30° | .025 | 40° | 1 |
| | 17080290 | 15/32 | Inner | 9/32 | .120 | 46° | — | 26° | .025 | 42° | 7/8 |
| | 17082291 | 15/32 | Inner | 9/32 | .120 | 46° | — | 26° | .025 | 42° | 7/8 |
| | 17082292 | 15/32 | Inner | 9/32 | .120 | 46° | — | 26° | .025 | 42° | 7/8 |
| | 17080298 | 3/8 | Inner | 9/32 | .120 | 37° | 23° | 30° | .025 | 40° | 1 |
| | 17080507 | 3/8 | Inner | 9/32 | .120 | 37° | 23° | 30° | .025 | 40° | 1 |
| | 17080512 | 3/8 | Inner | 9/32 | .120 | 46° | 24° | 30° | .025 | 40° | 3/4 |
| | 17080513 | 3/8 | Inner | 9/32 | .120 | 37° | 23° | 30° | .025 | 40° | 1 |
| | 17083220 | 13/32 | Inner | 9/32 | .120 | 46° | — | 24° | .025 | 39° | 7/8 |
| | 17083221 | 13/32 | Inner | 9/32 | .120 | 46° | — | 24° | .025 | 39° | 7/8 |
| | 17083222 | 13/32 | Inner | 9/32 | .120 | 46° | — | 24° | .025 | 39° | 7/8 |
| | 17083223 | 13/32 | Inner | 9/32 | .120 | 46° | — | 24° | .025 | 39° | 7/8 |
| | 17083224 | 13/32 | Inner | 9/32 | .120 | 46° | — | 24° | .025 | 39° | 7/8 |
| | 17083225 | 13/32 | Inner | 9/32 | .120 | 46° | — | 24° | .025 | 39° | 7/8 |
| | 17083226 | 13/32 | Inner | 9/32 | .120 | 46° | — | 24° | .025 | 39° | 7/8 |
| | 17083227 | 13/32 | Inner | 9/32 | .120 | 46° | — | 24° | .025 | 39° | 7/8 |
| | 17083230 | 13/32 | Inner | 9/32 | .120 | 46° | — | 24° | .025 | 39° | 7/8 |
| | 17083231 | 13/32 | Inner | 9/32 | .120 | 46° | — | 24° | .025 | 39° | 7/8 |
| | 17083234 | 13/32 | Inner | 9/32 | .120 | 46° | — | 24° | .025 | 39° | 7/8 |
| | 17083235 | 13/32 | Inner | 9/32 | .120 | 46° | — | 26° | .025 | 39° | 7/8 |
| | 17083290 | 13/32 | Inner | 9/32 | .120 | 46° | — | 24° | .025 | 39° | 7/8 |
| | 17083291 | 13/32 | Inner | 9/32 | .120 | 46° | — | 24° | .025 | 39° | 7/8 |
| | 17083292 | 13/32 | Inner | 9/32 | .120 | 46° | — | 24° | .025 | 39° | 7/8 |
| | 17083293 | 13/32 | Inner | 9/32 | .120 | 46° | — | 24° | .025 | 39° | 7/8 |
| | 17083298 | 3/8 | Inner | 9/32 | .120 | 37° | 23° | 30° | .025 | 40° | 1 |
| | 17083507 | 3/8 | Inner | 9/32 | .120 | 37° | 23° | 30° | .025 | 40° | 1 |
| 1984 | 170802012 | 3/8 | Inner | 9/32 | .120 | 46° | 24° | 30° | .025 | 40° | 3/4 |
| | 17080213 | 3/8 | Inner | 9/32 | .120 | 37° | 23° | 30° | .025 | 40° | 1 |
| | 17080298 | 3/8 | Inner | 9/32 | .120 | 37° | 23° | 30° | .025 | 40° | 1 |
| | 17082213 | 3/8 | Inner | 9/32 | .120 | 37° | 23° | 30° | .025 | 40° | 1 |
| | 17083298 | 3/8 | Inner | 9/32 | .120 | 37° | 23° | 30° | .025 | 40° | 1 |
| | 17084200 | 13/32 | Inner | 9/32 | .120 | 46° | — | 26° | .025 | 39° | 7/8 |
| | 17084206 | 13/32 | Inner | 9/32 | .120 | 46° | — | 26° | .025 | 39° | 7/8 |
| | 17084211 | 13/32 | Inner | 9/32 | .120 | 46° | — | 26° | .025 | 39° | 7/8 |
| | 17084220 | 13/32 | Inner | 9/32 | .120 | 46° | — | 26° | .025 | 39° | 7/8 |
| | 17084221 | 13/32 | Inner | 9/32 | .120 | 46° | — | 26° | .025 | 39° | 7/8 |
| | 17084226 | 13/32 | Inner | 9/32 | .120 | 46° | — | 24° | .025 | 39° | 7/8 |
| | 17084227 | 13/32 | Inner | 9/32 | .120 | 46° | — | 24° | .025 | 39° | 7/8 |
| | 17084228 | 13/32 | Inner | 9/32 | .120 | 46° | — | 26° | .025 | 39° | 7/8 |

## ADJUSTMENT SPECIFICATIONS—Continued

| Year | Carb. Production No. | Float Level | Pump Rod | | Choke Coil Lever | Choke Rod | Vacuum Break | | Air Valve Dashpot | Choke Unloader | Air Valve Spring (Turns) |
| | | | Hole | Adj. | | | Front | Rear | | | |
|---|---|---|---|---|---|---|---|---|---|---|---|
| 1984 | 17084229 | 13/32 | Inner | 9/32 | .120 | 46° | — | 26° | .025 | 39° | 7/8 |
| | 17084230 | 13/32 | Inner | 9/32 | .120 | 46° | — | 26° | .025 | 39° | 7/8 |
| | 17084231 | 13/32 | Inner | 9/32 | .120 | 46° | — | 26° | .025 | 39° | 7/8 |
| | 17084234 | 13/32 | Inner | 9/32 | .120 | 46° | — | 26° | .025 | 39° | 7/8 |
| | 17084235 | 13/32 | Inner | 9/32 | .120 | 46° | — | 26° | .025 | 39° | 7/8 |
| | 17084290 | 13/32 | Inner | 9/32 | .120 | 46° | — | 26° | .025 | 39° | 7/8 |
| | 17084291 | 13/32 | Inner | 9/32 | .120 | 46° | — | 26° | .025 | 39° | 7/8 |
| | 17084292 | 13/32 | Inner | 9/32 | .120 | 46° | — | 24° | .025 | 39° | 7/8 |
| | 17084293 | 13/32 | Inner | 9/32 | .120 | 46° | — | 26° | .025 | 39° | 7/8 |
| | 17084294 | 13/32 | Inner | 9/32 | .120 | 46° | — | 26° | .025 | 39° | 7/8 |
| | 17084298 | 13/32 | Inner | 9/32 | .120 | 46° | — | 26° | .025 | 39° | 7/8 |
| | 17084500 | 13/32 | Inner | 9/32 | .120 | 37° | 23° | 30° | .025 | 40° | 1 |
| | 17084501 | 13/32 | Inner | 9/32 | .120 | 37° | 23° | 30° | .025 | 40° | 1 |
| | 17084502 | 13/32 | Inner | 9/32 | .120 | 46° | 24° | 30° | .025 | 40° | 7/8 |
| 1985 | 17080212 | 3/8 | Inner | 9/32 | .120 | 46° | 24° | 30° | .025 | 40° | 3/4 |
| | 17080213 | 3/8 | Inner | 9/32 | .120 | 37° | 23° | 30° | .025 | 40° | 1 |
| | 17080298 | 3/8 | Inner | 9/32 | .120 | 37° | 23° | 30° | .025 | 40° | 1 |
| | 17082213 | 3/8 | Inner | 9/32 | .120 | 37° | 23° | 30° | .025 | 40° | 1 |
| | 17083298 | 3/8 | Inner | 9/32 | .120 | 37° | 23° | 30° | .025 | 40° | 1 |
| | 17084500 | 3/8 | Inner | 9/32 | .120 | 37° | 23° | 30° | .025 | 40° | 1 |
| | 17084501 | 3/8 | Inner | 9/32 | .120 | 37° | 23° | 30° | .025 | 40° | 1 |
| | 17084502 | 3/8 | Inner | 9/32 | .120 | 46° | 24° | 30° | .025 | 40° | 7/8 |
| | 17085000 | 3/8 | Inner | 9/32 | .120 | 46° | 24° | 30° | .025 | 40° | 7/8 |
| | 17085001 | 3/8 | Inner | 9/32 | .120 | 46° | 23° | 30° | 40° | .025 | 1 |
| | 17085003 | 13/32 | Inner | 9/32 | .120 | 46° | 23° | — | .025 | 35° | 7/8 |
| | 17085004 | 13/32 | Inner | 9/32 | .120 | 46° | 23° | — | .025 | 35° | 7/8 |
| | 17085205 | 13/32 | Inner | 9/32 | .120 | 20° | 26° | 38° | .025 | 39° | 7/8 |
| | 17085206 | 13/32 | Inner | 9/32 | .120 | 46° | — | 26° | .025 | 39° | 7/8 |
| | 17085208 | 13/32 | Inner | 9/32 | .120 | 20° | 26° | 38° | .025 | 39° | 7/8 |
| | 17085209 | 13/32 | Inner | 3/8 | .120 | 20° | 26° | 36° | .025 | 39° | 7/8 |
| | 17085210 | 13/32 | Inner | 9/32 | .120 | 20° | 26° | 38° | .025 | 39° | 7/8 |
| | 17085211 | 13/32 | Outer | 3/8 | .120 | 20° | 26° | 36° | .025 | 39° | 7/8 |
| | 17085212 | 13/32 | Inner | 9/32 | .120 | 46° | 23° | — | .025 | 35° | 7/8 |
| | 17085213 | 13/32 | Inner | 9/32 | .120 | 46° | 23° | — | .025 | 35° | 7/8 |
| | 17085215 | 13/32 | Inner | 9/32 | .120 | 46° | — | 26° | .025 | 32° | 7/8 |
| | 17085216 | 13/32 | Inner | 9/32 | .120 | 20° | 26° | 38° | .025 | 39° | 7/8 |
| | 17085217 | 13/32 | Inner | 3/8 | .120 | 20° | 26° | 36° | .025 | 39° | 1/2 |
| | 17085219 | 13/32 | Inner | 3/8 | .120 | 20° | 26° | 36° | .025 | 39° | 1/2 |
| | 17085220 | 13/32 | Outer | 3/8 | .120 | 20° | — | 26° | .025 | 32° | 7/8 |
| | 17085221 | 13/32 | Outer | 3/8 | .120 | 20° | — | 26° | .025 | 32° | 7/8 |
| | 17085222 | 13/32 | Inner | 9/32 | .120 | 20° | 26° | 36° | .025 | 39° | 1/2 |
| | 17085223 | 13/32 | Outer | 3/8 | .120 | 20° | 26° | 36° | .025 | 39° | 1/2 |
| | 17085224 | 13/32 | Inner | 9/32 | .120 | 20° | 26° | 36° | .025 | 39° | 1/2 |
| | 17085225 | 13/32 | Outer | 3/8 | .120 | 20° | 26° | 36° | .025 | 39° | 1/2 |
| | 17085226 | 13/32 | Inner | 9/32 | .120 | 20° | — | 24° | .025 | 32° | 7/8 |
| | 17085227 | 13/32 | Inner | 9/32 | .120 | 20° | — | 24° | .025 | 32° | 7/8 |
| | 17085228 | 13/32 | Inner | 9/32 | .120 | 46° | — | 24° | .025 | 39° | 7/8 |
| | 17085229 | 13/32 | Inner | 9/32 | .120 | 46° | — | 24° | .025 | 39° | 7/8 |

## ADJUSTMENT SPECIFICATIONS—Continued

| Year | Carb. Production No. | Float Level | Pump Rod | | Choke Coil Lever | Choke Rod | Vacuum Break | | Air Valve Dashpot | Choke Unloader | Air Valve Spring (Turns) |
| | | | Hole | Adj. | | | Front | Rear | | | |
|---|---|---|---|---|---|---|---|---|---|---|---|
| 1985 | 17085230 | 13/32 | Inner | 9/32 | .120 | 20° | — | 26° | .025 | 32° | 7/8 |
| | 17085231 | 13/32 | Inner | 9/32 | .120 | 20° | — | 26° | .025 | 32° | 7/8 |
| | 17085235 | 13/32 | Inner | 9/32 | .120 | 46° | — | 26° | .025 | 32° | 7/8 |
| | 17085238 | 13/32 | Outer | 9/32 | .120 | 20° | — | 26° | .025 | 32° | 7/8 |
| | 17085239 | 13/32 | Outer | 9/32 | .120 | 20° | — | 26° | .025 | 32° | 7/8 |
| | 17085290 | 13/32 | Inner | 9/32 | .120 | 46° | — | 24° | .025 | 39° | 7/8 |
| | 17085291 | 13/32 | Outer | 9/32 | .120 | 46° | — | 26° | .025 | 39° | 7/8 |
| | 17085292 | 13/32 | Inner | 9/32 | .120 | 46° | — | 24° | .025 | 39° | 7/8 |
| | 17085293 | 13/32 | Outer | 3/8 | .120 | 46° | — | 26° | .025 | 39° | 7/8 |
| | 17085294 | 13/32 | Inner | 9/32 | .120 | 46° | — | 26° | .025 | 39° | 7/8 |
| | 17085298 | 13/32 | Inner | 9/32 | .120 | 46° | — | 26° | .025 | 39° | 7/8 |
| 1986 | 17085000 | 3/8 | Inner | 9/32 | .120 | 46° | 24° | 30° | .025 | 40° | 7/8 |
| | 17085001 | 3/8 | Inner | 9/32 | .120 | 46° | 23° | 30° | .025 | 40° | 1 |
| | 17085003 | 13/32 | Inner | 9/32 | .120 | 46° | 23° | — | .025 | 35° | 7/8 |
| | 17085004 | 13/32 | Inner | 9/32 | .120 | 46° | 23° | — | .025 | 35° | 7/8 |
| | 17085206 | 13/32 | Inner | 9/32 | .120 | 46° | — | 26° | .025 | 39° | 7/8 |
| | 17085207 | 11/32 | Inner | 9/32 | .120 | 38° | 27° | — | .025 | 38° | 7/8 |
| | 17085208 | 13/32 | Inner | 9/32 | .120 | 20° | 26° | 38° | .025 | 39° | 7/8 |
| | 17085209 | 13/32 | Outer | 3/8 | .120 | 20° | 26° | 36° | .025 | 39° | 7/8 |
| | 17085210 | 13/32 | Inner | 9/32 | .120 | 20° | 26° | 38° | .025 | 39° | 7/8 |
| | 17085211 | 13/32 | Outer | 3/8 | .120 | 20° | 26° | 36° | .025 | 39° | 7/8 |
| | 17085215 | 13/32 | Inner | 9/32 | .120 | 46° | — | 26° | .025 | 32° | 7/8 |
| | 17085216 | 13/32 | Inner | 9/32 | .120 | 20° | 26° | 38° | .025 | 39° | 7/8 |
| | 17085217 | 13/32 | Inner | 9/32 | .120 | 20° | 26° | 36° | .025 | 39° | 7/8 |
| | 17085218 | 11/32 | — | — | .120 | 20° | 27° | — | .025 | 38° | 7/8 |
| | 17085219 | 13/32 | Inner | 9/32 | .120 | 20° | 26° | 36° | .025 | 39° | 1/2 |
| | 17085220 | 13/32 | Outer | 3/8 | .120 | 20° | — | 26° | .025 | 32° | 7/8 |
| | 17085221 | 13/32 | Outer | 3/8 | .120 | 20° | — | 26° | .025 | 32° | 7/8 |
| | 17085222 | 13/32 | Inner | 9/32 | .120 | 20° | 26° | 36° | .025 | 39° | 7/8 |
| | 170855223 | 13/32 | Outer | 3/8 | .120 | 20° | 26° | 36° | .025 | 39° | 1/2 |
| | 17085224 | 13/32 | Inner | 9/32 | .120 | 20° | 26° | 36° | .025 | 39° | 1/2 |
| | 17085225 | 13/32 | Outer | 3/8 | .120 | 20° | 26° | 36° | .025 | 39° | 1/2 |
| | 17085226 | 13/32 | Inner | 9/32 | .120 | 20° | — | 24° | .025 | 32° | 7/8 |
| | 17085227 | 13/32 | Inner | 9/32 | .120 | 20° | — | 24° | .025 | 32° | 7/8 |
| | 17085228 | 13/32 | Inner | 9/32 | .120 | 46° | — | 24° | .025 | 39° | 7/8 |
| | 17085229 | 13/32 | Inner | 9/32 | .120 | 46° | — | 24° | .025 | 39° | 7/8 |
| | 17085230 | 13/32 | Inner | 9/32 | .120 | 20° | — | 26° | .025 | 32° | 7/8 |
| | 17085231 | 13/32 | Inner | 9/32 | .120 | 20° | — | 26° | .025 | 32° | 7/8 |
| | 17085235 | 13/32 | Inner | 9/32 | .120 | 46° | — | 24° | .025 | 39° | 7/8 |
| | 17085238 | 13/32 | Outer | 3/8 | .120 | 20° | — | 26° | .025 | 32° | 7/8 |
| | 17085239 | 13/32 | Inner | 9/32 | .120 | 20° | — | 26° | .025 | 32° | 7/8 |
| | 17085283 | 13/32 | Inner | 9/32 | .120 | 20° | — | 24° | .025 | 32° | 7/8 |
| | 17085284 | 13/32 | Inner | 9/32 | .120 | 20° | — | 26° | .025 | 32° | 7/8 |
| | 17085285 | 13/32 | Inner | 9/32 | .120 | 20° | — | 24° | .025 | 32° | 7/8 |
| | 17085290 | 13/32 | Inner | 9/32 | .120 | 46° | — | 24° | .025 | 39° | 7/8 |
| | 17085291 | 13/32 | Outer | 3/8 | .120 | 46° | — | 26° | .025 | 39° | 7/8 |
| | 17085292 | 13/32 | Inner | 9/32 | .120 | 46° | — | 24° | .025 | 39° | 7/8 |

## ADJUSTMENT SPECIFICATIONS—Continued

| Year | Carb. Production No. | Float Level | Pump Rod | | Choke Coil Lever | Choke Rod | Vacuum Break | | Air Valve Dashpot | Choke Unloader | Air Valve Spring (Turns) |
| | | | Hole | Adj. | | | Front | Rear | | | |
|---|---|---|---|---|---|---|---|---|---|---|---|
| 1986 | 17085293 | 13/32 | Outer | 3/8 | .120 | 46° | — | 26° | .025 | 39° | 7/8 |
| | 17085294 | 13/32 | Inner | 9/32 | .120 | 46° | — | 26° | .025 | 39° | 7/8 |
| | 17085298 | 13/32 | Inner | 9/32 | .120 | 46° | — | 26° | .025 | 39° | 7/8 |
| | 17086044 | 17/32 | Inner | 9/32 | .120 | 20° | 26° | 38° | .025 | 39° | 7/8 |
| | 17086045 | 17/32 | Outer | 3/8 | .120 | 20° | 26° | 38° | .025 | 39° | 7/8 |
| | 17086046 | 17/32 | Inner | 9/32 | .120 | 20° | 26° | 38° | .025 | 39° | 7/8 |
| | 17086047 | 17/32 | Outer | 3/8 | .120 | 20° | 26° | 38° | .025 | 39° | 7/8 |
| | 17086048 | 17/32 | Inner | 9/32 | .120 | 20° | 26° | 38° | .025 | 39° | 7/8 |
| | 17086053 | 17/32 | Outer | 3/8 | .120 | 20° | 26° | 38° | .025 | 39° | 7/8 |
| | 17086054 | 17/32 | Inner | 9/32 | .120 | 20° | 26° | 38° | .025 | 39° | 7/8 |
| | 17086055 | 17/32 | Outer | 3/8 | .120 | 20° | 26° | 38° | .025 | 39° | 7/8 |
| 1987 | 17085000 | 3/8 | Inner | 9/32 | .120 | 46° | 24° | 30° | .025 | 40° | 7/8 |
| | 17085001 | 3/8 | Inner | 9/32 | .120 | 46° | 23° | 30° | .025 | 40° | 1 |
| | 17085003 | 13/32 | Inner | 9/32 | .120 | 46° | 27° | — | .025 | 35° | 7/8 |
| | 17085213 | 13/32 | Inner | 9/32 | .120 | 46° | 27° | — | .025 | 35° | 7/8 |
| 1987–89 | 17085004 | 13/32 | Inner | 9/32 | .120 | 46° | 23° | — | .025 | 35° | 7/8 |
| | 17085212 | 13/32 | Inner | 9/32 | .120 | 46° | 23° | — | .025 | 35° | 7/8 |
| 1988 | 17088040 | 13/32 | Inner | 9/32 | .120 | 46° | 27° | — | .025 | 35° | 7/8 |
| | 17088041 | 13/32 | Inner | 9/32 | .120 | 46° | 27° | — | .025 | 35° | 7/8 |

## IDENTIFICATION LOCATION

The carburetor identification number is stamped vertically on the left rear corner of the float bowl casting, adjacent to the secondary throttle lever, **Fig. 1**.

## DESCRIPTION

The M4M series (M4MC, M4ME, M4MED and M4MEF) Quadrajet carburetor is a four barrel, two stage unit consisting of three major assemblies: The air horn, float bowl and throttle body.

A single float chamber supplies the fuel to the four carburetor bores. A float, float needle and float seat are used to control the fuel level within the float chamber. A vacuum operated power piston and metering rods control the air/fuel metering in the primary throttle bores. The tapered metering rods are attached to the power valve piston assembly, moving in fixed metering jets to provide the various fuel flow requirements of the engine. A factory adjusted part throttle screw is used on all models to properly position the metering rods in the metering jets. The M4MEF model, in addition to the part throttle screw mentioned previously, also contains a rich stop adjusting bushing to position the enrichment portion of the metering rods in the jets. This bushing enables an adjustable wide open throttle mixture control capability. During wide open throttle operation, the air/fuel mixture in the secondary bores is controlled by air valves and tapered metering rods operating in fixed jets. On M4MEF models, the factory adjusted secondary well air bleed adjusting screw provides additional control of the air/fuel mixture during wide open throttle modes.

The accelerator pump system on all models uses a conventional throttle actuated pump plunger operating in a pump well, to provide additional fuel as needed. In addition, M4MED models are equipped with float bowl mounted dual capacity pump valve and solenoid assemblies. These assemblies provide a smoother transition from idle to part throttle operation during cold engine driving modes.

All carburetors use either electrically or hot air heated choke coils. The heated coils provide choke valve closing force for cold starts, as well as correct opening timing during warm-up. Vacuum break assemblies control initial choke valve opening during starting and warm-up periods.

Curb idle speeds are controlled, depending on engine and application, by either an idle speed adjusting screw or an idle speed solenoid. On vehicles without air conditioning, the idle speed solenoid provides desired idle speed, while preventing dieseling when the ignition switch is turned off. On vehicles with air conditioning, the solenoid maintains smooth idle during compressor clutch engagement. Vehicles without an idle speed solenoid are equipped with a throttle kicker assembly. The vacuum operated throttle kicker holds the throttle open during deceleration, thereby reducing exhaust emissions. On some engines, it is also used to increase idle speed depending on accessory load.

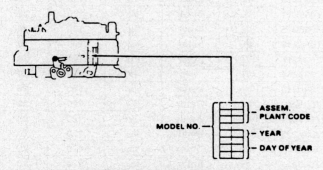

**Fig. 1  Carburetor identification number location**

## ADJUSTMENTS

### FLOAT LEVEL

1. Remove air horn, gasket, power piston/metering rod assembly and float bowl insert.
2. Attach base tool No. J-34817-1 or BT-8227A-1 to float bowl, **Fig. 2**.
3. Position tool J-34817-3 or BT-8227A into base, ensuring contact pin rests on outer edge of float lever.
4. Using adjustable T-scale shown, measure distance from top of casting to top of float, at a point 3/16 inch from

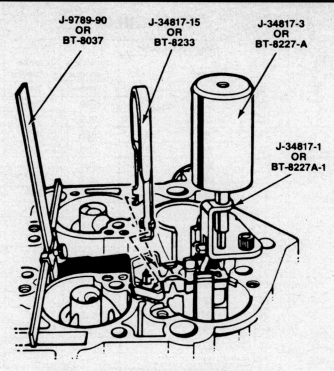

**Fig. 2   Float level Adjustment**

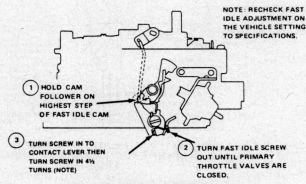

NOTE: RECHECK FAST IDLE ADJUSTMENT ON THE VEHICLE SETTING TO SPECIFICATIONS.

① HOLD CAM FOLLOWER ON HIGHEST STEP OF FAST IDLE CAM

③ TURN SCREW IN TO CONTACT LEVER THEN TURN SCREW IN 4½ TURNS (NOTE)

② TURN FAST IDLE SCREW OUT UNTIL PRIMARY THROTTLE VALVES ARE CLOSED.

**Fig. 3   Quadrajet M4M series pump rod adjustment**

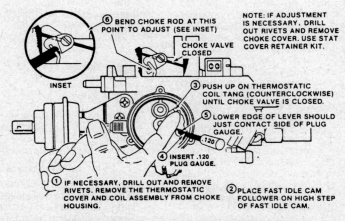

⑥ BEND CHOKE ROD AT THIS POINT TO ADJUST (SEE INSET)

INSET

CHOKE VALVE CLOSED

NOTE: IF ADJUSTMENT IS NECESSARY, DRILL OUT RIVETS AND REMOVE CHOKE COVER. USE STAT COVER RETAINER KIT.

③ PUSH UP ON THERMOSTATIC COIL TANG (COUNTERCLOCKWISE) UNTIL CHOKE VALVE IS CLOSED.

⑤ LOWER EDGE OF LEVER SHOULD JUST CONTACT SIDE OF PLUG GAUGE.

④ INSERT .120 PLUG GAUGE.

① IF NECESSARY, DRILL OUT AND REMOVE RIVETS. REMOVE THE THERMOSTATIC COVER AND COIL ASSEMBLY FROM CHOKE HOUSING.

② PLACE FAST IDLE CAM FOLLOWER ON HIGH STEP OF FAST IDLE CAM.

**Fig. 4   Choke coil lever adjustment**

large end of float. If float level deviates more than $^2/_{32}$ inch from specifications, bend float lever up or down as required with bending tool shown, **Fig. 2.**

5. Repeat procedure, check float alignment, then reassemble carburetor.

## PUMP ROD

With throttle valves completely closed and pump rod in specified hole, measure distance from top of choke valve wall (next to vent stack) to top of pump stem. Dimension should be as specified in the Specifications Chart. To adjust, bend pump lever, **Fig. 3.**

## CHOKE COIL LEVER

1. Remove choke cover retaining screws or drill out and remove rivets, then remove choke cover and thermostat.
2. Place fast idle cam on high step against follower lever and push up on choke lever to fully close choke valve.
3. Insert .120 inch gauge plug into hole in choke housing. Gauge should enter hole and just touch edge of lever.
4. Adjust as needed by bending choke link, **Fig. 4.**

## CHOKE ROD
### 1980–82 Units

1. Rotate degree scale until zero is opposite pointer, then with choke valve completely closed, place magnet on top of choke valve and rotate bubble until it is centered.
2. Rotate gauge to specified adjustment angle. Refer to specifications.
3. Place cam follower on second step of cam next to high step, **Fig. 5,** and close choke by pushing upward on choke coil lever.
4. To adjust bend tang on fast idle cam until bubble is centered, then remove gauge.

### 1983–89 Units

1. Attach rubber band to green tang of intermediate choke shaft.
2. Open throttle to allow choke valve to close, then rotate gauge to specified adjustment angle.
3. Position cam follower on second step of fast idle cam, next to high step, **Fig. 6.**
4. To adjust, bend tang of fast idle cam until bubble is centered, then remove gauge.

## FRONT VACUUM BREAK
### 1980–82 Units

1. Rotate degree scale until zero is opposite pointer. With choke valve completely closed, place gauge magnet on choke valve.
2. Rotate bubble until centered, then rotate degree scale until angle specified in Specifications Chart is opposite pointer.
3. Seat vacuum diaphragm using an external vacuum source. If equipped with air bleed, plug end cover with masking tape.
4. Close choke by pushing upward on

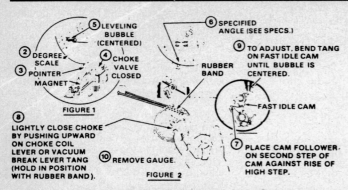

⑤ LEVELING BUBBLE (CENTERED)
② DEGREE SCALE
③ POINTER MAGNET
④ CHOKE VALVE CLOSED
⑥ SPECIFIED ANGLE (SEE SPECS.)
⑨ TO ADJUST, BEND TANG ON FAST IDLE CAM UNTIL BUBBLE IS CENTERED.
RUBBER BAND
FAST IDLE CAM
FIGURE 1
⑧ LIGHTLY CLOSE CHOKE BY PUSHING UPWARD ON CHOKE COIL LEVER OR VACUUM BREAK LEVER TANG (HOLD IN POSITION WITH RUBBER BAND).
⑩ REMOVE GAUGE.
⑦ PLACE CAM FOLLOWER ON SECOND STEP OF CAM AGAINST RISE OF HIGH STEP.
FIGURE 2

**Fig. 5   Choke rod adjustment (angle gauge method). 1980–82**

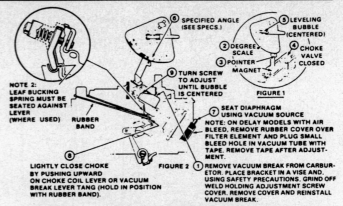

⑥ SPECIFIED ANGLE (SEE SPECS.)
⑤ LEVELING BUBBLE (CENTERED)
② DEGREE SCALE
③ POINTER MAGNET
④ CHOKE VALVE CLOSED
FIGURE 1
⑨ TURN SCREW TO ADJUST UNTIL BUBBLE IS CENTERED
NOTE 2: LEAF BUCKING SPRING MUST BE SEATED AGAINST LEVER (WHERE USED)
RUBBER BAND
⑦ SEAT DIAPHRAGM USING VACUUM SOURCE
NOTE: ON DELAY MODELS WITH AIR BLEED, REMOVE RUBBER COVER OVER FILTER ELEMENT AND PLUG SMALL BLEED HOLE IN VACUUM TUBE WITH TAPE. REMOVE TAPE AFTER ADJUSTMENT.
⑧ LIGHTLY CLOSE CHOKE BY PUSHING UPWARD ON CHOKE COIL LEVER OR VACUUM BREAK LEVER TANG (HOLD IN POSITION WITH RUBBER BAND).
FIGURE 2
⑩ REMOVE VACUUM BREAK FROM CARBURETOR. PLACE BRACKET IN A VISE AND, USING SAFETY PRECAUTIONS, GRIND OFF WELD HOLDING ADJUSTMENT SCREW COVER. REMOVE COVER AND REINSTALL VACUUM BREAK.
NOTE 1: MAKE CHOKE COIL LEVER AND FAST IDLE ADJUSTMENT (BENCH OR ON-THE-CAR SETTING). DO NOT REMOVE RIVETS AND CHOKE COVER TO PERFORM THIS ADJUSTMENT. USE RUBBER BAND ON VACUUM BREAK LEVER TANG TO HOLD CHOKE VALVE CLOSED (STEP 8).

**Fig. 6   Choke rod adjustment. 1983–89**

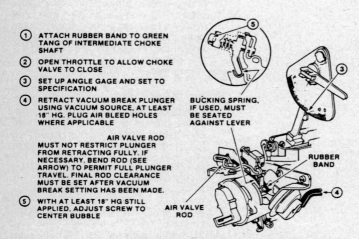

① ATTACH RUBBER BAND TO GREEN TANG OF INTERMEDIATE CHOKE SHAFT
② OPEN THROTTLE TO ALLOW CHOKE VALVE TO CLOSE
③ SET UP ANGLE GAGE AND SET TO SPECIFICATION
④ RETRACT VACUUM BREAK PLUNGER USING VACUUM SOURCE, AT LEAST 18" HG. PLUG AIR BLEED HOLES WHERE APPLICABLE

BUCKING SPRING, IF USED, MUST BE SEATED AGAINST LEVER

AIR VALVE ROD MUST NOT RESTRICT PLUNGER FROM RETRACTING FULLY. IF NECESSARY, BEND ROD (SEE ARROW) TO PERMIT FULL PLUNGER TRAVEL. FINAL ROD CLEARANCE MUST BE SET AFTER VACUUM BREAK SETTING HAS BEEN MADE.
RUBBER BAND
⑤ WITH AT LEAST 18" HG STILL APPLIED, ADJUST SCREW TO CENTER BUBBLE
AIR VALVE ROD

**Fig. 7   Front vacuum break adjustment (angle gauge method). 1980–82**

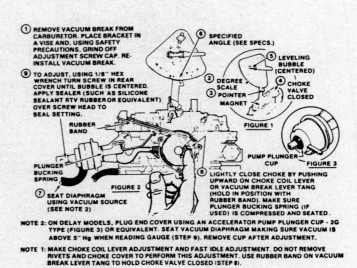

① REMOVE VACUUM BREAK FROM CARBURETOR. PLACE BRACKET IN A VISE AND, USING SAFETY PRECAUTIONS, GRIND OFF ADJUSTMENT SCREW CAP. REINSTALL VACUUM BREAK.
⑨ TO ADJUST, USING 1/8" HEX WRENCH TURN SCREW IN REAR COVER UNTIL BUBBLE IS CENTERED. APPLY SEALER (SUCH AS SILICONE SEALANT RTV RUBBER OR EQUIVALENT) OVER SCREW HEAD TO SEAL SETTING.
⑥ SPECIFIED ANGLE (SEE SPECS.)
⑤ LEVELING BUBBLE (CENTERED)
② DEGREE SCALE
③ POINTER MAGNET
④ CHOKE VALVE CLOSED
FIGURE 1
RUBBER BAND
PLUNGER BUCKING SPRING
PUMP PLUNGER CUP
FIGURE 3
⑦ SEAT DIAPHRAGM USING VACUUM SOURCE (SEE NOTE 2)
FIGURE 2
⑧ LIGHTLY CLOSE CHOKE BY PUSHING UPWARD ON CHOKE COIL LEVER OR VACUUM BREAK LEVER TANG (HOLD IN POSITION WITH RUBBER BAND). MAKE SURE PLUNGER BUCKING SPRING (IF USED) IS COMPRESSED AND SEATED.
NOTE 2: ON DELAY MODELS, PLUG END COVER USING AN ACCELERATOR PUMP PLUNGER CUP - 2G TYPE (FIGURE 3) OR EQUIVALENT. SEAT VACUUM DIAPHRAGM MAKING SURE VACUUM IS ABOVE 5" Hg WHEN READING GAUGE (STEP 9). REMOVE CUP AFTER ADJUSTMENT.
NOTE 1: MAKE CHOKE COIL LEVER ADJUSTMENT AND FAST IDLE ADJUSTMENT. DO NOT REMOVE RIVETS AND CHOKE COVER TO PERFORM THIS ADJUSTMENT. USE RUBBER BAND ON VACUUM BREAK LEVER TANG TO HOLD CHOKE VALVE CLOSED (STEP 8).

**Fig. 8   Front vacuum break adjustment. 1983–89**

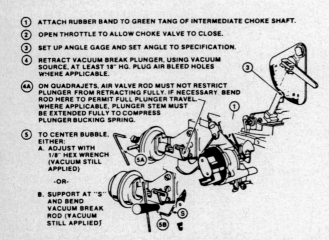

① ATTACH RUBBER BAND TO GREEN TANG OF INTERMEDIATE CHOKE SHAFT.
② OPEN THROTTLE TO ALLOW CHOKE VALVE TO CLOSE.
③ SET UP ANGLE GAGE AND SET ANGLE TO SPECIFICATION.
④ RETRACT VACUUM BREAK PLUNGER, USING VACUUM SOURCE, AT LEAST 18" HG. PLUG AIR BLEED HOLES WHERE APPLICABLE.
④A ON QUADRAJETS, AIR VALVE ROD MUST NOT RESTRICT PLUNGER FROM RETRACTING FULLY. IF NECESSARY, BEND ROD HERE TO PERMIT FULL PLUNGER TRAVEL. WHERE APPLICABLE, PLUNGER STEM MUST BE EXTENDED FULLY TO COMPRESS PLUNGER BUCKING SPRING.
⑤ TO CENTER BUBBLE, EITHER:
  A. ADJUST WITH 1/8" HEX WRENCH (VACUUM STILL APPLIED)
  -OR-
  B. SUPPORT AT "S" AND BEND VACUUM BREAK ROD (VACUUM STILL APPLIED)

**Fig. 9   Rear vacuum break adjustment. Late models (early models similar)**

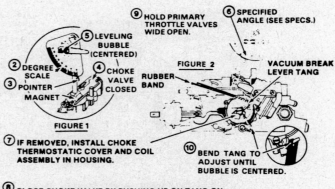

⑨ HOLD PRIMARY THROTTLE VALVES WIDE OPEN.
⑥ SPECIFIED ANGLE (SEE SPECS.)
⑤ LEVELING BUBBLE (CENTERED)
② DEGREE SCALE
③ POINTER MAGNET
④ CHOKE VALVE CLOSED
FIGURE 2
RUBBER BAND
VACUUM BREAK LEVER TANG
FIGURE 1
⑦ IF REMOVED, INSTALL CHOKE THERMOSTATIC COVER AND COIL ASSEMBLY IN HOUSING.
⑩ BEND TANG TO ADJUST UNTIL BUBBLE IS CENTERED.
⑧ CLOSE CHOKE VALVE BY PUSHING UP ON TANG ON VACUUM BREAK LEVER (HOLD IN POSITION WITH RUBBER BAND).

**Fig. 10   Air valve dashpot adjustment**

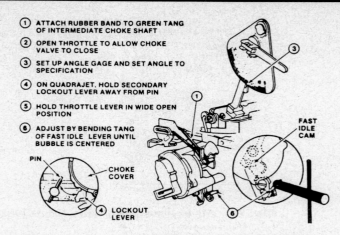

① ATTACH RUBBER BAND TO GREEN TANG OF INTERMEDIATE CHOKE SHAFT
② OPEN THROTTLE TO ALLOW CHOKE VALVE TO CLOSE
③ SET UP ANGLE GAGE AND SET ANGLE TO SPECIFICATION
④ ON QUADRAJET, HOLD SECONDARY LOCKOUT LEVER AWAY FROM PIN
⑤ HOLD THROTTLE LEVER IN WIDE OPEN POSITION
⑥ ADJUST BY BENDING TANG OF FAST IDLE LEVER UNTIL BUBBLE IS CENTERED

**Fig. 11   Unloader adjustment (angle gauge method). 1980–82**

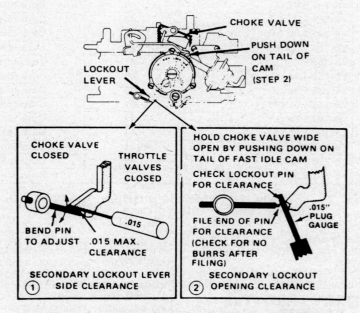

**Fig. 12   Unloader adjustment. 1983–89**

choke coil lever or vacuum break lever tang. If equipped with bucking spring, spring must be seated against lever.

5. To adjust, turn adjusting screw until bubble is centered, **Fig. 13**, then remove gauge.

### 1983–89 Units

1. Attach rubber band to green tang of intermediate choke shaft, then open throttle to allow choke valve to close.
2. Install angle gauge, **Fig. 8**, rotate degree scale until zero is opposite pointer, center leveling bubble, then rotate gauge to angle specified in Specifications Chart.
3. Seat vacuum break plunger using an external vacuum source of at least 18 inches Hg. If equipped with air bleed, plug bleed holes with masking tape. If equipped with bucking spring, spring must be seated against lever.
4. To adjust, rotate adjusting screw, with vacuum applied, until bubble is centered, **Fig. 8**, then remove gauge. Air valve rod must not restrict plunger from seating. If necessary, bend rod to permit full plunger travel.

## REAR VACUUM BREAK

1. Attach rubber band to green tang on intermediate choke shaft, the open throttle to allow choke to close.
2. Rotate degree scale until zero is opposite pointer, then with choke valve completely closed, place magnet on top of choke valve and rotate bubble until centered.
3. Rotate gauge to angle specified in Specifications Chart, then seat plunger using an external vacuum source. If equipped with air bleed, plug bleed holes with masking tape. Air valve rod must not restrict plunger from seating. If necessary, bend rod to permit full plunger travel.
4. If equipped with adjusting screw, rotate screw, using a suitable hex wrench, until bubble is centered, **Fig. 9**. On units less adjusting screw, bend link until bubble is centered as shown.

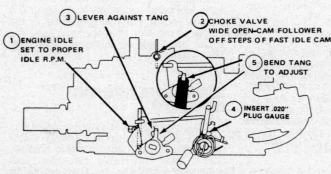

**Fig. 13   Secondary throttle valve lockout adjustment**

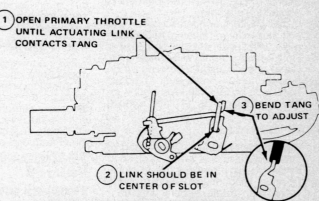

**Fig. 14   Secondary throttle valve closing adjustment**

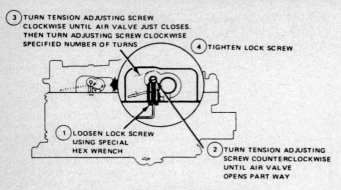

**Fig. 15  Secondary throttle valve opening adjustment**

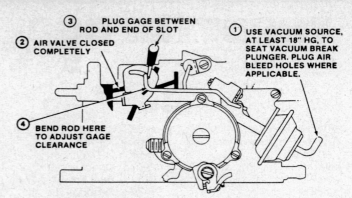

**Fig. 16  Air valve spring wind-up adjustment**

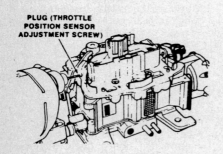

**Fig. 17  Throttle position sensor adjustment screw cover removal**

## AIR VALVE DASHPOT

Using an external vacuum source, seat vacuum diaphragm. With the air valve completely closed, place gauge specified in the Specifications Chart between air valve rod and end of slot in air valve lever. To adjust, bend rod at air valve end, **Fig. 10.**

## CHOKE UNLOADER

### 1980–82 Units

1. Rotate degree scale until zero is opposite pointer, then with choke valve completely closed, place magnet squarely on top of choke valve.
2. Rotate bubble until it is centered. Refer to Specifications and rotate scale until specified angle for adjustment is opposite the pointer.
3. Install choke thermostatic cover and coil assembly in housing. Align index mark with specified point on housing. Hold primary throttle valve wide open. Close choke valve by pushing up on tang on vacuum break lever. To adjust bend tang on fast idle lever until bubble is centered, **Fig. 11,** then remove gauge.

### 1983–89 Units

1. Attach rubber band to green tang of intermediate choke lever, then open throttle to allow choke valve to close.
2. Position magnet on top of choke valve, then rotate bubble until centered. Refer to Specifications and rotate scale until specified degree for adjustment is opposite pointer.

3. Hold secondary lockout lever away from pin, **Fig. 12,** then hold throttle wide open.
4. To adjust, bend tang on fast idle lever until bubble is centered.

## SECONDARY THROTTLE VALVE LOCKOUT

### Lockout Pin Clearance

With choke and throttle valves fully closed, measure clearance between lockout pin and lockout lever. Maximum clearance should not exceed .015 inch. To adjust, bend lockout pin, **Fig. 13.**

### Opening Clearance

Push downward on fast idle cam tail to open choke valve, then push lock-out lever counterclockwise so upper end of lever contacts the round pin in fast idle cam. Measure clearance between lockout pin and lockout lever toe. Clearance should be .015 inch. To obtain power clearance, file metal from end of lockout pin, **Fig. 13.**

## SECONDARY THROTTLE VALVES

### 1980–82 UNITS

#### Throttle Closing

With curb idle speed set, hold choke

| Year | Engine (VIN Code) | Voltage | Throttle Position |
|------|-------------------|---------|-------------------|
| 1983 | V8-305/5.0L (H) | .51 | Curb Idle |
| | V8-305/5.0L (F) | .40 | Curb Idle |
| | V8-350/5.7L (L) | .40 | Curb Idle |
| 1984 | V8-305/5.0L (H) | .48 | Curb Idle |
| | V8-305/5.0L (F) | .41 | Curb Idle |
| | V8-350/5.7L (L) | .41 | Curb Idle |
| 1985 | V6-262/4.3L (N) | .25 | Curb Idle |
| | V8-305/5.0L (H) | .48 | Curb Idle |
| | V8-305/5.0L (F) | .41 | Curb Idle |
| | V8-350/5.7L (L) | .41 | Curb Idle |
| 1986 | V8-305/5.0L (H) | .48 | Curb Idle |
| | V8-305/5.0L (F) | .41 | Curb Idle |
| | V8-350/5.7L (L) | .41 | Curb Idle |
| | V6-262/4.3L (N) | .25 | Curb Idle |

**Fig. 18  Throttle position sensor idle voltage**

valve open with cam follower lever off fast idle cam steps. Measure clearance between forward edge of slot in the secondary throttle valve pickup lever and the secondary actuating rod. On all units, clearance should be .020 inch. To adjust, bend secondary closing tang on primary throttle lever, **Fig. 14.**

### Throttle Opening

Open primary throttle lever until link lightly contacts secondary lever tang. The bottom end of the link should be in the center of the slot in secondary lever. To adjust, bend tang on secondary lever, **Fig. 15.**

## AIR VALVE SPRING WIND-UP

Loosen lock screw, using a suitable hex wrench. Rotate tension adjusting screw counterclockwise until air valve partially opens, then turn screw clockwise until valve just closes, **Fig. 16.** Turn adjusting screw clockwise specified number of turns listed in Specifications Chart, then tighten lock screw. Apply lithium based grease to contact area.

# THROTTLE BODY INJECTION (TBI) SYSTEM

## INDEX

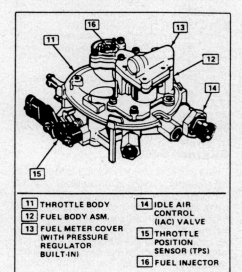

| | |
|---|---|
| **11** THROTTLE BODY | **14** IDLE AIR CONTROL (IAC) VALVE |
| **12** FUEL BODY ASM. | |
| **13** FUEL METER COVER (WITH PRESSURE REGULATOR BUILT-IN) | **15** THROTTLE POSITION SENSOR (TPS) |
| | **16** FUEL INJECTOR |

**Fig. 1   TBI unit. 4 cylinder engines**

## DESCRIPTION

The Throttle Body Fuel Injection System provide a means of fuel distribution for controlling exhaust emissions within the required limits by precisely controlling the air/fuel ratio under all operating conditions. This is accomplished by means of an Electronic Control Module (ECM) which receives electrical signals from various sensors indicating engine operating conditions, and varies the fuel delivery time (pulse width) of the injector(s) accordingly. The ECM may modify the fuel pulse to compensate for special operating conditions such as cranking, cold starting, altitude acceleration and deceleration. By in-

creasing the injector pulse, more fuel is delivered and the air/fuel mixture is enriched. When the injector pulse is decreased, the air/fuel ratio is decreased.

The ECM is capable of diagnosing faults with the various inputs and systems it controls. When the ECM detects a malfunction, a "Check Engine" or "Service Engine Soon" lamp in the instrument panel is illuminated, warning the driver to have the system checked.

In the fuel injection system used with the 4 cylinder engines, **Fig. 1**, the throttle body injector (TBI) is located on the intake manifold where fuel and air are distributed through a single bore in the throttle body, **Fig. 2**. Air for combustion is controlled by a single throttle valve which is connected to the accelerator pedal linkage by a throttle shaft and lever assembly. Fuel for combustion is supplied by a single fuel injector mounted on the TBI assembly, **Fig. 2**.

On fuel injected V6 and V8 applications, **Fig. 3**, the throttle body injector (TBI) is also located on the intake manifold where fuel and air are distributed through a double bore throttle body, **Fig. 2**. Combustion air is controlled by dual throttle valves while fuel is supplied by dual TBI unit mounted injectors. Both injectors are controlled by one ECM.

When the ignition key is turned on, the ECM will energize the fuel pump relay. The fuel tank mounted fuel pump pressurizes the system to approximately 10 psi. If a distributor reference pulse is not received by the ECM within two seconds, the fuel pump relay will be de-energized, turning off the fuel pump. If a distributor reference pulse is later received by the ECM, the fuel pump relay will be re-energized and the pump will resume operation.

If a fuel pump relay failure should occur, the oil pressure switch can also operate the fuel pump after the engine has built up approximately 4 psi of oil pressure.

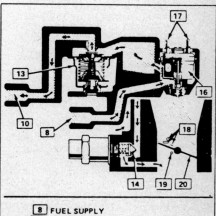

| | |
|---|---|
| **8** FUEL SUPPLY | |
| **10** FUEL RETURN | |
| **13** PRESSURE REGULATOR (PART OF FUEL METER COVER) | |
| **14** IDLE AIR CONTROL (IAC) VALVE (SHOWN OPEN) | |
| **16** FUEL INJECTOR | |
| **17** FUEL INJECTOR TERMINALS | |
| **18** PORTED VACUUM SOURCES* | |
| **19** MANIFOLD VACUUM SOURCE* | |
| **20** THROTTLE VALVE | |

*May Be Different on some Models.

**Fig. 2   TBI unit fuel metering schematic. 4 cylinder engines (similar to V6 & V8 engines).**

## SYSTEM COMPONENTS
### THROTTLE BODY INJECTOR UNIT

The Throttle Body Injector 700 (TBI 700) unit used on 4 cylinder engines is made up of two major castings: a throttle body and

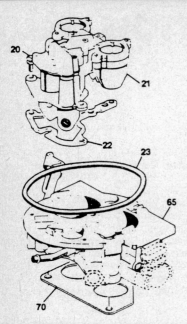

20 - SCREW ASSEMBLY - FUEL
     METER BODY - THROTTLE
     BODY ATTACHING
21 - FUEL METER BODY ASSEMBLY
22 - GASKET - THROTTLE BODY
     TO FUEL METER BODY
23 - GASKET - AIR FILTER
65 - THROTTLE BODY ASSEMBLY
70 - GASKET - FLANGE

**Fig. 3   TBI unit. V6 & V8
engines**

a fuel meter assembly. The throttle body contains an Idle Air Control (IAC) valve to control idle air flow and a throttle position sensor mounted on the throttle valve shaft. The fuel meter assembly contains a fuel pressure regulator to maintain constant fuel pressure and a fuel injector.

The Throttle Body Injector 220 (TBI 220) unit used on V6 and V8 engines is made up of three major castings: a throttle body, a fuel meter body, and a fuel meter cover. The throttle body contains an Idle Air Control (IAC) valve to control idle air flow, and a throttle position sensor mounted on the throttle valve shaft. The fuel meter body contains fuel injectors. The fuel meter cover, with an integral pressure regulator to maintain constant fuel pressure.

The throttle body portion of the TBI may also contain several ports located above or below the throttle valve(s) to provide vacuum signals to various vacuum operated equipment.

Each fuel injector is a solenoid operated device controlled by the ECM. Incoming fuel is directed towards the lower end of the injector assembly, **Fig. 2.** When the ECM actuates the injector solenoid, the normally closed ball valve is lifted off its seat and pressurized fuel is injected in a conical spray pattern at the TBI bore wall(s) above the throttle valve(s). Excess fuel is routed through the pressure regulator before being returned to the fuel tank.

The fuel pressure regulator is integral with the TBI fuel meter cover and is serviced as an assembly with the meter cover only.

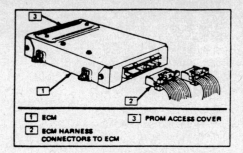

1. ECM
2. ECM HARNESS
   CONNECTORS TO ECM
3. PROM ACCESS COVER

**Fig. 4   ECM unit**

## IDLE AIR CONTROL (IAC) VALVE

The Idle Air Control (IAC) valve is located in the TBI unit and is used to control engine idle speed, **Fig. 2.** The valve operates by allowing air to bypass the throttle valve(s) in the TBI unit. If engine RPM is too low, the ECM will move the IAC conical valve in to allow more air to bypass the throttle valve(s). If engine RPM is too high, the ECM will move the IAC conical valve out to allow less air to bypass the throttle valve(s). If IAC connector is removed or installed with the engine running, the idle set RPM may be lost. Refer to "Idle Air Control (IAC) Valve, Replace" for valve reset procedure.

## ELECTRONIC CONTROL MODULE

The Electronic Control Module (ECM), located in the passenger compartment, is the control center of the fuel injection system. The ECM continually monitors and processes the input information and generates output commands to the various systems affecting vehicle performance.

A removable calibration unit (PROM) enables the ECM to recognize and adjust for vehicle variations (vehicle weight, axle ratio, etc.). There are specific ECM/PROM combinations for each specific vehicle which are not interchangeable, **Fig. 4.**

On V6 and V8 models, a CALPAK is also installed in the ECM. The CALPAK allows fuel delivery in the case that other parts of the ECM are damaged, **Fig. 5.**

On 4 cylinder engines, a MEM-CAL, performs the calibration functions in place of the PROM and CALPAK. The MEM-CAL also incorporates a backup fuel control circuit, which is operational if the ECM is damaged or faulty.

The ECM also performs the diagnostic function of the fuel injection system. When the ECM senses an operational problem, it will illuminate the "Check Engine" or "Service Engine Soon" light and store the appropriate code(s) to identify the problem area.

## DATA SENSORS

### Engine Coolant Temperature Sensor

The engine coolant temperature sensor is a thermistor that is located in the engine coolant flow. When the coolant temperature is low, the sensor produces a high resistance. When the coolant temperature is

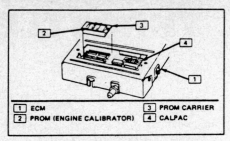

1. ECM
2. PROM (ENGINE CALIBRATOR)
3. PROM CARRIER
4. CALPAC

**Fig. 5   ECM unit showing
PROM & CALPAK locations**

high, the sensor produces a low resistance.

The ECM sends a 5 volt signal to the coolant temperature sensor through a resistor in the ECM and measures the voltage. A high voltage will be indicated when the coolant temperature is low, and low when the coolant temperature is high.

### Manifold Air Temperature Sensor (MAT)

The manifold air temperature sensor is a thermistor. The ECM sends a 5 volt signal to the MAT sensor, through a resistor in the ECM. The measurement of voltage tells the ECM the manifold air temperature. A high voltage, high resistance, will be indicated when the manifold air temperature is low, and a low voltage when the manifold air temperature is high.

The ECM utilizes the MAT sensor signal to delay EGR, until manifold temperature reaches approximately 40°F. A high ambient temperature signal, from the MAT sensor tells the ECM to slightly retard engine timing.

### Oxygen Sensor

The exhaust oxygen sensor is located in the exhaust system and monitors oxygen content in the exhaust gas stream. The oxygen content of the exhaust gas reacts with the oxygen sensor to produce a voltage output, **Fig. 6.** By monitoring the oxygen sensor output voltage, the ECM can determine the amount of oxygen in the exhaust gas and adjust the air/fuel mixture accordingly.

### Manifold Absolute Pressure Sensor

The Manifold Absolute Pressure (MAP) sensor measures changes in the intake manifold pressure resulting from engine load and speed changes and converts this to a voltage output, **Fig. 7.**

The ECM sends a 5 volt reference signal to the MAP sensor. As pressure changes in the intake manifold occur, the electrical resistance of the MAP sensor also changes. By monitoring the sensor output voltage, the ECM can determine the MAP. The higher the MAP, the lower the engine vacuum and the higher the sensor output, which requires more fuel. The lower the MAP, the higher the engine vacuum and the lower the sensor output, which requires less fuel.

### Vehicle Speed Sensor

The vehicle speed sensor (VSS) sends

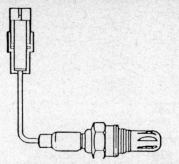

**Fig. 6  Oxygen sensor (typical)**

a pulsating voltage signal to the ECM, which the ECM converts to mph. This sensor mainly controls the operation of the transmission Torque Converter Clutch (TCC), shift light and cruise control (if equipped).

### Throttle Position Sensor

The Throttle Position Sensor (TPS) is connected to the throttle valve shaft in the throttle body unit. The TPS is a potentiometer with one connection to ground and the other to a ECM 5 volt voltage source. A third wire from the ECM is used to measure the voltage from the TPS. As the throttle angle changes, so does the TPS voltage output. By monitoring TPS voltage output, the ECM can determine fuel delivery rate based on throttle valve angle.

## ELECTRONIC SPARK TIMING

The Electronic Spark Timing (EST) distributor contains no vacuum or centrifugal advance mechanisms. In addition to the connectors normally found on HEI distributors, the HEI-EST distributor also has four wires going to a four terminal connector. A reference pulse, indicating engine RPM and crankshaft position is sent to the ECM. The ECM determines the proper spark advance for the engine operating conditions and sends an "EST" pulse to the distributor.

In the case of EST failure, a back-up spark advance system is incorporated in the module.

## ELECTRONIC SPARK CONTROL

Electronic Spark Control (ESC) is used on some models. The ESC system is used in conjunction with the EST system to provide additional spark retard during engine detonation. A knock sensor signals a separate ESC controller to retard the timing when it senses engine knock. The ESC controller signals the ECM which reduces spark advance until no more signals are received from the knock sensor.

## PARK/NEUTRAL SWITCH

The park/neutral switch indicates to the ECM when the transmission is in park or neutral. This information is used by the ECM for ignition timing, IAC operation and transmission Torque Converter Clutch (TCC) operation. Do not drive vehicle with park/neutral switch disconnected, as idle quality may be affected.

## CRANK SIGNAL

This signal is used to inform the ECM that the engine is cranking. The ECM uses this information to tell when the engine is in the cranking mode.

## AIR CONDITIONING "ON" SIGNAL

The air conditioning "On" signal informs the ECM the A/C selector switch is turned on, and the A/C pressure cycling switch is closed. Using this information, the ECM adjusts the engine idle speed as necessary to ensure a smooth idle.

## POWER STEERING PRESSURE SWITCH

The power steering pressure switch is used on 4 cylinder engines and opens during high pressure power steering situations. When the power steering switch is open, power to the A/C relay is shut off, resulting in compressor clutch disengagement. A signal is also sent to the ECM. The ECM uses this signal for idle control.

# OPERATION

## STARTING MODE

When the ignition switch is rotated to the "On" position, the ECM energizes the fuel pump for two seconds and fuel pressure is built up to the TBI unit. The ECM then checks the coolant temperature sensor, the TPS and determines the proper air/fuel mixture for starting.

The ECM controls the air/fuel ratio by changing the length of time the injectors are turned on and off. This is accomplished by "Pulsing" the injectors for short periods of time.

## CLEAR FLOOD MODE

A flooded engine is cleared by fully depressing the accelerator pedal, which causes the ECM to pulse the injectors at a air/fuel ratio of 20:1. The ECM will maintain this air/fuel ratio as long as the throttle is wide open and engine RPM is less than 600. If throttle position becomes less than 80% of wide open throttle, the ECM returns to "Starting Mode."

## RUN MODE

The Run Mode consists of two separate operating conditions; open loop and closed loop. The engine operates in open loop when it is first started and RPM is above 400 RPM. During open loop operation, the ECM disregards the oxygen sensor signal and determines air/fuel mixture primarily from the coolant and MAP sensors. The engine will continue to operate in open loop until the following conditions are met:

1. The oxygen sensor has varying voltage output, indicating it is hot enough to operate properly.
2. The Coolant sensor is above a specified temperature.
3. A specific amount of time has elapsed since the engine was started. The specified values for conditions mentioned above vary from model to model, and are stored in the ECM PROM.

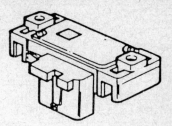

**Fig. 7  MAP sensor**

When the above conditions are met, the engine goes into closed loop operation. When operating in closed loop, the ECM determines the air/fuel ratio (injector pulse rate) based on signals from the oxygen sensor. This allows the air/fuel mixture to remain close to the optimum 14.7:1 ratio. During idling conditions, the V6-173/2.8L and V8-454/7.4L engines automatically goes into open loop operation.

## ACCELERATION MODE

In the Acceleration Mode, the ECM senses rapid change in throttle position and manifold pressure and provides a corresponding amount of added fuel.

## DECELERATION MODE

In the Deceleration Mode, the ECM senses changes in throttle position and manifold pressure and reduces fuel delivery. When decelerating very rapidly, the ECM can cut off fuel completely for short periods of time.

## BATTERY VOLTAGE CORRECTION MODE

When battery voltage is low, the ECM compensates to maintain acceptable system performance by increasing injector pulses, idle speed and ignition dwell time.

# DIAGNOSIS

A built-in, self diagnostic system will identify problems most likely to occur in the Throttle Body Fuel Injection System. When a problem is detected, the diagnostic system will illuminate a "Check Engine" or "Service Engine Soon" light in the instrument panel. The "Check Engine" light will flash a trouble code or codes when a trouble code "Test" terminal under the dash is grounded with ignition on and engine not running.

The "Check Engine" or "Service Engine Soon" light will illuminate with the ignition switch on and the engine not running. If the "Test" terminal is then grounded and the light flashes a Code 12, the self-diagnostic system is functioning properly. A Code 12 consists of one flash, a short pause, then two flashes in rapid succession. After a longer pause, the code will repeat two more times.

When the engine is started, the "Check Engine" or "Service Engine Soon" light should turn off. If the light remains lit, the self-diagnostic system has detected a problem. To determine where the problem exists, ground the "Test" terminal with ignition on and engine not running and ob-

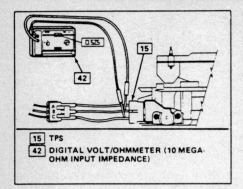

| 15 | TPS |
| 42 | DIGITAL VOLT/OHMMETER (10 MEGA-OHM INPUT IMPEDANCE) |

**Fig. 8  TPS adjustment check. 4 cylinder models (V6 models similar)**

serve trouble code display. Each trouble code will flash three times in numeric order. Each trouble code will indicate a fault in a particular circuit. To diagnose the problem, refer to procedure given for appropriate trouble code.

## TROUBLE CODE "TEST" LEAD

The trouble code "Test" lead is located in a 12 volt terminal connector under the dash. When this terminal is grounded, the ECM will flash any trouble codes stored in the memory. To ground the terminal, connect a jumper wire between the "Test" lead terminal and the adjacent ground terminal.

If the "Test" terminal is grounded with ignition on and engine not running, the system will enter the diagnostic mode. In the diagnostic mode, the ECM will flash a Code 12 and energize all ECM controlled relays.

If the "Test" terminal is grounded with the engine running, the system will enter the field service mode. In this mode, the "Check Engine" light will indicate whether the system is in open or closed loop operation. If the light flashes approximately twice per second, the system is in open loop operation. Closed loop operation is indicated by the light flashing approximately once per second.

## TROUBLE CODE MEMORY

When a problem develops in the system, the "Check Engine" or "Service Engine Soon" light will illuminate and a trouble code will be set in the ECM memory. If the problem is intermittent, the "Check Engine" or "Service Engine Soon" light will turn off after approximately ten seconds after the fault goes away. The trouble code, however, will be retained in the ECM memory until battery voltage to the ECM is removed. To clear all stored trouble codes, disconnect battery positive cable for thirty seconds and reconnect.

## CONNECTOR INSPECTION

Before replacing any system components, proceed as follows:
1. Disconnect connector(s) associated with suspected defective component and check for improper installation, bent, broken, or dirty terminals or mat-

ing tabs and repair or replace as required.
2. Reconnect all connectors and recheck the system to ensure that the problem has been corrected. **Any repairs made to wiring harness should be made with battery disconnected to prevent damaging the harness. Disconnecting battery will erase all trouble codes stored in the ECM.**

## TROUBLE CODE IDENTIFICATION

The "Check Engine" or "Service Engine Soon" light will turn On only if the following malfunctions occur during engine operation. If the malfunction clears, the light will go out and the code will store in the ECM memory. Code 12 does not store in the ECM memory. If the "Check Engine" or "Service Engine Soon" light illuminates intermittently, but no code is stored, refer to Intermittent "Check Engine" or "Service Engine Soon" Light Troubleshooting.

### Code 13
Code 13 indicates the oxygen sensor or oxygen sensor circuit was open while off idle for one minute or longer.

### Code 14
Code 14 indicates the coolant sensor is producing a low signal voltage. This code sets if the sensor or circuit becomes grounded for three seconds or more.

### Code 15
Code 15 indicates the coolant sensor is producing a high signal voltage. This code sets if the sensor or circuit becomes open for three seconds or more.

### Code 21
Code 21 indicates the TPS voltage is too high and will be set if the TPS voltage is greater than 2.5 volts for three seconds or more at 2000 RPM.

### Code 22
Code 22 indicates TPS voltage is too low and will be set if TPS is shorted to ground or circuit was open for more than three seconds.

### Code 23
Code 23 sets when MAT sensor connects or wire open for 3 seconds.

### Code 24
Code 24 is set when the ECM does not receive a speed signal from the Vehicle Speed Sensor (VSS).

### Code 25
Code 25 is set when MAT sensor or signal line becomes grounded for 3 seconds.

### Code 32
Code 32 indicates EGR switch is not operating properly.

### Code 33
Code 33 indicates the MAP sensor output voltage is too high for five seconds or more or the MAP sensor circuit is open.

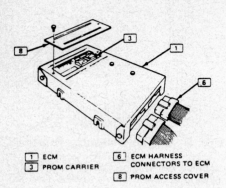

| 1 | ECM | 6 | ECM HARNESS CONNECTORS TO ECM |
| 3 | PROM CARRIER | 8 | PROM ACCESS COVER |

**Fig. 9  Access cover removal**

### Code 34
Code 34 is set when MAP sensor voltage is too low or there is no MAP sensor signal.

### Code 35
Code 35 indicates an error with the Idle Air Control (IAC) valve.

### Code 42
Code 42 indicates the ECM has detected an open or grounded EST or bypass circuit.

### Code 43
Code 43 is set when the ESC signal to the ECM has remained low for too long a time or the system has failed a functional test.

### Code 44
Code 44 indicates lean exhaust and is set when the oxygen sensor voltage has remained below .2 volts for approximately 20 seconds.

### Code 45
Code 45 indicates rich exhaust and is set when the oxygen sensor voltage has remained above .7 volts for approximately 60 seconds.

### Code 51
Code 51 indicates a faulty Programmable Read Only Memory (PROM) or ECM.

### Code 52
Code 52 indicates a faulty CALPAK.

### Code 53
Code 53 indicates a basic generator problem causing high system voltage.

### Code 54
Code 54 indicates low fuel pump voltage and is set when fuel pump voltage is less than 2 volts when reference pulses are being received.

### Code 55
Code 55 indicates a faulty ECM.

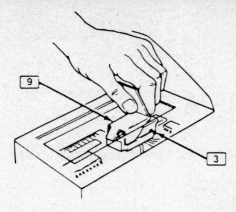

[3] PROM CARRIER
[9] PROM REMOVAL TOOL

**Fig. 10  Removing PROM**

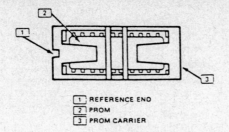

[1] REFERENCE END
[2] PROM
[3] PROM CARRIER

**Fig. 11  PROM or CALPAK installed in carrier**

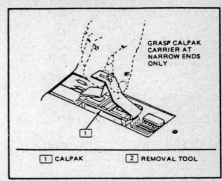

GRASP CALPAK CARRIER AT NARROW ENDS ONLY

[1] CALPAK   [2] REMOVAL TOOL

**Fig. 12  Removing CALPAK**

## ADJUSTMENTS

### THROTTLE POSITION SENSOR (TPS), ADJUST

#### 1985 Models

1. Remove air cleaner, then disconnect TPS electrical connector.
2. Remove TPS attaching screws, then apply suitable thread locking compound to screw threads and reinstall. Ensure TPS pickup lever is located above throttle actuator lever tang. Do not tighten screws at this time.
3. Install three jumper wires between TPS and TPS wire connector, **Fig. 8.**
4. With ignition "On" and engine not running, measure voltage between sensor terminals B and C on 4 cylinder engines or sensor terminals A and B on V6 engines with a digital voltmeter.
5. With throttle in the closed position, adjust TPS to obtain .525 ± .075 volts.
6. Tighten screws, then recheck adjustment to ensure it did not change.
7. Turn ignition "Off," then remove jumper wires and connect TPS wire connector.

#### 1986–89 Models Exc. 1988–89 V6-173/2.8L Engine

The TPS is not adjustable. The ECM utilizes the reading at idle for the zero reading, therefore no adjustment is necessary.

#### 1988–89 Models w/V6-173/2.8L Engine

Make adjustments, only after the minimum idle speed has been adjusted, or throttle body parts have been replaced.
1. Disconnect TPS connector. Connect a suitable digital voltmeter from TPS connector outside terminal A to center terminal B.
2. Turn ignition switch to the On position, but do not start the engine. TPS voltage should read less than 1.25 volts.
3. If voltage reading is higher then described, loosen the TPS retainer screw, then rotate the TPS, until a reading of 0.42-0.54 volts is obtained.
4. If voltage reading is satisfactory, tight-

en the retainer screw, then remove the voltmeter and reconnect the TPS connector.
5. If a proper voltage reading cannot be obtained, replace the TPS.

## COMPONENT REPLACEMENT

### • ECM, REPLACE

When replacing a production ECM with a service ECM, transfer the broadcast code and production number from the production unit to the service unit. Also, during replacement, the PROM, and if equipped, the CALPAK must be removed from the ECM being replaced and transferred to the new unit. Refer to "PROM, Replace" and "CALPAK, Replace" for procedure.
1. Disconnect battery ground cable.
2. Remove right side kick panel, then disconnect two ECM electrical connectors.
3. Remove ECM mounting hardware.
4. Remove ECM from passenger compartment.
5. Reverse procedure to install.

### PROM, REPLACE

1. Remove ECM from vehicle as described under "ECM, Replace."
2. Remove access cover, **Fig. 9.** Note position of PROM unit in ECM. PROMs are not interchangeable. Replacement PROMs must be installed in the same position and direction as defective PROM.
3. Grasp PROM carrier with PROM removal tool, **Fig. 10.**
4. Rock carrier side-to-side while applying a firm upward force, then remove PROM and carrier. Remove PROM from carrier. Inspect replacement PROM to ensure the part number is the same as the removed PROM.
5. Install replacement PROM in carrier, **Fig. 11.**
6. Position PROM and carrier assembly over PROM socket and press down firmly on top of carrier. Press down on carrier and ensure it seats squarely. Do not press on PROM. Press on carrier only.
7. Replace access cover, then install ECM in vehicle.
8. Start engine, enter self-diagnosis and check for code 51. If code 51 does not display, PROM is installed correctly. If code 51 is displayed, PROM is installed incorrectly and installation pro-

cedure must be repeated. If PROM is installed backwards, and ignition turned "On," it will be destroyed.

### CALPAK, REPLACE

1. Remove ECM from vehicle as described under "ECM, Replace."
2. Remove access cover, **Fig. 9.**
3. Remove Calpak, **Fig. 5,** using CALPAK removal tool, **Fig. 12.** Grasp CALPAK carrier at narrow ends only. To remove, gently rock the carrier from end to end while applying a firm upwards force.
4. Inspect CALPAK carrier reference end and set aside. Do not remove CALPAK from carrier unless necessary.
5. Install replacement CALPAK in carrier, **Fig. 11.**
6. Position replacement CALPAK and carrier assembly over CALPAK socket and press down firmly on top of carrier. Press down on carrier and ensure it seats squarely. Do not press on CALPAK. Press on carrier only.
7. Replace access cover, then install ECM in vehicle.

### MEM-CAL, REPLACE

#### Removal

1. Remove ECM from vehicle as described under "ECM, Replace."
2. Remove access cover.
3. Remove MEM-CAL by pulling the locking tabs apart, grasping MEM-CAL, and lifting it from the socket.
4. Inspect MEM-CAL, noting alignment marks. Do not open the MEM-CAL cover.

#### Installation

When installing the MEM-CAL, never press on the center of the unit, always press on the ends.
1. Position MEM-CAL to the socket. Ensure small notches of the MEM-CAL and socket are aligned.
   a. For early production models with solid locking tabs, press inward on the ends of the MEM-CAL, until the locking tabs snap into its sides.
   b. For late production models with hollow locking tabs, hold the locking tabs apart, then press inward on the ends of the MEM-CAL until seated.
2. On all models, press inward on the

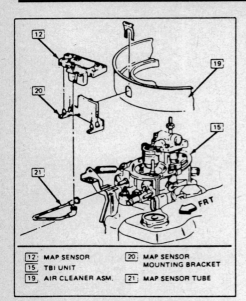

**Fig. 13   MAP sensor removal. 4 cylinder models (V6 models similar)**

| | | | |
|---|---|---|---|
| 12 | MAP SENSOR | 20 | MAP SENSOR MOUNTING BRACKET |
| 15 | TBI UNIT | | |
| 19 | AIR CLEANER ASM. | 21 | MAP SENSOR TUBE |

locking tabs, until they seat. Listen for a clicking noise.
4. Replace access cover, then install ECM in vehicle.

## COOLANT SENSOR, REPLACE

The coolant sensor must be handled carefully. If sensor is damaged, fuel injection operation will be affected.
1. Disconnect battery ground cable.
2. Drain coolant from radiator so level is below sensor.
3. Disconnect coolant sensor electrical connector.
4. Carefully back out coolant sensor and remove.
5. Reverse procedure to install.

## MAP SENSOR, REPLACE

The MAP sensor unit is not serviceable and must be replaced as a unit.
1. Disconnect vacuum hose from MAP sensor, then remove top of air cleaner assembly.
2. Remove MAP sensor unit retaining clip, then the sensor, Fig. 13.
3. Reverse procedure to install.

## MAT SENSOR, REPLACE

1. Disconnect battery ground cable.
2. Disconnect MAT sensor electrical connector, then loosen sensor and remove.
3. Reverse procedure to install. Apply a suitable sealer to sensor threads before installing.

## OXYGEN SENSOR, REPLACE

The following procedure should be performed with engine temperature over 120°F, otherwise the oxygen sensor may be difficult to remove.
1. Disconnect battery ground cable.
2. Disconnect oxygen sensor electrical connector, then carefully loosen oxy-

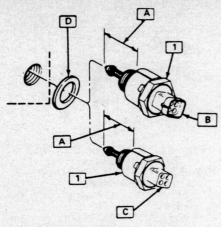

| | |
|---|---|
| 1 | IDLE AIR CONTROL VALVE |
| A | LESS THAN 28mm (1-1/8 IN.) |
| B | TYPE I (WITH COLLAR) |
| C | TYPE II (WITHOUT COLLAR) |
| D | GASKET (PART OF IAC VALVE SERVICE KIT) |

**Fig. 14   IAC thread type valve**

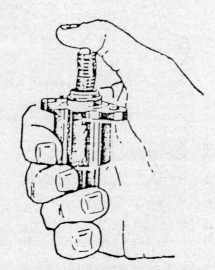

**Fig. 17   IAC flange type valve. Pintle adjustment**

gen sensor and remove.
3. Reverse procedure to install. Torque sensor to 30 ft. lbs. Replacement oxygen sensors should have a special anti-seize compound applied to threads. If replacement sensor is lacking anti-seize compound or original sensor is to be reinstalled, coat threads with suitable anti-seize compound.

## THROTTLE POSITION SENSOR, REPLACE

1. Disconnect TPS electrical connector.
2. Remove two TPS attaching screws, lockwashers and retainers.
3. If equipped, remove screw attaching TPS actuator lever to end of throttle.
4. Remove TPS.

| | |
|---|---|
| 1 | IACV ATTACHING SCREW ASSEMBLY |
| 2 | EXTERNAL IACV O-RING |
| 3 | GRIME SHIELD |

**Fig. 15   IAC flange type valve**

**Fig. 16   IAC thread type valve. Pintle adjustment**

5. With throttle valve(s) in normal closed idle position, install TPS. Ensure TPS pickup lever is located above tang on throttle actuator lever.
6. Apply suitable thread locking compound to screw threads, then install retainers, lockwashers and screws. Adjust TPS. Refer to "TPS, Adjust" for procedure.

## IDLE AIR CONTROL (IAC) VALVE, REPLACE

### Removal

1. Disconnect battery ground cable, then remove air cleaner assembly.
2. Disconnect IAC valve electrical connector.
   a. On thread mounted type IAC valve, Fig. 14. Using a suitable 1¼ inch wrench, remove valve, then discard gasket.
   b. On flange mounted type IAC valve, Fig. 15. Remove attaching screws, then the valve, and discard o-ring.

### Installation

Prior to installation, identify IAC valve as being either Type 1, Type 2, or flange type, Figs. 14, and 15. If dimension "A" is greater than 1⅛ inch, reduce as follows:
On Type 1 and flange type valve, Figs. 16 and 17, exert firm pressure with a side to side motion on valve pintle to retract it.
On Type 2, while turning IAC valve in clockwise direction, compress retaining spring. Return spring to original position with straight part of spring aligned with flat surface of valve.
1. Thoroughly clean valve mating surfaces, then install IAC valve in throttle

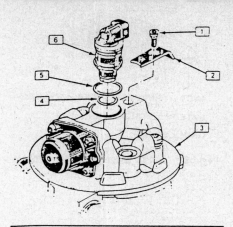

| 1 | SCREW ASSEMBLY |
| 2 | RETAINER |
| 3 | FUEL METER ASSEMBLY |
| 4 | LOWER "O" RING |
| 5 | UPPER "O" RING |
| 6 | INJECTOR |

**Fig. 18  Fuel injector assembly**

body using a new gasket or O-ring. Torque thread mounted valve to 13 ft. lbs. Torque flange mounted valve attaching screws to 28 inch lbs.
2. Connect IAC valve electrical connector.
3. Start engine and allow to reach operating temperature.
4. Reset the IAC valves as follows:
   a. On 1985 models, IAC valve will automatically reset idle speed after vehicle is driven over 30 mph on V6 engines, or over 35 mph on 4 cylinder engines.
   b. On 1986-87 models, IAC valve will automatically reset after engine has been turned Off.
   c. On 1988-89 models with V6 or V8 engines, the IAC valve will reset when the ignition switch is turned to the On position for ten seconds, then turned off.
   d. On 1988-89 models with 4 cylinder engine, the idle rpm is reset when the vehicle is driven above 30 mph.

## INJECTOR(S), REPLACE
### REMOVAL

1. Relieve fuel pressure. Refer to "Fuel Pressure Relief Procedure."
2. Disconnect battery ground cable, then remove air cleaner assembly.
3. Disconnect injector(s) electrical connector, then remove injectors as follows:
   a. On V6 and V8 models, remove fuel meter cover. Refer to "Fuel Meter Cover, Replace." Do not remove meter cover gasket from fuel meter body.
   b. On 4 cylinder engines, **Fig. 18**, remove attaching screw and retainer.
4. On all models, pry injector out of fuel meter body using a suitable screwdriver and bar stock, **Figs. 19 and 20**.
5. Remove and discard O-rings, wash-

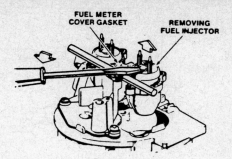

**Fig. 19  TBI 220 Fuel injector removal**

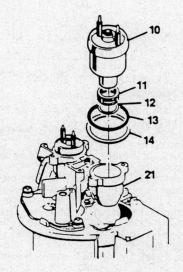

10 - INJECTOR - FUEL
11 - FILTER - FUEL INJECTOR INLET
12 - "O" RING - FUEL INJECTOR - LOWER
13 - "O" RING - FUEL INJECTOR - UPPER
14 - WASHER - FUEL INJECTOR
21 - FUEL METER BODY ASSEMBLY

**Fig. 21  Fuel injector installation. V6 & V8 engine. (4 cylinder models similar)**

ers, injector fuel filter and meter cover gasket.

## INSTALLATION
### V6 & V8 Engines

1. Using a twisting motion, install new injector filter on injector.
2. Lubricate replacement small O-ring with automatic transmission fluid, then push O-ring onto nozzle end of injector until seated against injector fuel filter.
3. Install meter body back-up washer in top counterbore of fuel meter body injector cavity, **Fig. 21**.
4. Lubricate replacement large O-ring with automatic transmission fluid,

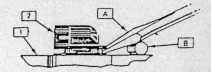

| 1 | FUEL METER BODY |
| 2 | FUEL INJECTOR |
| A | SCREWDRIVER |
| B | FULCRUM |

**Fig. 20  TBI 700 Fuel injector removal**

then install over meter body back-up washer in injector cavity. Ensure large O-ring is seated properly in cavity and is flush with top of fuel meter body casting surface.
5. Install injector in injector cavity, aligning raised lug on injector with notch in fuel meter body cavity.
6. Push down on injector until fully seated in cavity, **Fig. 22** At this time injector electrical terminals should be approximately parallel to throttle shaft.
7. Install fuel meter cover. Refer to "Fuel Meter Cover, Replace."
8. Connect electrical connector, then install air cleaner assembly.

### 4 Cylinder Engines

1. Lubricate new lower and upper O-rings with automatic transmission fluid.
2. Install O-rings to the injector. Seat lower O-ring flush to the filter and upper O-ring in the groove, **Fig. 18**.
3. Ensure injector electrical connector is facing the cutout of the fuel meter body and press the injector assembly into the cavity, **Fig. 21**.
4. Install the injector retainer. Apply a suitable locking compound to the retainer screw, then torque to 27 inch lbs.
5. Connect injector electrical connector. Turn ignition switch to the On position, and inspect injector assembly for leaks. If no leaks are found, install air cleaner assembly.

## FUEL METER COVER, REPLACE
### V6 & V8 Engines
#### Removal

The fuel meter cover contains the fuel pressure regulator and is serviced as a complete preset unit. Do not attempt to remove the four pressure regulator-to-fuel meter cover attaching screws as the pressure regulator is spring loaded and, if tension is released, could cause injury.
1. Perform steps 1 through 3 of "Injector(s), Replace" removal procedure.
2. Remove five screws securing meter cover-to-meter body. Note locations of two shorter screws.
3. Remove fuel meter cover. Do not immerse fuel meter cover/pressure regulator assembly in parts cleaner, as pressure regulator diaphragms and gaskets could be damaged.

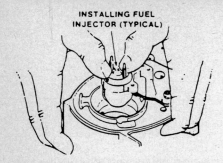

**Fig. 22  Seating fuel injector in throttle body**

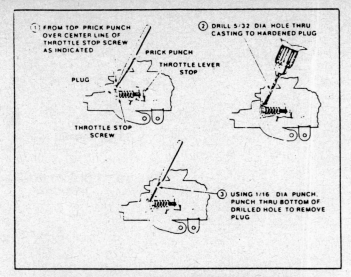

① FROM TOP PRICK PUNCH OVER CENTER LINE OF THROTTLE STOP SCREW AS INDICATED

② DRILL 5/32 DIA HOLE THRU CASTING TO HARDENED PLUG

PRICK PUNCH

THROTTLE LEVER STOP

PLUG

THROTTLE STOP SCREW

③ USING 1/16 DIA PUNCH. PUNCH THRU BOTTOM OF DRILLED HOLE TO REMOVE PLUG

**Fig. 24  Concealment plug removal**

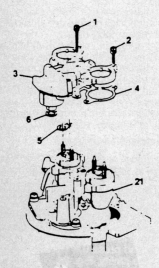

1 - SCREW ASSEMBLY - FUEL METER COVER ATTACHING - LONG
2 - SCREW ASSEMBLY - FUEL METER COVER ATTACHING - SHORT
3 - FUEL METER COVER ASSEMBLY
4 - GASKET - FUEL METER COVER
5 - GASKET - FUEL METER OUTLET
6 - SEAL - PRESSURE REGULATOR
21 - FUEL METER BODY ASSEMBLY

**Fig. 23  Fuel meter cover installation**

## Installation

1. Install a pressure regulator seal into fuel meter body recess, **Fig. 23.**
2. Install fuel meter outlet passage gasket on fuel meter cover.
3. Install fuel meter cover gasket on fuel meter cover.
4. Install fuel meter cover. Ensure pressure regulator seal and cover gaskets are properly installed. Apply suitable thread locking compound to meter cover-to-meter body attaching screws and install. Torque screws to 28 inch lbs. When applying thread locking compound to screw threads, use GM 1052624, Loctite 262 or equivalent. Use of a higher strength locking compound is not recommended as it may prevent attaching screw removal or screw head breakage if screws are removed again.

## FUEL PRESSURE REGULATOR, REPLACE

### 4 Cylinder Engines

Caution should be taken to avoid bodily injury when removing pressure regulator cover. Large spring in the assembly is under high compression and will release with force.

1. While keeping pressure regulator compressed, remove attaching screws.
2. Remove cover assembly, spring and seat, then the diaphragm assembly. Discard diaphragm.

3. Ensure the fuel meter body pressure regulator seat, is free of pitting or irregularities.
4. Reverse procedure to install, noting the following:
   a. Ensure new pressure regulator diaphragm assembly is fully seated in fuel meter body groove.
   b. Apply a suitable thread locking compound to meter cover-to-meter body attaching screws and install. Torque screws to 22 inch lbs.
   c. Turn ignition switch to the On position and inspect for leaks.

## CONCEALMENT PLUG REMOVAL

If necessary to adjust minimum idle speed, the concealment plug must first be removed. Refer to **Fig. 24** when removing plug.

## FUEL PRESSURE RELIEF PROCEDURE

1. Remove Fuel Pump fuse from fuse block.
2. Start engine and allow to run out of fuel, then crank engine an additional 3 seconds.
3. Service fuel system as necessary.